THE BATTLE OF FRANCE
THEN AND NOW

THE BATTLE OF FRANCE
THEN AND NOW
Peter D. Cornwell

Credits

ISBN: 9-781870-067652
© *After the Battle* 2007
Designed by Winston Ramsey, Editor-in-Chief

PUBLISHERS
Battle of Britain International Ltd
The Mews, Hobbs Cross House,
Hobbs Cross, Old Harlow, Essex CM17 0NN
Telephone: 01279 41 8833. Fax: 01279 41 9386

PRINTERS
Printed and bound in China by 1010 Printing
International Limited.

FRONT COVER
Hurricanes of No. 73 Squadron pictured over
eastern France in April 1940.

REAR COVER
A Fairey Battle of No. 142 Squadron brought
down at Rodange in Luxembourg on May 10,
1940, the opening day of the German offensive in the West.

FRONT ENDPAPER
Ground crew swarm to refuel and rearm a
Hurricane of B Flight, No. 73 Squadron,
flanked by a petrol bowser at Rouvres
aerodrome in May 1940.

REAR ENDPAPER
'In memory of a brave son and loving
husband — Pilot Officer H. J. Rennie Dunn,
RAF, who was killed on active service June
1, 1940. Per Ardua ad Astra.'

FRONTISPIECE (pages 2-3)
Flying Officer Bill Kain gives the thumbs-up
to Sergeant Tom Gallagher whereupon
'Gooney' Slater and Dave Dalziel begin to
wind up the Merlin of the 73 Squadron
Hurricane for a manual start.

THE AIR FORCES (pages 74-75)
A section of Fairey Battles from No. 88
Squadron under close escort by Curtiss
H-75As from the 1ère Escadrille GC I/5. In
reality, communication problems and poor
pre-flight briefing generally ensured such
bomber escorts, even by RAF fighters, were
a distinct rarity.

THE AIRCRAFT LOSSES (pages 90-91)
Detritus of defeat — June 1940. British and
French aircraft debris litters Poix airfield
now occupied by the Luftwaffe as a
Messerschmitt Bf109E of I./JG54 comes in
to land.

BLITZKRIEG! (pages 172-173)
A Staffel of Dornier Do17s heads off in classic
Verbandsflug. With improved defensive
armament, usually six Rheinmetall MG15
machine guns, and more powerful Bramo
Fafnir 323 radial engines, the Do17Z-2 was
the most popular and reliable German
bomber of the early war period. It equipped
four entire Kampfgeschwader at the opening
of the German offensive in the West.

ACKNOWLEDGEMENTS:
We are indebted to the following individuals
and organisations for their valuable help:
Sergio Andreanelli, Peter R. Arnold, Peter
Ayerst, Teresa Barnes of the Royal Air
Force Personnel Management Agency,
Adjudant Stephan Blommen and Korporaal-
Chef Eric Libotte of the Parachute Training
School at Schaffen, Robin Brooks, Alan
Brown, Guy Cassiman, Régis Decobeck,
Peter Devitt and Peter Elliott of the RAF
Museum, Susan Dickinson of the Air Histor-
ical Branch, RAF, John Foreman, F.
Gerdessen, Arnaud Gillet, Michael Ginns,
MBE, Chris Goss, Maria Choules, Peter
Holton and Derek Butler of the Common-
wealth War Graves Commission, Frans van
Humbeek, Roy Humphreys, Jeff Jefford, Jan
Jolie, Beate Kalbhenn of the Volksbund
Deutsche Kriegsgräberfürsorge, David List,
Phil Mertens, Yves Michelet, Lucien
Morareau, Hans Nauta, Bernard Paich, Mary
Parrott, Simon Parry, Tim Pearce of RAF
Cranwell, Jim Perry, Jean-Louis Roba, Chris
Shores, Johan Schuurman, Remi Tracanelli,
Kapitein-commandant Rob Troubleyn of the
Belgian War Graves Commission, Luc Ver-
voort, Dave Wadman, Neil Wakefield, Henk
Welting, Stephen Walton of the Imperial
War Museum, and Trevor A. Williams.

Special thanks are especially due to Karel
Margry, Editor of *After the Battle,* and Jean
Paul Pallud who took the majority of the
comparison photographs; Denis Bateman
Don Minterne, Gail Parker, Andy Saunders
and particularly to Peter Taghon, without
whose dedicated assistance the book would
be very much the poorer.

And our sincere appreciation to the
relatives of the airmen who died: Paul Adams,
Mrs Ruth Archer, Mrs E. B. Bazalgette, Mrs
Margaret Belcher, Mrs Pat Burrows, Jenny
Clare, Dave Cooper, John Corby, Anthony R.
Le Couteur, Aiden Cuthbert, Edwin Dodgson,
Mrs M. Dumbreck, Wilf Eggington, William
Hanna, Miss Wynne Hodges, Judy Pickard,
Sarah Pickles, Keith Robinson, Chris Sheldon,
Ann Thompson-Hill, David Thurgar, Shee-
lagh Tyrell, Roma Walsh, Derek L. Warwick,
Mrs Doreen Willis and Roger Wood.

Editorial Note

'Then and now' comparison photographs are the central theme of all
After the Battle publications yet the Battle of France presented particular
problems for us. During the 'Phoney War' period censorship was very strict
and there are no clues in the wartime captioning to identify places or determine the dates of individual crashes.

A good example is provided by the photo which appears on pages
500-501 and is simply described as 'funeral of British airmen in France'.
Only by a long process of elimination, and on-the-spot investigation, were
we able to discover where the picture had been taken: in Épernay, east of
Paris. By April 1940, several three-man crews had been buried in the
French National Cemetery in the town, all of whom were transferred after
the war to Terlincthun British Cemetery *(above)* at Wimille, near
Boulogne. Today 29 casualties of the battle lie there in Plot 19, gathered
together from isolated graves difficult to maintain.

Secondly, an army — or air force — in retreat does not spend time
taking photographs so for pictures of crashes once the Blitzkrieg started,
we have had to rely largely on those taken by German soldiery. The author
has collected several hundred snapshots, of varying quality, but again the
captioning is poor or non-existant.

A third problem with identification and the matching up of the crash
sites is that the main area over which the battle was fought was the wide
open countryside of eastern France — a flat terrain which makes comparison photography meaningless.

However, we are very fortunate that No. 73 Squadron was singled out
by the Press for special attention and we are grateful to the Mayor of
Rouvres, M. Romanello, also to the people of the village who were kind
enough to allow us into their homes to take comparison photographs, and to
the commander of the French airbase, Brigadier Maryline Furon and Lieutenant Pilippart, for allowing us to explore the squadron's former airfield,
albeit that it bears little relation to the aerodrome which existed in 1940.

WINSTON G. RAMSEY, Editor-in-Chief

Contents

6   Introduction

8   The Phoney War

74   THE AIR FORCES

90   THE AIRCRAFT LOSSES

1939

92   September

101 October

109 November

122 December

1940

130 January

137 February

143 March

155 April

166 May 1-9

172 BLITZKRIEG!

174 May 10-31

403 June 1-24

500 ROLL OF HONOUR

528 The Balance Sheet

530 RAF Aircraft Index

533 French Aircraft Index

536 Dutch Aircraft Index

537 Belgian Aircraft Index

538 Luftwaffe and Italian Aircraft Index

539 General Index

589 Photograph Credits

590 Addendum

592 Bibliography

Introduction

Pilots of No. 73 Squadron in France in 1940. Flying Officer — later Squadron Leader — Newell 'Fanny' Orton missing on September 17, 1941, aged 26, and Flying Officer Edgar 'Cobber' Kain, killed on June 7, 1940, aged 21.

This project resulted from a brief exchange with Winston Ramsey, Editor-in-Chief of *After the Battle*, in September 2002. Knowing of my abiding interest and long-term study of the air war of 1939-40, he floated the idea of a book covering the campaign in France. It would, he explained, act as an ideal companion to our earlier collaboration on *The Battle of Britain Then and Now* and act as a useful precursor to the momentous events described in that volume.

We discussed the scope of such a work, its key elements, and our joint 'venture into uncharted waters' as he described it. For, unlike the Battle of Britain where an Air Ministry Order specified precise dates for the beginning and end of the four-month battle, and set out the units deemed to have been involved, no such ruling was given for the six-week campaign that proceeded it: dubbed by Churchill, quoting Weygand, as 'The Battle of France'. We had to form our own criteria for the coverage of the book and decided, for completeness-sake, to begin the account in September 1939 and run through until the Armistice between France and Germany on June 24, 1940.

Similarly, we had to determine the criteria for inclusion in a Roll of Honour which we decided would include only those aircrew killed on operations or through enemy action while serving with the British Air Forces in France (BAFF) during the period. Inevitably applying criteria leads to many being omitted, either lost while flying from England, or at sea during the evacuation from France. All served and all paid the supreme sacrifice, but due to the chaotic nature of the closing stages of the battle no exact total exists in the surviving records.

With the fruits of years of research under my belt and most of the initial research already done, or so I thought, I blithely agreed to take it on — little appreciating the sheer enormity and complexities of the task ahead. But it soon became clear

that if I was to achieve the level of detail of my earlier work, much still remained to be done. A benchmark was set and I needed to meet the standards now expected by a new generation of readers who, thanks to the 'information highway' and improved access to official records, were much better informed than those of a quarter of a century before. Fortunately, my network of contacts proved equal to the task and their ready assistance is acknowledged elsewhere with grateful thanks. Some others deserve special mention.

My good friend, the Dutch air historian Jan Jolie, introduced me to other researchers on the Continent and to a wealth of material describing events during the *Meidagen*. A variety of Dutch Air Force studies document that traumatic period and are almost bewildering in the extent of detail they provide. Notable amongst them are the volumes compiled by Kolonel F. J. Molenaar that provide an essential foundation for any in-depth study of the subject. These I have supplemented with the work of Lieutenant-Kolonel E. H. Brongers while Fritz Gerdessen was also most helpful in answering questions on *Militaire Luchtvaart* losses. For details of the German airborne landings in Holland, I relied on another Dutch Air Force study, a detailed analysis compiled by Majoor J. E. van Zwieten. Combined with more of Brongers' work this provides a fairly accurate picture although, in the absence of reliable contemporary records, even van Zwieten apparently baulked at attempting to cover events at Waalhaven.

I was fortunate to have noted Belgian air historian Peter Taghon on hand for the duration of this project. His extensive knowledge and impressive photographic collection covering events in both his own country and further abroad made a significant contribution to the completed work. He has also been most helpful in referring my more obscure enquiries to the appropriate experts in the field.

For details of French Air Force operations I relied extensively on the work of Jacqueline and Paul Martin. Their impressive tome documenting the losses of the entire period incorporated valuable early research by Madame L'Herbier-Montagnon, an extraordinary woman who pioneered research into casualties of the French campaign and without whom much information would have been irrevocably lost. Complementing this source, the works of noted French air historian Arnaud Gillet, who has so thoroughly documented French fighter claims of the period, proved invaluable to this work. Pieter Hooijmans, a well-informed Dutch student of the period, also made a singular contribution by vetting my proofs for early May 1940, and sharing his views and offering alternative findings.

Luftwaffe losses were compiled from contemporary documents, principally the *Genst.Gen.Qu.6.Abt.(Ic)* returns and the *Namentliche Verlustmeldungen* of the individual units concerned. I am grateful to the staffs of the Deutsche Dienststelle WASt in Berlin and the Volksbund Deutche Kriegsgräberfürsorge, Kassel, for making this information available. Jim Perry provided a copy of his transcription of original German loss tables to cross-check against my own interpretation of details extracted from often murky microfilms while German fighter claims and losses were ably covered by the superb works of Jochen Prien.

Perversely, RAF records of the campaign in France are fragmentary in nature, those of the Air Component of the BEF famously so for, as one official account puts it, 'what survives . . . is entirely inadequate as a basis for an accurate account, and the historian in search of fuller documentary material . . . is regretfully referred to an indeterminate spot at the bottom of Boulogne harbour'. Reflecting the intense pressure under which most units were forced to operate during the rapid German advance, many squadron Operations Record Books are devoid of all detail for the crucial month of May 1940 or contain retrospectively compiled details taken from individual log-books, personal memories, or whatever sources were to hand. What survives was consulted at the National Archives at Kew, the *RAF Narrative of the Campaign in France* proving an excellent source for the daily accounts included in this work.

Never one to accept previously published works as a sole source, I trawled the records at Kew cross-referencing data from the Commonwealth War Graves Commission and other agencies. Any discrepancies revealed reflect the inherent difficulties of casualty reporting, difficulties that are perpetuated even in the modern conflicts of today, and all such apparent discrepancies are highlighted in the text.

I next compared my findings against those of other authors and was concerned to find that Brian Cull's exhaustive work on the subject contained far more detail of RAF aircraft losses, specifically aircraft serial numbers, than I was able to substantiate from examination of the available records. Clearly, I was ignoring a valuable source or, I reasoned, he had gained access to records of which I was unaware. For his patience in attempting to answer my rather pointed questions on the subject, I am grateful to him. He was also most generous in allowing me access to his correspondence files assembled during preparation of his own work.

From these, I concluded that the serial numbers originated with the late Heinrich Weiss, a fact confirmed when his archive later came into the possession of Larry Hickey. Thus, it transpires that many of the RAF serials as quoted by Cull come from Weiss' analysis of James Halley's work on the subject which, in the absence of any other source, is a legitimate device but a crude instrument prone to error. Further compounding any such errors, most of the serials are duplicated in Norman Franks' work on Fighter Command losses. Thus, my own loss lists will be found to be at odds with previously published accounts when I have evidence to the contrary, otherwise I have accepted others' findings in good faith though with reservation.

The difficulties in analysing the records of five independent air forces, written in four different languages, and across three separate time zones, introduced a certain level of complexity. Nor was I particularly well prepared for the fact that Diedenhofen and Thionville were one and the same place, as are Doornik and Tournai — the list is endless. Even differentiating between towns with similar or identical names posed an additional challenge.

Finally, sincere thanks to my wife Ann who supported me throughout, kept me firmly grounded when I was in imminent danger of going orbital, who helped me find my way out of some very dark places, and plucked me from the troughs of despond usually occasioned by the unwelcome machinations of Bill Gates and his cohorts. She has her husband back again.

PETER D. CORNWELL, FEBRUARY 2008

David Orton, son of Newell, and Judy Pickard, the sister of 'Cobber', at the dedication of a memorial plaque to the squadron at their old base in France at Rouvres on May 8, 2003.

Kain is buried in Choloy War Cemetery, where lie so many of the airmen killed in the Battle of France, and Orton is commemorated on the Runnymede Memorial.

The Phoney War

BY PILOT OFFICER EDWARD HALL, AFC

Just 21 years after the Royal Air Force left France at the end of the Great War, as it was then called, the RAF returned to defend the country against Germany once again. Here RAF officers lay a wreath at the most sacred shrine in France — the Tomb of the Unknown Soldier at the Arc de Triomphe in Paris.

Late September 1939 I was stacking away secret files in the Registry department of Adastral House. As an ex-officer, RFC and RAF, of the 1914-1918 war, I had secured — in my need, and apparently that of my country — a post as temporary clerk in the employ of the Air Ministry, when I was informed by a fellow clerk that I was wanted upon the telephone.

I wondered a little who could want me, until a somewhat blasé voice reminded me of my having made application in the previous May to be included in the Volunteer Officers' Reserve. As a result, I was commissioned in RAFVR as and from 19th September, and was to proceed overseas at once. Would I please report to so-and-so at Air Ministry, King Charles Street, for instructions!

And that was that — just that and no more. A 'dug-out' of the last war, superimposed upon a 'throw-out' of the Depression years, and, on top of it all, a period of 20 years as a thoroughly domesticated civilian to get out of my system, and forthwith. And what about my wife and three youngsters? Even if the Air Ministry hadn't time to consider their immediate reactions, or their future without me, I should have urgent occasion so to do.

Overseas too — and where was that likely to be? And suddenly I discovered that I was a most important man — almost in the first range of VIPs, in fact. Could I, would I, be ready to leave at once — for France! No, I couldn't; what about kit and uniform, for instance? Could I get through these formalities, say, in about three days? Yes, I thought perhaps I might. Right ho! You will leave by air from Hendon immediately thereafter.

And at 7 a.m., on the first day of October, 1939, goodbyes were wryly said upon a suburban platform; and in due course an RAF tender picked me up at Waterloo Station, and deposited me at Hendon before 8 o'clock. Here I found a few planes scattered around, but no sign of any particular activity — certainly none so far as I was concerned.

I approached a group of 'other ranks' at work in a hangar with all the diffidence and deference of a conscious ignoramus. Yes, a plane was going to France, but not before 10 a.m. Thereupon I wandered disconsolately about the huge, echoing, almost empty hangars, avoiding anything I saw which possessed rank braid wider than mine. I ventured into the palatial Officers' Mess, suffered a while the haughty stares of a small, high-ranking group who obviously resented

my intrusion, and shortly afterwards a Mess waiter promptly whisked me out of the only available unoccupied rooms.

Ten o'clock — and still no sign of life upon the 'drome — but, as I turned the corner of a depressing office block, I encountered an officer, displaying two gold rank-braids upon his great coat. I saluted — my one useful legacy from the last war — and desired to be informed, Sir, whether an aircraft was leaving for France? My salute created reciprocal embarrassment but the man was at least human, and could actually afford some information. A plane was leaving at 11 o'clock; and he would be piloting it. Accordingly, at 11 o'clock we met again beside a De Havilland Rapide, where yet more embarrassment awaited me. Was it absolutely necessary to wear that contraption and how did one get into it? More mystified than ever (I was sporting 'wings' and a row of medal ribbons), the grand object of the gold braid buckled the parachute around me, and, in a very short time, the Rapide was in the air. I was off, upon the great adventure into the unknown — very unknown — for, beyond a hint that I was to liaise between two fighter squadrons stationed vaguely in the north of France, that was all I had been permitted to know at this stage.

We touched down in a driving rain squall at Shoreham, and there some doubt was expressed as to the advisability of carrying on any farther for that day — doubts which were fully justified when, tentatively half-way across the Channel, we turned back, in low scud, almost at deck level. Over dinner later, the air was cleared somewhat. I admitted that I was somewhat of a fraud, and that it would be advisable to ignore any ribbons I was wearing — or at least to treat them for the anachronism they were; and, on his part, the pilot referred to the incident of the salute, and put me wise to the uniform of Western Airways, admittedly rather a barefaced copy of that of the RAF!

Over the Channel next morning, and in brilliant sunshine, we had it absolutely to ourselves. There was not even a surface craft to be seen. At Amiens, of course, I was unknown, unexpected, unwanted; but I had suspected that this sort of situation might possibly arise, and I proceeded to obtain a lift to the nearest Air Headquarters, where my case was broached and investigated at some hours' length.

And so, noon passed, the shadows lengthened, and I wished that I was back among the file racks of Secret Registry when, at long last, in rushed a diminutive officer wearing muddied flying boots, his hair blown awry, and carrying in his hand a flying helmet. Was I ready? Was I ready! A Magister (not that I knew its nomenclature) was revving slowly in a field close by, and I was once more adjusted into a parachute, my shame and embarrassment all the more

keen as I noticed that the officer had no fewer than two-and-a-half rank braids — and of the right colour, too! And either he was mad because of me, or just mad by nature, for we hedge-hopped the whole 50 miles or so to our destination — just to prove the alertness of the gun crews en route, as he subsequently informed me. And, certainly, the business-like manner in which one or two machineguns were trained on us, somewhat though in our rear, testified to the fact that this particular 'Maggy' was not unknown on this route. It was, perhaps, fortunate too that the war was really as 'phoney' then as much later it was designated and that probably none of the guns was loaded. With a magnificent surge upwards, followed by a significant feint-attack upon some unfortunates squatting cosily in a gun-pit on the edge of a large field in which were grounded a few fighter planes, we came to earth. 'Thanks very much for a most enjoyable trip', I idiotically muttered, and was at once chilled into silence by a malevolent glare which boded equally ill for the ground-gunners.

And now I realised whence the mud upon his flying boots must have come, as I walked, politely and diffidently, in the rear of this gentleman. Spaced along a minor country road, and separated from it by a much battered hedge, was a group of tents, settling down into the mud. My uncomfortably new black service shoes slithered, slipped, and gathered cold wet douches, as we approached a tent of somewhat larger proportions than the rest, and in which, before an untidily littered trestle-table,

was sitting a square-jawed, burly type, in all the anonymity of a huge white sweater, his rank not obvious, but his importance very much so. I was introduced . . . this officer had reported at Air Headquarters, Amiens, and, it was believed, in some connection with No. 1 Squadron.

Some connection indeed! And the supercilious emphasis upon the vagueness of my mission! However, the reception I was now accorded was relatively kind, and I proceeded to tell as much of myself as I judged would meet present circumstances and at once the CO (by name Halahan) grasped the situation — another 'dud' body to provide for and yet another Air Ministry bungle to straighten out. Meanwhile, I could take a look in at the Operations Tent and perhaps pick up the idea — I might conceivably be useful there.

I saluted smartly, picked up my hat (which the tent flap had promptly and spitefully removed) and wandered in search of the Ops Tent. Five minutes of the atmosphere of that place convinced me of my desperate situation. Those plotting charts; that huge board, a thing of queer squares and hieroglyphics; and, above all, those abominable field telephones — no, I could never face it. And everybody seemed so busy and so efficient, and so desperately polite and forebearing. I made my way to the Mess Tent, and sat there on a wooden form gloomily planning ahead. I had it all to myself, thank God, and my plans quickly matured. It was all a ghastly mistake and my job was probably still open at the Air Ministry.

The triumphal arch marks Napoleon's victories a century before; the tomb remembers the sacrifice of a generation of Frenchmen in the trenches of 1914-1918. Our comparison was taken at the Place de l'Etoile — the 'Square of the Star' — in April 2006.

In from the beginning was No. 73 Squadron. Here, the Adjutant Pilot Officer Edward 'Henry' Hall, is given a rousing welcome. 'Fanny' Orton leads the procession along the road leading to the aerodrome. According to the story which Henry told in the 73 Squadron Mess, he was awarded the Air Force Cross in the First World War for bombing an English lifeboat in June 1918! Before the war broke out he worked at the Air Ministry in London until he was recalled to the colours in October 1939.

Suddenly there was a noise of planes landing and, almost on top of this, a flood of the queerest objects swarmed into the tent, in all stages of undress — or so it appeared to me, who still thought that the modern aeroplane, spick and span, called for Number One dress uniform, and no less. Sweaters of all colours, torn trousers (some of grey flannel, too); scarves of silk and wool; and an occasional hat which looked as if it had been recently passed through the laundry in error. Pilots! My presence however in no way deterred them though some curious glances were cast in my direction. At last one of them came forward, introduced himself, and asked what I would have to drink. Alas, I had to confess that I did not drink but not so the others. There was a concerted shout for 'shampers' but not until the Mess Orderly responded had I the slightest idea what 'shampers' could mean. My astonishment upon seeing a case of champagne brought in, and the irregular removal of the corks of several bottles therefrom (apparently upon the scale of one bottle per pilot), was coupled with my embarrassment at being the only officer present without a glass of sorts in front of him. Port, if I remembered rightly, had been our significant drink in the last war — dare I order

one? Some good angel whispered 'no', definitely 'no', and I started on the downhill track with a foaming tankard of beer.

Immediately I was among friends. At last I had struck the right note. Obviously I must forget that I had been in a rut for so many years. I had another

The squadron moved from Norrent-Fontes to Rouvres on October 9, and it was from this airfield, 20 kilometres east of Verdun, that they fought the battle in France. Although it is difficult to be absolutely certain, this is the most likely spot where the picture was taken. The airfield lies on higher ground and they are coming down the old road to the village where the Officers' Mess was situated. (See map page 22.)

October 1939 . . . June 1940. In less than nine months the Battle of France was over, and 415 airmen of the Royal Air Force lay in graves across northern France or the tangled wreckage of their aircraft, together with hundreds of their counterparts from the air forces of France, Belgium and Holland. On May 10 Hitler launched his Blitzkreig attack in the West and in less than six weeks the battle had been lost and German troops had marched triumphantly into Paris.

beer, and learned more about the RAF in general during the next quarter of an hour or so, and of No. 1 Squadron in particular, than six months upon hot cocoa would ever have taught me.

Two beers had rendered me a little unsteady upon my feet but that was as nothing to the effect of a bottle of champagne on one or two others present. So this was the Royal Air Force? The noise and the tumult subsided, the Mess Tent thinned out, and I became too obvious once again. 'Oh, Hall' (no longer Mr, I noticed), 'we can't fix you up here tonight, so go down to Aire-sur-Lys for the night, and report back here at 9 o'clock tomorrow morning, and we'll see what we can do for you.'

A tender was just upon the point of leaving and I managed to clamber in, despite the overflow of junior officers, released from duty, and bent upon some nocturnal expedition, the details and possibilities of which were vociferously canvassed by the hilarious crowd. It was good to be among the juniors — I almost wished I was joining them, wherever they were going, but in due course they dropped me off in the 'black-out' of Aire-sur-Lys. It was still only 9 p.m. but the place was dead, and it was only after repeated hammerings upon a hotel door that a nightcap protruded from an upper window. Shortly afterwards I was ushered into a morgue of a bedroom, hung with hideously striped draperies, carpetless, and furnished with the bare necessaries in the way of furniture, including a kidney-shaped affair at the foot of the bed, the use of which I but vaguely divined. A monstrous crimson affair upon the bed was presumably the French notion of a quilt. As for breakfast the following morning, my request for bacon and eggs was firmly negatived in favour of coffee and rolls. Apparently I still had a deuce of a lot to learn.

At 9 o'clock, the RAF tender arrived and picked me up. I was due to report at that hour up at the camp, five miles distant! Whatever would they say? They said nothing — or rather, they told me to wander around for a bit. This 'wandering around' was getting to be the giddy limit. Was there a war on, or not? And what about the mud? Did it never occur to them that I was ill-equipped for 'wandering around'? And, as I could never be sufficiently distant from the Ops Tent, I edged round the huge field, towards what appeared to be the tented camp of a sister-squadron, of which I had heard somewhat last evening — No. 73, so they had said.

It was a fateful walk, for my career with No. 1 ended within a quarter of an hour of my tentatively reporting to the OC, No. 73 — an immense, beefy-faced, hoarse-voiced fellow, with a quite disarming smile, calculated to offset his rather abrupt manner and somewhat disconcertingly direct approach. Sartorially he was even more independent than any specimen of the RAF in the field that I had yet seen. His golf jacket exposed a knitted blue jersey, a scarf was loosely knotted round his thick neck, and his hefty size 10s were planted decisively upon his office table, as he elicited from me some indication of my plight, and the more important fact of my acquaintance with office routine. His hand flew to the field-telephone. 'Halahan? Oh, Knox here. This chap Hall — I'm bagging him as Adjutant. Any objections? No! Right!' And down went the receiver.

My fate was sealed. I was — or shortly would be — Adjutant to the first fighter squadron in the field; the squadron which was to make history, long before the actual war started; the squadron which would shortly be headline, front-page news, and the resort of Press correspondents from all over the world, but Germany; the squadron in which Flying Officer 'Cobber' Kain was a mere unit at present; the squadron, one of an inadequate allotment of four which would eventually pit themselves against the massed might of the German Air Force, and prove the Hurricane a match for anything that the Germans could produce, and incidentally pave the way for the successes of the Battle of Britain. *The* squadron, in fact! '73'! And I was to be its Adjutant! A job at long last — a *real* job.

Meanwhile it was a pretty browned-off squadron. Where was this confounded war, anyhow — why didn't it start?

Sheltered underneath the arch, the eternal flame at the Tomb of the Unknown Soldier burns on today as a memorial to a nation's losses in two world wars.

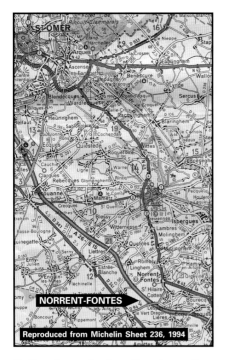

Reproduced from Michelin Sheet 236, 1994

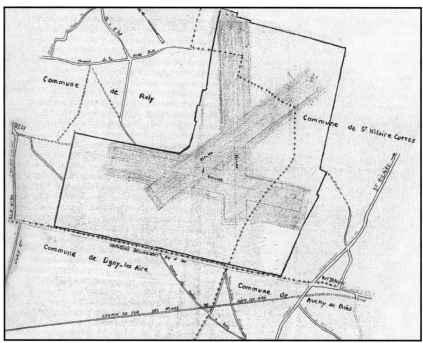

As the storm clouds gathered over Europe, it was recognised that with expanded air forces — on both sides of the Channel — more aerodromes and landing grounds would be required.

One such was Norrent-Fontes, 20 kilometres south of St Omer in the Pas de Calais, the land being requisitioned in January 1937. This plan was preserved by the mayor, Laurent Videlenne.

Norrent-Fontes

No. 73 Fighter Squadron had arrived, by air and sea, at Le Havre, in the course of the third week of September 1939, and, following a brief stay there (where its display of aerobatics had given the French an unbounded confidence in the RAF), it joined No. 1 Squadron further north, at the improvised aerodrome of Norrent Fontes, near Lille. Dull little villages, almost as lacking in taste in the expression of their domestic architecture, as in the hideous wrought iron tributes to their dead in the untidy graveyards, were scattered about slightly undulating countryside; and here and there, the headgear of a colliery indicated proximity to the more densely populated industrial areas around Lille.

No. 73 was separated from No. 1 by the breadth only of the flying field. Just down the country road which bordered its particular portion of it lay the hamlet of Rely, utterly destitute of anything in the way of diversion for either officer or 'other ranks'. The countryside was almost featureless, save in the peculiarity of its vast, undulating surface. Granted that the move was in the right direction geographically speaking, so far as possible business was concerned, Rely was a complete and utter bind, and every endeavour was made to escape to Lille, or other likely places, on off-duty hours — which tended more and more to be confused with duty hours, circumstances continuing to obtain of no hint of offensive action from the enemy.

The squadron flew the Hurricane, and though the pilots swore by it as the world's best, the fact that some of them were of the wooden 'prop' variety (as yet, no sign of the variable-pitch propel-

lor, of course) must have inspired many an unexpressed doubt when the latest development in the Me 109, or the possibilities of that unknown quantity, the Me 110 fighter-bomber, came under discussion. However, the pilots were there to do a job of work, and one for which they had been specially trained; and, come what may, they would get every ounce out of their machines. Let the enemy come; the sooner the better.

The squadron was led by a CO whose cure for a champagne headache was to graze — almost — the steeple of the local church with his wing tip, and who had positively exhausted all the possible aerobatics inherent in a Hurricane, and with Flight Commanders of the calibre respectively of Flight Lieutenant Lovett of 'A' Flight and Scouler of 'B', what might not the squadron achieve? Lovett, indeed, had not only flown the hush-hush Spitfire, but at night too, suitable to the secrecy still surrounding it; and there was hardly a pilot who could not turn his machine almost inside out, should the occasion demand it.

There they stood, the machines for the job — but where were the Me 109s and 110s? 'Come on, chaps, let's have a case of shampers; and who's for the highlights of Lille tonight?' And then the stentorian voice of Squadron Leader Knox would be heard booming across the camp, desiring the immediate presence of either his batman, or his Adjutant. The latter was a pilot acting by rotation in that capacity, but after about one week's intermittent and light-hearted juggling with figures and 'returns', he thrust the whole job upon me, never once to recur to the subject.

'Pissy' Paul was a red-headed (or rather, auburn) type, his hair naturally wavy, the crowning glory over what might by some be considered a hand-

some face, if one could ignore the slight blemish of a broken nose, tending somewhat to the appearance of a collegiate bruiser. An excellent pilot, he had performed the office work as and when he found time, or as and when Knox held an Orderly Room. At such times, 'Pissy' would bring along his writing pad, and also the Officers' Mess bar accounts, for which he was also responsible, and which certainly occasioned him far more concern than his more official appointment, he being directly responsible to Knox for this particular and unofficial 'return'. There pressed nevertheless, the recurrent problem of a certain official and statistical return — Form 765C — which seemed to be in rather a poorish way. How did one prepare it for Air Ministry? Petrol consumption, for instance — how did one arrive at that? 'Oh, ask one of the flight sergeants next time he is around.' And how about hours flown by pilots? 'Oh, multiply the numbers of gallons consumed by about eight; that's near enough for the Air Ministry. What the hell, anyhow; come and have a drink. Corporal Walker, the Orderly Room 'king', knows all about that sort of tripe; he'll keep you right.'

There was also the Official Record Book, or Squadron War Diary, Form 540 — the completest bind that ever was, or so I was informed. Who cared about the history of a squadron, which was like any other squadron, especially in lack of opportunity to do anything worth writing home about? Well, perhaps I, fresh from civilian life, and with some occasional experience in historical research, might be permitted to think otherwise, especially as being likely to see more of the game than those participating in it. And perhaps the shrewd CO had sensed this possibility when sizing up the relative values of an absolute ignoramus in all service matters. He had made his local decision without reference to Air Ministry, autocratically substituting me in the place of a valuable pilot and one who could now devote all his time to the main job, whilst I picked up the hang of the purely routine job of admin. And in the event he was justified, for Air Ministry had apparently forgotten about their projected liaison officer, and were forming No. 67 Wing to perform that particular task.

Meanwhile, there was little to do, and nothing operationally stirring; indeed, spare-time jobs had been created for the more junior of the pilots. 'Claudie' Wright (of distinctly lugubrious countenance, and whose father was of some consequence in the hierarchy of the RAF) was the Maps 'king', for instance; and 'Dickie' Martin, a recent posting to the squadron, a chubby-faced youngster, with an impish look which did not belie his character or subsequent record, kept various 'returns' not strictly proper to the Adjutant's job — as yet! And there was 'Tommy' Tucker, who was MT officer, was a privileged odd-jobber, provided he kept out of the way of Squadron Leader Knox and inevitable trouble. 'Tommy' was a man with a grievance. Aged 28, or thereabouts, and consequently senior in respect of age to the rest of the pilots, he was inclined to assert seniority and superiority on another but more debatable score; for was he not a pilot of standing — a 'week-end pilot', cer-

tainly, but one of several years' experience? And had he not been received, not to say swindled into the regular RAF, and with open arms by a Government eager to rope in all the material they could after the muck-up of Munich? Why should he remain a mere pilot officer, just like the bulk of the others? It was a shame, and he would redden round the rims where lurked just the suspicion of a tear, too. Poor 'Tommy' — not in the first class of pilots at any time; still, he did his stuff over London and the Channel a year later, and still bears the scars of a brush with the enemy.

There were not enough odd jobs to go round; but there was always one's Hurricane, and one's own pet servicing-crew, either to humour, or to tick off, just as occasion demanded. Jealousy, laudable jealousy, was rife in the squadron. Each crew claimed the best machine and though perhaps there may exist private doubts in the matter, they were never expressed when lauding the superiority of one's particular pilot. As for No. 1 Squadron over the way — well, they had the ill-luck to arrive a trifle later in France and, though the material, both officer and man, was undeniably good, well, there was no arguing — you simply couldn't beat good old 73, first everywhere, every time. Even the Class 'E' reservists, called back in August last, were imbued with laudable enthusiasm and keenness, eager to see the effects of their rather rusted

mechanical and technical knowledge translated into terms of blazing 'Jerries' falling all around, as undoubtedly must and would happen. The Hurricane had a 'punch' and one fine day, not far distant, those leading-edges would each show four circular holes, in place of the four virgin panels behind which at present lay concealed the Browning guns. God, what a punch — for somebody. Four of them per wing — eight guns in all!

From CO downwards, to the very batman I shared temporarily with Knox, I sensed this spirit, and it gripped me; but alas I was an interloper, a rank outsider, and how dared I hope to be assimilated, to be accepted, as one of 73. These youngsters, these keen pilots, slouching around, lolling against the rough-hewn bar in the Mess Marquee. They had trained together, 'binged' together, lived as one for months, shared the sporting side of the station life, courted the same girls. They spoke nostalgically of 'Butch', a dog, and tenderly, intimately, of a certain 'Beetle', and with possessive pride too. Who, or what, was this 'Beetle'? Another pedigree liver-spaniel, or what? It turned out that 'Beetle' was 'Bill' Kain's baby!

I retired to the privacy and obscurity of my tent more and more during the first few difficult days. How could I intrude, how could I hope possibly to fit in — I who but a week or so ago was a mere 'temporary' clerk at the Air Ministry, and was now masquerading under

Pilot Officer Hall claims that his squadron — No. 73 — was the first to go to France but records show that they were pipped to the post by No. 1 Squadron which arrived one day earlier at Le Havre. Nevertheless the tables were turned when No. 73 arrived first at Norrent-Fontes which was a staging post for both Hurricane Squadrons (see table pages 16-17). Here the commanding officer, Squadron Leader Brian 'Red' Knox in the greatcoat, takes stock of the squadron's 'wine cellar' with 'Cobber' Kain, glass in hand, at his rear; 'Claude' Wright on the extreme left, and 'Pissy' Paul behind the bar.

(I hoped not too palpably obvious) false colours. There was that pestiferous row of medal ribbons — it would be a 'crime' to take them down; it was a crime certainly to wear them. Everybody, almost, called me 'Sir' and though I was the elder by nearly ten years than the most senior member of the squadron — the CO — I knew that the tribute, so unsolicited and unwanted, was not to my age. The situation was ridiculous, for it was quite 20 years since I had piloted a plane. But if I could not be one of them, surely the distance could be bridged, in part, somehow. What in short was the matter with *me* — for obviously there lay the difficulty.

The drink issue paved the way. For a week I refused all proffers of drink. Why should I, after all these years? War should strengthen, not weaken one's character and I felt more than a little concerned when I saw 'Dickie' Martin, a little elevated after much whisky, go a purler over his camp bed with consequent damage to both himself and the bed. (I also saw him a little later emerge from an interview with Squadron Leader Knox; he would have been tenderly touching his posteriors but a year or two ago; this time there was nothing of that sort, but he was nevertheless distinctly hurt.) I was disturbed; was the war going to be won this way? The CO could take his drink in apparently unlimited quantities, his raucous voice soaring above everything and everyone but a look from him would be sufficient hint to any officer to lay off the booze at once. Do as I say, not as I do, in fact! Rarely did any officer get beyond the boisterously merry stage whilst in camp. Knox saw to that, all right. There was, too, the effect upon, or even the example to be shown No. 1 Squadron to be considered; where, despite my experience of the other afternoon, a pretty tight hand was reputed to be kept upon the younger pilots.

Gradually it dawned upon me that drink was not responsible for the 'bonhomie', the irrepressible cheerfulness, of the squadron. For instance, round about 9.30 a.m. I would hear a roar of laughter, and would look out of my tent flap. The 'Doc' had risen! There he was, taking the not too early air, yawning and stretching before his tent, and inadequately clad in a very short shirt. There was little preventable illness in the squadron; he saw to that all right, so a blind eye was turned upon this aspect of an indolent, but likeable nature. His genius was expressed in improvisation, and a subtle sense of the pulse of the squadron. His fat face would light up with a genial smile, whether it was officer or man for his attention; and he never grudged the use of his lumbering ambulance, indifferently either for a camouflaged trip to Lille, or for the conveyance of vegetables from a nearby farm. And you were sure to trip over a tame rabbit, or discover yourself, in decency, bound to sacrifice part of the milk from your morning coffee, if you did as the privileged did, take it in his Sick Quarters. Obviously, if there was anything to be alarmed about in his 'shampers' business, he was the proper

Pilot Officer 'Smooth' Holliday led the advance ground party to Norrent-Fontes (above) on September 26. Two days later the main body arrived and the aircraft flew in, everyone being put up under canvas around the 'drome. No. 1 Squadron arrived to join them on the 29th. Both squadrons then alternated at five minutes' readiness status, Air Vice-Marshal Charles Blount, the AOC-in-C of the British Expeditionary Force's Air Component, visiting the station on October 5. By then a move was being planned, not only to a new base 150 miles further east to Etain-Rouvres, but also a transfer to the Advanced Air Striking Force (AASF).

judge; and I watched him a little more carefully, and saw him give patient attention to a long tale of woe from 'Tommy' Tucker, meanwhile drawing that officer still farther and farther away from the Mess, towards his own tent.

On the other hand, he turned his attentions to me, of all persons. 'Have a drink, Hall, old boy.' 'No thanks "Doc" — awfully good of you, but I don't drink.' 'I don't blame you. Bring Mr Hall a beer — it *is* beer you prefer, isn't it? Not this 15 franc per bottle 'shampers' muck?' Curious eyes were turned upon both of us; and the CO, who had been consistently kind, but a little distant the last day or two, was not uninterested in the issue of this experiment in psychoanalysis. A cheer went up as the beer went down; obviously it was only a case of temporary suspension of good habits, and the type *was* decent after all.

The ice was broken, and I began to spend less and less time in my tent, and more in the mobile Orderly Room and the Mess. It would take a few more weeks (a little longer still in the case of 'Cobber' Kain) to do the trick; the day would arrive when it would no longer be 'Mr Hall', but 'Henry' Hall — or just 'Henry'. And, to anticipate a little, away flew yet one more pre-war prejudice with this re-christening; for, on my arrival at the squadron, I had quickly discovered that one of its composite virtues was not a love of high-brow music; and as the wireless could not be on all day, and as anyhow Henry Hall's dance band was not playing continu-

ously, its members had recourse to portable, and very wheezy gramophones, for the ubiquitous indulgence of their taste in dance music and the art of the 'crooner'. In particular, Squadron Leader Knox — whose taste, fortunately for the squadron, was apparently on a level with that of the latest joined (excluding myself) — had particular favourites; about four of them and he could, and did, suffer their repetition almost endlessly, whilst he, with a group of his pilots, would hang around the improvised bar. No matter how engrossed the party would be in the subject under discussion: No. 1 Squadron . . . the chances of contact with a roving Me . . . or the lost and dubious joys of Le Havre . . . the calculated omission would be detected, and a stentorian voice would roar out for 'J'attendrai' or 'Boom'.

What cannot be cured must usually be endured; nevertheless it was fairly obvious to the officers of '73' that Pilot Officer Hall might be cured of yet one more fanciful civilian fad. I was forthwith shepherded carefully into the net, and politely encouraged to state my views upon music. They were prepared to be decent in the matter. I should be granted a concession; there would be one portion of the day set apart on the wireless for my own particular diversion. Henry Hall had his hour; Pilot Officer Hall should have his half-hour. Yes, in future, it should be established as an institution — 'Henry' Hall's half-hour. A shade of something must have passed over my face, at finding myself thus bracketed with my *bête noire* in the world of music. It did not escape them; and though 'Henry' Hall's half-hour gradually, but inevitably, dwindled down to almost nothing. 'Henry' Hall as a soubriquet remained.

There was just one more link to bind me irrevocably to the 'boys'. It was Form 540, the official Squadron Diary. Historical research had been my passion (and escape from history unpleasantly in the making) for many years. I realised that the present lull was pregnant with signs and portents, perhaps insignificant at the time, which if not jotted down at once, and with relation to the squadron as a whole, might prove to be a valuable unit record lost; maybe, and remotely, even an officially sponsored history might prove the poorer for the omission. The job had been thrust upon me; it was part of the Adjutant's work, I was assured by the jubilant Paul, who did not trouble to confess that he was no writer — *that* was palpably evident. But was I competent to tackle a job bristling with such situations, and with technicalities of which I must forever remain chronically ignorant? I was aware of my limitations; but if I could not be *of* '73', perhaps I might yet capture and record the spirit of it in its minutiae, its work, its play, its personalities, its aims and achievements; and precise instructions existed as to the compiling of this record, sufficient in themselves to deter any but myself or an officer of some years standing and experience from undertaking the job.

I closed, firmly and finally, A.P.1301, (in which were embodied the Instructions), and, saying nothing to anybody as to my intention, I commenced upon a blank Form 540. Casually drifting into the office, one, and then another officer would cast a half-interested eye upon the daily record. 'Wrong there, aren't you, old chap — shouldn't it be so and so?' Then, one day the CO became mildly curious, and decided to exercise a long self-suspended right of 'vetting the record'. He had no comments to make, and from then on, the Air Ministry could have whistled for its lost liaison officer; and somewhat derogatory and doubtless ill-founded remarks upon the maintenance of F.540 by a certain other squadron reflected his satisfaction at the turn of events. No. 1 was all right in its way, but ! And so I became indispensable to 73 Squadron.

Nearly four years later, I heard semi-officially that the War Diary of 73 Squadron had proved useful in compiling a record of the Campaign in France, for the Official History. With such material, and with such folk, how could it have proved otherwise? Alas, of that frolic crowd who figured therein so often, and so much to their eternal credit, there were now few left. 'Reg' Lovett — his face and hands bearing terrible traces of burning consequent upon his being shot down in France, and later denied a sporting chance by the German Air Force as he descended, helpless in his parachute, during the early stages of the Battle of Britain. 'Fanny' Orton — 'missing', once again, but this time finally, after having already once shed his blood in, and for France. 'Claudie' Wright — hideous dent in his face, after an encounter with an Me, but nothing daunted, in due course continued his operations in England, until he too was posted as 'missing'. 'Wee' Brotchie — killed as a result of a taxying accident in England; his pal, 'Pete' Walker — killed in South Africa, as a result of a flying accident. 'Tubs' Perry — killed in France during the 'phoney war', as a result of a forced-landing following upon successful combat with the enemy. 'Cobber' Kain — alas that it should have to be recorded that *he* too was written off as a result of a flying accident — avoidable in his case, and at the height of his fame. Even the fat, genial 'Doc' himself, wary of having more than one foot off the ground at any one time — killed in a transport aircraft crash, out in distant Sicily in 1944.

And of the original sergeant pilots — what a list! Perry and Winn, the first to go, saddening our first Christmas in France, as also that of their relatives in England. Pyne and Dibden, casualties in the real battle of France. Pilkington — lost in a 'sweep' over enemy-occupied France, just over a year following our quitting its shores. Campbell, shot down by the Germans during the 'phoney war'; and shot down again by them a year or so later — and, this time, retained by them as prisoner until the end of the war. Humphris — shot down during the Blitz of May, and nearly sacrificed a leg in consequence of the wounds he had suffered.

Yes, both 'phoney' and 'real' war took toll of '73' — for, however 'phoney' one aspect of the far-flung war might appear to those upon the ground (or in other branches of the services, and particularly to those at home), events were soon to prove that, as far as concerned Nos. 1 and 73 Fighter Squadrons, the war had already commenced — their own private and very individual war.

'Henry' Hall's hand-written caption to this photo identifies both ground and aircrew: L-R: Bailey, Phillips, Healey, Pilkington (missing in action September 20, 1941), Campbell, Tucker, Sewell (missing March 19, 1944) and Pyne (killed May 14, 1940).

AIR COMPONENT (BEF)

September 1939 — May 1940

AOC-in-C: Air Vice Marshal C. H. B. Blount

HQ No.22 Group Farnborough to Laval then Le Mans 15.9.1939; to Maroeuil 2.10.1939

50 (ARMY CO-OP) WING
HQ Odiham to Athies 24.9.1939

4 SQUADRON
Lysander IIs (TV)

Odiham to Mons-en-Chaussée 2.10.1939
to Monchy-Lagache 3.10.1939

13 SQUADRON
Lysander IIs (OO)

Odiham to Mons-en-Chaussée 2.10.1939

53 SQUADRON
Blenheim IVs (PZ)

Odiham to Plivot 18.9.1939
to Poix 11.10.1939
transferred to 52 Wing 1.11.1939

51 (ARMY CO-OP) WING
HQ Andover to Abbeville 3.10.1939; to Dieppe (by 1.5.40)

2 SQUADRON
Lysander I & IIs (KO)

Hawkinge to Abbeville-Drucat 6.10.1939

26 SQUADRON
Lysander IIs (RM)

Catterick to Abbeville-Drucat 8.10.1939
to Dieppe (by 1.5.1940)

59 SQUADRON
Blenheim IVs (TR)

Andover to Poix 11.10.1939
transferred to 52 Wing 1.11.1939

52 (RECCE) WING
HQ at Maison Givord, Poix
to Château Courcelles 28.1.1940

53 SQUADRON
Blenheim IVs (PZ)

From 50 Wing 1.11.1939
Poix

59 SQUADRON
Blenheim IVs (TR)

From 51 Wing 1.11.1939
Poix

60 (FIGHTER) WING
Servicing Unit formed Debden 30.8.1939
HQ Allonville 5.9.1939
later 14 (FIGHTER) GROUP
HQ Achicourt from 20.1.1940

1 SQUADRON
Hurricane Is (JX)

Tangmere to Le Havre-Octeville 8.9.1939
to Norrent Fontes 29.9.1939
detached to AASF 9.10.1939

73 SQUADRON
Hurricane Is (TP)

Digby to Le Havre-Octeville 9.9.1939
to Caen 10.9.1939
return Le Havre-Octeville 11.9.1939
to Norrent Fontes 28.9.1939
detached to AASF 9.10.1939

60 (FIGHTER) WING
(Second formation)
HQ Lille-Seclin from 20.1.1940; to Amiens-Glisy 10.4.1940;
return Lille-Seclin 26.4.1940

85 SQUADRON
Hurricane Is (VY)

Debden to Rouen-Boos 9.9.1939
to Merville 29.9.1939
(detached flight at Norrent-Fontes)
to Lille-Seclin 5.11.1939
(flights at Le Touquet & St Inglevert)
to Mons-en-Chaussée 10.4.1940
to Lille-Seclin 26.4.1940

87 SQUADRON
Hurricane Is (LK)

Debden to Rouen-Boos 9.9.1939
to Merville 29.9.1939
(detached flight at Norrent-Fontes)
to Lille-Seclin 5.11.1939
(flights at Le Touquet & St Inglevert)
to Le Touquet 22.2.1940
return Lille-Seclin 9.3.1940
to Amiens-Glisy 10.4.1940
to Lille-Seclin 3.5.1940
(operating from Senon)

61 (FIGHTER) WING
Servicing Unit formed Hendon 23.9.1939
HQ to Nantes 4.10.1939
to Norrent-Fontes 9.10.1939
to Merville 4.11.1939
to Vitry-en-Artois 13.12.1939
to Abbeville 12.4.1940

607 SQUADRON
Gladiator I & IIs (AF)

to re-equip with
Hurricanes

Croydon to Merville 15.11.1939
to Vitry-en-Artois 13.12.1939
(detached flight at St Inglevert)
to Abbeville 12.4.1940
return Vitry-en-Artois 26.4.1940

615 SQUADRON
Gladiator I & IIs (KW)

to re-equip with
Hurricanes

Croydon to Merville 15.11.1939
to Vitry-en-Artois 13.12.1939
(detached flight at St Inglevert)
B Flight remain St Inglevert,
A Flight to Poix 12.4.1939
to Abbeville 27.4.1940
(A Flight detached to Le Touquet)

62 (FIGHTER) WING
(to receive two Hurricane squadrons)
Servicing Unit formed Hendon 13.10.1939
HQ to Rouen Boos 27.10.1939
to St Hilaire-le-Grand 25.3.1940

63 (FIGHTER) WING
(to receive two Hurricane squadrons)
Servicing Unit formed 1.1940
HQ to Lille-Seclin 3.1940

70 (BOMBER) WING
HQ Upper Heyford to Roye-Amy 30.9.1939

18 SQUADRON
Blenheim Is (WV)
Blenheim IVs (WV)
from 2.1940

Upper Heyford to Roye-Amy 30.9.1939
to Beauvraignes 30.9.1939
to Méharicourt 16.10.1939

57 SQUADRON
Blenheim Is (DX)
Blenheim IVs (DX)
from 2.1940

Upper Heyford to Roye-Amy 30.9.1939
to Rosières-en-Santerre 18.10.1939

Also under Air Component command:

16 (ARMY CO-OP) SQUADRON
Lysander IIs (UG)

Hawkinge to Bertangles
16.4.1940

**81 (COMMS)
SQUADRON**
Tiger Moths

Andover to Laval 17.9.1939
to Amiens-Mountjoie 1.10.1939

Karel Margry's comparison was taken from the upstairs window of Place de L'Eglise No. 6 (during the war Nos 15 and 18). The village has been almost untouched by the passage of time . . . but that was not always the case.

The laws regulating convoy distance hardly troubled us; and as for the law of the speed of the slowest vehicle, there did not seem to be any vehicle incapable of maintaining a steady average of 30 m.p.h. It was, indeed, an excruciating experience to find oneself in the relatively lordly 'tourer', subjected to the ordeal of endeavouring to pass the lumbering Orderly Room trailer whose alarming bouncings and lurchings might conceivably have served to instill a little more caution into our driver, a temporarily 'grounded' pilot. Cook-house, crane, petrol-bowser, each and all simply romped along the long highways and narrow winding village roads; and we in the staff car did our 70-plus, more than

once, halting occasionally to take potshots with a revolver at tame pheasants on the roadside, in default of the more legal, bit as yet invisible, German target.

If every village was impressively alive, turning temporarily from its avocations upon our passage through its midst, the towns seemed smitten with a sudden blight. Sedan especially was already brooding over impending doom; and it was an eerie experience to pass through that already partially-evacuated city, its tall houses shuttered up, its echoing streets deserted, save by stray cats and gendarmerie. Another prognostication of doom was the recurrent spectacle of long trains of horse-drawn munition wagons, and limbers of

forage and baggage; after working our way past so many of them, one had an uncanny feeling that one was back in the 1870s, and that Sedan was indeed the appropriate destination of these outmoded survivals from a bitter past. Poor blighters! The sight of a mechanised column passing along their roads must have astonished and excited others besides the French. The Germans had eyes, too; and the time was to come when, with a gesture of contempt, the temporarily absent enemy would reverse our direction, and we, now the van of British might, would have urgent occasion, if not always the opportunity, to maintain our present cool 30 mph! As it was, apparently unobserved, on this occasion we performed our long journey unmolested, and with every assistance from our enthusiastic Allies.

Three weeks after war broke out in Europe in 1914, Rouvres was entered by the I. Battalion of Infanterie-Regiment 130 during their battle against French forces in the Bois de Tilly north of the town of Etain, five kilometres further west. In the course of the attack on August 24, German troops opened fire on the inhabitants of the village who were trying to escape the fighting. Of the 56 killed, 13 were children. Rouvres was then put to the torch, completely destroying it. After the war when the people returned, the whole village was rebuilt from scratch, having been designed by one architect, Joseph Hornecker, which explains why most of the houses and public buildings — save for the church, school and Mairie — are of the same harmonious design with identical architectural features. This is the memorial to the 1914 massacre in which a total of 86 people died including 30 refugees from surrounding hamlets.

Verdun — a name which was synonymous with its bitter struggle for survival in 1916. *Left:* The Victory Monument was unveiled in 1929 and the Statue of Victory *(right)* by Rodin in 1939 but the latter has since been moved to another location.

We passed through historic Verdun in the late afternoon of a warm October day, the leaves yellowing on the ornamental trees or littering the broad pavements before the stark, staring stone monuments to this or that local folly, or almost forgotten tragedy of some few years back. And the deeper we penetrated into France, so curiously the more did I feel that I was coming into my own; that lone Corot in a provincial art gallery had somehow prepared me for this. I felt strangely akin; strange, that it has needed a war upon a European scale to bring me into my patrimony. Oh, that I could slip away for an hour or so, and steep myself in the beauty of that lovely secluded courtyard, or walk pensively along that avenue of evenly-spaced and carefully-dressed trees, down towards the château beside that strip of lake; or even be permitted to sip my French wine at a quiet table in a shaded corner of one of these roadside cafés! But I was the

Adjutant of a British fighter squadron; and we were accelerating once again, endeavouring to catch up with the mobile cookhouse, in order to tick off the driver of that shambling vehicle for prejudicing the chances of our next roadside meal.

There was a steady climb beyond the city of Verdun, over a range of shell-pocked hills, and with the burnt-out shells of barrack blocks on either side — far more realistic as war memorials than any stiff, staring *poilu* in perdurable stone just behind us. And suddenly, there, below and ahead of us, stretched a vast plain, dotted here and there with minor forests, black and solid in the distance — the countryside of Rouvres, our stepping stone to Germany, our dwelling place-to-be for the next seven months. It was as if that high maze of suffering, haunted hills that we had just surmounted was the dividing line between a France, beauti-

ful, bounteous, welcoming, hopeful, and a boundary or buffer state, would-be neutral or just simply apathetic, where not actively or passively pro-German! And the new rawness of resurrected villages, each with its pathetically absurd war memorial, to remind both it and us of the futility of all this. Here and there, we passed war cemeteries; some grand and imposing, showplaces for religious or political pilgrimage; others with a formal boundary of funereal trees surrounding a small paddock, where black German crossed declared the rigorously demarcated. And towering high above the charnel-house of one battlefield, that tremendous showpiece of Douamont, as fine a landmark in daytime for recce planes as any that could be devised. Indeed, the whole countryside seemed to breathe and exhale war, past and future, as the sun sank, obscuring Rouvres in a murk of blood-red haze. '73 had arrived!

The epitome of French sacrifice — the Ossuary at Douamont contains the remains of over 130,000 French and German dead.

The advance party had had its work cut out to provide accommodation out of the limitations of Rouvres. The 'Doc' fared best, as the guest of the local *Curé*; the CO, not so well off, in the house of a vinegarish widow, who never even trusted him with a door key, and frequently contrived to show her independence (and perhaps pro-German sympathies), by locking the door both on herself and him, when she went forth visiting, or shopping at the single retail store that the place boasted. Rouvres had been almost completely rebuilt after the last war, and always with strict attention to utilitarian dictates — the dictates of the peasant farmers. If any single peasant farmer of Rouvres was rich, his property certainly did not exhibit striking evidences of the fact; if he was poor, his cow was housed under the same roof as his family; an inconvenience perhaps less intolerable than the burden of children, as yet not qualifying in age to save him the expense of hired labour.

And in one such household, I found myself billeted. As I entered the door, I at once encountered in the narrow, bleak passage, a stench of penned cow, with a subtle commingling of unwashed humanity, sweated from dawn to dark. An apprehensive, prematurely-aged woman, and a silent man, her husband, were standing respectfully at the base of the stairway leading to my upper room. With a final half-hearted appeal from the woman, brusquely rejected by the French billeting official, acting in liaison with us, I was ushered into my room, where I was, though never so unwelcome, to be therefrom treated as an honoured guest. All that was evident of excruciatingly bad taste, but lovingly treasured as representative of hours and hours of arduous labour spent in the acquisition thereof, was assembled in that cheerless front bedchamber. Antimacassars; mean strips of carpet on a highly polished floor; a walnut wardrobe (locked); mirrors, draped with hanging lace and crocheted whatnots; an odd chair or two of forbidding rigidity; a night-commode; but above all, and the absolute apple of the woman's eye — the bed, *their* bed, crowned with an enormous red, silk-covered quilt, as the final convincing touch. I sensed, rather than observed, the combined emotions of fear and pride. What did the Englishman think of this? Would he respect the proprieties, or would he come in drunk, and abuse her confidence? Ah, these cruel wars! Once again — and not a hundred yards up the road was the monument, upon which the name of her own uncle figures — shot outside the village by the Germans in 1914! And now, after a hard struggle — and just when Simone was of an age to draw unwelcome attention upon her personable self, war had once again brought the threat of trouble over the village, and maybe into her home.

But war is war, and the inconveniences were not totally one-sided in this matter. Yes, the accommodation would, must suit all right. Meantime, I had a job to do; and, if only to take a long breath of air not impregnated with cow, I made my way down towards what appeared to be the centre of the village, the hub of our present and future activities. Here I found a small, triangular, sloping patch of green, at the head of which stood the *Mairie*, the only substantial building boasting any architectural pretension in the place — with the possible exception of the quite ugly modern church successor to the medieval relic which had failed to survive the last war. This gesture on the village green had doubtless cost the village dear; and doubtless its insistent bell still conjured the sous out of the pockets of the faithful, until, overruling all objections to the contrary by the *Curé*, we imposed a curfew upon it, and thrust upon it the office of improvised air raid alarm. And not even the threat of excommunication by the *Curé* could move Squadron Leader Knox upon this point — no bell, unless used as a raid alarm; and, *per contra*, if no bell, then, no hot water for the MO, billeted upon the *Curé*. *C'est la guerre!*

'As for the men, those who were in luck were also dispersed about the village . . .'
Henry Hall, Adjutant.

The right wing of the ground floor of the *Mairie* had been taken over as the Officers' Mess, the other wing having been permitted to continue functioning as the mixed school for the village children, so that one sometimes approached the Mess through a crowd of noisy kiddies of both sexes, the boys quite unselfconsciously attired in black pinafore overalls. The large room which was ours was totally devoid of furniture, and its only wall decoration was a framed Croix de Guerre, with its accompanying certificate, dusty, and hanging so high as to render quite undecipherable the panegyrics upon the brave Rouvrians of the last generation.

The mobile Orderly Room had arrived miraculously intact, and was now pitched upon the triangular green outside; and the assorted transport was housed in various open spaces about the village. As for the men, those who were in luck were also dispersed about the village, billeted on equal terms with the officers; those who were not so fortunate spent hours nailing the sides of discarded petrol tins over gaps in roofs, and across rat holes in floors, or set about the erection of make-shift screens, contrived out of hessian and wood battens; for already the night mists were creeping up from the water meadows, and some of the older men would soon complain of bitter cold in their draughty lofts and barns. There was only one alternative — tents! They had come from a first-class RAF Station, Digby, where everything had been 'laid on' for them, down to the detailed and very ample diet sheet, issued weekly in advance. And now — this perishing hole, where they were shoved away in lofts over cow byres, and fed in a stinking village hall, which had apparently never been cleaned out since it was built. And of amenities, or opportunities for recreation, what were there? North, south, east or west, just undulating, uninteresting countryside, dotted by lousy villages, with offensive refuse heaps rotting outside every house door. In due course, a 'liberty-wagon' was provided, in order to take small parties of the men to Verdun, or occasionally even to Metz; but this was the merest sop in the ocean of their initial discontent. For initial it fortunately proved to be.

'73' was more than a mere number to those boys. Certainly they had good reason to deplore their present lot but were they not members of a squadron which had been selected for the honour of a situation bang under the very nose of the enemy? They were 'priority number one'. If there was to be a war, who would stand the first chance of a crack at (or by) the enemy — '73' obviously! Who had the finest bunch of pilots — '73'! Who had the reputation for operational efficiency, second to none, solely (though this was frequently hotly contested by the MT section) made possible by the ground crews — why, '73'! Come on lads, let's push off down to the dining hall; beer 2d a glass — weak French muck, but better than nowt. Let's Roll out the Barrel; this so-and-so place gets you down.'

But it didn't, as was obvious during the exercise of our unsolicited, and frequently abused responsibility of letter-censoring. Here was *their* opportunity, and the airmen rose magnificently to it. Reference to much of their activities, for security reasons was necessarily forbidden them, so they got down to their individual grouses. To all appearances, '73' was in a pretty bad way — for about the first month; then, a tour of inspection of the quarters of the men revealed more hopeful indications, in instances, of the positive ingenuity with which they were adapting themselves to adverse circumstances. The gaping roofs were neatly lined with glittering silver sides of discarded 4-gallon petrol tins; packing cases had been adapted to the display of the private abundance of their owners; forbidden packs of cards were in evidence; musical instruments, and photographs of wives, sweethearts, and children appeared over almost every bed; or alternatively, and as a counter to all this respectability, there was an assorted array of the female body divine, and almost unadorned,

which, in the course of a tour of inspection of the billets, exacted something approximating an exercise in dispassionate survey.

The aerodrome was not particularly ideal, being possessed of treacherous hollows, but it was open on all sides, with the exception of one dense line of forest on the far side. Quickly an Ops Room was excavated, sandbagged and camouflaged. Camouflaged tents also sprung up, for the accommodation of stores; and Category 1 repairs were necessarily performed in the open, with the assistance of a static lorry and a mobile crane. The aircraft were of course carefully dispersed, and the unluckiest of the pilots might have a mile to walk (or run) to his machine. Defence posts sprang up, on the perimeter of the huge field, a batch of 'brassed-off' gunners, volunteers from England having joined us; and a system of 'stand-by flights' was initiated, OC Flights being accorded a large measure of individual responsibility, consistent with the CO's arrogation of final authority and responsibility.

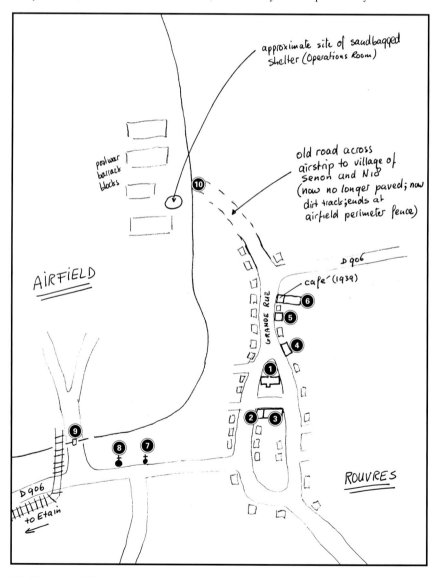

[1] Church. [2] Mairie (first Officers' Mess). [3] School. [4] Kain's billet. [5] Second Officers' Mess (No. 22). [6] Dining Hall (No. 26). [7] Memorial to 1914 massacre. [8] Village war memorial with plaque to No. 73 Squadron. [9] Present main gate to airfield. [10] Entrance to aerodrome in 1939.

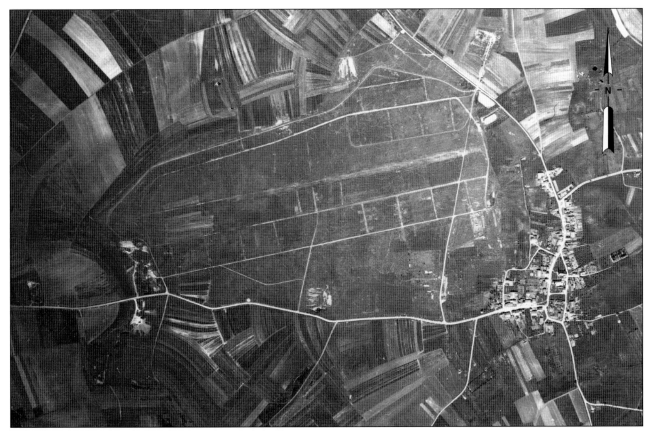

The aerodrome at Rouvres has been totally altered since the days that No. 73 were there. Still retaining its wartime appearance, this photograph was taken in 1951 with the direction of landing and take off running more or less east-west.

As for the countryside, that was one vast football field, suggesting that 'Roovers' *could* be made something of, and accordingly was. Nothing was overlooked as a possible source of distraction; the first signs of apprehension in the inhabitants at this sudden invasion of their village were quickly dispelled and the half-dozen or so passable females quickly disposed of parental objections and fears, or openly rebelled, as the Don Juans of '73' proceeded to become the envy of the less enterprising of their comrades. Those of the men who were billeted in houses were soon spouting pidgin French, playing with the children, or even helping to milk the cows; and in the long upper room which stretched above our Mess, where the irrepressible MT section was housed, the sound of revelry by night, frequently drowned that of the room below — no mean feat, with 'champers' still at 15 francs a bottle, and beer at an even more fantastically absurd figure — beer which was possessed of no particular potency, and only left one waterlogged, after ten or fifteen glasses of it. Long after the toil-worn villagers had retired for the night, and presumably the MT section up above were muttering in their dreams of home, a group of officers would be sitting at the improvised bar in the Mess, and anything up to 50 bottles, empty, would be neatly lined up, as we chatted away; and then, in would come the redoubtable Knox, rather 'fresh' from some expedition out either Verdun or Nancy way; and, with a characteristic sweep of the board with his arms, crash would go a dozen or so of the bottles, as he squared his huge bulk onto a high stool, and, with elbows planted on the sloppy American oil-

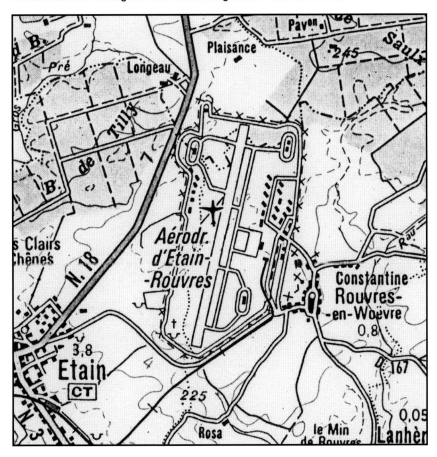

Security prevented us from obtaining a modern aerial photo as this is now a front-line base of the l'Armée de l'Air but the map shows how the present day runway has been completely realigned on a north-south axis.

23

Squadron Leader Brian 'Red' Knox, the dynamic head of No. 73 Squadron.

cloth, he would proceed to emphasise his points with a beer bottle, scarifying all and sundry. Then there would be a slight rumble overhead, and a few moments later he would descend the staircase leading from the MT billet, with a fist full of franc notes and silver — he had just put a summary conclusion to illegal gambling!

That was Knox — hardly a thing escaped his notice, whether at work or at play. Officer, NCO or other rank, hardly one of them escaped the lash of his tongue, or failed to quake at a glance from his stony, bloodshot eyes. His very bulk implied menace. He would bear down on some slacker, as if he were about to use violence; a few incisive, cutting remarks however, usually sufficed. And woe betide the inefficient NCO or mechanic who was responsible for the slightest defect or omission in an aircraft — particularly his own. Woe betide the Housey-housey 'king', too, if he suddenly formed the habit of remitting unaccountably large sums of money home. Woe betide any officer who let down the side. And above all — and for this the squadron could forgive him much — woe betide outside interference or criticism, from the AOC-in-C downwards. As visitors, all were welcome; but *he* was OC 73 Squadron, and there, responsibility to all intents and purposes began and ended. Be it a fracas in some low French village, or a scathing report upon the condition of a

Knox's deputy was Flight Lieutenant Reg Lovett, seen here examining a glass: is it half-full or half-empty! Flying Officer Orton, Pilot Officers 'Tommy' Tucker and 'Dickie' Martin are on the right, Pilot Officer George Brotchie left front with 'Doc' Outfin in the golf jacket.

The squadron dining room was located on the ground floor of the Mairie.

billet, submitted by a chance-visiting officer from HQ Rheims, he went at the unfortunates like a bull, risking all — and he lost all in the end — in defence of his 'boys' and of his prerogative. For a time, all 'liberties' would be stopped, and extra duties would be imposed upon all concerned in the fracas; and as regards the condition of the billets, it was whispered that, following upon one of Knox's surprise tours of inspection, two of the men had shown undeniable signs of fainting under the pressure of his presence and tongue. Notwithstanding, there was to come a day when the AOC-in-C himself would arrive specially, upon a visit to this amazing squadron — which had by then become known all over the world, by repute, if not by number; but by that time, Knox had gone, under a cloud, and a transient CO was there to reap the praise.

Meantime, the preliminaries were in process of being effected, and Knox was, par excellence, *the* man for the job, as he had been presumed to be when accorded the envied command. Certainly he was aggressive, self-opinionated, ruthless, bloody-minded, and impatient or intolerant of weaklings or sensitive types; but the squadron was in the process of being turned into a fighting force, with himself as the positive embodiment in the flesh of what a fighter indicated. He put the fear of God into the squadron, whilst on the ground; he divided the squadron into those who hoped for the best, and those who hoped for the worst, when he took to the air, and performed the most hair-raising stunts, over, almost through, the village. Farmers would give up their interminable field work for the time being, prepared for the fact that their horses would shortly attempt to career madly over the furrows, as the twisting, tortured machine hurtled towards them, or a burst of machine-gun fire sent spurts of ploughed earth into the air. He

knew, too, that there was approximately ten feet of clearance on either side of a Hurricane's wings, provided by the gap between the church steeple and the tower of the *Mairie*; and women (and men too) would cross themselves, as the roar of the engine grew louder, and suddenly, from below the level of the surrounding ring of houses, the green-grey object would rise slightly, and in a brief flash, would be visible from the windows of the Mess, as it zoomed away for a repetition of the feat.

The exercise cured his headache, but it gave another to many of the onlookers. Almost in an ecstacy of pride, whatever their grievances following upon their last contact with him, the men

would cease work — men who had grown up with the Hurricanes and their pilots. They would not have swapped such a man for any one of the lesser breed of decent, kindly, understanding COs — not them.

And Knox would get out of his machine, roar for his mechanic, and either tell him he was a bloody good type, or wither him with a look, an accusing finger pointed directly at the defect he had discovered during the gruelling test he had just given to the machine. Then he would roar for his personal driver, and proceed — no one knew whether; it might be for the night, it might be for the day following; or even the one after that. He had a deputy, and a most efficient deputy, in 'A' Flight commander, 'Reg' Lovett. He had also at last a full-time Adjutant. He, Knox, had set the wheels going, and he felt it due, both to himself and the squadron, to leave the latter to its own devices now and then.

It was a subtle, rather too subtle, piece of casuistry; for, unfortunately, there existed certain folk who did *not* regard '73' as being the personal property of Squadron Leader Knox, and who would icily suggest that he might include HQ Rheims in his next unofficial tour of inspection of the countryside; that is, if he still had a 'tourer' intact, after smashing two already in the course of his mad career. A lesser man would have been broken earlier in the game; but it was perhaps realised that it was not so much a man they were up against, as a force, that embodied the spirit of '73'. In an uncanny, unconstitutional sort of way, he had performed a miracle. Feared, admired, cursed (under the breath), there was not a member of the squadron but would have acknowledged the absolute identity of the man with the squadron, and of the absolute necessity (or so it appeared) of maintaining this paradoxical state of affairs.

Today the room has reverted to the Council Chamber but still with the original table. Note the aerial photo of the airfield on the far wall.

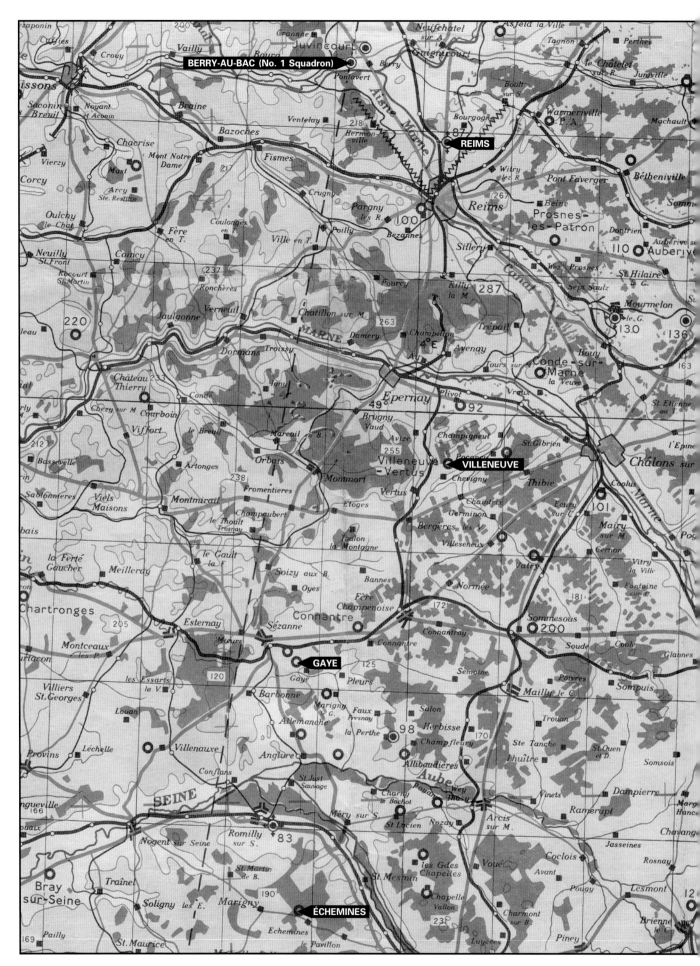

Extract from 1:500,000 Air Map published by the War Office in 1940 showing the myriad of aerodromes in this corner of France.

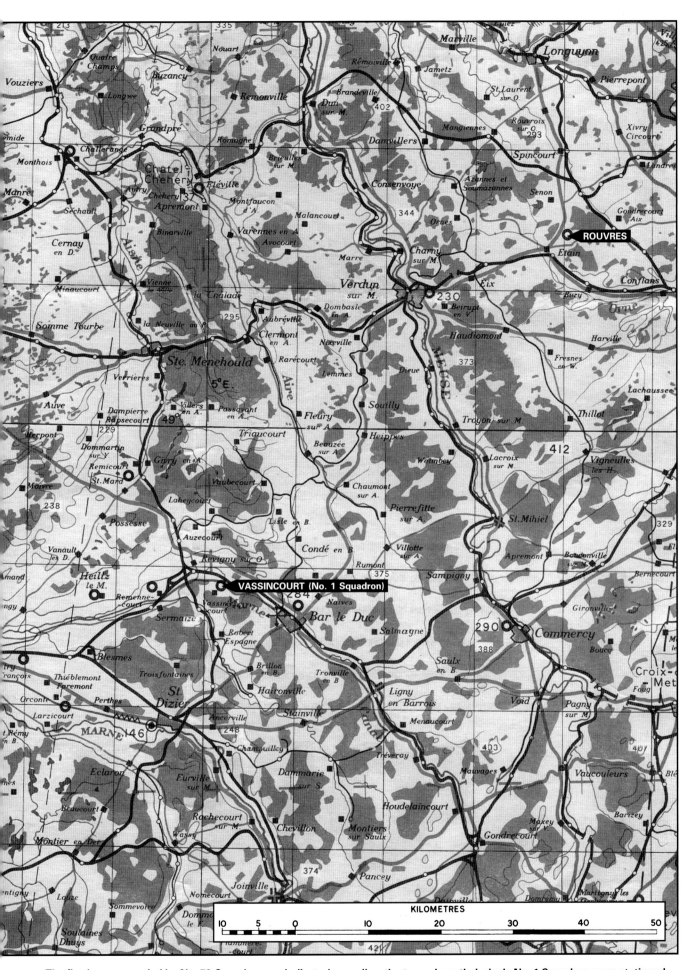

The five bases occupied by No. 73 Squadron are indicated as well as the two where their rivals No. 1 Squadron were stationed.

Due to a series of misfortunes, Flight Lieutenant Reg Lovett, the 'A' Flight commander, acquired the nick-name 'Unlucky'. On May 10, 1940, when the Battle of France began in earnest, he was shot down and badly burned on his face and hands. After weeks of treatment for his injuries in the UK, he rejoined No. 73 Squadron, then based at Church Fenton. On September 5 the squadron was posted south to Debden but within hours Ray had been shot down over Burnham, escaping by parachute. Then, two days later, he met his tragic end in combat over Essex.

'Reg' Lovett, OC 'A' Flight, was perhaps a fair match for Knox. He had quit a boring desk in a shipping office in order to take up the RAF as a career, and had required a considerable and varied flying experience whilst painstakingly mastering every detail of his duties as Flight Commander. Under a somewhat stiff and reserved manner, there existed a kindly, conscientious, though perhaps somewhat puritanical and inhabited individual. He had little sense of humour; was ambitious, and insistent on his prerogatives (one of which was the wearing of breeches and gaiters); exact, meticulous, and scrupulously fair in all his dealings, whether with officer or man. Provided they pulled their fair weight in the flight, very well — and if they didn't, his attitude towards them quickly brought them to a sense of duty, if nothing else. No one worked harder; and he could, and did, assume responsibility and control of the squadron, at a moment's notice. Characteristically, he neither shelved nor avoided admin work, and it was a refreshing change to find a CO (acting) who would pay a daily visit to his office, and there confer with the Adjutant upon current matters. 'Secret' files were confidently in their proper trays, and not heaped up in a pile at the end of the Officers' Mess bar, or permanently lost sight of in the CO's. billet. I had made my first contact with Lovett, at Rouvres itself, in his capacity of OC Advance party; and though for a considerable time he treated me as somewhat of an 'outsider', at last we became true and tried friends; but he could never unbend sufficiently to call me 'Henry', like the others, compromising always with 'Heinrich'.

'Ian' Scoular, of 'B' Flight, was the absolute opposite of Lovett, in almost every aspect; with him, however, he maintained the best of relations, whether on or off-duty, 'Ian' was a bit of an enigma; one never quite knew whether he was being either serious, or sarcastic; and he could be deucedly temperamental and moody. But it was in a quiet, unassuming way that he knit his flight together as one. He apparently had no particular ambition beyond his flight, and avoided direct responsibility outside it; but he would come out with amazingly practical ideas and suggestions, of considerable benefit to the squadron as a whole. He had, too, an uncanny sway over his men — trouble in the canteen simmered off when *he* appeared upon the scene. And he would devise lectures, illustrated by models of planes, or introduce a welcome scheme into Welfare. In the air, 'Reg' Lovett lost his calculating precision and reticence; a positive madness overtook him, and he would take desperate chances, leading his section (and woe betide the straggler or faint-heart) into the very heart of battle. But 'Ian' in the air was 'Ian' of the ground; cool as a cucumber, he took his measure of the odds, and though his score mounted slowly, it was deadly sure; and invariably he returned unscathed from action.

The officer next senior in rank under the CO was Flight Lieutenant 'Robin' Press, the Armaments Officer; he was non-operational now so far as flying was concerned, and with a somewhat crooked walk as a legacy of a bad crash in former operational days. An engaging personality, conversable upon literary topics, and happily in possession of a range of gramophone records, rigidly exclusive of jazz and the 'crooner'. He was the antithesis of Knox in almost every phase of his individuality — which inevitably led to clashes both inside and outside the Mess; and, in one such, I found myself rather unpleasantly involved. There had been a brush in the air with the enemy, and the results, owing to the enemy's numerical superiority (and one other regrettable factor upon the occasion), ought in theory to have proved bloodily disastrous for us. 'Cobber' had certainly shot off all his ammunition, but the reliable sergeant pilot with whom he was operating returned with his own ammo intact, and a complaint that there had been no response to his pressure upon the control button. This was serious, and Knox went into the matter with his customary thoroughness and ruthlessness. 'Robin' apparently had established, to his own satisfaction, that the guns of this particular aircraft *should* have functioned; and at once there arose the question of — yes, cowardice

The 'B' Flight commander was Flight Lieutenant John 'Ian' Scoular, credited with 3½ kills while serving with the squadron. He maintained an unofficial diary of squadron activities until he returned to the UK on June 7, 1940. In 1941 he was posted to command No. 250 Squadron in the Middle East. Ian Scoular survived the war and died in the 1980s.

Sergeant Basil 'Titch' Pyne watches the armourers reloading the guns of his early fixed-pitch Hurricane. Pyne was shot down in combat near Voncq, 11 kilometres north of Vouziers, and killed on May 14, 1940.

on the part of a pilot, in the face of the enemy' and, in the course of a little 'shop' being talked in the Mess that night, I, off the record, unfortunately touched upon this possible contingency.

Knox at once took me up. Was that my own impression, or had I got it from another source? I demurred, for I realised that the CO was upon the war path, and a coveted scalp was in the offing. 'Come on, out with it — Press, eh?' 'Well, sir, what other solution could be arrived at, in face of the result of his own personal examination of the guns' 'Get the Armament Officer on the phone, and ask him what the hell he means by casting such an aspersion upon one of my sergeant pilots.' With black mutiny in my heart, I went to the 'phone'. Press there? Oh, the CO wants to see you'. I had hardly replaced the receiver, when Knox dashed up to me in one of his towering rages. 'That was not what I told you to say. When I give an order, please obey it to the letter.'

I walked out of the Mess. Later that evening, the phone bell tinkled in my billet. That you, 'Henry'? Look here, you behaved a little childishly over the Press affair this evening, didn't you? It has all been cleared up, to everybody's satisfaction.' And then there was silence while he awaited my response. I was feeling very sore; I had nearly involved an officer and a sergeant pilot in a very nasty 'jam'; on the other hand, the CO had placed me in an invidious position, and subsequently publicly admonished me. Yet, here he was, subsequently admonished me. Yet, here he was, upon the verge of apologising to me — Knox, actually apologising!

'Henry, I am sorry if I hurt your feelings in the Mess tonight.' 'Thanks, sir', had been the churlish response.

And now, should I proceed with the application for a posting back to Home Establishment? Knox had apologised, had done an unprecedented thing; still, I felt unequal to this sort of thing, and perhaps it would be better for all concerned if I went. Yes, it should stand; and next morning, still feeling that I was in the right of it, I placed my application in the letter-rack, for Knox's attention. Two days later, I removed it; and only

then, over the bar, did Knox advert with a wicked wink, to a certain letter which had been 'overlooked' by him, in the letter-rack! Thereafter I credited my CO with a little more perception of character than in my own petty arrogance I had heretofore been prepared to accord him. And at least one good resulted from this storm in a tea-cup, for relations between the CO and his Armaments Officer noticeably improved. The latter's departure, on posting to Home Establishment in early spring of 1940, left a decided gap in the squadron.

Rouvres airfield — now the base of the 3ème Régiment d'Hélicoptères de Combat (3 RHC) — has changed out of all recognition and only the spire of the village church remains as a reference point.

It was quite a coincidence that there were two pilots on the squadron with the same name and both from New Zealand although not related. *Left:* Derek 'Bill' Kain and *(right)* Edgar 'Cobber' Kain. As we shall see, 'Cobber' lost his life in tragic circumstances in June 1940 but not before the British Press had hailed him as the hero of the batttle. By the time he died his score was ten confirmed kills.

There were two officers by the name of Kain in '73' and, by a curious coincidence, though in no way related, both hailed from Christchurch, New Zealand. First, 'Bill' Kain; and anything one might say of 'Bill' (his Christian name was Derek, by the way), must be subject to reservations and qualifications; for though he was the untidiest, slovenliest, most lackadaisical officer in the whole squadron, there were curious contradictions in his make-up and character, which took time to register and to assess in one's mind. I first met him under rather exciting circumstances, back at Rely. All the officers were talking of some absent officer familiarly referred to as 'Bill', and who had acquired the distinction of being the squadron's first casualty in action — French action! For the AA of our ally had recently shot him down into the sea, off Le Havre. He was now on his way back to the squadron; and in due course there was a howl of derisive laughter as a tall, angular, dishevelled figure appeared in the entrance to the Mess tent. He had nothing to tell (he never had, as I found later, to my infinite annoyance and impatience whilst acting as Intelligence-Officer-cum-Adjutant). 'Bill' on this occasion was immediately, but vainly plied with questions. He lolled — he always did — against anything handy, whether a tent pole or the bar, and accepted drinks.

Then he spotted me, hovering upon the perimeter of the mortified and envious group. He must have heard of my arrival, for he approached, sprang to attention (after a fashion), and punctiliously addressing me as 'Sir', extended his hand. It was an attention I could well have dispensed with; but not so with what obviously lay beneath the gesture. Coupled with dancing black eyes and a fascinatingly cracked and drawling speech, he had a heart of pure gold, and

a perception which penetrated at least *my* crying need; and I owe him a deep debt of gratitude for the manner in which he promptly assumed responsibility for my welfare, and gradually, by his example, broke down the reserve of the others — his pals, every one of them. As for the men, they idolised him, inevitably. The CO of course could not treat him as a responsible person, and had to adopt other and less forthright methods than those he usually adopted in connection with his other officers. And 'Bill' achieved the grade in his own way, and by methods not to be despised, but equally not to be copied; for only he could get away with.

And the other Kain — 'Cobber' Kain — what of him? My reception by him was rather intimidating, not to say unpromising. He, too, lolled around the place; but there, any resemblance between the two New Zealanders ended. Someone had had the pre-science, in Debden and Digby days, to prognosticate a startling future for this particular Dominions' pilot. And if those in authority had not noticed the fact, he could have assured them of its inherent possibility. For 'Cobber' had never hidden his light beneath the proverbial bushel (a snap is in existence of him, taken way back in 1938, bearing for caption, 'Cobber shoots a line'; and he was determined to get on; but unfortunately, being individual to the core, this fact somewhat militated against success as a prospective Flight Commander; and a tendency to put up 'blacks' on occasion was no recommendation either.

Perhaps no offence was intended in the fact of his so patently avoiding me at the outset. Was it because of that pestiferous row of ribbons, which both fascinated and repelled, by turns? Still not 21, he was a magnificent specimen of manhood, though traces of callow

youth, (which might by some be mistaken for stupidity, or even provincial boorishness) remained on his face; but that aggressive chin, that thick, loose, protruding lower lip — what did this combination indicate or portend? And the half-closed eyes, through which he superciliously sized one up! Here was the complete egotist and extrovert, obviously determined to override all obstacles. What *he* liked, what *he* wanted, *he* would have, and the others could either like it, or go to hell. Drink certainly discovered a weakness; he could not 'take it,' and he soon became silly-drunk but he was not unaware of this particular weakness, and he indulged only upon proper occasions, and usually in quantities just not sufficient to betray his Achilles' heel.

And if *he* did not know where to draw the line, Knox did; and it was with somewhat of a shamefaced air that 'Cobber' tendered his apologies — and a purloined hat-stand, the latter unlawfully abstracted property of the local host of some overnight's binge. Coming events, we are assured, cast their shadows before them; but at this stage, at any rate, he was by no means hail-fellow-well-met; and his modesty and reticence over his forthcoming early successes would be perfectly genuine and unassumed. 'Cobber' was a pilot, first and foremost, and ambitious as such. The RAF was his chosen career, to take up which he had come from the antipodes. He and his machine were going to prove themselves; make no mistake of that. 'Line-shoot Cobber, eh!' His chance — his great chance had arrived. And the arrival of a permanent Adjutant affected him only in so much as he would not have to perform his tour of duty in that menial capacity, and to the detriment of his duty by his aircraft.

Flying Officer Newell 'Fanny' Orton, awarded the Distinguished Flying Cross in May 1940 with ten confirmed kills equalling the victories of 'Cobber' as the squadron's top scorers. In July 1941, Squadron Leader Orton was appointed CO of No. 54 Squadron based at Hornchurch with Spitfires and it was on September 17 that year that he failed to return from a sweep over northern France. 'Fanny' is now commemorated on the Runnymede Memorial (Panel 28).

Of the other senior officer pilots there remained 'Fanny' Orton and 'Tubs' Perry for consideration — both since dead and the world demonstrably the poorer in consequence. 'Fanny' was temperamental, emotional, but this did not prevent his being a first-class pilot, contesting first place with 'Cobber' as the squadron's first 'ace'. Indeed, there were some who inclined to place him one ahead of 'Cobber'. A disciplinarian, fully respected and admired by his crew, he was unfortunately subject to startling and disturbing temperamental displays upon the slightest provocation. After a scene in the Mess one night, I stumbled over a prostrate body in the darkness of the road outside; it was 'Fanny', his home mail scattered around him in the mud, sobbing his heart out! There was not a more handsome fellow in the squadron; his 'Odol smile' would have made a small fortune for the discerning exploiter of it, could they but have overcome his detestation of them and their like. It was hinted that he was inclined to be a trifle 'near'; but the truth was that he could never balance his finances — which was inconvenient, as we all borrowed off one another when our only source of income — field pay — withered away towards the end of the month. Notwithstanding, there remained the fact of his undoubted all-around popularity, on general grounds. Well-bred, well-educated, and with the domestic background at home of a happy wife and child, he accepted this tribute naturally, and with no affectation of superiority. Time would show what grit and determination lay beneath a suspected instability of character.

What can one say about 'Tubs' Perry? One recalls a night in March, 1940, when the Adjutant, surrounded by empty beer bottles, was writing furiously in the *'UNOFFICIAL' SQUAD-RON DIARY*, upon the beer-soddened bar top. He *had* to write fast; but nothing would come from his pen which would satisfy the urge. How *could* he hope to do justice, whether drunk or sober, to the memory of that blithe spirit, whose six-foot body now stark, on a slab in a distant French mortuary?

Only a day or so back, after his first shared victory over a German plane, 'Tubs' had confided that he had been afraid of, and for, himself; but now — and it was exquisitely typical of the man — he felt that he was 'gaining confidence'. Gaining confidence! Ye Gods — would the Germans graduate their approach in battle to the measure of 'Tub's' improving self-confidence! And I silently prayed that either 'Cobber' or 'Fanny' would be around to shepherd this lovable specimen through the period of his probation, and perhaps beyond. He was 'Cobber's chum — so much so, that I once saw them fight out a difference in the Mess; but, for me, he reserved something far more precious than the knock-about associations and the raw intimacies of a fighter pilots' Mess. He was 21 — half of my then age; but he knew what I knew — that I was a fraud among them. I had no need to tell him that I had been in a rut for a long long time — ever since the last war, in fact! But now I had said goodbye to all that. Hitler had spoken, putting a decisive period to my bitter share of the Depression, and had now whisked me back into this second generation of flyers, into a dream-world beyond my most fantastic dreams. Hating war, yet I found it the portal to a new world; one far removed from that of bitter, and apparently unavailing struggle against the odds of civilian life.

Everybody sought the friendship of 'Tubs'. He was as near a butt in the Mess as any man could well approach, and yet not quite be. His follies were proverbial, and his good nature tripped him up continually. If he ever ceased to wreathe his face with that infectious smile of his, it must have been in his sleep. Women are born to be loved by the other sex; 'Tubs' Perry was loved by both sexes, all his short life; and one man, at least, cast himself upon his bed, and wept scalding tears over that untimely death.

The genial 'Tubs' Perry, possibly the most popular member of the squadron. On March 29, 1940 he force-landed on boggy ground but unfortunately the machine nosed over, breaking his neck.

'Cobber's' first victory took place on November 8 when a high-flying Dornier Do17P of Aufklarungs-Gruppe 123 piloted by Oberleutnant Hans Kutter was brought down in Lubey, just 13 kilometres east of Rouvres.

On that particular morning, during a break from office labours, I was gazing abstractedly out of the upstairs window (the mobile Orderly Room had recently given place to a requisitioned café), when suddenly I observed a large black object, plunging earthwards, beyond the black line of forest some miles distant. It surely was not, could not be, a Hurricane — no, by God; Oh boy, it *was* a Jerry! And in my excitement I yelled for the Orderly Room staff. There was no sign of either smoke or fire as it descended; but when it disappeared behind the screen of the forest a huge, slowly expanding and grey-black mushroom of smoke marked the spot of our first victory. Incidentally, and almost immediately, out attention was distracted by a curious phenomenon — that of a trail of black objects, emerging with a rush from the thick belt of woods. Wild boar! and where was 'Cobber' with his revolver? He who had sought them so often, and so vainly.

Yes, where was 'Cobber'? And where was 'Dickie' Martin? And for that matter, where was 'Bill' Kain, too? Then there was a tinkle upon the office 'phone. '"Cobber"'s done it! Just landed. Says he caught it at 27,000 feet. Shot it down promptly. A Do17. Afraid it fell into the middle of a village.' (Pause for breath). 'Will send him along as soon as his crew and the chaps down here will let him go.' The whole village was jubilant. The *salle* |*Boche*; one less, praise *le Bon Dieu*!

As there was no war except our own private one to bother about, everybody ceased work at once, and the village green fairly seethed with AC 'plonks', rubbing shoulders with officers, rank being agreeably sunk on this occasion. 'Cobber' was not unprepared for the reception he got. He was pleased, and very proud; the first honour to the squadron, his squadron, had come by way of him. And it had all been so damned easy, except for the real battle, that of beating 'Bill' Kain and 'Dickie' Martin, in the attempt to reach the blighter first. Skill, his skill, had told in the end, over both friends and foe.

There were others — it seemed that '73' had secured the pick of the bunch (with a doubtful or bad lot thrown in here and there, just to leaven it. *They* would go, whether officer or sergeant pilot, when their presence was no longer a distraction, but an absolute menace). Of the juniors worthy to be bracketed with such seniors, 'Dickie' Martin springs to the fore, just as he sprang into public and world-wide notice, almost as soon as we arrived at Rouvres. Not even the fact that 'Cobber' eclipsed 'Dickie's world-blazoned performance, by shooting down the enemy machine that 'Dickie' was after, could detract from the latter's performance — or its publicity!

It was a day of excitements, fraught with consequences which were to rock the squadron to its foundations — the consequences of unrestricted, undiluted, and wholly pernicious publicity for the individual, who was after all, but one of a team — as came to be emphasised and demonstrated, somewhat later. There was nothing, however, to indicate on that particular date, November 8th, 1939, that it would prove any more exciting or significant than any of the preceding days of this our first month's stay in Rouvres.

No. 1 Squadron had provokingly drawn first blood a day or two previously, having shot down a German plane (and later dined and wined their victim — with ensuing indications of official disapproval of their fraternal action). '73' was peeved; but their felicitations upon the excellent show of their sister squadron were sincere and acceptable. It was the more hard, as No.

1 were stationed at least 50 miles to the *rear* of us; and these blessed recce planes of the enemy, who usually took their course over our territory, were getting more than a bit cheeky now, penetrating ever deeper into French territory, but always at a ceiling well above that of the Hurricane. It was surmised that they flew 'light'; that is, not armed, in their necessity to do the job with the barest essentials of technical equipment, and subject themselves to a minimum of interference. But that fact remained to be proved; and it was sportingly hoped that the Hurricane would draw fire when the occasion arose.

| 1939 | AIRCRAFT | | PILOT, OR | 2ND PILOT, PUPIL | DUTY |
MONTH	DATE	Type	No.	1ST PILOT	OR PASSENGER	(INCLUDING RESULTS AND REMARKS)
						TOTALS BROUGHT FORWARD
Nov.	6	HURRICANE	P.	SELF.	—	To No I Sqdn. & Ret.
	7	"	X	"	—	Local Patrol.
	"	"	P	"	—	Patrol.
" X	8	"	P	"	—	Patrol. Brought down Dornier
	17	"	"	"	—	Interception Patrol. Metz.
	"	"	"	"	—	Patrol.
	22	"	P	"	—	Special Mission.
- X	23	"	Z	"	—	Interception Patrol.
	28	"	P	"	—	Local Patrol.

Extract from 'Cobber' Kain's log book — where he has marked his first two victories — both Do 17s — with an 'X'.

But what the hell, chaps, what's all the commotion about? Cut it out. But he flashed a significant wink in my direction, which I had no difficulty in interpreting. I shook him warmly by the hand, and he returned the pressure — doubly, painfully, for he had enormous hands. Next to 'Cobber', I was the proudest, happiest member of the squadron. I was fated thus — and alas — to dedicate myself as his first publicity-monger; and a rare hornets nest was I destined to stir up — and eventually to assist to smother! But to return to Rouvres.

'Bill' Kain duly turned up; and no one would have guessed the disappointment which lay beneath the honestly expressed tribute of appreciation to the better man, when the two Kains met. But there was still no sign of 'Dickie'. In the excitement of the individual endeavour to intercept, and, indifferent to the possible danger of enemy fighters, they had broken apart as a team, and neither Kain could say what had happened, or what might have happened, to 'Dickie'.

After a hurried lunch, a RAF tender took a privileged few of us to the scene of the crash, located in the village of Lubey, some seven miles distant. It was an amazing progress; from every point of the compass, disregarding crops, hedges, and ditches, men, women and children were converging upon the hitherto insignificant Lubey, above which a thin silver pall of smoke still hovered in the weak November sun. Gendarmes had already arrived, and were posted at the approaches to the village, to prevent further congestion by road traffic; and even we were stopped. Fortunately, 'Willie' Williams was one of our party, and a few incisive and curt phrases from him, in French, and a finger indicating the self-conscious, but delighted 'Cobber', sufficed; but — 'un moment' — had we a 'cigarette Anglaise' Not even the capture of Hitler himself would have rendered a French gendarme, at that stage of the war, forgetful of the opportunity to cadge an English cigarette.

We drew close to the scene of the tragedy; so nearly a tragedy for others

besides the late owners of those obscene chunks of charred flesh, which were still littered around, anonymous — that obscene object of a head, with the dark flying helmets still encasing it; the gunner who had just been separated from the twisted weapon which had impaled him; that sundered shoulder, still covered with grey-blue material, and a smart silver-piped epaulette.

It was simply miraculous how the village had escaped a frightful calamity. The bomber (turned photo-recce), plunging blindly earthwards, had hit exactly dead centre at the crossroads beside the signpost to Briey, where it had exploded, and disintegrated. Fortunately the explosion had travelled upwards and other than a no longer bedridden woman (who had suddenly found the use of her legs again), and burnt-out shed, there was little beyond a broken window here and there to record. But down there, in the deep trench in the road, there were splutterings and minor explosions, as machine-gun bullets exploded at intervals, and spurts of flame shot up from rolls of prematurely exposed photographic film; and, in the shed nearby, lay a few tattered shreds of uniform, and odd sections of human bodies, awaiting final resting place in the nearby village churchyard.

Official French photographers were already upon the scene, and a crowd of souvenir hunters ranged around, torn between the desire to trail the great handsome fellow who had done the job and the urge to collect souvenirs. We walked into the orchard, behind the old church, where an old woman was standing before an apple tree, still strung with human entrails. Soon the world would know of this second blow to German might and impudence; but one woman prayed for the souls, the families, of the crew of that one Do17 the less. She had lived through one major war, and perhaps even possessed childhood memories of yet another — of which the battlefield of Sedan, not far away, was of such bitter significance in the nation's annals.

New Zealander Brings Down German Plane

An R.A.F. pilot-officer, on November 8, proceeded to celebrate his 21st birthday by engaging a German plane in single-handed combat high in the sky behind the Maginot Line. This picture shows the result—the first enemy plane to be brought down by an Empire fighter at the Front. The wreckage you see here, strewn about a French village street, was a "flying pencil"

Dornier bomber. The young New Zealand pilot-officer engaged it at a height of 27,000 feet, his attention being first drawn towards it by British anti-aircraft shells that were bursting all around. The German pilot tried to play hide-and-seek among the clouds. But the New Zealander kept after him and brought him down with burst after burst of machine-gun fire.

At the end of a 600 m.p.h. nose-dive the German plane—the pilot had, apparently, been killed in mid-air—grazed a cottage with one of its wings and then 'hit the village road. The resultant explosion flung bits of the plane all round and high into the air. Fragments are seen here caught up in the tree.

This is a close-up of some of the fragments. Doubtless the victorious young New Zealand pilot-officer will keep a piece as a souvenir of this historic "first time" incident of the war. Now read "What I Saw at the Front," by Major Oliver Stewart.—Page 138. [Photo by Gaumont British News]

Although this was not the first aircraft shot down by the RAF in France (that honour had fallen to No. 103 Squadron on September 27), the Press made a big show of it being the first German credited to a pilot from the Empire. Oliver Stewart, the air correspondent of *The War* was at Rouvres that very morning: 'The conditions under which I was permitted by RAF headquarters to visit these stations preclude me from stating where this was and from mentioning the types of British machines that were concerned except in general terms. It was a single-handed action fought out in the old Royal Flying Corps traditions against a single German machine, but both machines were moving much faster, and they were both flying much higher than in any previous action of the kind.'

And what were the reactions of 'Cobber', in the presence of the mortal remains of his lawful prey? Dispassionately he surveyed them, as also the twisted remains of the beautifully designed plane, which he had last seen intact at 27,000 feet, bearing perhaps important information towards Germany. 'It was either him or me, and I gave him all I'd got.'

There was an amusing contretemps in the affair of the stricken Do17. On our way to Lubey, we had been signalled violently by an officer, in an approaching RAF tender, who had emerged there from hugging a blood-and-entrail-smeared Boche machine-gun — triumphantly claiming it as his by right of conquest. Its (temporary) claimant was the map-wallah, Pilot Officer 'Claudie' Wright and, until disabused on all sides, and the story of his own pretty staunch effort, correlated for him with an account of that of 'Cobber', he confidently expected to claim the squadron's first 'kill'. It was rather bad luck for 'Claudie', and he had our deepest sympathy. What had happened was that whilst still in the initial stage of our celebration of 'Cobber's' victory, another visual thrill had been provided for us; for, slowly gaining upon a German plane, and at a height which was all in its favour, a Hurricane was observed to be in pursuit of yet another of the enemy. Drunk with thrills and excitement, the mixed crowd surged round the church of Rouvres, in order to obtain a full-scale view. Yes, the Hurricane was gaining. Who could it be? It must be either 'Dickie', or 'Bill' or perhaps even 'Claudie', who had pushed off upon a lone hop. Whoever it was, he had it on toast, for a cert.

The distance between the two slowly lessened, and at last the Hurricane was within target distance — yes, he was firing. But, so were the French AA gunners; and, knowing their habits, a chill clutched us. True to their invariable and maddening technique, the gunners were shooting behind, overtaking the two aircraft. Height was promising; but what about the Hurricane, first in their line of fire? For Christ's sake, lay off, you blithering idiots; lay off we tell you. And then, a long-drawn Ah-h-h-h! from the whole crowd. They had got him — got the Hurricane! Would you bloody well credit it. And down it swooped, in a fearful curve, the machine seemingly out of control; but no, it slid off into a slower curve, gliding towards the ground, and was lost to our view — as was, blissfully enough, the apparently untouched enemy aircraft.

'Claudie's' luck was clean out, though he always believed that he had accounted for the other plane, before he himself became a target for the French. The AA had done considerable damage to his Hurricane; and though he would very much have liked to bale out, he could not do so, owing to the sliding panel overhead having become tightly jammed. And, what was worse, oil was now pouring over the perspex, reducing him to artificial twilight, and wedged, a prisoner in his cockpit — a fearful predicament! Fortunately a splinter of AA had punctured a tiny peep-hole, and through his he spied the ground, and actually performed quite a fair landing. Owing, however, to the damaged state of his machine, the undercarriage folded under him, and he was stunned and cut as a result; however, the upper panel had now become dislodged, and he was able to clamber out. An RAF tender which happened to be in the vicinity, promptly made its way to the scene, saluting 'Claudie' with the satisfactory, but in the event, false information, that his late antagonist had just crashed at Lubey. Leaving his damaged plane under a French guard, he was soon at Lubey, and the rear gunner was promptly separated — or part of him — from the twisted remains of 'Claudie's' lawful booty, his machine-gun. Thus it came about that 'Claudie' put up a brilliant show, coupled with the foulest luck that ever man had.

There was an amusing sequel to 'Claudie's' affair, in due course. By the time the French AA had shot down a third Hurricane (over Metz this time), it was decided that the 'amende honorable' was due, and an astonished sergeant-pilot of '73' was duly decorated with the Croix de Guerre — ostensibly for 'displaying extreme presence of mind and consummate bravery' in avoiding a village, whilst making his unpremeditated descent as a result of this constitutional error on the part of the French AA. And in order still further to cement the *entente cordiale* some of the officers of 73 Squadron were invited to partake of the hospitality of Army HQ at Metz, where they underwent the embarrassing satisfaction of witnessing certain officers of the French armed forces, in our honour, pelt with bread pellets the confused and mortified representatives of the French AA.

The 'enfant terrible' — Flying Officer 'Dickie' Martin.

And now for 'Dickie' Martin. Late that afternoon, there came another telephone message, this time from a French frontier post. A British machine had been seen to land in Luxembourg territory, just over the border. It was 'Dickie' all right; and that impish youngster must now be either eating his heart out in bitter resentment at this sudden termination of the war for him, or accepting bouquets from the hands of pretty maidens. Actually he was doing both.

The trouble with Pilot Officer Martin was that he *would* consider the RAF as an extension to, or in actual fact, a super-prep. school, with all rules and regulations to be treated in the spirit they would be by any rational youth at St Jim's — that is, ignored. For instance, that rule about oxygen masks — why should he take his with him this morning? It meant a trail back to his billet anyhow. So he set forth, hopefully, if ill-equipped, against the Hun; and as luck, or ill-luck, would have it, one such appeared, high up above him, and beetling for Germany, the bastard! Thereupon 'Dickie' did some rapid thinking. Competition, for instance. There was 'Bill'; there was 'Cobber'; and there was rarefied atmosphere to contend against (the enemy didn't count — or wouldn't, once 'Dickie' got near him). He was now at 17,000 feet, and breathing rather hard; but a quick climb up, then two or three short bursts, and down again — wouldn't that just do the trick? 'Dickie' recovered consciousness at about 3,000 feet, and in a dazed sort of way made towards a large aerodrome, lying almost immediately below him. Esch, or some such name, was displayed prominently upon it. He'd verify that when he landed.

Esch was less than five miles from the French frontier, but unfortunately, it was on the wrong side of it for 'Dickie', who now became that legendary figure, *THE PRISONER OF LUXEM-*

BOURG, featured in every newspaper, and photographed in mufti, standing beside an old gun, on the ramparts of the fortress of Luxembourg. We heard apocryphal tales, of course, about him; but knowing his habits rather better than the stunt Press, we credited but half of what we heard, and assumed the other half. Of one thing we did not doubt — that we should see 'Dickie' one day, on this side of the wire and not before long, either. Accordingly, and to anticipate a little, just before Christmas, the CO whispered to me that we were both to go secretly to a certain café in Metz, where a 'surprise' awaited us. Of course it was no surprise; we made straight for the table where the mufti-clad youngster was sitting. He was in no way altered; still the *'enfant terrible'*. A nickname handed to him by the charming wife of Marcel Festal, the proprietor of the elegant Hotel Vauban, in Verdun, who had soon become our very good friend.

When all the riot and tumult of his reception back to the Mess had subsided, and all but the original party at Metz had drifted away to bed, 'Dickie' sat upon a high stool, and related to the CO and myself some of his adventures, and how at last he had walked off, under cover of fog, to freedom. And we both failed to observe that talking induced a thirst, until, all of a sudden, the poised glass of whisky slid neatly over his shoulder, as 'Dickie' and the stool fell, in perfect alignment, to the floor. The CO and I exchanged glances. We ought to have known; perhaps ought to have felt a bit ashamed of ourselves. But judge of our astonishment when that irrepressible youth, calmly, and with as much dignity as he could assume, re-seated himself upon the high stool, and, as if there had been no 'incident', proceeded to carry on with his recital. Knox bellowed forth a roar of laughter, in which I joined; and that was the last we heard, for a week or two, of, or from, the Prisoner of Luxembourg, who departed upon a spot of well-earned home leave upon the day following.

ILLUSTRATED

Officer, poses for a photographer. While he was interned in the Grand Duchy he received every consideration from the authorities. Included was a regular weekly supply of ILLUSTRATED which Mr. Martin read regularly.

The Prisoner of Luxembourg

Lost in fog, forced down in the neutral territory of Luxembourg, interned on parole, then withdrawing his parole and escaping in another fog to Allied soil—this was the saga of the young R.A.F. pilot who made the first dramatic escape of the Nazi War. ILLUSTRATED now tells his story for the first time. Overleaf begins our cameraman's tour of Luxembourg, the little Duchy that lives under the menace of Nazi invasion

ON the morning of November 8 last year, the inhabitants of Luxembourg were given an unexpected thrill. Over the great iron producing centre of Esch appeared a military plane bearing the distinguishing marks of a machine of the Royal Air Force.

Over the aerodrome it circled, and then came slowly to earth to complete a perfect "three-point" landing. And, as the authorities hurried over the tarmac to investigate, there emerged from the cabin a young British officer who gave his name as R. John Martin.

He explained that he had lost his way while returning to his aerodrome "somewhere in France." Having seen the word "AERODROME," painted in large letters on the red ground, he assumed that

he was flying in safety over French territory.

Still believing that he was in France, he asked the bystanders to help him get his plane ready for taking off again, and then it was that disillusionment came. His sympathetic audience were, he discovered, unable to speak French.

As he was still trying vainly to make himself understood, a number of gendarmes arrived at the aerodrome in cars, and then it was that Martin realized that he had been misled by the French word into landing on neutral territory.

He was taken to the city of Luxembourg where he was interviewed by the authorities to whom he gave his parole. This enabled him to enjoy plenty of freedom and his captors did all in their power to make his lot as pleasant as possible.

But he had no intention of living a life of placid

inaction for the duration of the war, and a few weeks after landing in Luxembourg he outlined his parole. The authorities, realising that he would probably attempt to escape, kept him under careful observation, but even so the British airman was too clever for them.

Christmas Day dawned over the Grand Duchy with thick fog rolling over the countryside. Taking advantage of the fact that surveillance would be lax on that of all days, Martin slipped quietly away, eluding his guards.

Protected by the fog, he made good his escape, and by the time it was discovered that he had escaped, he was safely across the frontier. And behind him he left his mascot and photographs as mementoes of a visit that proved to be so brief as it was unexpected.

(continued overleaf)

ON 'ANTIC' SERVICE
THE 'LOST SQUADRON' (No. 73)

SOMEWHERE IN FRANCE — Concert in Airmen's Mess on 10.11.39

Programme

Corporal Byers	Envy of Charlie Kunz.
LAC Rodgers	Not quite George Formby.
LAC Cotterill	'Naughty but Nice' — 'Join up And Watch the Flares'.
LAC Blease	A Laddie from Yorkshire.
LAC Thomas	One of the Suffolks from the Sea.
LAC Smith	Always a good turn — LAC after his Tapes.
LAC Hart	Scotch, 'snuff said.
AC1 Reynolds	Imitations
LAC Randall	The Welsh Richard Tauber
Corporal Duncan and LAC Kerr	Larry Adler and Arthur Tolcher.

AC1 Teasdale	The Plumber's Representative.
Corporal Brehaut	That well-known Foreign Entertainer.
Corporal Anderson	A new arrival— (says he's Stanley Holloway — Let's see).

1st Res: AC2 Dallywaters Hints on how to Dodge Guards.

God Save The King

And upon the reverse of the programme, appeared the following notice:

TO ALL RANKS AIR RAID WARNING
In the event of the above taking place,
'ROLL OUT THE BARREL'

A couple of evenings later, the men sprang a concert. It was entirely their own affair; a spontaneous tribute to 'Cobber', and an assertion of their proper pride and sense of property in '73'. Not even the Adjutant was in the know, though under his very nose a programme was in process of being produced and without leave upon the Orderly Room stylograph; Le Veconte, Clerk GD, also improvised a neat job of Hurricanes in line astern, out of india-rubbers, as decoration for the borders of the programme.

Of course the actual programme bore very slight resemblance to that proposed. The men intended to have a little 'free and easy' sing-song, with lashings of beer to keep their throats from getting too dusty. The village hall, calculated to hold 150 comfortably, held, somewhat less comfortably, over 200, as we officers drifted in, following upon an early dinner. It was an appreciated, but quite a superfluous gesture, that of each officer putting himself down for a crate or two of La Slavia beer; for no one present seemed unprovided for. A narrow lane was opened for us to the stalls — forms in this case, and a trifle damp, as a result of beer having been slopped over some of them. At the piano (purchased out of PSI funds), that jovial Bradfordian, Corporal Myers, Signals, was performing, still in command of the keys, despite the presence of a bottle of beer on one side for him, and one in reserve on the other.

The F/Sgt. Discip. having called for order, and (the night being still young) rather surprisingly obtained it, the concert opened. Rodgers was certainly not *quite* George Formby, but decidedly one ahead of him in his 'asides'; and fortunately there were no ladies present to cramp Cotterill's style. Blease, with a face which had on occasion upset the dignity of Orderly Room parade, told an unprintable story which convulsed the house, and some of the beer which was going down, as promptly came up. The 'imitations' by 'Biff' Reynolds were not invariably successful; his rendering for instance (with the assistance of a glass globe), of a noise alleged to be that of a lion, was greeted with a wicked 'Oh, is it?' from some wag at the back of the hall. The Welsh Tauber unfortunately 'passed out' only a few minutes before he was due to substantiate his

claim; and, with the fun developing fast and furious in the body of the crowded, stuffy hall, it was now obvious that the concert had 'had it'. And in any case, some of the unsolicited 'turns' were tending to verge upon the personal, touching upon the supposed lapses of certain of the married men, strategically disposed in private billets, and rapidly acquiring a grasp of French which suggested dubious opportunities for the acquirement thereof.

And then, the star turn — 'Cobber'! The roof fairly reverberated, as he was shoved, vociferously protesting his unfitness, upon the platform. The reception he got was simply tremendous. The world was behind this privileged audience, as it almost danced, in an orgy of beer and uppishness for weren't they the boys of '73', and wouldn't they tell the world? Everybody knew what was coming, and a queer sort of hush descended upon the crowd, as 'Cobber' threw himself into those first contortions of face and figure which the preliminaries apparently to the Maori War Dance. There were two 'Cobbers' — the cold, calculating type who pressed the button of his firing mechanism at the precise moment indicated; and the savage, the primeval, which now fairly

exuded, as he forgot himself and his audience in this demoniac, unique performance — a performance which left him gasping and exhausted, and brought down the house.

Another officer was called for, and 'Pissy' staggered on to the platform, where he mumbled interminably, verse after verse concerning the behaviour (not particularly to her credit) of a certain 'Lady of Jerusalem', until he was prevailed upon to have a thirst-quencher, after approximately the fifteenth verse. And so, the whole affair came to a deafening and disorderly conclusion, reiterated cries of Order being drowned in distinct, but in the circumstances not very actionable, tokens of insubordination.

Tomorrow there would be the same old lowering grey skies; the same sodden fields would exhale their unhealthy mists; and the squadron would settle back to the same hard grind. But today, Rouvres, though unspecified by name, was in the world's eye; and 'Cobber', equally anonymous, had been accorded the one public ovation worth the having from the men of '73'! Tomorrow there would be a converging of uniformed specialists in publicity upon Rouvres; but tonight was *theirs*.

An original beer bottle label preserved from the concert in November 1939.

Concurrently with 'Cobber's' two victories — for he shot down another Do17 a fortnight later — the Mess was soon littered with relics of a Heinkel 111 in addition, contributed by 'Fanny' Orton — there came significant indications of what the Germans had prepared as an answer, or maybe more than an answer, to the Hurricane! The first indication provided a burst of laughter; the second wasn't quite so funny.

'Cobber's' next victim was photographed in detail by the Service Cinématographique de l'Armee. The Dornier was carrying out a reconnaissance over Reims on November 23 when Kain raked it from nose to tail. It crash-landed at La Besace near Rancourt and was fired by the crew. *Right:* Members of squadron were soon on the scene — here (L-R) are Henry Hall, 'Cobber' and Squadron Leader Knox.

Pilot Officer Peter Ayerst. He flew with No. 73 Squadron from the outbreak of war until May 1940 . . .

The most junior pilot of the squadron, Pilot Officer Ayerst, who was on 'aerodrome defence', had been vectored onto an enemy aircraft (sighted by units of the French Observer Corps operating with us). Having lost track of the objective, he was relieved to see a formation of nine aircraft below him, with which he promptly aligned himself, only to discover almost immediately and to his horror, that he was not among friends, as he had conjectured, but sailing alongside Nazi swastikas! Discretion being obviously the better part of valour in such a case, he disengaged himself from the formation with the minimum of self-advertisement, and boosted for the frontier for all he was worth, the Germans tally-ho-ing behind him; and it was fortunate for the lowered morale of the French that this decoy brought the hitherto somewhat shy enemy over their territory, as a result of which five were promptly shot down by French fighters, and without loss of themselves.

Ought he to have done battle, or had he performed no mean feat in out-manoeuvring vastly superior odds? Wisely, and with consequent benefit to his future operations, he inclined in the end to the latter verdict and the Mess, after its first doubts and laughter, inclined to agree with him. But the inci-

dent did not end there. Not a crumb which fell from our table in those days, but was snatched up by the Press, now in process of attaching themselves semi-permanently to the squadron. And so it happened that the public duly heard of the incident — suitably written up from Ayerst's own account, ex-

pounded and glorified; and though the Press could not as yet mention either the squadron by number, or an individual by name, the best scoop of all was secured by a provincial paper; one, by a perhaps not inexplicable coincidence, circulating in the home town of Ayerst himself!

. . . and 63 years later he returned to Rouvres for the dedication of the plaque recording the exploits of his squadron there.

But certain other provincial papers not long afterwards were in a position to indicate another aspect of the alertness of the enemy, and on this occasion, one hardly calculated to raise a smile; and the apposite reference was to be found in the obituary column! 'Pete' Walker leading, with sergeant-pilots Perry and Winn, set forth on patrol, just three days short of Christmas. Walker returned alone, a sadder and a wiser man — both sergeants had been shot down from the rear, in a surprise attack by the heretofore reasonably dreaded Me 109 and Walker had not been in a position to fire a single shot in return! It was devastatingly sudden — and a stern warning. Silk neck scarves now became not only the fashion but a painful necessity, and necks became raw with the unaccustomed and perpetual exercise they got. There were apparently other contacts to be made, besides those with high-flying, lightly-armed recce planes; and it was up to 73 Squadron to tackle the new menace.

With no hangarage on the aerodrome, all the servicing had to be carried out in the open. This was not too bad in the autumn of 1939 but disastrous when one of the worst winters on record closed in.

Above: **Peter Ayerst coming in to land and** *(below)* **the same view to the north-east today**.

For reasons beyond the control of either belligerent, however, the menace for some time showed no signs of developing. The province of Lorraine is notoriously the wettest in the whole of France, and it was not until February that the score of the squadron was increased. Meanwhile, incessant rain waterlogged the aerodrome; and this was followed by unprecedented falls of snow, accompanied by arctic cold, whilst blizzards swept over the plains, giving the snow a coating of treacherous sheet ice. But we had to be prepared; one never knew what the Germans might suddenly spring upon us and from such a short distance, too. So the officers left the comfort, such as it was, of the Mess and the men stamped, or ploughed, their way from their billets to that bitter place of purgatory, the 'drome. What little they could do, they did. Every machine was necessarily exposed to the elements; there were no hangars. Every machine must be ready to take to the air at a minute's notice, almost. What man could do, was done by the men of '73', all honour to them.

The cold was so intense that the rather dangerous expedient of heaters, inserted actually inside the cockpit and under the shrouded engine, was instituted, and proved successful. At home, the papers in due course enlarged upon the terrific winter they in England had

experienced; what happened at Rouvres in the first winter of the war will live in the memory of those who serviced Hurricanes under conditions proper to Russia; and their only reward was the rich one of the response of a Rolls-Royce engine to their command.

We had time to look around, and to prospect the amenities of the district — such as they were! Officers and men, weather and duties permitting, would proceed by road to Verdun; the officers favouring the Hotel Vauban, and the men the various cafés and estaminets with which the place seemed to abound. There was nothing which made our good friend Marcel Festal's face light up more certainly than a sudden influx of RAF officers round about dusk, eager for the luxury of a bath, and with an excellent dinner to follow. We soon had the run of the hotel, and the corridors would echo to the 'C'est defendus' of female bath-room attendants, or the giggle of a chambermaid at some preposterous suggestion put before her by a nondescript figure draped in a bath towel. Nevertheless, no scandal resulted, it was all good clean fun; indeed, months afterwards, and during the retreat across France, it was fairly reliably (and with some malicious zest) reported that at Troyes, not the least prepossessing of a batch of female refugees had inquired specifically, and even tenderly, after 'Monsieur Henri'!

But the source of most of our entertainment was almost upon our own doorstep, as we soon found. We were the only representatives of the RAF within a 50-mile radius, and there was not a French regimental or Air Force Mess which would remain satisfied until it had done us the honour of dining and wining us. A couple of French officers would pay us a call at the *Mairie*, shake hands with everybody to the accompaniment of a smart click of the heels and a bow, and thereupon formally invite the CO, and anything up to half a dozen of his officers, to do them the honour of a visit. At first competition was keen as to who should be the fortunate ones but after two or three gargantuan repasts, washed down by half a dozen carefully selected (not by us, fortunately) wines, our appetites began to pall, and we almost shivered with apprehension when yet another French car drew up outside the *Mairie*, and out stepped a kid-gloved colonel, accompanied by his aide.

Some of the regimental messes were poor, and their representatives, apologising in advance, would submit that we break humble bread with them? We did — six courses of it! As for the more exclusive and élite of the Messes, we would find a couple of bands to entertain us: the regimental one, and a dance band. The latter was not provided merely as a concession to the low tastes of the RAF for though (curiously enough) no ladies were ever invited, we were still expected to dance with an ally. And this once led to complications; for during our return from one such affair, 'Dickie' Martin suddenly inquired, 'What would you chaps do if a bloody Corsican bastard shoved a banknote into your hand?' We answered as one, 'Keep it'. I have responded 'Dickie'! But in the event it was not to prove quite so simple a transaction as all that. Next morning, the said Corsican paid an agitated visit to the Mess. 'Where is Monsieur "Dickie"?' No one knew; but it was drinks all round on 'Dickee' that evening; and a French banknote amply covered it.

At another Mess, a most elaborate menu had been prepared by an artist of some repute, and it was headed Rien a Faire — a reflection, or repercussion, of the reigning 'phoney war' phase, and one which we had no option at that particular time but to take in good part; and the night ended with 'bon accord', and the usual splitting headaches the following morning. Invitations even arrived from the Maginot Line, and parties of us were duly deposited in the bowels of the earth, where we all caught shocking colds as a consequence of passing from one temperature to another, along its draughty corridors. We were even permitted to operate the naval guns, listening politely, if not quite convinced, to all that was claimed on their behalf; and we ended the day at a dinner in a Mess strategically situated in a nearby wood. On this occasion, I found no fewer than seven intriguing wine glasses, of varying shapes and sizes, ranged beside my

cover, and I prepared for the worst. Fortunately, the resultant pastime of rubbing jam into one another's hair, was confined to our Allies, and was still in progress when we representatives of '73' staggered out into the night air, into the light of the weak searchlights which were frantically probing the starlit sky after a German plane. As for the facility with which these night intruders penetrated so deeply into French territory, the French had only themselves to blame. For instance, for some months after our arrival at Rouvres, two extremely flashing beacons operated in the direct path of our aerodrome — a guide, it was explained, to friendly machines returning from Germany. But it was soon apparent that they were by no means invariably French planes which made use of these so kindly beacons; and upon our urgent representations, they were eventually, though with obvious misgivings, dispensed with.

The original menu for the dinner hosted by the French Air Force on November 4.

Another publicity shot of a squadron which was becoming headline news which includes familiar faces in the Ops Room.

Here Lovett, the deputy CO, points out the day's patrol duties. Scoular, Orton, Kain and Pyne are all recognisable.

Henry Hall on the extreme left as Lovett briefs 'A' Flight gathered around the tail of one of its new three-bladed machines.

'Dickie' Martin takes his turn as Orderly Officer and inspects the cook house.

ment to those possessed of a purely military significance, one row almost sufficed — but it was a very creditable one. It transpired that a period of seven years as French master in a grammar school at Keighley, had provided him with the opportunity to acquire an accent indistinguishable from that of a local; and his passages with me, a fellow Yorkshireman, used to excite roars of laughter in the Mess.

As a mobile RAF unit in the field, we were hardly in a position to return the hospitality so lavishly thrust upon us by static French messes but our allies felt amply repaid in other directions, as for instance the opportunity to acquire English cigarettes in bulk. Indeed, in the end we had to restrict this convenience to 'friends of our friends', otherwise our stock would never have sufficed for our own needs and hospitalities. Walking up towards the Orderly Room one day, a large staff car drew in ahead of me, and out of it stepped a French officer of obviously high rank. I accordingly put on a spurt but he was already engaged in animated conversation with one of my clerks

A useful innovation, unprovided for upon the War Establishment of a mobile RAF fighter squadron, was the French sergeant-interpreter, now attached to the squadron and in due course succeeded by Sergeant Harman, ex-Cooks Tours, and destined to shepherd us across France in 1940. But the language question, as a matter of fact, presented no insuperable problem as almost every other French officer possessed some command of English, which was fortunate so far as the bulk of our own officers was concerned. At least one of the older French officers, with whom later we became so well acquainted, not only spoke fluent English, but had a perfect command of the Yorkshire dialect, so much so as to present a curious anomaly in his French uniform, his tunic strung with rows of decorations more or less appropriate, but on the whole indicative of long and honourable service on behalf of his country. Included in the medal ribbons upon his breast was that of a Doctor of Philosophy! Indeed, when he, quite without solicitation, reduced the assort-

We discovered that it had been located in Grand Rue No. 6, the actual room since having been sub-divided.

Left: In 1939-40, No. 26 was one of the village's cafes. The large room at the rear was used as the Other Ranks' dining room.

Right: Two of the original windows survive but the rear of the hall has now been converted into a garage.

when I arrived, who, with some embarrassment, divulged the nature of the august visitor's errand: could he be supplied with English cigarettes, please?

Inevitably the exchange of civilities extended itself to the interchange of regimental buttons, and the tunic of one officer of '73' was representative of the four French messes which he had recently visited, official regulations to the contrary notwithstanding. But our main ambition was to secure, by fair means or foul (much was allowable and forgiven towards the end of a French regimental dinner), one of the beautifully enamelled regimental badges which the French officers, exclusively, were privileged to wear upon their tunics. Some of these were unique specimens of the jeweller's art; and the gift of one such was not to be measured in terms only of the *entente cordiale*, especially as they were not a gratis issue to individual holders.

Metz was occasionally favoured with our presence; but the place was so fearful of what Germany had possibly in store for it that only the more questionable resorts offered any entertainment, suitably exorbitant, after dark; and the 'black-out' was 100 per cent. I have a lively memory of returning from Metz one night, when Knox, a little impatient at a prolonged halt at a level-crossing, poured the contents of his revolver into the presumably vacant lower storey of a signals box! The gates opened like magic, and we sped on.

For those camp-bound, a mobile cinema would pay a visit to Rouvres; and, still more occasionally, the mobile lecturer who revealed our only declared Communist, following upon one such lecturer's 'Any Questions?'

The most tiresome feature of this period of comparative inactivity was the impetus it gave to home correspond-

ence. From being the exclusive duty of the Orderly Officer of the day, censoring of private mail eventually saw whole afternoons devoted to the tedious job, by all available officers, and in the end we knew almost to a word what certain of the men would write; and 'Dickie' Martin always claimed the letters of one lovesick swain of his own crew, who

A wonderful discovery: the RAF wings still feintly visible on the end wall.

On November 26 — no doubt prompted by the publicity that No. 73 and its 'star' Cobber were receiving in the British Press — a party of journalists from Scandinavia arrived at Rouvres.

Prominent with the Danish pressmen are (L-R) Sergeants Bert Speake and Phillips, Lovett, Brotchie, Ayerst, Campbell, Holliday, Sergeants Humphris and Stuckey, 'Cobber', 'Tubs' and 'Fanny'.

regularly drew a tremendous heart, formed of X's, as a final convincing token of his imperishable devotion, in the centre of which 'Dickie' would proceed to add his signature as censoring officer! Very reprehensible, no doubt; but 'Dickie' knew his man, and the man knew his wife, so all was well. And it was sufficient punishment, anyhow, to have to read some of the letters. Those of the officers were at first censored by the writers themselves, a privilege which was temporarily withdrawn after 'Tommy' Tucker suffered the misfortune of having one of his letters opened at Base, in the course of which he had described, in sufficient detail, and to his aunt of all persons, the operational strength and activities of the squadron to which he had the honour to belong!

That was not the only aspect of 'security' which we tackled for on at least two occasions suspected spies were passed on by us for the attention of the French military authorities. One of these, obviously mistaking his men over an *estaminet* table, plied a number of our 'other-ranks' with questions upon the strength, equipment, and the possible future moves of the squadron. As he was wearing the uniform of a *poilu*, his auditors were at first prepared to allow that his questions might be construed in the light of the legitimate enthusiasm of an ally but, just in case, he was brought before me, and a pitiable spectacle he presented when informed that the affair was to be referred to the French military authorities. We never heard the result of their interrogation.

On the other occasion, it was observed that during the course of a practice football match in the vicinity of the dispersed aircraft on the 'drome, a French soldier was improving his collection of miscellaneous snaps by the inclusion of a series of the game in progress, all of which, on being developed by us, included, possibly by a coincidence, the Hurricane aircraft and the signals paraphernalia about the Ops Room! As there was a doubt about it in his case, the snaps were merely confiscated, and

any other action considered necessary referred to the French. In any case, the road which bordered two sides of the 'drome was public, and there was nothing to prevent any ill-disposed person taking all the notes or photographs he or she cared. For purposes of 'security', '73' was positively never to be referred to as such over the telephone, but always by the codeword 'Ibor' and, further to confuse the enemy, this was subsequently reversed by some smart individual at HQ into 'Robi'. So it was

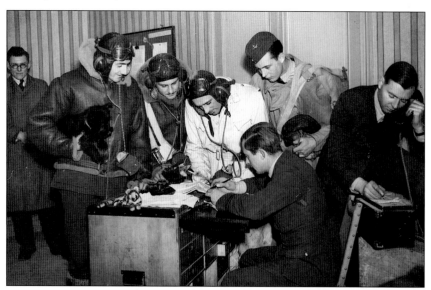

A flying display had been planned for the journalists but this had to be cancelled due to bad weather.

Christmas 1939 . . . high hopes with a huge bunch of mistletoe!

symbol of the regard which he was beginning to entertain on my behalf. Protruding from the brown paper wrapping in which I carried it, it proved a passport everywhere on the journey; and, had I been endeavouring to slip through with a whole crate of champagne under the noses of the customs officials, the attempt would have proved successful, I am sure. I also carried another weapon, gathered also from the wreckage of the first Do17. If there was one incentive above any other to shoot down a German plane, it was in order to secure the Mauser pistol which the pilot carried — a GAF weapon superior in every detail to the issue we personally received in the RAF. Unfortunately, in this case there was but the ruin of a Mauser to be had; but I was deputed to present it, *faut mieux* to the godfather of '73', and its CO during the last war, resident not very far from where I was to spend my leave.

perhaps as well that nobody present upon the occasion was likely to react with more than a roar of laughter when 'Fanny' Orton, over the none too inviolable service line, after repeatedly stating that he was 'Robi', exclaimed in a fit of impatience. '"Robi"', you know — 73 Squadron, "Robi!"!'

Only one of our men suffered as a result of direct contravention of security regulations and he plainly asked for it. Shortly after our arrival in France, the privileged 'Green Letter' was introduced. The contents of these private letters were not to be censored in the unit, but a small percentage of them were liable to be opened at Base. On the outside, the writer declared that the contents of the letter were purely private and personal, and contained nothing of service interest so, when a certain dimwit, wishfully thinking, or perhaps a victim of a cruel hoax, not only informed his wife that the squadron was shortly to move back to England (of all unlikely places), but actually gave the date of its indicated arrival at Southampton, he was obviously 'for it'; and in due course he was sentenced to 14 days Field Punishment.

But the greatest break of all for the squadron was the timely official reaction to the continued state of inactivity upon the war front, in the concession of 'home leave' which was instituted just in time for the first fortunate batch to spend Christmas of 1939 at home. A send-off party, almost as dense at that which had gathered to welcome the victor of November 8th, assembled upon the village green, and the first bus load departed to an accompanying chorus of reciprocal hoots and cat-calls. Thereafter, in batches of about 30, the officers and men proceeded, and without interference from the enemy, to indulge in a clear six days' spell at home, exclusive of travelling time' and almost without exception, at least one bottle of 'shampers' formed part of each individual's luggage.

In my own case, I proudly carried the twisted machine-gun, late the property of 'Cobber'Kain, but now mine, and a

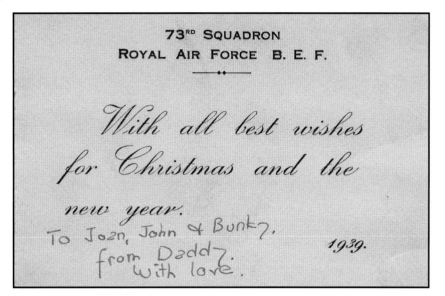

Henry Hall's Christmas card to his family and beloved daughter Joan.

This is the ground floor of the Mairie — the bar was in the corner of the same room we saw on page 25.

One for the folks back home. Pictured on the semi-sunken Duty Office are a line of Sergeant Pilots at the rear: Fred Perry, 'Humph' Humphris, Bert Speake, Donald Sewell, George Phillips, John Winn, Pilot Officer Henry Hall and Sergeants Ken Campbell and Sid Stuckey. The officers in front are 'Fanny' Orton, 'Tubs' Perry and Peter Ayerst on the left; George Brotchie and Reg Lovett in the centre, and Tommy Tucker, 'Smooth' Holliday and 'Cobber' on the right. 'The clue as to the date it was taken is the head of the Danish journalist just peeping over the sandbags . . . so November 26 . . . but less than a month later two of these men were dead. The squadron's first casualties occurred just before Christmas, when John Winn and Fred Perry were flying as wingmen to Pilot Officer Peter Walker, patrolling between Metz and Thionville. Suddenly they were bounced by four Bf109s from JG53 and both Winn and Perry were shot down. They were buried at Metz on Christmas Eve.

I had succumbed to the prevailing flu just about Christmas, and the 'Doc' had insisted that I should proceed upon the second leave draft. He felt that he had good reason, too; for, on receiving word one morning to the effect that I was laid up in my billet, he duly paid a call, performed a cursory inspection, and left with a succession of his customary puffings, and the remark that I had 'better cease malingering'. I was perhaps in a poor mood for being trifled with, and after pondering, in my then depressed state of mind, as to whether the 'Fin' was being either merely funny, or serious, I rashly inclined to the latter possibility, rose, dressed, and staggered out into the blinding snow. I just reached the Mess, and was promptly rushed back in the ambulance. In the meantime, the good old 'Doc' having made up a bottle of medicine, paid yet another personal call with it; and his astonishment and concern must have been worth the witnessing when he was met at the door by the woman of the house, arms thrown upwards, with the startling information: 'Ah, Monsier 'All, il est parti; il est mort!'

The interior of the underground Nissen hut. L-R: George Phillips, Peter Walker, Dickie Martin with Bert Speake on the phone to Ops.

Meantime, the period of quiescence produced an amazing crop of visitors to Rouvres. The Chief of the Air Staff, Marshal Sir Cyril Newall, arrived, unheralded, and spent a few hours with us one afternoon; and we were suitably impressed when, in response to a reasonable request for spare pilots, we were reminded that we were already up to strength, but assured that replacements would be forthcoming as and when there were 'wastages'! Mr Eden also blew in one day, hot and flushed after a visit to a French Mess. And a whole crowd of Dominions representatives, with their ciceroni, Major Astor, descended upon us on another occasion. Dignified and aloof Indians, too, in resplendent uniforms; the much-courted Turk, complete with fez; and civilians whose non-committal clothes were poor indication of their relative importance in the scheme of things. And always, the Press!

But the event of events was reserved for somewhat later, when, one December morning as I was gazing idly out of the window of the Mess, the untidy litter of the breakfast table behind me, I suddenly became aware of something unusual taking place on the green. Houses were emptying themselves of their French occupants, who were drawing respectfully near to a small party standing beside a handsome limousine. Pilot Officer Ayerst, still in flying gear, was in process of being interrogated; and then a couple of the party detached themselves and turned towards the Mess. It was — no, it couldn't possibly be and at this time of the morning — the Duke of Windsor!

'Hey, clear this table, somebody and send for Mr Lovett (the CO was absent upon one of his unexplained tours, and did *not* despite the detailed and somewhat fanciful account of the visit given by a certain Press correspondent, in his subsequent book devoted mainly to the activities of the two squadrons, act as cicerone upon the particular tour of inspection). And in he walked — the contemporary of my boyhood, the man I could never reconcile with my more adult plans for the disposal of royalty in my short-lived communistic phase. I was overcome for a few moments with confusion and embarrassment, but took the proferred hand, and muttered heaven knows what. Lovett, fortunately, was soon upon the scene; and, after offering the Duke a drink (which was politely but firmly declined), we proceeded towards the cookhouse, of all places. Meantime the news had spread like wildfire, and we passed along a double row of mixed French and English, a child or two timidly waving a Union Jack. Outside the Mess Hall, the cooks were busily giving a quick polish to Mess utensils; and some sensible individual had locked the door of a lean-to, from which though a decidedly unpleasant aroma floated.

He had brought, or rather, and inevitably, he was accompanied by, the Press; and we entered the grimy Mess Hall to the turning handles of cine-cameras. It was not our fault that the place was in such a disgusting state; Mess

Distinguished visitors. *Above:* **A party of representatives from the Dominions led by Major, the Hon. John Astor, the MP for the Dover division of Kent since 1922 and also Chairman of the Times Publishing Company. They visited the snowed-in squadron on January 21, 1940.**

orderlies were at a premium, and the passage thrice daily of between two and three hundred pairs of muddied boots left an impression hardly to be effaced from the floor — or from the memory of our visitor either, I surmise. Down at the bottom of the dreary hall, three men were engaged upon the job of peeling endless potatoes. I called them to attention and the Duke hove down upon them. As ill-luck would have it, he proceeded to address himself to perhaps the dourest, most nonchalant, of our redoubtable Lancashire contingent.

'You are a Mess Orderly?'
'Yes' — in broadest, most uncompromising Lancashire.
'Er — what is your name?'
'Broa-a-w-n.'
'Where do you come from?'
'Ma-a-a-nchester.'
'What were you in civil life?'
'Ba-a-a-ker.'

There was nothing more to be said, and, obviously nonplussed, the Duke withdrew. Unfortunately he could not spare the time to visit the 'drome, and he left to the further clicking of cine-cameras, and a rousing cheer.

But the visitor we craved was not forthcoming — a German — several Germans. An appropriate reception was guaranteed, and much time had been spent upon the preliminaries. And our French allies kept us upon our toes with their recurrent 'flaps' one of which, duly recorded in the *Unofficial Squadron Diary* will suffice as illustration.

January 4: Lest there be any doubt about it, the French informed us today that a 'secret wire' had been received, which declared a big advance to be imminent.

January 15: The French are still undecided about the great advance. At midnight it was 'off' — but at 6 a.m. it was 'on' again — indeed, 'more than ever', according to Sgt Pujot, our interpreter.

January 16: The 'flap' is off, and the snow has come. The new air-raid warning siren was tried out from the Orderly Room window — strident Klaxon horn, operated electrically, though not sufficiently penetrative to electrify the Officers Mess out of its customary afternoon's somnolence — 50 yards distant, too!

The Duke of Windsor had made a surprise visit on December 13 and caught the squadron having breakfast! Unfortunately we could not trace a photo taken that day — this is the Duke in France but with Air Vice-Marshal Blount.

Amusing perhaps — but just in case, and in order to be nearer the scene of our operational activities, I shifted my billet and the Orderly Room was moved nearer to the 'drome, whilst the Mess requisitioned a house from some less important French military unit. The Orderly Room certainly was a shabby, single-storied cottage — one room front, one back — but, on the other hand, the new Mess proved a decided improvement upon the *Mairie*. We were now self-contained, and with adequate provision for cooking, a dining room, an ante-room, a room for the pilots 'toggery' upstairs, and the bar in yet another room on that floor.

But why upstairs, moaned the pilots? Whose bloody idea was that? It was Knox's 'bloody idea', and it had firm foundation in his desire to impress visitors, whom he roughly divided into the sheep and he goats. The sheep were folded into the downstairs ante-room, where hot tea, and even cocoa on demand, earned their gratitude and approval, and they departed suitably impressed at the entire absence of any signs of strong drink around. The goats instinctively bypassed the ante-room, and in due course, 'Pissy' Paul or the 'Doc' were installed behind the upstairs bar, and all was well. They too departed — rather later in the day, or night, than the sheep, and also suitably impressed.

On January 18 the officers vacated the Mess in the Mairie and took over this house in Rouvres — Grand Rue No. 22. It has since been in the Morlet-Coppey family since 1977.

The New Year duly proceeded its crop of replacements for recent 'wastages'. R. M. Marchand filled the gap occasioned by Holliday's failure to return from Christmas leave and Sergeant Pilots Pilkington and Dibden, respectively, took the places of Winn and Perry. Of these replacements, Marchand and Dibden in due course qualified for places on the Roll of Hon-our of '73'; whilst Pilkington perished in September 1941, in the course of leading a 'sweep' over France, in which his squadron specialised at the time.

With regard to Marchand — 'Dim', as he came to be affectionately known by his fellow-pilots — he was the only son of a prominent Swiss watch-factor and wholesaler of Hatton Garden, and had recently thrown up a promising career

On February 6 'Cobber' bought a puppy from one of the villagers and gave it the squadron's code-name 'Ibor' although much fun was had in first teaching the dog English! In the picture Ibor is being held by Lovett with 'Hank' More and Dickie Martin.

The officers in the middle row are Don 'Scotty' Scott; 'Doc' Outfin, the MO; Henry Hall, Orton and Bill Kain. Tommy Tucker stands behind with Roy Marchand affectionately known as 'Dim' on the right. Members of the ground crew stand in the doorway.

as a medical student, in order to take up flying and, still more recently, he had been carefully selected from his OUT up in Scotland for the honour of joining '73'. A tall, handsome fellow, of fine physique, uncomfortable in either cap or hat on account of his mass of black hair, he was soon a familiar, and popular, figure on the 'drome, and invariably minus headgear. Conscious — too self-conscious, indeed — of his relative insignificance at the outset amongst such a bunch of operationally tried (almost) veterans, his reticence and modesty were inevitably his passport to the real regard of his flattered fellow pilots. And when in due course he overcame his initial shyness and, with increasing self-confidence, began to ply them with eager — and on occasion, sufficiently ingenuous — questions for operational 'gen', the cognomen of 'Dim' automatically obtained. He was the second 'Dim', in fact, to grace the squadron's annals for there had been 'Dimmy' Forshaw in the earlier days of the squadron's reforming. And, quite in keeping, when Marchand in due course contrived to shoot down not one, but *two* Me's, in the course of a single day, as his initial contribution to the squadron's record of 'bags', it was inevitable that 'Dim' should remain 'Dim' to his pals, although he now demonstrably had the best of that particular argument!

New recruits: Lionel Pilkington, centre, with Lovett and Orton. Pilkington went missing on September 20, 1941 when serving with No. 111 Squadron at North Weald.

He never got those medals — not even the advance in rank he was entitled to after he died — but if he was ever really desirous of either distinction, we of the squadron must have been even more blind than we are now prepared to admit that we were; no one could have been so utterly indifferent to such precious baubles. No one was more entitled to them than Roy Marchand. Not at heart interested to command such, he did better . . . he deserved them!

February brought the first signs of improvement in the weather, and with a recrudescence in enemy penetrations, which was promptly accepted as a decent gesture on the part of the Boche, and one to be suitably acknowledged. This is by no means an operational history of the squadron, so it is sufficient for the purpose of this record to note that thereafter the squadron's 'bag' steadily mounted, and that there was soon hardly a pilot who was not in a position to claim at least one 'kill' to his credit.

To those at home he was of course someone we had never known, and perhaps never quite did. His mother, refusing to be comforted, wrote in her too brief, palpitating memoir of him (penned shortly after his death, on the peak day of the Battle of Britain — 15th September 1940): 'He was so fine, so manly, so courageous at the thought of adventure, for which he had sacrificed the chance of an Instructor's job. To put it in his own words to one of his friends: 'To get a few medals, old boy'.

Pilot Officer Roy 'Dim' Marchand, second left. He was wounded on May 13 and did not rejoin the squadron until July. Three months later he was dead, his Hurricane being shot down in combat over Maidstone on September 15, the day which has now become known as Battle of Britain Day. With 'Dim' in this picture in the crew room are Ian Scoular on the cot, Peter Walker and Bill Kain.

Official censored caption: 'Sandwiched between two cannon-firing Messerschmitts, the 21-year-old New Zealand pilot won a brilliant success in a battle over the Siegfried Line on Saturday. He and a Sergeant Pilot were on patrol when engaged by Messerschmitt fighters escorting seven Heinkel bombers. The sergeant was unlucky, being hit by cannon fire very early in the fight. With his radiator damaged, he had to make a forced landing. The New Zealand pilot then took over single-handed. After a terrific battle he shot down one Messerschmitt. The other made off. It is believed that this machine also crashed. This is the third German to this young pilot's credit — possibly a fourth.' *Right:* 'Getting ready for more. The Sergeant Pilot helping the New Zealand Flying Officer to reload his machine with ammunition before resuming patrol.' *Below:* 'Walking to their machines to go on patrol hoping to meet more Germans in the air.'

And so it came about that visitors from HQ Rheims (who were classed as 'sheep', but who were no fools) first wondered, then became curious, and finally perhaps a little anxious, as to why the Press (a notoriously thirsty crowd) were so unanimous for '73'. And was it not a fact that any of the pilots who proceeded upon leave to Paris were sure of unconditional, and presumably free, accommodation in the service flats maintained by the respective Press correspondents?

It was curious, to say the least. Why this preference, why this concentration upon, and priority given to one particular squadron? Admittedly '73' was putting up a damned fine show but so was No. 1 and 'security' had clamped down so tightly upon the Press that the only sop gained by them so far had been permission, grudgingly enough given, to lift a corner of the cloak of 'Cobber's' concealment — the world being permitted to know that their hero was a New Zealander. But, reasoned Head-quarters, was all this publicity good for the pilots, either in general or in particular? Should there be such close liaison between the Press and '73' that a carload of them was upon the scene within a few hours of the latest victory!

This combat took place on March 2 and the RAF publicity machine was quick to take advantage, taking a series of pictures of 'Cobber' and Don Sewell although neither were named in the official captioning. And sorry to say, Luftwaffe records show that 'Cobber' failed to score that day. (Sewell later transferred to Bomber Command and his Lancaster crashed in the sea off Belgium while on an operation to Frankfurt on the night of March 18/19, 1944. His body was never found.)

Left: George 'Ian' Brotchie in his room in No. 22 Grand Rue. The wartime caption does not identify him by name but says: 'A Dundee Flying Officer (*sic*) who, while flying at 19,000 feet with another aircraft of his squadron, sighted a Dornier and, after his colleague had first engaged the enemy, attacked and saw the Dornier dive away with one engine out of action to 2,000 ft.

It is thought that the Dornier must have crashed inside the German frontier'. This combat took place on March 29 and both he and 'Tubs' Perry were credited with a probable although no Dornier is listed as having been lost that day. (Brotchie was killed at Debden in March 1942.) *Right:* Unfortunately all the fireplaces in the Morlet-Coppey home have been replaced with radiators.

For instance, 'Wee' Brotchie on one occasion failed to return with his section, and an anxious crowd upon the 'drome scoured the horizon, west and east, until at last — and not a minute too soon — a plane dived down towards us, significantly, however, omitting the customary circuit of the 'drome. And particular notice was taken of the black, gaping holes in the leading edges of the wing, where the gun panels were situated. But the pilot seemed to be in no hurry to get out of his plane, the prop of which too had gone 'dead' upon him, apparently. His crew dashed towards it, and were to be seen lifting him out of the cockpit. God, not so bad as *that* — and the 'Wee' Brotch, too! Fortunately it was not so bad as that; but his little adventure with an Me 109 was followed by a spell in hospital, where he was later to be joined by his bosom pal 'Pete' Walker.

And 'Tommy' Tucker thought that he too had a claim to advance. There were two versions of the affair. One was put forward with some heat by the other two pilots of the particular section involved, and to the effect that whilst they were making their approach towards an unsuspecting Do17, and meanwhile holding their fire, they suddenly became unpleasantly aware of a stream of tracer bullets passing between them, from the direction of 'Tommy' Tucker, well in the rear, but already in action! 'Tommy's' story in fact, closely corroborated that of the other two but he felt justified in the event which, he was increasingly positive, was in his favour. And he buttonholed me several times in the course of the next few days. Did I think he had 'got him'? 'Well, "Tommy", old boy, there seems to be a bit of a doubt about it; and you didn't quite make yourself excessively popular with the rest of the section, did you?'

'But I was within range.'

'*Extreme* range, according to the others.' And then 'Tommy' would fly

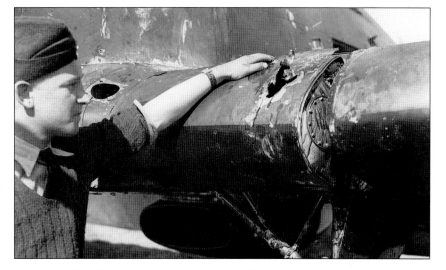

Damage to Brotchie's Hurricane being examined by an airframe fitter.

off into one of his very own particular brand of rages, and would smash down the bottle of HP sauce upon the table, in order to emphasise his argument and unfortunately the ceiling of the Mess would be spattered with nasty red blobs.

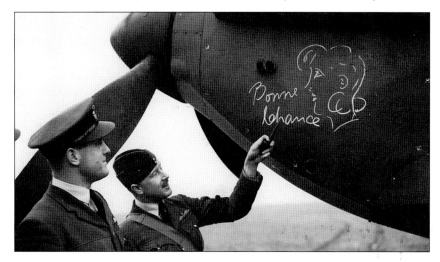

'Tommy' Tucker points out his mascot drawing to Peter Ayerst although there was a strict rule about no pipes in the vicinity of aircraft!

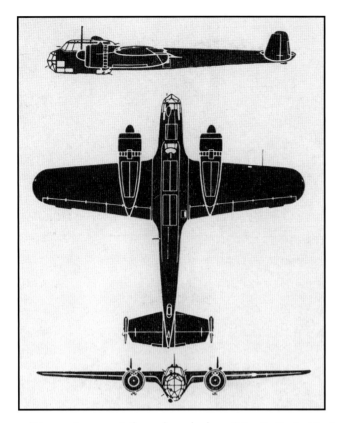 

'Tommy' was not the only unlucky one. Fate had already singled out, of all persons, 'Reg' Lovett for a particularly black mark in his pilot's log-book. News came through on the service line that he had shot down a German plane, some 70 miles distant, and had thereafter force-landed. As the whole of the operational pilots were otherwise engaged, the 'Doc' and I set forth in the 'tourer' to verify this claim, and to pick up Lovett. It was soon apparent that a machine had been shot down, but it was difficult to locate it, owing to the the unsatisfactory contacts we made with clods of French peasants. However, at last we obtained a clue — and most unpleasant misgivings struck into our hearts. No, there was no German plane around; but there *was* a French one, lying in the fields some miles distant. We neither of us said anything, but directed the driver towards a small group gathered upon a rounded knoll.

Alas, it was only too true; 'Reg' had shot down a French Potez in error; and the one survivor was in hospital with a broken hip! The splintered bone of a leg stood pitifully upright, from a blood-stained flying boot close by; and a gendarme was weeping silently beside the wreckage. Lovett was not present and we returned sadly enough. During the course of the same evening. Wing Commander Walter, of 67 Wing came over to open an investigation, and at the close of it he had the unpleasant duty of placing Lovett under open arrest in my presence, the CO being absent. Next day, I accompanied 'Reg' to the hospital where he nearly broke down before the injured pilot, who informed us that Lovett's machine-gun fire had killed the French rear gunner outright. *'C'est la guerre, c'est la guerre.* It was all a mistake. Don't worry. *Ça va!'*

Friendly fire incidents have always happened in war. It was on December 21 that one of the most embarrassing episodes befell No. 73 Squadron during the Phoney War . . . and the culprit was none other than the deputy commanding officer! *Left:* **The Dornier 17 and** *(right)* **the Potez 630 series. (See page 126.)**

'Reg' had the universal sympathy of both officers and men upon this occasion. After all, a Potez was not unlike a Dornier and the identification marks were not *so* obviously or prominently displayed either. And 'Reg' was not entirely to blame for a sergeant pilot of his section had finished off the Potez. Still it was unfortunate. It was not the first time a Potez had been shot up (serve it right, muttered the pilots, for barging in upon a dogfight). In due course, 'Reg' was ordered to report to HQ Rheims, and we feared the worst. He was due for his Flight Lieutenancy and perhaps he would have to forego this. But in the event it proved not quite so bad — the French were reasonable; they echoed the sentiments of the injured pilot. *'C'est la guerre'*; and 'Reg' came back with nothing more serious than an admonition and a request not to do it again. But there was a look in his keen eye which boded ill for the next Dornier he encountered — and there would be no mistake this time.

The 'phoney war' hardly suggests operations, so perhaps a selection from the authentic *Unofficial Diary* (more informative upon the operational aspect of our activities than the *Official* variant, the former having the advantage at this period of being maintained by Ian Scoular, one of the squadron's senior pilots) is indicated at this stage; the following entries are typical of brushes with the enemy.

February 20: Nice day in the morning, and some flying was done. Martin landed at Metz, having we think made a dash for Switzerland, but found the mountains too high. Major Norcott

arrived to stay with us for a few days, as he is in charge of a gang who are to make the one and only decent landing ground in France — we hope. In the evening, Claudie 'Harbinger' Wright pushed out a boat, having been promoted; and what a party ensued. Doc 'Fin' drank half-pints of champagne; and, what with soda syphon bottles, a good time was had by all — until waking up next morning.

March 2: Strong wind, and frost at night. Began with a patrol on the left front, and later six machines escorted a Potez upon a photographic job. One section was afterwards detached and flew on the front left patrol line — one of the three came back with oil-pressure trouble, while the other two, 'Cobber' and Sgt Sewell, closed two Me 109s and seven Heinkel 111s. Sgt Sewell was forced to land with engine trouble, while 'Cobber' hung on and brought down a Me 109; and although his aircraft was badly damaged, he managed to land it at Metz aerodrome. Sgt Sewell landed at Brulange. Tucker, returning from patrol, forced-landed near Abaucourt; and on our last patrol of the evening, Wright forced-landed near Metz, at a place called Noisseville, where he will be for the night, as we cannot fetch him tonight.

Alas for 'Claudie' — it was not to be quite so simple as all that; the forced-landing resulted in such a violent contact with his instrument dashboard that only after months of treatment from plastic and other surgeons was he at all fairly presentable for further operations, in England and that *final* combat which removed him from all but our memory.

'Is it friend . . . or foe?' Henry Hall's written caption for this picture was 'Enemy aircraft reported approaching'. The squadron sent a party to the funeral at Ansermet of the two French airmen, Lieutenant G. Castellana and Adjutant M. Pernot, who had been killed in the Potez crash. Robin Press who led the delegation recalled the 'controlled hostility of the assembled crowd as I felt that they regarded me as the culprit'. All four pictured outside the Mess were later killed: Reg Lovett, left, in the Battle of Britain on September 7; 'Cobber' Kain in an accident on June 7; Newell Orton went missing on September 17, 1941, and Basil Pyne was shot down on May 14.

The next entry (contributed by the Adjutant, in the temporary absence of Scoular) was, to anticipate a little, upon the occasion of the first change-over in command.

March 26: The squadron's great day — a farewell to its old CO, and welcome to the new S/Ldr McEwan) — and a few replacement pilots and aircraft indicated in Nazi Germany as a result of the day's efforts. Events have moved too swiftly to hope to give a coherent account; and, after a 'session' in the Sergeants Mess (in honour of the two COs), it is perhaps foolish to make the attempt at precisely 1.30 a.m. of the following day! However, at about 12.15 midday of yesterday, the Adjutant, uncomfortably cornered by the two COs, fortunately heard the noise of AA fire, and diverted the attention of his immediate superiors, from Secret (and non-existent) documents, to the fact of a beautiful enemy formation of three, heading from south-east straight over the 'drome, and followed at a discreet distance by French AA — as usual. Two Hurricanes, however, sufficed to break up the formation, and all disappeared into the blue, leaving us down below to calculate the odds. The F/Lt Lovett landed; and if ever man had the devil's own luck, Reggie was that man — with bullet holes a few inches from his petrol tanks, and even less from where he sits — and some of them more suggestive of cannon than bullets. For the third time in one month he had tackled the enemy, and still fate held out on him, with one enemy aircraft certainly damaged, and possibly fallen, but nothing conclusive to show for his efforts. Sgt Pilkington

had a bullet hole through his prop as evidence too of uncomfortably close connection with the enemy.

It was, however, reserved for the afternoons to produce a series of almost melodramatic thrills, with machines landing one after the other, in damaged condition; and the Orderly Room telephone tingling with impossible accounts of machines downed, and enemy pilots falling by parachute. Even the 'Fin' had to forego his afternoon nap, and duly appeared on the 'drome, in full war gear, and had to be led away from the vicinity of the Magister. As for the

Adjutant, he ran berserk with Forms 'F', and 'Gun Behaviour', and 'Personal Combats', flourishing them in the faces of pilots landing with nonchalant accounts of one, two, perhaps three Me 109's downed — Orton, Perry, Sgt Pyne. Orton a little pale, but otherwise the same old 'Fanny', and with certainly one, and perhaps two e/a to his credit. The genial J.G.P. (Perry), none more surprised than himself at having cornered a 'sitter' Me 109 — and violently sick on reflection; and Sgt Pyne, pleased as any overgrown boy would be at having brought the feared Me to earth. As for the planes, there they were, bullet-holed, and with a surging crowd of RAF personnel and French soldiers, examining holes and rents and dents. And of all the spectators, none more interested or pleased than S/Ldr MacEwan, who early made his appearance on the 'drome, and, as each machine coasted in, watched for the sign of gun-panels shot away. Indubitably no incoming CO ever had a better 'house-warming'.

But there was a note of apprehension throughout: what of 'Cobber' of whom it had been reported that he had last been seen about to land by parachute! All machines due were now landed but his, and it was not until 6 p.m. that word was received to the effect that he was safe and OK. Shortly afterwards, the Adjutant, whilst telephoning for his whereabouts, saw a French 'tourer' drive up, and in it was a rather soiled and crumpled object — but 'Cobber' none the less — hit in the leg and left hand, burnt on the face, and a bit washed-out — with two Me 109s to his credit, having dashed into a packet of nine of them, and achieved this notable result, here being accounted for himself. In his own words, as related to a crowd around the Mess bar, he had watched one machine go down in flames, and sent another to possibly a similar fate, when he suddenly found himself turning into the sun and a clear sky (excepting the machine, or machines, on his tail which he did not see). Then his emergency hood was

neatly removed by cannon, and a tidy fire originated, which he attempted to circumvent by bending down to switch off the petrol, and only reaped a burnt face for his efforts. After that there was little else to do but test the virtues of an Irving parachute, which he promptly put into effect, having first of all got out of the machine on the wrong side, and secondly forgotten to operate the release handle, so enamoured was he for a moment or two with the pleasant sensation of falling into nothing. He remembered nothing more until awakening in a beautiful white world (later recognised as prosaic cloud) and wondering if it was heaven! It, of course, was not, and the realities of a mundane existence were impressed on him as he descended earthwards with German soldiers taking pot shots at him. And it was either here, or whilst still in his machine, he received shrapnel wounds in his left calf, and a graze on his left knuckles. Having come to earth with a decided bump (he had already nearly castrated himself during the suddenly arrested course of his descent), he was menaced by a crowd of French soldiers, who fortunately had their zeal tempered a little by the timely arrival of a French officer; and so, by degrees, he arrived back into the bosom of 73.

Things were certainly beginning to hot up, now that spring was on the way. There had been various flaps, dating as far back as the previous November, and more than once I had been fetched out of bed to receive and to decode cypher messages of grave import, but still the war hung fire, and the occasional spots of bother only seemed to give point to the 'phoneyness' of it all. The war was in danger of becoming not so much a bore as the subject of grave misgiving, amounting almost to the hope that the whole affair would fizzle out, in our favour, too, for it was becoming increasingly obvious that we and the French were ill-prepared to withstand a heavy blow, if the defences (offensive action except in the air no longer entered our heads) strung out upon our portion of the French frontier were anything to go by, even taking into account too the fact of a reputed no fewer than 6,000 horses, limber and cavalry, stationed around Etain, a mile or two down the road towards Verdun!

Presumably this latter mean business but just what sort of business we shuddered to think of, in our capacity of a fighter squadron already picking up the notion of ground-strafing. It was significant, too, that the weary trail of horse-drawn transport usually elected to file past my office in the pitch dark of a rainy night as it headed towards the all-absorbing Maginot, or possibly the industrial area around Briey. And not only the French, but the British, our own lads, were taking up war positions in those areas. As they passed through, 'old-timers' looked upon them with almost fatherly, patronising interest. They had all their troubles before them, but would doubtless make the grade. And on their part they regarded us with flattering curiosity; wasn't this *the* squadron; and perhaps they might catch a glimpse of the great 'Cobber' himself. That would be something to write home about. And they did meet 'Cobber'; or rather, a certain junior officer of the artillery did, and doubtless will remember the incident — if he is still alive.

We were returning, a little elevated and merry, from an evening at the Vauban, and on the long flat stretch

towards Etain we caught up with a convoy of artillery proceeding at a snail's pace and quite commendably with no headlights. This was of course as it should be; there were orders to that effect but of course neither the French nor we bothered any more about such trifles at this stage of the war. We were making fair progress alongside the convoy, with the aid of our brilliant head-

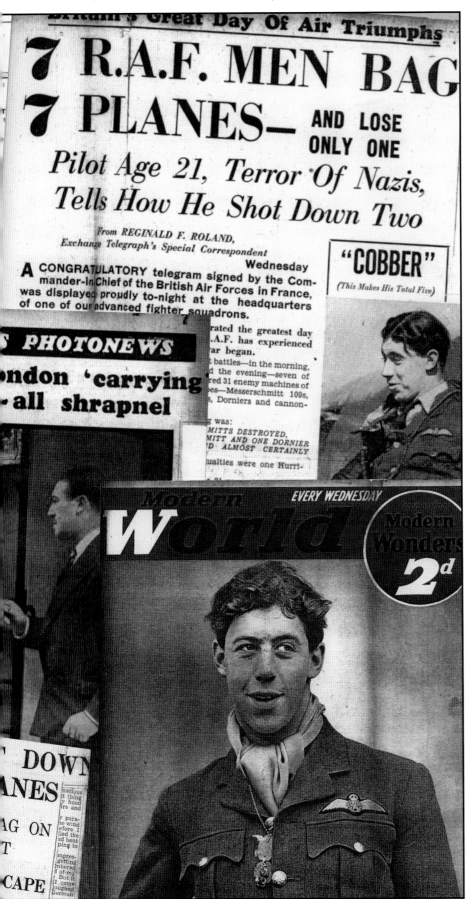

lights, when suddenly, as we drew near the head of the column, a figure stood forth, and with wildly waving arms, presumed we would halt. He was, of course, quite wrong in his presumption and just escaped in time.

Properly infuriated at this piece of impertinence, it was decided to prepare a reception for the uppish blighter. A stack of straw was abstracted from a barn in the village, and heaped up in the road along which the convoy must necessarily pass, and upon the approach of the vehicles, this was lit, with a resultant blazing bonfire. And a blazing young officer strutted importantly forward into the light of the dancing flames. 'Do you realise that you are imperilling the safety of my convoy?'

'Are we? Frightfully sorry, old chap; have a gasper?' With a gesture of combined irritation and utter contempt, he produced a note-book and a pencil, and, addressing 'Cobber', demanded his name. 'F/O. Joe Cod.' And went down 'J. Cod, F/O.' in the note-book. 'And this officer?' indicating 'Pissy' Paul. 'Joe Cod's brother.' The note-book was shut-to with a snap; only just in time, too, had the poor wretch but known it, for there was a glint in 'Cobber's' eyes which was not entirely that of the reflection of the fire.

For a week or two after his peppering with shrapnel, 'Cobber' hobbled around on sticks and it was during the convalescent period of enforced 'grounding' that I hazarded the suggestion that he might endeavour to prove himself in another line of action — that of Gas Officer, which was his particular 'odd job'. For months I had wasted my rhetoric upon him, in an endeavour to persuade him to show a good example to the rest of the squadron in the little matter of carrying his respirator about with him. "Cut it out, "Henry",' he would retort, 'you're too small to be awkward', as he made a playful pass at me. And as a result of his handling of the job — or rather mishandling — there occurred one dreadful contretemps. An expert, highly placed at HQ, came down in order to inspect our gas equipment and local preparations against gas attack. No one — with the possible exception of the CO (who was unfortunately absent) — knew the situation exactly of the Gas Hut and Decontamination Room and accordingly 'Cobber' was requested to report in person at the Orderly Room to the Adjutant, and whether operationally disposed or not. He came, not a little annoyed at this interference with his sky-gazing tactics (he would recline for hours in a deck chair, scanning the skies with a pair of binoculars). Would he show this visiting officer from HQ the Decontamination Room? 'Certainly!' — and 'Cobber' felt fairly happy, relying confidently on his Gas Squad. The party approached a low shed, which, to everybody's satisfaction was discovered to be approximately labelled as laid down in Regulations. There was even a neat row of empty petrol tins outside, and tins of bleaching powder were available. 'Cobber' took a confident pull at the door, and out walked . . . a cow!

March 26 was a red-letter day as far as No. 73 Squadron were concerned. The previous day a new CO, Squadron Leader Kenneth McEwan, had arrived to replace Knox who was to fill a position with No. 11 Group in the UK. On his first day on the job, his pilots claimed seven aircraft destroyed ('Cobber' two Bf 109s; Orton two Bf 109s; Perry Bf 109 and Do 17 probable; Lovett a Do 17, and Pyne a Do 17) but examination of the Luftwaffe losses for that day (see page 153) does not bear this out. Nevertheless 'Fanny' was awarded the Distinguished Flying Cross for his exploit and Kain recommended for the Victoria Cross. 'Cobber' never got the VC but here he congratulates 'Fanny' on the award of the DFC for — what was stated at the time — 'bagging his sixth enemy aircraft'.

among other songs appropriate to the occasion, and that sort of occasion only. But my abiding recollection is of being thrown, with quite unnecessary violence, out of 'Tubs' Perry's billet somewhat later, followed by a shower of flying boots, toilet articles, and eventually 'Tub's' small wireless set — all tokens of the high esteem in which I was now at liberty to presume he held me. And as I turned towards my own billet, and passed the lighted windows of 'Cobber's' particular bedroom, there *he* was, writing, writing, writing. What a job he must now have, to keep pace with his fan mail! And as I passed, I yelled out: *'Lumiére, lumiére!'*

Official recognition of the work of the pilots had one amusing repercussion; cheap notoriety was not necessarily confined to officers and/or NCO-pilots. A batch of British newspapers had arrived in the Mess, and from a perusal of one of the illustrated dailies, 'Willie' Williams suddenly started up with a jerk. 'Doc, isn't this one of your nursing orderlies?' and he passed the folded sheet over to the MO. There, upon the front page, was a photograph of an erstwhile 'other rank' of his Sick Quarters, suddenly become a full-blown corporal. Further, the medal ribbon of a sufficiently desirable decoration for gallantry, coyly advertised itself upon his breast. Still further, he had been caught (perhaps not without preconceived design) with a bride depend-

'Cobber' had now passed the 'ace' mark ('Fanny' was a close runner-up, but either his publicity was bad, or he was too distant in his manner with the Press, and consequently the public remained almost unaware of him or of his achievements) and now the French signified that they were disposed to make some sort of a decent gesture. Actually, 'Cobber' was awarded his DFC whilst the French were still sitting upon their recommendation and, as a result of the war — the *real* war butting in — neither 'Cobber', nor 'Ian', nor 'Pissy' got the French decoration for which they had been recommended. (Is it, perhaps, too much to invite the attention of our Ally to current and apposite files of that period, for appropriate action?) As for 'Cobber's' DFC, there were rumours that it was in the wind some weeks before the official intimation arrived, and it really began to look as if No. 1 would beat us to it. Good luck to them, of course but, oh heck, play the game, HQ, play the game.

And then, one night, as we were gathered around the largest of the dining tables at the Vauban, each with an ENSA girl (some a trifle long in the tooth, but charmers every one) at his side, from a 'show' which we had just attended, the news was broken to the party by the CO: 'Cobber' was DFC at long last! There were whoops and screams as the mixed crowd made a dash for him (had we but known it, the hero of the evening was sickening for German measles!). In self-defence he planted himself against a massive sideboard, piled high in successive rows with choice wines and liqueurs. There

> I led my section into an attacking position behind and below a gaggle of twelve 109s. They spotted us, and two turned to head for Germany. I pulled the boost override and got close enough to get in a burst at one which dived away emitting black smoke. I could not see if it crashed because I was attacked by another and we manoeuvred for about ten minutes when he pulled up sharply in front of me and I got in a good long burst, after which he turned on his back and dived steeply into the ground emitting a small amount of flame. I was again attacked, and I made my way home.
>
> PILOT OFFICER NEWELL ORTON,
> COMBAT REPORT, MARCH 26, 1940

was a scuffle; 'Cobber's' face exhibited several neat cupid's bows in lipstick; and, with a mighty crash, which brought Marcel in with a rush, at least £20 worth of damage had been done. But did Marcel care? At such a moment as this — *'c'est la guerre!'*

'Fanny's' DFC came a few weeks later, and was suitably celebrated and on that occasion, he and his brother officers were the guests of the Sergeants Mess, at a social held by them in an upper room at Rouvres. It would be convenient to place a row of dots here, to be interpreted or filled in by those who are acquainted with sergeants and their Messes. I suppose the affair was a success but I have only a hazy memory of the later stages of it. I certainly remember 'Fanny's' flushed face — flushed as much with pleasure as with liquor; and I remember his signing numerous autographs for the children of the married men of his Flight who would certainly treasure the memento. And I have a vague recollection of our singing 'For he's a jolly good fellow',

ing upon his arm as he posed outside a church door. Behind the couple, a small Page was casting confetti and for caption there appeared 'Gunner . . . is not afraid of an attack from the rear!' (Incidentally, the alleged Gunner had omitted to remove the tell-tale medical orderly badges from his tunic lapels.) Unfortunately for the bridegroom, who in due course and quite unsuspectingly returned from leave, he was of course not a corporal; nor was he the rightful possessor of a Croix de Guerre; nor was he a rear-gunner. He was, in plain fact, a mere and 'browned-off' A.C.1 Nursing Orderly and undeniably now a married one.

This was a most serious crime, and I commenced to prepare papers for a Summary of Evidence, with a view to possible court-martial for masquerading, etc. etc. I had no option — or thought I hadn't, until suddenly in puffed the 'Doc' — an unwanted honour, for in the ordinary course of affairs, he avoided the Orderly Room like the plague. 'What's all this about . . . ?'

'Bad case, "Doc". He's for it, I'm afraid.'

'He's hell as like. Who knows anything about it?'

'Well, for one thing, it is plain to be seen in the photograph that your unauthorised gunner is wearing the collar badges of a nursing orderly. Do you think that unlikely conjunction is apt to be overlooked?' The 'Doc's' response was composed of just one word, anatomical, and hardly polite. I took the papers out of my desk, and slowly tore them up.

'Come and have a drink, "Henry"; you've done enough work for one day.'

Knox was genuinely pleased. He was proud of his bunch of boys. He could look ahead with supreme confidence. Everything was running smoothly. There was hardly another improvement to suggest, a chink in the armour to indicate a weakness. The triumph was perfect but perhaps too facile. One of his temperament *must* come to grips with something, or somebody. These periods

The 73 Squadron 'Doc' mixes a draught!

No. 73 Squadron at Rouvres then: Pilkington, Paul, Orton and Kain . . .

map — the map of the world, too! It bucked the lads no end to feel that their efforts were appreciated. Perhaps not *all* the lads got the 'cover' they so richly deserved but how could they hope to with 'incidents' occurring so regularly nowadays, and the Hurricane a match for anything the Germans had put in the air, as yet? And at such surprisingly little cost, too! How many casualties had the squadron suffered up to date — four deaths, and one or two temporary 'non-operationals' through wounds.

But there was that interview with the AOC, followed by this persistent rumour of an impending change of command. Was there anything in it — was there anything behind it? Oh, snap out of it. 'Driver! Where the hell's my driver? Tell him I want him here at once.'

The *Unofficial Diary* is apposite enough for quotation at this juncture!

March 18: The CO beat up the aerodrome, and fired his guns fairly close to a man ploughing in a field by the side of the landing field; in fact, it was *too* close for him, for he packed up, and led his horses away — so we are now expecting a complaint concerning same tomorrow, but are confident that 'onest 'Enery can deal with it all right.

of bad weather, they got one down and, ten to one, some important phone call, some important (or would-be important) visitor happened upon the squadron, in his quite legitimate absences. That unpleasantness with the CO. of No. 1, too — damn it, he had a perfect right to visit Bar-le-Duc, even if unofficially, hadn't he? The 'show' given there *was* for the Forces, wasn't it; so why be so damned exclusive about it. And as for his squadron here — results, results — that's all that mattered! And hadn't he produced results? He and Lovett — one must be fair.

And there was the vexed question of the Press correspondents; as fine and jolly a bunch of fellows as one could ever hope to be associated with. Had not this association, sponsored and encouraged by him, put '73' on to the

. . . and Rouvres now . . . home of the 3ème Régiment d'Hélicoptères de Combat.

Left: **The squadron with 'Tubs' Perry's Hotchkiss 'Elizabeth'. Owned jointly with 'Claudie' Wright, it could seat eight on outings to Verdun and Metz. Peter Ayerst believes that after Perry was killed on March 29, and 'Claudie' returned to the UK, the car was left with a cafe owner in Nantes on June 17, 1940 when the squadron left France. These pictures were taken the** **previous December when an RAF photographer visited the station. 'Tubs' is at the wheel with Henry Hall and Peter Ayerst on the front bumper. Tucker, Orton and Lovett are on the right running board and Brotchie, 'Cobber' and 'Smooth' Holliday on the left.** *Right:* **Looking up the track which is all that is left of the old road to the airfield (see sketch page 22).**

Six months had passed since my arrival in France — six vital months. It was time to take stock of myself. The extrovert and the introvert seemed to be getting inextricably mixed, nowadays — besides, could I be both? And, endeavouring to collect myself, I would make towards a shallow depression in the water meadows, which lay in the rear of the village, and along which flowed a fussy little runlet, hardly a jump across in width, and bordered by green, flower-speckled banks. A mile or two distant, upon the crest of one of the lumbering, slow undulations which characterised the countryside in that direction, rose the spire of a village church — a pointer? But somehow I felt nearer to the communion I was seeking, enveloped in this pantheistic, mild expression of natural beauty.

My dearest Joan,

Don't laugh at the blunder above [I had inadvertently given my home address, instead of the BEF one] — my thoughts were far away, with 'Tubs' Perry, who has gone to his last account, and with him has taken God alone knows how much of me. Oh Suzie, how I loved that man at my time of life, to find that I could make a friend, and so effortlessly take him to my very heart, and so grieve at his loss — God has favoured me, and in taking him out of my life, has only consecrated that feeling I had for one of the sweetest natures ever produced. To us of the Mess he was known always as the genial J.G.P.' — that exactly summed him up. I can add little more, for he was so incapable of being anything else. Some would have called him a fool on his first acquaintance — but if he was a fool, it was to himself only — and we all loved him; not so much for his virtues as for his weaknesses. My own Orderly Room corporal begged permission to attend his funeral; and if the whole squadron could go to it, it would go as one man. It has been a heavy, a most bitter blow — and so tragically sudden.

As I was having breakfast, I heard the clatter of AA fire, and I rushed out, and there, shining in the sun, and silhouetted against a perfect frosty blue sky, were no fewer than six Do 17s — and after them were three of our machines! — Brotchie leading, Perry and a sergeant pilot with him. Later, Brotchie and the sergeant returned — but no Tubs'. It appeared that they tackled one, Perry gave it the first burst, followed by Brotchie, who put one of its engines out of the running and beat it down nearly to ground level, after killing its gunner. It just managed to scramble over the frontier, with the French ground fire peppering away at it. But Tubs had meanwhile disappeared lost himself, as he was somewhat in the habit of doing. Later on in the morning I heard *he had crashed and was injured; and I had just completed the official form to send off to HQ, when Lovett came on the 'phone — 'Sorry, old man — bad news!' He had no need to say more. It was enough, and I had lost the greatest gift that Hitler ever made in the wildest of his dreams of power.*

Poor 'Tubs' — he tried to land, hit a piece of marshy ground, turned turtle, and broke his neck. Some French soldiers rushed up and released him — he breathed once or twice and passed quietly away. God rest him, and help me to face up to a world without him in it. Yes, I have wept — bitterly, in the quiet of my Orderly Room, but now I feel calm; and 'Tubs' would have it so. I was twice his age, and perhaps it has come to very few to form such a queer friendship in such as short time, and with such a disparity in years. I have written to his mother, and paid a last tribute to him in the Official Diary. I have arranged about his coffin, the digging party, the funeral — and I shall pay my last respects at his burial on Sunday — and I hope I shall not break down — I must not. You know what he has meant to me — how he was to have come home on leave with me next week *— oh, it is all so horrible — but it must be borne, with what fortitude I can bring to bear.*

I know you will excuse more from me tonight, Suzie. I hope and know that you have enjoyed your holiday, and I hope to see you next week. I will send you a telegram as soon as I am in England; and I will try and get 'Cobber' to come down for an evening, as he will be in England too.

All my love. God bless you.

Yours ever
Dad xx

LETTER FROM PILOT OFFICER HENRY HALL
TO HIS DAUGHTER, MARCH 29, 1940

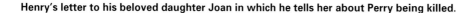

Henry's letter to his beloved daughter Joan in which he tells her about Perry being killed.

Left: Another shot in the series posed for the photographer. 'Tommy' Tucker prominent on the left. *Right:* The opposite view looking towards the aerodrome along the course of the old road. The houses are post-war married quarters for air base personnel.

More conventional transport from the Mess to the aerodrome. Sitting (L-R): Bill Kain, Basil 'Titch' Pyne, Harold 'Ginger' Paul and 'Tommy Tucker'. Behind: Roy 'Dim' Marchand, Peter Ayerst, Ian Scoular, 'Cobber' and Ken 'Tubby' Campbell.

At the top of the hill where originally it ran straight ahead, the road now turns right across the field to the aerodrome.

For the first months of the Phoney War, the RAF in France (as we have seen on the tables on pages 16-17) was split into two air forces with separate commands — the BEF Air Component and the Advanced Air Striking Force. No. 73 Squadron was switched from the former to the latter back in October but it soon became very evident that there was a need for an overall commander for the British Air Forces in France (BAFF).

Left: The commander appointed in January 1940 was Air Marshal Sir Arthur Barratt, seen here on the left with the AOC-in-C of the AASF, Air Vice-Marshal Playfair, visiting Rouvres on April 2. *Right:* No. 73 had only just received their new commanding officer, Squadron Leader Kenneth McEwan, although he lasted all of three weeks, being replaced on April 16 by Squadron Leader James More.

April, and sinister rumours. Was it *really* about to happen at long last? It certainly looked rather like it. The *Altmark* cutting out by the Navy had been a damned fine show, quite in the old tradition but, after all, it *was* a violation of neutral waters, surely?

April 2: Great preparations in all departments for the visit of the AOC-in-C, who duly arrived by air about 12.30 hours, at about the same time as the AOC (whose previous visits are likely to be remembered by those into whose affairs he enquired a little too closely). All, however, went well — a dinner, which was calculated to cost individual members of the Mess approximately forty francs, was so much appreciated by the visitors that payment was insisted upon, and the 'Fin' was reimbursed to the tune of twelve francs per, from the eight members of Headquarters Staff. The men were paraded on the 'drome, and the AOC-in-C, addressed them, praising the work of the squadron, both in the air and on the ground, and spoke also upon the twin topics of drunkenness and VD! Later he visited the Airmen's Mess, billets, and the Sick Quarters, and eventually departed, into very murky weather, at 15.00 hours. We now await, with what confidence we can command, the almost certain series of comments which will descend upon us from HQ in due course.

The second batch of leave from '73' was now in operation, and my turn had arrived again. The news came through of the invasion of Norway, as I waited impatiently upon the quayside at Boulogne. Blast Hitler! Would this mean the cancellation of all leave? My

luck was in, however, though it proved to be the last boat-load of leave personnel to England, and we were heavily escorted.

When I departed on leave the new CO Squadron Leader McEwan, had just replaced Knox and I arrived back at Rouvres to find him displaced by yet another! And at once I sensed a change. What was it? Certainly there had been some minor alterations effected in my office and it looked as if this new CO had taken possession in earnest. For instance, I had now been allotted a smaller table to myself, facing the wall; no longer would I be able to stare out of the window, mostly unseeingly, towards the distant black belt of woods. But this was perhaps all to the good — the time for day-dreaming had passed, or soon would — and I shook 'Dickie' warmly by the hand. He shook mine with a touching fervour, almost indeed as if he would wring it off. 'Thank God for that, "Henry". Thank Christ you are back.'

'Why, what's the matter, what's all the emotion about?'

'Well, I cease office as Deputy Adjutant; that's all — and it's good enough for me.'

'Good God, what's got you, "Dickie"? Is it as bad as all that?' Then suddenly "Dickie" got busy with his files, and I turned as I heard steps behind me. The new CO!

'Hall? Pleased to meet you. "Dickie" has been doing your job in your absence. Had a good leave? Oh, by the way, my name's More — "Hank" More. Been doing Operations up at HQ of late. My luck's in, and I've got the squadron.'

Got the squadron! — and a subtle inflexion over 'the'! I stole a look at him; tall, seemingly all arms and legs; and as he sat there, his feet were distributed at an angle of quite 90 degrees. Comic! His talk, too, was a series of jerks; and he would toss his head, and suddenly rise, and would have trouble with those extraordinary legs of his, dancing about the little room as if suffering from some uncontrollable nervous reflex. Suddenly he turned to 'Dickie', still standing there, unhappily cornered. 'Give me that file upon so and so, please.' He turned over a letter or two, and made an immediate decision. I later realised that it was the right one, though by no means the only possible one.

This was getting interesting. I looked up at the walls. Over his head were two pinned small notices — one bore the legend 'Raspberry', the other 'Chocolate' (I frequently had to help him out with his spelling later). The 'Raspberries' would soon melt away and I was also to learn that 'Chocolate' meant less than nothing to him. In the small room beyond, the Clerks G/D were industriously at it; even the windows had been washed and a neat row of white-washed stones now led up to the office door. He had been with the squadron exactly one week, I learned and the going was still decidedly hard, both domestic and operational. The short-lived (through no fault of his own) command of Knox's immediate successor had evoked a sympathy which came dangerously near to being indecently expressed and upon the very night of More's arrival, too. He had had the 'perception and decency', so I was informed, to efface himself whilst the boys took the dispossessed CO down to the Vauban for a farewell binge. They had seen More there — a lonely figure — and had left it at that. In their opinion, it was a 'job', an outrageous wangle that was what it was. More had worked it, or it had been worked for him by some of his pals up at HQ. With appalling swiftness and succession.

It was no mere case, either, of a new broom sweeping clean; it was simply uncanny how he managed to put his finger upon the weak spots, the tender spots, somehow as if he had been informed what to look for.

Perhaps he *had* been informed. For instance, there had been operational activity in my absence, involving some successes against the enemy and, to give the devil his due, 'Hank' More had shot down an Me on the very day but one after his arrival and no other confirmation was necessary than the visual one of the German pilot, wrapped in his parachute around the tail of his doomed machine. But where were the Press correspondents? Not a sign of them!

And his attitude in regard to the Orderly Room and his own particular Office — 'Why, "Henry", old cock, you know almost anybody could walk in and look at the files in Knox's day. Christ, you can't get inside the blessed office now without a written permit — almost. And when he's not in his office, he's up on the 'drome. We don't know where we are these days. Can't you do something about it? You know — give him the tip, sort of.'

'Cobber' was glumness personified — it had hit him, perhaps, hardest of the lot. 'Fanny' had nothing to say. 'Ian was non-committal — as ever. As for 'Pissy', he was deeply involved — in more senses than one — in his Bar accounts. Poor 'Tommy' Tucker had been made to stand guard, for six solid hours, in the rain, beside yet another machine he had crashed — this time near Verdun; and, what was more, he had been ordered to submit a 'report' upon the affair! In fact, everybody had to write reports nowadays. You'd have to seek permission shortly to go to the 'bog'.

The senior officers descend to inspect the Operations Room. McEwan follows.

With the help of two former 'Erks' who recalled using it as a guardhouse during cold duty nights, we pinpointed where the old Ops Room had stood, here beside the old road from the village to the aerodrome, just inside the airfield perimeter.

Before leaving, Air Marshal Barratt addressed the whole squadron. The trees on the left are the same ones we saw on page 39.

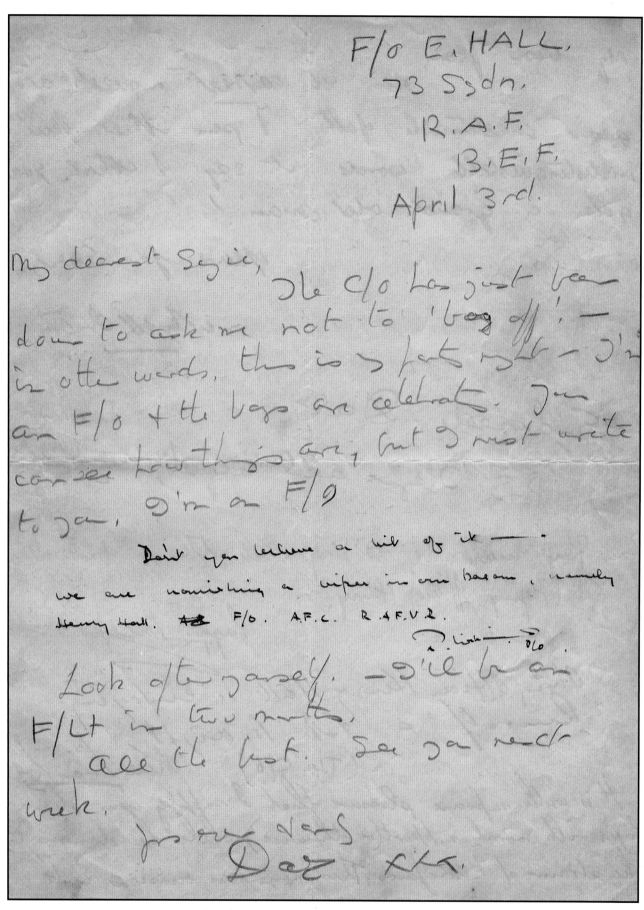

F/O E. HALL,
73 Sqdn.
R.A.F.
B.E.F.
April 3rd.

My dearest Sylvie, The C/O has just been down to ask me not to 'bag off'. — in other words, this is a fait accompli — I'm an F/O + the boys are celebrating. You can see how things are, but I must write to you, I'm an F/O

Don't you believe a bit of it —— we are nourishing a viper in our bosom, namely Henry Hall. F/O. A.F.C. R.A.F.V.R.

Look after yourself. — I'll be an F/Lt in two months. all the best. See you next week.

Yours very very
Dad xxx.

The day after the inspection tour Henry Hall wrote to his daughter to tell her of his promotion to Flying Officer and of his impending leave. This is the original letter which was autographed with congratulatory messages from many of the officers. 'Don't you believe a bit of it,' writes the Equipment Officer, Willie Williams. 'We are nourishing a viper in our harem, namely Henry Hall, F/O, A.F.C., R.A.F.V.R'. 'My wife accepted the situation', wrote Henry in his diary. 'She too was of 73 as half the letters she had received were from almost every member of the Mess, God protect those boys. Oh, God protect them'.

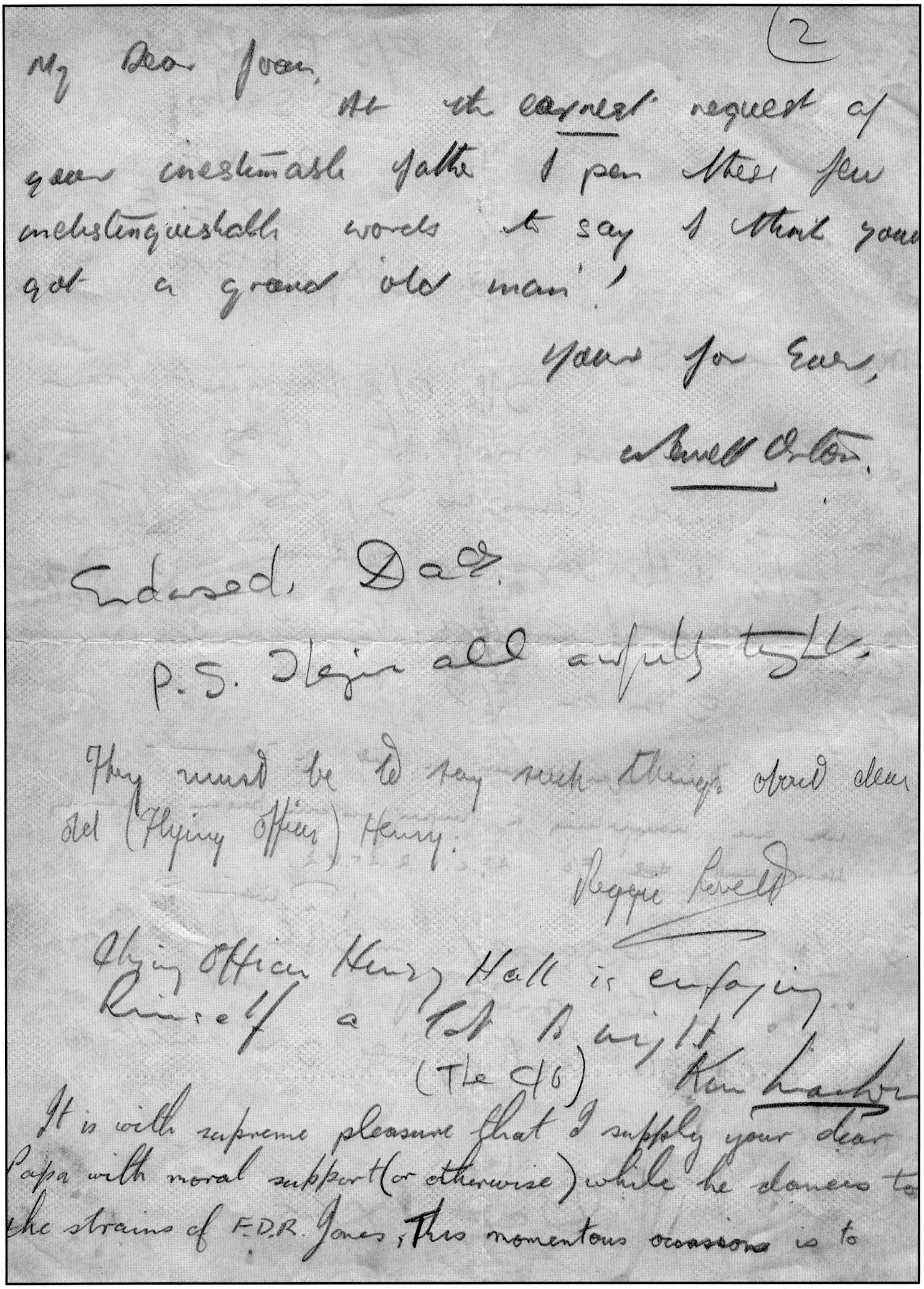

My Dear Joan,
                    At the earnest request of
your inestimable father I pen these few
indistinguishable words to say I think you
got a grand 'old man'.

                              Yours for Ears,

                                    Newell Orton.

Endorsed, Dad.

    P.S. They're all awfully tight.

They must be to say such things about dear
old (Flying Officer) Henry.

                                    Reggie Lovett

Flying Officer Henry Hall is enjoying
himself a lot tonight
                    (The CO)   Ken Marker

It is with supreme pleasure that I supply your dear
Papa with moral support (or otherwise) while he dances to
the strains of F.D.R. Jones, this momentous occasion is to

'My dear Joan', writes Newell Orton. 'At the earnest request of your inestimable father I pen these few indistinguishable words to say I think you've got a grand old man.' 'They must be to say such things about dear old (Flying Officer) Henry,' wrote Reg Lovett beneath Henry's comment that 'They're all awfully tight'.

The CO writes: 'Flying Officer Henry Hall is enjoying himself a lot tonight', and George Brotchie: 'It is with supreme pleasure that supply your dear Papa with moral support (or otherwise) while he dances to the strains of F.D.R. Jones. This momentous occasion is to celebrate his promotion to the exalted rank of F/O.'

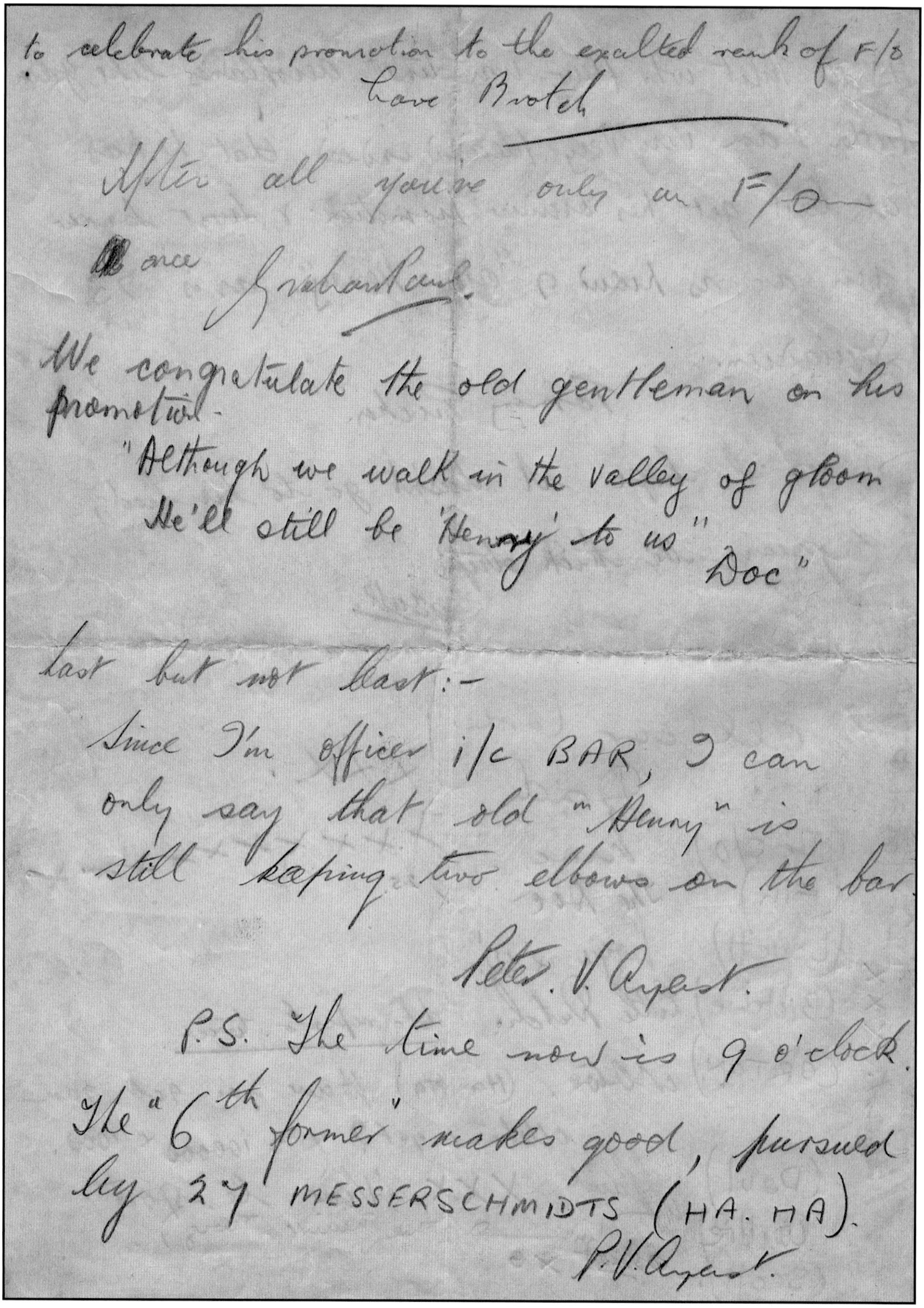

to celebrate his promotion to the exalted rank of F/O

Love Brotch

After all you're only an F/O once

Graham Paul

We congratulate the old gentleman on his promotion—

"Although we walk in the valley of gloom
He'll still be 'Henry' to us"

"Doc"

last but not least:—

Since I'm officer i/c BAR, I can only say that old "Henry" is still keeping two elbows on the bar.

Peter. V. Ayerst.

P.S. The time now is 9 o'clock.

The "6th former" makes good, pursued by 27 MESSERSCHMIDTS (HA. HA).

P.V. Ayerst.

Graham Paul writes: 'After all you're only an F/O once'. 'Doc' Finn: 'We congratulate the old gentleman on his promotion — "Although we walk in the valley of gloom, He'll still be 'Henry' to us".' Peter Ayerst follows with 'last but not least: — Since I'm officer i/c BAR, I can only say that old "Henry" is still keeping two elbows on the bar. P.S. The time is now 9 o'clock. The "6th former" makes good, pursued by 27 Messerschmitts (Ha Ha).'

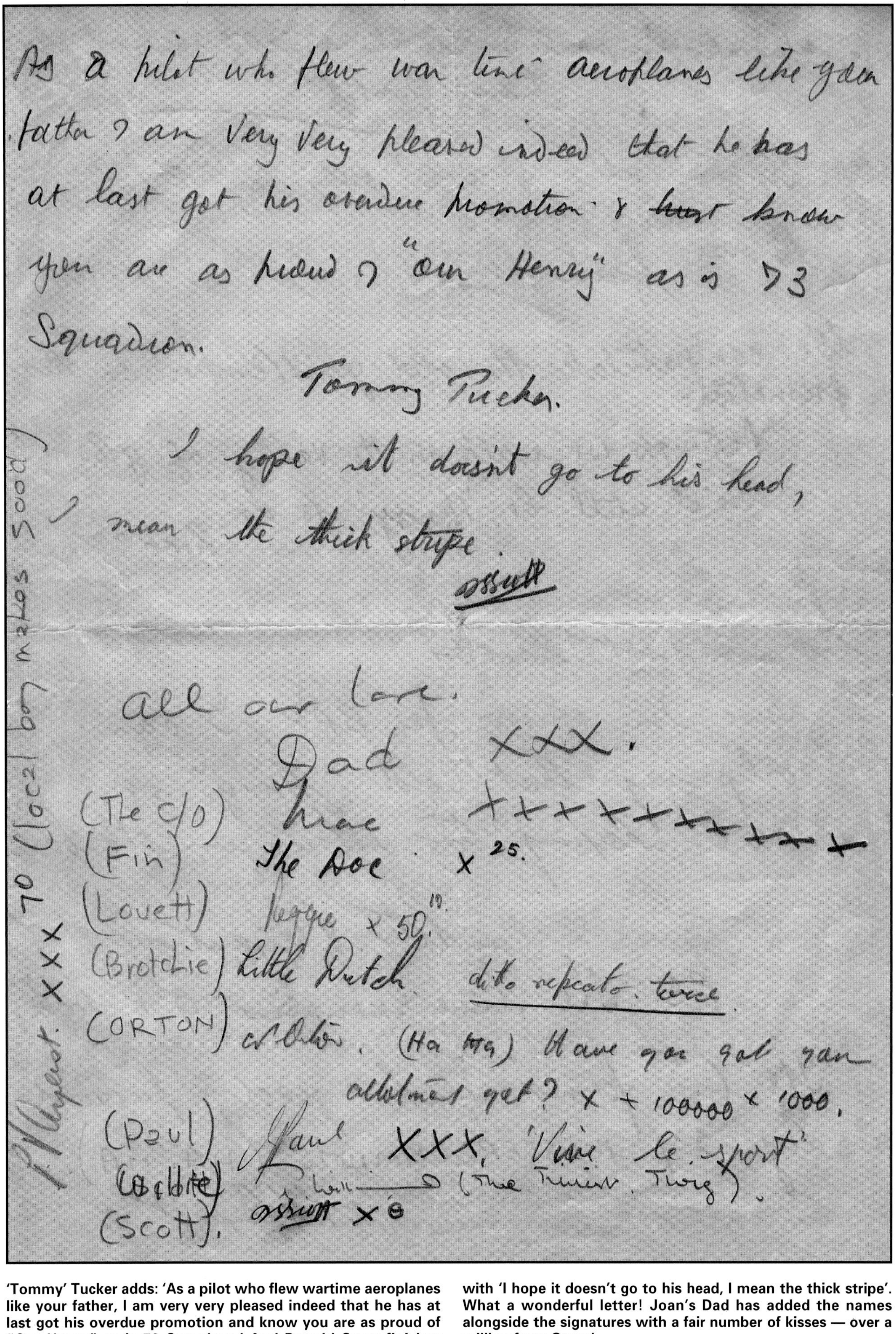

As a pilot who flew war time aeroplanes like your father I am very very pleased indeed that he has at last got his overdue promotion & ~~must~~ know you are as proud of "our Henry" as is 73 Squadron.

Tommy Tucker.

I hope it doesn't go to his head, I mean the thick stripe.

scott

all our love.
Dad   xxx.
(The C/O) Mac   xxxxxxxxxxxx
(Fin) The Doc x25.
(Lovett) Reggie x 5019.
(Brotchie) Little Dutch.   dito repeato. twice
(ORTON) orlton. (Ha Ha) Have you got yan
          allotmat yet? x + 100000 x 1000.
(Paul) Paul XXX, "Viva le. sport."
(Castle) .... (The Twins. Twig).
(Scott). scott x⊙

P. Whiplash. xxx 70 (local boy makes good)

'Tommy' Tucker adds: 'As a pilot who flew wartime aeroplanes like your father, I am very very pleased indeed that he has at last got his overdue promotion and know you are as proud of "Our Henry" as is 73 Squadron.' And Donald Scott finishes with 'I hope it doesn't go to his head, I mean the thick stripe'. What a wonderful letter! Joan's Dad has added the names alongside the signatures with a fair number of kisses — over a million from Orton!

65

As for myself, despite — or perhaps because he senses the almost entire lack of encouragement, and the difficulties under which I had laboured in the past — More found little to comment adversely upon. One or two suggestions, yes, and if ever he found the Clerks' billet, (situated behind the Orderly Room) in *that* state again, he would know the reason why.

'And now, "Henry", can you tell me what you know of the Press down here? Incidentally, I don't want any unpleasantness, though I am perfectly aware that I'm heading for trouble. I am not exactly blind and it *was* damned hard luck upon my immediate predecessor. That double shuffle of a posting was a silly mistake, which ought never to have occurred. But to revert to the other matter, I am arranging to have an officer down here from HQ, and I want to talk quite frankly with him upon this subject of the Press folk. Meantime, I have for-

On April 19 an RAF photographer arrived at Reims to take some air-to-air shots of the Hurricanes of No. 73 Squadron which flew in to rendezvous. Mr Devon, who was known to the pilots as 'Glorious', sat in the rear seat of a Fairey Battle.

The machines were piloted by Reg Lovett in 'D', Newell Orton in 'J' and Peter Walker in 'E'.

The next three weeks rocked the squadron to its foundations. The pilots could not help but admit that there *was* room for improvement; but now the fighting spirit was that of a mule — sullen, ready to kick viciously. And it was the unfortunate 'Tommy' Tucker who brought matters to a head. Not only was the new CO carrying on the disciplinary traditions of Knox, so far as the officers were concerned, but he even went some degrees further. 'Tommy' was apparently lazy, in addition to his other deficiencies; the report upon his recent crash was still not forthcoming. There was a cure for that — a run around the perimeter of the 'drome, once each morning! The 'Doc' promptly took an interest in the affair. Was 'Tommy' fit for the ordeal; for an ordeal it must prove, in the case of a man so palpably unfit. But, countered More, if Tucker was unfit to take not too excessive physical exercise, what was his state of fitness to continue as a pilot? Hotly the Mess canvassed the situation. Were they going to stand for it? 'Tommy' had

bidden the squadron to them. I am not interested in boosting up the individual as against the squadron. We are going into this job as a team, with me leading.'

The last sentence struck me. It was revolutionary, pregnant with meaning. If he could carry this thing off — and he did not seem to have any doubt about it — what a squadron it would be! A new note had been struck. The reign of individualism in '73' had usefully served its period, but had now been found wanting. Henceforward, '73' would only count as a whole, a team. The unit must subordinate itself to the welfare and efficiency of the majority. The part might still prove to be greater than the whole but it must not be allowed to impose itself upon the whole, nor to militate against unity by one false note of self-expression at the expense of the rest.

Identifiable aircraft are P2569, P2575 and N2359.

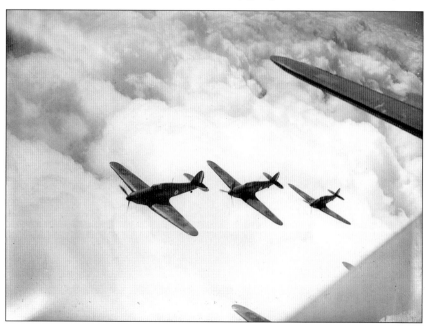

his weak points, admittedly, but the line must be drawn somewhere. Oh, come on fellows, let's go down to the Vauban.

But here arose another snag, 'Tommy' was confined to camp, pending production of the report. Meantime, I had forborne to interfere and, in any case, I too was rather under a cloud. The Adjutant obviously must have the CO's ear — how much did I know? And how much did the CO know through *my* instrumentality? How far was I prepared to go with the boys? 'Come on, "Henry", you're coming with us.'

'Not if "Tommy" goes.' The pilots concerned marched out in a body. Next morning I reported to Lovett. (Fortunately More was up at HQ, upon some business or other, and we had the battleground to ourselves.) 'Tommy' had accompanied the others, as I had guessed he would. Lovett taxed him with disobedience, and was met with a flat denial. Right!

"Doc", did Tucker go to the Vauban last night?' The 'Doc' who could lie like a trooper in what he considered a good cause, answered with an unblushing negative. There was apparently nothing to be done about it. But they had not reckoned with 'Reg', who was so particular where his prerogatives came in. His allegiance he owed to his CO and that CO should have it just as long as he proved himself worthy of it. On the other hand, Flight Lieutenant Lovett was for the time being acting CO, and the squadron was his to command. All officers would parade in the Mess at 07.30 hours the following morning — including the MO!

'Tommy' Tucker had his good points; he realised that he had involved the other officers in a nasty jam. He was frightened, of course, of Lovett, and had lied partly through fear of the consequences of telling the truth. Later that

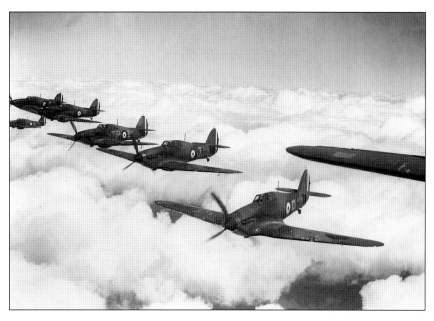

At the end of the session, Devon's Battle dived away into cloud losing a couple of the Hurricanes which then flew straight back to Rouvres to refuel.

day he sought out Lovett, and confessed. The meeting still held. Lovett spoke calmly, and with quiet dignity. Were the boys quite satisfied with their recent, their present, behaviour? It was not for him to apologise for his CO or to try and explain him away. More was the CO of the squadron, and nobody could yet accuse him of aught but a tightening-up of discipline and in that he felt he could support him to the hilt, and would. More had not interfered in any unconstitutional way with the legitimate exercise of any of the pilots' liberties. He had stood his rounds at the bar, and had certainly halved the responsibilities of individual flight commanders. It was obvious that his technique sprang from

an inside knowledge of operations and it was obvious, too, that he would expect no more from any pilot than he himself was both able and willing to perform. Nobody knew what might next happen on the war front and division in the squadron at a time like this would spell disaster if it was caught on the hop. As for the affair of the other night. Tucker had owned up, and nothing further would be done in the matter. As for Flying Officer Hall, as Adjutant he had had a most unpleasant duty to perform, and it should be realised that he owed his first duty to his CO. He did not beg the officers to do the decent thing either by the Adjutant or the CO. He expected it of them. Thank you, gentlemen!

At readiness in the crew room. Of these four only Don Scott on the right survived the war. Sid Stuckey, left, was killed on August 12 when he failed to return from a sortie over the Channel; Lionel Pilkington on September 20, 1941 and Reg Lovett September 7, 1940.

The CO in due course returned to his squadron. 'All well, "Henry".'

'Everything OK, Sir.'

'Tucker made out his report?'

'Yes, Sir.'

'Right, take him off Orderly Officer, I think we'll all go down to the Vauban tonight, and have a dinner on me. Just round up the boys, will you?'

It was a pretty successful dinner. Only the best sufficed for 'Hank' More — which also went for anybody with him. He scanned the wine list with the eye of a connoisseur, leaving the courses strictly to Marcel. And he exhibited a side of his character which as yet no one had a hint of on duty for he was possessed of that subtle thin, charm. Long before a stage of conviviality had been reached, as a result of good wine and choice food, he had the table with him. Considerable overseas service had been provided him with an inexhaustible flood of far from boring reminiscences, mostly service, and of some rather risqué stories; and he had already made decided conquests in our sphere of influence, the bathroom corridors! If there remained any feeling of animosity or resentment in the bosom of 'Dickie' Martin, it was absolutely obvious, from More's attitude to the boy, that the former was totally unaware of its existence. The 'enfant terrible' simply enchanted him. He thought him the absolute limit, and was in danger of spoiling him — off duty. He drew out the 'Doc' on his pet topic of psychoanalysis, and drink as affecting pilots. He chaffed Lovett to the boys. He had also discovered that 'Ian' Scoular had instituted, and was principal contributor to, the Unofficial Squadron Diary, and nothing would satisfy him now but to have the loan of it, in order to circulate it up at HQ.

The battle was on the way to being won, all right. Time would tell. It wasn't going to be all plain sailing, handling this bunch of lads — so highly individual, and some of them so highly strung. There had been a bad start, perhaps, but that was understandable in the circumstances. Let's forget it boys. There *had* been some wangling to get the squadron (the boys gasped), but what did anybody expect? There were fellows who would have put down £300 for the chance, including him. Could he speak fairer? Of course, he had his ideas as to how a squadron should be run. It wasn't his first command, but he was in

no hurry for another. He wanted to see his job through, with the boys who had already made '73' famous. 'And now, how about the driver waiting outside?' (That unfortunate individual had doubtless settled down to his usual prolonged vigil.) 'Some of us are on early turn tomorrow; I believe I am, am I not, Lovett?'

Shortly afterwards he left for London. The Press had revolted in a body. Who was this bloke who proposed to deny their public of news — of news of the first 'ace' of the war, 'Cobber'? For weeks now, not a word of Public Favourite No. 1; and at the rate things were going, public confidence would be undermined, and questions would have to be asked in Parliament. There was a conference in London, from which More duly returned, fully backed officially in his policy of exclusion. News would be released in future to the Press, but only through the proper channels. It was contrary to 'security' to have civilians, however accredited, associating too intimately with operational squadrons. And that was *that*!

But 'Cobber's' reaction, too, was prompt; henceforth, he was the recluse, spending an increasingly large proportion of his off-duty hours in his billet. His 'fan mail' we knew was tremendous; everybody was aware of that, and nothing could be done about it, in the circumstances. But was that all? Hardly, for after his death as the result of a flying accident I was deputised to make an inventory of his kit, in the course of which sad and revealing task I came across a magnificent specimen of a quarto-sized loose-leaf diary, obviously chosen for the purpose, and it was obvious from a cursory perusal that, in addition to current entries, 'Cobber' had been summarising back periods. 'Cobber' was no writer — it really was pitiful rubbish, stupid. Why had he written it? It oozed positively oozed, of the 'headliner,' the 'he-man'. Why? Oh why?

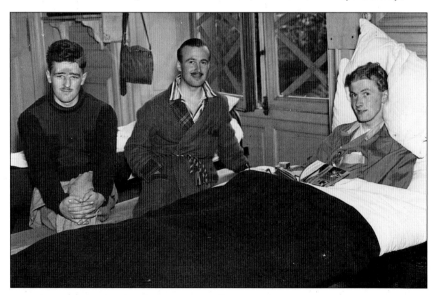

In the scrap on April 21, when 73 claimed six victories and four probables, Peter Walker (in bed) was wounded in the shoulder. 'Claudie' Wright on the left was still in the sick bay after he smashed his face when he force-landed on March 2, having undone his harness for a speedy exit, and Brotchie was still suffering from the splinters he received in his knee on April 7.

With Norway and Denmark having been invaded on April 9, the relative inactivity on the Western Front over the previous seven months was about to change. Hitler had issued a war directive about mounting an attack in the West against the French Army soon after the defeat of Poland the previous September. Yet the final plan, code-named 'Fall Gelb' (Plan Yellow), was not finalised until February 1940. The attack was scheduled for May 5 but weather conditions caused several postponements. Although the Allied air forces had a nominal strength of 3,500 aircraft to oppose 4,000 German machines, the latter were more modern types from a young air force which had already tested its equipment on active service in Spain and more recently on the Eastern Front. In this new scenario, the stalemate which had dogged the fighting in 1914-18 was to be swept aside in a new form of 'lightning' war in which ground and air forces worked together as one. Here pilots on dispersal wait for the signal to take off — Sergeant Stuckey in the centre, Dickie Martin nearest the camera.

It was not, however, until the return of the squadron to England that the mystery unravelled itself. A letter — a most fulsome letter — was received, addressed to the CO from a representative of an important pictorial daily. Would he please forward the diary lately maintained by Flying Officer 'Cobber' Kain, deceased? In the terms of a private arrangement entered into between the correspondent and 'Cobber', the former held first rights of publication. An answer in the negative was returned. And promptly there came a threat. Our friend had purchased it, and *loaned* it to 'Cobber'. It must be returned forthwith to him, otherwise he would refer the matter to higher authorities. There was one good, proper, and perfectly true answer to all this — the book now no longer existed; and we heard no more.

The reactions of the men to the new state of affairs were both prompt and spontaneous: More was one of them. Not only was he a live wire but had he not promptly shot down an Me on his arrival? He certainly knew his stuff; and he did not confine his attentions to the 'drome either. He would appear unheralded and unaccompanied in the airmen's Mess hall (of all places), thereby keeping them up to the mark, and would then pop equally inconsequently (and this time, undesired) into the sergeant pilots billets — unfortunately for them! And he not only sorted out the PSI accounts, but brought welfare assortments from HQ itself, at which place it was apparent he had a tremendous pull.

His jerky movements, the difficulty he had with the disposal of his long legs, might provoke a smile, but it was undeniable that they were dealing with a gentleman — and '73' was snobbish to a man. It was not only the 'bad hats' and the really skilled men (until recently in that order of priority), who would find themselves noticed and their names remembered, but the most unlikely types now found themselves not only singled out for attention, but called by their proper names — a prerogative and a gesture which they deeply valued. And if the CO had temporarily forgotten the name, or did not heretofore know it, there was an instant apology for his bad memory, and a painstaking registering of the name. Moreover, they were not now likely to be pulled up for some disorder in dress by an unbuttoned CO blatantly exposing his own jersey; for, despite the fact of his being a first-class fighter pilot, More was, singularly enough, the correctly-dressed officer — almost a parade type; the hint was sufficient. And, anyhow, it was worth tempting a return salute, for the energy he put into that gesture was a joy to see; indeed, it almost bordered upon a marionette show — he seemed to have so many joints all of a sudden, and all of them going into action.

And if there had been some bitterness over the compulsory wearing of gas respirators in the past, well, officers now significantly carried them (and it was remarked that the CO was the only exception to the new rule — a paradox which enhanced his prestige in their eyes, rather than the contrary). He also shared their disgust over the state of the Messing Hall and, the opportunity occurring of acquiring premises latterly in occupation by French troops as a canteen, he personally superintended the redecorating, and started the place going with beer all round, and that resultant social evening in which rank to all intents and purposes was sunk.

He was bitterly disappointed in certain of the NCOs — newcomers mostly to the squadron, and obviously the misfits or throw-outs of other units. Disregarding all regulations to the contrary, he immediately misemployed them; a sergeant would find himself detailed upon a perfect 'bind' of a job, and a specialist corporal would repent his ways under the jurisdiction of 'Willie' Williams — in whom More at once recognised the first-class Equipment Officer.

Wireless operators in the control trailer at Rouvres maintain contact with pilots aloft.

To sum up, in his case could be applied a pet warning of his own to all and sundry — 'Don't do anything I wouldn't do; that should give you plenty of scope.' But it was perhaps as well not to take him too literally in this advice; there was much that More did, to include which would have been inviting sheer disaster to the ordinary individual. And he reversed a famous adage — for his whole behaviour revealed that an occasional angel upon earth could rush in where fools feared to tread — and get away with it.

Finally, he killed two birds with one stone in the matter of Church Parades, which had heretofore been held, and with intent, in front of Knox's billet! The visiting padre was a decent type, and had pluckily, but to no purpose, shown his resentment. From then on, although the innovation resulted in a considerably reduced attendance, at least it was representative of the faithful and voluntary, even including an officer or two on occasion; and a man was no longer looked upon as either namby-pamby or letting down the side if he attended the mid-week talks instituted by Squadron Leader the Rev. Ensor.

It was reserved for Fate to play the shabbiest of tricks upon 'Hank' in the manner of his passing — lost in a Japanese PoW transport, attacked in error and sunk by our own men during a later phase of the war! *Vale et atque.*

Would there be time in which to lay a firm foundation which would resist the Nazi flood — now imminent? A revolt frequently signifies little in itself, and is usually over in a matter of days; its importance lies not too much in its immediate effect, as in its repercussions. Straighten these out, tie them up, and a revolution has been achieved. With regard to '73', it had passed through one minor revolt, and emerged therefrom with a fair degree of unanimity; and curiously the revolt had enhanced the prestige of the one man who was still blissfully unaware of what had happened.

But there still remained doubting Thomases and lipservers. Would they discover themselves, or would he discover them? (Did they but know it, he had never made a single enquiry into the past record of any single officer — his pride would have revolted at the very suggestion — even from the Adjutant, who was supposed, and suspected of 'having his ear'.) 'Dickie' Martin for instance, was blazing because I upheld the CO's decision in the matter of officers not being allowed to idly scan the files of official or semi-official correspondence. And 'Cobber' chafed under the intensified yoke of 'the team'. Hadn't most of his successes been procured as a direct result of free-lance work on his part? Quite apart from limiting his scope and tying his hands — probably at a vital moment — he questioned the wisdom of imposing leadership of a section upon *him*; as involving him in effect, in the responsibility for possible death or injury to one or other of his section. For, make no mistake about it, he was going to build up his 'score', team spirit or no, and somebody might get hurt in the process.

Henry, the Adjutant, left, writes at length in his diary about the squadron's new tough commanding officer, right, and his new broom. Squadron Leader James Winter Carmichael More — nick-named 'Hank, the Can-do' CO — ran the squadron from April 16 to August 30. After a chequered career from when he first joined the RAF in 1928, Wing Commander More failed to return on January 22, 1943 whilst with No. 615 Squadron in the Far East. He was taken prisoner and held at Malai camp by the Japanese. The charismatic Hank lost his life when the *Rakuyo Maru* on which he was being transported was torpedoed by the US submarine *Sealion* on September 12, 1944. Over 1,000 prisoners of war on board perished.

'Ian' was equable — as always; the 'Doc', constantly and fussily upon his guard against any further encroachment upon his territory, especially where it concerned the physical and nervous reactions of the pilots to flying — and drink. More had recently instituted a course of instructional training, which would inevitably bear heavily upon such of the pilots who might reasonably be expected to react on the lines confidently predicted by the 'Doc' — who insisted, not without reason, that what most of the pilots really were suffering from was strain, and that they needed either a complete rest, or a break of some sort.

The CO's hand looked like being forced when, all of a sudden, a trickle of new officers appeared upon the scene, and immediately everybody was satisfied; the 'Doc' was vindicated, the old-timers found the strain suddenly eased and a new note of admiration crept in — for there was no forecasting what might yet be done for the squadron by a CO with a pull such as this evidenced at HQ. Hadn't Marshal of the RAF Newall himself laid down, with positive finality, the condition attending upon the allotment of new bodies to the squadron — wastages! And had we not for instance been suffered to lose two sergeant-pilots before we got replacements earlier on in the year? And young Bishop, but three weeks with us, had had to go before we got Scott. And so it went on. But now — this! Four bodies for nothing.

And damned nice boys, too. One of them looked even more of a boy than 'Dickie' Martin. 'Chubby' Eliot was his name and on the face of it the nickname was certainly not inapposite. And could he fly! ('Of course he can fly,' whispered the CO in my ear; 'I know his antecedents and service history; that boy is going to be an acquisition to the squadron. You watch,' I did, and he *was* — none better, in fact.) One after another the new arrivals filed into my office for interview and for the purpose of having their particulars recorded. 'Langham-Hobart?' 'Sir,' Eliot?' 'Sir.' 'McFadden?' 'Sir.' A promising bunch; hand-picked — doubtless upon a suggestion in the right quarter by More. Only one fainted under the burden which was so shortly to be laid upon their immature shoulders; but then, better and more experienced men cracked under that strain.

Their admission into the Mess was timely, too. It was so obvious that they considered it a high honour to be of '73' — and their initial modesty almost amounted to positive self-abasement. The older — that is, in operational service — pilots were touched in their vanity. So it *was* really a fact, this cult for '73' in the outside world? And not only with the Press correspondent-fed public; for it had bitten the RAF, too, apparently! Obviously it wouldn't do to let the side down before these lads. And that supreme wrangler, 'Hank' More too, deserved a break; and by God he should have it. Wasn't it about time we returned that dinner upon him? 'Come on, chaps, who's for the Vauban? Give the CO a tinkle, "Henry", will you? Feel like joining us, you fellows?'

A nice series of pictures illustrating the refuelling and rearming of Ian Scoular's Hurricane by 'B' Flight mechanics.

April 23 was a fine day, with some cloud. First patrol went off, and as soon as they got on patrol, an Me 110 was sighted, and the chase began, with five Hurricanes strung out behind at different heights, depending on whether they were either variable pitch or 'fixed' props. In the end it was a duel between 'Cobber' and Scoular to see who could get up to it, and within range. 'Cobber' fired at it after we had chased it over Belgium, Luxemburg, and back into Germany, where one engine of it was disabled. In the meantime the rest of the formation found the pace too hot,

and Campbell and Pyne returned to the original patrol line, and were shot up by Me 109s with cannon. Campbell was shot in the leg and had to jump, while Pyne force-landed at Metz, with slight wounds in his arm and head. So on the whole it was not too good. P/O Walker was sent off to Épernay to be X-rayed.

April 26: Another 'dud' day, raining most of the time. Sergeants Campbell and Pyne arrived back after their expe-

riences with Me 109s. Campbell will not be fit for a week or two, owing to burns on the face. Pyne on the other hand seems full of beans, and has brought two amazing photos of his badly shot-up aircraft back with him. This afternoon was spent in telling Marchand what to do on his wedding day, the 'Doc' suggesting that we should have a 'dummy-run' tomorrow, with Martin as the bride, and 'Henry' giving 'her' away.

Ian about to clear his nose as he leaves the aircraft. Unfortunately the date when this photo was taken is not given, only that this series was not cleared for publication until January 31, 1941.

The tanks of the Hurricane normally held 75 gallons giving an effective range of 500 miles.

As I walked up to the Orderly Room, I counted no fewer than seven of the impudent blighters passing over the 'drome — recce planes, or decoys? It was a day in late April, and underneath the apple trees in the wire-fenced orchards a carpet of cowslips fluttered gaily in the breeze; it was beginning to look as if Rouvres had possibilities, grim as it was. I looked up again — the enemy aircraft were not going to be allowed to proceed with their reconnaissance — or whatever their business was — unmolested, apparently. Was there anything in the wind? Why this increased recce business; and how about those propaganda leaflets which had recently fluttered down onto the 'drome, in broad daylight, and addressed exclusively to our French allies! Well, let them come, and the more the merrier.

And, by the way, how did we stand with regard to our 'bag', to date. Not so dusty considering there was no war to speak of — as yet. Nineteen 'certs', and eight 'probables', including in the 'bag' Do's, He's, Me 109s, and event that dark horse, the Me 110 fighter-bomber. A truly amazing total, considering the relative paucity of opportunity offered. And the price paid — well, not so bad, either: out of less than a score of pilots operating, and as a result of actual action in the air, we had lost 'Tubs' Perry and Pilot Officer Bishop (presumed shot down by the enemy); 'Claudie' Wright, the 'Wee' Brocht and 'Pete' Walker wounded, and apparently permanently lost to the squadron. Of the sergeant pilots, two killed; Phillips, *Croix de Guerre*, slightly wounded, and absorbed into Home Establishment; Sergeant Campbell wounded but, fortunately for the squadron, only temporarily non-operational. Minor casualties, admittedly, had taken both officer and sergeant pilots off the active list now and again, but hardly affecting the operational efficiency. And as for the machines themselves, it was amazing what they would stand up to — simply amazing, or was it so amazing, backed by such ground personnel? Anyhow, machines were relatively of little consequence, as against the lives of pilots; you could patch up a Hurricane, provided you knew the job all right, but a u/s pilot was quite a different matter.

The recce planes were no longer in sight — dispersed, and probably not without loss to themselves. But some of them were bound to get back to Germany with valuable information. And why did the French so obligingly carry out their daylight tank trials; just behind the Maginot, too? And what about Lord 'Haw-Haw' and Rouvres? Everybody had had the information (from somebody else) that that gentleman had specially mentioned Rouvres in one of his recent broadcasts, specifying it as an objective which would in due course receive attention.

But what if they found the birds already flown? The cocky Germans were not the only folk who looked and planned ahead. We too had a plan; had indeed already tested it out in practice. The bulk of the squadron had spent a week or more in early April at the huge aerodrome of Reims-Champagne and if and when trouble started, it was more than likely that we should push back there, to cover possible bomber operations in the Low Countries. For we were not unaware either, of the German plans in that particular direction.

Meanwhile, we must certainly have proved a thorn in their side and, what was more, a surprise attack upon a comparatively unprotected aerodrome was in process of being discounted, for two batteries of Bofors had recently arrived as aerodrome defence (we already had our 40 machine-gunners — germ of the RAF Regiment) and had taken up positions around the 'drome. This looked like business; and could we please have one of their nice bright brass shell-cases as a gong for the Mess? Yes, with pleasure, but not until the war started, as they were strictly limited in ammunition, and couldn't even spare any for practice purposes — which made us ponder a little. Hadn't we been given several months' grace already in which to build up abundant stocks of ammunition? So why this! And when it concerned the lives of our own folks, it was not sufficient, either, to mutter — C'est la guerre!'

The eight Browning guns were each loaded with 332 rounds of .303 ammunition, which, at 20 rounds per second, would last just 17 seconds.

On Friday May 10, Hitler launched his long-awaited attack in the West (see *Blitzkrieg in the West Then and Now*) and the eight months of the 'Phoney' War entered the pages of history. At 4.35 a.m., without warning or provocation, German troops crossed the borders of the Netherlands, Belgium and Luxembourg, shattering those countries belief that their declarations of neutrality would protect them. Minutes earlier, German gliderborne troops had struck at the Belgian strong point of Fort Eben-Emael and the River Meuse bridges in nearby Maastricht, with further paratroop landings in the Ardennes in Belgium and at vital bridges in Holland. At 8.30 a.m. that morning, a signal was received by No. 73 Squadron to move west — so already on Day One the orders were being issued to pull back. Reims-Champagne aerodrome lay just to the north of the city with another airfield to the south-west (see map pages 26-27). Here 'Cobber' and friends are pictured in the barrack block area.

Obviously, something was in the wind. April gave place to May, and everybody was so busy that spring passed almost unnoticed. Down in the water meadows, the purple orchises buried themselves deep in lush grass; and the forgotten concrete dug-outs, gun emplacements and pillboxes left by the Germans from the last war were almost obliterated by spreading wild flowers, eager to hide traces of an error which surely existed only to be buried.

Spring had its religious festivals, too, and the church bells rang merrily across the undulating plain — for the ban upon them had been lifted, and the *Curé* was again our very good friend, and the 'Doc' (under sentence of posting back to Home Establishment, alas) got hot water on demand. The stairway to 'Claudie' Wright's late billet, and lolled in the sun; and everywhere the tangible signs of the real wealth of the inhabitants of Rouvres were being cultivated by their owners for all they were worth.

Would this monstrous thing happen? How could men in their generation be such fools, such criminals!

Security is tight at the military airfield today which is occupied by the l'Armée de l'Air but we were given permission for Jean Paul Pallud to visit the base in May 2006. He found that the picture had been taken in the Caserne Roisin — the barracks area on the western side — but that several of the old buildings had been demolished during modernisation. He could not find a building matching the particular arrangement of windows and doors seen in the wartime picture so took this shot of a similar building which now houses the photographic service.

THE AIR FORCES

The Royal Air Force

Pilots of No. 87 Squadron race to their Hurricanes for the benefit of the Press. The mixture of fixed and variable-pitch airscrews and the grass airfield are redolent of conditions on the Western Front during the so-called 'Sitzkrieg'.

At cessation of hostilities in 1918, Britain's newly-autonomous air force was the most powerful in the world with a strength of 23,000 aircraft, 188 operational squadrons, and close to 300,000 officers and men. Yet within a year, this once great force was reduced to a bare nucleus of 371 aircraft, 12 squadrons, and less than 32,000 personnel. After four years of debilitating war, the British Government was intent on cutting military spending and embraced a policy of retrenchment based on the false assumption that it was safe to do so, certainly for the next ten years, because the Treaty of Versailles precluded any chance of German re-armament.

Fortunately for the country, in March 1919, Air Chief Marshal Sir Hugh Trenchard, who had commanded both the Royal Flying Corps and the Independent Air Force during the Great War, was appointed RAF Chief of Air Staff, a post he was to occupy for the next decade. A firm adherent of the Douhet doctrine, that espoused that future wars would be won by air supremacy, Trenchard recognised that a powerful air force would act as a deterrent. He advocated passionately for an integrated, independent, organisation encompassing every aspect of aircraft provision, air and ground crew training, and ground control. This vision formed the basis of a White Paper presented to Parliament by Winston Churchill in December 1919, and provided the model on which the modern Royal Air Force would be based. Dubbed the 'Father of the RAF', Trenchard's legacy was to prove of crucial benefit to the nation within two decades.

Trenchard's foresight resulted in creation of an unparalleled training system, with a cadet college at Cranwell producing future air force commanders, and technical colleges at Halton and Flowerdown producing specialist ground staff. Flying training became standardised, adopting practices developed at the Central Flying School and, despite objections that military aviation was too complicated to be mastered by part-time volunteers, an Auxiliary Air Force was created to provide a constant reserve of trained pilots.

Yet, despite these important developments, Britain's air force remained small in comparison to its European neighbours, and particularly that of France with which political relations were then strained. This made Britain's air defence against the bomber a political as well as a military necessity. Consequently, in August 1922, a metropolitan air force of 14 bomber and nine fighter squadrons received government approval. Also, the following year, a sub-committee of the Committee of Imperial Defence chaired by Lord Salisbury finally spiked efforts by the Army and the Navy to regain political control over elements of the Air Force, and further recommended a Home Defence Air Force of at least 52 squadrons 'be created with as little delay as possible'. This was duly announced in the House of Commons by the Prime Minister, Stanley Baldwin, on June 20, 1923.

Despite such high ambition it was recognised that, realistically, this expansion programme, requiring 394 bombers and 204 fighters, could not be achieved before the end of 1928, but by the autumn of 1925 half the necessary squadrons were in place.

However, by then, relations with France had improved and appeasement was prevalent across Europe. Another defence committee under Lord Birkenhead therefore recommended that, in the interest of economy and international goodwill, the RAF expansion programme could be postponed and need not be completed before 1935-6. Despite strenuous objections to this delay Trenchard had no option but to bow to government policy.

Father of the Royal Air Force — Sir Hugh Trenchard.

Last of the RAF fighter biplanes, the Gloster Gladiator first flew in September 1934 and continued in production until April 1940 by which time it was already being superseded by more modern monoplane fighters. With fixed cantilever single-strut undercarriage and enclosed cockpit it was powered by a 840hp Bristol Mercury IX engine developing a top speed of 253 mph at 14,500ft, and a service ceiling of 33,000ft. Armament was twin synchronised 7.65mm Browning machine guns in the nose with another mounted under each wing. It was a feisty aircraft to fly and could prove temperamental, but when handled with skill it was a nimble fighter and a formidable opponent. No. 615 Squadron before being re-equipped with Hurricanes.

So as the League of Nations sought to achieve world peace and security, and futile disarmament conferences met in Geneva between 1932 and 1934, the RAF's role as Britain's first line of defence was yet again subordinated to financial constraints and government vacillation. The outcome of this political parsimony was that by 1933, when Adolf Hitler became Chancellor of Germany, the RAF remained ten squadrons short of the strength agreed nine years earlier.

However, largely due to 'Boom' Trenchard, who opposed every effort to stifle the infant service at birth, the RAF survived the austerity and political in-fighting of the 1920s. But if Trenchard was indeed 'Father of the RAF' then it was senior commanders that followed him, such as Air Marshal Sir Hugh Dowding, first Air Officer Commanding-in-Chief of Fighter Command, who would nurture the fledgling service during the truly formative years of the next decade.

By 1934 the worsening political situation in Europe and the rise of Nazi Germany demanded decisive Government action. Despite stormy opposition in the House of Commons, an air expansion programme was approved to increase the home defence force to 75 squadrons by the spring of 1939 and increasing first-line strength from 488 to 1,304 aircraft. This required decentralisation of the existing RAF control organisation and resulted, in June 1936, in the formation of four specialised commands: Bomber Command with headquarters at Uxbridge, Fighter Command HQ Stanmore, Coastal Command HQ Lee-on-Solent, and Training Command HQ Tern Hill.

Within a year, largely thanks to Dowding's tireless energy and total commitment, Britain had developed the nucleus of a unified air defence system incorporating fighter squadrons, RDF network, ground control, anti-aircraft guns, search-lights, and Observer Corps. Over the next two years this unique, complex organisation was refined, further developed, and tested in annual air defence exercises from which valuable experience was gained and important lessons learned.

The restrictions and financial constraints that dogged the growth of the RAF throughout the 1920s equally curtailed all aircraft development. With no government contracts there was little stimulus for Britain's aircraft industry to invest in new designs. Thus, by the mid-1930s, the air defence of Great Britain remained reliant upon Bristol Bulldog, Hawker Demon, and Hawker Fury biplane fighters not far removed from the Sopwith Snipes that had equipped fighter squadrons back in 1918. Britain's bomber force was similarly poorly equipped with mainly slow obsolescent types with limited range and bomb-loads.

The transition from the Gladiator to the Hurricane: a snapshot taken by Flight Lieutenant William Francis Blackadder with No. 607 Squadron at Vitry-en-Artois. Re-equipment took place in April 1940 for both the Gladiator squadrons of No. 61 Wing.

First flown in November 1935, the Hawker Hurricane formed the backbone of RAF fighter units based in France from September 1939 and was the principal British fighter with the Advanced Air Striking Force. Fitted with a Rolls-Royce Merlin II engine and Watts wooden two-bladed fixed-pitch propeller, the Hurricane had a top speed of 310 mph at 17,000ft, **a service ceiling of 32,000ft, with a range of 525 miles. Armament comprised eight .303in Browning machine guns. Later Hurricanes were fitted with three-bladed metal variable-pitch propellers. This is an early shot of machines of No. 85 Squadron, based at Lille-Seclin and Mons-en-Chaussée, before the introduction of rudder stripes.**

The international Schneider Trophy contest of the 1920s did, however, provide vital impetus for some radical developments in both aircraft and engine design that resulted in a new generation of fast, aerodynamic, monoplanes powered by liquid-cooled engines.

Applying experience gained from this contest, Reginald Mitchell, the chief designer at Supermarine, found government specification F7/30, issued in 1930 for a new fighter aircraft, too restrictive and insufficiently advanced in concept. So, on his own initiative, he exceeded the official brief and designed a gull-wing monoplane with retractable undercarriage, enclosed cockpit, and armed with four machine-guns. This 'interceptor-fighter' was to be powered by the new 750 hp. V-12 Merlin engine, also developed as a private venture by Rolls-Royce, that was just becoming available.

Meeting the same F7/30 specification, Sydney Camm, chief designer at the Hawker Aircraft Company, also produced a monoplane design based on the Hawker Fury biplane which was then entering RAF service. But availability of the new Merlin powerplant invited significant changes to this design which was further modified after an Air Ministry armament conference in July 1934. As a result of such developments, a fresh government specification F5/34 was issued calling for a monoplane fighter armed with eight Browning machine guns capable of catching the fastest bomber and destroying it with a two-second burst of gun-fire. This far-seeking requirement was to have profound consequences in the air defence of Britain barely six years later.

The Hawker Hurricane first flew on November 6, 1935, followed on March 5, 1936 by the Supermarine Type 300 Spitfire, and production orders for both types soon followed.

Employing traditional fabric-covered tubular steel construction methods the Hurricane was first to enter service in December 1937, the first Spitfires not being completed before August 1938 due to early manufacturing difficulties caused by its metal stressed-skin structure.

Other new bomber types were rapidly being developed, the Fairey Battle bomber being demonstrated for the first time on March 19, 1936, and the Bristol Blenheim, the outstanding performance of which caused a considerable stir when it first entered RAF service in 1937. The Bristol Type 142 was a privately-funded venture designed four years earlier as an all-metal eight-seat civil transport to out-perform similar American types. But when it became apparent that the aircraft had significant military potential as a fast medium bomber, the aircraft was gifted to the nation by its sponsor, Lord Rothermere, the wealthy newspaper proprietor.

The Munich Agreement of September 1938 allowed Great Britain a final year of grace. RAF Fighter Command was then still 'appallingly deficient' with 759 fighters, mostly Hawker Demons and Furies, Gloster Gladiators and Gauntlet biplanes, to oppose an estimated force of 1,200 long-range German bombers. A mere two squadrons of Hurricanes were then operational, and a single Spitfire in service. Yet within the next crucial twelve months, deliveries of both new fighters was accelerated, so that by the outbreak of war in September 1939, a total of 400 Hurricanes had been delivered and equipped 18 squadrons, while another nine squadrons were Spitfire-equipped. RAF Fighter Command was at last approaching the strength once deemed vital in order to adequately defend the country. It would have scant time to further prepare for the onslaught that followed.

The Fairey Battle — a clean low-wing monoplane — made its first flight in March 1936 and was ordered in quantity for the RAF as part of their expansion programme. Powered by a single Rolls-Royce Merlin III engine, it had a top speed of 241 mph at 13,000ft, a service ceiling of 23,500ft and carried a 1,000lb bomb-load in wing cells over a range of 1,050 miles. A crew of two (though provision could be made for a third man) was accommodated in a fully enclosed cockpit and defensive armament consisted of one forward-firing .303in Browning machine gun mounted in the starboard wing, and a single Vickers gas-operated machine-gun in the rear cockpit. Though it was still being produced in number, the Battle was sadly under-powered and already obsolescent by the outbreak of war. Lacking any newer types, it continued as a stop-gap to form the main equipment of many RAF bomber squadrons during the first year of the war. This particular aircraft belongs to No. 103 Squadron and was photographed at either Plivot or Bétheniville.

A British Blenheim of No. 139 Squadron at Bétheniville. Designed in 1933, and built for Press baron Lord Rothermere to promote interest in commercial aviation, the Bristol Type 135 all-metal, high-speed, civil transport first flew in April 1935. Its top speed of 307 mph exceeded that of RAF front-line fighters then in service so he generously gifted the prototype to the country for evaluation as a bomber. Considerably modified, the Blenheim Mark I first flew in June 1936 and was promptly ordered into production, first deliveries commencing in March 1937. Powered by two Bristol Mercury radial engines, and with a crew of three, the Blenheim carried a 1,000lb bomb-load and had a range of 1,125 miles. Defensive armament comprised a single .303inch browning in the port wing and a .303inch gas-operated Vickers K gun in a dorsal turret. With a service ceiling of 27,280 feet, endurance of 5½ hours, and top speed of 277 mph, it became the mainstay of Britain's light bomber force. A modified fighter version, the Blenheim IF, with four .303inch Brownings in a ventral gun pack was introduced in 1938. It proved a failure against modern single-seat fighters but was later usefully employed as a night fighter. In 1939 the 'long-nosed' Blenheim IV entered service carrying an extra 320lbs of bombs externally, and with extended range of 1,500 miles, increased endurance of 8½ hours, but reduced ceiling of 22,000 feet. On its introduction the Blenheim was a marked improvement on the light bombers then in service but found itself sorely tested when RAF daylight bombing policy met the challenges faced over France in 1940.

French Air Force

Once the most powerful air force in Europe, the Armée de l'Air had diminished significantly during the inter-war years, a victim of inadequate funds for the French aircraft industry following WWI. Economic uncertainty, and political instability due to frequent changes of government, reduced the quantity and quality of modern aircraft in the French Air Force. Like the RAF, it suddenly found itself ill-prepared to counter the potential military threat being posed by an emergent and dominant Germany.

The Munich crisis in September 1938 sounded alarm bells in Europe and prompted the French Chief of Air Staff, Général Joseph Vuillemin, to prepare a highly critical yet frank assessment of the forces then at his disposal for the defence of the country. In this report to the French government, he declared the Armée de l'Air obsolescent and announced urgent measures to introduce a wide programme of modernisation. Meantime, he restricted French bombers to night operations; daylight missions to be undertaken only in a dire emergency. Similar restrictions were imposed in the observation units which were forbidden to fly over 'the front line'; a policy that seriously limited their operational value. Later, however, this order would be partially revoked when better fighter protection for observation aircraft became available. These extraordinary measures were indicative of the parlous state of the French Air Force's readiness for war at that time.

Vuillemin's report triggered an ambitious construction programme (Plan V) that was to prove beyond the ability of the French aircraft industry to deliver. It would take two years for the industry to fully recover from the adverse effects of nationalisation and respond to demands; consequently, the modernisation programme was not fully initiated. Yet on August 26, 1939, a mere eight days before the outbreak of war, Vuillemin reported that re-equipment of the French fighter and reconnaissance force was almost complete, while the situation in French bombers units remained largely unchanged. Modern aircraft had not yet been delivered to the Groupes de Bombardement and he estimated that it would be another 4/5 months before they would become fully effective. In observation units the situation was even worse; re-equipment delayed for some further time to come.

On the outbreak of war in September 1939, the Armée de l'Air had over 3,600 aircraft based in France with its metropolitan air force, and an additional 350 aircraft (half of them shipborne) with the French Naval Air Arm, the Aéronautique Navale. But many of these aircraft were still not fully operational, and many units undergoing conversion training.

Having served in the French Air Force in the Great War, Général Joseph Vuillemin became Chief of the General Staff of the Armée de l'Air in April 1938.

In December 1939, in an effort to accelerate progress, all but two bomber units were withdrawn to southern France where a Groupement d'Instruction was established for their conversion and training. Army Observation units, some of which had already suffered heavy losses in the opening months of the war, were to be re-equipped with the Potez 63-11; twelve Groupes phasing in the new aircraft as a matter of urgency. It was determined that all Groupes de Bombardement and Groupes Aeriennes d'Observation should be fully converted by late April 1940. And, in a forlorn

The Dewoitine D520 was the best French fighter and was equal to the Messerschmitt 109. Deliveries commenced in January 1940

but only GC I/3 was operational by May 10, GC II/3 and GC II/7 hurriedly completing conversion before joining the action.

There were just short of 300 Morane MS-406 fighters *(left)* in service and nearly a hundred of the Curtiss H-75 *(right)* which was a machine imported from the United States while delivery of more modern French types was awaited.

effort to curb further losses in Groupes de Reconnaissance, it was ordered that only the Potez 637 was to be allowed across the enemy border in daylight.

By March 1940, with aircraft production rising steadily and rapidly, factories were delivering aircraft faster than the Armée de l'Air could train crews to fly them. Thus, by May 1940, the Armée de l'Air was better equipped, with over 85 per cent of its aircraft being modern types. And at the end of the Battle of France, despite all its losses, the Armée de l'Air would have more aircraft on strength than when the campaign opened on May 10, 1940.

The basic operational unit in the French Air Force was a Groupe, each normally comprising two Escadrilles, with two or more Groupes forming an Escadre; until reorganisation in September 1939, when the Escadres were replaced by Groupements. (See page 185 for Order of Battle on May 10, 1940.)

The statutory strength of each Groupe varied according to its function. In single-seat fighter Groupes de Chasse (GC) it was usually 26 aircraft, for multi-seat fighter (ECN) units 20 aircraft, bomber Groupes de Bombardement (GB) and Groupes de Reconnaissance (GR) each had 13, and Groupes Aériens d'Observation (GAO) units 11 aircraft. Some small, semi-autonomous Escadrilles operated fewer aircraft.

Organisation of the home-based Armée de l'Air reflected the deployment of French land forces and was concentrated in the north and east of the country defending the frontiers with Germany and Belgium. There were four zones of operations; the north, the east, the south, and one supporting the Armée des Alpes in the south-east.

Officers commanding each Zone d'Operations had the authority to direct all air units situated in their area, including fighter, reconnaissance and observation groups attached to the army, as well as the air forces retained under the direct control of Général Vuillemin. These 'independent' air forces included the remaining fighter units, strategic reconnaissance groups, and all bomber units. Experience would show this to be a recipe for disaster; any cohesive and concerted deployment of French air forces made difficult to achieve due to inconsistent and occasionally conflicting orders.

The Bloch 131 was first ordered as a fast day bomber but by September 1939 those in service were mainly consigned to strategic reconnaissance duties because of its poor performance.

The Potez 63/11 was a three-seat reconnaissance machine.

The elderly Amiot 143 could carry nearly 2,000lbs of bombs but, no match for fighters, it was largely relegated to night bombing.

Stefan Pawlikowski, who was well-known in France as a fighter pilot in the First World War, commanded the base for training Polish volunteers at Lyon-Bron. Conversion onto Morane MS-406 began in January 1940 at Montpellier *(above)*, the first Polish pilots joining regular French fighter units two months later.

Foreign Volunteers: The Czech and Polish Air Forces in France

On March 15, 1939, Germany marched into Czechoslovakia completing the occupation of the country that had started two years before with the Sudeten crisis. The subsequent Munich Agreement, that bought valuable time for France and Britain to prepare for war at the cost of Czechoslovak independence, deprived the Czechs of their small but effective air force, once considered the best equipped in Eastern Europe, so no organised military resistance was possible. Many Czech airmen, already witness of increasing German disruption of their air force organisation and occupation of their airfields in Hitler's Protectorate, had long concluded that any future resistance could only be achieved from abroad and finally left their homeland. Most of them made for Poland with hopes of joining the Polish Air Force, but, forbidden to fly on operations, few had their hopes realised when the Germans unleashed their attack on Poland on September 1, 1939, and plunged Europe into war.

The Polish Air Force put up a desperate defence of its homeland but with largely antiquated aircraft and against overwhelming numbers, the result was inevitable. So when Poland finally fell to the Germans in September 1939, the bulk of the Polish Air Force, including many Czechs, escaped into Rumania and Hungary in accordance with plans agreed during the first week of the German invasion. It was hoped that Russia and Rumania would maintain their neutrality until material support arrived from the West to enable the Poles to continue the fight in the south-eastern corner of the country, giving the Western allies time to intervene. But this was hope born of desperation. Ultimately, the Rumanian authorities, no doubt bowing to Russo-German influence, refused permission for Hurricane fighters and Fairey Battle light bombers that arrived from Britain by sea to be unloaded at Galatz, and all plans for further resistance were finally dashed when the Russian Army invaded eastern Poland.

Operations by the Polish Air Force continued until September 17 when its few remaining operational aircraft finally withdrew across the frontier into Rumania. Even then, a motley collection of machines continued flying from Mokotów, outside Warsaw, for another week. The air campaign in Poland had been short and ferocious, and its conclusion inevitable. In a little over two weeks of fighting the Polish Air Force ceased to exist as an effective force, having lost 90 per cent of its aircraft and some 70 per cent of aircrews in action. But despite inferior equipment and overwhelming odds, Polish airmen had managed to inflict serious losses on the Luftwaffe which had lost nearly 20 per cent of its forces deployed.

The bulk of Polish Air Force personnel now found themselves interned in, ostensibly, neutral countries and little time was lost in planning a mass evacuation of volunteers to Western Europe where, it was widely expected, Germany would make its next attack. Through the Polish Military Attaché's office in Bucharest, priority was given to evacuating as many airmen as possible to France where the Polish Government-in-exile was already located. There, discussions between British, French and Polish delegates, held at the French Air Ministry on October 25, determined that the Polish Air Force should be divided equally between Britain and France. So plans to evacuate the bulk of its personnel from Rumania immediately went ahead using four main routes; via the Black Sea ports to Syria or Marseille, through Yugoslavia, through Greece, and overland via Yugoslavia and northern Italy into France.

This mass movement continued until the end of December 1939, by which time severe restrictions were being imposed at the internment camps, and the Germans and Russians had established tighter border controls. During the next three months, small groups continued to make their way out through Rumania, Hungary, Latvia, or Estonia, some with the help of emergent underground organisations. By April 26, 1940, 8,678 Polish airmen had reached France or Britain, arriving in large groups, smaller parties, or as individuals. They all shared a common purpose — to continue the struggle.

The majority of Polish airmen reaching France arrived through Marseille and congregated at Lyon-Bron where the main Polish Air Force base in France was established. There they were quartered in barracks or the huge halls of the 'Foire' (industries fair), while officers were billeted in hotels in Lyon. At Bron, after screening and selection, an intense programme of training was initiated for pilots and groundcrew who were to serve in the Armée de l'Air, and in January 1940, a visiting RAF commission recruited an agreed 2,300 airmen for service in RAF Bomber Command.

Pilots from the training course were attached to French units, **Wladyslaw Gnys** *(above)* **joining CG III/1. He had already achieved fame as the first Allied airman to shoot down a German aircraft in the Second World War (on September 1, 1939), and on May 12, 1940 reputedly became the first Polish pilot to bring down a German in France. Portrait by the Polish artist Slawa Sadlowska.**

Being fewer in number, Czech Air Force personnel, who started arriving in France in December 1939, were simply absorbed into French Air Force units dispersed across France and even Syria. Earlier arrivals had already been taken into the French Foreign Legion as a pre-requisite to joining the French military, but the outbreak of war accelerated their acceptance into the Armée de l'Air. However, in spite of efforts to persuade the French High Command to keep them together, no plans were agreed for the formation of exclusively Czech Air Force units before June 1, 1940, when French Air Minister Laurent Eynac and Czech Lieutenant-General Sergej Ingr signed an agreement, but it came too late and the French collapse precluded its implementation.

Conversely, a Franco-Polish Air Agreement of January 4, 1940, had already provided for the formation of up to two Polish army co-operation squadrons in France plus two fighter squadrons, and the first of these fighter units, commanded by Captain Laszkiewicz, commenced training at Montpellier within a week of the agreement being signed. It was intended that pilots of this 'Montpellier Group' would form the cadre of a 2nd Polish Fighter Squadron to be equipped with Morane 406 fighters, but when they were eventually deployed on operations, on March 26, six sections of three aircraft were dispersed among regular French fighter units as follows:

Flight 1 led by Captain Stefan Laszkiewicz attached to GC III/2 at Cambrai-Niergnies
Flight 2 led by Captain Jan Pentz attached to GC II/6 at Anglure-Vouarces
Flight 3 led by Captain Mieczyslaw Sulerzycki attached to GC III/6 at Wez-Thuisy
Flight 4 led by Lieutenant Kazimierz Bursztyn attached to GC III/1 at Toul Croix-de-Metz
Flight 5 led by Lieutenant Jozef Brzezinski attached to GC I/2 at Xaffévillers
Flight 6 led by Captain Wladyslaw Göttel attached to GC II/7 at Luxeuil

During the following three months these flights were reinforced; a further three aircraft under Lieutenant Cebrzynski joining GC II/6 on May 16, and a section led by Lieutenant Baranski joining GC III/6 on 9 June. In the course of combat operations, the 'Montpellier Group' claimed 25 victories for the loss of three pilots.

Meantime remaining personnel of the 1st 'Warsaw' and 2nd 'Cracow-Poznan' Squadrons continued their training at Lyon-Bron where they were turning out up to 40 pilots a month, under the supervision of Commandant Alexandre Lionel de Marmier and Capitaine Pierre Rougevin Baville, the French commander of the Polish training unit.

With the numbers of Polish Air Force personnel now in France exceeding the requirements of the Franco-Polish agreement, a third fighter squadron was formed for operations in support of the Finns fighting the Russians during the 'Winter War'. Initially equipped with Morane 406 fighters, and stationed at Lyon-Bron, it was decided that the unit would be re-equipped with the Caudron C714 Cyclone aircraft and deliveries to DIAP, the Polish training unit, of this untried, under-powered, and less than robust type, commenced in February 1940. Commanded by Major Jozef Kepinski the unit was still in training when the armistice between the Soviet Union and Finland came into effect on March 13 so, consequently, it became Groupe de Chasse Polonais de Varsovie No. 145, or Polish Fighter Squadron 'Warsaw' GC 1/145.

Shortly after the German attack on May 10, 1940, the French authorities, concerned that GC 1/145 had not yet achieved combat readiness, decided that the unit should be dissolved and its pilots deployed to bolster existing French units. Vigorous objections were raised by the Poles, determined to retain some national identity, and the plan was ultimately dropped, GC 1/145 being dispatched to the front at Villacoublay on May 19. During the next four weeks, despite continuing technical problems with their Cyclone aircraft, largely due to the unreliability of the 450hp Renault 12R engines, GC 1/145 would complete 64 missions and claim eight enemy aircraft destroyed for the loss of four pilots, two more being wounded. Finally, on June 19, the squadron was withdrawn to the port of La Rochelle for evacuation to England, reluctantly abandoning its aircraft on the airfield at Rochefort.

Although GC 1/145 was the only exclusively Polish unit to see action during the French campaign, many Polish pilots also served in Armée de l'Air units and, like the 'Montpellier Group', several complete Polish flights or sections were attached to French Groupes de Chasse. Six pilots led by Captain Franciszek Jastrzebski were attached to GC II/1 on May 19, four more under Lieutenant Aleksander Gabszewicz joining GC III/10 on June 1, while six pilots led by Commandant Eugeniusz Wyrwicki joined GC II/10 on June 3, and five led by Commandant Edward Wieckowski went to GC III/9. Many Polish pilots also served in DAT flights.

Operations of Czech and Polish pilots in France during 1940 were generally confined to fighter units. Two Polish reconnaissance squadrons and a bomber squadron were planned but still in course of training or awaiting delivery of aircraft when the campaign ended, at which time plans for exclusively Czech units had only recently been agreed.

On June 19, 1940, with the fall of France imminent, the Polish High Command in London ordered all its forces to proceed to the nearest ports and seek evacuation to Britain. Units with operational aircraft, lacking the range to reach England direct, either flew to North Africa or abandoned their aircraft and made for the Atlantic coast. But with evacuation ports falling as the Germans advanced southwards it was a race against time. On June 24 an estimated 3,000 Polish airmen were finally evacuated from St Jean de Luz, near Biarritz, to join the 1,200 who escaped to Britain via St-Nazaire, Bordeaux, Le Vernon, and Bayonne. The bulk of Polish personnel from Lyon-Bron got away from Port Vendres, its aircraft flying to Perpignan from where they eventually made their way to Casablanca.

The majority of Czech pilots serving in France made their way to Bordeaux and Bayonne from where they were evacuated to Britain between June 18 and 20. Others escaped by air. A big Czech contingent sailed from Port Vendres on June 23, the last of their airmen in France, including the Czech Air Force High Command, leaving Bordeaux two days later.

The Royal Netherlands Air Force

Left: **Lieutenant-Generaal Petrus Best, Commander-in-Chief of the Royal Netherlands Air Force.** Above: **The nimble Fokker D XXI armed with four 7.92mm FN-Browning machine guns.**

The origins of the RNAF date back to July 1, 1913, when the Luchtvaart Afdeeling (LVA) was created by Royal decree as part of the Netherlands army. Formed at Soesterberg, its initial equipment comprised a single Brik aircraft on loan from Dutch pioneer pilot Marinus van Meel. By the outbreak of World War I in 1914, during which Holland remained neutral, the LVA consisted of only five machines; the original Brik, along with another improved version built by van Meel, and three Farman F.22s purchased from France.

Unable to promote any official interest for their aircraft designs in their homeland, two other early Dutch aviation pioneers, Anthony Fokker and Frits Koolhoven, were forced to move abroad to pursue their interests. Ignored in England, Fokker took his considerable talents to Germany where his designs subsequently made a significant contribution to the early successes of the Luftstreitkräfte. Meanwhile, Koolhoven chose to remain in England and ultimately founded a successful aircraft company.

During World War I, when Holland found further aircraft difficult to obtain, their Spijker motor company began building Farman F.22s under licence, any further limited expansion depending on the internment of a variety of British, French and German aircraft that happened to forced-land in Dutch territory. In 1917, when it again became possible to order aircraft from abroad, the LVA had close to 50 various types, and promptly engaged in a major expansion programme. Consequently, orders were placed with France for Nieuport 17C-1 fighters, and Caudron C.III reconnais-

sance aircraft, and with Germany for Fokker D III fighters, and Rumpler C Vs while, in Holland, the Trompenburg motor works started turning out Spijker training machines.

Immediately after the war, with the Dutch still pursuing a policy of strict neutrality, defence spending cuts resulted in a modest programme of modernisation of the Dutch Air Force. Fokker, returned from Germany and now with factories at Amsterdam and Veere, supplied the LVA with 20 of his successful D VII fighters and 65 Fokker C I reconnaissance machines, while designing several new types. Sixteen radical Thulin Type K monoplane fighters were also purchased from Sweden at this time.

By 1937, the emerging threat from German military expansion, resulted in further orders being placed for new aircraft for the LVA. Thirty-six Fokker D XXI fighters, 36 Fokker G 1A heavy fighters, 16 Fokker T V medium bombers, 20 Fokker C X reconnaissance-bombers, 24 Fokker S IX trainers, and 53 Koolhoven F. K. 51 observation machines were ordered, along with 18 Douglas DB-8A-3N bombers purchased from America. In addition, 35 Curtiss-Wright 21B fighters were also ordered from the USA but these were not delivered in time and eventually saw service in the Dutch East Indies.

Further expansion with more modern types was planned early in 1940, but when the Germans invaded the Netherlands on May 10, 1940, the LVA had only two front-line Air Regiments with a total strength of about 125 aircraft available to defend its neutrality. The outcome was inevitable. (See page 190 for Order of Battle in May 1940.)

Left: **The Fokker T V bomber was obsolescent by 1939 but the new G 1 Jachtkruiser** (right) **was a potent weapon.**

On its first flight in 1925, the clean and streamlined Fox two-seat day bomber *(right)* was able to outperform any contemporary day fighter, but severe financial restrictions had hampered its introduction into RAF service where it was soon superceded by the Hawker Hart. However, in 1931 the Aéronautique Militaire under Général-Major Paul Hiernaux *(left)* ordered an initial batch of 12 Fox IIs from Faireys, with further machines being produced under license by the Société Anonyme Belge at Gosselies. With supercharged Rolls Royce Kestrel IIS engine the Fox II had a top speed of 189 mph at 16,400ft, and could carry a 440lb bomb-load, but as its primary role in Belgian service was to be reconnaissance and army co-operation, armament was confined to a single forward-firing 7.62mm Vickers machine gun, with a Lewis gun mounted in the rear cockpit. A total of 40 Fox IIs, including two trainers, had been delivered to Belgian units by November 1933. The following month, the first Fairey Fox III was received carrying an additional 7.62mm forward-firing FN-Browning machine gun. This was progenitor of the Fox IIIC, with enclosed cockpits and fitted with bomb shackles beneath the lower mainplanes to meet its secondary role as light bomber, a total of 50 examples being delivered by May 1937. Powered by an Hispano-Suiza 12-cylinder liquid-cooled engine, the Fox IV was introduced in December 1934. After protracted testing, this developed into the Fox VIR reconnaissance aircraft, production of which took place alongside that of the Fox IIIC, with a total of 24 of the sub-type being delivered to the newly-formed IIIème Groupe de Chasse by the end of 1935. Hispano-powered aircraft achieved 224 mph at 13,120ft and had a service ceiling of 32,800ft. A two-seat fighter variant was also produced, designated the Fox VIC, the first of 52 to be built being completed in September 1935. By May 1939, when the last Fairey Fox VIII rolled off the assembly line at Gosselies, a total of 190 of this ubiquitous, though by then largely obsolete, aircraft had been produced by the Belgian factory.

Belgian Air Force

Belgian military aviation has its origins in the Compagnie des Ouvriers et Aérostiers formed in 1909 as a department of the Army. But surrounded as it was by two powerful European neighbours that were traditional enemies, France and Germany, and lacking adequate resources, Belgium adopted a policy of strict neutrality; its small metropolitan air forces only ever intended to protect its own air space, and provide support for the army.

Thus, at the outbreak of the First World War in 1914, the Belgian air arm consisted of four escadrilles equipped with a variety of aircraft purchased from abroad, mainly French Farman types used for reconnaissance and observation. By March 1915, when it was renamed the Militair Vliegwezen (Military Aviation), the Belgian air arm had expanded to a mere six escadrilles.

During the inter-war years Belgium maintained its strictly neutral stance and, by 1939, the Militair Vliegwezen, then still a branch of the Army, had expanded to three air regiments; one for Army Co-operation, another of Fighters, and a third of Bomber and Reconnaissance aircraft. With little or no aircraft industry, Belgium equipped its air arm with mainly British types like the Fairey Fox, Fairey Battle, Gloster Gladiator, and Hawker Hurricane, and by May 10, 1940, when its neutrality was once again violated, it had about 200 front-line aircraft the bulk of which were already approaching obsolescence.

Hurriedly ordered from Italy after negotiations to purchase Curtiss Hawk 75A fighters from the USA proved unsuccessful, the Fiat CR-42 *(left)* replaced the Fairey Firefly in Belgian fighter units during March 1940, equipping both escadrilles of the II Fighter Group at Nivelles. This rugged Italian biplane fighter with its fixed spatted undercarriage was fitted with a 840 hp Fiat A74 radial engine giving it a top speed of 270 mph at 13,100ft, a service ceiling of 32,000ft, and range of 460 miles. Armament comprised twin synchronised 12.7mm Breda-Safat machine guns mounted in the nose and although highly manoeuvrable and a pleasure to fly, the CR-42 was severely out-classed by more modern fighter monoplanes. *Right:* The Hurricane was ordered by the Belgian Government in April 1939, initial delivery from the first production batch of Hawker-built machines with fabric-covered wings being made to the Belgian Air Force that same month. Ultimately, a total of 20 aircraft were exported to Belgium, 15 of them equipping the 2/I/2 based at Schaffen.

The Luftwaffe

Hermann Göring . . . from First World War fighter pilot with the Jagdgeschwader Richthofen . . . to Commander-in-Chief of the Third Reich's Luftwaffe.

Following defeat in World War I, the Treaty of Versailles in June 1919 imposed punitive reparations on Germany and aimed to suppress its military aviation. Thus, under supervision of an Allied Control Commission, Germany was required to demobilise its Flying Corps, and surrender over 15,000 military aircraft and 27,000 engines along with all other aeronautical material. Under the terms of the treaty, the future manufacture and import of military aircraft, engines, and components, was also expressly forbidden.

Yet the ink on the document was barely dry when first steps were already being taken to resurrect the German air force. A nucleus of regular officers within the Reichswehrministerium under Chief of the Army Command, General Hans von Seeckt, was secretly preparing the ground for a future air force as an independent part of the German armed forces. This group included such officers as Helmuth Felmy, Albert Kesselring, Hugo Sperrle, Hans-Jürgen Stumpff, and Walther Wever; all later to become senior Luftwaffe commanders.

The Versailles treaty aimed to preclude any re-emergence of a German Air Force but was severely flawed in that it failed to prohibit Germany from obtaining or constructing civil aircraft, though certain limitations were subsequently imposed on both the size and numbers of such aircraft that could be produced. But by 1926 even these restrictions had been lifted and Germany allowed free rein in the development of its civil and commercial aviation. The opportunity was thus provided, and readily taken, for the rapid expansion within Germany of gliding clubs, a scheme promoted by Head of the Air Technical Branch of the Defence Ministry, Kurt Student. Commercial air lines, air transport services and flying training facilities all prospered. Germany fast became the most air-minded country in Europe, its Deutscher Luftsportverband, with membership exceeding 50,000 by the end of the decade, providing a solid foundation for the nascent air force.

During the early 1920s, restricted German aircraft manufacture was continued by designers such as Claude Dornier at Friedrichshafen, Heinrich Focke and Georg Wulf at Bremen, Ernst Heinkel at Warnemünde, Hugo Junkers at Dessau and

Willy Messerschmitt in Augsburg. So when the Paris Air Agreement of 1926 lifted restrictions on the manufacture of civil aircraft, Germany already possessed a highly efficient and technically advanced aircraft industry, capable of maintaining production rates as high as any country in Europe.

That same year a new state airways, Deutsche Lufthansa, was formed under the chairmanship of Erhard Milch, later to become a Luftwaffe Feldmarschall. Enjoying generous Government subsidies, this corporation proceeded to build airfields, and progress many technical developments in night-fly-

One of the Luftwaffe's most effective weapons — the Ju87 Stuka dive-bomber. Used as 'mobile artillery', it terrorised the skies of Belgium and France in May 1940 during the Blitzkrieg.

The German fighter force was spearheaded by the formidable single-seat Messerschmitt Bf109 which had first appeared in February 1937 on the strength of II./JG132 'Richthofen'.

The Luftwaffe were now able to field over 850 of them. This is Hauptmann 'Franzl' Lützow, commander of I./JG3, who claimed nine victories during the French campaign.

ing and blind-flying aids. Within short time Lufthansa became the best equipped and most efficient airline in Europe. Under the guise of its commercial flying training programme, a reserve of military pilots was steadily established far exceeding the number of service personnel permitted to fly by the strict terms of the Versailles treaty. Civil aircrews were similarly equipped to operate in a military role. Also, between 1928 and 1931, most of the officers later to hold high rank in the Luftwaffe attended a secret establishment at Lipetzk in Russia for military flying training.

When Hitler became Chancellor of Germany in January 1933, the aircraft industry was already developing military types, and production of these began in earnest the following year with the introduction of such aircraft as the Heinkel He51 biplane fighter. The Junkers Ju52, Junkers Ju86, and Heinkel He111 all soon followed, ostensibly as airliners for Lufthansa but with clear military capabilities as bombers. By March 1935, when the foundation of the new *Luftwaffe* was finally revealed to the world, it mustered some 20,000 officers and men and 1,888 aircraft, with German aircraft production increasing to 300 machines a month by the end of the year.

German rearmament and aggressive foreign policy between 1935 and 1938 determined that its aircraft industry expand to support volume production on a war basis. And more modern types, such as the Messerschmitt Bf109 and Bf110 fighters, Junkers Ju87 and Ju88 bombers, and the Dornier Do17 started being introduced into service.

In August 1936, the Spanish Civil War provided the perfect proving ground for the Luftwaffe to test new equipment and operational tactics in support of General Franco's Nationalist forces. Initially a small force of 20 Junkers Ju52s and six Heinkel He51 escort fighters was sent to Spain with 85 German volunteer air and groundcrews. But it soon became clear that a much larger force was required and consequently the *Legion Condor* was formed in November 1936 with an initial complement of 200 aircraft, under Generalmajor Sperrle. This campaign was to significantly shape future German Air Force strategy, with air bombardment in close support of ground troops being developed under Oberstleutnant Wolfram Freiherr von Richthofen, the new Henschel Hs123 and Junkers Ju87 dive-bombers making their first appearance in action over Spain late in 1937.

Although the Allied air forces had a theoretical strength of some 3,500 aircraft, they were faced by 4,000 German machines of the most modern types from a young air force not constrained by outdated thinking. The Luftwaffe's tactics and equipment had already been tested in action in Spain and fine-tuned in Poland just a few months earlier. Now they were ready to demonstrate a new form of 'lightning' war in which ground and air forces worked together as one. *Above:* Of the 1,200 fighters in the West, 355 were the twin-engined Messerschmitt Bf110 'Zerstörer' which first flew in May 1936. In this shot, Oberleutnant Helmut Florenz, Gruppe Signals Officer, leads a Rotte of the Stabscharm of II. ZG1.

The Dornier Do17 — dubbed the 'Flying Pencil' — was the Luftwaffe's older medium bomber blooded in the Spanish Civil War.

The latest, the Junkers Ju88, with normal bomb-load of 4,000lbs, served in a variety of roles throughout the Second World War.

During 1938, political events in Europe escalated when Germany annexed Austria and occupied the Sudeten area of Czechoslovakia, the Munich agreement of September 29 only securing brief postponement of the major European conflict that seemed sure to follow. At this time Luftwaffe strength stood at some 2,900 aircraft with only 57 per cent serviceability, but it overawed most of its European neighbours thanks in part to a successful campaign by the German Propaganda Ministry. In reality, the German Air Force, its rearmament programmes not yet completed, was still three years away from being the formidable force intended.

By the end of the civil war in Spain, in March 1939, the close tactical air-support doctrine soon to be known as Blitzkrieg, which would prove so devastatingly successful in the European campaigns of the early war years, was firmly established. The Luftwaffe had also developed effective fighter tactics and possessed modern, battle-proven, aircraft superior to any likely opponent, plus a cadre of pilots with invaluable combat experience. They were supremely confident, highly-motivated, and more than ready to demonstrate their superiority. They were soon to exploit their advantage.

The Heinkel He111 with a 4,400lb bomb-load and range of 1,224 miles remained in service even longer — right into the late 1960s.

September 2, 1939

Excludes Luftflotten 1 and 4, and units deployed in Poland.
Also, losses against Allied naval targets are omitted unless directly relevant to operations on the Western Front.

OBERBEFEHLSHABER DER LUFTWAFFE
HQ: Berlin-Werder

1 Westa/ObdL	Reg Rat Dr Kopp	8:8	He111J	Berlin-Gatow
8.(F)/LG2	Major Keienburg	12:10	Do17	Berlin-Werder
10.(F)/LG2	Major Wolff	12:10	Do18	Kiel-Holtenau

LUFTFLOTTE 2
General Felmy
HQ: Braunschweig

1.(F)/122	Hptmn Wappenhaus	12:10	Do17P	Goslar
		11:10	He111H	Goslar
2.(F)/122	Major Schneider	11:10	He111H	Münster
Westa 26	Oblt von Rotberg	6:6	Do17P	Braunschweig

3 Fliegerdivision
Generalmajor Putzier
HQ: Münster

Stab KG54	Oberst Lackner	6:6	He111P	Fritzlar
I./KG54	Major Höhne	33:30	He111P	Fritzlar
1./KG25	Hptmn Pohle	12:12	Ju88A	Jever
II./KG28	Major Koester	35:34	He111P	Gütersloh

4 Fliegerdivision
General Keller
HQ: Braunschweig

I./KG26	Major Loebel	36:32	He111H	Lübeck - Blankensee

Luftgaukommando XI
Generalleutnant Wolff
HQ: Hamburg

II./JG77	Major Schumacher	33:33	Bf109E	Nordholz
Stab ZG26	Oberst von Döring	3:1	Bf109D	Varel
I./ZG26	Hptmn Kaschka	43:39	Bf109D	Varel
III./ZG26	Hptmn Schalk	48:44	Bf109D	Neumünster

Luftgaukommando VI
Generalmajor Schmidt
HQ: Münster

Stab JG26	Oberst von Schleich	3:2	Bf109E	Odendorf
I./JG26	Major Handrick	48:48	Bf109E	Odendorf
II./JG26	Hptmn Knüppel	48:42	Bf109E	Bönninghardt
10.(N)/JG26	Oberlt Steinhoff	9:9	Bf109D	Bonn - Hangelar
I./JG52	Hptmn von Pfeil und Klein-Ellguth	48:34	Bf109E	Bonn - Hangelar
II./ZG26	Major Vollbracht	48:47	Bf109D	Werl

LUFTFLOTTE 3
General Sperrle
HQ: Roth b. Nürnberg

Westa 51	Oberlt Nissen	6:6	He111J	Roth
1.(F)/123		12:11	Do17P	Ansbach
2.(F)/123	Hptmn von Normann	12:12	Do17P	Würzburg

5 Fliegerdivision
Generalmajor Ritter von Greim
HQ: Gersthofen

Stab KG51	Oberst Dr Fisser	9:9	He111H	Landsberg
I./KG51	Oberstlt Korte	36:34	He111H	Memmingen
III./KG51	Oberst Stoeckl	36:33	He111H	Memmingen
I./ZG52	Hptmn Lessman	48:43	Bf109D	Biblis

6 Fliegerdivision
Generalmajor Dessloch
HQ: Frankfurt-Main

Stab KG53	Oberst Stahl	6:6	He111H	Schwäbisch Hall
II./KG53	Oberstlt Kohlbach	32:30	He111H	Schwäbisch Hall
III./KG53	Major von Braun	33:32	He111H	Giebelstadt
III./StG51	Major von Klitzing	3:3	Do17P	Wertheim
		31:29	Ju87B	Wertheim
II./ZG76	Hptmn Schmidt-Coste	48:39	Bf109D	Gablingen

Luftgaukommando VII
Generalleutnant Zenetti   HQ: München

I./JG51	Major von Berg	48:39	Bf109E	Eutingen
4./JG52	Oberlt H. Schumann	17:17	Bf109D	Böblingen
5./JG52	Oberlt A-W. Schumann	16:11	Ar68	Böblingen
2./JG71	Oberlt Fözö	12:9	Bf109D	Fürstenfeldbruck
Reserve St./JG71	Hptmn Tietzen	12:9	Bf109D	Fürstenfeldbruck
10.(N)/JG72	Oberlt Boenigk	12:12	Ar68	Mannheim-Stadt

Luftgaukommando XII
Generalmajor Dr Weissmann   HQ: Wiesbaden

Stab JG53	Oberstlt Junck	3:3	Bf109E	Wiesbaden-Erbenheim
I./JG53	Hptmn von Janson	48:41	Bf109E	Wiesbaden-Erbenheim
II./JG53	Hptmn von Maltzahn	48:41	Bf109E	Mannheim-Sandhofen

Luftgaukommando XIII
Generalmajor Heilingbrunner   HQ: Nürnberg

1./JG70	Oberlt Seiler	12:11	Bf109D	Herzogenaurach
2./JG70	Hpt v Cramon-Taubadel	12:10	Bf109D	Herzogenaurach

OBERBEFEHLSHABER DER MARINE
Generalmajor Ritter   HQ: Berlin

FdLUFT WEST
Generalmajor Bruch   HQ: Jever

Stab KüFlGr106	Oberstlt Jordan		HQ:	Norderney
1./KüFlGr106	Hptmn von Schrötter	10:10	He60	Norderney
2./KüFlGr106	Oberstlt Bischoff	12:12	Do18	Norderney
3./KüFlGr106	Major Horn	10:10	He59	Borkum
3./KüFlGr706	Hptmn Stein	12:12	He59	Norderney
Stab KüFlGr406	Major Minner		HQ:	List
1./KüFlGr406	Hptmn Wiesand	8:8	He115	List
2./KüFlGr406	Major Bartels	12:10	Do18	List
3./KüFlGr406	Hptmn Bergemann	9:9	He59	List
BoFlSt 1./196	Major Lessing	12:12	He60/ Ar196	Wilhelmshaven
BoFlSt 5./196	Hptmn Petersen	12:12	He60	Kiel-Holtenau

OBERBEFEHLSHABER DER HEER
Generalmajor Bogatsch   HQ: Berlin

KOLUFT HEERESGRUPPE C
Generalmajor Bieneck   HQ: Frankfurt-Rebstock

attached Heeresgruppe C
1.(F)/22		12:10	Do17P	Kassel-Rothwesten

attached XXX Armee Korps
4.(H)/12		12:7	He46	Rheinberg

attached V Armee Korps
3.(H)/13	Hptmn Schulz-Wiehenbrauck	12:8	Hs126	Villingen

attached 1 Armee
3.(F)/22	Major von Barsewitsch	12:10	Do17P	Koblenz-Karthausen

attached IX Armee Korps
1.(H)/13	Hptmn Göring	11:11	Hs126	Worms

attached XII Armee Korps
4.(H)/22	Hptmn Asmus	12:8	Hs126	Hoppstädten

attached Gen Kdo Saarpfalz
1.(H)/23	Major Heinsius	12:8	Hs126	Pferdsfeld

attached 5 Armee
2.(F)/22	Hptmn Blauensteiner	12:8	Do17P	Bonn-Hangelar

attached VI Armee Korps
2.(H)/12	Hptmn Wehl	12:10	Hs126	Rüdesheim

attached Gen Kdo Eifel
1.(H)/12		12:11	Hs126	Wengerohr

attached 7 Armee
7.(F)/LG2	Hptmn Gerndt	12:11	Do17P	Deckenpfronn

attached Gen Kdo Oberrhein
2.(H)/13	Hptmn Fischer	12:4	Hs126	Huchenfeld-Malmsheim

THE AIRCRAFT LOSSES

L9248

SEPTEMBER 1939

At readiness in France . . . waiting for 'the balloon to go up'. Fairey Battles of Nos. 71, 72, 74, 75 and 76 Bomber Wings were already on station on aerodromes in the Reims area (see map pages 26-27) when war was declared. Here, No. 218 Squadron stand by at Aubérive, some 30 kilometres east of Reims.

It is little known that when British Prime Minister Neville Chamberlain broadcast to the nation on September 3, 1939, solemnly announcing that we were 'once again at war with Germany', 160 Fairey Battles of the RAF Advanced Air Striking Force were already standing by in France ready for immediate offensive operations if so ordered.

Germany's attack on Poland two days before had prompted the general mobilisation of Britain and France, and triggered this transfer of British air forces to France as part of a general strategy agreed six months before. As early as the German occupation of the Rhineland in 1936, Britain, France, and initially also Belgium, had discussed naval, military and air collaboration in the event of further German aggression in Europe.

By September 1938 it had been agreed that an Advanced Air Striking Force of 20 squadrons of medium bombers from No. 1 Group RAF Bomber Command would transfer to airfields around Reims, with Nantes as their base port, reducing range to potential targets in Germany, and British bombs had been stockpiled in France from April 1939 disguised as sales to France. In the event, additional plans for No. 2 Group to follow were subsequently postponed, and later abandoned, due to lack of adequate airfields and facilities. It was further planned that an Air Component of the Field Force (later the RAF Component of the British Expeditionary Force) would also transfer to France in support of British ground forces, and No. 22 Group were earmarked for this duty.

This movement of RAF units to France was not accomplished without difficulty and much early chaos was reported. French preparations were insufficient, and lack of transport, basic facilities, and even billets, caused initial problems and not a little discomfort for some units. However, by September 12, with some reorganisation and relocation of units, the British air forces in France were established.

Little air activity took place over the Western Front, neither side wishing to provoke the massive air assaults so confidently predicted by pre-war strategists; both preferring to limit operations to reconnaissance sorties and attacks on naval targets. Besides which the main weight of the Luftwaffe was deployed against Poland until September 22 when, on conclusion of the Polish campaign, units could be transferred to the West.

The first recorded engagement on the Western Front took place on September 8 when six Curtis H-75As of GCII/4 clashed with Messerschmitt Bf109Es of I./JG53 in an inconclusive action over the Bienwald. The first engagement involving RAF aircraft took place 12 days later when Fairey Battles of No. 88 Squadron were badly mauled by German fighters west of Saarburg. As a result of these early actions, it was made abundantly clear to both the British and French High Commands that daylight bomber and reconnaissance sorties were proving very costly, French strategic reconnaissance units experiencing 'une Semaine Noire' towards the end of the month.

Saturday, September 30, saw the heaviest fighting yet over the Western Front. While French and German fighters disputed airspace over the frontier throughout the day, a formation of six Fairey Battles of No. 150 Squadron was decimated by predatory German fighters. As a result, further unescorted sorties by Battles were forbidden.

Solo reconnaissance flights resulted in many of the casualties experienced by all sides during the 'Drôle de Guerre' — the 'Phoney War'. This is all that remained of the Potez 637 belonging to GR 2/52 of the French Air Force which was brought down by a combination of attacks by Bf109s and anti-aircraft fire on September 26.

Saturday, September 2

BRITISH AIR FORCES IN FRANCE

40 SQUADRON Battle L4979. Suffered engine failure en-route to France and ditched in the Channel, 15 miles off Dieppe 2.15 p.m. Crew rescued by SS *Worthing*. Flight Lieutenant W. G. Moseby slightly concussed, admitted to Uxbridge hospital. Sergeant P. Cody and AC1 W. Furby both unhurt. Aircraft lost.

This was the first aircraft lost by the BAFF during transfer of RAF units to bases in France agreed months before. Both crewmen soon returned to operations, Willie Furby, by then promoted Sergeant, later reported missing on June 6, 1940.

105 SQUADRON Battle K9197. Wrecked in forced-landing near Poix due to engine failure during transfer flight to Reims 1.00 p.m. Sergeant B. F. Phillips and crew unhurt. Aircraft a write-off.

LUFTWAFFE

2./JG26 Messerschmitt Bf109E. Crashed at Cologne-Ostheim due to engine failure. Uffz J. Schuhbauer killed. Aircraft a write-off.

Wednesday, September 6

FRENCH AIR FORCE

GR 1/52 Potez 637 (47). Belly-landed near Trannes in bad weather during night sortie. Lt du Tertre, Sgt Canonne, and Sgt J. Melot unhurt. Aircraft damaged but repairable.

Thursday, September 7

FRENCH AIR FORCE

HS 2 Loire 130 (2). Disappeared from sortie off Brest; cause unknown but probably engine failure. EV1 de Tessières, Mt Rochefort, Mt Jacquiard, SM Monnet, and QM Coadic missing. Aircraft 2 lost.

Loss of this catapult floatplane from the battleship Dunkerque *resulted in the first casualties suffered by the French air forces in WWII.*

LUFTWAFFE

Fl.Div.7 Henschel Hs126. Wrecked when flew into trees while low-flying near Rathenow. Crew both injured. Aircraft a write-off.

Friday, September 8

FRENCH AIR FORCE

ECN 4/13 Potez 631 (114). Stalled during training flight and attempted a forced-landing at Villeneuve-St-Georges but crashed and caught fire. Sgt A. de Villoutreys killed. Lt Léonardo badly burned; died of injuries September 23. Adjt Fabre suffered badly broken legs. Aircraft a write-off.

GAO 553 Mureaux 115 (15). Shot down by Lt Gutbrod of 5./JG52 during photo-reconnaissance mission; crashed and burned out south-west of Karlsruhe 5.20 p.m. Lt J. Davier and Sgt S. Piaccentini both baled out but killed. Aircraft lost.

GC II/7 Potez 631. Crashed on take-off at Toul Croix-de-Metz, cause unknown. S/Lt J. Gauthier, Adjt Gresset, and Sgt R. Paratilla killed. Aircraft a write-off.

GR II/52 Potez 637 (52). Both engines badly damaged in attacks by Bf 109s of 3./JGr.152 west of Landau during reconnaissance sortie over Kaiserslautern. Crashed on landing at Herbéviller and burned out. S/Lt Vauthier, Aspirant Halle, and Cpl Bioletti unhurt. Aircraft a write-off.

HS 2 Loire 130 (5). Wrecked in forced-landing near Crozon due to fuel shortage. LV Lepeltier and crew slightly injured. Aircraft 1 a write-off.

LUFTWAFFE

1./JG53 Messerschmitt Bf109E. Overturned in forced-landing at Birkenfeld due to engine failure following combat with Curtiss H-75s of GC II/4 over the Bienwald near Schaidt 8.00 a.m. Hptmn W. Mölders *(Staffelkapitän)* injured. Aircraft damaged but repairable.

Saturday, September 9

FRENCH AIR FORCE

GAR 14 Bloch 131 (92). Shot down by Bf 109 of Oberfw Grimmling of 1./JG53 during photo reconnaissance of the German frontier defences near Zweibrücken. Crashed starboard engine in flames north-east of Saarbrücken 10.36 a.m. Capt. Fion, Sgt Bouvry, and Sgt M. Rayat killed. Sgt Trusson baled out badly wounded in legs. Aircraft a write-off.

SEPTEMBER 1939

The Mureaux 115 — a high-wing, all metal monoplane built by Les Ateliers de Constructions du Nord de la France et des Mureaux (ANF) — was designed as a long-range reconnaissance aircraft and could reach the somewhat incredible height of 33,000 feet. Equipped with racks for four 110lb bombs beneath the wings, and with two machine guns firing forward and two in the rear cockpit, this one was brought down on September 10 by Oberfeldwebel Walter Grimmling of 1. Staffel of JG53.

GAR 1/14 Bloch 131. Port engine set alight in attacks by Bf109s during photo reconnaissance over Saint-Ingbert and undercarriage collapsed in forced-landing at Martigny-les-Gerbonvaux. Cpl P. Martellière badly wounded, died two days later. Sgt Lacaille wounded. Capt. Frébillot (Commandant), and Adjt Thiebault unhurt. Aircraft damaged but repairable.

GB I/31 Bloch 200 (132). Shot down by Bf 109s over Saarbrücken during reconnaissance sortie to Sierck-les-Bains. Believed that claimed by Lt Hoffmann of 3./JG53. Crashed in flames near Zweibrücken 1.35 p.m. S/Lt Béranger, and Lt-Col. Enselem (Escadre Commandant) captured unhurt. Adjt Charpentier, Sgt Senot de la Londe, and Sgt Audoux captured wounded. Aircraft a write-off.

GB 1/31 Bloch 200. Badly damaged in attacks by Bf 109s of 3./JG53 over Zweibrücken during reconnaissance sortie to Sierck-les-Bains 1.40 p.m. Forced-landed at Haudimont-Manheulles. Capt. Villadier suffered badly injured back, Lt R. Hirsch and rest of crew unhurt. Aircraft a write-off.

GB II/31 Bloch 200 (163). Shot down by Bf 109s over Zweibrücken during reconnaissance sortie to Sierck-les-Bains. Believed that claimed by Oberlt Rhinow (Staffelkapitän) of 4./ZG76. Crashed in flames near Saarbrücken 1.45 p.m. Cmdt. E. Delozanne (Groupe Commandant), Lt M. Joly, S/Lt J. Charreire, Adjt G. Petton, and Adjt J. Gaillères killed. Aircraft lost.

GC II/4 Curtis H-75. Suffered engine failure shortly after take-off; crashed and burned out near Deinvillers. Sgt G. Jean killed. Aircraft a write-off.

GR I/52 Potez 637. Returned to base damaged by enemy fighters during reconnaissance sortie to Ulm. Adjt P. Mougel wounded, Cpl Dumas and rest of crew unhurt. Aircraft repairable.

Although this photograph was printed with a non-specific caption in October 1939, this funeral of two French airmen behind enemy lines could well show a crew from either of the other two Mureaux down that day.

BELGIAN AIR FORCE

4/II/2 Firefly. Returned to Nivelles damaged by return fire from a No. 102 Squadron Whitley while attempting to force it to land after it strayed over neutral Belgium 6.00 a.m. Sgt D. Leroy du Vivier unhurt. Aircraft repairable.
After the Belgian capitulation, Daniel Leroy du Vivier was one of over 70 Belgian airmen who escaped to England to join the RAF. He flew Hurricanes with No. 43 Squadron during the Battle of Britain, and in January 1943 became the first Belgian to command an RAF squadron when he was appointed their Squadron Leader.

5/III/2 Fox. Intercepted a Whitley (K8951) of No. 102 Squadron that strayed over Belgium during return from operations over Germany and attempted to force it to land. Hit by return fire and abandoned over Nouvelles; crashed on the estate of Count Gaston d'Oultrement 6.00 a.m. Adjt A. Genot baled out slightly wounded, Cpl R. Alaffe baled out and broke right shoulder on landing. Aircraft a write-off.

Sunday, September 10

BRITISH AIR FORCES IN FRANCE

73 SQUADRON Hurricane. Suffered broken tail wheel on landing at Caen. Squadron Leader B. W. Knox unhurt. Aircraft repairable.

FRENCH AIR FORCE

GAO 1/506 Mureaux 113 (4). Shot down during observation mission over Ensdorf by Bf109 of Oberlt Pingel (Staffelkapitän) of 2./JG53. Crashed near Saarlouis 1.15 p.m. Lt G. Leleu and S/Lt Moll killed. Aircraft a write-off.

GAO 1/520 Mureaux 115 (106). Shot down by Uffz Bezner of 1./JG53 during artillery ranging sortie for XXème Corps d'Armée. Crashed in flames near Zimming, 2 km north of Grosbliederstroff 5.30 p.m. Lt H. Potié and Sgt J. Tacquart killed. Aircraft a write-off.

GAO 1/520 Mureaux 115. Severely damaged in attack by Oberfw Grimmling of 1./JG53 and crash-landed behind enemy lines at Auersmacher 5.30 p.m. Sgt Lahaye unhurt, and Lt Cappoen injured; both evaded capture and reached French lines. Aircraft lost.

Monday, September 11

FRENCH AIR FORCE

GAO 3/551 Mureaux 117 (70). Shot down by AA fire during observation sortie between Perl and Apach, and crashed at Trassem. Capt. J. Rossignol and Lt J. Sueur killed. Aircraft lost.

2S1 Gourdou-Leseurre 812 (41). Failed to return from reconnaissance sortie to Finistère in deteriorating weather conditions and believed crashed in the sea off the Ile d'Ouessant. SM Kerambrun, QM Lavallée, and motor mechanic Le Friec missing. Aircraft seven lost.

Tuesday, September 12

FRENCH AIR FORCE

GAO 3/551 Mureaux 117. Hit by ground-fire during observation sortie and crashed inside French lines near Güdingen. Sgt Leclerc killed. Capt Boursaus *(Commandant)* escaped unhurt. Aircraft a write-off.

LUFTWAFFE

5./ZG76 Messerschmitt Bf109D-1. Crashed near Grosselfingen following engine failure. Uffz H. Oel killed. Aircraft a write-off.

Wednesday, September 13

DUTCH AIR FORCE

GVT2 Fokker T VIIIw (5586). Mistaken for an RAF aircraft and attacked by He115 of 1./106 off Ameland 1.30 p.m. Badly damaged and capsized attempting a landing in heavy seas. Lt van Rijn rescued wounded in shoulder, Sgt Buynink rescued wounded in foot. Kpl van Wingerden and Kpl Goudszwaard picked up unhurt. Aircraft R-5 lost.

This crew was picked up by their attacker, the He115 M2+LH, which after running repairs to a damaged float managed to take-off again at 5.00 p.m. and return with them to Nordeney. They were repatriated two days later following diplomatic exchanges. This incident prompted the Dutch to change the national markings on their aircraft from October 1 from a red, white and blue roundel, to a distinctive orange triangle to avoid further cases of mistaken identity.

LUFTWAFFE

2./KüFlGr.106 Dornier Do18D (718). Aborted routine patrol due to defective radio and damaged in landing to assist stranded He115 of 1./106 off Ameland 4.10 p.m. Attacked on the water by Fokker D XXIs of 1-II-1 and abandoned by crew. Lt zur See H. Rust, Fw O. Radons, Uffz O. Schenk, and Funkmaat H. Zieschang rowed ashore in dinghy and interned in Holland. Aircraft M2+LK a write-off.

The treatment of this crew compared to that of the Dutch crew above illustrates the niceties of international law relating to members of foreign armed forces interned by neutral countries in wartime. By the time Germany finally launched its offensive in the West, ten German and four British airmen had been interned in the Netherlands, while another five German, 19 British, and two French airmen had been interned in Belgium. Internees held by the Dutch were housed in Fort Spijkerboor, part of the First World War fortifications north of Amsterdam, but on May 10, 1940 all British internees were handed to the British Legation in Den Haag for immediate repatriation. Two days later the German internees were escorted to IJmuiden and later shipped to England from Scheveningen aboard the SS Proteus as prisoners of war along with another 623 enemy personnel captured in the fighting.

Thursday, September 14

FRENCH AIR FORCE

GAO 518 Breguet 270 (64). Crashed on take-off at Bray-sur-Seine. Cause not stated. Cmdt. Montaudie *(Commandant)* and Adjt Penclaud unhurt. Aircraft a write-off.

Saturday, September 16

LUFTWAFFE

4.(F)/122 Dornier Do17P. Crashed at Osteel, south of Norden, following engine fire. Three crew killed. Aircraft a write-off.

Sunday, September 17

FRENCH AIR FORCE

GR I/22 Bloch 131 (86). Intercepted by Bf 109s during reconnaissance of the Stenay-Sierck-Metz sector and shot down by Oberlt Balfanz of Stab I./JG53 over Morsbach 4.23 p.m. S/Lt Capdeville and Adjt Saron killed. Lt Rousset and S/Lt Leroy wounded. Aircraft a write-off.

Monday, September 18

FRENCH AIR FORCE

E 6 Latécoère 523. Run out of fuel after 12-hour reconnaissance flight and ditched south-east of Ile d'Ouessant, off Brest. Starboard wing and hull damaged against torpedo boat *Boulonnais* during rescue operations. LV Mathon and crew unhurt. Aircraft 'Algol' abandoned, sunk by naval gun-fire.

GC III/2 MS 406 (293). Destroyed in an accident, cause not stated. Sgt Billet unhurt. Aircraft a write-off.

LUFTWAFFE

I./JG53 Messerschmitt Bf109E. Wrecked in forced-landing at Lauterecken, cause not stated. Pilot unhurt. Aircraft a write-off.

Tuesday, September 19

FRENCH AIR FORCE

GB I/31 LeO 451 (9). Crashed due to engine failure on take-off from Connantre on reconnaissance sortie of the Strasbourg-Munich-Nuremberg sector. Cmdt. Dumas *(Commandant)* and Adjt Regnoux injured. Aircraft a write-off.

LUFTWAFFE

3./JG53 Messerschmitt Bf109E. Reported crashed 11.15 a.m. but no details recorded. Gefr G. Dill killed. Aircraft a write-off.

Wednesday, September 20

BRITISH AIR FORCES IN FRANCE

88 SQUADRON Battle K9242. Severely damaged by Bf109s during reconnaissance sortie over the German frontier and crash-landed on fire. Probably that claimed over Bitsch 10.46 a.m. by Lt Liedke of 5./JG 53. Flying Officer R. C. Graveley badly burned evacuated to RAF Halton Hospital. Sergeant W. S. Everett severely injured; leg amputated but died same day. AC1 D. J. John killed. Aircraft a write-off.

88 SQUADRON Battle K9245. Shot down by Bf109s during reconnaissance sortie and crashed and burned out at Guéblange, north-west of Sarrebourg. Probably that claimed over Bitsch 10.45 a.m. by Lt Richert of 5./JG 53. Flight Sergeant D. A. Page, Sergeant A. W. Eggington and AC1 E. A. W. Radford killed. Aircraft a write-off.

150 SQUADRON Battle L5225. Suffered engine failure shortly after take-off on local photo flight; crashed attempting forced-landing and caught fire 11.35 a.m. Pilot Officer J. L. Calvert critically injured, died in Chalons hospital same evening. Sergeant T. B. Woodmason, and AC1 J. L. Marsh killed. Aircraft a write-off.

218 SQUADRON Battle K9327. Landed at Gray, north-east of Dijon, slightly damaged in mid-air collision while descending through cloud in close formation. Flying Officer Hughes, Flight Sergeant Wavell, and AC Evans unhurt. Aircraft repairable.

FRENCH AIR FORCE

GAO 507 Mureaux 115 (21). Badly damaged by Bf109s during photo-reconnaissance over the Saar valley and forced-landed near Obergailbach. Possibly that claimed by Oberfw Hien of 3./JG53 10.15 a.m. Lt Bonal badly wounded in head and legs. Adjt Senne suffered leg wounds. Aircraft 'La Glandouille' a write-off.

GC II/5 Curtiss H-75 (21). Shot down by Hptmn Mölders *(Staffelkapitän)* of 1./JG53 during sector patrol between Apach and Büdingen, crashed and burned out west of Merzig 1.55 p.m. Sgt Quéguiner baled out with burns to face and hands. Aircraft a write-off.

GC II/5 Curtiss H-75. Believed badly damaged in attack by Uffz Freund of 1./JG53 west of Völkingen and belly-landed at St Mihiel 2.00 p.m. Sgt Pechaud unhurt. Aircraft a write-off.

GR 1/33 Potez 637 (25). Hit in the wing by AA fire during reconnaissance sortie to Pirmasens and crashed near Trèves. Capt. Schneider *(Commandant)* killed. S/Lt Noël and Sgt Le Plan both captured wounded. Aircraft a write-off.

LUFTWAFFE

3./JG53 Messerschmitt Bf109E. Shot down by Sgt Legrand of GC II/5 in combat west of Merzig and crash-landed in flames 1.55 p.m. Uffz M. Winkler badly burned, died four days later. Aircraft a write-off.

I./JG53 Messerschmitt Bf109E. Forced-landed at Hermeskeil damaged in combat with Curtiss H-75s of GC II/5 west of Merzig 1.55 p.m. Pilot unhurt. Aircraft damaged but repairable.

Thursday, September 21

BRITISH AIR FORCES IN FRANCE

40 SQUADRON Battle K9364. Returned slightly damaged by AA fire during photo-reconnaissance sortie over Losheim 12.30 p.m. Flight Lieutenant L. D. Wilson, Sergeant B. L. Harris, and AC1 H. Baguley unhurt. Aircraft repairable.

This Potez 637, serial 25, was brought down on September 20 by German anti-aircraft fire near Trèves (the French name for the German town Trier). Here Wachtmeister Stumm poses in front of their victory.

40 SQUADRON Battle L4982. Returned slightly damaged by AA fire during photo-reconnaissance sortie over Losheim 12.30 p.m. Pilot Officer G. D. Hill, Sergeant J. L. Alexander, and AC1 D. Goffe unhurt. Aircraft repairable.

FRENCH AIR FORCE

ECN 3/13 Potez 631 (30). Crashed at Bruyères-sur-Oise, cause not stated. Adjt Lepage and Sgt Collinot unhurt. Aircraft a write-off.

GAO 505 Potez 39 (50). Badly damaged in attacks by Bf109s of I./JG53 during observation sortie over the Rubenheim-Altheim-Hornbach sector 3.30 p.m. Forced-landed between Niedergailbach and Obergailbach. Capt. A. Léonard killed, Sgt Achaintre unhurt. Aircraft a write-off.

GAR 14 Bloch 131 (61). Lost bearings in fog on return from night reconnaissance and run out of fuel; belly-landed alongside the River Nièvre near Marcy a.m. Lt Josselin and crew unhurt. Aircraft repairable.

GC I/3 Morane 406. Shot down by Hptmn Dr Mix of Stab I./JG53 during escort sortie for Potez 39 of GAO 505 over Sarreguemines 3.15 p.m. S/Lt M. Baize baled out but parachute caught fire, fell dead at Bliesbruck. Aircraft a write-off.

Friday, September 22

FRENCH AIR FORCE

GC III/2 Morane 406 (295). Lost bearings during patrol over Vitry-le-François and landed in error at Saarbrücken-Ensheim. Sgt Duclos captured unhurt. Aircraft destroyed by French artillery fire.
Alternative sources suggest that this incident occurred on September 21.

GC II/6 Morane 406 (72). Crashed at Vouarces during training flight, circumstances unknown. Sgt Durouchard killed. Aircraft a write-off.

On the following day this Morane 406 was shot down in flames by Hauptmann Dr Erich Mix. Unfortunately the parachute of Sous-Lieutenant Marius Baize caught fire as he exited the aircraft and it failed to save him.

LUFTWAFFE

Stab JG52 Messerschmitt Bf109E-1 (3410). Wrecked in crash-landing at Karlsruhe following engine failure. Pilot injured. Aircraft a write-off.

Saturday, September 23

FRENCH AIR FORCE

GAO 502 Mureaux 115 (41). Crashed at Fagnon cause not stated. Capt. Trelluyer and S/Lt Duminil unhurt. Aircraft a write-off.

BELGIAN AIR FORCE

5/III/2 Fox (O.141). Crashed at Mettet, south-east of Charleroi, cause unknown. Pilot unhurt. Aircraft a write-off.

Sunday, September 24

BRITISH AIR FORCES IN FRANCE

73 SQUADRON Magister L8347. Propeller broken in forced-landing near Amiens during transit flight between Octeville and Norrent-Fontes. Flight Lieutenant R. Press and Warrant Officer Neale unhurt. Aircraft damaged but repairable.

FRENCH AIR FORCE

GAO 1/520 Mureaux 115 (107). Returned to Keskastel with elevators damaged in attack by Oberfw Kuhlmann of 3./JG53 during photo-reconnaissance sortie of the Scheid-Lanskirchen sector. Lt Bernard badly wounded, S/Lt E. Petit unhurt. Aircraft damaged but repairable.

GC I/3 Morane 406 (270). Engaged by Bf109s during escort sortie for Mureaux of GAO 1/520 and badly damaged. Pursued and shot down while attempting a forced-landing near Etting 1.00 p.m. Possibly that claimed by Oberlt Schnoor *(Staffelkapitän)* of 3./JGr.152. Sgt J. Garnier killed. Aircraft a write-off.

GC I/3 Morane 406. Shot down by Bf109s during escort sortie for Mureaux of GAO 1/520 west of Saarbrücken 1.00 p.m. Possibly that claimed by Lt Hagen of 3./JGr.152. Capt. R. Gérard baled out unhurt. Aircraft a write-off.

GC I/3 Morane 406. Damaged in combat with Bf109s during escort sortie for Mureaux of GAO 1/520 west of Saarbrücken and forced-landed 1.00 p.m. Possibly attacked by Oberfw Oertel of 3./JGr.152. Pilot believed unhurt. Aircraft a write-off.

GC I/3 Morane 406 (252). Shot down by Bf109s in combat west of Saarbrücken 1.00 p.m. Possibly one of those claimed by Lt Rosenkranz of 3./JGr.152. Adjt A. Combette baled out unhurt. Aircraft a write-off.

Censorship was extremely tight and the only information issued with this RAF official photograph was that it showed 'the violent end of one of Germany's much-vaunted Messerschmitt fighters shot down by French anti-aircraft fire on the Western Front'. It was published in *The War Illustrated* on October 21 and detailed examination of the Luftwaffe losses preceding that date indicates that it must show the Bf109 of Jagdgeschwader 152 shot down by Capitaine Gerard on September 24.

GC II/4 Curtiss H-75 (66). Shot down by Bf109s during escort sortie for Potez 637 of GR II/52 between Hornbach and Eppenbronn 2.40 p.m. Possibly that claimed by Fw Czikowsky of 6./JG53. Sgt A. de La Chapelle baled out unhurt. Aircraft a write-off.

GC II/4 Curtiss H-75. Returned badly damaged in attack by Bf109s during escort sortie for Potez 637 of GR II/52 between Hornbach and Eppenbronn 2.40 p.m. Possibly that claimed by Uffz Baun of 6./JG53. Adjt H. Dardaine unhurt. Aircraft damaged but repairable.

GC II/4 Curtiss H-75. Returned badly damaged in attack by Bf109s during escort sortie for Potez 637 of GR II/52 between Hornbach and Eppenbronn 2.40 p.m. Possibly that claimed by Lt Rupp of 1./JG53. S/Lt G. Duperret unhurt. Aircraft damaged but repairable.

GR 3/33 Potez 637 (7). Forced-landed at Orconte on one engine, damaged by flak and reportedly attacked by Bf109s during reconnaissance sortie between Oldendorf and Euskirchen. Lt Israël slightly wounded, Adjt A. Robert unhurt. Aircraft repairable.

LUFTWAFFE

3.(F)/22 Dornier Do17P. Engaged by own flak during reconnaissance sortie over Zweibrücken and shot down west of Neunkirchen. Fw E. Ragnit and Uffz K. Seiffert killed, another baled out unhurt. Aircraft a write-off.

10.(N)/JG26 Messerschmitt Bf109D-1 (538). Crashed at Hönningen following engine seizure. Pilot baled out unhurt. Aircraft a write-off.

JGr.152 Messerschmitt Bf109D-1. Shot down by Adjt Dardaine of GC II/4 in combat east of Hornbach, and crashed near Betviller, east of Sarreguemines 3.40 p.m. Oberlt Borth captured badly wounded. Aircraft a write-off.

2./JGr.152 Messerschmitt Bf109D-1. Shot down by Adjt Combette of GC I/3 and forced-landed 2 km north-east of Rimling, east of Sarreguemines 1.00 p.m. Gefr A. Hesselbach captured unhurt. Aircraft 9 + a write-off.
This aircraft was made serviceable for evaluation by the French but crashed on a test flight at Nancy on October 6. It is believed that it was subsequently repaired and passed to the RAF on December 22, being flown from Coulommiers to Tangmere, en-route to the A&AEE Boscombe Down, by W/C J.F.X. McKenna. Grounded at Tangmere by weather and refuelling problems it never arrived at Boscombe Down and its ultimate fate is unknown.

3./JGr.152 Messerschmitt Bf109D-1. Shot down by Capt Gérard of GC I/3 and belly-landed near Obergailbach, south-west of Saarbrücken 1.00 p.m. Lt K. Rosenkranz captured unhurt. Aircraft 12 + a write-off.

3./JGr.152 Messerschmitt Bf109D-1. Damaged in attacks by Adjt Plubeau and Adjt Tesseraud of GC II/4 in combat east of Hornbach, and belly-landed near Weilersbach 3.40 p.m. Lt H. Elstermann unhurt. Aircraft damaged but repairable.

3./JGr.152 Messerschmitt Bf109D-1. Damaged in attacks by S/Lt Plubeau and Adjt Tesseraud of GC II/4 in combat east of Hornbach, and forced-landed near Bingen 3.40 p.m. Lt H. Grasser unhurt. Aircraft damaged but repairable.

Monday, September 25

BRITISH AIR FORCES IN FRANCE

81 SQUADRON Tiger Moth N6843. Damaged on start-up at Entrepagny during ferry flight from Le Mans. Flying Officer A. J. Sayers unhurt. Aircraft damaged but repairable, later struck-off.

FRENCH AIR FORCE

GC 4/4 Curtiss H-75 (112). Set alight in attack by Bf109s south-east of Bad Bergzabern. Probably that claimed by Hptmn Pitcairn *(Staffelkapitän)* and Uffz Bär of 1./JG51 between Weissenburg and Lauterburg 11.07 a.m. Capt. P. Claude *(Commandant)* baled out but machine-gunned in his parachute landing near Soultz-sous-Forêts with right leg shattered and mortally wounded in the head — later died. Aircraft a write-off.

GC III/6 Morane 406 (238). Lost speed and crashed, exact cause unknown. Capt. Chainaut unhurt. Aircraft a write-off.

GC II/7 Morane 406. Abandoned when engine caught fire on return from operations. Sgt H. Grimaud baled out, hit tailplane and injured. Aircraft a write-off.

GR II/52 Potez 637 (31). Badly damaged by AA fire over Saarbrücken during photo-reconnaissance of the Landau-Pirmasens-Kaiserslautern sector. Also attacked by Bf109s of Stab I./JG53 over Bergzabern and port engine set alight by Hptmn von Janson *(Gruppenkommandeur)*. Crashed in flames on the banks of the Sarre, 3 km from Sarralbe 2.50 p.m. Lt Tissier badly wounded in shoulder, S/Lt Amarre burned and badly wounded in the leg, Sgt Genty wounded. Aircraft a write-off.

LUFTWAFFE

1./JG51 Messerschmitt Bf109E-1. Returned to Speyer with damage following combat with Curtiss H-75As over Weissenburg 11.20 a.m. Possibly one of those attacked by S/Lt Baptizet of GC II/4. Fw K. Schmid unhurt. Aircraft repairable.

1./JG51 Messerschmitt Bf109E-1. Returned to Speyer with damage following combat with Curtiss H-75As over Weissenburg 11.20 a.m. Possibly one of those attacked by Adjt Tesseraud of GC II/4. Fw J. Oglodek unhurt. Aircraft repairable.

6./JG53 Messerschmitt Bf109E. Shot down by S/Lt Verry of GC 1/4 and crashed in flames south-east of Bergzabern 11.20 a.m. Fw H. Helge killed. Aircraft a write-off.
The date of death of Heinz Helge is recorded as September 22 by the German War Graves Service.

6./JG53 Messerschmitt Bf109E. Badly damaged in combat with Moranes and crash-landed near Bergzabern 11.20 a.m. Possibly one of those attacked by S/Lt Verry of GC I/4. Pilot wounded. Aircraft damaged but repairable.

6./JG53 Messerschmitt Bf109E. Damaged in combat with Moranes of GC I/4 and GC II/4 and crash-landed near Bergzabern 11.25 a.m. Pilot wounded. Aircraft damaged but repairable.

Tuesday, September 26

BRITISH AIR FORCES IN FRANCE

40 SQUADRON Battle K9360. Returned aileron damaged by AA fire during photo-reconnaissance sortie over Saarbrücken, Neunkirchen and Altheim 10.15 a.m. Sergeant A. J. Roberton, Sergeant F. Nixon, and LAC T. F. S. Clark unhurt. Aircraft repairable.

Above: **Nice picture for the brag-book of Leutnant Werner Guth with easy identification of his first victory on September 26.**
Right: **Gefreiter Joseph Scherm's claim to fame was that he was the first German airman killed by the Royal Air Force in the Second World War. He was shot down on September 27 by point-blank return fire from Aircraftman John Ernest Summers, the gunner on Battle K9271 of No. 103 Squadron. Scherm fell into impenetrable woods near Bockweiler. Summers was later awarded the DFM for this action.**

81 SQUADRON Tiger Moth N6847. Damaged at Le Bourget during communications flight from Amiens-Glisy. Flying Officer J. W. Radbone unhurt. Aircraft damaged but repairable.

FRENCH AIR FORCE

GR 2/52 Potez 637 (46). Attacked by Bf109s and also hit by AA fire during reconnaissance sortie to Constance. Shot down by Lt Güth of 3./JGr.176 and crashed in flames near Sigmaringen 11.45 a.m. Adjt R. Lagarde baled out too low and killed. Sgt E. Heiltz killed during fighter attacks. Adjt Brard baled out and captured badly wounded in legs and shoulder. Aircraft a write-off.

GR II/55 Bloch 131 (80). Shot down by Oberlt Ehrlich of 2./JGr.176 during reconnaissance sortie and crashed outside Freiburg 11.30 a.m. S/Lt H. Folloroux killed. Sgt Crozon badly wounded. Capt. Evano and Adjt Girard believed unhurt. Aircraft a write-off.

DUTCH AIR FORCE

IV-2 Fokker C V (614). Oil system and airframe damaged by own AA fire over Blerick during interception of aircraft reported between Venlo and Helden, and forced-landed at Heierhoeve 7.10 p.m. Lt Benus wounded, Lt Paap unhurt. Aircraft damaged but repairable.

Vliegschool Haamstede Koolhoven F.K.51 (424). Crashed at Zonnemaire during training flight, cause not stated. Aro J. Jongkind and Aro. J. Hubregste killed. Aircraft a write-off.

Wednesday, September 27

BRITISH AIR FORCES IN FRANCE

103 SQUADRON Battle K9271. First attacked by French Curtiss H-75s then severely damaged by Bf109s of JGr.152 during photo-reconnaissance over the frontier between Bouzonville and the Rhine. Forced-landed on one wheel near Rohrbach 1.40 p.m. Flying Officer A. L. Vipan unhurt. Sergeant J. H. Vickers critically injured; died of wounds 5.10.39. AC1 J. E. Summers unhurt. Aircraft PM⊙G a write-off.

Sergeant Vickers, who was buried in the French Military Cemetery at St Louis-les-Bitche, was decorated with the French Medaille Militaire, the first such award to a member of the BEF. He was later reinterred in Choloy War Cemetery.

FRENCH AIR FORCE

GAO 2/508 Potez 25 (1700). Badly damaged in attacks by Bf109s of I./JG53 during reconnaissance mission over d'Elzange and crashed at Thionville 3.00 p.m. Lt Lambert wounded, and Lt Lequeu unhurt. Aircraft a write-off.

GR II/52 Potez 637 (4). Engaged by Bf109s of 1./JG53 north-east of Tenteling during reconnaissance sortie and caught fire under attack by Lt Heimbs. Broke up and fell between Sarreguemines and Forbach 3.20 p.m. Lt G. du Parc, Adjt K. Saudry, and Cpl Bioletti killed. Aircraft a write-off.

LUFTWAFFE

JGr.152 Messerschmitt Bf109D-1. Shot down by return fire during attack on No. 103 Squadron Battles west of Hornbach and crashed near Bockweiler 12.30 p.m. Gefr J. Scherm killed. Aircraft a write-off.
Joseph Scherm has the unenviable distinction of being the first RAF victory of the war.

JGr.176 Messerschmitt Bf109D-1. Forced-landed at Weisskirchen damaged in combat with Curtiss H-75As over Wolfersheim, east of Hornbach 1.25 p.m. Probably that attacked by Sgt de La Chappelle of GC II/4. Pilot unhurt. Aircraft repairable.

9./KG51 Heinkel He111. Destroyed when bombs with faulty fuses exploded during loading at Neuhausen airfield. Two ground-crew killed, five more injured. Aircraft 9K+LT a write-off.

Thursday, September 28

FRENCH AIR FORCE

GAO 553 Mureaux 115 (6). Shot down in flames by Lt Vogel of 4./JG53 during photo-reconnaissance sortie of Allied positions on La Wantzenau. Crashed 1 km north-east of Goersdorf 10.54 a.m. Lt B. Lapadu-Hargues killed. Adjt C. Georges baled out badly wounded in the head and chest, admitted to hospital in Haguenau where died of wounds. Aircraft a write-off.

LUFTWAFFE

2./JG26 Messerschmitt Bf109E-3. Badly damaged under attack by Sgt Hème of GC II/5 over Mettlach and belly-landed west of Perl 5.30 p.m. Lt J. Bürschgens wounded. Aircraft 5+ damaged but repairable.

2./JG51 Messerschmitt Bf109E-1 (3326). Forced-landed at 'Kirschacker', Geudertheim, 4 km east of Brumath, being lost and low on fuel. Uffz G. Pavenzinger captured unhurt. Aircraft 9 + a write-off.
This was the first intact Bf109E to fall into Allied hands.

I./JG71 Messerschmitt Bf109E. Belly-landed at Fürstenfeldbruck with undercarriage up. Pilot unhurt. Aircraft damaged but repairable.

3./JG77 Messerschmitt Bf109E-3. Collided with a balloon and crashed near Merseburg. Lt W. Gadow killed. Aircraft a write-off.
After the Polish campaign, I./JG77 transferred to Oedheim on this date under Hptmn Johannes Janke.

JGr.152 Messerschmitt Bf109D-1. Forced-landed near Ippesheim due to engine failure. Pilot unhurt. Aircraft damaged but repairable.

Friday, September 29

BRITISH AIR FORCES IN FRANCE

53 SQUADRON Blenheim L4840. Accidentally retracted undercarriage after landing at Villeneuve following night reconnaissance over Bremen, Osnabrück, and Münster 3.50 a.m. Pilot Officer J. A. A. Read, Sergeant Clayton, and AC Ferre unhurt. Aircraft damaged but repairable — later written-off.

53 SQUADRON Blenheim L4842. Lost bearings and low on fuel so forced-landed 3 miles south of Essertaux following reconnaissance over Bremen, Osnabrück, and Münster 5.15 a.m. Squadron Leader W. I. Clements, Sergeant W. J. Cronin, and AC L. H. Stryde unhurt. Aircraft PZ⊙E undamaged.

73 SQUADRON Hurricane L1588. Propeller shot off over Calais during familiarisation exercise for French AA gunners. Forced-landed on beach but swamped at high tide. Flying Officer D. W. Kain unhurt. Aircraft a write-off.
Derek 'Bill' Kain salvaged the spade grip as a memento and decades later it would be incorporated in a rebuilt Hurricane restored by Sir Tim Wallis for his collection of historic aircraft at Wanaka, in New Zealand.

FRENCH AIR FORCE

GR II/33 Potez 637 (15). Crashed on the runway at Orconte during training flight, cause unknown. Crew unhurt. Aircraft a write-off.

GR 4/36 Potez 540 (160). Hit an embankment on landing at Couvron from night sortie. Adjt A. Cathala and Capt. Hoquetis (*Commandant*) unhurt. Lt Genay and Adjt Matignon injured. Aircraft a write-off.

BELGIAN AIR FORCE

3/II/1 Fox (O.16). Crashed in Bruges, cause unknown. Pilot unhurt. Aircraft a write-off.

LUFTWAFFE

1./JGr.176 Messerschmitt Bf109D-1. Abandoned near Triberg following mid-air collision during attack on French aircraft over the Schwarzwald. Oberlt F-K. Rhinow (*Staffelkapitän*) baled out injured. Aircraft a write-off.

1./JGr.176 Messerschmitt Bf109D-1. Crashed near Triberg-im-Schwarzwald following mid-air collision during attack on French aircraft north-east of Freiburg. Uffz E. Köpke killed. Aircraft a write-off.
It is possible that these two losses occurred two days earlier in combat with GC II/4 but this is not confirmed in contemporary German records.

Saturday, September 30

BRITISH AIR FORCES IN FRANCE

81 SQUADRON Tiger Moth N6838. Wrecked in crash-landing during transit flight between Le Bourget and Amiens-Glisy. Sergeant Wheeldon unhurt. Aircraft a write-off.

150 SQUADRON Battle K9283. Badly damaged by Bf109s of 2./JG53 west of Saarbrücken during photo-reconnaissance sortie. Believed that attacked by Uffz Wurmheller 11.10 a.m. Returned to base but crashed on landing due to burst tyre and caught fire. Squadron Leader W. M. L. MacDonald unhurt. Sergeant F. H. Gardiner and AC1 A. Murcar both injured and burned, admitted to hospital in Châlons. Aircraft a write-off.
Gardiner received the BEM on December 8; MacDonald a DFC and Murcar a DFM the following February, the first crew decorated for a single action in WWII.

150 SQUADRON Battle N2093. Shot down by Bf109s of 2./JG53 during photo-reconnaissance sortie and abandoned over Merzig. Possibly that claimed by Stabsfw Prestele 10.53 a.m. Flight Lieutenant A. E. Hyde-Parker baled out and broke an ankle on landing. Sergeant W. F. L. Cole killed. AC1 D. E. Jones baled out clothing alight and badly burned — rescued by French Colonial troops. Aircraft a write-off.

150 SQUADRON Battle K9387. Shot down by Bf109s of 2./JG 53 west of Saarbrücken during photo-reconnaissance sortie. Possibly that attacked by Uffz Kaiser 10.57 a.m. Flying Officer F. M. C. Corelli and AC1 K. V. Gay killed. Sergeant L. B. Webber baled out injured over Morhange. Aircraft a write-off.

150 SQUADRON Battle N2028. Badly damaged by Bf109s of 2./JG 53 during photo-reconnaissance sortie south-west of Saarbrücken and abandoned over Morhange. Possibly that engaged by Uffz Kornatz 11.05 a.m. Pilot Officer M. A. Poulton, Sergeant T. A. Bates and AC1 H. E. A. Rose all baled out injured. Aircraft a write-off.

150 SQUADRON Battle K9484. Shot down by Bf109s south-west of Saarbrücken during photo-reconnaissance sortie. Possibly that claimed by Oberlt Pingel (*Staffelkapitän*) of 2./JG 53 10.50 a.m. Pilot Officer J. R. Saunders and AC1 D. L. Thomas killed. Sergeant G. J. Springett captured. Aircraft a write-off.

FRENCH AIR FORCE

GB I/31 LeO 451 (4). Crashed on take-off from Connantre, cause not stated. S/Lt Chaboureau and Adjt Magnan unhurt. Aircraft a write-off.

GC II/2 Morane 406 (321). Landing accident at Clermont-les-Fermes, cause not stated. Sgt J. Fortin unhurt. Aircraft a write-off.

GC III/3 Morane MS406. Crash-landed near Bischmisheim, south of Saarbrücken, badly damaged in combat with Bf109s of 3./JG53 during escort sortie for Potez 637 of GR II/52 over Wissembourg. Believed that credited to Oberfw Hien 1.30 p.m. Adjt M. Marias unhurt. Aircraft a write-off.

Orders had been given for an RAF patrol to reconnoitre a position behind the German line in the most strongly defended part of the Saar. Anti-aircraft batteries put up a fierce barrage, but the British aircraft went through it successfully.

When well over the frontier, at a height of over 20,000ft., the squadron-leader sighted the enemy. Out from behind a bank of cloud came nine Messerschmitt fighters. They approached from directly ahead, flying 2,000ft. higher. Away on the right another six swooped to attack. Breaking formation, the Germans concentrated mass fire on each British machine in turn.

Three of our machines were shot down. Another made a forced landing, but out of the 12 men forming the crews eight were seen to escape by parachute.

The squadron leader alone was left, but he flew on just the same to finish his job. Dodging, side-slipping and banking, he got away from the concentrated enemy fire, but he kept the course set for the reconnaissance. Meanwhile in the tail of the aircraft the air-gunner kept up a steady fire. A stream of bullets hit the engine of the leading Messerschmitt. The enemy machine swerved, and in a second burst into flames and plunged to earth. Keeping up his fire, the gunner landed further bursts into a second fighter. With black smoke pouring from the nose it went down in a spin. Two hundred and fifty rounds of ammunition had accounted for two enemy aircraft. Shaken by the gunner's steady and accurate fire, the 13 remaining Germans gave up the fight.

The aircraft, when it landed, had 80 bullet holes in the fabric, the ailerons and rudder were damaged, both petrol tanks were burst and flooding the inside of the fuselage with petrol and fumes. As they crossed the frontier the engine failed. From the starboard tank petrol poured through a bullet hole each time the aircraft banked, but by stopping up the hole with his handkerchief the pilot was able to save enough petrol to get home.

As the machine touched down it spun in a circle, cartwheeled over on one wing and caught fire. The navigator was flung out on his head with his clothes on fire. The gunner was jammed inside but the navigator hauled him out and smothered his blazing coat with bare hands. The squadron leader had been flung clear and was picked up dazed but not seriously hurt.

MINISTRY OF INFORMATION BULLETIN, OCTOBER 1, 1939

The official communique reporting on Squadron Leader MacDonald's reconnaissance on Sunday, September 30.

Back in 1939 commentators looked on the first month of the war on the Western Front as the 'Quiet War' or 'White War' as the predominant role of the British aircraft over Germany was to drop propaganda leaflets. People were unnerved by the absence of Hitler's much promised 'Lightning War' but in September German forces were concentrating their efforts to knock out their neighbour in the east. A surprise attack had been launched against Poland on September 1 which led to its defeat in less than four weeks, aided by the Soviet Union which joined in with

its own assault on the 17th to capture some of the spoils. As far as losses in the air war in the West were concerned, in September the French l'Armée de l'Air had lost 58 machines to the Luftwaffe's 27, with the British Air Forces in France suffering 14. The Belgians and Dutch, not yet in the fight, had lost four and two machines respectively. This was all that was left of the Belgian Renard R-31 which came down at Bierset, west of Liège, after it was abandoned by its crew. Adjutant Count du Monceau de Bergendael and Lieutenant Auguste Lemoine survived.

GC III/3 Morane MS406. Reportedly forced-landed south of Büdingen damaged by Bf109s of 3./JG53 in combat west of Merzig. Possibly that claimed by Oberlt Lippert and Oberfw Kuhlmann 2.45 p.m. Lt Patroux wounded in right arm. Aircraft a write-off.

GC I/5 Curtiss H-75 (15). Shot down by Bf109s west of Merzig during escort sortie for Potez 63s of GR II/22 and crashed near Launstroff 4.00 p.m. Possibly that credited to Lt Heimbs (Gruppenadjutant) of Stab I./JG53. S/Lt Y. Le Restif killed. Aircraft a write-off.

GC I/5 Curtiss H-75 (34). Shot down in combat with Bf109s west of Merzig during escort sortie for Potez 63s of GR II/22. Possibly that claimed by Oberlt Liensberger (Staffelkapitän) of 2./JGr.152 over Merzig 3.55 p.m. Sgt J. Lepreux killed. Aircraft a write-off.

GC I/5 Curtiss H-75. Landed at Toul badly damaged in combat with Bf109s west of Merzig during escort sortie for Potez 63s of GR II/22. Possibly that claimed by Fw Kuhl of 3./JG53 over Merzig 4.10 p.m. S/Lt H. Boitelet unhurt. Aircraft a write-off.

GC 4/5 Curtiss H-75 (118). Shot down by Bf109s over Merzig during close escort sortie for Potez 63s. Believed crashed near Weisskirchen 4.10 p.m. and possibly that claimed by Uffz Hinkeldey of 5./JG53. Sgt Magnez killed. Aircraft a write-off.

GC 6/6 Morane 406. Dropped flaps too early on landing approach, stalled and overturned. Sgt Grosdemanche badly injured admitted to St Vincent Hospital at Senlis with fractured skull. Aircraft a write-off.

GR II/52 Potez 637 (54). Shot down near Saarbrücken by Hptmn von Maltzahn (Gruppenkommandeur) of Stab II./JG53 during photo-reconnaissance over Wissembourg 10.34 a.m. Sgt Rituit killed. Adjt Mercy badly wounded. Capt. Dudezert baled out unhurt. Aircraft a write-off.

BELGIAN AIR FORCE

9/V/1 Renard R-31(N.29). Abandoned and crashed at Bierset, cause unknown. Adjt Count I. G. du Monceau de Bergendael and Lt A. Lemoine both baled out unhurt. Aircraft a write-off.

'Duke' du Monceau de Bergandael was another Belgian pilot who later flew with the RAF. Escaping from Belgium via Casablanca and Gibraltar, he reached England in July 1940, and flew Spitfires with No. 609 Squadron during 1941-42. As Major-General, CVO, DFC, he would command the post-war Belgian Tactical Air Force.

LUFTWAFFE

Stab I./JG53 Messerschmitt Bf109E-3. Shot down in combat with Curtiss H-75s of GC I/5 and GC II/5 west of Merzig 4.00 p.m. Possibly one of those claimed by Adjt Genty of GC I/5 between Wehingen and Bethingen. Lt K-W. Heimbs (Gruppenadjutant) killed. Aircraft a write-off.

1./JG53 Messerschmitt Bf109E-1. Crash-landed at Kirchberg-Hunsrück due to engine failure. Pilot unhurt. Aircraft 10 + a write-off.

2./JG53 Messerschmitt Bf109E. Returned fuel tank slightly damaged by return fire during attack on Fairey Battles of No. 150 Sqdn west of Saarbrücken 10.53 a.m. Stabsfw I. Prestele unhurt. Aircraft repairable.

2./JG53 Messerschmitt Bf109E. Returned slightly damaged by return fire during attack on Fairey Battles of No. 150 Sqdn west of Saarbrücken 10.50 a.m. Oberlt R. Pingel (Staffelkapitän) unhurt. Aircraft repairable.

3./JG53 Messerschmitt Bf109E-3. Believed shot down by Adjt Marias of GC III/3 in combat over Ensheim, east of Saarbrücken, and crashed near Bischmisheim 1.30 p.m. Oberfw W. Hien killed. Aircraft a write-off.

3./JG53 Messerschmitt Bf109E-3. Shot down in combat with Curtiss H-75s of GC I/5 and GC II/5 west of Merzig and crashed near Büdingen 4.00 p.m. Possibly that claimed north-west of Wehingen by Sgt Lachaux of GC II/5. Lt W. Hoffmann killed. Aircraft a write-off.

3./JG53 Messerschmitt Bf109E. Shot down in combat with Curtiss H-75s of GC I/5 and GC II/5 and abandoned west of Merzig 4.00 p.m. Possibly one of those claimed by Lt Huvet of GC II/5 between Wehingen and Bethingen. Uffz F. Kuhl baled out unhurt. Aircraft a write-off.

4./JG53 Messerschmitt Bf109E-3. Engine set alight in combat with Curtiss H-75s of GC II/4 east of Wissembourg and forced-landed near Karlsruhe 5.15 p.m. Possibly that claimed by Capt Guieu over Lauterbourg. Lt G. Schulze-Blank injured. Aircraft damaged but repairable.

5./JG53 Messerschmitt Bf109E-3. Shot down by Adjt Villey of GC II/4 in combat east of Wissembourg and exploded over the Bienwald, wreckage falling near Salmbach 5.00 p.m. Uffz R. Schmidt killed. Aircraft a write-off.

VY identifies this aircraft as belonging to No. 85 Squadron which flew to France from Debden on September 9 together with its sister squadron No. 87. The squadron claimed its first victory on November 21 when Flight Lieutenant 'Dickie' Lee shot a Heinkel into the sea off Cap Gris-Nez

OCTOBER 1939

Air activity on both sides of the Western Front was considerably reduced this month due, in part, to a deterioration in the weather which rendered several airfields waterlogged and severely restricted operations. The clear absence of any threat of an immediate offensive also reduced the need for constant reconnaissance sorties, though British and French reconnaissance units continued to suffer losses to both enemy flak and fighters. Indeed, such were casualties among French units equipped with the newly-introduced LeO 451 that they were withdrawn to complete their training.

Air Component strength increased with the arrival of four Lysander squadrons, and strategic reconnaissance bolstered by No. 59 Squadron which joined No. 53 Squadron at Poix. Meanwhile, French requests for an additional six RAF fighter squadrons to be based in France were being stoutly resisted, the British Chief of the Air Staff, Marshal of the Royal Air Force Sir Cyril Newall, voicing the opinion that French air defence plans were not as robust as the British, and citing inadequacies of the French fighter control system, compared to that of the British, as another important factor. The resulting controversy was to continue throughout the campaign in France and beyond.

As a compromise, preparations were made to receive two additional RAF fighter units should they be required, while two Air Component squadrons (Nos. 1 and 73) were transferred to the AASF area to provide fighter cover for the British Fairey Battle sorties. In the event, appearance of these unfamiliar fighters resulted in several mistaken attacks by French fighters, which prompted hurried application of distinctive rudder stripes to the British fighters.

Significant improvement in the weather on October 30 saw a resultant increase in reconnaissance flights and fighter activity.

The Lioré et Olivier 451, while an excellent bomber design, was compromised by being underpowered with engines fitted with propellers not suited to the power plants. Even so, the LeO could achieve a cruising speed of around 250 mph. On the outbreak of war the most modern aircraft in the French Air Force were the five LeO 451s transferred to Groupe de Bombardement 31 from the Experimental Flight based at Reims.

Sunday, October 1

LUFTWAFFE

3.(F)/122 Dornier Do17P. Overturned in high-speed landing at Uetersen due to brake failure. Crew unhurt. Aircraft damaged but repairable.

Monday, October 2

DUTCH AIR FORCE

Vliegschool Haamstede Koolhoven F.K.51. Crashed during training flight; circumstances not recorded. Crew believed unhurt. Aircraft a write-off.

Tuesday, October 3

BRITISH AIR FORCES IN FRANCE

88 SQUADRON Battle K9351. Belly-landed during low-level formation exercise, cause unknown 11.00 a.m. Pilot Officer R. M. C. de Lestang and crew unhurt. Aircraft damaged but repairable.

FRENCH AIR FORCE

GAO 502 Mureaux 115 (39). Destroyed in a flying accident at Attigny, details unknown. Adjt Catot and Capt. J. Gombeaud unhurt. Aircraft a write-off.

GC III/6 Morane 406 (577). Overturned in a landing accident 6.40 p.m. Sgt Laurent injured. Aircraft a write-off.

GR I/52 Potez 637 (39). Badly damaged by flak during reconnaissance sortie over Offenburg. Reached French lines and crashed near Obernai. Adjt H. Le Saoult, Adjt A. Véron, and Sgt J. Melot unhurt. Aircraft a write-off.

LUFTWAFFE

10.(N)/JG26 Arado Ar68 (1907). Abandoned due to petrol failure during night patrol and crashed west of Bunde. Fw H. Zimmermann baled out unhurt landing at Nieuweschans in Holland and interned. Aircraft a write-off.

I./JG77 Messerschmitt Bf109E. Lost control and crashed during emergency take-off at Oedheim. Pilot unhurt. Aircraft damaged but repairable.

Wednesday, October 4

LUFTWAFFE

4.(H)/22 Henschel Hs126. Returned slightly damaged in attacks by Adjt Cruchant of GC II/4 during observation sortie south-west of Pirmasens p.m. Oberlt H. Pape and Uffz W. Bodien slightly wounded. Aircraft repairable.

I./JG54 Messerschmitt Bf109E. Forced-landed at Sennfeld, near Schweinfurt, due to engine fire. Pilot unhurt. Aircraft damaged but repairable.

I./JG71 Messerschmitt Bf109E-1. Crashed near Eching following mid-air collision north of Munich. Pilot killed. Aircraft a write-off.

I./JG71 Messerschmitt Bf109E-1. Abandoned over Eching, north of Munich, following mid-air collision. Pilot baled out unhurt. Aircraft a write-off.

I.(Z)/LG1 Messerschmitt Bf110C. Flew into ferry-boat cable while low-flying at Gross-Heubach, south of Miltenberg. Oberlt Keller and gunner killed. Aircraft a write-off.

Thursday, October 5

BRITISH AIR FORCES IN FRANCE

87 SQUADRON Hurricane L1776. Lost speed and spun into the Forêt de Nieppe on breaking formation prior to landing at Merville following AA affiliation exercise 4.15 p.m. Sergeant G. G. Witty killed. Aircraft a write-off.

FRENCH AIR FORCE

GAR 14 Potez 63.11. Reported hit by flak and crashed near Nancy. Crew unhurt. Aircraft a write-off.

LUFTWAFFE

I./JG53 Messerschmitt Bf109E. Crashed near Wiesbaden following mid-air collision. Lt C. Hilbrandt killed. Aircraft a write-off.

I./JG53 Messerschmitt Bf109E. Crashed near Wiesbaden following mid-air collision. Lt Richardt killed. Aircraft a write-off.

III./StG51 Junkers Ju87B. Badly damaged while landing at Wertheim. Crew unhurt. Aircraft damaged but repairable.

However the loss of aircraft No. 6 on October 6, plus a spate of landing accidents, prompted the withdrawal of units equipped with the machine to carry out further intensive training in the south of France.

October 6: the seriously-wounded Maurice Aubert is treated on the field of battle.

Friday, October 6

BRITISH AIR FORCES IN FRANCE

18 SQUADRON Blenheim. Broke stern-frame on landing at Beauvraignes following local flight. No crew casualties. Aircraft damaged but repairable.

FRENCH AIR FORCE

GB 1/31 LeO 451 (6). Damaged in attacks by Bf109 flown by Lt Berthel of 2./JG52 south of Wachendorf during reconnaissance of the Rhine valley 12.40 p.m. Also engaged by flak *(Flakabt.84)* and crashed 9 km south of Euskirchen. Lt Col. Gérardot *(Escadre Commandant)*, Lt P. Aouach, and Aspirant Roy all captured wounded. Sgt M. Aubert also captured seriously wounded; died later after surgery. Aircraft a write-off.
This loss, plus a spate of recent landing accidents, prompted withdrawal of units equipped with the new LeO 451 to the south of France for further training.

Sunday, October 8

BRITISH AIR FORCES IN FRANCE

73 SQUADRON Hurricane L1569. Crashed on landing at Norrent-Fontes, cause not stated. Pilot unhurt. Aircraft damaged but repairable — later abandoned.

LUFTWAFFE

I./JG52 Messerschmitt Bf109E-3. Abandoned near Cochem due to petrol failure while flying in clouds. Pilot baled out unhurt. Aircraft a write-off.

Monday, October 9

BRITISH AIR FORCES IN FRANCE

73 SQUADRON Hurricane. Lost bearings in poor visibility during flight from Norrent-Fontes to Rouvres and propeller damaged in ground collision after forced-landing low on fuel north-east of Verdun 10.15 a.m. Pilot Officer P. B. Walker unhurt. Aircraft TP⊙F damaged but repairable.

73 SQUADRON Hurricane. Lost bearings in poor visibility during flight from Norrent-Fontes to Rouvres and wingtip damaged in ground collision after forced-landing low on fuel north-east of Verdun 10.15 a.m. Flying Officer E. J. Kain unhurt. Aircraft TP⊙P damaged but repairable.

73 SQUADRON Hurricane. Lost bearings in poor visibility during flight from Norrent-Fontes to Rouvres and tipped-up making dead-stick landing out of fuel near Verdun 10.30 a.m. Flying Officer N. Orton unhurt. Aircraft TP⊙C damaged but repairable.

73 SQUADRON Hurricane. Lost bearings in poor visibility during flight from Norrent-Fontes to Rouvres and stalled avoiding high-tension cables during low approach to Verdun airfield 10.35 a.m. Sergeant G. H. Phillips unhurt. Aircraft TP⊙W repairable.

LUFTWAFFE

I./KG51 Heinkel He111H. Involved in landing accident at Wörrishofen, cause not stated. Crew unhurt. Aircraft damaged but repairable.

Tuesday, October 10

LUFTWAFFE

1./JG26 Messerschmitt Bf109E. Got lost in fog and ran out of fuel, crashed at Albringhausen, near Velbert. Uffz F. Siebeck killed. Aircraft a write-off.

1./JG26 Messerschmitt Bf109E. Lost in bad weather and low on fuel, abandoned over Altena, south-west of Iserlohn. Lt E. Henrici baled out unhurt. Aircraft a write-off.

Wednesday, October 11

BRITISH AIR FORCES IN FRANCE

73 SQUADRON Hurricane. Propeller, undercarriage leg, and fuel tank damaged when tyre burst on take-off at Rouvres. Pilot Officer J. G. Perry unhurt. Aircraft damaged but repairable.

FRENCH AIR FORCE

GAO 553 Mureaux 115 (12). Shot down by Bf109 flown by Oberlt Priebe *(Staffelkapitän)* of 2./JG77 during photo-reconnaissance sortie over the Rhine bridges at Wörth. Crashed south of Lauterbourg 4.05 p.m. S/Lt Laluée captured wounded. Lt B. Hautière killed. Aircraft a write-off.

GBA I/54 Mureaux 115 (87). Flew into high-tension cable outside Coulmier-le-Sec during low-flying training and crashed. S/Lt Chauvet and Adjt Scourzic both injured and admitted to hospital. Aircraft a write-off.

GR II/55 Bloch 131. Crashed on landing at Lure-Malbouhans following reconnaissance sortie of the Freiburg, Rottweil, Villingen and Offenburg sectors. Lt Lory suffered head injuries. Aircraft a write-off.

LUFTWAFFE

2./JG53 Messerschmitt Bf109E-1. Damaged in forced-landing at Odenheim due to engine failure. Pilot unhurt. Aircraft damaged but repairable.

Thursday, October 12

LUFTWAFFE

1.(F)/123 Dornier Do17P. Crashed in flames at Göllheim, north of Kaiserslautern, cause unknown. Lt A. Kohler, Uffz K. Löw and Uffz E. Schönborn killed. Aircraft 4U+HK a write-off.

3./JGr.152 Messerschmitt Bf109D-1. Damaged during forced-landing at Friedrichsfeld, near Mannheim, due to faulty propeller pitch control. Pilot unhurt. Aircraft repairable.

Friday, October 13

BRITISH AIR FORCES IN FRANCE

57 SQUADRON Blenheim I L1138. Intercepted by Bf109s during reconnaissance sortie over Hamm — Hannover — Soest. Shot down by Oberfw Vollmer of 4./JG53 and exploded over Birkenfeld 1.05 p.m. Wing Commander H. M. A. Day *(Squadron Commander)* baled out and captured near Langweiler. Sergeant E. B. Hillier and AC2 F. G. Moller also baled out but parachutes caught fire and both killed. Aircraft a write-off.

'Wings' Day was a Royal Marine Officer who transferred to the Fleet Air Arm in 1924 and joined the RAF in 1930. Initially imprisoned in Spangenberg, and later Dulag Luft, he was to become a notorious escapee making seven escape attempts until eventually incarcerated in a condemned cell at Sachsenhausen. His outstanding courage and leadership while in captivity would be recognised in the award of a DSO and OBE in December 1945.

57 SQUADRON Blenheim I L1147. Met bad-weather over the North Sea on return from reconnaissance sortie to Münster and Bremen. Run out of fuel and crashed near Harpenden 4.50 p.m. Flying Officer C. T. Norman, Sergeant J. Edwards and AC1 T. J. Jervis unhurt. Aircraft a write-off.

114 SQUADRON Blenheim IV N6160. Shot down 3 km south-west of Duisburg by Lt Kirchner of 1./JG52 during reconnaissance sortie 1.40 p.m. Pilot Officer K. G. S. Thompson, Sergeant G. W. Marwood and AC2 A. Lumsden killed. Aircraft a write-off.

This aircraft took-off from Villeneuve-lès-Vertus having arrived there from Wyton the previous day. The squadron was not based in France with the AASF before early December.

LUFTWAFFE

10.(N)/JG26 Messerschmitt Bf109D-1. Wrecked in forced-landing at Lienen, near Mahlen, following engine failure. Pilot unhurt. Aircraft a write-off.

10.(N)/JG26 Messerschmitt Bf109D-1. Crash-landed at Bonn-Hangelar, cause not stated. Pilot unhurt. Aircraft a write-off.

Stab JG52 Messerschmitt Bf109E-1. Forced-landed at Sindelfingen due to petrol failure. Pilot unhurt. Aircraft damaged but repairable.

2./JG52 Messerschmitt Bf109E-1. Careered off runway at Crailsheim in high-speed landing. Pilot unhurt. Aircraft a write-off.

In an article published on April 16, 1940, *Der Adler* — the Luftwaffe house magazine — featured 'Oberstleutnant' Day in a story about Dulag Luft titled 'The Camp for those shot down'. Wing Commander Harry Day was brought down on October 13, the only survivor from his Blenheim of No. 57 Squadron.

Saturday, October 14

FRENCH AIR FORCE

SRC Levasseur PL7 (29). Crashed on landing at Villacoublay; cause not stated. No casualties. Aircraft a write-off.

The Section Réception et Convoyage was an Aéronautique Navale delivery unit based at Orly, and amalgamated with the Section Liaison et Entraînement (SLE) to form SCLE the following month.

DUTCH AIR FORCE

Vliegschool Vlissingen Fokker S IX (39). Crashed on take-off at Vlissingen, cause not stated. Lt W. Bakker and Sgt J. Smit believed unhurt. Aircraft a write-off.

Another Fokker S IV (100) crashed during training at Vlissingen sometime in October 1939, Sgt I. van Dijk and 2e Lt J. W. Y. Roeper Bosch both being unhurt.

LUFTWAFFE

4.(F)/121 Dornier Do17P. Forced-landed near Kulmbach due to fuel pump failure. Crew unhurt. Aircraft repairable.

7./JG53 Messerschmitt Bf109E-3. Abandoned over Hochheim, near Wiesbaden, following mid-air collision. Uffz F. Uhl baled out injured. Aircraft a write-off.

III./JG53 was formed at Wiesbaden-Erbenheim on September 26 under Hptmn Werner Mölders.

7./JG53 Messerschmitt Bf109E-3. Abandoned over Hochheim, near Wiesbaden, following mid-air collision. Uffz K. Sauer baled out unhurt. Aircraft a write-off.

Sunday, October 15

BRITISH AIR FORCES IN FRANCE

2 SQUADRON Lysander. Overturned forced-landing on soft ground at Frelinghien, near Lille 6.50 p.m. Flying Officer F. M. Benito unhurt. Corporal J. Crick concussed. Aircraft KO⊙U damaged but repairable.

81 SQUADRON Tiger Moth N9156. Met storm during communications flight between Arras and Amiens-Mountjoie and damaged propeller and engine cowling in forced-landing. Flying Officer R. A. G. Morgan unhurt. Aircraft repairable.

The wreck of French Amiot 143 of GB 2/34 — a rather ungainly looking aircraft which could carry 2,000lbs of bombs — brought down by flak during the early morning of October 15.

FRENCH AIR FORCE

GB 2/34 Amiot 143 (94). Hit by flak during night sortie and forced-landed near Mainz a.m. Lt Lamblin, Adjt Bondu, and Sgt Becqueret captured unhurt. Adjt Chable and Sgt Nomerange captured wounded. Aircraft a write-off.

GR 3/22 Potez 63.11 (53). Shot down by flak over Serrig and belly-landed near Sarrebourg. Capt. Quénet *(Commandant)* and crew unhurt. Aircraft a write-off.

LUFTWAFFE

10.(N)/JG72 Arado Ar68. Damaged in landing accident at Oedheim airfield, cause not stated. Pilot unhurt. Aircraft damaged but repairable.

Monday, October 16

BRITISH AIR FORCES IN FRANCE

57 SQUADRON Blenheim I L1141. Engaged on reconnaissance of railways in the Wesel — Bocholt sector and shot down by Lt Rosenboom of 3./JG1 over Fürstenau, north-west of Osnabrück 2.30 p.m. Flying Officer M. J. Casey, Sergeant A. G. Fripp and AC1 J. Nelson baled out and captured unhurt. Aircraft a write-off.

FRENCH AIR FORCE

GAO 1/520 Mureaux 115. Landed damaged at Morhange following attack by Morane 406 during photo-reconnaissance mission over the Sarre valley 12.30 p.m. Lt Ducasse wounded in leg. S/Lt Laurent unhurt. Aircraft repairable.

GR II/22 Potez 63.11. Reported hit by flak and crashed near Châtel-Chéhéry. Crew unhurt. Aircraft a write-off.

Another prisoner photographed at Dulag Luft was Flying Officer Michael Casey captured on October 16. He was one of the airmen executed by the Gestapo after the 'Great Escape' from Stalag Luft 3 in 1944.

Capitaine Quénet and his crew were unharmed when their Potez 63.11 from GR 3/22 force-landed near Sarrebourg on October 15.

Apart from the stencilled details, the characteristic twin tail identifies this wreck as a Potez of the 63 series — a twin-engined three-seat aircraft. In fact it is a 637 reconnaissance version operated by GR I/33 which was brought down near Darmstadt following a sortie over the Rhineland on October 16.

GR 1/33 Potez 637 (17). Hit by AA fire during reconnaissance over the Rhine valley near Mayenne and crashed in flames near Darmstadt. Sgt Arnion killed. Lt M. Caton (*Commandant*) fractured skull; died in hospital at Darmstadt after two days in a coma. Lt Laemmel captured badly wounded. Aircraft a write-off.

GR 4/52 Potez 637 (42). Engaged by Bf109s during photo-reconnaissance sortie of the Pirmasens — Kaiserslautern sector and shot down over Heltersberg by Hptmn Gerlitz (*Staffelkapitän*) of 3./JG51 3.05 p.m. Capt. H. Belbèze (*Commandant*) and Lt J-M. Pinczon du Sel killed. Sgt Vergne baled out and captured badly wounded. Aircraft a write-off.

2S4 Levasseur PL101 (51). Stalled on landing approach at La Baule Escoublac, Nantes. LV Blondeau (*Commandant*) killed, QM Amiel seriously injured. Aircraft 3 a write-off.

LUFTWAFFE

1./JG53 Messerschmitt Bf109E-1. Overturned on landing at Maisborn. Pilot unhurt. Aircraft a write-off.

7./JG53 Messerschmitt Bf109E-3. Damaged in forced-landing at Darmstadt-Griesheim following engine failure. Pilot unhurt. Aircraft damaged but repairable.

7./JG53 Messerschmitt Bf109E-1. Damaged in forced-landing at Wackernheim following engine failure. Pilot unhurt. Aircraft damaged but repairable.

7./JG53 Messerschmitt Bf109E-3. Damaged in landing collision at Wiesbaden-Erbenheim. Pilot unhurt. Aircraft damaged but repairable.

7./JG53 Messerschmitt Bf109E-3. Damaged in landing collision at Wiesbaden-Erbenheim. Pilot unhurt. Aircraft damaged but repairable.

Tuesday, October 17

BRITISH AIR FORCES IN FRANCE

57 SQUADRON Blenheim I. Suffered broken stern frame prior to take-off from Étain for reconnaissance sortie to Bremen; damage discovered on landing at Upper Heyford. Flight Lieutenant G. M. Wyatt, Sergeant W. J. Gardner, and LAC F. T. Russell unhurt. Aircraft repairable.

FRENCH AIR FORCE

GAO 504 Potez 390 (88). Destroyed in a landing accident north-east of Thuisy, circumstances unknown. Sgt Cornu and Aspirant Léon unhurt. Aircraft a write-off.

LUFTWAFFE

2.(F)/122 Heinkel He111H (2706). Forced-landed at Münster-Handorf due to port engine failure. Crew unhurt. Aircraft repairable.

13.(Z)/LG1 Messerschmitt Bf110C. Crash-landed at Niedermendig, south of Trier, port engine alight. Oberlt J. Glienke slightly injured. Aircraft a write-off.

After the Polish Campaign, V.(Z)/LG1 transferred to Würzburg on October 4 for operations on the Western Front.

Wednesday, October 18

DUTCH AIR FORCE

4-II-1 Fokker G 1 (314). Overturned during emergency take-off at Bergen due to soft ground. 1e Lt J. W. Thijssen and Sgt Wagener believed unhurt. Aircraft damaged but repairable.

LUFTWAFFE

1./JG21 Messerschmitt Bf109D-1. Crashed on take-off from Celle, cause not stated. Lt H. Lange unhurt. Aircraft repairable.

After the Polish campaign I/JG21 transferred to Plantlünne on October 14 for operations in north-west Germany.

JGr.176 Messerschmitt Bf109D-1. Wrecked in forced-landing at Eutingen following engine failure. Pilot unhurt. Aircraft a write-off.

Thursday, October 19

LUFTWAFFE

2./JG51 Messerschmitt Bf109E-3. Crashed on take-off from Speyer. Pilot unhurt. Aircraft a write-off.

I./KG54 Heinkel He111P. Collided with hangar at Detmold while taxying in slippery conditions. Crew unhurt. Aircraft damaged but repairable.

Friday, October 20

LUFTWAFFE

2.(H)/32 Henschel Hs126. Forced-landed at Lintach, near Amberg, following engine failure. Crew unhurt. Aircraft repairable.

10.(N)/JG72 Arado Ar68E-1. Crashed during ferry flight to Hochheim, cause not stated. Pilot unhurt. Aircraft a write-off.

3./KG77 Dornier Do17Z. Involved in landing collision at Nordhausen en-route to Werl. Oberlt Kirscheis killed, two crewmen injured. Aircraft damaged but repairable.

After the campaign in Poland, I/KG77 transferred from bases in Czechoslovakia on this date to airfields around Düsseldorf.

3./KG77 Dornier Do17Z. Involved in landing collision at Nordhausen. Two of crew injured. Aircraft damaged but repairable.

Saturday, October 21

BRITISH AIR FORCES IN FRANCE

73 SQUADRON Hurricane. Propeller and undercarriage leg damaged in forced-landing at Fort de Bruley, near Toul, after attacks by French Moranes and AA fire. Pilot Officer C. M. Wright unhurt. Aircraft a write-off.

FRENCH AIR FORCE

GR I/14 Potez 63.11. Landed at Delme, near Château-Salins, damaged by flak during reconnaissance sortie east of Saarbrücken 8.00 a.m. Lt Josselin shrapnel wounds to back. Adjt Thénard and Sgt R. Bernet unhurt. Aircraft damaged but repairable.

LUFTWAFFE

2./JGr.102 Messerschmitt Bf109D-1. Wrecked in forced-landing at Harthausen, south-east of Speyer, due to engine failure. Lt K. Wolf injured. Aircraft a write-off.

Operated in Poland as I./ZG2 before redesignation and transfer to Lachen-Speyerdorf on September 22 for the defence of south-west Germany and the Saarland.

Sunday, October 22

DUTCH AIR FORCE

4-II-1 Fokker G 1 (312). Overturned on take-off at Bergen due to soft ground. 1e Lt C. de Wijs and Sgt P. A. van der Starre unhurt. Aircraft damaged but repairable.

LUFTWAFFE

7./JG53 Messerschmitt Bf109E-1. Wrecked in forced-landing at Gross-Gerau/Wallerstädten following engine failure. Uffz Rybartzyk injured. Aircraft a write-off.

Monday, October 23

LUFTWAFFE

1.(H)/23 Henschel Hs126B. Returned to Pferdsfeld damaged by ground-fire following observation sortie south-west of Zweibrücken. Uffz E. Diebel wounded. Aircraft repairable.

2.(F)/123 Dornier Do17P. Hit a tree, crashed and burned out at Geiselbach-Neuss, 8 km south of Gelnhausen. Lt Dewing and two crewmen killed. Aircraft a write-off.

2.(F)/123 Dornier Do17P. Hit a tree, crashed and burned out north of the Oberursel-Schönberg road, near Frankfurt-Main. Lt Rebwinkel and two crewmen killed. Aircraft a write-off.

7./KG53 Junkers Ju52/3m. Crashed at Hartmannsdorf, south of Zwickau, cause unknown. Gefr H. Kronier, Gefr H. Baumann, and Gefr E. Hopper-Diestel killed. Aircraft a write-off.

Tuesday, October 24

LUFTWAFFE

3./JG54 Gotha Go145A-1 (1145). Damaged in hard landing at Fürth, cause not stated. Pilot unhurt. Aircraft D-IEGY damaged but repairable.

Wednesday, October 25

FRENCH AIR FORCE

GC III/7 Morane 406 (979). Crashed on take-off at Chaumont-Semoutiers, cause not stated. Adjt Lion injured head. Aircraft a write-off.

LUFTWAFFE

4.(H)/22 Henschel Hs126B. Returned to Hoppstädten hit by ground-fire during observation sortie. Oberfw K. Lachs killed, pilot unhurt. Aircraft repairable.

Thursday, October 26

LUFTWAFFE

4.(F)/122 Dornier Do17P (4052). Port engine failed during reconnaissance sortie to east coast of England. Attempted to reach base but crash-landed in Holland in the Noordpolder, at Uithuizen, west of Gröningse-Usquert, 7.25 p.m. Fw R. Diesterweg, Fw J. Hundenborn, and Uffz O. Wendt interned. Aircraft F6+HM a write-off.

This crew was interned in Fort Spijkerboor and handed over to the British following the German invasion of the Netherlands. The aircraft was taken to Soesterberg for examination by the RNAF.

1./JG53 Messerschmitt Bf109E-1. Crashed on landing at Kirchberg-Maisborn due to undercarriage failure. Pilot unhurt. Aircraft a write-off.

Friday, October 27

FRENCH AIR FORCE

GAO 2/514 Mureaux 115. Returned to Metz damaged by flak during reconnaissance sortie north of Bouzonville. S/Lt Broissand unhurt. Capt. Boignes seriously wounded. Aircraft repairable.

LUFTWAFFE

2./JG53 Messerschmitt Bf109E-1. Crashed on take-off at Speyer. Pilot unhurt. Aircraft damaged but repairable.

3./KG76 Junkers Ju52/3m (6463). Crashed on railway line near Crailsheim shortly after take-off due due to port engine failure and strong tail wind. Three crew injured. Aircraft a write-off.

I./KG76 moved from Leipheim to Crailsheim earlier in the month for operations on the Western Front.

Sunday, October 29

LUFTWAFFE

1./JG27 Messerschmitt Bf109E-1. Crashed 4km north of West-Bevern during combat practice, cause unknown. Uffz G. Loy killed. Aircraft a write-off.

Unit formed at Münster-Handorf on October 1 under Hptmn Helmut Riegel.

Monday, October 30

BRITISH AIR FORCES IN FRANCE

18 SQUADRON Blenheim I L1415. Attacked by Bf109s over Trier during reconnaissance between Hamm and Hannover and shot down by Hptmn Mölders of Stab III./JG53. Crashed on the Oberemmler Burg, near Klusserath 10.12 a.m. Flying Officer F. Elliott, Sergeant K. B. Crew and AC1 J. A. Garrick killed. Aircraft a write-off.

18 SQUADRON Blenheim I L6694. Attacked by Bf109s of II./JG53 during reconnaissance sortie of the Siegfried Line. Believed that claimed by Uffz Hinkeldey of 5./JG53 east of Trier 1.08 p.m. Flight Lieutenant A. A. Dilnot, Sergeant E. H. Crellin and AC1 J. S. Burrows killed. Aircraft a write-off.

57 SQUADRON Blenheim I L1246. Damaged in attacks by Bf109s during photo-reconnaissance west of Essen and an undercarriage leg collapsed on landing at Orly 5.15 p.m. Sergeant S. J. Farmer, Sergeant J. R. Proctor, and LAC R. T. W. Bartlow unhurt. Aircraft repairable.

FRENCH AIR FORCE

GR II/22 Potez 63.11 (36). Crippled by ground-fire during observation sortie over the Sarre and collided with a pylon while attempting a forced-landing at dusk. S/Lt M. Lechevrel, Sgt Fuhrer and Cpl Blanchot unhurt. Aircraft a write-off.

GR II/33 Potez 637 (6). Overshot runway and overturned on landing at Orconte. Adjt J. Josserand killed. Capt. Guillaume and Adjt Pernot both injured. Aircraft a write-off.

LUFTWAFFE

1.(H)/13 Henschel Hs126B. Believed that shot down near Rehlingen by Capt Reyne of GC II/5 during observation sortie to Creutzwald. Crew unhurt. Aircraft a write-off.

4.(H)/23 Henschel Hs126B. Believed that shot down near Bad Bergzabern by Lt Lechat, S/Lt Bardin, and Adjt Moret of GC III/3 during observation sortie to Wissembourg. Crew unhurt. Aircraft a write-off.

2.(F)/123 Dornier Do17P. Shot down by P/O Mould of No. 1 Squadron during photo-reconnaissance sortie south-west of Toul. Crashed and exploded at Traveron, north of Sauvigny 2.45 p.m. Hptmn B. von Normann und Audenhove *(Staffelkapitän)*, Oberlt H. Heisterbergk, and Fw F. Pfeuffer killed. Aircraft a write-off.

First enemy aircraft shot down over France by the RAF since 1918. Subject of post-war excavation when the remains of both BMW 132N radial engines were unearthed together with three corroded propeller blades, undercarriage unit, and various assorted relics and components.

2./JG52 Messerschmitt Bf109E-1. Wrecked in forced-landing at Böblingen due to engine failure. Pilot unhurt. Aircraft damaged but repairable.

4./ZG26 Messerschmitt Bf110D. Landed at Lippstadt with undercarriage retracted. Crew unhurt. Aircraft damaged but repairable.

OCTOBER 1939

Tuesday, October 31

BRITISH AIR FORCES IN FRANCE

73 SQUADRON Hurricane. Engine set alight by French AA fire during patrol between Bouzonville and Sarreguemines and abandoned over Inglance. Sergeant G. H. Phillips baled out and injured leg hitting the tailplane. Aircraft TP⊙B a write-off.

73 SQUADRON Hurricane. Clipped propeller and damaged radiator while low flying at Rouvres. Flying Officer E. J. Kain unhurt. Aircraft repairable.

87 SQUADRON Hurricane L1743. Crashed at Merville when engine cut on approach due to water in fuel. Flying Officer R. L. Glyde unhurt. Aircraft a write-off.

FRENCH AIR FORCE

GR 3/33 Potez 637 (5). Badly damaged in attacks by Bf109s over Trier during photo-reconnaissance of the Moselle valley, Coblenz, Remagen and Bitburg; forced-landed at Essey-lès-Nancy. Sgt Gurin and Lt Israël *(Commandant)* unhurt. Sgt Moreau wounded in chest, admitted to hospital. Aircraft damaged but repairable.

GR 1/35 Bloch 131 (73). Crashed at Brevans, near Dole-Tavaux during test flight. Adjt Chevassus, Sgt Thévinin, Sgt Chapuis, and Cpl Thomas all injured. Aircraft a write-off.

LUFTWAFFE

4.(H)/22 Henschel Hs126B. Believed shot down by S/Lt Plubeau of GC II/4 during observation sortie west of Creutzwald. Observer killed, pilot unhurt. Aircraft a write-off.

Despite its exceptional handling qualities, sturdy construction, and ease of maintenance, close to 150 of the ubiquitous Potez 63 series would be lost on operations prior to the French armistice — another 30 being destroyed in accidents. Two hundred crewmen would be lost and another 63 seriously injured flying this unspectacular though highly manoeuvrable type. *Right*: Potez 637, serial number 39, was lost on October 3.

When the book *Fighter Pilot* first appeared in 1941, it could not identify individuals and even the author, Paul Richey, was not named. But this is how he described No. 1 Squadron's first victory, 'Boy' being Pilot Officer Peter Mould *left*, although it was not as some claimed, the first RAF victory of the war; that had occured on September 27 when Joseph Scherm was brought down (see page 98). Richey: 'I cannot remember the exact date of our first victory, but I believe it was November 1. [It was in fact October 30.] It was a beautiful sunny day, with no low clouds but quite a lot of Cirrus and Cirrostratus, and a bit of Altocumulus. I was on the aerodrome by my machine when we heard the noise of unfamiliar aircraft engines. After a lot of neck-craning and squinting we saw it — a Dornier 17 immediately above the aerodrome at about 20,000 feet, travelling west and just visible in the thinner clouds. Like all German aircraft of the Luftwaffe it was painted light-blue underneath and was difficult to see. The French A.A. opened up but were nowhere near it. This was the first Hun we'd seen, and we were pretty excited. Sergeant Soper and I took off in pursuit, but of course had to watch our take-off and lost him. At 3,000 feet we saw him again, but lost him soon after. Up and up we clambered, turning gently from side to side and straining our eyes to find him. We never saw him again and at 25,000 feet, with our sights alight and gun-buttons on "Fire", we cursed like hell and came down after some 15 minutes' search. After lunch we went up to the aerodrome again. Not long afterwards a Hurricane dived across the field rocking its wings, turned, came back, and repeated the performance in an obviously excited manner. It turned out to be "Boy", who had come to the squadron in June. He had apparently just finished refuelling after a patrol over the aerodrome when the same Dornier went over. He took off immediately, without waiting for orders, pulled the "plug" (boost-override), lost the Hun, clambered up to about 18,000 feet — and found him. He did an ordinary straight astern attack, and fired one longish burst with his sights starting above the Dornier and moving slowly round the fuselage. The Hun caught fire immediately, went into a vertical spiral, and eventually made a large hole in the French countryside. It exploded on striking the ground, and there were no survivors. The remains of a gun from the machine, together with a bullet-pierced oxygen-bottle, from now on adorned our Mess as trophies of the first British fighter victory of the war — which was also the first fighter engagement — in France. The remains of the Nazi airmen — five hands — were given a funeral with military honours, at which the squadron was represented. Naturally we were all glad of our first trial, but we were sorry for the poor young devils we had downed. "Boy" got rather drunk that night, and said to me, "You know I'm damn' sorry I went and looked at the thing; and what gets me down is the thought that I did it . . ."'*Above*: L-R: Flying Officer Paul Richey, Squadron Leader Patrick 'Bull' Halahan, Sergeant Arthur 'Taffy' Clowes and, with a wary eye on the business end, Flight Lieutenant Peter Walker.

NOVEMBER 1939

It is difficult to be precise as to the location of this early morning shot of Hurricanes of No. 87 Squadron but in October 1939 they were based at Merville before a detachment moved to Lille-Seclin in November. Flight Lieutenant Voase Jeff claimed the squadron's first victory when he shot down an He 111 on November 2.

With successful completion of the Polish campaign, an influx of Luftwaffe units transferred to the Western Front with consequent increase in air activity over the frontier. More regular reconnaissance flights and offensive fighter patrols in some strength resulted in frequent contact with enemy aircraft, while both the Dutch and Belgians maintained a vigorous defence of their air space against intruders from both sides.

On November 2 one such reconnaissance sortie resulted in the first victory for RAF Air Component fighters. Four days later, French Curtiss Hawks ably demonstrated the glaring inadequacies of the Messerschmitt Bf109 Dora against modern fighter opposition in a disastrous engagement that, within the week, forced the withdrawal of JGr.102 back to Germany.

While the French High Command continued to press for more RAF fighter units to be based in France, intelligence reports of an impending German invasion of the Low Countries actually triggered the arrival of Nos. 607 and 615 Gladiators who flew in to the now water-logged Merville. With Norrent-Fontes by prior agreement reverting to French control, a chronic lack of suitable airfields in the Air Component area forced Nos. 85 and 87 Squadrons to move forward to Lille-Seclin which was an Advanced Landing Ground and not considered ideal as a permanent base. Its proximity to the Belgian border would also prove costly with the internment of three Hurricanes in a single week.

Also, to improve RAF strategic reconnaissance capabilities, aircraft of the Special Survey Flight — an off-shoot of the Photo Development Unit at Heston, arrived at Nancy and Lille-Seclin, amongst them the first Spitfire to be based in France.

Wednesday, November 1

FRENCH AIR FORCE

GR I/33 Potez 637. Returned to base following high-altitude reconnaissance sortie of the Mannheim — Neustadt sector with observer suffering from oxygen failure. S/Lt E. Sacchi later died in hospital. Cmdt. Valin and Adjt Brullot unhurt. Aircraft undamaged.

LUFTWAFFE

2./JG52 Messerschmitt Bf109E-1. Lost control and crashed on landing at Mannheim-Sandhofen. Pilot unhurt. Aircraft damaged but repairable.

7./JG53 Messerschmitt Bf109E-1. Wrecked in emergency landing outside Richen, near Darmstadt, in bad weather. Pilot unhurt. Aircraft a write-off.

7./JG53 Messerschmitt Bf109E-1. Belly-landed at Edesheim, near Lachen-Speyerdorf, due to bad weather. Pilot unhurt. Aircraft 9 + I repairable.

9./JG53 Messerschmitt Bf109E-3. Emergency belly-landing at Gernsheim, south of Darmstadt, due to bad weather. Pilot unhurt. Aircraft repairable.

As Nos. 1 and 73 Squadrons had been transferred to the Advanced Air Striking Force on October 9 to provide escort for the Fairey Battles of the AASF, this Heinkel was claimed as the first victory by a unit of the Air Component (see page 16). One of the long-range reconnaissance units attached to Luftflotte 2, the Heinkel He111s of 2.(F)/122 commanded by Major Roman Schneider, transferred from Goslar to Münster-Loddenheide on mobilisation and were engaged in strategic reconnaissance sorties over the North Sea, the east coast of Britain, north-eastern France, and the English Channel. They had suffered their first loss off the Yorkshire coast on October 17, 1939.

9./JG53 Messerschmitt Bf109E-3. Emergency belly-landing at Simmern, west of Bingen, due to bad weather. Pilot unhurt. Aircraft repairable.

10.(N)/JG72 Arado Ar68. Wrecked in landing accident at Speyer, cause not stated. Pilot unhurt. Aircraft a write-off.

Thursday, November 2

BRITISH AIR FORCES IN FRANCE

87 SQUADRON Hurricane L1965. Forced-landed at Lille-Seclin with petrol and oil lines damaged by return fire from 2.(F)/122 12.30 p.m. Pilot Officer C. C. D. Mackworth unhurt. Aircraft repairable.

87 SQUADRON Hurricane L1777. Returned with port wing-tip damaged by return fire from He111 of 2.(F)/122 engaged over Poperinghe 12.30 p.m. Pilot Officer W. D. David unhurt. Aircraft repairable.

87 SQUADRON Hurricane L1900. Crashed on landing at Merville, cause not stated 11.45 a.m. Pilot Officer St John unhurt. Aircraft a write-off.

LUFTWAFFE

2.(F)/122 Heinkel He111H-2 (5575). Landed at Münster-Handorf damaged in attacks by P/O David and P/O Mackworth of No. 87 Sqdn during reconnaissance sortie over northern France 12.50 p.m. Possibly also that attacked near the Boschplaat, east of Schiermonnikoog, by Lt de Grave of 1-II-1. Crew unhurt. Aircraft damaged but repairable.

2.(F)/122 Heinkel He111H-2 (5350). Shot down by F/L Voase Jeff of No. 87 Squadron and forced-landed at Staple, near Hazebrouck 11.00 a.m. Uffz F. Wezel captured badly wounded — later died. Fw W. Schmidt captured wounded. Oberlt W. Ohmsen and Uffz W. Jung captured unhurt. Aircraft F6+EK a write-off.

This was the first recorded victory for the Air Component of the BEF in recognition of which F/L Voase Jeff later received the French Croix de Guerre from Général Vuillemin.

The aircraft landed virtually intact behind Allied lines on November 2 and the French lost no time in dismantling the prize. Note how the Balkenkreuz has already been cut out of the fuselage for a souvenir.

Personnel from No. 87 Squadron proudly display their trophy for the crew room thanks to Flight Lieutenant 'Bobby' Voase Jeff . . .

Friday, November 3

DUTCH AIR FORCE

2-I-1 Fokker T V (860). Belly-landed near Beilen following engine failure during flight over northern Holland 10.50 a.m. Lt van Boekhout, Lt F. Peetoom, Lt Groen, Sgt P. Boon, and Sld A. J. Brands unhurt. Aircraft believed damaged but repairable.

Saturday, November 4

BELGIAN AIR FORCE

III/2 Fox. Abandoned during routine patrol, cause unknown. Crashed in the sea between Wenduine and De Haan. Sgt L. Mouzon baled out unhurt. Aircraft lost.

LUFTWAFFE

I./LG1 Junkers Ju88. Overturned and caught fire attempting landing at Osterbusen, near Greifswald. Oberlt K. Meyer and one crewman killed. Aircraft a write-off.

Sunday, November 5

FRENCH AIR FORCE

GR II/33 Potez 637 (3). Shot down west of Losheim by Oberlt Mayer *(Staffelkapitän)* of 1./JG53 during high-level photo-reconnaissance sortie over Aachen, Cologne, and the Ruhr valley. Crashed and burned out southeast of Sarrbourg 2.15 p.m. Lt M. Geoffroy and Adjt M. Bernard killed. Adjt A. Robert baled out and captured badly wounded. Aircraft a write-off.

LUFTWAFFE

III./KG51 2 Heinkel He111P. Damaged in taxying collision at Memmingen at night. No crew casualties. Aircraft both damaged but repairable.

II./KG55 Heinkel He111P. Collided with a He51 during night landing at Schleissheim. Crew unhurt. Aircraft damaged but repairable.
KG55 transferred from bases in Czechoslovakia late September before moving to Ingolstadt October 9.

Monday, November 6

BRITISH AIR FORCES IN FRANCE

73 SQUADRON Hurricane. Forced-landed at Nancy out of fuel and with tailplane badly damaged in attack by Bf109s of JGr.102 over the German frontier. Pilot Officer P. V. Ayerst unhurt. Aircraft damaged but repairable.

. . . who, following his victory on November 2, later received the French Croix de Guerre for his exploit together with the customary peck on both cheeks.

Stirring stuff . . . just what the public on both sides of the Channel wanted. Monday, November 6 saw the war's greatest air battle to date. However, although the claim was for nine enemy aircraft shot down, as will be seen from the losses recorded here, the total was actually eight.

73 SQUADRON Hurricane. Lost bearings during engagement with enemy aircraft and forced-landed at Charlemagne. Sergeant L. J. W. Humphris unhurt. Aircraft damaged but repairable.

57 SQUADRON Blenheim I L1145. Shot down by Lt Rott of 3./JG 53 during photo-reconnaissance sortie over Dutch-German frontier and crashed near Saulheim, Bad Kreuznach 10.11 a.m. Pilot Officer A. D. Morton, Sergeant G. Storr and AC1 F. A. Twinning killed. Aircraft a write-off.

FRENCH AIR FORCE

GAO 1/506 Mureaux 117 (66). Engaged by Uffz Koslowski of 9./JG53 during photo-reconnaissance of fortifications at Metz 9.45 a.m. and abandoned over Vigny. S/Lt Schmitt killed. Adjt Dillat baled out wounded. Aircraft a write-off.

GAO 2/506 Mureaux 117 (107). Abandoned over Plappeville during observation sortie of defences at Metz when set alight under attack by Lt Stoll of 9./JG53 1.35 p.m. Adjt Ruppert baled out badly burned landing south-east of Woippy church, Lt Gossard baled out unhurt. Aircraft a write-off.

GC II/5 Curtiss H-75 (57). Oil system damaged in combat with Bf109s of JGr.102 during escort sortie for Potez 63.11 of GR II/22 over the Sarre valley 3.00 p.m. and belly-landed at Toul Croix-de-Metz. Sgt R. Trémolet unhurt. Aircraft 3 damaged but repairable.

GC II/5 Curtiss H-75 Returned to base damaged following combat with Bf109s of JGr.102 during escort sortie for Potez 63.11 of GR II/22 over the Sarre valley 3.00 p.m. Lt P. Houzé unhurt. Aircraft repairable.

GC II/5 Curtiss H-75 Forced-landed at Lesse, 35 km east of Metz, out of fuel following combat with Bf109s of JGr.102 during escort sortie for Potez 63.11 over the Sarre valley 3.15 p.m. Sgt A. Legrand unhurt. Aircraft repairable.

LUFTWAFFE

1./JG21 Messerschmitt Bf109E-1. Crashed at Stoppelfeld shortly after take-off from Kassel-Waldau due to engine failure. Pilot injured. Aircraft a write-off.

Stab JGr.102 Messerschmitt Bf109D-1. Shot down by Asp Lefol of GC II/5 in combat south-west of Saarlautern and abandoned over Anzeling 3.00 p.m. Lt G. Voigt (Gruppennachrichtenoffizier) baled out and captured unhurt. Aircraft a write-off.

1./JGr.102 Messerschmitt Bf109D-1. Exploded under attack by Sgt Legrand of GC II/5 and crashed near Antilly, 10 km north of Metz 3.00 p.m. Oberlt W. von Roon (Staffelkapitän) badly wounded, died two days later. Aircraft a write-off.

1./JGr.102 Messerschmitt Bf109D-1. Shot down in combat with Curtiss H-75s of GC II/5 and crashed 30 km east of Metz 3.10 p.m. Believed that claimed by Sgt Salès near Eincheville. Fw F. Giehl baled out and captured unhurt. Aircraft a write-off.

ADMIRAL SIR R. BACON ON "GERMANY'S DOOMED BATTLESHIPS"

THE WAR
No. 4
3D WEEKLY

HOW 9 FRENCH PLANES BEAT 27 GERMANS

As a demonstration of Nazi air strength, 27 Messerschmitts flew over the French lines. Nine French chasers power-dived among them at 400 m.p.h., scattered them like chaff and sent nine Nazi planes crashing down in flames.

HITLER'S GENERALS GIVE TROUBLE
Guns That Guard Britain
HOLLAND AND BELGIUM—THE TRUTH

17th NOVEMBER, 1939

French communiqué: 'During a violent fight nine French fighters attacked a group of 27 German fighters. Nine of the latter were brought down, of which seven fell within our territory. Every one of our planes engaged in this encounter returned safely.'

2./JGr.102 Messerschmitt Bf109D-1. Belly-landed damaged following combat with Curtiss H-75s of GC II/5 over Metz 3.00 p.m. Possibly that damaged by Asp Lefol. Pilot unhurt. Aircraft 7 + repairable.

3./JGr.102 Messerschmitt Bf109D-1. Engine set alight under attack by Sgt Salès of GC II/5 east of Hesdorf and abandoned over Hunnenberg 3.00 p.m. Oberlt J. Kellner-Steinmetz (Staffelkapitän) baled out but killed. Aircraft a write-off.

JGr.102 Messerschmitt Bf109D-1. Crash-landed at Mannheim-Sandhofen badly damaged in combat with Curtiss H-75s of GC II/5 over Metz 3.00 p.m. Possibly that attacked by Sgt Trémolet. Uffz H. Hennings wounded. Aircraft a write-off.

JGr.102 Messerschmitt Bf109D-1. Returned damaged following combat with Curtiss H-75s of GC II/5 over Metz 3.00 p.m. Possibly that attacked by Adjt de Montgolfier. Pilot unhurt. Aircraft repairable.

JGr.102 Messerschmitt Bf109D-1. Returned damaged following combat with Curtiss H-75s of GC II/5 over Metz 3.00 p.m. Possibly that attacked by Sgt Bouhy. Pilot unhurt. Aircraft repairable.

Tuesday, November 7

BRITISH AIR FORCES IN FRANCE

18 SQUADRON Blenheim I L1435. Crashed on landing at Méharicourt following local flying practice, cause unknown. Sergeant Adam and crew believed unhurt. Aircraft a write-off.

57 SQUADRON Blenheim I L1325. Failed to return from photo-reconnaissance sortie over the Dutch-German border and shot down by Lt Müncheberg of Stab III./JG 26 south-west of Opladen 12.43 p.m. Pilot Officer H. R. Bewlay, Sergeant S. McIntyre and AC1 T. P. Adderley baled out and captured. Aircraft a write-off.

73 SQUADRON Hurricane. Forced-landed at Delme and bogged on soft ground. Sergeant T. B. G. Pyne unhurt. Aircraft repairable.

218 SQUADRON Battle K9273. Damaged on landing when one wheel unlocked following formation practice 3.30 p.m. Pilot Officer H. O. Forth, Sergeant P. Stubbs, and AC Forrester unhurt. Aircraft HA⊙R repairable.

FRENCH AIR FORCE

GR II/22 Potez 63.11 (31). Belly-landed at Metz-Frescaty damaged in attacks by Bf109s. Possibly that claimed over Völkingen by Oberlt Wilcke of 7./JG53 2.05 p.m. Cpl Cadoux killed. Adjt J-B. Le Bail and Adjt P. Marie unhurt. Aircraft damaged but repairable.

GR I/33 Potez 637 (18). Shot down by Bf109s of 9./JG53 during photo-reconnaissance sortie over the Sarre valley and crashed southeast of Boulay-Moselle 3.10 p.m. Capt. R. Hocqueviller, Adjt Trevis, and Sgt Waryn killed. Aircraft a write-off.

GR I/33 Potez 637 (26). Shot down by Bf109s of 9./JG53 during photo-reconnaissance sortie over the Sarre valley and crashed near Louvigny 3.15 p.m. Sgt Strub killed. Sgt Droitcourt baled out badly wounded. S/Lt Henry baled out wounded. Aircraft a write-off.

LUFTWAFFE

3.(F)/22 Dornier Do17P. Shot down south of Bleskastel by Sgt Salès of GC II/5 and crashed at Kahlenberg, between St Ingbert and Hassel. Oberfw H. Wagener, Oberfw H. Thor, and Oberfw A. Gerbig killed. Aircraft a write-off.

2./JG21 Messerschmitt Bf109D-1. Crashed on landing at Plantlünne. Gefr W. Nuhn unhurt. Aircraft 6+ repairable.

II./JG51 Messerschmitt Bf109E. Wrecked in forced-landing on emergency airstrip at Burlafingen in gathering darkness. Pilot unhurt. Aircraft a write-off.
Unit formed at Fürstenfeldbruck November 1 from elements of JG71 under Major Ernst Burggaller.

6./JG52 Messerschmitt Bf109E. Damaged in forced-landing near Wetzlar due to petrol failure. Pilot unhurt. Aircraft damaged but repairable.
Unit formed at Böblingen in September 1939 under Oberlt Werner Lederer.

I./JG54 Messerschmitt Bf109E-1. Parked aircraft involved in collision at Böblingen. No pilot casualty. Aircraft damaged but repairable.

2./JG54 Messerschmitt Bf109E-1. Collided with another Bf109 and crashed into the Klemmwerke hangar at Böblingen. Gefr J. Dörfler killed. Aircraft a write-off.

I./KG51 Heinkel He111H. Emergency landing at Ingolstadt following double engine failure. Crew unhurt. Aircraft damaged but repairable.
Major Otto Neuenfeld (Staffelkapitän) of 3./KG51 died of altitude sickness during a sortie over France on this day but returned in an undamaged aircraft.

Wednesday, November 8

BRITISH AIR FORCES IN FRANCE

73 SQUADRON Hurricane. Crashed on landing at Rouvres following attack on Do17P of 1.(F)/123 north-west of Metz 10.15 a.m. Sergeant L. J. W. Humphris unhurt. Aircraft a write-off.

This is the Curtiss H-75A-1 flown by Sergent Trémolet which crash-landed after the well-publicised '9-versus-27' battle of November 6. It later returned to service with GC I/5 and was destroyed in action on June 15.

The Story of the La Fayette Squadron

During the last war the most famous air fighters on the Allied side were the old La Fayette squadron. They were all Americans. At the beginning of this war a French squadron got permission from the Americans to use the old title and use the head of a Red Indian as the mascot. Here is the new leader of the La Fayette Squadron giving final orders to his pilots.

A pilot of the new La Fayette Squadron gives a final handshake to the mechanic who prepared his plane, before setting out on a "Jerry hunt."

Back from a hot battle over enemy lines the pilot surveys the wounds on his machine. The old Red Indian took a battering this time, but he will be ready for some more to-morrow.

Another trophy for the mess. It is one more feather in the cap of the old La Fayette Indian, for it means another Nazi plane has been brought down.

(Left) Traditions laid down by the old La Fayette boys in the last war say that a victory deserves a glass of whisky. There's a special bottle for the purpose and the new squadron keep up to the traditions. (Above) The original La Fayette Squadron presented their namesake with their old trophies and here they are side by side with the trophies of their new victories. Soon the trophy corner of the mess will have to be enlarged.

The French squadron involved in the battle was the Lafayette Groupe de Chasse II/5. Its origins stemmed from the American Lafayette Escadrille of Great War fame. After the war, the name was perpetuated in the French Air Force in recognition of the contribution given by the US airmen and the squadron adopted the Indian Head as its insignia. As we have seen, Sergent Pilote Legrand flying an American Curtiss Hawk scored the unit's first victory on September 20 (see page 95).

73 SQUADRON Hurricane. Glycol tank hit by French AA fire during pursuit of Do17 of 1.(F)/123 over Rouvres. Forced-landed on fire and later exploded. Pilot Officer C. M. Wright unhurt. Aircraft a write-off.

73 SQUADRON Hurricane L1959. Passed out at 20,000 feet due to oxygen failure during pursuit of Do17P of 1.(F)/123. Regained control but, low on fuel, forced-landed at Esch-sur-Alzette, in Luxembourg. Pilot Officer R. F. Martin interned. Aircraft a write-off.

Dickie Martin, dubbed 'The Prisoner of Luxembourg', evaded his guards while taking exercise on December 25 and escaped back across the French border. (See also page 35.)

FRENCH AIR FORCE

GB I/31 Bloch 200 (162). Shot down by AA fire at Brühl during night reconnaissance sortie over Coblenz a.m. S/Lt F. Berthaux, S/Lt M. Guisset, Sgt J. Terrel, Sgt H. Esnault, and Sgt W. Turbillon all killed. Aircraft a write-off.

GC 5/2 Morane 406. Became separated during sector patrol between Woerth and Haguenau and probably that shot down by Lt Faust of 5./JG52 north-east of Bitsch 1.22 p.m. Sgt Barbey baled out and captured badly wounded; later repatriated. Aircraft lost.

LUFTWAFFE

1.(F)/22 Dornier Do17P. Shot down by S/Lt Plubeau of GC II/4 during reconnaissance sortie south of Zweibrücken and exploded over the Forêt d'Hanviller, north-east of Bitche, 2.20 p.m. Oberlt H-J. Blankemeier killed. Fw A. Wawrock baled out and captured unhurt. Uffz C. Sieger baled out injured and rescued by German troops. Aircraft a write-off.

2.(H)/31 Henschel Hs126. Wrecked in collision with Ju52 at Fürth. Two crew injured. Aircraft a write-off.

The Ju52 involved, of an unrecorded unit, was also slightly damaged and two more personnel injured.

1.(F)/123 Dornier Do17P (4062). Shot down by F/O Kain of No. 73 Squadron during reconnaissance sortie and crashed in centre of Lubey, west of Briey 10.15 a.m. Oberlt H. Kutter, Oberfw G. Stühler, and Obergefr H. Schneidmüller killed. Aircraft a write-off.

7./JG53 Messerschmitt Bf109E. Damaged in forced-landing at Wengerohr, cause not stated. Uffz H-G. Schulte injured. Aircraft repairable.

Stab KG51 Focke-Wulf Fw58. Undercarriage accidentally retracted on the ground at Memmingen. Pilot injured. Aircraft a write-off.

Thursday, November 9

BRITISH AIR FORCES IN FRANCE

18 SQUADRON Blenheim. Crashed on landing at Worthy Down in bad weather following reconnaissance sortie over the German frontier. Flying Officer Langebear and crew believed unhurt. Aircraft damaged but repairable.

LUFTWAFFE

Stab JG53 Messerschmitt Bf109. Returned badly damaged by own flak over Nieder-Walluf, near Wiesbaden. Pilot unhurt. Aircraft a write-off.

Crashing in the village of Lubey on November 8, Kain's Dornier (see pages 32-33) attracted much interest from French servicemen.

KG53 Heinkel He111H. Crashed attempting forced-landing at Bielitz, near Kattewitz, in high winds. Crew unhurt. Aircraft a write-off.

I./KG76 Dornier Do17Z (2371). Crashed at Wien-Aspern while blind-flying. Four crew killed. Aircraft a write-off.

I./KG76 Dornier Do17Z. Hit a tree attempting forced- landing at Freschisdorf, west of Bomberg, at dusk. Crew unhurt. Aircraft damaged but repairable.

Friday, November 10

BRITISH AIR FORCES IN FRANCE

4 SQUADRON Lysander N1216. Overshot runway and overturned on landing at Croix-Moligneaux satellite airfield. Crew believed unhurt. Aircraft a write-off.

At this stage of the war, Belgium's neutrality had not been infringed so any pilot landing in that country would certainly be interned. However Pilot Officer Jimmy Dunn of No. 87 Squadron was soon able to make his escape after he force-landed at Aalbeke on the morning of Friday, November 10. Squadron Leader Coope and Flying Officer Glyde of No. 87 Squadron who came down in Belgium four days later (see overleaf) got away with him.

13 SQUADRON Lysander. Wrecked in forced-landing near Aix, cause unknown. Pilot Officer B. S. Jones unhurt. Lieutenant-Colonel H. F. Garnons-Williams (Royal Welch Fusiliers) killed. Aircraft a write-off.

87 SQUADRON Hurricane L1619. Ran out of fuel in pursuit of Do17P of 4.(F)/121 and forced-landed at Aalbeke, on the road between Courtrai and Mouscron, in neutral Belgium 11.30 a.m. Pilot Officer H. J. R. Dunn unhurt — interned. Aircraft LK⊙P impounded.

Pilot Officer Dunn, together with Squadron Leader Coope and Flying Officer Glyde of the same unit (see November 14) escaped from internment in Belgium on November 27 and returned to their unit. L1619 was impressed into service with Belgian Air Force unit 2/I/2 receiving serial H35.

FRENCH AIR FORCE

GC II/5 Curtiss H-75 (123). Shot down by return fire from Do17 engaged near Metz 10.00 a.m. Adjt J. Dugoujon baled out unhurt. Aircraft a write-off.

LUFTWAFFE

4.(F)/121 Dornier Do17P. Damaged in attacks by P/O Dunn of No. 87 Squadron during reconnaissance sortie and eventually crashed in woods by the autobahn at Echterdingen, south-east of Stuttgart 11.45 a.m. Oberlt H. Martinköwitz, Lt F. Langert, and Fw E. Frehse killed. Aircraft a write-off.

III./JG53 Messerschmitt Bf109E-1. Damaged in forced-landing at Rheinböllen, near Simmern, due to engine failure. Pilot unhurt. Aircraft damaged but repairable.

JGr.102 Messerschmitt Bf109D-1. Crashed near Lachen-Speyerdorf, following engine failure. Pilot injured. Aircraft a write-off.

JGr.102 Messerschmitt Bf109D-1. Crashed on landing at Bernburg due to undercarriage failure. Pilot injured. Aircraft damaged but repairable.

JGr.176 Messerschmitt Bf109D-1. Forced-landed at Tiefenbrunn, near Pforzheim, due to broken propeller pitch control. Pilot unhurt. Aircraft damaged but repairable.

II./KG4 Arado Ar66 and Messerschmitt Bf109. Wrecked in collision at air park Diepholz. Both pilots believed killed. Aircraft both write-offs.

II./KG54 Heinkel He111P (2314). Elevators damaged in collision with a truck on take-off, crash-landed 5 km south of Bistrup. Crew unhurt. Aircraft damaged but repairable.

3./KüFlGr.406 Dornier Do18 (804). Ditched and capsized following combat with Hudsons of No. 220 Squadron over the Dogger Bank. Oberlt zur See W. Lütjens killed, three crewmen rescued from dinghy by Dutch steamship *Jeanette* and landed at Vlieland. Aircraft K6+DL lost.

The survivors, picked up in international waters, were originally interned by the Dutch but later treated as 'shipwrecked mariners' and repatriated to Germany ten days later.

Saturday, November 11

LUFTWAFFE

3./JG54 Gotha Go145A-1 (1145). Crashed at Böblingen due to fractured wingspar. Lt H. Drossel killed, Hptmn Otte (of Stab I./JG54) injured. Aircraft D-IEGY a write-off.

Sunday, November 12

LUFTWAFFE

4.(F)/121 Dornier Do17P. Crashed when starboard engine failed on take-off from Stuttgart-Süd. One of crew injured. Aircraft damaged but repairable.

1./JG53 Messerschmitt Bf109E-1. Lost control at 20,000 feet and crashed near Sanddorf, east of Homburg; victim of oxygen failure. Fw G. Bleidorn killed. Aircraft a write-off.

2./JG53 2 Messerschmitt Bf109E. Badly damaged in forced-landing at Seligenstadt, near Hanau, in bad weather. Pilots unhurt. Aircraft both damaged but repairable.

4./KG27 Heinkel He111B (1403). Forced-landed at Karum, near Vechta, due to poor visibility. Crew unhurt. Aircraft 1G+BM damaged but repairable.

After the Polish campaign, KG27 had transferred to bases near Hannover in October 1939.

Monday, November 13

BRITISH AIR FORCES IN FRANCE

218 SQUADRON Battle K9356. Crashed near Aubérive-sur-Suippes when port wing collapsed in vertical dive during high dive-bombing practice 2.10 p.m. Pilot Officer R. Thynne, Sergeant R. C. L. Pike and AC1 V. W. L. Richardson killed. Aircraft a write-off.

FRENCH AIR FORCE

GB II/12 LeO 451 (1). Collided with a parked Bloch 210 (189) on take-off from Caen-Carpiquet 2.30 p.m. S/Lt Borgniet and Cmdt. Y. de la Herverie *(Commandant)* killed. Sgt Beuvin and Sgt Rozoy injured. Aircraft a write-off.

LUFTWAFFE

2./KG53 Heinkel He111H. Crashed and burned at Eltersdorf, north of Nuremberg, due to instrument failure. One of crew killed, Oberlt Barth, Oberlt Owe, and another crewman injured. Aircraft a write-off.

After the Polish campaign, I./KG53 moved to Giessen on September 9 for operations in the west.

2./KG53 Heinkel He111H. Crashed at Hansahafen-Nuremberg due to excessive landing speed. Crew unhurt. Aircraft damaged but repairable.

Tuesday, November 14

BRITISH AIR FORCES IN FRANCE

73 SQUADRON Hurricane. Forced-landed at Vistley following engine failure during transit flight from Rouvres to Reims for routine maintenance. Flying Officer H. G. G. Paul unhurt. Aircraft TP⊙S repairable.

87 SQUADRON Hurricane L1628. Forced-landed near De Panne in Belgium in deteriorating weather conditions 5.10 p.m. Squadron Leader W. E. Coope unhurt — interned. Aircraft LK⊙H impounded.

L1628 was impressed into service with Belgian Air Force unit 2/I/2 receiving serial H37.

87 SQUADRON Hurricane L1813. Forced-landed near Koksijde in Belgium in bad weather 2.00 p.m. Flying Officer R. L. Glyde unhurt — interned. Aircraft LK⊙O impounded.

Along with Pilot Officer Dunn (see November 10) both these pilots escaped on November 27 and returned to their unit. L1813 was impressed into service with Belgian Air Force unit 2/I/2 receiving serial H38.

LUFTWAFFE

2./JG21 Messerschmitt Bf109E-1 (3483). Damaged in accident at Hopsten. Gefr W. Nuhn unhurt. Aircraft 8+ repairable.

Fellow 87 Squadron pilot Dick Glyde interned along with his Hurricane, lived to fight another day when he escaped back to Allied lines on November 27.

A casualty from the fierce air battle which took place on Tuesday, November 21. As the loss list opposite shows, it was a particularly bad day for the Luftwaffe and, although this photo is not specifically captioned, the radial engine identifies it as the Dornier 17P reconnaissance aircraft downed at Eincheville.

Wednesday, November 15

BRITISH AIR FORCES IN FRANCE

57 SQUADRON Blenheim I L1246. Crashed in the River Seine near Villeneuve-St-Georges due to engine failure shortly after take-off from Orly, for return flight to Rosières-en-Santerre 4.15 p.m. Sergeant S. J. Farmer, Flight Sergeant F. S. Bowden and LAC I. R. T. W. Partlow killed. Aircraft a write-off.

LUFTWAFFE

II./JG51 2 Messerschmitt Bf109E. Damaged in taxying accident at Eutingen. Pilots unhurt. Aircraft repairable.

Thursday, November 16

BRITISH AIR FORCES IN FRANCE

57 SQUADRON Blenheim I L1148. Forced-landed on the Gent-Kortrijk road in Aalbeke, near Waregem, due to severe icing during reconnaissance to the Ruhr. Sergeant A. M. Gilmore, Sergeant B. R. Turnbridge and AC1 T. J. Jervis interned. Aircraft DX⊙H lost.

DUTCH AIR FORCE

IV-2 Fokker C V (602). Crashed in woods at Eindhoven, cause not stated. Sgt C. J. Merkelbach unhurt. Aircraft a write-off.

LUFTWAFFE

2./KG2 Dornier Do17Z. Emergency landing near Bamberg following engine failure. Crew unhurt. Aircraft damaged but repairable.
After the Polish campaign, KG2 were transferred to II./Fliegerkorps at Kitzingen on November 3.

2./LG1 Heinkel He111H-2 (5315). Wrecked in emergency landing at Klevendeich, near Ütersen, when both engines failed. Two of crew injured. Aircraft a write-off.

VIII. Fliegerkorps Fieseler Fi156C-1 (4207). Stalled and crashed from 100 feet on approach to Mönchengladbach. Pilot injured. Aircraft a write-off.

Friday, November 17

BRITISH AIR FORCES IN FRANCE

12 SQUADRON Battle. Undercarriage accidentally retracted while parked. No crew casualties. Aircraft damaged but repairable.

85 SQUADRON Hurricane L1778. Landed in error at Amiens-Montjoie and crashed on take-off following engine failure 8.30 a.m. Pilot Officer K. H. Blair unhurt. Aircraft a write-off.

DUTCH AIR FORCE

Vliegschool Haamstede Koolhoven F.K.51. Overturned and badly damaged; possibly due to stormy weather conditions. No casualties. Aircraft damage state not recorded.

Vliegschool Vlissingen 4 Fokker S IV & 3 Fokker S IX. Aircraft wrecked or damaged in storm at Vlissingen. No casualties. Aircraft damage states not recorded.

LUFTWAFFE

1.(F)/123 Dornier Do17P (3578). Lost bearings and blown off course in freak weather conditions, forced-landed and port engine damaged at Consugerne, near Bolzano, in Italy. Lt W. Vrancken, Oberfw F. Mende and Uffz M. Pietras unhurt. Aircraft abandoned.

1./JG26 Messerschmitt Bf109E. Belly-landed at Jever due to hydraulics failure. Pilot unhurt. Aircraft repairable.

1./KG51 Heinkel He111H. Took-off for leaflet-dropping mission between Nantes and Brest but became disorientated and blown off course in severe storm conditions and eventually crashed near Salzburg. Lt H. Domke, Fw Trautner, Uffz Tesch, and Uffz Altmann killed. Aircraft a write-off.

1./KG51 Heinkel He111. Took-off for leaflet-dropping mission between Nantes and Brest but became disorientated and blown off course in severe storm conditions, crashed at Marzia, north-west of Merano, in northern Italy. Oberlt K. Pfordte and two of crew killed, another badly injured. Aircraft a write-off.

3./KG51 Heinkel He111H. Returned with flaps and fuel tanks damaged in fighter attacks near Orléans. Crew unhurt. Aircraft repairable.

3./KG51 Heinkel He111H. Lost bearings due to severe storm conditions during leaflet-dropping sortie to Marseille and Bordeaux, and finally abandoned over the Austrian/Italian frontier near Untertillisch. Hptmn G. Ploeschke (*Staffelkapitän*) killed. Lt Henne baled out injured, rest of crew baled out unhurt. Aircraft a write-off.

1./KüFlGr.106 Heinkel He115. Returned to base one float damaged in attack by Sgt Hartkoren of 4-II-1 north of Terschelling 9.40 a.m. Crew unhurt. Aircraft M2+FH repairable.

Saturday, November 18

BRITISH AIR FORCES IN FRANCE

73 SQUADRON Magister. Tailwheel damaged on landing following ferry flight from Rouvres to Reims. Pilot Officer P. V. Ayerst unhurt. Aircraft repairable.

615 SQUADRON Gladiator. Overturned forced-landing in bad weather during transit flight from Lille-Seclin to Merville. Squadron Leader A. V. Harvey unhurt. Aircraft damaged but repairable.

615 SQUADRON Gladiator N5581. Damaged forced-landing in bad weather during transit flight from Lille-Seclin to Merville 12.15 p.m. Flight Lieutenant L. T. W. Thornley unhurt. Aircraft a write-off.

LUFTWAFFE

JGr.176 Messerschmitt Bf109D-1. Forced-landed at Eutingen with engine seized. Pilot unhurt. Aircraft damaged but repairable.

1./ZG76 Junkers Ju52/3m (6715). Crashed between Ibsenbüren and Osnabrück in bad weather. Five crew killed. Aircraft a write-off.

Ln.Staffel Braunschweig-Waggum Fieseler Fi156. Hit a tree while making a steep turn in bad weather, crashed and burned out at Lemmershagen. Two crew injured. Aircraft a write-off.

Sunday, November 19

DUTCH AIR FORCE

1-II-1 Fokker D XXI. Returned with engine cylinder damaged by return fire from He111 of 1.(F)/121 engaged over Schiermonnikoog 10.50 a.m. 2e Lt H. J. van Overvest unhurt. Aircraft repairable.

LUFTWAFFE

1.(F)/121 Heinkel He111H-2. Forced-landed at Borkum damaged by AA fire and in attacks by Fokker D XXIs of 1-II-1 east of Schiermonnikoog 10.50 a.m. following reconnaissance sortie over northern France. Crew unhurt. Aircraft 7A+CH damaged but repairable.

2.(F)/122 Dornier Do17Z. Hit an obstacle when wheel brake seized taxying at Münster-Loddenheide. Crew unhurt. Aircraft damaged but repairable.

1./JG2 Messerschmitt Bf109E. Aborted emergency take-off at Frankfurt-Rebstock due to high tailwind and run into boundary hedge. Pilot unhurt. Aircraft a write-off.
This unit had transferred from the defence of Berlin to Frankfurt-Rebstock on November 2.

4./KG27 Heinkel He111P. Crashed and exploded at Fusch in a snow storm during return from night sortie to Dijon a.m. Oberlt H. Rosenthal, Oberfw A. Wolff, Fw H. Bleich, and Uffz H. Reusch killed. Aircraft a write-off.

Monday, November 20

LUFTWAFFE

1./JG21 Messerschmitt Bf109E (0087). Lost bearings and crashed attempting forced-landing near the Kapellerlaan, at Roermond in Holland 11.10 a.m. Lt J. Rexin killed. Aircraft a write-off.

Tuesday, November 21

DUTCH AIR FORCE

2-V-2 Fokker D XVII (211). Taxied too fast and overturned prior to take-off at Soesterberg. Sgt P. J. Aarts unhurt. Aircraft a write-off.

LUFTWAFFE

3.(F)/22 Dornier Do17P. Engaged over Morhange by Sgt Salès and Sgt Trémolet of GC II/5 during reconnaissance sortie to Pont-à-Mousson and crashed north-east of Eincheville 11.10 a.m. Gefr A. Gerner killed. Oberlt W. Thiel and Fw L. Schneider captured. Aircraft 4N+EL a write-off.

Stab I./JG52 Messerschmitt Bf109E-3. Shot down in surprise attack by Sgt Casenobe of GC II/4 and abandoned over Hinterweidenthal, east of Pirmasens 3.10 p.m. Hptmn D. Graf von Pfeil und Klein-Ellguth *(Gruppenkommandeur)* baled out badly burned. Aircraft a write-off.

Stab I./JG52 Messerschmitt Bf109E-1. Radiator damaged in surprise attack by Adjt Villey of GC II/4 between Sturzelbronn and Ludwigswinkel and belly-landed at Hainfeld-Edenkoben, near Landau 3.10 p.m. Lt C. Geller *(Gruppenadjutant)* unhurt. Aircraft a write-off.

II./JG53 Messerschmitt Bf109E. Wrecked in forced-landing south of Pirmasens, cause unknown. Pilot believed unhurt. Aircraft a write-off.

9./JG53 Messerschmitt Bf109E. Returned to Wiesbaden-Erbenheim slightly damaged in combat with Curtiss H-75As of GC II/5 south of Saarbrücken 11.00 a.m. Pilot unhurt. Aircraft repairable.

9./JG53 Messerschmitt Bf109E. Returned to Wiesbaden-Erbenheim slightly damaged in combat with Curtiss H-75As of GC II/5 south of Saarbrücken 11.00 a.m. Pilot unhurt. Aircraft repairable.

9./JG53 Messerschmitt Bf109E. Returned to Wiesbaden-Erbenheim slightly damaged in combat with Curtiss H-75As of GC II/5 south of Saarbrücken 11.00 a.m. Pilot unhurt. Aircraft repairable.

III./JG53 Messerschmitt Bf109E. Damaged in landing accident at Wiesbaden-Erbenheim, cause not stated. Pilot unhurt. Aircraft repairable.

III./JG53 Messerschmitt Bf109E. Badly damaged in landing accident at Trier-Euren, cause unknown. Pilot unhurt. Aircraft damaged but repairable.

10.(N)/JG72 Arado Ar68F-1. Hit by Bf109 while landing at Mannheim-Sandhofen. Pilot unhurt. Aircraft damaged but repairable.

10.(N)/JG72 Messerschmitt Bf109D. Collided with Ar68 on take-off from Mannheim-Sandhofen. Pilot unhurt. Aircraft damaged but repairable.

I./JG77 Messerschmitt Bf109E. Crash-landed at Gegelsberg, 8 km north of Rufeld, cause not stated. Pilot injured. Aircraft damaged but repairable.

Stab KG4 Heinkel He111P (1567). Shot down by F/L Lee of No. 85 Squadron during reconnaissance sortie 10 miles north of Cap Gris Nez 11.00 a.m. Oberlt G. Schieckel, Lt K. Laudenbach, Oberfw E. Gründer, and Fw M. Hinterberger killed. Aircraft a write-off.

Wednesday, November 22

BRITISH AIR FORCES IN FRANCE

4 SQUADRON Lysander. Lost bearings and forced-landed near Roye out of fuel during photo-reconnaissance sortie over Fécamp. Crew unhurt. Aircraft repairable.

FRENCH AIR FORCE

GC I/1 Bloch 152s (124, 128, & 137). Forced-landed near 'Champsigny', St Léger du Bois, low on fuel during routine sortie. Sgt Harnard badly injured; other pilots unhurt. Aircraft repairable.

GC II/4 Curtiss H-75 (95). Shot down by Bf109s of 3./JG2 during escort sortie over Phalsbourg 11.20 a.m. Believed that claimed by Lt Wick. Crashed north-east of Quatre-Vents. Sgt P. Saillard badly wounded, baled out but fell dead. Aircraft a write-off.

GC II/4 Curtiss H-75 (169). Returned to Xaffévilers with rudder and elevators badly damaged in attack by Bf109s of 3./JG2 over Zweibrücken 11.20 a.m. Probably that claimed by Oberfw Kley. S/Lt C. Plubeau slightly wounded in face and leg. Aircraft 25 damaged but repairable.

GC II/6 Morane 406 (181). Hydraulics badly damaged in combat with Bf109s and crash-landed east of Freybouse 11.45 a.m. Possibly one of those claimed south of Saarbrücken by Hptmn Dr. Mix of Stab I./JG53. Adjt Schreiner unhurt. Aircraft a write-off.

GC III/7 Morane 406 (199). Shot down in combat over Houdemont, crash-landed and burned out near Heillecourt. Sgt J. Guillaume badly burned face and hands. Aircraft a write-off.

GC III/7 Morane 406 (165). Damaged in combat and crashed during high-speed forced-landing at Azelot. Adjt A. Littolff unhurt. Aircraft a write-off.

GC III/7 Morane 406 (182). Damaged in combat and wrecked landing at Ochey. Lt C. Lancrenon unhurt. Aircraft a write-off.
These GC III/7 losses may relate to three Moranes claimed over Zweibrücken by Lt Eberle and Lt Joppien of 1./JG51 and Lt Claus of III./JG53 at 2.25 p.m. on November 23.

GR II/33 Potez 637 (14). Crash-landed at Nevers slightly damaged by flak during reconnaissance sortie. Lt Sagen and crew unhurt. Aircraft repairable.

GR I/36 Bloch 131 (122). Attacked over Laon by Morane 406s of GC II/2 during return from photo-reconnaissance sortie and nosed-over forced-landing outside Beautor on approach to La Fère-Courbes airfield. Capt. P. Laurent and Sgt P. Clemenceau killed. Lt L. Pierrat and Adjt Loussalez wounded. Aircraft damaged but repairable.

SESBA Vought 156F (16). Crashed on take-off at Lanvéoc-Poulmic for first experience on type. SM Guesne killed. Aircraft a write-off.
This Section d'Entraînement et de Servitude was the advanced training school for Aéronautique Navale pilots for the aircraft carrier Béarn. It was later determined that the accident was largely due to lack of familiarity with the throttle controls which were reversed to those on French-built aircraft. As a result, all American types then in service were modified to conform with standard European practice.

DUTCH AIR FORCE

II-1 Fokker D XXI (237). Flew into fog during flight from Soesterberg to Waalhaven and unable to land eventually crashed in the Alexanderpolder at Duivenstein, near Hilligersberg. Aro. J. J. Clinge Doorenbosch killed. Aircraft a write-off.
This unit was based at Soesterberg under Lt F. van Breemen and undertook proving flights and operational development of the Fokker D XXI.

II-1 Fokker D XXI (229). Nosed-over in forced-landing near Sloterdijk having lost bearings in thick fog. Sgt J. Bik unhurt. Aircraft repairable.

LUFTWAFFE

3.(F)/121 Heinkel He111H. Badly damaged in attack by Sgt Delarue of GC III/7 during factory test flight over the frontier. Chase abandoned over Belgium but finally crashed at Dielkirchen, south of Bad Kreuznach. Oberfw H. Gräber, Fähnrich J. Schulz, Gefr A. May, and Oberprüfer O. Schulz killed. Aircraft a write-off.

4.(F)/121 Dornier Do17P. Engaged by Adjt Valentin, S/Lt Gauthier, S/Lt Gruyelle, and Sgt Lamblin of GC III/7 and pursued to Moos eventually forced-landing at Seefeld, west of Sulzburg. Lt R. Habermann died of injuries. Lt H. Böttcher and Gefr H. Gründling badly wounded. Aircraft a write-off.

1./JG51 Messerschmitt Bf109E-3. Damaged in attack by Sgt Jacquin of GC III/7 during combat south of Nancy and overturned on landing at Mannheim-Sandhofen. Lt H-F. Joppien unhurt. Aircraft 5+ a write-off.

2./JG51 Messerschmitt Bf109E-1 (1215). Lost bearings and forced-landed at Strasbourg-Neuhof. Oberfw H. Kloimüller captured unhurt. Aircraft 14 + lost.
This aircraft was flown to Toul on November 28, by Cmdt Konstantin Rozanoff a pre-war Villacoublay test-pilot, then commanding GC II/4. Arriving over Toul the Bf109 collided with one of its escorts, a Curtiss H-75 flown by S/Lt Baptizet of GC II/4, and lost its tail. Rozanoff baled out unhurt, but the opportunity to fully evaluate an intact 'Emil' was lost.

2./JG52 Messerschmitt Bf109E-1 (3372). Crashed south-east of Hatten, 17 km north-east of Haguenau, possibly due to petrol failure. Uffz H-J. Hellwig baled out but killed. Aircraft 4 + a write-off.

1./JG54 2 Messerschmitt Bf109Es. Damaged in forced-landings at Muellen, near Offenburg, out of fuel. Pilots unhurt. Aircraft both damaged but repairable.

1./JG76 Messerschmitt Bf109E-3 (1304). Shot down by S/Lt Thierry, Adjt Combette, and Sgt Bellefin of GC I/3 in combat between Hornsburg and Bitche and forced-landed at Goersdorf, 2 km north-east of Woerth, 11.45 a.m. Also attacked by S/Lt Cuffaut and Sgt de Bremond d'Ars of GC II/6. Fw K. Hier captured unhurt. Aircraft 1 + a write-off.

Repaired and first evaluated by the French at the Centre d'Essais en Vol at Orléans-Bricy, this aircraft was subsequently transferred to the RAF at Amiens in May 1940, where it was flown by Flying Officer Brown of No. 1 Squadron in mock combat against a Hurricane and a Curtiss Hawk. On May 4, it was escorted to A&AEE Boscombe Down for initial flight tests, before going to RAE Farnborough ten days later for general handling trials, where it was allotted RAF serial AE479. These trials, along with initial testing at Boscombe Down, confirmed a growing general belief that performance of the Hurricane, even when fitted with a Rotol airscrew, was inferior to the Bf109E in practically every respect apart from its turning circle and low-altitude manoeuvrability. On September 20, it was allocated to the AFDU Northolt, where the tail assembly was subsequently damaged in a crash-landing on January 5, 1941. After repair, using the tail unit from another captured Bf109E (W.Nr.1980), it was allotted to No. 1426 (Enemy Aircraft) Flight at Duxford on December 11, and eventually shipped to the USA on April 7, 1942 for evaluation at Wright Field. The following month, on May 14, it crashed during a test flight and was finally scrapped at Chanute Field on November 26, 1942.

3./JG76 Messerschmitt Bf109E-3 (1251). Shot down by Lt Lacombe, Adjt Havet, and Adjt Vinchon of GC I/3 in combat between Hornsburg and Bitche and crash-landed at Rémeling-lès-Puttelange, south-west of Merzig 11.45 a.m. Lt H. Schulz captured unhurt. Aircraft 11 + a write-off.

After the Polish campaign, I./JG76 returned to Vienna before transfer to Frankfurt/Rhein-Main on November 2 for operations on the Western Front. This aircraft was exhibited in the Place de la Concorde and at the Rond-Point in the Champs-Élysées, Paris, during January 1940.

The two lives of a German fighter. *Above:* **Messerschmitt Bf109E-3, White 1 of the 1. Staffel of Jagdgeschwader 76 flown by Feldwebel Karl Hier forced down behind Allied lines near Woerth and** *(below)* **under evaluation in RAF markings.**

After his release from French captivity, Karl Hier returned to his unit (by then re-designated 4./JG54), soon becoming one of its top scorers during the Battle of Britain. By the time he went missing in action on November 15, 1940, he had amassed a total of 15 victories. He is believed to have crashed in the sea off Shoeburyness in Essex.

II./JG77 Messerschmitt Bf109E. Reported shot down by AA fire near Haraucourt, 10 km south-east of Sedan. Uffz A. R. Edrich killed. Aircraft a write-off.

Unit based at Dünstekoven from October 31, to X. Fliegerkorps on November 29.

2./KG1 Heinkel He111H. Damaged in taxying accident at Eschwege. Crew unhurt. Aircraft damaged but repairable.

KG1 were transferred to Lüneburg and Fassberg on October 16.

2./KG1 Focke-Wulf Fw56. Forced-landed near Göttingen in bad weather. Pilot injured. Aircraft damaged but repairable.

1./KG2 Dornier Do17Z. Brakes failed and undercarriage collapsed on landing at Gelnhausen. Crew unhurt. Aircraft damaged but repairable.

2./KG2 Dornier Do17Z. Forced-landed near Bamberg, due to engine failure. Crew unhurt. Aircraft damaged but repairable.

Leutnant Heinz Schulz's Bf109 Yellow 11 of 3./JG76 also brought down by pilots of the GC I/3 on the morning of November 22.

As Schulz's machine was captured almost intact . . .

2./KG2 Gotha Go145. Forced-landed northwest of Amberg with engine trouble. Pilot unhurt. Aircraft damaged but repairable.

Stab KG4 Heinkel He111P. Intercepted at height over Calais and attacked over the Channel by Lt Weiss and Lt Hirschauer of GC I/4 and abandoned by three of crew. Pilot stayed aboard and crash-landed at 'Kruiskens' at Torhout. Lt F. Wischartz interned. Lt K. Wagner, Uffz H. Klein and Uffz W. Just baled out but killed. Aircraft 5J+FA a write-off.

V./KGzbV.1 Junkers Ju52/3m. Dead stick landing between Holzkirchen and Aibling when all three engines failed. No crew casualties. Aircraft repairable.

Thursday, November 23

BRITISH AIR FORCES IN FRANCE

1 SQUADRON Hurricane L1590. Hit in engine by return fire from Do17P of 4.(F)/122 engaged over Bar-le-Duc, and belly-landed near Moiremont, west of Verdun, 11.15 a.m. Flying Officer C. D. Palmer unhurt. Aircraft a write-off.

1 SQUADRON Hurricane L1842. One elevator and rudder badly damaged in collision with French H-75A of GC II/5 during attack on He111 of 2.(F)/122 over Saarbrücken, and nosed over in high-speed landing at Vassincourt 1.20 p.m. Sergeant A. V. Clowes unhurt. Aircraft ⊙G damaged but repairable.

57 SQUADRON Blenheim I L1129. Hit a tent while low-flying at Rosières-en-Santerre; gained height allowing crew to escape but lost control, stalled, and crashed. Pilot Officer O. C. Hume killed. Sergeant G. F. Couzens baled out unhurt. LAC Stevens baled out and sprained ankle on landing. Aircraft a write-off.

FRENCH AIR FORCE

GC 23 Curtiss H-75. Reported shot down by return fire during pursuit and attack on Do17 over Montmédy but possibly fell to Lt Methfessel of Stab V.(Z)/LG1. Crashed and burned out at Verneuil-Petit Lt-Col R. Mioche killed. Aircraft a write-off.
Robert Mioche, a 41-year-old staff officer with Groupement 23, had led the Bastille Day flypast over Paris the previous July 14.

DUTCH AIR FORCE

3-II-1 Fokker D XXI (227). Overturned landing at Soesterberg with brakes on. Sgt Sipkes unhurt. Aircraft repairable.

LUFTWAFFE

Aufkl.Gr.Ob.d.L Focke-Wulf Fw200V-10 (0001). Damaged in forced-landing at Jever following loss of both starboard engines on take-off. Crew unhurt. Aircraft BS+AF damaged but repairable.
This aircraft was specially modified for high-altitude photo-reconnaissance flights and was fitted with extra fuel tanks extending its range to 5,000 km.

3.(F)/22 Dornier Do17P. Shot down by S/L Halahan and F/O Brown of No. 1 Sqdn during reconnaissance sortie between Verdun and Metz; crashed and burned out near Haumont-lès-Lachaussée 2.00 p.m. Fw F. Hallauer, Fw S. Dressler, and Gefr W. Schulz killed. Aircraft a write-off.

1.(F)/122 Heinkel He111H. Forced-landed at Borkum damaged by Dutch fighters over Groningen 1.05 p.m. One of crew wounded. Aircraft damaged but repairable.

1.(F)/122 Heinkel He111H. Collided with lightning conductor while landing at Uetersen. Crew unhurt. Aircraft damaged but repairable.

. . . it was soon put on display in the French capital, giving Parisians their first close-up view of a German fighter.

On Thursday, November 23, between them Nos. 1 and 73 Squadrons accounted for six machines for the loss of one Hurricane. This is believed to be one of their victims, a Dornier 17, possibly that down at Raucourt. The Hurricane lost fell to return fire from a Dornier pilot, Arno Frankenberger, who was later entertained by No. 1 Squadron. 'We all admired and respected this German's guts. His machine had at least 500 bullets in it — not enough, we thought, considering three Hurricanes had been giving it their full attention. We later heard that to fire his final burst at Pussy he had to leave the pilot's seat and lock his gun in the fixed position. It was such a good effort that we determined to have him to dine with us in the mess.' Frankenberger was later released from French captivity and returned to his unit on June 30.

2.(F)/122 Heinkel He111H-2. Attacked near Saarbrücken by Hurricanes of No. 1 Squadron (F/Lt Plinston and Sgt Clowes), together with Curtiss H-75s of GC II/5 (Adjt de Montgolfier, Adjt Audrain, and Sgt Bouhy). Crashed at Koenigsmacker, north-east of Thionville, 12.00 p.m. Lt R. Aeckerle, Uffz A. Gumpp, Uffz T. Blattmann, and Obergefr A. Schidlitzki killed. Aircraft F6+FK a write-off.

3.(F)/122 Dornier Do17P. Shot down by F/O E. J. Kain of No. 73 Sqdn during photo-reconnaissance mission over Reims. Crash-landed ripping off starboard engine at 'Le Fond de Bériotte', La Besace, near Raucourt-et-Flaba 10.15 a.m. Oberfw B. Schlapp, Uffz H-H. Gründling, and Uffz A. Molek captured wounded, admitted to hospital in Le Chesne. Aircraft fired by crew.

4.(F)/122 Dornier Do17P. Both engines crippled in attacks by F/O Palmer of No. 1 Squadron over Écury-sur-Coole during photo-reconnaissance to Cambrai and forced-landed at Moiremont, north of Ste-Menehould 10.45 a.m. Also attacked by F/O Kilmartin and Sgt Soper. Uffz K. Ehlers baled out over Mairy-sur-Marne but fell dead. Uffz A. Roder also baled out and captured wounded in left leg, admitted to hospital in Châlons. Uffz A. Frankenberger captured unhurt. Aircraft F6+HM a write-off.

5.(F)/122 Dornier Do17P. Shot down by S/Lt Martin and Adjt Le Gloan of GC III/6 during reconnaissance of airfields between Avesnes and Mont Cornet and crashed at Bras-sur-Meuse, north of Verdun. Lt K. Behnke, Uffz H. Schrutek, and Uffz A. Herrmann believed baled out and captured unhurt. Aircraft a write-off.

1.(F)/123 Dornier Do17P. Shot down by Lt Bissoudre and Sgt Tourné of GC II/3 over Saône, east of Besançon, and belly-landed at Côtebrune, east of Bouclans 9.45 a.m. Fw L. Knoch, Uffz H. Pötzinger, and Uffz F. Böhle evaded capture and crossed the Swiss border near La Chaux-de-Fonds three days later and interned. Aircraft a write-off.

This crew was repatriated to Germany at Stetten-Lörrach on June 28.

1./JG51 Messerschmitt Bf109E-3. Damaged in combat with Moranes and overturned landing on burst tyres at Mannheim-Sandhofen. Lt H-F. Joppien unhurt. Aircraft 5+ a write-off.

Stab JG53 Messerschmitt Bf109E-3. Suffered undercarriage failure on landing at Frankfurt-Rebstock. Pilot unhurt. Aircraft repairable.

1./JG54 Messerschmitt Bf109E. Ground-looped when starboard tyre burst on landing at Böblingen. Pilot unhurt. Aircraft repairable.

JGr.102 Messerschmitt Bf109D-1. Belly-landed at Bonn-Hangelar due to undercarriage failure. Pilot unhurt. Aircraft damaged but repairable.

Stab KG2 Dornier Do17Z. Attacked by Curtiss H-75s over Fléville during photo-reconnaissance mission and badly damaged by Capt Accart of GC I/5. Then engaged south of Jarny by F/Lt Scoular and Sgt Winn of No. 73 Sqdn and pursued north to crash and burn out on the railway line between Audun-le-Roman and Trieux, at Sancy-le-Haut 1.10 p.m. Also attacked by Sergeant Campbell. Oberlt A. Winter and crew killed. Aircraft a write-off.

1./KG2 Dornier Do17Z. Lost control due to ice on runway at Gelnhausen. Crew unhurt. Aircraft damaged but repairable.

Stab KG53 Heinkel He111H-1 (5262). Shot down by F/O Orton of No. 73 Sqdn during reconnaissance sortie and exploded at Verize, south of Boulay-Moselle. Oberlt F-W. Franke and Oberfw A. Domanski captured wounded. A. Boormann and Uffz M. Wagner killed. Aircraft a write-off.

Friday, November 24

LUFTWAFFE

3./KG4 Heinkel He111P. Damaged in collision with blind-flying training aircraft at Vechta. No crew casualties. Aircraft damaged but repairable.

After the Polish campaign, KG4 transferred west at the end of September 1939.

Saturday, November 25

BRITISH AIR FORCES IN FRANCE

18 SQUADRON Blenheim. Forced-landed due to bad weather. Sergeant L. J. Sabin, Sergeant V. Harvey, and LAC W. S. Martin believed unhurt. Aircraft repairable.

87 SQUADRON Hurricane. Nosed-over on take-off at Le Touquet due to soft ground. Sergeant F. Howell unhurt. Aircraft repairable.

FRENCH AIR FORCE

GC III/6 Morane 406 (600). Met fog during routine patrol, lost bearings, and flew into the ground. Adjt L. Le Tallec killed. Aircraft a write-off.

GC III/6 Morane 406 (475). Met fog during routine patrol, lost bearings, and flew into the ground. Sgt P. Lamazou killed. Aircraft a write-off.

LUFTWAFFE

1./JG53 Messerschmitt Bf109E. Crashed at Mannheim-Sandhofen due to petrol failure. Pilot unhurt. Aircraft damaged but repairable.

Stab JG77 Messerschmitt Bf109E. Crashed near Arnsberg during ferry flight, cause unknown. Pilot believed unhurt. Aircraft a write-off.
  Unit formed at Neumünster on October 1 under Oberstlt Eitel Roediger von Manteuffel

Sunday, November 26

LUFTWAFFE

Kurierstaffel 9 Fieseler Fi 156. Stalled on take-off from Rhein-Main. Pilot injured. Aircraft a write-off.

Monday, November 27

LUFTWAFFE

Stab I./JG21 Messerschmitt Bf109E. Crashed following collision with Lt Schön over Lingen. Lt Bischoff (*Gruppennachrichtenoffizier*) killed. Aircraft a write-off.

2./JG21 Messerschmitt Bf109E. Abandoned following collision with Lt Bischoff over Lingen. Lt A. Schön baled out unhurt. Aircraft a write-off.

Tuesday, November 28

BRITISH AIR FORCES IN FRANCE

73 SQUADRON Hurricane. Propeller damaged hitting a fence during forced-landing at Manoncourt. Pilot Officer P. V. Ayerst unhurt. Aircraft damaged but repairable.

FRENCH AIR FORCE

GC II/3 Morane 406. Forced-landed at Morhange on return from routine patrol, cause not stated but probably mechanical failure. S/Lt Prayer unhurt. Aircraft a write-off.

GC II/7 Morane 406. Aircraft caught fire during routine patrol, cause unknown. Capt. Roy baled out badly burned on face and hands. Aircraft a write-off.

GC II/7 Morane 406. Abandoned when caught fire during routine patrol. Sgt H. Grimaud baled out with burns to face and hands. Aircraft a write-off.

LUFTWAFFE

2./KG27 Heinkel He111P. Crashed and burned out at Gablingen during night-flying practice 8.33 p.m. Hptmn K-J. Gerstenmeier (*Staffelkapitän*), Oberlt W. Schütz, Oberfw K. Volkmann, and Oberfw O. Hetzel killed. Aircraft 1G+KK a write-off.

Wednesday, November 29

LUFTWAFFE

3./KG77 Dornier Do17Z (3461). Belly-landed at Kuhnerwitz, near Görlitz, when both engines failed during landing circuit. Crew unhurt. Aircraft damaged but repairable.

"MEL" WITH THE A.A.S.F.—No. 1

NO. BLANK FIGHTER SQUADRON, R.A.F., SOMEWHERE IN FRANCE: By "MEL"

Les Brooks *(top)* **an armourer with No. 1 Squadron at Vassincourt, remembered that day and sent us this cartoon drawn by 'Mel' of the** *Tatler* **featuring the personalities of the squadron.**

GENERAL SWINTON : MY RECENT VISIT TO GERMANY

THE **WAR** No. 7 3ᴰ WEEKLY

A NEWNES PUBLICATION

R.A.F. BROUGHT DOWN THESE NAZIS [Picture by Gordon Nicols, R.I.]

When this bullet-riddled Dornier—one of four shot down by the R.A.F. on November 23—crashed in France, two of the Nazi crew jumped out, dragging with them their wounded gunner. One of the Nazis held up a French peasant with his revolver while another set fire to his machine. Then the French police arrived and the Germans surrendered.

GAMELIN'S RIGHT HAND MAN by BRIG.-GENERAL SPEARS

Finland's Next Move, by Bernard Newman

WONDERFUL MAPS, DIAGRAMS AND PICTURES

8th DECEMBER, 1939

DECEMBER 1939

Published on December 8, this artist's impression depicted the drama surrounding the capture of the crew of the Dornier brought down at La Besace by Flying Officer Kain on November 23 (see page 120). This was 'Cobber's' second victory — see also page 37.

Violent storms and the onset of the harshest winter weather for 50 years reduced all air activity on the Western Front of operations and resulted in several casualties. Both sides struggled to maintain a level of operations from airfields rendered increasingly unsuitable by the severe conditions.

Meanwhile, on December 18, a daylight armed-reconnaissance to Wilhelmshaven by 24 RAF Wellingtons would influence future Bomber Command strategy. Tracked by German naval radar as it approached the enemy coast, the formation

was decimated by enemy fighters. With little protection or defence against cannon-armed fighters, ten aircraft were shot down, two others ditching during the return flight, while six more limped back to England with severe damage. This sortie, together with similar experiences during the forthcoming Norwegian campaign, was to have a profound effect on RAF strategic bombing policy. Attacks by day were discontinued in favour of night bombing, a doctrine maintained by RAF Bomber Command for the rest of the war.

Friday, December 1

FRENCH AIR FORCE

GC III/7 Morane 406 (179). Collided with trees on rising ground and crashed into woods at Waltriche, 3 km south-west of Frouard. Lt C. Lancrenon killed. Aircraft a write-off.

BELGIAN AIR FORCE

2/I/2 Hurricanes (H.25, H.35). Nosed over on landing at Wevelgem. Pilots unhurt. Aircraft damaged but repairable.

LUFTWAFFE

JGr.152 Messerschmitt Bf108. Forced-landed at Cologne-Butzweilerhof, cause not stated. Pilot unhurt. Aircraft damaged but repairable.

2./KG2 Heinkel He111H. Forced-landed at Fürth airfield due to engine failure. Crew unhurt. Aircraft damaged but repairable.

Sunday, December 3

BRITISH AIR FORCES IN FRANCE

73 SQUADRON Hurricane. Damaged in forced-landing near Verdun, cause not stated. Ferry pilot slightly injured. Aircraft damaged but repairable.

81 SQUADRON Tiger Moth N9157. Forced-landed at Moyencourt during communications flight, cause not stated. Flying Officer J. W. Radbone unhurt. Aircraft damaged but repairable.

FRENCH AIR FORCE

GB II/35 Amiot 143 (110). Flew into a peak at Supt, 25 km from Pontarlier, in the Joux forest while flying in mist. Crashed and burned out. Sgt A. Balquier, S/Lt R. Lebrun, Sgt R. Ancard, Sgt R. Moisselin, and Sgt Charbonnier all killed. Aircraft a write-off.

The following week this picture was released for publication but, like most of the photography taken in France during this period, it was devoid of any location. However as the unit shield indicates that it belonged to Fernaufklärungsgruppe 122, this Heinkel could well be that brought down at Staple on November 2.

LUFTWAFFE

3.(F)/122 Heinkel He111H. Crashed and burned out at Arienheller, south of Linz 7.09 a.m. cause unknown. Oberfw H. Runkwitz, Fw F. Meyer, Uffz H. Förster, and Uffz H. Schröder killed. Aircraft a write-off.

II./JG51 Messerschmitt Bf109E. Overturned on take-off from Eutingen. Pilot unhurt. Aircraft damaged but repairable.

I./JG54 Messerschmitt Bf109E. Nosed-over at Eutingen. Pilot unhurt. Aircraft damaged but repairable.

Tuesday, December 5

LUFTWAFFE

III./KG27 Messerschmitt Bf108. Forced-landed at Maisach, near Fürstenfeldbruck, due to engine trouble. Oberlt Hartmann injured. Aircraft damaged but repairable.

1./KG53 Junkers W34. Crashed on take-off at Ansbach. Reg Rat W. Endres killed, and four crew injured. Aircraft a write-off.

This Hurricane of the Belgian Air Force was one of those that came a cropper on the waterlogged surface of Wevelgem aerodrome on December 1.

Wednesday, December 6

BRITISH AIR FORCES IN FRANCE

SQUADRON Hurricane. Lost bearings during ferry flight from Tangmere to Amiens-Glisy and crashed attempting landing at Amiens-Montjoie 2.30 p.m. Pilot Officer Stewart slightly injured. Aircraft repairable.
A replacement aircraft not allocated to unit.

13 SQUADRON Lysander L4763. Hit trees and crashed 1 mile south-west of Mons-en-Chaussée 11.05 a.m. Flight Lieutenant M. P. Skinner badly burned, died same night in Mondicourt hospital. LAC E. Whitehead killed. Aircraft a write-off.

LUFTWAFFE

1.(F)/122 Heinkel He111H (2709). Crashed on take-off at Uetersen. Lt H. Schierholz, Uffz W. Kunze, Uffz M. Strohschein and Obergefr G. Vogt killed. Aircraft a write-off.

1.(F)/122 Heinkel He111H (3154). Crashed in sea off Borkum. Fw H. Petersen, Uffz H. Weise, Uffz A. Kenzelmann and Flgr T. Beckmann killed. Aircraft a write-off.

II./JG53 Messerschmitt Bf109E-1. Lost control and side-slipped during practice emergency take-off from Mannheim-Sandhofen. Pilot injured. Aircraft a write-off.

1.(St)/186 Junkers Ju87B. Crashed through roof of sick quarters at Wertheim airfield due to late recovery during dive-bombing practice. Two crew killed. Aircraft a write-off.

Thursday, December 7

BRITISH AIR FORCES IN FRANCE

1 SQUADRON Hurricane L1971. Lost bearings and severely damaged in forced-landing at St-Dizier. Pilot Officer P. G. H. Matthews unhurt. Aircraft a write-off.

LUFTWAFFE

Stab KG1 Messerschmitt Bf108. Damaged in forced-landed at Mauden in bad weather. Pilot unhurt. Aircraft repairable.

III./KG53 Heinkel He111H. Stalled, crashed and burned out on take-off from Giebelstadt. Oberlt Hülse and another crewman killed. Aircraft a write-off.

Stab StG77 Dornier Do17M. Crashed and burned out at Eringerfeld while flying in poor visibility. Oberlt Jacobi and two crew killed. Aircraft a write-off.

Friday, December 8

BELGIAN AIR FORCE

5/III/3 Battle (T.59). Hit trees near Eeklo, north-west of Gent, during ground-attack exercise in bad weather. Capt. J. de Caters (*Commandant*) killed. Aircraft a write-off.

LUFTWAFFE

1./ZG1 Messerschmitt Bf110C. Crashed on landing at Gelsenkirchen-Buer due to under-carriage failure. Crew unhurt. Aircraft damaged but repairable.

Saturday, December 9

BRITISH AIR FORCES IN FRANCE

87 SQUADRON Hurricane N2361. Lost bearings in failing light and haze during delivery flight from Glisy to Lille-Seclin and forced-landed at La Ferme Blanche, near Esplechin in Belgium 4.15 p.m. Sergeant G. L. Nowell unhurt, escaped across the border, and returned to unit. Aircraft abandoned.
N2361 was impressed into service with Belgian Air Force unit 2/I/2 receiving serial H39. Damaged on March 2, 1940 it was under repair at Wevelgem when overtaken by the German advance in May 1940.

BELGIAN AIR FORCE

1/I/2 Gladiator (G.28). Dived vertically into the ground at Ingelmunster, due to malfunctioning oxygen supply. Sgt H. Dopagne killed. Aircraft a write-off.

Monday, December 11

LUFTWAFFE

Stab JG51 Messerschmitt Bf109E. Crash-landed at Essen-Mülheim following engine failure. Oberlt R. Freiherr von Barneckow (*Geschwaderadjutant*) unhurt. Aircraft a write-off.

3./KG76 Dornier Do17Z. Undercarriage collapsed on landing at Nidda. Crew unhurt. Aircraft damaged but repairable.

Tuesday, December 12

BRITISH AIR FORCES IN FRANCE

615 SQUADRON Gladiator. Forced-landed at Berck-sur-Mer due to engine trouble. Pilot Officer B. P. Young unhurt. Aircraft repairable.

LUFTWAFFE

II./JG51 Messerschmitt Bf109E-3. Pulled up too early and stalled on landing at Eutingen. Pilot unhurt. Aircraft damaged but repairable.

1./ZG1 Messerschmitt Bf110 (1344). Crashed into mountain at Deisterkamp, near Springe, while flying in cloud. Three crew killed. Aircraft a write-off.

3./StG51 Junkers Ju87B. Crashed and burned out near Forbach during ferry flight between Göttingen and Hahn. Lt Zahle and gunner killed. Aircraft a write-off.

Transportstaffel Luftflotte 2 Junkers Ju87. Crashed 2 km west of Badersleben during ferry flight, cause unknown. One crewman killed, another injured. Aircraft a write-off.

The awful scene at Ingelmunster where Sergeant Hubert Dopagne of the Belgian Air Force buried both himself and his Gladiator after crashing in a vertical dive on December 9, just a few days before his 20th birthday. He is now buried in the family grave in Jemeppe-sur-Meuse, just outside Liège.

Neville Chamberlain, September 1, 1939: 'I do not propose to say many words tonight. The time has come when action rather than speech is required'. Aviation historians on the trail of a Hurricane crash near St Hilaire-le-Grand stumbled on this fine comparison showing the British Prime Minister during his French tour in December 1939. His attire was rather bizarre, possibly adopted as a result of him suffering severely from gout — purple plus-fours!

LUFTWAFFE

III./KG76 Dornier Do17Z. Crashed and burned out attempting forced-landing at Pocking forward airfield. Three crew killed. Aircraft a write-off.

3./StG2 Junkers Ju87A. Forced-landed at Kattowitz with engine trouble. Crew unhurt. Aircraft damaged but repairable.

Friday, December 15

BRITISH AIR FORCES IN FRANCE

607 SQUADRON Gladiator. Ran into a dugout on landing at Douai and damaged propeller. Flying Officer Irving unhurt. Aircraft repairable.

LUFTWAFFE

3.(F)/122 Heinkel He111H (5457). Crashed and burned out at Münster-Loddenheide due to control failure. Crew unhurt. Aircraft a write-off.

II./KG3 Dornier Do17Z. Believed forced-landed 1 km south-east of Cochsheim due to cylinder head failure. Crew unhurt. Aircraft damaged but repairable.

Wednesday, December 13

LUFTWAFFE

II./JG53 Messerschmitt Bf109E. Forced-landed at Lachen-Speyerdorf with seized engine. Pilot unhurt. Aircraft damaged but repairable.

I./ZG76 Messerschmitt Bf110C (3006). Damaged in belly-landing at Gütersloh, cause not stated. Crew unhurt. Aircraft repairable.

Thursday, December 14

DUTCH AIR FORCE

2-II-1 Fokker D XXI (220). Badly damaged in a forced-landing believed near Boxtel; cause not stated. Sgt J. Roos unhurt. Aircraft damaged but repairable.

Group photo: on the left Air Vice-Marshal Playfair . . . and on the right . . . surely not Adolf!

No less sartorially challenged, Steve Whitehorn, Paul Cole and Andy Saunders outside the Hôtel de Ville.

Saturday, December 16

LUFTWAFFE

1./JG54 Messerschmitt Bf109E. Ground-looped when tyre burst on landing at Böblingen. Pilot unhurt. Aircraft damaged but repairable.

13.(Z)/LG1 Messerschmitt Bf110C. Crashed at Luisterberg, cause unknown. Fw G. Stern and Uffz W. Tietz killed. Aircraft a write-off.

Sunday, December 17

BRITISH AIR FORCES IN FRANCE

105 SQUADRON Battle K9185. Belly-landed near Thizay, south-west of Issoudun, during low-flying practice, cause unknown. Sergeant L. Wilson unhurt, AC1 A. C. Williams slightly injured. Aircraft a write-off.

Monday, December 18

BRITISH AIR FORCES IN FRANCE

615 SQUADRON Gladiator N5582. Escort for leave boat from Boulogne, stalled and crashed on landing approach to St Inglevert in bad visibility 1.40 p.m. Pilot Officer S. M. Wickham killed. Aircraft a write-off.

LUFTWAFFE

Stab KG55 Heinkel He111P. Crashed and burned out near Mainburg, cause not stated. One of crew killed, two others injured. Aircraft a write-off.

The Dornier wreck was put on display for the Prime Minister to inspect. His visit took place on December 17 but unfortunately the captions of the period are not very helpful and there are few clues to positively identify this particular Do17. However distinctive fuselage codes suggest that it is one of the reconnaissance machines lost by Aufklärungsgruppe 122 the previous month and, but for the discrepancy in the individual aircraft letter as reported, probably that brought down by No. 1 Squadron at Moiremont on November 23 (see p 120).

Wednesday, December 20

FRENCH AIR FORCE

GR I/33 Potez 637 (20). Shot down by Oberfw Willinger of 1./JG51 during high-level photo-reconnaissance sortie of Saarbrücken — Kaiserslautern — Pirmasens sector. Crashed and burned out near Landstuhl 1.33 p.m. Lt de Forges, Lt Navelet, and Adjt Tourel captured wounded. Aircraft a write-off.

LUFTWAFFE

1./KG4 Heinkel He111P (1877). Belly-landed at Hesepe due to undercarriage failure. Crew unhurt. Aircraft damaged but repairable.

Thursday, December 21

FRENCH AIR FORCE

GC III/2 Morane 406 (294). Wrecked in landing accident at Chaumont-Semoutiers; exact cause unknown. Sgt P. Chambon unhurt. Aircraft a write-off.

GC II/7 Morane 406 (91). Shot down by Major von Cramon-Taubadel (Gruppenkommandeur) of Stab I./JG54 during escort sortie for Potez 63.11 and combat over Breisach. Crash-landed near Artzenheim 11.15 a.m. S/Lt G. Gauthier badly wounded, admitted to hospital in Turckheim with fractured skull. Aircraft a write-off.

GC II/7 Morane 406 (93). Forced-landed badly damaged in attack by Major von Cramon-Taubadel (Gruppenkommandeur) of Stab I./JG54 during escort sortie for Potez 63.11 of GR I/55 east of Colmar 11.15 a.m. Sgt R. Panhard believed unhurt. Aircraft a write-off.

GR II/33 Potez 637 (14). Shot down by F/L Lovett of No. 73 Squadron west of Verdun on return from high-altitude reconnaissance sortie; crashed and burned out at Souilly. Lt Sagon baled out with burns and broken leg, admitted to hospital in Ansermet. Lt G. Castellana and Adjt M. Pernot killed. Aircraft a write-off.

GR I/52 Potez 637 (41). Failed to return from reconnaissance sortie and crashed and burned out in the Vosges mountains near Donon, north-west of Schirmeck 12.00 p.m. Adjt H. Le Saoult, Adjt A. Véron, and Sgt J. Melot killed. Aircraft a write-off.

LUFTWAFFE

3.(F)/121 Heinkel He111H. Stalled and crashed at Spöck, north-east of Karlsruhe during reconnaissance flight, exact cause unknown. Uffz K. Keller and Obergefr E. Otto killed, another crewman badly injured. Aircraft a write-off.

Stab I./JG54 Messerschmitt Bf109E. Returned damaged following combat with MS406s of GC II/7 over Breisach 11.15 a.m. Possibly that attacked by S/Lt de Fraville and Sgt Lamblin. Major H-J. von Cramon-Taubadel (Gruppenkommandeur) unhurt. Aircraft repairable.

2./JG54 Messerschmitt Bf109E. Believed shot down by S/Lt Gauthier of GC II/7 in combat over Breisach and crashed north-west of Gottenheim 11.15 a.m. Hptmn R. Paulitsch (*Staffelkapitän*) baled out splinter wounds in legs. Aircraft a write-off.

2./JG54 Messerschmitt Bf109E. Returned with starboard wing damaged following combat with MS406s of GC II/7 over Breisach 11.15 a.m. Possibly that claimed by Sgt Panhard. Uffz W. Wagner unhurt. Aircraft repairable.

2./JG54 Messerschmitt Bf109E. Returned damaged following combat with MS406s of GC II/7 east of Colmar 11.15 a.m. Fw E. Fricke unhurt. Aircraft repairable.

Friday, December 22

BRITISH AIR FORCES IN FRANCE

1 SQUADRON Hurricane. Forced-landed near Loxéville, west of Commercy, having lost bearings in bad weather 4.45 p.m. Flying Officer C. G. H. Crusoe unhurt. Aircraft repairable.

1 SQUADRON Hurricane L1960. Damaged in forced-landing near Loxéville, west of Commercy, having lost bearings in bad weather 4.45 p.m. Pilot Officer W. H. Stratton unhurt. Aircraft damaged but repairable.

18 SQUADRON 2 Blenheims. Stern-frames broken whilst taxying on frozen ground at Méharicourt. No crew casualties. Aircraft damaged but repairable.

73 SQUADRON Hurricane N2385. Shot down by Bf109s north-east of Metz and crashed at Homburg-Budange 2.30 p.m. Believed that claimed by Hptmn Mölders of III./JG53. Sergeant R. M. Perry killed. Aircraft a write-off.

73 SQUADRON Hurricane L1967. Shot down by Bf109s north-east of Metz and crashed at Altroff 2.30 p.m. Believed that claimed by Oberlt von Hahn of III./JG53. Sergeant J. Winn killed. Aircraft a write-off.

85 SQUADRON Hurricane L1653. Starboard undercarriage leg collapsed hitting a rut on landing at Le Touquet. Sergeant Faulkner unhurt. Aircraft repairable.

FRENCH AIR FORCE

AB2 L-N401. Wrecked in flying accident during familiarisation flight at Orly, cause not stated. SM A. Lansonneur killed. Aircraft a write-off.

GAO 2/520 Mureaux 115. Crashed on testflight; exact cause unknown. Sgt L. Engwiller and Sgt L. Lemaire killed. Aircraft a write-off.

GC III/7 Morane 406 (198). Suffered engine failure on take-off and crashed into trees at Vitry-le-François-Vauclerc. Sgt Mathieu injured. Aircraft a write-off.

LUFTWAFFE

1./JG51 Messerschmitt Bf109E. Lost bearings in bad weather and overturned attempting forced-landing near Schifferstadt, 9 km north-west of Speyer. Lt K. Gammel killed. Aircraft a write-off.

2./JG52 Messerschmitt Bf109E-3. Port wing hit barracks after landing at Lachen-Speyerdorf. Uffz K. Munz unhurt. Aircraft 3+ damaged but repairable.

3./JGr.102 Messerschmitt Bf109D-1. Bellylanded at Bonn-Hangelar due to control failure. Pilot unhurt. Aircraft repairable.

I./JGr.152 3 Messerschmitt Bf109D-1s. Damaged in landing accidents at Düsseldorf due to poor visibility. Pilots unhurt. Aircraft all damaged but repairable.

II./KG3 Dornier Do17Z. Lost control and crashed at Schweinfurt during take-off on one engine. Crew unhurt. Aircraft a write-off.
Unit transferred from Heiligenbeil to Schweinfurt and Würzburg in October 1939.

Saturday, December 23

BRITISH AIR FORCES IN FRANCE

85 SQUADRON Hurricane L1765. Crashed on take-off at Le Touquet due to icy conditions 7.15 a.m. Flying Officer J. R. M. Boothby unhurt. Aircraft a write-off.

85 SQUADRON Hurricane L1773. Crashed on take-off and burned out due to icy conditions at Le Touquet 7.45 a.m. Pilot Officer J. E. Marshall unhurt. Aircraft a write-off.

It is very interesting to compare the losses and claims as published in Britain at the end of 1939 as reproduced here with the actuality as wartime figures can hardly be relied upon for accuracy. Allied losses over the Western Front to the end of December were over 180 aircraft and, as far as the Luftwaffe were concerned, it is believed to have lost 151 aircraft by the end of the year.

FRENCH AIR FORCE

GAO 507 Mureaux 115. Crashed on take-off at Delme. Lt Picq killed. S/Lt Barbier injured. Aircraft a write-off.

LUFTWAFFE

4.(F)/122 Heinkel He111H. Returned to base when oxygen equipment failed at 27,000 feet during high-altitude reconnaissance sortie over north-east France. Lt F. Jordan died, rest of crew unhurt. Aircraft repairable.

II./JG51 Messerschmitt Bf109E. Parked aircraft damaged in landing accident at Eutingen. No pilot hurt. Aircraft damaged but repairable.

II./JG51 Messerschmitt Bf109E. Collided with another Bf109 on landing at Eutingen due to high tailwind. Pilot unhurt. Aircraft damaged but repairable.

Sunday, December 24

LUFTWAFFE

1./JG77 Messerschmitt Bf109E. Wrecked in landing accident at Bonn-Hangelar. Pilot unhurt. Aircraft a write-off.

Tuesday, December 26

LUFTWAFFE

5.(H)/13 Henschel Hs126. Emergency landing when observer suffered heart attack during high-altitude flight. Oberlt Jakob believed survived, pilot unhurt. Aircraft undamaged.

Wednesday, December 27

BRITISH AIR FORCES IN FRANCE

18 SQUADRON Blenheim IV L9040. Crashed at Champigny cause unknown. Sergeant L. J. Sabin, Sergeant V. Harvey, LAC W. S. Martin, and LAC J. Job (Fitter) killed. Aircraft a write-off.

As groundcrew distinct from aircrew, Jasen Job is not included in our BAFF Roll of Honour (see page 500). He is representative of the 277 British airmen lost in France without whose efforts and sacrifices, often endured under conditions of extreme danger, difficulty, or deprivation, aircraft could not continue to operate.

85 SQUADRON Hurricane L1835. Crashed on take-off at Le Touquet during night-flying practice 0.15 a.m. Flight Lieutenant R. L. Lorimer unhurt. Aircraft a write-off.

LUFTWAFFE

III./JG26 Messerschmitt Bf109E. Wrecked in crash-landing at Obertraubling following engine failure. Pilot injured. Aircraft a write-off.

ALLIED (Including Polish) LOSSES IN THE AIR

Date Announced	Place	Machines	Source.	Manner, etc.
Sept. 6	Poland.	6 Polish.	Official Polish communique.	
Sept. 9	Kiel Canal.	Half British Squadron.	Field Marshal Goering.	
Sept. 10		3 French.	German communique.	Shot down.
Sept. 15	Kiel Canal.	Germany claimed 12, but Ministry of Information stated considerably fewer.		
Sept. 18	Czernowitz, Rumania.	Nearly 500 Polish.		Flew over frontier and confiscated.
Sept. 21		120 Polish.	Soviet communique.	Captured war matl.
Sept. 21	Western Front.	8 aeroplanes. 3. observation balloons.	German war communique.	Brought down.
Sept. 23	Germany.	1 French.	Do. do.	Forced down A.A. fire.
Polish losses to date.		800 aeroplanes.	Do. do.	
Sept. 26		5 French mach., 2 observation balloons.	Do. do.	1 machine by A.A. fire.
Sept. 27	Freiberg and Sigmaringen.	2 French.	Do. do.	Shot down air battle.
Sept. 28	Saarbruecken.	1 machine.	Do. do.	Brought down air battle.
Sept. 28	Western Front. (Sept. 24).	2 French.	French Air Ministry.	Aerial battle.
Sept. 28	Western Front. (Sept. 25).	1 French fighter. 1 French reconn.	Official.	Aerial battle.
Sept. 29	Wissembourg.	1 French.	German communique.	Shot down.
Sept. 29	Osnabrueck.	1 British.	Do. do.	Do. do.
Sept. 29	Nr. Heligoland.	5 British.	Do. do.	
Oct. 1	Siegfried Line.	3 British and 1 forced landed.	Ministry of Information.	Shot down in battle with 15 Messerschmitts.
Oct. 1	Western Front.	5 British.	German report.	
Oct. 1	West.	2 French. 10 British.	German communique.	
	North Sea.	2 British.		
Oct. 2	Western Front.	1 British.	Do. do.	Shot down.
Oct. 2	Do. do. (Sept. 30).	3 French.	The Times.	Fights.
Oct. 7	Godesberg.	1 French.	German communique.	Shot down.
	Euskirchen.	1 French.		Forced down.
Oct. 12	Lauterburg.	1 French.	Ger. High Command.	Shot down.
Oct. 13	Western Front.	1 French.	Daily Telegraph.	Forced landed in France.
Oct. 14	Schleiden. Idar-Oberstein. Mayen.	2 machines.	Ger. High Command.	Fighters and A.A. fire.
Oct. 14	Terranova, Sardinia.	French 3-engined bomber.		Forced landed.
Oct. 15	Birkenfeld (Oct. 13).	1 machine.	German communique.	
Oct. 16	Mainz.	1 British bomber.	German news agency.	A.A. battery.
Oct. 16	Gemersheim.	1 French reconn.	Do. do.	Shot down.
Oct. 17	German territory.	3 French. 2 British.	German communique.	Do. do.
Oct. 17	Firth of Forth (Oct. 16).	2 British.	Official German news agency.	Do. do.
Oct. 17	Scapa Flow (Oct. 16).	1 British fighter.	Do. do.	Do. do.
Oct. 17	N.W. Germany.	1 British failed to return.	Air Ministry.	On reconnaissance.
Oct. 18	Emsland.	1 British.	Exchange.	Machine in flames.
Oct. 30	North Germany (Emsland).	1 British.	Air Ministry. (Exchange).	Failed to return. (Machine came down in flames.)
Oct. 31	Western Front.	4 machines.	Ger. High Command.	
Nov. 6	Saarburg.	1 French.	Do. do.	Brought down.
Nov. 6	W. Germany.	1 British.	Air Ministry.	Failed to return.
Nov. 7	Mainz.	1 British.	German communique.	Shot down air battle.
Nov. 7	Saarlautern.	2 French.	Do. do.	Do. do.
Nov. 8	N.W. Germany (Esch).	1 British.	Air Ministry	Failed to return.
Nov. 8	Upper-Rhine.	1 British.	German communique.	Aerial fight.
Nov. 8	Voelklingen.	1 French.	Do. do.	Do. do.
Nov. 8	Saarlautern.	3 machines.	Do. do.	Do. do.
Nov. 11	S.W. Germany.	1 British.	Air Ministry.	Failed to return.
Nov. 14	Shetlands.	2 seaplanes.	Ger. High Command.	
Nov. 17	Belgium.	3 machines.	Various.	Landed in error and interned.
Nov. 22	Shetlands.	1 seaplane.	Admiralty and Air Ministry.	Set on fire by enemy bombs.
Nov. 22	Western Front.	2 French (1 Curtiss).	Reuter.	Shot down.
Nov. 23	Near Sedan.	1 French.	German communique.	Shot down.
Nov. 23	Frontier.	4 French.	German communique.	Shot down.
Nov. 23.	Esbjerg.	1 British.	Daily Telegraph.	Wreckage picked up by fishing boat.
Nov. 23	Near Verdun.	1 British.		
	Near Saarbruecken.	1 British.	German communique.	A.A. guns.
	Near Zweibruecken.	1 French.		
Nov. 28	North Sea.	1 British.	German radio.	Forced down.
Nov. 29	North Sea.	1 Fleet Air Arm.	Manchester Guardian.	Came down with engine trouble.
Dec. 7	Texel.	1 British.	German High Command	Collided with German machine and fell into sea.
	North Sea.	1 British.	Air Ministry stated probably same machine as above.	Failed to return.
Dec. 9	Esplechain. (Belgium).	1 British fighter.	Associated Press.	Forced landed and pilot abandoned machine and crossed 200 yards to French frontier.
Dec. 12	Near Southampton.	1 Fleet Air Arm.	Admiralty communique.	Hit balloon barrage cable and crashed.

GERMAN LOSSES IN THE AIR

Date Announced	Place	Machines	Source	Manner, etc.
Sept. 6	Poland	35 machines	Official Polish communique.	Shot down.
Sept. 10	Poland.	15 bombers.	Warsaw radio.	Shot down.
Sept. 13	Warsaw.	15 machines.	Polish War communique.	A.A. fire.
Sept. 13	Holland.	1 machine.		Interned.
Sept. 14	Poland.	2 machines.	Polish war communique.	
Sept. 16	Poznan.	30 machines.	Warsaw broadcast.	Polish raid.
Sept. 21	Poland.	7 machines.	Yorkshire Post.	
Sept. 22	France.	1 fighter.	Ministry of Information.	Shot down by R.A.F.
Sept. 22	Swedish waters.	1 machine.		Engine trouble.
Sept. 23		1 machine.	German war communique.	Shot down in fight.
Sept. 24	Warsaw	4 machines.	Warsaw radio.	
Sept. 25	France	2 (prob. more).	French war communique.	Aerial combat.
Sept. 27	Warsaw.	8 machines.	Warsaw communique.	
Sept. 27	North Sea (Sept. 26).	2 and 1 badly damaged.	Mr. Churchill.	Attack on Home Fleet.
Sept. 28	Western Front (Sept. 24).	5 machines.	French Air Ministry.	Aerial combat.
Sept. 30	Nr. East Frisian Islands.	2 fighters.	German High Command.	Alighted on sea.
Oct. 1	Siegfried Line.	3 machines.	German communique.	Shot down.
Oct. 2	Western Front (Sept. 30).	5 machines. 7 machines.	The Times. Telegraph & Scotsman.	Fights.
Oct. 8	North Sea.	1 Flying-boat.	Air Ministry.	Shot down by R.A.F.
Oct. 9	Denmark.	2 machines.	Daily Telegraph.	1 forced landed, 1 destroyed by fire after North Sea battle.
Oct. 10	Norway.	1 machine.	Reuter.	
Oct. 13	Western Front.	4 Messerschmitts.	Daily Telegraph.	Aerial combat.
Oct. 13	North Sea.	4 machines.	Admiralty.	Aerial combat.
Oct. 16	Firth of Forth.	4 machines.	Admiralty and Air Ministry.	R.A.F. and A.A. fire.
Oct. 17	Scapa Flow.	1 destroyed, 1 prob. destroyed.	Mr. Chamberlain.	A.A. fire.
Oct. 17	Orkneys.	1 rep't'd dest'y'd.	Admiralty.	
Oct. 17	N.E. coast, Britain.	2 machines.	Admiralty.	Shot down R.A.F.
Oct. 17	Scapa Flow.	1 machine.	Confirmed by German News Agency.	Shot down by R.A.F.
Oct. 18	North Sea.	1 Heinkel. 1 flying-boat.	Scotsman.	Forced down.
Oct. 22	S.E. coast, Scotland.	1 machine.	Air Ministry.	Brought down R.A.F. fighters.
Oct. 22	Do., do.	1 Heinkel.	Scotsman.	Shot down.
Oct. 26	North Sea (Oct. 21).	7 machines.	Air Ministry.	
Oct. 28	Dalkeith.	1 machine.	Air Ministry.	Forced down.
Oct. 30	Western Front.	1 machine.	French communique.	Forced down A.A. fire.
Oct. 31	French territory (Oct. 30).	1 Dornier.	Air Ministry.	Shot down R.A.F.
Nov. 1	France.	2 machines.	Daily Telegraph.	Shot down.
Nov. 2	France	2 Heinkels.	Daily Telegraph.	Shot down.
Nov. 3	France (Nov. 2)	1 bomber.	Daily Telegraph.	Shot down.
Nov. 6	Western Front.	9 Messerschmitts.	French G.H.Q.	Shot down combat.
Nov. 8	North Sea.	1 machine.	Air Ministry.	Brought down R.A.F.
Nov. 8	Maginot Line.	1 Dornier.	Press Association.	Shot down.
Nov. 10	North Sea.	Dornier flying-boat.	Air Ministry.	Forced down.
Nov. 10	Liebersdorf (Nov. 8).	1 machine.	German communique.	Shot down.
Nov. 16	Dunkirk (Nov. 11).	1 machine.	Press Association.	A.A. fire.
Nov. 19	Egersund, Norway. Rudkoeping, Denmark.	2 machines.	Press Association, Reuter and B.U.P.	Hit in attack on British cruisers.
Nov. 19	Italy.	1 military mach.	Reuter.	Crashed.
Nov. 20	Limburg, near German fron.	1 military machine.	B.U.P.	Shot down by Dutch.
Nov. 21	Off Deal.	1 Dornier 17.	Air Ministry.	Shot down R.A.F.
Nov. 21	Western Front.	1 reconn. mach. 2 fighters. 1 Heinkel.	French communique.	
Nov. 22	North Sea (Nov. 20).	1 Heinkel III.	Air Ministry.	
Nov. 22	Off French coast.	1 Heinkel III.	The Times.	
Nov. 22	Off S.E. coast.	1 machine.	Air Ministry.	A.A. fire.
Nov. 22	Western front.	1 Heinkel III. 1 machine.	Reuter.	Shot down by British Hurricane. Shot down by French
Nov. 22	Strasbourg.	1 Messerschmitt.	Reuter.	Do. (fighters.
Nov. 22	Werth.	1 Messerschmitt.	Reuter.	Do.
Nov. 22	Remering.	1 Messerschmitt.	Reuter.	Do.
Nov. 22	Western Front.	1 machine.	Reuter.	Do.
Nov. 22	N. of Sedan.	1 Messerschmitt Me109.	Reuter.	Shot down French A.A. fire.
Nov. 22	Nancy.	1 Dornier.	Reuter.	Shot down.
Nov. 22	Near Ostend.	1 bomber.	Manchester Guardian.	Crashed.
Nov. 23	France.	4 Dornier DO17. 2 Heinkel HEIII. 1 machine.	Air Ministry.	Shot down.
Nov. 23	Belgium (Nov. 22).	1 rec. machine.	French communique.	Shot down.
Nov. 23	Freiburg.	1 machine.	German communique.	Forced to land by French fighters.
Nov. 24	Western France.	4 machines. 2 machines. 1 machine.	German official news agency.	Shot down. Forced landed. Missing.
Nov. 27	Western Front.	1 machine.	Official.	Landed behind Maginot Line.
Nov. 29	Near Mandal.	1 machine.	Press Association.	Forced landed and interned.
Nov. 29	Thorshaven (Faroe Islands).	1 machine.	Reuter.	Wrecked.
Nov. 29	Northumbrian coast.	1 Heinkel.	Various.	Shot down.
Nov. 30	North Sea (Nov. 29).	1 Dornier.	Air Ministry.	Shot down.

Thursday, December 28

LUFTWAFFE

3./JG26 Messerschmitt Bf109E. Forced-landed at Essen-Mülheim following engine trouble at 18,000 feet. Pilot unhurt. Aircraft damaged but repairable.

2./JG27 Messerschmitt Bf109E-1 (3299). Belly-landed at Plantlünne; cause not stated. Lt F. Keller unhurt. Aircraft 1+ repairable.

Friday, December 29

LUFTWAFFE

9./JG53 Messerschmitt Bf109E. Crash-landed at Trier-Euren due to technical fault. Lt J. Stoll injured. Aircraft damaged but repairable.

3./JG77 Messerschmitt Bf109E. Crashed near Wiesbaum-Schnee-Eifel due to oxygen failure during test flight. Lt V. Kisker killed. Aircraft a write-off.

II./KG53 Heinkel He111H. Run through boundary fence, caught fire, and burned out after landing at Döberitz en-route to Rechlin. Crew unhurt. Aircraft a write-off.

I.(J)/LG2 Messerschmitt Bf109E. Lost bearings in fog and forced-landed at Marienhave. Pilot unhurt. Aircraft damaged but repairable.
Unit had transferred from Jafü Deutsche Bucht on November 1 but was returning to Hage on this date.

I.(J)/LG2 Messerschmitt Bf109E. Damaged in aborted take-off at Cologne-Butzweilerhof. Pilot unhurt. Aircraft damaged but repairable.

II.(S)/LG2 Henschel Hs123. Forced-landed at Waggum due to petrol failure. Pilot unhurt. Aircraft damaged but repairable.

Saturday, December 30

LUFTWAFFE

II./LG2 Henschel Hs123. Damaged at Waggum due to control failure. Pilot unhurt. Aircraft damaged but repairable.

II./LG2 Henschel Hs123. Forced-landed at Waggum with engine seized due to oil line fracture. Pilot unhurt. Aircraft damaged but repairable.

Back in April, it had been estimated that Germany had a majority of aircraft over the Allies, some 3,700 fighters, bombers, army co-operation and reconnaissance aircraft against 2,600. But much more important were the personnel to fly them. Although the loss of RAF aircrew during the first four months of war had been minimal, a decision was taken that December which was to have a far-reaching effect on the final outcome of the war. On the 19th, an agreement was signed in Ottawa to set up the Empire Air Training Scheme. Under this, the United Kingdom was to supply all the aircraft and a nucleus of instructors while the Dominions — Australia, Canada and New Zealand — would set up training schools. By 1942 the organisation was capable of producing 11,000 pilots and 17,000 other aircrew each year.

JANUARY 1940

In January 1940, Bétheniville, some 25 kilometres east of Reims (see map pages 26-27), was the home of No. 71 Wing of the AASF, spearheaded by No. 139 Squadron, which, like No. 73, became a focus of attention from British and French photographers.

With the weather still impeding operations, both sides engaged in further redisposition and re-equipment of their air forces on the Western Front. As the French continued to re-equip units and reorganise their own command structure, the RAF established the British Air Forces in France (BAFF) under Air Marshal Barratt in a move designed to improve existing operational organisation of its air forces in France and to increase liaison between all Allied forces involved.

On January 10, the otherwise unremarkable forced-landing of a German light aircraft in neutral Belgium prompted immediate mobilisation of all Belgian and Dutch forces and a state of heightened readiness across the entire Western Front. Blown off course and in bad visibility, the Messerschmitt Bf108 suffered engine failure, and had put down near Mechelen. The passenger on board, en-route to a staff conference, was carrying a copy of German invasion plans set for January 17, and despite efforts to destroy them, they fell into Belgian hands. This breach of security resulted in the commander of Luftflotte 2, General Helmuth Felmy, being dismissed and replaced by General Albert Kesselring, as well as the widespread revision of German plans.

Because of the harsh weather at the beginning of 1940, the only operation of note carried out by No. 139 Squadron took place on Tuesday, January 2 when four Blenheims took to the air from Bétheniville for reconnaisance duties. Unfortunately the Operations Record Book does not specify which crew flew in E-XD pictured here. Despite adverse conditions, most squadrons managed to maintain a schedule of practice flights during the month.

Tuesday, January 2

BRITISH AIR FORCES IN FRANCE

73 SQUADRON Hurricane. Broken tail wheel due to frozen ground. Flying Officer H. G. G. Paul unhurt. Aircraft repairable.

73 SQUADRON Hurricane. Suffered sudden loss of oil pressure and broke tail bracket in forced-landing near Nancy. Sergeant D. A. Sewell unhurt. Aircraft repairable.

FRENCH AIR FORCE

GC III/2 Morane 406 (353). Crashed, undercarriage retracted, on take-off at Chaumont-Semoutiers. Adjt R. Prenez believed unhurt. Aircraft a write-off.

GC I/5 Curtiss H-75 (13). Suffered oxygen failure during high-level patrol and crashed into woods south of Malancourt. Cpl V. Vasek killed. Aircraft a write-off.
Vladimir Vasek was the first Czech pilot flying with the Armée de l'Air to be killed on active service. An alternative source gives serial 25 for the aircraft number.

LUFTWAFFE

1./JG53 Messerschmitt Bf109E. Damaged in combat with Curtiss H-75s of GC II/5 and forced-landed at Wiesbaden-Erbenheim 1.45 p.m. Lt W. Rupp unhurt. Aircraft 13+ repairable.

1./JG53 Messerschmitt Bf109E. Damaged in combat with Curtiss H-75s and forced-landed at Hoppstädten with engine alight. Possibly that attacked by Lt Huvet of GC II/5 1.45 p.m. Oberlt H. Ohly wounded. Aircraft 1+ repairable.

V.(Z)/LG1 Messerschmitt Bf110C (1358). Wrecked in forced-landing at Neuenkirchen, near Rheine, due to starboard engine fire. Crew unhurt. Aircraft a write-off.
This loss was reported as I./ZG1 in German records.

Wednesday, January 3

BRITISH AIR FORCES IN FRANCE

18 SQUADRON Blenheim I L1410. Escaped attack by Hurricanes undamaged but later shot down by Fw Goltzsche of 1./JG 77 during photo-reconnaissance sortie south of Aachen 9.10 a.m. Reached the Belgian border but crash-landed and burned out at Eynatten, north-east of Eupen. Flying Officer C. M. P. Kempster and Sergeant F. L. Smith both slightly injured, interned in hospital in Liège. LAC P. B. Harris baled out too low and killed. Aircraft WV⊙B a write-off.

85 SQUADRON Hurricane L1641. Suffered broken tail-wheel at Abbeville. Pilot unhurt. Aircraft repairable.

87 SQUADRON Hurricane N2353. Propeller and wing damaged in accident at Lille-Seclin following convoy patrol — selected wheels up instead of flaps up on landing 11.45 a.m. Flying Officer Joyce unhurt. Aircraft repairable.

615 SQUADRON Gladiator. Tailwheel damaged in forced-landing near Crécy due to broken oil pipe during affiliation exercise. Flying Officer J. R. H. Gayner unhurt. Aircraft repairable.

Bétheniville, like many of the airfields in the Champagne region of France, was simply a large grass-surfaced landing ground with no permanent buildings. It soon proved unsuitable for the heavy Blenheims and consequently in February the squadron had to be moved to Plivot, 30 kilometres south of Reims, where there were hard runways. They were forced to leave four aircraft behind immobilised by the weather.

FRENCH AIR FORCE

GC II/7 Morane 406 (66). Damaged during attack on Bf109s of JGr.176 over Märkt 11.12 a.m. and forced-landed at Colmar. Sgt Planchard unhurt. Aircraft repairable.

GC III/7 Morane 406 (76). Caught fire during routine patrol and dived vertically into the ground at Plichancourt 3.30 p.m. Exact cause unknown. Sgt G. Cahen killed. Aircraft a write-off.

LUFTWAFFE

1./JG21 Messerschmitt Bf109E. Damaged in heavy landing at Plantlünne. Lt J. Strauss unhurt. Aircraft damaged but repairable.

JGr.176 Messerschmitt Bf109D-1. Forced-landed at Schliengen, near Mühlhausen, due to engine failure. Probably that claimed by Moranes of GC II/7 in combat over Märkt 11.15 a.m. Pilot unhurt. Aircraft damaged but repairable.

1./ZG26 Messerschmitt Bf110C. Crashed near Deilinghofen, east of Iserlohn, when engine seized during transfer flight. Crew unhurt. Aircraft a write-off.

This Blenheim from No. 18 Squadron failed to make it back to base at Méharicourt on January 3.

Thursday, January 4

LUFTWAFFE

13.(Z)/LG1 Messerschmitt Bf110C. Crashed following collision over Randesacker, near Würzburg, during air combat practice 12.30 p.m. Uffz W. Landrock killed, Oberlt J. Glienke baled out injured. Aircraft a write-off.

13.(Z)/LG1 Messerschmitt Bf110C. Crashed following mid-air collision over Randesacker during air combat practice 12.30 p.m. Fw W. Kinzler and Obergefr P. Möller both fatally injured. Aircraft a write-off.

Friday, January 5

BRITISH AIR FORCES IN FRANCE

607 SQUADRON Gladiator. Tailwheel broken in landing at Mons-en-Chaussée during affiliation exercises with Lysanders. Flying Officer G. D. Craig unhurt. Aircraft repairable.
Two other squadron aircraft were similarly damaged during these exercises at Péronne.

DUTCH AIR FORCE

4-II-1 Fokker G 1 (306). Starboard rudder damaged in collision with D XXI over Graft 2.08 p.m. Crashed and burned out west of De Rijp. 2e Lt A. van Ulsen and Sgt P. J. Lok baled out unhurt. Aircraft a write-off.

II-1 Fokker D XXI (234). Landed on damaged undercarriage following collision with Fokker G 1 over Graft 2.08 p.m. Lt O. Thate unhurt. Aircraft damaged but repairable.

Saturday, January 6

LUFTWAFFE

1./JG53 Messerschmitt Bf109E-1. Belly-landed at Eich, near Gernsheim, following engine failure. Pilot unhurt. Aircraft damaged but repairable.

2./JG53 Messerschmitt Bf109E. Collided with parked aircraft during forced-landing at decoy airfield 'Petersen' due to petrol failure. Pilot unhurt. Aircraft damaged but repairable.
A redundant Messerschmitt Bf109C used as a decoy aircraft was also wrecked in this accident.

6./KG2 Dornier Do17Z. Crashed at Hopferstadt, near Ochsenfurt, during blind-flying practice 12.00 p.m. Fw H. Langer, Uffz H. Probst, Uffz P. Abeling, and Uffz O. Vogel killed. Aircraft a write-off.

It crashed between Eynatten and Raeren, eight kilometres north-east of Eupen quite close to the Belgian-German frontier.

The aircraft came in from the west, hit a tree and overhead tram wires, and crashed just beside the Eynattener Strasse.

2./StG2 Junkers Ju87B. Crashed at Bonn-Hangelar from 12,000 feet, cause unknown. Two crew killed. Aircraft a write-off.

Tuesday, January 9

LUFTWAFFE

VIII. Fliegerkorps Fieseler Fi 156. Slid off runway at Dyck, near Rheydt, and hit a tree. Pilot unhurt. Aircraft damaged but repairable.

2./StG2 Junkers Ju87B. Crashed near Burg Ahrental, cause unknown. Crew killed. Aircraft a write-off.

3./StG2 Junkers Ju87B (291). Crashed northeast of Rotenburg, cause unknown. One of crew killed. Aircraft a write-off.

Wednesday, January 10

BRITISH AIR FORCES IN FRANCE

1 SQUADRON Hurricane L1621. Forced-landed at Chambly with broken con-rod 2.30 p.m. Sergeant F. J. Soper unhurt. Aircraft damaged but repairable.

1 SQUADRON Hurricane L1689. Forced-landed at Ecury due to engine trouble 2.45 p.m. Sergeant R. A. Albonico unhurt. Aircraft repairable.

105 SQUADRON Battle K9198. Fuselage frame fractured in forced-landing near Poix due to glycol leak during tactical exercise. Flying Officer H. C. Tootal and crew unhurt. Aircraft a write-off.

218 SQUADRON Battle K9327. Damaged in forced-landing at Monchy, cause not stated. Crew unhurt. Aircraft repairable.

FRENCH AIR FORCE

GC III/7 Morane 406 (233). Forced-landed at Metz damaged in attack by Lt Radlick of Stab III./JG53 south of Perl 1.57 p.m. Sgt R. Delarue wounded in shoulder. Aircraft damaged but repairable.

GR 3/55 Potez 63.11 (184). Shot down by Oberlt Seiler *(Staffelkapitän)* of 1./JG54 during photo-reconnaissance mission over Grezhausen and crashed at Blotzheim 11.15 a.m. Lt R. Félix *(Commandant)*, Lt P. Boulard, and Sgt M. Chancrin killed. Aircraft a write-off.

LUFTWAFFE

2.(H)/10 Henschel Hs126. Crashed at Fassberg when propeller disintegrated. Crew unhurt. Aircraft a write-off.

1./JG2 Messerschmitt Bf109E-3. Badly damaged in attack by Sgt Legrand of GC II/5 over Ixheim and forced-landed south-west of Zweibrücken 1.15 p.m. Lt J. Seegert wounded. Aircraft a write-off.

1./JG2 Messerschmitt Bf109E-3. Belly-landed near Höchst-Main due to engine failure and possibly that claimed by Capt Portalis and S/Lt Villacèque of GC II/5 in combat over Zweibrücken 1.15 p.m. Pilot unhurt. Aircraft repairable.

1./JG51 Messerschmitt Bf109E-3. Abandoned due to engine fire and crashed near Soultz-sous-Forêts, east of Kutzenhausen 1.30 p.m. Oberfw W. von Balka baled out and captured badly injured. Aircraft a write-off.

Stab I./JG54 Messerschmitt Bf109E-3. Hit the ground during low-level pursuit of GR II/55, possibly hit by return fire. Crashed and burned out near Hirtzfelden, 20 km south-east of Colmar 11.15 a.m. Lt E. Schütz *(Gruppenadjutant)* killed. Aircraft a write-off.

1./JG76 Messerschmitt Bf109E-3. Dived vertically from 24,000 feet and crashed east of Bitburg; possible victim of oxygen failure. Lt C. von Bohlen-Halbach killed. Aircraft a write-off.

3./KG2 Dornier Do17Z. Crashed at Gross Dechsendorf, north of Erlangen, blinded by searchlight. Lt W. Schube, Uffz W. Teller, Uffz G. Aniol, and Flgr B. Kühn killed. Aircraft a write-off.

7. Flieger Division Messerschmitt Bf108. Lost bearings and run low on fuel, forced-landed at Maasmechelen, near Vucht. Major H. Reinberger and Major Dr E. Hoenmanns interned unhurt. Aircraft D-NF+AW a write-off.

Helmuth Reinberger, a communications officer on the staff of General Student, was en route from Münster to attend a conference at HQ 7. Fliegerdivision in Cologne, carrying a copy of the German invasion plans for Fall Gelb. Despite efforts to destroy them, the plans fell into Belgian hands and the full extent of German intentions in the West was revealed.

Thursday, January 11

LUFTWAFFE

3.(F)/11 Dornier Do17P. Engaged by Lt Marin La Meslée and S/Lt Rey of GC I/5 during reconnaissance sortie over Verdun and shot down at Haucourt-la-Rigole, near Spincourt, 9.45 a.m. Oberfw H. Erlbeck, Uffz H. Linsmayer, and Uffz J. Sticht captured. Aircraft a write-off.

Friday, January 12

BRITISH AIR FORCES IN FRANCE

114 SQUADRON Blenheim IV L8859. Starboard engine badly damaged in attack by Lt Malischewski of Stab I./JG 76 during reconnaissance of German airfields around Greimerath, Losheim, and Wahlen 12.45 p.m. Forced-landed at Metz. Pilot Officer G. R. Turner slightly injured. Sergeant W. J. Paul and AC1 S. G. Peplar unhurt. Aircraft damaged but repairable — later abandoned.

Aircraftman Peter Harris parachuted to his death some 200 yards from the wreck. He was buried in Robermont Cemetery **at Liège in the presence of his two crewmen. The old Baum family farm still stands but is now hidden by the trees.**

139 SQUADRON Blenheim IV. Forced-landed at Beauvais due to engine failure 6.00 a.m. Sergeant Parkinson, Sergeant Stokes, and LAC Crowley unhurt. Aircraft repairable.

218 SQUADRON Battle K9357. Forced-landed through a hedge at Pommiers during practice attacks on convoys 2.00 p.m. Flying Officer J. F. R. Crane, Sergeant W. H. Harris and AC1 J. A. Drummond unhurt. Aircraft a write-off.

218 SQUADRON Battle K9254. Forced-landed at Noyon, north-east of Compiègne, during practice attacks on convoys 2.00 p.m. Pilot Officer H. O. Forth, Sergeant P. Stubbs, and AC Forrester unhurt. Aircraft a write-off — abandoned at No. 21 Aircraft Depot, Château Bougon.

FRENCH AIR FORCE

GB 1/12 LeO 451 (17). Crashed and burned out near Sambruc, 20 km from Arles, during night navigation exercise 1.30 a.m. Cause unknown. Capt. Geerts *(Commandant)*, S/Lt C. Wemaere, Adjt Villemot, Adjt Vogel, and Sgt Hanotel killed. Aircraft a write-off.

LUFTWAFFE

I./JG26 Messerschmitt Bf109E. Belly-landed at Dortmund due to engine failure. Pilot unhurt. Aircraft a write-off.

Saturday, January 13

FRENCH AIR FORCE

GR II/22 Bloch 131. Abandoned when caught fire during night sortie; crashed and burned out near Douaumont. Adjt G. Lemoine baled out injured. Sgt Blanchard and Sgt Rigollier baled out unhurt. Adjt P. Marie baled out but fell dead with parachute alight. Aircraft a write-off.

This photo is a good example of the confusion with wartime captioning. This claimed that 'on 11th January 1940, three German reconnaissance planes were shot down within French lines' but this does not tie up with the losses recorded that day. Though the weather curtailed operations throughout the month each side strove to maintain a programme of all-important reconnaissance sorties. These resulted in fairly regular losses for those units involved with the British and French losing five reconnaissance machines between them against the Germans' six — doubtless considered small enough sacrifice for the information gathered.

LUFTWAFFE

1.(F)/Ob.d.L Dornier Do17S-0 (2502). Engaged at height over the Channel off Dover by Capt Barbier of GC 2/4 during photo-reconnaissance sortie to southern England. Engine damaged in attacks and belly-landed at Hemmes, near Calais-Marck, 1.18 p.m. Lt T. Rosarius, Gefr A. Schaal, and Uffz J. Kuge captured. Aircraft T5+FH a write-off. *One of only three examples built, (2184, 2501, and 2502) these specially-equipped aircraft were converted for use by the Versuchsstelle für Höhenflüge at Oranienburg — 'Kommando Rowehl'.*

2.(H)/21 Henschel Hs126. Crashed in turn during night landing at Windischenlaibach. Lt Jelinski and pilot injured. Aircraft a write-off.

1./JG2 Messerschmitt Bf109E-1. Undercarriage and propeller damaged on landing at Wengerohr due to poor state of airfield. Pilot unhurt. Aircraft damaged but repairable.

I.(J)/LG2 Messerschmitt Bf109E-3. Crash-landed near Wattenscheid during transit flight from Hage to Gymnich, cause not stated. Pilot injured. Aircraft a write-off.

Sunday, January 14

BRITISH AIR FORCES IN FRANCE

114 SQUADRON Blenheims N6153 and N6161. Stern-frames broken while taxying on frozen ground at Vraux airfield. No crew casualties. Aircraft damaged but repairable — later abandoned.

Wednesday, January 17

BRITISH AIR FORCES IN FRANCE

4 SQUADRON Lysander. Tailwheel damaged on landing at Douai. Flying Officer Fyffe unhurt. Aircraft TV⊙G damaged but repairable.

18 SQUADRON Blenheim I L1421. Stern-frame collapsed on landing at Upper Heyford on return from reconnaissance sortie over Cleve, Aarhus, and Gronau 1.00 p.m. Pilot Officer P. D. Smith, Sergeant Buckner, and LAC G. Hawkins unhurt. Aircraft damaged but repairable. *Alternative sources suggest that this accident may have occurred on January 12.*

Thursday, January 18

LUFTWAFFE

2./JG21 Messerschmitt Bf109E-1 (3490). Forced-landed at Münster-Handorf with boost control problems. Oberlt R. Hausmann unhurt. Aircraft 12+ repairable.

II./JG51 Messerschmitt Bf109E-1. Forced-landed near Freiburg due to engine failure. Pilot unhurt. Aircraft damaged but repairable.

II./KG1 Heinkel He111H. Forced-landed at Eisenach when both engines failed. Crew unhurt. Aircraft damaged but repairable.

However, this picture does match up. This particular Dornier was a rare prize, falling intact into Allied hands as it was one of only three special high-altitude models. A French pilot brought it down near Calais on January 13.

Friday, January 19

BRITISH AIR FORCES IN FRANCE

88 SQUADRON Battle. Flew into electricity lines at Illois, west of Aumale, during wireless exercise and returned with damaged fin. Pilot Officer Clark and crew unhurt. Aircraft repairable.

LUFTWAFFE

2.(H)/13 Dornier Do17M (2202). Shot down in flames over Bohain by Curtiss H-75s of GC II/5 during reconnaissance sortie and crashed at Wiernsheim, near Pforzheim. Fw P. Auer, Oberfw J. Kaspers, and Fw P. Dickfoss killed. Aircraft a write-off.

I./JG26 Messerschmitt Bf109E. Belly-landed at Dortmund following engine failure. Pilot unhurt. Aircraft a write-off.

2./JG54 Messerschmitt Bf109E-1. Undercarriage collapsed on landing at Böblingen. Possibly that attacked near Eschbach by S/Lt de Fraville of GC II/7 during combat north of Mühlhausen 11.15 a.m. Pilot unhurt. Aircraft damaged but repairable.

2./JG54 Messerschmitt Bf109E-1 (6037). Engaged on escort sortie for Hs126 and Do17 and shot down by S/Lt Gruyelle of GC II/7 in combat north-east of Mühlhausen. Abandoned over Grunhütte, south-east of Bantzenheim 11.15 a.m. Uffz W. Wagner badly wounded and burned, baled out and captured — transported to hospital at Cernay where left foot amputated. Aircraft 5 + a write-off.

Sunday, January 21

LUFTWAFFE

4.(F)/122 Heinkel He111H-2. Crash-landed at Osnabrück due to engine failure. Crew unhurt. Aircraft a write-off.

Wettererkundungsstaffel 51 Heinkel He111H. Disintegrated in mid-air over Unterjettingen, near Nagold, cause unknown. Oberlt von Loeben, Reg Rat Dr Etschel, and three crewmen killed. Aircraft a write-off.

Tuesday, January 23

BRITISH AIR FORCES IN FRANCE

218 SQUADRON Battle K9329. Flaps failed on landing from compass-swinging flight and collided with a stationary aircraft 10.05 a.m. Flying Officer I. G. Richmond sprained ankle. Sergeant C. M. Jennings and AC1 A. Ellis unhurt. Aircraft a write-off — abandoned at No. 21 Aircraft Depot, Château Bougon.

218 SQUADRON Battle K9327. Parked aircraft wrecked in collision with K9329 at Aubérive 10.05 a.m. No crew casualties. Aircraft a write-off — abandoned at No. 21 Aircraft Depot, Château Bougon.

Wednesday, January 24

LUFTWAFFE

10.(N)/JG72 Arado Ar68E. Crashed avoiding a landing collision at Grosselfingen. Pilot unhurt. Aircraft damaged but repairable.

Although the original censored caption to this picture published from a different source merely states 'a German bomber shot down in northern France', this is undoubtedly a close-up of the same aircraft.

2./StG77 Junkers Ju87B (5231). Crashed due to engine failure on final approach at Celle. Crew unhurt. Aircraft a write-off.

Thursday, January 25

BRITISH AIR FORCES IN FRANCE

57 SQUADRON Blenheim I L1280. Shot down by Fw Scherer of 2./JGr.102 during reconnaissance sortie over NW Germany. Crashed south of Duisburg 2.20 p.m. Pilot Officer J. N. O'Reilly-Blackwood, Sergeant D. J. Bendall and AC2 J. R. Hunter killed. Aircraft a write-off.

73 SQUADRON Hurricane L1975. Returned slightly damaged by return fire when guns froze during attack on He111 at 26,000 feet. Flying Officer E. J. Kain unhurt. Aircraft repairable.

73 SQUADRON Hurricane N2364. Returned propeller damaged by return fire when guns froze during attack on He111 at 26,000 feet. Sergeant S. G. Stuckey unhurt. Aircraft repairable.

LUFTWAFFE

3.(F)/10 Dornier Do17M. Crashed at Harsum, near Hildesheim, flying in thick haze. Lt K. Kremen, Fw E. Schwenk and Fw H. Wiere killed. Aircraft a write-off.

II./JG53 Messerschmitt Bf109E-1. Wrecked in forced-landing at Rockenhausen, cause unknown. Pilot unhurt. Aircraft a write-off.

7./JG53 Messerschmitt Bf109E-3. Wrecked in crash-landing south of Saarbrücken due to petrol failure. Uffz Zerning injured. Aircraft a write-off.

V.(Z)/LG1 Messerschmitt Bf110C. Collided with another Bf110 after landing at Würzburg on one engine. Crew unhurt. Aircraft damaged but repairable.

V.(Z)/LG1 Messerschmitt Bf110C. Parked aircraft damaged in landing collision at Würzburg. No crew casualties. Aircraft damaged but repairable.

Severe weather curtailed operations that January. Here mechanics clear snow and remove the cockpit cover from a Battle of an unnamed squadron.

Sunday, January 28

LUFTWAFFE

2./JG21 Messerschmitt Bf109E-1 (3491). Crashed and burned out on take-off from Münster-Handorf, cause unknown. Uffz W. Strassfeld killed. Aircraft a write-off.

Monday, January 29

BRITISH AIR FORCES IN FRANCE

1 SQUADRON Hurricane L1686. Forced-landed at Senoncourt-les-Maujouy, south of Verdun, due to engine failure 11.15 a.m. Pilot Officer Blomeley unhurt. Aircraft repairable.

LUFTWAFFE

1./KG27 Heinkel He111P. Crashed on landing at Leipheim due to undercarriage failure. No crew casualties reported. Aircraft 1G+DH damaged but repairable.

Wednesday, January 31

LUFTWAFFE

I./JG26 Messerschmitt Bf109E. Damaged in forced-landing west of Unna in deteriorating weather conditions. Pilot unhurt. Aircraft damaged but repairable.

3./KG2 Dornier Do17Z. Stalled and crashed at Gross-Langenheim after take-off from Kitzingen. Lt K. Kutz, Fw E. Zimmermann, Hauptgefr H. Machmer, and Gefr E. Riegel killed. Aircraft a write-off.

With no cockpit heating or heated flying clothing, aircrews needed to wrap up well against the harsh winter weather which severely restricted all flying. Even moving the aircraft from hardstandings along improvised taxiways was extremely hazardous and landing on frozen ground resulted in several instances of tail wheel damage. Maintaining aircraft parked out in the open under such conditions was equally difficult for long-suffering ground crews despite the use of engine tents into which warm air was blown. Engines also had to be started throughout the night to keep the oil hot and ensure they would start the following morning as and when required. But with operations so restricted this was rarely the case making the entire exercise seem fairly pointless. All in all, it was a bitterly uncomfortable period for an air force 'in the field'.

FEBRUARY 1940

Taking advantage of the further lull in air activity over the Western Front due to continuing poor weather, Air Marshal Barratt initiated reorganisation of his bomber forces with the disbandment of Nos. 72 and 74 Wings and redistribution of the squadrons involved. Meantime, No. 212 (PR) Squadron was established at Tigeaux, close to the headquarters of the British Air Forces in France, its eight, specially-modified, photo-reconnaissance Spitfires operating from advanced airfields as detached flights. A sister unit, the Photographic Development Unit based at Heston, also few regular high-altitude reconnaissance sorties over German naval targets.

First published in February 1940, the only clues are that this Dornier 17 was brought down in flames in Lorraine. The claim at the time was that 'not many German airmen have, so far, ventured to come within range of the French anti-aircraft guns or to make contact with French fighter planes'.

A planned programme to gradually re-equip all the Battle squadrons in France with Blenheims, which was initiated in October 1939, had been halted with only two squadrons re-equipped so far. Thus, the Fairey Battle, already generally recognised as obsolescent, and with serious shortcomings due to lack of speed at low level and lamentable fire-power, would remain in service with eight BAFF squadrons. It was, to quote an official RAF narrative, 'difficult to find any great volume of belief in its operational qualities'. Its crews were destined to pay a very high price indeed to confirm such misgivings.

Thursday, February 1

LUFTWAFFE

I./StG77 Junkers Ju87. Windscreen cracked and crashed attempting forced-landing in heavily wooded area at Gross Zehlen, near Celle. One of crew injured. Aircraft a write-off.

Friday, February 2

LUFTWAFFE

Stab II./JG51 Messerschmitt Bf109E-3. Hit the water of the Bodensee during air-to-ground firing practise and crashed into retaining wall at Immenstaad, 4 km east of Meersburg. Major E. G. Burggaller (Gruppenkommandeur) killed. Aircraft a write-off.

I./KG51 Heinkel He111H-2. Damaged in aborted take-off at Memmingen due to snow on airfield. Crew unhurt. Aircraft damaged but repairable.

Saturday, February 3

LUFTWAFFE

V.(Z)/LG1 Messerschmitt Bf110C-1 (2804). Crashed and burned out at Schlengerfeld, shortly after take-off from Marx on ferry flight, cause unknown. Both crew killed. Aircraft a write-off.

2./ZG26 Messerschmitt Bf110C-1. Crashed at Marx due to engine damage. Oberfw N. Flegel and Uffz E. Sauttler killed. Aircraft a write-off.

On February 1, His Majesty King George VI visited troops in France. Here he is pictured at Lille-Seclin aerodrome with the Hurricanes of No. 85 Squadron and No. 87 beyond. Gladiator Is and Blenheim IVs also on parade.

Sunday, February 4

LUFTWAFFE

1.(J)/LG2 Messerschmitt Bf109E-3. Stalled in steep turn, crashed and burned out west of Gymnich. Lt K. Seepold killed. Aircraft a write-off.

Monday, February 5

FRENCH AIR FORCE

T3 Latécoère 298 (20). Crashed into cliffs at Nez de Jobourg flying in fog on training flight west of Cherbourg 0.30 a.m. SM Viannès killed, and 2 crewmen badly injured. Aircraft 10 a write-off.

LUFTWAFFE

Stab StG1 Dornier Do17M. Crashed south of Wuppertal flying in thick fog. Three crew killed. Aircraft a write-off.

Tuesday, February 6

DUTCH AIR FORCE

2-I-1 Fokker C V (653). Experienced engine trouble during target-towing flight and landed on the beach at Wijk aan Zee. Later overturned while taxi-ing. 2e Lt A. de Waal Malefijt and J. van der Sleen believed unhurt. Aircraft a write-off.

LUFTWAFFE

Stab JG77 Messerschmitt Bf109E. Overturned on landing in thick snow at Peppenhoven. Pilot unhurt. Aircraft damaged but repairable.

Wednesday, February 7

BRITISH AIR FORCES IN FRANCE

607 SQUADRON Gladiator I K6137. Wrecked in forced-landing following engine failure on take-off at St Inglevert. Flying Officer G. D. Craig unhurt. Aircraft AF⊙Z a write-off.

Friday, February 9

LUFTWAFFE

II.(S)/LG2 Henschel Hs123. Forced-landed at Münster-Loddenheide due to engine failure. One crewman injured. Aircraft damaged but repairable.

I./StG2 Junkers Ju87B (6096). Crash-landed on Holsteiner-Heide out of fuel. Crew believed unhurt. Aircraft a write-off.

Saturday, February 10

LUFTWAFFE

AufklGr.156 Fieseler Fi156. Crashed on landing at Crailsheim. Pilot unhurt. Aircraft damaged but repairable.

I./JG1 Messerschmitt Bf109E-3 (5013). Abandoned over Moers due to engine fire. Pilot baled out unhurt. Aircraft a write-off.

After Poland, this unit moved to Lübeck-Blankensee for defence of north-west Germany, then Gymnich in January 1940 for operations on the Western Front.

I./JG26 Messerschmitt Bf109E-3 (710). Crashed on landing at Werl due to control failure. Pilot unhurt. Aircraft damaged but repairable.

III./KG3 Dornier Do17Z. Hit trees and crashed onto a house at Niederwerren, near Schweinfurt, shortly after take-off, probably due to icing. One of crew killed. Oberstlt Neubitler and Oberlt Niemann badly injured, later died. Another crewman badly injured. Aircraft a write-off.

I./KG77 Dornier Do17Z. Forced-landed near Lauf a.d. Pegnitz due to engine trouble. One of crew injured. Aircraft damaged but repairable.

Sunday, February 11

LUFTWAFFE

I./JG3 Messerschmitt Bf109E-1. Crashed on landing at Giessen on burst tyre. Pilot unhurt. Aircraft damaged but repairable.

Employed in the defence of central Germany, this unit transferred to Peppenhoven, north-west of Remagen, for operations on the Western Front January 13.

I./JG52 Messerschmitt Bf109E-1. Damaged one wing landing on icy ground at Lachen-Speyerdorf. Pilot unhurt. Aircraft repairable.

II./ZG26 Messerschmitt Bf110C. Belly-landed at Buer due to undercarriage failure. Crew unhurt. Aircraft damaged but repairable.

Monday, February 12

BRITISH AIR FORCES IN FRANCE

87 SQUADRON Hurricane L1613. Crashed at Pléchâtel, south-west of Rennes, having lost bearings in poor visibility. Sergeant P. F. H. Thurgar killed. Aircraft a write-off.

FRENCH AIR FORCE

GC III/2 Morane 406 (222). Crashed on landing at Cambrai-Niergnies. Sgt Monribot injured. Aircraft a write-off.

LUFTWAFFE

II./JG51 Messerschmitt Bf109E-1. Lost control and crashed on take-off from Eutingen. Pilot unhurt. Aircraft a write-off.

I./JG53 Messerschmitt Bf109E-1. Lost control and crashed on landing at Darmstadt-Griesheim. Pilot unhurt. Aircraft damaged but repairable.

I./JG53 Messerschmitt Bf109E-3. Damaged when undercarriage folded during take-off from Darmstadt-Griesheim. Pilot unhurt. Aircraft damaged but repairable.

Tuesday, February 13

FRENCH AIR FORCE

GC III/7 Morane 406 (209). Crashed at Laneuville-au-Pont, 10 km south of St Dizier, on return from sortie. S/Lt F. Pilâtre-Jacquin slightly injured. Aircraft a write-off.

DUTCH AIR FORCE

I-2 Fokker C V (595). Forced-landed near the German border, cause not stated. 1e Lt J. P. Schouw unhurt. Aircraft a write-off.

LUFTWAFFE

I./JG2 Messerschmitt Bf109E-1. Damaged taxying over runway light at Frankfurt-Rebstock. Pilot unhurt. Aircraft repairable.

II./JG26 Messerschmitt Bf109E. Stalled in steep turn and abandoned near Dortmund following engine failure. Pilot baled out landing injured. Aircraft a write-off.

2./KG53 Heinkel He111H. Caught in cross-wind and damaged landing in snow at Manching. Crew unhurt. Aircraft damaged but repairable.

Wednesday, February 14

FRENCH AIR FORCE

GAO 517 Potez 390 (30). Observer thrown from aircraft near Fayence during photo-reconnaissance sortie in high winds 2.40 p.m. S/Lt J. Poulain deployed parachute but blown out to sea and lost. Sgt Mougeot returned unhurt. Aircraft undamaged.

Thursday, February 15

BRITISH AIR FORCES IN FRANCE

105 SQUADRON Battle K9195. Wrecked in forced-landing at Beausse during transit flight to Nantes 12.30 p.m. Flying Officer R. N. Wall and crew unhurt. Aircraft abandoned at No. 21 Aircraft Depot, Château Bougon, June 1940.

BELGIAN AIR FORCE

1/I/1 Fox (O.33). Crashed and destroyed in landing accident. Sgt Flamion and Lt Ghysels both unhurt. Aircraft a write-off.

Friday, February 16

LUFTWAFFE

2./JG26 Messerschmitt Bf109E-3. Crash-landed at Neumünster due to control failure. Pilot unhurt. Aircraft a write-off.

Today the wartime aerodrome of Seclin has become the main civil airport at Lille, now known as Lesquin. The building in the right background of the wartime photo was demolished in the early 'sixties. During the war years there were six airfields located in the Lille area: Bondues, Lesquin-Enchémont, Marcq, Quatre-Ville, Ronchin and Seclin, and there has been much confusion over the locations as the names have also changed several times, Lesquin also being referred to as Vendeville which, after the invasion in 1944, became Allied airfield B51. Also Royal Air Force and Luftwaffe maps differ.

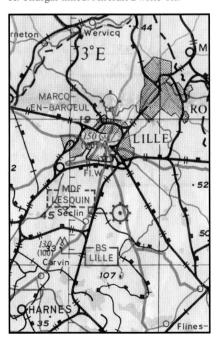

The winter scene at Mourmelon-le-Grand, 30 kilometres south-east of Reims, the home of the Battles of No. 88 Squadron.

6./JG52 Messerschmitt Bf109E-3. Hit a snow drift while landing at Speyer. Pilot unhurt. Aircraft damaged but repairable.

Saturday, February 17

LUFTWAFFE

II./JG26 Messerschmitt Bf109E-3. Abandoned following collision on take-off from Recklinghausen. Pilot baled out unhurt. Aircraft a write-off.
This aircraft crashed onto a house north of the airfield killing a woman and two children.

II./JG26 Messerschmitt Bf109E-3. Abandoned following collision on take-off from Recklinghausen. Pilot baled out unhurt. Aircraft a write-off.

III./KG51 Heinkel He111H-2. Stalled and crashed 2 km east of Memmingen flying in snow shower. Four crew killed. Aircraft a write-off.

II.(S)/LG2 Fieseler Fi156. Undercarriage damaged on landing at Dortmund due to poor state of airfield. Pilot unhurt. Aircraft repairable.

Sunday, February 18

BRITISH AIR FORCES IN FRANCE

139 SQUADRON Blenheim IV N6225. Starboard undercarriage damaged while taxying prior to take-off from Bétheniville . Pilot Officer Dundee and crew unhurt. Aircraft repairable.

LUFTWAFFE

3.(H)/14 Henschel Hs126B. Damaged in forced-landing at Maisebeck, 20 km northeast of Göttingen, following oxygen failure. Observer suffered oxygen sickness. Aircraft damaged but repairable.

1./JG21 Messerschmitt Bf109E-3. Abandoned over Rheydt due to engine fire. Fw F. Hartwich baled out unhurt. Aircraft a write-off.

2./JG21 Messerschmitt Bf109E-3 (1525). Forced-landed at Mönchengladbach with engine trouble. Uffz H. Jürgens unhurt. Aircraft 6+ repairable.

III./JG26 Messerschmitt Bf109E-3. Wrecked due to petrol failure during emergency take-off at Moors. Pilot unhurt. Aircraft a write-off.

8./ZG26 Messerschmitt Bf110C-1. Crashed at Braunschweig, cause unknown. Uffz H. Kaiser killed. Aircraft a write-off.

Monday, February 19

LUFTWAFFE

II./KG54 Heinkel He111P. Hit trees while forced-landing at Wietzenbruch, near Celle following engine fire. Crew unhurt. Aircraft a write-off.

Tuesday, February 20

BRITISH AIR FORCES IN FRANCE

105 SQUADRON Battle K9193. Crashed on beach between St Laurent and Villelongue de la Salanque, near Perpignan, during dive-bombing practice 11.30 a.m. Pilot Officer D. C. F. Murray and crew unhurt. Aircraft a write-off.

LUFTWAFFE

I./JG2 Messerschmitt Bf109E-1. Crash-landed at Kollweiler due to engine failure. Pilot unhurt. Aircraft a write-off.

3./JG3 Messerschmitt Bf109E. Belly-landed at Troisdorf, near Bonn-Hangelar, following engine failure. Lt E. von Fonderen unhurt. Aircraft 7+ damaged but repairable.

1./JG52 Messerschmitt Bf109E-1. Wrecked in crash-landing at Lachen-Speyerdorf following mid-air collision south of Ludwigshafen. Pilot unhurt. Aircraft a write-off.

1./JG52 Messerschmitt Bf109E-1. Crashed and burned out near Hockenheim, following mid-air collision south of Ludwigshafen. Pilot baled out unhurt. Aircraft a write-off.

Stab JG77 Messerschmitt Bf109E-1. Forced-landed at Bonn-Hangelar following engine failure. Pilot unhurt. Aircraft repairable.

2./JG77 Messerschmitt Bf109E-1. Crash-landed in woods near Bonn-Hangelar having shot off own propeller blades over Schweinheim firing range. Lt H. Mütherich injured. Aircraft 3+ a write-off.

1./ZG52 Messerschmitt Bf110C. Overturned on landing at Kaufbeuren due to snow on landing ground. Crew unhurt. Aircraft damaged but repairable.

Wednesday, February 21

FRENCH AIR FORCE

T3 Latécoère 298 (70). Wrecked in landing accident at Cherbourg, cause not stated. Crew unhurt. Aircraft a write-off.

LUFTWAFFE

I./JG3 Messerschmitt Bf109E. Belly-landed near Müntekoven due to engine failure. Uffz K. Gräf unhurt. Aircraft repairable.

I./JG53 Messerschmitt Bf109E-3. Undercarriage collapsed on take-off at Darmstadt-Griesheim. Pilot unhurt. Aircraft damaged but repairable.

I.(J)/LG2 Messerschmitt Bf109E-3. Abandoned near Cologne-Butzweilerhof during air test; cause not stated. Pilot baled out unhurt. Aircraft a write-off.

3./StG51 Junkers Ju87B. Forced-landed at Cologne-Wahn with engine trouble. Crew unhurt. Aircraft damaged but repairable.

Thursday, February 22

LUFTWAFFE

3.(H)/14 Henschel Hs126. Forced-landed at Vallendar due to engine trouble. Crew unhurt. Aircraft damaged but repairable.

1.(H)/21 Junkers W34. Crashed on take-off at Primstal. No casualties reported. Aircraft a write-off.

1./JG1 Messerschmitt Bf109E. Crashed on landing at Krefeld. Uffz K. Hoppe injured. Aircraft damaged but repairable.

4./JG53 Messerschmitt Bf109E-1. Wrecked in collision with Do17 of KG2 landing at Mannheim-Sandhofen. No pilot casualty. Aircraft 8 + a write-off.

II./KG2 Dornier Do17Z. Collided with Bf109 of II./JG53 on landing at Mannheim-Sandhofen. Fw K. Raatz injured. Aircraft damaged but repairable.

A quiet moment for the pilots of No. 88 Squadron in their Mess — according to BBC reporter Charles Gardner 'one of the best in the AASF'. The squadron had its origins in the First World War and when it was reformed in 1937 it adopted the wriggling serpent insignia of Escadrille 88 of the French Air Service in WWI. The badge is framed on the wall with its motto, 'En garde'.

III./KG77 Dornier Do17Z. Crash-landed at Werl, cause not stated. Crew unhurt. Aircraft damaged but repairable.

Friday, February 23

BRITISH AIR FORCES IN FRANCE

87 SQUADRON Hurricane. Nosed over on take-off at Le Touquet due to soft ground. Pilot unhurt. Aircraft repairable.

FRENCH AIR FORCE

GAO 553 Mureaux 115 (89). Returned to base damaged by flak *(Flakabt. 2/851)* during photo-reconnaissance sortie over La Wantzenau at Helmingen 1.45 p.m. Asp. de Lavergne unhurt. S/Lt Melchior wounded, admitted to hospital in Haguenau. Aircraft damaged but repairable.

DUTCH AIR FORCE

V-2 Fokker G 1 (341). Run into trees and damaged in landing accident at Soesterberg due to iced field. 2e Lt J. van Riemsdijk believed unhurt. Aircraft damaged but repairable.

LUFTWAFFE

I./JG2 Messerschmitt Bf109E-3. Forced-landed at Trier-Euren due to ruptured oil pipe. Pilot unhurt. Aircraft damaged but repairable.

7./JG53 Messerschmitt Bf109E-3. Forced-landed at Trier-Euren due to technical fault. Lt H. Riegel unhurt. Aircraft damaged but repairable.

JGr.176 2 Messerschmitt Bf109D. Damaged in landing collision at Nellingen due to state of landing field. Pilots unhurt. Aircraft both damaged but repairable.

II./KG2 Dornier Do17Z. Involved in landing collision with two parked Ju52s at Ansbach. No crew casualties. Aircraft damaged but repairable.
The Junkers Ju52s of an unspecified KGzbV were also both damaged but repairable.

Stab KG55 Heinkel He111P. Crash-landed at Leipheim, cause not stated. No crew casualties. Aircraft damaged but repairable.

II./KG77 3 Dornier Do17Z. Damaged in separate landing accidents at Werl due to soft ground. No crew casualties. Aircraft all damaged but repairable.

Saturday, February 24

BRITISH AIR FORCES IN FRANCE

85 SQUADRON Hurricane P2551. Nosed over on take-off at Le Touquet due to soft ground. Pilot Officer D. V. G. Mawhood unhurt. Aircraft VY⊙H repairable.

226 SQUADRON Battle. Damaged on landing at Perpignan. Crew unhurt. Aircraft damaged but repairable.

FRENCH AIR FORCE

GR I/35 Potez 63.11 (02). Lost control while low-flying during transit flight from Reims to St Omer. Crashed and burned out at Ecques. Lt Schaufelberger, Sgt Aris, and Sgt Tomasi injured. Aircraft a write-off.

DUTCH AIR FORCE

Jachtvliegschool Texel Fw58B-2 (199). Crashed at De Vlijt during training flight. Kapt J. L. Zegers *(Commandant 3LvR)* unhurt. Aircraft damaged but repairable.

LUFTWAFFE

I./JG51 Messerschmitt Bf109E-3. Hit an obstacle after landing at Darmstadt-Griesheim. Pilot unhurt. Aircraft damaged but repairable.

Sunday, February 25

BRITISH AIR FORCES IN FRANCE

18 SQUADRON Blenheim I L1444. Damaged by AA fire during reconnaissance sortie over north-west Germany and crashed attempting forced-landing in Burrell's Fields, Gosberton Risegate, Donna Nook, near North Coates, 3.10 p.m. Pilot Officer J. A. E. Monette badly injured legs. Sergeant J. A. H. Potter died of injuries. LAC A. C. Whitehill suffered severe shock. Aircraft a write-off.

73 SQUADRON Hurricane L1587. Crashed on take-off at Rouvres due to burst tyre. Sergeant T. B. G. Pyne unhurt. Aircraft TP⊙E damaged but repairable.

Monday, February 26

FRENCH AIR FORCE

GAO 553 Mureaux 115 (23). Crashed on landing at Haguenau following reconnaissance sortie. Crew unhurt. Aircraft a write-off.

DUTCH AIR FORCE

Vliegschool Haamstede Koolhoven F.K.51. Overturned during training flight; exact cause not stated. No crew casualties. Aircraft damaged but repairable.

One of two Koolhoven F.K.51 trainers reported damaged at Haamstede in February 1940, plus four more damaged the previous month, for which no details survive.

LUFTWAFFE

II./KG1 Heinkel He111H-2. Damaged in landing accident at Erfurt-Bindersleben. Crew unhurt. Aircraft repairable.

III./KG76 Dornier Do17Z. Damaged in landing accident at Gotha. Crew unhurt. Aircraft damaged but repairable.

III./KG76 Dornier Do17Z. Belly-landed due to undercarriage failure on landing at Gotha. Crew unhurt. Aircraft damaged but repairable.

Tuesday, February 27

BRITISH AIR FORCES IN FRANCE

114 SQUADRON Blenheim IV L8838. Lost control while flying in cloud during cross-country exercise and abandoned over Acheux-en-Amienois. Crashed at Mailly-Maillet. Pilot Officer H. Dodgson killed. Sergeant Hawkins and AC1 Barrow baled out unhurt. Aircraft a write-off.

FRENCH AIR FORCE

GC 3/6 Morane 406 (172). Wrecked in unknown circumstances. Adjt A. Deniau unhurt. Aircraft a write-off.

LUFTWAFFE

I./ZG2 Messerschmitt BF110C-1. Crashed and burned out at Straubling following port engine fire. Two crew injured. Aircraft a write-off.

Wednesday, February 28

FRENCH AIR FORCE

2S3 Levasseur PL101 (62). Wrecked in flying accident at Deauville; exact cause not stated. No crew casualties. Aircraft 6 a write-off.

BELGIAN AIR FORCE

2/I/2 Hurricane (H.28). Badly damaged in landing accident at Schaffen. Lt Drossaert unhurt. Aircraft a write-off.

DUTCH AIR FORCE

Vliegschool Vlissingen Fokker S IV (106). Emergency landing during training flight, cause unknown. 1e Lt D. Schröder believed unhurt. Aircraft a write-off.

LUFTWAFFE

1.(H)/13 Henschel Hs126. Crashed at Göppingen due to engine failure during night flight. Two crew killed. Aircraft a write-off.

Thursday, February 29

BRITISH AIR FORCES IN FRANCE

88 SQUADRON Battle K9441. Forced-landed on the ranges at Moronvilliers engine damaged by splinters during low-level bombing practice 10.20 a.m. Crew unhurt. Aircraft damaged but repairable — abandoned at No. 21 Aircraft Depot, Château Bougon.

BELGIAN AIR FORCE

1/I/1 Fox. Crashed at Sint-Job-in-'t-Goor, cause unknown. S/Lt E. Bossiroy and Cpl Labeau both injured. Aircraft a write-off.

LUFTWAFFE

I./JG53 Messerschmitt Bf109E-3. Involved in landing accident at Darmstadt-Griesheim. Pilot unhurt. Aircraft damaged but repairable.

I./JG53 Messerschmitt Bf109E-1. Involved in landing accident at Darmstadt-Griesheim. Pilot unhurt. Aircraft repairable.

Transportstaffel 1./V Fl.Korps Junkers Ju52/3m. Undercarriage collapsed on landing at Munich-Riem. Crew unhurt. Aircraft repairable.

An undated photograph of rather jaded-looking aircrews of No. 226 Squadron, then based at Reims. No. 226 (Bomber) Squadron was another First World War unit disbanded in 1918 and re-established in March 1937 under the RAF Expansion Scheme. It was equipped with the Fairey Battle with which the squadron went to war in October that year. This particular machine (L5468) survived the fighting in France and was later transferred to the Royal Canadian Air Force in 1942. Coincidentally, in June that year No. 226 hosted the very first American crew on operations by the United States Army Air Force in Europe during an operation to bomb marshalling yards at Hazebrouck.

MARCH 1940

French troops inspect a Heinkel from 3. Staffel Fernauf-klärungsgruppe 121 which came down near Forbach (see page 147). This was the sixth victory for No. 1 Squadron. Two crewmen survived and set the aircraft alight before escaping across no man's land where they were met by a German patrol.

The decision to employ BAFF Fairey Battles on night leaflet-dropping sorties, and the mine-laying of enemy waterways, initiated an intensive night-flying training programme. This resulted in a spate of fatal accidents reflecting a lack of instrument-flying skills, though most Battle crews were inclined to the belief that their aircraft was not suitable for night operations and particularly at low level. The first such 'Nickel' operation was flown by Nos. 88 and 226 Squadrons during the night of March 18/19.

As Luftwaffe units assigned to Fliegerkorps X prepared for Operation 'Weserübung', the occupation of Denmark and invasion of Norway, an improvement in weather conditions saw an increase in fighter patrols, some in strength, which resulted in several violent clashes over the Western Front. On March 29, the first confirmed victory over the Luftwaffe's vaunted Messerschmitt Bf110 fighter was claimed by No. 1 Squadron. The pilots involved were invited to celebrate the occasion with dinner in Paris hosted by Air Marshal Barratt, their contemporaries in No. 73 Squadron having missed the prize three days before.

On the last day of the month, French Moranes of GC III/7 were caught at a disadvantage and badly mauled by German fighters over Morhange. A savage reminder of the seemingly constant presence of predatory German fighters over the frontier.

A la pieuse et chère mémoire
de
XAVIER HENRARD
Sous-Lieutenant aviateur
Mort en plein ciel pour la Patrie
le 2 mars 1940
à l'âge de 25 ans
« Le Roi a daigné décerner au Lieutenant Xavier Henrard, tombé glorieusement en combat aérien, la croix de chevalier de l'ordre de Léopold. »

March 1940 began with the death of the first Belgian aviator. Although the country was still neutral, a Hurricane piloted by Sous Lieutenant Xavier Henrard was brought down at Hemroulle near Bastogne by the gunner of a Dornier 17.

Friday, March 1

BRITISH AIR FORCES IN FRANCE

218 SQUADRON Battle K9252. Crashed at Avot, 40 miles north of Dijon, during cross-country navigation exercise in bad weather. Flying Officer E. V. Hulbert broken ankle. Sergeant F. Dewar and AC1 R. F. J. Wiltshire killed. Aircraft a write-off — abandoned at No. 3 Salvage Section, Rosières.

LUFTWAFFE

I./JG53 Messerschmitt Bf109E-1. Damaged in take-off accident at Darmstadt-Griesheim. Pilot unhurt. Aircraft damaged but repairable.

8./JG53 Messerschmitt Bf109E-1. Wrecked in forced-landing at Hoppstädten following engine failure. Pilot unhurt. Aircraft a write-off.

I./KG76 Dornier Do17Z. Run out of fuel during night flight and abandoned over Gremsdorf, near Hoechstadt. Crew baled out, one injured. Aircraft a write-off.

III./KG76 Dornier Do17Z. Lost bearings when radio navigation system failed. Crashed and burned out at Karenthal, near Saalfeld. Oberlt H. G. Reisz and three crew killed. Aircraft a write-off.

III./ZG26 Messerschmitt Bf110C-2. Overturned landing on soft ground at Detmold. One of crew injured. Aircraft a write-off.

Saturday, March 2

BRITISH AIR FORCES IN FRANCE

1 SQUADRON Hurricane L1974. Propeller disintegrated during pursuit of Do17P of 4.(F)/11 over Metz and made dead-stick belly-landing at Nancy 11.15 a.m. Flying Officer M. H. Brown unhurt. Aircraft repairable.

1 SQUADRON Hurricane L1671. Engine damaged by return fire from Do17P of 4.(F)/11 engaged over Metz and crashed attempting forced-landing at Fénétrange, south of Sarre-Union, 12.00 p.m. Pilot Officer J. S. Mitchell killed. Aircraft a write-off.

73 SQUADRON Hurricane L1808. Shot down by Bf109s during pursuit of He111s over Saarbrücken. Possibly that claimed by Hptmn Mölders (Gruppenkommandeur) of Stab III./JG53 south of Bitche 12.15 p.m. Crash-landed outside Metz airfield. Flying Officer E. J. Kain unhurt. Aircraft damaged but repairable

73 SQUADRON Hurricane L1958. Engine badly damaged in attack by Bf109s of III./JG53 during pursuit of He111s over Saarbrücken. Possibly that claimed by Uffz Neuhoff of 7./JG53 south-east of Diedenhofen 12.20 p.m. Crashed attempting dead-stick landing near Brulange. Sergeant D. A. Sewell unhurt. Aircraft damaged but repairable.

73 SQUADRON Hurricane. Nosed-over forced-landing on soft ground at Noisseville following engine failure 12.15 p.m. Pilot Officer C. M. Wright admitted to hospital in Peltre badly injured. Aircraft damaged but repairable.

73 SQUADRON Hurricane. Forced-landed near Abaucourt, cause not stated. Pilot Officer A. B. Tucker unhurt. Aircraft repairable.

85 SQUADRON Hurricane P2563. Belly-landed at Lille-Seclin following engine failure during aerobatics practice 11.50 a.m. Flying Officer K. H. Blair unhurt. Aircraft VY⊙B a write-off.

103 SQUADRON Battle L5236. Hit a tree during forced-landing at Chandron, near Amboise, having lost bearings and run low on fuel during night cross-country exercise 3.00 a.m. Flying Officer A. J. Carver broken ankle, LAC Madkins broken wrist, and Sergeant Lloyd fractured skull; all admitted to hospital in Tours-sur-Loire. Aircraft a write-off.

Henrard was buried in the local cemetery of Sint Pieters Woluwe.

114 SQUADRON Blenheim IV N6157. Disorientated and lost control during night training exercise; abandoned by crew and crashed near Auxerre. Pilot Officer R. W. Farrow baled out but hit propeller and killed. Sergeant Wallis baled out unhurt. AC2 A. W. B. Sanders remained in the aircraft and killed. Aircraft a write-off.

Dates of death of Robert Farrow and Arthur Sanders both recorded as March 3 by the CWGC.

FRENCH AIR FORCE

GAO 544 Mureaux 115 (66). Landed at Bécourt damaged in attack by Uffz Reckers of 8./JG53 south-east of Diedenhofen during reconnaissance sortie over the German frontier 12.02 p.m. Sgt Foriel and crewman unhurt. Aircraft repairable.

GC 5/3 Morane 406. Badly damaged in combat with Bf109s during escort sortie for GAO 544 between Zweibrücken and Saarbrücken. Possibly that attacked by Oberlt Wilcke *(Staffelkapitän)* of 7./JG53 south of Bische 12.10 p.m. Forced-landed near Grostenquin. Sgt J. Ribo badly wounded in chest, died same evening in hospital at Morhange. Aircraft damaged but repairable.

BELGIAN AIR FORCE

1/I/1 Fox (O.12). Crashed following a collision over Ranst, east of Antwerp-Deurne. Lt E. Pigault de Beaupré killed. Aircraft a write-off.

1/I/1 Fox (O.30). Crashed following a collision over Ranst, east of Antwerp-Deurne. Pilot unhurt. Aircraft a write-off.

2/I/2 Hurricane (H.26). Shot down by Do17 of 1.(F)/22 intercepted over St Hubert. Crashed at Hemroulle, north of Bastogne. S/Lt X. Henrard killed. Aircraft a write-off.

Xavier Henrard was the first Belgian airman killed due to hostile action during WWII.

2/I/2 Hurricane (H.33). Hit by return fire from Do 17 of 1.(F)/22 intercepted over St Hubert and forced-landed at Achêne, near Ciney. Sgt E. Lieutenant unhurt. Aircraft repairable.

2/I/2 Hurricane (H.35). Returned damaged by Do 17 of 1.(F)/22 intercepted over St Hubert. Sgt Lelièvre unhurt. Aircraft repairable.

2/I/2 Hurricane (H.39). Ground-looped when port undercarriage collapsed in forced-landing at Bierset. Capt A. E. A. van den Hove d'Ertsenrijck injured. Aircraft a write-off.

Albert Émmanuel Alix van den Hove d'Ertsenrijck was another Belgian pilot who later flew Hurricanes with Nos. 501 and 43 Squadrons during the Battle of Britain until his death on September 15, 1940. Exhumed and repatriated to the Pelouse d'Honneur Cemetery at Brussels-Evere on October 20, 1949.

7/III/3 Fox (O.181). Crashed in southern outskirts of Brussels at Uccle-Calevoet during low-level aerobatics. Sgt J-P. Dejardin killed. Aircraft a write-off.

LUFTWAFFE

4.(F)/11 Dornier Do17P. Shot down by P/O Mitchell and Sgt Soper of No. 1 Sqdn and crashed at La Petite-Pierre 11.05 a.m. Oberlt A-J. Leupelt and Fw K. Lajczyk captured badly wounded. Fw H. Bür unhurt. Aircraft a write-off.

1.(F)/22 Dornier Do17P. Engaged by S/Lt Martin and Adjt Le Gloan of GC III/6 during photo-reconnaissance sortie between Achen and Wingen 10.30 a.m. Shot down in flames at Ferme Sainte-Marie, south-east of Bouzonville. Lt K-W. Barchfeld, Fw W. Will, and Obergefr F. Jabubeck captured. Aircraft a write-off.

1.(F)/22 Dornier Do17P. First intercepted near Puzieux by Adjt Gras, Adjt de Montgolfier, and Sgt Janoba of GC II/5 but escaped west of Völklingen. Later engaged over St Hubert by three Belgian Hurricanes of 2/I/2 and crippled all three with return fire, returning to base slightly damaged. One crewman wounded. Aircraft repairable.

4.(F)/121 Dornier Do17P. Intercepted by Sgt Doudies and Sgt Sonntag of GC II/7 over reconnaissance between Remiremont and Montbéliard. Shot down at Harol, west of Épinal 8.34 a.m. Uffz K-H. Jagielki and Uffz A. Matheus killed. Gefr K. Reschke baled out and captured wounded. Aircraft a write-off.

II./JG51 Messerschmitt Bf109E-1. Crashed on take-off from Böblingen. Pilot unhurt. Aircraft damaged but repairable.

II./KG1 Heinkel He111H-2. Crash-landed at Kirtorf, cause not stated. Crew unhurt. Aircraft damaged but repairable.

III./KG2 Dornier Do17Z. Taxied into a ditch after landing at Illesheim. Crew unhurt. Aircraft damaged but repairable.

III./KG76 Dornier Do17Z. Damaged in landing accident at Nidda. Crew unhurt. Aircraft damaged but repairable.

7.(F)/LG2 Dornier Do17P. Forced-landed at Münster-Handorf due to unrecorded engine trouble. Two crew injured. Aircraft a write-off.

III./ZG26 Messerschmitt Bf110C. Abandoned near Lippspringe due to engine fire. Pilot baled out unhurt, gunner killed. Aircraft a write-off.

In some cases a pilot was lucky and he could walk away from a crash but not so with this machine flown by Lieutenant Pigault de Beaupré. Here members of his squadron inspect the remains of the Fairey Fox in which he died on March 2. The 'Mouettes', 1e escadrille of Groupe I of Air Regiment 1, were based at Antwerp-Deurne and equipped with the Kestrel-engined Fairey Fox IIIC. The 'C' suffix indicated 'combat', this type being designed as a light bomber though its primary role in service remained reconnaissance and army co-operation. When the German offensive opened on May 10, 'the Seagulls' moved to their war station at Hingene where they remained until May 15 when ordered to Belsele-Waas. Two days later 1/I/1 was withdrawn to Ursel where they stayed until May 23 before leaving for Steene-Ostend where they continued operating until the Belgian capitulation.

FRENCH AIR FORCE

GC II/3 Morane 406. Belly-landed at Toul damaged in attack by Bf109s east of Metz . Possibly that claimed by Hptmn Mölders of Stab III./JG53 south-east of Diedenhofen 1.55 p.m. Cpl K. Korber wounded. Aircraft damaged but repairable.

LUFTWAFFE

2.(F)/22 Dornier Do17P. Hit a tree during emergency landing on one engine at Geldersheim following high-altitude navigation training flight. Fw W. Drebber and Gefr R. Dickfeld killed, Lt Noeliecke injured. Aircraft a write-off.

Two more aircraft from the Belgian Air Force came a cropper on March 2. *Above:* This is Sergeant Edmond Lieutenant's Hurricane which forced-landed at Achêne and *(below)* Capitaine Albert van den Hove d'Ertsenrijck's machine at Bierset.

Sunday, March 3

BRITISH AIR FORCES IN FRANCE

142 SQUADRON Battle L5240. Believed wrecked in taxying accident when hit a dung heap after landing from night flight. Crew unhurt. Aircraft a write-off.

150 SQUADRON Battle L4948. Overshot runway landing at Perpignan during night-flying practice. Crew unhurt. Aircraft damaged but repairable — later abandoned at No. 21 Aircraft Depot, Château Bougon.

Flying Officer Brown and Sergeant Soper of No. 1 Squadron hammered this Heinkel of 3.(F)/121, forcing it to belly-land south of Forbach at midday on March 3. Two of the crew were killed and another wounded. The wreck was set alight by the surviving crewman. Paul Richey's description of the action is interesting although not strictly accurate: 'The following day, the 3rd, came our sixth victory. Hilly and Sgt S—— were again concerned.

Between Nancy and Metz they sighted a He111K at about 24,000 feet. Hilly climbed beside and at some distance from it, but S—— tried to attack from underneath and spun. Hilly eventually got above it and attacked by diving from astern. Soon S—— was back again, and between them they set fire to both engines and saw the Heinkel forced-land between the French and German lines. Two men got out of it and ran for the German side.'

March 6 saw two more Belgian losses. This is the Renard which force-landed on the beach at Klemskerke.

3.(F)/121 Heinkel He111H. Both engines damaged in attacks by F/O Brown and Sgt Soper of No. 1 Squadron during reconnaissance sortie south and west of Metz. Belly-landed south of Forbach 12.00 p.m. Pilot unhurt. Obergefr A. Peter and Uffz G. Hedtke killed. Uffz F. Nagel wounded in left thigh, admitted to hospital in Salzbach. Aircraft a write-off.

I./JG1 Messerschmitt Bf109E-1. Crashlanded at Frechen due to engine failure. Pilot unhurt. Aircraft damaged but repairable.

1./JG2 Messerschmitt Bf109E-1. Damaged at Ippesheim when engine failed on landing. Pilot unhurt. Aircraft repairable.

I./JG3 Messerschmitt Bf109D. Crash-landed at Jever with engine seized. Pilot unhurt. Aircraft damaged but repairable.

I./JG20 Messerschmitt Bf109E. Abandoned near Wesel following mid-air collision with Bf110. Pilot baled out unhurt. Aircraft a write-off.
Employed in the defence of central Germany, this unit transferred to Bönninghardt on February 21 for defence of the frontier with Belgium and Holland. The Bf110, of an unreported unit, landed safely.

I./JG51 Messerschmitt Bf109E-1. Crash-landed at Mannheim-Sandhofen, cause not stated. Pilot unhurt. Aircraft repairable.

I./JG52 Messerschmitt Bf109E-3. Crash-landed at Lachen-Speyerdorf due to loss of control. Pilot unhurt. Aircraft damaged but repairable.

I./JG53 Messerschmitt Bf109E-1. Damaged in landing accident at Darmstadt-Griesheim. Pilot unhurt. Aircraft damaged but repairable.

II./JG53 Messerschmitt Bf109E-1. Rammed by another Bf109 landing at Wiesbaden-Erbenheim. No pilot casualty. Aircraft damaged but repairable.

I./JG76 Messerschmitt Bf109E-1. Crashed near Rüsselsheim following mid-air collision during combat practice. Gefr E. Engelbach killed. Aircraft a write-off.

I./JG76 Messerschmitt Bf109E. Slightly damaged in mid-air collision near Rüsselsheim; returned safely to base. Pilot unhurt. Aircraft repairable.

1./KG53 Heinkel He111H. Crashed in emergency landing at Frankfurt/Rhein-Main following engine failure. Crew unhurt. Aircraft damaged but repairable.

Monday, March 4

BRITISH AIR FORCES IN FRANCE

53 SQUADRON Blenheim IV L9190. Undercarriage raised in error after night landing at Poix. No crew casualties. Aircraft damaged but repairable — later abandoned at Château Bougon.

FRENCH AIR FORCE

ECN 1/13 Potez 540. Crashed near Meaux following night-flying exercise, cause unknown. Lt L. Audebaud badly injured and dead on arrival at hospital. Sgt Giloux suffered a broken leg. Aircraft a write-off.

GR I/133 Potez 63.11 (178). Crashed on landing at Verdun due to mechanical failure on return from photo-reconnaissance sortie. Crew unhurt. Aircraft a write-off.

DUTCH AIR FORCE

III-2 Koolhoven F.K.51 (417). Damaged at Gilze-Rijn, exact cause unknown. Pilot believed unhurt. Aircraft damaged but repairable.

Vliegschool Vlissingen Fokker S IV (120). Lost in fog and abandoned over Wester-schelde during training flight p.m. Korp. B. A. A. van Berkum jumped at 75 feet without a parachute and picked up unhurt by Greek steamer *Corinthiacos.* Aircraft lost.

LUFTWAFFE

I./JG51 Messerschmitt Bf109E-1. Crashed in a steep turn shortly after take-off from Mannheim-Sandhofen. Pilot killed. Aircraft a write-off.

Major Marcel Marchal and Capitaine Kurt Foerster were killed when their Fox nose-dived into the ground at Mamolle-Remicourt.

II./JG53 Messerschmitt Bf109E-1. Belly-landed near Blumental following engine failure. Pilot unhurt. Aircraft damaged but repairable.

I./JG76 Messerschmitt Bf109E-1. Slightly damaged in landing accident at Rhein-Main airfield, Frankfurt. Pilot unhurt. Aircraft repairable.

2./KG2 Dornier Do17Z. Port undercarriage collapsed on landing at Ansbach. Crew unhurt. Aircraft damaged but repairable.

Tuesday, March 5

BELGIAN AIR FORCE

1/I/1 Fox. Crash-landed at Gosselies, cause unknown. S/Lt P. J. Remy and Adjt Genin both injured. Aircraft damaged but repairable.

LUFTWAFFE

Flugbereitschaft Luftflotte 2 Focke-Wulf Fw58. Forced-landed at Ostbevern, northeast of Münster, due to engine failure, probably caused by dirty fuel. Crew unhurt. Aircraft damaged but repairable.

II.(S)/LG2 Henschel Hs123. Wrecked in forced-landing at Pulsheim due to petrol failure. One crewman injured. Aircraft a write-off.

Wednesday, March 6

BRITISH AIR FORCES IN FRANCE

13 SQUADRON Lysander L4766. Wrecked in forced-landing at Amy-Martin-Rieux during familiarisation flight. Pilot Officer True unhurt. Aircraft a write-off.

13 SQUADRON Lysander. Forced-landed 40 miles south-west of Rouen during familiarisation flight. Pilot Officer McCassey unhurt. Aircraft repairable.

85 SQUADRON Hurricane L1978. Suffered engine failure on take-off and crashed attempting down-wind landing at Mons-en-Chaussée during affiliation exercise with Lysanders 9.45 a.m. Sergeant S. W. Lenton killed. Aircraft VY⊙X a write-off.

BELGIAN AIR FORCE

11/VI/1 Renard R-31(N.31). Forced-landed on the beach at Klemskerke, and later swamped by incoming tide. Sgt E. Witmeur unhurt. Aircraft a write-off.

I/3 Fox (O.305). Nose-dived into the ground at Mamolle-Remicourt, cause unknown. Maj. M. L. Marchal and Capt K. A. Foerster killed. Aircraft a write-off.

Thursday, March 7

BRITISH AIR FORCES IN FRANCE

2 SQUADRON Lysander II P1722. Hit high-tension cables in low-flying practice and forced-landed at Graval 10.30 a.m. Pilot Officer G. Grant-Govan and observer unhurt. Aircraft damaged but repairable.

73 SQUADRON Hurricane. Damaged in heavy landing at Rouvres after familiarisation flight. Pilot Officer L. G. Bishop unhurt. Aircraft damaged but repairable.

DUTCH AIR FORCE

Jachtvliegschool Texel Fw 58B-2 (109). Belly-landed outside the airfield, cause not stated. Kapt J. L. Zegers *(Commandant 3LvR)* unhurt. Aircraft damaged but repairable.

LUFTWAFFE

2.(H)/31 Henschel Hs126. Crashed and burned out shortly after night take-off at Rotenburg. Uffz Berggräfe and Uffz Kallvuss both killed. Aircraft a write-off.

1.(F)/121 Heinkel He111H. Collided with He111 of Stab KG27 after landing at Münster-Handorf. No crew casualties. Aircraft damaged but repairable.

1./JG77 Messerschmitt Bf109E-1 (2521). Damaged in landing accident at Bonn-Hangelar due to undercarriage failure. Fw K. Schmid unhurt. Aircraft 2+ repairable.

I./JG77 Messerschmitt Bf109E-1 (2288). Belly-landed 6 km south of Siegburg following engine failure. Lt H. Schüller unhurt. Aircraft damaged but repairable.

Stab KG27 Heinkel He111H. Slightly damaged in collision with He111 of 1.(F)/121 landing at Münster-Handorf. No crew casualties. Aircraft repairable.

III./KG27 Heinkel He111P. Crashed and burned out at Kohlstädt during instrument flying. Four crew killed. Aircraft a write-off.

II./KG77 Dornier Do17Z. Damaged when crewman walked into revolving propeller at Düsseldorf. One crewman killed. Aircraft repairable.

Friday, March 8

DUTCH AIR FORCE

Vliegschool Vlissingen Fokker S IV. Forced-landed at Knokke during training flight, cause not stated. No casualties. Aircraft repairable.

Two more Fokker S IVs and a S IX were reported damaged in training accidents at Vlissingen during March 1940 but no details have been traced. Also, two Koolhoven F.K.51 trainers were reported damaged at Vliegschool Haamstede.

LUFTWAFFE

1.(H)/41 Henschel Hs126. Forced-landed at Bommerholz, near Witten, due to engine failure. Crew unhurt. Aircraft a write-off.

I./JG26 Messerschmitt Bf109E-3. Crashed on landing at Bönninghardt. Pilot injured. Aircraft damaged but repairable.

III./KG2 Dornier Do17E. Involved in taxying accident at Illesheim airfield. No crew casualties. Aircraft damaged but repairable.

Saturday, March 9

BRITISH AIR FORCES IN FRANCE

4 SQUADRON Lysander II L6852. Crashed on landing at Lille-Ronchin 9.45 a.m. Pilot Officer W. B. Adamson killed. LAC Satchell unhurt. Aircraft a write-off.

FRENCH AIR FORCE

CIC Morane 406. Crashed at Étampes during training flight, cause not stated. SM Monneyron killed. Aircraft a write-off.
Fighter training establishment (Cours Instruction de Chasse) of the l'Aéronautique Navale.

GC III/1 Morane 406. Forced-landed at Metz damaged following attack by Bf109s during escort sortie for photo-reconnaissance mission over Saarbrücken. Believed that claimed by Fw Jaenisch of 3./JG2 east of Diedenhofen 4.06 p.m. Adjt Guingo wounded in arm. Aircraft damaged but repairable.

GC II/6 Morane 406 (79). Wrecked in take-off accident at Anglure-Vouarces. Sgt Puget unhurt. Aircraft a write-off.

LUFTWAFFE

1.(H)/14 Henschel Hs126. Crashed at Kassel-Rothwesten, cause not stated. Oberlt H. Wokulat and Fw Kilimann both killed. Aircraft a write-off.

1./JG2 Messerschmitt Bf109E-3. Crash-landed at Wiesbaden-Erbenheim due to mechanical failure. Pilot unhurt. Aircraft damaged but repairable.

I./JG53 Messerschmitt Bf109E-1. Crash-landed at Darmstadt-Griesheim, cause not stated. Pilot unhurt. Aircraft damaged but repairable.

5./KG27 Heinkel He111P. Crashed and burned out north of Halen, near Osnabrück, shortly after take-off from Achmer. Lt J. Otto, Fw P. Nabinger, Fw Scholven, and Uffz Henrich killed. Aircraft 1G+LP a write-off.

II./KG54 Heinkel He111P-2. Taxied off runway at Celle-Wietzenbruch in snow storm. Crew unhurt. Aircraft damaged but repairable.

I./ZG52 Messerschmitt Bf110C. Forced-landed near Leipheim due to engine trouble. Crew unhurt. Aircraft repairable.

Monday, March 11

FRENCH AIR FORCE

GC I/6 Morane 406 (860). Suffered engine fire during patrol and finally abandoned while attempting a forced-landing. Crashed and burned out at Chissey, south-west of Dijon. Lt S. Janouch baled out under 200ft landing unhurt. Aircraft a write-off.

GR I/22 Potez 63.11 (22). Engaged in high-level photo-reconnaissance sortie over Metz and damaged in attack by Oberlt Wilcke *(Staffelkapitän)* of 7./JG53 north-east of Sierck 5.45 p.m. Crashed on landing at Metz-Frescaty. Lt Meitret wounded. Lt Parmentier and Cpl Hilt unhurt. Aircraft a write-off.

BELGIAN AIR FORCE

1/I/2 Gladiator (G.21). Crashed at Steene-Ostend airfield, cause unknown. Sgt Pipart killed. Aircraft a write-off.

LUFTWAFFE

I./JG21 Messerschmitt Bf109E. Lost control and crashed on landing at Mönchengladbach. Pilot unhurt. Aircraft damaged but repairable.

I./JG76 Messerschmitt Bf109E-1. Lost control and crashed during emergency take-off from Frankfurt/Rhein-Main. Pilot unhurt. Aircraft repairable.

Tuesday, March 12

BRITISH AIR FORCES IN FRANCE

73 SQUADRON Hurricane N2364. Dived vertically from 25,000 feet and crashed 2 km east of St-Privat-la-Montaigne, north-west of Metz; probably victim of oxygen failure 1.50 p.m. Pilot Officer L. G. Bishop killed. Aircraft a write-off.

73 SQUADRON Hurricane L1962. Crashed near Metz, cause not stated. Pilot believed unhurt. Aircraft a write-off.

BELGIAN AIR FORCE

2/I/2 Hurricane. Hit by return fire from Do 17 intercepted over Marche and damaged on landing at St Omer for fuel. Sgt van Strydonck unhurt. Aircraft damaged but repairable.

2/I/2 2 Hurricanes. Hit by return fire from Do17 intercepted over Marche and landed at St Omer to refuel. Capt Charlier and S/Lt de Hemricourt de Grune unhurt. Aircraft both repairable, returned to Schaffen.

DUTCH AIR FORCE

Jachtvliegschool Texel Fw 58B-2 (198). Lost bearings soon after take-off and landed on a sandbank in the Waddenzee during ferry flight from Texel to De Kooy 11.55 p.m. Kapt J. L. Zegers *(Commandant 3LvR)*, Adjt D. H. Lambermont, and H. W. van Dommelen unhurt, rescued next morning. Aircraft abandoned.

LUFTWAFFE

4.(H)/12 Henschel Hs126. Flew into power lines, crashed and burned out at Esch, near Cologne, while low-flying during army co-operation exercise. Pilot killed, Oberlt Lattke injured. Aircraft a write-off.

1.(F)/121 Heinkel He111H. Crashed into a mountain at Lämershagen, near Bielefeld. Oberlt F. Kohnke, Fw F. Grossmann, Uffz G. Kahlert, and Flgr H. Melzer killed. Aircraft a write-off.

I./JG3 Messerschmitt Bf109E-1. Hit by cross-wind and overturned on take-off from Bonn-Hangelar. Uffz Hering unhurt. Aircraft repairable.

I./JG51 Messerschmitt Bf109E-1. Belly-landed at Mannheim-Sandhofen due to engine failure. Pilot unhurt. Aircraft repairable.

III./JG53 Messerschmitt Bf109E-3. Damaged in take-off collision at Wiesbaden-Erbenheim. Pilot unhurt. Aircraft damaged but repairable.

III./JG53 Messerschmitt Bf109E-1. Crash-landed at Wiesbaden-Erbenheim; possibly result of collision on take-off. Pilot unhurt. Aircraft repairable.

V.(Z)/LG1 Messerschmitt Bf110C. Wrecked in crash-landing at Schliessheim following mid-air fire. Crew unhurt. Aircraft a write-off.

Wednesday, March 13

FRENCH AIR FORCE

GAO 548 Potez 63.11. Reported lost near Kehl on observation sortie, circumstances unknown. Lt J. Roussel slightly wounded; rest of crew unhurt. Aircraft a write-off.

LUFTWAFFE

I./KG27 Heinkel He111P. Reported damaged at Braunschweig, cause unknown. Crew believed unhurt. Aircraft damage state not recorded.

DAILY SKETCH, THURSDAY, MARCH 14, 1940.—Page 13

Sky 'Larks' Made Them Airmen

'Amateurs' Who Trained In Their Spare Time Now Fly In France

On March 14, the Press made a big splash on the pilots of the Auxiliary Air Force — the body of spare time airmen who spent their weekends learning to fly with the RAF. This composite montage shows pilots of No. 607 Squadron which went to France in November 1939 based at Vitry-en-Artois with Gladiators. At the time the censor prevented their names or the squadron appearing in print but featured are Johnny Sample, Peter Parrott and Willie Gore. The Auxiliary Air Force was first brought into being in 1924, the first four squadrons being formed the following year. Recruitment was by the County Territorial Army and Air Force Associations with members being drawn from the local district, hence the initial four squadrons were Nos. 600 (City of London), 601 (County of London), 602 (City of Glasgow) and 603 (City of Edinburgh). By September 1939 there were 20 Flying and 44 Balloon squadrons in existence. The weekend airmen attended a fortnight's camp once a year for intensive training. Before the war, officers were required to serve for a minimum period of five years on the active list, to be followed by a similar period on the Air Force Auxiliary Reserve. The AAF uniform was identical to that of the RAF with the exception that an 'A' badge was worn by officers on the collar of the jacket and on the shoulder straps of the greatcoat. Airmen wore the 'A' badge on the sleeve of their jackets and greatcoats immediately below the eagle insignia.

Thursday, March 14

BRITISH AIR FORCES IN FRANCE

139 SQUADRON Blenheim IV P4926. Crashed into the sea off Argelès-sur-Mer during training flight 8.20 a.m. Sergeant N. J. Price and Sergeant R. J. Stanley killed. LAC R. Brown slightly injured. Aircraft a write-off.

LUFTWAFFE

III./KG1 Heinkel He111. Damaged in forced-landing near Esperstädt one engine overheating. Crew unhurt. Aircraft damaged but repairable.

10./Ln.Regt.3 Junkers Ju52 and Junkers Ju86. Aircraft damaged in high winds while picketed at Munich-Oberwiesenfeld. No casualties. Aircraft both repairable.

Reserve Ob.d.L 12 Heinkel He111H. Aircraft picketed at Regensburg slightly damaged by strong winds. Aircraft all repairable.
Aircraft nominally on the strength of II./KG28 which was reformed from elements of KG27 on December 15 before moving to Kassel-Rothwesten in February.

II./KG76 Junkers Ju52. Parked aircraft damaged in storm at Wiener-Neustadt. No casualties. Aircraft repairable.
A Junkers W34 of III./KG54 and a Focke-Wulf Fw58 of Kurierstaffel 2 were also damaged.

Friday, March 15

BRITISH AIR FORCES IN FRANCE

57 SQUADRON Blenheim IV L9249. Failed to return from night reconnaissance sortie and possibly victim of Allied AA fire. Crashed near Orny, south-east of Metz, 11.45 p.m. Flying Officer W. W. Adam and AC1 F. J. Mantle killed. Sergeant G. Park baled out and slightly injured. Aircraft a write-off.

212 SQUADRON Spitfire I (PR) N3117. Damaged in landing accident on return to Lille-Seclin following photo-reconnaissance sortie over Oosterhout, north of Roosendaal. Flying Officer C. Milne unhurt. Aircraft damaged but repairable.

Flight Lieutenant William Blackadder, the OC of 'A' Flight, sent us the photo *(below)* of No. 607's Gladiators, the City of Durham squadron not being re-equipped with Hurricanes until April 1940.

One of two specially modified Spitfires I (Type B) operating in France under conditions of strict secrecy. Unarmed, but equipped with two F24 cameras in the wings and an extra 29-gallon fuel tank in the rear fuselage, they would photograph 5,000 square miles of enemy territory prior to the collapse of France.

FRENCH AIR FORCE

DIAP (CWL) Caudron C714 (8548). Damaged in landing accident at Lyon-Bron after oxygen cylinder exploded during training flight. S/Lt W. Lanowski unhurt. Aircraft I-206 damaged but repairable.
This unit of Polish volunteers, still in training, was formed to fly in support of the Finns. But with an armistice between the Soviet Union and Finland effective from March 13, it was ultimately deployed as Groupe de Chasse Polonais de Varsovie No. 145, or Polish Fighter Squadron 'Warsaw' GC 1/145. Caudron C714 (8546) I-204 also forced-landed during this training period but on a date unknown.

DUTCH AIR FORCE

3-V-2 Douglas DB-8A (386). High-speed stall during mock attacks on AA positions and spun into the ground at Ypenburg from 500 feet and burst into flames. 1e Lt H. F. J. M. Plasmans and Sgt G. Nijhuis both killed. Aircraft a write-off.

LUFTWAFFE

I./JG53 Messerschmitt Bf109E-3. Damaged in aborted take-off at Darmstadt-Griesheim. Pilot unhurt. Aircraft damaged but repairable.

Stab KG1 Heinkel He111H. Crash-landed at Giessen with engine trouble. Crew unhurt. Aircraft damaged bur repairable.

II./StG2 Junkers Ju87B-1. Crash-landed at Göttingen, cause not stated. Crew unhurt. Aircraft damaged but repairable.

I./ZG2 Messerschmitt Bf110C. Crashed following mid-air collision during combat training near Darmstadt-Griesheim. Two crew killed. Aircraft a write-off.

I./ZG2 Messerschmitt Bf110C. Abandoned following mid-air collision during combat training over Darmstadt-Griesheim. One crewman killed, another baled out unhurt. Aircraft a write-off.

Saturday, March 16

FRENCH AIR FORCE

GR I/52 Potez 637 (45). Hit by AA fire during photo-reconnaissance of airfields near Coblence 5.40 a.m. and pilot wounded. Observer took control and forced-landed at Nancy-Essey. Lt Layec wounded by shrapnel in leg and hand. Lt-Col. de Vitrolles *(Groupe Commandant)* and Sgt Raguant unhurt. Aircraft damaged but repairable.

LUFTWAFFE

I./JG3 Messerschmitt Bf109E. Hit an obstacle on landing at Bonn-Hangelar. Uffz Hering unhurt. Aircraft a write-off.

I./JG77 Messerschmitt Bf109E-1. Belly-landed at Bonn-Hangelar, cause not stated. Pilot unhurt. Aircraft repairable.

I./JG77 Messerschmitt Bf109D-1. Damaged in landing accident at Bonn-Hangelar. Pilot unhurt. Aircraft repairable.

Sunday, March 17

LUFTWAFFE

1./JG2 Messerschmitt Bf109E-3. Crashed on landing at Frankfurt-Rebstock. Pilot unhurt. Aircraft damaged but repairable.

Monday, March 18

BRITISH AIR FORCES IN FRANCE

59 SQUADRON Blenheim IV N6179. Wrecked attempting forced-landing at Querenaing, cause not stated. Pilot Officer R. N. Chudleigh and crew unhurt. Aircraft a write-off.

DUTCH AIR FORCE

V-2 Fokker D XVII (209). Slightly damaged; circumstances unknown. 1e Lt P. T. Bierema unhurt. Aircraft damaged but repairable.

Tuesday, March 19

LUFTWAFFE

4.(F)/14 Dornier Do17P. Run into boundary fence landing with high tail wind at Loddenheide. Crew unhurt. Aircraft damaged but repairable.

II./JG53 Messerschmitt Bf109E-1. Overturned on landing at Mannheim-Sandhofen. Pilot unhurt. Aircraft repairable.

I./KG1 Heinkel He111H-2. Crash-landed at Erfurt-Bindersleben, cause not stated. Crew unhurt. Aircraft damaged but repairable.

III./KG54 Heinkel He111P-2. Lost bearings and belly-landed near Celle in deteriorating weather conditions. Crew unhurt. Aircraft damaged but repairable.

Wednesday, March 20

LUFTWAFFE

I./JG51 Messerschmitt Bf109E-1. Wrecked in crash-landing at Mannheim-Sandhofen following engine failure. Pilot injured. Aircraft a write-off.

3./KüFlGr 806 Heinkel He111J. Engine damaged by AA fire during attack on fishing vessels and ditched off the Dutch coast northwest of the Waddeneilanden 4.50 p.m. Lt zur See H. Obermann, Oberfw A. Hubrich, Fw H. Kasch, and Uffz R. Mehnert rescued from dinghy by motor-cutter *Vier Gebroeders*, landed at IJmuiden next day. Aircraft M7+LE a write-off.
This crew was deemed 'ship-wrecked mariners' and later repatriated to Germany in accordance with international conventions.

3./KGrzbV.9 Junkers Ju52/3m. Hit another aircraft due to engine failure on take-off at Lippspringe. Crew unhurt. Aircraft damaged but repairable.

3./KGrzbV. 9 Junkers Ju52/3m. Damaged by another aircraft in take-off accident at Lippspringe. No crew casualties. Aircraft repairable.

Thursday, March 21

BRITISH AIR FORCES IN FRANCE

18 SQUADRON Blenheim I L1427. Lost bearings in fog and crashed on the South Downs between Mile Oak Farm and Fulking, outside Chichester, during transit flight from Rosières to Kemble via Tangmere 9.00 a.m. Pilot Officer H. S. P. Hulton and Sergeant O. W. Dumbreck killed. LAC I. B. Oultram slight burns and Corporal G. E. Lapwood (Fitter) badly injured. Aircraft a write-off.
Gerald Winter, who clambered into the burning wreckage and released the gunner, LAC Oultram, was later awarded the Empire Gallantry Medal, later exchanged for the George Medal.

FRENCH AIR FORCE

GR I/35 Potez 63.11 (255). Crashed at Barly, 10 km north-west of Doullens, due to engine failure. Lt L. Sorel, Sgt A. Bail, and Adjt J. Sicard killed. Aircraft a write-off.

Peter Parrott's picture was later used in a recruiting poster.

LUFTWAFFE

I./JG26 Messerschmitt Bf109E. Held off too high and crashed from 30 feet while landing at Bönninghardt. Pilot unhurt. Aircraft a write-off.

3./JG52 Messerschmitt Bf109E-3. Crashed on landing at Herxheim, south-east of Landau, on test flight following engine change. Lt M. Spenner injured. Aircraft a write-off.

2./KGrzbV.9 Junkers Ju52/3m (6023). Flew into a mountain near Iburg, cause unknown. Wreck found two days later. Three crew killed. Aircraft 9P+HK a write-off.

Friday, March 22

BRITISH AIR FORCES IN FRANCE

73 SQUADRON Hurricane P2542. Believed returned damaged following combat with Bf109s of III./JG53 over Bouzonville 2.10 p.m. Pilot believed unhurt. Aircraft TP⊙D damaged but repairable.

LUFTWAFFE

I./JG26 Messerschmitt Bf109E-3. Hit a tree while landing at Bönninghardt in high tail-wind. Pilot unhurt. Aircraft a write-off.

II./JG53 Messerschmitt Bf109E-3. Crashed on take-off from Mannheim-Sandhofen due to burst tyre. Pilot unhurt. Aircraft damaged but repairable.

8./JG53 Messerschmitt Bf109E. Forced-landed damaged in attack by F/L Lovett of No. 73 Sqdn during combat over Bouzonville 2.10 p.m. Fw A. Weigelt unhurt. Aircraft repairable.

On March 20, the C-in-C of the British Expeditionary Force toured the Air Component of the BEF (see page 16). Here General Lord Gort is pictured with officers of No. 70 (Bomber) Wing which operated Blenheims out of Méharicourt and Rosières-en-Santerre — both airfields lying some 35 kilometres south-east of Amiens. Though unconfirmed it is likely that the two officers on the left are Wing Commanders Garland and Opie the commanding officers of Nos. 18 and 57 Squadrons. Both units were employed on strategic reconnaissance for GHQ and had only recently re-equipped with Blenheim IVs which extended their range. In the first two months of the year No. 70 Wing flew 16 daylight sorties, only seven of them being successful, and had lost three aircraft.

I./JG54 Messerschmitt Bf109E-1. Crashed on take-off from Friedrichshafen due to engine failure. Pilot unhurt. Aircraft a write-off.

Saturday, March 23

BRITISH AIR FORCES IN FRANCE

607 SQUADRON Gladiator I K8030. Crashed following mid-air collision during training flight over Vitry-en-Artois 10.55 a.m. Flying Officer N. S. Graeme killed. Aircraft a write-off.

607 SQUADRON Gladiator I K8000. Crashed following mid-air collision during training flight over Vitry-en-Artois 10.55 a.m. Pilot Officer H. P. J. Radcliffe killed. Aircraft a write-off.

The dates of death of both these officers is recorded as March 24 in the Operations Record Book of No. 61 Wing and the records of the CWGC.

FRENCH AIR FORCE

T 1 Latécoère 298 (11). Hit the 'digue Carnot' barrier in Boulogne Harbour on take-off for training flight and bomb-load exploded 1.15 p.m. LV Desmons, SM Werle, and QM Renaud killed. Aircraft 3 a write-off.

Sunday, March 24

BRITISH AIR FORCES IN FRANCE

88 SQUADRON Battle P2247. Got low on fuel and abandoned over Pont-sur-Yonne having lost bearings due to radio failure during return from leaflet raid on Oppenheim 1.00 a.m. Flying Officer D. L. R. Halliday, Sergeant S. C. Boyton and LAC E. Wigglesworth baled out unhurt. Aircraft a write-off.

FRENCH AIR FORCE

GC II/3 Morane 406 (248). Engine caught fire during navigation exercise and attempted to reach Saint-Dizier but, overcome by smoke, lost control in a low-level turn and crashed . Sgt Viau injured. Aircraft a write-off.

GR I/52 Potez 637 (36). Starboard engine set alight in attacks by Uffz Griener and Uffz Zaunbrecher of 5./JG52 during reconnaissance sortie over Kaiserslautern. Crashed and burned out between the lines south of Rorbach-les-Dieuze 3.45 p.m. S/Lt E. Brugerolles killed. Sgt S. Dumas died of wounds. Adjt Barbier injured during landing, rescued by French infantry. Aircraft a write-off.

We were out on patrol. With me were a 23-year-old pilot officer from Devon and a 24-year-old sergeant-pilot from Hitchin. We saw some anti-aircraft fire ahead, and flew torwards it.

Then I saw some odd spots in the sky. I turned on the old radio telephone and said: 'Messerschmitts ahead'. We counted nine of them. I led in and the others followed. They tackled us in two lots of twos, and then the other five waded in. I got shot into one of the first two which attacked me and I saw it stall, and then go down with smoke pouring out of it. Then the fun got pretty furious. I looked for my other machines but saw only swastikas flashing by. I got a burst into one of them and saw it go down in a cloud of black smoke. Now comes my fade-out. Two or three German fighters were apparently above the rest. They waited there like hawks ready to pick off enemy machines. By this time the sky had cleared, and I looked round to see what was happening. There was nothing behind, and then — bang.

The cockpit covering was blown off. I did not have time to know what had happened, or where it came from. Flames and hot oil came up from the engine.

I passed out. I came to and put my left arm out of the cockpit and it seemed minutes before I could resist the wind pressure sufficiently to get it back.

Then I realised that I was in a steep dive. Bending forward to turn off the petrol, I got my face burned, and then I pulled back the stick to come out of the dive, undid my straps, rolled over and slipped out of the cockpit.

After getting my face scorched, the next thing I remember was feeling the air on my face as I fell and thinking how good and cool it was. Then I realised that I had not pulled the ripcord to release the parachute.

Owing to my glove being covered with oil I could not get hold of the grip. While I was tearing off my glove I fell through a large cloud. I could remember realising that everything all around me was white and very light.

For a moment I thought to myself 'This must be Heaven'; then I instinctively pulled the ripcord and I came out of the cloud hanging sideways on the parachute because my left shoulder strap had come loose.

As I floated down it was obvious that it was going to be touch and go whether I landed in Germany or France.

I came down with a wallop in no-man's-land. Picking myself up I ran like the devil to a small wood. A minute or two later a French officer came running up and presented his revolver at me.

THE WAR WEEKLY, APRIL 5, 1940

DUTCH AIR FORCE

MLD Fokker C XIVw (5608). Beached at Egmond aan Zee due to failing engine and mist. Sgt pilot unhurt. Aircraft F-16 undamaged — recovered next day.

Monday, March 25

BRITISH AIR FORCES IN FRANCE

103 SQUADRON Battle K9269. Returned to Bétheniville tail and port wing damaged by AA fire during leaflet raid on Frankfurt 1.10 a.m. Sergeant C. D. Perry, Sergeant Davison, and AC A. R. Layfield unhurt. Aircraft repairable.

FRENCH AIR FORCE

GC III/3 Morane 406 (756). Engaged by Bf109s during escort mission for Mureaux 115 of GAO 1/520 and badly damaged in attack by Oberlt Wilcke (*Staffelkapitän*) of 7./JG53. Crash-landed and burned out on the outskirts of Grostenquin 2.55 p.m. Adjt M. Marias slightly wounded. Aircraft a write-off.

LUFTWAFFE

I./JG21 Messerschmitt Bf109E. Crashed on landing at Mönchengladbach due to control failure. Pilot unhurt. Aircraft a write-off.

I./JG53 Messerschmitt Bf109E-3. Hit an obstruction landing at Darmstadt-Griesheim in darkness. Pilot unhurt. Aircraft a write-off.

7./JG53 Messerschmitt Bf109E. Returned damaged following combat with Moranes of GC III/3 south-west of Saarbrücken 2.00 p.m. Lt H. Riegel unhurt. Aircraft repairable.

I./KG1 Heinkel He111H-3. Lost formation during leaflet-dropping mission and forced-landed at Quedlinburg. Crew unhurt. Aircraft repairable.

III./KG55 Focke-Wulf Fw58. Stalled in steep turn and crashed near Gablingen during local flying. Uffz E. Schmidt and Lt Ortloff killed. Aircraft a write-off.

III./StG2 Junkers Ju87B. Wrecked in forced-landing near Nordhausen following engine failure. Crew unhurt. Aircraft a write-off.

Tuesday, March 26

'Cobber' was again in the news following the combat between No. 73 Squadron and Jagdgeschwader 53 on March 26.

BRITISH AIR FORCES IN FRANCE

73 SQUADRON Hurricane. Returned damaged following combat with Bf110s of V.(Z)/LG1 12.30 p.m. Flight Lieutenant R. E. Lovett unhurt. Aircraft repairable.

73 SQUADRON Hurricane. Returned damaged following combat with Bf109s of III./JG 53. Believed that claimed by Fw Weigelt west of Saarlautern 2.35 p.m. Flying Officer N. Orton unhurt. Aircraft repairable.

73 SQUADRON Hurricane L1766. Hood blown off and engine set alight in attack by Hptmn Mölders (*Gruppenkommandeur*) of Stab III./JG53 during combat west of Merzig, and abandoned over Ritzing 3.00 p.m. Flying Officer E. J. Kain baled out slightly burned right hand and splinter wounds in left leg, landing near Evendorff. Aircraft a write-off.

73 SQUADRON Hurricane N2404. Returned with propeller damaged by return fire from Do17. Sergeant L. S. Pilkington unhurt. Aircraft repairable.

87 SQUADRON Hurricane. Forced-landed near Lille-Seclin due to engine failure. Flight Lieutenant M. Lister-Robinson unhurt. Aircraft repairable.

87 SQUADRON Hurricane. Overshot runway due to change in wind direction during night-flying practice and nosed-over on landing at Lille-Seclin. Pilot unhurt. Aircraft repairable.

103 SQUADRON Battle P2256. Hit trees on take-off for night bombing exercise over the ranges at St-Hilaire-le-Grand. Crashed into woods near Moronvilliers and burned out 10.15 p.m. Pilot Officer I. P. Hinton, Sergeant D. C. Findlay and AC2 J. A. Sharpe killed. Aircraft a write-off.

I./ZG26 Messerschmitt Bf110C. Lost control and hit a wall on take-off at Langendiebach. One crewman injured. Aircraft a write-off.

105 SQUADRON Battle L4980. Crashed and burned out near 'Notre Dame', on the Châlons to Fère-Champenoise road west of Cheniers, during night cross-country training flight 9.15 p.m. Pilot Officer A. M. Edgar, Sergeant H. E. Pettit and Corporal A. E. Jones killed. Aircraft a write-off.

607 SQUADRON Gladiator I K7996. Abandoned near Courcelles-les-Lens when unable to land due to fog during night-flying practice. Pilot Officer W. H. R. Whitty baled out unhurt. Aircraft a write-off.

607 SQUADRON Gladiator I K7967. Lost bearings in bad weather and overturned in forced-landing at Athies, near Mons-en-Chaussée. Flying Officer G. D. Craig unhurt. Aircraft AF⊙L a write-off.

LUFTWAFFE

I./JG21 Messerschmitt Bf109E-1. Crashed on landing at Mönchengladbach due to control failure. Pilot unhurt. Aircraft a write-off.

8./JG26 Messerschmitt Bf109E. Crashed following mid-air collision over Essen-Mühlheim. Uffz B. Boy killed. Aircraft a write-off.

8./JG26 Messerschmitt Bf109E. Crashed following mid-air collision over Essen-Mühlheim. Pilot believed baled out unhurt. Aircraft a write-off.

4./JG52 Messerschmitt Bf109E-1. Crashed following collision on take-off at Speyer. Fw W. Hoops killed. Aircraft 4+ damaged but repairable.

4./JG52 Messerschmitt Bf109E-1. Forced-landed following collision on take-off from Speyer. Pilot unhurt. Aircraft 3+ damaged but repairable.

II./JG52 Messerschmitt Bf109E-3. Damaged in forced-landing at Schwetzingen, near Heidelberg, due to petrol failure. Pilot unhurt. Aircraft damaged but repairable.

III./JG53 Messerschmitt Bf109E-3. Forced-landed at Trier-Euren damaged by F/O Kain of No. 73 Sqdn in combat over Saarlautern 3.00 p.m. Pilot unhurt. Aircraft damaged but repairable.

III./JG53 Messerschmitt Bf109E-3. Forced-landed at Trier-Euren damaged by P/O Perry of No. 73 Sqdn in combat over Saarlautern 3.00 p.m. Pilot unhurt. Aircraft damaged but repairable.

III./JG53 Messerschmitt Bf109E-1. Forced-landed at Trier-Euren engine damaged by Sgt Pyne of No. 73 Sqdn in combat over Saarlautern 3.00 p.m. Pilot unhurt. Aircraft repairable.

I./KG1 Two Heinkel He111H-2. Damaged in separate taxying accidents at Giessen. No crew casualties. Aircraft both repairable.

I./StG2 Two Junkers Ju87B-1. Crashed near Bensberg following mid-air collision east of Cologne. Two crew killed and two injured. Aircraft both write-offs.

13.(Z)/LG1 Messerschmitt Bf110C. Forced-landed near Lutzerath both engines damaged in attacks by fighters during escort sortie over Verdun 12.15 p.m. Fw H. Datz and Uffz G. Lämmel unhurt. Aircraft repairable.

13.(Z)/LG1 Messerschmitt Bf110C. Forced-landed at Trier starboard engine damaged by fighters over Verdun 12.15 p.m. Uffz W. Petry badly wounded, died same day. Lt H. Gaffal unhurt. Aircraft repairable.

15.(Z)/LG1 Messerschmitt Bf110C. Forced-landed near Mainz one engine damaged in attack by F/L Lovett of No. 73 Sqdn during escort sortie for reconnaissance Dornier over Verdun 12.15 p.m. Fw A. Warrelmann and Uffz O. Kramp unhurt. Aircraft repairable.

Wednesday, March 27

LUFTWAFFE

Stab KG1 Heinkel He111H-2. Crashed and burned out at Sellnrod, 35 km east of Giessen, due to engine failure following combat sortie. Hptmn Tippmann (*Stabsstaffel-kapitän*) and three crewmen killed. Aircraft a write-off.

ZG26 Messerschmitt Bf110C. Nosed over on landing at Gelsenkirchen-Buer, cause not stated. Crew unhurt. Aircraft repairable.

Thursday, March 28

FRENCH AIR FORCE

GC 3/10 Bloch 151 (81). Overturned on landing at Rouen-Boos. Lt Possien unhurt. Aircraft repairable.

LUFTWAFFE

4.(F)/121 Dornier Do17P. Failed to return from reconnaissance of airfields south of Toul. Lt F. Böcher, Fw G. Mikusky, and Uffz F. Mückisch killed. Aircraft a write-off.

I./JG77 Messerschmitt Bf109E-3. Belly-landed at Bonn-Hangelar due to engine failure. Pilot unhurt. Aircraft damaged but repairable.

I./KG1 Heinkel He111H-3. Crashed and burned out at Erfurt-Bindersleben following engine failure. Three crew killed. Aircraft a write-off.

I./ZG2 Messerschmitt Bf110C. Crashed near Wiesbaden flying in snow shower. Oberlt A. Köhlisch and crewman killed. Aircraft a write-off.

Friday, March 29

BRITISH AIR FORCES IN FRANCE

73 SQUADRON Hurricane P2570. Shot down by Oberlt Boenigk of 9./JG53 during attack on Do17 of 2.(F)/22 and overturned forced-landing at Brienne-le-Château 9.15 a.m. Pilot Officer J. G. Perry killed. Aircraft a write-off.

LUFTWAFFE

7./JG53 Messerschmitt Bf109E-3. Wrecked in forced-landing at Mainz-Finthen due to petrol failure. Lt L. Magath injured. Aircraft a write-off.

9./JG53 Messerschmitt Bf109E-1. Damaged by F/O Richey of No. 1 Sqdn in combat over Bouzonville and forced-landed west of Saarburg 9.15 a.m. Lt J. Volk wounded. Aircraft damaged but repairable.

I./KG27 Heinkel He111P. Hit boundary fence while landing at Münster-Handorf. Crew unhurt. Aircraft damaged but repairable.

III./KG27 Heinkel He111P. Crashed and burned out at Hannover, cause unknown. Four crew killed. Aircraft a write-off.

14.(Z)/LG1 Messerschmitt Bf110C. One engine damaged by F/L Walker of No. 1 Sqdn in combat over Bouzonville, north-east of Metz, second engine set alight in attack by P/O Stratton. Retired east at low level and engaged by French AA crashing near Waldhouse, north of Bitche 3.10 p.m. Fw F. Lindemann baled out and captured wounded. Uffz K. Radeck killed. Aircraft a write-off.

Saturday, March 30

LUFTWAFFE

I./JG1 Messerschmitt Bf109E-1. Damaged in crash-landing at Frechen, near Cologne, following engine failure. Pilot unhurt. Aircraft damaged but repairable.

I./JG53 Messerschmitt Bf108. Undercarriage collapsed on landing at Darmstadt-Griesheim in cross-wind. Pilot unhurt. Aircraft damaged but repairable.

Sunday, March 31

BRITISH AIR FORCES IN FRANCE

105 SQUADRON Battle P2250. Lost control in steep turn and spun into the ground north-west of Champigneul-Champagne during AA co-operation exercise 4.35 a.m. Flight Lieutenant C. R. Mace and Corporal F. Coughtrey killed. Aircraft a write-off.

150 SQUADRON Battle P2244. Lost control in turn and flew into rising ground near St-Hilaire-le-Grand during low-bombing exercise in heavy ground mist 5.30 a.m. Flying Officer D. Devoto, Sergeant C. Wall and AC1 W. F. Taylor killed. Aircraft a write-off.

607 SQUADRON Gladiator I K7898. Forced-landed near Vitry-en-Artois with engine seized 6.50 p.m. Flying Officer W. E. Gore unhurt. Aircraft damaged but repairable.

FRENCH AIR FORCE

GC III/7 Morane 406 (971). Set alight in attack by Bf109s of II./JG53 during patrol between Saint-Avold and Hambach. Possibly that claimed by Hptmn von Maltzahn (*Gruppenkommandeur*). Crashed and burned out at Grostenquin, north of Morhange 3.55 p.m. Adjt R. Chavet killed. Aircraft a write-off.

GC III/7 Morane 406 (811). Set alight in attack by Bf109s of II./JG53 between Saint-Avold and Hambach 3.55 p.m. Possibly one of those claimed by Oberlt Bretnütz (*Staffelkapitän*) of 6./JG53. Abandoned over Grostenquin. S/Lt Y. Rupied baled out and admitted to hospital in Morhange with burns to face. Aircraft a write-off.

GC III/7 Morane 406 (212). Damaged in attack by Bf109s of II./JG53 between Saint-Avold and Hambach 3.55 p.m. Possibly one of those claimed by Oberlt Bretnütz (*Staffelkapitän*) of 6./JG53. Forced-landed at Morhange. S/Lt Renaud wounded in left hand. Aircraft damaged but repairable.

GC III/7 Morane 406 (177). Badly damaged in attack by Bf109s of II./JG53 between Saint-Avold and Hambach 3.55 p.m. Possibly that claimed by Uffz Kauffmann of 4./JG53. Crash-landed at Metz-Frescaty. Sgt R. Morlot unhurt. Aircraft a write-off.

GC III/7 Morane 406 (176). Set alight in attack by Bf109s of II./JG53 between Saint-Avold and Hambach and abandoned north of Morhange 3.55 p.m. Possibly that claimed by Fw Baun of 6./JG53. Sgt L'Hôpital-Navarre baled out badly wounded and admitted to hospital with broken leg and burns to face and hands. Aircraft a write-off.

GC III/7 Morane 406 (229). Badly damaged in attack by Bf109s of II./JG53 between Saint-Avold and Hambach 3.55 p.m. Possibly that claimed by Lt Michalski of Stab II./JG53. Forced-landed at Vitry-le-François-Vauclerc. Lt B. Dvorak wounded in left arm. Aircraft damaged but repairable.

GC III/7 Morane 406 (806). Returned with slight damage following attack by Bf109s of II./JG53 between Saint-Avold and Hambach 3.55 p.m. Sgt Bodin unhurt. Aircraft repairable.

LUFTWAFFE

5.(F)/122 Dornier Do17P. Crashed and burned out shortly after take-off from Cologne-Wahn on target practice flight for searchlights. Hptmn A. Dr. Schaefer killed. One of crew injured. Aircraft a write-off.

I./JG76 Messerschmitt Bf109E-1. Wrecked attempting forced-landing at Ottweiler due to engine failure. Pilot unhurt. Aircraft a write-off.

Wettererkundungsstaffel 26 Dornier Do17Z-2. Engaged off Orfordness and starboard engine badly damaged in attack by F/O Pearson of No. 54 Sqdn during weather reconnaissance sortie 12.25 p.m. Tried to reach base but crashed in the sea off Ameland. Reg Rat Dr J. Wille and Uffz H. Biester killed. Uffz G. Hertel and Uffz F. Jahn missing. Aircraft a write-off.
The bodies of meteorologist Dr Joseph Wille and radio operator Helmut Biester were washed ashore on the Dutch coast and buried in the nearby churchyard at Nes.

APRIL 1940

On April 11, French pilots brough down two aircraft before breakfast. This is the starboard outer wing section from the Heinkel of 3.(F)/121 which was shot down at Amifontaine. Three of the four-man crew were killed. The full code of the aircraft was 7A+GL

The German occupation of Denmark and invasion of Norway on April 9 significantly increased tension on the entire Western Front and a readiness alert, issued two days later, triggered some relocation of British fighter forces. This was reversed on April 19 when it became clear that there was no immediate threat of any German offensive.

On April 16, No. 98 Squadron joined the British forces in France, providing a valuable training facility for Fairey Battle crews plus a ready pool of operational reserves. Meantime, both Gladiator-equipped squadrons of No. 61 Wing (Nos. 607 and 615) accelerated plans for their re-equipment with Hurricanes.

Monday, April 1

BRITISH AIR FORCES IN FRANCE

1 SQUADRON Hurricane N2380. Forced-landed at Étain-Rouvres with port wing, main spar, petrol and oil tanks damaged in head-on attack by Bf110 of I./ZG26 between Thionville and Boulay 11.40 a.m. Flight Lieutenant P. P. Hanks unhurt. Aircraft ⊙S damaged but repairable.

FRENCH AIR FORCE

GC I/5 Curtiss H-75A. Hit by return fire from Do215 of 3.(F)/ObdL engaged near Longwy. S/Lt H. Boitelet unhurt. Aircraft repairable.

GB I/38 Amiot 143. Damaged by flak during night reconnaissance between Remagen and Cologne; forced-landed at Diekirch in Luxembourg and crew interned. Capt Faure *(Commandant)* and Adjt Herbier slightly wounded. Lt Kastler, Sgt Clavaud, and Sgt Kirsch unhurt. Aircraft destroyed by crew.

LUFTWAFFE

2./Aufkl.Gr.Ob.d.L. Dornier Do215. Forced-landed at Wiesbaden damaged in attacks by S/Lt Lefol and Sgt Girou of GC I/5 during reconnaissance sortie over Longwy. Oberlt E. Marquardt and Obergefr R. Fritsche wounded. Aircraft damaged but repairable.

4.(F)/11 Dornier Do17P (4033). Intercepted by Lt Cormouls and Adjt Blanchard of ECMJ 1/16 during photo-reconnaissance sortie and attacked between Rocroi and Flize. Then engaged over Signy forest by Adjt Renaudie and Sgt de la Gasnerie of GC II/2 and finally crashed into woods at 'La Fourche au Bouleau', near Mézières 12.10 p.m. Two crewmen killed, Uffz H-G. Altmann believed captured. Aircraft 6M+EM a write-off.

4.(F)/11 Dornier Do17P. Crashed near Kirchgoens during night flight, probably due to engine failure. Three crew killed. Aircraft a write-off.

I./JG26 Messerschmitt Bf109E-3. Crash-landed near Bönninghardt following engine failure. Pilot unhurt. Aircraft a write-off.

I./JG27 Messerschmitt Bf109E-3. Crashed on take-off from Krefeld. Pilot unhurt. Aircraft damaged but repairable.

I./JG51 Messerschmitt Bf109E-3. Crashed on landing at Mannheim-Sandhofen due to undercarriage failure. Pilot unhurt. Aircraft repairable.

II./JG51 Messerschmitt Bf109E-3. Left tyre burst on landing at Mannheim-Sandhofen. Pilot unhurt. Aircraft repairable.

II./JG51 Messerschmitt Bf109E-1. Crashed at Böblingen due to poor state of landing ground. Pilot unhurt. Aircraft damaged but repairable.

I./JG52 Messerschmitt Bf109E-1. Overturned on landing at Lachen-Speyerdorf due to control failure. Lt A-H. Waller injured. Aircraft a write-off.

I./JG53 Messerschmitt Bf109E-3. Crash-landed at Wengerohr, cause not stated. Pilot unhurt. Aircraft damaged but repairable.

III./KG51 Heinkel He111. Forced-landed at Gotha due to engine failure. Crew unhurt. Aircraft damaged but repairable.

The twisted wreckage of the Dornier which was brought down in woodland near Charleville-Mézières on the first day of the month.

I./ZG26 Messerschmitt Bf110C-1. Returned to Niedermendig damaged in combat with Hurricanes of No. 1 Sqdn between Thionville and Boulay 12.00 p.m. Oberfw E. Blass wounded. Aircraft damaged but repairable.

I./ZG26 Messerschmitt Bf110C-1. Undercarriage damaged on landing at Niedermendig following combat with Hurricanes of No. 1 Sqdn between Thionville and Boulay 12.00 p.m. Crew unhurt. Aircraft repairable.

Tuesday, April 2

BRITISH AIR FORCES IN FRANCE

1 SQUADRON Hurricane N2326. Reserve fuel tank blew up under attack by Hptmn Mölders *(Gruppenkommandeur)* of Stab III./JG53 in combat over Saint-Avold 11.10 a.m. Flying Officer C. D. Palmer baled out unhurt, rescued from no-man's land by French troops. Aircraft a write-off.

1 SQUADRON Hurricane L1681. Forced-landed at Metz low on fuel following combat with Bf109s of III./JG53 over Saint-Avold and broke tail wheel while taxying 11.45 a.m. Flying Officer P. H. M. Richey unhurt. Aircraft repairable.

26 SQUADRON Lysander L4775. Flew into high-tension cable and crashed. Crew believed unhurt. Aircraft a write-off.

FRENCH AIR FORCE

GC I/2 Morane 406 (681). Engine set alight by return fire from Do17 of 4.(F)/121 engaged over Saverne and hit a tree while attempting to land near Erstein; crashed and burned out 11.15 a.m. Adjt H. Bruckert killed. Aircraft a write-off.

GC 2/2 Morane 406 (439). Badly damaged in attack by Oberlt Methfessel *(Staffelkapitän)* of 14.(Z)/LG1 and overturned in forced-landing at Lunéville 11.00 a.m. Adjt J. Le Martelot wounded in left arm. Aircraft a write-off.

LUFTWAFFE

4.(F)/121 Dornier Do17. Forced-landed at Lahr, south of Offenburg, with engine damaged in attack by Capt Naudy of GC II/3 near Pirmasens, south-east of Zweibrücken 11.05 a.m. Crew unhurt. Aircraft damaged but repairable.

3.(F)/123 Dornier Do17P. Landed at Hanau-am-Main damaged by enemy fighters. Uffz J-P. Trümpener wounded. Aircraft repairable.

I./JG3 Messerschmitt Bf109E-1. Landing accident at Bonn-Hangelar. Pilot unhurt. Aircraft damaged but repairable.

II./JG52 Messerschmitt Bf109E-1. Forced-landed at Pirmasens damaged by F/O Kilmartin and F/O Clisby of No. 1 Sqdn in combat near St Avold 12.10 p.m. Pilot unhurt. Aircraft damaged but repairable.

III./JG53 Messerschmitt Bf109E-3. Wrecked in forced-landing near Simmern due to petrol failure during ferry flight. Pilot unhurt. Aircraft a write-off.

3./JG54 Messerschmitt Bf109E-1 (3454). Crashed near Mötzingen, near Nagold, during air-ground firing practice, cause unknown. Lt K. Ziegast killed. Aircraft 6+ a write-off.

15.(Z)/LG1 Messerschmitt Bf110. Shot down in combat with Moranes during escort sortie for Do17 of 4.(F)/121. Attacked in turn by Adjt Le Martelot of GC 2/2 and Lt Bissoudre of GC II/3. Crashed and burned out at Jolivet, north-east of Lunéville 12.13 p.m. Lt H. Busching and Uffz H. Arndt killed. Aircraft a write-off.

Wednesday, April 3

LUFTWAFFE

2./KG2 Dornier Do17Z. Hit HT lines shortly after take-off from Giebelstadt, crashed and burned out. Lt K. Ehlers, Uffz J. Kluch, and Uffz H. Heinze killed. Aircraft a write-off.

Thursday, April 4

LUFTWAFFE

2./JG77 Messerschmitt Bf109E-3. Abandoned near Mattenwalddorf due to technical fault Lt H. Lohoff baled out unhurt. Aircraft a write-off.

I./StG2 Junkers Ju87B. Crashed east of Cologne, cause unknown. Lt Allin and crewman killed. Aircraft a write-off.

These two Loire-Nieuport 40s came a cropper during a take-off on April 7 at the aerodrome at Berck-sur-Mer where the wrecks were later found by German forces.

Friday, April 5

BRITISH AIR FORCES IN FRANCE

59 SQUADRON Blenheim IV P6922. Crashed on take-off from Poix, cause unknown. No crew casualties. Aircraft damaged but repairable — later abandoned.

85 SQUADRON Hurricane P2552. Crashed on landing at Lille-Seclin, cause unknown. Pilot believed unhurt. Aircraft a write-off.

FRENCH AIR FORCE

F1C Potez 631 (38). Accidentally caught fire and burned out on the ground at Calais. No crew casualties. Aircraft a write-off.

LUFTWAFFE

1./JG26 Messerschmitt Bf109E-3. Damaged in taxying collision at Dortmund. Pilot unhurt. Aircraft damaged but repairable.

Saturday, April 6

LUFTWAFFE

1./JG2 Messerschmitt Bf109E-3. Lost control and crashed on take-off from Bassenheim. Pilot injured. Aircraft a write-off.

I./JG20 Messerschmitt Bf109E-1. Forced-landed at Bönninghardt with engine trouble. Pilot unhurt. Aircraft repairable.

I./JG26 Messerschmitt Bf109E-3. Crash-landed at Nörvenich due to fuel shortage. Lt F. Butterweck unhurt. Aircraft a write-off.

I./KG76 Dornier Do17Z-2. Crashed and burned out near Koblenz, cause unknown. Lt W. Engelhardt and three crew killed. Aircraft a write-off.

Sunday, April 7

BRITISH AIR FORCES IN FRANCE

73 SQUADRON Hurricane. Shot down by Oberlt Lippert *(Staffelkapitän)* of 3./JG 53 in action over Thionville 11.50 a.m. Flying Officer G. F. Brotchie baled out with splinter wounds in right knee, admitted to hospital in Épernay. Aircraft a write-off.

142 SQUADRON Battle N2088. Crashed at Houdilcourt, east of Neufchâtel, during night cross-country exercise 9.30 p.m. Exact cause unknown. Flying Officer P. A. L. Farrell, Sergeant L. A. Raper and Corporal C. E. Wilburn killed. Aircraft a write-off.
Patrick Farrell was found two miles from the crash site attached to his damaged parachute. It is thought that his shroud lines snagged the aircraft.

226 SQUADRON Battle P2265. Lost control and abandoned near La Preve during night training exercise 10.00 p.m. Sergeant J. R. Branton and LAC P. K. Davies killed. Flight Sergeant W. A. Dunn baled out landing with injured head. Aircraft MQ⊙B a write-off.

FRENCH AIR FORCE

AB2 Two L-N 40 (3 and 4). Wrecked in take-off accidents at Berck-sur-Mer; possibly due to collision. No crew casualties. Aircraft 11 and 12 both write-offs.

GC I/2 Morane 406 (379). Shot down by Oberlt Seiler *(Staffelkapitän)* of 1./JG54 south-east of Saverne during escort sortie for Potez 63.11 of GR I/36 to Wissembourg. Crashed 2 km north-east of Marmoutier 3.10 p.m. Capt M. Vidal wounded, attempted to bale out but harness fouled the aircraft and dragged to his death. Aircraft a write-off.

GC III/2 Morane 406. Hit by return fire from Do17 of 1.(F)/123 engaged north-east of Laon and crash-landed 8.15 a.m. Sgt Pizon believed unhurt. Aircraft a write-off.

GC III/3 Morane 406. Severely damaged in attack by Fw Lütjens of 4./JG53 during escort sortie for Potex 63.11 of GR I/36 between Bitsch and Saarbrücken 11.30 a.m. Crash-landed near Morhange and caught fire. Capt A. Richard killed. Aircraft a write-off.

GC I/5 Curtiss H-75 (161). Shot down by Bf110 of Hptmn Gentzen *(Gruppenkommandeur)* of Stab I./ZG2 in combat south of Sedan and crashed near Beaumont-en-Argonne p.m. Adjt A. Salmand killed. Aircraft a write-off.

GR II/36 Potez 63.11. Returned damaged by AA fire during reconnaissance sortie over Wissembourg. Lt Darre and crew unhurt. Aircraft damaged but repairable.

DUTCH AIR FORCE

3-II-1 Fokker G 1 (323). Landed with brakes on and ground-looped at Waalhaven 1.50 p.m. 1e Lt H. C. A. van Montfoort killed. Sgt C. H. F. van Lijff badly injured. Aircraft damaged but repairable.

LUFTWAFFE

1.(F)/123 Dornier Do17P. Returned to base on one engine after running fight with Moranes of GC III/2 and GC III/6 north-east of Laon 8.15 a.m. Crew unhurt. Aircraft repairable.

4./JG53 Messerschmitt Bf109E-1. Shot down by P/O Ayerst of No. 73 Sqdn in combat south-east of Diedenhofen and crashed at Ham-sous-Varsberg, south-east of Thionville, 11.50 a.m. Fw E. Weiss killed. Aircraft 4 + ~ a write-off.

Stab I./JG54 Messerschmitt Bf109E-3. Engine set alight under attack by Capt Hyvernaud of GC 2/2 and abandoned over Ernolsheim-Bruche, east of Strasbourg. Lt P-A. Stolte *(Gruppenadjutant)* baled out and captured unhurt. Aircraft a write-off.

I./KG1 Heinkel He111H-3. Hit a tree and crashed shortly after take-off from Giessen. Lt Zickelten, Lt Morgenstern, and one crewman killed. Aircraft a write-off.

3./ZG2 Messerschmitt Bf110 (3205). Shot down in combat with Curtiss H-75s of GC I/5 and Moranes of GC III/6 south of Sedan p.m. Possibly that claimed by Lt Dorance of GC I/5 at Stonne. Lt J. Kiel baled out and captured unhurt. Unterfw W. Ehm killed. Aircraft 3M+AL a write-off.

2./ZG2 Messerschmitt Bf110. Shot down by Curtiss H-75s of GC I/5 and Moranes of GC III/6 south of Sedan p.m. Possibly that claimed by S/Lt Warnier of GC I/5 at Beaumont-en-Argonne. Fw K. Müller and Uffz Neumann killed. Aircraft a write-off.

Fl.Komp.Ln.Regt.Ob.d.L. Junkers Ju52. Engaged over Lure by 16 Moranes of GC I/6 and GC II/7 during radio intercept mission and crashed south-east of Meurcourt 4.30 p.m. Oberlt L. Deutschenbaur and eight crewmen (of III./Ln.Regt.3) killed. Aircraft a write-off.

Monday, April 8

BRITISH AIR FORCES IN FRANCE

105 SQUADRON Battle. Landed on one wheel at Villeneuve-les-Vertus due to under-carriage failure 12.30 p.m. Pilot Officer H. E. White and crew unhurt. Aircraft repairable.

FRENCH AIR FORCE

GC II/7 Morane 406 (482). Belly-landed at Bessoncourt damaged in attack by Bf109s of I./JG76 over Colmar 11.35 a.m. Sgt R. Bret unhurt. Aircraft damaged but repairable.

LUFTWAFFE

3.(F)/123 Dornier Do17P (4043). Crashed at Hanau-am-Main during night flying. Oberlt G. Beisiegel and Obergefr J. Schadl killed. Aircraft a write-off.

4.(F)/123 Dornier Do17P. Collided with trees and crashed near Stommeln during air-ground firing practice. Fw A. Huberts, Uffz A. Früchtl and Uffz H. Bittkow killed. Aircraft 4U+DK a write-off.

1./JG3 Messerschmitt Bf109E. Collided with a steam roller while taxi-ing at Bonn-Hangelar. Fw F. Hessel unhurt. Aircraft repairable.

6./JG26 Messerschmitt Bf109E-3. Hit trees practicing low flying at Dortmund. Pilot unhurt. Aircraft repairable.

II./JG52 Two Messerschmitt Bf109E-3 (6003). Wrecked in taxi-ing collision at Speyer. Pilots both unhurt. Aircraft write-offs.

I./JG76 Messerschmitt Bf109E-1. Crashed on take-off from Frankfurt/Rhein-Main due to control failure. Pilot unhurt. Aircraft damaged but repairable.

II./KG28 Heinkel He111H. Belly-landed at Gotha airfield due to pilot error. No crew casualties. Aircraft damaged but repairable.

I./KG76 Dornier Do17Z. Taxied into a ditch at Merzhausen airfield. Crew unhurt. Aircraft damaged but repairable.

Tuesday, April 9

LUFTWAFFE

4./JG51 Messerschmitt Bf109E-3 (1162). Badly damaged by AA fire over Kehl and forced-landed at Baden-Oos. Pilot unhurt. Aircraft 4+ a write-off.

3./KG54 Heinkel He111P-2. Crashed at Badbergen during night exercise. Fw K. Schrader, Uffz H. Krüger, Obergefr H. Walter and Obergefr A. Maier killed. Aircraft a write-off.

Wednesday, April 10

FRENCH AIR FORCE

1S1 Loire 130 (62). Ditched off Courseulles-sur-Mer and wrecked in taxying onto the beach. Crew unhurt. Aircraft a write-off.

LUFTWAFFE

2.(H)/41 Henschel Hs126. Crashed near Marx during training. Crew both injured. Aircraft a write-off.

'GERMAN DORNIER AND HEINKEL MACHINES SHOT DOWN ON THE WESTERN FRONT. French fighters had a good morning [before breakfast] on Thursday when, in co-operation with the British anti-aircraft batteries, they shot down one Dornier and one Heinkel. The German machines crashed near each other after a short engagement with the French fighters. The part played by the British in this victory was that they cleverly guided the French to the enemy by firing just beneath them. A general view of the crashed Dornier, being guarded by French and British airmen.' So ran the official caption to the crash of the 5.(F)/122 machine on April 11.

I./JG3 Messerschmitt Bf109E-1. Crash-landed at Wiesbaden, cause not stated. Uffz Hinrichs unhurt. Aircraft damaged but repairable.

1./JG21 Messerschmitt Bf109E. Damaged while low-flying near Mönchengladbach. Uffz F. Schweser unhurt. Aircraft repairable.

Stab JG77 Messerschmitt Bf109E-1. Abandoned take-off at Bonn-Hangelar, cause not stated. Oberlt Dr. M. Otte injured. Aircraft damaged but repairable.

Thursday, April 11

BRITISH AIR FORCES IN FRANCE

57 SQUADRON Blenheim IV L9181. Lost control in turn and crashed at Foucacourt-en-Santerre, north of Lihons, shortly after take-off on night reconnaissance sortie 4.30 a.m. AC1 G. Lindsay killed. Flying Officer A. C. Stewart baled out but hit tailplane and broke leg. Sergeant C. Simpson baled out unhurt. Aircraft a write-off.

LUFTWAFFE

4.(H)/21 Henschel Hs126. Crashed near Essen following engine fire. Pilot unhurt. Aircraft a write-off.

3.(F)/121 Heinkel He111H (2305). Intercepted by S/Lt Villemin, Sgt Pimont, and Sgt Maigret of GC III/6 during reconnaissance of airfields between Verdun and Sedan and shot down at Amifontaine 8.00 a.m. Oberlt B. von Wühlisch, Uffz W. Nitsche, and Obergefr A. Loscher killed. Uffz H. Weichert captured wounded. Aircraft 7A+GL a write-off.

5.(F)/122 Dornier Do17P. Engaged by S/Lt Boitelet and Sgt Tallent of GC I/5, S/Lt Steunou and Sgt Boymond of GC III/6, and Sgt Delarue of GC III/7 between Chalons and Montmédy. Crashed at Ferme de Moscou, near Wez-Thuisy 7.30 a.m. Oberlt M. Guse, Uffz W. Heese, and Uffz P. Althaus killed. Aircraft 6M+AM a write-off.

I./JG3 Messerschmitt Bf109E-3. Crash-landed at Wiesbaden-Erbenheim, cause not stated. Pilot unhurt. Aircraft repairable.

II./JG53 Messerschmitt Bf109E-3. Burst tyre and collided with another Bf109 while landing at Darmstadt-Griesheim. Pilot unhurt. Aircraft damaged but repairable.

II./JG53 Messerschmitt Bf109E-1. Rammed by a Bf109 while landing at Darmstadt-Griesheim. Pilot unhurt. Aircraft damaged but repairable.

II.(S)/LG2 Henschel Hs123. Crashed at Düsseldorf airfield, cause not stated. Pilot injured. Aircraft a write-off.

Friday, April 12

FRENCH AIR FORCE

ECN 2/13 Potez 631 (22). Dived into the ground 12 km north of Melun, near Lissy, shortly after take-off 4.23 a.m. Circumstances unknown. Sgt Durand and Sgt Hermel killed. Aircraft a write-off.

DUTCH AIR FORCE

IV-2 Fokker C V (610). Crashed at Deurne, near Helmond, cause not stated. Sgt A. M. van Breugel believed unhurt. Aircraft damaged but repairable.

LUFTWAFFE

III./JG2 Messerschmitt Bf109E-1, Bf109E-3. Wrecked in forced-landings at Odenbach in bad weather. Pilots unhurt. Aircraft both write-offs.

Unit formed March 16 at Magdeburg-Ost under Major Dr Erich Mix moving to Frankfurt-Rebstock on April 10 for operations on the Western Front.

7./JG2 Messerschmitt Bf109E-1. Crashed south of Weilburg/Lahn during ferry flight, cause not stated. Uffz K. Elsner injured. Aircraft a write-off.

1./JG21 Messerschmitt Bf109E-1. Collided with Bf109 of 3./JG27 on landing at Mönchengladbach. Pilot unhurt. Aircraft damaged but repairable.

3./JG27 Messerschmitt Bf109E-3. Parked aircraft rammed by Bf109 of 1./JG21 at Mönchengladbach. Aircraft damaged but repairable.

2./StG77 Junkers Ju87B. Forced-landed at Marienloh, near Paderborn, with engine trouble during maintenance flight. Lt H. Sinn and gunner both injured. Aircraft damaged but repairable.

Saturday, April 13

FRENCH AIR FORCE

GC III/7 Morane 406 (218). Abandoned due to engine fire and crashed at Vouillers. Sgt L. Berthet baled out unhurt. Aircraft a write-off.

BELGIAN AIR FORCE

9/V/1 Renard R-31. Badly damaged, cause unknown. Lt J. Vandenbosch and Adjt Welkenhuyzen both slightly injured. Aircraft damaged but repairable.

LUFTWAFFE

3.(H)/41 Henschel Hs126. Hit trees while low-flying during combat training exercise at Marx. Observer killed, pilot injured. Aircraft a write-off.

3./JG26 Messerschmitt Bf109E-3. Crashed on landing at Essen-Mülheim due to high tail wind. Pilot unhurt. Aircraft damaged but repairable.

III./KG1 Heinkel He111H-3. Forced-landed near Nordhausen due to engine failure. No crew casualties. Aircraft damaged but repairable.

Sunday, April 14

BRITISH AIR FORCES IN FRANCE

57 SQUADRON Blenheim IV L9465. Attacked over Emmerich by Oberlt Lignitz of 3./JG20 during reconnaissance sortie over north-western Germany and crashed near Babberich, south-east of Arnhem, 4.40 p.m. Flying Officer H. G. Graham-Hogg, Sergeant J. R. Proctor and AC1 J. Shuttleworth killed. Aircraft a write-off.
Crash site subject of major excavation by the Royal Netherlands Air Force in May 1973.

DUTCH AIR FORCE

2-I-1 Fokker T V (864). Badly damaged in belly-landing at Haarlemmermeer due to engine failure. Pilot believed unhurt. Aircraft damaged but repairable.

3-II-1 Fokker G 1 (327). Starboard engine damaged by return fire during attack on French Vought 156s over Noordwijk and belly-landed near Spijkenisse. Sgt Maj J. J. Buwalda unhurt. Aircraft damaged but repairable.

MLD Fokker C Xw. Crashed in the sea between Camperduin and Petten during search mission for suspected German convoy 2.40 a.m. Sgt C. H. J. Knaapen and Off-Zeewrn. H. F. G. Langenhoff killed. Aircraft W-9 lost.

LUFTWAFFE

Stab JG52 Messerschmitt Bf109E-3. Damaged in taxying accident at Mannheim-Sandhofen. Pilot unhurt. Aircraft repairable.

Tuesday, April 16

BRITISH AIR FORCES IN FRANCE

4 SQUADRON Lysander L4750. Crashed on take-off at Padville following forced-landing. Pilot Officer A. F. B. Ramsay badly injured. LAC J. H. Gillham unhurt. Aircraft a write-off.
Alex Ramsay died in the French Military Hospital at Marcoing, south of Cambrai, four days later and was buried in Trefcon British Cemetery at Caulaincourt, where his date of death is recorded as April 21.

FRENCH AIR FORCE

GR 3/33 Bloch 174 (16). Shot down by Oberlt Rau and Lt Fiel of I./JG3 during high-level photo-reconnaissance of pontoon bridges over the Rhine between Duisburg and Bonn. Evaded attack but crashed and burned out at Longlier, north of Neufchâteau, in Belgium 9.00 a.m. Adjt L. Bagrel killed. S/Lt M. Bediez badly wounded, died same evening in Longlier clinic. Capt F. Laux (*Commandant*) interned badly wounded and burned. Aircraft a write-off.

LUFTWAFFE

I./JG26 Messerschmitt Bf109E. Abandoned following mid-air collision prior to landing at Wesel. Pilot baled out unhurt. Aircraft a write-off.

The wreckage of the Dornier which came down on Moscow Farm is picked over for souvenirs.

This is the wreckage of the second aircraft brought down by French pilots on April 11. Like the Dornier, great interest was shown in the wreck of the Heinkel from 3.(F)/121 which lay at Amifontaine (see page 155).

I./JG26 Messerschmitt Bf109E. Damaged in mid-air collision prior to landing at Wesel. Pilot unhurt. Aircraft repairable.

2./JG27 Messerschmitt Bf109E-3. Lost bearings and wrecked attempting forced-landing at Mentebrück, near Ziegen. Pilot unhurt. Aircraft a write-off.

4./KG2 Dornier Do17Z. Hit the ground during low-flying practice south of Ansbach. Oberfw L. Ommerborn killed. Lt A. Wieners and Flgr K. Hahn injured. Aircraft a write-off.

Wednesday, April 17

BRITISH AIR FORCES IN FRANCE

26 SQUADRON Lysander N1200. Wrecked in landing accident, cause unknown. Crew believed unhurt. Aircraft a write-off.

85 SQUADRON Hurricane L1637. Crash-landed at Carvin, north-east of Lens, probable engine failure. Sergeant G. Goodman admitted to hospital with concussion. Aircraft damaged but repairable — later abandoned.

218 SQUADRON Battle. Slightly damaged in one wheel landing at Aubérive-sur-Suippes. Flying Officer J. F. R. Crane, Sergeant Farmes, and LAC H. Baguley unhurt. Aircraft repairable.

LUFTWAFFE

Jagdfliegerführer 2 Focke-Wulf Fw58. Damaged in attack by Bf109s of I./JG20 and forced-landed near Orsey. Oberst K-B. von Döring, Oberlt Freiherr von Barneckow, and one other injured. Aircraft damaged but repairable.

Flakkorps I Dornier Do17. Taxying accident after landing at Koblenz-Karthausen. No crew casualties. Aircraft repairable.
A Junkers W34 and Messerschmitt Bf108 were also damaged in this incident.

I./KG1 Heinkel He111H-2. Hit an obstruction after landing at Nordhausen. Crew unhurt. Aircraft damaged but repairable.

Stab KG2 Dornier Do17Z. Ran off runway after landing at Babenhausen. No crew casualties. Aircraft damaged but repairable.

II./KG77 Messerschmitt Bf108. Crashed and burned out near Korbach flying in low cloud. Oberlt Hertling and passenger killed. Aircraft a write-off.

Thursday, April 18

BRITISH AIR FORCES IN FRANCE

4 SQUADRON Lysander L4741. Stalled and crashed on approach to Mons-en-Chaussée. Crew unhurt. Aircraft a write-off.

218 SQUADRON Battle L5245. Belly-landed at St-Christophe-à-Berry with burst glycol tank. Pilot Officer Meek and crew unhurt. Aircraft damaged but repairable.

BELGIAN AIR FORCE

7/III/3 Fox (O.184). Collided with the tower of the Abbaye d'Argenton during low-level patrol. S/Lt d'Alcantara de Querrieu and Lt Buyens both killed. Aircraft a write-off.

LUFTWAFFE

8./JG3 Messerschmitt Bf109D. Crashed and burned out near Halle after diving through cloud. Uffz G. Dietrich killed. Aircraft a write-off.
Unit formed March 1 under Hptmn Walter Kienitz, moving from Detmold to Hopsten on April 10.

8./JG3 Messerschmitt Bf109E-3. Wrecked attempting forced-landing near Recklinghausen in bad weather. Pilot unhurt. Aircraft a write-off.

I./JG27 Messerschmitt Bf109E. Lost bearings and wrecked in forced-landing at Siegen. Pilot unhurt. Aircraft a write-off.

4./JG52 Messerschmitt Bf109E-1. Involved in take-off collision at Speyer. Pilot unhurt. Aircraft 7+ damaged but repairable.

5./JG52 Messerschmitt Bf109E-1 (3403). Damaged in take-off collision at Speyer. Uffz L. Bielmeyer unhurt. Aircraft 8+ damaged but repairable.

III./JG52 Messerschmitt Bf109E-3. Crashed near Altripp following mid-air collision south of Mannheim. Oberlt A. Gerlach killed. Aircraft a write-off.
Unit formed at Strausberg March 1 under Major Wolf-Heinrich von Houwald moving to Mannheim-Sandhofen on April 6 for operational training subordinate to Stab JG53.

III./JG52 Messerschmitt Bf109E-3. Abandoned over Altripp following mid-air collision. Pilot baled out unhurt. Aircraft a write-off.

2./JG54 Messerschmitt Bf109E-1. Wrecked in crash-landing at Böblingen, cause not stated. Pilot unhurt. Aircraft a write-off.

II./KG28 Heinkel He111H-3. Collided with a tree after landing at Gotha. No crew casualties. Aircraft repairable.
This unit was reformed at Jesau on December 15 from elements of KG27, moving west to Kassel-Rothwesten in February 1940.

Friday, April 19

FRENCH AIR FORCE

GC 1/145 Caudron C-714. Run out of fuel on final approach following aerobatics practice; stalled and crashed outside Lyon-Bron airfield. S/Lt W. Dobrzynski killed. Aircraft a write-off.
Witold Dobrzynski, first Polish pilot to be killed on active service with the Armée de l'Air, was buried in La Guillotière Cemetery in Lyon.

BELGIAN AIR FORCE

1/I/2 Gladiator (G.35). Crashed in the sea, cause unknown. Pilot saved. Aircraft lost.

LUFTWAFFE

2.(H)/13 Henschel Hs126. Shot down by Moranes of GC II/7 during observation mission south of Neu-Breisach and crashed near Balgau. Lt W. Hellmann and Gefr H.Meissner killed. Aircraft 4E+BK a write-off.

4.(F)/121 Junkers Ju88. Believed that attacked by Capt Hugo and Sgt Planchard of GC II/7 over Biengen, south-west of Freiburg. Crew unhurt. Aircraft returned undamaged.

The shattered remains of the crew are recovered — today Bruno von Wühlisch, and Albert Loscher are buried in the cemetery at Fort-de-Malmaison.

2./JG2 Messerschmitt Bf109E-1. Crashed on landing at Bassenheim on burst tyre. Pilot unhurt. Aircraft damaged but repairable.

Stab JG52 Messerschmitt Bf109E-3. Damaged in taxi-ing accident at Mannheim-Stadt. Pilot unhurt. Aircraft damaged but repairable.

Saturday, April 20

BRITISH AIR FORCES IN FRANCE

1 SQUADRON Hurricane L1843. Hit by return fire from Ju88 of 4.(F)/121 engaged between Châlons and Reims, and belly-landed at Les Clérimois, north-east of Sens, with engine on fire 9.45 a.m. Flying Officer J. I. Kilmartin unhurt. Aircraft JX⊙H a write-off.

1 SQUADRON Hurricane. Dead stick landing back at Vassincourt after propeller disintegrated during pursuit of Ju88 of 4.(F)/121 between Châlons and Reims 9.45 a.m. Flying Officer P. H. M. Richey unhurt. Aircraft repairable.

87 SQUADRON Hurricane L1722. Wrecked in taxying accident at Amiens-Glisy. Pilot unhurt. Aircraft damaged but repairable — later abandoned.

218 SQUADRON Battle P2201. Failed to return from leaflet-dropping sortie over Worms and Mainz. Shot down by Oberfw Schmale of 12.(N)/JG2 north of Crailsheim 11.45 p.m. Pilot Officer H. D. Wardle captured. Sergeant E. Davison and AC1 A. Bailey killed. Aircraft a write-off.
   This was the first recorded victory of WWII for the Luftwaffe night fighter force. 'Hank' Wardle was later to join Pat Reid in a celebrated escape from Colditz in 1942.

FRENCH AIR FORCE

GC II/3 Morane 406. Suffered engine trouble during pursuit of a Do17 and forced-landed at Rosée, near Flavion, in Belgium. Cpl V. Cukr interned but later released. Aircraft impounded.

GC II/4 Curtiss H-75 (136). Engine and oil system badly damaged in attack by Hptmn Mölders *(Gruppenkommandeur)* of Stab III./JG53 during escort sortie for Potez 63.11 of GR II/36 over Wolmunster—Hornbach—Pirmasens sector. Crash-landed near Bliesbruck 10.54 a.m. Adjt Cruchant badly wounded admitted to hospital in Nancy. Aircraft destroyed by ground troops.

GC II/4 Curtiss H-75 (189). Forced-landed at Xaffévillers damaged following combat with Bf109s of III./JG53 near Hornbach 10.55 a.m. Sgt Casenobe unhurt. Aircraft repairable.

GR I/52 Bloch 174 (31). Shot down by Hptmn Tietzen *(Staffelkapitän)* of 5./JG51 over Lorquin during return from reconnaissance mission to Stuttgart and crashed north of Schirmeck 10.50 a.m. S/Lt P. Laneuze, S/Lt J. Février, and Adjt P. Mougel killed. Aircraft a write-off.

British and French servicemen help recover the heavy camera. Reformed at Prenzlau in November 1938, the 3. Staffel of Fernaufklärungsgruppe 121 was a long-range reconnaissance unit based at Frankfurt-Main.

LUFTWAFFE

4.(F)/14 Dornier Do17. Returned damaged in attack by Bf109s of 3./JG27 over Aachen. Oberlt Jähne wounded, rest of crew unhurt. Aircraft repairable.

4.(F)/121 Junkers Ju88A-1. Badly damaged in attack by F/O Kilmartin of No. 1 Squadron during reconnaissance of airfields and rail traffic between Saint-Dizier and Langres 9.45 a.m. Pursued from Beaune to Romilly where engaged by Asp Amouroux of GC III/9 and finally crashed at Ozolles. Oberlt K. Pritzel, Oberfw B. Hippel, Fw H. Kieler, and Uffz J. Adam captured unhurt. Aircraft a write-off.

1./JG2 Messerschmitt Bf109E-3. Hit by return fire from Potez 63 engaged over Saarlautern and forced-landed at Bassenheim. Uffz K. Geisler wounded. Aircraft repairable.

I./JG2 Messerschmitt Bf109E-1. Crashed on landing at Bassenheim, cause not stated. Pilot unhurt. Aircraft damaged but repairable.

III./JG2 Messerschmitt Bf109E-1. Forced-landed at Wittlich due to petrol failure. Pilot unhurt. Aircraft damaged but repairable.

4./JG52 Messerschmitt Bf109E-1. Wrecked in forced-landing at Landau due to petrol failure during frontier patrol. Lt P. Kranz injured. Aircraft 4+ a write-off.

8./JG52 Messerschmitt Bf109E-1. Starboard undercarriage leg collapsed on landing at Mannheim-Sandhofen. Pilot unhurt. Aircraft 10+ ~ repairable.

II./JG53 Messerschmitt Bf109E-1. Damaged in forced-landing at Gau-Bickelheim due to petrol failure. Pilot unhurt. Aircraft damaged but repairable.

7./JG53 Messerschmitt Bf109E-1. Shot down by F/L Walker of No. 1 Squadron in combat south-east of Diedenhofen and crashed at Kédange-sur-Canner, 15 km south-east of Thionville 12.30 p.m. Lt F. Sievers killed. Aircraft a write-off.

8./JG53 Messerschmitt Bf109E-3. Hit an obstruction on take-off from Hoppstädten. Fw A. Weigelt seriously injured, died next day. Aircraft a write-off.

8./JG53 Messerschmitt Bf109E-1. Crashed and burned out shortly after take-off from Hoppstädten due to poor state of runway. Pilot injured. Aircraft a write-off.

2./JG54 Messerschmitt Bf109E-3. Shot down by Sgt Boillot of GC II/7 in combat northeast of Belfort and exploded east of Lachapelle-sous-Chaux 6.55 a.m. Lt H. Hoch killed. Aircraft a write-off.

Stab KG1 Heinkel He111H-2 (2020). Attacked near Maubeuge by Sgt Cukr, S/Lt Troyes, S/Lt Codet, Adjt Poincourt, Sgt Vie, and Sgt Loï of GC II/3 during photo-reconnaissance sortie between Reims and Paris and chased into Belgium with port engine disabled. Then intercepted over Visé by Gladiators of 1/I/2 flown by Sgt Delorme, Sgt Verpoorten, and Sgt Van den Broeck and eventually belly-landed at Bunde in the Netherlands 11.40 a.m. Sonderführer F. Stern (*Kriegsbildberichter*) badly wounded, died next day. Lt P. Lehmann, Oberfw A. Wutz, Fw H-A. Kopitz, and Uffz K. Koschorreck interned. Aircraft V4+DA a write-off.
War correspondent Fritz Stern was buried with full military honours at Maastricht four days later.

Stab III./KG2 Dornier Do17Z-3. Lost bearings during night sortie and landed low on fuel at Basel-Birsfelden in Switzerland. Lt H. von der Groeben, Uffz O. Hermann, Uffz W. Schweinoch, and Uffz W. Böke interned. Aircraft U5+BD a write-off.
This aircraft was interned, made airworthy, and later flew in Swiss markings, but with the cessation of hostilities in France, it was returned to Germany by Oberlt Reinhard Hausin who flew from Altenrhein to Friedrichshafen on September 19, 1940. The crew was repatriated to Germany on June 28, 1940 at Stetten-Lörrach.

III./ZG26 Messerschmitt Bf110C-1. Crash-landed at Krefeld during courier flight, cause not stated. Crew unhurt. Aircraft a write-off.

Wettererkundungsstaffel 51 Dornier Do17U. Hit an obstruction on take-off at Langendiebach. No crew casualties. Aircraft damaged but repairable.

Sunday, April 21

BRITISH AIR FORCES IN FRANCE

73 SQUADRON Hurricane. Forced-landed with one wing badly damaged in attack by Oberlt Mayer (*Staffelkapitän*) of 1./JG53 during escort sortie for Mureaux observation machine north-west of Merzig 11.05 a.m. Pilot Officer P. B. Walker splinter wounds in shoulder. Aircraft damaged but repairable.

85 SQUADRON Hurricane N2363. Damaged in landing accident at Mons-en-Chaussée, circumstances not recorded. Pilot believed unhurt. Aircraft damaged but repairable — later abandoned.

212 SQUADRON Spitfire I (PR) N3071. Engine disabled over Böblingen by Bf109s of II./JG51 during photo-reconnaissance sortie and abandoned over Grossbettlingen, south-east of Stuttgart 5.55 p.m. Credited to Fw John of 4./JG51. Flying Officer C. Milne baled out and captured unhurt. Aircraft a write-off.
Believed to be the first loss of one of these specially modified aircraft when operating from France. The first actual loss occurred March 22 when N3069 of N Flight PDU at Heston was shot down over Kleve by Lt Jung of I./JG20 and crashed by the River Rhine at Lobith. P/O C. M. Wheatley baled out but was killed.

FRENCH AIR FORCE

GAO 1/520 Potez 63.11 (246). Crashed and burned out at Marzeville after engine failed on take-off during training flight. Adjt Grivel and Sgt Jérôme injured. Another crewman unhurt. Aircraft a write-off.

LUFTWAFFE

1.(F)/123 Dornier Do17P. Landed at Ansbach damaged in attacks by S/Lt Warnier and Sgt Tallent of GC I/5 over Stenay 11.20 a.m. One crewman wounded. Aircraft damaged but repairable.

I./JG2 Messerschmitt Bf109E-1. Set alight by F/O Orton of No. 73 Sqdn in combat over Tünsdorf p.m. Oberfw W. Höppner baled out but killed. Aircraft a write-off.

I./JG26 Messerschmitt Bf109E-3. Oil line fractured during wireless test flight and forced-landed at Rübenach. Pilot unhurt. Aircraft damaged but repairable.

II./JG51 Messerschmitt Bf109E-3 (5185). Wrecked in forced-landing at Böblingen following engine failure. Pilot unhurt. Aircraft a write-off.

2./JG76 Messerschmitt Bf109E-1. Shot down in flames by Hurricanes of No. 73 Sqdn during escort sortie for Hs126 and crashed at Bündingen, west of Merzig 12.15 p.m. Possibly that claimed by S/L More. Fw L. Wyhlidal killed. Aircraft a write-off.

I./ZG2 Messerschmitt Bf110C. Shot down in combat with Hurricanes of No. 73 Sqdn over Merzig p.m. Possibly that claimed by F/O Orton. Fw S. Fischer killed. Uffz E. Mayer baled out wounded. Aircraft a write-off.

I./ZG2 Messerschmitt Bf110C. Belly-landed at Hermeskeil damaged in combat with Hurricanes of No. 73 Sqdn over Merzig p.m. Possibly that claimed by F/L Lovett. Lt H. Nocher and Uffz A. Kirchof both wounded. Aircraft a write-off.

II./ZG76 Messerschmitt Bf110C. Damaged on landing at Rhein-Main due to undercarriage failure. Crew unhurt. Aircraft repairable.

Monday, April 22

BRITISH AIR FORCES IN FRANCE

150 SQUADRON Battle. Burned out on the ground at Ecury-sur-Coole when parachute flare ignited. No casualties. Aircraft a write-off.

LUFTWAFFE

3.(F)/11 Dornier Do17P. Shot down by S/Lt Rouquette, Adj Bouvard, and Sgt Morel of GC I/5 and crashed at 'Rechi', near Léglise, south-east of Neufchâteau 7.17 a.m. Uffz S. Beisbarth killed. Uffz G. Kratzmann, badly wounded and admitted to hospital in Longlier, and Fw W. Schulte-Umberg slightly wounded, both interned. Aircraft FN+GL a write-off.

I./JG3 Messerschmitt Bf109E-3. Aborted take-off from Bonn-Hangelar and undercarriage damaged. Pilot unhurt. Aircraft damaged but repairable.

6./JG51 Messerschmitt Bf109E-3 (5156). Wrecked in forced-landing at Böblingen following engine failure. Pilot unhurt. Aircraft a write-off.

6./JG51 Messerschmitt Bf109E-1 (6111). Forced-landed at Böblingen due to control failure. Pilot unhurt. Aircraft repairable.

III./JG53 Messerschmitt Bf109E-4. Crashed on landing at Wiesbaden-Erbenheim due to burst tyre. Pilot unhurt. Aircraft a write-off.

I./JG54 Messerschmitt Bf109E-3 (1225). Crash-landed at Eutingen following combat sortie. Pilot unhurt. Aircraft damaged but repairable.

I./JG76 Messerschmitt Bf109E-1. Crashed on landing at Ober-Olm due to undercarriage failure. Pilot unhurt. Aircraft damaged but repairable.

I./JG77 Messerschmitt Bf109E-1. Wrecked in forced-landing at Ludwigsburg due to petrol failure. Pilot unhurt. Aircraft a write-off.

III./KG28 Heinkel He111P. Wrecked in forced-landing at Siegen due to engine trouble. Two crew injured. Aircraft a write-off.

This Dornier came down at Léglise near Neufchâteau on April 22. Two crewmen were interned . . .

Stab KG53 Heinkel He111H. Slightly damaged when jacks collapsed at Schwäbisch-Hall. No crew casualties. Aircraft repairable.

15.(Z)/LG1 Messerschmitt Bf110C. Crashed near Mannheim-Sandhofen following engine failure on test flight. Oberlt W. Clausen (*Staffelkapitän*) and mechanic killed. Aircraft a write-off.

Aufklst. Flakkorps I Junkers W34. Damaged in taxying accident at Frankfurt-Rebstock. Crew unhurt. Aircraft repairable.

Tuesday, April 23

BRITISH AIR FORCES IN FRANCE

73 SQUADRON Hurricane P2576. 'Bounced' by Bf109s west of Merzig and gravity tank set alight in attack by Hptmn Mölders of III./JG53; abandoned over Thionville 10.14 a.m. Sergeant C. N. S. Campbell baled out burned on arms and face, and splinter wounds in right leg, admitted to hospital in Rombas. Aircraft a write-off.

73 SQUADRON Hurricane N2391. 'Bounced' by Bf109s west of Merzig and badly damaged in attack by Fw Gawlick of III./JG53 forced-landing near Sierck-les-Bains 10.30 a.m. Sergeant T. B. G. Pyne wounded in the shoulder, admitted to hospital in Metz. Aircraft a write-off.

FRENCH AIR FORCE

GC I/1 Bloch 152 (180). Crashed and burned out near Chantilly-les-Aigles when aircraft caught fire during training flight. Cpl J. Krakora killed. Aircraft a write-off.

GC II/5 Curtiss H-75. Returned damaged following combat with Bf109s of I./JG52 east of Metz 1.15 p.m. Adjt Delannoy believed unhurt. Aircraft repairable.

GC II/5 Curtiss H-75. Damaged by flak and forced-landed near Pont-à-Mousson 1.30 p.m. S/Lt Jaske believed unhurt. Aircraft damaged but repairable.

DUTCH AIR FORCE

Vliegschool Vlissingen Fokker S IV (127). Crashed during training flight, cause unknown. 1e Lt B. M. Aarts believed unhurt. Aircraft a write-off.

In addition, two Fokker S IVs and a Fokker S IX were also recorded as being damaged in accidents at Vlissingen in April 1940.

LUFTWAFFE

1.(H)/13 Dornier Do17P. Returned starboard engine damaged in attacks by Curtiss H-75s of GC II/5 during reconnaissance sortie southeast of Metz 1.15 p.m. Uffz A. Abele slightly wounded admitted to hospital in Neunkirchen. Aircraft damaged but repairable.

2.(H)/21 Henschel Hs126. Crashed near Rodder, cause unknown. Lt Klappert and another killed. Aircraft a write-off.

I./JG2 Messerschmitt Bf109E-1. Crashed on landing at Bassenheim due to undercarriage failure. Pilot unhurt. Aircraft damaged but repairable.

I./JG2 Messerschmitt Bf109E-3. Wrecked in crash-landing at Wengerohr, cause not stated. Pilot unhurt. Aircraft a write-off.

8./JG2 Messerschmitt Bf109E-1. Crashed on landing at Frankfurt-Rebstock when starboard undercarriage leg collapsed. Pilot unhurt. Aircraft 14 + ~ a write-off.

1./JG20 Messerschmitt Bf109E-1. Overturned attempting to take-off from Bönninghardt due to undercarriage failure. Lt H. Staiger unhurt. Aircraft 5+ damaged but repairable.

I./JG20 Messerschmitt Bf109E-1. Burst tyre on take-off from Bönninghardt. Pilot unhurt. Aircraft repairable.

. . . but Unteroffizier Siegfried Beisbarth was killed and was given full military honours at his funeral at Neufchâteau. He is now buried in the German War Cemetery at Lommel, Block 2, Grave 240.

6./JG51 Messerschmitt Bf109E-1 (3178). Lost control and crashed on take-off from Böblingen. Pilot unhurt. Aircraft a write-off.

2./JG52 Messerschmitt Bf109E-1. Damaged in combat with Curtiss H-75s of GC II/5 during escort sortie for 1.(H)/13 east of Metz. Possibly that claimed by S/Lt Klan which crash-landed at Tromborn, south-east of Bouzonville 1.15 p.m. Oberfw F. Essl wounded. Aircraft damaged but repairable.

2./JG52 Messerschmitt Bf109E-3. Damaged in combat with Curtiss H-75s of GC II/5 east of Metz during escort sortie for 1.(H)/13 and possibly that attacked by S/Lt Ruchoux. Forced-landed at St Wendel 1.15 p.m. Pilot unhurt. Aircraft damaged but repairable.

I./JG52 Messerschmitt Bf109E-3. Crash-landed at Lachen-Speyerdorf due to control failure. Pilot unhurt. Aircraft damaged but repairable.

8./JG53 Messerschmitt Bf109E-1. Crash-landed at Hoppstädten, cause not stated. Pilot injured. Aircraft damaged but repairable.

7./KG2 Dornier Do17Z. Crashed at Avenay, east of Épernay, cause unknown but possibly engine failure. Lt G. Karsten, Fw G. Zoller, Uffz H. Cybulski, and Gefr H. Miller killed. Aircraft a write-off.

2./KG27 Heinkel He111P. Crashed east of Münster-Handorf during night-landing practice, cause unknown. Uffz H. Schirrmacher killed, two crewmen injured. Aircraft 1G+BK a write-off.

II./KG27 2 Heinkel He111P. Aircraft damaged in taxiing accident at Gütersloh. No crew casualties. Aircraft both damaged but repairable.

I./ZG2 Messerschmitt Bf110C. Run into a slit trench on landing at Darmstadt-Griesheim. Crew unhurt. Aircraft repairable.

I./ZG2 Messerschmitt Bf110C. Forced-landed at Darmstadt-Griesheim with engine trouble. Crew unhurt. Aircraft damaged but repairable.

On April 25, the 4th Staffel of Reconnaissance Geschwader 121 lost a Dornier on a photo reconnaissance flight over eastern France. Believing they were over German territory, they landed at Tintigny whereupon the three-man crew were interned.

I./ZG52 Messerschmitt Bf110C. Tyre burst on landing at Neuhausen. Crew unhurt. Aircraft damaged but repairable.

Wednesday, April 24

FRENCH AIR FORCE

GAO 548 Mureaux 115 (83). Shot down by flak during photo-reconnaissance mission over Kehl p.m. Lt J. Roussel killed. Sgt Wibaux baled out badly wounded. Aircraft a write-off.

GC I/5 Curtiss H-75 (157). Crashed on perimeter of Suippes airfield on return from routine patrol; exact cause unknown. Adjt M. Emprin killed. Aircraft a write-off.

GC I/6 Morane 406. Crashed near Chissey-sur-Loue due to mechanical failure 12.45 p.m. Sgt B. Bertrand killed. Aircraft a write-off.

LUFTWAFFE

2./JG20 Messerschmitt Bf109E-1. Damaged in taxiing accident at Bönninghardt. Pilot unhurt. Aircraft repairable.

I./JG26 Messerschmitt Bf109E-3. Crash-landed at Bönninghardt due to control failure. Pilot unhurt. Aircraft damaged but repairable.

I./JG26 Messerschmitt Bf109E-3. Crash-landed at Bönninghardt during conversion flight. Pilot unhurt. Aircraft damaged but repairable.

5./JG26 Messerschmitt Bf109E-1. Forced-landed at Dortmund due to control failure. Pilot unhurt. Aircraft damaged but repairable.

I./JG77 Messerschmitt Bf109E-1. Crash-landed at Porz-Wahn, cause not stated. Pilot unhurt. Aircraft repairable.

I./KG1 Heinkel He111H. Crash-landed at Nordhausen airfield due to control failure. Crew unhurt. Aircraft a write-off.

Thursday, April 25

BRITISH AIR FORCES IN FRANCE

98 SQUADRON Battle. Landed at Nantes-Bougon with damage to port mainplane following mid-air collision during formation practice 11.40 a.m. Crew unhurt. Aircraft damaged but repairable.

LUFTWAFFE

1.(H)/21 Henschel Hs126. Hit the ground between Fraisen and Herschweiler, near Idar-Oberstein, during ferry flight in bad weather. Obergefr P. Karow badly injured, died next day in Baumholder surgical hospital, another crewman injured. Aircraft P2+MH a write-off.

4.(F)/121 Junkers Ju88A-1. Engine caught fire after landing at Stuttgart-Süd. Crew unhurt. Aircraft damaged but repairable.

4.(F)/121 Dornier Do17P (0173). Met bad weather during photo reconnaissance of railways between Neufchâteau and Mirecourt and landed in error near Ferme Ménil at Tintigny, Belgium 11.15 a.m. Oberlt P. Döring, Uffz E. Pristat, and Uffz G. Kriegenhofer interned — later handed to the British. Aircraft 7A+BM a write-off.

I./JG53 Messerschmitt Bf109E-1. Crashed on landing at Darmstadt-Griesheim when undercarriage collapsed. Pilot unhurt. Aircraft damaged but repairable.

I./JG77 Messerschmitt Bf109E-3. Lost control and crashed on landing at Porz-Wahn. Pilot unhurt. Aircraft a write-off.

As these pictures show, the machine was remarkably intact and a nice prize for the Belgians.

I./JG77 Messerschmitt Bf109E-1. Wrecked in forced-landing at Aachen following engine failure south of Cologne. Pilot unhurt. Aircraft a write-off.

I./StG2 Junkers Ju87B-1. Crashed following mid-air collision near Cologne. One of crew killed. Aircraft a write-off.
The other aircraft involved was undamaged and landed safely.

Friday, April 26

DUTCH AIR FORCE

Vliegschool Vlissingen Fokker S IV. Forced-landed at Grijpskerke during training flight, exact cause unknown. Pilot believed unhurt. Aircraft damage state not recorded.

LUFTWAFFE

4./JG51 Messerschmitt Bf109E-1 (6180). Involved in landing collision at Böblingen. Pilot unhurt. Aircraft damaged but repairable.

I./JG76 Messerschmitt Bf109E-1. Crashed on landing at Ober-Olm due to burst tyre. Pilot unhurt. Aircraft damaged but repairable.

II.(S)/LG2 Henschel Hs123A-1. Forced-landed near Mönchengladbach due to engine trouble. Pilot unhurt. Aircraft damaged but repairable.

Saturday, April 27

BRITISH AIR FORCES IN FRANCE

4 SQUADRON Lysander N1272. Undershot runway and crashed on landing at Mons-en-Chaussée. Crew believed unhurt. Aircraft a write-off.

BELGIAN AIR FORCE

2/I/2 Hurricane (H.25). Nosed-over landing on soft ground at Steene-Ostend. Pilot unhurt. Aircraft repairable.

LUFTWAFFE

II./JG51 Messerschmitt Bf109E-3 (683). Crashed on landing at Böblingen due to undercarriage failure. Pilot unhurt. Aircraft repairable.

I./KG76 Dornier Do17Z. Crashed near Nordhausen from 1,200 feet, pilot believed blinded by searchlights. Flgr P. G. Mirtschin and three crew killed. Aircraft a write-off.

II./ZG76 Messerschmitt Bf110C. Hit a tree, crashed and burned out, while low-flying near Hofheim. Crew both killed. Aircraft a write-off.

Monday, April 29

FRENCH AIR FORCE

DAT Châteauroux Romano R-82 (120). Engine seized during training flight; forced-landed between Le Grand Launay and Les Carrages, near Digoin 5.40 p.m. Lt M. Imiela unhurt. Aircraft a write-off.

GC II/7 Dewoitine 520 (26). Wrecked in an accident at Luxeuil airfield. Pilot unhurt. Aircraft a write-off.

LUFTWAFFE

I./JG77 Messerschmitt Bf109E-1. Undercarriage collapsed on landing at Porz-Wahn. Pilot unhurt. Aircraft damaged but repairable.

Tuesday, April 30

BRITISH AIR FORCES IN FRANCE

18 SQUADRON Blenheim IV L8875. Belly-landed at Brussels-Evere when compass failed having lost bearings in a storm during cloud-flying practice. Sergeant A. W. S. Thomas, Sergeant J. J. F. Talbot and LAC R. G. St James-Smith interned. Aircraft WV⊙S lost.

FRENCH AIR FORCE

GR 3/33 Bloch 174 (18). Stalled during training flight, crashed at Monceau-le-Waast. Adjt Sepet slightly injured with broken nose. Lt Israël *(Commandant)* and Cpl Blondel unhurt. Aircraft a write-off.

BELGIAN AIR FORCE

3/II/2 Fiat CR-42 (R.9). Lost control and crashed at Nivelles during dogfight practice. S/Lt W. Couturier killed. Aircraft a write-off.

LUFTWAFFE

1.(H)/11 Henschel Hs126. Tyre burst on landing at Schmidtheim after flak co-operation flight. Crew unhurt. Aircraft damaged but repairable.

4.(F)/122 Junkers Ju88A-1. Caught fire after landing at Münster-Loddenheide. No crew casualties. Aircraft a write-off.

I./JG2 2 Messerschmitt Bf109E. Slightly damaged landing at Bassenheim on burst tyres. Pilots unhurt. Aircraft both repairable.

II./JG53 Messerschmitt Bf109E-1. Crash-landed at Ippesheim, cause not stated. Pilot unhurt. Aircraft damaged but repairable.

10.(St)/LG1 Junkers Ju87B. Failed to recover from dive during dive-bombing practice at Kirchhellen, near Gladbeck. Uffz E. Piederstorfer and Uffz O. Wechel killed. Aircraft a write-off.

3./ZG26 Messerschmitt Bf110C. Undercarriage collapsed on landing at Krefeld. Crew unhurt. Aircraft damaged but repairable.

A photograph taken after the Luftwaffe had occupied Brussels-Evere airfield with the remains of No. 18 Squadron's Blenheim which came to grief on Tuesday, April 30 lying in the foreground.

MAY 1940

The land and air commanders in France General Gort *(left)*, the Commander-in-Chief of the British Expeditionary Force, and Air Marshal Barratt, commander of the Advanced Air Striking Force since January 15, pictured conferring at an undisclosed location.

If any significant lessons were learned by Allied commanders in the West from intelligence of German tactics employed during the recent invasion of Norway, there was scant time to put them into practice.

As tension in the West increased, long-range reconnaissance sorties now became almost continuous with mounting casualties among the strategic reconnaissance units. Rumours and reports of the imminence of a German attack were rife but, lacking the seeming novelty of all such earlier 'flaps', they now carried an ominous air of truth.

On the evening of May 7, Air Marshal Barratt telephoned Group Captain Strafford at Chauny to warn him to expect an alert being ordered. The same night, Strafford also received a warning from the French ZOAN Headquarters of air attacks expected at dawn but these failed to materialise.

At 2.15 a.m. on May 9, the Air Ministry telephoned Air Marshal Barratt's Headquarters at Coulommiers to inform him that Germany had issued an ultimatum to Holland. 'Readiness State No. 1' was consequently ordered throughout the British Air Forces in France.

Increasing reports of substantial German movements along its frontiers with the Low Countries continued throughout that night. Now, after eight months waiting, German intentions were suddenly beyond any further doubt.

The calm before the storm. Pilots relax in the back garden of their Mess at Pontavert. No. 1 Squadron moved to the nearby aerodrome at Juvincourt for a few days in mid-April before returning to Vassincourt. Putting their feet up are Flight Lieutenant P. R. 'Johnny' Walker, the 'A' Flight Commander, and Flying Officer M. H 'Killy' Brown, a Canadian in 'A' Flight who was killed in November 1941 on a low-level attack from Malta against a German airfield in Sicily.

Wednesday, May 1

BELGIAN AIR FORCE

3/II/1 Fox (O.61). Crashed at Schaffen, cause unknown. Sgt Deleers injured. Aircraft a write-off.

LUFTWAFFE

1./JG51 Messerschmitt Bf109E. Hit the ground low-flying and forced-landed at Krefeld. Fw H. Bär unhurt. Aircraft repairable.

I./JG77 Messerschmitt Bf109E-1. Forced-landed at Hoppstädten due to engine trouble. Pilot unhurt. Aircraft damaged but repairable.

Thursday, May 2

BELGIAN AIR FORCE

7/III/3 Stampe SV5 (N.25). Crashed on take-off at Steene-Ostend. Adjt F. Huenaerts and Adjt J. Barthels killed. Aircraft a write-off.

LUFTWAFFE

I./JG2 Messerschmitt Bf109E-3. Forced-landed at Bassenheim following engine failure. Pilot unhurt. Aircraft damaged but repairable.

I./JG53 Messerschmitt Bf109E-3. Overturned during take-off from Darmstadt-Griesheim. Pilot unhurt. Aircraft damaged but repairable.

The building still stands in Pontavert, the nearest village to the airfield (see map page 26-27), but as the rear garden is now hidden by trees planted close to the house, we had to be content with a photograph taken from the street side.

Friday, May 3

BRITISH AIR FORCES IN FRANCE

53 SQUADRON Blenheim IV L9329. Shot down near Hornisgrinde during reconnaissance sortie over the Ruhr 9.00 p.m. Pilot Officer J. L. G. Butterworth, Sergeant M. G. A. Pearce, and AC2 R. A. Wood killed. Aircraft TE⊙L a write-off.

DUTCH AIR FORCE

Vliegschool Vlissingen Fokker S IX (33). Crashed at West Souburg during training flight; exact cause unknown. Pilot believed unhurt. Aircraft a write-off.

LUFTWAFFE

1.(H)/23 Henschel 126. Crashed at Stallageberg, north of Cologne-Butzweilerhof, during training flight 4.15 p.m. Lt H-U. von Sichart and Lt E. Osten killed. Aircraft a write-off.

3./JG2 Messerschmitt Bf109E-1. Forced-landed at Trier-Euren due to engine failure. Uffz G. Seeger injured. Aircraft 12+ damaged but repairable.

2./JG26 Messerschmitt Bf109E-1. Damaged in take-off accident at Bönninghardt. Pilot unhurt. Aircraft damaged but repairable.

I./JG53 Messerschmitt Bf109E-1. Damaged in forced-landing at Saarbrücken following engine failure. Pilot injured. Aircraft damaged but repairable.

Saturday, May 4

BRITISH AIR FORCES IN FRANCE

59 SQUADRON Blenheim IV L4857. Crashed and burned out attempting night overshoot at Poix. Pilot Officer G. O. Arscott, Sergeant G. H. Barford, and AC2 P. W. Froom killed. Aircraft a write-off.

FRENCH AIR FORCE

GR I/55 Potez 63.11. Reported crashed near Villingen, cause unknown. Crew killed. Aircraft a write-off.

LUFTWAFFE

9./KG27 Heinkel He111P. Crashed near Osterfeine in the Dammer Bergen, south-west of Diepholz, during searchlight co-operation, cause unknown. Oberlt R. Paulsen, Fw W. Schilling, Fw G. Vogel, and Gefr J. Hallig killed. Aircraft a write-off.

II.(S)/LG2 Henschel Hs123A. Wrecked in explosion of 10kg bomb while loading at Kaarst airfield. One killed. Aircraft a write-off.
Another Hs123 and a Hs126 were also slightly damaged in this accident, but both repairable by unit.

No. 1 Squadron, under their charismatic Irish commanding officer Patrick Halahan 'The Bull', was based at Vassincourt. One of its 'A' Flight pilots, Paul Richey, kept a detailed diary of his experiences with the squadron in France that was later published as the seminal book *Fighter Pilot* in September 1941. He claimed a Bf109 near Saarburg on March 29 (see page 154) — the first of more than 11 victories. He died in 1989.

Sunday, May 5

BRITISH AIR FORCES IN FRANCE

2 SQUADRON Lysander. Overturned forced-landing at Rethel in bad weather during mail flight from Abbeville to Senon. Flight Lieutenant D. I. C. Ayres unhurt. Aircraft a write-off.

4 SQUADRON Lysander II L4749. Crashed at Lille-Ronchin due to engine failure 4.55 p.m. Pilot Officer MacDonald injured. Aircraft damaged but repairable — later abandoned.

LUFTWAFFE

3.(F)/121 Junkers Ju88A. Wrecked in belly-landing near Langendiebach when one engine failed. Crew unhurt. Aircraft a write-off.

Monday, May 6

BRITISH AIR FORCES IN FRANCE

87 SQUADRON Hurricane. Overturned due to poor state of airfield at Lille-Seclin. Squadron Leader J. S. Dewar injured, admitted to hospital. Aircraft repairable.

87 SQUADRON Master. Overturned when brakes seized while forced-landing at Lille-Seclin due to bad weather. Flight Lieutenant M. Lister-Robinson and Pilot Officer K. W. Tait both injured, admitted to hospital. Aircraft damage state not recorded.

88 SQUADRON Battle L5248. Crashed at Villiers-Charlemagne, east of Houssay, during endurance test; cause not stated. Sergeant N. F. F. Giddings and LAC C. J. Goddard killed. Sergeant Acock injured. Aircraft a write-off.

139 SQUADRON Blenheim IV N6224. Believed damaged by bird strike, circumstances not recorded. Pilot Officer D. G. Marshall lost right eye; rest of crew unhurt. Aircraft damaged but repairable — later abandoned.

FRENCH AIR FORCE

GAO 1/508 Potez 630 (70). Suffered loss of control during aerobatics and crashed at Marcilly-sur-Seine. Sgt Dupuy badly injured, Adjt Kulling unhurt. Lt Noir baled out injured. Aircraft a write-off.

BELGIAN AIR FORCE

2/I/2 Hurricane. Intercepted enemy aircraft between Mons and Ath and pursued over Colmar and Gérardmer eventually forced-landing at St Omer out of fuel 1.00 p.m. Sgt van Strydonck unhurt. Aircraft repairable.

2/I/2 2 Hurricanes. Intercepted enemy aircraft between Mons and Ath and pursued over Colmar and Gérardmer, eventually damaged in forced-landings at Diksmuide and Aartrijke 1.00 p.m. Pilots unhurt. Aircraft both damaged but repairable.

Vassincourt 65 years later. The airfield has had a colourful history for when it was captured the Germans sited a large market garden there to produce food for their troops, using imported Polish labourers. Then after the war the Americans set up a kennels to house security dogs for guarding military installations in the area including ammunition dumps in the Trois-Fontaines forest to the south-west. They also built a hospital on the northern part which is now used by an institution caring for disabled persons.

In his book Paul Richey includes this picture with the simple caption: 'The end of a Heinkel in a French field'. It is a British official picture (C1505) and one of a series titled 'First Bombs on French Soil'. Unfortunately the sequence is undated, the only clue being that the pictures were received in the UK on May 14, indicating that they would have been taken shortly before. However, even back as far as April 1, there is no Heinkel loss that fits the scenario.

This familiar series of photographs appeared in many publications of the period but without more detail it is not possible to identify the actual incident concerned. It is almost certainly one of the many Heinkels brought down in France during the opening days of the German offensive and would appear to have 'gone in' carrying its full bomb-load.

On the evening of May 7, Air Marshal Barratt advised Lieutenant-Colonel G. F. Hopkinson of No. 3 Mission that he should be ready for an immediate move into Belgium, the order to proceed being issued at 7.15 a.m. next morning. The function of No. 3 Air Mission was, in the event of a German invasion of the Low Countries, to move into Belgium, take up position alongside the Belgian GHQ, and gather information on the progress of the battle for transmission back to advanced headquarters of BAFF. Wing Commander J. M. Fairweather was in overall command while Lieutenant-Colonel Hopkinson commanded the Military Section which undertook ground reconnaissance duties.

LUFTWAFFE

I./KG1 Heinkel He111H. Crashed near Fürstenberg, cause unknown. Four crew killed. Aircraft a write-off.

I./ZG2 Messerschmitt Bf110C. Crashed on landing at Darmstadt-Griesheim due to undercarriage failure. Crew unhurt. Aircraft damaged but repairable.

Tuesday, May 7

BRITISH AIR FORCES IN FRANCE

18 SQUADRON Blenheim IV L9253. Crashed during night-flying practice 10.45 p.m. Pilot Officer G. F. Harding and crew unhurt. Aircraft a write-off.

FRENCH AIR FORCE

GR I/52 Bloch 174 (40). Crashed shortly after take-off from St-Dizier on reconnaissance sortie; caught fire and later exploded. Cdt. Faye *(Groupe Commandant)* slightly injured. Adjt J. Denain and Sgt Boulay unhurt. Aircraft a write-off.

LUFTWAFFE

2.(F)/122 Heinkel He111H-3. Crashed at Drensteinfurt, south of Münster, during searchlight co-operation, cause unknown. Oberfw F. Willuhn, Uffz E. Wessoly, Uffz H. Rucks, and Uffz G. Simon killed. Aircraft a write-off.

3.(F)/123 Dornier Do17P. Returned damaged by enemy fighters. No crew casualties. Aircraft damaged but repairable.

6./JG26 Messerschmitt Bf109E-3. Taxying accident at Dortmund. Pilot unhurt. Aircraft damaged but repairable.

II./JG53 Messerschmitt Bf109E-4. Undercarriage failure at Mannheim-Sandhofen. Pilot unhurt. Aircraft damaged but repairable.

Sergeant 'Ching' Friend's 73 Squadron Hurricane turned turtle at Rouvres on May 8.

I./JG77 Messerschmitt Bf109E-3. Damaged in take-off accident at Porz-Wahn. Pilot unhurt. Aircraft damaged but repairable.

III./KG2 Dornier Do17Z. Forced-landed near Uffenheim following engine failure. Crew unhurt. Aircraft damaged but repairable.

II./KG55 Junkers Ju52. Crash-landed at Leipheim, cause not stated. Crew unhurt. Aircraft damaged but repairable.

II./KG76 Dornier Do17Z. Lost control and crashed on landing at Gotha airfield. Crew unhurt. Aircraft repairable.

8./KG77 Dornier Do17Z. Belly-landed at Düsseldorf due to engine failure. Crew unhurt. Aircraft damaged but repairable.

Wettererkundungsstaffel 51 Dornier Do17Z. Damaged in taxi-ing accident at Langendiebach. Crew unhurt. Aircraft damaged but repairable.

Wednesday, May 8

BRITISH AIR FORCES IN FRANCE

18 SQUADRON Blenheim IV L9186. Run into a recently filled hole and crashed on landing at Méharicourt 11.15 a.m. Flight Lieutenant R. G. Wheldon and crew unhurt. Aircraft damaged but repairable.

73 SQUADRON Hurricane P2647. Braked hard to avoid collision with another aircraft and overturned on landing at Rouvres after practise flight. Sergeant L. Y. T. Friend unhurt. Aircraft TP⊙X damaged but repairable.

73 SQUADRON Hurricane. Undercarriage collapsed while taxi-ing at Rouvres. Squadron Leader J. W. C. More unhurt. Aircraft TP⊙W damaged but repairable.

During the night of May 9, Group Captain Strafford at Chauny received warning from his counterparts in the headquarters of the French Operations Zone (North) that German air attacks were expected at dawn. These failed to materialise in the sort of strength anticipated as the main German assault was directed against Holland and Belgium. At Senon airfield north-east of Verdun, a composite unit comprising No. 2 Squadron Lysanders and No. 87 Squadron Hurricanes detached for special duties over the Maginot line, was recalled to the BEF area. However, when later reports failed to confirm the German ultimatum to Holland, the order was cancelled before it could be executed. Nevertheless every BAFF unit remained at the highest state of readiness.

An unidentified Potez comes to grief . . . a portent of what was about to come to pass in France. Since the New Year, the French had lost a further 64 aircraft and the British 77 although the Germans had suffered a loss of 203 machines, more than double that of the Allies. (The Dutch had lost 10 aircraft and the Belgians 16.) So the score sheet for the entire Phoney War period looked like this: Netherlands 18; Belgium 23; Britain 133; France 175 and Germany 354.

FRENCH AIR FORCE

GC II/5 Curtiss H-75 (40). Collided with Sgt Sals during training exercise from Toul-Croix-de-Metz. Adjt Delannoy baled out unhurt. Aircraft a write-off.

GC II/5 Curtiss H-75 (58). Collided with Adjt Delannoy during collaboration exercise with a Potez 63.11. Sgt E. Salès baled out unhurt. Aircraft a write-off.

GC II/6 Morane 406 (98). Crashed on landing at Anglure-Vouarces, cause not stated. Sgt W. Dambrine unhurt. Aircraft a write-off.

GC II/7 Morane 406. Damaged by return fire during attack on He111 and forced-landed near Belfort. Lt W. Goettel unhurt. Aircraft damaged but repairable.
Wladyslaw Goettel was leader of No. 6 section, three Polish pilots from the 'Montpellier' squadron attached to GC II/7 for operations from March 29.

LUFTWAFFE

3.(F)/123 Dornier Do17P. Suffered engine trouble during reconnaissance sortie over southern England and returned over Holland where believed engaged by Fokker G 1s of 3-II-1 and damaged. Crew unhurt. Aircraft damaged but repairable.

8./KG77 Dornier Do17Z. Belly-landed at Düsseldorf following engine failure. Crew unhurt. Aircraft damaged but repairable.

Thursday, May 9

BRITISH AIR FORCES IN FRANCE

53 SQUADRON Blenheim IV L9331. Crashed at Poix due to ground mist on return from reconnaissance sortie over the German—Dutch border 1.30 a.m. Pilot Officer Wilson badly injured. Sergeant Ryan and AC Ferre slightly injured. Aircraft a write-off.

53 SQUADRON Blenheim IV R3634. Lost bearings due to ground mist on return from reconnaissance over Hamm and the Ruhr valley. Unable to locate airfield forced-landed at Laboissière, north-east of Montdidier, 2.45 a.m. Sergeant D. G. B. Falconer baled out but fell dead on road between Erches and Andechy. Squadron Leader W. B. Murray and AC Voules unhurt. Aircraft PZ⊙Y a write-off.

87 SQUADRON Hurricane N2362. Radiator damaged by return fire from Do17 of Stab KG2 engaged over Lille-Seclin and overturned attempting forced-landing near Rethel. Pilot Officer H. J. R. Dunn injured head, admitted to hospital. Aircraft a write-off.
Pilot Officer Dunn was evacuated back to England but succumbed to his injuries on June 1.

FRENCH AIR FORCE

GB I/11 LeO 451 (96). Stalled on landing approach and crashed at Arles-Mas-de-Rue. Lt-Col. Berthelon *(Groupement Commandant)* and Adjt Guiral killed. Aircraft a write-off.

GBA I/54 Breguet 693 (11). Crashed from 600ft shortly after take-off at Jouy-sur-Morin; exploded and burned out. Adjt B. Ferrand and Adjt H. Foucher killed. Aircraft a write-off.

British and French officers join together with Joan of Arc to celebrate her special day in Reims as back in 1920 the French Parliament decided to create a national day for Jeanne d'Arc to be held on the second Sunday in May.

DUTCH AIR FORCE

I-2 Fokker C V (600). Crashed at Hilversum, cause not stated. 1e Lt J. P. Schouw slightly injured. Aircraft damaged but repairable.

LUFTWAFFE

4.(F)/121 Dornier Do17P. Returned damaged by enemy fighters south of Lunéville during reconnaissance of French airfields 1.00 p.m. Believed that attacked by Sgt Nowell and P/O Dunn of No. 87 Sqdn. Oberlt W. Riebicke and Uffz H. Vogel unhurt. Uffz E. Just wounded. Aircraft damaged but repairable.

1.(F)/123 Junkers Ju88A. Suffered engine failure during reconnaissance of airfields between Chartres and Tours and belly-landed at Azy, north-east of Bourges. Lt F. Oswald, Stabsfw G. Kühhorn, Uffz E. Stratmann, and Uffz F. Bauer captured unhurt. Aircraft fired by crew.

I./JG2 Messerschmitt Bf109E-3. Crash-landed at Bassenheim, cause not stated. Pilot unhurt. Aircraft damaged but repairable.

6./JG27 Messerschmitt Bf109E-1. Tail damaged on landing at Bönninghardt. Pilot unhurt. Aircraft damaged but repairable.
Formed at Magdeburg-Ost on January 3 under Hptmn Werner Andres and deployed to Döberitz on February 16 for the defence of Berlin. Transferred to Bönninghardt May 3 for operations in the West.

Stab KG2 Dornier Do17Z. Wrecked in crash-landing at Homburg-Saar. Crew unhurt. Aircraft a write-off.

6./KG30 Junkers Ju88A. Crashed at Bad Zwischenahn due to engine failure. Crew injured. Aircraft a write-off.

V.(Z)/LG1 Messerschmitt Bf110C. Crash-landed near Katten out of fuel. Crew unhurt. Aircraft a write-off.

Later in the war, Maréchal Philippe Pétain, the leader of the collaborationist Vichy government, 'recruited' Jeanne to add support to his regime. After the war she was consequently rejected by many, particularly the Left, and it is now mainly the Right that continues to hold ceremonies on Jeanne d'Arc Day.

On airfields all over western Germany final preparations were now being made for the launch of 'Fall Gelb' and, before dawn, aircrews received their final briefings.

BLITZKRIEG!

Friday, May 10

Reinforcements for France. On May 10, three squadrons were sent from England to help stem the all-out German assault on the Western Front. No. 501 — formerly a bomber squadron which had converted to fighters in December 1938 — flew in its Hurricanes from Tangmere to Bétheniville.

The long-expected German offensive in the West opened at dawn with co-ordinated assaults across the frontiers of Holland, Belgium, and Luxembourg, combined with heavy air attacks on airfields and communications in all three countries, and in France.

In Holland, as German troops crossed the frontier, simultaneous large-scale air assaults on landing grounds around Rotterdam and Den Haag were launched by airborne and parachute troops. Airfields throughout the country were subjected to repeated bombing attacks and many Dutch aircraft destroyed or badly damaged on the ground. However, their early warning system allowed many others to get into the air where they offered courageous resistance to the overwhelming numbers of enemy aircraft encountered while inevitably suffering serious casualties.

Dutch ground forces provided equally fierce resistance along the Maas and the IJssel while confused fighting at Rotterdam and Den Haag would continue throughout the day. Despite determined Dutch counter-attacks, German paratroops clung tenaciously to Waalhaven airfield. Meantime, in accordance with pre-arranged plans, the French 7ème Armée advanced rapidly along the coast to occupy the island of Walcheren and secure the mouth of the Scheldt on the left flank of the Allied line.

Although the French continued to hold the southern border, the Germans soon occupied the Duchy of Luxembourg thus threatening an advance into Belgium through the Ardennes. Despite heavy ground-fire and fighter opposition, several French reconnaissance flights confirmed the

rapidly deteriorating situation and at 9.30 a.m. the Fairey Battles of No. 142 Squadron at Berry-au-Bac were ordered to 'Stand-By'. Hours then passed as German armoured columns advanced deeper into Luxembourg until, impatient at the French High Command's delay in issuing the necessary 'permission to bomb' order, Air Marshal Barratt finally despatched the bombers at noon acting on his own initiative.

Four waves of eight aircraft attacked enemy columns between Luxembourg and Dippach during the afternoon and early evening. Attacking from 250 feet with 4 × 250lb bombs fused for 11 seconds delay, an approach dictated by the absence of a fighter escort and vulnerability to enemy fighters, the Battles were met by withering ground-fire and suffered accordingly, a total of 13 Battles being lost, and the rest all returning with damage.

Elsewhere in Belgium the frontier defences were soon breached, with German airborne troops and paratroops again used to capture strategic crossings on the Maas and the Albert Canal to prevent their demolition. Aerodromes and landing fields across the country were systematically bombed and strafed from first light taking the defences by surprise and over 90 Belgian aircraft were destroyed on the ground with many others damaged. Three entire units were effectively wiped out in these initial attacks. As the Germans quickly exploited the ground situation, Franco-British forces moved into Belgium to take up positions on their planned line of resistance along the River Dyle between Antwerp and Namur.

At 7.15 a.m. North BAFF Headquarters at Chauny had ordered its No. 3 Mission to move forward into Belgium and at 7.40 a.m. signalled the Air Ministry, 'Triplets 0725 hours 10/5. Scratching and seeing only'. This coded signal indicated that the French High Command had granted authority for RAF fighter and reconnaissance flights over Holland, Belgium, and Luxembourg, but as yet not bombers.

Reconnaissance sorties over the advancing Allied troops were thus flown by No. 13 Squadron in support of I Corps, and No. 4 Squadron for II Corps, assisting military movements on roads already heavily congested with civilian refugee traffic. Airfields in Belgium were also reconnoitred for suitable landing places further forward than Lille, an essential element in Allied plans to counter the German offensive. Brussels-Evere and Courtrai were both examined from the air, the former being reported still serviceable despite the bomb damage.

Deeper penetrations into enemy territory by strategic and photo-reconnaissance aircraft also took place, the first RAF Component Blenheims taking off between 8.50 and 9.30 a.m. having been on 'Stand By' since 6.00 a.m.. Ten sorties were flown during the day resulting in mixed reports of the demolition of bridges, Dutch and Belgian columns moving East, but little positive news of enemy troop concentrations or movements, and resulted in the loss of three aircraft by No. 70 Wing over the northern area of operations. Also during the morning, No. 40 Squadron Blenheims, operating from England, reconnoitred north of the Lek with equally indecisive results losing one aircraft over Den Haag, while another crashed on landing back at Wyton. Another reconnaissance mission by two Blenheims of No. 15 Squadron from Wyton followed at 9.15 a.m..

Information derived from these reconnaissance sorties, scant though it was, was enough to trigger attacks on the massed German transport aircraft reported on Dutch aerodromes and the beaches near Den Haag. At 12.05 p.m. BAFF Headquarters requested that Bomber Command send a squadron to bomb Waalhaven, but this coincided with a disastrous attack on the airfield by six Blenheim IF fighters of No. 600 Squadron sent as result of a British Cabinet ruling that fighters rather than bombers be used to avoid possible casualties to Dutch civilians. Intercepted over the target by Bf110s only one aircraft returned to Manston. Later in mid-afternoon, responding to the earlier BAFF request, nine Blenheim bombers from No. 15 Squadron attacked Waalhaven and returned to Wyton without loss.

In response to further BAFF requests, attacks on German transports on Dutch airfields and beaches were ordered by Bomber Command during the afternoon and evening. Twelve Blenheims of No. 40 Squadron bombed Ypenburg around 4.50 p.m. losing three aircraft to Bf110 fighters, and an hour later beaches near Den Haag were attacked by No. 110 Squadron, all 12 Blenheims returning to Wattisham without loss. These 33 sorties represented the sum of British daylight offensive air operations over the northern sector of the front during the first day of the German invasion.

The situation at Waalhaven becoming critical, it was agreed with the Dutch High Command that 36 Wellingtons, despatched in four waves of nine aircraft, would attack the airfield throughout the night. This was to precede efforts by Dutch ground forces to recapture the airfield in a counter-attack timed for 3.00 a.m.

Across France an estimated 45 airfields had also been targetted and significant damage inflicted on installations with over 30 French aircraft destroyed and many others badly damaged in attacks. At Cambrai-Niergnies one French fighter unit caught on the ground suffered particularly serious losses. British-occupied airfields at Abbeville, Arras, Berry-au-Bac, Bétheniville, Le Touquet, Lille-Seclin, Mourmelon, Reims-Champagne and Senon were all attacked before 6.00 a.m. but escaped with only light casualties though serious damage was inflicted on hangars and workshops.

From first light the Hurricanes of Nos. 1 and 73 Squadrons, based forward of the main AASF area, were in almost constant action against usually small formations of unescorted German bombers aiming for airfields. In accordance with pre-arranged plans both squadrons were later withdrawn from their advanced position to Berry-au-Bac and Reims-Champagne to be better placed to defend AASF airfields and provide cover for Allied bombing operations. More German attacks followed around mid-day when Etain-Rouvres was again among airfields bombed only shortly after No. 73 Squadron had withdrawn. Meantime at 4.30 p.m., reinforcements arrived when No. 501 Squadron flew in to Bétheniville from Tangmere and were soon in action.

Further north, in the RAF Component area, the Hurricanes of No. 87 Squadron, operating from Senon when the German offensive opened, had also been heavily engaged since dawn before being recalled to Lille-Seclin. Here they would briefly join No. 85 Squadron which itself had been operating against small bomber raids over Belgium, around Ghent and Grammont, since first light. At Vitry-en-Artois, No. 607 Squadron was also in action against scattered forma-

tions of unescorted enemy bombers over the Belgian frontier throughout the day. Their sister unit No. 615 Squadron, still in process of re-equipping with Hurricanes, met with mixed fortune. Its Hurricane flight operating forward at Le Touquet was bombed during the morning attacks and forced to return to base at Abbeville leaving three damaged aircraft behind.

More reinforcements arrived from England during the afternoon with No. 3 Squadron and No. 79 Squadron flying in from Kenley and Biggin Hill to make up No. 63 Fighter Wing within the RAF Component.

In all, by the end of this first day of the German offensive, BAFF fighters had flown over 200 sorties, most pilots averaging three or four but some flying six or seven sorties throughout the day. Between them they laid claim to 42 enemy aircraft destroyed for the loss of five Hurricanes and ten badly damaged, with five more left in circumstances that would later result in them being abandoned. Three pilots had been injured. As Group Captain Fullard commanding No. 14 Fighter Group recorded, 'I have never seen squadrons so confident of success, so insensible to fatigue and so appreciative of their own aircraft'.

Overall, the success of British bombing operations on this first day of the German offensive varied considerably and apparently achieved very little by way of hindering the German advance. AASF daylight attacks in Luxembourg had resulted in a prohibitive loss rate of 40 per cent, while those by Bomber Command over Holland resulted in a more acceptable 9 per cent of sorties flown. However, by far the worst statistic of the day was the disastrous Fighter Command attack on Waalhaven which resulted in losses of 83 per cent, tersely described in one official narrative as 'an expensive failure'.

No. 501 was the first auxiliary squadron to join the Advanced Air Striking Force, the additional squadrons flown in to boost the strength of the Air Component being Nos. 3 and 79. Based at Merville, together they formed No. 63 (Fighter) Wing.

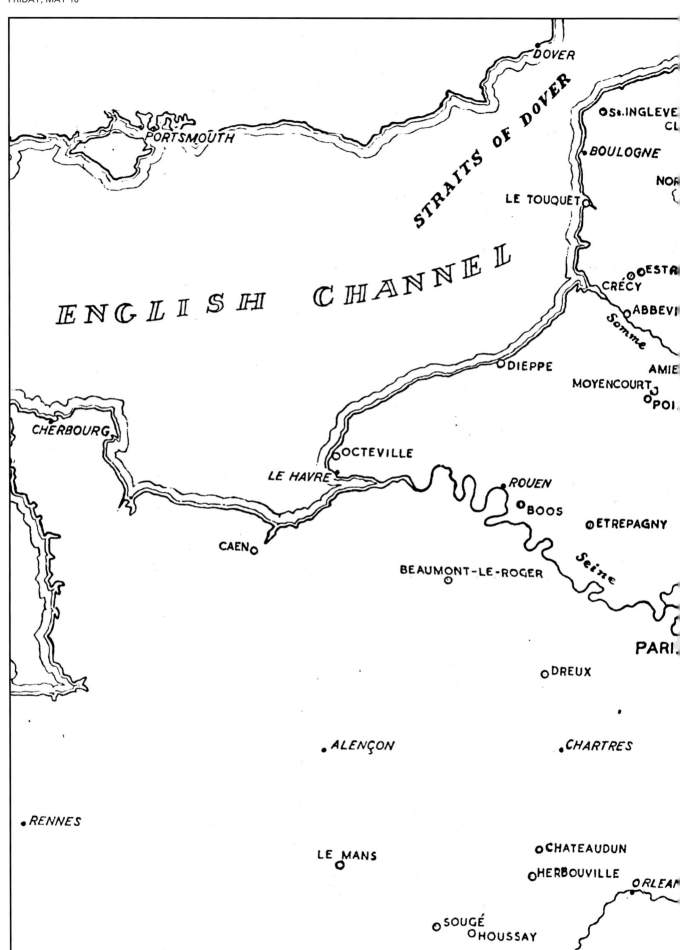

The battlefield for an aerial conflict, the like of which the world had never seen. Five countries and thousands of aircraft were involved.

This contemporary plan shows airfields in France and Belgium used by the British Air Forces from September 1939 to June 1940.

BRITISH AIR FORCES IN FRANCE (BAAF)
May 10 – June 19, 1940

AOC-in-C: Air Marshal A. S. Barratt —HQ: Coulommiers to Château Reze, Pornic 16.6.1940
OC: Group Captain C. S. Strafford — HQ (North): Chauny. OC: Squadron Leader R. Cleland — HQ (East): Nancy

212 (PR) Squadron   Squadron Leader MacPhall   HQ: Tigeaux with detached flights at Coulommiers,
Spitfire I (PR)s   Lille-Seclin & Nancy; withdrawn to Heston 14.6.1940

ADVANCED AIR STRIKING FORCE (AASF)

AOC-in-C: Air Vice Marshal P. H. L. Playfair — HQ: Château Polignac, Reims; to Troyes 15.5.1940;
to Muides, near Blois 3.6.1940; to Nantes 10.6.1940

67 (FIGHTER) WING
Wing Commander C. Walter — HQ: Bussy-la-Côte; to Cormicy
14.5.1940; to Château Fagnières, nr Châlons 16.5.40

1 SQUADRON Hurricanes (JX)
Squadron Leader P. J. H. Halahan
until 24.5.1940
Squadron Leader D. A. Pemberton

Vassincourt to Berry-au-Bac 10.5.1940;
to Conde-Vraux 17.5.1940;
to Anglure 18.5.1940;
to Châteaudun 4.6.1940;
to Le Mans 12.6.1940;
to Caen-Mathieu 13.6.1940;
to Nantes 14.6.1940;
to Tangmere 17.6.1940

73 SQUADRON Hurricanes (TP)
Squadron Leader J. W. C. More

Étain-Rouvres
to Reims-Champagne 10.5.1940; to Villeneuve-les-Vertus 16.5.1940;
to Gaye 18.5.1940;
to Echemines 3.6.1940;
to Ruaudin 7.6.1940;
to Nantes 15.6.1940;
to Church Fenton 18.6.1940

501 SQUADRON Hurricanes (SD)
Squadron Leader A. V. Clube

Tangmere to Bétheniville 10.5.1940;
to Anglure 16.5.1940;
to Ecury 17.5.1940;
to Mourmelon-le-Grand 19.5.1940;
to Le Mans 2.6.1940;
to Dinard 16.6.1940;
to St Helier, 18.6.1940;
to Croydon 20.6.1940

17 SQUADRON Hurricanes (YB)
Squadron Leader R. I. G. MacDougall

Hawkinge to Le Mans 8.6.1940; to Dinard 15.6.1940; to Jersey & Guernsey 17.6.1940;
to Debden via Tangmere 19.6.1940

242 SQUADRON Hurricanes (LE)
Squadron Leader F. M. Gobeil

to Le Mans en-route to Châteaudun 8.6.1940;
to Le Mans 14.6.1940;
to Nantes 15.6.1940;
to Coltishall via Tangmere 18.6.1940

71 (BOMBER) WING
Air Commodore R. M. Field — HQ: Château Fagnières,
near Châlons; to Abbeville 16.5.40; to Nantes 19.5.1940

105 SQUADRON Battles (GB)
Wing Commander J. D. Hawtrey

Villeneuve-les-Vertus;
to 76 Wing 17.5.1940;
return 71 Wing 23.5.40;
to Nantes 30.5.1940;
to Honington 11.6.1940

114 SQUADRON Blenheim IVs (FD)
Wing Commander P. W. M. Wright

Conde-Vraux
to Nantes 18.5.1940;
to Wattisham 29.5.1940

139 SQUADRON Blenheim IVs (XD)
Wing Commander L. W. Dickens

Plivot to Lannoy 15.5.40;
to Nantes 18.5.40;
to West Raynham 29.5.1940

---

150 SQUADRON Battles (JN)
Wing Commander A. Hesketh

Ecury-sur-Coole
to Pouan 15.5.1940;
to 75 Wing 15.5.1940

218 SQUADRON Battles (HA)
Wing Commander L. B. Duggan

from 75 Wing 23.5.40;
to Mildenhall 13.6.1940

75 (BOMBER) WING
Group Captain A. H. Wann — HQ: St Hilaire-le-Grand to
Méry-sur-Seine 16.5.1940; to Château Rocheux, Fréteval 3.6.1940;
to Nantes-Château Bougon 13.6.1940

88 SQUADRON Battles (RH)
Wing Commander C. S. Ellison

Mourmelon-le-Grand
to Les Grandes Chappelles 16.5.1940;
to Moisy 3.6.1940;
to Houssay 14.6.1940
to Driffield 15.6.1940

103 SQUADRON Battles (PM)
Wing Commander T. C. Dickens

Bétheniville
to St Lucien Ferme, Rhèges 16.5.1940;
to Ouzouer-le-Boyen 3.6.1940;
to Souge 14.6.1940;
to Abingdon 15.6.1940

150 SQUADRON Battles (JN)
Wing Commander A. Hesketh

from 71 Wing 15.5.1940;
to Houssay 3.6.1940;
to Abingdon 15.6.1940

218 SQUADRON Battles (HA)
Wing Commander L. B. Duggan

Auberive-sur-Suippes
to Moscou Ferme 15.5.1940;
to St Lucien Ferme, Rhèges 16.5.1940;
to Nantes 21.5.1940;
to 71 Wing 23.5.40

76 (BOMBER) WING
Group Captain H. S. Kerby — HQ: Neufchâtel
to Marigny-le-Châtel; to Montoire by 7.6.1940

12 SQUADRON Battles (PH)
Wing Commander A. G. Thackray

Amifontaine
to Echemines 16.5.1940;
to Souge 3.6.1940;
to Finningley 15.6.1940

105 SQUADRON Battles (GB)
Wing Commander J. C. Hawtrey

from 71 Wing 17.5.1940;
to Echemines 18.5.1940;
returned to 71 Wing 23.5.40

142 SQUADRON Battles (QT)
Wing Commander C. L. Falconer

Berry-au-Bac
to Faux-Villecerf 16.5.1940;
to Villers-Faux 6.6.1940;
to Waddington 15.6.1940

226 SQUADRON Battles (MQ)
Wing Commander H. C. Parker

Reims-Champagne
to Faux-Villecerf 16.5.1940;
to Artins 6.1940;
to Thirsk 16.6.1940

Also under AASF command:

98 (RESERVE) SQUADRON
Battles (OV)
Wing Commander G. R. Ashton

Nantes-Château Bougon;
to Gatwick 15.6.1940

RAF COMPONENT (BEF)
May 10 — May 24 1940
AOC-in-C: Air Vice Marshal C. H. B. Blount — HQ: Maroeuil to Arras 9.5.1940; to Hazebrouck 16.5.1940; withdrawn to UK 21/22.5.1940

14 (FIGHTER) GROUP
Group Captain P. F. Fullard — HQ: Achicourt

60 (FIGHTER) WING
Wing Commander J. A. Boret — HQ: Lille-Seclin
Wing Commander H. Broadhurst from 18.5.1940

85 SQUADRON Hurricanes (VY)
Squadron Leader J. O. W. Oliver — Lille-Seclin
Squadron Leader M. Peacock — to Merville 19.5.1940
+ 20.5.1940 — withdrawn to Manston
Squadron Leader P. Townsend — 20.5.40
re-inforced by:
A FLIGHT 242 SQUADRON
Hurricanes (LE) — from Church Fenton
Flight Lieutenant D. R. Miller — 16.5.40

87 SQUADRON Hurricanes (LK) — Lille-Seclin to Lille-
Squadron Leader J. S. Dewar — Marcq 10.5.1940
re-inforced by: — to Merville 19.5.1940
A FLIGHT 111 SQUADRON — withdrawn 20.5.1940
Hurricanes (JU)
Flight Lieutenant R. P. R. Powell — from Northolt 17.5.1940;

61 (FIGHTER) WING
Wing Commander R. Y. Eccles — HQ: Vitry-en-Artois

607 SQUADRON Hurricanes (AF)
Squadron Leader L. E. Smith — Vitry-en-Artois
+ 15.5.1940 — to Norrent Fontes
Squadron Leader G. Fidler — 18.5.1940
POW 19.5.1940 — withdrawn 20.5.1940
re-inforced by:
B FLIGHT 56 SQUADRON
Hurricanes (US)
Flight Lieutenant I. Soden — from North Weald
and: — 16.5.1940
B FLIGHT 229 SQUADRON
Hurricanes (RE)
Flight Lieutenant F. E. Rosier — from Digby 16.5.1940

615 SQUADRON Hurricanes (KW) — Abbeville, (A Flight) to
Squadron Leader J. R. Kayll — Vitry-en-Artois 12.5.1940
— to Moorseele 16.5.1940
— to Norrent Fontes
re-inforced by: — 20.5.1940
A FLIGHT 245 SQUADRON — withdrawn 20.5.1940
Hurricanes (DX)
Flight Lieutenant J. Thomson — from Manston 16.5.1940

504 SQUADRON Hurricanes (TM)
Squadron Leader J. B. Parnall — Tangmere to Lille-Marq
+ 14.5.1940 — 12.5.1940
Squadron Leader J. Hill w 19.5.1940 — to Norrent-Fontes
re-inforced by: — 19.5.1940
B FLIGHT 253 SQUADRON — withdrawn 20.5.1940
Hurricanes (SW)
Flight Lieutenant H. T. Anderson — from Kenley 16.5.1940

63 (FIGHTER) WING
Wing Commander E. S. Finch — HQ: Lille-Seclin

3 SQUADRON Hurricanes (QO)
Squadron Leader P. Gifford — Kenley to Merville
+ 16.5.1940 — 10.5.1940
Flight Lieutenant W. M. Churchill — withdrawn 20.5.1940
re-inforced by:
A FLIGHT 601 SQUADRON — from Tangmere
Hurricanes (UF) — 17.5.1940
Flight Lieutenant Sir A. P. Hope

79 SQUADRON Hurricanes (AL) — Biggin Hill to Merville
Squadron Leader R. V. Alexander — 10.5.1940, (B Flight)
— to Mons-en-Chaussée
— 11.5.1940, to Norrent
— Fontes 12.5.1940
re-inforced by: — to Merville 15.5.1940
B FLIGHT 213 SQUADRON — withdrawn 20.5.1940
Hurricanes (AK)
Flight Lieutenant D. Wight — from Manston 17.5.1940

50 (ARMY CO-OPERATION) WING:
Group Captain A. R. Churchman — HQ: Athies

4 SQUADRON Lysanders (TV) — Monchy-Lagache to
Wing Commander G. P. Charles — Lille-Ronchin 15.5.1940
— (A and C Flights) to
— Clairmarais 21.5.1940
— (A and C Flights)
— withdrawn to Hawkinge
— 22.5.1940
— (B Flight) to Clairmarais
— 23.5.1940
— (B Flight) withdrawn to
— Hawkinge 24.5.1940

13 SQUADRON Lysanders (OO) — Mons-en-Chaussée
Wing Commander S. H. C. Gray — to Authie 15.5.1940
— to Abbeville 19.5.1940
— (B and C Flights)
— withdrawn to Hawkinge
— 20.5.1940
— (A Flight) to Clairmarais
— 21.5.1940
— (A Flight) withdrawn
— to Hawkinge 22.5.1940

16 SQUADRON Lysanders (KJ) — Bertangles, withdrawn to
Wing Commander T. Humble — Lympne 19.5.1940

51 (ARMY CO-OPERATION) WING
Wing Commander A. H. Flower — HQ: Dieppe

2 SQUADRON Lysanders (KO) — Abbeville-Drucat
Wing Commander A. J. W. Geddes — to Bethune 15.5.1940
— withdrawn to Lympne
— 19.5.1940

26 SQUADRON Lysanders (RM) — Dieppe to Authie
Squadron Leader R. C. M. Ferrers — 15.5.1940, withdrawn to
— Lympne 19.5.1940

52 (RECONNAISSANCE) WING
Wing Commander A. F. Hutton — HQ: Courcelles

53 SQUADRON Blenheim IVs (PZ) — Poix
Squadron Leader W. B. Murray — to Crécy-en-Ponthieu
— 19.5.1940
— withdrawn to Lympne
— 19.5.1940

59 SQUADRON Blenheim IVs (TR) — Poix
Squadron Leader J. B. Fyfe — to Crécy-en-Ponthieu
— 19.5.1940
— withdrawn to Lympne
— 19.5.1940

70 (RECONNAISSANCE) WING
Wing Commander W. A. Opie — HQ: Rosières-en-Santerre
Wing Commander J. Cottle — to Château Courcelles,
from 15.5.1940 — Poix 17.5.1940
— to Crecy 19.5.1940

18 SQUADRON
Blenheim Is & IVs (WV)
Wing Commander W. A. Opie — Méharicourt
— to Goyencourt 17.5.40
— to Crecy 18.5.1940
— withdrawn to Lympne
— 19.5.1940

57 SQUADRON Blenheim IVs (DX)
Wing Commander A. H. Garland — Rosières-en-Santerre
— to Poix 17.5.1940;
— to Crecy-en-Ponthieu
— 18.5.1940;
— withdrawn to Lympne
— 19.5.1940

Also under Air Component command:

81 (COMMS) SQUADRON
Tiger Moths — Amiens-Montjoie
Squadron Leader J. H. Hill — withdrawn to Andover
— 19.5.1940

BRITISH AIR FORCES IN FRANCE

1 SQUADRON, VASSINCOURT

Hurricane P2649. Hit by return fire from Do17 engaged east of Rouvres 5.00 a.m. and returned with slight damage and punctured tyre. Pilot Officer P. W. O. Mould unhurt. Aircraft ⊙T damaged but repairable.

Hurricane N2382. Engine damaged by return fire from Do17 of Stab KG3 engaged near Metz and belly-landed east of Verdun 5.45 a.m. Flight Lieutenant P. R. Walker unhurt. Aircraft ⊙B abandoned.

Hurricane L1689. Hit by return fire and abandoned over Châlons-sur-Marne during attack on He111s 2.45 p.m. Flying Officer R. L. Lorimer baled out unhurt. Aircraft a write-off.

3 SQUADRON, MERVILLE

Hurricane L1923. Engine damaged by return fire from He111 of I./KG27 engaged over Lille and crashed in dead-stick landing in forest near Fiefs 9.30 p.m. Flying Officer R. B. Lines-Roberts unhurt. Aircraft a write-off.

Hurricane N2333. Abandoned over St Margarets Bay, off Dover, having lost bearings in dark after attack on He111 over Lille 10.30 p.m. Flying Officer A. R. Ball baled out unhurt. Aircraft lost.

12 SQUADRON, AMIFONTAINE

Battle L5249. Returned badly damaged by ground-fire during low-level attack on enemy armoured column on the Luxembourg — Junglinster road 5.30 p.m. Pilot Officer C. L. Hulse and LAC J. Aitken unhurt. Sergeant A. Young wounded in shoulder. Aircraft PH⊙D damaged but repairable — later abandoned.
Cecil Hulse died serving in France but not while flying on operations, hence his name does not appear in our Roll of Honour. He was admitted to base hospital on June 1 due to illness and transferred to hospital in Sens where he died three days later.

Battle P2243. Hit by ground-fire during sortie to attack enemy column between Luxembourg and Echternach and forced-landed at Haucourt-la-Rigole, west of Piennes, 5.30 p.m. Flight Lieutenant P. H. M. S. Hunt, Sergeant P. E. Wilks and LAC H. Cooke returned unhurt. Aircraft PH⊙U abandoned.

Battle L5190. Brought down by ground-fire during attack on enemy column on the Luxembourg — Junglinster road and belly-landed near Kirchberg 5.45 p.m. Pilot Officer A. W. Matthews, Sergeant A. A. Maderson and LAC J. C. Senior all captured wounded. Aircraft PH⊙P a write-off.

Day one of Hitler's Blitzkrieg war on the Western Front saw the demise of over 800 aircraft: 79 British; 68 French; 150 Dutch; 147 Belgian and 445 German. Here are just two: this is the Battle from No. 12 Squadron down at Kirchberg . . .

Battle L4949. Hit by intense ground-fire and engine set alight during low–level attack on enemy column 14 km north-east of Luxembourg. Crash-landed on fire at 'Mohimont', Sommethonne, north-west of Virton, 5.55 p.m. Flight Lieutenant W. Simpson seriously burned, and LAC R. T. Tomlinson burnt hands, both treated at emergency hospital near Verdun before transport to hospital in Bar-le-Duc where they were separated. Sergeant E. N. Odell unhurt. Aircraft PH⊙V a write-off.
William Simpson was later awarded the DFC, his crew both receiving the DFM. Simpson's wounds resulted in him being repatriated to England in November 1941.

18 SQUADRON, MÉHARICOURT

Blenheim IV L9185. Returned damaged by AA and attack by enemy fighter during low-level reconnaissance of the River Maas to Venlo 10.15 a.m. Pilot Officer P. D. Smith, Sergeant C. J. Hann and LAC Shepherd unhurt. Aircraft repairable.

Blenheim I L1405. Failed to return from reconnaissance of the River Maas to Venlo and believed crashed at Breyell 10.20 a.m. Possibly that claimed by Oberlt Steinhoff (Staffelkapitän) of 11.(N)/JG2 near Düsseldorf.Pilot Officer G. F. Harding and Sergeant K. N. Shrosbree killed. LAC R. B. H. Townsend-Coles captured. Aircraft a write-off.
Roland Townsend-Coles became a regular escapee and was amongst those reported executed by the Gestapo on July 15, 1944. He has no known grave. Dates of death of Geoffrey Harding and Kenneth Shrosbree recorded as May 11 by CWGC.

Blenheim IV L8860. Failed to return from low-level reconnaissance sortie and crashed on the banks of the Maas between Reuver and Kessel, south-west of Venlo, 6.00 p.m. Probably victim to ground-fire. Pilot Officer L. T. Dixon, Sergeant T. A. Peach and AC1 J. Townsley killed. Aircraft a write-off.

53 SQUADRON, POIX

Blenheim IV L4862. Aircraft caught on the ground at Metz in bombing attack. No crew casualties. Aircraft damaged but repairable — later abandoned.

Blenheim IV P6916. Aircraft caught on the ground at Metz in bombing attack. No crew casualties. Aircraft repairable.

Blenheim IV L9332. Damaged by AA fire during reconnaissance sortie over Belgium and landed at Vitry-en-Artois 11.40 a.m. Pilot Officer D. P. Massey, Sergeant Whetton, and AC1 Vickers unhurt. Aircraft PZ⊙Z damaged but repairable — later abandoned.

57 SQUADRON, ROSIÈRES-EN-SANTERRE

Blenheim IV L9246. Returned badly damaged from reconnaissance sortie north of 's-Hertogenbosch. Possibly that attacked by Oberlt Schäfer (Staffelkapitän) of 5./JG27 west of Nijmegen 12.50 p.m. Flight Lieutenant G. M. Wyatt wounded in arm, admitted to hospital. Sergeant W. J. Gardner and Corporal F. T. Russell both unhurt. Aircraft damaged but repairable.

. . . and this, the Blenheim from No. 53 Squadron, crash-landed at Vitry-en-Artois.

Blenheim IV L9246. Shot down during reconnaissance sortie and crashed at the Vogelenzangsebrug at Echteld, north-east of Tiel. Possibly that claimed by Lt Fluder of 5./JG27 west of Nijmegen 12.08 p.m. Pilot Officer A. Thomas and LAC L. F. Jordan killed. Sergeant P. L. Thomas baled out over Buurmalsen but killed. Aircraft a write-off.

Alban Thomas and Leslie Jordan were originally buried at Echteld but reinterred in Hook of Holland General Cemetery post-war. A lower torso later found in the River Linge near Zoelen, and buried there as an unknown airman, is also believed to be that of Alban Thomas. In March 1941, the remains of Sgt Penry Thomas were discovered between Buren and Buurmalsen and interred locally.

73 SQUADRON, ETAIN-ROUVRES

Hurricane N2318. Believed returned damaged by return fire from Do17 of 4./KG3 engaged near base 5.00 a.m. Sergeant L. J. W. Humphris unhurt. Aircraft damaged but repairable.

Hurricane P2575. Glycol system and windscreen damaged by return fire from Do17 of 4./KG3 engaged over base. Forced-landed near Conflans-en-Jarnisy 5.00 a.m. Flying Officer N. Orton unhurt. Aircraft ⊙J damaged but repairable.

Hurricane P2804. Hit in glycol system by concentrated cross-fire from Do17s of 4./KG3 attacked over base. crash-landed in flames at Puxe and exploded 5.20 a.m. Flight Lieutenant R. E. Lovett admitted to hospital burned on face and hands. Aircraft ⊙E lost.

85 SQUADRON, LILLE-SECLIN

Hurricane. Hit by return fire from Ju88 and forced-landed at Mons-en-Chaussée 4.45 a.m. Pilot Officer D. V. G. Mawhood seriously wounded, lost an eye. Aircraft VY⊙S damaged but repairable.

Hurricane L1779. Returned badly damaged by return fire from reported Ju88 engaged between Armentières and the Forêt-de-Nieppe 8.30 a.m. Flight Lieutenant R. H. A. Lee unhurt. Aircraft damaged but repairable.

Hurricane N2472. Forced-landed at Celles with engine seized and aircraft damaged by return fire from reported Ju88 engaged between Armentières and the Forêt-de-Nieppe 8.30 a.m. Flying Officer A. B. Angus unhurt. Aircraft abandoned.

Many of the photos taken of wrecked aircraft during the Lightning War are snapshots from German servicemen and they can only be identified by their squadron codes, the small serial numbers on the rear fuselage being too indistinct. *Above:* A Battle from No. 103 Squadron (PM) and *(below)* 'RH' on another denoting No. 88 Squadron. Two of their machines were damaged in the morning attack, and two more destroyed in a hangar during the afternoon.

87 SQUADRON, SENON

Hurricane. Forced-landed at Doncourt damaged by return fire from Do17 of 8./KG3 over Thionville 6.00 a.m. Flight Lieutenant R. Voase Jeff unhurt. Aircraft damaged but repairable.

Hurricane. Returned radiator badly damaged by crossfire from He111s of II./KG53 south of Thionville 12.30 p.m. Pilot Officer G. C. Saunders unhurt. Aircraft damaged but repairable.

Hurricane. Returned with engine seized and radiator damaged by return fire from He111s of II./KG53 engaged south-east of Thionville 12.30 p.m. Sergeant G. L. Nowell unhurt. Aircraft abandoned.
Gareth Nowell landed at Senon to find the squadron preparing to decamp to Lille-Marcq. He reached there in the back of the stores wagon.

87 SQUADRON LILLE-MARCQ

Hurricane. Returned slightly damaged by return fire from reported Ju88 engaged over Lille 6.55 p.m. Pilot Officer T. J. Edwards unhurt. Aircraft repairable.

88 SQUADRON, MOURMELON-LE-GRAND

Battles L4956, L5526, P2258 and P2355. Destroyed or badly damaged on the ground in bombing attacks by Do17s of III./KG2 5.35 a.m. and Do17s of III./KG3 6.40 p.m. No crew casualties. Aircraft all later abandoned on withdrawal on May 16.

103 SQUADRON, BÉTHENIVILLE

2 Battles. Reported slightly damaged in bombing by Do17s of II./KG2 4.45 a.m. No crew casualties. Aircraft repairable.

Battle K9264. Shot down by ground-fire during low-level bombing attack on enemy column east of Dippach. Crashed in flames at 'An der Jenken', Linger, north of Pétange, 3.00 p.m.. Pilot Officer K. J. Drabble, Sergeant T. D. Smith and LAC P. J. Lamble all killed. Aircraft PM⊙L a write-off.
Originally buried as three 'Unknowns' in Mont St Jean Cemetery, these airmen were correctly identified on reinterrment in Hotton War Cemetery on June 19, 1947.

Battle K9270. Hit by ground-fire and crashed on fire at 'Al Eisenbunnslinn', Linger, north of Pétange, during low-level bombing of enemy column east of Dippach 3.00 p.m. Sergeant C. H. Lowne captured. Sergeant C. J. S. Poole and LAC O. A. Hutchinson killed. Aircraft PM⊙O a write-off
Olaf Arthur Hutchinson is shown as Sergeant in CWGC records.

Battle K9372. Abandoned near Hautcharage after engine set alight and coolant tank hit by ground-fire during low-level bombing of enemy column east of Dippach 3.00 p.m. Flight Lieutenant M. C. Wells baled out and captured. Sergeant H. F. Bullock and LAC T. H. Bowen both baled out unhurt, evaded but eventually captured four days later. Aircraft PM⊙K a write-off.

Battle K9408. Returned to base badly damaged with wings, fuselage, and port fuel tank riddled by ground-fire during low-level bombing attack on enemy column east of Dippach 3.00 p.m. Flight Lieutenant J. A. Ingram and crew unhurt. Aircraft damaged but repairable.

German troopers inspect the fruits of victory. This is the remains of another of No. 142 Squadron's Battles (L5231) brought down by ground-fire just after midday.

Battle L5242. Returned badly damaged by heavy ground-fire during attack on enemy troops advancing on Dippach 12.40 p.m. Flying Officer A. D. Gosman, Sergeant Pollock both unhurt. LAC Cave slightly wounded in arm. Aircraft repairable — abandoned on withdrawal to Faux-Villecerf on May 16.

Battle L5578. Shot down by flak during attack on enemy troops advancing on Dippach and crashed near Pétange, south-west of Luxembourg 12.50 p.m. Pilot Officer F. S. Laws, Sergeant R. F. Miller and AC1 L. M. Langton killed. Aircraft a write-off.

Battle L5231. Hit by ground-fire during attack on enemy columns advancing on Dippach and belly-landed at Rodange, west of Pétange, 12.45 p.m. Flying Officer M. H. Roth, Sergeant W. F. Algie and AC H. Morris all captured. Aircraft QT⊙G a write-off.

Battle P5238. Damaged by ground-fire during attack on enemy troops advancing on Dippach and forced-landed at Colmey, north-west of Longuyon 12.50 p.m. Sergeant A. N. Spear, Sergeant S. J. Brooks and LAC R. H. Nugent unhurt. Aircraft repairable.

105 SQUADRON, VILLENEUVE-LES-VERTUS

Battle K9338. Returned badly damaged by ground-fire following attack on enemy column on the Echternach-Luxembourg road 4.15 p.m. Sergeant C. Bowles and Sergeant Radford unhurt. LAC Clegg slightly wounded. Aircraft damaged but repairable — later abandoned.

Battle P2200. Shot down by flak during attack on enemy column advancing along the Echternach-Luxembourg road and belly-landed at Clémency 4.15 p.m. Pilot Officer D. G. O'Brien captured unhurt, Sergeant D. F. Eastick and AC1 S. R. Wright both captured wounded. Aircraft GB⊙K a write-off.

Battle K9188. Returned badly damaged following attack on enemy troops on the Echternach-Luxembourg road 4.15 p.m. Sergeant Richardson and Sergeant Donlon unhurt, LAC R. W. McCarthy badly wounded. Aircraft damaged but repairable — abandoned on withdrawal to Échemines on May 18.

Admitted to No. 4 CCS at Épernay badly wounded in both legs and stomach, LAC McCarthy showed great fortitude during this action for which he was later awarded the DFM.

Battle P2190. Returned badly damaged following attack on enemy troops on the Echternach-Luxembourg road 4.15 p.m. Flying Officer R. N. Wall, Sergeant Woodhouse and Corporal Greenwood unhurt. Aircraft damaged but repairable — later abandoned at No. 21 Aircraft Depot, Château Bougon.

142 SQUADRON, BERRY-AU-BAC

Battles K7700 and K9366. Damaged on the ground in bombing attack 4.40 a.m. No crew casualties. Aircraft repairable — abandoned on withdrawal to Faux-Villecerf on May 16.

Alternative sources record five aircraft slightly damaged, plus another damaged in a further attack at 5.50 a.m.

Battle P2246. Returned damaged by ground-fire during attack on enemy troops near Dippach 12.40 p.m. Sergeant G. B. Irvine killed, Pilot Officer W. H. Corbett wounded ankle, LAC Gaston unhurt. Aircraft repairable.

 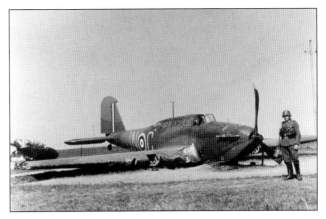

No. 150 Squadron lost four Battles on the first day; here are two of them. *Left:* **K9390** and *(right)* **L5540.**

150 SQUADRON, ECURY-SUR-COOLE

Battle K9369. Badly damaged by ground-fire over Differdange following low-level bombing attack on enemy column between Luxembourg and Grevenmacher 4.30 p.m. Returned to base, landing on burst tyres. Flying Officer W. M. Blom, Sergeant E. D. Martin and AC1 C. Cooper unhurt. Aircraft JN⊙G repairable — later abandoned.

Battle K9390. Shot down by ground-fire during low-level attack on enemy column between Luxembourg and Grevenmacher and belly-landed at Rue de la Barrière, Merl, 4.30 p.m. Flight Lieutenant E. Parker killed after landing. Sergeant J. Whalley captured unhurt. Corporal R. K. Rye captured wounded. Aircraft JN⊙I a write-off.

Battle L5540. Hit by ground-fire during low-level bombing attack on enemy column between Luxembourg and Grevenmacher and belly-landed at Bonnevoie 4.30 p.m. Flying Officer A. C. Roberts and Sergeant E. H. Ward captured unhurt. AC1 D. Meyrick captured wounded. Aircraft JN⊙C a write-off.

Battle L5539. Glycol and petrol tanks holed by ground-fire during low-level bombing of enemy column five miles west of Grevenmacher, and forced-landed 10 miles west of Thionville 4.30 p.m. Sergeant R. A. de C. White, Sergeant C. W. K. Booth and LAC R. H. Burrows unhurt. Aircraft a write-off.

218 SQUADRON, AUBÉRIVE-SUR-SUIPPES

Battle L5402. Returned badly damaged by ground-fire during attack on enemy columns on the Dippach-Luxembourg road 3.15 p.m. LAC H. Baguley killed; rest of crew unhurt. Aircraft damaged but repairable — later abandoned.

3 Battles. Returned damaged by ground-fire following attack on enemy transport on the Dippach-Luxembourg road 3.15 p.m. No crew casualties. Aircraft all repairable

226 SQUADRON, REIMS-CHAMPAGNE

Battle K9183. Hit by ground-fire during dive-bombing of enemy columns between Wallendorf and Diekirch and crashed at Hirzenhaff Farm, south of Bettendorf, 6.30 p.m. Flying Officer D. A. Cameron reportedly died of wounds in Diekirch hospital May 13. Sergeant C. S. Hart captured unhurt. AC1 J. G. Ward captured slightly wounded. Aircraft MQ⊙R a write-off.
The date of death of Douglas Cameron is recorded as May 10 by the CWGC and it is possible there may have been some confusion with the circumstances of the death of Brian Kerridge of the same squadron as detailed in the following entry.

Battle L5247. Shot down by ground-fire during dive-bombing attack on enemy columns between Wallendorf and Diekirch and crashed in the northern suburbs at Faubourg de Luxembourg, Weimerskirch 6.30 p.m. Flight Lieutenant B. R. Kerridge captured badly wounded, died May 15. Corporal G. H. Dixon captured badly burned. Sergeant D. I. Anthony captured unhurt. Aircraft a write-off.

Battle P2180. Returned damaged by ground-fire during dive-bombing attack on enemy columns between Wallendorf and Diekirch 6.20 p.m. Sergeant H. J. Barron wounded in left leg. Sergeant D. E. Bingham and Corporal L. Smith unhurt. Aircraft damaged but repairable — destroyed on evacuation May 16.

607 SQUADRON, VITRY-EN-ARTOIS

Hurricane P2572. Slightly damaged by AA fire from airfield defences on return to base after pursuit of He111s from Condé-sur-Lescaut to the Belgian border 5.00 a.m. Pilot Officer A. S. Dini unhurt. Aircraft AF⊙B repairable.

Hurricane P2536. Returned slightly damaged by return fire from Ju88s engaged near the Belgian border 5.45 a.m. Flight Lieutenant G. H. F. Plinston unhurt. Aircraft AF⊙R repairable.

Hurricane P2615. Shot down by crossfire from He111s of III./KG1 engaged west of St Quentin and abandoned over Laviéville 2.50 p.m. Flight Lieutenant J. Sample baled out spraining both ankles on landing. Aircraft lost.

Hurricane P2697. Hit by return fire from He111 of 3./LG1 and crash-landed near Ath 5.25 p.m. Pilot Officer C. R. Rowe injured. Aircraft abandoned.

Hurricane P2574. Forced-landed near Oudenaarde damaged by return fire from He111s of 6./KG27 engaged near Hundelgem 5.40 p.m. Flying Officer R. F. Weatherill unhurt. Aircraft AF⊙F repairable.

Hurricane P2573. Returned with oil tank damaged by return fire from He111s of III./KG54 intercepted near Roeselare 7.15 p.m. Pilot Officer H. P. Dixon unhurt. Aircraft AF⊙A repairable.

615 SQUADRON, LE TOUQUET

Three Hurricanes. Damaged in bombing by II./KG27 5.00 a.m. No pilot casualties. Aircraft all damaged but repairable.

Nice shot of the dismantling of K9369 of No. 150 Squadron — note the gentleman with the umbrella sporting a top hat!

UK-based aircraft lost or damaged on operations over the Western Front:

RAF BOMBER COMMAND

40 SQUADRON, WYTON
Armed-reconnaissance Dutch coast:

Blenheim IV L8776. Shot down near Den Haag 10.40 a.m. F/O R. M. Burns, Sgt J. R. Brooker, Cpl G. Hurford captured wounded. Aircraft BL⊙K lost.

Blenheim IV L8833. Damaged by Ju88 off the Dutch coast 10.40 a.m. and crash-landed on return. S/L B. Paddon, Sgt J. A. D. Beattie, P/O W. G. Edwards unhurt. Aircraft wrecked.

40 SQUADRON, WYTON
Attack on Ypenburg airfield:

Blenheim IV L8828. Shot down by Bf110s in sea off Rotterdam 5.30 p.m. F/O P. J. H. Rowan, Sgt G. Beardwood, Cpl T. F. S. Clark killed. Aircraft lost.

Blenheim IV L8831. Shot down by Bf110s near Den Haag 5.30 p.m. and possibly that reported down at Wateringen. Sgt I. L. Thomas, Sgt V. Spurr, LAC H. Bridson killed. Aircraft lost.

Blenheim IV P4901. Shot down by Bf110s near Voorburg 5.30 p.m. Sgt A. J. Robertson, Sgt F. Checkley killed. AC1 J. A. Webster captured. Aircraft lost.

Blenheim IV L8827. Returned damaged by Bf110s 5.30 p.m. F/L H. L. Smeddle, Sgt B. C. Wooldridge, LAC G. D. P. Quinn wounded. Aircraft repairable.

RAF COASTAL COMMAND

235 SQUADRON, BIRCHAM NEWTON
Reconnaissance Texel — Borkum:

Blenheim IV N6193. Belly-landed out of fuel on return 10.30 p.m. P/O R. L. Patterson, Lt Ogilvie RN, LAC A. G. Smith unhurt. Aircraft LA⊙N wrecked.

RAF FIGHTER COMMAND

600 SQUADRON, MANSTON
Attack on Waalhaven airfield:

Blenheim IF L1335. Shot down by Bf110s of I./ZG1 12.05 p.m. S/L J. M. Wells, Cpl B. A. Kidd killed. Sgt Davis captured. Aircraft BQ⊙R lost.

Blenheim IF L1401. Shot down by Bf110s of I./ZG1 and crashed near Piershil 12.05 p.m. P/O R. W. H. Echlin killed. F/O J. H. C. Rowe captured. Aircraft BQ⊙K lost.

Blenheim IF L1514. Shot down by Bf110s of I./ZG1 and crashed near Herkingen 12.05 p.m. F/O C. R Moore, Cpl L. D. Isaacs killed. Aircraft BQ⊙W lost.

Blenheim IF L1515. Shot down by Bf110s of I./ZG1 and crashed near Spijkenisse 12.05 p.m. P/O M. H. Anderson, LAC H. C. W. Hawkins killed. Aircraft BQ⊙L lost.

Blenheim IF L6616. Crash-landed between Pernis and Vondenlingenplaat damaged by Bf110s of I./ZG1 12.05 p.m. P/O R. C. Haine, P/O M. Kramer unhurt. Aircraft BQ⊙N lost.
These aircraft were IFF fitted, the prospect of this being captured caused much concern.

Blenheim IF. Returned damaged by Bf110s of I./ZG1 12.05 p.m. F/O T. N. Hayes, Cpl G. H. Holmes unhurt. Aircraft BQ⊙O damaged.

604 SQUADRON, NORTHOLT
Escort for No. 110 Sqdn to Ockenburg:

Blenheim IF L1517. Forced-landed on beach at Scheveningen damaged by flak 5.30 p.m. Crew unhurt. Aircraft abandoned.

Paul Richey of No. 1 Squadron landed at Rouvres to refuel after an early combat on May 10 and 'had a chat with some of 73's boys. Before leaving I admired the effect of a Hun bullet that had struck . . . a Hurricane's windscreen fair and square; the windscreen was just a big star, far from transparent, but the bullet had only penetrated about a quarter of an inch before flattening out — a most comforting sight'. All of which suggests that this splendid souvenir is from 'Fanny' Orton's aircraft hit that morning.

ARMÉE DE L'AIR — MAY 10, 1940

Excluding colonial air force units in Africa and Indo-China, and one ZOAA unit based in Corsica.
* Units in course of re-equipment or forming

C-in-C: Gen Vuillemin   HQ: St-Jean-les-Deux-Jumeaux

OC North-East: Gen Têtu   HQ: La Ferté-sous-Jouarre

AIR OPERATIONS NORTH
(ZONE D'OPÉRATIONS AÉRIENNES NORD — ZOAN)
Attached to 1éme Groupe d'Armées — General Billotte
C-in-C: Gen d'Astier de La Vigerie
HQ: Chauny

FIGHTERS

Groupement No 21
OC: Gen Pinsard
HQ: Chantilly-les-Aigles
Day defence of Paris

GC I/1	Bloch 152	Cdt Soviche	Chantilly-les-Aigles
GC II/1	Bloch 152	Cdt Robillon	Buc
GC III/3*	MS 406	Cne Le Bideau	Beauvais-Tillé
	D.520		5e Escadrille to Maubeuge 10.5.40
			6e Escadrille to Norrent-Fontès 10.5.40

Day defence of Basse-Seine

GC II/10	Bloch 151	Cdt Ronzet	Rouen-Boos
	Bloch 152		
GC III/10	Bloch 151	Cdt Risacher	Le Havre-Octeville
	Bloch 152		

Groupement No 23
OC: Gen Romatet
HQ: Laon-Chambry

GC II/2	MS 406	Cdt Bertrou	Laon-Chambry
GC III/2	MS 406	Cdt Geille	Cambrai-Niergnies
GC I/4	Curtiss H-75	Cdt Hertaut	Wez-Thuisy
			Dunkerque-Mardyck 10.5.40
GC I/5	Curtiss H-75	Cdt Murtin	Suippes
ECMJ 1/16	Potez 631	Cne Escudier	Wez-Thuisy

Groupement No 25
OC: Lt Col Augier de Moussac
HQ: Aire-sur-la-Lys

GC III/1	MS 406	Cdt Paoli	Norrent-Fontès
GC II/8	Bloch 152	Cdt de Ponton d'Amecourt	Calais-Marck

Groupement de Chasse de Nuit
Lt Col Dordilly
HQ: Meaux-Esbly
Night defence of Paris

ECN 1/13	Potez 631	Cne Treillard	Meaux-Esbly
ECN 2/13	Potez 631	Cne Petit de Mirbeck	Melun-Villaroche
ECN 3/13	Potez 631	Cne Comte	Le Plessis-Belleville
ECN 4/13	Potez 631	Cne Pouyade	Detz-Bouillancy

BOMBERS

1éme Division Aérienne
OC: Gen Escudier
HQ: Laon
Strategic Reconnaissance

GR II/33	Potez 637	Cdt Alias	Athies-sous-Laon
	Potez 63.11		
	Bloch 174		

Groupement No 6
OC: Col Lefort
HQ: Soissons

GB I/12	LeO 451	Cdt Malardel	Soissons-Saconin
GB II/12	LeO 451	Cdt de La Herverie	Persan-Beaumont

Groupement No 9
OC: Col François
HQ: Montdidier

GB I/34	Amiot 143	Cne Audin	Montdidier
	Amiot 354		La Ferté-Gaucher 10.5.40
GB II/34	Amiot 143	Lt Col Donzeau	Roye-Amy
	Amiot 354		Montdidier 10.5.40
	Bloch 131		

Groupement d'Assaut No 18
Gen Girier
HQ: La Ferté-Gaucher

GBA I/54	Breguet 693	Cdt Plou	La Ferté-Gaucher
GBA II/54	Breguet 693	Cdt Grenet	Nangis

RECONNAISSANCE & ARMY OBSERVATION

Attached to 1éme Armée — Gen Blanchard

GR I/14	Potez 63.11	Cdt Fayet	St Simon-Clastres
GAO 502	Mureaux 115	Cdt Rochard	La Fère-Courbes
	Potez 63.11		
GAO 503	Mureaux 115	Cdt de La	
	Potez 63.11	Genardière	Valenciennes-La Briquette
GAO 504	LeO C.30	Cdt Ginestet	Denain-Prouvy
	Potez 390		
	Potez 63.11		
GAO 505	Potez 390	Cne Petitjean	
	Potez 63.11	de Marcilly	Le Quesnoy-Vertain
GAO 544	Mureaux 115	Cne de Loisy	Villers-lès-Guise

Attached to 11éme Armée — Gen Huntziger

GR II/22	Potez 63.11	Cdt Barruet	Chatel-Chéhéry
GAO 507	Mureaux 115	Cdt Schwander	Attigny
	Potez 63.11		
GAO 510	Potez 390	Cdt Meyer-Jardin	Attigny
	Potez 63.11		
GAO 518	Breguet 270	Cdt Montaudie	Challerange
	Potez 63.11		
GAO 2/520	Mureaux 115	Cdt Delgée	Challerange
	Potez 63.11		

Attached to 7éme Armée — Gen Giraud

GR I/35	Potez 63.11	Cdt Deprez	St Omer-Longuenesse
GAO 501	Mureaux 115	Cdt Moguez	Dunkerque-Mardyck
	Potez 63.11		
GAO 516	Breguet 270	Cdt Durand	Calais-St Inglevert
	Potez 63.11		
GAO 552	Mureaux 117	Cdt Chauvet	St Omer-Wizernes
	Potez 63.11		

Attached to 9éme Armée — Gen Corap

GR II/52	Potez 637	Cdt Gourillon	Couvron
	Potez 63.11		
GAO 511	Potez 390	Cdt Mainguy	Villers-lès-Guise
	Potez 63.11		
GAO 545	Breguet 270	Cne Discors	Denain-Prouvy
	Potez 63.11		
GAO 547	Breguet 270	Cdt Lamey	La Malmaison
	Potez 63.11		
GAO 2/551	Mureaux 117	Cne Sacré	Tournès-Belval
	Potez 63.11		
GAO 4/551	Mureaux 117	Cne Ranon	
	Potez 63.11	de La Vergne	Romeries-Escarmain

ZOAN RESERVE

GAO 515	Mureaux 117 Potez 63.11	Cdt Fesnau	Connantre

AIR OPERATIONS EAST
(ZONE D'OPERATIONS AÉRIENNES EST — ZOAE)
Attached to 2éme Groupe d'Armées — Gen Prételat
C-in-C: Gen Bouscat
HQ: Nancy

FIGHTERS
Groupement No 22
OC: Col Dumèmes
HQ: Velaine-en-Haye

GC I/2	MS 406	Cdt Daru	Toul-Ochey
GC II/4	Curtiss H-75	Cdt Borne	Xaffévillers
GC II/5	Curtiss H-75	Cdt Hugues	Toul-Croix-de-Metz
GC II/6	MS 406	Cdt Fontanet	Anglure-Vouarces
GC III/7	MS 406	Cdt Crémont	Vitry-le-François-Vauclerc
GC I/8	Bloch 152	Cdt Collin	Velaine-en-Haye

BOMBERS
3éme Division Aérienne
OC: Gen Valin
HQ: Vitry-le-Francois
Strategic Reconnaissance

GR I/52	Potez 637 Potez 63.11 Bloch 174	Lt Col de Vitrolles	St Dizier

Groupement No 10
OC: Lt Col Aribaud
HQ: Troyes

GB I/38	Amiot 143 Bloch 200	Cdt Gougnon	Troyes-Barberey
GB II/38	Amiot 143 Bloch 200	Cdt Bodet	Chaumont-Semoutiers

Groupement No 15
OC: Col Moraglia
HQ: Reims

GB I/15	Farman 222	Cdt Quérat	Reims-Courcy
GB II/15	Farman 222	Cdt Guittery	Reims-Courcy

RECONNAISSANCE & ARMY OBSERVATION
Attached to 3éme Armée — Gen Condé

GR I/22	Potez 63.11	Lt Col Savart	Metz-Frescaty
GAO 1/506	Mureaux 113/115 Potez 63.11	Cne Robert	Doncourt-lès-Conflans
GAO 2/506	Mureaux 117 Potez 63.11	Cne de La Baume	Chambley-Bussières
GAO 2/508	Breguet 270 Potez 63.11	Cne Bussière	Mars-la-Tour
GAO 1/551	Mureaux 113/117 Potez 63.11	Cne Ternant	Étain-Busy
GAO 3/551	Mureaux 113/117 Potez 63.11	Cne Boursaus	Senon-Spincourt

Attached to 4éme Armée — Gen Réquin

GR I/36	Potez 63.11	Cdt Jouhaud	Martigny-les-Gerbonvaux
GAO 509	Breguet 270 Potez 63.11	Cne du Tertre	Delme
GAO 1/520	Mureaux 115 Potez 63.11	Cdt Rodet	Morhange Gueblange-les-Dieuze 10.5.40

Attached to 5éme Armée - Gen Bourret

GR II/36	Potez 63.11 Bloch 174	Cdt Bailly	Azelot
GAO 512	Potez 390 Potez 63.11	Cdt Leclèrc	La Perthe
GAO 517	Potez 390 Potez 63.11	Cne Michet de La Baume	Neufchâteau
GAO 548	Mureaux 115 Potez 63.11	Cdt Robert	Épinal-Dogneville
GAO 553	Mureaux 115	Cne de Grivel	Nancy-Azelot

ZOAE RESERVE

GAO 546	Potez 25 Breguet 270 Potez 63.11	Cdt Saget	Sézanne-St Remy
GM SGA	Potez 540 Hanriot 182	Cne Clapiers de Collanges	Reims

AIR OPERATIONS SOUTH
(ZONE D'OPERATIONS AÉRIENNES SUD — ZOAS)
Attached to 3éme Groupe d'Armées — Gen Besson
C-in-C: Gen Odic
HQ: Dôle

FIGHTERS
Groupement No 24
OC: Lt Col Lamon
HQ: Dijon-Longvic

GC I/3	D.520	Cne Thibaudet	Cannes-Mandelieu
GC II/3*	MS 406 D.520	Cdt Morlat	Le Luc
GC I/6	MS 406	Cdt Tricaud	Marseille-Marignane
GC III/6*	MS 406 D.520	Cdt Castanier	Chissey-sous-Loue
GC II/7*	MS 406 D.520	Cdt Durieux	Luxeuil-St Sauveur
GC II/9*	MS 406 Bloch 152	Cdt Rollet	Marseille-Marignane
GC III/9	Bloch 151	Cdt Viguier	Lyon-Bron
GC I/145*	Caudron 714	Cdt Kepinski	Lyon-Bron
ECN 5/13	Potez 631	Cne Perrolaz	Loyettes

RECONNAISSANCE & ARMY CO-OPERATION
6éme Division Aérienne
OC: Gen Hebrard
HQ: Pouilly-sur-Saone
Strategic Reconnaissance

GR I/33	Potez 637 Potez 63.11 Bloch 174	Cdt Dronneau	Dôle-Tavaux

Attached to 8éme Armée — Gen Garchery

GR I/55	Bloch 131 Potez 63.11	Cdt Bisson	Lure-Malbouhans
GAO 513	Breguet 270 Potez 390 Potez 63.11	Cne Perron	Belfort-Chaux
GAO 543	Breguet 270 Potez 63.11	Cne Duboscq	Luxeuil-St Sauveur Montbéliard

ZOAS RESERVE

GAO 1/508	Breguet 270 Potez 63.11	Cdt Levesque	Romilly-sur-Seine

AIR OPERATIONS ALPS
(ZONE D'OPERATIONS AÉRIENNES DES ALPES — ZOAA)
Attached to Armée des Alpes — Gen Olry
C-in-C: Gen Laurens
HQ: Valence

BOMBERS
Groupement d'Instruction de Bombardement du Sud-Est
OC: Gen Gama
HQ: Avignon

Groupement No 6
OC: Col Lefort
HQ: Soissons (ZOAN)

GB I/31	LeO 451	Cdt Schmitter	Lézignan
GB II/31	LeO 451	Cne de Chasseval	Lézignan

Groupement No 7
OC: Lt Col Ronin
HQ:

GB I/23	Bloch 210	Cdt Bordes	Istres-Le Paty
GB II/23	LeO 451	Cne Plique	Istres-Le Vallon

Groupement No 9
OC: Col François
HQ: Mont Didier (ZOAN)

GB I/21	Bloch 210 Amiot 351/354	Cdt Deperrois	Avignon-Châteaublanc
GB II/21	Bloch 210 Amiot 351/354	Cdt Dagan	Avignon-Châteaublanc

Groupement No 11
OC: Lt Col Chopin
HQ:

GB I/11	Bloch 210 LeO 451	Cdt Berdoulat	Arles-Mas de Rus
GB II/11	Bloch 210 LeO 451	Cdt Poupart	Arles-Mas de Rus

Groupement d'Assaut No 19
Lt Col De Castelets La Boulbène
HQ: Salon-de-Provence

GBA II/35	Breguet 691/693	Cne Férigoule	Briare
GBA I/51	Potez 633 Breguet 691/693	Cne Bernard	Salon-de-Provence
GBA II/51	Potez 633 Breguet 691	Cdt Davout d'Auerstaedt	Salon-de-Provence

RECONNAISSANCE & ARMY OBSERVATION

GR II/14	Potez 63.11	Cdt de La Vaissière de la Vergne	Chambaran-Marcilloles
GR II/55	Potez 63.11	Cdt Biron	Chambaran-Marcilloles
GAO 1/514	Potez 63.11 Mureaux 117	Cdt Chrétien	Touillon-lès-Montbard
GAO 2/514	Potez 63.11 Mureaux 115	Cdt Faidide	St Etienne-de-St Geoirs
GAO 1/584	Potez 63.11	Cne Suère	Valence-Chabeuil

Groupement de l'Infanterie de l'Air
Cdt Michel
HQ: Avignon-Pujaut

GIA 1/601	Potez 650 Farman 224	Cne Lanco	Calais-Marck (ZOAN)
GIA 1/602	Potez 650	Cne de Rugy	Montélimar

ZOAA RESERVE

GAO 581*	Potez 63.11	Cne Dupond	Marseille-Marignane
GAO 582*	Potez 63.11	Cne Henri	Valence-Chabeuil
GAO 1/589*	Potez 63.11	Cne Martin des Pallières	Fayence-Sisteron

DÉFENSE AÉRIENNE DU TERRITOIRE (DAT)

Local defence flights operating as small autonomous units, usually comprising no more than six aircraft, that provided local protection for key targets such as factories. Thus often termed 'Chimney Flights', DAT flights were also established to cover strategic targets.

DAT Angers	Bloch 152	
DAT Aulnat	FK 58, MS 406, Potez 63.11	Capt W. Jasionowski
DAT Avord	MS 406	
DAT Bourges	Curtiss H-75	Lt Col C. M. Haegelen
DAT Caen		
DAT Chartres	MS 406, MB 151, Fiat CR42	
DAT Châteaudun	Bloch 152	
DAT Châteauroux	Bloch 151, 152	Lt Z. K. Henneberg
DAT Cognac	Bloch 152	Lt J. P. Falkowski
DAT Étampes	MS 406, MB 151, Curtiss H-75	
Groupe I/55	MB 151, 152, 155, MS 406, D 520	Cdt Rabatel
DAT Guyancourt	Caudron 714	
DAT Istres	MS 406	
DAT La Rochelle	Bloch 151	Capt A. Kowalczyk
DAT Montpellier	MS 406, Fairey Firefly	
DAT Nantes	MS 406	
DAT Rennes	D 501	S/Lt A. Kolubinski
DAT Romorantin	MS 406	Col Olivain
DAT Salon	FK 58, MS 406, D 520	Capt W. Jasionowski
DAT Toulouse	D 520, MS 406	
DAT Tours	Bloch 151, 152	

AÉRONAUTIQUE NAVALE
Operational units based in Metropolitan France

1ére Région Maritime — Cherbourg

1S1	CAMS 55, Loire 130	Cherbourg-Chantereyne	LV Hourdin
3S2	LeO C301 autogyros	Deauville	EV1 Charre

5FT Flotille de Torpillage:
Cherbourg-Chantereyne
CC Suquet

T2	Latécoère 298	Cherbourg-Chantereyne	LV Amiot
T3	Latécoère 298	Cherbourg-Chantereyne	LV Marraud

2éme Région Maritime — Brest

B2	LeO H257b	Lanvéoc-Poulmic	LV Fournier
1S2	Latécoère 290 Gourdou-Leseurre 812	St Trojan Lanvéoc-Poulmic	LV Soulez
2S1	CAMS 55	St Trojan	LV Kervella
2S2	CAMS 37.11	St Trojan	EV1 Chouillet
2S4	Levasseur PL7, 10, 101, LeO 258	La Baule-Escoublac	LV Espouy
E2	Breguet 'Bizerte'	Lanvéoc-Poulmic	LV Duval
E6	Latécoère 521, 523	Lanvéoc-Poulmic	CF Bernard
E8	Potez-CAMS 141 'Antarès'	Lanvéoc-Poulmic	LV Bertin

3éme Région Maritime — Toulon

B3	LeO H257b	Berre	LV Echinard
3S1	LeO H43	St Mandrier	LV Normand

F1A Flotille du 'Béarn'
Lanvéoc-Poulmic
CC Corfmat

AB 1	Vought 156F	Hyères-Le Palyvestre	LV Mesny
AB 2	Loire-Nieuport 401	Berck-sur-Mer	LV Lorenzi
AB 3	Vought 156F	Boulogne-Alprech	LV Pierret
AB 4	Loire-Nieuport 411	Querqueville	LV Lâiné

F1C Flotille de Chasse:
Calais-Marck
CC Jozan

AC 1	Potez 631	Calais-Marck	LV Ferran
AC 2	Potez 631	Calais-Marck	LV Folliot

This Potez 63.11 (No. 570) was just one of over 60 aircraft lost by the Armée de l'Air on May 10. It belonged to Groupe Aérienne d'Observation 2/520 based at Challerange and crashed in Belgium.

FRENCH AIR FORCE

AB 3 Vought 156F (17, 19, 20, 21, 22, 23, 24, 25, 26, 27, 31 and 32). Destroyed in collapse of hangar at Alprech during bombing by He111s 4.30 a.m. No crew casualties. Aircraft 11, 12, 10, 5, 8, 6, 7, 3, 14, 9, 1, and 2 write-offs.
Caudron 635 (147) was also destroyed in this attack.

AC 1 Potez 631. Returned damaged following destruction of Ju52 over IJmuiden 10.00 a.m. EV1 P. de Scitivaux wounded in right arm. Aircraft repairable.

GAO 507 Potez 63.11 (437, 449 and 450). Damaged by machine-gun fire during low-level attack on Challerange 7.00 p.m. No crew casualties. Aircraft damaged but repairable.

GAO 510 Potez 390 (79). Damaged in enemy bombing attack on Attigny 2.30 p.m. No crew casualties. Aircraft damaged but repairable.

GAO 516 Two Potez 63.11. Destroyed in bombing at St Inglevert by He111s of KG54 5.00 a.m. Aircraft all write-offs.
Four Potez 39s also damaged in this attack.

GAO 518 Mureaux 115 (37). Destroyed in bombing attack on Laon-Couvron airfield by Do17s of KG76 5.30 a.m. No crew casualties. Aircraft a write-off.

GAO 2/520 Potez 63.11 (570). Shot down by flak during observation of enemy motorised columns and crash-landed near 'Kaaschboesch' at Ell, west of Redange, Luxembourg 1.20 p.m. Capt Fabia, Capt Francin *(Commandant)*, and Sgt Stizzel all captured badly wounded. Aircraft a write-off.

GAO 544 Potez 63.11 (201 and 429) and Mureaux 115 (35). Aircraft destroyed or badly damaged in bombing attack on Villers-lès-Guise by He111s 4.45 a.m. No crew casualties. Aircraft write-offs.

GAO 1/551 Mureaux 117 (132). Badly damaged on the ground at Étain-Buzy by enemy bombing. No crew casualties. Aircraft abandoned.

GAO 2/551 Potez 63.11 (318 and 577). Damaged on the ground in bombing attack by He111s 2.30 p.m. and abandoned on withdrawal from Tournes-Belval. No crew casualties. Aircraft abandoned.
Mureaux 115 (59) also crippled in this attack.

GB II/15 Two Farman 222. Damaged by bomb splinters during enemy attack on Reims-Champagne 3.45 p.m. No crew casualties. Aircraft both repairable.

GB II/21 Amiot 354 (6). Suffered engine failure during routine test flight and crashed south-west of Sougy. Lt Faure, Lt J. Spagnolo, Adjt Harent, and Adjt Domine killed. Aircraft a write-off.

GB I/34 Amiot 143. Landed at Mourmelon following night sortie over Mönchengladbach and damaged in bombing attack by Do17s of 8./KG2 5.35 a.m. Capt Véron and crew unhurt. Aircraft damaged but repairable.

GB II/34 Amiot 143 (85). Returned to Montdidier badly damaged by AA fire following night sortie over Mönchengladbach. Sgt Moreau wounded by shrapnel, Lt-Col. J. Dagnaux and rest of crew unhurt. Aircraft damaged but repairable.

GB I/38 Amiot 143 (63). Destroyed on the ground at Troyes-Barberey airfield by enemy bombing. No crew casualties. Aircraft a write-off.

GC II/1 Bloch 152. Returned to Buc damaged by return fire from He111 engaged east of Paris 5.20 a.m. Sgt A. Montfort slightly wounded in left leg. Aircraft repairable.

GC 6/1 Morane 406 (737). Engine damaged by return fire from He111 of II./KG27 engaged between Ghent and Termonde 6.00 p.m. Forced-landed near Labuissière, 7km south-east of Béthune, and hit a wall. S/Lt M. Goumy badly injured. Aircraft a write-off.

GC 6/1 Morane 406. Hit in oil system during attack on He111s of II./KG27 between Ghent and Termonde. Believed forced-landed at 'Le Fief', Ligny-lès-Aire, south of Norrent-Fontes 6.00 p.m. Sgt A. Durand unhurt. Aircraft a write-off.

GC 6/1 Morane 406. Believed crashed following engagement with He111s of II./KG27 between Ghent and Termonde 6.00 p.m. Adjt P. Déchanet unhurt. Aircraft a write-off.

GC I/2 Three Moranes 406. Slightly damaged on the ground at Toul-Ochey during enemy bombing attack. No pilot casualties. Aircraft all repairable.

GC I/2 Morane 406. Returned to Toul-Ochey with engine damaged by return fire from He111 of Stab III./KG55 engaged north-west of Toul 4.50 a.m. Lt J. de la Bretonnière unhurt. Aircraft repairable.

GC I/2 Morane 406. Returned to Toul-Ochey slightly damaged by return fire from He111 of Stab KG55 engaged south of Nancy 3.20 p.m. Lt G. Husson unhurt. Aircraft repairable.

GC II/2 Morane 406 (338). Hit by return fire and returned to Laon-Chambry with serious oil leak following attack on Do17s of II./KG76 south of Laon 5.00 a.m. Cmdt. P. Bertrou *(Commandant)* unhurt. Aircraft damaged but repairable.

GC II/2 Morane 406 (814). Oil system damaged by return fire during attack on Do17s of II./KG76 and forced-landed near Ferme de Granlup, north of Monceau-le-Wast 4.45 a.m. Lt H. de Rohan-Chabot unhurt. Aircraft damaged but repairable.

GC III/2 Morane 406. Crashed at Boyelles, 10 km south of Arras, damaged by return fire during attack on He111 of 5./KG1 near Bertincourt 1.15 p.m. Sgt F. Ravilly unhurt. Aircraft a write-off.

GC III/2 Morane 406. Landed at Méaulte badly damaged by return fire during attack on He111 of 5./KG1 over Bapaume 1.15 p.m. Adjt J. Nedelec unhurt. Aircraft a write-off.

GC III/2 Morane 406. Landed at Péronne badly damaged by return fire during attack on He111 of 5./KG1 over Bapaume 1.15 p.m. Pilot unhurt. Aircraft a write-off.

GC III/2 Eight Morane 406. Destroyed or burned out at Cambrai-Niergnies in bombing attack by He111s 4.30 a.m. No pilot casualties. Aircraft all write-offs.
Eighteen more MS406 were damaged, five seriously, during this attack. That evening the group was reinforced with aircraft from GC III/7, all serviceable aircraft dispersed overnight to Épinay.

GC I/4 Curtiss H-75 (71). Returned to Wez-Thuisy damaged by return fire from Do17s of II./KG2 engaged between Rocroi and Flize 5.30 a.m. Capt P. O'Byrne *(Commandant)* wounded in hand and admitted to hospital in Reims. Aircraft repairable.

GC 3/4 Curtiss H-75 (138). Shot down in combat with Bf110s over Lunéville 4.00 p.m. Crashed and burned out at Padoux, south of Rambervillers. S/Lt R. Tixier-Vignancourt killed. Aircraft a write-off.

GC 3/4 Curtiss H-75 (69). Abandoned over Epinal during combat with Bf110s 4.00 p.m. Sgt Ballin baled out badly burned and admitted to hospital in Nancy. Aircraft a write-off.

GC II/4 Curtiss H-75. (146) Emergency landing on burst tyre at Épinal with engine damaged and oil system riddled by return fire from He111 of 9./KG55 4.15 p.m. Sgt A. de La Chappelle unhurt. Aircraft a write-off.

GC I/5 Curtiss H-75 (159). Forced-landed back at Suippes badly damaged in solo attack on Bf110s of 3./ZG26 5.45 a.m. Sgt F. Morel unhurt. Aircraft a write-off.

GC I/5 Curtiss H-75. Hit by return fire during attack on a Do17 of 6./KG2 north of Mourmelon and forced-landed at Wez-Thuisy 6.30 a.m. S/Lt A. Goupy badly wounded in right thigh, admitted to hospital in Reims. Aircraft damaged but repairable.

GC I/5 Curtiss H-75 (26). Shot down by escort Bf110s during attack on Do17s of III./KG3 over Suippes 5.00 p.m. Sgt E. Preux baled out, face slightly burned. Aircraft a write-off.

GC III/6 Morane 406 (474). Shot down by return fire from He111s of I./KG51 engaged south of Dijon 3.30 p.m. Sgt R. Hardouin baled out unhurt over Forêt de Chaux. Aircraft a write-off.

GC III/6 Morane 406. Returned to Chissey-sur-Loue badly damaged by return fire from He111s of I./KG51 engaged south of Dijon 3.30 p.m. S/Lt R. Cavaroz unhurt. Aircraft damaged but repairable.

GC III/6 Morane 406 (413). Engine set on fire during attacks on He111 of I./KG51 engaged south of Dijon 3.30 p.m. Adjt C. Goujon baled out, landing unhurt near Citeaux. Aircraft a write-off.

GC II/7 Morane 406 (334). Shot down by Bf109s during attack on enemy bomber and crashed at Esmoulières, 5km from Faucogney 6.00 a.m. Cmdt. G. Clicquot de Mentque killed. Aircraft a write-off.

GC II/7 Four Moranes 406. Aircraft destroyed on the ground at Luxeuil in bombing by He111s. of I./KG51 5.00 a.m. No pilot casualties. Aircraft write-offs.

GC 3/7 Morane 406 (598). Engine set alight in combat with Bf110s north-east of Luxeuil and crashed into woods at Briaucourt 3.40 p.m. S/Lt R. Couillens seriously wounded, later died. Aircraft a write-off.

GC 3/7 Morane 406. Forced-landed with damage following combat with Bf110s north-east of Luxeuil 3.45 p.m. Lt H. Jeandet badly wounded. Aircraft a write-off.

GC III/7 Three Morane 406 (186, 228, and 392). Destroyed in bombing attack on Vitry-le-François by Do17s of 7./KG3 4.20 a.m. No pilot casualties. Aircraft all write-offs.
Two other MS406 were also reported damaged in this attack.

GC 6/7 Morane 406 (442). Engine damaged during attack on He111 near Châlons-en-Champagne and eventually caught fire so abandoned over Sézanne 6.00 a.m. Capt P. Bouvarre *(Commandant)* baled out with minor injuries. Aircraft a write-off.

GC 6/7 Morane 406 (813). Badly damaged by return fire from He111 engaged near Châlons-en-Champagne and overturned in crash-landing on rough ground at Avenay-Val-d'Or, north-west of Vitry-le-François 5.40 a.m. Cmdt. M. Arnoux injured face. Aircraft a write-off.

GC 2/8 Bloch 152 (545). Shot down by enemy fighters during attack on Do17s of 7./KG2 over Mars-la-Tour and crashed at Jaulny, 9km south of Chambley. Possibly that claimed by Oberlt Lippert of 3./JG53 south-east of Metz 2.55 p.m. Capt A. Astier *(Commandant)* killed. Aircraft a write-off.

GC III/9 Bloch 152. Landed at Lyon-Bron on burst tyre and with engine damaged by return fire from enemy aircraft engaged over base 4.45 a.m. Adjt Chapour unhurt. Aircraft damaged but repairable.

GR I/22 Potez 63.11 (425). Shot down by Oberlt Hauenschild of 3./JG2 during reconnaissance sortie over Luxembourg and the Sarre; crashed and burned out at Melickshoff Farm, near Echternach 8.20 a.m. S/Lt A. Chaumont, Sgt R. Pelletier, and Sgt A. Cattoen killed. Aircraft a write-off.

GR II/33 Potez 63.11 (7). Returned to Athies with starboard engine damaged by Belgian AA fire south of Liège. Lt Dutertre, S/Lt Hochedé, and Sgt Kinster unhurt. Aircraft repairable.

GR II/33 Potez 63.11 (154) and Bloch 174 (47). Destroyed in bombing attack on Athies-sous-Laon by Do17s of KG2 5.30 a.m. No crew casualties. Aircraft both write-offs.
Two Potez 63.11 (45 and 156) were also damaged during this attack, the latter being abandoned on withdrawal May 16.

GR I/36 Potez 63.11 (202). Forced-landed at Guéblange badly damaged by flak during reconnaissance sortie p.m. Lt Couderq unhurt. Capt Larmier wounded, baled out over enemy territory and captured. Aircraft damaged but repairable.

GRII/36 Three Potez 63.11 (174, 182 and 214) and two Bloch 174 (44 and 45). Destroyed in bombing at Neufchâteau. Aircraft all write-offs.
Five more Potez (48, 146, 209, 273 and 274) were also damaged in this attack.

GR II/52 Two Potez 63.11. Destroyed in bombing attack on Laon-Couvron airfield by Do17s of II./KG76 4.30 a.m. No crew casualties. Aircraft both write-offs.
Another Potez 63.11 and a Potez 637 were also reported damaged during this attack.

Down at Echternach in Luxembourg was another Potez 63.11 killing the three-man crew from Groupe de Reconnaissance I/22.

DUTCH AIR FORCE *(MILITAIRE LUCHTVAART)*

MAY 10, 1940

C-in-C: LtGen. P.W. Best — HQ: Den Haag

1st AIR REGIMENT (1e LVR)
OC: Majoor H.G. van Voorthuijsen — HQ: 'Kraaijveld', Schiphol

I (STRATEGIC) GROUP (I-1)
Majoor J.T.H. van Weeren   HQ: Schiphol

1 (RECCE) SQUADRON (1-I-1)
10 : 3 Fokker C Xs
Kapt J. van der Werff   Bergen

2 (BOMBER) SQUADRON (2-I-1)
9 : 3 Fokker T Vs
Kapt J. G. Sissingh   Schiphol

II (FIGHTER) GROUP (II-1)
Majoor H. van Weerden Poelman   HQ: Den Haag

1 SQUADRON (1-II-1)
11 : 1 Fokker D XXIs
Kapt H. M. Schmidt Crans   De Kooy

2 SQUADRON (2-II-1)
9 : 3 Fokker D XXIs
Kapt P.J.E. Janssens   Schiphol

3 SQUADRON (3-II-1)
11 : 1 Fokker G 1s
Kapt H. J. Scholtmeijer   Waalhaven

4 SQUADRON (4-II-1)
12 : 2 Fokker G 1s
Kapt T.J.A. Lamers   Bergen

2nd AIR REGIMENT (2e LVR)
OC: LtKol. J.H. Sar — HQ: Hotel Munzert, Zeist

I (RECCE) GROUP (I-2)
Attached IV Legerkorps
6 : 2 Fokker C Vs, 4 Koolhoven F.K.51s,
& 1 : 1 Fokker C X
Majoor H. van der Zanden   Hilversum

II (RECCE) GROUP (II-2)
Attached II Legerkorps
7 : 2 Fokker C Vs
& 5 : 1 Koolhoven F.K.51s
Kapt H.L.G. Lambert   Ypenburg

III (RECCE) GROUP (III-2)
Attached Brigades A and B
7 : 2 Fokker C Vs
& 3 Koolhoven F.K.51s
Majoor F. Raland   Ruigenhoek

IV (RECCE) GROUP (IV-2)
Attached III Legerkorps
7 : 1 Fokker C Vs
& 3 : 2 Koolhoven F.K.51s
Kapt A.W. de Ruyter van Steveninck   Gilze-Rijen

V (FIGHTER) GROUP (V-2)
'Jachtgroep Veldleger'
Kapt W.H. Wijnkamp — HQ: Ockenburg

1 SQUADRON (1-V-2)
8 : 1 Fokker D XXIs
Lt P.J.B. Ruijs de Perez   Ypenburg

3 SQUADRON (3-V-2)
11 : 1 Douglas DB-8As
Kapt J.A. Bach   Ypenburg

Note: Aircraft types are main equipment only and figures indicate serviceable : non-serviceable aircraft on strength May 10, 1940.

FLYING TRAINING

3rd AIR REGIMENT (3e LVR)
OC: Kapt J. L. Zegers — HQ: 'De Vlijt' Texel

ELEMENTARY FLYING TRAINING SCHOOL
(Elementaire Vliegschool)   Vlissingen (Souburg)
11 Fokker S IVs and 17 Fokker S IXs.

On May 14, apart from a Fokker S IX at Haamstede, and 3 unserviceable Fokker S IVs which were abandoned, all aircraft were evacuated to Berck-sur-Mer. The following day during a transit flight to Beauchamps, a Fokker S IX crashed at Héricourt-sur-Samson killing both crew: Sgt C. Sitters and Sgt C. J. van Hulzen.

ADVANCED FLYING TRAINING SCHOOL
(Voortgezette Vliegschool)   Haamstede
9 Fokker C Vs, 1 Fokker C IX, 1 Fokker F VIIA, 10 Koolhoven F.K.51s, and 2 Koolhoven F.K.56s.

At dawn on May 10, Haamstede was subjected to low-level attacks by Bf110s. In repeated attacks by enemy aircraft over successive days, half the aircraft were destroyed or seriously damaged. Four undamaged Fokker C Vs (603, 637, 648 and 652) were taken over by IV-2 who arrived from Gilze-Rijen on May 10.

FIGHTER SCHOOL *(Jachtvliegschool)* 'De Vlijt', Texel
1 Bücker Bü 131, 1 Fokker D XVI, 7 Fokker D XVIIs,
2 Fokker D XXIs, 1 Fokker G 1, 1 Fokker S II,
1 Fokker T V, 2 Focke-Wulf Fw58B-2s,
3 Koolhoven F.K.56s, and 1 North American NA27.

Six of the school's Fokker D XVII biplanes (202, 203, 205, 207, 209 and 210) were pressed into service with the composite unit 1/2-II-1 at Buiksloot on May 11, 1940. Most remaining aircraft were destroyed or damaged in repeated enemy fighter attacks.

NAVAL AIR SERVICE *(MARINE LUCHTVAART DIENST)*

DE MOK:
(Texel)   10 Fokker C VIIw
                         (L2 - L5, L7, L8, L13, L14, L17, and L18)
                         3 Fokker C VIIIw (G7 - G9)
                         1 Fokker T VIIIw (R4)
                         1 Fokker C XIw (W3)
                         10 Fokker C XIVw (F2, F4, F7 - F12, F14, and F19)

VEERE:
(Walcheren)   3 Fokker C VIIIw (G3, G5, and G6)
                         1 Fokker C XIw (W14)
                         4 Fokker C XIVw (F17, F21, F23, and F24)

SCHELLINGWOUDE:
(Amsterdam)   1 Fokker T VIIIw (R11)

ALKMAARDERMEER:
(near Akersloot)   10 Fokker C XIVw (F1, F3, F5, F6, F13, F15, F16, F18, F20 and F22)
BRAASSEMERMEER: 3 Fokker T VIIIw (R1 - R3)

WESTEINDERPLAS:
(near Kudelstaart)   3 Fokker C VIIIw (G1, G2 and G4)
                         3 Fokker T VIIIw (R6, R7 and R9)

On May 12, two more Fokker T VIIIw (R8 and R10) arrived direct from the Fokker works.

DE KOOY: 18 Fokker S III (S1 - S18) decoys
                         15 Fokker S IX (S20 - S34)
                         15 Koolhoven F.K.51 (E1 - E15)

Given the overwhelming air superiority of the *Luftwaffe*, and the nature of the German invasion, the *MLD* took little part in proceedings and there were few engagements with enemy aircraft. The majority of their aircraft were lost, either on the ground or at moorings, through repeated bombing and strafing attacks.

DUTCH AIR FORCE

1-I-1 Three Fokker C X (704, 707 and 710). Unserviceable machines burnt out in Hangar 2 at Bergen during bombing attack by 7./KG4 and 2./KGr.126 5.20 a.m. No crew casualties. Aircraft write-offs.

The squadron 'hack', a Fokker C V (654), was also badly damaged in this attack.

1-I-1 Fokker C X (709). Radiator and fuel tank damaged in attack by Bf109s of 7./JG3 following bombing of Waalhaven airfield and crash-landed at Dorpskade, near Wateringen 12.25 p.m. 1e Lt J. Pleij and 2e Lt M. G. A-Tjak unhurt. Aircraft a write-off.

1-I-1 Fokker C X (708). Damaged by Bf109s of 7./JG3 following bombing attack on Waalhaven airfield and forced-landed by the railway at Den Hoorn, near Abstwoude, south of Delft 12.55 p.m. 2e Lt S. J. Postma and 2e Lt H. J. Landman unhurt. Aircraft abandoned.

1-I-1 Fokker C X (712). Returned to Bergen slightly damaged by Bf109s of 7./JG3 following bombing attack on Waalhaven 12.25 p.m. 2e Lt W. H. Stein slightly wounded in foot. Kapt Dr. Ph. H. Kuenen badly wounded, admitted to Centraal Ziekenhuis in Alkmaar. Aircraft repairable.

1-I-1 Fokker C X (706). Returned to Bergen badly damaged by Bf109s of 7./JG3 following bombing attack on Waalhaven 12.25 p.m. 2e Lt J. F. de Laat unhurt. 1e Lt G. F. J. Jansen wounded, admitted to Centraal Ziekenhuis in Alkmaar. Aircraft repairable.

The Dutch Air Force was virtually crippled after the first day with 50 per cent of their aircraft destroyed on the ground or in combat. This is the remains of Fokker D XXI — the number 223 is still partly visible — shot down near the Hague.

1-I-1 Fokker C X (711). Returned to Bergen slightly damaged by Bf109s of 7./JG3 following bombing attack on Waalhaven 12.25 p.m. 1e Lt J. C. J. Vermeulen and 2e Lt H. A. M. van der Heyden unhurt. Aircraft repairable.

2-I-1 Fokker T V (859). Failed to take-off and caught in bombing attack on Schiphol by III./KG4 5.20 a.m. Hydraulic system damaged by splinters. No crew casualties. Aircraft abandoned.

2-I-1 4 Fokker T Vs (851, 857, 860 and 863). Unserviceable aircraft caught in bombing attack on Schiphol by III./KG4 and wrecked by splinters or burned out in hangars 5.20 a.m. No crew casualties. Aircraft write-offs.

2-I-1 Fokker T V (853). Emergency landing at Ruigenhoek due to engine failure 6.10 a.m. Lt W. F. Anceaux, Lt G. H. J. Ruygrok, Sgt O. W. Douwes Dekker, Sgt G. A. van Riemsdijk and Korp. A. J. Brands unhurt. Aircraft abandoned.

2-I-1 Fokker T V (858). Fuel tank and hydraulics damaged by Dutch AA fire over Veere following earlier attack on enemy aircraft over IJmuiden. Forced-landed at Haamstede 10.00 a.m. Lt J. J. Bak, Lt J. W. van Hengel, Sgt R. M. Draaisma, and Sold. J. W. Wevers unhurt. Aircraft damaged but repairable — later destroyed in bombing.

2-I-1 Fokker T V (865). Experienced undercarriage problems and forced-landed at De Kooy 5.50 a.m. Caught in bombing attack and burned out. Lt J. J. Mulder, Lt G. F. Verhage, Sgt J. L. van de As, Sgt G. Kroonsberg, and Sold. J. Wijnstra unhurt. Aircraft a write-off.

2-I-1 Fokker T V (855). Shot down by Bf110s after bombing enemy aircraft at Ockenburg and crashed in the sea between Terheide and Kijkduin 6.20 a.m. Possibly that claimed by Oberlt Mölders of 1./ZG1. 2e Lt A. H. Smoolenaars and Korp. A. Janse killed. 2e Lt N. Steenbeek and Korp. H. Vallentgoed believed baled out but lost. Lt B. Swagerman baled out and swam ashore. Aircraft lost.

The body of the pilot, 2e Lt Steenbeek, was washed ashore at 's-Gravenzande on June 1, 1940, that of the wireless operator, Korporaal Vallentgoed, at Zandvoort on June 15. They were both buried at Kijkduin.

2-I-1 Fokker T V (854). Attacked by Bf109s after bombing attack on Waalhaven and shot down over Langeweg, Oud-Beierland. Possibly that claimed by Uffz Uebe of 6./JG27 1.20 p.m. Sgt Maj. A. J. G. Oostindië, 1e Lt W. J. E. Künzel, 2e Lt F. H. Stoovelaar, and Sgt P. Boon killed. Sgt J. den Hartog baled out badly wounded. Aircraft a write-off.

2-I-1 Fokker T V (862). Attacked by Bf109s after bombing attack on Waalhaven and shot down over Langeweg, Oud-Beierland. Possibly that claimed by Lt Wenzel of 6./JG27 1.35 p.m. 1e Lt F. H. Groen, 1e Lt L. J. W. Blommesteijn, Sgt P. Espeet, and Sold. H. Kuiper killed. Aircraft a write-off.

1-II-1 Fokker D XXI (223). Separated from patrol and shot down during solo attack on He111s over Wassenaarse Slag 7.45 a.m. Wachtm. J. van Zuylen killed. Aircraft a write-off.

1-II-1 Fokker D XXI (241). Attacked by Bf109s of 5.(J)/TrGr.186 and engine set alight during landing approach at De Kooy, crashed on the airfield and burned out 7.45 a.m. Lt J. W. T. Bosch unhurt. Aircraft a write-off.

Fokker D XX1, serial 241, came to grief landing back on the aerodrome at De Kooy.

Of these D XXIs neatly lined up at Schiphol pre-war, 214 was lost on May 10 at De Kooy.

1-II-1 Fokker D XXI (219). Landed with instrument panel damaged in combat with Bf109s of 5.(J)/TrGr.186 over De Kooy 7.50 a.m. Further damaged in strafing attacks by Bf109s and Bf110s at 8.00 a.m. and again at 12.40 p.m. 2e Lt H. J. van Overvest unhurt. Aircraft repairable.

Thanks to incredible efforts by ground crews at De Kooy this aircraft was made serviceable later and joined the remnants of 1 and 2-II-1 at Buiksloot on May 12.

1-II-1 Fokker D XXI (214). Landed with undercarriage damaged following combat with Bf109s of 5.(J)/TrGr.186 over De Kooy 7.50 a.m. and lost when hangar set alight in subsequent strafing attack by Bf110s 12.00 p.m. 1e Lt H. A. J. Huddleston Slater unhurt. Aircraft a write-off.

1-II-1 6 Fokker D XXIs (218, 221, 233, 234, 240, and 242). Returned damaged following combat with Bf109s of 5.(J)/TrGr.186 over De Kooy 7.50 a.m. No pilot casualties. Aircraft repairable.

1-II-1 6 Fokker D XXIs (218, 221, 234, 240, 242 and 244). Caught on the ground at De Kooy and further damaged in strafing attack by Bf109s and Bf110s 8.40 a.m. 1e Lt H. A. J. Huddleston Slater wounded, admitted to hospital. Aircraft damaged but repairable.

Four aircraft (218, 221, 240, and 242) were further damaged in strafing by Bf110s at 12.00 p.m. but were repaired and joined remnants of 1 and 2-II-1 at Buiksloot next day.

1-II-1 2 Fokker D XXIs (233 and 234) and Fokker C IX (665). Destroyed at De Kooy in strafing by Bf110s 12.40 p.m. No casualties. Aircraft, two damaged in earlier attacks, all write-offs.

2-II-1 Fokker D XXI (245). Landed near Zwaagdijk after attack on Ju88s of I./KG30 bombing Schiphol 5.00 a.m. Sgt H. B. Bulten slightly wounded. Aircraft abandoned.

2-II-1 Fokker D XXI (235). Returned to Schiphol damaged in combat with Bf109s of 5./JG26 4.50 a.m. 2e Lt J. C. Plesman unhurt. Aircraft repairable.

2-II-1 Fokker D XXI (225). Returned to Schiphol with windscreen damaged by return fire from Ju52 attacked between Den Haag and Gouda 7.20 a.m. 1e Lt N. W. Sluijter wounded in the arm. Aircraft repairable.

2-II-1 Fokker D XXI (225). Believed shot down by Oberlt Seifert *(Staffelkapitän)* of 3./JG26 in combat over Ouderkerk aan de IJssel 9.15 a.m. Sgt F. C. H. Looijen killed, body recovered May 21. Aircraft a write-off.

The serial number of this aircraft is unconfirmed but believed to be correct as shown.

2-II-1 Fokker D XXI (238). Shot down in combat with Bf109s during escort sortie for 2-I-1 Fokker T-Vs attack on Waalhaven airfield. Possibly that claimed by Lt Neumann of 6./JG27 1.25 p.m. 1e Lt A. H. Bodaan killed. Aircraft a write-off.

2-II-1 Fokker D XXI (239). Returned to Schiphol with undercarriage and brakes badly damaged in combat with Bf109s during escort sortie for 2-I-1 Fokker TVs attack on Waalhaven. Possibly that attacked by Uffz Krenz of 6./JG27 1.20 p.m.. Sgt C. Ch. Steensma unhurt. Aircraft burned to prevent capture.

3-II-1 Fokker G I (319). Forced-landed on the perimeter of Waalhaven with port engine damaged by return fire from He 111s of 5./KG4 5.20 a.m. 1e Lt J. P. Kuipers and Sgt J. R. Venema unhurt. Aircraft abandoned.

Lt Kuipers escaped across the Maas by rowing boat. Sgt Jan Venema joined Dutch troops defending the airfield and was killed in action later in the day.

3-II-1 Fokker G 1 (309). Crashed in the Maas near Vlaardingen hit by return fire from He 111s of 5./KG4 attacked over Waalhaven 5.20 a.m. 2e Lt J. van der Jagt killed. Aircraft a write-off.

Van der Jagt took-off without his gunner, believed to be Sgt S. de Vos, who had been killed on the ground at Waalhaven.

3-II-1 Fokker G 1 (312). Forced-landed with starboard engine damaged by return fire from He111s of Stab KG4 engaged over Waalhaven 5.30 a.m. 1e Lt P. Noomen and Korp. H. de Vries unhurt. Aircraft abandoned.

3-II-1 4 Fokker G Is (302, 316, 334 and 335). Damaged on the ground at Waalhaven in repeated bombing attacks. No crew casualties. Aircraft abandoned.

On withdrawal, the unit also had to abandon a Focke-Wulf Fw58B-2 (195), Fokker C IX (664), Fokker C X (716), and 2 Koolhoven F.K.51s (19 and 417).

3-II-1 Fokker G 1 (347). Parked on the eastern perimeter at Waalhaven and destroyed in bombing attack by He111s of 5./KG4 5.20 a.m. No crew casualties. Aircraft a write-off.

One of 26 Fokker G 1s, powered by Wasp rather than Mercury engines, originally intended for the Spanish Republican Air Force. Ten were later accepted by the RNethAF with deliveries commencing January 1940, but not all are thought to have had their full armament fitted by May 10. Nine were captured (349, 350, 352, 354-357, 360 and 361).

3-II-1 Fokker G I (315). Slightly damaged hitting an obstruction at De Kooy where landed to refuel and rearm after combat over Waalhaven 7.30 a.m. 1e Lt A. van Oorschot and Sgt W. P. Wesly unhurt. Aircraft repairable.

3-II-1 Fokker G I (330). Badly damaged in combat with Bf109 over North Brabant following attack on He111s of I./KG4 over Waalhaven and forced-landed at Zevenbergen. Believed that claimed by Oberlt Leppla *(Staffelkapitän)* of 3./JG51 5.30 a.m. Sgt Maj. J. J. Buwalda unhurt, Sgt J. Wagner injured. Aircraft a write-off.

This Fokker G 1 (330) from 3-II-1 which came down at Zevenbergen is believed to have been the first victory of the Staffelkapitän of 3./JG51, Oberleutnant Richard Leppla.

3-II-1 Fokker G I (311). Forced-landed out of fuel on the shore near Oostvoorne after attack on Ju52s of III./KGzbV.1 and combat with Bf109s over Waalhaven 5.30 a.m. 2e Lt G. Sonderman and Sgt H. Holwerda unhurt. Aircraft undamaged.

3-II-1 Fokker G I (328). Forced-landed on the shore near Oostvoorne hydraulics damaged in attack on Ju52s of III./KGzbV.1 and combat with Bf109s over Waalhaven 5.30 a.m. Sgt H. F. Souffrée and Sgt J. C. de Man unhurt. Aircraft abandoned.

3-II-1 Fokker G I (329). Forced-landed out of fuel on the shore near Oostvoorne after attack on Ju87s of IV.(St)/LG1 and Ju52s of III./KGzbV.1 over Waalhaven 5.30 a.m. 1e Lt K. W. Woudenberg and Sgt J. A. Pouw unhurt. Aircraft undamaged.

4-II-1 Three Fokker G Is (304, 305, and 331). Badly damaged on the ground at Bergen in bombing by 7./KG4 and 2./KGr.126 5.20 a.m. No crew casualties. Aircraft damaged but repairable — later burned to prevent capture.

4-II-1 Two Fokker G Is (301 and 332). Badly damaged on the ground at Bergen in bombing by 7./KG4 and 2./KGr.126 5.20 a.m. No crew casualties. Aircraft abandoned and later captured.

4-II-1 Five Fokker G Is (308, 310, 318, 322, and 325). Badly damaged on the ground at Bergen by bombing from 7./KG4 and 2./KGr.126 5.20 a.m. No crew casualties. Aircraft repairable.

4-II-1 Two Fokker G Is (313 and 317). Unserviceable aircraft in Hangar 5 at Bergen destroyed by bombing from 7./KG4 and 2./KGr.126 5.20 a.m. No crew casualties. Aircraft write-offs.

4-II-1 Fokker G I (333). Burned out in front of Hangar 6 at Bergen by bombing from 7./KG4 and 2./KGr.126 5.20 a.m. 1e Lt A. D. Snitslaar unhurt. Aircraft a write-off.

I-2 Two Koolhoven F.K.51s (414 and 425), 2 Fokker C Vs (591 and 600), and Fokker C X (718). Unserviceable aircraft damaged in attack on Hilversum airfield 5.20 a.m. No crew casualties. Aircraft damaged but repairable.
These aircraft were left behind for repair when the unit moved to Middenmeer that evening. They were eventually abandoned or destroyed on final evacuation to De Zilk on May 13.

II-2 Two Fokker C Vs. Badly damaged on the ground at Ypenburg during enemy landings. No crew casualties. Aircraft damaged but repairable, later abandoned.

Many Dutch aircraft were destroyed on the ground in dawn attacks, Bergen being particularly badly hit by KG4. Fokker G 1, serial 301, was just one of the casualties.

III-2 Fokker C V (617). Hit by ground-fire during reconnaissance sortie over Valkenburg and returned to Ruigenhoek with oil-pipe shot through. 7.55 a.m. 2e Lt H. K. van Huizen and Sgt A. J. M. van Liempd unhurt. Aircraft damaged but repairable.

III-2 Fokker C V (621). Returned to Ruigenhoek damaged following low-level photo-reconnaissance of Valkenburg airfield 10.55 a.m. 1e Lt H. T. de Raaf and Sgt F. Fopma unhurt. Aircraft repairable.

III-2 Fokker C V (631). Returned to Ruigenhoek damaged by ground-fire following strafing of enemy transports on beaches between Katwijk and Scheveningen 4.20 p.m. 1e Lt H. T. de Raaf unhurt. Sgt L. J. M. Fiévez slightly wounded. Aircraft repairable.

III-2 Fokker C V (622). Damaged by enemy ground-fire during reconnaissance over the Moerdijk bridge and forced-landed near Hoge Zwaluwe 5.30 p.m. Sgt A. Muller and 2e Lt A. P. de Pauw unhurt. Aircraft damaged but repairable.

IV-2 Two Fokker C Vs (604 and 620) and two Koolhoven F.K.51 (415 and 421). Badly damaged on the ground at Gilze-Rijn by enemy bombing attacks between 5.20 and 7.25 a.m. No crew casualties. Aircraft abandoned on withdrawal to Haamstede.

IV-2 Fokker C V (625) and 2 Koolhoven F.K.51s (409 and 427). Unserviceable aircraft at Gilze-Rijn believed destroyed to prevent capture on withdrawal to Haamstede 10.10 a.m. No crew casualties. Aircraft write-offs.

IV-2 Fokker C V (606). Shot down in combat with Bf110s near Nieuwerkerk during sortie to bomb enemy landings at Waalhaven 1.28 p.m. 2e Lt W. Rooseboom killed. 1e Lt B. van Steenbergen baled out but shot in his parachute and seriously wounded — died May 19 in hospital at Noordgouwe. Aircraft a write-off.

IV-2 Fokker C V (614). Damaged in combat with Bf110s near Nieuwerkerk during sortie to bomb enemy landings at Waalhaven 1.20 p.m. Forced-landed at Sommelsdijk in the Oudelandspolder, south-west of Middelharnis, where bomb-load later exploded. Sgt K. Zwarthoed and 2e Lt W. H. Meulkens both unhurt. Aircraft a write-off.

1-V-2 Fokker D XXI (227). Unserviceable aircraft caught on the ground at Ypenburg in bombing by He111s of 1./KG4 5.35 a.m. No pilot casualty. Aircraft a write-off.

1-V-2 Fokker D XXI (222). Shot down over Westland following attack on enemy bombers. crash-landed between Monster and Terheyde 5.15 a.m. 1e Lt P. J. B. Ruijs de Perez *(Commandant)* wounded in the arm. Aircraft a write-off.

1-V-2 Fokker D XXI (216). Shot down in combat with Bf110s over Valkenburg and crashed near the Maaldrift by the Wassenaar — Leiden tramline at Den Deyl 6.15 a.m. Sgt G. K. P. Kiel wounded. Aircraft a write-off.
Guus Kiel remained trapped in the wreckage of his cockpit for four hours before being rescued and taken to the Ursula-Kliniek in Wassenaar.

Left: **Another G I of 4-II-1 destroyed at Bergen airfield was 333.**
Right: **The shambles inside the burned-out hangars.**

Two D XXIs, both from 1-V-2 . . . but having vastly different fates. Whereas aircraft 227 (left) was already unserviceable when it was a victim of the attack on Ypenburg airfield, this pile of wreckage of 216 (right) entombed the pilot for four hours. Sergeant Guus Kiel was shot down in the early morning and crashed at Den Deyl.

1-V-2 Fokker D XXI (247). Landed at Ypenburg to refuel and rearm 5.40 a.m. and destroyed on the ground in enemy attacks. Sgt J. Eden unhurt. Aircraft a write-off.

1-V-2 Fokker D XXI (215). Landed out of ammunition and fuel on the beach at Kijkduin 5.45 a.m. where later strafed by enemy fighters, set alight and burned out. 2e Lt G. Steen unhurt. Aircraft a write-off.

1-V-2 Fokker D XXI (246). Hit by Bf110s of II./ZG1 during attack on He111s over Delft 5.40 a.m. Abandoned over Klein-Delfgauw and crashed near Pijnacker. Sgt J. Linzel baled out wounded in thigh landing between Delft and Nootdorp. Aircraft a write-off.

1-V-2 Fokker D XXI (228). Landed at Ockenburg to refuel and rearm 5.40 a.m. and damaged in attack by Ju88s of 3./KG30. 2e Lt F. G. B. Droste unhurt. Aircraft abandoned.

1-V-2 Fokker D XXI (217). Landed at Ockenburg to refuel and rearm 5.40 a.m. and overtaken by enemy landings. Sgt P. J. Aarts unhurt. Aircraft abandoned.

3-V-2 Douglas DB-8A (382). Badly damaged in combat and abandoned over Honselersdijk 5.10 a.m. 2e Lt H. W. Guijt baled out and wounded while in parachute. 1e Lt J. Vonk killed. Aircraft a write-off.

3-V-2 Douglas DB-8A (384). Hit a sand ridge and nosed-over on landing at Rozenburg 6.05 a.m. Sgt D. Lub and Sgt F. Vijn unhurt. Aircraft abandoned.

3-V-2 Douglas DB-8A (387). Port wing damaged by bomb splinters during take-off and later collapsed during combat. Abandoned over Nootdorp 5.30 a.m. Sgt J. F. A. Jansen baled out unhurt, landing on van Buuren's Farm, Leerbroek. Sgt K. Beuving baled out injured, admitted to hospital in Den Haag. Aircraft a write-off.

3-V-2 Douglas DB-8A (388). Shot down in flames by Bf110s of II./ZG1 and crashed near 'Ter Horst' estate on the Papenlaan te Voorschoten 5.10 a.m. 2e Lt J. van Riemsdijk baled out wounded. Sgt G. Hagen killed. Aircraft a write-off.
Originally buried in a field grave alongside the wreckage of his aircraft Sergeant Hagen was reinterred in Het Lange Duin cemetery on July 13, 1940.

3-V-2 Douglas DB-8A (389). Landed at Ockenburg to refuel and rearm 5.25 a.m. Caught on the ground and set alight in enemy attacks and burned out. Sgt G. A. Hinrichs and Sgt J. C. Kentie unhurt. Aircraft a write-off.

3-V-2 Douglas DB-8A (390). Attacked by Bf110s of II./ZG1 and engine later hit by Dutch AA fire. Belly-landed on the Zouteveenseweg near Schipluiden 5.10 a.m. Sgt J. J. de Bruijn unhurt. 1e Lt H. F. H. van Boekhout wounded. Aircraft abandoned.

3-V-2 Douglas DB-8A (391). Landed at Ockenburg to refuel and rearm 5.25 a.m. Caught on the ground in attack. by enemy aircraft and burned out. 2e Lt J. H. Heijen and Sgt C. J. Nijveldt both unhurt. Aircraft a write-off.

3-V-2 Douglas DB-8A (392). Severely damaged in combat and shot down while seeking a forced-landing between Den Haag and Utrecht. Crashed and burned out on Highway 12 near Pijnacker 5.50 a.m. Sgt J. A. Kuhn baled out wounded in knee. Sgt J. Staal baled out unhurt and captured on return to Ypenburg. Aircraft a write-off.
Crash site at Pijnacker investigated in 1981 and items found confirming aircraft identity. Johannes Kuhn later became a Luftwaffe ferry pilot and defected to England in Focke-Wulf Fw190A-8 (171747) of 3./Überführungs Gruppe West on August 30, 1944.

3-V-2 Douglas DB-8A (393). Shot down in combat and abandoned by crew; dived into vegetable oil storage tank at Vlaardingen 5.10 a.m. 2e Lt H. Pauw and Korp. L. M. J. Ballangée both baled out but died of injuries. Aircraft a write-off.

3-V-2 Douglas DB-8A (381). Believed to have sustained undercarriage damage and attempting a belly-landing at Rozenburg when shot down by Bf110s of II./ZG1 and crashed in the sea north-west of the Hook of Holland 6.15 a.m. 1e Lt P. T. Bierema and 1e Lt M. Faber both killed. Aircraft lost.

3-V-2 Douglas DB-8A (385). Shot down in flames and crashed on the beach near Kijkduin 5.10 a.m. 2e Lt G. J. E. Scheepens and 2e Lt G. Vermeulen both killed. Aircraft a write-off.

3-V-2 Douglas DB-8A (383). Unserviceable aircraft caught on the ground at Ypenburg and badly damaged by machine-gun fire. No crew casualties. Aircraft abandoned.

3-V-2 5 Douglas DB-8As (394, 395, 396, 397, and 398). Unserviceable aircraft held in store at Ockenburg; damaged in attacks. No crew casualties. Aircraft abandoned and later captured.

MLD 18 Fokker S IIIs. Redundant aircraft used as decoys; destroyed or badly damaged in enemy attacks at De Kooy. No crew casualties. Aircraft S-1—S-18 all write-offs.

MLD 15 Fokker S IXs (5467-5478, 5482-4) and 15 Koolhoven F.K.51s (124, 13-16, 125, 53-61). Training aircraft destroyed or badly damaged by enemy bombing at De Kooy. No crew casualties. Aircraft S20 — S34, E1—E15 all write-offs or later burned to prevent capture.

MLD 10 Fokker C VIIw. Non-operational aircraft destroyed or badly damaged in successive enemy attacks at De Mok. No crew casualties. Aircraft L2—L5, L7, L8, L13, L14, L17, and L18 all write-offs.

MLD Fokker C VIIIw. Sent from De Mok in readiness to evacuate members of the Dutch government to England. Strafed by enemy aircraft and burned out on the beach at Scheveningen 9.55 a.m. No crew casualties. Aircraft G8 a write-off.

GVT 2 Fokker T VIIIw (5585). Sent from De Mok in readiness to evacuate members of the Dutch government to England. Strafed by enemy aircraft and burned out on the beach at Scheveningen 9.55 a.m. Off. J. M. Uijtenhoudt killed. Aircraft R4 a write-off.

MLD Fokker T VIIIw (5582). Damaged in attack by enemy aircraft during transit flight from Braassemermeer to Scheveningen to evacuate members of the Dutch government to England 9.10 a.m. Diverted to Schellingwoude to effect repairs. Crew unhurt. Aircraft R1 repairable.
Of the four aircraft allotted this mission, only Fokker T VIIIw (5584) R-3 got away safely from Scheveningen and landed off Brighton carrying the Dutch Foreign Minister, Dr Eelco van Kleffens and his wife, and the Dutch Colonial Minister, Charles Welter.

GVT 2 Fokker T VIIIw (5583). Engine badly damaged during attack on enemy aircraft and forced-landed on beach near Rozenburg where later fired by crew 1.10 p.m. Off. L. A. H. Rombeek and crewman unhurt. Aircraft R2 a write-off.

BELGIAN AIR FORCE (AERONAUTIQUE MILITAIRE BELGE)

MAY 10, 1940
C-in-C: Gén.-Maj. P. Hiernaux — HQ: Brussels-Evere

1 AIR REGIMENT
(ARMY CO-OPERATION)
Col. F. Foidart — HQ: Bierset   Thisnes

GROUPE I
(Attached IV and V Corps d'Armée)
Capt Cdt. F. Burniat

	Base	War Station
No. 1 Escadrille 'Mouette' (1/I/1) 10 Fairey Fox IIICs Capt L. Paulet	Antwerp-Deurne	Hingene

GROUPE II
(Attached II Corps d'Armée)
Cdt. G. Gobert

	Base	War Station
No. 3 Escadrille 'Feuille de Houx' (3/II/1) 12 Fairey Fox IIs & IIICs Capt P. Willemaers	Gossoncourt	Glabbeek

GROUPE III
(Attached III Corps d'Armée & Fortress Liège)
Capt Cdt. M. Tyou

	Base	War Station
No. 5 Escadrille 'Hirondelle' (5/III/1) 10 Fairey Fox IIICs Capt J. Wibin	Gossoncourt	Jeneffe

GROUPE IV
(Attached VII Corps d'Armée & Fortress Namur)
Capt Cdt. L. Lahaye

	Base	War Station
No. 7 Escadrille 'Diable' (7/IV/1) 9 Fairey Fox VICs Capt F. Vandenplassche	Gossoncourt	Lonzée

GROUPE V
(Attached Corps de Cavalerie)
Capt Cdt. M. Breulhez

	Base	War Station
No. 9 Escadrille 'Sioux Bleu' (9/V/1) 11 Renard R-31s Capt A. Lekeuche	Bierset	Wilderen-Duras

GROUPE VI
(Attached I & VI Corps d'Armée)
Capt Cdt. F. Dumonceau

	Base	War Station
No. 11 Escadrille 'Sioux Rouge' (11/VI/1) 10 Renard R-31s Capt P. H. de la Lindi	Bierset	Hannut-Thines

2 AIR REGIMENT:
(FIGHTER)
Col. F. de Woelmont HQ: Nivelles   Vissenaken

GROUPE I
Maj. J. Hendrickx

	Base	War Station
No. 1 Escadrille 'La Comète' (1/I/2) 15 Gloster Gladiator Is Capt M. Guisgand	Schaffen	Beauvechain
No. 2 Escadrille 'Le Chardon' (2/I/2) 11 Hawker Hurricane Is Capt M. Charlier	Schaffen	Beauvechain

	Base	War Station
GROUPE II Maj. J. Lamarche		
No. 3 Escadrille 'Cocotte Rouge' (3/II/2) 15 Fiat CR-42s Capt J. de Callataÿ	Nivelles	Brustem
No. 4 Escadrille 'Cocotte Blanche' (4/II/2) 9 Fiat CR-42s Capt T. d'Huart	Nivelles	Brustem
GROUPE III Maj. H. De Bock		
No. 5 Escadrille 'Épervier Bleu' (5/III/2) 15 Fairey Fox VIs & VIIIs Cdt. A. Boussa	Nivelles	Vissenaken
No. 6 Escadrille 'Épervier Rouge' (6/III/2) 14 Fairey Fox VIs & VIIIs Capt E. d'Hoore	Nivelles	Vissenaken

3 AIR REGIMENT
(BOMBER & RECONNAISSANCE)
Col. S. Hugon — HQ: Brussels-Evere   Neerwinden

Groupe I (Night Reconnaissance)
Maj. G. Duchâteau

	Base	War Station
No. 1 Escadrille 'Dragon Doré' (1/I/3) 14 Fairey Fox IIICs Capt D. Pottier	Brussels-Evere	Neerhespen
No. 3 Escadrille 'Dragon Argenté' (3/I/3) 14 Fairey Fox IIICs Cdt. N. Duchâtelet	Brussels-Evere	Neerhespen

Groupe II (Bomber)
(Unit being formed)
Maj. E. Weckers

	Base	War Station
No. 9 Escadrille (9/II/3) Fairey Fireflies and 1 Stampe-Vertongen SV5 *(aircraft & crews transferred to 5/III/3)* Capt E. Pierre	Brussels-Evere	Maldegem
No. 11 Escadrille (11/II/3) 1 LACAB, 2 Savoias and Morane-Saulnier MS236s Capt R. Nyssen	Brussels-Evere	Maldegem

Groupe III
(Day Reconnaissance)
Maj. J. Piot

	Base	War Station
No. 5 Escadrille 'Aigle Egyptien' (5/III/3) 8 Fairey Battle Is Capt C. de Hepcée	Brussels-Evere	Belsele
(Attached Corps de Cavalerie) No. 7 Escadrille 'Flèche Ailée' (7/III/3) 9 Fairey Fox VICs Capt M. Dörner	Brussels-Evere	Lonzée

FLYING TRAINING
Flying training in the Belgian Air Force was organised as follows:

Elementary Flying Training School
(École de Pilotage Elémentaire) comprised four *escadrilles* based at Antwerp-Deurne, Gosselies, St-Denijs-Westrem, and Wevelgem. They operated with a variety of Avro 504, Avro 626, Morane-Saulnier MS 236, and Stampe-Vertongen SV4B aircraft for basic flying training.

Advanced Flying Training Schools
(Écoles de Pilotage Avancé) based at Gossoncourt and Wevelgem were equipped with Breguet XIX, Fairey Firefly, Fairey Fox, Koolhoven F.K.56 and Potez 33 aircraft.

In addition, there was an **Air-firing School** *(École de Tir Aérien)* at Ostend-Steene, and the Belgian Air Force **School of Aeronautics** *(École Aéronautique)* based at Brussels-Evere and Le Zoute.

With the German intention of destroying as much of the opposition on the ground, devastating attacks were carried out against Belgian Air Force bases. For example at Schaffen, a message was telephoned through at 0305 hours from the 2e Régiment d'Aéronautique headquarters warning of an enemy attack at dawn and that all aircraft were to take off at sunrise. The first Gladiators managed to leave the ground just ten minutes before Dorniers hit the aerodrome with bombs and machine guns. For an hour, waves of German aircraft hit the airfield, killing 15 and destroying nearly a dozen aircraft including these two Hurricanes.

BELGIAN AIR FORCE

1/I/1 Two Foxes. Unserviceable aircraft abandoned at Antwerp-Deurne. No crew casualties. Aircraft both destroyed on withdrawal on May 13.

5/III/1 Fox (O.122). Damaged by AA fire during reconnaissance sortie over Eupen and crash-landed near Kettenis 9.15 a.m. Sgt R. Septroux and Lt G. Malchair both unhurt, evaded capture and reached the Belgian lines. Aircraft a write-off.

7/IV/1 Fox. Machine abandoned at Gossoncourt due to technical problems. No crew casualties. Aircraft a write-off.

9/V/1 Renard R-31(N.19). Starboard wing damaged by AA fire during reconnaissance sortie over Maaseik and nosed-over on landing back at Wilderen-Duras 10.00 a.m. S/Lt G. Duchesne and S/Lt L. Fontaine unhurt. Aircraft a write-off.

11/VI/1 Renard R-31 (N.1). Unserviceable machine destroyed on the ground at Brussels-Evere in bombing by He111s of KG27 5.15 a.m. No pilot casualty. Aircraft a write-off.

11/VI/1 Two Renard R-31s (N.14 and N.35). Unserviceable machines caught on the ground at Bierset in bombing attack. No pilot casualties. Aircraft both abandoned.
The unit also abandoned a Stampe SV 5 and a Morane 236 crashed at Hannut-Thisnes on withdrawal from Bierset this day.

11/VI/1 Renard R-31(N.9). Hit by ground-fire near Tongeren during reconnaissance sortie over the Albert Canal. Nosed-over on landing back at Hannut-Thisnes on burst tyre 1.00 p.m. Sgt J. Rigole and S/Lt E. Walch unhurt. Aircraft repairable — abandoned on withdrawal to Hingene next day.

1/I/2 Gladiator. Starboard tyre burst in emergency take-off from Schaffen during low-level strafing and bombing attack by Do17s of KG77 4.32 a.m. Collided with Hurricane of Capt Charlier of 2/I/2 and caught fire. S/Lt M. Wilmots shrapnel wound in leg. Aircraft a write-off.

1/I/2 Gladiator. Caught on the ground at Schaffen and destroyed in low-level attack by Do17s of KG77 4.32 a.m. No pilot casualty. Aircraft a write-off.

2/I/2 9 Hurricanes (H.20, H.21, H.22, H.27, H.30, H.31, H.32, H.34, and H.42). Caught on the ground at Schaffen and destroyed or badly damaged in low-level bombing and strafing attack by Do17s of KG77 4.32 a.m. Capt M. Charlier *(Commandant)*, Lt A. Drossaert, Sgt G. Philippo, and Sgt P. Libert all wounded. 8 aircraft write-offs, 1 aircraft damaged but repairable — destroyed the following day.

2/I/2 Hurricane (H.23). Landed at Beauvechain damaged by return fire from He111s of KG27 engaged near Brussels-Evere 5.15 a.m. Capt A. van den Hove d'Ertsenrijck unhurt. Aircraft damaged but repairable.

3/II/2 3 Fiat CR-42s (R.2, R.21, and R.27). Unserviceable machines in hangar at Nivelles damaged in bombing attack by Ju 87s of 4./StG2 5.30 a.m. Sgt E. van Zuylen van Nyevelt badly wounded in foot. Aircraft all damaged but repairable — later abandoned.
In addition to these aircraft, the unit also lost 4 Fairey Firefly (Y.28, Y.49, Y.66, and Y.67) and Morane 236 (M.17) trainers during this attack.

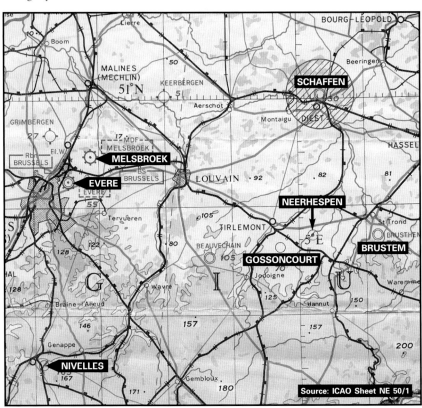

All told, nine Hurricanes and two Gladiators were lost and Hangar No. 1 burned out but two Hurricanes and 12 Gladiators managed to get airborne. The photos on the left show what the Germans found when they reached the abandoned airfield; those on the right the comparisons today.

Today Schaffen is the parachute training centre for the Belgian Army which is one of the few formations that still carry out initial training by jumping from a tethered barrage balloon.

For aircraft jumps, the soldiers board C-130s at Melsbroek (see map) and parachute into Schaffen which still remains a grass airfield.

Above: **It was the same story at the aerodrome at Brustem . . .**

3/II/2 14 Fiat CR-42s (R.1, R.3, R.4, R.6, R.7, R.8, R.11, R.14, R.16, R.17, R.18, R.19, R.20, and R.43). Caught on the ground at Brustem and destroyed or badly damaged in strafing by Bf109s 2.40 p.m. and bombing by Ju87s of I./StG2 3.25 p.m. No pilot casualties. Aircraft all write-offs.
Fiat CR-42 (R.43), usual aircraft of the commandant, Major Jacques Lamarche, had been renumbered and was originally serial R.13.

4/II/2 Fiat CR-42. Shot down in combat with Bf 109s over Brustem and crashed at Château Terkelen, near Melveren 6.25 a.m. 1/Sgt R. Delannay baled out, but badly wounded by ground-fire while in parachute and died in Sint-Trudostraat hospital, St Trond. Aircraft a write-off.

4/II/2 Fiat CR-42 (R.30). Overturned landing too fast at Brustem 5.05 a.m. 1/Sgt M. Michotte unhurt. Aircraft damaged but repairable — later abandoned.

5/III/2 Two Foxes (O.129 and O.146). Caught on the ground at Nivelles in bombing attack by Ju87s of 4./StG2 5.30 a.m. No pilot casualties. Aircraft both write-offs.
Six Fairey Fireflies (Y.26, Y.56, Y.63, Y.73, Y.79 and Y.81) and Morane-Saulnier MS 236 (M.18) were also destroyed or badly damaged in this attack.

. . . **and at Nivelles** *(above and below).*

5/III/2 Fox (O.123). Shot down in combat with Bf 109s between Tirlemont and St Trond 9.00 a.m. and possibly that claimed by Lt Axthelm of 3./JG27. Lt E. Dufossez baled out but killed due to parachute failure. Aircraft a write-off.

5/III/2 Fox (O.127). Petrol tank hit and set alight in combat with Bf109s between Tirlemont and St Trond and abandoned over Wellen, south of Hasselt 9.00 a.m. Possibly that claimed by Uffz Becher of 3./JG27. 1/Sgt C. F. J. Detal baled out badly burned, admitted to hospital. Aircraft a write-off.

Charles Detal was one of many Belgian Air Force pilots who later made their way to England to join the RAF. He flew Typhoons with No. 609 Squadron and was killed in an accident at Acklington in 1944.

5/III/2 Three Foxes (O.172, O.139 and O.179). Returned to Vissenaken damaged following combat with Bf109s of 3./JG27 between Tirlemont and St Trond 9.00 a.m. Sgt R. Godefroid, Adjt J. Schombroodt, and S/Lt E. Carpentier unhurt. Aircraft all damaged but repairable.

5/III/2 Fox (O.111). Abandoned under attack by Bf 109s of I./JG21 between St Trond and Landen and crashed at Wezerenberg, near the railway station at Gingelom 9.33 a.m. Possibly that claimed by Öberlt Schneider *(Staffelkapitän)* of 3./JG21. Lt A. Brel baled out but parachute failed and fell dead at rear of 4 Statiestraat, Montenaken. Aircraft a write-off.

5/III/2 Two Foxes (O.117 and O.135). Returned to Vissenaken damaged following attack on Do17s and combat with Bf109s of I./JG21 between Landen and St Trond 9.30 a.m. S/Lt M. D'Haes and Sgt Legros unhurt. Aircraft damaged but repairable.

6/III/2 Morane-Saulnier MS236. Destroyed in bombing attack on Knokke-Zoute by He111s of KG54. No pilot casualty. Aircraft a write-off.

This aircraft, on the strength of a Fairey Fox unit, was used for communications and liaison duties.

6/III/2 Two Foxes (O.106 and O.166). Unserviceable machines set alight in hangar during bombing attack on Knokke-Zoute by He111s of KG54 6.30 a.m. No pilot casualties. Aircraft write-offs.

Four Fairey Fireflies (Y.15, Y.32, Y.44, and Y.53) were also destroyed or badly damaged in this attack.

This is the Fox in which Captaine René Dethier was killed by shrapnel from a bomb-burst at Neerhespen aerodrome which lies between Tirlemont and Saint-Trond (see map page 196). He was originally buried in the Communal Cemetery at Schaarbeek but was transferred to the airmen's plot at Evere in August 1940.

I/3 Fox (O.306). Severely damaged in bombing attack by Do17s of KG77 while landing at Neerhespen 4.50 a.m. Capt R. Dethier killed. Aircraft damaged but repairable — later abandoned.

I/3 Four Foxes (O.69, O.70, O.81, and O.85). Destroyed in bombing attack on Neerhespen by Do17s of KG77 4.50 a.m. Lt A. Blanchart wounded. Aircraft all write-offs.

I/3 13 Foxes (O.67, O.68, O.71, O.73, O.75, O.78, O.84, O.86, O.88, O.90, O.96, O.300, and O.302). Damaged in bombing attack by Do17s of KG77 while landing at Neerhespen 4.50 a.m. No pilot casualties. Aircraft all damaged but repairable — most later abandoned.

Four of these aircraft (O.68, O.71, O.73, and O.75) were later destroyed in a strafing attack by Bf109s of JG27 at 6.00 p.m. The bulk of the remaining aircraft were abandoned on withdrawal to Zwevezele on May 12.

I/3 Six Foxes (O.66, O.76, O.87, O.93, O.301, and O.307). Unserviceable machines destroyed in hangar during bombing attack on Brussels-Evere by He 111s of KG27 5.15 a.m. No pilot casualties. Aircraft write-offs.

II/3 Stampe SV5 (N.1). Unserviceable machine slightly damaged during the bombing of Brussels-Evere by He 111s of KG27 5.15 a.m. No pilot casualty. Aircraft repairable — later abandoned.

A LACAB GR8 bomber was also wrecked in the collapse of a hangar during this attack, and several Moranes MS236 and Fairey Fireflys damaged — all abandoned on evacuation to Tours on May 13. The group's Fairey Battles all escaped damage, having transferred to the 5/III/3 at Belsele earlier.

5/III/3 Three Battles (T.63, T.65, and T.72). Unserviceable machines damaged in bombing of Brussels-Evere by He111s of KG27 5.15 a.m. No aircrew casualties. Aircraft damaged but repairable — destroyed on withdrawal May 17.

5/III/3 Battle (T.67). Wingtip damaged in taxying accident with T.65 at Brussels-Evere prior to take-off for Belsele 4.40 a.m. No aircrew casualties. Aircraft repairable.

5/III/3 Battle (T.66). Destroyed in bombing attack by He111s of KG27 while landing at Belsele 5.45 a.m. Adjt M. Vandevelde unhurt. Aircraft a write-off.

Four other Foxes were destroyed in the early morning attack on the airfield.

5/III/3 Battle (T.69). Slightly damaged in bombing attack on Belsele by He 111s of KG27 5.45 a.m. No crew casualties. Aircraft repairable.

7/III/3 7 Foxes (O.182, O.183, O.186, O.189, O.190, O.192 and O.193). Caught on the ground at Schaffen and destroyed in low-level bombing and strafing attack by Do 17s of KG77 4.32 a.m. Lt E. de Vuyst, Adjt W. Wallon, and Adjt J. Bodart all wounded. Aircraft write-offs.

2e Escadrille/École de Pilotage 10 Avro 504Ns. Aircraft destroyed or badly damaged in attack on Zwevezele airfield following move from Gosselies p.m. No personnel casualties. Aircraft all write-offs.

4e Escadrille/École de Pilotage 2 Koolhoven FK56 (K.105 and K.106). Badly damaged in attack on Gossoncourt by Do 17s of KG77 5.00 a.m. Adjt A. van Uffel badly wounded; died in hospital. Aircraft abandoned on evacuation to Tours on May 12.

At least five Fairey Fox trainers were also destroyed during this attack .

The skeletons of more Fairey Foxes caught on the ground at Schaffen. These machines belonged to 7/III/3.

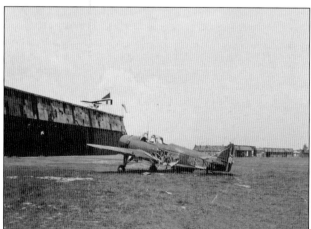

Centre and above: **These snapshots, taken by a German soldier, illustrate the carnage wrought at yet another Belgian aerodrome, this time Gossoncourt (also called Goetsenhoven). The airfield was the home of the 4th Flying Training School which operated both Koolhovens and Foxes as basic trainers. Dornier 17s of Kampfgeschwader 77 dealt the blow at 5 a.m. on May 10.**

Above: **The airfield was closed in 1996, until then it was the base of the Belgian Air Forces Elementaire Vliegschool (Elementary Flying Training School). Today it is only used during weekends by Belgian air cadets. The hangar is one of two, our comparison is taken looking west towards the control tower which was added after the war.**

5e and 6e Escadrille/École de Pilotage Five aircraft destroyed and 20 more damaged at Wevelgem in bombing by He111s of III./KG54 7.30 p.m. Aircraft all write-offs or abandoned on evacuation to Tours on May 12.

Germans pose amid the wreckage of Hangar No. 14 at Brussels-Evere where the LACAB GR8 of the 11e Escadrille of Groupe II, Air Regiment 3, stands crushed by the collapse of the roof (see page 199). This ungainly transport built by Les Ateliers de Construction Aéronautiques Belge had been converted for use as a bomber but was unserviceable and undergoing repair when the Heinkels of KG27 carpeted the airfield at dawn.

It was ironic — historically — because the Germans were bombing their own airfield having first built Evere for Zeppelin operations when they occupied the area in 1916. Between the wars the Belgian military used the Evere side of the aerodrome and civilian operators the end nearest to Haren where Charles Lindbergh landed his *Spirit of St Louis* a week after crossing the Atlantic in May 1927. The Germans re-occupied the airfield on May 17, 1940, expanding both it and the nearby landing ground at Melsbroek. After the cessation of hostilities, the latter airfield was developed in stages to become the main Brussels airport, Evere-Haren having disappeared, its surface now bisected by the Brussels-Zaventem autoroute. The site of the hangar, which was demolished after the war, is now occupied by the car park of the Kwartier Koningin Elisabeth — the military quarters adjacent to the NATO headquarters and housing the HQ of the Belgian armed forces. We identified the spot with the help of airport historian Frans van Humbeek and aviation enthusiast and contemporary witness Guy Cassiman.

LUFTWAFFE UNITS IN THE WEST

MAY 10, 1940

Excludes Luftflotten 1, 4, & 5, and units based in Denmark.

LUFTWAFFE HIGH COMMAND — HQ: Berlin				
1.(F)/ObdL	Oberlt Brix	16:11	various	Fritzlar
2.(F)/ObdL	Oberlt Kleine-Rüschkamp	12:3	Do215B	Berlin-Oranienburg
1.(F)/124	Hptmn Wolff	5:3	Do215B	Berlin-Tempelhof
Wekusta 1./ObdL	Oberlt Jonas	4:4	Do17Z	Berlin-Gatow
	Reg Rat Dr Schwerdtfeger	4:2	He111	Berlin-Gatow

9. FLIEGERDIVISION				
Generalmajor J. Coeler — HQ: Jever				
Divisiontransportstaffel		4:3	Ju52	Jever
KGr126	Hptmn G. Stein	36:24	He111H	Marx
Stab KüFlGr106	Oberstlt Jordan			HQ: Norderney
3./KüFlGr106	Hptmn Kannengiesser	12:10	He115B/C	Borkum
3./KüFlGr506	Hptmn Bergemann	11:11	He115B/C	Norderney
3./KüFlGr906	Hptmn Klümper	11:7	He111B	Norderney

This *Luftwaffe* Order of Battle only includes units in *Luftflotte* 2 and 3 available for deployment on the Western Front. Not all of the units shown were so deployed for the duration of the campaign.

Where included, figures shown indicate the individual units total establishment plus the number of serviceable aircraft on strength immediately prior to the opening of the German offensive.

ARMY HIGH COMMAND

Generalmajor Bongartz — HQ: Potsdam

HEERESGRUPPE A

2.(F)/11	Oberlt Höfer	Do17P	
attached **4. Armee**			
1.(H)/11(Pz)	Hptmn Heuser	Hs126B	
4.(F)/11	Hptmn Thiel	Do17P	Bonn-Hangelar
3.(H)/13		Hs126B	
1.(H)/21	Major Filips	Hs126B Do17M	
1.(H)/31	Hptmn Alberti	Hs126B	Ramscheiderhöhe
2.(H)/31(Pz)	Major Giesse	Hs126B	Vogelsang
4.(H)/31	Hptmn Nagel	Hs126B	Matzen
attached **12. Armee**			
2.(H)/12		Hs126B	
2.(H)/14(Pz)	Major Menzel	Hs126B	
2.(H)/21	Major Kubler	Hs126B	
1.(F)/22	Hptmn Dittrick	Do17P	Bad Kreuznach
attached **Panzergruppe von Kleist**			
3.(F)/10		Do17M/P	Eschweiler
1.(H)/14(Pz)	Major Bues	Hs126B	Steinborn
3.(H)/14	Major Stein	Hs126B	Seinsfeld
3.(H)/21	Hptmn Vinek	Hs126B	Blankenheim
2.(H)/23(Pz)		Hs126B	
3.(H)/41		Hs126B	
attached **16. Armee**			
1.(H)/10		Hs126B	Coefeld
1.(H)/12		Hs126B	
4.(H)/12		Hs126B Do17M	
2.(H)/13		Hs126B Do17M	
5.(H)/13	Hptmn Pinnow	Hs126B	Sandweiler
3.(F)/22	Hptmn Kaltz	Do17P	Wiesbaden

HEERESGRUPPE B

4.(F)/14	Hptmn Kusatz	Do17M/P	Vogelsang
attached **6. Armee**			
Kurierstaffel 5		Fi156	Oberbruch-Süd
3.(F)/11	Hptmn Tüttelmann	Do17P	
4.(H)/13(Pz)	Major Berger	Hs126B	Pütz
4.(H)/22	Hptmn Asmus	Hs126B	Holzweiler
1.(H)/23	Hptmn Heinsius	Hs126B	
1.(H)/41	Hptmn Stein	Hs126B	Hüchelhofen
2.(H)/41	Hptmn Haak	Hs126B	Hüchelhofen
9.(H)/LG2	Oberlt Wöbbeking	Hs126B	Münster-Handorf
		Do17	Münster-Handorf
		Fw189A	Münster-Handorf
attached **18. Armee**			
Kurierstaffel 7		Fi156 Ju52	Koblenz
1.(H)/10		Hs126B	Coefeld
2.(H)/10		Hs126B	Euskirchen
3.(H)/12(Pz)		Hs126B	
7.(F)/LG2		Do17P	Düsseldorf
		Do17M	Düsseldorf

HEERESGRUPPE C

3.(F)/31	Hptmn Schulze-Wiechenbrauch	Do17P	
attached **1. Armee**			
Fernaufklärungsstaffel		Do17P	
1.(H)/13		Hs126B Do17M	
4.(H)/21		Hs126B	
2.(H)/32		Hs126B	
3.(H)/32		Hs126B	
attached **7. Armee**			
2.(F)/22		Do17P	
4.(H)/23		Hs126B	

Küstenfliegergruppen were primarily engaged in maritime operations and coastal protection work. But their mine-laying and reconnaissance activities occasionally brought them within the scope of events covered by this book.

NAVAL HIGH COMMAND

Generalmajor Ritter — HQ: Berlin

FdLUFT WEST

Generalmajor Bruch — HQ: Jever

Stab KüFlGr406	Major Stockmann			HQ: Hörnum
1./KüFlGr406	Oberlt Kayser	10:6	Do18	Hörnum
		2:1	Bv139B	Hörnum
		3:2	Do26	Hörnum
2./KüFlGr406	Hptmn Tantzen	10:4	Do18	Hörnum

3./KüFlGr406	Hptmn von Roth	10:7	Do18	Hörnum
2./KüFlGr106	Hptmn Schrieck	9:4	Do18	Rantum
2./KüFlGr906	Hptmn von Laue	10:7	Do18	Hörnum
Stab KüFlGr806	Oberstlt von Wild			HQ: Uetersen
2./KüFlGr806	Hptmn Hahne	10:10	He111J	Uetersen
3./KüFlGr806	Hptmn Linke	10:6	He111J	Uetersen
BoFlSt 1./196	Hptmn Wiegmink	16:15	Ar196A	Wilhelmshaven

LUFTFLOTTE 2

General Kesselring— HQ: Münster

2.(F)/122	Oberlt Schwartz	7:5	He111H	Münster-Loddenheide
		5:4	Ju88A	Münster-Loddenheide
3.(F)/122	Major Keienburg	10:7	He111H	Münster-Loddenheide
		2:2	Ju88A	Münster-Loddenheide
4.(F)/122	Hptmn Pannwitz	7:5	He111H	Goslar
		5:3	Ju88A	Goslar
Wekusta 26	Hptmn von Rotberg	6:3	Do17Z	Münster-Loddenheide
	Reg Rat Dr Kopp	4:3	He111H	Münster-Loddenheide

LUFTLANDEKORPS: 7. FLIEGERDIVISION
Generalleutnant Student — HQ: Cologne

Korpsführungskette		6:5	Do17M	Cologne-Ostheim
Fernaufklst.	Oberlt Langhuth	4:3	Do17M	Cologne-Ostheim
II Flakkorps		4:4	Hs126B	Cologne-Ostheim
Stab KGzbV. 1	Oberstlt Morzik	1:1	Ju52	Loddenheide
I./KGzbV. 1	Major Witt	53:51	Ju52	Werl
II./KGzbV. 1	Major Drewes	53:53	Ju52	Loddenheide
III./KGzbV. 1	Hptmn Zeidler	53:50	Ju52	Handorf
IV./KGzbV. 1	Major Beckmann	53:53	Ju52	Loddenheide
Stab KGzbV. 2	Oberstlt Conrad	1:1	Ju52	HQ: Lippspringe
KGrzbV. 9	Major Janzen	53:53	Ju52	Lippspringe
KGrzbV. 11	Hptmn Fr von Hornbach	53:51	Ju52	Lippstadt
KGrzbV. 12	Oberstlt Wilke	53:51	Ju52	Störmede
I./KGzbV. 172	Hptmn Krause	51:48	Ju52	Paderborn
17./KGzbV.5	Hptmn Koch	52:48	Ju52	Cologne-Butzweilerhof
		50:50	DFS230	
		3:3	He111	
AufklstzbV.	Oberlt Florin	6:5	Do17M	Gütersloh
Sonderstaffel	Hptmn Schwilden	12:12	He59D	Bad Zwischenahn

FLIEGERKORPS zbV.2
Generalmajor Putzier — HQ: Bremen

KG4	Oberst Fiebig			Fassberg
Stabsstaffel	Hptmn Altvater	6:6	He111P	Fassberg
I./KG4	Oberstlt Rath	36:24	He111H	Gütersloh
II./KG4	Major Fr von Massenbach	35:18	He111P	Fassberg
III./KG4	Hptmn Bloedorn	23:11	He111P	Delmenhorst
		37:21	Ju88A	Delmenhorst
Stab KG54	Oberst Lackner	6:4	He111P	Quakenbrück
I./KG54	Oberstlt Höhne	36:33	He111P	Quakenbrück
II./KG54	Oberstlt Köster	29:26	He111P	Varrelbusch
III./KG54	Major Häring	35:27	He111P	Vechta
IV.(St)/LG1	Hptmn Kösl	39:37	Ju87B	Duisburg
AufklstzbV.2	Oberlt Sewing	5:4	Do17M	Bremen
		2:1	He111H	Bremen

JAGDFLIEGERFÜHRER 2
Generalmajor von Döring — HQ: Dortmund

Stabsschwarm	Oberst von Döring	4:2	Bf109E	Dortmund
Stab JG26	Major Witt	4:3	Bf109E	Dortmund
II./JG26	Hptmn Knüppel	47:36	Bf109E	Dortmund
III./JG26	Major Fr von Berg	42:22	Bf109E	Essen-Mülheim
III./JG3	Hptmn Kienitz	37:25	Bf109E	Hopsten
Stab JG51	Oberst Osterkamp	4:3	Bf109E	Bönninghardt
I./JG20	Hptmn Trautloft	48:36	Bf109E	Bönninghardt
I./JG26	Major Handrick	44:35	Bf109E	Bönninghardt

II./JG27	Hptmn Andres	32:23	Bf109E	Wesel
5./JG27	Oberlt Schäfer	16:12	Bf109E	Bönninghardt
I./JG51	Hptmn Brustellin	47:38	Bf109E	Krefeld
I./ZG1	Hptmn Falck	35:22	Bf110C/D	Kirchhellen
II./ZG1	Major Reichardt	37:26	Bf110C	Gelsenkirchen-Buer
Stab ZG26	Oberstlt Huth	3:3	Bf110C	Dortmund
I./ZG26	Hptmn Macrocki	34:11	Bf110C/D	Niedermendig
III./ZG26	Major Schalk	37:30	Bf110C/D	Krefeld

IV. FLIEGERKORPS
General Keller — HQ: Düsseldorf

Korpsführungskette		1:1	He111H	Düsseldorf
Stab KG27	Oberst Behrendt	5:4	He111P	Langenhagen
I./KG27	Oberstlt von Falkenstein	36:25	He111P	Langenhagen
II./KG27	Major Tamm	35:25	He111P	Delmenhorst
III./KG27	Hptmn Schirmer	38:32	He111P	Wunstorf
Stab KG30	Oberstlt Loebel	2:2	Ju88A	Oldenburg
I./KG30	Hptmn Doench	34:25	Ju88A	Oldenburg
II./KG30	Hptmn Hinkelbein	38:25	Ju88A	Oldenburg
III./KG30	Hptmn Kollewe	27:20	Ju88A	Marx
Stab LG1	Oberst Bülowius	5:4	He111H	Düsseldorf
I./LG1	Hptmn Kern	30:22	He111H	Düsseldorf
II./LG1	Major Debratz	26:18	He111H	Düsseldorf
		30:3	Ju88A	Düsseldorf
III./LG1	Major Dr Bormann	12:5	He111H	Düsseldorf
		35:11	Ju88A	Düsseldorf
1.(F)/121	Hptmn Fischer	3:2	Ju88A	Münster-Handorf
Korpstransportstaffel		9:7	He111H	Düsseldorf

VIII. FLIEGERKORPS
Generalmajor von Richthofen — HQ: Grevenbroich

Stab JG27	Oberstlt Ibel	4:4	Bf109E	Mönchengladbach
I./JG27	Hptmn Riegel	48:38	Bf109E	Mönchengladbach
I./JG1	Hptmn Schlichting	48:36	Bf109E	Gymnich
I./JG21	Hptmn Ultsch	46:37	Bf109E	Mönchengladbach
Stab KG77	Generalmajor von Stutterheim	8:6	Do17Z	Düsseldorf
I./KG77		35:28	Do17Z	Werl
II./KG77	Major Behrendt	35:28	Do17Z	Düsseldorf
III./KG77	Major Kless	34:21	Do17Z	Düsseldorf
II.(S)/LG2	Hptmn Weiss	49:38	Hs123	Lauffenberg b. Neuss
Stab StG2	Major Dinort	3:3	Ju87B	Cologne-Ostheim
Stabsstaffel StG2	Oberlt Metz	6:5	Do17M	Cologne-Ostheim
I./StG2	Hptmn Hitschold	40:33	Ju87B	Cologne-Ostheim
III./StG2	Major von Schönborn-Wesentheid	38:27	Ju87B	Nörvenich
I./StG76	Hptmn Sigel	39:34	Ju87B	Cologne-Ostheim
Stab StG77	Oberst Schwartzkopff	4:3	Ju87B	Cologne-Butzweilerhof
Stabsstaffel StG77	Oberlt Braunaus	6:5	Do17M	Cologne-Butzweilerhof
I./StG77	Hptmn von Dalwigk zu Lichtenfels	39:31	Ju87B	Cologne-Butzweilerhof
II./StG77	Hptmn Plewig	39:30	Ju87B	Cologne-Butzweilerhof
2.(F)/123	Hptmn Hurlin	12:10	Do17P	Mönchengladbach

LUFTFLOTTE 3

General Sperrle — HQ: Bad Orb

Unit	Commander	Strength	Aircraft	Base
1.(F)/123	Oberlt Sembritzki	8:6	Do17P	Langendiebach
		6:3	Ju88A	Langendiebach
3.(F)/123	Hptmn Liebe-Piderit	9:7	Do17P	Gelnhausen
		3:2	Ju88A	Gelnhausen
Wekusta 51	Oberlt Nissen	1:1	Do17U	Langendiebach
	Reg Rat Dr Reidat	4:3	He111H	Langendiebach

I. FLIEGERKORPS
General Grauert — HQ: Cologne

Unit	Commander	Strength	Aircraft	Base
Stab JG77	Oberstlt von Manteuffel	4:3	Bf109E	Peppenhoven
I./JG77	Hptmn Janke	48:35	Bf109E	Odendorf
Stab I./JG3	Hptmn Lützow	4:3	Bf109E	Bonn-Hangelar
1./JG3	Oberlt Keller	16:12	Bf109E	Peppenhoven
2./JG3	Hptmn Gärtner	16:12	Bf109E	Vogelsang
3./JG3	Hptmn Jänisch	16:11	Bf109E	Dünstekoven
Stab KG1	Oberst Exss	5:3	He111H	Gießen
I./KG1	Major Maier	34:25	He111H	Gießen
II./KG1	Oberstlt Kosch	35:23	He111H	Kirtorf
III./KG1	Major Schnelle	33:27	He111H	Ettinghausen
III./KG28	Major von Hoffmann	36:30	He111P	Bracht
Stab KG76	Oberstlt Fröhlich	4:4	Do17Z	Nidda
I./KG76	Major Schulz	36:32	Do17Z	Nidda
II./KG76	Major Hill	34:25	Do17Z	Nidda
III./KG76	Major Reuß	35:26	Do17Z	Nidda
III./StG51	Major von Klitzing	39:31	Ju87B	Cologne-Wahn
II./ZG26	Major von Rettberg	35:25	Bf110C/D	Kaarst/Neuss
Stab ZG76	Major Grabmann	3:3	Bf110C/D	Cologne-Wahn
II./ZG76	Major Groth	33:25	Bf110C/D	Cologne-Wahn
5.(F)/122	Hptmn Böhm	11:9	Do17P	Cologne-Wahn

II. FLIEGERKORPS
Generalleutnant Loerzer — HQ: Frankfurt/Main

Unit	Commander	Strength	Aircraft	Base
Stab KG2	Oberst Fink	7:5	Do17Z	Ansbach
I./KG2	Major Gutzmann	36:22	Do17Z	Giebelstadt
II./KG2	Oberstlt Weitkus	36:28	Do17Z	Ansbach
III./KG2	Major Kreipe	36:30	Do17Z	Illesheim
Stab KG3	Oberst von Chamier-Glisczinski	6:6	Do17Z	Würzburg
I./KG3	Oberstlt Gabelmann	35:31	Do17Z	Aschaffenburg
II./KG3	Oberst Jahn	36:27	Do17Z	Schweinfurt
III./KG3	Major von Kunowski	35:28	Do17Z	Würzburg
Stab KG53	Oberst Stahl	7:4	He111H	Roth
I./KG53	Oberstlt Mehnert	36:21	He111H	Roth
II./KG53	Oberstlt Kohlbach	36:24	He111H	Oedheim
III./KG53	Major Rohrbacher	36:26	He111H	Schwäbisch Hall
Stab StG1	Oberst Baier	3:3	Ju87B	Siegburg
Stabsstaffel StG1		6:5	Do17M	Siegburg
II./StG2	Major Enneccerus	38:33	Ju87B	Siegburg
I.(St)/TrGr186	Hptmn Hagen	39:36	Ju87B	Hemweiler
3.(F)/121	Oberlt Knapp	8:3	He111H	Frankfurt/Main
		3:2	Ju88A	Frankfurt/Main

V. FLIEGERKORPS
Generalleutnant von Greim — HQ: Gersthofen

Unit	Commander	Strength	Aircraft	Base
Stab JG52	Major von Bernegg	4:3	Bf109E	Mannheim-Sandhofen
I./JG52	Hptmn von Eschwege	48:36	Bf109E	Lachen-Speyerdorf
II./JG52	Hptmn von Kornatzki	48:33	Bf109E	Speyer
Stab JG54	Major Mettig	4:4	Bf109E	Böblingen
I./JG54	Hptmn von Bonin	48:29	Bf109E	Eutingen
II./JG51	Hptmn Matthes	48:35	Bf109E	Böblingen
Stab KG51	Oberst Kammhuber	1:1	He111H	Landsberg-Lech
		1:0	Ju88A	Landsberg-Lech
I./KG51	Major Schulz-Heyn	36:18	He111H	Lechfeld
		23:7	Ju88A	Lechfeld
II./KG51	Major Winkler	38:15	Ju88A	München-Riem
III./KG51	Major Kind	39:29	He111H	Landsberg-Lech
Stab KG55	Oberst Stoeckl	6:5	He111P	Leipheim
I./KG55	Major Marienfeld	35:25	He111P	Neuburg/Donau
II./KG55	Oberstlt von Lachemair	36:24	He111P	Leipheim
III./KG55	Major Schemmell	36:17	He111P	Gablingen
V.(Z)/LG1	Hptmn Liensberger	33:27	Bf110C/D	Mannheim-Sandhofen
I./ZG52	Hptmn Lessmann	35:23	Bf110C/D	Neuhausen ob Eck
4.(F)/121	Hptmn Kerber	10:7	Do17P	Gablingen
		2:1	Ju88A	Gablingen

JAGDFLIEGERFÜHRER 3
Oberst von Massow — HQ: Wiesbaden

Unit	Commander	Strength	Aircraft	Base
Stab JG2	Oberstlt von Bülow-Bothkamp	4:4	Bf109E	Frankfurt-Rebstock
I./JG2	Hptmn Roth	48:39	Bf109E	Bassenheim
III./JG2	Hptmn Dr Mix	48:23	Bf109E	Frankfurt-Rebstock
I./JG76	Major Kraut	48:43	Bf109E	Ober-Olm
Stab JG53	Major von Cramon-Taubadel	4:4	Bf109E	Wiesbaden-Erbenheim
I./JG53	Hptmn von Janson	48:40	Bf109E	Darmstadt-Griesheim
II./JG53	Hptmn von Maltzahn	48:45	Bf109E	Mannheim-Sandhofen
III./JG53	Hptmn Mölders	48:38	Bf109E	Trier-Euren
III./JG52	Hptmn von Houwald	48:30	Bf109E	Mannheim-Sandhofen
Stab ZG2	Oberstlt Vollbracht	3:2	Bf110C/D	Darmstadt-Griesheim
I./ZG2	Major Gentzen	32:22	Bf110C/D	Darmstadt-Griesheim

JAGDFLIEGERFÜHRER DEUTSCHE BUCHT
Oberstlt Schumacher — HQ: Jever

Unit	Commander	Strength	Aircraft	Base
Stab JG1	Oberstlt Schumacher	4:4	Bf109E	Jever
II./JG2	Hptmn Schellmann	47:35	Bf109E	Nordholz
Stab IV.(N)/JG2	Hptmn Blumensaat	4:3	Bf109D	Hopsten
10.(N)/JG2	Oberlt Bacsila	16:10	Bf109D	Hopsten
I.(J)/LG2	Hptmn Trübenbach	32:21	Bf109E	Wyk auf Föhr
3.(J)/LG2	Oberlt Graner	16:11	Bf109E	Esbjerg
II.(J)/TrGr186	Hptmn Seeliger	48:35	Bf109E	Wangerooge

Claims and counter-claims were all a part of the propaganda war. In releasing this picture, the Air Ministry captioned it: 'Five RAF pilots who got seven Germans before breakfast'. No date is given but we have narrowed it down to May 10 and named the pilots of No. 85 Squadron based at Lille-Seclin as (standing L-R): Flight Lieutenant Bob Boothby, Squadron Leader 'Doggy' Oliver, Pilot Officer John Lecky, Sergeant 'Sammy' Allard, with Pilot Officer Ken Blair crouching in front. Boothby and Blair shared an attack on a He111 of I./KG27 near Ghent and Oliver, Lecky and Allard an He111 of Stab I./KG27 downed at Borre (see page 210) but beyond that Peter Cornwell comments that 'the official caption stretches it somewhat!'

LUFTWAFFE

2./JG1 Messerschmitt Bf109E. Severely damaged in combat with Fiat CR-42s over Maastricht 6.30 a.m. Possibly that attacked by Lt Goffin of II/2. Abandoned over Aachen-Märzdorf during return flight. Leutnant E. Dutel baled out slightly wounded. Aircraft a write-off.

3./JG1 Messerschmitt Bf109E-1. Damaged in action over Maastricht and suffered engine failure near Düren on return flight. Obergefreiter J. Scheibe injured. Aircraft damaged but repairable.

I./JG2 Messerschmitt Bf109E. Nosed-over and wrecked while taxying at Bassenheim. No pilot casualty. Aircraft a write-off.

I./JG2 Messerschmitts Bf109E-1 & Bf109E-3. Damaged in taxying accidents at Bassenheim. No pilot casualties. Aircraft both damaged but repairable.

10.(N)/JG2 Messerschmitt Bf109D-1. Shot down by flak east of Rotterdam and wrecked in crash-landing 8.00 p.m. Feldwebel P. Keller captured. Aircraft a write-off.

I./JG3 Messerschmitt Bf109E-1. Damaged in forced-landing at Cologne-Ostheim due to petrol failure. Pilot unhurt. Aircraft damaged but repairable.

1./JG20 Messerschmitt Bf109E-3. Believed hit by flak over Kesteren-am-Rhein during escort sortie for Ju52s to Rotterdam and crashed in the Waal near Opijnen 1.40 p.m. Feldwebel W. Hoppe killed. Aircraft lost.

III./JG26 Messerschmitt Bf109E-1. Lost sight of the runway and crashed on landing. Pilot unhurt. Aircraft damaged but repairable.

III./JG26 Messerschmitt Bf109E-1. Crashed on take-off, cause not stated. Pilot unhurt. Aircraft damaged but repairable.

III./JG26 Messerschmitt Bf109E. Returned badly damaged following combat with Fokker T Vs south of Moerdijk 5.00 a.m. Pilot unhurt. Aircraft a write-off.

8./JG26 Messerschmitt Bf109E-3. Returned engine damaged following combat with Fokker T Vs over Etten 5.00 a.m. Pilot unhurt. Aircraft damaged but repairable.

9./JG26 Messerschmitt Bf109E-1 (3462). Shot down by flak over Ypenburg and belly-landed in dunes near Ockenburg 4.21 p.m. Leutnant W. Ludewig wounded. Aircraft 6 + I a write-off.

1./JG53 Messerschmitt Bf109E-1. Abandoned over Grevenmacher following mid-air collision with Gefr Reibel. Leutnant W. Rupp baled out and returned injured. Aircraft a write-off.

1./JG53 Messerschmitt Bf109E-3. Wrecked in forced-landing near Serrig-Saar following collision with Lt Rupp. Gefreiter L. Reibel believed unhurt. Aircraft a write-off.

1./JG53 Messerschmitt Bf109E-1. Forced-landed near Schweich, north-east of Trier, probable engine failure 12.30 p.m. Uffz Grothen injured. Aircraft damaged but repairable.

2./JG53 Messerschmitt Bf109E-4. Shot down by Adjt de Montgolfier of GC II/5 during escort mission and forced-landed south of Thionville 7.35 p.m. Leutnant G. Carnier captured wounded. Aircraft a write-off.

III./JG53 Messerschmitt Bf109E-3. Crashed on take-off at Wiesbaden-Erbenheim due to engine failure. Pilot unhurt. Aircraft damaged but repairable.

I./JG77 Messerschmitt Bf109E-3. Slightly damaged in forced-landing at Euskirchen due to petrol failure. Pilot unhurt. Aircraft repairable.

2./JG77 Messerschmitt Bf109E-1 (0703). Crashed on landing at Cologne-Wahn due to undercarriage failure. Uffz F. Möller unhurt. Aircraft 12+ damaged but repairable.

5./TrGr.186 Messerschmitt Bf109E-3 (1257). Shot down by 2e Lt van Overvest of 1-II-1 in combat over Den Helder and belly-landed at De Kooy 5.40 a.m. Hauptmann D. Robitzsch (Staffelkapitän) captured. Aircraft 1+ a write-off.

5./TrGr.186 Messerschmitt Bf109E-3. Shot down by Lt Doppenberg of 1-II-1 in combat over De Kooy and crashed at Anna Paulowna, Zwinweg, in Den Helder 5.40 a.m. Uffz W. Rudolf captured badly wounded, died May 14. Aircraft a write-off.

5./TrGr.186 Messerschmitt Bf109E-3. Forced-landed at Borkum engine damaged 5.40 a.m. Possibly that attacked by 1e Lt Focquin de Grave of 1-II-1 in combat over Den Helder. Pilot unhurt. Aircraft damaged but repairable.

2./Aufkl.Gr.Ob.d.L. Dornier Do215. Missing from reconnaissance sortie over western Belgium and believed crashed at Vlaardingen. Fw H-J. Schmidt missing. Uffz G. Hentschler killed. Lt H. Schierhold and Uffz E. Wittchen captured. Aircraft a write-off.

2./Aufkl.Gr.Ob.d.L. Dornier Do215. Brought down at Rossum, north of 's-Hertogenbosch, during reconnaissance sortie over western Holland. Uffz H. Kreutz killed. Oberfw H. Kaselowski, Uffz H. Krams, and Uffz R. Weinhold captured. Aircraft a write-off.

Aufkl.St. 7 Fl.Div. Dornier Do17Z (3474). Shot down over Nieuwkoop by 2e Lt van der Vaart of 1-V-2 during reconnaissance sortie to Den Haag. Crashed and burned out in Mijdrechtse Dwarsweg, Kagerplassen, at Wilnis 6.10 a.m. Oberlt E. Rättig, Uffz E. Müller, and Uffz A. Apholz baled out and captured wounded. Oberlt H-W. Florin (Staffelkapitän) baled out and captured unhurt. Aircraft a write-off.
Small items from this aircraft including Henschel component plate in possession of H.W. van Soest of Wilnis. Propeller hub and blade along with other souvenirs once owned by another local resident, G. Geerlof.

Aufkl.Gr.156 Sixteen Fieseler Fi156. Aircraft destroyed or abandoned after landing troops around Nives and Witry between 4.35 and 7.00 a.m. Two crewmen killed, two wounded, and one missing. Aircraft all write-offs.
This audacious airborne assault, codename Operation 'Niwi', landed troops behind the Allied lines to ease the advance of Gruppe von Kleist through the Ardennes east of Neufchâteau. 100 Storch aircraft took part, each carrying two men of Infanterie-Regiment 'Grossdeutschland', and making two round trips from bases at Dockendorf and Pützhöhe. Three Junkers Ju52s of Transportstaffel Fliegerkorps I were also assigned for supply. For a full account of this operation see Blitzkrieg in the West Then and Now.

Transportstaffel I. Fliegerkorps Junkers Ju52. Attacked by FT-13 tank after landing on supply mission in support of Operation 'Niwi'. Burned out near Grand-Rosière-Hottomont, north of Nives, 12.30 p.m. Gefr W. Pollmann killed. Oberfw W. Jung and Obergefr J. Hatting missing. Aircraft a write-off.

Staffel Schwilden Four Heinkel He59s (1830, 1995, 2593, and 2599). Wrecked after landing assault troops on the River Maas in Rotterdam harbour 6.30 a.m. Uffz Germann, Uffz Berthold, and Uffz H. Marschner captured. Three other crews picked up and returned. Aircraft all write-offs.
This airborne operation flew 120 men of 11 Kompanie, Infanterie-Regiment 16, and 2 Kompanie, Pionier-Bataillon 22, from Bad Zwischenahn and set them down in Rotterdam Harbour to secure the Koninginne and Willems bridges ahead of parachute landings. Formed on March 14 from a cadre of 3./KGrzbV.108, the unit was assigned 12 specially modified Heinkel He59 float-planes, drawn mainly from KüFlGr.606 under the overall command of Hptmn Horst Schwilden.

1.(H)/10 Henschel Hs126. Shot down by fighters 3 km east of Ingeldorf during observation sortie. Believed one of those claimed by Sgt Nowell of No. 87 Sqdn 6.30 a.m. Lt H. Schneider and Uffz A. Faulhaber killed. Aircraft a write-off.

4.(F)/11 Dornier Do17P (3521). Crashed on landing at Bonn-Hangelar airfield, cause not stated. Crew unhurt. Aircraft repairable.

2.(H)/12 Henschel Hs126. Returned damaged by F/Lt Lee, F/O Allen, and P/O Woods-Scawen of No. 85 Sqdn during observation sortie between Hosingen and Diekirch 4.35 a.m. Oberlt A. Daumling and Lt G. Troebs both wounded and admitted to hospital in Gerolstein. Aircraft a write-off.

2.(H)/12 Henschel Hs126. Shot down by F/Lt Lee, F/O Allen, and P/O Woods-Scawen of No. 85 Sqdn during observation sortie between Hosingen and Diekirch, crashed and burned out near Martelange, south of Bastogne 4.35 a.m. Oberlt P. Werle and Uffz H. Kohaut killed. Aircraft a write-off.

2.(H)/12 Henschel Hs126. Returned damaged by ground-fire near Fauvillers during observation sortie. Fw J. Larisch slightly wounded admitted to hospital in Gerolsheim. Aircraft damaged but repairable.

4.(H)/13 Henschel Hs126. Hit by ground-fire and landed near Maastricht. Lt E. Häckel wounded. Aircraft repairable.

3.(H)/14 Henschel Hs126. Shot down by fighters east of Nommern. Believed one of those claimed by Sgt Nowell of No. 87 Sqdn. 6.30 a.m. Lt P. Koll and Uffz H. Bieber killed. Aircraft a write-off.

1.(H)/41 Henschel Hs126. Returned damaged by ground-fire 10 km south-west of Maastricht. Lt R. Dietrich killed. Aircraft repairable.

2.(H)/41 Henschel Hs126. Returned damaged by ground-fire over Nederweert. Uffz H. Ringpfeil slightly wounded. Aircraft repairable.

3.(F)/121 Heinkel He111P. Shot down by S/L More of No. 73 Sqdn during photo-reconnaissance mission of airfields at Metz and Diedenhofen. Crashed and burned out near Chambley-Bussières, south-west of Metz 6.30 a.m. Oberlt K. Scheurich, Oberlt E. Horn, Fw H. Klein, and Uffz H. Bauer killed. Aircraft a write-off.

2.(F)/123 Dornier Do17P. Believed damaged in attack by Lt de Mérode of 3/II/2 during reconnaissance sortie over Brustem 3.05 p.m. Forced-landed near Mönchengladbach. Crew unhurt. Aircraft damaged but repairable.

3.(F)/123 Dornier Do17P. Petrol tank set alight by intense flak while under attack by Sgt Boymond and Sgt Gauthier of GC III/6 near Auxonne during reconnaissance sortie from Saonetal to the Swiss frontier. Abandoned north of Mouchard 7.45 a.m. Uffz L. Schwender baled out but separated from parachute and killed. Lt R. Fleissner baled out and captured badly burned, admitted to hospital in Dole. Fw L. Aigner baled out and captured unhurt. Aircraft 4U+JL a write-off.
The body of the unfortunate radio operator, Ludwig Schwender, was found in dense forest near Port-Lesney in March 1941.

Because Luftwaffe records during the Blitzkrieg period seldom include the markings or the serial number (Werk-Nummer), it takes a huge amount of detective work to identify particular losses and tie them to combat reports. Peter Taghon established that this picture shows the Heinkel of 3./KG1 listed below.

3./KG1 Heinkel He111H. Starboard engine disabled in attacks by Adjt Moret of GC III/2 following bombing of Cambrai-Niergnies airfield and belly-landed at 'Waremme', near Leugnies-Grandieu, south-west of Beaumont 5.10 a.m. Fw W. Wübbe killed. Lt W. Seel and Oberfw O. Odenbach captured unhurt. Fw W. Neuhaus captured wounded. Aircraft V4+KL a write-off.

5./KG1 Heinkel He111H. Port engine disabled in attacks by Adjt Nedelec, Sgt Zinnicker, and Sgt Ravilly of GC III/2 near Bapaume and believed crashed near Villers-Cotterêt 1.30 p.m. Oberfw R. Deicke, Uffz M. Wendler, and Gefr E. Langen killed. Uffz G. Kasten captured unhurt. Aircraft a write-off.

Stab III./KG1 Heinkel He111H. Shot down by F/O Weatherill of No. 607 Sqdn over Epehy during sortie to attack airfields near Albert, and railways between Cambrai and Peronne. Crashed in flames at Homblières, east of St Quentin 2.40 p.m. Major O. Schnelle (Gruppenkommandeur), Lt F. Hermann, Oberfw F-W. Meyer zu Düte, Oberfw H. Burmester, and Fw J. Stuhler killed. Aircraft V4+AD a write-off.

7./KG1 Heinkel He111H. Damaged by flak and engaged by Moranes south-east of Corbie during sortie to attack airfields near Albert. Believed that claimed by Adjt Romey and Sgt Pizon of GC III/2 but also attacked by P/O Parrott of No. 607 Sqdn and finally Sgt Allard of No. 85 Sqdn. Crashed and exploded at Gondécourt 2.40 p.m. Oberlt K-J. Schnaase, Oberfw E. Quarz, Uffz E. Bellgardt, and Uffz F. Marx killed. Aircraft a write-off.

7./KG1 Heinkel He111H. Shot down by Hurricanes of Nos. 85 and 607 Sqdns. south of St Quentin during sortie to attack airfields near Albert. Crashed and burned out between Benay and Hinacourt 3.00 p.m. Uffz P. Röder, Gefr F. Schirmer, and Flgr F. Marchelek killed. Oberfw K. Buchholz baled out over Essigny-le-Grand and captured badly wounded. Lt K-H. von Schmidt baled out between Ginchy and Maricourt and captured unhurt. Aircraft a write-off.

7./KG1 Heinkel He111H. Returned badly damaged by flak and Hurricanes of Nos. 85 and 607 Sqdns during sortie to attack airfields near Albert 2.50 p.m. Uffz W. Neumann and Gefr A. Scherer died of wounds. Uffz F. Neumeister and Uffz F. Grunewald both wounded, admitted to hospital in Bonn. Aircraft damaged but repairable.

9./KG1 Heinkel He111H. Port engine damaged in attacks by P/O Parrott and Sgt Townsend of No. 607 Sqdn during sortie to attack airfields near Albert. Crashed attempting forced-landing south-east of St Simon-Clastres airfield 3.00 p.m. Obergefr A. Freisberg captured wounded in head, admitted to Henri-Martin hospital in St-Quentin. Lt K. Neumann, Fw H. Oppermann, Flgr H. Pümpel and Flgr W. Pfeiffer captured unhurt. Aircraft a write-off.

9./KG1 Heinkel He111H. Engaged by Hurricanes of Nos. 85 and 607 Sqdns between Nesle and Curchy, south-east of Albert, during sortie to attack airfields and also hit by flak. Brought down near Benay 2.50 p.m. Uffz R. Naumann and Obergefr V. Eisenbach killed. Oberfw F. Schlotter and Fw H. Niemeyer captured wounded, admitted to hospital in Péronne. Uffz H. Heintzer captured wounded in right shoulder, sent to Henri-Martin hospital in St Quentin. Aircraft a write-off.

9./KG1 Heinkel He111H. Shot down by Hurricanes of Nos. 85 and 607 Sqdns during sortie to attack airfields and belly-landed near Albert 2.50 p.m. Fw W. Wappler captured wounded. Oberlt H. Braune, Fw W. Schön, Uffz A. Gottschalk, and Flgr E. Ernst captured unhurt. Aircraft V4+DT a write-off.

9./KG1 Heinkel He111H-3. Belly-landed at Bonn-Hangelar damaged by Hurricanes of Nos. 85 and 607 Sqdns and also hit by flak during sortie to attack airfields near Albert 2.50 p.m. Flgr F. Mitzkath badly wounded. Aircraft damaged but repairable.

Stab I./KG2 Dornier Do17Z. Damaged by AA fire during attack on Thionville airfield 5.00 a.m. Major M. Gutzmann *(Gruppenkommandeur)* and Oberlt H. Buchheim both badly wounded, admitted to hospital in Frankfurt. Aircraft repairable.

I./KG2 Dornier Do17Z. Undercarriage collapsed on landing at Lechfeld. No crew casualties. Aircraft repairable.

4./KG2 Dornier Do17Z. Returned damaged by Hurricanes over Châtel-Chéhéry following attack on Thionville airfield 4.45 a.m. and possibly that attacked by F/Lt Lovett and Sgt Humphris of No. 73 Sqdn Uffz G. Otterbeck slightly wounded. Aircraft damaged but repairable.

4./KG2 Dornier Do17Z. Engaged by F/O Mitchell of No. 87 Sqdn during sortie to attack Thionville airfield and shot down near Illange 4.30 a.m. Fw F. Schmid captured unhurt. Uffz E. Drong, Gefr O. Schär, and Gefr E. Züche captured wounded, admitted to Legouest hospital in Metz. Aircraft a write-off.

However, in this case there were nice sharp photos with clear markings making identifying this machine easy: the Heinkel of 9th Staffel of Kampfgeschwader 1 bearing the code V4+DT.

According to the story released by the Air Ministry with this series of photographs, George Muir (left) a local employee of the Imperial War Graves Commission, arrested the entire crew single-handed. 'He found the crew walking away from the crashed plane fully-armed and, with great bravery, asked them to hand over their arms, which they did; he then handed them over to the authorities.'

4./KG2 Dornier Do17Z. Badly damaged by Hurricanes over Châtel-Chéhéry during sortie to attack Thionville airfield 4.45 a.m. and possibly that attacked by F/Lt Hanks of No. 1 Sqdn. Believed crash-landed at Katzweiler, near Kaiserslautern. Uffz H. Stolle and Uffz W. Pfützenreuter killed. Uffz E. Strüven baled out but parachute fouled aircraft and killed. Uffz H. Veit slightly wounded. Aircraft a write-off.

4./KG2 Dornier Do17Z. Crash-landed at Ober-Esch badly damaged by flak and Hurricanes during sortie to attack Thionville airfield 4.30 a.m. Possibly that attacked by P/O Mould of No. 1 Sqdn. Uffz K. Schiweck and Uffz H. Suschka slightly wounded. Uffz H. Fischer unhurt. Fw J. Ottlik baled out over Châtel-Chéhéry and captured unhurt. Aircraft U5+HM a write-off.

6./KG2 Dornier Do17Z. Returned damaged by Curtiss H-75s of GC I/4 and GC I/5 during sortie to attack Reims-Champagne airfield 6.10 a.m. Obergefr A. Richter slightly wounded. Aircraft repairable.

6./KG2 Dornier Do17Z (3383). Badly damaged by flak during attack on Reims-Champagne airfield then engaged by Curtiss H-75s of GC I/4 and GC I/5 north of Suippes. Attacked by Capt Accart (*Commandant*) and Lt Perina of GC I/5 and belly-landed near Ferme de Cruzis, between Virginy and Ville-sur-Tourbe 5.30 a.m. Fw G. Passarge and Gefr G. Hochauf killed. Uffz W. Birkner and Uffz K. Volz captured unhurt. Aircraft U5+FP a write-off.

6./KG2 Dornier Do17Z. Shot down by Adjt Bouvard, S/Lt Goupy and S/Lt Rey of GC I/5 at 'Les Mayettes', outside Touret, north of Rethel, following attack on Reims-Champagne airfield 5.30 a.m. Uffz W. Heinrich, Uffz E. Burgdorf, Uffz A. Möllenbeck, and Obergefr E. Gerlach killed. Aircraft U5+KP a write-off.

7./KG2 Dornier Do17Z. Engaged by Curtiss H-75s of GC I/4 and GC I/5 during sortie to attack Challerange airfield and badly damaged in attacks by Sgt Bès and Sgt Lacroix of GC I/4 south of Châlons 6.15 a.m. Forced-landed near Kaiserslautern. Lt P. Krieger, Uffz K. Winter, Uffz H. Seifer, and Obergefr B. Schröder all wounded, admitted to hospital. Aircraft a write-off.

7./KG2 Dornier Do17Z. Damaged in attacks by GC I/8 east of Rouvres and possibly that attacked by Capt Astier over Mars-la-Tour. Forced-landed at Trier 2.30 p.m. Fw H. Olbrich badly wounded admitted to hospital. Lt J. Mumb and Uffz K. Aldenhoven slightly wounded. Aircraft repairable.

7./KG2 Dornier Do17Z. Returned damaged in attacks by GC I/8 east of Rouvres 1.30 p.m. Uffz W. Friedrich and Obergefr E. Nitzsche slightly wounded. Aircraft repairable.

9./KG2 Dornier Do17Z. Returned to base without mechanic who fell from aircraft over Thionville when hatch lock failed 4.10 a.m. cause unknown. Fw G. Glenz baled out unhurt. Aircraft undamaged.

Stab KG3 Dornier Do17Z. Shot down by F/Lt Walker, F/O Brown, F/O Kilmartin, F/O Richey, and Sgt Soper of No. 1 Sqdn during reconnaissance sortie over Etain-Rouvres and belly-landed at Mont-St-Martin, north of Longwy, 6.30 a.m. Uffz R. Wagner killed. Oberfw H. Schachtebeck, Oberfw K. Sommer, and Uffz W. Schmeis captured unhurt. Aircraft a write-off.

4./KG3 Dornier Do17Z. Badly damaged by F/O Lovett and F/O Orton of No. 73 Squadron near Rouvres and believed forced-landed near Baumholder 5.30 a.m. Oberfw H. Laube and Oberfw O. Vetter wounded, admitted to hospital. Aircraft a write-off.

4./KG3 Dornier Do17Z. Badly damaged by Hurricanes near Rouvres 5.30 a.m. and believed forced-landed near Hermeskeil. Possibly that engaged by F/O Paul of No. 73 Sqdn. Oberfw E. Kotulla and Uffz H. Pohl wounded, admitted to hospital. Aircraft a write-off.

4./KG3 Dornier Do17Z. Badly damaged by Hurricanes near Rouvres 5.30 a.m. and believed forced-landed near Simmern. Possibly that claimed by F/O E. J. Kain of No. 73 Sqdn. Oberfw W. Lange, Fw H. Kucz, Fw H. Berndt, and Uffz M. Beer badly wounded, all admitted to hospital. Aircraft a write-off.

4./KG3 Dornier Do17Z. Returned badly damaged by Hurricanes over Rouvres 5.30 a.m. and believed forced-landed at Zellhausen. Uffz H. Wünsch slightly wounded. Aircraft a write-off.

5./KG3 Dornier Do17Z. Hit by bomb from another aircraft during attack on Mourmelon and abandoned by crew. Crashed alongside the road from Suippes to Jonchery 4.00 p.m. Fw H. Schädlich, Uffz H. Rolle, and Uffz W. Pfau killed. Uffz R. Nötzold baled out and captured unhurt. Aircraft a write-off.
A claim was also filed for this aircraft by Sgt Vuillemain of GC I/5.

Stab III./KG3 Dornier Do17Z. Shot down by S/Lt Warnier and S/Lt Scotte of GC I/5 following attack on Suippes and crashed at Fontaine-en-Dormois, between Cernay and Bouconville 6.50 p.m. Oberlt W. Roemer and Oberfw E. Linke killed. Major G-W. von Kunowski (*Gruppenkommandeur*) and Fw G. Benseler captured unhurt. Aircraft a write-off.

7./KG3 Dornier Do17Z. Shot down by Capt Accart and Lt Perina of GC I/5 following attack on Suippes and crashed between Landres and Sainte-Georges, north of Sommerance 5.50 p.m. Uffz K. Köhler and Flgr R. Metz killed. Uffz W. Gräfe and Gefr H. Müller baled out and captured unhurt. Aircraft a write-off.

7./KG3 Two Dornier Do17Z. Returned damaged in attacks by Capt Accart and Lt Perina of GC I/5 over Villers-devant-Dun following bombing of Suippes 6.30 p.m. Uffz F. Goebel, Uffz W. Kriegel, and Uffz H. Henning slightly wounded. Aircraft both repairable.

8./KG3 Dornier Do17Z. Shot down by F/Lt Voase Jeff of No. 87 Sqdn during bombing attack on Thionville and crashed at Boulange 5.50 a.m. Fw W. Reichenbach and Fw R. Schneider captured wounded, admitted to hospital in Briey. Fw H. Hoffmann and Fw H. Schilling captured slightly wounded. Aircraft a write-off.

8./KG3 Dornier Do17Z. Forced-landed near St Wendel badly damaged in attacks by GC I/5 following attack on Suippes 5.30 p.m. Oberfw F. Thumser and Gefr J. Oster slightly wounded. Aircraft a write-off.

8./KG3 Dornier Do17Z. Belly-landed at Zellhausen damaged in attacks by GC I/5 following attack on Suippes 5.30 p.m. Uffz M. Duryn slightly wounded. Aircraft repairable.

This picture was published in the British press on May 24 claiming that it showed 'one of the Nazi planes which were shot down near Paris whilst attacking aerodromes on May 10'. The code 'T5' denotes that it belonged to the Aufklärungsgruppe Oberbefehlshaber der Luftwaffe — basically the Luftwaffe High Command's own reconnaissance unit — and 'H' that it was part of its 1st Staffel ('F' denotes the actual aircraft). However there are no losses on May 10 which fit this criteria . . . but look back at page 134! It just shows how inaccurate wartime captioning can be.

9./KG3 Dornier Do17Z. Shot down by F/O Mitchell of No. 87 Sqdn during attack on Thionville and crashed near Audun-le-Roman 6.00 a.m. Oberfw H. Schliwa captured wounded, admitted to hospital in Briey. Oberfw R. Richter and Fw O. Sprink captured wounded, admitted to Legouest hospital in Metz. Oberlt G. Hager captured unhurt. Aircraft a write-off.

9./KG3 Dornier Do17Z. Shot down by S/Lt Lefol of GC I/5 following attack on Suippes and crashed at Huldange 6.10 p.m. Oberfw A. Stopp, Fw W. Schaarschmidt, and Gefr H. Molderhauer killed. Fw E. Weinhold captured wounded. Aircraft a write-off.

9./KG3 Dornier Do17Z. Shot down by S/Lt Warnier of GC I/5 following attack on Suippes and crashed at Ville-sur-Tourbe, north-west of Ste-Menehould 5.50 p.m. Uffz H. Sowada, Gefr H. Lenz, and Gefr G. Brunken killed. Obergefr E. Jäckel baled out and captured wounded. Aircraft a write-off.

This Heinkel from the 2nd Staffel of KG27 was brought down just before 5 a.m. possibly by Flying Officer Bill Gore of No. 607 — the 'County of Durham' Squadron.

9./KG3 Dornier Do17Z. Shot down by Capt Accart and Lt Perina of GC I/5 following attack on Suippes and crashed at Perthes-les-Hurlus 6.00 p.m. Uffz H. Tacke killed. Uffz W. Zimmer baled out and captured wounded, admitted to hospital in Mourmelon. Gefr F. Ensle baled out and captured unhurt. Aircraft a write-off.

Stab KG4 Heinkel He111P (2909). Shot down by Fokker G 1s of 3-II-1 during sortie to Rotterdam and belly-landed in St Annapolder between Rockanje and Hellevoetsluis, south of Zwartedijk 4.15 a.m. Oberfw E-R. Frotscher killed. Oberst M. Fiebig (*Geschwaderkommodore*), Oberlt K. Born, Oberfw O. Hlubek, and Oberfw O. Blank captured unhurt. Aircraft 5J+DA a write-off.

Stab KG4 Heinkel He111P. Returned badly damaged by flak and Fokker G 1 of 3-II-1 (1e Lt Noomen and Korp de Vries) over Waalhaven 4.10 a.m. Oberlt Andersch unhurt. Fw P-K. Schiel badly wounded, admitted to hospital in Delmenhorst. Fw H. L. Romatowsky and Uffz H. Wiegand slightly wounded. Aircraft damaged but repairable.

1./KG4 Heinkel He111P. Crashed on take-off from Gütersloh for sortie to attack Ypenburg 3.15 a.m. Uffz K. Hirn and Uffz E. Richter killed. Uffz H. Trilling badly injured. Aircraft 5J+FH a write-off.

1./KG4 Heinkel He111P (1570). Returned damaged by flak and Fokker G 1 of 3-II-1 (1e Lt van Oorschot and Sgt Wesly) south of Dordrecht. Uffz H. Scharf badly wounded. Aircraft repairable.

2./KG4 Heinkel He111P (4570). Shot down by Fokker G 1s of 3-II-1 south of Dordrecht and crash-landed between Goudswaard and Piershil 4.15 a.m. Gefr H. Pälchen and Gefr K. Klemm badly wounded. Aircraft destroyed by crew.

4./KG4 Heinkel He111P. Hit by flak and believed collided with wingman. Crashed outside northern boundary of Soesterberg airfield 4.30 a.m. Lt A. Bohnenkamp, Uffz H. Heimsath, Hauptgefr W. Mittelhäuser, and Obergefr W. Römer killed. Aircraft a write-off.

4./KG4 Heinkel He111P. Believed brought down in collision with He111 hit by flak and crashed outside northern boundary of Soesterberg airfield 4.30 a.m. Oberlt P. von zu Mühlen, Uffz P. Kirsch, Obergefr W. Dreyer, and Gefr E. King killed. Aircraft a write-off.

5./KG4 Heinkel He111P-2 (3556). Believed shot down by Fokker G 1 of 3-II-1 (1e Lt Kuipers and Sgt Venema) and crashed south of Portugaal. Oberlt H. Roth, Uffz H. Heinig, and Obergefr E. Stephan captured slightly wounded. Aircraft 5J+DN a write-off.

5./KG4 Heinkel He111P. Returned hit by flak over Waalhaven. Oberfw F. Röhrborn slightly wounded. Aircraft repairable.

5./KG4 Heinkel He111P. Shot down by Fokker G 1 of 3-II-1 (Sgt Souffrée and Sgt de Man) and belly-landed south of Zevenbergschehoek 7.00 a.m. Oberfw H. Ganss killed. Oberlt R. Ganzert, Oberfw E. Tischer, and Gefr H. Dertinger captured unhurt. Aircraft 5J+KN a write-off.

5./KG4 Heinkel He111P. Shot down by Fokker G 1 of 3-II-1 (1e Lt Kuipers & Sgt Venema) and belly-landed at Rosmalen, north of 's-Hertogenbosch, 4.15 a.m. Uffz H. Zitzmann captured badly wounded, treated at Missiehuis Paters van Nuland. Uffz G. Klenk, Uffz W. Wiebke, and Gefr R. Schlegel captured unhurt. Aircraft 5J+JN a write-off.

7./KG4 Heinkel He111P (2633). Damaged by flak during attack on Schiphol and forced-landed at Zwanenburg 4.00 a.m. Lt V. Pollitz, Uffz B. Hintze, Uffz E. Schubert, and Obergefr H. Röthig captured unhurt. Aircraft 5J+PR a write-off.

7./KG4 Junkers Ju88A-1 (3040). Crashed at Gross-Mackenstedt shortly after take-off from Delmenhorst for attack on Bergen airfield; exact cause unknown. Lt H-J. Schwartz, Oberfw W. Voigt, and Obergefr H. Wilshaus killed. Uffz W. Grossmann mortally injured, later died. Aircraft a 5J+HR a write-off.

8./KG4 Junkers Ju88A-1. Shot down by own flak east of Arlon and crashed between Brouch and Reckange-lès-Mersch. Fw F. Wehrkoff and Fw W. Müller killed. Uffz W. Kunath baled out but killed. Aircraft a write-off.

9./KG4 Heinkel He111P (1591). Failed to return from attack on Bergen and crashed near Goudswaard, south-west of Rotterdam 4.15 a.m. Lt H-W. Paas, Uffz W. Hufnagel, Uffz F. Lewandofski, and Obergefr E. Stölzel believed captured. Aircraft 5J+ST a write-off.

9./KG4 Junkers Ju88A-1 (3041). Believed shot down by Fokker D XXI during dawn attack on Schiphol and crashed by the Hoofdweg, north of Hoofddorp, near Vijfhuizen 4.15 a.m. Gefr F. Strada killed. Oberlt F-K. Rinck, Oberfw W. Rüther, and Gefr F. Wissing captured unhurt. Aircraft 5J+GT a write-off.

9./KG4 Junkers Ju88A-1 (6018). Shot down during attack on Schiphol and crashed into lakes at the Kagerplassen 4.15 a.m. Lt R. Graf, Oberfw R. Mölle, Uffz O. Pälchen, and Obergefr G. Neuber killed. Aircraft 5J+AT lost.

9./KG4 Junkers Ju88A-1 (3035). Failed to return from dawn attack on Schiphol. Believed shot down by flak and crashed in the IJsselmeer off Sloten 4.15 a.m. Lt G. Hinsch, Obergefr K. Danzmair, and Obergefr A. Fölsch killed. Uffz E. Herzog missing. Aircraft 5J+IT lost.

Bill Gore (see also page 149), in the deckchair on the right, was an electrical engineer from Stockton-on-Tees. He was shot down on September 28 during the Battle of Britain, his Hurricane crashing into the Channel. His body was never recovered.

These two airmen from KG27 were both lost when their 3rd Staffel Heinkel was forced down by another 607 Squadron pilot, Flying Officer Bill Whitty. *Left:* The pilot was Otto Wehmeier, seen here wearing his marksman lanyard. *Right:* The radio operator, Manfred Kisker, pictured when a Gefreiter, was killed on his birthday.

Stab I./KG27 He111P. Attacked by S/L Oliver, P/O Lecky, and Sgt Allard of No. 85 Sqdn and possibly also engaged north-west of Lille by S/Lt Abrioux of GC 6/1. Crash-landed near Ferme Jourdain at Borre, east of Hazebrouck, 5.00 a.m. Uffz E. Glagow and Uffz E. Herpin killed. Oberlt R. Jenett *(Gruppen TO)* and Fw H. Müller captured unhurt. Aircraft 1G+CL a write-off.

This aircraft exploded 45 minutes later killing two of the crew, several bystanders, and injuring many more.

2./KG27 Heinkel He111P. Engaged by Hurricanes between Douai and Valenciennes during sortie to attack Hesdigneul and possibly that claimed by F/O Gore of No. 607 Sqdn. Belly-landed at 'La Taillette', near Notre-Dame d'Amour, east of Saint-Amand-les-Eaux 4.45 a.m. Uffz H. Glindemann killed. Fw F. Honig baled out and captured wounded. Oberlt G. Braunschweig captured wounded. Uffz P. Nashan captured unhurt. Aircraft 1G+DK a write-off.

3./KG27 Heinkel He111P. Crash-landed at Münster-Handorf airfield badly damaged in attacks by Hurricanes of No. 607 Sqdn and Moranes of GC III/1 near Lille-Seclin 5.15 a.m. Uffz W. Eckold badly wounded, Fw R. Boer and rest of crew unhurt. Aircraft 1G+BL damaged but repairable.

3./KG27 Heinkel He111P. Badly damaged by S/Lt Abrioux of GC 6/I during sortie to attack Lille-Seclin and also probably that attacked by F/O Whitty of No. 607 Sqdn. Belly-landed at Cambron-Casteau, south-east of Ath 5.15 a.m. Uffz M. Kisker killed. Uffz O. Wehmeier captured badly wounded, leg amputated but died May 30. Uffz A. Voigt captured wounded, admitted to hospital in Mons. Uffz O. Miklitz captured unhurt. Aircraft 1G+DL a write-off.

3./KG27 Heinkel He111P. Shot down by Moranes over Lille and possibly that attacked by Sgt Doublet of GC III/1 over Hazebrouck 5.20 a.m. Uffz H. Anders killed. Hptmn W. Bloem, Uffz H. Behrend, and Gefr U. Maddalena captured unhurt. Aircraft a write-off.

Walter Bloem was the pre-war novelist and screen-writer 'Kilian Koll'.

Stab II./KG27 Heinkel He111P-2. Shot down by fighters during sortie to attack Lille-Seclin and probably that claimed by F/L Sample, F/O Humpherson and F/O Bowen of No. 607 Sqdn. Crash-landed and burned out at Ormeignies, south-west of Ath 5.20 a.m. Lt H. W. Hover, Oberfw E. Lisse, Fw H. Walz, and Uffz F. Schlichting captured unhurt. Aircraft 1G+CC a write-off.

4./KG27 Heinkel He111P. Forced-landed at Cologne-Ostheim badly damaged by flak and fighters during sortie to attack rail targets between Brussels and Antwerp. Possibly that attacked by Sgt Vollières of GC III/1 5.50 p.m. Uffz E. Kortmann and Obergefr L. Merkel wounded. Aircraft 1G+GM damaged but repairable.

6./KG27 Heinkel He111P-2. Belly-landed at Achmer engine disabled in attacks by GC III/1 during sortie to attack rail targets around Ghent 5.50 p.m. Possibly that attacked by S/Lt du Boucher and Adjt Gagnaire near Roubaix, and also later attacked by F/O Weatherill and P/O Jay of No. 607 Sqdn near Oudenaarde. Uffz W. Pettke badly wounded. Lt H. Brandenberg and rest of crew unhurt. Aircraft 1G+AP damaged but repairable.

6./KG27 Heinkel He111P-2. Shot down by S/Lt Goumy, Sgt Lagrange of GC 6/1, and P/O Dini of No. 607 Sqdn, during sortie to attack rail targets around Ghent, and crashed at Munkzwalm 5.50 p.m. Uffz H. Zimmermann, Uffz G. Wackerhagen, Uffz H. Börnicke, and Uffz F. Beinhoff killed. Aircraft 1G+GP a write-off.

7./KG27 Heinkel He111P-2. Port engine disabled by flak during sortie to bomb airfield near Douai. Then engaged by Lt Tariel of GC 6/1 and Moranes of GC II/8 over Iseghem and belly-landed at Kweekstraat, Ingelmunster 5.50 p.m. Fw K. Berger, Fw F. Lange, Uffz A. Mozer, and Uffz R. Fromme captured unhurt. Aircraft 1G+JR destroyed by crew.

Karl Berger died in captivity when the French transport he was travelling in was destroyed at Dunkirk on May 30.

8./KG27 Heinkel He111P-2 (1430). Forced-landed at Münster-Loddenheide damaged in attacks by Moranes west of St-Quentin . Uffz F. Lösecke slightly wounded, Fw J. Oeckenpöhler and rest of crew unhurt. Aircraft 1G+ES damaged but repairable.

8./KG27 Heinkel He111P. Crashed at Münster-Handorf due to propeller failure. No crew casualties. Aircraft a write-off.

9./KG27 Heinkel He111P-2. Shot down by F/O Thompson and Sgt Townsend of No. 607 Sqdn during attack on Lille-Seclin and crashed near Péronnes-les-Antoing 5.15 a.m. Fw H. Schmelz, Uffz W. Stramm, and Uffz E. Leonhardt killed. Uffz W. Wingender baled out and captured unhurt. Aircraft a write-off.

Walter Wingender died aboard a French transport during an air attack at Dunkirk on May 30.

9./KG27 Heinkel He111P. Returned to base damaged in attack by fighters over Lille and possibly that attacked by Adjt Déchanet of GC 6/1 near Bruges 5.25 a.m. Uffz N. Jug slightly wounded, Fw K-E. Pohlmann, Fw J. Annen and another crewman unhurt. Aircraft 1G+KT repairable.

Stab I./KG30 Junkers Ju88A. Starboard engine damaged over Ede and abandoned by crew near Arnhem, pilot crash-landing in Rozendaalse Veld. Possibly attacked by Fokker D XXI of 1-II-1 7.45 a.m. Fw G. Hartmann captured unhurt. Fw K. Soldau and Gefr E. Gieseler baled out and captured slightly wounded. Uffz F. Lassen baled out too low and killed. Aircraft 4D+CB a write-off.

1./KG30 Junkers Ju88A-2 (2027). Cockpit hit by flak during armed reconnaissance south of Rotterdam 5.45 a.m. Uffz S. Weiss killed. Starboard engine failed and wrecked in heavy crash-landing west of Beek. Oberlt R. von Wartenberg, and Uffz H. Müller killed. Gefr D. Falcke captured with fractured jaw and head wound, admitted to Princenhage hospital. Aircraft 4D+IT a write-off.

1./KG30 Junkers Ju88A-2. One engine damaged by Bf109 following attack on cruiser in Rotterdam harbour. Belly-landed at Zevenhuizen 5.20 p.m. Oberlt W. Wülknitz, Obergefr H-W. Abt, and Obergefr H. Borchers captured unhurt. Gefr G. Manthei captured slightly wounded. Aircraft 4D+FT a write-off.

3./KG30 Junkers Ju88A. Badly damaged by light flak during low-level attack on Soesterberg and forced-landed at Rheine. Crew unhurt. Aircraft a write-off.

3./KG30 Junkers Ju88A. Returned badly damaged by Fokker G 1 of 3-II-1 (1e Lt K. W. Woudenberg and Sgt J. A. Pouw) east of Rotterdam during sortie to attack Ockenburg. Uffz H. Schreiber and Gefr E. Schröder badly wounded, died May 16. Uffz H. Hobik and Obergefr F. Baumgarten slightly wounded. Aircraft a write-off.

3./KG30 Junkers Ju88A-2. Shot down by flak during dive-bombing attack on Waalhaven and crashed at Ouderijn 11.30 a.m. Oberlt H-W. Magnussen, Uffz K. Roscher, and Uffz G. Richter baled out but killed. Oberfw L. Edmüller baled out and captured badly wounded, admitted to hospital in Rotterdam but later released. Aircraft a write-off.

4./KG30 Junkers Ju88A. Returned badly damaged following attack on Waalhaven. Oberfw H. Bloeck slightly wounded. Obergefr O. Zahnke badly wounded. Aircraft a write-off.

A 'then and now' comparison with a difference! This is Feldwebel Karl Berger's crew of the 7th Staffel of KG27 — before and after they were brought down by the French.

4./KG30 Junkers Ju88A. Returned damaged during attack on Waalhaven. Crew unhurt. Aircraft damaged but repairable.

4./KG30 Junkers Ju88A. Shot down by 2e Lt Droste of 1-V-2 during attack on AA positions near Den Haag. Abandoned by crew south of Ypenburg and crashed at Den Hoorn 6.15 a.m. Obergefr P. Müller killed. Fw A. Stahl baled out and captured badly wounded, admitted to St Anthoniushove hospital in Voorburg. Oberlt T. Beermann *(Staffelkapitän)* and Oberfw E. Maar baled out and captured unhurt. Aircraft 4D+AM a write-off.

5./KG30 Junkers Ju88A. Crashed into flak emplacement on take-off from Oldenburg, cause not stated. Gefr A. Sattelmacher badly injured, rest of crew unhurt. Aircraft a write-off.
Two flak personnel were killed and eight others injured in this accident.

5./KG30 Junkers Ju88A. Returned damaged by naval flak over Rotterdam. Gefr P. Casper badly wounded. Aircraft repairable.

7./KG30 Junkers Ju88A-2. Suffered direct hit by AA and exploded over Nijmegen main wreckage falling in the River Waal. Lt H. Begemann, Fw A. Herb, Uffz W. Haiges, and Flgr H. Müller killed. Aircraft 4D+KR a write-off.

8./KG30 Junkers Ju88A-1. Crashed on take-off at Marx, cause not stated. Uffz H. Landsberg, Obergefr H. Hoetz, and Gefr R. Alksaat killed. Uffz H. Haase badly injured. Aircraft a write-off.

8./KG30 Junkers Ju88A. Returned damaged. Gefr W. Raupach slightly wounded. Aircraft repairable.

Stab I./KG51 Heinkel He111H. Shot down by Capt Hugo, S/Lt Mangin, and Sgt Boillot of GC II/7 during photo-reconnaissance mission and crash-landed near the Swiss border northeast of Chavanatte 6.30 a.m. Uffz V. Spengler killed. Lt K. Haimerl, Fw P. Ehrfeld, and Uffz P. Heinze (of 2./KG51) captured slightly wounded, admitted to hospital in Dannemarie. Aircraft 9K+EB a write-off.
This aircraft belonged to the Gruppe-Aufklärungsschwarm and carried an automatic camera rather than ordnance in a specially modified bomb bay.

2./KG51 Heinkel He111H. Forced-landed with casualties and seriously damaged following running battle with Adjt Goujon and Sgt Hardouin of GC III/6 over Forêt d'Arbois 3.30 p.m. Uffz M. Freutle killed. Fw W. Kleinschmidt badly wounded. Aircraft a write-off.

Having fired their machine, the crew lined up for another snapshot!

The 8th Staffel of KG54 lost six aircraft on May 10, No. 607 Squadron contributing to their demise. Three are illustrated on these pages — this is Unteroffizier Walter Zenner's Heinkel at Hulste. He became a prisoner of the British.

II./KG51 Junkers Ju88A-1. Returned starboard engine damaged by flak and attack by S/Lt Couillens of GC 3/7 near Darney 5.55 a.m. No crew casualties. Aircraft repairable.

6./KG51 Junkers Ju88A-1. Crashed on take-off from Munich-Riem, cause not stated. Oberfw E. Kramer, Uffz G. Groke, and Obergefr K. Reins killed. Hptmn J. Berlin *(Staffelkapitän)* badly injured. Aircraft a write-off.

7./KG51 Heinkel He111H. Returned damaged by fighters over Lyon-Bron, possibly one of those engaged by GC III/9 4.45 a.m. Hptmn J. Poetter *(Staffelkapitän)* and Lt A. Fritsch slightly wounded. Aircraft damaged but repairable.

7./KG51 Heinkel He111H. Damaged in attack by Swiss Bf109 over the Toggenburg near Bütschwil, but escaped across the Bodensee following attack on Lyon-Bron 4.45 a.m.. Uffz A. Schäfer slightly wounded, rest of crew unhurt. Aircraft repairable.

8./KG51 Heinkel He111H. Shot down by flak during attack on Lyon-Bron and believed crashed near Brosses, Colombier-Saugnieu, 4.50 a.m. Fw J. Ellgass, Fw O. Wagner, Fw K. Bäuerle, Uffz H. Heiser, and Gefr J. Neumeyer captured wounded. Aircraft a write-off.

8./KG51 Heinkel He111H. Returned damaged by fighters south-east of Dole, following attack on Lyon-Bron 4.45 a.m. Possibly that attacked by Adjt Chapour of GC III/9. Fw K. Harenburg, Uffz R. Scheurich, and Obergefr R. Worsch slightly wounded. Aircraft repairable.

9./KG51 Heinkel He111H. Returned damaged following attack on Lyon-Bron 4.45 a.m. Possibly one of those engaged by GC III/9. Uffz L. Müller died of wounds, rest of crew unhurt. Aircraft repairable.

Stab KG53 Heinkel He111H. Landed at Frankfurt-Main damaged by fighters. Oberlt J. Schmitz *(Gruppenadjutant)* died of wounds. Aircraft repairable.

I./KG53 Two Heinkel He111H. Damaged in take-off collision at Roth airfield. No crew casualties. One aircraft a write-off, one damaged but repairable.

Stab II./KG53 Heinkel He111H. Forced-landed near Kochem damaged in attacks by Hurricanes of No. 87 Sqdn 12.05 p.m. Oberfw G. Träber and Uffz F. Freyinger killed. Oberst W. Kohlbach *(Gruppenkommandeur)* slightly wounded. Aircraft damaged but repairable.

Stab II./KG53 Heinkel He111H. Belly-landed at Ingolstadt damaged in combat 20 km south of Charleville-Mézières. Oberfw G. Lüders slightly wounded, rest of crew unhurt. Aircraft damaged but repairable.

5./KG53 Heinkel He111H. Shot down by Hurricanes of No. 87 Sqdn south of Thionville 12.25 p.m. Possibly that claimed by P/O David. Fw A. Hinze and Gefr T. Kappe killed. Uffz O. Simon baled out and missing. Oberlt W. Partl and Oberlt H. Mosbach baled out and captured unhurt. Aircraft a write-off.

5./KG53 Heinkel He111H. Shot down by Hurricanes of No. 87 Sqdn south of Thionville 12.25 p.m. Possibly that claimed by P/O Saunders. Fw T. Dietrich, Uffz F. Steinberg, Uffz A. Görtz, Uffz K. Beutel, and Gefr O. Kielwein captured unhurt. Aircraft a write-off.

5./KG53 Heinkel He111H. Returned damaged by Hurricanes of No. 87 Sqdn over Thionville 12.25 p.m. Possibly one of those claimed by Sgt Howell. Uffz J. Ballweg slightly wounded. Aircraft repairable.

III./KG53 Heinkel He111H. Belly-landed at Schwäbisch-Hall, cause not stated. No crew casualties. Aircraft damaged but repairable.

7./KG53 Heinkel He111H. Aircraft abandoned under attack by Adjt Hôtellier, Sgt Joire, and Sgt Bompain of GC I/4 and crashed at Ell, west of Redange, 5.30 a.m. Possibly also attacked by Potez 63 of GAO 2/520 (S/Lt Teissier, Capt de Devise, and Sgt Terse) of GAO 2/520 near Martelange. Fl-Stab-Ing. E. Issel (of Erp.Stelle Rechlin) baled out over Olizy-sur-Chiers and killed. Uffz W. Wolf baled out over Stenay and captured unhurt. Lt Franke captured wounded. Uffz Engelmann captured unhurt. Aircraft A1+AR a write-off.

4./KG54 Heinkel He111P. Belly-landed at Varelbusch due to engine failure, possible combat damage. Lt F. Gottschling injured. Aircraft repairable.

5./KG54 Heinkel He111P. Returned damaged following mission west of Antwerp. Gefr E. Strach killed. Obergefr H. Günther slightly wounded. Aircraft damage state not recorded.

6./KG54 Heinkel He111P. Returned damaged following operations over the Scheldt estuary. Fw A. Venhues badly wounded, died in Delmenhorst hospital. Fw Ritter and rest of crew unhurt. Aircraft B3+AP repairable.

6./KG54 Heinkel He111P. Returned damaged following operations over the Scheldt estuary. Obergefr H. Rudolph slightly wounded, rest of crew unhurt. Aircraft repairable.

Stab III./KG54 Two Heinkel He111Ps. Returned damaged in attacks by Hurricanes of Nos. 3, 85, and 607 Sqdns during sortie to attack Wevelgem airfield 7.30 p.m. Fw J. Kuhn, Uffz K. Schöneweiss, and Uffz E. Pollmann all slightly wounded. Aircraft both repairable.

8./KG54 Heinkel He111P. Damaged by Hurricanes of Nos. 3, 85 and 607 Sqdns south-west of Sluis and forced-landed in De Waterhoek Polder 7.45 p.m. Obergefr E. Luis killed. Uffz P. Hentschel captured wounded. Uffz A. Vogel and Uffz W. Pomorin captured unhurt. Aircraft a write-off.

This is the Heinkel of the Staffelkapitän, Hauptmann Fritz Stadelmayr.

8./KG54 Heinkel He111P. Both engines damaged in attacks by Hurricanes of Nos. 3, 85, and 607 Sqdns during sortie to attack Wevelgem airfield and believed crash-landed near Morkhoven 7.30 p.m. Lt A. Jansen, Obergefr H. Wittchen, Gefr K. Götz, and Flgr L. Dallmeier all captured badly wounded. Aircraft a write-off.

8./KG54 Heinkel He111P. Shot down by P/O Hemingway of No. 85 Sqdn and possibly also attacked by P/O Parrott of No. 607 Sqdn during sortie to attack Wevelgem airfield and crashed at Hulste 7.30 p.m. Gefr G. Mühlenbrink, Gefr H. Karing, and Gefr P. Grob killed. Uffz W. Zenner baled out and captured wounded. Aircraft a write-off.

8./KG54 Heinkel He111P. Shot down by Hurricanes of Nos. 3, 85 and 607 Sqdns during sortie to attack Wevelgem airfield and crashed at Ruiselede 7.30 p.m. Possibly that claimed by P/O Jay of No. 607 Sqdn. Obergefr G. Flehmer killed. Oberlt V. Riedesel Fr zu Eisenbach, Fw W. Joest, and Uffz E. Kreib captured wounded. Aircraft a write-off.

8./KG54 Heinkel He111P. Shot down by Hurricanes of Nos. 3, 85 and 607 Sqdns and believed crashed at Kampel, near Maldegem, 7.45 p.m. Stabsfw A. Huckelmann killed. Hptmn F. Stadelmayr (Staffelkapitän) and Fw O. Wolf captured wounded, admitted to hospital in Bruges. Oberlt F. Kriegeskotte captured unhurt. Aircraft B3+AS a write-off.

Unteroffizier Karl Reinhardt was hammered into the ground by the combined fire of aircraft from Nos. 3, 85 and 607 Squadrons.

8./KG54 Heinkel He111P. Both engines disabled in attacks by Hurricanes of Nos. 3, 85, and 607 Sqdns over Wevelgem and belly-landed and burned out at Merendree 7.35 p.m. Lt L. Heppe, Uffz G. Geppert, Uffz K. Reinhardt, and Uffz W. Reinhardt captured wounded. Aircraft B3+BS a write-off.

Stab KG55 Heinkel He111P. Returned badly damaged by flak and attacks by Lt Husson and Sgt Beda of GC I/2 south of Nancy 3.20 p.m. Fw K. Ander, Fw K. Rathmann, and Fw P. Müller seriously wounded. Aircraft a write-off.

5./KG55 Heinkel He111P. Returned badly damaged by flak and attacks by S/Lt Thollon and Sgt Liautard of GC I/8 over Château-Salins, east of Nancy 6.30 a.m. Fw W. Müller, Uffz K. Hauber, and Gefr S. Löffler badly wounded. Aircraft damaged but repairable.

Stab III./KG55 Heinkel He111P (2846). Port engine disabled by flak during sortie to Xaffévillers then attacked by Capt Hyvernaud, Lt de la Bretonnier, Sgt Meunier, and Sgt de Puybusque of GC I/2 and belly-landed at Vahl-les-Benestroff 5.45 a.m. Major P. Schemmel (Gruppenkommandeur), Oberlt F. Gräf (Gruppen TO), Oberlt H. Prüfer (Gruppen NO), and Oberfw F. Lehmann all captured. Fw E. Meyer killed. Aircraft G1+AD a write-off.

French sources report that this crew resisted capture and exchanged fire with troops of 414e Régiment de Pionniers who arrived within minutes of the crash. At least two wounded crewmen were later admitted to hospital in nearby Dieuze. Carrying so many staff officers in one crew was officially discouraged, though it was to be some months before specific orders were issued forbidding the practice.

Stab III./KG55 Heinkel He111P. One engine disabled in attacks by Capt Hyvernaud of GC 2/2 then engaged by Adjt Castel, Sgt Giordani, and Lt Lamaison of GC I/8 and belly-landed, under fire from ground defences, on Velaine-en-Haye airfield where fired by crew 5.40 a.m. Oberlt G. Hecker, Oberfw F. Glocke, Fw R. Labandowsky, Uffz H. Gentsch, and Gefr F. Günther all captured unhurt. Aircraft a write-off.

8./KG55 Heinkel He111P. Returned damaged by flak and fighters during sortie to Xaffévillers. Fw K. Neubacher and Gefr H. Pawlik wounded. Aircraft a write-off.

9./KG55 Heinkel He111P. Port engine set alight in attack by Sgt de La Chapelle of GC II/4 and abandoned over Luvigny, west of Donon 4.00 p.m. Oberfw H. Rohloff and Flgr N. Merkler killed. Lt G. Trosky and Uffz F. Stratmann baled out and captured unhurt. Gefr G. Kasischke also baled out but parachute failed. Aircraft G1+DT a write-off.

Stab KG76 Dornier Do17Z. Caught fire under attack by Sgt Cucumel, S/Lt Milbeau, and Sgt Forzy of GC I/4 during photo-reconnaissance sortie east of Cambrai. Crashed at 'Fond-Barré', Brieulles-sur-Bar, west of Buzancy 7.30 a.m. Lt O. Harms and Fw K. Baensch killed. Uffz H. Gauger baled out but parachute failed. Uffz W. Röbler baled out and captured badly wounded, died in St-Quentin hospital. Aircraft a write-off.

1./KG76 Dornier Do17Z. Returned damaged in attacks by Lt Fabre, S/Lt Ronin, Adjt Deniau, Adjt Gray, and Sgt de Bremond d'Ars of GC 3/6 between Hirson and Rocroi following sortie to bomb rail targets 6.40 p.m. Fw K. Frömer killed. Oberfw J. Berchermeier and Uffz G. Ehrhardt slightly wounded. Aircraft repairable.

6./KG76 2 Dornier Do17Z. Returned damaged in attacks by Moranes of GC II/2 south of Sedan during sortie to attack Athies-sous-Laon 5.20 a.m. One believed that attacked by Capt de Calonne and Sgt de la Gasnerie. Uffz H. Lehr and Fw K. Pfeifer slightly wounded. Aircraft both repairable.

6./KG76 Dornier Do17Z. Cockpit hit by flak between Sedan and Rethel during sortie to attack Athies-sous-Laon and crashed near Villers-devant-Orval 5.20 a.m. Oberlt J. Giesemann killed. Fw A. Trepl and Uffz W. Wirth missing. Fw A. Rist captured unhurt. Aircraft a write-off.

The observer, Julius Giesemann, was later discovered in woods and buried at Virton on September 6, 1940.

7./KG76 Dornier Do17Z. Rudder damaged by flak and both engines badly damaged in attacks by Lt de Rohan-Chabot and Adjt Dorcy of GC II/2 during sortie to attack Athies-sous-Laon. Belly-landed east of Fontaine-les-Vervins and burned out 5.30 a.m. Fw H. Sedlak killed. Fw W. Reiske, Fw E. Brauer, and Gefr K. Fritz captured unhurt. Aircraft F1+DR a write-off.

4./KG77 Dornier Do17Z. Returned damaged by ground-fire near Veldwezelt Fw G. Dittrich died of wounds, rest of crew unhurt. Aircraft repairable.

5./KG77 Dornier Do17Z. Returned damaged by ground-fire near Kesselt. Gefr K. Wellhausen died of wounds, rest of crew unhurt. Aircraft repairable.

5./KG77 Dornier Do17Z. Crashed near Vroenhoven reportedly shot down by flak but possibly attacked by Fiat CR-42s of II/2 flown by Sgt J. Maes and S/Lt J. Offenberg 6.30 a.m. Oberlt H. Bott, Lt R. Weib, Fw A. Baumgartner, and Oberfw H. Spohr killed. Aircraft a write-off.

6./KG77 Dornier Do17Z. Returned damaged by ground-fire near Eben-Emael. Uffz J. Stratmann slightly wounded. Aircraft repairable.

2./KGr.126 Two Heinkel He111H-4s (6179, 6970). Returned damaged by ground-fire during an attack on Bergen airfield 5.30 a.m. Fw R. Fries and Uffz A. Brendgen badly wounded. Aircraft both repairable.

2./KGr.126 Heinkel He111H-4 (7032). Returned damaged by flak during an attack on Bergen airfield 5.30 a.m. Obergefr E. Hühne slightly wounded. Aircraft 1T+FK repairable.

17./KGrzbV.5 Junkers Ju52. Believed shot down by Capt Callataÿ (Commandant) of 3/II/2 shortly after releasing DFS230 glider carrying airborne troops. Crashed and burned out at Vrusschenhuisken, near Simpelveld 6.30 a.m. Gefr H. Brunotte Killed, Uffz A. Göbel and rest of crew baled out and captured. Aircraft a write-off.

Formed in January 1939 for development of glider-borne operations, this unit was responsible for towing four assault groups of troops of Sturmabteilung Koch to attack Fort Eben-Emael, and bridges crossing the Albert Canal at Kanne, Veldwezelt, and Vroenhoven. The unit lost two more Ju52s but details are lacking though Oberlt Steinweg, Uffz W. Daum, Uffz B. Selle, and six crewmen were killed and nine more wounded on operations this day.

Lehrgeschwader 1 lost six machines. *Above:* **This is Unteroffizier Richard Bröer's Heinkel from Stab LG1.** *Right:* **Leutnant Otto-Friedrich Dörwald was the pilot of the second aircraft lost by the Geschwader Staff flight.**

3./KüFlGr. 506 Heinkel He115C. Crashed in fog on the Escamppolder near Loosduinen during night mine-laying sortie between Texel and Vlieland. Lt zur See E. Dirking, Uffz S. Graf, and Uffz R. Seipel killed. Aircraft a write-off.

Stab LG1 Heinkel He111H. Failed to return from armed-reconnaissance mission over Bruges and possibly that claimed by Lt de Mallmann and Adjt Saussol of GC III/1 near Dendermonde 5.35 p.m. Uffz R. Bröer captured badly wounded, died in hospital in Ghent. Uffz W. Kleint captured slightly wounded. Uffz W. Koch and Obergefr W. Hinrichs captured unhurt. Aircraft a write-off.

The wounded observer, Wilhelm Kleint, was held on the Saint Octave, *a French prison ship at Dunkirk, and was among 17 killed when the ship was damaged by artillery fire on May 29.*

Stab LG1 Heinkel He111H. Shot down during reconnaissance sortie and belly-landed at Meux, north of Namur, 1.30 p.m. Oberfw P. Fehlinger killed. Uffz A. Müller captured badly wounded, admitted to Zuydcoote hospital where died on May 31. Uffz E. Lehmann captured wounded. Lt O-F. Dörwald captured unhurt. Aircraft L1+BA a write-off.

1./LG1 Heinkel He111H. Shot down by Hurricanes of No. 607 Sqdn during armed reconnaissance and crashed at Fontenoy, northeast of Péronnes 5.15 p.m. Possibly that attacked by P/O Jay, P/O Dini, and P/O Dixon. Uffz H. Funke and Gefr H. Schneider killed. Oberfhr H-H. Thiessen and Uffz J. Meyer captured unhurt. Aircraft L1+IH a write-off.

1./LG1 Heinkel He111H. Returned damaged by flak. Oberfw W. Krüger badly wounded, rest of crew unhurt. Aircraft repairable.

2./LG1 Heinkel He111H. Returned damaged by P/O Ashton of No. 607 Sqdn near Äth 5.15 p.m. Uffz E. Hoffmann and Gefr K. Seelenmeyer wounded, rest of crew unhurt. Aircraft repairable.

3./LG1 Heinkel He111H. Shot down by Hurricane of No. 607 Sqdn during armed reconnaissance and crashed near Néchin, east of Lille 5.20 p.m. Possibly that claimed by P/O Le Breuilly and P/O Rowe. Uffz H. Saas killed. Fw W. Hartmann captured wounded. Fw W. Franz and Gefr M. Buhler captured unhurt. Aircraft L1+EL a write-off.

4./LG1 Heinkel He111H. Both engines disabled by Sgt Durand of GC 6/1 and Sgt Honorat of GC II/8 following attack on Berck-sur-Mer airfield. Also bracketed by flak prior to belly-landing on beach north of Calais-Marck 6.15 a.m. Fw R. Martin captured wounded. Oberlt H. Merkwitz, Lt E. Sy, and Fw B. Falkenhagen captured unhurt. Aircraft L1+EM a write-off.

8./LG1 Junkers Ju88A-1. Shot down over Hermaville, north-west of Arras. Fw E. Schade, Uffz G. Kronewitz, Uffz L. Hechmann, and Gefr H. Maiborn believed baled out and captured unhurt. Aircraft a write-off.

The gunner, Heinrich Maiborn, was later lost overboard en-route from England to Canada as a prisoner of war.

4.(S)/LG2 Henschel Hs123. Hit an obstruction on take-off from Oberbrück airfield. Pilot unhurt. Aircraft damaged but repairable.

4./StG2 Junkers Ju87B. Crashed and burned out at Siegburg due to control failure. Uffz H. Ramsbrock and Uffz R. Grauzow killed. Aircraft a write-off.

Left: 'He lived to fight another day.' **Leutnant Erwin Sy of the 4th Staffel was taken prisoner after his Heinkel came down on the beach at Calais but he was released from French captivity on May 31** *(right).* **Later, as Staffelkapitän with II./LG1, he was awarded the German Cross in Gold (seen below the right breast pocket of his tropical uniform) on January 2, 1942, and the Knight's Cross in May 1942. He was killed at Tobruk on December 2 that year.**

The Stuka was the much-vaunted terror weapon yet the wreckage of several littered the Belgian and Dutch countryside. Both these crashes were of 9./StG2 aircraft, this being the wreckage of Feldwebel Alfred Nitschke's machine down at Kapelle-op-den-Bos.

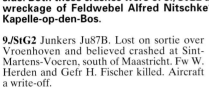

9./StG2 Junkers Ju87B. Lost on sortie over Vroenhoven and believed crashed at Sint-Martens-Voeren, south of Maastricht. Fw W. Herden and Gefr H. Fischer killed. Aircraft a write-off.

9./StG2 Junkers Ju87B. Lost on sortie over Vroenhoven and crashed near the Maaseik bridge, near Roosteren, north of Maastricht. Uffz E. Unger killed. Lt W. Kaiser returned wounded. Aircraft a write-off.

9./StG2 Junkers Ju87B. Crashed near Kapelle-op-den-Bos following possible collision during attack on roads near Antwerp 8.45 p.m. Fw A. Nitschke and Uffz E. Brückner killed. Aircraft a write-off.

9./StG2 Junkers Ju87B. Crashed near Kapelle-op-den-Bos following possible collision during attack on roads near Antwerp 8.45 p.m. Uffz U. Gilon killed. Obergefr H. Cechini captured unhurt. Aircraft T6+ET a write-off.

I./StG76 Junkers Ju87B. Crash-landed at Ferschweiler airfield, cause not stated. Crew unhurt. Aircraft damaged but repairable.

I./StG76 Two Junkers Ju87B. Damaged in flying accidents at Deggendorf airfield. No crew casualties. Aircraft both write-offs.

3./StG77 Junkers Ju87B. Shot down by flak and crashed near Vorselaer, 6 km north-west of Herentals during attack on Antwerp 7.15 p.m. Oberlt K. Hartmann (*Staffelkapitän*) and Fw W. Mische killed. Aircraft a write-off.

3./StG77 Junkers Ju87B. Crashed near Mopertingen after collision in the dive. Fw J. Becker and Uffz H. Behnert believed baled out unhurt. Aircraft a write off.

3./StG77 Junkers Ju87B. Crashed at Bilzenbaan, near Maastricht, after collision in the dive over Mopertingen. Uffz L. Bussenius and Uffz E. Albrecht killed. Aircraft a write-off.

4./ZG1 Messerschmitt Bf110C. Shot down by Vlissingen airfield defences and belly-landed at Goesche Sas 4.00 a.m. Uffz H. Vob captured wounded. Obergefr W. Steffen captured unhurt. Aircraft destroyed by crew.

3./ZG26 Messerschmitt Bf110C-2 (3011). Fuel tank holed in attack by Sgt Morel of GC I/5 south of Sedan and belly-landed at Létanne, north-east of Beaumont-en-Argonne 4.40 a.m. Obergefr H. Röwe killed. Fw H. Reimann captured. Aircraft U8+DL a write-off.

The rather pathetic grave at Maastricht of Feldwebel Werner Herden from one of the 9. Staffel's other Stukas. Today he lies in the German War Cemetery at Ysselstein (Block BZ, Row 4, Grave 90).

215

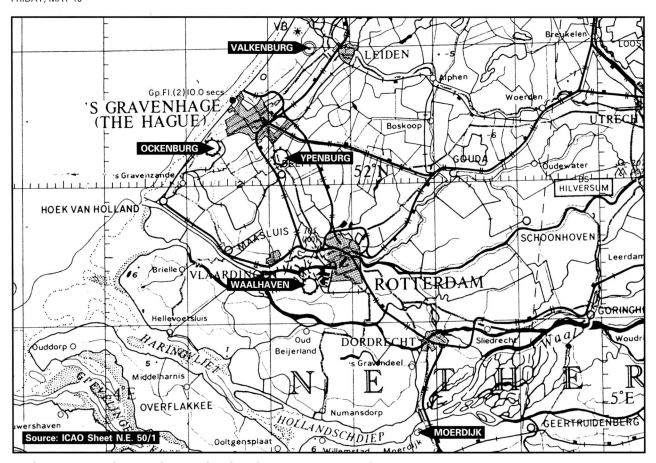

Source: ICAO Sheet N.E. 50/1

Airborne attacks on the Netherlands — German plans

To prevent a possible intervention by French and British troops through the Netherlands threatening the right flank of their advance into Belgium, revised plans for Fall Gelb were issued by the German High Command on January 30, 1940. These provided for a full-blown invasion of the Netherlands rather than a limited incursion by the 6. Armee across Limburg, in the south of the country around Maastricht, that had been originally planned.

Dutch preparations to counter an invasion were severely constrained by their strict policy of neutrality, and its forces poorly equipped to oppose the military might of Germany. Defence strategy therefore centred on Vesting Holland — Fortress Holland — the central provinces which included the cities of Amsterdam, Den Haag, Rotterdam and Utrecht. This region, already masked in the south by the water barriers of the Maas, Waal and Rhine rivers, could be virtually isolated from the rest of the country by deliberately flooding huge tracts of inland polder terrain to hinder the German advance. In the province of Zeeland, in the south-west of the country, the islands of Beveland and Walcheren were to be held leaving the Scheldt Estuary accessible for possible assistance from France and England.

Thus, on the eve of invasion, Dutch strategy was a holding campaign designed to delay any German advance for as long as possible, destroying river crossings and flooding the countryside, while withdrawing its forces within Vesting Holland.

German plans for the invasion of the Netherlands involved a three-pronged attack by the 18. Armee commanded by General der Artillerie Georg von Küchler. In the north, the 1. Kavallerie-Division was to advance into Friesland and cross the IJsselmeer (by means of the Afsluitdijk causeway that closed its northern end) to threaten Amsterdam from the north. In the

centre, a reinforced X. Armeekorps would thrust across Gelderland to take Utrecht while in the south, XXVI. Armeekorps would cross the River Maas and attack Vesting Holland from the south, while preventing intervention by the French army through Belgium. Well aware of the potential obstacles posed by the complex network of Dutch waterways, German plans incorporated ambitious airborne assaults on vital bridges and key river crossings.

These airborne operations were entrusted to Luftflotte 2 under General Albert Kesselring and special staff assigned to their detailed planning. Generalleutnant Kurt Student was appointed to command the Luftlandekorps — Air Landing Corps — formed from 3,500 paratroops of his own 7. Flieger-Division along with 12,000 men of the 22. Infanterie-Division who were to be air-lifted to support the initial parachute landings.

To transport these troops to their targets, two air transport wings of 430 Junkers Ju52s were assembled under the command of General Wilhelm Speidel, each wing comprising four groups (KGzbV.1 had I. II. III. and IV. Gruppe; the other wing consisted of KGzbV.9, 11, 12 and 172) of 53 aircraft able to transport the equivalent of a full battalion in a single mission. Support for the landings was to be provided by Fliegerkorps zbV.2 under Generalmajor Richard Putzier, a unit specially formed for this specific operation. They were to soften up the targets by heavy bombing ahead of the landings with any additional support required being made available by other units in Luftflotte 2.

The first wave of planned parachute landings aimed to capture the bridges between Moerdijk and Rotterdam, and seize four airfields at Rotterdam and Den Haag. Once these landing fields were secured, a second wave was to land elements of the 22. Infanterie-Division to support the paratroops already on the ground.

Three airfields around Den Haag formed the initial objectives for a reinforced battalion of paratroops from Fallschirmjäger-Regiment 2, with two regiments of the 22. Infanterie-Division standing by to follow the first wave of parachute landings as soon as the airfields were secured. The three targets were Valkenburg airfield, between Leiden and Den Haag, designated Landing Place I; Ockenburg to the south-west, Landing Place II; and Ypenburg, on the southern outskirts of the city, Landing Place III.

At Valkenburg (Landeplatz I) at 5.50 a.m. 12 Junkers Ju52s of I./KGrzbV.172 from Paderborn would drop 160 paratroops of the 6. Kompanie of Fallschirmjäger-Regiment 2 to seize the airfield. Once secured, the first wave of landings would follow at 6.20 a.m. when 53 Ju52s of KGrzbV.11 from Lippstadt started to ferry in 3,150 troops of III. Bataillon of Infanterie-Regiment 47.

Meanwhile, at Ockenburg (Landeplatz II) 14 Ju52s of IV./KGzbV.1 were to drop 160 men of the 3. Kompanie of Fallschirmjäger-Regiment 2 to secure the field. These would be reinforced from 6 a.m. by the first wave of landings by aircraft of KGrzbV.12 from Störmede air-lifting the battalion staff of II. Bataillon and the 5. Kompanie of Infanterie-Regiment 65.

Simultaneously, at Ypenburg (Landeplatz III), 390 men of I. Bataillon (minus 3. Kompanie) of Fallschirmjäger-Regiment 2 would drop at 5.48 a.m. from 40 Ju52s of IV./KGzbV.1 from Loddenheide. These would be followed, from 6.20 a.m., by landings planned by KGrzbV.12 to bring in the regimental staff and 6. and 8. Kompanie of Infanterie-Regiment 65 from Störmede.

Generalleutnant Hans von Sponeck, in overall command of the 22. Luftlande-Division, was in charge of these northern operations and according to plans was to have 9,300 troops in three pockets around Den Haag by the evening of May 10. He also had additional orders to enter the city, seize key government offices and buildings, and arrest the Dutch Royal Family.

Additional elements of this ambitious German airborne assault on the Netherlands were planned to the south-east; at Moerdijk, around Dordrecht, and on the southern outskirts of Rotterdam. These were under the command of General Student who, by the evening of May 10, planned to have 4,600 troops holding the main arterial highway and the river crossings between Rotterdam and Moerdijk.

The first stage of this part of the operation involved drops from 53 Ju52s of I./KGzbV.1 by about 700 paratroops of II. Bataillon of Fallschirmjäger-Regiment 1 to the north and south of the strategically important Moerdijk bridges that crossed the Hollands Diep south of Dordrecht. The paratroops were to seize the bridges while a second wave of 30 Ju52s from KGrzbV.172 dropped the bulk of I. Bataillon of Fallschirmjäger-Regiment 1, in all some 400 paratroops, between Moerdijk and Dordrecht to secure the main road to Rotterdam. At the same time, 12 more Ju52s from KGrzbV.172 were to drop 170 men of the 3. Kompanie of Fallschirmjäger-Regiment 1 to assault and capture both ends of the bridges crossing the Oude Maas at Dordrecht.

In addition to these landings, 53 Ju52s of II./KGzbV.1 would drop 700 paratroops of III. Bataillon of Fallschirmjäger-Regiment 1 on Waalhaven airfield (Landeplatz IV). Once the airfield was secured, 53 Ju52s from III./KGzbV.1 would then start airlifting III.Bataillon IR16, the first of 2,500 reinforcements from Infanterie-Regiment 16.

Co-inciding with the parachute landings at Waalhaven, 50 men of the 11. Kompanie of Fallschirmjäger-Regiment 1 were to be dropped by three Ju52s of II./KGzbV.1 around the Feyenoord football stadium and fight their way through the Rotterdam suburbs to seize the bridges spanning the River Maas at the Noordereiland in the heart of the city. Supporting this objective, 120 troops from the 11. Kompanie of Infanterie-Regiment 16 with engineers from Pionier-Bataillon 22, would directly assault the

bridges from 12 Heinkel He59 floatplanes that were to land on the Nieuwe Maas river right in the middle of the city. This assault group was to prevent demolition of the bridges, establish a bridgehead, and await the arrival of the 11. Kompanie of Fallschirmjäger-Regiment 1.

Widespread German use of airborne assault troops the previous month during Operation 'Weserübung' — the invasion of Denmark and Norway — alerted the Dutch High Command to the likely threat to airfields and other key installations. Consequently, ground defences at airfields throughout the Netherlands had been improved with a mobile force of M-36 light armoured cars being stationed at both Ypenburg and Schiphol. Late as they were, these measures were to prove most effective in countering German intentions when the time came.

Friday, May 10 was not a good day for the German airborne assault in Holland, particularly for the northern group. The men had been badly dispersed when they came in. By the evening more than half were casualties and the Dutch still held the three airfields. The 1,650 or so men still in action had assembled by then into five separate groups (denoted with the symbol ⊙). However operations were better in the south in the Rotterdam area where the paratroops had landed as planned (at locations marked O) and some 250 Ju52s had managed to bring reinforcements into Waalhaven.

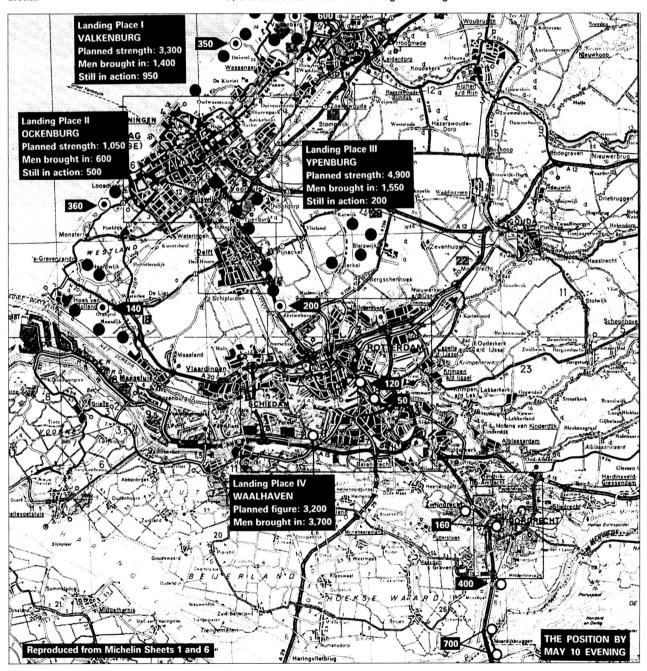

Landing Place I
VALKENBURG
Planned strength: 3,300
Men brought in: 1,400
Still in action: 950

Landing Place II
OCKENBURG
Planned strength: 1,050
Men brought in: 600
Still in action: 500

Landing Place III
YPENBURG
Planned strength: 4,900
Men brought in: 1,550
Still in action: 200

Landing Place IV
WAALHAVEN
Planned figure: 3,200
Men brought in: 3,700

Reproduced from Michelin Sheets 1 and 6

THE POSITION BY MAY 10 EVENING

Airborne landings at Den Haag

Over Den Haag on the morning of May 10, initial parachute drops went ahead as planned between 7.10 and 7.30 a.m. But the close formations of Ju52 transports were badly disrupted by intense AA fire on the way to their targets and, as a consequence, many paratroops dropped far from their designated landing zones.

Only at Valkenburg — Landeplatz I — did plans go relatively smoothly and the airfield was soon secured by the 6. Kompanie of Fallschirmjäger-Regiment 2. However, when the 50 Ju52s carrying the first wave of reinforcements landed around 6 a.m. many were unable to clear the runway as the landing ground was too soft and they quickly bogged down. As a further complication, seven aircraft of KGrzbV.12 arrived from Ypenburg where they had been unable to get down. Very soon the runway at Valkenburg became totally blocked so when the second wave of transports from I./KGzbV.1 arrived at around 10 a.m. there was nowhere for them to land.

Some of them set down on the beaches between Katwijk and Scheveningen, to the immediate north of Den Haag, where most soon became stranded in soft sand up to their axles and unable to take off again. The remainder had no option but to return to Werl with their loads intact. Another attempt to reinforce the troops on the ground at Valkenburg was made late in the afternoon when six transports from KGrzbv 9 arrived. One somehow managed to get down in the chaos at Ockenburg, but the others had to return with their loads to Lippspringe.

Swift to react, Dutch ground forces engaged the German positions at Valkenburg which was soon coming under increasingly heavy artillery fire. Throughout the rest of the day, determined counter-attacks by five battalions of Dutch troops split the occupying German forces into two main groups which were eventually forced to evacuate the airfield. One group of 600 men established a defensive position in the village to the north-east, while another 350 men of the 5. Kompanie of Infanterie-Regiment 47 dug in around Wassenaar, just west of the airfield. Repeated efforts failed to dislodge these pockets but by evening the airfield was back in Dutch hands.

At Ockenburg — Landeplatz II — the initial drop went badly, only about 40 men of 3. Kompanie of Fallschirmjäger-Regiment 2 actually landing on the airfield as planned. Five Ju52s overshot the drop point and

The Dutch air forces performed with great credit and accounted for 60 German aircraft during the campaign. The lumbering Ju52s were easy meat for both flak and fighters, and in this picture a Dutch Fokker G 1A, with its characteristic twin-boom tail, of 1e LVR has been caught by the camera after making a firing pass at a Ju52, just as the paratroops spill from their aircraft. It is a remarkable shot . . . or is it? The Dutch Air Historical Branch now consider that this picture has been faked!

dropped 70 men far to the west over 's-Gravenzande and it took these troops some time to join up with their unit at the airfield. Three more aircraft overshot even further west and off-loaded over Staalduinse Bos, ten kilometres away near the Hook of Holland, and the 40 or so paratroops of this group were contained in woods there for four days.

Despite this, the first wave of 17 Ju52s carrying reinforcements still managed to put down despite some getting stuck in the soft ground. However, the first aircraft of the second wave that landed around 6.45 a.m. crashed, completely blocking the runway. Ockenburg was effectively closed to any further landings and incoming aircraft were forced to put down where they could. Soon the area to the west of the airfield, the beach, and the dunes and meadows around Kijkduin and Ter Heijde, were littered with Ju52s.

Once off-loaded, some struggled to get airborne again, many returning to base carrying the crews of aircraft that had to be aban-

doned. But by the time the third wave of 12 Ju52s arrived at 10.05 a.m. the situation at Ockenburg was clearly impossible and two of them put down on the beaches near Wassenaar, to the north, while the others all headed for Waalhaven, Landeplatz IV.

Dutch artillery pounded Ockenburg throughout the afternoon and by evening Dutch ground forces had retaken the airfield capturing 130 prisoners. The remaining German forces, a few hundred men, fell back on Ockenrode where Generalleutnant von Sponeck had established a defensive position.

The situation at Ypenburg — Landeplatz III — proved even worse and was a complete disaster. The transports had been so badly mauled by AA fire en route that they completely missed their drop points and the paratroops of I. Bataillon (minus 3. Kompanie) of Fallschirmjäger-Regiment 2 were scattered over the surrounding countryside. With the first reinforcements scheduled to land around 6.10 a.m. this allowed no time to secure the landing area.

Two of the Ju 52s which diverted from Ypenburg to Ockenburg overflew The Hague, only to come under intense Dutch AA fire.

Both aircraft were brought down by 164e Batterij Lu.A, one of them crashing in Tweede Adelheidstraat.

As a result, when the first wave of 36 Ju52s carrying reinforcements attempted to land at Ypenburg they were greeted by intense fire from the ground — some coming from the two platoons of light armoured cars recently stationed there. Twelve transports were shot down within ten minutes while others circled above the flames, smoke, and total confusion. They attempted to land where they could; some at Berkel, others at Bleiswijk, seven diverting north to Valkenburg. Most of the remainder attempted landings nearby, either on or alongside the main road between Den Haag and Rotterdam, where they disgorged troops. Very few were able to take off again and were abandoned, leaving KGrzbV.12 with only two serviceable aircraft. The initial drop and first wave of landings at Ypenburg was a failure.

The second wave of 40 Ju52s from KGrzbV.9 arriving at Ypenburg fared little better. It lost several aircraft to heavy ground-fire as they attempted to set down on the airfield while others, desperate to find a landing place, put down on the highway south of Delft. The remainder, a dozen or so aircraft, diverted to Ockenburg, which took them directly over Den Haag where two more were promptly shot down by Dutch AA fire. One, carrying staff officers from the 22. Infanterie-Division, fell in the Tweede Adelheidstraat killing all on board, charred documents recovered from the wreckage revealing detailed plans to capture the Dutch Royal Family.

To complete the mayhem at Ypenburg, a third wave of transports from IV./KGzbV.1 arrived at 10.05 a.m. Few managed to get down, most of them diverting to Waalhaven, while others landed far to the west of the airfield, each side of the Nieuwe Waterweg, on Rozenburg Island and near Maasdijk. The entire fourth wave, brought in by KGrzbV.172 some three hours later, was forced to divert to Waalhaven.

Despite this, German forces still managed to gain control of most the airfield until late in the afternoon when concentrated artillery fire and persistent counter-attacks by Dutch troops eventually forced a withdrawal. Mop-

Tweede Adelheidstraat lay in the Bezuidenhout quarters of The Hague which was completely destroyed by the RAF bombing raid on the adjacent V2 launch site in Haagse Bos wood on March 3, 1945. The street has now been renamed Beatrixlaan and completely redeveloped.

ping-up continued into the evening when the last German position at Johannahoeve, just north of the airfield, was forced to surrender and a further 30 prisoners taken.

So as nightfall approached on May 10, Generalleutnant von Sponeck's command was in ruins. Not one of his three main objectives, the airfields at Valkenburg, Ockenburg, and Ypenburg, was in German hands and of the 9,300 men originally intended, only about 3,800 had been landed. Of these, 1,500 were already prisoners and many others wounded, leaving only about 1,650 still in action around Den Haag in five widely dispersed pockets. His position being considered hopeless, Luftflotte 2 ordered von Sponeck to move south and concentrate what was left of his command along the northern approaches to Rotterdam.

Communication problems delayed this move until the following night and, for the same reason, no contact could be established with troops still isolated at Valkenburg and Wassenaar. But early on May 12, von Sponeck's 360 men reached Wateringen where they commandeered transport, by-passed Delft, and arrived at Overschie, just north of Rotterdam, the next day. Here they joined up with the 200 survivors of the landings at Ypenburg who had moved south the previous day.

All four crew and 13 parachute troops on board were killed, but documents recovered from the blazing wreckage gave Dutch Intelligence an incredible windfall as the aircraft had been carrying members of the staff of 22. Infanterie-Division.

About 3,500 paratroops from the 7. Flieger-Division were to parachute into Vesting Holland, under the command of Generalleutnant Kurt Student, and this picture is reputed to have been taken on the morning of May 10.

Airborne landings between Rotterdam and Moerdijk

No such problems dogged the initial parachute landings at Rotterdam and to the south. The paratroops of Fallschirmjäger-Regiment 1 hit their six drop zones exactly as planned between 6 a.m. and 6.40 a.m.

At Moerdijk 700 men of II. Bataillon of Fallschirmjäger-Regiment 1 dropped north and south of the bridges, rounded up the local Dutch garrison, and captured both road and railway bridges which they found were mined for demolition but had no detonators in place. Further north, midway between Moerdijk and Dordrecht, 400 men of the Stab and of the 1. and 2. Kompanien of Fallschirmjäger-Regiment 1 dropped south-east of 's-Gravendeel and quickly neutralised the Dutch artillery battalion stationed there.

Meanwhile, at Dordrecht, 12 Ju52s dropped 170 men of the 3. Kompanie of Fallschirmjäger-Regiment 1 each side of the bridge; 50 landing on the north bank at Zwijndrecht, another 120 on the opposite bank. They suffered several losses from ground-fire, including the company commander, Oberleutnant Henning von Brandis, who was killed, but successfully stormed the bridge which quickly fell into German hands. The arterial route between Rotterdam and Moerdijk was secured.

Meanwhile at Waalhaven — Landeplatz IV — 700 paratroops of III. Bataillon of Fallschirmjäger-Regiment 1 dropped south and east of the airfield. Some came down in the nearby harbour and drowned, while others dropped onto buildings ablaze as a result of earlier bombing by II./KG4. Despite desperate Dutch resistance, the airfield was soon largely under German control and the first wave of transports from III./KGzbV.1 bringing in reinforcements from III. Bataillon of Infanterie-Regiment 16 began landing shortly before 6 a.m. Dutch AA fire at the airfield had not been entirely neutralised and the Ju52s suffered some losses plus the inevitable damage due to taxi-ing accidents.

By mid-morning, Waalhaven airfield was in German hands and a second sortie by III./KGzbV.1 arrived with additional troops. Heavy shelling by Dutch artillery situated in Kralingse Bos, north of the Maas in Rotterdam, could do little to prevent further landings during the afternoon so, by the end of the day, 3,700 men had been landed. This actually exceeded the figure originally planned as it included troops forced to divert from their landing places at Den Haag.

In central Rotterdam, 50 paratroops of the 11. Kompanie of Fallschirmjäger-Regiment 1 landed near the Feyenoord stadium around 6.30 a.m. as planned. Commandeering a passing tram, they ordered off the startled early-morning commuters and drove the short distance to the Maas bridges where they joined up with the troops who had landed by floatplane a short time earlier.

Twelve Heinkel He59s of Sonderstaffel Schwilden carrying 150 men of the 11. Kompanie of Infanterie-Regiment 16 had taken off from Zwischenhahn Lake and landed on the Maas both sides of the bridges at 6.30 a.m. They achieved total surprise and no shots were fired as the floatplanes taxied to the bridges. Four of them landed downstream and set their troops down at the northern end of the bridges where they quickly seized control.

The other eight landed upstream, some disembarking at Nassau Quay in the Koningshaven, while others landed near the Maas railway station. Calmly off-loading their equipment and inflatable dinghies while passing Dutch civilians looked on, the German troops set about establishing defensive strong points covering the southern approaches to the bridges. Here, a solitary Dutch policeman who attempted to intervene was killed. From Nassau Quay, the troops crossed the Koninginne Bridge to Noordereiland, the island in the middle of the river, and set up positions along its northern bank, before crossing the Willems Bridge to join up with the paratroops landing on the far side.

As they awaited the inevitable response from Dutch forces, the contingent of 50 paratroops arrived by tram from Feyenoord to reinforce the bridgeheads. Defensive positions were quickly established on and around the bridges, and in buildings overlooking the approaches. With the vital bridges in central Rotterdam now firmly in their hands, the small occupying force of less than 200 troops could do little but await developments and arrival of the main German advance.

The northern end of the bridges soon came under attack by a company of Dutch infantry that succeeded in breaking through the thinly-held German position. Also, machine gun positions on the right bank of the Maas were destroyed by grenades thrown by Dutch Marines from the roof of the Maas-Hotel, thus preventing capture of the Beurs railway station and effectively containing the German bridgehead.

By 8 a.m. the German-held positions were coming under close-range shelling and cannon fire from two Dutch boats that arrived from the Hook of Holland but, having expended their ammunition, both vessels withdrew badly damaged. Three more ships ordered to Rotterdam later in the afternoon were attacked by Stukas when near Vlaardingen and the destroyer Van Galen was badly damaged and later sank in Merwede Harbour.

Shortly after 10 a.m. next morning, two Fokker T Vs escorted by three Fokker D XXIs delivered attacks on the bridges but most of their bombs fell harmlessly in the river. This attack was repeated around noon with the same result.

Meantime on the ground, repeated Dutch counter-attacks, although piecemeal and uncoordinated, managed to contain the Germans occupying the bridges at the northern end. There the dwindling force of about 50 men, supplied by air, would continue to hold out for three days until the devastating air raid on the city and the Dutch surrender on May 14.

A flight of three Junkers Ju52s (a Kette) has just disgorged their loads — about 50 men — who are coming down at the northern end of the Moerdijk bridges. The railway bridge can be seen in the background. Though the poor quality of this picture might lend credence to the claim that it was genuinely taken at first light on the morning of May 10, it is more than likely that it was taken during a re-enactment the following month to provide film for propaganda purposes.

Valkenburg (Landeplatz I)

5.35 — 5.40 a.m. Eleven Junkers Ju52s of I./KGrzbV.172 drop 148 paratroops of 6./FJR2 north-west of the airfield and south-east towards the Haagse Schouw. One shot down prior to target, another missing, and one damaged during return flight.

I./KGrzbV.172 Junkers Ju52. Shot down, possibly by Fokker T-V of 2-I-1, en-route to Valkenburg and ditched in the sea south of Katwijk 5.30 a.m. Four crew and 14 men of III. Zug, 6./FJR2 captured. Aircraft a write-off.

I./KGrzbV.172 Junkers Ju52. Failed to return following paratroop drops at Valkenburg 5.35 a.m. Four crew and 13 men of 6./FJR2 missing. Aircraft a write-off.

I./KGrzbV.172 Junkers Ju52. Engine damaged by flak between Utrecht and Soesterberg following paratroop drops at Valkenburg 5.35 a.m. Crashed on landing back at Paderborn. Crew unhurt. Aircraft damaged but repairable.

6.00 a.m. First wave of 53 Junkers Ju52s of KGrzbV.11 arrives to land 783 men of III./IR47. One aircraft shot down before landing, another lands on beach at Katwijk, while a third diverts to Ockenburg. None return to Lippstadt.

KGrzbV.11 Junkers Ju52. Shot down en-route to Valkenburg and crashed and burned out near 'Rode Haan' at Slaperdijk, near Veenendaal 5.50 a.m. One crewman killed and three captured. 15 men of 10./IR47 missing. Aircraft a write-off.

Stab KGrzbV.11 Junkers Ju52. Landed 14 men of 10./IR47 on beach at Katwijk 6.28 a.m. Took-off later but forced to land near the railway crossing west of Gouda during return flight 8.39 a.m. Three crew captured. Aircraft a write-off.

KGrzbV.11 Two Junkers Ju52s. Badly damaged in landings at Valkenburg 6.12 a.m. Unable to take-off, aircraft are later caught on the ground in bombing by Dutch T Vs. Six crewmen missing, 30 men of Infanterie-Regiment 47 off-loaded. Aircraft both damaged but repairable.

KGrzbV.11 48 Junkers Ju52s. Destroyed or badly damaged during landings at Valkenburg 6.12 a.m. Unable to take-off, aircraft are later caught on the ground in bombing by Dutch T Vs. 152 crewmen missing, 753 men of Infanterie-Regiment 47 off-loaded. Aircraft all write-offs.

A total of 168 crewmen were reported missing on this mission, including almost the entire Gruppe command. The majority all later returned unhurt, but the following are believed to have been killed or died of wounds: Uffz Wilhelm Kzrykowski, Obergefr Herbert Schmidt, and Gefr Joseph Moraweck.

7.10 a.m. Seven Junkers Ju52s of KGrzbV.12 diverted from Ypenburg land 88 men of 6. and 8./IR65. Further take-offs or landings at Valkenburg now unlikely.

KGrzbV.12 Seven Junkers Ju52s. Destroyed or badly damaged after landing at Valkenburg 7.10 a.m. Twenty-one crewmen missing including Oberlt Otto Jacob (Gruppenadjutant). Aircraft all write-offs or abandoned.

10.05 a.m. Second wave of 37 Junkers Ju52s of 2, 3, and 4./KGzbV.1 arrives with II./IR47, two aircraft shot down en-route. One machine crashes while attempting to land, rest disperse to find alternate landings on beaches north of Den Haag, Twenty transports fail to land and return to base with troops still aboard. No further landings now possible.

2./KGzbV.1 Junkers Ju52 (6533). Believed shot down by AA fire en-route to target; crashed and burned out near Pottersbrug, between Ochten and IJzendoorn 9.50 a.m. Oberfw K. Rossner badly wounded. Two crew and 15 men of IR47 missing. Aircraft a write-off.

3./KGzbV.1 Junkers Ju52. Believed shot down by AA fire en-route to target, crashed at Kerk-Avezaath, near Zoelen 9.50 a.m. Uffz E. Grosse, two crew and 13 men of 6./IR47 all killed. Aircraft a write-off.

Stab I./KGzbV.1 Junkers Ju52. Crashed and burned out in meadow beyond the Maaldrift, near Leiden-Zuid, while attempting a landing at Valkenburg 10.10 a.m. Uffz O. Häberle, Fw P. Hätzel, Uffz K. Ramus, Gefr J. Simon, and 9 men of Stab II./IR47 killed. Aircraft a write-off.

I./KGzbV.1 Three Junkers Ju52s. Diverted from Valkenburg and landed on beaches between Scheveningen and Wassenaarse Slag 10.15 a.m. Nine crew and 45 men of 6./IR47 off-loaded. Aircraft abandoned.

Operating as 'Gruppe Lt Müller' these men remained in action along with other small pockets of troops in the area.

Of the 430 Ju52s involved in the invasion of Holland on May 10, the Luftwaffe lost upwards of 200 transports. The aircraft were scattered across and around the landing grounds . . . wrecks lay in fields . . .

I./KGzbV.1 Two Junkers Ju52s. Diverted from Valkenburg and landed on beaches between Scheveningen and Wassenaarse Slag 10.15 a.m. Six crew and 30 men of 7./IR47 off-loaded. Aircraft both abandoned.

Operating as 'Gruppe Lt Jennefeld' this group also remained in action.

I./KGzbV.1 Six Junkers Ju52s. Diverted from Valkenburg and landed on beaches north of the Wassenaarse Slag, north of Den Haag 10.25 a.m. Fifteen crew and 90 men of 5./IR47 off-loaded. Five aircraft abandoned.

One machine managed to take-off again at 12.35 p.m. and returned to Werl. The troops, operating as 'Gruppe Lt Erdmann', remained in action.

I./KGzbV.1 Junkers Ju52. Diverted from Valkenburg and landed on beach north of the Wassenaarse Slag, north of Den Haag 10.25 a.m. Three crew and 9 men of Nachrichtenzug Stab II./IR47 off-loaded. Aircraft abandoned.

This signals unit under Feldwebel Polyka continued to support operations by pockets of troops in the area.

I./KGzbV.1 Four Junkers Ju52s. Diverted from Valkenburg and landed on beaches south of Katwijk 10.35 a.m. Twelve crewmen, 30 men of 5./IR47 and 32 men of 6./IR47 off-loaded. Aircraft all abandoned.

These troops, together with 60 or more in the vicinity, stayed in action under overall command of Oberlt Voigt.

11.30 p.m. Third wave of landings by 53 Junkers Ju52s of KGrzbV.11 cancelled due to lack of aircraft, unit having suffered 100 per cent losses in landings at 6.00 a.m.

12.00 p.m. Three Fokker C Xs of 1-I-1 bomb the airfield and strafe the beaches at Katwijk damaging several Ju52s. These are followed by five Fokker D XXIs of 1-V-2 who also strafe the beaches causing additional damage and casualties among the German transports scattered there.

5.22 p.m. Led by Hptmn Blechschmidt, 6 Junkers Ju52s of KGrzbV.9 carrying 55 men of II./AR22 make final attempt to land but unable to do so. Five are forced to return to Lippspringe with troops still on board.

2./KGrzbV.9 Junkers Ju52. Unable to land at Valkenburg forced-landed on beach west of Ockenburg 5.40 p.m. Three crew and 9 men of Stab II./AR22 off-loaded. Aircraft abandoned.

These troops joined others in action with 'Gruppe Thoma' in the woods around Ockenrode.

7.05 p.m. During a solo reconnaissance Fokker C V of III-2 (2e Lt van de Weert and Kapt van Rooy) strafes the beaches at Katwijk further damaging 2 Ju52s.

Ockenburg (Landeplatz II)

5.35 — 6.00 a.m. Thirteen Junkers Ju52s of IV./KGzbV.1 miss their drop point and deposit 148 men of 3./FJR2 south-west of the airfield, north of the Staalduinse Bos, between 's-Gravenzande and Naaldwijk. One aircraft shot down prior to target.

IV./KGzbV.1 Junkers Ju52. Shot down by AA fire en-route to Ockenburg and crashed in the Woudse Polder, west of Delft 5.30 a.m. Possibly also that attacked by Douglas DB8A of 3-V-2 (Sgt J. J. de Bruijn and 1e Lt H. F. H. van Boekhout). Three crewmen and 14 paratroops of 3./FJR2 missing. Aircraft a write-off.

6.00 — 6.05 a.m. First wave of 17 Junkers Ju52s of KGrzbV.12 lands 221 men of Stab II./IR65 and 5./IR65. Seven transports believed write-offs, 2 badly damaged, and 7 more repairable.

Stab I./KGrzbV.12 Four Junkers Ju52s. Aircraft shot down or damaged by flak and unable to take-off, many later destroyed or badly damaged on the ground. Twelve crewmen missing. Uffz Friedrich Ladage, Uffz Rudolf Narat. Uffz Carl Schmitz killed. Oberlt Walter Lang, Uffz Karl Bitznat and Uffz Anton Schneider captured wounded. Aircraft abandoned.

3./KGrzbV.12 Twelve Junkers Ju52s. Aircraft shot down or damaged by flak and unable to take-off, many later destroyed or badly damaged on the ground. Thirty-six crewmen missing. Aircraft all abandoned.

The following crewmen were among those lost but individual aircraft allocation is not known: Fw Otto Halsmayr and Uffz Helmuth Winkler killed. Hptmn Gerhard Süssmann (Staffelkapitän), Oberfw Willi Schmidt, and Uffz Walter Böhner all died of wounds. Fw Ferdinand Molls captured unhurt. Oberfw Erich Waschke, Uffz Richard Lemke, Uffz Hugo Martin and Uffz Paul Quasdorf wounded.

3./KGrzbV.12 Junkers Ju52. Believed diverted from Ockenberg damaged by flak and forced-landed between Nijkampsweg and Lageweg at Klein Dochteren, near Lochem 6.10 a.m. Fw Willi Ulrich killed, rest of crew believed unhurt. Aircraft repairable.

5.50 — 6.20 a.m. A Junkers Ju52 of KGrzbV.11 intended for Valkenburg lands and is destroyed in bombing attacks by four Dutch Fokker T Vs of 2-I-1 who lose one machine to German fighters.

KGrzbV.11 Junkers Ju52. Aircraft diverted from Valkenburg caught on the ground and wrecked in bombing by Fokker T Vs 6.00 a.m. Three crew and 15 men of 10./IR47 missing. Aircraft a write-off.

6.45 a.m. Second wave of 15 Junkers Ju52s of I./KGrzbV.9 arrives carrying troops of I. and II. Zug Radf.Schw.2./A22. One aircraft shot down prior to landing.

1./KGrzbV.9 Junkers Ju52. Badly damaged by ground fire on approach to Ockenburg and forced-landed north of 'Bouwlust', south-west of the Houtweg, near Loosduinen 6.45 a.m. Three crew and 5 men of Stab 2./A22 captured. Aircraft a write-off.

1./KGrzbV.9 Junkers Ju52. Undercarriage wrecked on landing at Ockenburg under heavy ground fire 6.50 a.m. Later destroyed by artillery fire and bombing by Dutch aircraft. Five men of Stab Rdf.Schw. 2./A22 off-loaded. Aircraft a write-off.

This aircrew returned to Lippspringe aboard another aircraft.

1./KGrzbV.9 Four Junkers Ju52s. Landed at Ockenburg and 40 men of I. Zug Rdf.Schw. 2./A22 off-loaded under heavy ground fire 6.50 a.m. No crew casualties. Aircraft repairable.

These aircraft took-off between 9.14 a.m. and 9.35 a.m. for return to Lippspringe carrying 12 crewmen of aircraft abandoned at Ockenburg.

1./KGrzbV.9 Junkers Ju52. Landed at Ockenburg and 10 men of I. Zug Rdf.Schw. 2./A22 off-loaded 6.50 a.m. Despite damage by heavy ground fire, took-off again but forced to make an emergency landing at Wissel, east of Kleve, during return flight. No crew casualties. Aircraft damaged but repairable.

This aircraft carried 4 crewmen from other aircraft abandoned at Ockenburg.

1./KGrzbV.9 Junkers Ju52. Landed at Ockenburg and 9 men of I. Zug Rdf.Schw. 2./A22 off-loaded under heavy ground fire 6.50 a.m. Later destroyed in bombing by Dutch aircraft and artillery fire. No crew casualties. Aircraft a write-off.

This crew returned to Lippspringe aboard another aircraft.

1./KGrzbV.9 Junkers Ju52. Unable to land at Ockenburg, diverted and failed to return 6.50 a.m. Obergefr E. Richter killed, two crew and 10 men of 2./A22 missing. Aircraft a write-off.

1./KGrzbV.9 Three Junkers Ju52s. Damaged by ground fire and wrecked on landing outside western perimeter of Ockenburg 6.55 a.m. Later destroyed in bombing by Dutch aircraft. Fw R. Hoffmeister killed. Oberfw P. Brand, Oberfw F. Elgass, Oberfw F. Zigull, Fw W. Kaufhold, Fw H. Meister, Fw H. Stein, Fw J. Weberpals, Uffz H. Götz, and Uffz W. Seidenglanz wounded. Nine men of Stab 2./A22 and 20 men of II. Zug 2./A22 missing. Aircraft all write-offs.

1./KGrzbV.9 Three Junkers Ju52s. Unable to land at Ockenburg, forced-landed on beaches south of the Badhotel Kijkduin 6.55 a.m. Nine crew and 28 men of II. Zug 2./A22 missing. Aircraft abandoned.

Men from these aircraft stranded at Kijkduin took refuge in woods around Ockenrode where, operating as 'Gruppe Pollay', they remained in action until the Dutch surrender.

10.06 a.m. Third wave of 12 Junkers Ju52s of IV./KGzbV.1 arrive carrying 180 men of 7./IR65 but, unable to get down, most divert to land at Waalhaven. No further landings now possible.

IV./KGzbV.1 Two Junkers Ju52s (6508, 6607). Diverted from Ockenburg and tried landing at Valkenburg but fuel tanks and tyres shot through by ground fire. Attempted forced-landings on beach south of the Wassenaarse Slag, north of Scheveningen, 10.15 a.m. Six crew and 30 men of 7./IR65 missing. Aircraft both write-offs.

11.49 p.m. Planned landings by 13 Junkers Ju52s of KGrzbV.12 carrying Stab AR22 are cancelled due to lack of aircraft, unit having suffered 96 per cent losses 6.04 a.m.

1.29 p.m. Planned landings by 12 Junkers Ju52s of KGrzbV.9 carrying 13./IR65 cancelled due to lack of aircraft, unit having suffered 74 per cent losses 6.45 a.m.

5.30 p.m. Blenheims of No.110 Squadron, escorted by Blenheim IFs of No.604 Squadron, bomb and strafe the beaches at Kijkduin where four Junkers Ju52s are reported destroyed. One of the escorts is lost to ground fire.

. . . and alongside roads. This is the main Rotterdam highway . . .

Ypenburg (Landeplatz III)

5.35 — 6.00 a.m. Forty Junkers Ju52s of IV./KGzbV.1 drop paratroops of I./FJR2 on Ypenburg. One aircraft is shot down prior to target, two crash on landing back at Loddenheide where 18 more aircraft, all damaged by ground fire, are declared unserviceable on return.

13./KGzbV.1 Junkers Ju52. Shot down by AA fire (10e Bt.Lu.A) en-route to Ypenburg and crashed near Rhenen 5.20 a.m. Uffz O. Griesshaber killed. Two crewmen and 14 paratroops of 4./FJR2 missing. Aircraft a write-off.

13./KGzbV.1 Junkers Ju52 (6453). Shot down by AA fire (76e Bt.Lu.A) south of Rijswijk after drops over Ypenburg and crashed in the Schaapweipolder 5.40 a.m. Crew believed Uffz W. Schmaus, Obergefr W. Gropp, Gefr J. Deichmann, and Gefr K. Schaschek all killed. Aircraft a write-off.

13./KGzbV.1 Junkers Ju52 (6289). Shot down by AA fire after drops over Ypenburg and crashed near the 'Zuiderpark' on the Leiweg in Escamppolder 5.40 a.m. Fw E. Lorenz, Fw H. Krampitz, and Uffz K. H. Dupont killed. Aircraft a write-off.

14./KGzbV.1 Junkers Ju52. Possibly that hit by ground fire over Delft which crash-landed south-east of Den Hoorn 5.40 a.m. Uffz J. Schneider and Uffz W. Meissner captured wounded, admitted to hospital in Voorburg. Third crewman believed unhurt. Aircraft a write-off.

14./KGzbV.1 Junkers Ju52. Hit by ground fire near Den Haag and crashed near Zaltbommel during return flight Uffz O. Dieren badly wounded, died next day. Uffz H. Karow, Gefr W. Hüttenrauch, and Gefr E. Gläser baled out and captured. Aircraft a write-off.

Uffz Heinz Floer and Uffz Rolf Lehnert were among those killed. Hptmn Herbert Krause (Staffelkapitän), Fw Werner Tornow, and Uffz Wilhelm Busch were captured wounded.

14./KGzbV.1 Two Junkers Ju52s (5259). Damaged by AA fire between Utrecht and Soesterberg during return flight. Crashed on landing back at Münster-Loddenheide. Uffz M. Rolle and Uffz H. Thiel both badly wounded, admitted to hospital. Aircraft both damaged but repairable.

6.11 — 6.20 a.m. First wave of 36 Junkers Ju52s of KGrzbV.12 arrive carrying 429 men of IR65. Thirteen aircraft attempt to land and are destroyed by airfield defences, remainder divert elsewhere, seven reaching Valkenburg.

Stab I./KGrzbV.12 Junkers Ju52. Destroyed by airfield defences while attempting to land at Ypenburg 6.11 a.m. Hptmn Hans-Eberhard Fr von Hornstein *(Gruppenkommandeur)*, Fw W. Bludau and Uffz Leo Welticke captured. Eleven men of Nachrichtungszug IR65 missing. Aircraft G6+DB a write-off.

1./KGrzbV.12 Two Junkers Ju52s. Destroyed by airfield defences while attempting to land at Ypenburg 6.11 a.m. Six crew and 24 men of Stab Inf.Rgt.65 killed. Aircraft both write-offs.

1./KGrzbV.12 Six Junkers Ju52s. Destroyed by airfield defences while attempting to land at Ypenburg 6.18 a.m. Eighteen crew and 77 men of 6./IR65 killed. Aircraft all write-offs.

1./KGrzbV.12 Three Junkers Ju52s. Destroyed by airfield defences while attempting to land at Ypenburg 6.20 a.m. Nine crew and 43 men of 6./IR65 missing. Aircraft all write-offs.

2./KGrzbV.12 Junkers Ju52. Diverted from Ypenburg and forced-landed on eastern side of the Veesteeg, south of Beneden-Leeuwen 7.10 a.m. Fw W. Ochs badly wounded, died May 16. Oberlt G. Ehrhardt, two crew, and 7 men of 8./IR65 captured unhurt. Aircraft fired by crew.

2./KGrzbV.12 Three Junkers Ju52s. Diverted from Ypenburg and believed forced-landed in meadows east of the Delft — Rotterdam highway near Oude Leede, between Karitaat Molensloot and Overslag Molensloot, 7.02 a.m. Nine crew and 32 men of 8./IR65 missing. Aircraft abandoned.

2./KGrzbV.12 Junkers Ju52. Diverted from Ypenburg and damaged by ground fire south-west of Delft; possibly that forced-landed west of Abtswoude 7.10 a.m. Three crew and 11 men of 8./IR65 missing. Aircraft abandoned.

The unit lost the following aircrew but individual aircraft allocation has not been determined: Fw Heinrich Randelhoft, Uffz Walter Berner, and Uffz Joseph Ruh killed. Uffz August Hohlweg, Uffz Hans Hübner, Uffz Oskar Steffen, and Gefr Hans Pahl wounded. Fw F. Neumann, Uffz Heinz Fiedler and Uffz Kurt Strugalla captured unhurt.

4./KGrzbV.12 Junkers Ju52. Destroyed by airfield defences on landing at Ypenburg 6.20 a.m. Fw E. Welcher killed. Fw W. Heidenreich broken left leg, captured and admitted to hospital in Voorburg. Uffz A. Mertins captured wounded. Lt H. Meyer captured unhurt. Fifteen men of 6./IR65 killed or died of wounds. Aircraft G6+IM a write-off.

4./KGrzbV.12 Junkers Ju52. Hit by flak north-west Delft and forced-landed in the Plaspoelpolder, east of Spieringwetering, 6.35 a.m. Three crew and 10 men of Nachrichtungszug IR65 captured. Aircraft a write-off.

4./KGrzbV.12 Junkers Ju52. Shot down by ground fire north of Delft and crashed and burned out in the Plaspoelpolder, between the railway line to 's-Gravenhage and the Lange Kleiweg 6.36 a.m. Three crew and 11 men of Nachrichtungszug IR65 missing. Aircraft a write-off.

4./KGrzbV.12 Two Junkers Ju52s. Diverted from Ypenburg and landed in Noordpolder and the Overbuurtse Polder, north-west of Bleiswijk 6.50 a.m. Six crewmen later picked up by aircraft of KGzbV.9 and returned unhurt. Twenty-two men of 8./IR65 captured. Aircraft both abandoned.

4./KGrzbV.12 Junkers Ju52 (6377). Diverted from Ypenburg and forced-landed by the Korfwetering, in Bergboezem, south-west of Berkel station 6.55 a.m. Uffz H. Fösig, Uffz W. Matzel, and Uffz H. Pfortner killed. Eight men of Stab 8./IR65 missing. Aircraft a write-off.
Serial number believed correct as shown.

4./KGrzbV.12 Four Junkers Ju52s. Diverted from Ypenburg and forced-landed by the Delft — Rotterdam highway near the Karitaat Molensloot, and south of Ruivense bridge 7.05 a.m. Forty-four men of 8./IR65 off-loaded. Two aircraft abandoned.
Two of these aircraft later managed to take-off and returned to base with the crews. They were the sole survivors of 53 aircraft that left Störmede that morning.

4./KGrzbV.12 Two Junkers Ju52s. Diverted from Ypenburg and forced-landed in meadows between Karitaat Molensloot and Ruivense Molensloot, west of the road between Vliet and the Delft — Rotterdam highway 7.05 a.m. Uffz J. Altinger, Uffz W. Wolff, four crew and 22 men of 8./IR65 captured. Aircraft abandoned.

6.45 a.m. Second wave of 40 Junkers Ju52s of I./KGrzbV.9 arrives carrying 509 men, two aircraft of 4. Staffel having failed to start. Three attempt to land, two others putting down just outside the airfield. Remainder disperse to land where they can, many on or around the main highway between Delft and Rotterdam. One 4. Staffel machine, unable to land, returns with its load.

Stab I./KGrzbV.9 Junkers Ju52. Set alight by heavy ground fire on landing at Ypenburg 7.14 a.m. Uffz R. Ziegler unhurt, captured next day. Two crew and 16 men of Aufklärungszug IR65 missing. Aircraft 9P+EB a write-off.

Stab I./KGrzbV.9 Junkers Ju52. Destroyed by heavy ground fire on landing at Ypenburg 7.14 a.m. Uffz A. Mumb wounded. Two crew and 15 men of Aufklärungszug IR65 missing. Aircraft 9P+BB a write-off.

Stab I./KGrzbV.9 Junkers Ju52. Diverted from Ypenburg and badly damaged by ground fire, forced-landed on beaches near Terheyde 7.30 a.m. Uffz W. Laub (of 2./KGrzbV.9) killed by flak. Lt H. Einde and Uffz H. Werner unhurt. 13 men of 1. Zug 3./Pi.Btl.22 off-loaded. Aircraft 9P+HK abandoned.
This 2. Staffel machine was flying in the second Kette of the Stabschwarm on this mission.

Stab I./KGrzbV.9 Two Junkers Ju52s. Diverted from Ypenburg and badly damaged by ground fire, forced-landed on beaches near Terheyde 7.30 a.m. Oberlt Mersmann *(Stabsstaffelkapitän)*, Fw Glogner, Fw H. Griebsch, Uffz K-H. Knorr, Uffz Albrecht, and Gefr Bock unhurt. Twenty-five men of 1. Zug 3./Pi.Btl.22 off-loaded. Aircraft 9P+CB and another abandoned.

The crews of these aircraft joined ground troops and remained in action meeting the German advance at Overschie on May 14.

Stab I./KGrzbV.9 Junkers Ju52. Diverted from Ypenburg and believed forced-landed on beach between Kijkduin and Monster 7.30 a.m. Three crew and 12 men of Stab KGrzbV.9 landed. Aircraft repairable.

This aircraft, supposedly held in reserve until the landing place was secure, carried a landing control party led by Oberlt Knaach. It is believed to have taken off again later on a burst tyre and returned to Lippspringe carrying Hptmn Külbel, the acting Gruppen-kommandeur.

Stab I./KGrzbV.9 Junkers Ju52. Diverted from Ypenburg and forced-landed alongside the highway between Delft and Rotterdam, near the Ackersdijkseweg 7.52 a.m. Lt Scheels, two crewmen, and 16 men of 3./Fl.Kp.Ln.Regt.1 missing. Aircraft DF+ID abandoned.

This aircraft carried signals equipment and was intended to function as ground W/T station for the group. It formed part of the Stabschwarm of KGrzbV.9 on this mission.

Stab I./KGrzbV.9 Junkers Ju52. Diverted from Ypenburg under intense AA fire and crashed by the main highway from Rotterdam south of Delft 7.52 a.m. Fw H. Scharff wounded. Oberfw Seifert, Fw H. Jende, and 13 men of 1. Zug 3./Pi.Btl.22 missing. Aircraft 9P+DB a write-off.

2./KGrzbV.9 Junkers Ju52. Set alight by heavy ground fire on landing at Ypenburg 7.14 a.m. Uffz K. Jankowski killed. Uffz H. von zur Mühlen captured wounded in both legs, Uffz H. Seidel captured burned on left cheek and admitted to St Antoniushove hospital in Voorburg. Sixteen men of 2./Na.22 missing. Aircraft a write-off.

2./KGrzbV.9 Junkers Ju52. Set alight by heavy ground fire on landing at Ypenburg 7.14 a.m. Uffz H. Bosch killed in ground fighting. Uffz H. Schmitz captured wounded in left shoulder and admitted to St Antoniushove hospital in Voorburg. Uffz K. Umbeer captured unhurt. Sixteen men of 2./Na.22 missing. Aircraft a write-off.

2./KGrzbV.9 Junkers Ju52. Set alight by heavy ground fire while taxying at Ypenburg 7.14 a.m. Stabsfw H. Walden badly wounded, died 16 May. Oberfw W. Lieber and Fw W. Horter captured. Sixteen men of 2./Na.22 missing. Aircraft a write-off.

. . . and on the beaches . . . but the problem is that most cannot be identified as code-letters are either non-existant in German records or not visible in the photographs, most of which were snapshots taken by individual German soldiers.

2./KGrzbV.9 Junkers Ju52. Hit by ground fire and forced-landed at Sion, near Kitswoning in the Broekpolder, north-west of Delft 7.15 a.m. Three crew and 16 men of 2./Na.22 missing. Aircraft abandoned.

Survivors from this aircraft joined together with other troops who established a defensive position in a pumping station near the Woudse Polder.

2./KGrzbV.9 Junkers Ju52. Touched down at Ypenburg but under heavy ground fire took-off and landed on the highway to Den Haag, 2 km north of Delft 7.46 a.m. Seven men of Stab Na.22 off-loaded. Oberlt H. Ellerbrock *(Staffelkapitän)* wounded. Lt A.Wolff and one crewman unhurt. Aircraft 9P+AK undamaged.

This machine took-off 10 minutes later returning to Lippspringe carrying four passengers. August Wolff elected to remain with ground troops and met up with advancing German forces near Overschie on May 15.

2./KGrzbV.9 Two Junkers Ju52s. Diverted from Ypenburg and forced-landed on the main road to Rotterdam, south of Delft 7.52 a.m. Eighteen men of Stab Na.22 off-loaded. Aircraft undamaged.

These aircraft both managed to take-off again between 9.11 and 9.20 a.m. and returned to Lippspringe carrying the crews of other abandoned aircraft.

2./KGrzbV.9 Two Junkers Ju52s. Diverted from Ypenburg and forced-landed by the main road to Rotterdam, south of Delft 7.52 a.m. Thirty-two men of 2./Na.22 off-loaded. Aircraft abandoned.

Both these crews returned to Lippspringe aboard other aircraft.

2./KGrzbV.9 Junkers Ju52. Diverted from Ypenburg and damaged by ground fire. Crashed by electrical pumping station near Katwijk, north-east of Pijnacker 7.30 a.m. Oberfw M. Körner captured wounded in right leg, admitted to St Antoniushove hospital in Voorburg. Two other crewmen and 16 men of 2./Na.22 all captured. Aircraft a write-off.

In addition to those shown, 2./KGrzbV.9 reported the following casualties on this sortie:

Oberlt A. Lindloff, Fw O. d'Agostin, Fw G. Kornprobst, Uffz H. Büttner, Uffz H. Deisinger, Uffz F. Gratzel, Uffz M. Hengst, Uffz O. Jerzembeck, Uffz H. Liebscher, Uffz E. Podelleck, Uffz H. Moseler, Uffz H. Rateischak, and Uffz R. Schade captured. Uffz S. Bührig, Uffz E. Krause, and Gefr H. Hinz wounded.

3./KGrzbV.9 Junkers Ju52. Aircraft diverted from Ypenburg wrecked hitting a ditch while landing on beach at Terheyde 7.35 a.m. Oberlt L. Drengk *(Staffelkapitän)*, Lt H. Hahne and Oberfw H. Schlick unhurt. Twelve men of Feldgendarmerietrupp 22 landed. Aircraft 9P+AL a write-off.

This crew switched to the 9P+DL for the return flight.

We are indebted to Johan Schuurman for providing the pot-pourri reproduced on these pages from his collection.

3./KGrzbV.9 Junkers Ju52. Aircraft diverted from Ypenburg ripped off tail wheel on landing on beach at Terheyde 7.35 a.m. Oberfw F. Bauer, Fw M. Armbrust, and Uffz F. Seib unhurt. Fifteen men of Stab 22. Inf.Div. off-loaded. Aircraft 9P+DL repairable — later a write-off.

Despite heavy ground fire, this aircraft managed to take-off again at 8.32 a.m. carrying 5 crewmen of 3./KGrzbV.9 and a wounded Fallschirmjäger. Attacked by five Fokker D XXIs that put two engines out of action, it was finally shot down by 2e Lt Plesman of 2e JaVa and crashed at Stolwijk, south of Gouda, at 8.50 a.m. Among crewmen captured, Erich Rühl and Gustav Hensel were both admitted to the Van Iterson Ziekenhuizen in Gouda where Hensel died on May 13. Leo Drengk and Friedrich Bauer, both injured, were held in Fort Nieuwersluis at IJmuiden before transport to England aboard SS Protius on May 13/14.

3./KGrzbV.9 Junkers Ju52. Aircraft diverted from Ypenburg landed in meadows between Ockenburg and Ockenrode ripping off tail wheel and with starboard tyre shot through 7.42 a.m. Fw A. Mayer, Fw Radke, and Uffz J. Wagner unhurt. Gen.Lt Sponeck and 14 men of Stab 22. Inf.Div. off-loaded. Aircraft 9P+BL repairable.

Taking the tail wheel from the wreck of 9P+AL this aircraft taxied onto the nearby beach and took-off again at 12.00 p.m. carrying 6 passengers including 2 wounded. It landed back at Lippspringe out of fuel — the only 3. Staffel aircraft to return.

3./KGrzbV.9 Junkers Ju52. Diverted from Ypenburg and crashed into a drainage ditch landing between Ockenburg and Ockenrode 7.42 a.m. Fw E. Rühl slightly wounded by flak and Uffz G. Hensel wounded in leg. Fifteen men of Stab 22. Inf.Div. off-loaded. Aircraft abandoned.

The crew of this aircraft switched to 9P+DL for the return flight to Lippspringe.

3./KGrzbV.9 Three Junkers Ju52s. Diverted from Ypenburg and wrecked on landing at Ockenburg 7.42 a.m. Thirty-three men of Krad-Meldezug 22 missing. Aircraft abandoned.

One of these aircraft was subsequently used as an emergency field hospital. All three crews returned to Lippspringe aboard aircraft of 1./KGrzbV.9.

3./KGrzbV.9 Three Junkers Ju52s. Diverted from Ypenburg and forced-landed on and around the main road to Rotterdam, south of Delft 7.52 a.m. Lt R. Schmidt, 8 other crewmen and 44 men of Stab 22. Inf.Div. off-loaded. Aircraft abandoned.

This crew joined ground troops later moving south towards Overschie where Reinhard Schmidt was killed in ground fighting on May 13.

Badly damaged machines which could be salvaged were dismantled and transported back to Germany for repair. Minor repairs were effected in captured Dutch workshops.

3./KGrzbV.9 Junkers Ju52. Diverted from Ypenburg and shot down by AA fire (164e Bt.Lu.A) over Den Haag 7.15 a.m. Crashed and burned out in Tweede Adelheidstraat. Four crew and 13 men of Stab 22. Inf.Div. killed. Aircraft a write-off.

Documents detailing German attack plans were recovered from the wreckage of this aircraft.

3./KGrzbV.9 Junkers Ju52. Diverted from Ypenburg and shot down by AA fire (164e Bt.Lu.A) over Den Haag. Crashed and burned out by the Boslaan, in the Haagse Bos 7.35 a.m. Three crew and 15 men of Stab 22. Inf.Div. killed. Aircraft a write-off.

In addition to those shown, 3./KGrzbV.9 reported the following casualties on this sortie: Lt H. Noever, Oberfw K. Winkler, Fw E. Oellerking, Uffz E. Heuvelmann, Uffz E. Schmidt, and Obergefr E. Blietschau captured. Fw W. Muschert, Uffz E. Dubois de Luchat, and Uffz E. Schmidt wounded.

4./KGrzbV.9 Junkers Ju52. Damaged by flak and forced-landed east of Ypenburg, between Postenkade and Goo-Wetering 7.02 a.m. Fw M. Kaiss, Uffz K-H. Frensch, and another crewman captured May 12 along with 11 men of 13./IR47. Aircraft 9P+GM a write-off.

4./KGrzbV.9 Junkers Ju52. Forced-landed east of Ypenburg, near the Molentocht 7.02 a.m. Fw H. Hesse, Uffz F. Jacobi, Obergefr W. Hasselkus, and 11 men of 13./IR47 captured. Aircraft a write-off.

4./KGrzbV.9 Three Junkers Ju52s. Diverted from Ypenburg and landed in the Noordpolder, north-west of Bleiswijk 7.05 a.m. Nine men of Stab 13./IR47 and 22 men of 13./IR47 later captured. Aircraft undamaged.

All three transports took-off again and returned to Lippspringe with their crews.

4./KGrzbV.9 Junkers Ju52. Diverted from Ypenburg and forced-landed by the main road to Rotterdam, south of Delft 7.52 a.m. Thirteen men of Nachrichtenzug 13./IR47 off-loaded. Aircraft abandoned.

This crew returned to Lippspringe aboard another aircraft.

4./KGrzbV.9 Three Junkers Ju52s. Diverted from Ypenburg and forced-landed on and around the main road to Rotterdam, south of Delft 7.52 a.m. Nine crewmen and 32 men of 13./IR47 off-loaded. Aircraft repairable.

These aircraft managed to take-off again between 3.04 and 5.20 p.m. and returned to base carrying wounded troops and crewmen including pilot, Uffz E. Jobst.

10.06 a.m. Third wave of 26 Junkers Ju52s of IV./KGzbV.1 arrives carrying IR65, one aircraft having been shot down en-route. Unable to land they divert elsewhere, some eventually reaching Waalhaven. No further take-offs or landings at Ypenburg now possible.

The following aircraft are those that failed to return but crash locations are not established: 6135, 6220, 6243, 6248, 6260, 6393, 6419 and 6439.

One can just make out the code on this wreck — 9P+KL denotes that it was on the strength of the 3rd Staffel of Kampfgruppe zbV.9 but unfortunately this particular aircraft is not listed in the Luftwaffe Quartermaster General returns.

13./KGzbV.1 Junkers Ju52 (6513). Believed damaged by AA fire en-route to Ypenburg and belly-landed on the Houtse Steeg at Den Hout, north-east ot Oosterhout 10.30 a.m. Oberlt E. Zechlin *(Staffelkapitän)* captured wounded, Fw M. Lücke, and Fw R. Bratherig captured unhurt. Seven men of 2./IR65 also captured after heavy exchange of fire with Dutch troops. Aircraft 1Z+KX fired by crew.

15./KGzbV.1 Junkers Ju52 (6495). Unable to land at Ypenburg and hit by AA fire near Zaltbommel during return flight. Forced-landed near Afferden 10.33 a.m. Oberlt K. Lastig *(Staffelkapitän)* baled out landing in the Waal/Maas confluence and captured unhurt. Uffz G. Orschel killed. Fw A. Ridder and Uffz R. Breit captured with 12 troops of IR65. Aircraft 1Z+AZ a write-off.

IV./KGzbV.1 Junkers Ju52. Diverted from Ypenburg and tried to land at Ockenburg but shot down and crash-landed near Monster 10.40 a.m. Four crew and 8 men of Stab I./IR65 missing. Aircraft a write-off.

IV./KGzbV.1 Junkers Ju52. Diverted from Ypenburg and forced-landed on the highway south of Delft 10.46 a.m. Three crew and 15 men of 3./IR65 missing. Aircraft a write-off.

IV./KGzbV.1 Junkers Ju52. Diverted from Ypenburg tried Ockenburg but unable to land. Circled Hilwoning under heavy ground fire and finally landed near Rozenburg 10.48 a.m. Twelve men of 1. Kabeltrupp NA22 off-loaded but later captured and taken to Hook of Holland. Aircraft undamaged.
This aircraft took-off again almost immediately and returned to Loddenheide.

IV./KGzbV.1 Junkers Ju52. Diverted from Ypenburg tried Ockenburg but unable to land. Headed for Staalduinse Bos but hit by heavy ground fire, crashed and burned out near Hilwoning, Hook of Holland 11.00 a.m. Two killed, three crew, and 12 men of 1. Kabeltrupp NA22 captured. Aircraft a write-off.

IV./KGzbV.1 Two Junkers Ju52s. Diverted from Ypenburg and forced-landed in Nieuwlandse Polder between the railway line from Hook of Holland to Maassluis and the Nieuwe Oranjekanaal 12.05 p.m. Thirty men of 2./IR65 off-loaded. Aircraft undamaged.
These two aircraft took-off again almost immediately and returned to Loddenheide.

Stab IV./KGzbV.1 Two Junkers Ju52s. Diverted from Ypenburg and landed near Afgedamde Scheur on Rozenburg island, in the Bankpolder 12.09 p.m. Three crew and 24 men of Stab and 2./IR65 later captured and taken to Hook of Holland. One aircraft abandoned.
One of these aircraft took-off again at 12.52 p.m. and returned to Loddenheide carrying the badly wounded Uffz H. Breitscheidel who later died.

IV./KGzbV.1 Two Junkers Ju52s. Diverted from Ypenburg and forced-landed in Nieuwlandse Polder close to two other aircraft 12.05 p.m. Thirty men of 2./IR65 off-loaded. Aircraft undamaged.
These two aircraft also managed to take-off again, one almost immediately and the other about an hour later, both returning to Loddenheide.

IV./KGzbV.1 Junkers Ju52 (1327). Diverted from Ypenburg and taxied into a dyke after landing near Maashaven 12.12 p.m. Three crew and 15 men of 2./IR65 missing. Aircraft damaged but repairable — abandoned.

IV./KGzbV.1 Junkers Ju52. Diverted from Ypenburg and landed in 'De Lange Bonnen' Polder, south of Staalduinse Bos 12.30 p.m. Three crew and 14 men of 3./IR65 unhurt, later captured. Aircraft abandoned.

IV./KGzbV.1 Junkers Ju52. Diverted from Ypenburg and landed in 'De Lange Bonnen' Polder, south of Staalduinse Bos 12.30 p.m. Three crew and 15 men of 3./IR65 unhurt. Aircraft abandoned.
Troops from the two aircraft above, along with 60 men who landed in the Nieuwlandse Polder earlier, joined forces and operating as 'Gruppe Martin' remained in action.

11.49 p.m. Plans for fourth wave of 51 aircraft from KGrzbV.12 to air-lift 2./Fla.52 and 4./IR65 are shelved due to lack of aircraft, the unit having suffered 96 per cent losses earlier. Over an hour later, these troops arrive in 43 Junkers Ju52s hurriedly drawn from Stab KGzbV.2 and I./KGrzbV.172 but, unable to land, most must divert to Waalhaven.

1./KGrzbV.172 Junkers Ju52. Diverted from Ypenburg and forced-landed alongside the main road to Rotterdam, south of Delft 1.12 p.m. Hptmn H. Wiskandt *(Staffelkapitän)*, Fw H. Ehlers, and Uffz E. Löhr unhurt. Twelve men of Stab 2./Fla.52 off-loaded. Aircraft abandoned.

1.29 p.m. Fifth wave of 40 Junkers Ju52s of KGrzbV.9 carrying 5. and 6./IR65 and II./AR22 cancelled.

4.50 p.m. Twelve No.40 Squadron Blenheims from Wyton bomb the airfield causing considerable damage among the closely-packed Junkers Ju52s, and hitting one of the hangars but lost three aircraft to enemy fighters.

Waalhaven (Landeplatz IV)

5.30 — 5.40 a.m. After pre-assault bombing by He111s of II./KG4, 53 Junkers Ju52s of II./KGzbV.1 drop 700 men of III./FJR1 over Waalhaven.

5./KGzbV.1 Junkers Ju52 (5160). Damaged by ground fire over Waalhaven 5.35 a.m. and crash-landed at Loddenheide on return. Uffz A. Wiesgrill badly wounded. Aircraft a write-off.

5.50 a.m. 53 Junkers Ju52s of III./KGzbV.1 lands first wave of troops from Stab III./IR16 and 9./IR16 . Most off-load successfully and return to base.

9./KGzbV.1 Junkers Ju52 (6533). Hit by AA fire approaching Tiel en-route to Waalhaven and crashed near Druten 5.50 a.m. Uffz A. Fulte and Gefr H. Emmert killed, two other crew and 15 men of III./IR16 missing. Aircraft a write-off.

12./KGzbV.1 Junkers Ju52 (6320). Direct hit by AA fire and broke up over Waalhaven 5.55 a.m. Hptmn P. Dreikorn *(Staffelkapitän)* missing. Others possibly Fw K. Müller missing and Uffz N. Michels killed. Fifteen men of III./IR16 also missing. Aircraft a write-off.

III./KGzbV.1 Junkers Ju52 (5706). Two engines hit by AA fire, crash-landed on northern perimeter of Waalhaven 5.55 a.m. Four crew and 15 men of III./IR16 off-loaded. Aircraft abandoned – later destroyed by artillery fire.

Waalhaven airfield, located directly south of the docks at Rotterdam, was to be used for both the landing of paratroops and follow-up reinforcements brought in by Ju52 transports. The paratroopers were dropped south and east of the aerodrome with the first aircraft landing slightly before 6 a.m. This picture was taken by the Luftwaffe on May 10.

9./KGzbV.1 Junkers Ju52 (6404). Believed shot down by 2e Lt Sonderman of 3-II-1 over Waalhaven 5.50 a.m. and crashed at 'De Koning', north of Goidschalxoort ferry. Oberlt H. Kornagel, Gefr W. Lösch, two crewmen, and 15 men of III./IR16 captured. Aircraft a write-off.

9./KGzbV.1 Junkers Ju52 (6403). Believed attacked by Fokker G-1s and crash-landed at Waalhaven 5.50 a.m. Possibly that claimed by 1e Lt van Oorschot. Crew believed to be Uffz A. Balzer, Uffz W. Buchholz captured unhurt. Gefr W. Händel captured wounded, admitted to hospital in Leiden. Fifteen men of III./IR16 missing. Aircraft a write-off.

12./KGzbV.1 Junkers Ju52 (6526). Believed attacked by Fokker G-1s of 3-II-1 and crash-landed at Waalhaven 5.50 a.m. Possibly that claimed by 1e Lt Woudenberg. Crew believed to be Fw F. Unverdorben captured unhurt. Uffz K. Reichert and Fw G. Kupke captured badly wounded, admitted to hospital in Leiden where both later died. Fifteen men of III./IR16 missing. Aircraft a write-off.

III./KGzbV.1 Junkers Ju52 (6474). Believed shot down by Fokker G-1s of 3-II-1 over Waalhaven 5.50 a.m. Possibly attacked by 1e Lt Woudenberg. Four crew and 15 men of III./IR16 missing. Aircraft a write-off.

10.25 a.m. Twenty-two Junkers Ju52s of IV./KGzbV.1 diverted from Ockenburg and Ypenburg land 330 men of Infanterie Regiment 65. One aircraft destroyed while off-loading, rest take-off but another forced to land en-route to Loddenheide.

14./KGzbV.1 Junkers Ju52 (6319). Reported destroyed by artillery fire possibly after landing near Waalhaven 11.00 a.m. Oberlt W. Georg *(Staffelkapitän)* and three crew captured. Aircraft a write-off.

Bordfunker Fw Willi Birkelbach and Bord-mechaniker Uffz Günther Külpmann, who were both captured wounded, may also have been in this crew along with Hilfsabsetzer Gefr Olezynska..

IV./KGzbV.1 Junkers Ju52. Damaged by ground fire during landings at Waalhaven and forced-landed near Moordrecht during return flight 11.32 a.m. Three crew missing. Aircraft a write-off.

10.30 a.m. The second sortie carried out by III./KGzbV.1 lands more troops of III./IR16. One aircraft brought down by ground fire en-route. Additional landings by II./KGzbV.1 take place at intervals throughout the afternoon.

II./KGzbV.1 Six Junkers Ju52s (5203, 5288, 6006, 6009, 6016, 6146). Destroyed by artillery fire after landing at Waalhaven. Uffz D. Strahlendorf killed. Uffz E. Küster and Uffz A. Hartwig wounded, Gefr W. Leonhardt and rest of crews unhurt. Ninety men of III./IR16 off-loaded. Aircraft all write-offs.

II./KGzbV.1 Junkers Ju52 (5180). Damaged by ground-fire during landings at Waalhaven and believed forced-landed near Delft. One crewman believed killed, another wounded. Lt Schiffrer missing. Aircraft a write-off.

9./KGzbV.1 Junkers Ju52 (5156). Destroyed by artillery fire after landing at Waalhaven 10.30 a.m. Hptmn W. Eifler *(Staffelkapitän)*, and Fw F. Huber killed. Rest of crew and 15 men of III./IR16 missing. Aircraft a write-off.

10./KGzbV.1 Junkers Ju52 (5304). Shot down by ground fire on approach to Waalhaven and crash-landed 10.30 a.m. Fw M. Niederhofer, Uffz R. Pfeffer, Uffz A. Wrusch and Uffz O. Sixtus captured unhurt. Six men of III./IR16 missing. Aircraft 1Z+CU a write-off.

10./KGzbV.1 Junkers Ju52 (6785). Hit by ground fire over Waalhaven and crashed and burned out near 't Woud, south-west of Delft, 10.45 a.m. Hptmn G. Hauck *(Staffelkapitän)*, Oberfw H. Gorgas, Oberfw E. Niederer, and Uffz F. Fischer captured unhurt next day. One man of III./IR16 killed, five others missing. Aircraft 1Z+AU a write-off.

10./KGzbV.1 Junkers Ju52 (6476). Suffered direct hit by light AA over Waalhaven and set alight; forced-landed and burned out in the Westpolder, south-west of Berkel, 10.35 a.m. Uffz M. Lubbe killed during exchange of fire with Dutch troops of the Depot Wielrijders. Fw F. Felger, Uffz M. Schnalzger, and Uffz H. Schnittersmann captured unhurt. Ten men of III./IR16 captured, three of them wounded. Aircraft 1Z+JU a write-off.

10./KGzbV.1 Junkers Ju52 (6786). Hit by ground fire over Waalhaven and reportedly forced-landed near Den Haag 10.35 a.m. Fw W. Burger, Obergefr W. Wirth, Uffz W. Picha, and Uffz H. Heuer captured. Ten men of III./IR16 missing. Aircraft 1Z+LU a write-off.

III./KGzbV.1 Two Junkers Ju52s (3656, 5953). Undercarriages wrecked on landing at Waalhaven 10.30 a.m. Six crew and 30 men of III./IR16 off-loaded. Aircraft abandoned — later destroyed by artillery fire.

Ernst Schröder and Michael Roth (both of 10./KGzbV.1) were wounded and believed to have been among these crews.

III./KGzbV.1 Junkers Ju52 (5647). Landed at Waalhaven 10.30 a.m. Crew unhurt. Fifteen men of III./IR16 off-loaded. Aircraft later destroyed by artillery fire.

Stab III./KGzbV.1 Junkers Ju52 (5936). Believed landed at Waalhaven 10.35 a.m. and later destroyed by bombing. Lt G. Heckewerth, Fw E. Scheller and two crewmen wounded, 10 men of III./IR16 off-loaded. Aircraft a write-off.

12.05 p.m. Six Blenheim IFs from No.600 Squadron attack the airfield but are engaged by Messerschmitt Bf110s and only one returns to Manston.

12.25 p.m. Five Fokker C Xs of 1-I-1 attack Waalhaven losing two of their number to Messerschmitt Bf109s, the others returning to Bergen damaged.

1.12 p.m. Diverted from Ypenburg, 43 Junkers Ju52s of Stab KGzbV.2 and 1./KGrzbV.172 land 332 men of 4./IR65 and 2./Fla.52. Most take-off again and return to base with crews.

The paradox of warfare depicted in this peaceful country scene 'somewhere in Holland' with only the mechanical beasts of war to remind us that this is 1940.

Stab KGbV.2 Three Junkers Ju52s. Believed destroyed or badly damaged by bombing or artillery fire while off-loading 1.20 p.m. Uffz W. Paasch captured, two crewmen wounded, and six missing. Aircraft G6+CA and another write-offs.

4./KGrzbV.172 Two Junkers Ju52s. Shot down by airfield defences while landing at Waalhaven 1.20 p.m. Uffz G. Seyfert killed, four other crewmen missing. Aircraft both write-offs.

1.28 p.m. Fokker C Vs of IV-2 attack the airfield losing two machines to Messerschmitt Bf110s.

2.05 p.m. Fokker T Vs of 2-I-1, escorted by Fokker D-XXIs of 2-II-1, attack Waalhaven losing three aircraft to Messerschmitt Bf109s.

3.12 p.m. Forbidden to attempt further landings at airfields not in German hands, 7 Junkers Ju52s of KGrzbV.9 land 63 men of 14./IR65 and four 7.5cm guns on north-east side of airfield. One aircraft shot down prior to landing.

1./KGrzbV.9 Junkers Ju52. Shot down by AA fire on approach to Waalhaven and believed crashed and burned out in Charlois 3.12 p.m. Three crew and 9 men of 14./IR65 missing. Aircraft 9P+BH a write-off.

3.20 p.m. Nine Blenheims of No.15 Squadron bomb the airfield claiming 16 transports destroyed on the ground.

1./KGrzbV.9 Junkers Ju52. Destroyed in bombing while off-loading at Waalhaven. Crew believed unhurt. Aircraft a write-off.

9.30 p.m. — 3.00 a.m. Thirty-six No.3 Group Wellingtons attacking in four waves bomb Waalhaven during the night, in support of a Dutch counter-attack to retake the airfield next morning. This is the most intensive bombardment yet made by RAF aircraft in a single night.

OPERATIONS RECORD BOOK.

Appendix.................................... R.A.F. Form 541.

DETAIL OF WORK CARRIED OUT.

From 0315 hrs. 11 / 5 / 40. to ...... hrs. 11 / 5 / 40. By No. 73 Squadron "A" Flight   No. of pages used for day... 1

Aircraft Type and No.	Crew.	Duty.	Time Up.	Time Down.	Remarks.	References.
HURRICANE B	P/O TUCKER	PATROL	0545	0620	JU 88 brought down by F/O ORTON.	Operations Report.
L	F/O ORTON	"	0545	0620	F/O ORTON'S a/c damaged in action.	
K	P/O ELIOT	"	0545	0620	ME 111 brought down by P/O ELIOT.	
H	S/LDR MORE	"	0920	1035	DO 215 or 17 attacked, but got away, damaged.	
P1555 K	P/O ROE	"	0920	1200	P/O ROE got separated from the patrol & engaged	
D	P/O MARTIN	"	0920	1035	a DO (possibly the same one) which he damaged. His machine was damaged in the action.	
J	F/O ORTON	"	1130	1200		
C	SGT. PILKINGTON	"	1130	1200	ME11 brought down by P/O ELIOT	
E	P/O ELIOT	"	1130	1200		
J	F/O ORTON	"	1435	1530	F/O ORTON. D.F.C. (Twin-engine ?) Brought down.	
C	S/LDR MORE	"	1435	1535	HE111. Damaged port engine. P/O ELLIOT.	
B	P/O ELIOT	"	1435	1540		
D	SGT. PILKINGTON	"	1435	1530	ME 110 (?). damaged by Sgt PILKINGTON & probably crashed.	
E	SGT. HUMPHRIES	"	1435	1540	ME110. forced to jettison bomb-load by Sgt Humphries.	
C	SGT. DIBDEN	"	1720	1905		
K	SGT. FRIEND	"	1720	1905	ording patrol. No e/a encountered.	
J	F/O ORTON	"	1730	1740		
B	P/O MARTIN	"	1730	1740		

It is always fascinating to compare the written record produced at the time with the reality researched long after the event. *Above:* RAF Form 541 lists daily operations — in this case for 'A' Flight of No. 73 Squadron. *Below:* Squadron Leader More's report submitted to Wing Headquarters for May 11 — his own machine being hit by anti-aircraft fire.

Saturday, May 11

The German air assault continued as the previous day, with airfields the main targets for early morning attacks. Over a score of French bases bore the brunt, though it was at Condé-Vraux that the Luftwaffe enjoyed its greatest success of the morning, when a low-level attack at dawn all but eliminated the Blenheims of No. 114 Squadron.

In Holland, later that morning, 12 Ju52s of IV./KGzbV.1 dropped paratroops at Dordrecht to reinforce troops already holding the bridges, while additional landings at Delft posed a serious threat to Den Haag. Elsewhere, German troops were pressing on Utrecht and the main Dutch positions, while at Rotterdam, the German airborne invasion was making 'alarming progress', an early Dutch counter-attack at Waalhaven having failed to regain the airfield. During the afternoon, 35 Junkers Ju52s of KGrzbV.9 landed there with troops of Stab I./IR72 and Stab II./IR65 to further consolidate the position. By nightfall, the confused military situation in Holland would be deemed 'critical'.

With the defences of the Albert Canal and the Meuse effectively neutralised, German ground forces in Belgium were advancing in force from Maastricht towards Tongeren, and threatening the Belgian forward line. To stem this advance, successive attacks by Belgian, British, and French bombers, on bridges west of Maastricht were countered by German fighter patrols that were maintained throughout the day. This strong fighter presence also curtailed all reconnaissance sorties over the area due to repeated losses. Meanwhile, though hindered by enemy air attack, advance elements of the British and French armies started to reach their agreed positions on the Dyle.

```
                    C O P Y .
                    ---------
                                                    172

From :-    Officer Commanding, No. 73 Squadron, R.A.F.

To :-      Headquarters, No. 67 Wing, Royal Air Force.

Date :-    12th May, 1940.

Ref. :-    738/S.112/Air.

OPERATIONS - 11/5/40.
====================

        One section took off for aerodrome defence
at 06.15 and shot up one Ju.88, which was thought to
have crashed somewhere west of Reims.

        One flight took off 09.27 hours to carry out
a protective patrol in Luxemburg, for Battles bombing in
that area.   Seven D.O.17s. were passed flying in the
opposite direction, N.E. of VOUZIERS, at 7,000 feet.

        One D.O.17 was found and attacked near
ETTELBRUK and shot up.   The flight at this time was
flying at about 3,000 feet feet and experienced considerable
Anti-aircraft fire.   All pilots returned safely, but
one aircraft was written off as a result of attacking the
D.O.17.

        At 14.45 hours, eleven aircraft took off by
Sections and encountered large formation of H.E.111s.,
D.O.215s. and M.E.110s.   Five aircraft claimed fairly
confidently, two more were last seen with engines stopped
and one last seen with white smoke coming from the Port
Engine.

        Further patrols were carried out in the evening
but no enemy aircraft were contacted.


                    (Sgd.) J.W.C. MORE.

                    Squadron Leader,  Commanding,
                    No. 73 Squadron, Royal Air Force.
```

230

During the morning, attacks by AASF Fairey Battles aimed at halting an enemy column nearing Echternach resulted in the loss of all eight aircraft despatched. These casualties, plus those of the previous day, gave cause for grave anxiety, and brought into question the future of daylight bomber operations. That evening, Air Marshal Barratt contacted the Chief of Air Staff and explained that no such further attacks would take place in order to conserve his dwindling bomber force. Thus, on the second day of the German offensive, and with enemy concentrations all too readily found, the AASF was unable to afford the cost of attacking them.

German bombers were operating in larger numbers, many escorted by fighters, and these formations were proving difficult for the Allied fighters who opposed them, usually in much lesser strength. Lack of adequate early-warning, or effective fighter control systems, severely hampered any attempts to co-ordinate Allied fighter defence efforts.

Operating from England, Fighter Command flew four patrols over the Belgian and Dutch coasts during the afternoon and evening to provide cover for naval operations at Vlissingen. During one of these patrols, often the first combat sortie for many of the Fighter Command pilots involved, No. 17 Squadron lost five aircraft and four pilots. Tragically, it was a pattern repeated all too often in days to come as British pilots paid a high price to gain valuable combat experience and knowledge of fighter tactics.

BRITISH AIR FORCES IN FRANCE

1 SQUADRON, BERRY-AU-BAC

Hurricane L1679. Forced-landed at Tournes-Belval, north-west of Charleville-Mézières, low on fuel following attacks on Do17, believed to 3.(F)/31, and damaged port wing tip avoiding a bomb crater 9.15 a.m. Flying Officer P. H. M. Richey unhurt. Aircraft ⊙G damaged but repairable — destroyed in bombing May 14.

Hurricane L1685. Shot down in combat with Bf110s of I./ZG26 west of Charleville-Mézières and abandoned over Mont-St. Jean, north of Brunehamel 7.15 p.m. Flying Officer P. H. M. Richey baled out landing in woods unhurt. Aircraft a write-off.
Site excavated in 2000 by Anglo-French team. Engine recovered with fragments of wooden Watts propeller, gunsight, various cockpit items, and makers plate confirming serial 'L1685'. Items displayed in the Musée du Souvenir Militaire de Thiérache in nearby Martigny.

Half the Blenheims lost by the AASF in France would be lost on this day. Daylight attacks against the main German thrusts near Maastricht and Sedan were to cost AASF Blenheim units 48 per cent of all aircraft despatched and due to such losses in the air and destruction on the ground they would effectively cease to operate after May 17. Blenheims of No. 2 Group of Bomber Command operating from England would take up the fight.

18 SQUADRON, MÉHARICOURT

Blenheim IV L9255. Shot down by AA during low-level reconnaissance sortie over the Albert Canal and believed crash-landed east of Roermond 4.00 a.m. Sergeant E. E. B. Le Voi and Sergeant J. C. Sands both captured wounded. LAC R. D. Davies killed. Aircraft a write-off.

Blenheim IV R3590. Port engine and undercarriage damaged by enemy ground-fire and Belgian ground-fire during low-level reconnaissance sortie over the Albert Canal and Maastricht. Belly-landed near Vaucogne, north-east of Troyes 6.00 a.m. Pilot Officer M. P. C. Holmes wounded in eye. Sergeant F. Miller and Corporal B. M. Harding unhurt. Aircraft a write-off.

Blenheim IV L9192. Forced-landed at Vitry-en-Artois with tail and elevator damaged by Belgian AA fire during low-level reconnaissance sortie over the Albert Canal bridges 12.00 p.m. Pilot Officer J. R. Whelan, Sergeant T. J. Mongey, and LAC Brown unhurt. Aircraft repairable.

Blenheim IV L8861. Failed to return from reconnaissance sortie over the Albert Canal and crashed near Kanne, north-east of Tongeren 9.15 p.m. Flying Officer C. Bellis, Sergeant H. D. Welch and LAC K. Parry killed. Aircraft a write-off.
The dates of death of these three airmen are recorded as May 12 in the records of the CWGC. Aircraft lost on sorties late in the day would often be reported the next day once all hope of their return had gone.

No. 18 Squadron lost three aircraft on May 11, another returning damaged. This photograph may well show one of these casualties.

Two more Blenheims down that day were L9459 of No. 53 Squadron *(above)* **and** *(below)* **L4856 of No. 59 Squadron.**

53 SQUADRON, POIX

Blenheim IV L9459. Forced-landed and burned out near Borlez during photo-reconnaissance sortie over Belgium and possibly that claimed by Lt Braxator of 3./JG1 near Overijse 4.55 p.m. Flying Officer A. D. Panton and Sergeant W. A. Christie both wounded and evacuated to England. AC2 R. Bence severely wounded — leg amputated, and later captured. Aircraft PZ⊙C a write-off.

59 SQUADRON, POIX

Blenheim IV L4856. Forced-landed at Vitry with oil tank damaged and port engine destroyed by ground-fire west of Veghel during reconnaissance of the Eindhoven — Boxtel road 4.15 p.m. Flight Lieutenant G. V. Smithers, Sergeant R. Tull, and AC2 D. J. Pitcher unhurt. Aircraft TR⊙K repairable — burned at Poix on evacuation May 19.

73 SQUADRON, REIMS-CHAMPAGNE

Hurricane P2812. Returned oil tank and wing slightly damaged by return fire from enemy aircraft engaged over Reims 6.00 a.m. Flying Officer N. Orton unhurt. Aircraft ⊙L repairable.

Hurricane P2813. Landed badly damaged by AA fire during attack on Do17 near Vouziers 10.15 a.m. Squadron Leader J. W. C. More unhurt. Aircraft ⊙H repairable.

Hurricane P2535. Hit by return fire from Do17 attacked near Vouziers 10.15 a.m. and returned with slight damage. Pilot Officer V. Roe unhurt. Aircraft ⊙K repairable.

Hurricane P2569. Forced-landed at Rouvres badly damaged in engine and tailplane by Bf110 of I./ZG2 in combat over Mourmelon 3.30 p.m. Sergeant L. S. Pilkington unhurt. Aircraft ⊙D damaged but repairable — later abandoned.

Hurricane P2811. Riddled by cannon fire and radiator damaged in combat with Bf110s of I./ZG2 over Mourmelon 3.30 p.m. and forced-landed at Poilcourt. Pilot Officer A. McFadden unhurt. Aircraft abandoned.

79 SQUADRON, MERVILLE

Hurricane L2068. Set alight by return fire during attack on He111 of Stab KG1 near La Louvière, north-west of Mons, 6.00 a.m. Flight Lieutenant R. S. J. Edwards baled out with severe burns to arm. Aircraft a write-off.

Hurricane L2049. Damaged by return fire following attack on He111 of Stab KG1 over La Louvière and forced-landed at Le Touquet 6.00 a.m. Pilot Officer L. L. Appleton unhurt. Aircraft abandoned.

85 SQUADRON, LILLE-SECLIN

Hurricane N2388. Hit by AA fire over Maastricht during attack on Do17P of 2.(F)/123 1.00 p.m. Flight Lieutenant R. H. A. Lee baled out slightly wounded and evaded disguised as a civilian. Aircraft VY⊙R lost.

Hurricane. Returned damaged by ground-fire following attack on Do17P of 2.(F)/123 south of Nivelles 1.00 p.m. Flying Officer D. H. Allen unhurt. Aircraft repairable.

Hurricane L1979. Dead-stick landing outside Maastricht with engine damaged by ground-fire during pursuit of Fieseler Storch 1.30 p.m. Pilot Officer J. A. Hemingway slightly wounded in right leg. Aircraft VY⊙X abandoned.

Hurricane P2821. Returned hit by return fire during attack on He111s p.m. Squadron Leader J. O. W. Oliver slightly wounded. Aircraft repairable.

88 SQUADRON, MOURMELON-LE-GRAND

Battle P2261. Shot down by heavy ground-fire during attack on enemy column at Bouillon and crashed near Noville 10.30 a.m. Pilot Officer B. I. M. Skidmore, Sergeant R. A. P. Kirby and AC1 W. L. Parsons killed. Aircraft a write-off.
This crew was originally buried close to the crash site on Ferme Lambert Harcourt at Noville, but later reinterred in Hotton War Cemetery on November 28, 1946.

Battle P2202. Shot down by heavy ground-fire during attack on enemy column at Bouillon and crashed near Sainies 10.30 a.m. Pilot Officer A. W. Mungovan and Sergeant F. Robson captured. AC1 E. W. Maltby killed. Aircraft a write-off.
Remains of the wireless operator/air gunner, Eric Maltby, were recovered from a field grave in a wood and reinterred in Hotton War Cemetery on November 28, 1946.

Battle P2251. Badly damaged by ground-fire during attack on enemy column near Bouillon and belly-landed at 'Besagibet', between Vaux-sur-Sure and Bercheux, north of Juseret, 10.30 a.m. Flight Lieutenant A. J. Madge and Corporal A. C. Collyer captured. Sergeant E. J. M. Whittle killed. Aircraft RH⊙D a write-off.

Battle. Forced-landed at Vassincourt badly damaged by ground-fire during sortie to attack enemy column near Bouillon 10.30 a.m. Pilot Officer N. C. S. Riddell and crew unhurt. Aircraft damaged but repairable — later abandoned.

The latter machine managed to land at Vitry-en-Artois and, although it was repaired, it ended its days at Poix eight days later when the squadron abandoned that airfield, the ground crew setting fire to the lame ducks.

114 SQUADRON, CONDÉ-VRAUX

Blenheim IVs. Six aircraft destroyed on the ground during low-level bombing attack on the airfield by Do17s of 4. and 5./KG2 5.45 a.m. No crew casualties. Aircraft all write-offs.

All the squadron's aircraft were either destroyed or damaged in this attack, six crews transferring to Plivot three days later for operations with No. 139 Squadron. Records are incomplete, but the following aircraft, all recorded 'lost in France', are not listed elsewhere in our loss lists: L8857, L9177, L9178, L9398, N6148, N6154, N6159, N6162, N6232, P6885 and P6923.

150 SQUADRON, ECURY-SUR-COOLE

Battle P2334. Destroyed on the ground during bombing attack 6.10 a.m. No crew casualties. Aircraft a write-off.

Another aircraft was also reported damaged in this attack and later abandoned.

218 SQUADRON, AUBÉRIVE-SUR-SUIPPES

Battle K9325. Shot down by ground-fire during low-level sortie over St Vith 9.30 a.m. Flying Officer A. J. Hudson, Sergeant N. H. Thompson and AC1 A. Ellis captured unhurt. Aircraft a write-off.

Battle P2203. Hit by ground-fire over Basbellain during low-level attack on a bridge north of St Vith and crashed near Trois-Vierges, east of Houffalize 9.30 a.m. Sergeant C. J. E. Dockrill, Sergeant P. F. Dormer and AC1 K. G. Gregory killed. Aircraft a write-off.

Battle P2249. Shot down by intense ground-fire near Basbellain during low-level attack on a bridge north of St Vith 9.30 a.m. Pilot Officer H. M. Murray and AC2 I. G. Adams captured unhurt. Sergeant P. Stubbs captured wounded in right arm, admitted to hospital in Neuss. Aircraft HA⊙U a write-off.

Battle P2326. Shot down by ground-fire during low-level attack on a bridge and abandoned north of St Vith 9.30 a.m. Flying Officer C. A. R. Crews and Sergeant T. S. Evans baled out under 150 feet, landing in trees, and both captured unhurt. Sergeant C. M. Jennings also baled out over Amelscheid but killed. Aircraft a write-off.

501 SQUADRON, BÉTHENIVILLE

Hurricane L2045. Returned port wing damaged by cannon fire from Bf109s following solo reconnaissance over Sedan 4.30 p.m. Flying Officer E. J. Holden unhurt. Aircraft SD⊙A repairable.

Squadron personnel killed or injured in crash of Bristol Bombay L5183 of No. 271 (Transport) Squadron which stalled on approach to the airfield 5.10 p.m. Flying Officer A. C. J. Percy (Squadron Adjutant) and Sergeant H. J. Barnwell killed. Sergeant H. C. Adams, Flight Sergeant F. T. Avent, Sergeant D. B. Crabtree, Sergeant J. Davis, Pilot Officer B. L. Duckenfield, AC1 A. F. Holdsworth and LAC A. L. W. Holt all injured. Flying Officer B. J. R. Brady also seriously injured and evacuated to England where he died August 14. Sergeant W. H. Whitfield of No. 271 Squadron also killed.

607 SQUADRON, VITRY-EN-ARTOIS

Hurricane P2571. Hit by return fire from He111 of I./LG1 engaged south-east of Denain but returned safely to base 12.45 p.m. Pilot Officer D. T. Jay wounded in right knee. Aircraft AF⊙G repairable.

Hurricane P2573. Wrecked in forced-landing at airfield near Tirlemont out of fuel following pursuit of Bf110s 2.45 p.m. Pilot Officer H. P. Dixon unhurt. Aircraft AF⊙A a write-off.

Hurricane P3448. Forced-landed out of fuel following attack on Bf110s north-east of Brussels 2.05 p.m. Re-fuelled and returned to base 7.30 p.m. Flight Lieutenant W. F. Blackadder unhurt. Aircraft AF⊙H undamaged.

Blenheim L8857 was probably one of the aircraft lost by No. 114 Squadron during a bombing attack on their aerodrome at Condé-Vraux which lay some 30 kilometres south-east of Reims. The hulk proved a useful backdrop for snapshots by the victorious Wehrmacht.

UK-based aircraft lost or damaged on operations over the Western Front:

RAF BOMBER COMMAND

21 Squadron, Watton
Attack columns between Maastricht and Tongeren:

8 Blenheim IVs. Returned badly damaged by ground-fire 4.30 p.m. AC1 R. Charleton killed. Aircraft damaged.

3 Blenheim IVs. Returned hit by ground-fire 4.30 p.m. No crew casualties. Aircraft repairable.

49 Squadron, Scampton
Bomb communications at Mönchengladbach:

Hampden L4068. Crash-landed at Woignarue, north-east of le Tréport. P/O Drakes, P/O Fox, Sgt Fennell, AC1 Watson unhurt. Aircraft wrecked.

77 Squadron, Driffield
Bomb communications at Mönchengladbach:

Whitley N1366. Shot down by AA over target 11.00 p.m. F/O T. H. Parrott, Sgt T. T. Atchison, LAC T. Poad, AC2 T. Jones killed. F/O D. Blew captured. Aircraft lost.

110 Squadron, Wattisham
Attack Maastricht bridges:

Blenheim IV L9175. Believed that shot down by Oberlt Homuth of 3./JG27 at Kaggevinne, south-west of Diest 4.30 p.m. F/O G. R. Grattan, LAC F. J. Allam killed. Sgt T. Patterson captured. Aircraft lost.

Blenheim IV N6208. Belly-landed at Fouquières-lès-Béthune, damaged by fighters. Sgt A. Colling killed. Sgt G. C. Bennett, AC2 E. Hannah injured. Aircraft burned out.

144 Squadron, Hemswell
Bomb communications at Mönchengladbach:

Hampden P1326. Hit by AA over target 00.30 a.m. (May 12) — later crashed near Finnevaux north of Beauraing. W/C A. N. Luxmoore killed. P/O R. E. Allitt, Sgt H. Wathey, Cpl R. Jolly baled out unhurt. Aircraft lost.

RAF FIGHTER COMMAND

17 Squadron, Hawkinge
Patrol Den Haag – Delft – Rotterdam:

Hurricane N2407. Shot down by Bf109s south-west of Dordrecht 5.00 p.m. Possibly one of those claimed by Lt Terry of Stab I./JG51. P/O O. P. de L. Hulton-Harrop baled out and captured. Aircraft YB⊙N lost.

Hurricane N2547. Forced-landed at Hingene damaged by Bf109s south of Rotterdam 5.00 p.m. Possibly that claimed by Oberlt Schäter of 5./JG27. S/L G. C. Tomlinson unhurt. Aircraft abandoned.

Hurricane N2403. Shot down by Bf109s over Numansdorp 5.00 p.m. Possibly one of those claimed by Oberlt Krafft of 3./JG51. F/L M. S. Donne killed. Aircraft lost.

Hurricane P2758. Shot down by Bf109s in combat over Dordrecht 5.00 p.m. Possibly that claimed by Uffz Schreiter of 3./JG51. Sgt J. A. A. Luck captured. Aircraft lost.

Hurricane N2405. Shot down by Bf109s of I./JG51 over 's-Gravendeel 5.00 p.m. P/O G. W. Slee killed. Aircraft YB⊙Y lost.

Hurricane N2457. Returned damaged by Bf109s of I./JG51 in combat south of Rotterdam 5.00 p.m. F/O R. V. Meredith unhurt. Aircraft repairable.

FRENCH AIR FORCE

AC 2 Potez 631. Shot down over Biervliet by Oberfw Stahl of 4./ZG26 during attack on He111s of III./KG27 over Walcheren; crashed and burned out at Pyramide 6.00 p.m. LV Folliot *(Commandant)* and Mtre Frey both baled out wounded. Aircraft a write-off.

AC 2 Potez 631. Shot down by Oberfw Stahl of 4./ZG26 during attack on He111s of III./KG27 over Walcheren; crashed into a house at Nos. 159-161 Verkuyl Quakke-laarstraat in Vlissingen 6.00 p.m. PM G. Samery and QM E. Le Maresquier killed. Aircraft a write-off.

GAO 502 Potez 63.11 (224 and 233). Caught on the ground at Tournes-Belval during bombing and strafing attack by Do17s of 9./KG76 11.00 a.m. No crew casualties. Aircraft both write-offs.
A Potez 38 flown by S/Lt Bour and Sgt Fuselier was also destroyed in this attack.

GAO 507 Potez 63.11 (212). Oil tank holed by ground-fire over Sibret during reconnaissance sortie north of Neufchâteau 7.15 a.m. and port undercarriage collapsed in forced-landing at Chatel-Chéhéry. Lt Lapanne, Lt Clément, and Adjt Bergelin unhurt. Aircraft damaged but repairable — later abandoned.

GAO 511 Potez 39 (5). Damaged aircraft left at Villers-lès-Guise on withdrawal to Versigny 11.30 a.m. No crew casualties. Aircraft abandoned.

GAO 1/520 Potez 63.11. Hit by ground-fire during low-level ammunition supply drop to encircled troops at Emmerich 4.00 p.m. Returned to Guéblange-lès-Dieuze on one engine with fuselage and petrol tank holed. Adjt Vuillemin and crew unhurt. Aircraft damaged but repairable.

GAO 1/551 Potez 63.11 (774). Crashed on landing at Étain-Buzy damaged in attacks by Bf109s. Capt J. Riesser, Lt Lenclud, and Sgt Lombard unhurt. Aircraft a write-off.

GAO 2/551 Four Potez 63.11 (318). Destroyed or badly damaged on the ground at Tournes-Belval in bombing and strafing attack by Do17s of 9./KG76 11.00 a.m. No crew casualties. Aircraft all write-offs.
Two Mureaux 115 were also badly damaged in this attack which, along with earlier losses, rendered the unit ineffective. All unserviceable aircraft, including a Breguet 27, were destroyed on evacuation on May 13.

GB I/12 LeO 451 (63). Crashed on landing at Soissons-Saconin damaged by flak during sortie to attack enemy troop concentrations in Belgium 6.50 p.m. Adjt H. Chamaud unhurt. Lt Grandrémy and Sgt Ritz both baled out and captured unhurt. Aircraft a write-off.

GB II/12 LeO 451 (46). Damaged by AA fire then attacked by Fw Richter of 1./JG1 during sortie to bomb bridges over the Meuse at Maastricht 6.50 p.m. Crashed and burned out near Café des Essart at Grandville, alongside the road from St. Trond to Oreye. S/Lt L. Jacquet killed. S/Lt R. Morel badly burned taken to hospital in Maastricht where died of wounds May 28. Adjt J. Moquelet baled out too low and killed. Adjt M. Natta baled out and captured slightly wounded. Aircraft a write-off.

GB II/12 LeO 451 (45). Undercarriage damaged by flak on sortie to attack enemy troop concentrations in Belgium and crashed on landing back at Persan-Beaumont 6.50 p.m. Lt Ponson, Sgt Vasseur, and two other crewmen unhurt. Aircraft a write-off.

Here in a back street in Holland two French naval airmen died fighting for France.

GB 3/12 LeO 451 (43). Returned to Persan-Beaumont riddled by flak during sortie to attack enemy troop concentrations in Belgium 6.50 p.m. Capt Knipping *(Commandant)*, Adjt Orliac, and crew unhurt. Aircraft 35 damaged but repairable.

GB II/12 LeO 451 (40). Returned to Persan-Beaumont one wing badly damaged by flak during sortie to attack enemy troop concentrations in Belgium 6.50 p.m. Gunner wounded. Aircraft repairable.

GB I/15 Farman 222 (23). Engaged by French flak and crashed on landing at Saint-Yan on transfer flight from Romilly 5.30 a.m. Lt Avenard and crew unhurt. Aircraft a write-off.

GC 2/2 Morane 406 (946). Shot down by Bf109 of 1./JG53 during attack on Do17s near Longwy; crashed between Blénod-les-Toul and Ochey 6.50 a.m. Capt P. Hyvernaud tried to bale out but killed. Aircraft a write-off.
This loss has been credited to Oberfw Grimmling, but both Oberfw Müller and Oberlt Mayer filed equally valid claims following this combat. There is also compelling evidence to indicate Bloch 152s of GC I/8 were involved and suffered several losses.

GC II/2 Morane 406 (253). Hit by return fire during attack on He111; crashed and burned out at Champs Cornet, on the road to Champlon outside Ortho, south-east of La Roche-en-Ardenne, 4.50 a.m. Sgt J. Moreau killed. Aircraft a write-off.

GC 4/2 Morane 406 (281). Hit by return fire during attack on Do17 of 2.(F)/123 over Tirlemont and forced-landed at Vaulx, near Chimay, 5.15 a.m. Capt Alexandre *(Commandant)* unhurt. Aircraft lost.

GC III/2 Morane 406 (202). Shot down by Bf110s in action over Geluwe; crashed and burned out north-east of Fortress Dave, at Namur 7.05 p.m. Possibly that claimed by Hptmn Groth *(Gruppenkommandeur)* and Lt Peters *(Gruppenadjutant)* of Stab II./ZG76. S/Lt Y. Rupied (of GC III/7) baled out unhurt; arrested by Belgian troops but later released. Aircraft a write-off.
Several alternative sources suggest Rupied was attached to GCIII/3 and not as shown.

GC 6/2 Morane 406. Engine set alight under attack by Bf110s during combat between St-Trond and Namur, and crash-landed at Laon-Chambry 7.15 p.m. Possibly one of those claimed by Oberlt Christiansen of 4./ZG76. Sgt L. Flanek unhurt. Aircraft a write-off.

This is the spot where a Potez 631 carrier fighter of F1A Flotille du 'Bearn' crashed outside Nos. 159-161 (now Nos. 259-261) in Verkuyl Quakkelaarstraat in Vlissingen.

Eleven French airmen lost their lives on the Western Front on May 11. This is the grave in Belgium of Sergeant Fernand Lacroix of Groupe de Chasse No. 1/4 who was born in Paris just before the Armistice in 1918. He was initially buried in the cemetery at Meer *(above)* and on June 1, 1941 was accorded the honour of 'Mort pour la France'. In November 1949 his remains were returned to his home town of Aubervilliers in France to be buried by his family.

GC 6/2 Morane 406. Badly damaged in attack by Bf110 during action between St-Trond and Namur, and forced-landed at Maubeuge-Elesmes 7.10 p.m. Possibly that claimed by Uffz Stumpf of 4./ZG76. Sgt Monribot unhurt. Aircraft a write-off.

GC III/3 Morane 406 (546). Forced-landed between the lines near Namur severely damaged by Bf109s of I./JG1 west of Maastricht during escort sortie for LeO 451s of GB I/12 and GB II/12 attacking bridges over the Albert Canal 6.50 p.m. Sgt J. Hubacek badly wounded in shoulder and arm but evaded capture. Aircraft a write-off.

GC III/3 Morane 406. Crashed on landing at Marchovelette badly damaged in combat with Bf109s of I./JG1 west of Maastricht during escort sortie for LeO 451s of GB I/12 and GB II/12 attacking bridges over the Albert Canal 6.50 p.m. Lt Clostres unhurt. Aircraft a write-off.

GC I/4 Curtiss H-75 (172). Shot down by Bf109s of III./JG26 during pursuit of He111 of KGr.126 and crashed in the Meerheide, near Zoersel, 23 km north-east of Antwerp 4.50 p.m. Cmdt. A. Hertaut *(Groupe Commandant)* killed. Aircraft a write-off.
The body of André Hertaut was recovered by his comrades, transported to Dunkerque-Mardyck airfield on May 13, and buried two days later.

GC 1/4 Curtiss H-75 (116). Shot down in combat with Bf109s of III./JG26 near Antwerp; crashed and burned out between Wuustwezel and Zundert 4.45 p.m. Sgt F. Lacroix killed. Aircraft a write-off.

GC 1/4 Curtiss H-75 (75). Damaged in combat with Bf109s of III./JG26 and crash-landed near Sterreken 4.50 p.m. S/Lt Naudin wounded admitted to hospital in Antwerp. Aircraft a write-off.

GC 1/4 Curtiss H-75 (99). Shot down by Bf109s of III./JG26 in combat and abandoned over Brasschaat 4.50 p.m. S/Lt Verry baled out badly wounded in foot and fired on by Belgian troops; admitted to hospital in Antwerp where later captured. Aircraft a write-off.

GC 1/4 Curtiss H-75 (77). Belly-landed back at Mardyck damaged in combat with Bf109s of III./JG26 over Antwerp 4.45 p.m. Sgt C. Debéthune unhurt. Aircraft a write-off.

GC 2/4 Curtiss H-75. Returned to Mardyck damaged by Bf109s of III./JG26 during combat over Antwerp 5.00 p.m. Capt B. Barbier *(Commandant)* slightly wounded. Aircraft repairable.

GC II/6 Morane 406 (711). Engine hit by return fire from Do17 of II./KG76 south-east of Maubeuge 6.45 a.m. Crash-landed at Peissant, near Jeumont, careering across fields and into a sunken lane. Sgt J-F. Touret trapped in cockpit, released unhurt after 45 minutes. Aircraft a write-off.

GC II/6 Morane 406 (67). Engaged by Bf109s of I./JG1 during escort sortie for LeO 451s of GB I/12 and GB II/12 attacking bridges over the Albert Canal at Maastricht, and last seen in combat between Tongeren and Waremme 6.50 p.m. Adjt L. Leclercq missing. Aircraft lost.

GC 5/6 Morane 406 (412). Engine set alight by return fire from He111 of 7./KG55 engaged over Auxonne 6.30 p.m. Lt R. Martin baled out unhurt. Aircraft a write-off.

GC 5/6 Morane 406 (963). Set alight by return fire from He111 of 7./KG55 engaged over Auxonne 6.30 p.m. S/Lt G. Colonges baled out unhurt. Aircraft a write-off.

GC 5/6 Morane 406. Engine damaged by crossfire during attack on He111s of III./KG55 over Auxonne 6.30 p.m. Forced-landed near Broye-les-Pesmes. Adjt C. Goujon unhurt. Aircraft a write-off.

GC II/7 Morane 406. Crashed on landing, exact details unknown. Sgt Lefèvre badly injured and admitted to hospital. Aircraft a write-off.

GC II/7 Morane 406. Forced-landed due to combat damage. S/Lt J. Dussart slightly injured. Aircraft a write-off.

GC II/7 Two Moranes 406 (88 and 956) and Dewoitine D520. Aircraft destroyed on the ground at Luxeuil in bombing by He111s 8.00 a.m. No pilot casualties. Aircraft all write-offs.

GC III/7 Morane 406. Returned to Vitry-le-François slightly damaged by return fire from He111s of III./KG53 engaged near Sainte-Menehould 6.05 a.m. Lt Challe unhurt. Aircraft repairable — believed further damaged in later bombing.

GC III/7 Morane 406 (157). Hit by return fire from He111 near Vitry and forced-landed outside Brousseval, 2 km east of Wassy 12.00 p.m. S/Lt Martin unhurt. Aircraft a write-off.

GC I/8 Bloch 152 (369). Shot down by fighters during attack on He111s of I./KG53 between Toul and Nancy. Crashed and exploded at St-Germain-sur-Meuse, 6 km south-west of Pagny-sur-Meuse. Possibly that claimed by Oberlt Müller *(Staffelkapitän)* of 13.(Z)/LG1. S/Lt A. Flandi killed. Aircraft a write-off.

GC I/8 Bloch 152. Badly damaged in combat with fighters during attack on He111s of I./KG53 and crash-landed outside Toul 6.40 a.m. S/Lt R. Thollon unhurt. Aircraft a write-off.

GC I/8 Bloch 152 (537). Shot down by fighters during attack on He111s of I./KG53, and abandoned over Joinville 6.35 a.m. Cpl O. Spacek baled out unhurt. Aircraft a write-off.

GC I/8 Bloch 152. Returned to base damaged in combat with Bf110s of V.(Z)/LG1 over St Mihiel 6.30 a.m. Cpl A. Kralik unhurt. Aircraft damaged but repairable.

GC I/8 Bloch 152 (534). Damaged in combat with Bf110s of V.(Z)/LG1 over St Mihiel and crash-landed near Fort de Bruley 6.30 a.m. Adjt Guy wounded in head. Aircraft a write-off.

GR II/52 Potez 63.11 (163). Hit by French AA during reconnaissance over the Marche — Vielsalm — Houffalize — Rochefort sector and belly-landed in hospital grounds at Maison-Rouge, 10 km north of Viziers 6.30 a.m. S/Lt Colin and Sgt Millet both badly wounded. Sgt Martin unhurt. Aircraft a write-off.

DUTCH AIR FORCE

2-I-1 Fokker T V (850). Engaged by Bf110s of 3./ZG1 near Boskoop after bombing the northern Maas bridge at Rotterdam and abandoned over Waddinxveen 2.20 p.m. Lt J. J. Mulder, Lt G. F. Verhage, and Sold. J. Wijnstra baled out unhurt. Sgt J. L. van de As and Sgt L. Rozeboom killed. Aircraft a write-off.

Excavated by the Royal Netherlands Air Force on February 20, 1998, when minor components recovered. Re-excavated by the Stichting Aircraft Recovery Group March 11, 2000, and several larger parts found which are displayed at the Fort Veldhuis Museum at Heemskerk.

1/2-II-1 Fokker D XXI (244). Returned to Buiksloot damaged by ground-fire during escort sortie over de Grebbe 8.10 a.m. Wachtm. W. Hateboer (of 1-II-1) unhurt. Aircraft repairable.

This aircraft, originally on the strength of 1-II-1, was part of a composite unit formed from the remnants of 1 and 2-II-1 now operating from Buiksloot. From a total establishment of 20 Fokker D XXIs the II Fighter Group had lost nine aircraft, and another seven damaged, in actions on May 10. They also lost three pilots killed and three more wounded, but the survivors fought on for another three days flying hurriedly patched-up aircraft.

1/2-II-1 Fokker D XXI (213). Shot down in combat with Bf110s of 3./ZG1 during escort sortie for 2-I-1 Fokker T Vs attack on Maas bridge at Rotterdam 2.20 p.m. Overturned in forced-landing on the 's-Gravenhage — Utrecht road near Zevenhuisen. Lt F. L. M. Focquin de Grave (of 1-II-1) wounded, admitted to hospital in Gouda. Aircraft a write-off.

1/2-II-1 Fokker D XXI (229). Shot down in combat with Bf110s of 3./ZG1 during escort sortie for 2-I-1 Fokker T Vs attack on Maas bridge at Rotterdam and crashed at Nieuwkoop 2.20 p.m. Sgt J. Roos (of 2-II-1) badly wounded, admitted to hospital in Leiden. Aircraft a write-off.

Excavated June 22, 1993, by the Stichting Aircraft Recovery Group and items now displayed at the Fort Veldhuis Museum at Heemskerk.

Vliegschool Texel Fokker D XVII (202). Hit by Dutch AA fire during transit flight to Buiksloot and forced-landed in Balgzandpolder, near Den Helder 6.20 p.m. Sgt H. C. Schamhart unhurt. Aircraft abandoned.

Vliegschool Texel Fokker D XVII (203). Slightly damaged by Dutch AA fire during transit flight to Buiksloot and forced-landed at De Kooy 6.20 p.m. 2e Lt E. A. Roosenburg unhurt. Aircraft repairable.

Both D XVIIs above were in a formation of six elderly biplanes being transferred from the Fighter School at De Vlijt-Texel to reinforce the composite unit formed from the remnants of 1-II-1 and 2-II-1 based at Buiksloot where they were subjected to friendly fire.

4-II-1 Fokker G 1 (308). Propeller damaged on landing at Schiphol 10.55 a.m. 2e Lt B. Sandberg and Sgt J. van den Breemer unhurt. Aircraft repairable.

III-2 Fokker C V (639). Radiator damaged by Dutch AA over Utrecht and engine seized near Elst during reconnaissance sortie between Ede and Arnhem 7.55 a.m. Forced-landed between Driebergen and Zeist. 2e Lt N. J. Woensdregt and 1e Lt P. F. J. van Enckevort unhurt. Aircraft a write-off.

MLD Four Fokker C XIVw (5588, 5593, 5600 and 5610). Aircraft destroyed in bombing attacks at De Mok. No crew casualties. Aircraft F-2, F-7, F-8, and F-12 all write-offs.

Wiping out aircraft on the ground was all a part of the tactics of the Blitzkrieg method of warfare. Twisted burned out wreckage was all that was left on the airstrip at Jeneffe, an aerodrome 15 kilometres west of Liège.

BELGIAN AIR FORCE

3/II/1 Fox (O.9). Wrecked in take-off accident at Glabbeek due to poor state of ground 8.10 p.m. S/Lt J. Verheughe unhurt. Aircraft destroyed on withdrawal to Wilrijk, May 13.

5/III/1 Nine Foxes (O.114, O.162, O.163, O.168). Destroyed or badly damaged on the ground at Jeneffe in attack by Hs123s of II.(S)/LG2 at 2.20 p.m. and strafing by Bf 109s of I./JG1 4.00 p.m. No pilot casualties. Aircraft all write-offs or abandoned on withdrawal to St Denijs-Westrem.

9/V/1 Renard R-31 (N.7). Caught on the ground at Wilderen-Duras prior to take-off for Steenokkerzeel and badly damaged in attack by Hs123s of II.(S)/LG2 5.15 p.m. Adjt G. Salmon and Cpl G. Nossin both unhurt. Aircraft destroyed.

11/VI/1 Renard R-31 (N.18). Shot down by Bf 110s over Riemst during low-level reconnaissance sortie over the Albert Canal. Crash-landed and burned out at 's-Herenelderen east of the railway line between Tongeren and Bilsen 9.00 a.m. Sgt F. Boute and O/Lt C. Berhaut both unhurt. Aircraft a write-off.

1/I/2 Gladiator (G.31). Returned to Beauvechain badly damaged following combat with Bf109s of 1./JG1 west of Maastricht 5.50 a.m. Possibly that claimed by Uffz Gillert. Sgt A. Van den Broeck unhurt. Aircraft damaged but repairable.

1/I/2 Gladiator (G.27). Damaged in combat with Bf109s of 1./JG1 over Zichem during escort sortie for Battles of 5/III/3 and forced-landed at Faimes. Possibly that claimed by Lt Mann 5.50 a.m. Capt M. Guisgand (*Commandant*) wounded. Aircraft abandoned.

1/I/2 Gladiator (G.34). Shot down in combat with Bf109s of 1./JG1 over Zichem during escort sortie for Battles of 5/III/3 and crashed between Flexhe and Slins, north of Liege. Possibly that claimed by Lt Franzisket 5.53 a.m. 1/Sgt H. Clinquart killed. Aircraft a write-off.

1/I/2 Gladiator (G.22). Badly damaged in combat by Bf109s during escort sortie for Battles of 5/III/3 and finally abandoned over Heukelom 5.55 a.m. Possibly one of those claimed by Hptmn Balthasar (*Staffelkapitän*) of 1./JG1. 1/Sgt D. Rolin baled out unhurt but apprehended by Flemish soldiers and eventually captured by German troops. Aircraft a write-off.

More twisted wreckage, this time lying at s'Herenelderen where the Renard piloted by Sergeant Freddy Boute crash-landed after an encounter with German heavy fighters.

1/I/2 Gladiator (G.19). Failed to return following combat with Bf109s of 1./JG1 during escort sortie for Battles of 5/III/3 over the Albert Canal, west of Maastricht 5.55 a.m. Possibly one of those claimed by Hptmn Balthasar *(Staffelkapitän)*. Sgt A. Pirlot missing. Aircraft lost.

1/I/2 Gladiator (G.32). Returned to Beauvechain badly damaged following combat with Bf109s of 1./JG1 over Zichem. Possibly that attacked by Uffz Clade 6.01 a.m. 1/Sgt H. Winand unhurt. Aircraft damaged but repairable.

1/I/2 11 Gladiators (G.31, G.32, G.38). Destroyed or damaged on the ground at Le Culot in strafing attacks by Bf109s of I./JG1 at 2.10 p.m. and 4.30 p.m. No pilot casualties. Aircraft all write-offs or abandoned on withdrawal to Belsele that night.

2/I/2 3 Hurricanes (H.23, H.29). Destroyed or badly damaged on the ground at Le Culot in strafing attacks by Bf109s of I./JG1 at 2.10 p.m. and 4.30 p.m. No pilot casualties. Aircraft all write-offs or abandoned on withdrawal to Belsele that night.
A Caudron-Renault liaison machine was also destroyed during these attacks.

5/III/2 6 Foxes (O.101, O.102, O.140, O.143, O.152 and O.178). Caught on the ground at Vissenaken in attack by Ju87s of StG2 3.50 p.m. No pilot casualties. Aircraft all damaged — abandoned on withdrawal to Moerbeke same day

III/2 Fox (O.142). Badly damaged by ground-fire near Louvain during transfer flight from Vissenaken to Moerbeke 4.55 p.m. Pilot unhurt. Aircraft a write-off.

6/III/2 2 Foxes. Landed at Moerbeke damaged by ground-fire near Louvain during transfer flight from Vissenaken 4.55 p.m. Lt F. Capon and Capt E. Symaes unhurt. Aircraft both repairable.
III/2 was ordered to withdraw to Norrent-Fontes next day, handing its surviving aircraft over to the III/3 at Aalter. Later re-established at Fréjorgues, where they received eight Fairey Fireflys, III/2 flew further sorties against the Italians in defence of the Montpellier and Marseille region.

1/I/3 8 Foxes (O.78, O.84, O.86, O.88, O.90, O.300, O.302 and O.306). Aircraft damaged the previous day further damaged in attack on Neerhespen airfield. No pilot casualties. Aircraft all write-offs.
Morane-Saulnier MS236 (M.8) was also damaged in this attack and abandoned on withdrawal to Zwevezele next day.

On May 10, as the 4. Panzer-Division approached Maastricht, at around 6 a.m. Belgian engineers blew the strategic bridges the Germans were planning on using to cross the River Meuse. Although this gave the Belgian Ier Corps d'Armée a breathing space, within a day a pontoon bridge had been finished. Blenheims of No. 110 Squadron flying from Britain bombed the crossing sites, losing two aircraft (see page 233). There were still three bridges standing across the Albert Canal running just west of the city and these were targeted by Battles of the Belgian Air Force on May 11. Their escort was provided by Gladiators of 1ème Escadrille of the 2ème Régiment d'Aeronautique. *Left:* Its Commandant was Capitaine Max Guisgand who came down in G.27 near Faimes *(right)*.

This is purported to be the wreck of G.19 piloted by Sergeant André Pirlot *(below left)* who was also escorting the Battles. His body was never recovered and today he has a symbolic grave *(below right)* in the cemetery for Belgian aviators at Evere in Brussels.

The fate of the nine attacking aircraft *(left)* of the 5ème Escadrille was even worse with six failing to return. Three Battles were detailed to attack each bridge, Nos. T.58, T.60 and T.73 going to Veldwezelt; T.61, T.64 and T.70 to Vroenhoven, and T.62, T.68 and T.71 to the bridge at Briegden. Five men were killed including Capitaine André Glorie *(right)*, the second-in-command.

5/III/3 Battle (T.60). Severely damaged in attacks by Bf110s near Ghent during sortie to bomb Veldwezelt bridge. Crash-landed at Klein Antwerpen, near Lebbeke 6.30 a.m. Adjt D. Verbraeck (of 9/III/3) and Adjt J. Dôme both wounded, admitted to hospital in Dendermonde. Aircraft a write-off.

5/III/3 Battle (T.58). Shot down by Oberlt Redlich *(Staffelkapitän)* of 1./JG27 over Tongeren during sortie to attack the Veldwezelt bridge and crashed at Molsterveld, near 's-Hereneldern 6.40 a.m. Adjt G. Timmermans (of 9/III/3) and 1/Sgt G. Rolin-Hymans both killed. Aircraft lost.

5/III/3 Battle (T.73). Returned to Aalter damaged by AA fire during attack on Veldwezelt bridge 6.50 a.m. Capt E. Pierre *(Commandant* of 9/III/3) and Lt L. Cloquette both unhurt. Aircraft damaged but repairable.

5/III/3 Battle (T.70). Hit by intense AA fire and caught fire during attack on the Vroenhoven bridge. Crashed at Lafelt, near Vlijtingen, west of Maastricht 6.40 a.m. Capt A. Glorie killed. S/Lt J. Vandenbosch baled out under 500 feet and captured badly wounded. Aircraft lost.

5/III/3 Battle (T.61). Exploded under intense AA fire during attack on the Vroenhoven bridge and crashed near Veldwezelt 6.40 a.m. Adjt F. Delvigne killed. Sgt A. Moens believed baled out but fell dead in the target area. Aircraft lost.

5/III/3 Battle (T.64). Returned to Aalter damaged following attack on the Vroenhoven bridge 6.40 a.m. Adjt A. Binon and Kpl. G. H. Legrand both unhurt. Aircraft repairable.

5/III/3 Battle (T.71). Returned to Aalter hit by ground-fire from Belgian troops near Lier during sortie to attack Briegden bridge 6.40 a.m. Adjt M. Vandevelde unhurt. Cpl J. Bergmans wounded. Aircraft repairable.

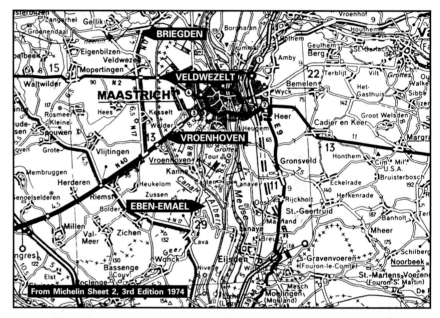

The three bridges at Maastricht are pinpointed on this early post-war Michelin map. Such were the improvisations in May 1940 that one signal despatched to No. 12 Squadron for an attack on two bridges over the Albert Canal stated: 'Additional information regarding targets obtained from Michelin guide for Belgium'.

5/III/3 Battle (T.62). Shot down by Belgian AA fire during sortie to attack the Briegden bridge and abandoned between Zonhoven and Diepenbeek after engine exploded 6.45 a.m. Adjt D. Jordens and Sgt X. de Ribaucourt both baled out, fired at by friendly troops, but avoided capture. Aircraft lost.

5/III/3 Battle (T.68). Crippled by AA fire during attack on the Briegden bridge and belly-landed near Schakkenbroek with bombs still in place due to defective bomb-release mechanism 6.50 a.m. 1/Sgt G. Wieseler unhurt. Adjt H. de Coninck baled out unhurt. Aircraft a write-off.

7/III/3 Fox (O.155). Attacked by German bombers during flight from Brussels-Evere to Lonzée and overturned attempting high-speed forced-landing at Gembloux. Sgt J. Coucke unhurt. Aircraft a write-off.

Two of the machines which failed to return from the Veldwezelt bridge. *Below left:* **Battle T.60 flown by Adjudants Désiré Verbraeck (of the 9éme Escadrille) and Jacques Dôme.** *Below:* **This is Battle T.58 in which both the pilot and the gunner, Adjudant Gustave Timmermans and Sergent Gustave Rolin-Hymans, were killed.**

LUFTWAFFE

AufklStaffel zbV. Luftflotte 2 Heinkel He111H. Returned damaged by flak following reconnaissance sortie over Antwerp. Uffz K. Schmidt slightly wounded. Aircraft repairable.

AufklStaffel zbV. Luftflotte 2 Heinkel He111H-2. Shot down by flak during reconnaissance sortie over Oostvoorne and crashed on the beach at Renesse, north of Haamstede 6.30 a.m. Uffz E. Steussloff, Uffz R. Wunderlich, and Uffz H. von Hoff killed. Obergefr S. Klug baled out and captured unhurt. Aircraft a write-off.

AufklSt. 7 Fliegerdivision Henschel Hs126B. Shot down by F/O Jefferies, and possibly also Sgt Wynn, of No. 17 Squadron and crashed at Pinksterhaven, near Piershil 7.10 p.m. Lt E. Francke killed. Fw H-J. Lindner died of wounds. Aircraft a write-off.

4.(H)/13 Henschel Hs126B. Reported crashed following collision with balloon. Lt Haeckel and another crewman believed killed. Aircraft a write-off.

1.(H)/14 Henschel Hs126. Returned damaged, believed due to ground-fire, following observation sortie over northern France. Lt L. Thomas badly wounded. Aircraft repairable.

3.(F)/31 Dornier Do17. Crashed at Aartal, near Bonn, while flying in fog. Lt B. Rumpelt and Uffz E. Schwär killed. Lt J. Kloppenburg badly injured. Aircraft a write-off.

3.(F)/31 Dornier Do17. Returned damaged in fighter attack during reconnaissance sortie over northern France. Possibly that engaged by F/O Richey of No. 1 Squadron north of Charleville-Mézières 8.40 a.m. Fw W. Vogt badly wounded in left arm, rest of crew unhurt. Aircraft repairable.

3.(F)/122 Junkers Ju88A-1. Shot down by No. 19 Squadron Spitfires during reconnaissance sortie off the English coast and ditched in sea east of Terschelling 3.00 p.m. Uffz H. Kunze drowned, rest of crew picked up by the *Bavaria*. Lt F. Meyer captured unhurt. Uffz R. Krulich and Uffz W. Höbel captured wounded. Aircraft lost.

2.(F)/123 Dornier Do17P. Returned riddled by Moranes of GC II/2 during reconnaissance sortie between Maastricht and Namur 5.10 a.m. Oberlt D. von Schaezler and Uffz W. Klaas both wounded. Oberfw Felgenhauer unhurt. Aircraft a write-off.

2.(F)/123 Dornier Do17P. Believed that attacked by No. 85 Squadron Hurricanes over Doenrade, during reconnaissance sortie and forced-landed at 't Rooth, near Schinnen 1.00 p.m. Lt H. Brosch and Fw H. Layher both wounded. Fw Steiner believed unhurt. Aircraft 4U+HK a write-off.

3./JG1 Messerschmitt Bf109E-3. Wrecked in forced-landing near Aachen out of fuel, following combat with fighters. Pilot believed unhurt. Aircraft a write-off.

4./JG2 Messerschmitt Bf109E. Overturned on landing following transfer to Hamminkeln. Leutnant J. Meimberg believed unhurt. Aircraft 1+ — damage state not recorded.

2./JG20 Messerschmitt Bf109E-4. Shot down by flak during offensive sortie over the Waal and crashed at Amerongen, north of Tiel 2.10 p.m. Oberleutnant A. Fr von Minnigerode (*Staffelkapitän*) captured. Aircraft a write-off.

I./JG26 Messerschmitt Bf109E. Damaged in combat with Moranes of GC I/4 south of Antwerp 4.45 p.m. and forced-landed near Erkelenz. Believed that attacked by Sgt Cucumel. Pilot unhurt. Aircraft a write-off.

2./JG26 Messerschmitt Bf109E-3. Shot down in combat with Moranes of GC I/4 south-west of Antwerp and believed crashed near Lier 4.40 p.m. Possibly that claimed by Sgt Debéthune or Adj Kesse. Feldwebel G. Herzog captured. Aircraft a write-off.

5./JG26 Messerschmitt Bf109E. Shot down during attack on flak battery south of the IJsselmeer and crashed near De Klomp. Oberleutnant H. von Holtey (*Staffelkapitän*) captured wounded. Aircraft 14+ — a write-off.

4./JG27 Messerschmitt Bf109E-3. Engine hit by flak during attack on Dutch battery near Tiel, and crashed at Almkerk, east of Kesteren, 8.00 a.m. Leutnant L. Scheffler believed baled out and captured. Aircraft a write-off.

3./JG51 Messerschmitt Bf109E. Believed shot down in combat with Hurricanes of No. 17 Squadron south of Rotterdam, and crashed at Lindtse Benedendijk, west of Zwijndrecht 5.10 p.m. Possibly that claimed by F/O Meredith. Uffz F. Schild killed. Aircraft a write-off.

3./JG51 Messerschmitt Bf109E. Believed shot down in combat with Hurricanes of No. 17 Squadron south of Rotterdam and crash-landed in the Merwedepolder east of Dordrecht 5.10 p.m. Possibly that attacked by Sgt Pavey. Uffz F. Schreiter captured wounded. Aircraft a write-off.

II./JG52 Messerschmitt Bf109E-1. Damaged in aborted take-off from Speyer. Pilot believed unhurt. Aircraft damaged but repairable.

9./JG53 Messerschmitt Bf109E-3. Crashed on take-off from Hoppstädten and burned out. Feldwebel Kahlmeier killed. Aircraft a write-off.

I./JG54 Messerschmitt Bf109E-3. Crash-landed at Horb-am-Neckar, near Eutingen, following escort sortie. Possibly that engaged by S/Lt Plubeau, Adjt Tesseraud, and Sgt Jaussaud of GC II/4 near Rambervillers 10.15 a.m. Pilot believed unhurt. Aircraft damaged but repairable.

I./JG76 Messerschmitt Bf109E-1. Wrecked in forced-landing at Retzerath following engine failure during transit flight from Ober-Olm to Wengerohr 9.15 a.m. Pilot believed unhurt. Aircraft a write-off.

6.(J)/TrGr.186 Messerschmitt Bf109E-3. Shot down by flak and crashed in the Waddenzee near the Afsluitdijk 3.30 p.m. Uffz W. Haase captured. Aircraft a write-off.

Stab KG1 Heinkel He111H. Believed shot down by anti-aircraft fire over Mastaing during reconnaissance sortie to Maubeuge and crashed into buildings at Avesnes-le-Sec 6.00 a.m. Uffz R. Diekmann, Uffz E. Türpitsch, and Gefr W. Brelage killed. Oberlt G. Schuster captured mortally wounded, died in Valenciennes military hospital. Uffz T. Gippert captured wounded. Aircraft V4+EA a write-off.

I./KG2 Four Dornier Do17Z. Returned damaged and with casualties caused by AA fire south of Sedan during low-level sortie between Montmédy, Stenay, and Remilly 6.15 a.m. Fw W. Baebenroth killed. Oberfw A. Heyer and Uffz H. Ohlrogge badly wounded. Fw R. Kunsch and Uffz K. Mackenstein slightly wounded. Aircraft all damaged but repairable.

1./KG2 Two Dornier Do17Z. Damaged by AA fire near Montmédy during sortie to attack La Malmaison airfield and crash-landed on return 5.30 a.m. Fw A. Schwengber killed. Oberfw K. Deekarm, Uffz W. Krüger, and Uffz H. Wolpers slightly wounded. Aircraft both repairable.

2./KG2 Dornier Do17Z. Shot down by F/Lt Williams, and possibly also Sgt Dafforn, of No. 501 Squadron during sortie to attack Malmaison airfield. Belly-landed and caught fire near Arcis-le-Ponsart 5.30 a.m. Fw F. Hauser baled out and captured wounded. Fw O. Müller captured unhurt. Fw F. Eyrich and Uffz P. Schuh captured wounded, admitted to Jeanne d'Arc Hospital in Reims. Aircraft a write-off.

4./KG2 Three Dornier Do17Z. Returned with flak damage and casualties caused by ground-fire south-west of Esch during sortie to attack Vraux airfield 5.30 a.m. Fw W. Hosemann and Gefr G. Weinhold both slightly wounded, admitted to hospital in Aschaffenburg. Uffz H. Veit believed unhurt. Aircraft all repairable.

4./KG2 Dornier Do17Z. Forced-landed at Frankfurt-Rebstock badly damaged by ground-fire south-west of Esch during sortie to attack Vraux airfield 5.30 a.m. Oberlt O. Reimers (*Staffelkapitän*) badly wounded, admitted to hospital in Frankfurt-am-Main. Oberfw Krüger, Fw Bredtmeier and Fw Lohrer unhurt. Aircraft U5+LM a write-off.

5./KG2 Dornier Do17Z. Returned damaged by ground-fire over Esch during sortie to attack Vraux airfield 5.30 a.m. Gefr K. Hadlich killed. Oberfw R. Brandes slightly wounded, admitted to hospital in Mannheim. Aircraft repairable.

III./KG2 Dornier Do17Z. Returned damaged in attacks by S/Lt Lefol, S/Lt Parnière, Sgt Tallent, and Sgt Girou of GC I/5 between Bulson and Chéhéry 6.20 a.m. No crew casualties. Aircraft damaged but repairable.

9./KG3 Dornier Do17Z. Crashed outside Langendiebach airfield during transit flight to Borstendorf 12.30 p.m. Cause not stated but probable engine failure. Fw S. Ganb, Uffz G. Lauckemann, and Gefr G. Richter (mechanic of Stab III./KG3) killed. Aircraft a write-off.

2./KG27 Heinkel He111P-2. Shot down near Tienen during sortie to Antwerp and possibly one of those attacked by Sgt Allard and S/L Oliver of No. 85 Squadron near Maastricht. Fw F. Ratzing and Fw W. Föcking captured wounded. Fw W. Efselmann and Uffz J. Schulz captured unhurt. Aircraft 1G+HK a write-off.

7./KG27 Heinkel He111P. Believed shot down by Capt Jozan of AC 1 over Vlissingen and crashed and burned out near Kapelle in Zuid-Beveland 7.00 p.m. Uffz W. Hettich captured badly wounded, later died. Uffz K. Migge captured wounded. Oberlt W. Bodenberger and Fw O. Fiedler both captured unhurt. Aircraft a write-off.

8./KG27 Heinkel He111P-2. Crashed and exploded in Steinhuder Meer on return from attack on shipping off Walcheren. Believed one of those attacked by Mtre Billottet, LV Folliot, and EV1 Craignic of AC 2 6.00 p.m. Uffz E. Eichler, Obergefr G. Lewioda, Gefr K-H. Becker, and Flgr W. Hammerschmidt killed. Aircraft 1G+BS a write-off.

Unteroffizier Emil Bohn was piloting his Heinkel from Stab KG54 when he was set upon by French Curtiss H-75s. Along with his observer, Oberleutnant Wilhelm Suborg, Bohn was captured but is believed to have died at Dunkirk en route to England on May 29. His other two comrades are both buried at Lommel. Twenty-six Curtiss H-75s of GC I/4 engaged bombers attacking Allied columns between Antwerp and Breda and claimed two He111s and three Bf109s destroyed, and another Bf109 damaged. However, it proved a costly action for they lost five H-75s including that piloted by the Groupe Commandant, and with the aircraft of the Commandant of 2e Escadrille returning damaged.

I./KG51 Heinkel He111H. Returned damaged following sortie to attack Châteauroux airfield 9.45 a.m. Possibly that engaged by Sgt Doudies and Sgt Grimaud of GC II/7. No crew casualties. Aircraft repairable.

1./KG51 Heinkel He111H. Starboard engine caught fire under attack by 9 Moranes of GC III/6 and GC II/7 during attack on Châteauroux airfield, jettisonned bombs and belly-landed north-west of Pirey 9.45 a.m. Believed credited to Adjt Le Gloan and Lt Legrand of GC III/6. Fw K. Zähnle captured slightly wounded, admitted to St Jacques hospital in Besançon. Fw H. Lenkeit, Uffz R. Lachmann, Uffz G. Geske, and Gefr J. Heyer captured unhurt. Aircraft 9K+GH a write-off.

II./KG51 3 Junkers Ju88A. Returned damaged in attacks by S/Lt Dussart, S/Lt Mangin, and Sgt Boillot of GC II/7 during attack on Lure-Malbouhans airfield 8.20 a.m. No crew casualties. Aircraft all damaged but repairable.

III./KG51 Heinkel He111H. Returned damaged in attacks by Moranes of GC II/7 between Dijon and Gray during sortie to attack Lyon-Bron airfield 9.30 a.m. No crew casualties. Aircraft repairable.

9./KG51 Heinkel He111H. Starboard engine set alight in attacks by 16 Moranes of GC II/7 between Dijon and Gray during sortie to attack Lyon-Bron airfield. Abandoned over Montsauche; crashed and exploded in Brassy 9.30 a.m. Uffz F. Niedermeyer killed. Gefr H. Hinrich baled out badly wounded, Gefr P. Riederer, Uffz E. Eden, and Gefr J. Zellner baled out slightly wounded. Crew captured near Poirot and La Fiolle, all admitted to hospital in Nevers. Aircraft 9K+MT a write-off.

Stabsstaffel KG53 Heinkel He111H. Both engines set alight in attacks by Capt Portalis, Sgt Salès, and Sgt Chabera of GC II/5 during photo-reconnaissance sortie. Crashed and exploded west of the railway line to Mars-la-Tour, north-east of Chambley, 7.45 a.m. Fw H. Zeep baled out too low and captured badly wounded; died Legouest Hospital June 8. Oberfw J. Beine and Uffz H. Jeschke killed. Oberlt J. von Horn and Uffz R. Mayer baled out and captured unhurt. Aircraft a write-off.

Stab I./KG53 Heinkel He111H (6808). Starboard engine damaged by flak during sortie over Toul then attacked by S/Lt Thollon and S/Lt Flandi of GC I/8, also Sgt Moulènes and Sgt Boyer of GC III/7. Belly-landed near Trondes 6.40 a.m. Oberlt M. Pröbst killed. Oberstlt K. Mehnert *(Gruppenkommandeur)*, Oberfw M. Winter, Oberfw G. Müller, and Fw F. Kempgens captured unhurt. Aircraft A1+JK fired by crew.

Stab I./KG53 Heinkel He111H (3327). Both engines disabled in attacks by GC I/8 and GC I/2 near Reims. Pursued by S/Lt Ruchoux of GC II/5, finally belly-landed and later exploded west of Recourt-le-Creux 7.30 a.m. Fw E. Bühler (of 3./KG53) killed. Oberlt A. Hufenreuter, Oberfw J. Schimpl, Oberfw G. Fegert, and Fw F. Puth captured wounded. Aircraft a write-off.

I./KG53 Heinkel He111H. Returned from sortie damaged by flak. No crew casualties. Aircraft repairable.

2./KG53 Heinkel He111H. Shot down by Adj Streiff, Lt Monty, Sgt Goile of GC I/2, and Lt Houzé, Sgt Janeba, Sgt Hanzlicek of GC II/5 near Montplonne, during sortie to Ste-Menehould. Crashed with port engine alight in the Bois de Chêne, west of Ligny-en-Barrois, and burned out. Gefr E. Plätschke, Gefr H. Ahrendt, Flgr K. Gilber, and Flgr H. Hiersemann killed. Uffz K-H. Menzel baled out and captured unhurt. Aircraft a write-off.

4./KG53 Heinkel He111. Both engines disabled in attacks by Capt Accart, Sgt Vuillemain, and Sgt Morel of GC I/5 following attacks on rail targets near Ste-Menehould. Crash-landed and burned out at Buxières-sous-les-Côtes 3.30 p.m. Uffz E. Hermann mortally wounded, died en-route to hospital. Uffz E. Landgraf captured wounded, admitted to Ste-Anne hospital in St Mihiel. Lt W. Wellstein and Uffz K. Kramer captured unhurt. Aircraft a write-off.

4./KG53 Heinkel He111. Shot down by Sgt Morel, Capt Accart, and Lt Perina of GC I/5 during sortie over Ste-Menehould. Crashed and burned out north-west of Ferme de Maivaux at Ville-sur-Cousances, east of Clermont-en-Argonne, 3.40 p.m. Uffz P. Volz, Uffz L. Bierfelder, Uffz R. Lyschick, Uffz M. Dudzinski, and Gefr E. Stäudner all killed. Aircraft A1+BM a write-off.

4./KG53 Heinkel He111H. Made dead-stick landing near Saarlautern both engines destroyed in attacks by Capt Accart of GC I/5 following sortie over Ste-Menehould 3.40 p.m. Uffz H. Weippert and Uffz H. Enghofer slightly wounded. Aircraft a write-off.

III./KG53 3 Heinkel He111H. Returned damaged in fighter attacks near Sedan. Possibly those claimed by Sgt Humphris of No. 73 Squadron, F/O Malfroy and F/Sgt Payne of No. 501 Squadron between Rethel and Charleville-Mézières 2.45 p.m. Gefr Hans Petzgall (of 7 Staffel) slightly wounded. Aircraft all repairable.

9./KG53 Heinkel He111H. Shot down by flak over Toul and crashed at Saint-Baussant 6.30 a.m. Uffz J. Zink, Obergefr A. Friebe, Gefr R. Müller, and Gefr F. Scholz killed. Uffz G. Lüders baled out and captured unhurt. Aircraft a write-off.

Stab KG54 Heinkel He111P. Attacked by eight Curtiss H-75s of GC I/4 during reconnaissance of roads between Breda and Antwerp, and shot down in the forest of Begijnenbos, near Zandhoven 5.00 p.m. Uffz H. Voges and Uffz W. Nahrgang killed. Oberlt W. Surborg and Uffz E. Bohn captured. Aircraft a write-off.

1./KG54 Heinkel He111P. Returned probably damaged in attacks by Moranes of GC I/4 north of St-Niklaas 4.50 p.m. Uffz K. Hansen slightly wounded. Aircraft repairable.

3./KG54 Heinkel He111P-2. Hit by flak and abandoned over Gorinchem 2.00 p.m. Fw W. Woszczyna baled out but fell dead in Arkel polder. Oberlt K. Brand baled out and captured wounded. Uffz B. Blankenfuland and Gefr H. Boegel both baled out and captured unhurt. Aircraft a write-off.

2./KG55 Heinkel He111P. Shot down by fighters and forced-landed near Illange, south of Thionville, 6.30 a.m. Fw E. George killed. Uffz H. Grosskreutz captured badly wounded, later died. Fw E. Beisser and Fw W. Dreffkorn captured unhurt. Aircraft a write-off.

3./KG55 Heinkel He111P. Returned damaged by ground-fire. Uffz H. Laag slightly wounded. Aircraft repairable.

First buried at Dunkirk, Unteroffizier Bohn now lies in the German War Graves Cemetery at Bourdon on the Somme west of Amiens.

6./KG55 2 Heinkel He111P. Returned damaged by flak and ground-fire over Baccarat following attack on Orléans-Bricy 12.30 p.m. Fw R. Kirchhoff, Uffz F. Mertz, and Uffz G. Pulver slightly wounded. Aircraft both repairable.

6./KG55 Heinkel He111P. Hit by intense flak and ground-fire near Baccarat following attack on Orléans-Bricy. Then port engine destroyed in attack by S/Lt Plubeau of GC II/4 and forced-landed and burned out at Hattigny 12.30 p.m. Oberlt W. Radünz and Oberfw W. Krups evaded in Forêt de Harcholins but surrendered at Niderhoff later that night. Fw R. Boiselle, Fw A. Meisel, and Obergefr O. Jäger baled out over Badonviller and captured unhurt. Aircraft a write-off.

III./KG55 Heinkel He111P. Returned damaged by flak and attacks by Moranes of GC III/6 during sortie to bomb airfield near Dijon 6.30 p.m. Probably that engaged by Adj Goujon and Sgt Hardouin. Oberfw K. Schwarze (of 9. Staffel) badly wounded. Aircraft damaged but repairable.

III./KG55 Heinkel He111P. Returned damaged, possibly by Moranes of GC III/6, following sortie to bomb airfield near Dijon 6.30 p.m. No crew casualties. Aircraft repairable.

7./KG55 Heinkel He111P (2800). Both engines destroyed in attacks by Lt Martin, S/Lt Colonges, and Adj Goujon of GC 5/6 north of Gray during sortie to bomb airfield near Dijon. Jettisonned bombs over Ste-Reine and belly-landed between Etuz and Gezier, north of Besançon 6.30 p.m. Gefr E. Rieger and Flgr E. Kiesenhofer killed reportedly resisting capture. Fw H. Rossmann, Obergefr H. Schenkenberg, and Gefr H-J. Schmahl wounded on capture. Aircraft G1+FR fired by crew.

After destroying the aircraft, this crew split into two groups in an effort to reach German-held territory. French reports state that three resisted capture and opened fired on gendarmes who returned fire killing both gunners, Emmerich Kiesenhofer and Ernst Rieger, and badly wounding the wireless operator, Hans-Joachim Schmahl. The pilot, Hans Rossmann, and gunner, Helmut Schenkenberg, who were both captured without resistance between Marnay and Brussey later that night, also suffered very rough treatment.

II./KG76 Dornier Do17Z. Returned damaged, possibly in attacks by Sgt Touret and S/Lt de Russé of GC II/6 south-east of Maubeuge 6.45 a.m. No crew casualties. Aircraft damaged but repairable.

III./KG76 Dornier Do17Z. Forced-landed at Fritzlar due to petrol failure. No crew casualties. Aircraft damaged but repairable.

3./KG77 Dornier Do17Z. Returned damaged by fighters over Valkenburg, east of Maastricht. Fw H. Beyer badly wounded. Aircraft damage state not recorded.

5./KG77 Dornier Do17Z. Returned damaged by ground-fire during sortie over Hasselt. Gefr H. Winkes slightly wounded. Aircraft damage state not recorded.

6./KG77 Two Dornier Do17Z. Returned hit by ground-fire near Tongeren. Uffz G. Brunke and Uffz H. Ullrich both slightly wounded. Aircraft damage state not recorded.

9./KG77 Dornier Do17Z. Returned damaged by flak and fighters. Gefr K. Weinberger wounded. Aircraft damage state not recorded.

3./KGr.126 Heinkel He111H-2. Believed shot down by Sgt Cucumel of GC I/4 near Antwerp during sortie to attack columns around Tilburg 5.00 p.m. Fw G. Vorbau, Uffz G. Grywatz, and Obergefr H. Hill captured wounded. Obergefr E. Wehner captured unhurt. Aircraft a write-off.

6./KGzbV.1 Junkers Ju52 (6462). Hit by ground-fire near Werkendam (24e Bt.Lu.A) during sortie to drop paratroops at Dordrecht and belly-landed in Lepelaar polder, south of Moordplaat in the Biesbosch 7.50 a.m. Obergefr R. Markert, Uffz T. Kierzynski, and Flgr M. Karhard captured. One Fallschirmjäger killed, 14 men of 3./FJR1 captured and taken to Sleeuwijk. Aircraft destroyed by crew.

14./KGzbV.1 Two Junkers Ju52 (6604, 6609). Shot down by flak south of Zaltbommel en-route to drop paratroops at Dordrecht and crashed near 's-Hertogenbosch 7.45 a.m. Oberlt K. Otto, Uffz O. Dieren, Uffz F. Tischer, Gefr J. Freese, Gefr M. Seeba, Gefr A. Busching, Gefr W. Knudsen, Gefr J-D. Schroder, Gefr J. Tischer, and Gefr J. Wohlgemuth all killed. Aircraft including 1Z+EY both write-offs.

3./KüFlGr. 506 Heinkel He115C. Crashed in sea off Norderney landing in fog following night mine-laying sortie off the Dutch coast. Oberfw F. Papner, Fw W. Rieck, and Gefr K. Pirrong killed. Aircraft a write-off.

3./KüFlGr. 506 Heinkel He115C. Crashed in fog at Baltrum following night mine-laying sortie off the Dutch coast. Oberlt zur See A. Friedrichs and Fw E. Gusikat both badly injured, admitted to hospital in Norderney. Radio operator unhurt. Aircraft a write-off.

3./KüFlGr. 906 Heinkel He115C. Crashed in fog on a building site at Norderney and burned out following night mine-laying sortie off the Dutch coast. Lt K-H. Schmidt, Oberfw O. zum Brook, and Uffz K. Mommertz killed. Aircraft a write-off.

Nine members of the Reichsarbeitsdienst were killed and 7 more injured in this accident.

3./KüFlGr. 906 Heinkel He115C. Crashed off Juist landing in fog following night mine-laying sortie off the Dutch coast. Lt zur See D. Lux and Fw W. Fiedler killed. Uffz H. Borgwedel slightly injured, admitted to hospital in Norderney. Aircraft a write-off.

3./KüFlGr. 906 Heinkel He115C. Forced-landed at Norderney in fog following night mine-laying sortie off the Dutch coast. Crew unhurt. Aircraft damaged but repairable.

1./LG1 Heinkel He111P. Shot down by P/O Appleton and P/O Wood of No. 79 Squadron and crashed on a house at Masnuy-St-Jean 5.00 a.m. Fw F. Heisel, Uffz A. Grunwald, Obergefr K. Winnat, and Gefr W. Kühne killed. Aircraft a write-off.

1./LG1 Heinkel He111P. Believed shot down by F/O Gore, P/O Jay and P/O Parrott of No. 607 Squadron and crashed near Heist-op-den-Berg 1.15 p.m. Fw H. Büchner, Uffz T. Rothfuss, Uffz J. Schmidt, and Uffz H. Klein-Altstedde killed. Aircraft a write-off.

1./LG1 Heinkel He111P. Returned damaged believed in attack by No. 607 Squadron Hurricanes near Brussels 1.15 p.m. Uffz G. Kunze killed. Aircraft damage state not recorded.

1./LG1 Heinkel He111P. Shot down by F/Lt Blackadder, F/O Bazin, F/O Thompson, P/O Dixon and P/O Dini of No. 607 Squadron and crashed at Wezembeek-Oppem, 10 km east of Brussels 6.45 p.m. Fw G. Fröhlich and Obergefr W. Rautmann killed. Obergefr R. Petermann captured wounded. Uffz K. Fürstenberg captured unhurt. Aircraft L1+FH a write-off.

8./LG1 Junkers Ju88A-1. Returned damaged in attack by Cdt. Bertrou, Capt de Gail, and S/Lt Robiaud of GC II/2 over Steenokkerzeel 7.00 p.m. Fw H. Peters badly wounded. Aircraft damage state not recorded.

14.(Z)/LG1 Messerschmitt Bf110C. Badly damaged in attack by Lt Zerovnicky of GC I/8 during escort sortie over St Mihiel. Caught fire during return flight, abandoned over Lenoncourt, and crashed at Cerville 6.35 a.m. Uffz W. Fabian killed. Lt H. Leickhardt baled out and captured badly wounded in the arm. Aircraft a write-off.

4.(S)/LG2 Henschel Hs123. Returned damaged by flak north of Liège 10.00 p.m. Fw B. Bludau slightly wounded. Aircraft damage state not recorded.

5.(S)/LG2 Henschel Hs123. Forced-landed damaged in attack by F/Lt Plinston of No. 607 Squadron south of Maastricht 4.00 p.m. No crew casualties. Aircraft damaged but repairable.

Stab StG2 Dornier Do17M. Believed shot down by S/L Dewar and F/O Mitchell of No. 87 Squadron during reconnaissance sortie over Tirlemont and belly-landed near St Trond 3.30 p.m. Uffz G. Muschner killed. Oberlt H. Metz *(Staffelkapitän) and* Fw H. Schindler captured unhurt. Aircraft a write-off.

Helmuth Schindler died May 30 in bombing at Dunkirk.

Stab StG2 Junkers Ju87B. Shot down by Hurricanes of No. 87 Squadron between Tirlemont and Leuven 3.30 p.m. Oberlt A. Kädtler and Uffz H. Grüneklee killed. Aircraft a write-off.

1./StG2 Junkers Ju87B. Returned severely damaged by Hurricanes of No. 87 Squadron over Tirlemont 3.30 p.m. Uffz H. Schneider killed, pilot unhurt. Aircraft repairable.

2./StG2 Junkers Ju87B. Shot down by Hurricanes of No. 87 Squadron over Tirlemont and crashed near St Trond 3.30 p.m. Uffz H. Lange and Obergefr A. Fischer killed. Aircraft a write-off.

2./StG2 Junkers Ju87B. Shot down by Hurricanes of No. 87 Squadron over Tirlemont and crashed at Attenhoven 3.30 p.m. Uffz R. Hahn killed. Lt S. Dryander captured unhurt. Aircraft a write-off.

2./StG2 Junkers Ju87B. Shot down by Hurricanes of No. 87 Squadron over Tirlemont 3.30 p.m. Uffz H. Werk and Uffz E. Chuchra killed. Aircraft a write-off.

2./StG2 Junkers Ju87B. Returned damaged by Hurricanes of No. 87 Squadron over Tirlemont 3.30 p.m. Gefr K-H. Schmidt badly wounded, pilot unhurt. Aircraft repairable.

3./StG2 Junkers Ju87B. Shot down by Hurricanes of No. 87 Squadron over Maastricht 3.30 p.m. Uffz H. Diegmann killed. Uffz F. Fiebranz captured wounded. Aircraft a write-off.

7./StG2 Junkers Ju87B. Returned damaged by No. 607 Squadron Hurricanes during attack on roads east of Tirlemont 4.35 p.m. Uffz F. Kulik killed, pilot unhurt. Aircraft damage state not recorded.

8./StG2 Junkers Ju87B. Shot down by No. 607 Squadron Hurricanes during attack on roads east of Tirlemont and crashed near Visé 4.35 p.m. Oberlt K. Janke and Uffz G. Gärtig both captured wounded. Aircraft T6+MS a write-off.

For the Luftwaffe, Saturday, May 11, 1940 ended somewhat inauspiciously with the loss of another 100-plus aircraft, whereas the four Allies only lost marginally more machines between them. Pilots of No. 87 Squadron forced down the Dornier of the Staffelkapitän of Stab StG2 in the mid-afternoon. Oberleutnant Hans Metz crash-landed his machine near St Trond. The Staff flight of every Stuka unit employed Do17s for pre-attack reconnaissance and post-strike evaluation of bombing results. Operating in small formations, or even singly, they would experience significant losses during the Blitzkrieg which relied so heavily on air-to-ground attacks.

8./StG2 Junkers Ju87B. Believed shot down by No. 607 Squadron Hurricanes during attack on roads east of Tirlemont and crash-landed near Maastricht 4.35 p.m. Oberlt L. Lau *(Staffelkapitän)* and Uffz F. Ochmanek captured badly wounded. Aircraft T6+AS a write-off.

8./StG2 Junkers Ju87B. Returned damaged by No. 607 Squadron Hurricanes south of Julémont during attack on roads east of Tirlemont 4.35 p.m. Lt H. Meyer and Uffz K. Gotzler slightly wounded. Aircraft damaged but repairable.

3.(St)/Tr.Gr.186 Junkers Ju87B. Damaged by flak during attack on enemy armour near Montmédy 6.30 a.m. and forced-landed near Steinbach. Fw W. Bornemann and Uffz H. Ulrich both unhurt. Aircraft a write-off.

3.(St)/Tr.Gr.186 Junkers Ju87B. Shot down by flak and crashed 1 km north of Montmédy during attack on enemy armour 6.30 a.m. Hptmn E. Blattner *(Staffelkapitän)* and Fw K. Fernholz killed. Aircraft a write-off.

Transportstaffel Fl.Korps II Junkers Ju52. Damaged in take-off accident. No crew casualties. Aircraft damaged but repairable.

3./ZG1 Messerschmitt Bf110C. Returned damaged by flak during escort sortie over Gorinchem 12.45 p.m. Pilot unhurt, Uffz L. Leidenbach badly wounded, admitted to hospital in Dorsten. Aircraft damage state not recorded.

3./ZG1 Messerschmitt Bf110C. Shot down by flak during escort sortie and crashed in flames at Grote Haar east of Gorinchem 12.45 p.m. Fw F. Stadler captured badly wounded, treated at the Missiehuis van de Paters Nuland. Obergefr K. Knuth captured unhurt. Aircraft a write-off.

6./ZG1 Messerschmitt Bf110C. Forced-landed at Liedern-bei-Bocholt badly damaged by ground-fire. Uffz A. Maske and Obergefr E. Schulze both slightly injured, admitted to hospital in Buer. Aircraft a write-off.

1./ZG2 Messerschmitt Bf110. Shot down by P/O Hulse and Sgt Morfill of No. 501 Squadron in action between Rethel and Charleville-Mézières during escort sortie for He111s of II./KG53. Crashed near Viel-St-Rémy, east of Novion-Porcien 3.15 p.m. Lt D. Moeller baled out over Machéroménil and captured with broken ankle. Gefr G. Kergel killed. Aircraft a write-off.

Major recovery by local landowner.

3./ZG2 Messerschmitt Bf110. Shot down by F/Lt Hanks and P/O Mould, and also attacked by F/O Clisby, of No. 1 Squadron in action between Rethel and Charleville-Mézières during escort sortie for He111s of II./KG53. Crash-landed outside Vendresse 3.15 p.m. Lt W. Maurer and Uffz S. Makera both captured unhurt. Aircraft a write-off.

1./ZG26 Messerschmitt Bf110C. Shot down by Hurricanes of No. 1 Squadron during escort sortie south-east of Hirson and believed that claimed by F/Lt Walker, F/O Brown, F/O Kilmartin, F/O Richey, and Sgt Soper. Crashed at 'la Planchette', between Aubenton and Ribeauvillé 7.15 p.m. Obergefr B. Hofeler killed. Lt F. Auinger baled out and captured wounded in left calf. Aircraft a write-off.

1./ZG26 Messerschmitt Bf110C. Shot down by Hurricanes of No. 1 Squadron during escort sortie south-east of Hirson and believed that claimed by F/Lt Walker, F/O Brown, F/O Kilmartin, F/O Richey, and Sgt Soper. Crashed into buildings at Rue-Larcher, west of Aubenton 7.15 p.m. Uffz E. Ebrecht killed. Uffz W. Weis baled out and captured unhurt. Aircraft a write-off.

Willi Weis escaped from French captivity and returned to his unit by May 20, only to be killed in action on June 13.

I./ZG52 Messerschmitt Bf110C. Damaged in taxying accident at Neuhausen airfield. Crew unhurt. Aircraft repairable.

II./ZG76 Messerschmitt Bf110C. Crash-landed near Wolfenbüttel with fuel tank damaged in attack by Sgt Flanek of GC 6/2 between St Trond and Namur 7.10 p.m. Crew unhurt. Aircraft damaged but repairable.

Sunday, May 12

Throughout the morning, 40 Junkers Ju52s of KGrzbV.9 flew in and out of Waalhaven with relative impunity bringing troops of Stab 2./AR22, 5. and 6. Batterien AR22, and 14./IR47. The relentless German advance continued in both Holland and Belgium as the British and French established defensive positions towards which Belgian forces withdrew. Luftwaffe activity was now mainly directed against communications in the immediate rear of the Allied forces, though airfields continued to attract attention but on a reduced scale.

RAF Component Lysanders, now flying regular contact patrols over British forward positions and observing enemy movements, reconnoitred several Belgian airfields where they reported wrecked aircraft and severe damage. French reconnaissance sorties over the Ardennes and Luxembourg, however, indicated an emerging and serious enemy thrust developing towards Sedan. But the gravity of the situation at Maastricht was considered to pose the greater threat and, as such, attracted most of the available air support during the morning.

Attacks were mounted against enemy columns advancing from Maastricht towards Tongeren and Gembloux, and, for the first time, AASF Blenheims were employed. Their losses were to prove equally disastrous as those suffered by the Fairey Battles. Only two of the nine aircraft despatched returned, the rest all falling victim to ever-present and increasing numbers of German fighters. French attacks in the same area provided even worse statistics, one bomber group losing nine Breguets to intense AA fire in a single sortie.

It was clear that, to try and stem this German advance, two bridges over the Albert Canal at Vroenhoven and Veldwezelt, southwest of Maastricht, had to be destroyed. An attack by Belgian Battles the previous day had met with calamitous results, and mindful of the AA and fighter defences in the area, Air Marshal Barratt determined that the mission should only be flown by volunteer crews drawn from the allotted No. 12 Squadron. In the event, every crew volunteered so the six crews were finally selected by drawing lots. Each bridge was to be attacked by a section of three Battles at 9.15 a.m. while 24 Bomber Command Blenheims hit the same targets shortly after. Fighter escort was to be provided by ten AASF Hurricanes plus two RAF Component squadrons.

What followed was a repeat of the disastrous Belgian attack of the previous day, but it passed into RAF legend. Fighting their way through heavy enemy fighter defence and pressing home their attacks in the teeth of intense AA fire, those Battles that reached the target each dropped four 250lb bombs from 2,000 feet. Only one of the aircraft returned. The posthumous award of the Victoria Cross to both Flying Officer Garland and Sergeant Gray, pilot and navigator of the lead aircraft in the first section, testament to what an official narrative described as 'the devoted heroism displayed by the crews in undertaking a virtually suicidal task'.

By afternoon, the German thrust through the Ardennes was fast becoming recognised as increasingly serious. More Battles were therefore despatched against a pontoon bridge at Bouillon and enemy troops advancing in the area. These attacks attracted further significant losses, mainly from the crippling AA fire that accompanied every German column.

Fighter Command support on the day was limited to three patrols over the Hook of Holland, one of which saw Spitfires and Defiants operating together over the Continent

Two days into the battle, the line of the Albert Canal, on which the Belgian defence had been based, was broken. On Sunday, May 12 they again made an urgent request for the bridges at Maastricht to be bombed. The first operation by Blenheims of No. 139 Squadron ended with seven of the nine aircraft failing to return. The next attempt by six Battles of No. 12 Squadron was equally disastrous, as was a later attempt to halt the German columns by the French 12ème and 54ème Escadres. Meanwhile the main German thrust was being set in motion, aimed at Sedan, 150 kilometres further south and, to this end, the VIII. Fliegerkorps was transferred to Luftflotte 3 in support. This area, which was weakly held by French reservists, would be hit by Gruppe von Kleist with close air support from VIII. Fliegerkorps. French air reconnaissance warnings of an impending attack went unheeded all attention being fixed on events in Belgium.

The screaming wail of the Stuka — produced by air-driven sirens fitted to the top of each undercarriage fairing — increased the fear of this weapon of 'aerial artillery' which epitomised the campaigns in Poland and the West. The awesome sound of these 'trumpets of Jericho' as wave after wave of Stukas plunged on their targets in near-vertical dives was deliberately intimidating, often creating panic and confusion on the ground, and particularly amongst already dispirited troops. As one British soldier stranded at Dunkirk remembers, 'Then came the Stukas with their bombs and machine guns and wingwailers. Unfortunately no RAF! All hell and no salvation'. This quality to inspire fear, together with the Stuka's near-legendary bombing accuracy, was fully exploited by the German Propaganda Ministry and widely reported in the European press. For close air support the Stuka was an extremely potent weapon provided it enjoyed total air superiority.

for the first time. And, to complete the agreed total of four squadrons to reinforce the RAF Component, No. 504 Squadron arrived from England that evening, landing at Vitry and Bapaume en route to Lille-Marcq.

Additional support was provided by Coastal Command Blenheims that flew several reconnaissance sorties over the Dutch coast in the morning, followed by an attack by Beauforts and Swordfish on Waalhaven airfield at night. Night operations by Bomber Command were on a reduced scale and again

directed against towns through which the German invasion was being supplied.

Losses to BAFF bombers on this, and on previous days, prompted an urgent despatch to Air Marshal Barratt from the Chief of Air Staff. '. . . we cannot continue indefinitely at this rate of intensity . . . If we expend all our effort in the early stages of the battle we shall not be able to operate effectively when the really critical phase comes . . .' It was abundantly clear that things were only expected to get worse.

This is Battle L5241 which Pilot Officer Tom Davy of No. 12 Squadron managed to put down at St-Germain-les-Mons. His target had been the Vroenhoven bridge.

BRITISH AIR FORCES IN FRANCE

1 SQUADRON, BERRY-AU-BAC

Hurricane. Belly-landed west of Maastricht engine damaged in combat with Bf109s of 2./JG27 during escort sortie for No. 12 Squadron Battles over the Albert Canal. Possibly that claimed by Oberlt Framm 9.35 a.m. Squadron Leader P. J. H. Halahan unhurt. Aircraft abandoned

Hurricane L1688. Set alight in combat with Bf109s of 2./JG27 over Maastricht during escort sortie for No. 12 Squadron Battles over the Albert Canal. Possibly that claimed by Lt von Weiher 9.15 a.m. F/O R. Lewis baled out slightly burned, locked in a cellar by local civilians but eventually released. Aircraft a write-off.

Hurricane. Returned badly damaged in combat with Bf109s of 2./JG27 near Maastricht during escort sortie for No. 12 Squadron Battles over the Albert Canal. Possibly that attacked by Fw Schröder near Glons 9.20 a.m. Flying Officer M. H. Brown unhurt. Aircraft damaged but repairable.

Hurricane. Returned starboard wing damaged in combat with Bf109s of 2./JG27 near Maastricht during escort sortie for No. 12 Squadron Battles over the Albert Canal. Possibly that attacked by Gefr Kaiser near Tongeren 9.20 a.m. Pilot Officer P. V. Boot unhurt. Aircraft repairable.

Hurricane L1686. Forced-landed on return damaged in combat with Bf109s of 2./JG27 near Maastricht during escort sortie for No. 12 Squadron Battles over the Albert Canal 9.20 a.m. Sergeant F. J. Soper unhurt. Aircraft damaged but repairable — later abandoned.

Hurricane P2807. Crashed attempting forced-landing 10 miles north of Coulommiers during ferry flight, cause unknown. Flying Officer J. R. Brown (of No. 4 Ferry Pilots Pool) killed. Aircraft a write-off.

Losses to ferry pilots are difficult to document as, in many cases, the aircraft was not allocated to a squadron. Also on this day, F/O R. H. Dingle of No. 4 FPP died when Fairey Battle L5289 dived into the ground en route to No. 1 ATS at Perpignan. He is buried at Mazargues War Cemetery, Marseille Plot 3, Row E, Grave 48. As such losses were not on operations or attributable to enemy action, they do not feature in our Roll of Honour.

12 SQUADRON, AMIFONTAINE

Battle L5241. Petrol tank set alight in attack by Fw Sawallisch of 2./JG27 during sortie to bomb the Vroenhoven bridge over the Albert Canal 9.35 a.m. Forced-landed at St-Germain-les-Mons. Pilot Officer T. D. H. Davy unhurt. Sergeant G. D. Mansell baled out north-east of Maastricht, returning unhurt. AC1 G. N. Patterson also baled out but hit the tail and slightly injured, landing outside the Hospital des Anglais in Liège where later captured. Aircraft PH⊙G later burned to prevent capture.

Battle P2332. Badly damaged by flak during bombing attack on the Vroenhoven bridge over the Albert Canal and forced-landed in the target area 9.20 a.m. Flying Officer N. M. Thomas, Sergeant B. T. P. Carey, and Corporal J. S. Campion all captured unhurt. Aircraft PH⊙F a write-off.

Battle L5227. Shot down by flak during low-level attack on the Veldwezelt bridge over the Albert Canal. Crashed and burned out at Eigenbilzen, north of Mopertingen, 9.15 a.m. Sergeant F. Marland, Sergeant K. D. Footner, and LAC J. L. Perrin killed. Aircraft PH⊙J a write-off.

These airmen were recovered from field graves outside the village of Eigenbilzen, north-west of Maastricht, on October 8, 1946 and reinterred in Heverlee War Cemetery, Leuven, where their dates of death are recorded as May 14, 1940.

Battle P2204. Shot down by flak during low-level attack on the Veldwezelt bridge over the Albert Canal 9.15 a.m. Crashed and burned out near Lanaken. Flying Officer D. E. Garland, Sergeant T. Gray, and LAC L. R. Reynolds killed. Aircraft PH⊙K a write-off.

The badly burnt remains of this crew was buried in two coffins in Lanaken Communal Cemetery, but later reinterred in Heverlee War Cemetery, Leuven.

Battle L5439. Set alight by ground-fire during low-level attack on the Veldwezelt bridge over the Albert Canal, jettisonned bombs and crash-landed at Neerharen 9.20 a.m. Pilot Officer I. A. McIntosh, Sergeant N. T. W. Harder, and LAC R. P. MacNaughton all captured unhurt. Aircraft PH⊙N a write-off.

59 SQUADRON, POIX

Blenheim IV L4859. Landed at Vitry damaged by Belgian AA fire during reconnaissance of the Maas between Roermond and Hasselt 4.15 a.m. Also hit by return fire from He111 over Turnhout 5.00 a.m. Flying Officer G. H. D. Evans, Sergeant Barry, and AC2 C. C. Cleland unhurt. Aircraft TR⊙W repairable.

Blenheim IV N6169. Landed at Vitry slightly damaged following reconnaissance sortie over Ronse 4.35 p.m. Pilot Officer J. S. Booth wounded in leg, rest of crew unhurt. Aircraft TR⊙M repairable.

73 SQUADRON, REIMS-CHAMPAGNE

Hurricane P2535. Returned starboard wing badly damaged by AA fire north-east of Naissin. Squadron Leader J. W. C. More slightly wounded above left eye. Aircraft ⊙K damaged but repairable.

And this is the second Battle attacking the same target: P2332 flown by Flying Officer Norman Thomas. It came down in the vicinity of the bridge.

Flying Officer Donald Garland (left) who led the raid and his observer Sergeant Tom Gray (right) were both posthumously awarded the Victoria Cross — the only VCs of the air battle in France in 1939-40. This is his citation published in *The London Gazette* on June 11, 1940: 'Flying Officer Garland was the pilot and Sergeant Gray the observer of the leading machine of a formation of five aircraft that were ordered to destroy at all costs a bridge over the Albert Canal which had not been demolished by the land forces and was allowing the Germans to advance into Belgium. In spite of very heavy defence of the area surrounding the bridge, the formation made a successful dive-bombing attack from the lowest practicable altitude. After releasing their bombs they were attacked by a large number of enemy fighters and only one aircraft of the five returned to its base. Much of the success of the operation must be attributed to the formation leader, Flying Officer Garland, and to the coolness and resource of Sergeant Gray, who navigated the leading aircraft under most difficult conditions in such a manner that the whole formation, although it subsequently suffered heavy losses, was able successfully to attack the target.' But the gunner on P2204, LAC Lawrence Reynolds, who also lost his life on the mission, was excluded from any award, even though all three airmen now share the same grave in Heverlee War Cemetery, near Leuven in Belgium. (See also page 513.)

79 SQUADRON, MERVILLE

Hurricane L2065. Shot down west of Maastricht by return fire during attack on Do17 of 8./KG77. Pilot Officer T. C. Parker baled out unhurt and evaded capture. Aircraft a write-off.

87 SQUADRON, LILLE-MARCQ

Hurricane L1630. Shot down by Bf109s of I./JG21, JG27 and 1.(J)/LG2 in combat west of Maastricht 9.15 a.m. Sergeant F. V. Howell baled out but parachute damaged and injured in heavy landing. Aircraft a write-off.

Hurricane L1970. Shot down by Bf109s of I./JG21, JG27 and 1.(J)/LG2 in combat west of Maastricht during escort sortie for No 2 Group Blenheims 9.20 a.m. Flying Officer J. A. Campbell killed. Aircraft a write-off.

103 SQUADRON, BÉTHENIVILLE

Battle L5512. Badly damaged by flak during attack on enemy columns between Bouillon and Sedan 5.15 p.m. Crashed attempting forced-landing at 'Fond-Wazelle', near Haraucourt, during return flight. Flying Officer G. B. Morgan-Dean and AC1 H. B. Sewell killed. Aircraft PM⊙L a write-off.

Battle P2193. Shot down by flak during attack on enemy columns between Bouillon and Sedan 5.15 p.m. Crashed and burned out at Curfoz, north of Bouillon. Pilot Officer E. E. Morton and AC1 A. S. Ross killed. Aircraft a write-off.

Two men died in this crash at Curfoz. The Battle, P2193 from No. 103 Squadron, was brought down during an attack on German troops advancing on Sedan. Pilot Officer Edgar Morton and AC1 Alex Ross were interred in the nearby village of Sensenruth together with the crew of Battle K9353 killed the same day. No. 218 Squadron were involved in the same attack on enemy transport in the Bouillon area when they lost two aircraft to flak. The graves of Flight Sergeant John Horner, Sergeant Leonard Flisher and LAC Leslie Davies lie in the cemetery on the eastern outskirts of the village (see page 247).

105 SQUADRON, VILLENEUVE-LES-VERTUS

Battle K9485. Hit by ground-fire and crashed at 'Hauteurs le Christ' during attack on bridge near Bouillon 3.05 p.m. Pilot Officer T. Hurst, Sergeant W. J. Anning, and LAC C. R. Wells killed. Aircraft a write-off.

Battle P2176. Returned damaged by ground-fire during attack on bridge near Bouillon 3.00 p.m. Flight Lieutenant H. C. Sammels, Sergeant F. B. Abbot, and LAC R. D. Hughes unhurt. Aircraft damaged but repairable — later abandoned.

Battle L5523. Returned damaged by ground-fire during attack on bridge near Bouillon 3.00 p.m. Pilot Officer D. C. F. Murray, Sergeant Hemingway, and AC Hill unhurt. Aircraft repairable.

139 SQUADRON, PLIVOT

Blenheim IV N6225. Returned badly damaged by Bf109s of 2./JG1 and 3./JG27 during attack on enemy columns between Maastricht and Tongeren 5.20 a.m. Wing Commander L. Dickens *(Squadron Commander)* and Sergeant J.R. Paine unhurt. LAC Crowley wounded, admitted to hospital where later captured. Aircraft abandoned on withdrawal May 15.
Wing Commander Louis Dickens and Sergeant James Paine subsequently received the DFC and DFM respectively following this action.

Blenheim IV L9416. Shot down by Bf109s of 2./JG1 and 3./JG27 during attack on enemy columns between Maastricht and Tongeren 5.20 a.m. Forced-landed at Hoepertingen. Flying Officer N. E. W. Pepper and Sergeant T. E. Hyde evaded capture. AC1 Hill captured wounded. Aircraft XD⊙A a write-off.
Relics from this machine were once displayed in the now defunct Historiek Centrum at St Truiden airbase.

Blenheim IV N6216. Shot down by Bf109s of 2/JG1 and 3./JG27 during attack on enemy columns between Maastricht and Tongeren, and crashed at Rekem, near Lanaken, 5.20 a.m. Squadron Leader W. I. Scott and LAC W. A. McFadden killed. Sergeant T. W. Davis missing. Aircraft XD⊙B a write-off.
Scott and McFadden were buried alongside an unidentified British airman who died the same day. Although there was no evidence to allow the authorities to make a positive identification, it seems likely that Sergeant Davis is the 'Unknown Airman' now occupying Grave 20 in Rekem Communal Cemetery.

Another casualty of the attacks at Bouillon. This Battle (K9485) of No. 105 Squadron crashed nearby killing the crew. Pilot Officer Tom Hurst, Sergeant Bill Anning and Leading Aircraftman Clifford Wells were buried in the north-western part of the local civilian cemetery.

Blenheim IV P4826. Shot down by Bf109s of 2./JG1 and 3./JG27 during attack on enemy columns between Maastricht and Tongeren 5.20 a.m. Flight Lieutenant A. W. Lee, Sergeant J. B. Keegan, and LAC C. C. Child missing. Aircraft lost.

Blenheim IV N6219. Shot down by Bf109s of 2./JG1 and 3./JG27 during attack on enemy columns between Maastricht and Tongeren 5.20 a.m. Flying Officer G. E. Grey-Smith captured. Sergeant P. C. Gray and Sergeant C. Taylor missing. Aircraft a write-off.

Blenheim IV N6215. Shot down by Bf109s of 2./JG1 and 3./JG27 during attack on enemy columns between Maastricht and Tongeren. Crashed near Lanaken 5.20 a.m. Flying Officer A. McPherson, Sergeant F. W. Gregory, and LAC H. F. Over killed. Aircraft a write-off.
Andrew McPherson was one of the first recipients of a DFC in Bomber Command during WWII. Gazetted on September 10, 1939, the award was in recognition of his efforts in photographing elements of the German Fleet at Wilhelmshaven prior to the first RAF bombing raid of the war on September 4, 1939.

Blenheim IV N6229. Shot down by Bf109s of 2./JG1 and 3./JG27 during attack on enemy columns between Maastricht and Tongeren 5.20 a.m. Crashed near Vroenhoven. Sergeant T. C. R. Harrison, Sergeant N. S. D. Jones, and LAC H. T. Garbett killed. Aircraft a write-off.

Blenheim IV P4923. Shot down by Bf109s of 2./JG1 and 3./JG27 during attack on enemy columns between Maastricht and Tongeren 5.20 a.m. Crash-landed between Herstal and Rhées, north-east of Liege. Possibly that claimed by Oberlt Homuth *(Staffelkapitän)* of 3./JG27. Squadron Leader T. G. Tideman and Sergeant Hale evaded capture. LAC J. Rooney killed. Aircraft a write-off.

142 SQUADRON, BERRY-AU-BAC

Battle K9259. Wrecked on the ground by enemy bombing 7.30 a.m. No crew casualties. Aircraft damaged but repairable.

150 SQUADRON, ECURY-SUR-COOLE

Battle P2336. Suffered direct hit by flak during attack on enemy column between Neufchâteau and Bertrix. Exploded south of Neufchâteau 3.00 p.m. Pilot Officer I. Campbell-Irons, Sergeant T. R. Barker, and LAC R. H. Hinder killed. Aircraft a write-off.

Below left: **Flying Officer Pepper of No. 139 Squadron managed to land his shot-up Blenheim *(below)* near Hoepertingen and he and his navigator, Sergeant Hyde, got back safely to Allied lines, although the wounded gunner, Aircraftman Hill, was captured.**

An all too familiar scene at AASF airfields in the days to come. Battle units suffered appalling losses during the first four days of the campaign, losing between 60-70 aircraft from some 130 sorties — a loss ratio of 50 per cent. In consequence of what the official campaign narrative would term 'this suicidal rate',

Fairey Battles were grounded for four days and urgent changes in RAF day-bombing policy effected. Low-level day-bombing by small formations was dropped in favour of individual attacks from much higher level and finally a switch to purely night operations was ordered.

Battle P2184. Returned to base badly damaged by AA fire during attack on enemy column between Neufchâteau and Bertrix 3.00 p.m. Sergeant S. E. Andrews and crew unhurt. Aircraft JN⊙P damaged but repairable — abandoned May 15.

218 SQUADRON, AUBÉRIVE-SUR-SUIPPES

Battle K9353. Starboard wing shot off by AA fire during attack on enemy column west of Bouillon. Crashed and burned out at Sensenruth 5.00 p.m. Flight Sergeant J. B. Horner, Sergeant L. C. Flisher, and LAC L. D. Davies killed. Aircraft HA⊙J a write-off.

Battle P2183. Shot down by ground-fire during attack on enemy column west of Bouillon and crash-landed at Ferme de l'Espérance, near Nouvion-sur-Meuse, 5.00 p.m. Pilot Officer F. S. Bazalgette died of wounds. Sergeant W. H. Harris and LAC H. B. Jones evaded capture unhurt. Aircraft a write-off.

501 SQUADRON, BÉTHENIVILLE

Hurricane L2054. Shot down by Oberlt Müller (*Staffelkapitän*) of 13.(Z)/LG1 during attack on He111s of II./KG53 east of Rethel. Crashed near 'Menu Champ' on the road to Mont-Laurent, south-east of Seuil 7.05 a.m. Flying Officer P. H. Rayner killed. Aircraft SD⊙E a write-off.

Hurricane L2050. Crash-landed near Beauvilliers engine damaged by return fire from Do17 attacked over St Étienne 8.00 a.m. Flying Officer E. J. Holden unhurt. Aircraft abandoned.

Hurricane L2053. Shot down during attack on Bf110s south of Sedan and abandoned over Artaise-le-Vivier 6.25 p.m. Believed that credited to Obergefr Pabius of 15.(Z)/LG1. Flying Officer M. F. C. Smith baled out too low and killed. Aircraft SD⊙M a write-off.

The body of Michael Smith was recovered by local inhabitants and placed in an empty piggery during general evacuation of the area. He was buried some weeks later as an 'Unknown RAF Fighter Pilot' in Artaise Communal Cemetery, and exhumed for reinterment in Choloy War Cemetery on September 26, 1963.

Hurricane L1910. Forced-landed at Mourmelon with engine bearers badly damaged by return fire during solo attack on Do17s of II./KG3 6.45 p.m. Pilot Officer K. N. T. Lee unhurt. Aircraft SD⊙N damaged but repairable.

Hurricane L1914. Damaged in action with Bf110s of V.(Z)/LG1 south of Sedan and forced-landed at Mourmelon 6.45 p.m. Flying Officer C. E. Malfroy unhurt. Aircraft repairable.

607 SQUADRON, VITRY-EN-ARTOIS

Hurricane P2616. Shot down by Bf109s and abandoned over Lens-St-Servais. Possibly that claimed by Oberlt Schneider (*Staffelkapitän*) of 3./JG21 near Jodoigne 9.10 a.m. Sergeant K. N. V. Townsend baled out with badly burned face and captured on landing west of Tourinne. Aircraft a write-off.

Site excavated May 1992 and remains of Rolls Royce Merlin engine, undercarriage, and various components recovered and displayed in Eben-Emael Museum.

Hurricane P2572. Shot down by return fire from He111s of 4./LG1 engaged over Lille 5.20 a.m. Flying Officer W. E. Gore baled out badly burned and admitted to hospital. Aircraft AF⊙B a write-off.

615 SQUADRON, VITRY-EN-ARTOIS

Hurricane P2564. Shot down in combat with Bf109s of I./JG21, JG27 and 1.(J)/LG2 between Liège and Tongeren; crashed and burned out at Wihogne. Possibly that claimed by Fw Schröder of 2./JG27 over Glons 9.20 a.m. Flying Officer L. Fredman killed. Aircraft a write-off.

UK-based aircraft lost or damaged on operations over the Western Front:

RAF BOMBER COMMAND

15 Squadron, Alconbury
Attack bridges at Maastricht:

Blenheim IV L8847. Shot down by flak or Bf109s of I./JG1 and 2./JG27 and crashed at Borgharen 9.25 a.m. F/O T. G. Bassett, Sgt N. C. Middlemass, LAC W. T. Cavanagh killed. Aircraft lost.

Blenheim IV L8849. Shot down by flak or Bf109s of I./JG1 and 2./JG27 and crashed at 73 Begeveld, at Beverst 9.25 a.m. F/O P. N. Douglass, Sgt W. O. Shortland killed. Sgt W. E. M. Davies captured. Aircraft LS⊙S lost.

Blenheim IV L8851. Returned damaged by flak and fighters 9.25 a.m. F/Lt P. F. Webster slightly wounded. Sgt R. A. M. Stone, LAC R. E. Hunter unhurt. Aircraft repairable.

Left: Easily recognisable — the tangled wreckage of Battle P2193 of No. 103 Squadron at Sensenruth with the grave of Pilot Officer

Morton and Aircraftman Ross alongside. *Right:* Now they lie with Horner, Flisher and Davies from K9353 of No. 218 Squadron.

247

Blenheim IV N6151. Shot down by flak or Bf109s of I./JG1 and 2./JG27 9.25 a.m. Sgt F. R. Pepper, Sgt R. Booth, LAC J. Scott captured. Aircraft lost.

Blenheim IV P6911. Shot down by flak or Bf109s of I./JG1 and 2./JG27. Crashed near Munsterbilzen 9.25 a.m. F/O A. E. Oakley, Sgt D. J. Avent, LAC D. V. Woods killed. Aircraft lost.

Blenheim IV P6912. Shot down by flak or Bf109s of I./JG1 and 2./JG27. Crashed near Kattevennen, east of Genk 9.25 a.m. P/O C. R. Frankish, Sgt E. G. Roberts, LAC E. W. L. Cooper killed. Aircraft lost.

Blenheim IV P6914. Shot down by flak or Bf109s of I./JG1 and 2./JG27. Crashed alongside canal at Kompfeld, near Gellik, 9.25 a.m. Sgt H. R. Hall, Sgt E. R. Perrin, LAC P. J. McDonnell killed. Aircraft lost.

Blenheim IV L8800. Bellylanded on return, hydraulics wrecked in attack by Bf109s of I./JG1 and 2./JG27 9.25 a.m. P/O C. H. Robinson, Sgt S. C. Readhead, LAC Horton unhurt. Aircraft damaged.

Blenheim L8850. Returned damaged by flak and Bf109s of I./JG1 and 2./JG27 9.25 a.m. F/O P. F. Eames wounded. Sgt Philips, LAC R. W. Austin unhurt. Aircraft damaged.

21 Squadron, Watton
Attack exits at Hasselt and Tongeren:

Blenheim IV L8739. Direct hit by flak, broke up over Tongeren 8.40 p.m. F/L A. D. Watson, Sgt A. L. F. Webb, LAC A. C. B. Burgess killed. Aircraft lost.

107 Squadron, Wattisham
Attack roads near Maastricht:

Blenheim IV L8733. Shot down by AA fire and crashed at Hodeige 9.25 a.m. P/O S. G. Thornton, Sgt K. Mellership, AC2 J. R. Mayor killed. Aircraft lost.

Blenheim IV L8748. Believed crash-landed at Casteau, south-west of Soignies, badly damaged by AA fire 9.25 a.m. F/O R. C. Rotheram unhurt. Sgt R. Brown wounded. LAC C. E. Coote badly injured, later captured in hospital. Aircraft OM⊙K lost.

Blenheim IV P4905. Shot down by Bf109s of I./JG1 and 2./JG27 over Bettenhoven 9.25 a.m. Possibly one of those claimed by Oberlt Framm. LAC W. E. Palmer killed. F/O W. H. Edwards, Sgt V. G. L. Luter captured. Aircraft lost.

Blenheim IV P4914. Shot down over Voroux-Goreux 9.25 a.m. by AA fire or Bf109s of I./JG1 and 2./JG27. P/O O. H. Keedwell, Sgt L. R. Merritt, AC2 L. A. Berridge killed. Aircraft lost.

Blenheim IV N6228. Belly-landed on return badly damaged by AA fire and Bf109s of I./JG1 and 2./JG27 9.25 a.m. F/O G. T. B. Clayton, Cpl L. Yeomans unhurt. Sgt M. Innes-Jones wounded. Aircraft damaged.

RAF COASTAL COMMAND

235 Squadron, Manston
Cover troop landings at Den Haag:

Blenheim IV L9189. Believed shot down by Bf109s of 4/JG27 near Oostvoorne 7.55 a.m. P/O N. A. Savill baled out and captured wounded admitted to Vlaardingen hospital. Sgt H. R. Sutherland, LAC R. H. Tyler killed. Aircraft LA⊙O lost.

Blenheim IV L9324. Believed shot down by Bf109s of 4./JG27 and crashed in the Nieuwlandse Polder 7.55 a.m. P/O N. A. L. Smith, Sgt J. C. Robertson, LAC T. J. Lowry killed. Aircraft LA⊙P lost.

815 (FAA) Squadron, Detling
Attack Waalhaven airfield:

Swordfish I. Hit by flak and crash-landed in Polder Oud Herkingen, at Overflakkee, 10.10 p.m. Lt A. S. Downes and crew unhurt. Aircraft a write-off.

From this sequence of German Army photographs, it would appear that a Fieseler Storch was overflying this crash of a French Mureaux when the pilot decided to land alongside to investigate. Such wrecks were becoming increasingly common in the immediate battle area but obviously still remained an attraction.

FRENCH AIR FORCE

GAO 502 Potez 63.11 (360). Unserviceable aircraft left behind on transfer from La Fère-Courbes to Villers-lès-Guise 5.00 p.m. No crew casualties. Aircraft abandoned.

GAO 511 Potez 63.11. Unserviceable aircraft destroyed on withdrawal from La Fère-Courbes to Signy-le-Petit. No crew casualties. Aircraft abandoned.

GAO 544 Mureaux 115 (42). Shot down by light flak during liaison mission at Pessoux; forced-landed near Leignon, south of Ciney, and burned out 2.30 p.m. Capt Montagnon and Lt Jean both captured unhurt. Aircraft a write-off.

GAO 544 Two Mureaux 115 (32 and 35). Damaged aircraft destroyed on withdrawal from Villers-lès-Guise to Brétigny-sur-Orge. No crew casualties. Aircraft both abandoned.

GAO 2/551 Breguet 27. Damaged in bombing at Tournes-Belval airfield 7.00 am. No crew casualties. Aircraft later abandoned on withdrawal to Bulgny.

GAO 553 Mureaux 115. Shot down by Fw Gasthaus of 4./JG51 during observation sortie east of Saverne 4.15 p.m. Lt Pinguet wounded. Lt-Col. Corsanini unhurt. Aircraft a write-off.

GBA 1/54 Breguet 693 (18). Shot down by flak during attack on mechanised columns near Tongeren; crashed and burned out at Vroenhoven, 4 km from Maastricht, 1.00 p.m. Lt R. Delattre (*Commandant*) and Adjt V. Di Matteo killed. Aircraft a write-off.

GBA I/54 Breguet 693 (10). Shot down by flak during attack on mechanised columns near Tongeren; crashed and burned out near the water tower between Roclenge-sur-Geer and Millen-Boirs 1.00 p.m. Adjt M. Renaudie killed. Adjt A. Richard captured wounded. Aircraft a write-off.

GBA I/54 Breguet 693 (7). Hit by intense flak during attack on mechanised columns near Tongeren and crashed in the target area 1.00 p.m. S/Lt E. Henry and S/Lt Besson-Guyard both captured unhurt. Aircraft a write-off.

GBA I/54 Breguet 693 (9). Hit by intense flak during attack on mechanised columns near Tongeren and crashed in the target area 1.00 p.m. Adjt Goyer captured unhurt. Sgt Tupin captured seriously wounded. Aircraft a write-off.

GBA I/54 Breguet 693 (4). Shot down by flak over the target during attack on mechanised columns near Tongeren 1.00 p.m. Adjt Boulanger captured unhurt. Sgt Roux captured badly wounded. Aircraft a write-off.

GBA I/54 Breguet 693 (14). Shot down by flak during attack on mechanised columns near Tongeren; crashed and burned out near Borgloon 1.00 p.m. Cmdt. Plou (*Groupe Commandant*) and Adjt Poitrot both captured unhurt. Aircraft a write-off.

GBA I/54 Breguet 693 (19). Hit by intense flak during attack on mechanised columns near Tongeren and abandoned over St Truiden 1.00 p.m. Lt Leleu baled out and captured unhurt. Sgt Massaux baled out and captured wounded. Aircraft a write-off.

GBA I/54 Breguet 693 (21). Crashed between Irles and Grévillers west of Bapaume crippled by ground-fire during attack on enemy columns near Tongeren 1.00 p.m. S/Lt Gady unhurt. Sgt Cabaret badly wounded. Aircraft a write-off.

GBA I/54 Breguet 693 (22). Returned badly damaged by ground-fire in attack on enemy columns near Tongeren 1.00 p.m. Sgt Normand and Sgt Voigard unhurt. Aircraft a write-off.

GBA II/54 Breguet 693 (34). Shot down by flak during attack on motorised columns between Liège and Tongeren and crashed at Ransberg 1.00 p.m. Sgt E. Fourdinier badly burned, transported to the Edith Cavell Hospital in Brussels. S/Lt M. de la Porte du Theil killed. Aircraft a write-off.

GBA II/54 Breguet 693 (32). Returned to Roye Beuvraignes damaged by flak during attack on motorised columns between Liège and Tongeren 1.00 p.m. Crew unhurt. Aircraft damaged but repairable.

GC 2/1 Bloch 152 (409). Shot down by Bf109s during free-lance patrol and abandoned between Moustier and Temploux. Possibly that claimed by Lt Schmidt of 3./JG21 over Namur 1.20 p.m. Adjt Levasseur believed baled out landing near Teills badly burned. Aircraft a write-off.

GC 2/1 Bloch 152. Landed at Couvron badly damaged possibly in combat with Bf109s of 3./JG21 during free-lance patrol over Namur 1.20 p.m. Sgt R. Starke unhurt. Aircraft a write-off.

GC 5/1 Morane 406 (1031). Belly-landed west of Antwerp with engine damaged by return fire from He111 of Stab KG54 engaged between Ghent and Wetteren 5.30 a.m. Lt K. Bursztyn slightly wounded in knee, treated in hospital in Ghent. Aircraft I a write-off.

GC 5/1 Morane 406 (759). Shot down in combat with Bf110s south-east of Antwerp and forced-landed at Mere, near Alost 12.45 p.m. Believed that claimed by Oberlt Meyer and Gefr Wengler of 8./ZG26. S/Lt Calmel wounded in leg, admitted to hospital where later captured. Aircraft 4 abandoned.

GC 6/1 Morane 406. Petrol tank caught fire in combat with Bf110s of III./ZG26 over Wetteren; crashed and burned out near Damstraat at Serskamp 7.20 a.m. Adjt Bassaguet baled out badly burned landing at Ferme Kadol, and admitted to hospital in Wetteren. Aircraft a write-off.

GC 6/1 Morane 406. Badly damaged in combat with Bf110s of III./ZG26 over Wetteren and crashed near Moerbeke airfield 7.30 a.m. Believed that claimed by Oberlt Baagoe of 8./ZG26 over Wachtebeke. Adjt P. Déchanet wounded admitted to hospital in Ghent. Aircraft a write-off.

GC 5/3 Morane 406. Shot down in combat with Bf110s of II./ZG76 over Schellebelle station, and crash-landed at Molenweg in Wetteren, alongside the Steenweg to Dendermonde 7.30 a.m. Lt J. Béran killed. Aircraft a write-off.

GC 6/3 Morane 406. Shot down by Bf110s of II./ZG76 during patrol over Maubeuge airfield 6.00 a.m. Crashed and burned out at Avesnes. S/Lt C. Isola killed. Aircraft a write-off.

GC II/4 Curtiss H-75 (74). Shot down by Bf109 on landing approach to Xaffévillers. Crashed south-east of Saint-Pierre Mont p.m. S/Lt G. Duperret killed. Aircraft a write-off.

GC 1/5 Curtiss H-75. Returned to Suippes damaged by return fire from Do17 near Sedan 9.15 a.m. Adjt Bouvard wounded in jaw, admitted to hospital. Aircraft damaged but repairable.

GC 1/5 Curtiss H-75 (151). Returned to Suippes with windscreen shattered by return fire from Do17 of Stab KG3 engaged near Sedan 10.15 a.m. Capt J-M. Accart (Commandant) splinter wounds to face. Aircraft repairable.

GC 1/5 Curtiss H-75 (193). Belly-landed at Vouziers with engine damaged following attack on Ju87s of I./StG76 over Forêt de Sedan 10.30 a.m. Sgt F. Morel unhurt. Aircraft damaged but repairable.

GC II/5 Curtiss H-75 (170). Hit by return fire from He111 and engine set alight; crash-landed blinded by smoke 12.30 p.m. S/Lt P. Villacèque wounded in face. Aircraft a write-off.

GC II/7 Four Morane 406s & 1 Dewoitine D520. Reported destroyed on the ground at Luxeuil in strafing by Bf109s. No pilot casualties. Aircraft all write-offs.

GC III/7 Morane 406 (171). Set alight during attack on Do17s of 3./KG3 near Blesme and abandoned over Chamouilley 1.20 p.m. Sgt A. Moulènes baled out unhurt. Aircraft a write-off.

GC III/7 Morane 406. Returned to Vitry-le-François-Vauclerc damaged by return fire following attack on Ju88s north of Bar-le-Duc 2.30 p.m. Adjt A. Littolff unhurt. Aircraft damaged but repairable.

GR I/14 Potez 63.11 (180). Starboard engine damaged in attack by Bf109s of I./JG21 and I./JG27 during reconnaissance sortie over Tongeren 9.30 a.m, Also hit by Allied ground-fire, crash-landed at 'Campagne du Pige', Mont-sur-Marchienne, near Charleroi. S/Lt Touret, S/Lt P. Moreau, and Sgt Bernet unhurt. Aircraft abandoned.

GR 2/22 Potez 63.11 (444). Engaged by Bf109s near Diekirch during photo-reconnaissance sortie and shot down by Oberlt Bretnütz (Staffelkapitän) of 6./JG53. Crash-landed south of Luxembourg with port engine in flames and burned out 11.00 a.m. Lt Detrie and Adjt Gres captured unhurt. Capt Lainey (Commandant) captured wounded in left arm. Aircraft a write-off.

GR II/33 Potez 637 (7). Returned to Athies-sous-Laon severely damaged by ground-fire during dawn reconnaissance sortie south of the Meuse and Albert Canal. Sgt M. Joannic killed. Capt Moreau badly wounded. S/Lt Hochedé unhurt. Aircraft a write-off.

GR I/35 Potez 63.11 (317). Shot down during reconnaissance between Tilburg and 's-Hertogenbosch by Lt Kolbow of 3./JG20 and belly-landed at St-Job-in-Goor, 12 km north-east of Antwerp 5.55 p.m. S/Lt Lamy, Sgt Sordet, and Sgt Vanaret all wounded and admitted to hospital at Zuydcoote. Aircraft a write-off.

GR I/35 Potez 63.11. Damaged by ground fire during reconnaissance mission over Breda. Capt Aubert unhurt, S/Lt Toni wounded by plexiglass splinters in the nose, Adjt Jeannin wounded in the arm. Aircraft damaged but repairable.

GR I/36 Potez 63.11 (80). Hit by flak during low-level reconnaissance sortie and crashed attempting a forced-landing at Pommérieux, south of Metz 6.00 a.m. S/Lt R. Marcusse and Adjt J. Haure killed. Sgt Cauquill unhurt. Aircraft a write-off.

GR II/52 Potez 63.11. Returned to Couvron damaged by ground-fire during reconnaissance sortie over Achêne and Emblève. Sgt Noël wounded, Capt Evrard and Sgt Serra both unhurt. Aircraft repairable.

GR II/52 Potez 63.11. Returned to Couvron hit by ground-fire during evening reconnaissance sortie east of the Meuse. Sgt Thierry, Adjt Charlier, and Sgt Rippe unhurt. Aircraft repairable.

It turned out to be the Mureaux No. 42 of Groupe Aérien d'Observation 544, the two crewmen having been taken prisoner. Flying in support of the French 1st Light Cavalry Division, the aircraft had come under fire from a motorised column near Ciney that damaged the engine and caused a fire. Surprisingly, this was one of only two vulnerable observation aircraft GAO 544 would lose during the entire campaign.

This is the Fokker C V of the IIIe Verkenningsgroep which force-landed at Slootdorp about 60 kilometres north of Amsterdam.

DUTCH AIR FORCE

1/2-II-1 Fokker D XXI (218). Met heavy ground-fire near Westervoort during escort sortie for Fokker C Vs of III-2 over Gelderland. Overturned on landing at Buiksloot due to locked brakes 6.45 a.m. Sgt C. Ch. Steensma slightly injured. Aircraft a write-off.

1/2-II-1 Fokker D XVII (203). Braked too hard and ground-looped on landing at Ruigenhoek airstrip after transfer flight from Buiksloot 2.50 p.m. 2e Lt E. A. Roosenburg unhurt. Aircraft a write-off.

1/2-II-1 Fokker D XVII (207). Undershot runway on landing at Ruigenhoek after transfer flight from Buiksloot 2.50 p.m. Sgt B. W. van der Heiden unhurt. Aircraft a write-off.

1/2-II-1 Fokker D XVII (205). Ran into barbed wire on landing at Ruigenhoek airstrip after transfer flight from Buiksloot 2.50 p.m. Sgt B. C. Moerkoert unhurt. Aircraft repairable.

1/2-II-1 Fokker D XVII (210). Landed at Soesterberg following escort sortie for Fokker C Vs over Wageningen 7.40 p.m. 2e Lt J. C. P. Stuy unhurt. Aircraft later abandoned due to engine trouble.

1/2-II-1 Fokker D XVII (205). Undercarriage damaged on landing at Soesterberg following escort sortie for Fokker C Vs over Wageningen 7.40 p.m. Sgt B. C. Moerkoert unhurt. Aircraft subsequently repaired using components cannibalised from D XVII (210).

4-II-1 Fokker G 1 (325). Landed at Soesterberg badly damaged by ground-fire during attack on enemy columns west of Wageningen 6.40 p.m. 1e Lt T. H. Leegstra unhurt, Sgt W. P. Wesly slightly wounded in hand. Aircraft repairable.

Oberst Theo Osterkamp (Geschwaderkommodore) of Stab JG51 was credited with a Fokker G 1 over Soesterberg but it has not proved possible to match this claim with certainty to any known loss.

4-II-1 Fokker G 1 (303). Landed at Soesterberg damaged by ground-fire during attack on enemy columns west of Wageningen 6.40 p.m. 1e Lt A. van Oorschot and Sgt M. W. Sonneveld unhurt. Aircraft repairable.

4-II-1 Fokker G 1 (322). Landed at Soesterberg petrol tank holed by ground-fire during attack on enemy columns west of Wageningen 6.40 p.m. Later returned to Schiphol. Sgt H. Hartkoren and Sgt P. J. Lok unhurt. Aircraft repairable.

I-2 Fokker C V (612). Damaged by flak during attack on German battery at Wageningen and forced-landed near Echteld 6.40 p.m. 2e Lt. J. van Meel and 1e Lt. H. C. Heideman unhurt. Aircraft abandoned.

I-2 Fokker C V (650). Landed at Soesterberg to refuel after attack on German battery at Wageningen 6.40 p.m. but unable to restart engine as no air compressor available. Sgt J. Zuger and 1e Lt L. Donkersloot unhurt. Aircraft abandoned on withdrawal to De Zilk next day.

I-2 Koolhoven F.K.51 (428). Forced-landed near Voorhout during transfer flight from Middenmeer to Ruigenhoek 7.10 p.m. Crew believed unhurt. Aircraft burned to prevent capture.

III-2 Fokker C V (631). Returned to Ruigenhoek with port wing badly damaged by ground-fire during reconnaissance sortie over Westervoort 6.40 a.m. Wachtm. W. P. Smits and 1e Lt R. E. van Duyl Schultz (II-2 crew) both unhurt. Aircraft repairable.

III-2 Fokker C V (645). Engine damaged by enemy fire and forced-landed at Slootdorp, near Middenmeer 5.10 p.m. 1e Lt E. M. Hoekstra and 2e Lt R. van den Heuvel (II-2 crew) unhurt. Aircraft abandoned.

III-2 Fokker C V (592). Shot down by Bf109s south of Wageningen and crash-landed near De Key at Opheusden 7.30 p.m. Believed that claimed by Lt Kohl of Stab II./JG27. Sgt G. F. Roeloffzen and Sgt J. L. Holtz both wounded and taken by lorry to hospital in Amsterdam. Aircraft a write-off.

III-2 Fokker C V (619). Shot down by Bf109s south of Wageningen and crashed at Rhenen 7.30 p.m. Believed that claimed by Hptmn Andres *(Gruppenkommandeur)* of Stab II./JG27. Sgt A. J. M. van Liempd shot by German troops. 2e Lt T. J. Vrins (of II-2) captured wounded in head. Aircraft a write-off.

IV-2 Fokker C V (603). Returned to Haamstede damaged over 's-Hertogenbosch during bombing sortie to Wageningen 7.10 p.m. Sgt J. A. Hartefelt and 2e Lt N. R. Baron van Hoëvell unhurt. Aircraft repairable.

IV-2 Fokker C V (652). Returned to Haamstede bomb-release damaged during sortie to Wageningen 7.10 p.m. Sgt J. Th. Reintjes and 2e Lt J. J. Cramer unhurt. Aircraft repairable.

The aircraft above were among four Fokker C Vs transferred to IV-2 from the Vliegschool Haamstede on May 10.

GVT3 Two Fokker C XIVw (5596 and 5599). Destroyed by enemy action while moored at Veere. No crew casualties. Aircraft F-21 and F-24 write-offs.

Two remaining Fokker C XIVs at Veere (5603 F-17 and 5598 F-23), together with those from Akersloot (5587 F-1, 5589 F-3, 5591 F-5, 5592 F-6, 5605 F-13, 5607 F-15, 5602 F-16, 5604 F-18 and 5597 F-22), were evacuated to France at 3.00 a.m. on May 14 and subsequently reached England. The bulk of them were later shipped abroad to serve in the Dutch East Indies.

MLD Two Fokker C VIIIw, six Fokker C XIVw (5590, 5601, 5608, 5609, 5606, and 5594), and Fokker C XIw (5421). Aircraft destroyed at De Mok in strafing attacks by Bf109s of II.(J)/TrGr.186. No crew casualties. Aircraft G-7 and G-9, F-4, F-9, F-10, F-11, F-14, and F-19 and W-3 all write-offs.

Damaged in combat, Fox O.175 of the 7/III/3 'Flèche Ailée' nosed over at the end of its landing run at Lonzée which lies on the road between Gembloux and Namur.

BELGIAN AIR FORCE

7/IV/1 2 Foxes. Unserviceable aircraft abandoned at Lonzée 11.00 a.m. No crew casualties. Aircraft destroyed on withdrawal to Fosses-Vitrival.

7/IV/1 Fox. Damaged by ground-fire during reconnaissance of enemy columns on road between Baillonville and Pessoux, 9.50 a.m. Adjt A. d'Hondt and S/Lt C. Mogenet both unhurt. Aircraft damaged but repairable — later abandoned.

5/III/3 Battle (T.71). Returned to Aalter badly damaged by ground-fire during reconnaissance of the Haacht — Kapellen sector 10.00 a.m. 1/Sgt M. Balasse and S/Lt M. Roël both unhurt. Aircraft a write-off.

5/III/3 Battle (T.64). Returned to Aalter hit by ground-fire during reconnaissance of Allied defence positions 10.15 a.m. Adjt J-P. Weynants and S/Lt F. Desclée both unhurt. Aircraft repairable.

7/III/3 Fox. Returned to Lonzée badly damaged by French ground-fire during reconnaissance sortie north of the Meuse 5.05 a.m. Sgt R. de Cannart d'Hamale and Lt P. Lippens both unhurt. Aircraft damaged but repairable.

7/III/3 Fox (O.175). Hit by French ground-fire on return from reconnaissance sortie to Marche and nosed over in forced-landing outside Lonzée 6.00 a.m. Adjt M. Vos and Lt A. Dulait both unhurt. Aircraft abandoned.

7/III/3 Fox (O.187). Shot down by S/Lt Bardin, S/Lt Dartevelle, Adj Romey of GC III/2, and Adj Boyer, Sgt Morlot of GC III/7, during reconnaissance sortie between Orval and Braives. With oil tank riddled, undercarriage collapsed during crash-landing at Ferme des Malheurs, near Forceilles 12.45 p.m. 1/Sgt G. Mot and Lt J. Lefebvre both unhurt. Aircraft destroyed by crew.
The Foxes above are believed to be among the III/2 aircraft that arrived from Sterreken to reinforce the depleted 7/III/3 on this day.

CISLA Avro 626 (N.4). Damaged in accident at Tours airfield after arrival from Zoute. Pilot unhurt. Aircraft damaged but repairable — recovered and transported to Pau.
Stampe-Vertongen SV-5 (N.24) was also damaged in a forced-landing at Douy during the flight to Tours on this date.

1ste Schoolsmaldeel Stampe-Vertongen SV-4B. Believed damaged in attack by Bf110 of III./ZG26 near St-Denijs-Westrem 7.30 a.m. Pilot unhurt. Aircraft damage state not recorded.
This aircraft of Escadrille 1 École de Pilotage Elementaire was among a number of trainers later reported abandoned on evacuation of various schools including the Breguet XIX (78) at Ostend, and Potez 33 (Z.8) and a Renard R-37 at Evere.

LUFTWAFFE

3.(F)/10 Dornier Do17. Reported wrecked in forced-landing near Maastricht. Lt H. Wrba and crew unhurt. Aircraft a write-off.

3.(F)/11 Dornier Do17. Lost on reconnaissance sortie, circumstances unknown. Oberlt Dr A. Müller and two crew killed. Aircraft a write-off.

1.(H)/13 Henschel Hs126. Returned damaged by ground-fire during observation sortie south of Saarbrücken. Oberlt G. Nell wounded. Aircraft repairable.

4.(H)/13 Henschel Hs126. Riddled by ground-fire and believed one of those attacked by F/O Clisby of No. 1 Squadron over Maastricht and crashed at emergency landing field at Neerbeek. Crew unhurt. Aircraft a write-off.

1.(H)/21 Dornier Do17M. Possibly that attacked by S/Lt Boudier and Sgt Héme of GC II/5 between Merzig and Saarelouis 6.00 a.m. Crashed with starboard engine alight at the Steinhomburger Berg, near Hilbringen. Fw L. Lieflander and Uffz J. Goldberg (both of 2.(H)/41) killed. Uffz P. Goldbach (of 4.(F)/11) wounded admitted to hospital in Merzig. Aircraft a write-off.

4.(H)/21 Henschel Hs126. Returned damaged by ground-fire during observation sortie over Gorinchem. One crewman killed. Oberlt von Schuler unhurt. Aircraft repairable.

1.(H)/23 Henschel Hs126. Believed shot down by F/Lt Churchill, F/O Stone and Sgt Wilkinson of No. 3 Squadron, and crashed at Linsmeau 11.00 a.m. Fw J. von Kienlin and Uffz W. Ulbrich killed. Aircraft a write-off.

3.(F)/31 Henschel Hs126. Believed returned damaged by ground fire during observation mission over Sedan and probably that engaged by F/O Kain of No. 73 Squadron between Bouillon and Noirefontaine 5.15 p.m. Lt Körig and observer unhurt. Aircraft damage state not recorded.

4.(H)/31 Henschel Hs126. Returned damaged, believed by ground-fire, during observation sortie over Ciney, south-east of Namur. Lt H-O. H. Wykowski killed. Aircraft repairable.

1.(H)/41 Henschel Hs126. Shot down by RAF Hurricane during observation sortie between Leuven and Gembloux and crashed at 'Les Trixnes', west of Bas-Oha 6.00 p.m. Probably that claimed by F/O Stone of No. 3 Squadron. Oberlt U. Strohm and Uffz H-W. Kübik killed. Aircraft a write-off.

1.(H)/41 Henschel Hs126. Believed shot down by F/O Adams, P/O Hallifax and Sgt Friendship of No. 3 Squadron during observation mission south-east of St Trond, and crashed at Waremme, south of Malines 11.00 a.m. Fw J. Poller and Fw W. Meyer killed. Aircraft a write-off.

1.(F)/121 Junkers Ju88A-1 (213). Both engines destroyed in attack by No. 85 Squadron Hurricane during reconnaissance of Belgian airfields. Crash-landed at 'Retranchement', in Zeeuws-Vlaanderen, 9.30 a.m. Fw K. Denner died of wounds. Lt E. Bruns captured badly wounded. Gefr G. Damazyn captured slightly wounded. Uffz A. Steinbock captured unhurt. Aircraft 7A+CH a write-off.

Another reconnaissance machine lost on May 12 was this Henschel of Heeres Aufklärungsstaffel 1.(H)/23 but in this case both the observer, Feldwebel Johannes von Kienlin and the pilot, Unteroffizier Wolfgang Ulbrich, were killed.

Two nice shots of the Dornier of 2. Staffel of long-range reconnaissance unit Fernaufklärungsgruppe 123 which was shot down by French pilots near Fosses-la-Ville.

2.(F)/122 Heinkel He111. Returned damaged following reconnaissance sortie over northern France. Gefr W. Strahl slightly wounded, admitted to hospital in Münster. Aircraft repairable.

2.(F)/123 Dornier Do17P (0147). Attacked by Capt de Calonne, Adjt Dorcy, Sgt Delisle, and Sgt Breitenstein of GC II/2 during reconnaissance mission between Louvain and Nivelles and belly-landed at 'Pont du Diable' at Mettet, south of Fosses-la-Ville 6.20 a.m. Oberlt H. Weicksel, Uffz H. Bournot, and Obergefr H. Richter captured unhurt. Aircraft 4U+EK a write-off.

11.(N)/JG2 Messerschmitt Bf109D-1. Shot down by AA over Holland. Pilot unhurt. Aircraft a write-off.

2./JG26 Messerschmitt Bf109E. Engine damaged by ground-fire and wrecked in forced-landing at Waalhaven. Pilot believed unhurt. Aircraft a write-off.
Alternative sources suggest this may have been May 11 and subject of late reporting.

2./JG27 Messerschmitt Bf109E. Damaged in combat with No. 1 Squadron Hurricanes over Maastricht 9.15 a.m. and undercarriage wrecked in forced-landing near Liège. Leutnant F. Keller unhurt. Aircraft 4 + damaged but repairable.

2./JG27 Messerschmitt Bf109E. Returned to base badly damaged over Maastricht, reportedly by flak, but possibly damaged in combat with No. 1 Squadron Hurricanes 9.20 a.m. Pilot unhurt. Aircraft a write-off.

Stab II./JG51 Messerschmitt Bf109E-4 (5095). Hit by flak over Haguenau and forced-landed near Rastatt. Hauptmann G. Matthes *(Gruppenkommandeur)* unhurt. Aircraft <<+ repairable.

6./JG51 Messerschmitt Bf109E-3 (5088). Returned to base slightly damaged by flak over Haguenau. Pilot unhurt. Aircraft repairable.

II./JG53 Messerschmitt Bf109E-1. Damaged in aborted take-off at Trier-Euren. Pilot unhurt. Aircraft repairable.

1./JG54 Messerschmitt Bf109E-3. Engine damaged by ground-fire during low-level attack on Luxeuil airfield and crash-landed at Frahier-et-Châtebier, north-east of Belfort. Lt A. Walter captured. Aircraft 1 + destroyed by pilot.

2./JG54 Messerschmitt Bf109E-1. Shot down by ground-fire during low-level attack on Herbéviller airfield and abandoned over Barbas, south of Blâmont. Lt H. Gödecke *(Staffelkapitän)* baled out too low and captured badly wounded, later died. Aircraft a write-off.

I./JG77 Messerschmitt Bf109E-1. Crashed on landing at Sourbrodt, north-east of Malmédy, probably damaged by AA fire during escort sortie for I./StG2 to Dinant. Pilot unhurt. Aircraft damaged but repairable.

I./JG77 Messerschmitt Bf109E-3. Involved in collision on take-off from Sourbrodt, north-east of Malmédy. Pilot baled out unhurt. Aircraft a write-off.

I./JG77 Messerschmitt Bf109E-3. Involved in take-off collision and abandoned near Sourbrodt. Pilot baled out unhurt. Aircraft a write-off.

II./KG1 Heinkel He111P. Returned damaged by fighters and possibly that attacked by S/L Gilbert of GC II/6 west of Dinant 8.00 a.m. Crew unhurt. Aircraft repairable.

7./KG2 Dornier Do17Z. Returned damaged by flak during sortie to attack Charleville-Mézières 6.20 p.m. Uffz E. Moser slightly wounded. Aircraft damaged but repairable.

7./KG2 Dornier Do17Z. Returned damaged by flak during sortie to attack Charleville-Mézières 6.10 p.m. Oberfw A. Chilla badly wounded, died same day in hospital in Mannheim. Aircraft repairable.

7./KG2 Dornier Do17Z (6036). Hit by flak over Charleville-Mézières and forced-landed near Vresse, 20 km west of Bertrix 6.10 p.m. Lt D. Giesecke, Fw W. Klöttschen, Fw H. Rösl, and Uffz P. Tillner all captured wounded. Aircraft a write-off.

8./KG2 Dornier Do17Z. Returned damaged by flak over Charleville during attack on Signy-l'Abbaye 6.10 p.m. Lt H. Frohn slightly wounded, admitted to hospital in Mannheim. Oberfw H. Schirr unhurt. Aircraft damage state not recorded.

8./KG2 Dornier Do17Z. Returned damaged by flak over Launois during sortie to attack Signy-l'Abbaye 6.10 p.m. Uffz H. Seifart, Gefr H. Behnke, and Gefr W. Eckert slightly wounded. Uffz R. Tiedemann unhurt. Aircraft damaged but repairable.

9./KG2 Dornier Do17Z. Belly-landed at Biblis damaged by flak during attack on roads near Poix-Terron 6.10 p.m. Crew unhurt. Aircraft damaged but repairable.

9./KG2 Dornier Do17Z. Belly-landed at Biblis damaged by flak during attack on roads near Poix-Terron 6.10 p.m. Oberlt B. Davids *(Staffelkapitän)*, Oberlt H. Ruess, and rest of crew unhurt. Aircraft damaged but repairable.

Stab KG3 Dornier Do17Z. Damaged by flak south-west of Compiègne and repeated attacks by Curtiss H-75s near Sedan and crashed at Redu 10.15 a.m. Credited to Capt Accart and Sgt Morel of GC I/5. Hptmn G. Altvater *(Staffelkapitän)* and Oberfw F. Schwede wounded, rest of crew unhurt. Aircraft a write-off.

I./KG3 Dornier Do17Z. Badly damaged in attacks by Sgt Boyer and Sgt Moulènes of GC III/7 near Blesmes and forced-landed in Belgium 1.15 p.m. No crew casualties. Aircraft damaged but repairable.

3./KG3 Dornier Do17Z. Hit by AA fire during attack on motorised columns between Stenay and Vouziers, then engaged by Moranes near Blesmes and starboard engine set alight in attacks by Capt Bouvarre, Sgt Bernadon, and Sgt Moulènes of GC III/7. Crashed in flames and exploded near the railway station at St-Dizier 1.00 p.m. Lt C. Zehge killed. Lt A. Paleit (of Stab I./KG3), Obergefr W. Schubert, and Gefr K. Jahraus all baled out low but captured unhurt. Aircraft 5K+EL a write-off.

Stab II./KG3 Dornier Do17Z. Returned damaged by fighters over Poix-Terron 6.30 p.m. Possibly one of those attacked by P/O Lee of No. 501 Squadron. Oberst A. Jahn *(Gruppenkommandeur)* killed. Aircraft repairable.

Stab II./KG3 Dornier Do17Z. Believed shot down by Hurricanes of No. 501 Squadron and crashed at 'La Glaux', between Sevigny-Waleppe and Dizy-le-Gros 8.00 a.m. Uffz H. Petereit and Oberfw W. Menzel killed. Lt R. Steingräber captured badly wounded, died next day. Fw W. Scheller captured badly wounded, admitted to hospital where leg amputated. Aircraft a write-off.

4./KG3 Dornier Do17Z. Shot down by P/O Lee of No. 501 Squadron during sortie over Izel and crash-landed near Arsfeld, north-west of Bitburg 6.35 p.m. Oberlt H. Martin *(Staffelkapitän)* badly wounded, admitted to hospital in Diekirch. Aircraft a write-off.

4./KG3 Dornier Do17Z. Returned damaged by Hurricanes of No. 501 Squadron following sortie over Charleville 6.00 p.m. Uffz W. Holzknecht and Gefr H. Maskolus slightly wounded. Aircraft repairable.

5./KG3 Dornier Do17Z. Shot down by Hurricanes of No. 501 Squadron and crash-landed at Maisoncelle-et-Villers, west of Raucourt-et-Flaba, 6.10 p.m. Uffz R. Fliegener killed. Oberlt H. Becker-Rob captured wounded. Fw W. Brinkmann and Fw A. Hansen captured unhurt. Aircraft a write-off.

5./KG30 Junkers 88A-1. Shot down while attacking shipping off IJmuiden by No. 264 Squadron Defiants and No. 66 Squadron Spitfires, and crashed with port engine alight at Hazerswoude 2.30 p.m. Flgr S. Lahm and Uffz W. Barowka killed. Fw T. Schwarz captured badly wounded, died of injuries May 21. Oberlt H. Schneider captured wounded. Aircraft a write-off.

Stab I./KG51 Heinkel He111H. Believed shot down by S/Lt Hutter of GC II/1 during reconnaissance sortie and belly-landed on Ferme de Pommard, 5 km south-east of Chablis 3.15 p.m. Possibly also attacked by Adj Dumas of DAT Châteaudun and Capt de Rivals-Mazères of CEAM. Oberfw K. Ernst, Oberfw M. Groth, Fw L. Gehring, and Fw J. Hofbauer all captured unhurt. Aircraft 9K+AA a write-off.

Stabsstaffel KG53 Heinkel He111H. Believed shot down by S/Lt Boitelet, Sgt Delporte, and Sgt Tallent of GC I/5 following attack on Mourmelon and belly-landed on the north bank of the Semois at Ste-Cécile, near Laiche, 7.00 a.m. Lt W. Ocker and Uffz H-J. Rissel captured wounded. Uffz H. Limburg, Uffz H. Fiedler, and Uffz K. Schrang believed captured unhurt. Aircraft fired by crew.
This crew resisted capture and opened fire on French troops who took them prisoner.

The Stab (staff) flight of Kampfgeschwader 3 was based at Schweinfurt. This particular Dornier ventured almost to Paris before repeated attacks by French pilots of Groupe de Chasse I/5 managed to bring it down just before it reached the border with Germany. The crew, including the Stabsstaffelkapitän Hauptmann Georgfriedrich Altvater, all made it back though the radio operator, Fritz Schwede, was badly wounded and admitted to hospital in Remagen.

2./KG53 Heinkel He111H. Shot down by F/O Rayner and P/O Sylvester of No. 501 Squadron following attack on Mourmelon and crashed 2 miles south-east of Beaumont-en-Argonne 7.15 a.m. Uffz W. Kortas killed. Fw L. Etzel, Uffz C. Wagner, Uffz G. Poppe, and Uffz W. Pahl captured unhurt. Aircraft A1+HK a write-off.

3./KG53 Heinkel He111H. Shot down by Lt Huvet and S/Lt Hebrard, but also attacked by S/Lt Angiolini and Sgt Trémolet of GC II/5 following attack on Mourmelon. Possibly also hit by AA fire, exploded between Ste-Marie and Sommepy-Tahure 7.05 a.m. Lt E. von Sazenhofen-Fuchsberg, Fw G. Stadler, and Gefr S. Holbein killed. Fw K. Ulrich and Uffz G. Eisenmann both blown out of the aircraft but landed by parachute and captured. Aircraft A1+EL a write-off.

3./KG53 Heinkel He111H. Returned damaged by Curtiss H-75s of GC II/5 and AA fire following attack on Mourmelon 7.00 a.m. Uffz F. Huber slightly wounded in hand. Aircraft damage state not recorded.

3./KG53 Heinkel He111H. Returned damaged by Curtiss H-75s of GC II/5 and AA fire following attack on Mourmelon 7.00 a.m. Uffz J. Maier slightly wounded. Aircraft damage state not recorded.

4./KG53 Heinkel He111H. Engaged near Vouziers by F/O Holden of No. 501 Squadron and port engine badly damaged, forced-landed at Hoppstädten 7.35 a.m. Uffz H. Engländer and Gefr F. Wollnitz both wounded, admitted to hospital in Birkenfeld. Aircraft A1+KM a write-off.

4./KG53 Heinkel He111H. Believed damaged in attack by Curtiss H-75s of GC II/5, then engaged near Vouziers by S/Lt Boitelet, Sgt Tallent, and Sgt Delporte of GC I/5. Finally crashed and burned out at Thonnelle, near Avioth, 7.35 a.m. Fw M. Siegle, Uffz P. Andreae, Uffz H. Moosbrugger, and Uffz H. Schien all killed. Oberlt K. Knorr baled out and captured unhurt. Aircraft A1+GM a write-off.

Stab KG54 Heinkel He111P. Shot down by 11 Moranes of GC 5/1 during photo-reconnaissance of troop movements between Brussels and Antwerp and ditched in the Scheldt near the Royerssluis, Antwerp Docks 6.30 a.m. Oberfw G. Köpp reported died of wounds May 30. Lt H. von Gundelach and Uffz K-H. Schuldt captured. Uffz G. Blombecker captured wounded. Aircraft a write-off.

2./KG54 Heinkel He111P. Both engines destroyed in attacks by No. 85 Squadron Hurricanes and belly-landed near Leuven 9.30 a.m. Possibly also attacked by No. 87 Squadron pilots. Obergefr K. Haase, Uffz F. Kotrade, Obergefr W. Kops, and Gefr W. Graubner captured unhurt. Aircraft B3+NK a write-off.
This aircraft was subjected to intense ground-fire from Belgian troops before the crew was eventually allowed to surrender. The pilot, Karl Haase, was later reportedly shot and seriously wounded while a prisoner under interrogation and eventually discovered by German troops in hospital at Zuydcoote on June 4.

2./KG54 Heinkel He111P. Crash-landed near Krefeld badly damaged by No. 85 Squadron Hurricanes over Deinze, south-west of Gent 9.30 a.m. Possibly also attacked by No. 87 Squadron pilots. Uffz F. Koch and Gefr W. Petersen both wounded. Aircraft a write-off.

4./KG55 Heinkel He111P. Attacked by Sgt Farnes, Sgt McKay, and Sgt Morfill of No. 501 Squadron south-west of St Hubert during sortie to bomb rail targets near Rethel. Pursued toward Maubeuge and finally crashed at 'Buisson Roualet', near Machault, 2.45 p.m. Lt H. Junk, Uffz H. Thöne, Uffz W. Ege, and Gefr H. Wendt killed. Uffz E. Rasper captured wounded. Aircraft G1+DM a write-off.

5./KG55 Heinkel He111P. Returned badly damaged by Sgt Farnes, Sgt McKay, and Sgt Morfill of No. 501 Squadron between St Hubert and Maubeuge following attack on rail targets near Rethel 2.40 p.m. Uffz I. Bartholmes wounded. Aircraft damaged but repairable.

6./KG76 Dornier Do17Z. Returned with observer injured when his MG15 overheated and a round exploded during action between Philippeville and Givet. Lt G. Gawlina slightly wounded. Aircraft undamaged.

8./KG77 Dornier Do17Z. Engaged by Hurricanes of No. 79 Squadron over Liège and badly damaged. Believed that pursued by P/O Parker which forced-landed at Crapoel, south-west of Gulpen. Lt K. Hengsbach, Uffz K. Pankau, Obergefr E. Hofmann, and Flgr K. Sprenger all seriously wounded and admitted to hospital in Aachen. Aircraft 3Z+CS damaged but repairable.

3./KGr.126 Heinkel He111H (3558). Shot down by 7 Moranes of GC III/3 during armed reconnaissance over South Beveland and the Scheldt Estuary. Crashed and burned out at Calfven, between Hoogerheide and Ossendrecht 8.10 p.m. Oberlt F-W. Sawade *(Staffelkapitän)*, Oberfw H. Klabunde, and Uffz J. Dethlefsen killed. Oberfw H. Widmayer baled out and captured badly wounded. Aircraft 1T+AL a write-off.

Site excavated by the RNLAF in June 1966.

3./KGr.126 Heinkel He111H (5571). Shot down by 7 Moranes of GC III/3 during armed reconnaissance over South Beveland and the Scheldt Estuary. Crashed and broke up at Doelstraat, Woensdrecht 8.10 p.m. Uffz E. Fischer and Uffz H. Gutteck killed. Uffz O. Kippschull and Oberfw P. Wittich captured wounded. Aircraft 1T+EL a write-off.

17./KGrzbV.5 Junkers Ju52. Wrecked in crash at Hildesheim due to engine failure. One crewman injured. Aircraft damaged but repairable.

4./KGrzbV.9 Two Junkers Ju52. Badly damaged by artillery fire while off-loading troops at Waalhaven 10.30 a.m. Uffz P. Polzin killed. Uffz H. Mutschter, Uffz H. Schirmer, Uffz H. Voigt, and Obergefr K. Unger badly wounded, admitted to hospital in Paderborn. Aircraft 9P+EM abandoned.

One of these aircraft got back to Lippspringe.

2./LG1 Heinkel He111H. Returned damaged by fighters. Probably that attacked by Blenheims of No. 235 Squadron off Texel 9.15 a.m. Gefr W. Jenderny killed. Aircraft repairable.

4./LG1 Heinkel He111H. Shot down by F/O Gore, F/O Weatherill, and P/O Stewart of No. 607 Squadron during sortie to bomb airfield near Lille and believed crashed near Armentières 6.00 a.m. Oberlt K. Sohler *(Staffelkapitän)*, Oberfw E. Staub, and Fw R. Dähne killed. Oberlt E. Hannen captured unhurt. Aircraft L1+BM a write-off.

4./LG1 Heinkel He111H. Shot down by F/O Gore, F/O Weatherill, and P/O Stewart of No. 607 Squadron during sortie to bomb airfield near Lille and believed crashed near Kemmel 6.00 a.m. Possibly also that attacked by P/O Cock of No. 87 Squadron. Uffz F. Gallina and Fw G. Häntsch killed. Lt W. Fleckenstein and Fw L. Hagedorn captured unhurt. Aircraft a write-off.

The observer, Ludwig Hagedorn, was killed in an air raid on the night of May 29/30 while on board ship in Dunkirk harbour en route to captivity in England.

4./LG1 Heinkel He111. Both engines destroyed in attacks by F/O Gore, F/O Weatherill, and P/O Stewart of No. 607 Squadron over Marquain during sortie to bomb airfield near Lille and forced-landed at Marquain, west of Tournai 6.00 a.m. Uffz R. Obst killed. Fw H-P. Piper and Uffz H. Szigat captured wounded. Fw E. Wolter captured unhurt. Aircraft L1+LM a write-off.

7./LG1 Junkers Ju88A-1. Returned damaged by Blenheims of No. 254 Squadron over Vlissingen during attack on shipping. Fw W. Flick badly wounded, admitted to hospital in Lingen where died of wounds that night. Aircraft damage state not recorded.

13.(Z)/LG1 Messerschmitt Bf110C. Pursued at low level by Sgt Bressieux of GC I/5 following attack on No. 501 Squadron Hurricane in combat over Vouziers, and overturned attempting high-speed forced-landing south-west of Chauvency-le-Château 7.20 a.m. Lt H. Schultze captured unhurt. Uffz G. Wiebe captured wounded. Aircraft L1+BH a write-off.

13.(Z)/LG1 Messerschmitt Bf110C. Exploded in mid-air between Thonne-les-Prés and Thonnelle, north of Montmédy, under attack by Lt Dorance of GC I/5 during escort sortie for KG53 to Mourmelon 7.15 a.m. Uffz K. Hartenstein and Obergefr G. Conrad killed. Aircraft a write-off.

13.(Z)/LG1 Messerschmitt Bf110C. Lost control in vertical dive avoiding attacks from S/Lt Boitelet and Sgt Tallent of GC I/5, also Sgt Guillaume of GC III/7, over Vouziers and hit trees at 'Nugimont', south of Blagny 7.15 a.m. Lt H. Gaffal thrown from aircraft and captured with fractured skull, admitted to hospital in Ste-Menehould. Uffz A. Dierkes also captured wounded. Aircraft L1+AH a write-off.

1.(J)/LG2 Messerschmitt Bf109E-1. Wrecked in aborted take-off at Nordholz. Pilot unhurt. Aircraft a write-off.

2.(J)/LG2 Messerschmitt Bf109E-3. Badly damaged by F/O Fowler of No. 615 Squadron in combat west of Tongeren 10.00 a.m. Pilot unhurt. Aircraft a write-off.

3.(J)/LG2 Messerschmitt Bf109E-4. Damaged due to burst tyre on take-off from Nordholz. Pilot unhurt. Aircraft damaged but repairable.

Stab II.(S)/LG2 Henschel Hs126. Returned damaged by ground-fire over St Truiden. Lt H. Rasch and Uffz P. Schnack both slightly wounded. Aircraft damage state not recorded.

Stab I./StG2 Junkers Ju87B (5136). Shot down by Hurricanes of No. 3 Squadron south-west of Hasselt and abandoned over Geetbets, north of Grazen, 8.30 a.m. Possibly one of those attacked by P/O Carey. Pilot believed baled out unhurt. Uffz H. Basler killed. Aircraft a write-off.

Major excavation by local enthusiasts 1990 recovered engine, propellor blades, section of fuselage, remains of undercarriage, cockpit canopy, armament, radio, maps, parachute- and scraps of uniform.

2./StG2 Junkers Ju87B. Shot down in combat with Hurricanes of No. 3 Squadron between Diest and Leuven and crashed at Lubbeek 8.30 a.m. Possibly one of those attacked by P/O Stephens. Uffz R. Stachowiak and Gefr E. Hummel killed. Aircraft a write-off.

7./StG2 Junkers Ju87B. Forced-landed east of St Truiden damaged, by No. 3 Squadron Hurricanes, during sortie to attack armour near Gembloux 5.30 a.m. Possibly one of those attacked by F/O Bowyer. One of crew wounded. Aircraft a write-off.

1./StG76 Junkers Ju87B. Returned damaged by Curtiss H-75s of GC I/5 during attack on Sedan 10.30 a.m. Uffz R. Kny badly wounded. Lt Haller unhurt. Aircraft damaged but repairable.

1./StG76 Junkers Ju87B. Damaged by Curtiss H-75s of GC I/5 during attack on Sedan 10.30 a.m. and believed forced-landed near Geroldstadt. Fw F. Petrick badly wounded. Oberlt Z. Unbehauen unhurt. Aircraft damaged but repairable.

2./StG76 Junkers Ju87B. Badly damaged by Curtiss H-75s of GC I/5 during attack on Sedan and crash-landed at Dohan, east of Bouillon 10.30 a.m. Uffz H. Gäth killed. Lt H. Migeot unhurt. Aircraft a write-off.

2./StG76 Junkers Ju87B. Badly damaged by Curtiss H-75s of GC I/5 during attack on Sedan and crash-landed behind the German lines 10.30 a.m. Gefr L. Kirner slightly wounded. Aircraft a write-off.

2./StG76 Junkers Ju87B. Shot down by Curtiss H-75s of GC I/5 during attack on Sedan and crashed in woods near Bouillon 10.30 a.m. Lt R. Schülze-Wimken and Uffz H. Rolland both captured wounded. Aircraft S1+DK a write-off.

4.(J)/TrGr.186 Messerschmitt Bf109E-1. Hit by flak north of Den Helder and crash-landed near Garijp, north-east of Leeuwarden 11.40 a.m. Pilot unhurt. Aircraft a write-off.

6.(J)/TrGr.186 Messerschmitt Bf109E-3. Damaged by flak over north end of Afsluitdijk and forced-landed between Pingjum and Wons, south of Harlingen. Pilot unhurt. Aircraft 12 + a write-off.

6.(J)/TrGr.186 Messerschmitt Bf109E-3. Damaged by flak over Texel during attack on De Mok air base and crash-landed at Groote Keeten, in the Oostpolder, south of Den Helder. Uffz G. Feld captured wounded. Aircraft a write-off.

4./ZG76 Messerschmitt Bf110C. Starboard engine damaged over Cambrai and crashed on landing at Zissenheim. Believed hit by ground-fire but possibly damaged in combat with Moranes of GC 6/3 over Avesnes 6.10 a.m. Lt O. Krause killed. Uffz F. Auerbach slightly wounded admitted to hospital in Bonn-Hangelar. Aircraft a write-off.

This Heinkel (5571) from the 3. Staffel of Kampfgruppe 126 spread itself across the Dutch landscape at Woensdrecht, courtesy of pilots of Groupe de Chasse III/3.

Monday, May 13 — Easter Monday in 1940 — has gone down in the annals of the Battle of France as 'The Day of the Defiants'. That morning a flight of six Boulton Paul Defiant fighters of No. 264 Squadron, on a combat mission over south-western Holland, was attacked by a swarm of enemy Messerschmitt Bf109 fighters just south-east of Rotterdam. In the ensuing dog-fight, five of the six Defiants were shot down, and of the ten airmen in the downed aircraft, three were killed, three became prisoners of war and four others evaded capture, eventually making their way back to Britain. Only one Defiant returned to base to report on the disastrous outcome of this, the squadron's first encounter with Bf109s. It was a devastating blow to the squadron and one that heralded little good for the final outcome of the air battle over the Continent. Later that summer, six Defiants of No. 264 were pictured at RAF Kirton-in-Lindsey, to where the squadron had transferred on July 23. In the cockpit of the aircraft nearest the camera is Pilot Officer Desmond Kay, the only pilot to come back from the ill-fated mission.

Monday, May 13

The Luftwaffe continued its assault on centres of communications well behind the front line during the day, while British reconnaissance flights were hampered by low cloud and intense ground-fire, much of it enemy. In Holland, German forces had penetrated the Dutch defences north of the Waal, between Wageningen and Rhenen, forcing French advance forces back through Breda and towards Bergen-op-Zoom. Thus, in an effort to relieve pressure on the retreating French 7ème Armée, No. 226 Squadron Battles, covered by No. 56 Squadron Hurricanes operating from England, bombed a road junction at Boeimeer mid-morning. Inconceivably, this was to be the only attack delivered by British aircraft throughout the entire day.

Earlier that morning, Fighter Command had despatched a flight of No. 264 Squadron Defiants, together with a flight of No. 66 Squadron Spitfires, over the Dutch coast north of Den Haag to attack stranded enemy troop transports. Venturing inland southeast of Rotterdam, they engaged Ju87s but fell victim to escort Bf109s and five Defiants were lost. This was the first time that the Defiant had encountered Bf109s and, although outnumbered, it clearly signalled its limitations. Regretably, the lesson went unheeded so had to be repeated eight weeks later over the English Channel with equally tragic results.

During the day, a Dutch Government signal to London confirmed that the Dutch Air Force no longer existed — though it continued to sacrifice both aircraft and crews. Without immediate Allied air support, if the German advance continued, the Dutch position would be hopeless and capitulation inevitable. Meantime, the Belgian Army continued its withdrawal to take up new defensive positions between Louvain and Antwerp forming part of an Allied line extending to Namur. But south of this axis, German ground forces, assisted by close support from Ju87s against strong points, were already crossing the Meuse north of Dinant — a surprise development first reported by a French reconnaissance flight. Far more alarming, major penetration of the French line at Sedan was now threatened.

More positively, increasingly urgent requests for fighter reinforcements in France resulted in an additional 32 Hurricanes and their pilots, detached from various squadrons in England, being ordered to France that afternoon. Also, assurances were given that deficiencies in the Hurricane squadrons would be made good without delay. These additions, welcome as they were, still left the Air Component one squadron short of what had been demanded, so it continued to press for more.

By evening the situation at Sedan was fast becoming critical, enemy forces crossing the Meuse to a depth of several miles to threaten the Allied right flank. As a consequence, all AASF units were warned of 'operations of vital importance' on the following day, and further instructed to consider plans for withdrawal in the event of a German breakthrough. While, such being the gravity of the situation in the Netherlands, plans were initiated to start evacuating the Dutch Royal Family and government from IJmuiden aboard the British destroyer HMS Codrington.

Night operations by Bomber Command were on a small scale but, of only twelve sorties despatched, seven of them failed to even reach or locate their targets, most returning with their bombs.

BRITISH AIR FORCES IN FRANCE

1 SQUADRON, BERRY-AU-BAC

Hurricane L1681. Forced-landed and burned out at St-Loup-Terrier, engine damaged by return fire during attack on He111 of 8./KG55 near Attigny 6.45 a.m. Flying Officer R. L. Lorimer unhurt. Aircraft a write-off.

Hurricane. Struck a deep furrow after landing near He111 of Stab KG55 brought down near 'Montachis' at Coulommes-les-Marqueny, north-west of Mazagran, 6.45 a.m. Flying Officer L. R. Clisby unhurt. Aircraft abandoned.
This aircraft is believed to have remained in situ for several years, slowly being stripped bare by scavengers.

Hurricane. Returning to base with oxygen failure, shot down by Bf110s during solo attack on Do17s and abandoned north-east of Perthes 7.15 a.m. Flying Officer B. Drake baled out wounded in back and legs, admitted to hospital in Rethel. Aircraft ⊙P a write-off.
A contemporary report of French 9ème Armée activities, and a letter in 1989 from Jean Logeart-Hans of Perthes, who attended the wounded British pilot and drove him to hospital, both record this event taking place on May 11. Surviving RAF records do not resolve the question, but most previously published accounts based upon Paul Richey's memoirs all accept that it was May 13.
Major excavation by Steve Vizard and fellow enthusiasts included in a BBC documentary broadcast in June 2004 about No. 1 Squadron in France, including the investigation of a Ju87 crash on May 14, 1940.
UK regulation has resulted in some British aviation archaeology groups now pursuing their interests abroad.

A line up of pilots from No. 1 Squadron. On the left stands Billy Drake who was shot down early on the morning of May 13. Beside him is Leslie Clisby, 'Lorry' Lorimer, 'Prosser' Hanks, 'Boy' Mould, the CO 'The Bull' Halahan, French interpreter Jean 'Moses' Demozay, 'Johnny' Walker, the MO 'Doc' Brown, Paul Richey, 'Killy' Kilmartin, 'Stratters' Stratton and the American, 'Pussy' Palmer. Clisby, Lorimer and Hanks all became casualties on May 14, only 'Prosser' surviving.

Hurricane. Returned hit by return fire from Do17 of 3.(F)/22 engaged near Reims 6.55 a.m. Sergeant L. S. Pilkington unhurt. Aircraft repairable.

Hurricane L1673. Oil and glycol tanks hit by return fire during attack on Do17 near Reims and crash-landed near Bétheniville 6.30 a.m. Pilot Officer R. A. Marchand slightly wounded in shoulder and perspex splinters in left eye. Aircraft a write-off.

85 SQUADRON, LILLE-SECLIN

Hurricane P2821. Shot down in combat with Bf109s of 8./JG3 south of Diest during offensive patrol over Belgium and possibly that attacked by Lt Schmidt 9.25 a.m. Squadron Leader J. O. W. Oliver baled out unhurt. Aircraft a write-off.

87 SQUADRON, LILLE-MARCQ

Hurricane L1930. Reported missing, circumstances not recorded. Pilot believed unhurt. Aircraft a write-off.

226 SQUADRON, REIMS-CHAMPAGNE

Battle P2353. Hit by ground-fire south-west of Wuestwezel during sortie to attack road junction at Boeimeer and forced-landed near Brussels 12.00 p.m. Pilot Officer M. W. Waddington slightly wounded. Sergeant G. Stephenson and LAC J. Hope unhurt. Aircraft abandoned.
This aircraft was subsequently impressed into the Belgian Air Force but was not flown in service as it used 100 octane petrol, Belgian Battles using lower-rated fuel.

Battle L5418. Flew into high tension cable during attack on road junction at Boeimeer 12.00 p.m. and returned damaged . Sergeant G. G. Martin, Sergeant N. Anderson, and AC H. K. Wyatt unhurt. Aircraft repairable — abandoned on withdrawal to Faux-Villecerf May 16.

3 SQUADRON, MERVILLE

Hurricane L1901. Crash-landed badly damaged in combat with Bf109s between Louvain and Wavre 1.30 p.m. Flying Officer A. R. Ball captured badly wounded in thigh, died of wounds June 4. Aircraft a write-off.

Hurricane N2654. Collided during return from patrol and crashed 5 miles from base 4.00 p.m. Flying Officer W. S. C. Adams killed. Aircraft a write-off.

Hurricane N2653. Collided while joining formation during return from patrol and exploded 5 miles from base 4.00 p.m. Flying Officer R. B. Lines-Roberts killed. Aircraft a write-off.

4 SQUADRON, MONCHY-LAGACHE

Lysander II P9063. Shot down by Lt Braxator of 2./JG1 during reconnaissance sortie near Hoogarde, and crashed alongside the road between Outgaarden and Goetsenhoeven 8.45 a.m. Pilot Officer P. W. Vaughan and AC2 E. Mold killed. Aircraft a write-off.

18 SQUADRON, MÉHARICOURT

Blenheim IV L8866. Returned slightly damaged by ground-fire during reconnaissance sortie over the Albert Canal 6.45 a.m. Flying Officer D. D. Rogers, Sergeant A. J. Gulliver, and LAC D. C. Moore unhurt. Aircraft repairable.

53 SQUADRON, POIX

Blenheim IV L4861. Damaged by ground-fire during reconnaissance sortie over Belgium and forced-landed on one engine at Vitry 7.35 a.m. Flight Lieutenant A. C. Brown and Sergeant Brooks unhurt. AC2 W. Cavett badly wounded in leg. Aircraft repairable.

57 SQUADRON, ROSIÈRES-EN-SANTERRE

Blenheim IV P6930. Shot down by AA fire during reconnaissance sortie over Belgium and crashed between Vlijtingen and Kesselt 8.00 p.m. Sergeant G. F. Couzens killed. Pilot Officer G. K. R. Drimmle and AC1 R. Shuttleworth both baled out and captured unhurt. Aircraft a write-off.
The date of death of Sergeant Couzens is recorded as May 12 by the CWGC.

59 SQUADRON, POIX

Blenheim IV L9266. Returned rudder damaged during reconnaissance sortie 2.15 p.m. Pilot Officer C. J. Hitch wounded in leg, rest of crew unhurt. Aircraft repairable.

Blenheim IV N6173. Shot down by flak during strategic reconnaissance sortie over Belgium and believed that crashed at Neerwinden 7.30 p.m. Pilot Officer C. J. E. Chamberlain, Sergeant G. E. Seldon, and AC1 F. Hands missing. Aircraft lost.
Possibly the three 'Unknown British Airmen' originally buried at Neerwinden and later reinterred in Hotton War Cemetery, Collective Grave VI.G.7. All recorded 'missing' on May 14 by the CWGC and commemorated so on the Runnymede Memorial.

73 SQUADRON, REIMS-CHAMPAGNE

Hurricane. Returned hit by return fire from Do17 of 3.(F)/22 engaged near Reims 6.55 a.m. Pilot Officer R. F. Martin unhurt. Aircraft repairable.

Hurricane. Returned hit by return fire from Do17 of 3.(F)/22 engaged near Reims 6.55 a.m. Pilot Officer D. S. Scott unhurt. Aircraft repairable.

Aviation historian Peter Arnold (right) shows Billy Drake the head armour from his Hurricane which was excavated in June 2004.

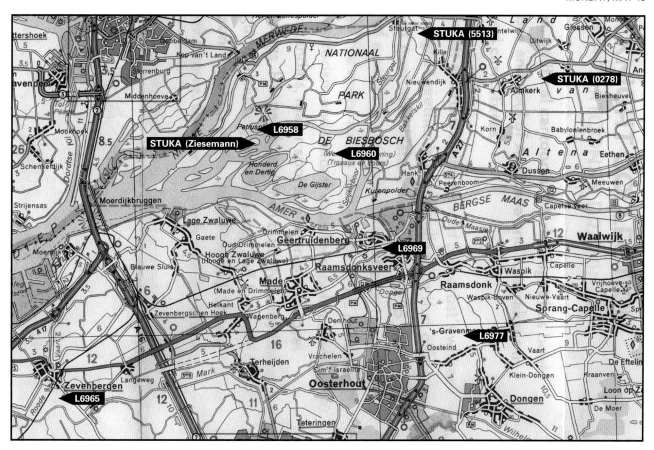

The graveyard of No. 264 Squadron's Defiants. All five aircraft were lost over the same general area of swampy wetlands — the Biesbosch — which lies between the Nieuwe Merwede and Amer rivers south-east of Rotterdam.

501 SQUADRON, BÉTHENIVILLE

Hurricanes L1605 and N2586. Damaged in enemy bombing at Bétheniville 6.00 a.m. No pilot casualties. Aircraft both damaged but repairable.

504 SQUADRON, LILLE-MARCQ

Hurricane. Broke a tail wheel on landing at Vitry-en-Artois. Pilot Officer B. van Mentz unhurt. Aircraft repairable.

607 SQUADRON, VITRY-EN-ARTOIS

Hurricane P3535. Returned radio and fuselage slightly damaged in surprise attack by Bf109s of I./JG1 south-east of Tienen 5.15 a.m. Pilot Officer P. L. Parrott unhurt. Aircraft AF⊙C repairable.

Hurricane P2620. Shot down in surprise attack by Bf109s south-east of Tienen and crashed at Landen 5.15 a.m. Possibly that claimed at Jodoigne by Hptmn Balthasar of I./JG1. Flying Officer M. H. B. Thompson killed. Aircraft a write-off.
Originally buried in Landen Convent Cloister, 'Monty' Thompson was reinterred in Heverlee War Cemetery at Leuven in January 1947.

Hurricane P3448. Returned damaged in combat with Bf109s of 8./JG3 south of Diest 9.30 a.m. Squadron Leader L. E. Smith unhurt. Aircraft AF⊙H repairable.

615 SQUADRON, VITRY-EN-ARTOIS

Hurricane. Returned damaged by ground-fire following escort sortie for No. 18 Squadron Blenheims on low-level reconnaissance over the Albert Canal. Flight Lieutenant L. T. W. Thornley unhurt. Aircraft repairable.

Hurricane L2035. Believed claimed by Lt Marchfelder of Stab II./ZG1 south-east of Namur, and crashed at Courrière p.m. Flying Officer P. N. Murton-Neale killed. Aircraft a write-off.
The date of death of Peter Norman Murton-Neale is recorded as May 14 by the Commonwealth War Graves Commission. Such contradictory dates are not unusual and only to be expected when completed by units operating 'in the field'.

UK-based aircraft lost or damaged on operations over the Western Front:

RAF FIGHTER COMMAND

56 Squadron, Martlesham Heath
Patrol Bergen — Turnhout:

Hurricane N2402. Landed at Manston damaged by ground-fire during cover patrol for No. 226 Squadron 11.00 a.m. S/L E. V. Knowles unhurt. Aircraft repairable.

Hurricane N2398. Landed at Manston damaged by ground-fire during cover patrol for No. 226 Squadron 11.00 a.m. Sgt C. Whitehead unhurt. Aircraft repairable.

66 Squadron, Martlesham Heath
Patrol IJmuiden — Den Haag:

Spitfire N3027. Badly damaged in combat with Bf109s of 5./JG26 and overturned landing on burst tyre at Aalter 6.00 a.m. P/O G. A. Brown unhurt. Aircraft wrecked.

264 Squadron, Martlesham Heath
Patrol IJmuiden — Den Haag:

Defiant L6974. Forced-landed at Aalter slightly damaged and low on fuel after combat with Bf109s of 5./JG26 over the Biesbosch 5.55 a.m. P/O D. H. S. Kay and LAC E. J. Jones unhurt. Aircraft repairable.

Defiant L6958. Shot down by Bf109s of 5./JG26 and crashed into creek 'Gat van de Kampen', south of Petrusplaat island, in the Biesbosch, 5.55 a.m. P/O S. R. Thomas baled out slightly wounded, LAC J. S. Bromley missing. Aircraft lost.
Wreckage recovered by Jaap Boddé assisted by Dutch authorities in 1994. Intact engine and other items displayed in the Biesboschmuseum at Werkendam. Partial human remains recovered were never formally identified nor buried. A full account of this action, by Dutch air historian Jan Jolie, was published in After the Battle No. 134.

Defiant L6969. Shot down by Bf109s of 5./JG26 and belly-landed on the banks of the Donge, south of Geertruidenberg, 5.55 a.m. F/L G. F. A. Skelton badly wounded, admitted to St Theresia Hospital, Ramsdonksveer, where captured. P/O J. E. Hatfield baled out wounded in elbow. Aircraft lost.

Defiant L6960. Exploded under attack by Bf109s of 5./JG26 and crashed into a creek 'Gat van de Zuiderklip' between Grote Turfzak and Moordplaat polders 5.55 a.m. P/O G. E. Chandler and LAC D. L. McLeish killed. Aircraft PS⊙M lost.

Defiant L6977. Shot down by Bf109s of 5./JG26 and belly-landed by the Rijsdijk, at Willemspolder, north of Oosteind, 5.55 a.m. P/O P. E. J. Greenhous captured, injured head on landing. Sgt F. D. Greenhalgh baled out, captured unhurt. Aircraft PS⊙U lost.

Defiant L6965. Set alight by Bf109s of 5./JG26 and crash-landed by the Hazeldonkse Zandweg, south of Zevenbergen, 5.55 a.m. P/O A. M. MacLeod and LAC W. E. Cox evaded capture. Aircraft burned out.

Defiant L6958 crashed in the 'Gat van de Kampen', a creek just south of Petrusplaat island in the Biesbosch marshland. Lost for over five decades, the wreck was accidentally found in July 1994. In a subsequent recovery operation by the Dutch Air Force in September, the engine and other parts of the aircraft were salvaged from the water.

Though badly wounded through the arms and legs, Flight Lieutenant George Skelton managed to crash-land L6969 in a strip of reeds bordering the Donge river south of the town of Geertruidenberg. He was taken to a Dutch hospital, then captured and sent to a POW camp hospital, from where he was eventually repatriated to Britain in 1943 due to his wounds.

Hit by fire from enemy fighters, L6960 exploded in mid-air, the aircraft breaking up and both Pilot Officer Gordon Chandler and LAC Douglas McLeish dying in the crash. The rear fuselage landed upside down in the 'Gat van de Zuiderklip', a narrow creek immediately west of Moordplaat island in the wetlands.

Here, three Dutchmen — A. Akkermans, the village policeman of Made; Jan van Strien, a local parish official; and Cees van den Diepstraten, a night-watchman from Drimmelen village — are pictured with the wreckage shortly after the crash. The squadron code of this Defiant was PS⊙M.

His aircraft hit by fire from two Bf109s, wounded in the head, and his engine stalled, Pilot Officer Patrick Greenhous, pilot of Defiant L6977, made a successful emergency landing in a meadow along the Rijsdijk dyke in the Willemspolder, some two miles east of the town of Oosterhout.

Pilot Officer Alex MacLeod force-landed L6965 near Zevenbergen. He and his gunner, LAC Walter Cox, joined up with a regiment of the Dutch Army that was chaotically retreating into Belgium and eventually reached Ostend from where they sailed to England aboard a British destroyer on May 17.

FRENCH AIR FORCE

AC 2 Bloch 151. Belly-landed at Calais-Marck due to undercarriage failure. Mt. Ley unhurt. Aircraft 4 damaged but repairable — later abandoned.
This was one of six Bloch fighters just arrived from Orly to reinforce Flotille de Chasse F1C.

ECMJ 1/16 Potez 631. Starboard wing and tail damaged in attack by Hurricane while engaging a Bf110 over Pontfaverger 7.10 a.m. Returned to Wez-Thuisy with aileron damage. Sgt P. Wurtz and crew unhurt. Aircraft repairable.

ECMJ 1/16 Potez 631. Damaged by Hurricane and reported further attack while landing at Wez-Thuisy following engagement with enemy aircraft over Pontfaverger 7.10 a.m. Capt G. Escudier *(Commandant)*, Lt Millot, and another crewman unhurt. Aircraft repairable.
It was later confirmed that these aircraft were engaged by No. 73 Squadron; F/O Paul stating that he fired one short deflection burst before recognising the aircraft as friendly, and P/O Marchand reporting that he had held fire. Both RAF pilots denied firing at an aircraft nearing the ground.

GAO 501 Potez 63.11 (297). Shot down by Lt Butterweck of 1./JG26 over Poppel during reconnaissance sortie between Breda and Eindhoven. Crashed and burned out at Kapeldijk, Oirschot, 5.45 p.m. Lt L. Coqueton, Capt A. Wiccaert, and Sgt L. Leygnac killed. Aircraft a write-off.

GAO 509 Potez 63.11. Returned to Delme damaged by ground-fire during reconnaissance of the sector La Grande Roselle — Forbach — Grosbliederstroff 6.10 a.m. S/Lt A. Giron and S/Lt H. Guillerme unhurt. Adjt R. Mary badly wounded, died later in hospital at Burthecourt. Aircraft damaged but repairable.

GAO 510 Potez 63.11 (393). Shot down by Lt Fischer of 3./JG53 during reconnaissance sortie over Givonne and crashed at Moulin Coquet, west of Cheveuges, south-west of Sedan 6.45 p.m. Lt Dubois and Sgt Rimlinger badly wounded. Capt Voituriez *(Commandant)* wounded. Aircraft a write-off.

GAO 511 Potez 63.11 (288). Shot down by flak during low-level reconnaissance over Anhée and Yvoir 12.30 p.m. Crashed and burned out at Champ Milcamp, by the road to Sommière at Bouvignes, near Dinant. Capt R. Peigné, S/Lt J-F. de la Rocque, and S/Lt J. Gessiaume killed. Aircraft a write-off.

GAO 511 2 Potez 63.11 (291 and 386). Destroyed on the ground at Signy-le-Petit in bombing and strafing attack by Do17s of II./KG76 5.00 p.m. No crew casualties reported. Aircraft both write-offs.
Two Potez 39s (13 and 29), and a Potez 58, were also destroyed in this attack which put the unit out of action. A single Potez 63.11 (390), airborne at the time of the attack, was the sole aircraft remaining.

GAO 552 Potez 63.11 (689). Damaged by flak during reconnaissance sortie and crashed in Nieuwkerken-Waas, 3 km from Sint-Niklaas airfield 10.00 a.m. Lt P. Colpin and Adjt J. Lux killed. Adjt R. Sacquepée badly wounded, died en route to hospital. Aircraft a write-off.

The remains of Potez 63.11, serial 393, shot down by Leutnant Fischer near Sedan.

GB 1/12 LeO 451 (47). Returned to Soissons-Saconin with starboard aileron damaged by flak during attack on enemy columns crossing the Meuse at Dinant 7.00 p.m. Lt de Saint-Victor *(Commandant)*, Adjt L. Leroy, Sgt Stevenel, and Sgt Guyon unhurt. Aircraft repairable.

GB 2/12 LeO 451. Returned to Soissons-Saconin starboard engine damaged by flak during attack on enemy columns crossing the Meuse at Dinant 7.00 p.m. Lt C. Raillard *(Commandant)* and crew unhurt. Aircraft repairable.

GB I/12 LeO 451 (54). Returned to Soissons-Saconin one engine damaged by flak during attack on enemy columns crossing the Meuse at Dinant 7.00 p.m. S/Lt Rousseau, Sgt Masset, Sgt Buisson, and Sgt Marty unhurt. Aircraft repairable.

GB I/12 LeO 451 (24). Returned to Soissons-Saconin damaged by flak during attack on enemy columns crossing the Meuse at Dinant 7.00 p.m. Sgt Blois wounded, Adjt Gobeau and rest of crew unhurt. Aircraft repairable.

GB 3/12 LeO 451 (49). Returned to Persan-Beaumont damaged by flak in aborted sortie to attack enemy columns crossing the Meuse at Dinant 7.00 p.m. Capt Knipping *(Commandant)* Adjt Orliac, Sgt Coant and S/Lt Charle unhurt. Aircraft repairable.

GB II/12 LeO 451 (52). Returned to Persan-Beaumont damaged by flak in aborted sortie to attack enemy columns crossing the Meuse at Dinant 7.00 p.m. Capt Lesueur, Adjt A. Michelet, Sgt A. Paumier, and Sgt Annon unhurt. Aircraft repairable.

GB I/34 Amiot 143. Damaged by flak and destroyed on evacuation of Mourmelon. No crew casualties. Aircraft a write-off.

GB II/34 Amiot 143 (118). Returned to Nangis with tail damaged by flak during night sortie. Cmdt. J. de Laubier *(Commandant)* Lt Ponsot, Adjt M. Lavolley, Adjt Allemin and Sgt Marsal unhurt. Aircraft repairable.

GB II/38 Amiot 143. Damaged on landing after night sortie, crew believed unhurt. Aircraft a write-off.

GC I/1 Bloch 152. Belly-landed with combat damage following escort sortie for GB I/12 and GB II/12 over Dinant 7.00 p.m. Sgt Fiala unhurt. Aircraft damaged but repairable.

GC 5/1 Morane 406 (532). Forced-landed near Moerbeke damaged by flak after combat with Bf109s of I./JG26 during patrol over Breda 9.50 a.m. Sgt G. Pralon unhurt. Aircraft destroyed to prevent capture.

GC 5/1 Morane 406. Landed at Maldegem damaged in attack by Lt Henrici of 1./JG26 south of Breda 9.50 a.m. Lt K. Bursztyn slightly wounded. Aircraft damaged but repairable.

GC II/2 Morane 406. Returned to Laon-Chambry slightly damaged by return fire during attack on Do17s between Charleville-Mézières and Givet 5.10 p.m. Pilot unhurt. Aircraft repairable.

GC II/2 Morane 406. Returned to Laon-Chambry with fuel lines severed by return fire during attack on Do17s of II./KG76 between Charleville-Mézières and Givet 5.10 p.m. Adjt A. Bernavon unhurt. Aircraft damaged but repairable.

GC II/2 Morane 406 (286). Shot down by Lt Guth of 6./ZG76 in combat south-west of Chimay 5.50 p.m. Crashed and exploded at the edge of Forêt Saint-Michel, south of Les Grands Riaux, north-east of Neuville-aux-Joûtes. Adjt M. Renaudie killed. Aircraft 4 a write-off.

GC II/2 Morane 406 (308). Shot down in combat with Bf110s of II./ZG76 south-west of Chimay 5.50 p.m. Crashed at 'Le Fourchis' alongside the Taillette road, 3 km west of Rocroi. Possibly another of those claimed by Lt Guth of 6./ZG76. Capt H. de Gail killed. Aircraft a write-off.

GC II/2 Morane 406 (164). Shot down in combat with Bf110s of II./ZG76 west of Rocroi 5.50 p.m. Possibly one of those claimed by Oberlt Nacke *(Staffelkapitän)* of 6./ZG76. Crashed near La Loge Rosette, west of Regniowez. Cmdt. P. Bertrou *(Commandant)* killed. Aircraft a write-off.
The wreckage of this aircraft remained undisturbed until its discovery in April 1941 when Paul Bertrou was finally laid to rest in Regniowez Cemetery on October 23, 1941.

GC III/2 Morane 406. Returned damaged by return fire from He111s engaged near Denain 5.30 a.m. Adjt J. Nedelec wounded. Aircraft damaged but repairable.

GC III/2 Two Morane 406. Returned damaged by return fire from He111s engaged near Denain 5.30 a.m. Pilots unhurt. Aircraft both repairable.

GC III/2 Morane 406 (634). Shot down by flak following attack on Hs126 near Landrecies during patrol north of Namur 3.30 p.m. Sgt P. Chambon baled out and captured badly burned. Aircraft a write-off.

GC 5/3 Morane 406 (549). Shot down by Lt Henrici of 1./JG26 in combat south of Breda and crashed at Hillekens, Etten-Leur 9.50 a.m. Capt R. Trouillard *(Commandant)* killed. Aircraft a write-off.

GC 6/3 Morane 406 (557). Shot down in combat with Bf109s of 1./JG21 over Namur 5.48 a.m. Possibly that claimed by Uffz Clerico. Adjt M. Marias unhurt. Aircraft a write-off.

GC 6/3 Morane 406 (767). Crash-landed badly damaged in combat with Bf109s of 1./JG21 and crash-landed near Namur 5.48 a.m. Possibly that claimed by Fw Frentzel-Beyme. Adjt M-E. Leblanc unhurt. Aircraft a write-off.

GC 6/3 Morane 406 (373). Badly damaged by flak during attack on Hs126 and later abandoned over Erquelinnes near Jeumont 2.00 p.m. Lt H. de Chezelles baled out wounded and fired on by French troops while in his parachute. Aircraft a write-off.

GC 1/4 Curtiss H-75. Damaged in attack on He111 of 2./KGr.126 over Rosendaal and belly-landed at De Clinge 6.25 p.m. Possibly that claimed by Oberlt Oesau of 1./JG20 over Halsteren. Lt J-L. Hirschauer unhurt. Aircraft damaged but repairable.

GC 1/5 Curtiss H-75. Returned to Suippes hit by return fire from Do17s 7.00 a.m. Adjt Bouvard wounded in jaw, admitted to hospital in Châlons-sur-Marne. Aircraft repairable.

GC 1/5 Curtiss H-75 (44). Crash-landed in open country, oil tank damaged by return fire from Do17s 7.00 a.m. Sgt G. Muselli injured face on gunsight. Aircraft abandoned.

GC 1/5 Curtiss H-75. Returned to Suippes damaged by return fire from Do17 of 3.(F)/22 engaged near Spincourt 6.40 a.m. S/Lt P. Scotte slightly wounded. Aircraft repairable.

GC 1/5 Curtiss H-75 (33). Shot down by Bf109s of 4./JG53 in combat near Saint-Pierremont and abandoned over Harricourt 11.05 a.m. Lt A. Vrana baled out unhurt landing south of Bar-les-Buzancy. Aircraft a write-off.

One of the 113 Czech airmen flying with the Armée de l'Air, Adolf Vrana was arrested by French troops and held in custody until his identity could be confirmed the following day.

GC II/6 Morane 406. Forced-landed near Guise following inconclusive attacks on He111 north of Florennes and Hs126 north of Namur 6.00 a.m. Sgt de Bremond d'Ars unhurt. Aircraft damaged but repairable.

GC II/6 Morane 406 (372). Damaged during attack on He111s of 3./KG54 south-east of Namur and belly-landed at Anhée 10.15 a.m. S/Lt J. Riss wounded. Aircraft abandoned.

GC 4/6 Morane 406 (628). Shot down by Oberlt Rau of Stab I./JG3 and belly-landed north-west of Dinant 10.30 a.m. S/Lt F. Gilbert captured wounded in foot. Aircraft a write-off.

GC II/6 Morane 406 (710). Forced-landed at Challerange following combat with Bf109s over Namur. Possibly one of those claimed by Uffz Wilhelm of 3./JG77 north-west of Dinant 10.30 a.m. S/Lt Sassard unhurt. Aircraft damaged but repairable

GC II/6 Morane 406 (932). Forced-landed at Verdun following combat with Bf109s near Namur. Possibly one of those claimed by Uffz Wilhelm of 3./JG77 in combat north-west of Dinant 10.30 a.m. S/Lt W. E. Karwowski unhurt. Aircraft damaged but repairable.

GC II/6 Morane 406 (703). Shot down by flak during patrol over Namur 2.10 p.m. Sgt W. Dambrine captured unhurt. Aircraft a write-off.

GC II/6 Morane 406 (728). Returned damaged by ground-fire during attack on Hs126 at low-level near Waremme 2.00 p.m. S/Lt M. Verdier unhurt. Aircraft repairable.

GC III/7 Morane 406 (791). Shot down by ground-fire during pursuit of Hs126 during sector patrol between Tirlemont and Namur. Believed crashed and burned out near Attenhoven 3.15 p.m. Adjt L. Boyer captured badly wounded and burned; repatriated in November 1940. Aircraft a write-off.

GC III/7 Morane 406 (200). Returned to Cambrai-Niergnies badly damaged by ground-fire during low-level pursuit of Hs126 during sector patrol Tirlemont—St Trond—Namur 3.15 p.m. Sgt R. Morlot unhurt. Aircraft damaged but repairable.

GR 3/33 Potez 637 (2). Believed that shot down by Oberlt Balfanz of Stab I./JG53 during low-level reconnaissance sortie over Givonne 5.45 p.m. Crashed and later exploded near Thénorgues, 16 km east of Vouziers. Lt Gavoille *(Commandant)*, Capt Vesin, and Cpl Saurt unhurt. Aircraft a write-off.

GR I/52 Bloch 174 (11). Believed attacked by Oberlt Hrabak of I./JG76 during reconnaissance sortie over Authe 10.05 a.m. Crashed at Nicey-sur-Aire, 19 km from Bar-le-Duc. Lt R. Brabant, Adjt J. Denain, and Adjt A. Labourdette killed. Aircraft a write-off.

GR II/52 Potez 63.11 (168). Crashed into a wood two km west of Couvron shortly after take-off on night reconnaissance sortie 12.50 a.m. Cause unknown, but probably engine failure. Lt L. Rouillon, Capt H. Baud, and Sgt G. Bour killed. Aircraft a write-off.

GR II/52 Potez 63.11. Returned to Couvron slightly damaged by ground-fire following reconnaissance sortie between Dinant and Ciney 12.00 p.m. Sgt Gray, Sgt Parat, and Sgt Frediani unhurt. Aircraft repairable.

GR II/52 Potez 63.11. Returned to Couvron slightly damaged by ground-fire following reconnaissance sortie between Dinant and Ciney 12.00 p.m. S/Lt Millard and Sgt Prévot unhurt. Aircraft repairable.

GR II/52 Potez 63.11. Returned to Couvron slightly damaged by ground-fire following reconnaissance sortie between Dinant and Ciney 12.00 p.m. S/Lt Kuehn, Sgt Duval, Sgt Granier, and Sgt Bayonne unhurt. Aircraft repairable.

GR II/52 Potez 63.11. Returned to Couvron slightly damaged by ground-fire following reconnaissance sortie between Dinant and Ciney 12.00 p.m. Lt Breton, Sgt Oliver, and Sgt Breton unhurt. Aircraft repairable.

There is some confusion as to precisely which unit this Morane 406 belonged to. It carries the emblem of GC 6/1 but is said to be the aircraft (532) flown by Sergeant G. Pralon of the 5th Escadrille. What is clear is that it was torched after landing.

Back in Holland later that summer, German engineers were clearing up the debris of war. Pilot Officer Greenhous's Defiant (L6977) was worth recovering and it was taken to the Seelig Artillery Barracks in the town of Breda.

DUTCH AIR FORCE

1-I-1 Fokker C X (705). Returned to Bergen slightly damaged by AA fire over Grebbe 12.40 p.m. 2e Lt S. J. Postma and 2e Lt M. G. A-Tjak unhurt. Aircraft repairable.

2-I-1 Fokker T V (858). Unserviceable aircraft destroyed on the ground at Haamstede in strafing attack by Bf110s of ZG1. No crew casualties. Aircraft a write-off.

2-I-1 Fokker T V (856). Shot down by Hptmn Ebbighausen *(Staffelkapitän)* of 4./JG26 during sortie to attack the Moerdijk bridge and crashed at 'Nieuwe Veer' near Ridderkerk 6.18 a.m. 1e Lt W. F. Anceaux, 2e Lt B. Swagerman, Sgt O. W. Douwes Dekker, Sgt G. A. van Riemsdijk, and Sold. J. Wijnstra killed. Aircraft a write-off.

1/2-II-1 Fokker D XVII (209). Hit an obstacle and wrecked during take-off from Soesterberg 6.40 p.m. 2e Lt J. C. Plesman (of 2-II-1) unhurt. Aircraft a write-off.

3-II-1 3 Fokker G 1s (311, 328 and 329). Destroyed in strafing attacks by Bf 109s on the beach at Oostvoorne where landed after combat with enemy bombers on May 10. No crew casualties. Aircraft all write-offs.

4-II-1 Fokker G 1 (310). Developed undercarriage fault shortly after take-off from Bergen during transfer to Schiphol and abandoned by crew over Badhoevedorp. Crashed in the Haarlemmermeerpolder 4.35 a.m. Sgt A. K. Bosman unhurt, Sgt R. M. Coene slightly injured. Aircraft a write-off.

4-II-1 Fokker G 1 (321). Returned to Bergen damaged by ground-fire over Wageningen after combat with Bf109s near Woerden 6.45 a.m. 2e Lt A. van Ulsen and Sgt K. Vermaat unhurt. Aircraft damaged but repairable — abandoned and later captured.

4-II-1 Fokker G 1 (318). Returned to Bergen damaged by ground-fire over Wageningen after combat with Bf109s near Woerden 6.45 a.m. 2e Lt F. Peetoom and Sgt G. J. M. Govers unhurt. Aircraft repairable.

4-II-1 Fokker G 1 (305). Shot down by Hptmn Ebbighausen *(Staffelkapitän)* of 4./JG26 over Ridderkerk during escort mission for Fokker T V (2-I-1) attack on the Moerdijk bridge. Crashed near Nieuw Lekkerland 6.20 a.m. 2e Lt P. C. Schoute killed. Sgt H. P. Lindner baled out badly wounded landing dead near De Wetering. Aircraft a write-off.

The serial number of this aircraft could be 304 or 305. Excavation by the Stichting Fokker G 1 group unearthed various fragments but nothing to confirm identity.

IV-2 6 Fokker C Vs (603, 618, 636, 637, 641 and 648), and 2 Koolhoven F.K.51s (411 and 415). Caught on the ground at Haamstede and badly damaged in attack by Bf110s 5.10 a.m. No crew casualties. Aircraft all damaged and later destroyed to prevent capture.

Three of these aircraft, (603, 637 and 648), came from the Vliegschool Haamstede on May 10 to make good losses. Another (652), the sole remaining aircraft in the group, was flown to Ruigenhoek to reinforce III-2 but eventually joined I-2 at De Zilk.

MLD Fokker C XIVw (5595) Destroyed by bombing in hangar at De Mok. No crew casualties. Aircraft F-20 a write-off.

BELGIAN AIR FORCE

7/IV/1 Fox (O.169). Hit by AA fire during reconnaissance over Les Fontaines and force-landed near Belgrade, south-west of Namur, 10.00 a.m. Sgt A. Van Werch and Adjt A. Taton both unhurt. Aircraft a write-off.

9/V/1 Renard R-31 (N.30). Returned to Grimbergen badly damaged by ground-fire during reconnaissance between Kwaad-mechelen and Diest 7.30 p.m. Adjt F. Breyre and Lt R. Lonthie both unhurt. Aircraft a write-off.

7/III/3 Fox (O.126). Shot down by flak during reconnaissance mission and forced-landed between Leuze and Longchamps, near d'Eghezée 1.45 p.m. Cpl J. Viroux and Sgt D. Dochain both unhurt. Aircraft a write-off.

7/III/3 Fox (O.133). Shot down by flak during reconnaissance of road between Hasselt and Beringen and forced-landed near Asse, west of Brussels, 3.30 p.m. Sgt J. Fromont and Sgt J. Pierre both unhurt. Aircraft a write-off.

The Seelig Barracks is no more having been redeveloped for housing.

Another post-battle picture showing the recovery of Feldwebel Johann Poller's Henschel of Heeresaufklärungsstaffel 1.(H)/41 shot down on May 12 (see page 251).

LUFTWAFFE

1.(H)/10 Henschel Hs126. Returned damaged by ground-fire during reconnaissance sortie over Escombres. Oberlt Fr-W. Berlin slightly wounded. Aircraft repairable.

3.(F)/11 Dornier Do17P. Returned from reconnaissance sortie badly damaged. Possibly that attacked by Bloch 152s of GC 1/1 over Namur 10.15 a.m. Lt Kempfen wounded. Aircraft a write-off.

4.(F)/11 Dornier Do17P. Failed to return from reconnaissance sortie north of Reims. Possibly that attacked by Capt Labit, Capt Alexandre, S/Lt Aquilina, Adj Bernavon, Sgt Fortin, and Sgt Desrumeaux of GC II/2 north of Givet, believed crashed at Vielsalm 5.50 a.m. Crew unhurt. Aircraft a write-off.

4.(F)/14 Dornier Do17P. Possibly that claimed by P/O Carey of No. 3 Squadron during reconnaissance sortie over Namur 1.30 p.m. Crew baled out over German-held territory. Aircraft a write-off.

3.(F)/22 Dornier Do17P. Repelled attacks by P/O Martin, P/O Scott, and Sgt Pilkington of No. 73 Squadron during reconnaissance sortie, but both engines crippled by S/Lt Warnier and S/Lt Scotte of GC I/5 over Spincourt. Belly-landed at Ferme Remenoncourt, near St Pierrevillers, south of Arrancy 7.30 a.m. Uffz H. Werth captured wounded in arm and shoulder. Oberlt R. Sauer and Fw K. Kroll captured unhurt. Aircraft 4N+TL a write-off.

2.(H)/41 Henschel Hs126. Oil pump damaged by Belgian ground-fire during reconnaissance of roads and forced-landed 10 km south of Turnhout 11.45 a.m. Uffz F. Schellack and Uffz W. Merzenich captured unhurt. Aircraft C2+KK a write-off.

I./JG1 Messerschmitt Bf109E-3. Crashed on take-off from Aachen-Merzbrück. Pilot believed unhurt. Aircraft damaged but repairable.

I./JG2 2 Messerschmitt Bf109E-4s. Crash-landed at Dockendorf, cause not stated. Pilots unhurt. Aircraft both damaged but repairable.

III./JG2 Messerschmitt Bf109E. Damaged in unspecified accident at Eschweiler airfield. No pilot casualty. Aircraft damage state not recorded.

I./JG3 Messerschmitt Bf109E. Crash-landed at Hargimont due to control failure. Pilot unhurt. Aircraft repairable.

8./JG3 Messerschmitt Bf109E-1. Believed shot down in combat with Hurricanes of No. 607 Squadron east of Brussels and abandoned over Tienen 9.25 a.m. Possibly that claimed by P/O Dini. Pilot baled out unhurt. Aircraft a write-off.

8./JG3 Messerschmitt Bf109E-1. Believed shot down in combat with Hurricanes of No. 607 Squadron east of Brussels and crashed at l'Ecluse, near Aarschot 9.25 a.m. Possibly that claimed by S/L Smith. Obergefreiter H. Schlandt killed. Aircraft a write-off

I./JG21 Messerschmitt Bf109E-3. Shot down by Adj Leniaud and Sgt Devin of GC II/6 in combat between Louvain and Namur, and crashed near Leuze 5.45 a.m. Leutnant A. Freiherr von Böselager (of Jagdfliegerschule 1) killed. Aircraft a write-off.

1./JG26 Messerschmitt Bf109E-1. Shot down by Moranes of GC III/3 in combat north of Breda and crashed by the pumping station on the Oude Dijk near Hoeven 10.40 a.m. Possibly one of those attacked by Sgt Le Nigen. Uffz H. Speck killed. Aircraft a write-off.
Tail trimming wheel, oxygen regulator, and various other components in Jan Jolie collection.

1./JG26 Messerschmitt Bf109E-3. Shot down by Adj Roger of GC III/3 in combat over West Polder and abandoned over Goed van IJkel 10.10 a.m. Feldwebel M. Frank baled out and captured, admitted to St Elizabeth Hospital in Breda with broken leg. Aircraft a write-off.

5./JG26 Messerschmitt Bf109E-3. Shot down in combat with No. 66 Squadron Spitfires and No. 264 Squadron Defiants and abandoned west of Dordrecht. Crashed at Oostmiddelweg, near Numansdorp 6.00 a.m. Leutnant K. Borris baled out and captured unhurt. Aircraft a write-off.
Major recovery by the RNLAF in May 1976.

I./JG53 Messerschmitt Bf109E-3. Belly-landed at Maisborn due to undercarriage failure. Pilot unhurt. Aircraft damaged but repairable.

I./JG53 Messerschmitt Bf109E-3. Crashed on take-off at Maisborn due to undercarriage failure. Pilot unhurt. Aircraft damaged but repairable.

II./JG53 Messerschmitt Bf109E-1. Damaged in forced-landing at Coulenberg due to petrol failure. Pilot unhurt. Aircraft damaged but repairable.

II./JG53 Messerschmitt Bf109E-3. Forced-landed at Caburg damaged in attack by Lt Marin-la-Meslée of GC I/5 in combat over Stonne 11.05 a.m. Pilot unhurt. Aircraft repairable.

I./JG76 Messerschmitt Bf109E-1. Rammed a Bf110 of I./ZG52 in aborted take-off at Wengerohr. Pilot unhurt. Aircraft damaged but repairable.

I./JG77 Messerschmitt Bf109E-3. Forced-landed at Sourbrodt due to engine failure. Pilot unhurt. Aircraft damaged but repairable.

Stab KG2 Dornier Do17Z. Returned damaged by flak south of Sedan. Uffz H. Genähr slightly wounded. Aircraft repairable.

1./KG4 Heinkel He111P. Hit by flak between Dordrecht and Middelburg and belly-landed in Lage Dijk between Jutphaas and Jaarsveld. Crew captured unhurt. Aircraft 5J+CH a write-off.

Stab II./KG4 Heinkel He111P. Attacked by Adj Hôtellier, Lt Weiss, and Sgt Joire of GC I/4 between Wuestwezel and St Leonhard during sortie to bomb troop concentrations at Ghent. Also hit by AA fire and crashed at Brecht, near Nollekens, 7.30 p.m. Oberlt E. Schacht (*Gruppennavigationsoffizier*) killed. Hauptgefr W. Peil and Gefr R. Winkelmann (both of 6. Staffel) killed. Oberlt E. Freiherr von Werthern (*Gruppenadjutant*) baled out and captured wounded. Aircraft a write-off.

5./KG4 Heinkel He111P. Hit by flak over Roosendaal and crash-landed with starboard engine on fire near Langeweg, between Zevenbergen and Terheijden, 6.00 p.m. Bomb load later exploded. Uffz F. Maas, Uffz H. Pieles, Uffz K. Kranich, and Gefr L. Korfhage captured unhurt. Aircraft 5J+FN a write-off.
Flight engineer Kurt Kranich was badly wounded in an air raid while aboard a ship in Dunkirk harbour while en route to captivity in England and he later died of his injuries on June 6.

5./KG4 Heinkel He111P. Shot down by Lt Hirschauer of GC I/4 and crash-landed 3 km east of Oudenbosch 6.00 p.m. Uffz A. Milhahn and Uffz K. Elbin captured wounded, admitted to hospital in Tilburg. Oberlt Röhl and Oberlt von Talkmann believed captured unhurt. Aircraft a write-off.

Stab I./KG27 Heinkel He111P. Returned riddled by flak and fighters following sortie south-west of Brussels. Oberfw K. Schütt slightly wounded. Aircraft 1G+BB a write-off.

5./KG27 Heinkel He111P. Returned damaged by AA fire north of Namur. Fw R. Haarmann badly wounded. Aircraft damage state not recorded.

7./KG28 Heinkel He111P. Failed to return from sortie west of Charleville and believed that attacked by S/L More of No. 73 Squadron which crashed at Beffu, north-east of Grandpré 7.15 a.m. Obergefr K. Funke killed. Fw H. Görke, Uffz O. Schulz, Uffz P. Schönhoff, and Uffz A. Wötzel believed baled out and captured unhurt. Aircraft a write-off.

8./KG30 Junkers Ju88A-2. Shot down by naval flak during attack on shipping and ditched in the Waddenzee off Texel, near Oudeschild 8.15 a.m. Lt A. Kleinmacher, Uffz M. Marmein, Gefr W. Gröber, and Gefr O. Beyer captured unhurt. Aircraft a write-off.
Wreck investigated in summer 1983 by amateur enthusiasts who recovered compass, navigation instruments, a camera and oxygen bottle. Later salvaged in May 1985 when an intact engine, cockpit framing and various components recovered.

II./KG51 Junkers Ju88A-1. Burst tyre on landing at Fürstenfeldbruck. Crew unhurt. Aircraft damaged but repairable.

Stabsstaffel KG53 Heinkel He111P. Landed at Mannheim-Sandhofen hit by flak over Sedan 12.40 p.m. Crew unhurt. Aircraft A1+BA repairable.

III./KG53 Heinkel He111H. Forced-landed at Mannheim-Sandhofen due to engine failure. Crew unhurt. Aircraft damaged but repairable.

3./KG54 Heinkel He111P. Engaged by Lt Fabre, S/Lt de Russé, Adjt Gaudon, S/Lt Riss, S/Lt Sassard and S/Lt Karwowski of GC II/6 north of Valenciennes during sortie to attack armoured columns between Namur and Gembloux, pursued over Maubeuge, and shot down north-west of Dinant 10.30 a.m. Gefr M. Engelmann and Flgr J. Wörz killed. Uffz G. Hoffmann and Gefr O. Reuter baled out and captured wounded. Aircraft a write-off.

Stab KG55 Heinkel He111P. Shot down by F/O Clisby of No. 1 Squadron during reconnaissance sortie between Charleville-Mézières and Ligny. Belly-landed at Coulommes-les-Marqueny, north-west of Mazagran, 6.45 a.m. Possibly one of those also attacked by Potez 631s of ECMJ 1/16. Obergefr H. Bell badly wounded in right thigh — died same day. Fw W. Wolter badly wounded by gendarmes while evading capture and dead on arrival at Mazarith de Vouziers emergency hospital. Oberlt D. Clemm von Hohenberg, Uffz H. Strobl, and Gefr F. Männer tried to reach German lines but captured at Coegny. Aircraft G1+GA a write-off.
According to a much-publicised account by Leslie Clisby, he landed alongside this aircraft and secured five prisoners whom he handed over to the French at Bourcq. It would appear, from evidence available, that this colourful version of events may have qualified for the squadron 'line book'.

3./KG55 Heinkel He111P. Returned damaged by ground-fire probably over Sedan. Uffz H. Eckhardt slightly wounded. Aircraft repairable.

Stab II./KG55 Heinkel He111P. Returned damaged by flak over Mouzon during sortie to attack road and rail targets between Reims and Rethel. Major O. von Lachemair *(Gruppenkommandeur)* and Oberlt S. Hensel *(Gruppennavigationsoffizier)* both slightly wounded. Aircraft damaged but repairable.

A fine study of a Luftwaffe airman of the 1940s, in this case rear gunner Flieger Jakob Wörz killed when his Heinkel of the 3. Staffel of KG54 was brought down near Valenciennes by six pilots of GC II/6. He is buried in the German War Cemetery at Lommel in Block 44, Grave 541. Here, Wörz wears a standard issue Siemens winter flying helmet, model LkpW100 with bakelite earphone housings, and Wagener und Rathenow model 295 flight goggles. The I. Gruppe of 'Totenkopf' Kampfgeschwader 54, under Gruppenkommandeur Oberstleutnant Otto Höhne, were to suffer the loss of 19 aircrew killed, 15 wounded, and 28 captured on operations during the campaign in the west up to the French armistice. The 3. Staffel was particularly hard hit, contributing 13 killed, two wounded, and two more captured, to the overall tally.

5./KG55 Heinkel He111P. Belly-landed at Attert damaged by AA fire and starboard engine destroyed in attacks by S/Lt Boutarel and S/Lt Salva of GC I/3 over Herbeumont 7.50 p.m. Oberlt G. Weigel, Fähnrich Ott, Uffz K. Gerdsmeier, and Gefr K. Geib unhurt. Aircraft damaged but repairable.
This crew was soon back on operations, the Bordmechaniker, Karl Gerdsmeier, being wounded five days later. Apart from Ott, they were shot down and captured on September 25, 1940.

6./KG55 Heinkel He111P. Shot down by Lt Dorance and S/Lt Parnière of GC I/5 during sortie to attack troop concentrations near Charleville-Mézières and finally crashed south of Puxe 7.45 a.m. Possibly one of those also attacked by Potez 631s of ECMJ 1/16. Obergefr K-H. Piur killed. Fw H. Winkelhaus died of wounds. Lt H. Köhler captured wounded. Fw P. Laufer and Fw G. Engel captured unhurt. Aircraft G1+GM a write-off.

6./KG55 Heinkel He111P. Attacked by Nos. 1 and 73 Squadron Hurricanes, then Lt Dorance, S/Lt Parnière, and Lt Vybiral of GC I/5 during sortie to bomb troop concentrations near Charleville-Mézières. Crashed and burned out at 'La Fosse', between Mairy and Amblimont 7.30 a.m. Possibly one of those also attacked by Potez 631s of ECMJ 1/16. Uffz A. Freitag, Obergefr P. Brandt, and Gefr H. Freiherr von Spiegel killed. Lt O-W. Pöhler and Obergefr F. Höfling captured wounded. Aircraft G1+HP a write-off.

6./KG55 Heinkel He111P. Shot down by No. 73 Squadron Hurricanes and Curtiss H-75s of GC I/5 between Biermes and Perthes during sortie to attack troop concentrations near Charleville-Mézières 7.45 a.m. Gefr J. Mittermaier killed. Uffz J. Schmidt captured badly wounded, died June 17. Uffz W. Zierau captured wounded. Lt R. Bertelsmann and Uffz H. Hänel captured unhurt. Aircraft a write-off.

Below: **His body is retrieved from its tangled parachute and loaded aboard French transport. The machine was brought down by pilots of Groupe de Chasse II/2, namely Sergent André Breitenstein, Adjudant Maurice Pollono, Adjudant-chef Pierre Dorcy and Sergent-chef de la Gasnerie. Breitenstein in his combat report believed he had fired on a Henschel 124: 'In the pursuit, the Henschel 124 turned slightly to the left, in a northerly direction with the two Moranes on the right. This manoeuvre enabled me to get closer to the enemy who then pulled upwards and turned to the left, with the intention of taking shelter in the cloud. He then turned towards me. At the moment he saw me he opened fire straight away, the burst passing 150 metres in front of me. I fired and the left engine of the Henschel 124 took fire instantaneously. I dived away and he did the same in climbing turn and I avoided him by the skin of my teeth. The plane pulled towards the cloud, the two men jumped with parachutes and then the plane dived vertically.'**

This smoking wreckage on the Louvry farm at Audigny is all that was left of Unteroffizier August Pfaff's Messerschmitt 110 of the 4. Staffel of Zerstörergeschwader 76. Pfaff himself was killed when he hit the tail of the aircraft on baling out.

The Battle with the Defiants was not all one-sided, as the escorting Spitfires helped even the score and the Luftwaffe lost five aircraft too. This is the wreck of Stuka L1+HW, which crashed near Werkendam (see the map on page 257), wounding the pilot, Unteroffizier Wilhelm Bienk, and killing the gunner, Gefreiter Günther Langner.

6./KG55 Heinkel He111P. Returned damaged by Nos. 1 and 73 Squadron Hurricanes and Curtiss H-75s of GC I/5 during sortie to attack troop concentrations near Charleville-Mézières 7.45 a.m. Uffz M. Stiller slightly wounded, rest of crew unhurt. Aircraft repairable.

8./KG55 Heinkel He111P. Shot down by F/L Hanks, F/O Lorimer, and P/O Goodman of No. 1 Squadron during sortie to bomb troop concentrations near Charleville-Mézières and crash-landed at Vendresse 6.30 a.m. Oberfw B. Hickel and Fw M. Hausdörfer unhurt. Fw W. Herzog, Gefr G. Arndt, and Gefr G. Bodenhagen wounded. Aircraft a write-off.

2./KG76 Dornier Do17Z. Returned damaged in attacks by GC II/2 during sortie to attack forward airfields north of Any 5.30 p.m. Uffz H. Knödler slightly wounded. Aircraft damage state not recorded.

6./KG76 Dornier Do17Z. Returned damaged in attacks by Adj Berland and Sgt Parent of GC II/2 between Philippeville and Givet 5.30 a.m. Fw H. Siedentopf slightly wounded. Aircraft damage state not recorded.

Stab I./KG77 Dornier Do17Z. Returned damaged by flak north of Charleville 12.45 p.m. Fw H. Reiche badly wounded, admitted to hospital in Cologne-Hohenlind. Aircraft damage state not recorded.

2./KGr.126 Heinkel He111H. Returned damaged by ground-fire during attack on road transport between Roosendaal and Breda. Uffz H. Müller slightly wounded. Aircraft damage state not recorded.

2./KGr.126 Heinkel He111H. Returned damaged by ground-fire during attack on road transport between Rosendaal and Breda. Fw G. Milbradt badly wounded. Aircraft damage state not recorded.

12.(St)/LG1 Junkers Ju87B (0278). Shot down by No.66 Squadron Spitfires over Wijngaarden, near Dordrecht, and crashed near Waardhuizense Brug, east of Almkerk 6.00 a.m. Uffz H. J. Kowatsch captured wounded. Uffz H. Jorzyck captured unhurt. Aircraft L1+AW a write-off.

12.(St)/LG1 Junkers Ju87B. Shot down in action with No. 264 Squadron Defiants and No. 66 Squadron Spitfires near Dordrecht and crashed on Buisjes island, Gat van de Kampen, in the Biesbosch 6.00 a.m. Fw K. Ziesemann and Uffz G. Jordan both baled out and captured. Aircraft a write-off.

12.(St)/LG1 Junkers Ju87B (5513). Shot down by P/O Brown of No. 66 Squadron east of Dordrecht, and crashed at Polder Bogers, south of Werkendam 6.00 a.m. Gefr G. Langner killed. Uffz W. Bienk captured wounded. Aircraft L1+HW a write-off.

12.(St)/LG1 Junkers Ju87B. Crash-landed at Neuenkamp airfield badly damaged in combat with No.66 Squadron Spitfires near Dordrecht 6.00 a.m. Lt G. Schmidt injured on landing, Uffz H. Witteborn wounded. Aircraft a write-off.

6.(S)/LG2 Henschel Hs123. Shot down by Sgt Wilkinson of No. 3 Squadron between Jauche and Piétrain, south of Tienen, during ground-attack sortie 1.00 p.m. Fw H. Knerr killed. Aircraft a write-off.

6.(S)/LG2 Henschel Hs123. Shot down by Sgt Allen of No. 3 Squadron over Orp-Jauche, south of Tienen, during ground-attack mission 1.00 p.m. Lt H-J. Fritz badly wounded. Aircraft a write-off.

9.(H)/LG2 Henschel Hs126N. Engaged by Lt de Chezelles, S/Lt Bevillard, Sgt Keprt, and Cpl Slouf of GC III/3 near Piétrain during observation sortie north of Pervez 5.30 a.m. Oberlt H. Staudenraus thrown from aircraft while evading attack and killed. Aircraft repairable.

The body of the unfortunate observer, Hans Staudenraus, was found with unopened parachute on a farm at Bolinne, north-east of Eghezée.

II./StG2 Junkers Ju87B. Returned damaged by flak. Crew unhurt. Aircraft repairable.

III./StG51 Junkers Ju87B. Damaged in ground loop while taxying at Odendorf airfield. Crew unhurt. Aircraft damaged but repairable.

3./StG76 Junkers Ju87B. Shot down by flak and crash-landed north-east of Bouillon 10.30 a.m. Oberfw A. Wollensack captured badly wounded, died in hospital. Fw J. Vogt believed baled out and captured wounded. Aircraft a write-off.

2./ZG1 Messerschmitt Bf110C. Returned with slight damage following combat over Gent. Obergefr P. Nick slightly wounded. Aircraft repairable.

5./ZG1 Messerschmitt Bf110C. Shot down by AA fire during sortie over Vlissingen and crashed by the harbour railway station 4.00 p.m. Hptmn R. Küppers *(Staffelkapitän)* and Fw E. Behrend killed. Aircraft a write-off.

3./ZG26 Messerschmitt Bf110. Shot down by Hurricanes of No. 1 and No. 73 Squadrons in combat west of Vouziers and crashed on Ferme de Merlan at 'Noue de Bétheniville', near La Neuville-en-Tourne-à-Fuy, south of Juniville 6.45 a.m. Lt F. Dunstheimer and Obergefr H. Büterhorn killed. Aircraft a write-off.

Lt Henri Cormouls of ECMJ 1/16, who visited this crash next day, noted the disrespect shown by locals for the remains of this crew. Another source also records that Heinz Büterhorn was shot while a prisoner at Ferme de Merlan.

3./ZG26 Messerschmitt Bf110. Shot down by Hurricanes of No. 1 and No. 73 Squadrons in combat west of Vouziers and crashed on a shed at Vaudétré, between Heutrégiville and Warmeriville, 6.45 a.m. Fw U. Ernst believed baled out but killed. Gefr T. Hoffmann baled out landing near 'Les Puisards' at Saint-Masmes and reportedly shot while resisting capture. Aircraft a write-off.

The exact fate of this crew also remains unclear.

I./ZG52 Messerschmitt Bf110C. Rammed by Bf109 of I./JG76 landing at Wengerohr airfield. No crew casualties. Aircraft damaged but repairable.

4./ZG76 Messerschmitt Bf110C. Shot down in combat with Moranes of GC II/2 during escort sortie for II./KG76 and abandoned over Guise 10.00 a.m. Possibly that attacked by Adj Pollono and also Sgt Breitenstein. Uffz A. Pfaff baled out but hit the tail and killed. Uffz F. Radzko baled out and captured wounded near Vervins. Aircraft a write-off.

This is the Stuka of Unteroffizier Hans Kowatsch and Hans Jorzyck that came down just east of Almkerk. Both Ju87s belonged to 12.(St)/LG1 led by Oberleutnant Hartmann Wendelin.

Tuesday, May 14

Despite stubborn resistance by Dutch ground forces, who continued to hold both the dyke across the IJsselmeer, and Zeeland province in the south, the military situation in The Netherlands was bleak. German troops were now advancing in strength through North Brabant to link up with the airborne troops who landed on the first day of the offensive and this already decided the issue.

To hasten the inevitable Dutch capitulation, Generalleutnant Rudolf Schmidt, commander of XXXIX. Armeekorps, part of the German force then preparing to assault Rotterdam, issued an ultimatum demanding surrender of the town by 2.10 p.m. 50 minutes before an artillery barrage and air raid preceding the German ground attack scheduled to commence at 3.30 p.m. The ultimatum was delivered to Kolonel Scharroo, Rotterdam town commander, at 11.10 a.m. but with a strong Dutch counter-attack on Overschie launched earlier that morning, the garrison at Rotterdam attempted to delay by seeking clarification of the surrender terms. At 2.15 p.m. Schmidt issued instructions that both the artillery barrage and air attack were to be postponed pending outcome of negotiations and further delayed expiry of his ultimatum until 6.00 p.m. Tragically, due to poor communications, the instruction to withhold the bombing attack was received by Luftflotte 2 too late as the bombers were already in the air, and repeated recall signals were unsuccessful.

Flying in two formations, and approaching Rotterdam from the east and south-east, 90 He111s of KG54 reached their aiming points north of the Maas opposite Noordereiland precisely on schedule. Mercifully, most of the south-eastern group, 36 aircraft of I./KG54 commanded by Oberstleutnant Otto Höhne, spotted red signal flares fired to indicate friendly forces on the ground and aborted their attack, apart from three leading aircraft of the Gruppenstabsschwarm that released their bombs. However, the entire eastern group, 54 aircraft commanded by Geschwaderkommodore Oberst Walter Lackner, failed to see the signals and delivered a devastating attack on the old town causing widespread damage and some 750 civilian casualties. Three hours later, Generaal Henri Winkelman, Commander of Vesting Holland, issued instructions to all Dutch forces, apart from those in Zeeland, to surrender.

Events in France were no less desperate. After heavy air bombardment, Namur was in serious danger of falling, while the German bridgehead north of Dinant now extended on a ten-mile front. The French defence line along the Meuse was crumbling from northeast of Chartres to south of Sedan, this critical situation provoking the heaviest RAF daylight bombing attacks of the entire campaign.

At dawn, following night attacks by French bombers, pontoon bridges across the Meuse and the Chiers near Sedan were bombed by six Fairey Battles of No. 103 Squadron but with inconclusive results. Two hours later, attacks were made on pontoon bridges northwest of Remilly-Aillicourt and north of Villers-devant-Mouzon by four aircraft from No. 150 Squadron. But by early afternoon the position around Sedan had deteriorated to such an extent that every available RAF bomber was readied for four waves of alternate attacks by French and British aircraft planned at three-hourly intervals.

The first attack was delivered by French aircraft around 12.30 p.m. and was to have been followed, between 3.00 and 3.45 p.m, by three waves of attacks on all five bridges south-east of Sedan by small formations of AASF bombers. Simultaneously, enemy columns advancing from Bouillon towards Givonne and Sedan were also targeted, a total of 71 Battles and Blenheims being despatched. Fighter protection, including some RAF Component Hurricanes detached for operations over the AASF area, proved ineffective and the bombers were decimated by intense enemy flak and prowling fighters. While it seems likely that hits were obtained on at least three of the bridges, and some delay caused to the enemy advance at Givonne, it was achieved at considerable cost. Surviving contemporary records are incomplete so an exact figure is difficult to assess, but RAF bomber losses over Sedan on this day have been variously estimated at between 50 per cent and 70 per cent of sorties flown. Certainly such losses, along with those already suffered on previous days, forced a rapid change of policy which resulted in the Fairey Battle being largely switched to night operations.

A subsequent wave of attacks planned by French aircraft was postponed until next morning while, a second wave of AASF bombers now being impossible due to losses, 28 Blenheims from Wattisham and Watton attacked the Bouillon to Sedan road between 6.00 and 6.45 p.m. with the river crossings at Sedan as alternate target. French heavies bombed the same area later that night.

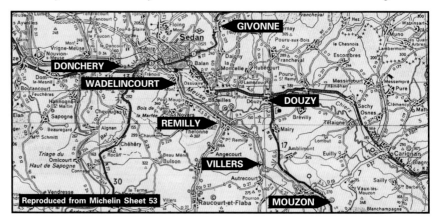

Reproduced from Michelin Sheet 53

Allied bombing attacks on the Meuse river crossings at Sedan on May 14, 1940

Time of attack: Target: Sorties:

5.30 a.m. Pontoons between Nouvion and Douzy by 6 Battles of No. 103 Squadron.

8.00 a.m. Pontoon north-west of Remilly-Aillicourt by 2 Battles of No. 150 Squadron and pontoon north of Villers-devant-Mouzon by 2 Battles of No. 150 Squadron.

10.00 a.m. Bazeilles and pontoon at Wadelincourt by 9 Breguet 693s of GBA I & II/54.

12.30-12.45 p.m. Bazeilles and Meuse crossings by 5 Amiot 143s of GB I & II/34, 6 Amiot 143s of GB II/38 and 5 Leo 451s of GB I & II/12.

1.00-1.15 p.m. Bridge No.1 at Wadelincourt by 4 Battles of No. 142 Squadron and Bridge No. 4 north of Villers-devant-Mouzon by 4 Battles of No. 142 Squadron.

3.00 p.m. First wave of attacks by No. 76 Wing (Nos. 12, 142 and 226 Squadrons) intended.

3.20 p.m. Second wave of attacks by No. 71 Wing (Nos. 105, 114, 139 and 150 Squadrons) intended.

3.20-3.30 p.m. Bridge No.1 at Wadelincourt by 2 Battles of No. 150 Squadron and Bridge No. 2 north-west of Remilly-Aillicourt by 2 Battles of No. 150 Squadron.

3.35 p.m. Third wave of attacks by No. 75 Wing (Nos. 88, 103 and 218 Sqdns) intended.

3.35-4.15 p.m. Bridge No.1 at Wadelincourt by 4 Battles of No. 218 Squadron.
Bridge No. 2 north-west of Remilly-Aillicourt by 4 Battles of No. 103 Squadron and 4 Battles of No. 105 Squadron*.
Bridge No. 3 at Douzy by 3 Battles of No. 105 Squadron* and 2 Battles of No. 226 Squadron*.
Bridge No. 4 north of Villers-devant-Mouzon by 4 Battles of No. 88 Squadron.
Bridge No. 5 at Mouzon by 4 Battles of No. 103 Squadron, 4 Battles of No. 105 Squadron* and 4 Battles of No. 226 Squadron*.
Columns between Bouillon and Givonne by 5 Battles of No. 12 Squadron*, 6 Battles of No. 88 Squadron, 4 Blenheims of No. 114 Squadron*, 4 Blenheims of No. 139 Squadron* and 7 Battles of No. 218 Squadron.

6.30-6.45 p.m. Columns between Bouillon and Givonne by 11 Blenheims of No. 21 Squadron, 6 Blenheims of No. 107 Squadron and 12 Blenheims of No. 110 Squadron.

8.50 p.m. Sedan by 2 Battles of No. 226 Squadron.

10.25-11.10 p.m. Sedan 6 by Farman 222s of GB I & II/15.

Night Sedan by 4 Amiot 143s of GB I & II/38.

Three phased attacks by AASF bombers was ordered for mid-afternoon against all five bridges but did not proceed as planned. Times shown indicate actual attacks, an asterisk (*) indicating those late over the target. Of the 71 aircraft despatched at least 37 were lost, and another six badly damaged. German fighters claimed 40 Allied bombers destroyed over Sedan during the afternoon. Flak-Regiment 102, attached to XIX. Armeekorps, was responsible for defence of the crossings. Motorised light flak units also accompanied the Panzer divisions across the Meuse between Donchery and Noyers-Pont-Maugis along with several army flak units. In total, the regiment would claim 150 Allied aircraft destroyed during the day, the commander, Oberst Walter von Hippel, being awarded a Ritterkreuz on July 29, 1940.

BRITISH AIR FORCES IN FRANCE

1 SQUADRON, BERRY-AU-BAC

Hurricane N2380. Gravity tank set alight in combat with Bf110s and abandoned over St Rémy-le-Petit, south-west of Rethel, 8.30 a.m. Flight Lieutenant P. P. Hanks baled out unhurt. Aircraft ⊙S a write-off.

Hurricane P2546. Shot down in combat with Bf110s south-west of Rethel and crashed near Ménil-lé-Pinois 8.30 a.m. Flying Officer L. R. Clisby killed. Aircraft a write-off.
Originally buried in the local communal cemetery, Leslie Clisby was exhumed in 1950 and reinterred in Choloy War Cemetery.

Hurricane L1676. Shot down in combat with Bf110s south-west of Rethel 8.30 a.m. Flying Officer R. L. Lorimer missing. Aircraft a write-off.
Despite exhaustive investigation by the Missing Research Enquiry Unit, 'Laurie' Lorimer's grave was never positively identified and he therefore remains officially 'missing'.

3 SQUADRON, MERVILLE

Hurricane N2441. Lost bearings en route to join unit from England and forced-landed near Lens a.m. Sergeant J. L. C. Williams (of No. 56 Squadron) unhurt. Aircraft repairable.

Hurricane L1932. Damaged by return fire from Do17 engaged south of Leuven and belly-landed at Morsaint, south of Hamme-Mille 6.30 a.m. Pilot Officer F. R. Carey wounded in leg. Aircraft a write-off.

Hurricane L1609. Forced-landed damaged by Bf109s of 1./JG53 during attack on Ju87s of I.(St)/TrGr.186 over Sedan 4.25 p.m. Pilot Officer N. D. Hallifax unhurt. Aircraft repairable.

Hurricane N2546. Reportedly forced-landed at Maubeuge damaged by Bf109s of 1./JG53 following attack on Ju87s of I.(St)/TrGr.186 over Sedan 4.25 p.m. Pilot Officer M. M. Stephens unhurt. Aircraft QO⊙S repairable.

Hurricane L1591. Shot down by Bf109s during attack on Ju87s of I.(St)/TrGr.186 over Sedan and crashed in dense forest 3 miles north-east of Villers-Cernay 4.25 p.m. Possibly that claimed by Oberlt Mayer (Staffelkapitän) of 1./JG53. Sergeant D. A. Allen killed. Aircraft a write-off.
Wreckage of this aircraft, still to be seen at the crash-site, was investigated July 17, 1999 by Jocelyn Leclercq, Pierre Roger, with members of the AASF Museum at Condé-Vraux, and several representative items recovered.

Hurricane L1908. Glycol tank damaged by fighters during attack on Ju87s of I.(St)/TrGr.186 and abandoned near Annelles, south of Rethel, 4.25 p.m. Possibly that claimed by Uffz Höhnisch of 1./JG53. Pilot Officer C. G. StD. Jefferies (of No. 253 Squadron) baled out unhurt. Aircraft a write-off.
Charles Jefferies was one of nine pilots attached from other squadrons who had arrived as reinforcements on this day.

4 SQUADRON, MONCHY-LAGACHE

Lysander II P1711. Crashed at Outer, near Aspelaere advanced landing ground 11.35 a.m. Pilot Officer Hankey and Sergeant Lewis believed unhurt. Aircraft a write-off.

Lysander II L4742. Believed shot down by Oberlt Kupka of 9./JG3 during sortie over Gembloux and crashed at 'Campagne du Reck', St Remigius Geest, near Jodoigne 6.30 p.m. Flying Officer T. C. Clarke and AC1 W. S. Rodulson killed. Aircraft TV⊙H a write-off.

Lysander II L4745. Failed to return from tactical reconnaissance sortie near Brussels 7.30 p.m. Pilot Officer D. M. Barbour and Corporal R. H. Waters missing. Aircraft lost.

12 SQUADRON, AMIFONTAINE

Battle L4950. Believed shot down by flak or Bf109s of 4./JG52 during attack on enemy columns between Bouillon and Givonne. Crashed and burned out at 'La Feudorie', Vrigne-aux-Bois 3.35 p.m. Flying Officer E. R. D. Vaughan and Sergeant C. Shelton-Jones killed. AC J. W. Wright captured. Aircraft PH⊙V a write-off.
Originally buried together in a field grave adjacent to the crash site, Vaughan and Shelton-Jones were exhumed in 1942 and reinterred in the local communal cemetery as three 'Unknown Airmen'.

Battle L5188. Believed shot down by flak or Bf109s of 4./JG52 during attack on enemy columns between Bouillon and Givonne 3.35 p.m. Sergeant H. R. W. Winkler, Sergeant M. D. Smalley, and AC L. R. Clarke all baled out and captured. Aircraft PH⊙C a write-off.

Battle L4952. Believed shot down by flak or Bf109s of 4./JG52 during attack on enemy columns between Bouillon and Givonne; crashed near Pouru-St-Rémy 3.35 p.m. Sergeant K. Alderson and AC1 R. T. Ainsworth killed. Flight Lieutenant G. D. Clancy captured. Aircraft PH⊙X a write-off.

Battle P5229. Believed shot down by flak or Bf109s of 4./JG52 during attack on enemy columns between Bouillon and Givonne; also crashed near Pouru-St-Rémy 3.35 p.m. Sergeant A. G. Johnson and Sergeant E. F. White killed. AC1 F. T. Spencer captured. Aircraft PH⊙O a write-off.

Battle L5538. Possibly damaged by flak or Bf109s of 4./JG52 prior to attack on enemy columns between Bouillon and Givonne 3.35 p.m. Jettisoned bombs and returned to base. Pilot Officer J. J. McElligott, Sergeant B. C. Long, and LAC T. O. Burgess unhurt. Aircraft PH⊙A repairable.

26 SQUADRON, DIEPPE

Lysander II L4777. Shot down at Arras during reconnaissance sortie 6.25 p.m. Pilot Officer Walker wounded in hand. LAC Brown unhurt. Aircraft a write-off.

May 14 — the day of the Meuse bridges — and an ominous portent of things to come. Reading between the lines of this signal from the Advanced Air Striking Force headquarters, the powers that be were already showing the first signs of retreat, if not defeat. The intention was 'to move all RAF units north-east of a line running through Laon—Reims—Châlons—Bar le Duc to the Troyes area'.

57 SQUADRON, ROSIÈRES-EN-SANTERRE

Blenheim IV L9180. Damaged by return fire from Do17 engaged during reconnaissance sortie over the Maas near Dinant and crash-landed alongside the Baasrode to Dendermonde road 8.10 a.m. AC2 O. R. Beaumont killed. Pilot Officer W. G. Spencer and Sergeant R. Pike both wounded. Aircraft fired by crew.

59 SQUADRON, POIX

Blenheim IV P6926. Failed to return from strategic reconnaissance sortie and possibly that claimed by Lt Malischewski of Stab I./JG76 over Sedan 12.40 p.m. Flying Officer P. A. Hawks, Sergeant F. J. J. Evans, and AC1 C. G. Shaw missing. Aircraft lost.

Peter Hawks is listed in the records of the CWGC as a Flight Lieutenant.

73 SQUADRON, REIMS-CHAMPAGNE

Hurricane L1891. Became separated from patrol and forced-landed damaged by return fire following attack on Do17 of 3./KG76 north-east of Sedan 5.40 a.m. Pilot Officer A. McFadden unhurt. Aircraft damaged but repairable — later abandoned.

Hurricane P2813. Returned oil tank damaged in combat with Bf110s of III./ZG26 near Namur 12.15 p.m. and believed crashed on landing. Flying Officer H. G. G. Paul unhurt. Aircraft ⊙H damaged but repairable.

Hurricane P2856. Shot down in combat with Bf110s of III./ZG26 and crashed in the Bois de Voncq, north of Vouziers 12.25 p.m. Sergeant T. B. G. Pyne believed baled out but killed. Aircraft a write-off.

Surviving squadron records give serial P2856 though one official post-war source indicates N2334. Originally buried in Voncq French Military Cemetery, Thomas Pyne was later reinterred in Choloy War Cemetery.

Hurricane P2812. Shot down in combat with Bf110s and crashed in the Bois de Voncq, north of Vouziers 12.25 p.m. Possibly one of those claimed by Lt Kuhrke of 8./ZG26. Pilot Officer V. D. M. Roe killed. Aircraft ⊙L a write-off.

Surviving squadron records give serial P2812 though one official post-war source indicates N2366. Originally buried near a French field dressing station on the road to Vouziers, Pilot Officer Valcourt Roe was later interred in Voncq French Military Cemetery, and subsequently reinterred in Choloy War Cemetery.

Hurricane P2689. Shot down by Bf109s of III./JG53 during attack on Ju87s of I./StG77 over Sedan, crashed and burned out in wood at 'La Haie Colette', north of Noirval, 3.30 p.m. Probably that claimed by Hptmn Mölders (Gruppenkommandeur) of Stab III./JG53. Sergeant L. G. M. Dibden killed. Aircraft a write-off.

Indicative of the problems facing MREU in their post-war investigations, the remains of Leon Dibden were originally buried at Noirval Churchyard in two separate plots both dated May 15, 1940; one marked 'From aircraft P2810' and the other as 'Unknown'. While P2810 was a No. 73 Squadron aircraft, it is not believed to be that shot down at Noirval although something clearly suggested so. Leon Dibden was exhumed to Choloy War Cemetery in August 1950.

79 SQUADRON, NORRENT-FONTES

Hurricane. Returned with windscreen damaged by return fire from Hs126 attacked near Louvain. Sergeant L.H.B. Pearce unhurt. Aircraft repairable.

Hurricane P2635. Believed shot down by return fire from He111 of 5./LG1 and reported crashed east of Renaix 7.00 p.m. Pilot Officer L. L. Appleton missing. Aircraft a write-off.

It is thought that 'Lew' Appleton may have crashed at Ninove, west of Brussels, but investigation by the MREU post-war was unable to locate and identify his burial.

Hurricane L1716. Returned with port main spar damaged by return fire from He111s of Stab II./LG1 engaged over Bierghes, south-west of Brussels, 7.00 p.m. Pilot Officer D. W. A. Stones unhurt. Aircraft repairable.

Hurricane N2490. Reported shot down by Bf110 during attack on Ju88 over Frasnes-lez-Buissenal, north of Leuze, 7.45 p.m. Pilot Officer J. E. R. Wood baled out wounded. Aircraft a write-off.

87 SQUADRON, LILLE-MARCQ

Hurricane L1612. Shot down during attack on He111s of KG 27 and crashed at Mainvault, north-west of Ath, 9.40 a.m. Pilot Officer G. C. Saunders killed. Aircraft a write-off.

Hurricane L1616. Shot down during attack on He111s of KG27 west of Maastricht 9.40 a.m. Pilot Officer P. L. Jarvis missing. Aircraft a write-off.

Hurricane L1834. Believed shot down by Lt Müncheberg of Stab III./JG26 in combat east of Ath 5.45 p.m. Crashed and burned at Ramegnies-Chin. Pilot Officer C. C. D. Mackworth baled out but parachute caught fire and killed. Aircraft a write-off.

Hurricane L1646. Badly damaged in combat with Bf109s and belly-landed south of Brussels 5.45 p.m. Possibly that attacked by Lt Westphal of Stab III./JG26. Flying Officer E. P. Joyce badly wounded, admitted to hospital in Amiens — leg amputated. Aircraft a write-off.

88 SQUADRON, MOURMELON-LE-GRAND

Battle L5581. Shot down by AA during sortie to attack bridge at Villers-devant-Mouzon and crashed in woods near St Menges 4.30 p.m. Sergeant W. G. Ross, Sergeant F. E. Beames, and LAC J. H. K. Gegg killed. Aircraft a write-off.

Battle L5233. Returned damaged by AA following sortie to attack bridge at Villers-devant-Mouzon 4.30 p.m. Crew believed unhurt. Aircraft damaged but repairable — abandoned on evacuation May 16.

103 SQUADRON, BÉTHENIVILLE

Battle P2191. Badly damaged by flak during attack on pontoon bridge over the Meuse and belly-landed at Cauroy during return flight 5.45 a.m. Sergeant C. D. Perry severely wounded in thigh and stomach, later died. AC A. R. Layfield unhurt. Aircraft PM⊙J a write-off.

Charles Perry was awarded the DFM on June 11 but died of his injuries three days later in hospital in England.

Battle K9374. Hit by intense flak during attack on bridge at Mouzon and forced-landed 3.40 p.m. Flying Officer T. B. Fitzgerald slightly wounded. Corporal Madkins unhurt. Aircraft a write-off.

Battle L5516. Shot down by Bf109s of 1./JG53 during attack on bridge at Mouzon and belly-landed south of Sedan 3.40 p.m. Possibly one of those claimed by Uffz Höhnisch. Sergeant G. Beardsley and LAC G. F. Lewis returned unhurt. Aircraft PM⊙N a write-off.

Battle L5465. Suffered a direct hit from intense flak during attack on bridge north-west of Remilly-Aillicourt and exploded over 'Le Chemin du Liry' 3.40 p.m. Pilot Officer V. A. Cunningham and AC1 L. J. Johnson killed. Aircraft a write-off.

The RAF death toll over the Western Front on May 14 was just one short of 100, the Battle crews bearing the brunt with 35 aircraft lost. The crew of L5581 of No. 88 Squadron were shot down near St Menges while attacking the Mouzon bridge. Sergeants Bill Ross, Frank Beames and Leading Aircraftman John Gegg were buried together in a single grave in the local cemetery. Such losses were clearly unsustainable and would result in the Fairey Battle being largely withdrawn from daytime operations.

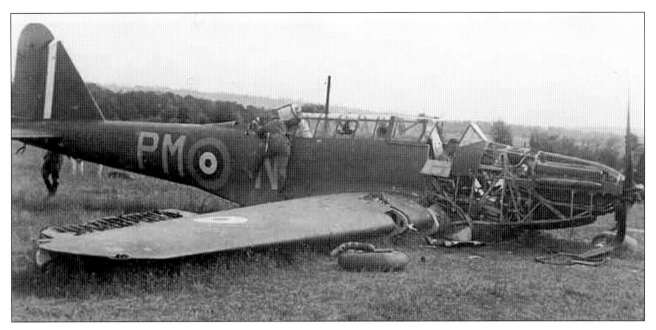

No. 103 Squadron lost four machines on the bridge attacks. On May 12 the squadron had decided that to preserve crews, their Battles would not carry an observer on future low-level raids. *Above:* Hence on May 14, L5516 just had a two-man crew, Sergeant Beardsley managing to bring his aircraft down safely.

Below: However at Remilly-Aillicourt lies a mystery. Joint Grave No. 2 in the local communal cemetery bears three headstones, that of Pilot Officer Vernon Cunningham and Aircraftman 1st Class Joe Johnson from L5465 plus an unknown but we know that No. 103 Squadron were only operating with two-man crews that day.

105 SQUADRON, VILLENEUVE-LES-VERTUS

Battle L5250. Forced-landed at Suippes badly damaged by AA during attack on bridge south-east of Sedan 4.15 p.m. Pilot Officer D. C. F. Murray, Sergeant Hemingway, and AC Hill unhurt. Aircraft abandoned.

Battle L5523. Failed to return following attack on bridge south-east of Sedan 4.15 p.m. Possibly that claimed by Oberlt Greisert of 2./JG2. Flight Lieutenant H. C. Sammels, Sergeant F. B. Abbot, and LAC R. D. Hughes missing. Aircraft lost.

Battle L5585. Shot down during attack on bridge at Remilly-Aillicourt and crashed at Noyers-Pont-Maugis 4.10 p.m. Possibly that claimed by Lt von Reden of 2./JG2. Flying Officer R. N. Wall, Sergeant A. C. Morgan, and LAC H. Hatton killed. Aircraft a write-off.

Battle K9186. Badly damaged by AA during attack on bridge at Sedan and crashed in woods at Lumes, south-east of Charleville-Mézières, 4.05 p.m. Flying Officer C. F. Gibson captured but escaped. Sergeant A. W. H. Hadley and AC1 W. Draper both captured badly concussed. Aircraft a write-off.
Flying Officer Gibson, slightly wounded during his escape, successfully evaded for four days while walking west. After swimming the Meuse he was fired on and badly wounded by French troops and admitted to hospital in Bordeaux where he was later captured. He was subsequently awarded a Military Cross and Croix de Guerre.

Battle K9342. Badly damaged by AA during attack on bridge at Mouzon, south-east of Sedan, and crashed at 'Bois de Sapins' near Villemontry 4.15 p.m. Pilot Officer F. A. G. Lascelles, Sergeant Ordway, and AC Weir returned unhurt. Aircraft GB⊙V 'NICKI' a write-off.

Right: **No. 105 Squadron on the other hand were still crewing their Battles with three men. This is the wreck of K9342 which crashed near Villemontry without casualty.**

Battle L5238. Shot down by AA during attack on bridges south-east of Sedan and crashed 150 metres upstream from Donchery bridge 4.05 p.m. Pilot Officer F. H. Ridley, Sergeant G. Atkinson, and AC J. S. Thomson killed. Aircraft a write-off.

Originally all buried near the wreck of their aircraft, two members of this crew were subsequently reinterred in Donchery cemetery as 'Unknown Airmen', the third crewman somehow being overlooked. On exhumation and transfer to Choloy War Cemetery in 1947, Ridley was formally identified but it would be another year before evidence from a German veteran allowed the MREU to locate the field grave of Gordon Atkinson and reunite him with his comrades.

Battle L5230. Shot down by AA during sortie to attack bridge south-east of Sedan and crashed near La Neuville-à-Maire 4.15 p.m. Pilot Officer H. E. White, Sergeant G. A. Cartwright, and AC1 J. Potter killed. Aircraft a write-off.

Only the pilot, Hugh Edgar White, was identified when this crew was originally buried at Bulson. They were all correctly identified on reinterrment in Choloy War Cemetery after the war.

Battle P2248. Hit by flak during attack on bridge south-east of Sedan and returned badly damaged 5.15 p.m. Sergeant A. J. C. Eagles, Sergeant John, and AC E. S. Rock unhurt. Aircraft a write-off.

114 SQUADRON, CONDÉ-VRAUX

Blenheim R3703. Returned starboard engine damaged by ground-fire near St Menges during reconnaissance sortie between Sedan and Bouillon 9.55 a.m. Pilot Officer N. Tasker, Sergeant Summers, and LAC Levack unhurt. Aircraft repairable.

114 SQUADRON, PLIVOT

Blenheim N6230. Shot down by Bf109s of I./JG53 during sortie to bomb enemy troop concentrations between Givonne and Bouillon. Crashed and burned out near La Cassine, south-west of Sedan, 3.40 p.m. Possibly one of those claimed by Oberlt Mayer (*Staffelkapitän*) of 1./JG53. Flying Officer J. H. Newberry and Sergeant R. Kendrick suffered slight burns. LAC H. R. Baker (of No. 139 Squadron) killed. Aircraft a write-off.

The serial number is correct as shown though several published accounts suggest N6223.

Blenheim L9466. Returned riddled by Bf109s of I./JG53 between Douzy and Pouru during attack on enemy troop concentrations around Givonne and Bouillon 3.40 p.m. Sergeant Potter and Sergeant Mulford unhurt. AC1 Longhorn believed wounded. Aircraft damaged but repairable.

The German inscription on the cross on the grave beside the wreck says 'Ein unbekannter Flieger, Flugzeug N6230' which ties it in with the Blenheim of No. 114 Squadron lost near Sedan. Due to recent losses they moved from Condé-Vraux to Plivot on this day to share operations with No. 139 Squadron, hence the grave will be that of Leading Aircraftman Harold Baker, now buried at Choloy War Cemetery.

Blenheim L9464. Shot down by Bf109s of I./JG53 during low-level attack on troop concentrations between Givonne and Bouillon; crashed and burned out at Glaire-et-Villette 3.45 p.m. Possibly that claimed by Oberlt Ohly of 1./JG53. Pilot Officer C. B. Jordan, Sergeant P. McK. Southwood, and LAC T. W. Brown killed. Aircraft a write-off.

Blenheim IV P4827. Shot down by Bf109s of I./JG53 south-west of Sedan during sortie to bomb troop concentrations between Givonne and Bouillon. Abandoned over Sauville and crashed in woods near La Cassine 3.30 p.m. Possibly that claimed by Lt Dittmar of Stab I./JG53. Sergeant Brady and Sergeant Willsher baled out unhurt. LAC S. A. Maddox (of No. 139 Squadron) killed. Aircraft a write-off.

139 SQUADRON, PLIVOT

Blenheim IV L9179. Shot down by Bf109s of I./JG53 south-west of Sedan during sortie to bomb troop concentrations between Givonne and Bouillon 3.40 p.m. Possibly claimed by Uffz Reibel of 1./JG53. Flying Officer R. H. de Montmorency and Sergeant H. B. Wallis killed. LAC V. S. G. Barlow (of No. 114 Squadron) baled out wounded in back and chest, admitted to hospital in Angers. Aircraft a write-off.

Recovered from the wreckage of the aircraft when it was finally cleared in June 1942, these airmen were buried as 'Unknowns' at Laneuville-sur-Meuse, near Stenay, but formally identified on exhumation in July 1947.

Blenheim IV P6902. Exploded under attack by Fw Stark of 1./JG53 south-west of Sedan during sortie to bomb troop concentrations between Givonne and Bouillon 3.40 p.m. Pilot Officer J. O'B. Power, Sergeant D. T. Stuart-Harris, and AC1 W. Parker missing. Aircraft a write-off.

The serial number is believed to be correct as shown though several post-war accounts cite N6230.

142 SQUADRON, BERRY-AU-BAC

Battle P2246. Shot down by Moranes of GC III/7 during sortie to bomb pontoon bridge between Sedan and Mouzon and both wings ripped off crash-landing through trees at Artaise-le-Vivier 12.54 p.m. Squadron Leader J. F. Hobler badly burned later evacuated to England. Sergeant R. V. T. Kitto and Corporal D. J. Barbrook unhurt. Aircraft a write-off.

Unaccountably mistaken for Henschel Hs126s, the tragic loss of these four aircraft to 'friendly fire' has been subject of rigorous investigation by noted French air historian Arnaud Gillet. The unfortunate French pilots involved were Capt Georges Lacombe (Commandant 5/7), Capt Pierre Bouvarre (Commandant 6/7), Adjt Jean Bertrand, Adjt Albert Littolff, S/Lt Marcel Billoin, S/Lt Yves Mourier, and Sgt Louis Berthet.

Four Battles from No. 142 Squadron were brought down in friendly fire incidents. Sergeant James Brookes and LAC Ron Nugent lie together in Choloy.

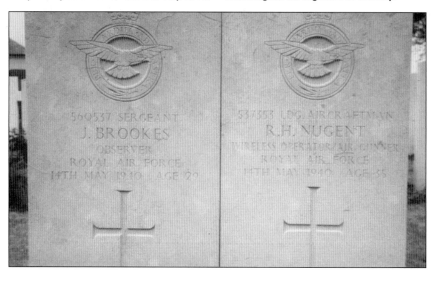

Left: **K9483 of No. 150 Squadron was another casualty of the bridge attacks. Its crew — Arthur Posselt, Don Bowen and Norman Vano — are buried in a collective grave at Choloy whereas their squadron fellows — John Boon, Tom Fortune and Syd Martin — lie in a single grave** *(right)* **in Douzy Communal Cemetery.**

Battle P2333. Tail shot off by Moranes of GC III/7 during sortie to bomb pontoon bridge between Sedan and Mouzon, crashed and burned out at Sauville 1.00 p.m. Sergeant J. Brookes and LAC R. H. Nugent both killed. Sergeant A. N. Spear baled out unhurt and evaded capture. Aircraft QT⊙P a write-off.
Originally buried in the nearby Military Cemetery at Mont Dieu, these airmen were both reinterred in Choloy War Cemetery post-war.

Battle K9333. Badly damaged by Moranes of GC III/7 over Vendresse during sortie to bomb pontoon bridge between Sedan and Mouzon 1.12 p.m. Belly-landed at Ecly, north-west of Rethel. Pilot Officer H. L. Oakley slightly injured. Sergeant Martin, and AC Preston unhurt. Aircraft QT⊙K a write-off.

Battle L5517. Shot down by Moranes of GC III/7 during sortie to bomb pontoon bridge between Sedan and Mouzon 1.25 p.m. Crashed between the road and River Bar near Chéhéry. Flight Lieutenant K. R. Rogers, Sergeant H. F. Trescothic, and Corporal H. Todd killed. Aircraft a write-off.

150 SQUADRON, ECURY-SUR-COOLE

Battle L4946. Believed shot down by Bf109s during attack on bridge at Wadelincourt and crashed at 'La Croix Piot', south of Donchery, 3.20 p.m. Possibly that claimed by Uffz Franke of 2./JG53. Flying Officer J. Ing, Sergeant J. D. Turner, and AC1 W. J. Nolan killed. Aircraft a write-off.

Battle K9483. Believed shot down by Bf109s during attack on pontoon bridge across the Meuse south of Sedan and crashed and burned out at 'le Petit Pont', Bulson 3.20 p.m. Possibly that claimed by Uffz Ghesla of 2./JG53. Pilot Officer A. F. Posselt, Sergeant D. J. Bowen, and AC2 N. V. Vano killed. Aircraft a write-off.

Battle P2182. Believed shot down by Bf109s during attack on bridge at Remilly-Aillicourt and crashed near 'La Rule', north of the Chiers, at Douzy 3.15 p.m. Possibly one of those attacked by Oberfw Stotz of I./JG76. Pilot Officer J. Boon, Sergeant T. Fortune, and AC1 S. Martin killed. Aircraft a write-off.

Battle P5232. Believed shot down by Bf109s during attack on pontoon bridge at Remilly-Aillicourt. Crashed and burned out in 'Bois de l'Arbre', near Raucourt-et-Flaba, 3.24 p.m. Possibly one of those claimed by Oberlt Mayer *(Staffelkapitän)* of 1./JG53. Flight Sergeant G. T. Barker and Sergeant J. D. F. Williams killed. LAC A. K. Summerson badly burned and wounded in leg evaded capture and admitted to hospital three days later. Aircraft JN⊙I a write-off.
Transferred to a variety of French hospitals ahead of the German advance, for some months Alan Summerson shared a room with Bill Simpson of No. 12 Squadron (see page 180) in the Hôpital Carnot at Chalon-sur-Saône. He would later receive the Medaille Militaire and Croix de Guerre from the French.

218 SQUADRON, AUBERIVE-SUR-SUIPPES

Battle P2360. Believed shot down by Bf109s during attack on the Meuse bridge at Wadelincourt 3.40 p.m. Possibly that claimed by Oberlt Ohly of 1./JG53. Pilot Officer R. T. L. Buttery and AC2 W. C. Waterston both missing. Aircraft lost.

Battle L5422. Believed shot down by Bf109s during attack on the Meuse bridge at Wadelincourt and crashed between Bulson and Noyers-Pont-Maugis 3.40 p.m. Possibly that claimed by Oberlt Balfanz of Stab I./JG53. Flying Officer J. F. R. Crane killed. AC1 T. W. Holloway captured. Aircraft a write-off.

Battle L5232. Set alight in attacks by Bf109s after bombing the Meuse bridge at Wadelincourt and crashed near cemetery at Sauville, north of Le Chesne, 3.40 p.m. Possibly that attacked by Oberlt Prestele of 1./JG53. Pilot Officer W. A. R. Harris baled out badly burned. Sergeant N. B. Herriott and AC1 W. Robinson both killed. Aircraft a write-off.

Battle L5235. Believed shot down by Bf109s during attack on columns between Bouillon and Givonne or the bridge at Wadelincourt and belly-landed near Thelonne, south of Sedan, 3.40 p.m. Possibly that claimed by Hptmn von Janson *(Gruppenkommandeur)* of Stab I./JG53. Pilot Officer A. M. Imrie captured. LAC A. J. Taylor seriously wounded, died shortly after capture. Aircraft HA⊙W a write-off.

No. 218 Squadron also sent four Battles to the bridge at Wadelincourt and another seven to attack troop concentrations in the Bouillon—Givonne area. Ten of the eleven aircraft were reported as failing to return but unfortunately the records are incomplete and it is only possible to detail the losses of five of their machines. This is L5235 down near Thelonne.

These are most probably two of the missing 218 Squadron Battles. *Left:* No serial is visible on HA⊙R and no clues as to exactly where the photo was taken. *Right:* To add to the enigma, here is another HA⊙R on which the serial is K9273.

Battle P2324. Believed shot down by Bf109s during attack on columns between Bouillon and Givonne or the bridge at Wadelincourt 3.40 p.m. Possibly that claimed by Oberstlt Kraut *(Gruppenkommandeur)* of Stab I./JG76. Flying Officer D. A. J. Foster and AC1 T. J. Bryan both captured. Aircraft a write-off.

Ten of the 11 aircraft despatched by No. 218 Squadron were reportedly lost in these attacks. This cannot be confirmed as official records are incomplete and details on five cannot be traced.

226 SQUADRON, REIMS-CHAMPAGNE

Battle P2267. Believed shot down by flak during attack on bridge at Douzy, south-east of Sedan, 4.00 p.m. Squadron Leader C. E. S. Lockett baled out and captured. Sergeant F. J. Percival and Corporal R. S. Clark missing. Aircraft lost.

No trace of the remains of Frederick Percival and Robert Clark were ever reported found. They are commemorated on the Runnymede Memorial where their date of death is recorded as May 15.

Battle P2254. Port aileron, tailplane, and bomb-release gear damaged by ground-fire during approach to bridge at Douzy 4.00 p.m. Attack aborted and returned to base. Sergeant R. S. Annan, Sergeant A. Livingston, and AC2 Jonas unhurt. Aircraft abandoned.

Battle L5438. Shot down during bombing attack on bridge at Mouzon and crashed near Mont Dieu 4.00 p.m. Flight Sergeant W. A. Dunn, Sergeant A. F. Sedgwick, and AC2 M. B. Millar killed. Aircraft a write-off.

Originally buried at Mont Dieu, this crew was exhumed in February 1947 and reinterred in Choloy War Cemetery where their dates of death are recorded as May 15.

Battle K9343. Failed to return from attack on bridge at Les Grandes-Armoises 4.00 p.m. Sergeant V. H. Moseley killed. Sergeant S. D. Hibberd and Corporal H. F. Little missing. Aircraft a write-off.

Only one body, together with a map marked 'Moseley', was recovered from this wreck and buried in Les Grandes-Armoises churchyard as an 'Aviateur Anglais. Avion Blenheim K9343'. Later formally identified as Victor Moseley, he was reinterred on February 11, 1947 in Choloy War Cemetery where his date of death is recorded as May 15 as are those of the other two crews above.

Battle K9345. Returned damaged by ground-fire during attack on bridge at Mouzon, south-east of Sedan, 3.48 p.m. Flight Lieutenant V. S. Butler, Sergeant Forsyth, and LAC J. P. Sullivan unhurt. Aircraft repairable.

Battle K9383. Returned with petrol tanks holed by ground-fire during attack on bridge at Mouzon, south-east of Sedan, 4.00 p.m. Sergeant E. E. Hopkins and Sergeant J. B. Callaghan unhurt. AC D. Barber injured ankle. Aircraft damaged but repairable — destroyed on evacuation May 16.

Battle K9176. Returned with petrol tanks holed by ground-fire during attack on transport between Ecly and Serincourt 10.40 p.m. Sergeant N. N. Hoyle, Sergeant Maguire, and AC Lewis unhurt. Aircraft repairable.

501 SQUADRON, BÉTHENIVILLE

Hurricane L1991. Returned damaged by return fire from He111 shot down over Reims 10.00 a.m. Sergeant J. E. Proctor unhurt. Aircraft SD⊙R repairable — later abandoned.

504 SQUADRON, LILLE-MARCQ

Hurricane L1941. Failed to return from patrol east of Brussels and believed victim of heavy ground-fire 1.00 p.m. Pilot Officer S. A. C. Sibley missing. Aircraft a write-off.

Hurricane L1639. Shot down in combat with Bf109s of III./JG26 and crashed at 'Hameau de Caillou', Chaussée-Notre-Dame-Louvignies 5.40 p.m. Possibly that claimed by Lt Blume of 7./JG26. Squadron Leader J. B. Parnall killed. Aircraft a write-off.

The dates of death of both officers above is recorded by the Commonwealth War Graves Commission as May 15.

Hurricane L1950. Shot down in combat with Bf109s of III./JG26 near Louvignies 5.40 p.m. Possibly that claimed by Lt Müller-Dühe of 7./JG26. Flying Officer M. E. A. Royce baled out unhurt. Aircraft a write-off.

Hurricane N2492. Shot down in combat with Bf109s of III./JG26 between Mons and Ath, crashed on the Congoberg, near Vollezele, 5.40 p.m. Possibly that claimed by Oberlt Wendt of 8./JG26. Sergeant S. Hamblett believed baled out wounded — later missing. Aircraft a write-off.

Stanley Hamblett was transported to the coast for evacuation to England but his ship lost to enemy action off Dunkirk. He is commemorated on the Runnymede memorial where his date of death is recorded as May 14. Crash-site excavated by the Belgian Aviation Historical Association in November 2001 when identity plate 'N2492' was recovered, now displayed in their collection at Erembodegem.

Hurricane L1916. Crash-landed damaged in action with Bf109s of III./JG26 between Mons and Ath 5.40 p.m. Pilot Officer B. E. G. White slightly wounded. Aircraft a write-off.

607 SQUADRON, VITRY-EN-ARTOIS

Hurricane P2621. Shot down by Oberlt Hahn *(Staffelkapitän)* of 4./JG2 over Corroy-le-Château during attack on Hs123s of II.(S)/LG2. Crashed and burned out at 'la Carrièrre', Perwez, north of Namur 10.55 a.m. Flight Lieutenant J. L. Sullivan (of No. 242 Squadron) killed. Aircraft a write-off.

One of four replacement pilots from No. 242 Squadron who arrived from England that morning, Sullivan was the first of his unit to die in action. Pilot Officers R. D. Grassick and W. L. McKnight were subsequently transferred to No. 615 Squadron at Moorsele, while Pilot Officer P. S. Turner remained with No. 607 Squadron; all three survivors returning to their original unit at Church Fenton on May 20.

Hurricane P2618. Shot down by Fw Harbauer of 4./JG2 over Corroy-le-Château during attack on Hs123s of II.(S)/LG2. Crashed at Aische-en-Refail, north of Namur, 10.55 a.m. Flying Officer G. I. Cuthbert killed. Aircraft a write-off.

Originally buried in the local communal cemetery, Gerald Cuthbert was subsequently reinterred in Hotton War Cemetery. A replacement pilot, he had arrived from No. 601 Squadron only the previous day.

Hurricane P2713. Shot down by Bf109s of 4./JG2 over Corroy-le-Château during attack on Hs123s of II.(S)/LG2 10.55 a.m. Possibly that claimed by Fw Schnell. Pilot Officer A. E. Le Breuilly missing. Aircraft lost.

UK-based aircraft lost or damaged on operations over the western front:

RAF BOMBER COMMAND

21 Squadron, Bodney
Troop concentrations near Sedan

Blenheim IV L8738. Shot down by Bf109s of 3./JG53 and forced-landed between l'Echelle and Aubigny-les-Pothées 6.40 p.m. Sgt J. J. Outhwaite, Sgt E. Broadland unhurt. AC1 J. E. Bartley wounded. Aircraft abandoned.

Blenheim IV L8742. Shot down by Bf109s of 3./JG53 and crashed in the Ardennes forest near Sugny, north of Sedan, 6.40 p.m. P/O R. G. M. Gilmore, Sgt T. R. A. D. Pearce, AC1 A. G. Wilson missing. Aircraft lost.

Blenheim IV P6890. Belly-landed on return, hydraulics badly damaged by Bf109s of 3./JG53 6.40 p.m. F/O J. C. G. Sarll and Sgt Jennings unhurt. AC1 L. H. Lightfoot wounded in shoulder. Aircraft wrecked.

44 Squadron, Waddington
Night attack on communications at Breda:

Hampden P4286. Shot down and crashed at 'Witte Weg', Den Hout. F/O L. J. Ashfield, P/O C. D. Crawley, Sgt F. W. McKinlay, Cpl F. Preston killed. Aircraft lost.
Originally buried in a field grave in Houteindsestraat, this crew was reinterred at Oosterhout in June 1941.

110 Squadron, Wattisham
Troop concentrations near Sedan:

Blenheim IV L9214. Shot down by Bf109s of 3./JG53 over Sedan 6.35 p.m. F/O G. O. M. Wright, Sgt J. Fancy, and LAC W. W. Street captured. Aircraft lost.

Blenheim IV L9217. Shot down by Bf109s of 3./JG53 and crashed in Boulevard Chanzy at Torcy, Sedan, 6.35 p.m. P/O E. R. Mullins and Sgt R. Lowe baled out and captured. AC2 P. Aherne killed. Aircraft lost.

Blenheim IV L9241. Badly damaged by Bf109s of 3./JG53 in the target area 6.15 p.m. and belly-landed near Orchies. Sgt A. R. Storrow, Sgt E. C. Parker, and LAC Rowlands unhurt. Aircraft abandoned.

Blenheim IV N6210. Shot down in the target area near Escombres 6.15 p.m. P/O S. G. Rose, Sgt D. A. Ashton, and LAC E. N. Edwards missing. Aircraft lost.
Incomplete and contradictory contemporary records do not allow positive identification, but it is possible that this was the crew originally buried as 'Unknowns' in the Communal Cemetery at Escombres-et-le-Chesnois and subsequently reinterred in Choloy War Cemetery Plots 1A.C.15-17.

Blenheim IV P6889. Hydraulics damaged in attacks by Bf109s of 3./JG53 and belly-landed at Ste-Vaubourg, near Attigny, 6.15 p.m. Sgt Cater, Sgt Crossland, AC1 Jones wounded. Aircraft lost.

FRENCH AIR FORCE

ECMJ 1/16 Potez 631 (140). Forced-landed at Aubérive damaged in attacks by P/O Sylvester and Sgt Farnes of No. 501 Squadron over Mourmelon 8.50 a.m. Sgt Sauvage, Sgt Simon, and Sgt Marmion unhurt. Aircraft repairable.

ECMJ 1/16 Potez 631 (127). Returned to Wez-Thuisy damaged in attacks by P/O Hairs of No. 501 Squadron over Mourmelon 8.50 a.m. Lt Cormouls slightly wounded, Sgt Desprette, and Adjt Bruyere unhurt. Aircraft repairable.

GAO 502 Potez 63.11 (349). Damaged by flak during observation sortie and crashed on landing at Villers-lès-Guise 7.45 a.m. Lt de Fay and crew unhurt. Aircraft a write-off.

GAO 502 Mureaux 115. Abandoned at Devant-les-Bois due to undercarriage damage 12.30 p.m. Crew unhurt, returned by road. Aircraft destroyed to prevent capture.

GAO 2/520 2 Potez 63.11 and two Mureaux 115. Damaged aircraft left behind at Challerange on withdrawal to Vassincourt p.m. No crew casualties. Aircraft abandoned.

GAO 545 Potez 63.11 (621). Shot down by Bf109s during observation sortie over Gembloux 10.45 a.m. Crash-landed in flames at Gourdinne, near Walcourt, where strafed and burned out. Capt Delove, S/Lt Perne, and Sgt Bouvay unhurt. Aircraft a write-off.

GAO 547 Potez 63.11 (381). Shot down by enemy fighters during low-level reconnaissance sortie over Monthermé. Crashed into forest near Roc-de-la-Tour, north-east of Château-Regnault 10.45 a.m. Lt C. Bertheux and Sgt A. Benech killed. Cpl Martin captured badly wounded. Aircraft a write-off.
The pilot and observer of this aircraft were originally buried alongside the aircraft but were exhumed on August 8, 1941, and reinterred in the cemetery of Croix-Sainte-Anne at Monthermé.

GAO 547 Potez 63.11 (579). Port fuel tank set alight by Bf110s of I./ZG52 over Mondigny on return from low-level reconnaissance of the Bar valley. Crashed and burned out at 'Marie-Barbe', near Ecogne in the Froidmont Forest, north-west of Gruyères 8.00 p.m. S/Lt C. Levasseur and Sgt A. Mougne killed. Capt M. Marrast badly burned, walked 5 km before rescue, and admitted to hospital in Laon where he died next day. Aircraft a write-off.

GB I/12 LeO 451 (48). Shot down by enemy fighters south of Sedan and exploded between Maisoncelle and Bulson 12.30 p.m. S/Lt P. Hugot and Adjt L. Leroy killed. Adjt Jacquemin and Sgt Lebeaupin both wounded, baled out and captured near Chémery. Aircraft a write-off.

GB II/12 LeO 451 (40). Returned damaged following sortie over Sedan 12.30 p.m. Capt A. Rocher, S/Lt A. Masclaud, Cpl Y. Le Goyat, and Adjt R. Lambert unhurt. Aircraft damaged but repairable.

GB 2/34 Amiot 143 (69). Damaged by flak and engaged by Bf109s during low-level attack on enemy concentrations near Givonne. Believed that claimed by Oberlt Schumann *(Staffelkapitän)* of 5./JG52. Crashed near Cernay-en-Dormois, south of Vouziers, 1.05 p.m. Capt Marie *(Commandant)*, Sgt Legrand, and Sgt Teyssier baled out unhurt. Adjt Speich and Sgt Thévenard baled out badly wounded. Aircraft a write-off.

GB I/34 Amiot 143 (80). Crash-landed at Bétheniville damaged by Bf109s of 5./JG52 following low-level attack in the Sedan — Bazeilles — Givonne sector 12.55 p.m. Capt J. Véron, Adjt Saulou, Sgt Milan, Sgt Carré, and Cpl Vandra unhurt. Aircraft damaged but repairable — abandoned May 16.

We have not been able to find any pictures of French Air Force aircraft down on May 14 — not surprising when one considers that photographing crashed aircraft would hardly have been a priority. Also one needs to be able to read either identifying letters or serials to tie a photo into the records. This is an example: a Dewoitine 520 of Groupe de Chasse I/3 which has made a successful belly-landing, so might it be Sous-Lieutenant Salva's aircraft or another of the 24 they lost in combat during the campaign?

GB I/34 Amiot 143 (30). Badly damaged by flak during attack on enemy concentrations near Givonne 1.00 p.m. and wrecked in heavy crash-landing back at La Ferté-Gaucher, Col François (*Commandant Groupement No. 9*) and crew unhurt. Aircraft a write-off.

GB I/34 Amiot 143 (57). Badly damaged by flak during attack on enemy concentrations near Givonne 1.00 p.m. and crashed on landing. Lt Carlier, S/Lts S. Poummeau, Faion, Cimbetti, and Dint unhurt. Aircraft a write-off.

GB II/34 Amiot 143 (56). Port engine set alight by flak during attack on enemy concentrations north of Sedan, crashed and exploded at l'Algérie', near Floing 12.45 p.m. Cmdt. J. de Laubier *(Commandant)*, and Lt J. Vauzelle killed. Sgt G. Occis baled out but killed. Sgt Gelly and Sgt R. Ankaoua baled out and captured unhurt. Aircraft a write-off.

GB II/34 Amiot 143 (85). Returned to Nangis badly damaged by Bf110s during attack on enemy concentrations near Sedan 12.55 p.m. Lt Fouchier and crew unhurt. Aircraft damaged but repairable.

GB II/38 Amiot 143 (29). Hit by flak and forced-landed at Souain with one engine on fire following attack on enemy columns north of Sedan 1.00 p.m. S/Lt Jeanne, Adjt Boussicaut, Sgt Azan, Sgt Laloncette, and Sgt Mercier unhurt. Aircraft a write-off.

GC I/1 Bloch 152 (371). Damaged in combat with Bf110s north of Dinant and belly-landed at Cuirieux, south-east of Marle, 10.00 a.m. Lt J. Schmidt unhurt. Aircraft destroyed by pilot.

GC 2/1 Bloch 152. Badly damaged in attack by Bf110 during patrol over Dinant and forced-landed at Aulnoye, 12 km south-east of Maubeuge 7.30 p.m. Capt G. Garde *(Commandant)* slightly wounded in left leg. Aircraft a write-off.

GC 4/1 Bloch 152 (504). Believed shot down by cross-fire during attack on Ju87s of I./StG76 between Flize and Sedan 10.30 a.m. but also possible victim of attack by Bf109 of 2./JG53. Cmdt. A. Coiral *(Commandant)* missing. Aircraft 1 a write-off.
This aircraft exploded at around 8,000 feet and no trace of its pilot was ever found.

GC II/1 Bloch 152 (570). Shot down in combat with Bf109s of 2./JG77 and Bf110s of II./ZG26 north of Dinant, during escort sortie for Potez 63.11 of GR II/52 3.10 p.m. Lt P. Maurin baled out wounded in arm and with burns to face. Aircraft a write-of.

GC II/1 Bloch 152 (172). Cockpit hood shattered in attack by Lt Mütherich of 2./JG77 during escort sortie for Potez 63.11 of GR II/52 between Dinant and Ciney. Pursued by enemy fighters, made high-speed belly-landing near Oret, south-west of Mettet, 3.10 p.m. Sgt R. Brisou wounded. Aircraft 9 abandoned.

GC II/1 Bloch 152. Engine damaged by Bf110s of I. and II./ZG26 in combat north of Dinant during escort sortie for Potez 63.11 of GR II/52. Believed forced-landed near Momignies 3.10 p.m. and destroyed on the ground by Bf110. Sgt J. Robert unhurt. Aircraft 12 a write-off.

GC II/1 Bloch 152. Damaged by Bf110s of I. and II./ZG26 in combat north of Dinant during escort sortie for Potez 63.11 of GR II/52 and belly-landed 3.10 p.m. Sgt Patoor unhurt. Aircraft 5 a write-off.

GC II/1 Bloch 152. Shot down in combat with Bf110s west of Charleroi and abandoned over Solre-le-Château, south-east of Maubeuge 7.00 p.m. Lt P. Matras baled out wounded in left arm. Aircraft a write-off.

GC II/2 Morane 406 (641). Returned to Laon-Chambry badly damaged in action during sector patrol over Namur—Dinant—Philippeville 7.30 a.m. Adjt G. Berland unhurt. Aircraft a write-off.

GC II/2 Morane 406. Belly-landed at Athies damaged by return fire from He111s engaged over Montcornet 9.00 a.m. Sgt Parent unhurt. Aircraft damaged but repairable.

GC II/2 Morane 406 (327). Hit by cross-fire during attack on Do17s escorted by Bf110s west of Dinant; crashed and exploded in woods at Cauderie, near Florennes 9.00 a.m. Lt H. de Rohan-Chabot killed. Aircraft 6 a write-off.

GC 5/2 Morane 406 (480). Landed at Cambrai-Niergnies damaged by Oberlt Keller (*Staffelkapitän*) of 1./JG3 in combat south-west of Namur 4.25 p.m. Adjt D. Danse badly wounded in head and arms. Aircraft repairable.

GC 5/2 Morane 406. Returned to Cambrai-Niergnies damaged in combat with Bf109s of 1./JG3 south-west of Namur 4.25 p.m. S/Lt J. Dartevelle unhurt. Aircraft repairable.

GC 5/2 Morane 406. Returned to Cambrai-Niergnies with windscreen shattered during combat with Bf109s of 1./JG3 south-west of Namur 4.25 p.m. Adjt Barrio unhurt. Aircraft repairable.

GC I/3 Dewoitine 520 (73). Shot down by Oberfw Schmidt of I./JG2 in action south-west of Sedan and crashed near Bois de la Marfée, between Cheveuges and Frénois, 9.10 a.m. Adjt A. Carrier killed. Aircraft 10 a write-off.
André Carrier died in this, his first air combat. His remains were eventually recovered on June 9, 1942, and buried in the communal cemetery at Frénois.

GC I/3 Dewoitine 520. Returned to Wez-Thuisy badly damaged by Lt Uhlhorn of 5./ZG76 during attack on Do17 north of Sedan 9.25 a.m. Capt B. Challe unhurt. Aircraft a write-off.

GC I/3 Dewoitine 520. Shot down by return fire during attack on He111 of 8./KG51 south-east of Ste-Menehould and abandoned between Villers-en-Argonne and Daucourt. Crashed and burned out behind Ferme de la Hotte, 1.30 p.m. S/Lt L-L. Potier baled out, mortally wounded by French ground-fire and landed dead at Châtrices. Aircraft a write-off.
Alternative accounts report that Lucien-Louis Potier became detached from his parachute and fell to his death. He received a posthumous Croix de Chevalier de la Legion d'Honneur, and Croix de Guerre with Palm on April 10, 1941. Site excavated April 2002 when engine, propeller blade and hub were among several items recovered.

GC I/3 Dewoitine 520. Dead-stick landing at emergency airstrip near Orconte with engine damaged by return fire following attack on He111 of 8./KG51 over Villers-Daucourt 1.30 p.m. S/Lt P. Salva unhurt. Aircraft a write-off.

GC 3/4 Curtiss H-75 (91). Shot down in head-on attack on Bf110 of III./ZG26 over Vendresse and crash-landed at speed near Omont, 8 km south-east of Poix-Terron, 6.40 p.m. S/Lt Cuny captured with serious head wounds. Aircraft a write-off.

GC I/5 Curtiss H-75 (92). Shot down by Oberfw Hauer of 1./JG76 south of Sedan and abandoned over 'Le Grand Fond' at Amblimont 11.30 a.m. Lt T. Hamsick baled out but parachute failed and fell dead near Mairy. Aircraft a write-off.

GC II/5 Curtiss H-75 (53). Shot down in combat with Bf110s of I./ZG52 south of Thionville and abandoned over Doncourt 4.15 p.m. Sgt A. Bouhy baled out unhurt Aircraft a write-off.

GC II/5 Curtiss H-75. Shot down in combat with Bf110s of I./ZG52 south of Thionville 4.25 p.m. S/Lt G. Ruchoux baled out unhurt. Aircraft a write-off.

GC II/6 Morane 406 (92). Landed at Maubeuge severely damaged in combat with Bf109s near Mons 10.15 a.m. Sgt Boyer unhurt. Aircraft a write-off.

GC 4/6 Morane 406 (86). Shot down in combat with Bf109s south-east of Mons, and crashed in Bois Grammaire field, near Bel Air Farm, Vellereille-les-Brayeux 10.15 a.m. Capt A. Gilbert *(Commandant)* killed. Aircraft a write-off.

GC II/6 Morane 406 (772). Set alight in combat with Bf110s during attack on He111s over Mons 7.00 p.m. Crashed and burned out near the canal north of St-Ghislain. Adjt M. Leniaud baled out badly burned, and fell to his death with his parachute alight. Aircraft a write-off.
Alternative accounts suggests that Marcel Leniaud fell victim to Belgian ground-fire while in his parachute. Taken to the casualty station at 'Les enfants des Bâteliers' he was later buried as an 'Unknown Airman' in the local graveyard. He was not formally identified until October 10, 1940.

GC III/6 Morane 406 (684). Shot down by return fire from Ju88 of 3./KG51 engaged over Longvic 11.45 a.m. Crashed into forest outside Prenois, 12 km north-west of Dijon. Sgt E. Boymond killed. Aircraft a write-off.
The people of Prenois erected a memorial to Emile Boymond where he is still remembered every year in a simple ceremony.

GC III/7 Morane 406. Radiator damaged by return fire from Do17 and forced-landed at Monthois 6.20 a.m. Sgt J. Guillaume unhurt. Aircraft destroyed by bombing later that afternoon.

GC I/8 Bloch 152 (506). Oil tank badly damaged in attack by Lt Hofer of 5./JG52 during escort sortie for Amiot 143s of GB I/34 over Sedan. Belly-landed alongside the road between Tahure and Suippes 1.05 p.m. S/Lt P. Gouachon-Noireault unhurt. Aircraft 10 a write-off.

GC I/8 Bloch 152 (531). Slightly damaged in combat with Bf109s of 5./JG52 during escort sortie for Amiot 143s of GB I/34 over Sedan and forced-landed at Bétheniville 1.05 p.m. Sgt H. Choulet unhurt. Aircraft 7 repairable.

GC 4/10 Bloch 152. Returned to base damaged in combat with Bf110s of I. and II./ZG26 over Dinant 7.30 p.m. Capt Dulac *(Commandant)* unhurt. Aircraft repairable.

GC II/10 Bloch 152. Belly-landed at Laon-Couvron following routine patrol over La Fère and Courbes 12.50 p.m. S/Lt Barbu unhurt. Aircraft damaged but repairable.

GC II/10 Bloch 152 (374). Shot down in engagement with Bf110s of I. and II./ZG26 over Dinant and crashed at Merbes-Sainte-Marie, south of Binche, 7.30 p.m. Sgt J. Hémery killed. Aircraft a write-off.

GC II/10 Bloch 152 (384). Badly damaged in combat with Bf110s of I. and II./ZG26 over Dinant and forced-landed out of fuel in Peissant, on the road to Erquelinnes 7.30 p.m. Adjt J. Couillard wounded, admitted to hospital in Lille. Aircraft a write-off.

GC II/10 Bloch 152 (120). Badly damaged in combat with Bf110s of I. and II./ZG26 over Dinant. Belly-landed outside La Bouteille, 7 km north-east of Vervins 7.30 p.m. Adjt Berger unhurt. Aircraft a write-off.

GC II/10 Bloch 152 (66). Belly-landed following combat with Bf110s of I. and II./ZG26 over Dinant 7.30 p.m. S/Lt Goetz believed unhurt. Aircraft damage state not recorded.

GC 6/10 Bloch 152. Badly damaged in combat with Bf109s of I./JG3 south-east of Charleroi and crashed attempting belly-landing alongside the road in Piéton, 12 km west of Charleroi, 7.45 p.m. Possibly that claimed by Lt Binder of 3./JG3. Capt G. Guizard *(Commandant)* wounded in left arm and leg. Aircraft 1 a write-off.

GC III/10 Bloch 152. Forced-landed at Noyon damaged after combat with Bf110s of I. and II./ZG26 over Dinant 7.30 p.m. Sgt C. Feldzer believed unhurt. Aircraft damaged state not recorded.

GC III/10 Bloch 152 (219). Shot down by Bf109s of I./JG3 during attack on Do17s south-east of Charleroi 7.30 p.m. Possibly one of those claimed by Hptmn Lützow *(Gruppenkommandeur)* of Stab I./JG3. Lt P. Martin baled out but seriously injured hitting the tailplane. Believed landed at 'Crapoto', Ragnies, and admitted to hospital where leg amputated. Aircraft a write-off.

GC III/10 Bloch 152 (170). Shot down by Bf109 of I./JG3 during attack on Do17s south-east of Charleroi 7.30 p.m. Possibly one of those claimed by Oberlt Rau of Stab I./JG3. Crashed at 'Perchoux', south-east of Thy-le-Château, near Dinant. Sgt J-M. Motte killed. Aircraft a write-off.

GC III/10 Bloch 152. Shot down by Bf109 of I./JG3 during attack on Do17s south-east of Charleroi, and crashed near St Quentin 7.30 p.m. Possibly that claimed by Lt Stange of 3./JG3. Sgt G. Martin badly wounded in the head, admitted to Marquion hospital in Cambrai but later transferred to the Golf Hospital in Le Touquet where captured. Aircraft a write-off.

GC III/10 Bloch 152 (235). Badly damaged in combat with Bf109s of I./JG3 south-east of Charleroi 7.30 p.m. Possibly one of those claimed by Oberlt Rau of Stab I./JG3. Crash-landed in a copse near Vieux-Mesnil, 8 km south-west of Maubeuge. Sgt Jere wounded face and hands. Aircraft a write-off.

Mort pour la France. Sergent-chef Jacques Hémery of Groupe de Chasse II/10 at rest in the French Military Cemetery at Chastres.

GC III/10 Bloch 152. Forced-landed near Le Hérie-la-Vieville out of fuel following combat with Bf109s of I./JG3 and attack on Do17s south-east of Charleroi 7.30 p.m. Possibly one of those claimed by Hptmn Lützow *(Gruppenkommandeur)* of Stab I./JG3. Adjt Schneider unhurt. Aircraft abandoned.

GR I/14 Potez 63.11 (188). Hit by flak during reconnaissance sortie over Namur and made emergency landing at Maubeuge 10.15 a.m. Lt N. Kervella badly wounded, later died. Sgt Rouch and Sgt Duffaud unhurt. Aircraft damaged but repairable.

GR II/22 Potez 63.11. Returned to Chatel-Chéhéry with starboard engine damaged by flak following reconnaissance sortie over Sedan 12.45 p.m. S/Lt Beau, Adjt Cedruix, and Sgt Fuhrer unhurt. Aircraft repairable.

GR II/22 Potez 63.11 (684). Lost flying speed, stalled and crashed on landing at Vassincourt 8.15 p.m. S/Lt F. Drouet, Adjt J-B. Le Bail, and Sgt Y. Le Cossec killed. Aircraft a write-off.

GR 1/36 Potez 63.11 (173). Badly damaged by flak during long-range reconnaissance sortie and crashed on approach to Martigny airfield. Crashed and burned out at Autigny-la-Tour 2.30 a.m. Lt L. Pierrat and Capt M. Louchard *(Commandant)* killed. Sgt Fèvre badly injured and admitted to hospital where later captured. Aircraft a write-off.

Left: **Following the devastating bombing of the centre of Rotterdam, the will to continue the fight in Holland collapsed. In 1940 the fear of aerial bombardment was coloured by horrific reports from Guernica destroyed in April 1937 during the Spanish Civil War and Warsaw razed in September 1939, although the Dutch figure announced of 30,000 dead was a** gross exaggeration, the actual total being closer to 900. Nevertheless General Henri Winkelman, the Dutch Army Commander-in-Chief, decided to surrender and at 6.30 p.m. on Tuesday evening he sent out instructions to that effect, save for that area in Zeeland which was occupied by a considerable number of French troops. *Right:* **The same view today.**

DUTCH AIR FORCE

1-I-1 Fokker C X (715). Unserviceable aircraft left on withdrawal from Bergen 8.00 a.m. No crew casualties. Aircraft abandoned — later captured.

1-I-1 Fokker C X (706). Returned to Ruigenhoek oil tank damaged by ground-fire over Oostendam after reconnaissance of bridges between Krimpen and Kralingen 12.50 p.m. Sgt R. M. van Luyk unhurt, 2e Lt J. H. M. ten Holder (both of III-2) splinter wound in leg. Aircraft repairable.

1-I-1 Five Fokker C Xs (706, 711, 712, 713 and 714). Aircraft burned at Ruigenhoek to prevent capture 6.40 p.m. No crew casualties. Aircraft write-offs.
The last two of the unit's aircraft escaped west on this day — (700) landed at Calais-Marck, its crew, 1e Lt H. van Linschoten and 2e Lt Jhr. J. E. van Panhuys (both of II-2), reaching England on May 22. The (705) landed on the beach at Zoutelande, eventually reaching Dunkirk on May 15, and was finally abandoned at Mardyck by its crew, 1e Lt E. M. Hoekstra (of II-2) and Kapt C. G. R. van Marcelis Hartsinck (of III-2).

1/2-II-1 Nine Fokker D XXIs (212, 219, 221, 224, 235, 240, 242, 243 and 244), and Fokker D XVII (205). Aircraft burned at Schiphol to prevent capture by enemy forces 5.40 p.m. Aircraft all write-offs.

1/2-II-1 Fokker D XXI (236). Engine thought to have been damaged by Dutch ground-fire during patrol east of Utrecht. Forced-landed at Vleuten near Breukelen and destroyed by the pilot 8.10 a.m. Lt H. B. Sitter (of 2-II-1) unhurt. Aircraft a write-off.

4-II-1 Fokker G 1 (346). Wheel locked on take-off at Schiphol and collided with G-1 (343) causing damage 7.45 a.m. Sgt C. R. Ottes and Sgt J. C. Kentie unhurt. Aircraft damaged but repairable — later abandoned.
This aircraft was one of 26 machines originally ordered for the Spanish Republican Air Force but production was delayed and the war in Spain over before deliveries were made. Fokker then tried to sell them to Finland and Estonia but negotiations failed. In January 1940, the Dutch began accepting delivery of 12 aircraft intended for a new unit 2-V-2, but when Germany invaded not every aircraft was fully armed, three hurriedly fitted with guns being pressed into service with 4-II-1.

4-II-1 Four Fokker G 1s (303, 308, 322 and 325). Serviceable aircraft burned at Schiphol to prevent capture by enemy forces 5.40 p.m. Aircraft all write-offs.

I-2 Three Fokker C Vs (594, 646 and 652), Fokker C X (719), and Koolhoven F.K.51 (407). Aircraft destroyed at De Zilk to prevent capture 7.40 p.m. No crew casualties. Aircraft all write-offs.

III-2 Fokker C V (631). Returned to Ruigenhoek damaged by enemy fighters over Doorn during reconnaissance sortie to Utrecht 1.10 p.m. Sgt N. J. Borgman and 1e Lt A. C. O. Mouthaan (II-2 crew) both unhurt. Aircraft repairable.

III-2 Four Fokker C Vs (593, 605, 621, and 631). Aircraft burned at Ruigenhoek to prevent capture 7.40 p.m. No crew casualties. Aircraft all write-offs.
Two unserviceable Fokker C Vs (615 and 622) and 3 Koolhoven F.K.51s (408, 419 and 426) were also destroyed.

MLD Fokker C VIIIw (5192). Wrecked in take-off accident at Westeinderplas on leaving for France. Crew believed unhurt. Aircraft G-4 a write-off.
Two remaining Fokker C VIIIs at Westeinderplas (5185 G-1 and 5190 G-2), and 3 more from GVT5 at Veere (5191 G-3, 5193 G-5 and 5194 G-6) together with Fokker C XIw (5465 W-14) of GVT3, were all evacuated to Cherbourg this day. On May 22 they flew on to Calshot later moving to Felixstowe. Seven surviving Fokker T VIIIs (5582 R-1, 5636 R-6, 5639 R-7, 5640 R-8, 5641 R-9, 5642 R-10, and 5643 R-11) from Schellingwoude and Westeinderplas also escaped to England where, along with the 5584 R-3 which landed off Brighton on May 10, they would later form 320 Squadron flying with British serials AV958 -AV965.

Left: **At 11.45 a.m. on May 15 the capitulation of the Netherlands was signed in the Rijsoord school where the German** airborne force had established a headquarters. *Right:* **Today a monument outside records an inglorious day in Dutch history.**

With Holland out of the conflict, Belgium would follow suit and lay down its arms two weeks hence. Meanwhile, this crowd of Belgian civilians at St Kruis-Winkel near Ghent were pleased to be pictured with their trophy of war: the remains of the Ju88 from the 1. Staffel of Fernaufklärungsgruppe 121 shot down by pilots of No. 504 Squadron.

BELGIAN AIR FORCE

1/I/1 Fox. Fuel tank hit by ground-fire during reconnaissance sortie over the Albert Canal between Campine and Herentals 3.30 p.m. Hit a high tension cable near Kasterlee and crashed at Lichtaart. Adjt H. de la Batista and S/Lt P. Remy both captured unhurt. Aircraft lost.

3/II/1 Fox (O.46). Wrecked in emergency landing near Herent during transfer flight from Hemiksem to Grimbergen 7.00 a.m. Capt P. Willemaers *(Commandant)* unhurt. Aircraft a write-off.

3/II/2 Firefly IIM. Engine damaged by Belgian ground-fire over Rijmenam and forced-landed at Keerbergen 3.50 p.m. Adjt D. Leroy du Vivier unhurt. Aircraft a write-off.
This aircraft was one of nine of these antiquated biplanes, a 1930 design still serving as advanced trainers, hurriedly pressed into service in an attempt to boost the morale of ground troops.

4/II/2 Fiat CR-42. Damaged in combat with Bf 109s of 8./JG3 over Fleurus and forced-landed at Nivelles 12.55 p.m. Adjt E. Francais unhurt. Aircraft damaged but repairable, later abandoned.

4/II/2 Fiat CR-42. Returned to Nieuwkerken-Waas with damage sustained in combat with Bf 109s of 8./JG3 over Fleurus, north-east of Charleroi 12.55 p.m. Pilot unhurt. Aircraft damaged but repairable, later abandoned.
Six remaining Fiats of 4/II/2 (including R.23, R.24, R.26, R.28 and R.29) were withdrawn two days later flying from Sterreken to Aalter but leaving there for Norrent-Fontes the same evening. They continued flying operations in defence of Chartres airfield, where R.26 was destroyed by bombing on May 19, and R.23 and R.28 also destroyed in bombing by I./KG76 on June 3. The survivors eventually reached Bordeaux-Mérignac where, reinforced by R.31, R.32 and R.33, they were finally overtaken by the German advance.

5/III/3 Battle (T.64). Returned to Aalter badly damaged by enemy and Allied ground-fire during reconnaissance mission in the Leuven — Aarschot — Diest — Tirlemont sector 11.30 a.m. Adjt L. Crooy and Capt P. Burtonboy both unhurt. Aircraft a write-off.

LUFTWAFFE

3.(H)/14 Henschel Hs126. Returned damaged by S/Lt Aquilina of GC II/2 over Wellin during reconnaissance sortie south-east of Dinant 8.40 a.m. Uffz F. Wucherer slightly wounded, observer unhurt. Aircraft repairable.

2.(H)/23 Henschel Hs126. Shot down by F/O Davies of No. 79 Squadron near Jehonville during reconnaissance sortie 7.45 p.m. Uffz F. Dörr reportedly slightly wounded, pilot unhurt. Aircraft a write-off.

1.(F)/121 Junkers Ju88A-1 (0165). Shot down by S/L Parnall, F/O Royce, and P/O van Mentz of No. 504 Squadron during reconnaissance sortie between Brussels and Antwerp. Crashed at St Kruis-Winkel, north-east of Gent, 6.00 a.m. Oberlt H. Spillmann, Oberfw R. Schnegotzki, Uffz W. Colleseus, and Uffz W. Gers killed. Aircraft 7A+BH a write-off.

3.(F)/122 Junkers Ju88A-1. Port engine damaged in attacks by F/O Fowler of No. 615 Squadron during reconnaissance of airfields along north French coast and belly-landed at Aalst 6.15 a.m. Uffz W. Reissmann killed. Fw F. Küttner, Fw E. Lauterbach, and Uffz E. Maxrath captured unhurt. Aircraft F6+BL a write-off.

2.(F)/123 Dornier Do17P (4112). Engaged by Capt Alexandre, Sgt Parent, and Adjt Berland of GC II/2 between Dinant and Namur during reconnaissance mission over north-west Belgium and shot down at Tourinnes-la-Grosse, south of Leuven, 9.00 a.m. Lt G. Pilhofer, Fw W. Alder, and Obergefr R. Blum killed. Aircraft 4U+BK a write-off.

I./JG2 Messerschmitt Bf109E-1. Shot down by S/Lt de Salaberry of GC I/3 in combat north of Sedan 9.20 a.m. Pilot unhurt. Aircraft a write-off.

I./JG2 Messerschmitt Bf109E-1. Shot down by Adjt Octave of GC I/3 in combat north of Sedan 9.20 a.m. Pilot unhurt. Aircraft a write-off.

1./JG2 Messerschmitt Bf109E-1. Badly damaged in combat with Bloch 152s of GC III/10 over Charleroi and belly-landed at Forge-Philippe 7.30 p.m. Possibly that claimed by Sgt Carbon. Leutnant W. Grübel unhurt. Aircraft 7+ a write-off.

Stab III./JG2 Messerschmitt Bf109E-1. Shot down by return fire during attack on Blenheim and abandoned east of Sedan. Lt E. Leie believed baled out unhurt. Aircraft a write-off.

3./JG21 Messerschmitt Bf109E-3. Wrecked in take-off accident at Vogelsang. Pilot believed unhurt. Aircraft a write-off.

I./JG26 2 Messerschmitt Bf109Es. Aircraft reportedly slightly damaged, circumstances not stated. Pilots unhurt. Aircraft both repairable.

II./JG51 Messerschmitt Bf109E-1. Belly-landed at Freiburg due to undercarriage failure. Pilot unhurt. Aircraft repairable.

II./JG52 Messerschmitt Bf109E-1. Belly-landed at Wengerohr, cause not stated. Pilot unhurt. Aircraft damaged but repairable.

4./JG52 Messerschmitt Bf109E-1. Hydraulics believed damaged by return fire from Fairey Battle attacked near Mouzon and overturned on landing at Wengerohr. Feldwebel H. Bauer killed. Aircraft 4 + a write-off.

Stab I./JG53 Messerschmitt Bf109E-3. Shot down in combat with No. 1 Squadron Hurricanes near Sedan 3.45 p.m. Oberlt W. Balfanz wounded. Aircraft a write-off.

I./JG53 Messerschmitt Bf109E-3. Wrecked in crash-landing at Esch, cause not stated. Pilot unhurt. Aircraft a write-off.

1./JG53 Messerschmitt Bf109E-1. Shot down in combat with No. 1 Squadron Hurricanes and crashed at 'Fond de Givonne', between Sedan and Bouillon, 3.45 p.m. Oberfw W. Grimmling killed. Aircraft a write-off.

1./JG53 Messerschmitt Bf109E-4. Collided with No. 139 Squadron Blenheim destroyed in combat over Remilly-Aillicourt 3.40 p.m. Fw A. Stark killed. Aircraft 3 + a write-off.

1./JG53 Messerschmitt Bf109E-3. Damaged in combat with No. 1 Squadron Hurricanes over Sedan 3.45 p.m. and belly-landed near Esch out of fuel. Uffz H. Tzschoppe believed unhurt. Aircraft a write-off.

1./JG53 Messerschmitt Bf109E-1. Damaged in combat with No. 1 Squadron Hurricanes over Sedan 3.45 p.m. and forced-landed at Niederbreisach out of fuel. Uffz Grothen unhurt. Aircraft repairable.

3./JG53 Messerschmitt Bf109E-3. Shot down in combat over Sedan and abandoned south of Bouillon 6.40 p.m. Lt W. Tonne baled out wounded. Aircraft a write-off.

8./JG53 Messerschmitt Bf109E-1. Shot down in combat with No. 1 Squadron Hurricanes west of Buzancy and believed crashed at 'La Gravière' near Doux, south-east of Rethel, 3.35 p.m. Fw J. Kröschel captured unhurt. Aircraft a write-off.

I./JG76 Messerschmitt Bf109E-3. Badly damaged in combat with No. 73 Squadron Hurricanes and wrecked in forced-landing 12.20 p.m. Pilot unhurt. Aircraft a write-off.

1./JG76 Messerschmitt Bf109E-3. Damaged in combat with No. 73 Squadron Hurricanes and belly-landed north of Sedan 11.45 a.m. Possibly that attacked by F/O Paul. Lt R. Ziegler unhurt. Aircraft a write-off.

Oberfeldwebel Walter Grimmling was retrieved from the remains of his Bf109 of 1./JG53, a victim of No. 1 Squadron.

3./JG76 Messerschmitt Bf109E-3. Believed shot down by F/O E. J. Kain of No. 73 Squadron in combat south-west of Neufchâteau and crashed at Pouru-St-Rémy, east of Sedan, 11.45 a.m. Fw W. Lohrer badly wounded, evacuated to hospital in Jamoigne where died of wounds May 16. Aircraft a write-off.

3./JG76 Messerschmitt Bf109E-1. Overturned on landing at Trier-Euren following combat with Hurricanes over Sedan 3.20 p.m. Lt D. Ziehl injured. Aircraft 2 + a write-off.

5./KG1 Heinkel He111. Crashed and burned out near Jülich following direct hit by flak south-west of Philippeville. Oberlt F. Kunkel, Fw E. Jordan, Fw F. Resch, and Uffz H. Holze all slightly wounded. Aircraft a write-off.

7./KG1 Heinkel He111. Returned damaged by AA fire over Arbre, south of Namur. Lt B. Krupczinski wounded admitted to hospital in Giessen. Aircraft repairable.

8./KG1 Heinkel He111. Returned damaged in attack by 11 Moranes of GC III/2 south-east of Philippeville 9.45 a.m. Gefr H. Schmitt killed, rest of crew believed unhurt. Aircraft repairable.

8./KG1 Heinkel He111. Returned both engines damaged in attacks by Sgt Pizon, S/Lt Lansoy, and Sgt Bouttier of GC III/2 east of Hannut 9.45 a.m. Uffz G. Büttner wounded, admitted to hospital in Butzweilerhof, rest of crew believed unhurt. Aircraft repairable.

Stab I./KG2 Dornier Do17Z. Returned damaged by ground-fire during attack on enemy columns north of Varennes. Lt L. Hofer badly wounded, admitted to hospital in Frankfurt. Aircraft repairable.

II./KG2 Dornier Do17Z. Returned damaged by flak near Grandpré during sortie over Vouziers. Crew unhurt. Aircraft repairable.

5./KG2 Dornier Do17Z. Returned damaged by ground-fire near Beaumont-en-Argonne. Uffz W. Häfele killed, rest of crew unhurt. Aircraft repairable.

6./KG2 Dornier Do17Z. Forced-landed near Neufchâteau damaged by flak south of Vouziers. Oberfw J. Spreter wounded, Oberlt G. Czernik and rest of crew unhurt. Aircraft repairable.

6./KG2 Dornier Do17Z. Returned damaged by ground-fire south-west of Sedan. Gefr G. Stein slightly wounded, rest of crew unhurt. Aircraft repairable.

6./KG2 Dornier Do17Z. Returned with crewman injured when MG15 round exploded in the barrel during action south-west of Sedan. Fw O. Liebold slightly wounded. Aircraft undamaged.

6./KG2 Dornier Do17Z. Badly damaged by ground-fire near Bouillon during sortie to Vouziers and forced-landed near Ste-Cécile 5.00 p.m. Oberlt A. Kindler, Oberfw H. Schirmer, and Uffz R. Leitgebel all slightly wounded. Aircraft a write-off.

2./KG27 Heinkel He111P. Returned damaged in attacks by Nos. 85 and 87 Squadron Hurricanes near Tirlemont 9.30 a.m. Uffz E. Mamsch killed, Gefr A. Hüttl slightly wounded, rest of crew unhurt. Aircraft damaged but repairable.

2./KG27 Heinkel He111P. Shot down by Nos. 85 and 87 Squadron Hurricanes over Tirlemont and crash-landed at 'Campagne du Tierse' between Lamontzée and Ville-en-Hesbaye 9.30 a.m. Fw R. Kleff killed. Fw W. Lütje and Obergefr G. Wulf slightly wounded. Lt J. Müller believed unhurt. Aircraft 1G+EK a write-off.

6./KG27 Heinkel He111P. Returned damaged by flak near Charlerois. Uffz J. Schaller and crew believed unhurt. Aircraft 1G+BP damage state not recorded.

7./KG27 Heinkel He111P. Damaged in attacks by Nos. 85 and 87 Squadron Hurricanes during sortie over Leuven and also hit by AA fire. Crash-landed south of Brussels 9.30 a.m. Fw W. Biskupski captured wounded. Uffz W. Heidbüchel, Uffz J. Kerstin, and Gefr A. Klöckner captured unhurt. Aircraft 1G+HR a write-off.

7./KG27 Heinkel He111P. Returned damaged by ground-fire and Nos. 85 and 87 Squadron Hurricanes during low-level reconnaissance between Liège and Leuven 9.30 a.m. Lt H-O. Heinert and crew believed unhurt. Aircraft 1G+ER damaged but repairable.

9./KG27 Heinkel He111P. Belly-landed with engine damaged by ground-fire and attacks by Nos. 85 and 87 Squadron Hurricanes over Leuven 9.30 a.m. Fw E. Heiner and crew believed unhurt. Aircraft a write-off.

9./KG27 Heinkel He111P. Forced-landed near Koersel, north of Hasselt, damaged in attacks by Nos. 85 and 87 Squadron Hurricanes over Leuven 9.30 a.m. Lt K. Häfele badly wounded. Fw O. Löken and rest of crew believed unhurt. Aircraft 1G+CD a write-off.

3./KG30 Junkers Ju88A. Returned damaged following attack on destroyer off Vlissingen. Crew unhurt. Aircraft damage state not recorded.

3./KG51 Junkers Ju88A (4008). Shot down by S/Lt Kawnik of GC III/6 following attack on Dijon airfield and belly-landed 1 km north of Preigney 12.10 p.m. Fw F. Würth, Fw R. Buck, Uffz G. Pfeuffer, and Uffz H. Seidel all captured. Aircraft 9K+EL fired by crew.

3./KG51 Junkers Ju88A. Both engines damaged in attacks by S/Lt Villemin and S/Lt Satge of GC III/6 east of Gray following attack on Dijon airfield 12.00 p.m. Eventually caught fire and abandoned near Zweifalten. Uffz F. Kröll, Uffz K. Schneider, and Gefr P. Holtfurth killed, Flgr K. Hinterhofer injured while baling out and admitted to hospital in Ehingen. Aircraft a write-off.

Stab III./KG51 Heinkel He111H (2648). Both engines damaged in attacks by S/Lt Steunou, Adjt Le Gloan, Sgt de Gervillier, and Sgt Trinel of GC III/6 during photo-reconnaissance over Dijon and crash-landed at Fougerolles 12.30 p.m. Uffz G. Schildt killed. Uffz H. Kazmierowski captured wounded. Oberlt S. Barth, Oberfw H. Matt, and Gefr F. Backhaus captured unhurt. Aircraft 9K+DD a write-off.

III./KG51 Heinkel He111H. Returned damaged in attacks by D520s of GC I/3 during sortie to attack the rail targets near Metz 1.30 p.m. Crew unhurt. Aircraft repairable.

8./KG51 Junkers Ju88A-1. Forced-landed at Neuhausen damaged by D520s of GC I/3 west of Verdun during sortie to attack the rail station at Revigny 1.30 p.m. Flgr F-K. Mayr slightly wounded. Aircraft 9K+CS a write-off.

8./KG51 Heinkel He111H. Starboard engine set alight in attack by D520s of GC I/3 over Ste-Menehould during sortie to attack the rail station at Revigny. Possibly that attacked by S/Lt Salva and S/Lt Potier. Crashed at Hennemont, south of Buzy, 1.25 p.m. Uffz W. Schäkel and Gefr W. Eckrich killed. Uffz V. Schüll, Uffz H. Fischer, and Uffz F. Knoch captured badly wounded, transported to Legouest military hospital in Metz. Aircraft 9K+BS a write-off.

9./KG51 Heinkel He111H. Forced-landed near Mannheim damaged by D520s of GC I/3 west of Verdun during sortie to attack the rail station at Aubréville 1.30 p.m. Gefr J. Heinrich badly wounded. Aircraft 9K+AT repairable.

2./KG53 Heinkel He111H. Hit by flak during sortie to attack rail targets between Dun and Verdun. Collided with Lt Anders aircraft and crashed at Thiaumont 4.30 p.m. Oberlt W. Kögl, Oberfw W. Schmidt, and Fw K. Acker killed. Major K. Wolfien (*Staffelkapitän*) and Fw A. Scherl baled out and captured unhurt. Aircraft a write-off.

2./KG53 Heinkel He111H. Rammed by Oberlt Kögl's damaged aircraft and crashed near Thiaumont 4.30 p.m. Fw W. Völter, and Flgr E. Rotter killed. Uffz E. Benkert, Lt K. Anders and Uffz E. Schmidt baled out and captured unhurt. Aircraft a write-off.

7./KG53 Heinkel He111H. Returned damaged by Capt Accart and Sgt Muselli of GC I/5 over Stenay during sortie to Suippes 10.30 a.m. Gefr H. Meiländer slightly wounded, admitted to hospital in Mannheim. Aircraft damage state not recorded.

I./KG55 Heinkel He111P. Forced-landed at Trier, damaged by No. 501 Squadron Hurricanes during attack on rail targets south of Sedan 10.00 a.m. Crew unhurt. Aircraft damaged but repairable.

I./KG55 Heinkel He111P. Forced-landed near Kreuznach damaged by S/Lt de Salaberry of GC I/3 and Hurricanes of No. 501 Squadron during sortie to attack rail targets south of Sedan 10.00 a.m. Crew unhurt. Aircraft damaged but repairable.

1./KG55 Heinkel He111. Returned damaged by No. 501 Squadron Hurricanes over Vouziers during attack on rail targets south of Sedan 10.00 a.m. Oberfw G. Kiessling and Fw F. Wurm badly wounded. Aircraft damage state not recorded.

7./KG55 Heinkel He111. Returned damaged by AA fire during attack on troops and rail targets near Metz 2.30 p.m. Lt H. Rockenhäuser and Gefr F. Lüdecke wounded by shell splinters. Aircraft repairable.

3./KG76 Dornier Do17Z. Returned damaged by flak during attack on enemy armour between Malmaison and Sissonne, north of Reims 5.40 a.m. Gefr G. Zipfler badly wounded, admitted to hospital in Cologne-Hohenlind. Oberlt W. Stoldt and Lt W. Fichtner slightly wounded. Aircraft damage state not recorded.

3./KG76 Dornier Do17Z. Returned damaged by F/O Orton and Sgt Pilkington of No. 73 Squadron east of Charleville during sortie to attack enemy armoured columns between Malmaison and Sissonne, north of Reims 5.30 a.m. Gefr H. Kohler killed. Gefr K. Hassler slightly wounded. Aircraft damage state not recorded.

5./KG76 Dornier Do17Z. Returned damaged by flak over Philippeville. Uffz F. Gaiser badly wounded, admitted to hospital in Cologne. Aircraft damage state not recorded.

6./KG76 Dornier Do17Z. Returned damaged by ground-fire during attack on enemy armour west of Dinant. Uffz K. Leissl badly wounded, admitted to hospital in Cologne. Oberlt W. Fundinger and rest of crew unhurt. Aircraft F1+CP damage state not recorded.

Stab III./KG76 Dornier Do17Z. Returned damaged by ground-fire following low-level reconnaissance over Macon, west of Chimay. Fw O. Waak slightly wounded. Aircraft damage state not recorded.

7./KG76 Dornier Do17Z. Returned damaged by ground-fire near Philippeville during low-level attack on enemy columns. Fw G. Schewe slightly wounded, admitted to hospital in Bonn. Aircraft damage state not recorded.

1./KGrzbV.9 Junkers Ju52. Destroyed by artillery fire while landing supplies for airfield command at Bierset 7.30 p.m. Fw R. Brennecke wounded. Aircraft 9P+KH a write-off.

V.(Z)/LG1 Messerschmitt Bf110C. Overturned on landing at Wengerohr. Crew unhurt. Aircraft a write-off.

Stab II./LG1 Heinkel He111. Attacked by P/O Stones and Sgt Cartwright of No. 79 Squadron between Enghien and Halle during armed-reconnaissance sortie and forced-landed at Wetteren, south-east of Gent 7.35 p.m. Fw K. Brakmann killed. Fw W. Krüger captured wounded admitted to hospital. Oberlt R. Müllauer and Oberfw H. Oberheide captured unhurt. Aircraft L1+UC a write-off.

Stab II./LG1 Heinkel He111. Attacked by P/O Stones of No. 79 Squadron between Enghien and Halle during armed-reconnaissance sortie and pursued to crash-landing at Boom, south of Antwerp, 7.45 p.m. Oberfw E. Eggert and Fw H. Düvel killed. Oberfw G. Fischer captured wounded and admitted to hospital. Oberlt G. Preub baled out and captured unhurt. Aircraft a write-off.

5./LG1 Heinkel He111. Believed shot down by P/O Appleton No.79 Squadron over Bierghes, south-west of Brussels, and crashed by the road between Enghien and Halle 7.30 p.m. Uffz F. Struwe and Gefr R. Freytag killed. Oberfw E. Weber baled out too low and killed. Fw B. Meining also baled out but parachute failed and fell dead near Haute-Croix. Aircraft L1+FN a write-off.
Site excavated in November 1997 and engines recovered with other major components. Items in Chièvres Air Museum.

9./LG1 Junkers Ju88A-1. Returned damaged in fighter attack over Mons. Uffz E. Krüger badly wounded, admitted to hospital in Wesendorf. Aircraft damage state not recorded.

5.(S)/LG2 Henschel Hs123. Shot down by No. 607 Squadron Hurricanes north of St Germain 10.55 a.m. Uffz K-S. Lückel wounded. Aircraft a write-off.

5.(S)/LG2 Henschel Hs123. Shot down by No. 607 Squadron Hurricanes north of St Germain 10.55 a.m. Lt G. Ritter believed wounded. Aircraft a write-off.

Stabsstaffel StG1 Dornier Do17M. Belly-landed at Dockendorf emergency airfield, north-west of Trier, damaged by No. 1 Squadron Hurricanes over Remilly-Aillicourt during photo-reconnaissance mission 3.45 p.m. Fw F. Fell slightly wounded. Aircraft a write-off.

II./StG2 Messerschmitt Bf108. Engine failed on take-off from Odendorf. Oberlt Steuer injured. Aircraft damaged but repairable.

II./StG2 Junkers Ju87R. Undercarriage failed on landing at Odendorf. Aircraft damaged but repairable.

7./StG51 Junkers Ju87. Returned badly damaged by flak over Torgny, south of Virton. Gefr K. Penninger badly wounded, died same day in Vogelsang hospital. Aircraft a write-off.

Stab I./StG76 Junkers Ju87B. Returned damaged by Bloch 152s of GC II/1 over Chémery, during attack on French armour south of Sedan 10.20 a.m. Major W. Sigel (*Gruppenkommandeur*) slightly wounded, Oberfw H. Herzog killed. Aircraft damaged but repairable.

2./StG76 Junkers Ju87B. Shot down by GC II/1 during attack on French armour south of Sedan and crash-landed near Malmy, between Vendresse and Chémery, 10.20 a.m. Possibly that claimed by Adjt Richardin. Lt K. Olbert and Uffz W. Günthert both wounded. Aircraft a write-off.

A Henschel 123 of 5.(S)/LG2 downed at 'Le Gibet' at Jausselette, east of Perwez, photographed by the late Jean Jauquet. Another Hs123 fell behind the Godechoul Farm on the road to Grand-Rosière-Hottomont, both victims of Hurricanes of No. 607 Squadron.

2./StG76 Junkers Ju87B. Shot down by GC II/1 during attack on French armour south of Sedan and crash-landed near Malmy, between Vendresse and Chémery, 10.20 a.m. Possibly that attacked by S/Lt Belland and Sgt Roquerbe. Pilot unhurt, Uffz W. Losensky badly wounded, later died. Aircraft a write-off.

2./StG76 Junkers Ju87B. Returned damaged by Bloch 152s of GC II/1 in action over Chémery during attack on French armour south of Sedan 10.20 a.m Crew believed unhurt. Aircraft damaged but repairable.

Stab StG77 Junkers Ju87B-2 (5328). Reportedly shot down by flak over Châtillon-sur-Bar, but also possible victim of Nos. 1 and 73 Squadron Hurricanes, following attack on enemy armour south-west of Le Chesne 3.45 p.m. Öberstlt G. Schwartzkopff *(Geschwaderkommodore)* and Fw H. Follmer killed. Aircraft S2+AA a write-off.

A most popular commander known throughout the Luftwaffe as 'Father of the Stukas', Günther Schwartzkopff was an early adherent of the dive-bombing concept and a keen pre-war exponent of the Stuka, perfecting techniques for its use as a close-support weapon. On Göring's order, issued that day, he was to relinquish command and return to a staff appointment in Berlin, but insisted on flying further operations. Post-humously promoted Generalmajor from May 1, his award of the Ritterkreuz followed on November 24.

2./StG77 Junkers Ju87B. Returned damaged in attacks by Nos. 1 and No. 73 Squadron Hurricanes south of Sedan following attack on enemy armour south-west of Le Chesne 3.45 p.m. Gefr H. Weidner badly wounded, admitted to hospital in Eupen. Aircraft repairable.

2./StG77 Junkers Ju87B. Shot down by Nos. 1 and No. 73 Squadron Hurricanes following attack on enemy armour south-west of Le Chesne 3.45 p.m. and crash-landed south of Sedan. Uffz R. Munk and gunner believed unhurt. Aircraft a write-off.

2./StG77 Junkers Ju87B. Shot down by Nos. 1 and 73 Squadron Hurricanes following attack on enemy armour south-west of Le Chesne 3.45 p.m. and crash-landed at Les Grandes-Armoises, south of Sedan. Lt H. Sinn and gunner believed unhurt. Aircraft write-off.

2./StG77 Junkers Ju87B. Believed shot down by P/O Martin of No. 73 Squadron between Singly and Malmy following attack on enemy armour south-west of Le Chesne 3.45 p.m. Oberlt W. Scherzinger killed. Uffz W. Rottländer baled out wounded. Aircraft a write-off.

2./StG77 Junkers Ju87B. Shot down by Nos. 1 and 73 Squadron Hurricanes 6 km south-west of Le Chesne following attack on enemy armour 3.45 p.m. Possibly that attacked by P/O Martin and Sgt Pilkington of No. 73 Squadron. Lt L. Kirchner and Gefr R. Zeilinger killed. Aircraft a write-off.

2./StG77 Junkers Ju87B. Crash-landed south of Le Chesne damaged in attacks by Nos. 1 and 73 Squadron Hurricanes following attack on enemy armour south-west of Le Chesne 3.45 p.m. Uffz J. Schneider and Uffz F. Wöllner both captured wounded. Aircraft a write-off.

Stab I.(St)/TrGr186 Junkers Ju87B. Shot down by No. 3 Squadron Hurricanes in combat over Florenville and crashed between Izel and Chiny 4.25 p.m. Oberlt M. Heyden and Lt H. Cords killed. Aircraft a write-off.

1.(St)/TrGr186 Junkers Ju87B. Shot down by No. 3 Squadron Hurricanes and crashed into 'Bois-la-Dame' at Matton, between Carignan and Florenville, 4.25 p.m. Uffz F. Hemken and Uffz O. Kopania killed. Aircraft a write-off.

1.(St)/TrGr186 Junkers Ju87B. Crash-landed near Malmédy damaged by No. 3 Squadron Hurricanes over Florenville 4.25 p.m. Crew believed unhurt. Aircraft damaged but repairable.

1.(St)/TrGr186 Junkers Ju87B. Crash-landed near Hemweiler damaged in attacks by No. 3 Squadron Hurricanes over Florenville 4.25 p.m. Crew unhurt. Aircraft damaged but repairable.

2.(St)/TrGr186 Junkers Ju87B. Over-turned in forced-landing near Ferschweiler damaged in attacks by No. 3 Squadron Hurricanes over Florenville 4.25 p.m. Crew unhurt. Aircraft damaged but repairable.

2.(St)/TrGr186 Junkers Ju87B. Shot down by No. 3 Squadron Hurricanes over Florenville and crashed between Les-Deux-Villes and Matton 4.25 p.m. Uffz O. Reuss and Uffz E. Hecht killed. Aircraft a write-off.

2.(St)/TrGr186 Junkers Ju87B. Shot down by No. 3 Squadron Hurricanes in action west of Florenville and believed crashed south of Brevilly 4.25 p.m. Fw W. Strehler and Gefr H. Hüsch killed. Aircraft a write-off.

3.(St)/TrGr186 Junkers Ju87B. Shot down in combat with No. 3 Squadron Hurricanes and crashed at Pin, east of Florenville, 4.25 p.m. Oberfhr H-J. Ellerlage and Uffz A. Froese killed. Aircraft a write-off.

1./ZG1 Messerschmitt Bf110C. Returned damaged following combat with French fighters of GC I/1, GC II/1, and GC III/10, 15 km north-east of Braine-l'Alleud 7.15 p.m. Lt W. Schenck unhurt, Uffz J. Kehren slightly wounded. Aircraft repairable.

2./ZG26 Messerschmitt Bf110C. Crashed south of Vogelsang airfield, possibly damaged in combat with French fighters of GC I/1, GC II/1, and GC III/10 east of Chimay 7.00 p.m. Oberlt K. Brückner and Gefr E. König killed. Aircraft a write-off.

2./ZG26 Messerschmitt Bf110C. Returned damaged following combat with French fighters of GC I/1, GC II/1, and GC III/10, east of Chimay 7.15 p.m. Lt H. Heisel slightly wounded. Aircraft damage state not recorded.

6./ZG26 Messerschmitt Bf110C. Believed shot down by Sgt Carbon of GC III/10 in combat over Solre-le-Château and crashed into Bois des Nielles, near 'l Ecrevisse, 7.00 p.m. Lt E. Josten and Uffz J. Stangl killed. Aircraft a write-off.

I./ZG52 Messerschmitt Bf110C. Forced-landed at Wengerohr damaged in combat with H-75s of GC II/5 south of Thionville 4.00 p.m. Possibly that attacked by S/Lt Ruchoux. Crew unhurt. Aircraft damaged but repairable.

I./ZG52 Messerschmitt Bf110C. Forced-landed at Wengerohr engine damaged in combat with H-75s of GC II/5 south of Thionville 4.00 p.m. Possibly that attacked by Sgt Chabera. Crew unhurt. Aircraft damaged but repairable.

1./ZG52 Messerschmitt Bf110C. Both engines set alight under attack by Sgt Salès of GC II/5 in combat south of Thionville and abandoned east of Fameck 4.00 p.m. Fw O. Weckbach baled out too low with damaged parachute and captured badly injured, died May 16. Uffz K. Klaus killed. Aircraft a write-off.

3./ZG52 Messerschmitt Bf110C. Shot down by Sgt Bouhy of GC II/5 in combat south of Thionville and crashed between Clouange and Rombas 4.00 p.m. Oberfw J. Oertel baled out and captured, believed shot and wounded after landing. Uffz W. Mentzel killed. Aircraft a write-off.

Left: **Before the war, Oberstleutnant Günther Schwartzkopff, the commander of Stukageschwader 77, had been instrumental in developing the concept of the Ju87 as a close-support weapon in a future war. His loss was keenly felt throughout the Luftwaffe, but a feather in the caps of No. 1 and 73 Squadrons who are believed to have brought him down.** *Right:* **He lies in the German Military Cemetery at Noyers-Pont-Maugis, just south of Sedan, together with over 25,000 of his countrymen.**

With so much strip farming in the Champagne district of eastern France, no wonder the AASF order of May 14 withdrawing its squadrons stated that 'units must send an advance party to indicate by a smudge fire where the aerodrome is and mark out a landing lane by ground strips'. *Above:* **No. 73 Squadron were initially ordered to Villeneuve-les-Vertus (see map page 26-27) some 35 kilometres south of Reims. Faint traces can still be detected at the top of this photograph taken in 1949.**

Wednesday, May 15

The struggle in the Netherlands, apart from Zuid Beveland and Walcheren, now being over, focus on the German advance switched to northern Belgium where Antwerp was threatened. Contact with enemy units was being reported by the BEF along the entire length of the Dyle positions, particularly heavy enemy pressure being exerted near Wavre where the French 1ème Armée was forced to yield ground. But the German breakthrough was making most alarming progress on a 70-mile front between Namur and Stenay, German armoured spearheads penetrating the Allied defences to a depth of up to 60 miles. Consequently, in accordance with pre-arranged plans to be executed only 'under extreme circumstances', Air Marshal Barratt that night ordered units of No. 67 Wing to move to No. 71 Wing airfields south of the Marne, while No. 76 Wing units retired to landing grounds in south Champagne.

Despite the additional 32 Hurricanes and pilots despatched to France two days before, increasingly urgent requests for further reinforcements continued to be received in London. Only the previous day, the French Prime Minister, Paul Reynaud, had telephoned Churchill asking for ten more squadrons to be sent 'at once' and the Chief of Air Staff, Cyril Newall, was consequently instructed to prepare for their early despatch. But Air Chief Marshal Dowding, most reluctant to divert more precious fighters from the air defence of Great Britain, took a step 'most unusual in military history' and requested he be allowed to state his views before a meeting of the War Cabinet.

To his surprise his request was granted, and during a highly-charged meeting, for news from the Continent was indeed grave, Dowding presented Churchill with figures to show, as he said to the meeting, that 'if the present rate of wastage continues for another fortnight we shall not have a single Hurricane left in France . . . or in this country'. Fortunately adding weight to his argument, the meeting had already agreed that Bomber Command initiate immediate attacks on targets in the Ruhr — thus raising the prospect of retaliatory attacks against Britain. So it was decided, contrary to Churchill's emotional view, but to Dowding's 'inexpressible relief', that 'no further fighter squadrons should, for the present, be sent to France'.

Yet more demands were to be made of Bomber Command for, with AASF Battles now diverted to night operations, it fell to No. 2 Group to undertake daylight missions over France. Thus, 12 Blenheims from Nos. 15 and 40 Squadrons attacked Dinant around 11.00 a.m. — the earliest time that adequate fighter cover could be arranged, and then only by using Nos. 3 and 615 Squadron Hurricanes ordered from the RAF Component area. Enemy fighters operating in strength covered the sector throughout the day and several major fighter actions resulted. Around 3.00 p.m., No. 82 Squadron Blenheims, escorted by Bloch 152s of GC II/1, attacked Monthermé in an effort to slow German passage of the Meuse, and these were shortly followed by four AASF Blenheims from No. 139 Squadron whose chances of survival were obviously rated somewhat higher than those of Fairey Battles. Attacks in and around Monthermé continued throughout the night, AASF Battles operating for the first time in their new role.

German air attacks during the day mainly centred upon rail targets disrupting movement of French reserves to sectors of the front that had collapsed. Communications behind the Allied lines around Ninove, Mons and Ghent, and a dozen or so airfields were also attacked, as was Allied shipping off the Dutch and Belgian coasts.

Two days later the squadron moved again, this time another 35 kilometres further south to Gaye. Although there is an airfield today just south of the village, exhaustive on the spot enquiries by Jean Paul Pallud indicated that the RAF used instead this field to the west, although there are no indications remaining today, even on an aerial photograph, of its former use. That Wednesday evening there was sadness in the Mess of 73 for Newell 'Fanny' Orton had been shot down during the afternoon and was in hospital. He was never to rejoin the squadron.

Pictures of aircraft like this one with no identifying squadron codes, no serial numbers visible, or even a date or location are very frustrating . . . but too good to leave out. This photo could show any one of the dozens of Hurricanes which forced-landed in France in May 1940.

BRITISH AIR FORCES IN FRANCE

1 SQUADRON, BERRY-AU-BAC

Hurricane L1943. Glycol tank set alight in combat with Bf110s of III./ZG26 east of Reims and abandoned over Beine-Nauroy 8.00 a.m. Flying Officer P. H. M. Richey baled out landing near St-Hilaire-le-Grand unhurt. Aircraft a write-off.

Paul Richey's memoirs place this action toward noon but all III./ZG26 claims northwest of Reims, albeit 'Moranes', are timed between 7.36 and 8.06 a.m. Also, the Flugbuch of Ernst Matthes, of 7. Staffel, notes combat with fighters around 7.50 a.m. during the first of three sorties flown this day.

Hurricane. Belly-landed at 'La Pierre Poiret' north of Pontfaverger, engine damaged by return fire from Bf110 of III./ZG26 pursued at low level from Vouziers 8.00 a.m. Flight Lieutenant P. R. Walker unhurt. Aircraft abandoned.

3 SQUADRON, MERVILLE

Hurricane L1610. Forced-landed at Wevelgem during patrol between Sedan and Dinant, probably due to engine failure 4.45 a.m. Squadron Leader P. Gifford unhurt. Aircraft repairable — later abandoned.

Hurricane L1846. Forced-landed at Vitry-en-Artois with starboard tank hit by return fire from Do17 engaged near Dinant 12.00 p.m. Flying Officer C. A. C. Stone unhurt. Aircraft QO⊙B repairable.

Hurricane N2534. Shot down by Bf109s near Maubeuge and possibly that claimed by Uffz Rosen south-east of Fourmies 12.40 p.m. Flight Lieutenant M. M. Carter killed. Aircraft a write-off.

Hurricane N2422. Shot down by Bf109s near Maubeuge and possibly that claimed by Lt Bauer of 2./JG77 1.10 p.m. Pilot Officer N. D. Hallifax captured wounded. Aircraft a write-off.

Likewise this Lysander being inspected by German personnel 'somewhere in France'. Although the 'Lizzie' appears ungainly, she had a top speed of over 200 mph and could be armed with three machine guns and 12 small anti-personnel bombs. The wheel-spat side panels have been removed to prevent the wheels binding.

Hurricane L1645. Believed shot down by Bf109s in combat near Dinant 12.40 p.m. Sergeant J. L. C. Williams missing. Aircraft a write-off.

Possibly occupant of the isolated field grave of an unknown RAF pilot 'killed 15.5.40' located at Corroy-le-Grand who, in 1946, was reinterred at Heverlee, Leuven (Louvain), where date of death is recorded as May 12. Despite post-war investigation by MREU it proved impossible to positively identify the pilot concerned. Three Hurricane pilots remain 'missing' following combats near Namur on this day.

Hurricane. Returned with minor damage following general engagement between Namur and Dinant 12.40 p.m. Sergeant R. Wilkinson slightly wounded. Aircraft repairable.

13 SQUADRON, AUTHIE

Lysander N1260. Crashed outside Bierbeek, near Leuven, during tactical reconnaissance sortie 10.00 a.m. Exact cause unknown but possibly that shot down by Oberlt Fronhöfer of 9./JG26. Pilot Officer A. C. Ollerenshaw and LAC C. F. Lucas killed. Aircraft a write-off.

26 SQUADRON, AUTHIE

Lysander II L4774. Crashed near Arras during reconnaissance sortie 4.45 a.m. Pilot Officer Clegg and Corporal Cassidy believed unhurt. Aircraft a write-off.

53 SQUADRON, POIX

Blenheim IV L9460. Returned slightly damaged by Bf109s during reconnaissance sortie 8.30 a.m. Pilot Officer R. I. C. MacPherson, Sergeant A. T. Moreland, and AC2 S. Robinson unhurt. Aircraft repairable.

Blenheim IV L9399. Shot down by F/L Owen of No. 504 Squadron over Tournai during reconnaissance sortie. Crashed and burned out near Couture de Froyennes, Ramegnies-Chin 8.50 a.m. Pilot Officer P. K. Bone and Sergeant W. J. Cronin killed. LAC J. Bromley missing. Aircraft a write-off.

The body of the gunner, Jack Bromley, was recovered from the molten remains of his aircraft but could not be identified and he was buried as an 'Unknown Airman' in Ramegnies-Chin cemetery.

Blenheim IV L4841. Crash-landed at Vitry damaged by Bf110s during reconnaissance sortie 9.15 a.m. Pilot Officer P. F. C. Villiers-Tuthill, Sergeant A. H. Payne, and LAC D. B. Mearns unhurt. Aircraft repairable.

Blenheim IV L4847. Damaged in attack by F/O E. J. Kain of No. 73 Squadron on return from photo-reconnaissance sortie 9.30 a.m. Flight Lieutenant B. B. St G. Daly, Sergeant W. R. B. Currie, and AC2 P. J. Blandford unhurt. Aircraft damaged but repairable.

59 SQUADRON, POIX

Blenheim IV. Shot down during strategic reconnaissance sortie between Dinant and Celles and crashed near Gembes 7.45 a.m. Flying Officer M. I. Murdoch captured. Sergeant C. A. Morgan killed. Aircraft a write-off.

73 SQUADRON, REIMS-CHAMPAGNE

Hurricane P2579. Shot down in combat with Bf110s of 6./ZG76 over Vouziers 2.30 p.m. Flying Officer N. Orton baled out at 600 feet, wounded in shoulder and burned, admitted to hospital in Bétheniville. Aircraft TP⊙J write-off.

Hurricane. Forced-landed at La Ferté damaged in combat with Bf110s of 6./ZG76 over Vouziers 2.30 p.m. Sergeant L. Y. T. Friend unhurt. Aircraft repairable — returned next day.

Hurricane. Returned with oil and glycol tanks badly damaged by crossfire from Do17s engaged south of Reims 6.40 p.m. Sergeant L. S. Pilkington unhurt. Aircraft damaged but repairable.

Hurricane L1693. Glycol, oil, and petrol tanks riddled by return fire during attack on Do17s near Reims 6.50 p.m. Sergeant L. J. W. Humphris baled out badly wounded in leg. Aircraft TP⊙K a write-off.

Hurricane P3279. Replacement aircraft hit a partially filled bomb crater and tipped up on landing damaging airscrew. P/O R. Ferguson (of No. 4 Continental Ferry Flight) unhurt. Aircraft repairable.

85 SQUADRON, LILLE-SECLIN

Hurricane P2818. Shot down in combat with Bf110s of 5./ZG26 during offensive patrol between Ath and Namur 1.15 p.m. Flying Officer D. H. Allen baled out unhurt. Aircraft a write-off.

Hurricane. Shot down in combat with Bf110s of 5./ZG26 during offensive patrol between Ath and Namur. Crash-landed on fire and burned out 1.15 p.m. Flying Officer T. G. Pace evacuated to hospital in England badly burned. Aircraft a write-off.

Hurricane L1775. Shot down in combat with Bf110s of 5./ZG26 during offensive patrol between Ath and Namur 1.15 p.m. Pilot Officer J. H. Ashton baled out unhurt. Aircraft a write-off.

87 SQUADRON, LILLE-MARCQ

Hurricane P2538. Believed that claimed by Lt Müncheberg of Stab III./JG26 over Overijse during action south-east of Brussels 12.00 p.m. Pilot Officer T. J. Edwards missing. Aircraft a write-off.
Possibly the aircraft excavated at Huldenberg by the Belgian Air Museum on September 11, 1982, when a shattered Rolls Royce Merlin engine was recovered along with undercarriage legs, instrument panel and fragments of fuselage and wings. Fragmentary human remains were also found together with the remains of a parachute and a pilot's boot and map but nothing to positively establish identity. Roland Beamont's autobiography Against the Sun (1955) records that 'an identity bracelet delivered by Royal Engineers confirmed the end of Taffy Edwards'. Relics from the excavation now held in the reserve collection of the Belgian Air Museum at Vissenaken.

103 SQUADRON, BÉTHENIVILLE

Battle K9404. Destroyed on the ground when bomb-load exploded during attack by Do17s of 5./KG3 7.30 a.m. No crew casualties. Aircraft a write-off.

218 SQUADRON, AUBÉRIVE-SUR-SUIPPES

Two Battles L5192, P2192. Damaged or unserviceable aircraft abandoned on withdrawal to Moscou-Ferme. No crew casualties. Aircraft HA⊙P and HA⊙E abandoned.
Other machines also abandoned may have included K9251 HA⊙K, K9256, K9273 HA⊙R, and P2189 — all aircraft the squadron reported 'lost in France' that do not appear elsewhere in our loss lists.

No. 218 Squadron had orders to move back from their aerodrome at Aubérive-sur-Suippes (30 kilometres north of Châlons-en-Champagne) to la Ferme de Moscou, closer to Aubérive, leaving behind the lame ducks. These are just two of them: HA⊙E (P2192) *(above)* and HA⊙K (K9251) *(below)*.

501 SQUADRON, BÉTHENIVILLE

Hurricane L1866. Damaged in landing accident following attack on Do17s of II./KG3 near Vouziers 8.30 a.m. Sergeant R. C. Dafforn unhurt. Aircraft SD⊙P repairable — abandoned next day.

Hurricane L2045. Returned badly damaged by return fire following attack on Do17s of II./KG3 near Vouziers 8.30 a.m. Sergeant Proctor unhurt. Aircraft SD⊙A damaged but repairable.

504 SQUADRON, LILLE-MARCQ

Hurricane. Lost bearings and forced-landed at St Simon-Clastres, south-west of St Quentin. Pilot Officer J. R. Hardacre unhurt. Aircraft repairable.

607 SQUADRON, VITRY-EN-ARTOIS

Hurricane P2870. Believed shot down by Hptmn Mölders (Gruppenkommandeur) of Stab III./JG53 near Charleville during cover mission for Blenheims between Givet and Dinant 12.00 p.m. Possibly also attacked by Oberlt Wittenberg. Squadron Leader L. E. Smith missing. Aircraft a write-off.

Hurricane P2619. Crash-landed following attack on He111s of 9./KG51 north-east of Reims 6.35 p.m. Flying Officer J. B. Russell slightly wounded, evacuated to UK. Aircraft AF⊙D a write-off.

Hurricane. High-speed landing without flaps due to damage by return fire from He111s of 9./KG51 engaged north-east of Reims 6.35 p.m. Pilot Officer H. P. Dixon unhurt. Aircraft AF⊙A repairable.

615 SQUADRON, VITRY-EN-ARTOIS

Hurricane P2622. Set alight in combat with Bf109s over Dinant during escort sortie for Blenheims. Possibly that claimed by Oberlt Eckerle (Staffelkapitän) of 3./JG76 11.00 a.m. Flying Officer H. N. Fowler baled out unhurt, joined French troops, but later captured. Aircraft a write-off.
An inveterate escapee, Bill Fowler escaped from Colditz in September 1942 eventually reaching Gibraltar via Spain. On his return to England he was awarded a Military Cross.

Hurrricane P2554. Hit by ground-fire during attack on Hs126 of 1.(H)/23 over Wavre and abandoned near Waterloo 4.00 p.m. Pilot Officer D. J. Looker baled out but hit tailplane and badly injured left leg. Aircraft a write-off.

With the loss of another 16 Hurricanes, the attrition rate was such that Fighter Command would cease to exist within eight to ten weeks. Yet the French had demanded that another ten squadrons be sent to France but Air Chief Marshal Dowding's strong objections 'against sending any fighters out of the country' were heeded and the British War Cabinet decided to send the equivalent of only four. Meantime, French losses were mounting. In this picture the remains of Potez 63.11, serial 223 of GAO 502, lies scattered on the airfield at Villers-lès-Guise. French observation and reconnaissance units paid a high price for the intelligence they gathered this day, nine of their aircraft falling to fighters and ground-fire with seven aircrew killed and another six captured.

UK-based aircraft lost or damaged on operations over the Western Front:

RAF BOMBER COMMAND

15 Squadron, Wyton
Communications at Dinant:

Blenheim IV L8856. Damaged by AA fire over the target. Propeller fell off during return flight, forced-landed in Grote Boom Polder, near Sint-Kruis, 11.15 a.m. P/O D. S. R. Harriman, Sgt J. R. Stanford, LAC Moorhouse unhurt. Aircraft abandoned.

40 Squadron, Wyton
Communications at Dinant:

Blenheim IV N6217. Shot down by Lt Haberland of 1./JG3 over Ecaussinnes-d'Enghien, north-west of Charleroi, 11.32 a.m. W/C E. C. Barlow, Sgt E. Clarke, LAC A. E. Millard killed. Aircraft lost.

Blenheim IV P4913. Shot down by Lt Sprenger of 1./JG3 near Ecaussinnes-d'Enghien, north-west of Charleroi, 11.32 a.m. F/O J. E. Edwards, Sgt C. T. White, LAC S. J. Johnson killed. Aircraft lost.

FRENCH AIR FORCE

E2 Breguet 'Bizerte' (30). Ditched due to engine failure and capsized under tow 90 miles south of Pointe de Penmarch. Wreck washed ashore two days later. Crew rescued unhurt. Aircraft 4 a write-off.

GAO 502 Potez 63.11 (223). Crippled by enemy fire during reconnaissance mission; crashed and burned out on landing at Villers-lès-Guise 7.30 a.m. Adjt Ratel, S/Lt Reverse, and Sgt Deremont unhurt. Aircraft a write-off.

GAO 502 Potez 63.11 (329). Returned to Villers-lès-Guise severely damaged and with fuel tanks holed by enemy fire 5.00 p.m. Cmdt. Rochard (*Commandant*), Sgt E. Bizet, and Sgt Nass unhurt. Aircraft destroyed on evacuation next day.

GAO 504 Potez 63.11 (388). Damaged by flak between Gembloux and Namur during low-level reconnaissance of roads south of Brussels 6.30 a.m. Tried to reach Allied lines but attacked by Bf109s and crash-landed at 'Champ de Maubeuge', Mignault. Capt J. de Montal killed. Sgt A. Chevalier and Sgt H. Soutif captured badly wounded. Aircraft a write-off.

GAO 510 2 Potez 63.11. Unserviceable aircraft left at Attigny on withdrawal to Suippes. No crew casualties. Aircraft both abandoned.

GAO 518 Potez 63.11 (601). Landed at Châtel-Chéhéry badly damaged in attacks by Bf109s during reconnaissance sortie over Malandry, south of Carignan. S/Lt J. Arino wounded in head and died en route to hospital. S/Lt Amarger wounded. Lt Monel unhurt. Aircraft a write-off.

GAO 546 Potez 63.11 (584). Shot down by Oberlt Führing of Stab I./JG77 south of Gerpinnes during reconnaissance sortie. Crashed and burned out on the road to Morialmé at St-Aubin 7.35 p.m. Lt Pradelle and Cpl Revelli wounded. Capt Compin unhurt. Aircraft a write-off.

GAO 1/551 Potez 63.11 (681). Shot down by Lt Temme of Stab I./JG2 during reconnaissance sortie over Raucourt-et-Flaba. Crashed and exploded in woods 2 km northwest of Vendresse 3.00 p.m. Capt J. Riesser killed. Lt H. Lebel baled out mortally wounded. Sgt L. Lombard captured wounded. Aircraft a write-off.
The pilot of this aircraft, Capitaine Jean Riesser, was originally buried alongside the wreckage of his machine but exhumed in March 1941 and re-interred in the nearby cemetery at Vendresse.

GAO 3/551 Potez 63.11 (389). Forced-landed badly damaged by Bf109s and destroyed in strafing attacks. Lt Lieb badly wounded. Lt Bragadir and Cpl Burcelin unhurt. Aircraft a write-off.

GAO 552 Potez 63.11 (606). Crashed at St-Nicolas shortly after take-off from St Omer-Wizernes due to engine failure 4.30 a.m. Lt de Villancourt injured, rest of crew unhurt. Aircraft a write-off.

GB II/12 2 LeO 451 (90, and 122). Returned with minor flak damage following attack on enemy troop concentrations east of Monthermé 6.45 p.m. Crews unhurt. Aircraft both repairable.
These aircraft from GB I/31 had flown in to Lézignan to reinforce Groupement No. 6 that morning.

GC 3/1 Bloch 152 (164). Shot down in combat with Bf109s of 3./JG53 during bomber escort sortie, and possibly that claimed by Oberfw Kuhlmann. Crashed in the Château-Regnault forest, at Les Woieries, 3 km northeast of Monthermé 3.10 p.m. Sgt R. Munier killed. Aircraft a write-off.
Capitaine Victor Veniel, Commandant of 3/1, claimed a Bf109 at this location during the combat but no such loss has been traced. The German unit involved did report the loss of two aircraft and another damaged, all due to petrol shortage, and possibly following this action. One of these may have been that attacked by Capitaine Veniel who then mistakenly witnessed the crash of his wingman René Munier.

GAO 502 left a second Potez on the airfield: this is the debris of machine 329.

GC 3/1 Bloch 152 (189). Shot down in combat with Bf109s near Monthermé during bomber escort sortie, possibly that claimed by Oberlt Lippert *(Staffelkapitän)* of 3./JG53. Crashed at La Neuville-aux-Haies, in the Bois de Fays 3.13 p.m. Adjt R. Autier killed. Aircraft a write-off.

GC 3/1 Bloch 152 (122). Badly damaged in combat with Bf109s during bomber escort sortie over Monthermé and forced-landed between the lines at 'Les-Petits-Hays', Raillimont, outside Rozoy-sur-Serre 3.22 p.m. Possibly that claimed by Lt Haase of 3./JG53. Lt Brun bruised left foot. Aircraft destroyed to prevent capture.

GC 3/1 Bloch 152. Returned to Laon-Couvron badly damaged in combat with Bf109s during bomber escort sortie over Monthermé 3.25 p.m. Possibly that attacked by Lt Haase of 3./JG53. Capt V. Veniel *(Commandant)* unhurt. Aircraft damaged but repairable.

GC II/2 Morane 406. Returned to Laon-Chambry seriously damaged by ground-fire following reconnaissance sortie over Liesse and Montcornet 4.00 p.m. Adjt R. Bricart unhurt. Aircraft damaged but repairable.

GC II/2 Morane 406. Returned to Laon-Chambry with wings badly damaged by ground-fire following reconnaissance sortie over Montcornet 7.40 p.m. S/Lt R. Milhiet unhurt. Aircraft damaged but repairable.

GC 5/2 Morane 406 (195). Shot down by Bf110s of III./ZG26 and crashed at 'La Petite Rue', Clairfontaine, 15 km south of Avesnes 8.00 a.m. Sgt H. d'Achon wounded. Aircraft a write-off.

GC 5/2 Morane 406 (1067). Damaged in attack by Bf110s of III./ZG26 and crash-landed at Mont-Dourlers, north-west of Sars-Poteries 8.00 a.m. Adjt R. Prenez slightly wounded. Aircraft a write-off.

GC 6/2 Morane 406 (750). Shot down by Bf110s of III./ZG26 and crashed at 'Trieux du Diable', Clairfayts, south-east of Solre-le-Château 8.00 a.m. S/Lt P. Voyer baled out unhurt. Aircraft a write-off.

GC I/3 Dewoitine 520 (115). Damaged by return fire from Do17 of KG2 engaged west of Ste-Menehould: belly-landed south of Soissons 7.30 a.m. S/Lt J. Parisse unhurt. Aircraft 8 destroyed to prevent capture.

GC I/3 Dewoitine 520. Engine damaged by return fire from Do17 engaged near Rethel and crash-landed at Beugneux, south of Soissons 7.45 a.m. S/Lt Boutarel unhurt. Aircraft 15 abandoned.

GC 1/3 Dewoitine 520 (124). Returned damaged in combat with Bf110s of III./ZG26 over Reims 8.00 a.m. Lt Lacombe *(Commandant)* unhurt. Aircraft repairable.

GC I/3 Dewoitine 520 (70). Returned damaged in combat with Bf110s of III./ZG26 over Reims 8.00 a.m. Sgt Bouffier unhurt. Aircraft 5 repairable.

GC I/3 Dewoitine 520. Damaged by return fire during attack on enemy bomber and forced-landed near Rethel 8.00 a.m. Adjt L. Bourbon unhurt. Aircraft abandoned.

GC I/3 Dewoitine 520 (122). Shot down in combat with Bf110s of III./ZG26 over Reims. Crash-landed with engine on fire and burned out opposite Fort de la Pompelle, near Wez-Thuisy 8.00 a.m. S/Lt É. Thierry unhurt. Aircraft 13 a write-off.

GC I/3 Dewoitine 520. Damaged in combat with Bf109s during escort sortie for Potez 63.11 of GR II/52 north of Namur and forced-landed in Belgium 1.45 p.m. Possibly that attacked by Lt Benz of 3./JG77. Sgt R. Barberis believed unhurt. Aircraft abandoned.

GC I/3 Dewoitine 520. Damaged in combat with Bf109s during escort sortie for Potez 63.11 of GR II/52 north of Namur and forced-landed in Belgium 1.45 p.m. Possibly that attacked by Fw Fleischhacker of 3./JG77. S/Lt M. Madon believed unhurt. Aircraft abandoned.

GC I/3 Dewoitine 520 (98). Shot down by Bf109s during escort sortie for Potez 63.11 of GR II/52 north of Namur 1.45 p.m. Possibly one of those claimed by Lt Hauck of 3./JG77. Crashed and burned out in woods at Cochenée, between Belvaux and Soulme, south-east of Dinant. Sgt A-P. Bellefin killed. Aircraft a write-off.

GC I/3 Dewoitine 520 (94). Shot down by Bf109s during escort sortie for Potez 63.11 of GR II/52 north of Namur 1.45 p.m. Possibly that claimed by Uffz Wilhelm of 3./JG77. Crashed and burned out in Champ Nicolas, alongside the road to Surice, at Latinne, south-east of Dinant. Sgt L. Rigalleau killed. Aircraft a write-off.

GC I/3 Dewoitine 520. Set alight in combat with Bf109s during escort sortie for Potez 63.11 of GR II/52 north of Namur and abandoned over Gochenée, near Dinant 1.45 p.m. Possibly that claimed by Oberlt Priebe of 2./JG77. Adjt A. Combette baled out and captured badly burned. Aircraft a write-off.

GC II/4 Curtiss H-75. Returned to Orconte badly damaged by Bf109s of 6./JG52 during attack on Do17s of III./KG2 south-east of Dinant 11.33 a.m. S/Lt C. Plubeau unhurt. Aircraft damaged but repairable.

GC 4/4 Curtiss H-75. Returned to Orconte fuel tank damaged by Bf109s of 6./JG52 during attack on Do17s of III./KG2 south-east of Dinant 11.33 a.m. Lt M. Vinçotte unhurt. Aircraft damaged but repairable.

GC II/5 Curtiss H-75 (180). Shot down by return fire from He111 of III./KG55 near Piennes and abandoned north-west of Briey 6.00 a.m. Capt G. Portalis baled out and fired at by French troops; admitted to hospital wounded in thigh. Aircraft a write-off.

GC II/5 Curtiss H-75 (145). Hit by return fire from He111 of III./KG55 and abandoned near Piennes 6.00 a.m. Adjt P. de Montgolfier baled out wounded and admitted to hospital. Aircraft a write-off.

GC II/6 Morane 406. Landed at Reims engine damaged by return fire from I./KG76 engaged over Nivelles 12.30 p.m. Cmdt. Fontanet *(Groupe Commandant)* unhurt. Aircraft repairable.

GC II/6 Morane 406 (75). Shot down by return fire from Do17 of I./KG76 engaged north-east of Maubeuge and abandoned over Elesmes 12.30 p.m. Sgt P. de Bremond d'Ars baled out unhurt. Aircraft a write-off.

GC II/6 Morane 406. Oil tank hit by return fire from Do17s of I./KG76 engaged north-east of Maubeuge; forced-landed before reaching base 12.30 p.m. Adjt A. Deniau unhurt. Aircraft abandoned.

GC III/7 Morane 406 (168). Hit by return fire during attack on Do17s of I./KG2 over Verdun and abandoned north of the Argonne, near Vouziers 8.15 a.m. Lt R. Challe baled out seriously wounded in chest and admitted to hospital. Aircraft a write-off.

GC III/7 Morane 406 (837). Shot down in combat with Bf109s of I./JG3 south-east of Charleroi 12.15 p.m. Possibly that claimed by Lt Bock of 3./JG3. Crashed and burned out beside the road from Morialmé to Florennes, near St-Aubin, 6 km north-east of Philippeville. Lt P. Costey killed. Aircraft a write-off.

A small monument dedicated to the memory of Paul Costey was erected at the crash site in May 1990.

GC III/7 Morane 406 (231). Shot down in combat with Bf109s of I./JG3 south-east of Charleroi 12.20 p.m. Possibly that claimed by Uffz Vollmer of 3./JG3. Crashed and burned out at Pont du Diable, near Somzée, 11 km north of Philippeville. Sgt R. Morlot killed. Aircraft a write-off.

GC III/7 Morane 406 (153). Shot down in combat with Bf109s of I./JG3 and abandoned near Charleroi 12.20 p.m. Possibly that claimed by Hptmn Lützow *(Gruppenkommandeur)* of Stab I./JG3. Sgt C. Boyer baled out unhurt. Aircraft a write-off.

This memorial was dedicated in 1990 to the memory of Lieutenant Paul Costey of GC III/7 who lost his life on this spot just after midday on May 15.

GC III/7 Morane 406. Crash-landed at Soissons damaged in combat with Bf109s of I./JG3 south-east of Charleroi. 12.15 p.m. Sgt A. Moulènes slightly wounded by shell splinters in arm. Aircraft a write-off.

GC III/7 Morane 406 (230). Shot down in combat over Reims 12.20 p.m. Sgt Deshons admitted to hospital with serious head wound. Aircraft a write-off.

GC II/10 Bloch 152 (100). Crash-landed at Laon-Couvron badly damaged by Bf110s during attack on He111s between Marle and Sissonne 1.55 p.m. Adjt Souche believed unhurt. Aircraft a write-off.

GC III/10 Bloch 152 (131). Forced-landed near Athies-sous-Laon out of fuel following routine patrol over Sissonne 4.00 p.m. Adjt E. Muller unhurt. Aircraft abandoned.

GR I/14 Potez 63.11 (192). Severely damaged by flak during reconnaissance sortie between Liège and Namur 6.00 a.m. Crash-landed at Kortenberg, outside Brussels-Evere airfield, ripping off undercarriage and starboard engine. Sgt Castres wounded. Lt Delaunay badly wounded in legs; admitted to hospital in Ostend where later captured. Sgt Bernet baled out unhurt near Waterloo and held by British troops. Aircraft a write-off.

GR II/22 Potez 63.11. Brakes failed on landing at Vassincourt following transit flight from Chatel-Chéhéry. Cmdt. Barruet and crew unhurt. Aircraft damaged but repairable.

GR II/22 Potez 63.11 (258). Shot down on reconnaissance sortie over Attigny and Stonne a.m. Crashed and burned out at 'La Crête', Sauville, 5 km north-east of Le Chesne. S/Lt M. Lechevrel, Adjt G. Lemoine, and Sgt C. Steildé killed. Aircraft a write-off.

GR II/52 Potez 63.11 (439). Hit by flak during reconnaissance sortie over Dinant and belly-landed at Sémeries, 5 km east of Avesnes. Capt Dudezert, S/Lt Bourhis, and Cpl Aperce unhurt. Aircraft a write-off.

BELGIAN AIR FORCE

1/I/1 Fox (O.64). Hit by ground-fire over Herenthals bridge during reconnaissance sortie and crash-landed near Olen. Lt L. Vandercruyssen evaded capture and reached the Belgian lines at Itegem but overtaken by the German advance and captured wounded — admitted to hospital at Mol. Sgt J. Beelen killed. Aircraft lost.

1/I/1 Fox (O.48). Shot down during reconnaissance sortie over the Albert Canal and crashed near Herentals. S/Lt P. de Theux de Meylandt et Montjardin and Lt E. Dierickx both badly wounded, admitted to hospital in Puurs. Aircraft lost.

1/I/1 Fox (O.8). Hit in fuel tank by AA fire during reconnaissance sortie and overturned in forced-landing south of Herentals 6.10 a.m. Adjt M. Brosteaux and S/Lt E. Bossiroy unhurt, evaded capture and reached the Belgian lines at Bouwel. Aircraft a write-off.

1/I/1 Fox. Returned to Hingene damaged by ground-fire during low-level reconnaissance over the Albert Canal 1.30 p.m. Sgt L. Bastin unhurt. Adjt E. Theysen wounded in rump. Aircraft repairable.

This Potez 63.11 of GR I/14 was on a reconnaissance flight over eastern Belgium when it was hit by anti-aircraft fire and made an emergency landing close to Evere aerodrome at Brussels. It was just an hour after this machine came down that the French Prime Minister Paul Reynaud telephoned Churchill in London telling him that the French counter-attack against the Germans at Sedan had failed and that 'the road to Paris was open'. Worse still, he was already saying that the battle was lost and openly spoke of 'giving up the struggle'.

3/II/1 Fox (O.15). Returned to Grimbergen badly damaged by ground-fire during reconnaissance sortie between Antwerp and Leuven 3.00 p.m. Sgt A. Blanco and Lt G. Desmeth both wounded admitted to hospital in Aalst. Aircraft abandoned on withdrawal to Maldegem next day.

3/II/1 Fox (O.32). Radiator damaged by ground-fire during reconnaissance sortie between Antwerp and Leuven 3.00 p.m. Overturned forced-landing near Sint-Katelijne-Waver. Sgt H. Bailly and Lt R. Ghyssels unhurt. Aircraft destroyed by crew.

7/IV/1 Fox. Unserviceable aircraft abandoned at Piéton. No crew casualties. Aircraft destroyed to prevent capture.

The remnants of 7/IV/1 were subsequently withdrawn to Tours from where they would continue flying operations until May 26.

9/V/1 Renard R-31(N.8). Returned to Hemiksen hit by ground-fire during reconnaissance over the Albert Canal 6.25 a.m. Adjt G. Salmon and S/Lt L. Fontaine unhurt. Aircraft repairable.

9/V/1 Renard R-31(N.16). Overshot runway and crashed into woods at Nieuwkerken-Waas 2.50 p.m. Sgt A. Mathieu unhurt. Aircraft a write-off.

9/V/1 Renard R-31(N.3). Returned to Hemiksen starboard wing badly damaged by AA fire over St Lenaerts following reconnaissance sortie over the Albert Canal 5.00 p.m. Adjt L. Boël and Lt G. Vanderbeck both unhurt. Aircraft disabled and abandoned.

5/III/3 Fox. Brought down by British ground-fire at Wezembeek during reconnaissance south of Brussels 6.30 a.m. Adjt A. Wetz and S/Lt R. Verlaine (of 5/III/2) both unhurt. Aircraft lost.

7/III/3 Fox (O.135). Shot down by AA fire during return from reconnaissance of the Antwerp-Breda sector and crash-landed near Hoogerheide 3.40 p.m. where crew came under fire from German infantry. Capt A. Maquet captured unhurt. Sgt J. de Thibault de Boesinghe captured badly wounded; died in hospital at Kleve on July 25. Aircraft a write-off.

7/III/3 Fox (O.185). Shot down by ground-fire during attack on German columns, crashed and burned out near Van Tilt Farm, Holsbeek 3.40 p.m. Sgt A. Soete and Capt G. de Briey baled out too low and killed. Aircraft lost.

In 1942, a memorial to these airmen was erected near the crash site alongside the Leuven road.

The burned-out wreckage of Sergent Albert Mathieu's Belgian Air Force Renard R.31 which came to grief after he overshot the runway and crashed at Nieuwkerken-Waas.

The death of Capitaine Count Guillaume de Briey was a bitter blow to the Belgians. His Fox, serial O.185, was hit by fire from the ground and both he and his observer/gunner, Sergent Albert Soete, baled out too low, striking the ground near the Van Tilt family château — the Kasteel van Hors — at Holsbeek, five kilometres north-east of Leuven.

Above: Here two men died for their country. *Right:* During the war a memorial to the two airmen was erected alongside the Leuvensebaan, next to a later monument to two sons of the Van Tilt family (their château lies in the background) who were executed by the Nazis in Breendonk prison (see *After the Battle* No. 51).

This sequence of British official photographs is a good example of the difficulty of identifying particular aircraft pictured during the Battle of France. They were taken by Mr Putnam of the War Office staff on May 12 so one might readily assume they show a crash on that date. The brief caption released with the pictures simply said: 'Wreckage of a Heinkel bomber brought down by a British anti-aircraft battery near Tournai [in Belgium]' yet one wartime caption changes this to 'French anti-aircraft units' and claimed that it 'crashed on French soil'.

LUFTWAFFE

1.(H)/10 Henschel Hs126. Attacked by seven Curtiss H-75s of GC I/5 during reconnaissance sortie south-east of Sedan and crashed at Lamouilly, north of Stenay, 10.50 a.m. Lt H. Kirschke and Uffz A. Wustmann killed. Aircraft a write-off.

2.(F)/11 Dornier Do17P (2419). Shot down during reconnaissance sortie from Courtrai to Charleroi and crashed at Mechelen and possibly that attacked by F/L Voase Jeff and P/O Beamont of No. 87 Squadron near Leuven 7.00 p.m. Uffz F. Höfer and Uffz J. Deutschle killed. Fw R. Karsten baled out and captured wounded. Aircraft 6M+LK a write-off.

3.(H)/12 Henschel Hs126. Believed shot down by ground-fire during observation sortie near Antwerp. Lt H. Hagans killed, Oberlt Dahinden wounded. Aircraft a write-off.

4.(H)/13 Henschel Hs126. Returned damaged by ground-fire during observation sortie. One crewman wounded. Aircraft damage state not recorded.

1.(H)/14 Henschel Hs126. Returned engine damaged and believed that attacked by Capt Guieu, S/Lt Baptizet, and Sgt Casenobe of GC II/4 over the Forêt de Signy-l'Abbaye 2.30 p.m. Oberlt Bues and Lt Matthes believed unhurt. Aircraft damaged but repairable.

3.(H)/14 Henschel Hs126. Returned damaged by ground-fire during observation sortie. Oberlt Bertram wounded. Aircraft damage state not recorded.

4.(F)/14 Dornier Do17P. Starboard engine set alight in attacks by Capt Coutaud, Sgt Coader, Sgt Teillet, and Cpl Pipa of GC I/1 north-east of Chimay, and crashed into woods near Givet 10.10 a.m. Oberfw O. Führer captured wounded, admitted to hospital Royallieu in Compiègne. Oberlt G. von Symonski and Fw A. Sommerla captured unhurt. Aircraft a write-off.

4.(H)/22 Henschel Hs126. Forced-landed north-west of Gembloux badly damaged in attacks by F/L Thornley, P/O Jackson, and P/O Looker of No. 615 Squadron during observation sortie over Leuven 3.30 p.m. Lt H. Ricke slightly wounded admitted to hospital in Tirlemont. Aircraft a write-off.

1.(H)/23 Henschel Hs126. Shot down during observation sortie north of Gembloux and believed crashed between Perwez and Orbais. Possibly that claimed by F/O Horne of No. 615 Squadron 4.00 p.m. Lt K-H. Küster died May 19. Lt F. Hach killed. Aircraft a write-off.

2.(H)/31 Henschel Hs126. Believed shot down by ground-fire during observation near Beaumont. Crew unhurt. Aircraft a write-off.

Stab Koluft Gruppe von Kleist Fieseler Fi56C. Wrecked in landing accident at Bellevaux, cause not stated. Kanonier R. Vorreiter badly injured. Aircraft a write-off.
This aircraft was engaged in preparing a suitable landing ground alongside the road between Aubigny-les-Pothées and Rozoy-sur-Serre for urgent supplies of petrol for 6. Panzer-Division to be flown in by Junkers Ju52s of III./KGzbV.1 over the next two days.

I./JG2 Messerschmitt Bf109E-1. Crashed on landing at Bastogne, cause not stated. Pilot unhurt. Aircraft damaged but repairable.

7./JG2 Messerschmitt Bf109E. Damaged in combat with Moranes and forced-landed at Ferschweiler. Oberfw H. Klee wounded. Aircraft repairable.

9./JG26 Messerschmitt Bf109E-3. Crashed on landing at St Trond, cause not stated. Pilot believed unhurt. Aircraft a write-off.

II./JG27 Messerschmitt Bf109E-1. Wrecked in forced-landing at Geldern following engine failure. Pilot believed unhurt. Aircraft a write-off.

II./JG51 2 Messerschmitt Bf109Es. Forced-landings at Baden-Baden and near Achern, cause not stated. Pilots both unhurt. Aircraft both repairable.

II./JG51 Messerschmitt Bf109E-1. Overturned on take-off, cause not stated. Pilot unhurt. Aircraft a write-off.

Stab I./JG52 Messerschmitt Bf109E-3. Shot down by F/O Whitty of No. 607 Squadron in combat with Hurricanes between Namur and Dinant. Abandoned near Charleville-Mézières and probably that reported crashed at Harcy sorting office 11.30 a.m. Leutnant K. Kirchner *(Gruppen TO)* baled out and captured. Aircraft a write-off.

Stab I./JG52 Messerschmitt Bf109E-3. Believed damaged in combat with Hurricanes of Nos. 3, 607, and 615 Squadrons between Namur and Dinant 11.30 a.m. Belly-landed near Liège and probably that attacked by P/O Grassick of No. 607 Squadron. Hptmn S. von Eschwege *(Gruppenkommandeur)* unhurt. Aircraft a write-off.

II./JG52 Messerschmitt Bf109E-1. Badly damaged in combat with GC II/4 near Vouziers 11.30 a.m. and forced-landed at Elsenborn airfield. Pilot unhurt. Aircraft a write-off.

II./JG52 Messerschmitt Bf109E-3. Forced-landed in Luxembourg out of fuel possibly damaged in combat with GC II/4 near Vouziers 11.30 a.m. Pilot unhurt. Aircraft damaged but repairable.

II./JG52 Messerschmitt Bf109E-3. Crashed on take-off due to undercarriage failure. Pilot unhurt. Aircraft damaged but repairable.

II./JG52 Messerschmitt Bf109E-3. Wrecked in taxying accident at Wengerohr. Pilot unhurt. Aircraft a write-off.

II./JG52 Messerschmitt Bf109E-1. Wrecked in aborted take-off at Lintgen-Luxembourg. Pilot believed unhurt. Aircraft a write-off.

III./JG52 Messerschmitt Bf109E-3. Burst tyre and crashed on landing at Ippesheim on transfer from Mannheim-Sandhofen. Pilot unhurt. Aircraft repairable.

I./JG53 Messerschmitt Bf109E-1. Crashed on take-off at Maisborn due to undercarriage failure. Pilot unhurt. Aircraft damaged but repairable.

I./JG53 Messerschmitt Bf109E-3. Crashed on take-off at Trier-Euren due to undercarriage failure. Pilot unhurt. Aircraft repairable.

3./JG53 Messerschmitt Bf109E-3. Abandoned north of Trier out of petrol after combat with GC II/1 near Château-Bogny, north of Charleville, 3.15 p.m. Uffz Hillmann baled out unhurt. Aircraft a write-off.

3./JG53 Messerschmitt Bf109E-1. Crash-landed at Wengerohr out of petrol possibly after combat with GC II/1 near Château-Bogny, north of Charleville, 3.15 p.m. Fw Krüger injured. Aircraft a write-off.

3./JG53 Messerschmitt Bf109E-1. Forced-landed at Niederbreisach out of petrol possibly after combat with GC II/1 near Château-Bogny, north of Charleville, 3.15 p.m. Pilot unhurt. Aircraft repairable.

Stab II./JG53 Messerschmitt Bf109E-3 (1347). Crashed on landing due to undercarriage failure. Hptmn G. von Maltzahn *(Gruppenkommandeur)* unhurt. Aircraft a write-off.

Reference to pages 251 to 254 listing the Luftwaffe losses for May 12 does not show a Heinkel being shot down by ground fire which fits that scenario, but this could be from one of the He111s of 4./LG1 downed by No. 607 Squadron that morning.

Stab I./JG77 Messerschmitt Bf109E. Nosed-over on landing at Sourbrodt, cause not stated, but possibly damaged in attack by Sgt Barberis of GC I/3 near Hastière-Lavaux, south-west of Dinant, 1.45 p.m. Oberlt K. Führing unhurt. Aircraft 15 + repairable.

2./JG77 Messerschmitt Bf109E. Shot down by Adj Octave of GC I/3 in combat south-west of Dinant and abandoned over Rosée 1.45 p.m. Uffz H. Klöpper baled out slightly wounded. Aircraft a write-off.

1./KG2 Dornier Do17Z. Returned damaged by No. 3 Squadron Hurricanes during sortie to attack rail targets between Challerange and Ste-Menehould. Possibly that engaged by F/O Stone. Gefr F. Hotz slightly wounded. Aircraft repairable.

1./KG2 Dornier Do17Z. Shot down by No. 3 Squadron Hurricanes between Sedan and Dinant 11.00 a.m. during sortie to attack rail targets between Challerange and Ste-Menehould. Possibly that claimed by F/L Carter. Lt J. Haupt killed. Gefr L. Miller, Uffz H. Richter (of Stab KG2), and Fw P. Oxe baled out over Carignan and captured slightly wounded. Aircraft a write-off.

2./KG2 Dornier Do17Z. Port engine set alight in attacks by No. 3 Squadron Hurricanes between Sedan and Dinant 11.00 a.m. during sortie to attack rail targets between Challerange and Ste-Menehould. Possibly that claimed by P/O Gardner. Uffz H. Tanzberger and Fw H. Schreyer captured wounded. Uffz V. Giessübel and Uffz K. Gerlach captured unhurt. Aircraft a write-off.

8./KG2 Dornier Do17Z. Forced-landed Mannheim damaged by D520s of GC I/3 north of Reims 9.00 a.m. Obergefr E. Hamma slightly wounded. Aircraft a write-off.

9./KG2 Dornier Do17Z. Returned damaged in attacks by S/Lt Plubeau, Lt Vinçotte, and Sgt Paulhan of GC II/4 over Bazancourt 11.50 a.m. Lt H. Stelzer, Fw H. Albach, and Fw K. Schettler unhurt. Uffz W. Klinkert slightly wounded. Aircraft U5+KT repairable.

5./KG3 Dornier Do17Z. Shot down by F/L Griffiths, P/O Hairs, and Sgt Morfill of No. 501 Squadron during sortie to Aubérive and crashed at St-Hilaire-le-Petit, west of Bétheniville, 8.15 a.m. Uffz H. Pfaff killed. Uffz F. Frey captured badly wounded, died two days later. Gefr W. Ewald and Gefr W. Rohde baled out and captured slightly wounded. Aircraft 5K+HN a write-off.

5./KG3 Dornier Do17Z. Believed badly damaged in attack by F/Sgt Payne of No. 501 Squadron near Bétheniville and crash-landed near Bertrix during return flight 8.30 a.m. Fw K. Falke and Uffz F. Kralemann slightly wounded, rest of crew unhurt. Aircraft a write-off.

6./KG3 Dornier Do17Z. Believed that attacked by Capt Coutaud, Sgt Couder, Sgt Teillet, Sgt Fiala, Sgt Tain, and Cpl Pipa of GC I/1 between Mézières and Sedan following sortie to Mourmelon and crash-landed in Luxembourg during return flight 6.50 p.m. Uffz A. Jungnickel badly wounded, rest of crew unhurt. Aircraft a write-off.

8./KG4 Junkers Ju88A. Failed to return from night attack on Ostend. Fw K-A. Liesenfeld killed. Fw H. Bartesch, Uffz J. Schmitt, and Gefr E. Döhla missing. Aircraft 5J+KS lost.

2./KG27 Heinkel He111H. Returned damaged by flak over Dunkirk. Uffz W. Matzke badly wounded — died May 22. Oberfw A. Bauer wounded. Oberlt Schlafke believed unhurt. Aircraft repairable.

2./KG30 Junkers Ju88A-2. Failed to return from low-level attack on shipping at Vlissingen and crashed into the Wester-schelde estuary off Beveland. Uffz L. Wengert, Uffz M. Stampfer, and Obergefr J. Wunder killed. Flgr A. Trinkl rescued by Dutch steamer badly wounded. Aircraft lost.
The body of gunner Josef Wunder was washed ashore at Borssele on May 29.

8./KG30 Junkers Ju88A. Returned from sortie damaged, circumstances unknown. Fw K. Fröhlich badly wounded. Aircraft damage state not recorded.

9./KG51 Heinkel He111H. Forced-landed on one engine, badly damaged by No. 85 Squadron Hurricanes north of Vitry-le-François a.m. Possibly that claimed by Sgt Allard. Gefr K. Landmann killed. Hptmn Brandt *(Staffelkapitän)* and rest of crew believed unhurt. Aircraft a write-off.

9./KG51 Heinkel He111H. Shot down by No. 85 Squadron Hurricanes north of Vitry-le-François a.m. Possibly one of those claimed by F/O Angus. Lt H. Klischat, Uffz H. Peper, Uffz A. Richter, and Uffz K. Hanff killed. Uffz A. Bracht captured wounded. Aircraft a write-off.

Many squadron messes, both Allied and German, sported such trophies (see pages 98, 108, 111 and 113). No. 1 Squadron boasted a particularly fine collection that adorned the walls of their mess at Berry-au-Bac as extracts from Paul Richey's diary confirms: 'The mangled remains of a gun together with a bullet-pierced oxygen bottle, trophies of the first British fighter victory of the war, a German eagle from a Dornier, a spinner from another'. On May 11, following combat with Bf110s, he acquired an equally handsome trophy of his own: 'The police presented me with one of the fins; with the black-and-white swastika pierced by two bullets, it made a respectable match for the two First War fins we had with the Black Cross emblems on them.' On June 18, the squadron had to abandon this trinket along with most of their kit and equipment when they evacuated Nantes.

9./KG51 Heinkel He111H. Shot down by No. 85 Squadron Hurricanes north of Vitry-le-François a.m. Possibly that claimed by F/L Lee. Fw J. Straub, Fw H. Flemming, and Fw G. Glufke killed. Fw E. Dimpfl baled out but reportedly shot at in his parachute and landed dead. Uffz G. Hien baled out and captured. Aircraft a write-off.

2./KG53 Heinkel He111H. Shot down by P/O Dixon and F/O Russell of No. 607 Squadron and crash-landed near Grandpré, south-east of Vouziers, 4.30 p.m. Oberfw W. Klaue and Uffz H. Kloha killed. Fw J. Wagner, Uffz W. Schulze and Gefr W. Grundmann captured. Aircraft A1+LK a write-off.

2./KG53 Heinkel He111H. Returned damaged following attack by P/O Dixon and F/O B. N. Russell of No. 607 Squadron near Grandpré, south-east of Vouziers, 4.30 p.m. Aircraft damaged but repairable.

9./KG53 Heinkel He111P. Forced-landed near Trier damaged by S/L More and F/L Scoular of No. 73 Squadron over Cheveuges-St-Aignan, south-west of Sedan 6.20 p.m. Gefr E. Ikert slightly wounded. Aircraft damaged but repairable.

1./KG54 Heinkel He111P. Reportedly set alight by AA fire over Hoeilaart, south of Brussels, during armed reconnaissance sortie but believed that attacked by Adjt Leblanc, S/Lt Bevillard, and Sgt Gouzi of GC III/3. Crash-landed and burned out at Huizingen 7.00 a.m. Lt H-B. Eymer, Gefr H. Huhle, Gefr A. Müller, and Flgr H. Meister captured unhurt. Aircraft B3+KH a write-off.

3./KG54 Heinkel He111P. Returned damaged in attacks by Adj Leblanc, S/Lt Bevillard, and Sgt Gouzi of GC III/3 between Tirlemont and St Trond 7.00 a.m. Uffz F. Göggel and Uffz K. Ilsemann slightly wounded admitted to hospital in Quakenbrück. Aircraft damaged but repairable.

Stab KG55 Heinkel He111. Forced-landed at Freibourg riddled in attacks by GC II/7 near Montagne du Larmont 12.00 p.m. Uffz H. Kalinna and Uffz W. Abbinghoff badly wounded. Fw H. Scheithauer, Fw F. Knecht and Uffz J. Möhn slightly wounded. Aircraft damage state not recorded.

8./KG55 Heinkel He111. Returned damaged by flak over Conflans. Flgr J. Schmidt died of wounds May 16. Gefr W. Manegold and Obergefr H. Schloms badly wounded. Aircraft damage state not recorded.

Stabsstaffel KG76 Dornier Do17Z. Possibly that shot down by S/Lt Thollon of GC I/8 reported overturned, caught fire, and burned out while attempting crash-landing south-east of Dinant 5.45 a.m. Fate of crew not known. Aircraft a write-off.

Stab I./KG76 Dornier Do17Z. Badly damaged in attack by Adj Deniau, and Sgt de Bremond d'Ars of GC II/6 east of Namur and crash-landed near Eupen 12.00 p.m. Oberlt H. Lütters died of wounds. Fw F. Klosterkemper badly wounded admitted to hospital in Eupen. Aircraft a write-off.

Stab III./KG76 Dornier Do17Z. Returned damaged by ground-fire following attack on motorised columns near La Capelle. Oberlt O. Hanssum and Oberfw A. Schreiweis badly wounded admitted to hospital in Bonn. Aircraft damaged but repairable.

8./KG76 Dornier Do17Z. Returned damaged by ground-fire during armed-reconnaissance near Namur. Uffz W. Arendt badly wounded — died in hospital in Mönchengladbach. Aircraft damaged but repairable.

5./KG77 Dornier Do17Z. Returned damaged by D520s of GC I/3 west of Sedan 8.50 a.m. Fw F. Moser slightly wounded. Aircraft repairable.

5./KG77 Dornier Do17Z. Returned damaged by D520s of GC I/3 north-west of Sedan 8.50 a.m. Oberfw A. Burghardt and Fw R. Meier slightly wounded. Aircraft repairable.

III./KGzbV.1 Junkers Ju52 (2820). Involved in taxying accident at Dockendorf. No crew casualties. Aircraft damaged but repairable.

11.(St)/LG1 Junkers Ju87B-1. Shot down by flak over Genappe 9.35 a.m. Uffz H. Schiller and Uffz W. Holz captured. Aircraft a write-off.

6.(S)/LG2 Henschel Hs123. Shot down by flak near Altiaux, 15 km south of Wavre. Gefr W. Krug killed. Aircraft a write-off.

2./StG2 Junkers Ju87B-1. Shot down by P/O Hardacre of No. 504 Squadron over Cortil-Noirmont, north-west of Gembloux, 10.45 a.m. Lt K. Brausch and Uffz R. Borrmann both badly wounded. Aircraft a write-off.

2./StG2 Junkers Ju87B-1. Set alight in attack by P/O van Mentz of No. 504 Squadron over Cortil-Noirmont, north-west of Gembloux, 10.45 a.m. Hptmn P. Mertz (Staffelkapitän) and Fw O. Wagner killed. Aircraft a write-off.

4./StG2 Junkers Ju87B. Shot down by ground-fire and crashed at Le Fraity, near Roly, south of Philippeville. Lt G. Bauerschäfer and Uffz E. Dräger killed. Aircraft a write-off.

9./StG2 Junkers Ju87B. Shot down by RAF fighters during attack on armour near Gentinnes, west of Gembloux 2.05 p.m. Uffz F. Urban and Obergefr A. Brandt killed. Aircraft a write-off.

4./StG77 Junkers Ju87B. Believed returned damaged by ground-fire over Cortil-Noirmont, south of Wavre, 1.30 p.m. Uffz H. Voigt wounded admitted to hospital in Cologne. Aircraft repairable.

1./ZG1 Messerschmitt Bf110C. Involved in collision south-west of Kirchhellen shortly after take-off. Uffz H. Braunsburger killed. Oberfw W. Gerstmann baled out but injured hitting the tailplane. Aircraft a write-off.

1./ZG1 Messerschmitt Bf110C. Involved in collision south-west of Kirchhellen shortly after take-off. Uffz H. Eberlein and Obergefr G. Schlender killed. Aircraft a write-off.

Stab I./ZG2 Messerschmitt Bf110C. Belly-landed near Trier out of fuel following combat with Hurricanes of No. 73 Squadron over Vouziers 2.00 p.m. Possibly that claimed by F/O Kain. Crew unhurt. Aircraft damaged but repairable.

3./ZG2 Messerschmitt Bf110C. Shot down by F/O Orton of No. 73 Squadron in combat over Vouziers and crashed in forest near Boult-au-Bois 2.00 p.m. Lt F. Mentzel and Gefr W. Oechsle both baled out and captured. Aircraft a write-off.

Stab I./ZG26 Messerschmitt Bf110C. Shot down by Adj Prenez of GC III/2 during escort sortie north of Chimay and crashed at Grandrieu, south-west of Beaumont, 7.55 a.m. Oberlt H-G. Koch (Gruppenadjutant) and Uffz K. Wolff killed. Aircraft a write-off.

2./ZG26 Messerschmitt Bf110C. Returned badly damaged following combat with Bloch 152s of GC I/8 between Fumay and Givet 11.10 a.m. Possibly that attacked by Sgt Liautard. Hptmn H. Kaminski (Staffelkapitän) and Obergefr K-H. Brockstedt both badly wounded, admitted to Marien-Hospital, Düsseldorf. Aircraft a write-off.

2./ZG26 Messerschmitt Bf110C. Shot down by Lt Lamaison, S/Lt de Castel, and Cpl Kralik of GC I/8 in combat south of Revin, and believed crashed in forest north-east of Rimogne 11.10 a.m. Possibly also attacked by S/Ldr Kayll of No. 615 Squadron. Lt K. Pertl and Gefr A. Steiner killed. Aircraft a write-off.

2./ZG26 Messerschmitt Bf110C. Shot down by Adj Michaud of GC I/8 south of Revin and crashed and exploded near Sécheval, north-east of Renwez, 11.10 a.m. Possibly also attacked by Sgt Louveau of GC I/8 and S/Ldr Kayll of No. 615 Squadron. One of crew attempted to bale out but parachute caught alight. Fw K. Friedrich and Gefr W. Neuburger killed. Aircraft a write-off.

II./ZG26 Messerschmitt Bf110C. Forced-landed possibly damaged in combat with No. 87 Squadron Hurricanes during escort sortie over Namur 6.45 p.m. Crew unhurt. Aircraft damaged but repairable.

7./ZG26 Messerschmitt Bf110C. Badly damaged in combat with No. 1 Squadron Hurricanes north of Reims 8.00 a.m. and abandoned near Arlon during return flight. Crew baled out unhurt. Aircraft a write-off.

8./ZG26 Messerschmitt Bf110C. Crashed near Kirchberg attempting emergency landing on one engine following combat with No. 1 Squadron Hurricanes north of Reims 8.00 a.m. Fw J. Kistler and Gefr K. Wengler killed. Aircraft a write-off.

9./ZG26 Messerschmitt Bf110C. Crash-landed near Liège damaged in combat with No. 1 Squadron Hurricanes north of Reims 8.00 a.m. Crew unhurt. Aircraft damaged but repairable.

9./ZG26 Messerschmitt Bf110C. Forced-landed at Maizborn damaged in combat with No. 1 Squadron Hurricanes near Reims 8.00 a.m. Crew unhurt. Aircraft damaged but repairable.

Stab I./ZG52 Messerschmitt Bf110C. Belly-landed at Wengerohr damaged in attack by Sgt Proctor of No. 501 Squadron during escort sortie for Do17s of 6./KG3 over Mourmelon 6.30 p.m. Crew unhurt. Aircraft damaged but repairable.

6./ZG76 Messerschmitt Bf110C. Returned damaged by Hurricanes of No. 73 Squadron during sortie to attack Montcornet airfield 2.30 p.m. Uffz H. Obert slightly wounded in right leg, admitted to hospital in Köln. Aircraft repairable.

6./ZG76 Messerschmitt Bf110C. Starboard engine damaged in combat with Hurricanes of No. 73 Squadron over Roizy during sortie to attack Montcornet airfield and belly-landed near Attigny 2.30 p.m. Possibly one of those claimed by F/O Orton but also engaged by French AA fire. Oberlt H-J. Knop and Uffz J. Neumayer both captured. Aircraft fired by crew.

6./ZG76 Messerschmitt Bf110C. Shot down in combat with No. 73 Squadron Hurricanes during sortie to attack Montcornet airfield 2.30 p.m. Possibly that claimed by P/O Scott. Lt G-U. Jaschob and Uffz F. Rigling both killed. Aircraft a write-off.

The squadron re-locate: No. 73 quit Reims after a stay of barely ten days.

The call came at 1 a.m. of the 16th and it was an eerie sight, the preparations for another trek being made in the rambling, draughty, dirty, but raid-proof night quarters of 73 Squadron in Fort de Brimont.

We proceeded first to the aerodrome where the work of destruction commenced. The air party had already taken off for some place called Villeneuve-les-Vertus but we of the ground were not due to leave much before 8 a.m. We guessed that very shortly the aerodrome would fall into the hands of the enemy, like the proverbial ripe plum. Here and there a French gendarme nursed his carbine as he stood moodily beside a gate, guarding he knew not why, against he knew not what.

We would indeed have liked to extend our fire-raising operations to the wooden block of offices but no — they were the property of the French! What utter 'cock', we thought! And theirs for how much longer, pray? Still orders were orders and we even swept out the rooms before we left.

Models of aircraft were smashed up and burned and not only models but the real thing, too. Five Hurricanes were lying there in more or less u/s state. One had arrived from England only yesterday and had unfortunately tipped upon its nose as a result of an imperfectly filled-in bomb-crater. One or two could have been rendered serviceable again within 24 hours but the enemy was not 24 miles away. The job of destruction had to be done.

A party of men savagely, mutinously, smashed open the tanks with pickaxes and a flood of petrol gushed out. The machines had been lugged together, nose to centre, and I stood there, hesitant, a flare in my hand, ready to ignite. Five Hurricanes — a £30,000 bonfire! Then I became aware of somebody standing beside me and I turned. An Air Commodore in person! 'What are you going to do?' 'Destroy these aircraft, Sir.' 'Is it absolutely necessary? Are you sure the Germans will get here?' 'I have my orders, sir.' 'Carry on, then,' and he turned wearily away. I flung the lighted flare and then ran like hell. There was a roar and a flash behind me.

And just at that precise moment the Germans decided to come over and make a superfluous demonstration of strength. Those Hurricanes, five of them, burning furiously beside that hangar, what havoc might they not have wreaked upon that crowd of impudent blighters?

The convoy of which I was in charge, had preceded us by half an hour, and I breathed a sigh of relief as we drew past the barrack blocks, having first responded to the absurd formality at the aerodrome gate over our papers.

We sped out of the city, the trend of road traffic entirely in our favour and shortly afterwards caught up with the convoy. For a time, it looked as if we would make a fair average along the entire route until we arrived at a road junction. There it became at once apparent that we had left Reims by a secondary road and were now at the main highway. An interminable, slow-moving, frequently-halting and pathetically futile train of refugees was heading south, away from Reims. A heterogenous collection of one-, two-, four- and six-wheeled vehicles comprised this semi-mobile column and mixed up inextricably with it were units of the British forces, heading, alas, southwards even as we hoped to do. What a target!

What did those poor fools think they were about? Had they the slightest idea of the range, the load-carrying capacity of a modern bomber? What earthly use was that double mattress, strapped on top of that saloon car, whose sides were at this moment being scarred by as equally speedy a donkey cart? Didn't they realise that even pilots had to be protected against armour-piercing bullets nowadays? An enormous farm-wagon had shed a wheel, pitching its varied load across the road. No one gave any help to the frenzied owners of the vehicle; everybody cursed the impediment to their progress. Impatient, utterly frustrated drivers, would use up all their battery-current in a cacophony of blowing their horn, and consume more petrol in a ten-mile stretch of road than would have sufficed for a normal journey halfway across France. Every mile was littered with its complement of fuel-less cars, abandoned completely by their owners who had proceeded on foot.

Somehow we gradually worked our way in the tightly-wedged phalanx, happily to discover that it occupied but two-thirds of the road, the remaining third being kept open by military police although with considerable difficulty, for the exclusive use of military traffic also bound south. As for any traffic proposing to travel north, well, that was palpably absurd.

We lost our way and had to swing back in a wide curve towards our destination. And as we drew near to it, what was our amazement to see a column of RAF personnel marching briskly along the road leading from it in the opposite direction to us. We stopped and enquired if we were all right for the 'drome only to be informed that they were just coming away from it — evacuating it in so much of a hurry that those for whom there was no transport had to take up their packs and walk.

FLYING OFFICER EDWARD HALL,
ADJUTANT NO. 73 SQUADRON

Jean Paul Pallud pictured the apron at Reims military airfield today.

Thursday, May 16

German columns continued to pour through the gap in the Allied line between Dinant and Sedan meeting little opposition in their rapid progress west, enemy units soon approaching Vervins and Laon. North BAAF advance headquarters at Chauny was duly abandoned, Air Marshal Barratt moving back to his main headquarters at Coulommiers early in the morning, while AASF headquarters retired south to Troyes. Further, in addition to squadron movements already underway, and communications becoming increasingly confused, No. 75 Wing units were now ordered to withdraw to the south Champagne area.

AASF daylight bombing efforts during the day were negligible, what remained of most units being occupied in switching airfields, but specific targets were difficult to confirm in the rapidly changing ground situation. By nightfall Allied troops in Belgium would initiate a planned withdrawal towards a line formed by the Terneuzen Canal and the River Escaut (Scheldt), while the French fell back on the Charleroi — Brussels Canal.

Meanwhile in England, a struggle of a different kind, but no less desperate, was taking place. Immediately upon his return to Fighter Command headquarters after the Cabinet meeting on the previous day, Dowding, with an innate distrust of politicians, set about drafting a statement to reflect his concerns at the continuing drain on his resources and its likely impact on the future defence of the country. His instincts were sound for, unknown to him, immediately after the meeting Churchill had reversed his decision and already issued instructions that four more squadrons be sent to France forthwith. In a well-intentioned but misguided effort to mitigate the impact of this further drain on RAF Fighter Command resources, eight separate flights, rather than four full squadrons, were ordered to France — six of them leaving that afternoon and two more the following morning. In addition, 20 experienced pilots were to be sent as replacements for RAF Component pilots exhausted by constant operations.

Dowding's statement became a two-page letter dated May 16, addressed to the Under Secretary of State, and one of the most eloquent and pivotal documents of the war. Without it, the Battle of Britain may well have been lost before it was fought.

As the situation in France deteriorated even further, Churchill flew to Paris to meet with Premier Reynaud who made a further passionate appeal for more RAF fighters. Despite all Dowding had said to him only 24 hours before, Churchill was swayed, and telegraphed the Cabinet in London to send out another six fighter squadrons at once. But mercifully, better sense now prevailed, and Chief of Air Staff Cyril Newall, doubtless persuaded by Dowding's argument, but equally mindful that British bases in northern France could only accommodate an additional three squadrons at best, persuaded the Cabinet to compromise. Instead of simply throwing six more squadrons into the cauldron of France, he proposed that they remain based at airfields in southern England for daily operations over France, where they would land to refuel and rearm, before returning each evening to their bases in England. These squadrons were promptly made ready for operations the following day.

Air Chief Marshal Dowding's crucial letter to Captain The Rt Hon. H. H. Balfour, the Under Secretary of State at the Air Ministry — a letter which would have far-reaching consequences for success in the forthcoming Battle of Britain.

Telephone Nos.: **WATFORD 9241 (10 lines).**
COLINDALE 5221 (4 lines).
PINNER 5691 (3 lines).
Telegraphic Address: " **AIRGENARCH, STANMORE** "

Reference: **FC/S.19048.**   SECRET

HEADQUARTERS, FIGHTER COMMAND,
ROYAL AIR FORCE,
BENTLEY PRIORY,
STANMORE,
MIDDLESEX.

16th May, 1940.

Sir,

I have the honour to refer to the very serious calls which have recently been made upon the Home Defence Fighter Units in an attempt to stem the German invasion on the Continent.

2.   I hope and believe that our Armies may yet be victorious in France and Belgium, but we have to face the possibility that they may be defeated.

3.   In this case I presume that there is no-one who will deny that England should fight on, even though the remainder of the Continent of Europe is dominated by the Germans.

4.   For this purpose it is necessary to retain some minimum fighter strength in this country and I must request that the Air Council will inform me what they consider this minimum strength to be, in order that I may make my dispositions accordingly.

5.   I would remind the Air Council that the last estimate which they made as to the force necessary to defend this country was 52 Squadrons, and my strength has now been reduced to the equivalent of 36 Squadrons.

6.   Once a decision has been reached as to the limit on which the Air Council and the Cabinet are prepared to stake the existence of the country, it should be made clear to the Allied Commanders on the Continent that not a single aeroplane from Fighter Command beyond the limit will be sent across the Channel, no matter how desperate the situation may become.

7.   It will, of course, be remembered that the estimate of 52 Squadrons was based on the assumption that the attack would come from the eastwards except in so far as the defences might be outflanked in flight. We have now to face the possibility that attacks may come from Spain or even from the North coast of France. The result is that our line is very much extended at the same time as our resources are reduced.

8.   I must point out that within the last few days the equivalent of 10 Squadrons have been sent to France, that the Hurricane Squadrons remaining in this country are seriously depleted, and that the more Squadrons which are sent to France the higher will be the wastage and the more insistent the demands for reinforcements.

9.   I must therefore request that as a matter of paramount urgency the Air Ministry will consider and decide what level of strength is to be left to the Fighter Command for the defences of this country, and will assure me that when this level has been reached, not one fighter will be sent across the Channel however urgent and insistent the appeals for help may be.

10.   I believe that, if an adequate fighter force is kept in this country, if the fleet remains in being, and if Home Forces are suitably organised to resist invasion, we should be able to carry on the war single handed for some time, if not indefinitely. But, if the Home Defence Force is drained away in desperate attempts to remedy the situation in France, defeat in France will involve the final, complete and irremediable defeat of this country.

I have the honour to be,
Sir,
Your obedient Servant,

Air Chief Marshal,
Air Officer Commanding-in-Chief,
Fighter Command, Royal Air Force.

BRITISH AIR FORCES IN FRANCE

3 SQUADRON, MERVILLE

Hurricane P2825. Shot down in combat with Bf110s of 1./ZG1 near Wavre 6.15 p.m. Squadron Leader P. Gifford missing. Aircraft a write-off.

4 SQUADRON, LILLE-RONCHIN

Lysander L4814. Forced-landed badly damaged by Bf110s during observation sortie. near Louvain. Pilot Officer Langley and LAC J. H. Gillham unhurt. Aircraft a write-off.

Lysander II P9064. Failed to return from tactical reconnaissance sortie 8.15 p.m. Flying Officer E. E. A. Wood missing. Corporal J. Bower believed unhurt. Aircraft lost.

Edward Wood is commemorated on the Runnymede Memorial where his date of death is given as May 17.

12 SQUADRON, AMIFONTAINE

Battle L4944. Failed to start for attack on columns around Monthermé the previous night and abandoned at Reims. No crew casualties. Aircraft destroyed on withdrawal.

13 SQUADRON, AUTHIE

Lysander L6885. Lost on tactical reconnaissance sortie and crashed near Vieux-Condé. Believed that claimed by Fw Bothfeld of 1./JG27 over La Chapelle 5.50 a.m. Pilot Officer T. H. Borg-Banks and LAC W. F. Lawes killed. ACI H. P. Moule suffered a broken arm. Aircraft a write-off.

18 SQUADRON, MÉHARICOURT

Blenheim IV L8863. Forced-landed at Vitry damaged by ground-fire during reconnaissance sortie 9.30 a.m. Sergeant A. W. S. Thomas badly wounded in neck, died two days later. Sergeant J. J. F. Talbot slightly wounded in left arm. LAC R. G. St James-Smith unhurt. Aircraft damaged but repairable.

Blenheim IV L9340. Returned from low-level reconnaissance sortie damaged by ground-fire. Sergeant R. N. Holland, Sergeant J. Chatterton, and LAC F. E. A. Greaney unhurt. Aircraft repairable — later abandoned.

Blenheim IV L9254. Shot down in flames by Bf110s during sortie to bomb enemy armour between Le Cateau and Cambrai 12.00 p.m. Crashed and burned out near Beaurevoir, east of Le Catelet. Flying Officer A. J. Stuart, Sergeant D. Borthwick, and LAC H. G. James killed. Aircraft a write-off.

In a corner of the cemetery at Crèvecoeur-sur-l'Escaut lies the grave of Flying Officer Arnold Stuart (left), Sergeant David Borthwick (centre) and Leading Aircraftman Horace James — the pilot, observer and gunner on Blenheim L9254 of No. 18 Squadron which crashed near Beaurevoir.

Blenheim IV L9187. Crash-landed near Gouy, east of Le Catelet, with port engine alight following attacks by Bf110s during sortie to bomb enemy armour between Le Cateau and Cambrai 12.00 p.m. Sergeant T. J. Mongey killed. Pilot Officer J. R. Whelan badly burned and broken arm. LAC Brown unhurt. Aircraft a write-off.

53 SQUADRON, POIX

Blenheim IV L4860. Shot down during strategic reconnaissance over the Albert Canal 6.00 a.m. Crash-landed at Wadelincourt, near Henegouwen. Pilot Officer M. Lovell wounded. Sergeant D. McLeod wounded. AC1 Kenneth unhurt. Aircraft PZ⊙W a write-off.

Blenheim IV L4843. Failed to return from strategic reconnaissance to Charleville-Mézières and reported crashed at Mainbressy, east of Rozoy, 11.00 a.m. Pilot Officer R. I. C. MacPherson, Sergeant A. T. Moreland, and AC2 S. Robinson captured. Aircraft a write-off.

Blenheim IV L4852. Engaged by Allied AA fire during reconnaissance sortie then starboard engine damaged in attack by Sergeant Crozier of No. 85 Squadron near Amiens. Crashed and burned out during emergency belly-landing at Glisy 4.30 p.m. Flight Lieutenant B. B. St G. Daly, Sergeant W. R. B. Currie, and AC2 P. J. Blandford badly burned. Aircraft a write-off.

59 SQUADRON, POIX

Blenheim IV N6168. Damaged by flak southeast of Louvain during strategic reconnaissance sortie then attacked by P/O Grassick of No. 615 Squadron over the Forêt de Meerdael and belly-landed at Vitry with port engine and hydraulics destroyed 6.25 a.m. Flight Lieutenant G. V. Smithers and Sergeant R. Tull unhurt. AC2 D. J. Pitcher slightly injured. Aircraft TR⊙A a write-off.

73 SQUADRON, REIMS-CHAMPAGNE

5 Hurricanes including N2404, P2810, P2813 and P3279. Unserviceable aircraft destroyed on evacuation to Villeneuve-les-Vertus 5.00 a.m. No pilot casualties. Aircraft all write-offs.

79 SQUADRON, MERVILLE

Hurricane N2426. Shot down by Oberlt Redlich *(Staffelkapitän)* of 1./JG27 during attack on Fw189 of 9.(H)/LG2 near Braine-le-Comte and crash-landed near 'Les Hayettes', at Rêves 8.30 p.m. Sergeant H. Cartwright believed unhurt. Aircraft abandoned.

Hurricane. Returned with tail damaged by ground-fire near Wavre p.m. Pilot Officer L. R. Dorrien-Smith unhurt. Aircraft repairable.

Hurricane. Returned hit in port wing by ground-fire near Wavre p.m. Flight Lieutenant R. Roberts unhurt. Aircraft repairable.

Local children explore the Blenheim of No. 53 Squadron which crash-landed at Wadelincourt.

85 SQUADRON, LILLE-SECLIN

Hurricane L1641. Shot down in combat with Bf109s of 5./JG2 and crashed near Fretin, south of Lille, 2.00 p.m. Possibly that claimed by Lt Schetelig. Flying Officer A. B. Angus killed. Aircraft a write-off.

Hurricane P2535. Shot down in combat with Bf109s of 5./JG2 south of Lille and crashed at Quiévrain 2.00 p.m. Possibly that claimed by Lt Hepe. P/O M. H. G. Rawlinson killed. Aircraft a write-off.

Hurricane N2389. Set alight in attack by Bf109s shortly after take-off and abandoned at 600 feet 2.00 p.m. Possibly that claimed by Uffz Hartwig of 5./JG2. Sergeant L. A. Crozier baled out badly burned. Aircraft a write-off.

Hurricane L1898. Unserviceable aircraft shot down by Bf109s shortly after take-off for Merville and crash-landed north-west of Lille 2.00 p.m. Possibly that claimed by Oberlt Bolz (Staffelkapitän) of 5./JG2. Sergeant H. H. Allgood wounded. Aircraft a write-off.

Hurricane P2824. Crash-landed damaged in attack by Hptmn Knüppel (Gruppenkommandeur) of Stab II./JG26 over Seclin 3.50 p.m. Pilot Officer H. D. Clark wounded. Aircraft a write-off.
Hugh Clark was one of two replacement pilots who arrived on attachment from No. 213 Squadron on May 14.

Hurricane L1640. Forced-landed damaged in attack by Lt Hillecke of Stab II./JG26 over Seclin 3.50 p.m. Flying Officer Count M. B. Czernin unhurt. Aircraft abandoned.

87 SQUADRON, LILLE-MARCQ

Hurricane L1614. Crash-landed near Goeferdinge with propeller shot off by return fire during attack on Do17s of 6./KG77 between Mons and St Ghislain a.m. Sergeant G. L. Nowell unhurt. Aircraft abandoned.

Hurricane. Failed to return following combat with Bf109s west of Mons and possibly that claimed by Uffz Dahmer of 4./JG26 northeast of Tournai 3.50 p.m. Sergeant A. N. Trice missing. Aircraft a write-off.
Alan Trice was one of four replacement pilots who had arrived on attachment from No. 151 Squadron earlier that morning.

88 SQUADRON, MOURMELON-LE-GRAND

Battles L5233 and L5243. Unserviceable aircraft abandoned on withdrawal to Les Grandes-Chapelles. No crew casualties. Aircraft both write-offs.

With the hurried exodus of the squadrons from the forward bases of the AASF, so many aircraft had to be left behind. Where possible — like L5243 of No. 88 Squadron — planes were set on fire before leaving . . .

. . . but No. 114 Squadron (code RT) left several intact specimens behind before moving to the coast.

103 SQUADRON, BÉTHENIVILLE

Battle L5234. Crashed on take-off on evacuation of airfield 7.00 a.m. No crew casualties. Aircraft PM⊙B abandoned.
Another unserviceable aircraft K9404 was also abandoned on withdrawal of the squadron to Rhèges.

114 SQUADRON, CONDÉ-VRAUX

Blenheim IV R3597. Returned with fuel tank damaged and one tyre holed following bombing sortie over Monthermé 6.35 a.m. Sergeant Seale, Sergeant Ellwood, and AC Gray unhurt. Aircraft repairable.
The squadron continued operations for a further two days until ordered to Nantes for evacuation to England. All remaining serviceable aircraft went to No. 18 Squadron at Crécy.

139 SQUADRON, PLIVOT

Blenheim IV L9411. Shot down by ground-fire during armed reconnaissance sortie over Monthermé and low-level attack on enemy convoy 4.00 p.m. Crashed near Floing. Pilot Officer K. M. A. de Souza, Sergeant E. W. Tough, and AC2 W. J. McCarthy killed. Aircraft a write-off.

Three Blenheim IVs. Returned badly damaged by ground-fire following low-level attack on enemy convoy near Monthermé 4.00 p.m. Aircraft abandoned later that day.

142 SQUADRON, BERRY-AU-BAC

Six Battles K7700, K9259, K9366, K9367, L5242 and L5440. Damaged or unserviceable aircraft abandoned on withdrawal to Faux-Villecerf. No casualties. Aircraft all write-offs.

212 SQUADRON, ÉTAMPES

Tiger Moth R5036. Crashed at St-Maixme-Hautrive, south-east of Dreux. Fate of pilot unknown. Aircraft a write-off.

226 SQUADRON, REIMS-CHAMPAGNE

Seven Battles K9180, K9330, K9345, K9383, L5418, P2180 and P2255. Damaged or unserviceable aircraft destroyed on withdrawal to Faux-Villecerf. No casualties. Aircraft MK⊙O, and MK⊙W all write-offs.

501 SQUADRON, BÉTHENIVILLE

Three Hurricanes L1866, L1953 and L1991. Aircraft believed left on withdrawal to Anglure. No pilot casualties. Aircraft SD⊙P, SD⊙F, and SD⊙R abandoned.
Seven unserviceable Hurricanes were reportedly abandoned, four later being made airworthy. P3453, an aircraft the unit reported 'lost in France', may have been one of these.

615 SQUADRON, VITRY-EN-ARTOIS

Hurricane N2335. Believed shot down by Oberlt Framm *(Staffelkapitän)* of 2./JG27 near Tirlemont in combat between Louvain and Wavre 1.40 p.m. Flight Lieutenant L. T. W. Thornley missing. Aircraft a write-off.

Hurricane. Shot down by Bf109s of 2./JG27 between Louvain and Wavre 1.40 p.m. Pilot Officer T. C. Jackson baled out wounded — captured and admitted to field hospital in Tirlemont. Aircraft a write-off.

Hurricane P2577. Brought down over Hekelgem during evening patrol over Brussels and crashed at the 'Hauwijk' at Essene p.m. Pilot Officer B. P. Young baled out badly burned but fired upon by British troops and further wounded — evacuated to UK. Aircraft a write-off.

The burned-out remains of L9477 which was on the strength of No. 139 Squadron; its fate is not specifically recorded other than 'lost in France'.

The remains of No. 142 Squadron's Battles at Berry-au-Bac.

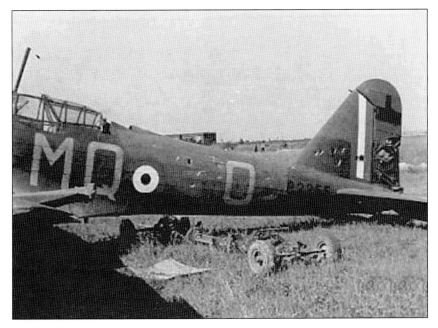

No. 226 Squadron — which shared Reims aerodrome with No. 73 — left behind six Battles including P2255.

FRENCH AIR FORCE

ECMJ 1/16 2 Potez 631. Destroyed on the ground at Wez-Thuisy in bombing attack by He111s 6.15 a.m. No crew casualties. Aircraft both write-offs.

A further nine unserviceable aircraft were abandoned on withdrawal to Meaux-Esbly later that morning. But a small team of mechanics returned and managed to repair six machines that eventually rejoined the unit on May 24.

GAO 503 Potez 63.11 (375). Hit by flak and starboard engine set alight during reconnaissance sortie over enemy armoured columns. Crashed and burned out near the goods station at Beert-Bellingen, between Soignies and Braine-le-Comte 3.20 p.m. S/Lt A. Mann dropped from aircraft at low level and seriously injured, taken to a clinic in Halle where died next day. Adjt Nourry baled out over Hennuyères but shot at by Allied troops and badly wounded, admitted to hospital in Binche. Adjt Gourdon baled out landing unhurt. Aircraft a write-off.

GAO 510 Potez 63.11 (619). Shot down by Oberfw Hauer of 1./JG76 during reconnaissance sortie north-east of Vouziers and crash-landed at 'Corbison', near Autruche 10.47 a.m. Lt R. Martin and Sgt A. Guesnel unhurt. Cpl Molinier wounded in foot. Aircraft a write-off.

GAO 547 Potez 63.11 and Breguet 270. Unserviceable aircraft abandoned at Vivaise on withdrawal to Compiègne at dawn. No crew casualties. Aircraft both write-offs.

GAO 1/551 Potez 63.11 (685). Hit by French AA fire during high-altitude reconnaissance over Fossé. Capt Luerruan, Sgt Jaulon, and Sgt Pegaz unhurt. Aircraft damaged but repairable.

GAO 4/551 2 Potez 63.11 (586). Unserviceable aircraft destroyed or damaged on the ground and abandoned on withdrawal from Romeries-Escarmain. No crew casualties. Aircraft both write-offs.

GAO 553 Potez 63.11. Returned to Nancy-Azelot damaged by light flak during reconnaissance sortie between Lauter and Acher. Capt Bachelot and Sgt Jeandel wounded. Aircraft damaged but repairable.

GB I/12 LeO 451 (54). Brought down by light flak and ground-fire during low-level bombing attack on armoured columns in the Montcornet — Dizy-le-Gros sector 8.00 a.m. Crashed on a house and exploded at Raillimont, 2 km from Rozoy-sur-Serre. S/Lt A. Devalez, Sgt A. Masset, Sgt M. Buisson, and Sgt J. Moity killed. Aircraft a write-off.

GB I/12 LeO 451 (105). Shot down by flak during solo attack on enemy concentrations between Rozoy and Montcornet and crashed at Bosmont-sur-Serre, 7 km east of Marle 9.30 a.m. Sgt H. Pironneau killed. Adjt Cherigié badly wounded; both arms and legs fractured. S/Lt Lemaire also wounded. Cpl Fourrier unhurt. Aircraft a write-off.

GB I/12 LeO 451. Returned to Soissons-Saconin with flak damage after solo attack on enemy concentrations between Rozoy-sur-Serre and Montcornet 10.45 a.m. S/Lt Rousseau and crew unhurt. Aircraft repairable.

GB I/12 LeO 451. Returned to Soissons-Saconin with flak damage after solo attack on enemy concentrations between Rozoy and Montcornet 10.45 a.m. Adjt A. Vuathelot and crew unhurt. Aircraft repairable.

The funeral pyre of Potez 63.11, serial 375, of Groupe Aérien d'Observation 503. One crewman baled out too low and another was shot and wounded by friendly troops.

GB 4/12 LeO 451 (42). Returned to Persan-Beaumont badly damaged by flak during low-level bombing attack on enemy armoured columns advancing along the Montcornet—Rozoy road 1.00 p.m. Collided with LeO 451 of GB I/31 due to damaged brakes and flaps. Capt Tonon *(Commandant)*, Adjt Brisset, and Sgt Chrétienne believed unhurt. Adjt Marsault badly wounded admitted to hospital in Senlis. Aircraft a write-off.

GB II/12 LeO 451 (80). Both engines set alight by flak during low-level bombing attack on enemy columns advancing along the Rozoy—Brunehamel road; forced-landed 3 km east of Soissons 1.30 p.m. Sgt Courréges, S/Lt Delacourt, Adjt Legros, and Cpl Florin unhurt. Aircraft abandoned — later destroyed.

GB II/12 LeO 451 (88). Aborted sortie to Montcornet due to accidental fire on board 6.00 p.m. Capt A. Rocher, S/Lt A. Masclaud, Adj R. Lambert, Cpl Y. Le Goyat unhurt. Aircraft repairable.

GB 1/31 LeO 451 (27). Hit by flak and set alight during attack on enemy armoured columns west of Montcornet and abandoned over Juvincourt. Crashed and burned out near Amifontaine station 7.15 a.m. S/Lt Raoul baled out badly wounded in shoulder. Capt R. Hirsch *(Commandant)* and Adjt Perrigouard baled out wounded. Sgt Meliguet baled out unhurt. Aircraft a write-off.

GB I/31 LeO 451 (78). Wrecked in collision with LeO 451 of GB II/12 at Persan-Beaumont airfield 11.50 a.m. No crew casualties. Aircraft a write-off.

GB I/31 LeO 451 (62). Crashed on take-off at Persan-Beaumont airfield due to undercarriage failure 10.00 a.m. No crew casualties. Aircraft repairable.

GB II/34 Amiot 143 (27). Returned to Nangis badly damaged by flak following repeated low-level attacks on enemy armour near Liart. Sgt Oeillard and Cpl Montel badly wounded. Lt Fiquet, Adjt Couzon, and Adjt Renard unhurt. Aircraft a write-off.

GB II/35 Breguet 693 (1008). Wrecked in an accident at Briare airfield, details unknown. No crew casualties. Aircraft a write-off.

GB II/38 Amiot 143 (136). Port engine failed shortly after take-off on night-bombing sortie. Dumped bombs at low level and crashed into the side of a hill at Bricon 11.15 p.m. Capt L. Destannes *(Groupe Commandant)* and Lt L. Vial killed. Adjt Leclerc badly injured. S/Lt Pons and Sgt Bauer unhurt. Aircraft a write-off.

GBA I/54 Breguet 693 (15). Returned to Montdidier badly damaged by flak during attack on enemy columns advancing along the Mezières — Laon road, north-east of Montcornet p.m. Sgt Codron badly wounded. Sgt Somedecoste unhurt. Aircraft 'Min de Rien' a write-off.

One of the Polish pilots flying wiith the French Air Force, Sous-Lieutenant Wladyslaw Chciuk, survived the crash of his Morane 406. He had a colourful journey to regain his unit, GC 5/1.

GBA 4/54 Breguet 693 (36). Forced-landed on perimeter of Montdidier airfield due to take-off accident. Lt de Béarn and Adjt Mercoeur unhurt. Aircraft a write-off.

GBA II/54 Breguet 693 (20). Suffered a direct hit by flak and exploded over Rocquigny during attack on enemy troop concentrations north of Chaumont-Porcien. Crashed and burned out in woods at Fontaine Barbette 5.30 p.m. S/Lt G. Chemineau and Sgt C. Guichon killed. Aircraft a write-off.

GBA II/54 Breguet 693 (30). Shot down by flak during attack on enemy columns northwest of Rethel. Crashed and burned out at Hannogne-Saint-Rémy 5.30 p.m. Sgt R. Lami and Sgt Giard rescued unhurt but captured later that night. Aircraft a write-off.

GC I/1 Bloch 152 (175). Belly-landed near Berneuil-sur-Aisne with combat damage 6.00 a.m. Lt J. Schmidt unhurt. Aircraft a write-off.

GC 5/1 Morane 406 (948). Engine damaged by return fire from Do17 engaged during patrol between Dendermonde and Bailleul 1.15 p.m. Crash-landed and burned out at Favarge, by the road from Petit Roeulx-les-Braine to Braine-le-Comte. S/Lt W. Chciuk unhurt. Aircraft III a write-off.
Speaking poor French, Wladyslaw Chciuk attempted to return on foot but was arrested twice as a spy and arrived back at Norrent-Fontes four days later to find the unit relocated to Plessis-Belleville. Overnight, enlisting the help of some mechanics, he cannibalised sufficient spares from several damaged machines to make an MS406 airworthy enough to risk flying to Le Bourget next morning.

GC II/2 Seven Morane 406. Unserviceable aircraft abandoned at Laon-Chambry on withdrawal to Plessis-Belleville 5.00 a.m. No pilot casualties. Aircraft all write-offs.

GC 5/2 Morane 406 (738). Shot down in combat with Bf110s of II./ZG76 and crashed at Wignehies, 5 km west of Fourmies 12.30 p.m. Possibly that claimed by Lt Guth of 6./ZG76 north of Avesnes. S/Lt P. Bardin killed. Aircraft a write-off.
It seems that this claim was not confirmed though German records do credit Uffz Helmut Jörke of 4./ZG76 with a Curtiss H-75 during this combat.

GC 5/2 Morane 406 (994). Pursued over the Bois de Couvin by Oberfw Anthony and Oberlt Borchers of II./ZG76. Undercarriage dropped near Signy-le-Petit airfield but fuel tank exploded under repeated attack. Finally crashed and disintegrated at La Neuville-aux-Tourneurs, south-west of Rocroi, 12.30 p.m. Sgt L. Flanek killed. Aircraft a write-off.
Originally buried in a field grave close to the crash site, Léopold Flanek was reinterred in Naz-Dar Cemetery, Neuville-St-Vaast, in 1963.

GC 6/2 Morane 406. Set alight in combat with Bf110s over Hirson and overturned attempting crash-landing at 'Ferme d'Angoutte', near Dizy-le-Gros, south of Montcornet, 12.30 p.m. Probably that claimed by Uffz Birndorfer of 6./ZG76. Adjt A. Moret slightly wounded. Aircraft a write-off.

GC 6/2 Morane 406 (923). Returned to Cambrai-Niergnies badly damaged in combat with Bf110s over Hirson 12.30 p.m. Capt Corniglion-Molinier unhurt. Aircraft 7 abandoned.

GC 6/2 Morane 406 (358). Returned to Cambrai-Niergnies badly damaged in combat with Bf110s over Hirson 12.30 p.m. S/Lt Lansoy unhurt. Aircraft abandoned.

GC III/2 10 Morane 406s including 926 and 931. Unserviceable or damaged aircraft destroyed on withdrawal from Cambrai-Niergnies. No pilot casualties. Aircraft all abandoned.
French Air Force GHQ returns indicate over 200 aircraft destroyed on the ground, or seriously damaged and abandoned due to enemy action, between May 10 and June 8, 1940. The same source gives a further 230 aircraft lost in accidents with 410 more destroyed in combat. While the accuracy of these figures may be questioned, it is clear that the Armée de l'Air was far from wiped out on the ground as has often been suggested.

GC I/3 Two Dewoitine 520. Destroyed on the ground at Wez-Thuisy in bombing attack by He111s 6.15 a.m. No pilot casualties. Aircraft both write-offs.
Nine more unserviceable D520s, some damaged in this attack, were burned on withdrawal to Meaux-Esbly at midday.

GC II/5 Curtiss H-75 (60). Damaged by Bf110 escort during attack on He111s near Verdun and forced-landed 3 km outside Damvillers 2.15 p.m. Lt J. Jaske wounded. Aircraft a write-off.

GC II/6 Morane 406 (771). Landed at Escarmain badly damaged by flak over Montcornet during low-level reconnaissance sortie 9.10 a.m. S/Lt M. Verdier badly wounded in thigh. Aircraft a write-off.

When German troops arrived at Cambrai-Niergnies aerodrome, the base of Groupe de Chasse III/2, they found several abandoned Moranes. This is 923 . . . before and after it was souvenired!

GC II/6 35 Moranes 406 including 78 and 668. Destroyed on the ground at Le Quesnoy-Vertain. No pilot casualties. Aircraft write-offs.

Decimated, the unit was immediately withdrawn to Beauvais, and later Châteauroux where it re-equipped with Bloch 152s, not returning to front-line operations until June 5.

GC 3/6 Morane 406 (943). Hit by flak during low-level reconnaissance sortie over Montcornet and belly-landed at Pontséricourt, west of Agnicourt 9.30 a.m. Capt Baché *(Commandant)* injured jaw. Aircraft a write-off.

GC II/7 Morane 406 (221). Destroyed on the ground at Luxeuil in strafing attack by Bf109s. No pilot casualty. Aircraft a write-off.

GC I/8 Bloch 152 (531). Shot down in combat with Bf110s of 15.(Z)/LG1 over Pontfaverger, north-east of Reims, 5.55 a.m. Crashed and burned out near Versigny. Sgt H. Choulet killed. Aircraft 7 a write-off.

GC I/8 3 Bloch 152. Damaged aircraft abandoned at La Fère-Courbes on withdrawal to Chantilly a.m. No pilot casualties. Aircraft all write-offs.

GC II/8 Bloch 152. Shot down in combat with Bf110s between Dendermonde and Willebroek 2.30 p.m. Adjt Curthelet baled out unhurt and captured by Belgian troops. Aircraft a write-off.

GC II/10 Bloch 152. Returned with oil tank damaged by return fire from He111s of 7./KG28 engaged over the forest of Mormal 6.30 p.m. S/Lt Dietrich unhurt. Aircraft repairable.

GC II/10 Bloch 152 (134). Forced-landed out of fuel at Beaurevoir, north of St Quentin, following extended patrol between Avesnes and Le Cateau 7.30 p.m. S/Lt Barbu unhurt. Aircraft abandoned.

BELGIAN AIR FORCE

3/II/1 Fox (O.96). Radiator hit and aircraft damaged by AA fire over Koningshooikt during reconnaissance sortie over the KW line. Crash-landed east of Putte 7.00 a.m. Sgt R. Van Lierde and Capt P. Willemaers *(Commandant)* both slightly wounded, returned to unit. Aircraft a write-off.

This machine was the 'Fox Royal', personal aircraft of King Leopold. Remi 'Mony' Van Lierde was one of many Belgian air force 'deserters' to fly with the RAF. He survived the war with six enemy aircraft and over 40 V1s to his credit being awarded the DFC and two bars. He died in 1983.

11/VI/1 Renard R-31. Engine damaged by ground-fire during photo-reconnaissance of the bridge at Werchter and crash-landed west of the canal at Kampenhout 9.00 a.m. Sgt J. Rigole and S/Lt E. Walch both unhurt. Aircraft a write-off.

Observation aircraft employed in support of army units, irrespective of nationality, tended to be slow, poorly armed, and extremely vulnerable to fighter attack; their low speed manoeuvrability close to the ground often their only salvation.

Operating from improvised landing strips close to enemy forward positions made them equally prone to ground fire. This Henschel Hs126 of 3.(H)/12 fell to Moranes south of Montcornet.

LUFTWAFFE

1.(H)/12 Henschel Hs126. Shot down by five Curtiss H 75s of GC II/5 and crashed at Foetz, between Esch-sur-Alzette and Mondercange, 10.45 a.m. Fw K. Jacob and Uffz H. Möller both wounded and admitted to hospital in Luxembourg. Aircraft a write-off.

3.(H)/12 Henschel Hs126. Shot down by six Moranes of GC III/2 and crashed between Lappion and Dizy-le-Gros 12.45 p.m. Oberlt H. Haase and crewman killed. Aircraft H1+GL a write-off.

Helmut Haase is reported to have died at Willerzie, west of Gedinne, on the following day and it is likely that, badly wounded, he was transported to a field hospital in the rear for emergency treatment. This unit also reported one man killed and another wounded during bombardment of the forward landing ground at Raillimont, including the attack described below.

5.(H)/12 Henschel Hs126. Shot down by Breguet 693 (S/Lt Menant and Sgt Voirgard) of GB II/54 during attack on the forward landing ground at Fraillicourt-Raillimont 12.45 p.m. One crewman killed. Aircraft a write-off.

4.(H)/13 Henschel Hs126. Possibly the aircraft attacked by Lt Marche, S/Lt Gnys, and S/Lt Chciuk of GC III/1 over Gembloux, south-east of Brussels, 2.10 p.m. Lt Kalweit killed. Aircraft damage state unknown.

1.(H)/14 Henschel 126. Reported forced-landed at Rillaer out of fuel during observation sortie between Boulzicourt and Mazerny but possibly that attacked by five Curtiss H 75s of GC I/5 near Chémery 7.20 p.m. Uffz Schulze and Uffz Baumgartner unhurt. Aircraft a write-off.

3.(H)/21 Henschel Hs126. Forced-landed badly damaged in attack by Sgt Flanek of GC III/2 over Mariembourg, near Couvin, 12.30 p.m. Oberfw H. Glantz and Uffz W. Redlich both badly wounded. Aircraft a write-off.

2.(F)/22 Dornier Do17. Shot down during reconnaissance sortie between Le Cateau and Guise, and crashed at Haybes, north of Fumay. Possibly that attacked by Adj Delegay, Sgt Starke, and Cpl Postolka of GC I/1 near Crépy, north-west of Laon, 6.10 a.m. Fw H. Meyer and Uffz A. Dröge killed. Lt E. Buraner badly wounded, died May 19. Aircraft a write-off.

1.(H)/23 Henschel Hs126. Failed to return from observation sortie over Wavre, probable victim of ground-fire. Fw H. Gross and Uffz H. Liebers missing. Aircraft a write-off.

2.(H)/31 Henschel Hs126. Shot down by Adj Gaudon of GC II/6 during observation sortie north-east of Chimay 10.30 a.m. Lt J. Horn and Uffz E. Prössel believed baled out and captured unhurt. Aircraft a write-off.

2.(H)/31 Henschel Hs126. Believed returned damaged following observation sortie over roads between Beaumont and Strée. Lt Leupold wounded. Aircraft damage state unknown.

3.(F)/31 Dornier Do17 (1630). Lost bearings in cloud during reconnaissance sortie and forced-landed near Altkirch, south-west of Mulhouse. Lt E. Grampp unhurt. Lt H-F. Schiemer (of IR19) captured badly injured. Gefr K-H. Thomas captured slightly injured. Aircraft 9K+LL a write-off.

1.(H)/41 Henschel Hs126. Returned damaged by flak during observation sortie over Bierges, south-west of Wavre. Fw H. Masching slightly wounded, admitted to hospital in Tirlemont. Aircraft repairable.

Left: **Hauptmann Egbert von Loesch was the Staffelkapitän of 1./KG30.** *Right:* **This was his grave at Westrode, pictured in August 1940 by his family; now he lies in the German War**

Cemetery at Lommel (Block 45, Grave 408). *Below:* **Items recovered from the crash site were given to the family at the time when they visited the grave. Now held by Peter Taghon.**

1.(F)/121 Heinkel He111. Believed shot down by F/L Lee and Sgt Allard of No. 85 Squadron near Tirlemont 5.00 p.m. Lt G. Fischer and crew baled out. Aircraft a write-off.

Aufklärungsstaffel I. Flakkorps Dornier Do17Z. Crash-landed near Ochamps, cause not stated. Lt Lenk killed, rest of crew believed unhurt. Aircraft damaged but repairable.

Stab VIII. Fliegerkorps Fieseler Fi156. Damaged in taxying accident at Neufchâteau. No casualties. Aircraft damaged but repairable.

1./JG2 Messerschmitt Bf109E-4. Shot down by return fire from LeO451 engaged east of Montcornet. Leutnant M. Jaczak captured unhurt. Aircraft a write-off.

I./JG3 Messerschmitt Bf109E-1. Belly-landed following control failure. Pilot unhurt. Aircraft damaged but repairable.

3./JG3 Messerschmitt Bf109E-4. Returned damaged by Do17 gunner south-east of Marche-en-Famenne. Oberleutnant W. Jänisch *(Staffelkapitän)* unhurt. Aircraft repairable.

I./JG21 Messerschmitt Bf109E-1. Wrecked in forced-landing at Elsenborn following engine failure. Pilot unhurt. Aircraft a write-off.

4./JG26 2 Messerschmitt Bf109E-3s. Forced-landed at Enschede out of fuel. Pilots unhurt. Aircraft both damaged but repairable.

5./JG26 Messerschmitt Bf109E-3. Shot down in combat with Hurricanes between Tournai and Lille during bomber escort sortie 3.50 p.m. Possibly that claimed by Sgt Deacon of No. 85 Squadron. Pilot believed unhurt. Aircraft a write-off.

5./JG26 Messerschmitt Bf109E-1. Shot down in combat with Hurricanes between Tournai and Lille during bomber escort sortie 3.50 p.m. Probably that claimed by F/O Rayner and P/O David of No. 87 Squadron. Crashed and burned out at Genech, south of Cysoing. Feldwebel E. Stolz killed. Aircraft a write-off.

9./JG26 Messerschmitt Bf109E-4. Shot down in combat north-west of Brussels and crashed at Buggenhout, north of Merchtem. Possibly that attacked by P/O van Mentz of No. 504 Squadron 6.00 p.m. Uffz M. Schröpfer baled out and captured. Aircraft a write-off.

I./JG27 Messerschmitt Bf109E-3. Returned damaged following combat with Hurricanes south-east of Brussels. Possibly that attacked by P/O Jackson of No. 615 Squadron over Tirlemont 1.40 p.m. Pilot unhurt. Aircraft damaged but repairable.

I./JG27 Messerschmitt Bf109E-1. Crashed on landing at Jeneffe due to undercarriage failure. Pilot unhurt. Aircraft damaged but repairable.

2./JG27 Messerschmitt BF109E-3. Shot down by P/O Grassick of No. 615 Squadron and abandoned south-east of Brussels 1.40 p.m. Fw O. Sawallisch baled out unhurt. Aircraft a write-off.

II./JG27 Messerschmitt Bf109E-4. Wrecked in forced-landing at Eindhoven due to petrol failure. Pilot believed unhurt. Aircraft a write-off.

Stab JG52 Bücker Bü131. Crashed in the Rhine near St Goar, circumstances not stated. Leutnant Stauffenberg and passenger both injured. Aircraft lost.

1./JG52 Messerschmitt Bf109E-1. Undercarriage collapsed on landing. Uffz F. Gilhaus unhurt. Aircraft 5 + repairable.

II./JG52 Messerschmitt Bf109E-3. Belly-landed at base, cause not stated. Pilot unhurt. Aircraft damaged but repairable.

III./JG53 Messerschmitt Bf109E-1. Forced-landed near Sedan damaged by friendly fire. Pilot unhurt. Aircraft damaged but repairable.

1./JG54 Messerschmitt Bf109E-3 (5083). Starboard radiator damaged by ground-fire during low-level attack on Luxeuil airfield and finally abandoned over Lutran, east of Belfort. Uffz F. Hotzelmann baled out and captured wounded. Aircraft 10 + a write-off.

Stabsstaffel KG2 Dornier Do17Z. Forced-landed at Gelnhausen damaged by Sgt Puda of GC II/4 near Berry-au-Bac, north of Reims, 1.00 p.m. No crew casualties. Aircraft damaged but repairable.

Stab II./KG2 Dornier Do17Z. Oil tank hit by flak south-west of Dun-sur-Meuse and starboard engine failed during sortie to Luxeuil 2.15 p.m. Crashed attempting forced-landing on one engine. Oberlt F. Dörwaldt, Oberfw M. Strobel, Uffz G. Mache, and Uffz R. Zöphel injured. Aircraft U5+BC a write-off.

5./KG2 Dornier Do17Z. Returned with wounded crewman after machine-gun barrel exploded during attacks by Curtiss H-75s of GC II/4 near Grandpré 1.15 p.m. Fw W. Lutz slightly injured. Aircraft undamaged.

6./KG2 Dornier Do17Z. Hit by flak west of Dun-sur-Meuse during sortie to Luxeuil and crashed in woods at Sommauthe 2.15 p.m. Flgr R. Wille killed. Oberlt F. Schwankert, Uffz G. Schubert, and Uffz H. Matussek captured wounded. Aircraft U5+GP a write-off.

2./KG4 Heinkel He111. Returned damaged by flak over Ath, south-west of Brussels. Uffz E. Börner badly wounded, admitted to hospital in Gütersloh. Aircraft repairable.

Not only is Switzerland the world's oldest democracy, its geographical position in the centre of Europe making it the guardian of the trans-Alpine route led to the establishment of its traditional neutrality. This was first enshrined in the Treaty of Westphalia in 1648 and reaffirmed by the League of Nations in 1920. Combatants landing in Switzerland were automatically interned like the crew of the 9./KG27 Heinkel 1G+HT.

2./KG4 Heinkel He111. Returned damaged by flak over Ath, south-west of Brussels. Gefr W. Modrzik badly wounded, admitted to hospital in Gütersloh. Aircraft repairable.

2./KG4 Heinkel He111. Returned damaged by fighters over Enghien, south-west of Brussels, and possibly that attacked by F/L Owen and P/O Renison of No. 504 Squadron 12.00 p.m. Fw W. Hellwig badly wounded, admitted to hospital in Gütersloh. Aircraft repairable.

9./KG27 Heinkel He111P. Blown off-course in snow storm over Épinal and strayed over the frontier near Montfaucon on return from sortie to Neufchâteau, and Troyes. Attacked over the Greifensee by Swiss Bf109s (Oberlt Streiff and Oberlt Kisling of FL.Kp.21) and belly-landed near Ottikon, east of Kempthal 5.45 p.m. Lt J. Riecker injured on back on landing, admitted to St Anna-Spital in Luzerne, Uffz H. Scholler captured unhurt. Fw G. Hobbie and Uffz A. Herzig baled out between Effretikon and Kempthal and captured badly wounded. Aircraft 1G+HT fired by crew.

This crew was interned by the Swiss authorities, the badly wounded Gerhard Hobbie and Hans Scholler being repatriated to Germany on June 28, Joachim Riecker and Alfred Herzig following on July 6.

7./KG28 Heinkel He111. Returned damaged in attack by S/Lt Dietrich of GC II/10 east of Berlaimont during against communications between Avesnes and Le Cateau 6.40 p.m. Uffz H. Rosenberger and Obergefr G. Triebstein slightly wounded. Aircraft repairable.

1./KG30 Junkers Ju88A. Shot down by flak during attack on roads west of Brussels and crashed east of Ramsdonk, south of the railway line from Dendermonde to Mechelen 12.00 p.m. Hptmn E. von Loesch *(Staffelkapitän)*, Fw W. Steffen, Uffz H. Feyen, and Gefr K-H. Teschner killed. Aircraft a write-off.

2./KG30 Junkers Ju88A-1. Hit by flak during attack on roads west of Brussels and crashed south of Wavre 12.00 p.m. Oberfw H. Strohmaier and Uffz W. Grazce killed. Uffz S. Sempert believed died of wounds. Hptmn K-F. Hielscher *(Staffelkapitän)* slightly wounded. Aircraft a write-off.

3./KG30 Junkers Ju88A-2. Port engine set alight in attack by P/O Parsons of No. 504 Squadron during attack on roads west of Brussels. Escaped into cloud but hit by AA and forced-landed at Ninove 12.00 p.m. Oberlt R. Bürner, Uffz A. Henkel, Uffz K. Schmitz, and Gefr D. Haase captured unhurt. Aircraft 4D+CL a write-off.

8./KG30 Junkers Ju88A. Hit high-tension cables and belly-landed shortly after take-off from Marx. Gefr K. Schmidt slightly injured. Aircraft damaged but repairable.

I./KG53 Heinkel He111H. Forced-landed near Trechtelfingen due to engine damage. No crew casualties. Aircraft damaged but repairable.

II./KG53 Heinkel He111H. Belly-landed near Ippesheim due to engine failure. No crew casualties. Aircraft damaged but repairable.

3./KG76 Dornier Do17Z. Returned damaged in attacks by No. 607 Squadron Hurricanes south of Vervins 3.15 p.m. Uffz H. Nöller killed. Aircraft repairable.

II./KG76 Dornier Do17Z. Damaged in forced-landing at Dortmund due to fuel shortage. No crew casualties. Aircraft damaged but repairable.

7./KG76 Dornier Do17Z. Returned damaged by ground-fire and possibly attacks by Moranes of GC III/2 during low-level attack on motorised columns near Maubeuge 12.30 p.m. Obergefr K. Kübler badly wounded, admitted to hospital at Bonn-Hangelar. Aircraft repairable.

7./KG76 Dornier Do17Z. Returned damaged by ground-fire and possibly attacks by Moranes of GC III/2 during low-level attack on motorised columns south of Charleroi 12.30 p.m. Oberfw H. von Dahlen killed. Aircraft repairable.

9./KG76 Dornier Do17Z. Returned damaged by ground-fire and possibly attacks by Moranes of GC III/2 during low-level attack on motorised columns near Beaumont 12.30 p.m. Uffz H. Müller badly wounded, admitted to hospital at Bonn-Hangelar. Aircraft repairable.

The 9th Staffel of KG76 was a low-level attack unit, their Dornier Do17Zs specially adapted for the role with extra armour protection fitted and a fixed 20mm MGFF cannon mounted in the nose. They enjoyed some spectacular successes during the campaign in the West developing the hedge-hopping techniques that would culminate in an audacious but ill-fated strike against Kenley airfield on August 18.

9./KG76 Dornier Do17Z. Badly damaged by ground-fire during low-level attack on motorised columns near Avesnes. Also believed attacked by Moranes of GC III/2 and crashed on railway at Beaumont, east of Maubeuge, 12.30 p.m. Uffz G. Elterich killed. Aircraft a write-off.

2./KG77 Dornier Do17Z. Reported shot down by fighters south of Tournai and possibly that attacked by Curtiss H-75s of GC I/5 east of Le Chesne 7.30 p.m. Oberfw W. Fischer, Uffz A. Reichert, Uffz E. Oberschelp, and Uffz W. Herst baled out and captured wounded. Aircraft a write-off.

6./KG77 Dornier Do17Z. Believed shot down by No. 87 Squadron Hurricanes east of Valenciennes a.m. Probably one of those attacked by Sgt Nowell. Crew believed captured wounded. Aircraft a write-off.

6./KG77 Dornier Do17Z. Returned damaged in attacks by No. 87 Squadron Hurricanes east of Valenciennes a.m. Probably one of those attacked by Sgt Nowell. Uffz H. Sonntag and Uffz L. Pragerstorfer wounded. Aircraft damage state not recorded.

I./KGzbV.1 Junkers Ju52 (5172). Crash-landed at Ochamps on supply mission. Crew believed unhurt. Aircraft a write-off.

III./KGzbV.1 Junkers Ju52 (5603). Crash-landed near Prez, east of Rumigny, during fuel supply mission. Crew believed unhurt. Aircraft damaged but repairable.

III./KGzbV.1 Junkers Ju52 (5738). Crashed on landing near Prez, east of Rumigny, during fuel supply mission. Crew believed unhurt. Aircraft a write-off.

Four aircraft, including the 1Z+ET, were lost in two days on these missions to airlift essential fuel supplies to German armour in the area.

2./LG1 Heinkel He111H. Shot down by own flak near Krefeld. Fw W. Dörenberg killed, rest of crew baled out unhurt. Aircraft a write-off.

11.(St)/LG1 Junkers Ju87B. Forced-landed damaged during sortie over Maubeuge 5.45 p.m. Crew believed unhurt. Aircraft a write-off.

11.(St)/LG1 Junkers Ju87B. Failed to return from sortie over Maubeuge 5.45 p.m. Crew believed unhurt. Aircraft a write-off.

15.(Z)/LG1 Messerschmitt Bf110C. Shot down by Lt Bouysse of GC I/8 in combat over La Fère during escort for reconnaissance sortie and crashed west of Rogécourt 5.55 a.m. Lt G. Schwarzer and Obergefr F. Petrich killed. Aircraft a write-off.

7.(F)/LG2 Dornier Do17P. Intercepted near Ghent by Lt Leenhardt, Adj Crémieu, and Sgt Cazade of GC III/1 and port fuel tank set alight during photo-reconnaissance between Brussels and Vlissingen. Belly-landed and burned out south-east of Spui, between Zaanslag and Magrette, south of Terneuzen, 1.10 p.m. Fw A. Schenkelberg, and Fw J. Gronn captured unhurt. Gefr H. Reiche captured wounded in thigh. Aircraft L2+GR a write-off.

9.(H)/LG2 Focke-Wulf Fw189A-0. Shot down by P/O Parker, P/O Clift, and Sgt Cartwright of No. 79 Squadron during observation sortie between Ernage and Orbais, north of Gembloux, 8.30 p.m. Oberlt G. Wöbbeking *(Staffelkapitän)* and Gefr B. Allmann badly wounded. Aircraft a write-off.

One of the pre-production examples of the Focke-Wulf Fw189 'Uhu' then undergoing operational evaluation with 9.(H)/LG2 prior to introduction into service. Unorthodox in design, it was to prove a remarkably successful reconnaissance type.

9.(H)/LG2 Focke-Wulf Fw189A-0. Shot down by P/O Parker, P/O Clift, and Sgt Cartwright of No. 79 Squadron and crashed near Ramillies-Offus, south-west of Hannut 8.30 p.m. Lt K. Seehase, Uffz H. Schmitz, and Gefr H. Kaven killed. Aircraft a write-off.

6./StG2 Junkers Ju87B. Shot down near Boncelles, south of Seraing. Uffz H. Hertung and Gefr H. Tritt killed. Aircraft a write-off.

4./StG77 Junkers Ju87B. Returned damaged by ground-fire. Crew believed unhurt. Aircraft damage state not recorded.

1./ZG1 Messerschmitt Bf110C. Returned damaged in combat with Hurricanes north-west of Brussels 6.00 p.m. Possibly that attacked by P/O Darwin of No. 87 Squadron. Lt W. Schenck slightly wounded admitted to hospital in Krefeld. Fw R. Jaschke believed unhurt. Aircraft damage state not recorded.

1./ZG1 Messerschmitt Bf110C. Shot down in combat with Hurricanes and crashed near Walemstraat in Mechelen, north-west of Brussels, 6.00 p.m. Possibly that claimed by F/O Rayner of No. 87 Squadron. Lt H. Bucksch and Gefr H-W. Roth killed. Aircraft 2N+HH a write-off.

8./ZG26 Messerschmitt Bf110C-2 (3096). Shot down by Sgt Casenobe and Cdt Rozanoff *(Commandant)* of GC II/4 in combat east of Fismes and crashed at Pévy, north-west of Reims, 2.45 p.m. Fw L. Grammann and Uffz K. Ehemann killed. Aircraft 3U+FS a write-off.

8./ZG26 Messerschmitt Bf110C. Returned damaged by Adj Villey of GC II/4 in combat east of Fismes 2.45 p.m. Obergefr P. Seidel badly wounded admitted to hospital in Simmern. Aircraft damage state not recorded.

Unfortunately not all comparisons are meaningful. When we saw the wartime shot in Peter Taghon's collection, it looked an ideal choice for a 'then and now' match but when Jean-Louis Roba reached the spot — some 200 metres south of the level crossing at La Graveline, a hamlet north of Beaumont — he found that the railway line to Charleroi had been lifted to be replaced by rampant vegetation!

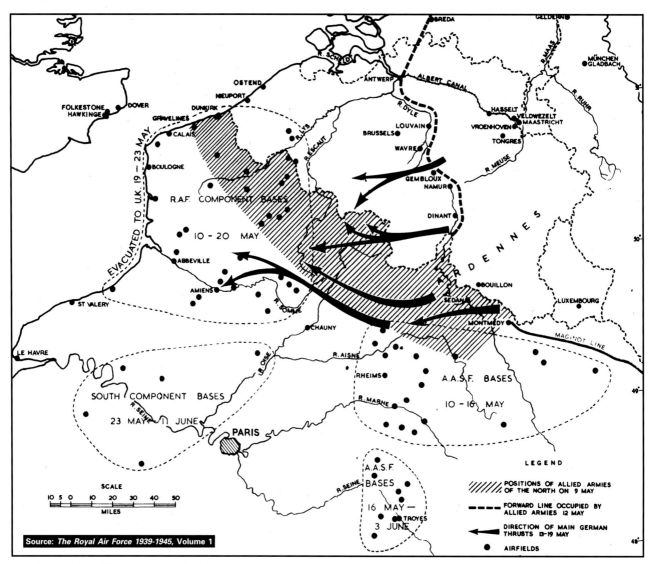

Source: *The Royal Air Force 1939-1945*, Volume 1

Friday, May 17

While Allied ground forces in Holland and Belgium continued to fall back and regroup in the face of enemy pressure, German forces in France exploited the gap in the French 1ère Armée line south-west of Maubeuge. Some French elements continued to hold Namur, Charleroi, and recaptured Montcornet, all well in advance of the main line, but only token forces now opposed the German advance between Maubeuge and Attigny.

RAF Component reconnaissance flights during the day attempted to establish the extent of enemy movements, but distinguishing German columns from retreating Allied columns proved difficult. This uncertainty, combined with rapidly deteriorating communications, inevitably resulted in confusion, cancelled orders, and several tragic errors. Late morning, 20 aircraft from Nos. 16, 18 and 57 Squadrons bombed a French column on the road between Le Cateau and Cambrai. And a further attack on the road between St Quentin and Péronne, by Nos. 18 and 57 Squadrons during late afternoon, is also thought to have been another French column. Meanwhile, further photo-reconnaissance flights by No. 53 Squadron were abandoned due to recent casualties inflicted by Hurricanes.

AASF bombers were unable to operate since no supplies of bombs or fuel had yet reached their new landing grounds. Consequently, at dawn, Bomber Command despatched 12 Blenheims of No. 82 Squadron to block the German advance through Gembloux. RAF Component fighters covered the target at the appointed time but the bombers never arrived. Coming under heavy and accurate AA fire before reaching the target area, the Blenheims had opened out into loose formation, and before they could close up again came under attack by Bf109s. Only one aircraft returned to base badly damaged, this disastrous raid prompting a further change in policy. That evening, BAFF HQ confirmed with the RAF Component that, in future, its Hurricanes would rendezvous with Bomber Command aircraft, escort them to the target, and cover them during the first stages of the return flight.

Operations by AASF fighters were also severely restricted during the day, partly due to their recent moves, but largely due to a serious lack of serviceable aircraft. By the end of the morning, there remained seven Hurricanes serviceable with No. 73 Squadron and only two with No. 1 Squadron. Replacements were available at Amiens-Glisy but collecting them was proving a problem. Easing the overall situation, reinforcing flights arriving in France were distributed amongst RAF Component squadrons desperately short of both pilots and aircraft. As such, they were used as replacements rather than reinforcements.

However, as result of the War Cabinet decision taken the previous day, six squadrons of Fighter Command Hurricanes, three of them composite units made up of flights from different squadrons, were now concentrated in southern England for operations over France. The original intention was for three to proceed to France for the morning 'shift', and be replaced by the other three during the afternoon. In fact, only one returned to England after morning operations, two of them enjoying considerable success against formations of Ju87s they encountered.

In addition, RAF Fighter Command flew two patrols of Spitfires over Ostend during the day while No. 604 Squadron maintained standing patrols between Béthune and St Omer by single Blenheims during the hours of darkness.

A threatened enemy advance on Cambrai and Arras now caused the RAF Component HQ to prepare for immediate withdrawal, similar instructions being issued to the headquarters staff remaining at Maroeuil and Achicourt. Several 'exposed' squadrons were also ordered to retire west to Poix and Moyencourt. Further changes would follow due to revised Air Ministry policy received by Air Marshal Barratt on this day that indicated the AASF should be reduced to a strength that could be maintained yet still allow full mobility. He therefore decided to preserve the three existing AASF fighter squadrons but reduce the bomber force to six Battle squadrons which resulted in further movements and reorganisation.

That night, 53 Bomber Command Wellingtons and Hampdens bombed the Meuse crossings at Namur, Yvoir-Anhée, Gembloux, Dinant and Givet following a War Cabinet directive issued the previous day. Twelve aircraft returned with their loads, unable to locate either primary or secondary targets.

Here, Sergeant Pilot Geoffrey Allard of No. 85 Squadron is being congratulated on his return to Lille-Seclin on May 10 having just shot down his second He111 of the day, the first shared with Squadron Leader Oliver and Pilot Officer Lecky (see page 210).

He went on to claim another probable at 8.35 p.m. that evening. His Hurricane N2319 lasted only a few more days before being lost on May 17 at the hands of Pilot Officer Patrick Woods-Scawen, who was later to lose his life in the Battle of Britain.

BRITISH AIR FORCES IN FRANCE

1 SQUADRON, CONDÉ-VRAUX

Hurricane P2820. Shot down by Fw Jentzsch of 13.(Z)/LG1 in combat over Vouziers 10.30 a.m. Flying Officer C. D. Palmer baled out unhurt. Aircraft a write-off.

Hurricane L1905. Returned badly damaged in combat with Bf110s of V.(Z)/LG1 over Vouziers 10.30 a.m. Sergeant F. J. Soper unhurt. Aircraft ⊙H damaged but repairable — destroyed on withdrawal to Anglure next day.

Hurricane. Returned wing and aileron damaged by cannon fire in combat with Bf110s of V.(Z)/LG1 over Vouziers 10.30 a.m. Flight Lieutenant P. R. Walker unhurt. Aircraft damaged but repairable — destroyed on withdrawal to Anglure next day.

2 SQUADRON, ABBEVILLE-DRUCAT

Lysander L4811. Landed at Douai damaged by Bf109 during reconnaissance flight. Possibly that attacked by Lt Kosse of 6./JG26 over Mons 5.30 p.m. Flying Officer C. H. Dearden and LAC Patterson unhurt. Aircraft KO⊙N damaged but repairable — later destroyed.

3 SQUADRON, MERVILLE

Hurricane L1899. Shot down by Lt Bucholz of 1./JG3 and crash-landed in flames near Vitry-en-Artois during attack on Do17s 6.15 p.m. Sergeant P. Hillwood badly burned hands and face. Aircraft a write-off.

Hurricane L1609. Shot down in combat with Bf109s of 1./JG3 and abandoned during attack on Do17s near Merville 6.30 p.m. Flying Officer D. A. E. Jones baled out unhurt. Aircraft a write-off.

16 SQUADRON, BERTANGLES

Lysander II L4796. Failed to return from tactical reconnaissance over St Quentin 2.30 p.m. and believed crashed near Doingt, south-east of Péronne. Pilot Officer L. M. Hamilton missing. LAC J. P. O'Reilly killed. Aircraft a write-off.

17 SQUADRON, MERVILLE

Hurricane. Shot down in combat with Bf109s of 8./JG26 following attack on Ju87s of IV.(St)/LG1 south-east of Brussels 5.15 p.m. Flying Officer A. P. Lines baled out unhurt. Aircraft a write-off.

Hurricane P3277. Stalled in steep turn during attack on Ju87s of IV.(St)/LG1 and crash-landed 15 miles south-east of Brussels 5.15 p.m. Squadron Leader G. C. Tomlinson injured. Aircraft destroyed by pilot.

18 SQUADRON, MÉHARICOURT

Two Blenheim IVs L9186, L9340. Unserviceable aircraft left on withdrawal to Goyencourt. No crew casualties. Aircraft both abandoned.

53 SQUADRON, POIX

Blenheim IV R3699. Returned starboard cowling damaged by light flak during reconnaissance sortie over Rethel and Vouziers 1.30 p.m. P/O S. G. Collins, Sergeant Service, and AC Cowling unhurt. Aircraft repairable.

B FLIGHT, 56 SQUADRON, VITRY-EN-ARTOIS

Hurricane N2553. Returned with wing and tail damaged by AA fire east of Lille 1.00 p.m. Sergeant C. Whitehead unhurt. Aircraft US⊙P damaged but repairable — abandoned on withdrawal to Norrent-Fontes next day.

Hurricane N2437. Lost port wing tip to AA fire east of Lille 1.00 p.m. Flight Lieutenant I. S. Soden unhurt. Aircraft US⊙L repairable.

57 SQUADRON, ROSIÈRES-EN-SANTERRE

Blenheim IV R3595. Forced-landed at Le Quesnel following reconnaissance sortie and strafed by Bf109s. Pilot Officer Ritchie and LAC G. C. P. Haines unhurt. Sergeant R. M. Wells wounded. Aircraft abandoned.

Blenheim IV L9245. Damaged aircraft dispersed at Lihons on withdrawal to Poix. No crew casualties. Aircraft abandoned.

79 SQUADRON, MERVILLE

Hurricane L2140. Failed to return from patrol between Vilvoorde and Braine-le-Comte and believed shot down by AA fire 8.30 p.m. Pilot Officer R. Herrick baled out and captured. Aircraft a write-off.

85 SQUADRON, LILLE-SECLIN

Hurricane N2319. Believed shot down in combat with Bf109s of II./JG26 west of Douai 4.00 p.m. Pilot Officer P. P. Woods-Scawen baled out slightly wounded. Aircraft a write-off.

151 SQUADRON, ABBEVILLE

Hurricane P3312. Forced-landed damaged by return fire from Ju87s of III./StG51 engaged over Valenciennes 11.00 a.m. Pilot Officer J. R. Hamar unhurt. Aircraft repairable.

B FLIGHT, 213 SQUADRON, MERVILLE

Hurricane. Became separated from patrol and lost bearings eventually forced-landing near Le Touquet 4.00 p.m. Sergeant A. F. C. Valentine broken arm, admitted to hospital. Aircraft AK⊙O a write-off.

Hurricane. Returned with one wing damaged by anti-aircraft fire over the Forêt-de-Nivelles during patrol between Vilvoorde and Braine-le-Comte 9.00 p.m. Flight Lieutenant D. Wight unhurt. Aircraft AK⊙S repairable.

A FLIGHT, 242 SQUADRON, LILLE-SECLIN

Hurricane. Forced-landed with damage to engine following combat with Bf109s of II./JG26 west of Douai 4.00 p.m. Pilot Officer D. G. MacQueen unhurt. Aircraft damaged but repairable.

A FLIGHT, 245 SQUADRON, MOORSELE

Hurricane N2501. Glycol tank damaged in combat with Bf109s between Ath and Brussels and crash-landed near Pottignies 7.40 p.m. Pilot Officer J. S. Southwell unhurt. Aircraft a write-off.

Hurricane N2702. Lost bearings during dusk patrol between Douai and Valenciennes and damaged in forced-landing near Dieppe 8.30 p.m. Sergeant R. W. E. Jarrett unhurt. Aircraft damaged but repairable — later abandoned.

A FLIGHT, 601 SQUADRON, MERVILLE

Hurricane N2435. Became separated from patrol in avoiding AA fire and lost bearings; forced-landed low on fuel near Aire, south-east of St Omer 8.15 p.m. Flying Officer G. R. Branch unhurt. Aircraft damaged but repairable.

Hurricane L2141. Wrecked in forced-landing near Bapaume damaged by return fire from Do17 engaged between Vilvoorde and Braine-le-Compte 9.15 p.m. Flight Lieutenant Sir A. P. Hope unhurt. Aircraft a write-off.

607 SQUADRON, VITRY-EN-ARTOIS

Hurricane P2874. Forced-landed at Amiens hit by return fire from He111s of I./KG54 engaged over Binche 2.50 p.m. Pilot Officer G. McK. Stewart unhurt. Aircraft AF⊙B repairable – returned later.

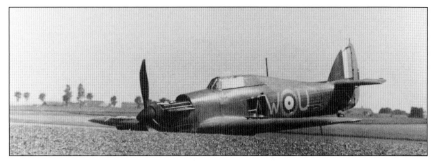

No positive proof but could this be Flight Lieutenant Sanders' Hurricane from No. 615 Squadron (code KW) which forced-landed near Lille?

615 SQUADRON, MOORSELE

Hurricane P2907. Lost bearings after attack on Hs126 of 3.(H)/41 and landed at Coulpiègne for directions. Wrecked in crash-landing through trees at Forges-les-Eaux when out of fuel 7.00 a.m. Pilot Officer M. Ravenhill (of No. 229 Squadron) unhurt. Aircraft a write-off.

Malcolm Ravenhill was one of three replacement pilots attached from No. 229 Squadron on May 14. Officially reported as 'missing', he returned to England on May 24 flying a Gladiator abandoned by No. 615 Squadron.

Hurricane. Forced-landed following attack on Ju88 of 7./LG1 near Lille 10.20 a.m. Flight Lieutenant J. G. Sanders unhurt. Aircraft repairable.

UK-based aircraft lost or damaged on operations over the Western Front:

RAF BOMBER COMMAND

82 Squadron, Watton
Armoured columns at Gembloux:

Blenheim IV L8830. Bomb-bay damaged by AA fire en route to target and believed abandoned over Rosseignies, north of Charleroi, 6.15 a.m. F/O R. J. McConnell baled out and captured. LAC H. Humphreys baled out wounded, taken to hospital where later captured. Sgt S. J. Fulbrook baled out unhurt, evaded capture and returned. Aircraft UX⊙T a write-off.

Blenheim IV L8858. Scuttled bombs and returned badly damaged in attacks by Bf109s of 1./JG3 en route to target 6.30 a.m. Sgt T. Morrison, Sgt Carbutt, and AC1 M. C. Cleary unhurt. Aircraft UX⊙W a write-off.

Blenheim IV L9210. Set alight in attack by Bf109s of 1./JG3 and crashed near Festieux, south-east of Laon, 6.30 a.m. P/O J. J. Greirson, Sgt J. W. Paul, and AC2 J. H. Patterson killed. Aircraft a write-off.

Claims by 1./JG3 report this action 'west of St Quentin' at around 7.20 a.m. While this location relates closely to that of identified casualties, it is difficult to understand why they were 120 km south-west of the prescribed target area.

Blenheim IV L9213. Shot down by Bf109s of 1./JG3 and crashed near Presles-et-Thierny, south of Laon, 6.30 a.m. F/L G. W. C. Watson, Sgt F. C. Wootten, and LAC A. G. Sims killed. Aircraft UX⊙M a write-off.

This crew, originally buried locally as 'Two Aviators RAF 17.5.40', was identified by the MREU following exhumation in 1948.

Blenheim IV P4838. Shot down by Bf109s of 1./JG3 6.30 a.m. F/O A. M. Gofton, Sgt F. S. Miller, and Cpl T. H. Cummins missing. Aircraft UX⊙R lost.

Blenheim IV P4851. Shot down by Bf109s of 1./JG3 6.30 a.m. Sgt F. Fearnley and Cpl A. G. Richards missing. F/O D. A. Fordham later returned. Aircraft lost.

Blenheim IV P4852. Shot down by Bf109s of 1./JG3 and crashed at Pancy-Courtecon, south-east of Laon, 6.30 a.m. P/O F. S. Jackson killed. S/L M. V. Delap wounded. Sgt R. F. Wyness baled out unhurt, evaded capture and returned. Aircraft a write-off.

Blenheim IV P4853. Shot down by Bf109s of 1./JG3 6.30 a.m. Sgt R. E. Newbatt, Sgt J. K. Crawley, and Sgt A. V. Knowles missing. Aircraft UX⊙D lost.

Blenheim IV P4854. Shot down by Bf109s of 1./JG3 6.30 a.m. Sgt A. G. B. Crouch and LAC R. Morris missing. P/O K. S. Toft captured. Aircraft UX⊙F lost.

Blenheim IV P4898. Shot down by Bf109s of 1./JG3 6.30 a.m. P/O S. Christensen, Sgt A. N. Phillips, and LAC P. R. V. Ettershank missing. Aircraft UX⊙Y lost.

Blenheim IV P4903. Shot down by Bf109s of 1./JG3 6.30 a.m. Sgt L. H. Wrightson, Sgt S. J. Beaumont, and AC1 K. A. Thomas later returned. Aircraft UX⊙U a write-off.

Blenheim IV P4904. Set alight in attacks by Bf109s of 1./JG3 and exploded between Merval and Lappion, south-east of Laon, 6.30 a.m. Sgt D. J. Lees and LAC K. G. Reed killed. Sgt T. J. Watkins blown from aircraft landing by parachute, evaded capture and returned. Aircraft a write-off.

RAF FIGHTER COMMAND

65 Squadron Hornchurch
Patrol Ostend:

Spitfire K9915. Returned wings damaged by return fire from Ju88 engaged off Vlissingen 9.00 a.m. F/O J. H. Welford unhurt. Aircraft repairable.

Certainly this is the remains of one of the Blenheims from No. 82 Squadron which suffered almost total wipe-out on its raid from Watton in Norfolk, to attack German forces at Gembloux in eastern Belgium. Twenty-two crewmen died in the attempt.

Sergent-Chef Cartier crash-landed his Curtiss H-75 (No. 84) of Groupe de Chasse 1/4 at Mardyck, just outside Dunkirk.

FRENCH AIR FORCE

AB 1 Vought 156F (4). Damaged during attack on Walcheren and crash-landed out of fuel on beach near Isigny. Mt. Claude and SM Le Guevel unhurt. Aircraft 2 a write-off.

AB 4 L-N 411 (2). Pulled out too late and crashed into the Baie d'Urville during dive-bombing practice off Cap Lévy a.m. SM Prigent killed. Aircraft 2 lost.

DAT Châteaudun Bloch 152. Forced-landed at Orléans reputedly damaged by return fire from Do17. Sgt S. Tomicki unhurt. Aircraft damaged but repairable.

DIAP (CWL) Caudron C-714 (8581). Forced-landed near Villiers-les-Dombes during training flight. Sgt M. Wedzik unhurt. Aircraft I-239 damaged but repairable, later abandoned.
This Polish unit based at Lyon-Bron trained fighter pilots for eventual service with GC 1/145.

ECN 2/13 Potez 631 (34). Shot down by flak during low-level attack on enemy motorised columns between Chimay and Trélon. Crashed and burned out in woods at 'Étangs-des-Moines', near Fourmies station, north of Hirson 8.40 a.m. Capt H. Petit de Myrbeck, Adjt H. Jouany, and Cpl J. Riche killed. Aircraft a write-off.

ECN 2/13 Potez 631 (71). Badly damaged by flak during strafing of enemy motorised columns between Chimay and Trélon; belly-landed near Chantilly 8.45 a.m. Adjt. Delmotte badly wounded. Adjt Le Cozannet wounded. Sgt Millot unhurt. Aircraft a write-off.

ECN 2/13 Potez 631. Engine hit by flak during low-level attack on enemy motorised columns between Chimay and Trélon; forced-landed near Laon 8.40 a.m. S/Lt Reyter and crew unhurt. Aircraft abandoned.

ECN 2/13 Potez 631. Shot down by flak during low-level attack on enemy motorised columns between Chimay and Trélon; forced-landed near Montceaux 8.45 a.m. Lt Guilier and Sgt Bal unhurt. Sgt Saint-Gall wounded. Aircraft abandoned.

ECN 3/13 Potez 631 (178). Shot down by flak during low-level attack on enemy armour between Fourmies and Chimay; crashed and burned out at 'Four Mathot', Macquenoise 10.30 a.m. Lt E. Rouyer and Adjt E. Chabert killed. Aircraft a write-off.

ECN 4/13 Potez 631. Hit by flak during low-level attack on enemy motorised columns between Chimay and Trélon; forced-landed near Cambrai 8.40 a.m. Adjt Cuiller badly wounded in knee; admitted to hospital in Amiens. Sgt Testu suffered severe shock. Aircraft a write-off.

ECN 4/13 Potez 631. Returned badly damaged by flak during attack on armoured columns between Chimay and Trélon 8.45 a.m. Adjt Martin and Sgt Fergue unhurt. Adjt R. Héritier mortally wounded, died during return flight. Aircraft damaged but repairable.

E2 Breguet 521 Bizerte. Forced-landed in the Gironde Estuary and sank off Verdon-sur-Mer. No crew casualties. Aircraft 4 lost.

GAO 4/551 5 Potez 63.11s (585). Aircraft destroyed or damaged on the ground at Bacqueville. No crew casualties. Aircraft all write-offs.

GB II/12 LeO 451 (40). Tail shot off by flak over Hauteville during bombing attack on motorised columns between Trélon and Chimay. Main wreckage fell at Macquigny, south-west of Guise 1.00 p.m. Capt A. Rocher, S/Lt A. Masclaud, Adjt R. Lambert, and Cpl Y. Le Goyat killed. Aircraft a write-off.
Eight other aircraft engaged on this sortie all returned to Persan-Beaumont with flak damage.

GB I/15 Farman 222 (32). Sortied to bomb road and rail targets between Hirson and Mezières but abandoned by crew over Montereau due to severe icing. Crashed at Misy-sur-Yonne 10.00 p.m. S/Lt S. Casse and Sgt P. Desroches baled out but killed due to parachute failure. Lt de Lagabre and four others baled out slightly injured. Aircraft a write-off.

GB I/15 Farman 222 (7). Crashed near Montagnon in severe weather conditions during night sortie to bomb road and rail targets between Hirson and Mezières 10.30 p.m. Lt Puissessau, S/Lt Humbert, S/Lt Lapeyre, Sgt Claret and two others unhurt. Aircraft a write-off.

GB I/31 LeO 451 (61). Shot down by Fw Rudorffer of 2./JG2 during sortie to attack armoured columns between Trélon and Chimay. Crashed at Le-Grand-Pré, near Floyon, north of La Capelle 1.20 p.m. S/Lt A. Rigourd, Sgt H. Bourgault, Adjt P. Fourneau, and Sgt J. Halma killed. Aircraft a write-off.

GB I/31 LeO 451 (122). Shot down by Bf109s during sortie to attack armoured columns between Trélon and Chimay. Possibly that attacked by Fw Keil or Fw Hermes of 2./JG2. Crashed and burned out at Esquéheries, north-east of Guise, 1.25 p.m. Sgt G. Gombert killed. Adjt L. Gast baled out but parachute failed and fell dead at Rocquigny. Lt G. Boudot baled out mortally wounded; died next day. Sgt Le Guellec baled out unhurt. Aircraft a write-off.

Left: **German troops examine their prizes on Cambrai airfield. The Morane 406** *(right)* **can be identified as No. 605 of Groupe de Chasse 5/2 which was damaged while taking off during a** raid on the aerodrome. The pilot, Sous-Lieutenant Lansoy, escaped unharmed but the plane was abandoned when the French pulled out.

GB I/31 LeO 451 (74). Shot down by Bf109s of 2./JG2 during sortie to attack armoured columns between Trélon and Chimay, possibly that claimed by Lt Hoffmann. Crashed in flames at Rogecourt, east of La Fère, 1.25 p.m. Cmdt. Schmitter *(Commandant)*, S/Lt Macombe, Sgt Veronet, and Sgt Panay wounded. Aircraft a write-off.

GC I/1 Bloch 152. Forced-landed at Noyon with damaged oil pump following combat with Bf109s of 1./JG3 over St Quentin 11.30 a.m. S/Lt P. Trébod unhurt. Aircraft repairable.

GC I/1 Bloch 152 (502). Propeller flew off during return from patrol over Maubeuge and Hirson 6.00 p.m. Crashed into trees bordering the runway at Chantilly. Adjt Monchanin injured. Aircraft a write-off.

GC II/1 Bloch 152 (255). Shot down by Bf109s of 1./JG1 during attack on Do17 south of St Quentin; crashed and burned out at Prémontré, 14 km west of Laon 12.10 p.m. Adjt H. Argueyrolles killed. Aircraft a write-off.

GC 6/1 Morane 406. Badly damaged in combat with enemy fighters during patrol over Ghent — Zelzate and forced-landed on Belgian airfield a.m. Sgt Castillon unhurt. Aircraft abandoned.
Another MS406 of GC III/1 was abandoned that evening on withdrawal from Norrent-Fontes to Plessis-Belleville.

GC I/2 Morane 406 (951). Suffered engine failure during patrol between Beaumont and Stenay; belly-landing at St-Vallier-sur-Marne, south-east of Langres 10.15 a.m. S/Lt S. Chalupa to hospital with badly injured head. Aircraft 6 a write-off.

GC III/2 Morane 406 (709). Forced-landed near Péronne following attack on Hs126 during patrol over Nivelles — Ligny — Charleroi sector 6.00 a.m. Sgt J. Linart unhurt. Aircraft a write-off.

GC 5/2 Morane 406 (605). Undercarriage damaged on take-off during bombing attack on Cambrai-Niergnies by Do17s 7.00 a.m. S/Lt A. Lansoy unhurt. Aircraft 10 damaged but repairable — later abandoned.

GC 1/4 Curtiss H-75. Shot down by Oberfw Dau of 1./JG20 during patrol over Beveland and crashed on a sandbank in the Westerschelde off Hoofdplaat 4.18 p.m. Lt J-L. Hirschauer wounded in foot, transported to hospital in Bruges. Aircraft a write-off.

GC 1/4 Curtiss H-75. Shot down by Fw Küll of 2./JG20 in combat over Walcheren, and abandoned north of Middelburg 4.15 p.m. Sgt D. Bompain baled out unhurt, reached Vlissingen and rejoined unit. Aircraft a write-off.

GC 1/4 Curtiss H-75 (84). Belly-landed at Mardyck damaged in combat with Bf109s of I./JG20 over Walcheren 4.15 p.m. Sgt Cartier unhurt. Aircraft 14 damaged but repairable.

GC I/8 Bloch 152 (508). Hit by light flak north of La Fère and crashed at 'Les Bruyères', near Moy-de-l'Aisne 2.30 p.m. Sgt P. Dupouy killed. Aircraft a write-off.
Originally buried alongside his aircraft by advancing German troops, Pierre Dupouy was exhumed on May 8, 1941, and reinterred in the local cemetery at Moy-de-l'Aisne.

GC I/8 Bloch 152 (548). Shot down by light flak south of St Quentin and crashed near 'Le Monument', north-east of Montescourt-Lizerolles 2.00 p.m. Lt J. Zerovnicky unhurt. Aircraft a write-off.
Jean Zerovnicky was taken in and hidden by locals. He spent the next four months masquerading as village idiot and working the land under German occupation. He later turned up at Montpellier where he was briefly reunited with comrades before moving on to Morocco where all trace of him was lost.

GC II/10 Bloch 152 (117). Shot down by Bf110s over Chauny and crashed at 'La Fontaine', Travecy, near La Fère 11.50 a.m. Possibly one of those claimed by Hptmn Groth *(Gruppenkommandeur)* of Stab II./ZG76. Lt R. Péronne killed. Aircraft a write-off.

GC II/10 Bloch 152 (42). Shot down by Bf110s over Chauny and crashed and burned out at Hinacourt, 11.50 a.m. Possibly one of those claimed by Hptmn Groth *(Gruppenkommandeur)* of Stab II./ZG76. S/Lt L. Thabuis killed. Aircraft a write-off.

GC II/10 Bloch 152 (193). Landed at Plessis-Belleville aileron damaged in combat with Bf110s between St Quentin and Chauny 12.00 p.m. Possibly that attacked by Oberlt Borchers of 4./ZG76. S/Lt L. Goetz unhurt. Aircraft damaged but repairable.

GC II/10 Bloch 152 (169). Shot down in combat with Bf110s over Chauny and abandoned over Plessis-Belleville 12.00 p.m. Possibly one of those attacked by Uffz Jörke of 4./ZG76. Adjt Souche baled out unhurt. Aircraft a write-off.

GC III/10 Bloch 152 (208). Shot down in combat with Bf110s of II./ZG76 and Bf109s of 1./JG3. Crashed alongside the railway at Pont d'Allemagne, near Canizy, 3 km west of Ham 12.00 p.m. Possibly one of those claimed by Oberfw Anthony of 4./ZG76. S/Lt R. Battut killed. Aircraft a write-off.

GC III/10 Bloch 152. Returned to Rouen-Boos with airframe and controls badly damaged following combat with Bf110s and Bf109s over Roye 12.00 p.m. Possibly that claimed by Oberlt Keller of 1./JG3. Sgt Y. Carbon unhurt. Aircraft a write-off.

GC III/10 Bloch 152 (185). Oil system damaged in combat with Bf110s and Bf109s over Roye, and possibly that claimed by Lt Bucholz of 1./JG3. Belly-landed south-east of Montescourt 12.00 p.m. Sgt R. Pinon unhurt. Aircraft a write-off.

GR I/14 Potez 63.11 (645). Badly damaged by flak during reconnaissance sortie over Walcourt and crashed on landing at Douai-Dechy 10.00 a.m. Capt d'Hennezel baled out and captured unhurt. Sgt Parmentier wounded in calf; admitted to hospital in Douai. Sgt Porchon unhurt. Aircraft a write-off.

GR II/22 Potez 63.11 (219). Forced-landed at Reims-Champagne with flak damage following reconnaissance sortie between Vervins and Liart 3.30 p.m. Capt Barse, Adjt Coudoux, and Adjt Crutel unhurt. Aircraft destroyed by crew.

GR II/33 Bloch 174 (9). Landed at Le Bourget damaged by ground-fire during low-level reconnaissance over armoured columns between Guise and Ribemont 5.00 a.m. S/Lt Hochedé and observer unhurt. Adjt G. Millet baled out over Grisy-les-Plâtres, hit the tailplane and fell mortally wounded. Aircraft a write-off.

GR I/36 Potez 63.11 (151). Landed at Martigny-les-Gerbonvaux badly damaged in attack by Bf110 during reconnaissance sortie to Landstuhl — Kaiserslautern — Husel. Crew unhurt. Aircraft a write-off.

BELGIAN AIR FORCE

1/I/1 Stampe-Vertongen SV-5. Unserviceable aircraft abandoned at Hingene on withdrawal to Ursel 7.00 a.m. Aircraft destroyed to prevent capture.

3/II/1 Fox (O.38). Returned to Aalter with longerons badly damaged by ground-fire during reconnaissance sortie over Walem, Duffel, and Lier 11.00 a.m. Adjt R. Uyttebroeckx and Lt M. Taymans both unhurt. Aircraft damaged but repairable — destroyed next day.

5/III/3 Battle (T.73). Returned to Aalter riddled by ground-fire following reconnaissance over the Leuven — Mechelen — Brussels sector and attack on enemy columns 6.45 p.m. Adjt A. Binon and S/Lt H. Dewit both unhurt. Aircraft damaged but repairable.

Parked in a revetment at the Belgian Air Force aerodrome at Aalter (between Ghent and Bruges), this Battle has suffered extensive damage and could well be the machine from 5/III/3 brought back by Adjutant Binon.

Oberleutnant Wolfgang Steudel *(left)* and Leutnant Peter Wintz *(right)* came to grief when their Henschel *(below)* was shot down by Groupe de Chasse I/1, but there is some discrepancy as to which unit the Germans belonged. Both officers were moved from their field grave *(centre)* to the cemetery at Fort-de-Malmaison (Block 7, Row 25, Graves 997 and 998).

LUFTWAFFE

1.(H)/14 Henschel Hs126. Shot down by Capt Garde, Sgt Starke, and Sgt Dubost of GC I/1 and crashed alongside the road to Origny-Ste-Benoîte, south-west of Guise, 5.45 p.m. Oberlt W. Steudel and Lt P. Wintz killed. Aircraft a write-off.

This loss is attributed to 3.(H)/41 in the Genst.Gen.Qu.6 Abt.(Ic) Luftwaffe General Quartermaster Returns.

2.(H)/14 Henschel Hs126. Shot down by Potez 631 gunner, Adj Le Cozannet, of ECN 2/13 and crashed near Coingt, between Vervins and Brunehamel, 11.30 a.m. Uffz L. Unterländer and Uffz H. Gehrke killed. Aircraft a write-off.

2.(H)/21 Henschel Hs126. Shot down by Capt Peyrègne and Cpl Sika, but also attacked by S/Lt Tanguy, of GC I/8 and forced-landed at La Capelle 5.40 p.m. Lt H. Lenne and Fw H-H. Broderson (both of 2.(H)/41) killed. Aircraft fired by crew.

German reports indicate that this crew was murdered after landing but no confirmation has been found.

1.(H)/23 Henschel Hs126. Returned damaged by Moranes of GC III/2 near Charleroi during observation sortie south-west of Leuven 5.30 a.m. and possibly that also attacked by P/O Parsons of No. 504 Squadron. Uffz H. Bauer slightly wounded. Aircraft damage state not recorded.

3.(F)/31 Dornier Do17. Wrecked in take-off accident. Crew believed injured. Aircraft a write-off.

4.(H)/31 Henschel Hs126. Shot down by S/Lt Tanguy and Sgt Liautard, but also attacked by Capt Peyrègne and S/Lt de Castel, of GC I/8 and crashed in flames near Ribemont 5.35 p.m. Lt Kranz wounded. Aircraft a write-off.

3.(H)/41 Henschel Hs126. Possibly that twice attacked and shot down by P/O Ravenhill of No. 615 Squadron north-west of Mons 6.40 a.m. One of crew believed killed. Oberlt Graf von der Schulenburg wounded. Aircraft a write-off.

1./JG3 Messerschmitt Bf109E. Badly damaged in combat with Bloch 152s of GC I/1 11.30 a.m. and crashed on landing at Hargimont. Possibly that attacked by Sgt Coader. Leutnant K. Haberland slightly wounded. Aircraft a write-off.

3./JG3 Messerschmitt Bf109E. Shot down by Sgt Teillet of GC I/1 in combat south-east of Cambrai and abandoned near Le Cateau 11.30 a.m. Leutnant H. Reumschüssel baled out unhurt. Aircraft a write-off.

1./JG20 Messerschmitt Bf109E-4. Fuel system damaged in attacks by nine Curtiss H-75s of GC I/4 and belly-landed between Vurste and Semmerzake, north of Gaverre, 4.15 p.m. Uffz W. Otterbeck captured. Aircraft 9 + destroyed.

2./JG20 Messerschmitt Bf109E-3. Believed shot down by Adj Hôtellier of GC I/4 in combat over Walcheren during low-level attack on batteries south of Middelburg and crashed at Nieuw-en-Sint-Joostland 4.15 p.m. Uffz M. Kazmaier killed. Aircraft a write-off.

I./JG21 Messerschmitt Bf109E-3. Damaged in taxying accident at Neufchâteau. Pilot unhurt. Aircraft damaged but repairable.

4./JG26 Messerschmitt Bf109E-3. Believed damaged in combat with Hurricanes west of Douai 4.40 p.m. and wrecked forced-landing at Bruges out of fuel. Possibly that claimed by P/O Wiens of No. 242 Squadron. Pilot believed unhurt. Aircraft a write-off.

4./JG26 Messerschmitt Bf109E-3. Believed shot down in combat with Hurricanes and abandoned west of Douai 4.40 p.m. Possibly one of those claimed by P/O Woods-Scawen of No. 85 Squadron. Oberfeldwebel H. Heidenpeter baled out and captured wounded. Aircraft a write-off.

1./JG51 Messerschmitt Bf109E. Forced-landed near base due to petrol failure. Feldwebel H. Bär unhurt. Aircraft repairable.

1./JG53 Messerschmitt Bf109E-1. Wrecked in forced-landing south of Büchenbeuren during transit flight to Ferschweiler. Uffz Grothen injured. Aircraft a write-off.

4./JG53 Messerschmitt Bf109E-4. Wrecked in take-off accident, cause not stated. Oberlt G. Schulze-Blanck unhurt. Aircraft a write-off.

I./JG76 Messerschmitt Bf109E-3. Returned damaged in combat with Moranes of GC I/5 between Hirson and Montcornet 5.30 p.m. Pilot unhurt. Aircraft damaged but repairable.

Backbone of the Heeresaufklärungsstaffeln during the French campaign, the parasol-winged Henschel Hs126 was a sound machine with excellent short take-off and landing capability and could absorb considerable punishment.

Unteroffizier Wilhelm Otterbeck of 1./JG20 escaped with his life when his Bf109 was hammered into submission by nine Curtiss H-75s.

I./JG76 Messerschmitt Bf109E-3. Damaged in combat with Moranes of GC I/5 south-east of Hirson and crashed on landing due to undercarriage failure 5.55 p.m. Pilot unhurt. Aircraft damaged but repairable.

2./JG76 Messerschmitt Bf109E-1. Shot down in combat with Moranes of GC I/5 and reported abandoned over Stonne, east of Le Chesne, 5.30 p.m. Lt B. Schulten baled out wounded. Aircraft a write-off.

1./JG77 Messerschmitt Bf109E. Lost during transit flight, circumstances not recorded. Uffz W. Evers unhurt. Aircraft a write-off.

6./KG1 Heinkel He111. Both engines damaged in attacks by Capt Peyrègne and Cpl Sika of GC I/8 between Le Cateau and Trélon, and forced-landed at Marchavenne, east of Bohain-en-Vermandois, 6.00 p.m. Uffz G. Aurich and Uffz W. Frank captured badly wounded. Flgr J. Güldens captured slightly wounded. Rest of crew unhurt. Aircraft a write-off.

Stabsstaffel KG2 Dornier Do17Z. Damaged in taxying accident at Ober-Olm. No crew casualties. Aircraft damaged but repairable.

1./KG2 Dornier Do17Z. Returned damaged following attack on railways between Challerange and Ste-Menehould. Gefr F. Hotz slightly wounded. Aircraft repairable.

3./KG2 Dornier Do17Z. Damaged in heavy landing at Geinsheim following night attack on Soissons. Uffz S. Stefanski slightly injured. Aircraft damaged but repairable.

II./KG2 Dornier Do17Z. Damaged in taxying accident after landing at Ober-Olm. Possible collision with Stab KG2 machine. No crew casualties. Aircraft damaged but repairable.

II./KG3 Dornier Do17Z. Damaged in fighter attack and forced-landed east of the railway between Laon and Soissons near Semilly. Possibly that attacked by Lt Le Gentil of GC I/1 over the Forêt de Laigue, north-east of Compiègne, 12.25 p.m. No crew casualties. Aircraft damaged but repairable.

III./KG3 Messerschmitt Bf108. Damaged in taxying accident at Dockendorf. No casualties. Aircraft damaged but repairable.

III./KG3 Junkers Ju52. Damaged in crash-landing near Niedermendig, cause not stated. No crew casualties. Aircraft damaged but repairable.

Stabsstaffel KG4 Heinkel He111P. Shot down by EV1 Prévost of AC 1 and crashed in the Scheldt Estuary, south of Westkapelle, during armed-reconnaissance of shipping south-west of Vlissingen 5.25 a.m. Also attacked by SM Domas of AC 2 and Lt Stiquel of GC I/4. Oberfw O. Geitz, Uffz W. Feller, Obergefr H. Schöning, and Gefr G. Kunze killed. Aircraft lost.

According to Lt Hirschauer of GC I/4 the aircraft attacked was an isolated Bristol Blenheim, but no such RAF loss has been identified. A suggestion that it could be one of the unresolved No. 82 Squadron losses is also doubted given the times of reported engagements.

Stabsstaffel KG4 Heinkel He111P. Shot down by AA and Sgt Joire of GC I/4 over Zuid Beveland during armed-reconnaissance of shipping south-west of Vlissingen and crashed off Ellewoutsdijk, west of Baarland, 5.25 a.m. Lt A. Bliesener, Uffz H. Hirschelmann, and Obergefr G. Förster killed. Aircraft lost.

Both Stab KG4 losses above have also been attributed to LV Folliot and Mt Billottet of AC 2 who claimed two He111s off Ostend at 9.00 a.m. on May 16. Given the differences in time, date, and location, it is difficult to reconcile these claims.

8./KG28 Heinkel He111. Returned damaged by flak near Le Cateau. Fw K. Warmuth slightly wounded. Aircraft repairable.

Stab III./KG30 Junkers Ju88A. Shot down by F/O Welford of No. 65 Squadron during anti-shipping sortie over Flushing and belly-landed on beach at Renesse, Schouwen Island, 10.15 a.m. Oberlt Wagner and crew missing. Aircraft 4D+CD a write-off.

2./KG54 Heinkel He111P. Shot down near Onnaing by Hurricanes of Nos. 56 and 607 Squadrons during reconnaissance between Valenciennes and Maubeuge 3.30 p.m. Uffz P. Ruppel and Obergefr L. Gfell killed. Uffz O. Schümann captured wounded. Gefr F. Matthes captured unhurt. Aircraft B3+HK a write-off.

3./KG54 Heinkel He111P. Shot down by Hurricanes of Nos. 56 and 607 Squadrons and forced-landed north-east of Valenciennes 3.30 p.m. Flgr F. Günther killed. Fw P. Lenz, Uffz W. Schlumpberger, and Obergefr G. Zirpel captured wounded. Aircraft a write-off.

3./KG54 Heinkel He111P. Shot down by Hurricanes of Nos. 56 and 607 Squadrons north-east of Valenciennes 3.30 p.m. Possibly that reported crashed and burned out at Onnaing. Gefr P. Petroschinski, Gefr B. Dau, and Flgr W. Kolbe killed. Fw A. Lau believed baled out and captured wounded. Aircraft a write-off.

3./KG54 Heinkel He111P. Possibly that reported forced-landed at Elouges damaged in attack by Hurricanes of Nos. 56 and 607 Squadrons north-east of Valenciennes 3.30 p.m. Fw W. Kümmel, Obergefr P. Friebe, Gefr K. Guhl, and Gefr J. Ebner captured. Aircraft a write-off.

4./KG76 Dornier Do17Z. Returned damaged by ground-fire during attack on roads between Cambrai and Bapaume. Also possibly attacked by Moranes of GC III/2 and Hurricanes of No. 607 Squadron. Uffz K. Pahlke and Oberfw E. Hofmeier both badly wounded. Aircraft damaged but repairable.

4./KG76 Dornier Do17Z. Returned damaged by ground-fire south of Valenciennes. Also possibly attacked by Moranes of GC III/2 and Hurricanes of No. 607 Squadron. Uffz K-H. Hipp died of wounds in hospital at Cologne-Hohenlind May 23. Aircraft damaged but repairable.

4./KG76 Dornier Do17Z. Returned damaged by ground-fire near Albert. Also possibly attacked by Moranes of GC III/2 and Hurricanes of No. 607 Squadron. Gefr W. Albert and Uffz E. Greiner wounded, admitted to hospital in Vogelsang. Aircraft damaged but repairable.

5./KG76 Dornier Do17Z. Returned damaged by ground-fire between Cambrai and Arras. Also possibly attacked by Moranes of GC III/2 and Hurricanes of No. 607 Squadron. Uffz K. Greulich slightly wounded, admitted to hospital in Vogelsang. Oberlt H. Weikert and rest of crew believed unhurt. Aircraft a write-off.

6./KG76 Dornier Do17Z. Shot down by F/L Soden of No. 56 Squadron and crashed outside Vitry-en-Artois 9.45 a.m. Lt O. Grüter, Uffz M. Perl, Gefr K. Kloster, and Uffz W. Scholz killed. Aircraft a write-off.

6./KG76 Dornier Do17Z. Set alight under attack by F/Sgt Higginson of No. 56 Squadron between Namur and Bapaume. Fw E. Hauser baled out but parachute failed. Uffz H. Koch, Oberfw J. Urban, and Gefr L. Paczinski baled out and captured unhurt. Aircraft a write-off.

7./KG76 Dornier Do17Z. Returned damaged by ground-fire during attack on motorised columns near Beaumont. Crew believed unhurt. Aircraft repairable.

9./KG76 Dornier Do17Z. Returned damaged by ground-fire during attack on motorised columns near Beaumont. Oberlt H. Neubert died of wounds in Venusberg hospital, Bonn. Aircraft damaged but repairable.

III./KGzbV.1 Junkers Ju52. Crashed on landing at a temporary airstrip near Prez, east of Rumigny, during fuel supply mission. No crew casualties. Aircraft a write-off.

III./KGzbV.1 Junkers Ju52 (6543). Crashed on landing at temporary airstrip near Prez, east of Rumigny, during fuel supply mission. No crew casualties. Aircraft damaged but repairable.

7./LG1 Junkers Ju88A-1. Returned to Düsseldorf damaged by flak and reported attack by biplane over Douai. Oberlt G. Richter and crew unhurt. Aircraft L1+CR damaged but repairable.

Possibly one of the recently discarded Gladiators of No. 615 Squadron distributed amongst squadrons for aerodrome defence with a few younger staff officers from RAF Component HQ to fly them.

7./LG1 Junkers Ju88A-1. Shot down by F/L Sanders of No. 615 Squadron and crashed at Flines-lez-Raches, north-east of Douai 10.15 a.m. Oberfw B. Hinke, Oberlt A. Dudek, and Gefr G. Salzmann killed. Oberlt E. Schwarz *(Staffelkapitän)* captured badly wounded. Aircraft L1+AR a write-off.

Ernst Schwarz was recovered from the aircraft and given emergency treatment by local Dr Antoine. Two gendarmes took him to hospital in Lille where he died of his injuries May 26.

10.(St)/LG1 Junkers Ju87B-1. Damaged in combat with Hurricanes of No. 17 Squadron over Grammont during sortie to attack Ninove and believed forced-landed 5.15 p.m. Pilot believed unhurt. Gefr E. Heller badly wounded, admitted to hospital in Liège where died June 3. Aircraft repairable.

11.(St)/LG1 Junkers Ju87B-1. Damaged in combat with Hurricanes of No. 17 Squadron south-west of Brussels during sortie to attack Ninove 5.15 p.m. Possibly one of those attacked by F/O Meredith. Crashed at Vaals, west of Aachen, on return flight. Gefr E. Gierger and Uffz J. Donderer killed. Aircraft a write-off.

12.(St)/LG1 Junkers Ju87B-1. Shot down by Hurricanes of No. 17 Squadron south-west of Brussels during sortie to attack Ninove. Crashed and burned out, 6 km north of Edingen, 5.15 p.m. Possibly that claimed by P/O Manger. Oberlt H. Wendelin *(Staffelkapitän)* and Fw A. Fleisch killed. Aircraft a write-off.

12.(St)/LG1 Junkers Ju87B-1. Shot down by Hurricanes of No. 17 Squadron south-west of Brussels during sortie to attack Ninove and crashed near Pepingen 5.15 p.m. Possibly that claimed by P/O Whittaker. Uffz S. Hofmann and Uffz H. Schmidt killed. Aircraft a write-off.

14.(Z)/LG1 Messerschmitt Bf110C. Shot down in combat with Hurricanes of No. 1 Squadron west of Reims during escort for KG2 10.35 a.m. Uffz F. Schmitt and Obergefr H. Schmidt killed. Aircraft a write-off.

14.(Z)/LG1 Messerschmitt Bf110C. Shot down in combat with Hurricanes of No. 1 Squadron west of Reims during escort for KG2 and believed crashed at Rosnay 10.35 a.m. Oberlt W. Methfessel *(Staffelkapitän)* and Uffz H. Resener killed. Aircraft a write-off.

14.(Z)/LG1 Messerschmitt Bf110C. Starboard engine damaged in combat with Hurricanes of No. 1 Squadron west of Reims and belly-landed near Florenville 10.35 a.m. Uffz K. Schalkhausser and Uffz J. Jäckel both baled out wounded. Aircraft L1+AK a write-off.

1.(J)/LG2 Messerschmitt Bf109E-3. Engaged by enemy flak and collided with Lt Thurz while taking avoiding action. Believed crashed at Boussois, east of Maubeuge. Oberlt H-E. Jäger *(Staffelkapitän)* killed. Aircraft a write-off.

1.(J)/LG2 Messerschmitt Bf109E-3. Collided with Oberlt Jäger and believed abandoned over Boussois, east of Maubeuge. Lt H. Thurz baled out, shot at by French troops while in his parachute and captured wounded — admitted to hospital in Valenciennes. Aircraft a write-off.

9./StG2 Junkers Ju87B. Crashed 2 km north-east of Ochamps airfield, cause not stated. Uffz H. Weinberg and Uffz H. Kunze both killed. Aircraft a write-off.

Stab III./StG51 Junkers Ju87B-2. Shot down by Hurricanes of No. 151 Squadron in combat north of Landrecies 10.30 a.m. Possibly one of those claimed by S/L Donaldson. Major H. von Klitzing *(Gruppenkommandeur)* and Uffz F. Zander both killed. Aircraft 6G+AD a write-off.

7./StG51 Junkers Ju87B. Shot down by Hurricanes of No. 151 Squadron in combat north-east of Landrecies 10.30 a.m. Possibly one of those claimed by S/L Donaldson. Oberlt W. Klemme *(Staffelkapitän)* and Uffz A. Jaspers captured wounded. Aircraft a write-off.

7./StG51 Junkers Ju87B. Crash-landed damaged by Hurricanes of No. 151 Squadron in combat north-east of Landrecies 10.30 a.m. Possibly that claimed by F/O Milne. Lt H. Glöckner and Uffz H. Pfauth both captured badly wounded. Aircraft a write-off.

8./StG51 Junkers Ju87B. Shot down by Hurricanes of No. 151 Squadron in combat over Boussois, north-east of Landrecies, 10.30 a.m. Possibly that claimed by P/O Wright. Pilot unhurt. Uffz K. Thismar killed. Aircraft a write-off.

8./StG51 Junkers Ju87B. Shot down by Hurricanes of No. 151 Squadron in combat north of Landrecies 10.30 a.m. Possibly that claimed by F/L Ives. Lt G. Wanke and Uffz S. Michl both killed. Aircraft a write-off.

8./StG51 Junkers Ju87B. Shot down by Hurricanes of No. 151 Squadron in combat and reported crashed near Aulnoye-Aymeries 10.30 a.m. Possibly that claimed by P/O Bushell. Lt M. Rentsch believed baled out unhurt. Uffz G. Feist killed. Aircraft a write-off.

9./StG51 Junkers Ju87B. Shot down by Hurricanes of No. 151 Squadron in combat north-east of Landrecies and reported crashed near Liniers 10.30 a.m. Possibly that attacked by P/O Hamar. Lt W. Schwarze and gunner believed baled out and rescued unhurt. Aircraft a write-off.

3./ZG1 Messerschmitt Bf110C. Shot down by S/Lt Goetz of GC II/10 and crashed at Wavrechain-sous-Faulx, south-east of Douai, 11.30 a.m. Lt H. Schwabedissen and Obergefr W. Chranowski both killed. Aircraft a write-off.

4./ZG76 Messerschmitt Bf110C. Belly-landed at Sovet emergency landing ground, west of Ciney, believed damaged in attacks by Adj Angibault of GC II/10 and Sgt Singeot of GC III/10 over Ham, south-east of Albert, 11.50 a.m. Crew unhurt. Aircraft M8+DM damaged but repairable.

4./ZG76 Messerschmitt Bf110C. Forced-landed at Philippeville damaged in combat with Bloch 152s during escort sortie for He111s south-east of Albert 11.50 a.m. Possibly that attacked by Sgt Carbon of GC III/10 over Roye. Oberfw G. Anthony and Uffz H. Nordmeier unhurt. Aircraft damaged but repairable.

Flieger Franz Günther was the only man killed in his Heinkel of 3. Staffel KG54 down near Valenciennes. He was initially buried in the cemetery at Elouges *(right)* **but has since been exhumed and transferred to Lommel (Block 59, Grave 376).**

Saturday, May 18

On the north of the front, and with little serious interference from the enemy, Belgian and British forces continued their withdrawal to defensive positions on a line formed by waterways between Terneuzen in the north and Tournai in the south. To complete the line, French forces also retired to take up positions from Tournai through Condé and Valenciennes, while the Franco-Belgian frontier was held east to Maubeuge.

South of this, the situation on the line formed by the rivers Sambre and Oise remained confused despite continuous reconnaissance flights throughout the day that often yielded conflicting information. French ground forces were reported 'holding firm' though, late in the day, it was acknowledged that two enemy thrusts had penetrated their lines at Landrecies and Origny, by-passing St Quentin for Péronne. The alarming fact emerged that German forces had crossed the Sambre at several points and were advancing north towards Le Quesnoy and west towards Le Cateau. The situation on the Oise, where four crossings were established, was equally serious, with St Quentin captured and enemy advance units already in Péronne.

AASF Battles were stood down, partly due to the lack of bombs at their new airfields, but mainly to prepare a major operation planned for the following day. Consequently, Blenheims from the Air Component and Bomber Command were prepared to attack advancing columns, the identity of which was often in some doubt. By mid-afternoon, a column east of Landrecies and at the eastern exits of Le Cateau was confirmed as enemy and Nos. 15, 21, and 40 Squadrons, along with No. 18 Squadron, were briefed to attack. The intention was that the No. 2 Group Blenheims would land at Abbeville and Poix, join up with No. 18 Squadron and get the latest target information, before rendezvousing over Douai with an escort provided by four RAF Component fighter squadrons.

Surviving records reflect the confusion that prevailed but certainly not every unit made the rendezvous as planned. No. 18 Squadron together with seven Blenheims of

As the squadrons in France pulled back, flights from England entered the fray. Eric Marsden was a mechanic with No. 145 Squadron based at Tangmere, later at Westhampnett where he took this photo. Eric commented that having worked on both Hurricanes and Spitfires, if 'we had had nothing but Spits we'd have lost in 1940 because the turn-round time on the ground was so poor. The Spit took 26 minutes to service, refuel and re-arm, and oxygen from down to up again compared to the Hurricane's nine minutes. One huge job my B Flight got before France was lost was to refuel and re-arm 100 Hurricanes which landed at Tangmere en route for France.'

No. 40 Squadron delivered their bombs on troops and transport at Le Cateau, all returning safely though one machine was slightly damaged. Late over Douai, six Blenheims of No. 15 Squadron proceeded without escort and bombed transport concentrated near Landrecies but lost half their number to enemy fighters, two returning to Poix seriously damaged. Accounts vary but No. 21 Squadron, which landed at Poix, was given the wrong take-off times and took no further part in events, returning to England just as 12 more aircraft from No. 2 Group were leaving to join them at Poix for a repeat attack that had been ordered. Growing general confusion, widespread communications breakdown, and the rapid German advance, all ensured arrangements went seriously awry and the second mission failed though Breguet 693s of GB II/35 and GB II/54 did attack the enemy column later.

Vitry-en-Artois was subjected to a number of heavy air attacks from mid-afternoon. Headquarters of No. 61 (Fighter) Wing, it was also a refuelling ground for visiting

Fighter Command squadrons, this concentration of often poorly-dispersed British fighters proving an attractive target. Countering these attacks, through afternoon and early evening, 11 Hurricanes were lost and five more damaged, four pilots being killed and two more wounded, while at least nine more aircraft were destroyed on the ground. Vitry was evacuated that night, units withdrawing to Norrent-Fontes. Similar attacks on Poix were less successful, bombing being inaccurate and the units based there already pulling out to Crécy.

RAF Fighter Command continued to mount daylight patrols over Ostend, losing one Blenheim to Allied fighters, while at night, a reduced Bomber Command effort of 24 aircraft was launched against the Meuse crossings claiming hits on two bridges and returning without loss.

As night fell on another day of bitter fighting, the stark reality was clear. There was no chance of barring further enemy advances — the Allied line had been breached and it was now a race to the Channel coast.

RAF FIGHTER UNITS BASED IN ENGLAND OPERATING IN FRANCE, MAY 17-22, 1940

17 SQUADRON
Hurricanes (YB)
Squadron Leader G. C. Tomlinson
injured 17.5.1940
Squadron Leader H. Edwardes-Jones

Hawkinge:
to Merville 17.5.1940
to Lille-Marcq 18.5.1940
to Norrent-Fontes
19.5.1940

32 SQUADRON
Hurricanes (GZ)
Squadron Leader J. Worrall

Biggin Hill:
to Abbeville 17.5.1940
to Moorsele 18.5.1940
to Merville 19.5.1940

151 SQUADRON
Hurricanes (DZ)
Squadron Leader E. M. Donaldson

Manston:
to Abbeville 17.5.1940
to Vitry-en-Artois
18.5.1940

Flights from different squadrons operating together:

A Flt. 56 SQUADRON
Hurricanes (US)
Squadron Leader E. V. Knowles
A Flt. 213 SQUADRON
Hurricanes (AK)
Flight Lieutenant E. G. Winning

Biggin Hill:
to Abbeville 17.5.1940
to Lille-Marcq 18.5.1940
to Lille-Seclin 19.5.1940
disbanded 20.5.1940

B Flt. 111 SQUADRON
Hurricanes (JU)
Squadron Leader J. M. Thompson
A Flt. 253 SQUADRON
Hurricanes (SW)
Flight Lieutenant G. Harris
wounded 19.5.1940

Kenley:
to Abbeville 17.5.1940
to Vitry-en-Artois
18.5.1940
to Valenciennes
19.5.1940
disbanded 19.5.1940

B Flt. 601 SQUADRON
Hurricanes (UF)
Squadron Leader T. L. E. Guinness
A Flt. 145 SQUADRON
Hurricanes (SO)
Flight Lieutenant R. G. Dutton

Tangmere:
(601) to Vitry 17.5.1940
(145) to Abbeville
17.5.1940
to Merville 18.5.1940
disbanded 22.5.1940

A Flt. 253 SQUADRON
Hurricanes (SW)
Squadron Leader E. D. Elliott
PoW 21.5.40
A Flt. 229 SQUADRON
Hurricanes (RE)
Flight Lieutenant F. N. Clouston

Kenley
formed 20.5.40
operated from Hawkinge
disbanded 24.5.40

Note: Five of these flights were from squadrons that had already sent one flight to join the RAF Component as part of the 'eight flights' reinforcement of May 16/17. Thus the equivalent of more than four additional squadrons were operating in France.

BRITISH AIR FORCES IN FRANCE

1 SQUADRON, CONDÉ-VRAUX

Hurricane L1856. Shot down by ground-fire and crash-landed near St Quentin during transfer flight to Anglure 6.30 a.m. Sergeant R. A. Albonico captured. Aircraft a write-off.

Hurricane. Belly-landed out of fuel outside Vraux after attacks on enemy aircraft during transfer flight to Anglure 6.30 a.m. Pilot Officer C. M. Stavert unhurt. Aircraft abandoned.

3 SQUADRON, MERVILLE

Hurricane N2464. Radiator and oil tank hit by return fire during attack on Do17s of 2./KG76 and forced-landed 10 miles south of Douai 7.00 a.m. Pilot Officer P. M. Gardner unhurt. Aircraft destroyed by pilot.

Hurricane L1940. Forced-landed south of Douai damaged by return fire during attack on Do17s of 2./KG76 during patrol east of St Quentin 7.00 a.m. Pilot Officer D. L. Bisgood unhurt. Aircraft damaged but repairable.

4 SQUADRON, LILLE-RONCHIN

Lysander N1263. Shot down by Bf109s during tactical reconnaissance sortie and crashed at Outer, near Ninove. Believed that claimed by Oberlt Rempel and Uffz Wischnewski of 6./JG2 south-east of Brussels 7.10 p.m. Flying Officer E. C. Ford and Flying Officer K. W. Graham killed. Aircraft a write-off.

13 SQUADRON, AUTHIE

Lysander N1221. Wrecked in explosion when bomb became detached on landing at Amiens. Pilot Officer J. H. Day believed badly wounded, evacuated but died in hospital at Le Tréport en route to England, May 20. Aircraft a write-off.

16 SQUADRON, BERTANGLES

Lysander II. Failed to return from tactical reconnaissance east of St Quentin and crashed near Creil. Possibly that claimed by Oberfw Schmid of 1./JG2 over Beauvais 8.15 a.m. Flying Officer T. W. Walker and Corporal E. T. Baillie killed. Aircraft a write-off.

18 SQUADRON, POIX

Blenheim IV. Returned with one wing badly damaged by AA fire following attack on enemy columns near Le Cateau 4.00 p.m. Pilot Officer P. D. Smith and crew unhurt. Aircraft abandoned.
L9193 is believed to have been among aircraft abandoned on evacuation to Crécy later this day.

53 SQUADRON, POIX

Blenheim IV L4861. Shot down during strategic reconnaissance and crash-landed in Belgium 6.15 a.m. Pilot Officer P. G. Royle and Sergeant E. F. Wood captured wounded. AC A. H. Malkin unhurt, evaded capture and discovered in Evesham Hospital on May 29. Aircraft a write-off.

Blenheim IV L4841. Failed to return from strategic reconnaissance and crashed near Frevent 6.30 a.m. Pilot Officer L. J. Huggett, Sergeant A. C. Gothard, and AC1 W. A. Christie killed. Aircraft a write-off.

Possibly this is one of those 100 Hurricanes serviced by Eric Marsden on their way to France as replacements because P2907 is not listed as being issued to any squadron, though one publication states that it was lost on May 17 with No. 615 Squadron.

Blenheim IV L9330. Landed at Vitry damaged by ground-fire during reconnaissance sortie over Belgium 6.45 a.m. Later destroyed in enemy bombing attacks 4.30 p.m. and 7.30 p.m. Pilot Officer Truscott, Sergeant Maguire, and AC McAndrew unhurt. Aircraft a write-off.

Blenheim IV P6916. Lost bearings during reconnaissance sortie and landed at Soissons 8.30 a.m. Later caught on the ground and destroyed by enemy bombing. Pilot Officer Bailey, Sergeant Evans, and AC1 A. A. Gillmore unhurt. Aircraft a write-off.

Blenheim IV L9460. Returned damaged by ground-fire during reconnaissance over Cambrai and Avesnes 8.20 a.m. Flying Officer I. H. Bartlett, Sergeant Aldridge, and AC Sheldrick unhurt. Aircraft repairable.
At dawn next day the squadron moved to Crécy from where remaining aircraft returned to Lympne later that evening. This aircraft, along with another, moved to Coulommiers for duties with BAFF headquarters.

B FLIGHT, 56 SQUADRON, VITRY-EN-ARTOIS

Hurricane L1992. Returned port mainplane damaged by return fire from Do17 of 4.(F)/14 engaged near Valenciennes 8.00 a.m. Pilot Officer F. B. Sutton unhurt. Aircraft US⊙C repairable.

Hurricane N2439. Shot down by Bf109s of II./JG26 north of Cambrai shortly after take-off on escort sortie and crashed at Brebières, south-west of Douai 3.30 p.m. Flying Officer F. C. Rose killed. Aircraft a write-off.

Hurricane L1992. Returned radiator and glycol tank damaged in attack by Bf109s of II./JG26 north of Cambrai shortly after take-off on escort sortie 3.30 p.m. Pilot Officer F. B. Sutton wounded in foot, later admitted to hospital in Frévent. Aircraft US⊙C damaged but repairable.

Two Hurricanes N2553, and N2437. Unserviceable aircraft destroyed or further damaged in low-level bombing attack by Do17s of III./KG76 4.30 p.m. No pilot casualties. Aircraft US⊙P and US⊙L later abandoned on withdrawal to Norrent-Fontes.

Hurricane N2430. Shot down by Bf110s of 5./ZG76 between Arras and Douai during attack on Do17s near base and crashed at Biache-St-Vaast 7.05 p.m. Flight Lieutenant I. S. Soden killed. Aircraft a write-off.

Another frustratingly anonymous Hurricane with no markings visible to identify it. The absence of squadron codes suggests a replacement aircraft en route to a unit or one only recently received. Even the tantalising partial serial on the rear fuselage fails to help identify this loss.

One of the four Blenheims left behind at Poix by No. 57 Squadron (code DX).

57 SQUADRON, POIX

Three Blenheim IVs L9182, L9248, and P6932. Returned to Poix damaged by ground-fire during bombing attacks on enemy armour near Le Cateau 8.40 p.m. No crew casualties. Aircraft all damaged but repairable — later abandoned.

Blenheim. Unserviceable aircraft left at Poix on withdrawal to Crecy. No crew casualties. Aircraft abandoned.
The following day the squadron was ordered to Boulogne for evacuation back to England, its five surviving aircraft flying from Crécy to Lympne.

59 SQUADRON, POIX

Blenheim IV R3702. Shot down by ground-fire during reconnaissance over enemy columns near Henegouwen, and crashed at Ribeaucourt Farm, Maubray 6.30 a.m. Pilot Officer R. A. Durie and Sergeant R. Burns killed. AC1 W. G. Murdoch believed wounded. Aircraft a write-off.

79 SQUADRON, MERVILLE

Hurricane. Returned with oil tank and main spar damaged by return fire from Do17 of 5./KG76 north-east of Arras 8.00 a.m. Pilot Officer T. C. Parker unhurt. Aircraft damaged but repairable.

Hurricane P3451. Oil tank damaged by return fire from Bf110 of 5./ZG76 and crash-landed near Vitry-en-Artois 7.15 p.m. Pilot Officer D. W. A. Stones slightly injured in face. Aircraft abandoned — later destroyed.
A despatch rider took 'Dimsie' Stones to Vitry where he was promptly ordered back to destroy the aircraft. He reached Norrent-Fontes early next morning.

85 SQUADRON, LILLE-SECLIN

Hurricane N2425. Shot down in combat with Bf110s of I./ZG26 during offensive patrol between Le Cateau and Cambrai 7.30 a.m. Flying Officer W. N. Lepine baled out and captured slightly wounded. Aircraft a write-off.

Hurricane P2701. Shot down in combat with Bf110s of I./ZG26 during offensive patrol between Le Cateau and Cambrai 7.30 a.m. Flying Officer D. H. Allen missing. Aircraft a write-off.
Derek Hurlstone Allen DFC is commemorated on the Runnymede Memorial where his date of death is recorded as May 15, 1940. He had been reported 'missing' by the squadron on that date but returned later.

A FLIGHT, 111 SQUADRON, LILLE-MARCQ

Hurricane L1607. Engine badly damaged in combat with Bf110s of 5./ZG26 near Douai and crash-landed north of Vimy 3.50 p.m. Sergeant J. T. Craig unhurt. Aircraft abandoned.

B FLIGHT, 111 SQUADRON, VITRY-EN-ARTOIS

Hurricane L2051. Shot down by Bf109s of II./JG26 south of Mons during escort sortie 3.40 p.m. Flight Lieutenant C. S. Darwood killed. Aircraft a write-off.

Two Hurricanes L1589 and L1718. Destroyed at dispersal during low-level bombing attack by Do17s of III./KG76 4.30 p.m. No pilot casualties. Aircraft both write-offs.

139 SQUADRON, LANNOY

Blenheim L8760. Unserviceable aircraft destroyed to prevent capture on withdrawal to Nantes. No crew casualties. Aircraft a write-off.
The squadron's last four surviving aircraft were handed to No. 57 Squadron at Poix prior to withdrawal to Nantes for evacuation.

A FLIGHT, 145 SQUADRON, MERVILLE

Hurricane N2600. Set alight by return fire during attack on He111 of II./KG4 over Ternat 4.45 p.m. Reportedly crashed and burned out in Stockmans orchard in Groenenboomgaardstraat at Pamel. P/O M. A. Newling baled out unhurt and evaded capture with help from local civilians. Aircraft a write-off.
Crash site excavated by the Belgian Aviation Historical Association in February 1997 and items now displayed at Erembodegem.

151 SQUADRON, VITRY-EN-ARTOIS

Hurricane P3315. Forced-landed at Le Touquet following combat with Bf110s of 5./ZG76 near Douai 7.00 p.m. Sergeant G. Atkinson unhurt. Aircraft repairable — returned next day.

Hurricane P3321. Returned damaged following combat with Bf110s of 5./ZG76 near Douai 7.00 p.m. Flying Officer R. M. Milne unhurt. Aircraft repairable.

B FLIGHT, 229 SQUADRON, VITRY-EN-ARTOIS

Hurricane P2729. Shot down in combat with Bf109s of II./JG2 between Brussels and Antwerp and possibly that claimed by Lt Hepe of 5./JG2 11.50 a.m. Pilot Officer M. A. Bussey baled out and captured. Aircraft a write-off.

Hurricane P2676. Shot down in combat with Bf109s of II./JG2 between Brussels and Antwerp and possibly that claimed by Fw Harbauer of 4./JG2 11.57 a.m. Pilot Officer D. de C. C. Gower baled out unhurt. Aircraft a write-off.

Hurricane L1802. Attacked by Bf109s of II./JG26 north of Cambrai shortly after take-off on escort sortie and crashed near Castillon Hill at Mons 3.30 p.m. Pilot Officer A. M. Dillon killed. Aircraft a write-off.
Tony Dillon was flying in No. 2 Section of B Flight, No. 56 Squadron. His date of death is recorded as May 17 by the CWGC.

Hurricane. Exploded under attack by Bf109s of II./JG26 shortly after take-off 3.30 p.m. Flight Lieutenant F. E. Rosier baled out badly burned, admitted to field hospital in Frévent. Aircraft a write-off.

A FLIGHT, 242 SQUADRON, LILLE-SECLIN

Hurricane L1665. Engine cooling system damaged in combat with Bf110s of I./ZG26 near Le Cateau and crashed into trees 7.30 a.m. Pilot Officer R. H. Wiens concussed and slightly wounded, evacuated to hospital in England. Aircraft a write-off.

Hurricane L1922. Exploded under attack by Bf110s of I./ZG26 during combat over Le Cateau 7.30 a.m. Pilot Officer L. E. Chambers baled out badly burned, admitted to hospital where captured next day. Aircraft a write-off.

Hurricane N2320. Shot down in combat with Bf110s of I./ZG26 near Le Cateau 7.30 a.m. Pilot Officer M. K. Brown baled out wounded in right leg, evacuated to hospital in England. Aircraft LE⊙H a write-off.

A FLIGHT, 253 SQUADRON, VITRY-EN-ARTOIS

Hurricane N2545. Crash-landed damaged in combat with escort Bf110s of 4./ZG26 south of Vitry during attack on He111s of II./KG1 4.00 p.m. Pilot Officer J. T. Strang unhurt. Aircraft a write-off.

Hurricane L1611. Shot down in combat with escort Bf110s of 4./ZG26 south of Vitry during attack on He111s of II./KG1 4.00 p.m. Pilot Officer J. D. Ford baled out unhurt. Aircraft a write-off.

Hurricane L1655. Shot down in combat with escort Bf110s of 4./ZG26 south of Vitry during attack on He111s of II./KG1 4.00 p.m. Pilot Officer D. B. Bell-Salter unhurt. Aircraft a write-off.

Hurricane L1667. Shot down in combat with escort Bf110s of 4./ZG26 south of Vitry during attack on He111s of II./KG1 4.00 p.m. Sergeant R. A. Brackley unhurt. Aircraft a write-off.

B FLIGHT, 253 SQUADRON, LILLE-MARCQ

Hurricane. Forced-landed at Amiens-Glisy with engine damaged by return fire from Do17 of 4./KG76 engaged near Denain 3.45 p.m. Pilot Officer D. Jenkins unhurt. Aircraft repairable.

504 SQUADRON, LILLE-MARCQ

Hurricane L1912. Shot down in combat with Bf109s of 2./JG3 south-east of Valenciennes during escort sortie for Blenheims of No. 18 Squadron 9.30 p.m. Possibly one of those claimed by Uffz Ehlers. Flight Lieutenant J. S. Owen baled out but reported killed while in parachute. Aircraft a write-off.

This is one of the five Blenheims lost by No. 15 Squadron on May 18. It is L8852 in which Flying Officer Francis Dawson Jones, Sergeant William Baxter and LAC Cyril Watts lost their lives. Their graves (below) **lie in the communal cemetery at Landrecies.**

Hurricane L1944. Shot down in combat with Bf109s of 2./JG3 south-east of Valenciennes during escort sortie for No. 18 Squadron Blenheims 9.30 p.m. Possibly that claimed by Lt Reumschüssel. Pilot Officer R. J. Renison baled out and captured. Aircraft a write-off.

A FLIGHT, 601 SQUADRON, MERVILLE

Hurricane N2605. Radiator and propeller damaged by return fire from Do17s of 2./KG76 engaged south of Douai and crash-landed at Grevillers, near Bapaume, 6.45 a.m. Flight Lieutenant Sir A. P. Hope unhurt. Aircraft abandoned.

Hurricane L2034. Returned badly damaged by return fire during attack on He111 near base 1.45 p.m. Squadron Leader T. L. E. Guinness unhurt. Aircraft damaged but repairable — later abandoned.

607 SQUADRON, NORRENT-FONTES

Hurricane P2873. Badly damaged in forced-landing at Vitry hit by return fire from Do17 of 3.(F)/10 engaged near Denain 8.00 a.m. Flight Lieutenant W. F. Blackadder unhurt. Aircraft AF⊙G a write-off.

Hurricane P2536. Shot down by Hptmn Mayer of 2./JG51 during tactical reconnaissance patrol and crashed at Seranvillers, south of Cambrai, 9.45 a.m. Flying Officer R. F. Weatherill killed. Aircraft AF⊙R a write-off.

Hurricane P3535. Forced-landed at Vitry slightly damaged in combat with Bf109s of II./JG26 3.30 p.m. Pilot Officer A. S. Dini unhurt. Aircraft AF⊙C repairable.

Magister P6343. Destroyed at Vitry-en-Artois in enemy bombing 4.30 pm and 7.30 p.m. No casualties. Aircraft a write-off.

615 SQUADRON, VITRY-EN-ARTOIS

4 Gladiators N2303, N2304, N2306, and N5899. Redundant aircraft awaiting disposal reported destroyed or badly damaged in enemy bombing 4.30 p.m. and 7.30 p.m. No pilot casualties. Aircraft all write-offs.

UK-based aircraft lost or damaged on operations over the Western Front:

RAF BOMBER COMMAND

15 Squadron, Wyton
Attack roads near Le Cateau:

Blenheim IV L8852. Shot down by Bf109s of 3./JG2 and crashed near Landrecies 4.05 p.m. Possibly one of those claimed by Uffz Stritzel. F/O F. D. Dawson Jones, Sgt W. Baxter, and LAC C. G. Watts killed. Aircraft a write-off.

Blenheim IV L8853. Shot down by Bf109s of 3./JG2 and crashed near Preux-au-Bois, north-west of Landrecies 4.05 p.m. Possibly that claimed by Oberfw Jaenisch. S/L H. Y. Lawrence and Sgt R. G. Hopkins killed. LAC E. L. H. Thomas captured. Aircraft a write-off.

Blenheim IV L9030. Landed at Poix badly damaged in attacks by Bf109s of 3./JG2 over Landrecies 4.05 p.m. Possibly that attacked by Oberfw Kley. P/O Robinson, Sgt Readhead, and LAC Horton unhurt. Aircraft damaged but repairable — later abandoned.

Blenheim IV P6917. Shot down by Bf109s of 3./JG2 and crashed near Landrecies 4.05 p.m. Possibly that claimed by Hptmn von Winterfeldt. F/L P. G. Chapman, Sgt C. E. Colbourn, and LAC E. J. Fagg killed. Aircraft a write-off.

Blenheim IV P6913. Landed at Poix badly damaged in attacks by Bf109s of 3./JG2 near Landrecies 4.05 p.m. F/O L. H. Trent, Sgt W. J. Stephens, and Cpl J. Sutcliffe unhurt. Aircraft repairable.

Grounded by the No. 59 Squadron Engineering Officer pending repairs, Leonard Trent ignored orders and coaxed this aircraft back to Mildenhall that evening once orders were received to evacuate Poix.

RAF COASTAL COMMAND

235 Squadron, Bircham Newton
Shipping protection Ostend:

Blenheim IV L9395. Shot down by S/Lt Jacquemet, Adjt Marchais, and Sgt Dietrich of GC II/8 and crashed in the sea off Nieuport 7.10 p.m. P/O C. S. Robinson, Sgt D. V. Moseley, and LAC A. E. Waddington missing. Aircraft lost.

Yet another tragic accident, despite the efforts of Adjt Henri Mir of GC II/8 who recognised the aircraft as a Blenheim and tried to alert attacking pilots who took it for an He111. Some accounts suggest that it was also attacked by an RAF Hurricane but no corresponding claim has been traced.

Similar problems of identification are present with French Air Force records at this time as both these Morane 406s — serials 337 and 924 — have not been traced as to their unit. However it appears obvious that they were both torched before the Luftwaffe arrived, this being Niergnies aerodrome just to the south of Cambrai.

FRENCH AIR FORCE

AC 2 Potez 631. Shot down by Blenheims of No. 248 Squadron following skirmish with a Ju88 of 8./KG30 and ditched in the sea off Nieuport 4.30 p.m. SM Domas and SM Le Thomas killed. Aircraft a write-off.

AC 2 Potez 631 (169). Shot down by Blenheims of No. 248 Squadron following skirmish with a Ju88 of 8./KG30 over Nieuport and crashed in flames in the sea off De Panne 4.30 p.m. Mtre J. Dupont missing. SM Le Bot baled out wounded, fired on by Allied troops while in his parachute and manhandled on landing, but treated at the Hôtel de l'Océan and later captured. Aircraft lost.

This was by no means an isolated or even uncommon occurrence. British crews involved in this tragic incident were convinced that they had attacked Bf110s, while the sole French survivor was equally sure that he had been shot down by Ju88s.

GAO 1/508 Potez 63.11 (626). Shot down by Oberlt Röders of 9./JG2 during observation sortie over the Neufchâtel — Rethel — Attigny sector 6.45 a.m. Crashed alongside the canal between Concevreux and Pontavert. Lt R. Le Goasguen and Capt P. Petit killed. Adjt Beauvallet badly wounded and burned. Aircraft a write-off.

GAO 3/551 Potez 63.11. Landed at Nangis having lost bearings during night reconnaissance sortie over Soissons and the Ardennes Canal 10.00 p.m. S/Lt Barlier baled out and believed landed unhurt. Adjt Ronot and Sgt Courmes unhurt. Aircraft undamaged.

GAO 552 Potez 63.11 (226). Port engine damaged during reconnaissance sortie northeast of Le Cateau. Attempted to reach Prouvy but starboard engine failed so forced-landed outside Maing, south-east of Prouvy, 7.00 p.m. S/Lt Ribereau-Gayon and Lt Versini unhurt. Cpl Doucet slightly wounded. Aircraft a write-off.

GB II/31 LeO 451 (94). Shot down by French ΛΛ fire near Meaux during transfer flight to Claye-Souilly. Crew baled out but Adjt R. Pioger fell in the River Marne and drowned. Aircraft a write-off.

GB II/34 Amiot 354 (29). Shot down by flak between Guise and Vervins during low-level sortie to attack enemy armour around Chimay. Crashed and exploded near the church in La-Vallée-aux-Blé 12.50 a.m. Lt-Col. J. Dagnaux and Adjt M. Lavolley missing Lt F. Frémond and Sgt Regnault both wounded, baled out and captured. Aircraft a write-off.

The bomb load exploded with such violence that no trace of the two dead crewmen was ever found.

GB II/35 Breguet 691 (39). Reportedly shot down by Bf109s during bombing sortie against enemy troops advancing between Landrecies and Avesnes. Crashed port engine on fire and burned out. Adjt Géraud and Lt Artola both captured unhurt. Aircraft a write-off.

No corresponding German claim has been traced in the surviving records. However, an inconclusive claim for a Do17 by No. 607 Squadron Hurricanes remains unresolved and may be connected.

GBA II/54 Breguet 693 (33). Returned to Briare damaged by flak during bombing attack on convoy between Landrecies and Avesnes 6.00 p.m. Sgt Lamour wounded. Lt de Béarn unhurt. Aircraft damaged but repairable.

GBA II/54 Breguet 693 (28). Shot down by flak during bombing attack on convoy between Landrecies and Avesnes. Crashed and burned out at Happegarbes, 2 km west of Landrecies 6.00 p.m. Cmdt. P. Grenet *(Groupe Commandant)* killed. Sgt Bouveret baled out over Bois l'Evêque and captured unhurt. Aircraft a write-off.

Pierre Grenet, originally buried in a field grave alongside his aircraft, was exhumed January 31, 1941 and reinterred in Landrecies cemetery.

GC 6/1 Morane 406 (752). Set alight by return fire from Do17 of 2.(F)/22 engaged north-west of Montcornet and belly-landed at Hary, south of Vervins, 11.20 a.m. Lt J. Tariel *(Commandant)* injured face. Aircraft a write-off.

GC III/2 Morane 406 (388). Shot down by Lt Stangl of I./JG76 in combat north of La Fère. Crashed and burned out near Château de Rouez, at Villequier-Aumont 9.10 a.m. Lt J. Peuto killed. Aircraft a write-off.

GC III/2 Morane 406 (653). Set alight in attack by Lt Stangl of I./JG76 in combat over Villequier-Aumont and abandoned north of Noyon 9.10 a.m. Sgt F. Vittini baled out and captured badly burned, spent the next year in hospital. Aircraft a write-off.

GC I/3 Dewoitine 520 (108). Engine set alight by return fire from Do17 of I./KG3 and hit trees, crashed and broke up at Bussiares, 12 km north-west of Château-Thierry. Sgt Bouffier slightly wounded. Aircraft a write-off.

GC 3/4 Curtiss H-75 (189). Forced-landed at Condé-Vraux badly damaged in combat with Bf109s of 1./JG76 near Rethel 3.25 p.m. Capt R. Guieu *(Commandant)* unhurt. Aircraft a write-off.

GC II/4 Curtiss H-75 (89). Returned to Orconte damaged in combat with Bf109s of 1./JG76 near Rethel 3.25 p.m. Adjt Paulhan unhurt. Aircraft damaged but repairable.

GC I/5 Curtiss H-75 (193). Shot down in flames by cross-fire during attack on He111s of II./KG55 north-east of Fismes and abandoned over Vierzy 3.00 p.m. Sgt F. Morel believed baled out unhurt but hit by ground-fire from French infantry and landed near Hartennes-et-Taux badly wounded in head — died in hospital at Chartres June 17. Aircraft a write-off.

GC I/5 Curtiss H-75 (204). Shot down in flames during attack on He111s of II./KG55 north-east of Fismes and forced-landed at Villers-sur-Fère, south-east of Fère-en-Tardenois 3.00 p.m. S/Lt J. Rey wounded in thigh, transported to hospital in Jaulgonne. Aircraft a write-off.

GC 1/5 Curtiss H-75 (158). Forced-landed at Suippes damaged following attack on He111s of II./KG55 north of Fismes 3.00 p.m. Lt Marin-la-Meslée unhurt. Aircraft a write-off.

GC II/5 Curtiss H-75 (144). Landed at Frescaty tailplane damaged in combat with Bf109s of 8./JG52 south of Metz 5.40 p.m. Cmdt M. Hugues *(Commandant)* unhurt. Aircraft damaged but repairable.

GC II/5 Curtiss H-75 (27). Set alight in combat with Bf109s of 8./JG52 east of Metz and abandoned over Nouilly 5.40 p.m. Probably that claimed by Lt Ehrlich. Sgt O. Hanzlicek baled out unhurt. Aircraft a write-off.

GC II/5 Curtiss H-75 (129). Belly-landed at Toul damaged in combat with Bf109s of 8./JG52 south of Metz 5.40 p.m. Lt P. Houzé unhurt. Aircraft damaged but repairable.

GC 1/6 Morane 406 (1053). Shot down by Oberfw Anthony of 4./ZG76 during solo attack on Do17s and abandoned north-east of Cambrai 2.45 p.m. Capt F. Mauvier *(Commandant)* wounded, baled out and captured. Aircraft a write-off.

GC I/6 Morane 406 (912). Damaged by return fire from Do17 and shot down during attack on flak positions north-east of Vermand. Crashed and burned out near Pontru 7.45 p.m. Capt G. Bruneau killed. Aircraft a write-off.

GC I/6 Morane 406. Damaged in attack on Do17s west of St Quentin 7.15 p.m. S/Lt J. Paturle wounded in shoulder admitted to hospital in Vincennes. Aircraft damaged but repairable.

GC I/6 Morane 406. Damaged in attack on Do17s west of St Quentin 7.15 p.m. Adjt Conte admitted to hospital suffering severe shock. Aircraft damaged but repairable.

GC I/8 Bloch 152 (527). Shot down by Lt Bauer of 1./JG77 in combat near Douai 2.45 p.m. Cpl A. Kralik baled out unhurt. Aircraft a write-off.

GC 3/10 Bloch 152 (129). Shot down by return fire from He111s and crashed in flames at Beuvraignes, 6 km south of Roye 2.45 p.m. Sgt J. Carletti killed. Aircraft a write-off.

BELGIAN AIR FORCE

3/II/1 9 Foxes (O.7, O.13, O.17, O.31, O.38, O.39, O.40, O.44 and O.49). Destroyed or badly damaged on the ground at Aalter in bombing attack by He 111s of I./KG4 7.40 a.m. No crew casualties. Aircraft all write-offs or destroyed on withdrawal to Norrent-Fontes same day.

9/V/1 Renard R-31(N.8). Engaged by Bf109 during approach to Zwevezele on return from reconnaissance sortie between Kallo and Terneuzen. Port wing hit the ground avoiding attack and crashed into a wood. Sgt M. Bruylants slightly wounded. Sgt A. Crabus killed. Aircraft a write-off.

9/V/1 Renard R-31(N.23). Returned to Zwevezele badly damaged from reconnaissance sortie of the Breskens-Terneuzen sector 3.30 p.m. Adjt F. Breyre and Lt R. Lonthie both unhurt. Aircraft damaged but repairable.

5/III/3 Five Battles (T.65, T.67, T.69, T72 and T.73). Unserviceable aircraft wrecked or damaged on the ground at Aalter in bombing attack by He 111s of I./KG4 7.40 a.m. Lt de Brabander slightly wounded. Aircraft all write-offs or abandoned.

7/III/3 Eight Foxes (O.108, O.148, O.149, O.188). Destroyed on the ground at Aalter in bombing attack by He 111s of I./KG4 7.40 a.m. No crew casualties. Aircraft all write-offs.

These losses include the last of the III/2 aircraft that arrived from Sterreken to reinforce the depleted III/3 at Aalter on May 12. The remnants of II/1 and III/3 were withdrawn to Norrent-Fontes later that evening.

Curtiss H-75 crash-landed after combat with Oberlt Lothar Ehrlich's 8./JG52. Lieutenant Pierre Houzé of the 4 Escadrille GC II/5 escaped unhurt only to be killed in action on June 6.

LUFTWAFFE

3.(F)/10 Dornier Do17P. Shot down during reconnaissance of airfields between Charleroi and Tournai and possibly that engaged by F/Lt Blackadder and P/O Stewart of No. 607 Squadron near Denain 8.00 a.m. Uffz H. Liebe, Uffz C. Kühnle, and Wmstr M. Volk (Army observer) all captured unhurt. Aircraft a write-off.

4.(F)/11 Dornier Do17. Believed that shot down by F/L Toyne, P/O Bird-Wilson, and F/O Adye of No. 17 Squadron, during reconnaissance sortie between Hazebrouck and Lille, which crashed south-east of Seclin 5.00 p.m. Oberlt O. von Dolega-Kozierowski, Fw C. Wiegand, and Uffz W. Hammann killed. Aircraft a write-off.

4.(F)/14 Dornier Do17P. Believed that attacked by F/L Soden, F/Sgt Higginson, and P/O Sutton of No. 56 Squadron during patrol between Brussels and Gent 8.00 a.m. Pursued at low level, careered across fields and crashed into trees at 'Sart Madame', Montignies-le-Tilleul, south of Charleroi. Lt A. Schreiner, Uffz H. Eggers, and Uffz W. Seefeldt killed. Aircraft a write-off.

4.(F)/14 Dornier Do17P. Failed to return from reconnaissance sortie and crashed in the Forêt de Mormal near Locquignol 6.30 p.m. Lt G. Losse, Lt F-J. Menge, and Uffz H. Ambrosch killed. Aircraft a write-off.

Two independent contemporary German sources both report this loss on May 18, yet another on the following day. Location and time also correspond exactly to a claim by Sgt Josef Stehlik of GC III/3 filed on May 19.

3.(F)/22 Dornier Do17P. Returned damaged by ground-fire between Nancy and Metz. Gefr R. Lackel slightly wounded. Aircraft repairable.

2.(H)/23 Henschel Hs126. Shot down by Capt Guieu, Cdt Rozanoff, S/Lt Rubin, and Sgt Paulhan of GC III/4 during observation sortie west of Rethel. Crashed on the banks of the Aisne at Nanteuil 3.12 p.m. Oberlt A. Hempel and Oberlt W. Raps killed. Aircraft a write-off.

2.(H)/23 Henschel Hs126. Returned damaged in attack by Adjt Leblanc of GC III/3 south of Péronne. One crewman wounded. Aircraft repairable.

2.(H)/31 Henschel Hs126. Believed that attacked by F/L Joslin of No. 56 Squadron near Mons 7.00 p.m. Lt Metzner wounded. Aircraft damaged but repairable.

2.(F)/22 Dornier Do17P. Both engines set alight in attacks by Lt Tariel, Adjt Saussol, and Sgt Durand of GC III/1 and Adjt Bernavon, Sgt Fortin, and Sgt Parent of GC II/2 during reconnaissance sortie north-east of Laon. Belly-landed and burned out at Gercy, south-west of Vervins, 11.25 a.m. Fw Krieger, Fw Schäfer, and Uffz Glas believed unhurt. Aircraft 4N+HK a write-off.

3.(H)/41 Henschel Hs126. Shot down by F/L Harris, P/O Bell-Salter, and P/O Ratford of No. 253 Squadron near Cambrai 11.00 a.m. Oberlt W. Erzleben and Fw F. Hösl believed killed. Aircraft a write-off.

3.(H)/41 Henschel Hs126. Shot down by S/L Thompson, F/L Darwood, and F/O Bruce of No. 111 Squadron near Cambrai 11.00 a.m. Fw O. Steeger and Uffz E. Müller both captured wounded. Aircraft a write-off.

3.(F)/121 Heinkel He111H. Shot down by Adjt Gagnaire and Sgt Paulhan of GC III/1 during reconnaissance of road and rail traffic, and crashed at Verberie, south-west of Compiègne, 2.45 p.m. Lt H. Horstmann killed. Uffz K. Mietzner, Uffz R. Schaarschmidt, and Obergefr H. Hartwig captured wounded, admitted to hospital in Senlis. Aircraft a write-off.

One contemporary German account states that Horstmann was shot attempting escape.

6./JG2 Messerschmitt Bf109E. Shot down in combat with Hurricanes over Brussels and crashed at Saintes, north-east of Tubize, 11.50 a.m. Probably that claimed by F/L Rosier of No. 229 Squadron and F/L Soden of No. 56 Squadron. Uffz W. Mub killed. Aircraft a write-off.

2./JG3 Messerschmitt Bf109E-1. Believed shot down in combat with Hurricanes of No. 504 Squadron between Valenciennes and Solesmes 7.30 p.m. Uffz H. Ehlers captured unhurt. Aircraft a write-off.

2./JG3 Messerschmitt Bf109E-1. Believed shot down in combat with Hurricanes of No. 504 Squadron between Valenciennes and Solesmes 7.30 p.m. Possibly that attacked by P/O van Mentz. Uffz K. Göhringer badly wounded in head. Aircraft a write-off.

This Dornier Do17 from 4.(F)/11, piloted by Unteroffizier Walter Hammann on reconnaissance duties, ended up crashing in a field near Seclin, believed to be a victim of pilots of No. 17 Squadron. All three crewmen were killed.

3./JG3 Messerschmitt Bf109E. Hit by ground-fire during low-level attack and forced-landed near Beaumont. Leutnant W. Binder unhurt. Aircraft repairable.

II./JG51 Messerschmitt Bf109E-3. Wrecked in forced-landing at Karlsruhe-Durlach due to petrol failure. Pilot believed unhurt. Aircraft a write-off.

Stab I./JG52 Messerschmitt Bf109E-3. Lost bearings and wrecked in forced-landing near Liège. Hauptmann S. von Eschwege (*Gruppenkommandeur*) unhurt. Aircraft a write-off.

8./JG52 Messerschmitt Bf109E-1. Belly-landed in a minefield at Werzlen, near Ulm, damaged by S/Lt Ruchoux of GC II/5 in combat over Stockholtz 5.45 p.m. Oberfw A. Walter unhurt. Aircraft damaged but repairable.

9./JG52 Messerschmitt Bf109E-3. Wrecked in forced-landing near Bad Kreuznach following engine failure. Pilot unhurt. Aircraft 7 + — a write-off.

7./JG53 Messerschmitt Bf109E-3. Believed shot down by S/Lt Plubeau of GC II/4 in combat west of Rethel and crashed at 'La Gravière', Doux, 3.25 p.m. Oberlt W-D. Wilcke (*Staffelkapitän*) baled out and captured unhurt. Aircraft a write-off.

I./JG76 Messerschmitt Bf109E-3. Lost on operations, circumstances not recorded. Possibly shot down in combat with Capt Engler, S/Lt Plubeau, Adjt Paulhan, and S/Lt Rubin of GC II/4 west of Rethel 3.25 p.m. Pilot believed unhurt. Aircraft a write-off.

2./JG76 Messerschmitt Bf109E-3. Believed shot down by Sgt Elmlinger of GC III/2 in combat north of La Fère 9.30 a.m. Uffz A. Mannske captured. Aircraft a write-off.

Stabsstaffel KG1 Heinkel He111H. Probably that engaged by F/O Coghlan and F/Sgt Elliott of No. 56 Squadron that crash-landed near Graux, south-west of Namur, during post-sortie reconnaissance mission 6.45 p.m. Uffz K. Jähser killed. Uffz K. Bernicke badly wounded, admitted to field hospital in Marche. Aircraft a write-off.

II./KG1 Heinkel He111H-2. Shot down in action with Hurricanes of Nos. 56, 151, and 253 Squadrons south of Vitry and crash-landed east of Valenciennes 4.00 p.m. Oberlt Kohlbruck, Oberlt Schmidt, and crew believed unhurt. Aircraft a write-off.

6./KG1 Heinkel He111H-2. Shot down in action with Hurricanes of Nos. 56, 151, and 253 Squadrons south of Vitry and crash-landed east of Le Cateau 4.00 p.m. Possibly that claimed by P/O Bird (of No. 4 Continental Ferry Flight). Crew unhurt. Aircraft a write-off.

6./KG1 Heinkel He111H-2. Shot down in action with Hurricanes of Nos. 56, 151, and 253 Squadrons south-west of Avesnes 4.00 p.m. Crew unhurt. Aircraft a write-off.

II./KG2 Dornier Do17Z. Returned damaged by flak and attack by Capt Bruneau, Cmdt Tricaud (*Groupe Commandant*), and Lt Jolicoeur of GC I/6 over St Quentin 3.00 p.m. No crew casualties. Aircraft repairable.

6./KG2 Dornier Do17Z (3613). Shot down by Capt Mauvier and Sgt Popelka of GC I/6 and crashed near Ognes, west of Chauny, 3.00 p.m. Fw O. Plähn, Uffz O. Frey, Uffz J. Eisenhut, and Uffz G. Berchtold killed. Aircraft U5+JP a write-off.

1./KG3 Dornier Do17Z. Returned damaged by Capt Schneider and Sgt Bouffier of GC I/3 following attack on enemy columns near La Ferté-Milon 12.15 p.m. Uffz G. Läthe killed. Aircraft damage state not recorded.

2./KG4 Heinkel He111P. Shot down by Hurricanes of Nos. 145 and 601 Squadrons north-east of Leuven and forced-landed at 'Gulledelle', south-east of Sint-Pieters-Rode, 4.45 p.m. Uffz J. Müller and Uffz W. Schneider killed. Fw R. Grebe slightly wounded admitted to hospital in Aachen. Lt H. Zeiss believed unhurt. Aircraft 5J+IK a write-off.

5./KG4 Heinkel He111P. Shot down by Hurricanes of Nos. 145 and 601 Squadrons north-east of Leuven and crash-landed near Beauvechain, south-west of Tirlemont 4.45 p.m. Lt Roepel, Lt Danzenberg, and crew believed wounded. Aircraft a write-off.

5./KG4 Heinkel He111P. Shot down by Hurricanes of Nos. 145 and 601 Squadrons west of Leuven and belly-landed at Kinderenbos, Vrebos, near Everberg 4.45 p.m. Uffz O. Noetzelmann killed. Oberfw K. Schorr badly wounded, died same day. Hptmn K. Leythäuser (*Staffelkapitän*) slightly wounded. Lt C. Nützel unhurt. Aircraft 5J+HN a write-off.

5./KG4 Heinkel He111P. Returned damaged in attacks by Hurricanes of Nos. 145 and 601 Squadrons near Brussels 4.45 p.m. Crew believed unhurt. Aircraft repairable.

4./KG27 Heinkel He111P-2 (1403). Crash-landed near Pirmasens port engine damaged in attacks by Lt Houzé and S/Lt Ruchoux of GC II/5 over Bouzonville 5.50 p.m. Oberlt H. Putz and crew believed unhurt. Aircraft 1G+BM a write-off.

6./KG27 Heinkel He111P. Hit by flak between Meaux and Couilly during sortie to bomb railway targets and crashed at Chelles, east of Paris, 4.45 p.m. Major R. Tamm (*Gruppenkommandeur*), Uffz J. Schmitz, Uffz W. Geck, Uffz P. Tappe, and Uffz K. Lyke believed baled out and captured unhurt. Aircraft 1G+EP a write-off.

III./KG28 Heinkel He111P. Damaged in collision at Wahn airfield. No crew casualties. Aircraft damaged but repairable.

1./KG30 Junkers Ju88A. Returned damaged by flak during anti-shipping sortie over Ostend. Crew believed unhurt. Aircraft damage state not recorded.

8./KG30 Junkers Ju88A. Shot down by flak and crashed in sea during attack on shipping off Dunkirk 5.30 p.m. Possibly that engaged earlier by Blenheims of No. 248 Squadron south-west of Nieuport. Obergefr T. König and Gefr W. Mebus killed. Lt S. Jung captured wounded. Flgr O. Barthels captured unhurt. Aircraft a write-off.

Stabsstaffel KG51 Junkers Ju88A. Crashed blind-flying at Lechfeld. Crew unhurt. Aircraft repairable.

I./KG51 Junkers Ju88A. Crash-landed at Lechfeld, cause unknown. Crew unhurt. Aircraft repairable.

Incidents of crews being murdered can be apocryphal but in the case of Heinkel B3+JT of 9./KG54 we have the testimony of Sergeant John Craig of No. 111 Squadron who had crash-landed his Hurricane nearby just minutes earlier (see page 312).

3./KG54 Heinkel He111P. Aircraft a write-off.

9./KG54 Heinkel He111P. Failed to return from sortie over Arras and possibly that shot down by F/L Soden of No. 56 Squadron that crash-landed near Bois de l'Emprunt, north of Vimy 4.00 p.m. Uffz O. Ellinghaus, Gefr E. Rzezniczek, Obergefr H. Jentzmik, and Gefr J. Bradac killed. Aircraft B3+JT a write-off.

According to Sergeant John Craig of No. 111 Squadron, who belly-landed in the next field, one of this crew had been shot by French troops on leaving the aircraft. On August 6, 1941, Lucien Delabasserue was executed at Doullens prison for his complicity in the murder of this crew.

I./KG55 Heinkel He111P. Crash-landed near Sedan badly damaged by French fighters during sortie to attack rail targets west of Fismes 3.40 p.m. Crew believed rescued by German troops. Aircraft a write-off.

4./KG55 Heinkel He111P. Returned damaged by French fighters during sortie to attack rail targets west of Fismes 3.30 p.m. Possibly one of those attacked west of Rethel by S/Lt Plubeau, Lt Girard, Capt Engler, Capt Guieu, S/Lt Rubin, and Adjt Paulhan of GC II/4. Uffz A. Kauder and Obergefr H. Hesse slightly wounded. Aircraft repairable.

4./KG55 Heinkel He111P. Attacked west of Rethel by S/Lt Plubeau, Lt Girard, Capt Engler, Capt Guieu, S/Lt Rubin, and Adjt Paulhan of GC II/4 during sortie to attack rail targets west of Fismes. Forced-landed with starboard engine alight at 'La Folie', near Vouziers 3.30 p.m. Lt K. Hertle, Uffz M. Zwenger, and Uffz K. Brüsch captured wounded. Uffz K. Held and Uffz E. Roggatz captured unhurt. Aircraft a write-off.

5./KG55 Heinkel He111P. Returned damaged by French fighters during sortie to attack rail targets west of Fismes 3.30 p.m. Uffz A. Strohschnitter slightly wounded. Aircraft repairable.

5./KG55 Heinkel He111P. Returned damaged by French fighters during sortie to attack rail targets west of Fismes 3.30 p.m. Uffz K. Gerdsmeier slightly wounded. Aircraft repairable.

6./KG55 Heinkel He111P. Shot down by Lt Marin-la-Meslée, S/Lt Rey, and Sgt Vuillemain of GC I/5 during sortie to attack rail targets west of Fismes and believed forced-landed at Taizy, south of Château-Porcien, 3.40 p.m. Fw J. Blase captured unhurt. Hptmn K-H. Schellmann *(Staffelkapitän)*, Oberfw M. Basmann, Fw P. Matz, and Oberfw O. Engel captured wounded. Aircraft a write-off.

6./KG55 Heinkel He111P. Shot down by Capt Accart, Capt Vasatko, Lt Marin-la-Meslée, S/Lt Rey, S/Lt Rouquette, Sgt Morel, and Sgt Museli of GC I/5 during sortie to attack rail targets west of Fismes. Both engines destroyed, belly-landed near Branges, north-east of Arcis-Ste-Restitue, 3.40 p.m. Believed also attacked on the ground by Potez 631s of ECN 1/13 and ECMJ 1/16. Gefr L. Thelen killed. Uffz H. Philipp mortally wounded. Uffz A. Kutsch captured wounded in left arm, Uffz S. Wiechers captured wounded in both legs, both admitted to hospital in Reims. Lt K. Klahn captured unhurt. Aircraft G1+JP a write-off.

6./KG55 Heinkel He111P (1523). Shot down by Capt Labit, Adjt Berland, and S/Lt Robiaud of GC II/2 during sortie to attack rail targets west of Fismes and belly-landed near Épernay 3.40 p.m. Fw F. Rotthauwe, Fw J. Köppel and Uffz F. Georgi killed, Lt E. Dörrfuss captured badly wounded — died later. Uffz H. Zenz captured wounded. Aircraft G1+CP a write-off.

Some of this crew died after capture and the Bordmechaniker, Hermann Zenz, later reported severe maltreatment.

III./KG55 Heinkel He111P. Crash-landed at Schwäbisch-Hall, cause not stated. No crew casualties. Aircraft damaged but repairable.

2./KG76 Dornier Do17Z. Crash-landed at Cologne-Ostheim damaged by Hurricanes between Cambrai and Arras 6.30 a.m. Possibly that attacked by P/O Gardner and P/O Bisgood of No. 3 Squadron. Fw N. Roch, Uffz N. Koch, and Uffz W. Knöchel badly wounded, admitted to hospital at Cologne-Hohenlind. Oberfw E. Neuffer slightly wounded, to hospital in Vogelsang. Aircraft damaged but repairable.

2./KG76 Dornier Do17Z. Starboard engine badly damaged in attacks by Hurricanes east of Arras 6.30 a.m. Possibly that attacked by F/L Hope and F/O Cleaver of No. 601 Squadron. Crash-landed near St Ghislain, west of Mons. Oberfw R. Richter, Oberfw W. Laurer, Gefr J. Buchholz, and Oberfw J. Huber captured unhurt. Aircraft a write-off.

2./KG76 Dornier Do17Z. Returned with damage following attacks by Hurricanes of Nos. 3 and 601 Squadrons near Cambrai 6.40 a.m. Crew believed unhurt. Aircraft repairable.

4./KG76 Dornier Do17Z. Forced-landed near Dinant damaged in attacks by Hurricanes of No. 253 Squadron near Valenciennes 4.00 p.m. Possibly that attacked by P/O Clifton. Obergefr E. Preiser slightly wounded, admitted to field hospital in Tirlemont. Aircraft a write-off.

4./KG76 Dornier Do17Z. Belly-landed near Wavre damaged in attacks by Hurricanes of No. 253 Squadron near Valenciennes 4.00 p.m. Possibly one of those attacked by P/O Jenkins. Uffz G. Schmidt slightly injured in landing, admitted to hospital in Hohenlind. Rest of crew unhurt. Aircraft a write-off.

4./KG76 Dornier Do17Z. Returned damaged by ground-fire near Vitry-en-Artois. Lt H. Rollberg slightly wounded, admitted to hospital in Vogelsang. Aircraft repairable.

5./KG76 Dornier Do17Z. Damaged by Hurricanes and crash-landed near Avesnes. Possibly that attacked by F/O Davies of No. 79 Squadron east of Arras 8.00 a.m. Crew rescued by German troops. Aircraft a write-off.

4./KGrzbV.9 Junkers Ju52. Crash-landed at Philippeville while delivering fuel supplies, cause not stated. Uffz Welch injured. Aircraft 9P+EM damage state not recorded.

1./KGrzbV.172 Junkers Ju52. One crewman wounded by infantry fire while off-loading supplies at Charleville. Aircraft undamaged.

III./LG1 Junkers Ju88A. Shot down by F/O Connors of No. 111 Squadron and crash-landed near Amiens 4.45 p.m. Crew unhurt, rescued by German troops. Aircraft a write-off.

1.(J)/LG2 Messerschmitt Bf109E. Shot down in combat with Hurricanes over Compiègne. Fw H. Pohland captured unhurt. Aircraft a write-off.

4./StG2 Junkers Ju87. Returned damaged in attacks by P/O Cock and P/O Tait of No. 87 Squadron east of Brussels 2.00 p.m. Pilot unhurt, Uffz K. Belensen slightly wounded. Aircraft repairable.

III./StG51 Junkers Ju160. Forced-landed near Euten damaged by own flak during courier flight. Aircraft a write-off.

1./ZG26 Messerschmitt Bf110C. Crash-landed at Cologne-Ostheim damaged in combat with Hurricanes of Nos. 85, 87, and 242 Squadrons south of Vitry 7.30 a.m. and possibly that attacked by Sgt Hampshire of No. 85 Squadron. Crew unhurt. Aircraft a write-off.

2./ZG26 Messerschmitt Bf110C. Belly-landed near Düren out of fuel following combat with Hurricanes south of Vitry 7.30 a.m. Possibly one of those attacked by P/O Wiens of No. 242 Squadron. Crew unhurt. Aircraft damaged but repairable.

2./ZG26 Messerschmitt Bf110C. Shot down by F/L Gleed, F/O Watson, and P/O Darwin of No. 87 Squadron south-west of Maubeuge 7.30 a.m. Lt H. Hensel and Gefr F. König killed. Aircraft a write-off.

Three crewmen lost their lives in this Dornier of 4.(F)/14 which lies at Montignies-le-Tilleul. Leutnant Alexander Schreiner, Unteroffiziere Hans Eggers and Wilhelm Seefeldt were first laid to rest in the local cemetery. Now they lie in the German War Cemetery at Lommel. All three are buried in Block 54, Schreiner and Seefeldt side by side in Graves 149 and 150 whereas Eggers has been interred in Grave 283.

3./ZG26 Messerschmitt Bf110C. Returned damaged in combat with Hurricanes south-east of Valenciennes 7.30 a.m. Possibly attacked by F/L Gleed, F/O Watson, and P/O Darwin of No. 87 Squadron. Lt W. Manhart unhurt. Uffz O. Bräutigam slightly wounded, admitted to hospital in Vogelsang. Aircraft repairable.

3./ZG26 Messerschmitt Bf110C. Crashed on landing at Vogelsang due to undercarriage damage. Possibly damaged in combat with Hurricanes of Nos. 85, 87, and 242 Squadrons south-east of Valenciennes 7.30 a.m. Crew unhurt. Aircraft a write-off.

4./ZG26 Messerschmitt Bf110C. Believed that attacked by F/O Bury and Sgt Craig of No. 111 Squadron in combat south-east of Douai, and finally shot down by P/O Simpson of No. 229 Squadron. Crashed between Monchecourt and Bugnicourt, 3.55 p.m. Uffz F. Mathis killed. Uffz E. Landgraf captured wounded. Aircraft U8+AM a write-off.

5./ZG26 Messerschmitt Bf110C. Shot down in combat with Hurricanes of Nos. 56, 111, and 151 Squadrons between Cambrai and Douai 5.00 p.m. Possibly that claimed by P/O Bushell of No. 151 Squadron. Hptmn E. d'Elsa *(Staffelkapitän)* and Uffz H. Rössler captured wounded. Aircraft 3U+AN a write-off.

5./ZG26 Messerschmitt Bf110C. Shot down in combat with Hurricanes of Nos. 56, 111, and 151 Squadrons between Cambrai and Amiens 5.00 p.m. Possibly that claimed by F/L Ironside of No. 151 Squadron. Uffz A. Komanns killed. Fw H. Schönthier believed baled out and captured. Aircraft a write-off.

5./ZG26 Messerschmitt Bf110C. Shot down in combat with Hurricanes of Nos. 56, 111, and 151 Squadrons south-west of Cambrai 5.00 p.m. Possibly that claimed by Sgt Aslin of No. 151 Squadron, believed also attacked by S/L Thompson of No. 111 Squadron. Lt L. Heckert and Uffz E. Berger believed baled out and captured. Aircraft U8+IN a write-off.

5./ZG26 Messerschmitt Bf110C. Crash-landed at Asch badly damaged in combat with Hurricanes of Nos. 56, 111, and 151 Squadrons east of Cambrai 5.00 p.m. Possibly one of those attacked by Sgt Whitehead of No. 56 Squadron. Fw W. Hamacher and gunner believed unhurt. Aircraft a write-off.

5./ZG26 Messerschmitt Bf110C. Landed at Asch damaged in combat with Hurricanes of Nos. 56, 111, and 151 Squadrons near Cambrai 5.00 p.m. Possibly that attacked by F/Sgt Higginson of No. 56 Squadron. Oberfw K. Rochel and Uffz W. Schöffler unhurt. Aircraft damaged but repairable.

5./ZG26 Messerschmitt Bf110C. Landed at Asch damaged in combat with Hurricanes of Nos. 56, 111, and 151 Squadrons near Cambrai 5.00 p.m. Possibly that claimed by F/O Ereminsky of No. 56 Squadron. Oberfw J. Auer unhurt. Uffz M. Nicoley slightly wounded, admitted to hospital in Neuss. Aircraft repairable.

5./ZG26 Messerschmitt Bf110C. Forced-landed at Asch one engine damaged in combat with Hurricanes of Nos. 56, 111, and 151 Squadrons over Cambrai 5.00 p.m. Possibly that attacked by S/L Donaldson of No. 151 Squadron. Oberlt A. Niebuhr and Uffz K. Theisen unhurt. Aircraft damaged but repairable.

Stab ZG76 Messerschmitt Bf110C. Shot down in combat with Hurricanes north-west of Douai 7.10 p.m. Possibly that attacked by P/O Atkinson of No. 213 Squadron. Major W. Grabmann *(Geschwaderkommodore)* captured. Fw R. Krone killed. Aircraft M8+XA a write-off.

4./ZG76 Messerschmitt Bf110C. Both engines damaged in combat with Hurricanes south of Denain 7.10 p.m. Possibly that claimed by F/O Duus of No. 79 Squadron. Uffz H. Jörke and Uffz G. Schablowski missing. Aircraft a write-off.

5./ZG76 Messerschmitt Bf110C. Shot down in combat with Hurricanes near Douai 7.10 p.m. Possibly one of those claimed by P/O Stones of No. 79 Squadron. Lt J. Uhlhorn and Gefr H. Neumann killed. Aircraft a write-off.

I speak to you for the first time as Prime Minister in a solemn hour in the life of our country, of our Empire, of our Allies, and above all, of the cause of freedom.

A tremendous battle is raging in France and Flanders. The Germans, by a remarkable combination of air bombing and heavily armoured tanks, have broken through the French defences north of the Maginot Line, and strong columns of their armoured vehicles are ravaging the open country which for the first day or two was without defenders.

They have penetrated deeply and spread alarm and confusion in their track. Behind them are now pouring infantry in lorries, and behind them again large masses are moving forward . . .

In the air, often at serious odds, even at odds hitherto thought overwhelming, we have been clawing down three or four to one of our enemies, and the relative balance of the British and German air forces is now considerably more favourable to us than at the beginning of the battle. In cutting down the German bombers we are fighting our own battle, as well as that of France . . .

Our task is not only to win the battle but to win the war. After this battle in France abates its force, there will come a battle for our island, for all that Britain is and all that Britain means. That will be the struggle . . .

If this is one of the most awe-striking periods in the long history of France and Britain this is also, beyond doubt, the most sublime . . . The British and French people have advanced to rescue not only Europe but mankind from the foulest and most soul-destroying tyranny that has ever darkened and stained the pages of history.

Behind them, behind us, behind the Armies and Fleets of Britain and France, gather a group of shattered States and bludgeoned races — the Czechs, the Poles, the Norwegians, the Danes, the Dutch, the Belgians — upon all of whom the long night of barbarism will descend unbroken even by a star of hope, unless we conquer, as conquer we must; as conquer we shall.

WINSTON CHURCHILL, MAY 19, 1940

Sunday, May 19

With an estimated 20 enemy divisions pouring through the gap in the Allied line and advancing towards the coast and the Somme estuary, British and French commanders rapidly formed new defensive lines to protect their exposed flanks. For the moment, Cambrai remained in Allied hands though Le Cateau had already fallen and Général Giraud, commanding 9ème Armée, captured along with several of his staff. The enemy penetration had effectively split the Allied armies and any attempt to reunite them clearly considered hopeless. Indeed, so desperate was the situation that discussions between GHQ and the War Office in London, initiated this day, started to consider the advisability of withdrawing on Dunkirk. Meanwhile, 'in consequence of the disaster which had met the French forces', Général Gamelin was relieved of his command and replaced as Allied C-in-C by Général Weygand.

It was further determined that the RAF Component should be controlled from England so orders were issued for the withdrawal of the main headquarters, already relocated to Hazebrouck, along with Nos. 52 and 70 Wings, plus Nos. 2, 16, and 26 Lysander Squadrons, who were ordered to fly to Lympne.

With many RAF units retiring to new bases, and others ordered back to England, communications between units was problematic — despatch riders often being used. Organised reconnaissance flights thus proved difficult and only three sorties by strategic reconnaissance Blenheims were flown all day, while French efforts attracted severe losses. However, one of these reported enemy concentrations north-west of Rethel which were attacked by some 33 Fairey Battles, covered by 26 AASF Hurricanes, around 10.40 a.m. Few worthwhile targets were found to balance the loss of five Battles with two more badly damaged. Later that evening, RAF Component Hurricanes were used for reconnaissance sorties.

On the morning of Sunday, May 19, the British War Cabinet met to discuss the options in France: to turn south and join with French forces retreating towards Paris or move north to the Channel ports to evacuate to Britain. The War Cabinet also agreed that the time had come for Churchill to broadcast to the nation, explaining in no uncertain terms that the country was in a tight fix and that the public would have to accept whatever measures were necessary to ensure final victory. To prepare for his first broadcast as Prime Minister, Churchill spent a few hours at Chartwell to prepare his speech which was to go out live that evening. Immediately after the broadcast, a conference was held at which Churchill made the irrevocable decision that no more fighters would leave Britain 'whatever the need in France', declaring that 'it makes no difference whether we strike down German bombers here or in France'. He decided that 'in the event of a withdrawal of the BEF or a collapse in France we should get a good many of our aircraft now fighting there back to Britain'.

Air combats over threatened ground between Arras, Douai, Valenciennes, Le Cateau, and Cambrai were heavy and numerous throughout the day with four major actions occurring. Both British and French fighters were heavily committed defending their respective sides of the German salient, with engagements spilling over each other and confused as units became dispersed and the action widespread. Some heavy bombing was experienced at Cambrai, Arras, and neighbouring towns, while Lille-Seclin airfield was attacked but escaped the damage experienced at Amiens. Nevertheless, acting on his own initiative, Group Captain Fullard, commanding No. 14 (Fighter) Group, immediately ordered evacuation of the Lille airfields, concentrating his forces at Merville and Norrent-Fontes. He also ordered the return of the eight reinforcing flights to England due to lack of adequate servicing equipment and personnel in France. These moves were clearly necessary, but it followed that No. 14 Group fighters no longer enjoyed operational information previously received from the filter-room at Arras, evacuated early that morning, and Operations Room at Achicourt, evacuated at midday. Also, Fighter Command aircraft would no longer be able to refuel at RAF Component airfields and would have to operate direct from England in future.

That night, Bomber Command Wellingtons were sent against Givet while others dropped incendiaries on forests around Fumay and Bouillon thought to harbour enemy troops and supply dumps, though precise results were impossible to observe.

Attacks were also carried out against road and rail targets at Gembloux, and bridges over the Brussels canal near Tubize and Nivelles, in an effort to hinder the German advance through Belgium. Nineteen heavies operated in support of the BEF, all returning without loss, though the bulk of Bomber Command effort that night was directed against oil targets in Germany reflecting a shift in policy most strenuously urged by the AOC-in-C of Bomber Command, Air Chief Marshal Portal.

An Air Staff conference on this day decided that 'in view of the prohibitive wastage rates by day' RAF medium bombers should only be used at night, while the heavy bomber force operate at maximum strength during favourable moon conditions against oil targets and marshalling yards in Germany. This prompted vigorous protest from Air Marshal Barratt, whose frustration can only be imagined, when he learned that No. 2 Group Blenheims were no longer available for daylight operations. But events in France would negate the decision within 24 hours and it would be agreed that day sorties could continue provided fighter protection was guaranteed and the latest target information made available — before any sorties were despatched.

The shortage of medium bombers was being felt equally by the French. During the afternoon, 20 Loire-Nieuports from naval bomber units AB 2 and AB 4 were thrown at the Sambre crossing at Berlaimont, southwest of Maubeuge and suffered crippling losses to AA defences concentrated in the area.

Rescued to fight another day . . . although in the case of L2045 when it arrived back in Britain it was relegated to a training role and ended its days as an instructional airframe. This Hurricane from No. 501 Squadron was damaged on May 15.

BRITISH AIR FORCES IN FRANCE

1 SQUADRON, ANGLURE

Hurricane P2694. Shot down by concentrated return fire from He111s of 8./KG27 engaged between Rethel and Reims, and belly-landed near Château-Thierry 11.30 a.m. Flying Officer P. H. M. Richey wounded in neck and admitted to hospital. Aircraft a write-off.

Hurricane L1925. Set alight by return fire from He111s of 8./KG27 engaged between Rethel and Reims. Extinguished fire in steep dive and belly-landed near Château-de-Pricory 11.30 a.m. Sergeant F. J. Soper slightly injured. Aircraft a write-off.

3 SQUADRON, MERVILLE

Hurricane N2535. Abandoned near Lille-Seclin during combat with Bf109s 3.45 p.m. Pilot Officer J. Rose baled out unhurt. Aircraft a write-off.
Jack Rose was one of four replacement pilots and aircraft attached from No. 32 Squadron on May 14.

4 SQUADRON, LILLE-RONCHIN

Lysander II. Shot down by Bf109s while making practice landings at Lille-Marcq. Possibly that claimed by Oberlt von Wangerov (Staffelkapitän) of 2.(J)/LG2 11.00 a.m. Pilot Officer J. A. Plumb and LAC R. J. Thornton killed. Aircraft a write-off.

Lysander II N1305. Shot down by Bf109s while making practice landings at Lille-Marcq. Possibly that claimed by Lt Tismar of 3.(J)/LG2 11.15 a.m. Flying Officer L. J. Oldacres and LAC C. Butterill killed. Aircraft a write-off.
This serial number is thought to be correct as shown. It was the aircraft flown by the same pilot the previous day on withdrawal from the advance landing ground at Aspelaere.

12 SQUADRON, ÉCHEMINES

Battle L5538. Port fuel tank set alight by Bf109s during attack on troop concentrations near St Fergeux and crashed into woods and burned out at 'Bois de la Corne', near Mesnil-Lépinois. Believed that claimed by Oberfw Sicking of 1./JG51 at La Neuville 11.10 a.m. Pilot Officer J. J. McElligott seriously wounded, died in Épernay hospital. LAC T. O. Burgess badly injured arm, also admitted to hospital. Sergeant B. C. Long returned unhurt. Aircraft PH⊙A a write-off.

Battle N2178. Badly damaged during attack on troop concentrations near Hannogne-Saint Rémy and crashed near Cauroy. Believed that claimed by Fw Schmid of 1./JG51 at La Neuville 11.15 a.m. Sergeant E. J. Belcher killed. Flying Officer P. R. Barr and LAC K. D. Rawlings both wounded admitted to hospital. Aircraft PH⊙I a write-off.

16 SQUADRON, BERTANGLES

Lysander. Failed to return from tactical reconnaissance sortie and possibly that shot down by Hptmn Schellmann (Gruppenkommandeur) of Stab II./JG2 west of Tournai 5.05 a.m. Flying Officer A. P. Reed and Pilot Officer I. Dromgoole missing. Aircraft lost.

Lysander. Forced-landed damaged by fighters during tactical reconnaissance. Possibly that attacked by Fw Kothmann of 2./JG27 near St Quentin 5.05 a.m. Pilot Officer Hughes wounded. Aircraft a write-off.

17 SQUADRON, NORRENT-FONTES

Hurricane N2408. Shot down by Hptmn von Winterfeldt of 3./JG2 in combat north-east of Cambrai and crashed at Noyelles-sur-Selle 5.10 p.m. Pilot Officer R. E. Harris killed. Aircraft a write-off.

Hurricane N2525. Shot down by Oberlt Hauenschild of 3./JG2 in combat north-east of Cambrai 5.10 p.m. Sergeant C. J. Pavey baled out and captured. Aircraft a write-off.

18 SQUADRON, CRÉCY

Blenheim IV L9191. Crashed on landing at Crécy 8.40 a.m. cause not stated. Flight Lieutenant R. G. Wheldon, Sergeant A. E. Craig, and Sergeant G. Hawkins unhurt. Aircraft abandoned.
The squadron's seven remaining Blenheims were withdrawn to the UK later this day, landing back at Lympne.

26 SQUADRON, AUTHIE

Lysander II N1290. Failed to return from tactical reconnaissance sortie and crashed west of Authie 5.30 a.m. Pilot Officer C. I. D. Halliday and LAC A. F. Church killed. Aircraft a write-off.
Wreckage excavated by local enthusiast Pierre Ben in December 2003. Complete Perseus XII engine, propeller hub and two blades recovered along with Vickers K machine gun, service revolver, intact control column, RPM counter, Ki-Gass priming pump, and various other relics.

Lysander II N1292. Returned to Authie damaged by ground-fire during reconnaissance sortie 7.55 a.m. Flying Officer Goodale unhurt. Pilot Officer Taylor wounded in leg. Aircraft repairable.

A Bristol Perseus recovered by Pierre Ben from the crash site of Lysander N1290 of No. 26 Squadron on display in Warloy in 2004.

Lysander II N1202. Shot down by Lt Strakel-jahn of Stab I.(J)/LG2 during tactical recon-naissance sortie; crashed and burned out at Neuvilly 1.30 p.m. Pilot Officer R. H. Clifford killed; LAC F. L. Bettany badly burned, admitted to hospital at Landrecies but later died. Aircraft a write-off.

A body, identified as LAC Bettany from papers found, and originally buried along-side the wreckage of the aircraft, was re-interred in Neuvilly cemetery on April 2, 1941. But, in September 1944, a local eye-wit-ness revealed that it had been the pilot who died, the gunner escaping the aircraft and throwing off his blazing tunic before being taken to a nearby German field hospital for emergency treatment. This was Fred Bettany who later died of his injuries but with no means of identification was buried at Lan-drecies as 'Unknown'. After thorough post-war investigation by No. 1 MREU both graves were correctly registered and relatives informed.

32 SQUADRON, MERVILLE

Hurricane N2462. Shot down in combat with Bf109s over the Forêt de Mormal, north-east of Le Cateau, 11.55 a.m. Possibly one of those claimed by Oberlt Bertram (*Staffelka-pitän*) of 1./JG2. Flying Officer J. C. Milner baled out and captured. Aircraft a write-off.

59 SQUADRON, POIX

Blenheim IV L9463. Returned tail wheel damaged by flak during reconnaissance sor-tie between La Fère and St Quentin 6.25 a.m. Pilot Officer C. M. M. Crece, Sergeant Davis, and AC Hurst unhurt. Aircraft TR⊙L repairable.

Blenheim IV L4856. Lost bearings during reconnaissance sortie over Lessines and Ath and force-landed low on fuel at St Vaast-en-Chaussée, north-west of Amiens, 7.00 p.m. where strafed by enemy aircraft. Pilot Officer C. R. Wylie and Sergeant Liddiard unhurt. Aircraft TR⊙K later returned but abandoned.

The squadron was withdrawn on this day, six surviving aircraft flying to Lympne.

73 SQUADRON, GAYE

Hurricane P2539. Forced-landed damaged by return fire following attack on Ju88s of II./KG51 11.30 a.m. Sergeant L. S. Pilkington unhurt. Aircraft ⊙D abandoned.

Hurricane P2543. Crash-landed damaged by Bf110s during attack on Ju88s of II./KG51 11.30 a.m. Pilot Officer N. C. Langham-Hobart injured knees. Aircraft a write-off.

Hurricane. Became separated during attack on Ju88s of II./KG51 and port wing badly damaged in combat with Bf110s 11.30 a.m. Hit a ditch forced-landing at Montargis and propeller and undercarriage wrecked. Pilot Officer J. E. P. Thompson slightly injured. Aircraft a write-off.

85 SQUADRON, MERVILLE

Hurricane P2562. Set alight in combat with Bf109s of I.(J)/LG2 and II./JG2 over Lille, crashed and burned out. Possibly that claimed by Lt Tismar of 3.(J)/LG2 11.02 a.m. Sergeant J. McG. Little missing. Aircraft a write-off.

Hurricane. N2601 Damaged on the ground during enemy bombing attack 4.00 p.m. Sergeant A. H. Deacon unhurt. Aircraft damaged but repairable — later abandoned.

Both crewmembers of another of the squadron's Lysanders lost their lives when N1202 crashed at Neuvilly yet they now lie in different cemeteries. The pilot, Ralph Clifford, was buried locally, while the gunner, Fred Bettany, who died from his injuries in a German field hospital without being identified, was interred at Landrecies.

Hurricane P2547. Shot down in combat with Bf109s south-east of Lille and believed that claimed by Uffz Wemhöner of 5./JG26 over Roubaix 4.40 p.m. Pilot Officer P. P. Woods-Scawen baled out slightly injured. Aircraft a write-off.

Hurricane P2551. Shot down in cross-fire from He111s of KG54 and abandoned east of Lille 5.00 p.m. Squadron Leader M. F. Pea-cock baled out unhurt. Aircraft VY⊙H a write-off.

87 SQUADRON, LILLE-MARCQ

Hurricane. Returned damaged by return fire from Hs126 of 1.(H)/11 attacked between Le Cateau and Cambrai 6.00 a.m. Flying Officer J. H. L. Allen slightly wounded in left arm. Aircraft repairable.

Hurricane P2687. Shot down in combat with Bf109s of 9./JG26 north-east of Tournai 10.30 a.m. Flying Officer J. M. Strickland baled out arms wounded and hit in legs by French ground-fire while in parachute. Air-craft a write-off.

Hurricane. Returned damaged in combat with Bf109s north-east of Tournai 10.30 a.m. Possibly that attacked by Oberlt Schöpfel (*Staffelkapitän*) of 9./JG26. Pilot Officer H. J. R. Dunn unhurt. Aircraft damage state not recorded.

Hurricane. Returned damaged in combat with Bf109s north-east of Tournai 10.30 a.m. Possibly that attacked by Uffz Eberz of 9./JG26. Flying Officer R. L. Glyde unhurt. Aircraft damage state not recorded.

Hurricane. Shot down by Bf109s of I.(J)/LG2 and II./JG2 and abandoned near Orchies. Possibly that claimed by Lt Müller of 6./JG2 over Tournai 11.50 a.m. Pilot Officer H. J. R. Dunn baled out with burns and admitted to hospital. Aircraft a write-off.

Hurricane P2819. Returned with control wires and main longerons badly damaged in combat with Bf109s of I.(J)/LG2 and II./JG2 11.45 a.m. Possibly that attacked by Lt Mertens of 1.(J)/LG2. Flying Officer R. F. Watson unhurt. Aircraft LK⊙G damaged but repairable — abandoned on withdrawal to Merville.

Hurricane P2683. Returned badly damaged by Bf109s in combat over Tournai 3.15 p.m. Flying Officer R. M. S. Rayner unhurt. Air-craft a write-off.

88 SQUADRON, LES GRANDES-CHAPELLES

Battle K9348. Returned damaged following bombing attack on Hirson 7.30 a.m. LAC E. Wigglesworth wounded, rest of crew unhurt. Aircraft damaged but repairable — later abandoned at No. 21 Aircraft Depot, Château-Bougon.

Another aircraft P2258 was also aban-doned by the unit around this time as were K9349 and K9352 for which details are unknown.

B FLIGHT, 111 SQUADRON, VALENCIENNES

Hurricane L1774. Shot down by Bf109s dur-ing attack on He111s of I./KG54 south-west of Douai and crashed at Gavrelle, east of Arras. Possibly that claimed by Lt Schmidt of 8./JG3 3.20 p.m. Flying Officer D. S. H. Bury killed. Aircraft a write-off.

Hurricane L1720. Shot down by Bf109s dur-ing attack on He111s of I./KG54 south-west of Douai and crashed at 'Le Guet', Sains-les-Marquion, west of Cambrai. Possibly that claimed by Fw Kuhn of 8./JG3 3.21 p.m. Pilot Officer I. C. Moorwood killed. Air-craft a write-off.

Hurricane L1733. Glycol tank damaged by Bf109s during attack on He111s of I./KG54 west of Cambrai and undercarriage collapsed on landing at Beauval, south of Doullens, with engine seized. Possibly that claimed by Lt Achleitner of 9./JG3 3.45 p.m. Squadron Leader J. M. Thompson unhurt. Aircraft a write-off.

Hurricane L1564. Landed damaged by return fire during attack on He111s of I./KG54 west of Cambrai 3.30 p.m. Flying Officer S. D. P. Connors unhurt. Aircraft repairable.

142 SQUADRON, FAUX-VILLECERF

Battle K7696. Failed to return from attack on targets west of Laon and believed victim of ground-fire 10.45 a.m. Pilot Officer H. H. Taylor, Sergeant S. Lang, and LAC H. Long all captured. Aircraft a write-off.

Battle L5226. Believed brought down by ground-fire during attack on targets west of Laon and crashed near Dagny-Lambercy 10.45 a.m. LAC W. D. Boyle killed. Sergeant A. J. Godsell and Sergeant B. A. Hopgood both captured. Aircraft a write-off.

Battle P5238. Damaged by ground-fire during attack on targets west of Laon and forced-landed south of Épernay 10.45 a.m. Sergeant T. Jones died of wounds. Sergeant G. H. Ebert and LAC R. S. Utteridge unhurt. Aircraft damaged but repairable — abandoned at No. 21 Aircraft Depot, Château-Bougon.

150 SQUADRON, POVAN

Battle P5235. Badly damaged during attack on enemy armour north of the Aisne west of Rethel and belly-landed near 'Chêne Tonneau' at Barby 11.15 a.m. Pilot Officer D. E. T. Osment, Sergeant G. W. Clifford, and AC2 W. G. Slade all captured. Aircraft JN⊙H a write-off.

Battle L5583. Forced-landed at Sommesous airfield damaged following attack on enemy armour north of the Aisne west of Rethel 11.25 a.m. Pilot Officer A. D. Frank and crew unhurt. Aircraft abandoned.

A FLIGHT, 213 SQUADRON, LILLE-SECLIN

Hurricane N2538. Believed shot down by French AA fire 12.05 p.m. Sergeant T. Boyd baled out unhurt. Aircraft a write-off.

Hurricane. Forced-landed at Nomain, north of Orchies, damaged by return fire from Ju88 engaged between Douai and St Amand 2.25 p.m. Pilot Officer L. G. B. Stone unhurt. Aircraft AK⊙K repairable.

226 SQUADRON, FAUX-VILLECERF

Battle L5452. Collided with Anson R3341 after landing at Povan in bad visibility. Sergeant F. Evans (of No. 4 Ferry Pilots Pool) unhurt. Aircraft repairable.

A FLIGHT, 242 SQUADRON, LILLE-SECLIN

Hurricane P2808. Returned port wing damaged in attack by Bf109s of I.(J)/LG2 and II./JG2 during action over Lille 12.30 p.m. Flight Lieutenant D. R. Miller unhurt. Aircraft repairable.

Hurricane. Landed at Manston oil tank holed by ground-fire during transit flight from Lille-Seclin. Flight Lieutenant D. R. Miller unhurt. Aircraft damaged but repairable.

A FLIGHT, 253 SQUADRON, VALENCIENNES

Hurricane N2590. Forced-landed at Dieppe damaged by Bf109s in action between Cambrai and Le Cateau. Possibly that attacked over Le Cateau by Fw Borchers of 1./JG77 3.15 p.m. Flight Lieutenant G. Harris wounded, admitted to hospital. Aircraft damaged but repairable.

Hurricane N2542. Shot down by Bf109s in combat between Cambrai and Arras and abandoned over Riencourt-lès-Cagnicourt. Possibly that claimed by Oberfw Leyerer of 2./JG77 south of Cambrai 4.10 p.m. Pilot Officer F. W. Ratford attempted to bale out but killed. Aircraft a write-off.

B FLIGHT, 253 SQUADRON, NORRENT-FONTES

Hurricane L1674. Shot down in combat with Bf109s of I.(J)/LG2 and II./JG2 south-east of Lille. Possibly that claimed by Oberlt Hahn of 4./JG2 over Tournai 11.18 a.m. Flight Lieutenant H. T. J. Anderson killed. Aircraft a write-off.

Hurricane. Shot down in combat with Bf109s of I.(J)/LG2 and II./JG2 south-east of Lille and crashed at Cysoing. Possibly that claimed by Lt Meimberg of 4./JG2 over Tournai 11.20 a.m. Sergeant G. MacKenzie killed. Aircraft a write-off.

504 SQUADRON, LILLE-MARCQ

Hurricane. Shot down in combat with Bf109s of I.(J)/LG2 and II./JG2 and abandoned east of Lille 11.15 a.m. Possibly one of those claimed by Fw Schmitz of 2.(J)/LG2. Pilot Officer J. R. Hardacre baled out unhurt. Aircraft a write-off.

Hurricane. Shot down in combat with Bf109s of I.(J)/LG2 and II./JG2 and abandoned east of Lille 11.15 a.m. Possibly that claimed by Oberfw Staege of 2.(J)/LG2. Squadron Leader J. H. Hill baled out but wounded in right leg by civilian ground-fire, mobbed on landing and admitted to hospital. Aircraft a write-off.

Hurricane N2355. Shot down by Bf109s of I.(J)/LG2 and II./JG2 over Lille-Seclin 11.30 a.m. Possibly that claimed by Oberfw Schott of 2.(J)/LG2. Sergeant M. V. Mapletoft baled out wounded. Aircraft a write-off.

A FLIGHT, 601 SQUADRON, MERVILLE

Hurricane P2800. Crash-landed south of Lille damaged by debris from He111 of KG54 attacked over Douai 2.30 p.m. Flying Officer G. N. S. Cleaver unhurt. Aircraft abandoned.

It is frustrating that of the dozens of snapshots by German soldiery of crashed aircraft, very few have any written identification on the reverse as to the date or place where they were taken. These two photos of Battles from No. 142 Squadron are a good example but with no serial number visible we cannot pinpoint the crash. All we can say is that the top photo was apparently taken at 'Audembert' while QT⊙L *(above)* features regularly in the photo albums of many Wehrmacht veterans.

607 SQUADRON, NORRENT-FONTES

Hurricane P3535. Badly damaged in combat with Bf109s near Cambrai and crashed at Bachy 4.30 p.m. Possibly that claimed by Oberlt Nordmann of Stab I./JG77. Squadron Leader G. M. Fidler killed. Aircraft AF⊙C a write-off.

615 SQUADRON, MOORSELE

Hurricane N2331. Shot down by Bf109s between Arras and Cambrai 6.15 p.m. Believed that claimed by Hptmn Lützow *(Gruppenkommandeur)* of Stab I./JG3. Flying Officer R. D. Pexton baled out slightly wounded. Aircraft a write-off.

Hurricane. Returned damaged during sortie over Douai, possibly that attacked by Lt von Cramon of Stab I./JG3 north-east of Cambrai 6.15 p.m. Pilot Officer W. L. McKnight (of No. 242 Squadron) unhurt. Aircraft KW⊙F damaged but repairable.

Combat Report and Log Book disagree on the date of this action.

That Sunday marked a turning point in the air war with many units of the British Air Forces in France being ordered to henceforth operate from airfields in the UK. Our criteria for the compilation of the BAFF Roll of Honour which is included on pages 500-529, is that it lists aircrew killed while serving in squadrons based in France. Thus, for example, Pilot Officer Kenneth Lucas killod on May 19 while on the strength of No. 145 Squadron (see entry below) is not included as on that particular day the squadron was flying from Manston. Nevertheless, the citizens of Warloy have accorded both him and Captain David Pinkney, who crashed in the area while attached to No. 662 AOP Squadron on September 1, 1944, this fitting memorial unveiled in 2004. (Both men are buried in the local Warloy-Baillon Cemetery, Plot 2, Row G, Graves 1 and 2.)

UK-based aircraft lost or damaged on operations over the Western Front:

RAF FIGHTER COMMAND

A Flight, 145 Squadron, Manston
Offensive patrol — Arras:

Hurricane N2711. Returned with pneumatics damaged by return fire from He111s of KG54 engaged south-west of Cambrai 3.30 p.m. Pilot Officer E. C. J. Wakeham unhurt. Aircraft SO⊙D repairable.

Hurricane N2713. Returned with propeller and windscreen damaged by return fire from He111s of KG54 engaged south-west of Cambrai 3.30 p.m. Pilot Officer A. Elson unhurt. Aircraft repairable.

Hurricane N2598. Shot down by Oberlt Homuth *(Staffelkapitän)* of 3./JG27 during attack on He111s of KG54, crashed and burned out between Warloy-Baillon and Varennes-en-Croix 3.30 p.m. Pilot Officer K. R. Lucas killed. Aircraft a write-off.

Site excavated by local enthusiast Pierre Ben in September 2003. Items recovered include aircraft identity plate confirming 'N2598', Rolls-Royce Merlin III engine plate '136692', oxygen bottle, one bent Browning machine gun, armour plate, KiGass priming pump, and various other corroded instruments and components. Like most RAF pilots of the time, Kenneth Lucas had little or no combat experience. He was first in his squadron to be killed in action.

B Flight, 601 Squadron, Manston
Offensive patrol — Douai:

Hurricane P2684. Forced-landed near Boyelles, south of Arras, badly damaged by Bf110s during attack on He111s over Douai 2.30 p.m. Flying Officer T. E. Hubbard unhurt. Aircraft destroyed by pilot.

Hurricane L2088. Forced-landed with reserve tank holed in attack on Bf110s near Douai 2.30 p.m. Flying Officer W. H. Rhodes-Moorhouse unhurt. Aircraft repairable.

Hurricane L2081. Shot down by Bf110 in combat over Douai 2.30 p.m. Flying Officer H. J. Riddle unhurt. Aircraft a write-off.

The French Air Force was desperately attempting to harass the German armoured columns and on the 19th called in help from the Navy. Eleven L-N 401 dive-bombers from AB 2 and nine L-N 411s from AB 4, both units based at Berck, launched a disastrous attack at Berlaimont which led to the loss of nearly a dozen aircraft. This is one of them — the Loire-Nieuport 401 of Lieutenant Vilbert of AB 2.

Shot down near Amiens on May 19, Commandant Henry Moguez and Sous-Lieutenant Victor Paquez succeeded in parachuting to safety, their hands badly burned as they abandoned their flaming Mureaux. They were taken to Niort, via Beauvais, where their burns were treated. They rejoined their unit, GAO 501, at Moissac where this picture was taken in July, Moguez and Paquez posing in front of a Mureaux 115.

FRENCH AIR FORCE

AB 2 L-N 401. Shot down by intense flak during attack on enemy armoured concentrations near Berlaimont. Mtre Pascal killed. Aircraft 9 a write-off.

AB 2 L-N 401 (8). Hit by flak during attack on enemy armoured columns near Berlaimont and belly-landed. LV Vilbert captured. Aircraft 4 a write-off.

AB 2 L-N 401 (7). Severely damaged by flak during attack on enemy armour around Berlaimont and belly-landed near Saint-Souplet. EV1 Douxami captured. Aircraft 7 a write-off.

AB 2 L-N 401(10). Damaged by flak during attack on enemy armour near Berlaimont, then attacked by Bf109s and belly-landed 10 km south of Cambrai. EV1 Faivre captured. Aircraft 10 a write-off.

AB 2 L-N 401. Damaged by flak during attack on enemy armour near Berlaimont and forced-landed during return flight. SM Bagot captured. Aircraft a write-off.

AB 2 L-N 401 (3). Believed returned severely damaged by flak during attack on enemy armour near Berlaimont. SM Bonnefoy believed unhurt. Aircraft 11 later abandoned.

AB 4 L-N 401. Suffered a direct hit from flak during attack on enemy armour near Berlaimont and crash-landed near Fontaine-au-Bois. Mtre Téoulet killed. Aircraft a write-off.

AB 4 L-N 411 (11). Shot down by French flak at Etreux having survived attack on enemy armoured columns at Berlaimont; belly-landed and burned out. SM Goasguen killed. Aircraft a write-off.

AB 4 L-N 411 (12). Badly damaged by flak during attack on armoured columns near Berlaimont; belly-landed and burned out. SM F. Jamais captured. Aircraft 12 a write-off.

AB 4 L-N 411. Hit by flak during attack on armoured columns near Berlaimont and forced-landed during return flight. SM Klein evaded capture and returned unhurt. Aircraft a write-off.

AB 4 L-N 411. Hit by flak during attack on armoured columns near Berlaimont and crash-landed. EV1 Decaix captured. Aircraft 10 a write-off.

ECN 4/13 Potez 631. Made emergency landing at Beauvais damaged by return fire from He111 between Creil and Beauvais 7.00 a.m.. Adjt Delage wounded in hand and leg. Aircraft repairable.

GAO 501 Mureaux 115 (57). Shot down by Bf109s during transfer flight to Mantes-Gassicourt and crashed at Boves, 6 km south-east of Amiens 12.50 p.m. Possibly that claimed by Lt Franzisket of 3./JG1. Sgt J. Canonne killed. Sgt Cocu badly wounded; admitted to Vernon hospital where right foot amputated. Aircraft a write-off.

GAO 501 Mureaux 115 (91). Shot down by Bf109s during transfer flight to Mantes-Gassicourt and crashed in flames outside Amiens 12.50 p.m. Possibly that claimed by Lt Mann of 1./JG1. Cmdt. H. Moguez (Groupe Commandant) and S/Lt V. Paquez baled out badly burned. Aircraft a write-off.

GAO 544 Potez 63.11 (200). Reported crashed at Brancourt-le-Grand, 5 km west of Bohain-en-Vermandois; circumstances not stated. Crew unhurt. Aircraft a write-off.

GAO 1/551 Potez 63.11 (678). Returned damaged by light flak following reconnaissance sortie over Signy-l'Abbaye, Montcornet, and Liart sector. Capt Massoni, S/Lt Deplanque, and Sgt Pegaz unhurt. Aircraft a write-off.

GAO 552 Potez 63.11 (637). Hit by flak and ground-fire during reconnaissance of enemy troop movements between Arras, Bethune, and Cambrai. Undercarriage damaged so belly-landed at St-Omer 8.30 a.m. Lt De Bort, Sgt Domain, and Sgt Plantier unhurt. Aircraft a write-off.

GB II/12 LeO 451 (11). Bomb load exploded during enemy bombing of Persan-Beaumont airfield 6.30 a.m. No crew casualties. Aircraft a write-off.
LeO 451 (88 and 104) were also reported damaged in this explosion.

GB II/15 Farman 221 (3). Caught fire on return flight after bombing enemy troop concentrations between Liart and Montcornet. Crash-landed and burned out at Versaugues, near Paray-le-Monial. Lt Charlan, S/Lt Balase, Sgt Boudin, Adj Kerbouch, Sgt Barbier, Sgt Gauvin, and Sgt Mille all slightly injured. Aircraft a write-off.

GC II/1 Bloch 152. Forced-landed at Chantilly-Les-Aigles damaged by return fire from Do17 1.45 p.m. S/Lt M. Hutter wounded in left arm. Aircraft damaged but repairable.

GC 5/1 Morane 406 (730). Shot down by Hptmn Mielke (Staffelkapitän) of 3.(J)/LG2 in combat over Guise 5.15 p.m. Crashed and burned out at Anizy-le-Château, 12 km south-west of Laon. Lt P. Marche (Commandant) killed. Aircraft a write-off.

This German snapshot does have a written inscription on the reverse although it merely states: 'Marine aircraft — Type unknown — French'. It is believed to be the L-N 401 flown by

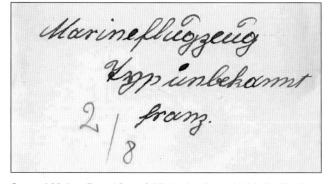

Second-Maître Bonnefoy of AB 4 who brought his badly damaged machine back to Berck where it lay propped on a trestle to await the German advance.

GC 5/1 Morane 406 (733). Forced-landed at Plessis-Belleville damaged in combat with Bf109s of 3.(J)/LG2 over Guise 5.15 p.m. Sgt G. Pralon seriously wounded in leg and arm. Aircraft a write-off.

GC 6/1 Morane 406. Belly-landed back at base badly damaged in combat with Bf109s of 3.(J)/LG2 over Guise 5.15 p.m. Sgt Pinochietti unhurt. Aircraft a write-off.

GC III/3 Morane 406. Forced-landed damaged by return fire from Do17s of II./KG3 near Estrées-St-Denis 10.30 a.m. Adjt M-E. Leblanc believed unhurt. Aircraft a write-off.

GC III/3 Morane 406. Set alight by return fire from Do17s of II./KG3 and abandoned over Beauvais-Tillé 10.30 a.m. Cpl V. Slouf baled out low but landed unhurt. Aircraft a write-off.

GC III/3 Morane 406 (467). Forced-landed damaged by flak 7.00 p.m. S/Lt P. Rebillat believed unhurt. Aircraft abandoned.

GC II/4 Curtiss H-75 (97). Returned to Orconte badly damaged in combat with Bf109s of III./JG53 north-east of Reims 8.35 a.m. Believed that attacked by Hptmn Mölders (Gruppenkommandeur) or Lt Altendorf of 7./JG53. Lt M. Vinçotte unhurt. Aircraft damaged but repairable — later abandoned.

GC I/8 Bloch 152 (522). Collided with Do17 of 8./KG2 during head-on attack over Creil and crashed at La Croix Sainte Jaunisse, outside Montepilloy, 5.45 a.m. S/Lt J. Ruby killed. Aircraft a write-off.

GR II/33 Potez 637 (11). Belly-landed shortly after take-off on low-level reconnaissance sortie, cause unknown. Crew unhurt. Aircraft a write-off.

This is the Potez 637 of Groupe de Reconnaissance II/33 which force-landed at Villers-St Christophe after being hit by anti-aircraft fire.

GR II/33 Potez 637 (69). Belly-landed at Villers-St Christophe, 4 km north of Ham, damaged by flak during reconnaissance sortie to Cambrai and Arras 5.30 a.m. Lt Mottez, Sgt Sausser and Sgt Genson (both of ECMJ 1/16) captured unhurt. Aircraft lost.

GR II/33 Potez 637 (129). Returned damaged by ground-fire from reconnaissance sortie over the Aisne valley 7.30 a.m. Lt Raby badly wounded. Adjt Blanchard and Sgt Prieur (both of ECMJ 1/16) unhurt. Aircraft damaged but repairable.
Both Potez 637s above (69 and 129) were from ECMJ 1/16 and had arrived at Le Bourget the previous day with their crews to reinforce GR II/33.

GR I/36 Potez 63.11 (580). Shot down by Fw Baun of 6./JG53 near Signy-l'Abbaye during reconnaissance sortie south-west of Sedan and crash-landed in flames at Connage 7.55 p.m. Capt Perrotte thrown from aircraft and captured badly wounded, leg later amputated. Sgt Cazenave and Sgt M. P. de Stampa captured unhurt. Aircraft a write-off.

GR I/52 Bloch 174 (8). Shot down by enemy aircraft during reconnaissance sortie to the Meuse valley to Maastricht. Crashed and exploded west of Vaudesincourt, 26 km east of Reims 8.00 p.m. Sgt M. Grand and Sgt E. Zinck killed. Lt J. Fulcrand fell from aircraft with unopened parachute and killed. Aircraft a write-off.

GR I/52 Bloch 174 (35). Returned to base badly damaged in attacks by Oberfw Leyerer of 2./JG77 over Le Quesnoy during reconnaissance sortie to the Ardennes and the Meuse valley 8.00 p.m. Sgt Cugnet and rest of crew unhurt. Aircraft damaged but repairable.

GR II/52 Potez 637. Shot down by Fw Galubinski of 7./JG53 during reconnaissance sortie for 9ème Armée and crash-landed on fire at Beaucourt-en-Santerre, 16 km north of Montdidier, 7.05 p.m. Adjt Charlier wounded in leg and shoulder, and Adjt Peltriaux wounded in thigh and face, both admitted to Beauvais hospital. Sgt Thierry unhurt. Aircraft a write-off.

GR II/52 Potez 637 (10). Believed shot down by Hptmn Galland of Stab JG27 near Méaulte, south of Albert, during reconnaissance sortie for 9ème Armée 7.45 p.m. Crash-landed and burned out. Lt Vuatrin and Adjt Thiebault wounded. Lt Escoffier unhurt. Aircraft a write-off.

GR II/55 Potez 63.11 (673). Shot down during low-level reconnaissance sortie to Arras and Cambrai, and crashed and burned out at St Germainmont, 20 km west of Rethel. Possibly that claimed by Hptmn Galland of Stab JG27 south-west of Hirson 8.45 p.m. Lt R. Durand, Sgt S. Rescoussie, and Sgt R. Brun killed. Aircraft a write-off.

BELGIAN AIR FORCE

11/VI/1 Renard R-31. Returned damaged by ground-fire following reconnaissance sortie south of Wetteren 4.00 p.m. Capt P. Henry de la Lindi (Commandant) and S/Lt A. Goedert unhurt. Aircraft damaged but repairable.

II/2 Fiat CR-42 (R.26). Destroyed on the ground in bombing attack on Chartres airfield. Pilot unhurt. Aircraft a write-off.

The demise of this Potez from GR II/52 is attributed to Adolf Galland of the staff flight of Jagdgeschwader 27.

LUFTWAFFE

An He111 brought down by Hurricanes during the morning combats of May 19. The complexity of the fighting makes it impossible to resolve individual actions with certainty, though it seems likely that No. 1 Squadron engaged the He111s of III./KG27 while No. 73 Squadron, whose aircraft recognition was not the best, attacked Ju88s of II./KG51. In reality, unit cohesion would have soon been lost as aircraft from all units became entangled.

1.(H)/11 Henschel Hs126. Attacked by ten H-75s of GC II/4 during observation sortie near Le Quesnoy then engaged by F/O Glyde, P/O Cock, F/O Ward, and F/O Allen of No. 87 Squadron. Tail broke off and crashed on fire alongside the road at Naves, north-east of Cambrai, 6.00 a.m. Oberlt H. Grether and Obergefr K-H. Kramer killed. Aircraft a write-off.

3.(F)/11 Dornier Do17P. Tail shot off by Sgt White of No. 32 Squadron during reconnaissance sortie and crashed near La Capelle 4.20 p.m. Lt R. Meyer, Uffz A. Winkert, and Uffz E. Schöbel killed. Aircraft a write-off.

3.(F)/11 Dornier Do17P. Believed damaged in attack south of Vervins by Lt Vinçotte of GC II/4 and forced-landed 7.50 a.m. One crewman wounded. Aircraft a write-off.

4.(F)/11 Dornier Do17P. Returned badly damaged by fighters near Marquion. Possibly that attacked by P/O Whittaker of No. 17 Squadron south of Cambrai 4.20 p.m. Alternatively, that engaged by Lt Cizek, Cpl Slouf, and Lt Behal of GC III/3 west of Valenciennes 6.00 p.m. One crewman slightly wounded. Aircraft a write-off.

2.(H)/12 Henschel Hs126. Believed shot down by Lt Dorance, Lt Rouquette, and Sgt Vuillemain of GC I/5 over Chémery and crashed at Stonne 7.45 a.m. Fw R. Helfrich mortally wounded, died in hospital at Sedan. Aircraft a write-off.
Two independently compiled Luftwaffe documents report this loss on May 20.

3.(H)/14 Henschel Hs126. Shot down by S/Lt Baptizet, Adj Tesseraud, and Sgt de La Chapelle of GC II/4 during observation sortie north of Laon and crashed at 'La Genette' near Raillimont airstrip 7.50 a.m. Fw G. Schröder killed. Lt Wölfing believed unhurt. Aircraft probable write-off.

2.(H)/23 Henschel Hs126. Returned damaged in attack by Adjt Furst of GC II/2 near Bellicourt 5.20 p.m. Lt Hundt wounded. Aircraft repairable.

1.(H)/41 Junkers W34. Forced-landed near Frauenbrück-Morelbusch shortly after take-off due to engine failure. No casualties. Aircraft damaged but repairable.

1.(H)/41 Henschel Hs126. Shot down by P/O Atkinson, P/O Sizer, and Sgt Butterfield of No. 213 Squadron during observation sortie between Pecq and Ath and crashed south-west of Peruwelz 12.40 p.m. Lt W. Bujalla and Uffz W. Ehemann killed. Aircraft a write-off.

2.(H)/41 Henschel Hs126. Shot down by F/L Wight, P/O Sizer, and P/O Atkinson of No. 213 Squadron during observation sortie over the Lys canal and crash-landed west of Aalst 6.15 p.m. Fw H. Carl and Uffz G. Meermann both wounded. Aircraft a write-off.

I./JG1 Messerschmitt Bf109E-3. Wrecked in forced-landing at St Quentin due to petrol failure. Pilot believed unhurt. Aircraft a write-off.

1./JG2 Messerschmitt Bf109E-3. Shot down by P/O Grice of No. 32 Squadron in combat south-east of Cambrai and crashed at Esnes 11.55 a.m. Leutnant W. Grübel killed. Aircraft a write-off.

1./JG2 Messerschmitt Bf109E-4 (677). Damaged by P/O Flinders of No. 32 Squadron in combat south-east of Cambrai 11.55 a.m. and undercarriage collapsed on landing at Beaulieu. Possibly also that attacked by F/L Brothers. Oberleutnant O. Bertram *(Staffelkapitän)* unhurt. Aircraft 1+ repairable.

4./JG2 Messerschmitt Bf109E. Shot down in combat with Hurricanes and broke its back in heavy crash-landing near Tournai 11.20 a.m. Possibly one of those claimed by P/O Lewis of No. 85 Squadron. Oberleutnant L. Krutein captured wounded. Aircraft 5 + — a write-off.

5./JG2 Messerschmitt Bf109E. Shot down by Hurricanes while returning to base with engine trouble 11.30 p.m. Possibly another of those claimed by P/O Lewis of No. 85 Squadron. Uffz H-J. Hartwig baled out and captured wounded. Aircraft 2 + — write-off.

1./JG3 Messerschmitt Bf109E-1. Crashed on landing at Philippeville following combat south-east of Valenciennes 3.40 p.m. Leutnant H. Schnabel badly wounded. Aircraft repairable.

3./JG3 Messerschmitt Bf109E-1. Reportedly collided with enemy fighter in action south-east of Valenciennes and crashed into the Forêt de Mormal near Englefontaine 6.30 a.m. Uffz L. Leicht baled out but killed. Aircraft a write-off.
The exact circumstances of this loss are controversial, German accounts reporting that Ludwig Leicht died following a collision with a 'Spitfire'. Surviving British records are incomplete but no corresponding loss or damage has been traced, nor was any engagement reported by Allied fighters in this area at the time.

9./JG3 Messerschmitt Bf109E-1. Forced-landed with radiator damaged in combat between Lille and Roubaix 4.15 p.m. Possibly one of those attacked by P/O Woods-Scawen of No. 85 Squadron. Uffz H. Stephan captured. Aircraft 2 + I a write-off.

3./JG20 Messerschmitt Bf109E. Suffered an engine fire at Eindhoven. Gefreiter K. Koch slightly injured. Aircraft damage state not recorded.

I./JG21 Messerschmitt Bf109E-1. Wrecked in forced-landing at Malincourt following engine failure. Pilot believed unhurt. Aircraft a write-off.

I./JG26 Messerschmitt Bf109E. Aircraft reportedly slightly damaged, cause not stated. Pilot unhurt. Aircraft repairable.

Stab II./JG26 Messerschmitt Bf109E-3 (1542). Shot down by F/O Eyre of No. 615 Squadron in combat east of Lille and crashed at Rumegies, south of Tournai, 7.40 p.m. Hauptmann H. Knüppel *(Gruppenkommandeur)* killed. Aircraft **<<+** — a write-off.
Herwig Knüppel was originally buried as 'Unknown' and not formally identified until the wreckage of his aircraft was properly investigated in February 1941.

4./JG26 Messerschmitt Bf109E-3. Forced-landed outside Lille damaged in attack by F/O Eyre of No. 615 Squadron 7.45 p.m. Possibly that belly-landed between Hallennes-lez-Haubourdin and Erquinghem-le-Sec. Hauptmann K. Ebbighausen *(Staffelkapitän)* slightly wounded. Aircraft **8 +** — a write-off.

4./JG26 Messerschmitt Bf109E-3. Forced-landed at Brussels following combat with No. 615 Squadron Hurricanes over Lille 7.40 p.m. Pilot unhurt. Aircraft damaged but repairable.

9./JG26 Messerschmitt Bf109E-3. Shot down in combat with No. 87 Squadron Hurricanes and abandoned north-east of Courtrai 10.30 a.m. Possibly that claimed by P/O Dunn. Leutnant H. Brucks baled out and captured. Aircraft a write-off.

5./JG27 Messerschmitt Bf109E-3. Engine set alight in combat with F/O Glyde of No. 87 Squadron over Lille 3.00 p.m. Oberleutnant H-C. Schäfer *(Staffelkapitän)* baled out south-east of La Bassée and captured badly wounded. Aircraft **1 +** — a write-off.

5./JG27 Messerschmitt Bf109E-1. Shot down in combat with Hurricanes and belly-landed east of Lille. Probably that claimed by P/O Stone of No. 213 Squadron 3.30 p.m. Leutnant H. Strobl evaded capture unhurt. Aircraft **2 +** — a write-off.

I./JG52 Messerschmitt Bf109E-1. Crash-landed at base, cause not stated. Pilot unhurt. Aircraft damaged but repairable.

III./JG52 Messerschmitt Bf109E-1. Damaged in take-off accident at Frankfurt/Rhein-Main. Pilot unhurt. Aircraft damaged but repairable.

II./JG53 Messerschmitt Bf109E-1. Damaged in crash-landing at base, cause not stated. Pilot unhurt. Aircraft damaged but repairable.

I./JG77 Fieseler Fi156C. Crash-landed at Philippeville, cause not stated. Pilot unhurt. Aircraft a write-off.

2./JG77 Messerschmitt Bf109E-1 (4072). Returned damaged following combat over Le Quesnoy 7.25 p.m. Oberlt E. Priebe *(Staffelkapitän)* wounded. Aircraft **1 +** damage state not recorded.

Stab KG2 Dornier Do17Z. Believed engine damaged in attack by F/O Kain of No. 73 Squadron east of Metz and forced-landed near Rehlingen 6.00 a.m. Crew unhurt. Aircraft damaged but repairable.

8./KG2 Dornier Do17Z. Collided with S/Lt Ruby of GC I/8 in head-on attack near Creil, crashed and burned out at Borest, south-east of Senlis, 5.45 a.m. Uffz R. Tiedemann, Uffz H. Seifart, and Gefr W. Eckert killed. Gefr H. Behnke baled out and captured unhurt. Aircraft a write-off.
Hans Behnke apparently remained at large until his capture at Pont-Ste-Maxence four days later.

Fortunately due to the dilligent research by Peter Taghon, we have these pictures of the end of the Heinkel of the 6th Staffel of Kampfgeschwader 4. One of a vic of three, it had dropped to 2,500 feet to avoid dense smoke from burning oil tanks at Antwerp and provided an ideal target for Belgian AA gunners.

Stab II./KG3 Dornier Do17Z. Forced-landed at Wiesbaden-Erbenheim damaged in sortie over Compiègne 10.30 a.m. Fw H. Zander wounded to hospital, rest of crew unhurt. Aircraft damaged but repairable.

II./KG3 Dornier Do17Z. Forced-landed near Trier damaged during sortie over Compiègne 10.30 a.m. No crew casualties. Aircraft damaged but repairable.

6./KG3 Dornier Do17Z. Shot down by Adjt Leblanc of GC III/3 over Estrées-St-Denis, north-west of Compiègne, 10.30 a.m. Gefr P. Dietze killed. Gefr A. Burghardt and Flgr R. Müller captured wounded. Lt G. Zein captured unhurt. Aircraft a write-off.

6./KG4 Heinkel He111. Port engine hit by flak during armed reconnaissance sortie. Caught fire and abandoned west of Lokeren 12.30 p.m. Lt F. Pieper killed. Uffz R. Schulze baled out and captured wounded. Uffz J. Kettner and Uffz K-H. Bringewat baled out and captured unhurt. Aircraft a write-off.

7./KG4 Junkers Ju88A-2 (5035). Shot down by flak and crash-landed during armed reconnaissance between Ostend and Boulogne. Hptmn E. Bloedorn *(Staffelkapitän)*, Oberfw H. Saure, Fw W. Stechardt, and Uffz R. Schaaf all injured. Aircraft 5J+FR a write-off.
Erich Bloedorn was also acting Gruppenkommandeur of III./KG4 at this time.

9./KG4 Junkers Ju88A (3036). Shot down during attack on flak positions at Le Havre. Oberfw W. Hansen captured wounded. Uffz G. Lewandowski, Uffz H. Krahn, and Gefr K. Rauchfuss captured unhurt. Aircraft 5J+HT a write-off.

8./KG27 Heinkel He111P. Shot down by Hurricanes of No. 1 Squadron and belly-landed near Chantilly 11.50 a.m. Possibly one of those credited to F/O Richey. Flgr O. Antelmann captured badly wounded — later died. Uffz F. Spickermann captured wounded. Fw F. Bürger, and Fw W. Brathauer captured unhurt. Aircraft 1G+HS a write-off.

8./KG27 Heinkel He111P. Shot down by F/O Brown of No. 1 Squadron and forced-landed west of Château-Thierry 11.40 a.m. Uffz F. Schmidt captured badly wounded, admitted to hospital. Oberlt K. Bormann, Oberfw J. Elster, and Uffz F. Berndt later captured unhurt. Aircraft fired by crew.
Leaving the mortally-wounded Bordmechaniker with the aircraft, this crew headed north. Travelling at night and using woods as cover they evaded until their eventual capture on the evening of May 24.

8./KG27 Heinkel He111P. Badly damaged in attacks by Hurricanes of No. 1 Squadron between Rethel and Reims 11.30 a.m. and abandoned over German-held territory. Possibly that attacked by F/O Brown and F/L Walker. Crew baled out and rescued unhurt. Aircraft a write-off.

9./KG27 Heinkel He111P. Shot down by D520s of GC I/3 south of Soissons and belly-landed near Épinal, north of Meaux, 5.30 a.m. Possibly that attacked by Sgt Barberis. Sonderführer E. Voigt (of Lw.Kr.Ber.Komp.2) killed. Fw A. Schäfer mortally wounded, died 4 June. Fw E. Heiner, Uffz F. Dietrich, and Gefr H. Bremer captured unhurt. Aircraft a write-off.
Eduard Voigt was a war correspondent covering operations with the unit.

9./KG27 Heinkel He111P. Shot down by D520s of GC I/3 south of Soissons and belly-landed near Grange-au-Bois at Thury-en-Valois, north of Meaux, 5.30 a.m. Fw K-E. Pohlmann killed. Fw G. Gass captured badly wounded. Gefr H. Annen and Gefr H. Moosbauer captured unhurt. Aircraft 1G+GT a write-off.
The pilot, Karl-Ernst Pohlmann, was killed at the controls and the aircraft successfully landed by another member of the crew believed to be the Bordmechaniker, Hans Moosbauer.

9./KG28 Heinkel He111P. Forced-landed damaged by Hurricanes near Douai. Fw E. R. Spoo and Fw J. Meyer both badly wounded, died in hospital. Uffz E. Zander badly wounded. Aircraft damaged but repairable.

9./KG28 Heinkel He111P. Returned damaged by Hurricanes near Douai. No crew casualties. Aircraft repairable.

2./KG51 Junkers Ju88A-1. Crashed at Böblingen airfield, cause not stated. Uffz S. Stretz, Uffz J. Putzbach, and Uffz H. Böttcher killed. Aircraft a write-off.

3./KG51 Junkers Ju88A-1. Believed shot down by 3 Potez 631s of ECN 1/13 and 4/13 north of Braine and crashed at Nampcel, between Soissons and Noyon, a.m. Fw M. Pfeiffer, and Uffz K. Lang killed. Oberlt W. Schallenberg baled out badly wounded, died later in hospital in Soissons. Fw M. Roggentin baled out and captured unhurt. Aircraft a write-off.

4./KG51 Junkers Ju88A-1. Forced-landed near Karlsruhe badly damaged by Hurricanes of No. 73 Squadron north-east of Reims 11.30 a.m. Possibly that attacked by F/O Paul. No crew casualties. Aircraft a write-off.

5./KG51 Junkers Ju88A-1. One engine damaged by flak during attack on Château-Thierry and shot down by Hurricanes of No. 73 Squadron east of Reims 11.30 a.m. Believed that claimed by F/L Scoular and Sgt Marshall. Oberlt V. Schnez, Oberfw H. Üllrich, Uffz O. Runge, and Obergefr H. Muhle captured unhurt. Aircraft a write-off.

5./KG51 Junkers Ju88A-1. Believed shot down by F/L Scoular of No. 73 Squadron after attack on Château-Thierry station and crashed near Courville, south of Fismes, 11.30 a.m. Lt F. Thelen and Fw H. Badura killed. Gefr H. Blicker baled out and captured wounded. Uffz R. Rüthrich captured unhurt. Aircraft a write-off.

6./KG51 Junkers Ju88A-1. Returned damaged by Hurricanes of No. 73 Squadron south-east of Reims 11.30 a.m. Possibly that claimed by F/O Kain. Flgr K-H. Bischoff badly wounded admitted to hospital in Karlsruhe. Aircraft repairable.

Aufklärungsschwarm III./KG51 Heinkel He111H. Badly damaged in fighter attack during reconnaissance sortie to Vitry-le-François and believed crashed near Seilles, east of Namur. Possibly that attacked S/Lt Marchelidon of GC I/2 1.45 p.m. Pilot believed unhurt. Uffz F. Weidenbach slightly wounded. Uffz E. de Mas, Uffz W. Heil, and Gefr E. Baake killed. Aircraft a write-off.

7./KG51 Heinkel He111H. Engaged by Lt Marin-la-Meslée and Lt Perina of GC I/5 over Ste-Menehould during sortie to Vitry-le-François. Crashed and burned out in the Forêt de Hesse, between Parois and Avocourt, 5.45 p.m. Flgr R. Graul and Flgr K. Lang killed. Fw A. Kellner captured at Montzéville wounded. Gefr A. Siller and Gefr F. Schulz captured unhurt. Aircraft 9K+ CR a write-off.

7./KG51 Heinkel He111H. Forced-landed damaged by Sgt Vuillemain of GC I/5 north of Attigny during sortie to Vitry-le-François 5.45 p.m. Fw G. Maier, Fw J. Wagner, Fw H. Müller, and Flgr J. Daxner wounded. Aircraft damaged but repairable.

7./KG53 Heinkel He111H. Caught fire under attack by 3 Potez 631s of ECN 1/13 and ECN 4/13 east of Compiègne during sortie to attack rail targets between Noyon and Montdidier. Crashed and burned out south-east of St Just-en-Chaussée 7.45 p.m. Fw L. Mauter and Gefr E. Gabler killed. Oberfw A. Link, Gefr H. Schmidt, and Fw H. Pöllath captured badly burned. Aircraft a write-off.

In this group line-up taken in Canada, the pilot, Unteroffizier Johann Kettner, is in the centre of the rear rank.

III./KG53 Heinkel He111H. Shot down by S/Lt Fontaine and Adj Crocq of GC II/1 south-east of Compiègne during sortie to attack rail targets at Creil. Crashed and burned out at Dives, north-west of Thiescourt, 10.30 a.m. Oberfw A. Gutschik, Fw H. Janker, Uffz M. Männer, and Uffz H. Marotzki killed. Aircraft a write-off.

Stabsstaffel KG54 Heinkel He111P. Engaged by Hurricanes north-east of Tournai during armed reconnaissance flight to Arras and shot down in the Forest-lez-Frasnes, 4.00 p.m. Obergefr J. Weiss and Obergefr H. Elias killed. Major J. Segschneider *(Stabsstaffelkapitän)* and Uffz H. Haferkamp captured wounded. Uffz H. Senft captured unhurt. Aircraft a write-off.

Aircraft of I./KG54 plus the Geschwaderstab took part in many heavy raids near Cambrai and Lille between 3.10 p.m. and 4.15 p.m. encountered by Hurricanes of Nos. 3, 85, 87, 111, 145, 213, 253, and 601 Squadrons. Given the complexity of the fighting, it has not been possible to attribute individual losses to the 18 claims for Heinkels submitted by British pilots.

Stabsstaffel KG54 Heinkel He111P. Engaged by Hurricanes north-east of Tournai during armed reconnaissance flight to Arras and shot down at Thun, north-east of Cambrai, 4.00 p.m. Oberst W. Lackner *(Geschwaderkommodore)* and Oberlt H. Howe *(Geschwaderadjutant)* baled out and captured wounded. Oberlt R. Sandstede *(Geschwadernachrichtenoffizier)*, Uffz T. Berz, Uffz W. Papendorf, and Uffz A. Mussgnug killed. Aircraft B3+AA a write-off.

Walter Lackner escaped from French captivity and returned home to a wave of press publicity while Heinrich Howe was shipped to England a prisoner of the British.

Stabsstaffel KG54 Heinkel He111P. Engaged by Hurricanes near Tournai during armed reconnaissance flight to Arras and shot down in Rue Parmentier at Onnaing, 4.00 p.m. Oberlt H. Fligge, Uffz T. Pannig, and Obergefr E. Schmidt killed. Uffz R. Wirthwein captured wounded. Aircraft a write-off.

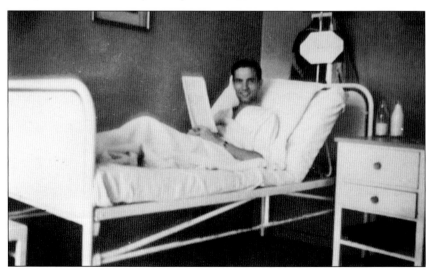

Although the RAF 'K' Report (the official investigation carried out into each German crash) states that the flight engineer, Unteroffizier Rudi Schulze, was uninjured, Peter found this picture of him recovering from his wounds.

1./KG54 Heinkel He111P. Shot down in action with Hurricanes during sortie to bomb railway near Arras and forced-landed near Douai 4.00 p.m. Possibly that claimed by F/O Aitken of No. 601 Squadron. Uffz H. Heringhaus killed. Fw F. Manske captured wounded. Lt A. Priebe and Fw A. Schultheiss captured unhurt. Aircraft B3+AH a write-off.

3./KG54 Heinkel He111P. Returned damaged by Hurricanes near Arras 4.00 p.m. Flgr H. Ogait badly wounded admitted to hospital in Hamm, died next day. Uffz K. Kleemann slightly wounded. Hptmn H. Widmann (*Staffelkapitän*) and rest of crew believed unhurt. Aircraft damaged but repairable.

3./KG54 Heinkel He111P. Shot down by Hurricanes near Arras and crash-landed south of Lille 4.00 p.m. Possibly that claimed by P/O Wakeham of No. 145 Squadron. Gefr K. Sichtar killed. Lt H. Fricke, Obergefr H. Pitz, and Flgr A. Hofer captured wounded. Aircraft a write-off.

3./KG54 Heinkel He111P. Exploded under attack by Hurricanes near Arras 4.00 p.m. Lt K. Brückhändler, Uffz W. Volz, Obergefr K. Sahlberg, and Gefr F. Mühlbauer killed. Aircraft a write-off.

4./KG54 Heinkel He111P. Damaged by Nos. 85, 87, and 242 Squadron Hurricanes near La Capelle 12.30 p.m. and crashed north-east of Solesmes attempting a forced-landing under fire from AA. Uffz E. Baum, Uffz T. Ziereisen, Gefr E. Lemm, and Flgr P. Welters killed. Aircraft a write-off.

4./KG54 Heinkel He111P. Belly-landed following attack by Nos. 85, 87, and 242 Squadron Hurricanes south-east of Lille 12.30 p.m. Uffz W. Czech and Gefr S. Fernes killed. Obergefr K. Hickel captured wounded. Uffz T. Kutsche captured unhurt. Aircraft B3+AM a write-off.
According to Theodor Kutsche, his pilot, Wilhelm Czech, was shot attempting to destroy the aircraft.

4./KG54 Heinkel He111P. Shot down by Hurricanes south-east of Lille 12.30 p.m. Possibly one of those credited to Sgt Little of No. 85 Squadron. Gefr W. Pernau captured badly wounded, later died. Uffz R. Michel captured wounded. Uffz K. Westerholt and Uffz W. Trompler captured unhurt. Aircraft B3+AM fired by crew.

4./KG54 Heinkel He111P. Shot down by Hurricanes south-east of Lille and possibly that claimed by Sgt Jowitt of No. 85 Squadron which crashed and exploded south of Templeuve 12.30 p.m. Oberlt H. Sauer and Uffz W. Nickel killed. Gefr H. Pönnighaus captured wounded. Lt F. Gottschling captured unhurt. Aircraft a write-off

6./KG54 Heinkel He111P. Both engines destroyed by F/L Gleed and F/O Rayner of No. 87 Squadron over Orchies after attack on Lille airfield. Lost control and abandoned after further attacks and crashed and exploded in woods near Elouges 12.45 p.m. Uffz G. Grondowski, Obergefr K. Scheid, and Gefr L. Schewe killed. Uffz A. Isselhorst baled out and captured unhurt. Aircraft B3+LP a write-off.

7./KG54 Heinkel He111P. Badly damaged by Nos. 85, 87, and 242 Squadron Hurricanes between Tournai and Lille during sortie to Arras 12.30 p.m. and believed abandoned near Tirlemont. Lt F. von Berlepsch, Uffz W. Marschall, Obergefr H. Angel, and Gefr O. Essig baled out and captured unhurt. Aircraft a write-off.

8./KG54 Heinkel He111P. Forced-landed near Mons damaged by Nos. 85, 87, and 242 Squadron Hurricanes during sortie to Arras 12.30 p.m. Lt G. Melhorn, Uffz H. Büchner, Uffz H. Tramm, and Gefr G. Bulkow believed captured wounded. Aircraft a write-off.

7./KG76 Dornier Do17Z. Returned damaged by ground-fire during attack on troop columns near Valenciennes. Gefr B. Gude badly wounded, admitted to hospital in Bonn-Hangelar. Rest of crew unhurt. Aircraft damage state not recorded.

9./KG76 Dornier Do17Z. Shot down by F/O Czernin of No. 85 Squadron during attack on troop columns and crashed into woods east of Valenciennes 8.00 a.m. Oberlt R. Strasser (*Staffelkapitän*), Lt W. Leonhardt, Uffz E. Feuchter, Obergefr H. Morneweg, and Gefr K. Hayeck killed. Aircraft a write-off.

9./KG76 Dornier Do17Z. Returned damaged in attack by F/O Czernin of No. 85 Squadron during attack on troop columns near Valenciennes 8.00 a.m. Fw W. Illg slightly wounded, admitted to St Augustin Hospital in Bonn. Aircraft repairable.

Stab KG77 Dornier Do17Z. Crash-landed at Sandweiler believed damaged in attack by Capt Patureau-Mirand of GC I/2 between Corbeny and Juvincourt during reconnaissance sortie to Amiens 5.25 a.m. No crew casualties. Aircraft a write-off.

3./KG77 Dornier Do17Z. Lost bearings and hit by ground-fire south-east of Bertrix during transfer flight from Cologne to Acremont. Uffz L. Fally wounded, admitted to hospital in Cologne-Hohenlind. Aircraft 3Z+CL repairable.

1.(J)/LG2 Messerschmitt Bf109E-1. Badly damaged in combat with Moranes over Compiègne and abandoned over German-held territory. Pilot baled out unhurt. Aircraft a write-off.

2.(J)/LG2 Messerschmitt Bf109E-3. Shot down in combat with Moranes over Compiègne. Lt F-W. Strakeljahn baled out and captured slightly wounded. Aircraft a write-off.

2.(J)/LG2 Messerschmitt Bf109E-3. Shot down by P/O Woods-Scawen of No. 85 Squadron and crashed at Hasnon, south-east of Lille, 11.20 a.m. Oberlt F. von Wangerov (*Staffelkapitän*) killed. Aircraft a write-off.

II./StG2 Junkers Ju87B. Returned with engine damage following sortie over Maubeuge. Crew unhurt. Aircraft damaged but repairable.

6./StG2 Junkers Ju87B. Returned damaged in reported fighter attack near Philippeville. Obergefr G. Redenz badly wounded. Aircraft damage state not recorded.

5./ZG26 Messerschmitt Bf110C. Damaged in combat on bomber escort sortie to Amiens and caught fire during return flight 3.30 p.m. Probably that attacked by F/O Ferriss of No. 111 Squadron. Oberlt A. Niebuhr baled out unhurt. Uffz K. Theisen baled out and captured wounded. Aircraft a write-off.

9./ZG26 Messerschmitt Bf110C. Shot down by Lt Dorance and Sgt Girou of GC I/5 and crashed into the 'Bois de la Vache', south-east of Beaumont-en-Argonne, 6.30 p.m. Fw F. Helbig and Uffz O. Pirschalek killed. Aircraft a write-off.

The observer, Leutnant Friedrich Pieper, now lies buried at Lommel in northern Belgium — the huge German War Graves Cemetery opened in 1959 which now contains nearly 40,000 graves concentrated from all over the Western Front.

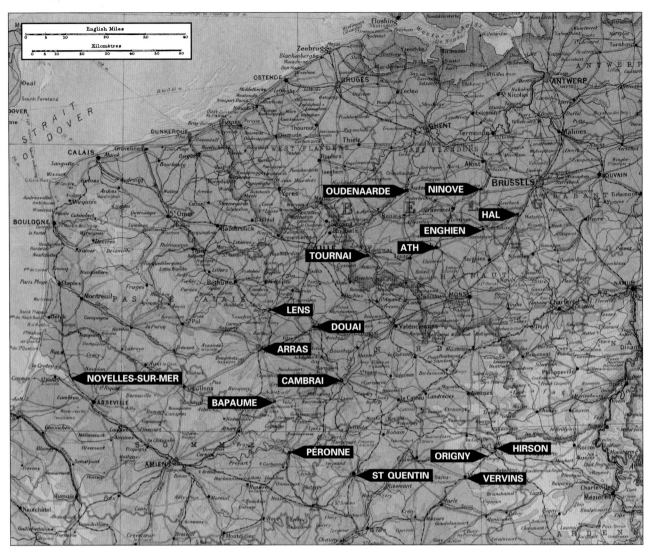

On May 20, the new Allied Commander-in-Chief, Général Maxime Weygand, met with the outgoing C-in-C, Général Maurice Gamelin, who had been dismissed as a scapegoat for his failure to understand, or effectively counter, the new form of fast-moving armour. That evening, the leading elements of 2. Panzer-Division reached the Channel coast at Noyelles-sur-Mer, effectively splitting the Allied force in two. Although Weygand was to propose a counter-attack, the British commander, General Gort, had already come to the realisation that evacuation was now the only practical course to save the BEF, regardless of what the French decided.

Monday, May 20

As German armour continued its advance towards Amiens, the northern front of the salient which contained the bulk of British and Belgian forces, remained relatively intact while, in the south, French positions on the Somme—Aisne line were hurriedly reinforced. Cambrai was overrun early in the day, but Bapaume and Arras were successfully defended so outflanked and bypassed by German advance units.

Apart from two No. 53 Squadron Blenheims retained for duties with BAFF Headquarters, the only British reconnaissance aircraft now remaining in France were the Lysanders of Nos. 4 and 13 Squadrons, so early morning tactical reconnaissance was again carried out by Hurricanes. Meanwhile, a rear headquarters 'Back Violet' was established at Hawkinge to control operations of the Corps reconnaissance units returning to England, their first sorties being flown early that afternoon, while Bomber Command assumed operational control of the Blenheims of Nos. 52 and 70 Wings.

RAF Component Hurricanes mounted offensive patrols over the BEF front between Oudenaarde and Tournai, and over the Arras—Douai—Lens sector where enemy fighters were encountered in strength. But so critical was the situation around Arras that Hurricanes were deployed on ground-strafing enemy troops and transport in the area, enjoying some considerable success. That evening, all surviving No. 14 Group Hurricanes were ordered back to England, as were the Lysanders of No. 13 Squadron — apart from one flight retained at St Omer for sorties on behalf of GHQ.

The German advance beyond Cambrai towards Arras, as reported by the early morning Hurricane flights, threatened the entire rear of the BEF position and this forced a rapid suspension of the British decision, taken less than 24 hours earlier, that no further attacks should be made by RAF medium bombers in daylight. Consequently, No. 107 Squadron Blenheims from Wattisham arrived over the area at 11.30 a.m. along with a close escort of three Fighter Command Hurricane squadrons, and they were followed within half an hour by the Blenheims of No. 21 Squadron from Watton. Untroubled by enemy fighters and subjected to sparse ground-fire, both units returned without loss. An hour later, a French attack on the Oise crossing at Origny-Ste-Benoite, east of St Quentin, by Vought 156F naval bombers met with less success, five aircraft falling prey to fighters.

French reconnaissance flights were maintained during the day and confirmed enemy forces nearing Arras from Bapaume which prompted an urgent request for continuous maximum bombing effort against German columns in the triangle Cambrai—Arras—Péronne. Nos. 21 and 107 Squadrons were again called upon and were over the target area, with escort Hurricanes, from 6.35 p.m. Again, both units returned without loss, seemingly vindicating the close-escort requirement.

Throughout the night, a total of 32 Bomber Command Wellingtons made continuous harrassing attacks on enemy troops in the area bounded by Cambrai, Hirson, Vervins, and St Quentin, while the French heavies concentrated their efforts against similar targets further west between Bapaume and Arras. In addition, 20 Whitleys and 18 Hampdens were despatched against the Oise and Sambre crossings. German lines of communication across the Meuse were also attacked by 38 AASF Battles, now operating primarily at night, but prevalent mist in the Meuse ravine made results difficult to observe.

In Belgium, 18 Blenheims, each operating independently, were sent against columns advancing between Oudenaarde and Grammont, and in an area west of Brussels bounded by Oudenaarde, Ninove, Hal, Enghien, and Ath. This night's bombing effort was achieved at little cost to the RAF for, from 130 sorties, only four aircraft failed to return.

Now, increasing numbers of aircraft were abandoned in France. *Left:* **This is No. 85 Squadron's communication aircraft — Miles Master N7577 — which they left behind at Merville on May 20.** *Right:* **Another of the squadron's machines appears to be in the process of being dismantled by the Germans. No. 85 Squadron's four remaining aircraft reached Manston next day, 29 Hurricanes having been written-off since they first arrived in France.**

BRITISH AIR FORCES IN FRANCE

79 SQUADRON, MERVILLE

Hurricane P2634. Shot down by ground-fire during attack on enemy armour and crash-landed west of Arras 2.30 p.m. Pilot Officer T. C. Parker unhurt. Aircraft a write-off.

Hurricane L2145. Shot down by ground-fire during attack on enemy armoured columns west of Arras 2.30 p.m. Pilot Officer L. R. Dorrien-Smith missing. Aircraft a write-off.

Lionel Roger Dorrien-Smith, a nephew of Lord Trenchard, the founding father of the Royal Air Force, has no known grave.

Hurricane. Returned damaged by ground-fire during attack on enemy armour west of Arras 2.30 p.m. Sergeant pilot unhurt. Aircraft repairable.

Hurricane. Returned damaged by ground-fire during attack on enemy armour west of Arras 2.30 p.m. Pilot Officer D. W. A. Stones unhurt. Aircraft repairable.

Hurricane. Returned wings hit by ground-fire during attack on enemy armour west of Arras 2.30 p.m. Sergeant H. Cartwright unhurt. Aircraft repairable.

Hurricane. Returned with windscreen shattered by ground-fire during attack on enemy armour west of Arras 2.30 p.m. Sergeant L. H. B. Pearce unhurt. Aircraft repairable.

85 SQUADRON, MERVILLE

Hurricane. Wrecked at dispersal during bombing attack 11.30 a.m. No pilot casualty. Aircraft a write-off.

Hurricane P2555. Shot down in combat with Bf110s and crash-landed near Abbeville 10.15 a.m. Sergeant H. N. Howes unhurt. Aircraft a write-off.

Hurricane. Shot down by Bf109s while ground strafing enemy columns east of Arras 3.30 p.m. Possibly one of those claimed by Hptmn von Selle of Stab II./JG3. Squadron Leader M. F. Peacock killed. Aircraft a write-off.

Hurricane. Shot down by Bf109s while ground strafing enemy columns east of Arras and crashed near Querrieu, north-east of Amiens, 3.30 p.m. Possibly that claimed by Lt von Werra of Stab II./JG3. Pilot Officer R. W. Burton killed. Aircraft a write-off.

Hurricane P3426. Shot down by Bf109s while ground strafing enemy columns east of Arras 3.30 p.m. Possibly that claimed by Lt Heymann of 4./JG3. Pilot Officer R. W. Shrewsbury killed. Aircraft a write-off.

87 SQUADRON, MERVILLE

Hurricane. Returned hit in wing and oil tank by return fire from Ju88 engaged near Arras 7.45 a.m. Pilot Officer P. W. Comeley unhurt. Aircraft repairable.

Hurricane. Shot down by Bf110s in combat over base and crashed north-west of Arras 10.00 a.m. Pilot Officer R. A. Sanders badly wounded — died May 23. Aircraft a write-off.

Richard Atheling Sanders of No. 145 Squadron had arrived at Lille-Marcq with a replacement aircraft a few days earlier and stayed to fly operations with No. 87 Squadron. Having survived this crash, and an air attack on the ambulance train to Dunkirk, he is believed to have died of injuries aboard the hospital ship Worthing *en route to England.*

Hurricane. Returned with starboard wing damaged by ground-fire while strafing enemy columns near Arras 4.15 p.m. Flight Lieutenant I. Gleed unhurt. Aircraft repairable.

Hurricane L1964. Crashed on landing following ground-strafing of enemy armoured columns near Arras 4.15 p.m. Pilot Officer H. J. R. Dunn believed unhurt. Aircraft LK⊙J abandoned on evacuation.

142 SQUADRON, FAUX-VILLECERF

Battle L5443. Accidentally set alight when parachute flare ignited prior to take-off and destroyed when bombs exploded 11.00 a.m. Pilot Officer Sutton, Sergeant Hall, and LAC Duckers escaped unhurt. Aircraft a write-off.

Four members of the duty fire crew were killed in this explosion; Corporal W. Passey, AC1 R. Bird, AC1 L. Jenkins, and AC1 J. McGrath. An onlooker, instrument repairer AC2 D. Knowlton, was seriously injured and died three days later. The driver of the fire tender, LAC Jarvis, was also injured and admitted to hospital where he was later captured. The dead were all buried in Perreuse Château Cemetery.

Could this be the remains of the Battle belonging to No. 142 Squadron which was destroyed when the bomb-load exploded at Faux-Villecerf? Material losses to the RAF in France were serious with a total of over 1,000 aircraft being lost.

B FLIGHT, 213 SQUADRON, MERVILLE

Hurricane. Crash-landed near La Panne following combat with Bf109s p.m. Pilot Officer W. M. Sizer slightly injured head. Aircraft abandoned.

Hurricane P2795. Returned starboard wing damaged following combat with Bf110s near Arras 5.15 p.m. Flight Lieutenant D. Wight unhurt. Aircraft repairable.

504 SQUADRON, NORRENT-FONTES

Hurricane P3586. Crash-landed damaged by ground-fire during attack on enemy columns between Cambrai and Arras 11.20 a.m. Pilot Officer M. Jebb wounded, admitted to hospital. Aircraft a write-off.

Hurricane. Crash-landed damaged by ground-fire during attack on enemy columns between Cambrai and Arras 11.20 a.m. Pilot Officer B. E. G. White wounded, admitted to hospital. Aircraft a write-off.

A FLIGHT, 601 SQUADRON, MERVILLE

Hurricane P2699. Hit by return fire during attack on Do17 of 3.(F)/10 and abandoned over Izel-les-Equerchin 6.30 a.m. Flying Officer G. R. Branch baled out unhurt. Aircraft UF⊙D a write-off.

Hurricane. Returned damaged by AA fire during attack on enemy columns between Arras and Marquion 10.45 a.m. Flight Lieutenant Sir A. P. Hope unhurt. Aircraft damage state not recorded.

Hurricane P3278. Returned badly damaged by AA fire during attack on enemy columns between Arras and Marquion 10.45 a.m. Flying Officer P. B. Robinson unhurt. Aircraft a write-off.

607 SQUADRON, NORRENT-FONTES

Hurricane P3448. Shot down by ground-fire during attack on enemy columns between Cambrai and Arras 11.00 a.m. Flying Officer R. E. W. Pumphrey baled out at low level and captured. Aircraft AF⊙H a write-off.

Hurricane N2671. Forced-landed at Merville damaged by ground-fire following attack on enemy columns between Cambrai and Arras 11.00 a.m. Pilot Officer R. S. Demetriadi (of No. 601 Squadron) unhurt. Aircraft AF⊙G repairable.

615 SQUADRON, NORRENT-FONTES

Hurricane L2060. Damaged by Bf110s of I./ZG26 during attack on Ju88s of III./LG1 over Aire and made dead-stick landing on return but overshot end of runway and wrecked undercarriage 1.30 p.m. Pilot Officer V. B. S. Verity (of No. 229 Squadron) unhurt. Aircraft abandoned.

UK-based aircraft lost or damaged on operations over the Western Front:

RAF AIR COMPONENT

26 Squadron, Lympne
Reconnaissance Calais:

Lysander L4773. Forced-landed on beach during evening reconnaissance sortie over Calais, 7.00 p.m. P/O Pennington and LAC Erskine believed captured. Aircraft lost.

RAF BOMBER COMMAND

77 Squadron, Driffield
Communications at Cambrai:

Whitley V N1384. Forced-landed at Abbeville 11.00 p.m. F/O D. D. Pryde, P/O A. W. Dunn, Sgt A. C. Thomas, AC1 T. B. Kenny, and AC1 F. Crawford unhurt. Aircraft abandoned.

102 Squadron, Driffield
Oise bridge at Ribemont:

Whitley V N1380. Believed hit by flak in the target area and crashed at Brissy-Hamégicourt, south-east of St Quentin, 11.30 p.m. F/L D. W. H. Owen, P/O D. F. S. Holbrook, Sgt D. H. J. Barrett, LAC R. J. Newberry, and AC2 M. D. Dolan killed. Aircraft a write-off.

RAF COASTAL COMMAND

48 Squadron, Detling
Patrol Dutch coast:

Anson I K8772. Hit by flak during attack on E-boats and ditched south-west of Texel 7.00 p.m. F/L S. Dodds, P/O B. S. Booth, LAC A. H. Gumbleton, and LAC N. E. Jacobs missing. Aircraft OY⊙G lost.
This aircraft and crew was attached for operations with No. 500 Squadron.

RAF FIGHTER COMMAND

32 Squadron, Manston
Escort sortie to Arras:

Hurricane N2583. Engine set alight by return fire during attack on Hs126, crash-landed and burned out south of Arras 6.30 p.m. Sgt G. North unhurt. Aircraft a write-off.

Although technically still part of the Air Component of the British Air Forces in France, No. 26 Squadron had been withdrawn from the continent on the 19th. This is their Lysander L4773 which forced-landed on the beach near Calais on its first day of operations carried out from Lympne. Both crewmen were believed made prisoner.

FRENCH AIR FORCE

AB 1 Vought 156F (14). Shot down by Bf109s of 3./JG2 during sortie to attack the bridge over the Sambre à l'Oise Canal at Origny-Ste-Benoite and crashed at Urvillers, south of St Quentin, 1.00 p.m. LV Martin and SM Jeandron killed. Aircraft 7 a write-off.

AB 1 Vought 156F (7). Shot down by Bf109s of 3./JG2 during sortie to attack the bridge over the Sambre à l'Oise Canal at Origny-Ste-Benoite and crashed at Croix-Moligneaux 1.00 p.m. EV Feltz and SM Nélias killed. Aircraft 4 a write-off.

A small monument commemorating this French crew was later erected near the crash site.

AB 1 Vought 156F (9). Shot down by Bf109s of 3./JG2 during sortie to attack the bridge over the Sambre à l'Oise Canal at Origny-Ste-Benoite and forced-landed 1.10 p.m. Mt Even evaded and returned unhurt. SM Walger baled out and also evaded. Aircraft 5 a write-off.

These Germans are obviously enjoying themselves posing in the Vought 156 (serial No. 5) of naval squadron AB 1 down at Villers-St-Christophe.

AB 1 Vought 156F (12). Shot down by Bf109s of 3./JG2 during sortie to attack the bridge over the Sambre à l'Oise Canal at Origny-Ste-Benoite and belly-landed outside Gury where strafed by Bf109s 1.00 p.m. SM Lafon killed and LV G. Léveillé wounded. Aircraft 11 a write-off.

AB 1 Vought 156F(5). Shot down by Bf109s of 3./JG2 during sortie to attack the bridge over the Sambre à l'Oise Canal at Origny-Ste-Benoite and belly-landed near Villers-St-Christophe 1.00 p.m. SM Lecoanet and SM Hirtz captured. Aircraft 2 a write-off.

AB 2 L-N 401. Hit by flak during attack on the bridge over the Sambre à l'Oise Canal and belly-landed near Villers-St-Christophe. SM Hautin captured. Aircraft 12 a write-off.

GAO 507 Potez 63.11 (440). Reported attacked by enemy fighters during photo-reconnaissance sortie between Le Chesne and Sedan, and crash-landed with both engines on fire near Chagny, north of Attigny, 12.45 p.m. Adjt Liebert captured badly wounded in arm and admitted to hospital in Sedan. Lt Louis and S/Lt Bikowetz captured slightly wounded. Aircraft a write-off.

GAO 2/520 Potez 63.11 (304). Badly damaged by flak south of Poix-Terron during low-level reconnaissance sortie and caught fire under attack by enemy fighters near La Horgne. Crash-landed near Alincourt, 12 km south of Rethel 1.00 p.m. Adjt L. Rougelet died of wounds. Lt Parisot and Adjt Cardon both wounded, admitted to Auban-Moët Hospital at Épernay. Aircraft a write-off.

Naval Squadron AB2 lost this Loire-Nieuport 401 in the same attack on the bridge over the canal at Origny-Ste-Benoite. Typical of the problems in identifying incidents, the reverse of this photograph states 'Villers-St-Christophe' but the number carried does not match published records.

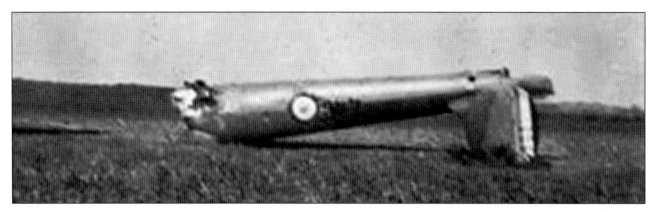

GAO 3/551 Potez 63.11 (365). Returned to Romilly-sur-Seine port wing tip damaged in collision with a Ju52 of III./KGzbV.1 engaged north-east of Laon during reconnaissance sortie between Ailette and St Gobain 6.30 a.m. Lt Ballet, Adjt Rossignol, and Sgt Courmes unhurt. Aircraft repairable.

GB I/12 LeO 451 (102). Flew into power cables while evading Bf109s during bombing of enemy armoured columns east of St Quentin, and crashed in flames near Guny, south of Chauny, 11.45 a.m. Adjt A. Vuathelot, Adjt J. MacGuiness, Adjt R. Maffat, and Sgt H. Legrand killed. Aircraft a write-off.
This crew was originally buried alongside the remains of the aircraft but exhumed on July 27, 1941, and reinterred in the communal cemetery at Guny.

GB II/12 LeO 451 (37). Shot down by Bf109s of 3./JG2 during sortie to bomb motorised columns near St Quentin. Crashed and burned out at Royat Paillard, Courjumelles, south-west of Guise 1.00 p.m. Adjt A. Michelet, Sgt Servais, Sgt G. Roques, and Adjt P. Auge killed. Aircraft a write-off.

GB I/15 Farman 222.1 (3). Hit by AA fire and starboard engine set alight; forced-landed between La Loge and Versaugues, south of Paray-le-Monial. Crew wounded. Aircraft a write-off.

GB I/31 LeO 451 (114). Damaged by flak and Bf109s of 3./JG2 during solo bombing of enemy columns between Guise and St Quentin. Forced-landed at Claye-Souilly 1.15 p.m. Sgt R. Ajam slightly wounded, rest of crew unhurt. Aircraft damaged but repairable.

GB 2/31 LeO 451 (95). Shot down by Hptmn Galland of Stab JG27 during sortie to attack enemy columns advancing between Albert and Amiens. Crashed and burned out alongside the road to Jumel at Berny-sur-Noye, 14 km south of Amiens, 7.50 p.m. Lt A. Sudres, Sgt P. Sommesous, Capt J. Moncheaux *(Commandant)* and Sgt C. Quideau killed. Aircraft a write-off.

GB I/31 LeO 451 (106). One engine destroyed by flak then intercepted by Bf109s of Stab JG27 during sortie to attack enemy columns advancing between Albert and Amiens. Abandoned over Lawarde-Mauger, south of Amiens 8.00 p.m. Lt Hourtic and Sgt Desneux baled out badly wounded. Sgt Tanchoux and Cpl Roger baled out slightly wounded. Aircraft a write-off.

GBA 2/51 Breguet 693 (65). Landed at Le Bourget damaged by flak over Péronne during bombing attack on enemy columns around Arras, Cambrai, and Bapaume 2.00 p.m. Capt Bernard unhurt. S/Lt Guimbretière badly wounded in foot, admitted to hospital in Bobigny. Aircraft damaged but repairable.

GBA II/51 Potez 633 (34). Hit by flak during attack on enemy columns south of Arras and crashed through trees in forced-landing at Gâtineau, near Berles-au-Bois, 18 km north-west of Bapaume 2.00 p.m. Sgt Dupond and Cpl Lacroix captured unhurt. Aircraft a write-off.

GC 1/1 Bloch 152 (391). Shot down by Bf110 during attack on He111 north-west of Senlis. Sgt L. Coader baled out but parachute failed and fell dead at Aumont-en-Halatte. Aircraft a write-off.

GC 1/2 Morane 406 (686). Oil system and flaps badly damaged in combat with Bf109s near Reims and forced-landed at Damblain 5.35 p.m. Possibly that claimed between Soissons and Laon by Hptmn Riegel *(Gruppenkommandeur)* of Stab I./JG27. Capt R. Williame *(Commandant)* unhurt. Aircraft 'Juliette' a write-off.

GC III/2 Morane 406 (404). Shot down by return fire during attack on He111s of I./KG53 north-west of Roye during patrol between Péronne and Ham, and crashed near Rosières-en-Santerre 11.10 a.m. Lt A. Lechat baled out unhurt. Aircraft a write-off.

GC III/2 Morane 406 (200). Damaged by escort Bf110s of III./ZG26 during attack on He111s bombing Beauvais-Tillé airfield 6.10 p.m. Forced-landed 15 km north of the airfield and possibly that attacked by Oberfw Dibowski of 7./ZG26. S/Lt J. Dartevelle injured in landing. Aircraft a write-off.

GC 5/3 Morane 406. Shot down by escort Bf110 of III./ZG26 during attack on He111s bombing Beauvais-Tillé airfield 6.10 p.m. Possibly that claimed by Uffz Kaufmann of 7./ZG26. Sgt A. Bekarian baled out unhurt. Aircraft a write-off.

GC 2/4 Curtiss H-75 (86). Shot down by Oberfw Schmid of I./JG2 during combat over Péronne and forced-landed behind enemy lines 5.40 p.m. Sgt J. Forzy captured wounded. Aircraft a write-off.

GC I/6 Morane 406 (862). Shot down in combat with Bf109s north of Villers-Bretonneux and crashed in marsh near the railway station at Heilly 5.20 p.m. Possibly that claimed by Lt Ostermann of 1./JG21. S/Lt Duchène-Marulaz badly burned on face, baled out landing at Franvillers, 16 km north-east of Amiens. Aircraft a write-off.
Excavated by a local enthusiast, Pierre Ben, in May 2005 and remains of Hispano Suiza engine, propeller hub with two blades, and various components recovered.

GC I/6 Morane 406 (844). Shot down in combat with Bf109s over Villers-Bretonneux and crashed by the River Luce between Demuin and Hangard 5.20 p.m. Possibly that claimed by Oberlt Scholz *(Staffelkapitän)* of 1./JG21. Sgt Pagès wounded, baled out and admitted to hospital in Beauvais. Aircraft a write-off.
Site on marsh excavated by Pierre Ben in July 2004. Hispano Suiza engine and three propeller blades recovered together with remains of various cockpit instruments and fuselage tubing. Aircraft identity plate confirming '844' also found.

GC I/6 Morane 406 (856). Engine damaged in combat with Bf109s of 1./JG21 over Villers-Bretonneux and forced-landed at Ailly-sur-Noye 5.25 p.m. Possibly that claimed by Uffz Marcks. S/Lt H. Raphenne unhurt. Aircraft damaged but repairable.

GC I/8 Bloch 152 (524). Shot down by Fw Schmid of 1./JG51 and abandoned over Crisolles, 5 km north of Noyon, 12.25 p.m. S/Lt A. Navratil baled out burned on face. Aircraft a write-off.

GC 3/10 Bloch 152 (52). Shot down by escort Bf110s during attack on enemy bombers north-west of Beauvais and crashed near Grémevillers 6.10 p.m. Possibly one of those claimed by Oberlt Heinrich *(Staffelkapitän)* of 7./ZG26. Capt A. Landeroin *(Commandant)* killed. Aircraft a write-off.

GR 3/52 Potez 637 (58). Believed damaged by flak during reconnaissance sortie between Beauvais and Amiens, and crashed on landing near Chantilly. Crew unhurt. Aircraft a write-off.

GR II/55 Potez 63.11 (430). Damaged by flak near Soissons during low-level reconnaissance sortie over Arras, Cambrai, and Valenciennes. Flew into high tension cables at Richebourg, Sainte-Marguerite, and crashed in flames near Bucy-le-Long. S/Lt G. Brune and Lt A. Rambault killed. Sgt Sève baled out landing unhurt at Missy-sur-Aisne. Aircraft a write-off.

BELGIAN AIR FORCE

7/IV/1 Fox (O.105). Damaged in taxying collision with Morane at Tours. Crew unhurt. Aircraft abandoned.

9/V/1 Renard R-31 (N.33). Returned to Zwevezele slightly damaged by AA fire following reconnaissance sortie over Ghent, Oudenaarde, and Zottegem 1.15 p.m. Adjt L. Boël and Lt G. Vanderbeck unhurt. Aircraft repairable.

This is the Potez 63.11 (No. 440) which was brought down near Chagny. The crew from GAO 507 were fortunate not to have been killed when the machine turned turtle. The 63.11 was an adaptable work-horse that equipped 52 reconnaissance and observation units. From the outbreak of war to the French capitulation a total of 127 of this popular aircraft would be lost: 56 in combat, 50 to AA fire, and a further 21 destroyed in accidents.

Towards evening on May 20, a Messerschmitt 110 belonging to the 9th Staffel of ZG26 crashed near Luchy, some 20 kilometres north of Beauvais. The roads leading south were crowded with refugees, intermingled with soldiers of the French Army. The two crewmen — one of whom was injured — were surrounded at which point a French non-commissioned officer pulled out his pistol and shot the uninjured pilot, Unteroffizier Wilhelm Ross, through the head. *Left:* Here the gunner, Gefreiter Alfred Welzel, is pictured besides Ross's field grave. *Right:* Later in the war, Ross was exhumed and transferred to a new war cemetery established by the Germans at Beauvais. His grave 101 lies in row 4 of block 2.

LUFTWAFFE

Aufklärungsstaffel I Flakkorps Dornier Do17M. Lost during reconnaissance sortie, details not recorded. Lt Engel and one crewman wounded. Aircraft a write-off.

3.(F)/Aufkl.Gr.Ob.d.L Dornier Do215. Intercepted during photo-reconnaissance sortie to Lille and shot down by F/L Wight, P/O Atkinson, and P/O Sizer of No. 213 Squadron south of Courtrai. Also attacked by Sgt Whitby of No. 79 Squadron and believed crashed into houses in Rue Guillaume Vanzeren in Moeskroen 7.45 a.m. Lt E. Kipple, Uffz K. Mertgen, and Gefr H. Schorn killed. Uffz E. Luther baled out and captured unhurt. Aircraft L2+MS a write-off.

3.(F)/10 Dornier Do17P. Damaged during reconnaissance sortie south of Arras and abandoned over German-held territory. Possibly that attacked by F/O Branch of No. 601 Squadron near Vitry-en-Artois 6.30 a.m. Fw F. Danapel baled out slightly wounded, admitted to hospital in Tirlemont. Rest of crew baled out unhurt. Aircraft a write-off.

3.(F)/10 Dornier Do17P. Starboard engine destroyed in attack by P/O Stephens of No. 3 Squadron during reconnaissance sortie between Valenciennes and Arras 6.00 a.m. Believed abandoned south-east of Douai and crashed near Bruille-lez-Marchiennes. Uffz W. Blaskowitz killed. Lt W. Ludwig and Uffz A. Romoth baled out and captured. Aircraft a write-off.

4.(F)/11 Dornier Do17P. Shot down by Adjt Beschet and Sgt Montfort of II/1 also Sgt Cucumel and Sgt Colomes of GC II/9 during reconnaissance sortie south of Compiègne. Crashed and burned out at Auger-St-Vincent, west of Crépy-en-Valois, 1.25 p.m. Fw P. Klafke, Uffz F. Harlander, and Obergefr M. Beer killed. Aircraft a write-off.

1.(F)/22 Dornier Do17P. Engaged during observation sortie west of Commercy by Cmdt Petitjean-Roget, Lt Houzé, S/Lt Ruchoux, Sgt Bouhy, and Sgt Legrand of GC II/5 and belly-landed at Crépey, south-east of Toul, 8.30 a.m. Fw M. Hecker, Fw F. Wagner, and Obergefr A. Ritte captured unhurt. Aircraft 4N+GH a write-off.

2.(F)/22 Dornier Do17P. Returned damaged in attack by Capt Garde of GC I/1 east of Verberie during reconnaissance sortie over Senlis 4.50 p.m. Gefr J. Weinrebe killed. Aircraft damaged but repairable.

4.(H)/22 Henschel Hs126. Returned damaged, believed by ground-fire, during observation sortie near Ghent but possibly that attacked by Sgt Wilkinson of No. 3 Squadron near Renaix 5.00 a.m. Uffz A. Danielsick slightly wounded. Aircraft damaged but repairable.

3.(F)/31 Dornier Do17P. Failed to return from reconnaissance sortie and possibly that engaged by P/O Gardner of No. 3 Squadron north of Merville 1.45 p.m. Fate of crew unknown. Aircraft a write-off.

3.(H)/41 Henschel Hs126. Believed first attacked by P/O Stephens of No. 3 Squadron during observation sortie south-east of Arras 7.00 a.m. Next engaged by F/O Czernin of No. 85 Squadron and believed crash-landed west of Cambrai where attacked on the ground 7.30 a.m. Lt W. von Reden killed. Lt Böhm wounded. Aircraft damaged but repairable.

3.(H)/41 Henschel Hs126. Shot down by P/O Stones, Sgt Pearce, and Sgt Cartwright of No. 79 Squadron, and also attacked by F/L Wight, P/O Atkinson, P/O Sizer, Sgt Butterfield, and F/O Gray of No. 213 Squadron 10.30 a.m. Crash-landed near Neuville-St-Vaast, north of Arras, where attacked on the ground. Oberlt Seppell wounded. Aircraft a write-off.

4.(F)/122 Junkers Ju88A. Crash-landed at Dülmen, west of Münster, cause not stated. Oberlt E. Gaul badly injured. Lt H. Doermer, Fw F. Bach, and Obergefr K. Lessmöllmann slightly injured. Aircraft a write-off.

5.(F)/122 Dornier Do17P. Believed shot down by Sgt Whitby of No. 79 Squadron south-east of Cambrai and crashed near Marquette, south-west of Denain, 5.10 p.m. Possibly that also engaged by Sgt Cartwright. Uffz K. Beyer and crew killed. Aircraft a write-off.

2.(F)/123 Dornier Do17P. Returned damaged in attack by S/Lt Janis and S/Lt Halgrin of GC I/6 over Ham during reconnaissance sortie west of Amiens and Beauvais 5.00 p.m. Fw W. Plotzitzka slightly wounded, admitted to hospital in Mönchengladbach. Aircraft repairable.

Flugbereitschaft I Fliegerkorps Fieseler Fi156. Hit by ground-fire over the Forêt de Mormal. Aircraft damaged but repairable.

I./JG1 Two Messerschmitt Bf109E-1s. Forced-landed at Namur out of fuel. Both pilots unhurt. Aircraft both damaged but repairable.

I./JG1 2 Messerschmitt Bf109E-3s. Forced-landed at Beaulieu, south of La Roche-en-Ardenne, out of fuel. Uffz A. Raab injured, other pilot unhurt. Aircraft both damaged but repairable.

1./JG1 Messerschmitt Bf109E-1. Forced-landed near Warzée, south-east of Esneux, out of fuel. Pilot unhurt. Aircraft 13 damaged but repairable.

3./JG1 Messerschmitt Bf109E. Shot down in combat with Moranes of GC I/6 and abandoned near Sains-en-Amiénois, south-east of Amiens, 7.30 a.m. Leutnant H. Braxator baled out but killed. Aircraft a write-off.

I./JG3 Messerschmitt Bf109E-3. Struck the ground during combat with Hurricanes near Arras 3.30 p.m. Possibly one of those claimed by P/O Tait of No. 87 Squadron. Fate of pilot unknown. Aircraft a write-off.

5./JG3 Messerschmitt Bf109E-3. Shot down by F/O Rayner of No. 87 Squadron during attack on No. 85 Squadron Hurricanes and believed crashed attempting forced-landing 3 km south of Arras 3.30 p.m. Leutnant P. Wisser killed. Aircraft a write-off.

I./JG51 Messerschmitt Bf109E-3. Believed shot down in combat with GC I/2 south of Laon 5.50 p.m. Pilot believed unhurt. Aircraft a write-off.

3./JG51 Messerschmitt Bf109E-3. Believed shot down in combat with GC I/2 south of Laon and abandoned over German-held territory 5.50 p.m. Possibly that claimed by Sgt de Puybusque. Pilot baled out unhurt. Aircraft a write-off.

335

When the Germans came to look into the murder, it is believed they received a tip-off from a man who had a grudge against Alfred Mullot, the owner of nearby Rouge-maison Farm. He was pulled in for interrogation having been seen in the vicinity of the crash with a firearm and was brought before an open-air military court. Here the accused stands between two Feldgendarmes.

III./JG52 Messerschmitt Bf109E-1. Under-carriage collapsed on take-off at Bassenheim. Pilot unhurt. Aircraft damaged but repairable.

III./JG52 Messerschmitt Bf109E-1. Damaged in aborted take-off at Bassenheim. Pilot unhurt. Aircraft damaged but repairable.

Stab II./JG53 Messerschmitt Bf109E-4 (5010). Returned with slight damage following combat with Curtiss H-75As south of Sedan. Hptmn G. von Maltzahn *(Gruppenkommandeur)* unhurt. Aircraft repairable.

II./KG2 Junkers Ju52. Forced-landed near Bastogne, cause not stated. No crew casualties. Aircraft damaged but repairable.

5./KG2 Dornier Do17Z. Hit by flak during attack on rail targets between Montdidier and Creil. Also attacked by Adjt Gilles of GC II/10 and Sgt Hiblot of GC III/10 over Breteuil 6.55 a.m. Crashed attempting emergency landing with damaged ailerons at Ober-Olm. Oberfw W. Kunze badly injured admitted to hospital in Mainz. Oberfw W. Herdina and Fw E. Ebert slightly injured. Aircraft a write-off.

3./KG3 Dornier Do17Z. Returned damaged by S/Lt Raphenne of GC I/6 following bombing attack on Amiens-Glisy 7.30 a.m. Obergefr A. Melcher wounded admitted to hospital in Neuwied. Aircraft damage state not recorded.

Stabsstaffel KG4 Heinkel He111. Returned damaged by flak near Ghent. Uffz G. Schindler wounded, rest of crew unhurt. Aircraft repairable.

4./KG4 Heinkel He111. Returned damaged by ground-fire near Oudenaarde. Crew believed unhurt. Aircraft damaged but repairable.

7./KG4 Junkers Ju88A (3051). Shot down in the sea off Zeebrugge by Lt d'Alançon, S/Lt de La Taille-Trétinville, and Sgt Lemare of GC I/4 during mine-laying sortie off Ostend and attack on shipping at Dunkirk a.m. Oberlt H. Camphausen and Uffz R. Gäbeler killed. Oberfw R. Rieck missing. Aircraft 5J+IR lost.

1./KG30 Junkers Ju88A. Returned damaged by flak near Ostend. Crew believed unhurt. Aircraft damage state not recorded.

3./KG51 Junkers Ju88A. Shot down by Adjt Saussol, S/Lt Abrioux, and Sgt Doublet of GC III/1 during dive-bombing attack on Compiègne 9.35 a.m. Also attacked by Lt de Mallmann, Sgt Durand, and Sgt Paulhan of GC III/1, plus Capt Coutaud and Sgt Teillet of GC I/1. Crashed and burned out on Venette football ground near Nourylande. Gefr E. Koschinski, Fw A. Frühling, and Uffz H. Rinn, and Flgr W. Gilgen baled out over Longueil-Ste-Marie and captured unhurt. Aircraft a write-off.

1./KG53 Heinkel He111. Shot down by Lt Lechat, Lt Leblanc, Adjt Romey, Sgt Élmlinger, and Sgt Monribot of GC III/2 during sortie to bomb road and rail targets between Amiens and Abbeville. Crashed in flames at Beauvois-en-Vermandois, west of St Quentin, 11.10 a.m. Uffz A. Schweighart killed. Oberlt K. Sauer, Oberfw E. Klenk, Uffz W. Weigle, and Uffz H. Methner baled out slightly wounded. Aircraft A1+EH a write-off.

2./KG53 Heinkel He111. Shot down by Lt Behal, Adjt Roger, Sgt Le Nigen, Adjt Marias, S/Lt Sauvage, and Sgt Kratkoruki of GC III/3 during sortie to bomb road and rail targets between Amiens and Abbeville. Crashed at Cléry-sur-Somme, north-west of Péronne, 10.30 a.m. Uffz G. Wissmeier and Flgr O. Dorer killed. Fw H. Querl, Uffz A. Truskowski, and Gefr H. Irrgang wounded. Aircraft A1+CK a write-off.

2./KG53 Heinkel He111. Shot down by AA fire during sortie to bomb road and rail targets between Amiens and Abbeville. Crashed and burned out at 'Le Vaucher', Bois de la Morue, near Bray-lès-Mareuil, south of Abbeville 10.45 a.m. Fw A. Bogdanski, Gefr H. Berner, Uffz R. Brucker, Uffz G. Wild, and Flgr E. Damböck killed. Aircraft A1+FK a write-off.
Site investigated by Simon Parry and surface fragments found.

2./KG55 Heinkel He111. Returned damaged in attacks by S/Lt Blanc, S/Lt Baptizet, and Sgt Puda of GC II/4 over Bétheniville following sortie to Châlons-sur-Marne. Fw H. Waschkowsky killed, rest of crew unhurt. Aircraft damage state not recorded.

II./KG55 Heinkel He111P. Forced-landed near Ludwigsburg due to engine fire. Crew unhurt. Aircraft a write-off.

1./KG76 Dornier Do17Z. Returned damaged by ground-fire during attack on enemy columns near Valenciennes 8.30 a.m. Lt H. Oelmann slightly wounded, admitted to hospital in Vogelsang. Aircraft repairable.

9./KG76 Dornier Do17Z. Believed returned damaged by enemy fire, circumstances unknown. Crew believed unhurt. Aircraft damage state not recorded.

Stabsstaffel KG77 Dornier Do17Z. Returned damaged in attack by Sgt Howes of No. 85 Squadron near Abbeville 9.45 a.m. Uffz O. Katzenberger and Gefr E. Eiseler slightly wounded. Aircraft damaged but repairable.

III./KGzbV.1 Junkers Ju52 (3085). Believed crashed in the Forêt de Samoussy, north-east of Laon, following collision with Potez 63.11 of GAO 3/551 6.30 a.m. Five crewmen killed. Aircraft a write-off.

The trial was held outside in front of the church at Luchy. Mullot was sentenced to death and, although this was commuted to five years' imprisonment with hard labour in October 1940, he was freed the following year. He died in 1980 — here Madame Mullot remembers.

2./LG1 Heinkel He111H. Shot down during armed reconnaissance sortie west of Lille and believed that attacked by F/O Duus of No. 79 Squadron 1.45 p.m. Fw E. Hackbarth, and Gefr H. Schönberg killed. Uffz M. Bröge captured badly wounded, died May 26. Fw E. Weber captured unhurt. Aircraft L1+GK a write-off.

6./LG1 Junkers Ju88A-1. Forced-landed at Beringen, north-east of Diest, reported damaged by flak. Oberfw W. Mehliss and Fw W. Hochwald badly wounded, Fw H. Sauer (of Stab II./LG1) and Uffz W. Kalusche slightly wounded, all admitted to hospital in Düsseldorf. Aircraft damaged but repairable.

Nachrichtenstaffel LnRgt.2 Junkers Ju52 (5042). Crashed on take-off from Braunschweig-Querum. Lt L. A. F. Ogger, four crew, and five passengers killed. Aircraft a write-off.

8./StG1 Junkers Ju87B. Shot down by Sgt Dekastello of GC I/8, and probably also that attacked by Sgt Giordani and Capt Peyrègne between La Fère and Courbes 12.35 p.m. Overturned attempting forced-landing near Jussy. Crew unhurt. Aircraft 6G+LS damaged but repairable.

III./StG51 Junkers Ju87B. Belly-landed at Jemelle, east of Rochefort, cause not stated. Crew unhurt. Aircraft a write-off.

1./ZG2 Messerschmitt Bf110C. Crashed and burned out at Ste-Marie, near Neufchâteau during escort sortie for I./KG3 over Amiens 7.30 a.m. Oberlt F. Lüders (Staffelkapitän) and Uffz L. Baron (of Stab I./ZG2) killed. Aircraft a write-off.

7./ZG26 Messerschmitt Bf110C. Belly-landed near Sedan badly damaged by Sgt Le Nigen of GC III/3 in combat north-east of Beauvais 6.10 p.m. Oberlt K-W. Heinrich (Staffelkapitän) badly wounded, died in hospital in Koblenz May 24. Gunner believed unhurt. Aircraft damaged but repairable.

9./ZG26 Messerschmitt Bf110C. Set alight in attacks by Sgt Le Nigen, Sgt Jeannaud, Sgt Beckarian, and Sgt Casaneuve of GC III/3 in combat north-east of Beauvais and abandoned over Rougemaison, south of Luchy. Crashed and burned out alongside the Amiens to Beauvais road 6.00 p.m. Uffz W. Ross baled out unhurt but killed. Gefr A. Welzel baled out and captured wounded. Aircraft a write-off.

Wilhelm Ross was shot in the head by a passing French NCO, one of many stragglers on the road. A full account by Jean Paul Pallud of the subsequent criminal trial at Luchy was published in 1986 in After the Battle *magazine No. 54.*

Ugly as they were, such incidents were by no means uncommon as traditional enmities surfaced during the bitter fighting that characterised the campaign in France. Several similar trials, some resulting in executions, followed the German occupation.

Tuesday, May 21

By May 21 the whole conduct of the RAF's battle in France had changed with the withdrawal of the majority of squadrons. Bomber Command's No. 2 Group — which operated from the closest airfields to France — joined in flying from its bases in East Anglia. These Blenheims of No. 40 Squadron were pictured at Wyton.

By early morning German forces had taken Amiens and were reported to be advancing on Abbeville with advance elements already at the coast and branching out towards Le Tréport and Montreuil. The Allied armies in the north were thus irretrievably separated from those to the south of the Somme and Aisne. Despite severe enemy pressure, Arras remained in Allied hands, but the situation on the main Belgian and BEF front along the Escaut was fast becoming untenable and forced further Allied retirements during the night.

The three squadrons of AASF fighters remaining in France flew uneventful local protection patrols during the day, while AASF bombers remained grounded. From England, No. 2 Group Blenheims continued to attack targets in France now selected by the Air Ministry and seemingly without even reference to BAFF HQ which prompted protest from Air Marshal Barratt.

First such attack of the day, escorted by two squadrons of fighters, was around 9.45 a.m. and against columns approaching Abbeville, six of the 12 aircraft involved returning slightly holed by intense flak over Auxi-le-Château. Crews reported roads so crowded with traffic that it was impossible to distinguish friend from foe. Soon after midday a second attack, again with Hurricane escort, was launched by nine Blenheims against columns heading for Montreuil, and Boulogne. This was followed at about 6.00 p.m. by a third attack in the same area by 24 Blenheims, with Hurricane escort, the final daylight attack of the day delivered by 12 Blenheims that bombed convoys north of Étaples at about 8.30 p.m. Unfortunately, one of their number was mistaken for an enemy bomber and shot down by a Spitfire during the return flight. But again, daylight bombing operations during the day were carried out at little cost, 58 sorties flown for the

loss of only two Blenheims, one of these to friendly fire, and was due in no small part to the strong fighter escort provided by Fighter Command Hurricanes.

Spitfires carried out shipping protection patrols and X-raid interceptions over Dunkirk and Calais throughout the day and engaged several formations of enemy bombers that remained unescorted for most of the day. At night, single Blenheim fighters maintained a constant presence over Boulogne.

At night, AASF and Bomber Command scheduled attacks on enemy communications with 41 bombers ordered against targets in the Upper Meuse area. But after only a dozen or so had taken off, the operation was

cancelled on Air Ministry instructions in favour of a possible attack on enemy tanks between Abbeville, Amiens and Arras to take place the following morning. This extraordinary intervention provoked further protest from Air Marshal Barratt who must have been becoming increasingly frustrated at what, to him, must surely have constituted unwarranted and possibly ill-advised interference in his command decisions. Meanwhile, RAF Bomber Command despatched 29 Wellingtons against crossings at Namur and Dinant, from which five aircraft failed to return, the bulk of their night effort being directed against rail targets deep in Western Germany.

No. 115 Squadron had already lost one of their Wellingtons on May 15 over Germany and then three more on the 21st in France, eventually suffering a total of 19 losses on operations during 1940, with four more lost in separate accidents.

BRITISH AIR FORCES IN FRANCE

4 SQUADRON, CLAIRMARAIS

Lysander N1296. Shot down by and crashed at Zudausques, west of St Omer. Believed that claimed by Lt Heinel of 4./JG2 east of Boulogne 2.10 p.m. Pilot Officer T. J. F. Davey and LAC J. H. Gillham killed. Aircraft a write-off.

B FLIGHT, 4 SQUADRON, LILLE-RONCHIN

Lysander N1298. Believed that claimed by Lt Lohoff of 3./JG77 during reconnaissance sortie and crashed at Bruyelle, south of Tournai, 8.00 a.m. Pilot Officer P. McL. Peace and Corporal R. A. Tamblin killed. Aircraft a write-off.

A FLIGHT, 13 SQUADRON, CLAIRMARAIS

Lysander. Took off on a liaison flight but shot down over St Omer and crashed in St. Martin-au-Laërt. Flight Lieutenant R. H. N. Graham and Pilot Officer R. E. C. Butterworth killed. Aircraft a write-off.

226 SQUADRON, FAUX-VILLECERF

Battle K9176. Failed to return from night attack on Montcornet 2.00 a.m. Sergeant R. S. Annan and AC2 R. J. Jones captured. Sergeant A. Livingston missing. Aircraft lost.

Alex Livingston is commemorated on the Runnymede Memorial where his date of death is recorded as May 22.

UK-based aircraft lost or damaged on operations over the Western Front:

RAF AIR COMPONENT

16 Squadron, Lympne
Tactical reconnaissance:

Lysander L4793. Returned tail and rudder badly damaged by Bf109s during sortie to Arras, Cambrai, and Amiens 6.45 p.m. Possibly that attacked by Uffz Lehmann of 2./JG51 near St-Pol-sur-Ternoise P/O Dexter and LAC Webb unhurt. Aircraft repairable.

RAF BOMBER COMMAND

15 Squadron, Wyton
Armoured columns near Boulogne:

Blenheim IV R3706. Damaged by flak over Montreuil and belly-landed on beach between Étaples and Boulogne during return flight 4.00 p.m. F/Lt P. F. Webster and LAC R. E. Hunter slightly injured. Sgt R. A. M. Stone unhurt. Aircraft a write-off.

Blenheim IV L8851 or L8855. Returned hit by flak between Montreuil and Boulogne 4.00 p.m. F/O L. H. Trent, Sgt W. J. Stephens, and Cpl J. Sutcliffe unhurt. Aircraft repairable.

18 Squadron, Watton
Railway junction near Boulogne:

Blenheim IV L9325. Failed to return from reconnaissance sortie over Douai—Arras—Amiens—Abbeville 3.00 p.m. P/O C. Light, Sgt A. E. Craig, and Sgt G. Hawkins missing. Aircraft lost.

No trace of this crew was reported found and they are commemorated on the Runnymede Memorial.

Blenheim IV L9185. Attacked by S/L A. L. Franks of No. 610 Squadron during return flight after bombing enemy columns near Étaples and belly-landed at Wimereux 5.45 p.m. P/O V. Rees, Sgt N. V. Pusey, and LAC K. E. Murray unhurt returned to Dover aboard HMS *Whitshed*. Aircraft fired by crew.

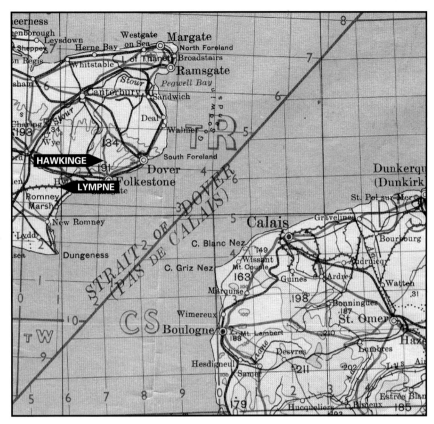

When the Air Component reconnaissance units were withdrawn from France to operate from aerodromes in south-east England, Hawkinge and Lympne were immediately earmarked. Early on the morning of May 20, Group Captain H. M. Fraser was sent from the Air Ministry to set up a rear headquarters for the Air Component at Hawkinge to control the operations of the units working from Britain. Group Captain John Vachell took over the following day, remaining until all the RAF component of the BEF had returned. Air Vice-Marshal Blount arrived on the evening of May 26. Air Marshal P. B. Joubert de la Ferté arrived on the morning of May 26, but his tenure was brief for Air Vice-Marshal C. H. B. Blount re-assumed command later that evening.

75 Squadron, Feltwell
Meuse crossings at Dinant:

Wellington IC R3157. Shot down and crashed near Kain, north-west of Tournai. P/O F. A. G. F. J. de Labouchere-Sparling killed. F/O J. N. Collins missing. F/L L. P. R. Hockey, Sgt J. S. Brooks, and Sgt G. Thorpe captured. Aircraft AA⊙H a write-off.

99 Squadron, Newmarket
Meuse crossings at Dinant:

Wellington IC L7803. Crashed near Belval, north-west of Charleville-Mézières. F/O J. P. Dyer, F/O O. L. Williams, Sgt J. H. Lawrenson, LAC C. R. A. Lovejoy, AC1 E. Morton, and AC1 S. C. Ogilvie killed. Aircraft a write-off.

115 Squadron, Marham
Troop concentrations near Cambrai:

Wellington IC P9298. Crashed in Belgium a.m. F/Sgt L. G. Moores, Sgt A. H. Hooper, Sgt K. W. Hughes, AC1 G. E. Flanigan, AC1 J. T. Packer, and AC2 D. Duggan all killed. Aircraft KO⊙H a write-off.

Wellington IC P9297. Forced-landed near Poix during sortie to bomb Meuse crossings near Dinant. F/O D. F. Laslett, P/O G. T. Dodgshun, P/O J. Whilton, Sgt W. L. Flower, AC1 H. D. Glendinning, and AC1 L. W. Ludlam captured. Aircraft KO⊙F a write-off.

Wellington IC R3152. Crashed near Le Havre during sortie to bomb Meuse crossings near Dinant. P/O D. W. W. Morris, Sgt F. A. G. Lowe, Sgt F. Williams, LAC H. G. Griffin, AC2 T. Kennedy, and AC2 A. Robinson killed. Aircraft KO⊙J a write-off.

RAF FIGHTER COMMAND

74 Squadron, Rochford
Patrol Dover — Calais:

Spitfire K9977. Forced-landed at Berck-sur-Mer, after attack on Ju88s near Calais. P/O R. D. Aubert unhurt. Aircraft abandoned.

A Flight, 229 Squadron, Hawkinge
Patrol Arras — Lens:

Hurricane P3546. Believed shot down by Bf110 of II./ZG76 and crashed near Étaples 7.30 p.m. Pilot Officer D. De C. C. Gower killed. Aircraft a write-off.

A Flight, 253 Squadron, Hawkinge
Patrol Arras — Lens:

Hurricane P3552. Believed shot down by Bf110 of II./ZG76 near Étaples 7.30 p.m. Squadron Leader E. D. Elliott captured. Aircraft a write-off.

A Flight, 601 Squadron, Hawkinge
Patrol Lens — Béthune:

Hurricane L2088. Suffered engine failure and lost bearings, crash-landing near Abbeville 2.30 p.m. Flying Officer C. J. Riddle unhurt. Aircraft abandoned.

FRENCH AIR FORCE

Another snapshot for the folks in the Fatherland. Unfortunately, although its serial is visible, we cannot trace the circumstances of the demise of this Bloch 174.

AB 1 Vought 156F (15). Caught fire and burned out at Boulogne when signal flare ignited prior to evacuation to Mardyck. SM Davonneau and SM P. Pennognon unhurt. Aircraft 8 a write-off.

AB 2 L-N 401. Forced-landed near Berck believed hit by return fire during attack on enemy bomber but possibly attacked by escort Bf110. SM Moulinier slightly wounded. Aircraft abandoned.

AB 2 L-N 401. Belly-landed near Caen en route to Cherbourg-Querqueville due to hasty repairs following damage on May 19. SM Niel unhurt. Aircraft abandoned.

AB 2 L-N 401 (3). Unserviceable aircraft abandoned at Berck-sur-Mer on withdrawal to Calais. No pilot casualty. Aircraft 11 burned.

AB 4 L-N 401. Belly-landed near Bayeux en route to Cherbourg-Querqueville on withdrawal from Berck-sur-Mer. Mt Billien unhurt. Aircraft abandoned.

AB 4 L-N 411. Shot down by flak and crash-landed during reconnaissance sortie to Hesdin. SM Jamet unhurt. Aircraft a write-off.
An alternative source suggests that EV1 de Rodellec de Porzic was pilot of this aircraft.

ECN 4/13 Potez 631. Returned starboard wing damaged in repeated attacks by S/Lt d'Harcourt of GC II/3 east of Creil 2.50 p.m. Adjt Martin and Adjt A. Guichard unhurt. Aircraft damaged but repairable.

GAO 518 Potez 63.11 (630). Shot down by Oberlt Bretnütz of 6./JG53 east of Montmédy during photo-reconnaissance mission to Thonne-le-Thil; crashed and burned out near Stenay 10.15 a.m. Sgt M. Rigal badly wounded in head, died same evening. Lt Frantz and Sgt Delpech wounded. Aircraft a write-off.

GB I/34 Amiot 143 (133). Shot down by flak south of St Quentin during night-bombing sortie. Crashed and burned out between Séraucourt-le-Grand and Essigny-le-Grand. Sgt G. Hoffmann and Adjt P. Minondo killed. Adjt Saulou wounded, baled out and captured. Capt Véron (*Commandant*) and Sgt Carré baled out and captured unhurt. Aircraft a write-off.

GBA 4/51 Potez 633 (36R). Badly damaged by flak during bombing of enemy motorised columns around Amiens and crash-landed at Étampes airfield. Capt J. Nicot (*Commandant*) and Adjt Irzen unhurt. Aircraft a write-off.

GBA I/54 Breguet 693 (17). Lost on sortie to attack enemy armour between Dieppe and Le Tréport. Crashed and exploded at Brétigny 7.00 p.m. probable victim of flak. S/Lt Rostand and Sgt Frin killed. Aircraft a write-off.

GC 1/1 Bloch 152. Crash-landed badly damaged in engine and wing following combat with Bf110s between Creil and Chantilly 6.30 a.m. Possibly that attacked by Lt Kuhrke of 8./ZG26. Lt Le Gentil unhurt. Aircraft a write-off.

GC 2/1 Bloch 152 (293). Badly damaged in attack by Bf110 of III./ZG26 and crashed on the outskirts of Chantilly 6.40 a.m. Possibly that attacked by Lt Konopka of 7./ZG26. Lt J. Schmidt badly wounded in both legs. Aircraft a write-off.

GC I/1 Bloch 152. Damaged in attack by Bf109 and crashed on landing p.m. Sgt Morel slightly injured. Aircraft a write-off.

GC 5/1 Morane 406 (857). Shot down by Bf109s and crashed and burned out at Cinqueux, 7 km north-east of Creil 7.10 a.m. Probably one of those claimed by Oberlt Leppla (*Staffelkapitän*) of 3./JG51. Sgt A. Paulhan killed. Aircraft a write-off.

GC 5/1 Morane 406 (613). Badly damaged in attack by Bf109s and crash-landed near Laigneville, north-west of Creil, 7.15 a.m. Possibly that claimed by Oberlt Krafft of 3./JG51. S/Lt J. du Boucher unhurt. Aircraft a write-off.

GC 5/1 Morane 406 (487). Shot down by return fire from Do17s east of Beauvais and forced-landed at Bulles p.m. S/Lt W. Chciuk unhurt. Aircraft a write-off.

GC II/2 Morane 406 (390). Forced-landed at Verneuil-en-Halatte following combat with Bf110s of III./ZG26 north-west of Creil 6.30 a.m. Adjt B. Furst wounded in left foot. Aircraft a write-off.

GC III/2 Morane 406 (478). Belly-landed at Bailleul-le-Sec engine damaged by Bf110 of V.(Z)/LG1 following attack on Do17s of KG2 west of Éstrées-St-Denis 6.55 p.m. S/Lt A. Lansoy wounded. Aircraft a write-off.

GC III/2 Morane 406. Forced-landed at Le Bourget engine damaged in combat with Bf110s of V.(Z)/LG1 following attack on Do17s of KG2 west of Éstrées-St-Denis 6.50 p.m. Sgt G. Bouttier unhurt. Aircraft damaged but repairable.

GC I/3 Dewoitine 520. Shot down by Major Mix (*Gruppenkommandeur*) of Stab III./JG2 in combat over Boussicourt, west of Roye, and belly-landed alongside the route to Punchy, near Fonches-Fonchette, 9.55 a.m. S/Lt J. Parisse badly wounded, died in hospital in Rennes. Aircraft a write-off.

GC I/3 Dewoitine 520. Shot down by flak over Hardecourt-aux-Bois, 10 km north-west of Péronne. Sgt G. Caussat baled out and captured. Aircraft 12 a write-off.

GC II/3 Dewoitine 520. Believed collided with Sgt Biard during attack on He111 and abandoned north of Douai 12.40 p.m. Adjt Dessault baled out unhurt. Aircraft a write-off.

GC II/3 Dewoitine 520. Abandoned north of Douai following suspected collision with Adjt Dessault during attack on He111 12.40 p.m. Adjt Biard baled out unhurt. Aircraft a write-off.

GC II/3 Dewoitine 520 (112). Shot down by return fire from Potez 631 of ECN 4/13 (Adjt Guichard and Adjt Martin) attacked in error during patrol between Soissons and Villers-Cotterêts. Crashed into forest at Verneuil-en-Halatte 3.00 p.m. S/Lt R. d'Harcourt killed. Aircraft a write-off.
Robert d'Harcourt, son of the Inspector General of the French fighter forces, was shot down during his fourth attack on the Potez.

GC II/3 Dewoitine 520. Engine set alight in combat with Bf110s of II./ZG1 between Villers-Cotterêts and Crépy en Valois; crash landed at Rethondes 4.45 p.m. Adjt S. Bouton admitted to hospital in Compiègne wounded in left arm. Aircraft a write-off.

GC I/5 Curtiss H-75 (38). Reportedly attacked by Bf109s over Beauclair and pursued at low level finally crashing north of Tailly, between Stenay and Buzancy, 5.30 p.m. Capt A. Malaval killed. Aircraft a write-off.
No corresponding German claim for this loss has been traced.

GC I/5 Curtiss H-75 (31). Suffered engine failure on delivery flight from Chantilly to St-Dizier and forced-landed behind enemy lines. Sgt E. Preux captured, believed unhurt. Aircraft a write-off.

GC I/6 Morane 406 (734). Shot down by Bf109s in combat east of Arras and abandoned over Cantin, 7 km south-east of Douai, 3.05 p.m. Believed that claimed by Hptmn Müller (*Staffelkapitän*) of 4./JG3. Cmdt. G. Tricaud (*Commandant de Groupe*) baled out unhurt. Aircraft a write-off.

GC 1/6 Morane 406 (896). Shot down by Bf109s of 4./JG3 following destruction of Fi156 at Cambrai-Niergnies and crashed near Bertincourt 3.10 p.m. Capt M. Silvestre de Sacy (*Commandant*) killed. Aircraft a write-off.

GC I/6 Morane 406. Returned to Lognes-Émerainville badly damaged in combat with Bf109s east of Arras 3.15 p.m. Possibly one of those claimed by Oberlt Keller (*Staffelkapitän*) of 1./JG3. S/Lt H. Raphenne unhurt. Aircraft damaged but repairable.

GC I/6 Morane 406. Returned to Lognes-Émerainville badly damaged in combat with Bf109s east of Arras 3.15 p.m. Possibly that claimed by Fw Hessel of 1./JG3. Adjt E. Senet unhurt. Aircraft damaged but repairable.

GC III/6 Morane 406 (803). Shot down in combat with enemy fighters south-west of Cambrai and crashed between Rue de la Vacquerie and Gonnelieu. Believed that claimed by Uffz Jürgens of 2./JG21 over Quéant 4.35 p.m. Sgt A. de Gervillier killed. Aircraft 11 a write-off.
Buried at depth, the remains of Sergent Arnould Thiroux, Comte de Gervillier, were not recovered until April 16, 1941, and interred in the cemetery at Gonnelieu. The tailplane from his aircraft is displayed at the Fort de la Pompelle museum, on the N44 south-east of Reims.

GC III/6 Morane 406 (462). Shot down in combat with enemy fighters and crashed at Hamel, 10 km south of Douai. Believed that claimed by Uffz Heinbockel of 2./JG21 over Cambrai 4.40 p.m. S/Lt J. Salaün badly wounded, baled out and captured. Aircraft a write-off.

GC III/6 Morane 406 (597). Forced-landed at Plessis Belleville believed damaged in attack by Hptmn Mölders of Stab III./JG53 following combat with Bf109s 4.30 p.m. south of Cambrai. S/Lt R. Cavaroz badly wounded in leg. Aircraft damaged but repairable.

GC III/6 Morane 406 (925). Believed damaged in attack by Hptmn Mölders of Stab III./JG53 and belly-landed north of Chantilly following combat with Bf109s of 2./JG21 south of Cambrai 4.30 p.m. Capt M. J. Sulerzycki unhurt. Aircraft a write-off.

GC III/7 Morane 406 (414). Damaged in combat with Bf109s of 1./JG2, 7./JG2, and III./JG53 between Montdidier and Compiègne 6.15 p.m. and belly-landed at Barbery, 6 km east of Senlis. Sgt L. Berthet badly wounded in leg. Aircraft a write-off.

GC III/7 Morane 406. Forced-landed at Orly badly damaged in combat with Bf109s of 1./JG2, 7./JG2, and III./JG53 between Montdidier and Compiègne 6.15 p.m. S/Lt Martin wounded in leg. Aircraft a write-off.

GC 5/7 Morane 406 (799). Shot down in combat with Bf109s of 1./JG2, 7./JG2, and III./JG53 and abandoned over Rémy, 4 km north-east of Éstrées-St-Denis, 6.15 p.m. Capt G. Lacombe (*Commandant*) badly wounded, baled out but killed due to parachute failure. Aircraft a write-off.

GC III/7 Morane 406 (758). Shot down in combat with Bf109s of 1./JG2, 7./JG2, and III./JG53 over Liqueur and hit trees attempting crash-landing at Cinqueux, near Creil, 6.15 p.m. Lt F. Dyma killed. Aircraft 27 a write-off.

GC III/7 Morane 406. Landed at Évreux damaged in combat with Bf109s of 1./JG2, 7./JG2, and III./JG53 between Montdidier and Compiègne 6.15 p.m. S/Lt Y. Rupied unhurt. Aircraft damaged but repairable.

GC III/7 Morane 406 (901). Shot down in combat with Bf109s of 1./JG2, 7./JG2, and III./JG53 north-west of Compiègne and abandoned over Mares-sur-Matz 6.15 p.m. S/Lt F. Pilâtre-Jacquin baled out wounded. Aircraft a write-off.

GC II/8 Bloch 152. Shot down in combat with Bf109s and abandoned over Péronne a.m. Possibly that claimed by Lt Stange of 3./JG3. Sgt P. Petitjean baled out severely wounded and burned. Aircraft a write-off.

GC II/8 Bloch 152. Landed at Villacoublay seriously damaged in combat with Bf109s during patrol between Arras and Cambrai a.m. Possibly that claimed by Uffz Vollmer of 3./JG3. Adjt Marchais unhurt. Aircraft a write-off.

GC II/9 Bloch 152. Landed at Chantilly one cylinder hit by return fire from Do17P of 4.(F)/11 attacked north-east of Creil 11.00 p.m. Sgt J. Tain unhurt. Aircraft repairable.

GC II/9 Bloch 152 (166). One of escort to Amiot 354 carrying Général Weygand on a tour of inspection; landed at deserted Norrent-Fontes but failed to leave due to mechanical failure 12.00 p.m. Lt Pascal unhurt. Aircraft abandoned.

GC III/10 Bloch 152 (144). Shot down by flak during repeated attacks on enemy armoured column near Abbeville 3.00 p.m. S/Lt R. Guay killed. Aircraft a write-off.
Originally buried in the garden of a café on the road to Crotoy, René Guay was exhumed on June 17, 1941, and re-interred in the military cemetery of Notre-Dame de la Chapelle at Abbeville.

GR II/55 Potez 63.11 (203). Hit by flak over the outskirts of Amiens during low-level reconnaissance of enemy armour 6.30 a.m. Crashed and burned out at La Croix-Quignon. Lt P. Germain, Sgt P. Dubois, and Sgt L. Pierre killed. Aircraft a write-off.
This crew, originally buried in a field grave near the Briquetterie at Croix-Quignon, was re-interred in the cemetery of Amiens-La Madeleine on June 18, 1941.

SAL 3/109 Caudron Simoun. Landed near the front to drop a liaison officer, and attacked on the ground by enemy aircraft. Capt de Roussy de Sales and S/Lt Costa de Beauregard unhurt. Aircraft destroyed to prevent capture.
This light communications aircraft was attached to the Section Aérienne de Liaisons HQ ZOAN.

BELGIAN AIR FORCE

1/I/1 Fox. Returned to Ursel damaged by ground-fire during reconnaissance sortie between Ghent and Terneuzen. Adjt H. Cartuyvels and S/Lt A. Watrin unhurt. Aircraft damaged but repairable.

9/V/1 Renard R-31 (N.33). Returned to Zwevezele slightly damaged by ground-fire during reconnaissance sortie between Gent and Zottegem 5.00 a.m. Sgt M. Bruylants and Cpl A. Charlier unhurt. Aircraft repairable.

LUFTWAFFE

4.(F)/11 Dornier Do17P. Intercepted north-east of Creil by Lt Escoffier of GC II/1, Sgt Tain of GC II/9, and S/Lt Boursain, Sgt Jobart, Sgt Post, and Adjt Boutillon of ECN 1/13 during photo-reconnaissance sortie between Senlis and Compiègne. Starboard engine damaged, belly-landed in a meadow in the Forêt d'Halatte, west of Fleurines, 11.00 a.m. Fw H. Rührschneck, Uffz J. Frank, and Gefr H. Hecht captured wounded. Aircraft 6M+CM a write-off.

5.(H)/13 Henschel Hs126. Shot down by Capt Destaillac, Cdt Petitjean-Roget, and Capt Monraisse of GC II/5 during photo-reconnaissance sortie south-east of Montmedy and crash-landed at Herméville-en-Woëvre, south-west of Etain, 10.00 a.m. Uffz H. Natthes and Uffz S. Hollatz captured unhurt. Aircraft a write-off.

1.(H)/14 Henschel Hs126. Exploded under attack by Sgt Atkinson of No. 151 Squadron during observation sortie near Boulogne 5.20 p.m. Both crewmen killed. Aircraft a write-off.

3.(H)/21 Fieseler Fi156C. Shot down in low-level attack by Capt de Sacy of GC I/6 during landing approach to Cambrai-Niergnies following courier flight from Florenville 3.05 p.m. Uffz F. Holzapfel killed. Aircraft a write-off.
This aircraft is believed to have been operating with Stab JG77, attached to I./JG3, whose fighters had occupied Cambrai on this date.

2.(H)/31 Henschel Hs126 (4229). Shot down by No. 17 Squadron Hurricanes north-east of Amiens and overturned attempting crash-landing near Vimy 10.45 a.m. Oberlt A. Köcher killed. Fw A. Herzig wounded. Aircraft 5D+DK a write-off.
This unit also reported two observers, Lt Wilhelm Leupold and Lt Kurt Metzner, wounded by enemy fire on this date, but as no related aircraft losses were notified it is likely these were ground casualties.

1.(F)/121 Heinkel He111 (5560). Shot down by Capt Naudy, Adjt Dessault, Adjt Biard, Capt Bissoudre, Sgt Tourné, and Cpl Körber of GC II/3 during sortie to observe troop movements between Lille and Orchies. Crashed and burned out at Roost-Warendin, north-east of Douai, 12.00 p.m. Lt G. Henke, Fw H. Marx, Uffz A. Neubert, and Uffz G. Gawron killed. Aircraft 7A+HH a write-off.

3.(F)/121 Junkers Ju88A. Starboard engine set alight in attacks by Adjt Richardin, Sgt Roquerbe, and Lt Trezebinski of GC II/1 during photo-reconnaissance of roads south of Amiens. Also attacked by S/Lt Faisandier, Sgt Bayle of GC II/9, abandoned over Estrées-St-Denis, and crashed at Rémy 12.30 p.m. Uffz R. Bomsdorf killed. Lt H. Wittmeyer and Obergefr W. Sauer baled out but killed. Lt O. Nitschke baled out and captured wounded in shoulder. Aircraft a write-off.

Sous-lieutenant Irumbery de Salaberry scored an important victory when he shot down the Kommandeur of III. Gruppe JG2. Born in 1898, Major Dr Erich Mix served in the infantry during the First World War transferring to the Air Service in 1917 and achieving three victories flying with Jasta 54. He added eight victories to his tally in WWII but was one of the veteran Gruppenkommandeuren replaced by younger officers in July 1940. He ended the war as Oberst Jagdfliegerführer Bretagne.

4.(F)/121 Junkers Ju88A. Forced-landed near Saargemünd due to electrical trouble and engine failure. Crew unhurt. Aircraft fired by crew.

Stab III./JG2 Messerschmitt Bf109E-3 (1526). Engine set alight by S/Lt de Salaberry of GC I/3 in combat between Boussicourt and Becquigny and belly-landed west of Roye 10.00 a.m. Major Dr E. Mix *(Gruppenkommandeur)* wounded. Aircraft << + ~ a write-off.

9./JG2 Messerschmitt Bf109E-3. Hit a tree and crashed on take-off from Signy-le-Petit. Leutnant J. Missfeldt injured. Aircraft 3 + ~ a write-off.

I./JG3 3 Messerschmitt Bf109Es. Damaged in landing accidents at base, cause not stated. No pilot casualties reported. Aircraft all damaged but repairable.
Flieger Wilhelm Maurer, who died this day and is buried at Lommel, may be related to these losses.

II./JG3 Messerschmitt Bf109E-3. Overturned on landing at Liège, cause not stated. Pilot unhurt. Aircraft a write-off.

4./JG3 Messerschmitt Bf109E. Shot down by Capt de Vaublanc, S/Lt Pelletier, and Sgt Husson of GC II/8 and abandoned southeast of Arras a.m. Leutnant E. Ewers baled out and captured wounded. Aircraft a write-off.

4./JG3 Messerschmitt Bf109E. Shot down by Capt de Vaublanc, S/Lt Pelletier, and Sgt Husson of GC II/8 and abandoned southeast of Arras a.m. Uffz R. Brüchert baled out and captured wounded. Aircraft a write-off.

6./JG3 Messerschmitt Bf109E. Crash-landed near Aachen following combat sortie. Leutnant G. Pollack killed. Aircraft a write-off.

1./JG26 Messerschmitt Bf109E-3. Wrecked in forced-landing at Antwerp due to petrol failure. Pilot unhurt. Aircraft a write-off.

2./JG26 Messerschmitt Bf109E-1. Ground-looped on take-off from Eindhoven, cause not stated. Pilot unhurt. Aircraft damaged but repairable.

2./JG26 Messerschmitt Bf109E-1. Crashed on take-off from Bergen-op-Zoom, cause unknown. Pilot unhurt. Aircraft damaged but repairable.

7./JG26 Messerschmitt Bf109E-4. Hit by flak during escort sortie between Lille and Tournai and attempted a forced-landing but hit a row of poplars and crashed between Haagstraat and Kouterstraat in Vrasene, east of Antwerp. Uffz H-D. Rudolph badly wounded, rescued by locals and taken to hospital in Antwerp. Aircraft a write-off.

6./JG27 Messerschmitt Bf109E-3. Damaged in combat and belly-landed alongside the railway between Gent and Mechelen at Buggenhout, near Merchtem. Lt J. Neumann unhurt. Aircraft 3 + - damaged but repairable.

6./JG51 Messerschmitt Bf109E-3 (5113). Damaged by flak and crash-landed at Rheinbischofsheim, near Kehl. Pilot unhurt. Aircraft 5 + repairable.

Stab II./JG53 Messerschmitt Bf109E-4. Returned damaged following combat with GC III/1 and GC III/7 over Pont-à-Mousson 6.30 p.m. Possibly that attacked by Adjt Gagnaire of GC III/1. Hptmn G. von Maltzahn *(Gruppenkommandeur)* unhurt. Aircraft damaged but repairable.

I./JG54 Messerschmitt Bf109E-1. Slightly damaged in take-off accident at Freiburg. Pilot unhurt. Aircraft repairable.

9./KG1 Heinkel He111. Shot down by P/O Simpson of No. 229 Squadron during sortie to Boulogne and believed belly-landed near 'Galgenbossen', between Elverdinge and Poperinge, 8.00 p.m. Uffz K. Rosshirt killed. Obergefr O. Saueressig captured wounded. Oberlt B. Staege, Gefr H-P. Marx, and Gefr K-H. von Dahlen captured unhurt. Aircraft V4+IT a write-off.

8./KG2 Dornier Do17Z. Returned damaged by ground-fire near Méru, north of Pontoise, 11.40 a.m. Oberfw A. Batz badly wounded, admitted to hospital in Trier. Aircraft repairable.

Stabsstaffel KG3 Dornier Do17Z. Forced-landed near Trier damaged in attack by Adjt Bouton of GC II/3 near Senlis, south-west of Compiègne, 5.30 p.m. Obergefr K. Rosenkranz badly wounded, admitted to hospital in Trier. Lt H. Hübner and Oberfw H. Bolowski slightly wounded. Aircraft damaged but repairable.

I./KG3 Dornier Do17Z. Belly-landed at Wiesbaden-Erbenheim damaged by flak. Crew unhurt. Aircraft damaged but repairable.

Stab I./KG27 Heinkel He111P. Returned damaged by Potez 631 of AC 1 over Calais 1.30 p.m. Fw W. Enigk slightly wounded. Aircraft 1G+BB damaged but repairable.

Stab I./KG27 Heinkel He111P. Landed at Hannover-Langenhagen damaged by flak north-west of Lille following sortie to Calais 1.30 p.m. Fw R. Linck killed. Fw L. Jäger slightly wounded. Aircraft 1G+CB damaged but repairable.

Stabsstaffel KG28 Heinkel He111. Returned damaged during sortie north-west of Béthune. Oberlt H-H. Sauer badly wounded, admitted to hospital at Neuwied. Aircraft repairable.

4./KG54 Heinkel He111P. Port engine damaged in fighter attack and tail hit by AA over Calais and crashed near Ooike, north-west of Oudenaarde, 8.40 p.m. Uffz W. Krause killed. Uffz J. Moors baled out and captured unhurt. Fw H. Bank and Uffz A. Albrecht believed baled out and captured. Aircraft B3+EM a write-off.

4./KG54 Heinkel He111P (2896). Badly damaged by flak over Calais and crashed near Scheldewindeke 8.40 p.m. Uffz W. Erkelens and Obergefr T. Keyzers killed. Hptmn W. Michel *(Staffelkapitän)* and Oberlt H-J. Willers slightly wounded. Aircraft B3+CM a write-off.

5./KG54 Heinkel He111P. Both engines damaged by solo Morane during sortie to bomb Calais harbour and crashed near Ypres 8.40 p.m. Uffz E. Hanstedt, Uffz H. Loest, and Gefr F. Pannekamp captured unhurt. Gefr W. Bethke captured wounded. Aircraft B3+HN a write-off.

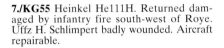

Bearing in mind the extent of the damage to his Heinkel of the 4th Staffel of KG54, Oberleutnant Hans-Jürgen Willers performed a remarkable crash-landing. The radio operator and the flight engineer were killed but he and the Staffelkapitän were only slightly wounded.

7./KG55 Heinkel He111H. Returned damaged by infantry fire south-west of Roye. Uffz H. Schlimpert badly wounded. Aircraft repairable.

Stabsstaffel KG76 Dornier Do17Z. Returned damaged during sortie to Arras. Crew believed unhurt. Aircraft repairable.

4./KG76 Dornier Do17Z. Returned damaged by flak and machine-gun fire during sortie to attack Norrent-Fontes airfield, north-west of Béthune. Fw J. Fuchssteiner killed. Fw R. Wolf died in Vogelsang hospital. Aircraft damaged but repairable.

8./KG76 Dornier Do17Z. Returned damaged by ground-fire over St Pol during weather sortie to Boulogne. Fw H. Thürich badly wounded, admitted St Augustin Hospital, Bonn. Aircraft repairable.

8./KG76 Dornier Do17Z. Returned damaged by ground-fire near Douai during sortie to attack enemy columns near Bruay. Uffz W. Onken and Gefr J. Streibel slightly wounded. Aircraft repairable.

1./KGr.126 Heinkel He111H-4. Failed to return from mine-laying sortie off Boulogne p.m. Hptmn G. Stein (*Gruppenkommandeur*), Oberlt W. Horten, Fw H. Thomas, and Obergefr H-L. Petersen missing. Aircraft lost.

1./KGr.126 Heinkel He111H-4. Failed to return from mine-laying sortie off Dunkirk p.m. Oberfw A. Eke, Obergefr W. Schröder, and Gefr W. Schirrmann killed. Uffz R. Kaufmann missing. Aircraft lost.

4./KGrzbV.1 Junkers Ju52 (6280). Crashed at Reinsfeld near Trier due to engine failure. Fw H-J. Meiser, Fw J. Anholt and Uffz P. Merle injured. Aircraft a write-off.

2./KGrzbV.9 Junkers Ju52. Damaged due to burst tyre at Charleville. No crew casualties. Aircraft repairable.

1./LG1 Heinkel He111H. Port engine damaged by flak during solo reconnaissance sortie over Dunkirk. Later attacked by Spitfires of No. 74 Squadron near Ostend and forced-landed at Groede. Obergefr K. Schneider badly wounded, died in hospital in Nieuwvliet. Gefr W. Knappe captured wounded, admitted to hospital in Calais. Oberfw H. Kassing and Obergefr G. Filla captured unhurt. Aircraft L1+BH a write-off.

6./LG1 Heinkel He111. Landed at Düsseldorf damaged possibly by No. 74 Squadron Spitfires during attack on shipping between Boulogne and Dunkirk 7.30 p.m. Crew believed unhurt. Aircraft repairable.

9./LG1 Junkers Ju88A-1. Crash-landed during sortie west of Boulogne, and possibly that attacked by F/L Leathart of No. 54 Squadron 1.57 p.m. Gefr H. Rose badly injured, admitted to hospital in Cambrai. Fw F-K. Meinshausen, Uffz G. Jakubowski, and Uffz R. Tilsner slightly injured. Aircraft a write-off.

13.(Z)/LG1 Messerschmitt Bf110C (3524). Elevators jammed causing crash on take-off from Ste-Marie on escort sortie for KG2 attack on Persan-Beaumont airfield 6.00 p.m. Oberfw A. Stegemann and Uffz G. Solluch killed. Aircraft a write-off.

9.(H)/LG2 Focke-Wulf Fw189. Returned damaged during sortie west of Valenciennes, cause not stated. Fw H. Bald slightly wounded. Aircraft repairable

6./StG77 Junkers Ju87B. Believed shot down during attack on roads near Montreuil 7.00 p.m. Fw E. Peter killed, other crewman believed unhurt. Aircraft a write-off.

Transportstaffel I Fliegerkorps Two Junkers Ju52s. Undercarriage damaged due to poor condition of landing ground at St-Aubin. Crew unhurt. Aircraft both damaged but repairable.

Transportstaffel I Fliegerkorps Junkers Ju52. Forced-landed at Le Quesnoy damaged by flak. Crew unhurt. Aircraft damaged but repairable.

Stab II./ZG1 Messerschmitt Bf110C. Shot down by S/Lt Codet, Sgt Killy, Lt Gleich, and S/Lt Troyes of GC II/3 during escort sortie for He111s south-west of Soissons and abandoned near Soucy 2.45 p.m. Lt D. Nülle (*Gruppenadjutant*) baled out and captured unhurt. Obergefr A. Hyrschke baled out over Coeuvre and captured wounded, admitted to hospital in Villers-Cotterêts. Aircraft a write-off.

7./ZG26 Messerschmitt Bf110C. Forced-landed at Charleroi damaged in combat with H-75s north-east of Beauvais. Believed that claimed by Adjt Bernavon and Sgt Fortin of GC II/2 over Crèvecoeur-le-Grand 6.30 a.m. Pilot unhurt, Uffz G. von Schemm badly wounded admitted to hospital in Mönchengladbach. Aircraft damaged but repairable.

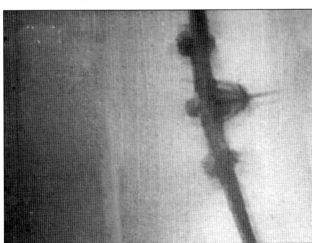

It was during an evening patrol over Dunkirk that No. 74 Squadron scored two victories — a Ju88 and an He111 — although at the time the pilots claimed another four 'unconfirmed'. The combat resulted in one of the most famous images of the battle of France, taken by the camera gun on Flight Lieutenant 'Sailor' Malan's Spitfire to record his first victory. Malan was the leader of 'A' Flight based at Hornchurch although flying out of Rochford to shorten the range.

On May 22, No. 607 Squadron arrived at their new UK base of Croydon aerodrome . . . together with one Hurricane which was to become the sole aircraft surviving today which fought in France during the battle (but see page 406). Hawker Hurricane P2617, which is now displayed in the Battle of Britain Museum at Hendon, was one of the first production batch of 500 aircraft built by the Gloster Aircraft Company at Brockworth in 1939 and was handed over to the Air Ministry in January 1940. On April 14 it was allocated to No. 615 Squadron, then in France equipped with Gladiators, but the following day switched to No. 607 at Abbeville. It remained with the squadron until it was ordered to leave France on May 20. The service-able aircraft including P2617 were flown to England the following day, the squadron re-assembling at Croydon. Although the Aeroplane Movement Card indicates that the Hurricane was undergoing repair between July and October, it *did* participate in the Battle of Britain. It suffered at least four accidents over the next four years before the Air Historical Branch of the RAF earmarked it for preservation in April 1944. In 1951 it appeared in the film *Angels One-Five* (above) and in *Reach For the Sky* in 1955. A further movie appearance came in 1968 when it was used in the filming of *Battle of Britain*. The Ministry of Defence transferred the machine to the RAF Museum at Hendon in 1972 and it was moved to the Battle of Britain extension in 1978.

Wednesday, May 22

As German armour pushed northwards from Montreuil and Hesdin, rain, low cloud, and mist over the entire front severely curtailed all air operations. To reinforce the defences at Boulogne and keep the port open for as long as possible, two Guards battalions were landed from England but by the end of the day the town would be isolated and the enemy within nine miles of Calais. Meanwhile, along the southern flank of the German penetration, they strengthened positions against possible French counter-attacks while their advance units neared Péronne.

With only one Air Component flight left in France, tactical reconnaissance and artillery observation flights were virtually impossible without direct fighter support. French reconnaissance flights had suffered equally serious losses so the bulk of reconnaissance sorties now had to be made by Back Component aircraft based at Hawkinge. Shortly after dawn, Air Vice-Marshal Blount, the AOC Air Component, left Merville flying the sole airworthy Tiger Moth to be found amongst the many wrecks abandoned there. The pitiful remnants of his command still remaining in France would soon follow.

At dawn, as ordered by the Air Ministry the previous evening, AASF Battles took off to locate and attack enemy armour in the Amiens—Abbeville—Arras sector. Twelve aircraft seem to have operated before the attack order was shelved, four returning due to bad weather, one returning with its bombs, three forced-landing elsewhere, and one falling to ground-fire. Two or three isolated attacks had been made, but without positive identification and purely on the basis that the aircraft were fired upon, and one tank was reported hit. Air Marshal Barratt's protests of the previous day on the advisability of such attacks seems more than well founded.

That afternoon, with some improvement in the weather, No. 2 Group Blenheims bombed enemy columns south of Samer around 5.00 p.m. They operated without fighter escort, and suffered several casualties to intense AA fire, but returned with much useful information on enemy movements in the area. Another attack was promptly launched two hours later, this time with fighter support over Abbeville, and returned without loss. This was followed by a third attack by 26 Blenheims in the same general area around 8.00 p.m. which coincided with a sortie by 11 Back Component Lysanders that bombed columns approaching Boulogne — a bold operation surely born of desperation.

During the night, 26 AASF bombers were despatched against Meuse crossings at Fumay and Château-Regnault and lines of approach in Belgium and Germany, nine aircraft returning without locating their targets due to the bad weather which continued to dog operations. Meantime, 27 Bomber Command aircraft attacked enemy lines of communication in France returning without loss.

Fighter Command Spitfires and Hurricanes covered the Channel ports of Boulogne, Calais, and Dunkirk from dawn to dusk reporting several engagements, and were joined by Blenheim fighters of No. 604 Squadron which had hitherto been operating mainly at night. In all, Fighter Command flew 198 sorties on the day indicating the growing extent to which RAF fighter resources were engaged over France. For their part, AASF fighters sent off two patrols to counter enemy bombers over south Champagne but no combats resulted.

Reflecting growing confusion, BAFF North HQ, unable to contact its No. 14 Group, requested French fighter support from ZOAN to counter dive-bombers in the Arras Cambrai area. Apparently BAFF was unaware that No. 14 Group fighters had returned to England and their headquarters evacuated the previous day.

BRITISH AIR FORCES IN FRANCE

103 SQUADRON, RHÈGES

Battle. Crash-landed damaged by ground-fire during attack on enemy armour between Amiens and Bernaville 5.30 a.m. Sergeant W. R. Crich and crewman unhurt. Aircraft a write-off.

142 SQUADRON, FAUX-VILLECERF

Battle. Forced-landed outside Paris in bad weather following attack on enemy tank between Amiens and Abbeville 5.30 a.m. Flying Officer A. D. Gosman, Sergeant Pollock, and LAC Gaston unhurt. Aircraft undamaged.

Battle. Lost bearings and forced-landed south of Paris during sortie to attack targets near Florenville 10.50 p.m. Pilot Officer Edwards, Sergeant Green, and LAC Welch unhurt. Aircraft abandoned.

UK-based aircraft lost or damaged on operations over the Western Front:

RAF AIR COMPONENT

2 Squadron, Bekesbourne
Columns south of Boulogne:

Lysander L6849. Shot down by ground-fire during bombing attack on roads between Étaples and Boulogne, and crashed near Pihen-lès-Guines 8.10 p.m. P/O M. L. G. Henderson killed. P/O V. B. Kelly believed unhurt. Aircraft a write-off.

Lysander P1672. Destroyed when unreleased bombs detached and exploded on return to Bekesbourne 8.30 p.m. P/O G. Grant-Govan unhurt. LAC H. G. Jones killed. Aircraft a write-off.

Lysander. Returned damaged by ground-fire during bombing attack on roads between Étaples and Boulogne 8.10 p.m. P/O E. L. Woolridge slightly wounded. LAC Jordan unhurt. Aircraft damaged but repairable.

RAF BOMBER COMMAND

15 Squadron, Wyton
Columns south of Boulogne:

Blenheim IV N6177. Returned damaged by AA fire 7.00 p.m. P/O D. Henderson and crew unhurt. Aircraft damaged but repairable.

53 Squadron, Hawkinge
Reconnaissance Arras — Péronne:

Blenheim R3596. Returned damaged by ground-fire and crashed on landing 6.15 a.m. P/O Triptree, Sgt Williamson, and LAC Jeffery unhurt. Aircraft a write-off.

57 Squadron, Hawkinge
Reconnaissance:

Blenheim IV L9184. Crashed alongside the Cambrai road at Haucourt, south-east of Arras. P/O R. L. Saunders, Sgt S. F. Simmons, and AC1 G. R. Pirie killed. Aircraft a write-off.
This crew was buried in a field grave adjacent to the crash site but reinterred together in the local communal cemetery in July 1942 along with the remains of Roi Saunders' dog which he had taken with him on his last flight. Diligent post-war investigation by No. 1 Missing Research and Enquiry Unit, involving two exhumations, finally resulted in all three crewmen being formally identified in May 1949.

Blenheim IV L9246. Crashed on landing at Rouen following ferry flight. P/O Herbert, Sgt Pope and AC Newberry unhurt. Aircraft damaged but repairable, later abandoned.
This aircraft was en route to unit after repair following damage suffered on May 10.

59 Squadron, Lympne
Reconnaissance:

Blenheim. Returned damaged by bird strike during sortie south of the Somme from Abbeville to Amiens p.m. F/O G. H. D. Evans and crew unhurt. Aircraft repairable.

Blenheim IV L9266. Shot down and crashed near Fricourt during sortie to Albert. F/O F. D. Bird, Sgt C. J. W. Brinn, and AC2 G. D. Coles killed. Aircraft a write-off.

82 Squadron, Watton
Transport Montreuil — Samer:

Blenheim IV P4828. Shot down by AA fire near Neufchâtel-Hardelot, south-west of Samer, 8.00 p.m. Sgt J. W. Hartfield, Sgt F. Phillipson, and AC2 A. W. Elliot killed. Aircraft UX⊙K a write-off.

107 Squadron, Wattisham
Transport south of Samer:

Blenheim IV P4925. One engine hit by flak over target area and ditched 7 miles off English coast when other engine failed during return flight 6.00 p.m. P/O J. A. Miller and Sgt R. J. Saunders rescued slightly wounded. LAC W. Stokell rescued unhurt. Aircraft lost.

110 Squadron, Wattisham
Transport Hesdin — St Pol:

Blenheim I L8761. Shot down by ground-fire during attack on enemy columns 5.00 p.m. S/L G. F. Hall, Sgt K. F. Quarrington, and LAC C. S. Torrance killed. Aircraft a write-off.

Blenheim IV L8749. Returned damaged by ground-fire during attack on enemy columns 5.00 p.m. P/O N. N. Ezekiel, Sgt Chaplin, and LAC Young unhurt. Aircraft repairable.

Having been pulled out of France on May 19, Blenheim squadrons Nos. 18, 53, 57 and 59 were now operating out of airfields in south-east England, and Nos. 114 and 139 would follow within ten days. This machine YH⊙P of No. 21 Squadron based at Watton as part of No. 79 Wing, is one of the many No. 2 Group aircraft lost on operations over northern France following the forced withdrawal of all BAFF Blenheims.

Blenheim IV L8755. Returned damaged by ground-fire during attack on enemy columns 5.00 p.m. F/L P. H. A. Simmons, Sgt Friendly, and LAC Smith unhurt. Aircraft repairable.

Blenheim IV N6207. Belly-landed on return, undercarriage damaged by ground-fire during attack on enemy columns 5.00 p.m. F/O G. O. Lings, Sgt Martin, and AC Bingham unhurt. Aircraft damaged but repairable.

Blenheim IV P4858. Returned damaged by ground-fire during attack on enemy columns 5.00 p.m. S/L J. S. Sabine, Sgt W. Evans, and Sgt J. V. West unhurt. Aircraft repairable.

Blenheim IV P4860. Returned damaged by ground-fire during attack on enemy columns 5.00 p.m. Sgt Miller, Sgt Duffy, and AC Greenwood unhurt. Aircraft repairable.

RAF FIGHTER COMMAND

32 Squadron, Manston
Patrol Arras — Merville:

Hurricane N2657. Shot down in combat with Bf109s near Arras 8.00 p.m. Sgt G. Turner unhurt. Aircraft a write-off.

56 Squadron, Manston
Patrol Arras — Cambrai:

Hurricane N2431. Hit by ground-fire during pursuit of Hs126 and forced-landed in enemy territory near the Belgian border 2.15 p.m. F/O B. J. Wicks unhurt, returned after evading for 12 days. Aircraft a write-off.

65 Squadron, Hornchurch
Patrol Arras:

Spitfire K9920. Suffered engine failure over the Channel, forced-landed and burned out near North Foreland. P/O K. G. Hart unhurt. Aircraft a write-off.

605 Squadron, Hawkinge
Patrol Arras:

Hurricane N2349. Shot down by Fw Lampskemper of 2./JG3 during attack on He111s of III./KG27 north of Arras and abandoned near Vermelles 12.10 p.m. F/O G. W. B. Austin baled out wounded in left leg, evacuated to hospital in England. Aircraft a write-off.

Hurricane L2058. Shot down by Lt Tiedmann of 2./JG3 during attack on He111s of III./KG27 west of Douai 12.10 p.m. Sgt Moffatt believed unhurt. Aircraft a write-off.

Hurricane P3575. Forced-landed oil system damaged in combat with Bf109s of 2./JG3 and attack on He111s of III./KG27 west of Douai 12.15 p.m. P/O C. F. Currant returned with broken nose. Aircraft destroyed by pilot.

Hurricane L2120. Shot down by return fire from He111 of III./KG27 over Arras and crashed near Berneville 12.20 p.m. F/O G. F. M. Wright killed. Aircraft a write-off.

FRENCH AIR FORCE

AB 3 Vought 156F (33). Crashed on landing at Lanvéoc-Poulmic, cause unknown. Crew unhurt. Aircraft a write-off.

GAO 1/514 Potez 63.11 (315). Shot down by Hptmn Mölders *(Gruppenkommandeur)* Stab III./JG53 during artillery observation sortie and crashed in wood between Isse and les Grandes Loges, south-east of Reims, 4.50 p.m. S/Lt J. Jacquet, S/Lt J. Marseille, and Sgt R. Pinatel killed. Aircraft a write-off.

GAO 516 Breguet 27 (53). Crashed in fog near Le Tréport during withdrawal from Rouen-Boos. Adjt Gilbertas and Sgt Nouvel both injured and admitted to hospital in Rouen. Aircraft a write-off.

GAO 516 Breguet 27 (94). Attacked by an enemy patrol during withdrawal from Rouen-Boos and evaded in coastal fog. Later suffered engine trouble and ditched off Fécamp. Crew rescued by trawler unhurt apart from Sgt Relat who could not be revived. Aircraft lost.

GB I/12 LeO 451 (57). Badly damaged on the ground at Orléans-Bricy in enemy bombing. No crew casualties. Aircraft abandoned.

GB II/19 Douglas DB-7 (29). Shot down by flak during attack on motorised columns between Cambrai and St Quentin p.m. S/Lt Mazon and Sgt Lacourie captured badly wounded. Sgt Guérin captured wounded. Aircraft a write-off.

GB II/19 Douglas DB-7 (23). Hit by flak over Doullens during sortie to attack enemy motorised columns between Cambrai and St Quentin p.m. Crash-landed at Évreux airfield. Sgt Malle wounded. Aircraft a write-off.

GBA I/51 Breguet 693 (25). Damaged by flak then engaged by Bf109s during attack on enemy armour between Cambrai and St Quentin. Crashed and burned out by the road to Benay, outside Essigny-le-Grand, and believed that claimed by Lt von Werra *(Gruppenadjutant)* of Stab II./JG3 11.52 a.m. S/Lt M. Rostand and Cpl A. Giraudon killed. Aircraft a write-off.

GBA II/51 Potez 633 (24). Shot down by Lt von Werra *(Gruppenadjutant)* of Stab II./JG3 during low-level attack on enemy armour between Cambrai and St Quentin. Crashed and burned out at Saudemont 11.36 a.m. Sgt P. Briançon killed. Sgt Hanras baled out and captured. Aircraft a write-off.

This Potez 637 from Groupe de Reconnaissance II/33 was hit by flak over Douai. The burned-out wreck was photographed by a German airman, his exposures revealing the all-important serial number, 582, so confirming the identity.

GBA II/51 Potez 633 (26). Shot down by Bf109s during attack on enemy armour between Cambrai and St Quentin; crashed and burned out near Bapaume. Believed that claimed by Lt Fiel of Stab I./JG3 near Arras 11.40 a.m. Lt Colle and S/Lt Bruckhardt both captured. Aircraft a write-off.

GB I/63 Martin 167F (117). Landed at Chartres damaged by flak during attack on motorised columns between Cambrai and Le Cateau 12.15 p.m. Adjt K. Carrera killed. Rest of crew unhurt. Aircraft damaged but repairable.

GB I/63 Martin 167F. Landed back at Évreux on one engine; damaged by flak during attack on motorised columns between Cambrai and Le Cateau 12.15 p.m. Crew unhurt. Aircraft repairable.

GC II/3 Dewoitine 520. Crashed on landing at Rouen following combat with Ju87s of I.(St)/TrGr.186 between Bapaume and Cambrai 5.15 p.m. Sgt H. Vie unhurt. Aircraft damaged but repairable.

GC II/3 Dewoitine 520 (128). Crash-landed near Betz-Bouillancy out of fuel and damaged following combat with Ju87s of I.(St)/TrGr.186 between Bapaume and Cambrai 5.15 p.m. Lt J. Gleich unhurt. Aircraft a write-off.

GC II/3 Dewoitine 520 (59). Shot down by Bf110s during combat with Ju87s of I.(St)/TrGr.186 and abandoned south-east of Arras 5.20 p.m. Crashed and burned out. Adjt Dessault baled out and captured unhurt. Aircraft a write-off.

GR 3/33 Potez 637 (49). Port engine hit by flak over the Somme valley on return from low-level reconnaissance sortie to Arras. Crashed in flames and later exploded south-east of Bapaume 6.45 a.m. Lt J. Israël *(Commandant)*, Adjt Guérin, and Sgt Hincker captured unhurt. Aircraft a write-off.

GR II/33 Potez 637 (582). Engine hit by flak near Douai during low-level reconnaissance sortie and belly-landed on fire 12.30 p.m. Lt B. de Reneville captured badly wounded; died in Cambrai hospital next day. Adjt Vaudaine thrown from cockpit and captured injured. S/Lt Andrès captured unhurt. Aircraft a write-off.

GR II/36 Potez 63.11. Hit by flak during low-level reconnaissance sortie over Landau and pilot mortally wounded. Observer took over controls, ordered the gunner to bale out, and returned to belly-land at Metz airfield. Adjt A. Cathala badly wounded, died same night. Sgt Delasseaux baled out unhurt. S/Lt Bourgoin unhurt. Aircraft damaged but repairable.

LUFTWAFFE

2.(H)/23 Henschel Hs126. Shot down by No. 56 Squadron Hurricanes during observation sortie, crashed and burned out at Bucamps, north of Hesdin, 2.15 p.m. Oberlt F. J. Schumann killed. Aircraft a write-off.

3.(F)/31 Dornier Do17P. Starboard engine destroyed in attacks by Adjt Hôtellier, Sgt Joire, and Sgt Bompain of GC I/4 and crashed near Pontru, north of St Quentin, 6.55 p.m. Oberlt H-H. Kaasch and two crewmen killed. Aircraft a write-off.

4.(H)/31 Henschel Hs126. Shot down by No. 56 Squadron Hurricanes during observation sortie and crashed at Lambus, west of Hesdin, 2.15 p.m. Oberlt W. Nogai and Oberfw H. Rische killed. Aircraft a write-off.

Flugbereitschaft I.Fliegerkorps I Fieseler Fi156. Undercarriage damaged in take-off accident at Sovet, north-east of Dinant. Pilot unhurt. Aircraft damaged but repairable.

3./JG1 Messerschmitt Bf109E-3. Shot down in combat with Hurricanes south-west of Béthune. Gefreiter W. Gent wounded. Aircraft a write-off.

3./JG1 Messerschmitt Bf109E-3. Shot down in combat with Hurricanes near Arras. Pilot unhurt. Aircraft a write-off.

Stab I./JG21 Messerschmitt Bf109E-3. Damaged by flak during attack on enemy armour and forced-landed at Abancourt, north of Cambrai, 9.00 a.m. Leutnant S. Schmidt captured. Aircraft repairable.

I./JG21 Messerschmitt Bf109E. Shot down by flak and forced-landed north-west of Cambrai. Pilot believed unhurt. Aircraft a write-off.

3./JG26 Messerschmitt Bf109E-3. Crashed on take-off from Woensdrecht, cause not stated. Pilot unhurt. Aircraft damaged but repairable.

I./JG27 Messerschmitt Bf109E-1. Shot down in combat with Hurricanes near Arras and crash-landed at St-Pol. Lt S. Schmidt believed unhurt. Aircraft a write-off.

2./JG51 Messerschmitt Bf109E. Shot down in combat with Hurricanes over Aire, south-west of Hazebrouck. Possibly that claimed by P/O Dixon of No. 145 Squadron near St Omer 7.10 p.m. Uffz E. Gerneth wounded. Aircraft a write-off.

2./JG51 Messerschmitt Bf109E-3. Landing accident — collided with a Ju87 of III./StG2 taking-off from Guise. Leutnant R. Beckert badly injured, died next day. Aircraft damaged but repairable.

Stab III./KG27 Heinkel He111P. Shot down by No. 605 Squadron Hurricanes south-west of Lens and crashed near Bouvigny-Boyeffles 12.10 p.m. Hptmn U. Schirmer *(Gruppenkommandeur)*, Oberfw G. Raudies, Fw W. Müller, and Gefr K. Mittelback killed. Fw A. Börgerding badly wounded. Aircraft a write-off.

8./KG27 Heinkel He111P. Shot down by No. 605 Squadron Hurricanes south-west of Lens and belly-landed 10 km north-west of Souchez 12.20 p.m. Uffz H. von Borstel killed. Uffz W. Kleinjohann wounded, admitted to hospital. Fw J. Oekenpöhler and Uffz E. Schreiber captured unhurt. Aircraft 1G+AS a write-off.

9./KG27 Heinkel He111P. Shot down by No. 605 Squadron Hurricanes south-west of Lens and crashed by the road to Aubigny south of Villers-Châtel 12.15 p.m. Fw R. Jansen captured wounded. Oberfw H. Hurst, Fw W. Recht, and Uffz F. Rottmann killed. Aircraft a write-off.

I./KG30 Junkers Ju88A. Shot down by own flak on approach to Schiphol and crashed at Osdorp 11.15 p.m. Oberlt H. Alisch, Fw B. Kowalski, Gefr M. Bornemann, and Gefr F. Lenke killed. Aircraft a write-off.
Site excavated by the RNLAF in April 1988 when various components recovered.

3./KG30 Junkers Ju88A-1. Shot down by Spitfires during armed reconnaissance over Dunkirk and crashed in the Channel. Probably that claimed by F/L Malan, F/O Freeborn, and Sgt Mould of No. 74 Squadron 5.45 a.m. Uffz W. Mattner, Uffz E. Klose, Uffz W. Gottlebe, and Gefr J. Corsepius missing. Aircraft lost.

8./KG30 Junkers Ju88A-1. Shot down by No. 151 Squadron Hurricanes over Dunkirk and crash-landed south of Calais 9.00 a.m. Uffz L. Georgi, Uffz K. Spura, and Gefr P. Wieczoreck slightly wounded. Aircraft a write-off.

II./KG53 Heinkel He111H. Forced-landed near Rouen damaged by fighters. Crew unhurt. Aircraft damaged but repairable.

5./KG76 Dornier Do17Z. Returned damaged in action near St Omer. Uffz O. Stephani wounded admitted to hospital in Vogelsang, rest of crew unhurt. Aircraft repairable.

6./KG76 Dornier Do17Z. Shot down by AA fire north of Lens. Oberlt G. Beyer captured wounded. Uffz W. Nikuth captured wounded. Oberlt W. Fundinger and Obergefr G. Fischer captured unhurt. Aircraft F1+HP a write-off.

6./KG76 Dornier Do17Z. Stalled on landing at Hargimont airfield following sortie, crashed and burned out. Hptmn W. Matuschek *(Staffelkapitän)*, Oberlt W. Helwig, Fw F. Janik, Uffz P. Haubensack, and Uffz J. Rieger killed. Aircraft a write-off.

6./KG76 Dornier Do17Z. Forced-landed near Huy on return flight damaged in action north of Lens. Uffz E. Beneder killed. Aircraft repairable.

8./LG1 Junkers Ju88A-1 (3025). Shot down by Spitfires during attack on shipping west of Boulogne and crashed in the sea off Wimereux. Probably that claimed by P/O Allen of No. 54 Squadron between Calais and Dunkirk 2.00 p.m. Gefr K. Pohle killed. Oberlt H. Dunse, Fw H. Kakanowski, and Gefr H. Przybyla missing. Aircraft L1+DS a write-off.

8./LG1 Junkers Ju88A-1. Starboard engine destroyed by Spitfires during attack on the tanker *Clairy* west of Boulogne, forced-landed and burned out near Montreuil. Probably that claimed by P/O Smart and F/Sgt Franklin of No. 65 Squadron off Calais 2.00 p.m. Gefr G. Glogger killed. Oberlt T. Hagen, Oberfw K-R. Britting, and Uffz H. Döring unhurt. Aircraft a write-off.

9./LG1 Junkers Ju88A-1. Landed at Düsseldorf badly damaged in attack by Spitfires west of Boulogne. Oberlt K. H. Schomann slightly wounded. Fw H. Jahn badly wounded, admitted to hospital. Aircraft a write-off.

III./StG2 Junkers Ju87B. Collided with a Bf109 of 2./JG51 on take-off from Guise. Crew unhurt. Aircraft a write-off.

9./StG2 Junkers Ju87B. Shot down by Hurricanes south-east of Arques and crashed at Roquetoire 7.25 p.m. Possibly one of those claimed by F/L Boyd of No. 145 Squadron. Lt P. Meyr and Uffz R. Ernst killed. Aircraft a write-off.

2./StG77 Junkers Ju87B-1. Crashed on take-off from Lippstadt on ferry flight, cause unknown. Uffz R. Ihle died of injuries. Uffz F. Rebholz (1./StG77 mechanic) badly injured, admitted to hospital. Aircraft a write-off.

4./StG77 Junkers Ju87B. Shot down by Hurricanes during attack on roads east of St Omer and crashed south of Cassel 7.30 p.m. Possibly one of those claimed by S/L Donaldson of No. 151 Squadron. Lt G. Kindermann and Uffz H. Reichart believed baled out and captured unhurt. Aircraft a write-off.

4./StG77 Junkers Ju87B. Crash-landed on return to Rocroi badly damaged by Hurricanes during attack on roads east of St Omer 7.30 p.m. Possibly one of those claimed by P/O Hamar of No. 151 Squadron. Fw F. Fischlein wounded. Aircraft damaged but repairable.

4./StG77 Junkers Ju87B. Shot down by Hurricanes during attack on roads east of St Omer 7.30 p.m. Possibly that claimed by Sgt Atkinson of No. 151 Squadron. Uffz F. Mutter killed, Fw F. Pawelka badly wounded. Aircraft a write-off.

4./StG77 Junkers Ju87B. Shot down by Hurricanes during attack on roads east of St Omer 7.30 p.m. Possibly that claimed by F/O Milne of No. 151 Squadron. Fw L. Brandt and Uffz H. Finzel believed baled out and captured unhurt. Aircraft a write-off.

I.(St)/TrGr.186 Junkers Ju87B. Forced-landed near Arras damaged in combat after attack on columns north of Cambrai 5.15 p.m. Possibly that attacked by Capt Clausse *(Commandant)* and Sgt Killy of GC 4/3. Crew unhurt. Aircraft a write-off.

2.(St)/TrGr.186 Junkers Ju87B. Shot down in combat with GC II/3 following attack on columns north of Cambrai and crash-landed south-east of Arras 5.20 p.m. Possibly one of those claimed by Sgt Tourné. Fw W. Bartsch slightly wounded in head and burned, Uffz W. Philipp also wounded and burned. Aircraft a write-off.

3.(St)/TrGr.186 Junkers Ju87B. Shot down in combat with GC II/3 following attack on columns north of Cambrai and crash-landed on fire at Duisans between Arras and Agnez 5.20 p.m. Possibly that claimed by Cmdt Morlat *(Commandant de Groupe)*. Uffz G. Wenzel killed. Lt O. Blumers badly wounded in back, evacuated to hospital in Aachen. Aircraft a write-off.
Eight Ju87s and two Hs126s were claimed destroyed in this action, these claims being more accurately assessed later as two confirmed, five probables, and one damaged.

1./ZG1 Messerschmitt Bf110C. Shot down by fighters south-east of Lille and crashed alongside the road to Roubaix at Lesquin. Uffz H. Walter and Obergefr G. Rothenberger killed. Aircraft a write-off.

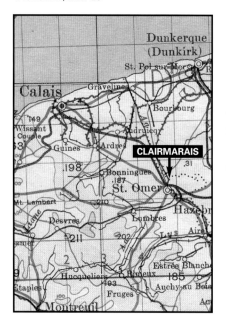

Clairmarais, just north of St Omer, was the last aerodrome to be occupied by the Air Component in France before evacuation to Britain. During the First World War this huge expanse of level grass was the home of 13 separate squadrons (Nos. 1, 15, 20, 27, 53, 54, 58, 65, 74, 98, 101, 149 and 209) of the Royal Flying Corps and the Royal Air Force established in April 1918.

At that time, the St Omer area hosted a number of other airfields including Ebblinghem, Hoog Huis, Boisdinghem, Quelmes, Esquerdes, and Longuenesse. So it was only natural that the RAF would return there in 1940. And when the Germans took over it became a fighter base for the Luftwaffe, this building serving as the combined station HQ/control tower.

Thursday, May 23

Despite increasingly desperate plans to re-establish contact, and Churchill's demand for immediate execution of the Weygand Plan which aimed to do just that, the Allied armies were irrevocably split. Events in the Belgian and British northern sector now centred upon retirement to the Channel ports and preparations for evacuation while, in the south, the crucial French defensive line formed by the Somme and the Aisne was urgently consolidated. The last British troops to be evacuated from Boulogne embarked at nightfall by which time Calais was already isolated leaving Dunkirk the only major port still available.

RAF operations from England were now almost exclusively in support of actions in the north, while AASF units based south of the German penetration had neither the range nor the detailed information needed to intervene effectively. The sole RAF Component aircraft in France, eight Lysanders of B Flight No 4 Squadron, arrived at Clairmarais from Lille-Ronchin with skeleton operations and maintenance staff — those of No. 13 Squadron having been withdrawn the day before. Apart from these, all that now remained of the RAF Air Component in northern France was a small HQ staff left behind to liaise with 'Back Violet' now established at Hawkinge. But such was the lack of information now being received from Army sources, and the difficulties of transmitting the results of air reconnaissance to the BEF, that the timeliness and overall value of air reconnaissance to British ground forces was negligible. But as a guide to air action in their support it continued to prove of use.

Enemy tanks and troops in the Forest of Boulogne were the alternative target attacked by 24 Blenheims of No. 2 Group during the morning, priority targets around Arras being obscured by cloud. Later sorties against the same target were unable to bomb accurately due to persistent British naval gun-fire. French naval aircraft directed against the same targets suffered severe losses to ever-present German fighters.

British fighters flew some 250 sorties over the northern coast of France on this day, many squadrons flying their first combat sortie of the war. During one early-morning skirmish, a British squadron leader was forced to land at Calais-Marck from where he was later picked up in a much-celebrated rescue mission. Later in the day, No. 92 Squadron was badly mauled in a ferocious action with Bf110s. Ten RAF fighter pilots were lost during the day and another three wounded.

At night, both British and French bombers struck enemy communications far beyond the front. Thirty-seven AASF Battles operated over the Upper Meuse, principally against Fumay and Monthermé, and also concentrations near Florenville and Libramont. At the same time, 49 Wellingtons attacked the Meuse crossings at Givet, Dinant, and Yvoir-Anhée and centres of communication further west between Liart and Charleroi, while 24 Whitleys attacked targets west of the Meuse. RAF bombing effort over France on the night of May 23/24 totalled 110 sorties at a cost of three aircraft and crews.

The Camels and the Pups, the Hurricanes and Lysanders, and the Messerschmitts have faded away . . . Clairmarais at peace today.

BRITISH AIR FORCES IN FRANCE

1 SQUADRON, ANGLURE

Hurricane. Returned badly damaged in attacks by Bf109s and probably that attacked by 2./JG3 north-west of Arras 3.15 p.m. Flight Lieutenant F. Warcup unhurt. Aircraft damaged but repairable.

88 SQUADRON, LES GRANDES-CHAPELLES

Battle P2356. Failed to return from night operations and crashed near Durnbach. Pilot Officer A. E. Wickham, Sergeant E. Hibbert, and AC2 M. Whelan killed. Aircraft a write-off.

UK-based aircraft lost or damaged on operations over the Western Front:

RAF BOMBER COMMAND

9 Squadron, Honington
Communications Namur:

Wellington L7777. Overshot runway on landing at Abingdon having strayed off-course during return flight 1.50 a.m. F/O K. H. V. Day, P/O Kaye, Sgt Cook, Sgt Read, Sgt McMahon, and Sgt Bowen unhurt. Aircraft a write-off.

15 Squadron, Wyton
Troop columns near Boulogne:

Blenheim IV L9403. Crashed near Morval, south-east of Bapaume, following attack on woods near Boulogne 2.30 p.m. P/O J. G. Masters, F/Sgt E. Tucker, and Sgt C. W. Thompson killed. Aircraft a write-off.

18 Squadron, Watton
Reconnaissance Channel ports:

Blenheim IV R3598. Shot down and crashed near Abbeville. Sgt F. Miller and Cpl B. M. Harding killed. P/O D. S. Dickins captured unhurt. Aircraft a write-off.
Frank Miller and Benjamin Harding are buried together at Abbeville Communal Cemetery Extension where their date of death is recorded as May 25.

Blenheim IV L9472. Returned damaged by light flak over Boulogne 4.25 p.m. P/O A. Hughes wounded in right hand, rest of crew unhurt. Aircraft repairable.

40 Squadron, Wyton
Columns Arras—Boulogne:

Blenheim IV P4909. Reported shot down by flak and crashed between Beuvry and Sailly-Labourse, south-east of Béthune, but possibly that claimed by Hptmn Gärtner (*Staffelkapitän*) of 2./JG3 12.20 p.m. W/Cdr J. G. Llewellyn and P/O W. G. Edwards killed. Sgt J. A. D. Beattie baled out unhurt. Aircraft a write-off.

Blenheim IV L8834. Shot down at Miraumont, north-east of Albert, and possibly that claimed by Lt Falkensamer and Fw Schmitt of 2./JG51 12.25 p.m. Sgt P. A. M. Burrell and LAC P. R. Whittle killed. F/O R. H. Jacoby believed baled out and captured. Aircraft a write-off.

Blenheim N3552. Belly-landed on return due to damaged hydraulics 12.45 p.m. Crew unhurt. Aircraft repairable.

53 Squadron, Hawkinge
Reconnaissance:

Blenheim R3691. Shot down during reconnaissance sortie 5.30 a.m. F/O S. G. L. Pepys, Sgt A. Haygreen, and AC H. Spear captured. Aircraft a write-off.

57 Squadron, Hawkinge
Ferry flight:

Blenheim IV L9243. Crashed on landing at Rouen due to small airfield. P/O Ritchie unhurt, Sgt R. M. Wells broken ankle, and LAC G. C. P. Haines concussed. Aircraft a write-off.

83 Squadron, Scampton
Communications Upper Meuse:

Hampden L4055. Flew into high ground south of Holmfirth in bad visibility on return flight 4.00 a.m. Sgt S. W. Jenkins, Sgt P. W. Josse, Sgt A. Marsh, and AC1 W. Thornton killed. Aircraft a write-off.

107 Squadron, Wattisham
Troop columns Boulogne:

Blenheim IV L8777. Port wing badly damaged by direct hit from AA west of Boulogne and forced-landed at Hawkinge 12.30 p.m. W/Cdr B. E. Embry and crew unhurt. Aircraft damaged but repairable.

RAF FIGHTER COMMAND

32 Squadron, Manston
Escort reconnaissance Blenheim:

Hurricane P3550. Believed shot down in combat with Bf109s and abandoned near Stavele-Brug at Beveren-IJzer, north-west of Ypres, 1.30 p.m. Possibly that claimed by Oberlt Keller (*Staffelkapitän*) of 1./JG3. Sergeant G. L. Nowell baled out badly burned, wounded in right arm and ankle. Aircraft a write-off.

54 Squadron, Hornchurch
Escort Magister to Calais-Marck:

Spitfire. Returned damaged following combat with Bf109s of I./JG1 over Calais-Marck 12.00 p.m. P/O J. L. Allen unhurt. Aircraft damage state not recorded.

56 Squadron, Manston
Patrol Dunkirk:

Hurricane. Returned wing badly damaged in combat with Bf110s over St Omer. F/L R. H. A. Lee unhurt. Aircraft repairable.

This is the Spitfire from No. 74 Squadron in which Squadron Leader Lawrence White made an emergency landing at Calais early on May 23. On return to Hornchurch, a hurried meeting was held after which the station commander, Group Captain C. A. 'Daddy' Bouchier, telephoned the AOC of No. 11 Group, Air Vice-Marshal Park, to suggest a rescue mission and, despite reservations on the size of the escort proposed, Park agreed. With No. 74 Squadron 'stood down' after a dawn patrol, No. 54 Squadron was allotted the job though 'Sailor' Malan argued, unsuccessfully, that it should be 'the Tigers' who rescued their CO. The tiny formation crossed the Channel at low level and arrived at Calais-Marck without incident but there was no sign of 'Droguer' White when Flight Lieutenant J. A. 'Prof' Leathart landed, so he took off only to set down again due to the sudden appearance of Bf109s. While his two escorts engaged the enemy fighters overhead he took cover in a nearby ditch where he found Squadron Leader White. After a hectic one-sided combat the Bf109s were driven off and the Master returned its passenger safely to Hornchurch.

74 Squadron, Rochford
Offensive patrol Calais—Dunkirk:

Spitfire K9867. Radiator hit by return fire during attack on Hs126 of 1.(H)/14 and landed at Calais-Marck with failing engine 6.00 a.m. S/L F. L. White unhurt. Aircraft ZP⊙J abandoned.
Two engine fitters, Corporal Higginbotham and LAC Cressey, were promptly despatched to Calais by Blenheim to effect repairs and were both subsequently reported 'missing' presumed captured. Laurie White was subject of a an audacious and well-publicised rescue sortie later in the day when a Miles Master piloted by F/L Leathart of No. 54 Squadron, with close escort of two Spitfires flown by P/O Allen and P/O Deere, landed at Calais around 12.00 p.m. Despite German fighters in the area, the Master was able to pick up the stranded pilot and return him safely to Hornchurch.

Spitfire P9441. Hit by AA fire and crash-landed near St Omer 6.00 a.m. F/O V. G. I. D. Byrne captured wounded in leg. Aircraft a write-off.
Two squadron histories published post-war suggest this loss occurred on May 21 but an analysis of aircraft serials and the Squadron Operations Record Book both indicate otherwise. Incarcerated in Stalag Luft 3 at Sagan 'Paddy' Byrne feigned prolonged mental illness until his eventual repatriation.

92 Squadron, Hornchurch
Offensive patrols:

Spitfire P9370. Shot down in combat with Bf109s of I./JG27, crashed and burned on beach near Cap Gris-Nez 11.30 a.m. Possibly that claimed by Oberlt Framm (*Staffelkapitän*) of 2./JG27. P/O P. A. G. Learmond missing. Aircraft a write-off.

Spitfire P9373. Shot down in combat with Bf110s of II./ZG76 and crashed vertically at Wierre-Effroy 6.05 p.m. Believed one of those claimed by Fw Hahn of 6./ZG76. Sgt P. H. Klipsch killed. Aircraft a write-off.
Subject of major recovery organised by noted aviation archaeologist and historian Steve Vizard filmed for the Channel 4 Time Team television programme in June 1999 and broadcast in February 2000.

With No. 11 Group fighters now actively supporting the battle, the Supermarine Spitfire was increasingly seen in the sky over France. No. 92 Squadron lost four machines on May 23 and some 59 years later the wreckage of one of them — P9373 — was excavated by Channel 4's Time Team. The crash site had been pinpointed by the late Alan Brown on the farm owned by Jacques Charlet at Wierre-Effroy, north-east of Boulogne. The pilot, Sergeant Paul Klipsch, was on his first combat flight and his remains had been recovered at the time and buried in the local cemetery. It was on June 1, 1999 that the film crew descended on the small French village. (All pictures by Peter Arnold.)

Veteran aviation archaeologist Steve Vizard was on hand with his own team of helpers to be able to advise and identify pieces of the aircraft as they were recovered. Although the Time Team had the intention of carrying out the excavation using traditional spade and trowel methods, with only three days allowed for the shoot, in the end a mechanical digger had to be brought in to finish the job. The Spitfire had hit the ground vertically crashing in excess of 300 mph and the 20-foot fuselage had been compressed into a tightly packed column of metal a third of that length.

On the evening of the second day, Charlie Brown flew his Spitfire Mk V to Calais to carry out a flypast in memory of the 24-year-old pilot 'killed in action' on this spot.

Left: **May 23 was also the day when Roger Bushell, formerly of No. 601 Squadron but since October 1939 the first commanding officer of No. 92 Squadron, was captured. Born in South Africa, before the war he had been a barrister; now a prisoner he put all his efforts into escaping. At Stalag Luft 3 he was in charge of the Escape Committee under Wing Commander Day (see page 104) and was shot by the Gestapo while en route from Saarbrücken** **to Mannheim on March 29, 1944 after having been recaptured following the 'Great Escape' from Sagan (see *After the Battle* No. 87). He was cremated at Neue Bremm concentration camp. Here Roger is pictured in happier days with an Avro 504 trainer.** *Right:* **His Spitfire QJ⊙Z crash-landed in open countryside near Boulogne and was fired by the pilot. In this picture the wreckage appears to have been tidied up, possibly by the land owner.**

Spitfire N3290. Shot down in combat with Bf110s of II./ZG76 6.07 p.m. Possibly one of those claimed by Uffz Huber of 6./ZG76. F/O J. Gillies captured. Aircraft a write-off.

Spitfire N3194. Damaged in combat with Bf110s of II./ZG76 and belly-landed east of Boulogne 6.20 p.m. Possibly one of those claimed by Fw Langenberg of 5./ZG76. S/L R. J. Bushell captured unhurt. Aircraft QJ⊙Z a write-off.

Roger Bushell became a key member of the escape committee at Dulag Luft and an inveterate escaper. Later, as 'Big X' at Stalag Luft 3 at Sagan, he master-minded the 'Great Escape' of 76 prisoners on the night of March 24/25, 1944 but was one of 50 escapers murdered after recapture.

Spitfire N3167. Forced-landed at Hawkinge badly damaged in combat with Bf110s of II./ZG76 and possibly that claimed by Hptmn Groth *(Gruppenkommandeur)* near Calais 6.25 p.m. F/L C. P. Green badly wounded in thigh, admitted to Shorncliffe Hospital. Aircraft damaged but repairable.

242 Squadron, Manston
Escort Blenheim to Cambrai:

Hurricane P2550. Shot down in combat with Bf109s of I./JG1 and abandoned south-west of Ypres 1.20 p.m. Possibly one of those claimed by Hptmn Balthasar *(Staffelkapitän)* of 1./JG1. P/O J. Benzie baled out wounded. Aircraft a write-off.

Hurricane P2809. Shot down by Bf109s of I./JG1 over Douai and crashed near Wancourt 1.20 p.m. Possibly one of those claimed by Lt Franzisket of 3./JG1. F/O J. W. Graafstra killed. Aircraft a write-off.

Hurricane P2730. Shot down by Bf109s of I./JG1 south-west of Ypres and crashed and exploded at Sailly-sur-Lys 1.20 p.m. Possibly one of those claimed by Hptmn Balthasar *(Staffelkapitän)* of 1./JG1. P/O G. A. Madore killed. Aircraft a write-off.

The aircraft exploded on impact making a crater 20-30 feet deep that burned for over 24 hours. A few remains were recovered on October 25 and buried as 'Unknown' in the British cemetery at Sailly. When the MREU investigated the site in 1946 the crater had been filled-in but a Browning machine gun found in the field assisted their enquiries and allowed a positive identification to be made.

Hurricane P3392. Shot down by Bf109s of I./JG1 south-west of Ypres and crashed at Ecques, south of St Omer, 1.20 p.m. Possibly that claimed by Lt Lass of 1./JG1. P/O J. W. Smiley wounded in head, baled out and captured. Aircraft a write-off.

Site investigated and subject of major recovery by local enthusiasts that revealed various components and remains of cockpit instruments. Aircraft serial plate also recovered confirming identity as 'P3392'.

253 Squadron, Kenley
Escort sortie:

Hurricane. Shot down in combat with Bf109s over Béthune 10.10 a.m. and probably that claimed by Fw Bär of 1./JG51. Pilot Officer J. D. Ford believed captured. Aircraft a write-off.

Hurricane. Forced-landed at Hawkinge damaged in combat with Bf109s over Béthune 10.10 a.m. and probably that attacked by Fw Oglodek of 1./JG51. Pilot Officer L. C. Murch unhurt. Aircraft damaged but repairable.

601 Squadron, Tangmere
Offensive patrol:

Hurricane L2057. Returned slightly damaged by AA fire 2.30 p.m. F/O T. E. Hubbard unhurt. Aircraft repairable.

605 Squadron, Hawkinge
Escort Blenheims to Arras:

Hurricane L2121. Shot down by AA fire and crashed near St-Pol. F/L P. G. Leeson captured badly wounded. Aircraft a write-off.

Although not recorded in the RAF losses, this aircraft was pictured by Heinrich Hoffmann, Hitler's personal photographer, albeit without being captioned but fortunately members of the Air Britain organisation came up with the answer. Alec Travers told us that 'it shows an Armstrong-Whitworth Ensign G-ADSZ "Elysian" which was shot up by Bf109s and burned out on Merville aerodrome on May 23. The lines under the registration letters are the red, white and blue underlining of civil registrations used on Imperial Airways and BOAC aircraft during the war years. The stripes on the tail are in similar colours'.

FRENCH AIR FORCE

AB 1 Vought 156F (10). Hit a pylon while taxying after landing at Deauville following attack on Fort de la Crèche, north of Boulogne, 6.00 p.m. Crew unhurt. Aircraft 9 repairable.

ECN 3/13 Potez 631. Attacked in error by Bloch 152s of GC I/1 and belly-landed badly damaged. Sgt Collinot seriously wounded, later died. Adjt Lepage also wounded. Aircraft a write-off.

F1C Bloch 151. Returned damaged by flak during escort sortie for AB 1 over Boulogne. Pilot unhurt. Aircraft damaged but repairable.

GAO 1/551 Potez 63.11 (687). Forced-landed at Remicourt with port engine and starboard wing damaged by flak during observation sortie between Raucourt and Le Chesne 11.00 a.m. Lt Rouig, Sgt Cotte, and Sgt Pegaz unhurt. Aircraft repairable.

GAO 1/551 Potez 63.11 (685). Returned to Hans damaged by ground-fire during observation sortie between Le Chesne and Mont-Dieu 3.45 p.m. Lt Ménard, Sgt Guilbert, and Sgt Capdevielle unhurt. Aircraft repairable.

GB I/21 Bloch 210 (53). Crashed on landing at La Ferté-Gaucher on return from bombing mission; circumstances not recorded. Crew unhurt. Aircraft a write-off.

GC 1/3 Dewoitine 520 (71). Set alight in combat with Bf109s of 1./JG51 during escort sortie for Bloch 174 of GR II/33 and abandoned north-west of Arras 3.30 p.m. Crashed and burned out at Mont-St-Éloi. Capt J. Schneider baled out badly burned, admitted to casualty station at Zuydcoote. Possibly that claimed by Hptmn Pitcairn (*Staffelkapitän*). Aircraft a write-off.

GC 1/3 Dewoitine 520 (70). Shot down in combat with Bf109s of 1./JG51 during escort sortie for Bloch 174 of GR II/33 and forced-landed at Angres, 14 km north of Arras, 3.30 p.m. Possibly that claimed by Oberlt Joppien. Capt J. Pape (*Commandant*) captured slightly wounded. Aircraft 5 fired by pilot.

As a ground-attack weapon the Stuka had the ability to create panic and confusion but in the same role the Latécoère 298 probably evoked feelings more akin to surprise and bewilderment. This slow and vulnerable torpedo floatplane, a 1936 design barely capable of 174 mph and with a single 7.5 mm Darne machine-gun in the rear cockpit, was ill-equipped for such work. Operating from Boulogne and Cherbourg, mainly on coastal patrols and anti-submarine work, so dire was the situation that they were now thrown into dive-bombing and strafing advancing German columns. The results were entirely predictable and, despite its ability to absorb considerable damage due to a sturdy construction, their lumbering formations were decimated. This is machine No. 4 of Escadrille de Torpillage T2 which forced-landed at Boisjean. Landing a floatplane on dry land is not without hazard and the remains of one float can be seen under the port wing.

GR 1/35 Potez 63.11. Attacked by Uffz Repple of 2./JG76 and also hit by ground-fire during reconnaissance sortie south of Arras 6.20 a.m. Forced-landed near Mantes-Gassicourt. Sgt J. Chapat seriously wounded; died later. Capt Neuville (*Commandant*) and Adjt De Bernardy unhurt. Aircraft damaged but repairable.

SAL 2/104 Caudron Simoun. Shot down by flak south-east of Boulogne during communications flight from Pierre-Levée, near Coulommiers, to the Lille pocket. Crashed at 'La Paturelle', Baincthun. Sgt Lespagnol and passenger killed. Aircraft a write-off.

T 2 Latécoère 298 (9). Damaged by flak then attacked by Bf109s of 3./JG27 over Hesdigneul during sortie to attack armour between Samer and Boulogne. Crash-landed at Boisjean, 15 km east of Berck, possibly that claimed by Lt Scherer north-west of Boulogne 11.50 a.m. QM Tassel badly wounded — died later. SM Halgand and SM Le Pezron both captured wounded. Aircraft 4 a write-off.

T 2 Latécoère 298 (3). Damaged by flak and attacked by Bf109s of 3./JG27 over Hesdigneul during sortie to attack armour between Samer and Boulogne. Forced-landed off-shore at Alprech where fired on by German troops and believed that claimed by Fw Kraus 11.30 a.m. QM Paul killed, SM Thénaizié badly wounded, and LV Lamiot (*Commandant*) unhurt. Aircraft 1 a write-off.

T 2 Latécoère 298 (4). Damaged by flak and attacked by Bf109s of 3./JG27 over Hesdigneul during sortie to attack enemy armour between Samer and Boulogne. Landed on Alprech beach in attempt to rescue Lamiot crew but crippled by machine-gun fire and EV1 Huet wounded 11.45 a.m. QM Coucal killed. Mt Cariou wounded, ordered to bale out over Boulogne. Aircraft 3 a write-off.

Four survivors from these two crews were later picked up from Boulogne by the trawler Fructidor.

T 2 Latécoère 298. Returned damaged by Bf109s of 3./JG27 over Hesdignuel during sortie to attack enemy armour between Samer and Boulogne 11.40 a.m. QM Payol badly wounded. PM Chauby and observer unhurt. Aircraft 2 damaged but repairable.

T 3 Latécoère 298 (68). Engine and floats damaged by flak over St Etienne-au-Mont during sortie to attack the rail bridge at Noyelles and forced-landed off Alprech 6.00 a.m. LV Marraud (*Commandant*) and crew unhurt, picked up by torpedo-boat *Mistral*. Aircraft 1 a write-off.

T 3 Latécoère 298. Returned to Cherbourg damaged by ground-fire during attack on targets between Samer and Montreuil 6.00 a.m. SM Etienne and crew unhurt. Aircraft 2 repairable.

T 3 Latécoère 298. Returned to Cherbourg with flak damage following attack on rail bridge at Noyelles 6.00 a.m. Crew unhurt. Aircraft repairable.

BELGIAN AIR FORCE

11/VI/1 Renard R-31. Brought down by ground-fire during reconnaissance east of the Lys between Desselgem and Lauwe, and crashed in flames at Pecq, east of Roubaix 5.30 p.m. 1/Sgt J. Bailly and Lt A. Warmont both killed. Aircraft lost.

11/VI/1 Stampe-Vertongen SV-5. Wrecked when undercarriage collapsed on landing at Zwevezele in poor visibility 8.30 p.m. Sgt P. Pirotte and Lt A. Henry both unhurt. Aircraft abandoned on withdrawal to Steene-Ostend 26 May.

The unit reported a second Stampe SV-5 abandoned at Ursel on withdrawal to Zwevezele this date.

This series of pictures — particularly this one depicting the entente cordiale between a Belgian soldier and an RAF airman — provides good copy, and appeared in the press during May but without any clues as to the date that the Heinkel was brought down.

LUFTWAFFE

Aufkl.Gr.Ob.d.L Dornier Do215. Forced-landed near Malmédy damaged. Crew unhurt. Aircraft damaged but repairable.

2.(H)/12 Henschel Hs126. Shot down by Lt Dorance, S/Lt Lefol, and Sgt Bressieux of GC I/5 during artillery observation mission north of Stonne and crashed south-east of Raucourt 11.15 a.m. Fw H. Bruns and Oberfw F. Peters killed. Aircraft a write-off.

1.(H)/14 Henschel Hs126. Shot down by S/Ldr White and F/O Measures of No. 74 Squadron during observation sortie south of Guines 6.00 a.m. Pilot killed, Lt Lindemann wounded. Aircraft a write-off.

5.(F)/122 Dornier Do17P. Reported shot down near Arras by own flak. Lt Bergener and crew killed. Aircraft a write-off.

1./JG1 Messerschmitt Bf109E. Shot down in combat with Spitfires of No. 54 Squadron and abandoned south-west of Calais 12.00 p.m. Believed that claimed by P/O Allen. Pilot baled out unhurt. Aircraft a write-off.

1./JG1 Messerschmitt Bf109E-1. Failed to return following combat with Spitfires of No. 54 Squadron over Calais and believed that claimed by P/O Deere which crashed just off-shore 12.00 p.m. Uffz H. Gillert missing. Aircraft lost.

2./JG1 Messerschmitt Bf109E-4. Shot down in combat with Hurricanes of No. 242 Squadron north-east of Cambrai 1.20 p.m. Pilot believed unhurt. Aircraft a write-off.

2./JG1 Messerschmitt Bf109E-4. Shot down in combat with Hurricanes of No. 242 Squadron north of Cambrai 1.20 p.m. Uffz P. Widmer killed. Aircraft a write-off.

1./JG27 Messerschmitt Bf109E-3. Shot down in combat with Spitfires of No. 92 Squadron between Boulogne and Dunkirk 11.30 a.m. Possibly that claimed by F/Lt Tuck. Oberfeldwebel W. Ahrens captured. Aircraft a write-off.

1./JG27 Messerschmitt Bf109E-1. Shot down in combat with Spitfires of No. 92 Squadron between Boulogne and Dunkirk 11.30 a.m. Possibly that claimed by P/O Bryson. Feldwebel A. Pötzsch captured. Aircraft a write-off.

2./JG27 Messerschmitt Bf109E-3. Believed shot down in combat with No. 253 Squadron Hurricanes east of Ypres 9.00 a.m. Possibly that claimed by P/O Ford. Leutnant H-W. von Weiher killed. Aircraft a write-off.

2./JG27 Messerschmitt Bf109E-1. Believed shot down in combat with No. 253 Squadron Hurricanes and forced-landed east of Ypres. Possibly that claimed by P/O Strang. Uffz E. Kaiser unhurt. Aircraft a write-off.

2./JG27 Messerschmitt Bf109E. Believed damaged in combat No. 253 Squadron Hurricanes near Merville and forced-landed near Hirson attempting to reach Guise 2.15 p.m. Possibly that claimed by F/Lt Clouston. Leutnant F. Keller unhurt. Aircraft 4+ damaged but repairable.

1./JG51 Messerschmitt Bf109E. Shot down in combat with Spitfires and crashed in the Channel off Dunkirk. Leutnant H. Strehl captured. Aircraft lost.

II./JG52 Messerschmitt Bf109E-1. Damaged during aborted take-off. Pilot unhurt. Aircraft damaged but repairable.

I./JG54 Messerschmitt Bf109E-1. Damaged in aborted take-off at Freiburg, cause not stated. Pilot unhurt. Aircraft repairable.

3./KG1 Heinkel He111. Returned damaged by flak near Orchies, north-west of St Amand. Gefr P. Grunze killed. Uffz K. Kühnel badly wounded, admitted to hospital in Antwerp. Rest of crew unhurt. Aircraft damaged but repairable.

3./KG1 Heinkel He111. Shot down by flak over Orchies, north-west of St Amand. Uffz B. Fröhling, Uffz E. Schirm, Uffz W. Heidig, Obergefr H. Kasper, and Obergefr A. Vinahl killed. Aircraft a write-off.

6./KG1 Heinkel He111. Crashed near Haillicourt, south-west of Béthune, due to icing. Uffz W. Dähling, Uffz B. Flassig, Uffz J. Kröll, and Obergefr J. Ruppel killed. Aircraft a write-off.

1./KG30 Junkers Ju88A. Returned damaged by own flak over Amsterdam. Two crewmen believed wounded, rest of crew unhurt. Aircraft damaged but repairable.

Stabsstaffel KG53 Heinkel He111H. Lost control and went into a spin, abandoned by crew near Paris. Crew baled out believed landed unhurt. Aircraft a write-off.

I./KG53 Heinkel He111H. Crashed on landing at Gross-Ostheim due to pilot error. Crew believed unhurt. Aircraft damaged but repairable.

5./KG55 Heinkel He111P. Forced-landed near Trier damaged by fighters during sortie to attack troop concentrations near Soissons. Probably that attacked by F/Lt Warcup, F/O Thorn, and Sgt Clowes of No. 1 Squadron plus unidentified French fighters. Pilot unhurt, Uffz M. Schiffer killed, Fw H. Volg and Uffz K. Gross slightly wounded. Aircraft damaged but repairable.

9./KG55 Heinkel He111P. Shot down during attack on La Ferté-Gaucher airfield and crashed near Barenton-Bugny, north of Laon. Uffz W. Elsner, Uffz A. Klingshirn, Uffz A. Hausenstein, Gefr K. Striebeck, and Flgr F. Sczepaniak killed. Aircraft a write-off.

6./KG76 Dornier Do17Z. Believed shot down in combat over Aubigny. Lt H. Krups killed, rest of crew unhurt. Aircraft damage state not recorded.

1./KGr.126 Heinkel He111H-4. Crashed in the IJsselmeer north of Huizen during night mine-laying sortie. Fw H. Laube, Uffz E. Raffler, and Obergefr H. Thiele killed. Lt zur See H. Spiegel missing. Aircraft lost. *The bodies of three of the crew were subsequently recovered from the sea. The flight mechanic, Hermann Thiele, was buried at Nieuwe Oosterbegraafplaats in Amsterdam on May 27, the pilot, Herbert Laube, at Bunschoten on May 31, and the radio operator, Erich Raffler, at Oosterbegraafplaats in Amsterdam on June 12. They were all later reinterred in IJsselstein. Wreck investigated by the Royal Netherlands Air Force in April 1976 and many small components recovered.*

Stab StG77 Dornier Do17M. Crashed on take-off on photo-reconnaissance sortie from Regniowez, near Rocroi, due to engine failure 8.30 a.m. Oberlt A. Hilmer and Fw R. Pieplow badly injured, admitted to hospital in Cologne. Aircraft a write-off.

I.(St)/TrGr.186 Junkers Ju87B. Forced-landed near Cambrai due to engine failure. Crew unhurt. Aircraft damaged but repairable.

Stab I./ZG26 Messerschmitt Bf110C. Returned damaged in combat with Spitfires between Boulogne and Calais and possibly one of those claimed by P/O Bartley of No. 92 Squadron 6.15 p.m. Lt G. Specht *(Gruppenadjutant)* and Uffz F. Fischer wounded. Aircraft U8+BB damaged but repairable.

3./ZG26 Messerschmitt Bf110C. Returned damaged in combat with Spitfires off Calais and possibly one of those claimed by P/O Holland of No. 92 Squadron 6.15 p.m. Pilot unhurt, Obergefr W. Kirberg slightly wounded, admitted to hospital in Vogelsang. Aircraft damaged but repairable.

6./ZG76 Messerschmitt Bf110C. Returned damaged in combat with Spitfires of No. 92 Squadron off Calais 6.15 p.m. Lt W. Guth slightly wounded, admitted to hospital in Kassel. Uffz K. Niedzwetski badly wounded, died in hospital in Trier May 29. Aircraft M8+GP damaged but repairable.

We believe that this He111, bearing the Werke-Nummer 2596, possibly belonged to KG27 as the overpainted characters appear to be the unit's pre-war '24' code. However, as serial numbers are not recorded in the German Quartermaster General returns at this early stage of the war, we cannot reliably link the crash to a particular loss.

Friday, May 24

At dawn, in an effort to drive a breach between the BEF and Belgian forces holding the Allied left, a fresh German attack was launched against the Belgian line along the River Lys near Courtrai. At the same time, seven Lysanders of No. 4 Squadron left St Omer-Clairmarais for Dunkirk en-route to Hawkinge — the last RAF Component aircraft in France.

Reconnaissance flights from England revealed few significant targets throughout the morning until Blenheims of No. 2 Group seeking columns approaching Calais found enemy armoured vehicles near St Inglevert at 9.45 a.m. These attracted further attacks during the day including one by six Fleet Air Arm Swordfish operating under Coastal Command who failed to locate their prescribed target — a troublesome enemy battery west of Calais. Calais was now by-passed by a considerable enemy force and at 4.45 p.m. some 200 tanks and transports were reported at Gravelines. This concentration was duly attacked around 6.00 p.m. by three Lysanders, all that could then be made available, and again shortly afterwards by ten Swordfish. Later that evening, 24 Blenheims of No. 2 Group attacked approach roads in the area and a bridge over the canal at Marck, east of Calais, but results were not possible to observe in the gathering darkness.

RAF Fighter Command was heavily involved during the day patrolling the north French coast and making shallow penetrations inland to St Omer, during which, another ten aircraft and six pilots were lost. The French were equally heavily engaged losing a total of 21 aircraft, at least two of them to Allied ground-fire.

At night, enemy communications were again attacked, with enemy-held airfields in Belgium and France as alternative targets, while eight Coastal Command Hudsons were directed against the oil storage tanks at Rotterdam. Forty-one AASF Battles visited the same targets as the night before with additional support from aircraft of Bomber Command. Conditions on the night May 24/25 were favourable, most aircraft reaching their targets, and with no losses.

Top: **Adolf Hitler's Ju52 circles the aerodrome just west of Charleville-Mézières.** *Above:* **He landed at 11.30 a.m. to be met by Generaloberst Gerd von Rundstedt, the commander of Heeresgruppe A, which was the army group responsible for the break-through. That same day Hitler had issued his Führer Directive No. 13 in which he ordered the Luftwaffe 'to break all enemy resistance on the part of the surrounded forces to prevent the escape of the English forces across the Channel and to protect the southern flank of Heeresgruppe A'. The directive went on to state that 'the enemy air force will be engaged whenever opportunity offers.'**

An unbelievable sight on the beach at Calais in January 1981 when the sea revealed a Mk 1 Spitfire which had been buried in the shifting sands since it crashed on May 24, 1940. Its pilot, Flying Officer Peter Cazenove of No. 92 Squadron, carried out a successful forced-landing on the beach after a cannon shell holed his radiator. Two days later he was captured, ending up in Stalag Luft 3. In December 1980, just when his Spitfire was emerging from the sand, Peter passed away, his lifelong desire to know what happened to his aircraft unanswered.

BRITISH AIR FORCES IN FRANCE

73 SQUADRON, ROUEN-BOOS

Hurricane. Crashed on landing after transfer flight from Gaye 8.35 a.m. Sergeant A. E. Scott believed unhurt. Aircraft damage state not recorded.

Hurricane P2803. Shot down in combat with Bf110s of V.(Z)/LG1 south-west of Amiens 1.30 p.m. Possibly that claimed by Fw Jentzsch and Oberfw Kobert. Flying Officer H. B. Bell-Syer baled out wounded in leg and badly burned face and hand, evacuated to hospital in Le-Grand-Lucé. Aircraft TP⊙L a write-off.

Hurricane P3274. Shot down in combat with Bf110s of V.(Z)/LG1 south-west of Amiens 1.30 p.m. Possibly that claimed by Lt Zobel. Pilot Officer P. E. G. Carter baled out unhurt. Aircraft TP⊙K a write-off.

501 SQUADRON, MOURMELON-LE-GRAND

Hurricane. Returned damaged by AA fire over Soissons. Flying Officer E. J. Holden unhurt. Aircraft repairable.

Hurricane. Returned damaged by AA fire over Soissons. Flight Lieutenant C. D. Griffiths unhurt. Aircraft repairable.

UK-based aircraft lost or damaged on operations over the Western Front:

RAF BOMBER COMMAND

15 Squadron, Wyton
Roads west of Calais:

Blenheim R3614. Spun into ground on return when port engine cut on final approach 9.00 p.m. P/O D. Henderson, Sgt A. N. Holmes, and LAC R. W. Austin killed. Aircraft a write-off.
    This accident was caused by the inexperienced pilot mishandling the fuel cocks.

21 Squadron, Watton
Concentrations near Calais:

Blenheim L8743. Landed at Manston with bomb bay damaged by flak during attack on armour between Calais and St Inglevert 12.30 p.m. LAC Lang wounded. P/O Rogers and rest of crew unhurt. Aircraft repairable.

57 Squadron, Hawkinge
Reconnaissance to Amiens:

Blenheim. Crashed on landing at Lympne hydraulics badly damaged in attacks by Bf110s 5.45 p.m. P/O W. Hutchings wounded in arm, Sgt Whitlam and Cpl A. Daley both unhurt. Aircraft damage state not recorded.

78 Squadron, Linton-on-Ouse
Communications:

Whitley V N1361. Crashed at Ochamps during night sortie early a.m. F/Lt I. L. McLaren, killed. Sgt J. R. Mirfin, Sgt J. Buckfield, LAC J. Spencer, and AC1 H. Wilkinson captured. Aircraft EY⊙F a write-off.

149 Squadron, Mildenhall
Communications:

Wellington P9270. Crashed near Barton Mills on return 3.15 a.m. F/Lt I. D. Grant-Crawford, AC1 E. Hewett, and AC2 J. Burton killed. F/O Holdsworth, Sgt Mundell, and AC1 Crook injured. Aircraft OJ⊙G a write-off.

RAF COASTAL COMMAND

825 (FAA) Squadron, Detling

Swordfish I K5955. Shot down by AA fire during bombing of column east of St Inglevert and believed crashed near Pihen-lès-Guines 4.15 p.m. Lt M. R. North killed, LAM C. A. Chichester missing. Aircraft G5L a write-off

Swordfish I K8380. Shot down by AA fire during dive-bombing attack on enemy armour west of Gravelines and believed crashed near Oye-Plage 6.30 p.m. Lt R. Carpmael and Lt K. P. Gurr killed. Aircraft G5A a write-off.

RAF FIGHTER COMMAND

54 Squadron, Hornchurch
Patrol Calais:

Spitfire P9455. Shot down by Fw Schmid of 1./JG51 and crashed south of Calais 5.10 p.m. F/O T. N. Linley killed. Aircraft a write-off.

Spitfire P9388. Oil system damaged by ground-fire following attack on enemy transports and caught fire, abandoned south of Calais 5.10 p.m. Sgt J. W. B. Phillips baled out and injured leg on landing. Aircraft a write-off.

74 Squadron, Rochford
Patrol Calais—Boulogne:

Spitfire K9952. Hit by return fire from He111s south of Dunkirk and caught fire, abandoned south-west of Bergues 7.30 a.m. Sgt E. A. Mould baled out unhurt. Aircraft a write-off.

Spitfire P9321. Glycol system damaged in attack on He111s and forced-landed at Calais-Marck 7.30 a.m. F/O D. S. Hoare captured. Aircraft a write-off.

Spitfire N3243. Shot down by Hptmn Ebbighausen *(Gruppenkommandeur)* of Stab II./JG26 in combat south of Dunkirk 3.55 p.m. P/O R. D. Aubert killed. Aircraft a write-off.

Spitfire K9992. Engine set alight in attack by Lt Hillecke of Stab II./JG26 and abandoned south of Dunkirk 3.55 p.m. F/L W. P. F. Treacy baled out unhurt. Aircraft a write-off.

Spitfire K9871. Returned damaged in combat south of Dunkirk and possibly one of those claimed by Oberlt Gäth *(Staffelkapitän)* of 8./JG3 between Lens and Douai 4.00 p.m. F/O J. Mungo-Park slightly wounded in left arm. Aircraft damaged but repairable.

92 Squadron, Hornchurch
Patrol Calais—Boulogne:

Spitfire P9374. Shot down by return fire from Do17s and belly-landed on beach outside Calais 9.00 a.m. F/O P. Cazenove unable to get on board destroyers and later captured. Aircraft a write-off.

Spitfire N3249. Returned slightly damaged by return fire and minus cockpit hood following attack on Do17s between Calais and Dunkirk 9.00 a.m. F/Lt R. R. S. Tuck slightly wounded in leg. Aircraft damaged but repairable.

Spitfire P9372. Returned damaged following combat with Bf110s over Calais 9.00 a.m. P/O A.C. Bartley unhurt. Aircraft repairable.

Spitfire N3193. Returned with one aileron damaged in combat with enemy fighters over Calais 9.00 a.m. P/O R. H. Holland unhurt. Aircraft repairable.

242 Squadron, Manston
Patrol Dunkirk—Boulogne:

Hurricane P3266. Collided with P/O Mitchell under AA fire and crashed in the Channel 12.45 p.m. P/O R. L. Hill killed. Aircraft lost.

Hurricane P3272. Collided with P/O Hill under AA fire and crashed in the Channel 12.45 p.m. P/O J. W. Mitchell killed. Aircraft lost.

News of the Spitfire was published in the local paper which led to the wreck being visited by hordes of sightseers and souvenir hunters. Realising the damage being caused to such a unique relic, the manager of the nearby hoverport organised a bulldozer to recover the wreck but instead of digging the sand away first, cables were fixed to the prop boss with the result that the engine was wrenched from its mountings and the wings were torn off. Nevertheless the seat, armour-plating, rudder pedals, control coumn, compass and odd instruments still remained in the cockpit. The clue to its identity was given by the .303 Brownings. Although three had been stolen, the serial numbers of the ones that remained matched those fitted in P9374. (For the full story of the recovery, see *After the Battle* No. 32.) Allocated British registration G-MKIA, remains now subject of a major restoration project by Historic Flying Limited based at Duxford.

FRENCH AIR FORCE

DAT Avord Morane 406 (722). Shot down by intense cross-fire from He111s of 8./KG51 engaged near Châteauroux and abandoned over Issoudun 10.30 a.m. Adjt P. Estan baled out slightly wounded, landing east of Ferme Bagneux near Ségry. Aircraft a write-off.

DAT Bourges Morane 406. Returned engine damaged by concentrated return fire from He11s of 8./KG51 in action over Châteauroux 10.30 a.m. Lt M. Wesolowski unhurt. Aircraft repairable.

DAT Bourges Morane 406 (131). Returned damaged by concentrated return fire from He11s of 8./KG51 in action over Châteauroux 10.30 a.m. Sgt V. Giermer unhurt. Aircraft repairable.

GAO 2/520 Potez 63.11 (571). Shot down by Oberfw Gawlick of 9./JG53 during low reconnaissance south of Sedan and belly-landed at La Neuville-à-Maire 3.45 p.m. Capt de Devise, S/Lt Teissier, and Sgt Vigoux captured wounded. Aircraft a write-off.

GB I/11 Two Leo 451s (86 and 134). Aircraft parked at Pont-sur-Yonne hit by Bloch 210 of GB I/23 and caught fire 2.00 a.m. No crew casualties. Aircraft both write-offs.

GB II/19 Douglas DB-7 (39). Shot down by Bf109s south-east of Doullens during sortie to attack enemy transport and possibly that claimed by Lt Hoffmann of 2./JG2 6.05 p.m. Crashed and exploded at Hameau des Essarts, Bucquoy, 16 km south of Arras. Adjt R. Mayer and Sgt H. Hyvert de Lignac killed. Sgt Delineau baled out and captured unhurt. Aircraft a write-off.

Due to the circumstances of the crash, the remains of Henri Hyvert de Lignac were never identified and he has no known grave. The body of Richard Mayer was found some distance from the aircraft and buried in Bucquoy cemetery.

GB II/19 Douglas DB-7 (37). Returned damaged by Bf109s south of Doullens during sortie to attack enemy transport 5.30 p.m. Sgt Bellocq wounded. Aircraft damaged but repairable.

GB 1/21 Amiot 354 (38). Shot down by flak during night reconnaissance sortie over Namur and Charleroi. Crashed between Vaurezis and Cuisy-en-Almond, 5 km north-west of Soissons 1.00 a.m. Lt P. Marchand *(Commandant)*, S/Lt M. Lafargue, Adjt G. Sère, and Sgt M. Galerneau killed. Aircraft a write-off.

GB I/21 Amiot 354 (34) and 2 Bloch 210s (104). Destroyed in enemy bombing attack on La Ferté-Gaucher 10.00 a.m. No crew casualties. Aircraft all write-offs.

GB II/21 2 Amiot 354s. Destroyed in enemy bombing attack on La Ferté-Gaucher 10.00 a.m. No crew casualties. Aircraft both write-offs.

GB I/23 Bloch 210. Hit two LeO 451s of GB I/11 and caught fire on landing at Pont-sur-Yonne after bombing sortie to Guise 2.00 a.m. S/Lt Roure died of injuries. Sgt Suau, Lt Terrien, Sgt Ficheux, and Cpl Gardiol all injured and admitted to hospital at Sens. Aircraft a write-off.

GB II/62 Martin 167F (45). Damaged by flak and attacked by fighters during bombing sortie over Péronne, Arras, and Bapaume. Crashed on landing on one engine and a burst tyre at St-Martin-la-Campagne, Eure, north-west of Évreux. Crew unhurt. Aircraft a write-off.

Groupe de Bombardement I/21 lost this Amiot 354 (serial 34) during a bombing attack on La Ferté-Gaucher.

GB 2/63 Martin 167F (61). Shot down by British AA fire on approach to Lille-Lesquin during transport flight. Crashed on fire at Lezennes 5.00 p.m. Capt J. Watrin *(Commandant)* and Sgt L. Grisonni killed. Sgt Le Gall baled out unhurt. Aircraft 1 a write-off.

GB I/63 Martin 167F (38). Shot down by British AA fire over Lesquin during transport flight between Le Bourget and Lille. Crashed and burned out at Gamand-Fretin, south of Lille-Ronchin airfield 5.00 p.m. S/Lt F. Maury, Sgt G. Eauclère, and Sgt G. Monthois killed. Aircraft a write-off.

GB II/63 Martin 167F (70). Shot down by enemy fighters during bombing sortie over Péronne, Arras, and Bapaume. Possibly that attacked by Fw Erdniss of 2./JG51 over St-Pol 5.35 p.m. Crashed and burned out at Bertangles, 8 km north of Amiens. Sgt S. Caputo killed. Lt Duffort and Sgt Derbey baled out and captured unhurt. Aircraft a write-off.

GC I/2 Morane 406 (607). Caught fire under attack by Bf109s of 8./JG53 and crashed and exploded north of Buzancy 5.15 p.m. Believed that claimed by Lt Fleitz. Sgt Gloanec baled out wounded in head and foot, admitted to hospital. Aircraft a write-off.

GC III/2 Morane 406 (569). Forced-landed at Clères badly damaged by flak during attack on enemy armour between Abbeville and St-Valéry-sur-Somme. 9.10 a.m. Adjt A. Moret unhurt. Aircraft a write-off.

GC III/2 Morane 406 (191). Crash-landed at St-Valéry-sur-Somme badly damaged by flak during attack on enemy armour around Cayeux 1.00 p.m. Sgt J. Linart unhurt. Aircraft a write-off.

GC III/2 Morane 406 (683). Forced-landed at Blangy-sur-Bresle with flak damage following attack on enemy armour around Cayeux 1.00 p.m. Adjt J. Nedelec slightly wounded. Aircraft abandoned.

GC 5/3 Morane 406 (768). Shot down in combat with Bf110s of Stab III./ZG26 east of Amiens 1.38 p.m. and crashed at Vaire-sous-Corbie. Sgt R. Firminhac killed. Aircraft 2 a write-off.

Raymond Firminhac was originally buried in a marked field grave near the crash site but the cross was displaced and his remains dispersed due to war operations during the occupation. A plaque, later replaced by a monument in Vaire, commemorates the lost pilot.

GC 5/3 Morane 406 (162). Shot down in combat with Bf110s of III./ZG26 south-west of Péronne 1.40 p.m. and crashed at Demuin, north-west of Moreuil. Possibly that claimed by Fw Klare of 8./ZG26. Sgt A. Bekarian killed. Aircraft a write-off.

GC 5/3 Morane 406. Badly damaged in combat with Bf110s of III./ZG26 south-east of Amiens and forced-landed between Compiègne and Éstrées-Saint-Denis 1.30 p.m. S/Lt Kruml unhurt. Aircraft a write-off.

GC II/5 Curtiss H-75. Forced-landed at Damblain damaged in combat with Bf109s of II./JG52 over Luxembourg 3.30 p.m. Lt P. Houzé unhurt. Aircraft repairable.

GC III/6 Morane 406. Forced-landed near Beauvais following combat with Bf110s of III./ZG26 east of Amiens 1.30 p.m. Sgt Pimont unhurt. Aircraft abandoned.

GC III/6 Morane 406. Retired damaged from combat with Bf110s of III./ZG26 east of Amiens and hit by French AA fire over Lambres-lès-Douai 1.40 p.m. Cmdt. P. Castanier *(Commandant)* baled out badly wounded; died in hospital at Lille next day. Aircraft a write-off.

GC III/6 Morane 406 (575). Set alight in combat with Bf109s and abandoned east of Amiens 1.55 p.m. S/Lt G. Colonges wounded, baled out and captured. Aircraft a write-off.

According to the Flugbuch of Lt Heinrich Sannemann of Stab II./JG3, he claimed a Morane at 4.55 p.m. on this date, the pilot being taken prisoner. S/Lt Colonges is the only Morane pilot known to have been captured on this day but according to French accounts was lost three hours earlier.

GC II/8 Potez 631. Believed wrecked in a landing accident at Mardyck 6.00 a.m. S/Lt de la Ménardière badly injured and captured in enemy advance. Aircraft a write-off.

GC II/9 Bloch 152. Pulled up too quickly on take-off from Buc; crashed and overturned catching fire. Sgt Tain thrown from aircraft and badly injured. Aircraft a write-off.

GC 1/145 Caudron C-714 (8563). Damaged in landing accident at Villacoublay. Pilot unhurt. Aircraft I-221 damaged but repairable, later abandoned.

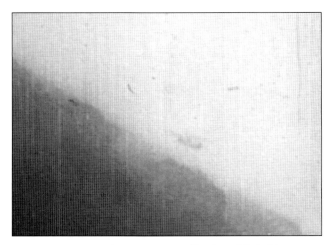 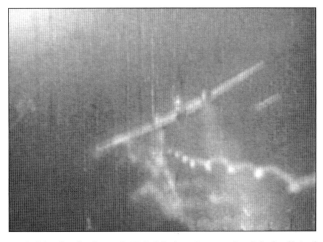

The rather poor quality camera gun film from Flight Lieutenant Treacy's Spitfire on May 24, is claimed to show him attacking a 'Henschel 126, Me110, Do17 and Ju88'. The latter was most probably the Junkers Ju88A-1 belonging to the 8th Staffel of Lehrgeschwader 1 which was a victory attributed to him at 10.30 a.m. that morning.

GR II/33 Potez 63.11 (607). Shot down by flak during low-level reconnaissance sortie between Amiens and Calais, crashed and burned out at Attaques 5.15 a.m. Lt A. Lenoir, Adjt M. Seguela, and Sgt V. Genest killed. Aircraft a write-off.

GR II/55 Potez 63.11 (432). Reportedly shot down by flak during low-level reconnaissance sortie between Lille and Amiens but possibly that claimed by Oberlt Schelcher of Stab I./JG21 south-west of Arras 5.30 p.m. Crashed and burned out at Sarton, 8 km south-east of Doullens. Capt A. Ceccaldi and Sgt A. Pfenninger killed. Sgt Rondeau seriously wounded. Aircraft a write-off.

1S1 Latécoère 298 (78). Attacked by Bf110 over Gravelines during courier flight from Cherbourg and shot down into the sea off Dunkirk by Hptmn Kaldrack *(Staffelkapitän)* of 4./ZG1. PM Lacheny wounded and drowned. PM Goret unhurt, rescued by minesweeper *Lucien Gougy*. Aircraft 2 a write-off.

2S4 Lioré et Olivier 258 (22). Wrecked in heavy landing during training flight. Crew unhurt. Aircraft a write-off.

BELGIAN AIR FORCE

1/I/1 Fox O.41. Failed to return from reconnaissance mission over Harelbeke 5.00 p.m. Sgt J. Degreef and Lt M. Keuleers missing. Aircraft lost.

9/V/1 Renard R-31 (N.10). Returned to Zwevezele damaged by Allied ground-fire during reconnaissance sortie between Harelbeke and Waregem 10.30 a.m. Lt G. Mersch and Sgt J. Danhiez unhurt. Aircraft repairable.

LUFTWAFFE

1./Aufkl.Gr.Ob.d.L Messerschmitt Bf110. Shot down during reconnaissance sortie over the English Channel and possibly that claimed by F/Lt Whitehouse and P/O Whitley of No. 264 Squadron south of Calais 1.05 p.m. Lt W. Kanz and Lt H-J. Heuermann wounded. Aircraft a write-off.

1.(H)/14 Henschel Hs126. Shot down during observation sortie south-east of Calais and believed crashed near Audricq. Possibly that claimed by F/L Saunders, P/O Smart, and F/Sgt Franklin of No. 65 Squadron 7.30 p.m. Lt E. Meyer and Uffz K. Boedecker killed. Aircraft a write-off.

2.(H)/14 Henschel Hs126. Returned damaged by fighters. Observer killed, pilot believed unhurt. Aircraft damaged but repairable.

2.(F)/22 Dornier Do17P. Reported crashed due to engine failure but possibly that attacked by Capt Naudy of GC II/3 over La Ferté-sous-Jouarre 9.50 a.m. Two crewmen wounded. Aircraft a write-off.

4.(H)/22 Henschel Hs126. Returned damaged by flak over Courtrai. Uffz F. Stevener slightly wounded. Aircraft repairable.

4.(H)/23 Henschel Hs126. Damaged in attack by Lt Marin-la-Meslée of GC I/5 over St-Loup-Terrier during observation sortie east of Rethel and forced-landed at Tannay, east of Le Chesne, 6.00 p.m. Pilot unhurt, Lt W. Buttler wounded. Aircraft repairable.

4.(H)/31 Henschel Hs126. Shot down during observation sortie south of Dunkirk and crashed between Bissezeele and Esquelbecq. Possibly that claimed by F/L Treacy, F/O Mungo-Park, and P/O Stephen of No. 74 Squadron 7.00 a.m. Wachtm Hans Grosse and Uffz W. Voss killed. Aircraft a write-off.

2.(F)/123 Dornier Do17P. Returned damaged by fighters south of St Omer during reconnaissance sortie. Possibly that attacked by P/O Cobden of No. 74 Squadron 10.25 a.m. Oberfw O. Karg and Fw H. Behrens slightly wounded. Aircraft damage state not recorded.

I./JG1 Messerschmitt Bf109E. Shot down in combat with Spitfires south of Calais. Pilot unhurt. Aircraft a write-off.

8./JG2 Messerschmitt Bf109E-3. Crashed on landing, cause not stated. Uffz K. Scheuermann injured. Aircraft 3 + ~ a write-off.

8./JG3 Messerschmitt Bf109E. Damaged by flak over Dunkirk and belly-landed near Tournai. Leutnant W. Schmidt wounded. Aircraft damaged but repairable.

2./JG21 Messerschmitt Bf109E. Returned damaged by flak. Uffz H. Jürgens unhurt. Aircraft 4 + repairable.

Stab JG27 2 Messerschmitt Bf109E-3s. Returned damaged in combat. Pilots unhurt. Aircraft both damaged but repairable.

Stab I./JG27 Messerschmitt Bf109E-3. Forced-landed at Courtrai cockpit damaged in combat. Hauptmann H. Riegel *(Gruppenkommandeur)* wounded. Aircraft damaged but repairable.

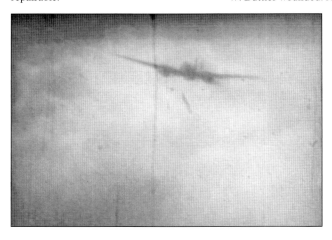 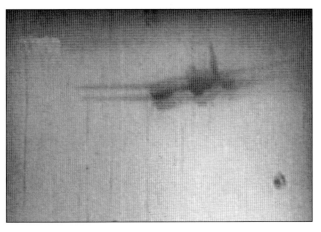

An interesting picture showing the He111 of 8./KG51 camouflaged after it belly-landed. The five-man crew were captured.

I./JG27 Messerschmitt Bf109E-1. Badly damaged in combat with Spitfires over Calais, forced-landed and burned out near Le Cateau. Pilot unhurt. Aircraft a write-off.

2./JG51 Messerschmitt Bf109E. Shot down in combat with No. 54 Squadron Spitfires and abandoned near Calais 5.10 p.m. Uffz A. Lindner baled out and captured badly wounded. Aircraft a write-off.

3./JG51 Messerschmitt Bf109E. Shot down in combat with No. 54 Squadron Spitfires and crash-landed near Calais 5.10 p.m. Oberleutnant H. Krafft captured wounded. Aircraft a write-off.

II./JG52 Two Messerschmitt Bf109E-3. Aircraft damaged in taxying collision. Pilots unhurt. One aircraft damaged but repairable, the other a write-off.

II./JG52 Messerschmitt Bf109E-3. Engine badly damaged in combat over Longuyon with Curtiss H-75s of GC II/5 and belly-landed near Arlon 7.10 p.m. Possibly that attacked by Lt Houzé. Pilot unhurt. Aircraft damaged but repairable.

4./JG52 Messerschmitt Bf109E-3. Shot down by Curtiss H-75s of GC II/5 over Longuyon and crashed near Longwy 7.10 p.m. Possibly that claimed by Adjt Audrain. Leutnant M. Mund killed. Aircraft a write-off.

1./KG1 Heinkel He111. Rammed two He111s of III./KG1 at Cologne-Butzweilerhof on landing after flight from Giessen. Fw E. Spiegelberg killed. Aircraft a write-off.

III./KG1 2 Heinkel He111s. Aircraft involved in landing collision above. No crew casualties. One aircraft a write-off the other damaged but repairable.

Stab II./KG2 Dornier Do17Z. Returned damaged by flak and attacked by Capt Kulhanek, S/Lt Raphenne, and Sgt Jicha of GC I/6 near Clermont, south of Montdidier, 11.00 a.m. Lt A. Lämmel slightly wounded and admitted to hospital in Mainz, rest of crew unhurt. Aircraft repairable.

6./KG2 Dornier Do17Z. Forced-landed west of St Quentin badly damaged by Capt Clausse, S/Lt Troyes, Sgt Killy, and Sgt Cukr of GC II/3 during sortie to attack columns near Montdidier 1.45 p.m. Flgr K. Hoffmann slightly wounded, Uffz Hermann and rest of crew unhurt. Aircraft a write-off.

9./KG4 Junkers Ju88A (3030). Crash-landed at Berge near Quakenbrück due to engine failure on take off for night sortie a.m. Hptmn M. Schumann (*Staffelkapitän*), Oberfw H. Laska, and Fw H. Wutkowski injured. Aircraft 5J+AT damaged but repairable.

I./KG51 Junkers Ju88A. Involved in landing accident at Lechfeld. Crew unhurt. Aircraft damaged but repairable.

8./KG51 Heinkel He111H. Shot down by Sgt Giermer, Sgt Kremski, and Lt Wesolowski of DAT Bourges during sortie to attack Châteauroux airfield and belly-landed between La Guerche-sur-l'Aubois and Sancoins, west of Nevers, 10.20 a.m. Uffz A. Körnig, Obergefr A. Meckelburg, and Gefr J. Demoliner captured wounded. Uffz E. Thiedemann and Gefr F. Puchstein captured unhurt. Aircraft 9K+NS a write-off.

8./KG51 Heinkel He111H (2636). Shot down by Capt Papin, Capt Hugo, S/Lt Pomier Layrargues, and S/Lt Krol of GC II/7 during attack on Châteauroux airfield. Jettisoned bombs after port engine failed and abandoned over Châtenois, west of Sélestat, 10.50 a.m. Fw H. Haisch, Fw W. Fittkau, Uffz L. Meyer, Uffz F. Goebel, and Gefr A. Dreyer baled out landing in the Hahenberg forest and captured unhurt. Aircraft 9K+BS a write-off.

The observer, Hugo Haisch, landed in thick forest, escaped immediate capture, and tried to reach the Swiss border but was arrested near Remiremont, 65 km from the crash site, on May 30. His comrades were less fortunate, receiving rough treatment on their capture by local troops and villagers from Kintzheim. This later resulted in a trial and severe reprisals after occupying German forces arrived.

1./KG54 Heinkel He111P. Returned damaged by fighters south of Dunkirk. Uffz K. Seitz and Flgr F. Grabmeier slightly wounded admitted to hospital in Hamm, rest of crew unhurt. Aircraft damaged but repairable.

1./KG54 Heinkel He111P. Attacked by fighters and both engines damaged near Cassel during sortie to Dunkirk. Believed crashed alongside the road between Dentergem and Meulbeke south of Bruges 4.45 p.m. Uffz R. Aschenbrenner and Obergefr H. Schröder captured unhurt. Uffz R. Lindenberg and Uffz W. Voss captured wounded. Aircraft B3+DH a write-off.

2./KG54 Heinkel He111P. Returned damaged by flak during attack on Dunkirk harbour. Lt F. Müngersdorff badly wounded, admitted to Marien Hospital in Düsseldorf, rest of crew unhurt. Aircraft damaged but repairable.

1./KG77 Dornier Do17Z. Shot down by Spitfires in action over Dunkirk and believed crashed near Fruges. Gefr W. Förster killed. Uffz S. Heilmann slightly wounded, admitted to hospital in St-Pol. Rest of crew unhurt. Aircraft a write-off.

3./KG77 Dornier Do17Z. Returned damaged by Spitfires in action over Dunkirk. Uffz G. Altmann slightly wounded, rest of crew unhurt. Aircraft damage state not recorded.

3./KG77 Dornier Do17Z. Returned damaged by Spitfires in action over Dunkirk. Uffz R. Kempte killed. Aircraft damage state not recorded.

3./KG77 Dornier Do17Z. Returned damaged by Spitfires in action over Dunkirk. Oberfw W. Preuss slightly wounded, rest of crew unhurt. Aircraft damage state not recorded.

2./KGr.126 Heinkel He111. Crash-landed at Neulanderfeld, near Bremen, on return from sortie in bad weather. Fw F. Dreyer slightly wounded, admitted to hospital in Hannover, rest of crew believed unhurt. Aircraft damaged but repairable.

8./LG1 Junkers Ju88A-1. Shot down by No. 74 Squadron Spitfires south of Ostend after attack on shipping off Dunkirk 10.30 a.m. Probably that claimed by F/Lt Treacy. Fw F. Plozitzka captured unhurt. Fw F. Prühs, Obergefr E. Cichos, and Gefr O. Röger captured badly wounded and admitted to St Josef Hospital in Bruges. Aircraft L1+IS a write-off.

I./StG77 Junkers Ju87B. Forced-landed near Guise due to engine failure. Aircraft damaged but repairable.

4./ZG1 Messerschmitt Bf110C. Overturned on landing at Trier-Euren due to undercarriage failure following sortie over Calais. Hptmn R. Kaldrack (*Staffelkapitän*) and Fw E. Hermanski injured, admitted to hospital in Trier. Aircraft a write-off.

I./ZG26 Messerschmitt Bf110C. Forced-landed near Ciney, cause unknown. Crew unhurt. Aircraft a write-off.

9./ZG26 Messerschmitt Bf110C. Dropped out of formation both engines damaged in combat with GC III/3 during bomber escort sortie south-east of Amiens and crashed at Wiencourt-l'Equipée 1.45 p.m. Probably that claimed by Capt Duval of GC 6/3. Fw H. Supke killed. Obergefr K. Schödl baled out wounded. Aircraft a write-off.

Heinz Supke was hastily buried in a nearby garden as the area was being evacuated by the civilian population. He was exhumed and reinterred in the local communal cemetery in July 1941.

3./ZG52 Messerschmitt Bf110C. Crashed during test flight at Metlach, cause unknown. Lt L. Hagen and Oberfw H. Hein killed. Aircraft a write-off.

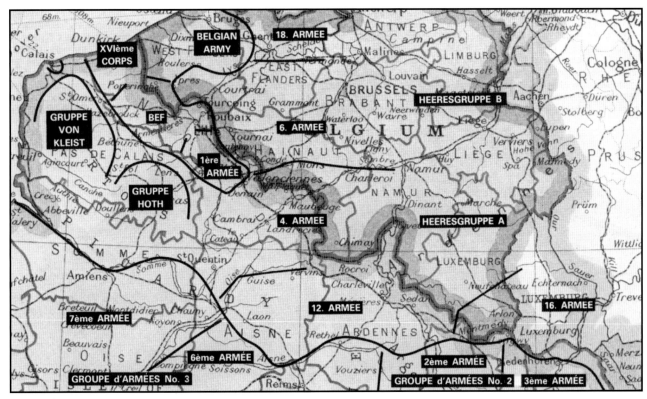

Saturday, May 25

German pressure on all fronts continued with the Belgians forced back towards Roulers creating a potential gap in the Allied line swiftly plugged by two British divisions previously earmarked for an attack south. This meant that any further BEF involvement in plans by Général Weygand to cut the German corridor to the coast and reunite the Allied armies was now a lost cause. Around 5.00 p.m. Blenheims of Nos. 21 and 107 Squadrons, responding to Belgian Army requests, pounded pontoon bridges over the River Lys between Menin and Courtrai — 'exceptionally unprofitable objectives' according to the vocal Wing Commander Basil Embry who led the attack.

Further east, enemy ground forces approaching Dunkirk from the south-west were subjected to bombing during the morning but, unlike the previous day, German fighters were in abundance and two Blenheims lost, several others returning damaged. This concentration of vehicles could not be found when a heavily escorted force of 11 Swordfish arrived later that afternoon and they were forced to squander their bombs on individual vehicles in the area. Early evening, Lysanders from No 613 Squadron, the optimistically titled 'reserve bombing force' formed under Back Component and comprising one flight of Lysanders and another of venerable Hawker Hectors, attempted to silence an enemy battery located near Sangatte, but smoke and dust from the first salvo of bombs totally obscured the target. The garrison at Calais remained completely isolated — its British defenders ordered to continue resisting 'for the sake of Allied solidarity'.

RAF Fighter Command flew 151 sorties over the Continent during the day, mainly close escort for bombing and reconnaissance missions, patrols over the Channel ports where attacks by Stukas were dispersed, and incursions further inland to Lille and Ypres. Several combats resulted and two pilots lost, along with another BAFF pilot lost on a sortie south of the Oise.

Saturday, May 25 was probably the most significant day in the whole battle of France. Not only had Hitler just confirmed von Rundstedt's controversial decision to stop the German panzers on the line Lens—Béthune—Aire—St Omer—Gravelines — the so-called 'Halt' order — but both General Gort in France and Churchill in London had almost simultaneously, but without the knowledge of the other, come to the same conclusion: the British Expeditionary Force would have to be evacuated from France. The German order to conserve their armoured forces for future operations had immense consequences as it made possible an organised withdrawal to the sea and the successful evacuation of over 300,000 men from Dunkirk. Von Rundstedt stated after the war that the armour was held back solely and exclusively on an explicit order from Hitler who feared that it would not be in sufficient strength for a second phase of the campaign; that his (Rundstedt's) headquarters objected, pointing out that it was more important to bring the first phase of the campaign to a successful conclusion; finally, that when he visited the headquarters later, Hitler stated that he had hoped to come to some rapid agreement with England if he let the British Expeditionary Force escape. However, from the memoirs of General Walter Warlimont who was the Deputy Chief of Operations of the Armed Forces High Command (OKW) under its head Generalmajor Alfred Jodl, we know that it was Hermann Göring who was indirectly responsible for persuading Hitler to hold the armour back from destroying the BEF.

On the southern, predominantly French, front the enemy launched an attack between Denain and Bouchain. Air activity over the entire front was accordingly increased with ten French fighters being lost, and others damaged, in the course of several fierce combats throughout the day. Five reconnaissance machines were also lost, while bad weather took a heavy toll of French night bombers.

Both French and British night bombing followed a similar pattern to the two previous nights but was widely disrupted by bad weather and half the RAF sorties despatched failed to even reach their targets.

Late in the afternoon of May 23, Göring was sitting at a heavy oak table beside his train wih his Chief-of-Staff [General Hans Jeschonnek] and his Chief Signals Officer, when the news arrived that the enemy in Flanders was almost surounded. Göring reacted in a flash. Banging his great fist on the table, he shouted 'This is a wonderful opportunity for the Luftwaffe. I must speak to the Führer at once. Get me on.'

In the telephone conversation which followed, he used every sort of language to persuade Hitler that this was a unique opportunity for his air force. If the Führer would give the order that this was an operation to be left to the Luftwaffe alone, he would give an unconditional assurance that he would annihilate the remnants of the enemy; all he wanted he said was a free run; in other words, the tanks must be withdrawn sufficiently far from the western side of the pocket to ensure that they were not in danger from our own bombing. Hitler was as quick as Göring to approve this plan without further consideration. Jeschonnek and Generalmajor Jodl [Chief of Operations of the OKW — the Armed Forces High Command] rapidly fixed the details, including the withdrawal of certain armoured units and the exact timing for the start of the air attack.

GENERAL WALTER WARLIMONT, 1962

BRITISH AIR FORCES IN FRANCE

1 SQUADRON, ANGLURE

Hurricane P2880. Shot down by AA fire during patrol between Laon and Chauny 3.15 p.m. Flying Officer D. S. Thom captured. Aircraft a write-off.

103 SQUADRON, RHÈGES

Battle. Shot down during attack on enemy columns near Abbeville 12.30 p.m. Sergeant G. Beardsley and LAC Lewis both evaded unhurt. Aircraft a write-off.

501 SQUADRON, MOURMELON-LE-GRAND

Hurricane L2124. Forced-landed at Limésy badly damaged by AA fire following patrol over Hesdin. Pilot Officer E. J. H. Sylvester unhurt. Aircraft SD⊙H damaged but repairable.

UK-based aircraft lost or damaged on operations over the Western Front:

RAF AIR COMPONENT

2 Squadron, Bekesbourne
Tactical Reconnaissance:

Lysander. Returned damaged by AA fire over Béthune 7.45 a.m. P/O E. N. Baker and LAC Galloway unhurt. Aircraft KO⊙L damaged but repairable.

Lysander. Returned slightly damaged by AA fire near Béthune 11.30 a.m. F/O E. J. M. Lang and LAC C. W. Evans unhurt. Aircraft KO⊙E repairable.

Lysander. Forced-landed at Hawkinge damaged by Bf109s over Boulogne 5.50 p.m. P/O Scotter and LAC C. W. Evans unhurt. Aircraft KO⊙X damaged but repairable.

RAF BOMBER COMMAND

15 Squadron, Wyton
Columns between Rety and Guines:

Blenheim IV P6913. Shot down by Oberlt Homuth *(Staffelkapitän)* of 3./JG27 near St Inglevert 11.30 a.m. P/O D. S. R. Harriman, P/O J. H. Gordon, and Sgt P. Bloomer killed. Aircraft a write-off.

21 Squadron, Watton
River Lys bridges:

Blenheim IV L8734. Shot down by AA fire during attack on pontoon crossings between Menin and Courtrai and crashed at Kezelberg, north-west of Wevelgem, 5.00 p.m. Sgt A. K. R. Keates and LAC D. V. Cleaver killed. Sgt H. Rowson captured badly wounded. Aircraft a write-off.

40 Squadron, Wyton
Columns between Rety and Guines:

Blenheim IV P4920. Shot down by Lt Axthelm of 3./JG27 near Rety, south-east of Marquise, 11.35 a.m. Sgt J. L. Alexander and LAC D. Goffe killed. Sgt S. I. Tonks captured. Aircraft a write-off.

Blenheim IV N6236. Returned hit by flak and Bf109s of 3./JG27 near Rety, south-east of Marquise, 11.35 a.m. F/O C. W. Bromley and crew unhurt. Aircraft repairable.

Blenheim IV L8827. Returned hit by flak and Bf109s of 3./JG27 near Rety, south-east of Marquise, 11.35 a.m. Sgt J. S. Morton and crew unhurt. Aircraft repairable.

Blenheim IV L8836. Returned hit by flak and Bf109s of 3./JG27 near Rety, south-east of Marquise, 11.35 a.m. F/Lt R. H. Batt and crew unhurt. Aircraft repairable.

Blenheim IV P4927. Returned hit by flak and Bf109s of 3./JG27 near Rety, south-east of Marquise, 11.35 a.m. F/O G. D. Hill and crew unhurt. Aircraft repairable.

53 Squadron, Hawkinge
Reconnaissance Neufchâtel — Rethel:

Blenheim IV R3694. Returned aileron damaged by light flak 5.30 p.m. F/O Rochfort, Sgt Clayton, and AC Roberts unhurt. Aircraft repairable.

57 Squadron, Hawkinge
Reconnaissance north-west of Lille:

Blenheim. Returned damaged by light flak over Ypres 6.00 a.m. Sgt A. G. Logan badly wounded, admitted to Shorncliffe Hospital where leg amputated. F/O E. F. Nind and Cpl F. T. Russell unhurt. Aircraft damage state not recorded.

59 Squadron, Andover
Reconnaissance Abbeville — St-Pol:

Blenheim IV L4859. Starboard engine failed during low reconnaissance and belly-landed near Étrépagny 4.05 p.m. P/O H. D. Carruthers, Sgt Shelton, and AC Salmon unhurt. Aircraft TR⊙W abandoned.

RAF COASTAL COMMAND

500 Squadron, Detling
Anti-shipping off Dutch coast:

Anson I N9731. Port engine hit by return fire during attack on E-boats and ditched 15 miles off Texel 7.12 p.m. P/O Grisenthwaite, P/O McLundie, LAC Bowers, and AC2 H. C. R. Hopwood all unhurt, rescued by HMS *Javelin*. Aircraft MK⊙U lost.

RAF FIGHTER COMMAND

17 Squadron, Hawkinge
Patrol Calais — Dunkirk:

Hurricane. Returned damaged by British AA fire 12.05 p.m. S/L G. D. Emms unhurt. Aircraft repairable.

Hurricane. Returned damaged by British AA fire 12.05 p.m. F/O R. V. Meredith unhurt. Aircraft repairable.

54 Squadron, Hornchurch
Escort Swordfish to Calais:

Spitfire N3188. Engine damaged in combat with Bf109s of I./JG76 and Bf110s of 6./ZG76 over Gravelines and caught fire, abandoned over the Channel 3.30 p.m. P/O J. L. Allen baled out unhurt, rescued by destroyer and landed at Dover. Aircraft lost.

Spitfire N3172. Returned badly damaged following combat with Bf109s of I./JG76 and Bf110s of 6./ZG76 over Gravelines 3.30 p.m. P/O C. F. Gray unhurt. Aircraft damaged but repairable.

Spitfire N3103. Belly-landed on beach outside Dunkirk damaged in combat with Bf109s of I./JG76 and Bf110s of 6./ZG76 over Gravelines 3.30 p.m. P/O G. D. Gribble unhurt. Radio salvaged and aircraft abandoned.

Spitfire N3096. Shot down in combat with Bf109s of I./JG76 and Bf110s of 6./ZG76 and believed crashed in the Channel off Gravelines 3.30 p.m. Sgt F. E. Buckland missing. Aircraft lost.

151 Squadron, Manston
Escort Blenheims to St Omer:

Hurricane P3323. Collided with F/L Ives in a turn and spun into the sea 12 miles off Ostend 5.15 p.m. P/O J. M. Bushell missing. Aircraft lost.

Hurricane P3319. Collided with P/O Bushell in a turn 12 miles off Ostend and headed for coast. Possibly that reported forced-landed at Noordhoek, near Wulveringen, 5.30 p.m. F/L F. A. Ives unhurt. Aircraft a write-off.
Freddy Ives made his way to Ostend and was assigned a place back to England on the SS Abukir but was not among 32 survivors of the 230 souls aboard when she was torpedoed on the night of May 28/29 (see also page 388).

605 Squadron, Hawkinge
Patrol Calais — Dunkirk:

Hurricane N2557. Starboard wing spar damaged by British AA on return to base 12.05 p.m. F/O G. R. Edge unhurt. Aircraft damaged but repairable.

This memorial is dedicated to the memory of Sergeant Arthur Keates and LAC Donald Cleaver whose Blenheim from No. 21 Squadron crashed near this spot in west Flanders.

| Time carried forward:— | 745.55 |

Date and Hour	Aeroplane Type and No.	Pilot	Passenger(s)	Time	Height	Course	REMARKS
20-5-40 18·55	Spitfire L	Self	Solo	50	6000	Northolt & district.	Target & attacks on section of storme.
22-5-40 14·20	Spitfire 3192	Self	Solo	15	3000	To Hawkinge	Offensive patrols.
22-5-40 21·25	Spitfire 3192	Self	Solo	15	3000	To Northolt	Returned at Dusk.
23-5-40 65·00	Spitfire 3192	Self	Solo	20	3000	To H'Church	For offensive patrols.
23-5-40 07·10	Spitfire 3192	Self	Solo	10	300	Local	Weather test.
23-5-40 10·45	Spitfire 3192	Self	Solo	2·00	15000	Dunkirk, Calais Bologne.	Offensive patrol. Shot down 1 Heinkel 109. Lost Pat Learmond.
23-5-40 17·20	Spitfire 3192	Self	Solo	1·45	15000	—"—	Offensive patrol. Shot down 2 ME.110. Lost Roger, John Collins, Paddy Green, & Sgt. Klipsch.
24-5-40 08·05	Spitfire 3249	Self	Solo	1·25	15000	—"—	Shot down 2 DO.17. Lost Peter Cazenove.
24-5-40 11·45	Spitfire 9434	Self	Solo	30	3000	To Northolt back	To Air Ministry to see D.H.O. Air Commodore Stevenson.
25-5-40 07·50	Spitfire 3192	Self	Solo	20	13000	To Manston	Investigating unidentified a/c.
25-5-40 11·30	Spitfire 3192	Self	Solo	2·20	22000	Dunkirk Calais Bologne.	Offensive patrol. Shot down 1 DO.17. Two of crew jumped.

| TOTAL TIME:— | 756·65 |

It is an interesting exercise to compare log-book victories to reality as inevitably there was much over-claiming in the heat of battle. These pages are reproduced from Flight Lieutenant Robert Stanford Tuck's log — at the time he had in excess of 750 hours flying on all types and was leading B Flight of No. 92 Squadron. As his log-book shows, the squadron got a rough reception on their combat debut over northern France on May 23 losing five pilots, including the CO and the A Flight Commander, in their first day's action. That evening Tuck was given acting command of the squadron which he led for the next three days until the arrival of their new CO, Squadron Leader 'Judy' Sanders. Characteristically, Tuck's log-book makes no mention of the fact that he was slightly wounded on May 24.

| Time carried forward:— | 760·15 |

Date and Hour	Aeroplane Type and No.	Pilot	Passenger(s)	Time	Height	Course	REMARKS
2-6-40 05·55	Spitfire L	Self	Solo.	20	3000	To Marthlesham Heath	Rendezvous for offensive patrol.
2-6-40 07·20	Spitfire L	Self	Solo.	2·00	20000	Dunkirk & Calais.	Sighted & attacked eight Heinkel 111. Shot down 1, & was attacked by 6-109. Shot down 1 ME.109 & returned having no ammo: left.
2-6-40 10·25	Spitfire 3248.	Self	Solo.	20	2000	To Duxford	Returned for repairs to a/c. Rather badly shot up.
2-6-40 20·30	Spitfire 3192	Self	Solo.	20	2000	To Marthlesham Heath.	Rendezvous for offensive patrol.
3-6-40 03·45	Spitfire 3192	Self	Solo.	15	1000	Local.	Took off for offensive patrol but weather extremely bad. Think went.
3-6-40 18·45	Spitfire 3192	Self	Solo.	25	2000	To Duxford.	Returned to base.
4-6-40 08·20	Spitfire 3192	Self	Solo	30	200.	To Northolt	Squadron move to new base. Extremely bad weather.
5-6-40 18·50	Spitfire 6596	Self	Solo	30	7000	Local.	Aerobatics & sighting practice.
7-6-40 18·20	Spitfire 9434	Self	Solo	20	6000	—"—	Aerobatics & sighting practice.
6-6-40 10·45	Spitfire 4436	Self	Solo.	15	2000	To Farnborough	For AFDU.

| TOTAL TIME:— | 765·30 |

FRENCH AIR FORCE

GAO 501 Potez 63.11 (350). Brought down by flak near Abbeville during observation sortie over the Somme and forced-landed behind enemy lines. Capt Gardeur captured wounded. Adjt Dufour and Adjt Legrand captured unhurt. Aircraft fired by crew.

GAO 546 Potez 63.11 (229). Port engine and tail-fin badly damaged by flak during reconnaissance sortie east of Roye then believed attacked by Uffz Gremm of 4./JG3 and crash-landed at Ognolles, outside Beaulieu-les-Fontaines, 7.45 p.m. Crew unhurt. Aircraft a write-off.

GAO 553 Potez 63.11 (177). Shot down by Fw Fernsebner of 7./JG52 during photo-reconnaissance mission over Rohrbach and Zweibrücken, and crashed south-west of Domfessel 12.35 p.m. Lt L. Kah killed. Adjt Jouandeau and Sgt Vercinger wounded. Aircraft a write-off.

GB I/21 Bloch 210 (185). Shot down by flak during night-bombing attack on the Cambrai — Douai road. Crashed at Graincourt-lès-Havrincourt, 10 km south-west of Cambrai a.m. S/Lt P. Emery, Sgt A. Moulinier, Adjt R. Paris, and Cpl P. Duclau killed. Aircraft a write-off.

GB I/21 Bloch 210 (10). Crashed on take-off on night-bombing sortie; probable engine failure. Crew unhurt. Aircraft a write-off.

GB I/21 Amiot 354 (37). Believed damaged on take-off from La Ferté-Gaucher in enemy bombing attack and belly-landed at Troyes on completion of sortie. Lt Marie and crew unhurt. Aircraft a write-off.

GB 4/21 Bloch 210 (14). Shot down by flak west of Soissons during night-bombing sortie and crashed at Pommiers, on the road to Pasly 11.00 p.m. Capt R. Pasteau *(Commandant)*, Sgt R. Gimel, Sgt R. Gonsalvez, and Sgt C. Roques killed. Aircraft a write-off.

GB II/21 Bloch 210 (188). Crashed into a farmhouse north-east of La Ferté-Gaucher shortly after take-off in bad weather and bomb-load exploded 10.00 p.m. S/Lt G. Mayerhoeffer, Adjt A. Guyot, Sgt R. Gibron, and Sgt E. Guidicelli killed. Aircraft a write-off.

GB I/23 Bloch 210 (25). Failed to lift off from Chaumont-Semoutiers and hit an Amiot 143 of GB 10. Caught fire and bomb-load exploded. S/Lt Lavenne, Adjt Laroche, and Sgt C. Verneret killed. Sgt Gautier and Sgt Kalensky injured. Aircraft a write-off.

GBA I/51 Breguet 693 (39). Shot down by Bf109s south of Péronne during sortie to attack enemy concentrations around St Quentin and crashed and burned out at Ennemain. Possibly that claimed by Oberlt Bethke of 2./JG2 7.35 p.m. S/Lt E. Drouelle baled out but killed. Sgt Carquin baled out and captured unhurt. Aircraft a write-off.

GBA I/51 Breguet 693 (66). Returned to Étampes badly damaged by flak during attack on enemy concentrations around St Quentin 7.00 p.m. Sgt Gionietti badly wounded. Lt Ancel unhurt. Aircraft damaged but repairable.

GBA II/54 Breguet 693 (13). Shot down by Bf109s west of Roye during attack on enemy motorised columns between St Quentin and Cambrai, and crash-landed between Erches and Guerbigny. Possibly that claimed by Fw Rudorffer of 2./JG2 7.35 p.m. Sgt Badel slightly wounded. Adjt Mitton unhurt. Aircraft a write-off.

The tangled wreckage of the Morane 406 in which Czech pilot Lieutenant Frantisek Bieberle of GC 2/6 lost his life at Havrincourt.

GC 5/1 Morane 406 (1047). Shot down by Oberlt Greisert and Fw Hermes of 2./JG2 during escort sortie for Potez 63 south of Bapaume 3.10 p.m. Crashed and burned out at Moyenneville, 12 km south of Arras. Lt K. J. A. Bursztyn killed. Aircraft 5 a write-off.
Kazimierz Bursztyn was leader of No. 4 'Bu' section of three Polish pilots from the 'Montpellier' group attached to GC III/1 for operations from March 29. Only that morning he returned from hospital as a result of wounds received on May 12. Originally buried in Moyenneville on June 2, he was reinterred post-war in 'La Targette' French Military Cemetery at Neuville-St-Vaast.

GC II/3 Dewoitine 520 (211). Shot down by Hptmn Mölders *(Gruppenkommandeur)* of Stab III./JG53 in combat south-west of Reims. Dived into the ground from high altitude and burned out at Ferme Berthenay, between Villers-Agron-Aiguizy and Romigny, 6.00 p.m. S/Lt A. Mikulasek killed. Aircraft a write-off.

GC II/3 Dewoitine 520. Returned to Betz-Bouillancy damaged by AA fire following emergency take-off and combat with Bf109s of III./JG53 south-west of Reims 6.00 p.m. Possibly that claimed by Lt Claus. S/Lt A. Troyes wounded. Aircraft damaged but repairable.

GC II/3 Dewoitine 520. Returned to Betz-Bouillancy damaged by AA fire following emergency take-off and combat with Bf109s of III./JG53 south-west of Reims 6.00 p.m. Possibly that claimed by Lt Radlick. S/Lt Fichepain wounded. Aircraft damaged but repairable.

GC 1/4 Curtiss H-75. Hit by return fire from Do17s of II./KG76 engaged between Saint-Pol and Hesdin 7.30 p.m. Forced-landed at Loeuilly, 15 km east of Poix. Sgt J. Joire wounded and admitted to hospital in Beauvais, later evacuated to England. Aircraft a write-off.

GC II/4 Curtiss H-75 (121). Collided with Sgt Dietrich under attack by Bf109s of 1./JG53 south of Attigny following escort sortie for GR I/52 and broke up over Machault, west of Vouziers, 11.05 a.m. Adjt P. Villey baled out but parachute failed to deploy and he fell dead at Cauroy. Aircraft a write-off.
One of these losses was credited to Oberlt Hans-Karl Mayer (Staffelkapitän) of 1./JG53 the other claim, a 'Staffelabschuss' being disallowed.

GC II/4 Curtiss H-75 (220). Collided with Adjt Villey west of Vouziers under attack by Bf109s of 1./JG53 and crashed at 'Mont Bernard', east of Machault, 11.30 a.m. Sgt F. Dietrich killed. Aircraft a write-off.

GC 2/6 Morane 406 (900). Shot down by Oberlt Schneider *(Staffelkapitän)* of 3./JG21 during attack on Bf109s of 9./JG2 between Noyon and Péronne 6.45 p.m. Crashed by the road to Trescault in Bois d'Havrincourt. Lt F. Bieberle killed. Aircraft a write-off.

GC I/6 Morane 406 (897). Shot down by Lt Bob of 3./JG21 during attack on Bf109s of 9./JG2 between Noyon and Péronne 6.45 p.m. Crash-landed behind enemy lines at Ferme Anthyme, Beaurains, south of Arras. Adjt R. Vantillard wounded in right arm and leg, evaded capture rejoining unit on July 18. Aircraft a write-off.

GC III/6 Morane 406 (458). Shot down by return fire from Do17 of 2.(F)/22 north of Soissons 7.20 a.m. Crash-landed near Ambleny and caught fire. S/Lt A. Villemin slightly wounded in hand. Aircraft a write-off.

GC III/6 Morane 406 (627). Shot down in combat with Bf110s of 13.(Z)/LG1 over Péronne 7.40 a.m. S/Lt de Rouffignac unhurt. Aircraft a write-off.

GC III/6 Morane 406 (524). Shot down by Bf110s of 13.(Z)/LG1 engaged near Péronne 7.45 a.m. Crashed at Travecy, 3 km north of La Fère. Sgt C. Maigret killed. Aircraft a write-off.

GC 1/145 Caudron C-714 (8572). Damaged in collision with 8580 at Villacoublay. Pilot believed unhurt. Aircraft I-230 a write-off.

GC 1/145 Caudron C-714 (8580). Wrecked in collision with 8572 at Villacoublay. S/Lt E. Fiedorczuk believed unhurt. Aircraft I-238 a write-off.

GR I/35 Potez 63.11 (265). Shot down by flak during reconnaissance sortie north of the Somme, crashed and burned out at Faubourg Thuison, Abbeville. Lt A. Galy, S/Lt R. Paneboeuf, and Sgt M. Valette killed. Aircraft a write-off.

GR I/52 Potez 637 (35). Crashed west of Attigny on return from reconnaissance along the River Aisne, cause unknown. Sgt J. Denain and Sgt P. Butz killed. S/Lt Brunerie injured. Aircraft a write-off.

As the British Expeditionary Force was retreating towards the coast, the number of sorties flown from England over northern France in support of the ground forces increased. General Franz Halder, the Chief of the Army General Staff, noted in his diary on May 24 that 'for the first time now enemy air superiority has been reported by [General Ewald] Kleist' (commanding Gruppe von Kleist). The same day the German XIX. Armeekorps war diary stated that 'Enemy fighter resistance was so strong that our own air reconnaisance was practically impossible', and by now Luftwaffe fighters were meeting for the first time the Supermarine Spitfire. In this picture, the Germans have occupied the airfield at Tournes-Belval where the burned-out wreck of a Potez 63.11 provides a suitable study for their scrapbooks. This particular machine, No. 233 of GAO 502 had been destroyed on the ground on May 11 (see page 234).

BELGIAN AIR FORCE

1/I/1 Fox (O.125). Landed at Steene-Ostend slightly damaged by enemy fighters during sortie to attack German observation balloon near Harelbeke. Lt G. Haubert unhurt. Aircraft repairable.

1/I/1 Fox. Returned to Steene-Ostend badly damaged by AA fire during photo-reconnaissance of the Maldegem to Eeklo road. Adjt L. Vandenweghe and S/Lt R. Delbroeck and both unhurt. Aircraft damaged but repairable.

1/I/3 Fox (O.171). Crashed in the sea off De Panne during liaison flight due to damaged fuel tank. Capt D. Potier *(Commandant)* and Adjt A. Colpaert rescued unhurt. Aircraft lost.

LUFTWAFFE

Aufkl.Gr.Ob.d.L Dornier Do215. Damaged in landing accident at Charleville. No crew casualties. Aircraft damaged but repairable.

2./Aufkl.Gr.Ob.d.L Dornier Do215. Damaged in landing accident at Charleville. No crew casualties. Aircraft damaged but repairable.

Aufklärungsstaffel z.b.V. Luftflotte 2 Dornier Do17Z. Crashed at Het Zoute, east of Zeebrugge, during reconnaissance sortie. Lt H. Dr Moegelin, Fw G. Dorowski, Uffz H. Metzger, and Uffz J. Steinhagen killed. Aircraft a write-off.

3.(F)/11 Dornier Do17. Crashed near Chimay and possibly that attacked by Sgt Loï of GC II/3 over Villers-Cotterêts 5.25 p.m. Fw W. Merrettig and Fw W. Schwarzkopf killed. Uffz R. Schillings captured. Aircraft a write-off

4.(H)/13 Henschel Hs126. Crashed near Armentières, cause not stated. Crew both wounded. Aircraft damage state not recorded.

1.(F)/22 Dornier Do17P. Returned damaged in attacks by Curtiss H-75s of GC II/5 engaged over Verdun and pursued to Luxembourg border near Angevillers 11.30 a.m. One crewman believed wounded. Aircraft damaged but repairable.

2.(F)/22 Dornier Do17P. Attacked over Vézaponin, north of Soissons, and port engine damaged by S/Lt Villemin and Sgt Maigret of GC III/6 during photo-reconnaissance over Meaux 7.20 a.m. Cabin fire broke out so belly-landed at Guise airfield. Obergefr Kinne badly wounded, Oberfw Zorn and rest of crew believed unhurt. Aircraft a write-off.

4.(H)/22 Henschel Hs126. Badly damaged by fighters over Courtrai and crashed at Wattripont airstrip, south-west of Renaix. Oberlt H. Niggel killed. Aircraft damage state not recorded.

2.(F)/122 Heinkel He111. Returned damaged by fighters during reconnaissance sortie over northern France. Uffz F. Barnickel and Gefr K. Herold slightly wounded, rest of crew unhurt. Aircraft damaged but repairable.

5.(F)/122 Dornier Do17P. Shot down during reconnaissance sortie, details unknown but possibly that attacked by S/L Gobell of No. 242 Squadron near Lille 8.30 a.m. Gefr J. Jockel killed. Lt H. Lemke and Uffz B. Lenz missing. Aircraft lost.

FlughafenbereichtsKdo. Jever Junkers Ju52. Crashed at Wangerooge, cause not stated. Uffz Bressel, Gefr A. Horlitz, and Gefr F. Heller (of JG1) and Uffz H. Moers, Obergefr H. Vordell, Gefr H. Günther, Uffz W. Rehbein, and Obergefr K. Walter (of II.(J)/TrGr.186) killed. Aircraft a write-off.
These airmen were all buried at Wangerooge, the dates of death of Unteroffizier Hans Moers and Gefreiter Fritz Heller being shown as April 25 in the records of the German War Graves Commission.

9./JG2 Messerschmitt Bf109E-1. Shot down by Adjt Vantillard of GC I/6 over Roye and crashed at Cizancourt, south of Péronne, 6.30 p.m. Uffz H. Grosser badly wounded, died May 28. Aircraft a write-off.

II./JG3 2 Messerschmitt Bf109Es. Returned damaged following combat sortie. Pilots believed unhurt. Aircraft both damaged but repairable.

The Commander-in-Chief of the Luftwaffe must have been sufficiently aware of the effect of almost three weeks of ceaseless operations on my airmen not to order an operation which could hardly be carried out successfully by fresh forces. I expressed this view very clearly to Göring and told him it could not be done even with the support of Fliegerkorps VIII. Jeschonnek told me he thought the same, but that Göring for some incomprehensible reason had pledged himself to the Führer to wipe out the English with his Luftwaffe. It is easier to excuse Hitler with so many operational tasks to occupy his mind for agreeing, than Göring for making this unrealistic offer. I pointed out to Göring that the modern Spitfires had recently appeared, making our air operations difficult and costly — and in the end it was the Spitfires which enabled the British and French to evacuate across the water.

GENERAL ALBERT KESSELRING, 1955

General Kesselring, the Commander-in-Chief of Luftflotte 2, was dismayed at the task of annihilating the Allied forces in the Pas de Calais, as was Göring's deputy, General Erhard Milch.

5./JG3 Messerschmitt Bf109E. Wrecked in landing collision at Montecouvez following ferry flight. Uffz M. Bücher killed. Aircraft a write-off.

5./JG3 Messerschmitt Bf109E-1. Involved in landing collision at Montecouvez following ferry flight. Pilot believed unhurt. Aircraft a write-off.

2./JG21 Messerschmitt Bf109E. Damaged in aborted take-off at Cambrai. Oberleutnant L. Eggers *(Staffelkapitän)* unhurt. Aircraft repairable.

I./JG27 Messerschmitt Bf109E-1. Forced-landed at Le Cateau due to petrol failure. Pilot unhurt. Aircraft damaged but repairable.

5./JG52 Messerschmitt Bf109E-3. Forced-landed at Rehlingen following engine failure. Uffz A. Griener unhurt. Aircraft 13 + damaged but repairable.

1./JG53 Messerschmitt Bf109E-1. Engine damaged in attacks by Adjt Villey and Sgt Dietrich of GC II/4 and forced-landed between Attigny and Ste-Vaubourg under intense ground-fire 11.05 a.m. Uffz L. Reibel captured unhurt. Aircraft a write-off.

III./JG53 Messerschmitt Bf109E-3. Forced-landed at Beaulieu, south of La Roche-en-Ardenne, due to petrol failure. Pilot unhurt. Aircraft damaged but repairable.

III./JG53 Messerschmitt Bf109E-3. Overturned on landing at Sissonne, cause not stated. Pilot unhurt. Aircraft a write-off.

I./JG76 Messerschmitt Bf109E-4. Believed shot down by P/O Gray and Sgt Norwell of No. 54 Squadron in combat over Gravelines 3.45 p.m. Fw O. Tschabuschnigg killed. Aircraft a write-off.

I./JG76 Messerschmitt Bf109E-1. Shot down by return fire from Breguet of GBA I/51 engaged north-east of Montdidier 7.15 p.m. Gefr R. Dabelow killed. Aircraft a write-off.

Stabsstaffel KG3 Dornier Do17Z. Shot down by Sgt Corrin and S/Lt Gouachon of GC I/8 and crashed at Allonville, north-east of Amiens, 7.15 p.m. Possibly also attacked by Cpl Sika. Fw K. Litzenberg killed. Oberlt Siebel and rest of crew believed baled out unhurt. Aircraft a write-off.

I./KG3 Dornier Do17Z. Crash-landed at Wiesbaden-Erbenheim believed due to pilot error. Crew believed unhurt. Aircraft a write-off.

1./KG3 Dornier Do17Z. Engaged by GC I/8 south-east of Amiens and shot down by Sgt Liautard and Sgt Maurel near Villers-Brûlin, north-east of Arras, 7.20 p.m. Fw S. Elsner killed. Obergefr W. Mergenthaler badly wounded. Fw H. Ketzscher and Fw H. Richter slightly wounded. Aircraft a write-off.

1./KG3 Dornier Do17Z. Returned damaged by Bloch 152s of GC I/8 south-east of Amiens 7.15 p.m. Obergefr A. Vakalopoulos slightly wounded, admitted to hospital in Wiesbaden. Rest of crew unhurt. Aircraft repairable.

2./KG3 Dornier Do17Z. Forced-landed at Cambrai badly damaged by Bloch 152s of GC I/8 between Poix and Amiens 7.15 p.m. Uffz H. Thierfelder and Uffz W. Liebscher badly wounded, rest of crew unhurt. Aircraft damaged but repairable.

3./KG3 Dornier Do17Z. Believed returned badly damaged in attacks by Bloch 152s of GC I/8 near Amiens 7.15 p.m. Uffz E. Jeromin baled out south-east of Valenciennes but parachute failed, rest of crew believed unhurt. Aircraft damage state not recorded.

Stabsstaffel II./KG51 Junkers Ju88A. Failed to recover from dive and crashed at Finsing, north-east of Munich, cause unknown. Uffz G. Stein and Gefr G. Lackinger killed. Aircraft a write-off.

Stabsstaffel KG53 Heinkel He111H. Belly-landed due to engine failure. Crew unhurt. Aircraft damaged but repairable.

Stab II./KG76 Dornier Do17Z. Engaged by GC I/4 north of Amiens and returned damaged in attacks near Douai 7.30 p.m. Possibly that attacked by Lt Weiss. Maj W. Hill *(Gruppenkommandeur)* slightly wounded, admitted to hospital in Vogelsang, rest of crew believed unhurt. Aircraft damage state not recorded.

4./KG76 Dornier Do17Z. Crashed from 150 feet between Vertain and Chapelle-d'Haussy following low-level attack on Escarmain airfield, probable victim of ground-fire. Lt A. Daubner, Uffz H. Lang, Uffz A. Flaig, and Gefr K. Posnanski killed. Aircraft a write-off.

4./KG76 Dornier Do17Z. Returned damaged in fighter attacks between Neuve Chapelle and Lille. Uffz J. Ladstätter and Gefr K. Winderlich badly wounded, admitted to hospital. Aircraft damaged but repairable.

5./KG76 Dornier Do17Z. Engaged by GC I/4 north of Amiens and returned damaged in attacks near Lens 7.30 p.m. Possibly that attacked by S/Lt Milbeau. Lt K. Schubert badly wounded, died in Vogelsang hospital May 29. Rest of crew unhurt. Aircraft damaged but repairable.

Stab LG1 Heinkel He111H. Returned damaged by flak over Wervik, north of Lille. Oberlt O. Patschkowski slightly wounded. Aircraft damage state not recorded.

3.(J)/LG2 Messerschmitt Bf109E-4. Damaged by return fire during attack on Potez 63 and forced-landed near Cambrai 7.30 p.m. Oberfw E. Clausen unhurt. Aircraft damaged but repairable.

Stabsstaffel StG2 Dornier Do17M (2236). Shot down by S/Ldr Emms, P/O Hanson, and P/O Manger of No. 17 Squadron and belly-landed near Calais 11.00 a.m. Fw J. Engler and rest of crew believed unhurt. Aircraft a write-off.

1./StG2 Junkers Ju87B. Shot down by Hurricanes of No. 17 Squadron during attack on shipping off Calais 11.15 a.m. Possibly that claimed by F/O Harper. Fw R. Oellrich wounded. Uffz K. Laux unhurt. Aircraft a write-off.

1./StG2 Junkers Ju87B. Shot down by Hurricanes of No. 17 Squadron during attack on shipping off Calais 11.15 a.m. Possibly that claimed by F/O Meredith. Fw A. Hausmann slightly wounded, gunner unhurt. Aircraft a write-off.

4./StG2 Junkers Ju87B. Believed shot down during attack on shipping off Calais. Oberlt G. Buchenau *(Staffelkapitän)* and Uffz M. Christ wounded. Aircraft a write-off.

4./StG2 Junkers Ju87B. Believed shot down by fighters near Arras during sortie to attack shipping off Calais. Uffz R. Mehl wounded. Fw S. Puschmann unhurt. Aircraft a write-off.

7./StG2 Junkers Ju87B. Shot down by Hurricanes of No. 17 Squadron during attack on shipping off Calais 11.15 a.m. Possibly that claimed by P/O Whittaker. Lt E. Keidel and Uffz A. Wiartalla unhurt. Aircraft damage state not reported.

11./KGzbV.1 Junkers Ju52. Shot down by Adjt Gagnaire of GC III/1 during supply mission to St Pol airfield and crash-landed near Gouzeaucourt, south-west of Cambrai, 3.20 p.m. Fw M. Schneider, Fw W. Polenz, Gefr L. Bernhard, and Gefr Thieme all slightly wounded. Aircraft a write-off.

11./KGzbV.1 Junkers Ju52. Landed to pick up crew above and damaged in attacks by Adjt Gagnaire of GC III/1 during supply mission 3.20 p.m. Tyre burst on landing later at St Pol. Uffz G. Kobelt and Uffz R. Mücke slightly wounded. Aircraft damaged but repairable.
Both aircraft operating as Transportstaffel VIII Fl.Korps

2./ZG26 Messerschmitt Bf110C. Forced-landed at Emptinne, north of Ciney, badly damaged by flak. Lt H-J. von Rochow and Uffz J. Benkelmann slightly wounded. Aircraft a write-off.

I./ZG52 Messerschmitt Bf110C. Forced-landed near Couvin out of fuel. Aircraft a write-off.

Stab II./ZG76 Messerschmitt Bf110C. Shot down by Spitfires of No. 54 Squadron in combat between Calais and Gravelines 3.45 p.m. Lt H. Peters *(Gruppenadjutant)* and Uffz A. Stumpf killed. Aircraft a write-off.

Operation 'Dynamo': May 26 – June 4

On May 19, in a conversation between the War Office and General H. R. Pownall, Lord Gort's Chief of Staff, the withdrawal of the BEF from its positions on the Escaut towards the coast was first discussed. Unable to verify that there were sufficient French reserves to stage an effective counter attack, and a retreat towards the lower Somme unlikely with the Germans already at Abbeville, Gort realized his only option was to retire north for the coast. This move was timely for six ports were then still available through which the BEF could be reinforced, supplied, or even evacuated: Zeebrugge, Ostend, Nieuport, on the Dutch and Belgian coasts and Dunkirk, Calais, and Boulogne on the French. So the problems of supplying the BEF via these ports was considered by the War Cabinet that day the meeting regarding the need for 'hazardous evacuation of very large forces' highly improbable.

But events moved quickly and the following day, May 20, Lord Gort ordered the evacuation of all non-fighting troops. Dover Command, the Admiralty, and Ministry of Shipping, therefore convened an immediate meeting at Dover to plan emergency evacuation from Calais, Boulogne, and Dunkirk. Using railway packet ships and passenger ferries it was estimated that 'allowing for moderate interference' 10,000 men could embark from each port every 24 hours, full-scale evacuation then still being viewed as 'unlikely'. Meanwhile, in an effort to hold the ports open for as long as possible, the 20th Guards Brigade was despatched to Boulogne, and the 3rd Royal Tank Regiment, with a newly created 30th Brigade, were ordered to Calais.

Next day, May 21, Vice-Admiral Ramsay, who as Flag Officer Commanding Dover was charged with planning and co-ordinating the evacuation efforts, requested continuous fighter cover over all three ports to prevent further enemy bombing. But, by that evening, badly damaged Boulogne was already under threat of occupation and enemy ground forces reported within nine miles of the equally battered harbour at Calais. This only left Dunkirk which was within effective fighter range of the east Kent airfields in No. 11 Group but not for fighters operating from forward airfields in Essex. Thus Ramsay's request posed difficulties for Fighter Command who were required to provide air cover over Dunkirk, least favourably situated of the three ports originally envisaged, as well as a protective umbrella for shipping concentrated in the Channel.

By May 23, the Guards holding Boulogne had been hurriedly withdrawn but the troops sent to Calais were now surrounded by German forces, while at Dunkirk air raids over the last three days finally made it impossible to land further supplies. The BEF encircled there, already without fresh water, went onto half rations. It was now that Vice-Admiral Ramsay was finally authorised to mount the greatest military evacuation since Gallipoli — Operation 'Dynamo' — the withdrawal of the BEF from Dunkirk. With a mere 16 specially-selected members of his staff, he immediately activated an operations room buried deep in the chalk cliffs at Dover.

Next day it was clear to the British authorities that the mili-

Vice-Admiral Sir Bertram Ramsay, as Flag Officer Commanding Dover, was tasked with masterminding the evacuation from his headquarters beneath Dover Castle.

tary situation in France was disintegrating fast and orderly withdrawal no longer possible. Far from the regular shuttle service from three French ports originally planned, there was now the very real prospect of having to rescue troops from a single ruined harbour, and the open beaches of northern France under enemy fire and constant air attack. Dunkirk Harbour alone remained open, though enemy bombing already made its continued use doubtful, when at 6.57 p.m. that evening, the Admiralty signalled that Operation 'Dynamo' is to commence'.

That same night Ramsay, whose contingency plans for full evacuation 'should it be required' were well advanced, issued an urgent demand for boats to Vice-Admiral Sir Lionel Preston who commanded the Small Vessels Pool and was responsible for auxiliary craft normally used for routine harbour work. Within days of the opening of the German offensive on May 10, it had been recognised that changes to the supply of the BEF may have to be improvised and the use of small vessels through Channel ports first considered. As a result, on May 14, the BBC had broadcast an order to all owners of self-propelled pleasure craft to register with the Admiralty and within 12 days vessels had been inspected, approved, and requisitioned for military use. These were the small boats that Ramsay now called upon but it was immediately recognised that these alone would not be enough, nor entirely suitable for operating from shallow beaches, so the Pool of London was also scoured for lifeboats and tugs.

Left: **Ramsay's historic 'cabin', complete with his bed, was swept away after the war when the tunnels were converted for use in the event of a nuclear war.** *Above:* **Ventilation plant was installed in his office, which lay at the far end of this chamber, which extracted through the window overlooking Dover harbour.**

The 'miracle of Dunkirk' is over . . . all that is left is the makeshift jetties and the abandoned vehicles like these photographed at De Panne. Yet the arguments over the role of the RAF were only just beginning. No. 11 Group mounted 101 patrols during the nine days of Operation 'Dynamo' which equates to 11 patrols each day — less than one flight per day by every squadron available. While such figures are over-simplistic, and do not accurately reflect individual squadrons' efforts, it remains the case that only two-thirds of all available fighters were employed, a level many considered inadequate.

On May 27, Lord Gort was informed that 'your sole task now is to evacuate to England maximum of your forces possible' but on this first full day of Operation 'Dynamo', a mere 7,669 troops embarked from Dunkirk harbour and its adjoining beaches. This pathetically inadequate total did little to engender any hope or confidence in a successful outcome with an estimated 300,000 men of the BEF left to evacuate. And adding to the general malaise, that night the Belgians capitulated and German artillery moved even closer to the evacuation beaches. Meantime, despite a break in the weather and the imminent threat of gales in the Channel, an armada of small boats headed for Dunkirk.

Over the next 48 hours things improved significantly with 17,804 and 47,310 troops returning on May 28 and May 29, so by midday on May 30 the remnants of the BEF were all contained within the Dunkirk perimeter and Lord Gort planning their final evacuation. He was also instructed to arrange his own withdrawal which was effected at 6.00 p.m. next evening when he handed command of the rearguard, less than 20,000 men of I Corps, to Major-General Harold Alexander and left for England aboard the Fleet minesweeper *Hebe* taking 'no more kit home than any private soldier'. He was one of 53,823 men who embarked that day.

On May 31, to the eternal credit of Allied seamen, 68,014 men were rescued from France and on June 1 another 64,429 men evacuated but it was clear that, despite the efforts of the RAF, the serious losses to shipping could no longer be sustained. Continued daylight operations were no longer possible even though it was anticipated that evacuation of the rearguard would be completed next day. Losses among the small craft had been enormous and Ramsay's original destroyer flotilla decimated by attack, collision, or other damage. His minesweepers also suffered crippling losses only made good by replacements drawn from other commands.

But with another 26,256 troops successfully embarked for England overnight, by dawn on June 2, the Senior Naval Officer at Dunkirk, Captain W. G. Tennant, had finally signalled 'BEF evacuated'. The main body of the BEF was safely away though some of the rearguard and other isolated parties, including stragglers, continued to reach the harbour and adjoining beaches over the next 48 hours. Thus 26,746 mainly French troops were brought away on June 3, followed by another 26,175 by dawn next morning. But at 9.00 a.m. on June 4, the estimated 30,000 French troops still left in Dunkirk, fighting house-to house and contesting every foot of ground, were finally forced to surrender. Within two hours Admiral Ramsay ordered the fleet of rescue ships to disperse and an Admiralty signal timed 2.23 p.m. that afternoon confirmed that 'Dynamo' was over. In the nine days of the official evacuation, far from the 45,000 men originally thought possible, a total of 338,226 had been delivered back to England.

Recriminations over the perceived lack of air cover began to surface during the evacuation itself and several ugly inter-service incidents were reported by shot-down pilots returning from France. The supposed absence of the RAF even

prompted a special message from Lieutenant-General Sir John Dill, the Vice-Chief of the Imperial General Staff, to all returning army units emphasising that the RAF had gone 'all-out' to supply cover. Of course fighter cover had been provided, but the resources employed were limited so their effect dissipated, and the intervals between patrols, described by the RAF as 'unavoidable', seem difficult to reconcile given the existing ground control system, three forward airfields, and the relatively concentrated patrol area involved.

Statistics quoted by Keith Park, Air Officer Commanding No. 11 Group, in a report dated July 8, 1940, show that 101 patrols were mounted over the Channel and Dunkirk bridgehead with 258 enemy aircraft destroyed and another 119 damaged in operations between May 26 and June 4. This for the loss of 141 RAF aircraft. It was celebrated as the first significant defeat for the Luftwaffe and, as such, a signal victory for the RAF. But, inevitably, whatever the level of RAF 'interference' achieved it was always going to be insufficient to prevent every Luftwaffe attack and consequent heavy naval losses. Yet it is indisputable that the perimeter defences around Dunkirk were not significantly weakened by the seemingly constant air attacks, nor were naval operations ever completely halted, although both factors can be viewed as more a failure of the Wehrmacht than a victory for the Royal Air Force.

The Royal Navy was most vocal on the inadequacy of air support that allowed unopposed German air attacks to interrupt naval traffic, prevent embarkation, and disrupt the marshalling of troops. This criticism is perhaps better understood, even justified, given the total of 228 vessels lost and another 45 badly damaged of the 765 involved, losses that ranged from small craft to naval ships and included six destroyers. Full air protection had been rightly expected and there was a genuine sense of disappointment and surprise at the seemingly puny efforts made by Fighter Command at the height of the evacuation. In the Royal Navy's view, RAF fighters were often so outnumbered that more were shot down than those of the enemy, contrary to accounts in the British press which engendered anger and disgust amongst those who experienced the harsh reality.

Historic facts, no matter how interpreted, cannot deny that Dunkirk formed part of a great military disaster, rightly viewed by many as a spectacular defeat, but the British are so obdurate in the face of such crises that, publicly at least, the possibility was never seriously considered, nor acknowledged, far less accepted. Overnight Dunkirk became synonymous with a remarkable deliverance. Indelibly stamped on the national psyche it kindled resurgence of patriotic spirit and awakened a fierce resolve. Though Britain now stood alone, the fight was not yet over and Fighter Command's greatest test to come.

NO. 11 GROUP SQUADRONS OPERATING OVER THE CONTINENT AND LATER IN SUPPORT OF OPERATION 'DYNAMO'

Squadron (Codes)	Base (Forward)	First sortie:	Movements:	Squadron (Codes)	Base (Forward)	First sortie:	Movements:
66 Spitfires (LZ)	Duxford (Manston)	May 12	to Horsham St Faith May 17	229 Hurricanes (RE)	Digby (Martlesham Heath)	May 28	to Wittering June 26
264 Defiants (PS)	Duxford (Manston)	May 12	to Kirton-in-Lindsey July 23	616 Spitfires (QJ)	Leconfield - detached (Rochford)	May 28	to Leconfield June 6
54 Spitfires (KL)	Hornchurch (Rochford)	May 16	to Catterick May 28	611 Spitfires (FY)	Digby (Martlesham Heath)	May 28	to Digby June 2
32 Hurricanes (GZ)	Biggin Hill (Manston)	May 17	to Wittering May 26	41 Spitfires (EB)	Hornchurch (Manston)	May 29	to Catterick June 8
65 Spitfires (FZ)	Hornchurch (Rochford)	May 17	to Kirton-in-Lindsey May 29	64 Spitfires (SH)	Kenley (Hawkinge)	May 29	to Leconfield August 19
145 Hurricanes (SO)	Tangmere (Manston)	May 19	to Westhampnett July 31	245 Hurricanes (DX)	Drem - detached (Hawkinge)	May 30	to Turnhouse June 6
151 Hurricanes (DZ)	North Weald (Manston)	May 19	to Stapleford August 29	609 Spitfires (PR)	Northolt (Biggin Hill)	May 30	to Middle Wallop July 5
74 Spitfires (ZP)	Hornchurch (Rochford)	May 21	to Leconfield May 27	66 Spitfires (LZ)	Kenley (Gravesend)	May 31	to Coltishall June 1
56 Hurricanes (US)	Biggin Hill (Manston)	May 22	to North Weald May 24		Coltishall (Martlesham Heath)	June 2	to Duxford June 3
	North Weald (Manston)	May 27	to Digby May 31		Duxford (Martlesham Heath)	June 3	to Kenley September 3
605 Hurricanes (UP)	Wick - detached (Hawkinge)	May 22	to Drem May 28	111 Hurricanes (JU)	North Weald (Hawkinge)	May 31	to Croydon June 4
92 Spitfires (QJ)	Hornchurch (Rochford)	May 23	to Duxford May 25		Croydon (Hawkinge)	June 6	to Debden August 19
242 Hurricanes (LE)	Biggin Hill (Manston)	May 23	to Ancenis June 13	43 Hurricanes (FT)	Tangmere (Manston)	June 1	to Northolt July 23
601 Hurricanes (UF)	Tangmere (Manston)	May 23	to Middle Wallop May 31	72 Spitfires (SD)	Gravesend (Manston)	June 2	to Acklington June 6
17 Hurricanes (YB)	Kenley (Hawkinge)	May 25	to Le Mans June 8	266 Spitfires (UO)	Wittering - detached (Martlesham Heath)	June 2	to Tangmere August 9
19 Spitfires (QV)	Hornchurch (Rochford)	May 26	to Duxford June 6	32 Hurricanes (GZ)	Biggin Hill (Manston)	June 8	to Acklington August 28
79 Hurricanes (AL)	Biggin Hill (Hawkinge)	May 27	to Digby May 27	615 Hurricanes (KW)	Kenley (Hawkinge)	June 8	to Prestwick August 29
610 Spitfires (DW)	Biggin Hill (Gravesend)	May 27	to Biggin Hill July 2				
213 Hurricanes (AK)	Biggin Hill (Manston)	May 28	to Wittering June 4				
222 Spitfires (ZD)	Digby (Martlesham Heath)	May 28	to Hornchurch May 28				
	Hornchurch (Rochford)	May 29	to Kirton-in-Lindsey June 4				

Note: With the evacuation of RAF Component squadrons, fighter units operating over France from bases in southern England needed airfields to refuel and rearm so, from May 19, Estrées-St-Denis, Etrepagny, and Rouen-Boos, were allocated, with additional landing grounds at Beaumont-le-Roger and Dreux becoming available later. On May 21, Air Commodore Cole Hamilton was detached from RAF Component HQ to command these facilities which were designated 'South Component'.

Sunday, May 26

One of the war's most evocative aerodromes, Hawkinge near Folkestone in Kent was relinquished by the RAF in 1964. Nevertheless in 1979 when this photo was taken, save for the removal of the hangars, the airfield still remained virtually intact. Air Vice-Marshal Blount arrived here on the evening of Sunday, May 26 (see page 339).

While enemy pressure on the Allied western flank made little progress, the continued German assault on the Belgian eastern flank further advanced on Ypres, Roulers, and Thielt, a separate thrust making equally good progress towards Bruges and the Belgian coast. The Belgian army was being driven north forcing a dangerous divide between them and the BEF. Anxious for reliable information of the current situation on the ground, three Blenheim reconnaissance sorties were sent off during the day but none of them returned. However, reports from No. 3 Air Mission, still operating in Belgium, triggered an attack by 18 Blenheims on enemy columns near Courtrai at 8.00 a.m. the aircraft all returning without loss.

Elsewhere, recognising the futility of holding onto the southern defensive line along the Escaut any longer, British forces retired north behind the River Lys in accordance with instructions 'to operate towards the coast forthwith in conjunction with the French and Belgian armies'. This thinly-veiled order had but one clear meaning — the prompt evacuation of the BEF.

Meantime, Calais had finally fallen and German artillery swiftly installed on the coast between Calais and Gravelines threatening the western approaches to Dunkirk. Following early reconnaissance of the area by Lysanders, a renewed attack was made on the enemy battery at Sangatte but this time by six Hectors of No. 613 Squadron. Once again, target identification was difficult and no definite results observed, but mercifully no fighter opposition was encountered. Incredibly it seems that no worthwhile targets were to be found inland, despite several

Hawkinge 30 years on. All protests over its preservation were in vain and now the historic flying field is covered in housing.

Accommodation at Hawkinge had to be quickly found for Back Violet (as the rear headquarters of the Air Component was called) and the Haskard Target, constructed in 1934, was selected. Its original purpose was to train No. 2 (AC) Squadron about battlefield tactics on a large hessian map supported some three feet above the floor. Back Component was to be responsible for arranging reconnaissance sorties by Lysanders and Blenheims recently returned from France and add information from other sources, such as returning bomber crews, and intelligence gathered by the Hawkinge wireless interception station. Timely communication of this information to the

British Expeditionary Force had always been a problem, the W/T link to General Headquarters often being overloaded with traffic, and once the Air Component left France on May 29, communication with BEF military units became even more difficult with messages having to be routed via London. Nevertheless, from May 26 until completion of Operation 'Dynamo' on June 4, this impromptu and make-shift headquarters, barely adequately staffed, was to become the nerve centre co-ordinating all RAF reconnaissance, bomber, and fighter operations in support of the evacuation of the British Expeditionary Force from Dunkirk.

reconnaissance flights, so 18 Blenheims despatched with fighter escort at 5.10 p.m. dropped their bombs on vehicles and troops near Hesdin, returning without loss.

Apart from bomber escort sorties, fighter operations were now almost exclusively devoted to patrols between Calais and Dunkirk, though two inland sweeps were flown during the day. Constant fighter cover over the French coast was maintained for most of the day with squadrons taking off from coastal airfields in England every 50 minutes between 4.30 a.m. and 7.30 p.m. Over 200 sorties were flown before 'close of play' and several combats took place over the coast of northern France and Channel during which eight British aircraft and pilots were lost, two pilots returning later. French fighters suffered similar losses on the day but with six of their pilots killed.

BRITISH AIR FORCES IN FRANCE

1 SQUADRON, ANGLURE

Hurricane. Hit by AA fire during patrol over Ochamps and crashed near Nancy on return flight. Pilot Officer R. Dibnah wounded in thigh. Aircraft a write-off.

73 SQUADRON, GAYE

Hurricane. Shot down by Hptmn Pingel (Staffelkapitän) of 2./JG53 and crashed and burned out at Chuffilly-Roche, north-west of Vouziers, 9.55 a.m. Pilot Officer F. Sydenham fell dead at 'Jardin Prosper'. Aircraft TP⊙H a write-off.

Hurricane. Collided with stationary aircraft on landing 10.50 a.m. Sergeant W. Millner unhurt. Aircraft TP⊙A repairable.

Hurricane. Parked aircraft subject of collision with Sgt Millner 10.50 a.m. No pilot casualty. Aircraft a write-off.

88 SQUADRON, LES GRANDES-CHAPELLES

Battle L5467. Failed to return from night operations north of Sedan and crashed in woods between Bulson and Haraucourt early a.m. Pilot Officer C. C. R. Anderson, Sergeant R. W. Butler, and Sergeant E. Wilks killed. Aircraft RH⊙L a write-off.

Top left: When we photographed the building in 1979 it was in a sad state of repair but it was hoped that because of its historical importance, it would be retained. Above: Sadly that was not to be and the building was suddenly demolished one day in the 1980s . . . but for what purpose when the site remains derelict 20 years later? Thus, once again, an important piece of Britain's wartime history was scrapped.

103 SQUADRON, RHÈGES

Battle L5514. Shot down by Oberfw Müller of 1./JG53 over Utimont during sortie to attack Luftwaffe HQ at Roumont, north-west of Bastogne, 10.15 a.m. Crashed at 'Le Tombeau du Géant' at Botassart. Flying Officer J. N. Leyden baled out and captured. Sergeant E. G. Hayward and Sergeant W. F. Hubbard killed. Aircraft a write-off.

Battle L5515. Belly-landed due to undercarriage failure following attack on Luftwaffe HQ at Roumont 10.17 a.m. Crew unhurt. Aircraft a write-off.

142 SQUADRON, FAUX-VILLECERF

Battle. Belly-landed due to undercarriage failure on return from attack on château at Roumont 10.15 a.m. Sergeant Heslop and Sergeant Hemmings unhurt. Aircraft a write-off.

150 SQUADRON, POVAN

Battle L5459. Damaged by Bf109s of 1./JG53 over Thonnelle during sortie to attack Luftwaffe HQ at Roumont and forced-landed near Avioth 10.20 a.m. Flying Officer J. E. Vernon evaded and returned unhurt. Sergeant G. Busby captured wounded in leg, LAC A. W. Rutland captured unhurt. Aircraft destroyed by crew.

UK-based aircraft lost or damaged on operations over the Western Front:

RAF AIR COMPONENT

16 Squadron, Lympne

Lysander. Attacked by P/O Stephen, F/Sgt Mayne, and P/O Cobden of No. 74 Squadron between Bourbourg and Bergues and crash-landed on return 7.45 a.m. AC1 H. G. Littlewood killed. P/O Hall believed unhurt. Aircraft damage state not recorded.

With the air battles now taking place nearer the coast there were a number of forced-landings on the beach — both British and German. This is Squadron Leader Stephenson's Spitfire N3200 from No. 19 Squadron — obviously photographed sometime long after the evacuation was over.

RAF BOMBER COMMAND

37 Squadron, Feltwell
Communications Courtrai — Brussels:

Wellington L7793. Hit by AA fire during sortie to bomb roads and rail targets west of Brussels and forced-landed at Steene, near Ostend. S/Ldr A. R. Glencross, P/O J. S. Cameron, Sgt R. C. Parkhouse, LAC G. A. Dear, and AC1 B. B. Stanhope all unhurt. Aircraft a write-off.
Arthur Glencross was among 31 RAF personnel lost while being evacuated to England from Ostend aboard the SS Abukir torpedoed off Dunkirk on May 28 by Schnellboot S-34 commanded by Oberlt zur See Obermeier. Stanhope and Dear both survived the sinking but John Cameron and Raymond Parkhouse were lost, both recorded missing on May 26 in CWGC records. Many members of No. 3 Air Mission, the RAF Component's advance unit in Belgium, were also lost.

53 Squadron, Hawkinge
Reconnaissance:

Blenheim L8863. Believed shot down by ground-fire and crashed near Bayenghem-les-Seninghem, near Lumbres, during reconnaissance to St Omer. P/O G. M. Bailey, Sgt W. J. K. Evans, and AC1 A. A. Gillmore killed. Aircraft a write-off.

57 Squadron, Hawkinge
Reconnaissance:

Blenheim IV. Returned badly damaged by ground-fire. S/L J. A. Roncoroni, Sgt Carter, and LAC Beagles unhurt. Aircraft damage state not recorded.

59 Squadron, Andover
Reconnaissance Amiens—Hesdin—St-Pol:

Blenheim R3613. Shot down and crashed near Warneton. P/O R. E. Shaw, Sgt G. L. Schwind, and AC2 A. C. Brogan killed. Aircraft a write-off.
At the request of the family, Richard Shaw was reinterred post-war in Jonkerbos Cemetery in Nijmegen in the Netherlands, alongside his brother S/L John Shaw killed on operations June 6, 1944.

Blenheim IV R3695. Elevator controls hit by AA fire near Abbeville and crew ordered out, but brought under control and belly-landed back at base 7.30 a.m. Sgt G. E. Kirk baled out and captured unhurt. P/O B. Reynolds and AC Pryde unhurt. Aircraft TR⊙A repairable.

We knew that this would be a difficult location to find as there has been much post-war building around Calais. We gave the task to Karel Margry, who trekked along the sand for a mile west of the town, but he found the whole coastline totally transformed.

The brunt of the air battle over Dunkirk and the evacuation beaches would be borne by Air Vice-Marshal Keith Park's No. 11 Group of RAF Fighter Command. In his subsequent report dated July 8, 1940, *Operations over France, May-June 1940*, he provided statistics which indicated that the Royal Air Force suffered 87 casualties between May 26 and June 4.

The losses detailed in this book show 74 Fighter Command aircrew killed, missing, or prisoners of war, with another 21 wounded, during that period. Park also reported 258 enemy aircraft confirmed destroyed and 119 more damaged — an over-optimistic total given the total lack of combat experience of most of the RAF pilots involved.

RAF COASTAL COMMAND

235 Squadron, Bircham Newton
Reconnaissance Zeebrugge:

Blenheim IV P6956. Lost control in cloud shortly after take-off and spun into ground at Docking 5.15 p.m. P/O A. H. Murphy and LAC E. P. Armstrong killed. P/O C. D. Wardle baled out unhurt. Aircraft a write-off.

825 (FAA) Squadron, Detling
Observation sortie Calais:

Swordfish I. Returned following attack by Bf109s north-west of Sangatte while spotting for guns from HMS *Galatea* 9.15 a.m. Lt G. N. Beaumont thrown from cockpit during violent evasive manoeuvres and missing, pilot unhurt. Aircraft 5H damage state not recorded.

RAF FIGHTER COMMAND

17 Squadron, Hawkinge
Offensive patrols:

Hurricane N2528. Shot down in combat over Calais 5.30 a.m. and possibly that claimed by Uffz Uht of 2./JG3. F/Sgt W. T. Jones killed. Aircraft a write-off.

Hurricane P3483. Shot down by Oberlt Keitel of Stab I./JG77 and crashed in sea off Dunkirk 11.20 a.m. F/Lt C. F. G. Adye baled out but missing. Aircraft lost.

19 Squadron, Hornchurch
Patrol Dunkirk—Calais:

Spitfire N3200. Radiator damaged in combat with Bf109s of I./JG1 and 2./JG2 following attack on Ju87s of 3./StG76 and belly-landed on beach west of Calais 8.45 a.m. Possibly one of those claimed by Fw Rudorffer of 2./JG2. S/L G. D. Stephenson captured. Aircraft a write-off.

Spitfire N3237. Shot down by Bf109s of I./JG1 and 2./JG2 during attack on Ju87s of 3./StG76 and abandoned near Calais 8.45 a.m. Possibly that claimed by Fw Clade of 1./JG1. P/O P. V. Watson baled out and captured badly wounded, died May 28. Aircraft a write-off.

Spitfire N3198. Shot down in combat with Bf109s of I./JG1 and 2./JG2 following attack on Ju87s of 3./StG76 off Calais 8.45 a.m. Possibly one of those claimed by Hptmn Balthasar *(Staffelkapitän)* of 1./JG1. F/O G. E. Ball wounded in head and arm. Aircraft QV⊙L damaged but repairable.

Spitfire N3040. Returned damaged by Bf109s of I./JG1 and 2./JG2 in combat off Calais 8.45 a.m. F/L B. J. E. Lane unhurt. Aircraft repairable.

Spitfire P9305. Shot down in combat with Bf109s of 1./JG2 south-west of Calais 4.00 p.m. Sgt C. A. Irwin killed. Aircraft a write-off.
Charles Irwin's date of death is recorded as May 28 by the CWGC.

Spitfire L1031. Damaged in combat with 1./JG2 and belly-landed on Walmer Beach, near Deal, 4.30 p.m. P/O M. D. Lyne wounded in leg. Aircraft damaged but repairable.

54 Squadron, Hornchurch
Patrol Calais:

Spitfire N3180. Returned hit in one wing by Bf109 during attack on Bf110s 5.35 a.m. P/O A. C. Deere unhurt. Aircraft KL⊙B repairable.

65 Squadron, Hornchurch
Patrol Dunkirk:

Spitfire P9437. Believed hit by AA on return from combat with Bf110s off Calais and crashed near Minster 6.05 a.m. F/O J. H. Welford baled out too low and killed. Aircraft a write-off.

Spitfire K9912. Starboard wing damaged in combat with Bf109s of I./JG1 and 2./JG2 off Calais and belly-landed on Dunkirk beach 9.00 a.m. Possibly one of those claimed by Hptmn Balthasar *(Staffelkapitän)* of 1./JG1. P/O K. G. Hart unhurt. Aircraft YT⊙O fired by pilot.

145 Squadron, Tangmere
Patrol Dunkirk—Boulogne:

Hurricane N2589. Radiator damaged by return fire from He111, engine seized and belly-landed at Little Mongeham, near Deal, 7.15 p.m. P/O P. L. Parrott unhurt. Aircraft damaged but repairable.

605 Squadron, Hawkinge
Patrol Dunkirk:

Hurricane N2346. Engine damaged by return fire from Bf110 of I./ZG1 and abandoned over Ostend while heading for Steene 2.15 p.m. P/O I. J. Muirhead baled out unhurt. Aircraft a write-off.
Fired on by Belgian troops while in his parachute and after landing, Ian Muirhead survived unhurt and reached Ostend where he managed to get a place on board the SS Abukir due to sail for England. The ship was torpedoed in mid-Channel on the night of May 28/29 but he was among 32 passengers and crew rescued by HMS Grenade. After a spell in hospital in Torquay he returned to operations with the squadron only to be killed in action on October 15, 1940.

FRENCH AIR FORCE

F1C Potez 631. Badly damaged by flak during reconnaissance sortie over St-Valéry-en-Caux harbour and forced-landed at Deauville. LV Lévis-Mirepoix unhurt. Aircraft a write-off.

GAO 2/506 Potez 63.11 (260). Returned to Chambley damaged by flak during reconnaissance sortie 12.00 p.m. S/Lt Dupont wounded. Col. Patanchon and Sgt Jousselin unhurt. Aircraft damaged but repairable.

GAO 1/508 Potez 63.11 (272). Shot down by Lt Leonhard of 3./JG53 west of Soissons during sortie to spot enemy artillery positions. Crashed onto an embankment bordering the main road at Mercin-et-Vaux, broke up and caught fire 1.58 p.m. Lt M. Couture, Sgt M. Guilloux, and Sgt R. Witry killed. Aircraft write-off.

GAO 512 Potez 63.11 (780). Engaged by Bf109s of 5./JG51 during reconnaissance sortie north-west of Strasbourg and attempted to reach Saverne-Steinbourg but pursued by Lt Lessing and shot down at Gimbrett 10.20 a.m. Lt J. Nodet, Cmdt. J. Leclère *(Commandant)*, and Sgt C. Licitri killed. Aircraft a write-off.

GBA II/51 Potez 633. Damaged by flak during attack on enemy motorised columns between La Fère and St Quentin and crashed on landing at Pithviers. Lt Collombet and Adjt Hervier unhurt. Aircraft a write-off.

Another beach wreck, in this case Spitfire K9912 of No. 65 Squadron. After he crash-landed, Pilot Officer Kenneth Hart set fire to his aircraft and returned to the UK by boat.

GB I/62 Martin 167F (39). Shot down by S/Lt Prayer of GC II/3 during sortie to attack enemy transport north-east of Amiens and crashed at Molliens-au-Bois 7.40 p.m. Sgt R. Terrié killed. Sgt L. Métraux baled out but killed. Sgt Tournié baled out and captured after spirited defence with his revolver. Aircraft a write-off.

Originally buried alongside their aircraft, Robert Terrié and Louis Métraux were reinterred in the communal cemetery at Molliens-au-Bois on April 24, 1941.

GB I/62 Martin 167F (89). Shot down by Sgt Loï and Sgt Cukr of GC II/3 south-east of Picquiny during sortie to attack enemy transport north-east of Amiens. Crashed and burned out at La Planquette, Ferrières, 7.45 p.m. Lt A. Mallet killed. Adjt Plantier wounded in knee, Sgt Segeat slightly burned. Aircraft a write-off.

GB I/62 Martin 167F (74). Returned damaged by flak during low-level attack on enemy transport north-east of Amiens 7.40 p.m. Lt Langlois slightly wounded, Adjt Gauche and rest of crew unhurt. Aircraft damaged but repairable.

GB I/62 Martin 167F (96). Returned damaged by GC II/3 during sortie to attack enemy transport north-east of Amiens 7.40 p.m. Sgt Marchand badly wounded in left thigh, Sgt Bazon and rest of crew unhurt. Aircraft damaged but repairable.

GB I/62 Martin 167F (129). Returned port wing damaged by GC II/3 during sortie to attack enemy transport north-east of Amiens 7.40 p.m. Crew believed unhurt. Aircraft repairable.

GC I/1 Bloch 152 (240). Shot down by Bf109 during patrol south-west of Creil and abandoned over Gouvieux 1.15 p.m. Sgt O. Fiala baled out wounded landing at Laversine, near Saint-Maximin, and admitted to hospital in Chantilly. Aircraft a write-off.

The only German fighter claim likely to relate to this loss was filed by Fw Alfons Bacher of 3./JG52 who claimed a Hawk-75A over Chantilly at 4.50 p.m. which suggests some error in surviving records.

GC 6/1 Morane 406 (260). Shot down in combat with Bf109s near Péronne during escort sortie for reconnaissance Potez and abandoned over Cambrai 8.30 a.m. Possibly that claimed by Oberlt Schneider *(Staffelkapitän)* of 3./JG21. Lt G. de Mallmann *(Commandant)* baled out wounded and captured. Aircraft a write-off.

GC 6/1 Morane 406 (783). Engine set alight in combat with Bf109s during escort sortie for reconnaissance Potez and belly-landed in flames at Nurlu, 8 km north-west of Péronne, 8.30 a.m. Possibly that claimed by Gefr Kempf of 2./JG21. Adjt R. Saussol captured wounded in left leg, and face badly burned, admitted to hospital in St Quentin. Aircraft a write-off.

GC II/3 Morane 406. Forced-landed damaged by AA fire over Villers-Bocage 7.50 a.m. Cpl K. Körber unhurt. Aircraft damaged but repairable.

GC 1/4 Curtiss H-75 (106). Shot down in combat with Bf109s south-west of Douai during escort sortie for reconnaissance Potez 8.30 a.m. Possibly one of those claimed by Uffz Clerico of 1./JG21. Crashed at Sailly-en-Ostrevent, near Étaing. Lt A. Stiquel killed. Aircraft a write-off.

GC 1/4 Curtiss H-75 (109). Shot down in combat with Bf109s during escort sortie for reconnaissance Potez 8.30 a.m. Crashed and burned out at Tortequesne, south-west of Douai. Possibly one of those claimed by Oberlt Scholz *(Staffelkapitän)* of 1./JG21. Adjt J. Hôtellier baled out and captured wounded and burned, admitted to hospital in Cambrai. Aircraft a write-off.

GC 1/4 Curtiss H-75 (84). Engine damaged in combat with Bf109s of I./JG21 south-west of Douai during escort sortie for Potez and belly-landed near Vitry-en-Artois 8.30 a.m. Possibly one of those claimed by Lt Behrens of 1./JG21. Sgt M. Bès captured wounded, admitted to hospital in Cambrai. Aircraft 14 a write-off.

GC I/5 Curtiss H-75. Returned with windscreen shattered by return fire from He111 of Stab/KG55 attacked near Vouziers 12.30 p.m. Capt L. Vasatko slightly wounded with splinters in face. Aircraft repairable.

GC I/6 Morane 406 (773). Shot down by Lt Sidow and Uffz Wissmann of 9./ZG26 during solo attack on enemy bombers north-west of Crépy-en-Valois 1.05 p.m. Belly-landed at Auger-Saint-Vincent, caught fire and burned out. S/Lt J. Halgrin killed. Aircraft a write-off.

GC II/9 Bloch 152 (556). Crashed on landing at Chantilly following combat 12.00 p.m. Pilot unhurt. Aircraft a write-off.

BELGIAN AIR FORCE

7/IV/1 Fox (O.170). Hit a concrete fence and crashed on landing at Steene-Ostend 7.00 p.m. Sgt M. Hodeige and S/Lt A. Rousseau both slightly injured. Aircraft a write-off.

9/V/1 Renard R-31 (N.10). Crashed on landing at Lombardzijde due to poor state of airfield 5.00 a.m. Sgt M. Bruylants unhurt. Aircraft damaged but repairable.

9/V/1 Renard R-31 (N.33). Damaged on landing at Lombardzijde due to poor state of airfield 5.00 a.m. Sgt M. Donnet unhurt. Aircraft damaged but repairable — later abandoned.

After the Belgian collapse, Mike Donnet was arrested by the Germans and held for seven months until his return to Belgium in January 1941. Along with another Belgian pilot, Leon Divoy, he found and made airworthy a Stampe-Vertongen SV-4b trainer in which they escaped to England on the night of July 4/5, 1941 landing near Thorpe-le-Soken after a three-hour flight. Both went on to fly Spitfires with No. 64 Squadron. Mike Donnet later commanded No. 350 (Belgian) Squadron and ended the war as a Wing Commander leading three squadrons of Mustangs with 375 sorties, four enemy aircraft destroyed and five more damaged to his credit. As Lieutenant-General Baron Mike Donnet he held high rank in the post-war Belgian Air Force.

9/V/1 Stampe-Vertongen SV-5. Crashed in emergency landing at Bredene, near Ostend, during transfer flight from Zwevezele to Lombardzijde 5.00 a.m. Pilot unhurt. Aircraft a write-off.

11/VI/1 Renard R-31. Returned to Zwevezele damaged by ground-fire during reconnaissance over the Mandel Canal 11.00 a.m. Capt P. Henry de la Lindi *(Commandant)* and S/Lt A. Goedert unhurt. Aircraft repairable.

At 5.30 a.m. on May 25, Belgian government ministers had met with King Leopold to implore him to relinquish command of the Army and go to France or England with them but he refused; his Order of the Day to his army was simply: 'Whatever may happen, I shall share your fate'. Nevertheless the time had come for Belgium to pull out of the war. This incongruous sight shows an antiquated Renard of 9/V/1 which came to grief when landing at Lombardzijde.

A German soldier pays his respects to a fallen enemy. This wreck is almost unrecognisable as a British Fairey Battle — and we know not where or when — only that a corner of this foreign field is now forever England.

LUFTWAFFE

4./Aufkl.Gr.Ob.d.L Dornier Do215. Believed returned damaged following sortie over Romilly. Flgr P. Düpong killed, rest of crew believed unhurt. Aircraft damaged but repairable.

3.(F)/10 Dornier Do17P (1091). Shot down near Gravelines by F/L Adye, P/O Whittaker, and P/O Manger of No. 17 Squadron during reconnaissance sortie to Lille and Ypres 5.00 a.m. Possibly also that attacked by F/L Toyne. Lt H. Wrba killed. Oberfw W. Hofmann captured badly wounded, died of injuries. Uffz H. Oelkers captured wounded. Aircraft T1+EL a write-off.

3.(H)/13 Henschel Hs126. Shot down by Capt Delfino, Lt Chesnais, Sgt Cucumel, Sgt Leschi, and Sgt Pinson of GC II/9 and forced-landed alongside the road at Sancourt, east of Ham, 9.15 a.m. Oberfw E. Bierwirth died of wounds, gunner baled out. Aircraft damaged but repairable.

4.(H)/21 Henschel Hs126. Attacked by S/Lt Abrioux and Sgt Cazade of GC III/1 near Albert and forced-landed 8.40 a.m. Fw A. Schmollinger wounded, gunner unhurt. Aircraft repairable.

4.(F)/121 Dornier Do17P. Shot down by Adjt Bernavon, Sgt Fortin, and Sgt Desrumeaux of GC II/2 during long-range reconnaissance of rail traffic between St Dié and Langres. Crashed and burned out at 'La Chevanne', north of Valdahon, 5.30 a.m. Lt F-K. Grünwald, Fw H. Vogel, and Uffz G. Nikolai killed. Aircraft a write-off.

1./JG1 Messerschmitt Bf109E-1. Shot down by F/O Ball of No. 19 Squadron in combat over the Channel off Calais during escort sortie for Ju87s of 3./StG76 8.45 a.m. Uffz R. Vogel killed. Aircraft lost.

The bent prop suggests a forced-landing but from the scattered wreckage it looks possible that the aircraft could have come down with its bomb load still intact. Field graves like this were usually soon re-interred to local communal cemeteries.

1./JG2 Messerschmitt Bf109E-3 (931). Shot down in combat with Spitfires of Nos. 19 and 65 Squadrons over Calais. Leutnant M. Jaczak baled out and captured wounded, admitted to hospital in Dunkirk. Aircraft a write-off.

Stab II./JG2 Messerschmitt Bf109E. Belly-landed damaged in combat with Spitfires over Dunkirk. Oberlt F. Liesendahl captured wounded. Aircraft a write-off.

9./JG2 Messerschmitt Bf109E-3. Shot down by Sgt Loï of GC II/3 and crashed north-east of Amiens 9.05 a.m. Possibly also attacked by Capt Delfino and Sgt Cucumel of GC II/9. Gefreiter E. Höhn baled out and captured. Aircraft a write-off.

1./JG21 Messerschmitt Bf109E-3. Shot down in combat with GC III/1 and GC I/4 over Cambrai 8.30 a.m. Possibly one of those claimed by Lt Guillaume of GC I/4. Feldwebel F. Hartwig believed baled out and captured unhurt. Aircraft a write-off.

Fridolin Hartwig is recorded killed at Zuydcoote and was probably a victim of German bombardment while a prisoner awaiting transport to England.

1./JG21 Messerschmitt Bf109E-1. Shot down in combat with GC III/1 and GC I/4 over Cambrai and overturned attempting forced-landing 8.30 a.m. Possibly one of those claimed by Adjt Saussol of GC III/1. Feldwebel K-E. Frentzel-Beyme captured wounded. Aircraft a write-off.

3./JG21 Messerschmitt Bf109E-1. Engine damaged in combat with GC III/1 and GC I/4 over Cambrai and forced-landed at St Pol 8.30 a.m. Possibly that engaged by S/Lt Abrioux of GC III/1. Oberleutnant G. Schneider *(Staffelkapitän)* unhurt. Aircraft a write-off.

2./JG51 Messerschmitt Bf109E-1. Crash-landed at St Pol during sortie, cause not stated but possibly combat damage. Uffz W. Bartsch wounded. Aircraft damaged but repairable.

II./JG52 Messerschmitt Bf109E-1. Wrecked in crash-landing at base, cause not stated. Pilot unhurt. Aircraft a write-off.

9./JG52 Messerschmitt Bf109E-1. Shot down over the Forêt-de-Moyeuvre by S/Lt Villacèque, S/Lt Boudier, and Adjt Audrain of GC II/5 during escort sortie for He111s, crashed and burned out at Briey, near Thionville, 5.25 a.m. Leutnant H. Planer killed. Aircraft a write-off.

Stab JG53 Messerschmitt Bf109E-4. Involved in a collision with a motorcycle at Couvron. No pilot casualty. Aircraft damaged but repairable.

II./JG53 Messerschmitt Bf109E-4. Crashed on landing at Sandweiler, cause not stated. Pilot unhurt. Aircraft a write-off.

4./JG53 Messerschmitt Bf109E-3. Collided with a Do17 during take-off on test flight. Oberlt K. Brändle badly injured. Aircraft a write-off.

9./KG2 Dornier Do17Z. Believed damaged over Ostend and crashed on landing due to poor conditions at Ste-Marie airfield. Lt O-W. Bechtle, Uffz W. Diller, and Uffz Quillitsch unhurt. Aircraft U5+BT damaged but repairable.

7./KG4 Junkers Ju88A-1 (3049). Shot down by P/O Cooper-Slipper of No. 605 Squadron during attack on Dunkirk and crashed in the sea 2.15 p.m. Fw F. Weigel killed. Hptmn H-J. Dr Rabe, Obergefr J. Koch and Gefr G. Thiel missing. Aircraft 5J+KR a write-off.
The body of flight mechanic Fritz Weigel was washed ashore near Wangerooge on July 30.

9./KG4 Junkers Ju88A-1. Shot down by F/L Crossley of No. 32 Squadron and abandoned near Dunkirk 2.15 p.m. Oberlt F. Podbielski, Fw H. Berkefeld, Uffz K. von Kidrowski, and Uffz O. Piontek baled out and rescued unhurt. Aircraft a write-off.

8./KG30 Junkers Ju88A. Crashed shortly after take-off from Schiphol on sortie to Dunkirk and bomb-load exploded 4.36 p.m. Uffz G. Dujardin, Uffz W. Bethe, Obergefr L. Burk, and Gefr J. Lippitsch killed. Aircraft a write-off.
Site investigated by the Stichting Aircraft Recovery Group in December 1998 and many minor components and engine cowling parts recovered.

2./KG53 Heinkel He111H. Shot down by S/Lt Codet of GC II/3 and Sgt Cazade of GC III/1 between Beauvais and Noailles, also attacked by Capt Kerangueven and S/Lt Lansoy of GC III/2. Crashed near Troussencourt where bombs later exploded 2.00 p.m. Lt S. von Goertz killed. Oberfw J. Fraitzl wounded in right arm, Fw F. Gruber, Uffz H. Knobloch, and Flgr W. Herrmann all baled out over La Haute Pommeraie and captured wounded, admitted to hospital in Chantilly. Aircraft A1+GK write-off.

6./KG53 Heinkel He111H. Crashed on landing approach and burned out at Hanauer-Haus, near Rückersbach, following combat sortie. Fw M. Unhold, Fw W. Hardecker, Fw G. Spatscheck, Uffz R. Berner, and Gefr H. Guhl killed. Aircraft a write-off.

III./KG54 Heinkel He111P. Crashed near Celle during test flight. Three civilians injured. Aircraft damaged but repairable.

Stabsstaffel KG55 Heinkel He111P. Landed at Trier-Euren believed damaged in attack by Capt Vasatko of GC I/5 near Vouziers during photo-reconnaissance sortie to Vitryle-François 12.30 p.m Oberlt W. Gottschalk and Uffz R. Fetzer badly wounded. Fw E. Hehs and Uffz K. Krümmel slightly wounded. Aircraft damaged but repairable.

2./KG55 Heinkel He111P. Shot down over Tannay, north-east of Le Chesne, by of GC I/5 during sortie to Vitry-le-François 12.10 p.m. Uffz W. Strothoff killed. Uffz H. Appelt, Uffz W. Fulda, Gefr H. Czaja, and Gefr A. Beigel captured. Aircraft a write-off.

2./KG55 Heinkel He111P. Shot down by Capt Accart, S/Lt Rouquette, Sgt Vuillemain, and Sgt Penzini of GC I/5 during sortie to Vitry-le-François and belly-landed south-east of Brieulles-sur-Bar, north of Germont, 12.30 p.m. Fw W. Kalz, Fw J. Jakobs, Fw K. Michel, Uffz W. Walz, and Uffz H. Henne believed captured. Aircraft G1+KK a write-off.

9./KG76 Dornier Do17Z. Returned damaged by ground-fire during attack on troop concentrations near Flines. Gefr W. Heumer badly wounded, admitted to hospital in Bonn. Aircraft damaged but repairable.

2./KG77 Dornier Do17Z. Suffered direct hit by flak 10 km south of Armentières, crashed and burned out north-east of Fromelles. Maj P-P. Pietrusky *(Staffelkapitän)* and Oberlt H. Möckel killed. Oberfw W. Exner and Fw G. Kästner baled out and believed captured unhurt. Aircraft a write-off.

III./KGzbV.1 Junkers Ju52 (5174). Forced-landed south of Fricourt following attack by S/Lt Abrioux and Sgt Doublet of GC III/1 8.45 a.m. Crew rescued wounded. Aircraft a write-off.

9./LG1 Junkers Ju88A-1 (4014). Shot down by P/O Bird-Wilson of No. 17 Squadron during attack on shipping off Calais. Also attacked by F/L Saunders and Sgt Kilner of No. 65 Squadron. Crashed one engine alight and burned out at Moulle, north-west of St Omer, 6.00 a.m. Oberfw F. Körnig, Uffz R. Kuke, Gefr C-H. Krüger, and Gefr H. Steinhagen killed. Aircraft a write-off.

7./StG2 Junkers Ju87B. Believed shot down by flak near Estaires, west of Lille. Uffz S. Bernrieder and Gefr E. Werner unhurt. Aircraft a write-off.

8./StG51 Junkers Ju87B. Crashed on take-off at Florennes probably due to engine failure. Lt E. Stumbler and Fw F. Zinner both injured. Aircraft a write-off.

3./StG76 Junkers Ju87B (5253). Shot down by No. 19 Squadron Spitfires during attack on shipping and crashed in sea off Calais 8.45 a.m. Lt H. Nietzschmann killed. Uffz K. Rieger missing. Aircraft S1+FL lost.

3./StG76 Junkers Ju87B (0450). Shot down by No. 19 Squadron Spitfires during attack on shipping and crashed in sea off Calais 8.45 a.m. Possibly one of those claimed by F/Lt Clouston. Fw H. Hartmann and Uffz R. Forster both missing. Aircraft S1+EL lost.

3./StG76 Junkers Ju87B. Shot down by No. 19 Squadron Spitfires during attack on shipping and crash-landed south of Calais 8.45 a.m. Uffz A. Knauber and Uffz W. Bock slightly wounded. Aircraft a write-off.

3./StG76 Junkers Ju87B. Landed at Guise damaged by No. 19 Squadron Spitfires during attack on shipping off Calais 8.45 a.m. Pilot unhurt, Fw R. Popp slightly wounded. Aircraft repairable.

I.(St)/TrGr.186 Junkers Ju87B. Returned engine damaged by AA fire over Dunkirk. Crew believed unhurt. Aircraft repairable.

I.(St)/TrGr.186 Junkers Ju87B. Crash-landed damaged by AA fire over Dunkirk, cause unknown. Lt Schimmelpfennig and gunner wounded. Aircraft a write-off.

I.(St)/TrGr.186 Junkers Ju87B. Controls damaged and engine set on fire by AA fire over Dunkirk. Crew believed unhurt. Aircraft a write-off.

I.(St)/TrGr.186 Junkers Ju87B. Returned damaged by AA fire over Dunkirk. Crew believed unhurt. Aircraft damaged but repairable.

Transportstaffel II. Fliegerkorps Junkers Ju52. Forced-landed near Termes damaged by fighters. Crew believed unhurt. Aircraft repairable.

Stab I./ZG1 Messerschmitt Bf110. Shot down in combat over Calais during escort sortie for Ju88s of III./KG4 and belly-landed at Bourbourg alongside the road to Gravelines 2.00 p.m. Oberlt K. Martin *(Gruppen TO)* killed. Fw H. Kräft captured wounded. Aircraft a write-off.

Stab I./ZG1 Messerschmitt Bf110C. Shot down in combat over Calais during escort sortie for Ju88s of III./KG4 and crash-landed south-west of Dunkirk 2.00 p.m. Lt W. Kleinecke and Uffz O. Schamberger captured wounded. Aircraft a write-off.

1./ZG1 Messerschmitt Bf110C. Shot down in combat south-west of Ostend during escort sortie for Ju88s of III./KG4 and crashed near Bourbourg 2.00 p.m. Possibly that claimed by F/O Edge of No. 605 Squadron. Lt G. Wölfle killed. Fw R. Schulze captured wounded. Aircraft a write-off.

1./ZG1 Messerschmitt Bf110C. Shot down in combat during escort sortie for Ju88s of III./KG4 and belly-landed south-west of Ostend 2.00 p.m. Obergefr O. Hoffmann killed. Uffz E. Michi captured wounded. Aircraft a write-off.

Stab I./ZG2 Messerschmitt Bf110C. Crashed into trees during emergency take-off during bombing attack on Neufchâteau airfield. Maj J. Gentzen *(Gruppenkommandeur)* and Lt H-B. Domeier *(Gruppenadjutant)* killed. Aircraft a write-off.

3./ZG2 Messerschmitt Bf110C. Control surfaces damaged by jettisonned canopy and crashed into truck on landing at Neufchâteau airfield. Obergefr H. Schröter badly injured, died May 27. Aircraft a write-off.

3./ZG2 Messerschmitt Bf110C. Crashed into Ju52 and exploded during cross-wind landing at Neufchâteau airfield on return from combat sortie. Lt H. Rosenkranz killed. Aircraft a write-off.

I./ZG26 Messerschmitt Bf110C. Belly-landed at Ciney engine damaged in attack by S/Lt Salva of GC I/3 during escort sortie for Do17s over Meaux-Esbly 1.00 p.m. Crew unhurt. Aircraft damaged but repairable.

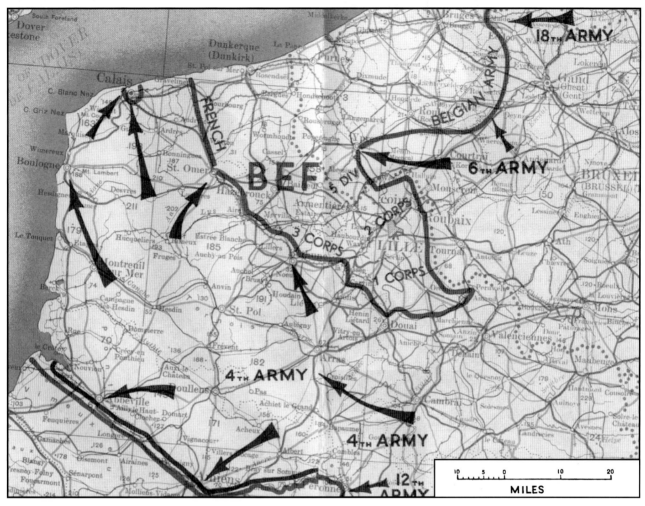

This map showing the situation on Sunday graphically illustrates the precarious position on the north-eastern flank of the British Expeditionary Force through the impending capitulation of the Belgians. In just over two weeks, the German armies had steam-rollered their way across Holland, Belgium, and France. Nearly 1,100 Allied airmen had lost their lives in a vain attempt to halt the advance, although the price for the Luftwaffe had been high with a loss of over 1,010 aircraft and 2,165 crewmen.

Monday, May 27

As full-scale evacuation of the BEF progressed, Dunkirk town and harbour was subjected to intensive air attacks that destroyed most of the town and set oil storage tanks ablaze resulting in the vast plume of black smoke which was to become one of the most enduring images of the war. German guns, recently installed at Gravelines, dominated the coast and prevented ships approaching Dunkirk from the west. This made a longer easterly approach necessary until a more direct central route could be cleared. The heavy air attacks made further embarkation from the harbour impossible, or so it was thought, and consequently British troops were forced onto the sand dunes and beaches outside the town which severely restricted evacuation plans. Meanwhile, the diminishing bridgehead remained under constant enemy pressure with German artillery already in positions little more than five miles distant and posing an increasing threat to both port and shipping.

Inland, the Anglo-French retirement north of the Lys had begun, exhausted and demoralised troops taking up new positions during the night. While on the Allied left flank, the situation suddenly deteriorated when the Belgian line through Roulers to Thielt finally collapsed under the weight of German air and ground attacks. At 5.45 p.m. Belgian GHQ announced that King Leopold had requested an armistice effective from mid-

night. This not altogether unexpected news effectively opened a 20-mile gap in the line on the left of the BEF between Ypres and the coast but, fortunately, the British were able to establish new defensive positions planned for in the event of a Belgian collapse.

At first light, 12 Lysanders dropped urgently needed water supplies to the beleaguered garrison at Calais, a further drop of ammunition following at around 10.00 a.m. Coinciding with this mission, nine Swordfish, plus the elderly Hectors of No. 613 Squadron, attacked enemy gun positions in the area. Three Lysanders were lost and one Hector crashed near Dover on return, these losses all the more regrettable as, unknown to Back Component, the Calais garrison had surrendered the previous evening.

From mid-afternoon, once news of the fall of Calais had finally reached Fighter Command, patrols became even more heavily concentrated on Dunkirk, with patrol lines primarily between Gravelines and Furnes but with incursions, by Hurricane squadrons, from Dunkirk or Furnes inland to St Omer. As far as possible, the bridgehead was constantly patrolled by at least one of the 16 squadrons involved from 5.00 a.m. to 9.30 p.m. — most units flying two, and sometimes three, sorties a day. When operating as single squadrons, RAF fighters occasionally found themselves outnumbered but still remained confident that they were inflicting greater losses on the enemy than they themselves suffered.

By nightfall, the Luftwaffe had launched at least a dozen heavy air attacks on Dunkirk during the day which seriously impeded

evacuation and which, despite their best efforts, RAF fighters had been unable to prevent — an impossible as it was implausible expectation. RAF fighter patrols surely limited enemy air activity in the Dunkirk area but, as the official narrative confirms, 'to what exact degree it is very difficult to say'. Fighter Command mounted a total of 287 sorties on the day from which 19 aircraft failed to return with the loss of 11 pilots, four more returning wounded.

With poor visibility reported early in the day, No. 2 Group Blenheims operated throughout the afternoon and early evening flying four separate attacks and finding no shortage of targets around St Omer. Thirty-six sorties were flown between 2.30 p.m. and 7.15 p.m., all without fighter protection, and two aircraft lost during an attack on vehicles south of St Omer and AA batteries near Clairmarais.

At night, the AASF despatched 36 Battles to targets across the south-west Ardennes, with ten Bomber Command Hampdens attacking the usual Meuse crossings while enemy communications further afield were visited by 35 Wellingtons. Bomber Command aircraft also operated against rail targets deeper in Germany making the total effort that night 159 sorties, all of which returned without loss. Meantime, single Blenheims of No. 604 Squadron maintained a constant vigil over the north French coast but were spread too thin to prevent He115s of KuFlGr.106 from sowing 24 mines off Dunkirk, Zeebrugge, and Ostend, while nine Ju88s of III./KG4 bombed Zeebrugge harbour installations.

BRITISH AIR FORCES IN FRANCE

1 SQUADRON, ANGLURE

2 Hurricanes. Returned from patrol slightly damaged by AA fire. Pilots unhurt. Aircraft both repairable.

88 SQUADRON, LES GRANDES-CHAPELLES

Battle L5333. Hit a tree on take-off for night operations and forced-landed. Sergeant D. Haywood unhurt. Sergeant J. R. A. Jones and LAC E. S. Williams both slightly injured. Aircraft damaged but repairable.

501 SQUADRON, MOURMELON-LE-GRAND

Hurricane P2714. Crashed on landing due to poor state of airfield after attack on He111s of 1./KG53 between Blargies and Abancourt 2.00 p.m. Sgt P. C. P. Farnes unhurt. Aircraft damaged but repairable — later abandoned.

Hurricane. Shot down during attack on He111s of 1./KG53 between Blargies and Abancourt and crash-landed near Rouen 2.05 p.m. Pilot Officer J. A. A. Gibson unhurt. Aircraft abandoned.

UK-based aircraft lost or damaged on operations over the Western Front:

RAF AIR COMPONENT

16 Squadron, Lympne
Supply drop Calais:

Lysander P1685. Badly damaged by AA fire during supply drop at Calais and crashed on return 5.45 a.m. F/Lt G. R. Shepley and Cpl Jones both wounded. Aircraft a write-off.

26 Squadron, Lympne
Reconnaissance / Supply drop Calais:

Lysander L4782. Shot down during armed reconnaissance and crashed near Sangatte 5.40 a.m. P/O H. D. Dixon and LAC D. McL. Nimmo killed. Aircraft a write-off.

At first light on Monday morning, Back Component sent 12 Lysanders on a supply-dropping mission to besieged Calais — not knowing that the Germans had over-run the town the night before. More aircraft followed later in an attempt to drop water and ammunition to the troops believed to be still holding out in the Citadel on the west side of Calais. Three aircraft failed to return, this Lysander crashing right on top of Fort Risban which controlled the entrance to the harbour. We believe this is L6863 of No. 26 Squadron in which Pilot Officer Ernest Howarth and Leading Aircraftman John Bolton were killed.

Lysander L6863. Shot down during supply drop and crashed east of Calais 10.20 a.m. P/O E. E. Howarth and LAC J. A. Bolton killed. Aircraft a write-off.

Lysander N1243. Shot down during supply drop at Calais 10.20 a.m. P/O J. H. Deas and Sgt T. McLoughlin killed. Aircraft a write-off.

613 Squadron, Lympne
Gun positions at Calais:

Hector K8116. Crashed in fog at Shakespeare Cliff, Dover, on return from bombing enemy artillery at Calais 10.30 a.m. P/O Kenkyns badly injured, LAC R. V. Brown died of injuries. Aircraft a write-off.

The scenes of brave deeds as they appear today. The fortress still stands abandoned with a camp site on its roof.

RAF BOMBER COMMAND

53 Squadron, Hawkinge
Reconnaissance:

Blenheim L8735. Shot down by Oberfw Labusga of 6./JG3 and crashed near Faumont, north of Douai, 6.35 a.m. P/O P. F. C. Villiers-Tuthill, Sgt D. B. Mearns, and Sgt A. H. Payne killed. Aircraft a write-off.

Blenheim R3703. Badly damaged by enemy fighters and abandoned over St Margarets, north of Dover, on return a.m. P/O Aldridge and AC Trafford baled out injured, Sgt McRae unhurt. Aircraft a write-off.

Blenheim R3735. Returned damaged by Bf109s between Hoogstade — Poperinge — St Omer 12.45 p.m. P/O Robinson, AC Couchen, and another all wounded. Aircraft repairable.

107 Squadron, Wattisham
Troop concentrations St Omer:

Blenheim IV L9391. Shot down by AA fire and crashed at Eperlecques, north-west of St Omer, 6.45 p.m. Cpl G. E. Lang killed. W/Cdr B. E. Embry *(Squadron Commander)* and P/O T. A. Whiting baled out and captured. Aircraft a write-off.
This was to have been Basil Embry's last sortie before relinquishing command on his appointment as Station Commander, West Raynham. He escaped two days later and evaded recapture returning via Paris, Madrid, and Gibraltar in early August 1940. His account Mission Completed *was published by Methuen in 1957.*

Blenheim IV N6192. Shot down by Bf109s of 5./JG53 and believed crashed near Calais-Marck 6.50 p.m. Sgt H. Warman, Sgt W. C. H. Paish, and LAC J. Mahoney missing. Aircraft lost.
No trace of this crew was reported found and they are now commemorated on the Runnymede Memorial.

RAF FIGHTER COMMAND

54 Squadron, Hornchurch
Patrol Dunkirk:

Spitfire N3030. Failed to return after attack on Ju88 over Dunkirk 5.30 a.m. F/L M. C. Pearson missing. Aircraft KL⊙T a write-off.

56 Squadron, Manston
Offensive patrols:

Hurricane P3478. Reported hit by Belgian flak during attack on He111s of KG54 but possibly that claimed by Uffz Philipp of 4./JG26. Abandoned near Ostend 4.15 p.m. P/O M. H. C. Maxwell baled out unhurt. Aircraft a write-off.

Hurricane P3311. Shot down by Bf109s during attack on He111s of KG54 and ditched in sea off Ostend 4.15 p.m. Possibly that claimed by Fw Lüders of 6./JG26. F/Lt R. H. A. Lee rescued unhurt. Aircraft a write-off.

Hurricane P3355. Forced-landed radiator damaged during combat with Bf110s of II./ZG1 and I./ZG52 over Dunkirk 7.20 p.m. F/O Fisher wounded, returned by sea and admitted to Margate Hospital. Aircraft a write-off.

Hurricane L2076. Returned fuel tank damaged during combat with Bf110s of II./ZG1 and I./ZG52 over Dunkirk 7.25 p.m. Sgt G. Smythe unhurt. Aircraft repairable.

65 Squadron, Hornchurch
Patrol Calais:

Spitfire N3128. Returned damaged by return fire from Do17 of KG2 engaged near Calais 7.40 a.m. F/O G. Proudman slightly wounded in left leg. Aircraft damaged but repairable.

74 Squadron, Rochford
Patrol Calais — Dunkirk:

Spitfire L1084. Radiator damaged by return fire from Do17 and belly-landed near Dunkirk 10.00 a.m. P/O P. C. F. Stevenson unhurt. Aircraft destroyed by pilot.
With singular dedication, Paddy Stevenson removed the blind-flying panel, reflector gunsight, and radio before setting fire to his aircraft and heading for Dunkirk. En route he also dismantled the blind-flying panel from Spitfire N3103 of No. 54 Squadron (see May 25, page 362) and arranged for removal of its guns and ammunition.

Spitfire K9875. Glycol tank holed by return fire during attack on Do17 of 3./KG3 and engaged by flak near Oye-Plage while seeking a landing place. Finally belly-landed near Gravelines 4.15 p.m. F/Lt W. P. F. Treacy captured unhurt, escaped but later recaptured. Aircraft a write-off.
Later that year 'Paddy' Treacy made another successful escape bid and eventually got back to England via Spain and Eire.

145 Squadron, Tangmere
Patrol Dunkirk — Calais:

Hurricane P2723. Shot down in the sea during combat with Bf110s and possibly one of those claimed by Oberlt Müller *(Staffelkapitän)* of 13.(Z)/LG1 south-west of Dunkirk 2.30 p.m. P/O A. Elson missing. Aircraft lost.

Hurricane N2713. Shot down in combat with Bf110s of V.(Z)/LG1 north-west of St Omer and possibly that claimed by Lt Beck of 13.(Z)/LG1 2.30 p.m. P/O P. H. O'C. Rainier killed. Aircraft a write-off.

Hurricane N2711. Shot down in combat with Bf110s of V.(Z)/LG1 south-west of Dunkirk and possibly that claimed by Oberlt Glienke of 13.(Z)/LG1 2.30 p.m. Sgt A. Bailey captured. Aircraft SO⊙D a write-off.

Hurricane N2710. Shot down in combat with Bf110s of II./ZG1 and I./ZG52 over Dunkirk 7.45 p.m. Possibly that claimed by Fw Lutter of 6./ZG1. P/O D. N. Forde slightly wounded. Aircraft a write-off.

Hurricane P3314. Shot down in combat with Bf110s of II./ZG1 and I./ZG52 over Dunkirk 7.45 p.m. Possibly that attacked by Uffz Maske of 6./ZG1. P/O E. C. J. Wakeham slightly wounded. Aircraft a write-off.

Hurricane. Shot down in combat with Bf110s of II./ZG1 and I./ZG52 over Dunkirk 7.45 p.m. Possibly that claimed by Lt Hermichen of 6./ZG1. P/O J. H. Ashton unhurt. Aircraft a write-off.

601 Squadron, Tangmere
Patrol Dunkirk:

Hurricane P3486. Shot down in combat with Bf110s of II./ZG1 and I./ZG52 over Diksmuide and crashed at Nieuwpoortstraat in Oostkerke 7.50 p.m. Possibly one of those claimed by Lt Schmid of I./ZG52. F/O C. A. Lee-Steere killed. Aircraft a write-off.

Hurricane P2568. Damaged in combat with Bf110s of II./ZG1 and I./ZG52 and belly-landed on beach east of Dunkirk 7.50 p.m. Possibly that claimed by Oberlt Grasser of 3./ZG52. F/Lt Sir A. P. Hope unhurt. Aircraft UF⊙R fired by pilot.

605 Squadron, Hawkinge
Escort Blenheims to St Omer:

Hurricane L2119. Went down over Poperinge following inconclusive attack on Do17 of KG2 and crash-landed 9.45 a.m. F/O N. Forbes captured. Aircraft a write-off.

Hurricane P3423. Shot down by Bf110s of 8./ZG26 during attack on Do17s of KG3 and crashed in sea off Dunkirk 3.10 p.m. Possibly one of those claimed by Oberlt Baagoe. S/L G. V. Perry missing. Aircraft lost.

Hurricane P3581. Shot down by Bf110s during attack on Do17s of KG3 and crashed in sea off Dunkirk 3.10 p.m. Possibly that claimed by Oberlt Meyer *(Staffelkapitän)* of 8./ZG26. F/O P. J. Danielson missing. Aircraft lost.

610 Squadron, Gravesend
Patrol Dunkirk — Furnes:

Spitfire L1016. Shot down in combat with Bf110s of II./ZG1 and I./ZG52 off Dunkirk 7.15 p.m. Possibly one of those claimed by Lt Marchfelder of Stab II./ZG1. F/O A. R. J. Medcalf missing. Aircraft DW⊙Q lost.

Spitfire L1003. Shot down in combat with Bf110s of II./ZG1 and I./ZG52 over Nieuport and crashed near Oostduinkerke 7.15 p.m. Possibly another claimed by Lt Marchfelder of Stab II./ZG1. Sgt W. T. Medway killed. Aircraft DW⊙J a write-off.

Spitfire. Nosed-over due to burst starboard tyre making dead-stick landing out of fuel after combat with Bf110s of II./ZG1 and I./ZG52 over Nieuport 7.45 p.m. F/O J. Kerr-Wilson unhurt. Aircraft repairable.

No. 601 Squadron lost two Hurricanes on May 27. One was burned out on the beach and the other some 12 kilometres inland near Diksmuide. There are no clues where the squdron lost this machine and no record in the Operations Record Book as to the fate of UF⊙B.

The attrition rate against the Luftwaffe was still very heavy with 43 aircraft lost and many more damaged. This is one of the write-offs — Unteroffizier Johann Rulfs' Dornier of 9./KG2 lying in a field at Maldegem near the Belgian-Dutch border.

FRENCH AIR FORCE

ECN 2/13 Potez 631 (33). Shot down by Fw Kornatz of 2./JG53 west of Noyon and crashed at Thiescourt 6.15 p.m. S/Lt J. Reyter, Adjt R. Baladier (of ECMJ 1/16), and Adjt E. Bourlon killed. Aircraft a write-off.

ECN 4/13 Potez 631 (146). Shot down by Bf109s and belly-landed at Chavigny, 5 km north of Soissons, where further strafed on the ground. Possibly that claimed by Fw Kaiser of 2./JG53 west of Noyon 6.16 p.m. Adjt A. Guichard badly wounded, died next day. S/Lt Odin and Sgt Ducancelle unhurt. Aircraft a write-off.

GAO 1/506 Potez 63.11 (413). Reportedly attacked by Bf109s during reconnaissance sortie over Virton and crashed outside Marville, 10 km south-east of Montmédy. S/Lt M. Coignier and Sgt J. Goetz killed. Lt. Sognet seriously wounded. Aircraft a write-off.

GAO 510 Potez 63.11 (623). Damaged by flak then attacked by Fw Frey of 1.(J)/LG2 during observation mission south of Amiens bridge. Crashed at Chaussoy-Épagny, 5 km south of Ailly-sur-Noye 12.10 p.m. Sgt P. Lucas killed. Capt Smet and Sgt A. Guesnel baled out unhurt. Aircraft a write-off.

GB I/11 LeO 451 (3001). Landed back at Étampes with tyre punctured by flak during bombing of troop concentrations near Bapaume 1.00 a.m. Crew unhurt. Aircraft repairable.

GB I/21 Bloch 210 (86). Crashed on take-off at Pont-sur-Yonne. Crew unhurt. Aircraft a write-off.

GB II/21 Amiot 354 (12). Returned to La Ferté-Gaucher damaged after night attack on Cambrai-Niergnies. No crew casualties. Aircraft repairable.

GC I/2 8 Morane 406s (667). Caught on the ground at Damblain airfield in enemy strafing attacks and burned out 1.20 p.m. No pilot casualties. Aircraft all write-offs.
Seven claims filed by 7./JG53 at this time remain unresolved. They were mainly for Moranes but '10 km south of Creil' a location that does not correspond to recorded French losses.

GC 2/8 Bloch 152 (555). 'Bounced' by Bf109s of III./JG53 over Amiens following escort sortie for Potez 63.11s between Albert and Valenciennes 8.10 a.m. Crashed and burned out at Le Quesnel, north of Montdidier and possibly that claimed by Lt Kunert of 8./JG53. Cpl A. Kralik killed. Aircraft a write-off.

GC 2/8 Bloch 152 (236). 'Bounced' by Bf109s over Amiens following escort sortie for Potez 63.11s between Albert and Valenciennes 8.10 a.m. Set alight and abandoned over Château Blin de Bourbon near Roye — one of those claimed by Hptmn Mölders (*Gruppenkommandeur*) of Stab III./JG53. S/Lt H. de Castel baled out badly burned on hands and face. Aircraft a write-off.

GC 2/8 Bloch 152. Returned to Claye-Souilly with port wing and aileron badly damaged in attack by Bf109s of III./JG53 over Amiens 8.10 a.m. Possibly that claimed by Lt Panten of 8./JG53. S/Lt P. Gouachon unhurt. Aircraft damaged but repairable.

GC II/8 Bloch 152. Damaged in landing accident at Deauville 8.10 p.m. Possibly result of a collision. Adjt Veyrunes unhurt. Aircraft damaged but repairable.

GC II/8 Bloch 152. Wrecked in landing accident at Deauville 8.10 p.m. Possibly result of a collision. S/Lt Mousset badly injured in face. Aircraft a write-off.

GC 1/145 Caudron C-714 (8576). Damaged at Villacoublay, exact circumstances not recorded. Pilot believed unhurt. Aircraft I-234 damaged but repairable.

GR 1/55 Potez 63.11 (679). Badly damaged by flak during reconnaissance sortie south of Neuf-Brisach then attacked by Lt Gehlhaar of 4./JG52 and crash-landed and later exploded at Heiteren 6.25 p.m. Lt Auzeing, Sgt Grancher, and Adjt Pouzol unhurt. Aircraft a write-off.

SESBR Caudron Goéland (215). Damaged in accident at Querqueville, cause unknown. No crew casualties. Aircraft repairable.
Section d'Entraînement et de Servitude Brest was training unit for navy pilots based at Lanvéoc-Poulmic.

BELGIAN AIR FORCE

9/V/1 Renard R-31. Returned to Lombardzijde seriously damaged by AA fire during reconnaissance over Eeklo 9.00 a.m. Sgt M. Bruylants and Cpl A. Charlier unhurt. Aircraft a write-off.

LUFTWAFFE

3.(F)/11 Dornier Do17P. Shot down by Sgt Tourné of GC II/3 during observation sortie east of Roye and crashed at Monceau-le-Neuf-et-Faucouzy, north of Laon, 7.05 a.m. Uffz G. Frenzel killed, Lt H. Veil and Uffz L. W. Lüttmann believed unhurt. Aircraft a write-off.

4.(H)/13 Fieseler Fi156. Crash-landed at Ruit during courier flight. Pilot believed unhurt. Aircraft a write-off.

4.(H)/22 Henschel Hs126. Shot down by F/O Brinsden and F/Sgt Unwin of No. 19 Squadron during observation sortie and crashed at Polincove, south-east of Ardres, 8.30 p.m. Lt K. Hauser slightly wounded. Aircraft a write-off.

4.(H)/22 Henschel Hs126. Crashed on transit flight to Paderborn. Lt Schumacher believed unhurt. Aircraft a write-off.

4.(F)/122 Junkers Ju88A-1. Forced-landed badly damaged by fighters south of Calais and probably that engaged by F/Lt Pearson of No. 54 Squadron 5.30 a.m. Uffz W. Becker and Gefr J. Speck slightly wounded, rest of crew unhurt. Aircraft a write-off.

3.(F)/123 Dornier Do17P. Port engine destroyed in attacks by Adjt Poincenot and Sgt Killy of GC II/3 during reconnaissance between Reims and La Fère, and forced-landed in flames near Amiens 7.15 a.m. Lt O. Schmidt, Uffz H. Wecker, and Uffz J. Eggl badly wounded, admitted to hospital. Aircraft a write-off.

3.(F)/123 Junkers Ju88A. Forced-landed at Langendiebach damaged by flak during reconnaissance between Amiens and Clermont. Uffz E. Riehle badly wounded. Aircraft damaged but repairable.

I./JG1 Messerschmitt Bf109E-3. Shot down in combat with Spitfires of No. 74 Squadron and Defiants of No. 264 Squadron east of Dunkirk 10.15 a.m. Pilot unhurt. Aircraft a write-off.

1./JG1 Messerschmitt Bf109E-3. Badly damaged in action with Spitfires of No. 74 Squadron and Defiants of No. 264 Squadron and abandoned east of Dunkirk 10.15 a.m. Leutnant H. Wasserzier baled out and captured wounded, admitted to hospital in Dunkirk. Aircraft 9 a write-off.

5./JG2 Messerschmitt Bf109E. Shot down by F/L Wight of No. 213 Squadron in combat east of Dunkirk and abandoned over Furnes 5.10 p.m. Feldwebel R. Heberlein baled out and captured wounded. Aircraft a write-off.

5./JG2 Messerschmitt Bf109E. Shot down by F/L Wight of No. 213 Squadron in combat east of Dunkirk and abandoned over Furnes 5.10 p.m. Leutnant W. Schetelig baled out but killed. Aircraft a write-off.

3./JG26 Messerschmitt Bf109E. Forced-landed at Boechout, south-east of Antwerp, following engine failure. Pilot unhurt. Aircraft damaged but repairable.

7./JG26 Messerschmitt Bf109E-3 (1202). Damaged in aborted take-off at Chièvres. Leutnant K. Mietusch unhurt. Aircraft damage state not recorded.

Stab JG27 Messerschmitt Bf109E-3. Returned damaged in combat with Spitfires of No. 74 Squadron and Defiants of No. 264 Squadron east of Dunkirk 10.15 a.m. Pilot unhurt. Aircraft damaged but repairable.

2./JG53 Messerschmitt Bf109E. Returned with cockpit damaged by return fire from Potez 631 of ECN 2/13 engaged west of Noyon 6.15 p.m. Fw H. Kornatz slightly wounded. Aircraft repairable.

3./KG1 Heinkel He111H. Returned damaged following sortie over Dunkirk 7.15 p.m. Possibly that attacked by F/O Smith of No. 610 Squadron. Obergefr J. Krause killed, rest of crew unhurt. Aircraft repairable.

Stabsstaffel KG2 Dornier Do17Z. Shot down over Oostvleteren during sortie to Nieuport and forced-landed south-west of Diksmuide. Hptmn J. Schulte-Frohlinde (*Staffelkapitän*) and Uffz W. Kirschmann (of 9./KG2) captured unhurt. Uffz K. Schütz and Obergefr R. Seidel (of 2./LNRgt.3) captured wounded in ground fighting. Aircraft a write-off.

3./KG2 Dornier Do17Z. Forced-landed at Trier-Euren badly damaged by S/Ldr Cooke and F/Sgt McPherson of No. 65 Squadron during sortie to attack harbour installations and roads between Ostend and Dunkirk 7.40 a.m. Gefr H. Heimann slightly wounded, admitted to hospital. Uffz P. Broich, Uffz W. Süptitz, and Uffz Sesner unhurt. Aircraft U5+CL damaged but repairable.

6./KG2 Dornier Do17Z. Force-landed near Giessen out of fuel following sortie over Ostend and Dunkirk 7.40 a.m. Possibly attacked by F/O Proudman of No. 65 Squadron. Oberfw H. Wolf and crew believed unhurt. Aircraft damaged but repairable.

8./KG2 Dornier Do17Z. Returned damaged in attack by No. 17 Squadron Hurricanes near Ostend 1.50 p.m. Lt Steudel and crew unhurt. Aircraft damaged but repairable.

8./KG2 Dornier Do17Z. Crashed on landing at Ste-Marie due to poor state of ground. Oberfw Wolff and crew unhurt. Aircraft damaged but repairable.

9./KG2 Dornier Do17Z. Badly damaged in attacks by No. 17 Squadron Hurricanes during sortie west of Ostend and belly-landed near Maldegem 2.00 p.m. Possibly that claimed by Sgt Steward. Gefr K. Gasser badly wounded, admitted to hospital. Uffz H. Glaser, Uffz J. Rulfs and Uffz F. Wieland slightly injured. Aircraft U5+CT a write-off.

9./KG2 Dornier Do17Z. Badly damaged in attack by No. 17 Squadron Hurricanes during sortie west of Ostend and crash-landed northeast of Schoondijke, south of Breskens, 2.00 p.m. Possibly that claimed by F/O Meredith. Lt W. Stöcker and Uffz J. Heutz slightly wounded, rest of crew unhurt. Aircraft a write-off.

I./KG3 Dornier Do17Z. Belly-landed damaged by fighters during sortie over Dunkirk. Crew believed unhurt. Aircraft damaged but repairable.

2./KG3 Dornier Do17Z. Shot down near Gravelines. Lt H. Hampel and Obergefr R. Lock killed. Uffz W. Köllner baled out wounded, another crewman also baled out unhurt. Aircraft a write-off.

3./KG3 Dornier Do17Z. Believed returned badly damaged by flak and fighters near Hondschoote, south-east of Dunkirk 4.00 p.m. Gefr J. Hölzle slightly wounded, admitted to hospital in Leipzig. Rest of crew believed unhurt. Aircraft a write-off.

3./KG3 Dornier Do17Z. Damaged by flak and ground-fire near Hondschoote, south-east of Dunkirk, and believed forced-landed near Brussels 4.15 p.m. Uffz H. Hirche killed during landing. Uffz W. Rohde badly injured, admitted to hospital. Uffz H. Zimmermann, Gefr F. Schäfer, and Gefr H. Brandt slightly wounded. Aircraft a write-off.

3./KG3 Dornier Do17Z. Believed shot down by F/L Treacy and P/O Stephen of No. 74 Squadron over Hondschoote, south-east of Dunkirk, crashed and burned out south-west of Fruges 4.00 p.m. Lt W. Kornblum and crew unhurt. Aircraft a write-off.

II./KG3 Dornier Do17Z. Returned damaged by fighters during sortie to Dunkirk 4.00 p.m. Crew believed unhurt. Aircraft damaged but repairable.

4./KG3 Dornier Do17Z. Badly damaged by AA fire over Dunkirk near Brussels 4.15 p.m. Fw H. Pippig badly wounded, admitted to hospital. Lt K. Dümler and rest of crew unhurt. Aircraft a write-off.

4./KG3 Dornier Do17Z. Shot down on sortie to Dunkirk and crashed at Melden, south-west of Oudenaarde 4.00 p.m. Fw E. Quosdorf, Uffz W. Brand, and Obergefr A. Latzel killed. Uffz K. Bergk badly wounded, died in hospital. Aircraft a write-off.

4./KG3 Dornier Do17Z. Shot down on sortie to Dunkirk and crash-landed near Moorslede 4.00 p.m. Uffz E. Willenbockel killed. Fw A. Vogel and Gefr K. Zauner badly wounded, admitted to hospital in Celles. Oberfw W. Stolle slightly wounded. Aircraft a write-off.

4./KG3 Dornier Do17Z. Shot down by flak over Ostend and crashed near Stabroeck, north of Antwerp 3.45 p.m. Gefr R. Brandt killed, rest of crew believed unhurt. Aircraft a write-off.

III./KG3 Dornier Do17Z. Returned damaged by fighters near Rombies-et-Marchipont, east of Valenciennes. Crew believed unhurt. Aircraft damaged but repairable.

7./KG3 Dornier Do17Z. Shot down by F/O Measures and P/O St John of No. 74 Squadron over Boulogne and crashed near Bécourt, south-east of Desvres 4.00 p.m. Lt H. Frenzel, Oberfw R. Bärthel, and Gefr W. Schmidt killed. Flgr R. Wetzel baled out badly wounded, admitted to hospital in Montreuil. Aircraft a write-off.

7./KG3 Dornier Do17Z. Returned damaged by flak and fighters over Senlecques, east of Desvres, during sortie over Boulogne 4.00 p.m. Uffz A. Heilmeier killed. Flgr J. Staffler badly wounded, rest of crew believed unhurt. Aircraft damage state not recorded.

7./KG3 Dornier Do17Z. Shot down by AA fire and crashed and burned out south of Ostend 3.45 p.m. Lt K. Kommoss and Uffz L. Kraus both badly wounded, admitted to hospital; rest of crew unhurt. Aircraft a write-off.

8./KG3 Dornier Do17Z. Believed returned badly damaged by fighters south-east of Diksmuide 4.00 p.m. Fw O. Kühn killed. Lt H. Grube badly wounded, admitted to hospital in Jülich-Aachen. Rest of crew believed unhurt. Aircraft a write-off.

9./KG3 Dornier Do17Z. Belly-landed Cologne-Ostheim damaged by flak over Ostend 3.45 p.m. Uffz E. Grunwald badly wounded, admitted to hospital in Hohenlind. Aircraft damaged but repairable.

9./KG3 Dornier Do17Z. Shot down by fighters over Boulogne and crash-landed between St Omer and St Pol where later exploded 4.30 p.m. Uffz G. Weiss and Uffz F. Ortmeier slightly wounded. Oberlt Guttmann and Oberlt Böcher believed unhurt. Aircraft a write-off.

Remarkably, Oberfeldwebel Johannes Groneberg's Heinkel 1G+EA from the staff flight of KG27 was listed in the records of the German Quartermaster as 'Repairable'!

Stab KG27 Heinkel He111. Damaged over Dunkirk and forced-landed near Sittard. Oberlt H. Schmid, Oberfw J. Groneberg and rest of crew unhurt. Aircraft 1G+EA damaged but repairable.

5./KG27 Heinkel He111P. Starboard engine hit by flak and abandoned by crew east of Diksmuide. Believed belly-landed at Krefeld airfield. Uffz L. Künast baled out but killed. Fw O. Kirch baled out and captured wounded. Uffz E. Steinhoff baled out and captured unhurt. Uffz H. Meyer believed unhurt. Aircraft damaged but repairable.

7./KG27 Heinkel He111P. Hit by flak over Roulers and abandoned near Beveren. Oberlt E. Bertelsmann baled out at 1,200 feet but killed. Obergefr H. Krause baled out and captured wounded, admitted to hospital. Lt O. Dold and another crewman believed baled out and both captured unhurt. Aircraft 1G+ER a write-off.
This crew was fired upon by Belgian troops while in their parachutes.

Stabsstaffel KG51 Junkers Ju88A. Belly-landed at Mannheim-Stadt with engine failure following sortie over Dunkirk. Crew unhurt. Aircraft damaged but repairable.

I./KG51 Junkers Ju88A. Forced-landed near Mannheim damaged by AA fire over Dunkirk. Crew unhurt. Aircraft a write-off.

I./KG51 Junkers Ju88A. Forced-landed near Brussels damaged by AA fire over Dunkirk. Crew unhurt. Aircraft damaged but repairable.

3./KG51 Junkers Ju88A. Belly-landed near Abbeville damaged by fighters over Dunkirk. Crew unhurt. Aircraft damaged but repairable.

2./KG51 Junkers Ju88A. Belly-landed at Brussels-Evere badly damaged by flak and fighters over Dunkirk. Lt A. Berger badly wounded, Uffz H. Puls slightly wounded, both admitted to hospital. Aircraft a write-off.

2./KG51 Junkers Ju88A. Forced-landed at Cologne-Wahn damaged in combat over Dunkirk. Crew unhurt. Aircraft damaged but repairable.

Stabsstaffel III./KG51 Heinkel He111. Returned damaged by Defiants of No. 264 Squadron during photo-reconnaissance over Dunkirk 12.20 p.m. Possibly that attacked by S/L Hunter, Sgt King, P/O Young and LAC Johnson. Gefr S. Beelitz slightly wounded, rest of crew unhurt. Aircraft damaged but repairable.

7./KG51 Heinkel He111P. Shot down by Defiants of No. 264 Squadron during attack on Dunkirk and crashed in sea 12.30 p.m. Probably that claimed by F/L Cooke and Cpl Lippett, P/O Welch and LAC Hayden, and P/O Whitley and LAC Turner. Lt R. Gild and Fw A. Göttlicher killed. Uffz H. Kannewurf, Gefr A. Kassegger, and Gefr P. Bartelt missing. Aircraft lost.

8./KG51 Heinkel He111. Returned damaged by Defiants of No. 264 Squadron in combat over Dunkirk 12.20 p.m. Possibly that attacked by F/L Whitehouse and P/O Scott. Uffz F. Schlupp slightly wounded, rest of crew unhurt. Aircraft damaged but repairable.

1./KG53 Heinkel He111H. Forced-landed on return damaged by No. 501 Squadron Hurricanes east of Forges-les-Eaux during sortie to bomb roads and railway between Amiens and Rouen 2.00 p.m. Gefr H. Hampel badly wounded, died in hospital August 26; rest of crew unhurt. Aircraft damaged but repairable.

Though anecdotal evidence is common, authenticated cases of German airmen being shot in their parachutes during the Battle of France are rare. Several reports by Allied pilots who baled out and came under fire leave no doubt that it was no isolated event and it is widely accepted that Oberleutnant Eberhard Bertelsmann of 7. Staffel of Kampfgeschwader 27 was one such helpless airman shot dead as he floated down to earth. This was reported by Cynrik De Decker and Jean-Louis Roba in 1993, citing Walter Cnudde, an eye-witness at Beveren, north of Roeslare, who recalled that three He111s appeared from the direction of Ardooie flying west towards Gitsberg and Hooglede and were engaged by 'intensive fire' from a mobile light AA unit stationed in the village. One was hit, four men baling out, the aircraft crashing nearby. A letter from Bertelsmann's brother Ernst, documented by De Decker and Roba, quotes an account by the local parish priest and testimony from the sexton stating that, 'The three airmen were fired at in their parachutes by Belgian soldiers. My brother hit the ground after his parachute folded up'. Yet Obergefreiter Heinz Krause, who also baled out at 1,200 feet, made no mention of the fact that they were fired at in their parachutes nor, apparently, did the other two crewmen, simply reporting that Bertelsmann 'probably' failed to open his parachute. Whatever the truth, he now rests in Block 42, Grave 110, at Lommel.

1./KG53 Heinkel He111H. Shot down by No. 501 Squadron Hurricanes east of Forges-les-Eaux during sortie to bomb roads and railway between Amiens and Rouen, and crashed at Neuville-Coppegueule 2.05 p.m. Gefr E. Tscherne killed. Uffz G. Berger seriously wounded. Oberfw J. Eberl, Fw H-H. Werner, and Gefr P. Klimaschka baled out and captured wounded, treated in hospital in Aumale. Aircraft A1+HH a write-off.

1./KG53 Heinkel He111H. Returned damaged by No. 501 Squadron Hurricanes east of Forges-les-Eaux during sortie to bomb roads and railway between Amiens and Rouen 2.00 p.m. Fw M. Eiblmeier slightly wounded, rest of crew. Aircraft damaged but repairable.

1./KG53 Heinkel He111H. Shot down by No. 501 Squadron Hurricanes east of Forges-les-Eaux during sortie to bomb roads and railway between Amiens and Rouen, jettisoned bombs and crash-landed at 'La Bucaille', south of Senarpont, 2.00 p.m. Oberlt H. Niklas (of Stab I./KG53) killed. Fw W. Haug and Fw H. Schrepfermann captured unhurt. Fw K. Helber captured wounded. Uffz E. Holdenried captured badly wounded. Aircraft A1+JH a write-off.

1./KG54 Heinkel He111P. Returned damaged by Hurricanes of No. 56 Squadron during attack on harbour installations at Zeebrugge and Nieuport 4.15 p.m. Possibly that attacked by F/Sgt Cooney. Gefr J. Reich wounded, rest of crew unhurt. Aircraft damaged but repairable.

Not much left of He111 A1+HH of 1./KG53 shot down by Hurricanes of No. 501 Squadron at Neuville-Coppegueule, a small village north of Aumale. Bringing up the rear of the Staffel formation it had come under attack by three Hurricanes during which both the wireless-operator, Gustav Berger, and gunner, Ernst Tscherne, were killed. The bombs were scuttled on a railway south-west of Neufchâtel-en-Bray before Fw Hans-Harro Werner ordered the crew to bale out. With an Iron Cross earned in Poland, and 200 flying hours to his credit, he was on his fourth sortie over France.

2./KG54 Heinkel He111P. Shot down by flak and Hurricanes of No. 56 Squadron during attack on harbour installations at Zeebrugge and Nieuport 4.15 p.m. Possibly that claimed by S/L Knowles. Uffz C. Konrad and Gefr K. Heimerl captured slightly wounded, admitted to hospital. Lt F. Hermann, Uffz P. Louis, and Gefr H. Bruns captured unhurt. Aircraft a write-off.

2./KG54 Heinkel He111P. Shot down by flak and Hurricanes of No. 56 Squadron during attack on harbour installations at Zeebrugge and Nieuport and crashed near Middelburg, north-east of Bruges, 4.20 p.m. Possibly that claimed by F/L Coghlan, F/O Fisher, and F/O Ereminsky. Uffz K. Reim and Flgr A. Hirsch killed. Oberfw H. Heussner, Uffz F. Werner, and Uffz F. Tölke slightly wounded. Aircraft a write-off.

5./KG54 Heinkel He111P. Badly damaged by Hurricanes of No. 56 Squadron over Nieuport and abandoned west of Bruges 4.20 p.m. Possibly that attacked by S/L Knowles and Sgt Baker. Uffz E. Stobbe captured badly wounded, died May 31. Uffz T. Bolle baled out and captured wounded. Oberlt W. Gerling and Uffz G. Ulke baled out and captured unhurt. Aircraft a write-off.

3./KG55 Heinkel He111P. Forced-landed near Langemark with starboard engine damaged by flak during sortie to attack roads west of Ypres 10.45 a.m. Oberfw E. Botzki, Fw H. Schmidt, Uffz H. Kaufhold, Uffz F. Wicklein, and Gefr W. Schwinn captured unhurt. Aircraft G1+CL a write-off.

4./LG1 Junkers Ju88A-1. Crash-landed at Düsseldorf-Lohausen following attack by fighters during sortie to Ostend. Hptmn H-D. von Kobylinski *(Staffelführer)* injured, admitted to hospital. Aircraft a write-off.

6./LG1 Junkers Ju88A-1. Believed badly damaged by fighters and flak during sortie to Ostend. Uffz G. Kunz believed wounded, rest of crew unhurt. Aircraft L1+KP a write-off.

5./ZG1 Messerschmitt Bf110C. Damaged in combat with No. 610 Squadron Spitfires north-west of Dunkirk and crash-landed near Avesnes 7.20 p.m. Pilot unhurt. Gefr H. Nickel wounded, admitted to field hospital. Aircraft a write-off.

1./ZG26 Messerschmitt Bf110C. Returned badly damaged following combat with No. 79 Squadron Hurricanes between Dunkirk and Furnes during escort sortie for Ju88s of KG51. Uffz K. Berndt killed, pilot unhurt. Aircraft a write-off.

Stab I./ZG52 Messerschmitt Bf110C. Shot down in combat with fighters of Nos. 56, 145, 601, and 610 Squadrons north-east of Calais 7.20 p.m. Lt C. F. von Neumann *(Gruppenadjutant)* killed. Uffz H. Laudemann baled out and captured wounded, admitted to hospital in Dunkirk. Aircraft a write-off.

I./ZG52 Messerschmitt Bf110C. Shot down in combat with fighters of Nos. 56, 145, 601, and 610 Squadrons north-east of Calais and abandoned over German-held territory 7.20 p.m. Crew baled out unhurt. Aircraft a write-off.

2./ZG52 Messerschmitt Bf110C. Shot down in combat with fighters of Nos. 56, 145, 601, and 610 Squadrons and crashed in the sea off Calais 7.20 p.m. Possibly that claimed by S/L Franks of No. 610 Squadron. Lt G. Borrmann and Uffz H. Riebesell killed. Aircraft lost.

The body of Gerhard Borrmann was washed ashore near Calais on June 8, that of Hans Riebesell coming ashore near De Panne 11 days later.

2./ZG52 Messerschmitt Bf110C. Shot down in combat with fighters of Nos. 56, 145, 601, and 610 Squadrons north of Calais and crashed in sea off De Panne 7.20 p.m. Uffz K. Kübler and Obergefr F. Günther killed. Aircraft a write-off.

The bodies of Karl Kübler and Fritz Günther were recovered and now lie in Block 42 at Lommel in Graves 299 and 367 respectively.

Mortally wounded, Unteroffizier Erwin Stobbe crash-landed inside Belgian lines, three of the crew having baled out and being taken prisoner, the wireless-operator, Theodor Bolle, also being injured. The flight engineer, Gerhard Ulke, and observer, Wilfried Gerling, were later released by advancing German troops and returned to duty the latter being killed in a flying accident on August 14, 1940. After the Polish campaign, II Gruppe of KG54 had moved to Celle before transferring to Aalborg for operations during the invasion of Norway. On transfer to the western front its 4, 5, and 6 Staffeln were based at Gütersloh, Varelbusch, and Diepholz respectively.

Tuesday, May 28

On May 28 Fighter Command was instructed to 'ensure the protection of Dunkirk beaches (three miles on either side) from first light until darkness by continuous fighter patrols in strength'.

Unlike the preceding day, and with the exception of one early-morning sortie escorting No. 2 Group Blenheims to St Omer, every Fighter Command patrol this day was at a strength of at least two squadrons. Given the forces and bases available, this resulted in rather fewer patrols and intervals when the bridgehead was not covered, but a record total of around 321 sorties was flown for the loss of 14 British fighters, nine others returning damaged.

Two large raids were encountered during the morning, one at 10.00 a.m. when a large force of enemy fighters was engaged, and another mixed formation, estimated up to 150 aircraft, about 40 minutes later. But during the afternoon and evening few engagements took place due to a welcome deterioration in the weather. Whatever the reason, Dunkirk was not so severely attacked as on the previous day prompting a signal from the Senior Naval Officer Dunkirk to Vice-Admiral Dover that night which confirmed that 'fighter protection has been invaluable, and . . . bombing only sporadic'.

Coastal Command, in addition to repeated patrols to counter enemy surface vessels, was now also made responsible for a constant daylight patrol of North Goodwins—Gravelines—Ostend. This was maintained, usually three aircraft at a time, by Blenheim IFs from Nos. 235 or 248 Squadron, Hudsons of Nos. 206 or 220 Squadrons, or Fleet Air Arm Rocs and Skuas from Nos. 801 and 806

Although the Belgian capitulation had been in the offing for several days, it was the timing which created much bitterness as the King surrendered against the advice of his ministers. *Left:* This is a copy of the Belgian response to the German terms: 'Lay down arms. Cease-fire on May 28 at 4.00 a.m. Belgian time. A parlementaire will cross the German lines at 5.00 a.m. Belgian time'. M. Hubert Pierlot, the Belgian Prime Minister, broadcast to the people that morning from Paris: 'Belgians! Overruling the formal and unanimous advice of the Government, the King has opened separate negotiations and has treated with the enemy. Belgium will be dumbfounded, but the guilt of one man cannot be imputed to the entire nation. Our army has not deserved the fate which has befallen it. The act which we deplore is without any legal validity. It does not bind the country. According to the terms of the Belgian Constitution, which the King swore to uphold, all the powers come from the people. They are exercised as laid down by the Constitution. No act of the King can be valid unless it bears the counter-signature of a Minister. The King, breaking the bond which bound him to his people, placed himself under the power of the invader.'

Squadrons. The appearance of such unfamiliar aircraft in the battle area resulted in yet another tragic incident when a flight of Skuas was attacked by Spitfires.

Night operations by 13 AASF Battles were hampered by the weather but again centred on the Meuse crossings at Givet and railway yards at Charleville and Libramont, while 14 Bomber Command Whitleys also struck Givet plus routes at Avesnes, Guise, and Hirson. From these sorties one Battle returned damaged by AA fire and one Whitley was lost. But main Bomber Command effort of the night was by 34 Wellingtons that aimed to disrupt enemy movements around Aire, Menin, Roulers, and St Omer. Almost half these sorties were hindered by low cloud but all aircraft returned without loss.

Beyond reconnaissance flights that resulted in several sporadic engagements, air activity over the line of the Somme and the Aisne remained ominously quiet. But German strategy was clear, and once Allied forces remaining in the north had been finally subdued, the full weight of the enemy offensive would again be turned upon the French armies in the south.

Today is likely to be the most critical day ever experienced by the British Army. The extreme gravity of the situation should be explained to all units. I am confident that all ranks will appreciate that it is the duty of the RAF to make their greatest effort today to assist their comrades of both the Army and the Navy.

SIGNAL FROM THE CHIEF OF AIR STAFF TO THE
HEADS OF ALL HOME OPERATIONAL COMMANDS:
MAY 28, 1940

No. 103 Squadron lost a Battle during the morning. Unfortunately the aircraft code-letter is not given in the records but here is one of the squadron's aircraft 'down in France'. It was photographed from all angles by passing German soldiery.

BRITISH AIR FORCES IN FRANCE

103 SQUADRON, RHÈGES

Battle. Forced-landed at Châlons engine badly damaged by flak during low-level attack on pontoon bridge near Abbeville 10.28 a.m. Flying Officer R. D. Max hit in left knee. Sgt D. Allen and LAC Dubois both wounded, admitted to hospital. Aircraft damaged but repairable — later abandoned.

UK-based aircraft lost or damaged on operations over the Western Front:

RAF AIR COMPONENT

16 Squadron, Lympne
Reconnaissance:

Lysander P1720. Believed shot down by ground-fire and crashed near Longuenesse 7.45 a.m. F/Lt W. R. Clapham and Sgt R. Brown killed. Aircraft a write-off.

RAF BOMBER COMMAND

21 Squadron, Watton
Clairmarais Forest:

Blenheim IV. Badly damaged by AA fire during attack on troop concentrations east of St Omer and belly-landed in beach-head area 2.00 p.m. Crew returned unhurt. Aircraft a write-off.

Blenheim IV L8744. Shot down by AA fire during attack on troop concentrations east of St Omer 2.00 p.m. Sgt A. E. D. Twamley killed. Sgt Bailes and AC1 S. C. Thompson believed baled out unhurt. Aircraft a write-off.

59 Squadron, Andover

Blenheim IV. Returned with port engine and tailplane damaged by AA fire during reconnaissance between Lambres and Merville 1.00 p.m. P/O R. W. Ayres, Sgt Roper, and AC Webb unhurt. Aircraft TR⊙P repairable.

Blenheim IV R3664. Shot down by AA fire and abandoned 15 miles south of Dunkirk 4.15 p.m. Sgt T. W. McDonagh and Sgt J. A. C. Finlayson baled out but both missing. P/O J. F. H. Peters baled out, parachute damaged by ground-fire during descent, but reached Dunkirk and returned aboard HMS *Pangbourne*. Aircraft TR⊙D a write-off.

Joseph Finlayson is believed to have fallen with an unopened parachute while the ultimate fate of Thomas McDonagh remains unknown. Both are commemorated on the Runnymede Memorial where their dates of death are recorded as May 29.

77 Squadron, Driffield
Hirson:

Whitley V N1432. Crashed and burned out at Campigneulles-les-Grandes, south-west of Montreuil-sur-Mer, 10.15 p.m. F/O T. J. Geach, Sgt L. J. Brooks, Sgt C. H. Butler, Sgt K. C. Chatfield, and Sgt A. Fryer killed. Aircraft a write-off.

RAF COASTAL COMMAND

806 (FAA) Squadron, Detling
Shipping protection:

Skua II. Shot down by No. 610 Squadron Spitfires and ditched in the Channel off Ostend. Crew rescued unhurt. Aircraft lost.

Skua II. Returned badly damaged by No. 610 Squadron Spitfires off Ostend. Pilot unhurt, LAM J. B. Burton badly wounded, died same day. Aircraft a write-off.

825 (FAA) Squadron, Detling
Bombing Calais—Boulogne:

Swordfish I K5982. Crashed in sea shortly after take-off. Crew rescued unhurt. Aircraft G5P lost.

Swordfish I K8865. Believed shot down by AA fire. Lt A. D. Neely and Lt R. G. Wood captured. Naval Airman V. S. A. Moore returned unhurt. Aircraft a write-off.

Alexander Neely was among escapees from Stalag Luft 3 during the 'Great Escape' but he returned to Sagan on his recapture and survived.

Swordfish I K6009. Ditched on the Goodwin Sands in bad visibility following sortie to attack E-boats reported off Ostend. Capt W. G. S. Aston rescued unhurt, S/Lt P. H. Rylands drowned. Aircraft G5B lost.

RAF FIGHTER COMMAND

19 Squadron, Hornchurch
Patrol Dunkirk:

Spitfire L1029. Returned damaged by cannon shell in cockpit following combat with Bf109s of I./JG26 north-west of Calais 9.45 a.m. Possibly that claimed by Oberlt Seifert *(Staffelkapitän)* of 3./JG26. F/O G. W. Petre shrapnel wound in leg. Aircraft damaged but repairable.

54 Squadron, Hornchurch
Patrol Dunkirk:

Spitfire N3180. Radiator hit by return fire in attack on Bf110 of 7.(F)/LG2, turned off engine and belly-landed on beach at De Panne 5.30 a.m. P/O A. C. Deere injured forehead. Aircraft KL⊙B fired by pilot.

Spitfire. Returned slightly damaged by return fire during pursuit of Bf110 of 7.(F)/LG2 from Westende towards Bruges 5.30 a.m. P/O D. A. P. McMullen unhurt. Aircraft repairable.

65 Squadron, Hornchurch
Patrol Calais:

Spitfire P9435. Forced-landed on beach outside Dunkirk glycol tank damaged by return fire from Do17s of III./KG77 10.00 a.m. P/O T Smart unhurt. Aircraft fired by pilot.

However, positively identified is this Spitfire which crash-landed on the beach in Belgium, fortunately inside Allied lines.

Pilot Officer Al Deere of No. 54 Squadron set fire to his aircraft before making it back to Hornchurch.

213 Squadron, Manston
Escort Blenheims to St Omer:

Hurricane P3354. Shot down in combat with Bf109s of 8./JG3 over Ostend and crashed near Langemark, north of Ypres, 6.45 a.m. F/Lt E. G. Winning killed. Aircraft AK⊙E a write-off.

Hurricane. Shot down in combat with Bf109s of 8./JG3 and crashed in sea off Ostend 6.45 a.m. Sgt T. Boyd rescued unhurt. Aircraft AK⊙B lost.

Hurricane P2721. Shot down in combat with Bf109s and crashed in sea off Dunkirk 11.45 a.m. Possibly that claimed by Oberlt Schmoller-Haldy (*Staffelkapitän*) of 3./JG54. Sgt S. L. Butterfield baled out and rescued by paddle steamer *Sundown* landing at Margate. Aircraft lost.

Hurricane P2792. Shot down in combat with Bf109s of 3./JG54 and crashed in sea off Dunkirk 11.45 a.m. Possibly that claimed by Uffz Kranz. P/O L. G. B. Stone missing. Aircraft AK⊙C lost.
  Laurence Stone was reported found and buried at sea by the Royal Navy.

Hurricane P2834. Shot down in combat with Bf109s of 3./JG54 and crashed in sea off Dunkirk 11.50 a.m. Possibly that claimed by Lt Witt. Sgt J. A. Lichman wounded in arm, rescued and admitted to Victoria Hospital in Dover. Aircraft AK⊙R lost.

229 Squadron, Biggin Hill
Patrol Ostend:

Hurricane N2551. Believed shot down by Bf109s of II./JG26 over the Channel southeast of Dover 11.40 a.m. Sgt S. A. Hillman killed. Aircraft lost.

242 Squadron, Manston
Patrol Ostend:

Hurricane N2651. Oil system destroyed in combat with Bf109s of III./JG26 and crash-landed near Ostend 11.30 a.m. Possibly that claimed by Lt Ebeling of 8./JG26. P/O A. H. Deacon wounded leg and face, later captured in Antwerp. Aircraft a write-off.

Hurricane L1746. Shot down in combat with Bf109s of 6./JG26 over Nieuport and believed crashed near Oostduinkerke 11.30 a.m. Possibly that claimed by Oberlt Beyer of 7./JG26. P/O D. F. Jones killed. Aircraft a write-off.

Hurricane. Returned with oil system badly damaged in combat with Bf109s of III./JG26 over Ostend 11.30 a.m. Possibly that claimed by Lt Müller-Dühe of 7./JG26. P/O W. L. McKnight unhurt. Aircraft damaged but repairable.

264 Squadron, Manston
Patrol Dunkirk—Calais:

Defiant L6959. Shot down in combat with Bf109s of 6./JG51 over the Channel north-west of Dunkirk 12.05 p.m. and probably one of those claimed by Oberlt Priller (*Staffelkapitän*). F/Lt E. H. Whitehouse missing and P/O H. Scott killed. Aircraft a write-off.

Defiant L7007. Shot down in combat with Bf109s of 6./JG51 over the Channel north-west of Dunkirk 12.05 p.m. and probably one of those claimed by Oberlt Priller (*Staffelkapitän*). P/O A. M. MacLeod missing and P/O J. E. Hatfield killed. Aircraft a write-off.

Defiant L6953. Shot down in combat with Bf109s of 6./JG51 over the Channel north-west of Dunkirk 12.05 p.m. Possibly that claimed by Lt Huppertz. Sgt L. C. W. Daisley and LAC H. Revill killed. Aircraft a write-off.

Defiant. Returned damaged in wings and tail in combat with Bf109s of 6./JG51 over the Channel north-west of Dunkirk 12.05 p.m. Possibly that claimed by Uffz Haase. Sgt E. R. Thorn and LAC F. J. Barker unhurt. Aircraft repairable.

611 Squadron, Martlesham Heath
Patrol Dunkirk:

Spitfire N3059. Swerved to avoid another aircraft and tipped up on landing in mist after transfer flight from Digby 5.20 a.m. P/O C. H. MacFie unhurt. Aircraft repairable.

616 Squadron, Rochford
Patrol Dunkirk:

Spitfire K9804. Shot down in combat with Bf109s of I./JG26 and believed ditched north-west of Calais 9.45 a.m. Possibly that claimed by Oberlt Losigkeit (*Staffelkapitän*) of 2./JG26. F/O R. O. Hellyer rescued unhurt. Aircraft a write-off.

Spitfire K9947. Returned damaged in combat with Bf109s of I./JG26 north-west of Calais 9.45 a.m. Sgt M. Ridley slightly wounded in head. Aircraft damaged but repairable.

Spitfire. Badly damaged in combat with Bf109s of I./JG26 north-west of Calais and crash-landed at Manston 10.00 a.m. S/Ldr M. Robinson unhurt. Aircraft damaged but repairable.

Spitfire. Returned damaged following combat with Bf109s of I./JG26 north-west of Calais 9.45 a.m. F/O G. E. Moberley unhurt. Aircraft repairable.

Spitfire. Returned hit in wings during combat with Bf109s of I./JG26 north-west of Calais 9.45 a.m. P/O E. W. S. Scott unhurt. Aircraft repairable.

Karel Margry found the location at De Panne on the extreme eastern end of the Dunkirk perimeter. 'Morning Star', the building with the conical tower, still stands today.

FRENCH AIR FORCE

DAT Tours Bloch 151 (426). Crashed on take-off at Tours, cause unknown. Sgt Staub unhurt. Aircraft 5 a write-off.

GAO 513 Potez 63.11 (448). Crashed on take-off at Lure-Malbouhans 8.20 a.m. S/Lt H. Clément killed. Sgt Poncet and Sgt Martinant-Surin injured. Aircraft a write-off.

GB I/21 Amiot 354 (33). Hit by flak during bombing attack on Cambrai-Niergnies airfield. Crashed on landing back at Pont-sur-Yonne and burned out. S/Lt Bouret, Adjt Baeckler, Sgt Houdenot, and Sgt Vauthier injured. Aircraft a write-off.

GB II/21 Amiot 354 (4). Collided with another Amiot 354 at La Ferté-Gaucher prior to take-off on night reconnaissance over Pas-de-Calais. Capt Fasso and crew unhurt. Aircraft repairable.

King Leopold's personal decision to surrender rather than lead his government into exile in London, laid the basis for a constitutional crisis and bitter post-war controversy over his return to the throne. During the early years of the war he was held prisoner by the Germans in his royal palace near Brussels until he was moved to Austria in 1944. Finally in 1950 he renounced his sovereignty in favour of his son, Baudouin. This is one of the many Belgian aircraft destroyed on the 28th — a Fairey Fox that appears to have been deliberately taxied into a convenient ditch at Steene-Ostend. Similar acts of destruction were taking place at airfields across Belgium during the hurried withdrawal of air force units to the West.

GB II/21 Amiot 354 (12). Unserviceable aircraft further damaged in collision with Amiot 354 at La Ferté-Gaucher. No crew casualties. Aircraft repairable.

GC II/8 Bloch 152. Crashed near St Gatiendes-Bois on approach to Deauville during training flight 3.45 p.m. Cpl L. Nowak killed. Aircraft a write-off.

BELGIAN AIR FORCE

1/I/1 Seven Foxes. Aircraft destroyed during evacuation of Steene-Ostend on withdrawal to Oudenburg 11.00 a.m. Aircraft all write-offs.

9/V/1 Four Renard R-31s. Aircraft destroyed at Lombardzijde to prevent capture. Aircraft all write-offs.

11/VI/1 Five Renard R-31s. Aircraft destroyed at Steene-Ostend to prevent capture. Aircraft all write-offs.

11/VI/1 Stampe-Vertongen SV-5. Suffered engine failure and crashed on take-off at Steene-Ostend attempting flight to England. Lt G. Haubert (of 1/I/1) and Lt G. Hoorickx unhurt. Aircraft a write-off.

Gabriel Haubert subsequently reached England and later served with the Special Operations Executive.

'Sunday-best' gathering around Unteroffizier Stobbe's machine which we saw on page 383.

LUFTWAFFE

2.(H)/21 Henschel Hs126. Hit a tree south of Château-Porcien avoiding attacks by S/Lt Baptizet and Sgt Puda of GC II/4 during observation sortie 5.30 a.m. Fw M. Hermann and Uffz K. Tietje killed. Aircraft a write-off.

1.(H)/22 Henschel Hs126. Returned damaged by Curtiss H-75s of GC II/5 near Nancy. Pilot unhurt, Fw H. May wounded. Aircraft damage state not recorded.

3.(F)/22 Dornier Do17. Returned damaged in attacks by Adjt Ponteins and Sgt Planchard of GC II/7 during long-range reconnaissance north of Chalindrey 6.50 a.m. Gefr R. Lackel wounded, rest of crew unhurt. Aircraft 4N+CL damage state not recorded.

4.(F)/121 Dornier Do17Z. Port wing hit by AA fire then starboard engine set alight in attacks by Capt Bissoudre, Capt Naudy, and S/Lt Codet of GC II/3 near Péronne during long-range reconnaissance between Roye and Soissons, and forced-landed near Athies 7.10 a.m. Obergefr K. Klauser killed, rest of crew believed unhurt. Aircraft damaged but repairable.

8./JG3 Messerschmitt Bf109E-3. Shot down by F/L Wight of No. 213 Squadron in combat between Nieuport and Ostend, and abandoned south of Middelkerke 6.45 a.m. Oberleutnant W. Gäth (Staffelkapitän) baled out and captured unhurt. Aircraft a write-off.

2./JG26 Messerschmitt Bf109E-3. Shot down in combat with Spitfires of Nos. 19 and 616 Squadrons north-west of Calais and abandoned over St-Pol-sur-Mer 9.45 a.m. Possibly that claimed by F/Sgt Steere of No. 19 Squadron. Feldwebel E. Biegert baled out badly wounded — later died. Aircraft 13 + a write-off.

II./JG51 Messerschmitt Bf109E-3. Wrecked in forced-landing at Thielt due to petrol failure. Pilot unhurt. Aircraft a write-off.

4./JG53 Messerschmitt Bf109E-1. Crashed on landing, cause not stated. Uffz E. Kuhlmann injured. Aircraft damaged but repairable.

1./KG27 Heinkel He111. Forced-landed at Frisoythe, near Oldenburg, reportedly badly damaged by night fighter over Dunkirk. Oberfw F. Witkowski slightly wounded. Fw H. Tötemeier badly wounded — died June 2, rest of crew unhurt. Aircraft 1G+HH a write-off.

8./KG30 Junkers Ju88A. Engine damaged by flak during armed reconnaissance sortie over the Channel and crashed in the sea. Uffz K. Geuthner and Gefr G. Follrichs killed. Two other crewmen swam ashore unhurt. Aircraft lost.
The body of Karl Geuthner was washed ashore on the Belgian coast June 20.

III./KG51 Heinkel He111H. Returned damaged following attack by F/L Wight and Sgt Butterfield of No. 213 Squadron over Nieuport 8.00 a.m. One crewman believed wounded. Aircraft repairable.

II./KG77 Dornier Do17Z. Crash-landed near Cologne due to engine failure. Crew believed unhurt but three civilians killed. Aircraft a write-off.

III./KG77 Dornier Do17Z. Believed forced-landed near Guines damaged by Spitfires of No. 65 Squadron 10.00 a.m. Crew unhurt. Aircraft damaged but repairable.

8./KG77 Dornier Do17Z. Reported shot down by AA fire near Lijssenthoek, south of Poperinge, during photo-reconnaissance to Lille but possibly that attacked by S/L Cooke of No. 65 Squadron 10.00 a.m. Hptmn H. Dannewitz (Staffelkapitän) and Oberfw A. Meinhardt killed. Lt J. Binder and Oberfw H. Kittner baled out and captured unhurt. Aircraft 3Z+CS a write-off.
The captured airmen were taken to England where, highly security-conscious, they gave fictitious names for the rest of the crew to prevent RAF Intelligence discovering the loss of their Staffelkapitän.

9./KG77 Dornier Do17Z. Returned damaged by Spitfires of No. 65 Squadron south of Poperinge 10.00 a.m. Possibly that attacked by F/Sgt Franklin and Sgt Kilner. Uffz E. Horbank and Gefr O. Czastka slightly wounded wounded, rest of crew unhurt. Aircraft damaged but repairable.

1./KGzbV.1 Junkers Ju52. Crashed at Ulmet, north-west of Kaiserslautern in a thunderstorm. Fw F. Seifert, Uffz K. Ludwig, Uffz K. Sommerfeld and Flgr H. Ruhnke killed. Aircraft a write-off.

IV./KGzbV.1 Junkers Ju52 (6216). Lost bearings and shot down by flak near St Pol. Crew unhurt. Aircraft a write-off.

5.(S)/LG2 Henschel Hs123. Returned damaged by ground-fire north of Bailleul. Lt G. Dörffel slightly wounded. Aircraft damage state not recorded.

II.(S)/LG2 Henschel Hs123. Crash-landed near St-Pol. Crew unhurt. Aircraft damaged but repairable.

7.(F)/LG2 Dornier Do17P. Engaged by P/O Macpherson and P/O Deere of No. 54 Squadron at Diksmuide during reconnaissance sortie to Ostend and chased towards Bruges belly-landing badly damaged on one engine 5.00 a.m. Oberlt H. Beckert, Uffz W. Butz, and Uffz K. Renner wounded. Aircraft a write-off.
Loss of this crew was recorded by 2.(H)/41, the parent unit from which they probably originated.

8./StG51 Junkers Ju87B. Crashed near Binche, cause unknown. Lt A. Sahnkow killed. Uffz J. Küppers injured. Aircraft damage state not recorded.

3./StG76 Junkers Ju87B. Shot down by flak and crashed in flames near Strazeele, between Bailleul and Hazebrouck. Oberlt H-J. von Doemming and Uffz H. Grenzow killed. Aircraft a write-off.

RAF PERSONNEL LOST ABOARD S.S. *ABUKIR* — MAY 28, 1940

ADAMS, AC1 F. V. Age 21.
Runnymede Memorial Panel 24.
BARRATT, Sergeant E. D. Age 19.
Runnymede Memorial Panel 11.
BARRATT, Pilot Officer F. A. Age 46.
Runnymede Memorial Panel 7.
BELLINGHAM, AC1 L. H. Age 32.
Runnymede Memorial Panel 24.
BURROWS, Flight Sergeant A. Age 39.
Runnymede Memorial Panel 10.
CHURCHARD, AC2 J.
Runnymede Memorial Panel 26.
CROSS, Pilot Officer E. H. Age 43. Sage War Cemetery - Oldenburg, Germany. Plot 5, Row C, Grave 11.
Originally buried in Juist Cemetery.
DAVIES, AC1 I. L. Age 32.
Runnymede Memorial Panel 25.
DICKSON, AC1 R. W.
Runnymede Memorial Panel 25.
GARDINER, AC1 H. H.
Runnymede Memorial Panel 25.
GLENCROSS, Squadron Leader A. R. No. 37 Squadron.
Runnymede Memorial Panel 4.

GLOVER, LAC A. Age 37.
Runnymede Memorial Panel 23.
GURNEY, Squadron Leader M. P. Age 46. Malo-les-Bains Communal Cemetery, Nord, France. Plot 2, Row A, Grave 16.
HUMPHREYS, LAC G. E. Age 22.
Runnymede Memorial Panel 23.
HUMPHREYS, Flying Officer W. H. Age 24. Runnymede Memorial Panel 6.
HUTCHISON, AC1 J. B. Age 20.
Runnymede Memorial Panel 25.
KEYTE, Corporal C. T. Age 26.
Runnymede Memorial Panel 22.
MACINTYRE, AC2 A. R. Age 27.
Runnymede Memorial Panel 27.
MURTON, Corporal C. V. Age 37. Dunkirk Town Cemetery, Nord, France. Plot 2, Row 2, Grave 29.
NEWMAN, Pilot Officer R. W. Sage War Cemetery, Oldenburg, Niedersachsen, Germany. Plot 4, Row B, Grave 3.
Washed ashore and originally buried in Esens Cemetery.
RUSSELL, LAC J. R. No.3 Air Mission. Age 20. Runnymede Memorial Panel 24.

SANDERS, Squadron Leader R. M. No.3 Air Mission.
Runnymede Memorial Panel 4.
SYMONS, Flight Lieutenant H. E. No.3 Air Mission. Age 40.
Runnymede Memorial Panel 5.
TOWNEND, AC2 H. Age 21.
Runnymede Memorial Panel 27.
TULLY, Sergeant M. L. Age 45.
Runnymede Memorial Panel 20.
WEBBER, LAC A. A. Age 19.
Runnymede Memorial Panel 24.
WHEELER, LAC A. Age 31.
Runnymede Memorial Panel 24.
WHITELAM, Sergeant J. T. Age 29.
Runnymede Memorial Panel 21.
WHITEMAN, LAC A. P. Age 42.
Runnymede Memorial Panel 24.
WOOLCOCK, Flying Officer A. H. Age 25.
Runnymede Memorial Panel 6.
ZECH, Flight Lieutenant G. L. P. Age 39.
Runnymede Memorial Panel 5.

The Egyptian Khedivial Mail Line coaster, the SS *Abukir*, came under the British flag early in the war when she was run by the General Steam Navigation Company. Late on the evening of May 27, under Captain Rowland Wolfenden, she departed from Ostend carrying over 200 passengers including some Belgian Nuns, a party of British schoolchildren who had been stranded on the Continent, together with 15 German prisoners of war.

She was intercepted by Oberleutnant zur See Obermaier of the S-34 who fired three torpedos. Captain Wolfenden tried to ram the E-Boat but the *Abukir* was struck by a fourth torpedo and sank within two minutes. The Royal Navy destroyers, HMS *Jaguar, Javelin, Codrington* and *Grenade* (the latter two also lost shortly afterwards), searched for survivors but only 21 passengers and five crew were found alive.

Wednesday, May 29

The southern flank of the Allied pocket was now shrinking fast as French and British troops poured into the Dunkirk perimeter adding to the already considerable congestion. By evening, demoralised troops of the French 1ère Armée isolated on the River Lys finally surrendered. Their compatriots who joined the withdrawal to within the perimeter alongside the BEF remained unaware that the British intention was total evacuation — the French Government having failed to advise their commander at Dunkirk, Admiral Abrial, of the fact. Meanwhile the evacuation was progressing well, a direct shipping route across the Channel from Dover now cleared of mines, and vessels once again using Dunkirk port by day though obviously subject to severe air attacks. The pace of the British evacuation quickened.

Air reconnaissance over both flanks of the BEF to locate suitable targets for bombers was hampered by poor weather and growing difficulties in distinguishing between Allied and enemy columns. Despite this, daylight operations were flown by No. 2 Group Blenheims and, early evening, ten Fleet Air Arm Swordfish were sent to attack an enemy battery reported shelling Dunkirk but they were unable to locate the target and lost half their number to enemy fighters. Further operations by Coastal Command during the day in support of the evacuation resulted in the loss of seven more aircraft.

To counter increasingly superior numbers of enemy aircraft met over Dunkirk in preceding days, Fighter Command was now despatching up to four squadrons on patrol at a time, though in practice two pairs operating together within a ten-mile radius of Dunkirk was the best that could be achieved. Thus the beach-head area was patrolled by RAF fighters from 4.40 a.m. to 9.10 p.m. while sections of three Coastal Command aircraft covered a line from the North Goodwins to Gravelines and Ostend throughout the day.

With an improvement in the weather, German attacks on the beaches and Dunkirk harbour commenced in earnest around midday and remained fairly continuous until 8.00 p.m. that evening. The Luftwaffe was swift to exploit gaps in the British fighter cover and mounted at least five major raids during the afternoon and evening, two of which went totally unopposed by RAF fighters. Of the three remaining major attacks, one was engaged before bombing, one during the actual attack, and one after the bombing was over. Fighter claims on the day were comparable, each side claiming over 60 enemy aircraft destroyed plus others probably destroyed or damaged, with Luftwaffe fighters claiming the destruction of 44 enemy fighters while the RAF claimed some 40 German fighters destroyed. Given the ferocity of the actions this degree of over-claiming, by both sides, was inevitable.

Despite these vicious engagements, German attacks remained fairly constant throughout the afternoon and early evening with eight vessels lost during the day though most of the more important naval losses were not due to enemy bombing but rather E-boat action and collisions. Nevertheless the Admiralty decided that the scale of enemy air attack was such that it was imprudent to risk the further use of its destroyers, two of which, HMS *Gregson* and HMS *Wakeful* were lost during the day. And later that evening a mistaken report that Dunkirk harbour was temporarily blocked prompted the Vice-Admiral Dover to order ships not to close the harbour thus inadvertently preventing large numbers of Allied troops from being evacuated under cover of darkness.

RAF night bombing was restricted by the continuing bad weather and of 23 aircraft despatched, three failed to return to base, four forced-landed, and another crashed on take-off.

Göring sent the Luftwaffe 'über Dunkirchen' with orders that the town be attacked 'in such a manner that further embarkations are reported to be impossible'. From a propaganda painting.

By intense effort Fighter Command maintained successive patrols over the scene, and fought the enemy at long odds. Hour after hour they bit into the German fighter and bomber squadrons, taking a heavy toll, scattering them and driving them away. Day after day this went on, till the glorious victory of the Royal Air Force was gained. Wherever German aircraft were encountered, sometimes in forties and fifties, they were instantly attacked, often by single squadrons or less, and shot down in scores, which presently added up into hundreds.

Unhappily, the troops on the beaches saw very little of this epic conflict in the air, often miles away or above the clouds. They knew nothing of the loss inflicted on the enemy. All they felt was the bombs scourging the beaches, cast by the foes who had got through, but did not perhaps return. There was even a bitter anger in the Army against the Air Force, and some of the troops landing at Dover or at Thames ports in their ignorance insulted men in Air Force uniform. They should have clasped their hands; but how could they know? In Parliament I took pains to spread the truth.

WINSTON S. CHURCHILL, 1949

BRITISH AIR FORCES IN FRANCE

88 SQUADRON, LES GRANDES-CHAPELLES

Battle P2313. Crashed shortly after take-off for night attack on fuel dump at Givet and bomb-load exploded. Flying Officer H. G. Evitt, Sergeant E. W. J. Chapman, and AC1 C. A. Edwards killed. Aircraft a write-off.

Two other aircraft lost contact with base in bad weather during a sortie to Charleville this night, F/O Halliday putting down safely at Vitry, while F/O Marriott set down at Avord.

103 SQUADRON, RHÈGES

Battle. Lost contact with base and forced-landed near Sens in bad weather during night bombing sortie to Charleville. Squadron Leader H. Lee and crew unhurt. Aircraft damaged but repairable.

F/L Tait's aircraft also lost contact but managed to land safely at Vitry.

UK-based aircraft also lost or damaged over the Western Front on this date:

RAF AIR COMPONENT

2 Squadron, Bekesbourne
Tactical reconnaissance:

Lysander. Forced-landed at Hawkinge starboard wing damaged by AA fire north-east of Dunkirk 6.45 a.m. P/O Chapman and Cpl Pickles unhurt. Aircraft KO⊙A damaged but repairable.

26 Squadron, Lympne
Tactical reconnaissance:

Lysander II P1689. Shot down and crashed in sea off Dunkirk p.m. F/Lt Bryant rescued slightly injured, P/O Stone unhurt. Aircraft lost.

RAF BOMBER COMMAND

21 Squadron, Watton
Enemy columns:

Blenheim IV P6886. Belly-landed on return hydraulics badly damaged by Lt Tiedmann and Uffz Küpper of 2./JG3 over Dunkirk 7.00 p.m. following low-level attack on troops and transport between Diksmuide and Torhout. P/O L. M. Blanckensee, Sgt A. Williams, and Sgt J. Guest unhurt. Aircraft a write-off.

RAF COASTAL COMMAND

48 Squadron, Detling
Shipping Patrol:

Anson I K8773. Wings and ailerons badly damaged in attack by Lt Hillecke of Stab II./JG26 off Zeebrugge and ditched off Deal when engine failed 6.05 p.m. LAC L. S. Dilnutt wounded, F/O S. Wherry, P/O G. Allington, and Cpl A. D. C. Harding unhurt, all rescued by drifter landing at Ramsgate. Aircraft OY⊙X lost.

235 Squadron, Detling
Offensive patrols:

Blenheim IV P6909. Hit trees and crashed near Sittingbourne returning to base due to bad weather 7.15 a.m. F/Lt R. P. Y. Cross and Sgt A. V. Slocombe killed. LAC J. North died of injuries. Aircraft a write-off.

Blenheim IV L9260. Shot down in sea by Bf109s of JG27 during patrol off Calais 12.00 p.m. Possibly one of those claimed by Hptmn Galland of Stab JG27 north of Gravelines. P/O J. R. Cronan, Sgt A. O. Lancaster, and LAC Peebles rescued from dinghy. Aircraft LA⊙E lost.

Blenheim IV L9397. Shot down in sea by Bf109s of JG27 during patrol off Calais 12.00 p.m. Possibly one of those claimed by Hptmn Galland of Stab JG27 north of Gravelines. P/O A. F. Booth, Sgt D. J. Elliott, and LAC E. R. Scott missing. Aircraft lost.

Blenheim IV L9401. Shot down in sea by Bf109s of JG27 during patrol north-west of Calais 12.00 p.m. Possibly that claimed by Lt Zirkenbach of 1./JG27. F/Lt G. A. P. Manwaring, Sgt I. MacPhail, and AC1 D. B. Murphy killed. Aircraft lost.

500 Squadron, Detling
Patrol Dutch coast:

Anson I N5227. Failed to return, cause unknown 11.00 a.m. P/O I. S. Wheelwright, F/Sgt R. G. T. Soper, and Sgt H. W. Johnson missing. LAC F. H. Giles killed. Aircraft MK⊙N lost.

Anson I N5065. Shot down by Fw Meyer of 6./JG26 and ditched off Ramsgate 6.05 p.m. P/O A. Leeson, Sgt J. H. Hoskins, Cpl R. G. Rogers, and LAC R. G. Honnor all wounded and rescued by *Royal Daffodil II*. Aircraft MK⊙L lost.

825 (FAA) Squadron, Hawkinge
Enemy battery:

Swordfish I L2828. Badly damaged by Bf109s of 3./JG54 and believed crashed near Bollezeele 7.00 p.m. Possibly that claimed by Oberlt Schmoller-Haldy *(Staffelkapitän)*. Sub Lt C. S. F. Hogg missing. Leading Naval Airman L. P. Gardner killed. Lt R. H. G. Grey captured. Aircraft G5C a write-off.

Swordfish I P4022. Shot down by Bf109s of 3./JG54 and overturned in forced-landing 7.00 p.m. Possibly one of those claimed by Lt Kitzinger. Lt Cdr J. B. Buckley (Squadron Commander) and Naval Airman F. G. Rumsey captured. Aircraft a write-off.

James Buckley was one of those who escaped Stalag Luft 3 during the 'Great Escape'. He reached the north German coast but drowned while attempting to reach Sweden by canoe on March 21, 1943.

Swordfish I L2756. Shot down by Bf109s of 3./JG54 and believed crashed in the Channel 7.00 p.m. Possibly one of those claimed by Lt Kitzinger. Pilot rescued unhurt, Leading Naval Airman H. K. Murrin missing. Aircraft lost.

Swordfish I P3997. Shot down by Bf109s of 3./JG54 and crash-landed 7.00 p.m. Possibly that claimed by Uffz Strohauer. Sub Lt J. T. Nicholson and Naval Airman V. S. A. Moore captured. Aircraft a write-off.

Swordfish I L9740. Shot down by Bf109s of 3./JG54 and crash-landed 7.00 p.m. Possibly that claimed by Uffz Windisch. Lt A. D. Neely and Lt R. G. Wood captured. Aircraft a write-off.

Swordfish I. Returned damaged by Bf109s of 3./JG54 during sortie to attack enemy battery 7.00 p.m. Pilot unhurt, gunner wounded. Aircraft damage state not recorded.

RAF FIGHTER COMMAND

17 Squadron, Hawkinge
Patrol Dunkirk:

Hurricane. Returned port wing damaged by return fire during attack on Bf110 of 5./ZG76 over Calais 1.00 p.m. P/O D. W. H. Hanson wounded in right leg. Aircraft repairable.

41 Squadron, Manston
Patrol Dunkirk:

Spitfire N3115. Forced-landed near Purfleet during return flight to Hornchurch 12.35 p.m. Sgt E. V. Darling unhurt. Aircraft a write-off.

56 Squadron, Manston
Patrol Dunkirk:

Hurricane N2659. Forced-landed on beach outside Dunkirk damaged by return fire during attack on Ju87s 3.30 p.m. Pilot Officer K. C. Dryden unhurt, returned by boat. Aircraft US⊙T a write-off.

Hurricane L1972. Shot down by return fire during attack on Ju87s over Dunkirk 3.30 p.m. F/Sgt J. W. Elliott missing. Aircraft lost.

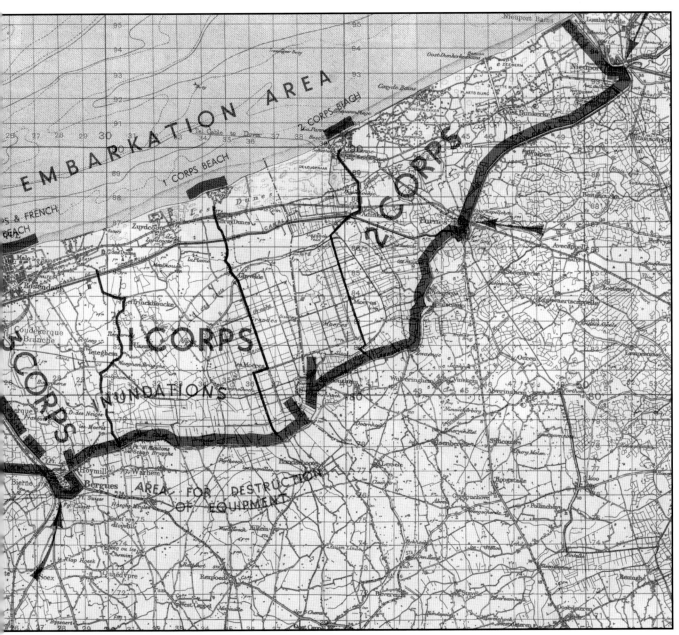

A Royal Engineer's plan of the Dunkirk perimeter as it appeared on May 28. 'On shore', wrote Major J. R. Blomfield, an officer with the Royal Engineers, 'we took a lot of notice of bombing and machine-gunning and dived frequently into the foxholes with which the beach was pockmarked. We collected all the light machine guns and ammunition we could find and set them up along the promenade at about ten-yard intervals. Anyone who cared was invited to have a shot. Our commander sat in a deck chair with a Bren and used an enormous amount of ammunition.'

64 Squadron, Kenley
Patrol Dunkirk:

Spitfire L1052. Shot down in combat with Bf109s 5.30 p.m. S/L E. G. Rogers missing. Aircraft lost.

Pilots of 4./JG3, III./JG3, Stab I./JG20, 6./JG20, 4./JG26, and III./JG26 claimed 20 Spitfires in combat with Nos. 64 and 610 Squadrons over Dunkirk between 5.10 and 6.15 p.m. this afternoon and it has not been possible to resolve individual claims.

Spitfire K9832. Shot down in combat with Bf109s 5.30 p.m. P/O R. T. George missing. Aircraft lost.

Spitfire N3272. Shot down in combat with Bf109s 5.30 p.m. P/O H. B. Hackney missing. Aircraft lost.

Spitfire K9813. Returned with electrical system damaged in combat with Bf109s 5.30 p.m. F/Sgt C. Flynn unhurt. Aircraft repairable.

151 Squadron, Manston
Escort Defiants to Dunkirk:

Hurricane. Returned badly damaged and airframe over-stressed due to violent evasive actions during combat with Bf110s of II./ZG76 off Calais 1.00 p.m. S/Ldr E. M. Donaldson unhurt. Aircraft damaged but repairable.

Hurricane P3303. Shot down by Oberlt Redlich of 1./JG27 and crashed in the sea off Dunkirk 7.30 p.m. F/O K. E. Newton baled out and rescued by hospital ship. Aircraft lost.

Hurricane P3321. Shot down by Fw Kothmann of 2./JG27 and crashed in sea off Dunkirk 7.30 p.m. P/O R. N. H. Courtney baled out wounded in neck and right leg, rescued by HMS *Shearwater* and landed at Ramsgate. Aircraft lost.

222 Squadron, Hornchurch
Patrol Dunkirk:

Spitfire P9376. Lost bearings in poor visibility, ran out of fuel, and belly-landed on return from patrol 6.40 a.m. P/O J. W. Broadhurst unhurt. Aircraft damaged but repairable.

229 Squadron,
Patrol Dunkirk:

Hurricane P3489. Shot down in combat with Bf109s of I.(J)/LG2 and crashed in sea off Dunkirk 5.30 p.m. F/Lt F. N. Clouston killed. Aircraft a write-off.

Hurricane P2636. Shot down in combat with Bf109s of I.(J)/LG2 off Dunkirk 5.30 p.m. F/Lt P. E. S. F. M. Browne missing. Aircraft lost.

Hurricane P2876. Shot down in combat with Bf109s of I.(J)/LG2 off Dunkirk 5.30 p.m. Sgt J. C. Harrison killed. Aircraft a write-off.

Pilot Officer Dryden managed to get down safely on the beach at Dunkirk. His Hurricane N2659 from No. 56 Squadron was operating from Manston.

Hurricane N2473. Shot down in combat with Bf109s of I.(J)/LG2 off Dunkirk 5.30 p.m. F/O W. G. New baled out unhurt. Aircraft a write-off.

Hurricane N2521. Shot down in combat with Bf109s of I.(J)/LG2 off Dunkirk 5.30 p.m. P/O A. S. Linney baled out and rescued unhurt. Aircraft a write-off.

Hurricane L1852. Believed returned damaged following combat with Bf109s of I.(J)/LG2 off Dunkirk 5.30 p.m. Pilot unhurt. Aircraft damaged but repairable.

242 Squadron, Manston
Patrol Dunkirk—Furnes:

Hurricane N2338. Crash-landed on return undercarriage damaged in combat with Bf109s of I.(J)/LG2 over Dunkirk 5.10 p.m. P/O J. B. Latta unhurt. Aircraft damaged but repairable.

Hurricane L1756. Crashed on take-off for return flight to Biggin Hill 7.30 p.m. cause unknown. P/O J. F. Howitt badly injured. Aircraft a write-off.

264 Squadron, Manston
Patrol Dunkirk—Calais:

Defiant L6957. Returned with starboard aileron and hydraulics badly damaged in combat over Dunkirk 3.45 p.m. P/O D. H. S. Kay unhurt, LAC E. J. Jones baled out but killed. Aircraft damaged but repairable.

Defiant L6956. Crashed landing on one wheel at Manston with damaged fuel tank after combat with Bf109s and Ju87s off Dunkirk 7.30 p.m. Sgt E. R. Thorn and LAC F. J. Barker unhurt. Aircraft damaged but repairable.

Defiant L7004. Returned damaged following combat over Dunkirk 3.45 p.m. Crew unhurt. Aircraft repairable.

610 Squadron, Gravesend
Patrol Dunkirk:

Spitfire L1006. Shot down in combat with Bf109s and crashed in sea off Dunkirk 5.40 p.m. F/O G. M. T. Kerr missing. Aircraft DW⊙R lost.

Spitfire N3289. Shot down in combat with Bf109s and crashed in sea off Dunkirk 5.40 p.m. F/O J. Kerr-Wilson missing. Aircraft lost.

Spitfire N3177. Shot down in combat with Bf109s and crashed in sea off Dunkirk 7.30 p.m. Probably that claimed by Oberlt Weber *(Staffelkapitän)* of 5.(J)/TrGr.186. S/L A. L. Franks killed. Aircraft DW⊙T lost.

Spitfire. Reportedly hit in port wing by naval AA fire and abandoned over the Channel but possibly that claimed by Uffz Schmetzer of 5.(J)/TrGr.186 north of Dunkirk 7.30 p.m. Sgt P. D. Jenkins baled out but missing. Aircraft DW⊙K lost.

FRENCH AIR FORCE

GB I/19 Douglas DB-7 (20). Hit by flak over Mesnil-Trois-Fêtus during low-level attack on bridges west of Amiens and forced-landed at Les Terres Noires, Bainast 8.00 p.m. Sgt Dupuis wounded; admitted to hospital in Beauvais. Aircraft a write-off.

GB I/21 Amiot 351 (60). Lost a wheel on take-off from Pont-sur-Yonne on night reconnaissance sortie over Arras and Valenciennes but landed safely. Crew unhurt. Aircraft repairable.

GB II/31 LeO 451 (128). Shot down by flak north of Abbeville; crashed and exploded at Grand Bois, between Cahon and Gouy. Lt P. Sabourdy, Adjt P. Tourres, Sgt F. Moser, killed. Sgt Bozon baled out and captured unhurt. Aircraft a write-off.

GC 3/4 Curtiss H-75 (279). Returned hit by return fire from Hs126 of 2.(H)/21 engaged near Rethel 3.00 p.m. Capt R. Guieu *(Commandant)* unhurt. Aircraft repairable.

LUFTWAFFE

2.(H)/21 Henschel Hs126. Returned damaged in attacks by Capt Guieu and Sgt Coisneau of GC II/4 west of Charleville during observation sortie over Rethel 3.00 p.m. Pilot unhurt, Oberlt Schünemann wounded. Aircraft repairable.

4.(H)/21 Henschel Hs126. Returned damaged by ground-fire during observation sortie over Amiens. Fw W. Groth slightly wounded. Aircraft damage state not reported.

3.(F)/22 Dornier Do17M. Returned damaged in attacks by Capt Destaillac, S/Lt Villacèque, S/Lt Boudier, and Sgt Svetlik of GC II/5 during high-altitude reconnaissance between Nancy and Metz 5.15 p.m. Uffz G. Ahrns killed. Aircraft damaged but repairable.

2.(H)/41 Henschel Hs126. Returned badly damaged by ground-fire near Furnes, south-west of Nieuport. Lt H. Brenken wounded. Aircraft a write-off.

5.(F)/122 Dornier Do17P-1. Crash-landed south-west of Dunkirk damaged by fighters during reconnaissance sortie. Uffz W. Kade believed wounded, rest of crew unhurt. Aircraft a write-off.

8./JG2 Messerschmitt Bf109E-3. Crashed near Beaulieu-en-Argonne following take-off collision. Uffz G. Häfner killed. Aircraft a write-off.

I./JG3 Messerschmitt Bf109E-3. Returned badly damaged following combat with No. 610 Squadron Spitfires during escort sortie for He111s of I./KG1 over Dunkirk 4.15 p.m. Pilot believed unhurt. Aircraft a write-off.

2./JG3 Messerschmitt Bf109E-3. Failed to return following combat with No. 610 Squadron Spitfires during escort sortie for He111s of I./KG1 over Dunkirk 4.15 p.m. Hauptmann H. Gärtner *(Staffelkapitän)* missing. Aircraft lost.

2./JG3 Messerschmitt Bf109E-1. Shot down in the Channel during combat with No. 610 Squadron Spitfires during escort sortie for He111s of I./KG1 over Dunkirk 4.15 p.m. Oberfeldwebel H. Beurer missing. Aircraft lost.

2./JG3 Messerschmitt Bf109E-3. Shot down in combat with No. 610 Squadron Spitfires during escort sortie for He111s of I./KG1 over Dunkirk 4.15 p.m. Feldwebel B. Lampskemper unhurt. Aircraft a write-off.

1./JG20 Messerschmitt Bf109E. Damaged by flak over Dunkirk and belly-landed at Merris, east of Hazebrouck p.m. Feldwebel L. Birk unhurt. Aircraft a write-off.

I./JG21 Messerschmitt Bf109E-3. Crash-landed at Monchy-Breton due to undercarriage failure. Pilot believed unhurt. Aircraft a write-off.

2./JG21 Messerschmitt Bf109E-1 (3471). Forced-landed near Roteux, cause not stated. Oberleutnant R. Hausmann unhurt. Aircraft 9 + repairable.

III./JG26 Messerschmitt Bf109E. Forced-landed at Beerst, north-east of Diksmuide, engine damaged in combat with Spitfires of Nos. 64 and 610 Squadrons over Dunkirk 5.45 p.m. Pilot unhurt. Aircraft damaged but repairable.

I./JG27 Messerschmitt Bf109E-1. Shot down by F/O Ereminsky of No. 56 Squadron in combat off Dunkirk 7.30 p.m. Pilot believed unhurt. Aircraft a write-off.

I./JG27 Messerschmitt Bf109E-3. Forced-landed at Desvres believed badly damaged in combat off Dunkirk 7.30 p.m. Possibly that claimed by F/Sgt Higginson of No. 56 Squadron. Pilot unhurt. Aircraft a write-off.

II./JG53 Messerschmitt Bf109E-1. Belly-landed near Ham, south-east of Ghent, following engine failure. Pilot unhurt. Aircraft damaged but repairable.

I./JG54 Messerschmitt Bf109E-1. Probably that forced-landed at Balham, north-east of Reims due to petrol failure. Pilot unhurt. Aircraft damaged but repairable.

1./KG1 Heinkel He111H. Set alight by No. 213 Squadron Hurricanes over Dunkirk and abandoned south of St Omer 4.20 p.m. Possibly that claimed by F/O Gray. Flgr S. Cimander killed. Fw F. Schöwer wounded. Uffz W. Johann, Gefr E. Mikeska, and Gefr H. Viehweger unhurt. Aircraft a write-off.

Another beach casualty, this time from the Luftwaffe, was Oberleutnant Alfred von Oelhaven, the Staffelkapitän of 6./LG1.

1./KG1 Heinkel He111H. Badly damaged by No. 213 Squadron Hurricanes over Dunkirk and crash-landed on fire south of Ostend 4.30 p.m. Possibly that claimed by P/O Sizer. Uffz F. Puzicha killed. Uffz H. Sonntag wounded. Lt H. Grunwald and Uffz F. Hogg unhurt. Aircraft a write-off.

1./KG1 Heinkel He111H. Badly damaged by No. 213 Squadron Hurricanes over Dunkirk 4.15 p.m. Engine caught fire during return flight and crash-landed near Ghent. Possibly that claimed by P/O Atkinson. Uffz E. Marczinke and Gefr R. Mysliwietz killed. Fw H-H. Zickmantel wounded and Fw G. Stier unhurt. Aircraft a write-off.

1./KG1 Heinkel He111H. Shot down by No. 213 Squadron Hurricanes and crash-landed south-west of Dunkirk 4.15 p.m. Possibly that claimed by F/Sgt Grayson. Fw A. Braun killed. Gefr H. Marcinek badly wounded, died in hospital June 2. Lt A. Zimmer, Oberfw S. Krewald, and Flgr J. Miedl unhurt. Aircraft a write-off.

1./KG1 Heinkel He111H. Returned damaged in attacks by No. 213 Squadron Hurricanes over Dunkirk 4.15 p.m. Crew believed unhurt. Aircraft repairable.

Stabsstaffel KG2 Dornier Do17Z. Returned badly damaged by Capt Canel and Sgt Courteville of GC II/9 over Amiens during reconnaissance sortie north of Breteuil-sur-Noye 7.40 a.m. Fw P. Gross slightly wounded, rest of crew unhurt. Aircraft a write-off.

5./LG1 Junkers Ju88A-1. Crashed near Mettmann during return from sortie, damaged in combat over Dunkirk 8.15 p.m. Oberfw A. Sasse and Fw H. Ruppel killed. Uffz H. Roewer and Uffz E. Berwanger slightly wounded. Aircraft a write-off.

6./LG1 Junkers Ju88A-1. Shot down by Hurricanes over Dunkirk and belly-landed on Nieuport beach 8.30 p.m. Possibly that claimed by S/L Donaldson and P/O Hamar of No. 151 Squadron. Oberfw F. Stobbe, and Flgr S. Tessmann killed. Oberlt A. von Oelhaven *(Staffelkapitän)* and Fw W. Notzke captured unhurt. Aircraft L1+AP a write-off.

6./LG1 Junkers Ju88A-1. Starboard engine damaged by AA fire during attack on shipping, belly-landed and burned out in Terhofstedepolder at Zuidzande 8.25 p.m. Gefr K. Meier slightly injured left hand. Oberfw Hahne, Fw H. Giessen, and Uffz Bronitzky believed unhurt. Aircraft L1+LP a write-off.

6./LG1 Junkers Ju88A-1. Shot down by fighters and crash-landed near Oudenburg, inland from Ostend 8.20 p.m. Possibly that attacked by five Defiants of No. 264 Squadron. Flgr H. Oehler killed. Fw M. Stapelberg, Uffz H. Rosenow, and Gefr H-J. Brömel badly wounded, admitted to hospital in Ghent. Aircraft a write-off.

9./LG1 Junkers Ju88A-1. Returned damaged following sortie over Dunkirk and possibly that attacked by three Skuas of No. 806 Squadron during attack on shipping north-east of Ostend 6.00 p.m. Oberlt H. Becker and Uffz R. Tilsner wounded, rest of crew unhurt. Aircraft repairable.

2./StG2 Junkers Ju87B. Shot down by No. 264 Squadron Defiants during attack on Dunkirk harbour 7.30 p.m. Oberlt E. Winschig *(Staffelführer)* and Uffz H. Albrecht killed. Aircraft a write-off.

2./StG2 Junkers Ju87B. Overturned in forced-landing at Ferques, north-east of Marquise, radiator and oil cooler damaged by flak over Dunkirk harbour 7.30 p.m. Uffz W. Kurtze slightly injured, gunner unhurt. Aircraft damage state not recorded.

II./StG2 Junkers Ju87R. Flew into another aircraft's slipstream, lost control, and crashed outside Cambrai airfield shortly after take-off 6.00 p.m. One crewman believed injured. Aircraft a write-off.

Stabsstaffel StG77 Junkers Ju87B. Damaged during attack on shipping in Dunkirk harbour and forced-landed south of Calais 7.55 p.m. Oberlt G. Bauhaus *(Stabsstaffelkapitän)* and Uffz E. Gimpel both slightly wounded. Aircraft damage state not recorded.

6./StG77 Junkers Ju87B. Shot down in the sea during attack on shipping in Dunkirk harbour 7.50 p.m. Lt F. Herlt and Gefr H. Scherber both missing. Aircraft lost.

6./StG77 Junkers Ju87B. Returned badly damaged during attack on shipping in Dunkirk harbour 7.50 p.m. Uffz H. Siems badly wounded, admitted to hospital. Aircraft a write-off.

Luftwaffe General Quartermaster Returns dated 2.6.40 lists these three StG77 losses on May 25, but personnel loss lists for the unit indicate otherwise.

I./ZG52 Messerschmitt Bf110C. Returned damaged, cause unknown. One crewman believed wounded. Aircraft damage state not recorded.

5./ZG76 Messerschmitt Bf110C. Believed belly-landed near St-André-sur-Orne, damaged in attack by Hurricanes of Nos. 17 and 245 Squadrons north-west of St Omer 1.00 p.m. Pilot unhurt, Uffz A. Links badly injured on landing, treated in field hospital at Erin. Aircraft M8+EN a write-off.

Peter Taghon knew the location which proved to be the beach at Nieuport.

Thursday, May 30

With heavy low cloud blanketing northern France and Belgium throughout the day, and mist and smoke over Dunkirk making operations hazardous, air activity was seriously reduced. This welcome respite from the almost constant bombing experienced in previous days allowed the pace of evacuation to markedly increase. So by nightfall it seemed almost possible that the last BEF troops might be evacuated within 24 hours provided Dunkirk harbour was used rather than the adjoining beaches which were now under threat from the enemy advance.

Efforts to hamper further enemy progress at Diksmuide and Nieuport were prevented by persistent low cloud and 11 Bomber Command Blenheims dispatched around mid-morning were forced to abandon the attack. But a further 48 sorties at 5.00 p.m. met with better success following slight improvement in weather conditions. The medium bombers of No. 2 Group flew 68 sorties without loss during the day but it was now clear that they had been operating at maximum effort, and suffering severe losses, for too long. So, while they would continue to support land operations, it was decided this would be on a reduced scale to allow replacement crews and aircraft to come up to strength.

Despite the appalling conditions (10/10 cloud between 300 and 3,000 feet with visibility down to 100 yards over the French coast reported at 10.50 a.m.), RAF fighters continued to patrol Dunkirk in strength flying 265 sorties during the day but finding few enemy

The exploits of No. 103 (Bomber) Squadron were specially commended by the Air Ministry — remember this was the unit that lost four Battles on May 14 in the vain attempt to destroy the bridges at Maastricht. On May 30 the squadron was allocated three decorations by the French so a shortlist of deserving aircrew was drawn up and the three recipients decided by the toss of a coin! Recommendations were duly put forward in the names of a pilot, Flying Officer Roy Max, an observer, Sergeant J. A. McCudden, and radio-operator air-gunner, Corporal Madkins. In this picture, the CO, Wing Commander T. C. Dickens (left) is congratulating Sergeant McCudden on his nomination for a 'gong'. In the event, the paperwork for the awards was lost during the collapse in France and the three medals never materialised.

aircraft in evidence. Further inland, where conditions were marginally better, French bombers also operated but were unfortunate to meet with German fighters though most losses experienced this day were due to the airman's common enemy: the weather.

They failed to return . . . a lonely grave beside a burned-out Battle.

Pictured somewhat earlier in the war at No. 99 Squadron's base at Newmarket, could this Wellington be LN⊙P which crashed near Chrishall?

ROYAL AIR FORCE

UK-based aircraft lost or damaged over the Western Front on this date:

RAF BOMBER COMMAND

15 Squadron, Wyton
Transport near Nieuport:

Blenheim IV N6156. Returned to Martlesham damaged by ground-fire 10.00 a.m. F/O Robertson wounded, rest of crew unhurt. Aircraft damaged but repairable.

99 Squadron, Newmarket
St Omer:

Wellington P9241. Run low on fuel on return from sortie, abandoned by crew, and crashed at Kilverstone Hall near Thetford 3.00 a.m. P/O J. C. Young baled out but killed, rest of crew unhurt. Aircraft a write-off.

Wellington P9282. Run low on fuel on return from sortie and abandoned by crew over Chrishall, north-west of Saffron Walden, 3.00 a.m. P/O J. Brain and crew baled out unhurt. Aircraft LN⊙P a write-off.

Wellington R3196. Run low on fuel on return from sortie and abandoned by crew over Brettenham, east of Thetford, 3.15 a.m. P/O C. J. A. C. Brain and crew baled out, two landing injured. Aircraft a write-off.

RAF COASTAL COMMAND

48 Squadron, Detling
Shipping Patrol:

Anson I N9919. Port engine damaged by AA fire from friendly trawler and ditched off Ramsgate 8.20 p.m. P/O Tilson, Sgt Ardenne, LAC O'Reilly, and LAC Smith rescued by HMS *Vega* landing at Sheerness. Aircraft ÓY⊙J lost.

RAF FIGHTER COMMAND

245 Squadron, Hawkinge
Patrol Dunkirk:

Hurricane. Returned with throttle jammed open and windscreen shattered by return fire from Do17 of I./KG3 over Dunkirk 1.15 p.m. F/Lt J. A. Thomson slightly wounded thigh. Aircraft repairable.

Hurricane N2496. Forced-landed in bad weather following aborted patrol over Dunkirk 2.00 p.m. Sgt P. Banks unhurt. Aircraft repairable.

Hurricane N2597. Forced-landed in bad weather following aborted patrol over Dunkirk 2.00 p.m. P/O G. Marsland unhurt. Aircraft repairable.

Hurricane N2709. Forced-landed in bad weather following aborted patrol over Dunkirk 2.00 p.m. P/O R. A. West unhurt. Aircraft repairable.

609 Squadron, Northolt
Patrol Dunkirk — Ostend:

Spitfire L1086. Run out of fuel on return from patrol and crashed into explosive works at Oakley, near Harwich, 4.15 p.m. F/O G. D. Ayre killed. Aircraft a write-off.

Spitfire L1063. Damaged a wing forced-landing at Frinton-on-Sea having lost bearings on return from patrol 4.15 p.m. F/O J. C. Dundas unhurt. Aircraft repairable.

Spitfire N3203. Forced-landed at Rochford out of fuel on return from patrol 4.15 p.m. F/O F. J. Howell unhurt. Aircraft repairable.

Spitfire. Forced-landing at Frinton-on-Sea having lost bearings on return from patrol 4.15 p.m. F/O J. Dawson unhurt. Aircraft repairable.

616 Squadron, Rochford
Weather Test:

Spitfire. Undercarriage collapsed on landing 11.30 a.m. F/Lt D. E. Gillam unhurt. Aircraft repairable.

FRENCH AIR FORCE

DAT Rennes. Crushed by taxying French bomber while sleeping in grass at Rennes airfield. Sgt J. Kedziora killed. No aircraft loss.

GAO 543 Potez 63.11 (677). Crashed making a forced-landing at Bergère-les-Vertus, south-west of Châlons-en-Champagne, due to engine failure during reconnaissance sortie over the Aisne. S/Lt Perret and S/Lt Garden unhurt. Sgt Orsat baled out breaking an arm and a leg. Aircraft a write-off.

GAO 1/551 Potez 63-11. Returned damaged by AA fire during reconnaissance sortie between Letanne and Les Grandes-Armoises 4.00 p.m. Adjt Langlois, S/Lt Estirac, Sgt R. Hild unhurt. Aircraft damaged but repairable.

GB I/11 LeO 451 (211). Returned to Étampes-Montdidier badly damaged by flak during attack on bridge over the Somme Canal 3.15 p.m. Crew unhurt. Aircraft damaged but repairable.

GB II/12 LeO 451 (53). Returned slightly damaged by flak during attack on bridges near Abbeville 6.15 p.m. Capt Risse and crew unhurt. Aircraft repairable.

GB 2/15 Farman 222 (25). Believed damaged by flak during bombing attack on Trier. Crashed and burned out at Les Riebles, near Lévigny during return flight. Capt T. Vanhoutte (*Commandant*), S/Lt R. Humbert, Lt J. Pailloux, Adjt R. Loyer, Sgt G. Seguin, and Adjt D. Servier killed. Sgt Simeoni badly injured leg. Aircraft a write-off.

GB II/38 Amiot 143. Suffered engine failure during night sortie to attack motorised columns north-west of La Fère and crashed on landing at Chaumont. Adjt J. Barrau de Lorde seriously injured; died next day. Rest of crew unhurt. Aircraft a write-off.

GB II/38 Amiot 143 (78). Wrecked in forced-landing near Genouilly; circumstances not recorded. Crew unhurt. Aircraft a write-off.

GBA 1/51 Breguet 693 (74). Shot down by Lt Adrian of 1./JG2 during bombing sortie north of Amiens; crashed and burned out near Rollot, south-east of Montdidier 5.07 p.m. Capt G. Hallopeau (*Commandant*) killed. Sgt C. Eugène badly wounded. Aircraft a write-off.

The aerodrome occupied heathland just north of the famous racecourse.

GBA II/51 Potez 633 (17). Shot down by Oberfw Schmid of 1./JG2 during bombing sortie south of Amiens and crashed outside Dury 5.05 p.m. Sgt Viger wounded. S/Lt Rolland unhurt. Aircraft a write-off.

GBA II/51 Breguet 693 (44). Damaged by Bf109s over Sacy-le-Grand during bombing sortie north of Amiens. Possibly that claimed by Lt Grote of 3./JG76 4.45 p.m. Sgt Ancelin and Sgt Lamy unhurt. Aircraft a write-off.

GC III/6 Moranes 406. Destroyed or badly damaged during enemy bombing attack on Coulommiers. No pilot casualties. Aircraft all write-offs.

GR II/33 Potez 63.11 (690). Undershot runway on landing from training flight and crashed at Orly. S/Lt Schutz badly injured shoulder. S/Lt Ysermann and Cpl Quellec slightly injured. Aircraft a write-off.

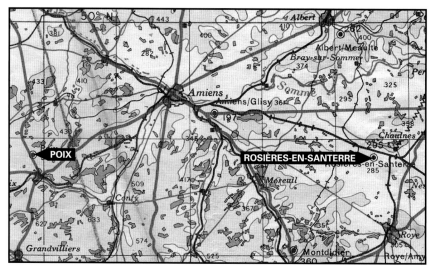

LUFTWAFFE

2.(H)/23 Henschel Hs126. Lost on reconnaissance over Montreuil. One crewman believed wounded. Aircraft a write-off.

1.(H)/41 Henschel Hs126. Returned damaged by own flak near St-Juliaan, north-west of Ypres. Oberlt P. Liesenhoff wounded. Aircraft repairable.

5.(F)/122 Dornier Do17P. Shot down by F/L Wight of No. 213 Squadron during reconnaissance sortie east of Dunkirk and crashed near Leisele, south-west of Furnes, 3.10 p.m. Lt W. Endemann and crew killed. Aircraft a write-off.

2./JG21 Messerschmitt Bf109E. Run into a trench on landing at Guise. Uffz R. Woick unhurt. Aircraft repairable.

1./JG76 Messerschmitt Bf109E-1 (3247). Lost bearings and landed in error at Orconte airfield. Uffz R. Hager captured unhurt. Aircraft 6 + a write-off.

5./KG2 Dornier Do17Z. Run out of fuel and abandoned over Wemmetsweiler, near Saarbrücken. Uffz J. Butz baled out landing slightly injured, rest of crew baled out unhurt. Aircraft a write-off.

I./KG3 Dornier Do17Z. Believed crash-landed badly damaged in attacks by F/L Thomson, P/O Pennington, and P/O Southwell of No. 245 Squadron over Dunkirk 1.10 p.m. Crew believed wounded. Aircraft a write-off.

Stabsstaffel KG27 Heinkel He111P. Forced-landed near Lille damaged by enemy fire. Crew unhurt. Aircraft a write-off.

1./KG30 Junkers Ju88A. Believed shot down by Coastal Command aircraft over Schouwen island during anti-shipping sortie. Three crewmen killed. Aircraft lost.

6./KG77 Dornier Do17Z. Flew into the ground south-west of Bras, north of Recogne, cause unknown. Oberfw G. Eschbaumer, Fw E. Pettinger, Fw H. Herzhauser, and Uffz B. Hopfenmüller killed. Aircraft a write-off.

16./KGzbV.1 Junkers Ju52. Aircraft leading formation drifted off course due to cross wind and low cloud during fuel supply flight from Libin to St-Pol. Lost height but damaged by ground-fire and forced to land south-east of Amiens 1.00 p.m. Fw H. Siegle, Uffz M. Wolgast, Uffz W. Bathe, and Gefr H. Sehr captured unhurt. Aircraft 1Z+DQ a write-off.

16./KGzbV.1 Junkers Ju52. Lost bearings during formation flight from Libin to St-Pol and forced-landed south-east of Amiens 1.00 p.m. Uffz P. Hemmerling, Uffz A. Klingebiel, Uffz K. Wenzel, and Obergefr G. Hornung captured unhurt. Aircraft 1Z+AQ a write-off.

16./KGzbV.1 Junkers Ju52. Lost bearings during formation flight from Libin to St-Pol and forced-landed south-east of Amiens 1.00 p.m. Uffz A. Filter and Uffz M. Ölschlegel, and both Uffz K. Nissen and H. Jäger of 14./KGzbV.1, captured unhurt. Aircraft 1Z+BQ a write-off.
The serial numbers of the three aircraft above were 6328, 6437 and 6438.

KGrzbV.172 Junkers Ju52 (5268). Crashed at Meyerode, south-east of Malmédy, cause unknown. Four crewmen killed, one injured. Aircraft a write-off.

5./ZG1 Messerschmitt Bf110C. Lost on transfer flight from Lachen-Speyerdorf to Trier-Euren. Lt E. Eichler, Gefr H. Book, and Uffz J. Schmitt killed. Aircraft a write-off.
This aircraft was found on June 3. The passenger, Josef Schmitt, was a mechanic with 2./JG51.

Picking over the fruits of victory at Poix or possibly at Rosières-en-Santerre as both aerodromes near Amiens were used by Morane units. Unfortunately these Morane 406 serials were not recorded so the wrecks cannot be identified.

Friday, May 31

Evacuation proceeded despite German artillery fire which now raked the beaches at De Panne and Bray-Dunes forcing troops gathered there to move further west within an increasingly shrinking beach-head. British and French troops were being taken off in roughly equal numbers and small motor-boats and towed craft were now arriving off-shore in considerable numbers. That evening, Lord Gort and his staff embarked for England having handed command of the reduced BEF to General Alexander.

RAF reconnaissance during the day was largely devoted to identifying enemy batteries shelling Dunkirk and several targets at Bergues, Furnes, and Nieuport were located. Enemy columns pressing towards Ostend from Diksmuide, and Furnes from Ypres, were bombed regularly from first light to early evening by No. 2 Group Blenheims, while an attack by six Albacores on road junctions near Westende just after 4.00 p.m. proved particularly successful in impeding enemy progress. Also, around 8.00 p.m. Fleet Air Arm Skuas attacked installations north-east of Nieuport.

With an improvement in the weather, increased Luftwaffe activity was to be expected though their attacks were aimed at shipping throughout the day, the port and town of Dunkirk not being targeted. Eight RAF fighter patrols, of three to four squadrons, covered Dunkirk from 5.10 a.m. to 8.10 p.m. and involving 289 sorties. However, this included four significant periods – a total of seven hours — when no fighter cover was in place.

Three major raids developed, the first around 2.15 p.m., another at 5.00 p.m. and the third at 7.00 p.m. though frequent attacks on the concentration of shipping, either by small formations or isolated aircraft, were a feature of the day and proved difficult to counter. A single minesweeper was sunk as a result of air attack, and two more damaged, while six destroyers were damaged in collisions.

Further south, following reconnaissance sorties mid-afternoon, French medium bombers struck at enemy concentrations between Amiens and Abbeville during the early evening. Activity on this front resulted in the loss of 21 French aircraft and five more damaged during the day.

At night, 33 AASF bombers struck at communications in the Ardennes and Meuse crossings though not all were able to find their targets due to unfavourable weather. RAF Bomber Command, operating on a reduced scale than usual, sent 30 Wellingtons to bomb roads approaching Nieuport and Bergues to relieve pressure on the Dunkirk perimeter.

The shelling of the De Panne beach — at the extreme eastern end of the encircled pocket — became so intense that it was decided that II Corps should pull back westwards (actually into France as the frontier ran right through the middle of the perimeter). This move was implemented on May 31 and by the following morning the last troops had left this sector.

The King's summer palace on the left has since been demolished. All that marks the site is rubble and a Belgian memorial.

What must have been some of the longest, most frustrating queues of all time formed up on the beaches east of Dunkirk. Although two-thirds of the troops embarked from the Continent did so from the port, nearly 100,000 men were lifted straight off the open beach. Apart from De Panne at the eastern end, there were two other loading points: Bray-Dunes (left) roughly in the centre for I Corps, and Malo-les-Bains close to the town of Dunkirk for III Corps and the French. *Right:* Empty beaches and windswept sand . . . where an army was saved to fight another day.

397

BRITISH AIR FORCES IN FRANCE

226 SQUADRON, FAUX-VILLECERF

Battle L5461. Returned damaged by AA fire during attack on Laon airfield in bad weather 11.45 a.m. AC1 H. G. Lewis wounded in leg and thigh, rest of crew unhurt. Aircraft damaged but repairable.

501 SQUADRON, MOURMELON-LE-GRAND

Hurricane L2056. Crashed on landing from patrol aborted due to bad weather 7.10 a.m. Sergeant J. E. Loverseed injured. Aircraft SD⊙G a write-off.

UK-based aircraft lost or damaged on operations over the Western Front:

RAF AIR COMPONENT

2 Squadron, Bekesbourne
Tactical reconnaissance:

Lysander. Believed crippled in attack by Uffz Busch of 2./JG20 during observation sortie between Nieuport and Ostend, retired west at low level but shot down by Lt Müncheberg of Stab III./JG26 between Furnes and Dunkirk 2.35 p.m. F/O C. H. Dearden killed. LAC A. O'N. McCoy missing. Aircraft KO⊙K lost.

16 Squadron, Lympne
Tactical reconnaissance:

Lysander P9127. Believed that claimed by Fw Witzel of 6./JG27 over Dunkirk 12.30 p.m. Crashed near Pihen-lès-Guines. F/Lt G. R. Shepley killed. P/O C. J. F. Hare missing. Aircraft a write-off.

Lysander L4793. Shot down by Major Freiherr von Berg *(Gruppenkommandeur)* of Stab III./JG26 and crashed in Channel between Dunkirk and Nieuport 7.20 p.m. P/O G. M. V. Biden and Sgt A. Beard both missing. Aircraft lost.

RAF BOMBER COMMAND

37 Squadron, Feltwell
Nieuport:

Wellington L7791. Crashed near Eringhem, south of Dunkirk, 11.30 p.m. P/O Sir A. T. Wilson and Sgt J. F. Brown killed. P/O W. A. Gray believed badly wounded, died June 9 at Cambrai. Sgt J. R. Axford and LAC E. R. Orland both captured. Aircraft a write-off.

Formerly a Lieutenant-Colonel in the 32nd Sikh Pioneers, Sir A T Wilson KCIE, CSI, CMG, DSO, was a holder of the King's Medal and Sandhurst Sword of Honour, and MP for Hitchin 1933-1940. Aged 56 years, he is thought to be the oldest and most highly decorated airman lost on bomber operations.

38 Squadron, Marham
Diksmuide:

Wellington R3162. Crashed at Furnes, southwest of Ostend, 12.30 a.m. F/O V. A. W. Rosewarne, P/O R. Baynes, Sgt J. Knight, Sgt D. D. G. Spencer, Sgt J. Dolan, and AC2 J. C. Adams killed. Aircraft a write-off.

RAF COASTAL COMMAND

500 Squadron, Detling
Enemy shipping off Boulogne:

Anson I R3389. Undershot landing on one engine, undercarriage collapsed, and crashed on the airfield 1.15 a.m. F/O R. D. C. Chambers killed in bomb explosion. P/O D. E. Bond rescued badly injured. Cpl Petts and LAC Smith unhurt. Aircraft MK⊙W a write-off.

Corporal Daphne Pearson stationed at Detling in Kent was the first woman to be awarded the George Cross — the highest decoration for bravery not in the face of the enemy. Unable to release his bombs, Pilot Officer Bond of No. 500 Squadron returned to base with one engine out and on landing the undercarriage of his Anson collapsed and fire broke out. When Corporal Pearson ran to the crash to pull the pilot from his seat, he muttered that there were still bombs on board and she just managed to drag him further away before they detonated, Flying Officer Richard Chambers, the navigator, being killed in the explosion. Daphne, later promoted to Assistant Section Officer, was awarded the Empire Gallantry Medal in July 1940 and, when the George Cross was instituted by King George VI on September 24 that year, holders of the EGM had to return their medals in exchange for the George Cross.

801 (FAA) Squadron, Detling
Pontoons over Nieuport Canal:

Skua L2917. Shot down by Bf109s of 3./JG20 after attack on piers and crashed in the Channel west of Nieuport. Believed one of those claimed by Oberlt Lignitz 8.00 p.m. Sub Lt J. B. Marsh and Naval Airman G. R. Nicholson missing. Aircraft lost.

Skua L3005. Shot down by Bf109s of 3./JG20 after attack on piers and crashed in sea off Nieuport. Possibly that claimed by Lt Kolbow 8.10 p.m. Lt R. L. Strange and Petty Officer N. R. Reid missing. Aircraft lost.

Skua L2881. Returned riddled by ground-fire and Bf109s of 3./JG20 after attack on piers at Nieuport and possibly that attacked by Uffz Heilmann 8.00 p.m. Sub Lt R. M. S. Martin and Naval Airman R. Hedger wounded. Aircraft damage state not recorded.

RAF FIGHTER COMMAND

64 Squadron, Kenley
Patrol Dunkirk:

Spitfire K9813. Shot down in combat with Bf109s of I./JG20 and Bf110s of 5./ZG26 off Dunkirk 5.00 p.m. F/Sgt G. H. Hatch captured badly wounded, died September 26. Aircraft a write-off.

Spitfire P9369. Returned damaged following combat with Bf109s of I./JG20 and Bf110s of 5./ZG26 off Dunkirk 5.00 p.m. F/Sgt C. Flynn unhurt. Aircraft repairable.

Spitfire. Returned damaged following combat with Bf109s of I./JG20 and Bf110s of 5./ZG26 off Dunkirk 5.00 p.m. Sgt A. E. Binham unhurt. Aircraft repairable.

111 Squadron, Hawkinge
Patrol Dunkirk:

Hurricane. Landed at Manston oil system, port wing, and tail damaged by return fire from He111s of KG27 engaged over Dunkirk 7.40 p.m. Sgt W. L. Dymond unhurt. Aircraft damaged but repairable.

Hurricane L1973. Landed at Manston damaged by return fire during attack on He111s of KG27 over Dunkirk 7.40 p.m. Sgt J. Robinson wounded in ankle. Aircraft repairable.

213 Squadron, Manston
Patrol Dunkirk:

Hurricane. Shot down in combat with Bf109s of III./JG26 and abandoned off Dunkirk 2.40 p.m. S/L H. D. McGregor baled out unhurt, landing in a minefield, rescued unhurt and landed at Dover. Aircraft AK⊙L lost.

No. 264 Squadron suffered another grievous loss on the last day of the month when five of their Defiants and three crews failed to return. Even so, they claimed four Bf109s and six He111s destroyed in the course of two vicious actions during the day.

Hurricane P2763. Shot down in combat with Bf109s of III./JG26 and abandoned over Dunkirk 2.40 p.m. F/O Robinson baled out unhurt. Aircraft AK⊙G a write-off.

Hurricane P3424. Set alight in combat with Bf109s of III./JG26 and crash-landed south of Dunkirk 2.40 p.m. P/O W. M. Sizer unhurt. Aircraft AK⊙P a write-off.

Hurricane P3361. Shot down in combat with Bf109s of III./JG26 over Dunkirk 2.40 p.m. F/O W. N. Gray killed. Aircraft AK⊙D a write-off.

Hurricane P3419. Shot down in combat with Bf109s of III./JG26 over Nieuport 2.40 p.m. Sgt T. Boyd killed. Aircraft AK⊙A a write-off.

222 Squadron, Hornchurch
Patrol Dunkirk:

Spitfire N3295. Engine damaged by anti-aircraft fire and belly-landed on beach near Fort Mardyck, west of Dunkirk, 6.00 a.m. P/O G. G. A. Davies unhurt. Aircraft ZD⊙G destroyed by pilot.

229 Squadron,
Patrol Dunkirk:

Hurricane L1982. Starboard aileron shot off in combat with Bf109s of I./JG20 and Bf110s of 5./ZG26 and went into an inverted spin, abandoned over the Channel 5.00 p.m. P/O V. B. S. Verity baled out unhurt and rescued by paddle steamer. Aircraft lost.

Hurricane P3553. Damaged in combat with Bf109s of I./JG20 and Bf110s of 5./ZG26 and crashed on landing approach 5.45 p.m. Sgt D. F. Edgehill badly wounded. Aircraft a write-off.

242 Squadron, Manston
Patrol Dunkirk — Furnes:

Hurricane P2732. Shot down in combat with Bf109s and crashed in the Channel. Possibly that claimed by Oberfw Dau of 1./JG20 north-west of Nieuport 8.15 p.m. P/O G. M. Stewart missing. Aircraft lost.

Hurricane P2884. Returned engine cowling damaged in combat with Bf109s of I./JG20 off Dunkirk 8.15 p.m. F/Lt G. H. F. Plinston unhurt. Aircraft repairable.

245 Squadron, Hawkinge
Patrol Dunkirk:

Hurricane P2902. Belly-landed on beach badly damaged by Lt Ulenberg of 2./JG26 in combat north-east of Dunkirk 1.20 p.m. P/O K. B. McGlashan wounded in thigh. Aircraft DX⊙R abandoned.
Wreckage recovered in 1988 and returned to UK where registered G-ROBT and subject of major restoration project 1994-2001 and returned to flying condition as DX⊙X.

264 Squadron, Duxford
Patrol Dunkirk — Calais:

Defiant L6968. Shot down in combat with Bf109s of III./JG26 off De Panne 2.40 p.m. P/O G. L. Hickman and LAC A. Fidler both believed baled out but killed. Aircraft lost.

Defiant L6961. Collided with P/O Young during combat with Bf109s of III./JG26 and crash-landed on beach near Dunkirk 2.40 p.m. P/O D. Whitley and LAC Turner unhurt. Aircraft abandoned.

Defiant L6980. Collided with P/O Whitley during combat with Bf109s of III./JG26 and disintegrated over Dunkirk 2.40 p.m P/O M. H. Young baled out unhurt. Sgt S. B. Johnson missing. Aircraft a write-off.

Defiant L6975. Shot down during attack on He111s of KG27 off Dunkirk 7.35 p.m. F/Lt N. G. Cooke and Cpl A. Lippett missing. Aircraft lost.

Defiant L6972. Damaged by return fire during attack on He111s of KG27 and ditched in sea five miles off Dover 7.40 p.m. P/O E. G. Barwell and P/O J. E. M. Williams rescued by a destroyer. Aircraft lost.

Defiant L7019. Badly damaged by return fire during attack on He111s of KG27 over Dunkirk 7.40 p.m. and crashed on landing at Manston. P/O R. W. Stokes unhurt. LAC Fairbrother baled out wounded. Aircraft damaged but repairable.

607 Squadron, Croydon

Hurricane. Believed crashed due to flying accident, details unknown. P/O A. S. Dini killed. Aircraft a write-off.

609 Squadron, Northolt
Patrol Dunkirk:

Spitfire N3202. Shot down by Bf109s of 9./JG26 off Dunkirk 2.45 p.m. F/Lt D. Persse-Joynt missing. Aircraft lost.

Spitfire L1081. Shot down in combat with Bf109s and crashed in sea off Dover 7.30 p.m. Possibly that claimed by Lt Müncheberg of Stab III./JG26. F/O J. C. Gilbert missing. Aircraft lost.

Spitfire L1087. Shot down in combat with Bf109s and ditched in sea 2 miles off Dover 7.30 p.m. Possibly that claimed by Lt Westphal of Stab III./JG26. Sgt G. C. Bennett wounded in right hand, rescued by minesweeper *Playboy*. Aircraft lost.

610 Squadron, Gravesend
Patrol Dunkirk:

Spitfire N3274. Shot down in combat with Bf109s of I./JG20 and Bf110s of 5./ZG26 and crashed in sea off Dunkirk 5.30 p.m. F/O G. L. Chambers missing. Aircraft lost.

Spitfire L1013. Shot down in combat with Bf109s of I./JG20 and Bf110s of 5./ZG26 and crashed in sea off Dunkirk 5.30 p.m. F/O G. Keighley baled out unhurt, rescued and landed at Ramsgate. Aircraft DW⊙E lost.

No. 610 Squadron flying from Gravesend (which ironically became the home of No. 264 in December 1940), lost two of its Spitfires to the combined efforts of the Bf109s of Jagdgeschwader 20 and the Bf110s of the 5th Staffel of Zerstörergeschwader 26.

One of the aircraft lost by the Armée de l'Air that Friday was this Dewoitine 520 which pancaked south-west of Abbeville.

FRENCH AIR FORCE

GB 2/11 LeO 451 (3001). Shot down by Bf109s of 2./JG2 and 9./JG53 during sortie to attack advancing enemy columns south of Amiens 7.30 p.m. Crashed and exploded at Sains-en-Amiénois. Cmdt. P. Berdoulat *(Groupe Commandant)* and Capt P. Maury *(Commandant)* killed. Sgt J. Salesses died of wounds in field hospital at Cempuis. Adjt Meyzonade baled out wounded. Aircraft a write-off.

GB I/11 LeO 451 (116). Shot down by Bf109s of 2./JG2 and 9./JG53 during sortie to attack advancing enemy columns south of Amiens 7.30 p.m. Crashed and burned out in Calmant Wood, Grattepanche. S/Lt A. Mazerolles and Adjt J. Daniel killed. Sgt M. Rose died in field hospital at Cempuis. Sgt P. Peyron baled out too low and fell dead near St-Fuscien. Aircraft a write-off.

GB I/11 LeO 451 (133). Shot down by Bf109s of 2./JG2 and 9./JG53 during sortie to attack enemy columns south of Amiens. Abandoned over Ressons-sur-Matz, 15 km northwest of Compiègne 7.30 p.m. S/Lt A. Bourges, Adjt H. Gauthier, Sgt G. Weber, and Sgt P. Michel all baled out too low and killed. Aircraft a write-off.

GB I/11 LeO 451 (56). Shot down by Bf109s of 2./JG2 and 9./JG53 during sortie to attack enemy columns south of Amiens. Crashed at Plessier-Rozainvillers, 15 km north-east of Montdidier 7.30 p.m. S/Lt J. Debrocq, Adjt R. Allaire, Adjt A. Blanquart, and Sgt P. Thouron killed. Aircraft a write-off. Aircraft a write-off.

GB I/12 LeO 451 (24). Believed shot down by Oberlt Wittenberg of Stab III./JG53 during sortie to attack enemy concentrations between Abbeville and Amiens 7.00 p.m. Crashed near Wanel, south-east of Abbeville, and later exploded. Lt E. Filippi and Cpl J. Dumont killed. Adjt Mathonnière wounded. Cpl Jacquemin unhurt. Aircraft a write-off.

GB 1/19 Douglas DB-7 (32). Believed that shot down by Oberlt Bethke of 2./JG2 south-west of Amiens during mission to attack roads near St Quentin 7.10 p.m. Crashed and exploded at Le Quesnel-Aubry. Lt H. Constant, Adjt H. Schoenherr, and Adjt A. Charoy killed. Aircraft a write-off.

GB I/19 Douglas DB-7 (10). Forced-landed at Gisors damaged by Bf109s of 2./JG53 during sortie to attack roads near St Quentin 6.50 p.m. Cdt. Chassandre-Patron *(Groupe Commandant)* and crew unhurt. Aircraft repairable.

GB I/19 Douglas DB-7 (46). Shot down by Bf109s of 2./JG53 south-east of Albert during sortie to attack roads near St Quentin 6.50 p.m. and possibly that attacked by Fw Heidmeier. Crashed beside the road from Bray-sur-Somme to Etinehem, outside Morlancourt. S/Lt F. Palmade killed. Lt F. Henry thrown from aircraft and died of injuries. Sgt Thyl baled out and captured unhurt. Aircraft a write-off.

GB I/19 Douglas DB-7 (42). Badly damaged by Bf109s of 2./JG53 during mission to attack roads near St Quentin and forced-landed near Auneuil, south-west of Beauvais 7.15 p.m. Possibly that claimed by Lt Schmid. Capt Couilleau *(Commandant)* and crew unhurt. Aircraft a write-off.

GB II/19 Douglas DB-7 (5). Believed shot down by Uffz Franke of 2./JG53 during attack on enemy armour and flak positions north of St Simon 7.12 p.m. Crashed and exploded alongside the canal at La Vallée du Pont, Artemps. Adjt J. Picart, Adjt L. Beynet, and Sgt P. Lajule killed. Aircraft a write-off.

The pilot and gunner of this aircraft, Louis Beynet and Pierre Lajule, were recovered by German troops and originally buried at the crash site but re-interred in the cemetery at Essigny-le-Grand on March 26, 1941. No trace of the observer, Joseph Picart, was found and he has no known grave.

GB I/31 LeO 451 (109). Shot down by Lt Volk of 9./JG53 south-east of St Just-en-Chaussée during low-level reconnaissance sortie to Abbeville. Crashed and burned out at Angivillers 3.45 p.m. S/Lt P. Scavizzi killed. Sgt J. Desesquelles and Sgt G. Champenois badly wounded, died in Agel hospital in Beauvais. Sgt Verna badly burned face. Aircraft a write-off.

GB I/31 LeO 451 (189). Returned to Chartres damaged by Bf109s during low-level reconnaissance over Abbeville and probably that attacked by Fw Ochsenkühn of 9./JG53 3.50 p.m. S/Lt Cassegrain and crew unhurt. Aircraft repairable.

GB II/31 LeO 451 (73). Set alight under attack from Bf109s of III./JG53 south of Abbeville and abandoned during bombing of enemy concentrations between Amiens and Abbeville. Possibly that claimed by Lt Claus 6.55 p.m. Sgt Callac and Sgt Le Mezo baled out wounded. S/Lt Rapoport and Adjt Loiseleux baled out unhurt. Aircraft a write-off.

GB II/31 LeO 451 (268). Shot down by Bf109s of III./JG53 south of Abbeville during bombing sortie and abandoned between Amiens and Abbeville. Possibly that claimed by Lt Radlick 6.55 p.m. Lt Millet, Adjt Magnan, Sgt Proteau, and Sgt Caudry baled out unhurt. Aircraft a write-off.

GB 4/31 LeO 451 (29). Crashed and burned out south of the Eu forest, between le Caule and Ste Beuve, and believed that claimed by Hptmn Mölders *(Gruppenkommandeur)* of Stab III./JG53 6.00 p.m. Sgt P. Dauge killed. Sgt A. Rey badly wounded. Lt G. de La Tour du Pin and Capt Irumbery de Salaberry *(Commandant)* unhurt. Aircraft a write-off.

GB II/34 Amiot 143 (64). Forced-landed at Malicorne, near Mans, damaged by flak during night supply drop over Ypres and Dunkirk. Cpl Léger wounded; rest of crew unhurt. Aircraft damaged but repairable.

GBA II/54 Breguet 693 (35). Shot down by Fw Heinzeller of 5./JG3 during low-level attack on enemy tanks on the road to Blangy-sur-Bresle, and crash-landed south-west of Abbeville 5.25 p.m. S/Lt P. Legrand unhurt. Adjt Poilbout baled out and captured unhurt. Aircraft a write-off.

GB I/62 Martin 167F (37). Shot down by Bf109s of 6./JG3 during attack on crossroads north of Abbeville and possibly that attacked by Oberlt Woitke *(Staffelkapitän)* of 6./JG3 at low level near Aumale 7.00 p.m. Cmdt. du Jonchay wounded, rest of crew unhurt. Aircraft a write-off.

GB II/62 Martin 167F (120). Crash-landed at Mantes-la-Jolie airfield badly damaged by Bf109s of 6./JG3 during attack on crossroads north of Abbeville 7.00 p.m. and possibly that attacked by Lt Westerhoff. Sgt Dezellis badly wounded in thigh; rest of crew unhurt. Aircraft a write-off.

GB II/62 Martin 167F (121). Forced-landed at Villacoublay damaged by Bf109s of 6./JG3 during attack on crossroads north of Abbeville 7.00 p.m. Lt Moron and crew unhurt. Aircraft repairable.

GB 4/63 Martin 167F (112). Returned to Évreux-Fauville badly damaged by flak during attack on crossroads north of Abbeville 7.40 p.m. Lt Vieugeot (*Commandant*) and Sgt Martin wounded. Aircraft damaged but repairable.

GC II/3 Dewoitine 520. Returned badly damaged in combat with Bf109s of I./JG3 and III./JG53 during patrol west of Abbeville 6.15 p.m. Sgt Tourné unhurt. Aircraft damaged but repairable.

GC II/3 Dewoitine 520 (131). Damaged in combat with Bf109s of I./JG3 and III./JG53 during patrol west of Abbeville and forced-landed at Ercourt 6.25 p.m. Possibly that claimed by Oberlt von Hahn (*Staffelkapitän*) of 8./JG53. S/Lt G. Prayer wounded in foot, admitted to hospital in Beauvais. Aircraft 3 a write-off.

GC 3/3 Dewoitine 520 (218). Shot down in combat with Bf109s of I./JG3 and III./JG53 and forced-landed west of Abbeville 6.20 p.m. Possibly one of those claimed by Lt Stoll of 9./JG53. Capt A. Naudy (*Commandant*) wounded in arm, admitted to hospital in Beauvais. Aircraft a write-off.

GC II/3 Dewoitine 520. Shot down in combat with Bf109s of I./JG3 and III./JG53 and crashed west of Abbeville 6.15 p.m. Possibly that claimed by Lt Fleitz of 8./JG53. Adjt J. Phénix fractured skull, died in hospital. Aircraft a write-off.

GC II/3 Dewoitine 520 (51). Set alight in combat with Bf109s of I./JG3 and III./JG53 and abandoned west of Abbeville 6.15 p.m. Possibly attacked by Oberlt Keller (*Staffelkapitän*) of 1./JG3. Sgt Boyer baled out slightly burned and admitted to hospital in Beauvais. Aircraft a write-off.

GC III/7 Morane 406 (795). Shot down by Bf109s of I./JG3 and III./JG53 and abandoned south of Abbeville 6.35 p.m. Possibly one of those claimed by Hptmn Lützow (*Gruppenkommandeur*) of Stab I./JG3. Adjt J. Bertrand baled out badly burned on face and hands. Aircraft a write-off.

Another May casualty of the French Air Force. This Dewoitine 520 is believed to be the machine flown by Sous-Lieutenant Jean Parisse of the 2nd Escadrille of GC I/3 which forced-landed near Soissons on May 15 (see page 285).

LUFTWAFFE

2./JG2 Messerschmitt Bf109E-4. Shot down by return fire from LeO 451s of GB I/11 engaged south-west of Amiens 7.30 p.m. Oberleutnant S. Bethke baled out wounded. Aircraft 7+ a write-off.

Stab I./JG20 Messerschmitt Bf109E-1. Believed shot down in combat with No. 242 Squadron Hurricanes during attack on No. 801 Squadron Skuas over Dunkirk 7.45 p.m. Oberlt C. Borries (Stabskompanie-Chef) killed. Aircraft a write-off.

3./JG20 Messerschmitt Bf109E-4. Believed shot down in combat with No. 242 Squadron Hurricanes during attack on No. 801 Squadron Skuas over Dunkirk 7.45 p.m. Uffz W. Franke killed. Aircraft a write-off.

3./JG20 Messerschmitt Bf109E. Believed shot down in combat with No. 242 Squadron Hurricanes during attack on No. 801 Squadron Skuas north-west of Dunkirk and belly-landed outside Calais 7.50 p.m. Leutnant H. Kolbow unhurt. Aircraft 2 + a write-off.

I./JG21 Messerschmitt Bf109E-3. Hit trees on take-off and crashed at Monchy-Breton. Pilot unhurt. Aircraft a write-off.

Stab I./JG26 Messerschmitt Bf109E-3. Shot down in combat with Hurricanes and abandoned over Nieuport 1.20 p.m. Believed that claimed by F/L Dutton and P/O Newling of No. 145 Squadron. Oberleutnant K. Pielmeyer (Gruppenadjutant) baled out but parachute failed and fell dead at Mannekensvere, south-east of Ostend. Aircraft a write-off.

2./JG26 Messerschmitt Bf109E-1. Shot down by P/O Manger of No. 17 Squadron in combat east of Dunkirk and crashed west of Nieuport 1.20 p.m. Uffz J. Richter killed. Aircraft a write-off.

7./JG26 Messerschmitt Bf109E-1. Set alight during combat with No. 213 Squadron Hurricanes and No. 264 Squadron Defiants and crashed on Dunkirk beach 2.40 p.m. Leutnant W. Hütter-Wallek killed. Aircraft a write-off.

8./JG26 Messerschmitt Bf109E-1. Shot down in combat with No. 213 Squadron Hurricanes and No. 264 Squadron Defiants and ditched off Dunkirk 2.40 p.m. Uffz H. Brügelmann badly wounded. Aircraft a write-off.

I./JG53 Messerschmitt Bf109E-3. Collided with crippled LeO 451 of GB I/11 in action west of Noyon 7.00 p.m. Pilot baled out unhurt. Aircraft a write-off.

6./JG53 Messerschmitt Bf109E. Shot down by return fire from LeO 451 of GB I/11 west of Noyon and crashed at Marquéglise, north-west of Compiègne, 7.00 p.m. Oberfw W. Czikowsky killed. Aircraft a write-off.

7./KG4 Junkers Ju88A-1. Dive brakes failed during attack on shipping off Dunkirk and port engine damaged by fighters – ditched off shore. Possibly that attacked by Sgt Robinson of No. 111 Squadron 7.15 p.m. Oberlt H. Herrmann (Staffelkapitän) and crew survived, two slightly wounded. Aircraft lost.

8./KG4 Junkers Ju88A-1. Returned badly damaged by flak and fighters following attack on shipping off Dunkirk. Possibly that attacked by F/L Plinston of No. 242 Squadron 5.00 p.m. Oberlt D. Marwitz badly wounded, admitted to hospital in Amsterdam. Rest of crew unhurt. Aircraft a write-off.

Stabsstaffel KG27 Heinkel He111H. Badly damaged in attacks by No. 264 Squadron Defiants and No. 609 Squadron Spitfires and last seen flying on one engine; believed crashed in the Channel off Dunkirk. Fw W. Bokelch, Fw E. Jagemann, Uffz G. Kostrzewski, Uffz H. Kredel, and Flgr J. Wittgen all missing. Aircraft lost.

1./KG27 Heinkel He111. Believed returned badly damaged in attacks by No. 264 Squadron Defiants and No. 609 Squadron Spitfires over the Channel off Dunkirk 7.25 p.m. Fw R. Petschke slightly wounded, rest of crew unhurt. Aircraft a write-off.

5./KG27 Heinkel He111P. Shot down by No. 264 Squadron Defiants and No. 609 Squadron Spitfires during attack on shipping and believed crashed near St Folquin, between Calais and Dunkirk 7.00 p.m. Uffz H. Meyer, Uffz A. Knapp, Gefr H. Jank, and Gefr G. Gersch all killed. Aircraft a write-off.

5./KG27 Heinkel He111P. Returned damaged in attacks by No. 264 Squadron Defiants and No. 609 Squadron Spitfires during attack on shipping off Dunkirk 7.00 p.m. Oberfw H. Lohmann badly wounded, died June 12 — rest of crew unhurt. Aircraft 1G+IN damaged but repairable.

5./KG27 Heinkel He111P. Returned damaged by No. 264 Squadron Defiants and No. 609 Squadron Spitfires during attack on shipping off Dunkirk 7.00 p.m. Obergefr M. Maass badly wounded. Oberlt Kalischewski, Lt Lüder, and Oberfw E. Anacker unhurt. Aircraft 1G+AN damaged but repairable.

6./KG27 Heinkel He111P. Landed at Krefeld damaged in attacks by No. 264 Squadron Defiants and No. 609 Squadron Spitfires over Dunkirk 7.00 p.m. Lt H. Brandenberg and crew unhurt. Aircraft 1G+BP damage state not recorded.

7./KG30 Junkers Ju88A. Shot down by flak and crashed in sea off Dunkirk. Fw W. Bergfeld, Fw H. Schmidt, Gefr E. Burmester, and Gefr S. Cytron killed. Aircraft lost.

The bodies of this crew were washed ashore at various points along the French and Belgian coasts in the coming weeks.

I./KG55 Heinkel He111P. Involved in take-off collision at Malmsheim airfield. Two crewmen injured. Aircraft a write-off.

I./KG55 Heinkel He111P. Damaged in take-off collision at Malmsheim airfield. No crew casualties. Aircraft repairable.

9./KG55 Heinkel He111. Crash-landed at Malmsheim during transfer flight, cause not stated. Uffz G. Mittelstädt and Uffz M. Lippert badly injured. Aircraft damage state not recorded.

2./LG1 Heinkel He111H. Shot down by fighters during attack on shipping off Dunkirk. Fw R. Wetzig, Uffz O. Hiller, and Gefr F. Grosser all badly wounded, admitted to hospital. Aircraft a write-off.

Radio operator Fritz Grosser died in hospital at Torhout on June 16.

Stab I.(J)/LG2 Messerschmitt Bf109E. Forced-landed near Doullens slightly damaged by flak. Hptmn H. Trübenbach (Gruppenkommandeur) unhurt. Aircraft << repairable.

Well, another day is gone, and with it a lot of grand blokes. Got another brace of 109s today, but the whole Luftwaffe seems to leap on us — we were hopelessly outnumbered. I was caught napping by a 109 in the middle of a dog fight, and got a couple of holes in the aircraft, one of them filled the office with smoke, but the Jerry overshot and he's dead. If anyone says anything to you in the future about the inefficiency of the R.A.F. — I believe the B.E.F. troops were booing the R.A.F. in Dover the other day — tell them from me we only wish we could do more. But without aircraft we can do no more than we have done — that is, our best, and that's fifty times better than the German best, though they are fighting under the most advantageous conditions. I know of no R.A.F. pilot who has refused combat yet — and that sometimes means combat with odds of more than fifty to one.

Three of us the other day had been having a fight, and were practically out of ammunition and juice when we saw more than eighty 109s with twelve Ju87s. All the same we gave them combat, so much so that they left us alone in the end — on their side of the Channel too. This is not a tale of stirring heroism. It is just the work that we all do.

One of my sergeants shot down three fighters and a bomber before they got him — and then he got back in a paddle steamer. So don't worry, we are going to win this war even if we have only one aeroplane and one pilot left — the Boche could produce the whole Luftwaffe and you would see the one pilot and the one aeroplane go into combat. All that sounds very involved, but I am trying to convey to you something of the spirit of 'Per ardua ad astra' today. The spirit of the average pilot has to be seen to be believed.

FLIGHT LIEUTENANT R. D. G. WIGHT
No. 213 SQUADRON,
LETTER TO HIS MOTHER, MAY 31, 1940

These poignant words written at the height of the evacuation indicate only too clearly the odds faced by RAF fighter pilots over Dunkirk. All too often sent on patrol in 'penny packets', and operating close to the limit of their effective range, when enemy formations were met it was invariably at a disadvantage and, consequently, the RAF fighter presence seriously compromised. No. 213 Squadron arrived at Biggin Hill from Wittering on May 26 and flew their first sortie, a Blenheim escort mission to St Omer, two days later. In four days action over Dunkirk before returning to Wittering on June 4, the squadron lost nine aircraft with four pilots killed or missing, and one wounded. The words are also sadly prophetic for on August 11, 1940, Ronald Wight, flying out of Exeter, failed to return from a combat over the Channel off Portland in which seven squadrons of British fighters were outnumbered two to one. Later his body was washed up in France and he was buried in Cayeux-sur-Mer Communal Cemetery.

JUNE 1940

From Germany to the Atlantic coast. Precisely four weeks to the day after the attack in the West was launched, an advance party from the 7. Panzer-Division drove onto the beach at the small seaside hamlet of Les Petites-Dalles, 15 kilometres east of Fécamp.

A scant three weeks after the enemy offensive in the West opened on May 10, the military situation for the Allied forces could only be described as grim and the outlook bleak. Holland and Belgium had capitulated and were overrun. The German breakthrough at Sedan and rapid armoured thrust across mainland France to Abbeville and the Channel coast cut a swathe through the British and French armies, and what remained of the BEF, some 39,000 men, were now hemmed into a 60-square-mile pocket at Dunkirk, reliant on the Royal Navy for evacuation. As Allied defences were consolidated along the Somme and the Aisne, the harsh reality remained that the campaign was a military disaster — a débâcle of monumental proportions.

In the preceding three weeks the Dutch and Belgian air forces had been wiped out and the entire AASF medium bomber force decimated, its remaining Fairey Battles relegated to night operations and rendered non-operational during their retirement to rear airfields in south Champagne. RAF daylight bombing in France was now almost entirely the remit of No. 2 Group Blenheims operating from eastern England. The Air Component of the BEF had been forced to evacuate to England, and plans already in hand for remaining AASF units to withdraw towards Le Mans and Orléans. German air attacks meanwhile continued across mainland France, as well as the south and east of the country, exerting pressure on the already hard-pressed French air defences.

Within days the Luftwaffe would launch a strategic attack against a still powerful French Air Force as a prelude to a renewed southern offensive which proved something of a relief to the British government which, until then, had no means of knowing if the next attack might not be directed across the Channel against southern England. These were desperate days for the survival of European democracy as the normally ebullient and pugnacious Churchill later confided to Anthony Eden, then Secretary of State for War: 'Normally I wake up buoyant to a new day. Then I awoke with dread in my heart.'

By the end of the month the world would witness the culmination of the German campaign in the west with a victorious Wehrmacht occupying Holland, Belgium, and France. Comprehensively defeated by the overwhelming weight of forces and lightning speed of the German assault, or simply outflanked, the Allied armies that opposed them were systematically routed. What could be saved of the British Expeditionary Force was snatched from complete disaster in the 'deliverance' at Dunkirk, though less fortunate bodies of troops were unsuccessful in getting away from Calais and St-Valéry-en-Caux. Yet others withdrew south and west ahead of the German advance to seek evacuation from French Atlantic or Mediterranean ports.

This month saw Britain alone surviving to continue the struggle. Fighter Command, charged with defence of the country, was suddenly confronted with new and daunting challenges for, quite apart from the imminent prospect of invasion, the world's largest air force was soon to be within one hour's flight of London. As an official history records, despite its losses in France the RAF 'emerged strong enough to fight, and win, the crucial battle of the war — not after long years of painful reconstruction, but within a few brief weeks'.

403

Saturday, June 1

On Saturday, June 1, the first of the four aircraft carrying Hitler and his staff to Brussels landed at the airfield at Evere. Hitler's Focke Wulf Fw200 Condor 'Immelmann III' was numbered D-2600 and was the prototype Fw200V-1 specially adapted and modified for executive use as the *Führermaschine*.

Dawn mist and low cloud over Dunkirk soon dispersed and the first German attacks of the day started at 4.15 a.m. shortly before RAF fighter cover had been requested. As on previous days, the Luftwaffe was quick to exploit gaps in the British fighter cover and heavy attacks were launched by Stukas against shipping off shore during the intervals between patrols. They met with considerable success for three destroyers, HMS *Basilisk, Keith* and *Skipjack*, were sunk and another, HMS *Ivanhoe*, badly damaged during one morning attack. Two of the three Coastal Command Blenheims on standing patrol that attempted to intervene fell to enemy fighters.

Fighter Command put eight patrols of three to four squadrons over Dunkirk throughout the day with maximum effort during the early morning and late evening when, it was planned, the bulk of shipping would either be leaving or approaching the harbour. Visibility declined over the Channel coast by late afternoon and, interceptions made difficult, the last fighter patrol of the day around 9.00 p.m. returned without meeting any enemy aircraft and reporting 'thick cloud'.

The perimeter at Dunkirk was shrinking fast under continuing enemy pressure and the newly-cleared direct sea route from Dover now came within range of German artillery at Gravelines. With all three sea approaches thus threatened by enemy shore batteries, and the weight of air attacks during the day inflicting serious losses to British shipping, Vice-Admiral Ramsay was forced to a decision that the evacuation could only continue at night.

Day bombing operations by No. 2 Group Blenheims had commenced at 6.00 a.m. and concentrated on enemy forces advancing near Bergues and Furnes, with an evening attack on concentrations near Hondschoote at 8.30 p.m. In all, 54 sorties were flown without loss while, later that night, 16 Bomber Command Wellingtons aimed at roads around Rexpoede, Socx, and Furnes but over half of them failed to locate their primary objectives due to the indifferent weather which had also caused the AASF to cancel operations entirely.

After five days of relative calm on the southern front, as the Luftwaffe concentrated on Dunkirk, German bombers struck at targets deep in mainland France prompting the hurried redeployment of several French fighter units. Two main waves of attacks struck at targets in Toulon, Marseille, and railways around Lyon. Harried by French fighters, some bombers sought refuge by crossing into Swiss air space where they triggered an equally determined reaction from Swiss Bf109Es.

AASF Hurricanes saw their first action after several days of inactivity in which some redeployment had taken place and replacement aircraft and pilots arrived. It proved something of a rude re-awakening.

This was a pivotal day — a day on which British fighter strategy, despite the sacrifice of another 17 precious aircraft and 12 pilots, clearly failed to prevent serious losses to Allied shipping, men, and material, and no doubt added considerable weight to a growing undercurrent of criticism that would eventually find voice in the taunt: 'Where was the RAF?'. Though certainly not the sole factor to influence the decision, particularly as enemy shore batteries now threatened all three sea lanes, it was abundantly clear that, after six days and nights of supremely costly effort, Operation 'Dynamo' would shortly be called to a halt.

The Führer was greeted by Generaloberst Fedor von Bock, the commander of Heeresgruppe B: 'I summarised the situation, development and present state of play at Dunkirk. The Führer thanked us and developed his ideas about the overall war situation and the new operation. He announced the imminent entry of Italy into the war. He said he was concerned about Paris from where he was expecting French counter-attacks. Afterwards the Führer drove through the city with me; only a few people recognised him, pointing at him excitedly. He knew more about Brussels than I did, presumably this was from the Great War.' The visit was not only to confer with his army commanders but to spend the weekend revisiting the battlefields in Flanders where Hitler had fought. (The full itinerary of his tour is described in *After the Battle* No. 117.)

BRITISH AIR FORCES IN FRANCE

73 SQUADRON, GAYE

Hurricane. Set alight in combat with Bf109s of 8./JG53 over La Malmaison, east of Laon, crashed and burned out at Plesnoy 7.10 p.m. Possibly that claimed by Lt Fleitz. Sergeant W. Millner killed. Aircraft TP⊙Ka write-off.

Originally buried near Plesnoy, Wilfred Millner was reinterred in Épernay on February 6, 1947 and subsequently moved to Terlincthun.

Hurricane. Shot down in combat with Bf109s of 8./JG53 near La Malmaison, east of Laon 7.10 p.m. Possibly that claimed by Lt Kunert. Pilot Officer I. C. G. Potts captured. Aircraft TP⊙E a write-off.

Hurricane. Returned via Orly where forced-landed with port wing and starboard aileron badly damaged by cannon fire in combat with Bf109s over La Malmaison, east of Laon 7.10p.m. Probably that attacked by Lt Stoll of 9./JG53. Pilot Officer D. S. Scott unhurt. Aircraft TP⊙D damaged but repairable.

UK-based aircraft lost or damaged on operations over the Western Front:

RAF AIR COMPONENT

2 Squadron, Bekesbourne
Tactical reconnaissance:

Lysander L4809. Shot down by Hptmn Schellmann (*Gruppenkommandeur*) of Stab II./JG2 and crashed in the Channel between Nieuport and De Panne 4.45 a.m. F/O A. F. Doidge and Sgt I. R. W. Michelmore missing. Aircraft KO⊙B lost.

26 Squadron, Lympne
Tactical reconnaissance:

Lysander N1253. Returned possibly damaged by AA fire and crashed on landing at Hawkinge 6.45 a.m. P/O J. C. Paterson and LAC A. Carter killed. Aircraft a write-off.

Lysander L4761. Shot down by Lt von Moller of 1./JG2 and crashed south of Furnes 8.40 a.m. P/O R. Wilson and LAC A. V. Fitzgerald killed. Aircraft a write-off.

RAF BOMBER COMMAND

37 Squadron, Feltwell
Nieuport:

Wellington P9288. Failed to return and believed crashed in the Channel early a.m. F/O R. C. Simmons, Sgt J. McLean, Sgt E. A. Downham, AC1 D. Atack, and AC1 J. Bridge missing. Aircraft lost.

RAF COASTAL COMMAND

254 Squadron, Detling
Patrol Goodwin Sands:

Blenheim IV L9481. Shot down by Oberlt Framm (*Staffelkapitän*) of 2./JG27 and crashed in the Channel 8.05 a.m. F/O J. W. Baird killed. Sgt R. Roskrow (of No. 48 Squadron) missing. P/O G. W. Spiers rescued unhurt. Aircraft QY⊙A lost.

Blenheim IV R3630. Shot down by Fw Sawallisch of 2./JG27 and crashed in the Channel 8.08 a.m. Sgt R. A. Bate, Sgt J. C. Love, and LAC W. T. Harrison missing. Aircraft QY⊙Q lost.

On 1st June 1940 I was on patrol with Red Section, No. 19 Squadron, and shortly after reaching the patrol line we found 12 Me 110's over Dunkirk. We moved into attack, whereupon they turned very quickly back over the town as if trying to escape. However, we soon engaged them and they broke up and most of them appeared to turn steeply to the left. This appeared to be the only means of escape they knew and they became quite easy to shoot at. I fired at several without apparent effect and then engaged one which had just begun a steep diving turn to the left. I had a full plan view of the top of the aircraft and opened fire at about 400 yards. I held my fire for almost eight seconds and could see my bullets going into the front half of the fuselage. At about 150 yards my ammunition ran out, and I had to avoid the shell-fire of another enemy aircraft which was firing at me from my port side. This evasion caused me to lose sight of the Me 110 I had attacked and, in spite of being able to state that my bullets had definitely registered, I cannot say whether it was disabled or not. I then started for home, diving with the 12lb boost in operation.

As I reached the outskirts of the fight a metallic 'bang' from my port side made me look at my port mainplane and I saw a hole about eight inches long and about two inches wide just above the position of the oil cooler. I did not realise that the oil cooler had been hit, and pursued a course of 310 degrees for home. About ten miles out from the coast the engine became very rough and oil and glycol smoke started to appear. Finally the engine seized up at about 4,000 feet and fifteen miles out from land. Previously I had glanced at the oil pressure gauge and found no pressure registering.

Looking round at the sea I saw a small boat and decided to land alongside it. I decided to stay with the aeroplane as the sea was very calm and I thought my chances of being picked up were greater if I landed alongside the boat than if I took to my parachute. I circled the boat at about fifty feet and then, being very close to the sea, straightened out to land. I did not drop the flaps. On the way down I had inflated my life jacket with three full breaths and removed the R/T plug from its socket. My Sutton harness I removed also in case the aircraft sank immediately.

On first touching the water the machine skimmed off again, and after one more such landing it dug its nose into the sea. I was flung forward and my forehead and nose met the reflector sight. However, I stood up in the cockpit and found the aircraft still afloat but it sank almost immediately. I should think it floated for a maximum of ten seconds. I had retained my parachute as it was reputed to be useful as a lifebuoy. As the aircraft sank I tried to get out but the parachute caught on the sliding hood and I was taken down with the aircraft. However, I was soon released and pushed off with my feet only to be struck by the tailplane as it went past. I started then to swim

upwards and eventually the colour of the water changed from black to green and I broke surface. The parachute proved very valuable, since it allowed me to float on my back holding the lower portion of my body up while the life jacket supported my head and chest. I had landed about fifty yards from the boat, which turned out to be a French fishing boat called Jolie Mascotte *carrying a crew of four. None of them could speak English. They were on their way to Dunkirk, but were lost, and I was able to tell them approximately what course to steer and gave them their approximate position on a chart. I was supplied by them with some dry clothing, food and drink.*

At last we approached Dunkirk and saw a British destroyer. A naval motor boat came out to us and a RNVR Lieutenant came aboard. He told me the destroyer was the Basilisk *and was out of action having been previously bombed. The engines and wireless were both out of order. Alongside the destroyer it was decided to try to tow the ship out to sea in order to escape the enemy bombers. She was loaded with troops. We attached a rope and succeeded in turning the destroyer partly in the right direction when I saw a large number of aircraft approaching. There were about thirty Dornier 17s and Heinkel 111s. Above them were about twenty-five Me 109s. I informed the Lieutenant that his ship was about to be bombed and we decided to cast off. At about three quarters of a mile from the destroyer we watched the bombing operations.*

The enemy aircraft did not appear to adopt any particular formation, but at about 3,000 feet turned singly over the target and jettisoned all their bombs. The bombs left the aircraft in a string of about ten. There appeared to be very little attempt at precision bombing, but rather as if they let all their bombs go hoping that one would hit. As they bombed, others opened fire with machine guns on the destroyer. During the course of the whole action they did not score a single hit despite the fact that the target was stationary and had only two pom-poms with no anti-aircraft shells.

We returned to the Basilisk *and once more started towing operations, but had to cast off again as about twenty Ju 87s dived very steeply to about four hundred feet and then released about four bombs. There were several hits. When the attack had finished the* Jolie Mascotte *returned to the warship. She was found to be sinking and the order was given to 'abandon ship'. We picked up about two hundred survivors, most of them troops, but also a large number of crew of the destroyer.*

When we had taken as many as possible aboard another destroyer appeared. We went alongside and told the commander of the other survivors. Then we set course for England and were able to see the relief destroyer shell the Basilisk *until it sank.*

SERGEANT JACK POTTER, JUNE 4, 1940.

Although Hurricane P2617 (see page 344) is the only genuine survivor of the battle from the period when the squadrons were based in France, L1592 *(above)*, now preserved in the Science Museum in London, had suffered damage on June 1 when it was brought back to Manston by Pilot Officer Tony Woods-Scawen of No. 43 Squadron. This particular aircraft was the 46th Hurricane to be built and was initially delivered to No. 56 Squadron on June 3, 1938. It passed through the hands of Nos. 17, 87, 43 and 152 Squadrons before it was shot up. After repair it served with No. 615 Squadron during the Battle of Britain, crash-landing at Croydon on August 18. It never flew again in anger, passing through the hands of several Training Units before being given to the museum in 1944. It appeared in a taxying role in *Angels One Five* in 1952 and, after being refurbished by Hawkers, was placed on display in the enlarged aviation gallery in 1963 wearing the codes of No. 615 (County of Surrey) Squadron.

RAF FIGHTER COMMAND

17 Squadron, Manston
Wing patrol Dunkirk:

Hurricane P3476. Glycol tank hit by cross-fire from Ju88s and abandoned off Dunkirk 7.30 p.m. P/O K. Manger baled out into the sea and rescued unhurt. Aircraft a write-off.

19 Squadron, Rochford
Wing patrol Dunkirk:

Spitfire K9836. Oil cooler damaged in combat with Bf110s of I./ZG1 and ditched in Channel near small boat 5.30 a.m. Sgt J. A. Potter rescued unhurt by the *Jolie Mascotte*, later transferred to RN coastal patrol boat and landed at Dover. Aircraft lost.

Spitfire K9807. Returned damaged by return fire from Do17s attacked over Dunkirk 10.00 a.m. F/Sgt H. Steere unhurt. Aircraft damaged but repairable.

41 Squadron, Manston
Wing patrol Dunkirk:

Spitfire N3234. Shot down during attack on bombers 10.00 a.m. P/O W. Stapleton captured. Aircraft a write-off.

Spitfire N3108. Shot down during attack on bombers 10.00 a.m. F/O W. E. Legard missing. Aircraft lost.

43 Squadron, Manston
Wing patrol Dunkirk:

Hurricane N2584. Shot down in combat with Bf109s of II./JG26 and crashed in Channel 11.45 a.m. P/O M. K. Carswell badly burned rescued by RN destroyer and landed at Dover. Aircraft lost.

Hurricane L1592. Returned riddled and with hydraulic system badly damaged in combat with Bf109s of II./JG26 north-west of Dunkirk 11.45 a.m. P/O C. A. Woods-Scawen unhurt. Aircraft FT⊙C damaged but repairable.
This aircraft is now preserved as a permanent exhibit in the Science Museum, London.

Hurricane L1758. Shot down in combat with Bf109s of II./JG26 and crashed in the Channel off Dunkirk 11.45 a.m. Sgt T. A. H. Gough missing. Aircraft lost.

64 Squadron, Hawkinge
Wing patrol Dunkirk:

Spitfire P9449. Shot down during attack on Ju87s over Dunkirk 4.45 p.m. P/O T. C. Hey killed. Aircraft a write-off.

Spitfire N3230. Returned damaged in action with Ju87s over Dunkirk 4.45 p.m. Sgt A. F. Laws unhurt. Aircraft damaged but repairable.

145 Squadron, Manston
Wing patrol Dunkirk:

Hurricane P2952. Shot down in combat with Bf109s of II./JG26 and Bf110s north-west of Dunkirk 11.45 a.m. P/O H. P. Dixon badly wounded, died June 3. Aircraft a write-off.

Hurricane N2497. Landed at Manston radiator damaged in combat with Bf109s of II./JG26 and Bf110s off Dunkirk 11.45 a.m. P/O L. D. M. Scott unhurt. Aircraft repairable.

222 Squadron, Hornchurch
Wing patrol Dunkirk:

Spitfire P9377. Engine damaged in combat with Bf109s of I./JG26 and Bf110s of I./ZG1 and belly-landed on beach east of Bray-Dunes 5.30 a.m. P/O R. A. L. Morant unhurt. Aircraft fired by pilot.

Spitfire P9317. Damaged in combat with Bf109s of I./JG26 and Bf110s of I./ZG1 and forced-landed at Le Touquet 5.40 a.m. P/O H. E. L. Falkust captured. Aircraft ZD⊙A a write-off.

Spitfire. Failed to return from combat with Bf109s of I./JG26 and Bf110s of I./ZG1 and believed crashed near Pihen-lès-Guines 5.40 a.m. Possibly that collided head-on with Oberlt Möller of 2./ZG1. P/O G. Massey-Sharpe killed. Aircraft a write-off.

Spitfire N3232. Shot down in combat with Bf109s of I./JG26 and Bf110s of I./ZG1; possibly that claimed by Uffz Wolf of 3./JG26 over Dunkirk 5.36 a.m. Sgt L. J. White killed. Aircraft a write-off.

245 Squadron, Hawkinge
Wing patrol Dunkirk:

Hurricane N2709. Shot down in combat with Bf109s of II./JG26 off Dunkirk 11.45 a.m. P/O R. A. West missing. Aircraft lost.

Hurricane N2658. Shot down in combat with Bf109s of II./JG26 north-west of Dunkirk 11.45 a.m. P/O A. L. Treanor missing. Aircraft lost.

609 Squadron, Biggin Hill
Wing patrol Dunkirk:

Spitfire L1058. Shot down by Oberlt Nacke of II./ZG76 in combat off Dunkirk 3.15 p.m. F/O I. B. N. Russell missing. Aircraft lost.

Spitfire N3222. Shot down by Bf110s during attack on He111s over Dunkirk 7.15 p.m. F/O J. Dawson killed. Aircraft a write-off.

616 Squadron, Rochford
Wing patrol Dunkirk:

Spitfire. Believed shot down by Oberlt Losigkeit (*Staffelkapitän*) of 2./JG26 and ditched in the Channel off Dunkirk 5.45 a.m. F/O J. S. Bell rescued unhurt by minesweeper HMS *Halcyon* and landed at Dover. Aircraft lost.

Spitfire. Crash-landed at Rochester out of fuel following combat with Bf109s of I./JG26 off Dunkirk 5.45 a.m. P/O K. Holden believed unhurt. Aircraft damaged but repairable.

Damaged but not preserved was Spitfire P9317 abandoned at Le Touquet.

FRENCH AIR FORCE

DAT Chartres Morane 406 (193). Wrecked in landing accident, cause not stated. Lt Sterbacouk injured. Aircraft a write-off.

DAT Lyon Morane 406. Returned damaged by return fire from He111 of 1./KG55 attacked over Vienne 12.30 p.m. Lt A. Gabszewicz unhurt. Aircraft repairable.

DAT Lyon Morane 406 (27). Shot down by return fire from He111s engaged south-west of Vienne and crashed at Chonas-l'Amballan 3.00 p.m. S/Lt R. Kalpas killed. Aircraft a write-off.
   This 'Groupe de Chasse Marche Polonais' based at Mions was formed from instructors and students of the Polish training establishment at Lyon-Bron and commanded by Captain W. Wiórkiewicz.

ECN 5/13 Potez 631. Landed back at Loyettes damaged by return fire from He111s of I./KG55 engaged over Vienne 12.00 p.m. Sgt David wounded in foot; rest of crew unhurt. Aircraft repairable.

GB I/63 Martin 167F (53). Damaged by flak during supply drop of medical supplies to troops encircled at Zuydcoote and crashed on landing back at Lympne p.m. Crew unhurt. Aircraft a write-off.

GC 1/5 Curtiss H-75 (151). Shot down by return fire during attack on He111s of 9./KG53 and abandoned near Frasne, southwest of Pontarlier, 4.30 p.m. Capt J-M. Accart *(Commandant)* baled out severely wounded landing near Frasne, and transported to hospital at Pontarlier. Aircraft a write-off.
   Crash site located by French air historians Marcel Dichamp and Arnaud Gillet in November 2002 and later excavated by Marcel Dichamp who recovered intact Twin Wasp engine and various other major components. Engine subsequently donated to the museum at Reims air base where Général Accart had been the commandant in 1952-55.

GC I/5 Curtiss H-75. Hit by return fire in attack on He111s of 9./KG53 over Pontarlier and crashed attempting forced-landing south-west of La Loge, near Germigney, 4.30 p.m. S/Lt Y. Le Calvez unhurt. Aircraft damaged but repairable.

GC II/8 Bloch 152. Returned port wing damaged following brief engagement with RAF fighters over Dunkirk 3.15 p.m. S/Lt Delocque-Fourcault unhurt. Aircraft repairable.
   This unit operated from Lympne, having arrived there from Deauville on May 30, but returned to France on June 12 on transfer to Estrées-la-Campagne.

GC III/9 Bloch 152. Returned to Lyon-Satolas damaged by return fire from Ju88 of II./KG51 engaged over Ambérieu during local defence of airfield. Adjt Pesant wounded in face and shoulder. Aircraft repairable.

GC 5/9 Bloch 152. Returned to Lyon-Satolas damaged by return fire from He111 of 4./KG53 engaged over Oyannax 3.40 p.m. Capt C. Billon *(Commandant)* wounded in right shoulder. Aircraft repairable.

GR II/55 Potez 63.11 (320). Shot down by flak during low-level reconnaissance east of Amiens and belly-landed with port engine on fire at Lamotte-Brebière 4.00 p.m. Lt Vallet and Sgt R. Lucas wounded. Sgt Gauthier unhurt. Aircraft a write-off.

(TRADUCTION)

Origine   :   Q.G., A.A.S.F. - Intelligence

Destinataires: ....
                     Mission Française auprès de l'A.A.S.F.

Date   :   Ier Juin 1940.

Référence   :   AASF/S.605/Int.

Interrogatoire de prisonniers de guerre.

   2 prisonniers du DO 17 abattu par les chasseurs français à 15 km. de TROYES ont été interrogés.
   Un membre de l'équipage a été tué. L'observateur Ober-Leutnant X, et le Pilote Feldwebel BOTTROP sont tous les deux blessés. L'appareil marqué 4 N + F H (F de couleur blanche) appartenait au 1 F/22, dont la base en temps de paix était CASSEL et peu après le début des hostilités FRANKFURT RHEIN MAIN, mais depuis décembre un aérodrome à environ 6 km. N. de BAD KREUZNACH.
   N° de la plaque d'identité 60004. Secteur postal N° 0115 L'escadrille (Staffel) comporte 9 ou peut-être 10 appareils. Un appareil qui manquait il y a trois ou quatre jours n'a pas encore été remplacé.
   Leur mission était de reconnaître l'activité sur voie ferrée, mais comme ils volaient à environ 8000 m., ils ne pouvaient effectuer leur mission que dans des régions libres de nuages. Ils commencèrent leur reconnaissance à BAR-le-DUC, mais TROYES avait été survolé à différentes reprises par des appareils de leur escadrille.
   Leurs pertes depuis le 10 Mai ne sont que d'un appareil porté manquant et deux hommes d'un autre appareil blessés. Le pilot a déjà pris part à 14 vols de reconnaissance au dessus de la France qu'il a également survolée de nuit en reconnaissance. C'était leur troisième sortie seulement depuis le 10 Mai par suite des condition météorologiques peu favorables.
   L'Officier commandant l'escadrille est le Hauptmann DITTRICK. L'observateur a été attaché pendant la bataille de Norvège à un groupe d'avions de transports Ju 52 et il a fait jusqu'à trois vols par jour d'Allemagne en Norvège. En Norvège, ils n'atterrissaient pas seulement sur lesaérodromes, mais aussi dans les champs. Il était à AALBORG au cours d'un de nos raids, et il a reconnu que les dégâts causés ont été considérables, en particulier aux apparei Il n'avait aucun renseignement de première main au sujet des dégâts causés à STAVANGER.
   Tous les deux déclaraient ne rien savoir d'autre au suje de nos attaques aériennes au dessus de l'Allemagne que ce qu'ils avaient lu dans les journaux, sauf qu'ils avaient entendu dire que 42 civils avaient été tués à BONN. Chaque fois qu'il y a une alerte de raid aérien, même la nuit, ils ont reçu l'ordre de gagner les abris. Ils ont eu une alerte au cours de la nuit du 31 Mai/Ier Juin (des bombardiers de l'A.A.S.F. se dirigeant sur RUDESHEIM).
   L'observateur a été en Espagne, et il est possible qu'il y ait piloté des appareils depuis le commencement des hostilités. L pilote appartient à l'escadrille depuis 4 ans. L'escadrille était à CASSEL en temps de paix avec la 2° et la 3° escadrilles, mais mai tenant elles ne font plus partie du Gruppe et constituent une unité indépendante.

(Signé) ....   pour le Wing

'Two prisoners from the Do17 shot down by French fighters, 15 km of Troyes, have been questioned. One of the crew was killed. Oberleutnant X, observer, and Feldwebel Bottrop, pilot, were both wounded. The aircraft, 4N+FH (F white in colour), belonged to 1.F/22 which was based in peacetime at Cassel [*sic*]; shortly after the beginning of the war, it moved to Frankfurt/Rhein-Main and since December to an airfield six kilometres north of Bad Kreuznach. Number of the ID plate 60004. Postal sector N° 0115***. The squadron (Staffel) had 9, possibly 10 aircraft. One aircraft missing for three or four days was not yet replaced. Their mission was to reconnoitre railway activities but as they flew at about 8000 metres they could only operate over areas free from clouds. They had started their reconnaissance at Bar-le-Duc but Troyes had already been surveyed on several occasions by aircraft of their unit. Since May 10, their losses are only one missing aircraft and two men wounded in another aircraft. The pilot had already flown 14 reconnaissance missions over France, including night flights. It was only their third mission over France since May 10 because of poor weather conditions. The officer commanding the Staffel is Hauptmann Dittrick. During the Norway operation the observer was attached to a group of Ju52 transport aircraft. They did up to three flights a day from Germany to Norway. In Norway, they not only landed on airfields, but also in fields. He was at Aalborg during one of our raids and he recognised that the damage done was considerable, particularly to the aircraft. He knew nothing first-hand as to damage done at Stavanger. As for our air attacks over Germany both said they knew nothing more than that they had read in the newspapers, but they had heard that 42 civilians have been killed in Bonn. Each time there was an air raid warning, even at night, they were ordered to make for the air raid shelter. They had had an alert during the night of May 31/June 1 (bombers from the AASF were going to Rüdesheim). The observer had been in Spain and it is possible that he had piloted aircraft since the beginning of hostilities. The pilot had belonged to the squadron for four years. The squadron was at Cassel [*sic*] in peace time with the 2nd and 3rd squadrons but these did not belong to the Gruppe any more and formed an independent unit.'

This particular Dornier 4N+FH of 1.(F)/22 came to grief near Troyes which lies 100-odd kilometres south of Reims. It is the last crash in France attended by a British official photographer being well out of the northern battle zone. In this picture, Squadron Leader Tommy Wisdom, a press officer, is inspecting the wreck lying at Jully-sur-Sarce on behalf of the RAF.

LUFTWAFFE

2.(H)/12 Henschel Hs126. Returned damaged in attack by Sgt Penzini of GC I/5 during observation sortie north of Laneuville-sur-Meuse and forced-landed at Martincourt 12.55 p.m. Fw J. Hofmeister slightly wounded. Aircraft repairable.

1.(F)/22 Dornier Do17P. Shot down by Lt Dorance, Lt Vybiral, and Sgt Bressieux of GC I/5 during reconnaissance of rail traffic and broke up between Bourguignon and Jully-sur-Sarce, south-east of Troyes, 5.45 a.m. Fw S. Post baled out too low and killed. Oberlt K. Opderbeck baled out and captured badly wounded, landing between Avaleur and Villemorien. Fw J. König baled out and captured badly wounded, landing at Sèche-Fontaine. Aircraft 4N+FH a write-off.
'Fw Bottrop' quoted in the French report is an error, Bottrop was the birth place of Fw Johann König.

4.(F)/121 Junkers Ju88A. Shot down by Adjt Dorcy, Sgt Delisle, and Sgt Plzak of GC II/2 during photo-reconnaissance between Besançon and Dijon; crash-landed and burned out in 'Marais du Goutterot' at La Rivière-Drugeon, south-west of Pontarlier, 4.05 p.m. Also engaged by S/Lt Gragelle, S/Lt Krol, Sgt Grimaud, and Cpl Nowakiewicz of GC II/7 prior to landing. Oberlt H-W. von Niebelschütz, Oberfw E. Winkler, Uffz H. Maiwald, and Uffz A. Dobschall captured. Aircraft 7A+PM a write-off.

2.(F)/122 Junkers Ju88A. Failed to return from recce over Dunkirk and possibly that shot down in the Channel by F/O Moberley of No. 616 Squadron 10.00 a.m. Lt R. Hey, Fw E. Lange-Gläscher, Fw E. Kiess, and Uffz W. Giesa captured unhurt. Aircraft F6+DK a write-off.

1.(F)/123 Dornier Do17P. Forced-landed near Trier out of fuel. No crew casualties. Aircraft damaged but repairable.

3.(F)/123 Junkers Ju88A. Returned damaged in attack by S/Ldr Donaldson of No. 151 Squadron and believed also engaged by Adjt Marchais and Adjt Nicole of GC II/8 near Bray-Dunes on reconnaissance sortie to Dunkirk 3.00 p.m. Crew unhurt. Aircraft repairable.

III./JG3 Messerschmitt Bf109E. Shot down in combat and crashed near Douai. Pilot believed unhurt. Aircraft a write-off.

1./JG20 Messerschmitt Bf109E. Returned badly damaged by return fire during attack on No. 500 Squadron Anson near Dunkirk 10.55 a.m. Uffz W. Bielefeldt wounded in left shoulder. Aircraft 2 + a write-off.
Werner Bielefeldt fell prey to two .303 inch Brownings fitted as additional side armament to P/O Peters' MK⊗V fitted on the initiative of the squadron gunnery officer, F/O H. Jones.

Lfb. Nr.	Ort und Tag des Verlustes	Staffel usw.	Dienst-grad	Vorname	Familienname, Truppenteil, Nr. der Erkennungs-marke	Geburt			Verwundet Körperstelle und Waffe		Vermißt		Gestorben außerhalb der Lazarettbehandlung infolge von				Abgegeben an welche Feinbee (Krankenhaus) und weshalb	Bemerkung (3. B. Grablage oder bei 17 vermutlich übergelaufen)
						Tag	Ort	llen*)	schwer	leicht	gefangen	sonstiges	Ver-wun-bung)*	Krankheit	Unfall	Selbst-mord		
1	2	3	4	5	6	7	8	10	11	12	13	14	15	16	17	18	19	20
1	Südl. von Troyes (Frankreich) am 1.Juni 1940	1.(F)/22	Feld-webel	Siegfried	P o s t 1.(F)/22 Nr.38 (60004)	1.12. 1914	Marien-burg	Oa	1.6. 1940 L.A.	gefallen		-	-	-	-	-	-	-	-

The partially-burned record lists the death of Feldwebel Siegfried Post who baled out too low.

I./JG21 Messerschmitt Bf109E-1. Belly-landed at Crupilly, north-east of Guise, due to undercarriage failure. Pilot unhurt. Aircraft damaged but repairable.

I./JG26 Messerschmitt Bf109E-3. Shot down in combat with Spitfires of Nos. 19, 222, and 616 Squadrons over Dunkirk 5.40 a.m. Pilot believed unhurt. Aircraft a write-off.

3./JG26 Messerschmitt Bf109E-1. Shot down in combat with Spitfires of Nos. 19, 222, and 616 Squadrons over Dunkirk and crashed at Pervijze, east of Furnes 5.45 a.m. Leutnant S. Gruel killed. Aircraft a write-off.

3./JG26 Messerschmitt Bf109E-3. Shot down in combat with Spitfires of Nos. 19, 222, and 616 Squadrons over Dunkirk and forced-landed near Furnes 5.45 a.m. Oberleutnant R. Germeroth wounded. Aircraft a write-off.

6./JG26 Messerschmitt Bf109E-3. Belly-landed near Langemark badly damaged in combat with Hurricanes of Nos. 43, 145, and 245 Squadrons north-west of Dunkirk 11.40 a.m. Pilot believed unhurt. Aircraft 12 + — damaged but repairable.

6./JG26 Messerschmitt Bf109E-3. Shot down in combat with Hurricanes of Nos. 43, 145, and 245 Squadrons off Dunkirk 11.40 a.m. Oberleutnant A. Pomaska (Staffelkapitän) killed. Aircraft a write-off.

6./JG26 Messerschmitt Bf109E-1. Shot down in combat with Hurricanes of Nos. 43, 145, and 245 Squadrons and crashed between Dunkirk and Calais 11.40 a.m. Oberfeldwebel P. Keller baled out and captured badly burned. Aircraft a write-off.

6./JG26 Messerschmitt Bf109E-3 (1937). Damaged in combat with Hurricanes of Nos. 43, 145, and 245 Squadrons over Dunkirk and belly-landed near Langemark, north of Ypres 11.45 a.m. Pilot believed unhurt Aircraft 9 + - repairable.

8./JG26 Messerschmitt Bf109E-1. Shot down in combat and abandoned over Furnes. Leutnant G. Sprick baled out unhurt. Aircraft a write-off.

9./JG26 Messerschmitt Bf109E-3. Hit by ground-fire during transit flight from Krefeld to Brussels and forced-landed outside Crépigny, west of Chauny, 9.30 a.m. Uffz A. Beese captured unhurt. Aircraft 2 + I a write-off.

I./JG27 2 Messerschmitt Bf109E-1s. Damaged in taxying accident at Guise. Pilots unhurt. Aircraft both repairable.

I./JG27 Messerschmitt Bf109E-1. Crash-landed at Guise due to technical fault Pilot unhurt. Aircraft damaged but repairable.

Stab I./JG52 Messerschmitt Bf109E-3. Abandoned following take-off collision with Gefr Bokel at Trier. Feldwebel K. Munz baled out injured. Aircraft a write-off.

2./JG52 Messerschmitt Bf109E. Wrecked in collision with Fw Munz on take-off from Trier. Gefreiter K-H. Bokel unhurt. Aircraft a write-off.

Stab II./JG52 Messerschmitt Bf109E-3 (5097). Hit an electricity pylon south-east of Pouilly-sur-Meuse while low-flying in bad weather and belly-landed west of Belval-Bois-des-Dames. Leutnant P. Gutbrod reportedly killed after landing by French colonial troops. Aircraft a write-off.

II./JG52 Messerschmitt Bf109E-1. Forced-landed at Sandweiler due to engine failure. Pilot unhurt. Aircraft damaged but repairable.

III./JG52 Messerschmitt Bf109E-1. Crashed on landing at Trier-Euren, cause not stated. Pilot unhurt. Aircraft damaged but repairable.

1./KG4 Heinkel He111. Returned damaged by fighters west of Dunkirk. Uffz M. Fisch-gräbe slightly wounded, rest of crew unhurt. Aircraft damage state not recorded.

I./KG4 Heinkel He111. Forced-landed damaged near Münster. No crew casualties. Aircraft damaged but repairable.

1./KG4 Heinkel He111P. Shot down by fighters over Dunkirk. Lt K. Leither, Fw H. Tromsdorf, Uffz H. Fünfstück, and Uffz R. W. Patzer killed. Aircraft a write-off.

4./KG51 Junkers Ju88A (8004). Engaged over Lac de Paladru by Adjt Baritel of GC III/9 during sortie to Marseille and pursued north-east eventually forced-landing near Ruffieux with port engine feathered 1.45 p.m. Fw R. Müller, Uffz P. Dickhut, Gefr B. Sartor, and Gefr H. Spiess captured unhurt. Aircraft 9K+DM a write-off.

3./KG53 Heinkel He111H (5474). Crossed the Swiss border and intercepted by Swiss Bf109s (Lt Schenk and Hptmn Lindecker (Commandant) of Fl.Komp.15) between the Freibergen and Les Rangiers mountains in the Jura range after bombing the railway between Rives and Marcilloles. Both engines set alight and pursued back over the frontier where attacked by Cdt Mümler of GC II/7 finally belly-landing near Ferme de Lai-hausen, south-west of Bettlach, and burned out 5.30 p.m. Lt G. Siegfried and Fw H. Arnold captured unhurt, Uffz A. Offinger, Uffz E. Hanft, and Gefr E. Haag captured wounded. Aircraft A1+EL a write-off.

4./KG53 Heinkel He111H. Believed damaged in attack by Capt Billon (Commandant) of GC III/9 near Oyonnax 3.40 p.m. Crossed the Swiss frontier and engaged by Swiss Bf109s (Lt Wachter and Hptmn Roubaty (Commandant) of Fl.Komp.6) over Neu-châtel. Shot down and exploded in woods at Serroue, north-west of Lignières, on the Bielersee 4.20 p.m. Fw A. Nöss, Fw H. Kaltenbach, Uffz E. Heimann, Gefr O. Müller, and Gefr E. Plötz killed. Aircraft A1+DM a write-off.

His body lies partially covered with hay. He is now buried in Grave 17, Row 1, Block 2 of Solers German War Cemetery.

9./KG53 Heinkel He111H. Returned badly damaged in attacks by GC II/7 between Dole and Besançon during sortie to bomb targets at Ambérieu-en-Bugey 12.30 p.m. Possibly that attacked by Adjt Ponteins. Fw H. Kehrer, Uffz A. Ranftl, and Gefr F. Hopfgartner wounded. Aircraft a write-off.

9./KG53 Heinkel He111H. Returned damaged in attack by GC II/7 west of Besançon during sortie to bomb targets at Ambérieu-en-Bugey 12.30 p.m. Possibly that attacked by Sgt Planchard. Fw E. Krumm and Fw G. Kubis badly wounded, admitted to hospital in Frankfurt-am-Main. Aircraft a write-off.

9./KG53 Heinkel He111H. Returned badly damaged in attacks by GC II/7 west of Besançon during sortie to bomb targets at Ambérieu-en-Bugey 12.30 p.m. Possibly that attacked by Sgt Lamblin. Gefr W. Borisch and Gefr H. Wagner wounded. Aircraft a write-off.

9./KG53 Heinkel He111H. Both engines damaged and caught fire under attack by S/Lt Le Calvez, Lt Perina, and Capt Accart *(Commandant)* of GC I/5 south-east of Vesoul during sortie to bomb railway targets near Ambérieu-en-Bugey. Abandoned south-west of Belfort under further attack by seven D520s of GC II/7 and crashed at Grand-Crochet in the Forêt du Cherimont, south of Champagney, 5.15 p.m. Uffz G. Leppin and Gefr E. Ickert killed. Uffz W. Hohe slightly wounded, Uffz F. Lenk badly wounded, and Gefr R. Biedenkapp baled out and captured unhurt. Aircraft A1+CT a write-off.
The radio operator, Fritz Lenk, landed on the roof of the Schwob factory at Héricourt and was only rescued from lynching by prompt action by local police and military. During the German occupation, seven locals were arrested and interned for several months, four being charged for this offence.

1./KG55 Heinkel He111P. Attacked by Lt Gabszewicz of DAT Lyon near Vienne during sortie to Valence and believed crashed near Dagneux, north-east of Lyon, 12.40 p.m. Also attacked by S/Lt Radomski and Lt Baranski of DAT Lyon, Capt Billon of GC III/9, and three Potez 631s of ECN 5/13. Gefr J. Getz killed. Lt H. Will, Oberfw O. Dettke, Fw B. Marquardt, and Uffz A. Lohr captured. Aircraft a write-off.

Leutnant Günther Siegfried strayed over the French frontier into Switzerland and was consequently set upon by Messerschmitt Bf109s of the Swiss Air Force. On mobilisation late August 1939, the Swiss already had 41 Messerschmitt Bf109s equipping Fliegerkompanie 6 based at Thun, Fl.Komp.15 at Payerne, and Fl.Komp.21 at Dübendorf. By February 1940, Fliegerkompanie 7, 8, and 9 were also converted to the type another 50 aircraft arriving from the manufacturer by the end of April. The following month, 113 violations of Swiss air space were recorded, many of them countered by Swiss Bf109Es resulting in casualties to Luftwaffe aircraft. Göring's reaction to this vigorous defence of Swiss neutrality was to add Bf110 escorts to German bomber formations over-flying Switzerland in early June 1940. Backbone of the Swiss air defences throughout the war, the Bf109 was finally withdrawn from service on December 28, 1949, a single survivor (J-355) now displayed at the Swiss Air Force Museum at Dübendorf.

8./KG55 Heinkel He111. Returned damaged by flak and fighters during sortie to bomb rail targets between Lyon and St Valier 4.30 p.m. Fw U. Flügge wounded, rest of crew unhurt. Aircraft damaged but repairable.

4./KG76 Dornier Do17Z. Damaged by fighters while bombing shipping off Dunkirk and crashed within own lines. Possibly one of those claimed by F/L Webster of No. 41 Squadron 10.45 a.m. Uffz H. Fortmüller and Uffz J. Wörlein killed. Oberlt E. Moll and Fw E. Mössner wounded. Aircraft F1+FM a write-off.

4./LG1 Junkers Ju88A-1. Returned damaged by Spitfires of No. 616 Squadron during attack on shipping off Dunkirk 10.00 a.m. Possibly that attacked by F/L Gillam. Oberlt J. Helbig slightly wounded, Uffz H. Fliescher and rest of crew unhurt. Aircraft L1+EM damaged but repairable.

I./StG77 Junkers Ju87B. Forced-landed damaged by flak over Béthune. Crew unhurt. Aircraft damaged but repairable.

5./StG77 Junkers Ju87B. Shot down by naval AA fire during attack on shipping and crashed in the Channel between Furnes and Dunkirk 12.00 p.m. Oberlt E. Weiser and Uffz H. Ruckdeschel missing. Aircraft lost.

I.(St)/TrGr.186 Junkers Ju87B. Shot down in combat involving Nos. 64, 220, 229, and 242 Squadrons during attack on shipping off Dunkirk 4.45 p.m. Oberlt D. Troll and Fw W. Rampf missing. Aircraft lost.

2.(St)/TrGr.186 Junkers Ju87B. Returned damaged following combat involving Nos. 64, 220, 229, and 242 Squadrons during attack on shipping off Dunkirk 4.45 p.m. Pilot unhurt, Uffz J. Müller badly wounded. Aircraft damaged but repairable.

3.(St)/TrGr.186 Junkers Ju87B. Shot down in combat involving Nos. 64, 220, 229, and 242 Squadrons during attack on shipping off Dunkirk 4.45 p.m. Lt W. Stengel killed. Uffz P. Horstmann wounded. Aircraft a write-off.

4.(J)/TrGr.186 Messerschmitt Bf109E. Damaged in combat with Spitfires of Nos. 19, 222, and 616 Squadrons over Dunkirk and forced-landed near Furnes 5.40 a.m. Oberlt O. Hintze *(Staffelkapitän)* unhurt. Aircraft 5 + a write-off.

Wettererkundungsstaffel 26. Dornier Do17Z. Forced-landed damaged by fighters over Calais. Crew believed unhurt. Aircraft damaged but repairable.

1./ZG1 Messerschmitt Bf110C. Shot down in combat with Spitfires over Nieuport and crashed alongside the road from Koksijde to Oostduinkerke 5.30 a.m. Probably that claimed by P/O Sinclair of No. 19 Squadron. Uffz M. Rutz killed, pilot unhurt. Aircraft a write-off.

1./ZG1 Messerschmitt Bf110C. Returned damaged Spitfires of Nos. 19 and 222 Squadrons over Dunkirk 5.30 a.m. Pilot unhurt, Uffz G. Richter slightly wounded, admitted to hospital in Brussels. Aircraft damaged but repairable.

2./ZG1 Messerschmitt Bf110C. Collided head-on with No. 222 Squadron Spitfire during combat east of Dunkirk and lost starboard wing 5.30 a.m. Oberlt J. Möller and Uffz K. Schieferstein baled out and captured unhurt. Aircraft a write-off.

3./ZG1 Messerschmitt Bf110C. Shot down in combat with Spitfires of Nos. 19 and 222 Squadrons over Dunkirk 5.30 a.m. Uffz R. Müller and Uffz H. Dietsch killed. Aircraft a write-off.

Sunday, June 2

Despite enemy shelling, evacuation proceeded during the night of June 1/2 until daybreak, shipping now only being present in the Dunkirk area between 9.00 p.m. and 3.30 a.m.

Seven reconnaissance sorties were flown by Back Component during the day and proved successful in locating several enemy batteries, all crews returning safely though one aircraft was forced to ditch on return. Among batteries pinpointed were two at les Huttes and le Clipon, between Gravelines and Mardyck, that threatened the direct approach to Dunkirk, and these were attacked by successive sections of Blenheims between dawn and 7.45 a.m. In all 24 sorties were flown and timed to coincide with a concentration of shipping approaching the harbour. No bombers were lost but they met intense AA fire and three crashed on landing. By night, 16 Wellingtons attacked roads beyond the Dunkirk perimeter while 17 AASF Battles struck at enemy communications and airfields at Givet, Mézières, and Trier. All aircraft returned without loss.

Fighter patrols were now concentrated at dawn and dusk when Allied shipping was either approaching or leaving Dunkirk, and the first two patrols of the day, both of four squadrons, encountered no enemy aircraft in the early morning haze that blanketed the area. However, a third patrol of five squadrons that covered Dunkirk from 7.45 a.m. to 8.45 a.m. engaged considerable enemy forces and fought three separate combats. Around 8.00 a.m. No. 32 Squadron engaged about 20 bombers and fighters while Nos. 92 and 611 Squadrons became involved with a larger formation. Half an hour later, Nos. 66 and 266 Squadrons met a separate formation of 60-plus bombers and fighters. In all, 18 bombers and ten fighters were claimed for the loss of seven Spitfires and one Hurricane, but no attacks on shipping were reported. No. 611 Squadron, in their first and only action over Dunkirk, suffered significant losses to enemy fighters and returned to Digby that evening.

Another major engagement took place around 8.10 p.m. when a four-squadron patrol met a large formation of bombers and fighters claiming three Stukas and three Messerschmitts in the ensuing combat for the loss of two more fighters.

German bombers again struck deep into mainland France with morning attacks on airfields between Orléans and Tours, and a heavy raid on harbour installations and oil refineries at Marseille. This latter raid provoked violent reaction from defending French fighters and the enemy formations met with spirited resistance near Lyon on the return flight forcing further violations of Swiss air space.

At dusk Allied troops again began to embark from the harbour and the beaches just east of Dunkirk and by 11.30 p.m. that night the Senior Naval Officer at Dunkirk was finally able to send the long-awaited signal to Vice-Admiral Ramsay in Dover, 'BEF evacuated'. There still remained, however, an unknown number of French troops yet to embark but they were, understandably, far from a constant flow of men — many of them naturally reluctant to leave their homeland whatever the circumstances.

UK-based aircraft lost or damaged on operations over the Western Front:

RAF BOMBER COMMAND

53 Squadron, Eastchurch
Reconnaissance Dunkirk:

Blenheim IV L9476. Starboard propeller damaged by hitting a sand-dune when low-flying to avoid light flak. Belly-landed on the Goodwin Sands during return flight 5.25 a.m. F/L A. C. Brown, Sgt Brooks, and AC Voules rescued unhurt. Aircraft abandoned.

107 Squadron, Wattisham
Batteries at Gravelines:

Blenheim IV N6190. Returned damaged by flak and crashed on landing 7.15 a.m. F/O J. W. Stephens, Sgt W. J. Barrett, and LAC E. C. White unhurt. Aircraft a write-off.

Blenheim IV P4919. Crash-landed on return to base damaged by flak 7.00 a.m. F/Sgt H. J. Ratcliffe, Sgt P. J. Crowley, and LAC D. S. Harrison unhurt. Aircraft a write-off.

Blenheim IV R3683. Returned damaged by flak and overturned on landing 7.15 a.m. Sgt R. S. Gunning, Sgt W. G. Brinn, and AC1 D. L. Leonard unhurt. Aircraft a write-off.

RAF FIGHTER COMMAND

32 Squadron, Manston
Wing Patrol Dunkirk:

Hurricane P2727. Shot down in combat with Bf109s and Bf110s over Dunkirk 8.10 a.m. Sgt D. Flynn captured. Aircraft a write-off.
German fighter units 2./JG2, Stab II./JG2, I./JG27, II./JG26, III./JG26, and II./ZG76 filed claims for a total of 18 Spitfires and five Hurricanes in combats involving Nos. 32, 66, 92, 266, and 611 Squadrons between 8.00 a.m. and 8.30 a.m. RAF claims were equally ambitious with six German fighters confirmed destroyed, ten more probably destroyed, and nine others assessed as damaged. Due to the complexity of the action it has not been possible to resolve individual claims with any certainty.

66 Squadron, Martlesham Heath
Wing Patrol Dunkirk:

Spitfire N3047. Shot down in combat with Bf109s and Bf110s over Dunkirk 8.10 a.m. F/Sgt M. W. Hayman killed. Aircraft a write-off.

Spitfire N3028. Shot down in combat with Bf109s and Bf110s and abandoned inland from Dunkirk 8.10 a.m. Sgt D. A. C. Hunt baled out unhurt. Aircraft a write-off.

Spitfire N3033. Starboard aileron shot off in combat with Bf109s and Bf110s west of Dunkirk 8.10 a.m. Sgt F. N. Robertson baled out slightly wounded in leg. Aircraft a write-off.

72 Squadron, Manston
Wing Patrol Dunkirk:

Spitfire K9924. Belly-landed at Gravesend with starboard wing, port aileron, and air pressure system damaged by return fire from Ju87 of II./StG2 attacked over Dunkirk 7.00 p.m. F/O O. St J. Pigg slightly wounded in leg. Aircraft damaged but repairable.

92 Squadron, Martlesham Heath
Wing Patrol Dunkirk:

Spitfire N3248. Returned damaged by Bf109s in combat between Calais and Dunkirk 8.00 a.m. F/L R. R. S. Tuck unhurt. Aircraft QJ⊙L repairable.

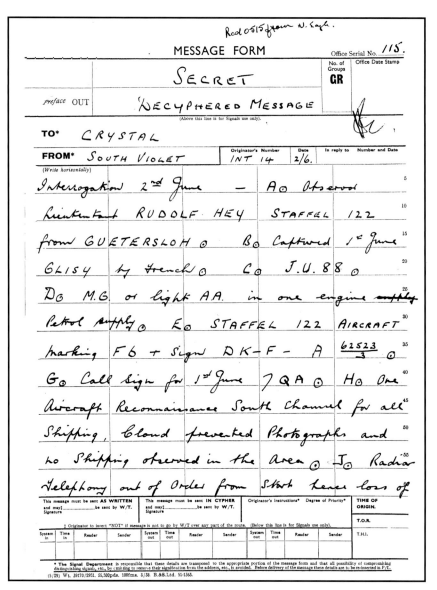

111 Squadron, Hawkinge
Wing Patrol Dunkirk:

Hurricane L1564. Believed badly damaged in attacks by Oberlt Priller *(Staffelkapitän)* and Uffz Haase of 6./JG51 and abandoned over the Channel off North Foreland 8.15 p.m. P/O R. R. Wilson baled out unhurt landing near Manston airfield. Aircraft lost.

266 Squadron, Martlesham Heath
Wing Patrol Dunkirk:

Spitfire N3197. Shot down in combat with Bf109s over Dunkirk 8.30 a.m. P/O J. W. B. Stevenson missing. Aircraft lost.

Spitfire N3092. Shot down in combat with Bf109s over Dunkirk 8.30 a.m. Sgt R. T. Kidman killed. Aircraft a write-off.

Spitfire N3169. Returned with wings and engine damaged following attack by Bf109s over Dunkirk 8.30 a.m. P/O N. G. Bowen unhurt. Aircraft damaged but repairable.

611 Squadron, Martlesham Heath
Wing Patrol Dunkirk:

Spitfire N3064. Shot down in combat with Bf109s and Bf110s over Dunkirk 8.15 a.m. F/O R. K. Crompton killed. Aircraft a write-off.

Spitfire N3055. Shot down in combat with Bf109s and Bf110s over Dunkirk 8.15 a.m. F/O T. D. Little killed. Aircraft a write-off.

Spitfire N3050. Returned with port wing and airscrew damaged following combat with Bf109s and Bf110s over Dunkirk 8.15 a.m. P/O C. A. T. Jones unhurt. Aircraft damaged but repairable.

Spitfire N3056. Landed on burst tyre at Southend with port wing and tailplane damaged in combat with Bf109s and Bf110s over Dunkirk 8.15 a.m. P/O M. P. Brown unhurt. Aircraft damaged but repairable.

Spitfire N3058. Returned badly damaged in combat with Bf109s and Bf110s over Dunkirk 8.15 a.m. F/L K. M. Stoddart unhurt. Aircraft damaged but repairable.

Spitfire N3066. Returned slightly damaged following combat with Bf109s and Bf110s over Dunkirk 8.15 a.m. P/O D. A. Adams unhurt. Aircraft repairable.

Spitfire. Nosed up taxying on soft ground at North Weald where landed to refuel after combat with Bf109s and Bf110s over Dunkirk 8.15 a.m. S/L J. E. McComb unhurt. Aircraft repairable.

Spitfire N3054. Landed at Duxford damaged in combat with Bf109s and Bf110s over Dunkirk 8.15 a.m. F/L W. J. Leather unhurt. Aircraft damaged but repairable.

MESSAGE FORM

96A. (Naval).

Office Serial No..................

Call IN
and :—
Preface OUT

No. of Groups **GR**

Office Date Stamp

(Above this line is for Signals use only).

TO*

FROM*

Originator's Number | Date | In reply to | Number and Date

(Write horizontally)

direction ⊙ Three M.G.'s only ⊙ I ⊙ Ignorant
of Casualties but would consider 300 to 400
in last fortnight light ⊙ Only highly
trained Personnel used for these reconnaissances
Pilots 13ᵗʰ ⊙ Morale Good ⊙ M⊙ Pilot
states JU 88 rely on speed only and
orders not to fire or engage in combat unless
inevitable ⊙ Air (Bends)? FELDWEBEL ERWIN
KREISS AUSWEIS Book No 119 and W/T Operator
WILHELM GIESA AUSWEIS BOOK 108 added nothing ⊙
U/O LANGE Pilot imprisoned separately by French
therefore not interrogated ⊙

This message must be sent AS WRITTEN and may.............be sent by W/T. Signature | This message must be sent IN CYPHER and.............be sent by W/T. Signature | Originator's Instructions* | Degree of Priority* | TIME OF ORIGIN.

‡ Originator to insert "NOT" if message is not to go by W/T over any part of the route. (Below this line is for Signals use only). | T.O.R.

System in | Time in | Reader | Sender | System out | Time out | Reader | Sender | System out | Time out | Reader | Sender | T.H.I.

* The Signal Department is responsible that these details are transposed to the appropriate portion of the message form and that all possibility of compromising distinguishing signals, etc., by omitting to remove their signification from the address, etc., is avoided. Before delivery of the message these details are to be re-inserted in P/L.
(5/29) Wt. 39170/2951. 55,500pds. 100fms. 3/38. B.&B.Ltd. 51-1363.

FRENCH AIR FORCE

DAT Étampes Bloch 151. Forced-landed damaged by return fire from He111s of III./KG55 engaged near Lyon 9.00 a.m. Adjt R. Doucet badly wounded in left arm. Aircraft damaged but repairable.

DAT Étampes Bloch 151 (370). Hit by return fire and caught fire during attack on He111s of III./KG55 near of Lyon. Crash-landed and burned out near Marcilloles 9.00 a.m. Adjt J. Vopalecky badly burned and wounded left arm and hand. Aircraft a write-off.

Josef Vopalecky was one of three Czechs serving with Polish pilots commanded by Major Zdzislaw Krasnodebski attached to Groupe de Chasse de Defense I/55 at Châteaudun from May 17. Five days later they moved to Étampes for local defence duties where relations with resident French personnel proved difficult. The unit moved to Orléans-Bricy on June 14 shortly after which Vopalecky was one of four pilots transferred to Châteauroux. After the French collapse he made his way to England where he joined No. 310 (Czech) Squadron flying Hurricanes.

ECN 4/13 Potez 631 (192). Hit by flak and set alight, belly-landing alongside the Soissons to Villers-Cotterêts road between Gravancourt and Verte-Feuille. Adjt Pigeon badly burned, and Sgt Allonzo, wounded in right hand, both admitted to hospital in Croisy. Capt P. Pouyade (Commandant) slightly burned on right hand and face. Aircraft a write-off.

GAO 1/589 Potez 63.11 (804). Reported shot down by flak during reconnaissance sortie between Montcornet and Rethel but possibly that claimed by Lt Kunert of 8./JG53 over La Selve 11.45 a.m. Lt J. Cheysson and Sgt B. de Barbeyrac killed. Sgt Denis badly wounded. Aircraft a write-off.

GB I/21 Bloch 210. Flew into high-tension cable and crashed outside Pont-sur-Yonne shortly after take-off on sortie to attack Couvron airfield p.m. Crew escaped unhurt. Aircraft a write-off.

GB II/21 Amiot 354 (8). Went into a vertical stall at 1,000 feet and crashed at St-Florentin during training flight p.m. Adjt P. Carteron, Sgt M. Decombes, and Sgt Clément killed. Aircraft a write-off.

GC I/2 Morane 406 (676). Set alight by return fire from He111s engaged near Montbéliard and abandoned over St Hippolyte 10.15 a.m. Sgt J. de Puybusque baled out unhurt. Aircraft 15 a write-off.

GC II/2 Morane 406. Returned to Chissey hit by return fire in attack on He111s over Lons-le-Saulnier 8.30 a.m. S/Lt Aquilina wounded in leg. Aircraft repairable.

GC 5/3 Dewoitine 520 (246). Crashed on take-off at Toulouse-Francazal for transit flight to Cormeilles-en-Vexin, cause not stated. Sgt J. Novak killed. Aircraft a write-off.

This interrogation report despatched from the field to the southern headquarters of the Air Component covers the Ju88 lost by the 2nd Staffel of Fernaufklärungsgruppe 122 on June 1 (see page 408).

GC II/7 Dewoitine 520. Hit by return fire and abandoned after attack on He111s of III./KG55 engaged east of Bourg-en-Bresse 9.10 a.m. Pilot baled out unhurt. Aircraft a write-off.

GC II/7 Dewoitine 520. Shot down by return fire during attack on He111s of III./KG55 engaged east of Bourg-en-Bresse 9.10 a.m. Pilot killed. Aircraft a write-off.

GC II/7 Dewoitine 520. Returned slightly damaged by return fire from He111s of III./KG55 engaged east of Bourg-en-Bresse 9.10 a.m. Cpl E. Nowakiewicz unhurt. Aircraft repairable.

GC III/9 Bloch 151 (91). Forced-landed at Chambarrand-Marseilles severely damaged by Bf110s during attack on Ju88s of 3./KG51 intercepted east of Bourg-en-Bresse 8.30 a.m. Adjt Baritel badly wounded in right arm. Aircraft a write-off.

GR 1/52 Bloch 174 (29). Spun from 15,000 feet during engine test; crashed and burned out alongside the runway at Pleurs, 10 km south-east of Sézanne. Capt M. Bertaux (Commandant), Sgt L. Hubin, and Sgt H. Blanchot killed. Aircraft a write-off.

LUFTWAFFE

II./JG2 Messerschmitt Bf109E-3. Belly-landed at Évreux due to undercarriage failure. Pilot unhurt. Aircraft damaged but repairable.

II./JG26 Messerschmitt Bf109E-1. Badly damaged in combat with RAF fighters and belly-landed near Ypres. Pilot unhurt. Aircraft damaged but repairable.

I./JG27 Messerschmitt Bf109E-1. Returned damaged following combat with RAF fighters over Dunkirk. Pilot unhurt. Aircraft damaged but repairable.

3./JG27 Messerschmitt Bf109E-1. Shot down in combat with RAF fighters south of Dunkirk and crashed at Rubrouck, 11 km north-east of St Omer. Feldwebel J. Kraus captured wounded. Aircraft a write-off.

1./JG54 Arado Ar66. Lost bearings during transit flight from Trier and landed behind enemy lines. Gefr L. Hegwein captured injured. Aircraft a write-off.

8./KG1 Heinkel He111. Returned damaged by ground-fire near Noyon while transporting bombs to advanced landing ground. Gefr J. Schreiner wounded, rest of crew unhurt. Aircraft damaged but repairable.

9./KG27 Heinkel He111. Hydraulics damaged in attack by Adjt Balmer of DAT Étampes over Provins during sortie to attack airfields at Tours, Blois, and Orléans. Forced-landed on abandoned French airstrip on the outskirts of Paris 3.00 p.m. Uffz W. Schalles, Uffz Timmermanns, Uffz Karsten, and another crewman unhurt. Aircraft 1G+AT repairable.

After running repairs this aircraft was able to take off again five hours later and returned to Lille.

I./KG51 Junkers Ju88A. Forced-landed at Augsburg airfield due to fuel problem and ground mist. No crew casualties. Aircraft damaged but repairable.

413

3./KG51 Junkers Ju88A. Shot down by S/Lt Picot of GC III/9 between Nantua and Belle-garde-sur-Valserine and crashed near Dagneux, north-east of Lyon, following attack on Marseille 9.10 a.m. Oberlt P. Kibele, Oberfw M. Schulzki, Fw G. Köppel, and Uffz R. Bauer killed. Aircraft a write-off.

8./KG51 Heinkel He111. Returned damaged by French fighters following attack on Marseille 9.10 a.m. Obergefr H. Schulze slightly wounded, rest of crew unhurt. Aircraft 9K+CT damage state not recorded.

1./KG54 Heinkel He111P. Shot down by No. 92 Squadron Spitfires over Dunkirk 8.00 a.m. Obergefr J. Müller killed. Flgr M. Plank wounded, rest of crew unhurt. Aircraft a write-off.

4./KG54 Heinkel He111P. Badly damaged by No. 92 Squadron Spitfires over Dunkirk and belly-landed on beach at Middlekerke 8.00 a.m. Uffz F. Härter killed. Uffz H. Bayer and Uffz K. Fiedler wounded. Oberlt G. Seubert unhurt. Aircraft B3+JMa write-off.

4./KG54 Heinkel He111P. Believed shot down by No. 92 Squadron Spitfires over Dunkirk 8.00 a.m. Obergefr K. Braun and Uffz K. Wissussek wounded. Hptmn L. Maiwald *(Staffelkapitän)* and Uffz F. Becker unhurt. Aircraft a write-off.

4./KG54 Heinkel He111P. Believed returned badly damaged by No. 92 Squadron Spitfires over Dunkirk 8.00 a.m. Flgr O. Kaschel wounded, Oberlt Berg and rest of crew unhurt. Aircraft a write-off.

6./KG54 Heinkel He111P. Shot down by No. 92 Squadron Spitfires over Dunkirk and believed forced-landed 8.00 a.m. Uffz H. Knobloch killed. Oberlt G. Schmidt, Fw W. Fister and Obergefr E. Sprung unhurt. Aircraft a write-off.

9./KG54 Heinkel He111P. Shot down by No. 92 Squadron Spitfires over Dunkirk and belly-landed at Oudekapelle, south-west of Dixmude 8.00 a.m. Obergefr A. Beiersdorf killed. Gefr F. Dreschler wounded. Lt E. Petzold and Gefr B. Okuniewski unhurt. Aircraft a write-off.

8./KG55 Heinkel He111P (1705). Engaged by Capt Papin, S/Lt Krol, Sgt Doudies, Sgt Gauffre, and Sgt Grimaud of GC II/7 following attack on Lyon-Bron airfield; also attacked by Potez 631 of ECN 5/13 (Sgt Farriol and Adjt Birembaut) and one engine damaged. Escaped over the Swiss frontier near Bernex but attacked by Swiss Bf109s (Hptmn Lindecker and Lt Aschwanden of Fl.Komp.15) over Yverdon and belly-landed south of Ursins 9.20 a.m. Gefr H. Lindner badly wounded in head, died same night in hospital at Yverdon. Uffz W. Schubert slightly wounded while attempting to destroy the aircraft and interned along with Uffz H. Mahnert, Uffz H. Söhner, and Uffz M. Volkmer. Aircraft G1+HS interned.
The crew was prevented from destroying the aircraft and the four survivors repatriated to Germany at Stetten-Lörrach on June 28, 1940.

9./KG55 Heinkel He111P. Landed at Stuttgart-Süd damaged by French fighters following attack on Lyon-Bron airfield 9.10 a.m. Possibly that claimed by Adjt Benausse of DAT Étampes. Fw A. Veith, Fw H. Ehrentreich, and Fw L. Schuderer badly wounded. Oberfw Schied and Uffz L. Huber unhurt. Aircraft G1+ET damage state not recorded.

1./StG2 Junkers Ju87B. Shot down by No. 611 Squadron Spitfires during attack on shipping and crashed in the Channel east of Dunkirk 8.00 a.m. Possibly that claimed by P/O MacFie. Uffz W. Bierfreund killed, Uffz H. Schlöffel missing. Aircraft a write-off.

II./StG2 Junkers Ju87B. Believed badly damaged by Sgt Douthwaite of No. 72 Squadron during attack on shipping off Dunkirk and crash-landed near St Quentin 7.00 p.m. Crew unhurt. Aircraft a write-off.

II./StG2 Junkers Ju87R. Shot down by F/O Elsdon of No. 72 Squadron during attack on shipping off Dunkirk and abandoned over Fort-Philippe at Gravelines 7.00 p.m. Crew baled out unhurt. Aircraft a write-off.

II./StG2 Junkers Ju87B. Returned damaged by No. 72 Squadron Spitfires during attack on shipping off Dunkirk 7.00 p.m. Crew unhurt. Aircraft damaged but repairable.

II./StG2 Junkers Ju87B. Returned damaged by No. 72 Squadron Spitfires during attack on shipping off Dunkirk 7.00 p.m. Crew unhurt. Aircraft damaged but repairable.

5./StG2 Junkers Ju87R. Shot down by S/L Lees of No. 72 Squadron during attack on shipping off Dunkirk and crashed near Coudekerque 7.00 p.m. Lt H-H. Busch and Gefr E. Roock killed. Aircraft a write-off.

III./StG51 Junkers Ju87B. Crash-landed at Wertheim airfield during training flight, cause unknown. No crew casualties. Aircraft a write-off.

Stab I./ZG26 Messerschmitt Bf110C. Crashed at Le Transloy during practice flight from Cambrai, cause unknown. Oberlt H-J. Kirchhoff *(Gruppe TO)* and Oberfw H. Mette slightly wounded, admitted to hospital in Bapaume. Aircraft a write-off.

I./ZG52 Messerschmitt Bf110C. Crash-landed near Freiburg badly damaged by ground-fire. Crew believed unhurt. Aircraft a write-off.

I./ZG52 Messerschmitt Bf110C. Crash-landed at Freiburg airfield badly damaged by ground-fire. Uffz E. Flug injured, gunner unhurt. Aircraft a write-off.

4./ZG76 Messerschmitt Bf110C. Crashed on landing, both engines damaged in fighter attack over Haynecourt, north-west of Cambrai. Oberlt G. Christiansen slightly wounded, admitted to hospital in Munich; gunner unhurt. Aircraft a write-off.

Pilots of No. 92 Squadron were responsible for bringing down Lieutenant Ernst Petzold and his crew in their Heinkel from 9./KG54. Flight Lieutenant Tuck, the CO, whose Spitfire was damaged over Dunkirk entered in his log book: 'Sighted and attacked eight Heinkel 111. Shot down 1 and was attacked by 6-109. Shot down 1 Me 109 and returned having no ammo left'.

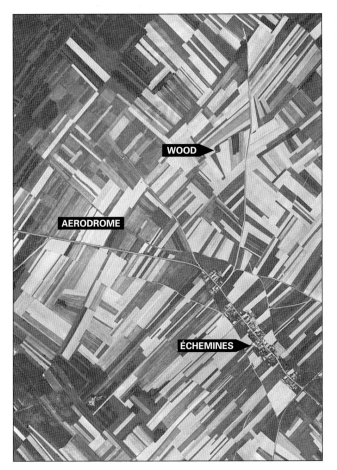

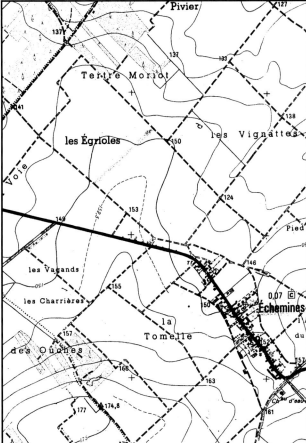

At the beginning of June preparations began for those squadrons still remaining in the south to begin leap-frogging from aerodrome to aerodrome towards the Atlantic coast. No. 73 Squadron at Gaye moved further south to Échemines (see map page 26) on June 3. The airfield lay beside the D442 to the north-west of the village and had been occupied by Battles of No. 12 Squadron that left for Sougé. *Left:* No trace of the aerodrome is apparent on this aerial photo taken in 1948. *Right:* Even more changes since with several roads and tracks expunged on the present-day map.

Monday, June 3

Since June 1, a large-scale enemy assault on French Air Force targets in and around Paris had been expected, full details of German plans for this Operation 'Paula', other than its actual date, having been known to the Allies for some time through intelligence sources and wireless intercepts. French defences were accordingly reinforced and organised, and interception plans prepared, under a French counter-operation code-named 'Tapir'. But when Operation 'Paula' was launched early in the afternoon of June 3, the alerts transmitted by the French communications centre located at the Fifel Tower were subjected to heavy and most-effective German radio interference. Consequently, the first warning of impending attack that most French fighter units received was the sound of French AA defences and the detonation of German bombs.

Serious failings in telephone communications prevented No. 67 Wing Hurricanes from making any significant contribution to the defence of the French capital. Surviving records are fragmentary and confused, but No. 501 Squadron Hurricanes are believed to have encountered Bf109s of 9./JG53 north of Creil around 8.50 a.m. while No. 73 Squadron, airborne as escort to French reconnaissance along the Aisne between Neufchâtel and Rethel, also reported contact with enemy aircraft and claimed one escort fighter destroyed, and another probable, for the loss of one Hurricane in action west of Épernay early afternoon. The enemy bomber formation, variously reported as 200 plus and approaching Paris from Rethel and Reims, proceeded towards Melun unhindered by the British fighters.

Simultaneously, another enemy formation estimated at 100 aircraft approached from Cambrai before turning south at Beauvais, while a third wave flew direct for Paris via St Quentin and Crépy-en-Valois. According to German sources, a total of 600 bombers escorted by 460 fighters drawn from both Luftflotten was involved in this major effort to destroy French Air Force potential before the inevitable offensive along the Somme-Aisne line was launched. For the first time, the full weight of the German air weapon was directed against a strategic objective and, given the material effort they had already expended in the preceding weeks, it was a chilling demonstration of aerial power.

Whatever the actual number of aircraft employed, they attacked a wide variety of targets including 16 airfields around Paris, three air parks, several aircraft factories, marshalling yards, and railways where widespread serious damage was caused; 22 stations hit and several main lines cut. Despite Luftwaffe claims of 42 French aircraft destroyed on the ground, surprisingly few seem to have been destroyed or damaged in the attacks but casualties were high with some 250 killed and 650 injured. And while the bombing failed to cause any civilian panic, its effect on the French Government must have been considerable.

Close to 250 French fighters rose to defend Paris and, ordered to concentrate their attacks on enemy bombers, found this difficult to achieve due to superior numbers of enemy fighters. This overwhelming German fighter presence, plus the element of surprise achieved by the enemy, placed *La Chasse* at a considerable disadvantage and, though French fighters fought with total commitment and great aggression, by the end of the day fewer than ten enemy aircraft destroyed could be claimed, seven of which were later confirmed. The Luftwaffe claimed a total of 95 victories, over 50 of them by the swarming fighter units, but as can be seen from the loss lists this optimistic tally was far in excess of reality.

Meanwhile, evacuation of French troops still awaiting embarkation from Dunkirk, along with British stragglers, continued during the hours of darkness and further low-level attacks by 18 Blenheims on the German guns near Pointe de Gravelines took place early in the morning. These attacks were continued through the night by 12 Wellingtons that also bombed Bergues which had fallen to German troops during the day. Coastal Command also despatched seven Beauforts and eight Hudsons to bomb oil storage facilities at Ghent and Rotterdam.

Haze and heavy ground mist in the Dunkirk area had hampered fighter operations throughout the morning but there was little enemy activity, attention having switched to Paris, and only sporadic engagements were reported. Consequently, no patrols were flown after 9.30 a.m. though RAF fighters remained at constant readiness to respond to any requests for cover. Meanwhile, an estimated 20,000-30,000 French troops, including many non-combatants their food and ammunition largely expended, crowded into the Dunkirk pocket to await the arrival of German infantry units now occupying the outer suburbs of Mardyck, Bergues, and Rosendael.

415

BRITISH AIR FORCES IN FRANCE

73 SQUADRON, ÉCHEMINES

Hurricane. Believed shot down in combat with Bf109s of 1./JG76 west of Épernay and crashed near Dormans 2.20 p.m. Pilot Officer I. D. Hawken killed. Aircraft a write-off.

Originally buried in the communal cemetery at Dormans, Ian Hawken was reinterred in Épernay on October 10, 1947 and subsequently moved to Terlincthun.

501 SQUADRON, ROUEN-BOOS

Hurricane P2867. Believed shot down in combat with Bf109s of 9./JG53 north of Creil 8.50 a.m. Pilot believed unhurt. Aircraft a write-off.

German claims cite three Hurricanes destroyed at this time and place by Lt Jakob Stoll, Lt Horst von Weegmann, and Uffz Kurt Sauer, but surviving RAF records do not clarify further than to confirm this serial was destroyed 'due to enemy action' on this date.

UK-based aircraft lost or damaged on operations over the Western Front:

RAF FIGHTER COMMAND

17 Squadron, Manston
Wing Patrol Dunkirk:

Hurricane P3477. Shot down by Bf109s of 5./JG3 in combat over Dunkirk and possibly that claimed by Lt Buddenhagen 7.40 a.m. F/O R. V. Meredith killed. Aircraft a write-off.

Hurricane. Returned port wing damaged by cannon fire during attack on Ju87s and possibly that claimed by Uffz Freitag of 5./JG3 over Dunkirk 7.45 a.m. P/O D. W. H. Hanson wounded in left leg. Aircraft damaged but repairable.

FRENCH AIR FORCE

DAT Chartres Two Fiat CR42s (R23 and R28). Caught on the ground at Chartres in bombing by Do17s of I./KG76 1.45 p.m. No pilot casualties. Aircraft both damaged but repairable.

Two of six Belgian Fiats of II/2 that arrived from Norrent-Fontes, via Tours, with 12 pilots on May 19.

ECN 1/13 Potez 631 (117). Shot down by Lt Altendorf of 7./JG53 during patrol over Lassigny and Vic-sur-Aisne. Crashed and burned out north of Gournay-sur-Aronde, 15 km north-west of Compiègne, 9.35 a.m. S/Lt S. Biger, Adjt E. Gobert, and Sgt P. Duffour killed. Aircraft a write-off.

F1C Three Dewoitine 520 (285, 286, and 298). Aircraft destroyed in bombing attack on Orly airfield. No pilot casualties. Aircraft all write-offs.

These D520s had arrived to reinforce the Aéronautique Navale Flotille de Chasse the previous day.

GAO 582 Potez 63.11. Crashed on landing at Connantre from routine reconnaissance training flight 2.45 p.m. Lt H. Gruningre, Sgt P. Busschaert, and Sgt J. Cornu killed. Aircraft a write-off.

GB I/11 Two LeO 451s. Damaged in bombing of Étampes-Montdésir airfield by KG51 2.15 p.m. No crew casualties. Aircraft both damaged but repairable.

GB II/34 Amiot 143 and Amiot 351 (58). Unserviceable aircraft destroyed in enemy bombing attack on Nangis airfield. No crew casualties. Aircraft both write-offs.

On June 3, No. 73 Squadron lost Pilot Officer Ian Hawken. This picture shows Hurricane TP⊙Z down 'somewhere in France' but unfortunately only 'A' Flight code-letters were logged in the squadron ORB. This particular machine was from 'B' Flight but exhaustive investigation by Don Minterne, the squadron historian, has failed to identify this particular casualty.

GB II/35 Breguet 691 (60). Hit the ground and caught fire at Montierchaume during training flight, cause unknown. Sgt Simon and Sgt Poulitou killed. Aircraft a write-off.

GC 2/1 Bloch 152 (593). Caught by Bf109s of 6./JG3 shortly after emergency take-off from Chantilly and shot down at Saint-Leu-d'Esserent. Believed that claimed by Oberfw Labusga 1.40 p.m. Capt B. Maréchal killed. Aircraft a write-off.

GC 2/1 Bloch 152 (427). Caught by Bf109s of 6./JG3 over Senlis after emergency take-off from Chantilly and exploded in mid-air between Barbery and Ognon. Believed that claimed by Oberlt Woitke *(Staffelkapitän)* 1.40 p.m. Lt A. Le Gentil baled out badly burned. Aircraft a write-off.

GC 2/1 Bloch 152 (551). Caught by Bf109s of 6./JG3 over Boran-sur-Oise shortly after emergency take-off from Chantilly and shot down at 'Le Grand Terrier' between Crouy-en-Thelle and Morangles. Believed that claimed by Oberfw Labusga 1.41 p.m. S/Lt P. Trébod killed. Aircraft a write-off.

GC II/1 Bloch 152. Shot down by Oberlt Lippert *(Staffelkapitän)* of 3./JG53 during attack on enemy bombers over Brétigny-sur-Orge airfield 1.20 p.m. Sgt Guitard baled out badly wounded. Aircraft a write-off.

GC II/1 Bloch 152 (578). Crippled during attack on enemy bombers over Brétigny-sur-Orge airfield and belly-landed 3 km east of Gonesse 1.30 p.m. Adjt J. Crocq slightly wounded. Aircraft a write-off.

GC I/3 Dewoitine 520 (114). Shot down by Lt Zeis of 1./JG53 following attack on Do17s of II./KG76 north of Tournan-en-Brie and crashed and burned out at 'Les Trente Arpents', Favières, 1.45 p.m. Sgt R. Robert killed. Aircraft a write-off.

GC I/3 Dewoitine 520 (225). Shot down by Lt Fleitz of 8./JG53 during attack on Do17s of II./KG76 west of Meaux and crashed and burned out at 'Le Charton', Charmentray, 1.50 p.m. Adjt J. Vinchon killed. Aircraft a write-off.

A sorry sight on the aerodrome at Chartres, the target of a German bombing attack early afternoon. Two Belgian Fiat CR42s (R23 and R28) were hit.

GC I/3 Dewoitine 520. Returned to Meaux-Esbly damaged during attack on Do17s of II./KG76 1.30 p.m. S/Lt Silvan slightly wounded. Aircraft repairable.

GC I/3 Dewoitine 520. Badly damaged by Bf109s during attack on Do17s near Meaux of II./KG76 and overturned attempting emergency landing at Lognes-Émerainville airfield 1.40 p.m. Sgt F. Glauder escaped unhurt. Aircraft a write-off.

GC I/5 Curtiss H-75 (49). Wing shot off by Bf109 during attack on enemy bombers between Reims and Épernay 1.45 p.m. Crashed and burned out near Dormans. S/Lt P. Scotte killed. Aircraft a write-off.

GC I/5 Curtiss H-75 (85). Forced-landed badly damaged by Bf109 during attack on enemy bombers engaged between Reims and Épernay 2.15 p.m. S/Lt M. Parnière seriously wounded in left leg and foot admitted to hospital in Épernay. Aircraft a write-off.

GC I/5 Curtiss H-75. Belly-landed at La Ferté-Gaucher badly damaged by Bf110s of III./ZG26 during attack on enemy bombers between Reims and Épernay 2.15 p.m. Lt F. Perina wounded in arm and leg, admitted to hospital. Aircraft damaged but repairable.

GC I/5 Curtiss H-75 (200). Belly-landed near St-Dizier damaged by Bf110s of III./ZG26 during attack on enemy bombers between Reims and Épernay 2.15 p.m. S/Lt Warnier unhurt. Aircraft abandoned.

GC I/5 Curtiss H-75. Returned badly damaged by Bf110 of III./ZG26 during attack on Do17s near Épernay 2.15 p.m. Sgt Delparte unhurt. Aircraft damaged but repairable.

GC I/6 Morane 406. Forced-landed damaged in combat with fighters near Lagny-sur-Marne 1.35 p.m. Sgt J. de Lestapis severely wounded in chest, died undergoing surgery. Aircraft damaged but repairable.

GC I/6 Morane 406 (693). Shot down by Hptmn Mölders *(Gruppenkommandeur)* of Stab III./JG53 in combat over Ozoir-la-Ferrière and crashed and burned out at Monthéty 1.30 p.m. Sgt S. Popelka killed. Aircraft a write-off.

GC I/6 Morane 406 (1022). Shot down by Hptmn Mölders *(Gruppenkommandeur)* of Stab III./JG53 in combat over Ozoir-la-Ferrière 1.40 p.m. Sgt Jost badly wounded, baled out but hit the aircraft and landed heavily; admitted to hospital in Corbeil with broken thigh. Aircraft a write-off.

GC III/7 Morane 406 (351). Returned to Coulommiers damaged by fighters during attack on He111s. S/Lt Martin admitted to hospital wounded in left leg. Aircraft repairable.

GC I/8 Bloch 152. Returned damaged in action with Bf109s 9.30 a.m. Possibly that attacked by Fw Galubinski of 7./JG53 over Montdidier. Sgt Maurel wounded. Aircraft repairable.

GC I/8 Bloch 152 (567). Crashed on landing at Claye-Souilly damaged in action with Bf109s 9.30 a.m. Possibly that attacked by Uffz Neuhoff of 7./JG53 west of Creil. Sgt J. Dekastello killed. Aircraft a write-off.

GC I/8 Bloch 152. Forced-landed at Brétigny damaged in attack by Bf109s between Crécy and Combs-la-Ville during pursuit of Ju88s of I./KG51 2.10 p.m. Lt R. Bouysse unhurt. Aircraft repairable.

GC I/8 Bloch 152. Forced-landed south of Lagny damaged by Bf109s during attack on Ju88s of I./KG51 2.10 p.m. Possibly that attacked by Oberlt von Hahn of 8./JG53. S/Lt V. Tanguy unhurt. Aircraft damaged but repairable.

GC 3/9 Bloch 152 (608). Shot down by Bf109s of 2.(J)/LG2 shortly after take-off from Chantilly and crashed and burned out at Rivecourt, 9 km south-west of Compiègne. Possibly that claimed by Oberfw Schott 1.32 p.m. Capt Canel *(Commandant)* baled out wounded and badly burned. Aircraft a write-off.

GC II/9 Bloch 152 (601). Shot down by Bf109s of 2.(J)/LG2 shortly after take-off from Chantilly and crashed and burned out at Verberie. Possibly that claimed by Fw Görbing 1.34 p.m. Sgt J. Sibiril-Lefèbre killed. Aircraft a write-off.

GC II/9 Bloch 152 (600). Shot down by Bf109s of 2.(J)/LG2 east of Senlis shortly after take-off from Chantilly and crashed at Montepilloy. Possibly that claimed by Uffz Schiller 1.40 p.m. Sgt J. Mairesse-Lebrun killed. Aircraft a write-off.

GC II/9 Bloch 152 (604). Shot down by Bf109s of 2.(J)/LG2 in combat north-east of Chantilly and crashed and burned out at Roberval. Possibly that claimed by Oberfw Staege 1.46 p.m. Sgt M. Bailly killed. Aircraft a write-off.

GC II/9 Bloch 152 (647). Shot down in combat with Bf109s north of Chantilly 2.00 p.m. Crashed at St Maximin. Lt J. Daval killed. Aircraft a write-off.

GC II/9 Bloch 152. Landed back at Chantilly seriously damaged in attack by enemy fighters north of the airfield 2.00 p.m. Sgt Lepage unhurt. Aircraft 63 damaged but repairable.

GC II/9 Bloch 152. Landed with port elevator destroyed in attack by enemy fighters north of Chantilly 2.00 p.m. Sgt P. Bayle unhurt. Aircraft damaged but repairable.

GC II/9 Bloch 152. Crippled by return fire during attack on Do17s near Épernay and forced-landed near Mareuil-sur-Ay. S/Lt Bardet slightly wounded. Aircraft damaged but repairable.

GIA I/601 Potez 650. Crashed following mid-air collision with another Potez 650 during night sortie from Montargis-Vimory. Adjt R. Renouard, Adjt F. Rigaill, and Sgt M. Melot killed. Aircraft a write-off.

3S2 LeO C301 (4). Wrecked in accident at Dinard. No reported casualties. Autogyro a write-off.

LUFTWAFFE

Aufkl.Gr.Ob.d.L. Junkers Ju88A. Crash-landed at Charleville due to technical failure. No crew casualties recorded. Aircraft damaged but repairable.

I./JG2 Messerschmitt Bf109E-4. Badly damaged in combat with GC I/5 and belly-landed south of Reims 2.00 p.m. Possibly that claimed by S/Lt Parnière. Pilot unhurt. Aircraft a write-off.

9./JG2 Messerschmitt Bf109E-1. Engine set alight by Sgt Bressieux of GC I/5 and abandoned over Oeuilly, west of Épernay, 2.10 p.m. Leutnant K. Schade baled out wounded. Aircraft 8 + ~ a write-off.

4./JG26 Messerschmitt Bf109E-3. Shot down by S/Lt Fontaine and Adjt Crocq of GC II/1 and abandoned between Creil and Château de Laversine, north of Chantilly, 1.30 p.m. Feldwebel W. Roth baled out and captured unhurt. Aircraft 5 + - a write-off.

II./JG52 Messerschmitt Bf109E-3. Damaged in aborted take-off. Pilot unhurt. Aircraft damaged but repairable.

II./JG53 Messerschmitt Bf109E-4. Shot down in combat south-east of Reims and possibly that claimed by P/O Eliot of No. 73 Squadron 2.00 p.m. Pilot believed unhurt. Aircraft a write-off.

4./JG53 Messerschmitt Bf109E-3. Badly damaged by S/Lt Raphenne of GC I/6 in combat north of Lagny and engaged by flak north of Noyon during return flight. Abandoned over Crisolles and crashed at Bussy 1.45 p.m. Oberfw E. Vollmer killed. Aircraft a write-off.

Ernst Vollmer is reported to have been shot while in his parachute by French territorial troops.

8./JG53 Messerschmitt Bf109E-3. Engine badly damaged by S/Lt Raphenne of GC I/6 in combat over Claye-Souilly and belly-landed at Dammartin-en-Goële, near Rouvres, 1.55 p.m. Lt H. Fleitz badly wounded, died June 8. Aircraft 6 + I a write-off.

Stab Luftflotte 3 Messerschmitt Bf109E-3. Believed crash-landed at Rouy-le-Grand, south-west of St Quentin, damaged in attack by S/Lt Thollon of GC I/8 over Roye 9.25 a.m. Oberst G. von Massow *(Jagdfliegerführer 3)* captured. Aircraft a write-off.

Previously Geschwaderkommodore of JG2 'Richthofen', Gerd von Massow was in overall command of the combined Luftwaffe fighter forces deployed for Operation 'Paula'. After the French capitulation he was released from captivity and survived the war as a Generalmajor. He died on June 29, 1967.

3./KG3 Dornier Do17Z. Returned damaged in attacks by GC I/5 and GC II/9 near Reims 1.45 p.m. Fw W. Schuler slightly wounded admitted to hospital in Bernkastel. Aircraft damaged but repairable.

8./KG4 Junkers Ju88A. Damaged hitting a balloon cable during night sortie over Le Havre and belly-landed back at Schiphol. Hptmn W. Storp *(Staffelkapitän)* injured, admitted to Wilhelmina Hospital in Amsterdam. Aircraft a write-off.

Stab KG51 Junkers Ju88A. Dive brakes failed to retract after dive-bombing Étampes airfield then both engines set alight in attacks by S/Lt Salva of GC I/3 and S/Lt Thollon of GC I/8 near Claye-Souilly and belly-landed south of Cocherel 2.00 p.m. Oberst J. Kammhuber *(Geschwaderkommodore)*, Lt H. Kroesch, and Lt W. Lüderitz captured unhurt. Uffz K. Schneider captured wounded in leg. Aircraft 9K+AA a write-off.

I./KG51 Junkers Ju88A. Returned damaged by flak and fighters during attack on Étampes airfield 2.15 p.m. and possibly that claimed by S/Lt Tanguy of GC I/8. One of crew wounded. Aircraft repairable.

III./KG51 Heinkel He111H. Returned damaged in fighter attacks. One of crew wounded. Aircraft repairable.

Stabsstaffel I./KG76 Dornier Do17Z. Shot down by Potez 631 of ECN 2/13 north-east of the Compiègne forest during pre-attack reconnaissance and crashed near Cuise-la-Motte 10.30 a.m. Oberlt H. Heinz, Oberfw E. Hoyer, Fw H. Schmid, and Fw W. Schütz killed. Aircraft a write-off.

Stab I./KG76 Dornier Do17Z. Returned damaged in attacks by GC II/1, DAT Étampes, and Belgian Fiat CR42s south of Ham during sortie to attack Chartres airfield 1.10 p.m. Believed that attacked by S/Lt Dumonceau of DAT Chartres. Major L. Schulz *(Gruppenkommandeur)* slightly wounded, admitted to hospital in Vogelsang. Aircraft repairable.

1./KG76 Dornier Do17Z. Returned badly damaged in attacks by GC II/1, DAT Étampes, and Belgian Fiat CR42s of DAT Chartres south of Ham during sortie to attack Chartres airfield 1.10 p.m. Possibly one of those claimed by Adjt Balmer of DAT Étampes. Hptmn W. Riedinger *(Staffelkapitän)* badly wounded — died en-route to hospital in Cambrai, rest of crew believed unhurt. Aircraft a write-off.

1./KG76 Dornier Do17Z. Returned badly damaged in attacks by GC II/1, DAT Étampes, and Belgian Fiat CR42s of DAT Chartres south of Ham during sortie to attack Chartres airfield 1.10 p.m. Possibly that claimed by Adjt Benausse or Sgt Karubin of DAT Étampes. Uffz R. Stühmer killed. Uffz G. Zeilmann badly wounded, died in hospital in Vogelsang June 5. Uffz L. Bauer slightly wounded. Aircraft a write-off.

3./KG76 Dornier Do17Z. Returned damaged in attacks by GC II/1, DAT Étampes, and Belgian Fiat CR42s of DAT Chartres south of Ham during sortie to attack Chartres airfield 1.10 p.m. Believed that attacked by Sgt Jottard and Lt Goffin of DAT Chartres. Uffz H. Bungardt slightly wounded, admitted to hospital in Vogelsang. Aircraft repairable.

4./KG76 Dornier Do17Z. Returned damaged in attacks by D520s of GC I/3 southeast of Paris during attack on Chelles airfield 1.30 p.m. Probably that attacked by Capt Challe and Adjt Bourbon. Fw F. Schmalzbauer and Uffz F. Gerstner slightly wounded, rest of crew unhurt. Aircraft damaged but repairable.

6./KG76 Dornier Do17Z. Shot down by Sgt Cucumel and Sgt Daunizeau of GC II/9 during attack to attack Chelles airfield 2.00 p.m. Abandoned over Ferme St-Antoine at Mardeuil and crashed in the eastern suburbs of Épernay 2.00 p.m. Obergefr C. Bang killed. Gefr E. Grossmann-Hermann missing. Gefr A. Bräutigam baled out and captured wounded. Uffz K. Hoffmann and Uffz J. Hinterberger baled out and captured unhurt. Aircraft a write-off.

This aircraft crashed at 5 Rue Lochet and later exploded badly damaging neighbouring buildings and killing three people and injuring ten others.

Stab III./KG76 Dornier Do17Z. Returned badly damaged in attacks by GC II/1, DAT Étampes, and Belgian Fiat CR42s of DAT Chartres over Compiègne during low-level sortie to attack Claye-Souilly airfield 1.30 p.m. Possibly that claimed by S/Lt Fontaine and Adjt Crocq of GC II/1. Major F. Reuss *(Gruppenkommandeur)* badly wounded, admitted to hospital in Bonn; rest of crew unhurt. Aircraft damage state not recorded.

7./KG76 Dornier Do17Z. Returned damaged in attacks by GC II/1, DAT Étampes, and Belgian Fiat CR42s of DAT Chartres south of Ham during low-level sortie to attack Claye-Souilly airfield 1.30 p.m. Uffz E. Musiolik slightly wounded, rest of crew unhurt. Aircraft repairable.

8./KG76 Dornier Do17Z. Returned damaged in attacks by GC II/1, DAT Étampes, and Belgian Fiat CR42s of DAT Chartres over Noyon during low-level sortie to attack Claye-Souilly airfield 1.30 p.m. Possibly that attacked by Adjt Richardin near Cuvilly. Fw M. Friedrich badly wounded, died June 7 in hospital in Düsseldorf; rest of crew unhurt. Aircraft damaged but repairable.

9./ZG26 Messerschmitt Bf110C. Badly damaged in combat with Hurricanes of No. 73 Squadron and H-75s of GC I/5 between Reims and Épernay and overturned attempting forced-landing at Ste-Marie-Chevigny airfield, near Libramont, 2.15 p.m. Probably that claimed by F/Lt Nicholls but possibly also attacked by Cdt Murtin *(Groupe Commandant)* and S/Lt Parnière. Uffz E. Ahrens and Gefr A. Fiedler killed. Aircraft a write-off.

After bombing Étampes aerodrome, this Ju88 of Stab KG51 failed to return having been brought down by French pilots.

Tuesday, June 4

On completion of the early morning embarkation, Admiral Abrial, the French garrison commander at Dunkirk, acknowledged that further resistance was useless and consequently, during the afternoon, Operation 'Dynamo' was officially terminated at 2.23 p.m. RAF Air Component Rear HQ at Hawkinge promptly disbanded.

Three reconnaissance sorties north of the Somme found little of any consequence to report so no daylight bombing operations were ordered, but at night the AASF continued to attack communications and enemy concentrations in the upper Meuse. Nineteen sorties were flown and incendiaries dropped on woods at Givet and Hirson believed to be German holding areas.

Fighter Command covered the Dunkirk approaches from first light until 6.00 a.m. when it was intended that Coastal Command aircraft would take over but this was prevented by thick fog over the Channel. Deteriorating weather conditions, that caused a fatal accident at Rochford, forced returning fighters to land at Tangmere, the only airfield in No. 11 Group to have clear visibility.

Conditions over the Channel were so dire that, though unconfirmed by the Operations Record Book, Spitfires of No. 72 Squadron, trying to find Manston in the thickening clag, nearly flew into cliffs at the North Foreland. With Littlestone and Hawkinge both fogbound, they apparently lost four aircraft in a further vain attempt to get in at Manston while three others are reported to have landed safely at Shoreham, and a fourth put down in a field. As the official RAF Narrative succinctly puts it, 'With this unfortunate anti-climax, the fighter patrols over Dunkirk came to an end'.

BRITISH AIR FORCES IN FRANCE

1 SQUADRON, ROUEN-BOOS

Hurricane. Crash-landed on fire, radiator damaged in combat with escort Bf110s during attack on He111s west of Rouen 6.30 a.m. Pilot Officer H. B. L. Hillcoat unhurt. Aircraft a write-off.

Hurricane. Returned to Boos with radiator shot away by concentrated return fire during attack on He111s west of Rouen 6.30 a.m. Sergeant J. Arbuthnot unhurt. Aircraft repairable.

Hurricane. Crashed on landing following combat with escort Bf110s during attack on He111s west of Rouen 6.30 a.m. Pilot Officer N. P. W. Hancock unhurt. Aircraft a write-off.

No. 67 (Fighter) Wing records indicated that this action took place on June 5.

UK-based aircraft lost or damaged on operations over the Western Front:

RAF BOMBER COMMAND

59 Squadron, Andover
Reconnaissance:

Blenheim IV. Crashed on take-off from Hawkinge, cause unknown but probably engine failure 12.30 p.m. P/O S. W. Ashton and crew unhurt. Aircraft damage state not recorded.

Blenheim IV R3697. Belly-landed outside Eastchurch airfield, hydraulic undercarriage lock damaged by ground-fire during reconnaissance north of the Somme 5.10 p.m. F/O G. H. D. Evans, Sergeant Barry and AC2 C. C. Cleland unhurt. Aircraft a write-off.

RAF FIGHTER COMMAND

616 Squadron, Rochford
Patrol Dunkirk:

Spitfire N3130. Crashed attempting landing in bad weather 4.17 a.m. P/O E. W. S. Scott killed. Aircraft a write-off.

FRENCH AIR FORCE

AB 1 Vought 156F (1). Forgot to lower undercarriage and wrecked in belly-landing at Maupertus. LV Mesny *(Commandant)* and crewman unhurt. Aircraft 1 a write-off.

AB 4 L-N 411 (9). Engine set alight over Vierzon in mistaken attack by S/Lt J. Daszewski of DAT Romorantin during transit flight from Querqueville to Hyères 8.45 a.m. SM Rochon baled out wounded. Aircraft a write-off.

GAO 2/506 Potez 63.11 (772). Returned to Chambley badly damaged in attack by Oberlt Lederer of 6./JG52 east of Luxembourg during observation of roads and railways between Apach and Trier 4.20 a.m. S/Lt P. Bolle seriously wounded, died in hospital same night. Sgt Jousselin slightly wounded in left cheek. Sgt Demuyter unhurt. Aircraft a write-off.

By now the wrecks of hundreds of downed aircraft littered the countryside of northern France. The circumstances surrounding the loss of many of them cannot be reliably established — like this Potez 63.11, serial 366.

GAO 517 Potez 63.11 (327). Shot down by Lt von Aspern of 1./JG76 during flight from Bray-sur-Seine to Monthiers, 12 km north west of Château-Thierry, and crashed in Montmirail 8.40 a.m. Adjt M. Fonvielle killed. S/Lt J. Caujolles severely wounded, died June 9. S/Lt Collomb wounded. Aircraft a write-off

GB I/12 LeO 451 (19). Crashed with full bomb-load and exploded at Glamondans during night attack on the BMW aero-engine works north of Munich early a.m. Lt C. Raillard, Adjt H. Chamaud, Adjt G. Delacroix, and Sgt P. Verdy killed. Aircraft a write-off.

GB I/15 Farman 222.2 (34). Damaged by AA fire during sortie to bomb the BWM engine works at Munich. Lost fuel and crashed in St Sernin forest, between Les Germenets and Croix-Brenot, during return flight. Crew believed baled out unhurt. Aircraft a write-off.

GB II/21 Bloch 210 (15). Wrecked in forced-landing due to petrol failure during night sortie to attack enemy convoys near Péronne and Cambrai. Crew unhurt. Aircraft a write-off.

GR I/33 Bloch 174 (17). Crashed and caught fire on take-off from Tavaux for transfer flight to Martigny-les-Gerbonvaux. Lt B. Germette, Sgt Rebois, and Sgt Vaillant killed. Aircraft a write-off.

GR 2/35 Potez 63.11 (620). Shot down by Uffz Schulte of 8./JG53 south-west of Crépy-en-Valois during photo-reconnaissance sortie and crashed near Ormoy-Villers 5.15 p.m. Capt J. Robert *(Commandant)* and S/Lt S. Larpent killed. Adjt Jannin seriously wounded knees. Aircraft a write-off.

SCLE Potez 56 (3713). Aircraft left at Orly on withdrawal to Rochefort. No crew casualties. Aircraft abandoned.
Service de Convoyage, Liaison et Entraînement was the ferry and delivery flight for the Aéronautique Navale.

LUFTWAFFE

Flugbereitschaft II. Fliegerkorps Fieseler Fi156. Hit trees while landing at Château-Thierry. One injured. Aircraft a write-off.

4./KG1 Heinkel He111. Lifted off too late and crashed on take-off for transfer flight from Cologne-Wahn. Uffz G. Priemer badly injured admitted to hospital in Hohenlind, Uffz W. Henke, Uffz H. Küchler, Uffz H. Pries, Uffz W. Schlosser, and Uffz A. Werner all slightly injured. Aircraft a write-off.

Stabsstaffel KG55 Heinkel He111P. Returned damaged in attacks by Adjt Hervé, Sgt Tomicki, and Sgt Kowalski of DAT Châteaudun during reconnaissance sortie between Tours and Chartres 6.00 a.m. Gefr F. Schmied badly wounded, admitted to hospital at Schwäbisch-Hall; rest of crew unhurt. Aircraft repairable.

3./KG76 Dornier Do17Z. Crashed 15 km south-west of Cambrai prior to landing from transfer flight, cause unknown 8.45 p.m. Fw E. Müller, Uffz K-H. Hambrecht, Uffz L. Gohr, and Uffz W. Hartzsch killed. Aircraft a write-off.
Mechanic Uffz Walter Pflüger, who was passenger in the aircraft, also died in this accident.

7.(F)/LG2 Dornier Do17. Believed damaged by AA fire during reconnaissance sortie and crash-landed at Voyenne, near Marle. Uffz H. Pinske wounded, treated in field hospital at St Quentin; gunner unhurt. Aircraft damaged but repairable.

II./StG2 Junkers Ju87B. Propeller and wing damaged on landing at Remaisnil. Crew unhurt. Aircraft damaged but repairable.

6./ZG1 Messerschmitt Bf110C. Violated neutral air space and engaged by Swiss Bf109s of Fl.Komp.6 and Fl.Komp.15. Badly damaged in attacks and abandoned just inside the French border over Fournet-Blancheroche, south of Charquemont, 3.45 p.m. Uffz A. Killermann and Uffz G. Wöhl baled out too low and killed. Aircraft a write-off.
One Swiss Bf109C (J-310) was lost in this encounter, its pilot killed when his parachute failed to open.

Stab I./ZG52 Messerschmitt Bf110C. Crashed at Maizey both engines destroyed in attacks by Lt Huvet, S/Lt Hebrard, and Sgt Hème of GC II/5 north of St Mihiel 8.10 a.m. Oberlt H. Ziebarth *(Gruppenadjutant)* baled out and captured. Uffz J. Sisterhenn killed. Aircraft a write-off.

From the moment that the French defences at Sedan and on the Meuse were broken at the end of the second week of May, only a rapid retreat to Amiens and the south could have saved the British and French Armies who had entered Belgium at the appeal of the Belgian King; but this strategic fact was not immediately realised. The French High Command hoped they would be able to close the gap, and the armies of the north were under their orders. Moreover, a retirement of this kind would have involved almost certainly the destruction of the fine Belgian Army of over 20 divisions and the abandonment of the whole of Belgium. Therefore, when the force and scope of the German penetration were realised and when a new French Generalissimo, Général Weygand, assumed command in place of Général Gamelin, an effort was made by the French and British armies in Belgium to keep on holding the right hand of the Belgians and to give their own right hand to a newly created French Army which was to have advanced across the Somme in great strength to grasp it.

However, the German eruption swept like a sharp scythe around the right and rear of the armies of the north. Eight or nine armoured divisions, each of about 400 armoured vehicles of different kinds, but carefully assorted to be complementary and divisible into small self-contained units, cut off all communications between us and the main French armies. It severed our own communications for food and ammunition, which ran first to Amiens and afterwards through Abbeville, and it shore its way up the coast to Boulogne and Calais, and almost to Dunkirk. Behind this armoured and mechanised onslaught came a number of German divisions in lorries, and behind them again there plodded comparatively slowly the dull brute mass of the ordinary German Army and German people, always so ready to be led to the trampling down in other lands of liberties and comforts which they have never known in their own.

I have said this armoured scythe-stroke almost reached Dunkirk — almost but not quite. Boulogne and Calais were the scenes of desperate fighting. The Guards defended Boulogne for a while and were then withdrawn by orders from this country. The Rifle Brigade, the 60th Rifles, and the Queen Victoria's Rifles, with a battalion of British tanks and 1,000 Frenchmen, in all about 4,000-strong, defended Calais to the last. The British brigadier was given

an hour to surrender. He spurned the offer, and four days of intense street fighting passed before silence reigned over Calais, which marked the end of a memorable resistance. Only 30 unwounded survivors were brought off by the Navy, and we do not know the fate of their comrades. Their sacrifice, however, was not in vain. At least two armoured divisions, which otherwise would have been turned against the British Expeditionary Force, had to be sent to overcome them. They have added another page to the glories of the light divisions, and the time gained enabled the Gravelines water lines to be flooded and to be held by the French troops.

When, a week ago today, I asked the House to fix this afternoon as the occasion for a statement, I feared it would be my hard lot to announce the greatest military disaster in our long history. I thought — and some good judges agreed with me — that perhaps 20,000 or 30,000 men might be re-embarked. But it certainly seemed that the whole of the French First Army and the whole of the British Expeditionary Force north of the Amiens-Abbeville gap would be broken up in the open field or else would have to capitulate for lack of food and ammunition. These were the hard and heavy tidings for which I called upon the House and the nation to prepare themselves a week ago. The whole root and core and brain of the British Army, on which and around which we were to build, and are to build, the great British Armies in the later years of the war, seemed about to perish upon the field or to be led into an ignominious and starving captivity.

The enemy attacked on all sides with great strength and fierceness, and their main power, the power of their far more numerous air force, was thrown into the battle or else concentrated upon Dunkirk and the beaches. Pressing in upon the narrow exit, both from the east and from the west, the enemy began to fire with cannon upon the beaches by which alone the shipping could approach or depart. They sowed magnetic mines in the channels and seas; they sent repeated waves of hostile aircraft, sometimes more than a hundred strong in one formation, to cast their bombs upon the single pier that remained, and upon the sand dunes upon which the troops had their eyes for shelter. Their U-Boats, one of which was sunk, and their motor launches took their toll of the vast traffic which now began. For four or five days an intense struggle reigned. All their armoured divisions — or what was left of them — together with great masses of infantry and artillery, hurled themselves in vain upon the ever-narrowing, ever-contracting appendix within which the British and French armies fought.

Meanwhile, the Royal Navy, with the willing help of countless merchant seamen, strained every nerve to embark the British and Allied troops; 220 light warships and 650 other vessels were engaged. They had to operate upon the difficult coast, often in adverse weather, under an almost ceaseless hail of bombs and an increasing concentration of artillery fire. Nor were the seas, as I have said, themselves free from mines and torpedoes. It was in conditions such as these that our men carried on, with little or no rest, for days and nights on end, making trip after trip across the dangerous waters, bringing with them always men whom they had rescued. The numbers they have brought back are the measure of their devotion and their courage. The hospital ships, which brought off many thousands of British and French wounded, being so plainly marked were a special target for Nazi bombs; but the men and women on board them never faltered in their duty.

Meanwhile, the Royal Air Force, which had already been intervening in the battle, so far as its range would allow, from home bases, now used part of its main metropolitan fighter strength, and struck at the German bombers and at the fighters which in large numbers protected them. This struggle was protracted and fierce. Suddenly the scene has cleared, the crash and thunder has for the moment — but only for the moment — died away. A miracle of deliverance,

On Tuesday, June 4, Churchill carried out the promise he had made a week previously to give the House of Commons — and thereby the British people — a statement about the result of the Dunkirk evacuation; an unenviable occasion which, he confided, might 'result in my hard lot to announce the greatest military defeat in our long history'. Instead his address, given to a packed house and lasting just over 30 minutes, centred on 'the miracle of deliverance'.

achieved by valour, by perseverance, by perfect discipline, by faultless service, by resource, by skill, by unconquerable fidelity, is manifest to us all. The enemy was hurled back by the retreating British and French troops. He was so roughly handled that he did not hurry their departure seriously. The Royal Air Force engaged the main strength of the German Air Force, and inflicted upon them losses of at least four to one; and the Navy, using nearly 1,000 ships of all kinds, carried over 335,000 men, French and British, out of the jaws of death and shame, to their native land and to the tasks which lie immediately ahead.

We must be very careful not to assign to this deliverance the attributes of a victory. Wars are not won by evacuations. But there was a victory inside this deliverance, which should be noted. It was gained by the Air Force. Many of our soldiers coming back have not seen the Air Force at work; they saw only the bombers which escaped its protective attack. They underrate its achievements. I have heard much talk of this; that is why I go out of my way to say this. I will tell you about it.

This was a great trial of strength between the British and German Air Forces. Can you conceive a greater objective for the Germans in the air than to make evacuation from these beaches impossible, and to sink all these ships which were displayed, almost to the extent of thousands? Could there have been an objective of greater military importance and significance for the whole purpose of the war than this? They tried hard, and they were beaten back; they were frustrated in their task. We got the army away; and they have paid fourfold for any losses which they have inflicted.

Very large formations of German aeroplanes — and we know that they are a very brave race — have turned on several occasions from the attack of one-quarter of their number of the Royal Air Force, and have dispersed in different directions. Twelve aeroplanes have been hunted by two. One aeroplane was driven into the water and cast away by the mere charge of a British aeroplane, which had no more ammunition. All of our types — the Hurricane, the Spitfire and the new Defiant — and all our pilots have been vindicated as superior to what they have at present to face.

When we consider how much greater would be our advantage in defending the air above this island against an overseas attack, I must say that I find in these facts a sure basis upon which practical and reassuring thoughts may rest. I will pay my tribute to these young airmen. The great French Army was very largely, for the time being, cast back and disturbed by the onrush of a few thousands of armoured vehicles. May it not also be that the cause of civilisation itself will be defended by the skill and devotion of a few thousand airmen?

I return to the Army. In the long series of very fierce battles, now on this front, now on that, fighting on three fronts at once, battles fought by two or three divisions against an equal or somewhat larger number of the enemy, and fought fiercely on some of the old grounds that so many of us knew so well, in these battles our losses in men have exceeded 30,000 killed, wounded and missing. I take occasion to express the sympathy of the House to all who have suffered bereavement or who are still anxious. The President of the Board of Trade [Sir Andrew Duncan] is not here today. His son has been killed, and many in the House have felt the pangs of affliction in the sharpest form. But I will say this about the missing: We have had a large number of wounded come home safely to this country, but I would say about the missing that there may be very many reported missing who will come back home, some day, in one way or another. In the confusion of this fight it is inevitable that many have been left in positions where honour required no further resistance from them.

Nevertheless, our thankfulness at the escape of our army and so many men, whose loved ones have passed through an agonising week, must not blind us to the fact that what has happened in France and Belgium is a colossal military disas-

ter. The French Army has been weakened, the Belgian Army has been lost, a large part of those fortified lines upon which so much faith had been reposed is gone, many valuable mining districts and factories have passed into the enemy's possession, the whole of the Channel ports are in his hands, with all the tragic consequences that follow from that, and we must expect another blow to be struck almost immediately at us or at France.

We are told that Herr Hitler has a plan for invading the British Isles. This has often been thought of before. When Napoleon lay at Boulogne for a year with his flat-bottomed boats and his Grand Army, he was told by someone: 'There are bitter weeds in England'. There are certainly a great many more of them since the British Expeditionary Force returned.

I have, myself, full confidence that if all do their duty, if nothing is neglected, and if the best arrangements are made, as they are being made, we shall prove ourselves once again able to defend our island home, to ride out the storm of war, and to outlive the menace of tyranny, if necessary for years, if necessary alone. At any rate, that is what we are going to try to do. That is the resolve of His Majesty's Government — every man of them. That is the will of Parliament and the nation. The British Empire and the French Republic, linked together in their cause and in their need, will defend to the death their native soil, aiding each other like good comrades to the utmost of their strength.

Even though large tracts of Europe and many old and famous States have fallen or may fall into the grip of the Gestapo and all the odious apparatus of Nazi rule, we shall not flag or fail. We shall go on to the end, we shall fight in France, we shall fight on the seas and oceans, we shall fight with growing confidence and growing strength in the air, we shall defend our island, whatever the cost may be, we shall fight on the beaches, we shall fight on the landing grounds, we shall fight in the fields and in the streets, we shall fight in the hills; we shall never surrender, and even if, which I do not for a moment believe, this island or a large part of it were subjugated and starving, then our Empire beyond the seas, armed and guarded by the British Fleet, would carry on the struggle, until, in God's good time, the New World, with all its power and might, steps forth to the rescue and the liberation of the old.

WINSTON CHURCHILL, JUNE 4, 1940

'We must be very careful not to assign to this deliverance the attributes of a victory. Wars are not won by evacuations. But there was a victory inside this deliverance, which should be noted. It was gained by the Air Force'. Churchill closed with a stirring rallying call: 'We shall defend our island whatever the cost may be, we shall fight on the beaches, we shall fight on the landing grounds, we shall fight in the fields and in the streets, we shall fight in the hills; we shall never surrender'.

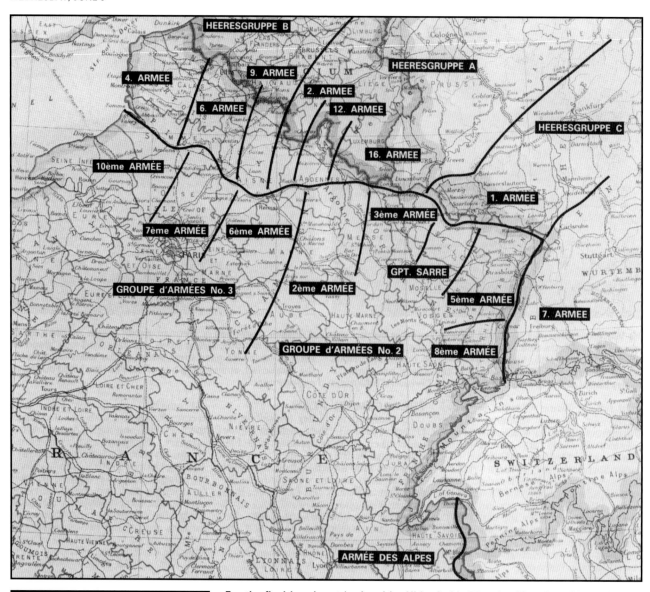

Wednesday, June 5

For the final knock-out (ordered by Hitler in his Directive No. 13 on May 24) code-named 'Fall Rot', the Germans deployed 143 divisions, seven more than for 'Fall Gelb' on May 10. Facing this huge force were 60 French divisions, many demoralised by the swiftness of the German assault which within three weeks had wiped out Belgium and the Netherlands; seen off the British Army, and dealt the French Army a mortal blow.

At 5.00 a.m., after violent artillery bombardment, Heeresgruppe B finally launched 'Fall Rot', the long-expected German offensive against remaining Allied forces in France. The main attacks along the Somme—Aisne line were directed southwest from St-Valéry-sur-Somme and Abbeville, with two major armoured thrusts south from Amiens and south-west from Péronne, crossings of the Crozat Canal near Chauny, and advances south-west from Laon. The immediate threat to the Lower Seine was clear as was their main objective: Paris.

Undaunted by an estimated 250 enemy fighters opposing them, the French fighter units fought with fierce courage and determination. By the end of the day they would have flown a staggering 487 sorties and amassed their highest score of the entire campaign with 23 confirmed plus 35 unconfirmed victories for the declared loss of 19 aircraft. For their part, the German fighter units would claim over 58 Allied aircraft destroyed for the loss of 12 fighters. If the Luftwaffe entertained any thoughts that the campaign in the West was all but won, then this was the day that the Armée de l'Air starkly signalled otherwise.

All three AASF fighter squadrons were seriously under strength, awaiting replacement aircraft and pilots that would not start arriving in any numbers before next day, so each of the 18 serviceable Hurricanes available were now flying up to four sorties a day. Correctly anticipating attacks on Rouen, a key military centre for both the British and French, Hurricanes of No. 1 Squadron, together with Bloch 152s of GC II/10, were in the air early. They engaged a large formation of He111s of I./KG27 escorted by Bf110s of I./ZG1 and Bf109s of I./JG20 around 6.00 a.m. but were unable to prevent the bombers reaching their targets at Rouen where the airfield at Boos and Rouvray camp were both hit. According to one official RAF source, four Hurricanes were 'definitely lost' in this engagement but such is the parlous state of surviving squadron records that these cannot be identified.

This raid was repeated later in the evening when a smaller formation of Ju88s of III./LG1, again escorted by Bf110s, was intercepted around 7.00 p.m. by the Bloch 152s of GC II/10 and Hurricanes of No. 501 Squadron. Meanwhile further east, No. 73 Squadron patrolled the Reims area throughout the day but met with little opposition.

Reconnaissance flights had confirmed enemy armour advancing between Amiens and Montdidier and on roads from Péronne to Roye but it was not before early evening that they were scheduled for attack by 11 AASF Battles. Arriving that late in the target area the Battles, unsurprisingly, found no panzers but bombed the designated roads and attacked any vehicles they could find. Regretably this included French tanks moving west at Tricot which prompted intervention by Moranes patrolling the area, but fortunately without any casualties.

Around the same time that evening, Bomber Command despatched 24 Blenheims against enemy concentrations north of the Somme between Albert and Péronne. They were escorted by two Fighter Command squadrons that made a sweep of the Abbeville area on the return leg, practically the sole appearance by Fighter Command aircraft over France during the entire day.

That night, in an effort to hinder German reinforcements arriving from the north, 48 British heavies pounded communications at Cambrai, Le Cateau, Bapaume, and Doullens, while 11 AASF Battles, operating from the advanced landing ground at Échemines, attacked roads around Givet, Hirson, and Guise where the airfield also received some bombs. One aircraft was lost.

Oldest extant RAF aircraft of the campaign, Supermarine Spitfire K9942 was delivered to No. 72 Squadron at Church Fenton on April 14, 1939. Allocated to 'A' Flight it was regularly flown by Flying Officer James Nicolson, later the sole Fighter Command recipient of the Victoria Cross for valour. Damaged in a crash-landing at Gravesend on June 5, 1940, K9942 went to No. 4 MU Ruislip for repair after which it passed through a number of Maintenance and Operational Training Units, and was twice more damaged, before being earmarked for static display on August 28, 1944. Later refurbished in No. 72 Squadron markings, it was finally incorporated in the RAF Museum permanent collection on November 9, 1971, and is currently maintained at Cosford.

BRITISH AIR FORCES IN FRANCE

1 SQUADRON, CHÂTEAUDUN

Hurricane. Shot down during attack on He111s and combat with Bf110s over Rouen 6.15 a.m. Pilot Officer J. A. Shepherd killed. Aircraft a write-off.

12 SQUADRON, SOUGÉ

Battle L5458. Returned damaged in mistaken attack by S/Lt Paturle of GC I/6 during attack on French tanks near Tricot 8.00 p.m. Pilot Officer J. F. McPhie, Sgt C. S. G. Beevers, and LAC J. G. Thomson unhurt. Aircraft repairable.

Battle L5568. Crash-landed at Faux-Villecerf damaged in mistaken attack by S/Lt Paturle of GC I/6 during attack on French tanks near Tricot 8.00 p.m. Pilot Officer G. M. Hayton, Sgt Simpson, and LAC J. Tracy unhurt. Aircraft repairable.

This aircraft would again suffer a similar tragic accident on the night of July 31/August 1 when it was shot down by a Blenheim night fighter of No. 29 Squadron off Skegness with the loss of the entire crew.

Battle L5520. Crash-landed at Vaux-Villaine following night attack on convoys near Hirson and in woods north of St Michel. Pilot Officer P. C. D. Eaton, Sergeant J. S. Willis, and LAC J. Pickering unhurt. Aircraft PH⊙N abandoned.

Battle L5383. Forced-landed at Chaumont airfield with magneto drive-pin sheared following night attack on convoys near Hirson and in woods north of St Michel. Pilot Officer J. S. Shorthouse and crew unhurt. Aircraft PH⊙F repairable.

73 SQUADRON, ÉCHEMINES

Hurricane. Returned slightly damaged in combat with Bf109s of 7./JG53 following attack on Do17 south-east of Reims 6.50 a.m. Possibly that claimed by Uffz Neuhoff over Poix. Flying Officer E. J. Kain unhurt. Aircraft repairable.

Hurricane. Returned slightly damaged in combat with Bf109s of 7./JG53 following attack on Do17 south-east of Reims 6.50 a.m. Possibly that claimed by Fw Galubinski over Poix. Squadron Leader J. W. C. More unhurt. Aircraft repairable.

Magister P6351. Lost bearings and forced-landed at La Bouëxière during transfer flight from Échemines to Ruaudin and crashed attempting take-off on boggy ground. Pilot Officer P. E. G. Carter and Pilot Officer N. C. Langham-Hobart unhurt. Aircraft a write-off.

103 SQUADRON, ÉCHEMINES

Battle. Damaged by AA fire during night attack on enemy columns and Guise airfield, belly-landed at Château-Thierry 8.00 a.m. Pilot Officer Harper unhurt. Sergeant Stead and LAC Ramsay both ordered to bale out and landed unhurt. Aircraft a write-off.

2 Battles. Parked aircraft badly damaged in enemy bombing attacks. No crew casualties. Aircraft both damaged but repairable.

501 SQUADRON, ROUEN-BOOS

Hurricane. Shot down during attack on He111s of III./LG1 and combat with Bf110s over Rouen 6.30 p.m. Pilot Officer A. J. Claydon killed. Aircraft a write-off.

UK-based aircraft lost or damaged on operations over the Western Front:

RAF AIR COMPONENT

26 Squadron, Lympne
Tactical Reconnaissance:

Lysander N1211. Shot down by Hptmn Müller *(Staffelkapitän)* of 4./JG3 south-west of Abbeville and crashed near Ercourt 12.10 p.m. P/O D. G. Fevez and Sgt R. D. K. Cochrane killed. Aircraft a write-off.

RAF BOMBER COMMAND

107 Squadron, Wattisham
Armour south of Bapaume:

Blenheim N6191. Forced-landed at Hawkinge en route to base damaged by flak and fighters 8.40 p.m. P/O K. D'A. Taute shrapnel wounds in legs and Sgt J. R. Waterhouse badly wounded, both admitted to hospital. Sgt L. S. Fearnley unhurt. Aircraft repairable.

110 Squadron, Wattisham
Armour south of Bapaume:

Blenheim. Crashed on take-off, cause unknown, 7.50 p.m. F/L H. D. H. Cooper and crew believed unhurt. Aircraft damage state not recorded.

RAF FIGHTER COMMAND

72 Squadron, Gravesend
Patrol Dungeness:

Spitfire K9942. Belly-landed following routine patrol 9.52 p.m. Cause unknown. Sgt R. F. Hamlyn unhurt. Aircraft damaged but repairable.
This aircraft is preserved as a permanent exhibit in the RAF Museum, Cosford.

Spitfire L1056. Collided with F/O Thompson while taxying 9.55 p.m. Sgt P. Else unhurt. Aircraft damaged but repairable.

Spitfire P9460. Subject of taxying collision with Sgt Else 9.55 p.m. F/O R. A. Thompson unhurt. Aircraft damaged but repairable.

June 5, 1940 stands as a red-letter day in the annals of the French Air Force. Facing numerically superior odds its pilots gave of their utmost, claiming more enemy aircraft than on any other day in the entire war. The cost was high with 37 aircraft lost in combat, 32 airmen killed, and another 30 wounded. Depicted here are an assortment of types lost by the Armée de l'Air: this being the wreckage of a Breguet 693.

FRENCH AIR FORCE

DAT Bourges Curtiss H-75 (183). Returned to base damaged by return fire during attack on He111s of KG55 near Bourges airfield 1.30 p.m. Lt-Col. C. M. Haegelen wounded in shoulder. Aircraft damaged but repairable.

Base Commandant at Bourges, Claude Marcel Haegelen was a celebrated French ace who had shot down ten enemy aircraft and 12 balloons while flying with Escadrille 103 during WWI. He claimed another victory during this action to bring his overall score to 23 and would end the war a Chevalier of the Légion d'Honneur, holder of the Médaille Militaire, Croix de Guerre with 15 palms and three stars, and a British Distinguished Service Order.

DAT Châteauroux Bloch 151 (93). Suffered oxygen failure shortly after take-off against He111s of 5./KG55 and wrecked in forced-landing north of Issoudin 1.45 p.m. Sgt R. Lewczynski unhurt. Aircraft a write-off.

Alternative sources incorrectly suggest Cpl Jozef Larczycki was pilot of this aircraft, and record his death in action.

DIAP Morane 406. Crashed during training flight at Lyon-Bron, exact circumstances not recorded. S/Lt S. Kogut killed. Aircraft a write-off.

GAO 501 Potez 63.11 (250). Shot down north of Senlis by Hptmn Mölders (*Gruppenkommandeur*) of Stab III./JG53 during photo-reconnaissance sortie to Chaulnes and Péronne. Crashed and burned out at Sarron, 2 km north-east of Pont-Sainte-Maxence 10.23 a.m. S/Lt M. Benoist, Sgt H. Cuvillier, and Sgt J. Rabuel killed. Aircraft a write-off.

GAO 2/508 Potez 63.11 (306). Shot down by Uffz Holdermann of 5./JG53 during photo-reconnaissance sortie west of Vouziers and crashed and burned out at Mars-sous-Bourcq 12.35 p.m. Sgt Aries grievously wounded. Lt Lescuyer wounded, admitted to hospital in Épernay. S/Lt Pesch unhurt. Aircraft a write-off.

GAO 509 Potez 63.11 (592). Badly damaged in attack by Bf109s during sortie to photograph German troop concentrations north of the Somme and possibly that attacked by Oberfw Götz of 5./JG3 over Beauvais 3.45 p.m. Crashed at Thil-Manneville, north of Bacqueville-en-Caux. S/Lt H. Guillerme, S/Lt A. Giron, and Lt E. Dutartre killed. Aircraft a write-off.

GAO 509 Potez 63.11 (588). Believed shot down by Bf109s of 3.(J)/LG2 during reconnaissance sortie between Abbeville and St-Valéry-en-Caux, and crashed at 'Bois de la Croix Parrières', near Campneuseville, north-west of Aumale 3.00 p.m. S/Lt E. Boudinier, S/Lt P. Colin, and S/Lt M. Blanchet killed. Aircraft a write-off.

GAO 510 Potez 63.11 (493). Shot down by Bf109s during observation sortie, crashed and burned out at Brassy, south-east of Poix-de-Picardie 3.00 p.m. Possibly that claimed by Lt Landry and Lt Kloiber of 2./JG3 near Amiens. Lt L. Noiret and Adjt Rage killed. Sgt Desbordes wounded, baled out and captured. Aircraft a write-off.

GAO 3/551 Potez 63.11 (365). Shot down by Hptmn von Selle (*Gruppenkommandeur*) of Stab II./JG3 during reconnaissance sortie over enemy armour south-west of Abbeville 11.40 a.m. Crashed and burned out at Eu, south of Le Tréport. Lt Debladis, Capt Boursaus (*Commandant*), and Sgt Lhoste all wounded, admitted to hospital in Eu. Aircraft a write-off.

GAO 3/551 Potez 63.11 (796). Reported shot down into the sea north-east of Le Tréport by Bf109s during observation sortie and crashed offshore near the Ault lighthouse 2.30 p.m. S/Lt R. Jost, Sgt P. Neuville, and Sgt A. Quilico killed. Aircraft a write-off.

GB I/15 Farman 222 (13). Swerved off runway at Saint-Yan during take-off on night bombing sortie to Cologne station p.m. Crew unhurt. Aircraft repairable.

GB I/19 Douglas DB-7 (31). Shot down by Bf110s over Formerie during sortie to attack enemy armour north of Rouen. Crashed and burned out on the banks of the Seine at Houppeville 7.00 p.m. Lt J. Delperie, Adjt V. Raveneau, and Sgt M. Beguier killed. Aircraft a write-off.

GBA I/51 Breguet 693 (78). Shot down by Bf109s of 1./JG1 over Roye during bombing mission to Chaulnes and Péronne. Crashed in the grounds of Château Davenescourt, north of Montdidier 9.45 a.m. Possibly one of those claimed by Hptmn Balthasar (*Staffelkapitän*). Sgt J. Lefroid and Sgt E. de Catalano killed. Aircraft a write-off.

GBA I/51 Breguet 693 (31). Damaged by Bf109s of 1./JG1 over Roye during bombing mission to Chaulnes and Péronne 9.45 a.m. Starboard undercarriage collapsed on landing at Beauvais airfield. Sgt Jonoux wounded. Sgt Fetiveau unhurt. Aircraft a write-off.

GBA 2/51 Breguet 693 (86). Shot down by Bf109s of 1./JG1 over Roye during bombing mission to Chaulnes and Péronne 9.45 a.m. Crashed at Domart-sur-la-Luce, south-east of Amiens. Possibly one of those claimed by Hptmn Balthasar (*Staffelkapitän*). Capt P. Chocheprat (*Commandant*) and S/Lt R. Pascaly killed. Aircraft a write-off.

GBA II/51 Breguet 693 (40). Shot down by Bf109s of 1./JG1 over Roye during sortie to bomb enemy armoured columns around Chaulnes, Marchélepot, and Ablaincourt. Crashed and burned out between Erches and Guerbigny, north-east of Montdidier 9.45 a.m. Possibly one of those claimed by Lt Franzisket. S/Lt G. De Saint Marceaux and Sgt Beda wounded. Aircraft a write-off.

GBA II/51 Breguet 693 (61). Badly damaged by Bf109s of 1./JG1 over Roye during sortie to bomb enemy armoured columns around Chaulnes, Marchélepot, and Ablaincourt 9.45 a.m. Crashed on landing at Bouard, north of Orléans. Possibly that attacked by Lt Lass. Cpl Godineau badly wounded. Sgt Le Goff unhurt. Aircraft a write-off.

A Bloch 152, but the aircraft number '30' does not appear in French Air Force records. Three Bloch 152s were lost in combat on this day.

GBA II/54 Breguet 693 (5). Shot down by Bf109s of 1./JG1 during sortie to attack enemy tanks between Amiens and St Quentin 9.45 a.m. Crashed at Hattencourt, north of Roye. Possibly one of those claimed by Hptmn Balthasar *(Staffelkapitän)*. S/Lt R. Brunet baled out but parachute failed and he fell into woods north-east of Hattencourt and was killed. Sgt J. Matuchet killed. Aircraft a write-off.

Due to intense shelling in the area, it proved impossible to recover the body of Raymond Brunet and he was never found. He has no known grave.

GBA 3/54 Breguet 693 (32). Shot down by Bf109s of 1./JG1 over Roye during sortie to attack enemy tanks between Amiens and St Quentin 9.45 a.m. Crashed and burned out at Folies, north-east of Montdidier. Possibly one of those claimed by Lt Franzisket. Capt M. Jeunet and Sgt Ducas both badly wounded. Aircraft a write-off.

GB I/62 Martin 167F (74). Shot down by Bf109s during attack on enemy armour around Roye and Péronne and crashed near Montdidier 1.50 p.m. Possibly that claimed by Lt Terry of Stab I./JG51. Adjt Gauche badly burned on face and hands, rest of crew unhurt. Aircraft a write-off.

GB II/62 Martin 167F (128). Returned to St-Martin-la-Campagne damaged by flak during attack on enemy armoured columns between Roye and Péronne 1.45 p.m. Sgt Marc wounded in right thigh; rest of crew unhurt. Aircraft damaged but repairable.

GB II/62 Martin 167F (28). Returned to St-Martin-la-Campagne damaged by Bf109s of Stab I./JG51 during sortie to attack armoured columns between Roye and Péronne 1.45 p.m. Crew unhurt. Aircraft repairable.

GB I/63 Martin 167F (68). Shot down by Bf109s during sortie to bomb enemy armour around Roye and Péronne, and possibly that claimed by Hptmn Brustellin *(Gruppenkommandeur)* of Stab I./JG51. Crash-landed in flames and later exploded at Marissel, near Beauvais 1.55 p.m. Sgt R. Chieusse died of wounds. S/Lt Vaux and Adjt Mony badly burned. Aircraft a write-off.

GC I/1 Bloch 152. Returned to Chantilly-les-Aigles damaged in combat with Bf109s west of Compiègne 2.35 p.m. Cpl J. Pipa believed unhurt. Aircraft damaged but repairable.

GC I/1 Bloch 152. Forced-landed at Gouvieux badly damaged in combat with Bf109s west of Compiègne 2.35 p.m. Cpl H. Postolka believed unhurt. Aircraft a write-off.

This Curtiss H-75A bearing the insignia of 'Les Sioux' denotes it belonged to the 3rd Escadrille of GC II/5.

GC II/2 Morane 406 (249). Shot down by flak west of Péronne during attack on enemy armour around Berny-en-Santerre and Marchélepot 7.00 p.m. S/Lt R. Milhiet baled out over Herbecourt, badly burned on face and hands. Aircraft a write-off.

GC I/3 Dewoitine 520 (126). Shot down by Oberlt Wandel of 2./JG76 in combat east of Amiens and crashed near Argoeuves 10.00 a.m. S/Lt O. Korek baled out too low and killed. Aircraft a write-off.

GC I/3 Dewoitine 520. Shot down by Lt Stangl of 2./JG76 east of Amiens and abandoned over Péronne 9.35 a.m. S/Lt Prévost baled out badly wounded. Aircraft a write-off.

GC III/3 Dewoitine 520 (260). Set alight by Fw Gräf of 3./JG51 in combat near Estrées-St-Denis 1.40 p.m. Sgt J. Casaneuve baled out over Compiègne badly burned. Aircraft a write-off.

GC 5/3 Dewoitine 520. Returned to Cormeilles-en-Vexin cockpit damaged in combat with Bf109s over Estrées-St-Denis 1.40 p.m. Possibly that attacked by Oberlt Joppien of 1./JG51 near Breteuil. Sgt E. Le Nigen slightly wounded by plexiglass splinters. Aircraft repairable.

GC 2/4 Curtiss H-75. Believed one of those claimed by Uffz Keil or Uffz Saborowski of 8./JG3 in combat west of Amiens 7.45 a.m. Crashed at Beaucamps-le-Vieux, north of Aumale. Lt P. Meyzonnier killed. Aircraft a write-off.

GC II/5 Curtiss H-75. Returned to Connantre damaged following bomber escort sortie between Ham and Roye 3.00 p.m. S/Lt J. Burger wounded in foot. Aircraft damaged but repairable.

GC II/5 Curtiss H-75 (42). Belly-landed at Connantre following bomber escort sortie between Ham and Roye 3.00 p.m. S/Lt G. Le Stum unhurt. Aircraft a write-off.

GC I/6 Morane 406 (1035). Shot down by Bf109s between Montdidier and Creil 11.40 a.m. Crashed and exploded at Laneuvilleroy, north-west of Compiègne. Sgt J. Hranicka killed. Aircraft a write-off.

GC 2/6 Morane 406. Returned to Lognes-Émerainville damaged by flak during attack on enemy armour around Chaulnes and Marchélepot 3.10 p.m. Capt J. Kulhanek *(Commandant)* slightly wounded. Aircraft damaged but repairable.

GC I/6 Morane 406. Returned to Lognes-Émerainville damaged by flak during attack on enemy armour around Chaulnes and Marchélepot 3.10 p.m. Adjt Gaudry slightly wounded. Aircraft damaged but repairable.

GC I/6 Morane 406 (456). Petrol tank set alight by flak during low-level attack on enemy tanks north-east of Chaulnes and abandoned over Marchélepot 7.00 p.m. Adjt Senet baled out with badly burned face and admitted to hospital in Marcoing where later captured. Aircraft a write-off.

GC II/6 Bloch 152. Returned slightly damaged by return fire during attack on He111s of 5./KG55 north of Châteauroux 1.30 p.m. Lt A. Cebrzynski unhurt. Aircraft 6 repairable.

GC II/6 Bloch 152. Forced-landed damaged by return fire from He111s of 5./KG55 north of Châteauroux 1.30 p.m. Cpl M. Brzezowski unhurt. Aircraft 16 repairable.

GC II/7 Dewoitine 520 (273). Caught fire under attack by Bf109s of I./JG27 and 8./JG53 between Compiègne and Estrées-St-Denis during bomber escort sortie 5.20 p.m. Crashed and burned out between Chaussoy and Épagny, north of Breteuil. Adjt D. Ponteins baled out badly wounded landing near Berny-sur-Noye. Aircraft a write-off.

GC II/7 Dewoitine 520. Crash-landed at Évreux damaged in combat with Bf109s of I./JG27 and 8./JG53 between Compiègne and Estrées-St-Denis during bomber escort sortie 5.20 p.m. Sgt R. Bret seriously wounded. Aircraft a write-off.

A Potez 63.11 on which the number '617' can vaguely be discerned under a magnifying glass. But where and when?

GC II/7 Dewoitine 520 (266). Shot down in combat with Bf109s of I./JG27 and 8./JG53 between Compiègne and Estrées-St-Denis during bomber escort sortie. Possibly that claimed by Oberlt Homuth *(Staffelkapitän)* of 3./JG27 5.15 p.m. Crashed and burned out at Marissel on the outskirts of Beauvais. S/Lt R. Pomier Layrargues killed. Aircraft a write-off.

GC II/7 Dewoitine 520 (240). Shot down in combat with Bf109s of I./JG27 and 8./JG53 between Compiègne and Estrées-St-Denis during bomber escort sortie. Crashed and burned out at 'Le Bouleau Méru', near Quesnel-Aubrey. Believed that claimed by Oberlt Homuth *(Staffelkapitän)* of 3./JG27 5.20 p.m. S/Lt C. Louis killed. Aircraft a write-off.

GC II/7 Dewoitine 520 (233). Shot down by Bf109s of I./JG1 during escort sortie for aircraft dropping supplies to encircled Allied troops between Marchélepot and Pertain 8.20 p.m. S/Lt W. S. Strzembosz badly wounded, admitted to hospital in Libourne. Aircraft a write-off.

Wiktor Strzembosz was one of a section of three Polish pilots from the Polish 'Montpellier' group, under Capt W. Goettel, flying operations with GC II/7.

GC III/7 Morane 406 (144). Shot down in combat east of Amiens. Crashed and burned out by the main road between Amiens and St Quentin, near Vaire-sous-Corbie. Cpl J. Kosnar killed. Aircraft a write-off.

GC I/8 Bloch 152 (651). Belly-landed at 'Montvient', south of Pontpoint, starboard aileron badly damaged in combat with Bf109s of III./JG53 during escort sortie for Potez 63.11 of GAO 501 over Ham and Péronne 10.20 a.m. Sgt J. Louveau slightly injured. Aircraft a write-off.

GC II/10 Bloch 152 (607). Badly damaged in combat with Bf110s during attack on He111s of III./LG1 and forced-landed at Rouen-Boos 6.30 p.m. S/Lt Dietrich unhurt. Aircraft burned to prevent capture.

A Dewoitine 520 of the 4th Escadrille of GCII/3. When the German offensive opened, GC II/3 was at Le Luc converting onto the D520 before moving to Betz-Bouillancy on May 19. They fell back to La Ferté-Gaucher on June 1 gradually retiring south until their evacuation to Maison-Blanche in Algeria shortly before the Armistice.

GR I/36 Potez 63.11 (595). Shot down by Bf109s on return from photo-reconnaissance sortie to Évreux, Rouen, and Le Havre. Crashed in flames at Saint-Ouen-du-Tilleul, south of Rouen, and possibly that claimed by Lt Westerhoff of 6./JG3 3.05 p.m. Sgt G. de Monts de Savasse and Sgt G. Guille killed. Aircraft a write-off.

Originally buried in field graves adjacent to the crash site, Gérard de Monts de Savasse and Gaston Guille were reinterred in nearby La Londe on June 6, 1941. Sous-Lieutenant Hautecoeur, believed to be the observer in this aircraft, survived, having been landed at Étrépagny with the photos during the return flight to Octeville.

GR II/22 Potez 63.11 (216). Severely damaged by Bf109 during photo-reconnaissance sortie, crash-landed and burned out at Rouvroy-sur-Audry, west of Charleville-Mezières, 1.30 p.m. Believed that claimed by Oberfw Götz of 7./JG53. Sgt Quenolle severely injured and Capt Demimuid wounded in the head; both admitted to hospital in Épernay. Sgt Blanchard unhurt. Aircraft a write-off.

This is — or rather was — a LeO 451 but with nothing to identify the unit or location. Some 47 aircraft of this type were lost on operations, a further 20 being destroyed in accidents.

WERNER MÖLDERS CLAIMS — FRENCH CAMPAIGN

1.9.39	***Hptmn and Staffelkapitän 1./JG53:***		
20.9.39	H-75A	Sierck	07.45 (?)
26.9.39	***Hptmn and Gruppenkommandeur Stab III./JG53:***		
30.10.39	Blenheim	Klüsserath	11.12
22.12.39	Hurricane	NE of Metz	15.05
2.3.40	Hurricane	S of Bitsch	12.15
3.3.40	Morane	SE of Diedenhofen	13.55
26.3.40	Morane	Wolkenfeld	15.00
2.4.40	Hurricane	S of Saargemünd	12.10
20.4.40	H-75A	W of Saargemünd	11.54
23.4.40	Hurricane	S of Diedenhofen	11.14
14.5.40	Hurricane	Sedan	16.30
15.5.40	Hurricane	Charleville	13.05
19.5.40	Bloch 152	NE of Reims	09.35
20.5.40	Wellesley	Compiègne	19.15
21.5.40	Morane 406	SW of Compiègne	17.30
21.5.40	Morane 406	SW of Compiègne	17.50
21.5.40	Morane 406	SW of Compiègne	19.18
22.5.40	Potez 63	SW of Mourmelon-le-Grand	17.50
25.5.40	Morane 406	Forêt de Compiègne	18.55
27.5.40	H-75A	W of Amiens	09.10
27.5.40	H-75A	W of Amiens	09.11
29.5.40	***First fighter pilot awarded the Ritterkreuz***		
31.5.40	LeO 451	S of Abbeville	19.00
3.6.40	H-75A	Paris	14.30
3.6.40	H-75A	SE of Paris	14.40
5.6.40	Bloch	W of Compiègne	11.20
5.6.40	Potez 63	NW of Pont-Ste-Maxence	11.23
5.6.40	***Shot down west of Compiègne and French PoW***		
30.6.40	***Returned from captivity***		

Note: To illustrate the problems in analysing such claims they are shown here as recorded in contemporary German documents.

Werner Mölders was Kommandeur of the III Gruppe of Jagdgeschwader 53 throughout the French campaign. He had flown with the Condor Legion in Spain succeeding Adolf Galland as Staffelkapitän of 3./JGr.88, and claimed 14 victories between July 15 and November 3, 1938 to become the highest scoring German pilot of that war. 'Vati' (Daddy) Mölders claimed another 25 victories before his capture by the French on June 5, 1940.

LUFTWAFFE

4./Aufkl.Gr.Ob.d.L. Dornier Do215 (022). Failed to return from reconnaissance sortie to Nantes and crashed near Warloy-Baillon, north-east of Amiens, cause unknown. Uffz R. König and Uffz W. Lichtenberger killed. Lt F. von Brandt and Oberfw E. Schneider wounded. Aircraft G2+HH a write-off.

3.(H)/13 Henschel Hs126. Shot down by nine H-75s of GC II/5 during reconnaissance sortie of sector south-west of St Quentin to Verberie and crashed between the Oise and the canal east of Ourscamps 4.30 p.m. Oberlt F. Lamm and Fw F. Neufang killed. Aircraft a write-off.

3.(F)/22 Dornier Do17P. Forced-landed both engines damaged in attacks by S/L More and F/O Kain of No. 73 Squadron during reconnaissance over Reims. Lt W. Felge, Fw W. Rössler, and Obergefr J. Heims captured unhurt. Aircraft a write-off.

4.(H)/22 Henschel Hs126. Shot down by Cpl Truhlar of GC II/4 during low-level reconnaissance over Chauny and crashed near St-Paul-aux-Bois 3.10 p.m. Lt Walter captured unhurt. Uffz H. Hoffmann captured slightly wounded. Aircraft a write-off.

1.(H)/23 Henschel Hs126. Shot down by Adjt Feuillat of GC I/4 during observation sortie between Picquigny and Amiens 7.45 a.m. and believed crashed near Bovelles. Oberlt W. Staudinger and Uffz F. Drexl badly wounded. Aircraft a write-off.

1.(H)/31 Henschel Hs126. Collided with balloon at Vignacourt. Crewmen believed unhurt. Aircraft damaged but repairable.

2.(F)/122 Junkers Ju88A. Hit an obstruction on take-off at Cologne-Ostheim. Lt J. Nolte, Uffz B. Renken, and Obergefr K-H. Rott killed. Gefr L. Hase badly injured, died in Hohenlind hospital June 7. Aircraft a write-off.

1.(F)/123 Junkers Ju88A. Undercarriage damaged on landing at Langendiebach. No crew casualties. Aircraft damaged but repairable.

3.(F)/123 Dornier Do17P. Undercarriage damaged on landing at Gelnhausen. No crew casualties. Aircraft damaged but repairable.

1./JG1 Messerschmitt Bf109E-1. Shot down by S/Lt Milhiet, Adjt Bricart, Adjt Dorcy, Adjt Marconnet, and Sgt Plzak of GC II/2 in combat north-west of Roye and abandoned over Lamotte-Warfusée, 8.20 p.m. Uffz A. Tismer baled out and captured unhurt. Aircraft a write-off.

2./JG2 Messerschmitt Bf109E-3. Shot down by S/Lt Baptizet of GC II/4 in combat north-east of Soissons and crashed at Vailly-sur-Aisne 9.45 a.m. Leutnant E. von Reden killed. Aircraft a write-off.

8./JG3 Messerschmitt Bf109E-3. Shot down by Capt Barbier, Lt d'Alançon, Lt de Montravel, and Lt Guillaume of GC I/4 in combat west of Amiens and abandoned over Vraignes-lès-Hornoy 7.45 a.m. Possibly that reported down near Campneuseville. Uffz R. Saborowski baled out and captured. Aircraft a write-off.

8./JG3 Messerschmitt Bf109E-3. Shot down in combat with H-75s of GC I/4 west of Amiens and crash-landed near Vraignes-lès-Hornoy 7.45 a.m. Uffz J. Keil captured. Aircraft 8 + I a write-off.

4./JG26 Messerschmitt Bf109E-3. Lost during transit flight between Le Touquet and Chièvres. Uffz P. Leisse killed. Aircraft 9 + - a write-off.

Three months later, the grave of an 'Unknown German Airman' reported found at Les-Grande-Ventes, east of Longueville-sur-Scie, was exhumed and identified as that of Paul Leisse — lost on his first operational flight. His loss is recorded on June 6 in the Luftwaffe General Quartermaster's returns.

2./JG27 Messerschmitt Bf109E-1. Believed shot down by Lt Lacombe of GC I/3 in combat east of Clermont 5.15 p.m. Feldwebel E. Schröder baled out and captured slightly burned. Aircraft 2 + a write-off.

5./JG27 Messerschmitt Bf109E-1. Set alight in attacks by Capt Portalis, Adjt Dugoujon, and Sgt Chabera of GC II/5 east of Montdidier and crash-landed in woods near Thiescourt, south of Lassigny 3.00 p.m. Oberleutnant W. Roos *(Staffelkapitän)* captured badly burned on face and arms. Aircraft a write-off.

2./JG51 Messerschmitt Bf109E-1. Shot down by Sgt Casaneuve of GC III/3 over Estrées-St-Denis 1.45 p.m. Leutnant E. Falkensamer captured. Aircraft a write-off.

I./JG53 Messerschmitt Bf109E-3. Crashed on take-off, cause not stated. Pilot unhurt. Aircraft damaged but repairable.

II./JG53 Messerschmitt Bf109E-1. Forced-landed at Thin-le-Moutier, west of Sedan, due to engine failure. Pilot unhurt. Aircraft damaged but repairable.

Stab III./JG53 Messerschmitt Bf109E-3. Forced-landed at Laon due to engine failure and possibly damaged in combat with GC I/8 over Pont-Ste-Maxence 10.20 a.m. Pilot unhurt. Aircraft damaged but repairable.

Stab III./JG53 Messerschmitt Bf109E-4. Shot down by S/Lt Pommier-Layrargues of GC II/7 and crashed and exploded at edge of woods on 'Ferme du Villerseau' at Canly, west of Compiègne, 5.15 p.m. Hptmn W. Mölders *(Gruppenkommandeur)* baled out landing between Blincourt and Sacy-le-Petit and captured unhurt. Aircraft << + I a write-off

1./KG27 Heinkel He111P. Crash-landed damaged by Blochs of GC II/10 during attack on Rouen 6.15 a.m. Uffz C. Nuhn and Oberfw E. List killed. Lt H. Lavallée and Uffz F. Deimling captured unhurt. Aircraft 1G+DH a write-off.

1./KG27 Heinkel He111P. Shot down by Blochs of GC II/10 during attack on Rouen 6.15 a.m. Fw H. Grube (of Stab I./KG27), Uffz H. Richter, and Uffz K-H. Pioszyk baled out and captured badly wounded. Uffz P. Herbold baled out and captured unhurt. Aircraft 1G+KH a write-off.

1./KG27 Heinkel He111P. Shot down by Blochs of GC II/10 during attack on Rouen 6.15 a.m. Fw K-H. Hofmann, Uffz H. Bertram, Uffz M. Töpper, and Gefr R. Ahrenholz captured unhurt. Aircraft 1G+AH a write-off.

It was Sous-Lieutenant René Pomier Layrargues who brought down Mölders (left) near Compiègne just before he was himself shot down and killed. Two weeks later, on the signing of the Armistice, Mölders was liberated and returned to Germany to receive promotion to Major and command of JG51. He would achieve a further 43 victories in operations against England to overtake his contemporary, Major Adolf Galland (right) the Kommodore of JG26 who matched his total of 68 victories on June 21, 1941. That month, JG51 transferred to the Eastern Front where Mölders became the first pilot in history to reach the milestone figure of 100 victories. This achievement earned him the Diamonds – the first German serviceman to receive this award – to add to his Ritterkreuz, already adorned with Oakleaves and Swords. Ironically, he lost his life on November 22, 1941 when flying as a passenger in a Heinkel He111 en-route to attend the funeral of Ernst Udet.

We take-off at 17.15 hours [German summer time]. Aircraft above us. We can't identify them. We climb to 7000 metres but they are 109s so we go down a little and get ready to fly home. But suddenly we see six Moranes. I prepare to attack but right in the middle of my attack I see two unknown Staffeln of 109s which are attacking the same aircraft from behind and above.

I watch this fight for a while, then I attack a Morane at which three 109s are firing but all the time in vain as he is in a turn. I get him for a moment in my sights but he breaks immediately although he has not had enough yet. He suddenly climbs again below me — I lose sight of him below my wings — then he comes again from the side, lower. Donnerwetter! And what's more, this Morane is firing but at an extreme range.

I break briefly then climb towards the sun. He probably lost me for he turns in the opposite direction and disappears southwards. Below two 109s are still attacking a single Morane. I watch this fight which goes down to hedge-hopping level, the Morane preventing effective shooting by continual turns. I glance behind and upwards to see 109s still wheeling about everywhere.

I am flying approximately at a height of 800 metres when suddenly there are explosions and sparks in my cockpit, so much so that I am totally stunned! The throttle lever is destroyed and the control column jumps forward and I am in a vertical dive. I grab the cockpit jettison lever and the hood flies away. My machine levels out one last time giving me an opportunity to undo my straps and raise myself from the seat. Then I am free and the parachute has already opened. I see my aircraft falling out of control, its left wing breaking up. Just before it hits the ground it pulls up once more as if it refuses to be beaten despite everything after 25 victories. Then it crashes vertically.

Hanging under the parachute I look round for my adversary but I can only see 109s which are circling me. I am

silently floating towards the ground, ground that is still being held by the enemy as I am 60 kilometres behind the front line, west of Compiègne. I draw my pistol and having cocked it put it into the pocket of my trousers.

The ground is coming up fast so I bend my knees slightly and the impact is relatively soft. I immediately free myself from the parachute and run towards a wood. Frenchmen are running towards me from all sides and as I reach the edge of the wood a bullet flies past my ears. I throw away my fur-lined flight jacket and run breathlessly to the other end of the wood. A large field of lupins lies in front of me so I crawl into it.

Suddenly I hear a powerful explosion nearby and I see a thick cloud of blue smoke rising. My aircraft, having caught fire as it crashed, has just blown up and been completely destroyed. For about an hour I manage to stay hidden but suddenly I realise that this field is being searched too and the men are closing in. I lie totally flat and a farmer walks past ten meters away without seeing me. I am already believing that I am out of danger when I am challenged from behind. I stand up and raise my arms. Only now do I see soldiers and farmers everywhere. While I am standing still one of the Poilus fires again but without hitting me.

In the twinkling of an eye I am surrounded by about 50 people with five bayonets menacingly pointing towards me. Eventually an officer arrives who relieves me of all my possessions, including my Ritterkreuz, but fortunately I don't have much on me. Wearing a shirt and a sleeveless sweater I am standing in the middle of a growing number of troops and the mood is hardly friendly. I explain that I am an Air Force officer and I have barely turned around to walk towards a road when the first kick lands on my rear. I think 'Stay calm' as I receive another blow in the small of my back. A little gnome of a farmer walking beside me berates me with no uncertain words until the officer intervenes and they escort me to a car with a few last blows.

HAUPTMANN WERNER MÖLDERS

3./KG27 Heinkel He111H. Shot down by Hurricanes of No. 1 Squadron during sortie to attack Rouen 6.15 a.m. Lt G. Franck, Fw J. Scheunemann, Uffz W. Forster, and Uffz A. Jenau captured unhurt. Aircraft a write-off.

3./KG27 Heinkel He111P. Shot down by Hurricanes of No. 1 Squadron during sortie to attack Rouen 6.15 a.m. Uffz K. Meier and Uffz F. Wolff killed. Oberlt H-G. Bätcher *(Gruppenadjutant)* and Oberlt S. Scholz *(Gruppen NO)* both captured unhurt. Aircraft a write-off.

3./KG27 Heinkel He111P. Returned damaged by Hurricanes of No. 1 Squadron during sortie to Rouen 6.15 a.m. Uffz A. Ullmann slightly wounded. Fw R. Boer, Fw H. Hegemann, and another crewman believed unhurt. Aircraft repairable.

Stab I./KG51 Junkers Ju88A. Shot down by Capt Opulski and Sgt Krawczynski of DAT Romorantin during attack on Romorantin-Prunières and belly-landed near l'Angélus at Presly where burned out 2.00 p.m. Also attacked by S/Lt de Seynes, Sgt Delhoume, S/Lt Riss, and Adjt Couffon of GC II/6 and S/Lt Wingert and M. Desmazières of DAT Châteauroux. Fw K. Diekert, Fw H. Wagner, Uffz W. Krichbaum, and Gefr W. Schindler captured unhurt. Aircraft a write-off.
Pierre-François Desmazières was a civilian flying operations with the Châteauroux defence flight.

4./KG51 Junkers Ju88A (29). Shot down by Capt Williame, Lt Husson, S/Lt Audebert, and Sgt de Puybusque of GC I/2 south of Troyes during sortie to attack Tours airfield and belly-landed between Treix and Andelot, north-east of Chaumont, 1.45 p.m. Lt H-J. Zobel captured unhurt. Oberlt P. Herr, Fw E. Tocha, and Oberfw K. Graffenberger captured unhurt. Aircraft 9K+HM a write-off.

4./KG51 Junkers Ju88A (5018). Shot down by Capt Williame, Lt Pichon, Lt de la Bretonnière, Adjt Weber, and Sgt de Puybusque of GC I/2 over Recey-sur-Ource during sortie to attack Tours airfield and broke up in heavy belly-landing south of Arbot 1.50 p.m. Oberlt F. Hohenstein and Fw R. Hepp killed. Fw H. Kroll captured wounded admitted to hospital in Langres. Fw H. Ludwig captured unhurt. Aircraft 9K+KM a write-off.

5./KG51 Junkers Ju88A. Shot down by Lt Pichon, Adjt Weber, Sgt de Puybusque, and Sgt Beda of GC I/2 and abandoned south of Troyes during sortie to attack Tours airfield. Exploded and burned out in forest at Clairvaux south of La Borde 1.15 p.m. Uffz A. Schopf remained in aircraft and killed. Fw G. Doege baled out landing unhurt but shot dead by French officer. Uffz E. Werner baled out but separated from parachute and fell dead north-east of Champignol. Oberlt H. Kohl baled out and discovered with badly injured legs in 'Le Bois de Morlieu', west of Clairvaux, three days later. Aircraft a write-off.
Commandant Reverseau, CO of the 3ème Battaillon of Régiment d'Infanterie 108, would later report that the gunner, Gustav Doege, was arrogant and threatening, and was shot when he put a hand in his pocket as if reaching for a weapon.

II./KG53 Heinkel He111H. Forced-landed near Mainz due to engine fire. Crew unhurt. Aircraft a write-off.

7./KG53 Heinkel He111H. Returned damaged in attacks by Capt Delfino and S/Lt Faisandier of GC II/9 near Noyon 6.30 p.m. Gefr A. Dittrich slightly wounded, admitted to hospital at Frankfurt-am-Main. Aircraft damage state not recorded

Stabsstaffel KG55 Heinkel He111. Returned badly damaged over La-Ferté-St-Aubin, south of Orléans. Fw P. Badura, Oberfw H. Stern, and Fw K. Rathmann badly wounded. Oberfw A. Spiewack slightly wounded. Aircraft damaged but repairable.

5./KG55 Heinkel He111P. Returned damaged by fighters over Bourges during sortie to attack Châteauroux-la-Martinerie airfield 12.00 p.m. Gefr H. Müller slightly wounded, rest of crew unhurt. Aircraft repairable.

5./KG55 Heinkel He111P. Shot down by S/Lt Wingert of DAT Châteauroux and S/Lt Riss, S/Lt de Seynes, Adjt Couffon, and Sgt Delhoume of GC I/6 over Bourges during sortie to attack Châteauroux-la-Martinerie airfield and abandoned near Anthien, north-east of Corbigny, 12.00 p.m. Fw H. Belles, Fw W. Harland, and Uffz E. John baled out and captured wounded, admitted to hospital in Auxerre. Fw F. Hölterscheidt and Obergefr B. Stengel baled out and captured unhurt. Aircraft G1+FN a write-off.
This crew received rough treatment at the hands of local civilians and André Gautheron and Roger Moulinot, who were members of the territorial defence force, were later arrested by the Germans for their part in their capture. Gautheron was subsequently released with Moulinot being transported to Germany where he died.

5./KG55 Heinkel He111P. Shot down by Lt Henneberg of DAT Châteauroux and Lt Cebrzynski of GC II/6 over Bourges during sortie to attack Châteauroux-la-Martinerie airfield. Also attacked by S/Lt Wingert of DAT Châteauroux and belly-landed at St Florentin, west of Vatan, 1.45 p.m. Oberfw A. Rudisele, Oberfw H. Guddasch, Fw F. Teika, Uffz H. Herrmann, and Gefr W. Klär captured unhurt. Aircraft G1+AN fired by crew.

7./KG55 Heinkel He111. Returned damaged by flak and fighters during attack on Nevers-Sermoise airfield, south-east of Bourges, 2.15 p.m. Uffz W. Manger badly wounded, died July 8; rest of crew unhurt. Aircraft repairable.

9./KG55 Heinkel He111. Crashed near Aachen damaged by flak and fighters during attack on Nevers-Sermoise airfield 2.15 p.m. Fw P. Knetsch badly wounded. Aircraft a write-off.

9./KG55 Heinkel He111P. Crashed at Böblingen badly damaged by flak and fighters during attack on Nevers-Sermoise airfield 2.15 p.m.. Oberfw G. Geissler, Fw J. Brammer, Obergefr G. Hemmerle, and Uffz P. Brzoska all badly wounded. Aircraft a write-off.

KG76 Dornier Do17Z. Involved in taxying accident at St Leger. No crew casualties. Aircraft damaged but repairable.

3./KG76 Dornier Do17Z. Starboard engine damaged in attacks by Lt Morin of GC III/3 near Mantes-la-Jolie, north-west of Paris, and belly-landed near Auxi-le-Château 3.00 p.m. Probably also attacked by Sgt Le Nigen. Lt J. Hübner died of wounds, rest of crew unhurt. Aircraft a write-off.

9./KG76 Dornier Do17Z. Returned damaged by ground-fire during low-level sortie over Aumale. Gefr T. Grandy slightly wounded, admitted to hospital in Bonn-Hangelar; rest of crew unhurt. Aircraft damage state not recorded.

Stab III./LG1 Junkers Ju88A. Shot down by GC II/10 and No. 501 Squadron during attack on railway targets south of Rouen 6.30 p.m. Uffz G. Weimann and Oberfw J. Tiedemann captured wounded. Fw K. Brammann and Obergefr K. Franz captured unhurt. Aircraft a write-off.

7./LG1 Junkers Ju88A. Shot down by GC II/10 and No. 501 Squadron on railway targets south of Rouen 6.30 p.m. Fw J. Jankowski and Uffz K. Zipperling captured wounded. Obergefr G. Sirlin and Gefr H. Plate captured unhurt. Aircraft a write-off.

II.(S)/LG2 Henschel Hs123. Crashed on take-off from Monceau. Pilot unhurt. Aircraft repairable.

II.(S)/LG2 Henschel Hs123. Forced-landed near Mons-en-Chaussée oil cooler damaged in attack by GC I/6 near Chaulnes 10.30 a.m. Possibly that claimed by Lt Fejfar. Pilot unhurt. Aircraft damaged but repairable.

4.(S)/LG2 Henschel Hs123. Damaged in take-off collision at Puisieux airfield. Uffz A. Eisenmann slightly injured, admitted to hospital in Guise. Aircraft a write-off.

4.(S)/LG2 Henschel Hs123. Shot down by GC I/6 near Chaulnes and crashed near Hallu, south of Chaulnes 10.30 a.m. Possibly that claimed by S/Lt Janis. Lt S. Panten died of wounds. Aircraft a write-off.

4.(S)/LG2 Henschel Hs123. Engaged by GC I/6 near Chaulnes, pursued by Lt Janouch and shot down at Mennessis 10.35 a.m. Uffz K. Heinz killed. Aircraft a write-off.

Stab III./StG2 Junkers Ju87B. Badly damaged in attack by S/Lt Baptizet and Lt Hlobil of GC II/4 during sortie to attack troops near Morchain and crash-landed in flames south of Monceau-le-Neuf 9.40 a.m. Uffz B. Selck killed. Lt R. Schaffner *(Gruppenadjutant)* died of wounds in Laon hospital. Aircraft a write-off.
Bruno Selck was originally buried in a field grave adjacent to the crash site south-west of the D64 and D967 crossroads but was reinterred post-war in Fort-de-Malmaison War Cemetery; Block 6, Row 14, Grave 633.

3.(St)/TrGr.186 Junkers Ju87B. Shot down by flak north-west of Corbie 4.30 a.m. Fw H. Idel and Obergefr H. Dziallas killed. Aircraft a write-off.

Transportstaffel I. Fliegerkorps Junkers Ju52 (5230). Crash-landed at Vitry-en-Artois. Aircraft damaged but repairable.

1./ZG1 Messerschmitt Bf110C. Collided with Uffz Rinke during attack on Lt Possien of GC II/10 north-east of Rouen and crashed near Moliens 6.30 a.m. Fw F. Duensing baled out and broke ankle on landing. Uffz R. Ander killed. Aircraft a write-off.

3./ZG1 Messerschmitt Bf110C. Collided with Fw Duensing during attack on Lt Possien of GC II/10 north-east of Rouen 6.30 a.m. Uffz J. Rinke and Uffz H. Meyer killed. Aircraft a write-off.

7./ZG26 Messerschmitt Bf110C. Belly-landed at Ste-Marie airfield with port engine destroyed in attack by Sgt Maurel of GC I/8 over Nangis, during escort sortie south-east of Paris, 2.50 p.m. Oberlt E. Matthes and Uffz Pfäfflin unhurt. Aircraft a write-off.

Thursday, June 6

At several points along the Somme—Aisne front, German armoured units were successful in penetrating French lines and bypassing pockets of resistance which they left in their rear creating a fluid and, for the Allies, a highly confused situation. Only south of Amiens were French forces able to contain the relentless German advance.

During the day Blenheims of No. 2 Group attacked German troop concentrations advancing on the River Bresle between Le Tréport and Blangy where the British 51st (Highland) Division was fighting a desperate rearguard action. The first attack by 12 aircraft of No. 40 Squadron was delivered around 10.00 a.m. and met with heavy and accurate AA fire and enemy fighters. Despite a fighter escort provided by Nos. 17 and 111 Squadrons, five of the Blenheims and two Hurricanes were lost. A further attack in the same area took place around 5.15 p.m. this time without loss.

Hitler had conducted the campaign in the West from a purpose-built headquarters complex near Bad Münstereifel code-named 'Felsennest', but with the advance proceeding at a pace that probably even amazed the Führer, he wanted to move closer to the action. On May 22 a little Belgian village named Brûly-de-Peche, some 25 kilometres north-west of Charleville, was selected for the new HQ to be known as 'Wolfsschlucht' and a concrete bunker hastily constructed in the adjacent wood. The nearest airfield was just over the frontier in France at Gros-Caillou but Fieseler Storch communications aircraft could set down in the large field in the foreground.

Fighter cover for the hard-pressed British troops had been provided from first light by No. 501 Squadron but no AASF fighters were available to continue such patrols, No. 1 Squadron now being reduced to six serviceable aircraft. Thus Nos. 56 and 151 Squadrons were detailed from North Weald for afternoon and evening patrols over the area, both units landing at Rouen-Boos to refuel and rearm. A joint operation planned with the locally-based Hurricanes had to be dropped due to 'tactical and R/T difficulties'.

French medium bombers made several determined attacks on German mechanised forces advancing from Péronne towards Roye throughout the afternoon and evening, suffering considerable losses to the ever-present enemy flak and fighters. They were

joined, at around 4.30 p.m. by nine AASF Battles who reported considerable numbers of enemy aircraft in the area.

At night, Bomber Command flew 28 sorties against communications to the rear of the German lines attacking railheads and roads at Hirson, Avesnes, Béthune, and Le Cateau, while convoys and troop concentrations around Hesdin and between Abbeville and Étaples also came under attack. Endorsing the British decision not to send any more fighter reinforcements to France, at the risk of Britain's security, and certainly not until the Germans had committed themselves to a fresh offensive, 134 enemy aircraft were plotted over England during the night. It was a further portent of the changing nature of the campaign in the West.

BRITISH AIR FORCES IN FRANCE

212 SQUADRON, MEAUX

Spitfire IC (PR) P9331. Experienced glycol leak during sortie to Liège and forced-landed at Reims-Champagne. Pilot unhurt. Aircraft repairable — later abandoned.

British attempts to repair and salvage this aircraft proved unsuccessful so it was abandoned on the understanding that the French authorities would destroy it. It was subsequently captured intact (see page 437).

UK-based aircraft lost or damaged on operations over the Western Front:

RAF BOMBER COMMAND

21 Squadron, Watton
Bridges at Abbeville:

Blenheim IV R3761. Belly-landed on return, hydraulics damaged by ground-fire over the target 5.30 p.m. Sgt Parker shrapnel wounds in leg, Sgt Walters and Sgt Burt unhurt. Aircraft damaged but repairable.

40 Squadron, Wyton
Columns near St-Valéry-sur-Somme:

Blenheim. Returned damaged by flak and fighters following dawn reconnaissance of movements around St-Valéry. F/L R. H. Batt and Sgt E. G. Neville unhurt. Sgt A. Spencer wounded. Aircraft damage state not recorded.

Blenheim IV L8827. Shot down by Bf109s during attack on troops advancing between St-Valéry and Abbeville 10.00 a.m. Possibly that attacked by Hptmn Lützow (*Gruppenkommandeur*) of Stab I./JG3. Sgt T. A. Foreman and Sgt V. C. Salvage captured. S/L B. Paddon evaded capture and returned unhurt. Aircraft a write-off.

Blenheim IV L9410. Shot down by Bf109s between St-Valéry and Abbeville 10.00 a.m. and possibly that claimed by Lt Bock of 3./JG3. P/O B. B. James, Sgt J. E. Garcka, and Sgt W. Furby missing. Aircraft lost.

Blenheim IV P4917. Badly damaged in attacks by Bf109s of I./JG3 and forced-landed in Allied territory 10.00 a.m. Sgt Baker badly wounded detained in hospital in France. P/O P. F. T. Wakeford and Sgt Wallace wounded but evacuated to England. Aircraft a write-off.

Blenheim IV P4927. Shot down by Bf109s between St-Valéry and Abbeville 10.00 a.m. and possibly that claimed by Uffz Hofelich of 3./JG3. Sgt D. J. Rice, Sgt R. C. Moffatt, and Sgt D. E. Peters captured. Aircraft a write-off.

Blenheim IV R3692. Forced-landed badly damaged by Bf109s during attack on troops advancing between St-Valéry and Abbeville 10.00 a.m. and possibly that attacked by Lt Rohwer of Stab I./JG3. Sgt M. R. Chouler and Sgt D. Liddle both wounded and captured. P/O V. G. W. Engstrom wounded, evaded capture, and later admitted to hospital in Uxbridge. Aircraft a write-off.

53 Squadron, Eastchurch

Blenheim IV. Returned to Rouen-Boos badly damaged by ground-fire during reconnaissance of sector Soissons—Laon—Noyon 5.30 a.m. F/O Rochfort and Sgt Clayton slightly wounded. AC Roberts unhurt. Aircraft TR⊙X damage state not recorded.

An aircraft on loan from No. 59 Squadron. Both strategic reconnaissance squadrons borrowed aircraft from each other to alleviate serviceability problems.

Blenheim IV R3602. Returned to Rouen-Boos badly damaged by Bf109s during reconnaissance between Dreuil-lès-Amiens and Ault. Possibly that claimed by Oberlt Kupka of 9./JG3 between Hiermont and Yvrench 10.15 a.m. P/O J. N. Bethell and Sgt Randall unhurt. Sgt H. H. Wilson wounded in head. Aircraft PZ⊙N abandoned.

Both sorties were flown from Rouen-Boos though the squadron was based at Eastchurch. Henry Wilson was evacuated to England where he died of his wounds on August 7.

77 Squadron, Driffield

Whitley V. Forced-landed at Finningley and burned out after flare ignited causing fire soon after take-off 10.00 p.m. P/O A. W. Dunn unhurt. AC1 A. L. Kennedy baled out and injured back in landing. P/O C. J. D. Montagu, Sgt Lucas, and AC2 Martin baled out unhurt. Aircraft a write-off.

No. 40 Squadron suffered grievously on June 6 with five aircraft failing to return. This is one of their severely damaged Blenheims which forced-landed on the beach but the serial is too indistinct to determine exactly where and when.

RAF FIGHTER COMMAND

17 Squadron, Hawkinge
Blenheim escort:

Hurricane P3360. Believed shot down by Lt von Perthes of 3.(J)/LG2 in combat east of Abbeville 10.10 a.m. Sgt S. H. Holman missing. Aircraft lost.

Last seen under attack by Bf109s 20 miles east of Abbeville, no trace of Holman was ever reported found and he has no known grave.

111 Squadron, Hawkinge
Blenheim escort:

Hurricane P2885. Engine set alight in combat in attacks by Oberlt Kijewski and Uffz Heckmann of 5./JG3 over Abbeville 10.10 a.m. Sgt R. J. W. Brown baled out, returned with injured thigh. Aircraft a write-off.

151 Squadron, Manston
Wing patrol Abbeville — Amiens:

Hurricane. Forced-landed near Rouen damaged in attack by Bf109 and possibly that claimed by Fw Bauer of 7./JG3 west of Aumale 3.10 p.m. F/O C. F. Atkinson unhurt. Aircraft repairable returned later.

No. 53 Squadron was now based in England operating from forward airfields or, as on this day, from French airfields closer to BAFF HQ. It is unclear whether R3602 belly-landed on return to Rouen-Boos or if the undercarriage was deliberately retracted when it was finally abandoned.

We could not trace a photo of one of the ten LeO 451s lost on June 6; this particular machine not being listed in French records.

FRENCH AIR FORCE

GB I/11 LeO 451 (3007). Shot down by Bf109s of I./JG1 and I./JG51 during sortie to attack enemy tanks around Chaulnes. Crashed and exploded at Fransart, 8 km north of Roye 3.00 p.m. Lt R. Puech, Adjt J. Colomer, Adjt P. Labiche, and Sgt A. Dartiges killed. Aircraft a write-off.

GB I/11 LeO 451 (150). Exploded under attack by Bf109s of I./JG1 and I./JG51 during sortie to attack enemy tanks around Chaulnes. Broke up and fell between Remaugies and Onvillers, 7 km east of Montdidier 3.00 p.m. S/Lt G. Paulet, Adjt M. Gatinois, Sgt L. Laberty, and Sgt R. Midonnet killed. Aircraft a write-off.

GB I/11 LeO 451 (3022). Engine and fuselage set alight in attack by Bf109s of I./JG1 and I./JG51 during sortie to bomb enemy tanks around Chaulnes 3.00 p.m. Crash-landed at Warvillers, 10 km north-west of Roye, and later exploded. Capt Tournes *(Groupe Commandant)*, Adjt Cros, Adjt Henquel, and Sgt Barras all wounded. Aircraft a write-off.

GB I/11 LeO 451 (183). Damaged by Bf109s of I./JG1 and I./JG51 during attack on armour near Chaulnes and belly-landed between Mantes-la-Jolie and Gassicourt, north-west of Paris, 3.00 p.m. Sgt M. Contant badly wounded — left foot amputated. Sgt Grandchamp wounded in arm. Lt Tourret and Sgt Mas unhurt. Aircraft a write-off.

GB II/12 LeO 451 (38). Shot down by Bf109s of I./JG1 and I./JG51 north-west of Roye during sortie to bomb enemy armoured columns. Crashed and exploded between Mézières and Beaucourt-en-Santerre 4.15 p.m. Lt Y. Saussine, Sgt M. Gentier and Sgt M. Arachequesne killed. Sgt A. Paumier baled out but machine-gunned in his parachute and killed. Aircraft a write-off.
This aircraft exploded on impact and only the gunner, Maurice Arachequesne, was identifiable. The observer, Yves Saussine, and radio operator, Maurice Gentier, have no known grave.

GB II/12 LeO 451 (151). Shot down by Bf109s of I./JG1 and I./JG51 south-east of Moreuil during sortie to bomb enemy armoured columns, and crashed at 'La Vallée des Sauvillers', Braches 4.15 p.m. Lt R. Genty and Sgt Petit both baled out slightly injured. Sgt C. Jacquot and Sgt L. Caillet killed. Aircraft a write-off.
Charles Jacquot and Lucien Caillet were buried together in a field grave alongside the wreckage of their aircraft until March 4, 1941, when they were both reinterred in the cemetery at Braches.

GB II/12 LeO 451 (152). Shot down by Bf109s of I./JG1 and I./JG51 during sortie to bomb enemy armoured columns and abandoned south-west of Montdidier 4.15 p.m. Crashed and burned out north-east of Bois de Maignelay. Lt Mayer, Sgt Cadiou, Sgt Verlet, and Sgt Baert all baled out badly wounded, landing around Ferrières-Dompierre. Aircraft a write-off.

GB II/15 Farman 222 (17). Returned to St-Yan crippled by flak during night attack on enemy barracks at Mainz and Bonn a.m. Crew unhurt. Aircraft damaged but repairable.

GB 3/23 LeO 451 (260). Shot down by flak and Bf109s of I./JG1 and I./JG51 during bombing attack on motorised columns around Roye-Chaulnes. Crashed and exploded near the road to Crémery at Gruny, 4 km north-east of Roye 3.00 p.m. Capt J. Bienvenu *(Commandant)*, Adjt M. Canaux, and Adjt A. Jean killed. Adjt Favre-Bulle baled out and captured wounded. Aircraft a write-off.

GB 3/23 LeO 451 (214). Damaged by flak then set alight by Bf109s of I./JG1 and I./JG51 during bombing attack on motorised columns around Roye and Poix 3.00 p.m. Abandoned near Ognolles. Sgt D. Defendini and Adjt M. Mariani killed. Capt Marchand baled out badly wounded. Cpl Boileau baled out badly wounded landing at Campagne; treated at Beaulieu-les-Fontaines casualty station. Aircraft a write-off.

GB II/31 LeO 451 (271). Shot down by Bf109s of I./JG1 and I./JG51 during bombing sortie against enemy armour advancing on roads around Chaulnes. Crashed at Beauvraignes, 6 km south of Roye. Sgt Caudry badly wounded. Lt Millet, Adjt Magnan, and Sgt Proteau unhurt. Aircraft a write-off.

GB I/62 Martin 167F (147). Suffered a direct hit by flak during sortie to attack armour north of Roye and exploded over Haut-Matz Ferme, Ricquebourg, 7.45 p.m. S/Lt M. Rigaux, and Sgt M. Hardy killed. S/Lt P. Painchaux badly wounded, landed by parachute near Cuvilly but later died of wounds. Aircraft a write-off.

GB I/62 Martin 167F (75). Returned to Damville damaged by Bf109s of 2./JG2 during sortie to attack enemy armour north of Roye. Possibly one of those claimed by Oberfw Rudorffer 7.45 p.m. Sgt Bontemps injured in violent evasive manoeuvres, rest of crew unhurt. Aircraft repairable.

GB I/62 Martin 167F (25). Returned to Damville severely damaged by flak and Bf109s of 2./JG2 during sortie to attack enemy armour north of Roye 7.45 p.m. Possibly that claimed by Oberfw Sass or Fw Keil. Lt Selva wounded, rest of crew unhurt. Aircraft a write-off.

A German trooper just captioned this snapshot 'shot-down enemy machine'. Just another anonymous example of the 47 LeO 451s lost in action during the French campaign.

GBA I/51 Breguet 693 (27). Shot down by Bf109s of I./JG1 and I./JG51 during attack on enemy tank concentrations north of Chaulnes 3.20 p.m. Crashed and burned out at Arvillers, north-west of Roye. Sgt G. Bousquet killed. Sgt Le Coq de Kerland wounded, transported to hospital. Aircraft a write-off.

GBA I/51 Breguet 693 (63). Badly damaged by Bf109s of I./JG1 and I./JG51 during attack on enemy tank concentrations north of Chaulnes 3.20 p.m. and crashed at Pont-Ste-Maxence. Cpl B. Barbron died of wounds. Sgt Nièvremont unhurt. Aircraft a write-off.

GBA II/51 Breguet 691. Wrecked in a landing accident at Bouard during training flight. Lt Collombet injured. Sgt Chaillon unhurt. Aircraft a write-off.

GBA II/54 Breguet 693 (29). Shot down by Bf109s of I./JG1 and I./JG51 during attack on enemy tank concentrations north of Chaulnes and crashed in forest near Chantilly 3.40 p.m. Adjt Mitton and Sgt Uteza badly wounded. Aircraft a write-off.

GBA II/54 Breguet 693 (1013). Returned to Chartres damaged by Bf109s of I./JG1 and I./JG51 during attack on enemy tank concentrations north of Chaulnes 3.30 p.m. Pilot unhurt. Sgt Badel wounded. Aircraft damaged but repairable.

GC II/1 Bloch 152 (379). Shot down in combat with Bf109s of 7./JG53 south-east of Soissons and abandoned near Acy 8.55 a.m. Probably one of those claimed by Fw Galubinski. Sgt P. Chénelot baled out but parachute caught fire and he fell to his death. Aircraft a write-off.

GC II/1 Bloch 152 (621). Badly damaged in combat with Bf109s of 7./JG53 south-east of Soissons 8.55 a.m. Possibly that claimed by Oberfw Götz. Attempted to reach base but crashed at Plessis-Pâté, 2 km short of Bretigny airfield. Sgt M. Gaudon killed. Aircraft a write-off.

GC II/1 Bloch 152. Shot down in combat with Bf109s of 7./JG53 south-east of Soissons, possibly that attacked by Lt Riegel 8.55 a.m. Believed crashed in flames near Coeuvres-et-Valsery. Capt Jastrzebski wounded, baled out landing at Taillefontaine. Aircraft a write-off.

GC I/3 Dewoitine 520 (84). Caught fire under attack by Bf109s of 3./JG2 in action between Péronne and Ham 11.20 a.m. and belly-landed at Rethondes, near Compiègne. Adjt L. Bourbon wounded. Aircraft a write-off.

GC 5/3 Morane 406. Returned damaged during escort sortie for Breguet 693 of GB I/51 and GB II/54 3.40 p.m. Believed that attacked by Lt Krafftschick of 1./JG27 near Clermont. Lt J. Morin slightly wounded. Aircraft damaged but repairable.

GC I/4 Curtiss H-75. Forced-landed near Bernay following combat with Bf109s of I./JG3, 4./JG3, and I./JG76 during escort mission for reconnaissance Potez 63.11 of GR I/36 west of Amiens 8.00 p.m. Possibly one of those claimed by Oberfw Hauer of 1./JG76. Lt F. Burda unhurt. Aircraft repairable.

GC I/4 Curtiss H-75 (221). Damaged in combat with Bf109s of I./JG3, 4./JG3, and I./JG76 during escort mission for reconnaissance Potez 63.11 of GR I/36 west of Amiens 8.00 p.m. Possibly one of those claimed by Uffz Schätzel of 1./JG76. Crashed attempting forced-landing at Beuzevilette, 5 km east of Bolbec. Cpl F. Sticka wounded. Aircraft a write-off.

GC 2/4 Curtiss H-75 (260). Shot down by Bf109s of I./JG3, 4./JG3, and I./JG76 during escort mission for Potez 63.11 of GR I/36 west of Amiens 8.00 p.m. Possibly one of those claimed by Lt von Aspern of 1./JG76. Crashed at Morvillers, 5 km east of Aumale. Lt E. Audemar d'Alançon killed. Aircraft a write-off.

GC I/4 Curtiss H-75 (124). Shot down by Bf109s of I./JG3, 4./JG3, and I./JG76 during escort mission for Potez 63.11 west of Amiens, 12 km south of Rouen, 8.00 p.m. Possibly one of those claimed by Oberfw Stotz of 3./JG76. S/Lt H. de La Taille-Trétinville baled out badly burned but parachute failed and killed. Aircraft a write-off.

GC I/4 Curtiss H-75 (265). Last seen in combat with Bf109s of I./JG3, 4./JG3, and I./JG76 during escort mission for Potez 63.11 west of Amiens 8.00 p.m. Possibly that claimed by Oberlt Hrabak (Staffelkapitän) of 1./JG76. Lt A. Weiss missing. Aircraft lost.

GC II/4 Curtiss H-75 (276). Badly damaged in combat with Bf109s of 2./JG76 during patrol over the Aisne bridges and crash-landed near Cocherel, west of Château-Thierry, 7.45 a.m. Probably that claimed by Oberfw Donninger near Crépy-en-Valois. Adjt J. Paulhan unhurt. Aircraft a write-off.

GC II/4 Curtiss H-75. Damaged in combat with Bf109s during patrol over Soissons and belly-landed at Cocherel. S/Lt Fauconnet wounded in leg. Aircraft a write-off.

GC II/5 Curtiss H-75 (197). Shot down by Bf109s of 2./JG2 during escort sortie for GB II/62 and GB II/63 and abandoned north-east of Soissons 12.15 p.m. Possibly one of those claimed by Fw Hermes. Lt P. Houzé baled out landing unhurt, joined ground troops and killed later that afternoon resisting the German advance near Besme. Aircraft a write-off.

GC II/5 Curtiss H-75. Returned to Connantre damaged in combat with Bf109s of 2./JG2 north-east of Soissons during escort sortie for GB II/62 and GB II/63 12.15 p.m. Possibly that attacked by Oberlt Greisert (Staffelkapitän). Sgt L. Hème wounded in left leg. Aircraft damaged but repairable.

GC II/5 Curtiss H-75 (56). Severely damaged in combat with Bf109s of 2./JG2 north-east of Soissons during escort sortie for GB II/62 and GB II/63 and forced-landed at Missy-sur-Aisne 12.15 p.m. Possibly that claimed by Oberfw Rudorffer. Sgt J. Janeba unhurt. Aircraft 6 a write-off.

GC II/6 Bloch 152. Returned damaged by Lt Hoffmann of 7./JG2 during attack on Do17s of KG76 near Roye 2.45 p.m. Adjt Schreiner unhurt. Aircraft repairable.

GC II/6 Bloch 152 (677). Badly damaged in combat west of Montmirail and belly-landed at Viels-Maisons p.m. Sgt Geillon wounded admitted to hospital in Sézanne. Aircraft 23 a write-off.

GC III/7 Morane 406 (132). Believed shot down by Hptmn Balthasar (Staffelkapitän) of 1./JG1 during escort sortie for Breguet 693 of GB I/51 and GB II/54. Attempted to land but hit the top of a hill and lost control, crashing inverted and catching fire alongside the D36 road near Angivillers, south-east of St-Just-en-Chaussée. Cmdt M. Arnoux killed. Aircraft a write-off.

GC 1/8 Bloch 152 (303). Believed shot down by Bf109s during attack on Do17s in the Roye — Chaulnes — Noyon sector 7.40 p.m. Possibly that claimed by Oberlt Steidle of Stab III./JG2. Crashed near Bois Defoy at Assainvillers, south-east of Montdidier. Capt M. Peyrègne (Commandant) killed. Aircraft a write-off.

The remains of Marcel Peyrègne were not recovered until September 20, 1942, when he was finally laid to rest in the cemetery at Assainvillers.

GC II/9 Bloch 152 (612). Shot down during offensive patrol north-east of Soissons and crashed into trees and burned out in 'Semilly' suburb of Laon 12.30 p.m. Probably that claimed by Lt Hoffmann of 2./JG2. Sgt J. Cucumel captured badly wounded and admitted to hospital in St Quentin. Aircraft a write-off.

GR I/36 Potez 63.11 (161). Shot down by Fw Müller of 4./JG3 during photo-reconnaissance sortie west of Amiens 8.05 p.m. Crashed and burned out between Cavillon and Fourdrinoy. Capt M. Chastenet and Sgt R. Jost killed. Adjt A. Mayençon seriously wounded; died in hospital at Cambrai. Aircraft a write-off.

A Bloch 152 now under new management.

LUFTWAFFE

2.(F)/11 Two Dornier Do17P. Reported damaged at Ham, south-west of St Quentin, cause not stated. Two wounded. No aircraft damage state recorded.

Three men of 2./Leicht Abt. 86 slightly wounded at Thieulloy l'Abbaye and Namps are among losses reported by 1.(H)/11 on this date and may be associated with these entries.

2.(H)/12 Henschel Hs126. Returned to Daigny airfield reportedly damaged by fighters. Uffz H. Belz slightly wounded, other crewman unhurt. Aircraft damage state not recorded.

4.(H)/12 Henschel Hs126. Engaged by Adjt Paulhan of GC II/4 during observation sortie over Fourdrain and shot down at Samoussy, north-east of Laon, 7.20 a.m. Lt G. Warda and Uffz O. Wichert killed. Aircraft a write-off.

4.(H)/12 Henschel Hs126. Returned damaged following sortie over Soupir, east of Soissons. Lt Schimmelpfennig wounded, another crewman unhurt. Aircraft damage state not recorded.

3.(H)/14 Henschel Hs126. Returned damaged by own ground-fire over St-Fuscien, south of Amiens. Oberlt H. Bertram killed. Oberlt Meyer wounded. Aircraft repairable.

3.(H)/21 Henschel Hs126. Returned to Doullens, north of Amiens, damaged in attack by F/O Bruce of No. 111 Squadron during observation sortie over Abbeville 6.40 a.m. Oberlt B. Dobner killed, pilot unhurt. Aircraft damaged but repairable.

4.(H)/22 Henschel Hs126. Shot down by Capt Delfino, Lt Chesnais, Adjt Rebière, Sgt Cucumel, and Sgt Paris of GC II/9 during observation sortie over Coucy-le-Château, north of Soissons, 12.15 p.m. Oberlt U. Schlichting and Oberfw H. Köhler killed. Aircraft a write-off.

Originally buried on the western perimeter of Mesbrecourt airfield, Ulrich Schlichting and Horst Köhler are now both interred in the German War Cemetery at Fort-de-Malmaison.

I./JG1 Messerschmitt Bf109E-4. Failed to return from operations, circumstances unknown. Lt H. Hammerschmidt missing. Aircraft lost.

1./JG1 Messerschmitt Bf109E-1. Ground-looped during take-off at Tupigny. Lt H. Lass injured. Aircraft damaged but repairable.

2./JG2 Messerschmitt Bf109E-4. Failed to return following combat south of Roye and possibly that claimed by Sgt Quéguiner of GC II/5 in combat north-east of Soissons 12.15 p.m. Lt H. Hoffmann missing. Aircraft lost.

Stab JG3 Messerschmitt Bf109E-1. Badly damaged in combat with H-75s of GC I/4 north-west of Amiens and believed crashed south-east of Candas. Possibly one of those claimed by Adjt Dagbert 8.00 p.m. Major T. Quandt killed. Aircraft a write-off.

Born in 1897, Theodor Quandt was a veteran WWI pilot having flown in FAA270 and Jasta 36 before taking command of Jasta 53 in December 1917. He was credited with at least 15 victories during WWI.

I./JG3 Four Messerschmitt Bf109Es. Returned damaged following combat with H-75s of GC I/4 over Ferrières, west of Amiens, 8.00 p.m. Probably those claimed by Lt Guillaume, Sgt Collard, and Sgt Lemare. No pilot casualties. Aircraft all repairable.

1./JG3 Messerschmitt Bf109E-1. Shot down by H-75s of GC I/4 and crashed at Vignacourt, north-west of Amiens 8.00 p.m. Possibly that claimed by Lt Guillaume. Uffz A. Schneider killed. Aircraft a write-off.

4./JG3 Messerschmitt Bf109E-3 (862). Shot down in combat with H-75s of GC I/4 and abandoned over Picquigny, north-east of Cavillon 8.10 p.m. Possibly that claimed by Lt Burda. Lt R. Heymann baled out too low and killed. Aircraft 13+ – a write-off.

4./JG3 Messerschmitt Bf109E-3. Damaged by return fire during attack on Potez 63-11 of GR I/36 west of Amiens 8.05 p.m. and crash-landed near St Sauflieu. Fw A-W. Müller wounded. Aircraft a write-off.

4./JG3 Messerschmitt Bf109E-3. Shot down by Sgt Teillet of GC I/1 in combat south of Montdidier and crashed at 'La Sablonnière, north-west of Le-Quesnel-Aubry, 5.30 p.m. Fw E. Dickow badly burned — died. Aircraft a write-off.

I./JG26 Messerschmitt Bf109E-3. Damaged in taxying accident at Hesdin. Pilot unhurt. Aircraft repairable.

2./JG27 Messerschmitt Bf109E-1. Shot down in combat with D520s of GC I/3 south-west of Roye and belly-landed between Rollot and Conchy-les-Pots 7.45 p.m. Lt J. Unterberger captured. Aircraft a write-off.

5./JG27 Messerschmitt Bf109E-3. Burned out following take-off accident at Guise-Nord. Leutnant E. Daig injured. Aircraft 13 + – a write-off.

II./JG52 Two Messerschmitt Bf109E-1s. Damaged in take-off accidents. Pilots unhurt. One aircraft a write-off, the other damaged but repairable.

On June 6, the Luftwaffe lost one of its celebrated pilots, Major Theodor Quandt, and ex-WWI fighter pilot with 15 victories to his credit and decorated with the Knight's Cross with Swords of the Hohenzollern House Order. A regular army officer, he transferred to the German Air Service in July 1916 and all his victories were gained while flying with Jasta 36 which he joined on April 1, 1917. He rose to command the unit from August 14, 1918 and was their second highest scorer. He now lies in Champigny-St André Cemetery, Block 9, Row 12, Grave 815.

III./JG52 Arado Ar66C. Crashed during transit flight from Tupigny, cause not stated. Gefr G. Deinzer injured. Aircraft a write-off.

I./JG53 Messerschmitt Bf109E-1. Wrecked in taxying accident. Pilot unhurt. Aircraft a write-off.

1./JG53 Messerschmitt Bf109E-1 (1346). Engaged by ground-fire near Metz during transit flight from Wiesbaden to Charleville and lost bearings. Belly-landed north of Faverolles, north-west of Langres. Uffz P. Grond evaded but captured four days later at La Neuville-sous-Monfort. Aircraft 8 + a write-off.

7./JG53 Messerschmitt Bf109E-1. Shot down by Adjt Crocq of GC II/1 in combat south-east of Soissons and crashed north of Belleu 8.50 a.m. Fw H. Galubinski baled out and captured wounded. Aircraft a write-off.

3./KG27 Heinkel He111. Returned to Vechta reportedly damaged by fighters. Fw R. Boer believed wounded. Aircraft damage state not recorded.

Stabsstaffel KG76 Dornier Do17Z. Shot down by S/Lt Thollon of GC I/8 during attack on infantry columns between Éramecourt and Famechon, south-west of Amiens, 3.00 p.m. Possibly also that attacked by Adjt Schreiner of GC II/6. Uffz J. Parszyk killed. Fw H. Häussler badly wounded, died June 7. Oberfw H. Schildt and Uffz O. Ochs badly wounded, admitted to field hospital in Bapaume. Aircraft a write-off.

4./KG76 Dornier Do17Z. Returned damaged by fighters during sortie to Beauvais and possibly that attacked by S/Lt Madon of GC I/3 and S/Lt Ronin of GC II/6 near Rosières-en-Santerre 7.40 p.m. Uffz R. Kampichler badly wounded, died in hospital in Cambrai June 7. Rest of crew unhurt. Aircraft damage state not recorded.

7./KG76 Dornier Do17Z. Shot down by P/O Lee of No. 501 Squadron south of Abbeville during attack on roads between Blangy and Aumale 6.20 a.m. Uffz H. Mitschke killed. Uffz L. Menges captured wounded. Lt F. Taucar and Uffz H. Wagner captured unhurt. Aircraft a write-off.

7./KG76 Dornier Do17Z. Returned damaged by Sgt Proctor of No. 501 Squadron south of Abbeville during attack on roads between Blangy and Aumale 6.20 a.m. Uffz J. Dandorfer badly wounded, Fw O. Wilbrich and Uffz R. Carl slightly wounded, rest of crew unhurt. Aircraft damage state not recorded.

3.(J)/LG2 Messerschmitt Bf109E-3. Shot down by F/L Toyne of No. 17 Squadron in combat south-east of Abbeville 10.15 a.m. Oberfw K. Bühler killed. Aircraft a write-off.

II.(S)/LG2 Two Henschel Hs123s. Involved in landing collision at Monceau. Pilots unhurt. Aircraft both damaged but repairable.

II.(S)/LG2 Henschel Hs123. Damaged in landing accident at Monceau. Pilot unhurt. Aircraft damaged but repairable.

6./ZG1 Messerschmitt Bf110C. Shot down by Capt Coutaud *(Commandant)* of GC I/1 during bomber escort sortie and crashed in Ruelle St Sauveur in Crcil 5.45 p.m. Uffz A. Maske killed. Obergefr E. Schulze baled out but parachute failed to open and killed. Aircraft a write-off.

Friday, June 7

Though French reports reaching London suggested that little enemy progress was being made, the stark truth was that a gap had been forced through the French 10ème Armée lines between Liomer and Poix on the Allied left. Exploiting this advantage, German armoured units soon reached Formerie and Argeuil forcing British forces to retire from Neufchâtel and Forges-les-Eaux. The road to Rouen now lay open and the British 51st Division becoming ever more isolated. Elsewhere, enemy forces were also threatening Beauvais and by the end of the day were moving south of Grandvilliers to link up with other formations making steady advances from the direction of Amiens.

This German advance towards the Seine compelled withdrawal of the RAF refuelling and servicing facilities at Rouen-Boos and Étrépagny, including Southern Component HQ, which hurriedly evacuated to Dreux and Beaumont-le-Roger respectively. This was not achieved without casualties for the road convoys were attacked by enemy aircraft en route and 12 airmen killed and 40 wounded.

Early in the afternoon 18 Bomber Command Blenheims, with an escort of 24 Hurricanes, struck at the German columns advancing on the Seine, while French medium bombers attacked others moving south from Péronne. A further attack by 36 Blenheims of No. 2 Group delivered later in the afternoon found little in the designated target area either side of the road between Abbeville and Blangy for the speed of the German advance was outpacing information gained from air reconnaissance. For once, enemy fighters were notably absent and the Blenheims returned safely to base. However, AASF Battles did find worthwhile targets near Hornoy and Poix around 6.30 p.m. but also encountered Bf109s. Fighter cover for this operation was provided by a flight of No. 1 Squadron Hurricanes plus Nos. 43 and 601 Squadrons, both of which had refuelled at Beaumont-le-Roger, but as they were all using different R/T frequencies it proved ineffective though a large formation of enemy fighters was engaged near Aumale.

In addition to these 34 escort sorties, RAF fighter effort throughout the afternoon was directed towards protection of British troops, including the 51st Division, who were fighting a desperate rearguard action along the River Bresle between Le Tréport and Aumale. A total of 84 sorties was flown over the area between 2.00 and 8.00 p.m. by Nos. 17, 56, 111, and 151 Squadrons operating in pairs and three major combats resulted. But, reflecting the changing nature of the air war in France, Armée de l'Air casualties on this day exceeded those of the RAF.

Luftwaffe bombing effort was concentrated on railways and marshalling yards behind the Allied lines to interfere with lines of communication and hinder the movement of reinforcements, though Évreux airfield and the port of Cherbourg were also targeted.

At night, 24 Bomber Command Wellingtons struck at Somme river crossings claiming hits on bridges at St-Valéry, Abbeville, and Bray-sur-Somme — targets also visited by 12 AASF Battles. Six Whitleys were also despatched to bomb the railhead at Hirson while eight AASF Battles attacked the airfield at Laon and the Forêt de Gobain, thought to be harbouring enemy troops, each aircraft carrying extra incendiary bombs loose in the cockpits.

He therefore decided against billeting any of the personnel on the airfield itself, save for the ground defence and wireless, so accommodation was found in the nearby village of Ruaudin.

On June 1 the CO of No. 73 Squadron had flown to Le Mans to inspect the next aerodrome in the line of retreat. Squadron Leader More's considered opinion was that 'it is certainly an excellent target with its works buildings and railway sidings alongside'.

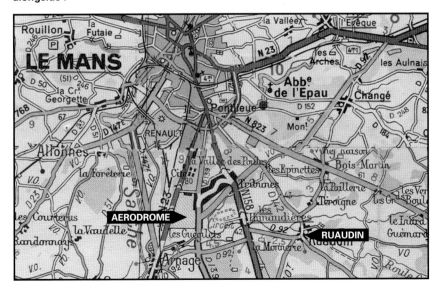

Left: **Adjutant Henry Hall: 'The Orderly Room is accommodated in an empty, rather tumble-down cottage' although unfortunately Hall does not identify the staff in his photo.**

Right: **We put Jean Paul Pallud on the case and he was able to trace the house just in time as it was about to be demolished as part of a plan to enlarge the town centre.**

BRITISH AIR FORCES IN FRANCE

12 SQUADRON, SOUGÉ

Battle P2162. Shot down by Bf109s of 5./JG3 during attack on armoured columns near Poix, crashed and burned out near St-Valéry 6.10 p.m. Possibly that claimed by Fw Heinzeller or Uffz Freitag. Sergeant F. J. Field, Sergeant H. C. C. Bevan, and Sergeant J. F. W. MacKrell killed. Aircraft PH⊙Q a write-off.

Battle L5415. Returned with port wing, elevator, and tailplane damaged by Bf109s of 5./JG3 during attack on armoured columns near Poix 6.10 p.m. Possibly that attacked by Uffz Nelleskamp. Sergeant G. R. Wheeldon, Sergeant E. Shone, and LAC J. Taylor unhurt. Aircraft PH⊙O repairable.

73 SQUADRON, ÉCHEMINES

Hurricane L1826. Stalled during series of flick rolls at 800 feet shortly after take-off for Le Mans; crashed and burned out 11.20 a.m. Flying Officer E. J. Kain thrown from the aircraft and killed. Aircraft TP⊙B a write-off.

But the move from Échemines on June 7 was marred by a tragic accident. The previous day orders had been received that Flight Lieutenant Scoular and Flying Officer Kain (Cobber) were to return to the UK as soon as replacements arrived. That evening at 9 p.m. a tender drew up outside the Café de l'Hippodrome in Le Mans where the officers were dining and out of it stepped 15 officer and sergeant pilots. Thus, overjoyed at the prospect of an immediate return to England, Cobber prepared to leave. The following day, back at Échemines, Adjutant Hall explained that, 'his exhuberance got the better of his judgement and skill and he terminated his brief and brilliant service career in a display of aerobatics. It is particularly sad considering that the only two officer pilots of the original squadron who lost their lives in France, have come to grief in flying accidents not attributable to enemy action. [The other was Pilot Officer Lloyd Bishop — see page 149] Both were firm friends and exceedingly popular with all of us. Kain's loss will be regretted by a wide circle outside the service after the phenominal press publicity he received.'

```
                                               214

From:-    Officer Commanding, No. 73 Squadron, R.A.F.

To  :-    Headquarters A.A.S.F. Royal Air Force.
          Base Personnel Staff Officer. H.Q.NO.2 Base Area.
          Headquarters No. 67 Wing, Royal Air Force.


Date:-    12th June, 1940.

Ref.:-    73S/209/6/P.1.


          Flying Officer E.J. KAIN - 39534. D.F.C.

               With reference to this units signal P. 56 dated
7th June, 1940, herewith report on accident.

          Flying Officer E.J. KAIN took off from Echmines
in a fixed pitch Hurricane at approximately 11.15 hours
on 7th June, 1940, en route for LE MANS.  He passed over
the aerodrome at about 800 feet and went into a series of
"Flick" Rolls to the left.    At the third roll the
aircraft lost speed very rapidly and went into a spin to the
right.    The spin was very fast and the aircraft straight-
ened with a burst of engine, but was completely stalled and
hit the ground.

          The aircraft burst into flames on impact and the
pilot was thrown out some distance ahead of it.

          Death was instantaneous from Head injuries.


               (Signed)  J.W.C. MORE

                         Squadron Leader, Commanding,
                         No. 73 Squadron,  R.A.F.
                         ===============================
```

Specially modified for high-level photo-graphic-reconnaissance, this Spitfire IC (PR) P9331 suffered a glycol leak on June 6 and was forced to put down at Reims-Champagne where it was abandoned and later captured intact (see page 431). Records for the unit are incomplete, but its last documented mission had been from Stradishall three days earlier when Flight Lieutenant Corbishley flew it on a sortie to Wilhelmshaven. This flush-riveted, highly-glossed, exotic bright blue machine must have proved a handsome prize for Luftwaffe Technical Intelligence.

88 SQUADRON, MOISY

Battle. Damaged on the ground by splinters during enemy bombing 12.20 a.m. Flying Officer D. G. S. Honor unhurt. Sergeant C. T. Lewis badly injured — later died. Aircraft damaged but repairable.

Cecil Lewis, a Wireless Operator/Air Gunner, was critically injured when he ran into a turning propeller while seeking cover and died six hours later.

Battle. Damaged on the ground by splinters during enemy bombing 1.00 a.m. Flying Officer D. L. R. Halliday and crew unhurt. Aircraft damaged but repairable.

Battle. Damaged on the ground by splinters during enemy bombing 1.00 a.m. Sergeant D. Haywood and crew unhurt. Aircraft repairable.

103 SQUADRON, HERBOUVILLE

Battle. Forced-landed damaged in attacks by Bf109s p.m. Pilot Officer Roberts and crew unhurt. Aircraft repairable.

Battle. Forced-landed damaged in attacks by Bf109s p.m. Sergeant Brams and crew unhurt. Aircraft repairable.

142 SQUADRON, VILLIERSFAUX

Battle. Abandoned near Châteauneuf having lost bearings and run low on fuel during aborted night sortie to bomb St Hubert airfield. Pilot Officer H. L. Oakley, Sergeant Martin, and Sgt J. H. Ledson baled out unhurt. Aircraft a write-off.

150 SQUADRON, HOUSSAY

Battle L5288. Brought down by AA fire during sortie to attack convoys between Poix and Abbeville and crashed near Vergies 7.15 p.m. Flying Officer J. E. Vernon, Sergeant G. W. Clawley, and Sergeant J. F. Atkins killed. Aircraft a write-off.

Battle L5579. Returned with one wing damaged by AA fire during attack on crossroads near Poix-de-Picardie 7.15 p.m. P/O A. D. Frank and crew unhurt. Aircraft repairable.

226 SQUADRON, SOUGÉ

Battle L5450. Reported missing following attack on enemy columns between Poix and Abbeville. Crew believed returned later unhurt. Aircraft a write-off.

UK-based aircraft lost or damaged on operations over the Western Front:

RAF BOMBER COMMAND

82 Squadron, Wattisham
Reconnaissance:

Blenheim IV P6915. Returned badly damaged in attack by Lt Schmidt of 8./JG3 over the Somme estuary during reconnaissance between Abbeville and St-Valéry 1.30 p.m. Sgt A. E. Merritt, F/Sgt Robertson, and Cpl Harris unhurt. Aircraft UX⊙A a write-off.

107 Squadron, Wattisham
Reconnaissance Somme estuary:

Blenheim IV R3686. Starboard engine hit by ground-fire and belly-landed near Longueville-sur-Scie, south of Dieppe. F/L H. P. Pleasance wounded in right leg, Sgt G. A. Wilson and Sgt P. E. F. Adams unhurt. Aircraft fired by crew.

RAF FIGHTER COMMAND

17 Squadron, Hawkinge
Wing Patrol Le Tréport:

Hurricane P3472. Shot down by cross-fire during attack on Do17s near Bernaville 1.30 p.m. S/L G. D. Emms missing. Aircraft lost.

Hurricane P2905. Shot down by Bf109s north-east of Airaines and believed one of those claimed by Lt Wedding of Stab III./JG3 between Le Tréport and Aumale 1.40 p.m. P/O R. C. Whittaker missing. Aircraft lost.

Both these losses are recorded by the CWGC on June 6, a date confirmed by the Aircraft Accident Cards. Yet the Squadron Operations Record Book reports as shown, details that correspond with the official RAF narrative and relate closely to German fighter claims.

43 Squadron, Manston
Wing Patrol Le Tréport:

Hurricane L1931. Set alight under attack by Bf109s east of Dieppe and crashed at Puisenval 11.00 a.m. Possibly that claimed by Lt Tiedmann of 2./JG3. F/O J. D. Edmonds killed. Aircraft a write-off.

John Edmonds was recovered by the MREU on October 15, 1947, his aircraft being identified from the engine number. Site later excavated by team led by Simon Parry and Andy Saunders in October 2004. Corroded propeller hub recovered deep in chalk and presented to the local Maire to form the basis of a memorial.

Hurricane L1847. Shot down in combat with Bf109s east of Dieppe and exploded on impact at Gremonval, Bailleul-Neuville 11.00 a.m. Possibly that claimed by Fw Lampskemper of 2./JG3. F/O W. C. Wilkinson killed. Aircraft FT⊙J a write-off.

Originally buried in a field grave adjacent to the crash site, William Wilkinson was reinterred as an 'Unknown RAF Airman' on February 17, 1941, and not formally identified until 1947. Site later investigated by team led by Simon Parry and Andy Saunders in October 2004 and widely scattered surface fragments found.

Hurricane L2116. Shot down by Bf109s east of Dieppe and believed abandoned over Ste-Agathe-d'Aliermont 11.00 a.m. Possibly that claimed by Lt Bock of 3./JG3. F/L T. Rowland baled out wounded. Aircraft a write-off.

Hurricane N2585. Shot down by Bf109s and abandoned between Dieppe and Abbeville 11.00 a.m. Possibly that claimed by Lt Meckel of 2./JG3. Sgt H. J. L. Hallowes baled out and dislocated ankle on landing. Aircraft a write-off.

43 Squadron, Beaumont-le-Roger
Wing Patrol Abbeville:

Hurricane L1726. Shot down in combat with Bf109s and possibly one of those claimed by Uffz Dahmer of 4./JG26 south of Dieppe 6.35 p.m. P/O C. A. Woods-Scawen baled out unhurt. Aircraft a write-off.

This sortie was flown from Beaumont-le-Roger where the Hurricanes of Nos. 43 and 601 Squadrons had refuelled and rearmed following an earlier patrol, the remnants of both units returning to Tangmere that evening.

Hurricane L1737. Badly damaged in combat with Bf109s of 1./JG20 and 4./JG26 south-east of Dieppe and crashed on landing at Rouen-Boos 6.35 p.m. Sgt C. A. H. Ayling unhurt. Aircraft a write-off.

Hurricane L1608. Header tank exploded under attack by Bf109s south-east of Dieppe and abandoned over 'Beaumont', Wanchy-Capval 6.35 p.m. Possibly that claimed by Lt Bildau of 1./JG20. Sgt P. G. Ottewill baled out badly burned. Aircraft a write-off.

Major recovery by team led by Simon Parry and Andy Saunders in October 2004. Fairly intact Rolls Royce Merlin engine recovered with propeller blade, remains of tail and tail-wheel, fuselage, fabric wing covering, control column, various components, together with evidence of partial serial. Engine gifted to local group and now displayed in car showroom.

79 Squadron, Biggin Hill

Hurricane. Crash-landed at Hawkinge following engine failure. S/L J. D. C. Joslin unhurt. Aircraft a write-off.

151 Squadron, Manston
Wing Patrol Amiens:

Hurricane P3529. Shot down by Fw Albert of 7./JG3 in combat over St-Valéry-sur-Somme, west of Abbeville, 1.58 p.m. P/O J. F. Pettigrew missing. Aircraft a write-off.

264 Squadron, Duxford

Defiant L7004. Abandoned east of airfield due to loss of control and crashed at Hadstock. P/O W. F. Carnaby baled out unhurt. P/O C. C. Ellery baled out seriously injured and admitted to Littleport hospital. Aircraft a write-off.

Accident investigators later determined that this loss was due to bad repairs on unit to damage sustained in combat on May 29, 1940.

601 Squadron, Beaumont-le-Roger
Patrol Abbeville:

Hurricane P3484. Shot down in combat with Bf109s and possibly that claimed by Uffz Philipp of 4./JG26 east of Dieppe 6.30 p.m. F/O T. E. Hubbard unhurt. Aircraft a write-off.

Hurricane P3490. Shot down in combat with Bf109s and possibly one of those claimed by Uffz Dahmer of 4./JG26 south of Dieppe 6.35 p.m. F/O P. B. Robinson wounded. Aircraft a write-off.

"COBBER" — top-scoring ace of the R.A.F., now on leave in England—is pictured above with Miss Joyce Phillips, aged twenty, back-stage in the Empire Theatre, Peterborough, where Miss Phillips is appearing in "The Importance of Being Earnest."

There was a green room celebration in his honour.

"We aren't engaged — officially," said Joyce yesterday. "Anyway, I don't believe in getting married until the war is over."

A great welcome is being prepared at Rose Farm, Great Mollington, near Chester, where "Cobber"—Flying Officer E. J. Kain, D.F.C., of New Zealand—ranks as one of the family. Rose Farm is the home of Mr. Percy Phillips—and of Joyce.

KILLED

FIRST D.F.C. PILOT OF THE WAR

Flyg. Offr. E. J. Kain, the famous New Zealand pilot, known as "Cobber," has been killed in a flying accident on active service.

Kain, who was 22, was the first airman to win distinction in France. He was awarded the D.F.C. in March for his gallantry in attacking, with another aircraft, seven enemy bombers and chasing them into German territory.

Previously he had shot down five enemy machines — two Dornier bombers and three Messerschmitt fighters.

When on leave in April he announced his engagement to Miss Joyce Phillips, a 23-year-old actress, then appearing at the Repertory Theatre, Peterborough. They had hoped to be married in July.

NARROW ESCAPES

During the air fight which won him the D.F.C. Kain brought his badly damaged Hurricane back to the Allied lines with the cockpit thick with smoke and oil fumes. In another battle he shot down two Messerschmitts and was himself shot down. Wounded and with his fighter out of control and in flames, he bailed out within half a mile of the German lines and landed safely in no-man's land.

Cobber" was taken to New Zealand by his English parents soon after the Armistice. He came to England two years ago to take a short-service commission in the R.A.F. and soon gained a reputation for fearlessness.

COBBER KAIN IS KILLED IN ACTION

Evening Standard Reporter

Flying-officer E. J. ("Cobber") Kain, Britain's first air "ace" of this war, has been killed in action, it was learned in London to-day.

He was to have been married within a few days to Miss Joyce Phillips, an actress, at Great Mollington, Cheshire, parish church, near her parents' farm.

Mrs. Phillips, her mother, received the first news by cable from the fighter-pilot's father in Auckland, New Zealand.

Kain's mother and sister set off three weeks ago to be present at the wedding.

Kain proposed to Miss Phillips in April after she had been playing in "The Importance of Being Earnest" at Peterborough. The couple next day drove to London by buy the engagement ring.

Kain, 6ft. 3ins., 22 years old, was awarded the D.F.C. in March for his gallantry in attacking, seven enemy bombers, and chasing them into German territory

He had previously shot down five enemy machines.

WAS REJECTED

In the air fight which won him the D.F.C., he brought his badly-damaged Hurricane back to the Allied lines with the cockpit thick with smoke and oil fumes

In another battle Kain shot down two Messerschmitts and was himself shot down Wounded, he took to his parachute.

When he first tried to join the R.A.F. Kain was turned down. He came to England four years ago to take a short service commission in the R.A.F.

Kain's parents are English. They took him to New Zealand soon after the Armistice.

The death of Cobber Kain — who was, in the public's eyes, the RAF's leading ace — was felt throughout the Empire, Peter Fraser, the New Zealand Prime Minister, declaring that his death had 'caused the deepest sorrow throughout the Dominion'. *Above:* The aerodrome where Kain came to grief is no more. Like so many of the temporary airfields in France, Échemines has reverted to farmland but fortunately the place where Kain crashed has not been lost to history. When Jean Paul Pallud arrived to pay our respects, he discovered that in 1970 the secretary at the local Mairie had questioned all those who lived in the village in 1940, several of whom saw Kain crash in a small copse of trees (see aerial photo page 415), which was cut down in the 1980s. She also believed that the British removed all of the wreckage and none of the villagers have ever found any fragments. Cobber was first buried in the town cemetery at Troyes but was transferred after the war to Choloy War Cemetery *(right)*.

It is Friday, June 7, 1940. On a dusty emergency aerodrome near Troyes in France a two-seater Magister communications plane is being loaded up with kit by an orderly. A tin helmet and a gas-mask complete the loading, and the orderly reports to a group of young pilots wearing the uniform of the Royal Air Force chatting gaily a few yards away:

'Gear aboard. Good luck sir.'

A tall, broad-shouldered, black-haired Flying Officer, with the ribbon of the Distinguished Flying Cross newly sewn below his wings, leaves the group and walks to the waiting plane. He calls, 'Cheerio, chaps! Be good' to his colleagues and climbs into the cockpit, settles himself, gives a mechanic the thumbs-up. The engine roars.

Suddenly a mischievous grin spreads over the face of the young giant in the Magister. On the port side of him he has caught sight of a Hurricane fighter. It is his old ship. Only yesterday at 20,000 feet over Reims he had 'squeezed the teat' that controlled its eight machine-guns, and down went his twenty-fifth Nazi.

So he uncurls his long legs from the cockpit of the Magister and, going across to the Hurricane, wedges himself into the cockpit. 'One more beat up, me lads', he calls, and he is off across the aerodrome in a cloud of hot dust.

The Magister's engine is left ticking over nicely.

With a roar like a thunderclap the Hurricane comes back over the 'drome, above the heads of the little group of officers — only just above their heads, because it is barely twenty feet off the ground, is upside down, and travelling at 350 miles an hour. The boys call this a 'beat up'.

Still upside down, the Hurricane shoots up to 1,500 feet in less than a minute, turns right side up, then starts a series of rolls earthward.

That is just how the young man in the Hurricane is feeling, rolling about in the thin air. The little Magister below, with its engine ticking over nicely, is going to take him home to England for special duties.

Two rolls are completed. The group of R.A.F. officers suddenly stop laughing and chattering. One says anxiously, 'What the hell?' as the Hurricane goes into a third roll. His experienced eye can see this will bring it mighty close to mother earth.

Then three or four of them yell 'Cobber! Cobber!' They start running. There is a crash. The Hurricane does not quite complete the third roll. Its port wing touches the ground. The young officers lift their dead comrade from the wreckage. A mechanic climbs into the cockpit of the Magister. He switches off the engine . . .

NOEL MONKS, *SQUADRONS UP*, 1940

It was in November 1940 that Noel Monks, the *Daily Mail's* war correspondent in France, published his tribute to the pilots of Nos. 1 and 73 Squadrons. Kain had become a close friend and as they parted for the last time after a dinner at Maxim's in Paris, Cobber confided to him. 'Don't put it in the paper but I'm getting married next week. That is if I am alive.' A week to the day he was dead. Monks: 'His courage, his fighting heart, and his life were at Britain's service. His friendship was mine'.

So who was the RAF's leading 'ace' in France? At the time of his death Cobber Kain (*left*) was top scorer credited with 17 enemy aircraft destroyed and two damaged. However, 'Fanny' Orton (*centre*) was giving him a good run for his money being ahead of him credited with 15 victories up to May 15 (ten confirmed plus one shared, one probable, and one damaged plus one shared) when he was wounded in action and so took no further part in proceedings. At that date Kain's score stood at 11 destroyed and two damaged so it was a close-run thing. *Right:* Leslie Clisby of No. 1 Squadron had the edge on both of them, having 16 victories (one source suggests 19) at the time of his death on May 14 (see page 267).

FRENCH AIR FORCE

GAO 1/589 Potez 63-11. Returned to
Romilly-sur-Seine damaged in attacks by
Bf109s of 1./JG2 and 6./JG53 during recon-
naissance sortie between Soissons and
Coucy-le-Château 6.00 a.m. Lt Tabas, Lt de
Thuisy, and Sgt Fonteneau unhurt. Aircraft
damaged but repairable.

GB I/12 LeO 451 (130). Wrecked in forced-
landing near St-Paterne-Racan having run
out of fuel on return from raid on Ham 7.45
p.m. Adjt Gobeau and crew unhurt. Aircraft
a write-off.

GB I/19 Douglas DB-7 (33). Shot down by
flak during attack on enemy armour south-
west of Roye. Crashed and exploded on the
road at 'La Ruelle', outside St-Mard 6.45
p.m. S/Lt A. Bellin, Sgt G. Le Goff, and Sgt
G. Descamps killed. Aircraft a write-off.
*Georges Le Goff was originally buried
alongside his aircraft by advancing German
troops. Later, on October 24, 1940, the body
of Guy Descamps was discovered in a nearby
pond and buried in St-Mard. The remains of
André Bellin were never reported found and
he has no known grave.*

GB I/31 LeO 451 (3006). Hit by flak and
instruments destroyed during sortie to bomb
enemy barracks near Ham 7.30 p.m. Wandered off course and abandoned over the sea
off Sables-d'Olonne. Lt J. Colleter, Sgt R.
Ajam, and Adjt M. Oliveres baled out but
drowned. Sgt Renard baled out and rescued
unhurt. Aircraft lost.

On June 7, four Polish and seven French
pilots of Groupe de Chasse II/10 based at
Bernay, south-west of Rouen, clashed
with a force of Bf110s from II./ZG76 over
Neufchâtel-en-Bray. Commandant Eugeniusz Wyrwicki and Sous-Lieutenants
Hieronim Dudwal and Jerzy Poniatowski
were shot down in the ensuing combat
and now lie buried in Aubérive Cemetery
Grave Nos. 284, 253, and 193 respectively.
Of the four Polish pilots involved, only
Sous Lieutenant Jerzy Radomski survived
to return and report what happened.

GB II/62 Martin 167F (63). Destroyed on the
ground at Évreux-Fauville by enemy fighter
attacks p.m. No crew casualties. Aircraft a
write-off.

GB II/62 Martin 167F (59). Unserviceable
aircraft left behind on withdrawal from St-
Martin-la-Campagne. No crew casualties.
Aircraft abandoned.

GB I/63 Martin 167F (46). Returned to St-
André-de-l'Eure with flak damage following
attack on enemy armour between Roye and
Puzeaux 3.00 p.m. Crew unhurt. Aircraft
repairable.

GB II/63 Martin 167F (95). Destroyed on the
ground at Évreux-Fauville by enemy fighter
attacks p.m. No crew casualties. Aircraft a
write-off.

GB II/63 Martin 167F (26). Shot down by
flak south of Roye and crashed at Laucourt
6.55 p.m. S/Lt Y. Le Marchand-de-Trigon,
Sgt H. Bufferne, and Sgt H. Chommeloux
killed. Aircraft a write-off.

GB II/63 Martin 167F (69). Returned to
Droisy damaged by ground-fire during
attack on enemy armour south of Roye 7.00
p.m. Crew unhurt. Aircraft repairable.

GBA I/51 Breguet 693 (67). Hit by flak and
badly damaged during attack on enemy
armour around Chaulnes 7.30 a.m. Belly-
landed at Le Bourget. Lt Lebourg and Sgt
Mitard unhurt. Aircraft a write-off.

GBA II/51 Breguet 693 (77). Damaged by
flak and crashed on landing at Bouard. Sgt
Ancelin and Sgt Lamy unhurt. Aircraft a
write-off.

GBA II/54 Breguet 693 (1). Shot down by
Bf109s of 9./JG3 during attack on armoured
column on the road between Poix and
Airines. Possibly that claimed by Uffz von
Boremski 11.05 a.m. Crashed and burned out
6 km north-east of Grandvillers at 'Le Mon-
toir', on the outskirts of Laverrière and Sommereux. S/Lt P. Legrand killed. Sgt J. Verge
thrown from aircraft and died of fractured
skull. Aircraft a write-off.
*This crew was originally buried in simple
field graves as two 'unknown airmen', but on
investigation, their aircraft was finally identified and Pierre Legrand and Jean Verge
exhumed on July 23, 1941, for reinterrment in
nearby Laverrière Cemetery.*

GBA II/54 Breguet 693 (54). Shot down by
Bf109s of 9./JG3 during attack on armoured
column on the road between Poix and
Airines; possibly that claimed by Oberfw
Heitmann 11.00 a.m. Crashed and burned
out 7 km from Forges-les-Eaux. Sgt Sannier
and Sgt Renault badly wounded. Aircraft a
write-off.

GBA II/54 Breguet 693 (33). Severely damaged by Bf109s of 9./JG3 during attack on
armoured column on the road between Poix
and Airines 11.00 a.m. Finally abandoned over
woods at Parc, Saint-Just-des-Marais, 2 km
west of Beauvais. S/Lt Devin and Sgt Lebert
both baled out unhurt. Aircraft a write-off.

GBA II/54 Breguet 693 (1011). Forced-
landed at St-André-de-l'Eure damaged by
flak following attack on road convoys
between Roye, St-Mard, and Warsy 6.00 p.m.
Adjt Coiffard badly wounded; rest of crew
unhurt. Aircraft damaged but repairable.

GBA II/54 Breguet 693 (3). Crashed on landing at Chartres during training flight. Adjt
Walser killed. Général L. F. A. Girier (*Commandant Groupement 18*) injured legs. Aircraft a write-off.

GC II/3 Dewoitine 520. Shot down by Lt
Angeli of 3./JG54 south-west of Péronne
during bomber escort sortie and crash-
landed at Francières, north-east of Estrées-
Saint-Denis, 6.30 p.m. Capt M. Bissoudre
slightly injured. Aircraft 2 a write-off.

GC 3/4 Curtiss H-75 (213). Shot down in
combat with Bf109s of 6./JG53 during escort
sortie for Potez 63.11 of GAO 1/589 south-
west of Soissons. Crashed and burned out at
Ferme de Vaubéron at Morte-Fontaine 6.10
a.m. Capt R. Guieu (*Commandant*) killed.
Aircraft a write-off.
*The serial is believed correct as shown as a
plate owned by a local farmer, Mr Guy Ferté,
carried serial number '213', an aircraft regularly flown by Régis Guieu, though research
by Mme L'Herbier-Montagnon indicated
serial 196. Also, this loss has been credited to
Lt Werner Voigt of 5./JG3 who claimed an
H-75A at Vénizel, east of Soissons, at 5.25
a.m. However, given that GC II/4 are reported
to have taken off at 5.30 a.m., it is difficult to
reconcile this when 6./JG53 filed three claims,
albeit for Bloch 151s, east of Compiègne at
around 6.07 a.m.*

GC I/6 Morane 406 (908). Shot down by intense flak during low-level attack on enemy armour around Formerie and impacted near Frettemolle, south-west of Poix, 6.30 p.m. S/Lt J. Paturle killed. Aircraft a write-off.

GC I/6 Morane 406 (898). Shot down by intense flak west of Grandvilliers during ground-attack mission against enemy armour around Formerie and exploded over Moliens 6.30 p.m. Sgt J. Bendl killed. Aircraft a write-off.

GC I/6 Morane 406. Returned with aircraft riddled by intense flak during low-level attack on enemy armour around Formerie 6.30 p.m. Lt S. Janouch wounded in leg. Aircraft a write-off.

GC II/6 Bloch 152. Belly-landed back at base due to undercarriage failure following routine patrol 6.20 a.m. Adjt Laguet unhurt. Aircraft a write-off.

GC I/8 Bloch 152. Belly-landed out of fuel following attack on Hs126 of 4.(H)/21 near Amiens 7.00 p.m. Sgt E. Prchal unhurt. Aircraft damaged but repairable.

GC II/10 Bloch 152 (115). Shot down in combat with Bf110s of II./ZG76 during ground-support mission over Neufchâtel-en-Bray and crash-landed at 'Le Bois de Tout Vent', Fresnoy-Folny, south of Eu 5.25 a.m. Possibly that claimed by Lt Jabs of 6./ZG76. Cmdt E. Wyrwicki critically wounded in head, died en route to hospital in Rouen. Aircraft 2 a write-off.
Eugeniusz Wyrwicki was leader of No. 7 'Wy' flight of six Polish pilots from the 'Montpellier' group attached to GC II/10 only four days before — half of them were killed in this action and now lie buried in the Polish Military Cemetery at Aubérive-sur-Suippes. This wreck was later buried in a nearby bomb crater and, on June 16, 1997, excavated by the Association Normande du Souvenir Aérien who recovered large sections of wing and airframe, undercarriage leg, and engine.

GC II/10 Bloch 152 (130). Shot down in combat with Bf110s of II./ZG76 during ground-support mission and exploded in woods at 'La Marre', near St-Germain-sur-Eaulne, north-east of Neufchâtel-en-Bray, 5.25 a.m. Possibly that claimed by Oberlt Weeber of Stab II./ZG76. S/Lt H. Dudwal killed. Aircraft 10 a write-off.
The body of Hieronim Dudwal was recovered from the wreckage of his aircraft on September 1, 1940, but defied identification and he was originally buried as an 'unknown airman' in the village cemetery at St-Germain-sur-Eaulne.

GC II/10 Bloch 152 (688). Shot down in combat with Bf110s of II./ZG76 during ground-support mission over Neufchâtel-en-Bray and crashed at Fontaine-le-Sec, south of Abbeville, 5.30 a.m. Possibly that claimed by Lt Helmer of 5./ZG76. S/Lt J. Poniatowski killed. Aircraft a write-off.

GC II/10 Bloch 152 (687). Badly damaged in combat with Bf110s of II./ZG76 during ground-support mission over Neufchâtel-en-Bray and crash-landed at St-Germain-des-Essourts 5.20 a.m. S/Lt L. Sperat badly wounded in right ankle. Aircraft a write-off.

GC II/10 Bloch 152. Belly-landed out of fuel following combat with Bf109s of 5./JG3 east of Amiens 6.00 p.m. Sgt K. Sztramko unhurt. Aircraft a write-off.

GC III/10 Bloch 152 (192). Badly damaged in combat with Bf110s of II./ZG76 during offensive patrol over Neufchâtel-en-Bray and belly-landed at Nesle-Hodeng 5.30 a.m. Adjt A. Gaulard slightly wounded. Aircraft a write-off.

GC III/10 Bloch 152 (14). Badly damaged in combat with Bf110s of II./ZG76 during offensive patrol and crashed attempting forced-landing near Bellencombre, west of Neufchâtel-en-Bray, 5.30 a.m. Sgt A. Hiblot unhurt. Aircraft a write-off.

GR I/35 Potez 63.11 (827). Shot down by Fw Kauffmann of 4./JG53 during reconnaissance sortie between Chaulnes and Roye. Crashed in the Arve near Damouy Tannery, Roye 10.05 a.m. Lt P. Regis, Sgt M. Prini, and Sgt R. Mathelin killed. Aircraft a write-off.

LUFTWAFFE

2.(H)/12 Henschel Hs126 (3128). Shot down by Lt Dorance, S/Lt Lefol, and Sgt Girou of GC I/5 during observation sortie over the Aisne between Monthois and Grandpré. Crashed and burned out south of Olizy-Primat 8.15 p.m. Oberlt A. Graf von Plettenberg and Uffz U. Schneider killed. Aircraft H1+LH a write-off.

2.(H)/14 Henschel Hs126. Landed damaged in attacks by Lt Marin-la-Meslée, Lt Vrana, and Sgt Muselli of GC I/5 south of Chièvres-Val during observation sortie east of Soissons 10.00 a.m. Lt E. Martin slightly wounded, observer unhurt. Aircraft repairable.

4.(H)/21 Henschel Hs126. Returned reportedly damaged by flak but possibly that attacked by Sgt Prchal of GC I/8 near Amiens 7.00 p.m. One crewman reported wounded. Aircraft repairable.

2.(F)/123 Dornier Do17P. Believed shot down by Capt Guieu and Cpl Truhlar of GC II/4 south-west of Soissons during reconnaissance sortie and crashed east of Thiescourt 6.10 a.m. Oberlt D. von Schäzler *(Gruppe NO)*, Oberfw H. Lang, and Uffz G. Sell killed. Aircraft a write-off.

II./JG2 Messerschmitt Bf109E-1. Crash-landed at Laon-Athies, cause not stated. Pilot believed unhurt. Aircraft damaged but repairable.

III./JG2 Messerschmitt Bf109E-3. Wrecked in forced-landing at Laon-Athies, cause not stated. Pilot believed unhurt. Aircraft a write-off.

III./JG3 Messerschmitt Bf109E. Shot down in combat with Hurricanes of Nos. 32 and 79 Squadrons and abandoned near Abbeville 1.15 p.m. Possibly one of those claimed by P/O Parker. Pilot believed unhurt. Aircraft a write-off.

7./JG3 Messerschmitt Bf109E-3. Shot down in combat with Hurricanes of Nos. 32 and 79 Squadrons south of Abbeville 1.15 p.m. Possibly that claimed by Sgt MacQueen. Uffz M. Seidler wounded. Aircraft a write-off.

8./JG3 Messerschmitt Bf109E-3. Shot down in combat with Hurricanes of Nos. 32 and 79 Squadrons and abandoned north-west of Abbeville 1.15 p.m. Possibly that claimed by F/O Davies. Oberleutnant K-H. Sandmann *(Staffelkapitän)* baled out wounded. Aircraft a write-off.

8./JG3 Messerschmitt Bf109E-1. Shot down in combat with Hurricanes of Nos. 32 and 79 Squadrons and abandoned north-west of Abbeville 1.15 p.m. Possibly that claimed by P/O Stones. Leutnant W. Schmidt baled out wounded. Aircraft a write-off.

8./JG3 Messerschmitt Bf109E-3. Returned damaged following combat with Hurricanes of Nos. 32 and 79 Squadrons north-west of Abbeville 1.15 p.m. Possibly that attacked by F/L Roberts. Pilot unhurt. Aircraft repairable.

4./JG26 Messerschmitt Bf109E-3 (1541). Shot down in combat with No. 43 Squadron Hurricanes and crashed at Douvrend, near Envermeu, south-east of Dieppe, 6.35 p.m. Possibly one of those claimed by F/Lt Simpson. Uffz R. Iberle killed. Aircraft 13 + - a write-off.
Site excavated by Simon Parry in 2001 when fragments of shattered DB601 engine, parachute release box, and various small items recovered from a shallow crater in an orchard.

4./JG26 Messerschmitt Bf109E-3. Shot down by F/Lt Simpson of No. 43 Squadron and abandoned over Dieppe 6.35 p.m. Uffz W. Philipp baled out wounded. Aircraft a write-off.

5./JG26 Messerschmitt Bf109E-3. Shot down by return fire from Blenheim engaged south-east of Montreuil and crashed at 'La Palette', Beaumerie-St-Martin. Oberfeldwebel F. Lorenz killed. Aircraft a write-off.
Site identified and investigated by Simon Parry but nothing significant found.

III./JG52 Arado Ar66. Crashed at Basse-Ham during transfer flight from Tupigny to Hoppstädten, cause unknown. Gefr G. Deinzer captured unhurt. Aircraft a write-off.

8./JG53 Messerschmitt Bf109E. Shot down in combat with fighters over Compiègne 3.53 p.m. and possibly that claimed by Sgt Barberis of GC I/3. Fw H. Veith killed. Aircraft a write-off.

1./JG76 Messerschmitt Bf109E-3 (1250). Damaged by enemy fire and forced-landed near Londinières, north of Neufchâtel-en-Bray. Oberlt D. Hrabak *(Staffelkapitän)* unhurt. Aircraft repairable.

7./KG1 Heinkel He111H-3. Returned to Butzweilerhof both engines damaged in attacks by Capt Hugo, Sgt Panhard, and Sgt Boillot of GC II/7 over Chantilly during sortie to Beauvais 6.30 p.m. Uffz J. Mohr badly wounded, rest of crew unhurt. Aircraft damage state not recorded.

8./KG2 Dornier Do17Z. Crashed into parked Ju52 on take-off from Kirchberg-Maisborn 11.30 a.m. Hptmn J. Willigmann *(Staffelkapitän)*, Oberlt I. Holleck-Weithmann, Fw O. Hartge, and Uffz A. Witte badly injured, admitted to hospital in Simmern. Oberfw K. Gross slightly injured admitted to hospital in Kirchberg. Aircraft a write-off.

Stabsstaffel KG28 Heinkel He111H-3. Returned both engines damaged in attacks by Capt Dulac and S/Lt Barbu of GC II/10 over Abbeville 6.15 a.m. No crew casualties. Aircraft damaged but repairable.

II./KG53 Heinkel He111H. Forced-landed near Sedan damaged by fighters. No crew casualties. Aircraft damaged but repairable.

Stabsstaffel KG55 Heinkel He111P. Returned badly damaged in attacks by GC I/5 north-east of Soissons during sortie to attack troop concentrations between Soissons and Compiègne 10.15 a.m. Possibly that attacked by Lt Marin-la-Meslée, S/Lt Rouquette, S/Lt Le Calvez, and Sgt Penzini. Uffz J. Geiger and Gefr O. Unterstab slightly wounded, admitted to hospital in Schwäbisch-Hall; rest of crew unhurt. Aircraft a write-off.

II./KG55 Heinkel He111P. Forced-landed badly damaged in attacks by GC I/5 south-west of Laon during sortie to attack troop concentrations between Soissons and Compiègne 10.15 a.m. No crew casualties. Aircraft a write-off.

4./KG55 Heinkel He111P. Returned badly damaged in attacks by GC I/5 north-east of Soissons during sortie to attack troop concentrations between Soissons and Compiègne 10.15 a.m. Possibly that attacked by Capt Vasatko, Lt Vrana, Lt Rouquette, and Sgt Vuillemain. Uffz H. Förster slightly wounded. Aircraft a write-off.

III./KG55 Heinkel He111P. Belly-landed at Eutingen following sortie to attack roads between Compiègne and Crépy-en-Valois 6.30 p.m. No crew casualties. Aircraft damaged but repairable.

7./KG55 Heinkel He111P. Returned damaged by enemy fire during sortie to attack roads between Compiègne and Crépy-en-Valois 6.30 p.m. Gefr J. Leonhardt killed, rest of crew unhurt. Aircraft damage state not recorded.

7./KG55 Heinkel He111P. Both engines damaged by flak during attack roads east of Compiègne then engaged by S/Lt Codet and Sgt Cukr of GC II/3. Belly-landed near Dury, east of Ham, 6.45 p.m. Fw A. Hedoch killed. Oberfw R. Homuth, Uffz K. Schraps, and Flgr H. Hennessen badly wounded. Uffz Frimberger unhurt. Aircraft G1+CR a write-off.

Bordmechaniker Alfred Hedoch was originally buried in the garden of Gutshofe Ferme at Verlaines but is now interred in Bourdon Cemetery, Block 37, Row 11, Grave 425.

2./KG76 Dornier Do17Z. Returned damaged by flak and H-75s of GC I/4 during sortie south of Amiens 6.15 p.m. Gefr J. Hauffe badly wounded, admitted to hospital in Doullens. Oberfw K. Kusenberger and Fw W. Braito slightly wounded, pilot unhurt. Aircraft damage state not recorded.

2./KG76 Dornier Do17Z. Returned damaged by flak and H-75s of GC I/4 during sortie south-west of Amiens 6.00 p.m. Fw W. Schmidt slightly wounded, admitted to hospital in Vogelsang. Rest of crew unhurt. Aircraft damage state not recorded.

KGrzbV.105 Junkers Ju52 (5365). Crashed near Charleville, cause not stated. Crew killed. Aircraft a write-off.

KGrzbV.105 Junkers Ju52 (6266). Crashed near Koblenz shortly after take-off. Three crewmen injured. Aircraft a write-off.

KGrzbV.105 Junkers Ju52 (6461). Crashed on take-off from Mannheim-Ostheim. One crewman killed and another injured. Aircraft a write-off.

3.(J)/LG2 Messerschmitt Bf109E-4. Shot down by flak north of Évreux. Oberfw E. Clausen baled out unhurt. Aircraft a write-off.

3.(J)/LG2 Messerschmitt Bf109E-4. Shot down in combat with Moranes north of Pontoise. Hptmn B. Mielke *(Staffelkapitän)* captured. Aircraft a write-off.

3.(J)/LG2 Messerschmitt Bf109E. Returned damaged following combat with Moranes north of Pontoise. Oberfw S. Krause unhurt. Aircraft repairable.

9./StG2 Junkers Ju87B. Damaged by ground-fire over Grécourt, south-east of Ham, and forced-landed near Hombleux. Lt C. Banke badly wounded, admitted to hospital in St Quentin; gunner unhurt. Aircraft damaged but repairable.

9./StG51 Junkers Ju87B. Radiator hit by ground-fire and forced-landed between woods and the road between Senarpont and Campneuseville. Oberlt H. Arndt *(Staffelkapitän)* attempted to evade but killed by infantry fire. Fw A. Kaupper captured unhurt. Aircraft damaged but repairable.

At Bourdon overlooking the River Somme lies the huge German War Cemetery which contains over 22,000 dead having been concentrated here in the early 1960s. Among them is Feldwebel Alfred Hedoch of the 7. Staffel of Kampfgeschwader 55 who was exhumed from a field grave in a private garden at Verlaines where he was originally buried in 1940. Bourdon Cemetery was begun in 1961 and was inaugurated in September 1967.

Saturday, June 8

German forces continued their advance towards Rouen forcing opposing British troops to retire before them. By midday the enemy had crossed the Andelle river between Nolléval and Rouvray-Catillon and by evening was within ten miles of Rouen itself. On the left of the British line the remains of the BEF, mainly the 51st Division, were also in retreat but being forced towards Le Havre rather than Rouen and in clear danger of becoming entrapped in the area between Dieppe and Fécamp. Evacuation from here, according to a signal from the General Staff, 'could not be contemplated'.

North of Beauvais the French attempted to establish a defensive line but by nightfall German troops were north of Clermont threatening both Beauvais and Compiègne. While, further to the right of the French line, 12 German infantry divisions that had crossed the Aisne on the previous day would, by evening, have penetrated as far as Saponay, south-east of Soissons, only ten miles short of the Marne. This forced the move of General d'Astier's ZOAN headquarters to Orléans and, to avoid the approaching threat to Coulommiers, Air Marshal Barratt also abandoned his advance headquarters which withdrew to Olivet.

To bolster AASF fighter strength, the Hurricanes of No. 17 Squadron arrived from Hawkinge to join Nos. 73 and 501 Squadrons at Le Mans, while No. 242 Squadron also landed at Le Mans en route to join No. 1 Squadron at Châteaudun. Both squadrons arrived with some maintenance facilities but with no dedicated servicing unit which inevitably created additional demands on those existing in France.

RAF bomber effort during the day was almost entirely directed against German troop movements around Poix and, with the restriction on the use of Bomber Command Blenheims imposed on May 30 now lifted, Air Marshal Barratt once again had the full resources of No. 2 Group available to him.

First strike of the day was delivered around 12.00 p.m. by 18 Blenheims which attacked columns in the area north of Poix-de-Picardie. An escort of 22 Fighter Command Hurricanes prevented any interference by enemy fighters but the bombers were subjected to very heavy AA fire. Targets in this area being plentiful, a further attack by 36 Blenheims was made around 4.30 p.m. This went ahead without planned fighter cover, the escort of 21 Hurricanes having failed to make rendezvous, and three aircraft were lost but mainly to the intense ground-fire.

Twelve AASF Battles attacked similar targets at around 1.45 p.m. with instructions not to bomb from lower than 5,000 feet but, with a weak escort of only seven Hurricanes of No. 501 Squadron operating from Dreux, they were unfortunate enough to meet a very strong enemy formation and suffered several casualties. Mid-afternoon 11 AASF Battles again struck at enemy columns between Poix and Aumale, their promised fighter cover from No. 1 Squadron having failed to materialise due to refuelling difficulties at Beaumont-le-Roger.

French bombers were similarly occupied during the day striking at armour and motorised columns around Forges-les-Eaux and suffering serious losses to both ground-fire and enemy fighters. French fighters were equally heavily engaged flying some 430 sorties and fighting a series of violent actions along the entire front between Fère-en-Tardenois and Rouen during which they claimed 11 victories but lost 16 fighters with six pilots killed.

The Führer and Supreme   Führer Headquarters,
Commander of the Armed Forces   8th June 1940

Directive No. 14

1. The enemy is offering stiff resistance on our right flank and in the centre of 6. Armee.

2. Therefore, according to the proposal of Commander-in-Chief Army, I approve the orders given this morning by Heeresgruppe B. viz.:

   (a) Merely to hold down the enemy on the 6. Armee front.
   (b) To transfer XIV. Armeekorps to the left flank of 4. Armee.
   (c) To strike a crushing blow at the strong enemy forces on the 6. Armee front by increasing the pressure exerted by the bulk of 4. Armee south-eastwards and by the left flank of 6. Armee south-westwards.

3. I further order:

(a) The basic intention as laid down in Directive No. 13 [see page 355] viz.: to destroy enemy forces in the Château-Thierry—Metz—Belfort triangle, and to bring about the collapse of the Maginot Line, remains valid.
   However, since Phase 1 of the operation is not yet ended, and extremely strong resistance is being offered north of Paris, stronger forces must be employed on the lower Seine and against Paris than had originally been contemplated.

(b) Heeresgruppe A will move to the attack on the 9th June south-south-westwards as ordered in Directive No. 13.

(c) 9. Armee will thrust southwards towards the Marne. It will be reinforced as soon as possible by XVI. Armeekorps (including attached SS units and the SS-Totenkopf-Division). Strong reserve forces must back up the juncture of the two Heeresgruppen.

(d) I reserve to myself the decisiton as to the direction of any further thrust by 9. Armee or whether it is to be left with Heeresgruppe B or put under command of Heeresgruppe A.

4. **The task of the Luftwaffe**. In addition to what has been laid down in Directive No. 13. is as follows:

   (a) To support the concentric attack on the flanks of the main enemy forces facing Heeresgruppe B.
   (b) To keep under observation and under strong fighter cover the coast on the right flank of Heeresgruppe B and the area south-west of the Bresle sector.
   (c) To help the advance of Heeresgruppe A at the focal point.

ADOLF HITLER

On June 8 Hitler was forced to issue a further directive to cope with the unexpected French resistance facing the attack launched by his 6. Armee three days earlier. Generaloberst Fedor von Bock, the Heeresgruppe B commander, summarised the situation on June 6 as 'a hard day, rich in crises — it seems that we are brought to a stand-still'. Meanwhile in Britain, Churchill was still receiving demands from the French for more fighters. During the afternoon of June 8, the Defence Committee met to take a final decision, Churchill summing up the two alternatives: 'We could regard the present battle as decisive for France and ourselves, and throw in the whole of our fighter resources in an attempt to save the situation, and bring about victory. If we failed, we should then have to surrender. Alternatively, we should recognise that whereas the present land battle was of great importance, it would not be decisive one way or the other for Great Britain. If it were lost, and France was forced to submit, we could continue the struggle with good hopes of ultimate victory, provided we ensured that our fighter defences in this country were not impaired; but if we cast away our defence the war would be lost, even if the front in France were stabilised, since Germany would be free to turn her air force against this country, and would have us at her mercy.'

British fighters, apart from the bomber escort sorties mentioned, flew patrols between Le Tréport and Aumale during the day to cover BEF forces in the area. Four squadrons operated from England, three of them landing at Dreux to refuel, and flew a total of 68 sorties between 8.20 a.m. and 7.30 p.m.

However, it was decided that evening that fighters operating from England should no longer land in France except in an emergency. This meant that the servicing and refuelling airfields currently operated by South Component would be for the AASF alone thus relieving very considerable pressure on an already over-stretched facility. Also, in view of their precarious position given the continuing German advance, further retreat would necessarily be southwards

putting them out of range of British fighters from England.

German aircraft again violated neutral Swiss airspace during the course of the afternoon, the Bf110s of II./ZG1 deliberately 'trailing their coats' to provoke the Swiss air defences. They were not disappointed and provoked a costly exchange that was not repeated and would keep diplomatic channels engaged for many weeks to come.

At night 50 RAF bombers operating in small formations attacked a wide variety of targets along the lower Somme. A further 19 aircraft were despatched against enemy concentrations north of Soissons while some 50 sorties were directed against road and rail junctions at Avesnes, Aulnoye, Charleville, and Hirson.

BRITISH AIR FORCES IN FRANCE

12 SQUADRON, SOUGÉ

Battle L5546. Shot down by Hptmn Trüben-bach of Stab I.(J)/LG2 during attack on armoured columns west of Aumale. Crashed and burned out at Rue de Bettembos, Lamaronde, 3.15 p.m. Sergeant J. P. Boddington and LAC C. S. Burt killed. Flying Officer T. F. S. Brereton baled out and captured near Meigneux. Aircraft PH⊙U a write-off.

Calcified remains discovered when the wreckage was cleared by the Germans on June 2, 1941, were originally buried as two 'Unknown Airmen' in the local communal cemetery. However, a report to the French Red Cross dated February 2, 1943, based on local research by Madame L'Herbier, together with post-war investigation of the site, confirmed the aircraft identity 'L5546'. Thus John Boddington and Charles Burt could be formally identified and reinterred together at Abbeville.

A major recovery on June 28, 2005 organised by Simon Parry recovered the Rolls Royce Merlin engine, propeller hub and two blades, control column, blind flying panel, rudder bar pedals, armour plate, flare pistol, and various other cockpit instruments and components. A propeller blade and memorial plaque was unveiled at Lamaronde on May 8, 2006, in a ceremony attended by relatives of the crew, several veterans, No. 12 Squadron ground party, and civil and military dignitaries.

It was in 2004 that a group of British aviation archaeologists organised by Simon Parry investigated the crash site of a Fairey Battle which had crashed at Lamaronde — a small village ten kilometres north-east of Aumale. *Above:* A decision was made to carry out a full excavation which took place in June 2005. *Below left:* The Rolls-Royce Merlin was recovered and evidence of its last action could be seen by bullet holes in one of the propeller blades *(below right)*.

The following year a ceremony was held to unveil a memorial plaque on the wall of the Mairie at Lamaronde.

The wreckage of two Bristol Blenheims — B-Baker and U-Uncle — which failed to return. Unfortunately the squadrons to which each belonged cannot be determined.

103 SQUADRON, HERBOUVILLE

Battle P2315. Forced-landed south of Paris damaged by Bf109s during attack on Ju87s over Poix-de-Picardie 1.50 p.m. Possibly that claimed by Lt Ulenberg of 2./JG26. Pilot Officer G. W. Thorougood and Sergeant Assop unhurt. Pilot Officer Webber wounded. Aircraft damaged but repairable.

Battle N2253. Shot down by Bf109s during attack on Ju87s and possibly that claimed by Oberlt Seifert *(Staffelkapitän)* of 3./JG26 north of Beauvais 1.50 p.m. Sergeant G. Beardsley, Sergeant G. Avery, and LAC G. F. Lewis captured. Aircraft a write-off.

150 SQUADRON, HOUSSAY

Battle L5112. Shot down by ground-fire during attack on armoured column near Hornoy and crashed at Fallencourt, south of Blangy 1.45 p.m. Flight Lieutenant R. A. Weeks, Sergeant W. D. P. Pittar, and LAC L. O. Grant killed. Aircraft a write-off.

501 SQUADRON, LE MANS

Hurricane. Shot down in combat with Bf109s during escort sortie for Fairey Battles and crashed inverted into woods at Sentelie, south of Poix-de-Picardie 1.50 p.m. Possibly one of those claimed by Fw Müller of 3./JG26. Pilot Officer R. G. Hulse killed. Aircraft a write-off.
Excavated August 1996.

UK-based aircraft lost or damaged on operations over the Western Front:

RAF BOMBER COMMAND

15 Squadron, Wyton
Columns between Amiens and Poix:

Blenheim IV R3746. Shot down at Guerville, south-west of Gamaches, 4.50 p.m. Possibly one of those claimed by Lt Troha or Uffz Schentke of III./JG3 near Abbeville. S/L W. I. H. Burke, P/O R. Moffat, and Sgt G. Thompson killed. Aircraft a write-off.

Blenheim IV R3704. Returned cockpit damaged by ground-fire during attack on armoured vehicles near Poix 4.50 p.m. Sgt A. Box badly wounded in leg. F/O W. H. George and Sgt O'Donnell unhurt. Aircraft damaged but repairable.

21 Squadron, Bodney
Armoured columns near Abbeville:

Blenheim IV L9023. Believed shot down by flak during attack on concentrations between Hornoy-le-Bourg and Poix-de-Picardie but possibly that claimed by Hptmn Lützow *(Gruppenkommandeur)* of Stab I./JG3 12.05 p.m. F/O H. D. S. Dunford-Wood, Sgt E. Jones, and Sgt D. R. C. MacLagan killed. Aircraft a write-off.

49 Squadron, Scampton
Northern approaches to Amiens:

Hampden L4044. Crash-landed on Carlton Hill, near North Carlton, north-west of Lincoln shortly after take-off on night sortie. P/O E. D. Parker, P/O Lockhead, Sgt Lloyd, and Sgt Robinson all injured. Aircraft a write-off.

59 Squadron, Odiham
Reconnaissance:

Blenheim IV. Lost bearings flying in poor visibility, forced-landed low on fuel near Moncerf 6.40 a.m. P/O B. Everton-Jones, Sgt Morton, and Sgt F. V. W. Thake believed unhurt. Aircraft TR*L abandoned.
Aircraft temporarily detached to Rouen-Boos for reconnaissance duties for HQ BAFF.

82 Squadron, Watton
Columns between Hornoy and Poix:

Blenheim IV R3618. Believed shot down by ground-fire and crashed near Éplessier, north-west of Poix-de-Picardie, but possibly that attacked by Uffz Mayerl of 2./JG20 12.10 p.m. Sgt J. H. Cooper killed. P/O R. C. D. McKenzie and Sgt Crozier captured. Aircraft UX⊙N a write-off

Blenheim R3754. Believed returned damaged in attacks by Bf109s of Stab II./JG51 during sortie to attack petrol dump at Bois Watte, north-east of Abbeville 6.05 p.m. Sgt J. Byatt killed. P/O Percival and Sgt Dodrill believed unhurt. Aircraft a write-off.

Blenheim IV R3709. Shot down by Oberlt Priller *(Staffelkapitän)* of 6./JG51 and crashed at Lamotte-Buleux during sortie to attack petrol dump at Bois Watte, north-east of Abbeville, 6.05 p.m. Sgt B. W. Burt killed. P/O G. P. Robertson and Sgt J. Hounston captured. Aircraft UX⊙F a write-off.

A Potez 63.11 has come to grief . . .

107 Squadron, Wattisham
Columns between Amiens and Poix:

3 Blenheim IVs. Returned hit by ground-fire during attack on armour and troops near Amiens 4.30 p.m. No crew casualties. Aircraft all repairable.

110 Squadron, Wattisham
Columns between Amiens and Poix:

Blenheim IV R3670. Shot down by ground-fire in the target area 4.30 p.m. P/O P. V. Arderne, Sgt G. Robson, and Cpl J. Tippett unhurt. Aircraft a write-off.

Blenheim IV. Forced-landed at Le Havre damaged by ground-fire during attack on armour and troops near Amiens 4.30 p.m. Sgt Sims and crew unhurt. Aircraft abandoned.

RAF FIGHTER COMMAND

32 Squadron, Manston
Wing patrol Le Tréport—Aumale:

Hurricane P3353. Shot down by Bf109s of III./JG26 during attack on He111s of I./KG1 between Rouen and Neufchâtel-en-Bray and crash-landed behind Allied lines 9.25 a.m. P/O D. H. Grice unhurt. Aircraft a write-off.

Hurricane N2582. Shot down by Bf109s of III./JG26 during attack on He111s of I./KG1 over Rouen and crashed at Fief-Thoubert, Saint-Saëns, 9.25 a.m. P/O G. I. Cherrington killed. Aircraft a write-off.
The remains of Geoffrey Cherrington, originally buried alongside the crash site, were reinterred as an 'Unknown Airman' on June 4, 1941, but post-war excavation of the site by the MREU in October 1947 discovered aircraft serial N2582 thus confirming his identity.

Hurricane N2406. Shot down by Bf109s of III./JG26 during attack on He111s of I./KG1 south-east of Rouen and crashed near Houville-en-Vexin 9.30 a.m. P/O K. Kirkcaldie killed. Aircraft a write-off.

151 Squadron, Manston
Escort Blenheims to Amiens:

Hurricane P3315. Hit by AA fire and set alight, abandoned south-west of Amiens 12.15 p.m. P/O D. H. Blomely baled out unhurt. Aircraft a write-off.

Hurricane. Returned to North Weald damaged in combat with Bf109s near Amiens 4.30 p.m. P/O Maxwell wounded in leg. Aircraft damaged but repairable.

266 Squadron, Martlesham Heath
Interception patrol:

Spitfire N3244. Damaged in landing accident following patrol over Peterborough 10.40 a.m. P/O R. J. B. Roach unhurt. Aircraft damaged but repairable.

615 Squadron, Hawkinge
Wing patrol:

Hurricane P3380. Damaged propeller on landing at Dreux to refuel 2.15 p.m. P/O Evans unhurt. Aircraft repairable.

FRENCH AIR FORCE

GAO 510 Potez 63.11 (494). Shot down by flak during reconnaissance sortie over enemy armour south of La Hortoy and Poix. Crashed into woods at Ferme de la Motte, Bois Lainé 5.30 a.m. Lt R. Martin and Sgt A. Guesnel killed. Sgt Menet captured wounded. Aircraft a write-off.

GAO 517 Potez 63.11 (331). Shot down by Bf109s of 4./JG53 and crash-landed in flames south of Château-Thierry 10.50 a.m. Possibly that claimed by Fw Litjens. Lt Plaud and Cpl Barbarin badly wounded. S/Lt Battle wounded. Aircraft a write-off.

GAO 543 Potez 63.11 (336). Crashed on landing back at base due to flak damage, after reconnaissance sortie over the Aisne. S/Lt Faugeras badly injured. Capt F. Berveiller and Sgt Molle unhurt. Aircraft a write-off.

GAO 1/551 Potez 63.11 (284). One engine set alight in attacks by Bf109s of 4./JG53 during artillery observation sortie over La Besace and crashed in flames at Vaux-en-Dieulet, north of Buzancy, 10.50 a.m. Possibly that claimed by Fw Kauffmann. Sgt R. Hild seriously wounded, died next day. Lt J. Rouig badly wounded and burned. Sgt Cotte badly wounded. Aircraft a write-off.

GAO 1/584 Potez 63.11 (404). Returned with starboard aileron badly damaged in attacks by Bf110s of II./ZG1 over Damprichard near the Swiss frontier 12.30 p.m. Lt Confuron, Sgt Bayle, and Sgt Minaro unhurt. Aircraft a write-off.

GB I/11 Two LeO 451s (89). Damaged in night take-off accident at Étampes-Montdidier; possibly collided while taxi-ing. No crew casualties. Both aircraft repairable.

GB 4/19 Douglas DB-7 (26). Shot down by flak south of Pommiers during attack on enemy armour near Pasly. Crashed at La Chaussée Romaine at Mercin-et-Vaux, west of Soissons, 3.00 p.m. Adjt F. Montrozier killed. Sgt D. Follaci baled out, but fell dead in fields at Figeonville with unopened parachute. Capt Provoost (*Commandant*) unhurt. Aircraft a write-off.

GB I/21 Bloch 210 (55). Shot down by flak during night attack on pontoon bridge at Péronne. Crashed and exploded in marshes at La Germaine, Offoy. S/Lt R. Colombo, Lt J. Soltner, Adjt P. Veit, Sgt P. Beaufrère, and Sgt M. Hirsch killed. Aircraft a write-off.
The recovery of this crew was extremely difficult, the remains of four being recovered in August 1940. A fifth body was recovered over two years later, on September 30, 1942, and only formally identified as being that of the gunner, Paul Veit, after two years further research.

GB I/21 Amiot 354 (40). Forced-landed near Montdidier damaged by own bomb blasts during low-level night attack on pontoon bridge at Péronne. Crew unhurt. Aircraft repairable.

. . . and closer inspection suggests its serial is either '336' or possibly '386' although the damage is far too severe for it to be the machine of GAO 543 which was reported crashed when landing on June 8.

GB II/23 LeO 451 (206). Shot down by flak during night-bombing sortie against enemy troop concentrations and roads near Poix. Crashed on the outskirts of Fontenay-Torcy, 9 km north of Gournay-en-Bray. Sgt E. Grange died of head wounds. Lt Blanchard, Adjt Voisine, and Cpl Conquet captured badly wounded. Aircraft a write-off.

GB II/23 LeO 451 (258). Hit by flak during night-bombing sortie against enemy troop concentrations and roads near Poix and crash-landed at Chantilly. Lt Clerc wounded. Adjt Chuzeville, Adjt Mauret, and Adjt R. Terrières unhurt. Aircraft a write-off.

GB II/35 Breguet 691 (57). Crashed shortly after take-off from Châteauroux on training flight. Sgt Bellogrote killed. Aircraft a write-off.

GB I/63 Martin 167F (71). Landed at Vernon with flak damage after attack on armoured columns between Forges-les-Eaux and Gournay-en-Bray. Adjt J. Habourdin seriously injured, died of wounds. Aircraft damaged but repairable.

GBA I/51 Breguet 693 (1017). Seriously damaged by flak during attack on enemy armour and crashed south of Soissons 2.15 p.m. Adjt C. Darriet seriously wounded in head, died next day. Sgt Mitifeux unhurt. Aircraft a write-off.

GBA II/51 Breguet 693 (52). Damaged by flak and crashed on landing back at Bouard following attack on enemy armour around Fontenoy, Condé-sur-Aisne, and Berzy-le-Sec 6.30 p.m. S/Lt R. Rolland and Sgt des Courtis unhurt. Aircraft a write-off.

GBA II/51 Breguet 693 (48). Damaged by flak and crashed on landing back at Bouard following attack on enemy armour around Fontenoy, Condé-sur-Aisne, and Berzy-le-Sec 6.30 p.m. Adjt Hervier injured. Lt Collombet unhurt. Aircraft a write-off.

GBA I/54 Breguet 693 (6). Badly damaged by flak and crashed on landing near Meaux following attack on enemy armour attempting to cross the River Aisne at Condé-sur-Aisne, Missy, and Vailly-sur-Aisne 2.15 p.m. Sgt Conill badly wounded in leg. Lt Blondy unhurt. Aircraft a write-off.

GC I/1 Bloch 152. Shot down by Hptmn von Bonin (Gruppenkommandeur) of Stab I./JG54 between Noailles and Méru 7.50 p.m. Lt J. Kral killed. Aircraft a write-off.

GC I/2 Morane 406 (225). Last seen in low-level pursuit of a Ju87 of StG2 over the Ourcq river during offensive patrol between Soissons and Attichy. Believed fell victim to Bf109s of 3./JG2 and possibly that claimed by Oberfw Jaenisch south-west of Soissons 8.08 p.m. Crashed in the forest of Retz near Corcy, east of Villers-Cotterêts. Lt A. Monty killed. Aircraft a write-off.
André Monty's grave and the substantial remains of his aircraft are still situated just off the road from Corcy to Longpont as a lasting tribute. His memorial stone is inscribed: 'Lieutenant André Monty. Pilote de Chasse Groupe I/2. Tué en combat aérien le 3 Juin 1940'.

GC I/2 Morane 406 (1044). Damaged by return fire from Ju87s of StG2 during offensive patrol between Soissons and Attichy, and possibly also attacked by Bf109s of 3./JG2. Wrecked in forced-landing south of Soissons 8.05 p.m. Sgt A. Goile unhurt. Aircraft a write-off.

GC II/2 Morane 406 (712). Shot down by flak during low level attack on enemy armour south of Forêt de Bray 8.30 a.m. Broke up between Saumont and La Poterie, south-east of Forges-les-Eaux. Capt C. d'Abbadie d'Arrast killed. Aircraft a write-off.

GC II/2 Morane 406 (244). Shot down by flak during low-level attack on enemy armour south of Forêt de Bray and crashed at Guizancourt, south of Poix-de-Picardie, 8.30 a.m. Adjt R. Marconnet killed. Aircraft a write-off.
René Marconnet was originally buried alongside his aircraft but reinterred in the local communal cemetery on February 26, 1941.

GC II/2 Morane 406 (555). Shot down by flak during low-level attack on enemy armour south of Forêt de Bray 8.30 a.m. S/Lt J. Robiaud unhurt. Aircraft a write-off.

GC III/2 Curtiss H-75 (246). Badly damaged by flak during offensive patrol and forced-landed near Lesges, south of Braine, 9.30 a.m. Adjt M. Romey unhurt. Aircraft destroyed to prevent capture.

GC III/2 Curtiss H-75 (231). Shot down during attack on enemy bombers near Château-Thierry 5.45 p.m. Crashed and burned out on a hill outside Nesles-la-Montagne. Sgt P. Zinnicker killed. Aircraft a write-off.

GC II/3 Dewoitine 520. Damaged by flak and wrecked in forced-landing at Montlhéry 6.15 a.m. Cpl K. Körber unhurt. Aircraft a write-off.

GC II/3 Dewoitine 520. Badly damaged by Fw Potthast of 5./JG52 in combat over Vailly-sur-Aisne and belly-landed at Cramaille, north-west of Fère-en-Tardenois, 2.55 p.m. Sgt V. Cukr wounded in head, admitted to hospital in Sézanne. Aircraft a write-off.

GC I/5 Curtiss H-75. Believed badly damaged by Oberlt Borchers of 4./ZG76 during attacks on Ju87s of II./StG2 over Rouen 3.40 p.m. and belly-landed back at Évreux-Fauville. Capt L. Vasatko unhurt. Aircraft a write-off.

GC I/5 Curtiss H-75 (125). Badly damaged in forced-landing due to petrol failure during attack on Ju87s of II./StG2 over Rouen 3.30 p.m. S/Lt M. Rouquette unhurt. Aircraft a write-off.

GC I/6 Morane 406 (804). Hit by ground-fire during low-level attack on enemy tanks south-east of Forges-les-Eaux 5.15 p.m. Crashed and burned out at 'Les Mefrequennes' at Haussez. Capt X. Poilloue de Saint-Mars killed. Aircraft a write-off.

GC 4/6 Bloch 152 (664). Shot down by Bf109s of 3./JG2 in combat between Soissons and Attichy and abandoned over Crepy-en-Valois 8.05 p.m. Possibly one of those claimed by Lt Wick. Lt Y. Vié (Commandant) wounded in thigh, baled out but hit aircraft and badly injured knee, admitted to Saint-Martin-du-Tertre Hospital in Senlis. Aircraft a write-off.

GC II/6 Bloch 152 (640). Badly damaged in combat with Bf109s of 3./JG2 between Soissons and Attichy 8.10 p.m. and possibly also that attacked by Hptmn von Ankum-Frank of Stab JG27 over the Forêt de Compiègne. Belly-landed alongside the River Aisne at Rethondes. Lt Sassard unhurt. Aircraft a write-off.

Although the serial '555' on the tail fin is rather indistinct in the photo, this is the Morane 406 of Groupe de Chasse II/2 brought down by flak at breakfast time.

GC III/7 Morane 406 (584). Seriously damaged by flak during low-level attack on enemy armour near Forges-les-Eaux and belly-landed near Gournay-en-Bray 5.15 p.m. Sgt Mathieu unhurt. Aircraft a write-off.

GC II/10 Bloch 152. Lost bearings and forced-landed out of fuel following patrol over Rouen. Sgt M. Adamek unhurt. Aircraft undamaged.

GR I/35 Potez 63.11 (691). One engine destroyed by ground-fire during armed-reconnaissance of enemy armoured concentrations east of Roye 10.15 a.m. Crash-landed on the banks of the Oise near Houdancourt, 17 km south-west of Compiègne. Lt Montantème, Capt Monigard, and Adjt Châtillon unhurt. Aircraft a write-off.

GR II/55 Potez 63.11 (800). Collided with a Morane 406 on take-off on reconnaissance sortie, caught fire and burned out. S/Lt Chareyre, Sgt Morier, and Adjt A. Jacquemart unhurt. Aircraft a write-off.

LUFTWAFFE

7./JG3 Messerschmitt Bf109E-3. Shot down by Capt Williame, S/Lt Audebert, and S/Lt Chalupa of GC I/2 during escort sortie for Do17s north-east of Beauvais and crashed at Nivillers 4.25 p.m. Feldwebel F. Albert killed. Aircraft a write-off.

2./JG26 Messerschmitt Bf109E-3. Shot down by Sgt Chapera of GC II/5 in combat east of Poix-de-Picardie and crashed into woods near Taisnil, south-west of Amiens, 11.00 a.m. Leutnant W. Reimer killed. Aircraft a write-off.

The body of Walter Reimer was discovered by German military in the wreckage of his aircraft on July 22, 1940, and buried in a field grave adjacent to the crash site. Today he lies in Bourdon Germany War Cemetery, Block 43, Row 7, Grave 256.

3./JG26 Messerschmitt Bf109E-3. Shot down by Adjt Lachaux of GC II/5 in combat west of Beauvais and abandoned between Marseille-en-Beauvaisis and Songeons 11.00 a.m. Feldwebel A. Burkhardt baled out and captured wounded. Aircraft a write-off.

III./JG26 Messerschmitt Bf109E-1. Returned damaged following combat with Hurricanes of Nos. 32 and 79 Squadrons near Conches-en-Ouche during escort sortie for He111s of I./KG1 9.30 a.m. Pilot unhurt. Aircraft repairable.

7./JG26 Messerschmitt Bf109E-1. Shot down by Hurricanes of Nos. 32 and 79 Squadrons south-west of Neufchâtel-en-Bray during escort sortie for He111s of I./KG1 and crashed at 'Vaudichon', near Saint-Saëns, 9.30 a.m. Oberfw H. Dörr killed. Aircraft a write-off.

Hermann Dörr was buried by locals in a field grave alongside the road between Bellencombre and Saint-Saëns. Six months later he was located and reinterred thanks largely to enquiries pursued by his comrade Klaus Mietusch who was shot down the same day. Site bordering local golf course investigated by Simon Parry.

7./JG26 Messerschmitt Bf109E-3 (2746). Shot down in combat with Hurricanes of Nos. 32 and 79 Squadrons during escort sortie south-west of Dieppe and forced-landed at Offranville 9.30 a.m. Leutnant K. Mietusch captured wounded. Aircraft a write-off.

8./JG26 Messerschmitt Bf109E-1. Returned damaged following combat with Hurricanes of Nos. 32 and 79 Squadrons during escort sortie for He111s of I./KG1 9.30 a.m. Leutnant H. Ripke wounded. Aircraft damaged but repairable.

2./KG1 Heinkel He111H-3. Shot down by Hurricanes of Nos. 32 and 79 Squadrons over Rouen 9.30 a.m. Flgr C. Jetter killed. Gefr O. Kaluza captured wounded. Lt H. Wasserberg and Uffz K. Gundlach captured unhurt. Aircraft a write-off.

3./KG1 Heinkel He111H-3. Returned slightly damaged in attacks by Hurricanes of Nos. 32 and 79 Squadrons between Neufchâtel-en-Bray and Rouen 9.20 a.m. Flgr E. Huber badly wounded, rest of crew unhurt. Aircraft repairable.

3./KG1 Heinkel He111H-3. Returned damaged by Hurricanes of Nos. 32 and 79 Squadrons over Neufchâtel-en-Bray 9.20 a.m. Uffz G. Lewioda killed, Fw O. Jung badly wounded, rest of crew unhurt. Aircraft damaged but repairable.

3./KG1 Heinkel He111H-3. Shot down by Hurricanes of Nos. 32 and 79 Squadrons east of Neufchâtel-en-Bray 9.15 a.m. Fw H. Wunnicke, Fw K. Rogoss, Uffz P. Schuckliess, Uffz H. Jütte, and Flgr K. Kugler unhurt. Aircraft a write-off.

4./KG4 Heinkel He111. Returned reportedly damaged by flak near Merville. Uffz W. Brinken badly wounded, admitted to hospital in Dorsten; rest of crew unhurt. Aircraft damage state not recorded.

4./KG4 Heinkel He111. Returned damaged by flak over Vernon, north-west of Paris. Uffz O. Steinbrück and Uffz H. Beutel slightly wounded, admitted to hospital in Dorsten; rest of crew unhurt. Aircraft damage state not recorded.

This is the Bf110 from 5./ZG1 which violated Swiss airspace . . . to its cost.

5./KG76 Dornier Do17Z. Shot down north-west of Aumale and crashed at St-Martin-le-Gaillard. Lt D. Schmidt, Oberfw A. Wiest, Fw J. Sättele, and Uffz H. Immel *(Waffen-Oberfw)* killed. Uffz N. Schwab baled out and captured unhurt. Aircraft a write-off.

IV.(St)/LG1 Junkers Ju87R. Believed shot down by Adjt Poincenot and Sgt Killy of GC II/3 in action south of Vailly 3.05 p.m. Lt J. Fürnweger and gunner unhurt. Aircraft a write-off.

12.(St)/LG1 Junkers Ju87B. Believed badly damaged in attack by Cdt Morlat *(Commandant)* of GC II/3 south of Vailly and forced-landed north of the Canal de l'Oise 3.05 p.m. Fw H. Werner wounded, admitted to hospital in St Quentin; gunner unhurt. Aircraft damage state not recorded.

1./StG2 Junkers Ju87B. Shot down by Capt Williame of GC I/2 over Longpont, south-west of Soissons, and believed crashed and exploded in woods north-east of Villers-Cotterêts 7.50 p.m. Lt H-W. Koslik and Uffz O. Spitta killed. Aircraft a write-off.

1./StG2 Junkers Ju87B. Believed that attacked by S/Lt Chalupa, Lt Monty, and Sgt de Puybusque of GC I/2 near Longpont and crash-landed east of Soissons 7.55 p.m. Crew believed unhurt. Aircraft a write-off.

1./StG2 Junkers Ju87B. Returned damaged in attacks by Moranes of GC I/2 near Longpont, south-west of Soissons, 7.45 p.m. Possibly that attacked by S/Lt Chalupa and Sgt Beda. Crew unhurt. Aircraft a write-off.

1./StG2 Junkers Ju87B. Returned damaged in attacks by Moranes of GC I/2 near Longpont, south-west of Soissons, 7.45 p.m. Possibly that claimed by Capt Williame and Lt Monty. Lt F. Lang badly wounded, gunner unhurt. Aircraft T6+HH damage state not recorded.

II./StG2 Junkers Ju87R. Over-turned on landing at Remaisnil badly damaged in attacks by S/Lt Rouquette of GC I/5 east of Elbeuf 3.30 p.m. Crew unhurt. Aircraft a write-off.

5./StG2 Junkers Ju87R. Shot down by Capt Vasatko and S/Lt Rouquette of GC I/5 east of Elbeuf, and crashed and burned out at Freneuse 3.30 p.m. Lt J. Pfannenstein and Uffz J. Wurz killed. Aircraft a write-off.

Stab III./StG2 Junkers Ju87B. Shot down by Moranes of GC III/2 south of Soissons during attack on Vierzy and crashed at Mareuil-en-Dôle 8.00 p.m. Gefr H. Schreiber killed. Oberlt K. Hamann *(Gruppenadjutant)* baled out and captured wounded. Aircraft a write-off.

4./ZG1 Messerschmitt Bf110C. Badly damaged in attacks by Swiss Bf109s (of Fl.Kp.6, Fl.Kp.15 and Fl.Kp.21) over Réchésy, north of Bonfol, during bomber escort sortie to Lyon and crashed at Friesen, south of Dannemarie, 12.40 p.m. Fw O. Beiter killed. Obergefr R. Hink captured slightly wounded. Aircraft a write-off.

This deliberate violation of neutral air space by II./ZG1 was intended to provoke Swiss fighter reaction and inflict casualties in retaliation for the loss of three Luftwaffe aircraft over Switzerland since May 16. For the further loss of three Messerschmitt Bf110s, one Swiss Bf109C (J.328) of Fl.Kp.15 was badly damaged in combat over Tramelan, its badly-wounded pilot, Oberlt Homberger, managing to get down at Biel-Bözingen. Oberlt E. Gürtler and Lt R. Meuli of Fl.Kp.10 were both killed when their C-35 reconnaissance machine was shot down between Porrentruy and Alle at 11.42 a.m.

4./ZG1 Messerschmitt Bf110C (2124). Shot down by Swiss Bf109s (Oberlt Streiff, Lt Köpfli, and Lt Mühlemann of Fl.Kp.21) and crashed and burned out at Triengen 12.55 p.m. Uffz A. Scholz and Obergefr W. Hofmann killed. Aircraft a write-off.

5./ZG1 Messerschmitt Bf110C (2881). Port engine damaged in attack on Potez 63.11 of GAO 1/584 during escort sortie to Besançon and crossed into Swiss air space on return flight. Further damaged in combat with Swiss Bf109s (of Fl.Kp.6, Fl.Kp.15 and Fl.Kp.21) and both engines put out of action. Finally engaged by AA fire (Flab.Det. 80) near Wahlen prior to belly-landing south of Oberkirch church, east of Breitenbach, 12.40 p.m. Fw M. Dähne interned unhurt. Obergefr H. Klinke interned, injured left hand. Aircraft 2N+GN interned.

Manfred Dähne and Herbert Klinke were both repatriated at Stetten-Lörrach on June 28, 1940, their slightly damaged aircraft being returned to Germany on September 12.

6./ZG1 Messerschmitt Bf110C. Returned badly damaged in combat with Swiss Bf109s (of Fl.Kp.6, Fl.Kp.15 and Fl.Kp.21) 12.45 p.m. Oberlt G. Kadow *(Staffelkapitän)* wounded, admitted to hospital in Freiburg. Uffz F. Wunnicke killed. Aircraft a write-off.

Sunday, June 9

During the day further German advances were made, their forward units reaching the Seine between Vernon and Rouen which was evacuated, its bridges blown, and fuel and oil stores fired. This now placed the British 51st Division and accompanying troops on the left of the Allied line in an increasingly precarious situation, already threatened by enemy infantry from the east and now mechanised forces from the south. With Dieppe about to be blocked this isolated pocket of troops was forced to retire towards Le Havre, the nearest port available that offered any hope of evacuation. Moving at night, it was estimated that they would not reach Le Havre until June 13, if at all, and signals received in London impressed the desperate need for air support. 'Essential that air delay enemy movement mostly AFVs to south of Saint-Saëns—Bolbec road, also his infantry advance from east. Air support requested to prevent unrestrained bombing'.

This dictated RAF fighter activities for the day and two patrols, each of four squadrons, were flown by Fighter Command between Le Tréport and Crèvecoeur around midday and late afternoon both proving uneventful. Three squadrons of AASF Hurricanes also provided protection for Allied ground forces during the day, as indeed did four French Groupes de Chasse, and several engagements were reported though results were mixed due to poor visibility in the area caused by the dense palls of smoke rising from Rouen and Beauvais.

Elsewhere along the Aisne the situation also continued to deteriorate despite resolute opposition by the French who were unable to prevent several enemy crossings either side of Rethel. French fighters were active over this area for most of the day flying patrols in support of their ground forces and several engagements with German fighters resulted with serious losses on both sides. By the end of the day, French fighter units would have flown 280 sorties, claiming 29 enemy aircraft destroyed plus another 11 probables, for the loss of 17 of their own fighters. Reflecting the increasing change of focus in the air campaign over France this may be compared to RAF fighter claims on the day for two Bf109s destroyed and another probable for the loss of three Hurricanes.

AASF Battles stood by all day pending instructions for an attack which was cancelled late afternoon as no fighter support could be provided. Thus the entire British bombing effort on the day was provided by No. 2 Group and was concentrated in the area around Formerie and Forges-les-Eaux where German armoured vehicles were reported to be making most progress. French medium bombers also struck at these targets mid-morning losing three aircraft to ground-fire and fighters. This was followed by an attack at midday by 18 Blenheims escorted by 24 Hurricanes but they found few targets and also lost three aircraft to the ever-present heavy ground-fire. A further attack around 6.00 p.m. by two formations of 15 Blenheims, again escorted by 24 Hurricanes, met with more success and bombed enemy columns near Conteville that were advancing towards Neufchâtel-en-Bray.

At night, ten AASF Battles operated against river crossings at St-Valéry, Abbeville, and Amiens, while 20 or so Whitleys attacked similar targets in the lower Somme. Woods believed to be sheltering German transport and enemy communications from Laon to the Ardennes Forest were targets for nine Battles and 30 Wellingtons, while 21 Whitleys attacked towns in the Meuse valley.

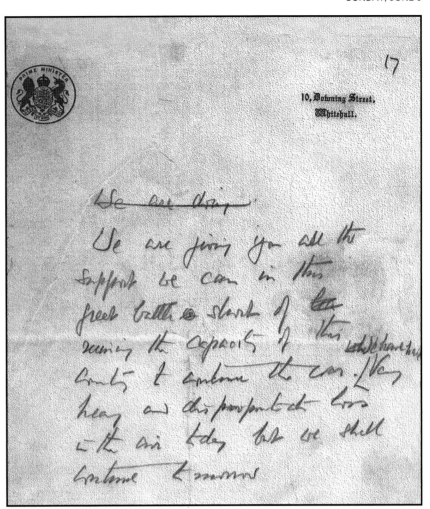

An interesting insight in the behind-the-scene dealings between the leaders of Britain and France at this critical time. Following the meeting of the Defence Committee held on the evening of June 8, this was the message that was drafted *(above)* and finally sent *(below)* from Churchill via the Foreign Office to the French Prime Minister at 8.20 p.m. On Sunday afternoon Churchill met Charles de Gaulle for the first time when the Prime Minister told the French Général bluntly that he 'no longer believed in the possibility of a victory in France'.

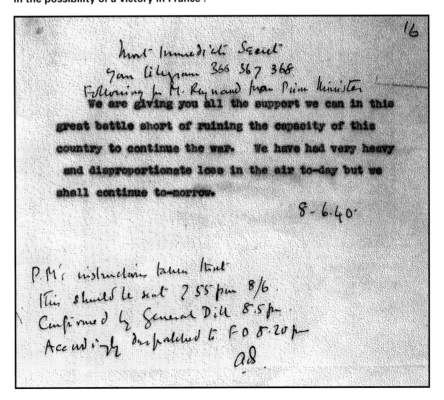

A snapshot taken by a German soldier records a poignant scene. The battle has passed by to leave a warrior's grave beside his stricken aircraft. It is sad that we cannot put a name to the unfortunate crew of this Battle from No. 142 Squadron but the code-letters QT-Q are not listed in the surviving records. The flat open countryside of much of France makes it virtually impossible to identify locations without some sort of further clue.

Analysis of No. 142 Squadron casualties suggests this may be an aircraft lost on May 19, 1940, during a sortie west of Laon. Two were lost in circumstances that match our photograph, each involving a single casualty; L5226 that crashed near Dagny-Lambercy, and P5238 that forced-landed ten miles south of Épernay. Of the two L5226 seems the more likely so, while impossible to resolve, is this the field grave of William Donald Boyle?

BRITISH AIR FORCES IN FRANCE

17 SQUADRON, LE MANS

Hurricane. Forced-landed during patrol over Rouen 4.30 p.m. Cause not stated, probably engine failure. Pilot Officer D. C. Leary unhurt, arrested on landing but later returned. Aircraft a write-off.

103 SQUADRON, OUZOUER-LE-DOYEN

Battle L5246. Unable to locate airfield with failing engine during night operations and abandoned over Verdres. Squadron Leader H. Lee baled out and evacuated to hospital in Le Mans with compound fracture of right leg. Sergeant D. Norrington and LAC Werner both baled out landing unhurt. Aircraft PM⊙Q a write-off.

242 SQUADRON, CHÂTEAUDUN

Hurricane P2767. Shot down by Lt Gehlhaar of 4./JG52 in attack over Châlons-sur-Marne and crashed near Courtisols 4.35 p.m. Pilot Officer D. G. MacQueen killed. Aircraft a write-off.

Donald Garfield MacQueen from High River, Alberta, joined the all-Canadian No. 242 Squadron on November 6, 1939, and was one of six 'A' Flight pilots ordered to France on May 16, 1940. In four days of intense fighting during which he hardly ate, never washed, and slept 'an hour here and there' they were recalled to England. He was killed in action the day after their return to France.

501 SQUADRON, LE MANS

Hurricane. Engine damaged during inconclusive combat over Le Havre and ground-looped attempting forced-landing on marshy ground near Sougé. Sergeant J. H. Lacey injured head. Aircraft a write-off.

UK-based aircraft lost or damaged on operations over the Western Front:

RAF BOMBER COMMAND

53 Squadron, Eastchurch
Reconnaissance Fismes—Crécy:

Blenheim IV R3632. Returned tail damaged by AA fire near Laon 7.00 a.m. P/O S. G. Collins, Sgt Irvine, and AC Cowling unhurt. Aircraft repairable.
Temporarily detached to Rouen-Boos for operations in France.

82 Squadron, Watton
Columns near Poix:

Blenheim IV P6925. Returned hit by ground-fire during attack on enemy transport between Poix and Grandvilliers. Sgt Thripp slightly wounded. P/O D. M. Wellings and another crewman unhurt. Aircraft UX⊙Z repairable.

2 Blenheim IVs. Returned hit by ground-fire during attack on enemy transport between Poix and Grandvilliers. No crew casualties. Aircraft both repairable.

107 Squadron, Wattisham
Armoured columns:

Blenheim IV L9323. Shot down by flak during attack on enemy armour in the Forêt-de-Bray at Forges-les-Eaux, and crashed in flames near Torcy-le-Petit, south-east of Dieppe, 12.00 p.m. F/O C. P. Bomford and Sgt R. A. Bowman killed. P/O F. E. Frayn thrown from the aircraft badly burned and admitted to hospital. Aircraft a write-off.

Blenheim IV R3685. Shot down by flak during sortie to bomb armour between Hornoy-le-Bourg and Forges-les-Eaux 12.00 p.m. P/O R. H. M. Bennett, Sgt A. E. Langford, and Sgt H. T. Denison unhurt. Aircraft a write-off.

Blenheim IV R3739. Shot down by flak during sortie to bomb enemy armour between Formerie and Forges-les-Eaux, and crashed near Rouen 12.00 p.m. P/O C. Campbell killed. F/O C. Y. Buckley and Sgt E. H. B. Cotton captured. Aircraft a write-off.

RAF FIGHTER COMMAND

111 Squadron, Hawkinge
Wing patrol:

Hurricane. Slightly damaged hitting a gun emplacement while landing at Dreux to refuel. Sgt R. Carnall unhurt. Aircraft damaged but repairable.

FRENCH AIR FORCE

AB 1 Vought 156F (8). Believed shot down by ground-fire near Forges-les-Eaux following attack on motorised columns advancing between Abbeville and Rouen 4.40 p.m. Forced-landed on the banks of the Seine near Deauville. SM Buhot-Launay and EV1 du Bessey de Contenson unhurt. Aircraft 6 a write-off.

EGAN CAMS 55 (85). Shot down by flak south of Rouen during ferry flight and crashed at Cléon. PM Corrège killed, his mechanic baled out unhurt. Aircraft a write-off.
This elderly machine was on the strength of the Établissement Général de l'Aéronautique Navale.

GAO 543 Potez 63.11 (682). Engaged by Bf109s near Braisne during photo-reconnaissance sortie and pursued at low-level towards Épernay. Finally shot down in flames and burned out in forest near the road junction between Boursault and St-Martin-d'Ablois 7.45 p.m. Believed that credited to Oberfw Maden of 4./JG52. Lt F. Gonzales, Capt F. Berveiller, and Cpl J. Delorme killed. Aircraft a write-off.
This crew was buried in field graves adjacent to the crash site until April 17, 1941, when they were reinterred in the communal cemetery at Épernay.

GAO 546 Potez 63.11 (702). Returned to La Colombe damaged following reconnaissance sortie over Gournay and possibly that attacked by Oberlt Seifert *(Staffelkapitän)* of 3./JG26 south-east of Rouen 10.10 a.m. Sgt Lecorre badly wounded thigh; rest of crew unhurt. Aircraft damaged but repairable.

GB I/21 Amiot 351 (65). Abandoned over Nogent-sur-Saône due to mid-air fire during night sortie to Soissons. Fire brought under control and aircraft returned safely to base. Sgt Geiger baled out unhurt. Aircraft repairable.

GB I/31 LeO 451 (142). Returned to Chalon-sur-Saône damaged by French AA during night sortie to attack road junctions at Mézières and Signy-l'Abbaye. Capt Hirsch *(Commandant)*, Lt Dupre, Sgt Meliguet, and Sgt Marion unhurt. Aircraft repairable.

GB II/62 Martin 167F. Returned to St-Martin-la-Campagne with flak damage following photo-reconnaissance sortie over the Seine and Andelle valleys a.m. Crew unhurt. Aircraft repairable.

GB I/63 Martin 167F (140). Shot down by Fw Keil of 2./JG2 during sortie to attack convoys at Pont-Arcy between Braine and Fère-en-Tardenois. Crashed and exploded in woods at 'Richebourg', Bucy-le-Long, north-east of Soissons, 8.40 p.m. Lt G. Pollet killed. Sgt M. Rey baled out too low and killed, falling at Missy-sur-Aisne. Sgt Martin baled out and captured unhurt. Aircraft a write-off.

Picking over the spoils of war, these two airmen may just have inspected Potez 63.11 '625' out of interest . . . or did they have a hand in its demise and had deliberately sought out a souvenir of their victory? However the absence of any engine wreckage suggests this was simply one of many unserviceable, and mostly unrecorded, airframes that were torched on airfields across France during the final collapse and abandoned to await the arrival of occupying Luftwaffe units.

GBA I/51 Breguet 693 (1016). Shot down by flak during attack on enemy armour north of Les Andelys and crashed at Saint-Jacques-sur-Darnetal, east of Rouen, 10.00 a.m. Sgt G. Denis and Cpl A. Masse killed. Aircraft a write-off.

GBA II/51 Breguet 693 (69). Shot down by fighters during sortie to attack enemy tanks between Forges-les-Eaux and Gournay-en-Bray 10.00 a.m. Believed fell in the Seine at Cléon, south of Rouen. Lt F. Maurel and Sgt P. Rochais killed. Aircraft a write-off.

GBA II/51 Breguet 693 (49). Shot down by fighters during sortie to attack enemy tanks between Forges-les-Eaux and Gournay-en-Bray 10.00 a.m. Crashed in the Forêt de Lyons near Fleury-sur-Andelle. S/Lt Rolland wounded, evaded eventually reaching Toulouse. Sgt des Courtis captured unhurt. Aircraft a write-off.

GBA 2/54 Breguet 693 (12). Crash-landed with starboard wheel retracted at Bessay airfield. S/Lt Chauvet and crewman unhurt. Aircraft repairable, later abandoned.

GBA II/54 Breguet 693 (92). Shot down by Lt Zirkenbach of 1./JG27 during mission to bomb armoured columns south-east of Soissons and crashed at Villers-Cotterêts 3.35 p.m. Sgt A. Lelong killed. S/Lt Mayadoux wounded. Aircraft a write-off.

GBA II/54 Breguet 693 (58). Shot down by Lt Krafftschick of 1./JG27 over Sommelans, 12 km north-west of Château-Thierry during mission to bomb armoured columns south-east of Soissons 3.35 p.m. Lt J. Dupuy and S/Lt G. Beaud killed. Aircraft a write-off.

GBA II/54 Breguet 693 (46). Shot down by flak during mission to bomb armoured columns south-east of Soissons. Crashed and burned out in forest at Villers-Cotterêts 3.30 p.m. Sgt de Thannberg and Adjt Delporte unhurt. Aircraft a write-off.

GBA II/54 Breguet 693 (70). Damaged by flak during bombing of armoured columns south-east of Soissons, and crash-landed at Courmont, south-east of Fère-en-Tardenois. S/Lt Girard and Sgt Plessiez wounded. Aircraft a write-off.

GC I/1 Bloch 152. Shot down near St Quentin, circumstances unknown. Cpl Novacek baled out wounded. Aircraft a write-off.

GC III/2 Curtiss H-75 (244). Landed at Mourmelon damaged by return fire from Do17 attacked near Reims 11.15 a.m. S/Lt A. Lansoy unhurt. Aircraft abandoned.

GC III/2 Curtiss H-75. Set alight in attack by Hptmn Galland of Stab JG27 east of Rosoy-en-Multien during escort sortie for reconnaissance Potez and crashed in flames into forest west of Château-Thierry 2.55 p.m. Sgt G. Elmlinger wounded. Aircraft a write-off.

GC I/3 Dewoitine 520 (133). Badly damaged in combat with Bf109s of II./JG27 near La Ferté-sous-Jouarre and forced-landed near Hervillers, south of La Ferté-Milon, 12.45 p.m. Possibly that claimed by Hptmn Andres *(Gruppenkommandeur)*. Adjt Guillaume unhurt. Aircraft a write-off.

GC II/4 Curtiss H-75 (206). Shot down by Bf109s of 7./JG53 in combat between Rethel and Attigny, abandoned north of Moronvilliers and crashed through trees at 'Les Carmélites' 9.15 a.m. Possibly that claimed by Oberfw Götz. S/Lt Blanc baled out wounded in leg. Aircraft a write-off.

GC II/4 Curtiss H-75 (89). Shot down by Bf109s of 7./JG53 in combat between Rethel and Attigny and belly-landed south-east of Bouy 9.15 a.m. Possibly that claimed by Uffz Neuhoff. Adjt J. Paulhan badly wounded, admitted to hospital in Troyes. Aircraft a write-off.

GC II/4 Curtiss H-75. Returned damaged following combat with Bf109s of 7./JG53 between Rethel and Attigny 9.15 a.m. Lt M. Vinçotte unhurt. Aircraft damaged but repairable.

GC II/4 Curtiss H-75 (218). Shot down during attack on Do17s of 2./KG2 south-west of Rethel, crashed and burned out between Roizy and Sault-Saint-Remy. Possibly that claimed by Oberlt Lippert *(Staffelkapitän)* of 3./JG53 over Boult-sur-Suippe 1.50 p.m. S/Lt C. Plubeau baled out badly burned. Aircraft a write-off.

GC II/4 Curtiss H-75 (215). Returned to Orconte damaged in combat with Bf109s during attack on Do17s of 2./KG2 south-west of Rethel and believed that claimed by Lt Tonne of 3./JG53 near St Dizier 1.40 p.m. S/Lt Guillou wounded, admitted to hospital. Aircraft a write-off.

GC II/6 Bloch 152 (681). Crashed on landing at Reims damaged by Bf109s near Neufchâtel-sur-Aisne 2.00 p.m. and possibly that claimed by Uffz Höhnisch of 1./JG53. Adjt A. Laguet wounded in neck and back, admitted to hospital in Épernay. Aircraft a write-off.

GC II/6 Bloch 152 (673). Forced-landed at Reims following combat with Bf109s of 1./JG53 near Neufchâtel-sur-Aisne 1.50 p.m. S/Lt J. Riss unhurt. Aircraft a write-off.

Now host to new visitors, a Heinkel 111 of Stab KG55 (G1+BA) stands on Cambrai airfield alongside the burned-out remains of Morane 406, serial 337 of GC III/2. A military aerodrome at Cambrai was first mooted in 1931 but when it opened four years later, it was only used by civilian aircraft. The Germans enlarged it and laid down two concrete runways over 1500 metres long. In 1945 the Americans occupied it briefly before it returned once again to civilian use.

GC III/7 Morane 406. Caught on the ground and wrecked in strafing attack on Coulommiers airfield 3.00 p.m. Sgt C. Boyer badly wounded in shoulder. Aircraft a write-off.

GC III/7 Morane 406. Caught on the ground in strafing attack on Coulommiers airfield 3.00 p.m. Adjt Lion slightly wounded in right hand. Aircraft a write-off.

One source indicates that 12 aircraft were destroyed in this attack and several others damaged.

GC II/8 Bloch 152. Shot down by Bf109 and abandoned near Rouen during escort sortie for attack on motorised columns at Forges-les-Eaux by Vought 156Fs of AB 1 4.40 p.m. Believed that claimed by Uffz Heinbockel of 2./JG21. Adjt Nicolle baled out but attacked in his parachute and wounded in head. Aircraft a write-off.

This unit had been based at Lympne since May 30 and flew several escort missions for French aircraft operating in support of Allied troops at Dunkirk.

GC I/145 Caudron C-714. Shot down in engagement with Do17s escorted by Bf109s of III./JG26 near Vernon. Possibly that claimed by Lt Bürschgens of 7./JG26 2.15 p.m. Lt J. Obuchowski killed. Aircraft a write-off.

GC I/145 Caudron C-714 (8552). Shot down in engagement with Do17s escorted by Bf109s of III./JG26 near Vernon. Possibly that claimed by Lt Ebeling of 8./JG26 over Rouen 2.30 p.m S/Lt L. Lachowicki-Czechowicz killed. Aircraft I-210 a write-off.

GC I/145 Caudron C-714 (8557). Shot down in engagement with Do17s escorted by Bf109s of III./JG26 near Vernon. Possibly that claimed by Fw Gärtner of 8./JG26 between Mantes and Les Andelys 2.35 p.m. Crashed at Villiers-en-Désoeuvre, south-east of Pacy-sur-Eure. Cpl E. Uchto killed. Aircraft I-215 a write-off.

Two C714s from Flight II of GC I/145 were reported 'crashed' on this date, but the names of the pilots not recorded. Thus the serials above could be reversed.

GC I/145 Caudron C-714. Forced-landed at Évreux with engine damage following attack on Do17s escorted by Bf109s of III./JG26 near Vernon 2.30 p.m. Lt Z. Zadrozinski unhurt. Aircraft abandoned.

GC I/145 Caudron C-714. Returned to Bernay damaged following attack on Do17s escorted by Bf109s of III./JG26 near Vernon 2.30 p.m. Lt J. Kowalski slightly wounded in arm. Aircraft a write-off.

GC I/145 Caudron C-714. Forced-landed damaged following attack on Do17s escorted by Bf109s of III./JG26 near Vernon 2.30 p.m. S/Lt B. Skibinski unhurt. Aircraft damaged but repairable.

GC I/145 Caudron C-714. Forced-landed at Villacoublay damaged following attack on Do17s escorted by Bf109s of III./JG26 near Vernon 2.30 p.m. S/Lt J. Godlewski unhurt. Aircraft a write-off.

Jerzy Godlewski was reported 'missing in action' during the withdrawal from France but reached England where he later served in No. 72 Squadron. He was lost over the Channel on April 10, 1941.

GC I/145 Caudron C-714. Forced-landed at Évreux oil system damaged in combat with Bf109s of III./JG26 over Les Andelys 2.45 p.m. S/Lt C. Glówczynski unhurt. Aircraft repairable.

GC I/145 Caudron C-714. Forced-landed at Évreux following attack on Do17s escorted by Bf109s of III./JG26 near Vernon 2.30 p.m. S/Lt J. Czerniak unhurt. Aircraft undamaged.

GR II/33 Potez 63.11 (665). Shot down by flak during low-level reconnaissance mission along the Aisne valley to Soissons, and the Ailette canal to Laon. S/Lt Ysermann, S/Lt Collot, and Cpl Blondel captured wounded. Aircraft a write-off.

GR II/55 Potez 63.11 (198). Crash-landed at Buc airfield seriously damaged by intense flak over Formerie, and again over Poix, during low-level reconnaissance sortie 2.45 p.m. Lt Roupain and Sgt André wounded. Sgt Lefèvre unhurt. Aircraft a write-off.

T 3 Latécoère 298 (14). Failed to return from night attack on the rail bridge at Noyelles-sur-Mer and believed shot down by flak over the Somme Bay 2.45 a.m. PM Grand and QM G. Tanguy missing. Aircraft lost.

LUFTWAFFE

2.(H)/10 Henschel Hs126. Landed near Avricourt badly damaged by ground-fire during observation sortie over Compiègne. Oberlt G. Meuser killed, pilot unhurt. Aircraft damage state not recorded.

2.(H)/12 Henschel Hs126. Returned reportedly damaged by ground-fire during observation sortie but believed that attacked by S/Lt Codet of GC II/3 near Asfeld, south-west of Rethel, 2.20 p.m. Crew unhurt. Aircraft damaged but repairable.

1.(H)/31 Henschel Hs126. Shot down by Capt Delfino, S/Lt Faisandier, Lt Chenais, Adjt Rebière, and Sgt Pinson of GC II/9 during a photo-reconnaissance sortie and hit a hedge attempting a crash-landing near Gancourt, south of Formerie, 11.30 a.m. Uffz W. Jakob killed, Fw H. Mattes thrown from aircraft and rescued badly wounded. Aircraft a write-off.

This loss is recorded on June 10 in the Luftwaffe Quartermaster General Returns. Walter Jakob was originally buried in a field grave west of the road to St Etienne, 500 metres south of Gancourt, but later reinterred in Champigny-St-André German War Cemetery.

1.(H)/41 Henschel Hs126. Badly damaged in attacks by Lt Dubreuil and Lt Leblanc of GC III/2 during observation sortie south-east of Fismes and landed between Marle and Montcornet 2.20 p.m. Lt W. Deimann killed, pilot unhurt. Aircraft damage state not recorded.

II./JG3 2 Messerschmitt Bf109Es. Wrecked in landing collision at Valheureux. Pilots believed unhurt. Aircraft both write-offs.

3./JG26 Messerschmitt Bf109E. Shot down by Lt Lamaison of GC I/8 following attack on Potez 63 south-east of Rouen 10.20 a.m. Oberleutnant J. Seifert (*Staffelkapitän*) wounded. Aircraft a write-off.

Stab II./JG27 Messerschmitt Bf109E-3. Badly damaged in combat with D520s of GC I/3 over Villers-Cotterêts and wrecked in crash-landing at Montdidier 12.40 p.m. Hauptmann W. Andres (*Gruppenkommandeur*) unhurt. Aircraft a write-off.

Stab II./JG27 Messerschmitt Bf109E-1. Engine badly damaged in combat with D520s of GC I/3 over Villers-Cotterêts and belly-landed at Croutoy 12.30 p.m. Possibly claimed by Adjt Guillaume. Leutnant H. Bosch captured wounded in left calf. Aircraft a write-off.

4./JG27 Messerschmitt Bf109E-1. Engine damaged in combat with D520s of GC I/3 east of Villers-Cotterêts and abandoned near Oulchy-le-Château 12.40 p.m. Believed that claimed by Capt Gérard. Feldwebel K-H. Kranich baled out and captured wounded but later escaped. Aircraft a write-off.

5./JG27 Messerschmitt Bf109E-1. Shot down in combat with D520s of GC I/3 and crashed in the Forêt d'Halatte, east of Creil, 12.40 p.m. Possibly claimed by Adjt Guillaume. Uffz H. Siegemund killed. Aircraft a write-off.

5./JG27 Messerschmitt Bf109E-1. Shot down in combat with D520s of GC I/3 and forced-landed north of Villers-Cotterêts 12.40 p.m. Fw E. Krenzke captured. Aircraft a write-off.

6./JG27 Messerschmitt Bf109E-3. Shot down in combat with D520s of GC I/3 over Crépy-en-Valois and crashed near La Ferté-Milon 12.45 p.m. Uffz L. Hettmer killed. Aircraft a write-off.

4./JG52 Messerschmitt Bf109E-1. Flew into a high tension cable during low-level pursuit of Potez 63.11 of GAO543 and believed crashed at St-Martin-d'Ablois, south-west of Épernay, 7.45 p.m. Oberfw W. Maden killed. Aircraft a write-off.

Stab II./JG53 Messerschmitt Bf109E-3. Shot down by Capt Patureau-Mirand and Lt Laurent of GC I/2 in combat between Attigny and Stenay and abandoned over Stonne 6.05 p.m. Oberlt O. Böhner (*Gruppen TO*) baled out and captured unhurt. Aircraft < O + – a write-off.

2./KG2 Dornier Do17Z. Returned badly damaged in attacks by GC II/4 and GC I/5 over Cormicy during sortie to attack artillery positions near Trigny, north-west of Reims. Fw J. Förster slightly wounded, admitted to hospital in Trier. Aircraft a write-off.

2./KG2 Dornier Do17Z. Forced-landed at Charleville-Mézières badly damaged in attacks by GC II/4 and GC I/5 over Cormicy during sortie to attack artillery positions near Trigny, north-west of Reims. Fw F. Lübbing killed. Gefr H. Kanow badly wounded, admitted to hospital in Charleville. Aircraft a write-off.

II./KG2 Dornier Do17Z. Undercarriage collapsed on landing at Signy-le-Petit following sortie to Reims. No crew casualties. Aircraft damaged but repairable.

II./KG2 Dornier Do17Z. Undercarriage damaged on landing at Signy-le-Petit following sortie over Reims. No crew casualties. Aircraft damaged but repairable.

III./KG2 Dornier Do17Z. Forced-landed near Morch due to engine trouble. No crew casualties. Aircraft a write-off.

I./KG3 Dornier Do17Z. Returned damaged by flak. Crew believed unhurt. Aircraft damaged but repairable.

2./KG51 Two Junkers Ju88A. Crashed from 1,000 feet following collision during formation flying practice at Lechfeld. Lt H. Kaun, Uffz G. Müller, Uffz G. Hauptmeier, and Gefr A. Frey (mechanic of Stabsstaffel KG51) all killed. Both aircraft write-offs.
Two aircraft mechanics, Gefr O. Wühle and Flgr H-B. Klötzer of 2.FBK/KG51, were also reported killed at Lechfeld on this date and may have been involved in this accident.

German officers examine burned-out DFS 230 glider wrecks, most possibly on the roof of the Belgian fortress at Eben-Emael assaulted during the opening hours of the offensive in the West.

II./KG51 Junkers Ju88A. Crash-landed at Stuttgart-Süd, cause unknown. No crew casualties. Aircraft damaged but repairable.

III./KG55 Heinkel He111P. Belly-landed, cause not stated. No crew casualties. Aircraft a write-off.

4./KG76 Dornier Do17Z. Returned damaged by ground-fire near Le Havre. Fw K. Häcker, Uffz A. Lepp, and Uffz R. Kania badly wounded. Aircraft damage state not recorded.

4./KG77 Dornier Do17Z. Forced-landed at Charleville-Mézières damaged in attacks by H-75s of GC II/4 during sortie to Reims 9.00 a.m. Uffz W. Drescher badly wounded. Uffz S. Nies, Obergefr A. Kolodzig, and another crewman unhurt. Aircraft 3Z+LM damage state not recorded

6./KG77 Dornier Do17Z. Returned damaged in attacks by H-75s of GC II/4 northeast of Reims during sortie to Nogent-l'Abbesse 9.00 a.m. Fw J. Gehring slightly wounded, rest of crew unhurt. Aircraft damage state not recorded.

Stab StG1 Junkers Ju87B. Shot down by S/Lt Blanck and Sgt Glauder of GC I/3 over Liancourt during attack on Pont-Ste-Maxence and crashed at Brenouille, north-east of Creil, 6.30 p.m. Oberlt F-W. Schaefer (*Geschwaderadjutant*) and Uffz H. Janz killed. Aircraft a write-off.

Stabsstaffel StG1 Dornier Do17M. Shot down by Capt Challe, S/Lt Salaberry, and S/Lt Boutarel of GC I/3 east of Verberie during reconnaissance sortie over Pont-Ste-Maxence 6.15 p.m. Oberlt W. Pöppler and Uffz H-G. Venner captured wounded. Oberfw V. Gnan captured unhurt. Aircraft a write-off.

I./ZG2 Two Messerschmitt Bf110C. Involved in taxying collision prior to take-off. No crew casualties. Both aircraft repairable.

I./ZG2 Messerschmitt Bf110C. Belly-landed following engine failure. Oberlt Vohwinkel and gunner believed unhurt. Aircraft a write-off.

I./ZG52 Messerschmitt Bf110C. Reported collided with Bf109, details unknown. No crew casualties. Aircraft damaged but repairable.

Monday, June 10

British and French air reconnaissance during the day confirmed the dismal fact that German troops had crossed the Seine and established bridgeheads at Elbeuf and Louviers. They were also reported south of the river at Courcelles and Vernon making an advance on Paris from three sides inevitable. Reflecting the gravity of the military situation the French government vacated the capital for Tours.

Elsewhere along the entire French front the situation was generally bleak despite several pockets of determined resistance that the Germans simply bypassed and encircled while continuing their advance. An enemy thrust from north of Paris continued to progress, as well as another advance from Soissons towards Château-Thierry. Further east, German forces now reached Dormans making Reims vulnerable and, though the French checked enemy pressure on the Aisne Canal and launched a violent and heroic counter-attack south of Perthes, the battle for Champagne was lost. Also, there were growing indications of an imminent fresh German assault being readied along the Saar—Rhine front.

Thus it was, with French and British forces stretched to the limit, that Italy finally entered the arena and formally declared war on the Allies.

This probability had long been foreseen and plans for bombing Italian targets prepared even before the opening of the German offensive on May 10. It was proposed that up to four squadrons of Wellingtons should be based in the south of France for operations against the industrial centres of Genoa, Milan, Turin, and Venice. Air Marshal Barratt, who doubted that sufficient weight of attack on Italy could be maintained given the already desperate situation in France, did not welcome this added responsibility and voiced his concerns. The French

Since coming to power in October 1922, Benito Mussolini had striven to recreate in Italy the glory of the old Roman empire. He launched an attack to conquer Abyssinia in 1936; lent support to General Franco in the Spanish Civil War, and in April 1939 Il Duce invaded Albania. Just over a year later he stood on the balcony of the Palazzo Venezia in Rome to proclaim a new war: 'Fighting men of the land, the sea and the air, Blackshirts of the Revolution and of the Legions, men and women of Italy, of the Empire and of the Kingdom of Albania, hearken! An hour marked by destiny is striking in the sky of our country; the hour of irrevocable decisions. We are entering the lists against the plutocratic and reactionary democracies of the West, who have always hindered the advance and often plotted against the very existence of the Italian people. At a memorable meeting in Berlin I said that, according to the laws of Fascist morality, when one has a friend one goes with him to the very end. We have done this and will do this with Germany, with her people, with her victorious armed forces. Proletarian and Fascist Italy is for the third time on her feet, strong, proud and united as never before. The single and categoric watchword is binding on us all. Already it is flying through the air and kindling hearts from the Alps to the Indian Ocean — to conquer. And we will conquer. And we will give finally a long period of peace with justice to Italy, to Europe and to the world. People of Italy, to arms! Show your courage, your tenacity and your worth.'

Hitler's 'palace' in Berlin, with its balcony designed by Albert Speer overlooking the Wilhelmplatz, was destroyed after the war, but Mussolini's Palazzo Venezia still survives as a national museum complete with its historic balcony.

ITALIAN AIR FORCE *(REGIA AERONAUTICA)* June 10, 1940
Units based in north-west Italy for deployment against France

1st Air Region	HQ — Milan		**43 Stormo:**	HQ — Cameri
			98 Gruppo	
2 (Fighter) Division 'Borea'	HQ — Turin-Caselle		(240, 241 Squadriglia) 16 Fiat BR20	Cameri
			99 Gruppo	
3 Stormo:	HQ — Novi Ligure		(242, 243 Squadriglia) 16 Fiat BR20	Cameri
18 Gruppo				
(83, 85, 95 Squadriglia) 17 Fiat CR42	Novi Ligure			
23 Gruppo			**RECONNAISSANCE UNITS**	
(70, 74, 75 Squadriglia) 25 Fiat CR42	Cervere			
53 Stormo:	HQ — Turin-Caselle		**Attached Army GHQ:**	
150 Gruppo			1 Gruppo	
(363, 364, 365 Squadriglia) 20 Fiat CR42	Turin-Caselle		(27, 121 Squadriglia) 10 Meridionali Ro37	Arezzo
151 Gruppo				
(366, 367, 368 Squadriglia) 19 Fiat CR42	Casabianca		**Attached Army Group West:**	
			5 Gruppo	
4 (Bomber) Division 'Drago'	HQ — Novara		(31, 39, 40 Squadriglia) 27 Meridionali Ro37	Venaria Reale
7 Stormo:	HQ — Lonate Pozzolo		69 Gruppo	
4 Gruppo			(118, 123 Squadriglia) 14 Meridionali Ro37	Levaldigi & Novi Ligure
(14, 15 Squadriglia) 16 Fiat BR20	Lonate Pozzolo		72 Gruppo	
25 Gruppo			(119, 129 Squadriglia) 9 Caproni Ca311	Albenga & Mondovi
(8, 9 Squadriglia) 16 Fiat BR20	Ghemme			
13 Stormo:	HQ — Piacenza		33 Squadriglia 4 Meridionali Ro37	Bresso
11 Gruppo				
(1, 4 Squadriglia) 17 Fiat BR20	Piacenza		114 Squadriglia 4 Meridionali Ro37	Turin-Mirafiori
43 Gruppo				
(3, 5 Squadriglia) 16 Fiat BR20	Cascina Vega			

also had serious misgivings believing that any air attacks should only be retaliatory. It was nevertheless agreed at a meeting of the Supreme War Council in Paris on June 3 that, in the event of an Italian declaration of war, the Allies would bomb industrial and oil targets in north-west Italy at the earliest possible moment.

Operational responsibility for this new enterprise, code-named 'Haddock', fell to Air Commodore Field and the personnel of No. 71 Wing then at Nantes. They promptly proceeded to the airfields of Le Vallon and Salon, north-west of Marseille, with two servicing flights. Fighter defences were to be provided by three French Groupes de Chasse, GC III/1 already ordered from Rozay-en-Brie to Valence to bolster defences in the area. It was further proposed that three more Groupes could be released provided the RAF sent another 20 fighter squadrons to northern France. This was as optimistic as it was fanciful so by June 10, when the 'Haddock' airfields were declared ready for operations, local fighter defences were still negligible and AA defences largely non-existent.

In mainland France, RAF bombing operations concentrated on German crossings over the Seine and included two major attacks by AASF Battles that apparently operated without fighter escort. Mercifully, Luftwaffe fighters were not in evidence but the formation was nevertheless attacked and lost two aircraft to French fighters. Mid-afternoon 33 Blenheims, escorted by 20 Hurricanes, hit enemy troop concentrations and transport between Rouen and Les Andelys while another attack around 5.00 p.m. by 12 Battles struck at the already damaged bridges at Vironvay and Pont-de-l'Arche. But it was becoming abundantly clear to the British and French bomber crews involved that German combat engineers could repair bridges and ford rivers almost as quickly as the Allied air forces could destroy the existing crossings.

The main body of the British 51st Division along with the French IXème Corps d'Armée were now fully enveloped between Dieppe and St-Valéry-en-Caux. Only some 4,000 troops sent ahead to cover withdrawal of the main body towards Le Havre would reach safety. German forces now held Veulettes-sur-Mer and Cany-Barville and unless the beleaguered Allied troops could fight their way through to Le Havre the only alternative to evacuation from the beaches and quay at St-Valéry-en-Caux, was surrender. So with their options clear, some of the more seriously wounded embarked that night.

Fighter Command flew a total of 63 sorties over the coast between Le Tréport and Fécamp now occupied by the remnants of the 51st Division while AASF Hurricanes were tasked with a series of patrols to cover evacuation of British and French troops from Le Havre, the aim being to maintain at least one squadron over the port all day. As far as surviving records allow this seems to have been achieved for Nos. 1, 17, 73, 242, and 501 Squadrons flew at least 12 patrols between them. According to the official narrative 'a very considerable effort was made' using the airfields at Dreux and Beaumont-le-Roger although the latter had to be evacuated during the afternoon. Its servicing crews, along with those at Évreux, were ordered to Caen-Mathieu where the French promised facilities and which was to be readied for three squadron sorties next day. Dreux, further south, was not immediately threatened and, for the moment, would be maintained.

Poor visibility and haze over France seriously hampered RAF night bombing efforts and of 81 sorties despatched, 14 aircraft returned with their bombs, while 15 more were unable to locate their primary targets.

BRITISH AIR FORCES IN FRANCE

1 SQUADRON, ROUEN-BOOS

Hurricane. Crashed at Orléans, cause not stated. Flying Officer P. G. H. Matthews unhurt. Aircraft damage state not recorded.

88 SQUADRON, MOISY

Battle. Forced-landed during night operations, cause not stated. Pilot Officer J. M. Talman and Sergeant Dixon unhurt. Aircraft abandoned.

103 SQUADRON, OUZOUER-LE-DOYEN

Battle P2328. Crashed near Gasny following attack by Caudron 714s of GC 1/145 during sortie to bomb bridges near Vernon 11.30 a.m. Pilot Officer C. V. Thomas and Sergeant P. I. Bligh killed. Aircraft a write-off.

Battle. Landed badly damaged following attack by Caudron 714s of GC 1/145 during sortie to bomb bridges near Vernon 11.30 a.m. Flying Officer D. D. A. Kelly and crewman unhurt. Aircraft a write-off.

Battle K9409. Returned severely damaged by AA over Pont de l'Arche 5.30 p.m. Sergeant W. R. Critch and crewman unhurt. Aircraft PM⊙P a write-off.

501 SQUADRON, LE MANS

Hurricane. Abandoned near Le Mans following combat with Bf109s of I./JG76 over Le Havre. Pilot Officer J. A. A. Gibson baled out unhurt. Aircraft a write-off.

UK-based aircraft lost or damaged on operations over the Western Front:

RAF BOMBER COMMAND

77 Squadron, Driffield
Somme bridges:

Whitley V N1372. Aborted mission following engine failure over the Channel and crashed attempting forced-landing at Abingdon 2.30 a.m. AC1 A. L. Kennedy injured. P/O A. W. Dunn, P/O C. J. D. Montagu, Sgt Lucas, and AC2 Martin unhurt. Aircraft KN⊙O a write-off.

FRENCH AIR FORCE

GAO 1/514 Potez 63.11 (333). Forced-landed at Villeneuve-les-Vertus port engine damaged by flak during photo-reconnaissance sortie over Asfeld, north of Reims. Lt Rix wounded in face. Sgt Mazeron and Sgt Laurent unhurt. Aircraft repairable.

GAO 1/589 Potez 63.11. Returned hit by AA fire during reconnaissance between Château-Thierry and Condé-sur-Marne. S/Lt Labas, Lt de Thuisy, Sgt Fonteneau unhurt. Aircraft repairable.

GB I/12 LeO 451 (14). Shot down west of Rethel during sortie to attack enemy armour between Château-Porcien and Avançon 3.15 p.m. Crashed and burned out at 'Le Brignet', Tagnon, near Juniville. S/Lt P. Riche, Sgt G. Ménard de Chabannes, and Sgt R. Weiler killed. Cpl L. Vridaud believed baled out too low and captured seriously injured, died next day in hospital at Herbigny. Aircraft 11 a write-off.

GB II/12 LeO 451 (208). Lost bearings and run out of fuel after night attack on Mézières and Signy-l'Abbaye. Abandoned north-east of Besançon 2.30 a.m. Adjt Domo and Adjt Mahaut baled out unhurt. Adjt Prenez and Sgt Bonnet baled out injured. Aircraft a write-off.

GB 2/19 Douglas DB-7 (41). Shot down south-west of Rethel during sortie to attack advancing enemy armour, and crashed alongside the road between Neuflize and Tagnon 7.00 a.m. S/Lt J. Gillet, Capt P. Dupont (Commandant), and Adjt A. Arnulphy killed. Aircraft a write-off.

GB II/21 Bloch 210 (92). Landed at St-Florentin damaged in attack by Oberlt Lederer of 6./JG52 on return from sortie over the Aisne between Soissons and Château-Porcien 2.30 p.m. S/Lt Mendels, Sgt Vallée, Sgt Comme, and Sgt Demede unhurt. Aircraft damaged but repairable.

GB 4/23 LeO 451 (93). Belly-landed at Étampes-Montdidier damaged by flak during night-bombing sortie over Mousteron and collided with an aircraft of GB I/11. Capt Guionnet, Adjt Moroy, Adjt J. Bauer, and Adjt R. Terrières unhurt. Aircraft a write-off.

GBA I/51 Breguet 693 (38). Badly damaged during sortie to attack pontoon bridges over the Seine near Les Andelys and crash-landed near Blois. Sgt Metifeu and Cpl Genre unhurt. Aircraft a write-off.

GC 5/1 Morane 406 (618). Reported shot down by ground-fire during low-level patrol west of Fère-en-Tardenois and crashed at Corbeny Farm, near Bruyères-sur-Fère. Adjt E. Gagnaire killed. Aircraft a write-off.

GC 5/1 Morane 406 (792). Reported set alight by ground-fire during low-level patrol and crash-landed at Monthiers, north-west of Château-Thierry. Sgt Péllissier captured unhurt near Soissons. Aircraft a write-off.

GC I/5 Curtiss H-75A. Returned badly damaged by return fire from He111s of I./KG53 attacked near Vouziers 5.45 p.m. S/Lt Y. Le Calvez unhurt. Aircraft a write-off.

GC 1/145 Caudron C-714 (8565). Mistakenly joined formation of Bf109s following attack on Do17s and shot down by Oberlt Keller (Staffelkapitan) of 1./JG3. Belly-landed back at Dreux 8.40 a.m. Cmdt J. Kepinski (Commandant) badly wounded in left arm, admitted to hospital in Chartres. Aircraft I-223 a write-off.
Within days the hospital was evacuated further south, Jozef Kepinski eventually reaching England four months later via Vichy, Spain, and Portugal.

GC 1/145 Caudron C-714 (8550). Forced-landed at Dreux with engine badly damaged in attack by Oberlt Keller (Staffelkapitän) of 1./JG3 during combat south of the airfield 8.45 a.m. S/Lt M. Lukaszewicz unhurt. Aircraft I-208 a write-off.

GR 1/33 Potez 63.11 (426). Stalled and crashed into woods at Martigny-les-Gerbonvaux shortly after take-off 1.30 a.m. Lt X. Bisch killed. Capt R. Pécou (Commandant) badly burned, died same day at Saint-Esprit Hospital in Neufchâteau. Sgt A. Moxica badly burned, died of injuries June 15. Aircraft a write-off.

GR II/33 Potez 63.11 (50). Returned to base badly damaged by flak during low-level reconnaissance sortie. S/Lt Frisou, Adjt Constantin, and Adjt Magnin unhurt. Aircraft a write-off.

1S2 Latécoère 290 (26). Wrecked on alighting at Lanvéoc-Poulmic, cause of accident not stated. SM Le Bihan killed. Aircraft a write-off.

T 2 Latécoère 298 (76). Shot down by naval AA fire from French *Chasseur 7* during reconnaissance sortie over Seine Bay and crashed in the sea off Honfleur. PM Gobert and crew rescued unhurt. Aircraft 9 lost.

T 3 Latécoère 298 (73). Forced-landed at St-Nazaire with engine trouble during withdrawal to Berre. Crew unhurt. Aircraft repairable — destroyed by enemy action June 19.

LUFTWAFFE

2.(F)/11 Dornier Do17. Failed to return from reconnaissance sortie to Rambouillet and crashed at Boullay-les-Troux, north of Limours, 6.00 a.m. Possibly that claimed by S/Lt Zukowski, S/Lt Lukaszewicz, and S/Lt Czerniak of GC 1/145. Oberlt K. Stecher, Fw H. Sehlmacher, and Fw J. Hermann killed. Aircraft a write-off.

4.(F)/11 Dornier Do17P (4137). One engine set alight by AA fire during reconnaissance sortie north-east of Soissons and also attacked by Capt Delfino, Lt Chesnais, and S/Lt Faisandier of GC II/9 near Chamouille. Crash-landed on fire south of Oulchy-la-Ville. Lt G. Büss killed, Oberlt H. Lenzer died of wounds, and Uffz O. Lietzau captured wounded. Aircraft 6M+BM a write-off.

1.(H)/13 Dornier Do17P. Shot down by seven H-75s of GC II/5 north-east of Nancy and crash-landed with starboard engine on fire south-east of Sornéville 6.20 p.m. Oberfw W. Sauerborn and Uffz G. Lehmann killed, Uffz A. Prestel captured wounded admitted to Sédillot Military Hospital at Nancy. Aircraft a write-off.

5.(H)/13 Henschel Hs126. Engaged during observation sortie near Le Thour by Lt Chesnais, Adjt Rebière, and Sgt Courteville of GC II/9 and shot down at Pargny-Resson, east of Rethel, 3.50 p.m. Oberlt W. Wieser and Fw J. Blatz killed. Aircraft a write-off.

1.(H)/14 Henschel Hs126. Crashed on landing at Vervins possibly damaged by ground-fire. Two killed. Aircraft a write-off.

3.(H)/21 Henschel Hs126. Shot down during observation sortie over the Channel coast. Lt Kirchner and 1 killed. Aircraft a write-off.

4.(F)/121 Dornier Do17P. Crashed following collision with Ju52 of 1./KGzbV.1 shortly after take-off from Mannheim-Sandhofen. Oberlt W. Riebicke, Uffz H. Zielke, and Uffz H. Kramer killed. Aircraft a write-off.

1.(F)/123 Dornier Do17P. Shot down by Adjt Valentin, Capt Papin, and Sgt Lamblin of GC II/7 during reconnaissance sortie over the Vosges and exploded in woods at Chaume, Le Haut-du-Them, 5.45 p.m. Two crewmen missing, Fw Heck baled out and later captured. Aircraft a write-off.

7./JG2 Messerschmitt Bf109E. Crashed at Vivaise, north-west of Laon, due to flying accident. Flgr E. Fiedler killed. Aircraft a write-off.

II./JG3 Messerschmitt Bf109E-3. Returned badly damaged following combat with Caudrons 714s of GC 1/145 north-east of Vernon 8.40 a.m. Possibly that claimed by Capt Laguna. Pilot believed unhurt. Aircraft a write-off.

2./JG20 Klemm Kl35B. Landed damaged by own flak between Cassel and St Omer during ferry flight. Gefr F. Reinhold wounded. Aircraft repairable.

I./JG76 Messerschmitt Bf109E-1. Damaged by P/O Gibson of No. 501 Squadron near Le Havre and belly-landed at Yvrench. Pilot unhurt. Aircraft a write-off.

I./JG76 Messerschmitt Bf109E-1. Returned damaged following combat with No. 501 Squadron Hurricanes near Le Havre. Pilot unhurt. Aircraft damaged but repairable.

I./JG76 Messerschmitt Bf109E-1. Damaged in aborted take-off from Loge-Wactiaux on transfer flight to Conteville. Pilot unhurt. Aircraft damage state not recorded.

4./KG2 Dornier Do17Z. Returned damaged in attacks by Lt Marin-la-Meslée, Capt Vasatko, Lt Le Calvez, S/Lt Rouquette, and Sgt Penzini of GC I/5 near Châtillon-sur-Bar during sortie to Reims 5.00 a.m. Uffz L. Steuernagel badly wounded, admitted to hospital in Trier; rest of crew unhurt. Aircraft damage state not recorded.

7./KG2 Dornier Do17Z. Returned damaged by flak over Épernay during sortie to Reims 1.15 p.m. Uffz K. Rosenbrock badly wounded, admitted to hospital in Trier; rest of crew unhurt. Aircraft repairable.

1./KGzbV.1 Junkers Ju52 (5719). Crashed following collision with Do17P of 4.(F)/121 shortly after take-off on a test flight from Mannheim-Sandhofen. Uffz F. Slomka, Uffz P. Woitzig and Prüfmstr W. Jensch (of Stab I./KGzbV.1) killed. Aircraft a write-off.

4./KGrzbV.9 Junkers Ju52. Crashed at Norrent-Fontes, cause not stated. Crew believed unhurt. Aircraft 9P+AM a write-off.

1.(J)/LG2 Messerschmitt Bf109E-3 (707). Crashed on landing, cause not stated. Uffz W. Goetting unhurt. Aircraft 11 + damaged but repairable.

1./StG76 Junkers Ju87B. Crashed following mid-air collision west of Crécy. Uffz J. Haas and Uffz J. Rupp killed. Aircraft a write-off.

1./StG76 Junkers Ju87B. Crashed following mid-air collision west of Crécy. Uffz H. Mahnert badly injured, pilot unhurt. Aircraft a write-off.

II./ZG1 Messerschmitt Bf110C. Forced-landed at Vlissingen damaged by flak. Crew unhurt. Aircraft a write-off.

I./ZG26 Junkers Ju52 (5326). Forced-landed near Cambrai, cause unknown. Crew unhurt. Aircraft damaged but repairable.

I./ZG26 Messerschmitt Bf110C. Damaged in bombing at Amiens. No crew casualties. Aircraft damaged but repairable.

5./ZG76 Messerschmitt Bf110C. Shot down by own AA fire near Verneuil. Fw W. Klöpping and Uffz W. Görlitzer killed. Aircraft a write-off.

Tuesday, June 11

While German forces consolidated their bridgeheads across the Seine and continued to make further ground between Chantilly and the Ourcq, east of Château-Thierry their advance units crossed the Marne threatening Paris from yet another direction. Further east, considerable armoured forces were now across the Aisne near Rethel and advancing on the Marne, so Reims was clearly lost. But, it was recognised, should this rapid enemy advance towards Châlons decide to swing east, rather than west for Paris, the rear of the Maginot Line would be exposed — a direct frontal assault on this massive defensive complex by massing German forces already believed to be imminent.

These movements forced the retirement of Southern Component HQ from heavily-bombed Dreux to Laigné, south-west of Le Mans, its servicing commandos moving to Châteaudun. The enemy advance across the Marne also forced the withdrawal of the AASF advance landing ground at Échemines which was moved to Le Mans. French fighter units were similarly disorganised by a spate of movement orders withdrawing them south.

An intention that the British 51st Division and French IXème Corps d'Armée form a perimeter around St-Valéry-en-Caux and gradually retire there for evacuation at night was prevented by German forces who occupied Fécamp during the morning putting pressure on the western defensive screen. Ships approaching the harbour were attacked by Stukas and came under fire from artillery installed in cliff-top positions, the quayside itself now well within range of enemy mortars. Consequently, that night the order was given to destroy all vehicles and heavy equipment and proceed to the harbour for evacuation early next morning by 207 assorted vessels that were assembled off the coast. Meanwhile, at Le Havre, despite heavy bombing throughout the day and into the night, evacuation of troops to Cherbourg went ahead and would continue for another two nights while the Germans were kept occupied at St-Valéry-en-Caux.

Cover for the evacuations accounted for almost all 59 sorties flown by AASF fighters during the day, as well as the 147 sorties put up by Fighter Command between 9.30 a.m. and 9.20 p.m. operating at an average strength of 21 aircraft per patrol. Discounting the time spent gaining height and reaching their patrol lines between Le Tréport and Fécamp, this level of effort only provided protection for about seven hours in total which was obviously not enough to meet the needs of the beleaguered troops below. But, it was argued, more-frequent patrols would have meant operating in less strength which would have proved costly and ineffective. Also, many squadrons were still recuperating from the fighting over Dunkirk and Fighter Command's prime responsibility remained the defence of Britain.

RAF bombing during the day and throughout the night concentrated on the Seine crossings, most effort being directed against Les Andelys, though 46 night sorties were despatched to attack communications between the Ardennes and the Meuse to hamper movement of German reinforcements. However, the main change in British bombing policy this night was the despatch of 48 aircraft against objectives in Italy.

Thirty-six Whitleys of No. 4 Group flew to Jersey where they refuelled prior to an attack on the Fiat works at Turin. They met with mixed fortunes, only six aircraft claiming to have bombed the primary target, five more attacking alternate objectives in Turin and Genoa, while another delivered its

On the afternoon of June 11, Churchill once again flew to France. By now the French government had left Paris (which was to be declared an 'open city') for Tours, some 200 kilometres south of the capital. The meeting between the British and French delegations was held at Général Weygand's headquarters which had relocated in the small town of Briare on the River Loire. Here in the Château du Muguet *(above)* the inevitable fate of France was debated exactly one month after the Blitzkrieg had commenced. Weygand described the military situation, stating that there was no hope of halting the German drive on Paris or beyond. There were no reserves left. 'C'est la dislocation', he declared, 'the break-up'. Although the British delegation tried to raise the spirits of the French, they had little to offer in the way of positive support when the French need was immediate. Churchill was pressed for every fighter in England to be sent to France, but his answer reflected the view already agreed by the War Cabinet; that if Britain sacrificed any more aircraft she would be unable to counter the German offensive against the British Isles when that began. A sour note was added to the proceedings when Churchill received a call during dinner from Air Marshal Barratt informing him that 'the local French authorities will not allow my bombers at Salon to take off against Italy'. Although Prime Minister Reynaud undertook to send orders to allow the raid to proceed, early next morning Barratt, having driven to Briare through the night, arrived at the château in a rage to report personally that obstructions had been put in place to stop his aircraft taking off. This refusal by the French to permit the operation was the last straw, particularly when, during the morning conference, Reynaud backtracked, now saying that he supported the move to block the British aircraft, declaring that any such attacks on Italy should take place from England.

bombs over the target area at estimated time of arrival. Most of the aircraft despatched did not even reach Italy due to heavy storms over the Alps which forced 23 aircraft to abort the mission, another failing to return.

The experiences of the 12 Wellingtons of No. 3 Group sent out to Salon as part of 'Haddock Force' proved equally unsatisfactory. Arriving at Salon at 3.30 p.m. they found that Général Gama, who commanded French bomber forces in the area, had communicated to Air Commodore Field that no operations against Italy were to be carried out. Thus, while the aircraft were readied for the operation, much confusion ensued, until 7.25 p.m. when the executive order for the mission was received from BAFF headquarters. Over the next five hours, Air Commodore Field would receive 'a large number of telephone messages from various French authorities' all insisting that the operation was expressly forbidden. Higher echelons were soon involved and at 9.45 p.m. Air Marshal Barratt received a message from Général Vuillemin requesting that operations against Italy should be stopped. Barratt immediately contacted the Air Ministry and was advised to contact Churchill who was then in France at the Château du Muguet, Général Weygand's headquarters, near Briare. Unsurprisingly, the Prime Minister's view was that operations should proceed and this was communicated to Air Marshal Barratt who

instructed Air Commodore Field accordingly.

Consequently, at 12.27 a.m. the first Wellington began to taxy into position for take-off at Salon when numbers of French military lorries were suddenly driven onto the airfield and dispersed to prevent the aircraft from taking off. This bizarre stand-off was on the orders of the local French air commander who was instructed to prevent British aircraft from taking off at all costs. Given that the time of the operation was by now far advanced, and with the weather over the Alps deteriorating, plus the inescapable fact that French interference could only be countered by using force, Air Commodore Field cancelled the operation.

Exactly what prompted French actions this night remains unclear. Certainly they had their hands full opposing the German invasion and it is reasonable to assume that they had no desire to provoke more Italian activity than was necessary. They had argued, unsuccessfully, for restricting air attacks on Italy to solely retaliatory operations but a clear agreement had been reached on offensive action at the earliest possible moment and, clearly, this was violated. But before any recriminations could follow this extraordinary incident, and they were 'fairly bitter', more urgent matters arose, Churchill being informed privately by the French Prime Minister, Paul Reynaud, that Marshal Pétain had already decided to seek an armistice.

BRITISH AIR FORCES IN FRANCE

88 SQUADRON, MOISY

Battle L5519. Shot down by ground-fire during attack on troop concentrations in the Forêt de Bizy and crashed near Perdreauville, south-west of Mantes, 6.00 p.m. Pilot Officer J. D. W. Gillam and Sergeant R. C. Caldwell killed. Aircraft a write-off.

142 SQUADRON, VILLIERSFAUX

Battle. Returned damaged by ground-fire following attack on pontoon bridges over the Seine between Les Andelys and St Pierre. Pilot Officer Sutton and LAC Duckers unhurt. Sergeant Hall wounded in hand. Aircraft repairable.

Battle L5200. Shot down by AA south of Rouen during attack on pontoon bridges over the Seine at Le Manoir. Sergeant J. N. Fraser and Sergeant J. H. Ledson killed. Pilot Officer B. W. Peryman captured. Aircraft a write-off.

226 SQUADRON, FAUX-VILLECERF

Battle P6598. Shot down by Bf109s of 4./JG3 during attack on Vernon and crashed near St Pierre-d'Autils. Sergeant G. P. McLoughlin, Sergeant E. Marrows, and Flight Sergeant J. A. Russell killed. Aircraft a write-off.

UK-based aircraft lost or damaged on operations over the Western Front:

RAF BOMBER COMMAND

10 Squadron, Dishforth
Communications:

Whitley V P4954. Crashed near Abbeville, probably victim of AA fire 10.00 p.m. P/O D. F. Braham, Sgt L. A. Keast, Sgt J. J.Myers, Sgt J. McD. Black, and LAC R. R. H. Nuttall killed. Aircraft ZA⊙T a write-off.

15 Squadron, Wyton
Troop concentrations near Les Andelys:

Blenheim IV L8851. Collided with F/O Clark while flying in cloud south-east of Le Havre and lost one wing. Crashed near Pont-Audemer 12.30 p.m. P/O R. H. Werner, Sgt M. G. Jones, and Sgt R. Spencer killed. Aircraft a write-off.

Blenheim IV L9024. Collided with P/O Werner while flying in cloud south-east of Le Havre, finally lost starboard engine and crashed at Freneuse-sur-Risle 12.35 p.m. F/O R. B. G. E. Clark killed. Sgt T. J. W. Maloney and Sgt B. S. J. Piff baled out unhurt. Aircraft a write-off.

Blenheim IV N3588. Badly damaged by ground-fire and forced-landed near Cherbourg 1.00 p.m. P/O Myland, Sgt Pirks, and Sgt P. J. Petrie unhurt. Aircraft damaged but repairable.

21 Squadron, Bodney
Concentrations at La Mare:

Blenheim IV L8743. Shot down by Lt Schnell of 3./JG20 south-east of Rouen 6.35 p.m. P/O Rogers, Sgt Huckins, and Sgt Bradshaw believed captured. Aircraft a write-off.

Blenheim IV R3674. Shot down by Uffz Heilmann of 3./JG20 and crashed near Boulleville, west of Pont-Audemer, 6.35 p.m. Sgt J. J. Outhwaite, Sgt J. P. Waters, and Sgt J. M. Sculfer killed. Aircraft a write-off.

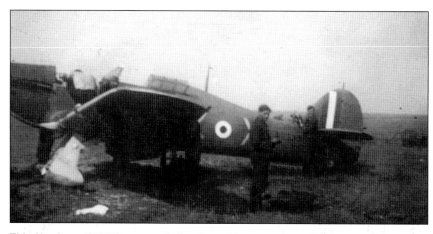

This Hurricane N2533 went missing from Manston on the afternoon of June 11. Sergeant Jones from No. 32 Squadron made a decent forced-landing and was believed captured unhurt.

Blenheim IV L8746. Shot down by Lt Senoner of 3./JG20 and crashed at St-Aubin-sur-Scie, south-west of Dieppe, 7.00 p.m. Sgt G. Lewis and Sgt A. G. Murray killed. F/Lt D. MacDonald captured. Aircraft a write-off.

Blenheim IV L8745. Belly-landed on return badly damaged by Bf109s of 3/JG20 south-east of Rouen 6.45 p.m. F/O S. L. Sigurdson, Sgt Bailey, and Sgt Trew unhurt. Aircraft damaged but repairable.

44 Squadron, Waddington
Meuse—Ardennes communications:

Hampden P1325. Crashed near Le Paradis, north of Béthune, cause unknown. F/Sgt C. L. Sumpster, Sgt W. Jeffrey, Sgt J. F. Sandall, and Sgt J. Simpson killed. Aircraft a write-off.

77 Squadron, Jersey
Fiat works at Turin:

Whitley V N1362. Crashed and burned out between Lignières-Orgères and Pré-en-Pail, north-west of Alençon, during return flight 10.30 p.m. Sgt N. M. Songest, Sgt P. H. J. Budden, Sgt A. Findlay, Sgt R. C. Astbury, and Sgt E. Ombler killed. Aircraft a write-off.

149 Squadron, Mildenhall
Communications at Soissons:

Wellington L7800. Lost bearings and crashed in the North Sea off Belgium, possibly damaged by AA fire. F/O J. S. Douglas-Cooper, P/O M. B. Dawson, P/O J. R. Swift, Sgt G. B. Fleming, Sgt R. Donaldson, and Sgt M. Murphy all missing. Aircraft lost.

RAF FIGHTER COMMAND

32 Squadron, Manston
Wing patrol Le Tréport—Dieppe:

Hurricane N2533. Failed to return following attack on Hs126 over Dieppe and forced-landed in France 2.00 p.m. Sgt Jones believed captured. Aircraft GZ⊙X lost.

264 Squadron, Duxford

Defiant. Crashed attempting forced-landing at Duxford following engine failure. P/O G. A. Hutcheson killed. LAC Robinson injured. Aircraft a write-off.

609 Squadron, Northolt

Spitfire R6637. Port wing damaged when incendiary ammunition exploded in the feed chute while on the ground. F/O P. Drummond-Hay unhurt. Aircraft repairable.

FRENCH AIR FORCE

GAO 501 Potez 63.11 (347). Crashed and broke up on take-off from St-André-de-l'Eure on transfer flight to Voves-Baignolet. S/Lt B. Rousseau killed. Aircraft a write-off.

GAO 518 Potez 63.11 (609). Forced-landed at Sommesous damaged, circumstances unclear. Crew believed unhurt. Aircraft damaged but repairable.

GB II/21 Amiot 354 (39). Damaged during enemy attack on St Florentin airfield 2.55 a.m. No crew casualties. Aircraft damaged but repairable.

GB II/34 Amiot 143 (85). Collided with a Potez 63 after night landing at Avord. Crew unhurt. Aircraft repairable.

GB 4/38 Amiot 143 (113). Caught in a storm on return from night attack on German airfields at Neustadt and Frankfurt so forced-landed near Sombernon, west of Dijon, a.m. Lt Benoît and Lt Jacob *(Commandant)* baled out unhurt. Aircraft repairable — abandoned.

GC II/1 Bloch 152 (618). Reportedly shot down by Bf109 during patrol over Château-Thierry. Lt Brun wounded chin. Aircraft a write-off.

GC 6/1 Morane 406. Destroyed in bombing by Do17s while taking off from Connantre 3.30 p.m. Sgt K. Doublet legs crushed and badly wounded, died next day in Sézanne hospital. Aircraft a write-off.

GC I/2 Morane 406 (947). Damaged in combat with Bf110s attacking Damblain airfield 7.00 a.m. and crashed on landing. Sgt A. Beda wounded. Aircraft a write-off.

GC 2/4 Curtiss H-75A. Forced-landed east of Évreux damaged by ground-fire during reconnaissance sortie between Bolbec and Yvetot 12.00 p.m. Capt B. Barbier *(Commandant)* wounded in foot, admitted to hospital in Chartres. Aircraft a write-off.

GC I/6 Morane 406 (821). Shot down in combat with Bf109s of III./JG53 and abandoned over Loivre, north of Reims, 10.55 a.m. Possibly one of those claimed by Hptmn Pingel *(Gruppenkommandeur)*. Capt Lefoyer baled out and captured wounded and burned. Aircraft a write-off.

GC I/6 Morane 406 (431). Badly damaged in combat with Bf109s of III./JG53 during sector patrol between Guignicourt and Berry-au-Bac and overturned in forced-landing 11.00 a.m. Possibly that claimed by Lt Claus. Sgt Standera injured. Aircraft a write-off.

Sous-Lieutenant Rousseau of GAO 501 lost his life when his Potez 63.11 spread itself across the landscape. Here German forces inspect the remains on St-André-de-l'Eure aerodrome.

GC I/6 Dewoitine 520 (49). Shot down in combat with Bf109s of III./JG53 and crashed near Épernay 11.10 a.m. Possibly one of those claimed by Hptmn Pingel (Gruppenkommandeur). Capt G. de Rivals-Mazères wounded in foot. Aircraft 10 a write-off.

Guillaume de Rivals-Mazères, a test pilot with the Centre d'Expérimentations Aériennes Militaires based at Orléans-Bricy, was on temporary attachment to GC I/6 flying operational trials with this modified anti-tank version of the D520 equipped with 13mm cannon.

GC I/6 Morane 406. Returned to Connantre damaged in combat with Bf109s of III./JG53 near Épernay 11.00 a.m. Sgt G. Kucera wounded. Aircraft believed damaged but repairable.

GC I/6 Morane 406. Returned to Connantre damaged in combat with Bf109s of III./JG53 near Épernay 11.00 a.m. Sgt V. Horsky wounded. Aircraft believed damaged but repairable.

GC I/6 Two Morane 406. Destroyed on the ground at Connantre in attack by Do17s and Bf110s 4.00 p.m. No pilot casualties. Aircraft both write-offs.

GC II/9 Bloch 152 (516). Engine damaged in combat with Bf109s of III./JG53 and crashed attempting forced-landing near Crugny, south-east of Fismes, 10.55 a.m. Possibly that claimed by Oberfw Götz of 7./JG53. Lt P. Pascal killed. Aircraft a write-off.

GC II/9 Bloch 152 (695). Abandoned near Reims during combat with Bf109s of III./JG53 10.40 a.m. Possibly that claimed by Lt Riegel of 7./JG53. S/Lt Ponneau baled out badly wounded and burned on face and hands. Aircraft a write-off.

GC II/9 Bloch 152. Badly damaged in combat with Bf109s of III./JG53 during sector patrol between Guignicourt and Berry-au-Bac. Possibly that claimed by Uffz Neuhoff of 7./JG53. Forced-landed north of the Marne outside Châlons-en-Champagne 11.03 a.m. Sgt Daunizeau unhurt. Aircraft abandoned.

GC II/9 Bloch 152. Lost bearings and forced-landed following pursuit of Do17s that bombed Connantre. Sgt Bernard unhurt. Aircraft damaged but repairable.

T 3 Latécoère 298. Crashed in fog on the Montagne Noire at St-Salvy-de-la-Balme, near Castres during withdrawal from Hourtin to Berre. SM Le Louarn, Mt G. Tanguy, and QM Gaston killed. Aircraft 6 a write-off.

T 3 Latécoère 298. Suffered engine trouble during flight from Hourtin to Berre and forced-landed on the Garonne at Pont-Jumeau, near Toulouse, where wrecked on a submerged cable. SM Etienne and crew unhurt. Aircraft 2 a write-off.

LUFTWAFFE

1.(H)/14 Henschel Hs126. Shot down by H-75s of GC II/4 during observation sortie south-east of Rethel 11.10 a.m. Possibly that claimed by S/Lt Cordier, S/Lt Baptizet, Sgt de la Flechère, and Sgt Posta near Annelles. Lt Schreiber wounded, Fw Wendler unhurt. Aircraft a write-off.

4.(F)/14 Dornier Do17P. Returned damaged by in attack by F/O Higgs of No. 111 Squadron during reconnaissance sortie over Le Havre 1.30 p.m. Fw F. Epp slightly wounded, rest of crew unhurt. Aircraft damage state not reported.

2.(H)/23 Henschel Hs126. Shot down by H-75s of GC II/4 during observation sortie south-east of Rethel 11.15 a.m. Possibly that claimed by S/Lt Cordier, Adjt Tesseraud, Sgt de La Chapelle, Sgt Puda, and Sgt Jaussaud near Annelles. Lt G. Peters wounded, pilot unhurt. Aircraft a write-off.

2.(H)/41 Henschel Hs126. Returned damaged in attack by Adjt Nedelec of GC III/2 near Ronchères during observation sortie between Puisieulx and Warmeriville, east of Reims, 10.30 a.m. Wachmeister E. Werner badly wounded, pilot unhurt. Aircraft damage state not recorded.

5.(F)/122 Dornier Do17P. Returned damaged in attack by Sgt Zavoral of DAT Chartres over Ablis. Hptmn Böhm (Staffelkapitän) wounded, rest of crew unhurt. Aircraft damage state not reported.

12.(N)/JG2 Messerschmitt Bf109D-1. Wrecked in flying accident at Mönchengladbach. Fw H. Tschauner killed. Aircraft a write-off.

2./JG3 Two Messerschmitt Bf109E-1s. Crash-landed badly damaged in combat with No. 111 Squadron Hurricanes during escort sortie north of Le Havre 1.30 p.m. Pilots unhurt. Aircraft both write-offs.

2./JG3 Messerschmitt Bf109E-1. Shot down in combat with No. 111 Squadron Hurricanes during escort sortie and crashed on coast between Berneval-le-Grand and Belleville-sur-Mer 1.30 p.m. Uffz L. Uth killed. Aircraft a write-off.

3./JG20 Messerschmitt Bf109E-1. Returned damaged by return fire following attack on No. 21 Squadron Blenheims south-east of Rouen 6.35 p.m. Pilot unhurt. Aircraft damaged but repairable.

6./JG26 Klemm Kl35B. Crashed near Écuires, south of Montreuil, when port wing collapsed during local weather flight. Lt K. Klammer and Stabarzt Dr F. Axmacher (of Stab II./JG26) both killed. Aircraft a write-off.

II./JG52 Messerschmitt Bf109E-1. Damaged in taxying accident. Pilot unhurt. Aircraft damaged but repairable.

I./KG1 Heinkel He111H. Returned to Ettinghausen damaged by fighters. No crew casualties. Aircraft damaged but repairable.

Stab II./KG2 Dornier Do17Z. Forced-landed with engine damaged by ground-fire during attack on roads south of Reims 9.00 a.m. No crew casualties. Aircraft U5+AC damaged but repairable.

4./KG2 Dornier Do17Z. Returned damaged by ground-fire and in attack by Lt Fabre of GC II/6 during attack on roads near Damery, south of Reims, 9.00 a.m. No crew casualties. Aircraft repairable.

4./KG2 Dornier Do17Z. Returned damaged by flak and in attack by Lt Fabre of GC II/6 during attack on roads near Damery, south of Reims, 9.00 a.m. No crew casualties. Aircraft damaged but repairable.

Stabsstaffel KG28 Dornier Do17M. Lost on sortie to Le Havre and possibly that attacked by S/L Thompson of No. 111 Squadron 1.30 p.m. Crew believed unhurt. Aircraft a write-off.

Stabsstaffel KG28 Dornier Do17M. Crash-landed damaged by fighters and flak. Possibly that attacked by F/O Bruce of No. 111 Squadron near Le Havre 1.30 p.m. Crew believed unhurt. Aircraft damaged but repairable.

I./KG51 Junkers Ju88A. Crash-landed at Mannheim damaged by flak. Crew unhurt. Aircraft damaged but repairable.

II./KG51 Junkers Ju88A. Crash-landed at Nellingen due to engine failure. Crew unhurt. Aircraft repairable.

8./KG55 Heinkel He111P. Shot down during attack on troop concentrations between Esternay and Trayes. Fw J. Markl, Uffz E. Ens, Uffz J. Ehrensberger, Uffz E. Herber, and Gefr H. Pawlik unhurt. Aircraft a write-off.

4./LG1 Junkers Ju88A. Crashed at Hannover-Langenhagen during night training flight, cause unknown. Fw W. Scholl and Flgr P. Müller badly injured, died next day. Fw W. Dester badly injured, died June 13. Uffz P. Tibusch badly injured, admitted to hospital in Hannover. Aircraft L1+FM a write-off.

9./StG51 Junkers Ju87B. Failed to return from sortie, details unknown. Crew unhurt. Aircraft a write-off.

5./ZG1 Messerschmitt Bf110C. Crashed near Haslach during return from sortie, cause unknown. Oberlt G. Schmidt (Staffelkapitän) and Uffz A. Lotz injured, admitted to hospital in Donaueschingen. Aircraft a write-off.

II./ZG1 Messerschmitt Bf110C. Forced-landed at Essen-Bochold damaged by flak. Crew unhurt. Aircraft a write-off.

Whereas Operation 'Dynamo' had run its course, the Royal Navy were now preparing Operation 'Clyde' to evacuate those north of the River Seine. At first it was hoped to use Le Havre but when it became clear that British and French troops would not be able to reach the port, the evacuation was switched 50 kilometres further up the coast to St-Valéry-en-Caux. Général Marcel Ihler, commanding the IXème Corps d'Armée, had some 40,000 men bottled up of whom around 8,000 were British — mainly from the 51st (Highland) Division under Major-General Victor Fortune. The German formation surrounding St Valery was the 7. Panzer-Division led by Generalmajor Erwin Rommel. They soon pushed through to occupy the cliffs overlooking the town which they then began to shell. The whole evacuation plan was in jeopardy when the promised ships failed to arrive during the night of June 11/12 and with the Germans breaking through the perimeter defences, there was no alternative but to surrender. Therefore, at 8 a.m. Général Ihler decided to order a cease-fire.

Wednesday, June 12

At St-Valéry-en-Caux, 24,000 British and French troops awaiting evacuation waited in vain. Their 'last possible chance', as the OC 51st Division, Major-General Fortune, described it, cruelly thwarted by fog which prevented ships from approaching the coast. A few small parties were lifted from the beach at Veules-les-Roses but the main body, now practically disarmed and unable to resist further, finally surrendered at 10.30 a.m. Unfortunately this was not known by higher command and consequently considerable effort continued to be expended by British air and naval forces in the area. Strenuous efforts to provide continuous air cover were made by Fighter Command with a total of 180 sorties flown over St-Valéry-en-Caux between 5.05 a.m. and 9.25 p.m. This, their biggest effort since the height of the Dunkirk evacuation, was achieved without engaging a single enemy aircraft — and the bulk of the effort (119 sorties) completely wasted from the point of view of the land forces.

Meantime, embarkation of French and British troops from Le Havre proceeded steadily throughout the day and into the night, and would be completed the following morning, some 24,000 troops eventually evacuated to Cherbourg where a newly-constituted BEF under Sir Alan Brooke was now concentrated.

From Vernon, German forces had penetrated to Évreux. The ring was gradually closing on Paris with the enemy across the defensive obstacles of the Seine, Marne, and Oise rivers, and now 50 miles to the west, less than 50 miles to the east, and within 20 miles to the north of the French capital. Mindful of the destruction inflicted on the cities of Warsaw and Rotterdam, Général Weygand declared Paris an open city at 1.15 p.m. all routes south out of the city clogged with traffic fleeing the German advance.

During the day British bombing effort again centred on the Seine crossings, starting with an attack by nine AASF Battles at dawn and followed by four further attacks by Battles and Blenheims, a total of 66 sorties, most of them against targets around Les Andelys. Also, around 9.30 a.m., 12 AASF Battles, responding to French requests, attacked pontoon bridges across the Oise near Verberie, Pontpoint, and south of Chevrières. Two aircraft were lost to the customary intense ground-fire but hits were claimed on all three targets.

Rommel: 'The tanks rolled slowly down the narrow winding roads, nearer and nearer to the first houses, until finally they entered the western quarter of the town. Fifty to a hundred yards away from us stood a number of British and French soldiers, irresolute, with their rifles grounded. Fires were blazing all over the farther side of the town and there was war material lying about everywhere, including large numbers of vehicles. Shortly afterwards an NCO reported to me that a high-ranking French general had been taken prisoner on the eastern side of the town and was asking to see me. A few minutes later the French Général Ihler came up to me wearing an ordinary plain military overcoat. When I asked the General what division he commanded, he replied in broken German: "No division, I command IXème Corps d'Armée".' Above: Rommel listens as an interpreter speaks to Général Ihler; General Fortune stands on the right.

At night, AASF Battles continued operations over Les Andelys while Bomber Command despatched eight Whitleys to Amiens and Aulnoye and 30 Hampdens against railway targets, roads, and river crossings, at Laon, Neufchâtel, Villers-Cotterêts, Charleville, Hirson, Recoigne, and Rethel. Fourteen aircraft failed to find their targets and one Hampden was lost when it flew into the balloon barrage at Harwich with predictable results.

With the military situation in France this day described by Général Weygand as, 'worse than dreadful: it was hopeless . . . a cessation of hostilities is compulsory . . . The war is definitely lost . . . an armistice is imperative', French intentions were abundantly clear. Neatly anticipating this possibility, a letter to Air Marshal Barratt from the Air Staff dated this day suggested preparations be made for evacuation of RAF forces. In part it read: 'You should start to make your preparations for a quick withdrawal from France . . . take all possible steps to ensure that items of equipment (including large AA guns) of which there is a particular shortage will be got out first . . . make certain that there is a refuelling base for your fighters somewhere near the coast . . . All these steps should be taken as unostentatiously as possible, as it is obvious that we should not give the French any impression that we are preparing to leave them in the lurch. The CAS feels, however, that we should be foolish not to take precautions for any unfortunate contingency that may arise . . . In the meantime every possible step is to be taken to keep your squadrons, both bombers and fighters, up to strength in aircraft and crews during the ensuing period of operations.'

Here on the quayside the drama of yesterday was played out.

BRITISH AIR FORCES IN FRANCE

88 SQUADRON, MOISY

Battle. Fuel tanks and hydraulics badly damaged by AA during attack on pontoon bridges at Verberie and Pontpoint and forced-landed on Mitry-Mory airfield 9.30 a.m. Pilot Officer J. M. Talman and Sergeant Dixon believed unhurt. Aircraft destroyed.

Battle L5334. Shot down by AA during attack on pontoon bridges at Verberie and Pontpoint and crashed near Beaurepaire 9.30 a.m. Flight Lieutenant A. L. Pitfield and Sergeant J. Ballantyne killed. Aircraft a write-off.

UK-based aircraft lost or damaged on operations over the Western Front:

RAF BOMBER COMMAND

15 Squadron, Wyton
Transport at Le Bourget:

Blenheim IV R3747. Shot down by ground-fire at Malleville-les-Grès, south-west of St-Valéry-en-Caux 12.45 p.m. P/O A. Takideli, Sgt F. V. Gunning, and Sgt D. H. Peulevé killed. Aircraft a write-off.

40 Squadron, Wyton
Battery at St Valéry-en-Caux:

Blenheim IV R3893. Shot down by flak at Életot, north-east of Fécamp, 1.30 p.m. Sgt D. L. Dorris missing. Sgt C. D. W. Bartlam and Sgt E. Rodgers baled out and captured. Aircraft a write-off.

59 Squadron, Odiham
Reconnaissance Châlons—Reims:

Blenheim IV. Forced down by Moranes during reconnaissance sortie over the Marne valley. P/O A. D. Hopkin and crew unhurt. Aircraft abandoned
Six aircraft and crews on detachment from Odiham operating from Le Mans for reconnaissance sorties over France

107 Squadron Wattisham
Concentrations at La Mare:

Blenheim IV R3810. Shot down by AA fire and crashed south-east of Rouen 11.00 a.m. P/O B. D. G. H. Reid, Sgt R. W. Lawrence, and Sgt C. A. Bartlett killed. Aircraft a write-off.

144 Squadron, Hemswell
Communications:

Hampden P4345. Collided with balloon cable near Ipswich and crashed into a flour mill at Felixstowe. W/C J. J. Watts, P/O J. F. E. Andrews, Sgt A. Winstanley, and Sgt R. Jolly killed. Aircraft a write-off.

FRENCH AIR FORCE

GAO 1/589 Potez 63.11 (309). Returned with starboard aileron damaged by ground-fire during dawn reconnaissance between Château-Thierry and Dormans. Capt M. des Pallières *(Commandant)*, S/Lt Michon, and Sgt Hamon unhurt. Aircraft repairable.

GB I/62 Martin 167F (161). Shot down by flak during bombing mission against enemy convoys around Laon, Montcornet, Rethel, and Reims. Crashed and burned out at Vézilly, east of Fère-en-Tardenois. Adjt P. Bonnefous killed. Lt Langlois and Sgt Pourkat captured wounded. Aircraft a write-off.

GB I/62 Martin 167F (34). Crash-landed on Romilly airfield, damaged by flak during sortie to attack road convoys around Laon, Montcornet, Rethel, and Reims. Cpl Vanwormhoudt slightly wounded. Sgt Bazon and Cpl Frazier unhurt. Aircraft a write-off.

GB II/62 Martin 167F (154). Shot down by flak during low-level attack on enemy columns north of Château-Thierry. Crashed at Château de Jouvence, Brécy. Lt E. Séguin and Sgt J. Masson killed. Sgt Guenou baled out and captured badly wounded, admitted to hospital Foch in Laon. Aircraft a write-off.

GB II/62 Martin 167F (133). Shot down by flak during attack on enemy columns north of Château-Thierry. Crashed at Beugneux, north-east of Oulchy-le-Château. Adjt M. Barraud and Sgt H. Panier killed. Sgt Davan captured badly wounded. Aircraft a write-off.

GB II/62 Martin 167F (60). Hit by flak during low-level attack on enemy columns north of Château-Thierry and forced-landed behind French lines. Sgt Chauvin, Adjt Chautard, and Sgt Pons wounded. Aircraft destroyed by crew.

GB II/62 Martin 167F (191). Destroyed in landing accident at Châteauroux-La Martinerie. Sgt Lousori, S/Lt Baraque, and Sgt Jaubert injured. Aircraft a write-off.

GB II/63 Martin 167F. Returned to Châteauroux-Déols with flak damage. Sgt Veneroso wounded, rest of crew unhurt. Aircraft repairable.

GBA II/51 Breguet 693 (68). Shot down by flak south of Reims during sortie to attack enemy armour between Berry-au-Bac and Bétheny 10.30 a.m. Sgt Lamy wounded. Sgt Ancelin unhurt. Aircraft a write-off.

GBA II/51 Breguet 693. Hit by flak south of Reims during sortie to attack enemy armour between Berry-au-Bac and Bétheny 10.30 a.m. Forced-landed in flames at Soudron, south-west of Châlons-en-Champagne, and burned out. Adjt Hegron and Adjt Hervier unhurt. Aircraft a write-off.

GC III/2 Curtiss H-75. Shot down by flak during reconnaissance sortie a.m. Cmdt F. Geille *(Commandant)* unhurt. Aircraft a write-off.

GC I/8 Bloch 152 (542). Destroyed in flying accident between Chaumont and Troyes 7.00 a.m. Exact circumstances not recorded; possible collision. Sgt H. Liautard slightly injured, admitted to hospital in Troyes. Aircraft a write-off.

Prior to its recovery, this Bloch 152 (serial 506) was photographed by the Germans on June 12 although it had been downed on May 14. As can be seen from the entry on page 274, **Sous-Lieutenant Pierre Gouachon-Noireault crash-landed his machine from GC I/8 beside the Suippes road near Souain. Later, unknown hands have inscribed it with reverse swastikas.**

With the fighting in the north virtually over, there was now time to examine the fruits of victory. This is the remains of the

Potez 63.11, serial 425, of Groupe de Reconnaissance I/22 which we have already seen on page 189.

GC I/8 Bloch 152. 7.00 a.m. Destroyed in flying accident between Chaumont and Troyes 7.00 a.m. Circumstances not recorded. Cpl Spacek slightly injured, admitted to hospital in Troyes. Aircraft a write-off.

GIA I/601 Farman 224 (5). Lost during transfer flight to Algiers-Maison Blanche and crashed into forest between Clairefontaine-en-Yvelines and Rambouillet. Adjt G. Lepage, Sgt P. Petriconne, and Sgt N. Gardenier killed. Adjt Dumont, Sgt Maffat, and Adjt Pinardi wounded. Soldat Rival unhurt. Aircraft a write-off.

GR I/14 Potez 63.11 (720). Fuselage collapsed on landing at Plancy-l'Abbaye due to flak damage; crashed and burned out. Sgt Le Bras, S/Lt Valin, and Sgt de Quillac unhurt. Aircraft a write-off.

GR I/14 Potez 63.11. Destroyed on the ground at Plancy-l'Abbaye; circumstances not recorded. No crew casualties. Aircraft a write-off.

LUFTWAFFE

2.(H)/12 Henschel Hs126. Returned to Daigny badly damaged by ground-fire. Obergefr H. Reiche slightly wounded, treated in hospital in Sedan. Aircraft a write-off.

2.(F)/123 Dornier Do17P. Shot down by own flak, details not recorded. Crew believed unhurt. Aircraft a write-off.

Flugbereitschaft Luftflotte 2 Heinkel He111. Crash-landed at Brussels-Evere due to engine damage. Aircraft a write-off.

III./JG53 Messerschmitt Bf109E-4. Forced-landed at Nordhausen damaged, details not recorded. Pilot unhurt. Aircraft a write-off.

III./KG1 Heinkel He111H. Undercarriage damaged on landing at Nordhausen. No crew casualties. Aircraft damaged but repairable.

I./KG51 Junkers Ju88A. Forced-landed at Lechfeld airfield due to engine failure. Lt Modrach and one crewman injured, rest of crew unhurt. Aircraft a write-off.

II./KG51 Junkers Ju88A. Forced-landed near Maisach, north of Fürstenfeldbruck, due to engine failure. No crew casualties. Aircraft damaged but repairable.

II./KG53 Heinkel He111H. Forced-landed damaged by flak near Châlons. Crew unhurt. Aircraft damaged but repairable.

Stab KG54 Heinkel He111. Shot down by Hurricanes of Nos. 17 and 242 Squadrons over Le Havre. Possibly that claimed by F/O Czernin. Oberlt Erdmann, Oberlt Meyer, and two crewmen captured. Aircraft a write-off.

Stab KG54 Heinkel He111. Shot down by Hurricanes of Nos. 17 and 242 Squadrons near Le Havre. Possibly that claimed by P/O Leary. Oberlt Winkler, Oberlt Schletz, and two crew men believed captured. Aircraft a write-off.

Stab KG54 Heinkel He111. Forced-landed damaged by Hurricanes of Nos. 17 and 242 Squadrons near Le Havre. No crew casualties. Aircraft a write-off.

III./KG54 Heinkel He111P. Crash-landed at Cologne-Ostheim. Crew unhurt. Aircraft a write-off.

8./KG76 Dornier Do17Z. Crashed on landing at Cologne-Butzweilerhof following sortie to bomb Dreux railway station. Lt A. Hotz and Fw H. Krug killed. Uffz W. Weingärtner and Uffz E. Tomczak slightly wounded, admitted to hospital in Cologne-Nippes. Aircraft a write-off.

Stab IV.(St)/LG1 Junkers Ju87B. Forced-landed at Turnhout out of petrol. Oberlt L. Schimitschek and Fw M. Heck injured. Aircraft a write-off.

II.(S)/LG2 Henschel Hs123. Hit a mine in forced-landing near Berry-au-Bois. Pilot unhurt. Aircraft damaged but repairable.

II.(S)/LG2 Henschel Hs123. Forced-landed near Soilly, south of Dormans, due to engine failure but possibly that attacked by Capt Corniglion Molinier of GC III/2. Pilot unhurt. Aircraft repairable.

I.(St)/TrGr.186 Junkers Ju87B. Hit by ground-fire north of Esternay. Oberfw H. Obermeier badly wounded, admitted to field hospital in Soissons; pilot unhurt. Aircraft damage state not reported.

Wettererkundungsstaffel 51 Heinkel He111H. Shot down by Spitfires of Nos. 64 and 610 Squadrons during weather reconnaissance over the Thames estuary 7.10 a.m. Oberlt Nissen and one crewman missing. Reg Rat Freurienberg and two crewmen killed. Aircraft a write-off.

ITALIAN AIR FORCE

14 Squadriglia, 4 Gruppo, 7 Stormo Fiat BR20. Damaged by fighters during reconnaissance sortie over Cannet des Maures, Cuers-Pierrefeu and Hyères airfields, and the port of Toulon. Crash-landed near Bergamo. Sottotenente de Michelis and crew believed unhurt. Aircraft damaged but repairable.

More visitors to the wreck of GR I/14's Potez which had lain for the last month near the perimeter of Brussels-Evere aerodrome. We last saw it on page 286.

Thursday, June 13

British forces in France were all now south of the Seine as, indeed, were forward elements of the German advance. The line defending Paris to the north had fallen back considerably and would retire even further south of the city during the night while, on a 40-mile front along the Marne between Brabant-le-Roi and Buzancy, French positions were seriously compromised. Their last lines of defence were already penetrated in two places and, unwilling to see Paris bombarded, the French High Command was pressing Prime Minister Reynaud to sue for peace.

So critical was the situation that the Air Ministry directed Air Marshal Barratt that in the event of a decisive enemy breakthrough BAFF forces should retire towards Nantes or Bordeaux. 'Your subsequent action must be dictated by the course of events, but so long as the French army is fighting you should endeavour to continue to render support. In such an event evacuation must not take place without instructions from the British government. In the event of a sudden cessation of hostilities by France you may take immediate action at your own discretion to evacuate your force as rapidly as possible to UK.'

Retirement to Nantes, the BAFF base port, would enable the five British fighter and six bomber squadrons left in France to continue operating free from any immediate threat to their airfields, and was obviously also convenient for evacuation when the time came. But it distanced what was left of the British Air Forces in France from the French Air Forces which were then retiring to the south of Orléans. Even so, by evening, Barratt ordered evacuation of his forward airfields at Châteaudun and Herbouville which were both vulnerable should the Germans chose to advance south from Dreux. The Battles of No. 75 Wing consequently made immediate preparations for the move while the Hurricanes of Nos. 1 and 242 Squadrons were instructed to proceed temporarily to Caen until a suitable airfield could be found for them near Nantes.

The scale of British daylight bombing efforts was today dictated by Churchill's undertaking to the French High Command that the RAF would provide the 'fullest air support' to slow the German advance. But the 102 sorties flown by AASF Battles and No. 2 Group Blenheims throughout the day were hampered by bad weather and countered by flak and enemy fighters which, due to the apparent absence of any Allied fighter cover, resulted in the loss of 18 bombers. French medium bombers also struck at advancing German columns throughout the day losing 12 aircraft.

Surviving records are incomplete but it seems that BAFF fighter operations were severely hampered by the weather apart from sorties from Caen that patrolled the Seine and over Le Havre. Wasteful cover flights also continued over St Valéry-en-Caux until the evening when news of the surrender of the 51st Division finally reached BAFF headquarters. Fighter Command effort was also drastically reduced from that of the previous day, its fighters being held in readiness for anticipated raids on Cherbourg which did not materialise. In direct contrast, French fighters flew a total of 116 sorties and lost six fighters, one of the pilots being killed and another four wounded.

Meantime, on the southern front, the Italian Air Force launched two well-planned attacks on the French airfields at Fayence and Hyères to precede a bombing raid on nearby Toulon. Fiat CR42 fighters of 23 Gruppo strafed Fayence while those of 151 Gruppo attacked Hyères together claiming

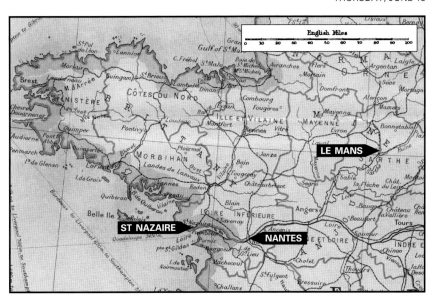

Nantes was now the evacuation base for the remaining RAF squadrons in France.

over 20 French aircraft destroyed on the ground. Lack of co-ordination resulted in the BR20 bombers of 11 and 43 Gruppi arriving over the airfields 15 minutes after these preliminary attacks when French fighters were fully alerted. Two BR20s were lost from the force attacking Hyères, another returning damaged, while the follow-up attack on Toulon went largely unhindered though two more BR20s of 4 Gruppo returned with minor damage. Thus, recognising that Italy was not going to remain passive, Général Vuillemin indicated that 'Haddock Force' could resume operations, so recall to England of the RAF Wellingtons based in southern France for operations against Italy was cancelled.

AASF Battles, already stretched beyond the limit, did not operate this night having exceeded their maximum effort during the day, but Bomber Command despatched 164 heavy bombers over the Seine and Marne fronts, making their biggest effort of the campaign to date. One Wellington was lost.

French troop redispositions during the night made Paris an open city, the French decision not to defend their capital also prohibiting British aircraft over-flying it. More seriously, these troop movements also weakened the Allied line between Caen and Tours. It was clear that the remnants of the BEF still positioned around Le Mans would be insufficient to counter an enemy advance from that direction and this made Nantes vulnerable. This disturbing development left Barratt no option but to recommend the immediate withdrawal of what remained of the British Air Forces in France

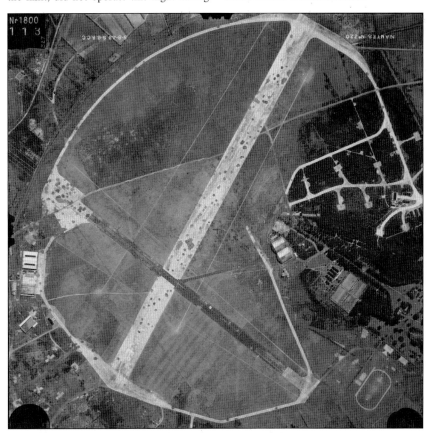

This photograph from 1949 shows much evidence of wartime bombing.

BRITISH AIR FORCES IN FRANCE

12 SQUADRON, SOUGÉ

Battle L5580. Shot down by ground-fire and Bf109s of I./JG27 during attack on enemy armour reported in the Forêt de Gault and belly-landed at Château de la Noue, north of Sézanne. Possibly that claimed by Fw Arnold of 2./JG27 near Montmirail 6.55 p.m. Pilot Officer R. C. L. Parkhouse, Sergeant A. R. Morris, and LAC D. A. MacDonald captured. Aircraft PH⊙X a write-off.

Battle L5324. Shot down by ground-fire and Bf109s of I./JG27 during attack on enemy armour in the Forêt de Gault; crashed and burned out near St Barthélémy. Possibly that claimed by Oberlt Redlich (Staffelkapitän) of 1./JG27 near Montmirail 7.05 p.m. Sergeant N. C. Cotterell killed. Pilot Officer J. S. Shorthouse and LAC Copley both admitted to hospital badly burned. Aircraft PH⊙A a write-off.

Battle L5531. Shot down by ground-fire and Bf109s of I./JG27 during attack on enemy armour in the Forêt de Gault and belly-landed by the road between Esternay and St-Martin-du-Boschet 7.00 p.m. Pilot Officer J. F. McPhie, Sergeant C. S. G. Beevers, and LAC J. G. Thomson captured. Aircraft fired by crew.

73 SQUADRON, RUAUDIN

Hurricane. Wrecked in landing accident following routine patrol. Pilot Officer D. N. W. L. Anthony badly injured, died next day. Aircraft a write-off.

88 SQUADRON, MOISY

Battle. Shot down over Provins by Uffz Neef and Oberlt Redlich (Staffelkapitän) of 1./JG27 during sortie to attack enemy armour reported in the Forêt de Gault 3.35 p.m. Sergeant D. Haywood and Sergeant J. R. A. Jones both captured wounded, admitted to hospital in Sens. Aircraft a write-off.

Just like tourists in a foreign country, this party of sightseers seize an opportunity for a photo posing on the remains of a British Battle. This is the remains of L5397 of No. 142 Squadron which returned slightly damaged on June 13 and was further damaged next day. It was one of three aircraft that were destroyed to prevent capture when Villiersfaux was evacuated two days later.

142 SQUADRON, VILLIERSFAUX

Battle. Failed to return from night attack on Gisors and crashed near Les Corvées-les-Yys, south-west of Chartres, early a.m. Flight Lieutenant A. D. J. Martin, Sergeant E. F. W. Curtis, and Sergeant G. H. Kettlewell killed. Aircraft a write-off.

Battle. Shot down by fighters east of Évreux during attack on enemy columns between Pacy and Vernon; crash-landed with port fuel tank in flames. Possibly that claimed by Lt Sprick of 8./JG26 near Paris 11.39 a.m. Flight Lieutenant J. M. Hewson unhurt. LAC R. S. Utteridge wounded in head admitted to hospital in Chartres where later captured. Sergeant R. V. T. Kitto baled out unhurt, reached England via St Malo. Aircraft a write-off.

Battle. Shot down by fighters east of Évreux during attack on enemy columns between Pacy and Vernon and possibly that claimed by Lt Ebeling of 8./JG26 near Paris 11.40 a.m. Pilot Officer K. R. Sutton believed unhurt. Sergeant Rudd wounded in head and Sergeant B. J. Rowe wounded left leg, both admitted to hospital. Aircraft a write-off.

Battle L5397. Returned damaged by fighters during sortie to attack enemy columns between Pacy and Vernon 11.45 a.m. Pilot Officer W. D. K. Franklin, and LAC Rounds unhurt. Sergeant Pollock wounded in legs admitted to hospital. Aircraft repairable.

Battle. Failed to return from attack on armoured columns near Montmirail and believed that claimed by Lt Strobl of 5./JG27 over Romilly-sur-Seine 5.30 p.m. Sergeant D. J. Holliday, Sergeant D. A. Whiting, and AC T. Greenall captured. Aircraft a write-off.

150 SQUADRON, HOUSSAY

Battle L5524. Shot down by Uffz Vollmer of 3./JG3 during attack on enemy columns between Vernon and Évreux, crash-landed and burned out near Aigleville 9.30 a.m. Pilot Officer A. R. Gulley killed. Sergeant H. Berry and LAC D. L. Phillips both captured. Aircraft a write-off.

The date of death of Alfred Gulley is recorded by the Commonwealth War Graves Commission as June 14. LAC Donald Phillips was later reported a prisoner in hospital in Amiens but subsequently escaped and successfully evaded eventually returning to England via Gibraltar. He was the first RAF airman to be awarded the Military Medal for escape and evasion.

Battle L5437. Shot down by Lt Stange of 3./JG3 during attack on enemy columns between Vernon and Évreux, and crashed at Merey 9.30 a.m. Pilot Officer R. C. Beale, Sergeant H. J. F. Tutt, and Sergeant D. B. Carter killed. Aircraft a write-off.

Battle L5474. Returned badly damaged by Bf109s of I./JG27 during attack on enemy armour in the Forêt de Gault Possibly that claimed by Fw Kothmann of 2./JG27 over Montmirail 7.31 p.m. Pilot Officer C. H. Elliott, Sergeant Gupwell, and LAC Kirk unhurt. Aircraft damaged but repairable — later abandoned.

Battle L5591. Set alight by Bf109s of I./JG27 during attack on enemy armour in the Forêt de Gault and crash-landed on fire north of Rebais. Possibly that claimed by Fw Mitsdörffer of 1./JG27 over Montmirail 7.55 p.m. Squadron Leader R. M. Bradley slightly wounded in leg and arm, Flight Sergeant A. Leitch unhurt. LAC Rickard badly wounded in arm and leg, admitted to hospital. Aircraft a write-off.

The wreckage of Battle L5524 in which the pilot was killed is guarded, possibly pending the removal of his body. Pilot Officer Alfred Gulley of No. 150 Squadron crashed on June 13 although his death is recorded on his headstone in Aigleville Churchyard, 12 miles east of Évreux, as June 14.

226 SQUADRON, FAUX-VILLECERF

Battle P2161. Shot down during attack on enemy troop concentrations south-west of Montmirail and crashed near La Chapelle-Moutils. Possibly that claimed by Lt Wick of 3./JG2 between Montpothier and Provins 8.10 p.m. Sergeant E. E. Hopkins captured unhurt. Sergeant J. B. Callaghan and Sergeant L. Turner both killed. Aircraft a write-off.

UK-based aircraft lost or damaged on operations over the Western Front:

RAF BOMBER COMMAND

21 Squadron, Bodney
Armour in Forêt de Gault:

Blenheim IV L9269. Forced-landed damaged by ground-fire 4.30 p.m. F/Lt L. V. E. Petley, Sgt Hart, and Sgt Norris believed captured unhurt. Aircraft abandoned.

Blenheim IV R3676. Shot down by ground-fire and crashed at St Hilliers, north-west of Provins, 4.50 p.m. P/O L. M. Blanckensee, Sgt A. Williams, and Sgt J. Guest killed. Aircraft a write-off.

82 Squadron, Watton
Armour in Forêt de Gault:

Blenheim IV L8829. Crashed in the North Sea during return from sortie 4.00 p.m. Sgt A. E. Merritt and Sgt N. W. Carlile killed. Sgt L. D. Nineham missing. Aircraft UX⊙P lost.
The bodies of Albert Merritt and Neville Carlile were both later recovered from the sea and are now interred at Sage in Germany and Harlingen in Holland respectively, but Leslie Nineham has no known grave.

Blenheim IV P6910. Shot down by Hptmn Balthasar *(Staffelkapitän)* of 1./JG1 and crashed at Courgivaux, south-west of Esternay, 5.20 p.m. Sgt K. H. Harris killed. F/Lt J. C. Breese and Sgt H. H. Williams captured. Aircraft UX⊙X a write-off.

Blenheim IV P6925. Shot down by Hptmn Gerlitz of 1./JG1 during sortie to attack armoured columns north-west of Sézanne 5.20 p.m. P/O R. E. Williams, Sgt D. Carbutt, and Sgt A. S. Beeby believed unhurt. Aircraft UX⊙Z a write-off.

107 Squadron, Wattisham
Seine Bridge at Vernon:

Blenheim R3616. Believed shot down by Uffz Nelleskamp of 5./JG3 and crashed near Caugé, west of Évreux, 3.45 p.m. P/O A. F. Stidtson, Sgt F. C. Higgins, and Sgt J. R. Browning killed. Aircraft a write-off.

RAF COASTAL COMMAND

500 Squadron, Detling

Anson I N5225. Crashed in the North Sea during convoy escort sortie, circumstances unknown, 10.00 p.m. F/O R. K. Curzon, Sgt N. J. Sparks, LAC G. A. Mitchell, and AC1 L. V. Pepper missing. Aircraft MK⊙M lost.
The rank of George Mitchell is recorded by the CWGC as Sergeant.

RAF FIGHTER COMMAND

266 Squadron, Martlesham Heath

Spitfire N3094. Overshot runway on landing. Sgt F. B. Hawley unhurt. Aircraft damaged but repairable.

FRENCH AIR FORCE

AB 3 Vought 156F (6). Shot down by Fiat CR42s of 151 Gruppo and crashed on beach while landing at Hyères following training flight 11.15 a.m. SM Le Droucpeet and QM Lucas killed. Aircraft a write-off.

GAO 518 Potez 63.11. Damaged by flak and forced-landed during reconnaissance sortie over sector Stenay, Montmédy, Longuyon and Verdun. Adjt Ecalle and crew unhurt. Aircraft destroyed to prevent capture.

GAO 3/551 Potez 63.11 (384). Shot down during observation of enemy troop movements around Évreux and crashed near the Beaumont forest at Sainte-Marguerite-en-Ouche. Possibly that claimed by Oberlt Oesau *(Staffelkapitän)* of 1./JG20 south-west of Les Andelys 2.41 p.m. Lt E. de Ginestet, Adjt R. Berland, and Sgt L. Girard killed. Aircraft a write-off.

GAO 581 Potez 63.11. Returned severely damaged by flak during low-level observation of enemy movements south of Montmirail 1.30 p.m. Capt F. Mermet badly wounded, died in hospital at Troyes. Sgt Varet and Cpl Duval unhurt. Aircraft a write-off.

GAO 1/589 Potez 63.11 (309). Returned damaged after hitting a telegraph pole while low-flying to avoid ground-fire near Montmirail. Lt Lallou, Sgt Rousseau, and Sgt L'Heritier unhurt. Aircraft damaged but repairable.

GB 1/11 LeO 451 (276). Shot down by Hptmn Balthasar *(Staffelkapitän)* of 1./JG1 during attack on motorised column near Châlons-en-Champagne and crashed west of Quincey church, 2 km south-east of St Aubin 4.50 p.m. S/Lt A. Lefage baled out but parachute failed and killed. Capt Heriard-Dubreuil *(Commandant)* baled out unhurt. Adjt Colin and Adjt Gourron baled out wounded, admitted to hospital at Nogent-sur-Seine. Aircraft a write-off.
Due to evacuation of the local population, the body of André Lefage was not recovered for burial at St Aubin until June 21.

Another British fatality on June 13 was that of Sergeant Kenneth Harris when Blenheim P6910 of No. 82 Squadron was brought down by the German ace Hauptmann Wilhelm Balthasar of JG1. (As No. 82 was a Bomber Command unit operating from the UK, his name does not appear on our Roll of Honour on pages 500-529 which lists only those killed while flying from French soil.)

Although several years behind their British counterparts whose frantic exploits at investigating and excavating crashed aircraft dominated the years between 1970 and 1990, French aviation archaeologists have not been idle. These finds were made by Pierre Ben from French aircraft losses which came down on May 20. Discovery of the serial plate is paramount to proving the identity of a crash site and in the case of the Morane 406 of Sergeant Pagès of GC I/6, Pierre came up trumps (see page 334).

GB II/11 Bloch 210. Failed to return from night-bombing sortie to attack oil reservoirs at Vado-Ligure, Italy. S/Lt Poher, Sgt Rannoux, Adjt Senciel, and Sgt Yvernault missing. Aircraft lost.

GB I/19 Douglas DB-7 (10). Forced-landed on one wheel at Lissay-Lochy damaged by Bf110 during sortie to attack road convoys between Montmirail and Compiègne 3.00 p.m. Capt Couilleau (Commandant), S/Lt Guelin, and Sgt Caneau unhurt. Aircraft a write-off.

GB I/19 Douglas DB-7 (43). Forced-landed near Provins during sortie to attack road convoys between Montmirail and Compiègne 7.15 p.m. Crew unhurt. Aircraft destroyed by crew.

GB II/19 Douglas DB-7 (35). Shot down by Oberlt Homuth (Staffelkapitän) of 3./JG27 and crash-landed with starboard engine on fire, hit high-tension cables and overturned outside Léchelle, north-east of Provins, 7.20 p.m. S/Lt P. Defaye and Sgt F. Estève killed. Sgt Vincent badly wounded, admitted to hospital in Moulins and later captured. Aircraft a write-off.

GB I/21 Amiot 354 (7). Wrecked in forced-landing after attack on motorised column near Châlons-en-Champagne. Lt Descamp injured. Adjt Bordenet, Sgt Puivif, and Sgt Armanet unhurt. Aircraft a write-off.

GB I/21 Amiot 354 (64). Damaged by flak during evening attack on enemy armour south of Montmirail and crashed into a hill near Sancerre. Lt E. Turrel killed, Adjt Sabourault badly wounded, rest of crew unhurt. Aircraft a write-off.

GB I/21 Amiot 354 (12). Shot down by flak during evening attack on armour south of Montmirail and crashed near Avord. S/Lt Dupont, S/Lt Dumond, Sgt Raoul, and Sgt Chaltet killed. Aircraft a write-off.

GB 4/23 LeO 451 (154). Suffered direct hit by flak and exploded at 'L'Aubrot' outside Couvrot, north of Vitry-le-François, during bombing attack on road to Châlons-sur-Marne. Capt A. Lachaux (Commandant), Adjt J. Bauer, and Adjt R. Terrières killed. Sgt Petermann baled out and captured wounded in legs and with burns to face. Aircraft a write-off.

GB II/31 LeO 451 (275). Badly damaged by flak during low-level bombing attack on armoured columns near Mourmelon and crashed on landing. Lt Pré, Sgt Alexandre, Sgt Mesples, and Cpl Bardon unhurt. Aircraft a write-off.

GBA I/51 Breguet 693. Shot down by flak during attack on motorised columns north-east of Esternay 3.30 p.m. Crashed and burned out near Saint-Bon. Sgt Névraumont and Sgt Douzet unhurt. Aircraft a write-off.

GBA I/54 Breguet 693 (79). Shot down by intense flak during bombing attack on motorised columns south of Reims 8.45 a.m. Crashed and burned out at Fontenailles, west of Nangis. Sgt J. Paulin and Adjt G. Moroge killed. Aircraft a write-off.

GBA I/54 Breguet 693 (53). Port engine hit by flak during bombing attack on motorised columns south of Reims 8.45 a.m. Crash-landed alongside the road between La Ferté-Gaucher and Courtacon. Sgt Petitpain wounded in right leg. Capt Petitguillaume unhurt. Aircraft destroyed by crew.

GC III/2 Curtiss H-75 (262). Forced-landed at Vaupoisson, south-east of Arcis-sur-Aube, due to engine failure 8.15 a.m. S/Lt Dartevelle unhurt. Aircraft abandoned.

GC III/2 Curtiss H-75 (247). Shot down in attack on Ju87s of II./StG77 and combat with Bf109s of 2./JG27 between Montmirail and Esternay 11.30 a.m. Crashed and burned out at Montceaux-lès-Provins. Possibly that claimed by Uffz Brehm of Stab StG77. Cmdt F. Geille (Commandant) baled out badly burned on face, admitted to Auxerre hospital. Aircraft a write-off.

GC III/2 Curtiss H-75 (236). Badly damaged during attack on Ju87s of II./StG77 and combat with Bf109s of 2./JG27 south of Montmirail and crash-landed at La Noue 11.30 a.m. S/Lt A. Lansoy wounded in left arm. Aircraft a write-off.

GC III/2 Curtiss H-75 (264). Shot down by Uffz Kaiser of 2./JG27 in combat south of Montmirail, crashed and burned out near Champguyon 11.20 a.m. Adjt M. Romey killed. Aircraft a write-off.
Maurice Romey was eventually recovered and buried at Champguyon on October 17, 1942.

GC 6/2 Curtiss H-75. Returned to Auxerre with cockpit damaged following patrol north of Esternay 11.30 a.m. Lt Dubreuil unhurt. Aircraft repairable.

GC II/3 Dewoitine 520. Badly damaged in combat with Bf110s over Montmirail and forced-landed south of Nogent-sur-Seine 4.30 p.m. S/Lt de Solminihac wounded. Aircraft a write-off.

GC II/3 Dewoitine 520. Destroyed in landing accident following transit flight 6.00 p.m. Lt J. Gleich killed. Aircraft a write-off.

GC III/3 Dewoitine 520 (171). Badly damaged by Bf110 during attack on Ju87 over Troyes and forced-landed near Romilly. Sgt R. Claireaux wounded in head and hand. Aircraft a write-off.

GC II/10 Bloch 152 (690). Shot down by flak near Aigle during reconnaissance sortie p.m. S/Lt Goetz unhurt. Aircraft a write-off.

GR I/14 Potez 63.11 (205). Returned riddled by ground-fire during reconnaissance sortie and crashed on landing at Troyes-Barberey. Adjt Prual badly wounded. Lt Meric and S/Lt Pommares unhurt. Aircraft a write-off.

GR II/55 Potez 63.11 (355). Returned to Blois badly damaged by flak during reconnaissance sortie over Vernon. S/Lt Salles wounded in head and back. Sgt Granier slightly wounded. Sgt Avon unhurt. Aircraft a write-off.

Likewise he found the serial number on wreckage of a second Morane — the one flown by Sous-Lieutenant Duchène-Marulaz.

LUFTWAFFE

Aufklärungsstaffel I. Fliegerkorps Dornier Do17P. Shot down during reconnaissance near Château-Thierry. Hptmn H. Lorenz and Oberlt K-W. Konradt killed, another crewman wounded. Aircraft a write-off.

Flugbereitschaft I. Fliegerkorps Bücker Bü131. Crash-landed near Bézu-la-Forêt, south-west of Gournay-en-Bray. No casualties reported. Aircraft damaged but repairable.

2./JG27 Messerschmitt Bf109E-4. Shot down in combat with H-75s of GC III/2 over Montmirail during escort sortie for Ju87s of II./StG77 to Esternay 11.35 a.m. Uffz E. Kaiser captured unhurt. Aircraft a write-off.
This loss is recorded on June 12 in the Luftwaffe General Quartermaster's Returns.

II./JG53 Messerschmitt Bf109E-1. Belly-landed at Dinant, cause not stated. Pilot unhurt. Aircraft a write-off.

III./KG1 Heinkel He111H. Crash-landed at Poix due to engine failure. No crew casualties. Aircraft damaged but repairable.

II./KG3 Dornier Do17Z. Returned damaged by flak. No crew casualties. Aircraft repairable.

9./KG4 Junkers Ju88A-1 (0244). Crashed near Amsterdam, cause unknown. Fw R. Haeberle, Fw H-O. Steeger, Uffz O. Pacholleck, and Uffz W. Streubel killed. Aircraft 5J+JT a write-off.

4./KG27 Heinkel He111P. One engine damaged in attacks by P/O Eliot and other Hurricanes of No. 73 Squadron during sortie to attack shipping at Le Havre and crashed-landed north of Bolbec. Uffz W. Krause badly wounded, died June 16. Uffz W. Müller also badly wounded, rest of crew unhurt. Aircraft 1G+DM damaged but repairable..

2./KGr.126 Heinkel He111H. Reportedly attacked by night-fighter during mine-laying sortie and both engines damaged. Crash-landed at Dranouter, north-east of Hazebrouck, 12.30 a.m. Lt G. Schulz, Lt zur See H. Müller, Uffz K-W. Schlegel, Uffz H. Müller, and Oberfw H. Kaselitz (of 1./KG4) badly wounded, admitted to hospital in Ypres. Aircraft a write-off.

IV./KGzbV.1 Junkers Ju52 (6499). Crash-landed Laon, cause unknown. Crew believed unhurt. Aircraft damage state not reported.

IV./KGzbV.1 Junkers Ju52 (5373). Crash-landed Esternay, cause unknown. Crew believed unhurt. Aircraft damaged but repairable.

5.(S)/LG2 Henschel Hs123. Returned damaged by ground-fire over Montmort, south of Reims. Hptmn E. Thiem *(Staffelkapitän)* slightly wounded. Aircraft damaged but repairable.

6./StG77 Junkers Ju87B. Shot down by H-75s of GC III/2 south of Montmirail during sortie to attack Esternay railway station 11.35 a.m. Fw R. Barthle slightly wounded and Uffz W. Nolte badly wounded, both captured and admitted to hospital. Aircraft a write-off.

1./ZG26 Messerschmitt Bf110C (3258). Shot down by AA fire and crashed near La Houssoye, south-west of Beauvais. Fw W. Weis and Uffz H. Bornkessel killed. Aircraft U8+EH a write-off.

1./ZG26 Messerschmitt Bf110C. Shot down by AA fire near Chartres. Crew unhurt. Aircraft a write-off.

I./ZG26 Messerschmitt Bf110C. Returned damaged by AA fire over Chartres. Aircraft damaged but repairable.

The Italian Regia Aeronautica possessed over 200 Fiat BR20s — the twin-engined light bomber which had first seen service in the Spanish Civil War.

ITALIAN AIR FORCE

3 Squadriglia, 43 Gruppo, 13 Stormo Fiat BR20 (MM21503). Engaged by GC III/6 over Porquerolles during sortie to attack Hyères airfield and badly damaged in attacks by Adjt Le Gloan and Adjt Goujon. Ditched in the sea off Arma di Taggia 11. 30 a.m. Tenente S. Catalano, Sgt Ferrari, and Cpl Gaeta killed. Maresciallo Aliani and Cpl Farris rescued by fishing boat and captured unhurt. Aircraft lost.
Remains of this aircraft, still relatively intact, located sitting on its belly on the sea bed.

3 Squadriglia, 43 Gruppo, 13 Stormo Fiat BR20 (MM21504). Returned damaged by Adjt Le Gloan, Lt Martin, and Adjt Goujon of GC III/6 engaged near Porquerolles during sortie to attack Hyères airfield 11.15 a.m. Sottotenente Rondinelli died of wounds, two other crewmen wounded, rest of crew unhurt. Aircraft damaged but repairable.

3 Squadriglia, 43 Gruppo, 13 Stormo Fiat BR20 (MM21505). Engaged by GC III/6 over Porquerolles during sortie to attack Hyères airfield and shot down in sea off Agay by Adjt Le Gloan and Adjt Goujon 11. 30 a.m. Tenente A. Sammartano baled out but believed drowned. Sgt G. Goracci and Sgt M. Costa baled out but killed. Cpl N. Vannuzzo baled out and captured wounded. Cpl R. Mangiarotti baled out and captured unhurt. Aircraft lost.
Mario Costa was shot while in his parachute and Giuseppe Goracci lynched on landing by a frenzied mob.

15 Squadriglia, 4 Gruppo, 7 Stormo Fiat BR20 (MM21917). Returned damaged in attack by six Bloch 151s of AC 3 over Hyères during sortie to bomb Toulon 11.40 a.m. One crewman wounded. Aircraft damaged but repairable.

15 Squadriglia, 4 Gruppo, 7 Stormo Fiat BR20. Returned starboard engine damaged in attack by six Bloch 151s of AC 3 over Hyères during sortie to bomb Toulon 11.40 a.m. Tenente Zucconi and crew believed unhurt. Aircraft damaged but repairable.

BR20 (MM21503) from the 3rd Squadron of the 43rd Group attacked by GC III/6 off Hyères and forced to ditch in the sea. Sixty years later, its remains were discovered by professional divers and photographed by Patrice Strazzera lying on the seabed.

Friday, June 14

At 5.30 a.m. the German 9. Infanterie-Division entered Paris, a triumphal parade down the Champs Elysées taking place that same afternoon. Elsewhere, enemy forces were pressing the now disparate French armies to retire further south of the Seine. And though a German assault on the Saar front was repulsed, and Italian troops made no progress in the south-east, this offered little consolation to the now routed French army.

As British forces in France prepared to evacuate, ships were sent from England to Cherbourg, Brest, St-Nazaire, and St Malo. General Brooke and Air Marshal Barratt were instructed that they were no longer under French military control and should withdraw their forces to convenient ports and evacuate all surplus personnel and stores. And, apart from a night attack on Italy by 'Haddock Force', the BAFF was forthwith relieved from any further co-operation with the French and instructed to concentrate exclusively on protecting the BEF withdrawal.

British daylight bombing thus aimed at German penetrations around Évreux but bad weather again prevented any decisive results and enemy fighters, now operating as far south as Chartres from recently occupied French airfields, contributed to the loss of six Battles and three Blenheims during the day.

Fighter Command despatched 190 sorties over northern France between 4.25 a.m. and 9.15 p.m., their maximum effort since Dunkirk. The ten squadrons involved each flew two sorties but, apparently, without engaging enemy aircraft for no combats resulted. AASF Hurricanes reported several combats during the day but surviving records are fragmentary and unreliable — a reflection of the uncertain times. French fighters flew 120 sorties claiming three victories for the loss of two aircraft in combat.

At night the Seine crossings at Pont-de-l'Arche, Les Andelys, and Vernon, were each visited by a single British heavy bomber, plans to despatch ten aircraft against these targets being scrubbed due to bad weather and the possibility of intense operations the following night. Similarly, a single Whitley delivered its attack on Soissons while another visited Château-Thierry, five others being recalled after take-off.

The approach to Saumur seethed with a mass of refugees, walking, pushing heavily-laden bicycles and wheel-barrows, or making what speed was possible on cars, which were little recognisable as such under their considerable top hamper of luggage and household gear. Under a blazing sun, progress at the rate of approximately one m.p.h. was made towards the two bridges spanning the Loire at this point but which, owing to the mining activities taking place at this eleventh hour, could only accommodate a single, one-way stream of traffic. There was also the danger from bombed and burned-out buildings falling upon passing traffic but the biggest nuisance of all was the poor, scared refugees, so much so, that 73 Squadron had to take over traffic control. Three motor-cycle despatch riders spread themselves out abreast at the head of the inextricably mixed column of service vehicles, farm waggons, old cars laden to the limit and beyond, limousines dragging trailers, motor-coaches full of sick, aged persons and children in a triple tightly-wedged column, heading urgently in one direction.

At long last the bridges were negotiated and the convoy managed to proceed towards the aerodrome perched high up on a sun-baked plateau where a French training squadron was already hastily packing up, prior to evacuation. The aerodrome and city were absolutely at the mercy of the enemy bombers, one of which was at this moment circling lazily overhead with not a single puff of A.A. fire even to disturb its business of taking notes.

There was little natural cover for our dispersed vehicles and our aircraft were not to join us, either, having been detailed to operate from Nantes. The magnificent, uncamouflaged target of newly-built hutments beside the aerodrome were viewed askance. At any other time the men would have rushed at such tempting billets, especially after suffering so long in tents, barns and lofts, but now the stifling interior of a camouflaged tent, removed from the aerodrome, held far greater attraction. Tired as they were, the old familiar game of trench-digging recommenced but we found, after nine months of wartime and warning, that there was only provision for one hundred men, in two covered trench systems. Granted, it must have proved devilish hard work to dig even these; for shale and rock lay immediately under the thin layer of turf but with provision made in those huts for one thousand men or so, surely it was criminal to have forced them to depend upon the shelter of the hedgeside for protection.

FLYING OFFICER HENRY HALL, No. 73 SQUADRON, JUNE 1940

BRITISH AIR FORCES IN FRANCE

1 SQUADRON, NANTES-CHÂTEAU BOUGON

Hurricane. Failed to return from shipping escort patrol over St-Nazaire, details not recorded. Flight Lieutenant F. Warcup baled out and captured. Aircraft a write-off.

Hurricane. Failed to return from shipping escort patrol over St-Nazaire, details not recorded. Flight Lieutenant M. H. Brown baled out unhurt. Aircraft a write-off.

12 SQUADRON, SOUGÉ

Battle L5396. Badly damaged by Bf109 during attack on woods south-east of Évreux and crashed near Coulonges-Ardennes 4.00 p.m. Probably that claimed by Lt Landry of 2./JG3. Sergeant D. L. Grant killed. Pilot Officer P. H. Blowfield unhurt, evaded but later killed in ground fighting near Les Minières. Sergeant J. J. C. Batty evaded successfully and returned unhurt. Aircraft a write-off.

Battle L5383. Shot down by Bf109s during attack on woods south-east of Évreux and crashed near Pacy-sur-Eure 4.00 p.m. Probably that claimed by Lt Tiedmann of 2./JG3. Sergeant R. J. Willcox, Sergeant G. H. Emery, and Flight Sergeant J. Hislop killed. Aircraft PH⊙F a write-off.

Battle. Caught fire during night bombing attack on the airfield. No crew casualties. Aircraft a write-off.

Squadron records are incomplete, but three aircraft (L5328, N2150, PH⊙Y, and P5231) were reported 'lost in France' for which no further details are known. Nine surviving aircraft left for England next day.

88 SQUADRON, SOUGÉ

Battle. Destroyed in night bombing attack on the airfield. No crew casualties. Aircraft a write-off.

103 SQUADRON, SOUGÉ

Battle. Believed shot down by Hptmn Tietzen of 5./JG51 during attack on armoured column in woods south-west of Évreux 7.15 p.m. Flying Officer R. Hawkins and Pilot Officer F. Hugill captured unhurt. Aircraft a write-off.

Hawkins managed to escape and evaded successfully through Vichy France, eventually reaching England via neutral Spain.

Battle. Badly damaged in attack on armoured column in woods south-west of Évreux and crash-landed in an orchard near Laval during return flight 7.30 p.m. Sgt Brumby, Sgt Hedley, and LAC Werner unhurt. Aircraft a write-off.

Four Battles. Destroyed or badly damaged in low-level attack on airfield by Bf110s 5.00 p.m. Sergeant Bone wounded. Aircraft all write-offs — abandoned on evacuation next day.

142 SQUADRON, VILLIERSFAUX

Battle L5397. Returned badly damaged following attack on enemy aircraft at Évreux. Crew believed unhurt. Aircraft a write-off.

A Potez 63.11 sits abandoned on an unidentified French airfield to provide the ideal backdrop for a snapshot for another member of the victorious Wehrmacht. Its colourful rudder canvas has already proved irresistible to souvenir hunters.

226 SQUADRON, FAUX-VILLECERF

Battle P2335. Failed to return from attack on enemy armour and believed crashed near Breux-sur-Avre. Possibly that claimed by Hptmn Ebbighausen (*Staffelkapitän*) of 4./JG26 south of Vernon 4.53 p.m. Flying Officer K. N. Rea killed. Sergeant F. Nixon missing. Sergeant H. P. White captured seriously wounded, died in Doullens hospital August 2, 1940. Aircraft WT⊙N a write-off.

242 SQUADRON, LE MANS

Hurricane. Became separated and lost bearings following combat with Bf110s of 9./ZG26 over Conches 4.05 p.m. Wrecked undercarriage by hitting a ditch during forced-landing near Blain, north of Nantes. Pilot Officer N. K. Stansfeld unhurt. Aircraft a write-off.

UK-based aircraft lost or damaged on operations over the Western Front:

RAF BOMBER COMMAND

9 Squadron, Honington
Seine River crossings:

Wellington L7787. Crashed at Drosay, northwest of Doudeville, during night sortie to bomb Pont-de-l'Arche, south of Rouen, early a.m. Sgt R. Hewitt, Sgt F. R. Edwards, Sgt L. W. Routledge, Sgt F. D. Hardy, Sgt S. F. Youngson, and Sgt C. B. Kircher killed. Aircraft WS⊙J a write-off.

21 Squadron, Bodney
Merville airfield:

Blenheim IV R3742. Last seen pursued by Bf109s following attack on Merville airfield 6.36 p.m. P/O W. A. Saunders missing. Sgt W. H. Eden and Sgt C. Webb captured. Aircraft a write-off.

Despite bombs being seen to fall amongst aircraft on the ground in what the RAF narrative describes as this 'very successful' attack by 24 Blenheims, no record of any losses or casualties has been found in German records.

40 Squadron, Wyton
Troop concentrations Évreux — Vernon:

Blenheim IV N3592. Shot down by Hptmn Galland (*Gruppenkommandeur*) of Stab III./JG26 and crashed near Fresney, south-east of Évreux, 4.15 p.m. S/L G. W. C. Gleed, Sgt R. W. Burge, and Sgt A. F. W. Sammells killed. Aircraft BL⊙C a write-off.

Blenheim IV R3693. Crashed near Garancières-en-Drouais following attack by Lt Blume of 7./JG26 near Dreux 4.40 p.m. and possibly that earlier attacked by Hptmn Galland (*Gruppenkommandeur*) of Stab III./JG26 south of Évreux. P/O Lewis and Sgt Currie believed captured. Sgt S. W. Johnson killed. Aircraft a write-off.

Blenheim IV R3745. Forced-landed at Bicester with oil tank damaged en route to target 3.30 p.m. P/O Bowler, Sgt Coburn, and Sgt Shawyers unhurt. Aircraft repairable.

53 Squadron, Gatwick
Reconnaissance:

Blenheim IV R3632. Returned damaged by ground fire near Elbeuf 2.30 p.m. F/Lt A. D. Panton, Sgt McRae, and Sgt Nisbett unhurt. Aircraft repairable.

Aircraft detached for reconnaissance duties in France and operating from Nantes for HQ BAFF.

FRENCH AIR FORCE

DAT Châteaudun Bloch 152. Forced-landed due to engine failure following engagement with Bf109s over Étampes. Sgt M. Machowiak unhurt. Aircraft damaged but repairable.

DAT Tours Bloch 151 (422). Shot down by Bf110s in combat near Tours 4.30 p.m. Adjt Verrier badly wounded, admitted to Saint-Gatien Hospital at Tours. Aircraft a write-off.

DAT Tours Potez 631. Shot down near Mantes, south-east of Vernon. Adjt Morizot and crew believed baled out and captured. Aircraft a write-off.

GAO 1/506 Two Potez 63.11. Returned to base seriously damaged by flak during reconnaissance sorties. Crews unhurt. Aircraft both damaged but repairable.

GAO 1/508 Potez 63.11 (634). Crashed into a quarry shortly after take-off from Troyes-Barberey 4.15 a.m. Cause unknown but probably engine failure. Lt Noir and Sgt Brias injured admitted to hospital in Auxerre. S/Lt Chiers unhurt. Aircraft a write-off.

GAO 581 Potez 63.11 (837). Shot down by Lt Schneider and Uffz Grimpe of 1./JG1 during observation sortie and crashed between Romilly and Nogent-sur-Seine 1.30 p.m. Capt Vénard, Sgt Gautron, and Adjt Giroud captured badly wounded. Aircraft a write-off.

GB II/21 Bloch 210 (12). Lost in fog and also possibly damaged by AA fire, crashed near Farges-en-Septaine 2.15 a.m. S/Lt Dupont, S/Lt Dumond, Sgt Raoul, and Sgt Chaltet killed. Aircraft a write-off.

GBA II/51 Breguet 693. Crashed on landing at Orléans-Bricy seriously damaged in attack by Bf109 during reconnaissance sortie over Melun and Fontainebleau a.m. Adjt Izern badly wounded. Capt J. Nicot unhurt. Aircraft a write-off.

GBA II/51 Breguet 693 (80). Set alight in attacks by enemy fighters during bombing sortie north of Romilly-sur-Seine and crashed on Nantes-Bouguenais airfield. Possibly that claimed by Oberfw Umbach of 3./JG1 over Romilly 1.30 p.m. Cpl Malouet badly wounded. S/Lt du Tertre unhurt. Aircraft a write-off.

GBA II/61 Bloch 210. Run out of fuel and abandoned during return from night sortie over Épernay and Châlons-sur-Marne. S/Lt Trioux, Sgt Darcy, Sgt Camus, and Cpl Ferry baled out unhurt. Aircraft a write-off.

GC I/4 Curtiss H-75 (257). Stalled and crashed at Fonts-Puis, Déols; cause unknown. S/Lt Blondeau killed. Aircraft a write-off.

GC III/2 Curtiss H-75. Forced-landed near Romilly-sur-Seine damaged by flak. Capt S. Laszkiewicz unhurt. Aircraft abandoned.

GR I/14 Potez 63.11 (604). Shot down by Hptmn von Ankum-Frank (Staffelkapitän) of 5./JG27 during reconnaissance sortie over Troyes, Châlons-sur-Marne, Épernay, and Romilly. Crashed and burned out at Buchères 3.45 p.m. S/Lt L. Fournier and Sgt P. de Quillac killed. S/Lt Moreaux baled out wounded. Aircraft a write-off.

GR 3/22 Potez 63.11 (716). Failed to return from reconnaissance sortie over Troyes, Brienne, St-Dizier, and Bar-le-Duc. Adjt Kerbrat, Capt Sagon (Commandant), and Sgt Guérin captured unhurt. Aircraft a write-off.

LUFTWAFFE

2.(H)/10 Henschel Hs126. Shot down by six D520s of GC I/3 during observation sortie east of Paris and crashed at Grisy-Suisnes, south-east of Brie-Comte-Robert. Lt F. Bauer and Uffz H. Krahe killed. Aircraft a write-off.

2.(H)/10 Henschel Hs126. Returned badly damaged in attack by S/Lt Madon and Sgt Glauder of GC I/3 during observation sortie over Lagny-le-Sec, north-east of Paris. Uffz H. Brock slightly wounded, pilot unhurt. Aircraft a write-off.

4.(F)/11 Dornier Do17. Failed to return from reconnaissance sortie and possibly that claimed by Sgt Wurtz of ECMJ 1/16 near Tours 5.00 p.m. Crew believed killed. Aircraft a write-off.

2.(H)/23 Henschel Hs126. Shot down by ground fire during observation sortie to Langres and believed crashed at Lafauche south-west of Neufchâteau. Unterfw H. Hummenberger killed, another crewman wounded. Aircraft damage state not reported.

2.(H)/32 Henschel Hs126. Returned damaged by flak over Ingeweiler near Niederbronn. Fw H. Baumeler slightly wounded, pilot unhurt. Aircraft damaged but repairable.

I./JG1 Messerschmitt Bf109E-1. Returned damaged following combat with fighters over Calais-Marck. Pilot unhurt. Aircraft damaged but repairable.

1./JG1 Messerschmitt Bf109E-4. Crashed near Cutry during emergency take-off, cause not stated. Obergefr W. Hillgruber injured. Aircraft a write-off.

I./JG2 Messerschmitt Bf109E-4. Wrecked in taxying accident at Oulchy. Pilot unhurt. Aircraft a write-off.

1./JG20 Klemm Kl35B. Wrecked in flying accident at Darnétal, east of Rouen, due to engine failure. Uffz H. Ensch killed. Gefr Limpert unhurt. Aircraft a write-off.

8./JG26 Messerschmitt Bf109E. Shot down in combat with fighters south-west of Évreux and forced-landed at 'La Noë Allain', near La Vieille-Lyre, south of Beaumesnil, 4.50 p.m. Lt G. Sprick slightly wounded. Aircraft a write-off.

I./JG27 Messerschmitt Bf109E-1. Forced-landed at Soissons due to engine failure. Pilot unhurt. Aircraft damaged but repairable.

3./JG54 Messerschmitt Bf109E-4. Believed shot down in combat with No. 17 Squadron Hurricanes near Évreux during bomber escort sortie 3.30 p.m. Lt H-E. Angeli killed. Aircraft a write-off.

3./KG1 Heinkel He111H. Landed on one engine following collision with Oberlt Feilitzsch between Chartres and Nogent-le-Rotrou. Uffz G. Rensinghoff, Uffz H. Kuhn, Uffz K. Schmidt, Gefr J. Michel, and Flgr P. Hartmann unhurt. Aircraft V4+FL damaged but repairable.

3./KG1 Heinkel He111H. Collided with Uffz Rensinghoff and crashed between Chartres and Nogent-le-Rotrou. Oberlt W. Feilitzsch, Fw H. Bertelsmeyer, Uffz H. Wolfs, Uffz W. Schubert, and Gefr R. Hart captured unhurt. Aircraft V4+GL a write-off.

8./KG1 Heinkel He111H. Returned damaged in attack by Bloch 152s of DAT Châteaudun and also hit by flak over Orléans. Oberfw H. Burian and Gefr E. Glockner badly wounded, admitted to hospital in Cologne-Nippes; rest of crew unhurt. Aircraft damaged but repairable.

3./KG2 Dornier Do17Z (3314). Shot down by ground-fire during low-level attack on enemy columns west of Neufchâteau. Fw G. Mader, Fw A. Berger, Uffz W. Schlicht, and Uffz W. Grande killed. Aircraft U5+IL a write-off.

2./KG51 Junkers Ju88A. Returned damaged by flak over Puttelange. Flgr J. Zieger badly wounded, died in hospital in Speyer; rest of crew unhurt. Aircraft repairable.

5./KG51 Junkers Ju88A. Crash-landed at Wiesloch, near Heidelberg, with engine damage. Gefr R. Möricke badly injured, died in hospital in Wiesloch. Uffz H. Deil, Uffz E. Ruhland, and Uffz R. Krauss also badly injured. Aircraft a write-off.

III./KG51 Junkers Ju88A. Belly-landed on Regensburg airfield due to engine failure. No crew casualties. Aircraft damaged but repairable.

8./KG53 Heinkel He111. Returned damaged by fighters and flak. Uffz W. Scharfscheer badly wounded, died in hospital in Frankfurt on August 4. Uffz H. Hebig and Gefr W. Hassmann also badly wounded, rest of crew unhurt. Aircraft damage state not recorded.

Stab KG55 Heinkel He111P. Shot down by AA fire and crashed in flames near Frémestroff during reconnaissance sortie between St Avold and Puttelange. Oberlt W. Müller, Hauptfw H. Witt, Oberfw K. Franz, Fw K. Ander, and Uffz H. Behrens killed. Aircraft a write-off.

Stab KG55 Heinkel He111P. Belly-landed at Schwäbisch-Hall airfield. Crew unhurt. Aircraft damaged but repairable.

Stab KG77 Dornier Do17Z. Shot down by Capt Huvet, Lt Durod, Adjt Lachaux, and Sgt Quéguiner of GC II/5 during reconnaissance sortie south of Nancy and also hit by AA fire over Bricon. Crashed and exploded in forest near Braux-le-Châtel, south of Chaumont, 7.00 a.m. Oberlt H. Reuter, Fw K. Dreier, and Uffz A. Tix killed. Fw H. Golombek unhurt. Aircraft a write-off.

Stab IV.(St)/LG1 Junkers Ju87B. Shot down by AA fire during attack on defences at Valette, south-west of Saarbrücken, and crashed near Cappel 10.00 a.m. Hptmn P. Kögl (Gruppenkommandeur) and Oberfw E. Stichel killed. Aircraft a write-off.

3./StG76 Junkers Ju87B. Shot down over La Chapelle, north of Romilly. Uffz F. im Spring and Uffz F. Krohn captured unhurt. Aircraft a write-off.

9./ZG26 Messerschmitt Bf110C. Believed shot down by No. 242 Squadron Hurricanes in combat north of Conches-en-Ouche, south-west of Évreux, 4.05 p.m. Possibly that claimed by P/O Stansfeld. Lt W. Kuhlke and Gefr P. Eckert captured wounded. Aircraft a write-off.

9./ZG26 Messerschmitt Bf110C. Believed shot down by No. 242 Squadron Hurricanes north of Conches-en-Ouche and crashed near Marbeuf, 4.05 p.m. Possibly one of those claimed by P/O McKnight. Uffz K. Wissmann and Obergefr W. Bülow killed. Aircraft a write-off.

This time it is the Germans inspecting one of their own casualties. This is believed to be the Henschel of 2.(H)/23 brought down by pilots of Groupe de Chasse II/4 near Rethel on June 11 (see page 459).

Saturday, June 15

As BAFF units moved to new locations around Angers, Nantes, Rennes, and Saumur, the latest directive received by Air Marshal Barratt instructing him to cover the military evacuation and evacuate his own surplus personnel and equipment posed certain difficulties. Airfields near the western ports were in short supply and already severely congested putting extreme pressure on any refuelling and servicing facilities. With the collapse of France imminent, and the ever-present threat from the German advance, he decided to order the remaining six Battle squadrons of Nos. 75 and 76 Wings back to England immediately. Any further delay would only have placed withdrawal of their ground echelons in jeopardy. Despatch riders conveyed his orders to the squadrons already in convoy en route to Rennes and Nantes, and diverted them to Brest for immediate embarkation, the aircraft leaving for England over the next two days after completing any scheduled sorties.

What remained of Barratt's command in France, five depleted squadrons of Hurricanes comprising No. 67 Wing, were now required to cover the evacuation ports of Brest, La Pallice, and St Malo, as well as Cherbourg, Nantes, and St-Nazaire, these three already well within range of German forces. Nos. 1, 73, and 242 Squadrons were therefore ordered to Nantes for operations under BAFF headquarters, while Nos. 17 and 501 Squadrons were placed under South Component command and covered Cherbourg and St Malo. At Nantes-Château Bougon No. 1 Squadron found 'so many aircraft on it that it looked like several Empire Air Days all at once'.

The military situation remained grim. The French 10ème Armée was retreating towards Britanny, as German forces poured through a gap south-west of Chartres, while another enemy thrust pushed the French line back towards the Loire. Verdun was reported to have fallen and a frontal assault on the Maginot Line, repulsed the previous day, finally penetrated the fixed defences between St Avold and Sarralbe. Such was the confusion as the Allied lines crumbled under this relentless German pressure that the British War Office Intelligence Summary had to quote intercepted German communiqués as the only source of information on the ground situation in certain areas.

Before their departure for England, AASF Battles attacked targets between Dreux and Évreux losing another two aircraft to the customary intense AA fire and enemy fighters. German air attacks on BAFF airfields, by now stripped of all but the lightest AA defences, also accounted for several more losses before the last of approximately 65 Fairey Battles then left in France took off for England.

N2150 was a replacement Battle which was allocated to No. 12 Squadron on May 23. It was never brought back to the UK and it is believed that it was abandoned at or near Nantes (see page 469).

Given the inevitable upheaval caused by French units vacating their airfields in the region of Paris and redeploying south, the Escadrilles de Chasse nevertheless achieved 200 sorties during the day, their heaviest effort in almost a week. They would claim 15 victories for the loss of nine fighters, five of the pilots being killed and, despite the now clearly hopeless military situation, French aircrews continued to fight with determination and courage in defence of their homeland. A sacrifice apparently little recognised by their British allies whose attention, understandably, now centred exclusively on their own evacuation.

Bomber Command despatched two formations of six Blenheims to Évreux during the day, but both returned without delivering attacks, the cloud cover they had been instructed to use in place of non-existent fighter protection being deemed insufficient. Fighter Command operations on the day were similarly limited, 22 aircraft from Tang-

mere patrolling Cherbourg without incident, but the campaign in France was gradually moving ever further out of range of RAF fighters based in England.

Overnight the French Navy sent one long-range heavy bomber against targets in Rome and near Venice, the Italians responding with further attacks on French airfields at Cuers-Pierrefeu, Le Luc, and St Raphaël around midday. These raids were opposed by GC III/6 and French Navy Blochs who inflicted several losses but were themselves caught at a disadvantage and attacked shortly after take-off losing three aircraft.

Later, night operations by Bomber Command were cancelled due to bad weather apart from the first foray by 'Haddock Force' which despatched eight Wellingtons from Salon to bomb aircraft works in Genoa. Heavy thunderstorms prevented most of them reaching the target area and only one aircraft reported hits on the Ansaldo factory.

Still no news! The despatch-rider failed to return and yet another was on the point of being sent out when all downed tools to the welcome note of a Hurricane engine. A servicing crew dashed out, and out of the plane stepped the recently appointed commander of 'B' Flight, Flying Officer Drake, ex-test-pilot, who forthwith handed a hastily scribbled message from the CO to the Adjutant: 'Pack up, and make for Nantes immediately'.

Within two hours, the convoy was heading down the narrow, twisting country road, and with never a backward look.

Once clear of Saumur and its dense fringe of refugees, the road was comparitively free of obstacles to our progress and once again, convoy-wise, there was no sign of enemy aircraft. It was only upon approaching Nantes in the evening that the

main stream of refugees was again encountered and this time, significantly enough, fleeing in the contrary direction, away from the port. We had anticipated trouble ahead, but all we encountered was a severe thunderstorm, with rain of such density that the convoy quickly got swallowed up and lost in Nantes itself, sections of it taking considerable time to locate the field in which we were directed to park ourselves and our vehicles. Here (at Bois Cholet, a mile or two past the aerodrome), Squadron Leader More met the convoy, and with the perhaps not unexpected, but still breath-taking news, that the bulk of the men were to proceed almost immediately to nearby ports, homeward bound for the UK!

FLYING OFFICER HENRY HALL, JUNE 1940

AMESBURY
WAR CASUALTIES

Mr. and Mrs. P. Godfray, of New Barn, Amesbury, have received a telegram from the Air Ministry stating that their only son, Ldg.-A.-C. Roy Godfray, R.A.F., has been killed in action. He had been serving as an air gunner in France since the outbreak of war. Ldg.-A.-C. Godfray, who was 26 years of age, attended Amesbury Church of England School until 1927, when he proceeded to the Bishop Wordsworth's School, Salisbury. For some years prior to joining the R.A.F. he was employed as a motor mechanic by Messrs. H. Norman Pitt and Co. He was home on leave shortly after Easter.

The parents of the following Amesbury men, all former scholars of Amesbury Church of England School, have been informed officially that their sons are posted as missing :—Pte. Frank Brooks, Royal Tank Regiment, aged 22, of Coldharbour ; Fus. Hector Hibbs, Royal Fusiliers, aged 21, of 23, Lynchets-road ; and Pte. Douglas Kett, Wilts Regiment, aged 21, of 2, Edward's-road.

An enigma lost to history. When Mr and Mrs Percy Godfray received a telegram informing them of their son's death it just told them that he had been killed in action in France. And therein lies the mystery. LAC Roy Godfray certainly served with No. 12 Squadron and Leading Aircraftmen were employed as air gunners, but in Roy's case no aircraft or trade details confirm this in the surviving personnel records. His loss is simply given as 'bombing casualty, Sauge, approx. 1030 hours'. Two other airmen appear to have been injured in the same incident: AC1 Byron Ellis and LAC Victor Thomas McFarlane. Roy is now buried in the Communal Cemetery at Sougé-sur-Braye. His death is an example of the many airmen who failed to return from the battle in France although only aircrew killed due to enemy action while based in France are included in our listing of the casualties.

BRITISH AIR FORCES IN FRANCE

73 SQUADRON, CHÂTEAU BOUGON

Hurricane. Shot down by Bf109 following cover patrol for Battles over Les Andelys and belly-landed north of Le Mans 6.00 a.m. Sergeant A. L. McNay wounded in shoulder. aircraft TP⊙D a write-off.

Alex McNay's own account dates this event June 13 although surviving squadron records and Squadron Leader More's report covering operations in France both indicate otherwise.

98 SQUADRON, CHÂTEAU BOUGON

Five Battles K9201, K9202, K9218 and K9452. Aircraft believed burned on evacuation. No crew casualties. Aircraft all write-offs.

103 SQUADRON, SOUGÉ

Battle. Briefed for offensive patrol south of the Seine between Vernon and Dreux, but reportedly hit by AA over Laval and crashed near Vitré 9.45 a.m. Sergeant Brumby, Sergeant Hedley, and LAC Werner unhurt. Aircraft a write-off.

Three Battles. Destroyed or badly damaged in bombing attack on airfield 12.00 p.m. Sergeant A. N. Dowling killed in shelter trench. Aircraft all write-offs — abandoned on evacuation.

Nine surviving aircraft took off for England just before this attack. One of the aircraft destroyed was that of the squadron CO, Wing Commander Dickens, who was making a final inspection before leaving. With two of his pilots, he nevertheless reached Nantes flying an unserviceable machine. Fifteen ground crew casualties were reported in this and other attacks later in the day.

142 SQUADRON, VILLIERSFAUX

Three Battles. Damaged or unserviceable aircraft destroyed on evacuation to Rennes 1.00 p.m. No crew casualties. Aircraft all write-offs.

Battle. Forced-landed near Rennes due to engine failure en route to England. Pilot Officer Kirby and crew believed unhurt. Aircraft abandoned.

150 SQUADRON, HOUSSAY

Battle L5541. Badly damaged by Lt Landry of 2./JG3 over St-André-de-l'Éure during attack on troop concentrations south-east of Évreux and crash-landed near La Ferté-Vidame 5.30 a.m. Pilot Officer Benjamin and Sergeant Armstrong unhurt. LAC Hillyard wounded admitted to hospital. Aircraft destroyed by crew.

UK-based aircraft lost or damaged on operations over the Western Front:

43 Squadron, Tangmere
Combat training:

Hurricane N2615. Lost control and crashed in the Channel 5 miles off Shoreham while making practice attacks 6.45 p.m. Sgt W. T. Pratt killed. Aircraft lost.

FRENCH AIR FORCE

AB 3 Six Vought 156Fs. Destroyed on the ground at Cuers-Pierrefeu airfield in attack by Fiat CR42s 12.00 p.m. No pilot casualties. Aircraft all write-offs.

AC 3 Bloch 151 (51). Shot down shortly after take-off during attack on Cuers-Pierrefeu by Fiat CR42s 12.00 p.m. Adjt Hourcade killed. Aircraft 15 a write-off.

AC 3 Bloch 151 (348). Crash-landed badly damaged in combat with Fiat CR42s shortly after take-off from Cuers-Pierrefeu 12.00 p.m. SM Soulimont unhurt. Aircraft 8 a write-off.

AC 3 Bloch 151 (37). Damaged on take-off during attack on Cuers-Pierrefeu and shot down in combat with Fiat CR42s 12.00 p.m. Crashed into a ravine near Rocbaron. SM Le Bihan badly wounded, died same day in Brignolles hospital. Aircraft 9 a write-off.

AC 3 Bloch 151 (77). Crash-landed damaged in attack by Fiat CR42s while gaining height after take-off from Cuers-Pierrefeu 12.00 p.m. LV Ziegler (*Commandant*) wounded. Aircraft damaged but repairable.

On the morning of Thursday, the 13th June, I took off in Hurricane 'D' to carry out a patrol in the area of Les Andelys. Due to 'Yellow' leader being unable to start his engine, we flew in two formations of four aircraft. Towards the end of the patrol I had the feeling, although I saw nothing, that we were being stalked from the cover of the sun. I therefore fell behind and climbed above the squadron slightly, and zig-zagged to watch our rear.

The patrol finished, and we commenced to descend from our altitude of 23,000 feet towards Le Mans, our base. Nothing happened until at 12,000 feet I felt a jerk on my controls. Thinking I was under fire I did a steep turn to the left but saw and felt nothing more. The sky was apparently empty so, completing my turn, I began to chase the remainder of the patrol which was now about a mile or so away. After about a minute, when I was at 10,000 feet, I saw tracer shooting past, and as I swung away from the burst I felt a sting in my shoulder. Looking up I saw two single-engined machines coming down on me. I think it was their leader who hit me as they seemed to be too far away for such close-grouped accurate fire as the burst which got me. I couldn't see more than two, but knowing myself to be hit, I decided not to linger. I banged my controls as far into the left-hand corner as I could, and with full throttle went down to the tree-tops and, by luck more than good judgement, came out of my dive, heading west.

Satisfied I had shaken off pursuit, I tried to find where I was but my compass was broken by a bullet which had ricocheted off the inside of my windscreen, and I could not trust my gyro. I continued to fly west by the sun but unable to pick up any landmark, I force-landed in the first available field. I noticed that the machine was apparently undamaged, except for a shot which had broken the runner of the sliding hood, entered the cockpit, and broken the compass; and a clean hole in the hump-back where the shot which hit me had entered. Some men from a French battery came to my assistance. On learning that I was wounded, they insisted that I see their M.O.

When the M.O. saw my shoulder, he forbade me to try and fly the machine to Le Mans, but I took no notice of what he said until he began to clean my wound. I felt no pain as my shoulder was numb but I began to feel faint — probably just reaction but, as the bullet was in my shoulder and not just a graze as I at first thought, I changed my mind. An officer volunteered to phone my squadron so I gave him their location, and my name. I was bundled into an ambulance and commenced a circular tour of French hospitals before he returned, so I was left to assume the squadron would salvage the machine.

We visited three hospitals before we got to one which was not evacuated.

They took me in and cleaned and dressed my wound properly. I spent about three or four hours there, before they took me to a hospital at Laval. It was about half an hour's journey by ambulance. We reached Laval at 21.00 hours and were just in time to meet the patients walking out of the hospital — evacuating! I was getting used to evacuation by this time. We went up to the station, and having all boarded the train, we were told to hop out again as the train was not moving off until next morning.

Next morning, after a breakfast of a mouthful of black coffee and a piece of bread, an English Tank Corps chap and myself decided to go and hunt up a supply of food. We wandered back armed with long loaves and other odds and ends only to find that the ambulance train had gone! When we were about to see about commandeering a car, we spotted a train which turned out to be ours in another siding. Once we were aboard, it took off but, instead of going direct to Nantes, it went via Rennes, taking two days as it took three or four hours rest for every half-hour's run.

We at last arrived at Nantes, and I was sent to Broussais Hospital, as I was still waiting to have the bullet extracted. My shoulder was X-rayed on the morning of my arrival which was Sunday. By Monday dinnertime I was nearly crazy with trying to speak French all the time and watching Hurricanes sailing over the town. I went to the Commandant and asked to be sent to the English hospital at La Boule. He willingly gave me permission to go but had no transport. When outside, I decided to try and see my squadron M.O. I made my way out towards the Nantes aerodrome at Château-Bougon. When about half way there, I was told that all the English squadrons had gone that morning! I jumped on to the tail-board of a lorry which was going back to Nantes and from there I managed to hitch-hike to La Boule.

Before I entered St-Nazaire, I saw at least a thousand motor vehicles, including Ford V-8s, Bren-gun carriers, and heavy lorries. French people were bringing up petrol, filling the tanks, and driving them off. I myself was given a lift from the dump to La Boule in one of our own lorries.

Having reached La Boule, I found the hospital had packed up and gone back to England two days before. I then considered picking up a motor launch and sailing to England if I could get enough petrol. I decided first of all to try La Boule-les-Pins aerodrome to see if I could get a lift to Britain in a French bomber. While wandering along the promenade, I was stopped by a Special Constable. I had no papers except my Broussais discharge paper and he was all for running me in, but a French boy who could speak a little English helped me

to explain what I was doing there and what my intentions were. Another French lad, who was a member of the 'defense passive', told me to wait, and he dashed off to return a few minutes later with a car. He insisted on running me up to the aerodrome, and he dashed around trying to help.

I was soon the centre of a gaping crowd of Armée de l'Air pilots and ground staff. They were all asking questions and I was tied in a knot trying to answer them. I met a Yankee at the 'drome and I was never more pleased to hear an English voice. He was an employee of the Lockheed Company and was assembling the civil version of our Hudsons so that the civilian ground staff could clear out to Toulouse. He told me about some Harvards which were to be burned, so that Jerry would not get them and he suggested that the owner would be only too glad if I would fly one away.

I next saw the C.O. of the French squadron who said that his machines were fighters. He couldn't help me but said that it would be a good idea to fly a Harvard if possible. I returned to the civilian hangars and after a grand meal I had a sleep in the Lockheed's cabin. I was wakened at about one o'clock, in time to watch a raid on St-Nazaire. Whoever the raiders were, they were unchallenged as not a shot was fired at them. I returned to the machine and slept again until about five o'clock. The owner of the Harvards turned up shortly afterwards and he willingly gave me a machine.

My first intention was to go north to Brest, refuel there, and then cross the Channel. I was very strongly advised not to risk it as this was Tuesday morning and by that time the Boche were probably there. One of the ground staff wanted to go to Bordeaux to join his father, who was a major in the French Army so I decided to go south to Bordeaux. As I had not flown a Harvard before, I had to do some lightning calculations to make sure of my airspeed in miles per hour, particularly on coming in to land as they were supposed to be vicious at lowish speeds. I had to land at a 'drome near the mouth of the Garonne to check my course but I could hardly get her down as she preferred to float along.

When I reached Bordeaux, I found, after two ineffectual attempts at landing, that the rule of the road there was 'just barge in' and let the other fellow clear out of the way. This time I closed my throttle completely and, gliding in at about 90 m.p.h., found the Harvard handling like a Tiger Moth.

I arrived there at about 11.00 hours, and the manager of the Potez hangars very kindly put a car at my disposal to go down to the town to have my shoulder dressed. While I was in hospital the driver went to the docks and made enquiries about a boat for England. There was no boat so I returned to the

---

The records are also adrift concerning the loss of Sergeant Alex McNay of No. 73 Squadron who failed to return from a flight early on June 15. There was no news of his fate until he arrived in Britain two weeks later.

aerodrome. I had spotted a de Havil-land Rapide sitting on the 'drome. Apparently the pilots, who were English, had left two four-engined buses and two twin-engined while they cleared off to England by boat. I thought of trying to fly the four-engined machine to Britain, but four engines rather scared me as I had never even flown a twin-engined machine. The machine I chose was an eight-seater, or nine including the pilot. It hadn't the range to reach home but I thought of going to Marseilles and from there to Morocco if I couldn't get a boat.

While sitting there, I saw a Potez bomber take off in a stalled condition, and as soon as the pilot tried to turn he half-rolled into the deck from about 100 feet. The full petrol tanks simply blew up, and this didn't cheer me any, as I was about to do my first trip in a twin, and with umpteen passengers. I heard later that there was a boat going from Bayonne, which is 20 or 30 kilos from the Spanish frontier so I changed my plan and had as a result only one passenger.

I took off about 7.15 on Tuesday evening and decided to follow the shore, because my map was about 50 miles to the inch and showed no landmarks, only Imperial Airways European routes. After about an hour's flying, I ran into violent rain, and I was scared stiff because my port engine wasn't running too well, and I did not fancy spinning-in from a low altitude. I ran out of it, and reached Biarritz, but saw no aerodrome. I kept on as the aerodrome was supposed to be practically on the shore. I reached St Jean-de-Luz, and was sure I had crossed the frontier, as the coast was running east to west, which on my map was wrong. Turning back, I was forced down by low cloud, and I saw lightning flashes, which I didn't like because I had a large aerial out. When I was ready to force-land, I saw a largish field, which on inspection proved to be Biarritz aerodrome. I attempted to land as though I was flying a Hurricane. I shot across the fields at about 90 miles per hour, drifting like the deuce because the landing 'T' was dead across a fairly stiff breeze. I repeated my attempt, but this time at about 70 miles per hour and got in with no bother. I had hardly got in when a Potez came along to land. It was quite dark by this time and he hit a ridge in the field, collapsed his undercart, and practically stood on his nose. The crew were alright and no damage was done.

I reported to the Consul in Bayonne whom I reached in the only available transport — an ambulance. He told me to come back the following morning so I and my ex-passenger searched around for a bed. The place was choked with refugees but finally we bedded down in an ambulance in the garage. Next morning, when I turned up, I met an RAF officer who took me into the Consul and I found myself

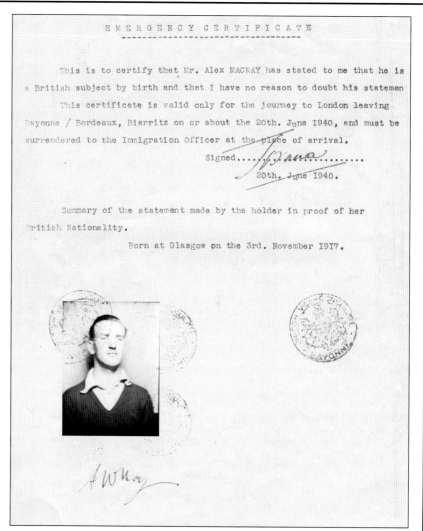

Alex McNay returned to his squadron only to go missing in action during the Battle of Britain on September 5, 1940. His name is now commemorated on the Runnymede Memorial, Panel 17. He was 22 years of age.

helping on the Consular staff. There was no need for panic but the way in which a number of middle-aged Britishers fought to get to the door was sickening. However, it was interesting work, and I managed to get a bed with the F/O driver in Biarritz. He got away on the first boat but I was remaining as I was going to fly my machine to Toulouse, destroy it there, and pick up a decent French military machine which I would take on to Morocco. How I would get home from there I had not thought about, or the fact that I was still the unwilling host of a bullet.

The day I was going to leave for Toulouse, my machine's battery was u/s, so we arranged with the French to charge it and we would call for it after lunch. Even if it hadn't been serviceable I would have taken a new Stinson Reliant which was on the 'drome instead. However, we had a puncture, and by the time we had it mended and reached the Consul's office, we found a bit of a panic on. We were rushed to the boat and there we sat for two days in the harbour, doing nothing. It was decided to mount guards on the ship, as we had a number of known, and

suspected, 'fifth column' on board. All arms were collected, including those of the Polish officers.

The voyage home was uneventful. I had to stay an extra night on board on arriving at Plymouth because of the guard business. Exactly 14 days from the time of being wounded, I got to a decent hospital. I was X-rayed on Thursday evening, and on Friday morning they decided to operate. In the hospital I met one of the squadron, who had been on the Lancastria when it was bombed and sunk by the Germans, and from him I gathered that the squadron didn't know what had happened to me. I got definite news of the report when my telegrams home were answered. As I could not write for a day or two after the operation, I asked the authorities to notify the Air Ministry and my squadron. I spent a week in Stoke Military Hospital, and I was then sent up to Victoria Hospital, Glasgow, as an out-patient until my shoulder had progressed sufficiently to allow me to return to my squadron, on July 21st.

SERGEANT ALEX McNAY, 1940

Pilots of GC II/5 brought down a Heinkel of the 3. Staffel of Kampfgeschwader 53 which scattered itself across a field between Mornay and Champlitte, north-east of Dijon. A local Frenchman, Gustave Henry, had film in his camera to record the scene.

AC 3 Bloch 151. Returned damaged in attack by Fiat CR42s while gaining height after take-off from Cuers-Pierrefeu 12.00 p.m. SM Briet unhurt. Aircraft repairable.

AC 3 Bloch 151 (69). Force-landed at Hyères damaged in combat with Fiat CR42s 12.00 p.m. SM Miramond unhurt. Aircraft repairable.

GAO 518 Potez 63.11 (382). Shot down by fighters south-west of Troyes during reconnaissance sortie over Chaumont, Vitry, and Romilly. Crashed and burned out at St-Germain. Sgt G. Leynaud and Lt M. Robert killed. Sgt R. Sainte Marie badly burned, died in hospital at Troyes. Aircraft a write-off.

Originally buried in field graves alongside the wreckage of their aircraft, pilot Georges Leynaud and his observer Marius Robert were reinterred in the cemetery at St-Germain on September 14, 1941.

GAO 518 Mureaux 115. Seriously damaged in attacks by Bf109s following communications flight to Bourbonne-les-Bains and crash-landed near Nevers. S/Lt Terral badly wounded. S/Lt Tixerand wounded. Aircraft a write-off.

GB I/25 LeO 451 (3011). Suffered engine failure and crashed near Miramas, south-west of Salon-de-Provence, on return from sortie to Turin. Cpl Diguet killed, rest of crew unhurt. Aircraft a write-off.

GB II/31 LeO 451 (132). Unserviceable aircraft left behind on withdrawal from Dole-Tavaux. No crew casualties. Aircraft abandoned.

GBA I/54 Breguet 693. Landed at Avord with one engine on fire, hit by flak during attack on motorised columns south and west of Troyes 1.00 p.m. Adjt Hugonnier wounded in thigh. Adjt Chevallet unhurt. Aircraft a write-off.

GBA II/54 Breguet 695 (7). Crashed on landing at Châteauroux following attack on mechanised columns north of Troyes. S/Lt A. de Dampierre killed. Capt Lacat (*Groupe Commandant*) injured. Aircraft a write-off.

GC 2/4 Curtiss H-75 (65). Reportedly shot down by flak during low-level reconnaissance south of Chartres and last seen near Voves. Crashed south of Loches, between Le Bois-Long and Le Loriot and possibly that claimed by Oberlt Greisert of 2./JG2 6.45 a.m. Sgt A. Keller seriously wounded baled out landing dead near Bonville. Aircraft a write-off.

GC I/5 Curtiss H-75 (57). Forced-landed outside Heuilley le Grand, south-east of Langres, due to petrol failure 5.00 p.m. Subsequently crashed shortly after take-off and burned out at Rouillot. Sgt E. Moravek killed. Aircraft a write-off.

GC II/7 Dewoitine 520 (235). Forced-landed badly damaged by flak over Pont-St-Vincent 10.00 a.m. Sgt Lamblin unhurt. Aircraft a write-off.

GC II/7 Dewoitine 520 (242). Damaged by return fire from Do17 and forced-landed near Gray 4.00 p.m. Cmdt M. Mümler unhurt. Aircraft a write-off.

GC II/7 Dewoitine 520 (238). Shot down by Bf109s during solo reconnaissance over Langres and Châtillon-sur-Seine, and crashed near Humes, north-west of Langres. Possibly that claimed by Lt Roth of 9./JG2. Cmdt R. Pépin killed. Aircraft a write-off.

The body of René Pépin was not recovered until October 29, 1941.

GC III/7 Morane 406 (356). Wrecked in landing accident at Vichy-Rhue airfield. S/Lt Rupied slightly injured. Aircraft a write-off.

GR I/52 Bloch 174. Returned to Bourges damaged by flak during reconnaissance sortie over enemy armoured columns around Autin, Chaumont, Troyes, and Melun p.m. Capt Martre wounded in leg. Lt Layec unhurt. Aircraft damaged but repairable.

GR II/55 Potez 63.11 (857). Belly-landed north-west of Courville both engines damaged by flak during reconnaissance sortie south of the Seine 7.30 a.m. S/Lt Bayle, Lt D'Anglejan, and Sgt About unhurt. Aircraft fired by crew.

LUFTWAFFE

2.(H)/10 Henschel Hs126. Shot down by Capt Garde, S/Lt Pebrel, and Sgt Starke of GC I/1 during observation sortie east of Orléans and broke up over Rue des Moulins at Mardié 11.10 a.m. Oberlt R. Knüpfer and Uffz F. Hauser both baled out and captured. Aircraft a write-off.

3.(H)/13 Henschel Hs126. Shot down by S/Lt Madon of GC I/3 during reconnaissance sortie west of Melun and crashed near Le Mée-sur-Seine. Oberlt W. Glitz and Lt H. Bergemann killed. Aircraft a write-off.

1.(H)/21 Dornier Do17P. Believed badly damaged during reconnaissance sortie to Nancy and crashed near Mössingen on return flight 7.20 p.m. Wachtmstr H. Trenkler, Uffz H. Kutsch, and Uffz W. Watta killed. Aircraft a write-off.

1.(H)/21 Henschel Hs126. Shot down by S/Lt Valentin of GC II/7 during observation sortie to Nancy and believed crashed near Guessling-Hémering, south-west of St Avold, 9.00 a.m. Oberlt H. Schumann and Lt F. Weiss killed. Aircraft a write-off.

4.(H)/21 Henschel Hs126. Shot down during reconnaissance sortie near Troyes and believed that claimed by six Moranes of GC II/6 south-east of Estissac 7.12 p.m. Fw G. Stegmann badly wounded, admitted to Marien Hospital in Düsseldorf. Fw A. Kaldart slightly wounded. Aircraft a write-off.

2.(H)/23 Henschel Hs126. Shot down during observation sortie south of Langres and probably that claimed by Capt Vasatko, S/Lt Brian, Sgt Tallent, and Cpl Kothera of GC I/5 north of Les Riceys 7.20 a.m. Wachtmstr J. Schmidt killed, pilot unhurt. Aircraft a write-off.

KG1 Junkers Ju52 (6019). Forced-landed at Domberg, near Steinhagen, with engine trouble. No crew casualties. Aircraft a write-off.

II./KG2 Dornier Do17Z. Returned damaged by fighters. Crew believed unhurt. Aircraft damaged but repairable.

5./KG2 Dornier Do17Z. Returned damaged by ground-fire near Thiaucourt. Uffz G. Godl badly wounded, admitted to hospital in St Quentin. Aircraft damaged but repairable.

5./KG2 Dornier Do17Z. Shot down by flak over Chaillon, north-east of St Mihiel. Oberlt K-H. Marten, Fw W. Starker, Oberfw S. Schwickart, and Gefr E. Leitner unhurt. Aircraft a write-off.

6./KG2 Dornier Do17Z. Returned damaged by AA fire south of Sedan. Fw R. Spies slightly wounded, Oberlt G. Czernik and rest of crew unhurt. Aircraft damaged but repairable.

8./KG3 Dornier Do17Z. Belly-landed at Trier-Euren damaged by fighters over Bar-le-Duc. Possibly that abandoned by S/Lt Valentin, Sgt Lamblin, Sgt Boillot, and Cpl Nowakiewicz of GC II/7 with one engine on fire over the Forêt-de-la-Warndt, east of Forbach. Fw O. Wohlgemuth killed, rest of crew unhurt. Aircraft damaged but repairable.

8./KG4 Junkers Ju88A-1 (0044). Sortied to bomb Loire bridges east of Orléans and shot down by S/Lt Thollon of GC I/8 during attack on bridge at Jargeau 6.15 p.m. Crashed and exploded near Fay-aux-Loges. Lt J. Reiners, Uffz R. Haase, Uffz W. Püschel, and Uffz W. Thier killed. Aircraft 5J+GS a write-off.

9./KG4 Junkers Ju88A. Forced-landed damaged during sortie over Paris. Lt Sommer and crew unhurt. Aircraft a write-off.

4./KG27 Heinkel He111P. Reported belly-landed at Marcq-en-Baroeul damaged by flak. No crew casualties. Aircraft 1G+LM damaged but repairable.

7./KG30 Junkers Ju88A. Crash-landed at Münster due to bad weather during transfer flight. Crew unhurt. Aircraft damaged but repairable.

7./KG30 Junkers Ju88A. Crash-landed at Loddenheide in bad weather during transfer flight. Crew unhurt. Aircraft a write-off

7./KG30 Junkers Ju88A. Crash-landed at Münster in bad weather during transfer flight. Crew unhurt. Aircraft damaged but repairable.

Stabsstaffel KG53 Heinkel He111H. Crashed into a quarry near Heidelberg flying through low cloud. Crew reported killed. Aircraft a write-off.

3./KG53 Heinkel He111H. Reportedly shot down by fighters near Jussey. Oberlt H. Wegner, Fw F. Fern, Uffz J. Hertle, Uffz P. Kraft, and Gefr H. Thiele unhurt. Aircraft a write-off.

3./KG53 Heinkel He111H. Shot down by fighters near Jussey and possibly that attacked by Sgt Salès and Adjt Dugoujon of GC II/5 between Langres and Vesoul. Hptmn B. Schwarz (Staffelkapitän), Lt Schoeppler, Oberfw F. Weidenhammer, Fw A. Burger, and Uffz K. Berninger killed. Aircraft a write-off.

3./KG53 Heinkel He111H. Shot down by Capt Monraisse, Capt Duda, S/Lt Klan, Lt Hebrard, Adjt Gras, and Sgt Svetlik of GC II/5 and broke up over 'Le Puiseau' between Mornay and Champlitte, north-east of Dijon, 7.15 a.m. Uffz K. Berrang, Uffz O. Haas, and Uffz H. Deringer killed. Oberfw H. Röthemeier baled out wounded, and Fw H. Mayer baled out unhurt, both captured on landing near Fontaine-Française. Aircraft a write-off.

Stab III./KG53 Heinkel He111H. Returned damaged following sortie over Langres. Uffz J. Antholzner killed, rest of crew unhurt. Aircraft damage state not recorded.

Stabsstaffel KG54 Heinkel He111P. Crash-landed at Cologne-Ostheim, cause not stated. Crew unhurt. Aircraft damaged but repairable.

1./KG76 Dornier Do17Z. Crash-landed damaged by flak north-east of Pontoise 6.00 a.m. Fw P. Licht badly wounded. Oberlt A. Molenaar and Lt W. Riedl slightly wounded. Aircraft damage state not recorded.

One of the awful images Gustave Henry captured was that of the smouldering body of one of the crew.

With the battle lost, and little help from the British, the exploits of French airmen, even at this stage, was exemplary, fighting to the bitter end and bravely risking their lives for La France. In the conflict on June 15 one man stands supreme: Adjutant Pierre Le Gloan of Groupe de Chasse III/6 who downed four Italian aircraft and damaged another.

Stabsstaffel KG77 Dornier Do17Z. Believed shot down by Cdt Mümler, S/Lt Valentin, Sgt Grimaud, Sgt Martin, and Sgt Passemard of GC II/7 west of Neufchâteau and crash-landed near Leurville 3.15 p.m. Gen-Major W. von Stutterheim *(Kommodore)* badly wounded treated in field hospital at St-Dizier, airlifted to Berlin next day but died of injuries December 3. Oberlt G. Esch slightly wounded. Lt R. Gaude baled out landing slightly wounded near Taliseul and captured next day. Fw H. Herrig also baled out but killed by fighters while in his parachute. Fw O. Jelinek died in the aircraft. Aircraft a write-off.

I./KG77 Dornier Do17Z. Lost during sortie, details not recorded. Crew later returned unhurt. Aircraft a write-off.

5./KG77 Dornier Do17Z. Engaged by nine Moranes of GC II/2 between Bayon and Lunéville during sortie to attack columns between Épinal and Thaon-les-Vosges, and belly-landed near Neufchâteau 3.15 p.m. Fw J. Schweiger and Gefr L. Hopf captured wounded. Fw K. Zimmer and Uffz J. Anschau captured unhurt. Aircraft a write-off.
On vacating the aircraft this crew was fired upon by French troops and two of them wounded, they were all roughly treated after capture.

I./KGzbV.1 Junkers Ju52 (5205). Damaged in taxying accident at Esternay, west of Sézanne. Crew believed unhurt. Aircraft TA+QA damaged but repairable.

IV./KGzbV.1 Junkers Ju52 (5373). Crash-landed at Esternay, west of Sézanne, cause not stated. Crew believed unhurt. Aircraft damaged but repairable.

7./StG2 Junkers Ju87B. Shot down by ground-fire during attack on targets between St Sérotin and Voulx, north-west of Sens, 9.00 a.m. Oberlt W. Schröder *(Staffelkapitän)* killed. Uffz W. Neuschwander unhurt. Aircraft a write-off.

7./StG2 Junkers Ju87B. Shot down by ground-fire during attack on targets between St Sérotin and Voulx, north-west of Sens, 9.00 a.m. Lt H. von Stromberg and Uffz E. Müller unhurt. Aircraft a write-off.

Wettererkundungsstaffel 51 Dornier Do17P. Crashed at Alzenau, east of Hanau, cause unknown. Oberlt Wilckens and crew killed. Aircraft a write-off.

ITALIAN AIR FORCE

83 Squadriglia, 18 Gruppo, 3 Stormo Fiat CR42 (MM 4366). Shot down by Adjt Le Gloan of GC III/6 during cover sortie for attack on Le Cannet-des-Maures airfield and crashed near Fermes des Termes 12.20 p.m. Maresciallo F. Colombo killed. Aircraft a write-off.

83 Squadriglia, 18 Gruppo, 3 Stormo Fiat CR42 (MM 4449). Shot down by Adjt Le Gloan and Capt Bernache-Assolant of GC III/6 during cover sortie for attack on Le Cannet-des-Maures airfield and crashed at St Amé, near Pampelonne 12.15 p.m. Sgt Maj E. Parmiggiani baled out and captured. Aircraft a write-off.

83 Squadriglia, 18 Gruppo, 3 Stormo Fiat CR42. Returned to Villanova d'Albenga top wing badly damaged in combat during cover sortie for attacks on Cuers-Pierrefeu and Le Luc airfields 12.00 p.m. Maresciallo G. Bortolini unhurt. Aircraft repairable.

85 Squadriglia, 18 Gruppo, 3 Stormo Fiat CR42 (MM 4372). Badly damaged in attack by EV1 Carmeille of AC 3 during cover sortie for attacks on Cuers-Pierrefeu and Le Luc airfields 12.00 p.m. and undercarriage wrecked in heavy forced-landing at Dorniella, near Grosseto. Capt G. Anelli *(Commandante)* unhurt. Aircraft a write-off.
Two more Fiat CR42s were later damaged in landing accidents at Villanova d'Albenga due to bad weather and not as a result of this action.

74 Squadriglia, 23 Gruppo, 3 Stormo Fiat CR42. Returned to Cervere lower wing badly damaged during cover sortie for attack on Le Cannet-des-Maures airfield 12.00 p.m. Tenente L. Viale unhurt. Aircraft damaged but repairable.

75 Squadriglia, 23 Gruppo, 3 Stormo Fiat CR42 (MM 4361). Shot down by Adjt Le Gloan of GC III/6 following strafing attack on Le Cannet-des-Maures airfield and abandoned over Ramatuelle, south of St Tropez, 12.00 p.m. Capt L. Filippi *(Commandante)* baled out and captured. Aircraft a write-off.

75 Squadriglia, 23 Gruppo, 3 Stormo Fiat CR42. Returned to Cervere damaged following attack by Adjt Le Gloan of GC III/6 south of Grimaud following strafing attack on Le Cannet-des-Maures airfield 12.00 p.m. Tenente L. Pasquetti wounded. Aircraft damaged but repairable.

75 Squadriglia, 23 Gruppo, 3 Stormo Fiat CR42. Returned to Cervere damaged following strafing attack on Le Cannet-des-Maures airfield 12.00 p.m. Tenente M. Rigatti unhurt. Aircraft repairable.

75 Squadriglia, 23 Gruppo, 3 Stormo Fiat CR42. Returned to Cervere damaged following strafing attack on Le Cannet-des-Maures airfield 12.00 p.m. Sottotenente Malvezzi unhurt. Aircraft repairable.

364 Squadriglia, 150 Gruppo, 53 Stormo Fiat CR42 (MM 5590). Forced-landed at Cuers-Pierrefeu with broken throttle control during cover sortie for attack on the airfield 12.00 p.m. Tenente G. E. Zuffi captured unhurt. Aircraft lost.

365 Squadriglia, 150 Gruppo, 53 Stormo Fiat CR42 (MM 5579). Shot down by SM Miramond and SM Le Bihan of AC 3 during cover sortie for attack on Cuers-Pierrefeu airfield and crashed near Rocbaron 12.00 p.m. Capt N. Caselli killed. Aircraft a write-off.

365 Squadriglia, 150 Gruppo, 53 Stormo Fiat CR42. Returned to Villanova d'Albenga damaged in combat following strafing of Cuers-Pierrefeu airfield 12.00 p.m. Capt G. Graffer *(Commandante)* unhurt. Aircraft repairable.

365 Squadriglia, 150 Gruppo, 53 Stormo Fiat CR42. Returned to Villanova d'Albenga damaged in combat following strafing of Cuers-Pierrefeu airfield 12.00 p.m. Sottotenente L. Clerici unhurt. Aircraft repairable.

172 Squadriglia, Ricognizione Strategica Fiat BR20 (MM 21873). Shot down by Adjt Le Gloan of GC III/6 during post-attack photo-reconnaissance sortie and crashed at Ferme Moulin Rouge near Le Luc airfield, south-west of Vidauban, 12.25 p.m. Aviere G. Bonanno and Aviere E. Di Croce killed. Maj M. Salvadori, Capt G. Parodi *(Commandante)*, and Aviere A. Imparator baled out and captured wounded. Aircraft a write-off.
Mario Salvadori was an intelligence officer on the staff of Regia Aeronautica headquarters.

Sunday, June 16

Evacuation of British troops proceeded swiftly during the day, some 50,000 men embarking from Brest, Cherbourg, Nantes, and St-Nazaire, the bulk of the returning AASF ground personnel leaving Brest on board SS *Vienna* and reaching Plymouth next day. By mid-afternoon, revised plans to evacuate all that remained of the BAFF in France were well advanced, as a signal to the Air Ministry in London from Air Marshal Barratt's headquarters confirms, 'French have been told officially that we are removing the surplus – in fact we intend to remove the lot. Air Ministry is requested to clear up the situation.' Whatever the politicians may have agreed, British commanders in France had clearly reached the decision that it was time to cut their losses and withdraw.

French military resistance was now on the verge of collapse while the German advance spread further throughout France. That night French ministers rejected a British offer of political union and Prime Minister Paul Reynaud resigned to be replaced by Maréchal Philippe Pétain whose first action was to seek terms of an armistice.

Indifferent weather impeded air operations throughout the day but, despite early fog which resulted in some cancelled sorties, AASF Hurricanes flew squadron patrols over the ports of embarkation from dawn to dusk with half-an-hour's interval between patrols. Enemy aircraft also operated over the ports for they were successful in seeding the Loire Estuary with mines and made several attacks on shipping. French efforts were similarly adversely affected by the weather though their airmen continued to pay a high price in defence of a now lost cause. As French airfields in the south and west of the country became swamped with aircraft retreating ahead of the German advance, choice targets ignored for the moment by the Luftwaffe, French Air Force units began evacuation to bases in North Africa.

The only RAF bombing operations this night were flown by 'Haddock Force' which despatched nine Wellingtons to attack a variety of Italian targets. Four aircraft were prevented from bombing by intense darkness and low cloud and, on return, the Wellingtons based at Salon were all ordered back to England. This was the last British bombing operation of the campaign in France.

ROYAL AIR FORCE

UK-based aircraft lost or damaged on operations over the Western Front:

43 Squadron, Tangmere
Local flying:

Hurricane. Crashed on landing following radio test flight 10.45 a.m. P/O James admitted to Royal West Sussex Hospital with concussion. Aircraft damage state unknown.

FRENCH AIR FORCE

DAT Clermont-Ferrand Koolhoven F.K.58. Lost on delivery flight from Nevers 3.00 p.m. S/Lt W. Czaplinski missing. Aircraft lost.

DAT Clermont-Ferrand Koolhoven F.K.58. Attacked by Bf109s while landing at Nevers to pick up spares p.m. Lt B. Grzeszczak unhurt. Aircraft a write-off.

GAO 502 Potez 63.11 (844). Shot down by flak during attack on enemy columns; crashed and burned out at 'Le Rougemont', near Étampes 10.30 a.m. Sgt E. Bizet and S/Lt R. Balbiano killed. Sgt Nass captured badly wounded. Aircraft a write-off.

GAO 502 Potez 63.11 (845). Landed on one wheel south of Civry, east of Châteaudun, both engines damaged by ground-fire south of Rambouillet 11.30 a.m. Sgt Hourcade, Lt de Ketautem, and Sgt Navers unhurt. Aircraft destroyed by crew.

GAO 510 Potez 63.11 (415). Hit by flak and belly-landed, one engine on fire, at Teillay-St Benoit, 4 km north of Neuville-aux-Bois. Adjt Girard, Lt Roulland, and Cpl Bonnet unhurt, captured three days later near Le Mans. Aircraft destroyed by crew.

GB I/11 LeO 451. Unserviceable aircraft left behind on withdrawal from Tours. No crew casualties. Aircraft abandoned.

GB II/15 Farman 221 (8). Aircraft abandoned on evacuation of Saint-Yan airfield. Aircraft a write-off.

GB II/35 Breguet 691 (49). Crashed on take-off at Châteauroux-la-Martinerie on transit flight to Bourgneuf. Lt Antoine, Adjt R. Todoli, and Sgt Thonin killed. Aircraft a write-off.

GC II/2 Morane 406. Believed shot down by flak during solo attack on enemy column on the road between Langres and Dijon. Crashed close to Vingeanne reservoir, near Vesvres-sous-Prangey 3.00 p.m. Lt P. Boissel killed. Aircraft a write-off.

GC I/3 Dewoitine 520. Shot down by return fire from He111 over Orléans. Adjt Boileau baled out unhurt. Aircraft a write-off.

GC I/3 Dewoitine 520 (35). Hit by flak during low-level reconnaissance of traffic between La Charité-sur-Loire and Nevers; belly-landed on fire outside La Charité. S/Lt P. Salva unhurt. Aircraft a write-off.

GC II/4 Curtiss H-75 (98). Shot down by Bf109s during solo reconnaissance of enemy armour near Châtillon-sur-Seine 1.00 p.m. Crashed through trees and burst into flames outside Avallon. Cmdt A. Borne *(Commandant)* killed. Aircraft a write-off.

GC II/7 Two Dewoitine 520s (231 and 251). Wrecked in accidents at Lézignan airfield during move to Carcassonne; cause not stated but possible collision. Pilots unhurt. Aircraft both write-offs.

GR II/33 Potez 63.11 (718). Forced-landed at Vievy-le-Raye, north of Oucques, after propellers hit ground during low-level reconnaissance sortie 9.00 a.m. Sgt Créput, Lt Hébrad, and Sgt Mot unhurt. Aircraft abandoned.

GR I/35 Potez 63.11 (610). Shot down by Oberlt Hollweg *(Staffelkapitän)* of 4./JG27 over St Hillaire-lès-Andresis during low-level reconnaissance of the Yonne bridges 7.30 p.m. S/Lt Allaire and S/Lt Toni captured wounded but escaped two days later. Sgt Ploye captured badly wounded in head and right leg, admitted to hospital. Aircraft a write-off.

Lying where it had fallen on May 21, the Dornier 6M+CM of the 4. Staffel of Fernaufklärungs 11 presents a sorry sight east of Creil. All three crewmen were taken prisoner by the French (see page 341) after they met six Armée de l'Air fighters during a wide-ranging reconnaissance of airfields north and east of Paris. Though two of the fighters were out of ammunition, Johann Frank lost no time in setting his aircraft down to escape the unwelcome attention of the others.

LUFTWAFFE

1.(H)/12 Henschel Hs126. Returned badly damaged by flak during observation sortie over Dammerie-lè-Lys, south of Melun. Lt S. Steinberger slightly wounded, observer unhurt. Aircraft a write-off.

3.(H)/12 Henschel Hs126. Shot down by AA fire south of Toul during observation sortie to Joinville and crashed near Uruffe alongside the road to Colombey-les-Belles. Oberlt P. Raabe and Oberlt A. Ohms killed. Aircraft a write-off.

4.(H)/21 Henschel Hs126. Shot down by S/Lt Lefol, Sgt Bressieux, and Sgt Girou of GC I/5 during reconnaissance sortie over Lucy-sur-Yonne, north-east of Clamecy, 11.00 a.m. Fw J. Ottersbach and Fw E. Loets both slightly wounded. Aircraft a write-off.

3.(F)/22 Dornier Do17P. Returned reportedly damaged by ground-fire west of Cosne, north-west of Dijon, but believed to be that attacked by S/Lt Janis and S/Lt Demoulin of GC I/6 south-east of Cosne 1.15 p.m. Uffz F. Heim slightly wounded, admitted to hospital in Reims, rest of crew unhurt. Aircraft damage state not recorded.
This casualty is recorded on June 17 in the Luftwaffe Quartermaster General's Returns.

2.(F)/123 Dornier Do17P. Collided with Bf109s of I./JG27 in emergency landing during strafing by D520s of GC III/3 at Auxerre airfield 3.00 p.m. No crew casualties. Aircraft 4U+EK a write-off.

Flugbereitschaft VIII. Fliegerkorps Junkers Ju87. Badly damaged in attack by D520s of GC III/3 on take-off from Auxerre 3.00 p.m. Lt Goblet wounded. Aircraft damage state not recorded.

2./JG1 Messerschmitt Bf109E-4. Collided with Uffz Stahn during low-level strafing attack on Châteauroux airfield. Uffz H. Brandt killed. Aircraft a write-off.

2./JG1 Messerschmitt Bf109E-1. Collided with Uffz Brandt during low-level attack on Châteauroux. Uffz F. Stahn killed. Aircraft a write-off.

I./JG26 Messerschmitt Bf109E. Damaged in forced-landing at Quevauvillers, south-west of Amiens, cause not stated. Pilot unhurt. Aircraft repairable.

1./JG27 Three Messerschmitt Bf109E-1s. Parked aircraft rammed by Do17 of 2.(F)/123 making emergency landing at Auxerre 3.00 p.m. No casualties. Aircraft all write-offs.

6./JG51 Messerschmitt Bf109E-1. Shot down by flak near Chartres. Gefr A. Madler captured wounded. Aircraft a write-off.

5./KG1 Heinkel He111H. Returned damaged by AA fire over Lonneval. Fw G. Geissler killed, rest of crew unhurt. Aircraft damage state not recorded.

8./KG4 Junkers Ju88A-1 (6042). Crashed near Vendeville during routine ferry flight, probably due to engine failure. Oberlt P. Grüner, Fw A. Picking, Gefr R. Hornbogen, Gefr F. Gessner, and Fw R. Dowjatow (mechanic) killed. Aircraft 5J+BS a write-off.

3./KG27 Heinkel He111. Reported crash-landed at Merville due to engine failure. Oberfw Klause and rest of crew believed unhurt. Aircraft 1G+BL a write-off.

4./KG27 Heinkel He111P. Returned damaged by flak over Jargeau during attack on Loire bridges east of Orléans. Possibly also that attacked by S/Lt Madon of GC I/3. Obergefr W. Strecke slightly wounded, rest of crew unhurt. Aircraft damaged but repairable.

5./KG30 Junkers Ju88A. Hit by flak and also attacked by Adjt Bastien of DAT Tours and crashed at Flée during return flight. Fw K. Hacker, Uffz F. Richers, and Flgr D. Flessner killed. Lt W. Mann badly wounded, admitted to hospital in Cologne. Aircraft a write-off.

9./KG54 Heinkel He111P. Believed that attacked by Capt Gérard of GC I/3 during sortie south of Orléans and crashed east of Melun, at La Mée-sur-Seine, 10.30 a.m. Fw K. Wifling, Uffz E. Rieg, Uffz P. Orasch, and Gefr H. Biedermann killed. Aircraft a write-off.

During an emergency landing at Auxerre a Dornier of the 2. Staffel of Fernaufklärungsgruppe 123 collided spectacularly with three Bf 109s!

II./KG55 Heinkel He111P. Returned damaged by flak. No crew casualties. Aircraft damaged but repairable.

9./KG55 Heinkel He111P. Returned damaged by flak during attack on rail targets north of Lyon between Louhans, Macon, and Bourg-en-Bresse, 4.00 p.m. Possibly also that attacked by Capt Monraisse, Lt Fabre, and S/Lt Klan of GC II/5 near Marennes. Obergefr W. Teske badly wounded, died next day. Rest of crew unhurt. Aircraft damaged but repairable.

3./KGr.126 Heinkel He111H. Crashed at Heinrichsdorf, near Winterberg, on return from mine-laying sortie. Oberlt E. Gunz, Fw W. Flohr, and Gefr J. Frittum killed. Aircraft a write-off.

KGrzbV.101 Junkers Ju52. Forced-landed at Rouen following engine failure. One of crew killed. Aircraft a write-off.

3.(St)/TrGr.186 Junkers Ju87B. Lost during attack on railway at Beaune, west of Dijon, details not recorded. Fw R. Dietz and Uffz H. Kortenhaus killed. Aircraft a write-off.

3.(St)/TrGr.186 Junkers Ju87B. Lost during attack on railway at Beaune, west of Dijon. Uffz H. Ulrich and Obergefr H. Heine killed. Aircraft a write-off.

1./ZG26 Messerschmitt Bf110C. Forced-landed south-west of Quevauvillers, cause unknown. Pilot unhurt, Uffz H. Wilkening (Mechanic) badly injured, admitted to hospital in Amiens. Aircraft damage state not recorded.

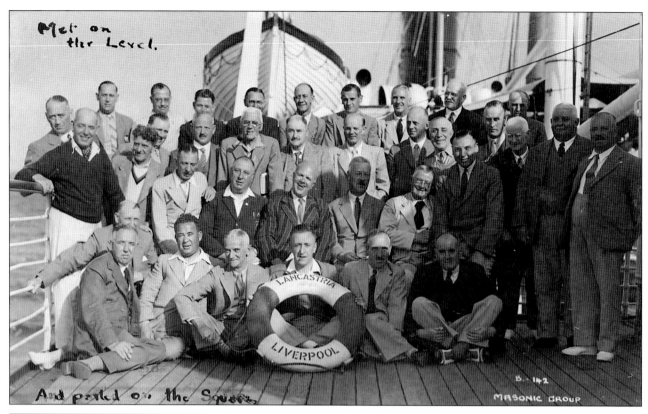

Met on the Level.

And parked on the Squate,

B.-142

MASONIC GROUP

Monday, June 17

Happier days aboard the liner *Lancastria*. By an amazing coincidence, this picture of a Masonic group, led by Bill Ramsey in the striped blazer, enjoying a cruise in 1937 was taken on July 17. Three years later all but a month she went to the bottom . . . and with her between 3,000 and 4,000 servicemen were sent to their deaths.

First intimation that the French were seeking an armistice reached British commanders in France at 12.30 p.m. when Maréchal Pétain broadcast the fact on the radio while, ten minutes later in London, the British Cabinet received news that the French had ceased fire. As the loss lists show this was far from being so, for negotiations had yet to take place, but much confusion resulted within an already dispirited, demoralised, and defeated French army.

Complete evacuation of all British forces was now ordered, the main elements still in the north embarked or sailed from Cherbourg by the following morning, Fighter Command providing cover over the port and ships returning escorted by aircraft of Coastal Command. To ensure continued protection of the port, both AASF fighter squadrons operating under South Component, Nos. 17 and 501, were transferred from Dinard to Jersey, in the Channel Islands, where facilities had been prepared in advance and an operations room opened there at 11.30 p.m.

Meantime, the approaches to Nantes and St-Nazaire were now so seriously congested that several rear parties were diverted to La Rochelle, thought to be less chaotic, and where embarkation proved uneventful, the British parties sailing in the colliers *Thistle Glen* and *Philip M* around 7.00 p.m. At Brest, evacuation also proceeded without incident, the final parties leaving that same evening aboard the vessels *Strathlaird* and *Bactria* and arriving at Plymouth the following morning. Among the estimated 31,000 men evacuated here was Air Vice-Marshal 'Pip' Playfair, Air Officer Commanding the AASF, with the remnants of his headquarters staff. As one former airman recorded, 'On the quay alongside the coaler *Bactria* was a senior officer whose bearing gave confidence to the motley, shattered air men as they boarded this little ship, and sat on the coal still on the deck. This was Air Vice-Marshal Playfair. For the next five

years of the war the example shown by (him) was a morale booster for me, and I am sure for all those airmen who saw him.'

At St-Nazaire it was fast becoming impossible to enter the assembly area, an estimated 10,000 personnel crowded into transit camps by noon, and approach roads jammed with traffic for up to three miles. Despite the desperation and confusion, military order prevailed, and most of the RAF personnel eventually embarked by tender on the *Lancastria* which, along with the *Oronsay*, lay off St-Nazaire in the Loire estuary. By noon, 5,000 soldiers and airmen were crowded aboard — more than twice her normal capacity. At 2.00 p.m. a German air attack took place using cloud cover and the *Oronsay* was hit on the bridge. In a further attack at around 3.30 p.m. bombs missed the *Lancastria* by 50 yards but during a third attack delivered at

3.45 p.m. two bombs struck the ship which sank in under 30 minutes with great loss of life.

At Nantes at 4.30 p.m. Air Marshal Barratt issued his last orders before himself leaving by air for Heston an hour later, Air Vice-Marshal Evill remaining to command. Barratt's orders directed Wing Commander Walter, OC No. 67 Wing, to cover Nantes and St-Nazaire with his fighters until embarkation was completed, probably later that night or early the following morning, when all remaining aircraft could return to England — the ground staff leaving in civil aircraft being organised for the purpose. Thus, by nightfall, all that remained of the once confident and optimistic British Air Force that landed in France nine months before, were three squadrons of Hurricanes and their skeleton ground crews.

Lazing on the Lancastria

B.135

ROYAL AIR FORCE

UK-based aircraft lost or damaged on operations over the Western Front:

RAF FIGHTER COMMAND

56 Squadron, North Weald

Hurricane. Crashed into the roof of a house near Guildford flying in poor visibility a.m. F/O L. Ereminsky killed. Aircraft a write-off.
Leonid Ereminsky is recorded being with No. 151 Squadron by the CWGC.

FRENCH AIR FORCE

DAT Bourges Curtiss H-75s. Damaged and unserviceable aircraft destroyed on withdrawal to Perpignan 10.00 a.m. No pilot casualties. Aircraft all write-offs.

DAT Romorantin Morane 406. Crashed on take-off due to undercarriage failure. Capt T. Opulski unhurt. Aircraft a write-off.

AC 2 Potez 631 (177). Shot down by Uffz Mias of 5./JG3 during reconnaissance sortie between Caen and Lisieux, and crashed near Lecaude 4.35 p.m. EV1 Jacoubet and SM Scouezec missing. Aircraft a write-off.

GAO 1/584 Potez 63.11 (396). Tail badly damaged by flak over Saulieu during reconnaissance sortie 8.30 a.m. Forced-landed at Bron without flaps or brakes. Lt Confuron, Sgt Cases, and Sgt de Benuchamp unhurt. Aircraft a write-off.

GBA II/54 Breguet 691 (69). Wrecked in take-off accident at Dampierre. Capt Cassagnou injured. S/Lt Billon du Plan unhurt. Aircraft a write-off.

GC 2/2 Morane 406 (989). Shot down by flak during reconnaissance sortie and crashed on an island near La Charité-sur-Loire 11.45 a.m. Capt R. Patureau-Mirand *(Commandant)* killed. Aircraft a write-off.
With the river in spate, the body of Raoul Patureau-Mirand was not recovered until August 11.

GR I/33 Potez 63.11 (454). Shot down by flak during reconnaissance of enemy armour around Auxerre, crashed and burned out between Clamecy and Avallon. S/Lt C. Levy killed. Sgt Josserand captured badly wounded. Sgt Monneret captured wounded. Aircraft a write-off.

GR I/55 Potez 63.11. Landed at Feurs damaged by flak during reconnaissance of enemy movements around Roanne, Digoin, and Montbard 2.00 p.m. Lt R. de Lessans killed, rest of crew unhurt. Aircraft damaged but repairable.

LUFTWAFFE

2.(H)/31 Fieseler Fi156. Crashed near Mortagne, west of St Dié, due to engine failure. Hptmn H. Sorge and Uffz H. Pless both injured. Aircraft a write-off.

4.(H)/32 Henschel Hs126. Returned damaged by flak during observation sortie near Toul. Oberlt Klaus believed wounded. Aircraft damage state not recorded.

1./KG26 Heinkel He111. Returned reportedly damaged by fighters between Toul and Nancy. Uffz K. Magerkurth badly wounded, admitted to hospital in Frankfurt; rest of crew unhurt. Aircraft damage state not recorded.

3./KG30 Junkers Ju88A. Returned damaged by flak over the Loire estuary and also attacked by F/Sgt Berry of No. 1 Squadron during armed-reconnaissance and attack on shipping off St-Nazaire 3.45 p.m. Believed also engaged by PM Barbé of AC 5. Oberfw L. Edmüller killed, Fw F. Erdel and Obergefr H. Krauss slightly wounded, Oberlt S-U. Freiherr von Gravenreuth *(Staffelkapitän of 1./KG30)* unhurt. Aircraft damaged but repairable.

Possibly the aircraft that attacked the Lancastria, von Gravenreuth's logbook noting a direct hit on a 10,000-ton transport, but other aircraft of I./KG30 were operating and also attacked shipping in the estuary, as did Oberleutnant Suin de Boutemard of 4./LG1. Standing patrols of Allied fighters may have provided some small sense of security to troops on the vessels below but were clearly unable to prevent such attacks — as British experience at Dunkirk should have proved.

In spite of much speculation, the German pilot who scored hits on the *Lancastria* has never been positively identified. This is the OKL report of operations by KG30:

SECRET. Reports received by the Luftwaffe General Staff during 18.6.40. The attack against shipping gathered in the Loire Estuary reported on 17.6 was carried out by the Ju88 units of IV. Fliegerkorps, in which units of KG30 had especially great success. The summary report of results gave the following overview:

2 hits SC500 amidships on fully-loaded transport entering the Loire Estuary. Transport similar in plan to a battleship. Size about 30,000t, stern flew into the air, ship capsized. 2 hits SC500 on transport ship of 20,000t, one direct hit on the deck, one hit amidships. Heavy smoke and fire resulted. Bows went under water. 3 hits SC250 on big 1,000t transport. Ship lowered boats and capsized. 2 hits SC500 on tanker, one hit amidships, one hit 10m to starboard behind the stern. Heavy side impact, fire apparent and smoke developed. Hit on front of 10-12,000t transport. One hit 5m ahead of the bow. Effect of fire as well as side impact on the bow. 4 hits SC250 on freighter of about 10,000t. Ship stopped and burning. 1 hit amidships, one direct hit on the deck SC500 m.V. (delayed action) on large conspicuous transport, estimated 30,000t. Smoke resulted and firmly established.

At approximately 0600 hours 17.6.40, a detachment of one officer and 60 airmen from 73 Squadron embarked on this troopship.

At approximately 15.45 hours the ship was attacked by enemy aircraft, two bombs being dropped in the sea in close proximity of the ship. The raid alarm was sounded and the ship commenced to list to port. On a second attack a second bomb hit the ship approximately midships. The ship then turned slowly on to her port side and began to sink.

It was impossible then for most of the lifeboats to be launched owing to the list of the boat. A considerable number of men must have been trapped on the lower decks as the ship turned over.

At this time the ship was again attacked, the enemy aircraft using machine guns on the decks and also on men who had already jumped into the water.

It appeared that the oil tanks were either opened or burst as the surface of the sea was being covered by a thick layer of oil which spread all around the ship. I among considerable numbers of men, then slid off the side of the ship into the water. Two more machine gun attacks were made by the enemy aircraft. After a considerable time, which later I worked out to be two and a half hours, I was picked up by a rowing boat and taken on board a small French flower boat.

WARRANT OFFICER W. H. NEALE,
No. 73 SQUADRON, JULY 2, 1940

Extract from No. 67 Wing Operations Record Book, June 17, 1940: 'Wing fighters were several times seen overhead but at approximately 1400 hours an attack was launched on both ships by enemy aircraft which dived out of the clouds. Air raid warnings were sounded on the S.S. *Lancastria* and one bomb was seen to strike the bridge of the S.S. *Oronsay*. Soon after the Hurricanes returned and the loading of the S.S. *Oronsay* continued. Both ships still remained stationary and at 1550 hours enemy aircraft dived out of the clouds and executed another bombing attack. In spite of heavy anti-aircraft fire from both ships and a destroyer stationed nearby, the attack was pressed home and a large bomb fell down the main hatchway of the S.S. *Lancastria*. The resultant explosion in the bowels of the ship created terrible havoc and blew a large hole in her side below the water line. She immediately began to settle by the stern and assumed a most serious list. This situation, coupled with the rapidity with which she was sinking, made it extremely difficult to launch the lifeboats but some success was achieved in this direction. Rafts and any wooden articles were thrown overboard but to the grimness of the situation was now added the further peril of fuel oil which gushed out from the engine room and covered the surrounding water. In a quarter of an hour the S.S. *Lancastria* had disappeared and sterling work was performed by small French boats and the lifeboats from the destroyer which came to the rescue. Some two to three hours elapsed before all the survivors were picked up. In addition to those killed on board, many lives were lost by drowning, a large number of these deaths being directly attributable to the floating oil. A considerable quantity of A.A. shell splinters and machine gun bullets also struck the water and several casualties were doubtless caused thereby. Very shortly after the attack the Hurricanes returned and drew off the enemy. Although favoured by clouds one Ju88 was shot down and two others seriously damaged. It is believed that a further bomber was destroyed by A.A. fire. Finally, the survivors were taken to the S.S. *Oronsay*, which by this time had moved out to sea and also to a large cargo ship inshore. Everything possible was there done to help and at approximately 2000 hours the S.S. *Oronsay* set sail for England the cargo ship following later.'

Flight Sergeant George Berry of B Flight, No. 1 Squadron, fought with distinction throughout the campaign in France, claiming three enemy aircraft destroyed, and was leading a section of three Hurricanes over St-Nazaire on June 17, 1940, when he was credited with the 'Heinkel He111' that sunk the *Lancastria*. This action was widely publicised by a British Press starved of positive news from the dismal events then unfolding in France.

We were all on board ready to sail at 8 o'clock in the morning but we remained at anchor until the bomb hit us. This means that we were stationary from over seven hours, even though the harbour had been bombed twice during the previous day. Why did we have to wait so long?

Most of our men were asleep in the hold when the ship was successfully bombed and, according to the Wireless Operator, the stairs leading from this hold to the higher decks were destroyed so that escape from this hold must have been extremely difficult if not impossible. He himself used a porthole.

At least two previous bombs had missed the ship by perhaps twenty yards but even then we felt the concussion as the blast travelled through the water to strike the ship, and these were of sufficient strength to compel me to don my helmet and life jacket.

The bomb hit the ship whilst I was standing in a corridor not far from two watertight doors, and the blast flung me nearer to these two doors. During that ordeal I was conscious of breaking glass and burning and cracking wood and my own helplessness to prevent myself from moving. When I finally stopped I was bleeding from nose and mouth and from wounds in the legs, and the more serious of these I bound with my handkerchief before I swung into the water.

The ship heeled over to the port first, so that there was a general rush to the port safety doors. Then she came over to the starboard side and it was from the starboard doors that I swung myself into the comparative safety of the sea.

I swam perhaps fifty yards before I turned around just to see how she would take her final plunge. By this time her bows were well under and her screw at least ten feet off the surface. I watched her until she had nearly disappeared. Even at this time there were hundreds of people sitting on the ship singing 'Roll out the Barrel'.

I never saw her sink for when I clambered aboard a minesweeper she had already gone, and the sea around a mass of oil, spars and bodies. I was in the water perhaps half an hour and on the ship a good half hour before I jumped so that she sank within an hour after being hit.

LAC C. CROSS, No. 73 SQUADRON, JULY 2, 1940

The death toll for the sinking has never been reliably established. Churchill forbade publication saying that 'the newspapers have got quite enough disaster for today at least'. He explained that 'I had intended to release the news a few days later, but events crowded upon us so black and so quickly that I forgot to lift the ban, and it was some time before the knowledge of this horror became public.' (The Ministry of Information announced the loss of the ship on July 26 following a report in *The Times* the previous day.) What is known is that the Admiralty put the loss figure at 2,823 and Churchill 'upwards of 3,000 men'.

The total number of troops on board has been estimated at 6,000-8,000 of whom some 2,500 were rescued. The registers of the Commonwealth War Graves Commission identify 1,816 as having died on the *Lancastria* and the following pages list those who were serving with the Royal Air Force. No. 73 Squadron lost 37 men of whom 31 have no grave but the sea compared with 12 pilots killed during the previous ten months in France. (In the annals of naval disasters, this death toll was only surpassed by the sinking of the *Wilhelm Gustloff* off Danzig in January 1945, when an estimated 7,000-plus lost their lives.)

RAF PERSONNEL LOST ABOARD S.S. *LANCASTRIA* — JUNE 17, 1940

ADAMS, AC1 A. A. Age 27.
Runnymede Memorial. Panel 24.

ALSTON, Flight Sergeant H. D. 98 Sqdn.
Pornic War Cemetery, Loire-Atlantique,
France. Special Memorial. 2.F.14.

APPLEBY, AC2 W. Age 26.
Runnymede Memorial. Panel 26.

APPLIN, AC2 E. C. S. 98 Sqdn. Age 20.
Runnymede Memorial. Panel 26.

ARDERN, Sergeant W. 98 Sqdn.
Runnymede Memorial. Panel 11.

ASHARD, AC2 E. F. 98 Sqdn. Age 19.
Runnymede Memorial. Panel 26.

ASHBY, AC2 K. W. Age 23.
Runnymede Memorial. Panel 26.

ASHLEY, Corporal A. 73 Sqdn. Age 38.
Pornic War Cemetery, Loire-
Atlantique, France. Grave 2.A.18.

BAKER, Sergeant L. G. 98 Sqdn. Age
19. La Bernerie-en-Retz Communal
Cemetery, Loire-Atlantique, France.
Row C. Grave 12.

BARDGETT, AC1 J. E. C. 73 Sqdn. Age 20.
Runnymede Memorial. Panel 24.

BARRIE, LAC G. W. 98 Sqdn. Age 22.
Runnymede Memorial. Panel 22.

BASSAM, LAC G. W. 73 Sqdn. Age 30.
Runnymede Memorial. Panel 22.

BATEMAN, LAC G. 98 Sqdn.
Runnymede Memorial. Panel 22.

BAXTER, Corporal J. R. 73 Sqdn. Age 32.
Runnymede Memorial. Panel 21.

BELL, LAC E. Age 39.
Runnymede Memorial. Panel 22.

BELL, Sergeant J. D. Age 23.
Runnymede Memorial. Panel 11.

BELLAMY, AC2 C. V. 98 Sqdn. Age 20.
Runnymede Memorial. Panel 26.

BLACKETT, AC1 G. 98 Sqdn. Age 24.
Runnymede Memorial. Panel 24.

BLACKWELL, LAC F. J. 98 Sqdn. Age 34.
Runnymede Memorial. Panel 22.

BODDEN, Corporal R. R. Age 32.
Runnymede Memorial. Panel 21.

BONIFACE, Sergeant R. J. 98 Sqdn.
Ste Marie Communal Cemetery,
Loire-Atlantique, France. Collective
Grave 1.

BOOTH, AC1 T. G. 73 Sqdn. Age 20.
Runnymede Memorial. Panel 24.

BOTT, AC2 K. V. 98 Sqdn. Age 25.
Runnymede Memorial. Panel 26.

BOUMPHREY, AC1 A. 73 Sqdn. Age 22.
Runnymede Memorial. Panel 24.

BROADBENT, LAC R. RAF.
Runnymede Memorial. Panel 22.

BROWN, AC2 D. 98 Sqdn.
Runnymede Memorial. Panel 26.

BROWN, AC2 G. O. 98 Sqdn.
Runnymede Memorial. Panel 26.

BRUNTON, AC2 J. 98 Sqdn. Age 23.
Runnymede Memorial. Panel 26.

BURROWS, AC2 H. 98 Sqdn. Age 18.
Runnymede Memorial. Panel 26.

CANNAR, AC1 B. R. 73 Sqdn.
Runnymede Memorial. Panel 24.

CARTWRIGHT, Corporal J. 98 Sqdn.
Age 32.
Runnymede Memorial. Panel 21.

CHART, AC2 G. A.
Runnymede Memorial. Panel 26.

CHAVE, AC1 F. S. H.
Runnymede Memorial. Panel 25.

CHILDS, AC2 T. H. 98 Sqdn. Age 20.
Prefailles Communal Cemetery, Loire-
Atlantique, France. Grave 41.

CHRISTIE, AC1 J. B. Age 19.
Runnymede Memorial. Panel 25.

CLARKE, AC1 D. B. 98 Sqdn.
Runnymede Memorial. Panel 25.

CLARKE, Corporal H. Age 26.
Runnymede Memorial. Panel 21.

CLARKE, LAC S. 98 Sqdn. Age 25.
Runnymede Memorial. Panel 22.

CLIFFORD, Corporal N. J. Age 27.
Noirmoutier-en-l'Île Communal Cemetery,
Vendee, France. Row 2. Grave 16.

COCKING, Corporal N. Age 21.
Runnymede Memorial. Panel 21.

COOK, Corporal A. C. 98 Sqdn. Age 24.
Runnymede Memorial. Panel 21.

COOPER, AC1 J. W. 98 Sqdn.
Runnymede Memorial. Panel 25.

CORMACK-BEATSON, LAC C. E.
98 Sqdn.
Runnymede Memorial. Panel 22.

CRANE, LAC L. J. 73 Sqdn. Age 43. La
Plaine-sur-Mer Communal Cemetery,
Loire-Atlantique, France. Grave 17.

CRANSTON, AC1 J. Age 19. Château-
d'Olonne Churchyard, Vendée, France.
Grave 3.

CROSS, LAC R. A. R. 98 Sqdn. Age 39.
Runnymede Memorial. Panel 22.

DANIEL, Corporal H. 98 Sqdn. Age 21.
Runnymede Memorial. Panel 21.

DEAN, AC2 H. W. Age 19.
Runnymede Memorial. Panel 26.

DENTON, Sergeant T. F. 98 Sqdn. Age 34.
Runnymede Memorial. Panel 13.

DERWIN, LAC H. D. 73 Sqdn. Age 33.
Runnymede Memorial. Panel 22.

DIAMOND, LAC G. M. Age 23.
Runnymede Memorial. Panel 22.

DIGNAN, AC2 G. A. 98 Sqdn. Age 19.
Runnymede Memorial. Panel 26.

DOWDING, LAC J. H. 98 Sqdn.
Runnymede Memorial. Panel 22.

EDWARDS, LAC H. G.
Runnymede Memorial. Panel 22.

ELDRED, Corporal W. G.
Runnymede Memorial. Panel 21.

FISHER, AC1 H. Age 27.
Runnymede Memorial. Panel 25.

FISHER, LAC H. 98 Sqdn. Age 20.
Runnymede Memorial. Panel 23.

FITZPATRICK, AC1 T. 98 Sqdn. Age 20.
Runnymede Memorial. Panel 25.

FOTHERGILL, AC1 J. E. 73 Sqdn. Age 46.
Runnymede Memorial. Panel 25.

FROST, Corporal J. 73 Sqdn. Age 34.
Runnymede Memorial. Panel 21.

GARSIDE, AC2 C. 98 Sqdn. Age 23.
Runnymede Memorial. Panel 26.

GAVIN, AC1 P. 98 Sqdn. Age 19.
Runnymede Memorial. Panel 25.

GLEAVE, LAC W.
Runnymede Memorial. Panel 23.

GLOVER, LAC D. W. Age 20.
Runnymede Memorial. Panel 23.

GOLDING, Corporal C. A. 73 Sqdn. Age 31.
Runnymede Memorial. Panel 21.

GORDON, Corporal F. L. 98 Sqdn. Age 31.
Runnymede Memorial. Panel 21.

GREENMAN, AC2 W. J. 98 Sqdn. Age
20. Runnymede Memorial. Panel 26.

GRIFFIN, AC2 K. W. 98 Sqdn. Age 19.
Runnymede Memorial. Panel 26.

GRIFFITHS, AC2 D. M. 98 Sqdn. Age
24. L'Aiguillon-sur-Mer Communal
Cemetery, Vendée, France. North Plot.
Row 17. Grave 14.

GROVE, Corporal R. G. B. 73 Sqdn. Age 31.
Runnymede Memorial. Panel 21

GROVES, AC1 G. E. 98 Sqdn. Age 20.
Runnymede Memorial. Panel 25.

GUNN, AC1 H. C. Age 33.
Runnymede Memorial. Panel 25.

GUYMER, LAC H. P. F. 98 Sqdn. Age
33. St Trojan-les-Bains Communal
Cemetery, Charente-Maritime, France.
Row 4. Grave 2.

HALL, Corporal G. T.
Runnymede Memorial. Panel 21.

HAMILTON, Corporal A. G. 73 Sqdn.
Age 29.
Runnymede Memorial. Panel 21.

HARDISTY, LAC W. 73 Sqdn. Age 23.
Runnymede Memorial. Panel 23.

HARPHAM, AC1 W. 98 Sqdn.
Runnymede Memorial. Panel 25.

HARRIS, Sergeant S. L. 98 Sqdn. Age 20.
Runnymede Memorial. Panel 15.

HATHERLY, AC2 F. H. La Bernerie-en-
Retz Communal Cemetery, Loire-
Atlantique, France. Row B. Grave 21.

HAYES, AC1 T. A. 73 Sqdn. Age 34.
Runnymede Memorial. Panel 25.

HEDGER, AC2 H. J.
Runnymede Memorial. Panel 26.

HEPPLEWHITE, LAC J. I. Age 21.
Runnymede Memorial. Panel 23.

HIGGINS, AC1 J. Le Clion-sur-Mer
Communal Cemetery, Loire-
Atlantique, France. Collective Grave 4.

HILL, AC2 A. D. 98 Sqdn. Age 20.
Runnymede Memorial. Panel 27.

HILLS, Sergeant G. G. S, 98 Sqdn. Age 24.
Runnymede Memorial. Panel 15.

HODGETTS, AC2 A. H. J. 98 Sqdn. Age 23.
Runnymede Memorial. Panel 27.

HOE, Corporal A. F. G. Age 25.
Runnymede Memorial. Panel 22.

HOLLAND, LAC R. A. 73 Sqdn. Age 40.
Runnymede Memorial. Panel 23.

HONDERWOOD, LAC W. S. 73 Sqdn.
Age 20.
Runnymede Memorial. Panel 23.

HOPKINSON, AC2 J. F. Age 20.
Runnymede Memorial. Panel 27.

HOSKINS, Sergeant E. D. C. 98 Sqdn.
Age 19. Le Clion-sur-Mer Communal
Cemetery, Loire-Atlantique, France.
Collective Grave 4.

HOW, AC1 V. H. 98 Sqdn. Age 19.
Runnymede Memorial. Panel 25.

HOWELL, AC1 R. Age 20.
Runnymede Memorial. Panel 25.

HUMPHREYS, AC1 O. 73 Sqdn. Age 21.
Runnymede Memorial. Panel 25.

HUNTER, LAC R. W. Age 21.
Runnymede Memorial. Panel 23.

HUTCHISON, LAC J. 73 Sqdn. Age 34.
Runnymede Memorial. Panel 23.

I'ANSON, Corporal L. A. Age 23.
Runnymede Memorial. Panel 22.

INGRAHAM, LAC I. 98 Sqdn.
Runnymede Memorial. Pancl 23.

JAMIESON, AC2 R. W. Age 24.
Runnymede Memorial. Panel 27.

JARVIS, AC2 P. J. 98 Sqdn. Age 20.
(Served as William Henry KIRK).
Runnymede Memorial. Panel 27.

JARY, LAC R. S. Age 21.
Runnymede Memorial. Panel 23.

JONES, Sergeant C. P. 98 Sqdn.
Runnymede Memorial. Panel 16.

JONES, LAC D. W. 98 Sqdn.
Runnymede Memorial. Panel 23.

JONES, LAC R. T. Age 22.
Runnymede Memorial. Panel 23.

JONES, Corporal T. D. 98 Sqdn.
Runnymede Memorial. Panel 22.

JOY, Corporal F. 73 Sqdn. Age 38.
Runnymede Memorial. Panel 22.

KELLY, LAC R. M. Age 24.
Runnymede Memorial. Panel 23.

KENT, AC1 J. E. 73 Sqdn. Age 34.
Pornic War Cemetery, Loire-
Atlantique, France. Grave 1.A.9.

KERR, AC1 J. Age 22.
Runnymede Memorial. Panel 25.

KEVAN, Corporal R. 98 Sqdn. Age 26.
Pornic War Cemetery,
Loire-Atlantique, France. Special Memorial.
1.D.7.

KING, Corporal G. R. 98 Sqdn. Age 26.
Runnymede Memorial. Panel 22.

LANSDOWNE, AC1 M. M. 73 Sqdn.
Age 40.
Runnymede Memorial. Panel 25.

LATTER, LAC G. A. 98 Sqdn. Age 20.
Runnymede Memorial. Panel 23.

LAWSON, AC2 T. E.
Runnymede Memorial. Panel 27.

LLOYD, AC1 T. D. S. 73 Sqdn. Age 19.
Runnymede Memorial. Panel 25.

LUNNUN, AC2 W. E. Age 24.
Runnymede Memorial. Panel 27.

LUNT, AC2 H. 98 Sqdn.
Runnymede Memorial. Panel 27.

LUSTY, AC1 W. Age 20. Préfailles
Communal Cemetery, Loire-
Atlantique, France. Grave 3.

MACAULEY, AC1 A.
Runnymede Memorial. Panel 25.

MACPHERSON, LAC W. 98 Sqdn. Age 19.
Runnymede Memorial. Panel 23.

MARRON, LAC S. J. 73 Sqdn. Age 25.
Runnymede Memorial. Panel 23.

MARTIN, AC2 W. W. 98 Sqdn. Age 38.
Runnymede Memorial. Panel 27.

MAWSON, AC2 J. H. 73 Sqdn. Age 38.
Runnymede Memorial. Panel 27.

McFARLANE, AC2 J. 98 Sqdn. Age 23.
Runnymede Memorial. Panel 27.

McKELVIE, Sergeant J. 98 Sqdn. Age 27.
Préfailles Communal Cemetery,
Loire-Atlantique, France. Grave 65.

McLEOD, AC1 H. G. 98 Sqdn. Age 21.
Runnymede Memorial. Panel 25.

McMAHON, Corporal R. P. W. Age 19.
Runnymede Memorial. Panel 22.

McNAUGHTON, LAC N. 98 Sqdn.
Runnymede Memorial. Panel 23.

MITCHELL, AC2 W. R.
Runnymede Memorial. Panel 27.

MOORE, Corporal A. W. Age 26.
Runnymede Memorial. Panel 22.

MOORE, Corporal R. 73 Sqdn. Age 30.
Pornic War Cemetery, Loire-
Atlantique, France. Grave 2.B.10.

NIALL, AC1 J. D. Age 19.
Runnymede Memorial. Panel 25.

NORRIS, AC1 J. H. Age 21.
Runnymede Memorial. Panel 25.

ODGERS, LAC J. A. Age 24.
Runnymede Memorial. Panel 23.

OLSEN, AC2 N. W.
Runnymede Memorial. Panel 27.

PARK, Corporal A. 98 Sqdn.
Runnymede Memorial. Panel 22.

PARTON, AC1 F. Age 43. St Palais-sur-
Mer Communal Cemetery, Charente-
Maritime, France. Row 3. Grave 3.

PEARSON, AC2 H. V. 98 Sqdn. Age 27.
Runnymede Memorial. Panel 27.

PETERS, AC2 J. E. 98 Sqdn. Age 20.
Runnymede Memorial. Panel 27.

PETRIE, Corporal E. 73 Sqdn. Age 36.
Runnymede Memorial. Panel 22.

PLUMB, AC1 E. G. 98 Sqdn.
Runnymede Memorial. Panel 25.

PRICE, AC2 T. Age 20. Pornic War
Cemetery, Loire-Atlantique.
Grave 2.J.14.

PUGH, AC1 W. 98 Sqdn. Age 20.
Runnymede Memorial. Panel 25.

RADFORD, AC1 W. E. 98 Sqdn.
Runnymede Memorial. Panel 25.

RAMSEY, AC1 D. J. 73 Sqdn.
Runnymede Memorial. Panel 25.

RANSON, AC2 M. W. J. 98 Sqdn.
Runnymede Memorial. Panel 27.

RAYNER, LAC E. E. 73 Sqdn.
Runnymede Memorial. Panel 23.

READING, AC2 G. 98 Sqdn. Age 23.
Runnymede Memorial. Panel 27.

READING, LAC R. G. Age 36.
Runnymede Memorial. Panel 23.

RECORD, LAC G. A. T.
Runnymede Memorial. Panel 23.

REDFERN, AC2 L. 98 Sqdn. Age 21.
Runnymede Memorial. Panel 27.

REEVES, AC2 E. C. 98 Sqdn. Age 23.
l'Île-d'Yeu (Port Joinville) Communal
Cemetery, Vendée, France.
Plot F. Row 1. Grave 93.

ROXBOROUGH, Corporal J. H. 98 Sqdn.
Runnymede Memorial. Panel 22.

RUCK, AC2 G. 98 Sqdn. Age 22.
Runnymede Memorial. Panel 27.

RUSHTON, Corporal W. C. Age 25.
St Nazaire-sur-Charente Communal
Cemetery, Charente-Maritime, France.

RICHARDSON, LAC W. Age 38.
Runnymede Memorial. Panel 24.

RIDDELL, LAC R. 98 Sqdn. Age 19.
Runnymede Memorial. Panel 24.

RIGBY, Corporal G. A. 98 Sqdn. Age 23.
Runnymede Memorial. Panel 22.

RIGBY, Corporal G. H. 73 Sqdn.
Runnymede Memorial. Panel 22.

ROBINSON, AC1 H. 98 Sqdn.
Runnymede Memorial. Panel 26.

RODGERS, Corporal J. B. 73 Sqdn. Age 41.
Runnymede Memorial. Panel 22.

ROE, LAC A. G. 73 Sqdn. Age 43.
Runnymede Memorial. Panel 24.

ROGERS, AC1 J. 98 Sqdn. Age 18.
Runnymede Memorial. Panel 26.

SARGENT, LAC H. V. Age 20.
Runnymede Memorial. Panel 24.

SAUNDERS, AC1 P. W.
Runnymede Memorial. Panel 26.

SCOTT-KIDDIE, AC2 A. J. 98 Sqdn.
Age 24.
Runnymede Memorial. Panel 27.

SELLICK, AC1 H. W. B. 73 Sqdn. Age 22.
Runnymede Memorial. Panel 26.

SIBBORN, AC2 J. A. 98 Sqdn. Age 21.
Runnymede Memorial. Panel 27.

SLATER, AC1 C. F. 98 Sqdn. Age 19.
Runnymede Memorial. Panel 26.

SMALL, AC1 W. L. 98 Sqdn. Age 22.
Runnymede Memorial. Panel 26.

SMITH, AC2 F. H. 98 Sqdn. Age 19.
Runnymede Memorial. Panel 27.

SMITH, AC1 H. V. Age 26.
Runnymede Memorial. Panel 26.

SMITH, Sergeant J. T. 98 Sqdn. Age 27.
Pornic War Cemetery, Loire-
Atlantique, France. Grave 2.A.13.

SMITH, AC2 S. Age 22.
Runnymede Memorial. Panel 27.

SMYTH, AC1 N. Age 20.
Runnymede Memorial. Panel 26.

STOCKER, LAC F. 98 Sqdn. Age 20.
Runnymede Memorial. Panel 24.

STOKES, Sergeant L. J. 98 Sqdn. Age 27.
Pornic War Cemetery, Loire-
Atlantique, France. Grave 1.A.7.

STONES, AC1 D. 98 Sqdn.
Runnymede Memorial. Panel 26.

STORRAR, LAC J. R.
Runnymede Memorial. Panel 24.

SYMMONDS, AC1 A. L. 98 Sqdn. Age
21. Runnymede Memorial. Panel 26.

TAWS, LAC S. 98 Sqdn.
Runnymede Memorial. Panel 24.

TAYLOR, LAC A. J. Age 36.
Runnymede Memorial. Panel 24.

THOMAS, LAC J. V. L. Age 28.
Runnymede Memorial. Panel 24.

TIDY, Flight Sergeant G. K. Age 28.
Runnymede Memorial. Panel 11.

TIMMS, AC2 C. 98 Sqdn. Age 19.
Runnymede Memorial. Panel 27.

TRAHEARN, LAC H. C. 73 Sqdn. Age
30. Escoublac-La-Baule War Cemetery,
Loire-Atlantique, France. Grave 1.F.17.

TREDGETT, AC1 E. 73 Sqdn. Age 21.
Pornic War Cemetery, Loire-Atlantique,
France. Special Memorial 1.D.8.

WAITE, LAC J. A. 98 Sqdn.
Runnymede Memorial. Panel 24.

WALKER, AC1 K. M. 73 Sqdn. Age 18.
Runnymede Memorial. Panel 26.

WARD, AC1 W. A. Age 22.
Runnymede Memorial. Panel 26.

WATKIN, LAC F. W. 98 Sqdn. Age 19.
Préfailles Communal Cemetery, Loire-
Atlantique, France. Grave 52.

WATSON, AC1 A. 98 Sqdn. Age 23.
Runnymede Memorial. Panel 26.

WATTS, Corporal A. J. Age 22.
L'Épine Communal Cemetery, Vendée,
Row 3. Grave 3.

WAYMAN, LAC A. W. Age 20.
Runnymede Memorial. Panel 24.

WHITMARSH, LAC K. R. 98 Sqdn. Age 32.
Runnymede Memorial. Panel 24.

WHITTET, Corporal J. Age 20.
Runnymede Memorial. Panel 22.

WILLIAMSON, LAC J. A. Age 22.
Runnymede Memorial. Panel 24.

WILLIAMSON, LAC W. J. 98 Sqdn. Age 23.
Runnymede Memorial. Panel 24.

WILSON, AC1 F. J. 98 Sqdn. Age 19.
Runnymede Memorial. Panel 26.

WILSON, Corporal W. Age 20.
Noirmoutier-en-l'Île (L'Herbaudière)
Communal Cemetery, Vendee, France.
Row B. Grave 6.

WRIGHT, AC2 J. N. 98 Sqdn.
Runnymede Memorial. Panel 27.

WYATT, AC2 K. L. 98 Sqdn.
Runnymede Memorial. Panel 27.

Flying Officer Hall: '73 Squadron was destined to be the last to leave France. First in, last out . . . it was as it should be'.

Tuesday, June 18

This would be the last day of the campaign to see RAF operations from French soil. Air Vice-Marshal Evill was recalled to England and left Nantes by air at about 9.00 a.m. By midday, having completed their last patrols over Nantes and St-Nazaire, the Hurricanes of Nos. 1 and 242 Squadrons had also left. The final troop embarkations at St Nazaire which had been expected around 1.00 p.m. were not completed until later, happily without interference from the Luftwaffe, after which the last BAFF operational aircraft to leave France, seven Hurricanes of No. 73 Squadron, took-off from Nantes-Château Bougon around 2.45 p.m. The rear ground party followed in a Handley Page Harrow soon afterwards, climbing away through dense smoke from the wrecked and burning aircraft, vehicles, and equipment abandoned on the now deserted airfield. The last British aircraft away was an Avro Anson carrying the staff of No. 67 Wing, including Wing Commander Walter, that took off just before the first German armoured vehicles arrived.

Meanwhile, evacuation of British forces from Cherbourg also proceeded relatively unhindered with cover provided by the two BAFF Hurricane squadrons now based in the Channel Islands which flew a total of 27 sorties over the port during the day. In response to a request from ground forces in the area for some 'pretty hefty bombing', six Blenheims attacked enemy vehicles approaching Les Pieux, some 15 miles to the southwest, around 3.45 p.m. This modest effort representing the only British bombing of the entire day. Fighters operating from Tangmere sent 75 sorties over Cherbourg between 4.30 a.m. and 6.30 p.m. and met a German air attack on assembled shipping around 4.00 p.m. For the loss of two Hurricanes and pilots, this raid proved unsuccess-

ful in preventing the last main body of British troops from sailing aboard the SS *Manxman*.

The bulk of the French armies were now in full retreat, but with armistice negotiations yet to begin, the conflict in France continued albeit on a much reduced scale. While Général de Gaulle broadcast from London exhorting continued resistance, more French Air Force units withdrew to the south, still others already leaving for North Africa.

That afternoon, Churchill addressed a sombre House of Commons: 'We do not yet know what will happen in France, or whether France's resistance will be prolonged, both in France and in the French Empire overseas. The French government will be throwing away great opportunities and casting away all their future if they do not continue the war in accordance with their treaty obligations, from which we have not felt able to release them. However matters may go in France, or with the French government, we in this island and in the British Empire will never lose our sense of comradeship with the French people. If we are now called upon to

endure what they have suffered we shall emulate their courage and, if final victory rewards our toils, they shall share the gains.'

Thus the campaign in France, at least from a British perspective, came to an inglorious end. And though RAF aircraft operating from England continued to attack French targets, notably Channel ports and enemy-occupied airfields where most Luftwaffe casualties were to take place during the next few days, it was clear that a new phase in the war between Britain and Germany had already begun. Luftwaffe activity over mainland Britain was increasing as more German bomber and reconnaissance units settled into newly-occupied bases in Holland and Belgium. RAF Fighter Command, meantime, marshalled its depleted resources and prepared to defend Britain against the full onslaught of the German air weapon which must now surely follow. Doubtless, however resolute and determined RAF pilots and aircrew may have been, there were those among them that now recognised, and only too well, just how desperately close-fought the coming air battle would be.

What Général Weygand called the Battle of France is over. I expect that the Battle of Britain is about to begin. Upon this battle depends the survival of Christian civilisation. Upon it depends our own British life, and the long continuity of our institutions and our Empire. The whole fury and might of the enemy must very soon be turned on us. Hitler knows that he will have to break us in this island or lose the war. If we can stand up to him, all Europe may be free and the life of the world may move forward into broad, sunlit uplands. But if we fail, then the whole world, including the United States, including all that we have known and cared for, will sink into the abyss of a new dark age made more sinister and perhaps more protracted by the lights of perverted science. Let us therefore brace ourselves to our duties, and so bear ourselves that, if the British Empire and its Commonwealth last for a thousand years, men will say, 'This was their finest hour.'

WINSTON CHURCHILL, JUNE 18, 1940

(05.10 hours). The Squadron was at readiness at dawn. P.O. Eliot and P.O. McGaw left for Guernsey and Tangmere at 04.15, to deliver messages for A.V.M. Evill, McGaw distinguishing himself by missing Guernsey and fetching up at Lands End!

The C.O. took off at dawn, and carried out a low flying reconnaissance, to try and locate enemy tanks and armoured vehicles, which were rumoured to be approaching Nantes. He went up to just north of Le Mans, via Angers, returning via Tours, but saw nothing of more interest then several agitated female refugee cyclists, who rode into a ditch on his approach, thinking he was an enemy machine.

(07.00 hours). 'A' and 'B' Flights last six aircraft took off, and carried out covering patrols over St-Nazaire and Nantes. No enemy aircraft were seen, and the patrol of an hour and a half was carried out uneventfully.

(11.30 hours). At 11.30, 'A' and 'B' Flights, led by F/Lt. Nicholls and the C.O. respectively, took off to carry out the last patrols in France, over Nantes and St-Nazaire. Nothing was seen and at 13.00 hours they left their patrol lines and returned to refuel. On landing, they discovered that another patrol of one flight of aircraft had been asked for over St-Nazaire, and this was led by F/O Drake who took off at 13.15 hours, leading a patrol of five aircraft. The patrol was carried out without incident, and landed at

14.30. In the meantime, there were various alarms and excursions, and reports of approaching tanks. No. 1 Squadron had already left, and we began to wonder if we should get away in time.

(14.15 hours). Accordingly, F/Lt. Nicholls and nine other pilots left for U.K., as soon as they were refuelled, at 14.15 hours. The rear party prepared to refuel the patrolling aircraft immediately they landed, and F/Lt. Brown of 67 Wing went round, firing the unserviceable and crashed aircraft on the aerodrome.

F/O Drake's patrol landed at about 14.30, and was at once refuelled. The Bombay, which was to take the rear party, consisting of Sgt. Gallagher and fourteen men, was started up, as also was W/Cdr. Walter's Anson. At 15.00 hours, the remaining six aircraft took off, led by the C.O., for Tangmere — the last Squadron to leave France.

We thus severed our very pleasant connection with 67 Wing and A.A.S.F. The C.O's party had a very uneventful trip to Tangmere, via Cherbourg. F/Lt Nicholls refuelled at Boscombe Down and then came on to Tangmere.

At Tangmere, the Squadron found instructions to proceed to Church Fenton, and proceeded there after refuelling pilots and machines.

SQUADRON LEADER J. W. C. MORE, JUNE 18, 1940

BRITISH AIR FORCES IN FRANCE

1 SQUADRON, NANTES-CHÂTEAU BOUGON

Three Hurricanes L1757, L1974, and P3045. Unserviceable aircraft burned on evacuation to England 11.45 a.m. No pilot casualties. Aircraft all write-offs.

242 SQUADRON, NANTES-CHÂTEAU BOUGON

Three Hurricanes N2381 LE⊙X, P3683, and P3779. Unserviceable aircraft burned on evacuation to England 11.00 a.m. No pilot casualties. Aircraft all write-offs.

Hurricane P2985. Run low on fuel during return from Nantes and damaged tail wheel and rudder in forced-landing on Dunster Beach, Minehead, 2.00 p.m. Pilot Officer R. D. Grassick unhurt. Aircraft damaged but repairable.

Hurricane P3149. Run low on fuel during return from Nantes and nosed-over damaging propeller in forced-landing on Dunster Beach, Minehead, 2.00 p.m. Pilot Officer N. N. Campbell unhurt. Aircraft LE⊙N repairable.

Hurricane P3719. Run low on fuel during return from Nantes and tore off tail wheel and rudder in forced-landing on Dunster Beach, Minehead, 2.00 p.m. Sergeant E. Richardson unhurt. Aircraft damaged but repairable.

UK-based aircraft lost or damaged on operations over the Western Front:

RAF COASTAL COMMAND

801 Squadron (FAA), Detling
Reconnaissance French coast:

Skua II. Returned with windscreen smashed by AA fire during photo-reconnaissance between Boulogne and Calais 4.45 a.m. Lt Savage injured face, Lt Hayes unhurt. Aircraft F repairable.

RAF FIGHTER COMMAND

151 Squadron, Manston
Escort Blenheims:

Hurricane P3313. Shot down by return fire during attack on He111s of 5./KG1 and abandoned off Cherbourg 4.10 p.m. P/O L. Wright baled out but died. Aircraft a write-off.

Hurricane P3324. Shot down by return fire during attack on He111s of 5./KG1 off Cherbourg 4.10 p.m. Sgt M. R. Aslin killed. Aircraft a write-off.

4 (Continental) Ferry Flight, Tangmere
Transfer flight to Middle East:

Hurricane. Lost formation flying in cloud and reportedly attacked by enemy aircraft. Hit a hedge and overturned forced-landing near Loudon 10.00 a.m. P/O A. G. Maycock unhurt. Aircraft destroyed.

Five Blenheims were also lost on this flight meeting severe storm conditions north-west of Limoges; L9317 crashed near Charroux, L9318 at Crozon-sur-Vauvre, L9315 at Hiesse, L9314 at Prunières, and L9351 near Mazarques, with the loss of all 15 crewmen.

'The Battle of France is over . . . the Battle of Britain is about to begin.' **A Hurricane shorn of any identification markings, lies abandoned on a French airfield as the Stukas prepare for their next campaign.**

FRENCH AIR FORCE

AC 2 Potez 631. Damaged by French AA fire during withdrawal from Calais-Marck to Lanvéoc-Poulmic. Mtre Chaume and crew unhurt. Aircraft damaged but repairable — later abandoned.

AC 2 Bloch 151 (15). Shot down by Oberlt Herget of 6./ZG76 over Auvers, west of Carentan, during escort flight from Calais-Marck to Lanvéoc-Poulmic 8.05 a.m. SM Amory missing. Aircraft 6 lost.

AC 2 Bloch 151 (61). Damaged by French AA fire during escort flight from Calais-Marck to Lanvéoc-Poulmic. Pilot unhurt. Aircraft 3 damaged — later abandoned.

E 2 Breguet 'Bizerte'. Forced-landed at Hourtin out of fuel en route to Berre on withdrawal from Lanvéoc-Poulmic. Crew unhurt. Aircraft abandoned.

E 6 Latécoère 523. Flying boat undergoing major modifications scuttled by crew on withdrawal from Lanvéoc-Poulmic. LV Jolivet de Riencourt and crew unhurt. Aircraft 'Aldebaran' a write-off.

Over 30 aircraft were abandoned on the evacuation of the Aéronautique Navale base at Lanvéoc-Poulmic on this date; 4 Dewoitine 373s (4, 11, 12 and 13), Dewoitine 376 (32), 3 Loire 130s (30, 56 and 63), Gourdou-Leseurre 813 (66), and Gourdou-Leseurre 832 (14), all of the base establishment. Also, 7 North American 57s (103, 104, 107, 108, 110, 119 and 120), 2 Caudron Goélands (211 and 219), and 2 MS230s (452 and 457) of the Cours de Perfectionnement training school, together with 2 CAMS 37.11s (64 and 95), 2 Caudron Goélands (214 and 215), 3 Schreck FBA 17s (207, 208 and 218), Gourdou-Leseurre 812 (62), and Potez 567 (3) belonging to the Section d'Entraînement et Servitudes Brest.

GAO 2/514 Potez 63.11. Crashed on take-off at St Étienne-de-St-Geoirs on withdrawal to Sisteron p.m. S/Lt A. Klein, Adjt L. Coullet, and Sgt P. Tenin killed. Aircraft a write-off.

GB I/23 Bloch 210 (154). Port engine caught fire during night bombing attack on Coni airfield in Italy. Abandoned on regaining French territory. S/Lt N'Guyen and crew baled out unhurt. Aircraft a write-off.

1S2 Gourdou-Leseurre 812. Suffered engine failure and forced-landed at St-Denis-d'Oléron during withdrawal from Lanvéoc-Poulmic to St Trojan. SM Cartigny unhurt. Aircraft burned to prevent capture.

3S2 Two LeO C301s (6 and 7). Burned on withdrawal from Lanvéoc-Poulmic. No crew casualties. Autogyros both write-offs.

SESBA Caudron Goéland (209). Crashed at Villeneuve-sur-Lot airfield during evacuation from Lanvéoc-Poulmic, cause unknown. Mt Gérard, Mot Mariema, and Mot Davau killed. Aircraft a write-off.

Section d'Entraînement et de Servitude was the advanced training school for navy pilots from the aircraft carrier Béarn.

SESCB CAMS 37.11 (52). Aircraft abandoned on withdrawal from Cherbourg. No crew casualties. Aircraft a write-off.

Section d'Entraînement et de Servitude Cherbourg also left 2 Romano 82s (36 and 58), and North American NA57 (113) at Lessay on this date, plus another NA57 (130), and Caudron 635 Simoun (7795) abandoned at Querqueville.

LUFTWAFFE

2.(H)/41 Henschel Hs126. Believed returned damaged following observation sortie near Prosnes. Oberlt Dr Raber and Lt Übele wounded. Aircraft damage state not recorded.

JG1 Messerschmitt Bf109E-3. Forced-landed at Amdorf, cause not stated. Pilot believed unhurt. Aircraft damaged but repairable

II./JG53 Messerschmitt Bf109E-1. Wrecked in a taxying accident at Vraux. Pilot unhurt. Aircraft a write-off.

II./JG53 Messerschmitt Bf109E-1. Wrecked in forced-landing near Châlons-sur-Marne due to engine failure. Pilot unhurt. Aircraft a write-off.

4./JG53 Messerschmitt Bf109E-1. Hit a tractor on landing at Vraux. Gefr A. Appel injured. Aircraft damaged but repairable.

III./JG53 Messerschmitt Bf109E-1. Forced-landed at Châlons-sur-Marne due to engine failure. Pilot unhurt. Aircraft damaged but repairable.

III./JG53 Messerschmitt Bf109E-1. Damaged in combat and belly-landed near Metz. Pilot unhurt. Aircraft damaged but repairable.

III./JG53 Messerschmitt Bf109E-1. Damaged by ground-fire and belly-landed at Metz. Pilot unhurt. Aircraft damaged but repairable.

5./KG1 Heinkel He111H-2. Shot down by W/C Beamish of No. 151 Squadron and crashed in the Channel off Cherbourg 4.10 p.m. Fw H. Strahl and Uffz S. Auerswald killed, Fw A. Dennerl, Uffz H. Kling, and Uffz W. Zeyer captured wounded. Aircraft a write-off.

5./KG1 Heinkel He111H. Returned damaged in attack by Hurricanes of No. 151 Squadron over the Channel off Cherbourg 4.10 p.m. Uffz W. Schneeberger badly wounded, admitted to hospital in Essen-Mülheim; rest of crew unhurt. Aircraft damage state not recorded.

Stabsstaffel KG27 Heinkel He111P. Port engine damaged by flak during sortie south of Orléans and belly-landed near Salbris, north of Bourges. Oberlt H. Schmidt, Oberfw J. Groeneberg, Fw F. Reichel, Uffz P. Baums, and Flgr K. Lindemann captured unhurt. Aircraft a write-off.

Top and above: **Sergent-Chef Stanislav Plzak and Adjudant Pierre Dorcy of GC II/2 proudly claim their victory on June 1 (see page 408).**

The German armed forces had secured an incredible victory in little over four weeks yet the price was high. Over 3,000 airmen had been lost and the Luftwaffe was down by over 1,800 aircraft.

This Junkers Ju88 (9K+HM) belonging to the 4. Staffel of Kampfgruppe 51 was a victory of GC I/2 on the day that French pilots brought down Hauptmann Mölders (see page 429).

I./KG51 Junkers Ju88A-1. Forced-landed at Neuhausen due to engine failure. Crew unhurt. Aircraft damaged but repairable.

2./KG51 Junkers Ju88A-1. Forced-landed near Lyon following engine failure. Oberlt E. Freiherr von Dalwigk, Fw W. Herrmann, Gefr J. Brandl, and Gefr J. Steinleitner believed captured unhurt. Aircraft a write-off.

III./KG55 Heinkel He111P. Returned from attack on enemy concentrations between Épinal and St Dié, south-east of Nancy, 6.20 p.m. Gefr W. Haselsteiner wounded when round in his MG15 exploded. Aircraft undamaged.

KGrzbV.172 Junkers Ju52. Damaged in taxying accident after landing at Escorpain, west of Dreux. Crew believed unhurt. Aircraft damaged but repairable.

KGrzbV.9 Junkers Ju52. Crashed at Le Bourget, cause not stated. Crew believed unhurt. Aircraft 9P+EP damage state not recorded.

9./LG1 Junkers Ju88A-1. Shot down by flak west of Brest. Oberst A. Bülowius (*Kommodore*), Oberlt F-W Schaumann (*Staffelkapitän*), and two crewmen captured. Aircraft a write-off.

9./LG1 Junkers Ju88A-1. Shot down by flak west of Brest. Major Dr Kranz and Oberlt K. Sodemann captured wounded, two other crewmen believed captured unhurt. Aircraft a write-off.

5./StG2 Junkers Ju87B. Crashed following collision over Nivillers, north of Beauvais. Uffz R. Raddant killed, pilot believed baled out unhurt. Aircraft a write-off.

5./StG2 Junkers Ju87B. Crashed following collision over Nivillers, north of Beauvais. Lt G. Lohfink and Obergefr A. Heinemann killed. Aircraft a write-off.

Another KG51 victim of GC I/2 that day lies smashed on a French hillside. This is Oberleutnant Fritz Hohenstein's Ju88 (9K+KM) which cartwheeled attempting a crash-landing near Arbot on June 5 (see page 429).

Wednesday, June 19

At 6.30 a.m. on June 19, in an approach made through the Spanish ambassador, the German High Command advised the French government that they were prepared to discuss armistice terms. Général Charles Huntziger, commander of Groupe d'Armées 4, was consequently appointed to lead the French delegation which left for Tours the following afternoon to open negotiations.

Meantime the fighting carried on with German panzers reaching Brest, Cherbourg, and Nantes, while Luftflotte 2 bombers struck at Bordeaux, Lorient, and St-Nazaire. Only now did the last BAFF aircraft finally return to England, these being the Hurricanes of No. 501 Squadron that carried on operating from the Channel Islands until their eventual withdrawal on June 20. Yet operations over France continued for another four days with further losses as detailed in the loss lists that follow.

ROYAL AIR FORCE

UK-based aircraft lost or damaged on operations over the Western Front:

RAF COASTAL COMMAND

801 Squadron (FAA), Detling
Reconnaissance French coast:

Skua II. Landed at Manston port wing damaged by AA fire during photo-reconnaissance between Boulogne and Calais 10.15 a.m. Crew unhurt. Aircraft P repairable.

RAF FIGHTER COMMAND

615 Squadron, Hawkinge
Escort Blenheims:

Hurricane P2793. Forced-landed at Wilmington out of fuel following escort sortie to Rouen 3.55 p.m. F/O A. Eyre unhurt. Aircraft damaged but repairable.

TELEPHONE No. : **Edgware 2361.** ~~GERRARD 9234~~

TRUNK CALLS AND
TELEGRAPHIC ADDRESS :} "AIR MINISTRY LONDON"

AIR MINISTRY,
(Casualty Branch)
~~73-77, OXFORD STREET~~,
~~LONDON, W.1.~~

London Road,
Stanmore,
Middlesex.

30th May, 1949.

P352731/S.14 Cas.A.1.

Madam,

     I am directed to refer to your letter dated 26th May, 1949, and to say that according to the available information, your son's photograph album was found by Monsieur R. Caoudal, 16 rue du Chapeau, Quimper, Department of Finistere, in June, 1940, at which time he was serving in the French Marine.

     I am, Madam,
     Your obedient Servant,

Mrs. N. M. Kain,
Cathedral Guest House,
Canterbury,
Kent.

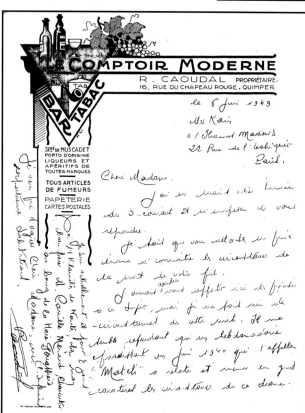

On June 18, No. 73 Squadron — whose fortunes we have followed in these pages since the previous September — quit France. But there was an incredible sequel — but one that would not be played out until after the war. *Above:* It was in May 1949 that Cobber Kain's mother received this letter from the Casualty Branch of the Air Ministry which informed her that her son's photograph album had been found. The Frenchman who had discovered the album was a shop-keeper in Quimper, a city some 200 kilometres north-west of Nantes. Mrs Kain promptly wrote to Monsieur Caoudal. This was the reply she received: 'Dear Mrs Kain, I have your letter of June 3rd and hasten to answer you. I know it means a very great deal to you to learn the circumstances of your son's death. I would have liked to give you particulars on that subject, but I do not know any details about his death. However, I seem to remember that in June 1940 a weekly publication called *Matels* reported, in large print, the circumstances of that drama. For my part, I can only confirm to you what I told the person to whom I handed over the album. In June 1940 the English forces went to La Pallice (near La Rochelle, in Charente Maritime), to embark for England. In their great haste they left everything behind in order to save themselves. Ahead the advancing German army, our officers ordered us to collect and hide from the Germans as much as we could: trucks, motorcycles, provisions, tools, etc. At that time I was in the navy, working as a seaman/secretary in a building near the port, which in wartime was occupied by the offices of various groups: the Staff of the Coastal Artillery, the Centre for Armaments on Merchant Navy ships, Police navigation, etc, and it was on this occasion that I went into an English truck and discovered the souvenir album which I had sent to you. As soon as the Germans had been defeated, I advertised in the *Les Fimes* (?) newspaper in order to hand the memento back to his family. Unfortunately, dear Mrs Kain, that is all I can tell you. I would like to give you whatever information I can; if there is anything more I can tell you, please don't hesitate to write to me. Right now and for another week I am staying 14km outside Nantes, with my brother-in-law, Mr Camille Mènard, who is a pork butcher in the borough of La Haie Fouattière (C. Inférieur). Yours faithfully, R. Caoudal.'

So we could not resist taking some comparisons to match Cobber's own photographs taken at the time the squadron was stationed in Rouvres. *Above:* He took this shot of his billet in No. 10 Grande Rue (see plan page 22). His room was on the first floor on the right. *Right:* Today the house, little changed, is the residence of Yves and Micheline Bedin.

Looking out from his first-floor window he could see the church with the Mairie beyond on the far side of the square.

Cobber's two snapshots show the whole aspect with troops drawn up on parade over on the right.

Even before any surrender negotiations had begun, orders had been issued on July 15 by the 170. Infanterie-Division instructing its Infanterie-Regiment 391 to proceed to Compiègne — where the Armistice had been signed ending the First World War — to prepare the site ready for Hitler to turn the tables on the French. Here the engineers march onto the Clairière de l'Armistice which had been dedicated in 1922. In the foreground the inscribed slab rests between the railway lines on which Maréchal Foch's Compagnie des Wagon Lits carriage had stood on November 11, 1918.

FRENCH AIR FORCE

AB 4 Loire-Nieuport LN 411. Failed to return from night attack over the Gulf of Genoa. Mt Billien missing. Aircraft lost.

AB 4 Loire-Nieuport LN 411. Failed to return from night attack over the Gulf of Genoa. SM Ricquier missing. Aircraft lost.

Five days later, mere hours before the French armistice, all surviving aircraft left for Ajaccio in Corsica, en-route to Bône in Algeria.

AC 5 Morane 406 (1062). Aircraft abandoned on withdrawal from Rochefort. Pilot unhurt. Aircraft a write-off.

Cours de Chasse Morane 406 (1059). Forced-landed at Escoublac badly damaged by French AA fire during attack on He111s over St-Nazaire. Pilot unhurt. Aircraft C37 abandoned.

This was one of five aircraft from the advanced training school for l'Aéronautique Navale fighter pilots at Hourtin-Louley detached to cover withdrawal of the battleship Jean Bart.

DAT Clermont-Ferrand Koolhoven F.K.58. Engine unserviceable on withdrawal to Rodez. Asp. B. Muth unhurt. Aircraft abandoned.

DAT Tours Bloch 151. Stalled and crashed on landing at Bordeaux. Sgt Lepezel killed. Aircraft a write-off.

GAO 515 Potez 63.11 (730). Forced-landed damaged by flak during observation sortie near Tours. Lt Becker badly wounded admitted to hospital in Châteauroux. Sgt Baron and Sgt Gauze unhurt. Aircraft repairable.

GC III/3 Bloch 174 (101). Collided with LeO 451 and caught fire in take-off accident at Perpignan during transit flight. Capt A. Le Bideau *(Commandant)* seriously injured, died same day; rest of crew unhurt. Aircraft a write-off.

GC 1/145 11 Caudron C714s and 2 Bloch 152s. Aircraft abandoned at Rochefort on withdrawal of ground unit to La Rochelle for evacuation to England. No pilot casualties. Aircraft abandoned.

GR II/14 Potez 63.11 (196). Lost control in poor visibility over the Rhône valley and abandoned by crew. Crashed and burned out at Ardèche 6.30 a.m. Sgt P. Coulommier baled out but fell dead with parachute on fire. Lt Cochetel and Sgt Frayssines baled out unhurt. Aircraft a write-off.

GR II/55 Potez 63.11 (197). Crippled by flak east of Cerizay during reconnaissance sortie. Attempted a belly-landing but hit trees and struck the roof of a house before disintegrating beside the road at La Génetrie, near Cirières 7.45 a.m. S/Lt B. Chaudel, Sgt E. Chantelou, and Cpl A. Vasseur killed. Aircraft a write-off.

T 2 Latécoère 298 (93). Crashed in fog at Fougax-et-Barrineuf during withdrawal from Hourtin to Berre. SM Sébire and Mt Lemoine killed. Aircraft a write-off.

T 3 Latécoère 298 (73). Unserviceable aircraft destroyed in bombing attack on St-Nazaire where forced-landed during transfer to Berre on June 10. No crew casualties. Aircraft a write-off.

Left: **The original coach was preserved in a purpose-built museum building which had been financed by an American** benefactor 'Arthur H. Fleming' in 1927 *(right).* **It was Hitler's intention to have the French sign in the same carriage.**

Having blasted an opening in the end wall of the museum building . . .

LUFTWAFFE

2.(H)/31 Two Fieseler Fi156, and a Henschel Hs126. Damaged in attack on Rennes airfield by Bf110s. Hptmn H. Friedrich badly wounded. Aircraft all damaged but repairable.

Five ground crew were also wounded in this attack.

5./JG3 Messerschmitt Bf109E. Shot down by P/O Carey of No. 3 Squadron in combat south of Cherbourg and forced-landed near Brezolles. Uffz F. Mias believed captured. Aircraft a write-off.

Stab II./JG26 Messerschmitt Bf109E-3. Believed collided with an high-tension cable while evading ground-fire and crashed at 'Les Écharbeaux', near St Maur during low-level strafing attack on enemy columns west of Châteauroux. Lt P. Blohm *(Gruppen-adjutant)* killed. Aircraft a write-off.

6./JG26 Messerschmitt Bf109E-3. Believed collided with an high-tension cable and crashed at 'Les Écharbeaux', near St Maur during low-level strafing attack on enemy columns west of Châteauroux. Uffz J. Ganster killed. Aircraft a write-off.

5./JG52 Messerschmitt Bf109E-1. Crashed south-east of Karlsruhe following engine failure during proving flight. Lt W. Hofer baled out but killed. Aircraft 10 + a write-off.

III./KG2 Dornier Do17Z. Crashed near Châlons shortly after take-off. No crew casualties. Aircraft a write-off.

7./KG2 Junkers Ju52. Damaged in accident at Gros-Caillou emergency landing ground east of Rocroi 12.25 p.m. Uffz H. Klehn badly injured, died June 25. Gefr R. Schumann slightly injured, admitted to hospital in Charleville. Aircraft damaged but repairable.

KG4 lost six Heinkel He111s with two more returning damaged during night attacks on RAF airfields. As these losses took place over mainland Britain they have not been included. For further details see The Blitz Then and Now *Volume I (pages 108-110).*

. . . the coach was pulled out and placed in position over the commemorative slab. All was now ready for Hitler to humiliate the French.

I./KG51 Junkers Ju88A. Crashed at Stuttgart when starboard tyre burst on landing. No crew casualties. Aircraft damaged but repairable.

1./KG51 Junkers Ju88A. Suffered engine fire and crashed and burned out at Weilheim attempting forced-landing on return from sortie. Fw K. Swoboda and Uffz K. Freisewinkel killed. Fw A. Vischer and Fw K. Stölzle badly injured, admitted to hospital in Göppingen. Aircraft a write-off.

Stabsstaffel KG53 Heinkel He111H. Reportedly forced-landed north of Tournon damaged in attack by Lt Tariel of GC III/1 during reconnaissance sortie over Dompierre 11.10 a.m. No crew casualties. Aircraft damaged but repairable.

4./KG55 Heinkel He111P. Returned damaged by flak and ground-fire during attack on enemy columns near Rambervillers, south-east of Nancy. Uffz R. Märtin slightly wounded, rest of crew unhurt. Aircraft repairable.

1./KGrzbV.101 Junkers Ju52 (5847). Forced-landed at Laon with engine trouble. Crew believed unhurt. Aircraft damaged but repairable.

6./ZG26 Messerschmitt Bf110C. Destroyed in bombing attack on Rouen-Boos airfield by Blenheims of Nos. 15 and 40 Squadrons. Oberlt A-W. Bier *(Staffelführer)* and Uffz G. Schultz both badly wounded. Aircraft a write-off.

One electrical mechanic was killed during this attack and another five ground crew badly wounded.

III./ZG26 Two Messerschmitt Bf110C. Destroyed in bombing attack on Rouen-Boos airfield by Blenheims of Nos. 15 and 40 Squadrons. No crew casualties. Aircraft both write-offs.

Two members of 7. Flug-Betriebs-Kompanie were wounded during this attack.

9./ZG26 Messerschmitt Bf110C. Damaged in bombing attack on Rouen-Boos airfield by Blenheims of Nos. 15 and 40 Squadrons. No crew casualties. Aircraft damaged but repairable.

Four members of the Staffel ground crew were killed during this attack.

1./ZG52 Messerschmitt Bf110C. Returned damaged during low-level attack on enemy troop concentrations. Lt W. Hoffmann badly wounded, admitted to hospital in Karlsruhe. Aircraft damaged but repairable.

II./ZG76 Messerschmitt Bf110C. Destroyed in bombing attack. No crew casualties. Aircraft damaged but repairable.

Thursday, June 20

BRITISH AIR FORCES IN FRANCE

501 SQUADRON, ST HELIER

Hurricane P3347. Unserviceable aircraft left on evacuation to England. No pilot casualty. Aircraft abandoned.

Five more airframes reported 'lost' on the following day (L1624, L1911, P3450, P3491, and P3542) were either similarly abandoned or earlier casualties finally 'struck-off' the squadron inventory.

UK-based aircraft lost or damaged on operations over the Western Front:

RAF COASTAL COMMAND

235 Squadron, Thorney Island

Blenheim IV N3534. Reported crashed, details unknown. Crew believed unhurt. Aircraft LA⊙X a write-off.

236 Squadron, Middle Wallop
Training:

Blenheim IV L1334. Belly-landed when undercarriage jammed. F/O W. S. Moore and crew unhurt. Aircraft a write-off.

French people! I have asked the enemy to put an end to hostilities. The Government yesterday appointed plenipotentiaries to receive their conditions. I took this decision with the stout heart of a soldier because the military situation imposed it.

We had hoped to resist on the Somme-Aisne line. Général Weygand had regrouped our forces, and his name alone presaged victory. The line yielded, however, under the pressure of the enemy and our troops were forced to retreat. From June 13 the request for an armistice was inevitable. The blow surprised you, and remembering 1914-18, you sought the reasons for it. I am going to give you them.

On May 1, 1917, we still had 3,280,000 men under arms in spite of three years of murderous fighting. On the eve of the present battle we had 500,000 fewer. In May 1918, we had 85 British divisions; in May 1940, we only had ten. In 1918 we had with us 58 Italian divisions and 42 American divisions.

The inferiority of our matériel was even greater than that of our effectives. French aviation has fought at odds of one to six. Not so strong as 22 years ago, we had also fewer friends, too few children, too few arms, too few allies. This is the cause of our defeat.

The French people do not deny the blow. All peoples have known ups and downs. It is by the way they react that they show themselves to be weak or great. We will learn a lesson from the battle which has been lost. Since victory the spirit of pleasure has prevailed over the spirit of sacrifice. People have demanded more than they have given, they have wanted to spare themselves effort. Today misfortune comes.

I was with you in the glorious days. As head of Government I will remain with you in the dark days. Stand by me. The fight still goes on. It is for France, the soil of her sons.

MARÉCHAL PHILIPPE PÉTAIN, FRENCH PRIME MINISTER,
BROADCAST, JUNE 20, 1940

FRENCH AIR FORCE

AB 3 Vought 156F. Crashed in the sea, cause unknown. SM Perdomo and QM Cabon unhurt. Aircraft a write-off.

AC 2 Dewoitine 520 (292). Aircraft destroyed on withdrawal from Orly. No pilot casualty. Aircraft a write-off.

AC 2 Dewoitine 520. Lost bearings in bad weather and overturned in attempted forced-landing near Béage during withdrawal to Hyères. LV Folliot *(Commandant)* injured. Aircraft a write-off.

AC 2 Dewoitine 520. Forced-landed near Béage in bad weather during withdrawal to Hyères. Mtre Leclerq unhurt. Aircraft a write-off.

AC 2 Dewoitine 520. Forced-landed near Béage in bad weather during withdrawal to Hyères. Mtre Chaume unhurt. Aircraft a write-off.

GB I/34 Amiot 354 (28). Lost during transit flight from Lézignan to Oran, crashed in sea. Sgt G. Lefèvre killed. Capt P. Gémon, Lt M. Molliet-Billiet, Adjt E. Foisset, and Sgt R. Pech missing. Aircraft lost.

On February 7, 1941, a Spanish fishing boat recovered the body of the mechanic, Germain Lefèvre, from the sea off Premia. By a remarkable coincidence, the same boat trawled up a valise belonging to the observer, Paul Gémon, at Vaillet de Fora on May 28, 1941.

Left: **The opening in the end of the coach shed, visible in the background, has been boarded up ready for the big day; this would appear to be a dress rehearsal.** *Below:* **The statue of Maréchal Foch looks down on the parade. The plinth on which the officers are standing is engraved with the words: 'Here on the Eleventh of November 1918 succumbed the criminal pride of the German Empire — vanquished by the free peoples which it tried to enslave'.**

This Heinkel of the 7. Staffel of Kampfgeschwader 1 was shot down by the combined attacks of five French pilots.

GC I/1 Bloch 152. Collided with Bloch 152 of GC I/8 and crashed near Saujon 7.00 p.m. Sgt R. Starke killed. Aircraft a write-off.

GC I/8 Bloch 152. Broke up in mid-air over Saujon following collision with Bloch 152 of GC I/1 after attack on He111s over Royan 7.00 p.m. S/Lt Porodo landed by parachute unhurt. Aircraft a write-off.

GR II/55 Potez 63.11 (719). Shot down by flak on reconnaissance sortie between Tours and Nantes, and broke up north-east of Lire. Rear fuselage fell at Vieille Cour, main wreckage falling at Le Patiou. S/Lt E. Jacques and Adjt A. Jacquemart killed. Sgt H. Robert badly wounded, died in Ancenis hospital on June 30. Aircraft a write-off.

2S4 Levasseur PL101 (69). Crashed in bad weather during transfer from Rochefort to Agen. SM Boucher and Mot Pointel killed. Aircraft a write-off.

2S4 Three LeO 258s (3, 7 and 18) Aircraft abandoned on withdrawal from Rochefort to Agen. No crew casualties. Aircraft all write-offs.

More than a dozen aircraft were destroyed by bombing or abandoned during evacuation of Rochefort Aéronautique Navale base over the next few days including FBA 294 (2), and three Romano 82s (7, 18 and 45) of the Section d'Entraînement Rochefort, plus Farman NC471 (01), LeO 258 (8), Levasseur PL101 (70), MS 230s (223 and 228), and Potez 542 (128). Also two Caudron Goélands (422 and 423), North American NA57 (111), and Potez 540 (236) of the Service de Convoyage, Liaison et Entraînement.

LUFTWAFFE

4.(H)/22 Henschel Hs126 (3365). Shot down by Capt Coutaud, S/Lt De Fins, Adjt Verots, Sgt Teillet, Sgt Montchamin, and Sgt Le-provost of GC I/1 during observation sortie between Valençay and Argenton-sur-Creuse, west of Bourges. Crashed and burned out at Ferme de la Grand-Métairie, at Tendu 8.00 p.m. Lt K. Hauser and Lt H. Ricke killed. Aircraft 4N+AM a write-off.

8./JG3 Messerschmitt Bf109E-1. Crash-landed in the Ardennes due to engine failure during transit flight to Douai. Obergefr W. Bässell injured. Aircraft a write-off.

7./KG1 Heinkel He111H. Starboard engine set alight by Capt Garde, S/Lt Pebrel, Adjt Delegay, and Sgt Dubost of GC I/1 and S/Lt Porodo of GC I/8 during sortie to attack oil refineries at Pauillac, north of Bordeaux, and crash-landed at Saujon, south of Rochefort, 7.45 p.m. Fw K. Popp killed. Uffz W. Gerspacher baled out badly wounded, died next day. Uffz L. Muegge baled out and captured wounded, admitted to hospital. Fw R. Hemmelmann and Uffz A. Ragutt baled out and captured unhurt. Aircraft a write-off.

Ludwig Muegge was roughly handled by French civilians after landing.

9./KG1 Heinkel He111H. Returned damaged by GC I/55 and flak during sortie to attack oil refineries at Pauillac, north of Bordeaux, 7.45 p.m. Gefr M. Taberry died of wounds, Obergefr A. Knust badly wounded, rest of crew unhurt. Aircraft damage state not recorded.

9./KG1 Heinkel He111H. Crash-landed damaged by fighters and flak during sortie to attack oil refineries at Pauillac, north of Bordeaux, 7.45 p.m. Possibly that attacked by S/Lt Souviat of GC I/55 and EV Castel of AC 5. Flgr W. Borrmann captured badly wounded. Uffz H. Steincke, Uffz W. Hirsch, Obergefr E. Kramer, and Flgr K. Uthke captured unhurt. Aircraft a write-off.

Stabsstaffel KG77 Dornier Do17Z. Returned damaged by ground-fire near Vignory, south of St-Dizier. Uffz A. Linder slightly wounded, rest of crew unhurt. Aircraft damaged but repairable.

I./KGrzbV.172 Junkers Ju52 (5423). Damaged in bombing attack on Schiphol airfield. No crew casualties. Aircraft damaged but repairable.

III./ZG26 Two Messerschmitts Bf110C. Destroyed in bombing attack on Rouen-Boos airfield by Blenheims of Nos. 107 and 110 Squadrons. No crew casualties. Aircraft both write-offs.

Eight ground crew were killed and 11 more wounded in this attack.

Unteroffizier Ludwig Muegge: 'Our plane, a Heinkel He 111, was shot down on June 20, at about 8.30 p.m. in the area of Bordeaux. Our pilot, Feldwebel Karl Popp, was badly wounded by the first burst and he was unable to leave the plane. The remainder of the crew took to their parachutes. After I landed, I was taken under fire by machine guns and tried in vain to escape. Unteroffizier Walter Gerspacher was wounded when landing and he succumbed to his injuries the next morning. I had a splinter in my face but the remainder of the crew were unscathed.'

Friday, June 21

Reaching Tours early on June 21, the French delegation was escorted to Rethondes in the Forêt de Compiègne, and to the exact spot where, on November 11, 1918, the armistice had been signed ending the First World War. With great sense of occasion, deliberately intended to humiliate the French and restore German pride, the railway carriage in which that earlier ceremony took place had been restored to its original position and it was here, later that afternoon, that the French met the German delegation headed by an exultant Adolf Hitler.

Generaloberst Wilhelm Keitel led discussions from the German side and it soon became abundantly clear that there was little scope for any negotiation. Nevertheless, discussions went on until dusk when Général Huntziger telephoned details of the 24 articles of the German armistice terms to the French government back in Bordeaux.

In the meantime, Italian mountain troops opened an offensive in the French Alps and Italian aircraft struck at the French Mediterranean airfields at Cannes, Marseille, and St Raphaël.

ROYAL AIR FORCE

UK-based aircraft lost or damaged on operations over the Western Front:

RAF COASTAL COMMAND

801 (FAA) Squadron, Detling
Gun positions Cap Gris Nez:

Roc I. Believed shot down by ground-fire during dive-bombing attack and crashed in sea 2.40 p.m. but possibly that claimed by Oberfw Buhl of 1.(J)/LG2 over Étaples. Sub Lt A. V. M. Day and Naval Airman F. Berry missing. Aircraft H lost.

826 (FAA) Squadron, Bircham Newton
Dutch airfields:

Albacore I L7081. Shot down in flames during attack on De Kooy and Den Helder, and crashed near Oosterend in Eierlandse Polder, Texel. Possibly that claimed by Uffz Schreiter of 3./JG51 north of Texel 2.55 p.m Lt J. L. M. Bell, Sub Lt F. B. Hookins, and Naval Airman R. G. Poole killed. Aircraft a write-off.

Albacore I L7089. Shot down during attack on De Kooy and Den Helder, and crash-landed on De Slufter beach, Texel. Possibly that claimed by Fw Gräf of 3./JG51 north of Texel 3.12 p.m. Sub Lt V. J. Dyke captured badly wounded, died of injuries. Sub Lt W. S. Butterworth and Naval Airman R. J. Jackson captured. Aircraft lost.

Albacore I L7111. Returned damaged in attack by Bf109s of 3./JG51 during attack on De Kooy and Den Helder. Possibly that attacked by Gefr zur Lage north of Texel 3.02 p.m. Naval Airman C. J. C. Homer wounded. Sub Lt P. D. Urwin and Sub Lt G. S. Dormad unhurt. Aircraft damaged but repairable.

FRENCH AIR FORCE

DAT Clermont-Ferrand Eight Koolhoven F.K.58s. Abandoned at Perpignan on evacuation to England. No pilot casualties. Aircraft abandoned.

GC II/8 Bloch 152. Hit a Morane 406 of GC III/1 during emergency take-off at Marignane. Pilot unhurt. Aircraft a write-off.

GR 1/22 Potez 63.11. Crashed and burned out between Grau and Lançon shortly after take-off from Salon. Lt A. Merceur (*Commandant*), Adjt J. Guarneri, and Sgt H. Jocquel killed. Aircraft a write-off.

GR II/55 Potez 63.11 (489). Shot down by flak and crashed at La Métairie, south-east of St Sébastien-sur-Loire 4.00 p.m. Lt A. Marty and S/Lt J. Auge killed. Sgt A. Thierry baled out badly burned, died of wounds in hospital at St Jacques on June 25. Aircraft a write-off.

On June 21, Hitler arrived at Compiègne at 3.15 p.m. American newsman William Shirer watched as he approached the memorial: 'Hitler reads it and Göring reads it. They all read it, standing there in the June sun and the silence. I look for the expression in Hitler's face. It is afire with scorn, anger, hate, revenge, triumph. He steps off the monument and contrives to make even this gesture a masterpiece of contempt. He glances back at it, contemptuous, angry — angry, you can almost feel, because he cannot wipe out the awful, provoking lettering with one sweep of his high Prussian boot. He glances slowly around the clearing, and now, as his eyes meet ours, you grasp the depth of his hatred. But there is triumph there too — revengeful, triumphant hate. Suddenly, as though his face were not giving quite complete expression to his feelings, he throws his whole body into harmony with his mood. He swiftly snaps his hands on his hips, arches his shoulders, planted his feet wide apart. It is a magnificent gesture of defiance of burning contempt for the place and all that it has stood for in the 22 years since it witnessed the humbling of the German Empire.'

LUFTWAFFE

2.(F)/122 Junkers Ju88A. Hit the ground in a turn while low flying near Brussels. Lt O. Marschik, Uffz H. Seggelke, Uffz B. Reuter, and Uffz A. Seith killed. Aircraft a write-off.

3./JG3 Messerschmitt Bf109E. Belly-landed near Évreux due to petrol failure. Pilot unhurt. Aircraft damaged but repairable.

I./JG51 Messerschmitt Bf109E-1. Forced-landed at De Kooy, damaged by return fire from No. 826 Squadron Albacores attacked over Den Helder 3.00 p.m. Pilot unhurt. Aircraft damaged but repairable.

3./JG51 Messerschmitt Bf109E. Forced-landed at Amsterdam damaged by return fire from No. 826 Squadron Albacores attacked over Den Helder 3.00 p.m. Pilot unhurt. Aircraft repairable.

3./JG76 Messerschmitt Bf109E. Shot down during attack on No. 826 Squadron Albacores over Den Helder, and crashed northwest of Texel, 3.00 p.m. Lt E. Marquard killed. Aircraft a write-off.

I./KG53 Heinkel He111H. Wrecked in landing accident at Gross-Ostheim, cause not stated. No crew casualties. Aircraft a write-off.

III./KG53 Heinkel He111H. Reported wrecked, circumstances unknown. No crew casualties. Aircraft a write-off.

6./LG1 Junkers Ju88A. Crashed near Vendeville during proving flight. Prüfer F. Kuhlmann (of Stab II./LG1) badly injured, died undergoing surgery in Lille hospital next day. Fw F. Wohlgemuth suffered a broken shin. Obergefr G. Dressel (Mechanic) slightly injured. Aircraft a write-off.

Saturday, June 22

Over the next 24 hours, the French delegation attempted to negotiate more favourable terms but by 5.00 p.m. on June 22 it was clear that further discussions were useless and the armistice was finally signed by Huntziger and Keitel at 5.50 p.m. It would come into force once France concluded an armistice with Italy so the French team left for Rome early the next morning in three Luftwaffe transport aircraft.

ROYAL AIR FORCE

UK-based aircraft lost or damaged on operations over the Western Front:

RAF FIGHTER COMMAND

615 Squadron, Kenley
Patrol Abbeville — Dieppe:

Hurricane P2764. Shot down by Lt Konopka of 7./ZG26 during attack on He111s of III./KG1 west of Rouen and crashed near La Mailleraye-sur-Seine 8.10 a.m. P/O J. R. Lloyd killed. Aircraft a write-off.

Hurricane P3487. Forced-landed on the Isle of Wight during return from patrol due to petrol shortage. F/Lt J. G. Sanders unhurt. Aircraft undamaged.

FRENCH AIR FORCE

AC 5 Morane 406. Forced-landed at Hourtin damaged during attack on He111s and probably that claimed by Oberlt Borchers of 4./ZG76 4.50 p.m. PM Chaffurin unhurt. Aircraft damaged but repairable.

AC 5 Four Morane 406s. Destroyed or badly damaged at Hourtin airfield in bombing by He111s and strafing by Oberlt Nacke (*Staffelkapitän*) and Fw Wagner of 6./ZG76 4.30 p.m. No pilot casualties. Aircraft all write-offs.

This attack prompted total evacuation of the Aéronautique Navale base at Hourtin over following days. Over 70 naval training machines were abandoned at Hourtin and adjacent Louley on June 24 including 34 FBA 17s, 15 CAMS 37s, and 11 Farman NC.470s. Also the following:

AB 1 Two Vought 156F (11 and 13). Aircraft abandoned on evacuation of Hourtin-Louley. No crew casualties. Aircraft 11, and 12 both write-offs.

E 2 Breguet 521 Bizerte (34). Abandoned at Hourtin-Louley. No crew casualties. Aircraft 4 a write-off.

1 S2 Latécoère 290 (10), Gourdou-Leseurre 810 (19), 811 (26), 812 (63), and 813 (64). Aircraft destroyed at Pointe de Piqueyrot, Hourtin to prevent capture. No crew casualties. Aircraft all write-offs.

2 S1 Six CAMS 55 (86, 88, 89, 102, 104, and 105). Aircraft abandoned on evacuation of Hourtin. No crew casualties. Aircraft all write-offs.

SCLE Breguet 521 Bizerte (11), and Potez 567 (15). Aircraft abandoned at Hourtin-Louley. No crew casualties. Aircraft both write-offs.

LUFTWAFFE

4.(F)/122 Junkers Ju88A. Crashed at Calais following engine failure. Crew unhurt. Aircraft a write-off.

2.(H)/23 Gotha Go145. Crashed at Choye, south-east of Gray, cause unknown. Fw H. Vögelein and Lt A. Gamber killed. Aircraft a write-off.

Flugbereitschaft I. Fliegerkorps Messerschmitt Bf108. Destroyed by enemy fire on the ground at Vannes. No crew casualties. Aircraft a write-off.

3./JG2 Messerschmitt Bf109E-4. Lost control and crashed on take-off at Marigny. Gefreiter L. Becker killed. Aircraft a write-off.

II./JG2 Messerschmitt Bf109E-1. Crashed on landing at Évreux due to control failure. Pilot unhurt. Aircraft damaged but repairable.

I./JG21 Caudron 445. Crashed near Brussels during transit flight, cause unknown. Uffz O. Wolz and Obergefr F. Baukus killed. Aircraft a write-off.

I./JG26 Messerschmitt Bf109E. Crash-landed at Nevers due to unspecified technical fault. Pilot unhurt. Aircraft damaged but repairable.

II./JG52 Messerschmitt Bf109E-1. Forced-landed following engine failure. Pilot unhurt. Aircraft damaged but repairable.

III./KG1 Heinkel He111H. Crash-landed possibly damaged in attacks by S/L Kayll and P/O Lofts of No. 615 Squadron west of Rouen 8.00 a.m. Crew believed unhurt. Aircraft damaged but repairable.

I./KG30 Junkers Ju88A. Crash-landed, circumstances unknown. Crew believed unhurt. Aircraft damaged but repairable.

With Hitler having taken Foch's old seat (extreme left) facing the French delegation led by Général Charles Huntziger, Generaloberst Wilhelm Keitel, the Chief of the Army High Command, stands beside him to read a prepared statement putting the blame for the new war fairly and squarely on the Allies. Göring (C-in-C Luftwaffe), Raeder (C-in-C Kriegsmarine) and von Ribbentrop (Foreign Minister) have their backs to the camera, with von Brauchitsch (C-in-C Army) and Rudolf Hess (Deputy Führer) sitting at the far end. Hitler then left the coach, leaving Keitel in charge of the negotiations. The French tried many stalling tactics and the discussions continued for the rest of that Friday and into Saturday. finally, at 5.00 p.m. with his patience at an end, Keitel issued an ultimatum: the French must either accept or reject the terms without further argument by 6.30 p.m.

Sunday, June 23

ROYAL AIR FORCE

UK-based aircraft lost or damaged:

RAF FIGHTER COMMAND

79 Squadron, Biggin Hill

Hurricane P2698. Descended through fog and landed off the runway colliding with gun emplacement 11.00 p.m. P/O D. W. A. Stones unhurt. Aircraft a write-off.

FRENCH AIR FORCE

ECN 4/13 Potez 631. Returned to Nîmes-Garons damaged by ground-fire during low-level attack on armour near St Égrève, north of Grenoble. Lt de Golbery wounded, rest of crew unhurt. Aircraft repairable.

GC II/6 Bloch 152 (630). Shot down by flak during low-level attack on motorised columns near Tain-l'Hermitage and crash-landed on Romans airfield. Sgt C. Boyer captured unhurt. Aircraft a write-off.

LUFTWAFFE

II./JG2 Messerschmitt Bf109E-1. Damaged in crash-landing, cause not stated. Pilot unhurt. Aircraft repairable.

I./JG3 Messerschmitt Bf109E. Wrecked in forced-landing near Le Mans, cause not stated. Pilot injured. Aircraft a write-off.

3./JG51 Messerschmitt Bf109E-4. Belly-landed at De Kooy, possibly damaged in attack on Blenheims south of Leeuwarden 2.50 p.m. Pilot unhurt. Aircraft 2 + damaged but repairable.

I./KGzbV.1 Junkers Ju52 (5477). Crashed west of Birkenfeld, cause not stated. Fw W. Janotta, Uffz H. Eichmüller, Uffz R. Koch, and Uffz A. Raab killed. Aircraft a write-off.
  Fw E. Gross and Uffz A. Schmidt (both ground-crew of Stab II./KG51) also died in this accident..

I./KGrzbV.172 Junkers Ju52 (5347). Destroyed in bombing attack on Schiphol airfield 7.30 p.m. Aircraft a write-off.

Once the Armistice had been signed the railway carriage was transported to Berlin as a museum piece, while at Compiègne engineers set about razing the whole area.

Charges were placed against the walls and ceiling of the railway shed bringing down the roof.

Monday, June 24

The last victory. Fighting to the bitter end, the Armée de l'Air shot down this Henschel 126 just hours before the Armistice came into effect. The pilot, Oberleutnant Christoph Jahn, was also the last German airman killed in action in the Battle of France.

Negotiations with the Italians went better, their terms being less onerous, but given their experiences over the preceding 24 hours the French delegation would scarcely have viewed them otherwise. The Italian armistice was duly signed in the Villa Incisa outside Rome at 6.15 p.m. on June 24, news being communicated to the German High Command shortly afterwards for, under the terms of the Franco-German armistice, a general cease-fire would come into effect six hours later. Thus, at 12.35 a.m. on June 25 the Battle of France lurched to its tragic conclusion. But for many soldiers and citizens of France the misery was far from over for they now faced an uncertain future under German occupation. They would endure this bleak prospect for the next four years.

FRENCH AIR FORCE

AB 1 Two Vought 156F. Lost in bad weather during transit flight between Hourtin and St-Laurent-de-la-Salanque. No crew casualties. Aircraft both write-offs.

AC 5 Morane 406. Shot down by flak during strafing of Fort du Chay at Royan 2.30 p.m. SM Pivet killed. Aircraft a write-off.

Cours de Chasse Morane 406 (970), Wrecked in an accident at Hourtin, exact cause not stated. Pilot unhurt. Aircraft 36 a write-off.

GB II/11 LeO 451 (386). Wrecked in accident at Montpensier, cause not specified. Crew unhurt. Aircraft a write-off.

GC II/1 Bloch 152. Returned to Valensole badly damaged by flak during attack on enemy column between Hauterive and Romans-sur-Isère. S/Lt H. Fontaine unhurt. Aircraft a write-off.

GC 6/1 Morane 406. Hit by ground-fire and engine caught fire after attack on vehicles north of Romans-sur-Isère and abandoned over Grignan, south-east of Montélimar. Sgt J. Lagrange baled out, sprained ankle on landing. Aircraft a write-off.

GC 1/6 Morane 406 (1056). Shot down by flak north-east of Romans-sur-Isère during ground-attack sortie, crashed at 'Les Perrières' Mours-Saint-Eusèbe, 7.30 p.m. S/Lt H. Raphenne *(Commandant)* killed. Aircraft a write-off.
Henri Raphenne was the last member of the Armée de l'Air to be killed in action during the French campaign. Cessation of hostilities between France and Germany became effective five hours later.

GR II/14 Potez 63.11 (187). Attacked by fighters during low-level reconnaissance of the Rhône-Isère to Grenoble, crash-landed and burned out at Montélimar. Sgt Martin wounded in thigh. S/Lt Debaris and Sgt Robin unhurt. Aircraft a write-off.

SRC Morane 230 (455). Wrecked in accident at Chartres, cause not stated. Pilot unhurt. Aircraft a write-off.
The Section Réception et Convoyage was the delivery flight for Aéronautique Navale aircraft.

LUFTWAFFE

5.(H)/13 Henschel Hs126. Shot down by S/Lt Marchelidon of GC I/2 during observation sortie between Romans and Valence, and crash-landed by the Isère at Ferme Chatain, Beaumont-Monteux, 6.15 p.m. Fw H-J. Lessing killed. Oberlt C. Jahn badly wounded, admitted to field hospital at Saint-Donat but died next day. Aircraft 4E+BN a write-off.
This was the last German aircraft shot down by French fighters prior to the armistice.

II./JG2 Messerschmitt Bf109E-1. Damaged in crash-landing at Caen, cause not stated. Pilot unhurt. Aircraft damaged but repairable.

3./JG51 Messerschmitt Bf109E-1. Belly-landed at Leeuwarden, cause not stated. Oberlt R. Leppla *(Staffelkapitän)* unhurt. Aircraft 1 + damaged but repairable.

II./JG52 Messerschmitt Bf109E-1. Stationary aircraft rammed by Junkers W34 on take-off at Karlsruhe. No pilot casualty. Aircraft damaged but repairable.

6./KG54 Junkers Ju88A. Forced-landed at Celle due to engine trouble. No crew casualties. Aircraft a write-off.

2./LG1 Junkers Ju88A. Crashed at Hannover-Langenhagen attempting forced-landing due to engine trouble on training flight. Lt H. Müller-Rabe killed. Oberlt W. Lüben and rest of crew believed unhurt. Aircraft L1+DK a write-off.

I./StG1 Dornier Do17M. Forced-landed near Caen due to engine trouble. Crew unhurt. Aircraft damaged but repairable.

The last casualty . . . here Sous-Lieutenant Henri Raphenne lost his life.

ROLL OF HONOUR

'If I should die, think only this of me: That there's some corner of a foreign field, That is forever England.' How many times would Rupert Brooke's immortal words from *The Soldier* ring out across the battlefield. All those airmen of the British Air Forces in France who lost their lives, save for those missing and six airmen who are buried in the UK, lie in cemeteries spread right across the Continent from the Channel coast to the soil of Germany. Although this sequence of photographs is undated, and the location not given, we have established that it shows a funeral procession in Épernay, most probably that of Sergeant Richard Pike, Pilot Officer Robert Thynne and AC1 Vivian Richardson of No. 218 Squadron who were killed on November 13, 1939 (see page 115).

RAF aircrew lost on operations or to enemy action while serving with the British Air Forces in France from September 3, 1939 to June 24, 1940

ABBOTT, Sgt. F. B. No. 105 Squadron 14:5:40 Age 28. Runnymede Memorial Panel 11.

ADAM, F/O W. W. No. 57 Squadron 15:3:40 Age 25. Chambières French National Cemetery, Metz, Moselle, France. Grave 14.

ADAMS, F/O W. S. C. No. 3 Squadron 13:5:40 Age 33. Cité Bonjean Military Cemetery, Armentières, Nord, France. Plot 11. Row B. Grave 6.

ADAMSON, P/O W. B. No. 4 Squadron 9:3:40 Age 22. Cité Bonjean Military Cemetery, Armentières, Nord, France. Plot 11. Row A. Grave 13.

AINSWORTH, AC1. R. T. No. 12 Squadron 14:5:40 Age 20. Pouru-St-Rémy Communal Cemetery, Ardennes, France. Joint Grave 3.

ALDERSON, Sgt. K. No. 12 Squadron 14:5:40 Age 27. Pouru-St-Rémy Communal Cemetery, Ardennes, France. Joint Grave 3.

ALLEN, Sgt D. A. No. 3 Squadron 14:5:40 Age 20. Villers-Cernay Communal Cemetery, Ardennes, France.

ALLEN, F/O D. H. No. 85 Squadron 18:5:40 22. Runnymede Memorial Panel 5.

ANDERSON, P/O C. C. R. No. 88 Squadron 26:5:40 Age 22. Haraucourt Churchyard, Ardennes, France. Joint Grave 1-2.

ANDERSON, F/Lt. H. T. J. No. 253 Squadron 19:5:40 Lille Southern Cemetery, Nord, France. Plot 5. Row A. Grave 13.

ANGUS, F/O A. B. No. 85 Squadron 16:5:40 Age 22. Fretin Communal Cemetery, Nord, France. Grave 3.

ANNING, Sgt. W. J. No. 105 Squadron 12:05:40 Age 26. Bouillon Communal Cemetery, Bouillon, Luxembourg.

ANTHONY, P/O D. N. W. L. No. 73 Squadron. Injured 13:6:40, died 14:6:40 Château Renault Communal Cemetery, Indre-et-Loire, France. Military Plot. Grave 9.

APPLETON, P/O L. L. No. 79 Squadron 14:5:40 Age 23. Runnymede Memorial Panel 71.

ARSCOTT, P/O G. O. No. 59 Squadron 4:5:40 Age Age 19. Dieppe Canadian War Cemetery, Seine-Maritime, France. Grave A.65.

ATKINS, Sgt. J. F. No. 150 Squadron 7:6:40 Age 20. Vergies Communal Cemetery, Somme, France. Row 1. Joint Grave 19-20

The funeral procession moved down Avenue de Champagne — the picture on the preceding pages being taken in front of the famous Moët & Chandon building — before reaching the main cemetery. Three other crews were also buried there (Pilot Officer Ian Hinton, Sergeant Duncan Findlay and AC2 John Sharpe of No. 103 Squadron; Pilot Officer Alan Edgar, Sergeant Hugh Pettit and Corporal Alex Jones of No. 105 Squadron, all killed on March 26; and Flying Officer David Devoto, Sergeant Clifford Wall and AC1 William Taylor of No. 150 Squadron killed on March 31). All were exhumed and reburied in Terlincthun British Cemetery near Boulogne after the war (see page 4).

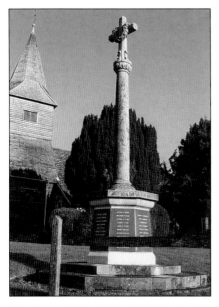
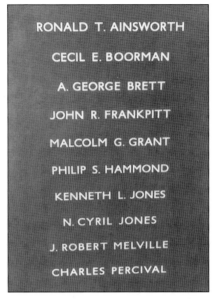

RONALD T. AINSWORTH

CECIL E. BOORMAN

A. GEORGE BRETT

JOHN R. FRANKPITT

MALCOLM G. GRANT

PHILIP S. HAMMOND

KENNETH L. JONES

N. CYRIL JONES

J. ROBERT MELVILLE

CHARLES PERCIVAL

The Ainsworth family lived at Woodlands, Newdigate Road in Beare Green in Surrey and attended the local church. Ronald is remembered by Mollie Posner, who still lives in the village, as 'a delightful young man, dressed in uniform whom she looked up to in awe'. Although buried in France, his name now appears on the Newdigate War Memorial.

Albert Ball, writing to his family: 'This is our ordinary Service Dress. Now that we are qualified as pilots we sport a pair of silver wings on our tunics.'

ATKINSON, Sgt. G. No. 105 Squadron 14:5:40 Age 19. Donchery Communal Cemetery, Ardennes, France. Joint Grave 7-8.

BAGULEY, LAC H. No. 218 Squadron 10:5:40 Age 22. Terlincthun British Cemetery, Wimille, Pas de Calais, France. Plot 19. Row B. Grave 9.

BAILEY, AC1 A. No. 218 Squadron 20:4:40 Durnbach War Cemetery, Bad Tölz, Germany. Grave 7. D. 24.

BAILLIE, Cpl. E. T. No. 16 Squadron 18:5:40 Age 31. Creil Communal Cemetery, Oise, France. Plot 1. Joint Grave 380.

BAKER, LAC H. R. No. 139 Squadron 14:5:40 Age 22. Choloy War Cemetery, Meurthe-et-Moselle, France. Grave 1A.A.13.

BALL, F/O A. R. No. 3 Squadron. Badly wounded 13:5:40, died 4:6:40 Reichswald Forest War Cemetery, Kleve, Nordrhein-Westfalen, Germany. Grave 28.E.13.

BALLANTYNE, Sgt. J. No. 88 Squadron 12:6:40 Age 23. Beaurepaire Communal Cemetery, Oise, France.

BARBOUR, P/O D. M. No. 4 Squadron 14:5:40 Age 19. Runnymede Memorial Panel 7.

BARFORD Sgt. G. H. No. 59 Squadron. 4:5:40 Age 29. Dieppe Canadian War Cemetery, Seine-Maritime, France. Grave A.68.

BARKER, F/Sgt. G. T. No. 150 Squadron 14:5:40 Age 27. Choloy War Cemetery, Meurthe-et-Moselle, France. Joint Grave 1A.A.14-15.

The Royal Air Force College at Cranwell in Lincolnshire was established in 1920 as the world's first military air academy. On the outbreak of war, the college was closed to become one of several Service Flying Training Schools which were set up in the UK and Commonwealth to expand the RAF. Then the only means of entry into the service was by enlistment in the Volunteer Reserve which had been established in 1936 with a target of producing 800 new pilots each year which brought pilot strength in the RAFVR to over 6,500 by September 1, 1939. The records of those individuals who passed out at Cranwell prior to December 1939, when the college became a Service Flying Training Squadron (SFTS), are still preserved. David Barbour went missing on May 14, 1940 but, as the entry shows, he was not officially listed as 'killed in action' until January 2, 1941.

After attacking an enemy column on May 12, Pilot Officer Freddie Bazalgette of No. 218 Squadron managed to crash-land his Battle at Nouvion-sur-Meuse to save the lives of his two crewmen, only to die in the attempt.

Another Fairey Battle crew killed in the desperate attempt to halt the German breakthrough was that of Sergeant Frank Beames, Sergeant William Ross and Leading Aircraftman John Gegg of No. 88 Squadron. They were attacking the bridge at Villers-devant-Mouzon on May 14 when they were shot down near St Menges. Their mortal remains could not be individually identified so they lie in a joint grave in the local cemetery.

BARKER, Sgt. T. R. No. 150 Squadron 12:5:40 Neufchâteau Communal Cemetery, Neufchâteau, Luxembourg, Belgium. Joint Grave 2.

BAZALGETTE, P/O F. S. No. 218 Squadron 12:5:40 Age 22. Nouvion-sur-Meuse Communal Cemetery, Ardennes, France.

BEALE, P/O R. C. No. 150 Squadron 13:6:40 Age 26. Merey Communal Cemetery, Eure, France. Collective Grave.

BEAMES, Sgt. F. E. No. 88 Squadron 14:5:40 St Menges Communal Cemetery, Ardennes, France. Collective Grave.

BEAUMONT, AC2 O. R. No. 57 Squadron 14:5:40 Age 18. Dendermonde Communal Cemetery, Dendermonde, Oost-Vlaanderen, Belgium. Grave 83.

BELCHER, Sgt. E. J. No. 12 Squadron 19:5:40 Age 20. Choloy War Cemetery, Meurthe-et-Moselle, France. Grave 2.G.9.

BELLIS, F/O C. No. 18 Squadron 11:5:40 Cement House Cemetery, Langemark-Poelkapelle, West-Vlaanderen, Belgium. Section XXIA. Collective Grave 16-17.

BENDALL, Sgt. D. J. No. 57 Squadron 25:1:40 Reichswald Forest War Cemetery, Kleve, Germany. Coll. Grave 11. A. 5-7.

BETTANY, LAC F. L. No. 26 Squadron 19:5:40 Age 19. Landrecies Communal Cemetery, Nord, France. Row C. Grave 2.

BEVAN, Sgt. H. C. C. No. 12 Squadron 7:6:40 Age 26. St Valery-en-Caux Franco-British Cemetery, Seine-Maritime, France. Collective Grave A24-26.

BISHOP, P/O L. G. No. 73 Squadron 12:3:40. Chambières French National Cemetery, Metz, Moselle, France. Grave 13.

BLIGH, Sgt. P. I. No. 103 Squadron 10:6:40 Age 20. Gasny Communal Cemetery, Eure, France. Plot B. Joint Grave 175.

BLOWFIELD, P/O P. H. No. 12 Squadron 14:6:40 Age 20. Les Minières Communal Cemetery, Eure, France.

BODDINGTON, Sgt. J. P. No. 12 Squadron 8:6:40 Age 27. Abbeville Communal Cemetery Extension, Somme, France. Plot 8. Row A. Joint Grave 5-6.

On May 19, two Battles from No. 12 Squadron were lost during attacks on troop concentrations in eastern France. Sergeant Edward Belcher was first buried in Cauroy Communal Cemetery but was moved to Choloy (see page 507) in October 1947.

On October 30, 1939, Blenheims from No. 18 Squadron were on a reconnaissance mission along the German frontier when they were attacked by II./JG53. One aircraft fell to the guns of Hauptmann Mölders (see page 427), the other possibly to Unteroffizier Hinkeldey. All the crews were killed including Aircraftman 1st Class John Burrows (left) and all are buried in Cologne Southern Cemetery (above) which lies within a large civil cemetery known locally as Köln Südfriedhof on the Höninger Platz.

BONE, P/O P. K. No. 53 Squadron 15:5:40 Age 27. Templeuve Communal Cemetery, Tournai, Belgium. Row A. Grave 2.

BOON, P/O J. No. 150 Squadron 14:5:40 Age 27. Douzy Communal Cemetery, Ardennes, France. Collective Grave.

BORG-BANKS, P/O T. H. No. 13 Squadron 16:5:40 Age 19. Vieux-Condé Communal Cemetery, Pas de Calais, France. Joint Grave.

BORTHWICK, Sgt. D. No. 18 Squadron 16:5:40 Age 26. Crèvecoeur-sur-l'Escaut Communal Cemetery, France. Grave 2.

BOWDEN, F/Sgt. F. S. No. 57 Squadron 15:11:39 Age 32. Villeneuve-St Georges Old Communal Cemetery, Val de Marne, France. Grave 119.

BOWEN, Sgt. D. J. No. 150 Squadron 14:5:40 Age 22. Choloy War Cemetery, Meurthe-et-Moselle, France. Collective Grave 1A.A.10-12.

BOYLE, LAC W. D. No. 142 Squadron 19:5:40 Age 19. Dagny-Lambercy Churchyard, Aisne, France.

BRANTON, Sgt. J. R. No. 226 Squadron 7:4:40 Terlincthun British Cemetery, Wimille. Plot 19. Row E. Grave 5.

BROMLEY, LAC J. No. 53 Squadron 15:5:40 Age 20. Runnymede Memorial Panel 22.

BROOKES, Sgt. J. No. 142 Squadron 14:5:40 Age 29. Choloy War Cemetery, Meurthe-et-Moselle, France. Joint Grave 2A.A.6.

BROWN, LAC T. W. No. 114 Squadron 14:5:40 Age 21. Glaire-et-Villette Communal Cemetery, Ardennes, France. Collective Grave.

BURNS, Sgt. R. No. 59 Squadron 18:5:40 Allied Extension of Tournai Communal Cemetery, Tournai, Hainaut, Belgium. Section VI. Grave C10.

BURROWS, AC1 J. S. No. 18 Squadron 30:10:39 Age 20. Cologne Southern Cemetery, Nordrhein-Westfalen, Germany. Plot 4. Row AA. Coll. Grave 16-18.

BURT, LAC C. S. No. 12 Squadron 8:6:40 Age 20. Abbeville Communal Cemetery Extension, Somme, France. Plot 8. Row A. Joint Grave 5-6.

BURTON, P/O R. W. No. 85 Squadron 20:5:40 Querrieu British Cemetery, Somme, France. Row E. Grave 15.

BURY, F/O D. S. H. No. 111 Squadron 19:5:40 Chili Trench Cemetery, Gavrelle, Pas de Calais, France. Row AA. Grave 1.

BUTLER, Sgt. R. W. No. 88 Squadron 26:5:40 Age 24. Haraucourt Churchyard, Ardennes, France. Joint Grave 1-2.

One of the first to die. On August 26, 1939, Pilot Officer Jimmy Calvert married Eileen Morgan at the Register Office in Kensington, London. Less than a month later, Jimmy was dead. He was at the controls of a Fairey Battle of No. 150 Squadron which suffered engine failure after take-off. Jimmy was mortally wounded and his two fellow crewmen, Sergeant Tom Woodmason and Aircraftman 1st Class John Marsh killed outright. That day, Wednesday, September 20, was a bad day for the British Air Forces in France which had suffered eight deaths by nightfall (see pages 95 and 511).

The awful cost in lives during the western campaign of 1939-40 is reflected in the many military cemeteries scattered throughout Holland, Belgium, Luxembourg and France, most of them established to accommodate the carnage of the First World War. Casualties from the later conflict were often hurriedly buried close to where they fell only to be reinterred in local communal cemeteries long after the fighting was over, but post-war the majority were recovered and concentrated in military cemeteries such as Choloy War Cemetery *(above)* where maintenance of their graves could be better assured. Of the 415 RAF airmen included in our BAFF Roll of Honour, 409 remain buried abroad — 48 of them still officially listed as 'missing' though some of these are commemorated as 'Unknown'. By 1950, the Commonwealth War Graves Commission had moved more than 100 graves to Choloy, and there are now 32 named burials in the cemetery from the Battle of France including Flying Officer Leslie Clisby *(bottom)* of No. 1 Squadron whom we saw on page 439. He was moved there from his first grave in the Communal Cemetery at Ménil-Lépinois.

BUTTERILL, LAC C. No. 4 Squadron 19:5:40 Age 38. St André Communal Cemetery, Nord, France. Row AA. Grave 4.

BUTTERWORTH, P/O J. L. G. No. 53 Squadron 3:5:40 Age 21. Durnbach War Cemetery, Bad Tölz, Germany. Grave 11. E. 20.

BUTTERWORTH, P/O R. E. C. No. 13 Squadron 21:5:40 Age 33. St Martin-au-Laërt Churchyard, Pas de Calais, France. Grave 2.

BUTTERY, P/O R. T. L. No. 218 Squadron 14:5:40 Runnymede Memorial Panel 7.

CALDWELL, Sgt. R. C. No. 88 Squadron 11:6:40 Age 26. Perdreauville Communal Cemetery, Yvelines, France.

CALLAGHAN, Sgt. J. B. No. 226 Squadron 13:6:40 Age 25. La Chapelle-Véronge Communal Cemetery, Seine-et-Marne, France.

CALVERT, P/O J. L. No. 150 Squadron 20:9:39 Clichy Northern Cemetery, France. Plot 16. Row 10. Grave 16.

CAMERON, F/O D. A. No. 226 Squadron. Critically wounded 10:5:40, died 13:5:40 Age 25. Diekirch Communal Cemetery, Luxembourg.

CAMPBELL, F/O J. A. No. 87 Squadron 12:5:40 Maastricht General Cemetery, Limburg, Netherlands. Row 3. Grave 140.

CAMPBELL-IRONS, P/O I. No. 150 Squadron 12:5:40 Neufchâteau Communal Cemetery, Neufchâteau, Luxembourg, Belgium. Grave 3.

CARTER, Sgt. D. B. No. 150 Squadron 13:6:40 Age 22. Merey Communal Cemetery, Eure, France. Collective Grave.

CARTER, F/Lt. M. M. No. 3 Squadron 15:5:40 Age 27. Maubeuge-Centre Cemetery, Nord, France. Row B. Grave 27.

CARTWRIGHT, Sgt. G. A. No. 105 Squadron 14:5:40 Age 23. Choloy War Cemetery, Meurthe-et-Moselle, France. Collective Grave 1A.A.7-9.

CHAMBERLAIN, P/O C. J. E. No. 59 Squadron 13:5:40. Age 20. Runnymede Memorial Panel 7.

CHAPMAN, Sgt. E. W. J. No. 88 Squadron 29:5:40 Age 23. Choloy War Cemetery, Meurthe-et-Moselle, France. Grave 1A.C.10.

CHILD, LAC C. C. No. 139 Squadron 12:5:40 Age 20. Runnymede Memorial Panel 22.

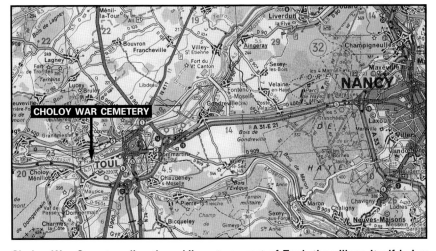

Choloy War Cemetery lies three kilometres west of Toul, the village itself being located 28 kilometres west of Nancy.

CHRISTIE, AC1 W. A. No. 53 Squadron 18:5:40 Age 18. St Hilaire Cemetery, Frévent, Pas de Calais, France. Plot 2. Row E. Grave 7.

CHURCH, LAC A. F. No. 26 Squadron 19:5:40 Age 25, Authie Churchyard, Somme, France.

CLARK, Cpl. R. S. No. 226 Squadron 14:5:40 Runnymede Memorial Panel 21.

CLARKE, F/O T. C. No. 4 Squadron 14:5:40 Age 25. St-Rémy-Geest Churchyard, Jodoigne, Brabant Wallon, Belgium. Grave 1.

CLAWLEY, Sgt. G. W. No. 150 Squadron 7:6:40 Vergies Communal Cemetery, Somme, France. Row 1. Joint Grave 19-20.

CLAYDON, P/O A. J. No. 501 Squadron 5:6:40 St Sever Cemetery Extension, Rouen, Seine-Maritime, France. Block S. Plot 4. Row S. Grave 1.

CLIFFORD, P/O R. H. No. 26 Squadron 19:5:40 Neuvilly Communal Cemetery Extension, Nord, France. Row C. Grave 13.

CLISBY, F/O L. R. DFC No. 1 Squadron 14:5:40 Choloy War Cemetery, Meurthe-et-Moselle, France. Grave 2.G.8.

Battle pilot Flying Officer John Crane of No. 218 Squadron lost his life on May 14 while attacking the bridge across the Meuse at Wadelincourt.

Flying Officer Gerald Cuthbert, a Hurricane pilot, was killed the same day. He had only just arrived at Vitry-en-Artois to join No. 607 Squadron.

COLE, Sgt. W. F. L. No. No. 150 Squadron 30:9:39 Metzing Communal Cemetery, France.

CORELLI, F/O F. M. C. No. 150 Squadron 30:9:39 Clichy Northern Cemetery, France. Plot 16. Row 10. Grave 14.

COTTERELL, Sgt. N. C. No. 12 Squadron 13:6:40 Age 20. St Barthélemy Communal Cemetery, Seine-et-Marne, France.

COUGHTREY, Cpl. F. No. 105 Squadron 31:3:40 Terlincthun British Cemetery, Wimille, France. Plot 19. Row E. Grave 7.

COUZENS, Sgt. G. F. No. 57 Squadron 13:5:40 Age 26. By entrance to Vlijtingen Churchyard, Riemst, Limburg, Belgium.

CRANE, F/O J. F. R. No. 218 Squadron 14:5:40 Noyers-Pont-Maugis French National Cemetery, Ardennes, France. Grave 500.

CRELLIN, Sgt. E. H. No. 18 Squadron 30:10:39. Age 27. Cologne Southern Cemetery, Germany. Plot 4. Row AA. Coll. Grave 16-18.

CREW, Sgt. K. B. No. 18 Squadron 30:10:39. Cologne Southern Cemetery, Germany. Plot 4. Row AA. Grave 2.

CRONIN, Sgt. W. J. DFM No. 53 Squadron 15:5:40 Age 31. Templeuve Communal Cemetery, Tournai, Hainaut, Belgium. Row A. Grave 3.

CUNNINGHAM, P/O V. A. No. 103 Squadron 14:5:40 Age 24. Rémilly-et-Aillicourt Communal Cemetery, Ardennes, France. Joint Grave 2.

CURTIS, Sgt. E. F. W. No. 142 Squadron 13:6:40 Les Corvées-les-Yys Churchyard, Eure-et-Loir, France. Grave 2.

CUTHBERT, F/O G. I. No. 607 Squadron 14:5:40 Hotton War Cemetery, Hotton, Luxembourg, Belgium. Section IX. Grave C1.

DARWOOD, F/Lt. C. S. No. 111 Squadron 18:5:40 Longuenesse (St Omer) Souvenir Cemetery, Pas de Calais, France. Plot 8. Row B. Grave 31.

Left: Charles Darwood was educated at Beaumont School, a Jesuit Catholic public school in Windsor. He was married to Betty Simpson in August 1938 and his daughter Jane *(centre)* was born in 1939. On May 18, Flight Lieutenant Darwood was a member of B Flight of No. 111 Squadron based at Vitry-en-Artois when he was shot down south of Mons. *Right:* His wife received this photo from a local priest of his initial grave on a canal bank near the crash site. Charles never lived to see his second daughter, Ann, born in September 1940.

DAVEY, P/O T. J. F. No. 4 Squadron 21:5:40 Age 20. Zudausques Churchyard, Pas de Calais, France. Grave 1.

DAVIES, LAC L. D. No. 218 Squadron 12:5:40 Age 21. Senseruth (Curfoz) Communal Cemetery, Bouillon, Luxembourg, Belgium. Collective Grave 3-4.

DAVIES, LAC P. K. No. 226 Squadron 7:4:40 Terlincthun British Cemetery, Wimille, France. Plot 19. Row E. Grave 4.

DAVIES, LAC R. D. No. 18 Squadron 11:5:40 Age 21. Reichswald Forest War Cemetery, Kleve, Nordrhein-Westfalen, Germany. Grave 25.D.18.

DAVIS, Sgt. T. W. No. 139 Squadron 12:5:40 Age 22. Runnymede Memorial Panel 13.

DAVISON, Sgt. E. No. 218 Squadron. 20:4:40 Durnbach War Cemetery, Bad Tölz, Germany. Grave 7.D.25.

DAY, P/O J. H. No. 13 Squadron. Wounded 18:5:40, died 20:5:40 Mont-Huon Military Cemetery, Le Tréport, Seine-Maritime, France. Section VI. Row L. Grave 2.

DE MONTMORENCY, F/O R. H. No. 139 Squadron 14:5:40 Age 23. Laneuville-sur-Meuse Communal Cemetery, Meuse, France. Joint Grave 1.

DE SOUZA, P/O K. M. A. No. 139 Squadron 16:5:40 Floing Communal Cemetery, Ardennes, France. Grave 3.

DEVOTO, F/O D. No. 150 Squadron 31:3:40 Terlincthun British Cemetery, Wimille, France. Plot 19. Row D. Grave 4.

DEWAR, Sgt. F. No. 218 Squadron 1:3:40 Terlincthun British Cemetery, Wimille, France. Plot 19. Row D. Grave 13.

DIBDEN, Sgt. L. G. M. No. 73 Squadron 14:5:40 Age 21. Choloy War Cemetery, Meurthe-et-Moselle, France. Grave 2.G.10.

DILLON, P/O A. M. No. 229 Squadron 18:5:40 Age 18. Mons Communal Cemetery, Mons, Hainaut, Belgium. Section X. Grave C32.

DILNOT, F/Lt. A. A. No. 18 Squadron 30:10:39 Cologne Southern Cemetery, Germany. Plot 4. Row AA. Coll. Grave 16-18.

DIXON, P/O L. T. No. 18 Squadron 10:5:40 Jonkerbos War Cemetery, Nijmegen, The Netherlands. Grave 8.I.1.

DOCKRILL, Sgt. C. J. E. No. 218 Squadron 11:5:40 Age 26. Troisvierges (Bas-Bellain) Churchyard, Luxembourg. Collective Grave.

Cranwell . . . the name synonymous with the Royal Air Force. Before the officer training college in Lincolnshire was taken over for an SFTS the duration, individual 'class' photographs were taken outside the main entrance *(above)* at the end of each term. *Top:* This was the passing-out photograph for December 1937 and the officer cadet with the broad grin, fourth from the right in the front row, is Raymond de Montmorency. Born on June 11, 1916, he had studied at Wellesley House School at Broadstairs before going to Eton College. He enrolled at Cranwell in September 1935 and his commission on December 18, 1937 saw him posted to No. 114 (Bomber) Squadron at RAF Wyton. Promoted to Flying Officer in June 1939, joining No. 139 Squadron with Blenheims, he became another casualty during the desperate attempts to stem the relentless German assault on May 14. He was officially listed as missing on May 23 but not until March 1941 was he officially classified as being killed in action. However, the Germans did not recover the remains from the crash site until June 1942 when they were buried in Laneuville-sur-Meuse Communal Cemetery as two unknown airmen (see page 527).

509

Left: **Pilot Officer Harold Dodgson, proudly sporting his coveted wings, was killed when his Blenheim of No. 114 Squadron came to grief on February 27, 1940.** *Centre:* **His observer, Sergeant** Hawkins who survived, took this picture of him on that Tuesday morning, before they took off. *Right:* **Harold's grave lies in Bienvillers Military Cemetery, 18 kilometres south-west of Arras.**

DODGSON, P/O H. No. 114 Squadron 27:2:40 Age 20. Bienvillers Military Cemetery, France. Plot 14. Row D. Grave 15.

DORMER, Sgt. P. F. No. 218 Squadron 11:5:40 Age 27. Troisvierges (Bas-Bellain) Churchyard, Luxembourg. Collective Grave.

DORRIEN-SMITH, P/O L. R. No. 79 Squadron 20:5:40 Age 21. Runnymede Memorial Panel 8.

DOWLING, Sgt. A. N. No. 103 Squadron 15:6:40 Age 24. Sougé-sur-Braye Communal Cemetery, Loir-et-Cher, France. Military Plot. Row 1. Collective Grave 5-7.

DRABBLE, P/O K. J. No. 103 Squadron 10:5:40 Age 20. Hotton War Cemetery, Hotton, Luxembourg, Belgium. Section IV. Grave C11.

DROMGOOLE, P/O I. No. 16 Squadron 19:5:40 Age 25. Runnymede Memorial Panel 8.

DUMBRECK, Sgt. O. W. No. 18 Squadron 21:3:40 Age 26. Kirkcaldy (Dysart) Cemetery, Fifeshire. Plot 59. Middle. Grave 3.

Right: **Lionel Roger Dorrien-Smith was born at Kings Hill House, Berkhamstead, on June 2, 1918, the fifth child of Major Arthur and Eleanor Dorrien-Smith. When Lionel was two months old, his parents inherited the Isles of Scilly which were held on a 99-year lease from the Duchy of Cornwall. His home then became Tresco Abbey. In the autumn of 1926 Lionel went to Sunningdale Preparatory School and then on to Eton College later in 1931. In October 1937 he went up to University College in Oxford, joining the Royal Air Force in 1938. The Dorrien-Smith family suffered a double blow on May 20, 1940 when both Lionel and his brother Robert were killed on the very same day; Lionel with No. 79 Squadron and Robert with the 15th/19th King's Royal Hussars, and at exactly the same location — Arras. Lionel's body was never found and he is now remembered on the Runnymede Memorial. His brother was buried in Lapugnoy Military Cemetery, six kilometres west of Béthune. The Dorrien-Smith family were to suffer a third loss in 1944 when another son, Francis, a major in the 1st Batallion, Rifle Brigade, was killed on June 20 in Normandy. His grave lies in Bayeux Eastern Cemetery.**

On March 21, 1940, a Blenheim from No. 18 Squadron took off from Rosières-en-Santerre to fly back to Kemble via Tangmere, but the crew lost their bearings in fog and crashed on the South Downs. The aircraft burst into flames but, in spite of the exploding ammunition, Gerald Winter *(left)*, who was working nearby, ran to the wreck. He pulled out an airman from the rear of the plane but the pilot, Henry Hulton, and the observer, Sergeant Oliver Dumbreck (seen *centre* in his Scout uniform), were trapped in the cockpit. Mr Winter climbed into the wreck and tried to pull the two men to safety but the heat drove him back. On June 28, 1940 *The London Gazette* announced his award of the Empire Gallantry Medal (later exchanged for the George Cross). *Right:* Sergeant Dumbreck was interred in the family grave in Dysart Cemetery in Kirkcaldy, Scotland.

DUNN, P/O H. J. R. No. 87 Squadron. Wounded 9:5:40, died 1:6:40. Age 23. Henham (St Mary) Churchyard, Henham, Essex.

DUNN, F/Sgt. W. A. No. 226 Squadron 14:5:40 Choloy War Cemetery, Meurthe-et-Moselle, France. Joint Grave 2A.A.2-3.

DURIE, P/O R. A. No. 59 Squadron 18:5:40 Age 19. Allied Extension of Tournai Communal Cemetery, Tournai, Hainaut, Belgium. Section VI. Grave C9.

EDGAR, P/O A. M. No. 105 Squadron 26:3:40 Terlincthun British Cemetery, Wimille, France. Plot 19. Row C. Grave 2.

EDWARDS, AC1 C. A. No. 88 Squadron 29:5:40 Choloy War Cemetery, Meurthe-et-Moselle, France. Grave 1A.C.11.

EDWARDS, P/O T. J. No. 87 Squadron 15:5:40 Runnymede Memorial Panel 8.

EGGINGTON, Sgt. A. W. No. 88 Squadron 20:9:39 Choloy War Cemetery, Meurthe-et-Moselle, France. Grave 2A. C. 14.

ELLIOTT, F/O D. F. No. 18 Squadron 30:10:39 Age 23. Cologne Southern Cemetery, Germany. Plot 4. Row AA. Grave 1.

EMERY, Sgt. G. H. No 12 Squadron 14:6:40 Age 26. Pacy-sur-Eure Communal Cemetery, Eure, France. Grave 3.

EVANS, Sgt. F. J. J. No. 59 Squadron 14:5:40 Age 29. Runnymede Memorial Panel 14.

EVERETT, Sgt. W. S. No. 88 Squadron 20:9:39 Choloy War Cemetery, Meurthe-et-Moselle, France. Grave 2A. C. 19.

EVITT, F/O H. G. No. 88 Squadron 29:5:40 Age 26. Choloy War Cemetery, Meurthe-et-Moselle, France. Grave 1A.C.9.

FALCONER, Sgt. D. G. B. No. 53 Squadron 09:05:40 Age 28. Dieppe Canadian War Cemetery, France. Grave B. 73.

FARMER, Sgt. S. J. No. 57 Squadron 15:11:39 Age 25. Villeneuve-St Georges Old Communal Cemetery, Val de Marne, France. Grave 120.

FARRELL, F/O P. A. L. No 142 Squadron. 7:4:40 Terlincthun British Cemetery, Wimille, France. Plot 19. Row D. Grave 3.

FARROW, P/O R. W. No. 114 Squadron 2:3:40 Age 25. Terlincthun British Cemetery, France. Plot 19. Row D. Grave 7.

Left: Alfred Eggington was born on December 21, 1913 at Durrington, Wiltshire. He was the eldest son of Ernest Eggington, a NAAFI canteen manager, and Eliza, being one of nine children. Alf's elementary education was at Durrington Parochial School from where he won a scholarship to attend Bishop Wordsworth School in Salisbury. Due to his enthusiasm for both aircraft and woodworking, on leaving school Alf secured a place at the Apprentice Training School at RAF Halton. He became a craftsman working on wooden aircraft structures, and as a Leading Aircraftman served overseas at the RAF stations at Singapore and Heliopolis, Egypt. In 1938 Alf applied for and was accepted to train as a navigator/observer. As a sergeant navigator he was posted to a Fairey Battle squadron at Boscombe Down. On the day after war was declared, No. 88 Squadron flew to France and on September 20, the squadron mounted a reconnaissance of the German frontier when two of its machines were brought down by the 5. Staffel of JG53. Five of their men lost their lives that day, the very first of the Battle of France (see also page 506). *Right:* After the war, Sergeant Eggington's grave was moved from Le-Val-de-Guéblange to Choloy War Cemetery, where all eight casualties of Nos. 88 and 150 Squadrons from that day are buried.

A postcard from the past. Leading Aircraftman Harry Garbett (centre front row) lived at the White House, Follyfields, Cheddington, and he was the first local man to be killed in the Second World War — his name now being commemorated on the town war memorial *(below)*. He was the wireless operator/air gunner on one of seven Blenheims lost during the dawn attacks in the Maastricht area on May 12. On the reverse of the postcard, Harry lists the other individuals as (rear L-R): 'Jimson, Hibbert, Petersen, Lewis, Hunter, Jusley(?); (centre) Hare, Edwards, McClymont; (front) James, Me, Wilson'.

FIDLER, S/Ldr G. M. No. 607 Squadron 19:5:40 Bachy Communal Cemetery, Nord, France.

FIELD, Sgt. F. J. No. 12 Squadron 7:6:40 Age 24. St Valery-en-Caux Franco-British Cemetery, Seine-Maritime, France. Collective Grave A24-26.

FINDLAY, Sgt. D. C. No. 103 Squadron 26:3:40 Terlincthun British Cemetery, Wimille, France. Plot 19. Row E. Grave 9.

FLISHER, Sgt. L. C. No. 218 Squadron 12:5:40 Age 26. Senseruth (Curfoz) Communal Cemetery, Bouillon, Luxembourg, Belgium. Collective Grave 3-4.

FOOTNER, Sgt. K. D. No. 12 Squadron 12:5:40 Age 24. Heverlee War Cemetery, Leuven, Vlaams-Brabant, Belgium. Grave 8.J.5.

FORD, F/O E. C. No. 4 Squadron 18:5:40 Age 24. Outer Communal Cemetery, Ninove, Oost-Vlaanderen, Belgium. Grave 261.

FORTUNE, Sgt. T. No. 150 Squadron 14:5:40 Douzy Communal Cemetery, Ardennes, France. Collective Grave.

FRASER, Sgt. J. N. No. 142 Squadron 11:6:40 Age 19. St Sever Cemetery Extension, Rouen, Seine-Maritime, France. Block S. Plot 4. Row T. Joint Grave 9.

FREDMAN, F/O L. No. 615 Squadron. 12:5:40 Wihogne Churchyard, Juprelle, Liège, Belgium. Grave 9.

FROOM AC2 P. W. No. 59 Squadron. 4:5:40 Dieppe Canadian War Cemetery, Seine-Maritime, France. Grave A.69.

GARBETT, LAC H. T. No. 139 Squadron 12:5:40 Age 24. Heverlee War Cemetery, Leuven, Vlaams-Brabant, Belgium. Collective Grave 10.F.8-10.

GARLAND, F/O D. E. No. 12 Squadron 12:5:40 Age 21. Heverlee War Cemetery, Leuven, Vlaams-Brabant, Belgium. Collective Grave 6.F.14-16.

GARNONS-WILLIAMS, Lt-Col. (Royal Welch Fusiliers) H. F. No. 13 Squadron 10:11:39 Age 43. Douai Communal Cemetery, Nord, France. Row K. Grave 8.

GARRICK, AC1 J. A. No. 18 Squadron 30:10:39 Cologne Southern Cemetery, Germany. Plot 4. Row AA. Grave 3.

GAY, AC1 K. V. No. 150 Squadron. 30:9:39 Clichy Northern Cemetery, France. Plot 16. Row 10. Grave 12.

The first VCs of the air war. On May 12, as we have seen on pages 244-245, No. 12 Squadron carried out an attack on the bridges at Maastricht, a suicidal operation from which only one aircraft returned. Crews of two of the Battles perished, all six men lying buried in Heverlee War Cemetery near Leuven in Belgium. *Above:* These are the graves of the crew of Battle P2204, the headstones of Flying Officer Garland (left) and Sergeant Gray being inscribed with the Victoria Cross. Yet Leading Aircraftman Lawrence Reynolds was given no decoration so we searched out the official paperwork to try to discover the reason why. The recommendation for the award of the VC was prepared by the AOC-in-C of the BAFF, Air Marshal Barratt, and sent to the Air Ministry in London on May 26. From the facsimile reproductions below we can see the chain of command right up to King George VI, and also that it was a 'symbolic' award to the formation leader and his navigator, although why Lawrence Reynolds was omitted is not explained.

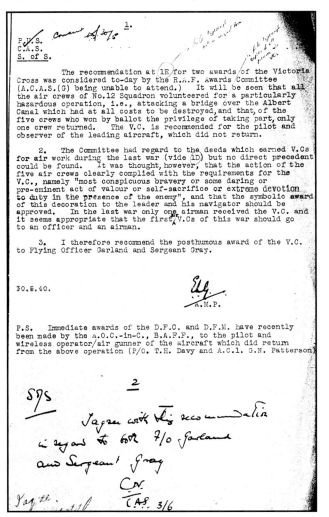

Of the Cranwell class of July 1939, four men were killed in the Battle of France. Sitting on the extreme right of the front row is Pilot Officer Robert Harris who lost his life on May 19. He lived in Stert, Wiltshire, and had initially been posted to No. 56 Squadron in July 1939. Second from the right in the third row is Pilot Officer Henry Hulton, the son of Lieutenant-Colonel Hulton, DSO, the Government Secretary in Jersey. Henry was posted to the School of Army Co-operation at Old Sarum in September 1939. In the back row Geoffrey Harding stands second from the left. After leaving Clifton College in Bristol in 1937, he went to Cranwell as a Prize Cadet. He also was posted to Old Sarum as a Pilot Officer in September 1939, being killed on the morning the German attack in the West was launched. (The fourth officer killed from the Sixth Term was Pilot Officer Christopher Halliday on May 19 but he was unfortunately sick on the day this group photo was taken.)

GEGG, LAC J. H. K. No. 88 Squadron 14:5:40 Age 20. St Menges Communal Cemetery, Ardennes, France. Collective Grave.

GIDDINGS, Sgt. N. F. F. No. 88 Squadron. 6:5:40 Age 26. Le Grand-Luce War Cemetery, France. Row A. Grave 4.

GIFFORD, S/L P. No. 3 Squadron 16:5:40 Runnymede Memorial Panel 4.

GILLAM, P/O J. D. W. No. 88 Squadron 11:6:40 Age 21. Perdreauville Communal Cemetery, Yvelines, France.

GILLHAM, LAC J. H. No. 4 Squadron 21:5:40 Age 21. Zudausques Churchyard, Pas de Calais, France. Grave 2.

GODDARD, LAC C. J. No. 88 Squadron. 6:5:40 Age 19. Le Grand-Luce War Cemetery, France. Row A. Grave 5.

GOTHARD, Sgt. A. C. No. 53 Squadron 18:5:40 St Hilaire Cemetery, Frévent, Pas de Calais, France. Plot 2. Row E. Grave 6.

GRAEME, F/O N. S. No. 607 Squadron 23:3:40 Douai Communal Cemetery, Nord, France. Row L. Grave 12.

GRAHAM, F/O K. W. No. 4 Squadron 18:5:40 Age 36. Outer Communal Cemetery, Ninove, Oost-Vlaanderen, Belgium. Grave 262.

GRAHAM, F/Lt. R. H. N. No. 13 Squadron 21:5:40 Age 34. St Martin-au-Laërt Churchyard, Pas de Calais, France. Grave 1.

GRAHAM-HOGG, F/O H. G. No. 57 Squadron 14:4:40 Age 27. Arnhem (Moscowa) General Cemetery, Netherlands. Coll. Grave 1.

GRANT, Sgt. D. L. No. 12 Squadron 14:6:40 Age 26. Coulonges Churchyard, Eure, France.

GRANT, LAC L. O. No. 150 Squadron 8:6:40 Fallencourt Communal Cemetery, Seine-Maritime, France. Collective Grave.

GRAY, Sgt. P. C. No. 139 Squadron 12:5:40 Runnymede Memorial Panel 14.

GRAY, Sgt. T. No. 12 Squadron 12:5:40 Age 26. Heverlee War Cemetery, Leuven, Vlaams-Brabant, Belgium. Collective Grave 6.F.14-16.

GREGORY, Sgt. F. W. No. 139 Squadron 12:5:40 Age 23. Heverlee War Cemetery, Leuven, Vlaams-Brabant, Belgium. Collective Grave 6.F.17-19.

GREGORY, AC1 K. G. No. 218 Squadron 11:5:40 Age 20. Troisvierges (Bas-Bellain) Churchyard, Luxembourg. Collective Grave.

GULLEY, P/O A. R. No. 150 Squadron 13:6:40 Age 21. Aigleville Churchyard, Eure, France.

HALLIDAY, P/O C. I. D. No. 26 Squadron 19:5:40 Authie Churchyard, Somme, France.

HAMBLETT, Sgt. S. No. 504 Squadron 14:5:40 Runnymede Memorial Panel 15.

HAMILTON, P/O L. M. No. 16 Squadron 17:5:40 Age 35. Runnymede Memorial Panel 8.

HANDS, AC1 F. No. 59 Squadron 13:5:40 Age 21. Runnymede Memorial Panel 25.

HARDING, P/O G. F. No. 18 Squadron 10:5:40 Age 21. Reichswald Forest War Cemetery, Kleve, Nordrhein-Westfalen, Germany. Grave 20.D.5.

Henry Hulton was killed together with Oliver Dumbreck (see page 511). His family laid him to rest in St Brelade's Churchyard in Jersey.

Pilot Officer Paul Jarvis was shot down early on the morning of May 14 west of Maastricht. His Hurricane was never found and his name is now commemorated on the Memorial to the Missing at Runnymede.

HARRIS, LAC P. B. No. 18 Squadron 3:1:40 Age 20. Liège (Robermont) Cemetery, Belgium. Grave 51.

HARRIS, P/O R. E. No. 17 Squadron 19:5:40 Noyelles-sur-Selle Communal Cemetery, Nord, France. Grave 4 A.

HARRISON, Sgt. T. C. R. No. 139 Squadron 12:5:40 Age 25. Heverlee War Cemetery, Leuven, Vlaams-Brabant, Belgium. Collective Grave 10.F.8-10.

HARVEY, Sgt. V. No. 18 Squadron 27:12:39 Age 19. Le Quesnel Communal Cemetery Extension. Row B. Grave 10.

HATTON, LAC H. No. 105 Squadron 14:5:40 Age 22. Noyers-Pont-Maugis French National Cemetery, Ardennes, France. Grave 503.

HAWKEN, P/O I. D. No. 73 Squadron 3:6:40 Age 24. Terlincthun British Cemetery, Wimille, Pas de Calais, France. Plot 19. Row D. Grave 8.

HAWKS, F/O P. A. No. 59 Squadron 14:5:40 Age 25. Runnymede Memorial Panel 4.

HAYWARD, Sgt. E. G. No. 103 Squadron 26:5:40 Age 25. Ucimont Churchyard, Bouillon, Luxembourg, Belgium. Grave 11.

HERRIOT, Sgt. N. B. No. 218 Squadron 14:5:40 Age 22. Sauville Communal Cemetery, Ardennes, France.

HIBBERD, Sgt. S. D. No. 226 Squadron 14:5:40 Age 26. Runnymede Memorial Panel 15.

HIBBERT, Sgt. E. No. 88 Squadron 23:5:40 Durnbach War Cemetery, Bad Tölz, Bayern, Germany. Collective Grave 6.B.17-19.

HILLIER, Sgt. E. B. No. 57 Squadron 13:10:39 Age 23. Rheinberg War Cemetery, Germany. Row 9. Section G. Grave 4.

HINDER, LAC R. H. No. 150 Squadron 12:5:40 Age 20. Neufchâteau Communal Cemetery, Neufchâteau, Luxembourg, Belgium. Joint Grave 2.

HINTON, P/O I. P. No. 103 Squadron. 26:3:40 Terlincthun British Cemetery, Wimille, France. Plot 19. Row E. Grave 8.

HISLOP, F/Sgt. J. No. 12 Squadron 14:6:40 Age 19. Pacy-sur-Eure Communal Cemetery, Eure, France. Grave 2.

HORNER, F/Sgt. J. B. No. 218 Squadron 12:5:40 Age 24. Senseruth (Curfoz) Communal Cemetery, Bouillon, Luxembourg, Belgium. Collective Grave 3-4.

HUBBARD, Sgt. W. F. No. 103 Squadron 26:5:40 Age 25. Ucimont Churchyard, Bouillon, Luxembourg, Belgium. Grave 12.

HUGGETT, P/O L. J. No. 53 Squadron 18:5:40 St Hilaire Cemetery, Frévent, Pas de Calais, France. Plot 2. Row F. Grave 7.

HUGHES, LAC R. D. No. 105 Squadron 14:5:40 Age 20. Runnymede Memorial Panel 23.

HULSE, P/O R. G. No. 501 Squadron 8:6:40 Sentelie Churchyard, Somme, France.

HULTON, P/O H. S. P. No. 18 Squadron 21:3:40 Age 20. St Brelade's Churchyard, Jersey. Grave 452 North.

HUME, P/O O. C. No. 57 Squadron 23:11:39 Age 20. Le Quesnel Communal Cemetery Extension. Row B. Grave 8.

HUNTER, AC2 J. R. No. 57 Squadron 25:1:40 Reichswald Forest War Cemetery, Kleve, Germany. Coll. Grave 11. A. 5-7.

HURST, P/O T. No. 105 Squadron 12:5:40 Age 22. Bouillon Communal Cemetery, Bouillon, Luxembourg, Belgium.

HUTCHINSON, LAC O. A. No. 103 Squadron 10:5:40 Age 23. Hotton War Cemetery, Hotton, Luxembourg, Belgium. Section III. Grave E11.

ING, F/O J. No. 150 Squadron 14:5:40 Donchery Communal Cemetery, Ardennes, France. Grave 12.

IRVINE, Sgt. G. B. No. 142 Squadron 10:5:40 Age 21. Terlincthun British Cemetery, Wimille, Pas de Calais, France. Plot 19. Row C. Grave 5.

JAMES, LAC H. G. No. 18 Squadron 16:5:40 Crevecouer-sur-L'Escaut Communal Cemetery, Nord, France. Grave 3.

JARVIS, P/O P. L. No. 87 Squadron 14:5:40 Runnymede Memorial Panel 8.

JENNINGS, Sgt. C. M. No. 218 Squadron 11:5:40 Age 20. Heverlee War Cemetery, Leuven, Belgium. Grave 1.J.11.

JOHN, AC1 D. J. No. 88 Squadron. 20:9:39 Choloy War Cemetery, Meurthe-et-Moselle, France. Grave 2A. C. 20.

JOHNSON, Sgt. A. G. No. 12 Squadron 14:5:40 Age 27. Pouru-St-Rémy Communal Cemetery, Ardennes, France. Grave 2.

JOHNSON, AC1 J. No. 103 Squadron 14:5:40 Age 20. Rémilly-et-Aillicourt Communal Cemetery, Ardennes, France. Joint Grave 2.

JONES, Cpl. A. E. No. 105 Squadron 26:3:40 Terlincthun British Cemetery, Wimille, France. Plot 19. Row C. Grave 11.

JONES, Sgt. N. S. D. No. 139 Squadron 12:5:40 Heverlee War Cemetery, Leuven, Vlaams-Brabant, Belgium. Collective Grave 10.F.8-10.

Another casualty in the early attempts to stall the German attack was Sergeant Cedric Jennings. His Battle was hit by ground fire near St Vith but he baled out too low.

JONES, Sgt. T. No. 142 Squadron 19:5:40 Age 29. Terlincthun British Cemetery, Wimille, Pas de Calais, France. Plot 19. Row E. Grave 1.

JORDAN, P/O C. B. No. 114 Squadron 14:5:40 Age 27. Glaire-et-Villette Communal Cemetery, Ardennes, France. Collective Grave.

JORDAN, LAC L. F. No. 57 Squadron 10:5:40 Age 27. Hook of Holland General Cemetery, Zuid-Holland, The Netherlands. Row G. Grave 6.

KAIN, F/O E. J. DFC No. 73 Squadron 7:6:40 Age 21. Choloy War Cemetery, Meurthe-et-Moselle, France. Grave 1A.C.8.

KEEGAN, Sgt. J. B. No. 139 Squadron 12:5:40 Runnymede Memorial Panel 16.

KERRIDGE, F/Lt. B. R. No. 226 Squadron. Seriously wounded 10:5:40, died 15:5:40 Age 27. Luxembourg (Hollerich) Communal Cemetery, Luxembourg. Grave 4.

KETTLEWELL, Sgt. G. H. No. 142 Squadron 13:6:40 Age 20. Les Corvées-les-Yys Churchyard, Eure-et-Loir, France. Grave 3.

KIRBY, Sergeant R. A. P. No. 88 Squadron 11:5:40 Age 24. Hotton War Cemetery, Hotton, Luxembourg, Belgium. Section I. Coll. Grave B3-5.

LAMBLE, LAC P. J. No. 103 Squadron 10:5:40 Age 20. Hotton War Cemetery, Hotton, Luxembourg, Belgium. Section IV. Grave C10.

LANGTON, AC1 L. M. No. 142 Squadron 10:5:40 Pétange (La Madelaine) Communal Cemetery, Luxembourg. Grave 27.

LAWES, LAC W. F. No. 13 Squadron 16:5:40 Vieux-Condé Communal Cemetery, Pas de Calais, France. Joint Grave.

LAWS, P/O F. S. No. 142 Squadron. 10:5:40 Pétange (La Madelaine) Communal Cemetery, Luxembourg. Grave 29.

LE BREUILLY, P/O A. E. No. 607 Squadron 14:5:40 Runnymede Memorial Panel 9.

LEDSON, Sgt. J. H. No. 142 Squadron 11:6:40 Age 21. St Sever Cemetery Extension, Rouen, Seine-Maritime, France. Block S. Plot 4. Row T. Joint Grave 9.

LEE, F/Lt. A. W. No. 139 Squadron 12:5:40 Runnymede Memorial Panel 4.

LENTON, Sgt. S. W. No. 85 Squadron 6:3:40 Péronne Communal Cemetery Extension, France. Plot 5. Row G. Grave 25.

LEWIS, Sgt. C. T. No. 88 Squadron 7:6:40 Age 21. Moisy Communal Cemetery, Loir-et-Cher, France.

LINDSAY, AC1 G. No. 57 Squadron 11:4:40 Age 19. Le Quesnel Communal Cemetery Extension. Row B. Grave 13.

LINES-ROBERTS, F/O R. B. No. 3 Squadron 13:5:40 Cité Bonjean Military Cemetery, Armentières, Nord, France. Plot 11. Row B. Grave 5.

LITTLE, Cpl. H. F. No. 226 Squadron 14:5:40 Age 27. Runnymede Memorial Panel 22.

LITTLE, Sgt. J. McG. No. 85 Squadron 19:5:40 Age 22. Runnymede Memorial Panel 16.

LIVINGSTON, Sgt. A. No. 226 Squadron 21:5:40 Age 29. Runnymede Memorial Panel 16.

LORIMER, F/O R. L. No. 1 Squadron 14:5:40 Runnymede Memorial Panel 6.

LUCAS, LAC C. F. No. 13 Squadron 15:5:40 Age 23. Leuven Communal Cemetery, Leuven, Vlaams-Brabant, Belgium. Row A. Grave 7.

LUMSDEN, AC2 A. No. 114 Squadron 13:10:39. Age 21. Rheinberg War Cemetery, Germany. Row 1. Section A. Grave 3.

MACE, F/Lt. C. R. No. 105 Squadron 31:3:40 Terlincthun British Cemetery, Wimille, France. Plot 19. Row E. Grave 6.

MacKENZIE, Sgt. G. No. 253 Squadron 19:5:40 Cysoing Communal Cemetery, Nord, France. Grave 5.

MacKRELL, Sgt. J. F. W. No. 12 Squadron 7:6:40 St Valery-en-Caux Franco-British Cemetery, Seine-Maritime, France. Collective Grave A24-26.

Heverlee War Cemetery *(above)* lies 30 kilometres from Brussels and three from Leuven. Here lie two more casualties from May 12: Sergeant Fred Marland *(left)* of No. 12 Squadron shot down while attacking the Veldwezelt bridge, and Flying Officer Andrew McPherson *(right)* of No. 139 Squadron whose Blenheim was brought down near Lanaken. He had already been awarded the Distinguished Flying Cross — one of the first of the war — for a reconnaissance flight over Germany on September 3, 1939.

MACKWORTH, P/O C. C. D. No. 87 Squadron 14:5:40 Bruyelle War Cemetery, Antoing, Hainault, Belgium. Section I. Grave B21.

MACQUEEN, P/O D. G. No. 242 Squadron 9:6:40 Courtisols (St Memmie) Churchyard, Marne, France. Military Plot. Row 1. Grave 5.

MADDOX, LAC S. A. No. 139 Squadron 14:5:40 Age 19. La Cassine Communal Cemetery, Ardennes, France.

MALTBY, AC1 E. W. No. 88 Squadron 11:5:40 Age 19. Hotton War Cemetery, Hotton, Luxembourg, Belgium. Section I. Grave B2.

MANTLE, AC1 F. J. No. 57 Squadron 15:3:40 Age 25. Chambières French National Cemetery, Metz, France. Grave 15.

MARLAND, Sgt. F. No. 12 Squadron 12:5:40 Age 28. Heverlee War Cemetery, Leuven, Vlaams-Brabant, Belgium. Grave 8.J.4.

MARROWS, Sgt. E. No. 226 Squadron 11:6:40 St Pierre-D'Autils Communal Cemetery, Eure, France. Collective Grave.

MARSH, AC1 J. L. No. 150 Squadron 20:9:39 Clichy Northern Cemetery, France. Plot 16. Row 10. Grave 13.

MARTIN, F/Lt. A. D. J. No. 142 Squadron 13:6:40 Age 23. Les Corvées-les-Yys Churchyard, Eure-et-Loir, France. Grave 1.

MARTIN, AC1 S. No. 150 Squadron 14:5:40 Douzy Communal Cemetery, Ardennes, France. Collective Grave.

MARTIN, LAC W. S. No. 18 Squadron 27:12:39 Age 21. Le Quesnel Communal Cemetery Extension. Row B. Grave 12.

MARWOOD, Sgt. G. W. No. 114 Squadron 13:10:39 Age 25. Rheinberg War Cemetery, Germany. Row 1. Section A. Grave 1.

McCARTHY, AC2 W. J. No. 139 Squadron 16:5:40 Age 23. Floing Communal Cemetery, Ardennes, France. Grave 1.

McELLIGOTT, P/O J. J. No. 12 Squadron 19:5:40 Age 24. Terlincthun British Cemetery, Wimille, Pas de Calais, France. Plot 19. Row D. Grave 10.

McFADDEN, LAC W. A. No. 139 Squadron 12:5:40 Rekem Communal Cemetery, Lanaken, Limburg, Belgium. Grave 22.

McLOUGHLIN, Sgt. G. P. No. 226 Squadron 11:6:40 Age 19. St Pierre-D'Autils Communal Cemetery, Eure, France. Collective Grave.

McPHERSON, F/O A. DFC No. 139 Squadron 12:5:40 Age 22. Heverlee War Cemetery, Leuven, Vlaams-Brabant, Belgium. Collective Grave 6.F.17-19.

MILLAR, AC2 M. B. No. 226 Squadron 14:5:40 Age 24. Choloy War Cemetery, Meurthe-et-Moselle, France. Joint Grave 2A.A.2-3.

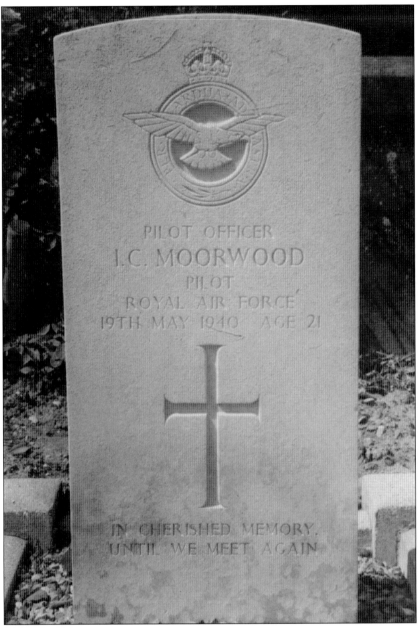

MOLD, AC2 E. No. 4 Squadron 13:5:40 Age 23. Outgaarden Communal Cemetery, Hoegaarden, Vlaams-Brabant, Belgium. Grave 2.

MOLLER, AC2 F. G. No. 57 Squadron 13:10:39 Rheinberg War Cemetery, Germany. Row 9. Section G. Grave 5.

MONGEY, Sgt. T. J. No. 18 Squadron 16:5:40 Prospect Hill Cemetery, Gouy, Aisne, France. Plot 1. Row A. Grave 1A.

MOORWOOD, P/O I. C. No. 111 Squadron 19:5:40 Sains-les-Marquion Churchyard, Pas de Calais, France.

MORGAN, Sgt. A. C. No. 105 Squadron 14:5:40 Age 28. Noyers-Pont-Maugis French National Cemetery, Ardennes, France. Grave 502.

MORGAN, Sgt. C. A. No. 59 Squadron 15:5:40 Age 22. North-east corner of Gembes Churchyard, Gembes, Luxembourg, Belgium.

MORGAN-DEAN, F/O G. B. No. 103 Squadron 12:5:40 Age 23. Haraucourt Churchyard, Ardennes, France. Grave 4.

MORTON, P/O A. D. No. 57 Squadron 6:11:39. Age 27. Rheinberg War Cemetery, Germany. Grave 18. D. 3.

MORTON, P/O E. E. No. 103 Squadron 12:5:40 Age 25. Senseruth (Curfoz) Communal Cemetery, Bouillon, Luxembourg, Belgium. Joint Grave 1-2.

MOSELEY, Sgt. V. H. No. 226 Squadron 14:5:40 Age 26. Choloy War Cemetery, Meurthe-et-Moselle, France. Grave 1A.A.21.

MURTON-NEALE, F/O P. N. No. 615 Squadron 13:5:40 South-east corner of Courriere Churchyard, Assesse, Namur, Belgium.

NIXON, Sgt. F. No. 226 Squadron 14:6:40 Age 21. Runnymede Memorial Panel 18.

NOLAN, AC1 W. J. No. 150 Squadron 14:5:40 Age 20. Donchery Communal Cemetery, Ardennes, France. Grave 11.

NUGENT, LAC R. H. No. 142 Squadron 14:5:40 Age 35. Choloy War Cemetery, Meurthe-et-Moselle, France. Joint Grave 2A.A.6.

OLDACRES, F/O L. J. No. 4 Squadron 19:5:40 Age 23. St André Communal Cemetery, Nord, France. Row AA. Grave 7.

OLLERENSHAW, P/O A. C. No. 13 Squadron 15:5:40 Age 19. Leuven Communal Cemetery, Leuven, Vlaams-Brabant, Belgium. Row A. Grave 6.

O'REILLY, LAC J. P. No. 16 Squadron 17:5:40. Age 20. Doingt Communal Cemetery Extension, Péronne, Somme, France.

Treble-One Squadron lost two pilots on May 19, Flying Officer David Bury and Pilot Officer Iain Moorwood, both victims of Messerschmitt Bf109s during an attack on Heinkels of I./KG54. Both are buried in the Pas de Calais area, David Bury in what is now called Chili Trench Cemetery although it was formerly known as Fampoux Cemetery or Gavrelle Road Cemetery after the nearby village of that name located ten kilometres north-east of Arras. He is one of 196 burials at the cemetery although he is the only airman of the Second World War interred there. Iain Moorwood on the other hand, lies quite alone, the only British burial in Sains-les-Marquion Churchyard, 12 kilometres north-west of Cambrai (above).

MILLER, Sgt. R. F. No. 142 Squadron 10:5:40 Age 31. Pétange (La Madelaine) Communal Cemetery, Luxembourg. Grave 28.

MILLNER, Sgt. W. No. 73 Squadron 1:6:40 Terlincthun British Cemetery, Wimille, Pas de Calais, France. Plot 19. Row D. Grave 9.

MITCHELL, P/O J. S. No. 1 Squadron 2:3:40 Chambières French National Cemetery, Metz, Moselle, France. Grave 12.

The cemetery at Doingt on the eastern outskirts of Péronne, was established in the First World War for both Commonwealth and American graves (the latter since removed by the American Graves Registration Service). There are two burials from the Second World War, one being Leading Aircraftman John O'Reilly who was killed when his Lysander of No. 16 Squadron failed to return. His pilot, Pilot Officer Leslie Hamilton, remains missing. (The other grave at Doingt is that of LAC Leonard Laurie, the records simply stating that he was killed on June 25, 1940 'during the evacuation from France'.)

Chambières French National Cemetery on the northern outskirts of the city of Metz holds a special place in the annals of No. 73 Squadron for it was here that four of their earliest casualties are buried. Sergeants Reg Perry and John Winn killed on December 22, 1939; Pilot Officer Lloyd Bishop on March 12, 1940 and Pilot Officer James Perry on March 29.

O'REILLY-BLACKWOOD, P/O J. N. No. 57 Squadron 25:1:40. Reichswald Forest War Cemetery, Kleve, Germany. Coll. Grave 11. A. 5-7.

OVER, LAC H. F. No. 139 Squadron 12:5:40 Age 19. Heverlee War Cemetery, Leuven, Vlaams-Brabant, Belgium. Collective Grave 6.F.17-19.

OWEN, F/Lt. J. S. No. 504 Squadron 18:5:40 Cambrai (Route De Solesmes) Communal Cemetery, Nord, France. Plot 2. Row A. Grave 12.

PAGE, F/Sgt. D. A. No. 88 Squadron. 20:9:39 Choloy War Cemetery, Meurthe-et-Moselle, France. Grave 2A. C. 15.

PARKER, F/Lt. E. No. 150 Squadron 10:5:40 Luxembourg (Hollerich) Communal Cemetery, Luxembourg. Grave 7.

PARKER, AC1 W. No. 139 Squadron 14:5:40 Runnymede Memorial Panel 25.

PARNALL, S/L J. B. No. 504 Squadron 14:5:40 Rear left of Chaussée-Notre-Dame-Louvignies Communal Cemetery, Soignies, Hainaut, Belgium.

PARRY, LAC K. No. 18 Squadron 11:5:40 Age 20. Cement House Cemetery, Langemark-Poelkapelle, West-Vlaanderen, Belgium. Section XXIA. Coll. Grave 16-17.

PARSONS, AC1 W. L. No. 88 Squadron 11:5:40 Hotton War Cemetery, Hotton, Luxembourg, Belgium. Section I. Collective Grave B3-5.

PARTLOW, LAC I. R. T. W. No. 57 Squadron 15:11:39 Age 25. Villeneuve-St Georges Old Communal Cemetery, Val de Marne, France. Grave 121.

PEACE, P/O P. McL. No. 4 Squadron 21:5:40 Bruyelle War Cemetery, Antoing, Hainault, Belgium. Section II. Grave B2.

PEACH, Sgt. T. A. No. 18 Squadron 10:5:40 Age 24. Jonkerbos War Cemetery, Nijmegen, The Netherlands. Grave 18.G.8.

PEACOCK, S/Ldr M. F. No. 85 Squadron 20:5:40 Age 28. Arras Communal Cemetery, Pas de Calais, France. Plot Y. Row 1. Joint Grave 64-65.

PEARCE, Sgt M. G. A. No. 53 Squadron 3:5:40 Age 24. Durnbach War Cemetery, Bad Tölz, Germany. Grave 11. E. 21.

PERCIVAL, Sgt. F. J. No. 226 Squadron 14:5:40 Age 27. Runnymede Memorial Panel 18.

PERRIN, LAC J. L. No. 12 Squadron 12:5:40 Age 22. Heverlee War Cemetery, Leuven, Vlaams-Brabant, Belgium. Grave 8.J.6.

PERRY, Sgt C. D. No. 103 Squadron. Wounded 14:5:40, died 14:6:40. Age 29. St Helen's Churchyard Extension, Benson (or Bensington), Oxfordshire. Row E. Grave 7.

PERRY, P/O J. G. No. 73 Squadron 29:3:40. Age 22. Chambières French National Cemetery, Metz, France. Grave 17.

PERRY, Sgt R. M. No. 73 Squadron 22:12:39. Chambières French National Cemetery, Metz, France. Grave 1.

PETTIT, Sgt. H. E. No. 105 Squadron 26:3:40 Terlincthun British Cemetery, Wimille, France. Plot 19. Row C. Grave 3.

PIKE, Sgt. R. C. L. No. 218 Squadron 13:11:39 Terlincthun British Cemetery, Wimille, France. Plot 19. Row C. Grave 1.

PITFIELD, F/Lt. A. L. No. 88 Squadron 12:6:40 Age 22. Beaurepaire Communal Cemetery, Oise, France.

PITTAR, Sgt. W. D. P. No. 150 Squadron 8:6:40 Age 23. Fallencourt Communal Cemetery, Seine-Maritime, France. Collective Grave.

PLUMB, P/O J. A. No. 4 Squadron 19:5:40 St André Communal Cemetery, Nord, France. Row AA. Grave 5.

POOLE, Sgt. C. J. S. No. 103 Squadron 10:5:40 Age 20. Hotton War Cemetery, Hotton, Luxembourg, Belgium. Section III. Grave E10.

POSSELT, P/O A. F. No. 150 Squadron 14:5:40 Age 21. Choloy War Cemetery, Meurthe-et-Moselle, France. Collective Grave 1A.A.10-12.

POTTER, AC1 J. No. 105 Squadron 14:5:40 Choloy War Cemetery, Meurthe-et-Moselle, France. Collective Grave 1A.A.7-9.

POTTER, Sgt J. A. H. No. 18 Squadron 25:2:40 Age 28. East Grinstead (Mount Noddy) Cemetery, Sussex. Sec. 3. Cons. Grave 210.

POWER, P/O J. O'B. No. 139 Squadron 14:5:40 Runnymede Memorial Panel 9.

PRICE, Sgt. N. J. No. 139 Squadron 14:3:40 Age 25. Mazargues War Cemetery, Marseille, France. Plot 3. Row E. Grave 46.

PROCTOR, Sgt. J. R. No. 57 Squadron 14:4:40 Age 26. Arnhem (Moscowa) General Cemetery, Netherlands. Coll. Grave 1.

PYNE, Sgt. T. B. G. No. 73 Squadron 14:5:40 Age 24. Choloy War Cemetery, Meurthe-et-Moselle, France. Grave 2.J.9.

RADCLIFFE, P/O H. P. J. No. 607 Squadron 23:3:40 Douai Communal Cemetery, Nord, France. Row L. Grave 11.

RADFORD, AC1 E. A. W. No. 88 Squadron 20:9:39 Choloy War Cemetery, Meurthe-et-Moselle, France. Grave 2A. C. 13.

RAMSAY P/O A. F. B. No. 4 Squadron. Seriously injured 16:4:40, died 21:4:40 Age 19. Trefcon British Cemetery, Caulaincourt, France. Plot 1. Row D. Grave 64.

Sergeant Charles Perry of No. 103 Squadron was severely wounded while attacking a pontoon bridge over the Meuse on May 14. He was transferred to hospital in Britain but died exactly a month later. He was laid to rest in the station plot in the old cemetery in Benson, Oxfordshire, to lie in perpetuity with airmen and women from Britain, Canada, Czechoslovakia, New Zealand and South Africa.

Of the 415 casualties of the British Air Forces in France, all but six lie buried on the Continent or are commemorated at Runnymede. Those airmen buried in the United Kingdom are Sergeant Oliver Dumbreck whose grave lies in Scotland (see page 511), Pilot Officer Horatio Dunn in Essex (see rear endpaper), Pilot Officer Henry Hulton in Jersey (page 514); Sergeant Charles Perry in Oxfordshire (opposite page); Pilot Officer Richard Sanders in Kent (page 520) and Sergeant John Potter in Sussex. He lived in East Grinstead and after he died on February 25, 1940 as a result of injuries received while on a reconnaissance flight over Germany, his wife Enid had him buried locally in Mount Noddy Cemetery (above).

RAPER, Sgt. L. A. No. 142 Squadron. 7:4:40 Terlincthun British Cemetery, Wimille, France. Plot 19. Row D. Grave 2.

RATFORD, P/O F. W. No. 253 Squadron 19:5:40 Riencourt-lès-Cagnicourt Communal Cemetery, Pas de Calais, France.

RAWLINSON, P/O M. H. G. No. 85 Squadron 16:5:40 Adegem Canadian War Cemetery, Maldegem, Oost-Vlaanderen, Belgium. Section XI. Grave J8.

RAYNER, F/O P. H. No. 501 Squadron 12:5:40. Seuil Churchyard, Ardennes, France.

REA, F/O K. N. No. 226 Squadron 14:6:40 Age 27. Breux-sur-Avre Communal Cemetery, Eure, France. Grave 3.

REED, F/O A. P. No. 16 Squadron 19:5:40 Age 27. Runnymede Memorial Panel 6.

REYNOLDS, LAC L. R. No. 12 Squadron 12:5:40 Age 20. Heverlee War Cemetery, Leuven, Vlaams-Brabant, Belgium. Collective Grave 6.F.14-16.

RICHARDSON, AC1 V. W. L. No. 218 Squadron 13:11:39 Terlincthun British Cemetery, Wimille, France. Plot 19. Row B. Grave 15.

RIDLEY, P/O F. H. No. 105 Squadron 14:5:40 Donchery Communal Cemetery, Ardennes, France. Grave 9.

ROBINSON, AC1 W. No. 218 Squadron 14:5:40 Age 20. Sauville Communal Cemetery, Ardennes, France.

No. 218 Squadron suffered grievously on May 14, losing the five Battles listed in these pages — possibly more as the records for this unit are incomplete. What is certain is that five men were killed, among them Aircraftman Bill Robinson (right), and five made prisoners of war.

RODULSON, AC1 W. S. No. 4 Squadron 14:5:40 St-Rémy-Geest Churchyard, Jodoigne, Brabant Wallon, Belgium. Grave 2.

ROE, P/O V. D. M. No. 73 Squadron 14:5:40 Age 28. Choloy War Cemetery, Meurthe-et-Moselle, France. Grave 2.J.8.

ROGERS, F/Lt. K. R. No. 142 Squadron 14:5:40 Age 23. Chéhery Communal Cemetery, Ardennes, France. Grave 1.

ROONEY, LAC J. No. 139 Squadron 12:5:40 Age 20. In Belgian plot of Herstal (Rhees) Communal Cemetery, Herstal, Liège, Belgium.

ROSE, F/O F. C. No. 56 Squadron 18:5:40 Longuenesse (St Omer) Souvenir Cemetery, Pas de Calais, France. Plot 8. Row B. Grave 33.

ROSS, AC1 A. S. No. 103 Squadron 12:5:40 Age 19. Senseruth (Curfoz) Communal Cemetery, Bouillon, Luxembourg, Belgium. Joint Grave 1-2.

ROSS, Sgt. W. G. No. 88 Squadron 14:5:40 Age 26. St Menges Communal Cemetery, Ardennes, France. Collective Grave.

RUSSELL, F/Sgt. J. A. No. 226 Squadron 11:6:40 St Pierre-D'Autils Communal Cemetery, Eure, France. Collective Grave.

SABIN, Sgt. L. J. No. 18 Squadron 27:12:39 Age 23. Le Quesnel Communal Cemetery Extension. Row B. Grave 9.

SAMMELS, F/Lt. H. C. No. 105 Squadron 14:5:40 Age 24. Runnymede Memorial Panel 5.

SANDERS, AC2 A. W. B. No. 114 Squadron 2:3:40 Age 25. Terlincthun British Cemetery, Wimille Plot 19. Row C. Grave 9.

SANDERS, P/O R. A. No. 87 Squadron. Badly wounded 20:5:40, died 23:5:40 Age 20. Shorncliffe Military Cemetery, Kent. Section M. Grave 1066.

SAUNDERS, P/O G. C. No. 87 Squadron 14:5:40 Fenain Communal Cemetery, Nord, France.

SAUNDERS, P/O J. R. No. 150 Squadron 30:9:39 Rheinberg War Cemetery, Germany. Grave 8. J. 7.

SCOTT, S/Ldr W. I. No. 139 Squadron 12:5:40 Rekem Communal Cemetery, Lanaken, Limburg, Belgium. Grave 21.

SEDGWICK, Sgt. A. F. No. 226 Squadron 14:5:40 Age 31. Choloy War Cemetery, Meurthe-et-Moselle, France. Grave 2A.A.1.

SELDON, Sgt. G. E. No. 59 Squadron 13:5:40 Age 26. Runnymede Memorial Panel 19.

SEWELL, AC1 H. B. No. 103 Squadron 12:5:40 Age 21. Haraucourt Churchyard, Ardennes, France. Grave 5.

SHARPE, AC2 J. A. No. 103 Squadron 26:3:40 Terlincthun British Cemetery, Wimille, France. Plot 19. Row E. Grave 10.

The sixth Battle of France grave in Britain lies here in Shorncliffe Military Cemetery overlooking the English Channel near Folkestone. Pilot Officer Richard Sanders came from Llandrindod Wells in Radnorshire but is believed to have died of his wounds aboard a hospital ship bound for Britain (see page 331).

The faded image of Sergeant George Seldon who remains missing together with his two crewmen, Pilot Officer Croyden Chamberlain from Auckland, New Zealand, and Aircraftman Frank Hands from Bideford-on-Avon, Warwickshire. According to the Operations Record Book of No. 59 Squadron, they took off from Poix aerodrome in their Blenheim at 6.30 p.m. on May 13 on a reconnaissance sortie but just failed to return. However, as we have commented several times in these pages, their loss was not reported until the following day, hence their date of death has been recorded as May 14. George had joined the RAF as an apprentice engine fitter in 1929 and spent seven years with No. 17 Squadron and served in the Middle East before returning in 1939 as an air observer.

'My brother John was only 19 years of age when he died', writes Aircraftman John Sharpe's sister Ruth from Ireland. 'John loved and was very proud of his RAF uniform — he is second from the left in the middle row of this group photograph. On his last visit home I remember him saying that he would like to have been wearing it for us to see but it was not allowed. We saw him off on the boat at Dún Laoghaire Pier in County Wicklow. The following week the telegram arrived with tragic news: he had been on No. 103 Squadron's first leaflet-dropping mission over Germany and had been hit with ack-ack fire. The 'plane managed to limp back but crashed close to base in Reims on March 26. All the crew were lost. It was for our mother a very harrowing time as our father had died only three years earlier. John's RAF Commemorative Scroll, framed, is still hanging in the same place here in our home since our mother died in 1973. The first photo (below left), sent to us by the Air Ministry, shows his original grave in Épernay and they sent us the second picture (below right) taken after he was moved to Terlincthun British Cemetery in 1964'.

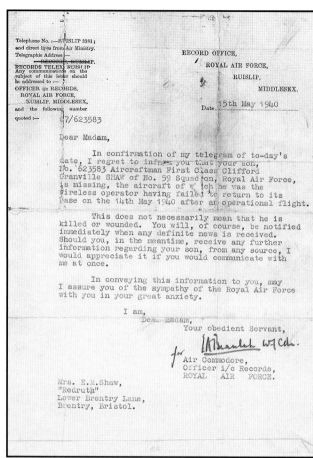

Telephone No. :—RUISLIP 3381;
and direct lines from Air Ministry.
Telegraphic Address :—
RECORDS, RUISLIP.
RECORDS TELEX RUISLIP
Any communication on the
subject of this letter should
be addressed to :—
OFFICER i/c RECORDS,
ROYAL AIR FORCE,
RUISLIP, MIDDLESEX,
and the following number
quoted :— C7/623583

RECORD OFFICE,
ROYAL AIR FORCE,
RUISLIP,
MIDDLESEX.

Date..15th May 1940

Dear Madam,

In confirmation of my telegram of to-day's date, I regret to inform you that your son, No. 623583 Aircraftman First Class Clifford Granville SHAW of No. 59 Squadron, Royal Air Force, is missing, the aircraft of which he was the wireless operator having failed to return to its base on the 14th May 1940 after an operational flight.

This does not necessarily mean that he is killed or wounded. You will, of course, be notified immediately when any definite news is received. Should you, in the meantime, receive any further information regarding your son, from any source, I would appreciate it if you would communicate with me at once.

In conveying this information to you, may I assure you of the sympathy of the Royal Air Force with you in your great anxiety.

I am,

Dear Madam,

Your obedient Servant,

[signature]

for Air Commodore,
Officer i/c Records,
ROYAL AIR FORCE.

Mrs. E.M.Shaw,
"Redruth"
Lower Brentry Lane,
Brentry, Bristol.

---

3 De Vaux Place
Salisbury
Wilts
29th July

Dear Mrs Shaw

Please forgive me for troubling you — but I am most anxious to know if you have heard any further news of A.C. Shaw (No 623583) reported missing on May 15th? My husband Flying Officer P. A. Hawks, was the pilot of the plane — also for I have not been able to find out anything, except that they were doing a special reconnaissance over the Albert Canal area in Belgium — The C.O. of 59 squadron gave me the names of the crew, which I sent with my husband's

2

To the Red Cross — but I have heard nothing further — Should you hear any news I'd be most grateful if you could let me know — It's a very sad & anxious time for us all & I sincerely hope we may yet hear good news —

Yrs Sincerely
E. Hawks.

These interesting documents were sent to *After the Battle* by Anthony Le Couteur, a cousin of Aircraftman Clifford Shaw *(top left)*, and another casualty of No. 59 Squadron missing on May 14 (see page 268). In her letter, Mrs Elizabeth Hawks was seeking any information on her husband, Flying Officer Peter Hawks, but all three crewmen remain missing to this day.

SHAW, AC1 C. G. No. 59 Squadron 14:5:40 Age 19. Runnymede Memorial Panel 26.

SHELTON-JONES, Sgt. C. No. 12 Squadron 14:5:40 Choloy War Cemetery, Meurthe-et-Moselle, France. Grave 1A.C.20.

SHEPHERD, P/O J. A. No. 1 Squadron 5:6:40 St Sever Cemetery Extension, Rouen, Seine-Maritime, France. Block S. Plot 4. Row O. Grave 4.

SHREWSBURY, P/O R. W. No. 85 Squadron 20:5:40 Arras Communal Cemetery, Pas de Calais, France. Plot Y. Row 1. Joint Grave 64-65.

SHROSBREE, Sgt. K. N. No. 18 Squadron 10:5:40 Age 25. Reichswald Forest War Cemetery, Kleve, Nordrhein-Westfalen, Germany. Grave 20.D.4.

SHUTTLEWORTH, AC1 J. No. 57 Squadron 14:4:40 21. Arnhem (Moscowa) General Cemetery, Netherlands. Coll. Grave 1.

SIBLEY, P/O S. A. C. No. 504 Squadron 14:5:40 Runnymede Memorial Panel 10.

SKIDMORE, P/O B. I. M. No. 88 Squadron 11:5:40 Age 20. Hotton War Cemetery, Hotton, Luxembourg, Belgium. Section I. Collective Grave B3-5.

SKINNER, F/Lt. M. P. No. 13 Squadron 6:12:39 Péronne Communal Cemetery Extension. Plot 5. Row G. Grave 23.

A promising career cut short in its prime. Malcolm Skinner entered Cranwell in January 1934 and he passed out with flying colours in December the following year having been awarded the Sword of Honour. He was promoted to Flying Officer in June 1937 and to Flight Lieutenant in June 1939 only to lose his life six months later.

Gale & Polden Ltd., Aldershot.

PRIZE WINNERS, ROYAL AIR FORCE COLLEGE
CRANWELL, DECEMBER, 1935

F/C. J. A. Chorlton   F/C. R. K. Jefferies   F/C. Cpl. E. Banthorpe   F/C. Sgt. A. R. Atkins
(English and History)   (Science)   (Service Subjects)   (Engineering)

F/C. Sgt. G. Elsmie   F/C. U/O. M. P. Skinner   F/C. Cpl. P. J. K. Pike
(Flying)   (Sword of Honour)   (King's Medal)

I met Michael at a hunt ball in Brockley Coombe in early 1939. We obviously were attracted because after that he rang me and we went out. He was full of fun. Typical of what you might think a fighter pilot might be, and certainly there was a great glamour attached to the squadron. We were engaged in the early summer of 1939 and, because the war was imminent, we got married. Obviously he knew the dangers much more than I. You see, I was only 21 and I must admit the thought of war — awful to say it now — was a little bit on the glamorous side. There was a sort of frisson of excitement about it all. But he knew the dangers much more than I of course, it never occurred to me.

He was at Filton for some time and I think they went to Tangmere in about October, after we were married in September. There was no accommodation, of course, for wives at that time. I went down before Christmas, about November and we had digs in Chichester when he was off duty.

It was very difficult being apart because we were both very young. He was only 27 and I was 21, so it was tough. I used to go down sometimes for 48 hours until I eventually went down and lived in Chichester. And I was still working as a physiotherapist. We did write to each other, of course. We used to watch the postman come, he there and I here. I can't think it was daily, because of course they were on duty, and they were night flying and all the rest of it. But it was certainly three or four letters a week we used to write to each other. We were very newly married, you see, so we were telling each other how much we missed each other, and how much we loved each other, and how long it would be before we saw each other, all that sort of thing, as newly-weds would. I wasn't worried about Michael. It never occurred to me somehow that anything would happen. It shows how naïve I was at that age. Funnily enough, Michael was on 24 hours' leave and the phone went and he said, 'I bet that's the mess,' and it was. That was May 11, 1940 and they flew out to France that afternoon.

MARY LALONDE, formerly Mrs MARY SMITH, 2005

SMITH, S/L L. E. No. 607 Squadron 15:5:40 Runnymede Memorial Panel 4.

SMITH, F/O M. F. C. No. 501 Squadron 12:5:40 Choloy War Cemetery, Meurthe-et-Moselle, France. Grave 4.A.22.

SMITH, Sgt. T. D. No. 103 Squadron 10:5:40 Hotton War Cemetery, Hotton, Luxembourg, Belgium. Section IV. Grave C12.

SODEN, F/Lt. I. S. No. 56 Squadron 18:5:40 Biache-St-Vaast Communal Cemetery, Pas de Calais, France. Grave 2.

SOUTHWOOD, Sgt. P. McK. No. 114 Squadron 14:5:40 Age 23. Glaire-et-Villette Communal Cemetery, Ardennes, France. Collective Grave.

Mary Lalonde's evocative description of how she met and married Michael Smith was told to Nick Maddocks and reproduced in *The West at War*. Michael and Mary were married in St Barnabas Church, Temple Cloud, in Somerset, on September 30, 1939. The bride's father, the Reverend Israel Westhead, conducted the ceremony and No. 501 Squadron organised a flypast, dipping their wings in salute as the couple left the church. The 'County of Gloucester' squadron arrived in France on May 10 taking up station on the aerodrome at Bétheniville and was launched straightaway into the thick of the action. In the course of several combats over the next two days the squadron would claim over 20 enemy aircraft destroyed against the loss of two pilots on May 12 — their first combat losses of the war. *Below left:* Sixty-two years after Michael's Hurricane plunged into the French countryside, his crash site was excavated in the presence of members of the Hurricane Society. *Below right:* Mary Lalonde pictured with the control column that her husband last held on May 12, 1940. 'I was very proud of him. He gave his life for the country, for me, and he thought, I'm sure, for peace for evermore'.

STANLEY, Sergeant R. J. No. 139 Squadron 14:3:40 Age 25. Mazargues War Cemetery, Marseille, France. Plot 3. Row E. Grave 47.

STORR, Sgt. G. No. 57 Squadron 6:11:39 Age 26. Rheinberg War Cemetery, Germany. Grave 18. D. 4.

STUART, F/O A. J. No. 18 Squadron 16:5:40 Age 29. Crevecouer-sur-L'Escaut Communal Cemetery, Nord, France. Grave 1.

STUART-HARRIS, Sgt. D. T. No. 139 Squadron 14:5:40 Age 20. Runnymede Memorial Panel 19.

SULLIVAN, F/Lt. J. L. No. 242 Squadron 14:5:40 Military plot Perwez Churchyard, Perwez, Brabant Wallon, Belgium. Row A. Grave 4.

SYDENHAM, P/O F. No. 73 Squadron 26:5:40 Age 26. Chuffilly-Roche Communal Cemetery, Ardennes, France. Grave 63.

TAMBLIN, Cpl. R. A. No. 4 Squadron 21:5:40 Bruyelle War Cemetery, Antoing, Hainault, Belgium. Section I. Grave C16.

TAYLOR, LAC A. J. No. 218 Squadron 14:5:40 Age 21. Thelonne Communal Cemetery, Ardennes, France.

TAYLOR, Sgt. C. No. 139 Squadron 12:5:40 Age 23. Runnymede Memorial Panel 20.

TAYLOR, AC1 W. F. No. 150 Squadron 31:3:40 Terlincthun British Cemetery, Wimille, France. Plot 19. Row D. Grave C6.

THOMAS, P/O A. No. 57 Squadron 10:5:40 Hook of Holland General Cemetery, Zuid-Holland, The Netherlands. Row G. Grave 7.

THOMAS, Sgt. A. W. S. No. 18 Squadron. Seriously injured 16:5:40, died of wounds 18:5:40 Age 28. Houchin British Cemetery, Pas de Calais, France. Plot 4. Row B. Grave 3.

B Flight of No. 56 Squadron at North Weald in 1937 at the start of the air exercises on August 13. L-R standing: Flight Sergeant Bentall, NCO i/c Maintenance; Pilot Officer Eustace 'Gus' Holden and Pilot Officer Ian S. Soden, Adjutant. L-R seated: Flight Sergeant Webb, Sergeant Evetts, Pilot Officer G. Horne, Flight Commander; Petty Officer Pluiston, FAA on attachment, and Sergeant Thomas. Ian Soden was a Prize Cadet to RAF Cranwell following his education at Woodbridge School in Suffolk. He was posted to No. 56 Squadron on receiving his commission in December 1936 and promoted to Flying Officer in June 1938. Ian died in combat on May 18 and on June 28 *The London Gazette* announced that he had been posthumously appointed a Companion of the Distinguished Service Order in recognition of gallantry displayed in flying operations against the enemy.

Sheelagh Taylor (now Mrs Tyrell): 'This photo was taken in our house at Benson aerodrome just before the war broke out. We were amongst the very first families who moved into Benson and the building wasn't finished. A number of photos were taken for a recruiting brochure to encourage young fellows to join up. I love the one of me with my father and the cat.'

When interviewed by the *Irish Independent*, the father of 'Wally' Taylor, serving with No. 150 Squadron, told the reporter that 'I received a letter from him only yesterday in reply to a telegram which I had sent him to tell him that his mother Gwendoline died on March 21. My son was looking forward to getting leave on April 16 or 17 and he intended to come to Dublin.'

Two early casualties of the Battle. On September 27, 1939, a Battle of No. 103 Squadron was attacked by both French and German fighters. Flying Officer Vipan managed to get the aircraft down in one piece but Sergeant John Vickers *(left)* had been severely wounded. He died on October 5, just days before he was to be awarded the Medaille Militaire — the first decoration to be given to a member of the British Expeditionary Force by the French. *Right:* Young Percy Thurgar, a sergeant pilot with No. 87 Squadron, came to grief after losing his bearings in poor visibility on February 12, 1940.

THOMAS, P/O C. V. No. 103 Squadron 10:6:40 Age 19. Gasny Communal Cemetery, Eure, France. Plot B. Joint Grave 175.

THOMAS, AC1 D. L. No. 150 Squadron 30:9:39 Rheinberg War Cemetery, Germany. 8. J. 6.

THOMAS, Sgt. P. L. No. 57 Squadron 10:5:40 Age 27. Buurmalsen General Cemetery, Gelderland, The Netherlands.

THOMPSON, P/O K. G. S. No. 114 Squadron 13:10:39. Age 19. Rheinberg War Cemetery. Row 1. Section A. Grave 2.

THOMPSON, F/O M. H. B. No. 607 Squadron 13:5:40 Heverlee War Cemetery, Leuven, Vlaams-Brabant, Belgium. Grave 7.B.1.

THOMSON, AC1 J. S. No. 105 Squadron 14:5:40 Donchery Communal Cemetery, Ardennes, France. Joint Grave 7-8.

THORNLEY, F/Lt. L. T. W. No. 615 Squadron 16:5:40 Runnymede Memorial Panel 5.

THORNTON, LAC R. J. No. 4 Squadron 19:5:40 Age 23. St André Communal Cemetery, Nord, France. Row AA. Grave 6.

THURGAR, Sgt. P. F. H. No. 87 Squadron 12:2:40 Rennes Eastern Communal Cemetery, France. Section 18. Plot 2. Row F. Grave 2.

THYNNE, P/O R. No. 218 Squadron 13:11:39 Terlincthun British Cemetery, Wimille, France. Plot 19. Row C. Grave 4.

TODD, Cpl. H. No. 142 Squadron 14:5:40 Age 21. Chéhery Communal Cemetery, Ardennes, France. Grave 3.

TOUGH, Sgt. E. W. No. 139 Squadron 16:5:40 Age 23. Floing Communal Cemetery, Ardennes, France. Grave 2.

TOWNSLEY, AC1 J. No. 18 Squadron 10:5:40 Age 18. Jonkerbos War Cemetery, Nijmegen, The Netherlands. Grave 8.I.2.

TRESCOTHIC, Sgt. H. F. No. 142 Squadron 14:5:40 Age 25. Chéhery Communal Cemetery, Ardennes, France. Grave 2.

TRICE, Sgt. A. N. No. 87 Squadron 16:5:40 Runnymede Memorial Panel 20.

TURNER, Sgt. J. D. No. 150 Squadron 14:5:40 Donchery Communal Cemetery, Ardennes, France. Grave 10.

TURNER, Sgt. L. No. 226 Squadron 13:6:40 Age 21. La Chapelle-Véronge Communal Cemetery, Seine-et-Marne, France.

TUTT, Sgt. H. J. F. No. 150 Squadron 13:6:40 Age 32. Merey Communal Cemetery, Eure, France. Collective Grave.

TWINNING, AC1 F. A. No. 57 Squadron 6:11:39 Age 19. Rheinberg War Cemetery, Germany. Grave 18. D. 5.

VANO, AC2 N. V. No. 150 Squadron 14:5:40 Age 18. Choloy War Cemetery, Meurthe-et-Moselle, France. Collective Grave 1A.A.10-12.

VAUGHAN, F/O E. R. D. No. 12 Squadron 14:5:40 Age 22. Choloy War Cemetery, Meurthe-et-Moselle, France. Grave 1A.C.19.

VAUGHAN, P/O P. W. No. 4 Squadron 13:5:40 Outgaarden Communal Cemetery, Hoegaarden, Vlaams-Brabant, Belgium. Grave 1.

VERNON, F/O J. E. No. 150 Squadron 7:6:40 Age 24. Vergies Communal Cemetery, Somme, France. Row 1. Grave 21.

VICKERS, Sgt. J. H. No. 103 Squadron. Critically injured 27:9:39, died of wounds 5:10:39 Choloy War Cemetery, Meurthe-et-Moselle, France. Grave 1A. B. 14.

WALKER, F/O T. W. No. 16 Squadron 18:5:40 Age 32. Creil Communal Cemetery, Oise, France. Plot 1. Joint Grave 380.

WALL, Sgt. C. No. 150 Squadron 31:3:40 Terlincthun British Cemetery, Wimille, France. Plot 19. Row D. Grave 5.

WALL, F/O R. N. No. 105 Squadron 14:5:40 Age 25. Noyers-Pont-Maugis French National Cemetery, Ardennes, France. Grave 515.

WALLIS, Sgt. H. B. No. 139 Squadron 14:5:40 Age 22. Laneuville-sur-Meuse Communal Cemetery, Meuse, France. Joint Grave 1.

WATERS, Cpl. R. H. No. 4 Squadron 14:5:40 Runnymede Memorial Panel 22.

WATERSTON, AC2 W. C. No. 218 Squadron 14:5:40 Runnymede Memorial Panel 27.

WEATHERILL, F/O R. F. No. 607 Squadron 18:5:40 Cambrai (Route De Solesmes) Communal Cemetery, Nord, France. Plot 2. Row A. Grave 13.

WEEKS, F/Lt. R. A. No. 150 Squadron 8:6:40 Age 27. Fallencourt Communal Cemetery, Seine-Maritime, France. Collective Grave.

WELCH, Sgt. H. D. No. 18 Squadron 11:5:40 Cement House Cemetery, Langemark-Poelkapelle, West-Vlaanderen, Belgium. Section XXIA. Collective Grave 16-17.

WELLS, LAC C. R. No. 105 Squadron 12:5:40 Age 19. Bouillon Communal Cemetery, Bouillon, Luxembourg, Belgium.

WHELAN, AC2 M. No. 88 Squadron 23:5:40 Age 19. Durnbach War Cemetery, Bad Tölz, Bayern, Germany. Collective Grave 6.B.17-19.

WHITE, Sgt. E. F. No. 12 Squadron 14:5:40 Age 20. Pouru-St-Rémy Communal Cemetery, Ardennes, France. Grave 1.

WHITE, P/O H. E. No. 105 Squadron 14:5:40 Age 26. Choloy War Cemetery, Meurthe-et-Moselle, France. Collective Grave 1A.A.7-9.

WHITE, Sgt. H. P. No. 226 Squadron. Seriously wounded 14:6:40, died 2:8:40 Age 22. Doullens Communal Cemetery, France. Section 4. Grave 10.

WHITEHEAD, LAC E. No. 13 Squadron 6:12:39. Péronne Communal Cemetery Extension. Plot 5. Row G. Grave 21.

WHITTLE, Sgt. E. J. M. No. 88 Squadron 11:5:40 Age 26. Juseret (Bercheux) New Communal Cemetery, Vaux-sur-Sure, Luxembourg, Belgium.

WICKHAM, P/O A. E. No. 88 Squadron 23:5:40 Age 22. Durnbach War Cemetery, Bad Tölz, Bayern, Germany. Collective Grave 6.B.17-19.

WICKHAM, P/O S. M. No. 615 Squadron 18:12:39 Douai Communal Cemetery, Nord, France. Row K. Grave 1.

Right: Corporal Clifford Wilburn of No. 142 Squadron. He lost his life together with his fellow crewmen, Flying Officer Patrick Farrell and Sergeant Leslie Raper, on April 7 when their Fairey Battle came to grief during a night cross-country exercise (see page 157).

WILBURN, Cpl. C. E. No. 142 Squadron 7:4:40 Terlincthun British Cemetery, Wimille, France. Plot 19. Row B. Grave 14.

WILKS, Sgt. E. No. 88 Squadron 26:5:40 Age 25. Haraucourt Churchyard, Ardennes, France. Grave 3.

WILLCOX, Sgt. R. J. No. 12 Squadron 14:6:40 Age 24. Pacy-sur-Eure Communal Cemetery, Eure, France. Grave 1.

WILLIAMS, Sgt. J. D. F. No. 150 Squadron 14:5:40 Age 27. Choloy War Cemetery, Meurthe-et-Moselle, France. Joint Grave 1A.A.14-15.

WILLIAMS, Sgt. J. L. C. No. 3 Squadron 15:5:40 Runnymede Memorial Panel 21.

WILTSHIRE, AC1 R. F. J. No. 218 Squadron 1:3:40 Terlincthun British Cemetery, Wimille, France. Plot 19. Row D. Grave 1.

WINN, Sgt J. No. 73 Squadron 22:12:39. Chambières French National Cemetery, Metz, Moselle, France. Grave 2.

WITTY, Sgt. G. G. No. 87 Squadron 5:10:39 Merville Communal Cemetery Extension, Nord, France. Plot 3. Row A. Grave 32A.

WOOD, F/O E. E. A. No. 4 Squadron 16:5:40 Age 26. Runnymede Memorial Panel 6.

WOOD, AC2 R. A. No. 53 Squadron 3:5:40 Age 21. Durnbach War Cemetery, Bad Tölz, Germany. Grave 11. E. 19.

WOODMASON, Sgt. T. B. No. 150 Squadron 20:9:39 Clichy Northern Cemetery, France. Plot 16. Row 10. Grave 15.

On May 14 a Blenheim of No. 139 Squadron was shot down while attempting to halt the German breakthrough at Sedan. One of the crewmen baled out but the other two were killed in the crash. At the time their identities could not be confirmed so they were buried in the local cemetery at Laneuville-sur-Meuse as unknown. It was only when the Missing Research and Enquiry Unit opened the grave during their investigations in July 1947 that the remains were positively identified as Flying Officer Raymond de Montmorency (see page 509) and Sergeant Howard Wallis *(left)*.

The Dutch accorded full military honours to the crew of the Blenheim of No. 57 Squadron which crashed at Babberich on April 14 following a reconnaissance sortie over north-western Germany (see page 159). Flying Officer Horace Graham-Hogg, Sergeant John Proctor and Aircraftman 1st Class James Shuttleworth were laid to rest in Arnhem's Moscowa General Cemetery.

The Balance Sheet

While official records of the period are often fragmentary, unreliable, and contradictory, the losses detailed in the accompanying tables are believed to be the most accurate yet published in a single volume. However, while the following totals provide a more balanced overview of the casualties suffered by respective air forces in air operations over the western front, due to the nature of the source material consulted in their preparation, it is recognised that they cannot be accepted as statistically valid.

The first figure under each heading is the total number of aircraft destroyed, missing, or abandoned, due to all causes in the period shown, as reflected in the accompanying tables of losses. This does not include those aircraft considered repairable 'off-unit', or where the damage state was not fully assessed or recorded in contemporary documents, many of which may subsequently have been declared 'write-offs'. Thus, totals shown are inevitably lower than the actual losses suffered.

Similarly, the second figure under each heading is the total number of aircrew recorded as missing, killed, or died of wounds, or those reported captured, in the accompanying tables of losses. These do not include those wounded in action, however seriously. It should also be noted that many captured *Luftwaffe* aircrew were released during the German advance or directly following the French armistice. All totals are cumulative.

	British		French		Dutch		Belgian		German	
	Aircraft	*Personnel*	*Aircraft*	*Personnel*	*Aircraft*	*Personnel*	*Aircraft*	*Personnel*	*Aircraft*	*Personnel*
1939										
September:	15	15	58	60	2	2	4	0	27	25
October:	11	16	20	19	3	0	-	-	33	28
November:	19	21	21	24	3	1	1	0	67	102
December:	11	8	12	18	-	-	2	2	24	36
Total:	**56**	**60**	**111**	**121**	**8**	**3**	**7**	**2**	**151**	**191**
1940										
January:	9	6	6	6	1	0	-	-	31	44
February:	7	3	8	2	3	0	3	0	28	19
March:	28	28	16	11	3	2	8	6	53	74
April:	23	17	26	16	2	3	3	3	81	98
1 - 9 May:	10	9	8	7	1	0	2	2	10	19
Total:	**133**	**123**	**175**	**163**	**18**	**8**	**23**	**13**	**354**	**445**

MAY 1940

	British		French		Dutch		Belgian		German	
	Aircraft	Personnel	Aircraft	Personnel	Aircraft	Personnel	Aircraft	Personnel	Aircraft	Personnel
May 10:	54	67	63	15	149	28	144	5	353	904
May 11:	41	43	48	15	9	2	52	9	68	179
May 12:	49	89	37	27	20	2	9	0	54	118
May 13:	22	19	30	24	16	7	4	0	35	77
May 14:	81	118	48	33	34	0	6	2	59	91
May 15:	31	19	41	18			11	6	52	81
May 16:	57	20	104	15			2	0	40	64
May 17:	33	28	42	26			2	0	46	81
May 18:	54	36	21	21			23	1	54	89
May 19:	52	33	33	24			1	0	60	150
May 20:	22	17	26	31			1	0	28	55
May 21:	16	43	42	23			0	0	28	54
May 22:	18	15	14	22			0	0	29	54
May 23:	22	31	9	10			3	2	18	33
May 24:	16	21	33	30			1	2	23	32
May 25:	12	12	25	32			1	0	26	36
May 26:	20	29	14	16			3	0	37	67
May 27:	30	27	17	8			1	0	43	70
May 28:	25	25	4	2			17	0	12	18
May 29:	33	38	2	4					25	21
May 30:	5	2	11	9					13	29
May 31:	31	35	21	32					19	21
Total:	**857**	**891**	**860**	**600**	**246**	**47**	**304**	**40**	**1476**	**2769**

JUNE 1940

	British		French		German		Italian	
	Aircraft	Personnel	Aircraft	Personnel	Aircraft	Personnel	Aircraft	Personnel
June 1:	25	30	5	1	32	55		
June 2:	13	6	11	10	19	19		
June 3:	3	2	29	23	14	23		
June 4:	4	1	10	12	5	8		
June 5:	6	4	38	34	40	87		
June 6:	10	12	33	34	19	25		
June 7:	21	9	27	21	22	17		
June 8:	17	25	32	24	19	28		
June 9:	7	6	34	23	21	19		
June 10:	6	2	14	13	17	29		
June 11:	14	43	16	7	13	7		
June 12:	6	15	14	9	12	15		
June 13:	21	45	27	27	8	12	2	11
June 14:	19	26	12	16	17	35		
June 15:	15	2	22	10	21	42	7	10
June 16:			16	15	18	27		
June 17:	1	1	6	7	1	1		
June 18:	9	2	46	7	9	25		
June 19:			24	10	9	6		
June 20:	8	0	25	11	6	14		
June 21:	3	8	11	6	5	6		
June 22:	1	1	80	0	5	5		
June 23:	1	0	1	1	3	2		
June 24:	-	-	10	2	3	3		
Grand Total:	**1067**	**1127**	**1403**	**923**	**1814**	**3278**	**9**	**21**

RAF Aircraft Index

The remains of Pilot Officer Greenhous's Defiant, serial L6977, are loaded aboard German transport for salvaging (see page 261). Recycling such debris would stretch both sides' salvage organisations for several months to come.

ARMSTRONG		L1141	105	L8834	349	L9329	167	N6229	246
WHITWORTH		L1145	112	L8836	362	L9330	311	N6230	270
ENSIGN		L1147	104	L8838	142	L9331	171	N6232	233
G-ADSZ 351		L1148	116	L8847	247	L9332	180	N6236	362
		L1246	107, 116	L8849	247	L9340	293, 303	P4826	246
ARMSTRONG		L1280	136	L8850	248	L9391	379	P4827	270
WHITWORTH		L1325	112	L8851	247, 339, 458	L9395	313	P4828	345
WHITLEY		L1334	494	L8852	313	L9397	390	P4838	304
N1361	356	L1335	184	L8853	313	L9398	233	P4851	304
N1362	458	L1401	184	L8855	339	L9399	282	P4852	304
N1366	233	L1405	180	L8856	284	L9401	390	P4853	304
N1372	455	L1410	131	L8857	233	L9403	349	P4854	304
N1380	332	L1415	107	L8858	304	L9410	431	P4858	345
N1384	332	L1421	134	L8860	180	L9411	295	P4860	345
N1432	385	L1427	151	L8861	231	L9416	246	P4898	304
P4954	458	L1435	112	L8863	293, 372	L9459	232	P4901	184
		L1444	141	L8866	256	L9460	282, 311	P4903	304
AVRO ANSON		L1514	184	L8875	165	L9463	321	P4904	304
K8772	332	L1515	184	L8859	133	L9464	270	P4905	248
K8773	390	L1517	184	L9023	445	L9465	159	P4909	349
N5065	390	L4840	99	L9024	458	L9466	270	P4913	284
N5225	465	L4841	282, 311	L9030	313	L9472	349	P4914	248
N5227	390	L4842	99	L9040	128	L9476	412	P4917	431
N9731	362	L4843	293	L9175	233	L9481	405	P4919	412
N9919	395	L4847	282	L9177	233	N3534	494	P4920	362
R3341	322	L4852	293	L9178	233	N3552	349	P4923	246
R3389	398	L4856	232, 321	L9179	270	N3588	458	P4925	345
		L4857	167	L9180	268	N3592	469	P4926	150
BLACKBURN SKUA		L4859	244, 362	L9181	158	N6148	233	P4927	362, 431
L2881	398	L4860	293	L9182	312	N6151	248	P6885	233
L2917	398	L4861	256, 311	L9184	345	N6153	134	P6886	390
L3005	398	L4862	180	L9185	180	N6154	233	P6889	273
		L6616	184	L9185	339	N6156	395	P6890	272
BOULTON PAUL		L6694	107	L9186	170, 303	N6157	145	P6902	270
DEFIANT		L8733	248	L9187	293	N6159	233	P6909	390
L6953	386	L8734	362	L9189	248	N6160	104	P6910	465
L6956	392	L8735	378	L9190	147	N6161	134	P6911	248
L6957	392	L8738	272	L9191	320	N6162	233	P6912	248
L6958	257	L8739	248	L9192	231	N6168	293	P6913	313, 362
L6959	386	L8742	272	L9193	311	N6169	244	P6914	248
L6960	257	L8743	356, 458	L9210	304	N6173	256	P6915	437
L6961	399	L8744	385	L9213	304	N6177	345	P6916	180, 311
L6965	257	L8745	458	L9214	273	N6179	151	P6917	313
L6968	399	L8746	458	L9217	273	N6190	412	P6922	157
L6969	257	L8748	248	L9241	273	N6191	423	P6923	233
L6972	399	L8749	345	L9243	349	N6192	379	P6925	450, 465
L6974	257	L8755	345	L9245	180, 303	N6193	184	P6926	268
L6975	399	L8760	312	L9246	181, 345	N6207	345	P6930	256
L6977	257	L8761	345	L9248	312	N6208	233	P6932	312
L6980	399	L8776	184	L9253	170	N6210	273	P6956	373
L7004	392, 437	L8777	349	L9254	293	N6215	246	P9249	150
L7007	386	L8800	248	L9255	231	N6216	246	R3590	231
L7019	399	L8827	184, 362, 431	L9260	390	N6217	284	R3595	303
		L8828	184	L9266	256, 345	N6219	246	R3596	345
BRISTOL		L8829	465	L9269	465	N6223	270	R3597	294
BLENHEIM		L8830	304	L9323	450	N6224	168	R3598	349
L1129	119	L8831	184	L9324	248	N6225	140, 246	R3602	431
L1138	104	L8833	184	L9325	339	N6228	248	R3613	372

Serial	Ref		Serial	Ref		Serial	Ref		Serial	Ref		Serial	Ref
R3614	356		K9342	269		L5474	464		K5982	385		L1726	437
R3616	465		K9343	272		L5512	245		K6009	385		L1733	321
R3618	445		K9345	272, 295		L5514	371		K8380	356		L1737	437
R3630	405		K9348	321		L5515	371		K8865	385		L1743	108
R3632	450, 469		K9349	321		L5516	268		L2756	390		L1746	386
R3634	171		K9351	102		L5517	271		L2828	390		L1756	392
R3664	385		K9352	321		L5519	458		L9740	390		L1757	487
R3670	446		K9353	247		L5520	423		P3997	390		L1758	406
R3674	458		K9356	115		L5523	246, 269		P4022	390		L1765	127
R3676	465		K9357	134		L5524	464, 465					L1773	127
R3683	412		K9360	97		L5526	181		**GLOSTER**			L1774	321
R3685	450		K9364	95		L5531	464		**GLADIATOR**			L1775	283
R3686	437		K9366	182, 295		L5534	461		K6137	138		L1776	102
R3691	349		K9367	295		L5538	267, 320		K7898	154		L1777	110
R3692	431		K9369	183		L5539	183		K7967	153		L1778	116
R3693	469		K9372	181		L5540	183		K7996	153		L1779	181
R3694	362		K9374	268		L5541	472		K8000	152		L1802	312
R3695	372		K9383	272, 295		L5546	444		K8030	152		L1808	144
R3697	419		K9387	99		L5568	423		N2303	313		L1813	115
R3699	303		K9390	183		L5578	182		N2304	313		L1826	436
R3702	312		K9404	283		L5579	437		N2306	313		L1834	268
R3703	270, 378		K9408	181		L5580	464		N5581	116		L1835	128
R3704	445		K9409	455		L5581	268		N5582	126		L1842	119
R3706	339		K9441	142		L5583	322		N5899	313		L1843	161
R3709	445		K9452	472		L5585	269					L1846	282
R3735	378		K9483	271		L5591	464		**HANDLEY PAGE**			L1847	437
R3739	450		K9484	99		N2028	99		**HAMPDEN**			L1852	392
R3742	469		K9485	246		N2088	157		L4044	445		L1856	311
R3745	469		L4944	293		N2093	99		L4055	349		L1866	283, 295
R3746	445		L4946	271		N2150	469, 471		L4068	233		L1891	268
R3747	461		L4948	146		N2178	320		P1325	458		L1898	294
R3754	445		L4949	180		N2253	445		P1326	233		L1899	303
R3761	431		L4950	267		P2161	465		P4286	273		L1900	110
R3810	461		L4952	267		P2162	436		P4345	461		L1901	256
R3893	461		L4956	181		P2176	246					L1905	303
			L4979	93		P2180	183, 295		**HAWKER HECTOR**			L1911	494
BRISTOL BOMBAY			L4980	153		P2182	271		K8116	378		L1950	272
L5183	233		L4982	96		P2183	247					L1908	267
			L5112	445		P2184	247		**HAWKER**			L1910	247
DE HAVILLAND			L5188	267		P2189	283		**HURRICANE**			L1912	312
TIGER MOTH			L5190	180		P2190	182		L1564	321, 412		L1914	247
N6838	99		L5192	283		P2191	268		L1569	103		L1916	272
N6843	97		L5200	458		P2192	283		L1587	141		L1922	312
N6847	98		L5225	95		P2193	245		L1588	99		L1923	180
N9156	104		L5226	322, 450		P2200	182		L1589	312		L1925	320
N9157	123		L5227	244		P2201	161		L1590	119		L1930	256
R5036	295		L5230	270		P2202	232		L1591	267		L1931	437
			L5231	182		P2203	233		L1592	406		L1932	267
FAIREY ALBACORE			L5232	271		P2204	244		L1605	257		L1940	311
L7089	496		L5233	268, 294		P2243	180		L1607	312		L1941	272
L7081	496		L5234	294		P2244	154		L1608	437		L1943	282
L7111	496		L5235	271		P2246	182, 270		L1609	267, 303		L1944	313
			L5236	144		P2247	152		L1610	282		L1953	295
FAIREY BATTLE			L5238	270, 450		P2248	270		L1611	312		L1958	144
K7696	322		L5240	146		P2249	233		L1612	268		L1959	114
K7700	182, 295		L5241	244		P2250	154		L1613	139		L1960	127
K9176	272, 339		L5242	182, 295		P2251	232		L1614	294		L1962	149
K9180	295		L5243	294		P2254	272		L1616	268		L1964	331
K9183	183		L5245	160		P2255	295		L1619	115		L1965	110
K9185	126		L5246	450		P2256	153		L1621	133		L1967	127
K9186	269		L5247	183		P2258	181, 321		L1624	494		L1970	245
K9188	182		L5248	168		P2261	232		L1628	115		L1971	124
K9193	140		L5249	180		P2265	157		L1630	245		L1972	390
K9195	139		L5250	269		P2267	272		L1637	160		L1973	398
K9197	93		L5288	437		P2313	390		L1639	272		L1974	144, 487
K9198	133		L5289	244		P2315	445		L1640	294		L1975	136
K9201	472		L5328	469		P2324	272		L1641	131, 294		L1978	148
K9202	472		L5324	464		P2326	233		L1645	282		L1979	232
K9218	472		L5333	378		P2328	455		L1646	268		L1982	399
K9242	95		L5383	423, 469		P2332	244		L1653	127		L1991	272, 295
K9245	95		L5396	469		P2333	271		L1655	312		L1992	311
K9251	283		L5397	464, 469		P2334	233		L1665	312		L2034	313
K9252	144		L5402	183		P2335	469		L1671	144		L2035	257
K9254	134		L5415	436		P2336	246		L1673	256		L2045	233, 283, 320
K9256	283		L5418	256, 295		P2353	256		L1674	322		L2049	232
K9259	246, 295		L5422	271		P2355	181		L1676	267		L2050	247
K9264	181		L5437	464		P2356	349		L1679	231		L2051	312
K9269	153		L5438	272		P2360	271		L1681	156, 255		L2053	247
K9270	181		L5439	244		P5229	267		L1685	231		L2054	247
K9271	98		L5440	295		P5231	469		L1686	136, 244		L2056	398
K9273	112, 283		L5443	331		P5232	271		L1688	244		L2057	351
K9283	99		L5450	437		P5235	322		L1689	133, 180		L2058	345
K9325	233		L5452	322		P5238	182, 322		L1693	283		L2060	332
K9327	95, 133, 135		L5458	423		P6598	458		L1716	268		L2065	245
K9329	135		L5459	371					L1718	312		L2068	232
K9330	295		L5461	398		**FAIREY**			L1720	321		L2076	379
K9333	271		L5465	268		**SWORDFISH**			L1722	161		L2081	323
K9338	182		L5467	371		K5955	356					L2088	323, 339

Serial	Page(s)	Serial	Page(s)	Serial	Page(s)	Serial	Page(s)	Serial	Page(s)
L2116	437	N2651	386	P2813	232, 268, 293	**SUPERMARINE SPITFIRE**		P9317	406
L2119	379	N2653	256	P2818	283	K9804	386	P9321	356
L2120	345	N2654	256	P2819	321	K9807	406	P9331	431, 437
L2121	351	N2657	345	P2820	303	K9813	391, 398	P9369	398
L2124	362	N2658	406	P2821	232, 256	K9832	391	P9370	349
L2140	303	N2659	390, 392	P2824	294	K9836	406	P9372	356
L2141	304	N2671	332	P2825	293	K9867	349	P9373	349
L2145	331	N2702	304	P2834	386	K9871	356	P9374	356, 357
N2318	181	N2709	395, 406	P2856	268	K9875	379	P9376	391
N2319	303	N2710	379	P2867	416	K9912	373	P9377	406
N2320	312	N2711	323, 379	P2870	283	K9915	304	P9388	356
N2326	156	N2713	323, 379	P2873	313	K9920	345	P9434	363
N2331	323	P2535	232, 244, 294	P2874	304	K9924	412	P9435	385
N2333	180	P2536	183, 313	P2876	391	K9942	423	P9437	373
N2334	268	P2538	283	P2880	362	K9947	386	P9441	349, 350
N2335	295	P2539	321	P2884	399	K9952	356	P9449	406
N2338	392	P2542	152	P2885	431	K9977	339	P9455	356
N2346	373	P2543	321	P2902	399	K9992	356	P9460	423
N2349	345	P2546	267	P2907	304, 311	L1003	379	R6637	458
N2353	131	P2547	321	P2952	406	L1006	392		
N2355	322	P2550	351	P2985	487	L1013	399	**VICKERS WELLINGTON**	
N2361	124	P2551	141, 321	P3045	487	L1016	379	L7777	349
N2362	171	P2552	157	P3149	487	L1029	385	L7787	469
N2363	162	P2554	283	P3266	357	L1031	373	L7791	398
N2364	136, 149	P2555	331	P3272	357	L1052	391	L7793	372
N2366	268	P2562	321	P3274	356	L1056	423	L7800	458
N2380	156, 267	P2563	144	P3277	303	L1058	406	L7803	339
N2381	487	P2564	247	P3278	332	L1063	395	P9241	395
N2382	180	P2568	379	P3279	283, 293	L1081	399	P9270	356
N2385	127	P2569	232	P3303	391	L1084	395	P9282	395
N2388	232	P2570	154	P3311	379	L1086	395	P9288	405
N2389	294	P2571	233	P3312	303	L1087	399	P9297	339
N2391	163	P2572	183, 247	P3313	487	N3027	257	P9298	339
N2398	257	P2573	183, 233	P3314	379	N3028	412	R3152	339
N2402	257	P2574	183	P3315	312, 446	N3030	379	R3157	339
N2403	233	P2575	181	P3319	362	N3033	412	R3162	398
N2404	293	P2576	163	P3321	312, 391	N3040	373	R3196	395
N2405	233	P2577	295	P3323	362	N3047	412		
N2406	446	P2579	282	P3324	487	N3050	412	**WESTLAND LYSANDER**	
N2407	233	P2615	183	P3353	446	N3054	412	L4741	160
N2408	320	P2616	247	P3354	386	N3055	412	L4742	267
N2422	282	P2617	344, 406	P3355	379	N3056	412	L4745	267
N2425	312	P2618	272	P3360	431	N3058	412	L4749	168
N2426	293	P2619	283	P3361	399	N3059	386	L4750	159
N2430	311	P2620	257	P3380	446	N3064	412	L4761	405
N2431	345	P2621	272	P3392	351	N3066	412	L4763	124
N2435	304	P2622	283	P3419	399	N3069	162	L4766	148
N2437	303, 311	P2634	331	P3423	379	N3071	162	L4773	332
N2439	311	P2635	268	P3424	399	N3092	412	L4774	282
N2441	267	P2636	391	P3426	331	N3094	465	L4775	156
N2457	233	P2647	170	P3347	494	N3096	362	L4777	267
N2462	321	P2649	180	P3448	233, 257, 332	N3103	362, 379	L4782	378
N2464	311	P2676	312	P3450	494	N3108	406	L4793	339, 398
N2472	181	P2683	321	P3451	312	N3115	390	L4796	303
N2473	392	P2684	323	P3453	295	N3117	150	L4809	405
N2490	268	P2687	321	P3472	437	N3128	379	L4811	303
N2492	272	P2689	268	P3476	406	N3130	419	L4814	293
N2496	395	P2694	320	P3477	416	N3167	351	L6849	345
N2497	406	P2697	183	P3478	379	N3169	412	L6852	148
N2501	304	P2698	498	P3483	373	N3172	362	L6863	378
N2521	392	P2699	332	P3484	437	N3177	392	L6885	293
N2525	320	P2701	312	P3486	379	N3180	373, 385	N1200	160
N2528	373	P2713	272	P3487	497	N3188	362	N1202	321
N2533	458	P2714	378	P3489	391	N3192	363	N1211	423
N2534	282	P2721	386	P3490	437	N3193	356	N1216	114
N2535	320	P2723	379	P3491	494	N3194	351	N1221	311
N2538	322	P2727	412	P3529	437	N3197	412	N1243	378
N2542	322	P2729	312	P3535	257, 313, 323	N3198	373	N1253	405
N2545	312	P2730	351	P3542	494	N3200	373	N1260	282
N2546	267	P2732	399	P3546	339	N3202	399	N1263	311
N2547	233	P2758	233	P3550	349	N3203	395	N1272	165
N2551	386	P2763	399	P3552	339	N3222	406	N1290	320
N2553	303, 311	P2764	497	P3553	399	N3230	406	N1292	320
N2557	362	P2767	450	P3575	345	N3232	406	N1296	339
N2582	446	P2792	386	P3581	379	N3234	406	N1298	339
N2583	332	P2793	490	P3586	332	N3237	373	N1305	320
N2584	406	P2795	332	P3683	487	N3243	356	P1672	345
N2585	437	P2800	322	P3719	487	N3244	446	P1685	378
N2586	257	P2803	356	P3779	487	N3248	363, 412	P1689	390
N2589	373	P2804	181			N3249	356	P1711	267
N2590	322	P2805	437	**MILES MAGISTER**		N3272	391	P1720	385
N2597	395	P2807	244	L8347	96	N3274	399	P1722	148
N2598	323	P2808	322	P6343	313	N3289	392	P9063	256
N2600	312	P2809	351	P6351	423	N3290	351	P9064	293
N2601	321	P2810	268, 293			N3295	399	P9127	398
N2605	313	P2811	232	**MILES MASTER**		P9305	373		
N2615	472	P2812	232, 268	N7577	331				

French Aircraft Index

Details of this Potez 63.11 serial number 732 are lost to history.

AMIOT 143
27	296
29	274
30	274
56	274
57	274
63	188
64	400
69	273
78	395
80	273
85	188, 274, 458
94	105
110	123
113	458
118	259
133	340
136	296

AMIOT 351
58	416
60	392
65	451

AMIOT 354
4	387
6	188
7	466
8	413
12	380, 387, 466
28	494
29	314
33	387
34	358
37	364
38	358
39	458
40	446
64	466

BLOCH 131
61	96
73	108
80	98
86	95
92	93
122	117

BLOCH 151
15	488
37	472
51	472
61	488
69	475
77	472
81	154
91	413
93	424
348	472
370	413
422	469
426	387

BLOCH 152
14	441
42	306
52	334
66	275
100	286
115	441
117	306
120	275
122	285
124	117
128	117
129	315
130	441
131	286
134	298
137	117
144	341
164	284
166	341

169	306
170	275
172	274
175	297
180	163
185	306
189	285
192	441
193	306
208	306
219	275
235	275
236	380
240	374
255	306
293	340
303	433
369	235
371	274
374	275
379	433
384	275
391	334
409	249
427	416
502	306
504	274
506	274, 461
508	306
516	459
522	325
524	334
527	315
531	274, 298
534	235
537	235
542	461
545	189
548	306
551	416
555	380
556	374
567	417
570	274
578	416
593	416
600	417
601	417
604	417
607	426
608	417
612	433
618	458
621	433
630	498
640	447
647	417
651	426
664	447
673	451
677	433
681	451
687	441
688	441
690	466
695	459

BLOCH 174
8	325
9	306
11	260
16	159
17	419
18	165
19	340
29	413
31	161
35	325
40	170
44	189
45	189
47	189
101	492

BLOCH 200
132	94
162	114
163	94

BLOCH 210
10	364
12	469
14	364
15	419
25	364
53	352
55	446
86	380
92	456
104	358
154	488
185	364
188	364
189	115

BREGUET 27
53	346
94	346

BREGUET 270
64	95

BREGUET 521 'BIZERTE'
11	497
30	284
34	497

BREGUET 691
39	314
49	478
57	447
60	416
69	481

BREGUET 693
1	440
3	440
4	248
5	425
6	447
7	248
9	248
10	248
11	171
12	451
13	364
14	248
15	296
17	340
18	248
19	248
20	297
21	248
22	248
25	346
27	433
28	314
29	433
30	297
31	424

32	249, 425
33	314, 440
34	249
35	400
36	297
38	456
39	364
40	424
44	396
46	451
48	447
49	451
52	447
53	466
54	440
58	451
61	424
63	433
65	334
66	364
67	440
68	461
69	451
70	451
74	395
77	440
78	424
79	466
80	470
86	424
92	451
1008	296
1011	440
1013	433
1016	451
1017	447

BREGUET 695
7	475

CAMS 37.11
52	488
64	488
95	488

CAMS 55
85	451
86	497
88	497
89	497
102	497
104	497
105	497

CAUDRON C714
8546	150
8548	150
8550	456
8552	452
8557	452
8563	358
8565	456
8572	364
8576	380
8580	364
8581	305

CAUDRON GOELAND
209	488
211	488
214	488
215	380, 488
219	488
422	495
423	495

CAUDRON 635
147	188
7795	488

CURTISS H-75
13	131
15	100
21	95
25	131
26	189
27	315
31	341
33	260
34	100
38	341
40	171
42	425
44	260
49	417
53	274
56	433
57	112, 475
58	171
60	297
65	475
66	97
69	188
71	188
74	249
75	235
77	235
84	306, 374
85	417
86	334
89	314, 451
91	274
92	274
95	117
97	325
98	478
99	235
106	374
109	374
112	97
116	235
118	100
121	364
123	115
124	433
125	447
129	315
136	161
138	188
144	314
145	285
146	188
151	249, 407
157	164

158 314
159 188
161 157
169 117
170 249
172 235
180 285
183 424
189 161, 314
193 249, 314
197 433
200 417
204 314
206 451
213 440
215 451
218 451
220 364
221 433
231 447
236 466
244 451
246 447
247 466
257 470
260 433
262 466
264 466
265 433
276 433
279 392

DEWOITINE 373
4 488
11 488
12 488
13 488

DEWOITINE 376
32 488

DEWOITINE 520
26 165
35 478
49 459
51 401
59 346
70 285, 352
71 352
73 274
84 433
94 285
98 285
108 314
112 340
114 416
115 285
122 285
124 285
126 425
128 346
131 401
133 451
144 426
171 466
211 364
218 401
225 416
231 478
233 426
235 475
238 475
240 426
242 475
246 413
251 478
260 425
266 426
273 425
285 416
286 416
292 494
298 416

DOUGLAS DB-7
5 400
10 400, 466
20 392

23 346
26 446
29 346
31 424
32 400
33 440
35 466
37 358
39 358
41 456
42 400
43 466
46 400

FARMAN 221
3 324
8 478

FARMAN 222
3 334
7 305
13 424
17 432
23 234
25 395
32 305
34 419

FARMAN NC471
1 495

SCHRECK FBA 17
207 488
208 488
218 488

SCHRECK FBA 294
2 495

GOURDOU-LESEURRE 810
19 497

GOURDOU-LESEURRE 811
26 497

GOURDOU-LESEURRE 812
41 94
62 488
63 497

GOURDOU-LESEURRE 813
64 497
65 488

GOURDOU-LESEURRE 832
14 488

LATECOERE 290
10 497
26 456

LATECOERE 298
3 352
4 352
9 352
11 152
14 452
20 138
68 352
70 140
73 456, 492
76 456
78 359
93 492

LEVASSEUR PL7
29 104

LEVASSEUR PL101
51 106
62 142
69 495
70 495

LOIRE 130
2 93
5 93
30 488
56 488
62 158
63 488

LOIRE-ET-OLIVIER 258
3 495
7 495
8 495
18 495
22 359

LOIRE-ET-OLIVIER C301
4 417
6 488
7 488

LOIRE-ET-OLIVIER 451
1 115
4 99
6 103
9 95
11 324
14 456
17 134
19 419
24 259, 400
27 296
29 400
37 334
38 432
40 234, 273, 305
42 296
43 234
45 234
46 234
47 259
48 273
49 259
52 259
53 395
54 259, 296
56 400
57 346
61 305
62 296
63 234
73 400
74 306
78 296
80 296
86 358
88 296
89 446
90 284
93 456
94 314
95 334
96 171
102 334
105 296
106 334
109 400
114 334
116 400
122 284, 305
128 392
130 440
132 475
133 400
134 358
142 451
150 432
151 432
152 432
154 466
183 432
189 400
206 447
208 456
211 395
214 432

258 447
260 432
268 400
271 432
275 466
276 465
386 499
3001 380, 400
3006 440
3007 432
3011 475
3022 432

LOIRE-NIEUPORT L-N 40
3 157
4 157

LOIRE-NIEUPORT L-N 401
3 324, 340
7 324
8 324
10 324

LOIRE-NIEUPORT L-N 411
2 305
9 419
11 324
12 324

MARTIN 167F
25 432
26 440
28 425
34 461
37 400
38 358
39 374
45 358
46 440
53 407
59 440
60 461
61 358
63 440
68 425
69 440
70 358
71 447
74 374, 425
75 432
89 374
95 440
96 374
112 401
117 346
120 400
121 401
128 425
129 374
133 461
140 451
147 432
154 461
161 461
191 461

MORANE-SAULNIER 230
223 495
228 495
452 488
455 499
457 488

MORANE-SAULNIER 406
27 407
66 132
67 235
72 96
75 285
76 132
78 298
79 148
86 274

88 235
91 126
92 274
93 126
98 171
131 358
132 433
153 285
157 235
162 358
164 259
165 117
168 285
171 249
172 142
176 154
177 154
179 123
181 117
182 117
186 189
191 358
193 407
195 285
199 117
200 260, 334
202 234
209 139
212 154
218 159
222 139
225 447
228 189
229 154
230 286
231 285
233 133
238 97
244 447
248 152
249 425
252 96
253 234
260 374
270 96
281 234
286 259
293 95
294 126
295 96
308 259
321 99
327 274
334 189
337 314, 452
338 188
351 417
353 131
356 475
358 297
372 260
373 260
379 157
388 314
390 340
392 189
404 334
412 235
413 189
414 341
431 458
439 156
442 189
456 425
458 364
462 341
467 325
474 189
475 121
478 340
480 274
482 158
487 340
524 364
532 259
546 235
549 260
555 447

557 260
569 358
575 358
577 102
584 447
597 341
598 189
600 121
605 306
607 358
613 340
618 456
627 364
628 260
634 260
641 274
653 314
667 380
668 298
676 413
681 156
683 358
684 274
686 334
693 417
703 260
709 306
710 260
711 235
712 447
722 358
728 260
730 324
733 325
734 341
737 188
738 297
750 285
752 314
756 153
758 341
759 249
767 260
768 358
771 297
772 274
773 374
783 374
791 260
792 456
795 401
799 341
803 341
804 447
806 154
811 154
813 189
814 188
821 458
837 285
844 334, 466
856 334
857 340
860 148
862 334, 466
896 341
897 364
898 441
900 364
901 341
908 441
912 315
923 297
924 314
925 341
926 297
931 297
932 260
943 298
946 234
947 458
948 297
951 306
956 235
963 235
970 499
971 154
979 107
989 481
994 297
1022 417
1031 249
1035 425
1044 447
1047 364
1053 315
1056 499
1059 492
1062 492
1067 285

MUREAUX 113
4 94

MUREAUX 115
6 98
12 103
15 93
21 95
23 141
32 248
35 248
37 188
39 102
41 96
42 248, 249
57 324
59 188
66 145
83 164
87 103
89 141
91 324
106 94
107 96

MUREAUX 117
66 112
70 94
107 112
132 188

NORTH AMERICAN 57
103 488
104 488
107 488
108 488
110 488
111 495
113 488
119 488
120 488
130 488

POTEZ 25
1700 98

POTEZ 39
5 234
13 259
29 259
50 96

POTEZ 56
3713 419

POTEZ 390
30 139
79 188
88 106

POTEZ 540
160 99
236 495

POTEZ 542
128 495

POTEZ 567
15 497

POTEZ 63.11
02 141
7 189
22 148
31 113
36 107
45 189
48 189
50 456
53 105
80 249
146 189
151 306
154 189
156 189
161 433
163 235
168 260
173 275
174 189
177 364
178 147
180 249
182 189
184 133
187 499
188 275
192 286
196 492
197 492
198 452
200 324
201 188
202 189
203 341
205 466
209 189
212 234
214 189
216 426
219 306
223 284
224 234
226 314
229 364
233 234, 365
246 162
250 424
255 151
258 286
260 373
265 364
272 373
273 189
274 189
284 446
288 259
291 259
297 259
304 333
306 424
309 461, 465
315 346
317 249
318 188, 234
320 407
327 419
329 284
331 446
333 455
336 446
347 458
349 273
350 364
355 466
360 248
365 334, 424
366 419
375 296
381 273
382 475
384 465
386 259, 446
388 284
389 284
390 259
393 259
396 481
404 446
413 380
415 478
425 189
426 456
429 188
430 334
432 359
437 188
439 286
440 333, 334
444 249
448 387
449 188
450 188
454 481
489 496
493 424
494 446
570 188
571 358
577 188
579 273
580 325
584 284
585 305
586 296
588 424
592 424
595 426
601 284
604 470
606 284
607 359
609 458
610 478
617 425
619 296
620 419
621 273
623 380
625 451
626 314
630 340
634 469
637 324
645 306
665 452
673 325
677 395
678 324
679 380
681 284
682 451
684 275
685 296, 352
687 352
689 259
690 396
691 447
702 451
716 470
718 478
719 495
730 492
772 419
774 234
780 373
796 424
800 447
804 413
827 441
837 469
844 478
845 478
857 475

POTEZ 567
3 488

POTEZ 630
70 168

POTEZ 631
22 158
30 96
33 380
34 305
71 305
114 93
117 416
127 273
140 273
146 380
169 314
177 481
178 305
192 413

POTEZ 633
17 396
24 346
26 346
34 334
36R 340

POTEZ 637
2 260
3 111
4 98
5 108
6 107
7 97, 249
10 325
11 325
14 117, 126
15 99
17 106
18 113
20 126
25 95, 96
26 113
31 97
35 364
36 152
38 157
39 102, 108
41 126
42 106
45 151
46 98
47 93
49 346
52 93
54 100
58 334
69 325
129 325
582 346

ROMANO 82
7 495
18 495
36 488
45 495
58 488
120 165

VOUGHT 156F
1 419
4 305
5 333
6 465
7 333
8 451
9 333
10 352
11 497
12 333
13 497
14 333
15 340
16 117
17 188
19 188
20 188
21 188
22 188
23 188
24 188
25 188
26 188
27 188
31 188
32 188
33 346

Dutch Aircraft Index

Fokker G1 serial number 312 of 3-II-1 bogged down at Waalhaven on May 10 (see page 192). The entire unit was put out of action in the first two hours of the German assault.

DOUGLAS DB-8A	
381	194
382	194
383	194
384	194
385	194
386	150
387	194
388	194
389	194
390	194
391	194
392	194
393	194
394	194
395	194
396	194
397	194
398	194

FOCKE-WULF 58	
109	148
195	192
198	149
199	141

FOKKER C V	
591	193
592	250
593	276
594	276
595	139
600	171, 193
602	116
603	250, 261
604	193
605	276
606	193
610	158
612	250
614	98, 193
615	276
617	193
618	261
619	250
620	193
621	193, 276
622	193, 276
625	193
631	193, 250, 276
636	261
637	261
639	236
641	261
645	250
646	276
648	261
650	250
652	250, 261, 276

653	138
654	191

FOKKER C VIIIW	
5185	276
5190	276
5191	276
5192	276
5193	276
5194	276

FOKKER C IX	
664	192
665	192

FOKKER C X	
700	276
704	191
705	261, 276
706	191, 276
707	191
708	191
709	191
710	191
711	191, 276
712	191, 276
713	276
714	276
715	276
716	192
718	193
719	276

FOKKER C XIW	
5421	250
5465	276

FOKKER C XIVW	
5587	250
5588	236
5589	250
5590	250
5591	250
5592	250
5593	236
5594	250
5595	261
5596	250
5597	250
5598	250
5599	250
5600	236
5601	250
5602	250
5603	250
5604	250
5605	250
5606	250
5607	250

5608	153, 250
5609	250
5610	236

FOKKER D XVII	
202	236
203	236, 250
205	250, 276
207	250
209	151, 261
210	250
211	117

FOKKER D XXI	
212	276
213	236
214	192
215	194
216	193, 194
217	194
218	192, 250
219	192, 276
220	125
221	192, 276
222	193
223	191
224	276
225	192
227	119, 193, 194
228	194
229	117, 236
233	192
234	132, 192
235	192, 276
236	276
237	117
238	192
239	192
240	192, 276
241	191
242	192, 276
243	276
244	192, 236, 276
245	192
246	194
247	194

FOKKER G 1	
301	193
302	192
303	250, 276
304	193, 261
305	193, 261
306	132
308	193, 236, 276
309	192
310	193, 261
311	193, 261
312	107, 192

313	193
314	106
315	192
316	192
317	193
318	193, 261
319	192
321	261
322	193, 250, 276
323	157
325	193, 250, 276
327	159
328	193, 261
329	193, 261
330	192
331	193
332	193
333	193
334	192
335	192
341	141
346	276
347	192
349	192
350	192
352	192
354	192
355	192
356	192
357	192
360	192
361	192

FOKKER S IV	
100	104
106	142
120	147
127	163

FOKKER S IX	
33	167
39	104
5467	194
5468	194
5469	194
5470	194
5471	194
5472	194
5473	194
5474	194
5475	194
5476	194
5477	194
5478	194
5482	194
5483	194
5484	194

FOKKER T V	
850	236
851	191
853	191
854	191
855	191
856	261
857	191
858	191, 261
859	191
860	111, 191
862	191
863	191
864	159
865	191

FOKKER T VIIIW	
5582	194, 276
5583	194
5584	194, 276
5585	194
5586	95
5636	276
5639	276
5640	276
5641	276
5642	276
5643	276

KOOLHOVEN FK 51	
13	194
14	194
15	194
16	194
19	192
53	194
54	194
55	194
56	194
57	194
58	194
59	194
60	194
61	194
124	194
125	194
407	276
408	276
409	193
411	261
414	193
415	193, 261
417	147, 192
419	276
424	98
425	193
426	276
427	193
428	250

Belgian Aircraft Index

Another unrecorded casualty, a crash-landed Fairey Fox mars the Belgian pastoral idyll. Over half of all Foxes were destroyed in the first 48 hours of 'Fall Gelb', the survivors flying a total of 65 sorties before the final collapse.

AVRO 626
4	251

BREGUET XIX
78	251

FAIREY BATTLE
58	238
59	124
60	238
61	238
62	238
63	199
64	238, 251, 277
65	199, 315
66	199
67	199, 315
68	238
69	200, 315
70	238
71	238, 251
72	199, 315
73	238, 306, 315

FAIREY FIREFLY
15	199
26	198
28	196
32	199
44	199
49	196
53	199
56	198
63	198
66	196
67	196
73	198
79	198
81	198

FAIREY FOX
7	315
8	286
9	236
12	145
13	315
15	286
16	99

17	315
30	145
31	315
32	286
33	139
38	306, 315
39	315
40	315
41	359
44	315
46	277
48	286
49	315
61	167
64	286
66	199
67	199
68	199
69	199
70	199
71	199
73	199
75	199
76	199
78	199, 237
81	199
84	199, 237
85	199
86	199, 237
87	199
88	199, 237
90	199, 237
93	199
96	199, 298
101	237
102	237
105	334
106	199
108	315
111	199
114	236
117	199
122	196
123	199
125	365
126	261
127	199
129	198

133	261
135	199, 286
139	199
140	237
141	96
142	237
143	237
146	198
148	315
149	315
152	237
155	238
162	236
163	236
166	199
168	236
169	261
170	374
171	365
172	199
175	251
178	237
179	199
181	145
182	200
183	200
184	160
185	286
186	200
187	251
188	315
189	200
190	200
192	200
193	200
300	199, 237
301	199
302	237
305	148
306	199, 237
307	199

FIAT CR-42
1	198
2	196
3	198
4	198
6	198

7	198
8	198
9	165
11	198
13	198
14	198
16	198
17	198
18	198
19	198
20	198
21	196
23	277, 416
24	277
26	277, 325
27	196
28	277, 416
29	277
30	198
31	277
32	277
33	277
43	198

GLOSTER GLADIATOR
19	237
21	148
22	236
27	236, 237
28	124
31	236, 237
32	237
34	236
35	160
38	237

HAWKER HURRICANE
20	196
21	196
22	196
23	196, 237
25	123, 165
26	145
27	196
28	142
29	237

30	196
31	196
32	196
33	145
34	196
35	123, 145
39	145
42	196

KOOLHOVEN FK 56
105	200
106	200

MORANE-SAULNIER MS 236
8	237
17	196
18	198

POTEZ 33
8	251

RENARD R-31
1	196
3	286
7	236
8	286, 315
9	196
10	359, 374
14	196
16	286
18	236
19	196
23	315
29	100
30	261
31	148
33	334, 341, 374
35	196

STAMPE-VERTONGEN SV 5
1	199
24	251
25	167

Luftwaffe Aircraft Index

Uncharacteristically, very few serial numbers were recorded by the Luftwaffe for its losses during the early part of the war. Thus Heinkel He111 Werk Nummer 5543 does not appear in German records of the period.

ARADO 68
1907	102

DORNIER 17M
2202	135
2236	366

DORNIER 17P
0147	252
0173	164
1091	375
1630	298
2419	288
3521	206
3578	116
4033	156
4043	158
4052	107
4062	114
4112	277
4137	456

DORNIER 17S
2184	134
2501	134
2502	134

DORNIER 17Z
2371	114
3314	470
3383	208
3461	121
3474	206
3613	316
6036	252

DORNIER 18D
718	95
804	115

DORNIER 215
022	427

FIESELER 156C
4207	116

GOTHA 145A
1145	115

HEINKEL 59
1830	206
1995	206
2593	206
2599	206

HEINKEL 111B
1403	115

HEINKEL 111H
2020	162

2305	158
2596	354
2636	360
2648	278
2706	106
2709	124
3154	124
3327	240
3558	254
5315	116
5350	110
5457	125
5474	409
5560	341
5571	254
5575	110
6179	213
6808	240
6970	213
7032	213

HEINKEL 111P
1403	316
1430	210
1523	317
1567	117
1570	209
1591	209
1705	414
1877	126
2314	115
2633	209
2800	241
2846	213
2896	342
2909	209
3556	209
4570	209

HENSCHEL 126
3128	441
3365	495
4229	341

JUNKERS JU52
1327	227
2820	290
3085	336
3656	229
5042	337
5156	229
5160	229
5172	301
5174	376
5180	229
5203	229
5205	477
5230	429
5259	224
5268	396
5288	229

5304	229
5326	456
5347	498
5365	442
5373	467, 477
5423	495
5477	498
5603	301
5647	229
5706	228
5719	456
5738	301
5847	493
5936	229
5953	229
6006	229
6009	229
6016	229
6019	476
6023	152
6146	229
6216	388
6266	442
6280	343
6289	223
6319	228
6320	228
6377	224
6403	228
6404	228
6453	223
6461	442
6462	241
6463	107
6474	228
6476	229
6495	227
6499	467
6508	223
6513	227
6526	228
6533	228
6543	309
6604	241
6607	223
6609	241
6715	116
6785	229
6786	229

JUNKERS 87B
278	265
291	133
450	376
5136	254
5231	136
5253	376
5328	280
5513	265
6096	138

JUNKERS 88A
029	429
044	476
165	277
213	251
244	467
2027	211
3025	347
3030	360
3035	209
3036	327
3040	209
3041	209
3049	376
3051	336
4008	278
4014	376
5018	429
5035	327
6018	209
6042	479
8004	409

MESSERSCHMITT 109D
538	97

MESSERSCHMITT 109E
087	117
677	326
683	165
703	205
707	456
710	139
862	434
931	375
1162	158
1202	381
1215	117
1225	162
1250	441
1251	118
1257	205
1304	118
1346	434
1347	288
1525	140
1526	342

1541	441
1542	327
1937	409
1980	118
2288	148
2521	148
2746	448
3178	164
3247	396
3299	129
3326	99
3372	118
3403	160
3410	96
3454	156
3462	205
3471	392
3483	115
3490	134
3491	136
4072	327
5010	336
5013	139
5083	300
5088	252
5095	252
5097	409
5113	342
5156	162
5185	162
6003	158
6037	135
6111	162
6180	165

MESSERSCHMITT 110C
1344	124
1358	131
2124	448
2804	138
2881	448
3006	125
3011	215
3096	301
3205	157
3524	343
3528	467

Italian Aircraft Index

FIAT BR20
21503	467
21504	467
21505	467
21873	477
21917	467

FIAT CR42
4361	477
4366	477
4372	477
4779	477
5579	477
5590	477

A Junkers Ju88 down in the British sector comes under close scrutiny by RAF airmen. Unfortunately, this series of British Official photographs (see also page 550) is undated and the accompanying captions offer no clues that allow us to establish its exact identity. Like the Messerschmitt Bf110, the Junkers Ju88 was a relatively new type in Luftwaffe service so a fairly intact example was of considerable interest to RAF Technical Intelligence.

INDEX

COMPILED BY PETER B. GUNN

Notes:

1. Page numbers in *italics* refer to illustrations. There may also be textual references on these pages.

2. The word *passim* following page numbers (e.g. 124-129 *passim*) indicates several mentions of an entry over a range of pages.

3. In some cases units have been added in brackets after the names of personnel, mostly to distinguish between individuals with similar names.

4. Orders of Battle are not indexed in detail but are indicated under UNITS.

5. The **ROLL OF HONOUR** is not indexed but is to be found from pages 502-527.

LOCATIONS

Aachen, 165, 239, 253, 316, 342, 347
Aachen-Merzbrück, 262
Aalbeke, *114*, 115, 116
Aalborg, *383*, *407*
Aalst/Alost, 277, 326
Aalter, 237, 238, 251, 257, 277, *306*, 315
Aartal, 239
Aartrijke, 168
Abancourt, 347
Abaucourt, 52, 144
Abbaye d'Argenton, 160
Abbeville, 131, 175, 303, 310, 331, 332, 336, 338, 339, 341, *344*, 345, 349, 358, 362, 364, 367, 372, 382, 385, 392, 395, 397, *400*, 401, 403, 420, 422, 424, 430, 431, 434, 435, 437, 441, 444, 445, 449, 451, 458, 497
    Communal Cemetery Extension, 349, 444
    Faubourg Thuison, 364
    Notre-Dame de la Chapelle cemetery, 341
Abbeville-Drucat, 303
Abingdon, 349, 455
Ablaincourt, 424
Ablis, 459
Achêne, 145, *146*
Achicourt, 302, 319
Achmer, 148, 210
Acklington, 199
Acy, 433
Afferden, 227
Agay, 467
Agen, 495
Aigle, 466
Aigleville, 464, *465*
Ailette canal, 452
Ailly-sur-Noye, 334
Aire-sur-Lys, 11, 304, *361*, 384
Aische-en-Refail, 272
Aisne, River, 315, 330, 338, 348, 364, 384, 395, 403, 415, 422, 430, 433, 443, 446, 447, 449, 456, 457, 494

Aisne Canal, 454
Aisne valley, 325, 452
Aix, 115
Ajaccio, Corsica, 492
Akersloot, 250
Albert, 308, 309, 375, 422
Albert Canal, 174, 196, 213, 230, 231, 235, 236, *237*, *238*, *243*, 244, *245*, 256, 257, 277, 286, 293
Albringhausen, 103
Alconbury, 247-248
Algiers-Maison Blanche, *426*, 462
Alincourt, 333
Alkmaar, 191
Allonville, 366
Almkerk, 239, *265*
Alost/Aalst, 286
Alprech, 188, 352
Altenrhein, 162
Altiaux, 290
Altkirch, 298
Altroff, 127
Alzenau, 477
Ambérieu-en-Bugey, 407, 410
Ambleny, 364
Amblimont, 'Le Grand Fond', 274
Amdorf, 488
Ameland, 154
Amerongen, 239
Amiens, 9, 96, 118, 268, 293, 304, 305, 311, 317, 319, *324*, 329, 330, 337, 338, 339, 340, 341, 344, 356, 358, 359, 372, 374, 375, 380, 392, *396*, 397, 400, 420, 422, 424, 431, 433, 434, 435, 437, 445, 446, 449, 456, 460, 464, 479
Amiens-Glisy, 161, 302, 312, 336
Amiens-La Madeleine cemetery, 341

Amiens-Montjoie, 116, 124
Amifontaine, *155*, 158, *160*, 180, 244, 267, 293, 296
Amsterdam, 84, 216, 250, 353, 467, 496
    Nieuve-Ooster, 353
    Osterbegaarplatz, 353
    Wilhelmina Hospital, 418
Amsterdam-Rijnkanal, 181
Amy-Martin-Rieux, 148
Ancenis, 495
Andelle, River, 443
Andelle valley, 451
Andover, 362, 372, 385, 419
Angers, 270, 471, 487
Angevillers, 365
Angivillers, 400, 433
Anglure, 303, 320, 349, 362, 371, 378
Anglure-Vouarces, 83, 148, 171, 295
Angres, 352
Anhée, 260
Anizy-le-Château, 324
Anna Paulowna, Zwinweg, Den Helder, 205
Annelles, 267, 459
Ansbach, 123, 141, 148, 160, 162
Ansermet, *53*, 126
Anthien, 429
Antilly, 112
Antwerp, 215, 235, 253, 255, 281, 288, *327*, 342, 353, 386
Antwerp-Deurne, *145*, 196
Apach-Trèves, 419
Arbot, 429, *489*
Arbre, 278
Ardèche, 492
Ardennes, 325, 397, 457, 458, 495

Ardennes Forest, 272, 449
Ardooie, *382*
Argelès-sur-Mer, 150
Argenton-sur-Creuse, 495
Argoeuves, 425
Argueil, 435
Arienheller, 123
Arkel polder, 240
Arles-Mas-de-Rue, 171
Arlon, 290, 360
Arma di Taggia, 467
Armentières, 254, 365, 376
Arnhem, 211
Arnsberg, 121
Arques, 347
Arras, 175, 267, 282, 302, 319, 325,
328, 329, 330, 331, 332, 334, 335,
338, 339, 343, 344, 345, 347, 349,
351, 352, 353, 358, 366, *510*
Arsfeld, 253
Artaise-le-Vivier, 247, 270
Artemps, La Vallée du Pont, 400
Artzenheim, 126
Arvillers, 433
Asch, 318
Aschaffenburg, 239
Asfeld, 452, 455
Aspelaere, 320
Assainvillers, Bois Defoy, 433
Asse, 261
Ath, 300, 330
Athies, 153, 274, 388
Athies-sous-Laon, 189, 213, 249,
286
Attaques, 359
Attenhoven, 242, 260
Attert, 263
Attigny, 102, 188, 284, 286, 290,
302
Aubenton, 242
Aubérive-sur-Suippes, *92*, 115, 135,
160, 183, 233, 247, 271, 273, *283*,
289, *440*, 441
Aubervilliers, *235*
Aubigny, 353
Aubréville, 279
Auckland, NZ, *520*
Audembert, *322*
Audigny, Louvry farm, *264*
Audricq, 359
Audun-le-Roman, 208
Auersmacher, 94
Auger-Saint-Vincent, 335, 374
Augsburg, 86, 413
Aulnoye-Aymeries, 274, 275, 309,
443, 460
Ault, 431
Ault lighthouse, 424
Aumale, 400, 429, 434, 435, 443,
444, 446
Aumont-en-Halatte, 334
Auneuil, 400
Authie, 282, 293, 311, 320-321
Autigny-la-Tour, 275
Autin, 475
Autruche, 'Corbison', 296
Auxerre, 145, 429, 466, 469, *479*,
481
Auxi-le-Château, 338, 429
Avallon, 478, 481
Avenay, 164, 189
Avesnes, 301, 317, 383, 384, 430,
443
Avesnes-le-Sec, 239, 249
Avesnes-sur-Helpe, 286, 314
Avioth, 371
Avord, 390, 458, 466, 475
Avricourt, 452
Azelot, 117

Babberich, 159
Babenhausen, 160
Baccarat, 241
Bachy, 323
Bacqueville, 305
Bad Bergzabern, 107
Bad Kreuznach, 316, *407*
Bad Münstereifel, 'Felsennest', *430*
Bad Zwischenahn, 171, 206
Badbergen, 158

Baden-Baden, 288
Baden-Oos, 158
Baie d'Urville, 305
Bailleul, 388
Bailleul Neuville, 437
Bainast, Les Terres Noires, 392
Baincthun, 'La Paturelle', 352
Balgau, 160
Balgzandpolder, 236
Balham, 392
Baltrum, 241
Bamberg, 116
Bapaume, 243, 304, 330, 334, 346,
349, 358, 380, 414, 422, 423, 434
Bar-le-Duc, 18, 57, 180, *407*, 470,
476
Bar-les-Buzancy, 260
Barbery, 341
Barby, 'Chêne Tonneau', 322
Barenton-Bugny, 353
Barton Mills, 356
Basel-Birsfelden, 162
Basse-Ham, 441
Bassenheim, 157, 161, 162, 163,
165, 167, 205, 336
Bastogne, 288, 336
Baumholder, 164, 208
Bayenghem-les-Seninghem, 372
Bayeux, 340
     Eastern Cemetery, *510*
Bayonne, 83, 474
Bazeilles, 266
Béage, 494
Beare Green, Surrey, *503*
Beauchamps-le-Vieux, 425
Beaucourt-en-Santerre, 325, 432
Beaulieu, 326, 335, 366
Beaulieu-en-Argonne, 392
Beaulieu-les-Fontaines, 432
Beaumerie-St-Martin, 441
Beaumont, 288, 300, *301*, 308, 316
Beaumont forest, 465
Beaumont School, Windsor, *508*
Beaumont-en-Argonne, 157, 253,
278
     'Bois de la Vache', 329
Beaumont-le-Roger, 435, 437, 443,
455
Beaumont-Monteux, Ferme
Chatain, 499
Beaune, 479
Beaurains, Ferme Anthyme, 364
Beaurepaire, 461
Beaurevoir, *293*, 298
Beausse, 139
Beautor, 117
Beauvais, 134, 298, 311, *324*, 325,
334, *335*, 358, 364, 392, 401, 415,
424, 434, 435, 441, 443, 449
     Agel hospital, 400
Beauvais-Tillé, 325, 334
Beauval, 321
Beauvechain, 196, 316
Beauvilliers, 247
Beauvois-en-Vermandois, 336
Beauvraignes, 103, 432
Bécourt, 145, 381
Beek, 211
Beerst, 392
Beert-Bellingen, 296
Begijnenbos, 240
Beilen, 111
Beine-Nauroy, 282
Bekesbourne, 345, 362, 390, 398,
405
Belfort, 171, 410, 443
Belgrade, 261
Bellencombre, 441
Belleu, 434
Bellevaux, 288
Belsele, 199, 200, 237
Belval, 339
Benay, 207
Benson, *518*, *525*
Bercheux, 232
Berck-sur-Mer, 124, *157*, 214, *324*,
339, 340
Bergamo, 462
Bergboezem, 224
Berge, 360

Bergen, 106, 107, 191, *193*, 209,
213, 229, 261, 276
Bergen-op-Zoom, 255, 342
Bergère-les-Vertus, 395
Bergues, 356, 397, 404, 415
Bergzabern, 97
Beringen, 337
Berkel, 219
Berlaimont, 319, *324*
Berlin, 171, *454*, *498*
Bernaville, 437
Bernay, *440*, 452
Bernburg, 115
Berneuil-sur-Aisne, 297
Berneville, 345
Bernex, 414
Bernkastel, 418
Berny-en-Santerre, 425
Berny-sur-Noye, 334, 425
Berre, 456, 459, 488, 492
Berry-au-Bac, 174, 175, 182,
231, 244, 246, 255, 267, 270, 282,
289, *295*, 300, 461
Berry-au-Bois, 462
Bertangles, 303, 311, 320, 358
Bertincourt, 341
Bertrix, 289, 329
Berzy-le-Sec, 447
'Besagibet', Vaux-sur-
Sure/Bercheux, 232
Besançon, 448
     St Jacques hospital, 240
Besme, 433
Bessay, 451
Bessoncourt, 158
Bétheniville, *79*, *130*, *131*, 140, *174*,
175, 181, 233, 245, 247, 256, 257,
268, 272, 273, 274, 282, 283, 294,
295, 336, *524*
Bétheny, 461
Béthune, 302, 339, 343, 347, 349,
351, 361, 362, 410, 430
Bettlach, 409
Betviller, 97
Betz-Bouillancy, 346, 364, *426*
Beugneux, 285, 461
Beuvraignes, 315
Beuzevilette, 433
Beveland island, 216
Beveren, *382*
Beveren-IJzer, 349
Beverst, 247
Bézu-la-Forêt, 467
Biache-St-Vaast, 311
Biarritz, 474
Biblis, 252
Bicester, 469
Bideford-on-Avon, *520*
Biel-Bözingen, 448
Bielitz, 114
Bienvillers Military Cemetery, *510*
Bierbeek, 282
Bierset, *100*, 145, *146*, 196, 279
Biesbosch, the, 241, *257-258*, 265
Biggin Hill, 175, 310, 386, 392, *402*,
406, 437, 498
Bilzenbaan, 215
Binche, 296, 388
Bingen, 97
Bircham Newton, 184, 313, 373,
496
Birkenfeld, 93, 104, 253, 498
Birkham Newton, 184, 313, 373,
Bischmisheim, 99, 100
Bistrup, 115
Bitsch, 427
Blain, 469
Blangy, 430, 434, 435
Blangy-sur-Bresle, 358
Bleiswijk, 219
Blesmes, 252
Bliesbruck, 96, 161
Blois, 413, 456
Blotzheim, 133
Blumental, 148
Bobigny, 334
Böblingen, 107, 113, 115, 120, 126,
135, 145, 156, 160, 162, 165, 328,
429
Bochold, 459
Bockweiler, *98*

Bodensee, the, 138, 212
Bodney, 272, 445, 458, 465, 469
Boechout, 380
Boeimeer, 255, 256
Bois Cholet, 471
Bois de Chêne, 240
Bois de Fays, 285
Bois de la Marfée, 274
Bois de la Morue, Bray lès
Marueil, 336
Bois de l'Emprunt, 317
Bois de Voncq, 268
Bois des Nielles, 280
Bois d'Havrincourt, 364
Bois Lainé, Ferme de la Motte, 446
Bois l'Evêque, 314
Bois Watte, 445
Boisdinghem, *348*
Boisjean, *352*
Boissois, 309
Bolbec, 449, 467
Bolinne, 265
Bollezeele, 390
Bommerholz, 148
Boncelles, 301
Bondues *see* Lille-Bondues
Bône, Algeria, 492
Bonn, 206, 279, 290, 376, *407*, 418,
432
     St Augustin Hospital, 329, 343
     Venusberg hospital, 308
Bonn-Hangelar, 104, 120, 127, 128,
133, 140, 148, 149, 151, 154, 156,
158, 162, 206, 207, 254, 300, 329,
429
Bonnevoie, 183
Bönninghardt, 147, 148, 152, 156,
157, 163, 164, 167, 171
Boom, 279
Boos *see* Rouen-Boos
Bordeaux, 83, 269, 463, 473, 490,
492, *495*, 496
Bordeaux-Mérignac, 277
Borest, 327
Borgharen, 247
Borgloon, 248
Borkum, 116, 119, 124, 205
Borlez, 232
Borre, *205*
     Ferme Jourdain, 210
Borssele, 289
Borstendorf, 239
Boschplaat, 110
Boscombe Down, 97, 118, 487, *511*
Boslaan, the, Haagse Bos, 226
Bosmont-sur-Serre, 296
Botassart, 'Le Tombeau du
Géant', 371
Bouard, 424, 433, 440, 447
Bouchain, 361
Bouillon, 243, *245*, *246*, 254, 265,
266, 270, *271*, 272, 278, 319
Boulange, 208
Boulay-Moselle, 113
Boullay-les-Troux, 456
Boulleville, 458
Boulogne, 126, 152, 312, 338, 339,
340, 342, 343, 344, 345, 347, 348,
349, *350*, *351*, *352*, 354, 356, 357,
362, 367, 373, 381, 385, 398, 420,
421, 487, 490, *502*
Boult-au-Bois, 290
Boult-sur-Suippe, 451
Bourbonne-les-Bains, 475
Bourbourg, 376
Bourcq, 263
Bourdon, German War Cemetery,
241, *442*
Bourg-en-Bresse, 479
Bourges, 171, 358, 360, 424, 429,
475, 481
Bourgneuf, 478
Boussicourt, 340
Bouvigny-Boyeffles, 347
Bouwel, 286
Bovelles, 427
Boves, 324
Boxtel, 125
Boyelles, 188, 323
Braassemermeer, 194

Brabant-le-Roi, 463
Braches, 'La Vallée des Sauvillers', 432
Braine-le-Comte, 293, 303
Braisne, 451
Brancourt-le-Grand, 324
Branges, 317
Bras-sur-Meuse, 120
Brassy, 240
Braunschweig, 140, 149
Braunschweig-Querum, 337
Braux-le-Châtel, 470
Bray lès Mareuil, Bois de la Morue, 336
Bray-Dunes, *397*, 406, 408
Bray-sur-Seine, 95, 419
Bray-sur-Somme, 435
Brebières, 311
Brecht, 262
Brécy, Château de Jouvence, 461
Breda, 255, 273
    St Elizabeth hospital, 262
    Seelig Barracks, *261*
Bredene, 374
Breendonk prison, *287*
Bremen, 86
Brenouille, 453
Bresle, River, 430, 435
Brest, 380, 468, 471, 473, 478, 480, 488, 490
Brétigny, 340, 417, 433
Brétigny-sur-Orge, 248, 416
Brettenham, 395
Breux-sur-Avre, 469
Brevans, 108
Breyell, 180
Brezolles, 493
Briare, 296, 314, *457*
Briaucourt, 189
Bricon, 296, 470
Briegden, *238*
Brienne-le-Château, 154, 470
Brieulles-sur-Bar, 'Fond-Barré', 213
Briey, 33, 54, 208, 285, 376
Brighton, 194, 276
Brignolles, 472
Brissy-Hamégicourt, 332
Bristol, Clifton College, *514*
Brockworth, Gloster Aircraft Company, *344*
Broekpolder, the, 225
Brosses, Colombier-Saugnieu, 212
Brousseval, 235
Broye-les-Pesmes, 235
Bruay, 343
Bruges/Brugge, 99, 213, 306, 307, 360, 370, 385, 388
    St Josef Hospital, 360
Brühl, 114
Bruille-lez-Marchiennes, 335
Brulange, 52, 144
Brûly-de-Peche, 'Wolfsschlucht', *430*
Brussels, 292, 319, 327, 330, 372, 381, 382, *387*, *404*, 410, 496, 497
    Edith Cavell Hospital, 249
    Sint Pieters Woluwe Cemetery, *144*
Brussels-Evere, *165*, 174, 196, 199, *201*, 238, *286*, 382, *462*
    Pelouse d'Honneur Cemetery, 145, *199*, *237*
Brussels-Zaventem, *201*
Brustem, *198*
Bruyelle, 339
Bruyères-sur-Fère, Corbeny Farm, 456
Bruyères-sur-Oise, 96
Buc, 188, 358, 452
Bucharest, 82
Büchenbeuren, 307
Buchères, 470
Bucquoy, Hameau des Essarts, 358
Bucy-le-Long, 334
    'Richebourg', 451
Büdingen, 100
Buer, 139
Buggenhout, 299, 342
Buiksloot, 192, 236

Buisjes island, 265
Bulgny, 248
Bulles, 340
Bulson, 270, 271
Bunde, 162
Bündingen, 162
Bunschoten, 353
Burg Ahrental, 133
Burlafingen, 113
Burnham, *28*
Burthecourt, 259
Bussiares, 314
Bussy, 418
Butzweilerhof, 278
Buxières-sous-les-Côtes, 240
Buzancy, 358, 463

Caburg, 262
Caen, 94, 340, 463, 481, 499
Caen-Carpiquet, 115
Caen-Mathieu, 455
Calais, 99, *135*, 157, *214*, *332*, 338, 339, 340, 342, 343, 344, 347, 348, *349*, *350*, 351, 353, 354, 355, *356-357*, 360, 361, 362, 366, 367, 370, 371, *372*, 373, 375, 376, 377, *378*, 379, 383, 385, 386, 390, 392, 393, 399, 402, 403, 410, 420, 487, 490, 497
Calais-Marck, 214, 259, 276, 348, *349*, 355, 356, 379, 470, 488
Calfven, 254
Calshot, 276
Cambrai, 302, *305*, 311, 312, 315, 317, 318, 319, 320, 323, 325, 328, 330, 332, 334, 339, 341, 343, 344, 374, 375, 376, 393, 398, 414, 415, 418, 419, 422, 433, 434, *452*, 456
    Marquion Hospital, 275
Cambrai-Niergnies, 83, 139, 175, 188, 206, 260, 274, *297*, 306, *314*, 341, 380, 387
Cambron-Casteau, 210
Campagne, 432
'Campagne du Tierse', Lamontzée/Ville-en-Hesbaye, 278
Campigneulles-les-Grandes, 385
Campneuseville, 424, 427
Canal de l'Oise, 448
Candas, 434
Canly, 'Ferme du Villerseau', 428
Cannes, 496
Cannet des Maures, 462
Cany-Barville, 455
Cap Gris-Nez, *101*, 349, 496
Cap Lévy, 305
Cappel, 470
Carcassonne, 478
Carlton Hill, North Carlton, 445
Casablanca, 83
Cassel, 360, *407*, 456
Casteau, 248
Castres, 459
Cauderie, 274
Caugé, 465
Caulaincourt, Trefcon British Cemetery, 159
Cauroy, 268, 320, *505*
Čayeux, 358
Cayeux-sur-Mer, Communal Cemetery, *402*
Celle, 106, 136, 151, 376, *383*, 499
Celle-Ziezenbruch, 148
Celles, 181, 381
Cempuis, 400
Cerizay, 492
Cernay, 135
Cernay-en-Dormois, 273
Cervere, 477
Cerville, 241
Chablis, Ferme de Pommard, 253
Chagny, 333, *334*
Chaillon, 476
Challerange, *188*, 208, 260, 273
Chalon-sur-Saône, 271, 451
Châlons-en-Champagne (-sur-Marne), 120, 189, 260, *283*, 336, 385, 395, 457, 459, 461, 462, 465, 466, 470, 488, 493

Chambarrand-Marseilles, 413
Chambières French National Cemetery, Metz, *518*
Chambley, 373, 419
Chambley-Bussières, 206
Chambly, 133
Chamouilley, 249
Champ Milcamp, 259
Champagne, *281*, 292, 403, 454
Champguyon, 466
Champigny, 128
Champigny-St André Cemetery, *434*, 452
Champlitte, *475*, 476
Champs Cornet, 234
Chandron, 144
Channel Islands, 457, 458, 480, 486, 487, 490, 494, *514*, *519*
Chantilly, 298, 305, 306, 327, 334, 340, 341, 374, 376, 416, 417, 418, 433, 441, 447, 457
Chantilly-les-Aigles, 163, 324, 425
Chanute Field, 118
Charité-sur-Loire, 481
Charlemagne, 112
Charleroi, 249, 275, 285, 292, *301*, 302, 307, 343, 348
Charleville-Mézières, *156*, 212, 239, 252, 259, 263, 265, 283, 288, 293, 317, 343, *355*, 365, 384, 390, 411, 417, 432, 442, 443, 451, 453, 456, 460, 493
Charlois, 229
Charmentray, 'Le Charton', 416
Charroux, 487
Chartres, 266, 277, 314, 325, 400, 407, 416, *417*, 418, 419, 433, 440, 456, 458, 459, 464, 467, 468, 470, 471, 479, 499
Chartwell, *319*
Chastres, French Military Cemetery, *275*
Château Blin de Bourbon, Roye, 380
Château Bougon, 134, 135, 139, 142, 146, 147, 164, 469, 470, 471, 472, 473, 486, 487
    No. 21 Aircraft Depot, 182, 321, 322
Château Davenescourt, 424
Château de Jouvence, Brécy, 461
Château de la Noue, 464
Château de Muguet, *457*
Château de Rouez, 314
Château Terkelen, 198
Château-Bogny, 288
Château-de-Pricory, 320
Château-Regnault, 344
Château-Regnault forest, 284
Château-Thierry, 320, 327, 328, 419, 423, 443, 446, 447, 451, 454, 457, 458, 461, 467, 468
Châteaudun, 253, 305, 413, 419, 423, 443, 450, 457, 463, 469, 470
Châteauneuf, 437
Châteauroux, 165, 240, 298, 358, 360, 413, 424, 429, 447, 475, 479, 492, 493
Châteauroux Déols, 461
Chateauroux-la-Martinerie, 429, 461, 478
Chatel-Chéhéry, 105, 234, 275, 284, 286
Châtenois, 360
Châtillon-sur-Bar, 280, 456
Châtillon-sur-Seine, 475, 478
Châtrices, 274
Chaulnes, 424, 425, 429, 432, 433, 440
Chaume, Le Haut du Them, 456
Chaumont, 395, 423, 429, 475
Chaumont-Semoutiers, 107, 126, 131, 364
Chauny, 306, 422
    BAFF HQ, 166, *170*, 174, 292
Chaussée-Notre-Dame-Louvignies, 272
Chaussoy-Épagny, 380, 425
Chauvency-le-Château, 254
Chavigny, 380

Cheddington, *512*
Chéhéry, 271
Chelles, 316, 418
Chémery, 273, 298, 326
Cherbourg, 140, 276, *352*, 435, 457, 458, 463, 468, 471, 478, 480, 486, 487, 488, 490
Cherbourg-Querqueville, 340
Chevrières, 460
Chichester, 151, 524
Chiers, River, 266
Chièvres, 381, 427
Chili Trench Cemetery (formerly Fampoux/Gavrelle Road Cemetery), *517*
Chimay, 314, 365
Chissey-sur-Loue, 148, 164, 189, 413
Choloy War Cemetery, 7, 98, 247, 267, 268, *270*, *271*, 272, 273, *438*, *505*, *507*, *511*
Chonas-l'Amballan, 407
Choye, 497
Chrishall, *395*
Chuffilly-Roche, 371
Church Fenton, *28*, 272, 487
Ciney, 248, *249*, 309, 360, 376
Cinqueux, 340, 341
Cirières, La Génetrie, 492
Civry, 478
Cizancourt, 365
Clairfayts, 285
Clairfontaine, 285
Clairmarais, 339, *348*, 355, 377
Clairmarais Forest, 385
Clairvaux, 429
Clamecy, 481
Claye-Souilly, 314, 334, 380, 417, 418
Clémency, 182
Cléon, 451
Clères, 358
Clermont, 360, 433, 443
Clermont-Ferrand, 478, 492, 496
Clermont-les-Fermes, 99
Cléry-sur-Somme, 336
Coblenz, 114, 151, 157, 337, 442
Coblenz-Karthausen, 160
Cochem, 103
Cochenée, 285
Cocherel, 433
Coegny, 263
Coeuvres-et-Valsery, 433
Coingt, 307
Colditz, 161, 283
Colmar, 132
Colmey, 182
Cologne, 133, 279, 290, 353, 388, 424, 479
    Southern Cemetery (Köln Südfriedhof), *506*
Cologne-Butzweilerhof, 123, 129, 360, 462
Cologne-Hohenlind, 265, 279, 308, 317, 329, 381, 419, 427
Cologne-Nippes, 462, 470
Cologne-Ostheim, 93, 205, 210, 317, 381, 427, 462, 476
Cologne-Wahn, 140, 154, 205, 382, 419
Colombey-les-Belles, 479
Compiègne, 296, 317, 327, 329, 336, 340, 425, 428, 440, 441, 442, 443, 452, 466, *492-494*, *496-498*
    Clairière de l'Armistice, *492*
    hospital Royallieu, 288
Conches-en-Ouche, 448, 469, 470
Conchy-les-Pots, 434
Condé-sur-Aisne, 447
Condé-Vraux, 230, *233*, 270, 294, 303, 310, 311, 314
    AASF Museum, 267
Conflans, 290
Conflans-en-Jarnisy, 181
Congoberg, the, 272
Coni, 488
Connage, 325
Connantre, 95, 99, 425, 433, 458, 459
Consugerne, 116

Conteville, 449, 456
Corbeil, 417
Corbie, 429
Corcy, 447
Cormeilles-en-Vexin, 413, 425
Cormicy, 453
Corroy-le-Grand, 282
Cosford, RAF Museum, 423
Côtebrune, 120
Coucy-le-Château, 434
Coudekerque, 414
Coulenberg, 262
Coulmier-le-Sec, 103
Coulommes-les-Marqueny, 255, 263
Coulommiers, 166, 292, 311, 396, 417, 443, 452
Coulonges-Ardennes, 469
Coulpiègne, 304
Courcelles, 454
Courgivaux, 465
Courjumelles, Royat Paillard, 334
Courmont, 451
Courrière, 257
Courseulles-sur-Mer, 158
Courtacon, 466
Courtisols, 450
Courtrai/Kortrijk, 174, 355, 359, 361, 365, 370, 372
Courville, 328, 475
Couvin, 366
Couvron, 99, 249, 260, 376, 413
Couvrot, 466
Crailsheim, 104, 107, 138
Cramaille, 447
Cranwell, RAF College, 76, 503, 509, 514, 523, 525
Crapoel, 253
Crécy, 131, 294, 310, 311, 312, 320, 450, 456
Creil, 311, 325, 328, 416
    Ruelle St Sauveur, 434
Crépey, 335
Crépigny, 409
Crépy-en-Laonnois, 298
Crépy-en-Valois, 374, 415, 433, 442, 447
Crèvecoeur, 449
Crèvecoeur-le-Grand, 343
Crèvecoeur-sur-l'Escaut, cemetery, 293
Croisy, 413
Croix-Moligneaux, 114, 333
Croutoy, 453
Crouy-en-Thelle, 416
Croydon, 344, 399, 406
Crozat canal, 422
Crozon, 93
Crozon-sur-Vauvre, 487
Crugny, 459
Crupilly, 409
Cuers-Pierrefeu, 462, 471, 472, 475, 477
Cuirieux, 274
Cuise-la-Motte, 418
Curfoz, 245
Cutry, 470
Cuvilly, 418, 432
Cysoing, 322

Dagneux, 410, 414
Dagny-Lambercy, 322, 450
Daigny, 434, 462
Damblain, 334, 358, 380, 458
Damery, 459
Dammartin-en-Goële, 418
Dammerie-lè-Lys, 479
Dampierre, 481
Damprichard, 446
Damville, 432
Damvillers, 297
Dannemarie, 211
Danzig, 483
Darmstadt, 106
Darmstadt-Griesheim, 106, 139, 140, 141, 142, 144, 147, 148, 150, 151, 153, 154, 158, 164, 167, 170
Darnétal, 470
Darney, 212
De Clinge, 260

De Klomp, 239
De Kooy, 191, 192, 194, 205, 236, 496, 498
'De Lange Bonnen' Polder, 227
De Mok, 194, 236, 250, 254, 261
De Panne (La Panne), 115, 332, 365, 368, 383, 385, 397, 399
    Hôtel de l'Océan, 314
De Stufter beach, 496
De Vlijt, 141
De Waterhoek Polder, 212
De Wetering, 261
De Zilk, 193, 250, 261, 276
Deal, 390
Deauville, 142, 352, 373, 380, 387, 407, 451
Debden, 28, 30, 51, 101
Deggendorf, 215
Deilinghofen, 132
Deisterkamp, 124
Delft, 219, 223, 229, 230
Delme, 107, 112, 128, 259
Delmenhorst, 209, 212
Demuin, 358
Den Deyl, 193, 194
Den Haag (The Hague), 95, 174, 175, 184, 191, 194, 211, 216, 218-219, 220, 221, 223, 226, 229, 230, 248, 255
Den Helder, 205, 496
Den Hoorn, 191, 211
Den Hout, 227
    'Witte Weg', 273
Denain, 313, 315, 318, 361
Dendermonde, 214, 238
Déols, Fonts-Puis, 470
Dessau, 86
Desvres, 392
Detling, 248, 332, 356, 362, 373, 385, 390, 395, 398, 405, 465, 487, 490, 496
Detmold, 106, 144, 160
Deurne, 158
    see also Antwerp-Deurne
Devant-les-Bois, 273
Diedenhofen see Thionville
Diekirch, 156, 183, 253
Dielkirchen, 117
Diepholz, 115, 383
Dieppe, 267, 304, 322, 437, 441, 443, 449, 455, 458, 497
Dieuze, 213
Digby, 22, 30, 386, 411
Digoin, 165, 481
Dijon, 148, 278, 478
Diksmuide, 168, 379, 381, 388, 390, 394, 397, 398
Dinant, 259, 266, 268, 281, 282, 284, 285, 292, 302, 317, 338, 339, 348, 467
Dinard, 417, 480
Dippach, 174, 182
Dishforth, 458
Dives, 328
Dizy-le-Gros, 297
Döberitz, 129, 171
Dockendorf, 206, 262, 279, 290, 308
Docking, 373
Dohan, 254
Doingt, Péronne, 303, 517
Dole, 206, 212
Dole-Tavaux, 108, 475
Domart-sur-la-Luce, 424
Domberg, 476
Domfessel, 364
Donaueschingen, 459
Donchery, 266, 270, 271
Donge, River, 257, 258
Donna Nook, North Coates, 141
Doornik/Tournai, 282
Dordrecht, 217, 220, 230, 241
Dormans, 416, 417, 454
Dorniella, 477
Dorpskade, 191
Dorsten, 242, 448
Dortmund, 134, 135, 139, 140, 157, 158, 164, 170, 300
Douai, 125, 134, 210, 303, 306, 310, 311, 318, 319, 323, 327, 328, 329, 330, 340, 346, 408

Douai-Dechy, 306
Douaumont, 134
Doullens, 346, 358, 402, 422, 434, 442, 469
    prison, 317
Douvrend, 441
Doux, 277
    'La Gravière', 316
Douy, 251
Douzy, 266, 271, 272
    Communal Cemetery, 271
Dover, 339, 367, 377, 386, 389, 398, 399, 402, 404, 406, 411
    Castle, 367
    St Margaret's Bay, 180, 378
    Shakespeare Cliff, 378
    Victoria Hospital, 386
Dranouter, 467
Drensteinfurt, 170
Dreuil-lès-Amiens, 431
Dreux, 295, 435, 443, 446, 450, 455, 456, 457, 462, 463, 469, 471, 472
Driffield, 233, 332, 385, 431, 455
Drimmelen, 258
Droisy, 440
Drosay, 469
Druten, 228
Dübendorf, Swiss Air Force Museum, 410
Duisans, 347
Duisburg, 104
Duivenstein, 117
Dulag Luft, 104, 105
Dülmen, 335
Dungeness, 423
Dunkerque-Mardyck, 235
Dunkirk (Dunkerque), 210, 240, 241, 254, 262, 272, 276, 289, 316, 319, 331, 336, 338, 343, 344, 347, 348, 349, 353, 355, 356, 357, 359, 360, 361, 362, 367, 368, 369, 370, 371, 372, 373, 375, 376, 377, 379, 380, 381, 382, 383, 384, 385, 386, 388, 389-421 passim, 452, 457, 460, 468, 481
    Saint Octave (prison ship), 214
Dünstekoven, 118
Düren, 317
Durnbach, 349
Durrington, 511
Dury, 396, 442
Düsseldorf, 106, 127, 148, 158, 170, 171, 180, 309, 337, 343, 347, 418
    Marien Hospital, 290, 360, 476
Düsseldorf-Lohausen, 383
Duxford, 118, 399, 412, 437, 458
Dyck, 133
Dyle, River, 174, 230, 281

East Grinstead, 519
    Mount Noddy Cemetery, 519
Eastchurch, 412, 419, 431, 450
Ebblinghem, 348
Eben-Emael
    Fort see Fort Eben-Emael
    Museum, 247
Ecaussinnes-d'Enghien, 284
Échemines, 26, 182, 293, 320, 415, 416, 422, 423, 436, 438, 457
Eching, 102
Echteld, 181, 250
    Vogelenzangsebrug, 181
Echterdingen, 115
Echternach, 231
    Melickshoff Farm, 189
Ecly, 271
Ecogne, Froidmont Forest, 273
Ecqnes, 141, 351
Ecuires, 459
Ecury-sur-Coole, 120, 133, 162, 183, 233, 246, 271
Edesheim, 110
Edingen, 309
Eeklo, 124, 380
Eghezée, 265
Egmond aan Zee, 153
Ehingen, 278
Eich, 132
Eigenbilzen, 244
Eincheville, 116, 117

Eindhoven, 116, 300, 326, 342
Eisenach, 134
Elbeuf, 454, 469
Elesmes, 285
Életot, 461
Ell, 212
    'Kaaschboesch', 188
Ellewoutsdijk, 308
Elouges, 308, 309, 329
Elsenborn, 288, 299
Enschede, 299
Eltersdorf, 115
Emmerich, 234
Emptinne, 366
Enghien, 330
Ennemain, 364
Enschede, 299
Entrepagny, 97
Éperlecques, 379
Épernay, 71, 157, 317, 320, 322, 405, 415, 416, 417, 418, 424, 426, 450, 451, 456, 459, 470, 502, 521
    Auban-Moët Hospital, 333
    No. 4 CCS, 333
Épinal, 145, 188, 300, 327, 477, 489
Éplessier, 445
Ercourt, 401, 423
Erembodegem, Belgian Aviation Historical Association, 272, 312
Erfurt-Bindersleben, 142, 151, 154
Erin, 393
Eringerfeld, 124
Eringhem, 398
Erkelenz, 239
Erstein, 156
Esampolder, 223
Escarmain, 297, 366
Escaut, River, 292, 338, 367, 370
Esch, 35, 149, 277
Esch-sur-Alzette, 114
Eschwege, 118
Eschweiler, 262
Escombres-et-les-Chesnois, 273
Escorpain, 489
Escoublac, 492
Esmoulières, 189
Esnes, 326
Esperstädt, 150
Esquéheries, 305
Esquerdes, 348
Essen-Mülheim, 124, 129, 159, 488
Essene, 295
Essertaux, 99
Essey-lès-Nancy, 108
Essigny-le-Grand, 346, 400
Estaires, 376
Esternay, 464, 466, 467, 477
Estrées-la-Campagne, 407
Estrées-St-Denis, 325, 327, 340, 425, 427
Étain, 54-55, 106
Étain-Buzy, 188, 234
Étain-Rouvres, 14, 18-73 passim, 156, 175, 181
Étampes, 148, 295, 340, 364, 380, 413, 414, 418, 469, 478
Étampes-Montdésir, 416
Étampes-Montdidier, 395, 446, 456
Étaples, 338, 339, 345, 430, 496
Eton College, 509, 510
Étrépagny, 362, 426, 435
Etten-Leur, 260
Etting, 96
Ettinghausen, 459
Eu, 424
Eu forest, 400
Eupen, 290
Euskirchen, 205
Euten, 317
Eutingen, 106, 116, 123, 124, 128, 139, 162, 442
Evendorff, 153
Everberg, 316
Evere, 251, 404
    airmen's cemetery see Brussels-Evere (Pelouse d'Honneur Cemetery)
Evere-Haren (now Kwartier Koningin Elisabeth: Belgian HQ), 201

Evesham, 311
Évreux, 341, 346, 413, 425, 426, 435, 442, 452, 455, 458, 460, 464, *465*, 468, 469, 470, 471, 472, 496, 497
Évreux-Fauville, 401, 440, 447
Exeter, *402*
Eynatten, 131, *132*

Fagnon, 96
Faimes, 236, *237*
Fallencourt, 445
Fampoux Cemetery *see* Chili Trench Cemetery
Farges-en-Septaine, 469
Farnborough, 118
Fassberg, 118, 133
Faubourg de Luxembourg, Weimerskirch, 183
Faubourg Thuison, Abbeville, 364
Faumont, 378
Faux-Villecerf, 182, 256, 295, 322, *331*, 339, 345, 371, 398, 423, 458, 465, 469
Favarge, 297
Faverolles, 434
Favières, 'Les Trente Arpents', 416
Fay-aux-Loges, 476
Fayence, 139, 463
Fécamp, 346, *403*, 443, 455, 457, 461
Felixstowe, 276, 461
Feltwell, 339, 372, 398, 405
Fénétrange, 144
Fère-en-Tardenois, 443
Ferme Berthenay, Villers-Agron-Aiguizy/Romigny, 364
Ferme de Cruzis, 208
Ferme de Granlup, 188
Ferme de la Grand-Métairie, Tendu, 495
Ferme de la Hotte, 274
Ferme de Laihausen, Bettlach, 409
Ferme de l'Espérance, Nouvion-sur-Meuse, 247
Ferme de Merlan, 'Noue de Bétheniville', 265
Ferme de Moscou (Moscow Farm), 158, *159*, *283*
Ferme de Pommard, Chablis, 253
Ferme Remenoncourt, St-Pierre-villers, 262
Ferme Sainte-Marie, 145
Fermes des Termes, 477
Ferques, 393
Ferrières, 434
    La Planquette, 374
Ferrières-Dompierre, 432
Ferschweiler, 215, 280, 288, 307
Festieux, 304
Feurs, 481
Fiefs, 180
Figeonville, 446
Filton, 524
Finnevaux, 233
Finningley, 431
Finsing, 366
Fismes, 317, 450
Flée, 479
Fleury-sur-Andelle, 451
Flines, 376
Flines-lez-Raches, 309
Floing, 274, 295
Florennes, 376
Florenville, 280, 309, 345, 348
Flowerdown, 76
Flushing/Vlissingen, 304, 306, 308
Foetz, 298
Folies, 425
Fontaine Barbette, 297
Fontaine-au-Bois, 324
Fontaine-en-Dormois, 208
Fontaine-Française, 476
Fontaine-le-Sec, 441
Fontainebleau, 469
Fontenailles, 466
Fontenay-Torcy, 447
Fontenoy, 214, 447
Forbach, 124, *143*, *146*, 147
Forceilles, Ferme des Malheurs, 251

Forest-lez-Frasnes, 328
Forêt d'Arbois, 211
Forêt de Bizy, 458
Forêt de Bray, 447, 450
Forêt de Chaux, 189
Forêt de Compiègne, 447, 496
Forêt de Gault, 464, 465
Forêt de Harcholins, 241
Forêt de Hesse, 328
Forêt de Laigue, 308
Forêt de Meerdael, 293
Forêt de Mormal, 315, 321, 326, 335
Forêt de Nieppe, 102
Forêt de Nivelles, 304
Forêt de Samoussy, 336
Forêt de Sedan, 249
Forêt de Signy-l'Abbaye, 288
Forêt d'Halatte, 341, 453
Forêt d'Hanviller, 114
Forêt du Cherimont, 410
Forêt Saint-Michel, 259
Forêt-de-Gobain, 435
Forêt-de-la-Warndt, 476
Forêt-de-Moyeuvre, 376
Forge-Philippe, 277
Forges-les-Eaux, 304, 382, 435, 440, 443, 447, 449, 450, 451, 452
Formerie, 424, 435, 441, 449, 450, 452
Fort de Brimont, 291
Fort de Bruley, 107, 235
Fort de la Crèche, 352
Fort de la Pompelle, 285
    museum, 341
Fort du Chay, Royan, 499
Fort Eben-Emael, *73*, 213, *453*
Fort Mardyck, 399
Fort Nieuwersluis, 226
Fort Risban, *378*
Fort Spijkerboor, 95, 107
Fort Veldhuis Museum, Heemskerk, 236
Fort-de-Malmaison, *161*, *307*, 429, 434
Fort-Philippe, Gravelines, 414
Fossé, 296
Fosses-la-Ville, *252*
Fosses-Vitrival, 251
Foucacourt-en-Santerre, 158
Fougax-et-Barrineuf, 492
Fougerolles, 278
Fouquières-lès-Béthune, 233
Fourmies station, 'Étangs-des-Moines', 305
Fournet-Blancheroche, 419
Frahier-et-Châtebier, 252
Fraillicourt-Raillimont, 298
Francières, 440
Frankfurt, 207, 278, 458, 470, 481
Frankfurt-Main, 107, *161*, 212, 239, 410, 429
Frankfurt-Rebstock, 117, 120, 139, 151, 158, 163, 239
Frankfurt/Rhein-Main, 118, 121, 147, 148, 149, 158, 162, 327, *407*
Fransart, 432
Franvillers, 334
Frasne, 407
Frauenbrück Morelbusch, 326
Frechen, 147, 154
Freiburg, 98, 103, 134, 277, 342, 353, 414, 448
Fréjorgues, 237
Frelinghien, 104
Frémestroff, 470
Freneuse, 448
Freneuse-sur-Risle, 458
Frénois cemetery, 274
Frescaty, 314
Freschisdorf, 114
Fresney, 469
Fresnoy-Folny, 441
Fretin, 294
Frettemolle, 441
Frévent, 311, 312
Fricourt, 345, 376
Friedrichsfeld, 104
Friedrichshafen, 86, 152, 162
Friesen, 448

Friesland, 216
Frinton-on-Sea, 395
Frisoythe, 388
Fritzlar, 241
Fruges, 381
Fumay, 319, 344, 348
Furnes, 377, 379, 380, 392, 397, 398, 399, 404, 405, 409, 410
Fürstenfeldbruck, 99, 113, 263
Fürth, 107, 114, 123
Fusch, 117

Gablingen, 121, 153
Galatz, 82
Gamand-Fretin, 358
Gancourt, 452
Garancières-en-Drouais, 469
Garijp, 254
Garonne, River, 459, 473
Gasny, 455
Gassicourt, 432
Gâtineau, 334
Gatwick, 469
Gau-Bickelheim, 162
Gavrelle, 321, *517*
Gaye, *26*, *281*, 321, 371, 405, *415*
Geertruidenberg, 257, *258*
Gegelsberg, 117
Geinsheim, 308
Geiselbach-Neuss, 107
Geldern, 288
Geldersheim, 146
Gelnhausen, 118, 120, 300, 427
Gelsenkirchen-Buer, 124, 154
Gembes, 282
Gembloux, 238, 243, 254, 288, 298, 302, *304*, 319
Genech, 299
Genoa, 454, 457, 471
    Gulf of, 492
Genouilly, 395
Gentinnes, 290
Gercy, 315
Gernsheim, 110
Geroldstadt, 254
Gerolsheim, 206
Gerolstein, 206
Geudertheim, 99
Ghent, 175, 210, 214, 238, 249, 253, 262, *277*, 281, 301, 306, 334, 336, 393, 415
Giebelstadt, 124, 156
Giessen, 115, 139, 150, 154, 157, 278, 360, 381
Gilze-Rijen, 147, 193
Gimbrett, 373
Gingelom, 199
Gironde Estuary, 305
Gisors, 464
Gitsberg, *382*
Givet, 288, 302, 348, 384, 390, 411, 419, 422
Givonne, 266, 270, *271*, 272, 273, 274
Glabbeek, 236
Glaire-et-Villette, 270
Glamondans, 419
Glasgow, Victoria Hospital, 474
Glisy, 293
Goehence, 285
Goeferdinge, 294
Goersdorf, 118
Goesche Sas, 215
Göllheim, 104
Gondécourt, 206
Gonnelieu, 341
Goodwin Sands, 385, 405, 412
Gooimeer, the, 353
Göppingen, 142, 493
Goslar, *110*
Gosselies, *85*, 148, 200
Gossoncourt (Goetsenhoven), 196, *200*
Gotha, 142, 156, 158, 160, 170
Göttingen, 118, 150
Gouda, 236
    Van Iterson Ziekenhuizen, 226
Goudswaard, 209
Gourdinne, 273
Gournay-en-Bray, 447, 451, 467

Gournay-sur-Aronde, 416
Gouvieux, 374, 425
Gouy, 293
Gouzeaucourt, 366
Goyencourt, 303
Graincourt-lès-Havrincourt, 364
Grammont, 175, 330
Grand Bois, 392
Grand-Crochet, 410
Grand-Rosière-Hottomont, 206, *279*
Grandpré, 278, 290, 300
Grandrieu, 290
Grandville, Café des Essart, 234
Grandvilliers, 435, 441, 450
Grange-au-Bois, 327
Grattepanche, Calmant Wood, 400
Grau, 496
Graux, 316
Graval, 148
Gravelines, 355, 356, 359, *361*, 362, 366, 370, 375, 377, 379, 381, 389, 390, 404, 411, 412, 415
    Fort-Philippe, 414
Gravesend, 379, 392, *399*, 412, 423
Gray, 475
Grécourt, 442
Grémevillers, 334
Gremonval, 437
Gremsdorf, 144
Grenoble, 499
Grevillers, 313
Grignan, 499
Grijpskerke, 165
Grimbergen, 261
Grisy-Suisnes, 470
Groede, 343
Groote Keeten, 254
Gros-Caillou, *430*, 493
Gross Dechsendorf, 133
Gross Zehlen, 138
Gross-Gerau/Wallerstädten, 107
Gross-Heubach, 102
Gross-Langenheim, 136
Gross-Mackenstedt, 209
Gross-Ostheim, 353, 496
Grosselfingen, 95, 135
Grostenquin, 145, 153, 154
Grote Boom Polder, Sint-Kruis, 284
Grote Haar, Gorinchem, 242
Güdingen, 95
Guéblange-lès-Dieuze, 95, 189, 234
Guernica, *276*
Guernsey, 487
Guerville, 445
Guessling-Hémering, 476
Guildford, 481
Guillotière Cemetery, Lyon, 160
Guines, 362, 388
Guise, 260, 265, 325, 347, 353, 358, 360, 365, 376, 384, 396, 409, 422, 423, 429
Guise-Nord, 434
Guizancourt, 447
Guny, 334
Gury, 333
Gütersloh, 125, 164, 209, 300, *383*
Gymnich, 139

Haamstede, 191, 193, 250, 261
    see also Units, Dutch (Vliegschool Haamstede)
Haarlemmermeerpolder, the, 159, 261
Hadstock, 437
Hage, 96
Haguenau, 98, 141
Hahenberg forest, 360
Haillicourt, 353
Hainfeld-Edenkoben, 117
Hal, 330
Halen, 148
Halle, 296
Hallu, 429
Halton, RAF Apprentice Training School, 76, *511*
Ham, 309, 334, 335, 392, 418, 434, 440
Ham-sous-Varsberg, 157

Hamel, 341
Hamm, 329, 360
Hamme-Mille, 267
Hamminkeln, 239
Hanau-am-Main, 156, 158
Hanauer-Haus, Rückersbach, 376
Hannogne-Saint-Rémy, 297, 320
Hannover, 154, 360, 459
Hannover-Langenhagen, 342, 459, 499
Hannut-Thisnes, 196
Hans, 352
Hansahafen-Nuremberg, 115
Happegarbes, 314
Haraucourt, 'Fond-Wazelle', 245
Harcy, 288
Hardecourt-au-Bois, 340
Harelbeke, 359
Haren see Evere-Haren
Hargimont, 262, 307, 347
Harlingen, 465
Harol, 145
Harpenden, 104
Harsum, 136
Hartennes-et-Taux, 314
Harthausen, 107
Hartmannsdorf, 107
Harwich, 395, 460
Hary, 314
Haslach, 459
Hasnon, 329
Hasselt, 248
Hastière-Lavaux, 289
Hattencourt, 425
Hattigny, 241
Haucourt, 345
Haucourt-la-Rigole, 133, 180
Haudimont-Manheulles, 94
Haumont-lès-Lachaussée, 119
Haute-Croix, 279
Hauterive, 499
'Hauteurs le Christ', nr Bouillon, 246
Havrincourt, 364
Hawkinge, 233, 310, 330, 339, 344, 345, 348, 349, 351, 355, 356, 362, 370-371, 372, 373, 378, 379, 390, 395, 398, 399, 405, 406, 412, 419, 423, 431, 437, 446, 450, 490
Haybes, 298
Haynecourt, 414
Hazebrouck, 142, 319
Hazerswoude, 253
Heemskerk, Fort Veldhuis Museum, 236
Heidelberg, 476
Heierhoeve, 98
Heiligenbeil, 127
Heillecourt, 117
Heilly, 334
Heinrichsdorf, 479
Heiteren, 380
Hekelgem, 295
Helmingen, 141
Hemiksen, 286
Hemmes, 134
Hemroulle, 144, 145
Hemswell, 233, 461
Hemweiler, 280
Hendon, 8
  RAF Museum, 344
Henegouwen, 312
Hennemont, 278
Hennuyères, 296
Herbecourt, 425
Herbéviller, 93, 252
Herbigny, 456
Herbouville, 437, 445, 463
Herent, 277
Herenthals, 286
Héricourt, Schwob factory, 410
Hérie-la-Vieville, 275
Herkingen, 184
Hermeskeil, 162, 208
Herméville-en-Woëvre, 341
Hervillers, 451
Herxheim, 152
Hesdigneul, 210
Hesdin, 340, 344, 371, 372, 430, 434
Hesepe, 126

Heston, 109, 137, 162, 480
Het Lange Duin cemetery, 194
Het Zoute, Zeebrugge, 365
Heuilley le Grand, 475
Heverlee War Cemetery, Leuven (Louvain), 244, 245, 257, 282, 513, 516
Hiesse, 487
Hildesheim, 254
Hilversum, 171, 193
Hinacourt, 306
Hingene, 196, 233, 286, 306
Hirson, 242, 297, 308, 321, 325, 330, 353, 384, 385, 419, 422, 423, 430, 435, 443, 460
Hirtzfelden, 133
Hirzenhaff Farm, 183
Hochheim, 104
Höchst-Main, 133
Hockenheim, 140
Hodeige, 248
Hoeilaart, 290
Hoepertingen, 246
Hoeven, Oude Dijk, 262
Hofheim, 165
Holmfirth, 349
Holsbeek, Van Tilt Farm, 286, 287
Holsteiner-Heide, 138
Hombleux, 442
Hombières, 206
Homburg-Budange, 127
Homburg-Saar, 171
Hondschoote, 381, 404
Honfleur, 456
Honington, 349, 469
Hönningen, 97
Hoofdplaat, 306
Hoog Huis, 348
Hoogerheide, 286
Hooglede, 382
Hoogstade, 378
Hook of Holland (Hoek van Holland), 194, 218, 220, 227, 243
  General Cemetery, 181
Hopferstadt, 132
Hoppstädten, 107, 131, 144, 162, 164, 167, 239, 253
Hopsten, 115, 160
Horb-am-Neckar, 239
Hornchurch, 31, 304, 343, 345, 349, 356, 362, 373, 379, 385, 386, 391, 399, 406
Hornisgrinde, 167
Hornoy-le-Bourg, 435, 445, 450
Hotton War Cemetery, 181, 232, 256, 272
Houdancourt, 447
Houppeville, 424
Hourtin, 459, 488, 492, 497, 499
Hourtin-Louley, 492, 497
Houssay, 437, 445, 464, 472
Houville-en-Vexin, 446
Huizingen, 290
Huldange, 208
Huldenberg, 283
Hulste, 212, 213
Humes, 475
Huy, 247
Hyères, 419, 462, 463, 465, 467, 475, 494

Iburg, 152
Idar-Oberstein, 164
IJmuiden, 151, 223, 226, 253, 255
IJssel, 174
IJsselmeer/Zuyder Zee, 209, 216
IJsselstein, 353
Ile d'Ouessant, 94
Illesheim, 145, 148
Illois, 135
Immenstaad, 138
Ingelmunster, 124, 210
Ingeweiler, 470
Ingolstadt, 113, 212
Ippesheim, 99, 147, 165, 288, 300
Ipswich, 461
Isère, River, 499
Isigny, 305
Isle of Wight, 497
Isles of Scilly, 510

Issoudin, 424
Izel-les-Equerchin, 332

Jamoigne, 278
Jargeau, 476, 479
Jaulgonne, 314
Jaulny, 189
Jausselette, 'Le Gibet', 279
Jemelle, 337
Jemeppe-sur-Meuse, 124
Jeneffe, 236, 299
Jersey, 457, 458, 480, 494, 514
  St Brelade's Churchyard, 514, 519
Jesau, 160
Jever, 116, 119, 147
Jodenville, 212
Jodoigne, 257, 267
Joinville, 479
Jolivet, 156
Jonkerbos Cemetery, 372
Joux forest, 123
Jouy-sur-Morin, 171
Jülich-Aachen, 381
Jully-sur-Sarce, 408
Juniville, 456
Jussey, 476
Jussy, 337
Juvincourt, 167

Kaarst, 167
Kaggevinne, 233
Kahlenberg, 113
Kagerplassen, 209
Kain, 339
Kaiserslautern, 208, 388
Kampel, 213
Kampenhout, 298
Kanne, 213, 231
Kapelle, Zuid-Beveland, 239
Kapelle-op-den-Bos, 215
Kapellerlaan, 117
Karethal, 144
Karlsruhe, 96, 100, 328, 493, 499
Karlsruhe-Durlach, 316
Karum, 115
Kassel, 354
Kassel-Rothwesten, 148, 150, 160
Kassel-Waldau, 112
Kasteel van Hors, Holsbeek, 287
Kasterlee, 277
Katten, 171
Kattowitz, 125
Katwijk, 221, 222, 225
Katzweiler, 208
Kaufbeuren, 140
Kédange-sur-Canner, 162
Keerbergen, 277
Keighley, 42
Kemble, 511
Kemmel, 254
Kenley, 175, 301, 310, 351, 391, 398, 497
Kerk-Avezaath, 221
Kessel, 180
Kesselt, 213
Kettenis, 196
Kezelberg, 362
Kijkduin, 191, 194, 223
Kilverstone Hall, Thetford, 395
Kintzheim, 360
Kirchberg, 180, 290, 441
Kirchberg-Hunsrück, 100
Kirchberg-Maisborn, 107, 441
Kirchgoens, 156
Kirchhellen, 165, 290
Kirkcaldy, Dysart Cemetery, 511
Kirton-in-Lindsey, 255
Kirtorf, 145
Kitzingen, 116, 136
Klein Antwerpen, 238
Klemskerke, 147, 148
Kleve, 286
Klevendeich, 116
Klusserath, 107
Knokke, 148
Knokke-Zoute, 199
Kochem, 212
Koenigsmacker, 120
Koersel, 278

Kohlstädt, 148
Koksijde, 115, 410
Kollweiler, 140
Kompfeld, 248
Kortenberg, 286
Kortrijk, see Courtrai
Krefeld, 140, 156, 162, 165, 167, 253, 301, 382, 402
Kreuznach, 279
Kuhnerwitz, 121
Kulmbach, 104

La Baule Escoublac, Nantes, 106
La Besace, 'Le Fond de Bériotte', 37, 120, 122
La Bouëxière, 423
La Boule, 473
La Boule-les-Pins, 473
La Bouteille, 275
La Capelle, 290, 307, 326, 329
La Cassine, 270
La Chapelle, 293, 470
La Chapelle-Moutils, 465
La Charité sur Loire, 478
La Chaux-de-Fonds, 120
La Colombe, 451
La Croix Sainte Jaunisse, 325
La Croix-Quignon, 341
La Fère, 306, 314, 321, 364, 395
La Fère-Courbes, 117, 248, 298, 301
La Ferme Blanche, 124
La Ferté-Gaucher, 274, 352, 353, 358, 364, 380, 387, 417, 426, 466
La Ferté-Milon, 316, 453
La Ferté-sous-Jouarre, 359, 451
La Ferté-Vidame, 472
La Graveline, 301
La Haie Fouattière, 490
La Horgne, 333
La Houssoye, 467
La Loge, 334, 407
La Loge Rosette, 259
La Londe, 426
La Louvière, 232
La Mailleraye-sur-Seine, 497
La Malmaison, 239, 405
La Mare, 458, 461
La Mée-sur-Seine, 479
La Métairie, 496
La Neuville-à-Maire, 270, 358
La Neuville-aux-Haies, 285
La Neuville-aux-Tourneurs, 297
La Neuville-en-Tourne-à-Fuy, 265, 320
La Neuville-sous-Monfort, 434
La Noue, 466
La Pallice, 471, 490
La Panne see De Panne
La Petite-Pierre, 145
'La Pierre Poiret', Pontfaverger, 282
'la Planchette', Aubenton/Ribeauvillé, 242
La Poterie, 447
La Rivière-Drugeon, 408
La Rochelle, 83, 480, 490, 492
La Vieille-Lyre, 470
La-Ferté-St-Aubin, 429
La-Roche-en-Ardenne, 335
La-Vallée-aux-Blé, 314
Laboissière, 171
Lac de Paladru, 409
Lachen-Speyerdorf, 107, 115, 125, 127, 139, 140, 147, 156, 164, 396
Lafauche, 470
Lafelt, 238
Lagny-le-Sec, 470
Lagny-sur-Marne, 417
Lahr, 156
Laigné, 457
Laigneville, 340
Lamaronde, 444
Lambres-lès-Douai, 358
Lambus, 347
Lämershagen, 149
Lamontzée, 278
Lamotte-Brebière, 407
Lamotte-Buleux, 445
Lamotte-Warfusée, 427

Lamouilly, 288
Lanaken, 244, 246, *516*
Lançon, 496
Landau, 162, 346
Landen, 257
Landrecies, 260, 309, 310, *313*, 314, *321*
Landstuhl, 126
Laneuville-au-Pont, 139
Laneuville-sur-Meuse Communal Cemetery, 270, *509*, *527*
Laneuvilleroy, 425
Langemark, 383, 386, 409
Langendiebach, 153, 162, 168, 170, 239, 380, 427
Langeweg, 262
Langres, 429, 470, 475, 476, 478
Langweiler, 104
Lannoy, 312
Lanvéoc-Poulmic, 117, 346, 380, 456, 488
Laon, 273, 292, 305, 335, 398, 422, 428, 429, 435, 449, *450*, 452, 460, 461, 467, 493
  hospital Foch, 461
  'Semilly', 433
Laon-Athies, 441
Laon-Chambry, 188, 234, 259, 274, 285, 297
Laon-Couvron, 188, 189, 275, 285, 286
Lapugnoy Military Cemetery, *510*
Latinne, 285
Laucourt, 440
Lauf a.d. Pegnitz, 139
Launstroff, 100
Lauterecken, 95
Laval, 472, 473
Laverrière, 440
Laversine, 374
Laviéville, 183
Lawarde-Mauger, 334
Le Bois-Long, 475
Le Bourget, 98, 297, 306, 325, 334, 340, 358, 440, 461, 489
Le Cannet-des-Maures, 477
Le Cateau, 302, 307, 308, 310, 311, 312, 313, 319, 322, 346, 360, 366, 422, 430
Le Chesne, 120, 280, 301, 376
Le Culot, 237
Le Fraity, 290
'Le Grand Terrier', Crouy-en-Thelle/Morangles, 416
Le Havre, 12, *13*, 14, 30, 327, 339, 418, 426, 443, 446, 449, 450, 453, 455, 456, 457, 459, *460*, 462, 463, 467
Le Loriot, 475
Le Luc, *426*, 471, 477
  Ferme Moulin Rouge, 477
Le Manoir, 458
Le Mans, 403, *435*, 443, 445, 450, 455, 457, 461, 463, 469, 472, 473, 478, 487, 498
  Café de l'Hippodrome, *436*
Le Mée-sur-Seine, 476
'Le Monument', Montescourt-Lizerolles, 306
Le Paradis, 458
Le Patiou, 495
Le Quesnel, 303, 380
Le Quesnel-Aubry, 400, 434
Le Quesnoy, 310, 325, 326, 327, 343
Le Quesnoy-Vertain, 298
Le Thour, 456
Le Touquet, 120, 127, 128, 141, 175, 183, 232, 304, 312, *406*, 427
  Golf Hospital, 275
Le Transloy, 414
Le Tréport, 311, 338, 346, 424, 430, 435, 437, 443, 446, 449, 455, 457, 458
Le Vallon, 455
Le Vernon, 83
Le-Grand-Lucé, 356
Le-Grand-Pré, 305
Le-Val-de-Guéblange, *511*
Lecaude, 481
Léchelle, 466

Lechfeld, 207, 316, 360, 453, 462
l'Ecluse, 262
Lee-on-Solent, RAF Coastal Command HQ, 77
Leerbroek, van Buuren's Farm, 194
Leeuwarden, 499
Léglise, 162, 163
Leiden, 228, 236
Leiden-Zuid, 221
Leipheim, 107, 136, 141, 148, 170
Leipzig, 381
Leisele, 396
Lek, 174
Lemmershagen, 116
Lens, 267, 330, 339, *361*, 366
Lepelaar Polder, 241
Les Andelys, 452, 455, 456, 457, 458, 460, 465, 468, 472, 473
'Les Carmélites', Moronvilliers, 451
Les Clérimois, 161
Les Grandes-Armoises, 272, 280
Les Grandes-Chapelles, 294, 321, 349, 371, 378, 390
Les Mefrequennes à Haussez, 447
Les Minières, 469
Les Petites-Dalles, *403*
Les Pieux, 486
Les Riebles, near Lévigny, 395
'Les Trixnes', Bas-Oha, 251
Les Woieries, 284
Les-Corvées-les-Yys, 464
Les-Grandes-Ventes, 427
Lesges, 447
Lesquin, 347, 358
  see also Lille-Seclin; Vendeville
Lesquin-Enchémont, *139*
Lessay, 488
Lesse, 112
Létanne, 215
Leugnies-Grandieu, 'Waremme', 206
Leurville, 477
Leuven/Louvain, 237, 253, 255, 268, 278, 288
  Heverlee War Cemetery, 244, *245*, 257, 282, *513*, *516*
Leuze, 261, 262
Lezennes, 358
Lézignan, 284, 478, 494
Liancourt, 453
Liart, 296, 324, 348
Libourne, 426
Libramont, 348, 384, 418
Lichtaart, 277
Liedern-bei-Bocholt, 242
Liège/Lüttich, 131, *132*, 252, 288, 290, 309, 342, 431
  Hospital des Anglais, 244
  Robermont Cemetery, *133*
Lienen, 104
Lier, 239
Lignières-Orgères, 458
Ligny-lès-Aire, 'Le Fief', 188
Lihons, 303
Lijssenthoek, 388
Lille/Rijsel, 174, 275, *304*, 309, 319, 327, 328, 329, 335, 347, 352, 358, 359, 361, 362, 375, 396, 413, 496
Lille-Bondues, *139*
Lille-Marcq, *139*, 181, 243, 245, 256, 257, 268, 272, 283, 294, 310, 312-313, 320, 321, 322
Lille-Quatre-Ville, *139*
Lille-Ronchin, *139*, 148, 168, 293, 311, 320, 339, 348
Lille-Seclin (now Lesquin), *78*, *109*, 110, 131, *138*, *139*, 144, 150, 153, 157, 168, 171, 175, 181, *205*, 210, 232, 256, 283, 294, *303*, 304, 310, 312, 319, 320, 322
Limburg, 216
Limésy, 362
Limoges, 487
Lindtse Benedendijk, 239
Linge, River, 181
Lingen, 254
Linger
  'Al Eisenbunnslinn', 181
  'An der Jenken', 181
Liniers, 309

Linsmeau, 251
Lintach, 106
Lintgen-Luxembourg, 288
Linton-on-Ouse, 356
Liomer, 435
Lipetzk, 87
Lippspringe, 145, 151, 218, 222, 225, 226, 254
Lippstadt, 107, 216, 221, 347
Lisieux, 481
Lissay-Lochy, 466
Lissy, 158
Little Mongeham, 373
Littleport hospital, 437
Littlestone, 419
Llandrindod Wells, *520*
Lobith, 162
Lochem, 222
Locquignol, 315
Loddenheide, 151, 216, 223, 227, 228, 476
Loeuilly, 364
Loge-Wactiaux, 456
Lognes-Émerainville, 341, 417, 425
Loire, River, *457*, 468, 471, 476, 479
Loire Estuary, 478, *481*
Loivre, 458
Lombardzijde, *374*, 380, 387
Lommel, German War Cemetery, *163*, *240*, *263*, 299, *309*, *318*, *329*, 342, *382*, 383
Londinières, 441
London, 292, 319, *387*, 435, 480
  Pool of, 367
  Science Museum, *406*
Longchamps, 261
Longlier, 159, 162
Longpont, 447, 448
Longueil-Ste-Marie, 336
Longuenesse, *348*, 385
Longueville-sur-Scie, 437
Longuyon, 360, 465
Longwy, 360
Lonneval, 479
Lons-le-Saulnier, 413
Lonzée, *251*
Loosduinen, 222
  Escamppolder, the, 214
Lorient, 490
Loudon, 487
Louhans, 479
Louvain *see* Leuven
Louviers, 454
Louvignies, 272
Louvigny, 113
Loxéville, 127
Loyettes, 407
Lubbeek, 254
Lübeck-Blankensee, 139
Lubey, *32*, 33, 34, *114*
Luce, River, 334
Luchy, *335*, *336*, 337
Lucy-sur-Yonne, 479
Ludwigsburg, 162, 336
Lumes, 269
Lüneburg, 118
Lunéville, 156
Lure-Malbouhans, 103, 240, 387
Lüttich/Liège, 316
Luxembourg, 174, 175, *243*, 288, 289, 298
Luxeuil, 83, 165, 189, 235, 249, 252, 298, 300
Luzerne, St Anna-Spital, 300
Lympne, 311, 312, 319, 320, 321, *332*, *339*, 345, 356, 371, 378, 385, 390, 398, 405, 407, 423, 452
Lyon, *82*, 404, 407, 410, 411, 413, 448, 479, 489
Lyon-Bron, 82, 83, 150, 160, 189, 212, 240, 305, 407, 414, 424, 481
Lyon-Satolas, 407
Lyons forest, 451
Lys, River, 361, 362, 370, 377, 389
Lys canal, 326

Maas, River, 174, 180, 192, 206, 216, 217, 220, 227, 236, 244
  see also Meuse, River

Maasdijk, 219
Maashaven, 227
Maasmechelen, 133
Maastricht, *73*, 162, 205, *215*, 216, 230, *231*, 232, 233, 234, 235, *237*, *238*, 242, *243*, 247, 248, 251, 325, *394*, *512*, *513*, *515*
Machault, 253
  'Mont Bernard', 364
Macon, 279, 479
Macquenoise, 'Four Mathot', 305
Macquigny, 305
Made, *258*
Magdeburg-Ost, 158, 171
Maginot Line, 319, 443, 457, 471
Mailly-Maillet, 142
Mainbressy, 293
Maing, 314
Mainvault, 268
Mainz/Mayenne, 105, 106, 336, 360, 429, 432
Mainz-Finthen, 154
Mairy, 274
Maisach, 123, 462
Maisborn, 106, 262, 288
Maisebeck, 140
Maison-Blanche, *426*, 462
Maison-Rouge, 235
Maisoncelle-et-Villers, 253
Maizborn, 290
Maizey, 419
Malai camp, *70*
Malandry, 284
Maldegem, 259, 286, *380*, 381
Malicorne, Mans, 400
Malincourt, 326
Malleville-les-Grès, 461
Malmédy, 280, 353, 396
Malmsheim, 402
Malmy, 279, 280
Malo-les-Bains, *397*, *411*
Mamolle-Remicourt, *147*, 148
Manching, 139
Mandel Canal, 374
Mannekensvere, 402
Mannheim, 239, 252, 279, 289, *351*, 382, 459
Mannheim-Ostheim, 442
Mannheim-Sandhofen, 110, 112, 117, 120, 121, 124, 140, 147, 149, 151, 152, 156, 159, 160, 162, 163, 170, 263, 288, 456
Mannheim-Stadt, 161, 382
Manoncourt, 121
Manston, 175, 184, 229, 248, 257, 310, 322, *323*, *331*, 332, 345, 349, 351, 356, 357, 362, 379, 386, 390, 391, *392*, 398-399, *406*, 412, 416, 419, 431, 437, 446, *458*, 487, 490
Mantes, 469
Mantes-Gassicourt, 324, 352
Mantes-la-Jolie, 400, 429, 432
Marbeuf, 470
Marchavenne, 308
Marche, 316
Marchélepot, 424, 425
Marchovelette, 235
Marcilloles, 413
Marcilly-sur-Seine, 168
Marck *see* Calais-Marck
Marcoing, 159, 425
Marcq *see* Lille-Marcq
Marcq-en-Baroeul, 476
Marcy, 96
Mardeuil, Ferme St-Antoine, 418
Mardié, 476
Mardyck, 276, *305*, 306, 340, 358, 399, 411, 415
  see also Dunkerque-Mardyck
Marennes, 479
Mares-sur-Matz, 341
Mareuil-en-Dôle, 448
Mareuil-sur-Ay, 417
Margate, 386
  Hospital, 379
Marham, 339, 398
Marienhave, 129
Marienloh, 159
Marignane, 496
Marigny, 497

Marissel, 425, 426
Marne, River, 314, 443, 457, 460, 463
Marne valley, 461
Maroeuil, 302
Marquain, 254
Marquéglise, 402
Marquette, 335
Marquoin, 326, 332
Mars-sous-Bourcq, 424
Marseille, 82, 404, 409, 411, 414, 474, 496
    Mazargues War Cemetery, 244
Martelange, 206, 212
Martigny, 275
    Musée du Souvenir Militaire de Thiérache, 231
Martigny-les-Gerbonvaux, 94, 306, 419, 456
Martincourt, 408
Martlesham Heath, 257, 386, 395, 412, 446, 465
Marville, 380
Marx, 138, 158, 159, 211, 300
Marzeville, 162
Marzia, 116
Masnuy-St-Jean, 241
Mastaing, 239
Mattenwalddorf, 156
Matton, 'Bois-la-Dame', 280
Maubeuge, 249, 267, 274, 275, 282, 300, 301, 302, 310, 317, 319, 329
Maubeuge-Elesmes, 235
Maubray, Ribeaucourt Farm, 312
Mauden, 124
Maupertus, 419
Mayenne, *see* Mainz
Mazarith de Vouziers, 263
Mazarques, 487
Méaulte, 188, 325
Meaux, 147, 314, 431, 447
Meaux-Esbly, 296, 297, 376, 417
Mechelen, 130, 288
Meerheide, the, 235
Méharicourt, 112, 127, *132, 152,* 170, 180, 231, 256, 293, 303
Meigneux, 444
Melden, 381
Melsbroek, *197, 201*
Melun, 415, 469, 475
Memmingen, 111, 114, 138
Ménil-Lépinois, 267, *507*
Menin, 361, 384
Mennessis, 429
Mentebrück, 160
'Menu Champ', Mont-Laurent road, 247
Merbes-Sainte-Marie, 275
Mercin-et-Vaux, 373
    La Chaussée Romaine, 446
Mere, 249
Merendree, 213
Merey, 464
Merl, 183
Merris, 392
Merseburg, 99
Méru, 342, 447
Merville, 102, 108, *109,* 110, *175,* 180, 232, 245, 256, 267, 282, 293, 294, 303, 304, 310, 311, 312, 313, 319, 320, 321, 322, *331,* 332, 335, 344, 345, *351,* 353, 448, 469, 479
Merwedepolder, the, 239
Merzhausen, 158
Merzig, 99, 100, 251
Mesbrecourt, 434
Mesnil-Lépinois, 320
Mesnil-Trois-Fêtus, 392
Metlach, 360
Mettet, 96
Mettmann, 393
Metz, 22, 34, 35, 43, *46,* 52, *58,* 71, 107, 133, 144, 148, 156, 163, 278, 346, 434, 443, 488
    Chambieres French National Cemetery, *518*
    Leghouest military hospital, 207, 208, 240, 278

Metz-Frescaty, 113, 148, 154
Meuse, River, *73,* 230, 234, *237,* 255, 259, *266, 267,* 268, 269, 271, 281, 302, 310, 330, 338, 339, 344, 348, 349, 377, 384, 397, 419, 420, 457, 458, *508, 518*
    see also Maas, River
Meuse valley, 325, 449
Meux, 214
Meyerode, 396
Mézières *see* Charleville-Mézières
Middelkerke, 388
Middenmeer, 193
Middle Wallop, 494
Middlekerke, 414
Mignault, 'Champ de Maubeuge', 284
Milan, 454
Mildenhall, 313, 356, 458
Minehead, Dunster Beach, 487
Minster, 373
Mions, 407
Miramas, 475
Miraumont, 349
Missy-sur-Aisne, 334, 433, 447, 451
Misy-sur-Yonne, 305
Mitry Mory, 461
Moerbeke, 237, 249, 259
Moerdijk, 216, 217, *220,* 261
Moers, 139
Moeskroen, 335
Moiremont, 119, 120, *126*
Moissac, *324*
Moisy, 437, 455, 458, 461, 464
Mokotów, 82
Mol, 286
Moliens, 429
Molliens-au-Bois, 374
Momignies, 274
Monceau, 429, 434
Monceau-le-Neuf-et-Faucouzy, 380, 429
Monceau-le-Waast, 165
Moncerf, 445
Mönchengladbach, 116, 140, 148, 153, 158, 159, 165, 188, 206, 233, 290, 335, 343, 459
Monchy-Breton, 392, 402
Monchy-Lagache, 133, 256, 267
Mondicourt, 124
Mons, 210, 274, 281, 303
    Castillon Hill, 312
Mons-en-Chaussée, *78,* 132, 148, 160, 162, 165, 181, 429
Monster, 227
Mont Dieu, 272
    Military Cemetery, 271
Mont St Jean Cemetery, 181
Mont-Dourlers, 285
Mont-St Éloi, 352
Mont-St-Martin, 208
Mont-sur-Marchienne, 'Campagne du Pige', 249
Montagne du Larmont, 290
Montagne Noire, 459
Montagnon, 305
Montargis, 321
Montargis-Vimory, 417
Montbard, 481
Montceaux, 305
Montceaux-lès-Provins, 466
Montcornet, 285, 290, 296, 297, *298,* 302, 324, 339, 461
Montdidier, 188, 296, 297, 360, 422, 424, 425, 432, 446, 453
Montecouvez, 366
Montélimar, 499
Montenaken, 4 Statiestraat, 199
Montepilloy, 417
Montereau, 305
Montescourt, 306
Monthermé, 281, 285, 293, 294, 295, 348
    Croix-Sainte-Anne Cemetery, 273
Monthéty, 417
Monthiers, 419, 456
Monthois, 274
Montierchaume, 416
Montignies-le-Tilleul, 315, *318*
Montlhéry, 447

Montmédy, 465
Montmirail, 419, 464, 465, 466, 467
Montmort, 467
Montpellier, *82,* 306
Montpensier, 499
Montplonne, 240
Montreuil, 338, 339, 343, 344, 345, 347, 381, 396, 441
Montzéville, 328
Moordrecht, 228
Moors, 140
Moorsele, 272, 304, 310, 323
Moorslede, 381
Mopertingen, 215
Morangles, 416
Morch, 453
Morchain, 429
Morhange, 99, 105, 121, 143, 145, 154, 157
Morkhoven, 213
Morlancourt, 400
Mormal, 298
    see also Forêt de Mormal
Mornay, *475,* 476
Moronvilliers, 142, 153, 451
Morsaint, 262
Morsbach, 95
Mortagne, 481
Morte-Fontaine, Ferme de Vaubéron, 440
Morval, 349
Morvillers, 433
Moscou-Ferme (Moscow Farm) *see* Ferme de Moscou
Mössingen, 476
Mosterveld, 238
Mötzingen, 156
Moulin Coquet, 259
Moulins, 466
Moulle, 376
Mourmelon-le-Grand, *140,* 175, 181, 188, 208, 209, 232, 247, 253, 254, 259, 268, 273, 289, 290, 294, 356, 362, 378, 398, 451, 466
Mours-Saint-Eusèbe, 499
Mouzon, *266, 268,* 269, 272, 277
Moy-de-l'Aisne, 306
Moyencourt, 123, 302
Moyenneville, 364
Muellen, 118
Mühlhausen, 135
Munich, 414, 419
Munich-Oberwiesenfeld, 150
Munich-Riem, 142, 212
Munkzwalm, 210
Münster, 133, 252, 409, 476
Münster-Handorf, 106, 107, 110, 134, 136, 145, 148, 154, 210
Münster-Loddenheide, *110,* 117, 125, 138, 165, 210, 224
Müntekoven, 140

Nampcel, 328
Namps, 434
Namur, 234, 255, 257, 260, 266, 281, 282, 285, 290, 302, 335, 338, 349
Nancy, 23, 97, 102, 109, 111, 131, 145, 161, 188, 371, 476, 481
    Sédillot Hospital, 456
Nancy Azelot, 296
Nancy-Essey, 151
Nangis, 274, 296, 314, 416, 429
Nantes, *58, 289,* 294, 312, 427, 455, *463,* 468, 469, *471,* 473, 478, 480, 486, 487, *490,* 495
    see also Château Bougon
Nanteuil, 315
Naves, 326
Naz-Dar Cemetery, Neuville St Vaast, 297
Néchin, 214
Nederweert, 206
Neerbeek, 251
Neerharen, 244
Neerhespen, *199,* 237
Neerwinden, 256
Nellingen, 141, 459
Nes, 154
Nesle-Hodeng, 441
Nesles-la-Montagne, 447

Neue Bremm concentration camp, *351*
Neuenkamp, 265
Neuenkirchen, 131
Neufchâteau, 162, *163,* 189, 246, 278, 299, 300, 307, 337, 376, 477
Neufchâtel-en-Bray, *383,* 435, *440,* 441, 448, 449
Neufchâtel-Hardelot, 345
Neufchâtel-sur-Aisne, 362, 415, 451, 460
Neuhausen, 98, 164, 242, 278, 489
Neulanderfeld, 360
Neumünster, 121, 139
Neunkirchen, 163
Neuss, 233, 318
Neustadt, 458
Neuville-Coppegueule, 382, *383*
Neuville-St-Vaast, 335
    'La Targette' French Military Cemetery, 364
    Naz-Dar Cemetery, 297
Neuvilly, *321*
Neuwied, 336, 342
Nevers-Sermoise, 117, 240, 429, 475, 478, 497
Newdigate War Memorial, *503*
Newmarket, 339, *395*
Nez de Jobourg, 138
Nicey-sur-Aire, 260
Nidda, 124, 145
Niderhoff, 241
Niederbreisach, 277, 288
Niedermendig, 106, 156, 308
Niederwerren, 139
Niergnies *see* Cambrai-Niergnies
Nieuport, 313, 314, 367, 379, 382, 383, *386,* 388, *393,* 394, 395, 397, 398, 399, 402, 405
Nieuport Canal, 398
Nieuw Lekkerland, 261
Nieuw-en-Sint-Joostland, 307
Nieuwerkerk, 193
Nieuweschans, 102
Nieuwkerken-Waas, 259, 277, *286*
Nieuwkoop, 236
Nieuwlandse Polder, 227, 248
Nieuwvliet, 343
Nièvre, River, 96
Nijmegen, 211
Nîmes-Garons, 498
Ninove, 268, 281, 300, 309, 330
Niort, *324*
Nivelles, *85,* 94, 165, 196, *198,* 277, 285, 304, 319
    see also Forêt de Nivelles
Nives, 206
Nivillers, 448, 489
Noailles, 447
Nogent-l'Abbesse, 453
Nogent-le-Rotrou, 470
Nogent-sur-Seine, 465, 466, 469
Noirval, 268
Noisseville, 52, 144
Nolléval, 443
Nomain, 322
Noordgouwe, 193
Noordhoek, 362
Noordpolder, 224
Noorpolder, the, 226
Norderney, 241
Nordhausen, 106, 153, 159, 160, 164, 165, 462
Nordholz, 254
Norrent-Fontes, *10, 12, 13, 14,* 18, 103, 109, 237, 268, 277, 297, 303, 306, 310, 311, 312, 313, 315, 319, 320, 322, 323, 332, 341, 343, 416, 456
North Foreland, 345
North Weald, *49,* 412, 430, 446, 481, *525*
Northolt, 118, 184, 395, 399, 458
Nörvenich, 157
Notre-Dame d'Amour, 'La Tail-lette', 210
Nouilly, 315
Nourylande, Venette football ground, 336
Nouvion-sur-Meuse, *504*
    Ferme de l'Espérance, 247

Noville, Ferme Lambert Harcourt, 232
Noyelles, 352
Noyelles-sur-Mer, *330*, 452
Noyelles-sur-Selle, 320
Noyers-Pont-Maugis, *266*, 269
  German Military Cemetery, *280*
Noyon, 134, 275, 306, 413, 429
Nuland, Missiehuis van de Paters, 209, 242
Numansdorp, 262
Nurlu, 374

Oakley, near Harwich, 395
Ober-Esch, 208
Ober-Olm, 162, 165, 239, 308, 336
Oberbrück, 214
Obergailbach, 95, 97
Oberkirch church, 448
Obernai, 102
Obertraubling, 128
Ochamps, 299, 301, 309, 356, 371
Ochey, 117
Ockenburg, 184, 191, 194, 211, 216, *218*, 219, 221, 222-223, 226, 227
Ockenrode, 218, 222
Octeville, 426
Odenbach, 158
Odendorf, 265, 279
Odenheim, 104
Odiham, 445, 461
Oedheim, 99, 102, 105
Oeuilly, 418
Offoy, La Germaine, 446
Offranville, 448
Ognes, 316
Ognolles, 364, 432
Oirschot, 259
Oise, River, 310, 330, 332, 361, 447, 460
Old Sarum, *514*
Oldenburg, 211
Olen, 286
Olivet, 443
Olizy-Primat, 441
Olizy-sur-Chiers, 212
Omont, 274
Onnaing, 308, 328
Oostduinkerke, 379, 386
Oosterend, 496
Oosterhout, *258*, 273
Oostkerke, 379
Oostvoorne, 193, 261
Opheusden, 250
Opijnen, 205
Oran, 494
Oranienburg, 134
Orchies, 273, 321, 329, 353
Orconte, 97, 99, 107, 274, 285, 396
Oret, 274
Orfordness, 154
Origny, 310
Origny-Ste-Benoite, 330, *333*
Orival, 433
Orléans, 116, 305, 403, 411, 413, 443, 463, 470, 478, 479
Orléans-Bricy, 118, 241, 346, 413, 469
  CEAM at, 459
Orly, 104, 107, 116, 127, 259, 341, 396, 405, 416, 419, 494
Ormeignies, 210
Ormoy-Villers, 419
Orny, 150
Orsey, 160
Osdorp, 347
Osnabrück, 135
Ostbevern, 148
Osteel, 95
Ostend, 251, *258*, 286, 289, 302, 304, 308, 310, 313, 316, 336, 360, 362, 367, 372, 373, 376, 377, 379, 381, 383, 385, 386, 388, 389, 395, 397
Osterbusen, 111
Osterfeine, 167
Ottawa, 129
Ottikon, 300
Ottweiler, 154
Oude Dijk, Hoeven, 262

Oudekapelle, 414
Oudenaarde (Audenarde), 183, 330, 334, 336
Oudenburg, 387, 393
Ouderijn, 211
Oudeschild, 263
Oulchy-la-Ville, 456
Oulchy-le-Château, 453, 470
Ounaing, 308
Ourcq, River, 447, 457
Ourscamps, 427
Outer, 267, 311
Ouzouer-le-Doyen, 450, 455
Overbuurtse Polder, 224
Overflakkee, Polder Oud Herkingen, 248
Overijse, 232
Overschie, 219, 225, 226, 266
Oye-Plage, 356, 379
Oyonnax, 409
Ozolles, 162

Pacy-sur-Eure, 452, 464, 469
Paderborn, 216, 221, 380
Padoux, 188
Padville, 159
Pamel, 312
Pancy-Courtecon, 304
Papenlaan te Voorschoten, 'Ter Horst' Estate, 194
Pargny-Resson, 456
Paris, 118, *119*, *286*, 292, 353, *384*, *404*, 413, 415, 422, 443, 454, 455, *457*, 460, 463, 471, 476
  Arc de Triomphe, *8-9*, *11*
  Champs Elysées, 468
  Maxim's, *439*
Pasly, 446
Pauillac, 495
Payerne, *410*
Pecq, 352
Peissant, 235, 275
Peltre, 144
Pepingen, 309
Peppenhoven, 138, 139
Perdreauville, 458
Pernis, 184
Péronne, 132, 188, 207, 302, 303, 306, 310, 315, 330, 334, 341, 344, 345, 358, 364, 374, 388, 419, 422, 424, 425, 430, 435, 446, *517*
Péronnes-les-Antoing, 210
Perpignan, 83, 140, 141, 146, 244, 481, 492, 496
Perreuse Château Cemetery, 331
Persan-Beaumont, 234, 259, 296, 305, 324, 343
Perthes, 255, 454
Perthes-les-Hurlus, 209
Pervijze, 409
Perwez, 'la Carrièrre', 272
Pessoux, 248
Peterborough, 446
'Petersen' (decoy airfield), 132
Petrusplaat island, 257, *258*
Pévy, 301
Pferdsfeld, 107
Philippeville, 309, 317, 326, 327, 329
Picquigny, 434
Piennes, 285
Pierre-Levée, 352
Piershil, 184
Piéton, 275, 286
Pihen-lès-Guines, 345, 356, 398, 406
Pijnacker, 194
Pin, 280
Pinksterhaven, 239
Pirmasens, 156, 316
Pithviers, 373
Plancy-l'Abbaye, 462
Plantlünne, 106, 113, 129, 132
Plaspoelpolder, the, 224
Pléchâtel, 139
Plesnoy, 405
Plessier-Rozainvillers, 400
Plessis-Belleville, 297, 306, 325, 341
Plessis-Pâté, 433
Pleurs, 413

Plichancourt, 132
Plivot, *79*, *131*, 233, 246, *270*, 295
Plymouth, 474, 478, 480
Pocking, 125
Poilcourt, 232
Poix, 133, 147, 157, 167, 180, 232, 244, 256, 268, 282, 293, 302, 303, 310, 311, *312*, 313, 321, 339, *396*, 423, 432, 435, 436, 443, 445, 446, 447, 450, 467, *520*
Poix-de-Picardie, 424, 437, 443, 445, 447
Poix-Terron, 252, 333
Polincove, 380
Pommérieux, 249
Pommiers, 134, 364
Pont d'Allemagne, Canizy, 306
Pont du Diable, Somzée, 285
Pont-à-Mousson, 163, 342
Pont-Arcy, 451
Pont-Audemer, 458
Pont-de-l'Arche, 455, 468, 469
Pont-Jumeau, Toulouse, 459
Pont-Ste-Maxence, 327, 433, 453
Pont-St Vincent, 475
Pont-sur-Yonne, 358, 380, 387, 392, 413
Pontarlier, 407
Pontavert, *167*
Pontfaverger, 298
Pontpoint, 426, 460, 461
Pontru, 347
Pontséricourt, 298
Pouru-St-Rémy, 267, 278
Povan, 322, 371
Pré-en-Pail, 458
Preigney, 278
Prémontré, 306
Prenois, 274
Prenzlau, *161*
Presles-et-Thierny, 304
Presly, 429
Preux-au-Bois, 313
Prez, 301, 308, 309
Primstal, 140
Prosnes, 488
Prouvy, 314
Prunières, 487
Puisenval, 437
Puisieux, 429
Pulsheim, 148
Punchy, 340
Purfleet, 390
Pussy, *120*
Puttelange, 470
Pützhöhe, 206
Puurs, 286
Puxe, 181
Pyramide, 234

Quatre-Ville *see* Lille-Quatre-Ville
Quedlinburg, 153
Quelmes, *348*
Querenaing, 151
Querqueville, 380, 419, 488
Querrieu, 331
Quesnel-Aubrey, 426
Quevauvillers, 479
Quiévrain, 294
Quimper, *490*

Ragnies, 275
Raillimont, 285, 296, 298, 326
Ramatuelle, 477
Rambervillers, 493
Rambouillet, 456
Ramegnies-Chin, 268, 282
  cemetery, 282
Ramillies-Offus, 301
Ramsdonk, 300
Ramsdonksveer, St Theresia Hospital, 257

Ramsgate, 390, 391, 395, 399
Rancimont, 162, *163*
Randesacker, 132
Ransberg, 249
Rastatt, 252
Rathenow, 93
Raucourt-et-Flaba, *120*, 271, 353
Rebais, 464
Réchésy, 448
Reckange-lès-Mersch, 209
Recklinghausen, 140, 160
Recoigne, 460
Redu, 252
Regensburg, 150, 470
Regniowez, 353
  Cemetery, 259
Rehlingen, 327, 366
Reims, 25, *26*, 50, 52, *66*, *102*, *142*, *171*, 188, 239, 262, *281*, 285, 286, 290, *291*, 293, *295*, 317, 407, *408*, 415, 418, 422, 423, 439, 451, 453, 454, 456, 457, 459, 461, 479, *521*
Reims-Champagne, 72, *73*, 175, 183, 188, 208, 232, 244, 256, 268, 272, 282-283, 293, 295, 306, 431
Reinsfeld, 343
Rekem, Communal Cemetery, 246
Rely, 12, 18
Remagen, *253*
Remaisnil, 419, 448
Rémeling-lès-Puttelange, 118
Remicourt, 352
Remilly-Aillicourt, 266, 268, *269*, 271, 279
Remiremont, 360
Rémy, 341
Renesse, Schouwen Island, 239, 308
Rennes, 340, 395, 471, 472, 473, 493
Ressons-sur-Matz, 400
Rethel, 171, 253, 255, 297, 303, 314, 322, 362, 392, 415, 449, 451, 457, 459, 460, 461, *470*
Rethondes, 340, 433, 447, 496
Rety, 362
Retz, forest of, 447
Retzerath, 239
Reuver, 180
Rêves, 'Les Hayettes', 293
Revigny, 278
Rexpoede, 404
Rhèges, 294, 345, 362, 371, 385, 390
Rheinbischofsheim, 342
Rheinböllen, 115
Rheine, 211
Rhenen, 223, 250
Rhine, River, 216, 300
Rhône valley, 492
Rhône-Isère, 499
Ribeaucourt Farm, Maubray, 312
Ribemont, 307, 332
Richebourg, Sainte-Marguerite, 334
Richen, 110
Ricquebourg, Haut-Matz-Ferme, 432
Ridderkerk, 261
Riencourt-lès-Cagnicourt, 322
Rijsdijk, Willemspolder, 257, 258
Rijsoord School, Rotterdam, 276
Rillaer, 298
Rimling, 97
Rimogne, 290
Rivecourt, 417
Roanne, 481
Roberval, 417
Roc-de-la-Tour, 273
Rocbaron, 472, 477
Rochefort, 83, 492, 495
Rochester, 406
Rochford, 339, *343*, 349, 356, 379, 386, 395, 406, 419
Rockenhausen, 136
Rocquigny, 297, 305
Rocroi, 259, 347
Rodange, 182
Rodder, 163
Rodez, 492
Rogecourt, 306

Rohrbach, 98
Roizy, 451
Rollot, 395, 434
Romans-sur-Isère, 498, 499
Rombas, 163
Rombies-et-Marchipont, 381
Rome, 471
    Palazzo Venezia, *454*
    Villa Incisa, 499
Romeries-Escarmain, 296
Romilly-sur-Seine, 334, 375, 440,
461, 464, 466, 469, 470, 475
Romorantin, 419, 429, 481
Romorantin-Prunières, 429
Ronchières, 459
Ronchin *see* Lille-Ronchin
Roost-Warendin, 341
Roosteren, Maaseik bridge, 215
Roquetoire, 347
Rorbach-les-Dieuze, 152
Rosée, 161
Rosendael, 415
Rosières-en-Santerre, 119, 144,
152, 180-181, 256, 268, 303, 334,
396, 434, *511*
Rosmalen, 209
Rossum, 206
Rosnay, 309
Rotenburg, 133, 148
Roteux, 392
Roth, 212
Rotterdam, 174, 184, 206, 211, 216,
217, 219, *220*, 229, 230, 236, *255*,
266, 355, 415, 460
    Rijsoord School, *276*
Rouen, 345, 346, 347, 349, 378, 422,
423, 426, 428, 429, 431, 435, 441,
443, 446, 447, 449, 450, 451, 452,
455, 479, 490
Rouen-Boos, 154, 306, 346, 356,
416, 419, 422, 423, 426, 430, *431*,
435, 437, 445, 450, 455, 493, 495
Rougemaison, Luchy, *336*, 337
Rouillot, 475
Roulers, 361, 370, 377, 384
Roumont, Luftwaffe HQ, 371
Rouvray, 422
Rouvray-Catillon, 443
Rouvres, *7*, *10*, 18-73 *passim*, 103,
108, 113, 141, 148, *170*, *184*, 232,
491
    see also Étain-Rouvres
Rouvroy-sur-Audry, 426
Rouy-le-Grand, 418
Royan, 495
    Fort du Chay, 499
Roye, 117, 422, 424, 425, 430, 432
    Château Blin de Bourbon, 380
    Damouy Tannery, 441
Roye Beuvraignes, 249
Rozay-en-Brie, 455
Rozenburg, 194, 227
Rozenburg Island, 219, 227
Rozendaalse Veld, Arnhem, 211
Ruaudin, 423, *435*, 464
Rübenach, 162
Rubrouck, 413
Rückersbach, 376
Rudesheim, *407*
Ruffieux, 409
Ruigenhoek, 191, 193, 250, 261,
276
Ruiselede, 213
Ruit, 380
Rumegies, 327
Runnymede, Memorial to the
Missing, *7*, *31*, 180, 272, 312, 339,
379, 385, *474*, *510*, *515*, *519*
Rüsselheim, 147

'S-Gravendeel, 220, 233
'S-Gravenzande, 191, 218
Saarbrücken, 100, 167, *168*, *351*
Saargemünd, 342, 427
Saarlouis, 94, 251
Sables-d'Olonne, 440
Sachsenhausen, 104
Sacy-le-Grand, 396
Sagan, Stalag Luft 3, *105*, 349, *351*,
356, 385, 390

Sage, 465
Sailly-en-Ostrevent, 374
Sailly-sur-Lys, 351
Sains-en-Amiénois, 335, 400
Sains-les-Marquion, 321
    Churchyard, *517*
Ste-Agathe-d'Aliermont, 437
St-Amé, 477
St-André-de-l'Eure, 440, 458, *459*,
472
St-André-sur-Orne, 393
St Annapolder, 209
St-Aubin, 284, 285, 343, 465
St-Aubin-sur-Scie, 458
St Avold, 470, 471
St Barthélémy, 464
Saint-Baussant, 240
Saint-Bon, 466
Ste-Cécile, *253*, 278
St-Christophe-à-Berry, 160
St-Denijs-Westrem, 236, 251
St-Denis-d'Oléron, 488
St-Dié, 489
St-Dizier, 124, 170, 252, 341, 417,
451, 470, 477
Saint-Donat, 499
Saint-Égrève, 498
St-Esprit de Neufchâteau, clinic,
456
St-Étienne-de-St-Geoirs, 488
St Fergeux, 320
St-Florentin, 413, 429, 456, 458
St-Folquin, 402
St-Fuscien, 400, 434
St Gatien-des-Bois, 387
Saint-Germain, 279, 475
St-Germain-des-Essourts, 441
St Germain-les-Mons, *244*
St-Germain-sur-Eaulne, 441
St-Germain-sur-Meuse, 235
St-Germainmont, 325
St-Ghislain, 274, 317
St Goar, 300
St Helier, 494
St-Hilaire-le-Grand, *125*, 153, 154,
282
St-Hilaire-le-Petit, 289
St Hillaire-lès-Andresis, 478
St-Hilliers, 465
St Hippolyte, 413
St Hubert, 437
St Inglevert, 126, 138, 188, 355,
356, 362
St-Jacques, 496
Saint-Jacques-sur-Darnetal, 451
St Jean de Luz, 83, 474
St-Job-in-Goor, 249
St-Juliaan, 396
Saint-Just-des-Marais, 440
St Just-en-Chaussée, 328
St Kruis-Winkel, *277*
St-Laurent-de-la-Salanque, 499
St Leger, 429
St Léger du Bois, 117
St Lenaerts, 286
Saint-Leu-d'Esserent, 416
St Louis-lès-Bitche French Mili-
tary Cemetery, 98
St-Loup-Terrier, *255*, 359
St-Maixme-Hautrive, 295
St Malo, 464, 468, 471
Saint-Mard, 440
St Margaret's Bay, Dover, 180, 378
Sainte-Marguerite, 334
Sainte-Marguerite-en-Ouche, 465
Ste-Marie, 337, 343, 376, 381, 429
Ste-Marie-Chevigny, 418
St Martin-au-Laërt, 339
St-Martin-d'Ablois, 453
St-Martin-du-Boschet, 464
St-Martin-la-Campagne, 358, 425,
440, 451
St-Martin-le-Gaillard, 448
Saint-Masmes, 265
Saint-Maur, 493
St Maximin, 417
Ste-Menehould, 240, 254, 278, 285,
328
St Menges, *268*, 270, *505*
St-Mihiel, Ste-Anne hospital, 240

St-Nazaire, 83, 456, 468, 469, 471,
473, 478, 480, 481, *483*, 486, 487,
490, 492
St Nicolas, 284
St Omer, 149, 168, 302, 324, 330,
339, 347, *348*, 349, 355, 359, *361*,
362, 372, 377, 378, 379, 384, 385,
386, 392, 395, *402*, 456
St Omer-Wizernes, 284
Saint-Ouen-du-Tilleul, 426
St-Paterne-Racan, 440
St-Paul-aux-Bois, 427
St Pierre-d'Autils, 458
St-Pol, 347, 351, 358, 360, 362, 366,
372, 376
St-Pol-sur-Mer, 388
St-Pol-sur-Ternoise, 339
St Quentin, 210, 213, 275, 302, 303,
304, 306, 310, 311, 315, 316, 320,
321, 326, 330, 332, 334, 346, 360,
364, 374, 400, 414, 415, 419, 433,
442, 448, 451, 476
    Henri-Martin hospital, 207
St-Raphaël, 471, 496
St Remigius Geest, 267
Saint-Saëns, 449
    Fief-Thoubert, 446
    'Vaudichon', 448
St-Salvy-de-la-Balme, 459
St Sauflieu, 434
St Sernin forest, 419
St Sérotin, 477
St Simon-Clastres, 283
Saint-Souplet, 324
St Trojan, 488
St Trond, *242*, 288
    Sint-Trudostraat hospital, 198
St Truiden, Historiek Centrum
(former), 246
St Vaast-en-Chaussée, 321
St-Valéry-en-Caux, 373, 403, 449,
455, 457, *460*, 461, 463
St-Valéry-sur-Somme, 358, 422,
431, 435, 436, 437
Saint-Vallier-sur-Marne, 306
Ste-Vaubourg, 273
St Vith, *515*
St Wendel, 164, 208
Saint-Yan, 234, 424, 432, 478
Saintes, 315
Salbris, 488
Salisbury, Bishop Wordsworth
School, *511*
Salmbach, 100
Salon, 455, *457*, 471, 478, 496
Salzburg, 116, 147
Sambre à l'Oise canal, 333
Sambre, River, 310, 319, 330
Sambruc, 134
Samer, 345
Samoussy, 434
Sancerre, 466
Sancourt, 375
Sancy-le-Haut, 120
Sandweiler, 329, 376, 409
Sangatte, 361, 370, 373
Saponay, 443
Sarralbe, 97, 471
Sarre, River, 97
Sarrebourg, 95, *105*
Sarrebrücken-Ensheim, 96
Sarron, 424
Sarton, 359
Saudemont, 346
Saujon, 495
Saulheim, 112
Saulieu, 481
Sault-Saint-Remy, 451
Saumont, 447
Saumur, 468, 471
Sauville, 271
    'La Crête', 286
Saverne-Steinbourg, 373
Scampton, 233, 349, 445
Schaapweipolder, the, 223
Schaarbeek, Communal Cemetery,
199
Schaffen, *85*, 142, 149, 167, *196*,
197, *200*
Scheldt, River, 174, *253*

Scheldt Estuary, 212, 216, 254,
308
Schellingwoude, 194, 276
Scheveningen, 184, 194
Schiphol, 191, *192*, 209, 217, 236,
250, 261, 276, 347, 376, 495, 498
Schipluiden, 194
Schleissheim, 111
Schlengerfeld, 138
Schliengen, 132
Schliessheim, 149
Schmidtheim, 165
Schouwen Island, 239, 308, 396
Schwäbisch-Hall, 163, 212, 317,
419, 442, 470
Schweinfurt, 127, *253*
Schwetzingen, 153
Sèche-Fontaine, 408
Seclin, 315, *316*
    see also Lille-Seclin
Sedan, 19, 33, *231*, *243*, *245*, 254,
255, *259*, 263, *266*, 267, 268, 269,
270, 272, 273, 274, 279, *286*, 288,
292, 300, 317, 326, 333, 336, 337,
403, 420, 441, 462, *527*
Seefeld, 117
Ségry, 358
Seilles, 328
Seine, River, 116, 422, 435, 443,
449, 451, 454, 455, 456, 457, 458,
460, 463, 465, 468, 469, 475
Seine Bay, 456
Seine valley, 451
Seligenstadt, 115
Sellnrod, 154
Semilly, 308
Séméries, 286
Semilly, 308
Senarpont, 'La Bucaille', 382
Senlecques, 381
Senlis, 100, 296, 315, 334, 416
    Saint-Martin-du-Tertre Hos-
    pital, 447
Sennfeld, 102
Senon, *170*, 175, 181
Senoncourt-les-Maujouy, 136
Sens, 180, 358, 390, 464
Sensenruth, *245*, *247*
Sentelie, 445
Seranvillers, 313
Serroue, 409
Serskamp, 249
Sézanne, 189, 433, 447, 458, 465
Sheerness, 395
's-Herenelderen, *236*
's-Hertogenbosch, 206, 241
Shoreham, 9, 419, 472
Shorncliffe
    Hospital, 351, 362
    Military Cemetery, *520*
Siegburg, 214
Siegen, 160, 162
Sierck-les-Bains, 163
Sigmaringen, 98
Signy-l'Abbaye, 248, 252, 324, 325,
451, 456
    Forêt de, 288
Signy-le-Petit, *259*, 297, 342, 453
Simmern, 110, 156, 208, 301, 441
Sindelfingen, 104
Sint-Job-in-'t-Goor, 142
Sint-Katelijne-Waver, 286
Sint-Martens-Voeren, 215
Sint-Niklaas, 259
Sint-Pieters-Rode, 316
Sion, 225
Sissonne, 286, 366
Sisteron, 488
Sittard, 382
Sittingbourne, 390
Skegness, 423
Slaperdijk, 'Rode Haan', 221
Sleeuwijk, 241
Slootdorp, *250*
Sloten, 209
Sloterdijk, 117
Socx, 404
Soesterberg, 84, 107, 117, 119, 141,
209, 211, 250, 261
Soilly, 462
Soire-le-Château, 280

Soissons, 285, 286, 308, 311, 328, 334, 353, 356, *401*, 433, 442, 443, 447, 451, 452, 454, 456, 458, 462, 468, 470
Soissons-Saconin, 234, 259, 296
Solers, German War Cemetery, *409*
Solre-le-Château, 274
Sombernon, 458
Sommauthe, 300
Somme, River, 330, 338, 348, 364, 367, 384, 395, 403, 415, 420, 422, 430, 435, *442*, 443, 449, 452, 455, 494
Somme estuary, 319, 437
Sommelsdijk, the Oudeland-spolder, 193
Sommereux, 440
Sommesous, 322, 458
Sommethonne, 'Mohimont', 180
Sornéville, 456
Souain, 274, *461*
Souchez, 347
Soucy, 343
Soudron, 461
Sougé, *415*, 423, 436, 437, 450, 464, 469, 472
Sougé-sur-Braye, Communal Cemetery, *472*
Souilly, 126
Soultz-sous-Forêts, 97, 133
Soupir, 434
Sourbrodt, 252, 262, 289
Southend, 412
Sovet, 309, 347
Speyer, 97, 106, 107, 110, 140, 153, 158, 160, 239, 470
Spijkenisse, 159, 184
Spöck, 126
Stabroeck, 381
Stalag Luft 3 *see* Sagan
Stallageberg, 167
Stanmore, RAF Fighter Command HQ, 77
Staple, 110, *123*
Stavanger, *407*
Steene-Ostend, 148, 165, 167, 352, 365, 372, 373, 374, *387*
Steenokkerzeel, 236
Steinbach, 242
Steinhomburger Berg, 251
Steinhuder Meer, 239
Stenay, 212, 270, 281, 340, 465
Sterreken, 277, 315
Stert, *514*
Stetten-Lörrach, 120, 162, 414, 448
Stichting Aircraft Recovery Group, 236, 261, 376
Stockton-on-Tees, *209*
Stoke Military Hospital, 474
Stolwijk, 226
Stommeln, 158
Stonne, 157, 286, 308, 326, 353, 453
Stoppelfeld, 112
Störmede, 216, 224
Stradishall, *437*
Strasbourg, 373
Strasbourg-Neuhof, 117
Straubling, 142
Strausberg, 160
Strazeele, 388
Stuttgart, 493
Stuttgart-Süd, 115, 164, 414, 453
Sugny, Ardennes Forest, 272
Suippes, 164, 188, 208, 209, 249, 260, 269, 279, 284, 314
Supt, 123

't Woud, 229
Tagnon, Juniville, 456
Taillefontaine, 433
Tailly, 341
Tain-l'Hermitage, 498
Taisnil, 448
Taizy, 317
Taliseul, 477
Tangmere, 97, 175, *310*, 351, 373, 379, 419, 437, 471, 472, 478, 486, 487, *511*, 524
Tannay, 359, 376
Tavaux, 419

Teillay-St-Benoit, 478
Teills, 249
Temple Cloud, Somerset, *524*
Templeuve, 329
Tendu, 495
Terheyde, 225, 226
Terlinchun, 405, 416, *502*, *521*
Termes, 376
Tern Hill, RAF Training Command HQ, 77
Ternat, 312
Terneuzen, 310
Terneuzen Canal, 292
Texel, 362, 496
   Waddenzee, 263
   see also Units, Dutch (Vliegschool Texel)
Thaon-les-Vosges, 477
The Hague *see* Den Haag
Thelonne, *271*
Thénorgues, 260
Thetford, 395
Thiaucourt, 476
Thiaumont, 279
Thielt, 370, 377, 388
Thiescourt, 380, 427
Thieulloy l'Abbaye, 434
Thil-Manneville, 424
Thin-le-Moutier, 428
Thionville/Diedenhofen, 98, 205, 207, 208, 212, 280
Thonne-le-Thil, 340
Thonnelle, 253
Thorney Island, 494
Thorpe-le-Soken, 374
Thun, *410*
Thury-en-Valois, 327
Thy-le-Château, 275
Tiefenbrunn, 115
Tiel, 239
Tigeaux, 137
Tilburg, 241, 262
Tillement, 233, 242, 288, 295, 298, 299, 317, 329, 335
Tintigny, *164*
Tirlemont, 233, 242, 288, 295, 298, 299, 317, 329, 335
Tobruk, *214*
Toggenburg, the, near Bütschwil, 212
Tongeren, 230, 243, 244, 248
Torcy, Sedan, 273
Torcy-le-Petit, 450
Torhout, 119, 402
Torquay, 373
Tortequesne, 374
Toul, 481
Toul Croix-de-Metz, 83, 93, 100, 112, 117, 146, 171
Toul-Ochey, 188
Toulon, 404, 462, 463, 467
Toulouse, 451, 459, 473, 474
Toulouse-Francazal, 413
Touret, 'Les Mayettes', 208
Tourinnes-la-Grosse, 277
Tournai/Doornik, *288*, 310, 326, 330, 359
Tournes-Belval, 188, 231, 234, 248, *365*
Tournon, 493
Tours, 199, 200, 201, 251, 286, 334, 387, 411, 413, 416, 419, 429, 454, *457*, *463*, *469*, 470, 478, 479, 487, 490, 492, 495, 496
   Saint-Gatien Hospital, 469
Tours-sur-Loire, 144
Tramelan, 448
Trannes, 93
Trassem, 94
Travecy, 306, 364
Traveron, 107
Trechtelfingen, 300
Tresco, Isles of Scilly, *510*
Trèves/Trier, 95, *96*, 154, 208, 279, 288, 290, 327, 342, 353, 354, 360, 395, 408, 409, 411, 453, 456
Triberg-im-Schwarzwald, 99
Tricot, 422, 423
Triengen, 448
Trier *see* Trèves
Trier-Euren, 117, 129, 141, 153, 154, 167, 252, 278, 288, 360, 376, 381, 396, 409, 476

Trigny, 453
Trois-Fontaines, *168*
Troisdorf, 140
Tromborn, 164
Trondes, 240
't Rooth, 239
Trossencourt, 376
Troyes, 40, 300, 364, *407*, *408*, 429, *438*, 439, 451, 461, 462, 465, 470, 475, 476
   AASF HQ, 292
Troyes-Barberey, 188, 466, 469
Tubize, 319
Tupigny, 434
Turckheim, 126
Turin, 454, 475
   Fiat works, 457, 458

Uccle-Calevoet, Brussels, 145
Uetersen, 102, 119, 124
Uffenheim, 170
Uithuizen, the Noordpolder, 107
Untertillisch, 116
Upper Heyford, 106, 134
Ursel, 306, 341, 352
Ursins, 414
Uruffe, 479
Urvillers, 333
Utrecht, 216, 276
Uxbridge, 431
   RAF Bomber Command HQ, 77

Vaals, 309
Vado-Ligure, 466
Vahl-les-Benestroff, 213
Vailly-sur-Aisne, 427, 447, 448
Vaire-sous-Corbie, 358, 426
Valdahon, 'La Chevanne', 375
Valençay, 495
Valence, 455, 499
Valenciennes, 239, *263*, 303, 308, *309*, 310, 311, 316, 317, 319, 321, 322, 329, 334, 336
Valensole, 499
Valette, 470
Valheureux, 452
Valkenburg, 193, 216, 218, 219, 221-222, 223, 224
Vallendar, 140
Vanderlingenplaat, 184
Vannes, 497
Varelbusch, *383*
Vassincourt, *27*, 119, *121*, *167*, *168*, 180, 232, 273, 275, 286
Vaucogne, 231
Vaudesincourt, 325
Vaudétré, 265
Vaulx, 234
Vaupoisson, 466
Vaux-en-Dieulet, 446
Vaux-sur-Sure, 232
Vaux-Villaine, 423
Vechta, 120, 434
Veere, 84, 250, 276
Velaine-en-Haye, 213
Veldwezelt, 213, *238*, 243, 244, *516*
Vellereille-les-Brayeux, 274
Vendeville (Allied airfield B51), *139*, 479, 496
   see also Lille-Seclin (Lesquin)
Vendresse, 242, 265, 284
Venice, 454, 471
Vénizel, 440
Verberie, 315, 417, 460, 461
Verdon-sur-Mer, 305
Verdres, 450
Verdun, 18, *20*, 22, 23, 35, 40, 54, 56, *58*, 61, 67, 70, 103, 123, 147, 260, 297, 465, 471
Vergies, 437
Verize, 120
Verlaines, Gutshofe Ferme, *442*
Vermand, 315
Vermelles, 345
Verneuil, 456
Verneuil-en-Halatte, 340
Verneuil-Petit, 119
Vernon, 324, 447, 448, 449, 452, 454, 455, 458, 460, 464, 465, 468, 469, 472

Versaugues, 324, 334
Versigny, 234, 298
Vervins, 265, 292, 330, 456
Vesvres-sous-Prangey, 478
Veules-les-Roses, 460
Veulettes-sur-Mer, 455
Vézaponin, 365
Vézilly, 461
Vichy-Rhue, 475
Vieille Cour, 495
Viel-St-Rémy, 242
Viels-Maisons, 433
Vielsalm, 262
Vienna, 118
Vierzon, 419
Vierzy, 314
Vieux-Condé, 293
Vieux-Mesnil, 275
Vievy-le-Raye, 478
Vignacourt, 427, 434
Vignory, 495
Villacoublay, 83, 104, 117, 341, 358, 364, 380, 401, 452
Villanova d'Albenga, 477
Ville-en-Hesbaye, 278
Ville-sur-Cousances, 240
Ville-sur-Tourbe, 208
Villemontry, *269*
Villeneuve, *26*, 99
Villeneuve-lès-Vertus, 104, 158, 182, 246, 269, *281*, 291, 293, 455
Villeneuve-St-Georges, 93, 116
Villeneuve-sur-Lot, 488
Villequier-Aumont, 314
Villers-Agron-Aiguizy/Romigny, Ferme Berthenay, 364
Villers-Bocage, 374
Villers-Bretonneux, 334
Villers-Brûlin, 366
Villers-Cernay, 267
Villers-Châtel, 347
Villers-Cotterêts, 343, 448, 451, 453, 460
Villers-devant-Mouzon, 266, 268, *505*
Villers-devant-Orval, 213
Villers-les-Dombes, 305
Villers-lès-Guise, 73, 188, 234, 248, *284*
Villers-St-Christophe, *325*, *333*
Villers-sur-Fère, 314
Villiers-Charlemagne, 168
Villiers-en-Désoeuvre, 452
Villiersfaux, 437, 458, *464*, 469, 472
Villingen, 167
Vimy, 341
Vincennes, 315
Vingeanne reservoir, 478
Vironvay, 455
Virton Cemetery, 213
Visé, 242
Vissenaken, 199, 237
   Belgian Air Museum, 283
Vistley, 115
Vitré, 472
Vitry, 293, 390, 475
Vitry-en-Artois, *77*, *149*, 152, 154, 175, *180*, 183, 231, *232*, 233, 243, 244, 247, 256, 257, 272, 282, 283, 295, 303, 304, 308, 310, 311, 312, 313, 317, 335, 374, 429, *508*
Vitry-le-François-Vaucler, 127, 154, 189, 235, 249, 289, 290, 328, 376
Vivaise, 296, 456
Vivoorde, 303
Vlaardingen, 194, 206, 220, 248
Vleuten, nr Breukelen, 276
Vlieland, 115
Vlissingen/Flushing, 104, 116, 148, 163, 215, 231, *234*, 265, 278, 289, 308, 456
   see also Units, Dutch (Vliegschool Vlissingen)
Vogelsang, 277, 279, 308, 317, 318, 336, 343, 347, 354, 366, 418, 442
Vollezele, 272
Voncq, *29*, 268
   French Military Cemetery, 268

Voorburg, 223, 224
   St Anthoniushove hospital, 211,
   225
Vorselaer, 215
Vosges mountains, 126
Vouarces, 96
Vouillers, 159
Voulx, 477
Vouziers, *29*, 249, 265, 268, 278,
282, 283, 288, 290, 303, 317, 374,
376, 456
Voves, 475
Voyenne, 419
Vraignes-lès-Hornoy, 427
Vrasene, 342
Vraux, 134, 239, 488
Vrebos, 316
Vresse, 252
Vrigne-aux-Bois, 267
Vroenhoven, 213, *238*, 243, *244*,
246, 248
Vrusschenhuisken, 213

Waal, River, 211, 216, 227
Waalhaven, 157, 174, 175, 184, 191,
192, 193, 211, *217*, 219, 220, 223,
226, 227, 228-229, *228*, 230, 243,
248, 252, 254
Wackernheim, 106
Waddeneilanden, the, 151
Waddenzee, the, 149, 239
Waddington, 273, 458
Wadelincourt, 266, *271*, 272, *293*, *508*
Wageningen, 250
Waggum, 129
Wahlen, 448
Wahn, 316
Walcheren island, 174, 216, 239,
281, 305, 307
Waldhouse, 154
Walmer Beach, Deal, 373
Waltriche, 123
Wanchy-Capval, 437
Wancourt, 351
Wanel, 400
Wangerooge, 365, 376

Waremme, 251, 260
Warloy, *320*, *323*
Warloy-Baillon, 427
   Cemetery, *323*
Warnemünde, 86
Warneton, 372
Warsaw, 82, *276*, 460
Warvillers, 432
Warzée, 335
Wassenaar, 193, 218, 219
   Ursula-Kliniek, 193
Wateringen, 184, 219
Waterloo, 283, 286
Watripont, 365
Wattenscheid, 134
Wattisham, 175, 233, 248, 266, 273,
330, 345, 349, 379, 412, 423, 437,
446, 450, 461, 465
Watton, 233, 248, 266, *304*, 330,
339, 345, 349, 356, 362, 385, 390,
431, 445, 450, 465
Wavre, 281, 283, 293, 298, 300
Wavrechain-sous-Faulx, 309
Weilersbach, 97
Weilheim, 493
Weisendorf, 279
Weisskirchen, 98, 100
Wellen, 199
Wengerohr, 114, 134, 156, 163,
239, 262, 265, 277, 279, 280, 288,
290
Werchter, 298
Werkendam, 241, *265*
   Biesboschmuseum, 257
Werl, 139, 141, 218, 222
Wertheim, 102, 124, 414
Wervik, 366
Werzlen, 316
Wesel, 159, 160
West Raynham, 379
West Souburg, 167
Westeinderplas, 276
Westende, 397
Westerschelde, 289, 306
Westhampnett, *310*
Westpolder, the, 229

Westrode, *299*
Wetteren, 249, 279
Wetzlar, 113
Wevelgem, *123*, 124, 201, 212, 213,
282
Wez-Thuisy, 83, 188, 259, 273, 274,
285, 296, 297
Wezembeek-Oppem, 241, 286
Wezerenberg, 199
Wien-Aspern, 114
Wiencourt-l'Equipée, 360
Wiener-Neustadt, 150
Wiernsheim, 135
Wierre-Effroy, 349, *350*
Wiesbaden, 102, 104, 158, 366
Wiesbaden-Erbenheim, 104, 106,
117, 131, 147, 148, 149, 158, 162,
205, 327, 342, 366
Wiesbaum-Schnee-Eifel, 129
Wiesloch, 470
Wietzenbruch, 140, 148
Wignehies, 297
Wihogne, 247
Wijk aan Zee, 138
Wilderen-Duras, 196, 236
Wilhelmshaven, 122, 246, *437*
Willerzie, 298
Wilmington, 490
Wilnis, 206
Wilrijk, 236
Wimereux, 339, 347
Windischenlaibach, 134
Wissel, 222
Witry, 206
Wittering, *402*
Wittlich, 162
Woensdrecht, *254*, 347
Woerth, *118*
Woignarue, 233
Woippy, 112
Wolfenbüttel, 242
Wörrishofen, 103
Worthy Down, 114
Woudse Polder, 222, 225
Wright Field, 118
Würzburg, 106, 127, 136

Wyton, 175, 184, 227, 284, 313, *338*,
339, 345, 349, 356, 362, 395, 431,
445, 458, 461, 469, *509*

Xaffévillers, 83, 117, 161, 213, 249
Yonne bridges, 478
Ypenburg, 150, 175, 184, 193, *194*,
209, 216, 217, *218*, 219, 221, 223-
227, 229
Ypres, 342, 351, 361, 362, 370, 375,
377, 397, 400, 413, 467
Ysselstein, German War Ceme-
tery, *215*
Yverdon, 414
Yvoir-Anhée, 302, 348
Yvrench, 456

Zaltbommel, 223
Zandvoort, 191
Zeebrugge, 336, 365, 367, 373, 377,
382, 383
Zeeland (province), 216, 266, *276*
Zeeuws-Vlaanderen, 'Retranche-
ment', 251
Zellhausen, 208
Zevenbergen, *192*, 257, *258*
Zevenbergschehoek, 209
Zevenhuizen, 211
Zissenheim, 254
Zonnemaire, 98
Zottegem, 334
Zoute, 251
Zoutelande, 276
Zudausques, 339
Zuid Beveland, 281, 308
Zuidzande, Terhofstedepolder,
393
Zuydcoote, 214, 249, 253, 352,
375, 407
Zuyder Zee/IJsselmeer, 266
Zwaagdijk, 192
Zwanenburg, 209
Zweifalten, 278
Zwevezele, 199, 200, 237, 315,
334, 341, 352, 359, 374
Zwischenhahn Lake, 220

Internal components of a Junkers Ju88 (see page 539) are dismantled for unscheduled inspection.

PERSONNEL

ROLL OF HONOUR, *501-527*
SS *Abukir* losses, 372, 373, *388*
SS *Lancastria* losses, 474, *480-483*, 484-485
A-Tjak, 2e Lt M. G., 191, 261
Aarts, 1e Lt B. M., 163
Aarts, Sgt P. J., 117, 194
Abbinghoff, Uffz W., 290
Abbot, Sgt F. B., 246, 269
Abele, Uffz A., 163
Abeling, Uffz P., 132
About, Sgt (GR II/55), 475
Abrial, Adm., 389, 419
Abrioux, S/Lt (GC III/1), 210, 336, 375, 376
Abt, Obergefr H-W., 211
Accart, Capt. J-M. (GC I/5), 120, 208, 209, 240, 249, 252, 279, 317, 376, 407, 410
Achaintre, Sgt, 96
Achleitner, Lt (JG3), 321
Acker, Fw K., 279
Acock, Sgt, 168
Adam, F/O W. W., 150
Adam, Sgt, 112
Adam, Uffz J., 162
Adamek, Sgt M. (GC II/10), 447
Adams, AC2 I. G. (218 Sqn), 233
Adams, AC2 J. C. (38 Sqn), 398
Adams, F/O W. S. C. (3 Sqn), 251, 256
Adams, P/O D. A. (611 Sqn), 412
Adams, Sgt H. C., 233
Adams, Sgt P. E. F. (107 Sqn), 437
Adamson, P/O W. B., 148
Adderley, AC1 T. P., 112
Adrian, Lt (1./JG2), 395
Adye, F/Lt C. F. G. (17 Sqn), 315, 373, 375
Aeckerle, Lt R., 120
Aherne, AC2 P., 273
Ahrendt, Gefr H., 240
Ahrenholz, Gefr R. (1./KG27), 428
Ahrens, Oberfw W. (1./JG27), 353
Ahrens, Uffz E. (9./ZG26), 418
Ahrns, Uffz G. (3.(F)/22), 392
Aigner, Fw L., 206
Ainsworth, AC1 R. T., 267, *503*
Ainsworth family, *503*
Aitken, F/O (601 Sqn), 329
Aitken, LAC J., 180
Ajam, Sgt R. (GB I/31), 440
Akkermans, A., *258*
Alaffe, Cpl R., 94
Albach, Fw H., 289
Albert, Fw F. (7./JG3), 437, 448
Albert, Gefr W. (4./KG76), 308
Albonico, Sgt R. A., 133, 311
Albrecht, Uffz A. (4./KG54), 342
Albrecht, Uffz E. (3./StG77), 215
Albrecht, Uffz H. (2./StG2), 393
Albrecht, Uffz (KGrzbV.9), 225
Aldenhoven, Uffz K., 208
Alder, Fw W., 277
Alderson, Sgt K., 267
Aldridge, P/O (53 Sqn), 378
Aldridge, Sgt (53 Sqn), 311
Alexander, Maj.-Gen. Harold, 368, 397
Alexander, Sgt J. L. (40 Sqn), 96, 362
Alexandre, Capt. (GC II/2), 234, 262, 277
Alexandre, Sgt (GB II/31), 466
Algie, Sgt W. F., 182
Aliani, Maresciallo (43 Gruppo), 467
Alisch, Oberlt H. (I./KG30), 347
Alksaat, Gefr R., 211
Allaire, Adjt R. (GB I/11), 400
Allaire, S/Lt (GR I/35), 478
Allam, LAC F. J., 233
Allard, Sgt Geoffrey 'Sammy', *205*, 206, 210, 239, 289, 299, *303*
Allemin, Adjt, 259
Allen, F/O Derek Hurlstone, DFC (85 Sqn), 206, 232, 283, 312
Allen, F/O J. H. L. (87 Sqn), 321, 326

Allen, P/O J. L. (54 Sqn), 347, 349, 353, 362
Allen, Sgt D. (103 Sqn), 385
Allen, Sgt D. A. (3 Sqn), 265, 267
Allgood, Sgt H. H., 294
Allin, Lt, 156
Allington, P/O G. (48 Sqn), 390
Allitt, P/O R. E., 233
Allmann, Gefr B., 301
Allonzo, Sgt (ECN 4/13), 413
Altendorf, Lt (7./JG53), 325, 416
Althaus, Uffz P., 158
Altinger, Uffz Josef, 224
Altmann, Uffz G. (3./KG77), 360
Altmann, Uffz H-G. (4.(F)/11), 156
Altmann, Uffz (KG51), 116
Altvater, Hptmn Georgfriedrich, 252, *253*
Amarger, S/Lt, 284
Amarre, S/Lt, 97
Ambrosch, Uffz H., 315
Amiel, QM, 106
Amory, SM (AC 2), 488
Amouroux, Asp., 162
Anacker, Oberfw E. (5./KG22), 402
Ancard, Sgt R., 123
Anceaux, Lt W. F., 191, 261
Ancel, Lt (GBA I/51), 364
Ancelin, Sgt (GBA II/51), 396, 440, 461
Ander, Fw K. (Stab KG55), 213, 470
Ander, Uffz R. (1./ZG1), 429
Anders, Lt K., 279
Anders, Uffz H., 210
Andersch, Oberlt, 209
Anderson, F/Lt H. T. J. (253 Sqn), 322
Anderson, P/O C. C. R. (88 Sqn), 371
Anderson, P/O M. H. (600 Sqn), 184
Anderson, Sgt N., 256
André, Sgt (GR II/55), 452
Andreae, Uffz P., 253
Andres, Hptmn Werner (II./JG27), 171, 250, 451, 453

Andrès, S/Lt (GR II/33), 346
Andrews, P/O J. F. E. (144 Sqn), 461
Andrews, Sgt S. E., 247
Anelli, Capt. G., 477
Angel, Obergefr H. (KG54), 329
Angeli, Lt H-E. (3./JG54), 470
Angibault, Adjt, 309
Angiolini, S/Lt, 253
Angus, F/O A. B., 181, 289, 294
Anholt, Fw J., 343
Aniol, Uffz G., 133
Ankaoua, Sgt R., 274
Ankum-Frank, Hptmn von (JG27), 447, 470
Annan, Sgt R. S. (226 Sqn), 272, 339
Annen, Gefr H. (KG27), 327
Anning, Sgt W. J., *246*
Annon, Sgt, 259
Anschau, Uffz J. (5./KG77), 477
Antelmann, Flgr O., 327
Antholzner, Uffz J. (Stab III./KG53), 476
Anthony, Oberfw G. (ZG76), 297, 306, 309, 315
Anthony, P/O D. N. W. L. (73 Sqn), 464
Anthony, Sgt D. I. (226 Sqn), 183
Antoine, Dr, 309
Antoine, Lt (GB II/35), 478
Aouach, Lt P., 103
Aperce, Cpl, 286
Apholz, Uffz A., 206
Appel, Gefr A. (4./JG53), 488
Appelt, Uffz H. (2./KG55), 376
Appleton, P/O L. L. 'Lew', 232, 241, 268, 279
Aquilina, S/Lt (GC II/2), 262, 277, 413
Arachequesne, Sgt Maurice (GB II/12), 432
Arbuthnot, Sgt J. (1 Sqn), 419
Ardenne, Sgt (48 Sqn), 395
Arderne, P/O P. V. (110 Sqn), 446
Arendt, Uffz W., 290
Argueyrolles, Adjt H., 306
Aries, Sgt (GAO 2/508), 424

Arino, S/Lt J., 284
Aris, Sgt, 141
Armanet, Sgt (GB I/21), 466
Armbrust, Fw M., 226
Armstrong, LAC P. (235 Sqn), 373
Armstrong, Sgt (150 Sqn), 472
Arndt, Gefr G. (8./KG55), 265
Arndt, Oberlt H. (9./StG51), 442
Arndt, Uffz H. (15.(Z)/LG1), 156
Arnion, Sgt, 106
Arnold, Fw (2./JG27), 464
Arnold, Fw H. (3./KG53), 409
Arnold, Peter (historian), *256*
Arnoux, Cmdt M. (GC III/7), 189, 433
Arnulphy, Adjt A. (GB 2/19), 456
Arscott, P/O G. O., 167
Artola, Lt, 314
As, Sgt J. L. van de, 191, 236
Aschenbrenner, Uffz R. (1./KG54), 360
Aschwanden, Lt (Swiss Fl.Komp.15), 414
Ashfield, F/O L. J., 273
Ashton, P/O J. B. (607 Sqn), 214
Ashton, P/O J. H. (85 Sqn/145 Sqn), 283, 379
Ashton, P/O G. W. (59 Sqn), 419
Ashton, Sgt D. A. (110 Sqn), 273
Aslin, Sgt M. R. (151 Sqn), 318, 487
Aspern, Lt von (1./JG76), 419, 433
Assop, Sgt (103 Sqn), 445
Astbury, Sgt R. C. (77 Sqn), 458
Astier, Capt. A., 189, 208
Aston, Capt. W. G. S. (825 FAA Sqn), 385
Astor, Maj. the Hon. John, *47*
Atack, AC1 D. (37 Sqn), 405
Atchison, Sgt T. T., 233
Atkins, Sgt J. F. (150 Sqn), 437
Atkinson, F/O C. F. (151 Sqn), 431
Atkinson, P/O (213 Sqn), 318, 326, 335, 393
Atkinson, Sgt G. (151 Sqn), 312, 341, 347
Atkinson, Sgt Gordon (105 Sqn), 270

Two stalwarts of No. 85 Squadron who lived to fight another day. Flight Lieutenant 'Dickie' Lee (left) was decorated with the Distinguished Service Order and Distinguished Flying Cross by the King on June 26, 1940 for 'great powers of leadership and a keen fighting spirit' during the Battle of France. Shot down on May 11, he had escaped from behind enemy lines and according to Pilot Officer Lewis, a member of his flight, he had 'that magic quality to evoke unquestioning loyalty, which tolerated the sometimes hair-raising demands he made of those who flew with him'. He was killed on August 18, 1940 during the Battle of Britain. Flying Officer Kenneth Blair (right) received his DFC for 'exceptional keenness' in action.

Aubert, Capt. (GR I/35), 249
Aubert, P/O R. D. (74 Sqn), 339, 356
Aubert, Sgt M. (GB 1/31), *103*
Audebaud, Lt L. (ECN 1/13), 147
Audebert, S/Lt (GC I/2), 429, 448
Audenhove, Hptmn B. von Normann und, 107
Audoux, Sgt, 94
Audrain, Adjt (GC II/5), 120, 360, 376
Auer, Fw P., 135
Auer, Oberfw J., 318
Auerbach, Uffz F., 254
Auerswald, Uffz S. (5./KG1), 488
Auge, Adjt P. (GB II/12), 334
Auge, S/Lt J. (GR II/55), 496
Auinger, Lt F., 242
Aurich, Uffz G., 308
Austin, F/O G. W. B. (605 Sqn), 345
Austin, LAC R. W. (15 Sqn), 248, 356
Autier, Adjt R., 285
Auzeing, Lt (GR 1/55), 380
Avenard, Lt, 234
Avent, F/Sgt F. T., 233
Avent, Sgt D. J., 248
Avery, Sgt G. (103 Sqn), 445
Avon, Sgt (GR II/55), 466
Axford, Sgt J. R. (37 Sqn), 398
Axmacher, Stabarzt Dr F. (Stab II./JG26), 459
Axthelm, Lt (3./JG27), 199, 362
Ayerst, P/O P. V., *38-39, 44, 46, 47, 51, 58, 59, 64,* 111, 116, 121, 157
Ayling, Sgt C. A. H. (43 Sqn), 437
Ayre, F/O G. D. (609 Sqn), 395
Ayres, F/Lt D. I. C. (2 Sqn), 168
Ayres, P/O R. W. (59 Sqn), 385
Azan, Sgt, 274

Baagoe, Oberlt (8./ZG26), 249, 379
Baake, Gefr E. (KG51), 328
Bach, Fw F. (4.(F)/122), 335
Baché, Capt., 298
Bachelot, Capt., 296
Bacher, Fw Alfons (3./JG52), 374
Backhaus, Gefr F., 278
Badel, Sgt (GBA II/54), 364, 433
Badura, Fw H. (KG51), 328
Badura, Fw P. (Stab KG55), 429
Baebenroth, Fw W., 239
Baeckler, Adjt (GB I/21), 387
Baensch, Fw K., 213
Baert, Sgt (GB II/12), 432
Bagot, SM, 324
Bagrel, Adjt L., 159
Baguley, AC1 H., 95
Baguley, LAC H., 160, 183
Bailes, Sgt (21 Sqn), 385
Bailey, AC1 A. (218 Sqn), 161
Bailey, P/O G. M. (53 Sqn), 311, 372
Bailey, Sgt (21 Sqn), 458
Bailey, Sgt A. (145 Sqn), 379
Baillie, Cpl E. T., 311
Bailly, 1/Sgt J. (11/VI/1), 352
Bailly, Sgt H. (3/II/1), 286
Bailly, Sgt M. (GC II/9), 417
Baird, F/O J. W. (254 Sqn), 405
Baize, S/Lt M., *96*
Bak, Lt J. J., 191
Baker, LAC Harold R. (139 Sqn), *270*
Baker, P/O E. N. (2 Sqn), 362
Baker, Sgt (40 Sqn), 431
Baker, Sgt (56 Sqn), 383
Bakker, Lt W., 104
Bal, Sgt, 305
Baladier, Adjt R. (ECMJ 1/16), 380
Balase, S/Lt., 324
Balasse, 1/Sgt M., 251
Balbiano, S/Lt R. (GAO 502), 478
Bald, Fw H. (9.(H)/LG2), 343
Baldwin, Stanley, 76
Balfanz, Oberlt W., 95, 260, 271, 277
Balfour, Capt. The Rt Hon. H. H., *292*

Balka, Oberfw W. von, 133
Ball, F/O Albert R. (3 Sqn), 180, 256, *503*
Ball, F/O G. E. (19 Sqn), 373, 375
Ballangée, Korp. L. M. J., 194
Ballantyne, Sgt J. (88 Sqn), 461
Ballet, Lt (GAO 3/551), 334
Ballin, Sgt, 188
Ballweg, Uffz J., 212
Balmer, Adjt (DAT Étampes), 413, 418
Balquier, Sgt A., 123
Balthasar, Hptmn Wilhelm (1./JG1), 236, 237, 257, 351, 373, 424, 425, 433, *465*
Balzer, Uffz A., 228
Bang, Obergefr C. (6./KG76), 418
Bank, Fw H. (4./KG54), 342
Banke, Lt C. (9./StG2), 442
Banks, Sgt P. (245 Sqn), 395
Baptizet, S/Lt (GC II/4), 97, 117, 288, 326, 336, 388, 427, 429, 459
Bär, Uffz (later Fw) H. (JG51), 97, 167, 307, 351
Baranski, Lt (DAT Lyon & GC III/6), 83, 410
Baraque, S/Lt (GB II/62), 461
Barbarin, Cpl (GAO 517), 446
Barbé, PM (AC 5), 481
Barber, AC D., 272
Barberis, Sgt R. (GC I/3), 285, 289, 327, 441
Barbey, Sgt (GC 5/2), 114
Barbeyrac, Sgt B. de (GAO 1/589), 413
Barbier, Adjt (GR I/52), 152
Barbier, Capt. B. (GC I/4), 134, 235, 427, 458
Barbier, S/Lt (GAO 507), 128
Barbier, S/Lt (GB II/15), 324
Barbour, P/O David M., 267, *503*
Barbron, Cpl B. (GBA I/51), 433
Barbrook, Cpl D. J., 270
Barbu, S/Lt (GC II/10), 275, 298, 441
Barchfeld, Lt K-W., 145
Bardet, S/Lt (GC II/9), 417
Bardin, S/Lt P., 107, 251, 297
Bardon, Cpl (GB II/31), 466
Barford, Sgt G. H., 167
Baritel, Adjt (GC III/9), 409, 413
Barker, F/Sgt G. T. (150 Sqn), 271
Barker, LAC F. J. (264 Sqn), 386, 392
Barker, Sgt T. R. (150 Sqn), 246
Barlier, S/Lt, 314
Barlow, LAC V. S. G., 270
Barlow, W/Cdr E. C., 284
Barneckow, Oberlt R. Fr von, 124, 160
Barnickel, Uffz F. (2.(F)/122), 365
Barnwell, Sgt H. J., 233
Baron, Sgt (GAO 515), 492
Baron, Uffz L. (Stab I./ZG2), 337
Barowka, Uffz W., 253
Barr, F/O P. R. (12 Sqn), 320
Barras, Sgt (GB I/11), 432
Barratt, AM Sir Arthur, *60, 61,* 130, 137, 143, *166, 169,* 174, 231, 243, 281, 292, 302, 319, 338, 344, 443, 454, *457,* 460, 463, 468, 471, 478, 480, *513*
Barraud, Adjt M. (GB II/62), 461
Barrett, Sgt D. H. J. (102 Sqn), 332
Barrett, Sgt W. J. (107 Sqn), 412
Barrio, Adjt, 274
Barron, Sgt H. J., 183
Barrow, AC1, 142
Barruet, Cmdt, 286
Barry, Sgt (59 Sqn), 244, 419
Barse, Capt., 306
Bartelt, Gefr P. (7./KG51), 382
Bartesch, Fw H., 289
Barth, Oberlt (KG53), 115
Barth, Oberlt S. (KG51), 278
Bärthel, Oberfw R. (7./KG3), 381
Barthels, Adjt J., 167
Barthels, Flgr O., 316
Barthle, Fw R. (6./StG77), 467
Bartholmes, Uffz J., 253

Bartlam, Sgt C. D. W. (40 Sqn), 461
Bartlett, F/O I. H., 311
Bartlett, Sgt C. A. (107 Sqn), 461
Bartley, AC1 J. E., 272
Bartley, P/O A. C. (92 Sqn), 354, 356
Bartlow, LAC R. T. W., 107
Bartsch, Fw W. (TrGr.186), 347
Bartsch, Uffz W. (2./JG51), 376
Barwell, P/O E. G. (264 Sqn), 399
Basler, Uffz H., 254
Basmann, Oberfw M., 317
Bassaguet, Adjt, 249
Bässell, Obergefr W. (8./JG3), 495
Bassett, F/O T. G., 247
Bastien, Adjt (DAT Tours), 479
Bastin, Sgt L. (1/I/1), 286
Bätcher, Oberlt H-G. (3./KG27), 429
Bate, Sgt R. A. (254 Sqn), 405
Bates, Sgt T. A. (150 Sqn), 99
Bathe, Uffz W. (16./KGzbV.1), 396
Batt, F/Lt R. H. (40 Sqn), 362, 431
Battle, S/Lt (GAO 517), 446
Battut, S/Lt R., 306
Batty, Sgt J. J. C. (12 Sqn), 469
Batz, Oberfw A. (8./KG2), 342
Baud, Capt. H., 260
Baudouin (heir to King Leopold), *387*
Bauer, Adjt J. (GB 4/23), 456, 466
Bauer, Fw (7./JG3), 431
Bauer, Fw H. (4./JG52), 277
Bauer, Lt F. (2.(H)/10), 470
Bauer, Lt (JG77), 282, 315
Bauer, Oberfw A. (2./KG27), 289
Bauer, Oberfw Friedrich (KGrzbV.9), 226
Bauer, Sgt (GB II/38), 296
Bauer, Uffz F. (1.(F)/123), 171
Bauer, Uffz H. (1.(H)/23), 307
Bauer, Uffz H. (3.(F)/121), 206
Bauer, Uffz L. (1./KG76), 418
Bauer, Uffz R. (3./KG51), 414
Bäuerle, Fw K., 212
Bauerschäfer, Lt G., 290
Bauhaus, Oberlt G. (Stab StG77), 393
Baukus, Obergefr F. (I./JG21), 497
Baum, Lt E. (KG54), 329
Baumann, Gefr H., 107
Baumeler, Fw H. (2.(H)/32), 470
Baumgarten, Obergefr F., 211
Baumgartner, Fw A., 213
Baumgartner, Uffz, 298
Baums, Uffz P. (Stab KG27), 488
Baun, Uffz (later Fw) (JG53), 97, 154, 325
Baville, Capt. Pierre Rougevin, 83
Baxter, Sgt William, *313*
Bayer, Uffz H. (4./KG54), 414
Bayle, S/Lt (GR II/55), 475
Bayle, Sgt (GAO 1/584), 446
Bayle, Sgt P. (GC II/9), 341, 417
Baynes, P/O R. (38 Sqn), 398
Bayonne, Sgt, 260
Bazalgette, P/O Freddie S., 247, *504*
Bazin, F/O, 241
Bazon, Sgt (GB I/62), 374, 461
Beagles, LAC (57 Sqn), 372
Beale, P/O R. C. (150 Sqn), 464
Beames, Sgt Frank E., *268, 505*
Beamish, W/Cdr (151 Sqn), 488
Beamont, P/O Roland 283, 288
Beard, Sgt A. (16 Sqn), 398
Beardsley, Sgt G. (103 Sqn), 268, *269,* 362, 445
Beardwood, Sgt G. (40 Sqn), 184
Béarn, Lt de, 297, 314
Beattie, Sgt J. A. D. (40 Sqn), 184, 349
Beau, S/Lt (GR II/22), 275
Beaud, S/Lt G. (GBA II/54), 451
Beaufrère, Sgt P. (GB I/21), 446
Beaumont, AC2 O. R., 268
Beaumont, Lt G. (825 FAA Sqn), 373

Beaumont, Sgt S. J., 304
Beaupré, Lt E. Pigault de, *145*
Beauregard, S/Lt Costa de (SAL 3/109), 341
Beauvallet, Adjt, 314
Becher, Uffz, 199
Bechtle, Lt O-W. (9./KG2), 376
Beck, Lt (13.(Z)/LG1), 379
Beckarian, Sgt (GC III/3), 337
Becker, Fw J. (StG77), 215
Becker, Gefr K-H. (8./KG27), 239
Becker, Gefr L. (3./JG2), 497
Becker, Lt (GAO 515), 492
Becker, Oberlt H. (9./LG1), 393
Becker, Uffz F. (4./KG54), 414
Becker, Uffz W. (4.(F)/122), 380
Becker-Rob, Oberlt H. (5./KG3), 253
Beckert, Lt R. (2./JG51), 347
Beckert, Oberlt H. (7.(F)/LG2), 388
Beckmann, Flgr T., 124
Becqueret, Sgt, 105
Beda, Sgt A. (GC I/2), 213, 429, 448, 458
Beda, Sgt (GBA II/51), 424
Bediez, S/Lt M., 159
Bedin, Micheline, *491*
Bedin, Yves, *491*
Beeby, Sgt A. S. (82 Sqn), 465
Beelen, Sgt J., 286
Beelitz, Gefr S. (Stab III./KG51), 382
Beer, Obergefr M. (4.(F)/11), 335
Beer, Uffz M. (4./KG3), 208
Beermann, Oberlt T., 211
Beese, Uffz A. (9./JG26), 409
Beevers, Sgt C. S. G. (12 Sqn), 423, 464
Begemann, Lt H., 211
Beguier, Sgt M. (GB I/19), 424
Behal, Lt (GC III/3), 326, 336
Behnert, Uffz H., 215
Behnke, Gefr Hans (8./KG2), 252, 327
Behnke, Lt K., 120
Behrend, Fw E. (5./ZG1), 265
Behrend, Uffz H., 210
Behrens, Fw H. (2.(F)/123), 359
Behrens, Lt (1./JG21), 374
Behrens, Uffz H. (Stab KG55), 470
Beiersdorf, Obergefr A. (9./KG54), 414
Beigel, Gefr A. (2./KG55), 376
Beine, Oberfw J., 240
Beinhoff, Uffz F., 210
Beisbarth, Uffz Siegfried, 162, *163*
Beisiegel, Oberlt G., 158
Beisser, Fw E., 240
Beiter, Fw O. (4./ZG1), 448
Bekarian, Sgt A. (GC 5/3), 334, 358
Belbèze, Capt. H., 106
Belcher, Sgt Edward J. (12 Sqn), 320, *505*
Belensen, Uffz K., 317
Bell, F/O J. S. (616 Sqn), 406
Bell, Lt J. L. M. (826 FAA Sqn), 496
Bell, Obergefr H., 263
Bell-Salter, P/O D. B., 312, 315
Bell-Syer, F/O H. B. (73 Sqn), 356
Belland, S/Lt, 280
Bellefin, Sgt A-P., 118, 285
Belles, Fw H. (5./KG55), 429
Bellgardt, Uffz E., 206
Bellin, S/Lt André (GB I/19), 440
Bellis, F/O C., 231
Bellocq, Sgt (GB II/19), 358
Bellogrote, Sgt (GB II/35), 447
Belz, Uffz H. (2.(H)/12), 434
Ben, Pierre, *320,* 323, 334, *466*
Benausse, Adjt (DAT Étampes), 414, 418
Bence, AC2 R., 232
Bendall, Sgt D. J., 136
Bendl, Sgt J. (GC I/6), 441
Benech, Sgt A., 273
Beneder, Uffz E. (6./KG76), 347
Benito, F/O F. M., 104

Benjamin, P/O (150 Sqn), 472
Benkelmann, Uffz J. (2./ZG26), 366
Benkert, Uffz E., 279
Bennett, P/O R. H. M. (107 Sqn), 450
Bennett, Sgt G. C. (110 Sqn), 233
Bennett, Sgt G. C. (609 Sqn), 399
Benoist, S/Lt M. (GAO 501), 424
Benoît, Lt (GB 4/38), 458
Benseler, Fw G., 208
Bentall, F/Sgt, 525
Benuchamp, Sgt de (GAO 1/584), 481
Benus, Lt, 98
Benz, Lt, 285
Benzie, P/O J. (242 Sqn), 351
Béran, Lt J., 249
Béranger, S/Lt, 94
Berchermeier, Oberfw J., 213
Berchtold, Uffz G., 316
Berdoulat, Cmdt P. (GB 2/11), 400
Berg, Maj. Ernst Fr. von (Stab III./JG26), 398
Berg, Oberlt (4./KG54), 414
Bergelin, Adjt, 234
Bergemann, Lt H. (3.(H)/13), 476
Bergendael, Adjt (later Maj.-Gen.) Count I. G. du Monceau de, 100
Bergener, Lt (5.(F)/122), 353
Berger, Adjt (GC II/10), 275
Berger, Fw A. (3./KG2), 470
Berger, Fw Karl (7./KG27), 210, 211
Berger, Lt A. (2./KG51), 382
Berger, Uffz E. (5./ZG26), 318
Berger, Uffz Gustav (1./KG53), 382, 383
Bergfeld, Fw W. (7./KG30), 402
Berggräfe, Uffz, 148
Bergk, Uffz K. (4./KG3), 381
Bergmans, Cpl J., 238
Berhaut, O/Lt C., 236
Berkefeld, Fw H. (9./KG4), 376
Berkum, Korp. B. A. A. van, 147
Berland, Adjt G. (GC II/2), 265, 274, 277, 317
Berland, Adjt R. (GAO 3/551), 465
Berlepsch, Lt F. von (KG54), 329
Berlin, Hptmn J., 212
Berlin, Oberlt Fr-W., 262
Bernache-Assollant, Capt. (GC III/6), 477
Bernadon, Sgt, 252
Bernard, Adjt M. (GR II/33), 111
Bernard, Capt. (GBA 2/51), 334
Bernard, Lt (GAO 1/520), 96
Bernard, Sgt (GC II/9), 459
Bernardy, Adjt De (GR 1/35), 352
Bernavon, Adjt A. (GC II/2), 259, 262, 315, 343, 375
Berndt, Fw H. (4./KG3), 208
Berndt, Uffz F. (8./KG27), 327
Berndt, Uffz K. (1./ZG26), 383
Berner, Gefr H. (2./KG53), 336
Berner, Uffz R. (6./KG53), 376
Berner, Uffz Walter (KGrzbV.12), 224
Bernet, Sgt R., 107, 249, 286
Bernhard, Gefr L., 366
Bernicke, Uffz K., 316
Berninger, Uffz K. (3./KG53), 476
Bernrieder, Uffz S. (7./StG2), 376
Berrang, Uffz K. (3./KG53), 476
Berridge, AC2 L. A., 248
Berry, F/Sgt George (1 Sqn), 481, 483
Berry, Naval Airman F. (801 FAA Sqn), 496
Berry, Sgt H. (150 Sqn), 464
Bertaux, Capt. M. (GR 1/52), 413
Bertelsmann, Ernst, 382
Bertelsmann, Lt R. (6./KG55), 263
Bertelsmann, Oberlt Eberhard (7./KG27), 382
Bertelsmeyer, Fw H. (3./KG1), 470
Berthaux, S/Lt F., 114
Berthel, Lt, 103
Berthelon, Lt-Col, 171
Berthet, Sgt Louis (GC III/7), 159, 270, 341

Bertheux, Lt C., 273
Berthold, Uffz, 206
Bertram, Oberlt H. (3.(H)/14), 288, 434
Bertram, Oberlt Otto (1./JG2), 321, 326
Bertram, Uffz H. (1./KG27), 428
Bertrand, Adjt Jean (GC III/7), 270, 401
Bertrand, Sgt B., 164
Bertrou, Cmdt Paul, 188, 241, 259
Berveiller, Capt. F. (GAO 543), 446, 451
Berwanger, Uffz E. (5./LG1), 393
Berz, Uffz T. (KG54), 328
Bès, Sgt M. (GC I/4), 208, 374
Beschet, Adjt (GC II/1), 335
Besson-Guyard, S/Lt, 248
Best, Lt Gen. Petrus, 84
Bethe, Uffz W. (8./KG30), 376
Bethell, P/O J. N. (53 Sqn), 431
Bethke, Gefr W. (5./KG54), 342
Bethke, Oberlt S. (2./JG2), 364, 400, 402
Bettany, LAC Fred L. (26 Sqn), 321
Beurer, Oberfw H. (2./JG3), 392
Beutel, Uffz H. (4./KG4), 448
Beutel, Uffz K. (5./KG53), 212
Beuvin, Sgt, 115
Beuving, Sgt K., 194
Bevan, Sgt H. C. C. (12 Sqn), 436
Bevillard, S/Lt, 265, 290
Bewlay, P/O H. R., 112
Beyer, Fw H. (3./KG77), 241
Beyer, Gefr O. (8./KG30), 263
Beyer, Oberlt (7./JG26), 386
Beyer, Oberlt G. (6./KG76), 347
Beyer, Uffz K. (5.(F)/122), 335
Beynet, Adjt Louis (GB II/19), 400
Bezner, Uffz, 94
Biard, Adjt (GC II/3), 340, 341
Biden, P/O G. M. V. (16 Sqn), 398
Bieber, Uffz H., 206
Bieberle, Lt Frantisek (GC 2/6), 364
Biedenkapp, Gefr R. (9./KG53), 410
Biedermann, Gefr H. (9./KG54), 479
Biegert, Fw E. (2./JG26), 388
Bielefeldt, Uffz Werner (1./JG20), 408
Bielmeyer, Uffz L., 160
Bienk, Uffz Wilhelm, 265
Bienvenu, Capt. J. (GB 3/23), 432
Bier, Oberlt A-W. (6./ZG26), 493
Bierema, 1e Lt P. T., 151, 194
Bierfelder, Uffz L., 240
Bierfreund, Uffz W. (1./StG2), 414
Bierwirth, Oberfw E. (3.(H)/13), 375
Biester, Uffz Helmut, 154
Biger, S/Lt S. (ECN 1/13), 416
Bik, Sgt J., 117
Bikowetz, S/Lt (GAO 507), 333
Bildau, Lt (1./JG20), 437
Billet, Sgt, 95
Billien, Mt (AB 4), 340, 492
Billoin, S/Lt Marcel, 270
Billon, Capt. C. (GC III/9), 407, 409, 410
Billottet, Mt, 239, 308
Binder, Lt J. (8./KG77), 388
Binder, Lt W. (3./JG3), 275, 316
Bingham, AC (110 Sqn), 345
Bingham, Sgt D.R. (226 Sqn), 183
Binham, Sgt A. E. (64 Sqn), 398
Binon, Adjt A., 238, 306
Bioletti, Cpl, 93, 98
Bird, AC1 R., 331
Bird, F/O F. D. (59 Sqn), 345
Bird, P/O (4 Continental Ferry Flt), 316
Bird-Wilson, P/O (17 Sqn), 315, 376
Birembaut, Adjt (ECN 5/13), 414
Birk, Fw L. (1./JG20), 392
Birkelbach, Bordfunker Fw Willi, 228

Birkenhead, Lord, 76
Birkner, Uffz W., 208
Birndorfer, Uffz, 297
Bisch, Lt X. (GR 1/33), 456
Bischoff, Flgr K-H. (KG51), 328
Bischoff, Lt (JG21), 121
Bisgood, P/O D. L. (3 Sqn), 311, 317
Bishop, P/O Lloyd G. (73 Sqn), 70, 72, 148, 149, 436, 518
Biskupski, Fw W., 278
Bissoudre, Lt (later Capt.) M. (GC II/3), 120, 156, 341, 388, 440
Bittkow, Uffz H., 158
Bitznat, Uffz Karl, 222
Bizet, Sgt E. (GAO 502), 284, 478
Black, Sgt J. McD. (10 Sqn), 458
Blackadder, F/Lt William Francis (607 Sqn), 77, 150, 233, 241, 313, 315
Blair, P/O (later F/O) K. H., 116, 144, 206
Blanc, S/Lt (GC II/4), 336, 451
Blanchard, Adjt (ECMJ I/16), 156, 325
Blanchard, Lt (GB II/23), 447
Blanchard, Sgt (GR II/22), 134, 426
Blanchart, Lt A. (I/3), 199
Blanchet, S/Lt M. (GAO 509), 424
Blanchot, Cpl (GR II/22), 107
Blanchot, Sgt H. (GR 1/52), 413
Blanck, S/Lt (GC I/3), 453
Blanckensee, P/O L. M. (21 Sqn), 390, 465
Blanco, Sgt A., 286
Blandford, AC2 P. J., 282, 293
Blank, Oberfw O., 209
Blankemeier, Oberlt H-J., 114
Blankenfuland, Uffz B., 240
Blanquart, Adjt A. (GB I/11), 400
Blase, Fw J., 317
Blaskowitz, Uffz W. (3.(F)/10), 335
Blass, Oberfw, 156
Blattmann, Uffz T., 120
Blattner, Hptmn E., 242
Blatz, Fw J. (5.(H)/13), 456
Blease, LAC, 36
Blechschmidt, Hptmn, 222
Bleich, Fw H., 117
Bleidorn, Fw G., 115
Blerage, Gefr W., 239
Blew, F/O D., 233
Blicker, Gefr H. (KG51), 328
Bliesener, Lt A., 308
Blietschau, Obergefr E., 226
Bligh, Sgt P. I. (103 Sqn), 455
Bloeck, Oberfw H., 211
Bloedorn, Hptmn Erich (III./KG4), 327
Bloem, Hptmn Walter (3./KG27), 210
Blohm, Lt P. (Stab II./JG26), 493
Blois, Sgt, 259
Blom, F/O W. M., 183
Blombecker, Uffz G., 253
Blomeley, P/O (1 Sqn), 136
Blomely, P/O D. H. (151 Sqn), 446
Blomfield, Maj. J. R., 391
Blommesteijn, 1e Lt L. J. W., 191
Blondeau, LV (2S4), 106
Blondeau, S/Lt (GC I/4), 470
Blondel, Cpl (GR II/33), 165, 452
Blondy, Lt (GBA I/54), 447
Bloomer, Sgt P. (15 Sqn), 362
Blount, AVM Charles H. B., 14, 16, 17, 47, 339, 344, 370
Blowfield, P/O P. H. (12 Sqn), 469
Bludau, Fw B. (LG2), 241
Bludau, Fw W. (KGrzbV.12), 224
Blum, Obergefr R., 277
Blume, Lt (7./JG26), 272, 469
Blumers, Lt O. (TrGr.186), 347
Bob, Lt (3./JG21), 364
Böcher, Lt F. (4.(F)/121), 154
Böcher, Oberlt (9./KG3), 381
Bock, Gefr (KGrzbV.9), 225
Bock, Genoberst Fedor von, 404, 443
Bock, Lt (3./JG3), 285, 431, 437

Bock, Uffz W. (3./StG76), 376
Bodaan, 1e Lt A. H., 192
Bodart, Adjt J., 200
Boddé, Jaap, 257
Boddington, Sgt John P. (12 Sqn), 444
Bodenberger, Oberlt W., 239
Bodenhagen, Gefr G., 265
Bodien, Uffz W., 102
Bodin, Sgt, 154
Boedecker, Uffz K. (1.(H)/14), 359
Boegel, Gefr H., 240
Boekhout, 1e Lt H. F. H. van (3-V-2), 194, 222
Boekhout, Lt van (2-I-1), 111
Boël, Adjt L. (9/V/1), 286, 334
Boenigk, Oberlt, 154
Boer, Fw R. (3./KG27), 210, 429, 434
Boesinghe, Sgt J. de Thibault de, 286
Bogdanski, Fw A. (2./KG53), 336
Bohle, Uffz F., 120
Bohlen-Halbach, Lt C. von, 133
Böhm, Hptmn (5.(F)/122), 459
Böhm, Lt (3.(H)/41), 335
Bohn, Uffz Emil, 240, 241
Bohnenkamp, Lt A., 209
Böhner, Oberlt O. (Stab II./JG53), 453
Böhner, Uffz Walter, 222
Boignes, Capt., 107
Boileau, Adjt (GC I/3), 478
Boileau, Cpl (GB 3/23), 432
Boillot, Sgt (GC II/7), 162, 211, 240, 441, 476
Boiselle, Fw R., 241
Boissel, Lt P. (GC II/2), 478
Boitelet, S/Lt H., 100, 156, 158, 253, 254
Böke, Uffz W., 162
Bokel, Gefr K-H. (2./JG52), 409
Bokelch, Fw W. (Stab KG27), 402
Bolle, S/Lt P. (GAO 2/506), 419
Bolle, Uffz Theodor (5./KG54), 383
Bolowski, Oberfw H. (Stab KG3), 342
Bolton, LAC John A. (26 Sqn), 378
Bolz, Oberlt, 294
Bomford, F/O C. P. (107 Sqn), 450
Bompain, Sgt D. (GC I/4), 212, 306, 347
Bomsdorf, Uffz R. (3.(F)/121), 341
Bonal Lt, 95
Bonanno, Aviere G., 477
Bond, P/O D. E. (500 Sqn), 398
Bondu, Adjt, 105
Bone, P/O P. K. (53 Sqn), 282
Bone, Sgt (103 Sqn), 469
Bonin, Hptmn von (Stab I./JG54), 447
Bonnefous, Adjt P. (GB I/62), 461
Bonnefoy, SM (AB 4), 324
Bonnet, Cpl (GAO 510), 478
Bonnet, Sgt (GB II/12), 456
Bontemps, Sgt (GB I/62), 432
Book, Gefr H. (5./ZG1), 396
Boon, P/O John, 271
Boon, Sgt P., 111, 191
Boormann, A., 120
Boot, P/O P. V., 244
Booth, P/O A. F. (235 Sqn), 390
Booth, P/O B. S. (48 Sqn), 332
Booth, P/O J. S. (59 Sqn), 244
Booth, Sgt C. W. K., 183
Booth, Sgt R., 248
Boothby, F/O (later F/Lt) J. R. M. 'Bob', 127, 205
Borchers, Fw (1./JG77), 322
Borchers, Obergefr H. (KG30), 211
Borchers, Oberlt (ZG76), 297, 306, 447, 497
Bordenet, Adjt (GB I/21), 466
Boremski, Uffz von (9./JG3), 440
Borg-Banks, P/O T. H., 293
Börgerding, Fw A. (Stab III./KG27), 347

Borgman, Sgt N. J., 276
Borgniet, S/Lt, 115
Borgwedel, Uffz H., 241
Borisch, Gefr W. (9./KG53), 410
Bormann, Oberlt K. (8./KG27), 327
Born, Oberlt K., 209
Borne, Cmdt A. (GC II/4), 478
Bornemann, Fw W. (TrGr.186), 242
Bornemann, Gefr M. (I./KG30), 347
Börner, Uffz E., 300
Börnicke, Uffz H., 210
Bornkessel, Uffz H. (1./ZG26), 467
Borries, Oberlt C. (Stab I./JG20), 402
Borris, Lt K., 262
Borrmann, Flgr W. (9./KG1), 495
Borrmann, Lt Gerhard (2./ZG52), 383
Borrmann, Uffz R., 290
Borstel, Uffz H. von (8./KG27), 347
Borth, Oberlt, 97
Borthwick, Sgt David, 293
Bortolini, Maresciallo G., 477
Bosch, Lt H. (Stab II./JG27), 453
Bosch, Lt J. W. T. (1-II-1), 191
Bosch, Uffz H. (KGrzbV.9), 225
Böselager, Lt A. Fr von, 262
Bosman, Sgt A. K., 261
Bossiroy, S/Lt E., 142, 286
Bothfeld, Fw, 293
Bott, Oberlt H., 213
Böttcher, Lt H. (4.(F)/121), 117
Böttcher, Uffz H. (KG51), 328
'Bottrop,' Fw (1.(F)/22), 407, 408
Botzki, Oberfw E. (3./KG55), 383
Boucher, S/Lt J. du (GC III/1), 210, 340
Boucher, SM (2S4), 495
Bouchier, G/Capt. C. A. 'Daddy', 349
Boudier, S/Lt (GC II/5), 251, 376, 392
Boudin, Sgt, 324
Boudinier, S/Lt E. (GAO 509), 424
Bouffier, Sgt, 285, 314, 316
Bouhy, Sgt A. (GC II/5), 112, 120, 274, 280, 335
Boulanger, Adjt, 248
Boulard, Lt P., 133
Boulay, Sgt, 170
Bour, S/Lt, 234
Bour, Sgt G., 260
Bourbon, Adjt L. (GC I/3), 285, 418, 433
Bourdot, Lt G., 305
Bouret, S/Lt (GB I/21), 387
Bourgault, Sgt H., 305
Bourges, S/Lt A. (GB I/11), 400
Bourgoin, S/Lt (GR II/36), 346
Bourhis, S/Lt, 286
Bourlon, Adjt E. (ECN 2/13), 380
Bournot, Uffz H., 252
Boursain, S/Lt (ECN 1/13), 341
Boursaus, Capt. (GAO 3/551), 95, 424
Bousquet, Sgt G. (GBA I/51), 433
Boussicaut, Adjt, 274
Boutarel, S/Lt (GC I/3), 263, 285, 453
Boute, Sgt Freddy, 236
Boutemard, Oberlt Suin de (4./LG1), 481
Boutillon, Adjt (ECN 1/13), 341
Bouton, Adjt S. (GC II/3), 340, 342
Bouttier, Sgt G. (GC III/2), 278, 340
Bouvard, Adjt, 162, 208, 249, 260
Bouvarre, Capt. Pierre, 189, 252, 270
Bouvay, Sgt, 273
Bouveret, Sgt, 314
Bouvry, Sgt, 93
Bouysse, Lt R. (GC I/8), 301, 417
Bowden, Sgt F. S., 116
Bowen, F/O (607 Sqn), 210
Bowen, LAC T. H. (103 Sqn), 181

Bowen, P/O N. G. (266 Sqn), 412
Bowen, Sgt (9 Sqn), 349
Bowen, Sgt Don J. (150 Sqn), 271
Bower, Cpl J., 293
Bowers, LAC (500 Sqn), 362
Bowler, P/O (40 Sqn), 469
Bowman, Sgt R. A. (107 Sqn), 450
Bowyer, F/O, 254
Box, Sgt A. (15 Sqn), 445
Boy, Uffz B., 153
Boyd, F/Lt (145 Sqn), 347
Boyd, Sgt T. (213 Sqn), 322, 386, 399
Boyer, Adjt Léo (GC III/7), 251, 260
Boyer, Sgt C. (GC II/6), 274, 498
Boyer, Sgt C. (GC III/7), 240, 252, 285, 452
Boyer, Sgt (GC II/3), 401
Boyle, LAC William Donald (142 Sqn), 322, 450
Boymond, Sgt Emile, 158, 206, 274
Boyton, Sgt S. C., 152
Bozon, Sgt (GB II/31), 392
Brabander, Lt de, 315
Brabant, Lt R., 260
Bracht, Uffz A., 289
Brackley, Sgt R. A., 312
Bradac, Gefr J., 317
Bradley, S/Ldr R. M. (150 Sqn), 464
Bradshaw, Sgt (21 Sqn), 458
Brady, F/O B. J. R., 233
Brady, Sgt, 270
Bragadir, Lt, 284
Braham, P/O D. F. (10 Sqn), 458
Brain, P/O C. J. A. C. (99 Sqn), 395
Brain, P/O J. (99 Sqn), 395
Braito, Fw W. (2./KG76), 442
Brakmann, Fw K., 279
Bramman, Fw K. (Stab III./LG1), 429
Brammer, Fw J. (9./KG55), 429
Brams, Sgt (103 Sqn), 437
Branch, F/O G. R. (601 Sqn), 304, 332, 335
Brand, Oberfw D., 223
Brand, Oberlt K., 240
Brand, Uffz W. (4./KG3), 381
Brandenberg, Lt H. (6./KG27), 210, 402
Brandes, Oberfw R., 239
Brandis, Oberlt Henning von, 220
Brandl, Gefr J. (2./KG51), 489
Brändle, Oberlt K. (4./JG53), 376
Brands, Sld (later Korp.) A. J., 111, 191
Brandt, Fw L. (4./StG77), 347
Brandt, Gefr H. (3./KG3), 381
Brandt, Gefr R. (4./KG3), 381
Brandt, Hptmn (9./KG51), 289
Brandt, Lt F. von (AufklGr.Ob.d.L), 427
Brandt, Obergefr A. (StG2), 290
Brandt, Obergefr P. (6./KG55), 263
Brandt, Uffz H. (2./JG1), 479
Branton, Sgt J. R., 157
Brard, Adjt, 98
Brathauer, Fw W. (8./KG27), 327
Bratherig, Fw R., 227
Brauchitsch, Gen. Walter von, 497
Brauer, Fw E., 213
Braun, Fw A. (1./KG1), 393
Braun, Obergefr K. (4./KG54), 414
Braune, Oberlt H., 207
Braunsburger, Uffz H., 290
Braunschweig, Oberlt G., 210
Brausch, Lt K., 290
Bräutigam, Gefr A. (6./KG76), 418
Bräutigam, Uffz O. (3./ZG26), 318
Braxator, Lt H. (JG1), 232, 256, 335
Bredtmeier, Fw, 239
Breemen, Lt F. van, 117
Breemer, Sgt J. van den, 236
Breese, F/Lt J. C. (82 Sqn), 465
Brehm, Uffz (Stab StG77), 466

Breit, Uffz R., 227
Breitenstein, Sgt André, 252, 264, 265
Breitscheidel, Uffz, H., 227
Brel, Lt A., 199
Bremer, Gefr H. (9./KG27), 327
Bremond d'Ars, Sgt P. de, 118, 213, 260, 285, 290
Brendgen, Uffz A., 213
Brenken, Lt H. (2.(H)/41), 392
Brennecke, Fw R., 279
Brereton, F/O T. F. S. (12 Sqn), 444
Bressel, Uffz (JG1), 365
Bressieux, Sgt (GC I/5), 254, 353, 408, 418, 479
Bret, Sgt R. (GC II/7), 158, 425
Bretnütz, Oberlt (6./JG53), 154, 249, 340
Breton, Lt (GR II/52), 260
Breton, Sgt (GR II/52), 260
Bretonnière, Lt J. de la (GC I/2), 188, 213, 429
Breugel, Sgt A. M. van, 158
Breyre, Adjt F., 261, 315
Brian, S/Lt (GC I/5), 476
Briançon, Sgt P. (GBA II/51), 346
Brias, Sgt (GAO 1/508), 469
Bricart, Adjt R. (GC II/2), 285, 427
Bridge, AC1 J. (37 Sqn), 405
Bridson, LAC R., 184
Briet, SM (AC 3), 475
Briey, Capt. Count Guillaume de, 286, 287
Bringewat, Uffz K-H. (6./KG4), 327
Brinken, Uffz W. (4./KG4), 448
Brinkmann, Fw W., 253
Brinn, Sgt C. J. W. (59 Sqn), 345
Brinn, Sgt W. G. (107 Sqn), 412
Brinsden, F/O (19 Sqn), 380
Brisou, Sgt R., 274
Brisset, Adjt, 296
Britting, Oberfw K-R. (8./LG1), 347
Broadhurst, P/O J. W. (222 Sqn), 391
Broadland, Sgt E., 272
Brock, Uffz H. (2.(H)/10), 470
Brockstedt, Obergefr K-H., 290
Broderson, Fw H-H., 307
Broeck, Sgt A. Van den, 162, 236
Bröer, Uffz Richard, 214
Brogan, AC2 A. C. (59 Sqn), 372
Bröge, Uffz M. (2./LG1), 337
Broich, Uffz P. (3./KG2), 381
Broissand, S/Lt, 107
Brömel, Gefr H-J. (6./LG1), 393
Bromley, F/O C. W. (40 Sqn), 362
Bromley, LAC J. S. (264 Sqn), 257
Bromley, LAC Jack (53 Sqn), 282
Bronitzky, Uffz (6./LG1), 393
Brook, Oberfw O. zum, 241
Brooke, Gen. Sir Alan, 460, 468
Brooker, Sgt J. R., 184
Brookes, Sgt James (142 Sqn), 270, 271
Brooks, Les (1 Sqn), 121
Brooks, Sgt (53 Sqn), 256, 412
Brooks, Sgt J. S. (75 Sqn), 339
Brooks, Sgt L. J. (77 Sqn), 385
Brooks, Sgt S. J. (142 Sqn), 182
Brosch, Lt H., 239
Brosteaux, Adjt M., 286
Brotchie, P/O (later F/O) George F. 'Ian', 15, 24, 44, 46, 51, 58, 63, 68, 72, 157
Brothers, F/Lt, 326
Brown, Alan, 350
Brown, Charlie, 350
Brown, 'Doc' (MO), 256
Brown, F/Lt (67 Wing), 487
Brown, F/Lt A. C. (53 Sqn), 256, 412
Brown, F/O J. R. (No. 4 FPP), 244
Brown, F/O (later F/Lt) M. H. 'Killy' (1 Sqn), 118, 119, 144, 146, 147, 167, 208, 242, 244, 327, 469
Brown, LAC (18 Sqn), 231, 293
Brown, LAC (26 Sqn), 267

Brown, LAC R. (139 Sqn), 150
Brown, LAC R. V. (613 Sqn), 378
Brown, LAC T. W. (114 Sqn), 270
Brown, P/O G. A. (66 Sqn), 257, 265
Brown, P/O M. K. (242 Sqn), 312
Brown, P/O M. P. (611 Sqn), 412
Brown, Sgt J. F. (37 Sqn), 398
Brown, Sgt R. (16 Sqn), 385
Brown, Sgt R. (107 Sqn), 248
Brown, Sgt R. J. W. (111 Sqn), 431
Browne, F/Lt P. E. S. F. M. (229 Sqn), 391
Browning, Sgt J. R. (107 Sqn), 465
Bruce, F/O (111 Sqn), 315, 434, 459
Brüchert, Uffz R. (4./JG3), 342
Brucker, Uffz R. (2./KG53), 336
Bruckert, Adjt H. (GC I/2), 156
Brückhändler, Lt K. (KG54), 329
Bruckhardt, S/Lt (GBA II/51), 346
Brückner, Oberlt K., 280
Brückner, Uffz E., 215
Brucks, Lt H. (JG26), 327
Brügelmann, Uffz H. (8./JG26), 402
Brugerolles, S/Lt E., 152
Bruijn, Sgt J. J. de, 194, 222
Brullot, Adjt, 110
Brumby, Sgt (103 Sqn), 469, 472
Brun, Lt (GC II/1), 285, 458
Brun, Sgt R. (GR II/55), 325
Brune, S/Lt G. (GR II/55), 334
Bruneau, Capt. G., 315, 316
Brunerie, S/Lt (GR I/52), 364
Brunet, S/Lt Raymond (GBA II/54), 425
Brunke, Uffz G., 241
Brunken, Gefr G., 208
Brunotte, Gefr H., 213
Bruns, Fw H. (2.(H)/12), 353
Bruns, Gefr H. (2./KG54), 383
Bruns, Lt E., 251
Brüsch, Uffz K., 317
Brustellin, Hptmn (Stab I./JG51), 425
Bruyere, Adjt, 273
Bruylants, Sgt M. (9/V/1), 315, 341, 374, 380
Bryan, AC1 T. J., 272
Bryant, F/Lt (26 Sqn), 390
Bryson, P/O (92 Sqn), 353
Brzezinski, Lt Jozef, 83
Brzezowski, Cpl M. (GC II/6), 425
Brzoska, Uffz P. (9./KG55), 429
Buchenau, Oberlt G. (4./StG2), 366
Bücher, Uffz M. (5./JG3), 366
Buchheim, Oberlt H., 207
Buchholz, Gefr J., 317
Buchholz, Oberfw K., 206
Buchholz, Uffz W., 228
Büchner, Fw H. (LG1), 241
Büchner, Uffz H. (KG54), 329
Bucholz, Lt, 303, 306
Buck, Fw R., 278
Buckfield, Sgt J. (78 Sqn), 356
Buckland, Sgt F. E. (54 Sqn), 362
Buckley, F/O C. Y. (107 Sqn), 450
Buckley, Lt Cdr James B. (825 FAA Sqn), 390
Buckner, Sgt, 134
Bucksch, Lt H., 301
Budden, Sgt P. H. J. (77 Sqn), 458
Buddenhagen, Lt (5./JG3), 416
Bues, Oberlt, 288
Bufferne, Sgt H. (GB II/63), 440
Buhl, Oberfw (1.(J)/LG2), 496
Bühler, Fw E. (3./KG53), 240
Buhler, Gefr M. (3./LG1), 214
Bühler, Oberfw K. (3.(J)/LG2), 434
Bührig, Uffz S., 225
Buisson, Sgt M., 259, 296
Bujalla, Lt W., 326
Bulkow, Gefr G. (KG54), 329
Bullock, Sgt H. F., 181
Bülow, Obergefr W. (9./ZG26), 470
Bülowius, Oberst A. (9./LG1), 489

Bulten, Sgt H. B., 192
Bungardt, Uffz H. (3./KG76), 418
Bür, Fw H., 145
Burcelin, Cpl, 284
Burda, Lt F. (GC I/4), 433, 434
Burgdorf, Uffz E., 208
Burge, Sgt R. W. (40 Sqn), 469
Burger, Fw A. (3./KG53), 476
Bürger, Fw F. (8./KG27), 327
Burger, Fw Wolfgang (KGzbV.1), 229
Burger, S/Lt J. (GC II/5), 425
Burgess, LAC A. C. B. (21 Sqn), 248
Burgess, LAC T. O. (12 Sqn), 267, 320
Burggaller, Maj. Ernst G., 113, 138
Burghardt, Gefr A. (6./KG3), 327
Burghardt, Oberfw A. (5./KG77), 290
Burian, Oberfw H. (8./KG1), 470
Burk, Obergefr L. (8./KG30), 376
Burke, S/Ldr W. I. H. (15 Sqn), 445
Burkhardt, Fw A. (3./JG26), 448
Burmester, Gefr E. (7./KG30), 402
Burmester, Oberfw H. (Stab III./KG1), 206
Bürner, Oberlt R., 300
Burns, F/O R. M., 184
Burns, Sgt R., 312
Burrell, Sgt P. A. M. (40 Sqn), 349
Burrows, AC1 John S., 107, 506
Burrows, LAC R. H., 183
Bürschgens, Lt J. (2./JG26 & 7./JG26), 99, 452
Bursztyn, Lt Kazimierz ('Montpellier Group' - GC III/1), 83, 249, 259, 364
Burt, LAC Charles S. (12 Sqn), 444
Burt, Sgt (21 Sqn), 431
Burt, Sgt B. W. (82 Sqn), 445
Burton, AC2 J. (149 Sqn), 356
Burton, LAM J. B. (806 FAA Sqn), 385
Burton, P/O R. W. (85 Sqn), 331
Burtonboy, Capt. P., 277
Bury, F/O David S. H. (111 Sqn), 318, 321, 517
Busby, Sgt G. (150 Sqn), 371
Busch, Lt H-H. (5./StG2), 414
Busch, Uffz (2./JG20), 398
Busch, Uffz Wilhelm (KGrzbV.12), 224
Busching, Gefr A., 241
Busching, Lt, 156
Bushell, P/O J. M. (151 Sqn), 309, 318, 362
Bushell, S/Ldr Roger J. (92 Sqn), 351
Büss, Lt G. (4.(F)/11), 456
Busschaert, Sgt P. (GAO 582), 416
Bussenius, Uffz L., 215
Bussey, P/O M. A., 312
Büterhorn, Obergefr Heinz, 265
Butler, F/Lt V. S., 272
Butler, Sgt C. H. (77 Sqn), 385
Butler, Sgt R. W. (88 Sqn), 371
Büttner, Uffz H., 225
Butterfield, Sgt S. L. (213 Sqn), 326, 335, 386, 388
Butterill, LAC C. (4 Sqn), 320
Butterweck, Lt F., 157, 259
Butterworth, P/O J. L. G. (53 Sqn), 167
Butterworth, P/O R. E. C. (13 Sqn), 339
Butterworth, Sub Lt W. S. (826 FAA Sqn), 496
Buttery, P/O R. T. L., 271
Buttler, Lt W. (4.(H)/23), 359
Büttner, Uffz G., 278
Butz, Sgt P. (GR I/52), 364
Butz, Uffz J. (5./KG2), 396
Butz, Uffz W. (7.(F)/LG2), 388
Buwalda, Sgt Maj. J. J., 159, 192
Buyens, Lt, 160
Byatt, Sgt J. (82 Sqn), 445
Byrne, F/O V. G. I. D. 'Paddy' (74 Sqn), 349

Cabaret, Sgt, 248
Cabon, QM (AB 3), 494
Cadiou, Sgt (GB II/12), 432
Cadoux, Cpl (GR II/22), 113
Cahen, Sgt G., 132
Caillet, Sgt Lucien (GB II/12), 432
Caldwell, Sgt R. C. (88 Sqn), 458
Callac, Sgt (GB II/31), 400
Callaghan, Sgt J. B. (226 Sqn), 272, 465
Callataÿ, Capt., 213
Calmel, S/Lt, 249
Calonne, Capt. de, 213, 252
Calvert, Eileen (née Morgan), 506
Calvert, P/O Jimmy L., 95, 506
Cameron, F/O D. A. (226 Sqn), 183
Cameron, P/O John S. (37 Sqn), 372
Camm, Sydney, 78
Campbell, F/O J. A., 245
Campbell, P/O C. (107 Sqn), 450
Campbell, P/O N. N. (242 Sqn), 487
Campbell, Sgt C. N. 'Ken' S., 15, 44, 46, 59, 71, 72, 120, 163
Campbell-Irons, P/O I., 246
Camphausen, Oberlt H. (7./KG4), 336
Campion, Cpl J. S., 244
Camus, Sgt (GBA II/61), 470
Canaux, Adjt M. (GB 3/23), 432
Caneau, Sgt (GB 1/19), 466
Canel, Capt. (GC II/9), 393, 417
Canonne, Sgt (GR 1/52), 93
Canonne, Sgt J. (GAO 501), 324
Caoudal, R., 490
Capdevielle, Sgt (GAO 1/551), 352
Capdeville, S/Lt (GR I/22), 95
Capon, Lt F., 237
Cappoen, Lt, 94
Capuro, Sgt S. (GB II/63), 358
Carbon, Sgt Y., 277, 280, 306, 309
Carbutt, Sgt D. (82 Sqn), 304, 465
Cardon, Adjt (GAO 2/520), 333
Carey, P/O F. R. (3 Sqn), 254, 262, 267, 493
Carey, Sgt B. T. P. (12 Sqn), 244
Cariou, Mt (T 2), 352
Carl, Fw H., 326
Carl, Uffz R. (7./KG76), 434
Carletti, Sgt J., 315
Carlier, Lt, 274
Carlile, Sgt Neville W. (82 Sqn), 465
Carmeille, EV1 (AC 3), 477
Carnaby, P/O W. F. (264 Sqn), 437
Carnall, Sgt R. (111 Sqn), 450
Carnier, Lt G., 205
Carpentier, S/Lt E., 199
Carpmael, Lt R. (825 FAA Sqn), 356
Carquin, Sgt (GBA I/51), 364
Carré, Sgt G. (GB I/34), 273, 340
Carrera, Adjt K. (GB I/63), 346
Carrier, Adjt André, 274
Carruthers, P/O H. D. (59 Sqn), 362
Carswell, P/O M. K. (43 Sqn), 406
Carter, F/Lt M. M., 282, 289
Carter, LAC A. (26 Sqn), 405
Carter, P/O P. E. G. (73 Sqn), 356, 423
Carter, Sgt (57 Sqn), 372
Carter, Sgt D. B. (150 Sqn), 464
Carteron, Adjt P. (GB II/21), 413
Cartier, Sgt, 305, 306
Cartigny, SM (1S2), 488
Cartwright, Sgt G. A. (105 Sqn), 270
Cartwright, Sgt H. (79 Sqn), 279, 293, 301, 331, 335
Carver, F/O A. J., 144
Casaneuve, Sgt J. (GC III/3), 337, 425, 427
Caselli, Capt. N., 477
Casenobe, Sgt (GC II/4), 117, 161, 288, 301
Cases, Sgt (GAO 1/584), 481

Casey, F/O M. J., 105
Casper, Gefr P., 211
Cassagnou, Capt. (GBA II/54), 481
Casse, S/Lt S., 305
Cassegrain, S/Lt (GB I/31), 400
Cassidy, Cpl, 282
Castanier, Cmdt P. (GC III/6), 358
Castel, EV (AC 5), 495
Castel, S/Lt H. de (GC I/8), 213, 290, 307, 380
Castellana, Lt G., 53, 126
Castillon, Sgt, 306
Castres, Sgt, 286
Catalano, Sgt E. de (GBA I/51), 424
Catalano, Tenente S., 467
Cater, Sgt, 273
Caters, Capt. J. de, 124
Cathala, Adjt A. (GR II/36), 99, 346
Caton, Lt M., 106
Catot, Adjt, 102
Cattoen, Sgt A., 189
Caudry, Sgt (GB II/31), 400, 432
Caujolles, S/Lt J. (GAO 517), 419
Cauquill, Sgt, 249
Caussat, Sgt G. (GC I/3), 340
Cavanagh, LAC W. T., 247
Cavaroz, S/Lt R. (GC III/6), 189, 341
Cave, LAC, 182
Cavett, AC2 W., 256
Cazade, Sgt (GC III/1), 301, 375, 376
Cazenave, Sgt (GR I/36), 325
Cazenove, F/O Peter (92 Sqn), 356
Cebrzynski, Lt A. (GC II/6), 83, 425, 429
Ceccaldi, Capt. A. (GR II/55), 359
Cechini, Obergefr H., 215
Cedruix, Adjt, 275
Chabannes, Sgt G. Ménard de (GB I/12), 456
Chabera, Sgt (GC II/5), 240, 280, 427
Chabert, Adjt E., 305
Chable, Adjt, 105
Chaboureau, S/Lt, 99
Chaffurin, PM (AC 5), 497
Chaillon, Sgt (GBA II/51), 433
Chainaut, Capt., 97
Challe, Capt. B. (GC I/3), 274, 418, 453
Challe, Lt R. (GC III/7), 235, 285
Chaltet, Sgt (GB II/21), 466, 469
Chalupa, S/Lt S. (GC I/2), 306, 448
Chamaud, Adjt H. (GB I/12), 234, 419
Chamberlain, Neville, 92, 125
Chamberlain, P/O Croyden J. E., 256, 520
Chambers, F/O G. L. (610 Sqn), 399
Chambers, F/O Richard D. C. (500 Sqn), 398
Chambers, P/O L. E. (242 Sqn), 312
Chambon, Sgt P., 126, 260
Champenois, Sgt G. (GB I/31), 400
Chancrin, Sgt M., 133
Chandler, P/O Gordon E., 257, 258
Chantelou, Sgt E. (GR II/55), 492
Chapat, Sgt J. (GR I/35), 352
Chapelle, Sgt A. de La (GC II/4), 97, 98, 188, 213, 326, 459
Chapera, Sgt (GC II/5), 448
Chaplin, Sgt (110 Sqn), 345
Chapman, F/Lt P. G. (15 Sqn), 313
Chapman, P/O (2 Sqn), 390
Chapman, Sgt E. W. J. (88 Sqn), 390
Chapour, Adjt, 189, 212
Chapuis, Sgt (GR 1/35), 108
Charbonnier, Sgt, 123
Chareyre, S/Lt (GR II/55), 447
Charlan, Lt, 324
Charle, S/Lt, 259
Charlet, Jacques, 350
Charleton, AC1 R., 233

Charlier, Adjt (GR II/52), 249, 325
Charlier, Capt. M. (2/I/2), 149, 196
Charlier, Cpl A. (9/V/1), 341, 380
Charoy, Adjt A. (GB 1/19), 400
Charpentier, Adjt, 94
Charreire, S/Lt J., 94
Chassandre-Patron, Cmdt (GB I/19), 400
Chastenet, Capt. M. (GR I/36), 433
Chatfield, Sgt K. C. (77 Sqn), 385
Châtillon, Adjt (GR I/35), 447
Chatterton, Sgt J., 293
Chauby, PM (T 2), 352
Chaudel, S/Lt B. (GR II/55), 492
Chaume, Mtre (AC 2), 488, 494
Chaumont, S/Lt A., 189
Chautard, Adjt (GB II/62), 461
Chauvet, S/Lt (GBA I/54), 103, 451
Chauvin, Sgt (GB II/62), 461
Chavet, Adjt R., 154
Chciuk, S/Lt Wladyslaw (GC 5/1), 297, 298, 340
Checkley, Sgt F., 184
Chemineau, S/Lt G., 297
Chenais, Lt (GC II/9), 452
Chénelot, Sgt P. (GC II/1), 433
Cherigié, Adjt, 296
Cherrington, P/O Geoffrey I. (32 Sqn), 446
Chesnais, Lt (GC II/9), 375, 434, 456
Chevalier, Sgt A., 284
Chevallet, Adjt (GBA I/54), 475
Chevassus, Adjt (GR I/35), 108
Cheysson, Lt J. (GAO 1/589), 413
Chezelles, Lt H. de, 260, 265
Chichester, LAM C. A. (825 FAA Sqn), 356
Chiers, S/Lt (GAO 1/508), 469
Chieusse, Sgt R. (GB I/63), 425
Child, LAC C. C., 246
Chilla, Oberfw A., 252
Chocheprat, Capt. P. (GBA 2/51), 424
Chommeloux, Sgt H. (GB II/63), 440
Chouler, Sgt M. R. (40 Sqn), 431
Choulet, Sgt H. (GC I/8), 274, 298
Chranowski, Obergefr W., 309
Chrétienne, Sgt, 296
Christ, Uffz M. (4./StG2), 366
Christensen, P/O S., 304
Christiansen, Oberlt G. (4./ZG76), 234, 414
Christie, AC1 W. A. (53 Sqn), 311
Christie, Sgt W. A. (53 Sqn), 232
Chuchra, Uffz E., 242
Chudleigh, P/O R. N., 151
Church, LAC A. F. (26 Sqn), 320
Churchill, F/Lt, 251
Churchill, Winston, 76, 281, 286, 292, 319, 348, 361, 389, 403, 420-421, 443, 449, 457, 463, 483, 486
Chuzeville, Adjt (GB II/23), 447
Cichos, Obergefr E. (8./LG1), 360
Cimander, Flgr S. (1./KG1), 392
Cimbetti, S/Lt, 274
Cizek, Lt (GC III/3), 326
Clade, Fw (1./JG1), 237, 373
Claireaux, Sgt R. (GC III/3), 466
Clancy, F/Lt G. D., 267
Clapham, F/Lt W. R. (16 Sqn), 385
Claret, Sgt, 305
Clark, Cpl R. S., 272
Clark, F/O R. B. G. E. (15 Sqn), 458
Clark, LAC (later Cpl) T. F. S., 97, 184
Clark, P/O (88 Sqn), 135
Clark, P/O Hugh D. (85 Sqn), 294
Clarke, AC L. R., 267
Clarke, F/O T. C. (4 Sqn), 267
Clarke, Sgt E., 284
Claude, Capt. P., 97
Claude, Mt (AB 1), 305
Claus, Lt (III./JG53), 117, 364, 400, 458
Clausen, Oberfw E. (3.(J)/LG2), 366, 442

Clausen, Oberlt (15.(Z)./LG1), 163
Clausse, Capt. (GC II/3), 347, 360
Clavaud, Sgt, 156
Clawley, Sgt G. W. (150 Sqn), 437
Claydon, P/O A. J. (501 Sqn), 423
Clayton, F/O G. T. B. (107 Sqn), 248
Clayton, Sgt (53 Sqn), 99, 362, 431
Cleary, AC1 M. C., 304
Cleaver, F/O G. N. S. (601 Sqn), 317, 322
Cleaver, LAC Donald V. (21 Sqn), *362*
Clegg, LAC, 182
Clegg, P/O, 282
Cleland, AC2 C. C. (59 Sqn), 244, 419
Clemenceau, Sgt P., 117
Clément, Lt (GAO 507), 234
Clément, S/Lt H. (GAO 513), 387
Clément, Sgt (GB II/21), 413
Clements, S/Ldr W. I., 99
Clerc, Lt (GB II/23), 447
Clerici, Sottotenente L., 477
Clerico, Uffz (1./JG21), 260, 374
Clifford, P/O Ralph H. (26 Sqn), *321*
Clifford, Sgt G. W. (150 Sqn), 322
Clift, P/O, 301
Clifton, P/O, 317
Clinquart, 1/Sgt H., 236
Clisby, F/O Leslie R., 156, 242, 251, 255, *256*, 263, 267, *439, 507*
Cloquette, Lt L., 238
Clostres, Lt, 235
Clouston, F/Lt F. N. (229/253 Sqn), 310, 353, 391
Clouston, F/Lt W. G. (19 Sqn), 376
Clowes, Sgt Arthur V. 'Taffy' (1 Sqn), *108*, 119, 120, 353
Cnudde, Walter, *382*
Coader, Sgt L. (GC I/1), 288, 307, 334
Coadic, QM, 93
Coant, Sgt, 259
Cobden, P/O (74 Sqn), 359, 371
Coburn, Sgt (40 Sqn), 469
Cochetel, Lt (GR II/14), 492
Cochrane, Sgt R. D. K. (26 Sqn), 423
Cock, P/O (87 Sqn), 254, 317, 326
Cocu, Sgt, 324
Codet, S/Lt (GC II/3), 162, 343, 376, 388, 442, 452
Codron, Sgt, 296
Cody, Sgt P., 93
Coene, Sgt R. M., 261
Coghlan, F/Lt (56 Sqn), 383
Coiffard, Adjt (GBA II/54), 440
Coignier, S/Lt M. (GAO 1/506), 380
Coiral, Cmdt A., 274
Coisneau, Sgt (GC II/4), 392
Colbourn, Sgt C. E., 313
Cole, Paul, *125*
Cole, Sgt W. F. L., 99
Coles, AC2 G. D. (59 Sqn), 345
Colin, Adjt (GB 1/11), 465
Colin, S/Lt (GR II/52), 235
Colin, S/Lt P. (GAO 509), 424
Collard, Sgt (GC I/4), 434
Colle, Lt (GBA II/51), 346
Colleseus, Uffz W., 277
Colleter, Lt J. (GB I/31), 440
Colling, Sgt A., 233
Collinot, Sgt (ECN 3/13), 96, 352
Collins, F/O J. N. (75 Sqn), 339
Collins, P/O S. G. (53 Sqn), 303, 450
Collomb, S/Lt (GAO 517), 419
Collombet, Lt (GBA II/51), 373, 433, 447
Collot, S/Lt (GR II/33), 452
Collyer, Cpl A. C., 232
Colombo, Maresciallo F., 477
Colombo, S/Lt R. (GB I/21), 446
Colomer, Adjt J. (GB I/11), 432
Colomes, Sgt (GC II/9), 335
Colonges, S/Lt G. (GC III/6), 235, 241, 358

Colpaert, Adjt A. (1/I/3), 365
Colpin, Lt P., 259
Combette, Adjt A., 96, 97, 118, 285
Comeley, P/O P. W. (87 Sqn), 331
Comme, Sgt (GB II/21), 456
Compin, Capt., 284
Confuron, Lt (GAO 1/584), 446, 481
Conill, Sgt (GBA I/54), 447
Coninck, Adjt H. de, 238
Connors, F/O S. D. P. (111 Sqn), 317, 321
Conquet, Cpl (GB II/23), 447
Conrad, Obergefr G., 254
Constant, Lt H. (GB 1/19), 400
Constantin, Adjt (GR II/33), 456
Contant, Sgt M. (GB I/11), 432
Conte, Adjt, 315
Contenson, EV1 du Bessey de (AB 1), 451
Cook, Sgt (9 Sqn), 349
Cooke, F/Lt N. G. (264 Sqn), 382, 399
Cooke, LAC H. (12 Sqn), 180
Cooke, S/Ldr (65 Sqn), 381, 388
Cooney, F/Sgt (56 Sqn), 382
Coope, S/Ldr W. E., 115
Cooper, AC1 C., 183
Cooper, F/Lt H. D. H. (110 Sqn), 423
Cooper, LAC E. W. L., 248
Cooper, Sgt J. H. (82 Sqn), 445
Cooper-Slipper, P/O (605 Sqn), 376
Coote, LAC C. E., 248
Copley, LAC (12 Sqn), 464
Coqueton, Lt L., 259
Corbett, P/O W. H., 182
Corbishley, F/Lt (PDU), *437*
Cordier, S/Lt (GC II/4), 459
Cords, Lt H., 280
Corelli, F/O F. M. C., 99
Cormouls, Lt Henri, 156, 265, 273
Corniglion-Molinier, Capt., 297
Cornu, Sgt (GAO 504), 106
Cornu, Sgt J. (GAO 582), 416
Corrège, PM (EGAN), 451
Corrin, Sgt (GC I/8), 366
Corsanini, Lt-Col, 248
Corsepius, Gefr J. (3./KG30), 347
Costa, Sgt M. (Gruppo 43), 467
Costey, Lt Paul, *285*
Cotte, Sgt (GAO 1/551), 352, 446
Cotterell, Sgt N. C. (12 Sqn), 464
Cotton, Sgt E. H. B. (107 Sqn), 450
Coucal, QM (T 2), 352
Couchen, AC (53 Sqn), 378
Coucke, Sgt J., 238
Couder, Sgt, 289
Couderq, Lt, 189
Coudoux, Adjt, 306
Couffon, Adjt (GC II/6), 429
Coughlan, P/O, 316
Couillard, Adjt J. (GC II/10), 275
Couilleau, Capt. (GB 1/19), 400, 466
Couillens, S/Lt R., 189, 212
Coullet, Adjt L. (GAO 2/514), 488
Coulommier, Sgt P. (GR II/14), 492
Courmes, Sgt (GAO 3/551), 314, 334
Courréges, Sgt, 296
Courteville, Sgt (GC II/9), 393, 456
Courtis, Sgt des (GBA II/51), 447, 451
Courtney, P/O R. N. H. (151 Sqn), 391
Coutaud, Capt. (GC I/1), 288, 289, 336, 434, 495
Couteur, Anthony le, *522*
Couture, Lt M. (GAO 1/508), 373
Couturier, S/Lt W., 165
Couzens, Sgt G. F., 119, 256
Couzon, Adjt, 296
Cowling, AC (53 Sqn), 303, 450
Cox, LAC Walter E., 257, *258*
Crabtree, Sgt D. P., 233
Crabus, Sgt A., 315

Craig, F/O G. D., 132, 138, 153
Craig, Sgt A. E. (18 Sqn), 320, 339
Craig, Sgt John T. (111 Sqn), 312, *317*, 318
Craignic, EV1, 239
Cramer, 2e Lt J. J., 250
Cramon, Lt von (Stab I./JG3), 323
Cramon-Taubadel, Maj. von, 126
Crane, F/O John F. R., 134, 160, 271, *508*
Crawford, AC1 F. (77 Sqn), 332
Crawley, P/O C. D., 273
Crawley, Sgt J. K., 304
Crece, P/O C. M. M. (59 Sqn), 321
Crellin, Sgt E. H., 107
Crémieu, Adjt, 301
Créput, Sgt (GR II/33), 478
Cressey, LAC, 349
Crew, Sgt K. B., 107
Crews, F/O C. A. R., 233
Crich, Sgt W. R. (103 Sqn), 345
Crick, Cpl J., 104
Critch, Sgt W. R. (103 Sqn), 455
Crocq, Adjt J. (GC II/1), 328, 416, 418, 434
Crompton, F/O R. K. (611 Sqn), 412
Cronan, P/O J. R. (235 Sqn), 390
Cronin, Sgt W. J., 99, 282
Crook, AC1 (149 Sqn), 356
Crooy, Adjt L., 277
Cros, Adjt (GB I/11), 432
Cross, F/Lt R. P. Y. (235 Sqn), 390
Cross, LAC C. (73 Sqn), 483
Crossland, Sgt, 273
Crossley, F/Lt (32 Sqn), 376
Crouch, Sgt A. G. B., 304
Crowley, LAC (139 Sqn), 134, 246
Crowley, Sgt P. J. (107 Sqn), 412
Crozier, Sgt (82 Sqn), 445
Crozier, Sgt L. A. (85 Sqn), 293, 294
Crozon, Sgt, 98
Cruchant, Adjt, 102, 161
Crusoe, F/O C. G. H., 127
Crutel, Adjt, 306
Cucumel, Sgt Johannès (GC I/4 & GC II/9), 213, 239, 241, 335, 375, 418, 433, 434
Cuffaut, S/Lt, 118
Cugnet, Sgt (GR I/52), 325
Cuiller, Adjt, 305
Cukr, Sgt V. (GC II/3), 161, 162, 360, 374, 442, 447
Cummins, Cpl T. H., 304
Cunningham, P/O Vernon A., 268, *269*
Cuny, S/Lt, 274
Currant, P/O C. F. (605 Sqn), 345
Currie, Sgt (40 Sqn), 469
Currie, Sgt W. R. B. (53 Sqn), 282, 293
Curthelet, Adjt, 298
Curtis, Sgt E. F. W. (142 Sqn), 464
Curzon, F/O R. K. (500 Sqn), 465
Cuthbert, F/O Gerald I., 272, *508*
Cuvillier, Sgt H. (GAO 501), 424
Cybulski, Uffz H., 164
Cytron, Gefr S. (7./KG30), 402
Czaja, Gefr H. (2./KG55), 376
Czaplinski, S/Lt W. (DAT Clermont-Ferrand), 419
Czastka, Gefr O. (9./KG77), 388
Czech, Uffz Wilhelm (KG54), 329
Czerniak, S/Lt J. (GC I/145), 452, 456
Czernik, Oberlt G. (6./KG2), 278, 476
Czernin, F/O Count M. B., 294, 329, 335, 462
Czikowsky, Oberfw W. (6./JG53), 97, 402

Dabelow, Gefr R. (I./JG76), 366
d'Achon, Sgt H., 285
Dafforn, Sgt R. C., 239, 283
Dagbert, Adjt (GC I/4), 434
Dagnaux, Lt-Col J., 188, 314
d'Agostin, Fw O., 225
Dahinden, Oberlt, 288

Dahlen, Gefr K-H. von (9./KG1), 342
Dahlen, Oberfw H. von (7./KG76), 300
Dähling, Uffz W. (6./KG1), 353
Dahmer, Uffz (4./JG26), 294, 437
Dähne, Fw Manfred (5./ZG1), 448
Dähne, Fw R. (4./LG1), 254
Daig, Lt E. (5./JG27), 434
Daisley, Sgt L. C. W. (264 Sqn), 386
d'Alançon, Lt E. Audemar (GC I/4), 336, 427, 433
Daley, Cpl A. (57 Sqn), 356
Dallmeier, Flgr L., 213
Dalwigk, Oberlt E. Fr von (2./KG51), 489
Daly, F/Lt B. B. St G., 282, 293
Damazyn, Gefr G., 251
Dambock, Flgr E. (2./KG53), 336
Dambrine, Sgt W., 171, 260
Dampierre, S/Lt A. de (GBA II/54), 475
Danapel, Fw F. (3.(F)/10), 335
Dandorfer, Uffz J. (7./KG76), 434
D'Anglejan, Lt (GR I/55), 475
Danhiez, Sgt J. (9/V/1), 359
Daniel, Adjt J. (GB I/11), 400
Danielsick, Uffz A. (4.(H)/22), 335
Danielson, F/O P. J. (605 Sqn), 379
Dannewitz, Hptmn H. (8./KG77), 388
Danse, Adjt D., 274
Danzenberg, Lt, 316
Danzmair, Obergefr K., 209
Darcy, Sgt (GBA II/61), 470
Dardaine, Adjt H., 97
Darling, Sgt E. V. (41 Sqn), 390
d'Arrast, Capt. C. d'Abbadie (GC II/2), 447
Darre, Lt, 157
Darriet, Adjt C. (GBA I/51), 447
d'Ars, Sgt de Bremond *see* Bremond d'Ars, Sgt P. de
Dartevelle, S/Lt J. (GC III/2), 251, 274, 334, 466
Dartiges, Sgt A. (GB I/11), 432
Darwin, P/O (87 Sqn), 301, 317, 318
Darwood, Betty (née Simpson), *508*
Darwood, F/Lt Charles S., 312, 315, *508*
d'Astier, Gen., 443
Daszewski, S/Lt J. (DAT Romorantin), 419
Datz, Fw H., 154
Dau, Gefr B. (3./KG54), 308
Dau, Oberfw (1./JG20), 306, 399
Daubner, Lt A. (4./KG76), 366
Dauge, Sgt P. (GB 4/31), 400
Daum, Uffz W., 213
Daumling, Oberlt A., 206
Daunizeau, Sgt (GC II/9), 418, 459
Daval, Lt J. (GC II/9), 417
Davan, Sgt (GB II/62), 461
Davau, Mot (SESBA), 488
Davey, P/O T. J. F. (4 Sqn), 339
David, P/O W. D., 110, 212, 299
David, Sgt (ECN 5/13), 407
Davids, Oberlt B., 252
Davier, Lt J., 93
Davies, F/O (79 Sqn), 277, 317, 441
Davies, LAC Leslie D. (218 Sqn), *245, 247*
Davies, LAC P. K. (226 Sqn), 157
Davies, LAC R. D. (18 Sqn), 231
Davies, P/O G. G. A. (222 Sqn), 399
Davies, Sgt W. E. M. (15 Sqn), 247
Davis, Sgt (59 Sqn), 321
Davis, Sgt (600 Sqn), 184
Davis, Sgt J. (271 Sqn), 233
Davis, Sgt T. W. (139 Sqn), 246
Davison, Sgt (103 Sqn), 153
Davison, Sgt E. (218 Sqn), 161
Davonneau, SM (AB 1), 340
Davy, P/O Tom D. H., *244*
Dawson, F/O J. (609 Sqn), 395, 406
Dawson, P/O M. B. (149 Sqn), 458

Daxner, Flgr J. (7./KG51), 328
Day, F/O K. H. V. (9 Sqn), 349
Day, P/O J. H. (13 Sqn), 311
Day, Sub-Lt A. V. M. (801 FAA Sqn), 496
Day, W/Cdr Harry M. A. 'Wings' (57 Sqn), *104, 351*
De Bort, Lt, 324
de Gaulle, Gén. Charles, *449*, 486
Deacon, P/O A. H. (242 Sqn), 386
Deacon, Sgt A. H. (85 Sqn), 299, 321
Dear, LAC G. A. (37 Sqn), 372
Dearden, F/O C. H. (2 Sqn), 303, 398
Deas, P/O J. H. (26 Sqn), 378
Debaris, S/Lt (GR II/14), 499
Debéthune, Sgt C., 235, 239
Debladis, Lt (GAO 3/551), 424
Debrocq, S/Lt J. (GB I/11), 400
Decaix, EV1, 324
Déchanet, Adjt P., 188, 211, 249
Decker, Cynrik De, *382*
Decombes, Sgt M. (GB II/21), 413
Deekarm, Oberfw K., 239
Deelers, Sgt, 167
Deere, P/O A. C. (54 Sqn), 349, 353, 373, 385, *386*, 388
Defaye, S/Lt P. (GB II/19), 466
Defendini, Sgt D. (GB 3/23), 432
Degreef, Sgt J. (1/I/1), 359
Deichmann, Gefr J., 223
Deicke, Oberfw R., 206
Deil, Uffz M. (5./KG51), 470
Deimann, Lt W. (1.(H)/41), 452
Deimling, Uffz F. (1./KG27), 428
Deinzer, Gefr G. (III./JG52), 434, 441
Deisinger, Uffz H., 225
Dejardin, Sgt J-P., 145
Dekastello, Sgt J. (GC I/8), 337, 417
Dekker, Sgt O. W. Douwes, 191, 261
Delabasserue, Lucien, 317
Delacourt, S/Lt, 296
Delacroix, Adjt G. (GB I/12), 419
Delage, Adjt, 324
Delannay, 1/Sgt R., 198
Delannoy, Adjt, 163, 171
Delap, S/Ldr M. V., 304
Delarue, Sgt R., 117, 133, 158
Delasseaux, Sgt (GR II/36), 346
Delattre, Lt R., 248
Delaunay, Lt, 286
Delbroeck, S/Lt R. (1/I/1), 365
Delegay, Adjt (GC I/1), 298, 495
Delfino, Capt. (GC II/9), 375, 429, 434, 452, 456
Delhoume, Sgt (GC II/6), 429
Delineau, Sgt (GB II/19), 358
Delisle, Sgt (GC II/2), 252, 408
Delmotte, Adjt, 305
Delocque-Fourcault, S/Lt (GC II/8), 407
Delorme, Cpl J. (GAO 543), 451
Delorme, Sgt (1/I/2), 162
Delove, Capt., 273
Delozanne, Cmdt E., 94
Delparte, Sgt (GC I/5), 253, 417
Delpech, Sgt (GAO 518), 340
Delperie, Lt J. (GB I/19), 424
Delporte, Adjt (GBA II/54), 451
d'Elsa, Hptmn E., 318
Delvigne, Adjt F., 238
Demede, Sgt (GB II/21), 456
Demetriadi, P/O R. S. (601 Sqn), 332
Demimuid, Capt. (GR II/22), 426
Demoliner, Gefr J. (8./KG51), 360
Demoulin, S/Lt (GC I/6), 479
Demozay, Jean 'Moses', *256*
Demuyter, Sgt (GAO 2/506), 419
Denain, Adjt J. (GR I/52), 170, 260
Denain, Sgt J. (GR I/52), 364
Deniau, Adjt A. (GC II/6), 142, 213, 285, 290
Denis, Sgt (GBA I/51), 451
Denis, Sgt (GAO 1/589), 413

Denison, Sgt H. T. (107 Sqn), 450
Denner, Fw K., 251
Dennerl, Fw A. (5./KG1), 488
Deplanque, S/Lt (GAO 1/551), 324
Derbey, Sgt (GB II/63), 358
Deremont, Sgt, 284
Deringer, Uffz H. (3./KG53), 476
Dertinger, Gefr H., 209
d'Ertsenrijck, Capt. A. E. A. van den Hove, 145, *146*, 196
Desbordes, Sgt (GAO 510), 424
Descamp, Lt (GB I/21), 466
Descamps, Sgt Guy (GB I/19), 440
Desclée, S/Lt F., 251
Desesquelles, Sgt J. (GB I/31), 400
Deshons, Sgt, 286
Desmazières, Pierre-François (DAT Châteauroux), 429
Desmeth, Lt G., 286
Desmons, LV, 152
Desneux, Sgt (GB I/31), 334
Desprette, Sgt, 273
Desroches, Sgt P., 305
Desrumeaux, Sgt (GC II/2), 262, 375
Dessault, Adjt (GC II/3), 340, 341, 346
Destaillac, Capt. (GC II/5), 341, 392
Destannes, Capt. L., 296
Dester, Fw W. (4./LG1), 459
Detal, 1/Sgt Charles F. J., 199
Dethier, Capt. René, *199*
Dethlefsen, Uffz J., 254
Detrie, Lt, 249
Dettke, Oberfw O. (1./KG55), 410
Deutschenbaur, Oberlt L., 157
Deutschle, Uffz J., 288
Devalez, S/Lt, 296
Devin, S/Lt (GBA II/54), 440
Devin, Sgt (GC II/6), 262
Devise, Capt. de (GAO 2/520), 212, 358
Devon, Mr, *66, 67*
Devoto, F/O D., 154, *502*
Dewar, S/Ldr J. S., 168, 242
Dewar, Sgt F., 144
Dewing, Lt, 107
Dewit, S/Lt H., 306
Dexter, P/O (16 Sqn), 339
Dezellis, Sgt (GB II/62), 400
D'Haes, S/Lt M., 199
d'Hamale, Sgt R. de Cannart, 251
d'Harcourt, S/Lt Robert (GC II/3), 340
d'Hennezel, Capt., 306
d'Hondt, Adjt A., 251
Di Croce, Aviere E., 477
Dibden, Sgt Leon G. M., 15, 48, 268
Dibnah, P/O R. (1 Sqn), 371
Dibowski, Oberfw (7./ZG26), 334
Dichamp, Marcel, 407
Dickens, W/Cdr Louis W., DFC (139 Sqn), 246
Dickens, W/Cdr T. C. (103 Sqn), *394*, 472
Dickfeld, Gefr R., 146
Dickfoss, Fw P., 135
Dickhut, Uffz P. (4./KG51), 409
Dickins, P/O D. S. (18 Sqn), 349
Dicklow, Fw E. (4./JG3), 434
Diebel, Uffz E., 107
Diegmann, Uffz H., 242
Diekert, Fw K. (Stab I./KG51), 429
Diekmann, Uffz R., 239
Diepstraten, Cees van den, *258*
Dieren, Uffz O., 241
Dierickx, Lt E., 286
Dierkes, Uffz A., 254
Diesterweg, Fw R., 107
Dietrich, Fw T. (5./KG53), 212
Dietrich, Lt R. (1.(H)/41), 206
Dietrich, S/Lt (GC II/10), 298, 300, 426
Dietrich, Sgt F. (GC II/4), 364, 366
Dietrich, Sgt (GC II/8), 313
Dietrich, Uffz F. (9./KG27), 327
Dietrich, Uffz G. (JG3), 160
Dietsch, Uffz H. (3./ZG1), 410

Dietz, Fw R. (TrGr.186), 479
Dietze, Gefr P., 327
Diguet, Cpl (GB I/25), 475
Dijk, Sgt I. van, 104
Dill, Gefr G., 95
Dill, Lt-Gen. Sir John, 369
Diller, Uffz W. (9./JG2), 376
Dillon, P/O A. M. 'Tony', 312
Dilnot, F/Lt A. A., 107
Dilnutt, LAC L. S. (48 Sqn), 390
Dimpfl, Fw E., 290
Dingle, F/O R. H., 244
Dini, P/O A. S. (607 Sqn), 183, 210, 214, 241, 262, 313, 399
Dint, S/Lt, 274
Dirking, Lt zur See E., 214
Dittmar, Lt, 270
Dittrich, Fw G. (4./KG77), 213
Dittrich, Gefr A. (7./KG53), 429
Dittrick, Hptmn (1.(F)/22), *407*
Divoy, Leon, 374
Dixon, Cpl G. H. (226 Sqn), 183
Dixon, P/O H. D. (26 Sqn), 378
Dixon, P/O H. P. (607 Sqn/145 Sqn), 183, 214, 233, 241, 283, 290, 347, 406
Dixon, P/O L. T. (18 Sqn), 180
Dixon, Sgt (88 Sqn), 455, 461
Dobner, Oberlt B. (3.(H)/21), 434
Dobrzynski, S/Lt Witold, 160
Dobschall, Uffz A. (4.(F)/121), 408
Dochain, Sgt D., 261
Dockrill, Sgt C. J. E., 233
Dodds, F/Lt S. (48 Sqn), 332
Dodgshun, P/O G. T. (115 Sqn), 339
Dodgson, P/O Harold, 142, *510*
Dodrill, Sgt (82 Sqn), 445
Doege, Fw Gustav (5./KG51), 429
Doemming, Oberlt H-J. von (3./StG76), 388
Doermer, St H. (4.(F)/122), 335
Döhla, Gefr E., 289
Doidge, F/O A. F. (2 Sqn), 405
Dolan, AC2 M. D. (102 Sqn), 332
Dolan, Sgt J. (38 Sqn), 398
Dold, Lt O. (7./KG27), 382
Dolega-Kozierowski, Oberlt O. von, 315
Domain, Sgt, 324
Domanski, Oberfw A., 120
Domas, SM, 308, 314
Dôme, Adjt Jacques, *238*
Domeier, Lt H-B. (Stab I./ZG2), 376
Domine, Adjt, 188
Domke, Lt H., 116
Dommelen, H. W. van, 149
Domminger, Oberfw (2./JG76), 433
Domo, Adjt (GB II/12), 456
Donaldson, S/Ldr E. M. (151 Sqn), 309, 310, 318, 347, 391, 393, 408
Donaldson, Sgt R. (149 Sqn), 458
Donderer, Uffz J., 309
Donkersloot, 1e Lt L., 250
Donlon, Sgt, 182
Donne, F/Lt M. S., 233
Donnet, Sgt Mike (later Lt Gen. Baron), 374
Doominger, Oberfw (2./JG76), 433
Doorenbosch, Aro. J. J. Clinge, 117
Dopagne, Sgt Hubert, *124*
Doppenberg, Lt, 205
Dorance, Lt (GC I/5), 157, 254, 263, 326, 329, 353, 408, 441
Dorcy, Adjt Pierre (GC II/2), 213, 252, 264, 408, 427, *488*
Dörenberg, Fw W., 301
Dorer, Flgr O. (2./KG53), 336
Dörffel, Lt G. (5.(S)/LG2), 388
Dörfler, Gefr J., 113
Döring, Oberlt P., 164
Döring, Oberst K-B. von, 160
Döring, Uffz H. (8./LG1), 347
Dormad, Sub Lt G. S. (826 FAA Sqn), 496
Dormer, Sgt P. F., 233
Dornier, Claude, 86
Dorowski, Fw G. (AufklSt.z.b.V), 365

Dörr, Oberfw Hermann (7./JG26), 448
Dörr, Uffz F. (2.(H)/23), 277
Dörrfuss, Lt E., 317
Dorrien-Smith, Francis, *510*
Dorrien-Smith, P/O Lionel R. (79 Sqn), 293, 331, *510*
Dorrien-Smith, Robert, *510*
Dorris, Sgt D. L. (40 Sqn), 461
Dörwald, Lt Otto-Friedrich (Stab LG1), *214*
Dörwaldt, Oberlt F. (Stab II./KG2), 300
Doublet, Sgt K. (GC III/1), 210, 336, 376, 458
Doucet, Adjt R. (DAT Étampes), 413
Doucet, Cpl (GAO 552), 314
Doudies, Sgt (GC II/7), 145, 240, 414
Douglas-Cooper, F/O J. S. (149 Sqn), 458
Douglass, F/O P. N., 247
d'Oultrement, Count Gaston, 94
Douthwaite, Sgt (72 Sqn), 414
Douxami, EV1, 324
Douzet, Sgt (GBA I/51), 466
Dowding, ACM Sir Hugh, 77, 281, *284, 292*
Dowjatow, Fw R. (8./KG4), 479
Dowling, Sgt A. N. (103 Sqn), 472
Downes, Lt A. S., 248
Downham, Sgt E. A. (37 Sqn), 405
Draaisma, Sgt R. M., 191
Drabble, P/O K. J., 181
Dräger, Uffz E., 290
Drake, F/O (73 Sqn), 471, 487
Drake, F/O Billy (1 Sqn), 255, *256*
Drakes, P/O (49 Sqn), 233
Draper, AC1 W., 269
Drebber, Fw W., 146
Dreffkorn, Fw W., 240
Dreier, Fw K. (Stab KG77), 470
Dreikorn, Hptmn P., 228
Drengk, Oberlt Leo, 225, 226
Drescher, Uffz W. (4./KG77), 453
Dreschler, Gefr F. (9./KG54), 414
Dressel, Obergefr E. (6./LG1), 496
Dressler, Fw S., 119
Drexl, Uffz F. (1.(H)/23), 427
Dreyer, Fw F. (2./KG126), 360
Dreyer, Gefr A. (8./KG51), 360
Dreyer, Obergefr W. (4./KG4), 209
Drimmle, P/O G. K. R., 256
Dröge, Uffz A., 298
Droitcourt, Sgt, 113
Dromgoole, P/O I. (16 Sqn), 320
Drong, Uffz E., 207
Drossaert, Lt A., 142, 196
Drossel, Lt H., 115
Droste, 2e Lt F. G. B., 194, 211
Drouelle, S/Lt E. (GBA I/51), 364
Drouet, S/Lt F., 275
Drummond, AC1 J. A., 134
Drummond-Hay, F/O P. (609 Sqn), 458
Dryander, Lt S., 242
Dryden, P/O K. C. (56 Sqn), 390, *392*
Dubois de Luchat, Uffz E., 226
Dubois, LAC (103 Sqn), 385
Dubois, Lt (GAO 510), 259
Dubois, Sgt P. (GR II/55), 341
Dubost, Sgt (GC I/1), 307, 495
Dubreuil, Lt (GC III/2), 452, 466
Ducancelle, Sgt (ECN 4/13), 380
Ducas, Sgt (GBA 3/54), 425
Ducasse, Lt, 105
Duchène-Marulaz, S/Lt (GC I/6), 334, *466*
Duchesne, S/Lt G., 196
Duckenfield, P/O B. L., 233
Duckers, LAC (142 Sqn), 331, 458
Duclau, Cpl P. (GB I/21), 364
Duclos, Sgt, 96
Duda, Capt. (GC II/5), 476
Dudek, Oberfw A., 309
Dudezert, Capt., 100, 286
Dudwal, S/Lt Hieronim (GC II/10), *440, 441*

Dudzinski, Uffz M., 240
Duensing, Fw F. (1./ZG1), 429
Duffaud, Sgt, 275
Duffort, Lt (GB II/63), 358
Duffour, Sgt P. (ECN 1/13), 416
Duffy, Sgt (110 Sqn), 345
Dufossez, Lt E., 199
Dufour, Adjt (GAO 501), 364
Duggan, AC2 D. (115 Sqn), 339
Dugoujon, Adjt J. (GC II/5), 115, 427, 476
Dujardin, Uffz G. (8./KG30), 376
Dulac, Capt. (GC II/10), 274, 441
Dulait, Lt A., 251
Dumas, Adjt, 253
Dumas, Cmdt, 95
Dumas, Cpl, 94
Dumas, Sgt S., 152
Dumbreck, Sgt O. W., 151, *511, 514, 519*
Duminil, S/Lt, 96
Dümler, Lt K. (4./KG3), 381
Dumonceau, S/Lt (DAT Chartres), 418
Dumond, S/Lt (GB II/21), 466, 469
Dumont, Adjt (GIA I/601), 462
Dumont, Cpl J. (GB I/12), 400
Duncan, Sir Andrew, 421
Dundas, F/O J. C. (609 Sqn), 395
Dundee, P/O, 140
Dunford-Wood, F/O H. D. S. (21 Sqn), 445
Dunn, F/Sgt W. A. (226 Sqn), 157, 272
Dunn, P/O A. W. (77 Sqn), 332, 431, 455
Dunn, P/O H. J. R. (87 Sqn), *114*, 115, 171, 321, 327, 331
Dunse, Oberlt H. (8./LG1), 347
Dunstheimer, Lt F., 265
Duperret, S/Lt G., 97, 249
Dupond, Sgt (GBA II/51), 334
Düpong, Flgr P. (AufKl.Gr.Ob.d.L.), 375
Dupont, Capt. P. (GB 2/19), 456
Dupont, Mtre J. (AC 2), 314
Dupont, S/Lt (GAO 2/506), 373
Dupont, S/Lt (GB II/21), 466, 469
Dupont, Uffz K-H., 223
Dupouy, Sgt Pierre (GC I/8), 306
Dupre, Lt (GB 1/31), 451
Dupuis, Sgt (GB I/19), 392
Dupuy, Lt J. (GBA II/54), 451
Dupuy, Sgt (GAO 1/508), 168
Durand, Lt R. (GR II/55), 325
Durand, Sgt A. (GC III/1), 188, 214, 315, 336
Durand, Sgt (ECN 2/13), 158
Durie, P/O R. A., 312
Durod, Lt (GC II/5), 470
Durouchard, Sgt, 96
Duryn, Uffz M., 208
Dussart, S/Lt J., 235, 240
Dutartre, Lt E. (GAO 509), 424
Düte, Oberfw F-W. Meyer zu, 206
Dutel, Lt E., 205
Dutertre, Lt, 189
Dutton, F/Lt R. G. (145 Sqn), 310, 402
Duus, F/O (79 Sqn), 318, 337
Duval, Capt. (GC 6/3), 360
Duval, Cpl (GAO 581), 465
Duval, Sgt (GR II/52), 260
Düvel, Fw H., 279
Dvorak, Lt B., 154
Dyer, F/O J. P. (99 Sqn), 339
Dyke, Sub Lt V. J. (826 FAA Sqn), 496
Dyma, Lt F. (GC III/7), 341
Dymond, Sgt W. L. (111 Sqn), 398
Dziallas, Obergefr H. (3.(St)/TrGr.186), 429

Eagles, Sgt A. J. C., 270
Eames, F/O P. F., 248
Eastick, Sgt D. F., 182
Eaton, P/O P. C. D. (12 Sqn), 423
Eauclère, Sgt G. (GB I/63), 358
Ebbighausen, Hptmn K. (II./JG26), 261, 327, 356, 469

Ebeling, Lt (8./JG26), 386, 452, 464
Eberl, Oberfw J. (1./KG53), 382
Eberle, Lt (1./JG51), 117
Eberlein, Uffz H., 290
Ebert, Fw E. (5./KG2), 336
Ebert, Sgt G. H. (142 Sqn), 322
Eberz, Uffz, 321
Ebner, Gefr J., 308
Ebrecht, Uffz E., 242
Ecalle, Adjt (GAO 518), 465
Echlin, P/O R. W. H., 184
Eckerle, Oberlt, 283
Eckert, Gefr P. (9./ZG26), 470
Eckert, Uffz W. (8./KG2), 252, 327
Eckhardt, Uffz H., 263
Eckold, Uffz W., 210
Eckrich, Gefr W., 278
Eden, Anthony, 47, 403
Eden, Sgt J. (1-V-2), 194
Eden, Sgt W. H. (21 Sqn), 469
Eden, Uffz E., 240
Edgar, P/O Alan M., 153, *502*
Edge, F/O G. R. (605 Sqn), 362, 376
Edgehill, Sgt D. F. (229 Sqn), 399
Edmonds, F/O John D. (43 Sqn), 437
Edmüller, Oberfw L. (3./KG30), 211, 481
Edrich, Uffz A. R., 118
Edwardes-Jones, S/Ldr H., 310
Edwards, AC1 C. A. (88 Sqn), 390
Edwards, F/Lt R. S. J. (79 Sqn), 232
Edwards, F/O J. E. (40 Sqn), 284
Edwards, F/O W. H. (107 Sqn), 248
Edwards, LAC E. N. (110 Sqn), 273
Edwards, P/O (142 Sqn), 345
Edwards, P/O T. J. 'Taffy' (87 Sqn), 181, 283
Edwards, P/O W. G. (40 Sqn), 184, 349
Edwards, Sgt F. R. (9 Sqn), 469
Edwards, Sgt J. (57 Sqn), 104
Efselmann, Fw W., 239
Ege, Uffz W., 253
Eggers, Oberlt L. (2./JG21), 366
Eggers, Uffz Hans, 315, *318*
Eggert, Oberfw E., 279
Eggington, Sgt Alfred W., 95, *511*
Eggl, Uffz J. (3.(F)/123), 380
Ehemann, Uffz K. (ZG26), 301
Ehemann, Uffz W. (1.(H)/41), 326
Ehlers, Lt K. (KG2), 316
Ehlers, Fw H. (1./KGrzbV.172), 227
Ehlers, Uffz H. (JG3), 312, 315
Ehlers, Uffz K. (4.(F)/122), 120
Ehm, Unterfw W., 157
Ehrensberger, Uffz J. (8./KG55), 459
Ehrentreich, Fw H. (9./KG55), 414
Ehrfeld, Fw P., 211
Ehrhardt, Oberlt G., 224
Ehrhardt, Uffz G., 213
Ehrlich, Lt (JG52), 315
Ehrlich, Oberlt (JGr.176), 98
Eiblmeier, Fw M. (1./KG53), 382
Eichler, Lt E. (5./ZG1), 396
Eichler, Uffz E. (8./KG27), 239
Eichmüller, Uffz H., 498
Eifler, Hptmn W., 229
Einde, Lt H., 224
Eiseler, Gefr E. (Stab KG77), 336
Eisenbach, Obergefr V., 207
Eisenbach, Oberlt V. Riedesel Fr zu, 213
Eisenhut, Uffz J., 316
Eisenmann, Uffz A. (4.(S)/LG2), 429
Eisenmann, Uffz G. (3./KG53), 253
Eke, Oberfw A. (1./KGr.126), 343
Elbin, Uffz K., 262
Elgass Oberfw F., 223
Elias, Obergefr H. (KG54), 328
Eliot, P/O 'Chubby' (73 Sqn), 70, 418, 467, 487

Ellerbrock, Oberlt H., 225
Ellerlage, Oberfhr H-J., 280
Ellery, P/O C. C. (264 Sqn), 437
Ellgass, Fw J., 212
Ellinghaus, Uffz O., 317
Elliot, AC2 A. W. (82 Sqn), 345
Elliott, F/O D. F. (18 Sqn), 107
Elliott, F/Sgt J. W. (56 Sqn), 316, 390
Elliott, P/O C. H. (150 Sqn), 464
Elliott, S/Ldr E. D. (253 Sqn), 310, 339
Elliott, Sgt D. J. (235 Sqn), 390
Ellis, AC1 A. (218 Sqn), 135, 233
Ellis, AC1 Byron, *472*
Ellwood, Sgt, 294
Elmlinger, Sgt G. (GC III/2), 316, 336, 451
Elsdon, F/O (72 Sqn), 414
Else, Sgt P. (72 Sqn), 423
Elsner, Fw S. (1./KG3), 366
Elsner, Uffz K. (7./JG2), 158
Elsner, Uffz W. (9./KG55), 353
Elson, P/O A. (145 Sqn), 323, 379
Elster, Oberfw J. (8./KG27), 327
Elterich, Uffz G., 301
Embry, W/Cdr Basil E. (107 Sqn), 349, 361, 379
Emery, S/Lt P. (GB I/21), 364
Emery, Sgt G. H. (12 Sqn), 469
Emmert, Gefr H., 228
Emms, S/Ldr G. D. (17 Sqn), 362, 366, 437
Emprin, Adjt M., 164
Enckevort, 1e Lt P. F. J., 236
Endemann, Lt W. (5.(F)/122), 396
Endres, Reg Rat W., 123
Engel, Fw G. (6./KG55), 263
Engel, Lt (Aufkl. I Flakkorps), 335
Engel, Oberfw O. (6./KG55), 317
Engelbach, Gefr E., 147
Engelhardt, Lt W., 157
Engelmann, Gefr M., 263
Engelmann, Uffz, 212
Enghofer, Uffz H., 240
Engländer, Uffz H., 253
Engler, Capt. (GC II/4), 316, 317
Engler, Fw J. (Stab StG2), 366
Engstrom, P/O V. G. W. (40 Sqn), 431
Engwiller, Sgt L., 127
Enigk, Fw W. (Stab I./KG27), 342
Ens, Uffz E. (8./KG55), 459
Ensch, Uffz H. (1./JG20), 470
Enselem, Lt-Col, 94
Ensle, Gefr F., 209
Ensor, S/Ldr the Rev., 70
Epp, Fw F. (4.(F)/14), 459
Erdel, Fw F. (3./KG30), 481
Erdmann, Oberlt (Stab KG54), 462
Erdniss, Fw (2./JG51), 358
Ereminsky, F/O L., 318, 383, 392, 481
Erkelens, Uffz W. (4./KG54), 342
Erlbeck, Oberfw H., 133
Ernst, Flgr E., 207
Ernst, Fw U., 265
Ernst, Oberfw K., 253
Ernst, Uffz R. (9./StG2), 347
Erskine, LAC (26 Sqn), 332
Erzleben, Oberlt W., 315
Esch, Oberlt G. (Stab KG77), 477
Eschbaumer, Oberfw G. (6./KG77), 396
Eschwege, Hptmn S. von, 288, 316
Escoffier, Lt (GC II/1), 341
Escoffier, Lt (GR II/52), 325
Escudier, Capt. G., 259
Esnault, Sgt H., 114
Espeet, Sgt P., 191
Essig, Gefr O. (KG54), 329
Essl, Oberfw F., 164
Estan, Adjt P. (DAT Avord), 358
Estève, Sgt F. (GB II/19), 466
Estirac, S/Lt (GAO 1/551), 395
Etienne, SM (T 3), 352, 459
Etschel, Reg Rat Dr, 135
Ettershank, LAC P. R. V., 304

Etzel, Fw L., 253
Eugène, Sgt C. (GBA 1/51), 395
Evano, Capt., 98
Evans, AC (218 Sqn), 95
Evans, F/O G. H. D. (59 Sqn), 244, 345, 419
Evans, LAC C. W. (2 Sqn), 362
Evans, P/O (615 Sqn), 446
Evans, Sgt F. (Ferry Pilots Pool), 322
Evans, Sgt F. J. J. (59 Sqn), 268
Evans, Sgt T. S. (218 Sqn), 233
Evans, Sgt W. (110 Sqn), 345
Evans, Sgt W. J. K. (53 Sqn), 311, 372
Even, Mt (AB 1), 333
Everett, Sgt W. S., 95
Evers, Uffz W., 308
Everton-Jones, P/O B. (59 Sqn), 445
Evetts, Sgt (56 Sqn), *525*
Evill, AVM, 480, 486, 487
Evitt, F/O H. G. (88 Sqn), 390
Evrard, Capt., 249
Ewald, Gefr W., 289
Ewers, Lt E. (4./JG3), 342
Exner, Oberfw W. (2./KG77), 376
Eymer, Lt H-B., 290
Eynac, Laurent, 83
Eyre, F/O A. (615 Sqn), 327, 490
Eyrich, Fw F., 239
Ezekiel, P/O N. N. (110 Sqn), 345

Faber, 1e Lt M., 194
Fabia, Capt., 188
Fabian, Uffz W., 241
Fabre, Adjt (ECN 4/13), 93
Fabre, Lt Albert (GC II/6), 213, 263, 469
Fabre, Lt Yves (GC II/5), 479
Fagg, LAC E. J., 313
Faion, S/Lt, 274
Fairbrother, LAC (264 Sqn), 399
Fairweather, W/Cdr J. M., *169*
Faisandier, S/Lt (GC II/9), 341, 429, 452, 456
Faivre, EV1, 324
Falcke, Gefr D., 211
Falconer, Sgt D. G. B., 171
Falke, Fw K., 289
Falkenhagen, Fw B., 214
Falkensamer, Lt E. (2./JG51), 349, 427
Falkust, P/O H. E. L. (222 Sqn), 406
Fally, Uffz L. (KG77), 329
Fancy, Sgt J., 273
Farmer, Sgt S. J., 107, 116
Farmes, Sgt (218 Sqn), 160
Farnes, Sgt P. C. P. (501 Sqn), 253, 273, 378
Farrell, F/O Patrick A. L., 157, *527*
Farriol, Sgt (ECN 5/13), 414
Farris, Cpl (43 Gruppo), 467
Farrow, P/O R. W., 145
Fasso, Capt. (GB II/21), 387
Fauconnet, S/Lt (GC II/4), 433
Faugeras, S/Lt (GAO 543), 446
Faulhaber, Uffz A., 206
Faulkner, Sgt, 127
Faure, Capt., 156
Faure, Lt, 188
Favre-Bulle, Adjt (GB 3/23), 432
Fay, Lt de, 273
Faye, Cmdt, 170
Fearnley, Sgt F. (82 Sqn), 304
Fearnley, Sgt L. S. (107 Sqn), 423
Fegert, Oberfw G., 240
Fehlinger, Oberfw P., 214
Feilitzsch, Oberlt W. (3./KG1), 470
Feist, Uffz G., 309
Fejfar, Lt (GC I/6), 429
Feld, Uffz G., 254
Feldzer, Sgt C., 275
Felge, Lt W. (3.(F)/22), 427
Felgenhauer, Oberfw, 239
Felger, Fw F., 229
Félix, Lt R., 133
Fell, Fw F., 279

Feller, Uffz W., 308
Felmy, Gen. Helmuth, 86, 130
Feltz, EV (AB 1), 333
Fennell, Sgt, 233
Fergue, Sgt, 305
Ferguson, P/O R., 283
Fern, Fw F. (3./KG53), 476
Fernes, Gefr S. (KG54), 329
Fernholz, Fw K., 242
Fernsebner, Fw (7./JG52), 364
Ferrand, Adjt B., 171
Ferrari, Sgt (43 Gruppo), 467
Ferre, AC, 99, 171
Ferriss, F/O (111 Sqn), 329
Ferry, Cpl (GBA II/61), 470
Ferté, AM P. B. Joubert de la, 339
Ferté, Guy, 440
Festal, Marcel, 35, 40, 56, 68
Fetiveau, Sgt (GBA I/51), 424
Fetzer, Uffz R. (Stab KG55), 376
Feuchter, Uffz E. (KG76), 329
Feuillat, Adjt (GC I/4), 427
Fevez, P/O D. G. (26 Sqn), 423
Fèvre, Sgt, 275
Février, S/Lt J., 161
Feyen, Uffz H., 300
Fiala, Sgt O. (GC I/1), 259, 289, 374
Fichepain, S/Lt (GC II/3), 364
Ficheux, Sgt (GB I/23), 358
Fichtner, Lt W., 279
Fidler, LAC A. (264 Sqn), 399
Fidler, S/Ldr G. M. (607 Sqn), 323
Fiebig, Oberst M., 209
Fiebranz, Uffz F., 242
Fiedler, , Flgr E. (7./JG2), 456
Fiedler, Fw O. (7./KG27), 239
Fiedler, Fw W. (KüFlGr.906), 241
Fiedler, Gefr A. (9./ZG26), 418
Fiedler, Uffz H. (KG53), 253
Fiedler, Uffz Heinz (KGrzbV.12), 224
Fiedler, Uffz K. (4./KG54), 414
Fiedorczuk, S/Lt E. (GC 1/145), 364
Fiel, Lt (Stab I./JG3), 159, 346
Field, Air Comm., 455, 457
Field, Sgt F. J. (12 Sqn), 436
Fiévez, Sgt L. J. M., 193
Filippi, Capt. L., 477
Filippi, Lt E. (GB I/12), 400
Filla, Obergefr G. (1./LG1), 343
Filter, Uffz A. (16./KGzbV.1), 396
Findlay, Sgt A. (77 Sqn), 458
Findlay, Sgt Duncan O. (103 Sqn), 153, 502
Finlayson, Sgt Joseph A. C. (59 Sqn), 385
Finzel, Uffz H. (4./StG77), 347
Fion, Capt., 93
Fiquet, Lt, 296
Firminhac, Sgt Raymond (GC 5/3), 358
Fischer, Fw S. (I./ZG2), 162
Fischer, Gefr H. (9./StG2), 215
Fischer, Lt G. (1.(F)/121), 299
Fischer, Lt (JG53), 259
Fischer, Oberfw G. (Stab II./LG1), 279
Fischer, Oberfw W. (2./KG77), 301
Fischer, Obergefr A. (2./StG2), 242
Fischer, Obergefr G. (6./KG76), 347
Fischer, Uffz E. (3./KGr.126), 254
Fischer, Uffz F. (I./ZG26), 354
Fischer, Uffz H. (KG2), 208
Fischer, Uffz H. (KG51), 278
Fischer, Uffz F. (KGzbV.1), 229
Fischgräbe, Uffz M. (1./KG4), 409
Fischlein, Fw F. (4./StG77), 347
Fisher, F/O (56 Sqn), 379, 383
Fister, Fw W. (6./KG54), 414
Fittkau, Fw W. (8./KG51), 360
Fitzgerald, F/O T. B., 268
Fitzgerald, LAC A. V. (26 Sqn), 405
Flaig, Uffz A. (4./KG76), 366
Flamion, Sgt, 139
Flandi, S/Lt A. (GC I/8), 235, 240
Flanek, Sgt Léopold, 234, 242, 297, 298

Flanigan, AC1 G. E. (115 Sqn), 339
Flassig, Uffz B. (6./KG1), 353
Flechère, Sgt de la (GC II/4), 459
Fleckenstein, Lt W., 254
Flegel, Oberfw N., 138
Flehmer, Obergefr G., 213
Fleisch, Fw A., 309
Fleischhacker, Fw, 285
Fleissner, Lt R., 206
Fleitz, Lt H. (8./JG53), 358, 401, 405, 416, 418
Fleming, Arthur H., 492
Fleming, Sgt (149 Sqn), 458
Flemming, Fw H., 290
Flessner, Flgr D. (5./KG30), 479
Flick, Fw W., 254
Fliegener, Uffz R., 253
Fliescher, Uffz H. (4./LG1), 410
Fligge, Oberlt H. (KG54), 328
Flinders, P/O (32 Sqn), 326
Flisher, Sgt Leonard C., 245, 247
Floer, Uffz Heinz, 224
Flohr, Fw W. (3./KGr.126), 479
Florin, Cpl, 296
Florin, Oberlt H-W., 206
Flower, Sgt W. L. (115 Sqn), 339
Fluder, Lt, 181
Flug, Uffz E. (1./ZG52), 414
Flügge, Fw U. (8./KG55), 410
Flynn, F/Sgt C. (64 Sqn), 391, 398
Flynn, Sgt D. (32 Sqn), 412
Foch, Maréchal, 492, 494, 497
Focke, Heinrich, 86
Föcking, Fw W., 239
Foerster, Capt. Kurt A., 147, 148
Foisset, Adjt E. (GB I/34), 494
Fokker, Anthony, 84
Follaci, Sgt D. (GB 4/19), 446
Folliot, LV (AC 2), 234, 239, 308, 494
Folloroux, S/Lt, 98
Follrichs, Gefr G. (8./KG30), 388
Folmer, Fw H., 280
Fölsch, Obergefr A., 209
Fonderen, Lt E. von, 140
Fontaine, S/Lt H. (GC II/1), 328, 418, 499
Fontaine, S/Lt L. (9/V/1), 196, 286
Fontanet, Cmdt, 285
Fonteneau, Sgt (GAO 1/589), 440, 456
Fonvielle, Adjt M. (GAO 517), 419
Footner, Sgt K. D., 244
Fopma, Sgt F., 193
Forbes, F/O N. (605 Sqn), 379
Ford, F/O E. C. (4 Sqn), 311
Ford, P/O J. D. (253 Sqn), 312, 351, 353
Forde, P/O D. N. (145 Sqn), 379
Fordham, F/O D. A., 304
Foreman, Sgt T. A. (40 Sqn), 431
Forges, Lt de, 126
Foriel, Sgt, 145
Forrester, AC, 112, 134
Forshaw, 'Dimmy', 49
Förster, Fw J. (2./KG2), 453
Förster, Gefr W. (1./KG77), 360
Förster, Obergefr G. (Stab KG4), 308
Förster, Uffz H. (3.(F)/122), 123
Förster, Uffz H. (4./KG55), 442
Forster, Uffz R. (3./StG76), 376
Forster, Uffz W. (3./KG27), 429
Forsyth, Sgt, 272
Forth, P/O H. O., 112, 134
Fortin, Sgt J. (GC II/2), 99, 262, 315, 343, 375
Fortmüller, Uffz H. (4./KG76), 410
Fortune, Maj.-Gen. Victor, 460
Fortune, Sgt Tom, 271
Forzy, Sgt J. (GC I/4), 213, 334
Fösig, Uffz H., 224
Foster, F/O D. A. J., 272
Foucher, Adjt H., 171
Fouchier, Lt, 274
Fourdinier, Sgt E., 249
Fourneau, Adjt P., 305
Fournier, S/Lt L. (GR I/14), 470
Fourrier, Cpl, 296

Fowler, F/O H. N. 'Bill', 254, 277, 283
Fox, P/O, 233
Fraitzl, Oberfw J. (2./KG53), 376
Framm, Oberlt (2./JG27), 244, 248, 295, 349, 405
Francais, Adjt E., 277
Francin, Capt., 188
Franck, Lt G. (3./KG27), 429
Francke, Lt A., 239
Franco, Gen. Francisco, 87, 454
Frank, Fw M. (1./JG26), 262
Frank, P/O A. D. (150 Sqn), 322, 437
Frank, Uffz J. (4.(F)/11), 341, 478
Frank, Uffz W. (6./KG1), 308
Franke, Lt (7./KG53), 212
Franke, Oberlt F-W. (Stab KG53), 120
Franke, Uffz (2./JG53), 271, 400
Franke, Uffz W. (3./JG20), 402
Frankenberger, Uffz Arno, 120
Frankish, P/O C. R., 248
Franklin, F/Sgt (65 Sqn), 347, 359, 388
Franklin, P/O W. D. K. (142 Sqn), 464
Franks, S/Ldr A. L. (610 Sqn), 339, 383, 392
Frantz, Lt (GAO 518), 340
Franz, Fw W. (3./LG1), 214
Franz, Oberfw K. (Stab KG55), 470
Franz, Obergefr K. (Stab III./LG1), 429
Franzisket, Lt (1./JG1 & 3./JG1), 236, 324, 351, 424, 425
Fraser, G/Capt. H. M., 339
Fraser, Peter (NZ Prime Minister), 438
Fraser, Sgt J. N. (142 Sqn), 458
Fraville, Sgt de, 126, 135
Frayn, P/O F. E. (107 Sqn), 450
Frayssines, Sgt (GR II/14), 492
Frazier, Cpl (GB I/62), 461
Frébillot, Capt., 94
Frediani, Sgt, 260
Fredman, F/O L., 247
Freeborn, F/O (74 Sqn), 347
Freese, Gefr J., 241
Frehse, Fw E., 115
Freisberg, Obergefr A., 207
Freisewinkel, Uffz K. (1./KG51), 493
Freitag, Uffz (5./JG3), 416, 436
Freitag, Uffz A. (6./KG55), 263
Frémont, Lt F., 314
Frensch, Uffz K-H., 226
Frentzel-Beyme, Fw K-E. (1./JG21), 260, 375
Frenzel, Lt H. (7./KG3), 381
Frenzel, Uffz G. (3.(F)/11), 380
Freund, Uffz H., 95
Freurienberg, Reg Rat, 462
Freutle, Uffz M., 211
Frey, Fw (1.(J)/LG2), 380
Frey, Gefr A. (Stab KG51), 453
Frey, Mtre (AC 2), 234
Frey, Uffz F. (5./KG3), 289
Frey, Uffz O. (6./KG2), 316
Freyinger, Uffz F., 212
Freytag, Gefr R., 279
Fricke, Fw E., 127
Fricke, Lt H. (KG54), 329
Friebe, Obergefr A. (KG53), 240
Friebe, Obergefr P. (KG54), 308
Friedrich, Fw K., 290
Friedrich, Hptmn H. (2.(H)/31), 493
Friedrich, Uffz W., 208
Friedrichs, Oberlt zur See A., 241
Friend, Sgt L. Y. T. 'Ching' (73 Sqn), 170, 283
Friendly, Sgt (110 Sqn), 345
Friendship, Sgt (3 Sqn), 251
Fries, Fw R., 213
Frimberger, Uffz (7./KG55), 442
Frin, Sgt (GBA I/54), 340
Fripp, Sgt A. G., 105

Frisou, S/Lt (GR II/33), 456
Fritsch, Lt A., 212
Fritsche, Obergefr R., 156
Frittum, Gefr J. (3./KGr.126), 479
Fritz, Gefr K., 213
Fritz, Lt H-J., 265
Froese, Uffz A., 280
Fröhlich, Fw G., 241
Fröhlich, Fw K., 289
Fröhling, Uffz B. (3./KG1), 353
Frohn, Lt H., 252
Frömer, Fw K., 213
Fromme, Uffz R., 210
Fromont, Sgt J., 261
Fronhöfer, Oberlt, 282
Froom, AC2 P. W., 167
Frotscher, Oberfw E-R., 209
Früchtl, Uffz A., 158
Frühling, Fw A. (3./KG51), 336
Fryer, Sgt A. (77 Sqn), 385
Fuchssteiner, Fw J. (4./KG76), 343
Führer, Oberfw O., 288
Fuhrer, Sgt, 107, 275
Führing, Oberlt K., 284, 289
Fulbrook, Sgt S. J., 304
Fulcrand, Lt J. (GR I/52), 325
Fulda, Uffz W. (2./KG55), 376
Fullard, G/Capt. P. F., 175, 319
Fulte, Uffz A., 221, 228
Fundinger, Oberlt W. (6./KG76), 279, 347
Fünfstück, Uffz H. (1./KG4), 409
Funke, Obergefr K., 263
Funke, Uffz H., 214
Furby, AC1 (later Sgt) Willie (40 Sqn), 93, 431
Fürnweger, Lt J. (IV.(St)/LG1), 448
Furst, Adjt B. (GC II/2), 326, 340
Fürstenberg, Uffz K., 241
Fuselier, Sgt, 234
Fyffe, F/O, 134

Gäbeler, Uffz R. (7./KG4), 336
Gabler, Gefr E. (KG53), 328
Gabszewicz, Lt Aleksander (GC III/10 & DAT Lyons), 83, 407, 410
Gadow, Lt W., 99
Gady, S/Lt, 248
Gaeta, Cpl (43 Gruppo), 467
Gaffal, Lt H., 154, 254
Gagnaire, Adjt E. (GC III/1), 210, 315, 342, 366, 456
Gail, Capt. H. de, 241, 259
Gaillères, Adjt A., 94
Gaiser, Uffz F., 279
Galerneau, Sgt M. (GB 1/21), 358
Galland, Hptmn, (later Maj.) Adolf, 325, 334, 390, 427, 428, 451, 469
Gallina, Uffz F., 254
Galloway, LAC (2 Sqn), 362
Galubinski, Fw H. (7./JG53), 325, 417, 423, 433, 434
Galy, Lt A. (GR I/35), 364
Gama, Gen., 457
Gamber, Lt A. (2.(H)/23), 497
Gamelin, Gén. Maurice, 319, 330, 420
Gammel, Lt K., 127
Ganb, Fw S., 239
Ganss, Oberfw H., 209
Ganzert, Oberlt R., 209
Garbett, LAC Harry T., 246, 512
Garcka, Sgt J. E. (40 Sqn), 431
Garde, Capt. G. (GC I/1), 274, 307, 335, 476, 495
Garden, S/Lt (GAO 543), 395
Gardeur, Capt. (GAO 501), 364
Gardiner, Sgt F. H., 99
Gardinier, Sgt N. (GIA I/601), 462
Gardiol, Cpl (GB I/23), 358
Gardner, Charles, 141
Gardner, Leading Naval Airman L. P. (825 FAA Sqn), 390
Gardner, P/O P. M. (3 Sqn), 289, 311, 317, 335
Garland, F/O Donald E., VC, 243, 244, 245, 513

Garland, W/Cdr, *152*
Garnier, Sgt J., 96
Garnons-Williams, Lt-Col H. F., 115
Garrick, AC1 J. A., 107
Gärtig, Uffz G., 242
Gärtner, Fw (8./JG26), 452
Gärtner, Hptmn H. (2./JG3), 349, 392
Gasnerie, Sgt de la, 156, 213, *264*
Gass, Fw G. (KG27), 327
Gasser, Gefr K. (9./KG2), 381
Gast, Adjt L., 305
Gasthaus, Fw, 248
Gaston, LAC (142 Sqn), 182, 345
Gaston, QM (T 3), 459
Gäth, Oberlt W. (8./JG3), 356, 388
Gäth, Uffz H. (2./StG76), 254
Gatinois, Adjt M. (GB I/11), 432
Gauche, Adjt (GB I/62), 374, 425
Gaude, Lt R. (Stab KG77), 477
Gaudon, Adjt (GC II/6), 263, 298
Gaudon, Sgt M. (GC II/1), 433
Gaudry, Adjt (GC I/6), 425
Gauffre, Sgt (GC II/7), 414
Gauger, Uffz H., 213
Gaul, Oberlt E. (4.(F)/122), 335
Gaulard, Adjt A. (GC III/10), 441
Gautheron, André, 429
Gauthier, Adjt H. (GB I/11), 400
Gauthier, S/Lt G. (GC II/7), 117, 126, 127
Gauthier, S/Lt J. (GC II/7), 93
Gauthier, Sgt (GC III/6), 206
Gauthier, Sgt (GR II/55), 407
Gautier, Sgt (GB I/23), 364
Gautron, Sgt (GAO 581), 469
Gauvin, Sgt (GB I/15), 324
Gauze, Sgt (GAO 515), 492
Gavoille, Lt, 260
Gawlick, Oberfw (III./JG53), 163, 358
Gawlina, Lt G., 253
Gawron, Uffz G. (1.(F)/121), 341
Gay, AC1 K. V., 99
Gayner, F/O J. R. H., 131
Geach, F/O T. J. (77 Sqn), 385
Geck, Uffz W., 316
Geerlof, G., 206
Geerts, Capt., 134
Gegg, LAC John H. K., *268*, *505*
Gehlhaar, Lt (4./JG52), 380, 450
Gehring, Fw J. (6./KG77), 453
Gehring, Fw L. (Stab I./KG51), 253
Gehrke, Uffz H., 307
Geib, Gefr K., 263
Geiger, Sgt (GB I/21), 451
Geiger, Uffz J. (Stab KG55), 442
Geille, Cmdt F. (GC III/2), 461, 466
Geillon, Sgt (GC II/6), 433
Geisler, Uffz K., 162
Geissler, Fw G. (5./KG1), 479
Geissler, Oberfw G. (9./KG55), 429
Geitz, Oberfw O., 308
Geller, Lt C., 117
Gelly, Sgt, 274
Gémon, Capt. Paul (GB I/34), 494
Genähr, Uffz H., 262
Genay, Lt, 99
Genest, Sgt V. (GR II/33), 359
Genin, Adjt, 148
Genot, Adjt A., 94
Genre, Cpl (GBA I/51), 456
Genson, Sgt, 325
Gent, Gefr W. (3./JG1), 347
Gentier, Sgt Maurice (GB II/12), 432
Gentsch, Uffz H., 213
Genty, Adjt (GC I/5), 100
Genty, Lt R. (GB II/12), 432
Genty, Sgt (GR II/52), 97
Gentzen, Maj. J. (Stab I./ZG2), 157, 376
Geoffroy, Lt M., 111
Georg, Oberlt W., 228
George, F/O W. H. (15 Sqn), 445
George, Fw E., 240

George, P/O R. T. (64 Sqn), 391
George VI, King, *138*, *398*, *513*
Georges, Adjt C., 98
Georgi, Uffz F. (6./KG55), 317
Georgi, Uffz L. (8./KG30), 347
Geppert, Uffz G., 213
Gérard, Capt. R. (GC I/3), 96, *97*, 453, 479
Gérard, Mt (SESBA), 488
Gérardot, Lt Col, 103
Géraud, Adjt, 314
Gerbig, Oberfw A., 113
Gerdsmeier, Uffz Karl, 263, 317
Gerlach, Obergefr E., 208
Gerlach, Oberlt A., 160
Gerlach, Uffz K., 289
Gerling, Oberlt Wilfried (5./KG54), *383*
Gerlitz, Hptmn (3./JG51 & 1./JG1), 106, 465
Germain, Lt P. (GR II/55), 341
Germann, Uffz, 206
Germeroth, Oberlt R. (3./JG26), 409
Germette, Lt B. (GR I/33), 419
Gerner, Gefr A., 117
Gerneth, Uffz E. (2./JG51), 347
Gers, Uffz W., 277
Gersch, Gefr G. (5./KG27), 402
Gerspacher, Uffz Walter (7./KG1), *495*
Gerstenmeier, Hptmn K-J., 121
Gerstmann, Oberfw W., 290
Gerstncr, Uffz F. (4./KG76), 418
Gervillier, Comte de *see* Thiroux, Sgt Arnould
Geske, Uffz G., 240
Gessiaume, S/Lt J., 259
Gessner, Gefr F. (8./KG4), 479
Getz, Gefr J. (1./KG55), 410
Geuthner, Uffz Karl (8./KG30), 388
Gfell, Obergefr L., 308
Ghesla, Uffz, 271
Ghysels, Lt, 139
Ghyssels, Lt R., 286
Giard, Sgt, 297
Gibron, Sgt R. (GB II/21), 364
Gibson, F/O C. F. (105 Sqn), 269
Gibson, P/O J. A. A. (501 Sqn), 378, 455, 456
Giddings, Sgt N. F. F., 168
Giehl, Fw F., 112
Gierger, Gefr E., 309
Giermer, Sgt V. (DAT Bourges), 358, 360
Giesa, Uffz W. (2.(F)/122), 408
Giesecke, Lt D., 252
Gieseler, Gefr E., 211
Giesemann, Oberlt Julius, 213
Giessen, Fw H. (6./LG1), 393
Giessübel, Uffz V., 289
Gifford, S/Ldr P., 282, 293
Gilber, Flgr K., 240
Gilbert, Capt. A., 274
Gilbert, F/O J. C. (609 Sqn), 399
Gilbert, S/Lt F., 252, 260
Gilbertas, Adjt (GAO 516), 346
Gild, Lt R. (7./KG51), 382
Giles, LAC F. H. (500 Sqn), 390
Gilgen, Flgr W. (3./KG51), 336
Gilhaus, Uffz F., 300
Gillam, F/Lt D. E. (616 Sqn), 395, 410
Gillam, P/O J. D. W. (88 Sqn), 458
Gillert, Uffz H. (1./JG1), 236, 353
Gilles, Adjt (GC II/10), 336
Gillet, Arnaud (historian), 270, 407
Gillet, S/Lt J. (GB 2/19), 456
Gillham, LAC J. H. (4 Sqn), 159, 293, 339
Gillies, F/O J. (92 Sqn), 351
Gillmore, AC1 A. A. (53 Sqn), 311, 372
Gilmore, P/O R. G. M. (21 Sqn), 272
Gilmore, Sgt A. M., 116
Gilon, Uffz U., 215
Giloux, Sgt, 147
Gimel, Sgt R. (GB 4/21), 364

Gimpel, Uffz E. (Stab StG77), 393
Ginestet, Lt E. de (GAO 3/551), 465
Gionietti, Sgt (GBA I/51), 364
Giordani, Sgt (GC I/8), 213, 337
Gippert, Uffz T., 239
Girard, Adjt (GAO 510), 478
Girard, Adjt (GR II/55), 98
Girard, Lt (GC II/4), 317
Girard, S/Lt (GBA II/54), 451
Girard, Sgt L. (GAO 3/551), 465
Giraud, Gen. Henri, 319
Giraudon, Cpl A. (GBA I/51), 346
Girier, Gén. L. F. A., 440
Giron, S/Lt A. (GAO 509), 259, 424
Girou, Sgt (GC I/5), 156, 239, 329, 441, 479
Giroud, Adjt (GAO 581), 469
Glagow, Uffz E., 210
Glantz, Oberfw H., 298
Glas, Uffz, 315
Gläser, Gefr E., 223
Glaser, Uffz H. (9./KG2), 381
Glauder, Sgt F. (GC I/3), 417, 453, 470
Gleed, F/Lt I. (87 Sqn), 317, 318, 329, 331
Gleed, S/Ldr G. W. C. (40 Sqn), 469
Gleich, Lt J. (GC II/3), 343, 346, 466
Glencross, S/Ldr Arthur R. (37 Sqn), 372
Glendinning, AC1 H. D. (115 Sqn), 339
Glenz, Fw G., 208
Glienke, Oberlt J. (13.(Z)/LG1), 106, 132, 379
Glindemann, Uffz H., 210
Glitz, Oberlt W. (3.(H)/13), 476
Gloanec, Sgt (GC I/2), 358
Glocke, Oberfw F., 213
Glockner, Gefr E. (8./KG1), 470
Glöckner, Lt H., 309
Glogger, Gefr G. (8./LG1), 347
Glogner, Fw, 225
Glorie, Capt. André, *238*
Glówczynski, S/Lt C. (GC I/145), 452
Glufke, Fw G., 290
Glyde, F/O Richard L. (87 Sqn), 108, *114*, *115*, 321, 326, 327
Gnan, Oberfw V. (Stab StG1), 453
Gnys, S/Lt, 298
Goasguen, SM, 324
Gobeau, Adjt (GB I/12), 259, 440
Göbel, Uffz A., 213
Gobell, S/Ldr (242 Sqn), 365
Gobert, Adjt E. (ECN 1/13), 416
Gobert, PM (T 2), 456
Goblet, Lt (Flug.Fl.Korps VIII), 479
Goddard, LAC C. J., 168
Gödecke, Lt H., 252
Godefroid, Sgt R., 199
Godfray, LAC Roy (12 Sqn), *472*
Godfray, Mr and Mrs Percy, *472*
Godineau, Cpl (GBA I/51), 424
Godl, Uffz G. (5./KG2), 476
Godlewski, S/Lt Jerzy (GC I/145), 452
Godsell, Sgt A. J. (142 Sqn), 322
Goebel, Uffz F. (7./KG3), 208
Goebel, Uffz F. (8./KG51), 360
Goedert, S/Lt A. (11/VI/1), 325, 374
Goertz, Lt S. von (2./KG53), 376
Goettel, Lt (later Capt.) Wladyslaw ('Montpelier' Gp), 171, 426
Goetting, Uffz W. (1.(J)/LG2), 456
Goetz, S/Lt L. (GC II/10), 275, 306, 309, 466
Goetz, Sgt J. (GAO 1/506), 380
Goffe, LAC D. (40 Sqn), 96, 362
Goffin, Lt (II/2 & DAT Chartres), 205, 418
Gofton, F/O A. M., 304
Göggel, Uffz F., 290
Gohr, Uffz L. (3./KG76), 419

Göhringer, Uffz K., 315
Goile, Sgt A. (GC I/2), 240, 447
Goissard, Lt, 112
Golbery, Lt de (ECN 4/13), 498
Goldbach, Uffz P., 251
Goldberg, Uffz J., 251
Golombek, Fw H. (Stab KG77), 470
Goltzsche, Fw, 131
Gombeaud, Capt. J., 102
Gombert, Sgt G., 305
Gonsalvez, Sgt R. (GB 4/21), 364
Gonzales, Lt F. (GAO 543), 451
Goodale, F/O (26 Sqn), 320
Goodman, P/O (1 Sqn), 265
Goodman, Sgt G. (85 Sqn), 160
Goracci, Sgt Guiseppe (Gruppo 43), 467
Görbing, Fw (2.(J)/LG2), 417
Gordon, P/O J. H. (15 Sqn), 362
Gore, F/O W. E., *149*, 154, *209*, 210, 241, 247, 254
Goret, PM (1S1), 359
Gorgas Oberfw H., 229
Göring, Hermann, *86*, 280, *361*, *366*, *389*, *410*, *496*, *497*
Görke, Fw H., 263
Görlitzer, Uffz W. (5./ZG76), 456
Gort, Gen. Lord, *152*, *166*, *330*, *361*, 367, 368, 397
Görtz, Uffz A., 212
Gosman, F/O A. D. (142 Sqn), 182, 345
Gothard, Sgt A. C., 311
Göttel, Capt. Wladyslaw, 83
Gottlebe, Uffz W. (3./KG30), 347
Göttlicher, Fw A. (7./KG51), 382
Gottschalk, Oberlt W. (Stab KG55), 376
Gottschalk, Uffz A., 207
Gottschling, Lt F. (KG54), 212, 329
Götz Uffz H. (1./KGrzbV.9), 223
Götz, Gefr K. (8./KG54), 213
Götz, Oberfw Franz (7./JG53), 426, 433, 451, 459
Götz, Oberfw Horst (5./JG3), 424
Gotzler, Uffz K., 242
Gouachon-Noireault, S/Lt Pierre (GC I/8), 274, 366, 380, *461*
Goudszwaard, Kpl, 95
Gough, Sgt T. A. H. (43 Sqn), 406
Goujon, Adjt C. (GC III/6), 189, 211, 235, 241, 467
Goumy, S/Lt M., 188, 210
Goupy, S/Lt A., 188, 208
Gourdon, Adjt (GAO 503), 296
Gourron, Adjt (GB I/11), 465
Gouzi, Sgt, 290
Govers, Sgt G. J. M., 261
Gower, P/O D. de C. C. (229 Sqn), 312, 339
Goyer, Adjt, 248
Graafstra, F/O J. W. (242 Sqn), 351
Gräber, Oberfw H., 117
Grabmann, Maj. W., 318
Grabmeier, Flgr F. (1./KG54), 360
Graeme, F/O N. S., 152
Gräf, Fw (3./JG51), 425, 496
Graf, Lt R. (KG4), 209
Gräf, Oberlt F. (KG55), 213
Gräf, Uffz K. (JG3), 140
Graf, Uffz S. (KüFlGr.506), 214
Gräfe, Uffz W. (7./KG3), 208
Graffenberger, Oberfw K. (4./KG51), 429
Graffer, Capt. G., 477
Gragelle, S/Lt (GC II/7), 408
Graham, F/Lt R. H. N. (13 Sqn), 339
Graham, F/O K. W., 311
Graham-Hogg, F/O H. G., 159
Grammann, Fw L., 301
Grampp, Lt E., 298
Grancher, Sgt (GR I/55), 380
Grand, PM (T 3), 452
Grand, Sgt M. (GR I/52), 325
Grandchamp, Sgt (GB I/11), 432
Grande, Uffz W. (3./KG2), 470
Grandrémy, Lt, 234

Grandy, Gefr T. (9./KG76), 429
Grange, Sgt E. (GB II/23), 447
Granier, Sgt (GR II/52), 260
Granier, Sgt (GR II/55), 466
Grant, LAC L. O. (150 Sqn), 445
Grant, Sgt D. L. (12 Sqn), 469
Grant-Crawford, F/Lt I. D. (149 Sqn), 356
Grant-Govan, P/O G. (2 Sqn), 148, 345
Gras, Adjt (GC II/5), 145, 476
Grasser, Lt H. (3./JGr.152), 97
Grasser, Oberlt (3./ZG52), 379
Grassick, P/O R. D., 272, 288, 293, 299, 487
Grattan, F/O G. R., 233
Gratzel, Uffz F., 225
Graubner, Gefr W., 253
Graul, Flgr R. (KG51), 328
Grauzow, Uffz R., 214
Grave, 1e Lt F. L. M. Focquin de, 110, 205, 236
Graveley, F/O R. C., 95
Gravenreuth, Oberlt S-U. Fr von (3./KG30), 481
Gray, AC (114 Sqn), 294
Gray, Adjt (GC 3/6), 213
Gray, F/O W. N. (213 Sqn), 335, 392, 399
Gray, P/O C. F. (54 Sqn), 362, 366
Gray, P/O W. A. (37 Sqn), 398
Gray, Sgt (GR II/52), 260
Gray, Sgt P. C. (139 Sqn), 246
Gray, Sgt Tom, VC (12 Sqn), 243, 244, 245, 513
Grayson, F/Sgt (213 Sqn), 393
Grazce, Uffz W., 300
Greaney, LAC F. E. A., 293
Grebe, Fw R., 316
Green, Sgt (142 Sqn), 345
Greenall, AC T. (142 Sqn), 464
Greenhalgh, Sgt F. D., 257
Greenhous, P/O Patrick E. J., 257, 258, 261
Greenwood, AC (110 Sqn), 345
Greenwood, Cpl (105 Sqn), 182
Gregory, AC1 K. G., 233
Gregory, Sgt F. W., 246
Greiner, Uffz E., 308
Greirson, P/O J. J., 304
Greisert, Oberlt (2./JG2), 269, 364, 433, 475
Gremm, Uffz (4./JG3), 364
Grenet, Cmdt Pierre, 314
Grenzow, Uffz H. (3./StG76), 388
Gres, Adjt, 249
Gresset, Adjt, 93
Grether, Oberlt H., 326
Greulich, Uffz K., 308
Grey, Lt R. H. G. (825 FAA Sqn), 390
Grey-Smith, F/O G. E., 246
Gribble, P/O G. D. (54 Sqn), 362
Grice, P/O D. H. (32 Sqn), 326, 446
Griebsch, Fw H., 225
Griener, Uffz A. (5./JG52), 152, 366
Griesshaber, Uffz O., 223
Griffin, LAC H. G. (115 Sqn), 339
Griffiths, F/Lt C. D. (501 Sqn), 289, 356
Grimaud, Sgt H. (GC II/7), 97, 121, 240, 408, 414, 477
Grimmling, Oberfw Walter, 93, 94, 234, 277, 278
Grimpe, Uffz (1./JG1), 469
Grisenthwaite, P/O (500 Sqn), 362
Grisonni, Sgt L. (GB 2/63), 358
Grivel, Adjt, 162
Grob, Gefr P., 213
Gröber, Gefr W., 263
Groeben, Lt H. von der, 162
Groen, 1e Lt F. H., 191
Groen, Lt, 111
Groeneberg, Oberfw J. (Stab KG27), 488
Groke, Uffz G., 212
Grond, Uffz P. (1./JG53), 434
Grondowski, Uffz G. (KG54), 329
Groneberg, Oberfw Johannes (Stab KG27), 381, 382

Gronn, Fw J., 301
Gropp, Obergefr W., 223
Grosdemanche, Sgt, 100
Gross, Fw E. (Stab II./KG51), 498
Gross, Fw H. (1.(H)/23), 298
Gross, Fw P. (Stab KG2), 393
Gross, Oberfw K. (8./KG2), 441
Gross, Uffz K. (5./KG55), 353
Grosse, Fw E. (KGzbV.1), 221
Grosse, Wachm. Hans (4.(H)/31), 359
Grosser, Gefr Fritz (2./LG1), 402
Grosser, Uffz H. (9./JG2), 365
Grosskreutz, Uffz H., 240
Grossmann, Fw F., 149
Grossmann, Uffz W., 209
Grossmannn-Hermann, Gefr E. (6./KG76), 418
Grote, Lt (3./JG76), 396
Groth, Fw W. (4.(H)/21), 392
Groth, Hptmn (II./ZG76), 234, 306, 351
Groth, Oberfw M. (Stab I./KG51), 253
Grothen, Uffz, 205, 277, 307
Grube, Fw H. (Stab I./KG27), 428
Grube, Lt H. (8./KG3), 381
Grübel, Lt W. (JG2), 277, 326
Gruber, Fw F. (2./KG53), 376
Gruel, Lt S. (3./JG26), 409
Gründer, Oberfw E., 117
Gründling, Gefr H. (4.(F)/121), 117
Gründling, Uffz H-H. (3.(F)/122), 120
Grundmann, Gefr W., 290
Grune, S/Lt de Hemricourt de, 149
Grüneklee, Uffz H., 242
Grüner, Oberlt P. (8./KG4), 479
Grunewald, Uffz F. (7./KG1), 206
Gruningre, Lt H. (GAO 582), 416
Grünwald, Lt F-K. (4.(F)/121), 375
Grunwald, Lt H. (1./KG1), 393
Grunwald, Uffz A. (1./LG1), 241
Grunwald, Uffz E. (9./KG3), 381
Grunze, Gefr P. (3./KG1), 353
Grüter, Lt O., 308
Gruyelle, S/Lt, 117, 135
Grywatz, Uffz G., 241
Grzeszczak, Lt B. (DAT Clermont-Ferrand), 478
Guarneri, Adjt J. (GR 1/22), 496
Guay, S/Lt René (GC III/10), 341
Guddasch, Oberfw H. (5./KG55), 429
Gude, Gefr B. (KG76), 329
Guelin, S/Lt (GB 1/19), 466
Guenou, Sgt (GB II/62), 461
Guérin, Adjt (GR 3/33), 346
Guérin, Sgt (GB II/19), 346
Guérin, Sgt (GR 3/22), 470
Guesne, SM (SESBA), 117
Guesnel, Sgt A. (GAO 510), 296, 380, 446
Guest, Sgt J. (21 Sqn), 390, 465
Guhl, Gefr H. (6./KG53), 376
Guhl, Gefr K. (3./KG54), 308
Guichard, Adjt A. (ECN 4/13), 340, 380
Guichon, Sgt C., 297
Guidicelli, Sgt E. (GB II/21), 364
Guieu, Capt. R. (GC II/4), 100, 288, 314, 315, 317, 392, 440, 441
Guijt, 2e Lt H. W., 194
Guilbert, Sgt (GAO 1/551), 352
Guilier, Lt, 305
Guillaume, Adjt (GC I/3), 451, 453
Guillaume, Capt. (GR II/33), 107
Guillaume, Lt (GC I/4), 375, 427, 434
Guillaume, Sgt J. (GC III/7), 117, 254, 274
Guille, Sgt Gaston (GR I/36), 426
Guillerme, S/Lt H. (GAO 509), 259, 424
Guillou, Lt (GC II/4), 451
Guilloux, Sgt M. (GAO 1/508), 373
Guimbretière, S/Lt (GBA 2/51), 334
Guingo, Adjt, 148

Guinness, S/Ldr T. L. E., 310, 313
Guionnet, Capt. (GB 4/23), 456
Guiral, Adjt, 171
Guisgand, Capt. Max, 236, 237
Guisset, S/Lt M., 114
Guitard, Sgt (GC II/1), 416
Guizard, Capt. G., 275
Güldens, Flgr J., 308
Gulley, P/O Alfred R. (150 Sqn), 464, 465
Gulliver, Sgt A. J., 256
Gumbleton, LAC A. H. (48 Sqn), 332
Gumpp, Uffz A., 120
Gundelach, Lt H. von, 253
Gundlach, Uffz K. (2./KG1), 448
Gunning, Sgt F. V. (15 Sqn), 461
Gunning, Sgt R. S. (107 Sqn), 412
Günther, Flgr Franz (3./KG54), 308, 309
Günther, Gefr F. (KG55), 213
Günther, Gefr H. (TrGr.186), 365
Günther, Obergefr Fritz (2./ZG52), 383
Günther, Obergefr H. (5./KG54), 212
Günthert, Uffz W., 279
Gunz, Oberlt E. (3./KGr.126), 479
Gupwell, Sgt (150 Sqn), 464
Gurin, Sgt, 108
Gurr, Lt K. P. (825 FAA Sqn), 356
Gürtler, Oberlt E. (Swiss Fl.Kp.10), 448
Guse, Oberlt M., 158
Gusikat, Fw E., 241
Gutbrod, Lt P. (5./JG52 & Stab II./JG52), 93, 409
Guth, Lt W. (6./ZG76), 98, 259, 297, 354
Gutschik, Oberfw A. (KG53), 328
Gutteck, Uffz H., 254
Guttmann, Oberlt (9./KG3), 381
Gutzmann, Maj. M., 207
Guy, Adjt, 235
Guyon, Sgt (GB 1/12), 259
Guyot, Adjt A. (GB II/21), 364
Guys, Wladyslaw, 83

Haag, Gefr E. (3./KG53), 409
Haarmann, Fw R., 263
Haas, Uffz J. (1./StG76), 456
Haas, Uffz O. (3./KG53), 476
Haase, Gefr D. (3./KG30), 300
Haase, Lt (3./JG53), 285
Haase, Obergefr Karl (2./KG54), 253
Haase, Oberlt Helmut (3.(H)/12), 298
Haase, Uffz (6./JG51), 386, 412
Haase, Uffz H. (8./KG30), 211
Haase, Uffz R. (8./KG4), 476
Haase, Uffz W. (TrGr.186), 239
Haberland, Lt K., 284, 307
Häberle, Uffz O., 221
Habermann, Lt R., 117
Habourdin, Adjt J. (GB I/63), 447
Hach, Lt F., 288
Hackbarth, Fw E. (2./LG1), 337
Häckel, Lt E., 206
Häcker, Fw K. (4./KG76), 453
Hacker, Fw K. (5./KG30), 479
Hackney, P/O H. B. (64 Sqn), 391
Hadley, Sgt A. W. H. (105 Sqn), 269
Hadlich, Gefr K., 239
Haeberle, Fw R. (9./KG4), 467
Haeckel, Lt, 239
Haegelen, Lt-Col Claude Marcel (DAT Bourges), 424
Häfele, Lt K., 278
Häfele, Uffz W., 278
Haferkamp, Uffz H. (KG54), 328
Häfner, Uffz G. (8./JG2), 392
Hagedorn, Fw Ludwig, 254
Hagen, Lt (JGr.152), 96
Hagen, Lt L. (3./ZG52), 360
Hagen, Oberlt T. (8./LG1), 347
Hagen, Sgt G. (3-V-2), 194
Hagens, Lt H. (3.(H)/12), 288
Hager, Oberlt G., 208

Hager, Uffz R. (1./JG76), 396
Hahn, Flgr K. (4./KG2), 160
Hahn, Fw (6./ZG76), 349
Hahn, Oberlt (4./JG2), 272, 322
Hahn, Oberlt von (III./JG53 - 8./JG53), 127, 401, 417
Hahn, Uffz R. (2./StG2), 242
Hahne, Lt H. (KGrzbV.9), 225
Hahne, Oberfw (6./LG1), 393
Haiges, Uffz W., 211
Haimerl, Lt K., 211
Haine, P/O R. C., 184
Haines, LAC G. C. P. (57 Sqn), 303, 349
Hairs, P/O, 273, 289
Haisch, Fw Hugo (8./KG51), 360
Halahan, S/Ldr Patrick 'Bull', 9, 11, 108, 119, 168, 244, 256
Halder, Gen. Franz, 365
Hale, Sgt, 246
Halgand, SM (T 2), 352
Halgrin, S/Lt J. (GC I/6), 335, 374
Hall, P/O (16 Sqn), 371
Hall, P/O (later F/O) Edward 'Henry' (73 Sqn), 8-73, 291, 436, 468, 471, 486
Hall, S/Ldr G. F. (110 Sqn), 345
Hall, Sgt (142 Sqn), 331, 458
Hall, Sgt H. R. (15 Sqn), 248
Hallauer, Fw W., 119
Halle, Aspirant, 93
Haller, Lt, 254
Halliday, F/O D. L. R. (88 Sqn), 152, 390, 437
Halliday, P/O Christopher I. D. (26 Sqn), 320, 514
Hallifax, P/O N. D., 251, 267, 282
Hallig, Gefr J., 167
Hallopeau, Capt. G. (GBA 1/51), 395
Hallowes, Sgt H. J. L. (43 Sqn), 437
Halma, Sgt J., 305
Halsmayr, Fw Otto, 222
Hamacher, Fw W., 318
Hamblett, Sgt Stanley, 272
Hambrecht, Uffz K-H. (3./KG76), 419
Hamilton, P/O Leslie M., 303, 517
Hamlyn, Sgt R. F. (72 Sqn), 423
Hamma, Obergefr E., 289
Hammann, Uffz Walter, 315, 316
Hammerschmidt, Flgr W. (8./KG27), 239
Hammerschmidt, Lt H. (I./JG1), 434
Hamon, Sgt (GAO 1/589), 461
Hampel, Gefr H. (1./KG53), 382
Hampel, Lt H. (2./KG3), 381
Hampshire, Sgt (85 Sqn), 317
Hamsick, Lt T., 274
Hancock, P/O N. P. W. (1 Sqn), 419
Händel, Gefr W., 228
Hands, AC1 Frank, 256, 520
Hänel, Uffz H., 263
Hanff, Uffz K. (9./KG51), 289
Hanft, Uffz E. (3./KG53), 409
Hankey, P/O, 267
Hanks, F/Lt P. P. 'Prosser', 156, 208, 242, 256, 265, 267
Hann, Sgt C. J., 180
Hannah, AC2 E., 233
Hannen, Oberlt E., 254
Hanotel, Sgt, 134
Hanras, Sgt (GBA II/51), 346
Hansen, Fw A., 253
Hansen, Oberfw W. (9./KG4), 327
Hansen, Uffz K., 240
Hanson, P/O D. W. H. (17 Sqn), 366, 390, 416
Hanssum, Oberlt O., 290
Hanstedt, Uffz E. (5./KG54), 342
Häntsch, Fw G., 254
Hanzlicek, Sgt Otto (GC II/5), 240, 315

Harbauer, Fw, 272, 312
Hardacre, P/O J. R. (504 Sqn), 283, 290, 322
Hardecker, Fw W. (6./KG53), 376
Harder, Sgt N. T. W., 244
Harding, Cpl A. D. C. (48 Sqn), 390
Harding, Cpl Benjamin M. (18 Sqn), 231, 349
Harding, P/O Geoffrey F., 170, 180, *514*
Hardouin, Sgt R., 189, 211, 241
Hardy, Sgt F. D. (9 Sqn), 469
Hardy, Sgt M. (GB I/62), 432
Hare, P/O C. J. F. (16 Sqn), 398
Harenburg, Fw K., 212
Harent, Adjt, 188
Harland, Fw W. (5./KG55), 429
Harlander, Uffz F. (4.(F)/11), 335
Harman, Sgt, 42
Harms, Lt O., 213
Harnard, Sgt, 117
Harper, F/O (17 Sqn), 366
Harper, P/O (103 Sqn), 423
Harriman, P/O D. S. R. (15 Sqn), 284, 362
Harris, Cpl (82 Sqn), 437
Harris, F/Lt G. (253 Sqn), 310, 315, 322
Harris, LAC P. B. (18 Sqn), 131, *133*
Harris, P/O Robert E. (17 Sqn), 320, *514*
Harris, P/O W. A. R. (218 Sqn), 271
Harris, Sgt B. L. (40 Sqn), 95
Harris, Sgt Kenneth H. (82 Sqn), *465*
Harris, Sgt W. H. (218 Sqn), 134, 247
Harrison, LAC D. S. (107 Sqn), 412
Harrison, LAC W. T. (254 Sqn), 405
Harrison, Sgt J. C. (229 Sqn), 391
Harrison, Sgt T. C. R. (139 Sqn), 246
Hart, Gefr R. (3./KG1), 470
Hart, P/O Kenneth G. (65 Sqn), 345, *373*
Hart, Sgt (21 Sqn), 465
Hart, Sgt C. S. (226 Sqn), 183
Hartefelt, Sgt J. A., 250
Hartenstein, Uffz K., 254
Härter, Uffz F. (4./KG54), 414
Hartfield, Sgt J. W. (82 Sqn), 345
Hartge, Fw O. (8./KG2), 441
Hartkoren, Sgt H., 116, 250
Hartmann, Flgr P. (3./KG1), 470
Hartmann, Fw G. (Stab I./KG30), 211
Hartmann, Fw H. (3./StG76), 376
Hartmann, Fw W. (3./LG1), 214
Hartmann, Oberlt (III./KG27), 123
Hartmann, Oberlt K. (3./StG77), 215
Hartog, Sgt J. den, 191
Hartsinck, Kapt. C. G. R. van Marcelis, 276
Hartwich, Fw F., 140
Hartwig, Fw Fridolin (1./JG21), 375
Hartwig, Obergefr H. (3.(F)/121), 315
Hartwig, Uffz A. (KGzbV.1), 229
Hartwig, Uffz H-J. (5./JG2), 294, 326
Hartzsch, Uffz W. (3./KG76), 419
Harvey, S/Ldr A. V., 116
Harvey, Sgt V., 121, 128
Hase, Gefr L. (2.(F)/122), 427
Haselsteiner, Gefr W. (III./KG55), 489
Hasselkus, Obergefr W., 226
Hassler, Gefr K., 279
Hassmann, Gefr W. (8./KG53), 470
Hatch, F/Sgt G. H. (64 Sqn), 398
Hateboer, Wachtm. W., 236
Hatfield, P/O J. E. (264 Sqn), 257, 386

Hatting, Obergefr J., 206
Hatton, LAC H., 269
Hätzel, Fw P., 221
Haubensack, Uffz P. (6./KG76), 347
Hauber, Uffz K., 213
Haubert, Lt Gabriel (1/I/1), 365, 387
Hauck, Hptmn G., 229
Hauck, Lt, 285
Hauenschild, Oberlt (3./JG2), 189, 320
Hauer, Oberfw (1./JG76), 274, 296, 433
Hauffe, Gefr J. (2./KG76), 442
Haufhold, Fw W., 225
Haug, Fw W. (1./KG53), 382
Haupt, Lt J., 289
Hauptmeier, Uffz G. (2./KG51), 453
Haure, Adjt J., 249
Hausdörfer, Fw M., 265
Hausenstein, Uffz A. (9./KG55), 353
Hauser, Fw E. (KG76), 308
Hauser, Fw F. (KG2), 239
Hauser, Lt K. (4.(H)/22), 380, 495
Hauser, Uffz F. (2.(H)/10), 476
Hausin, Oberlt Reinhard, 162
Hausmann, Fw A. (1./StG2), 366
Hausmann, Oberlt R. (2./JG21), 134, 392
Häussler, Fw H. (Stab KG76), 434
Hautecoeur, S/Lt (GR I/36), *126*
Hautière, Lt B., 103
Hautin, SM (AB 1), 333
Havet, Adjt, 118
Hawken, P/O Ian D. (73 Sqn), *416*
Hawkins, F/O R. (103 Sqn), 469
Hawkins, LAC G. (18 Sqn), 134
Hawkins, LAC H. C. W. (600 Sqn), 184
Hawkins, Sgt (114 Sqn), 142, *510*
Hawkins, Sgt G. (18 Sqn), 320, 339
Hawks, F/O Peter A., 268, *522*
Hawks, Mrs Elizabeth, *522*
Hawley, Sgt F. B. (266 Sqn), 465
Hayden, LAC (264 Sqn), 382
Hayeck, Gefr K. (KG76), 329
Hayes, F/O T. N. (600 Sqn), 184
Hayes, Lt (801 FAA Sqn), 487
Haygreen, Sgt A. (53 Sqn), 349
Hayman, F/Sgt M. W. (66 Sqn), 412
Hayton, P/O G. M. (12 Sqn), 423
Hayward, Sgt E. G. (103 Sqn), 371
Haywood, Sgt D. (88 Sqn), 378, 437, 464
Heberlein, Fw R. (5./JG2), 380
Hebig, Uffz H. (8./KG53), 470
Hébrad, Lt (GR II/33), 478
Hebrard, Lt (GC II/5), 253, 419, 476
Hecht, Gefr H. (4.(F)/11), 341
Hecht, Uffz E., 280
Heck, Fw (1.(F)/123), 456
Hecker, Fw M. (1.(F)/22), 335
Hecker, Oberlt G., 213
Heckert, Lt L., 318
Heckewert, Lt G., 229
Heckmann, Uffz (5./JG3), 431
Hedger, Naval Airman R. (801 FAA Sqn), 398
Hedley, Sgt (103 Sqn), 469, 472
Hedoch, Fw Alfred (7./KG55), *442*
Hedtke, Uffz G., 147
Heese, Uffz W., 158
Hegemann, Fw H. (3./KG27), 429
Hegron, Adjt (GBA II/51), 461
Hegwein, Gefr L. (1./JG54), 413
Hehs, Fw E. (Stab KG55), 376
Heidbüchel, Uffz W., 278
Heideman, 1e Lt H. C., 250
Heiden, Sgt B. W. van der, 250
Heidenpeter, Oberfw H., 307
Heidenreich, Fw W., 224
Heidig, Uffz W. (3./KG1), 353
Heidmeier, Fw (2./JG53), 400
Heijen, 2e Lt J. H., 194
Heil, Uffz W. (KG51), 328

Heilmann, Uffz (3./JG20), 398, 458
Heilmann, Uffz S. (1./KG77), 360
Heilmeier, Uffz A. (7./KG3), 381
Heiltz, Sgt E., 98
Heim, Uffz F. (3.(F)/22), 479
Heimann, Gefr H. (3./KG2), 381
Heimann, Uffz E. (4./KG53), 409
Heimbs, Lt K-W., 98, 100
Heimerl, Gefr K. (2./KG54), 383
Heims, Obergefr J. (3.(F)/22), 427
Heimsath, Uffz H., 209
Hein, Oberfw H. (3./ZG52), 360
Heinbockel, Uffz (2./JG21), 341, 452
Heine, Obergefr H. (TrGr.186), 479
Heinel, Lt (4./JG2), 339
Heinemann, Obergefr A. (5./StG2), 489
Heiner, Fw E. (9./KG27), 278, 327
Heinert, Lt H-O., 278
Heinig, Uffz H., 209
Heinkel, Ernst, 86
Heinrich, Gefr J., 279
Heinrich, Oberlt K-W. (7./ZG26), 334, 337
Heinrich, Uffz W., 208
Heintzer, Uffz H., 207
Heinz, Oberlt H. (Stab I./KG76), 418
Heinz, Uffz K. (4.(S)/LG2), 429
Heinze, Uffz H., 156
Heinze, Uffz P., 211
Heinzeller, Fw (5./JG3), 400, 436
Heisel, Fw F., 241
Heisel, Lt H., 280
Heiser, Uffz H., 212
Heisterbergk, Oberlt H., 107
Heitmann, Oberfw (9./JG3), 440
Helber, Fw K. (1./KG53), 382
Helbig, Fw F. (ZG26), 329
Helbig, Oberlt J. (4./LG1), 410
Held, Uffz K., 317
Helfrich, Fw R., 326
Helge, Fw H., 97
Heller, Gefr E. (10.(St)/LG1), 309
Heller, Gefr Fritz (JG1), 365
Hellmann, Lt W., 160
Hellwig, Fw W., 300
Hellwig, Uffz H-J., 118
Hellyer, F/O R. O. (616 Sqn), 386
Helmer, Lt (5./ZG76), 441
Helwig, Oberlt W. (6./KG76), 347
Hème, Sgt L. (GC II/5), 99, 251, 419, 433
Hémery, Sgt Jacques, *275*
Hemingway, P/O J. A., 213, 232
Hemingway, Sgt, 246, 269
Hemken, Uffz F., 280
Hemmelmann, Fw R. (7./KG1), 495
Hemmerle, Obergefr G. (9./KG55), 429
Hemmerling, Uffz P. (16./KGzbV.1), 396
Hemmings, Sgt (142 Sqn), 371
Hempel, Oberlt A., 315
Henderson, P/O D. (15 Sqn), 345, 356
Henderson, P/O M. L. G. (2 Sqn), 345
Hengel, Lt J. W. van, 191
Hengsbach, Lt K., 253
Hengst, Uffz M., 225
Henke, Lt G. (1.(F)/121), 341
Henke, Uffz W. (4./KG1), 419
Henkel, Uffz A., 300
Henne, Lt, 116
Henne, Uffz H. (2./KG55), 376
Henneberg, Lt (DAT Château-roux), 429
Hennessen, Flgr H. (7./KG55), 442
Henning, Uffz H. (7./KG3), 208
Hennings, Uffz H. (JGr.102), 112
Henquel, Adjt (GB I/11), 432
Henrard, S/Lt X., *144*, 145
Henrich, Uffz, 148
Henrici, Lt E., 103, 259, 260
Henry, Gustave, *475*, *476*
Henry, Lt A. (11/VI/1), 352

Henry, Lt F. (GB 1/19), 400
Henry, S/Lt E. (GBA I/54), 248
Henry, S/Lt (GR I/33), 113
Hensel, Lt H., 317
Hensel, Oberlt S., 263
Hensel, Uffz Gustav, 226
Hentschel, Uffz P., 212
Hentschler, Uffz G., 206
Hepe, Lt (5./JG2), 294, 312
Hepp, Fw R. (4./KG51), 429
Heppe, Lt L. (8./KG54), 213
Herb, Fw A., 211
Herber, Uffz E. (8./KG55), 459
Herbert, P/O (57 Sqn), 345
Herbier, Adjt, 156
Herbold, Uffz P. (1./KG27), 428
Herden, Fw Werner, *215*
Herdina, Oberfw W. (5./JG2), 336
Herget, Oberlt (6./ZG76), 488
Heriard-Dubreuil, Capt. (GB 1/11), 465
Hering, Uffz, 149, 151
Heringhaus, Uffz H. (KG54), 329
Héritier, Adjt R., 305
Herlt, Lt F. (6./StG77), 393
Hermann, Fw J. (2.(F)/11), 456
Hermann, Fw M. (2.(H)/21), 388
Hermann, Lt F. (2./KG54), 383
Hermann, Lt F. (Stab III./KG1), 206
Hermann, Uffz (6./KG2), 360
Hermann, Uffz E. (4./KG53), 240
Hermann, Uffz O. (Stab III./KG2), 162
Hermanski, Fw E. (4./ZG1), 360
Hermel, Sgt, 158
Hermes, Fw (2./JG2), 305, 364, 433
Hermichen, Lt (6./ZG1), 379
Herold, Gefr K. (2.(F)/122), 365
Herpin, Uffz E., 210
Herr, Oberlt P. (4./KG51), 429
Herrick, P/O R., 303
Herrig, Fw H. (Stab KG77), 477
Herriott, Sgt N. B., 271
Herrmann, Flgr W. (2./KG53), 376
Herrmann, Fw W. (2./KG51), 489
Herrmann, Oberlt H. (7./KG4), 402
Herrmann, Uffz A. (5.(F)/122), 120
Herrmann, Uffz H. (5./KG55), 429
Herst, Uffz W., 301
Hertaut, Cmdt André, 235
Hertel, Uffz G., 154
Hertle, Lt K., 317
Hertle, Uffz J. (3./KG53), 476
Hertling, Oberlt, 160
Hertung, Uffz H., 301
Hervé, Adjt (DAT Châteaudun), 419
Herverie, Cmdt Y. de la, 115
Hervier, Adjt (GBA II/51), 373, 447, 461
Herzhauser, Fw H. (6./KG77), 396
Herzig, Fw A. (2.(H)/31), 341
Herzig, Uffz Alfred (9./KG27), 300
Herzog, Fw G., 239
Herzog, Fw W., 265
Herzog, Oberfw H., 279
Herzog, Uffz E., 209
Heslop, Sgt (142 Sqn), 371
Hess, Rudolf, *497*
Hesse, Fw R., 226
Hesse, Obergefr H., 317
Hessel, Fw F. (1./JG3), 158, 341
Hesselbach, Gefr A., 97
Hettich, Uffz W., 239
Hettmer, Uffz L. (6./JG27), 453
Hetzel, Oberfw O., 121
Heuer Uffz H., 229
Heuermann, Lt H-J. (Aufkl.Gr.Ob.d.L), 359
Heumer, Gefr W. (9./KG76), 376
Heussner, Oberfw H. (2./KG54), 383
Heutz, Uffz J. (9./KG2), 381
Heuvel, 2e Lt R. van den, 250
Heuvelmann, Uffz E., 226
Hewett, AC1 E. (149 Sqn), 356
Hewitt, Sgt R. (9 Sqn), 469
Hewson, F/Lt J. M. (142 Sqn), 464

Hey, Lt R. (2.(F)/122), 408, 412
Hey, P/O T. C. (64 Sqn), 406
Heyden, 2e Lt H. A. M. van der, 191
Heyden, Oberlt M., 280
Heyer, Gefr J., 240
Heyer, Oberfw A., 239
Heymann, Lt R. (4./JG3), 331, 434
Hibberd, Sgt S. D. (226 Sqn), 272
Hibbert, Sgt E. (88 Sqn), 349
Hiblot, Sgt A. (GC III/10), 336, 441
Hickel, Oberfw B. (KG55), 265
Hickel, Obergefr K. (KG54), 329
Hickman, P/O G. L. (264 Sqn), 399
Hielscher, Hptmn K-F., 300
Hien, Oberfw W., 95, 99, 100
Hien, Uffz G., 290
Hier, Fw Karl, *118*
Hiernaux, Gén.-Maj. Paul, *85*
Hiersemann, Flgr H., 240
Higginbotham, Cpl, 349
Higgins, Sgt F. C. (107 Sqn), 465
Higginson, F/Sgt (56 Sqn), 308, 315, 318, 392
Higgs, F/O (111 Sqn), 459
Hilbrandt, Lt C., 102
Hild, Sgt R. (GAO 1/551), 395, 446
Hill, AC (105 Sqn), 246, 269
Hill, AC (139 Sqn), *246*
Hill, F/O G. D. (40 Sqn), 96, 362
Hill, Maj. W. (Stab II./KG76), 366
Hill, Obergefr H., 241
Hill, P/O R. L. (242 Sqn), 357
Hill, S/Ldr J. H. (504 Sqn), 322
Hillcoat, P/O H. B. L. (1 Sqn), 419
Hillecke, Lt (Stab II./JG26), 294, 356, 390
Hiller, Uffz O. (2./LG1), 402
Hillgruber, Obergefr W. (1./JG1), 470
Hillier, Sgt E. B., 104
Hillman, Sgt S. A. (229 Sqn), 386
Hillmann, Uffz, 288
Hillwood, Sgt P., 303
Hillyard, LAC (150 Sqn), 472
Hilmer, Oberlt A. (Stab StG77), 353
Hilt, Cpl, 148
Hincker, Sgt (GR 3/33), 346
Hinder, LAC R. H., 246
Hink, Obergefr R. (4./ZG1), 448
Hinke, Oberfw B., 309
Hinkeldey, Uffz, 100, 107, *506*
Hinrich, Gefr H., 240
Hinrichs, Obergefr W., 214
Hinrichs, Sgt G. A., 194
Hinrichs, Uffz, 158
Hinsch, Lt G., 209
Hinterberger, Fw M., 117
Hinterberger, Uffz J. (6./KG76), 418
Hinterhofer, Flgr K., 278
Hinton, P/O Ian P., 153, *502*
Hintze, Oberlt O. (4.(J)/TrGr.186), 410
Hintze, Uffz B. (7./KG4), 209
Hinz, Gefr H., 225
Hinze, Fw A., 212
Hlpp, Uffz K-H., 308
Hippel, Oberfw B., 162
Hippel, Oberst Walter von, *266*
Hirche, Uffz H. (3./KG3), 381
Hirn, Uffz K., 209
Hirsch, Capt. R. (GB 1/31), 94, 296, 451
Hirsch, Flgr A. (2./KG54), 383
Hirsch, Sgt M. (GB I/21), 446
Hirsch, Uffz W. (9./KG1), 495
Hirschauer, Lt J-L., 119, 260, 262, 306, 308
Hirschelmann, Uffz H., 308
Hirtz, SM (AB 1), 333
Hislop, F/Sgt J. (12 Sqn), 469
Hitch, P/O C. J., 256
Hitler, Adolf, *11*, *69*, *73*, 77, 82, 87, *351*, *355*, *361*, 366, *404*, 421, *422*, *430*, *443*, *454*, 486, *492*, *493*, *496-497*
Hlobil, Lt (GC II/4), 429
Hlubek, Oberfw O., 209

Hoare, F/O D. S. (74 Sqn), 356
Hobbie, Fw Gerhard, 300
Höbel, Uffz W., 239
Hobik, Uffz H., 211
Hobler, S/Ldr J. F., 270
Hoch, Lt H., 162
Hochauf, Gefr G., 208
Hochedé, S/Lt, 189, 249, 306
Hochwald, Fw W. (6./LG1), 337
Hockey, F/Lt L. P. R. (75 Sqn), 339
Hocqueviller, Capt. R., 113
Hodeige, Sgt M. (7/IV/1), 374
Hoekstra, 1e Lt E. M., 250, 276
Hoenmanns, Maj. Dr E., 133
Hoetz, Obergefr H., 211
Hoëvell, 2e Lt N. R. Baron van, 250
Hofbauer, Fw J., 253
Hofeler, Obergefr B., 242
Hofelich, Uffz (3./JG3), 431
Hofer, Flgr A. (KG54), 329
Hofer, Lt L. (KG2), 278
Hofer, Lt W. (5./JG52), 274, 493
Höfer, Uffz F., 288
Hoff, Uffz H. von, 239
Hoffmann, Flgr K. (6./KG2), 360
Hoffmann, Fw H. (8./KG3), 208
Hoffmann, Gefr T. (3./ZG26), 265
Hoffmann, Heinrich (photographer), *351*
Hoffmann, Lt (7./JG2), 433
Hoffmann, Lt H. (2./JG2), 306, 358, 433, 434
Hoffmann, Lt W. (1./JG52), 493
Hoffmann, Lt W. (JG53), 94, 100
Hoffmann, Obergefr O. (1./ZG1), 376
Hoffmann, Sgt G. (GB I/34), 340
Hoffmann, Uffz E. (2./LG1), 214
Hoffmann, Uffz G. (3./KG54), 263
Hoffmann, Uffz H. (4.(H)/22), 427
Hoffmann, Uffz K. (6./KG76), 418
Hoffmann, Uffz S. (12.(St)/LG1), 309
Hoffmeister Fw R., 223
Höfling, Obergefr F., 263
Hofmann, Fw K-H. (1./KG27), 428
Hofmann, Oberfw W. (3.(F)/10), 375
Hofmann, Obergefr E. (8./KG77), 253
Hofmann, Obergefr W. (4./ZG1), 448
Hofmeier, Oberfw E., 308
Hofmeister, Fw J. (2.(H)/12), 408
Hogg, Sub Lt C. S. F. (825 FAA Sqn), 390
Hogg, Uffz F. (1./KG1), 393
Hohe, Uffz W. (9./KG53), 410
Hohenberg, Oberlt D. Clemm von, 263
Hohenstein, Oberlt Fritz (4./KG51), 429, *489*
Hohlweg, Uffz August, 224
Höhn, Gefr E. (9./JG2), 375
Höhne, Oberstlt Otto, *263*, 266
Höhnisch, Uffz (1./JG53), 267, 268, 451
Holbein, Gefr S., 253
Holbrook, P/O D. F. S. (102 Sqn), 332
Holden, F/O E. J. (501 Sqn), 233, 247, 253, 356
Holden, P/O Eustace 'Gus' (56 Sqn), *525*
Holden, P/O K. (616 Sqn), 406
Holdenried, Uffz E. (1./KG53), 382
Holder, 2e Lt J. H. M. ten, 276
Holdermann, Uffz (5./JG53), 424
Holdsworth, AC1 A. F., 233
Holdsworth, F/O (149 Sqn), 356
Holland, P/O R. H. (92 Sqn), 354, 356
Holland, Sgt R. N. (18 Sqn), 293
Hollatz, Uffz S. (5.(H)/13), 341
Holleck-Weithmann, Oberlt I. (8./KG2), 441
Holliday, P/O 'Smooth', *14*, *44*, *46*, *58*

Holliday, Sgt D. J. (142 Sqn), 464
Holloway, AC1 T. W., 271
Hollweg, Oberlt (4./JG27), 478
Holman, Sgt S. H. (17 Sqn), 431
Holmes, Cpl G. H., 184
Holmes, P/O M. P. C., 231
Holmes, Sgt A. N. (15 Sqn), 356
Holt, LAC A. L. W., 233
Hölterscheidt, Fw F. (5./KG55), 429
Holtey, Oberlt H. von, 239
Holtfurth, Gefr P., 278
Holtz, Sgt J. L., 250
Holwerda, Sgt H., 193
Holz, Uffz W., 290
Holzapfel, Uffz F. (3.(H)/21), 341
Holze, Uffz H., 278
Holzknecht, Uffz W., 253
Hölzle, Gefr J. (3./KG3), 381
Homberger, Oberlt (Swiss Fl.Kp.15), 448
Homer, Naval Airman C. J. C. (826 FAA Sqn), 496
Homuth, Oberfw R. (7./KG55), 442
Homuth, Oberlt (3./JG27), 233, 246, 323, 362, 426, 466
Honig, Fw F., 210
Honnor, LAC R. G. (500 Sqn), 390
Honor, F/O D. G. S. (88 Sqn), 437
Honorat, Sgt, 214
Hookins, Sub Lt F. B. (826 FAA Sqn), 496
Hooper, Sgt A. H. (115 Sqn), 339
Hoops, Fw W., 153
Hoorickx, Lt G. (11/VI/1), 387
Hope, F/Lt Sir A. P. (601 Sqn), 304, 313, 317, 332, 379
Hope, LAC J., 256
Hopf, Gefr L. (5./KG77), 477
Hopfenmüller, Uffz B. (6./KG77), 396
Hopfgartner, Gefr F. (9./KG53), 410
Hopgood, Sgt B. A. (142 Sqn), 322
Hopkin, P/O A. D. (59 Sqn), 461
Hopkins, Sgt E. E. (226 Sqn), 272, 465
Hopkins, Sgt R. G., 313
Hopkinson, Lt-Col G. F., *169*
Hoppe, Fw W., 205
Hoppe, Uffz K., 140
Hopper-Diestel, Gefr E., 107
Höppner, Oberfw W., 162
Hopwood, AC2 H. C. R. (500 Sqn), 362
Hoquetis, Capt., 99
Horbank, Uffz E. (9./KG77), 388
Horlitz, Gefr A. (JG1), 365
Horn, Lt J. (2.(H)/31), 298
Horn, Oberlt E. (3.(F)/121), 206
Horn, Oberlt J. von (Stab kG53), 240
Hornbogen, Gefr R. (8./KG4), 479
Horne, F/O (615 Sqn), 288
Horne, P/O G. (56 Sqn), *525*
Horner, F/Sgt John B., *245*, *247*
Hornstein, Hptmn Hans-Eberhard Fr von, 224
Hornung, Obergefr G. (16./KGzbV.1), 396
Horsky, Sgt V. (GC I/6), 459
Horstmann, Lt H. (3.(F)/121), 315
Horstmann, Uffz P. (3.(St)/TrGr.186), 410
Horten, Oberlt W. (1./KGr.126), 343
Horter, Fw W., 225
Horton, LAC, 248, 313
Hosemann, Fw W., 239
Hoskins, Sgt J. H. (500 Sqn), 390
Hösl, Fw F., 315
Hôtellier, Adjt J. (GC I/4), 212, 262, 307, 347, 374
Hotz, Gefr F., 289, 308
Hotz, Lt A. (8./KG76), 462
Hotzelmann, Uffz F., 300
Houdenot, Sgt (GB I/21), 387
Houlihan, AC (59 Sqn), 321
Hounston, Sgt J. (82 Sqn), 445

Hourcade, Adjt (AC 3), 472
Hourcade, Sgt (GAO 502), 478
Hourtic, Lt (GB I/31), 334
Houwald, Maj. Wolf-Heinrich von, 160
Houzé, Lt P. (GC II/5), 112, 240, *315*, 316, 335, 358, 360, 433
Hover, Lt H. W., 210
Howarth, P/O Ernest E. (26 Sqn), *378*
Howe, Oberlt Heinrich (KG54), 328
Howell, F/O F. J. (609 Sqn), 395
Howell, Sgt F. V. (87 Sqn), 121, 212, 245
Howes, Sgt H. N. (85 Sqn), 331, 336
Howitt, P/O J. F. (242 Sqn), 392
Hoyer, Oberfw E. (Stab I./KG76), 418
Hoyle, Sgt N. N. (226 Sqn), 272
Hrabak, Oberlt D. (I./JG76), 260, 433, 441
Hranicka, Sgt J. (GC I/6), 425
Hubacek, Sgt J., 235
Hubbard, F/O T. E. (601 Sqn), 323, 351, 437
Hubbard, Sgt W. F. (103 Sqn), 371
Huber, Flgr E. (3./KG1), 448
Huber, Fw F. (9./KGzbV.1), 229
Huber, Oberfw J. (2./KG76), 317
Huber, Uffz (6./ZG76), 351
Huber, Uffz F. (3./KG53), 253
Huber, Uffz L. (9./KG55), 414
Huberts, Fw A., 158
Hubin, Sgt L. (GR 1/52), 413
Hübner, Lt H. (Stab KG3), 342
Hübner, Lt J. (3./KG76), 429
Hubner, Uffz Hans, 224
Hubregste, Aro J., 98
Hubrich, Oberfw A., 151
Huckelmann, Stabsfw A., 213
Huckins, Sgt (21 Sqn), 458
Hudson, F/O A. J., 233
Huenaerts, Adjt F., 167
Huet, EV1 (T 2), 352
Hufenreuter, Oberlt A., 240
Hufnagel, Uffz W., 209
Huggett, P/O L. J., 311
Hughes, F/O (218 Sqn), 95
Hughes, LAC R. D. 246, 269
Hughes, P/O (16 Sqn), 320
Hughes, P/O A. (18 Sqn), 349
Hughes, Sgt K. W. (115 Sqn), 339
Hugill, P/O F. (103 Sqn), 469
Hugo, Capt. (GC II/7), 160, 211, 360, 441
Hugonnier, Adjt (GBA I/54), 475
Hugot, S/Lt P. (GB I/12), 273
Hugues, Cmdt M., 314
Huhle, Gefr H., 290
Hühne, Obergefr E., 213
Huizen, 2e Lt H. K. van, 193
Hulbert, F/O E. V., 144
Hülse, Oberlt, 124
Hulse, P/O Cecil L. (12 Sqn), 180
Hulse, P/O R. G. (501 Sqn), 242, 445
Hulton, Lt-Col, DSO, *514*
Hulton, P/O Henry S. P., 151, *511*, *514*, *519*
Hulton-Harrop, P/O O. P. de L., 233
Humbeek, Frans van, *201*
Humbert, S/Lt R. (GB I/15), 305, 395
Hume, P/O O. C., 119
Hummel, Gefr E., 254
Hummenberger, Unterfw H. (2.(H)/23), 470
Humpherson, F/O, 210
Humphreys, LAC H., 304
Humphris, Sgt L. J. W., 15, *44*, *46*, 112, 113, 181, 207, 240, 283
Hundenborn, Fw J., 107
Hundt, Lt, 326
Hunt, F/Lt P. H. M. S., 180
Hunt, Sgt D. A. C. (66 Sqn), 412
Hunter, AC2 J. R., 136
Hunter, LAC R. E. (15 Sqn), 247, 339

Hunter, S/Ldr (264 Sqn), 382
Huntziger, Gén. Charles, 490, 496, *497*
Huppertz, Lt (6./JG51), 386
Hurford, Cpl G., 184
Hurst, AC (59 Sqn), 321
Hurst, Oberfw H. (9./KG27), 347
Hurst, P/O Tom, *246*
Hüsch, Gefr H., 280
Husson, Lt G. (GC I/2), 188, 213, 429
Husson, Sgt (GC II/8), 342
Hutcheson, P/O G. A. (264 Sqn), 458
Hutchings, P/O W. (57 Sqn), 356
Hutchinson, LAC O. A., 181
Hüttenranch, Gefr W., 223
Hutter, S/Lt M. (GC II/1), 253, 324
Hütter-Wallek, Lt W. (7./JG26), 402
Hüttl, Gefr A., 278
Huvet, Lt (later Capt.) (GC II/5), 100, 131, 253, 419, 470
Hyde, Sgt T. E., *246*
Hyde-Parker, F/Lt A. E., 99
Hyrschke, Obergefr A. (Stab II./ZG1), 343
Hyvernaud, Capt. P., 157, 213, 234

Iberle, Uffz R. (4./JG26), 441
Ickert, Gefr E. (9./KG53), 410
Idel, Fw H. (3.(St)/TrGr.186), 429
Ihle, Uffz R. (2./StG77), 347
Ihlcr, Gén. Marccl, *460*
Ikert, Gefr E., 290
Illg, Fw W. (KG76), 329
Ilsemann, Uffz K., 290
Imiela, Lt M., 165
Immel, Uffz H. (5./KG76), 448
Imparator, Aviere A., 477
Imrie, P/O A. M., 271
Ing, F/O J., 271
Ingr, Lt Gen. Sergej, 83
Ingram, F/Lt J. A., 181
Innes-Jones, Sgt M., 248
Ironside, F/Lt (151 Sqn), 318
Irrgang, Gefr H. (2./KG53), 336
Irvine, Sgt (53 Sqn), 450
Irvine, Sgt G. B. (142 Sqn), 182
Irving, F/O (607 Sqn), 125
Irwin, Sgt Charles A. (19 Sqn), 373
Irzen, Adjt (GBA 4/51), 340
Isaacs, Cpl L. D., 184
Isola, S/Lt C., 249
Israël, Lt J. (GR 3/33), 97, 108, 165, 346
Issel, Fl-Stab-Ing. E., 212
Isselhorst, Uffz A. (KG54), 329
Ives, F/Lt Freddy A. (151 Sqn), 309, 362
Izern, Adjt (GBA II/51), 469

Jabs, Lt (6./ZG76), 441
Jabubeck, Obergefr F., 145
Jäckel, Obergefr E., 208
Jäckel, Uffz J., 309
Jackson, Naval Airman R. J. (826 FAA Sqn), 496
Jackson, P/O F. S., 304
Jackson, P/O T. C., 288, 295, 299
Jacob, Fw K., 298
Jacob Oberlt Otto, 221
Jacob, Lt (GB 4/38), 458
Jacobi, Oberlt, 124
Jacobi, Uffz, 226
Jacobs, LAC N. E. (48 Sqn), 332
Jacoby, F/O R. H. (40 Sqn), 349
Jacoubet, EV1 (AC 2), 481
Jacquemart, Adjt A. (GR II/55), 447, 495
Jacquemet, S/Lt (GC II/8), 313
Jacquemin, Adjt (GB I/12), 273
Jacquemin, Cpl (GB I/12), 400
Jacques, S/Lt E. (GR I/55), 495
Jacquet, S/Lt J. (GAO 1/514), 346
Jacquet, S/Lt L. (GB II/12), 234
Jacquiard, Mt, 93
Jacquin, Sgt, 117
Jacquot, Sgt Charles (GB II/12), 432
Jaczak, Lt M. (1./JG2), 299, 375

Jaenisch, Oberfw (3./JG2), 148, 313, 447
Jagemann, Fw E. (Stab KG27), 402
Jäger, Fw L. (Stab I./KG27), 342
Jäger, Obergefr O., 241
Jäger, Oberlt H-E., 309
Jäger, Uffz H. (16./KGzbV.1), 396
Jagielki, Uffz K-H., 145
Jagt, 2e Lt J. van der, 192
Jahn, Fw H. (9./LG1), 347
Jahn, Oberlt Christoph (5.(H)/13), *499*
Jahn, Oberst A., 253
Jahn, Uffz F., 154
Jähne, Oberlt, 162
Jahraus, Gefr K., 252
Jähser, Uffz K., 316
Jakob, Oberlt (5.(H)/13), 128
Jakob, Uffz Walter (1.(H)/31), 452
Jakobs, Fw J. (2./KG55), 376
Jakubowski, Uffz G. (9./LG1), 343
Jamais, SM F., 324
James, LAC Horace G., *293*
James, P/O (43 Sqn), 478
James, P/O B. B. (40 Sqn), 431
Jamet, SM (AB 4), 340
Janeba, Sgt J. (GC II/5), 240, 433
Janik, Fw F. (6./KG76), 347
Janis, S/Lt (GC I/6), 335, 429, 479
Jänisch, Oberlt W., 299
Jank, Gefr H. (5./KG27), 402
Janke, Hptmn J., 99
Janke, Oberlt K., 242
Janker, Fw H. (KG53), 328
Jankowski, Fw J. (7./LG1), 429
Jankowski, Uffz K. (KGrzbV.9), 225
Janoba, Sgt, 145
Janotta, Fw W., 498
Janouch, Lt S. (GC I/6), 148, 429, 441
Janse, Korp. A., 191
Jansen, Fw R. (9./KG27), 347
Jansen, Lt A., 213
Jansen, Sgt J. F. A., 194
Janson, Hptmn von, 97, 271
Janz, Uffz H. (Stab StG1), 453
Jarrett, Sgt R. W. E., 304
Jarvis, LAC, 331
Jarvis, P/O Paul L., 268, *515*
Jaschke, Fw R., 301
Jaschob, Lt G-U., 290
Jaske, S/Lt, 163
Jaspers, Uffz A., 309
Jastrzebski, Capt. Franciezk (GC II/1), 83, 433
Jaubert, Sgt (GB II/62), 461
Jaulon, Sgt, 296
Jaussaud, Sgt (GC II/4), 239, 459
Jay, P/O D. T., 210, 213, 214, 233, 241
Jean, Adjt A. (GB 3/23), 432
Jean, Lt (GAO 544), 248
Jean, Sgt G. (GC II/4), 94
Jeandel, Sgt, 296
Jeandet, Lt H., 189
Jeandron, SM (AB 1), 333
Jeannaud, Sgt (GC III/3), 337
Jeanne, S/Lt, 274
Jeannin, Adjt, 249
Jebb, P/O M. (504 Sqn), 332
Jeff, F/Lt R. Voase, *109*, 110, *111*, 181, 208, 288
Jefferies, F/O (17 Sqn), 239
Jefferies, P/O Charles G. StD. (253 Sqn), 267
Jeffery, LAC (53 Sqn), 345
Jeffrey, Sgt W. (44 Sqn), 458
Jelinek, Fw O. (Stab KG77), 477
Jelinski, Lt, 134
Jenau, Uffz A. (3./KG27), 429
Jende, Fw H., 225
Jenderny, Gefr W., 254
Jenett, Oberlt R., 210
Jenkins, AC1 L., 331
Jenkins, P/O D. (253 Sqn), 312, 317
Jenkins, Sgt P. D. (610 Sqn), 392
Jenkins, Sgt S. W. (83 Sqn), 349
Jennings, Sgt (21 Sqn), 272
Jennings, Sgt Cedric M. (218 Sqn), 135, 233, *515*

Jensch, Prüfmstr W., 456
Jentzmik, Obergefr H., 317
Jentzsch, Fw (V.(Z)/LG1), 303, 356
Jere, Sgt, 275
Jérôme, Sgt, 162
Jeromin, Uffz E. (3./KG3), 366
Jervis, AC1 T. J., 104, 116
Jerzembeck, Uffz O., 225
Jeschke, Uffz H., 240
Jeschonnek, Gen. Hans, 361, 366
Jetter, Flgr C. (2./KG1), 448
Jeunet, Capt. M. (GBA 3/54), 425
Jicha, Sgt (GC I/6), 360
Joannic, Sgt M., 249
Job, LAC J., 128
Jobart, Sgt (ECN 1/13), 341
Jobst, Uffz E., 316
Jockel, Gefr J. (5.(F)/122), 365
Jocquel, Sgt H. (GR 1/22), 496
Jodl, Genmaj. Alfred, *361*
Joest, Fw W., 213
Johann, Uffz W. (1./KG1), 392
John, AC1 D. J. (88 Sqn), 95
John, Fw (4./JG51), 162
John, Sgt (105 Sqn), 270
John, Uffz E. (5./KG55), 429
Johnson, AC1 L. J. 'Joe' (103 Sqn), 268, *269*
Johnson, LAC S. J. (40 Sqn), 284
Johnson, Sgt A. G. (12 Sqn), 267
Johnson, Sgt H. W. (500 Sqn), 390
Johnson, Sgt S. B. (264 Sqn), 382, 399
Johnson, Sgt S. W. (40 Sqn), 469
Joire, Sgt J. (GC I/4), 212, 262, 308, 347, 364
Jolicoeur, Lt, 316
Jolie, Jan, 257, 262
Jolly, Cpl (later Sgt) R. (144 Sqn), 233, 461
Joly, Lt M., 94
Jonas, AC2, 272
Jonchay, Cmdt du (GB I/62), 400
Jones, AC1 (44 Sqn), 273
Jones, AC1 D. E. (150 Sqn), 99
Jones, AC2 R. J. (226 Sqn), 339
Jones, AC2 T. (77 Sqn), 233
Jones, Cpl (16 Sqn), 378
Jones, Cpl A. E. (105 Sqn), 153, *502*
Jones, F/O D. A. E. (3 Sqn), 303
Jones, F/O Francis D. Dawson (15 Sqn), *313*
Jones, F/O H. (500 Sqn), 408
Jones, F/Sgt W. T. (17 Sqn), 373
Jones, LAC E. J. (264 Sqn), 257, 392
Jones, LAC H. B. (218 Sqn), 247
Jones, LAC H. G. (2 Sqn), 345
Jones, P/O B. S. (13 Sqn), 115
Jones, P/O C. A. T. (611 Sqn), 412
Jones, P/O D. F. (242 Sqn), 386
Jones, Sgt (32 Sqn), *458*
Jones, Sgt E. (21 Sqn), 445
Jones, Sgt J. R. A. (88 Sqn), 378, 464
Jones, Sgt M. G. (15 Sqn), 458
Jones, Sgt N. S. D. (139 Sqn), 246
Jones, Sgt T. (142 Sqn), 322
Jongkind, Aro J., 98
Jonoux, Sgt (GBA I/51), 424
Joppien, Oberlt H-F. (1./JG51), 117, 120, 352, 425
Jordan, Fw E., 278
Jordan, LAC (2 Sqn), 345
Jordan, LAC Leslie F. (57 Sqn), 181
Jordan, Lt F., 128
Jordan, P/O C. B., 270
Jordan, Uffz G., 265
Jordens, Adjt D., 238
Jörke, Uffz Helmut, 297, 306, 318
Jorzyck, Uffz Hans, *265*
Joslin, F/Lt (later S/Ldr) J. D. C. (56 Sqn & 79 Sqns), 315, 437
Josse, Sgt P. W. (83 Sqn), 349
Josselin, Lt, 96, 107
Josserand, Adjt J. (GR II/33), 107
Josserand, Sgt (GR I/33), 481

Jost, S/Lt R. (GAO 3/551), 424
Jost, Sgt (GC I/6), 417
Jost, Sgt R. (GR I/36), 433
Josten, Lt E., 280
Jottard, Sgt (DAT Chartres), 418
Jouandeau, Adjt (GAO 553), 364
Jouany, Adjt H., 305
Joubert de la Ferté, AM P. B., *339*
Jousselin, Sgt (GAO 2/506), 373, 419
Jowitt, Sgt (85 Sqn), 329
Joyce, F/O E. P., 131, 268
Jozan, Capt., 239
Jug, Uffz N., 211
Jung, Fw O. (3./KG1), 448
Jung, Lt S., 316
Jung, Oberfw W., 206
Jung, Uffz W., 110
Jungnickel, Uffz A., 289
Junk, Lt H., 253
Junkers, Hugo, 86
Jürgens, Uffz H. (2./JG21), 140, 341, 359
Just, Uffz E., 171
Just, Uffz W., 119
Jütte, Uffz H. (3./KG1), 448

Kaasch, Oberlt H-H. (3.(F)/31), 347
Kade, Uffz W. (5.(F)/122), 392
Kadow, Oberlt G. (6./ZG1), 448
Kädtler, Oberlt A., 242
Kah, Lt L. (GAO 553), 364
Kahlert, Uffz G., 149
Kahlmeier, Fw, 239
Kain, F/O Derek W. 'Bill', 13, *30*, 32, 33, 35, *48*, *49*, *59*, 99
Kain, F/O Edgar J. 'Cobber', *6-7*, 11, *13*, 14, 15, *18*, 22, 28, *30-33*, 34-37, *37*, *41*, *44*, 45, *46*, *48*, *50*, 52-59, 61, 68-71, *73*, 103, 108, *114*, 120, *122*, 136, 144, *153*, 208, 251, 278, 282, 290, 327, 328, 423, 427, *436*, *438-439*, *490-491*
Kain, Mrs (Cobber's mother), *490*
Kaiser, Fw (2./JG53), 99, 380
Kaiser, Lt W. (9./StG2), 215
Kaiser, Oberfw F. (KGrzbV.9), 226
Kaiser, Uffz E. (2./JG27), 244, 353, 466, 467
Kaiser, Uffz H. (ZG26), 140
Kaisz, Fw M., 226
Kakanowski, Fw H. (8./LG1), 347
Kaldart, Fw A. (4.(H)/21), 476
Kaldrack, Hptmn R. (4./ZG1), 359, 360
Kalensky, Sgt (GB I/23), 364
Kalinna, Uffz H., 290
Kalischewski, Oberlt (5./KG27), 402
Kallvuss, Uffz, 148
Kalpas, S/Lt R. (DAT Lyons), 407
Kaltenbach, Fw H. (4./KG53), 409
Kalusche, Uffz W. (6./LG1), 337
Kaluza, Gefr O. (2./KG1), 448
Kalweit, Lt, 298
Kalz, Fw W. (2./KG55), 376
Kaminski, Hptmn, 290
Kammhuber, Oberst J. (Stab KG51), 418
Kampichler, Uffz R. (4./KG76), 434
Kania, Uffz R. (4./KG76), 453
Kannewurf, Uffz H. (7./KG51), 382
Kanow, Gefr H. (2./KG2), 453
Kanz, Lt W. (Aufkl.Gr.Ob.d.L.), 359
Kappe, Gefr T., 212
Karg, Oberfw O. (2.(F)/123), 359
Karhard, Flgr M. (KGzbV.1), 241
Karing, Gefr H., 213
Karow, Uffz H., 223
Karow, Obergefr P., 164
Karsten, Fw R. (2.(F)/11), 288
Karsten, Lt G. (7./KG2), 164
Karsten, Uffz (9./KG27), 413
Karubin, Sgt (DAT Étampes), 418
Karwowski, S/Lt W. E., 260, 263

Kasch, Fw H., 151
Kaschel, Flgr O. (4./KG54), 414
Kaselitz, Oberfw H. (1./KG4), 467
Kaselowski, Oberfw H., 206
Kasischke, Gefr G., 213
Kasper, Obergefr H. (3./KG1), 353
Kaspers, Oberfw J., 135
Kassegger, Gefr A. (7./KG51), 382
Kassing, Oberfw H. (1./LG1), 343
Kasten, Uffz G., 206
Kastler, Lt, 156
Kästner, Fw G. (2./KG77), 376
Katzenberger, Uffz O. (Stab KG77), 336
Kauder, Uffz A., 317
Kauffmann, Fw (4./JG53), 154, 441, 446
Kaufhold, Uffz H. (3./KG55), 383
Kaufhold, Fw W. (1./KGrzbV.9), 223
Kaufmann, Uffz (7./ZG26), 334
Kaufmann, Uffz R. (1./KGr.126), 343
Kaun, Lt H. (2./KG51), 453
Kaupper, Fw A. (9./StG51), 442
Kaven, Gefr H., 301
Kawnik, S/Lt, 278
Kay, P/O Desmond H. S. (264 Sqn), *255*, 257, 392
Kaye, P/O (9 Sqn), 349
Kayll, S/Ldr (615 Sqn), 290, 497
Kazmaier, Uffz M., 307
Kazmierowski, Uffz H., 278
Keast, Sgt L. A. (10 Sqn), 458
Keates, Sgt Arthur K. R. (21 Sqn), *362*
Kedziora, Sgt J. (DAT Rennes), 395
Keedwell, P/O O. H., 248
Keegan, Sgt J. B., 246
Kehren, Uffz J., 280
Kehrer, Fw H. (9./KG53), 410
Keidel, Lt E. (7./StG2), 366
Keighley, F/O G. (610 Sqn), 399
Keil, Fw (2./JG2), 305, 432, 451
Keil, Uffz J. (8./JG3), 425, 427
Keitel, Genoberst Wilhelm, 496, *497*
Keitel, Oberlt (Stab I./JG77), 373
Keller, Fw P. (JG2), 205
Keller, Lt F. (2./JG27), 129, 252, 353
Keller, Oberfw P. (6./JG26), 409
Keller, Oberlt (1./JG3), 274, 306, 341, 349, 401, 456
Keller, Oberlt (I.(Z)/LG1), 102
Keller, Sgt A. (GC 2/4), 475
Keller, Uffz K. (3.(F)/121), 126
Kellner, Fw A. (7./KG51), 328
Kellner-Steinmetz, Oberlt J., 112
Kelly, F/O D. D. A. (103 Sqn), 455
Kelly, P/O V. B. (2 Sqn), 345
Kempf, Gefr (2./JG21), 374
Kempfen, Lt, 262
Kempgens, Fw F., 240
Kempster, F/O C. M. P., 131
Kempte, Uffz R. (3./KG77), 360
Kendrick, Sgt R., 270
Kenkyns, P/O (613 Sqn), 378
Kennedy, AC1 A. L. (77 Sqn), 451, 455
Kennedy, AC2 T. (115 Sqn), 339
Kenneth, AC1 (53 Sqn), 293
Kenny, AC1 T. B. (77 Sqn), 332
Kentie, Sgt J. C., 194, 276
Kenzelmann, Uffz A., 124
Kepinski, Cmdt (Maj.) Jozef (GC 1/145), 83, 456
Keprt, Sgt, 265
Kerambrun, SM, 94
Kerangueven, Capt. (GC III/2), 376
Kerbouch, Adjt, 324
Kerbrat, Adjt (GR 3/22), 470
Kergel, Gefr G., 242
Kerland, Sgt Le Coq de (GBA I/51), 433
Kerr, F/O G. M. T. (610 Sqn), 392
Kerr-Wilson, F/O J. (610 Sqn), 379, 392

Kerridge, F/Lt B. R., 183
Kerstin, Uffz J., 278
Kervella, Lt N., 275
Kesse, Adjt, 239
Kesselring, Gen. Albert, 86, 130, 216, *366*
Ketautem, Lt de (GAO 502), 478
Kettlewell, Sgt Flgr H. (142 Sqn), 464
Kettner, Uffz Johann (6./KG4), 327, *328*
Ketzscher, Fw H. (1./KG3), 366
Keuleers, Lt M. (1/I/1), 359
Keyzers, Obergefr T. (4./KG54), 342
Kibele, Oberlt P. (3./KG51), 414
Kidd, Cpl B. A., 184
Kidman, Sgt R. T. (266 Sqn), 412
Kidrowski, Uffz K. von (9./KG4), 376
Kiel, Lt J., 157
Kiel, Sgt Guus K. P., 193, *194*
Kieler, Fw H., 162
Kielwein, Gefr O., 212
Kienitz, Hptmn Walter, 160
Kienlin, Fw Johannes von, *251*
Kierzynski, Uffz T. (KGzbV.1), 241
Kiesenhofer, Flgr Emmerich, 241
Kiess, Fw E. (2.(F)/122), 408
Kiessling, Oberfw G., 279
Kijewski, Oberlt (5./JG3), 431
Kilimann, Fw, 148
Killermann, Uffz A. (6./ZG1), 419
Killy, Sgt (GC II/3), 343, 347, 360, 380, 448
Kilmartin, F/O J. I., 120, 156, 161, 162, 208, 242, *256*
Kilner, Sgt (65 Sqn), 376, 388
Kindermann, Lt G. (4./StG77), 347
Kindler, Oberlt Alfred, 278
Kindler, Uffz E., 229
King, Gefr E., 209
King, Sgt (264 Sqn), 382
Kinne, Obergefr (2.(F)/22), 365
Kinster, Sgt, 189
Kinzler, Fw W., 132
Kipple, Lt E. (Aufkl.Gr.Ob.d.L), 335
Kippschull, Uffz O., 254
Kirberg, Obergefr W. (3./ZG26), 354
Kirby, P/O (142 Sqn), 472
Kirby, Sgt R. A. P. (88 Sqn), 232
Kirch, Fw O. (5./KG27), 382
Kircher, Sgt C. B. (9 Sqn), 469
Kirchhoff, Fw R., 241
Kirchhoff, Oberlt H-J. (Stab I./ZG26), 414
Kirchner, Lt (3.(H)/21), 456
Kirchner, Uffz K. (JG52), 104, 288
Kirchner, Lt L. (StG77), 280
Kirchof, Uffz A., 162
Kirk, LAC (150 Sqn), 464
Kirk, Sgt G. E. (59 Sqn), 372
Kirkcaldie, P/O K. (32 Sqn), 446
Kirner, Gefr L., 254
Kirsch, Sgt, 156
Kirsch, Uffz P., 209
Kirscheis, Oberlt, 106
Kirschke, Lt H., 288
Kirschmann, Uffz W. (9./KG2), 381
Kisker, Lt V., 129
Kisker, Uffz Manfred, *210*
Kisling, Oberlt, 300
Kistler, Fw J., 290
Kittner, Oberfw H. (8./KG77), 388
Kitto, Sgt R. V. T. (142 Sqn), 270, 464
Kitzinger, Lt (3./JG54), 390
Klaas, Uffz W., 239
Klabunde, Oberfw H., 254
Klafke, Fw P. (4.(F)/11), 335
Klahn, Lt K., 317
Klammer, Lt K. (6./JG26), 459
Klan, S/Lt (GC II/5), 164, 476, 479
Klappert, Lt, 163
Klär, Gefr W. (5./KG55), 429
Klare, Fw (8./ZG26), 358

Klaue, Oberfw W., 290
Klaus, Oberlt (4.(H)/32), 481
Klaus, Uffz K., 280
Klause, Oberfw (3./KG27), 479
Klauser, Obergefr K. (4.(F)/121), 388
Klee, Oberfw H., 288
Kleemann, Uffz K. (KG54), 329
Kleff, Fw R., 278
Kleffens, Dr Eelco van, 194
Klehn, Uffz H. (7./KG2), 493
Klein, Fw H. (3.(F)/121), 206
Klein, S/Lt A. (GAO 2/514), 488
Klein, SM (AB 4), 324
Klein, Uffz H., 119
Klein-Altstedde, Uffz H., 241
Klein-Ellguth, Hptmn D. Graf von Pfeil und, 117
Kleinecke, Lt W. (Stab I./ZG1), 376
Kleinjohann, Uffz W. (8./KG27), 347
Kleinmacher, Lt A., 263
Kleinschmidt, Fw W., 211
Kleint, Uffz Wilhelm, 214
Kleist, Gen. Ewald, *365*
Klemm, Gefr K., 209
Klemme, Oberlt W., 309
Klenk, Oberfw E. (1./KG53), 336
Klenk, Uffz G., 209
Kley, Oberfw, 117, 313
Klimaschka, Gefr P. (1./KG53), 382
Kling, Uffz H. (5./KG1), 488
Klingebiel, Uffz A. (16./KGzbV.1), 396
Klingshirn, Uffz A. (9./KG55), 353
Klinke, Obergefr Herbert (5./ZG1), 448
Klinkert, Uffz W., 289
Klipsch, Sgt Paul H. (92 Sqn), 349, *350*
Klischat, Lt H., 289
Klitzing, Maj. H. von, 309
Klöckner, Gefr A., 278
Kloha, Uffz H., 290
Kloiber, Lt (2./JG3), 424
Kloimüller, Oberfw H., 117
Kloppenburg, Lt J., 239
Klöpper, Uffz H., 289
Klöpping, Fw W. (5./ZG76), 456
Klose, Uffz E. (3./KG30), 347
Kloster, Gefr K., 308
Klosterkemper, Fw F., 290
Klöttschen, Fw W., 252
Klötzer, Flgr H-B. (KG51), 453
Kluch, Lt J., 156
Klug, Obergefr S., 239
Knaach, Oberlt, 225
Knaapen, Sgt C. H. J., 159
Knapp, Uffz A. (5./KG27), 402
Knappe, Gefr W. (1./LG1), 343
Knauber, Uffz A. (3./StG76), 376
Knecht, Fw F., 290
Knerr, Fw H., 265
Knetsch, Fw P. (9./KG55), 429
Knight, Sgt J. (38 Sqn), 398
Knipping, Capt., 234, 259
Knobloch, Uffz H. (2.(F)/KG53), 376
Knobloch, Uffz H. (6./KG54), 414
Knoch, Fw L., 120
Knoch, Uffz F., 278
Knöchel, Uffz W., 317
Knödler, Uffz H., 265
Knop, Oberlt H-J., 290
Knorr, Oberlt K., 253
Knorr, Uffz K-H., 225
Knowles, S/Ldr E. V. (56 Sqn), 257, 310, 383
Knowles, Sgt A. V., 304
Knowlton, AC2 D., 331
Knox, S/Ldr Brian W. 'Red', 11, 12, *13*, 14, 21, 23, 24-25, *24*, 28-29, 30, 35, *37*, 43, *56*, 57, 60, 66, 70, 94
Knudsen, Gefr D., 241
Knüpfer, Oberlt R. (2.(H)/10), 476
Knüppel, Hptmn Herwig (Stab II./JG26), 294, 327
Knust, Obergefr A. (9./KG1), 495
Knuth, Obergefr K., 242

Kny, Uffz R., 254
Kobelt, Uffz G., 366
Kobert, Oberfw (V.(Z)/LG1), 356
Kobylinski, Hptmn H-D. von (4./LG1), 383
Koch, Gefr K. (3./JG20), 326
Koch, Obergefr J. (7./KG4), 376
Koch, Oberlt H-G. (ZG26), 290
Koch, Uffz F. (KG54), 253
Koch, Uffz H. (6./KG76), 308
Koch, Uffz N. (2./KG76), 317
Koch, Uffz R., 498
Koch, Uffz W. (LG1), 214
Köcher, Oberlt A. (2.(H)/31), 341
Kögl, Hptmn P. (Stab IV.(St)/LG1), 470
Kögl, Oberlt W. (2./JG53), 279
Kogut, S/Lt S. (DIAP), 424
Kohaut, Uffz H., 206
Kohl, Lt (Stab II./JG27), 250
Kohl, Oberlt H. (5./KG51), 429
Kohlbach, Oberst W., 212
Kohlbruck, Oberlt, 316
Kohler, Gefr H. (3./KG76), 279
Kohler, Lt A. (2.(F)/123), 104
Köhler, Lt H. (6./KG55), 263
Köhler, Oberfw Horst (4.(H)/22), 434
Köhler, Uffz K. (7./KG3), 208
Köhlisch, Oberlt A., 154
Kohnke, Oberlt F., 149
Kolbe, Flgr W., 308
Kolbow, Lt H. (3./JG20), 249, 398, 402
'Koll, Kilian' (Hptmn W. Bloem), 210
Koll, Lt P., 206
Köllner, Uffz W. (2./KG3), 381
Kolodzig, Obergefr A. (4./KG77), 453
Komanns, Uffz A., 318
Kommoss, Lt K. (7./KG3), 381
König, Fw Johann (1.(F)/22), 408
König, Gefr E. (2./ZG26), 280
König, Gefr F. (2./ZG26), 317
König, Obergefr T. (8./KG30), 316
König, Uffz R. (AufklGr.Ob.d.L), 427
Konopka, Lt (7./ZG26), 340, 497
Konrad, Uffz C. (2./KG54), 383
Konradt, Oberlt K-W. (Aufklst Fl.K. I), 467
Koolhoven, Frits, 84
Kopania, Uffz O., 280
Köpfli, Lt (Swiss Fl.Kp.21), 448
Kopitz, Fw H-A., 162
Köpke, Uffz E., 99
Köpp, Oberfw G., 253
Köppel, Fw G. (3./KG51), 414
Köppel, Fw J. (6./KG55), 317
Kops, Obergefr W., 253
Körber, Cpl K. (GC II/3), 146, 341, 374, 447
Korek, S/Lt O. (GC I/3), 425
Korfhage, Gefr L., 262
Körig, Lt, 251
Kornagel, Oberlt H., 228
Kornatz, Fw H. (2./JG53), 99, 380, 381
Kornblum, Lt W. (3./KG3), 381
Körner, Oberfw M., 225
Körnig, Oberfw F. (9./LG1), 376
Körnig, Uffz A. (8./KG51), 360
Kornprobst, Fw G., 225
Kortas, Uffz W., 253
Kortenhaus, Uffz H. (TrGr.186), 479
Kortmann, Uffz E., 210
Koschinski, Gefr E. (3./KG51), 336
Koschorreck, Uffz K., 162
Koslik, Lt H-W. (1./StG2), 448
Koslowski, Uffz, 112
Kosnar, Cpl J. (GC III/7), 426
Kosse, Lt, 303
Kostrzewski, Uffz G. (Stab KG27), 402
Kothera, Cpl (GC I/5), 476
Kothmann, Fw (2./JG27), 320, 391, 464
Kotrade, Uffz F., 253

Kotulla, Oberfw E., 208
Kowalski, Fw B. (I./KG30), 347
Kowalski, Lt Julian (GC I/145), 452
Kowalski, Sgt Henryk (DAT Châteaudun), 419
Kowatsch, Uffz Hans J., 265
Krafft, Oberlt H. (3./JG51), 233, 340, 360
Krafftschick, Lt (1./JG27), 433, 451
Kräft, Fw H. (Stab I./ZG1), 376
Kraft, Uffz P. (3./KG53), 476
Krahe, Uffz H. (2.(H)/10), 470
Krahn, Uffz H. (9./KG4), 327
Krakora, Cpl J., 163
Kral, Lt J. (GC I/1), 447
Kralemann, Uffz F., 289
Kralik, Cpl A. (GC I/8), 235, 290, 315, 380
Kramer, Oberfw E. (6./KG51), 212
Kramer, Obergefr E. (9./KG1), 495
Kramer, Obergefr K-H. (1.(H)/11), 326
Kramer, P/O M. (600 Sqn), 184
Kramer, Uffz H. (4.(F)/121), 456
Kramer, Uffz K. (4./KG53), 240
Kramp, Uffz O., 154
Krampitz, Fw H., 223
Krams, Uffz H., 206
Kranich, Fw K-H. (4./JG27), 453
Kranich, Uffz Kurt (5./KG4), 262
Kranz, Lt (4.(H)/31), 307
Kranz, Lt P. (JG52), 162
Kranz, Maj. Dr (9./LG1), 489
Kranz, Uffz J. (3./JG54), 386
Krasnodebski, Maj. Zdzislaw, 413
Kratkoruki, Sgt (GC III/3), 336
Kratzmann, Uffz G., 162
Kraus, Fw J. (3./JG27), 352, 413
Kraus, Uffz L. (7./KG3), 381
Krause, Hptmn Herbert (KGrzbV.12), 224
Krause, Lt O. (4./ZG76), 254
Krause, Oberfw S. (3.(J)/LG2), 442
Krause, Obergefr Heinz (7./KG27), 382
Krause, Obergefr J. (3./KG1), 381
Krause, Uffz E. (KrzbV.9), 225
Krause, Uffz W. (4./KG27), 467
Krause, Uffz W. (4./KG54), 342
Krauss, Obergefr H. (3./KG30), 481
Krauss, Uffz R. (5./KG51), 470
Kraut, Oberstlt, 272
Krawczynski, Sgt (DAT Romorantin), 419
Kredel, Uffz H. (Stab KG27), 402
Kreib, Uffz E., 213
Kremer, Lt K., 136
Kremski, Sgt (DAT Bourges), 360
Krenz, Uffz Herbert (6./JG27), 192
Krenzke, Fw Erich (5./JG27), 453
Kreutz, Uffz H., 206
Krewald, Oberfw S. (1./KG1), 393
Krichbaum, Uffz W. (Stab I./KG51), 429
Kriegel, Uffz W., 208
Kriegenhofer, Uffz G., 164
Krieger, Fw, 315
Krieger, Lt P., 208
Kriegeskotte, Oberlt F., 213
Kroesch, Lt H. (Stab KG51), 418
Krohn, Uffz F. (3./StG76), 470
Krol, S/Lt (GC II/7), 360, 408, 414
Kroll, Fw H. (4./KG51), 429
Kroll, Fw K. (3.(F)/22), 262
Kröll, Uffz F. (6./KG1), 278
Kröll, Uffz J. (6./KG1), 353
Krone, Fw R., 318
Kronier, Gefr H., 107
Kroonsberg, Sgt G., 191
Kröschel, Fw J., 277
Krug, Fw H. (8./KG76), 462
Krug, Gefr W. (LG2), 290
Krüger, Fw J. (3./JG53), 288
Krüger, Fw W. (Stab II./LG1), 279
Krüger, Gefr C-H. (9./LG1), 376
Krüger, Oberfw (4./KG2), 239
Krüger, Oberfw W. (1./LG1), 214
Krüger, Uffz E. (9./LG1), 279

Krüger, Uffz H. (3./KG54), 158
Krüger, Uffz W. (1./KG2), 239
Krulich, Uffz R., 239
Kruml, S/Lt (GC 5/3), 358
Krumm, Fw E. (9./KG53), 410
Krümmel, Uffz K. (Stab KG55), 376
Krupczinski, Lt B., 278
Krups, Lt H. (6./KG76), 353
Krups, Oberfw W., 241
Krutein, Oberlt L. (JG2), 326
Kübik, Uffz H-W., 251
Kubis, Fw G. (9./KG53), 410
Kübler, Obergefr K. (7./KG76), 300
Kübler, Uffz Karl (2./ZG52), 383
Kucera, Sgt G. (GC I/6), 459
Küchler, Gen. Georg von, 216
Küchler, Uffz H. (4./KG1), 419
Kucz, Fw H., 208
Kuehn, S/Lt, 260
Kuenen, Kapt. Dr Ph. H., 191
Kuge, Uffz J., 154
Kugler, Flgr K. (3./KG1), 448
Kühhorn, Stabsfw G., 171
Kuhl, Fw F., 100
Kuhlke, Lt W. (9./ZG26), 470
Kuhlmann, Oberfw (3./JG53), 96, 100, 284
Kuhlmann, Prüfer F. (Stab II./LG1), 496
Kuhlmann, Uffz E. (4./JG53), 388
Kühn, Flgr B. (3./KG2), 133
Kuhn, Fw (8./JG3), 321
Kulin, Fw J. (KG54), 212
Kühn, Fw O. (4./JG3), 381
Kuhn, Sgt Johannes A. (3-V-2), 194
Kuhn, Uffz H. (3./KG1), 470
Kühne, Oberfw W., 241
Kühnel, Uffz K. (3./KG1), 353
Kühnle, Uffz C., 315
Kuhrke, Lt (8./ZG26), 268, 340
Kuiper, Sold. H., 191
Kuipers, 1e Lt J. P., 192, 209
Kuke, Uffz R. (9./LG1), 376
Külbel, Hptmn, 225
Kulhanek, Capt. J. (GC I/6), 360, 425
Kulik, Uffz F., 242
Küll, Fw, 306
Kulling, Adjt, 168
Külpmann, Bordmechanic Uffz Günther, 228
Kümmel, Fw W., 308
Künast, Uffz L. (5./KG27), 382
Kunath, Uffz W., 209
Kunert, Lt (8./JG53), 380, 405, 413
Kunkel, Oberlt F., 278
Kunowski, Maj. G-W. von, 208
Kunsch, Fw R., 239
Kunz, Uffz G. (6./LG1), 383
Kunze, Gefr G. (KG4), 308
Kunze, Oberfw W. (5./KG2), 336
Kunze, Uffz G. (1./LG1), 241
Kunze, Uffz H. (3.(F)/122), 239
Kunze, Uffz H. (9./StG2), 309
Kunze Uffz W. (1.(F)/122), 124
Künzel, 1e Lt W. J. E., 191
Kupka, Oberlt (9./JG3), 267, 431
Kupke, Fw G., 228
Küpper, Uffz (2./JG3), 390
Küppers, Hptmn R., 265
Küppers, Uffz J. (8./StG51), 388
Kurtze, Uffz W. (2./StG2), 393
Kusenberger, Oberfw K. (2./KG76), 442
Küster, Uffz E. (II./KGzbV.1), 228
Küster, Lt K-H., 288
Kutsch, Uffz A. (6./KG55), 317
Kutsch, Uffz H. (1.(H)/21), 476
Kutsche, Uffz Theodor (KG54), 329
Kutter, Oberlt Hans, 32, 114
Küttner, Fw F., 277
Kutz, Lt K., 136
Kzrykowski, Uffz Wilhelm, 221

Laag, Uffz H., 240
Labandowsky, Fw R., 213
Labas, S/Lt (GAO 1/589), 456

Labeau, Cpl, 142
Laberty, Sgt L. (GB I/11), 432
Labiche, Adjt P. (GB I/11), 432
Labit, Capt., 262, 317
Labouchere-Sparling, P/O F. A. G. F. J. de (75 Sqn), 339
Labourdette, Adjt A., 260
Labusga, Oberfw (6./JG3), 378, 416
Lacaille, Sgt, 94
Lacat, Capt. (GBA II/54), 475
Lacey, Sgt J. H. (501 Sqn), 450
Lachaux, Capt. A. (GB 4/23), 466
Lachaux, Sgt (later Adjt) (GC II/5), 100, 448, 470
Lachemair, Maj. O. von, 263
Lacheny, PM (1S1), 359
Lachmann, Uffz R., 240
Lachowicki-Czechowicz, S/Lt L. (GC I/145), 452
Lachs, Oberfw K., 107
Lackel, Gefr R. (3.(F)/22), 315, 388
Lackinger, Gefr G. (Stab II./KG51), 366
Lackner, Oberst Walter (KG54), 266, 328
Lacombe, Capt. Georges (GC 5/7), 270, 341
Lacombe, Lt (GC I/3), 118, 285, 427
Lacourie, Sgt (GB II/19), 346
Lacroix, Cpl (GBA II/51), 334
Lacroix, Sgt F. (GC I/4), 208, 235
Ladage, Uffz Friedrich, 222
Ladstätter, Uffz J. (4./KG76), 366
Laemmel, Lt, 106
Lafargue, S/Lt M. (GB I/21), 358
Lafon, SM (AB 1), 333
Lagabre, Lt de, 305
Lagarde, Adjt R., 98
Lage, Gefr zur (JG51), 496
Lagrange, Sgt J. (GC 6/1), 210, 499
Laguet, Adjt A. (GC II/6), 441, 451
Laguna, Capt. (GC 1/145), 456
Lahaye, Sgt, 94
Lahm, Flgr S., 253
Lainey, Capt., 249
Lajczyk, Fw K., 145
Lajule, Sgt Pierre (GB II/19), 400
Lallou, Lt (GAO 1/589), 465
Laloncette, Sgt, 274
Lalonde, Mary (Michael Smith's widow), 524
Laluée, S/Lt, 103
Lamaison, Lt (GC I/8), 213, 290, 452
Lamarche, Maj. Jacques, 198
Lamazou, Sgt P., 121
Lambermont, Adjt D. H., 149
Lambert, Adjt R. (GB II/12), 273, 296, 305
Lambert, Lt (GAO 2/508), 98
Lamble, LAC P. J., 191
Lamblin, Lt (GB 2/34), 105
Lamblin, Sgt (GC II/7), 117, 126, 410, 456, 475, 476
Lami, Sgt R., 297
Lamiot, LV (T 2), 352
Lamm, Oberlt F. (3.(H)/13), 427
Lämmel, Lt A. (Stab II./KG2), 360
Lämmel, Uffz G., 154
Lamour, Sgt, 314
Lampskemper, Fw B. (2./JG3), 345, 392, 437
Lamy, S/Lt (GR I/35), 249
Lamy, Sgt (GBA II/51), 396, 440, 461
Lancaster, Sgt A. O. (235 Sqn), 390
Lancrenon, Lt C., 117, 123
Landeroin, Capt. A. (GC 3/10), 334
Landgraf, Uffz E. (4./KG53), 240
Landgraf, Uffz E. (4./ZG26), 318
Landman, 2e Lt H. J., 191
Landmann, Uffz W., 132
Landmann, Gefr K., 289
Landrock, Uffz W., 132
Landry, Lt (2./JG3), 424, 469, 472
Landsberg, Uffz H., 211
Lane, F/Lt B. J. E. (19 Sqn), 373

Laneuze, S/Lt P., 161
Lang, Cpl G. E. (107 Sqn), 379
Lang, F/O E. J. M. (2 Sqn), 362
Lang, Flgr K. (7./KG51), 328
Lang, LAC (21 Sqn), 356
Lang, Lt F. (1./StG2), 448
Lang, Oberfw H. (2.(F)/123), 441
Lang, Sgt S. (142 Sqn), 322
Lang, Uffz H. (4./KG76), 366
Lang, Uffz K. (3./KG51), 328
Lang Oberlt Walter (Stab I./KGrzbV.12), 222
Lange, Fw F. (7./KG27), 210
Lange, Lt H. (1./JG21), 106
Lange, Oberfw W. (4./KG3), 208
Lange, Uffz H. (2./StG2), 242
Lange-Gläscher, Fw E. (2.(F)/122), 408
Langebear, F/O, 114
Langen, Gefr E., 206
Langenberg, Fw (5./ZG76), 351
Langenhoff, Off-Zeewrn. H. F. G., 159
Langer, Fw H., 132
Langert, Lt F., 115
Langford, Sgt A. E. (107 Sqn), 450
Langham-Hobart, P/O N. C. (73 Sqn), 70, 321, 423
Langley, P/O, 293
Langlois, Adjt (GAO 1/551), 395
Langlois, Lt (GB I/62), 374, 461
Langner, Gefr Günther, 265
Langton, AC1 L. M., 182
Lanowski, S/Lt W., 150
Lansonneur, SM A., 127
Lansoy, S/Lt A. (GC III/2 & GC 5/2), 278, 297, 305, 306, 340, 376, 451, 466
Lapadu-Hargues, Lt B., 98
Lapanne, Lt, 234
Lapeyre, S/Lt, 305
Lapwood, Cpl G. E., 151
Larczycki, Cpl Jozef, 424
Larisch, Fw J., 206
Larmier, Capt., 189
Laroche, Adjt (GB I/23), 364
Larpent, S/Lt S. (GR 2/35), 419
Lascelles, P/O F. A. G., 269
Laska, Oberfw H. (9./KG4), 360
Laslett, F/O D. F. (115 Sqn), 339
Lass, Lt H. (1./JG1), 351, 424, 434
Lassen, Uffz F., 211
Lastig, Oberlt K., 227
Laszkiewicz, Capt. Stefan (GC III/2), 83, 470
Läthe, Uffz G., 316
Latta, P/O J. B. (242 Sqn), 392
Lattke, Oberlt, 149
Latzel, Obergefr A. (4./KG3), 381
Lau, Fw A., 308
Lau, Oberlt L., 242
Laub, Uffz W., 224
Laube, Fw Herbert (1./KGr.126), 353
Laube, Oberfw H. (4./KG3), 208
Laubier, Cmdt J. de, 259, 274
Lauckemann, Uffz G., 239
Laudemann, Uffz H. (Stab I./ZG52), 383
Laudenbach, Lt K., 117
Laufer, Fw P., 263
Laurent, Capt. P. (GR I/36), 117
Laurent, Lt (GC I/2), 453
Laurent, S/Lt (GAO 1/520), 105
Laurent, Sgt (GAO 1/514), 455
Laurent, Sgt (GC III/6), 102
Laurer, Oberfw W., 317
Laurie, LAC Leonard, 517
Lauterbach, Fw E., 277
Laux, Capt. F., 159
Laux, Uffz K. (1./StG2), 366
Lavallé, QM, 94
Lavallée, Lt H. (1./KG27), 428
Lavenne, S/Lt (GB I/23), 364
Lavergne, Asp. de, 141
Lavolley, Adjt M., 259, 314
Lawes, LAC W. F., 293
Lawrence, S/Ldr H. Y., 313
Lawrence, Sgt R. W. (107 Sqn), 461

Lawrenson, Sgt J. H. (99 Sqn), 339
Laws, P/O F. S. (142 Sqn), 182
Laws, Sgt A. F. (64 Sqn), 406
Layec, Lt (GR I/52), 151, 475
Layfield, AC A. R., 153, 268
Layher, Fw H., 239
Le Bail, Adjt J-B., 113, 275
Le Bideau, Capt. A. (GC III/3), 492
Le Bihan, SM (1S2), 456
Le Bihan, SM (AC 3), 472, 477
Le Bot, SM, 314
Le Bras, Sgt (GR I/14), 462
Le Breuilly, P/O A. E., 214, 272
Le Calvez, S/Lt Y. (GC I/5), 407, 410, 442, 456
Le Cossec, Sgt Y., 275
Le Cozannet, Adjt, 305, 307
Le Droucpeet, SM (AB 3), 465
Le Friec, 94
Le Gall, Sgt (GB 2/63), 358
Le Gentil, Lt A. (GC I/1), 308, 340, 416
Le Gloan, Adjt Pierre (GC III/6), 120, 145, 240, 278, 467, 477
Le Goasguen, Lt R., 314
Le Goff, Sgt (GBA II/51), 424
Le Goff, Sgt Georges (GB I/19), 440
Le Goyat, Cpl Y. (GB II/12), 273, 296, 305
Le Guellec, Sgt, 305
Le Guevel, SM, 305
Le Louarn, SM (T 3), 459
Le Marchand-de-Trigon, S/Lt Y. (GB II/63), 440
Le Maresquier, QM E., 234
Le Martelot, Adjt J., 156
Le Mezo, Sgt (GB II/31), 400
Le Nigen, Sgt E. (GC III/3), 145, 262, 336, 337, 425, 429
Le Pezron, SM (T 2), 352
Le Plan, Sgt, 95
Le Saoult, Adjt H., 102, 126
Le Stum, S/Lt G. (GC II/5), 425
Le Thomas, SM, 314
Le Voi, Sgt E. E. B., 231
Learmond, P/O P. A. G. (92 Sqn), 349
Leary, P/O D. C. (17 Sqn), 450, 462
Leathart, F/Lt J. A. 'Prof' (54 Sqn), 343, 349
Leather, F/Lt W. J. (611 Sqn), 412
Lebeaupin, Sgt, 273
Lebel, Lt H., 284
Lebert, Sgt (GBA II/54), 440
Leblanc, Adjt M-E. (GC III/3), 260, 290, 315, 325, 327
Leblanc, Lt (GC III/2), 336, 452
Lebourg, Lt (GBA I/51), 440
Lebrun, S/Lt R., 123
Lechat, Lt A. (GC III/2), 107, 334, 336
Lechevrel, S/Lt M., 107, 286
Lecky, P/O John, 205, 210, 303
Leclerc, Adjt (GB II/38), 296
Leclerc, Mtre (AC 2), 494
Leclerc, Sgt (GAO 3/551), 95
Leclercq, Adjt L. (GC II/6), 235
Leclercq, Jocelyn, 261
Leclère, Cmdt J. (GAO 512), 373
Lecoanet, SM (AB 1), 333
Lecorre, Sgt (GAO 546), 451
Lederer, Oberlt Werner (6./JG52), 113, 419, 456
Ledson, Sgt J. H. (142 Sqn), 437, 458
Lee, F/Lt A. W. (139 Sqn), 246
Lee, F/Lt R. H. A. 'Dickie' (85 Sqn/56 Sqn), 101, 117, 181, 206, 232, 290, 299, 349, 379
Lee, P/O K. N. T. (501 Sqn), 247, 253, 434
Lee, S/Ldr H. (103 Sqn), 390, 450
Lee-Steere, F/O C. A. (601 Sqn), 379
Leegstra, 1e Lt T. H., 250
Leenhardt, Lt, 301
Lees, S/Ldr (72 Sqn), 414
Lees, Sgt D. J. (82 Sqn), 304

Leeson, F/Lt P. G. (605 Sqn), 351
Leeson, P/O A. (500 Sqn), 390
Lefage, S/Lt André (GB I/11), 465
Lefebvre, Lt J. (7/III/3), 251
Lefèvre, Sgt (GC II/7), 235
Lefèvre, Sgt Germain (GB I/34), 494
Lefèvre, Sgt (GR II/55), 452
Lefol, S/Lt (GC I/5 & II/5), 112, 156, 208, 239, 353, 441, 479
Lefoyer, Capt. (GC I/6), 458
Lefroid, Sgt J. (GBA I/51), 424
Legard, F/O W. E. (41 Sqn), 406
Léger, Cpl (GB II/34), 400
Legrand, Adjt (GAO 501), 364
Legrand, Kpl G. H. (5/III/3), 238
Legrand, Lt (GC III/6), 240
Legrand, S/Lt Pierre (GBA II/54), 400, 440
Legrand, Sgt A. (GC II/5), 95, 112, 113, 133, 335
Legrand, Sgt (GB 2/34), 273
Legrand, Sgt H. (GB I/12), 334
Legros, Adjt (GB II/12), 296
Legros, Sgt (5/III/2), 199
Lehmann, Lt P. (Stab KG1), 162
Lehmann, Oberfw F. (Stab III./KG55), 213
Lehmann, Uffz (2./JG51), 339
Lehmann, Uffz E. (Stab LG1), 214
Lehmann, Uffz G. (1.(H)/13), 456
Lehnert, Uffz Rolf, 224
Lehr, Uffz H., 213
Leicht, Uffz Ludwig (3./JG3), 326
Leickhardt, Lt H., 241
Leidenbach, Uffz L., 242
Leie, Lt E., 277
Leisse, Uffz Paul (4./JG26), 427
Leissl, Uffz K., 279
Leitch, F/Sgt A. (150 Sqn), 464
Leitgebel, Uffz Rudolf, 278
Leither, Lt K. (1./KG4), 409
Leitner, Gefr E. (5./KG2), 476
Leleu, LV G. (GAO 1/506), 94
Leleu, Lt (GBA I/54), 248
Lelièvre, Sgt, 145
Lelong, Sgt A. (GBA II/54), 451
Lemaire, S/Lt (GB I/12), 296
Lemaire, Sgt L. (GAO 2/520), 127
Lemare, Sgt (GC I/4), 336, 434
Lemke, Lt H. (5.(F)/122), 365
Lemke, Uffz Richard, 222
Lemm, Gefr E. (KG54), 329
Lemoine, Adjt G. (GR II/22), 134, 286
Lemoine, Lt Auguste, 100
Lemoine, Mt (T 2), 492
Lenclud, Lt, 234
Leniaud, Adjt Marcel, 262, 274
Lenk, Lt, 299
Lenk, Uffz Fritz (9./KG53), 410
Lenke, Gefr F. (1./KG30), 347
Lenkeit, Fw H., 240
Lenne, Lt H., 307
Lenoir, Lt A. (GR II/33), 359
Lenton, Sgt S. W., 148
Lenz, Fw P., 308
Lenz, Gefr H., 208
Lenz, Uffz B. (5.(F)/122), 365
Lenzer, Oberlt H. (4.(F)/11), 456
Léon, Aspirant, 106
Leonard, AC1 D. L. (107 Sqn), 412
Léonard, Capt. A., 96
Léonardo, Lt, 93
Leonhard, Lt (3./JG53), 373
Leonhardt, Gefr J. (7./KG55), 442
Leonhardt Gefr W. (KGzbV.1), 229
Leonhardt, Lt W. (KG76), 329
Leonhardt, Uffz E. (KG27), 210
Leopold, King, 298, 374, 377, 384, 387, 397, 400
Lepage, Adjt (ECN 3/13), 96, 352
Lepage, Sgt (GC II/9), 417
Lepeltier, LV, 93
Lepezel, Sgt (DAT Tours), 492
Lepine, F/O W. N., 312
Lepp, Uffz A. (4./KG76), 453
Leppage, Adjt G. (GIA I/601), 462
Leppin, Uffz G. (9./KG53), 410

Leppla, Oberlt Richard (3./JG51), 192, 340, 499
Lepreux, Sgt J., 100
Leprovost, Sgt (GC I/1), 495
Lequeu, Lt, 98
Leroy, Adjt L., 259, 273
Leroy, S/Lt, 95
Leschi, Sgt (GC II/9), 375
Lescuyer, Lt (GAO 2/508), 424
Lespagnol, Sgt (SAL 2/104), 352
Lessans, Lt R. de (GR I/55), 481
Lesueur, Capt., 259
Lessing, Fw H-J. (5.(H)/13), 499
Lessing, Lt, 373
Lessmöllmann, Obergefr K. (4.(F)/122), 335
Lestang, P/O R. M. C. de, 102
Lestapis, Sgt J. de (GC I/6), 417
Levack, LAC, 270
Levasseur, Adjt, 249
Levasseur, S/Lt C., 273
Léveillé, LV G. (AB 1), 333
Lévis-Mirepoix, LV (F1C), 373
Levy, S/Lt C. (GR I/33), 481
Lewandofski, Uffz F. (9./KG4), 209
Lewandowski, Uffz G. (9./KG4), 327
Lewczynski, Sgt R. (DAT Châteauroux), 424
Lewioda, Obergefr G. (8./KG27), 239
Lewioda, Uffz G. (3./KG1), 448
Lewis, AC (226 Sqn), 272
Lewis, AC1 H. G. (226 Sqn), 398
Lewis, F/O R. (1 Sqn), 244
Lewis, LAC G. F. (103 Sqn), 268, 362, 445
Lewis, P/O (40 Sqn), 469
Lewis, P/O (85 Sqn), 326
Lewis, Sgt (4 Sqn), 267
Lewis, Sgt Cecil T. (88 Sqn), 437
Lewis, Sgt G. (21 Sqn), 458
Ley, Mt., 259
Leyden, F/O J. N. (103 Sqn), 371
Leyerer, Oberfw (2./JG77), 322, 325
Leygnac, Sgt L., 259
Leynaud, Sgt Georges (GAO 518), 475
Leythäuser, Hptmn K., 316
L'Herbier-Montagnon, Mme, 440, 444
L'Heritier, Sgt (GAO 1/589), 465
L'Hôpital-Navarre, Sgt, 154
Lhoste, Sgt (GAO 3/551), 424
Liautard, Sgt A. J. M. (GC I/8), 213, 290, 307, 366, 461
Libert, Sgt P., 196
Lichman, Sgt J. A. (213 Sqn), 386
Licht, Fw P. (1./KG76), 476
Lichtenberger, Uffz W. (AufklGr.Ob.d.L), 427
Licitri, Sgt C. (GAO 512), 373
Liddiard, Sgt (59 Sqn), 321
Liddle, Sgt D. (40 Sqn), 431
Lieb, Lt, 284
Liebe, Uffz H., 315
Lieber, Oberfw W., 225
Liebers, Uffz H., 298
Liebert, Adjt (GAO 507), 333
Liebold, Fw O., 278
Liebscher, Uffz H. (3./KGrzbV.9), 225
Liebscher, Uffz W. (2./KG3), 366
Liedke, Lt, 95
Lieflander, Fw L., 251
Liempd, Sgt A. J. M. van, 193, 250
Liensberger, Oberlt, 100
Lierde, Sgt Remi 'Mony' Van, 298
Liesendahl, Oberlt F. (Stab II./JG2), 375
Liesenfeld, Fw K-A., 289
Liesenhoff, Oberlt P. (1.(H)/41), 396
Lietzau, Uffz O. (4.(F)/11), 456
Lieutenant, Sgt E., 145, 146

Light, P/O C. (18 Sqn), 339
Lightfoot, AC1 L. H., 272
Lignac, Sgt Henri Hyvert de (GB II/19), 358
Lignitz, Oberlt (3./JG20), 159, 398
Lijff, Sgt C. H. F., 157
Limburg, Uffz H., 253
Limpert, Gefr (1./JG20), 470
Linart, Sgt J. (GC III/2), 306, 358
Linck, Fw R. (Stab I./KG27), 342
Lindbergh, Charles, 201
Lindecker, Hptmn (Swiss Fl.Komp.15), 409, 414
Lindemann, Flgr K. (Stab KG27), 488
Lindemann, Fw F., 154
Lindemann, Lt (1.(H)/14), 353
Lindenberg, Uffz R. (1./KG54), 360
Linder, Uffz A. (Stab KG77), 495
Lindi, Capt. P. Henry de la (11/VI/1), 325, 374
Lindloff, Oberlt R., 225
Lindner, Gefr H. (8./KG55), 414
Lindner, Sgt H. P., 261
Lindner, Uffz A. (2./JG51), 360
Lindsay, AC1 G., 158
Lines, F/O A. P., 303
Lines-Roberts, F/O R. B., 180, 256
Lings, F/O G. O. (110 Sqn), 345
Link, Oberfw A. (KG53), 328
Linke, Oberfw E. (Stab III./KG3), 208
Links, Uffz A. (5./ZG76), 393
Linley, F/O T. N. (54 Sqn), 356
Linney, P/O A. S. (229 Sqn), 392
Linschoten, 1e Lt H. van, 276
Linsmayer, Uffz H., 133
Linzel, Sgt J., 194
Lion, Adjt (GC III/7), 107, 452
Lippens, Lt P., 251
Lippert, Oberlt (3./JG53), 100, 157, 189, 285, 416, 451
Lippert, Uffz M. (9./KG55), 402
Lippett, Cpl A. (264 Sqn), 382, 399
Lippitsch, Gefr J. (8./KG30), 376
Lisse, Oberfw E., 210
List, Oberfw E. (1./KG27), 428
Lister-Robinson, F/Lt M., 153, 168
Litjens, Fw (4./JG53), 446
Litzenberg, Fw K. (Stab KG3), 366
Little, Cpl H. F. (226 Sqn), 272
Little, F/O T. D. (611 Sqn), 412
Little, Sgt J. McG. (85 Sqn), 321, 329
Littlewood, AC1 H. G. (16 Sqn), 371
Littolff, Adjt Albert, 117, 249, 270
Livingston, Sgt A. (226 Sqn), 272, 339
Llewellyn, W/Cdr J. G. (40 Sqn), 349
Lloyd, P/O J. R. (615 Sqn), 497
Lloyd, Sgt (49 Sqn), 445
Lloyd, Sgt (103 Sqn), 144
Lock, Obergefr R. (2./KG3), 381
Lockett, S/Ldr C. E. S., 272
Lockhead, P/O (49 Sqn), 445
Loeben, Oberlt von, 135
Loesch, Hptmn Egbert von, 299, 300
Loest, Uffz H. (5./KG54), 342
Loets, Fw E. (4.(H)/21), 479
Löffler, Gefr S., 213
Lofts, P/O (615 Sqn), 497
Logan, Sgt A. G. (57 Sqn), 362
Logeart-Hans, Jean, 255
Lohfink, Lt G. (5./StG2), 489
Lohmann, Oberfw H. (5./KG27), 402
Lohoff, Lt H. (JG77), 156, 339
Lohr, Uffz A. (1./KG55), 410
Löhr Uffz E. (1./KGrzvV.172), 227
Lohrer, Fw (KG2), 239
Lohrer, Fw W. (JG76), 278
Loï, Sgt (GC II/3), 162, 365, 374, 375
Loiseleux, Adjt (GB II/31), 400

Lok, Sgt P. J., 132, 250
Löken, Fw O., 278
Lombard, Sgt L., 234, 284
Long, LAC H. (142 Sqn), 322
Long, Sgt B. C. (12 Sqn), 267, 320
Longhorn, AC1, 270
Lonthie, Lt R., 261, 315
Looijen, Sgt F. C. H., 192
Looker, P/O D. J., 283, 288
Lorde, Adjt J. Barrau de (GB II/38), 395
Lorenz, Fw E. (KGzbV.1), 223
Lorenz, Hptmn H. (Aufklst Fl.K. I), 467
Lorenz, Oberfw (5./JG26), 441
Lorimer, F/Lt R. L. (85 Sqn), 128
Lorimer, F/O R. L. 'Laurie' (1 Sqn), 180, 255, 256, 265, 267
Lory, Lt, 103
Lösch, Gefr W., 228
Loscher, Obergefr Albert, 158, 161
Lösecke, Uffz F., 210
Losensky, Uffz W., 280
Losigkeit, Oberlt (2./JG26), 386, 406
Losse, Lt G., 315
Lotz, Uffz A. (5./ZG1), 459
Louchard, Capt. M., 275
Louis, Lt (GAO 507), 333
Louis, S/Lt C. (GC II/7), 426
Louis, Uffz P. (2./KG54), 383
Lousori, Sgt (GB II/62), 461
Loussalez, Adjt, 117
Louveau, Sgt J. (GC I/8), 290, 426
Love, Sgt J. C. (254 Sqn), 405
Lovejoy, LAC C. R. A. (99 Sqn), 339
Lovell, P/O M., 293
Loverseed, Sgt J. E. (501 Sqn), 398
Lovett, F/O (later F/Lt) R. E. 'Reg', 12, 15, 24, 25, 28, 41, 44, 46, 47, 48, 49, 52-53, 56, 57, 58, 63, 66, 67, 68, 126, 152, 153, 154, 162, 181, 207, 208
Löw, Uffz K., 104
Lowe, Sgt F. A. G. (115 Sqn), 339
Lowe, Sgt R. (110 Sqn), 273
Lowne, Sgt C. H., 181
Lowry, LAC T. J., 248
Loy, Uffz G., 107
Loyer, Adjt R. (GB 2/15), 395
Lub, Sgt D., 194
Lubbe, Uffz M., 229
Lübbing, Fw F. (2./KG2), 453
Lüben, Oberlt W. (2./LG1), 499
Lucas, LAC C. F. (13 Sqn), 282
Lucas, P/O Kenneth R. (145 Sqn), 323
Lucas, QM (AB 3), 465
Lucas, Sgt (77 Sqn), 431, 455
Lucas, Sgt P. (GAO 510), 380
Lucas, Sgt R. (GR II/55), 407
Luck, Sgt J. A. A., 233
Lücke, Fw M., 227
Lückel, Uffz K-S., 279
Lüdecke, Gefr F., 279
Lüder, Lt (5./KG27), 402
Lüderitz, S/Lt W. (Stab KG51), 418
Lüders, Fw (6./JG26), 379
Lüders, Oberfw Georg (Stab II./KG53), 212
Lüders, Oberlt F. (1./ZG2), 337
Lüders, Uffz Gustav (9./KG53), 240
Ludewig, Lt W., 205
Ludlam, AC1 L. W. (115 Sqn), 339
Ludwig, Fw H. (4./KG51), 429
Ludwig, Lt W. (3.(F)/10), 335
Ludwig, Uffz K., 388
Luerruan, Capt., 296
Luis, Obergefr E., 212
Lukaszewicz, S/Lt M. (GC 1/145), 456
Lumsden, AC2 A., 104
Luter, Sgt V. G. L., 248
Luther, Uffz E. (Aufkl.Gr.Ob.d.L.), 335
Lütje, Fw W., 278
Lütjens, Fw, 157
Lütjens, Oberlt zur See W., 115

Lutter, Fw (6./ZG1), 379
Lütters, Oberlt H., 290
Lüttmann, Uffz L. W. (3.(F)/11), 380
Lutz, Fw W., 300
Lützow, Hptmn (Stab I./JG3), 275, 285, 323, 401, 431, 445
Lux, Adjt J., 259
Lux, Lt zur See D., 241
Luxmoore, W/Cdr A. N., 233
Luyk, Sgt R. M. van, 276
Lyke, Uffz K., 316
Lyne, P/O M. D. (19 Sqn), 373
Lys, River, 355
Lyschick, Uffz R., 240

Maar, Oberfw E., 211
Maas, Uffz F., 262
Maass, Obergefr M. (5./KG27), 402
McAndrew, AC, 311
McCarthy, AC2 W. J., 295
McCarthy, LAC R. W., DFM, 182
McCassey, P/O, 148
McComb, S/Ldr J. E. (611 Sqn), 412
McConnell, F/O R. J., 304
McCoy, LAC A. O'N. (2 Sqn), 398
McCudden, Sgt J. A. (103 Sqn), 394
McDonagh, Sgt Thomas W. (59 Sqn), 385
MacDonald, F/Lt D. (21 Sqn), 458
MacDonald, LAC D. A. (12 Sqn), 464
MacDonald, P/O (4 Sqn), 168
MacDonald, S/Ldr W. M. L., 99
McDonnell, LAC P. J., 248
Mace, F/Lt C. R., 154
McElligott, P/O J. J. (12 Sqn), 267, 320
McEwan, S/Ldr Kenneth, 53, 56, 60, 61
McFadden, LAC W. A., 246
McFadden, P/O A., 70, 232, 268
McFarlane, LAC Victor Thomas, 472
MacFie, P/O C. H. (611 Sqn), 386, 414
McGaw, P/O (73 Sqn), 487
McGlashan, P/O K. B. (245 Sqn), 399
McGrath, AC1 J., 331
McGregor, S/Ldr H. D. (213 Sqn), 398
MacGuiness, Adjt J. (GB I/12), 334
Mache, Uffz G., 300
Machmer, Hauptgefr H., 136
Machowiak, Sgt M. (DAT Châteaudun), 469
McIntosh, P/O I. A., 244
McIntyre, Sgt S., 112
McKenna, W/Cdr J. F. X., 97
Mackenstein, Uffz K., 239
McKenzie, P/O R. C. D. (82 Sqn), 445
MacKenzie, Sgt G. (253 Sqn), 322
McKinlay, Sgt F. W., 273
McKnight, P/O W. L. (242/615 Sqn), 272, 323, 386, 470
MacKrell, Sgt J. F. W. (12 Sqn), 436
Mackworth, P/O C. C. D., 110, 268
MacLagan, Sgt D. R. C. (21 Sqn), 445
McLaren, F/Lt I. L. (78 Sqn), 356
McLean, Sgt J. (37 Sqn), 405
McLeish, LAC Douglas L., 257, 258
MacLeod, P/O Alex M. (264 Sqn), 257, 258, 386
McLeod, Sgt D., 293
McLoughlin, Sgt G. P. (226 Sqn), 458
McLoughlin, Sgt T. (26 Sqn), 378
McLundie, P/O (500 Sqn), 362
McMahon, Sgt (9 Sqn), 349
McMullen, P/O D. A. P. (54 Sqn), 385

MacNaughton, LAC R. P., 244
McNay, Sgt Alex L. (73 Sqn), 472, 473-474
Macombe, S/Lt, 306
MacPhail, Sgt I. (235 Sqn), 390
McPherson, F/O Andrew, DFC (139 Sqn), 246, 516
Macpherson, P/O (54 Sqn), 388
MacPherson, P/O R. I. C. (53 Sqn), 282, 293
McPhie, P/O J. F. (12 Sqn), 423, 464
MacQueen, P/O Donald Garfield (242 Sqn), 304, 450
MacQueen, Sgt R. R. (79 Sqn), 441
McRae, Sgt (53 Sqn), 378, 469
Maddalena, S/Lt U., 210
Maddocks, Nick, 524
Maddox, LAC S. A., 270
Maden, Oberfw W. (4./JG52), 451, 453
Mader, Fw G. (3./KG2), 470
Maderson, Sgt A. A., 180
Madge, F/Lt A. J., 232
Madkins, LAC (later Cpl) (103 Sqn), 144, 268, 394
Madler, Gefr A. (6./JG51), 479
Madon, S/Lt M. (GC I/3), 285, 434, 470, 476, 479
Madore, P/O G. A. (242 Sqn), 351
Maes, Sgt J., 213
Maffat, Adjt R. (GB I/12), 334
Maffat, Sgt (GIA I/601), 462
Magath, Lt L., 154
Magerkurth, Uffz K. (1./KG26), 481
Magnan, Adjt (GB I/31), 99
Magnan, Adjt (GB II/31), 400, 432
Magnez, Sgt, 100
Magnin, Adjt (GR II/33), 456
Magnussen, Oberlt H-W., 211
Maguire, Sgt (53 Sqn), 311
Maguire, Sgt (226 Sqn), 272
Mahaut, Adjt (GB II/12), 456
Mahnert, Uffz H. (1./StG76), 456
Mahnert, Uffz H. (8./KG55), 414
Mahoney, LAC J. (107 Sqn), 379
Maiborn, Gefr Heinrich, 214
Maier, Fw G. (KG51), 328
Maier, Obergefr A. (3./KG54), 158
Maier, Uffz J., 253
Maigret, Sgt C. (GC III/6), 158, 364, 365
Mairesse-Lebrun, Sgt J. (GC II/9), 417
Maiwald, Hptmn L. (4./KG54), 414
Maiwald, Uffz H. (4.(F)/121), 408
Makera, Uffz S., 242
Malan, F/Lt 'Sailor' (74 Sqn), 343, 347, 349
Malaval, Capt. A. (GC I/5), 341
Malchair, Lt G., 196
Malefijt, 2e Lt A. de Waal, 138
Malfroy, F/O C. E., 240, 247
Malischewski, Lt, 133, 268
Malkin, AC A. H., 311
Malle, Sgt (GB II/19), 346
Mallet, Lt A. (GB I/62), 374
Mallmann, Lt G. de (GC III/1), 214, 336, 374
Maloney, Sgt T. J. W. (15 Sqn), 458
Malouet, Cpl (GBA II/51), 470
Maltby, AC1 Eric W., 232
Maltzahn, Hptmn G. von (Stab II./JG53), 100, 154, 288, 336, 342
Malvezzi, Sottotenente, 477
Mamsch, Uffz E., 278
Man, Sgt J. C. de, 193, 209
Manegold, Gefr W., 290
Manger, P/O K. (17 Sqn), 309, 366, 375, 402, 406
Manger, Uffz W. (7./KG55), 429
Mangiarotti, Cpl R. (Gruppo 43), 467
Mangin, S/Lt, 211, 240
Manhart, Lt W., 318
Mann, Lt (1./JG1), 236, 324
Mann, Lt W. (5./KG30), 479
Mann, S/Lt A., 296

Männer, Gefr F., 263
Männer, Uffz M. (KG53), 328
Mannske, Uffz A., 316
Mansell, Sgt G. D., 244
Manske, Fw F. (KG54), 329
Manteuffel, Oberstlt Eitel Roediger von, 121
Manthei, Gefr G., 211
Mantle, AC1 F. J., 150
Manwaring, F/Lt G. A. P. (235 Sqn), 390
Mapletoft, Sgt M. V. (504 Sqn), 322
Maquet, Capt. A., 286
Marc, Sgt (GB II/62), 425
Marchais, Adjt (GC II/8), 313, 341, 408
Marchand, Capt. (GB 3/23), 432
Marchand, Lt P. (GB 1/21), 358
Marchand, P/O Roy 'Dim', 48-49, 59, 71, 256, 259
Marchand, Sgt (GB I/62), 374
Marche, Lt P. (GC III/1 & 5/1), 298, 324
Marchelek, Flgr F., 206
Marchelidon, S/Lt (GC I/2), 328, 499
Marchfelder, Lt (Stab II./ZG1), 257, 379
Marcinek, Gefr H. (1./KG1), 393
Marcks, Uffz (1./JG21), 334
Marconnet, Adjt René (GC II/2), 427, 447
Marcusse, S/Lt R., 249
Marczinke, Uffz E. (1./KG1), 393
Maréchal, Capt. B. (GC 2/1), 416
Mariani, Adjt M. (GB 3/23), 432
Marias, Adjt M. (GC III/3), 99, 100, 153, 260, 336
Marie, Adjt P. (GR II/22), 113, 134
Marie, Capt. (GB 2/34), 273
Marie, Lt (GB I/21), 364
Mariema, Mot (SESBA), 488
Marin-la-Meslée, Lt (GC I/5), 262, 314, 317, 328, 359, 441, 442, 456
Marion, Sgt (GB 1/31), 451
Markert, Oberfw R. (KGzbV.1), 241
Markl, Fw J. (8./KG55), 459
Marland, Sgt Fred, 244, 516
Marmein, Uffz M., 263
Marmier, Cmdt Alexandre Lionel de, 83
Marmion, Sgt, 273
Marotzki, Uffz H. (KG53), 328
Marquard, Lt E. (3./JG76), 496
Marquardt, Fw B. (1./KG55), 410
Marquardt, Oberlt E. (AufklGr.Ob.d.L.), 156
Marrast, Capt. M., 273
Marraud, LV (T 3), 352
Marriott, F/O (88 Sqn), 390
Marrows, Sgt E. (226 Sqn), 458
Marsal, Sgt, 259
Marsault, Adjt, 296
Marschall, Uffz W. (KG54), 329
Marschik, Lt O. (2.(F)/122), 496
Marschner, Uffz H., 206
Marsden, Eric, 310, 311
Marseille, S/Lt J. (GAO 1/514), 346
Marsh, AC1 John L. (150 Sqn), 95, 506
Marsh, Sgt A. (83 Sqn), 349
Marsh, Sub Lt J. B. (801 FAA Sqn), 398
Marshall, P/O D. G. (139 Sqn), 168
Marshall, P/O J. E. (85 Sqn), 127
Marshall, Sgt (73 Sqn), 328
Marsland, P/O G. (245 Sqn), 395
Martellières, Cpl P., 94
Marten, Oberlt K-H. (5./KG2), 476
Martin, AC1 Syd (150 Sqn), 271
Martin, AC2 (77 Sqn), 431, 455
Martin, Adjt (ECN 4/13), 305, 340
Martin, Cpl (GAO 547), 273
Martin, F/Lt A. D. J. (142 Sqn), 464
Martin, Fw R. (LG1), 214
Martin, LAC W. S. (18 Sqn), 121, 128

Martin, Lt E. (2.(H)/14), 441
Martin, Lt P. (GC III/10), 275
Martin, Lt R. (GAO 510), 296, 446
Martin, Lt R. (GC III/6), 120, 145, 235, 241, 467
Martin, LV (AB 1), 333
Martin, Oberlt K. (Stab I./ZG1), 376
Martin, Oberlt R. (KG3), 253
Martin, P/O R. F. 'Dickie' (73 Sqn), 13, 14, *24*, 32, 33, 34, *35*, 40, *42*, 43-44, *46*, *48*, 60, 68, *69*, 70, 71, 114, 256, 262, 280
Martin, S/Lt (GC III/7), 235, 341, 417
Martin, Sgt (110 Sqn), 345
Martin, Sgt (142 Sqn), 271, 437
Martin, Sgt E. D. (150 Sqn), 183
Martin, Sgt G. G. (226 Sqn), 256
Martin, Sgt G. (GC III/10), 275
Martin, Sgt (GB 4/63), 401
Martin, Sgt (GB I/63), 451
Martin, Sgt (GC II/7), 477
Martin, Sgt (GR II/14), 499
Martin, Sgt (GR II/52), 235
Martin, Sub Lt R. M. S. (801 FAA Sqn), 398
Martin, Uffz Hugo (KGrzbV.12), 222
Märtin, Uffz R. (4./KG55), 493
Martinant-Surin, Sgt (GAO 513), 387
Martinköwitz, Oberlt H., 115
Martre, Capt. (GR I/52), 475
Marty, Lt A. (GR II/55), 496
Marty, Sgt (GB I/12), 259
Marwitz, Oberlt D. (8./KG4), 402
Marwood, Sgt G. W., 104
Marx, Fw H. (1.(F)/121), 341
Marx, Gefr H-P. (9./KG1), 342
Marx, Uffz F. (7./KG1), 206
Mary, Adjt R., 259
Mas, Sgt (GB I/11), 432
Mas, Uffz E. de (KG51), 328
Masching, Fw H., 298
Masclaud, S/Lt A. (GB II/12), 273, 296, 305
Maske, Uffz A. (6./ZG1), 242, 379, 434
Maskolus, Gefr H., 253
Massaux, Sgt, 248
Masse, Cpl A. (GBA I/51), 451
Masset, Sgt A., 259, 296
Massey, P/O D. P. (53 Sqn), 180
Massey-Sharpe, P/O G. (222 Sqn), 406
Masson, Sgt J. (GB II/62), 461
Massoni, Capt. (GAO 1/551), 324
Massow, Oberst Gerd von (Stab Luftflotte 3), 418
Masters, P/O J. G. (15 Sqn), 349
Mathelin, Sgt R. (GR I/35), 441
Matheus, Uffz A., 145
Mathieu, Sgt Albert (9./V/1), *286*
Mathieu, Sgt (GC III/7), 127, 447
Mathis, Uffz F., 318
Mathon, LV, 95
Mathonière, Adjt (GB I/12), 400
Matignon, Adjt, 99
Matras, Lt P., 274
Matt, Oberfw H., 278
Matteo, Adjt V. Di, 248
Mattes, Fw H. (1.(H)/31), 452
Matthes, Gefr F., 308
Matthes, Hptmn G. (Stab II./JG51), 252
Matthes, Lt (1.(H)/14), 288
Matthes, Oberlt Ernst. (7./ZG26), 282, 429
Matthews, F/O P. G. H. (1 Sqn), 124, 455
Matthews, P/O A. W. (12 Sqn), 180
Mattner, Uffz W. (3./KG30), 347
Matuchet, Sgt J. (GBA II/54), 425
Matuschek, Hptmn W. (6./KG76), 347
Matussek, Uffz H., 300
Matz, Fw P., 317
Matzel, Uffz Walter, 224
Matzke, Uffz W., 289

Maurel, Lt F. (GBA II/51), 451
Maurel, Sgt (GC I/8), 366, 417, 429
Maurer, Flgr Wilhelm, 342
Maurer, Lt W. (ZG2), 242
Mauret, Adjt (GB II/23), 447
Maurin, Lt P., 274
Maury, Capt. P. (GB 2/11), 400
Maury, S/Lt F. (GB I/63), 358
Mauter, Fw L. (KG53), 328
Mauvier, Capt. F., 315, 316
Mawhood, P/O D. V. G., 141, 181
Max, F/O Roy D. (103 Sqn), 385, *394*
Maxrath, Uffz E., 277
Maxwell, P/O (151 Sqn), 446
Maxwell, P/O M. H. C. (56 Sqn), 379
May, Fw H. (1.(H)/22), 388
May, Gefr A., 117
Mayadoux, S/Lt (GBA II/54), 451
Maycock, P/O A. G. (No. 4 (Cont.) Ferry Flt), 487
Mayençon, Adjt A. (GR I/36), 433
Mayer, Adjt Richard (GB II/19), 358
Mayer, Fw A. (3./KGrzbV.9), 226
Mayer, Fw H. (3./KG53), 476
Mayer, Hptmn (2./JG51), 313
Mayer, Lt (GB II/12), 432
Mayer, Oberlt Hans-Karl (1./JG53), 111, 162, 267, 270, 271, 364
Mayer, Uffz E. (I./ZG2), 162
Mayer, Uffz R. (Stab KG53), 240
Mayerl, Uffz (2./JG20), 445
Mayerrhoeffer, S/Lt G. (GB II/21), 364
Mayne, F/Sgt (74 Sqn), 371
Mayor, AC2 J. R., 248
Mayr, Flgr F-K., 278
Mazerolles, S/Lt A. (GB I/11), 400
Mazeron, Sgt (GAO 1/514), 455
Mazon, S/Lt (GB II/19), 346
Mearns, LAC D. B. (53 Sqn), 282, 378
Measures, F/O (74 Sqn), 353, 381
Mebus, Gefr W., 316
Meckel, Lt (2./JG3), 437
Meckelburg, Obergefr A. (8./KG51), 360
Medcalf, F/O A. R. J. (610 Sqn), 379
Medway, Sgt W. T. (610 Sqn), 379
Meek, P/O, 160
Meel, 2e Lt J. van, 250
Meel, Marinus van, 84
Meermann, Uffz G., 326
Mehl, Uffz R. (4./StG2), 366
Mehliss, Oberfw W. (6./LG1), 337
Mehnert, Oberstlt K., 240
Mehnert, Uffz R., 151
Meier, Fw R. (5./KG77), 290
Meier, Gefr K. (6./LG1), 393
Meier, Uffz K. (3./KG27), 429
Meiländer, Gefr H., 279
Meimberg, Lt J. (4./JG2), 239, 322
Meinhardt, Oberfw A. (8./KG77), 388
Meining, Fw B., 279
Meinshausen, Fw F-K. (9./LG1), 343
Meisel, Fw A., 241
Meiser, Fw H-J., 343
Meissner, Gefr H., 160
Meissner, Uffz W., 223
Meister, Flgr H., 290
Meister, Fw H. (I./LG1), 223
Meitret, Lt, 148
Melcher, Obergefr A. (3./KG3), 336
Melchior, S/Lt, 141
Melhorn, Lt G. (KG54), 329
Meliguet, Sgt (GB 1/31), 296, 451
Mellership, Sgt K., 248
Melot, Sgt J. (GR I/52), 93, 102, 126
Melot, Sgt M. (GIA I/601), 417
Melzer, Flgr H., 149
Menant, S/Lt, 298
Ménard, Camille, *490*

Ménard, Lt (GAO 1/551), 352
Ménardière, S/Lt de la (GC II/8), 358
Mende, Oberfw F., 116
Mendels, S/Lt (GB II/21), 456
Menet, Sgt (GAO 510), 446
Menge, Lt F-J., 315
Menges, Uffz L. (7./KG76), 434
Mentque, Cmdt G. Clicquot de, 189
Mentz, P/O B. van, 257, 277, 290, 299, 315
Mentzel, Lt F., 290
Mentzel, Uffz W., 280
Menzel, Oberfw W., 253
Menzel, Uffz K-H., 240
Merceur, Lt A. (GR 1/22), 496
Mercier, Sgt, 274
Mercoeur, Adjt, 297
Mercy, Adjt, 100
Meredith, F/O R. V. (17 Sqn), 233, 239, 309, 362, 366, 381, 416
Mergenthaler, Obergefr W. (1./KG3), 366
Meric, Lt (GR I/14), 466
Merkel, Obergefr L., 210
Merkelbach, Sgt C. J., 116
Merkler, Flgr N., 213
Merkwitz, Oberlt H., 214
Merle, Uffz P., 343
Mermet, Capt. F. (GAO 581), 465
Mérode, Lt de, 206
Merrettig, Fw W. (3.(F)/11), 365
Merritt, Sgt Albert E. (82 Sqn), 437, 465
Merritt, Sgt L. R. (107 Sqn), 248
Mersch, Lt G. (9/V/1), 359
Mersmann, Oberlt, 225
Mertens, Lt, 321
Mertgen, Uffz K. (Aufkl.Gr.Ob.d.L.), 335
Mertins, Uffz A., 224
Mertz, Hptmn P., 290
Mertz, Uffz F., 241
Merzenich, Uffz W., 262
Meslée, Lt Marin La, 133
Mesny, LV (AB 1), 419
Mesples, Sgt (GB II/31), 466
Messerschmitt, Willy, 86
Methfessel, Oberlt W., 119, 309
Methner, Uffz H. (1./KG53), 336
Metifeu, Sgt (GBA I/51), 451
Metraux, Sgt Louis (GB I/62), 374
Mette, Oberfw H. (Stab I./ZG26), 414
Metz, Flgr R., 208
Metz, Oberlt Hans, *242*
Metzger, Uffz H. (AufklSt.z.b.V), 365
Metzner, Lt Kurt (2.(H)/31), 315, 341
Meuli, Lt R. (Swiss Fl.Kp.10), 448
Meulkens, 2e Lt W. H., 193
Meunier, Sgt, 213
Meuser, Oberlt G. (2.(H)/10), 452
Meyer, Fw (6./JG26), 390
Meyer, Fw E. (KG55), 213
Meyer, Fw F. (3.(F)/122), 123
Meyer, Fw H. (2.(F)/22), 298
Meyer, Fw J. (9./KG28), 327
Meyer, Fw W. (1.(H)/41), 251
Meyer, Lt E. (1.(H)/14), 359
Meyer, Lt F. (3.(F)/122), 239
Meyer, Lt H. (KGrzbV.12), 224
Meyer, Lt H. (StG2), 242
Meyer, Lt R. (3.(F)/11), 326
Meyer, Oberlt (3.(H)/14), 434
Meyer, Oberlt (8./ZG26), 249, 379
Meyer, Oberlt K. (I./LG1), 111
Meyer, Oberlt (Stab KG54), 462
Meyer, Uffz H. (3./ZG1), 429
Meyer, Uffz H. (5./KG27), 382, 402
Meyer, Uffz J. (1./LG1), 214
Meyer, Uffz L. (8./KG51), 360
Meylandt et Montjardin, S/Lt P. de Theux de, 286
Meyr, Lt P. (9./StG2), 347
Meyrick, AC1 D., 183
Meyzonade, Adjt (GB 2/11), 400
Meyzonnier, Lt P. (GC 2/4), 425
Mias, Uffz F. (5./JG3), 481, 493
Michalski, Lt, 154

Michaud, Adjt, 290
Michel, Fw K. (2./KG55), 376
Michel, Gefr J. (3./KG1), 470
Michel, Hptmn W. (4./KG54), 342
Michel, Sgt P. (GB I/11), 400
Michel, Uffz R. (4./KG54), 329
Michelet, Adjt A. (GB II/12), 259, 334
Michelis, Sottotenente de, 462
Michelmore, Sgt I. R. W. (2 Sqn), 405
Michels, Uffz N., 228
Michi, Uffz E. (1./ZG1), 376
Michl, Uffz S., 309
Michon, S/Lt (GAO 1/589), 461
Michotte, 1/Sgt M., 198
Middlemass, Sgt N. C., 247
Midonnet, Sgt R. (GB I/11), 432
Miedl, Flgr J. (1./KG1), 393
Mielke, Hptmn B. (3.(J)/LG2), 324, 442
Mietusch, Lt Klaus (7./JG26), 381, 448
Mietzner, Uffz K., 315
Migeot, Lt H., 254
Migge, Uffz K., 239
Mikeska, Gefr E. (1./KG1), 392
Miklitz, Uffz O., 210
Mikulasek, S/Lt A. (GC II/3), 364
Mikusky, Fw G., 154
Milan, Sgt, 273
Milbeau, S/Lt (GC I/4), 213, 366
Milbradt, Fw G., 265
Milch, Gen. Erhard, 86, *366*
Milhahn, Uffz A., 262
Milhiet, S/Lt R. (GC II/2), 285, 425, 427
Millar, AC2 M. B., 272
Millard, LAC A. E., 284
Millard, S/Lt, 260
Mille, Sgt (GB II/15), 324
Miller, F/Lt D. R. (242 Sqn), 322
Miller, Gefr H. (7./KG2), 164
Miller, Gefr L. (1./KG2), 289
Miller, P/O J. A. (107 Sqn), 345
Miller, Sgt (110 Sqn), 345
Miller, Sgt F. S. (82 Sqn), 304
Miller, Sgt Frank (18 Sqn), 231, 349
Miller, Sgt R. F. (142 Sqn), 182
Millet, Adjt G. (GB I/33), 306
Millet, Lt (GB II/31), 400, 432
Millet, Sgt (GR II/52), 235
Millner, Sgt Wilfred (73 Sqn), 371, 405
Millot, Lt (ECMJ 1/16), 259
Millot, Sgt (ECN 2/13), 305
Milne, F/O C. (212 Sqn), 150, 162
Milne, F/O R. M. (151 Sqn), 309, 312, 347
Milner, F/O J. C. (32 Sqn), 321
Minaro, Sgt (GAO 1/584), 446
Minnigerode, Oberlt A. Fr von, 239
Minondo, Adjt P. (GB I/34), 340
Minterne, Don, *416*
Mioche, Lt Col R., 119
Mir, Adjt Henri, 313
Miramond, SM (AC 3), 475, 477
Mirfin, Sgt J. R. (78 Sqn), 356
Mirsche, Fw W., 215
Missfeldt, Lt J. (9./JG2), 342
Mitard, Sgt (GBA I/51), 440
Mitchell, F/O (87 Sqn), 207, 208, 242
Mitchell, LAC (Sgt) George A. (500 Sqn), 465
Mitchell, P/O J. S. (1 Sqn), 144, 145
Mitchell, P/O J. W. (242 Sqn), 357
Mitchell, Reginald, 78
Mitifeux, Sgt (GBA I/51), 447
Mitschke, Uffz H. (7./KG76), 434
Mitsdörffer, Fw (1./JG27), 464
Mittelback, Gefr K. (Stab III./KG27), 347
Mittelhäuser, Hauptgefr W., 209
Mittelstädt, Uffz G. (9./KG55), 402
Mittermaier, Gefr J., 263
Mitton, Adjt (GBA II/54), 364, 433

569

Mitzkath, Flgr F., 207
Mix, Hptmn (later Oberst) Dr Erich (JG53/JG2), *96*, 117, 158, 340, *342*
Moberley, F/O G. E. (616 Sqn), 386, 408
Möckel, Oberlt H. (2./KG77), 376
Modrach, Lt (I./KG51), 462
Modrzik, Gefr W., 300
Moegelin, Lt H. Dr (AufklSt.z.b.V), 365
Moeller, Lt D., 242
Moens, Sgt A., 238
Moerkoert, Sgt B. C., 250
Moers, Uffz Hans (TrGr.186), 365
Moffat, P/O R. (15 Sqn), 445
Moffatt, Sgt (605 Sqn), 345
Moffatt, Sgt R. C. (40 Sqn), 431
Mogenet, S/Lt C., 251
Moguez, Cmdt Henry, *324*
Möhn, Uffz J., 290
Mohr, Uffz J. (7./KG1), 441
Moisselin, Sgt R., 123
Moity, Sgt J., 296
Mold, AC2 E., 256
Molderhauer, Gefr H., 208
Mölders, Hptmn Werner, 93, 95, 104, 107, 127, 144, 146, 153, 156, 161, 163, 268, 283, 325, 341, 346, 364, 380, 400, 417, 424, *427*, *428*, *489*, *506*
Mölders, Oberlt Viktor, 191
Molek, Uffz A., 120
Molcnaar, Oberlt A. (1./KG76), 476
Molinier, Capt. Corniglion (GC III/2), 462
Molinier, Cpl (GAO 510), 296
Moll, Oberlt E. (4./KG76), 410
Moll, S/Lt (GAO 1/506), 94
Mölle, Oberfw R., 209
Molle, Sgt (GAO 543), 446
Möllenbeck, Uffz A., 208
Moller, AC2 F. G., 104
Moller, Lt von (1./JG2), 405
Möller, Obergefr P. (13.(Z)/LG1), 132
Möller, Oberlt J. (2./ZG1), 406, 410
Möller, Uffz F. (2./JG77), 205
Möller, Uffz H. (1.(H)/12), 298
Molliet-Billiet, Lt M. (GB I/34), 494
Molls, Fw Ferdinand, 222
Mommertz, Uffz K., 241
Monchanin, Adjt, 306
Moncheaux, Capt. J. (GB 2/31), 334
Monel, Lt, 284
Monette, P/O J. A. E., 141
Mongey, Sgt T. J., 231, 293
Monigard, Capt. (GR I/35), 447
Monks, Noel (*Daily Mail*), *439*
Monneret, Sgt (GR I/33), 481
Monnet, SM, 93
Monneyron, SM, 148
Monraisse, Capt. (GC II/5), 341, 476, 479
Monribot, Sgt (GC III/2), 139, 235, 336
Montagnon, Capt., 248
Montagu, P/O C. J. D. (77 Sqn), 431, 455
Montal, Capt. J. de, 284
Montantème, Lt (GR I/35), 447
Montaudie, Cmdt, 95
Montchamin, Sgt (GC I/1), 495
Montel, Cpl, 296
Montfoort, 1e Lt H. C. A., 157
Montfort, Sgt A. (GC II/1), 188, 335
Montgolfier, Adjt P. de, 112, 120, 145, 205, 285
Monthois, Sgt G. (GB I/63), 358
Montjardin *see* Meylandt et Montjardin, S/Lt P. de Theux de
Montmorency, F/O Raymond H. de, 270, *509*, *527*
Montravel, Lt de (GC I/4), 427
Montrozier, Adjt F. (GB 4/19), 446

Monty, Lt André (GC I/2), 240, 447, 448
Mony, Adjt (GB I/63), 425
Moore, F/O C. R., 184
Moore, F/O W. S. (236 Sqn), 494
Moore, LAC D. C., 256
Moore, Naval Airman V. S. A. (825 FAA Sqn), 385, 390
Moores, F/Sgt L. G. (115 Sqn), 339
Moorhouse, LAC, 284
Moors, Uffz J. (4./KG54), 342
Moorwood, P/O Iain C. (111 Sqn), 321, *517*
Moosbauer, Gefr Hans (KG27), 327
Moosbrugger, Uffz H., 253
Moquelet, Adjt J., 234
Morant, P/O R. A. L. (222 Sqn), 406
Moravek, Sgt E. (GC I/5), 475
Moraweck, Gefr Joseph, 221
Moreau, Capt. (GR II/33), 249
Moreau, S/Lt P. (GR I/14), 249
Moreau, Sgt (GB II/34), 188
Moreau, Sgt (GR 3/33), 108
Moreau, Sgt J. (GC I/2), 234
Moreaux, S/Lt (GR I/14), 470
Morel, S/Lt R. (GB II/12), 234
Morel, Sgt F. (GC I/5), 162, 188, 215, 240, 249, 252, 314, 317
Morel, Sgt (GC I/1), 340
Moreland, SGT A. T., 282, 293
Moret, Adjt A. (GC III/2), 107, 206, 297, 358
Morfill, Sgt, 242, 253, 289
Morgan, F/O R. A. G., 104
Morgan, Sgt A. C. (105 Sqn), 269
Morgan, Sgt C. A. (59 Sqn), 282
Morgan-Dean, F/O G. B., 245
Morgenstern, Lt, 157
Möricke, Gefr R. (5./KG51), 470
Morier, Sgt (GR II/55), 447
Morin, Lt J. (GC III/3), 429, 433
Morizot, Adjt (DAT Tours), 469
Morlat, Cmdt (GC II/3), 347, 448
Morlet-Coppey family, *48*, *51*
Morlot, Sgt R., 154, 251, 260, 285
Morneweg, Obergefr H. (KG76), 329
Moroge, Adjt G. (GBA I/54), 466
Moron, Lt (GB I/62), 401
Moroy, Adjt (GB 4/23), 456
Morris, AC H. (142 Sqn), 182
Morris, LAC R. (82 Sqn), 304
Morris, P/O D. W. W. (115 Sqn), 339
Morris, Sgt A. R. (12 Sqn), 464
Morrison, Sgt T., 304
Morton, AC1 E. (99 Sqn), 339
Morton, P/O A. D., 112
Morton, P/O Edgar E., *245*, *247*
Morton, Sgt (59 Sqn), 445
Morton, Sgt J. S. (40 Sqn), 362
Mosbach, Oberlt H., 212
Moseler, Uffz H., 225
Moseley, Sgt D. V., 313
Moseley, Sgt Victor H., 272
Moser, Fw F. (5./KG77), 290
Moser, Sgt F. (GB II/31), 392
Moser, Uffz E. (7./KG2), 252
Mosesby, F/Lt W. G., 93
Mössner, Fw E. (4./KG76), 410
Mot, 1/Sgt G. (7/III/3), 251
Mot, Sgt (GR II/33), 478
Motte, Sgt J-M., 275
Mottez, Lt, 325
Mougel, Adjt P., 94, 161
Mougeot, Sgt, 139
Mougne, Sgt A., 273
Mould, P/O P. W. O. 'Boy' (1 Sqn), 107, *108*, 180, 208, 242, *256*
Mould, Sgt E. A. (74 Sqn), 347, 356
Moule, AC1 H. P., 293
Moulènes, Sgt A., 240, 249, 252, 286
Moulinier, Sgt A. (GB I/21), 364

Moulinier, SM (AB 2), 340
Moulinot, Roger, 429
Mourier, S/Lt Yves, 270
Mousset, S/Lt (GC II/8), 380
Mouthaan, 1e Lt A. C. O., 276
Mouzon, Sgt L., 111
Moxica, Sgt A. (GR 1/33), 456
Mozer, Uffz A., 210
Mub, Uffz W., 315
Mücke, Uffz R., 366
Mückisch, Uffz F., 154
Muegge, Uffz Ludwig (7./KG1), *495*
Mühlbauer, Gefr F. (KG54), 329
Muhle, Obergefr H. (KG51), 328
Mühlemann, Lt (Swiss Fl.Kp.21), 448
Mühlen, Oberlt P. von zu, 209
Mühlen, Uffz H. von zur, 225
Mühlenbrink, Gefr G., 213
Muir, George (IWGC), *207*
Muirhead, P/O Ian J. (605 Sqn), 373
Mulder, Lt J. J., 191, 236
Mulford, Sgt, 270
Müllauer, Oberlt R., 279
Muller, Adjt E., 286
Müller, Flgr H. (7./KG30), 211
Müller, Flgr P. (4./LG1), 459
Müller, Flgr R. (6./KG3), 327
Müller, Fw (3./JG26), 445
Müller, Fw A-W. (4./JG3), 433, 434
Müller, Fw E. (3./KG76), 419
Müller, Fw H. (7./KG51), 328
Müller, Fw H. (Stab I./KG27), 210
Müller, Fw K. (KGzbV 1), 228
Müller, Fw K. (ZG2), 157
Müller, Fw O. (KG2), 239
Müller, Fw P. (KG55), 213
Müller, Fw R. (4./KG51), 409
Müller, Fw W. (KG4), 209
Müller, Fw W. (KG55), 213
Müller, Fw W. (Stab III./KG27), 347
Müller, Gefr A. (1./KG54), 290
Müller, Gefr H. (5./KG55), 429
Müller, Gefr H. (KG3), 208
Müller, Gefr O. (4./KG53), 409
Müller, Gefr P. (9./KG53), 240
Müller, Hptmn (4./JG3), 341, 423
Müller, Lt (6./JG2), 321
Müller, Lt J. (2./KG27), 278
Müller, Lt zur See H. (2./KGr.126), 467
Müller, Oberfw (1./JG53), 234, 371
Müller, Oberfw G. (Stab I./KG53), 240
Müller, Obergefr J. (1./KG54), 414
Müller, Obergefr P. (5./KG30), 211
Müller, Oberlt (13.(Z)/LG1), 235, 247, 379
Müller, Oberlt Dr A. (3.(F)/11), 251
Müller, Oberlt W. (Stab KG55), 470
Muller, Sgt A. (III-2), 193
Müller, Uffz A. (Stab LG1), 214
Müller, Uffz E. (3.(H)/41), 315
Müller, Uffz E. (7./StG2), 477
Müller, Uffz E. (AufklSt. 7 Fl.Div.), 206
Müller, Uffz G. (2./KG51), 453
Müller, Uffz H. (1./KG30), 211
Müller, Uffz H. (2./KGr.126), 265, 467
Müller, Uffz H. (9./KG76), 300
Müller, Uffz J. (2./KG4), 316
Müller, Uffz J. (2.(St)/TrGr.186), 410
Müller, Uffz L. (9./KG51), 212
Müller, Uffz R. (3./ZG1), 410
Müller, Uffz W. (4./KG27), 467
Müller-Dühe, Lt (7./JG26), 272, 386
Müller-Rabe, Uffz Lt H. (2./LG1), 499
Mullins, P/O E. R., 273
Mullot, Alfred, *336*
Mullot, Mme, *336*
Mumb, Uffz A., 224
Mumb, Lt J., 208
Mümler, Cmdt M. (GC I/7), 409, 475, 477
Müncheberg, Lt (Stab III./JG26), 112, 268, 283, 398, 399

Mund, Lt M. (4./JG52), 360
Mundell, Sgt (149 Sqn), 356
Müngersdorff, Lt F. (2./KG54), 360
Mungo-Park, F/O J. (74 Sqn), 356, 359
Mungovan, P/O A. W., 232
Munier, Sgt René, 284
Munk, Uffz R., 280
Munz, Fw K. (2./JG52 & Stab I./JG52), 127, 409
Murcar, AC1 A., 99
Murch, P/O L. C. (253 Sqn), 351
Murdoch, AC1 W. G., 312
Murdoch, F/O M. I., 282
Murphy, AC1 D. B. (235 Sqn), 390
Murphy, P/O A. H. (235 Sqn), 373
Murphy, Sgt M. (149 Sqn), 458
Murray, LAC K. E., 339
Murray, P/O D. C. F., 140, 246, 269
Murray, P/O H. M., 233
Murray, S/Ldr W. B., 171
Murray, Sgt A. G. (21 Sqn), 458
Murrin, Leading Naval Airman H. K. (825 FAA Sqn), 390
Murtin, Cmdt (GC I/5), 418
Murton-Neale, F/O Peter Norman, 257
Muschert Fw W., 226
Muschner, Uffz G., 242
Muselli, Sgt G. (GC I/5), 260, 279, 317, 441
Musiolik, Uffz E. (7./KG76), 418
Mussgnug, Uffz A. (KG54), 328
Mussolini, Benito, *454*
Muth, Asp. B. (DAT Clermont-Ferrand), 492
Mütherich, Lt H., 140, 274
Mutschter, Uffz, 254
Mutter, Uffz F. (4./StG77), 347
Myers, Cpl, 36
Myers, Sgt J. J. (10 Sqn), 458
Myland, P/O (15 Sqn), 458
Myrbeck, Capt. H. Petit de, 305
Mysliwietz, Gefr R. (1./KG1), 393

Nabinger, Fw P., 148
Nacke, Oberlt (II./ZG76), 259, 406, 497
Nagel, Uffz F., 147
Nahrgang, Uffz W., 240
Narat, Uffz Rudolf, 222
Nashan, Uffz P., 210
Nass, Sgt (GAO 502), 284, 478
Natta, Adjt M., 234
Natthes, Uffz H. (5.(H)/13), 341
Naudin, S/Lt, 235
Naudy, Capt. A. (GC II/3), 156, 341, 359, 388, 401
Naumann, Uffz R., 207
Navelet, Lt, 126
Navers, Sgt (GAO 502), 478
Navratil, S/Lt A. (GC I/8), 334
Neale, WO W. H. (73 Sqn), 96, 482
Nedelec, Adjt J. (GC III/2), 188, 206, 259, 358, 459
Neef, Uffz (1./JG27), 464
Neely, Lt Alexander D. (825 FAA Sqn), 385, 390
Nélias, SM (AB 1), 333
Nell, Oberlt G., 251
Nelleskamp, Uffz (5./JG3), 436, 465
Nelson, AC1 J., 105
Neubacher, Fw K., 213
Neuber, Obergefr G., 209
Neubert, Oberlt H., 308
Neubert, Uffz A. (1.(F)/121), 341
Neubitler, Oberstlt, 139
Neuburger, Gefr W., 290
Neuenfeld, Maj. Otto, 113
Neufang, Fw F. (3.(H)/13), 427
Neuffer, Oberfw E., 317
Neuhaus, Fw W., 206
Neuhoff, Uffz (7./JG53), 144, 417, 423, 451, 459
Neumann, Fw F. (2./KGrzbV.12), 224
Neumann, Gefr H. (ZG76), 318
Neumann, Lt C. F. von (Stab I./ZG52), 383
Neumann, Lt J. (6./JG27), 192, 342

Neumann, Lt K. (9./KG1), 207
Neumann, Uffz (2./ZG2), 157
Neumann, Uffz W. (7./KG1), 206
Neumayer, Uffz J., 290
Neumeister, Uffz F., 206
Neumeyer, Gefr J., 212
Neuschwander, Uffz W. (7./StG2), 477
Neuville, Capt. (GR 1/35), 352
Neuville, Sgt P. (GAO 3/551), 424
Neville, Sgt E. G. (40 Sqn), 431
Névraumont, Sgt (GBA I/51), 466
New, F/O W. G. (229 Sqn), 392
Newall, MRAF Sir Cyril, 47, 70, 101, 281, 292
Newbatt, Sgt R. E., 304
Newberry, AC (57 Sqn), 345
Newberry, F/O J. H., 270
Newberry, LAC R. J. (102 Sqn), 332
Newling, P/O M. A. (145 Sqn), 312, 402
Newton, F/O K. E. (151 Sqn), 391
N'Guyen, S/Lt (GB I/23), 488
Nicholls, F/Lt (73 Sqn), 418, 487
Nicholson, Naval Airman G. R. (801 FAA Sqn), 398
Nicholson, Sub Lt J. T. (825 FAA Sqn), 390
Nick, Obergefr P., 265
Nickel, Gefr H. (5./ZG1), 383
Nickel, Uffz W. (KG54), 329
Nicole, Adjt (GC II/8), 408
Nicoley, Uffz M., 318
Nicolle, Adjt (GC II/8), 452
Nicot, Capt. J. (GBA II/51), 340, 469
Niebelschütz, Oberlt H-W. von (4.(F)/121), 408
Niebuhr, Oberlt A. (5./ZG26), 318, 329
Niederer, Fw E., 229
Niederhofer, Fw, 229
Niedermeyer, Uffz F., 240
Niedzwetski, Uffz K. (6./ZG76), 354
Niel, SM (AB 2), 340
Niemann, Oberlt, 139
Niemeyer, Fw H., 207
Nies, Uffz S. (4./KG77), 453
Nietzschmann, Lt H. (3./StG76), 376
Nièvremont, Sgt (GBA I/51), 433
Nigen, Sgt E. Le see Le Nigen
Niggel, Oberlt H. (4.(H)/22), 365
Nijhuis, Sgt G., 150
Nijveldt, Sgt C. J., 194
Niklas, Oberlt H. (Stab I./KG53), 382
Nikolai, Uffz G. (4.(F)/121), 375
Nikuth, Uffz W. (6./KG76), 347
Nimmo, LAC D. McL. (26 Sqn), 378
Nind, F/O E. F. (57 Sqn), 362
Nineham, Sgt Leslie D. (82 Sqn), 465
Nisbett, Sgt (53 Sqn), 469
Nissen, Oberlt (Wettererkundungsst. 51), 462
Nissen, Uffz K. (16./KGzbV.1), 396
Nitsche, Uffz W., 158
Nitschke, Fw Alfred, 215
Nitschke, Lt O. (3.(F)/121), 341
Nitzsche, Obergefr E., 208
Nixon, Sgt F. (40 Sqn), 97
Nixon, Sgt F. (226 Sqn), 469
Nocher, Lt H., 162
Nodet, Lt J. (GAO 512), 373
Noël, S/Lt (GR 1/33), 95
Noël, Sgt (GR II/52), 249
Noeliecke, Lt, 146
Noetzelmann, Uffz O., 316
Noever, Lt H., 226
Nogai, Oberlt W. (4.(H)/31), 347
Noir, Lt (GAO 1/508), 168, 469
Noiret, Lt L. (GAO 510), 424
Nolan, AC1 W. J., 271
Nöller, Uffz H., 300
Nolte, Lt J. (2.(F)/122), 427

Nolte, Uffz W. (6./StG77), 467
Nomerange, Sgt, 105
Noomen, 1e Lt P., 192, 209
Norcott, Maj., 52
Nordmann, Oberlt (JG77), 323
Nordmeier, Uffz H., 309
Norman, F/O C. T., 104
Normand, Sgt, 248
Norrington, Sgt D. (103 Sqn), 450
Norris, Sgt (21 Sqn), 465
North, LAC J. (235 Sqn), 390
North, Lt M. R. (825 FAA Sqn), 356
North, Sgt G. (32 Sqn), 332
Norwell, Sgt (54 Sqn), 366
Nöss, Fw A. (4./KG53), 409
Nossin, Cpl G., 236
Notzke, Fw W. (6./LG1), 393
Nötzold, Uffz R., 208
Nourry, Adjt, 296
Nouvel, Sgt (GAO 516), 346
Novacek, Cpl (GC I/1), 451
Novak, Sgt J. (GC 5/3), 413
Nowak, Cpl L. (GC II/8), 387
Nowakiewicz, Cpl E. (GC II/7), 408, 413, 476
Nowell, Sgt Gareth L. (87 Sqn/32 Sqn), 124, 171, 181, 206, 294, 301, 349
Nugent, LAC Ron H., 182, 270, 271
Nuhn, Gefr W. (2./JG21), 113, 115
Nuhn, Uffz C. (1./KG27), 428
Nülle, Lt D. (Stab II./ZG1), 343
Nuttall, LAC R. R. H. (10 Sqn), 458
Nützel, Lt C., 316
Nyevelt, Sgt E. van Zuylen van, 196

Oakley, F/O A. E. (15 Sqn), 248
Oakley, P/O H. L. (142 Sqn), 271, 437
Oberheide, Oberfw H., 279
Obermann, Lt zur See H. (3./KüFlGr.806), 151
Obermeier, Oberfw H. (TrGr.186), 462
Obermeier, Oberlt zur See (S-34), 372, 388
Oberschelp, Uffz E., 301
Obert, Uffz H., 290
O'Brien, P/O D. G., 182
Obst, Uffz R., 254
Obuchowski, Lt J. (GC I/145), 452
O'Byrne, Capt. P., 188
Occis, Sgt G., 274
Ochmanek, Uffz F., 242
Ochs, Fw W. (KGrzbV.12), 224
Ochs, Uffz O. (Stab KG76), 434
Ochsenkühn, Fw (9./JG53), 400
Ocker, Lt W., 253
Octave, Adjt, 277, 289
Odell, Sgt R. N., 180
Odenbach, Fw W. O., 206
Odin, S/Lt (ECN 4/13), 380
O'Donnell, Sgt (15 Sqn), 445
Oechsle, Sgt G., 274
Oeckenpöhler, Fw J., 210
Oehler, Flgr H. (6./LG1), 393
Oeillard, Sgt, 296
Oekenpöhler, Fw J. (8./KG27), 347
Oel, Uffz H., 95
Oelhaven, Oberlt Alfred von (6./LG1), 393
Oelkers, Uffz H. (3.(F)/10), 375
Oellerking, Fw E., 226
Oellrich, Fw R. (1./StG2), 366
Oelmann, Lt H. (1./KG76), 336
Oertel, Oberfw J. (ZG52), 280
Oertel, Oberfw (JGr.152), 96
Oesau, Oberlt (1./JG20), 260, 465
Offenberg, S/Lt J., 213
Offinger, Uffz A. (3./KG53), 409
Ogait, Flgr H. (KG54), 329
Ogger, Lt L. A. F. (Nachtrichtungsst. Ln.Regt. 2), 337
Ogilvie, AC1 S. C. (99 Sqn), 339
Ogilvie, Lt, RN, 184
Oglodek, Fw J. (1./JG51), 97, 351

Ohlrogge, Uffz H., 239
Ohly, Oberlt H., 131, 270, 271
Ohms, Oberlt A. (3.(H)/12), 479
Ohmsen, Oberlt W., 110
Okuniewski, Gefr B. (9./KG54), 414
Olbert, Lt K., 279
Olbrich, Fw H., 208
Oldacres, F/O L. J. (4 Sqn), 320
Olezynska, Gefr, 228
Oliver, S/Ldr J. O. W. 'Doggy', 205, 210, 232, 239, 256, 303
Oliver, Sgt, 260
Oliveres, Adjt M. (GB I/31), 440
Ollerenshaw, P/O A. C., 282
Olschlegel, Uffz M. (16./KGzbV.1), 396
Ombler, Sgt E. (77 Sqn), 458
Ommerborn, Oberfw L., 160
Onken, Uffz W. (8./KG76), 343
Oorschot, 1e Lt A. van, 192, 209, 250
Oostindië, Sgt Maj. A. J. G., 191
Opderbeck, Oberlt K. (1.(F)/22), 408
Opie, W/Cdr, 152
Oppermann, Fw H., 207
Opulski, Capt. (DAT Romorantin), 429, 481
Orasch, Uffz P. (9./KG54), 479
Ordway, Sgt, 269
O'Reilly, LAC (48 Sqn), 395
O'Reilly, LAC J. P. (16 Sqn), 303, 517
O'Reilly-Blackwood, P/O J. N., 136
Orland, LAC E. R. (37 Sqn), 398
Orliac, Adjt, 234, 259
Orsat, Sgt (GAO 543), 395
Orschel, Uffz G., 227
Ortloff, Lt, 153
Ortmeier, Uffz F. (9./KG3), 381
Orton, F/O (later S/Ldr) Newell 'Fanny', DFC, 6-7, 10, 15, 24, 31, 37, 41, 44, 45, 46, 48, 49, 53, 56, 57, 58, 61, 63, 65, 66, 103, 120, 153, 162, 181, 184, 208, 232, 279, 281, 282, 290, 439
Osment, P/O D. E. T. (150 Sqn), 322
Osten, Lt E., 167
Oster, Gefr J., 208
Osterkamp, Oberst Theo, 250
Ostermann, Lt (1./JG21), 334
Oswald, Lt F., 171
Ott, Fähnrich, 263
Otte, Hptmn, 115
Otte, Oberlt Dr M., 158
Otterbeck, Uffz G. (KG2), 207
Otterbeck, Uffz Wilhelm (JG20), 307, 308
Ottersbach, Fw J. (4.(H)/21), 479
Ottes, Sgt C. R., 276
Ottewill, Sgt P. G. (43 Sqn), 437
Ottlick, Fw J., 208
Otto, Lt J., 148
Otto, Obergefr E., 126
Otto, Oberlt K., 241
Oultram, LAC I. B., 151
Outfin, F/Lt R. M. 'Doc', 15, 21, 24, 46, 48, 52, 56-57, 57, 64, 66, 67, 68, 70, 71, 73
Outhwaite, Sgt J. J. (21 Sqn), 272, 458
Over, LAC H. F., 246
Overvest, 2e Lt H. J. van, 116, 192, 205
Owe, Oberlt, 115
Owen, F/Lt J. S. (504 Sqn), 282, 300, 312
Owen, F/Lt W. H. (102 Sqn), 332
Oxe, Fw P., 289

Paap, Lt, 98
Paas, Lt H-W., 209
Paasch, Uffz W., 229
Pabius, Obergefr, 247
Pace, F/O T. G., 283
Pacholleck, Uffz O. (9./KG4), 467
Packer, AC1 J. T. (115 Sqn), 339

Paczinski, Gefr L., 308
Paddon, S/Ldr B. (40 Sqn), 184, 431
Page, F/Sgt D. A., 95
Pagès, Sgt (GC I/6), 334, 466
Pahl, Gefr Hans, 224
Pahl, Uffz W., 253
Pahlke, Uffz K., 308
Pailloux, Lt J. (GB 2/15), 395
Painchaux, S/Lt P. (GB I/62), 432
Paine, Sgt James R., DFM, 246
Paish, Sgt W. C. H. (107 Sqn), 379
Pälchen, Gefr H., 209
Pälchen, Uffz O., 209
Paleit, Lt A., 252
Pallières, Capt. M. des (GAO 1/589), 461
Palmade, S/Lt F. (GB 1/19), 400
Palmer, F/O C. D. 'Pussy', 119, 120, 156, 256, 303
Palmer, LAC W. E., 248
Panay, Sgt, 306
Paneboeuf, S/Lt R. (GR I/35), 364
Panhard, Sgt R. (GC II/7), 126, 127, 441
Panhuys, 2e Lt Jhr. J. E. van, 276
Panier, Sgt H. (GB II/62), 461
Pankau, Uffz K., 253
Pannekamp, Gefr F. (5./KG54), 342
Pannig, Uffz T. (KG54), 328
Panten, Lt (8./JG53), 380
Panten, Lt S. (4.(S)/LG2), 429
Panton, F/O (later F/Lt) A. D. (53 Sqn), 232, 469
Pape, Capt. J. (GC 1/3), 352
Pape, Oberlt H., 102
Papendorf, Uffz W. (KG54), 328
Papin, Capt. (GC II/7), 360, 414, 456
Papner, Oberfw F., 241
Paquez, S/Lt Victor, 324
Parat, Sgt, 260
Paratilla, Sgt R., 93
Parc, Lt G. du, 98
Parent, Sgt, 265, 274, 277, 315
Paris, Adjt R. (GB I/21), 364
Paris, Sgt (GC II/9), 434
Parisot, Lt (GAO 2/520), 333
Parisse, S/Lt Jean (GC I/3), 285, 340, 401
Park, AVM (later AM Sir) Keith, 349, 369, 372
Park, Sgt G., 150
Parker, AC1 W. (139 Sqn), 270
Parker, F/Lt E. (150 Sqn), 183
Parker, P/O E. D. (49 Sqn), 445
Parker, P/O T. C. (79 Sqn), 245, 253, 301, 312, 331, 441
Parker, Sgt (21 Sqn), 431
Parker, Sgt E. C. (110 Sqn), 273
Parkhouse, P/O R. C. L. (12 Sqn), 464
Parkhouse, Sgt Raymond C. (37 Sqn), 372
Parkinson, Sgt, 134
Parmentier, Lt (GR I/22), 148
Parmentier, Sgt (GR I/14), 306
Parmiggiani, Sgt Maj. E., 477
Parodi, Capt. G., 477
Parnall, S/Ldr J. D., 272, 277
Parnière, S/Lt M. (GC I/5), 239, 263, 417, 418
Parodi, Capt. G., 477
Parrott, F/O T. H. (77 Sqn), 233
Parrott, P/O Peter L. (607 Sqn/145 Sqn), 149, 151, 206, 207, 213, 241, 257, 373
Parry, LAC K., 231
Parry, Simon, 336, 437, 441, 444, 448
Parsons, AC1 W. L., 232
Parsons, P/O, 300, 307
Parszyk, Uffz J. (Stab KG76), 434
Partl, Oberlt W., 212
Partlow, LAC I. R. T. W., 116
Pascal, Lt P. (GC II/9), 341, 459
Pascal, Mtre (AB 2), 324
Pascaly, S/Lt R. (GBA 2/51), 424
Passarge, Fw G., 208
Passemard, Sgt (GC II/7), 477

Passey, Cpl W., 331
Pasteau, Capt. R. (GB 4/21), 364
Patanchon, Col (GAO 2/506), 373
Paterson, P/O J. C. (26 Sqn), 405
Patoor, Sgt, 274
Patroux, Lt, 100
Patschkowski, Oberlt O. (Stab LG1), 366
Patterson, AC1 G. N. (12 Sqn), 244
Patterson, AC2 J. H. (82 Sqn), 304
Patterson, LAC (2 Sqn), 303
Patterson, P/O R. L. (235 Sqn), 184
Patterson, Sgt T. (110 Sqn), 233
Patureau-Mirand, Capt. Raoul (GC I/2), 329, 453, 481
Paturle, S/Lt J. (GC I/6), 315, 423, 441
Patzer, Uffz R. W. (1./KG4), 409
Paul, F/O H. G. G. (73 Sqn), 12, *13*, 15, 36, 48, 55, 56, *57*, *59*, 61, *64*, 115, 131, 208, 259, 268, 277, 328
Paul, QM (T 2), 352
Paul, Sgt J. W. (82 Sqn), 304
Paul, Sgt W. J. (114 Sqn), 133
Paulet, S/Lt G. (GB I/11), 432
Paulhan, Adjt Jean (GC II/4), 289, 314, 315, 316, 317, 433, 434, 451
Paulhan, Sgt Auguste (GC III/1), 315, 336, 340
Paulin, Sgt J. (GBA I/54), 466
Paulitsch, Hptmn R., 127
Paulsen, Oberlt R., 167
Paumier, Sgt A. (GB II/12), 259, 432
Pauw, 2e Lt A. P. de, 193
Pauw, 2e Lt H., 194
Pavenzinger, Uffz G., 99
Pavey, Sgt C. J. (17 Sqn), 239, 320
Pawelka, Fw F. (4./StG77), 347
Pawlik, Gefr H. (8./KG55), 213, 459
Pawlikowski, Stefan, *82*
Payne, F/Sgt (501 Sqn), 240, 289
Payne, Sgt A. H. (53 Sqn), 282, 378
Payol, QM (T 2), 352
Peace, P/O P. McL. (4 Sqn), 339
Peach, Sgt T. A., 180
Peacock, S/Ldr M. F. (85 Sqn), 321, 331
Pearce, Sgt L. H. B. (79 Sqn), 268, 331, 335
Pearce, Sgt M. G. A. (53 Sqn), 167
Pearce, Sgt T. R. A. D. (21 Sqn), 272
Pearson, Cpl Daphne, *398*
Pearson, F/Lt M. C. (54 Sqn), 154, 379, 380
Pebrel, S/Lt (GC I/1), 476, 495
Pech, Sgt R. (GB I/34), 494
Pechaud, Sgt, 95
Pécou, Capt. R. (GR 1/33), 456
Peebles, LAC (235 Sqn), 390
Peetoom, Lt F., 111, 261
Pegaz, Sgt (GAO 1/551), 296, 324, 352
Peigné, Capt. R., 259
Peil, Hauptgefr W., 262
Pelletier, S/Lt (GC II/8), 342
Pelletier, Sgt R. (GR I/22), 189
Péllissier, Sgt (GC 5/1), 456
Peltriaux, Adjt (GR II/52), 325
Penclaud, Adjt, 95
Penninger, Gefr K., 279
Pennington, P/O (26 Sqn), 332
Pennington, P/O (245 Sqn), 396
Pennognon, SM P. (AB 1), 340
Pentz, Capt. Jan, 83
Penzini, Sgt (GC I/5), 376, 408, 442, 456
Peper, Uffz H., 289
Pépin, Cmdt René (GC II/7), 475
Peplar, AC1 S. G., 133
Pepper, AC1 L. V. (500 Sqn), 465
Pepper, F/O N. E. W., *246*
Pepper, Sgt F. R., 248
Pepys, F/O S. G. L. (53 Sqn), 349
Percival, P/O (82 Sqn), 445
Percival, Sgt F. J. (226 Sqn), 272
Percy, F/O A. C. J., 233
Perdomo, SM (AB 3), 494

Perez, 1e Lt P. J. B. Ruijs de, 193
Perina, Lt F. (GC I/5), 208, 209, 240, 328, 410, 417
Perl, Uffz M., 308
Pernau, Gefr W. (KG54), 329
Perne, S/Lt, 273
Pernot, Adjt M., *53*, 107, 126
Péronne, Lt R., 306
Perret, S/Lt (GAO 543), 395
Perrigouard, Adjt, 296
Perrin, LAC J. L., 244
Perrin, Sgt E. R., 248
Perrotte, Capt. (GR I/36), 325
Perry, P/O J. G. 'Tubs' (73 Sqn), *31*, *44*, *46*, *51*, 53, 56, *58*, 72, 103, 154, *518*
Perry, S/Ldr G. V. (605 Sqn), 379
Perry, Sgt Charles D., DFM (103 Sqn), 153, 268, *518*, *519*
Perry, Sgt R. M. (73 Sqn), 15, 39, *46*, 48, 127, *518*
Persse-Joynt, F/Lt D. (609 Sqn), 399
Perthes, Lt von (3.(J)/LG2), 431
Pertl, Lt K., 290
Peryman, P/O B. W. (142 Sqn), 458
Pesant, Adjt (GC III/9), 407
Pesch, S/Lt (GAO 2/508), 424
Pétain, Maréchal Philippe, *171*, 457, 478, 480, 494
Peter, Fw E. (6./StG77), 343
Peter, Obergefr A., 147
Petereit, Uffz H., 253
Petermann, Obergefr R., 241
Petermann, Sgt (GB 4/23), 466
Peters, Fw H. (8./LG1), 241
Peters, Lt G. (2.(H)/23), 459
Peters, Lt H. (II./ZG76), 234, 366
Peters, Oberfw F. (2.(H)/12), 353
Peters, P/O (500 Sqn), 408
Peters, P/O J. F. H. (59 Sqn), 385
Peters, Sgt D. E. (40 Sqn), 431
Petersen, Fw H. (1.(F)/122), 124
Petersen, Gefr W. (2./KG54), 253
Petersen, Obergefr H-L. (1./KGr.126), 343
Petit, Capt. P. (GAO 1/508), 314
Petit, S/Lt E. (GAO 1/520), 96
Petit, Sgt (GB II/12), 432
Petitguillaume, Capt. (GBA I/54), 466
Petitjean, Sgt P. (GC II/8), 341
Petitjean-Roget, Cmdt (GC II/5), 335, 341
Petitpain, Sgt (GBA I/54), 466
Petley, F/Lt L. V. E. (21 Sqn), 465
Petre, F/O G. W. (19 Sqn), 385
Petrich, Obergefr F., 301
Petrick, Fw F., 254
Petriconne, Sgt P. (GIA I/601), 462
Petrie, Sgt P. J. (15 Sqn), 458
Petroschinski, Gefr P., 308
Petry, Uffz W., 154
Petschke, Fw R. (1./KG27), 402
Pettigrew, P/O J. F. (151 Sqn), 437
Pettinger, Fw E. (6./KG77), 396
Pettit, Sgt Hugh E., 153, *502*
Pettke, Uffz W., 210
Petton, Adjt G., 94
Petts, Cpl (500 Sqn), 398
Petzgall, Gefr Hans, 240
Petzold, Lt Ernst (9./KG54), *414*
Peulevé, Sgt D. H. (15 Sqn), 461
Peuto, Lt J., 314
Pexton, F/O R. D. (615 Sqn), 323
Peyrègne, Capt. Marcel (GC I/8), 307, 308, 337, 433
Peyron, Sgt P. (GB I/11), 400
Pfaff, Uffz August (4./ZG76), *264*, 265
Pfaff, Uffz H. (5./KG3), 289
Pfäfflin, Uffz (7./ZG26), 429
Pfannenstein, Lt J. (5./StG2), 448
Pfau, Uffz W., 208
Pfauth, Uffz H., 309
Pfeffer, Uffz R., 229
Pfeifer, Fw K., 213
Pfeiffer, Flgr W., 207
Pfeiffer, Fw M. (KG51), 328
Pfenninger, Sgt A. (GR II/55), 359
Pfeuffer, Fw F., 107

Pfeuffer, Uffz G., 278
Pflüger, Uffz Walter, 419
Pfordte, Oberlt K., 116
Pfortner, Uffz H., 224
Pfützenreuter, Uffz W., 208
Phénix, Adjt J. (GC II/3), 401
Philipp, Uffz H. (6./KG55), 317
Philipp, Uffz W. (4./JG26), 379, 437, 441
Philipp, Uffz W. (TrGr.186), 347
Philippo, Sgt G., 196
Philips, Sgt (15 Sqn), 248
Phillips, LAC Donald L. (150 Sqn), 464
Phillips, Sgt A. N. (82 Sqn), 304
Phillips, Sgt B. F. (105 Sqn), 93
Phillips, Sgt George H. (73 Sqn), *15*, *44*, *46*, 72, 103, 108
Phillips, Sgt J. W. B. (54 Sqn), 356
Phillipson, Sgt F. (82 Sqn), 345
Piaccentini, Sgt S., 93
Picart, Adjt Joseph (GB II/19), 400
Picha Uffz W., 229
Pichon, Lt (GC I/2), 429
Pickering, LAC J. (12 Sqn), 423
Picking, Fw A. (8./KG4), 479
Pickles, Cpl (2 Sqn), 390
Picot, S/Lt (GC III/9), 414
Picq, Lt, 128
Piederstorfer, Uffz E., 165
Pieles, Uffz H., 262
Pielmeyer, Oberlt K. (Stab I./JG26), 402
Pieper, Lt Friedrich, 327, *329*
Pieplow, Fw R. (Stab StG77), 353
Pierlot, M. Hubert, *384*
Pierrat, Lt L., 117, 275
Pierre, Capt. E. (9/III/3), 238
Pierre, Sgt J. (7/III/3), 261
Pierre, Sgt L. (GR I/55), 341
Pietras, Uffz M., 116
Pietrusky, Maj. P-P. (2./KG77), 376
Piff, Sgt B. S. J. (15 Sqn), 458
Pigeon, Adjt (ECN 4/13), 413
Pigg, F/O O. St J. (72 Sqn), 412
Pike, Sgt R. (57 Sqn), 268
Pike, Sgt Richard C. L. (218 Sqn), 115, *502*
Pilâtre-Jacquin, S/Lt F. (GC III/7), 139, 341
Pilhofer, Lt G., 277
Pilkington, Sgt Lionel S. (73 Sqn), *15*, 48, *49*, 53, *57*, *68*, 153, 232, 256, 262, 279, 280, 283, 321
Pimont, Sgt (GC III/6), 158, 358
Pinardi, Adjt (GIA I/601), 462
Pinatel, Sgt R. (GAO 1/514), 346
Pinczon du Sel, Lt J-M, 106
Pingel, Hptmn R-P. (2./JG53 & III./JG53), 94, 99, 100, 371, 458, 459
Pinguet, Lt, 248
Pinkney, Capt. David E. (662 AOP Sqn), *323*
Pinochietti, Sgt (GC 6/1), 325
Pinon, Sgt R. (GC III/10), 306
Pinske, Uffz H. (7.(F)/LG2), 419
Pinson, Sgt (GC III/9), 375, 452
Pioger, Adjt R., 314
Piontek, Uffz O. (9./KG4), 376
Pioszyk, Uffz K-H. (1./KG27), 428
Pipa, Cpl J. (GC I/1), 288, 289, 425
Pipart, Sgt, 148
Piper, Fw H-P., 254
Pippig, Fw H. (4./KG3), 381
Pirie, AC1 G. R. (57 Sqn), 345
Pirks, Sgt (15 Sqn), 458
Pirlot, Sgt André, *237*
Pironneau, Sgt H., 296
Pirotte, Sgt P. (11/VI/1), 352
Pirrong, Gefr K., 241
Pirschalek, Uffz O. (ZG26), 329
Pitcairn, Hptmn (1./JG51), 97, 352
Pitcher, AC2 D. J., 232, 293
Pitfield, F/Lt A. L. (88 Sqn), 461
Pittar, Sgt W. D. P. (150 Sqn), 445
Pitz, Obergefr H. (KG54), 329
Piur, Obergefr K-H., 263
Pizon, Sgt, 157, 206, 278

Plähn, Fw O., 316
Plan, S/Lt Billon du (GBA II/54), 481
Planchard, Sgt (GC II/7), 132, 160, 388, 410
Planer, Lt H. (9./JG52), 376
Plank, Flgr M. (1./KG54), 414
Plantier, Adjt (GB I/62), 374
Plantier, Sgt (GAO 552), 324
Plasmans, 1e Lt H. F. J. M., 150
Plate, Gefr H. (7./LG1), 429
Plätschke, Gefr E., 240
Plaud, Lt (GAO 517), 446
Playfair, AVM Patrick H. L., *17*, *60*, *125*, 480
Pleasance, F/Lt H. P. (107 Sqn), 437
Pleij, 1e Lt J., 191
Plesman, 2e Lt J. C., 192, 226, 261
Pless, Uffz H. (2.(H)/31), 481
Plessiez, Sgt (GBA II/54), 451
Plettenberg, Oberlt A. Graf von (2.(H)/12), 441
Plinston, F/Lt G. H. F. (1 Sqn/607 Sqn/242 Sqn), 120, 183, 241, 399, 402
Ploeschke, Hptmn G., 116
Plötz, Gefr E. (4./KG53), 409
Plotzitzka, Fw W. (2.(F)/123), 335
Plou, Cmdt, 248
Ploye, Sgt (GR I/35), 478
Plozitzka, Fw F. (8./LG1), 360
Plubeau, S/Lt C. (GC II/4), 97, 108, 114, 117, 239, 241, 285, 289, 316, 317, 451
Pluiston, Petty Off. (FAA), *525*
Plumb, P/O J. A. (4 Sqn), 320
Plzak, Sgt Stanislav (GC II/2), 408, 427, *488*
Poad, LAC T., 233
Podbielski, Oberlt F. (9./KG4), 376
Podelleck, Uffz E., 225
Poetter, Hptmn J., 212
Poher, S/Lt (GB II/11), 466
Pohl, Uffz H., 208
Pohland, Fw H., 317
Pohle, Gefr K. (8./LG1), 347
Pöhler, Lt O-W., 263
Pohlmann, Fw Karl-Ernst (KG27), 211, 327
Poilbout, Adjt (GBA II/54), 400
Poincenot, Adjt (GC II/3), 162, 380, 448
Pointel, Mot (2S4), 495
Poitrot, Adjt, 248
Polenz, Fw W., 366
Pollack, Lt G. (6./JG3), 342
Pöllath, Fw H. (7./KG53), 328
Poller, Fw Johann, 251, *262*
Pollet, Lt G. (GB I/63), 451
Pollitz, Lt V., 209
Pollmann, Gefr W., 206
Pollmann, Uffz E., 212
Pollock, Sgt (142 Sqn), 182, 345, 464
Pollono, Adjt Maurice, *264*, 265
Polyka, Fw, 222
Polzin, Uffz P., 254
Pomaska, Oberlt A. (6./JG26), 409
Pommares, S/Lt (GR I/14), 466
Pomier Layrargues, S/Lt René (GC II/7), 360, 426, *428*
Pomorin, Uffz W., 212
Poncet, Sgt (GAO 513), 387
Poniatowski, S/Lt Jerzy (GC II/10), *440*, 441
Ponneau, S/Lt (GC II/9), 459
Pönnighaus, Gefr H. (KG54), 329
Pons, S/Lt (GB II/38), 296
Pons, Sgt (GB II/62), 461
Ponson, Lt (GB II/12), 234
Ponsot, Lt (GB II/34), 259
Ponteins, Adjt D. (GC II/7), 388, 410, 425
Poole, Naval Airman R. G. (826 FAA Sqn), 496
Poole, Sgt C. J. S., 181
Pope, Sgt (57 Sqn), 345
Popelka, Sgt S. (GC I/6), 316, 417
Popp, Fw Karl (7./KG1), *495*

Popp, Fw R. (3./StG76), 376
Poppe, Uffz G., 253
Pöppler, Oberlt W. (Stab StG1), 453
Porchon, Sgt, 306
Porodo, S/Lt (GC I/8), 495
Portal, ACM Sir Charles, 319
Portalis, Capt. G. (GC II/5), 133, 240, 285, 427
Porzic, EV1 de Rodellec de, 340
Posnanski, Gefr K. (4./KG76), 366
Posner, Mollie, *503*
Posselt, P/O Arthur F., *271*
Possien, Lt (GC II/10), 154, 429
Post, Fw Siegfried (1.(F)/22), 408, *409*
Post, Sgt (ECN 1/13), 341
Posta, Sgt (GC II/4), 459
Postma, 2e Lt S. J., 191, 261
Postolka, Cpl H. (GC I/1), 298, 425
Potié, Lt H., 94
Potier, Capt. D. (1/I/3), 365
Potier, S/Lt Lucien-Louis (GC I/3), 274, 278
Potter, AC1 J. (105 Sqn), 270
Potter, Enid (widow of J. A. H.), *519*
Potter, Sgt (114 Sqn), 270
Potter, Sgt J. A. H. (18 Sqn), 141, *519*
Potter, Sgt Jack A. (19 Sqn), 405, 406
Potthast, Fw (5./JG52), 447
Potts, P/O I. C. G. (73 Sqn), 405
Pötzinger, Uffz H., 120
Pötzsch, Fw A. (1./JG27), 353
Poulain, S/Lt J., 139
Poulitou, Sgt (GB II/35), 416
Poulton, P/O M. A., 99
Poummeau, S/Lt, 274
Pourkat, Sgt (GB I/62), 461
Pouw, Sgt J. A., 193, 211
Pouyade, Capt. P. (ECN 4/13), 413
Pouzol, Adjt (GR 1/55), 380
Power, P/O J. O'B., 270
Pownall, Gen. H. R., 367
Pradelle, Lt, 284
Pragerstorfer, Uffz L., 301
Pralon, Sgt G. (GC 5/1), 259, *260*, 325
Pratt, Sgt W. T. (43 Sqn), 472
Prayer, S/Lt G. (GC II/3), 121, 374, 401
Prchal, Sgt E. (GC I/8), 441
Pré, Lt (GB I/31), 466
Preiser, Obergefr E., 317
Prenez, Adjt (GB II/12), 456
Prenez, Adjt R. (GC III/2), 131, 285, 290
Press, F/Lt R., 28, 29, *53*, 96
Prestel, Uffz A. (1.(H)/13), 456
Prestele, Stabsfw (later Oberlt) I., 99, 100, 271
Preston, AC, 271
Preston, Cpl F., 273
Preston, Vice-Adm. Sir Lionel, 367
Preub, Oberlt G., 279
Preuss, Oberfw W. (3./KG77), 360
Preux, Sgt E. (GC I/5), 189, 341
Prévost, EV1 (AC 1), 308
Prévost, S/Lt (GC I/3), 425
Prévot, Sgt (GR II/52), 260
Price, Sgt N. J., 150
Priebe, Lt A. (KG54), 329
Priebe, Oberlt E. (2./JG77), 103, 285, 327
Priemer, Uffz G. (4./KG1), 419
Pries, Uffz H. (4./KG1), 419
Prieur, Sgt (ECMJ I/16), 325
Prigent, SM, 305
Priller, Oberlt (6./JG51), 386, 412, 445
Prini, Sgt M. (GR I/35), 441
Pristat, Uffz E., 164
Pritzel, Oberlt K., 162
Pröbst, Oberlt M., 240
Probst, Uffz H., 132
Proctor, Sgt J. E. (501 Sqn), 272, 283, 290, 434
Proctor, Sgt J. R. (57 Sqn), 107, 159

Prössel, Uffz E., 298
Proteau, Sgt (GB II/31), 400, 432
Proudman, F/O G. (65 Sqn), 379, 381
Provoost, Capt. (GB 4/19), 446
Prual, Adjt (GR I/14), 466
Prüfer, Oberlt H., 213
Prühs, Fw F. (8./LG1), 360
Pryde, AC (59 Sqn), 372
Pryde, F/O D. D. (77 Sqn), 332
Przybyla, Gefr H. (8./LG1), 347
Puchstein, Gefr F. (8./KG51), 360
Puda, Sgt (GC II/4), 300, 336, 388, 459
Puech, Lt R. (GB I/11), 432
Puget, Sgt, 148
Puissessau, Lt, 305
Puivif, Sgt (GB I/21), 466
Pujot, Sgt, 47
Puls, Uffz H. (2./KG51), 382
Pulver, Uffz G., 241
Pümpel, Flgr H., 207
Pumphrey, F/O R. E. W. (607 Sqn), 332
Püschel, Uffz W. (8./KG4), 476
Puschmann, Fw S. (4./StG2), 366
Pusey, Sgt N. V., 339
Puth, Fw F., 240
Putnam, Mr, *288*
Putz, Oberlt H., 316
Putzbach, Uffz J. (KG51), 328
Putzier, Genmaj. Richard, 216
Puybusque, Sgt J. de (GC I/2), 213, 335, 413, 429, 448
Puzicha, Uffz F. (1./KG1), 393
Pyne, Sgt Thomas B. G., *15*, *29*, *41*, *53*, *56*, *59*, 71, 112, 141, 154, 163, 268

Quandt, Maj. Theodor (Stab JG3), *434*
Quarrington, Sgt K. F. (110 Sqn), 345
Quarz, Oberfw E., 206
Quasdorf, Uffz Paul, 222
Quéguiner, Sgt (GC II/5), 95, 434, 470
Quellec, Cpl (GR II/33), 396
Quénet, Capt., *105*
Quenolle, Sgt (GR II/22), 426
Querl, Fw H. (2./KG53), 336
Querrieu, S/Lt d'Alcantara de, 160
Quideau, Sgt C. (GB 2/31), 334
Quilico, Sgt A. (GAO 3/551), 424
Quillac, Sgt P. de (GR I/14), 462, 470
Quillitsch, Uffz (9./KG2), 376
Quinn, LAC G. D. P., 184
Quosdorf, Fw E. (4./KG3), 381

Raab, Uffz A. (I./JG1), 335
Raab, Uffz A. (I./KGzbV.1), 498
Raabe, Oberlt P. (3.(H)/12), 479
Raaf, 1e Lt H. T. de, 193
Raatz, Fw K., 140
Rabe, Hptmn H-J. Dr (7./KG4), 376
Raber, Oberlt Dr (2.(H)/41), 488
Rabuel, Sgt J. (GAO 501), 424
Raby, Lt, 325
Radbone, F/O J. W., 98, 123
Raddant, Uffz R. (5./StG2), 489
Radek, Uffz K., 154
Radford, AC1 E. A., 95
Radford, Sgt, 182
Radke, Fw, 226
Radlick, Lt (III./JG53), 133, 364, 400
Radliffe, P/O H. P. J., 152
Radomski, S/Lt Jerzy (DAT Lyons & GC II/10), 410, *440*
Radons, Fw O., 95
Radünz, Oberlt W., 241
Radzko, Uffz F., 265
Raeder, Adm. Erich, *497*
Raffler, Uffz Erich (1./KGr.126), 353
Rage, Adjt (GAO 510), 424
Ragnit, Fw E., 97
Raguant, Sgt, 151
Ragutt, Uffz A. (7./KG1), 495
Raillard, Lt C. (GB I/12), 259, 419
Rainier, P/O P. H. O'C. (145 Sqn), 379

Rambault, Lt A. (GR II/55), 334
Rampf, Fw W. (I.(St)/TrGr.186), 410
Ramsay, LAC (103 Sqn), 423
Ramsay, P/O Alex F. B., 159
Ramsay, Vice-Adm. Sir Bertram, *367*, 368, 404, 411
Ramsbrock, Uffz H., 214
Ramsey, Bill, *480*
Ramus, Uffz Karl, 221
Randall, Sgt (53 Sqn), 431
Randelhoft, Fw Heinrich, 224
Ranftl, Uffz A. (9./KG53), 410
Rannoux, Sgt (GB II/11), 466
Raoul, S/Lt (GB 1/31), 296
Raoul, Sgt (GB II/21), 466, 469
Raper, Sgt Leslie A., 157, *527*
Raphenne, S/Lt Henri (GC I/6), 334, 336, 341, 360, 418, *499*
Rapoport, S/Lt (GB II/31), 400
Raps, Oberlt W., 315
Rasch, Lt H., 254
Rasper, Uffz E., 253
Ratcliffe, F/Sgt H. J. (107 Sqn), 412
Ratel, Adjt, 284
Ratenschak, Uffz H., 225
Ratford, P/O F. W. (253 Sqn), 315, 322
Rathmann, Fw K. (Stab KG55), 213, 429
Rättig, Oberfw E., 206
Ratzing, Fw F., 239
Rau, Oberlt, 159, 260, 275
Rauch, Oberlt W., 241
Rauchfuss, Gefr K. (9./KG4), 327
Raudies, Oberfw G. (Stab III./KG27), 347
Raupach, Gefr W., 211
Rautmann, Obergefr W., 241
Raveneau, Adjt V. (GB I/19), 424
Ravenhill, P/O Malcolm, 304, 307
Ravilly, Sgt F., 188, 206
Rawlings, LAC K. D. (12 Sqn), 320
Rawlinson, P/O M. H. G., 294
Rayat, Sgt M., 93
Rayner, F/O P. H. (501 Sqn), 247, 253
Rayner, F/O R. M. S. (87 Sqn), 299, 301, 321, 329, 335
Rea, F/O K. N. (226 Sqn), 469
Read, P/O J. A. A. (53 Sqn), 99
Read, Sgt (9 Sqn), 349
Readhead, Sgt S. C., 248, 313
Rebholz, Uffz F. (2./StG77), 347
Rebière, Adjt (GC II/9), 434, 452, 456
Rebillat, S/Lt P. (GC III/3), 325
Rebois, Sgt (GR I/33), 419
Rebwinkel, Lt, 107
Recht, Fw W. (9./KG27), 347
Reckers, Uffz, 145
Reden, Lt E. von (2./JG2), 269, 427
Reden, Lt W. von (3.(H)/41), 335
Redenz, Obergefr G. (StG2), 329
Redlich, Oberlt (1./JG27), 238, 293, 391, 464
Redlich, Uffz W. (3.(H)/21), 298
Reed, F/O J. W., 98, 123
Reed, F/O A. P. (16 Sqn), 320
Reed, LAC K. G., 304
Rees, P/O V., 339
Regis, Lt P. (GR I/35), 441
Regnault, Sgt (GB II/34), 314
Regnoux, Adjt (GB I/31), 95
Rehbein, Uffz W. (TrGr.186), 365
Reibel, Gefr. (later Uffz) L. (1./JG53), 205, 270, 366
Reich, Gefr J. (1./KG54), 382
Reichart, Uffz H. (4./StG77), 347
Reiche, Fw H. (Stab I./KG77), 265
Reiche, Gefr H. (7.(F)/LG2), 301
Reiche, Obergefr H. (2.(H)/12), 462
Reichel, Fw F. (Stab KG27), 488
Reichenbach, Fw W., 208
Reichert, Uffz A. (KG77), 301
Reichert, Uffz K. (III./KGzbV.1), 228
Reid, P/O B. D. G. H. (107 Sqn), 461
Reid, Pat, 161

Reid, Petty Off. N. R. (801 FAA Sqn), 398
Reim, Uffz K. (2./KG54), 383
Reimann, Fw H., 215
Reimer, Lt Walter (2./JG26), 448
Reimers, Oberlt O., 239
Reinberger, Maj. Helmuth, 133
Reiners, Lt J. (8./KG4), 476
Reinhardt, Uffz Karl, *213*
Reinhardt, Uffz W., 213
Reinhold, Gefr F. (2./JG20), 456
Reins, Obergefr K., 212
Reintjes, Sgt J. Th., 250
Reiske, Fw W., 213
Reissmann, Uffz W., 277
Reisz, Oberlt H. G., 144
Relat, Sgt (GAO 516), 346
Rempel, Oberlt, 311
Remy, S/Lt P. J., 148, 277
Renard, Adjt (GB II/34), 296
Renard, Sgt (GB I/31), 440
Renaud, QM (T1), 152
Renaud, S/Lt (GC III/7), 154
Renaudie, Adjt M. (GBA I/54), 248
Renaudie, Adjt M. (GC II/2), 156, 259
Renault, Sgt (GBA II/54), 440
Reneville, Lt B. de (GR II/33), 346
Renison, P/O R. J. (504 Sqn), 300, 313
Renken, Uffz B. (2.(F)/122), 427
Renner, Uffz K. (7.(F)/LG2), 388
Renouard, Adjt R. (GIA I/601), 417
Rensinghoff, Uffz G. (3./KG1), 470
Rentsch, Lt M., 309
Repple, Uffz (2./JG76), 352
Resch, Fw F., 278
Reschke, Gefr K., 145
Rescoussie, Sgt S. (GR II/55), 325
Resener, Uffz H., 309
Restif, S/Lt Y. Le, 100
Reumschüssel, Lt H., 307, 313
Reusch, Uffz H., 117
Reuss, Maj. F. (Stab III./KG76), 418
Reuss, Uffz O., 280
Reuter, Gefr O., 263
Reuter, Oberlt H. (Stab KG77), 470
Reuter, Uffz B. (2.(F)/122), 496
Revelli, Cpl, 284
Reverse, S/Lt, 284
Reverseau, Cmdt (108e Inf. Regt), 429
Revill, LAC H. (264 Sqn), 386
Rexin, Lt J., 117
Rey, S/Lt J. (GC I/5), 133, 208, 314, 317
Rey, Sgt A. (GB 4/31), 400
Rey, Sgt M. (GB I/63), 451
Reynaud, Paul (Prime Minister), 281, *286*, 292, *457*, 463, 478
Reyne, Capt., 107
Reynolds, AC1 (73 Sqn), 36
Reynolds, LAC Lawrence R., 244, *245*, *513*
Reynolds, P/O B. (59 Sqn), 372
Reyter, S/Lt J. (ECN 2/13), 305, 380
Rhinow, Oberlt F-K., 94, 99
Rhodes-Moorhouse, F/O W. H. (601 Sqn), 323
Ribaucourt, Sgt X. de, 238
Ribbentrop, Joachim von, *497*
Ribereau-Gayon, S/Lt, 314
Ribo, Sgt J., 145
Rice, Sgt D. J. (40 Sqn), 431
Richard, Adjt A. (GBA I/54), 248
Richard, Capt. A. (GC III/3), 157
Richardin, Adjt (GC II/1), 279, 341, 418
Richards, Cpl A. G., 304
Richardson, AC1 Vivian W. L. (218 Sqn), 115, *502*
Richardson, Sgt (105 Sqn), 182
Richardson, Sgt E. (242 Sqn), 487
Richardt, Lt, 102
Riche, Cpl J. (ECN 2/13), 305

Riche, S/Lt P. (GB I/12), 456
Richers, Uffz F. (5./KG30), 479
Richert, Lt, 95
Richey, F/O Paul H. M., *108*, *146*, 154, 156, 161, *168*, *169*, *184*, 208, 231, 239, 242, 255, *256*, 282, *289*, 320, 327
Richmond, F/O I. G., 135
Richter, Fw (1./JG1), 234
Richter, Fw H. (1./KG3), 366
Richter, Mech. G. (Stab III./KG3), 239
Richter, Oberfw R. (2./KG76), 317
Richter, Oberfw R. (9./KG3), 208
Richter, Obergefr A. (6./KG2), 208
Richter, Obergefr Egon (1./KGrzbV.12), 223
Richter, Obergefr H. (2.(F)/123), 252
Richter, Oberlt G. (7./LG1), 309
Richter, Uffz A. (KG51), 289
Richter, Uffz E. (KG4), 209
Richter, Uffz G. (1./ZG1), 410
Richter, Uffz G. (KG30), 211
Richter, Uffz H. (Stab I./KG27), 428
Richter, Uffz H. (5./KG2), 289
Richter, Uffz J. (2./JG26), 402
Richthofen, Oberstlt Wolfram Freiherr von, 87
Rickard, LAC (150 Sqn), 464
Ricke, Lt H. (4.(H)/22), 288, 495
Ricquier, SM (AB 4), 492
Riddell, P/O N. C. S., 232
Ridder, Fw A., 227
Riddle, F/O C. J. (A Flt, 601 Sqn), 339
Riddle, F/O H. J. (B Flt, 601 Sqn), 323
Ridley, P/O F. H., 270
Ridley, Sgt M. (616 Sqn), 386
Riebesell, Uffz Hans (2./ZG52), 383
Riebicke, Oberlt W. (4.(F)/121), 171, 456
Rieck, Fw W. (3./KüFlGr.506), 241
Rieck, Oberfw R. (7./KG4), 336
Riecker, Lt Joachim, 300
Riederer, Gefr P., 240
Riedinger, Hptmn W. (1./KG76), 418
Riedl, Lt W. (1./KG76), 476
Rieg, Uffz E. (9./KG54), 479
Riegel, Gefr E., 136
Riegel, Hptmn Helmut (Stab I./JG27), 107, 334, 359
Riegel, Lt H. (7./JG53), 141, 153, 433, 459
Rieger, Gefr Ernst, 241
Rieger, Uffz J. (6./KG76), 347
Rieger, Uffz K. (3./StG76), 376
Riehle, Uffz E. (3.(F)/123), 380
Riemsdijk, 2e Lt J. van, 141, 194
Riemsdijk, Sgt G. A. van, 191, 261
Riencourt, LV Jolivet de (E 6), 488
Riesser, Capt. Jean, 234, 284
Rigaill, Adjt F. (GIA I/601), 417
Rigal, Sgt M. (GAO 518), 340
Rigalleau, Sgt L., 285
Rigatti, Tenente M., 477
Rigaux, S/Lt M. (GB I/62), 432
Rigling, Uffz F., 290
Rigole, Sgt J., 196, 298
Rigollier, Sgt, 134
Rigourd, S/Lt A., 305
Rijn, Lt van, 95
Rimlinger, Sgt, 259
Rinck, Oberlt F-K., 209
Ringpfeil, Uffz H., 206
Rinke, Uffz J. (3./ZG1), 429
Rinn, Uffz H. (3./KG51), 336
Ripke, Lt H. (8./JG26), 448
Rippe, Sgt, 249
Rische, Oberfw H. (4.(H)/31), 347
Riss, S/Lt J. (GC II/6), 260, 263, 429, 451
Risse, Capt. (GB II/12), 395
Rissel, Uffz H-J., 253
Rist, Fw A., 213
Ritchie, P/O (57 Sqn), 303, 349
Ritte, Obergefr A. (1.(F)/22), 335

Ritter, Fw, 212
Ritter, Lt G., 279
Rituit, Sgt, 100
Ritz, Sgt, 234
Rival, Soldat (GIA I/601), 462
Rivals-Mazères, Capt. Guillaume de (CEAM & GC I/6), 253, 459
Rix, Lt (GAO 1/514), 455
Roach, P/O R. J. B. (266 Sqn), 446
Roba, Jean-Louis, *301*, *382*
Robert, Adjt A. (GR II/33), 97, 111
Robert, Capt. J. (GR 2/35), 419
Robert, Lt Marius (GAO 518), 475
Robert, Sgt H. (GR II/55), 495
Robert, Sgt J. (GC II/1), 274
Robert, Sgt R. (GC I/3), 416
Roberton, Sgt A. J., 97
Roberts, AC (53 Sqn), 362, 431
Roberts, F/Lt R. (79 Sqn), 293, 441
Roberts, F/O A. C. (150 Sqn), 183
Roberts, P/O (103 Sqn), 437
Roberts, Sgt E. G. (15 Sqn), 248
Robertson, F/O (15 Sqn), 395
Robertson, F/Sgt R. (82 Sqn), 437
Robertson, P/O G. P. (82 Sqn), 445
Robertson, Sgt A. J. (40 Sqn), 184
Robertson, Sgt F. N. (66 Sqn), 412
Robertson, Sgt J. C. (235 Sqn), 248
Robiaud, S/Lt J. (GC II/2), 241, 317, 447
Robin, Sgt (GR II/14), 499
Robinson, AC1 W. (218 Sqn), 271, *519*
Robinson, AC2 A. (115 Sqn), 339
Robinson, AC2 S. (53 Sqn), 282, 293
Robinson, F/O (213 Sqn), 399
Robinson, F/O P. B. (601 Sqn), 332, 437
Robinson, LAC (264 Sqn), 458
Robinson, P/O (53 Sqn), 378
Robinson, P/O C. H. (15 Sqn), 248, 313
Robinson, P/O C. S. (235 Sqn), 313
Robinson, S/Ldr M. (616 Sqn), 386
Robinson, Sgt (49 Sqn), 445
Robinson, Sgt J. (111 Sqn), 398, 402
Robitzsch, Hptmn D., 205
Röbler, Uffz W., 213
Robson, Sgt F. (88 Sqn), 232
Robson, Sgt G. (110 Sqn), 446
Roch, Fw N., 317
Rochais, Sgt P. (GBA II/51), 451
Rochard, Cmdt, 284
Rochefort, Mt, 93
Rochel, Oberfw K., 318
Rocher, Capt. A. (GB II/12), 273, 296, 305
Rochfort, F/O (53 Sqn), 362, 431
Rochon, SM (AB 1), 419
Rochow, Lt H-J. von (2./ZG26), 366
Rock, AC E. S., 270
Rockenhäuser, Lt H., 279
Rocque, S/Lt J-F. de la, 259
Röder, Uffz A., 120
Röder, Uffz P., 206
Röders, Oberlt, 314
Rodgers, LAC (73 Sqn), 36
Rodgers, Sgt E. (40 Sqn), 461
Rodulson, AC1 W. S., 267
Roe, P/O V. D. M., 232, 268
Roël, S/Lt M., 251
Roeloffzen, Sgt G. F., 250
Roemer, Oberlt W., 208
Roepel, Lt, 316
Roeper Bosch, 2e Lt J. W. Y., 104
Roewer, Uffz H. (5./LG1), 393
Roger, Adjt (GC III/3), 262, 336
Roger, Cpl (GB I/31), 334
Röger, Gefr O. (8./LG1), 360
Roger, Pierre, 267
Rogers, Cpl R. G. (500 Sqn), 390
Rogers, F/Lt K. R. (142 Sqn), 271
Rogers, F/O D. D. (18 Sqn), 256
Rogers, P/O (21 Sqn), 356, 458
Rogers, S/Ldr E. G. (64 Sqn), 391
Roggatz, Uffz E., 317

Roggentin, Fw M. (KG51), 328
Rogoss, Fw K. (3./KG1), 448
Rohan-Chabot, Lt H. de, 188, 213, 274
Rohde, Gefr W. (5./KG3), 289
Rohde, Uffz W. (3./KG3), 381
Röhl, Oberlt, 262
Röhrborn, Oberfw F., 209
Rohloff, Oberfw H., 213
Rohwer, Lt (Stab I./JG3), 431
Rolin, 1/Sgt D., 236
Rolin-Hymans, 1/Sgt Gustave, *238*
Rolland, S/Lt R. (GBA II/51), 396, 447, 451
Rolland, Uffz H., 254
Rollberg, Lt H., 317
Rolle, Uffz H., 208
Rolle, Uffz M., 224
Romatowsky, Fw H. L., 209
Rombeeck, Off. L. A. H., 194
Römer, Obergefr W., 209
Romey, Adjt Maurice (GC III/2), 206, 251, 336, 447, 466
Rommel, Genmaj. Erwin, *460*
Romoth, Uffz A. (3.(F)/10), 335
Roncoroni, S/Ldr J. A. (57 Sqn), 372
Rondeau, Sgt (GR II/55), 359
Rondinelli, Sottotenente (Gruppo 43), 467
Ronin, S/Lt (GC II/6), 213, 434
Ronot, Adjt, 314
Roock, Gefr E. (5./StG2), 414
Roon, Oberlt W. von, 112
Rooney, LAC J., 246
Roos, Oberlt W. (5./JG27), 427
Roos, Sgt J., 125, 236
Rooseboom, 2e Lt W., 193
Roosenburg, 2e Lt E. A., 236, 250
Rooy, Kapt. van, 222
Roper, Sgt (59 Sqn), 385
Roquerbe, Sgt (GC II/1), 280, 341
Roques, Sgt C. (GB 4/21), 364
Roques, Sgt G. (GB II/12), 334
Rosarius, Lt T., 134
Roscher, Uffz K., 211
Rose, AC1 H. E. A., 99
Rose, F/O F. C. (56 Sqn), 311
Rose, Gefr H. (9./LG1), 343
Rose, P/O Jack (3 Sqn, ex-32 Sqn), 320
Rose, P/O S. G. (110 Sqn), 273
Rose, Sgt M. (GB I/11), 400
Rosen, Uffz, 282
Rosenberger, Uffz H., 300
Rosenboom, Lt, 105
Rosenbrock, Uffz K. (7./KG2), 456
Rosenkranz, Lt H. (3./ZG2), 376
Rosenkranz, Lt K. (3./JGr.152), 96, 97
Rosenkranz, Obergefr K. (Stab KG3), 342
Rosenow, Uffz H. (6./LG1), 393
Rosenthal, Oberlt H., 117
Rosewarne, F/O V. A. W. (38 Sqn), 398
Rosier, F/Lt F. E., 312, 315
Roskrow, Sgt R. (48 Sqn), 405
Rösl, Fw H., 252
Ross, AC1 Alex S., *245*, *247*
Ross, Sgt William G., *268*, *505*
Ross, Uffz Wilhelm (9./ZG26), *335*, 337
Rosshirt, Uffz K. (9./KG1), 342
Rossignol, Adjt (GAO 3/551), 334
Rossignol, Capt. J. (GAO 3/551), 94
Rössler, Fw W. (3.(F)/22), 427
Rössler, Uffz H., 318
Rossmann, Fw Hans, 241
Rossner Oberfw K., 221
Rostand, S/Lt (GBA I/54), 340
Rostand, S/Lt M. (GBA I/51), 346
Roth, F/O M. H., 182
Roth, Fw W. (4./JG26), 418
Roth, Gefr H-W. (1./ZG1), 301
Roth, Lt (9./JG2), 475
Roth, Michael (KGzbV.1), 229
Roth, Oberlt H. (5./KG4), 209
Röthemeier, Oberfw H. (3./KG53), 476

Rothenberger, Obergefr G. (1./ZG1), 347
Rotheram, F/O R. C., 248
Rothermere, Lord, 78, *79*
Rothfuss, Uffz T., 241
Röthig, Obergefr H., 209
Rott, Lt (3./JG53), 112
Rott, Obergefr K-H. (2.(F)/122), 427
Rotter, Flgr E., 279
Rotthauwe, Fw F., 317
Rottländer, Uffz W., 280
Rottmann, Uffz F. (9./KG27), 347
Roubaty, Hptmn (Swiss Fl.Komp.6), 409
Rouch, Sgt, 275
Rougelet, Adjt L. (GAO 2/520), 333
Rouig, Lt J. (GAO 1/551), 352, 446
Rouillon, Lt L. (GR II/52), 260
Roulland, Lt (GAO 510), 478
Rounds, LAC (142 Sqn), 464
Roupain, Lt (GR II/55), 452
Rouquette, S/Lt Marcel (GC I/5), 162, 317, 326, 376, 442, 447, 448, 456
Roure, S/Lt (GB I/23), 358
Rousseau, S/Lt A. (7/IV/1), 374
Rousseau, S/Lt B. (GAO 501), 458, *459*
Rousseau, S/Lt (GB I/12), 259, 296
Rousseau, Sgt (GAO 1/589), 465
Roussel, Lt J., 149, 164
Rousset, Lt, 95
Routledge, Sgt L. W. (9 Sqn), 469
Roux, Sgt, 248
Rouyer, Lt E., 305
Rowan, F/O P. J. H., 184
Rowe, F/O J. H. C., 184
Röwe, Obergefr H., 215
Rowe, P/O C. R., 183, 214
Rowe, Sgt B. J. (142 Sqn), 464
Rowland, F/Lt T. (43 Sqn), 437
Rowlands, LAC, 273
Rowson, Sgt H. (21 Sqn), 362
Roy, Aspirant, 103
Roy, Capt., 121
Royce, F/O M. E. A., 272, 277
Royle, P/O P. G., 311
Rozanoff, Cmdt Konstantin, 117, 301, 315
Rozeboom, Sgt L., 236
Rozoy, Sgt, 115
Rubin, S/Lt (GC II/4), 315, 316, 317
Ruby, S/Lt J. (GC I/8), 325, 327
Ruchoux, S/Lt G. (GC II/5), 164, 240, 274, 280, 316, 335
Ruckdeschel, Uffz H. (5./StG77), 410
Rucks, Uffz H., 170
Rudd, Sgt (142 Sqn), 464
Rudisele, Oberfw A. (5./KG55), 429
Rudolf, Uffz W. (TrGr.186), 205
Rudolph, Obergefr H. (6./KG54), 212
Rudolph, Uffz H-D. (7./JG26), 342
Rudorffer, Oberfw (2./JG2), 305, 364, 373, 432, 433
Ruess, Oberlt H., 252
Ruh, Uffz Joseph, 224
Rühl, Fw Erich, 226
Ruhland, Uffz E. (5./KG51), 470
Ruhnke, Flgr H., 388
Rührschneck, Fw H. (4.(F)/11), 341
Rulfs, Uffz Johann (9./KG2), *380*, 381
Rumpelt, Lt B., 239
Rumsey, Naval Airman F. G. (825 FAA Sqn), 390
Rundstedt, Generaloberst Gerd von, *355*, *361*
Runge, Uffz O. (KG51), 328
Runkwitz, Oberfw H., 123
Rupied, S/Lt Y. (GC III/7), 154, 234, 341, 475
Rupp, Lt W. (1./JG53), 97, 131, 205
Rupp, Uffz J. (1./StG76), 456

Ruppel, Fw H. (5./LG1), 393
Ruppel, Obergefr J. (6./KG1), 353
Ruppel, Uffz P. (2./KG54), 308
Ruppert, Adjt, 112
Russé, S/Lt de, 241, 263
Russell, F/O I. B. N. (609 Sqn), 406
Russell, F/O J. B. (607 Sqn), 283, 290
Russell, F/Sgt J. A. (226 Sqn), 458
Russell, LAC (later Cpl) F. T. (57
Sqn), 106, 180, 362
Rust, Lt zur See H., 95
Rüther, Oberfw W., 209
Rüthrich, Uffz R. (KG51), 328
Rutland, LAC A. W. (150 Sqn),
371
Rutz, Uffz M. (1./ZG1), 410
Ruygrok, Lt G. H. J., 191
Ryan, Sgt, 171
Rybartzyk, Uffz, 107
Rye, Cpl R. K., 183
Rylands, S/Lt P. H. (825 FAA
Sqn), 385
Rzezniczek, Gefr E., 317

Saas, Uffz H., 214
Sabin, Sgt L. J., 121, 128
Sabine, S/Ldr J. S. (110 Sqn), 345
Saborowski, Uffz R. (8./JG3), 425,
427
Sabourault, Adjt (GB I/21), 466
Sabourdy, Lt P. (GB II/31), 392
Sacchi, S/Lt E., 110
Sacquepée, Adjt R., 259
Sacy, Capt. M. Silvestre de (GC
1/6), 341
Sadlowska, Slawa, 83
Sagon, Capt. (GR 3/22), 470
Sagon, Lt (GR II/33), 117, 126
Sahlberg, Obergefr K. (KG54), 329
Sahnkow, Lt A. (8./StG51), 388
Saillard, Sgt P., 117
Saint-Gall, Sgt, 305
St James-Smith, LAC R. G., 165, 293
St John, P/O (74 Sqn), 381
St John, P/O (87 Sqn), 110
Saint Marceaux, S/Lt G. De (GBA
II/51), 424
Saint-Mars, Capt. X. Poilloue de
(GC I/6), 447
Saint-Victor, Lt de, 259
Sainte Marie, Sgt R. (GAO 518),
475
Salaberry, Capt. Irumbery de (GB
4/31), 400
Salaberry, S/Lt Irumbery de (GC
I/3), 277, 279, 342, 453
Salaün, S/Lt (GC III/6), 341
Sales, Capt. de Roussy de (SAL
3/109), 341
Salès, Sgt E. (GC II/5), 112, 113,
117, 171, 240, 280, 476
Salesses, Sgt J. (GB 2/11), 400
Salisbury, Lord, 76
Salles, Sgt (GR II/55), 466
Salmand, Adjt A., 157
Salmon, AC (59 Sqn), 362
Salmon, Adjt G., 236, 286
Sals, Sgt, 171
Salva, S/Lt P. (GC I/3), 263, 273,
274, 278, 376, 418, 478
Salvadori, Maj. Mario, 477
Salvage, Sgt V. C. (40 Sqn), 431
Salzmann, Gefr G., 309
Samery, PM G., 234
Sammartano, Tenente A. (Gruppo
43), 467
Sammells, Sgt A. F. W. (40 Sqn),
469
Sammels, F/Lt H. C. (105 Sqn),
246, 269
Sample, F/Lt Johnny, 149, 183, 210
Sandall, Sgt J. F. (44 Sqn), 458
Sandberg, 2e Lt B., 236
Sanders, AC2 A. W. B., 145
Sanders, F/Lt J. G. (615 Sqn), 304,
309, 497
Sanders, P/O Richard A. (145/87
Sqn), 331, 519, 520
Sanders, S/Ldr P. J. 'Judy' (92
Sqn), 363

Sandmann, Oberlt K-H. (8./JG3),
441
Sands, Sgt J. C., 231
Sandstede, Oberlt R. (KG54), 328
Sannemann, Lt Heinrich (Stab
II./JG3), 358
Sannier, Sgt (GBA II/54), 440
Sarll, F/O J. C. G., 272
Saron, Adjt, 95
Sartor, Gefr B. (4./KG51), 409
Sass, Oberfw (2./JG2), 432
Sassard, Lt (GC II/6), 260, 263, 447
Sasse, Oberfw A. (5./LG1), 393
Satchell, LAC, 148
Satge, S/Lt, 278
Sättele, Fw J. (5./KG76), 448
Sattelmacher, Gefr A., 211
Saudry, Adjt K., 98
Sauer, Fw H. (Stab II./LG1), 337
Sauer, Obergefr W. (3.(F)/121),
341
Sauer, Oberlt H. (KG54), 329
Sauer, Oberlt H-H. (Stab KG28),
342
Sauer, Oberlt K. (1./KG53), 336
Sauer, Oberlt R. (3.(F)/22), 262
Sauer, Uffz Kurt (7. & 9./JG53),
104, 416
Sauerborn, Oberfw A. (1.(H)/13),
456
Saueressig, Obergefr O. (9./KG1),
342
Saulou, Adjt (GB I/34), 273, 340
Saunders, Andy, 125, 437
Saunders, F/Lt (65 Sqn), 359, 376
Saunders, P/O G. C. (87 Sqn), 181,
212, 268
Saunders, P/O J. R. (150 Sqn), 99
Saunders, P/O R. L. (57 Sqn), 345
Saunders, P/O W. A. (21 Sqn), 469
Saunders, Sgt R. J. (107 Sqn), 345
Saure, Oberfw H. (7./KG4), 327
Saurt, Cpl, 260
Sausser, Sgt, 325
Saussine, Lt Yves (GB II/12), 432
Saussol, Adjt R. (GC III/1), 214,
315, 336, 374, 375
Sauttler, Uffz E., 138
Sauvage, S/Lt (GC III/3), 336
Sauvage, Sgt (ECMJ 1/16), 273
Savage, Lt (801 FAA Sqn), 487
Savasse, Sgt Gérard de Monts de
(GR I/36), 426
Savill, P/O N. A., 248
Sawade, Oberlt F-W., 254
Sawallisch, Fw O. (2./JG27), 244,
299, 405
Sayers, F/O A. J., 97
Sazenhofen-Fuchsberg, Lt E. von,
253
Scavizzi, S/Lt P. (GB I/31), 400
Schaaf, Uffz R. (7./KG4), 327
Schaal, Gefr A., 134
Schaarschmidt, Fw W., 208
Schaarschmidt, Uffz R., 315
Schablowski, Uffz G., 318
Schacht, Oberlt E., 262
Schachtebeck, Oberfw H., 208
Schade, Fw E., 214
Schade, Lt K. (9./JG2), 418
Schade, Uffz R., 225
Schadl, Obergefr J., 158
Schädlich, Fw H., 208
Schaefer, Hptmn A. Dr
(5.(F)/122), 154
Schaefer, Oberlt F-W. (Stab
StG1), 453
Schaezler, Oberlt D. von, 239
Schäfer, Fw (2.(F)/22), 315
Schäfer, Fw A. (9./KG27), 327
Schäfer, Gefr F. (3./KG3), 381
Schäfer, Oberlt H-C. (5./JG27),
180, 233, 327
Schäfer, Uffz A. (7./KG51), 212
Schaffner, Lt R. (Stab III./StG2),
429
Schäkel, Uffz W., 278
Schalkhausser, Uffz K., 309
Schallenberg, Oberlt W. (KG51),
328

Schaller, Uffz J., 278
Schalles, Uffz W. (9./KG27), 413
Schamberger, Uffz O. (Stab
I./ZG1), 376
Schamhart, Sgt H. C., 236
Schansky, Oberlt, 224
Schär, Gefr O., 207
Scharf, Uffz H., 209
Scharff, Fw H., 225
Scharfscheer, Uffz W. (8./KG53),
470
Scharroo, Kol, 266
Schaschek, Gefr K., 223
Schätzel, Uffz (1./JG76), 433
Schaufelberger, Lt, 141
Schaumann, Oberlt F-W. (9./LG1),
489
Schäzler, Oberlt D. von
(2.(F)/123), 441
Scheels, Lt, 225
Scheepens, 2e Lt G. J. E., 194
Scheffler, Lt L., 239
Scheibe, Obergefr. J., 205
Scheid, Obergefr K. (KG54), 329
Scheithauer, Fw H., 290
Schelcher, Oberlt (Stab I./JG21),
359
Schellack, Uffz F., 262
Scheller, Fw E. (KGzbV.1), 229
Scheller, Fw W. (KG3), 253
Schellmann, Hptmn K-H.
(6./KG55), 317
Schellmann, Hptmn (Stab II./JG2),
320, 405
Schemm, Uffz G. von (7./ZG26),
343
Schemmel, Maj. P., 213
Schenk, Lt (1./ZG1) W., 280, 301
Schenk, Lt (Swiss Fl.Komp.15),
409
Schenk, Uffz O. (KüFlGr.106), 95
Schenkelberg, Fw A., 301
Schenkenberg, Obergefr Helmut,
241
Schentke, Uffz (III./JG3), 445
Scherber, Gefr H. (6./StG77), 393
Scherer, Fw, 136
Scherer, Gefr A., 206
Scherer, Lt (3./JG27), 352
Scherl, Fw A., 279
Scherm, Gefr J., 98, 108
Scherzinger, Oberlt W., 280
Schetelig, Lt W. (5./JG2), 294, 380
Schettler, Fw K., 289
Scheuermann, Uffz K. (8./JG2),
359
Scheunemann, Fw J. (3./KG27), 429
Scheurich, Oberlt K., 206
Scheurich, Uffz R., 212
Schewe, Fw G., 279
Schewe, Gefr L. (KG54), 329
Schidlitzki, Obergefr A., 120
Schieckel, Oberlt G., 117
Schied, Oberfw (9./KG55), 414
Schieferstein, Uffz K. (2./ZG1),
410
Schiel, Fw P-K., 209
Schiemer, Lt H-F., 298
Schien, Uffz H., 253
Schierhold, Lt H., 206
Schierholz, Lt H., 124
Schiffer, Uffz M. (5./KG55), 353
Schiffrer, Lt, 229
Schild, Uffz F., 239
Schildt, Oberfw H. (Stab KG76),
434
Schildt, Uffz G., 278
Schiller, Uffz (2.(J)/LG2), 417
Schiller, Uffz H. (11.(St)/LG1), 290
Schilling, Fw H., 208
Schilling, Fw W., 167
Schillings, Uffz R. (3.(F)/11), 365
Schimmelpfennig, Lt (4.(H)/12),
434
Schimmelpfennig, Lt
(I.(St)/TrGr.186), 376
Schimpl, Oberfw J., 240
Schindler, Fw H. (Stab StG2), 242
Schindler, Gefr W. (Stab I./KG51),
429

Schindler, Uffz E. (KGzbV.1), 229
Schindler, Uffz G. (Stab KG4), 336
Schirm, Uffz E. (3./KG1), 353
Schirmer, Gefr F., 206
Schirmer, Hptmn U. (Stab
III./KG27), 347
Schirmer, Oberfw Herbert, 278
Schirmer, Uffz, 254
Schirr, Oberfw H., 252
Schirrmacher, Uffz H., 164
Schirrmann, Gefr W. (1./KGr.126),
343
Schiweck, Uffz K., 208
Schlafke, Oberlt, 289
Schlandt, Obergefr H., 262
Schlapp, Oberfw B., 120
Schlegel, Gefr R., 209
Schlegel, Uffz K-W. (2./KGr.126),
467
Schlender, Obergefr G., 290
Schletz, Oberlt (Stab KG54), 462
Schlicht, Uffz W. (3./KG2), 470
Schlichting, Oberlt Ulrich
(4.(H)/22), 434
Schlichting, Uffz F. (Stab
II./KG27), 210
Schlick, Oberfw H., 225
Schlimpert, Uffz H. (7./KG55), 343
Schliwa, Oberfw H., 208
Schlöffel, Uffz H. (1./StG2), 414
Schloms, Obergefr H., 290
Schlosser, Uffz W. (4./KG1), 419
Schlotter, Oberfw F., 207
Schlumpberger, Uffz W., 308
Schlupp, Uffz F. (8./KG51), 382
Schmahl, Gefr Hans-Joachim, 241
Schmale, Oberfw, 161
Schmalzbauer, Fw F. (4./KG76), 418
Schmaus, Uffz W., 223
Schmeis, Uffz W., 208
Schmelz, Fw H., 210
Schmetzer, Uffz (TrGr.186), 392
Schmid, Fw F. (KG), 207
Schmid, Fw H. (Stab I./KG76), 418
Schmid, Fw K. (1./JG51), 97, 320,
334, 356
Schmid, Fw K. (1./JG77), 148
Schmid, Lt (2./JG53), 400
Schmid, Lt (I./ZG52), 379
Schmid, Oberfw (I./JG2), 311, 334,
396
Schmid, Oberlt H. (Stab KG27),
382
Schmidt, Flgr J. (8./KG55), 290
Schmidt, Fw H. (3./KG55), 383
Schmidt, Fw H. (KG30), 402
Schmidt, Fw H-J.
(AufklGr.ObdL), 206
Schmidt, Fw W. (2./KG76), 442
Schmidt, Fw W. (2.(F)/122), 110
Schmidt, Gefr H. (7./KG53), 328
Schmidt, Gefr K. (8./KG30), 300
Schmidt, Gefr K-H. (StG2), 242
Schmidt, Gefr W. (7./KG3), 381
Schmidt, Genlt Rudolf (XXXIX
Armeekorps), 266
Schmidt, Lt D. (5./KG76), 448
Schmidt, Lt G. (St)/LG1, 265
Schmidt, Lt J. (GC I/1), 274, 297,
340
Schmidt, Lt K-H. (KüFlGr. 906),
241
Schmidt, Lt K-H. von (7./KG1),
206
Schmidt, Lt O. (3.(F)/123), 380
Schmidt, Lt Reinhard (KGrzbV.9),
226
Schmidt, Lt S. (I./JG21), 249, 347
Schmidt, Lt S. (I./JG27), 347
Schmidt, Lt W. (8./JG3), 256, 321,
359, 437, 440
Schmidt, Oberfw (I./JG2), 274
Schmidt, Oberfw W. (2./KG53),
279
Schmidt, Oberfw Willi
(KGrzbV.12), 222
Schmidt, Obergefr E. (Stab
KG54), 328
Schmidt, Obergefr H.
(14.(Z)/LG1), 309

Schmidt, Obergefr Herbert (KGrzbV.11), 221
Schmidt, Oberlt G. (5./ZG1), 459
Schmidt, Oberlt G. (6./KG54), 414
Schmidt, Oberlt H. (Stab KG27), 488
Schmidt, Oberlt (II./KG1), 316
Schmidt, Uffz A. (Stab II./KG51), 498
Schmidt, Uffz E. (2./KG53), 279
Schmidt, Uffz E. (III./KG55), 153
Schmidt, Uffz Ed (3./KGrzbV.9), 226
Schmidt, Uffz Erich (3./KGrzbV.9), 226
Schmidt, Uffz F. (8./KG27), 327
Schmidt, Uffz G. (4./KG76), 317
Schmidt, Uffz H. (12.(St)LG1), 309
Schmidt, Uffz J. (1./LG1), 241
Schmidt, Uffz J. (6./KG55), 263
Schmidt, Uffz K. (3./KG1), 470
Schmidt, Uffz K. (AufklSt zbv), 239
Schmidt, Uffz R. (JG53), 100
Schmidt, Wachtmstr J. (2.(H)/23), 476
Schmied, Gefr F. (Stab KG55), 419
Schmitt, Fw (2./JG51), 349
Schmitt, Gefr H. (8./KG1), 278
Schmitt, S/Lt (GAO 1/506), 112
Schmitt, Uffz F. (LG1), 309
Schmitt, Uffz J. (8./KG4), 289
Schmitt, Uffz Josef (2./JG51), 396
Schmitter, Cmdt, 306
Schmitz, Uffz Carl (KGrzbV.12), 222
Schmitz, Fw (2.(J)/LG2), 322
Schmitz, Oberlt J. (Stab KG53), 212
Schmitz, Uffz H. (2./KGrzbV.9), 225
Schmitz, Uffz H. (9./LG2), 301
Schmitz, Uffz J. (KG27), 316
Schmitz, Uffz K. (KG30), 300
Schmoller-Haldy, Oberlt (3./JG54), 386, 390
Schmollinger, Fw A. (4.(H)/21), 375
Schnaase, Oberlt K-J., 206
Schnabel, Lt H. (1./JG3), 326
Schnack, Uffz P., 254
Schnalzger, Uffz M., 229
Schneeberger, Uffz W. (5./KG1), 488
Schnegotzki, Oberfw R., 277
Schneider, Adjt (GC III/10), 275
Schneider, Capt. (GR 1/33), 95
Schneider, Capt. J. (GC I/3), 316, 352
Schneider, Fw L. (3.(F)/22), 117
Schneider, Fw M. (11./KGrzbV.1), 366
Schneider, Fw R. (8./KG3), 208
Schneider, Gefr H. (1./LG1), 214
Schneider, Lt (1./JG1), 469
Schneider, Lt H. (1.(H)/10), 206
Schneider, Maj. Roman (2.(F)/122), 110
Schneider, Oberfw E. (AufklGr.Ob.d.L), 427
Schneider, Obergefr K. (1./LG1), 343
Schneider, Oberlt G. (3./JG21), 199, 247, 364, 374, 376
Schneider, Oberlt H. (KG30), 253
Schneider, Uffz A. (1./JG3), 434
Schneider, Uffz Anton (KGrzbV.12), 222
Schneider, Uffz H. (1./StG2), 242
Schneider, Uffz J. (KGzbV.1), 223
Schneider, Uffz J. (StG77), 280
Schneider, Uffz K. (3./KG51), 278
Schneider, Uffz K. (Stab KG51), 418
Schneider, Uffz U. (2.(H)/12), 441
Schneider, Uffz W. (2./KG4), 316
Schneidmüller, Obergefr H., 114
Schnell, Fw (4./JG2), 272
Schnell, Lt (3./JG20), 458
Schnelle, Maj. O. (Stab III./KG1), 206

Schnez, Oberlt V. (KG51), 328
Schnittersmann, Uffz H., 229
Schnoor, Oberlt, 96
Schöbel, Uffz E. (3.(F)/11), 326
Schödl, Obergefr K. (9./ZG26), 360
Schoenherr, Adjt H. (GB 1/19), 400
Schoeppler, Lt (3./KG53), 476
Schöffler, Uffz W., 318
Scholl, Fw W. (4./LG1), 459
Scholler, Uffz Hans, 300
Scholven, Fw, 148
Scholz, Gefr F. (9./KG53), 240
Scholz, Oberlt (1./JG21), 334, 374
Scholz, Oberlt S. (3./KG27), 429
Scholz, Uffz A. (4./ZG1), 448
Scholz, Uffz W. (6./KG76), 308
Schomann, Oberlt K. H. (9./LG1), 347
Schombroodt, Adjt J., 199
Schön, Fw W., 207
Schön, Lt, 121
Schönberg, Gefr H. (2./LG1), 337
Schönborn, Uffz E., 104
Schöneweiss, Uffz K., 212
Schönhoff, Uffz P., 263
Schöning, Obergefr H., 308
Schönthier, Fw H., 318
Schopf, Uffz A. (5./KG51), 429
Schöpfel, Oberlt (JG26), 321
Schorn, Gefr H. (Aufkl.Gr.Ob.d.L), 335
Schorr, Oberfw K., 316
Schott, Oberfw (2.(J)/LG2), 322, 417
Schoute, 2e Lt P. C., 261
Schouw, 1e Lt J. P., 139, 171
Schöwer, Fw F. (1./KG1), 392
Schrader, Fw K., 158
Schrang, Uffz K., 253
Schraps, Uffz K. (7./KG55), 442
Schreiber, Gefr H. (Stab III./StG2), 448
Schreiber, Lt (1.(H)/14), 459
Schreiber, Uffz E. (8./KG27), 347
Schreiber, Uffz H. (3./KG30), 211
Schreiner, Adjt (GC II/6), 117, 433, 434
Schreiner, Gefr J. (8./KG1), 413
Schreiner, Lt Alexander (4.(F)/14), 315, 318
Schreiter, Uffz F. (3./JG51), 233, 239, 496
Schreiweis, Oberfw A., 290
Schrepfermann, Fw H. (1./KG53), 382
Schreyer, Fw H., 289
Schröder, 1e Lt D., 142
Schröder, Ernst (KGzbV.1), 229
Schröder, Fw E. (2./JG27), 244, 247, 427
Schröder, Fw G. (3.(H)/14), 326
Schröder, Gefr E. (KG30), 211
Schroder, Gefr J-D. (KGzbV.1), 241
Schröder, Obergefr B. (KG2), 208
Schröder, Obergefr H. (1./KG54), 360
Schröder, Obergefr W. (1./KGr.126), 343
Schröder, Oberlt W. (7./StG2), 477
Schröder, Uffz H. (3.(F)/122), 123
Schröpfer, Uffz M., 299
Schröter, Obergefr H. (3./ZG2), 376
Schrutek, Uffz H., 120
Schube, Lt W., 133
Schubert, Lt K. (5./KG76), 366
Schubert, Obergefr W. (3./KG3), 252
Schubert, Uffz E. (7./KG4), 209
Schubert, Uffz G. (6./KG2), 300
Schubert, Uffz W. (3./KG1), 470
Schubert, Uffz W. (8./KG55), 414
Schuckliess, Uffz P. (3./KG1), 448
Schuderer, Fw L. (9./KG55), 414
Schuh, Uffz P., 239
Schuhbauer, Uffz J., 93
Schuldt, Uffz K-H., 253
Schulenburg, Oberlt Graf von der, 307

Schuler, Fw W. (3./KG3), 418
Schuler, Oberlt von, 251
Schüll, Uffz V., 278
Schüller, Lt H., 148
Schulte, Uffz H-G. (7. & 8./JG53), 114, 419
Schulte-Frohlinde, Hptmn J. (Stab KG2), 381
Schulte-Umberg, Fw W., 162
Schulten, Lt B., 308
Schultheiss, Fw A. (KG54), 329
Schultz, 1e Lt R. E. van Duyl, 250
Schultz, Uffz G. (6./ZG26), 493
Schultze, Lt H. (LG1), 254
Schulz, Fähnrich J. (3.(F)/121), 117
Schulz, Gefr F. (KG51), 328
Schulz, Gefr W. (3.(F)/22), 119
Schulz, Lt G. (2./KGr.126), 467
Schulz, Lt Heinz (JG76), 118, 119
Schulz, Maj. L. (Stab I./KG76), 418
Schulz, Oberprüfer O., 117
Schulz, Uffz J. (KG27), 239
Schulz, Uffz O. (KG28), 263
Schulze, Fw R. (1./ZG1), 376
Schulze, Obergefr E. (6./ZG1), 242, 434
Schulze, Obergefr H. (8./KG51), 414
Schulze, Uffz (1.(H)/14), 298
Schulze, Uffz Rudi (6./KG4), 327, 328
Schulze, Uffz W. (2./KG53), 290
Schulze-Blanck, Oberlt G., 100, 307
Schülze-Wimken, Lt R., 254
Schulzki, Oberfw M. (3./KG51), 414
Schumacher, Lt (4.(H)/22), 380
Schumann, Gefr R. (7./KG2), 493
Schumann, Hptmn M. (9./KG4), 360
Schumann, Oberlt (5./JG52), 273
Schumann, Oberlt F. J. (2.(H)/23), 347
Schumann, Oberlt H. (1.(H)/21), 476
Schümann, Uffz O., 308
Schünemann, Oberlt (2.(H)/21), 392
Schuster, Oberlt G., 239
Schütt, Oberfw K., 262
Schütz, Fw W. (Stab I./KG76), 418
Schütz, Lt E. (Stab I./JG54), 133
Schütz, Oberlt W. (2./KG27), 121
Schutz, S/Lt (GR II/33), 396
Schütz, Uffz K. (LNRegt.3), 381
Schuurman, Johan, 225
Schwab, Uffz N. (5./KG76), 448
Schwabedissen, Lt H., 309
Schwankert, Oberlt F., 300
Schwär, Uffz E., 239
Schwartz, Lt H-J., 209
Schwartzkopff, Oberstlt Günther, 280
Schwarz, Fw T., 253
Schwarz, Hptmn B. (3./KG53), 476
Schwarz, Oberlt Ernst, 309
Schwarze, Lt W., 309
Schwarze, Oberfw K., 241
Schwarzer, Lt G., 301
Schwarzkopf, Fw W. (3.(F)/11), 365
Schwede, Oberfw Fritz, 252, 253
Schweiger, Fw J. (5./KG77), 477
Schweighart, Uffz A. (1./KG53), 336
Schweinoch, Uffz W., 162
Schwender, Uffz Ludwig, 206
Schwengber, Fw A., 239
Schwenk, Fw E., 136
Schweser, Uffz F., 158
Schwickart, Oberfw S. (5./KG2), 476
Schwilden, Hptmn Horst, 206
Schwind, Sgt G. L. (59 Sqn), 372
Schwinn, Gefr W. (3./KG55), 383
Scitivaux, EV1 Philippe de, 188
Scott, LAC E. R. (235 Sqn), 390
Scott, LAC J. (15 Sqn), 248
Scott, P/O D. S. Don 'Scotty' (73 Sqn), 48, 65, 68, 70, 256, 262, 290

Scott, P/O E. W. S. (616 Sqn), 386, 419
Scott, P/O H. (264 Sqn), 382, 386
Scott, P/O L. D. M. (145 Sqn), 406
Scott, S/Ldr W. I. (139 Sqn), 246
Scott, Sgt A. E. (73 Sqn), 356
Scotte, S/Lt P. (GC I/5), 208, 260, 262, 417
Scotter, P/O (2 Sqn), 362
Scouezec, SM (AC 2), 481
Scoular, F/Lt John 'Ian' (73 Sqn), 12, 28, 41, 49, 52, 53, 56, 59, 61, 68, 70, 71, 120, 290, 328, 436
Scourzic, Adjt, 103
Sculfer, Sgt J. M. (21 Sqn), 458
Sczepaniak, Flgr F. (9./KG55), 353
Seale, Sgt, 294
Sébire, SM (T 2), 492
Sedgwick, Sgt A. F., 272
Sedlak, Fw H., 213
Seeba, Gefr M., 241
Seeckt, Gen. Hans von, 86
Seefeldt, Uffz Wilhelm, 315, 318
Seeger, Uffz G., 167
Seegert, Lt J., 133
Seehase, Lt K., 301
Seel, Lt W., 206
Seelenmeyer, Gefr K., 214
Seepold, Lt K., 138
Segeat, Sgt (GB I/62), 374
Seggelke, Uffz H. (2.(F)/122), 496
Segschneider, Maj. J. (KG54), 328
Seguela, Adjt M. (GR II/33), 359
Séguin, Lt E. (GB I/62), 461
Seguin, Sgt G. (GB 2/15), 395
Sehlmacher, Fw H. (2.(F)/11), 456
Sehr, Gefr H. (16./KGzbV.1), 396
Seib, Uffz F., 226
Seidel, Obergefr P. (8./ZG26), 301
Seidel, Obergefr R. (LnRegt.3), 381
Seidel, Uffz H. (KG51), 278
Seidel, Uffz H. (KGrzbV.9), 225
Seidenglanz, Uffz W., 223
Seidler, Uffz M. (7./JG3), 441
Seifart, Uffz H. (8./KG2), 252, 327
Seifer, Uffz H., 208
Seifert, Fw F., 388
Seifert, Oberfw (KGrzbV.9), 225
Seifert, Oberlt J. (3./JG26), 192, 385, 445, 451, 452
Seiffert, Uffz K. (3.(F)/22), 97
Seiler, Oberlt, 133, 157
Seipel, Uffz R., 214
Seith, Uffz A. (2.(F)/122), 496
Seitz, Uffz K. (1./KG54), 360
Selck, Uffz Bruno (Stab III./StG2), 429
Seldon, Sgt George E., 256, 520
Sell, Uffz G. (2.(F)/123), 441
Selle, Hptmn von (Stab II./JG3), 331, 424
Selle, Uffz B., 213
Selva, Lt (GB I/62), 432
Sempert, Uffz S., 300
Senciel, Adjt (GB II/11), 466
Senet, Adjt E. (GC I/6), 341, 425
Senft, Uffz H. (KG54), 328
Senior, LAC J. C., 180
Senne, Adjt, 95
Senoner, Lt (3./JG20), 458
Senot de la Londe, Sgt, 94
Sepet, Adjt, 165
Seppell, Oberlt (3.(H)/41), 335
Septroux, Sgt R., 196
Sère, Adjt G. (GB 1/21), 358
Serra, Sgt, 249
Servais, Sgt (GB II/12), 334
Service, Sgt (53 Sqn), 303
Servier, Adjt D. (GB 2/15), 395
Sesner, Uffz (3./KG2), 381
Seubert, Oberlt G. (4./KG54), 414
Sève, Sgt (GR II/55), 334
Sewell, AC1 H. B., 245
Sewell, Sgt Donald A., 15, 46, 50, 52, 131, 144
Seyfert, Uffz G., 228
Seynes, S/Lt de (GC II/6), 429
Sharpe, AC2 John A., 153, 502, 521

Shaw, AC1 Clifford G., 268, *522*
Shaw, P/O Richard E. (59 Sqn), 372
Shaw, S/Ldr John, 372
Shawyers, Sgt (40 Sqn), 469
Sheldrick, AC, 311
Shelton, Sgt (59 Sqn), 362
Shelton-Jones, Sgt C. (12 Sqn), 267
Shepherd, LAC, 180
Shepherd, P/O J. A. (1 Sqn), 423
Shepley, F/Lt G. R. (16 Sqn), 378, 398
Shirer, William, *496*
Shone, Sgt E. (12 Sqn), 436
Shorthouse, P/O J. S. (12 Sqn), 423, 464
Shortland, Sgt W. O., 247
Shrewsbury, P/O R. W. (85 Sqn), 331
Shrosbree, Sgt K. N., 180
Shuttleworth, AC1 J. (57 Sqn), 159
Shuttleworth, AC1 R. (57 Sqn), 256
Sibiril-Lefèbre, Sgt J. (GC II/9), 417
Sibley, P/O S. A. C., 272
Sichart, Lt H-U. von, 167
Sichtar, Gefr K. (KG54), 329
Sicking, Oberfw, 320
Sidow, Lt (9./ZG26), 374
Siebeck, Uffz, 103
Siebel, Oberlt (Stab KG3), 366
Siedentopf, Fw H., 265
Siegemund, Uffz H. (5./JG27), 453
Sieger, Uffz C., 114
Siegfried, Lt Günther (3./KG53), 409, *410*
Siegle, Fw H. (16./KGzbV.1), 396
Siegle, Fw M. (4./KG53), 253
Siems, Uffz H. (6./StG77), 393
Sievers, Lt F., 162
Sigel, Maj. W., 279
Sigurdson, F/O S. L. (21 Sqn), 458
Sika, Cpl (GC I/8), 307, 308, 366
Siller, Gefr A. (KG51), 328
Silvan, S/Lt (GC I/3), 417
Simeoni, Sgt (GB 2/15), 395
Simmons, F/Lt P. H. A. (110 Sqn), 345
Simmons, F/O R. C. (37 Sqn), 405
Simmons, Sgt S. F. (57 Sqn), 345
Simon, Sgt (ECMJ 1/16), 273
Simon, Sgt (GB II/35), 416
Simon, Uffz G., 170
Simon Gefr J., 221
Simon, Uffz O., 212
Simpson, F/Lt (43 Sqn), 441
Simpson, F/Lt William (12 Sqn), 180, 271
Simpson, P/O (229 Sqn), 318, 342
Simpson, Sgt (12 Sqn), 423
Simpson, Sgt C. (57 Sqn), 158
Simpson, Sgt J. (44 Sqn), 458
Sims, LAC A. G. (82 Sqn), 304
Sims, Sgt (110 Sqn), 446
Sinclair, P/O (19 Sqn), 410
Singeot, Sgt, 309
Sinn, Lt H., 159, 280
Sipkes, Sgt, 119
Sirlin, Obergefr G. (7./LG1), 429
Sisterhenn, Uffz J. (Stab I./ZG52), 419
Sitter, Lt H. B., 276
Sixtus, Uffz O., 229
Sizer, P/O W. M. (213 Sqn), 326, 332, 335, 393, 399
Skelton, F/Lt George F. A., 257, *258*
Skibinski, S/Lt B. (GC I/145), 452
Skidmore, P/O B. I. M., 232
Skinner, F/Lt Malcolm P., 124, *523*
Slade, AC2 W. G. (150 Sqn), 322
Slater, 1e Lt H. A. J. Huddleston, 192
Slee, P/O G. W., 233
Sleen, J. van der, 138
Slocombe, Sgt A. V. (235 Sqn), 390
Slomka, Uffz F., 456
Slouf, Cpl V. (GC III/3), 265, 325, 326

Sluijter, 1e Lt N. W., 192
Smalley, Sgt M. D., 267
Smart, P/O T. (65 Sqn), 347, 359, 385
Smeddle, F/Lt H. L., 184
Smet, Capt. (GAO 510), 380
Smiley, P/O J. W. (242 Sqn), 351
Smit, Sgt J., 104
Smith, Cpl L. (226 Sqn), 183
Smith, F/O (610 Sqn), 381
Smith, F/O Michael F. C. (501 Sqn), 247, *524*
Smith, LAC (48 Sqn), 395
Smith, LAC (110 Sqn), 345
Smith, LAC (500 Sqn), 398
Smith, LAC A. G. (235 Sqn), 184
Smith, Mary (now Lalonde), *524*
Smith, P/O N. A. L. (235 Sqn), 248
Smith, P/O P. D. (18 Sqn), 134, 180, 311
Smith, S/Ldr L. E. (607 Sqn), 257, 262, 283
Smith, Sgt F. L. (18 Sqn), 131
Smith, Sgt T. D. (103 Sqn), 181
Smithers, F/Lt G. V., 232, 293
Smits, Wachtm. W. P., 250
Smoolenaars, 2e Lt A. H., 191
Smythe, Sgt G. (56 Sqn), 379
Snitslaar, 1e Lt A. D., 193
Sodemann, Oberlt K. (9./LG1), 489
Soden, F/Lt Ian S., 303, 308, 311, 315, 317, *525*
Soest, H. W. van, 206
Soete, Sgt Albert, 286, *287*
Sognet, Lt (GAO 1/506), 380
Sohler, Oberlt K., 254
Söhner, Uffz H. (8./KG55), 414
Soldau, Fw K., 211
Solluch, Uffz G. (13.(Z)/LG1), 343
Solminihac, S/Lt de (GC II/3), 466
Soltner, Lt J. (GB I/21), 446
Somedecoste, Sgt, 296
Sommer, Lt (9./KG4), 476
Sommer, Oberfw K. (Stab KG3), 208
Sommerfeld, Uffz K., 388
Sommerla, Fw A., 288
Sommesous, Sgt P. (GB 2/31), 334
Sonderman, 2e Lt G., 193, 228
Songest, Sgt N. M. (77 Sqn), 458
Sonneveld, Sgt M. W., 250
Sonntag, Sgt (GC II/7), 145
Sonntag, Uffz H. (1./KG1), 393
Sonntag, Uffz H. (6./KG77), 301
Soper, F/Sgt R. G. T. (500 Sqn), 390
Soper, Sgt F. J. (1 Sqn), *108*, 120, 133, 145, *146*, 147, 208, 242, 244, 303, 320
Sordet, Sgt, 249
Sorge, Hptmn H. (2.(H)/31), 481
Souche, Adjt, 286, 306
Souffrée, Sgt H. F., 193, 209
Soulimont, SM (AC 3), 472
Southwell, P/O J. S. (245 Sqn), 304, 396
Southwood, Sgt P. McK., 270
Soutif, Sgt H., 284
Souviat, S/Lt (GC I/55), 495
Souza, P/O K. M. A. de, 295
Sowada, Uffz H., 208
Spacek, Cpl O. (GC I/8), 235, 462
Spagnolo, Lt J., 188
Sparks, Sgt N. J. (500 Sqn), 465
Spatscheck, Fw G. (6./KG53), 376
Speake, Sgt Bert, *44*, *46*
Spear, AC H. (53 Sqn), 349
Spear, Sgt A. N. (142 Sqn), 182, 271
Specht, Lt G. (I./ZG26), 354
Speck, Gefr J. (4.(F)/122), 380
Speck, Uffz H., 262
Speer, Albert, *454*
Speich, Adjt, 274
Speidel, Gen. Wilhelm, 216
Spencer, AC1 F. T. (12 Sqn), 267
Spencer, LAC J. (78 Sqn), 356
Spencer, P/O W. G. (57 Sqn), 268
Spencer, Sgt A. (40 Sqn), 431

Spencer, Sgt D. D. G. (38 Sqn), 398
Spencer, Sgt R. (15 Sqn), 458
Spengler, Uffz V., 211
Spenner, Lt M., 152
Sperat, S/Lt L. (GC II/10), 441
Sperrle, Genmaj. Hugo, 86, 87
Spickermann, Uffz F., 327
Spiegel, Gefr H. Fr. von (6./KG55), 263
Spiegel, Lt zur See H. (1./KGr.126), 353
Spiegelberg, Fw E. (1./KG1), 360
Spiers, P/O G W. (254 Sqn), 405
Spies, Fw R. (6./KG2), 476
Spiess, Gefr H. (4./KG51), 409
Spiewack, Oberfw A. (Stab KG55), 429
Spillmann, Oberlt H., 277
Spitta, Uffz O. (1./StG2), 448
Spohr, Oberfw H., 213
Sponeck, Genlt Hans von, 216, 218, 219, 226
Spoo, Fw E. R., 327
Sprenger, Flgr K., 253
Sprenger, Lt, 284
Spreter, Oberfw J., 278
Sprick, Lt G. (8./JG26), 409, 464, 470
Spring, Uffz F. im (3./StG76), 470
Springett, Sgt G. J., 99
Sprink, Fw O., 208
Sprung, Obergefr E. (6./KG54), 414
Spura, Uffz K. (8./KG30), 347
Spurr, Sgt V., 184
Staal, Sgt J., 194
Stachowiak, Uffz R., 254
Stadelmayr, Hptmn Fritz, *212*, 213
Stadler, Fw F., 242
Stadler, Fw G., 253
Staege, Oberfw (2.(J)/LG2), 322, 417
Staege, Oberlt B. (9./KG1), 342
Staffler, Flgr J. (7./KG3), 381
Stahl, Fw A., 211
Stahl, Oberfw, 234
Stahn, Uffz F. (2./JG1), 479
Staiger, Lt H., 163
Stampa, Sgt M. P. de (GR I/36), 325
Stampfer, Uffz M., 289
Standera, Sgt (GC I/6), 458
Stanford, Sgt J. R., 284
Stange, Lt (3./JG3), 275, 341, 464
Stangl, Lt (I./JG76), 314, 425
Stangl, Uffz J., 280
Stanhope, AC1 B. B. (37 Sqn), 372
Stanley, Sgt R. J., 150
Stansfeld, P/O N. K. (242 Sqn), 469, 470
Stapelberg, Fw M. (6./LG1), 393
Stapleton, P/O W. (41 Sqn), 406
Stark, Fw A., 270, 277
Starke, Sgt R., 249, 298, 307, 476, 495
Starker, Fw W. (5./KG2), 476
Starre, Sgt P. A. van der, 107
Staub, Oberfw E., 254
Staub, Sgt (DAT Tours), 387
Staudenraus, Oberlt Hans, 265
Staudinger, Oberlt W. (1.(H)/23), 427
Stäudner, Gefr E., 240
Stauffenberg, Lt, 300
Stavert, P/O C. M., 311
Stead, Sgt (103 Sqn), 423
Stechardt, Fw W. (7./KG4), 327
Stecher, Oberlt K. (2.(F)/11), 456
Steeger, Fw H-O. (9./KG4), 467
Steeger, Fw O. (3.(H)/41), 315
Steen, 2e Lt G., 194
Steenbeck, 2e Lt N., 191
Steenbergen, 1e Lt B. van, 193
Steensma, Sgt C. Ch., 192, 250
Steere, F/Sgt H. (19 Sqn), 388, 406
Stefanski, Uffz S., 308
Steffen, Fw W., 300
Steffen, Obergefr W., 215
Steffen, Uffz Oskar, 224

Stegemann, Oberfw A. (13.(Z)/LG1), 343
Stegmann, Fw G. (4.(H)/21), 476
Stehlik, Sgt Josef, 315
Steidle, Oberlt (Stab III./JG2), 433
Steildé, Sgt C., 286
Stein, 2e Lt W. H., 191
Stein, Gefr G. (6./KG2), 278
Stein, Hptmn G. (KGr.126), 343
Stein, Uffz G. (Stab II./KG51), 366
Stein Fw H. (1./KGrzbV.9), 223
Steinberg, Uffz F., 212
Steinberger, Lt S. (1.(H)/12), 479
Steinbock, Uffz A., 251
Steinbrück, Uffz O. (4./KG4), 448
Steincke, Uffz H. (9./KG1), 495
Steiner, Fw, 239
Steiner, Gefr A., 290
Steingräber, Lt R., 253
Steinhagen, Gefr H. (9./LG1), 376
Steinhagen, Uffz J. (AufklSt.z.b.V.), 365
Steinhoff, Oberlt (11.(N)/JG2), 180
Steinhoff, Uffz E. (5./KG27), 382
Steinleitner, Gefr J. (2./KG51), 489
Steinweg, Oberlt, 213
Stelzer, Lt H., 289
Stengel, Lt W. (3.(St)/TrGr.186), 410
Stengel, Obergefr B. (5./KG55), 429
Stephan, Obergefr E., 209
Stephan, Uffz H. (JG3), 326
Stephani, Uffz O. (5./KG76), 347
Stephen, P/O (74 Sqn), 359, 371, 381
Stephens, F/O J. W. (107 Sqn), 412
Stephens, P/O M. M. (3 Sqn), 254, 267, 335
Stephens, Sgt W. J. (15 Sqn), 313, 339
Stephenson, S/Ldr G. D. (19 Sqn), *372*, 373
Stephenson, Sgt G. (226 Sqn), 256
Sterbacouk, Lt (DAT Chartres), 407
Stern, Fw G., 126
Stern, Oberfw H. (Stab KG55), 429
Stern, Sonderf. Fritz, 162
Steudel, Lt (8./KG2), 381
Steudel, Oberlt Wolfgang (1.(H)/14), *307*
Steuer, Oberlt, 279
Steuernagel, Uffz L. (4./KG2), 456
Steunou, S/Lt, 158, 278
Steussloff, Uffz E., 239
Stevenel, Sgt, 259
Stevener, Uffz F. (4.(H)/22), 359
Stevens, LAC, 119
Stevenson, P/O J. W. B. (266 Sqn), 412
Stevenson, P/O Paddy C. F. (74 Sqn), 379
Steward, Sgt (17 Sqn), 381
Stewart, F/O A. C. (57 Sqn), 158
Stewart, Oliver, *34*
Stewart, P/O, 124
Stewart, P/O G. M. (242 Sqn), 399
Stewart, P/O G. McK. (607 Sqn), 254, 304, 315
Stichel, Oberfw E. (Stab IV.(St)/LG1), 470
Sticht, Uffz J., 133
Sticka, Cpl F. (GC I/4), 433
Stidtson, P/O A. F. (107 Sqn), 465
Stier, Fw G. (1./KG1), 393
Stiller, Uffz M., 265
Stiquel, Lt A. (GC I/4), 308, 374
Stizzel, Sgt, 188
Stobbe, Oberfw F. (6./LG1), 393
Stobbe, Uffz Erwin (5./KG54), *383*, *387*
Stöcker, Lt W. (9./KG2), 381
Stoddart, F/Lt K. M. (611 Sqn), 412
Stokell, LAC W. (107 Sqn), 345
Stokes, P/O R. W. (264 Sqn), 399
Stokes, Sgt (139 Sqn), 134
Stoldt, Oberlt W., 279

Stoll, Lt Jakob (9./JG53), 112, 129, 401, 405, 416
Stolle, Oberfw W. (4./KG3), 381
Stolle, Uffz H., 208
Stolte, Lt P-A., 157
Stolz, Fw E., 299
Stölzel, Obergefr E., 209
Stölzle, Fw K. (1./KG51), 493
Stone, F/O C. A. C. (3 Sqn), 251, 282, 289
Stone, P/O (26 Sqn), 390
Stone, P/O Laurence G. B. (213 Sqn), 322, 327, 386
Stone, Sgt R. A. M. (15 Sqn), 247, 339
Stones, P/O D. W. A. 'Dimsie' (79 Sqn), 268, 279, 312, 318, 331, 335, 441, 498
Stoovelaar, 2e Lt F. H., 191
Stopp, Oberfw A., 208
Storp, Hptmn W. (8./KG4), 418
Storr, Sgt G., 112
Storrow, Sgt A. R., 273
Stotz, Oberfw (I./JG76), 271, 433
Strach, Gefr E., 212
Strada, Gefr F., 209
Strafford, G/Capt., 166, 170
Strahl, Fw H. (5./KG1), 488
Strahl, Gefr W., 252
Strahlendorf, Uffz D., 229
Strakeljahn, Lt F-W. (LG2), 39, 321
Stramm, Uffz W., 210
Strang, P/O J. T. (253 Sqn), 312, 353
Strange, Lt R. L. (801 FAA Sqn), 398
Strasser, Oberlt R. (KG76), 329
Strassfeld, Uffz W., 136
Stratmann, Uffz E., 171
Stratmann, Uffz F., 213
Stratmann, Uffz J., 213
Stratton, P/O W. H., 127, 154, 256
Straub, Fw J., 290
Strauss, Lt J., 132
Strazzera, Patrice, 467
Strecke, Obergefr W. (4./KG27), 479
Street, LAC W. W., 273
Strehl, Lt H. (1./JG51), 353
Strehler, Fw W., 280
Streibel, Gefr J. (8./KG76), 343
Streiff, Adjt (GC I/2), 240
Streiff, Oberlt (Swiss Fl.Kp.21), 300, 448
Stretz, Uffz S. (KG51), 328
Streubel, Uffz W. (9./KG4), 467
Strickland, F/O J. M. (87 Sqn), 321
Striebeck, Gefr K. (9./KG55), 353
Strien, Jan van, 258
Stritzel, Uffz, 313
Strobel, Oberfw M., 300
Strobl, Lt H. (5./KG77), 327, 464
Strobl, Uffz H. (Stab KG55), 263
Strohauer, Uffz (3./JG54), 390
Strohm, Oberlt U., 251
Strohmaier, Oberfw H., 300
Strohschein, Uffz M., 124
Strohschnitter, Uffz A., 317
Stromberg, Lt H. von (7./StG2), 477
Strothoff, Uffz W. (2./KG55), 376
Strub, Sgt, 113
Strugalla, Uffz Kurt, 224
Strüven, Uffz E., 208
Struwe, Uffz F., 279
Stryde, AC L. H., 99
Strydonck, Sgt van, 149, 168
Strzembosz, S/Lt Wiktor S. (GC II/7), 426
Stuart, F/O Arnold J., 293
Stuart-Harris, Sgt D. T., 270
Stubbs, Sgt P., 112, 134, 233
Stuckey, Sgt Sid G., 44, 46, 68, 69, 136
Student, Genlt Kurt, 86, 133, 216, 217, 220
Stuhler, Fw J., 206
Stühler, Oberfw G., 114
Stühmer, Uffz R. (1./KG76), 418

Stumbler, Lt E. (8./StG51), 376
Stumm, Wachtmeister, 96
Stumpf, Uffz A. (4./ZG76 & Stab II./ZG76), 235, 366
Stumpff, Hans-Jürgen, 86
Stutterheim, Genmaj. W. von, 477
Stuy, 2e Lt J. C. P., 250
Suau, Sgt (GB I/23), 358
Sudres, Lt A. (GB 2/31), 334
Sueur, Lt J., 94
Sulerzycki, Capt. Mieczyslaw (GC III/6), 83, 341
Sullivan, F/Lt J. L., 272
Sullivan, LAC J. P., 272
Summers, AC1 J. E., 98
Summers, Sgt, 270
Summerson, LAC Alan K., 271
Sumpster, F/Sgt C. L. (44 Sqn), 458
Supke, Fw Heinz (9./ZG26), 360
Süptitz, Uffz W. (3./KG2), 381
Surborg, Oberlt Wilhelm, 240
Suschka, Uffz H., 208
Süssmann, Hptmn Gerhard, 222
Sutcliffe, Cpl J. (15 Sqn), 313, 339
Sutherland, Sgt H. R., 248
Sutton, P/O F. B. (56 Sqn), 311, 315
Sutton, P/O K. R. (142 Sqn), 331, 458, 464
Svetlik, Sgt (GC II/5), 392, 476
Swagerman, Lt B., 191, 261
Swift, P/O J. R. (149 Sqn), 458
Swoboda, Fw K. (1./KG51), 493
Sy, Lt Erwin, 214
Sydenham, P/O F. (73 Sqn), 371
Sylvester, P/O E. J. H. (501 Sqn), 253, 273, 362
Symaes, Capt. E., 237
Symonski, Oberlt G. von, 288
Szigat, Uffz H., 254
Sztramko, Sgt K. (GC II/10), 441

Tabas, Lt (GAO 1/589), 440
Tacke, Uffz H., 209
Tacquart, Sgt J., 94
Taghon, Peter, 299, 301, 327, 386, 393
Taille-Trétinville, S/Lt H. de La (GC I/4), 336, 433
Tain, Sgt (GC I/1), 289
Tain, Sgt J. (GC II/9), 341, 358
Tait, F/Lt (103 Sqn), 390
Tait, P/O K. W. (87 Sqn), 168, 317, 335
Takideli, P/O A. (15 Sqn), 461
Talbot, Sgt J. J. F., 165, 293
Talkmann, Oberlt von, 262
Tallec, Adjt L. Le, 121
Tallent, Sgt (GC I/5), 158, 162, 239, 253, 254, 476
Talman, P/O J. M. (88 Sqn), 455, 461
Tamblin, Cpl R. A. (4 Sqn), 339
Tamm, Maj. R., 316
Tanchoux, Sgt (GB I/31), 334
Tanguy, Mt Gabriel (T 3), 459
Tanguy, QM Georges (T 3), 452
Tanguy, S/Lt V. (GC I/8), 307, 417, 418
Tanzberger, Uffz H., 289
Tappe, Uffz P., 316
Tarberry, Gefr M. (9./KG1), 495
Tariel, Lt J. (GC III/1), 210, 314, 315, 493
Tasker, P/O N., 270
Tassel, QM (T 2), 352
Taton, Adjt A., 261
Taucar, Lt F. (7./KG76), 434
Taute, P/O K. D'A. (107 Sqn), 423
Taylor, AC1 W. F. (150 Sqn), 154, 502, 525
Taylor, LAC A. J. (218 Sqn), 271
Taylor, LAC J. (12 Sqn), 436
Taylor, P/O (26 Sqn), 320
Taylor, P/O H. H. (142 Sqn), 322
Taylor, Sgt C. (139 Sqn), 246
Taylor, Sheelagh (now Mrs Tyrell), 525
Taymans, Lt M., 306
Teika, Fw F. (5./KG55), 429

Teillet, Sgt (GC I/1), 288, 289, 307, 336, 434, 495
Teissier, S/Lt (GAO 2/520), 212, 358
Teller, Uffz W., 133
Temme, Lt, 284
Tenin, Sgt P. (GAO 2/514), 488
Tennant, Capt. W. G., 368
Téoulet, Lt A. (GB 2/31), 334
Terral, S/Lt (GAO 518), 475
Terrel, Sgt J., 114
Terrié, Sgt Robert (GB I/62), 374
Terrien, Lt (GB I/23), 358
Terrières, Adjt R. (GB II/23), 447, 456, 466
Terry, Lt (Stab I./JG51), 233, 425
Terse, Sgt, 212
Tertre, Lt du, 93
Tesch, Uffz, 116
Teschner, Gefr K-H., 300
Teske, Obergefr W. (9./KG55), 479
Tesseraud, Adjt (GC II/4), 97, 239, 326, 459
Tessières, EV1 de, 93
Tessmann, Flgr S. (6./LG1), 393
Testu, Sgt, 305
Tetre, S/Lt du (GBA II/51), 470
Teyssier, Sgt, 273
Thabuis, S/Lt L., 306
Thake, Sgt F. V. W.(59 Sqn), 445
Thannberg, Sgt de (GBA II/54), 451
Thate, Lt O., 132
Theil, S/Lt M. de la Porte du, 249
Theisen, Uffz K. (5./ZG26), 318, 329
Thelen, Gefr L., 317
Thelen, Lt F. (KG51), 328
Thénaizié, SM (T 2), 352
Thénard, Adjt, 107
Thévenard, Sgt, 273
Thévinin, Sgt (GR 1/35), 108
Theysen, Adjt E., 286
Thiebault, Adjt (GAR 1/14), 94
Thiebault, Adjt (GR II/52), 325
Thiedemann, Uffz E. (8./KG51), 360
Thiel, Gefr G. (7./KG4), 376
Thiel, Oberlt W. (3.(F)/22), 117
Thiel, Uffz H. (KGzbV.1), 224
Thiele, Gefr H. (3./KG53), 476
Thiele, Obergefr Hermann (1./KGr.126), 353
Thiem, Hptmn E, (5.(S)/LG2), 467
Thieme, Gefr, 366
Thier, Uffz W. (8./KG4), 476
Thierfelder, Uffz H. (2./KG3), 366
Thierry, S/Lt E. (GC I/3), 118, 285
Thierry, Sgt A. (GR II/55), 496
Thierry, Sgt (GR II/52), 249, 325
Thiessen, Oberfhr H-H., 214
Thijssen, Lt J. W., 106
Thiroux, Sgt Arnould (Comte de Gervillier) (GC III/6), 278, 341
Thismar, Uffz K., 309
Thollon, S/Lt (GC III/7), 240
Thollon, S/Lt R. (GC I/8), 213, 235, 290, 418, 434, 476
Thom, F/O D. S. (1 Sqn), 362
Thomas, AC1 D. L., 99
Thomas, AC1 K. A., 304
Thomas, Cpl (GR I/35), 108
Thomas, F/O Norman M., 244
Thomas, Fw H. (1./KGr.126), 343
Thomas, Gefr K-H., 298
Thomas, LAC E. L. H., 313
Thomas, Lt L., 239
Thomas, Oberfw Alfred, 221
Thomas, P/O Alban, 181
Thomas, P/O C. V. (103 Sqn), 455
Thomas, P/O S. R., 257
Thomas, Sgt (56 Sqn), 525
Thomas, Sgt A. C. (77 Sqn), 332
Thomas, Sgt A. W. S. (18 Sqn), 165, 293
Thomas, Sgt I. L. (40 Sqn), 184
Thomas, Sgt Penry L. (57 Sqn), 181
Thompson, AC1 S. C. (21 Sqn), 385

Thompson, F/O M. H. B. 'Monty' (607 Sqn), 210, 241, 257
Thompson, F/O R. A. (72 Sqn), 423
Thompson, P/O J. E. P. (73 Sqn), 321
Thompson, P/O K. G. S. (114 Sqn), 104
Thompson, S/Ldr J. M. (111 Sqn), 310, 315, 318, 321, 459
Thompson, Sgt C. W. (15 Sqn), 349
Thompson, Sgt G. (15 Sqn), 445
Thompson, Sgt N. H. (218 Sqn), 233
Thomson, AC J. S. (105 Sqn), 270
Thomson, F/Lt J. A. (245 Sqn), 395, 396
Thomson, LAC J. G. (12 Sqn), 423, 464
Thöne, Uffz H., 253
Thonin, Sgt (GB II/35), 478
Thor, Oberfw H., 113
Thorn, F/O (1 Sqn), 353
Thorn, Sgt E. R. (264 Sqn), 386, 392
Thornley, F/Lt L. T. W., 116, 257, 288, 295
Thornton, AC1 W. (83 Sqn), 349
Thornton, LAC R. J. (4 Sqn), 320
Thornton, P/O S. G., 248
Thorougood, P/O G. W. (103 Sqn), 445
Thorpe, Sgt G. (75 Sqn), 339
Thouron, Sgt P. (GB I/11), 400
Thripp, Sgt (82 Sqn), 450
Thuisy, Lt de (GAO 1/589), 440, 456
Thumser, Oberfw F., 208
Thurgar, Sgt Percy F. H., 139, 526
Thürich, Fw H. (8./KG76), 343
Thurz, Lt H., 309
Thyl, Sgt (GB 1/19), 400
Thynne, P/O Robert (218 Sqn), 115, 502
Tibusch, Uffz P. (4./LG1), 459
Tideman, S/Ldr T. G., 246
Tiedemann, Oberfw J. (Stab III./LG1), 429
Tiedemann, Uffz R. (8./KG2), 252, 327
Tiedmann, Lt (2./JG3), 345, 390, 437, 469
Tietje, Uffz K. (2.(H)/21), 388
Tietz, Uffz W. (13.(Z)/LG1), 126
Tietzen, Hptmn (5./JG51), 161, 469
Tillner, Uffz F., 252
Tilsner, Uffz R. (9./LG1), 343, 393
Tilson, P/O (48 Sqn), 395
Timmermanns, Uffz (9./KG27), 413
Timmermans, Adjt Gustave, 238
Tippett, Cpl J. (110 Sqn), 446
Tippmann, Hptmn, 154
Tischer, Gefr J., 241
Tischer, Oberfw E., 209
Tischer, Uffz F., 241
Tismar, Lt (3.(J)/LG2), 320, 321
Tismer, Uffz A. (1./JG1), 427
Tissier, Lt, 97
Tix, Uffz A. (Stab KG77), 470
Tixerand, S/Lt (GAO 518), 475
Tixier-Vignancourt, S/Lt R., 188
Tocha, Fw E. (4./KG51), 429
Todd, Cpl H., 271
Todoli, Adjt R. (GB II/35), 478
Toft, P/O K. S., 304
Tölke, Uffz F. (2./KG54), 383
Tomasi, Sgt, 141
Tomczak, Uffz E. (8./KG76), 462
Tomicki, Sgt S. (DAT Châteaudun), 305, 419
Tomlinson, LAC R. T., 180
Tomlinson, S/Ldr G. C., 233, 303, 310
Toni, S/Lt (GR I/35), 249, 478
Tonks, Sgt S. I. (40 Sqn), 362
Tonne, Lt W. (3./JG53), 277, 451
Tonon, Capt., 296
Tootal, F/O H. C., 133
Töpper, Uffz M. (1./KG27), 428

Tornow, Fw Werner, 224
Torrance, LAC C. S. (110 Sqn), 345
Tötemeier, Fw H. (1./KG27), 388
Tough, Sgt E. W., 295
Tour du Pin, Lt G. de La (GB 4/31), 400
Tourel, Adjt (GR I/33), 126
Touret, Lt (GB I/11), 432
Touret, S/Lt (GR I/14), 249
Touret, Sgt J-F. (GC II/6), 235, 241
Tourné, Sgt (GC II/3), 120, 341, 347, 380, 401
Tournes, Capt. (GB I/11), 432
Tournié, Sgt (GB I/62), 374
Tourres, Adjt P. (GB II/31), 392
Townsend, Sgt K. N. V., 207, 210, 247
Townsend-Coles, LAC Roland B. H., 180
Townsley, AC1 J., 180
Toyne, F/Lt (17 Sqn), 315, 375, 434
Träber, Oberfw G., 212
Tracy, LAC J. (12 Sqn), 423
Trafford, AC (53 Sqn), 378
Tramm, Uffz H. (KG54), 329
Trautner, Fw, 116
Travers, Alec, *351*
Treacy, F/Lt W. P. F. 'Paddy' (74 Sqn), 356, *359*, 360, 379, 381
Treanor, P/O A. L. (245 Sqn), 406
Trébod, S/Lt P. (GC I/1), 306, 416
Trelluyer, Capt., 96
Trémolet, Sgt R., 112, *113*, 117, 253
Trenchard, ACM Sir Hugh 'Boom' (later Lord), *76*, 77, 331
Trenkler, Wachtmstr H. (1.(H)/21), 476
Trent, F/O Leonard H. (15 Sqn), 313, 339
Trepl, Fw A., 213
Trescothic, Sgt H. F., 271
Trevis, Adjt, 113
Trew, Sgt (21 Sqn), 458
Trezebinski, Lt (GC II/1), 341
Tricaud, Cmdt G. (GC I/6), 316, 341
Trice, Sgt Alan N., 294
Triebstein, Obergefr G., 300
Trilling, Uffz H., 209
Trinel, Sgt, 306
Trinkl, Flgr A., 289
Trioux, S/Lt (GBA II/61), 470
Triptree, P/O (53 Sqn), 345
Tritt, Gefr H., 301
Troebs, Lt G., 206
Troha, Lt (III./JG3), 445
Troll, Oberlt D. (I.(St)/TrGr.186), 410
Trompler, Uffz W. (KG54), 329
Tromsdorf, Fw H. (1./KG4), 409
Trosky, Lt G., 213
Trouillard, Capt. R., 260
Troyes, S/Lt A. (GC II/3), 162, 343, 360, 364
Trübenbach, Hptmn H. (Stab I.(J)/LG2), 402, 444
True, P/O, 148
Truhlar, Cpl (GC II/4), 427, 441
Trümpener, Uffz J-P., 156
Truscott, P/O, 311
Truskowski, Uffz A. (2./KG53), 336
Trusson Sgt, 93
Tschabuschnigg, Fw O. (I./JG76), 366
Tschauner, Fw H. (12.(N)/JG2), 459
Tscherne, Gefr Ernst (1./KG53), *382*, *383*
Tuck, F/Lt Robert Stanford (92 Sqn), 353, 356, *363*, 412, *414*
Tucker, F/Sgt E. (15 Sqn), 349
Tucker, P/O A. B. 'Tommy', 13, 14, *15*, 24, 44, 46, *48*, *51*, 52, *58*, *59*, 61, *65*, 66-67, 144
Tull, Sgt R., 232, 293
Tupin, Sgt, 248
Turbillon, Sgt W., 114
Turnbridge, Sgt B. R., 116

Turner, LAC (264 Sqn), 382, 399
Turner, Sgt L. (226 Sqn), 465
Turner, P/O G. R. (114 Sqn), 133
Turner, P/O P. S. (607 Sqn), 272
Turner, Sgt G. (32 Sqn), 345
Turner, Sgt J. D. (150 Sqn), 271
Türpitsch, Uffz E., 239
Turrel, Lt E. (GB I/21), 466
Tutt, Sgt H. J. F. (150 Sqn), 464
Twamley, Sgt A. E. D. (21 Sqn), 385
Twinning, AC1 F. A., 112
Tyler, LAC R. H., 248
Tzschoppe, Uffz H., 277

Übele, Lt (2.(H)/41), 488
Uchto, Cpl E. (GC I/145), 452
Udet, Genlt Ernst, *428*
Uebe, Uffz, 191
Uffel, Adjt A. van, 200
Uhl, Uffz F., 104
Uhlhorn, Lt J., 274, 318
Uht, Uffz (2./JG3), 373
Uijtenhoudt, Off. J. M., 194
Ulbrich, Uffz Wolfgang, *251*
Ulenberg, Lt (2./JG26), 399, 445
Ulke, Uffz Gerhard (5./KG54), *383*
Ullmann, Uffz A. (3./KG27), 429
Ullrich, Oberfw H. (KG51), 328
Ullrich, Uffz H. (KG77), 241
Ulrich, Fw K. (KG53), 253
Ulrich, Uffz H. (TrGr.186), 242, 479
Ulrich, Fw Willi (KGrzbV.12), 222
Ulsen, 2e Lt A. van, 132, 261
Umbach, Oberfw (3./JG1), 470
Umbeer, Uffz K., 225
Unbehauen, Oberlt Z., 254
Unger, Uffz E. (StG2), 215
Unger, Uffz (KGrzbV.9), 254
Unhold, Fw M. (6./JG53), 376
Unterberger, Lt J. (2./JG27), 434
Unterländer, Uffz L., 307
Unterstab, Gefr O. (Stab KG55), 442
Unverdorben, Fw F., 228
Unwin, F/Sgt (19 Sqn), 380
Urban, Oberfw J., 308
Urban, Uffz F., 290
Urwin, Sub Lt P. D. (826 FAA Sqn), 496
Uteza, Sgt (GBA II/54), 433
Uth, Uffz L. (2./JG3), 459
Uthke, Flgr K. (9./KG1), 495
Utteridge, LAC R. S. (142 Sqn), 322, 464
Uyttebroeckx, Adjt R., 306

Vaart, 2e Lt van der, 206
Vachell, G/Capt. J., *339*
Vaillant, Sgt (GR I/33), 419
Vakalopoulus, Obergefr A. (1./KG3), 366
Valentin, Adjt (later S/Lt) (GC II/7), 117, 456, 476, 477
Valentine, Sgt A. F. C., 304
Valette, Sgt M. (GR I/35), 364
Valin, Cmdt (GR I/33), 110
Valin, S/Lt (GR I/14), 462
Vallet, Lt (GR II/55), 407
Vallée, Sgt (GB II/21), 456
Vallentgoed, Korp. H., 191
Van Tilt family, 286, *287*
Vanaret, Sgt, 249
Vandenbosch, Lt J. (9./V/1), 159
Vandenbosch, Lt J. (5./III/3), 238
Vandenweghe, Adjt L. (1/I/1), 365
Vanderbeck, Lt G. (9./V/1), 286, 334
Vandercruyssen, Lt L., 286
Vandevelde, Adjt M., 199, 238
Vandra, Cpl, 273
Vanhoutte, Capt T. (GB 2/15), 395
Vano, AC2 Norman V., *271*
Vantillard, Adjt R. (GC I/6), 364, 365
Vanuzzo, Cpl N. (Gruppo 43), 467
Vanwormhoudt, Cpl (GB I/62), 461
Varet, Sgt (GAO 581), 465

Vasatko, Capt. L. (GC I/5), 317, 374, 376, 442, 447, 448, 456, 476
Vasek, Cpl Vladimir, 131
Vasseur, Cpl A. (GR II/55), 492
Vasseur, Sgt (GB II/12), 234
Vaublanc, Capt. de (GC II/8), 342
Vaudaine, Adjt (GR II/33), 346
Vaughan, F/O E. R. D., 267
Vaughan, P/O P. W., 256
Vauthier, S/Lt (GR II/52), 93
Vauthier, Sgt (GB I/21), 387
Vaux, S/Lt (GB I/63), 425
Vauzelle, Lt J., 274
Veil, Lt H. (3.(F)/11), 380
Veit, Adjt Paul (GB I/21), 446
Veit, Uffz H. (4./KG2), 208, 239
Veith, Fw A. (9./KG55), 414
Veith, Fw H. (8./JG53), 441
Vénard, Capt. (GAO 581), 469
Venema, Sgt Jan R., 192, 209
Veneroso, Sgt (GB II/63), 461
Venhues, Fw A., 212
Venier, Uffz H-G. (Stab StG1), 453
Venner, Uffz H-G. (Stab StG1), 453
Verbraeck, Adjt Désiré, *238*
Vercinger, Sgt (GAO 553), 364
Verdier, S/Lt M., 260, 297
Verdy, Sgt P. (GB I/12), 419
Verge, Sgt Jean (GBA II/54), 440
Vergne, Sgt, 106
Verhage, Lt G. F., 191, 236
Verheughe, S/Lt J., 236
Verhage, Lt G. F., 191, 236
Verity, P/O V. B. S. (229 Sqn), 332, 399
Verlaine, S/Lt R., 286
Verlet, Sgt (GB II/12), 432
Vermaat, Sgt K., 261
Vermeulen, 1e Lt J. C. J., 191
Vermeulen, 2e Lt G., 194
Verna, Sgt (GB I/31), 400
Verneret, Sgt C. (GB I/23), 364
Vernon, F/O J. E. (150 Sqn), 371, 437
Véron, Adjt A. (GR I/52), 102, 126
Véron, Capt. J. (GB I/34), 188, 273, 340
Veronet, Sgt, 306
Verots, Adjt (GC I/1), 495
Verpoorten, Sgt, 162
Verrier, Adjt (DAT Tours), 469
Verry, S/Lt, 97, 235
Versini, Lt, 314
Vesin, Capt., 260
Vetter, Oberfw O., 208
Veyrunes, Adjt (GC II/8), 380
Vial, Lt L., 296
Viale, Tenente L., 477
Viannès, SM, 138
Viau, Sgt, 152
Vickers, AC1, 180
Vickers, Sgt John H., 98, *526*
Vidal, Capt. M., 157
Videlenne, Laurent, *12*
Vié, Lt Y. (GC 4/6), 447
Vie, Sgt H. (GC II/3), 162, 346
Viehweger, Gefr H. (1./KG1), 392
Vieugeot, Lt (GB 4/63), 401
Viger, Sgt (GBA II/51), 396
Vigoux, Sgt (GAO 2/520), 358
Vijn, Sgt F., 194
Vilbert, Lt (AB 2), *324*
Villacèque, S/Lt P. (GC II/5), 133, 249, 376, 392
Villadier, Capt., 94
Villancourt, Lt de, 284
Villemin, S/Lt A. (GC III/6), 158, 278, 364, 365
Villemot, Adjt, 134
Villey, Adjt P. (GC II/4), 100, 117, 301, 364, 366
Villiers-Tuthill, P/O P. F. C. (53 Sqn), 282, 378
Villoutreys, Sgt A. de, 93
Vinahl, Obergefr A. (3./KG1), 353
Vincent, Sgt (GB II/19), 466
Vinchon, Adjt J. (GC I/3), 118, 416
Vinçotte, Lt M. (GC II/4), 285, 289, 325, 326, 451
Vipan, F/O A. L., 98, *526*

Viroux, Cpl J., 261
Vischer, Fw A. (1./KG51), 493
Vitrolles, Lt-Col de, 151
Vittini, Sgt F., 314
Vivier, Sgt (later S/Ldr, RAF) Daniel Leroy du, 94, 277
Vizard, Steve, 255, 349, *350*
Vob, Uffz H., 215
Vogel, Adjt, 134
Vogel, Fw A. (4./KG3), 381
Vogel, Fw G. (9./KG27), 167
Vogel, Fw H. (4.(F)/121), 171, 375
Vogel, Lt (4./JG53), 98
Vogel, Uffz A. (8./KG54), 212
Vogel, Uffz O. (6./KG2), 132
Vogel, Uffz R. (1./JG1), 375
Vögelein, Fw H. (2.(H)/23), 497
Voges, Uffz H., 240
Vogt, Obergefr G. (1.(F)/122), 124
Vogt, Fw J., 265
Vogt, Fw W., 239
Vogt, Uffz, 254
Vohwinkel, Oberlt (I./ZG2), 453
Voigard, Sgt, 248
Voigt, Lt (Stab JGr.102), 112
Voigt, Lt Werner (5./JG3), 440
Voigt, Oberfw W., 209
Voigt, Oberlt, 222
Voigt, Sonderf. Eduard, 327
Voigt, Uffz A., 210
Voigt, Uffz H., 290
Voirgard, Sgt, 298
Voisine, Adjt (GB II/23), 447
Voituriez, Capt., 259
Volg, Fw H. (5./KG55), 353
Volk, Lt J. (9./JG53), 154, 400
Volk, Wmstr M., 315
Volkmann, Oberfw K., 121
Volkmer, Uffz M. (8./KG55), 414
Vollières, Sgt, 210
Vollmer, Oberfw Ernst (4./JG53), 104, 418
Vollmer, Uffz (3./JG3), 285, 341, 464
Völter, Fw W., 279
Volz, Uffz K. (KG2), 208
Volz, Uffz P. (KG53), 240
Volz, Uffz W. (KG54), 329
Vonk, 1e Lt J., 194
Vopalecky, Adjt Josef (DAT Étampes), 413
Vorbau, Fw G., 241
Vordell, Obergefr H. (TrGr.186), 365
Vorreiter, Kanonier R., 288
Vos, Adjt M., 251
Vos, Sgt S. de, 192
Voss, Uffz W. (1./KG54), 360
Voss, Uffz W. (4.(H)/31), 359
Voules, AC (53 Sqn), 171, 412
Voyer, S/Lt P., 285
Vrana, Lt Adolf (GC I/5), 260, 441, 442
Vrancken, Lt W., 116
Vridaud, Cpl L. (GB I/12), 456
Vries, Korp. H. de, 192, 209
Vrins, 2e Lt T. J., 250
Vuathelot, Adjt A. (GB I/12), 296, 334
Vuatrin, Lt (GR II/52), *325*
Vuillemain, Sgt (GC I/5), 208, 240, 317, 326, 328, 376, 442
Vuillemin, Adjt (GAO 1/520), 234
Vuillemin, Gén. Joseph, *80*, 81, 110, 457, 463
Vuyst, Lt E. de, 200
Vybiral, Lt (GC I/5), 263, 408

Waak, Fw O., 279
Wachter, Lt (Swiss Fl.Komp.6), 409
Wackerhagen, Uffz G., 210
Waddington, LAC A. E., 313
Waddington, P/O M. W., 256
Wagener, Oberfw H., 113
Wagener, Sgt, 106
Wagner, Fw (6./ZG76), 497
Wagner, Fw F. (1.(F)/22), 335
Wagner, Fw H. (Stab I./KG51), 429

Wagner, Fw J. (2./KG53), 290
Wagner, Fw J. (7./KG51), 328
Wagner, Fw O. (2./StG2), 290
Wagner, Fw O. (8./KG51), 212
Wagner, Gefr H. (9./KG53), 410
Wagner, Lt K. (Stab KG4), 119
Wagner, Oberlt (Stab III./KG30), 308
Wagner, Sgt J. (3-II-1), 192
Wagner, Uffz C. (2./KG53), 253
Wagner, Uffz H. (7./KG76), 434
Wagner, Uffz J.(KGrzbV.9), 226
Wagner, Uffz M. (Stab KG53), 120
Wagner, Uffz R. (Stab KG3), 208
Wagner, Uffz W. (JG54), 127, 135
Wakeford, P/O P. F. T. (40 Sqn), 431
Wakeham, P/O E. C. J. (145 Sqn), 323, 329, 379
Walch, S/Lt E., 196, 298
Walden, Stabsfw H., 225
Walger, SM (AB 1), 333
Walker, Cpl, 12
Walker, F/Lt P. R. 'Johnny' (1 Sqn), 108, 154, 167, 180, 208, 242, 256, 282, 303, 327
Walker, F/O T. W. (16 Sqn), 311
Walker, P/O (26 Sqn), 267
Walker, P/O Peter B. (73 Sqn), 15, 39, 46, 49, 51, 66, 68, 71, 72, 103, 162
Wall, F/O R. N., 139, 182, 269
Wall, Sgt C., 154, 502
Wallace, Sgt (40 Sqn), 431
Waller, Lt A-H., 156
Wallis, Sgt (114 Sqn), 145
Wallis, Sgt Howard B., 270, 527
Wallis, Sir Tim, 99
Wallon, Adjt W., 200
Walser, Adjt (GBA II/54), 440
Walter, Lt (4.(H)/22), 427
Walter, Lt A. (JG54), 252
Walter, Oberfw A. (JG52), 316
Walter Obergefr H. (3./KG53), 158
Walter, Obergefr K. (II.(J)/TrGr.186), 365
Walter, Uffz H. (1./JG1), 347
Walter, W/Cdr (67 Wing), 52, 480, 486, 487
Walters, Sgt (21 Sqn), 431
Walz, Fw H., 210
Walz, Uffz W. (2./KG55), 376
Wandel, Oberlt (2./JG76), 425
Wangerov, Oberlt F. von (LG2), 320, 329
Wanke, Lt G., 309
Wappler, Fw W., 207
Warcup, F/Lt F. (1 Sqn), 349, 353, 469
Ward, AC1 J. G., 183
Ward, F/O (87 Sqn), 326
Ward, Sgt E. H., 183
Warda, Lt G. (4.(H)/12), 434
Wardle, P/O C. D. (235 Sqn), 373
Wardle, P/O H. D. 'Hank' (218 Sqn), 161
Warlimont, Gen. Walter, 361
Warman, Sgt H. (107 Sqn), 379
Warmont, Lt A. (11/VI/1), 352
Warmuth, Fw K., 308
Warnier, S/Lt (GC I/5), 157, 162, 208, 262, 417
Warrelmann, Fw A., 154
Wartenberg, Oberlt R. von, 211
Waryn, Sgt, 113
Waschke, Oberfw Erich, 222
Waschkowsky, Fw H. (2./KG55), 336
Wasserberg, Lt H. (2./KG1), 448
Wasserzier, Lt H. (1./JG1), 380
Waterhouse, Sgt J. R. (107 Sqn), 423
Waters, Cpl R. H., 267
Waters, Sgt J. P. (21 Sqn), 458
Waterston, AC2 W. C., 271
Wathey, Sgt H., 233
Watkins, Sgt T. J., 304
Watrin, Capt. J. (GB 2/63), 358
Watrin, S/Lt A. (1/I/1), 341
Watson, AC1, 233

Watson, F/Lt A. D. (21 Sqn), 248
Watson, F/Lt G. W. C. (82 Sqn), 304
Watson, F/O R. F. (87 Sqn), 317, 318, 321
Watson, P/O P. V. (19 Sqn), 373
Watta, Uffz W. (1.(H)/21), 476
Watts, LAC Cyril G. (15 Sqn), 313
Watts, W/Cdr J. J. (144 Sqn), 461
Wavell, F/Sgt, 95
Wawrock, Fw A., 114
Weatherill, F/O R. F., 183, 206, 210, 254, 313
Webb, AC (59 Sqn), 385
Webb, F/Sgt (56 Sqn), 525
Webb, LAC (16 Sqn), 339
Webb, Sgt A. L. F. (21 Sqn), 248
Webb, Sgt C. (21 Sqn), 469
Webber, P/O (103 Sqn), 445
Webber, Sgt L. B., 99
Weber, Adjt (GC I/2), 429
Weber, Fw E. (2./LG1), 337
Weber, Oberfw E. (5./LG1), 279
Weber, Oberlt (5.(J)/TrGr.186), 392
Weber, Sgt G. (GB I/11), 400
Webster, AC1 J. A., 184
Webster, F/Lt J. T. (41 Sqn), 410
Webster, F/Lt P. F. (15 Sqn), 247, 339
Weburpals, Fw J., 225
Wechel, Uffz O., 165
Weckbach, Fw O., 280
Wecker, Uffz H. (3.(F)/123), 380
Wedding, Lt (Stab III./JG3), 437
Wedzik, Sgt M., 305
Weeber, Oberlt (Stab II./ZG76), 441
Weegmann, Lt Horst von (9./JG53), 416
Weeks, F/Lt R. A. (150 Sqn), 445
Weert, 2e Lt van de, 222
Wegner, Oberlt H. (3./KG53), 476
Wehmeier, Uffz Otto, 210
Wehner, Obergefr E., 241
Wehrkoff, Fw F., 209
Weib, Lt R., 213
Weichert, Uffz H., 158
Weicksel, Oberlt H., 252
Weidenbach, Uffz F. (KG51), 328
Weidenhammer, Oberfw F. (3./KG53), 476
Weidner, Gefr H., 280
Weigel, Fw Fritz (7./KG4), 376
Weigel, Oberlt G., 263
Weigelt, Fw A., 152, 153, 162
Weigle, Uffz W. (1./KG53), 336
Weiher, Lt H-W. von (2./JG27), 244, 353
Weikert, Oberlt H., 308
Weiler, Sgt R. (GB I/12), 456
Weimann, Uffz G. (Stab III./LG1), 429
Weinberg, Uffz H., 309
Weinberger, Gefr K., 241
Weingärtner, Uffz W. (8./KG76), 462
Weinhold, Fw E., 208
Weinhold, Gefr G., 239
Weinhold, Uffz R., 206
Weinrebe, Gefr J. (2.(F)/22), 335
Weippert, Uffz H., 240
Weir, AC, 269
Weis, Uffz (later Fw) Willi (1./ZG26), 242, 467
Weise, Uffz H., 124
Weiser, Oberlt E. (5./StG77), 410
Weiss, Fw E. (4./JG53), 157
Weiss, Lt A. (GC I/4), 119, 262, 366, 433
Weiss, Lt F. (1.(H)/21), 476
Weiss, Obergefr J. (KG54), 328
Weiss, Uffz G. (9./KG3), 381
Weiss, Uffz S. (1./KG30), 211
Welch, LAC (142 Sqn), 345
Welch, P/O (264 Sqn), 382
Welch, Sgt H. D. (18 Sqn), 231
Welch, Uffz, 317
Welcher, Fw E., 224
Welford, F/O J. H. (65 Sqn), 304, 308, 373

Welkenhuyzen, Adjt, 159
Wellhausen, Gefr K., 213
Wellings, P/O D. M. (82 Sqn), 450
Wells, F/Lt M. C., 181
Wells, LAC Clifford R., 246
Wells, S/Ldr J. M., 184
Wells, Sgt R. M. (57 Sqn), 303, 349
Wellstein, Lt W., 240
Welter, Charles, 194
Welters, Flgr P. (KG54), 329
Welticke, Uffz Leo, 224
Welzel, Gefr Alfred (9./ZG26), 335, 337
Wemaere, S/Lt C., 134
Wemhöner, Uffz (JG26), 321
Wendelin, Oberlt Hartmann, 265, 309
Wendler, Uffz M., 206
Wendt, Gefr H., 253
Wendt, Oberlt, 272
Wendt, Uffz O., 107
Wengert, Uffz L., 289
Wengler, Gefr K., 249, 290
Wenzel, Lt, 191
Wenzel, Uffz G. (TrGr.186), 347
Wenzel, Uffz K. (16./KGzbV.1), 396
Werch, Sgt A. Van, 261
Werk, Uffz H., 242
Werle, Oberlt P., 206
Werle, SM, 152
Werner, Fw H. (12.(St)/LG1), 448
Werner, Fw Hans-Harro (1./KG53), 382, 383
Werner, Gefr E. (7./StG2), 376
Werner, LAC (103 Sqn), 450, 469, 472
Werner, P/O R. H. (15 Sqn), 458
Werner, Uffz A. (4./KG1), 419
Werner, Uffz E. (5./KG51), 429
Werner, Uffz F. (2./KG54), 383
Werner, Uffz H. (Stab KGrzbV.9), 224
Werner, Wachtm. E. (2.(H)/41), 459
Werra, Lt von (Stab II./JG3), 331, 346
Werth, Uffz H., 262
Werthern, Oberlt E. Fr von, 262
Wesly, Sgt W. P., 192, 209, 250
Wesolowski, Lt M. (DAT Bourges), 358, 360
Wessoly, Uffz E., 170
West, P/O R. A. (245 Sqn), 395, 406
West, Sgt J. V. (110 Sqn), 345
Westerhoff, Lt (6./JG3), 400, 426
Westerholt, Uffz K. (KG54), 329
Westhead, the Rev. Israel, 524
Westhal, Lt (Stab III./JG26), 268, 399
Wetz, Adjt A., 286
Wetzel, Flgr R. (7./KG3), 381
Wetzig, Fw R. (2./LG1), 402
Wever, Walther, 86
Wevers, Sold. J. W., 191
Weygand, Gén. Maxime, 319, 330, 341, 348, 361, 420, 457, 460, 486, 494
Weynants, Adjt J-P., 251
Wezel, Uffz F., 110
Whalley, Sgt J., 183
Wheatley, P/O C. M., 162
Wheeldon, Sgt (81 Sqn), 99
Wheeldon, Sgt G. R. (12 Sqn), 436
Wheelwright, P/O I. S. (500 Sqn), 390
Whelan, AC2 M. (88 Sqn), 349
Whelan, P/O J. R., 231, 293
Wheldon, F/Lt R. G. (18 Sqn), 170, 320
Wherry, F/O S. (48 Sqn), 390
Whetton, Sgt, 180
Whilton, P/O J. (115 Sqn), 339
Whitby, Sgt (79 Sqn), 335
White, LAC E. C. (107 Sqn), 412
White, P/O B. E. G. (504 Sqn), 272, 332
White, P/O Hugh Edgar (105 Sqn), 158, 270
White, S/Ldr F. L. (Lawrence) (74 Sqn), 349, 353

White, Sgt (32 Sqn), 326
White, Sgt C. T. (40 Sqn), 284
White, Sgt E. F. (12 Sqn), 267
White, Sgt H. P. (226 Sqn), 469
White, Sgt L. J. (222 Sqn), 406
White, Sgt R. A. de C. (150 Sqn), 183
Whitehead, LAC E., 124
Whitehead, Sgt C. (56 Sqn), 257, 303, 318
Whitehill, LAC A. C., 141
Whitehorn, Steve, 125
Whitehouse, F/Lt E. H. (264 Sqn), 359, 382, 386
Whitfield, Sgt W. H., 233
Whiting, P/O T. A. (107 Sqn), 379
Whiting, Sgt D. A. (142 Sqn), 464
Whitlam, Sgt (57 Sqn), 356
Whitley, P/O D. (264 Sqn), 359, 382, 399
Whittaker, P/O R. C. (17 Sqn), 309, 326, 366, 375, 437
Whittle, LAC P. R. (40 Sqn), 349
Whittle, Sgt E. J. M. (88 Sqn), 232
Whitty, P/O (later F/O) W. H. R., 153, 210, 288
Wiartalla, Uffz A. (7./StG2), 366
Wibaux, Sgt, 164
Wiccaert, Capt. A., 259
Wichert, Uffz O. (4.(H)/12), 434
Wick, Lt (3./JG2), 117, 447, 465
Wickham, P/O A. E. (88 Sqn), 349
Wickham, P/O S. M. (615 Sqn), 126
Wicklein, Uffz F. (3./KG55), 383
Wicks, F/O B. J. (56 Sqn), 345
Widmann, Hptmn H. (KG54), 329
Widmayer, Oberfw H., 254
Widmer, Uffz P. (2./JG1), 353
Wiebe, Uffz G., 254
Wiebke, Uffz W., 209
Wiechers, Uffz S., 317
Wieckowski, Cmdt Edward, 83
Wieczoreck, Gefr P. (8./KG30), 347
Wiegand, Fw C., 315
Wiegand, Uffz H., 209
Wieland, Uffz F. (9./KG2), 381
Wieners, Lt A., 160
Wiens, P/O R. H. (242 Sqn), 307, 312, 317
Wiere, Fw H., 136
Wieseler, 1/Sgt G., 238
Wieser, Oberlt W. (5.(H)/13), 456
Wiest, Oberfw A. (5./KG76), 448
Wifling, Fw K. (9./KG54), 479
Wigglesworth, LAC E. (88 Sqn), 152, 321
Wight, F/Lt Ronald D. G. (213 Sqn), 304, 326, 332, 335, 380, 388, 396, 402
Wijnstra, Sold. J., 191, 236, 261
Wijs, 1e Lt C. de, 107
Wilbrich, Fw O. (7./KG76), 434
Wilburn, Cpl Clifford E., 157, 527
Wilcke, Oberlt W-D., 113, 145, 148, 153, 316
Wilckens, Oberlt (Wettererkundungsst. 51), 477
Wild, Uffz G. (2./KG53), 336
Wilhelm, Uffz, 260, 285
Wilkening, Uffz H. (1./ZG26), 479
Wilkinson, AC1 H. (78 Sqn), 356
Wilkinson, F/O William C. (43 Sqn), 437
Wilkinson, Sgt R. (3 Sqn), 251, 265, 282, 335
Wilks, Sgt E. (88 Sqn), 371
Wilks, Sgt P. E. (12 Sqn), 180
Will, Fw W., 145
Will, Lt H. (1./KG55), 410
Willcox, Sgt R. J. (12 Sqn), 469
Wille, Dr Joseph, 154
Wille, Flgr R., 300
Willemaers, Capt. P., 277, 298
Willenbockel, Uffz E. (4./KG3), 381
Willers, Oberlt Hans-Jürgen (4./KG54), 342, 343
Williame, Capt. R. (GC I/2), 334, 429, 448

Williams, AC1 A. C. (105 Sqn), 126
Williams, F/Lt (501 Sqn), 239
Williams, F/O O. L. (99 Sqn), 339
Williams, LAC E. S. (88 Sqn), 378
Williams, P/O J. E. M. (264 Sqn), 399
Williams, P/O R. E. (82 Sqn), 465
Williams, Sgt A. (21 Sqn), 390, 465
Williams, Sgt F. (115 Sqn), 339
Williams, Sgt H. H. (82 Sqn), 465
Williams, Sgt J. D. F. (150 Sqn), 271
Williams, Sgt J. L. C. (56 Sqn/3 Sqn), 267, 282
Williams, Willie, 33, 56, 62, 69
Williamson, Sgt (53 Sqn), 345
Willigmann, Hptmn J. (8./KG2), 441
Willinger, Oberfw, 126
Willis, Sgt J. S. (12 Sqn), 423
Willsher, Sgt, 270
Willuhn, Oberfw F., 170
Wilmots, S/Lt M., 196
Wilshaus, Obergefr H., 209
Wilson, AC1 A. G. (21 Sqn), 272
Wilson, F/Lt L. D. (40 Sqn), 95
Wilson, P/O (53 Sqn), 171
Wilson, P/O R. (26 Sqn), 405
Wilson, P/O R. R. (111 Sqn), 412
Wilson, P/O Sir A. T. (37 Sqn), 398
Wilson, Sgt H. H. (53 Sqn), 431
Wilson, Sgt G. A. (107 Sqn), 437
Wilson, Sgt S. L. (105 Sqn), 126
Wiltshire, AC1 R. F. J., 144
Winand, 1/Sgt H., 237
Winderlich, Gefr K. (4./KG76), 366
Windisch, Uffz (3./JG54), 390
Windsor, The Duke of, 47
Wingender, Uffz Walter, 210
Wingerden, Kpl van, 95
Wingert, S/Lt (DAT Château-roux), 429
Winkelhaus, Fw H., 263
Winkelman, Gen. Henri, 266, 276
Winkelmann, Gefr R., 262
Winkert, Uffz A. (3.(F)/11), 326
Winkes, Gefr H., 241
Winkler, Oberfw E. (4.(F)/121), 408
Winkler, Oberfw K. (KGrzbV.9), 226
Winkler, Oberlt (Stab KG54), 462
Winkler, Sgt H. R. W., 267
Winkler, Uffz Helmuth (KGrzbV.12), 222
Winkler, Uffz M. (3./JG53), 95
Winn, Sgt John, 15, 39, 46, 48, 120, 127, 518
Winnat, Obergefr K., 241
Winning, F/Lt E. G. (213 Sqn), 310, 386
Winschig, Oberlt E. (2./StG2), 393
Winstanley, Sgt A. (144 Sqn), 461
Winter, Gerald, GM, 151, 511
Winter, Oberfw M., 240
Winter, Oberlt A., 120
Winter, Uffz K., 208
Winterfeldt, Hptmn von (3./JG2), 313, 320
Wintz, Lt Peter, 307
Wiórkiewicz, Capt. W., 407
Wirth, Obergefr W. (KGzbV.1), 229
Wirth, Uffz W. (6./KG76), 213
Wirthwein, Uffz R. (Stab KG54), 328
Wischartz, Lt F., 119
Wischnewski, Uffz, 311
Wisdom, S/Ldr Tommy, 408
Wiskandt, Hptmn H., 227
Wisser, Lt P. (5./JG3), 335
Wissing, Gefr F., 209
Wissmann, Uffz K. (9./ZG26), 374, 470
Wissmeier, Uffz G. (2./KG53), 336
Wissussek, Uffz K. (4./KG54), 414
Witkowski, Oberfw F. (1./KG27), 388
Witmeur, Sgt, 148
Witry, Sgt R. (GAO 1/508), 373
Witt, Hauptm H. (Stab KG55), 470
Witt, Lt (3./JG54), 386

Wittchen, Obergefr H., 213
Wittchen, Uffz E., 206
Witte, Uffz A. (8./KG2), 441
Witteborn, Uffz H., 265
Wittenberg, Oberlt (Stab III./JG53), 283, 400
Wittgen, Flgr J. (Stab KG27), 402
Wittich, Oberfw P., 254
Wittmeyer, Lt H. (3.(F)/121), 341
Witty, Sgt G. G., 102
Witzel, Fw (6./JG27), 398
Wöbbeking, Oberlt G., 301
Woensdregt, 2e Lt N. J., 236
Wöhl, Uffz G. (6./ZG1), 419
Wohlgemuth, Fw F. (6./LG1), 496
Wohlgemuth, Fw O. (8./KG3), 476
Wohlgemuth, Gefr J. (KGzbV.1), 241
Woick, Uffz R. (2./JG21), 396
Woitke, Oberlt (6./JG3), 400, 416
Woitzig, Uffz P., 456
Wokulat, Oberlt H., 148
Wolf, Fw O. (8./KG54), 213
Wolf, Fw R. (4./KG76), 343
Wolf, Lt K. (JGr.102), 107
Wolf, Oberfw H. (6./KG2), 381
Wolf, Uffz (3./JG26), 406
Wolf, Uffz W. (7./KG53), 212
Wolfenden, Capt. Rowland (SS Abukir), 388
Wolff, Lt August (KGrzbV.9), 225
Wolff, Oberfw (8./KG2), 381
Wolff, Oberfw A. (4./KG27), 117
Wolff, Uffz F. (3./KG27), 429
Wolff, Uffz K. (Stab I./ZG26), 290
Wolff, Uffz Wilhelm (KGrzbV.12), 224
Wolfien, Maj. K., 279
Wölfing, Lt (3.(H)/14), 326
Wölfle, Lt G. (1./ZG1), 376
Wolfs, Uffz H. (3./KG1), 470
Wolgast, Uffz M. (16./KGzbV.1), 396
Wollensack, Oberfw A., 265
Wöllner, Uffz A., 280
Wollnitz, Gefr F., 253
Wolpers, Uffz H., 239
Wolter, Fw E., 254
Wolter, Fw W., 263
Wolz, Uffz O. (I./JG21), 497
Wood, AC2 R. A., 167
Wood, F/O E. E. A. (4 Sqn), 293
Wood, Lt R. G. (825 FAA Sqn), 385, 390
Wood, P/O J. E. R. (79 Sqn), 241, 268
Wood, Sgt E. F., 311
Woodhouse, Sgt, 182
Woodmason, Sgt Tom B., 95, 506
Woods, LAC D. V., 248
Woods-Scawen, P/O C. A. (43 Sqn), 406, 437
Woods-Scawen, P/O Patrick P. (85 Sqn), 206, 303, 307, 321, 326, 329
Wooldridge, Sgt B. C. (40 Sqn), 184
Woolridge, P/O E. L. (2 Sqn), 345
Wootten, Sgt F. C., 304
Wörlein, Uffz J. (4./KG76), 410
Worrall, S/Ldr J., 310
Worsch, Obergefr R., 212
Wörz, Flgr Jakob, 263
Wosczyna, Fw W., 240
Wötzel, Uffz A., 263
Woudenberg, 1e Lt K. W., 193, 211, 228
Wrba, Lt H. (3.(F)/10), 251, 375
Wright, AC1 S. R., 182
Wright, F/O G. F. M. (605 Sqn), 345
Wright, F/O G. O. M. (110 Sqn), 273
Wright, P/O C. M. 'Claude' ('Claudie') (73 Sqn), 13, 15, 34, 52, 58, 68, 72, 73, 107, 114, 144
Wright, P/O L. (151 Sqn), 309, 487
Wrightson, Sgt L. H., 304
Wrusch, Uffz A., 229
Wübbe, Fw W., 206
Wucherer, Uffz F., 277
Wühle, Gefr O. (KG51), 453

Wühlisch, Oberlt Bruno von, 158, 161
Wulf, Georg, 86
Wulf, Obergefr G., 278
Wülknitz, Oberlt W., 211
Wunder, Obergefr Josef, 289
Wunderlich, Uffz R., 239
Wunnicke, Fw H. (3./KG1), 448
Wunnicke, Uffz F. (6./ZG1), 448
Wünsch, Uffz H., 208
Wurm, Fw F., 279
Wurmheller, Uffz, 99
Würth, Fw F., 278
Wurtz, Uffz G. (ECMJ 1/16), 259, 470
Wurz, Uffz J. (5./StG2), 448
Wustmann, Uffz A., 288
Wutkowski, Fw H. (9./KG4), 360
Wutz, Oberfw A., 162
Wyatt, AC H. K., 256
Wyatt, F/Lt G. M., 106, 180
Wyhlidal, Fw L., 162
Wykowski, Lt H-O. H., 251
Wylie, P/O C. R. (59 Sqn), 321
Wyness, Sgt R. F., 304
Wynn, Sgt, 239
Wyrwicki, Cmdt Eugeniusz (GC II/10), 83, 440, 441

Yeomans, Cpl L., 248
Young, LAC (110 Sqn), 345
Young, P/O B. P. (615 Sqn), 124, 295
Young, P/O J. C. (99 Sqn), 395
Young, P/O M. H. (264 Sqn), 382, 399
Young, Sgt A. (12 Sqn), 180
Youngson, Sgt S. F. (9 Sqn), 469
Ysermann, S/Lt (GR II/33), 396, 452
Yvernault, Sgt (GB II/11), 466

Zadrozinski, Lt Z. (GC 1/145), 452
Zahle, Lt, 124
Zahnke, Obergefr O., 211
Zähnle, Fw K., 240
Zander, Fw H. (Stab II./KG3), 327
Zander, Uffz E. (KG28), 327
Zander, Uffz F. (StG51), 309
Zaunbrecher, Uffz, 152
Zauner, Gefr A. (4./KG3), 381
Zavoral, Sgt (DAT Chartres), 459
Zechlin, Oberlt E., 227
Zeep, Fw H., 240
Zegers, Kapt. J. L., 141, 148, 149
Zehge, Lt C., 252
Zeilinger, Gefr R., 280
Zeilmann, Uffz G. (1./KG76), 418
Zein, Lt G. (6./KG3), 327

Zeis, Lt (1./JG53), 416
Zeiss, Lt H. (2./KG4), 316
Zellner, Gefr J., 240
Zenner, Uffz Walter, 212, 213
Zenz, Uffz Hermann, 317
Zerning, Uffz, 136
Zerovnicky, Lt, 241, 306
Zeyer, Uffz W. (5./KG1), 488
Zickelten, Lt, 157
Zickmantel, Fw H-H. (1./KG1), 393
Ziebarth, Oberlt H. (Stab I./ZG52), 419
Ziegast, Lt K., 156
Zieger, Flgr J. (2./KG51), 470
Ziegler, Lt R., 277
Ziegler, LV (AC 3), 472
Ziegler, Uffz R., 224
Ziehl, Lt D., 278
Zielke, Uffz H. (4.(F)/121), 456
Zierau, Uffz W., 263
Ziereisen, Uffz T. (KG54), 329
Zieschang, Funkmaat H., 95
Ziesemann, Fw K., 265
Zigull Oberfw F., 223
Zimmer, Fw K. (5./KG77), 477
Zimmer, Lt A. (1./KG1), 393
Zimmer, Uffz W., 209
Zimmermann, Fw E., 136
Zimmermann, Fw H., 102
Zimmermann, Uffz H. (3./KG3), 381
Zimmermann, Uffz H. (6./KG27), 210
Zinck, Sgt E. (GR I/52), 325
Zink, Uffz J., 240
Zinner, Fw F. (8./StG51), 376
Zinnicker, Sgt P. (GC III/2), 206, 447
Zipfler, Gefr G., 279
Zipperling, Uffz K. (7./LG1), 429
Zirkenbach, Lt (1./JG27), 390, 451
Zirpel, Obergefr G., 308
Zitzmann, Uffz H., 209
Zobel, Lt H-J. (4./KG51), 429
Zobel, Lt (V.(Z)/LG1), 356
Zoller, Fw G., 164
Zöphel, Uffz R., 300
Zorn, Oberfw (2.(F)/22), 365
Zucconi, Tenente (4 Gruppo), 467
Züche, Gefr E., 207
Zuffi, Tenente G. E., 477
Zuger, Sgt J., 250
Zukowski, S/Lt (GC 1/145), 456
Zuylen, Wachtm. J. van, 191
Zwarthoed, Sgt K., 193
Zwenger, Uffz M., 317

The last to die. Sous-Lieutenant Henri Raphenne of GC I/6 was the last Frenchman to be killed in the Battle of France when he was shot down on June 24 (see page 499).

On May 13, Potez 63-11 number 689 of Groupe d'Aérienne Observation 552 crashed just outside the Sint-Niklaas airfield in Belgium. The crew of three were killed in the crash (see page 259). They were initially buried in the local cemetery but their remains were transferred to France when hostilities had ceased. In September 2007 this memorial headstone was inaugurated in Sint-Niklaas (Tereken) cemetery on the exact location of the original grave.

UNITS

Belgian

Order of Battle, 195
1/I/1, 139, 142, *145*, 148, 196, 277, 286, 306, 341, 359, 365, 387
II/1, 315
3/II/1, 99, 167, 171, 236, 277, 286, 298, 306, 315
5/III/1, 196, 236
7/IV/1, 196, 251, 261, 286, 334, 374
9/V/1, 100, 159, 196, 236, 261, 286, 315, 334, 341, 359, *374*, 380, 387
11/VI/1, 148, 196, 236, 298, 325, 352, 374, 387
1/I/2, 124, 148, 160, 162, 196, 236-237, *237*
2/I/2, 115, 123, 124, 142, 145, 149, 165, 168, 196, 237
II/2, 205, 325, 416
3/II/2, 165, 196, 198, 213, 277
4/II/2, 94, 198, 277
III/2, 111, 237, 315
5/III/2, 94, 96, 198, 199, 237, 286
6/III/2, 199, 237
I/3, 148, 199
1/I/3, 237, 365
II/3, 199
11/II/3, *201*
III/3, 237, 315
5/III/3, 124, 199, 200, 236, 237, *238*, 251, 277, 286, *306*, 315
7/III/3, 145, 160, 167, *200*, 238, *251*, 261, 286, 315
9/III/3, *238*
II Fighter Gp, *85*
CISLA (Centre d'Instruction des Sous Lieutenants d'Active), 251
Ier Corps d'Armée, *237*
2e Régt d'Aéronautique, *196*
1e Escadrille/École de Pilotage, 251
2e Escadrille/École de Pilotage, 200
4e Escadrille/École de Pilotage, *200*
5e Escadrille/École de Pilotage, 201
6e Escadrille/École de Pilotage, 201
Militaire Vliegwezen, 85

British

Advanced Air Striking Force (AASF), *60*, *78*, *175*, *231*, 243, 255, *266*, *267*, *281*, 292, *294*, 302, 310, 319, 330, 338, 344, 348, 355, 377, 384, 397, 403, 404, *407*, 411, 419, 422, 430, 435, 443, 445, 449, 455, 457, 460, 463, 468, 471, 478, 480, 487
Museum at Condé-Vraux, 267
Order of Battle, 17, 178
Air Component (BEF), *17*, *60*, *110*, *152*, *175*, 243, 255, 266, 292, 302, 310, 319, 330, *332*, *339*, 345, *348*, *371*, 403, *413*, 419
No. 3 Air Mission, 370, 372
Order of Battle, 16, *179*
British Air Forces In France (BAAF), 292, 302, *323*, 330, 338, 344, *345*, 361, *431*, 457, 463, 468, 469, 471, 478, 486, 490
Order of Battle, 178-179
1 Gp (later AASF), *17*, 92
2 (Bomber) Gp, *17*, 92, *231*, 245, 281, 310, 319, *338*, 344, *345*, 348, 355, 377, 384, 389, 394, 397, 403, 404, 430, 435, 443, 449, 463
3 Gp, 229, 457
4 Gp, 457
11 Gp, *56*, *349*, *350*, 367, *368*, *372*, 419
Order of Battle, 369
14 (Fighter) Gp, 175, 319, 330, 344
22 Gp, 92
52 Wing, 319, 330
61 (Fighter) Wing, *77*, 152, 155, 310

Units, British—continued

63 (Fighter) Wing, *175*
67 (Fighter) Wing, 13, 18, 52, *230*, 281, 415, 471, 480, *482*, 486, 487
70 (Bomber) Wing, *152*, 174, 319, 330
71 (Bomber) Wing, *92*, *130*, 266, 281, 455
72 Wing, *92*, 137
74 Wing, *92*, 137
75 (Bomber) Wing, *92*, 266, 292, 463, 471
76 (Bomber) Wing, *92*, 266, 281, 471
79 Wing, *345*
1 Sqn, 9, 11-15, *13*, *14*, 18, *27*, 32, 50, 56, 57, 101, 107, *108*, *110*, 118, 119, *120*, *121*, 124, *126*, 127, 133, 136, *143*, 144-147, *146*, 154, 156, 161, 162, *167*, *168*, 175, 180, *184*, 208, 231, 239, 242, 244, 251, 252, 255, *256*, 263, 265, 267, 277, *278*, 279, *280*, 282, *289*, 290, 302, 303, 309, 311, 320, *326*, 327, 349, 353, 362, 371, 378, 419, 422, 423, 429, 430, 435, *439*, 443, 455, 463, 469, 471, 481, *483*, 486, 487, *507*
2 (AC) Sqn, 104, 148, 168, *170*, 303, 319, 345, 362, *371*, 390, 398, 405
3 Sqn, *175*, 180, 212, *213*, 251, 254, 256, 262, 265, 267, 280, 281, 282, 288, 289, 293, 303, 311, 317, 320, 328, 335, 493
4 Sqn, 114, 117, 134, 148, 159, 160, 165, 168, 174, 256, 267, 293, 311, 320, 330, 339, 355
'B' Flt, 339, 348
9 Sqn, 349, 469
10 Sqn, 458
12 Sqn, 116, *180*, *238*, *243-245*, 266, 267, 271, 293, 320, *415*, 423, 436, 444, 464, 469, *471*, *472*, *505*, *513*, *516*
13 Sqn, 115, 124, 148, 174, 282, 293, 311, 330, 348
15 Sqn, 175, 229, 247-248, 281, 284, 310, *313*, 339, 345, 349, 356, 362, 395, 445, 458, 461, 493
16 Sqn, 302, 303, 311, 319, 320, 339, 371, 378, 385, 398, *517*
17 Sqn, 231, 233, 239, 303, 309, 310, 315, *316*, 320, 326, 341, 362, 366, 373, 375, 376, 381, 390, 393, 402, *406*, 416, 430, 431, 434, 435, 437, 443, 450, 455, 462, 470, 471, 480, *520*
18 Sqn, 103, 107, 112, 114, 121, 127, 128, 131, *132*, 134, 141, 151, *152*, *165*, 170, 180, *231*, 256, 257, *293*, 294, 302, 303, 310, 311, 312, 313, 320, 339, *345*, 349, *506*, *511*
19 Sqn, 239, *372*, 373, 375, 376, 380, 385, 388, 405, 406, 409, 410
21 Sqn, 233, 248, 266, 272, 310, 330, *345*, 356, 361, *362*, 385, 390, 431, 445, 458, 459, 465, 469
26 Sqn, 156, 160, 267, 282, 319, *320-321*, *332*, 378, 390, 405, 423
29 Sqn, 423
32 Sqn, 310, 320, 321, 326, 332, 345, 349, 376, 411, 412, 441, 446, 448, *458*
37 Sqn, 372, 398, 405
38 Sqn, 398
40 Sqn, 93, 95, 96, 97, 174, 175, 184, 227, 281, 284, 310, *338*, 349, 362, 430, *431*, 461, 469, 493
41 Sqn, 390, 406, 410
43 Sqn, 94, 145, *406*, 409, 435, 437, 441, 472, 478
44 Sqn, 273, 458
48 Sqn, 332, 390, 395, 405
49 Sqn, 233, 445
53 Sqn, 99, 101, 147, 167, 171, *180*, *232*, 256, 282, *293*, 302, 303, 311, 330, *345*, 349, 362, 372, 378, 412, *431*, 450, 469

Units, British—continued

54 Sqn, *31*, 154, 343, 347, *349*, 353, 356, 360, 362, 366, 373, 379, 380, 385, *386*, 388
56 Sqn, 255, 257, 267, 308, 315, 316, 317, 318, 345, 347, 349, 379, 382, 383, 390, *392*, *406*, 430, 435, *514*, *525*
A Flt, 310
B Flt, 303, 311, 312
57 Sqn, *104*, 105, 106, 107, 112, 116, 119, 136, 150, *152*, 158, 159, 180-181, 256, 268, 302, 303, *312*, *345*, 349, 356, 362, 372
59 Sqn, 101, 151, 157, 167, *232*, 244, 256, 268, 282, 293, 312, 313, 321, 345, 362, 372, 385, 419, 431, 445, 461, *520*, *522*
64 Sqn, 374, 391, 392, 398, 406, 410, 462
65 Sqn, 304, 308, 345, 347, 359, *373*, 375, 376, 379, 381, 385, 388
66 Sqn, 253, 255, 257, 262, 265, 411, 412
72 Sqn, 412, 414, 419, 423, 452
73 Sqn, 6-73 *passim*, 94, 96, 99, 101, 103, 107-116 *passim*, *120*, 121, 123, 126, 127, *130*, 131, 136, 141, 143, 144, 148-149, 152-154, 157, 162, 163, *170*, 175, 181, *184*, 206-208, *230*, 232, 240, 244, 251, 256, 259, 262, 263, 265, 268, 277-283, 290-293, *295*, 302, 321, *326*, 327, 328, 356, 371, 405, *415-416*, 418, 422, 423, 427, *435-436*, *439*, 443, 455, 464, 467, 468, 471, 472, *473-474*, 482-483, *486*, *490*, *518*
74 Sqn, 339, *343*, 347, *349*, 353, 356, 359, 360, 371, 379, 380, 381
75 Sqn, 339
77 Sqn, 233, 332, 385, 431, 455, 458
78 Sqn, 356
79 Sqn, *175*, 232, 241, 245, 253, 268, 277, 279, 293, 301, 303, 312, 317, 318, 331, 335, 337, 383, 437, 441, 448, 498
81 Sqn, 97, 98, 99, 104, 123
82 Sqn, 281, 302, *304*, 308, 345, 437, 445, 450, *465*
83 Sqn, 349
85 Sqn, *78*, *101*, 109, 116, 117, 127, 128, 131, *138*, 141, 144, 148, 157, 160, 162, 175, 181, *205*, 206, 207, 210, 212, *213*, 232, 239, 251, 253, 256, 278, 283, 289, 290, 293, 294, 299, *303*, 307, 312, 317, 318, 321, 326, 328, 329, *331*, 335, 336
87 Sqn, *76*, *101*, 102, 108, *109*, 110, *111*, *114*, *115*, 121, 124, 131, *138*, 139, 141, 153, 161, 168, *170*, 171, 175, 181, 206, 207, 208, 212, *242*, 245, 253, 254, 256, 268, 278, 283, 288, 290, 294, 299, 301, 317, 318, 321, 326, 327, 328, 329, 331, 335, *406*, *526*
88 Sqn, 92, 95, 102, 135, *140*, *141*, 142, 143, 152, 168, *181*, 232, 266, *268*, *294*, 321, 349, 371, 378, 390, 437, 455, 458, 461, 464, 469, *505*, *511*
92 Sqn, 348, 349-351, *350-351*, 353, 354, *356*, *363*, 411, 412, *414*
98 Sqn, 155, 164, 472
99 Sqn, 339, *395*
102 Sqn, 94, 332
103 Sqn, *34*, *79*, *98*, 144, 153, *181*, *245*, *247*, 266, 268, *269*, 283, 294, 345, 362, 371, *385*, 390, *394*, 423, 437, 445, 450, 455, 469, 472, *518*, *521*, *526*
105 Sqn, 93, 126, 133, 139, 140, 153, 154, 158, 182, *246*, 266, 269-270, *269*
107 Sqn, 248, 266, 330, 345, 349, 361, 379, 412, 423, 446, 450, 461, 465, 495
110 Sqn, 175, 184, 223, 233, *237*, 266, 273, 345, 423, 446, 495

Units, British—continued

111 Sqn, *49*, 315, *317*, 318, 328, 329, 398, 402, 412, 430, 431, 434, 435, 450, 459, *508*, *517*
A Flt, 312
B Flt, 310, 312, 321
114 Sqn, 104, 133, 134, 142, 145, 230, *233*, 266, *270*, *294*, *345*, *509*, *510*
115 Sqn, *338*, 339
139 Sqn, *79*, *130*, *131*, 134, 140, 150, 168, 233, *243*, *246*, 266, *270*, 277, 281, *295*, 312, *345*, *516*, *527*
142 Sqn, 146, 157, 174, *182*, 246, 266, 270-271, *270*, *295*, *322*, *331*, 345, 371, 437, *450*, 458, *464*, 469, 472, *527*
144 Sqn, 233, 461
145 Sqn, *310*, 316, *323*, 328, 329, 331, 347, 373, 379, 383, 402, 406, 409
A Flt, 310, 312, 323
149 Sqn, 356, 458
150 Sqn, 92, 95, 99, 100, 146, 154, 162, *183*, 233, 246-247, 266, *271*, 322, 371, 437, 445, 464, *465*, 472, *506*, *525*
151 Sqn, 294, 303, 309, 310, 312, 316, 318, 341, 347, 362, 391, 393, 408, 430, 431, 435, 437, 446, 481, 487, 488
152 Sqn, *406*
206 Sqn, 384
212 (PR) Sqn, 137, 150, 162, 295, 431
213 Sqn, 294, 318, 326, 327, 328, 335, 380, 386, 388, 392, 393, 396, 398-399, *402*
A Flt, 310, 322
B Flt, 304, 332
218 Sqn, *92*, 95, 112, 115, 133, 134, 135, 144, 160, 161, 183, 233, *245*, *247*, 266, *271-272*, *283*, *502*, *504*, *508*, *519*
220 Sqn, 115, 384, 410
222 Sqn, 391, 399, 406, 409, 410
226 Sqn, 141, *142*, 143, 157, 183, 255, 256, 257, 266, 272, *295*, 322, 339, 398, 437, 458, 465, 469
229 Sqn, 304, 315, 318, 332, 342, 386, 391-392, 399, 410
A Flt, 310, 339
B Flt, 312
235 Sqn, 184, 248, 254, 313, 373, 384, 390, 494
236 Sqn, 494
242 Sqn, 272, 307, 317, 318, 323, 329, 351, 353, 357, 365, 386, 392, 399, 402, 410, 443, 450, 455, 462, 463, 469, 470, 471, 486, 487
A Flt, 304, 312, 322, 450
245 Sqn, 393, 395, 396, 399, 406, 409
A Flt, 304
248 Sqn, 314, 316, 384
250 Sqn, *28*
253 Sqn, 267, 315, 316, 317, 328, 351, 353
A Flt, 310, 312, 322, 339
B Flt, 312, 322
254 Sqn, *254*, 405
264 Sqn, 253, *255*, *257-258*, *261*, 262, 265, 359, 380, 381, 382, 386, 392, 393, *399*, 402, 437, 458
266 Sqn, 411, 412, 446, 465
271 (Transport) Sqn, 233
310 (Czech) Sqn, 413
320 Sqn, 276
350 (Belgian) Sqn, 374
500 Sqn, 332, 362, 390, *398*, 408, 465
501 Sqn, 145, *174*, *175*, 233, 239, 240, 242, 247, 253, 254, 257, 272, 273, 279, 283, 289, 290, 295, *320*, 356, 362, 378, 382, *383*, 398, 415, 416, 422, 423, 429, 430, 434, 443, 445, 450, 456, 471, 480, 490, 494, *524*
504 Sqn, 243, 257, 272, *277*, 282, 283, 290, 299, 300, 307, 312-313, 315, 322, 332

Units, British—continued
600 (City of London) Sqn, *149*, 175, 184, 229
601 (County of London) Sqn, *149*, 272, 316, 317, 328, 329, 335, *351*, *379*, 383, 435, 437
    A Flt, 304, 313, 322, 332, 339
    B Flt, 310, 323
602 (City of Glasgow) Sqn, *149*
603 (City of Edinburgh) Sqn, *149*
604 Sqn, 184, 223, 302, 344, 377
605 Sqn, 345, 347, 351, 362, 373, 376, 379
607 (County of Durham) Sqn, *77*, 109, 125, 132, 138, *149*, *150*, 152, 153, 154, 155, 175, 183, 206, 207, *209*, *210*, *212*, *213*, 214, 233, 241, 242, 247, 254, 257, 262, 272, *279*, 283, 288, *289*, 290, 300, 304, 308, 313, 314, 315, 323, 332, *344*, 399, *508*
609 Sqn, 100, 199, 395, 399, 402, 406, 458
610 Sqn, 339, 379, 381, 383, 385, 391, 392, *399*, 462
611 Sqn, 386, 411, 412, 414
613 Sqn, 361, 370, 377, 378
615 (County of Surrey) Sqn, *77*, 109, 116, 124, 126, 131, 155, 175, 183, 247, 254, 257, 272, 277, 281, 283, 288, 290, 293, 295, 299, *304*, 307, 309, 313, 323, 327, 332, *344*, *406*, 446, 490, 497
616 Sqn, 386, 388, 395, 406, 408, 409, 410, 419
662 AOP Sqn, *323*
801 (FAA) Sqn, 384, 398, 402, 487, 490, 496
806 (FAA) Sqn, 384, 385, 393
815 (FAA) Sqn, 248
825 (FAA) Sqn, 356, 373, 385, 390
826 (FAA) Sqn, 496
AFDU, 118
Missing Research & Enquiry Unit (MREU), 267, 268, 270, 282, 304, 351, 437, 446, *527*
    No. 1 MREU, 321, 345
No. 1 ATS (Armament Training Station), 244
No. 4 (Continental) Ferry Flt, 283, 316, 487
No. 4 Ferry Pilots Pool, 244, 322
No. 21 Aircraft Depot, Château Bougon, 182, 321, 322
No. 1426 (Enemy Aircraft) Flt, 118
Photographic Development Unit (PDU), 109, 137, 162, *437*
SOE (Special Operations Executive), 387
Special Survey Flight, 109
I Corps, 174, 368, *397*
II Corps, 174, *397*
III Corps, *397*
51st Highland Div., 430, 435, 443, 449, 455, 457, *460*, 463
20th Guards Bde, 367
30th Bde, 367
3rd Royal Tank Regt, 367
60th Rifles, 420
King's Royal Hussars, *510*
Queen Victoria's Rifles, 420
The Rifle Bde, 420

Dutch
Dutch Air Force, *84*
    Order of Battle, 190
1-I-1, 191, 222, 229, 261, 276
2-I-1, 111, 138, 159, 191, 192, 221, 222, 229, 236, 261
1-II-1, 110, 116, 191, 192, 205, 211, 236
1/2-II-1, 236, 250, 261, 276
2-II-1 (2e JaVa), 125, 192, 226, 229, 236, 261
3-II-1, 119, 157, 159, *192*, 193, 209, 211, 228, 261
4-II-1, 106, 107, 116, 132, *193*, 236, 250, 261, 276

Units, Dutch—continued
I-2, 139, 171, 193, 250, 261, 276
II-1, 117, 119, 132
II-2, 193, 250, 276
3-II-2, 206
III-2, 147, 193, 222, 236, *250*, 261, 276
IV-2, 98, 116, 158, 193, 229, 250, 261
V-2, 141, 151
1-V-2, 193, *194*, 206, 211, 222
2-V-2, 117, 276
3-V-2, 150, 194, 222
GVT2, 95, 194
GVT3, 250, 276
GVT5, 276
10e Batterij Lu.A, 223
24e Batterij Lu.A, 241
76e Batterij Lu.A, 223
164e Batterij Lu.A, *219*, 226
Depot Wielrijders, 229
Jachtvliegschool Texel, 141, 148, 149
Luchtvaart Afdeeling (LVA), 84
Marine Luchtvaart Dienst (MLD), 153, 159, 194, 236, 250, 261, 276
    Order of Battle, 190
Vliegschool Haamstede, 98, 102, 116, 142, 148, 250, 261
Vliegschool Texel, 236
Vliegschool Vlissingen, 104, 116, 142, 147, 148, 163, 165, 167

French
Armée de l'Air
    Order of Battle, 185-187
    organisation, 80-81
CEAM (Experimental Centre), 253, 459
CIC, 148
Défense Aérienne du Territoire (DAT)
    DAT Avord, 358
    DAT Bourges, 358, 360, 424, 481
    DAT Chartres, 407, 416, 418, 459
    DAT Châteaudun, 253, 305, 419, 469, 470
    DAT Châteauroux, 165, 424, 429
    DAT Clermont-Ferrand, 478, 492, 496
    DAT Étampes, 413, 414, 418
    DAT Lyon, 407, 410
    DAT Rennes, 395
    DAT Romorantin, 419, 429, 481
    DAT Tours, 387, 469, 479, 492
    Order of Battle, 187
DIAP (CWL), 150, 305, 424
ECMJ 1/16, 156, 259, 263, 265, 273, 296, 317, 325, 380, 470
ECN 1/13, 147, 317, 328, 341, 416
ECN 2/13, 158, 305, 307, 380, 381, 418
ECN 3/13, 96, 305, 352
ECN 4/13, 93, 305, 324, 328, 340, 380, 413, 498
ECN 5/13, 407, 410, 414
GAO 501, 259, *324*, 364, 424, 426, 458
GAO 502, 96, 102, 234, 248, 273, *284*, 478
GAO 503, *296*
GAO 504, 106, 284
GAO 505, 96
GAO 506
    GAO 1/506, 94, 112, 380, 469
    GAO 2/506, 112, 373, 419
GAO 507, 95, 128, 188, 234, 333, *334*
GAO 508
    GAO 1/508, 168, 314, 373, 469
    GAO 2/508, 98, 424
GAO 509, 259, 424
GAO 510, 188, 259, 284, 296, 380, 424, 446, 478
GAO 511, 234, 248, 259
GAO 512, 373

Units, French—continued
GAO 513, 387
GAO 514
    GAO 1/514, 346, 455
    GAO 2/514, 107, 488
GAO 515, 492
GAO 516, 188, 346
GAO 517, 139, 419, 446
GAO 518, 95, 188, 284, 340, 458, 465, 475
GAO 520
    GAO 1/520, 94, 96, 105, 153, 162, 234
    GAO 2/520, 127, *188*, 212, 273, 333, 358
GAO 543, 395, *446*, 451, 453
GAO 544, 145, 188, 248, *249*, 324
GAO 545, 273
GAO 546, 284, 364, 451
GAO 547, 273, 296
GAO 548, 149, 164
GAO 551
    GAO 1/551, 188, 234, 284, 296, 324, 352, 395, 446
    GAO 2/551, 188, 234, 248
    GAO 3/551, 94, 95, 284, 314, 334, 336, 424, 465
    GAO 4/551, 296, 305
GAO 552, 259, 284, 314, 324
GAO 553, 93, 98, 103, 141, 248, 296, 364
GAO 581, 465, 469
GAO 582, 416
GAO 584, GAO 1/584, 446, 448, 481
GAO 589, GAO 1/589, 413, 440, 456, 461, 465
GAR 14, 93, 96, 102
GAR 1/14, 94
GB 10, 364
GB I/11, 171, 358, 380, 395, 400, 402, 416, 432, 446, 456, 478
GB 1/11, 465
GB 2/11, 400
GB II/11, 466, 499
GB I/12, 234, 235, 259, 266, 273, 296, 334, 346, 400, 419, 440, 456
GB 1/12, 134, 259
GB 2/12, 259
GB II/12, 115, 234, 235, 259, 266, 273, 284, 296, 305, 324, 334, 395, 432, 456
GB 3/12, 234, 259
GB 4/12, 296
GB I/15, 234, 266, 305, 334, 419, 424
GB 2/15, 395
GB II/15, 188, 266, 324, 432, 478
GB I/19, 392, 400, 424, 440, 466
GB 1/19, 400, 466
GB 2/19, 456
GB II/19, 346, 358, 400, 466
GB 4/19, 446
GB I/21, 352, *358*, 364, 380, 387, 392, 413, 446, 451, 466
GB 1/21, 358
GB II/21, 188, 358, 364, 380, 387, 413, 419, 456, 458, 466, 469
GB 4/21, 364
GB I/23, 358, 364, 488
GB II/23, 447
GB 3/23, 432
GB 4/23, 456, 466
GB I/25, 475
GB 31, *102*
GB I/31, 95, 99, 114, 284, 296, 305-306, 334, 400, 440, 451
GB 1/31, 94, 103, 296
GB 2/31, 334
GB II/31, 94, 314, 392, 400, 432, 466, 475
GB 4/31, 400
GB I/34, 188, 259, 266, 273-274, 340, 494
GB 2/34, *105*, 273
GB II/34, 188, 259, 266, 274, 296, 314, 400, 416, 458
GB II/35, 123, 296, 310, 314, 416, 447, 478

Units, French—continued
GB I/38, 156, 188, 266
GB II/38, 259, 266, 274, 296, 395
GB 4/38, 458
GB I/51, 433
GB II/54, 298, 304, 310, 314, 433
GB I/62, 374, 400, 425, 432, 461
GB II/62, 358, 400-401, 425, 433, 440, 451, 461
GB I/63, 346, 358, 407, 425, 440, 447, 451
GB 2/63, 358
GB II/63, 358, 433, 440, 461
GB 4/63, 401
GBA I/51, 346, 364, 366, 424, 433, 440, 447, 451, 456, 466
GBA 1/51, 395
GBA 2/51, 334, 424
GBA II/51, 334, 346, 373, 396, 424, 433, 440, 447, 451, 461, 469-470
GBA 4/51, 340
GBA I/54, 103, 171, 248, 266, 296, 340, 447, 466, 475
GBA 1/54, 248
GBA 2/54, 451
GBA II/54, 249, 266, 297, 364, 400, 425, 433, 440, 451, 475, 481
GBA 3/54, 425
GBA 4/54, 297
GBA II/61, 470
GC I/1, 117, 163, 259, 274, 280, 288, 289, 297, 298, 306, *307*, 308, 335, 336, 340, 352, 374, 425, 434, 447, 451, 476, 495
GC 1/1, 262, 334, 340
GC 2/1, 249, 274, 340, 416
GC II/1, 83, 188, 253, 274, 279, 280, 281, 288, 306, 324, 328, 335, 341, 416, 418, 433, 434, 458, 499
GC 3/1, 284-285
GC 4/1, 274
GC III/1, *83*, 148, 188, 210, 214, 298, 301, 306, 315, 336, 342, 364, 366, 375, 376, 455, 493, 496
GC 5/1, 249, 253, 259, *260*, *297*, 324-325, 340, 364, 456
GC 6/1, 188, 210, 211, 214, 249, *260*, 306, 314, 325, 374, 458, 499
GC I/2, 83, 156, 157, 188, 213, 240, 306, 328, 329, 335, 358, 380, 413, 429, 447, 448, 453, 458, *489*, 499
GC 1/2, 334
GC 2/2, 156, 157, 213, 234, 481
GC II/2, 99, 117, 156, 188, 213, 234, 239, 241, 252, 259, 262, *264*, 265, 274, 277, 285, 297, 315, 317, 326, 340, 343, 375, 408, 413, 425, 427, *447*, 477, 478, *488*
GC 4/2, 234
GC III/2, 83, 95, 96, 107, 126, 131, 139, 157, 188, 206, 234, 251, 259, 260, 278, 290, *297*, 298, 300, 301, 306, 307, 308, 314, 316, 334, 336, 340, 358, 376, 447, 448, 451, *452*, 459, 461, 462, 466, 467, 470
GC 5/2, 114, 274, 285, 297, *305*, 306
GC 6/2, 234, 235, 242, 285, 297, 466
GC I/3, 96, 97, *118*, 263, *273*, 274, 277, 278, 279, 285, 289, 290, 297, 314, 316, 327, 340, 342, 376, *401*, 416, 417, 418, 425, 427, 433, 434, 441, 451, 453, 470, 476, 478, 479
GC 1/3, 285, 352
GC II/3, 120, 121, 146, 152, 156, 161, 162, 340, 341, 342, 343, 346, 347, 359, 360, 364, 365, 374, 375, 376, 380, 388, 401, *426*, 440, 442, 447, 448, 452, 466
GC 3/3, 401
GC 4/3, 347
GC III/3, 99, 100, 153, 157, 234, 235, *254*, 262, 265, 290, 315, 325, 326, 327, 336, 337, 360, 425, 427, 429, 466, 479, 492
GC 5/3, 145, 249, 260, 334, 358, 413, 425, 433

Units, French—continued
GC 6/3, 249, 254, 260, 360
GC I/4, 97, 119, 208, 212, 213, 235, 239, *240*, 241, 262, 307, 308, 336, 347, 366, 375, 376, 427, 433, 434, 442, 470
GC 1/4, 97, 188, *235*, 260, *305*, 306, 364, 374
GC 2/4, 134, 235, 334, 425, 433, 458, 475
GC II/4, 92, 93, 94, 97, 98, 99, 100, 102, 108, 114, 117, 161, 188, 213, 239, 241, 249, 285, 288, 289, 300, 301, 314, 315, 316, 317, 325, 326, 336, 364, 366, 388, 392, 427, 429, 433, 434, 440, 441, 451, 453, 459, *470*, 478
GC 3/4, 188, 274, 314, 392, 440
GC 4/4, 97, 285
GC I/5, 100, *113*, 120, 131, 133, 156, 157, 158, 162, 164, 188, 189, 208, 209, 215, 240, 252, *253*, 254, 260, 262, 263, 265, 274, 279, 288, 298, 301, 307, 308, 314, 317, 326, 328, 329, 341, 353, 359, 374, 376, 407, 408, 410, 417, 418, 441, 442, 447, 448, 453, 456, 475, 476, 479
GC 1/5, 249, 260, 407
GC II/5 (Lafayette), 95, 99, 100, 107, 112, *113*, 115, 117, 119, 120, 131, 133, 135, 145, 163, 164, 171, 205, 240, 249, 251, 253, 274, 280, 285, 297, 298, 314-315, *315*, 316, 335, 341, 358, 360, 365, 376, 388, 392, 419, *425*, 427, 433, 434, 448, 456, 470, *475*, 476, 479
GC 4/5, 100
GC I/6, 148, 157, 164, 315, 316, 334, 335, 336, 341, 360, 364, 365, 374, 417, 418, 423, 425, 429, 441, 447, 458-459, *466*, 479
GC 1/6, 315, 341, 499
GC 2/6, *364*, 425
GC II/6, 83, 96, 117, 118, 148, 171, 235, 241, 252, 260, 262, *263*, 274, 285, 290, 297-298, 425, 429, 433, 434, 441, 447, 451, 459, 476, 498
GC 3/6, 142, 213, 298
GC 4/6, 260, 274, 447
GC III/6, 83, 97, 102, 120, 121, 145, 157, 158, 189, 206, 211, 235, 240, 241, 274, 278, 341, 358, 364, 365, 396, *467*, 471, *477*
GC 5/6, 235, 241
GC 6/6, 100
GC II/7, 83, 93, 97, 117, 121, 126, 127, 132, 135, 145, 157, 158, 160, 165, 171, 189, 211, 235, 240, 249, 290, 298, 360, 388, 408, 409, 410, 413, 414, 425-426, 428, 441, 456, 475, 476, 477, 478
GC 3/7, 189, 212
GC III/7, 107, 117, 123, 127, 132, 133, 139, 143, 154, 158, 159, 162, 188, 189, 234, 235, 240, 249, 251, 252, 254, 260, 270, 271, 274, 285-286, *285*, 341, 342, 401, 417, 426, 433, 447, 452, 475
GC 5/7, 270, 341
GC 6/7, 189, 270
GC I/8, 208, 213, 234, 235, 240, 241, 274, 290, 298, 301, 306, 307, 308, 315, 325, 327, 334, 337, 366, 417, 418, 426, 428, 429, 433, 434, 441, 452, 461-462, *461*, 476, 495
GC 2/8, 189, 380
GC II/8, 210, 214, 298, 313, 341, 342, 358, 380, 387, 407, 408, 452, 496
GC II/9, 335, 341, 358, 374, 375, 393, 417, 418, 429, 433, 434, 452, 456, 459
GC 3/9, 417
GC III/9, 83, 162, 189, 212, 407, 409, 410, 413, 414
GC 5/9, 407
GC II/10, 83, *275*, 286, 298, 300, 306, 309, 336, 422, 426, 428, 429, *440*, 441, 447, 466

Units, French—continued
GC 3/10, 154, 315, 334
GC 4/10, 274
GC III/10, 83, 275, 277, 280, 286, 306, 309, 336, 341, 441
GC 6/10, 275
GC 23, 119
GC I/55, 413, 495
GC I/145 (Polish Fighter Sqn 'Warsaw'), 83, 452
GC 1/145, 150, 160, 305, 358, 364, 380, 452, 455, 456, 492
GIA I/601, 417, 462
GR I/14, 107, 249, 275, *286*, 306, *462*, 466, 470
GR II/14, 492, 499
GR I/22, 95, 148, *189*, *462*
GR 1/22, 496
GR 2/22, 249
GR II/22, 100, 105, 107, 112, 113, 134, 275, 286, 306, 426
GR 3/22, *105*, 470
GR I/33, 110, 113, 126, 419, 481
GR 1/33, 95, *106*, 456
GR II/33, 99, 107, 111, 117, 126, 189, 249, 306, 325, 346, *346*, 352, 359, 396, 452, 456, 478
GR 3/33, 97, 108, 159, 165, 260, 346
GR I/35, 478
GR 1/35, 108, 141, 249, 352, 364, 441, 447
GR 2/35, 419
GR I/36, 117, 157, 189, 249, 306, 325, 426, 433, 434
GR 1/36, 275
GR II/36, 157, 161, 189, 346
GR 4/36, 99
GR I/52, 94, 102, 126, 151, 152, 161, 170, 260, 325, 364, 475
GR 1/52, 93, 413
GR 2/52, *93*, 98
GR II/52, 93, 97, 98, 99, 100, 189, 235, 249, 260, 274, 285, 286, *325*
GR 3/52, 334
GR 4/52, 106
GR I/55, 126, 167, 481
GR 1/55, 380
GR II/55, 98, 103, 133, 325, 334, 341, 359, 407, 447, 452, 466, 475, 492, 495, 496
GR 3/55, 133
GR I/133, 147
'Groupe de Chasse Marche Polonais', 407
'Montpellier Group', 83, 171, 364, 426, 441
SAL 2/104, 352
SAL 3/109, 341
Aéronautique Navale, 80
Order of Battle, 187
1S1, 158, 359
2S1, 94, 497
1S2, 456, 488, 497
3S2, 417, 488
2S3, 142
2S4, 106, 359, 495
AB 1, *305*, *333*, 340, 352, 419, 451, 452, 492, 497, 499
AB 2, 127, 157, 319, *324*, *333*, 340
AB 3, 188, 346, 465, 472, 494
AB 4, 305, 319, *324*, 340, 419, 492
AC 1, 188, 223, 239, 308, 342
AC 2, 234, 239, 259, 308, 314, 481, 488, 494
AC 3, 467, 472, 475, 477
AC 5, 481, 492, 495, 497, 499
Cours de Chasse, 492, 499
E2, 284, 305, 488, 497
E6, 95, 488
EGAN, 451
F1C Flotille de Chasse, 157, 259, 352, 373, 416
SCLE, 419, 497
HS 2, 93
SESBA, 117, 488

Units, French—continued
SESBR, 380
SESCB, 488
SRC (later SLE and SCLE), 104, 499
T1, 152
T2, *352*, 456, 492
T3, 138, 140, 352, 452, 456, 459, 492
Groupe d'Armées 4, 490
1ère Armée, 281, 302, 389
7ème Armée, 174, 255
9ème Armée, 255, 319, 325
10ème Armée, 435, 471
IX Corps d'Armée, 455, 457, *460*
XX Corps d'Armée, 94
1st Light Cavalry Div., *249*
3ème Régt d'Hélicoptères de Combat (3 RHC), *29*, *57*
108e Inf. Regt, 429
414e Régt de Pionniers, 213

German
Luftwaffe Order of Battle, 89, 202-204
1.(F)/Ob.d.L, 134
3.(F)/Ob.d.L, 156
1.(H)/10, 206, 262, 288
2.(H)/10, 133, 452, 470, 476
3.(F)/10, 136, 251, 313, 315, 332, 335, 375
1.(H)/11, 165, 321, 326, 434
2.(F)/11, 288, 434, 456
3.(F)/11, 133, 162, 251, 262, 326, 365, 380
4.(F)/11, 144, 145, 156, 206, 251, 262, 315, *316*, 326, 335, 341, 456, 470, *478*
1.(H)/12, 298, 479
2.(H)/12, 206, 326, 353, 408, 434, 441, 452, 462
3.(H)/12, 288, *298*, 456, 479
4.(H)/12, 149, 434
5.(H)/12, 298
1.(H)/13, 107, 142, 163, 164, 251, 456
2.(H)/13, 135, 160
3.(H)/13, 375, 427, 476
4.(H)/13, 206, 239, 251, 288, 298, 365, 380
5.(H)/13, 128, 341, 456, 499
1.(H)/14, 148, 239, 288, 298, 307, 341, 349, 353, 359, 456, 459
2.(H)/14, 307, 359, 441
3.(H)/14, 140, 206, 277, 288, 307, 326, 434
4.(F)/14, 151, 162, 262, 288, 311, 315, *318*, 459
1.(H)/21, 140, 164, 251, 476
2.(H)/21, 134, 163, 307, 388, 392
3.(H)/21, 298, 341, 434
4.(H)/21, 158, 251, 375, 392, 441, 476, 479
1.(F)/22, 114, 145, 335, 365, *407*, *408*, 409
1.(H)/22, 388
2.(F)/22, 146, 154, 298, 314, 315, 335, 359, 364, 365
3.(F)/22, 97, 133, 117, 119, 256, 260, 262, 315, 388, 392, 427, 479
4.(H)/22, 102, 107, 108, 288, 335, 359, 365, 380, 427, 434, 495
1.(H)/23, 107, 167, *251*, 283, 288, 298, 307, 427
2.(H)/23, 277, 315, 326, 347, 396, 459, *470*, 476, 497
4.(H)/23, 107, 359
1.(H)/31, 427, 452
2.(H)/31, 114, 148, 288, 298, 315, 341, 481, 493
3.(F)/31, 231, 239, 251, 298, 307, 335, 347
4.(H)/31, 251, 307, 347, 359
2.(H)/32, 106, 470
4.(H)/32, 481
1.(H)/41, 148, 206, 251, *262*, 298, 326, 396, 452
2.(H)/41, 158, 206, 251, 262, 307, 326, 388, 392, 459, 488
3.(H)/41, 159, 304, 307, 315, 335

Units, German—continued
1.(F)/121, 116, 148, 149, 251, *277*, 299, 341
3.(F)/121, 117, 126, *143*, *146*, 147, *155*, 158, *160*, *161*, 168, 206, 315, 341
4.(F)/121, 104, 115, 117, 145, 154, 156, 160, 161, 162, *164*, 171, 342, 375, 388, 408, 456
1.(F)/122, 119, 124
2.(F)/122, 106, *110*, 117, 119, 120, *123*, 170, 252, 365, 408, *412-413*, 427, 496
3.(F)/122, 102, 120, 123, 125, 239, 277
4.(F)/122, 95, 107, 119, 120, 128, 135, 165, 335, 380, 497
5.(F)/122, 120, 154, *158*, 335, 353, 365, 392, 396, 459
1.(F)/123, *32*, 104, 113, 114, 116, 120, 157, 162, 171, 408, 427, 456
2.(F)/123, 107, 206, 232, 234, 239, *252*, 277, 335, 359, 441, 462, *479*
3.(F)/123, 156, 158, 170, 171, 206, 380, 408, 427
4.(F)/123, 158
Aufkl.Gr. 122, *126*
Aufkl.Gr. 156, 138, 206
Aufkl.Gr.Ob.d.L, 119, 353, 365, 417
1./Aufkl.Gr.Ob.d.L, *208*, 359
2./Aufkl.Gr.Ob.d.L, 156, 206, 365
3.(F)/Aufkl.Gr.Ob.d.L, 335
4./Aufkl.Gr.Ob.d.L, 375, 427
AufklStaffel zbV. Luftflotte 2, 239, 365
Erp.Stelle Rechlin (Luftwaffe test facility), 212
Feldgendarmerietrupp 22, 225
Flakabt. 2/851, 141
Flakabt. 84, 103
Flakkorps I, 160
Aufklst. Flakkorps I, 163, 299, 335
Flakkorps VIII, Stab Flakkorps VIII, 299
Fliegerkorps
I. Fliegerkorps Aufklst, 467
I. Fliegerkorps Flugbere-itschaft, 335, 347, 467, 497
II. Fliegerkorps Flugbereitschaft, 419
VIII. Fliegerkorps Flugbereitschaft, 479
Fliegerkorps zbV 2, 216
II. Fliegerkorps, 116
IV. Fliegerkorps, *481*
Transportstaffel 1./V Fliegerkorps, 142
Transportstaffel Fl.Korps I, 206, 343, 429
Transportstaffel Fliegerkorps II, 242, 376
VIII. Fliegerkorps, 116, 133, *243*, 376
X. Fliegerkorps, 118, 143
Flugabwehrabt. 52 (Fla.52), 227, 229
FlughafenbereichsKdo. Jever, 365
Jafü Deutsche Bucht, 129
JagdfliegerFührer 2, 160
Jagdfliegerschule 1, 262
JG1, 365, 488
I./JG1, 139, 147, 154, 235, 236, 237, 247, 248, 257, 262, 326, 335, 349, 351, 359, 373, 380, 426, 432, 433, 434, 470
1./JG1, 140, 234, 236, 237, 257, 306, 324, 335, 351, 353, 373, 375, 380, 424, 425, 427, 433, 434, 465, 469, 470
2./JG1, 205, 246, 256, 353, 479
3./JG1, 105, 205, 232, 239, 324, 335, 347, 351, 470
JG2
Stab I./JG2, 284
I./JG2, 133, 139, 140, 141, 162, 163, 165, 167, 171, 205, 262, 274, 277, 288, 334, 417, 470

Units, German—continued

1./JG2, 117, 133, 134, 147, 148, 151, 157, 162, 277, 299, 311, 321, 326, 341, 373, 375, 395, 396, 405, 440
2./JG2, 161, 269, 305, 306, 358, 364, 373, 400, 402, 412, 427, 432, 433, 434, 451, 475
3./JG2, 117, 148, 167, 313, 320, 333, 334, 433, 447, 465, 497
Stab II./JG2, 375, 405, 412
II./JG2, 312, 320, 321, 322, 413, 441, 497, 498, 499
4./JG2, 239, 272, 312, 322, 326, 339
5./JG2, 294, 312, 326, 380
6./JG2, 311, 315, 321
Stab III./JG2, 277, 340, *342*, 433
III./JG2, 158, 162, 262, 441
7./JG2, 158, 288, 341, 433, 456
8./JG2, 163, 359, 392
9./JG2, 314, 342, 364, 365, 375, 418, 475
10.(N)/JG2, 205
11.(N)/JG2, 252
12.(N)/JG2, 161, 459
JG3
Stab JG3, 434
Stab I./JG3, 260, 275, 285, 323, 346, 401, 431, 445
I./JG3, 139, 140, 147, 149, 151, 156, 158, 159, 162, 205, 262, 275, 285, 299, 335, 341, 342, 392, 401, 431, 433, 434, 498
1./JG3, 158, 274, 284, 286, 303, 304, 306, 307, 326, 341, 349, 434, 456
2./JG3, 312, 313, 315, 345, 349, 373, 390, 392, 424, 437, 459, 469, 472
3./JG3, 140, 275, 285, 299, 307, 316, 326, 341, 431, 437, 464, 496
Stab II./JG3, 331, 346, 358, 424
II./JG3, 342, 365, 452, 456
4./JG3, 331, 341, 342, 364, 391, 423, 433, 434, 458
5./JG3, 335, 366, 400, 416, 424, 431, 436, 440, 441, 465, 481, 493
6./JG3, 342, 378, 400, 401, 416, 426
Stab III./JG3, 437
III./JG3, 391, 408, 441, 445
7./JG3, 191, 431, 437, 441, 448
8./JG3, 160, 256, 257, 262, 277, 321, 356, 359, 386, 388, 425, 427, 437, 441, 495
9./JG3, 267, 321, 326, 431, 440
JG20, *399*
Stab I./JG20, 391, 402
I./JG20, 147, 157, 160, 162, 163, 306, 398, 399, 422
1./JG20, 163, 205, 260, 306, 307, *308*, 392, 399, 408, 437, 465, 470
2./JG20, 164, 239, 306, 307, 398, 445, 456
3./JG20, 159, 249, 326, 398, 402, 458, 459
6./JG20, 391
JG21
Stab I./JG21, 121, 347, 359
I./JG21, 106, 148, 153, 199, 245, 247, 249, 262, 299, 307, 326, 347, 374, 392, 402, 409, 497
1./JG21, 106, 112, 117, 132, 140, 158, 159, 260, 334, 374, 375
2./JG21, 113, 115, 121, 134, 136, 140, 341, 359, 366, 374, 392, 396, 452
3./JG21, 199, 247, 249, 277, 364, 374, 376
JG26, *428*
Stab I./JG26, 402
I./JG26, 134, 135, 136, 139, 148, 152, 156, 157, 159, 160, 162, 164, 239, 259, 277, 327, 385, 386, 406, 409, 434, 479, 497

Units, German—continued

1./JG26, 103, 116, 259, 260, 262, 342
2./JG26, 93, 99, 139, 167, 239, 252, 312, 342, 386, 388, 399, 402, 406, 445, 448
3./JG26, 129, 159, 192, 347, 380, 385, 406, 409, 445, 448, 451, 452
Stab II./JG26, 294, 327, 356, 390, 459, 493
II./JG26, 139, 140, 157, 303, 304, 311, 312, 313, 386, 406, 412, 413
4./JG26, 261, 294, 299, 307, 327, 379, 391, 418, 427, 437, 441, 469
5./JG26, 164, 192, 239, 257, 262, 299, 321, 441
6./JG26, 158, 170, 303, 379, 390, 409, 459, 493
Stab III./JG26, 112, 268, 283, 398, 399, 469
III./JG26, 128, 140, 205, 235, 272, 386, 391, 392, 398, 399, 412, 446, 448, 452
7./JG26, 272, 342, 381, 386, 402, 448, 452, 469
8./JG26, 153, 205, 272, 303, 386, 402, 409, 448, 452, 464, 470
9./JG26, 205, 282, 288, 299, 321, 327, 399, 409
10.(N)/JG26, 97, 102, 104
JG27, 245, 247, 390
Stab JG27, *325*, 334, 359, 381, 390, 447, 451
Stab I./JG27, 334, 359
I./JG27, 156, 160, 244, 299, 347, 349, 360, 366, 392, 409, 412, 413, 425, 426, 464, 470, 479
1./JG27, 107, 238, 293, 353, 390, 391, 433, 451, 464, 479
2./JG27, 129, 156, 160, 244, 247, 248, 252, 295, 299, 320, 349, 353, 391, 405, 427, 434, 464, 466, 467
3./JG27, 159, 162, 199, 233, 246, 323, 352, 362, 413, 426, 466
Stab II./JG27, 250, 453
II./JG27, 288, 300, 451
4./JG27, 239, 248, 453, 478
5./JG27, 180, 181, 233, 327, 427, 434, 453, 464, 470
6./JG27, 171, 191, 192, 342, 398, 453
JG51, *428*
Stab JG51, 124, 250
Stab I./JG51, 233, 425
I./JG51, 141, 147, 149, 151, 156, 233, 335, 432, 433, 496
1./JG51, 97, 117, 120, 126, 127, 133, 167, 307, 320, 334, 351, 352, 353, 356, 425
2./JG51, 99, 106, 117, 313, 339, 347, 349, 358, 360, 376, 396, 427
3./JG51, 106, *192*, 233, 239, 335, 340, 360, 425, 496, 498, 499
Stab II./JG51, 138, 252, 445
II./JG51, 113, 116, 123, 124, 128, 134, 139, 145, 156, 162, 165, 277, 288, 316, 388
4./JG51, 158, 162, 165, 248
5./JG51, 161, 373, 469
6./JG51, 162, 164, 252, 342, 386, 412, 445, 479
JG52, *315*
Stab JG52, 96, 104, 159, 161, 300
Stab I./JG52, 117, 288, 316, 409
I./JG52, 103, 139, 147, 156, 163, 164, 327
1./JG52, 104, 140, 300
2./JG52, 103, 104, 107, 110, 118, 127, 164, 409

Units, German—continued

3./JG52, 152, 374
Stab II./JG52, 409
II./JG52, 153, 156, 158, 239, 277, 288, 300, 353, 358, 360, 376, 409, 418, 434, 459, 497, 499
4./JG52, 153, 160, 162, 267, 277, 360, 380, 450, 451, 453
5./JG52, 93, 114, 152, 160, 273, 274, 366, 447, 493
6./JG52, 113, 140, 285, 419, 456
III./JG52, 160, 288, 327, 336, 409, 434, 441
7./JG52, 364
8./JG52, 162, 314, 315, 316
9./JG52, 316, 376
JG53, *506*
Stab JG53, 114, 120, 376
Stab I./JG53, 95, 97, 100, 117, 157, 260, 270, 271, 277
I./JG53, 92, 95, 96, 98, 102, 139, 140, 142, 144, 147, 148, 150, 153, 154, 156, 164, 167, 262, 270, 277, 288, 402, 428, 434
1./JG53, 93, *94*, 95, 97, 100, 106, 107, 110, 115, 121, 131, 132, 162, 205, 234, 267, 268, 270, 271, 277, *278*, 307, 364, 366, 371, 416, *427*, 434, 451
2./JG53, 94, 99, 100, 104, 107, 115, 132, 205, 271, 274, 371, 380, 381, 400
3./JG53, 94, 95, 96, 99, 100, 112, 189, 259, 272, 273, 277, 284, 285, 288, 373, 416, 451, 470
Stab II./JG53, 100, 154, 288, 336, 342, 453
II./JG53, 107, 117, 124, 125, 136, 140, 147, 148, 151, 152, 154, 158, 162, 165, 170, 252, 262, 327, 376, 392, 418, 428, 467, 488
4./JG53, 98, 100, 104, 140, 154, 157, 260, 307, 376, 388, 418, 441, 446, 488
5./JG53, 95, 100, 107, 379, 424, *511*
6./JG53, 97, 154, 249, 325, 340, 402, 440
Stab III./JG53, 107, 133, 144, 146, *153*, 156, 161, 283, 346, 364, 380, 400, 417, 424, *427*, 428
III./JG53, *46*, 104, 115, 117, 127, 144, 145, 149, 152, 153, 154, 156, 161, 162, 163, 205, 268, 300, 325, 341, 364, 366, 380, 400, 401, 426, 458, 459, 462, 488
7./JG53, 104, 106, 107, 110, 113, 114, 136, 141, 144, 145, 148, 153, 154, 162, 316, 325, 380, 416, 417, 423, 426, 433, 434, 451, 459
8./JG53, 144, 145, 152, 162, 164, 277, 358, 380, 401, 405, 413, 416, 417, 418, 419, 425, 426, 441
9./JG53, 110, 112, 113, 117, 129, 154, 239, 358, 400, 401, 405, 415, 416
JG54
Stab I./JG54, 115, 126, 133, 157, 447
I./JG54, 102, 113, 123, 152, 162, 239, 342, 353, 392
1./JG54, 118, 120, 126, 133, 157, 252, 300, 413
2./JG54, 113, 127, 135, 160, 162, 252
3./JG54, 107, 115, 156, 386, 390, 440
4./JG54, *118*
JG71, 113
I./JG71, 99, 102
JG72, 10.(N)/JG72, 105, 106, 110, 117, 135

Units, German—continued

JG76
Stab I./JG76, 133, 272
I./JG76, 118, 147, 148, 149, 154, 158, 162, 165, 239, 260, 262, 265, 268, 271, 277, 307-308, 314, 316, 362, 366, 416, 433, 455, 456
1./JG76, *118*, 133, 158, 274, 277, 296, 314, 396, 419, 433, 441
2./JG76, 162, 308, 316, 352, 425, 433
3./JG76, *118*, 278, 283, 396, 433, 496
JG77
Stab JG77, 121, 138, 140, 158, 341
Stab I./JG77, 284, 289, 323, 373
I./JG77, 99, 102, 117, 148, 151, 154, 162, 164, 165, 167, 170, 205, 252, 262, 327
1./JG77, 128, 131, 148, 308, 315, 322
2./JG77, 103, 140, 205, 274, 282, 285, 289, 322, 325, 327
3./JG77, 99, 129, 260, 285, 339
II./JG77, 118
JG132, II./JG132, *87*
JGr.88, 3./JGr.88, *427*
JGr.102, 109, 111, 112, 115, 120
StabJGr.102, 112
I./JGr.102, 127
1./JGr.102, 112
2./JGr.102 (formerly I./ZG2), 107, 112, 136
3./JGr.102, 112, 127
JGr.152, 97, 98, 99, 123
2./JGr.152, 97, 100
3./JGr.152, 93, 96, *97*, 104
JGr.176, 98, 106, 115, 116, 132, 141
1./JGr176, 99
2./JGr176, 98
3./JGr.176, 98
KG1, 476
Stab KG1, 124, 150, 154, 162, 232, 239, 316
I./KG1, 151, 153, 154, 157, 160, 164, 170, 392, 446, 448, 459
1./KG1, 360, 392-393
2./KG1, 118, 448
3./KG1, *206*, 353, 381, 448, 470
II./KG1, 134, 142, 145, 252, 312, 316
4./KG1, 419
5./KG1, 188, 206, 278, 479, 487, 488
6./KG1, 308, 316, 353
Stab III./KG1, 206
III./KG1, 150, 159, 360, 462, 467, 497
7./KG1, 206, 278, 441, *495*
8./KG1, 278, 413, 470
9./KG1, *207*, 342, 495
KG2, 140, 189, 285, 309, 340, 343, 379
Stab KG2, 120, 160, 171, 262, 289, 300, 308, 327, 381, 393
Stab I./KG2, 278
I./KG2, 239, 285
1./KG2, 118, 120, 239, 289, 308
2./KG2, 116, 118, 119, 123, 148, 156, 239, 289, 451, 453, 470
3./KG2, 133, 136, 308, 381
Stab II./KG2, 300, 360, 459
II./KG2, 140, 141, 181, 188, 278, 308, 316, 336, 453, 476
4./KG2, 160, 208, 233, 239, 456, 459
5./KG2, 233, 239, 278, 300, 336, 396, 476
6./KG2, 132, 188, 208, 278, 300, 316, 360, 381, 476
Stab III./KG2, 162
III./KG2, 145, 148, 170, 181, 239, 285, 453, 493
7./KG2, 164, 189, 208, 252, 456, 493

Units, German—continued

8./KG2, 188, 252, 289, 325, 327, 342, 381, 441
9./KG2, 208, 252, 289, 376, *380*, 381
KG3
Stab KG3, 180, 208, 249, 252, 342, 366
Stab I./KG3, 252
I./KG3, 252, 314, 337, 342, 366, 381, 395, 396, 453
1./KG3, 316, 366, 379
2./KG3, 366, 381
3./KG3, 249, 252, 336, 366, 379, 381, 418
Stab II./KG3, 253, 327
II./KG3, 125, 127, 247, 283, 308, 325, 327, 381
4./KG3, 181, 208, 253, 381
5./KG3, 208, 253, 283, 289
6./KG3, 289, 290, 327
Stab III./KG3, 208, 239
III./KG3, 139, 181, 189, 308, 381
7./KG3, 189, 208, 381
8./KG3, 181, 208, 381, 476
9./KG3, 208, 209, 239, 381
KG4, *193*, 493
Stab KG4, 117, 119, 192, 209, 308, 336
I./KG4, 192, 315, 409
1./KG4, 126, 193, 209, 262, 409, 467
2./KG4, 209, 300, 316
3./KG4, 120
Stab II./KG4, 262
II./KG4, 115, 220, 228, 312
4./KG4, 209, 336, 448
5./KG4, 192, 209, 262, 316
6./KG4, 262, *327*
III./KG4, 191, 327, 376, 377
7./KG4, 191, 193, 209, 327, 336, 376, 402
8./KG4, 209, 289, 402, 418, 476, 479
9./KG4, 209, 327, 360, 376, 467, 476
KG26, 1./KG26, 481
KG27, 150, 160, 196, 199, 200, *201*, 268, *354*, 398, 399
Stab KG27, 148, *381*, 382, 396, 402, 488
Stab I./KG27, *205*, 210, 262, 342, 428
I./KG27, 149, 154, 180, *205*, 422
1./KG27, 136, 388, 402, 428
2./KG27, 121, 164, *209*, 210, 239, 278, 289
3./KG27, *210*, 429, 434, 479
Stab II./KG27, 210
II./KG27, 164, 183, 188
4./KG27, 115, 117, 210, 316, 467, 476, 479
5./KG27, 148, 263, 382, 402
6./KG27, 183, 210, 278, 316, 402
Stab III./KG27, 347
III./KG27, 123, 148, 154, 234, *326*, 345
7./KG27, 210, *211*, 239, 278, *382*
8./KG27, 210, 239, 320, 327, 347
9./KG27, 167, 210-211, 278, *300*, 327, 347, 413
KG28
Stab KG28, 342, 441, 459
II./KG28, 150, 158, 160
III./KG28, 162, 316
7./KG28, 263, 298, 300
8./KG28, 308
9./KG28, 327-328
KG30, *481*
Stab I./KG30, 211
I./KG30, 192, 347, 497
1./KG30, 211, 299, 300, 316, 336, 353, 396, 481
2./KG30, 289, 300
3./KG30, 194, 211, 278, 300, 347, 481

4./KG30, 211
5./KG30, 211, 253, 479
6./KG30, 171
Stab III./KG30, 308
7./KG30, 211, 402, 476
8./KG30, 211, 263, 289, 300, 314, 316, 347, 376, 388
KG51, 383, 416, 453
Stab KG51, 114, 316, 382, *418*, 453
Stab I./KG51, 211, 253, 429
Aufkl.Schwarm Stab I./KG51, 211
I./KG51, 103, 113, 138, 189, 240, 316, 360, 382, 413, 417, 418, 459, 462, 489, 493
1./KG51, 116, 240, 493
2./KG51, 211, 328, 382, 453, 470, 489
3./KG51, 113, 116, 274, 278, 328, 336, 382, 413, 414
Stab II./KG51, 366, 498
II./KG51, 212, 240, 263, 321, *326*, 407, 453, 459, 462
4./KG51, 328, 409, 429, *489*
5./KG51, 328, 429, 470
6./KG51, 212, 328
Stab III./KG51, 278, 382
III./KG51, 111, 140, 156, 240, 278, 388, 418, 470
Aufkl.Schwarm III./KG51, 328
7./KG51, 212, 328, 382
8./KG51, 212, 274, 278, 358, *360*, 382, 414
9./KG51, 98, 212, 240, 279, 283, 289-290
KG53, 114, 254
Stab KG53, 120, 163, 212, 240, 253, 263, 353, 366, 476, 493
Stab I./KG53, 240, 382
I./KG53, 115, 212, 235, 240, 300, 334, 353, 456, 496
1./KG53, 123, 147, 336, 378, 382, *383*
2./KG53, 115, 139, 240, 253, 279, 290, 336, 376
3./KG53, 240, 253, 409, *475*, 476
Stab II./KG53, 212
II./KG53, 129, 181, 242, 247, 300, 347, 429, 441, 462
4./KG53, 240, 253, 407, 409
5./KG53, 212
6./KG53, 376
Stab III./KG53, 476
III./KG53, 124, 212, 240, 263, 328, 496
7./KG53, 107, 212, 279, 328, 429
8./KG53, 470
9./KG53, 240, 290, 407, 410
KG54, 188, 199, 266, 322, 323, 379
Stab KG54, *240*, 249, 253, 328, 462, 476
I./KG54, 106, *263*, 266, 304, 321, 328, *517*
1./KG54, 240, 290, 329, 360, 382, 414
2./KG54, 253, 308, 360, 383
3./KG54, 158, 240, 260, *263*, 290, 308, *309*, 317, 329
II./KG54, 140, 148, *383*
4./KG54, 212, 329, 342, *343*, *383*, 414
5./KG54, 212, 342, *383*
6./KG54, 212, 329, *383*, 414, 499
Stab III./KG54, 212
III./KG54, 150, 151, 183, 201, 376, 462
7./KG54, 329
8./KG54, *212*, 213, 329
9./KG54, 317, *414*, 479
KG55, 424
Stab KG55, 126, 141, 188, 213, 255, 263, 290, 374, 376, 419, 429, 442, *452*, 470

I./KG55, 279, 317, 402, 407
1./KG55, 279, 407, 410
2./KG55, 240, 336, 376
3./KG55, 240, 263, 383
Stab II./KG55, 263
II./KG55, 111, 170, 314, 336, 442, 479
4./KG55, 253, 317, 442, 493
5./KG55, 213, 253, 263, 317, 353, 424, 425, 429
6./KG55, 241, 263, 265, 317
Stab III./KG55, 213
III./KG55, 153, 188, 235, 241, 285, 317, 413, 442, 453, 489
7./KG55, 235, 241, 279, 343, 429, *442*
8./KG55, 213, 255, 265, 290, 410, 414, 459
9./KG55, 188, 213, 353, 402, 414, 429, 479
KG76, 188, 429, 433
Stab KG76, 213, 290, 343, 434
Stab I./KG76, 290, 418
I./KG76, 107, 114, 144, 157, 158, 165, 277, 285, 416
1./KG76, 213, 336, 418, 476
2./KG76, 265, 311, 313, 317, 442
3./KG76, 107, 124, 268, 279, 300, 418, 419, 429
Stab II./KG76, 366
II./KG76, 150, 170, 188, 189, 235, 241, 259, 265, 300, 364, 416, 417
4./KG76, 308, 312, 317, 343, 366, 410, 418, 434, 453
5./KG76, 279, 308, 312, 317, 347, 366, 448
6./KG76, 213, 253, 265, 279, 308, 347, 353, 418
Stab III./KG76, 279, 290, 418
III./KG76, 125, 142, 144, 145, 241, 311, 312
7./KG76, 213, 279, 300, 308, 329, 418, 434
8./KG76, 290, 343, 418, 462
9./KG76, 234, 300-301, *301*, 308, 329, 336, 376, 429
KG77, 196, 199, *200*
Stab KG77, 329, 336, 470, 477, 495
Stab I./KG77, 265
I./KG77, 106, 139, 477
1./KG77, 360
2./KG77, 301, 376
3./KG77, 106, 121, 241, 329, 360
II./KG77, 141, 148, 160, 388
4./KG77, 213, 453
5./KG77, 213, 241, 290, 477
6./KG77, 213, 241, 294, 301, 396, 453
III./KG77, 141, 385, 388
8./KG77, 170, 171, 245, 253, 388
9./KG77, 241, 388
KGr.126
1./KGr.126, 343, 353
2./KGr.126, 191, 193, 213, 235, 260, 265, 360, 467
3./KGr.126, 241, *254*, 479
KGrzbV.5, 17./KGrzbV.5, 213, 254
KGrzbV.9, 216, 218, 219, 222, 223, 224, 227, 229, 230, 243, 489
Stab KGrzbV.9, 224-225
1./KGrzbV.9, 222-223, 226, 229, 279
2./KGrzbV.9, 152, 222, 224, 225, 343
3./KGrzbV.9, 151, 225-226, *226*
4./KGrzbV.9, 224, 226, 254, 317, 456
KGrzbV.11, 216, 221, 222
Stab KGrzbV.11, 221
KGrzbV.12, 216, 218, 219, 221, 222, 223, 224, 227
Stab KGrzbV.12, 222, 224

1./KGrzbV.12, 224
2./KGrzbV.12, 224
3./KGrzbV.12, 222
4./KGrzbV.12, 224
KGrzbV.101, 479
1./KGrzbV.101, 493
KGrzbV.105, 442
KGrzbV.108, 3./KGrzbV.108, 206
KGrzbV.172, 216, 217, 219, 396, 489
I./KGrzbv.172, 216, 221, 227, 229, 495, 498
1./KGrzbv.172, 221, 227, 317
4./KGrzbv.172, 228
KGzbV.1
I./KGzbV.1, 216, 217, 218, 221-222, 228, 301, 343, 388, 477, 498
1./KGzbV.1, 456
2./KGzbV.1, 221
3./KGzbV.1, 221
4./KGzbV.1, 221
II./KGzbV.1, 216, 217, 228, 229
6./KGzbV.1, 241
III./KGzbV.1, 193, 216, 220, 228, 229, 288, 290, 301, 308-309, 334, 336, 376
9./KGzbV.1, 228, 229
10./KGzbV.1, 229
11./KGzbV.1, 228, 366
12./KGzbV.1, 228
IV./KGzbV.1, 216, 219, 222, 223, 226, 227, 228, 229, 230, 388, 467, 477
13./KGzbV.1, 223, 227
14./KGzbV.1, 223-224, 228, 241
15./KGzbV.1, 227
16./KGzbV.1, 396
V./KGzbV.1, 119
KGzbV.2
Stab KGzbV.2, 227, 229
3./KGzbV.2, 229
KüFlGr.106, 377
1./KüFlGr.106, 95, 116
2./KüFlGr.106, 95
KüFlGr.406, 3./KüFlGr.406, 115
KüFlGr.506, 3./KüFlGr.506, 214, 241
KüFlGr.606, 206
KüFlGr.806, 3./KüFlGr.806, 151
KüFlGr.906, 3./KüFlGr.906, 241
Kurierstaffel 2, 150
Kurierstaffel 9, 121
LG1
Stab LG1, *214*, 366
I./LG1, 111, 233
1./LG1, 214, 241, 343
2./LG1, 116, 214, 254, 301, 337, 402, 499
3./LG1, 183, 214
Stab II./LG1, 279, 337, 496
II./LG1, *214*, 268
4./LG1, *214*, 254, *289*, 383, 410, 459, 481
5./LG1, 268, 279, 393
6./LG1, 337, 343, 383, 393, 496
Stab III./LG1, 429
III./LG1, 317, 332, 422, 423, 426
7./LG1, 254, 304, 309, 429
8./LG1, 214, 241, 347, *359*, 360
9./LG1, 279, 343, 347, 376, 393, 489
Stab IV.(St)/LG1, 462, 470
IV.(St)/LG1, 193, 303, 448
10.(St)/LG1, 165, 309
11.(St)/LG1, 290, 301, 309
12.(St)/LG1, *265*, 309, 448
I.(Z)/LG1, 102
Stab V.(Z)/LG1, 119
V.(Z)/LG1, 106, 131, 136, 138, 149, 153, 171, 235, 247, 279, 303, 340, 356, 379
13.(Z)/LG1, 106, 126, 132, 154, 235, 247, 254, 303, 343, 364, 379

Units, German—continued

14.(Z)/LG1, 154, 156, 241, 309
15.(Z)/LG1, 154, 156, 163, 247, 298, 301
LG2
Stab I.(J)/LG2, 321, 402, 444
I.(J)/LG2, 129, 134, 138, 140, 321, 322, 392
1.(J)/LG2, 245, 247, 254, 309, 317, 321, 329, 380, 391, 456, 496
2.(J)/LG2, 254, 320, 322, 329, 417
3.(J)/LG2, 254, 320, 321, 324, 325, 366, 424, 431, 434, 442
Stab II.(S)/LG2, 254
II.(S)/LG2, 129, 138, 140, 148, 158, 165, 167, 236, 272, 388, 429, 434, 462
4.(S)/LG2, 214, 241, 429
5.(S)/LG2, 241, *279*, 388, 467
6.(S)/LG2, 265, 290
7.(F)/LG2, 145, 301, 385, 388, 419
9.(H)/LG2, 265, 293, 301, 343
2./Leicht Abt. 86, 434
Ln.Regt. 1, 225
Ln.Regt. 2, Nachrichtungsst., 337
Ln.Regt. 3
2./Ln.Regt. 3, 381
10./Ln.Regt. 3, 150
III./Ln.Regt. 3, 157
Ln.Regt.Ob.d.L.,
Fl.Komp.Ln.Regt.Ob.d.L., 157
Ln.St. Braunschweig-Waggum, 116
Luftflotte 2, *110*, 130, 216, 219, 266, *366*, 490
    Flugbereitschaft, 148, 462
    Transportstaffel, 124
Luftflotte 3, *243*
    Stab Luftflotte 3, 418
Luftlandekorps, 216
Luftwaffe Kriegsberichter Komp. 2, 327
Reserve Ob.d.L, 150
Sonderstaffel Schwilden, 206, 220
StG1
    Stab StG1, 138, 279, 453
    I./StG1, 499
    8./StG1, 337
StG2, 237, 447
    Stab StG2, *242*, 366
    Stab I./StG2, 254
    I./StG2, 138, 154, 156, 165, 198, 252
    1./StG2, 242, 366, 414, 448
    2./StG2, 133, 242, 254, 290, 393
    3./StG2, 125, 133, 242
    II./StG2, 150, 265, 279, 329, 393, 412, 414, 419, 447, 448
    4./StG2, 196, 198, 214, 290, 317, 366
    5./StG2, 414, 448, 489
    6./StG2, 301, 329
    Stab III./StG2, 429, 448
    III./StG2, 153, 347
    7./StG2, 242, 254, 366, 376, 477
    8./StG2, 242
    9./StG2, *215*, 290, 309, 347, 442
StG51

Units, German—continued

3./StG51, 124, 140
Stab III./StG51, 309
III./StG51, 102, 265, 303, 317, 337, 414
7./StG51, 279, 309
8./StG51, 309, 376, 388
9./StG51, 309, 442, 459
StG76
    Stab I./StG76, 279
    I./StG76, 215, 249, 274
    1./StG76, 254, 456
    2./StG76, 254, 279, 280
    3./StG76, 265, 373, 375, 376, 388, 470
StG77, 393
    Stab StG77, 124, *280*, 353, 393, 466
    I./StG77, 138, 268, 360, 410
    1./StG77, 347
    2./StG77, 136, 159, 280, 347
    3./StG77, 215
    II./StG77, 466, 467
    4./StG77, 290, 301, 347
    5./StG77, 410
    6./StG77, 343, 393, 467
Sturmabt. Koch, 213
TrGr.186
    Stab I.(St)/TrGr.186, 280
    I.(St)/TrGr.186, 267, 346, 347, 353, 376, 410, 462
    1.(St)/TrGr.186, 124, 280
    2.(St)/TrGr.186, 280, 347, 410
    3.(St)/TrGr.186, 242, 280, 347, 410, 429, 479
    II.(J)/TrGr.186, 365
    4.(J)/TrGr.186, 254, 410
    5.(J)/TrGr.186, 191, 192, 205, 392
    6.(J)/TrGr.186, 239, 254
Überführungs Gruppe West,
3./Überführungs Gruppe West, 194
Wettererkundungsstaffel 26, 154, 410
Wettererkundungsstaffel 51, 135, 162, 170, 462, 477
ZG1, 261
    Stab I./ZG1, 376
    I./ZG1, 131, 184, 373, 406, 422
    1./ZG1, 124, 191, 280, 290, 293, 301, 347, 376, 410, 429
    2./ZG1, 265, 406, 410
    3./ZG1, 236, 242, 309, 410, 429
    Stab II./ZG1, 257, 343, 379
    II./ZG1, 194, 340, 379, 443, 446, 448, 456, 459
    4./ZG1, 215, 359, 360, 448
    5./ZG1, 265, 383, 396, *448*, 459
    6./ZG1, 242, 379, 419, 434, 448
ZG2
    Stab I./ZG2, 157, 290, 337, 376
    I./ZG2 (later 2./JGr.102), 107, 142, 151, 154, 162, 164, 170, 232, 453
    1./ZG2, 242, 337
    2./ZG2, 157
    3./ZG2, 157, 242, 290, 376
ZG26, 154
    Stab I./ZG26, 290, 354, 414
    I./ZG26, 153, 156, 274, 275, 312, 332, 360, 376, 456, 467
    1./ZG26, 132, 156, 242, 317, 383, 467, 479

Units, German—continued

2./ZG26, 138, 139, 280, 290, 317, 366
3./ZG26, 165, 188, 215, 265, 318, 354
II./ZG26, 274, 275, 290
4./ZG26, 107, 234, 312, 318
5./ZG26, 312, 318, 329, 398, *399*
6./ZG26, 280, 493
Stab III./ZG26, 358
III./ZG26, 144, 145, 162, 249, 251, 268, 282, 285, 334, 340, 358, 417, 493, 495
7./ZG26, 290, 334, 337, 340, 343, 429, 497
8./ZG26, 140, 249, 268, 290, 301, 340, 358, 379
9./ZG26, 290, 329, *335*, 337, 360, 374, 418, 469, 470, 493
ZG52
    Stab I./ZG52, 290, 383, 419
    I./ZG52, 148, 164, 242, 262, 265, 273, 274, 280, 366, 379, 383, 393, 414, 453
    1./ZG52, 140, 280, 414, 493
    2./ZG52, 383
    3./ZG52, 280, 360, 379
ZG76
    Stab ZG76, 318
    I./ZG76, 125
    1./ZG76, 116
    Stab II./ZG76, 234, 306, 366, 441
    II./ZG76, 162, 165, 242, 249, 259, 297, 306, 339, 349, 351, 391, 406, 412, *440*, 441, 493
    4./ZG76, 94, 234, 235, 254, *264*, 265, 297, 306, 309, 315, 318, 414, 447, 497
    5./ZG76, 95, 274, 283, 311, 312, 318, 351, 390, 393, 441, 456
    6./ZG76, 259, 282, 283, 290, 297, 351, 354, 362, 441, 488, 497
    III./ZG76, 274
OKW (Armed Forces High Command), *361*
Heeresgruppe A, *355*, 443
Heeresgruppe B, *404*, 422, *443*
4. Armee, 443
6. Armee, 216, *443*
9. Armee, 443
18. Armee, 216
X. Armeekorps, 216
XIV. Armeekorps, 443
XVI. Armeekorps, 443
XIX.Armeekorps, *266*, *365*
XXVI. Armeekorps, 216
XXXIX. Armeekorps, 266
1. Kavallerie-Division, 216
2. Panzer-Division, *330*
4. Panzer-Division, *237*
6. Panzer-Division, 288
7. Flieger-Division, 93, 133, 216, *220*
    AufklSt., 206, 239
7. Panzer-Division, *403*, *460*
9. Infanterie-Division, 468
22. Infanterie-Division, 216, *219*, 226
22. Luftlande-Division, 216
170. Infanterie-Division, *492*

Units, German—continued

SS-Totenkopf Division, 443
Artillerie-Regt 22 (AR22), 222, 223, 227, 243
Fallschirmjäger-Regt 1 (FJR1), 217, 220, 228, 241
Fallschirmjäger-Regt 2 (FJR2), 216, 218, 221, 222, 223
Flak Regt 102, *266*
'Gruppe Lt Erdmann' (Inf.-Regt 47), 222
'Gruppe Lt Jennefeld' (Inf.-Regt 47), 222
'Gruppe Lt Müller' (Inf.-Regt 47), 221
'Gruppe Pollay' (Artillerie-Regt 22), 223
'Gruppe Thoma' (Artillerie-Regt 22), 222
Gruppe von Kleist, 206, *243*, *365*
    Stab Koluft, 288
Infanterie-Regt 16 (IR16), 206, 217, 220, 228, 229
Infanterie-Regt 19 (IR19), 298
Infanterie-Regt 22 (IR22), Nachrichtenabt. 22, 225, 227
Infanterie-Regt 47 (IR47), 216, 218, 221, 222, 226, 243
Infanterie-Regt 65 (IR65), 216, 221, 222, 223, 224, 226, 227, 228, 229, 230
Infanterie-Regt 72 (IR72), 230
Infanterie-Regt 130 (IR130), *19*
Infanterie-Regt 391, *492*
Infanterie-Regt 'Gross Deutsch-land', 206
Pionier-Bn 22, 206, 217, 224, 225
Condor Legion, 87, *427*

Italian (*Regia Aeronautica*)
Order of Battle, 455
3 Stormo, 477
7 Stormo, 462, 467
13 Stormo, *467*
53 Stormo, 477
Ricognizione Strategica, 477
    172 Squadriglia, 477
4 Gruppo, 463
    14 Squadriglia, 462
    15 Squadriglia, 467
11 Gruppo, 463
18 Gruppo
    83 Squadriglia, 477
    85 Squadriglia, 477
23 Gruppo, 463
    74 Squadriglia, 477
43 Gruppo, 463
    3 Squadriglia, *467*
150 Gruppo
    364 Squadriglia, 477
    365 Squadriglia, 477
151 Gruppo, 463, 465

Swiss
Flab.Det.80, 448
Flieger Komp. 6, 409, *410*, 419, 448
Flieger Komp. 7, *410*
Flieger Komp. 8, *410*
Flieger Komp. 9, *410*
Flieger Komp. 10, 448
Flieger Komp. 15, 409, *410*, 414, 419, 448
Flieger Komp. 21, 300, *410*, 448

Photograph Credits

Both Junkers Jumo 211 radial engines of a Ju88 (see also pages 539, 550 and 592) are hoisted onto a low-loader for onward transmission we know not where. The resources available for this recovery suggest a loss relatively early early in the campaign.

Copyright/source is indicated for all original illustrations where known. All other photographs, including present-day comparisons, are the copyright of After the Battle *unless stated otherwise.*

Peter R. Arnold: 256 bottom, 350 all, 444 all.
Associated Press: 482, 483 bottom.
Peter Ayerst: 38 top and bottom.
Michael Balass: 270 top left and right.
Jean-François Beaumin: 434.
Belgian War Graves Commission: 144 bottom.
Pierre Ben: 466 all.
William Blackadder: 77 bottom, 150 bottom.
British Aerospace: 406 top.
Les Brooks: 121 both.
Robin Brooks: 398, 399 both.
Charles E. Brown: 351 top left.
Bundesarchiv: 88 top and bottom, 172-173, 276 bottom left, 430 top and bottom left.
Commonwealth War Graves Commission: 247 bottom right, 506 top right, 507 top, 516 centre, 518 top.
Rose E. B. Coombs: 20 top left and bottom.
Cornwallis Collection: 80 bottom, 81 all, 82, 83, 85 all, 86 all, 92, 93, 94 both, 96 both, 97, 98, 105, 108 bottom, 111 bottom, 113 bottom, 114 top, 116, 118 all, 119 all, 120, 123 top, 134, 135 both, 136 both, 137, 146 top and centre, 157 both, 165 bottom, 170 bottom, 180 both, 181 both, 182 top, 183 top left, 191 both, 192 both, 193 both, 194 both, 208, 231 both, 232 bottom, 233, 250, 259, 269 top and bottom, 271 top left and bottom, 272 both, 283 both, 284 both, 294 top and bottom, 295 middle and bottom, 304 bottom, 310, 311 both, 312, 313 top, 315, 322 both, 324 bottom left and right, 325 both, 331 top left, 334, 340, 345, 346 both, 349, 351 top right, 358, 360, 365, 372 top and centre, 375 both, 379, 385 all, 386 top and bottom left, 394 bottom, 400, 401 bottom, 406 bottom, 416 both, 419, 424 both, 425 both, 426 both, 431 both, 432 both, 433, 437, 445 both, 446 both, 447, 450, 451 both, 458, 459, 461, 462 all, 465 both, 467, 469, 470, 471 both, 479 both, 487, 488 both, 489 top, 499 bottom, 528, 530, 533, 536, 537.
Lewis E. Deal, MBE: 423.
Régis Decobeck: 279.
Jacques van Dijke: 276 top and bottom right.
ECPAD, Paris: 37 top, bottom left and right, 88 centre, 90-91, 110 bottom left and right, 143 both, 146 bottom, 155, 156, 160 top left, 245 bottom, 248, 249, 282 bottom, 305 bottom left and right, 314, 332, 335 top left, 336 top 351 bottom, 373, 378 top, 396 bottom, 411 top, 452.
Bryn Elliott: 320 bottom, 323.
Kerry Foster: 282 top.
FotoFlite Imaging: 370 bottom.
Roger Freeman Collection: 338 both, 395 top.

Jean-Pol Galichet: 440.
Gemeentearchief Den Hague: 215 bottom, 218 bottom, 219 top and centre, 220 bottom.
Michael Ginns, MBE: 514 bottom
Chris Goss: 317.
Peter Grimm: 528
Henry Hall: 58 bottom, 62, 63, 64, 65.
Steve Hall: 87 bottom.
Gustav Henry: 475 both, 476 all.
Lawrence J. Hickey (EOE Archive): 351 right.
Imperial War Museum: 2-3 (C742), 8 (C165), 17 top left (C228), 21 bottom (C180), 25 top (C187), 28 top (C1328), bottom (C1280), 29 top (C737), 30 left (C738) right (C1144), 31 top (C186), bottom (C189), 35 top (C1287), 41 top (C747), bottom (C190), 46 (C748), 47 (C732), 49 top (C1324), 50 top (C876), bottom (C879), 51 top left (C1108), centre (C1135), 56 (C1563), 57 top (C1323), centre (C1565), 58 top left (C169), 59 top left (C172), centre (C743), 60 left (C1128), right (C1127), 61 top (C1130), bottom (C1134), 66 (C1288), centre (C1289), bottom (C1295), 67 (C1290), bottom (C1291), 69 top (C746), bottom (C741), 71 top (C1551), 72 top (C1550), bottom (C1549), 74-75 (C649), 76 top (C468), bottom (E18091), 77 top (C511), 78 (C1153), 79 top (C790), bottom (C346), 101 (C460), 108 top left (C1592), 109 (C465), 111 top (C457), 126 (C112), 127 (C113), 130 (C355), 131 top (C347), 138 (F2344B), 140 (C583), 141 (C891), 142 (C1700), 150 top (C907), 152 (C1031), 158 (C1195), 159 (C1205), 160 top right (C1197), 161 top (C1202), centre (C1201), bottom (C1203), 166 (C435), 169 top (C1505), centre left (C1510), centre right (C1508), bottom (C1509), 171 top (C1441), 174 (C1731), 175 (C1688), 184 (C1656), 205 (C1513), 207 top (C1528), centre (C1529), bottom (C1524), 209 bottom (C840), 246 bottom left (C1469), 288 (F4413), 289 top (F4415), bottom (F4416), 296 (F4493), 303 (C1512), 320 top (C1674), 326 (C1578), 353 (C1572), 354 top (C1579), centre (C1573), bottom (C1580), 367 bottom left (A9904), 394 top (C1675), 408 top (C1774), bottom (C1770), 409 bottom (C1713), 439 top (B188), bottom left (C749), centre (C1329), 500-501 (C273), 502 top (C271), 539 (C1495), 550 (C1491), 551 (CH433), 590 (C1492), 592 (CH1494).
Institut Géographique National: 14, 23 top, 281 top, 415 top left, 435 top, 463 bottom.
Jan Jolie: 255, 261 top, 265 both, 530.
E. J. Kain: 491 top left, middle left, centre and bottom left.
Francis Leroy: 502 bottom.
Günther Lützow (via Dr Jochen Prien): 87 top.
Nick Maddocks: 524 bottom left and right.
Don Minterne: 35 bottom, 70 top, 170 top, 291 top.

No. 1 Squadron: 167 top, 168 top, 256, 439 bottom right, 483 top.
No. 73 Squadron: 6, 10 top, 13, 15, 18 top, 24 top and bottom, 32 top, 33 bottom, 37 top and bottom left and right, 39 top and centre, 40, 42 top, 43 top, 44 top, 45 top and centre, 46 top, 47 top, 48 bottom, 49 bottom, 51 both, 53 top, 68 both, 71 bottom, 73 top, 436 top left, 468, 486.
Jean Paul Pallud: 110, 139, 167 bottom, 168 bottom, 171 bottom, 218 top, 219 top and centre, 220 top, 238 top left and right, 276 top left, 291 bottom, 324 top left and right, 335 top right, 336 bottom, 337, 384 both, 403, 411 both, 436 top right, 438 bottom left, 457, 460 bottom.
R. Potié: 411 bottom.
Jean-Louis Roba: 301 bottom.
Andy Saunders: 125 all, 268, 269 centre, 270 bottom, 271 top right, 293 top, 295 top, 313 bottom left, centre and right, 321 both, 356 both, 357 both, 438 bottom right, 505 top left, centre and right, 507 bottom right, 509 bottom right, 511 bottom right, 517 both.
Johan Schuurman: 221 all, 222 both, 223 both, 224 both, 225 all, 226 both, 227 both, 228, 229, 590.
Service Historique de la Defense: 264 all, 298, 477, 478, 495 both, 499 top, 538, 581.
Hans-Heiri Stapfer: 300, 448.
Patrice Strazzera: 467 bottom.
Peter Taghon: 100, 102 top and bottom, 103, 106, 114 bottom, 115, 123 bottom, 124 bottom, 132 both, 144 top left and right, 145, 147 both, 163 both, 164, 165 top, 182 bottom, 183 top right and bottom, 188, 189, 196, 197 left, top, centre, middle and bottom, 198 all, 199 both, 200 top, centre, bottom left, 201 top, 206, 209 top, 210 both, 211 both, 212 both, 213, 214 all, 215 all, 232 top, 234 top, 235, 236 both, 237 all, 238 bottom left and right, 240 both, 241 both, 242, 244 both, 246 top and bottom right, 247 top left, right and bottom left, 251 all, 252 all, 253, 254, 260, 262, 263, 273, 275 both, 277, 278 both, 280 both, 285, 286 both, 287 top and centre, 293 bottom, 294 middle, 297 all, 299 all, 301 top, 304 top, 305 top, 306, 307 all, 308, 309 both, 316, 318 both, 327, 328 both, 329 bottom left, 331 top right and bottom, 333 both, 342 both, 343 top left and right, 352, 364, 374, 380, 381, 382, 383 both, 387 both, 392, 393 top, 410, 414 both, 417 both, 489 bottom.
US National Archives: 403, 460 top.
Luc Vervoort: 362, 582.
T. Visser: 258 top left.
Volksbund Deutsche Kriegsgräberfürsorge: 442.
Bas Zijlmans: 258 top right.

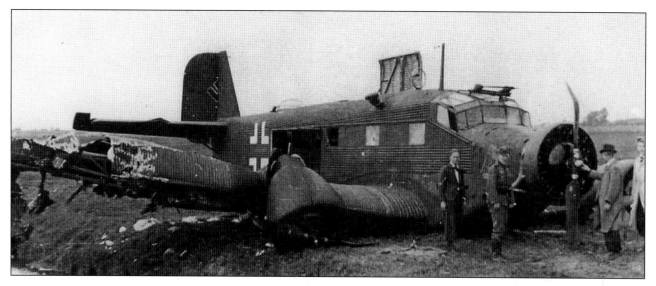

Nearly 200 troop-carrying Junkers Ju52s were lost on Day One of the German invasion of Holland. Such heavy losses would have seriously hampered any subsequent German invasion plans for England.

Addendum

With any research project, particularly one as extensive and complex as this, it is frustrating when information comes to light too late for incorporation. But when a complete listing of personnel losses of the *Transportverbände* engaged in the airborne landings in the Netherlands surfaced recently amongst documents in the archive of the late Heinrich Weiss, we were nearing final production stage. The author is indebted to Larry Hickey for affording access to these papers and to Wim de Meester for his prompt response to my request for copies. Thus, in the interests of adding to the published record, casualties reported in addition to those already listed (see pages 221-229) were as follows:

Stab I./KGzbV.1

Stabsfw Karl Hübner missing — returned to unit May 19.
Oberfw Waldemar Nieswandt missing — returned to unit May 20.
Oberfw Alfred Thomas killed. Buried at Kruisweg, Valkenburg, now in Ysselsteyn Grave CN-5-104.
Fw Wilhelm Janotta missing — returned to unit May 19.
Uffz Albert Dietrich missing — returned to unit May 19.
Uffz Hans Eichmüller missing — returned to unit May 24.
Uffz Otto Girnth missing — returned to unit May 19.
Uffz Kurt Meier missing — returned to unit May 24.
Gefr Max Kathe missing — returned to unit May 24.
Gefr Erwin Witt missing — returned to unit May 24.
Flgr Erich Becker missing — returned to unit May 19.

1./KGzbV.1

Fw Kurt Sacher badly wounded, admitted to hospital in Buer.

2./KGzbV.1

Lt Friedrich Ebert missing — returned to unit May 24.
Oberfw Kurt Scherfling missing — returned to unit May 24.
Uffz Ernst Greve captured near Gouda.

Uffz Adam Herbig badly wounded, admitted to hospital in Hamm.
Uffz Siegfried Maass captured.
Uffz Hans Müller badly wounded, admitted to hospital in Hamm.
Uffz Robert Obst captured near Gouda.
Uffz Heinz Schmidt killed. Buried West Duin, Den Haag, now in IJsselstein Grave BH-7-166.
Uffz Emil Spalleck slightly wounded, admitted to hospital in Hamm.
Uffz Walter Volmer captured near Gouda.

3./KGzbV.1

Uffz Karl Berger missing — returned to unit May 19.
Uffz Horst Erdmann badly wounded, treated in Onze Lieue Vrouwe Gasthuis, Amsterdam.
Uffz Siegmund Horkl missing — returned to unit May 24.
Uffz Eberhard Klein missing — returned to unit May 19.
Uffz Willi Lichy missing — returned to unit May 24.
Gefr Bernhard Brodkorb slightly wounded.
Gefr Hermann Hofmann missing — returned to unit May 19.
Gefr Otto Pielicke missing — returned to unit May 24.

4./KGzbV.1

Lt Hans-Walter Fiehn missing — returned to unit May 24.
Fw Wilhelm Gigl badly wounded, admitted to Academisch Ziekenhuis, Leiden.
Fw Alfred Lau missing — returned to unit May 19.
Uffz Emil Ranta missing — returned to unit May 19.
Uffz Fritz Schiedler missing — returned to unit May 24.
Uffz Ernst Weidenmüller badly wounded, admitted to Diakonessenhuis, Leiden.
Uffz Karl Wissing missing — returned to unit May 24.
Obergefr Hermann Trossen badly wounded, admitted to Diakonessenhuis, Leiden.

9./KGzbV.1

Oberfw Hans Burzlauer captured.
Oberfw Otto Günther captured.
Oberfw Karl Klaus missing — returned to unit May 18.
Oberfw Karl Presch missing — returned to unit May 18.
Fw Reinhard Klingelhöfer slightly wounded.
Fw Georg Lippert missing — returned to unit May 18.

Fw Friedrich Vedder badly wounded, died in hospital in Dortmund.
Uffz Herrmann Gutsche slightly wounded.
Uffz Helmut Hanns captured.
Uffz Justus Krein killed.
Uffz Wilhelm Maier badly wounded, died next day in hospital in Dortmund.
Uffz Johann Siebertz missing — returned to unit May 18.
Uffz Wilhelm Wittemann slightly wounded.
Flgr Christian Caisberger slightly wounded.

10./KGzbV.1

Oberfw Dietrich Gropp missing — returned to unit May 18.
Oberfw Paul Zinke captured.
Fw Paul-Friedrich Hecht missing — returned to unit May 18.
Fw Alfred Maier slightly wounded, admitted to hospital in Münster-Loddenheide.
Uffz Werner Rödel missing — returned to unit May 18.

13./KGzbV.1

Oberfw Alfred Petermann captured near Gouda.
Fw Heinz Aude missing — returned later.
Fw Heinrich Delp captured.
Fw Stephan Koller killed. Buried Crooswijk, Rotterdam, now in IJsselstein Grave BU-4-087.
Fw Friedrich Kleschnitzki captured.
Uffz Karl-Heinz Dietrich missing — returned later.
Uffz Hermann Günther captured.
Uffz Georg Köhler missing — returned later.
Uffz Walter Kurzbach captured near Gouda.
Uffz Kurt Pscheidl captured.
Uffz Josef Schäfer missing — returned later.
Uffz Claudius Struve captured near Gouda.
Uffz Rudi Zickenberg missing — returned later.
Uffz Bernhard Ziebe missing — returned later.
Hptgefr Waldemar Brenner captured.
Obergefr Ehrhard Deinser missing — returned later.
Obergefr Paul Gottschlich captured.
Gefr Kurt Wehnes captured near Gouda.

15./KGzbV.1

Uffz Willi Pischzur wounded, admitted to Noordhospitaal, Vlietstraat, Voorburg.
Gefr Helmut Asmus missing — returned later.
Gefr Josef Gross missing — returned later.
Gefr Gerhard Kleinert missing — returned later.

16./KGzbV.1

Oberfw Kurt Bonnemann missing — returned later.
Fw Hans Prieff reported killed.
Fw Karl Sammet captured.
Fw Paul Zebhauser badly wounded, died in hospital in Münster-Loddenheide.
Uffz Hermann Bachinger slightly wounded.
Uffz Karl Blumberger missing — returned later.
Uffz Josef Borg missing — returned later.
Uffz Ernst Dümesnil wounded, admitted to St Antoniushove Centraal Hospitaal, Voorburg.
Uffz Erich Glatz captured, held at Borneostraat, Den Haag.
Uffz Heinz Grotke captured.
Uffz Johann Hasslinger killed. Buried at Kanaalweg, Delft, now in IJsselstein Grave AA-11-251.
Uffz Herbert Oertelt captured.
Uffz Hermann Juffa captured.
Uffz Hermann Mayer missing — returned later.
Uffz Günther Mesters captured, held at Borneostraat, Den Haag.
Uffz Paul Remling captured, held at Borneostraat, Den Haag.
Uffz Heinrich Schmölz captured.
Uffz Siegfried von Bonin wounded, admitted to St Antoniushove Centraal Hospitaal, Voorburg..
Gefr Jakob Fleischmann badly wounded, died in hospital in Münster-Loddenheide.
Gefr Heinrich Forger wounded, admitted to St Antoniushove Centraal Hospitaal, Voorburg.
Gefr Karl Metzner captured, held at Borneostraat, Den Haag.
Gefr Helmut Weil badly wounded, died in hospital in Münster-Loddenheide.

Stab I./KGrzbV.9

Uffz Hans Grotzinger badly wounded.
Gefr Fritz Fuhlke captured.

Stab I./KGrzbV.11

Oberstlt Gustav Wilke (Gruppenkommandeur) missing.
Hptmn Eugen Staehle (attached to Stab I./KGrzbV.172) badly wounded, died in hospital in Lippstadt.
Oberlt Hermann Roser missing.
Lt Werner Stein missing.
Oberfw Franz Hopke missing.
Oberfw Rudolf Sperling missing.
Oberfw Heinz Zeegmann missing.
Fw Heinz Fimmers missing.
Uffz Heinz Beines missing — returned later.
Uffz Willy Corts missing.
Uffz Bernhard Dominiak captured, held at Nieuwe Frederikkazerne, Den Haag.
Uffz Karl Keck missing — returned later.
Uffz Alfons Kurse missing.
Uffz Ernst Schumacher missing.
Obergefr August Vietje missing — returned later.
Gefr Siegfried Schick missing.

1./KGrzbV.11

Hptmn Willy Gutsche (Staffelkapitän) missing.
Lt Karl Hausknecht missing.
Lt Walter Pulz missing — returned later.
Oberfw Walter Reiser missing.
Oberfw Karl Schmidt missing.
Oberfw Karl von Prietz missing.
Fw Willy Knapp missing.
Fw Hermann Steeb missing.
Fw Hermann Volte missing.
Fw Erich Winkler missing.
Uffz Otto-Wilhelm Bertelsmann captured, held at Nieuwe Frederikkazerne, Den Haag.
Uffz Herbert Bayer missing.
Uffz Franz Busch captured, held at Nieuwe Frederikkazerne, Den Haag.

Uffz Konrad Feldhammer missing.
Uffz Ernst-August Heimplätzer missing.
Uffz Karl Herzberg died of wounds.
Uffz Heinz Klar missing.
Uffz Arno Knoch missing.
Uffz Hans Kretschmer missing — returned later.
Uffz Adolf Landau captured, held at Nieuwe Frederikkazerne, Den Haag.
Uffz Erich Liebig missing.
Uffz Friedrich Trimpel missing.
Uffz Alfred Wichert missing.
Hptgefr Josef Neumann missing — returned later.
Obergefr Ludwig Tenser missing.
Gefr Helmut Baumann missing.
Gefr Otto Holst missing.
Gefr Kurt Schwenke missing.
Gefr Helmut Talberger missing.
Gefr Paul Wulf missing.

2./KGrzbV.11

Hptmn Albert-Heinz Fr von Beust (Staffelkapitän) missing.
Hptmn Karl-Heinrich Pickerott missing.
Lt Raimund Reissmüller missing — returned later.
Lt Hans Schmidt missing.
Oberfw Georg Lors missing — returned later.
Fw Gerhard Baier missing.
Fw Gerhard Berndt missing — returned later.
Fw Wilhelm Gerlach missing.
Fw Karl Hanke captured, held at Nieuwe Frederikkazerne, Den Haag.
Fw Anton Henn missing.
Fw Hermann Kaiser captured, held at Nieuwe Frederikkazerne, Den Haag.
Fw Hans Retske missing.
Fw Christian Sieger missing.
Fw Dietrich Weber missing.
Uffz Herbert Beyer missing.
Uffz Willi Glatz captured, held at Borneostraat, Den Haag.
Uffz Erwin Hübner missing — returned later.
Uffz Alfred Römke captured, held at Nieuwe Frederikkazerne, Den Haag.
Uffz Gerhard Schneider missing — returned later.
Uffz Alfons Sempert captured, held at Nieuwe Frederikkazerne, Den Haag.

3./KGrzbV.11

Lt Günter Zorn died of wounds, May 10.

4./KGrzbV.11

Uffz Heinrich Sonntag captured.
Uffz Friedhelm Weber missing.

Stab I./KGrzbV.12

Oberfw Karl Biehl captured.
Oberfw Georg Kühnel captured.
Fw Gebhard Berendes slightly wounded, admitted to Elisabeth Ziekenhuis, Leiden.
Fw Erich Haas captured.
Uffz Gerhardt Böhme killed. Buried at IJsselstein as 'Unknown'.
Uffz Herbert Schareimm captured.
Gefr Siegfried Koch captured.
Gefr Hermann Kröger killed. Buried in IJsselstein Grave BU-9-209.

1./KGrzbV.12

Oberlt Friedrich Bolte slightly wounded, admitted to hospital in Hannover.
Fw Georg Wahl captured, held at Nieuwe Frederikkazerne, Den Haag.
Uffz Paul Behr captured.
Uffz Erich Fuchs captured, held at Nieuwe Frederikkazerne, Den Haag.
Uffz Bruno John captured, held at Nieuwe Frederikkazerne, Den Haag.
Uffz Gerhardt Klein captured, held at Nieuwe Frederikkazerne, Den Haag.

Uffz Oskar Kopp badly wounded, admitted to hospital in Dorsten.
Uffz Hans Liche badly wounded, admitted to hospital in Hameln.
Uffz Hans Schmidtmann badly wounded, admitted to hospital in Dortmund.
Uffz Kurt Wendrich badly wounded, admitted to hospital in Lippstadt.

3./KGrzbV.12

Oberfw Georg Häussler killed. Buried in IJsselstein BI-11-274.
Fw Werner Baganz captured.
Fw Werner Morgenstern captured.
Fw Adolf Rastetter captured.
Fw Ernst Weber captured.
Uffz Hugo Dreyer badly wounded, admitted to hospital in Paderborn.
Uffz Heinrich Velten captured.

4./KGrzbV.12

Lt Fritz Hasenmayer captured near Gouda.
Lt Helmuth Schultz badly wounded, admitted to Academisch Ziekenhuis, Leiden.
Oberfw Fritz Zigler captured.
Fw Ernst Deeg captured.
Fw Hans Gilly captured.
Fw Ernst Lösche badly wounded, admitted to hospital in Rotterdam.
Fw Herbert Novotzin captured.
Fw Willi Schrage captured.
Fw Paul Ulrich badly wounded, admitted to hospital in Minden.
Uffz Josef Beymore killed. Buried at IJsselstein as 'Unknown'.
Uffz Max Dölker captured.
Uffz Heinrich Fritsch killed. Buried at Kerkhoflaan, Den Haag, now in IJsselstein BK-1-1.
Uffz Hans Groneberg captured.
Uffz Benno Huber captured near Gouda.
Uffz Alfons Michalski captured.
Uffz Franz Neumann missing.
Uffz Rudolf Schuster captured.
Uffz Eduart Steinhauser badly wounded, admitted to hospital in Delft.
Uffz Otto Traps captured.

1./KGrzbV.101

Uffz Ernst Theophil Schindler killed. Buried at Crooswijk, Rotterdam, now in IJsselstein Grave BW-3-62.
Gefr Wilhelm Basson badly wounded.

Stab I./KGrzbV.172

Fw Walter Elsermann slightly wounded, admitted to hospital in Paderborn.
Fw Hans-Dietrich Korn reported killed.
Uffz Karl Schubert missing — returned later.
Uffz Alfred Zilm missing — returned later.
Gefr Heinrich Kubischke missing — returned later.
Flgr Heinz Schulze slightly wounded, admitted to hospital in Paderborn.

1./KGrzbV.172

Fw Erich Bork missing — returned later.
Uffz Walter Redecker missing — returned later.
Uffz Werner Ross missing — returned later.
Uffz Fritz Weber missing — returned later.
Uffz Wilhelm Wentzlaff missing — returned later.
Gefr Walter Blaser slightly wounded.
Gefr Günther Stiller slightly wounded.

4./KGrzbV.172

Oberfw Erich Flader died of wounds in Bürder Hospital, Paderborn.
Uffz Werner Zinke badly wounded, admitted to hospital in Cologne.
Gefr Konrad Göbell slightly wounded, admitted to hospital in Paderborn.

Bibliography

Auwerda, Frans (Ed.): *Bulletin Air War No. 247, Speciale Editie: Verlieslijst 1939–1941* (Studiegroep Luchtoorlog 1939-1945: Baarle-Nassau, 2002).

Balke, Ulf: *Der Luftkrieg in Europa 1939–1941. Die Einsätze des Kampfgeschwaders 2* (Bechtermünz Verlag: Augsburg, 1997).

Beedle, J.: *43 Squadron RFC, RAF: History of the Fighting Cocks 1916-66* (Beaumont Aviation: London, 1966).

Belcarz, Bartlomiej: *GC 1/145 in France 1940* (Sandomierz: Mushroom Model Publications, 2002).

Bruin, Rob de & Grimm, Peter & Hoiting, Henk & Luijten, Peter & van Vliet, Jaap & Zwaaf, Leo: *Illusies en Incidenten. De Militaire Luchtvaart en de neutraliteitshandhaving tot 10 mei 1940* (Koninklijke Luchtmacht: Den Haag, 1988).

Chorley, W. R.: *Bomber Command Losses*, Vol. 1 (Midland Counties: Hinckley, 1992).

Clayton, Eric: *What if the Heavens Fall. Reminiscences of 56 (F) Squadron in the Battle of Britain* (Wye College Press: London, 1995).

Cull, Brian & Lander, Bruce & Weiss, Heinrich: *Twelve Days in May* (Grub Street: London, 1995).

De Decker, Cynrik & Roba, Jean Louis: *Mei 1940 boven België* (De Krijger: Erpe, 1993).

Deere, Alan C.: *Nine Lives* (Hodder & Stoughton: London, 1959).

Divine, David: *Dunkirk* (Faber & Faber: London, 1945).

Ellis, Major L. F.: *The War in France and Flanders 1939-1940* (HMSO: London, 1953).

Foreman, John: *RAF Fighter Command Victory Claims*, Vol. 1 (Red Kite: Walton on Thames, 2003).

Forrester, Larry: *Fly For Your Life. The Story of R. R. Stanford Tuck, DSO, DFC* (Frederick Muller: London, 1956).

Franks, Norman: *Double Mission. RAF Fighter Ace and SOE Agent Manfred Czerin, DSO, MC, DFC* (William Kimber: London, 1976).

———: *Valiant Wings. The Battle and Blenheim Squadrons over France, 1940* (William Kimber: London, 1988).

———: *Fighter Command Losses*, Vol. 1 (Midland Counties: Hinckley, 1997).

———: *Air Battle Dunkirk* (Grub Street: London, 2000).

Halley, James J.: *RAF Aircraft Serials* (Air-Britain: Staplefield, 1976-80).

———: *The Squadrons of the Royal Air Force* (Air-Britain: Staplefield, 1980).

Halliday, Hugh A.: *No. 242 Squadron. The Canadian Years. The Story of the RAF's 'All-Canadian' Fighter Squadron* (Canada's Wings: Stittsville, 1981).

Jolie, Jan: *Luchtgevechten boven West-Brabant en de Biesbosch* (Lorelax: Muiderberg, 2000).

Gardner, Charles: *A.A.S.F. The Full Story of Our Advanced Air Striking Force in France* (Hutchinson: London, 1940).

Gillet, Arnaud: *Les Victoires de l'Aviation de Chasse Francaise*, 3 Vols. (Imprimerie Félix Vouziers, 2003–2005).

Marsh, Alan E.: *Flying Marines. A Record of Royal Marine Aviators who flew Fixed Wing Aircraft in the Royal Naval Air Service and Fleet Air Arm* (1980).

Martin, Jacqueline & Paul: *Ils étaient là… (l'Armée de l'Air, Septembre 39-Juin 40)* (Aéro Éditions: Fleurance, 2001).

McNeill, Ross: *Coastal Command Losses*, Vol. 1 (Midland Counties: Hinckley, 2003).

Minterne, Don: *The History of 73 Squadron, Part 1: 1917 to November 1940* (Tutor Publications: Dorchester, 1994).

Monks, Noel: *Squadrons Up!* (Victor Gollancz: London, 1941).

Molenaar, Kolonel F. J.: *De Luchtverdediging in de Meidagen 1940* (Staatsuitgeverij: Den Haag, 1971).

Morareau, Lucien: *L'Aéronautique Navale Française de septembre 1939 à juin 1940 (Avions, Hors-Série No.1)* (Lela Presse: Boulogne-sur-Mer, 1994).

Narracott, Arthur H.: *War News had Wings. A Record of the RAF in France* (Frederick Muller: London, 1941).

Pallud, Jean Paul: *Blitzkrieg in the West Then and Now* (After the Battle: London, 1991).

Richey, Paul: *Fighter Pilot. A Personal Record of the Campaign in France, Sept 8th 1939-June 13th 1940* (Batsford: London, 1941).

Roger, Françoise & Pierre: *Combats Aériens sur la Meuse et la Semoy, 10-14 mai 1940 (Liège-Bouillon-Sedan)* (Musée de L'AASF de Vraux, Imprimerie SOPAIC: Charleville-Mézières, 1998).

———: *Combats Oubliés du Ciel des Ardennes et de la Marne, 15 mai-14 juin 1940. (Monthermé-Rethel-Reims-Sedan-Châlons-Montmirail)* (Musée de L'AASF de Vraux, Imprimerie SOPAIC: Charleville-Mézières, 2001).

Sacré, Jacques & Gillet, Arnaud: *Bataille Aérienne et Rupture sur la Meuse. Quadrilatère: Namur-Cambrai-Troyes-Luxembourg (10-18 mai 1940)* (Les Éditions du Plateau de Rocroi, 2004).

Schuurman, Johan: *Vliegveld Bergen, NH 1938–1945* (Uitgeverij De Coogh: Bergen, 2001).

Shail, Sidney: *The Battle File* (Air-Britain: Staplefield, 1997).

Shaw, Michael: *Twice Vertical. The History of No. 1 (Fighter) Squadron RAF* (MacDonald: London, 1971).

Shores, Christopher, et al.: *Fledgling Eagles. The Complete Account of Air Operations during the Phoney War and the Norwegian Campaign, 1940* (Grub Street: London, 1991).

Smith, Peter C.: *Stuka Squadron. Stukagruppe 77 – The Luftwaffe's Fire Brigade* (Patrick Stephens: Wellingtonborough, 1990).

Stones, Donald: *Dimsie. Memoirs of a Pilot from Air to Ground – A Trilogy* (Wingham Press: Canterbury, 1991).

Slizewski, Grzegorz: *The Lost Hopes. Polish Fighters over France in 1940* (FH Panda, Koszalin, 2000).

Sutton, Barry: *The Way of a Pilot. A Personal Record* (MacMillan: London, 1942).

Taghon, Peter: *L'Aéronautique Militaire Belge en Mai-Juin 1940 (Avions, Hors-Série No.18)* (Lela Presse: Outreau, 2006).

Prien, Jochen & Stemmer, Gerhard & Rodeike, Peter & Bock, Winfried: *Die Jagdfliegerverbände der Deutschen Luftwaffe 1934 bis 1945*, Vols. 1-4 (Struve-Druck: Eutin, 2000-2002).

Watteeuw, Pierre: *Les Pertes de la Chasse de Jour Allemande en France 1939-1945*, Vol. 1 *(Avions, Hors-Série No.10)* (Lela Presse: Outreau, 2002).

———: *Les Pertes de la Chasse de Jour Allemande en Belgique 1940-1945*, Vol. 1 (De Krijger: Erpe, 1999).

Winter, Vincent Adams: *Resurgam: The Story of Flight Lieutenant G. L. Nowell, DFM & Bar, AE 'The Best Fighter Pilot of Them All'* (Privately printed, Melbourne, 1985).

Zwieten, Majoor J. E. van: *Duitse Luchtlandingen in Nederland, Mei 1940* (Koninklijke Luchtmacht: Den Haag, 1967).